The Sporting News

COMPLETE HOCKEY BOOK

1994-95 EDITION

Editors / Complete Hockey Book
CRAIG CARTER
GEORGE PURO
KYLE VELTROP

Contributing Editor / Complete Hockey Book
LARRY WIGGE

D1601666

The Sporting News
PUBLISHING CO.

Francis P. Pandolfi, Chairman and Chief Executive Officer; Nicholas H. Niles, President; John D. Rawlings, Editorial Director; Kathy Kinkeade, Vice President/Production; Mike Nahrstedt, Managing Editor; Joe Hoppel, Senior Editor; Tom Dienhart and Dave Sloan, Associate Editors; Craig Carter, Statistical Editor; George Puro and Kyle Veltrop, Assistant Editors; Jim Bender, Josh Gotthelf, Raman Kansal, David Kantor and Lenny Steber, Editorial Assistants; Fred Barnes, Director of Graphics; Michael Bruner, Art Director/Yearbooks and Books; Steve Levin, Photo Editor; Gary Levy, Special Projects Editor; Gary Brinker, Director of Electronic Information Development; Vern Kasal, Composing Room Supervisor.

A Times Mirror
Company

CONTENTS

ON THE COVER: New York Rangers goaltender Mike Richter led the NHL with 42 victories last season, then led the Rangers to the Stanley Cup championship with 16 victories, four shutouts and a 2.07 goals-against average in 23 playoff games. (Photo by John Giamundo/Bruce Bennett Studios)

Editorial assistance provided by Igor Kuperman of the Winnipeg Jets.

ISBN: 0-89204-498-5 (perfect-bound)
    0-89204-499-3 (comb-bound)

10 9 8 7 6 5 4 3 2 1

1994-95 NHL SEASON

NHL directory

Team information

Schedule

NHL DIRECTORY

LEAGUE OFFICES

OFFICERS

Commissioner
Gary B. Bettman
Senior V.P. and chief operating officer
Stephen Solomon
Senior V.P. and dir. of hockey operations
Brian P. Burke
Senior vice president and general counsel
Jeffrey Pash
Vice president and chief financial officer
John M. Houston
Vice president, public relations
Arthur Pincus
Vice president, corporate communications
Bernadette Mansur
Vice president, broadcasting
Glenn Adamo
Vice president, team service and television
Ellis T. "Skip" Prince

NHL ENTERPRISES

Senior V.P. and chief operating officer
Richard Dudley
Senior V.P. and general counsel
Richard Zahnd
Vice president, corporate Marketing
Edward Horne

Vice president, retail licensing
Fred Scalera

PUBLIC RELATIONS

Vice president, public relations
Arthur Pincus
Director, public relations
Gary Meagher
Mgr., public relations and news services
Andrew McGowan
Manager, media relations
Susan Aglietti
Manager, news services
Greg Inglis
Statistician
Benny Ercolani
Communications assistant
David Keon
News service assistant
Tamir Lipton
Administrative assistants
Karen Levine
Kay Merritts

NEW YORK OFFICE (NHL and NHLE)

Address
1251 Avenue of the Americas
47th Floor
New York, NY 10020

Phone
212-789-2000
FAX
212-789-2020

TORONTO OFFICE

Address
75 International Blvd.
Suite 300
Rexdale, Ont. M9W 6L9
Phone
416-798-0809
FAX
416-798-0852

MONTREAL OFFICE

Address
1800 McGill College Avenue
Suite 2600
Montreal, Que., Canada H3A 3J6
Phone
514-288-9220
FAX
514-284-0300

BOARD OF GOVERNORS

Anaheim
Michael D. Eisner
Boston
Jeremy M. Jacobs
Buffalo
Seymour H. Knox III
Calgary
Harley N. Hotchkiss
Chicago
William W. Wirtz
Dallas
Norman N. Green
Detroit
Michael Ilitch

Edmonton
Peter Pocklington
Florida
William A. Torrey
Hartford
Peter Karmanos Jr.
Los Angeles
Bruce P. McNall
Montreal
Ronald L. Corey
New Jersey
Dr. John J. McMullen
New York Islanders
Bob Rosenthal

New York Rangers
Neil Smith
Ottawa
Roderick M. Bryden
Philadelphia
Bob Clarke
Pittsburgh
Howard L. Baldwin
Quebec
Marcel Aubut
St. Louis
Michael F. Shanahan

San Jose
George Gund III
Tampa Bay
David E. LeFevre
Toronto
Steve A. Stavro
Vancouver
Arthur R. Griffiths
Washington
Abe Pollin
Winnipeg
Barry L. Shenkarow

DIVISIONAL ALIGNMENT

EASTERN CONFERENCE

ATLANTIC DIVISION
Florida Panthers
New Jersey Devils
New York Islanders
New York Rangers
Philadelphia Flyers
Tampa Bay Lightning
Washington Capitals

NORTHEAST DIVISION
Boston Bruins
Buffalo Sabres
Hartford Whalers
Montreal Canadiens
Ottawa Senators
Pittsburgh Penguins
Quebec Nordiques

WESTERN CONFERENCE

CENTRAL DIVISION
Chicago Blackhawks
Dallas Stars
Detroit Red Wings
St. Louis Blues
Toronto Maple Leafs
Winnipeg Jets

PACIFIC DIVISION
Mighty Ducks of Anaheim
Calgary Flames
Edmonton Oilers
Los Angeles Kings
San Jose Sharks
Vancouver Canucks

MIGHTY DUCKS OF ANAHEIM
WESTERN CONFERENCE/PACIFIC DIVISION

1994-95 SCHEDULE

Home games shaded.
* — All-Star Game at San Jose Arena.
† — At Las Vegas.
Δ — At San Antonio.
D — Day game.

OCTOBER

SUN	MON	TUE	WED	THU	FRI	SAT
						1 DAL
2	3	4	5 EDM	6	7 VAN	8
9 CAL	10	11	12 VAN	13	14 BOS	15
16	17 EDM	18	19 EDM	20 CAL	21	22
23 WIN	24	25 DET	26	27 CHI	28	29
30 STL	31					

NOVEMBER

SUN	MON	TUE	WED	THU	FRI	SAT
		1	2 NYR	3	4 NJ	5
6	7	8 LA	9	10 SJ	11 VAN	12
13 CAL	14	15 BUF	16	17 VAN	18	19
20 CHI	21	22	23 SJ	24	25 D BOS	26 D HAR
27	28	29 PIT	30 TOR			

DECEMBER

SUN	MON	TUE	WED	THU	FRI	SAT
				1	2 NYR	3
4 CHI	5	6	7 WAS	8	9 SJ	10
11 TOR	12	13 PIT	14	15	16 SJ	17
18 NYI	19	20	21 WIN	22 CAL	23	24
25	26 LA	27	28 LA	29	30 CHI	31

JANUARY

SUN	MON	TUE	WED	THU	FRI	SAT
1	2 MGN	D 3	4	5	6 BUF	7 NJ
8	9 PHI	10	11 DET	12 TOR	13	14
15 OTT	16	17 QUE	18 MON	19	20	21°
22	23	24	25 DAL	26	27 WIN	28
29	30	31 STL				

FEBRUARY

SUN	MON	TUE	WED	THU	FRI	SAT
			1	2	3 DET	4
5 EDM	D 6	7	8 CAL	9† STL	10	11
12 EDM	D 13 CAL	14	15 QUE	16	17 OTT	18
19 LA	20	21 LA	22 PHI	23	24 SJ	25
26 VAN	D 27	28				

MARCH

SUN	MON	TUE	WED	THU	FRI	SAT
			1 TB	2	3 DAL	4
5 FLA	6 TB	7	8	9 DET	10	11Δ DAL
12	13	14	15 HAR	16	17 TOR	18
19 STL	D 20	21 FLA	22	23 STL	24	25 D WAS
26 NYI	D 27	28	29 WIN	30	31 VAN	

APRIL

SUN	MON	TUE	WED	THU	FRI	SAT
						1
2 SJ	D 3	4	5 EDM	6	7 DAL	8
9 LA	D 10	11	12	13	14	15

1994-95 SEASON

CLUB DIRECTORY

Governor
Michael Eisner
President and alternate governor
Tony Tavares
Vice president and general manager
Jack Ferreira
Vice president of finance/administration
Andy Roundtree
Assistant general manager
Pierre Gauthier
Head coach
Ron Wilson
Assistant coaches
Tim Army
Al Sims
Director of hockey operations
Kevin Gilmore
Director of player personnel
David McNab

Pro scout
Paul Fenton
Regional scouts
Al Godfrey
Richard Green
Trainer
Blynn DeNiro
Equipment manager
Mark O'Neill
Director of sales and marketing
Bill Holford
Director of public relations
Bill Robertson
Controller
Marc Serrio
Manager of administration
Jenny Price
Manager of premium ticketing services
Anne McNiff

DRAFT CHOICES

Rd.—Player	H/W	Overall	Pos.	Last team
1—Oleg Tverdovsky	6-0/183	2	D	Krylja Sovetov, CIS
2—Johan Davidsson	5-11/170	28	C	Jonkoping, Sweden
3—Craig Reichert	6-0/195	67	RW	Red Deer (WHL)
4—Byron Briske	6-2/194	80	D	Red Deer (WHL)
5—Pavel Trnka	6-3/187	106	D	Skoda Pizen, Czech.
6—Jon Battaglia	6-0/175	132	RW	Caledon (Jr. A)
7—Mark Welsing	6-2/205	158	D	Wisconsin (Jr. A)
8—John Brad Englehart	5-11/180	184	LW	Kimball Un. Acad. (Mass.)
10—Tommi Miettinen	5-10/165	236	C	Kalpa Kuopio, Finland
11—Jeremy Stevenson	6-1/208	262	LW	Sault Ste. Marie (OHL)

MISCELLANEOUS DATA

Home ice (capacity)
Anaheim Arena—The Pond
(17,250)
Address
2695 E. Katella Avenue
P.O. Box 61077
Anaheim, CA 92803-6177

Business phone
714-704-2700
Rink dimensions
200 feet by 85 feet
Club colors
Purple, jade, silver and white

TRAINING CAMP ROSTER

No.	FORWARDS	Ht./Wt.	Place	BORN Date	NHL exp.	1993-94 clubs
	Maxim Bets (LW)	6-1/185	Chelyabinsk, U.S.S.R.	1-31-74	1	Spokane (WHL), Anaheim, San Diego (IHL)
	Patrik Carnback (LW)	6-0/187	Goteborg, Sweden	2-1-68	2	Anaheim
	Bob Corkum (C/RW)	6-2/212	Salisbury, Mass.	12-18-67	4	Anaheim
16	Peter Douris (RW)	6-1/195	Toronto	2-19-66	8	Anaheim
	Dean Ewen (LW)	6-2/225	St. Albert, Alta.	2-28-69	0	San Diego (IHL)
36	Todd Ewen (RW)	6-2/220	Saskatoon, Sask.	3-22-66	8	Anaheim
	Stu Grimson (LW)	6-5/227	Kamloops, B.C.	5-20-65	6	Anaheim
	Paul Kariya (LW)	5-11/157	Vancouver, B.C.	10-16-74	0	Canadian national team (Int'l), Canadian Olympic Team (Int'l), Univ. of Maine (Hockey East)
	Valeri Karpov (LW/RW)	5-10/176	Chelyabinsk, U.S.S.R.	8-5-71	0	Traktor Chelyabinsk (CIS), Russian Olympic team (Int'l)
	Steven King (RW)	6-0/195	East Greenwich, R.I.	7-22-69	2	Anaheim
	Stephan Lebeau (C)	5-10/173	Sherbrooke, Que.	2-28-68	6	Montreal, Anaheim
48	John Lilley (RW)	5-0/170	Wakefield, Mass.	8-3-72	1	U.S. national team (Int'l), U.S. Olympic Team (Int'l), San Diego (IHL), Anaheim
	Mike Maneluk (LW)	5-11/188	Winnipeg, Man.	10-1-73	0	Brandon (WHL), San Diego (IHL)
	Steve Rucchin (C)	6-3/210	London, Ont.	7-4-71	0	U. of Western Ontario (OUAA)
24	Joe Sacco (LW)	6-1/195	Medford, Mass.	2-4-69	4	Anaheim
	Anatoli Semenov (C/LW)	6-2/190	Moscow, U.S.S.R.	3-5-62	5	Anaheim
41	Tim Sweeney (C)	5-11/185	Boston	4-12-67	4	Anaheim
	Jim Thomson (RW)	6-1/220	Edmonton, Alta.	12-30-65	7	Anaheim
	Garry Valk (LW/RW)	6-1/205	Edmonton, Alta.	11-27-67	4	Anaheim
	Shaun Van Allen (C)	6-1/200	Shaunavon, Sask.	8-29-67	3	Anaheim
	Terry Yake (RW)	5-11/175	New Westminster, B.C.	10-22-68	6	Anaheim
	DEFENSEMEN					
	Robert Dirk	6-4/218	Regina, Sask.	8-20-66	7	Vancouver, Chicago
38	Bobby Dollas	6-2/212	Montreal	1-31-65	9	Anaheim
45	Anatoli Fedotov	5-11/178	Saratov, U.S.S.R.	5-11-66	2	San Diego (IHL), Anaheim
	Mark Ferner	6-0/193	Regina, Sask.	9-5-65	5	Anaheim
	Bill Houlder	6-3/218	Thunder Bay, Ont.	3-11-67	7	Anaheim
	Tom Kurvers	6-1/197	Minneapolis	9-14-62	10	New York Islanders
	Randy Ladouceur	6-2/220	Brockville, Ont.	6-30-60	12	Anaheim
	Don McSween	5-11/197	Detroit	6-9-64	3	San Diego (IHL), Anaheim
	Myles O'Connor	5-11/190	Calgary, Alta.	4-2-67	4	Anaheim, San Diego (IHL)
	Nikolai Tsulygan	6-3/196	Ufa, U.S.S.R.	5-29-75	0	Salavat (CIS)
	Oleg Tverdovsky	6-0/183	Donetsk, U.S.S.R.	5-18-76	0	Soviet Wings (CIS)
3	David Williams	6-2/195	Plainfield, N.J.	8-25-67	3	San Diego (IHL), Anaheim
	GOALTENDERS					
	Guy Hebert	5-11/185	Troy, N.Y.	1-7-67	3	Anaheim
	Mikhail Shtalenkov	6-2/180	Moscow, U.S.S.R.	10-20-65	1	San Diego (IHL), Anaheim
	John Tanner	6-3/182	Cambridge, Ont.	3-17-71	3	Cornwall (AHL), San Diego (IHL)

1993-94 REVIEW

INDIVIDUAL STATISTICS

SCORING

	Games	G	A	Pts.	PIM	+/-	PPG	SHG	Shots	Shooting Pct.
Terry Yake	82	21	31	52	44	2	5	0	188	11.2
Bob Corkum	76	23	28	51	18	4	3	3	180	12.8
Garry Valk	78	18	27	45	100	8	4	1	165	10.9
Tim Sweeney	78	16	27	43	49	3	6	1	114	14.0
Bill Houlder	80	14	25	39	40	-18	3	0	187	7.5
Joe Sacco	84	19	18	37	61	-11	3	1	206	9.2
Peter Douris	74	12	22	34	21	-5	1	0	142	8.5
Shaun Van Allen	80	8	25	33	64	0	2	2	104	7.7
Anatoli Semenov	49	11	19	30	12	-4	4	0	103	10.7
Sean Hill	68	7	20	27	78	-12	2	1	165	4.2
Patrik Carnback	73	12	11	23	54	-8	3	0	81	14.8
Alexei Kasatonov*	55	4	18	22	43	-8	1	0	81	4.9
Bobby Dollas	77	9	11	20	55	20	1	0	121	7.4
David Williams	56	5	15	20	42	8	2	0	74	6.8
Troy Loney	62	13	6	19	88	-5	6	0	93	14.0
Todd Ewen	76	9	9	18	272	-7	0	0	59	15.3
Don McSween	32	3	9	12	39	4	1	0	43	7.0
Steven King	36	8	3	11	44	-7	3	0	50	16.0

	Games	G	A	Pts.	PIM	+/-	PPG	SHG	Shots	Shooting Pct.
Stephan Lebeau*	22	6	4	10	14	-5	2	0	37	16.2
Randy Ladouceur	81	1	9	10	74	7	0	0	66	1.5
Jarrod Skalde	20	5	4	9	10	-3	2	0	25	20.0
Mark Ferner	50	3	5	8	30	-16	0	0	44	6.8
John Lilley	13	1	6	7	8	1	0	0	20	5.0
Stu Grimson	77	1	5	6	199	-6	0	0	34	2.9
Myles O'Connor	5	0	1	1	6	0	0	0	7	0.0
Robin Bawa	12	0	1	1	7	-3	0	0	1	0.0
Scott McKay	1	0	0	0	0	0	0	0	1	0.0
Maxim Bets	3	0	0	0	0	-3	0	0	1	0.0
Anatoli Fedotov	3	0	0	0	0	-1	0	0	1	0.0
Lonnie Loach	3	0	0	0	2	-2	0	0	8	0.0
Jim Thomson	6	0	0	0	5	0	0	0	1	0.0
Mikhail Shtalenkov (goalie)	10	0	0	0	0	0	0	0	0	0.0
Ron Tugnutt* (goalie)	28	0	0	0	2	0	0	0	0	0.0
Guy Hebert (goalie)	52	0	0	0	2	0	0	0	0	0.0

GOALTENDING

	Games	Min.	Goals	SO	Avg.	W	L	T	Shots	Sv. Pct.
Mikhail Shtalenkov	10	543	24	0	2.65	3	4	1	265	.909
Guy Hebert	52	2991	141	2	2.83	20	27	3	1513	.907
Ron Tugnutt*	28	1520	76	1	3.00	10	15	1	828	.908

Empty-net goals (do not count against a goaltender's average): Hebert 5, Tugnutt 4, Shtalenkov 1.
*Played with two or more NHL teams.

RESULTS

OCTOBER

8—Detroit	L		2-7
10—N.Y. Islanders	L		*3-4
13—Edmonton	W		4-3
15—Boston	T		*1-1
17—Calgary	T		*2-2
19—At N.Y. Rangers	W		4-2
20—At New Jersey	L		0-4
23—At Montreal	L		1-4
25—At Ottawa	L		1-4
28—At San Jose	L		3-4
29—Washington	L		2-5
31—San Jose	L		*1-2

NOVEMBER

3—Dallas	W		5-4
5—New Jersey	L		3-6
7—Pittsburgh	L		4-5
9—Dallas†	W		4-2
11—At Calgary	L		4-5
14—At Vancouver	L		2-3
17—Toronto	L		3-4
19—At Vancouver	W		6-3
21—At Edmonton	W		4-2
22—At Calgary	W		2-1
24—At Winnipeg	W		2-1
26—San Jose	L		3-4
27—At San Jose	L		0-1

DECEMBER

1—Winnipeg	W		5-2
2—At Los Angeles	L		2-3
5—Tampa Bay	L		2-4
7—Florida	L		2-3

12—St. Louis	W	*2-1
14—At Detroit	L	2-5
15—At Toronto	W	1-0
17—At Dallas	W	3-2
19—At Chicago	L	0-2
20—At Winnipeg	W	7-5
22—Dallas	L	*2-3
26—Los Angeles	L	2-3
28—At N.Y. Islanders	W	3-0
30—At Washington	L	0-3

JANUARY

1—At Florida	L	2-4
2—Tampa Bay‡	W	4-1
6—At Chicago	W	6-2
8—At St. Louis	W	5-3
10—Detroit	L	4-6
12—San Jose	L	2-5
14—Hartford	W	6-3
16—Vancouver	L	3-4
18—At Toronto	T	*3-3
19—At Detroit	T	*4-4
24—St. Louis	L	*2-3
26—Winnipeg	W	3-1
28—N.Y. Rangers	W	3-2
29—At Los Angeles	L	1-5

FEBRUARY

2—Calgary	L	2-4
4—Vancouver	W	3-0
6—Chicago	L	2-3
11—Los Angeles	L	3-5
13—At Edmonton	W	6-3
16—Philadelphia	W	6-3

18—Quebec	L	0-1
20—At St. Louis	L	1-4
23—At Buffalo	L	2-4
24—At Pittsburgh	T	*2-2
26—At Quebec	W	6-3

MARCH

2—Montreal	L	2-5
4—Edmonton	W	4-1
6—At San Jose	L	0-6
8—Chicago†	L	0-3
9—Buffalo	L	0-3
11—Chicago	L	2-3
13—Ottawa	W	5-1
16—Los Angeles	W	5-2
22—At Dallas	L	3-4
24—At Boston	L	3-5
26—At Hartford	W	3-2
27—At Philadelphia	W	*3-2
30—At Los Angeles	W	5-2
31—Edmonton	L	*2-3

APRIL

2—Toronto	W	3-1
6—At Calgary	L	2-4
8—At Edmonton	W	3-1
9—At Vancouver	W	3-1
11—Calgary	L	0-3
13—Vancouver	L	1-2

*Denotes overtime game.
†At Phoenix.
‡At Orlando, Fla.

BOSTON BRUINS
EASTERN CONFERENCE/NORTHEAST DIVISION

1994-95 SCHEDULE

☐ Home games shaded.
* — All-Star Game at San Jose Arena.
† — At Minneapolis.
∆ — At Hamilton, Ont.
D — Day game.

OCTOBER

SUN	MON	TUE	WED	THU	FRI	SAT
						1 MON
2	3 OTT	4	5	6 QUE	7	8 TOR
9	10 D FLA	11	12 SJ	13	14 ANA	15 LA
16	17	18	19 VAN	20	21 EDM	22 CAL
23	24	25	26	27 MON	28	29 BUF
30	31					

NOVEMBER

SUN	MON	TUE	WED	THU	FRI	SAT
		1	2	3 PIT	4	5 CHI
6	7 OTT	8	9	10 QUE	11	12 D NJ
13 FLA	14	15	16	17 STL	18	19 WAS
20	21 PIT	22	23 BUF	24	25 D ANA	26
27 VAN	28	29 NYI	30			

DECEMBER

SUN	MON	TUE	WED	THU	FRI	SAT
				1 HAR	2	3 PIT
4 HAR	5	6 DET	7	8 EDM	9	10 CAL
11	12	13	14 MON	15	16 WAS	17 BUF
18	19	20	21 NYR	22 DAL	23	24
25	26 D WIN	27	28	29 WIN	30	31 TOR

JANUARY

SUN	MON	TUE	WED	THU	FRI	SAT
1	2 TB	3 D	4	5 PHI	6	7 DET
8	9	10	11 OTT	12 WIN	13	14 QUE
15	16 D WAS	17	18 PIT	19	20	21*
22	23	24	25 NYR	26 NJ	27	28 PHI
29	30 FLA	31				

FEBRUARY

SUN	MON	TUE	WED	THU	FRI	SAT
			1	2 OTT	3	4 D NYI
5	6	7 NYR	8	9 SJ	10	11 D LA
12 BUF	13	14	15 DAL	16	17 TB	18
19 FLA	20	21	22 HAR	23	24	25 QUE
26	27	28 QUE				

MARCH

SUN	MON	TUE	WED	THU	FRI	SAT
			1	2 NJ	3	4 D OTT
5 HAR	6	7	8	9† TB	10	11
12 D WAS	13	14∆ BUF	15	16 MON	17	18 D BUF
19 NJ	20	21	22 MON	23	24 TB	25
26 STL	27	28 NYI	29	30 PIT	31	

APRIL

SUN	MON	TUE	WED	THU	FRI	SAT
						1 D NYR
2 PHI	3 D	4 PHI	5	6 NYI	7	8 D TB
9 D CHI	10	11	12	13	14	15

1994-95 SEASON

CLUB DIRECTORY

Owner and governor
Jeremy M. Jacobs
Alternative governor
Louis Jacobs
Alternate governor, president and G.M.
Harry Sinden
Vice president
Tom Johnson
Assistant to the president
Nate Greenberg
Director of administration
Dale Hamilton
Coach
Brian Sutter
Assistant coach
Tom McVie
**Coord. of minor league player personnel/
scouting**
Bob Tindall
Director of player evaluation
Bart Bradley

Scouting staff
Jim Morrison
Andre Lachapelle
Joe Lyons
Don Saatzer
Gordie Clark
Lars Waldner
Marcel Pelletier
Jean Ratelle
Harvey Keck
Sven-Ake Svensson
Controller
Bob Vogel
Trainer
Don DelNegro
Assistant trainer
Mike Murphy
Equipment manager
Ken Fleger
Director of media relations
Heidi Holland

DRAFT CHOICES

Rd.—Player	H/W	Overall	Pos.	Last team
1—Evgeni Ryabchikov...	5-11/167	21	G	Molot Perm, CIS
2—Daniel Goneau............	6-0/184	47	LW	Laval (QMJHL)
4—Eric Nickulas............	5-11/190	99	C	Cushing Academy (Mass.)
5—Darren Wright..........	6-1/182	125	D	Prince Albert (WHL)
6—Andre Roy	6-3/178	151	LW	Chicoutimi (QMJHL)
7—Jeremy Schaefer.......	6-3/195	177	LW	Medicine Hat (WHL)
9—John Grahame.........	6-2/195	229	G	Sioux City (Jr. A)
10—Heil Savary...............	6-0/169	255	G	Hull (QMJHL)
11—Andrei Yakhanov......	5-11/187	281	D	Salavat Yulayev Ufa, CIS

MISCELLANEOUS DATA

Home ice (capacity)
Boston Garden (14,448)
Address
150 Causeway Street
Boston, MA 02114
Business phone
617-557-1351

Rink dimensions
191 feet by 83 feet
Club colors
Gold, black and white

TRAINING CAMP ROSTER

No.	FORWARDS	Ht./Wt.	Place	Date	NHL exp.	1993-94 clubs
	Clayton Beddoes (C)	5-10/180	Bentley, Alta.	11-10-70	0	Lake Superior State (CCHA)
19	Mariusz Czerkawski	5-11/185	Radomski, Poland	4-13-72	1	Boston
21	Ted Donato (C)	5-10/170	Dedham, Mass.	4-28-68	3	Boston
23	Steve Heinze (RW)	5-11/180	Lawrence, Mass.	1-30-70	3	Boston
42	Brent Hughes (LW)	5-11/180	New Westminster, B.C.	4-5-66	5	Providence (AHL), Boston
48	Fred Knipscheer (C)	5-11/185	Ft. Wayne, Ind.	9-3-69	1	Boston, Providence (AHL)
27	Steve Leach (RW)	5-11/200	Cambridge, Mass.	1-16-66	9	Boston
	Mikko Makela (LW)	6-2/200	Tampere, Finland	2-28-65	6	Finland Olympic Team (Int'l)
17	Daniel Marois (RW)	6-0/190	Montreal	10-3-68	7	Boston, Providence (AHL)
9	Jon Morris (C)	6-0/175	Lowell, Mass.	5-6-66	6	Kansas City (IHL), Providence (AHL), Boston
44	Glen Murray (RW)	6-2/200	Halifax, N.S.	11-1-72	3	Boston
8	Cam Neely (RW)	6-1/210	Comox, B.C.	6-6-65	11	Boston
12	Adam Oates (C)	5-11/190	Weston, Ont.	8-27-62	9	Boston
13	Grigori Panteleev	5-9/194	Riga, U.S.S.R.	11-13-72	2	Providence (AHL), Boston
	Marc Potvin (RW)	6-1/215	Ottawa	1-29-67	4	Los Angeles, Hartford
17	David Reid (LW)	6-1/205	Toronto	5-15-64	11	Boston
20	Bryan Smolinski (C)	6-0/185	Toledo, O.	12-27-71	2	Boston
	Cam Stewart (C)	5-10/188	Kitchener, Ont.	9-18-71	1	Boston, Providence (AHL)
22	Jozef Stumpel (LW)	6-1/190	Nitra, Czechoslovakia	6-20-72	3	Boston, Providence (AHL)
11	Sergei Zholtok (LW)	6-0/185	Riga, U.S.S.R.	12-2-72	2	Providence (AHL), Boston
	DEFENSEMEN					
77	Ray Bourque	5-11/210	Montreal	12-28-60	15	Boston
6	Glen Featherstone	6-4/215	Toronto	7-8-68	6	Boston
29	John Gruden	6-0/180	Hastings, Minn.	4-6-70	1	Ferris State (CCHA), Boston
34	Al Iafrate	6-3/220	Dearborn, Mich.	3-21-66	10	Washington, Boston
	Alexei Kasatonov	6-1/215	Leningrad, U.S.S.R.	10-14-59	5	Anaheim, St. Louis
14	Gord Roberts	6-1/195	Detroit	10-2-57	15	Boston
	Jon Rohloff	6-0/200	Mankato, Minn.	10-3-69	0	Providence (AHL)
	Andrei Sapozhnikov	6-1/185	Chelyabinsk, U.S.S.R.	6-15-71	0	Traktor Chelyabinsk (CIS)
34	David Shaw	6-2/204	St. Thomas, Ont.	5-25-64	12	Boston
23	Paul Stanton	6-1/200	Boston	6-22-67	4	Boston
32	Don Sweeney	5-11/170	St. Stephen, N.B.	8-17-66	6	Boston
26	Glen Wesley	6-1/195	Red Deer, Alta.	10-2-68	7	Boston
	GOALTENDERS					
39	John Blue	5-10/185	Huntington Beach, Calif.	2-9-66	2	Boston, Providence (AHL)
	Blaine Lacher	6-1/205	Medicine Hat, Alta.	9-5-70	0	Lake Superior State (CCHA)
37	Vince Riendeau	5-10/185	St. Hyacinthe, Que.	4-20-66	7	Detroit, Adirondack (AHL), Boston
	Yevgeni Ryabchikov	5-11/167	Yaroslavl, U.S.S.R.	1-16-74	0	Molot Perm (CIS)

1993-94 REVIEW

INDIVIDUAL STATISTICS

SCORING

	Games	G	A	Pts.	PIM	+/-	PPG	SHG	Shots	Shooting Pct.
Adam Oates	77	32	80	112	45	10	16	2	197	16.2
Ray Bourque	72	20	71	91	58	26	10	3	386	5.2
Cam Neely	49	50	24	74	54	12	20	0	185	†27.0
Joe Juneau*	63	14	58	72	35	11	4	0	142	9.9
Glen Wesley	81	14	44	58	64	1	6	1	265	5.3
Ted Donato	84	22	32	54	59	0	9	2	158	13.9
Bryan Smolinski	83	31	20	51	82	4	4	3	179	17.3
Glen Murray	81	18	13	31	48	-1	0	0	114	15.8
Brent Hughes	77	13	11	24	143	10	1	0	100	13.0
Jozef Stumpel	59	8	15	23	14	4	0	0	62	12.9
Dave Reid	83	6	17	23	25	10	0	2	145	4.1
Stephen Heinze	77	10	11	21	32	-2	0	2	183	5.5
Don Sweeney	75	6	15	21	50	29	1	2	136	4.4
Dmitri Kvartalnov	39	12	7	19	10	-9	4	0	68	17.6
Stephen Leach	42	5	10	15	74	-10	1	0	89	5.6
Al Iafrate*	12	5	8	13	20	6	2	0	47	10.6
Dan Marois	22	7	3	10	18	-4	3	0	32	21.9
Paul Stanton	71	3	7	10	54	-7	1	0	136	2.2
David Shaw	55	1	9	10	85	-11	0	0	107	0.9
Cameron Stewart	57	3	6	9	66	-6	0	0	55	5.5
Glen Featherstone	58	1	8	9	152	-5	0	0	55	1.8
Gordie Roberts	59	1	6	7	40	-13	0	0	19	5.3

	Games	G	A	Pts.	PIM	+/-	PPG	SHG	Shots	Shooting Pct.
Fred Knipscheer	11	3	2	5	14	3	0	0	15	20.0
Mariusz Czerkawski	4	2	1	3	0	-2	1	0	11	18.2
Sergei Zholtok	24	2	1	3	2	-7	1	0	25	8.0
Jon Casey (goalie)	57	0	2	2	14	0	0	0	0	0.0
Darren Banks	4	0	1	1	9	0	0	0	3	0.0
John Gruden	7	0	1	1	2	-3	0	0	8	0.0
Vincent Riendeau* (goalie)	18	0	1	1	0	0	0	0	0	0.0
Andrew McKim	29	0	1	1	4	-10	0	0	22	0.0
Jamie Huscroft	36	0	1	1	144	-2	0	0	13	0.0
Mikhail Tatarinov	2	0	0	0	2	0	0	0	4	0.0
Jon Morris	4	0	0	0	0	-2	0	0	3	0.0
Jim Wiemer	4	0	0	0	2	-3	0	0	8	0.0
Grigori Panteleev	10	0	0	0	0	-2	0	0	8	0.0
John Blue (goalie)	18	0	0	0	7	0	0	0	0	0.0

GOALTENDING

	Games	Min.	Goals	SO	Avg.	W	L	T	Shots	Sv. Pct.
Jon Casey	57	3192	153	4	2.88	30	15	9	1289	.881
John Blue	18	944	47	0	2.99	5	8	3	407	.885
Vincent Riendeau*	18	976	50	1	3.07	7	6	1	415	.880

Empty-net goals (do not count against a goaltender's average): Blue 1, Casey 1.
*Played with two or more NHL teams.
†Led league.

RESULTS

OCTOBER

5—At N.Y. Rangers	W	4-3
7—Buffalo	L	3-5
9—Quebec	W	7-3
11—Montreal	T	*1-1
15—At Anaheim	T	*1-1
16—At San Jose	T	*1-1
19—At Vancouver	L	4-5
22—At Edmonton	W	3-1
23—At Calgary	T	*3-3
28—Ottawa	W	6-2
30—St. Louis	L	1-2

NOVEMBER

2—At Detroit	L	1-6
4—Calgary	W	6-3
6—Tampa Bay	T	*1-1
7—At Buffalo	W	4-3
8—Edmonton	W	5-1
13—At N.Y. Islanders	W	5-2
17—At Hartford	W	4-2
18—San Jose	W	3-1
20—Philadelphia	T	*5-5
24—At Pittsburgh	L	3-7
26—Florida	W	3-2
27—At Toronto	L	2-4
30—At Quebec	W	5-2

DECEMBER

2—N.Y. Islanders	W	7-3
4—Montreal	L	1-8
5—At Buffalo	L	1-3
9—Vancouver	L	*2-3
11—Chicago	L	4-5

12—Hartford	T	*2-2
15—At New Jersey	W	5-4
18—At Tampa Bay	W	5-3
19—At Florida	W	*2-1
23—Pittsburgh	L	3-4
27—At Ottawa	W	5-3
31—Philadelphia†	L	3-4

JANUARY

2—Washington	W	8-2
6—Winnipeg	W	5-4
8—Florida	T	*2-2
10—Toronto	L	0-3
11—At Pittsburgh	L	*4-5
13—At Philadelphia	L	2-6
15—Detroit	L	2-3
17—Hartford	W	5-3
19—At Montreal	T	*3-3
24—At Hartford	W	2-1
25—At Washington	W	3-1
28—At N.Y. Islanders	W	3-0
29—N.Y. Islanders	W	2-1
31—Quebec	W	4-3

FEBRUARY

3—N.Y. Rangers	L	0-3
5—Philadelphia	W	4-0
6—At Florida	L	0-3
8—At Quebec	W	6-1
10—Buffalo	T	*3-3
12—New Jersey	W	5-3
14—At Los Angeles	W	*3-2
16—At Dallas	W	3-0
18—At St. Louis	L	1-3

20—At Tampa Bay	T	*2-2
23—At N.Y. Rangers	W	6-3
25—At Winnipeg	W	7-6
27—At Chicago	W	4-0

MARCH

3—Los Angeles	W	6-4
5—Ottawa	W	6-1
7—Washington	W	6-3
8—At Pittsburgh	L	3-7
10—N.Y. Rangers	T	*2-2
12—At New Jersey	L	1-2
14—At Montreal	L	4-5
17—Pittsburgh	L	2-4
19—New Jersey	L	6-8
22—At Quebec	L	3-5
24—Anaheim	W	5-3
26—Montreal	W	6-3
27—At Washington	W	6-4
31—Dallas	T	*2-2

APRIL

1—At Buffalo	L	0-5
3—Pittsburgh‡	L	2-6
7—Ottawa	W	5-4
9—Tampa Bay	L	0-3
10—At Philadelphia	L	4-3
13—At Ottawa	W	8-0
14—Hartford	L	2-3

*Denotes overtime game.
†At Minneapolis.
‡At Cleveland.

BUFFALO SABRES
EASTERN CONFERENCE/NORTHEAST DIVISION

1994-95 SCHEDULE

- ☐ Home games shaded.
- * — All-Star Game at San Jose Arena.
- † — At Minneapolis.
- ∆ — At Hamilton, Ont.
- D — Day game.

OCTOBER

SUN	MON	TUE	WED	THU	FRI	SAT
						1 QUE
2	3	4	5 PIT	6	7 MON	8 MON
9	10 TOR	11	12 DET	13	14 HAR	15 WAS
16	17	18	19	20	21 FLA	22
23 QUE	24	25	26	27 FLA	28	29 BOS
30	31					

NOVEMBER

SUN	MON	TUE	WED	THU	FRI	SAT
		1	2 CHI	3	4 PHI	5 PHI
6	7	8 TB	9	10 OTT	11	12 SJ
13	14	15 ANA	16	17 LA	18	19
20	21 DAL	22	23 BOS	24	25 VAN	26
27 NYI	28	29	30 NYR			

DECEMBER

SUN	MON	TUE	WED	THU	FRI	SAT
				1	2 LA	3 NYI
4	5	6	7 PIT	8	9 HAR	10 PIT
11	12	13	14 TB	15	16 MON	17 BOS
18	19 OTT	20	21 MON	22	23 HAR	24
25	26 NJ	27 NJ	28	29 PIT	30	31 PHI

JANUARY

SUN	MON	TUE	WED	THU	FRI	SAT
1	2	3	4	5	6 ANA	7 HAR
8	9 NYI	10	11 WAS	12	13 CAL	14
15 EDM	16	17	18 VAN	19	20	21*
22	23 OTT	24	25 NJ	26	27 QUE	28 OTT
29	30	31				

FEBRUARY

SUN	MON	TUE	WED	THU	FRI	SAT
			1	2 NJ	3	4 PHI
5	6	7 DAL	8	9 FLA	10	11 TOR
12 BOS	13	14	15 NYR	16	17 FLA	18 TB
19	20 WIN	21	22 NYI	23	24	25 HAR
26 NYR	27	28 SJ				

MARCH

SUN	MON	TUE	WED	THU	FRI	SAT
			1	2 CHI	3	4 QUE
5 CAL	6	7	8 NYR	9	10 WIN	11
12 STL	13	14∆ BOS	15	16 DET	17	18 D BOS
19 TB	20 D	21 PIT	22	23	24 QUE	25 MON
26	27	28	29 EDM	30	31	

APRIL

SUN	MON	TUE	WED	THU	FRI	SAT
					1 NYI	1 D
2 OTT	3	4 STL	5	6	7 WAS	8 WAS
9	10	11	12	13	14	15

1994-95 SEASON

CLUB DIRECTORY

Chairman of the board and president
Seymour H. Knox III
Vice chairman of the board and counsel
Robert O. Swados
Vice chairman of the board
Robert E. Rich Jr.
Treasurer
Joseph T.J. Stewart
Assistant to the president
Seymour H. Knox IV
Senior vice president, administration
George Bergantz
V.P. of finance and chief financial officer
Dan DiPofi
Exec. V.P. for sports operations
Gerry Meehan
General manager and coach
John Muckler
Assistant coaches
John Tortorella
Don Lever
Director of player evaluation
Larry Carriere
Director of player personnel
Don Luce
Director of scouting
Rudy Migay

Pro scout
Joe Crozier
Scouting staff
Don Barrie
Jack Bowman
Larry Carriere
Boris Janicek
Dennis McIvor
Paul Merritt
Mike Racicot
Gleb Tchistyakov
Frank Zywiec
Director of communications
Paul Wieland
Director of public relations
Steve Rossi
Public relations assistant
Bruce Wawrzyniak
Media relations assistant
Jeff Holbrook
Head athletic trainer
Jim Pizzutelli
Trainer
Rip Simonick
Equipment supervisor
George Babcock

DRAFT CHOICES

Rd.—Player	H/W	Overall	Pos.	Last team
1—Wayne Primeau	6-3/193	17	C	Owen Sound (OHL)
2—Curtis Brown	6-0/182	43	C	Moose Jaw (WHL)
3—Rumun Ndur	6-2/200	69	D	Guelph (OHL)
5—Sergei Klimentjev	5-11/200	121	D	Medicine Hat (WHL)
6—Cal Benazic	6-3/187	147	D	Medicine Hat (WHL)
7—Steve Plouffe	5-11/167	168	G	Granby (QMJHL)
7—Shane Hnidy	6-1/200	173	D	Prince Albert (WHL)
7—Steve Webb	5-11/205	176	RW	Peterborough (OHL)
8—Bob Westerby	6-1/195	199	LW	Kamloops (WHL)
9—Craig Millar	6-2/198	225	D	Swift Current (WHL)
10—Mark Polak	6-0/178	251	C	Medicine Hat (WHL)
11—Shanye Wright	5-11/189	277	D	Owen Sound (OHL)

MISCELLANEOUS DATA

Home ice (capacity)
Memorial Auditorium
(16,284, including standees)
Address
Memorial Auditorium
140 Main St.
Buffalo, NY 14202

Business phone
716-856-7300 or 800-333-7825
Rink dimensions
193 feet by 84 feet
Club colors
Blue, white and gold

TRAINING CAMP ROSTER

		BORN		NHL	
No. FORWARDS	Ht./Wt.	Place	Date	exp.	1993-94 clubs
28 Donald Audette (RW)....	5-8/175	Laval, Que.	9-23-69	5	Buffalo
36 Matthew Barnaby (LW)	6-0/170	Ottawa	5-4-73	2	Buffalo, Rochester (AHL)
Jason Dawe (RW)	5-10/195	North York, Ont.	5-29-73	1	Rochester (AHL), Buffalo
9 Viktor Gordiouk (RW) ...	5-10/176	Moscow, U.S.S.R.	4-11-70	1	Rochester (AHL)
14 Dave Hannan (C)......	5-10/185	Sudbury, Ont.	11-26-61	13	Buffalo
10 Dale Hawerchuk (C)......	5-11/190	Toronto	4-4-63	13	Buffalo
13 Yuri Khmylev (LW)	6-1/189	Moscow, U.S.S.R.	8-9-64	2	Buffalo
16 Pat LaFontaine (C)	5-10/177	St. Louis	2-22-65	11	Buffalo
44 Doug MacDonald (LW) .	6-0/192	Port Moody, B.C.	2-8-69	2	Rochester (AHL), Buffalo
27 Brad May (LW)	6-0/200	Toronto	11-29-71	3	Buffalo
89 Alexander Mogilny (RW).	5-11/187	Khabarovsk, U.S.S.R.	2-18-69	5	Buffalo
Sergei Petrenko (LW) ...	5-11/167	Kharkov, U.S.S.R.	9-10-68	1	Buffalo, Rochester (AHL)
Derek Plante (C)...........	5-11/160	Cloquet, Minn.	1-17-71	1	U.S. national team (Int'l), Buffalo
Wayne Presley (RW).....	5-11/180	Dearborn, Mich.	3-23-65	10	Buffalo
Wayne Primeau (C)........	6-3/193	Scarborough, Ont.	6-4-76	0	Owen Sound (OHL)
32 Rob Ray (LW)	6-0/203	Stirling, Ont.	6-8-68	5	Buffalo
Brad Rubachuk (C)	5-11/180	Winnipeg, Man.	6-11-70	0	Buffalo
17 Todd Simon (C)	5-10/188	Toronto	4-21-72	1	Rochester (AHL), Buffalo
Craig Simpson (LW)	6-2/195	London, Ont.	2-15-67	9	Buffalo
20 Bob Sweeney (C)	6-3/200	Boxborough, Mass.	1-25-64	8	Buffalo
21 Scott Thomas (RW)	6-2/195	Buffalo, N.Y.	1-18-70	2	Buffalo
19 Randy Wood (LW)........	6-0/195	Princeton, N.J.	10-12-63	8	Buffalo
Jason Young (LW)	5-10/197	Sudbury, Ont.	12-16-72	0	Rochester (AHL)
DEFENSEMEN					
Mark Astley	5-11/185	Calgary, Alta.	3-30-69	1	Canadian national team (Int'l), Canadian Olympic Team (Int'l), Buffalo
8 Doug Bodger...............	6-2/213	Chemainus, B.C.	6-18-66	10	Buffalo
4 Philippe Boucher	6-2/188	St. Apollnaire, Que.	3-24-73	2	Buffalo, Rochester (AHL)
David Cooper	6-1/190	Ottawa	11-2-73	0	Rochester (AHL)
Doug Houda	6-2/190	Blairmore, Alta.	6-3-66	8	Hartford, Los Angeles
Dean Melanson..............	6-0/213	Antigonish, N.S.	11-19-73	0	Rochester (AHL)
Craig Muni..................	6-3/200	Toronto	7-19-62	12	Chicago, Buffalo
42 Richard Smehlik	6-3/208	Ostrava, Czechoslovakia	1-23-70	2	Buffalo
41 Ken Sutton	6-0/198	Edmonton, Alta.	5-11-69	4	Buffalo
7 Petr Svoboda	6-1/175	Most, Czechoslovakia	2-14-66	10	Buffalo
Denis Tsygurov	6-3/198	Chelyabinsk, U.S.S.R.	2-26-71	1	Buffalo, Rochester (AHL)
GOALTENDERS					
31 Grant Fuhr	5-9/190	Spruce Grove, Alta.	9-28-62	13	Buffalo, Rochester (AHL)
39 Dominik Hasek	5-11/168	Pardubice, Czech.	1-29-65	4	Buffalo
Markus Ketterer............	5-11/169	Helsinki, Finland	8-23-67	0	Rochester (AHL)

1993-94 REVIEW

INDIVIDUAL STATISTICS

SCORING

	Games	G	A	Pts.	PIM	+/-	PPG	SHG	Shots	Shooting Pct.
Dale Hawerchuk	81	35	51	86	91	10	13	1	227	15.4
Alexander Mogilny	66	32	47	79	22	8	17	0	258	12.4
Donald Audette	77	29	30	59	41	2	16	1	207	14.0
Yuri Khmylev	72	27	31	58	49	13	11	0	171	15.8
Derek Plante	77	21	35	56	24	4	8	1	147	14.3
Brad May	84	18	27	45	171	-6	3	0	166	10.8
Richard Smehlik	84	14	27	41	69	22	3	3	106	13.2
Doug Bodger	75	7	32	39	76	8	5	1	144	4.9
Randy Wood	84	22	16	38	71	11	2	2	161	13.7
Wayne Presley	65	17	8	25	103	18	1	5	93	18.3
Bob Sweeney	60	11	14	25	94	3	3	3	76	14.5
Ken Sutton	78	4	20	24	71	-6	1	0	95	4.2
Dave Hannan	83	6	15	21	53	10	0	3	40	15.0
Pat LaFontaine	16	5	13	18	2	-4	1	0	40	12.5
Craig Simpson	22	8	8	16	8	-3	2	0	28	28.6
Petr Svoboda	60	2	14	16	89	11	1	0	80	2.5
Philippe Boucher	38	6	8	14	29	-1	4	0	67	9.0
Jason Dawe	32	6	7	13	12	1	3	0	35	17.1
Randy Moller.....................	78	2	11	13	154	-5	0	0	77	2.6
Craig Muni*	73	2	8	10	62	28	0	1	39	5.1
Rob Ray...........................	82	3	4	7	274	2	0	0	34	8.8
Matthew Barnaby................	35	2	4	6	106	-7	1	0	13	15.4

	Games	G	A	Pts.	PIM	+/-	PPG	SHG	Shots	Shooting Pct.
Scott Thomas	32	2	2	4	8	-6	1	0	26	7.7
Keith Carney*	7	1	3	4	4	-1	0	0	6	16.7
Sergei Petrenko	14	0	4	4	0	-3	0	0	7	0.0
Grant Fuhr (goalie)	32	0	4	4	16	0	0	0	0	0.0
Dominik Hasek (goalie)	58	0	3	3	6	0	0	0	0	0.0
Todd Simon	15	0	1	1	0	-3	0	0	14	0.0
Mark Astley	1	0	0	0	0	-1	0	0	2	0.0
James Black*	2	0	0	0	0	0	0	0	2	0.0
Doug MacDonald	4	0	0	0	0	-2	0	0	3	0.0
Gord Donnelly*	7	0	0	0	31	1	0	0	2	0.0
Denis Tsygurov	8	0	0	0	8	-1	0	0	3	0.0

GOALTENDING

	Games	Min.	Goals	SO	Avg.	W	L	T	Shots	Sv. Pct.
Dominik Hasek	58	3358	109	‡7	†1.95	30	20	6	1552	†.930
Grant Fuhr	32	1726	106	2	3.68	13	12	3	907	.883

Empty-net goals (do not count against a goaltender's average): Hasek 3.
*Played with two or more NHL teams.
†Led league.
‡Tied for league lead.

RESULTS

OCTOBER
7—At Boston	W	5-3
9—At Montreal	L	4-7
10—Hartford	L	2-3
12—At Philadelphia	L	3-5
15—N.Y. Rangers	L	2-5
16—At Washington	L	3-4
18—Detroit	L	4-6
22—Pittsburgh	L	2-4
23—At Hartford	T	*3-3
27—At Calgary	W	5-3
29—At Edmonton	W	6-3
30—At Vancouver	W	6-3

NOVEMBER
3—Pittsburgh†	L	2-6
7—Boston	L	3-4
10—Philadelphia	L	3-5
13—At Philadelphia	W	7-2
17—At New Jersey	L	0-4
19—Winnipeg	W	6-0
21—San Jose	W	6-5
22—At Ottawa	W	5-2
24—New Jersey	L	3-5
26—Ottawa	W	5-2
27—At Quebec	T	*2-2
29—At Toronto	W	3-0

DECEMBER
1—At Tampa Bay	W	3-0
2—At Florida	L	*1-2
5—Boston	W	3-1
8—At Ottawa	W	3-1
10—Calgary	W	6-2
11—At Hartford	W	3-0
13—At N.Y. Rangers	L	0-2
16—At Pittsburgh	L	1-2
17—Los Angeles	W	2-0
19—Tampa Bay	T	*3-3
23—Montreal	W	5-0
26—At N.Y. Islanders	L	*3-4
27—Philadelphia	L	0-2
31—N.Y. Rangers	W	4-1

JANUARY
2—Toronto	T	*3-3
7—Pittsburgh	L	*3-4
9—Vancouver	W	5-3
11—At Chicago	W	5-2
12—At Winnipeg	L	2-3
15—At St. Louis	L	1-2
16—At Dallas	W	4-2
19—Edmonton	T	*1-1
24—Tampa Bay‡	L	0-4
27—Washington	W	7-2
29—At Montreal	W	3-2
30—Florida	L	2-3

FEBRUARY
2—At New Jersey	W	3-2
4—At Florida	W	7-2
6—N.Y. Islanders	W	4-1
8—At N.Y. Islanders	L	1-3
10—At Boston	T	*3-3
11—Montreal	W	5-1
13—Dallas	L	3-5
16—At Hartford	W	5-3
18—Florida	W	4-1

MARCH (left column continued)
20—At Washington	T	*3-3
21—Quebec	W	2-1
23—Anaheim	W	4-2
25—Chicago	L	1-3
26—At Pittsburgh	L	3-4

MARCH
2—At Ottawa	W	7-2
4—Pittsburgh	W	2-1
6—At Detroit	W	3-2
8—At San Jose	T	*4-4
9—At Anaheim	W	3-0
12—At Los Angeles	W	5-3
17—New Jersey	L	1-6
18—N.Y. Islanders§	T	*2-2
20—Ottawa	W	6-2
23—St. Louis	L	2-3
25—Hartford	W	6-3
27—N.Y. Islanders	W	4-1
30—Tampa Bay	L	*2-3

APRIL
1—Boston	W	5-0
2—At Quebec	W	6-2
4—At Quebec	L	4-6
8—Montreal	W	1-0
10—Quebec	W	4-1
12—At N.Y. Rangers	L	2-3
14—Washington	L	2-3

*Denotes overtime game.
†At Sacramento, Calif.
‡At Orlando, Fla.
§At Minneapolis.

CALGARY FLAMES
WESTERN CONFERENCE/PACIFIC DIVISION

1994-95 SCHEDULE

- ☐ Home games shaded.
- * — All-Star Game at San Jose Arena.
- † — At Phoenix.
- D — Day game.

OCTOBER

SUN	MON	TUE	WED	THU	FRI	SAT
						1 VAN
2	3	4 DAL	5	6	7	8 LA
9 ANA	10	11	12 EDM	13	14 SJ	15
16 PHI	17	18 WIN	19	20 ANA	21	22 BOS
23	24 TOR	25	26 NJ	27	28 NYR	29 NYI
30	31					

NOVEMBER

SUN	MON	TUE	WED	THU	FRI	SAT
		1 WAS	2	3	4 EDM	5
6 FLA	7	8 STL	9	10 LA	11	12
13 ANA	14	15 SJ	16	17	18 EDM	19 VAN
20	21	22 LA	23	24 CHI	25	26 EDM
27	28	29	30			

DECEMBER

SUN	MON	TUE	WED	THU	FRI	SAT
				1	2 DET	3
4 OTT	5	6 QUE	7 MON	8	9	10 BOS
11	12 HAR	13	14	15 TOR	16	17
18 NYR	19	20 STL	21	22 ANA	23	24
25	26	27 WIN	28	29 VAN	30	31 MON

JANUARY

SUN	MON	TUE	WED	THU	FRI	SAT
1	2	3 DET	4	5 CHI	6	7 SJ D
8 QUE	9	10 TB	11	12 CHI	13 BUF	14
15	16 LA	17	18 WIN	19	20	21*
22	23 EDM	24	25 TB	26 FLA	27	28 STL
29	30	31				

FEBRUARY

SUN	MON	TUE	WED	THU	FRI	SAT
			1 DET	2	3 HAR	4 TOR
5	6	7	8 ANA	9	10 DAL	11 STL
12	13 ANA	14	15 WIN	16	17	18 DAL
19	20 DAL	21	22† SJ	23	24	25 LA
26	27	28 EDM				

MARCH

SUN	MON	TUE	WED	THU	FRI	SAT
			1	2 PIT	3	4 TOR
5 BUF	6	7 WAS	8	9 PHI	10	11 PIT D
12 CHI D	13	14	15 OTT	16	17 SJ	18
19 NYI	20	21 DET	22	23† NYR	24 NJ	25
26 VAN	27	28	29	30	31 SJ	

APRIL

SUN	MON	TUE	WED	THU	FRI	SAT
						1
2 VAN	D 3	4	5 SJ	6	7 LA	8 VAN
9	10	11	12	13	14	15

1994-95 SEASON

CLUB DIRECTORY

Owners
Harley N. Hotchkiss
Norman L. Kwong
Sonia Scurfield
Byron J. Seaman
Daryl K. Seaman
President and alternate governor
W.C. "Bill" Hay
General manager
Doug Risebrough
Vice president, business and finance
Clare Rhyasen
Director, hockey operations
Al MacNeil
Consultant to president
Leo Ornest
Vice president, marketing
Lanny McDonald
Assistant general manager
Al Coates
Head Coach
Dave King
Assistant coaches
Guy Charron
Jamie Hislop
Slavomir Lener
Goaltending consultant
Glenn Hall

Director of public relations
Rick Skaggs
Assistant public relations director
Mike Burke
Scouts
Ray Clearwater
Jiri Hrdina
Guy Lapointe
Ian McKenzie
Nick Polano
Larry Popein
Scouting staff
Ron Ferguson
Glen Giovanacci
Paul MacIntosh
Anders Steen
Tom Thompson
Jarmo Tolvanen
Ernie Vargus
Controller
Lynne Tosh
Trainer
Jim "Bearcat" Murray
Equipment manager
Bobby Stewart
Physiotherapist
James Gattinger

DRAFT CHOICES

Rd.—Player	H/W	Overall	Pos.	Last team
1—Chris Dingman	6-3/231	19	LW	Brandon (WHL)
2—Dmitri Ryabykin	6-1/183	45	D	Dynamo Moscow, CIS
3—Chris Clark	6-0/190	77	RW	Springfield (Jr. B)
4—Ryan Duthie	5-10/178	91	C	Spokane (WHL)
4—Johan Finnstrom	6-3/205	97	D	Rogle Angelholm, Sweden
5—Nils Ekman	5-11/167	107	RW	Stockholm Hammarby, Swe.
5—Frank Appel	6-4/207	123	D	Dusseldorf, Germany
6—Patrik Haltia	6-1/176	149	G	Farjestad Grums, Sweden
7—Ladislav Kohn	5-10/172	175	RW	Swift Current (WHL)
8—Keith McCambridge	6-2/204	201	D	Swift Current (WHL)
9—Jorgen Jonsson	6-0/183	227	C	Rogle, Sweden
10—Mike Peluso	6-1/205	253	C	Omaha (Jr. A)
11—Pavel Torgayev	6-1/187	279	LW	TPS Turku, CIS

MISCELLANEOUS DATA

Home ice (capacity)
Olympic Saddledome (20,230)
Address
P.O. Box 1540
Station M
Calgary, Alta. T2P 3B9
Business phone
403-261-0475

Rink dimensions
200 feet by 85 feet
Club colors
Red, white and gold

No.	FORWARDS	Ht./Wt.	Place	Date	NHL exp.	1993-94 clubs
	Ryan Duthie (C)	5-10/180	Strathmore, Alta.	9-2-74	0	Spokane (WHL)
	Neil Eisenhut (C)	6-1/190	Osoyoos, B.C.	2-9-67	1	Hamilton (AHL), Vancouver
14	Theo Fleury (C/RW)	5-6/160	Oxbow, Sask.	6-29-68	6	Calgary
	Todd Hlushko (LW)	5-11/185	Toronto	2-7-70	1	Canadian national team (Int'l), Canadian Olympic Team (Int'l), Hershey (AHL), Philadelphia
11	Kelly Kisio (C)	5-10/185	Peace River, Alta.	9-18-59	12	Calgary
12	Paul Kruse (LW)	6-0/202	Merritt, B.C.	3-15-70	4	Calgary
	Jesper Mattsson (C)	6-0/173	Malmo, Sweden	5-13-75	0	Malmo (Sweden)
	Sandy McCarthy (RW)	6-3/225	Toronto	6-15-72	1	Calgary
25	Joe Nieuwendyk (C)	6-1/195	Oshawa, Ont.	9-10-66	8	Calgary
36	Mikael Nylander (C)	5-11/190	Stockholm, Sweden	10-3-72	2	Hartford, Springfield (AHL), Calgary
29	Joel Otto (C)	6-4/220	Elk River, Minn.	10-29-61	10	Calgary
23	Greg Paslawski (RW)	5-11/190	Kindersley, Sask.	8-25-61	11	Calgary, Peoria (IHL)
26	Robert Reichel (C)	5-10/185	Litvinov, Czechoslovakia	6-25-71	4	Calgary
10	Gary Roberts (LW)	6-1/190	North York, Ont.	5-23-66	8	Calgary
22	Ronnie Stern (RW)	6-0/195	Ste. Agatha Des Mont, Que.	1-11-67	7	Calgary
	Cory Stillman (C)	6-0/185	Peterborough, Ont.	12-20-73	0	Saint John (AHL)
33	David Struch (C)	5-10/180	Calgary, Alta.	2-11-71	1	Saint John (AHL), Calgary
32	Mike Sullivan (LW)	6-2/190	Marshfield, Mass.	2-28-68	3	San Jose, Kansas City (IHL), Saint John (AHL), Calgary
13	German Titov (C)	6-0/190	Borovsk, U.S.S.R.	10-16-65	1	Calgary
	Vesa Vitakoski (LW)	6-3/210	Lappeenranta, Finland	2-13-71	1	Calgary, Saint John (AHL)
	Wes Walz (C)	5-10/185	Calgary, Alta.	5-15-70	4	Calgary, Saint John (AHL)
	DEFENSEMEN					
	Steve Chiasson	6-1/205	Barrie, Ont.	4-14-67	8	Detroit
4	Kevin Dahl	5-11/190	Regina, Sask.	12-30-68	2	Calgary, Saint John (AHL)
	Sami Helenius	6-5/220	Helsinki, Finland	1-22-74	0	Reipas Lahti (Finland)
	Phil Housley	5-10/185	St. Paul, Minn.	3-9-64	12	St. Louis
	Roger Johansson	6-3/190	Ljungby, Sweden	4-17-67	3	Leksand (Sweden), Swedish Olympic Team (Int'l)
37	Dan Keczmer	6-1/190	Mt. Clemens, Mich.	5-25-68	4	Hartford, Springfield (AHL), Calgary
	Bobby Marshall	6-1/190	North York, Ontario	4-11-72	0	Miami of Ohio (CCHA)
	Frank Musil	6-3/215	Pardubice, Czechoslovakia	12-17-64	8	Calgary
	James Patrick	6-2/200	Winnipeg, Man.	6-14-63	11	New York Rangers, Hartford, Calgary
18	Trent Yawney	6-3/195	Hudson Bay, Sask.	9-29-65	7	Calgary
3	Zarley Zalapski	6-1/215	Edmonton, Alta.	4-22-68	7	Hartford, Calgary
	GOALTENDERS					
	Trevor Kidd	6-2/190	St. Boniface, Man.	3-29-72	2	Calgary
	Jason Muzzatti	6-1/190	Toronto	2-3-70	1	Calgary, Saint John (AHL)
1	Andrei Trefilov	6-0/180	Moscow, U.S.S.R.	8-31-69	2	Saint John (AHL), Calgary

1993-94 REVIEW

INDIVIDUAL STATISTICS

SCORING

	Games	G	A	Pts.	PIM	+/-	PPG	SHG	Shots	Shooting Pct.
Robert Reichel	84	40	53	93	58	20	14	0	249	16.1
Theoren Fleury	83	40	45	85	186	30	16	1	278	14.4
Gary Roberts	73	41	43	84	145	37	12	3	202	20.3
Al MacInnis	75	28	54	82	95	35	12	1	324	8.6
Joe Nieuwendyk	64	36	39	75	51	19	14	1	191	18.8
German Titov	76	27	18	45	28	20	8	3	153	17.6
Wes Walz	53	11	27	38	16	20	1	0	79	13.9
James Patrick	68	10	25	35	40	-5	5	1	91	11.0
Kelly Kisio	51	7	23	30	28	-6	1	0	62	11.3
Ronnie Stern	71	9	20	29	243	6	0	1	105	8.6
Paul Ranheim*	67	10	14	24	20	-7	0	2	110	9.1
Joel Otto	81	11	12	23	92	-17	3	1	108	10.2
Michel Petit	63	2	21	23	110	5	0	0	103	1.9
Trent Yawney	58	6	15	21	60	21	1	1	62	9.7
Dan Keczmer*	57	1	20	21	48	-2	0	0	104	1.0
Gary Suter*	25	4	9	13	20	-3	2	1	51	7.8
Ted Drury*	34	5	7	12	26	-5	0	1	43	11.6
Chris Dahlquist	77	1	11	12	52	5	0	0	57	1.8

	Games	G	A	Pts.	PIM	+/-	PPG	SHG	Shots	Shooting Pct.
Paul Kruse	68	3	8	11	185	-6	0	0	52	5.8
Michael Nylander*	15	2	9	11	6	10	0	0	21	9.5
Sandy McCarthy	79	5	5	10	173	-3	0	0	39	12.8
Zarley Zalapski*	13	3	7	10	18	0	1	0	35	8.6
Frank Musil	75	1	8	9	50	38	0	0	65	1.5
Brad Schlegel	26	1	6	7	4	-4	0	0	24	4.2
Mike Sullivan*	19	2	3	5	6	2	0	0	27	7.4
James Patrick*	15	2	2	4	6	6	1	0	20	10.0
Trevor Kidd (goalie)	31	0	4	4	4	0	0	0	0	0.0
Vesa Viitakoski	8	1	2	3	0	0	0	1	15	6.7
Leonard Esau	6	0	3	3	7	-1	0	0	4	0.0
Kevin Dahl	33	0	3	3	23	-2	0	0	20	0.0
Greg Paslawski	15	2	0	2	2	-4	0	0	13	15.4
David Haas	2	1	1	2	7	2	0	0	3	33.3
Guy Larose*	7	0	1	1	4	-3	0	0	3	0.0
Brad Miller	8	0	1	1	14	-2	0	0	2	0.0
Lee Norwood	16	0	1	1	16	3	0	0	10	0.0
Jason Muzzatti (goalie)	1	0	0	0	0	0	0	0	0	0.0
Jeff Reese* (goalie)	1	0	0	0	0	0	0	0	0	0.0
Mark Freer	2	0	0	0	4	0	0	0	0	0.0
Peter Ahola	2	0	0	0	0	0	0	0	1	0.0
David Struch	4	0	0	0	4	-2	0	0	3	0.0
Kevin Wortman	5	0	0	0	2	1	0	0	2	0.0
Andrei Trefilov (goalie)	11	0	0	0	4	0	0	0	0	0.0
Mike Vernon (goalie)	48	0	0	0	14	0	0	0	0	0.0

GOALTENDING

	Games	Min.	Goals	SO	Avg.	W	L	T	Shots	Sv. Pct.
Andrei Trefilov	11	623	26	2	2.50	3	4	2	305	.915
Mike Vernon	48	2798	131	3	2.81	26	17	5	1209	.892
Trevor Kidd	31	1614	85	0	3.16	13	7	6	752	.887
Jeff Reese*	1	13	1	0	4.62	0	0	0	5	.800
Jason Muzzatti	1	60	8	0	8.00	0	1	0	35	.771

Empty-net goals (do not count against a goaltender's average): Vernon 4, Trefilov 1.
*Played with two or more NHL teams.

RESULTS

OCTOBER

5—N.Y. Islanders	W	2-1	
7—San Jose	W	6-2	
9—At Vancouver	W	5-1	
14—At San Jose	W	2-1	
16—At Los Angeles	L	4-8	
17—At Anaheim	T	*2-2	
20—At Edmonton	W	5-3	
21—Vancouver	L	3-6	
23—Boston	T	*3-3	
25—Washington	W	*3-2	
27—Buffalo	L	3-5	
30—Edmonton	W	4-1	
31—At Winnipeg	W	4-3	

NOVEMBER

3—At Hartford	W	6-3
4—At Boston	L	3-6
6—At Montreal	W	4-3
9—Los Angeles	W	3-2
11—Anaheim	W	5-4
13—Vancouver	W	4-3
15—Winnipeg	W	7-2
18—At St. Louis	T	*3-3
20—At Dallas	L	3-4
22—Anaheim	L	1-2
24—Toronto	W	5-3
26—Chicago	L	3-6
30—Dallas	T	*2-2

DECEMBER

4—Philadelphia	W	6-0
6—At Ottawa	W	6-1
7—At Quebec	T	*4-4

10—At Buffalo	L	2-6
11—At Toronto	L	1-3
14—Vancouver	W	8-4
17—St. Louis	L	3-4
18—Winnipeg	W	*5-4
20—Los Angeles	L	*4-5
22—At Edmonton	L	3-7
23—Vancouver†	L	3-4
28—At San Jose	T	*3-3
30—Edmonton	W	7-1
31—Montreal	L	2-5

JANUARY

2—At St. Louis	L	*3-4
5—At N.Y. Rangers	W	4-1
7—At N.Y. Islanders	L	2-6
8—At Pittsburgh	T	*2-2
11—Quebec	W	1-0
15—Ottawa	W	10-0
17—At San Jose	L	2-3
19—At Vancouver	W	4-3
24—Los Angeles‡	T	*3-3
26—Dallas	L	2-3
28—New Jersey	T	*2-2
29—St. Louis	L	3-5

FEBRUARY

2—At Anaheim	W	4-2
5—At Los Angeles	W	*5-4
7—Edmonton	W	4-3
9—At Edmonton	W	6-1
11—Hartford	W	4-1
12—Toronto	W	3-2
14—Chicago	L	2-4

18—At Dallas	L	2-4
20—At Winnipeg	W	5-2
22—At Vancouver	T	*4-4
24—Tampa Bay	L	0-4
26—Los Angeles	W	4-2

MARCH

1—At Detroit	L	2-5
3—At Chicago	L	2-4
5—At New Jersey	L	3-6
6—At Washington	T	*4-4
9—Detroit	L	1-5
11—Florida	W	4-2
12—San Jose	W	2-0
15—At Tampa Bay	W	7-3
16—At Florida	L	1-2
20—At Toronto	W	6-3
22—N.Y. Rangers	T	*4-4
26—Pittsburgh	W	5-3
31—At Philadelphia	W	4-1

APRIL

2—At Detroit	T	*3-3
3—At Chicago	L	1-2
6—Anaheim	W	4-2
8—San Jose	W	5-2
9—Detroit	W	4-2
11—At Anaheim	W	3-0
13—At Los Angeles	L	4-6

*Denotes overtime game.
†At Saskatoon, Sask.
‡At Phoenix.

CHICAGO BLACKHAWKS
WESTERN CONFERENCE/CENTRAL DIVISION

1994-95 SCHEDULE

☐ Home games shaded.
* — All-Star Game at San Jose Arena.
† — At Phoenix.
D — Day game.

OCTOBER

SUN	MON	TUE	WED	THU	FRI	SAT
						1 PIT
2 STL	3	4	5	6 NJ	7	8 DAL
9 EDM	10	11 STL	12	13 WIN	14	15 QUE
16	17 MON	18	19	20 SJ	21	22 WIN
23 LA	24	25	26	27 ANA	28	29
30 TB	31					

NOVEMBER

SUN	MON	TUE	WED	THU	FRI	SAT
		1	2 BUF	3	4	5 BOS
6 DAL	7	8	9	10 TOR	11	12 WIN
13 STL	14	15 LA	16	17	18	19
20 ANA	21	22 SJ	23	24 CAL	25 EDM	26
27	28	29	30			

DECEMBER

SUN	MON	TUE	WED	THU	FRI	SAT
				1 MON	2	3 FLA
4 ANA	5	6	7	8 VAN	9 DAL	10
11 FLA	12	13	14 DAL	15	16 TB	17
18 PHI	19	20 NYI	21 TOR	22	23 DET	24
25	26 DET	27 STL	28	29	30 ANA	31

JANUARY

SUN	MON	TUE	WED	THU	FRI	SAT
1 SJ	2	3 NYI	4	5 CAL	6 DET	7
8 LA	9	10	11 VAN	12 CAL	13	14
15 HAR	16	17 TOR	18	19	20	21°
22	23	24	25 EDM	26	27 TOR	28
29 WAS	D 30	31 PHI				

FEBRUARY

SUN	MON	TUE	WED	THU	FRI	SAT
			1	2 NYR	3	4 D NJ
5	6	7	8 EDM	9 VAN	10	11
12	13	14	15 TOR	16 PIT	17	18
19 WIN	D 20	21 OTT	22	23 WAS	24	25 STL
26 DET	27	28 OTT				

MARCH

SUN	MON	TUE	WED	THU	FRI	SAT
			1	2 BUF	3	4 D HAR
5 STL	D 6	7 WIN	8	9† OTT	10	11
12 CAL	D 13	14 DET	15	16 VAN	17	18† HAR
19	20	21 SJ	22	23 LA	24	25
26 DAL	D 27 DAL	28	29 DET	30	31 QUE	

APRIL

SUN	MON	TUE	WED	THU	FRI	SAT
						1
2 NYR	D 3	4	5 WIN	6 TOR	7	8
9 BOS	D 10	11	12	13	14	15

1994-95 SEASON

CLUB DIRECTORY

President
  William W. Wirtz
Vice president
  Arthur M. Wirtz Jr.
Vice president and asst. to the president
  Thomas N. Ivan
Senior vice president/general manager
  Bob Pulford
Director of player personnel
  Bob Murray
Head coach
  Darryl Sutter
Assistant coaches
  Rich Preston
  Paul Baxter

Scouts
  Jimmy Walker
  Dave Lucas
  Kerry Davison
  Bruce Franklin
  Michel Dumas
  Jim Pappin
  Steve Lyons
Public relations
  Jim DeMaria
Trainer
  Mike Gapski
  Lou Varga
  Randy Lacey

DRAFT CHOICES

Rd.—Player	H/W	Overall	Pos.	Last team
1—Ethan Moreau	6-2/205	14	LW	Niagara Falls (OHL)
2—Jean-Yves Leroux	6-2/193	40	LW	Beauport (QMJHL)
4—Steve McLaren	6-0/194	85	D	North Bay (OHL)
5—Marc Dupuis	5-11/176	118	D	Belleville (OHL)
6—Jim Ensom	6-3/191	144	C	North Bay (OHL)
7—Tyler Prosofsky	5-11/175	170	C	Tacoma (WHL)
8—Mike Josephson	5-11/195	196	LW	Kamloops (WHL)
9—Lubomir Jandera	5-11/180	222	D	Chemopetrol (Czech Jrs.)
10—Lars Weibel	6-0/178	248	G	Lugano, Switzerland
11—Rob Hara	6-1/175	263	RW	Belmont Hill H.S. (Mass.)

MISCELLANEOUS DATA

Home ice (capacity)
  United Center (17,742)
Address
  1901 W. Madison Street
  Chicago, IL 60612
Business phone
  312-455-7000

Rink dimensions
  200 feet by 85 feet
Club colors
  Red, black and white

TRAINING CAMP ROSTER

No.	FORWARDS	Ht./Wt.	Place (BORN)	Date	NHL exp.	1993-94 clubs
	Tony Amonte (RW)	6-0/186	Weymouth, Mass.	8-2-70	4	New York Rangers, Chicago
	Zac Boyer (RW)	6-1/185	Inuvik, N.W.T.	10-25-71	0	Indianapolis (IHL)
	Rob Cimetta (LW)	6-0/190	Toronto	2-15-70	4	Indianapolis (IHL)
32	Steve Dubinsky (C)	6-0/190	Montreal	7-9-70	1	Chicago, Indianapolis (IHL)
16	Michel Goulet (LW)	6-1/195	Peribonqua, Que.	4-21-60	15	Chicago
33	Dirk Graham (LW/RW).	5-11/198	Regina, Sask.	7-29-59	11	Chicago
	Brent Grieve (LW)	6-1/205	Oshawa, Ont.	5-9-69	1	Salt Lake City (IHL), New York Islanders, Cape Breton (AHL), Edmonton
29	Darin Kimble (RW)	6-2/205	Lucky Lake, Sask.	11-22-68	6	Chicago
	Sergei Klimovich (C)	6-2/189	Novosibirsk, U.S.S.R.	5-8-74	0	Dynamo Moscow (CIS)
59	Sergei Krivokrasov.	5-11/175	Angarsk, U.S.S.R.	4-15-74	2	Indianapolis (IHL), Chicago
	Eric Lecompte (LW)	6-4/190	Montreal	4-4-75	0	Hull (QMJHL)
	Andy MacIntyre (LW)	6-2/195	Thunder Bay, Ont.	4-16-74	0	Saskatoon (WHL)
	Eric Manlow (C)	6-0/190	Belleville, Ont.	4-7-75	0	Kitchener (OHL)
	Ethan Moreau (LW)	6-2/205	Orillia, Ont.	9-22-75	0	Niagara Falls (OHL)
17	Joe Murphy (RW)	6-1/190	London, Ont.	10-16-67	8	Chicago
	Bernie Nicholls (C)	6-0/185	Haliburton, Ont.	6-24-61	13	New Jersey
24	Patrick Poulin (LW)	6-1/208	Vanier, Que.	4-23-73	3	Hartford, Chicago
	Bob Probert (LW)	6-3/215	Windsor, Ont.	6-5-65	9	Detroit
27	Jeremy Roenick (C)	6-0/170	Boston	1-17-70	6	Chicago
22	Christian Ruuttu (C)	5-11/192	Lappeenranta, Finland	2-20-64	8	Chicago
	Jeff Shantz (C)	6-0/185	Edmonton, Alta.	10-10-73	1	Chicago, Indianapolis (IHL)
12	Brent Sutter (C)	5-11/180	Viking, Alta.	6-10-62	14	Chicago
23	Rich Sutter (RW)	5-11/188	Viking, Alta.	12-2-63	12	Chicago
21	Paul Ysebaert (LW)	6-1/190	Sarnia, Ont.	5-15-66	6	Winnipeg, Chicago

No.	DEFENSEMEN	Ht./Wt.	Place	Date	NHL exp.	1993-94 clubs
	Keith Carney	6-2/205	Pawtucket, R.I.	2-3-70	3	Louisville (ECHL), Buffalo, Indianapolis (IHL), Chicago
7	Chris Chelios	6-1/186	Chicago	1-25-62	11	Chicago
	Ivan Droppa	6-2/209	Lip. Mikulas, Czech.	2-1-72	1	Indianapolis (IHL), Chicago
	Karl Dykhuis	6-3/195	Sept-Iles, Que.	7-8-72	2	Indianapolis (IHL)
8	Cam Russell	6-4/206	Halifax, N.S.	1-12-69	5	Chicago
5	Steve Smith	6-4/215	Glasgow, Scotland	4-30-63	10	Chicago
	Greg Smyth	6-3/212	Oakville, Ont.	4-23-66	8	Florida, Toronto, Chicago
20	Gary Suter	6-0/190	Madison, Wis.	6-24-64	9	Calgary, Chicago
5	Eric Weinrich	6-0/210	Roanoke, Va.	12-19-66	6	Hartford, Chicago

No.	GOALTENDERS	Ht./Wt.	Place	Date	NHL exp.	1993-94 clubs
30	Ed Belfour	5-11/182	Carman, Man.	4-21-65	6	Chicago
	Jeff Hackett	6-1/185	London, Ont.	6-1-68	5	Chicago
	Chris Rogles	5-11/175	St. Louis	1-22-69	0	Indianapolis (IHL)
	Christian Soucy	5-11/160	Gatineau, Que.	9-14-70	1	Indianapolis (IHL), Chicago

1993-94 REVIEW

INDIVIDUAL STATISTICS

SCORING

	Games	G	A	Pts.	PIM	+/-	PPG	SHG	Shots	Shooting Pct.
Jeremy Roenick	84	46	61	107	125	21	24	5	281	16.4
Joe Murphy	81	31	39	70	111	1	7	4	222	14.0
Chris Chelios	76	16	44	60	212	12	7	1	219	7.3
Brent Sutter *	73	9	29	38	43	17	3	2	127	7.1
Brian Noonan*	64	14	21	35	57	2	8	0	134	10.4
Dirk Graham	67	15	18	33	45	13	0	2	122	12.3
Stephane Matteau*	65	15	16	31	55	10	2	0	113	13.3
Michel Goulet	56	16	14	30	26	1	3	0	120	13.3
Christian Ruuttu	54	9	20	29	68	-4	1	1	96	9.4
Steve Smith	57	5	22	27	174	-5	1	0	89	5.6
Rich Sutter	83	12	14	26	108	-8	0	0	122	9.8
Eric Weinrich*	54	3	23	26	31	6	1	0	105	2.9
Patrick Poulin*	58	12	13	25	40	0	1	0	83	14.5
Jocelyn Lemieux*	66	12	8	20	63	5	0	0	129	9.3
Frantisek Kucera *	60	4	13	17	34	9	2	0	90	4.4
Jeff Shantz	52	3	13	16	30	-14	0	0	56	5.4
Neil Wilkinson	72	3	9	12	116	2	1	0	72	4.2
Kevin Todd *	35	5	6	11	16	-2	1	0	49	10.2
Paul Ysebaert*	11	5	3	8	8	1	2	0	31	16.1
Keith Carney*	30	3	5	8	35	15	0	0	31	9.7
Steve Dubinsky	27	2	6	8	16	1	0	0	20	10.0

— 18 —

	Games	G	A	Pts.	PIM	+/-	PPG	SHG	Shots	Shooting Pct.
Cam Russell	67	1	7	8	200	10	0	0	41	2.4
Randy Cunneyworth*	16	4	3	7	13	1	0	0	33	12.1
Darin Kimble	65	4	2	6	133	2	0	0	17	23.5
Gary Suter*	16	2	3	5	18	-9	2	0	35	5.7
Bryan Marchment*	13	1	4	5	42	-2	0	0	18	5.6
Tony Amonte*	7	1	3	4	6	-5	1	0	16	6.3
Craig Muni*	9	0	4	4	4	3	0	0	6	0.0
Ed Belfour (goalie)	70	0	4	4	61	0	0	0	0	0.0
Dave Christian	9	0	3	3	0	0	0	0	6	0.0
Sergei Krivokrasov	9	1	0	1	4	-2	0	0	7	14.3
Ivan Droppa	12	0	1	1	12	2	0	0	13	0.0
Troy Murray*	12	0	1	1	6	1	0	0	7	0.0
Jeff Hackett (goalie)	22	0	1	1	2	0	0	0	0	0.0
Christian Soucy (goalie)	1	0	0	0	0	0	0	0	0	0.0
Robert Dirk*	6	0	0	0	26	0	0	0	4	0.0
Tony Horacek	7	0	0	0	53	1	0	0	2	0.0
Greg Smyth*	38	0	0	0	108	-2	0	0	29	0.0

GOALTENDING

	Games	Min.	Goals	SO	Avg.	W	L	T	Shots	Sv. Pct.
Christian Soucy	1	3	0	0	0.00	0	0	0	0	.000
Ed Belfour	70	3998	178	‡7	2.67	37	24	6	1892	.906
Jeff Hackett	22	1084	62	0	3.43	2	12	3	566	.890

Empty-net goals (do not count against a goaltender's average): None.
*Played with two or more NHL teams.
‡Tied for league lead.

RESULTS

OCTOBER
6—Florida	T	*4-4
9—At Toronto	L	1-2
10—Winnipeg	W	*4-3
12—At Dallas	T	*3-3
14—Hartford	L	2-6
16—At Winnipeg	L	*0-1
18—Dallas	L	3-5
21—Quebec	W	3-2
23—Detroit	W	4-2
26—St. Louis	W	9-2
28—Toronto	L	2-4
30—At Pittsburgh	L	3-4
31—Philadelphia	L	6-9

NOVEMBER
4—N.Y. Islanders	W	4-2
7—Edmonton	W	3-0
11—Pittsburgh	W	4-1
13—At Toronto	W	3-2
14—Dallas	W	4-1
18—At Florida	W	3-2
20—At Tampa Bay	L	3-4
24—At Edmonton	W	3-1
26—At Calgary	W	6-3
29—At Vancouver	L	*1-2

DECEMBER
4—At New Jersey	T	*2-2
7—At St. Louis	L	2-3
11—At Boston	W	5-4
12—At San Jose	W	2-1
15—At Dallas	W	3-2
18—At Philadelphia	T	*2-2

19—Anaheim	W	2-0
21—At Detroit	L	1-5
23—San Jose	W	5-3
26—At St. Louis	L	2-3
27—Toronto	W	5-2
29—At Winnipeg	L	2-3
31—Dallas	L	2-5

JANUARY
2—Winnipeg	W	5-1
4—At Dallas	W	*2-1
6—Anaheim	L	2-6
8—At Washington	L	1-4
9—Edmonton	L	2-4
11—Buffalo	L	2-5
13—Tampa Bay	W	1-0
15—At N.Y. Islanders	T	*5-5
16—N.Y. Rangers	L	1-5
25—At Detroit	W	5-0
27—Detroit	L	*3-4
29—Ottawa	T	*3-3
31—At Ottawa	W	1-0

FEBRUARY
2—At Vancouver	L	4-6
4—At Edmonton	W	3-1
6—At Anaheim	W	3-2
8—San Jose†	L	3-4
9—At Los Angeles	L	2-4
11—At San Jose	L	3-4
13—At San Jose	L	0-1
14—At Calgary	W	4-2
17—Vancouver	L	2-4
18—At Winnipeg	W	7-2

20—New Jersey	T	*1-1
24—Winnipeg	W	6-3
25—At Buffalo	W	3-1
27—Boston	L	0-4

MARCH
3—Calgary	W	4-2
6—Los Angeles	T	*3-3
8—Anaheim‡	W	3-0
9—At Los Angeles	W	4-0
11—At Anaheim	W	3-2
13—Vancouver	W	5-2
14—At Quebec	L	1-5
16—At Montreal	L	3-5
18—At N.Y. Rangers	W	7-3
20—St. Louis	L	*3-4
22—At Detroit	L	1-3
24—Montreal	T	*5-5
27—Detroit	L	1-3
30—At Hartford	L	*2-3
31—Washington	L	3-6

APRIL
3—Calgary	W	2-1
5—At St. Louis	L	1-5
8—St. Louis	W	6-1
10—Los Angeles	W	2-1
12—At Toronto	W	4-3
14—Toronto	L	4-6

*Denotes overtime game.
†At Sacramento, Calif.
‡At Phoenix.

DALLAS STARS
WESTERN CONFERENCE/CENTRAL DIVISION

1994-95 SCHEDULE

- ▨ Home games shaded.
- * — All-Star Game at San Jose Arena.
- † — At Denver.
- △ — At San Antonio.
- D — Day game.

OCTOBER

SUN	MON	TUE	WED	THU	FRI	SAT
						1 ANA
2	3	4 CAL	5	6	7	8 CHI
9	10	11 WIN	12	13	14	15 OTT
16	17 DET	18	19 WIN	20	21 VAN	22
23 EDM	24	25 PIT	26 NYR	27	28	29 QUE
30	31					

NOVEMBER

SUN	MON	TUE	WED	THU	FRI	SAT
		1 NYI	2	3	4 WIN	5
6 CHI	7 NYI	8	9	10 PIT	11	12 DET
13 PHI	14	15 WAS	16 NJ	17	18 SJ	19
20	21 BUF	22	23 QUE	24	25	26 STL
27	28 TOR	29	30			

DECEMBER

SUN	MON	TUE	WED	THU	FRI	SAT
				1	2 VAN	3
4	5 SJ	6	7 STL	8	9 CHI	10 STL
11	12	13 DET	14 CHI	15	16	17 NJ
18	19 TOR	20	21 HAR	22 BOS	23	24
25	26 STL	27	28 DET	29 TOR	30	31 STL

JANUARY

SUN	MON	TUE	WED	THU	FRI	SAT
1	2 LA	3	4	5	6 TB	7 WIN
8	9 EDM	10	11 SJ	12	13	14 LA
15	16 HAR	17	18† HAR	19	20	21*
22	23	24 LA	25 ANA	26	27	28 SJ D
29	30	31				

FEBRUARY

SUN	MON	TUE	WED	THU	FRI	SAT
			1	2 TB	3	4 STL
5 FLA	6	7 BUF	8	9	10 CAL	11 DET
12	13 TOR	14	15 BOS	16	17 WIN	18 CAL
19	20 CAL	21	22 EDM	23	24 VAN	25
26	27	28				

MARCH

SUN	MON	TUE	WED	THU	FRI	SAT
			1 MON	2	3 ANA	4
5	6 LA	7	8 WIN	9	10	11△ ANA
12	13 TOR	14	15 PHI	16	17	18 MON
19 OTT	20	21 NYR	22	23 EDM	24	25
26 D CHI	27 CHI	28	29 TOR	30	31	

APRIL

SUN	MON	TUE	WED	THU	FRI	SAT
						1 D DET
2 D WAS	3	4 VAN	5	6	7 ANA	8
9 D FLA	10	11	12	13	14	15

1994-95 SEASON

CLUB DIRECTORY

Owner and governor
Norman N. Green
President
Jim Lites
Vice president/g.m. and head coach
Bob Gainey
V.P of advertising and promotion
Jeff Cogen
Vice president of finance
Rick McLaughlin
Vice president of marketing
Bill Strong
Assistant coaches
Doug Jarvis
Rick Wilson
Director of player personnel
Les Jackson
Director of amateur scouting
Craig Button

Assistant to the general manager
Doug Armstrong
Assistant to the hockey department
Dan Stuchal
Director of public relations
Larry Kelly
Director of merchandising
Jason Siegel
Director of ticket sales
Brian Byrnes
Head trainer
Dave Surprenant
Assistant trainer
Dave Smith
Equipment manager
Lance Vogt

DRAFT CHOICES

Rd.—Player	H/W	Overall	Pos.	Last team
1—Jason Botterill	6-3/205	20	LW	Univ. of Michigan (CCHA)
2—Lee Jinman	5-10/155	46	C	North Bay (OHL)
4—Jamie Wright	5-11/172	98	LW	Guelph (OHL)
5—Marty Turco	5-11/175	124	G	Cambridge (Jr. B)
6—Yevgeny Petrochinin	5-9/165	150	D	Spartak Moscow, CIS
9—Marty Flichel	5-10/168	228	RW	Tacoma (WHL)
10—Jimmy Roy	5-11/170	254	C	Thunder Bay (Jr. A)
11—Chris Szysky	5-10/180	280	RW	Swift Current (WHL)

MISCELLANEOUS DATA

Home ice (capacity)
Reunion Arena (16,914)
Address
901 Main Street
Suite 2301
Dallas, TX 75202

Business phone
214-712-2890
Rink dimensions
200 feet by 85 feet
Club colors
Black, gold, green and white

TRAINING CAMP ROSTER

No.	FORWARDS	Ht./Wt.	Place	Date	NHL exp.	1993-94 clubs
11	Dave Barr (RW)	6-1/195	Edmonton, Alta.	11-30-60	13	Dallas, Kalamazoo (IHL)
7	Neal Broten (C)	5-9/170	Roseau, Minn.	11-29-59	14	Dallas
37	Paul Broten (RW)	5-11/190	Roseau, Minn.	10-27-65	5	Dallas
27	Shane Churla (RW)	6-1/200	Fernie, B.C.	6-24-65	8	Dallas
26	Russ Courtnall (RW)	5-11/185	Victoria, B.C.	6-3-65	11	Dallas
34	Gord Donnelly (D/RW)	6-1/202	Montreal	4-5-62	11	Buffalo, Dallas
16	Dean Evason (C)	5-10/180	Flin Flon, Man.	8-22-64	11	Dallas
15	Dave Gagner (C)	5-10/180	Chatham, Ont.	12-11-64	10	Dallas
41	Brent Gilchrist (LW)	5-11/185	Moose Jaw, Sask.	4-3-67	6	Dallas
	Todd Harvey (C)	5-11/190	Hamilton, Ont.	2-17-75	0	Detroit (OHL)
29	Trent Klatt (RW)	6-1/205	Robbinsdale, Minn.	1-30-71	3	Dallas, Kalamazoo (IHL)
	Jamie Langenbrunner (C)	5-11/170	Edmonton, Alta.	4-21-75	0	Peterborough (OHL)
	Jere Lehtinen (RW)	6-0/180	Espoo, Finland	6-24-73	0	TPS Turku (Finland), Finland Olympic Team (Int'l)
23	Alan May (RW)	6-1/200	Swan Hills, Alta.	1-14-65	7	Washington, Dallas
17	Mike McPhee (LW)	6-1/205	Sydney, N.S.	2-14-60	11	Dallas
	Mitch Messier (C/RW)	6-2/210	Regina, Sask.	8-21-65	4	Fort Wayne (IHL)
9	Mike Modano (RW/C)	6-3/190	Livonia, Mich.	6-7-70	6	Dallas
33	Mike Needham (RW)	5-10/185	Calgary, Alta.	4-4-70	3	Pittsburgh, Cleveland (IHL), Dallas
18	Chris Tancill (C)	5-10/185	Livonia, Mich.	2-7-68	4	Dallas, Kalamazoo (IHL)
	Jarkko Varvio (LW)	5-9/172	Tampere, Finland	4-28-72	1	Dallas, Kalamazoo (IHL)
	DEFENSEMEN					
5	Brad Berry	6-2/190	Bashaw, Alta.	4-1-65	8	Dallas, Kalamazoo (IHL)
14	Paul Cavallini	6-1/202	Toronto	10-13-65	8	Dallas
2	Derian Hatcher	6-5/225	Sterling Heights, Mich.	6-4-72	3	Dallas
22	Mike Lalor	6-0/200	Fort Erie, Ont.	3-8-63	9	San Jose, Dallas
12	Grant Ledyard	6-2/195	Winnipeg, Man.	11-19-61	10	Dallas
3	Craig Ludwig	6-3/217	Rhinelander, Wis.	3-15-61	12	Dallas
4	Richard Matvichuk	6-2/190	Edmonton, Alta.	2-5-73	2	Kalamazoo (IHL), Dallas
23	Mark Osiecki	6-2/200	St. Paul, Minn.	7-23-68	2	Kalamazoo (IHL)
	Travis Richards	6-2/195	Crystal, Minn.	3-22-70	0	U.S. national team (Int'l), U.S. Olympic Team (Int'l)
24	Mark Tinordi	6-4/205	Red Deer, Alta.	5-9-66	7	Dallas
5	Doug Zmolek	6-2/220	Rochester, Minn.	11-3-70	2	San Jose, Dallas
	GOALTENDERS					
	Emmanuel Fernandez	6-0/173	Etobicoke, Ont.	8-27-74	0	Laval (QMJHL)
	Troy Gamble	5-11/195	New Glasgow, N.S.	4-7-67	4	Kalamazoo (IHL)
	Chad Lang	5-10/188	Newmarket, Ont.	2-11-75	0	Peterborough (OHL)
35	Andy Moog	5-8/170	Penticton, B.C.	2-18-60	14	Dallas
	Marty Turco	5-11/175	Sault Ste. Marie, Ont.	8-13-75	0	Cambridge Jr. B (OHA)
34	Darcy Wakaluk	5-11/180	Pincher Creek, Alta.	3-14-66	5	Dallas

1993-94 REVIEW

INDIVIDUAL STATISTICS

SCORING

	Games	G	A	Pts.	PIM	+/-	PPG	SHG	Shots	Shooting Pct.
Mike Modano	76	50	43	93	54	-8	18	0	281	17.8
Russ Courtnall	84	23	57	80	59	6	5	0	231	10.0
Dave Gagner	76	32	29	61	83	13	10	0	213	15.0
Ulf Dahlen*	65	19	38	57	10	-1	12	0	147	12.9
Neal Broten	79	17	35	52	62	10	2	1	153	11.1
Grant Ledyard	84	9	37	46	42	7	6	0	177	5.1
Paul Cavallini	74	11	33	44	82	13	6	0	145	7.6
Dean Evason	80	11	33	44	66	-12	3	2	118	9.3
Trent Klatt	61	14	24	38	30	13	3	0	86	16.3
Mike Craig	72	13	24	37	139	-14	3	0	150	8.7
Mike McPhee	79	20	15	35	36	8	1	3	115	17.4
Brent Gilchrist	76	17	14	31	31	0	3	1	103	16.5
Derian Hatcher	83	12	19	31	211	19	2	1	132	9.1
Paul Broten	64	12	12	24	30	18	0	0	76	15.8
Mark Tinordi	61	6	18	24	143	6	1	0	112	5.4
Craig Ludwig	84	1	13	14	123	-1	1	0	65	1.5
Shane Churla	69	6	7	13	333	-8	3	0	62	9.7
Dave Barr	20	2	5	7	21	-6	0	0	20	10.0
Jim Johnson*	53	0	7	7	51	-6	0	0	44	0.0

	Games	G	A	Pts.	PIM	+/-	PPG	SHG	Shots	Shooting Pct.
Jarkko Varvio	8	2	3	5	4	1	0	0	17	11.8
James Black*	13	2	3	5	2	-4	2	0	16	12.5
Jim McKenzie*	34	2	3	5	63	4	0	0	18	11.1
Chris Tancill	12	1	3	4	8	-7	0	0	18	5.6
Pelle Eklund*	5	2	1	3	2	-1	0	0	4	50.0
Richard Matvichuk	25	0	3	3	22	1	0	0	18	0.0
Tommy Sjodin*	7	0	2	2	4	-1	0	0	8	0.0
Darcy Wakaluk (goalie)	36	0	2	2	34	0	0	0	0	0.0
Doug Zmolek	7	1	0	1	11	1	0	0	3	33.3
Alan May*	8	1	0	1	18	-1	0	0	7	14.3
Neil Brady	5	0	1	1	21	-1	0	0	1	0.0
Mike Lalor*	12	0	1	1	6	-5	0	0	3	0.0
Gord Donnelly*	18	0	1	1	66	-4	0	0	5	0.0
Andy Moog (goalie)	55	0	1	1	16	0	0	0	0	0.0
Rob Brown	1	0	0	0	0	-1	0	0	1	0.0
Derrick Smith	1	0	0	0	0	-1	0	0	1	0.0
Duane Joyce	3	0	0	0	0	0	0	0	1	0.0
Mike Needham*	5	0	0	0	0	-2	0	0	3	0.0
Brad Berry	8	0	0	0	12	-2	0	0	4	0.0

GOALTENDING

	Games	Min.	Goals	SO	Avg.	W	L	T	Shots	Sv. Pct.
Darcy Wakaluk	36	2000	88	3	2.64	18	9	6	978	.910
Andy Moog	55	3121	170	2	3.27	24	20	7	1604	.894

Empty-net goals (do not count against a goaltender's average): Moog 7.
*Played with two or more NHL teams.

RESULTS

OCTOBER

5—Detroit	W	6-4
7—At Toronto	L	3-6
9—Winnipeg	T	*3-3
12—Chicago	T	*3-3
16—St. Louis	W	4-0
18—At Chicago	W	5-3
20—At Montreal	L	2-5
21—At Ottawa	W	*6-5
23—At Quebec	L	2-3
25—At Detroit	W	5-3
27—Hartford	W	5-1
30—Ottawa	L	*4-5

NOVEMBER

1—Toronto	T	*3-3
3—At Anaheim	L	4-5
5—At San Jose	L	2-4
7—Winnipeg	T	*1-1
9—Anaheim†	L	2-4
11—San Jose	W	4-0
13—At Winnipeg	W	3-2
14—At Chicago	L	1-4
17—Tampa Bay	W	4-3
20—Calgary	W	4-3
21—Los Angeles	W	7-4
24—N.Y. Islanders	T	*2-2
27—At Detroit	L	4-10
29—At Edmonton	W	*6-5
30—At Calgary	T	*2-2

DECEMBER

4—At St. Louis	L	3-4
5—Edmonton	W	4-3
8—Pittsburgh	W	3-2
9—Ottawa‡	W	6-1
12—Florida	T	*4-4
15—Chicago	L	2-3
17—Anaheim	L	2-3
19—At Vancouver	W	3-1
22—At Anaheim	W	*3-2
23—At Los Angeles	W	2-1
27—Detroit	L	0-6
29—Toronto	W	4-0
31—At Chicago	W	5-2

JANUARY

2—Quebec	L	4-6
4—Chicago	L	*1-2
6—Philadelphia	W	8-0
9—St. Louis	W	2-1
11—Edmonton	W	5-2
13—At Toronto	L	*3-4
14—At Detroit	L	3-9
16—Buffalo	L	2-4
18—Los Angeles	W	5-3
24—New Jersey	L	2-6
26—At Calgary	W	3-2
27—At Vancouver	W	*3-2
29—At Edmonton	W	5-3

FEBRUARY

2—At Winnipeg	W	7-3
6—San Jose	L	1-7
9—Winnipeg	W	4-2
12—At Pittsburgh	W	9-3
13—At Buffalo	W	5-3
16—Boston	L	0-3
18—Calgary	W	4-2
21—At San Jose	W	6-3
23—At Los Angeles	T	*0-0
26—N.Y. Rangers	W	3-1

MARCH

2—At Winnipeg	L	2-4
4—Vancouver	L	1-4
6—Montreal	T	*2-2
8—At Philadelphia	W	*4-3
9—At Toronto	L	2-4
12—At Hartford	T	*2-2
13—At New Jersey	L	0-4
18—Washington	W	6-2
20—Vancouver	W	*2-1
22—Anaheim	W	4-3
25—At St. Louis	L	3-5
27—At Tampa Bay	T	*2-2
28—At Florida	W	5-4
31—At Boston	T	*2-2

APRIL

1—At N.Y. Rangers	L	0-3
3—At Washington	W	6-3
5—Toronto	L	4-6
8—At N.Y. Islanders	L	1-5
10—At St. Louis	T	*2-2
12—St. Louis	W	9-5
14—Detroit	W	4-3

*Denotes overtime game.
†At Phoenix.
‡At Minneapolis.

DETROIT RED WINGS
WESTERN CONFERENCE/CENTRAL DIVISION

1994-95 SCHEDULE

■ Home games shaded.
* — All-Star Game at San Jose Arena.
† — At Hamilton, Ont.
∆ — At Denver.
D — Day game.

OCTOBER

SUN	MON	TUE	WED	THU	FRI	SAT
						1 STL
2	3	4	5 LA	6	7 SJ	8
9	10	11	12 BUF	13	14 FLA	15 NYI
16	17	18	19 MON	20	21 PIT	22 QUE
23	24	25 ANA	26	27	28 LA	29 OTT
30	31					

NOVEMBER

SUN	MON	TUE	WED	THU	FRI	SAT
		1 HAR	2	3	4 TOR	5 TOR
6	7	8 WIN	9	10	11	12 DAL
13	14	15	16 TB	17 FLA	18	19
20 PHI	21	22	23 STL	24	25	26 D NJ
27	28 SJ	29	30 PHI			

DECEMBER

SUN	MON	TUE	WED	THU	FRI	SAT
				1	2 CAL	3 MON
4	5	6 BOS	7 HAR	8	9 NJ	10
11 STL	12	13 DAL	14	15 QUE	16	17 D WIN
18 WIN	19	20 PIT	21	22	23 CHI	24
25	26 CHI	27	28 DAL	29	30	31 SJ

JANUARY

SUN	MON	TUE	WED	THU	FRI	SAT
1	2	3 CAL	4	5	6 CHI	7 BOS
8	9	10	11 ANA	12	13 WIN	14 TOR
15	16	17 NYR	18 TOR	19	20	21*
22	23	24 VAN	25	26	27	28 D EDM
29	30 EDM	31				

FEBRUARY

SUN	MON	TUE	WED	THU	FRI	SAT
			1 CAL	2	3 ANA	4 LA
5	6† TB	7	8	9 LA	10	11 DAL
12 STL	13	14	15 EDM	16	17 WAS	18 WAS
19	20 NYI	21	22 TB	23	24 WIN	25
26 CHI	27	28				

MARCH

SUN	MON	TUE	WED	THU	FRI	SAT
			1 OTT	2	3 TOR	4
5 EDM	D 6 VAN	7	8	9 ANA	10 SJ	11
12∆ FLA	13	14 CHI	15	16 BUF	17 VAN	18
19	20	21 CAL	22 WIN	23	24	25 VAN
26	27	28 NYR	29 CHI	30	31	

APRIL

SUN	MON	TUE	WED	THU	FRI	SAT
						1 D DAL
2 STL	D 3	4	5	6 STL	7	8 TOR
9	10	11	12	13	14	15

1994-95 SEASON

CLUB DIRECTORY

Owner and president
  Michael Ilitch
Owner and secretary/treasurer
  Marian Ilitch
Senior vice president
  Jim Devellano
Dir. of player personnel/head coach
  Scott Bowman
Assistant general manager
  Ken Holland
Assistant coaches
  Dave Lewis
  Barry Smith
Pro scouting director
  Dan Belisle
USA scouting director
  Billy Dea
Western hockey league scout
  Wayne Meier
Western USA scout
  Chris Coury

Eastern USA scout
  To be announced
Ontario scout
  Paul Crowley
Eastern Canada scout
  To be announced
Quebec scout
  Tim Murray
European scouts
  Hakan Andersson
  Vladimir Havluj
Director of public relations
  Bill Jamieson
Director of advertising sales
  Jack Johnson
Athletic trainer
  John Wharton
Equipment manager/trainer
  Mark Brennan
Assistant equipment manager
  Tim Abbott

DRAFT CHOICES

Rd.—Player	H/W	Overall	Pos.	Last team
1—Yan Golubovsky	6-3/183	23	D	CSKA Moscow, CIS
2—Mathieu Dandenault	6-0/174	49	RW	Sherbrooke (QMJHL)
3—Sean Gillam	6-1/187	75	D	Spokane (WHL)
5—Frederic Deschenes	5-9/164	114	G	Granby (QMJHL)
5—Doug Battaglia	6-0/185	127	LW	Brockville (Tier II, Jr. A)
6—Pavel Agarkov	5-11/167	153	RW	Krylja Sovetov, CIS
8—Jason Elliot	6-2/183	205	G	Kimberley (Jr. A)
9—Jeff Mikesch	6-0/175	231	C	Michigan Tech
10—Tomas Holmstrom	5-11/198	257	RW	Boden, Sweden
11—Toivo Suursoo	5-10/176	283	LW	Krylja Sovetov, CIS

MISCELLANEOUS DATA

Home ice (capacity)
  Joe Louis Arena (19,275)
Address
  600 Civic Center Drive
  Detroit, MI 48226
Business phone
  313-396-7544

Rink dimensions
  200 feet by 85 feet
Club colors
  Red and white

TRAINING CAMP ROSTER

No.	FORWARDS	Ht./Wt.	Place	BORN Date	NHL exp.	1993-94 clubs
	Micah Aivazoff (C/LW)	6-0/185	Powell River, B.C.	5-4-69	1	Detroit
	Curt Bowen (LW)	6-1/190	Kenora, Ont.	3-24-74	0	Ottawa (OHL)
11	Shawn Burr (LW)	6-1/195	Sarnia, Ont.	7-1-66	10	Detroit
22	Dino Ciccarelli (RW)	5-10/175	Sarnia, Ont.	2-8-60	14	Detroit
	Sylvain Cloutier (C)	6-0/195	Mt. Laurier, Que.	2-13-74	0	Guelph (OHL), Adirondack (AHL)
	Sylvain Couturier (C)	6-2/205	Greenfield Park, Que.	4-23-68	3	Milwaukee (IHL)
	Kris Draper (C/LW)	5-11/190	Toronto	5-24-71	4	Adirondack (AHL), Detroit
91	Sergei Fedorov (C)	6-1/191	Minsk, U.S.S.R.	12-13-69	4	Detroit
	Greg Johnson (C)	5-10/174	Thunder Bay, Ont.	3-16-71	1	Canadian national team (Int'l), Canadian Olympic Team (Int'l), Adirondack (AHL), Detroit
13	Slava Kozlov (LW)	5-10/175	Voskresensk, U.S.S.R.	5-3-72	3	Detroit, Adirondack (AHL)
	Mike Krushelnyski (C)	6-2/200	Montreal	4-27-60	13	Toronto
20	Martin Lapointe (RW)	5-11/200	Lachine, Que.	9-12-73	3	Adirondack (AHL), Detroit
	Darren McCarty (RW)	6-1/214	Burnaby, B.C.	4-1-72	1	Detroit
55	Keith Primeau (C/LW)	6-4/220	Toronto	11-24-71	4	Detroit
26	Ray Sheppard (RW)	6-1/190	Pembroke, Ont.	5-27-66	7	Detroit
23	Mike Sillinger (C)	5-10/191	Regina, Sask.	6-29-71	4	Detroit
	Tim Taylor (C)	6-1/180	Stratford, Ont.	2-6-69	1	Adirondack (AHL), Detroit
19	Steve Yzerman (C)	5-11/185	Cranbrook, B.C.	5-9-65	11	Detroit
	DEFENSEMEN					
	Sergei Bautin	6-3/218	Murmansk, U.S.S.R.	3-11-67	2	Winnipeg, Detroit, Adirondack (AHL)
29	Terry Carkner	6-3/212	Smith Falls, Ont.	3-7-66	8	Detroit
77	Paul Coffey	6-1/195	Weston, Ont.	6-1-61	14	Detroit
	Anders Eriksson	6-3/218	Bollnas, Sweden	1-9-75	0	MoDo (Sweden)
	Yan Golubovsky	6-3/185	Novosibirsk, U.S.S.R.	3-9-76	0	Russian Penguins (IHL), Dynamo-2 Moscow (CIS Div. III)
	Bob Halkidis	5-11/200	Toronto	3-5-66	9	Adirondack (AHL), Detroit
16	Vladimir Konstantinov	5-11/176	Murmansk, U.S.S.R.	3-19-67	3	Detroit
8	Gord Kruppke	6-1/200	Edmonton, Alta.	4-2-69	3	Adirondack (AHL), Detroit
5	Nicklas Lidstrom	6-2/180	Vasteras, Sweden	4-28-70	3	Detroit
	Dimitri Motkov	6-3/190	Moscow, U.S.S.R.	2-23-71	0	Adirondack (AHL)
	Jamie Pushor	6-3/192	Lethbridge, Alta.	2-11-73	0	Adirondack (AHL)
	Mike Ramsey	6-3/195	Minneapolis	12-3-60	15	Pittsburgh
	Aaron Ward	6-2/200	Windsor, Ont.	1-17-73	1	Detroit, Adirondack (AHL)
38	Jason York	6-1/192	Nepean, Ont.	5-20-70	2	Adirondack (AHL), Detroit
	GOALTENDERS					
	Bob Essensa	6-0/180	Toronto	1-14-65	6	Winnipeg, Detroit
	Kevin Hodson	6-0/182	Winnipeg, Man.	3-27-72	0	Adirondack (AHL)
	Norm Maracle	5-9/175	Belleville, Ont.	10-2-74	0	Saskatoon (WHL)
	Chris Osgood	5-10/160	Peace River, Alta.	11-26-72	1	Adirondack (AHL), Detroit
	Mike Vernon	5-9/170	Calgary, Alta.	2-24-63	11	Calgary

1993-94 REVIEW

INDIVIDUAL STATISTICS

SCORING

	Games	G	A	Pts.	PIM	+/-	PPG	SHG	Shots	Shooting Pct.
Sergei Fedorov	82	56	64	120	34	48	13	4	337	16.6
Ray Sheppard	82	52	41	93	26	13	19	0	260	20.0
Steve Yzerman	58	24	58	82	36	11	7	3	217	11.1
Paul Coffey	80	14	63	77	106	28	5	0	278	5.0
Vyacheslav Kozlov	77	34	39	73	50	27	8	2	202	16.8
Keith Primeau	78	31	42	73	173	34	7	3	155	20.0
Dino Ciccarelli	66	28	29	57	73	10	12	0	153	18.3
Nicklas Lidstrom	84	10	46	56	26	43	4	0	200	5.0
Steve Chiasson	82	13	33	46	122	17	4	1	238	5.5
Vladimir Konstantinov	80	12	21	33	138	30	1	3	97	12.4
Dallas Drake*	47	10	22	32	37	5	0	1	78	12.8
Mike Sillinger	62	8	21	29	10	2	0	1	91	8.8
Darren McCarty	67	9	17	26	181	12	0	0	81	11.1
Mark Howe	44	4	20	24	8	16	1	0	72	5.6
Shawn Burr	51	10	12	22	31	12	0	1	64	15.6
Bob Probert	66	7	10	17	275	-1	1	0	105	6.7
Greg Johnson	52	6	11	17	22	-7	1	1	48	12.5
Martin Lapointe	50	8	8	16	55	7	2	0	45	17.8
Sheldon Kennedy	61	6	7	13	30	-2	0	1	60	10.0
Kris Draper	39	5	8	13	31	11	0	0	55	9.1
Micah Aivazoff	59	4	4	8	38	-1	0	0	52	7.7

	Games	G	A	Pts.	PIM	+/-	PPG	SHG	Shots	Shooting Pct.
Terry Carkner	68	1	6	7	130	13	0	0	32	3.1
Bob Halkidis	28	1	4	5	93	-1	0	0	35	2.9
Jason York	7	1	2	3	2	0	0	0	9	11.1
Bob Essensa* (goalie)	13	0	2	2	0	0	0	0	0	0.0
Tim Taylor	1	1	0	1	0	-1	0	0	4	25.0
Aaron Ward	5	1	0	1	4	2	0	0	3	33.3
Steve Maltais	4	0	1	1	0	-1	0	0	2	0.0
Tim Cheveldae* (goalie)	30	0	1	1	0	0	0	0	0	0.0
Sergei Bautin*	1	0	0	0	0	1	0	0	0	0.0
Mark Pederson	2	0	0	0	2	-1	0	0	0	0.0
Peter Ing (goalie)	3	0	0	0	0	0	0	0	0	0.0
Vincent Riendeau* (goalie)	8	0	0	0	0	0	0	0	0	0.0
Gord Kruppke	9	0	0	0	12	-4	0	0	5	0.0
Steve Konroyd*	19	0	0	0	10	1	0	0	12	0.0
Chris Osgood (goalie)	41	0	0	0	2	0	0	0	0	0.0

GOALTENDING

	Games	Min.	Goals	SO	Avg.	W	L	T	Shots	Sv. Pct.
Bob Essensa*	13	778	34	1	2.62	4	7	2	337	.899
Chris Osgood	41	2206	105	2	2.86	23	8	5	999	.895
Tim Cheveldae*	30	1572	91	1	3.47	16	9	1	727	.875
Vincent Riendeau*	8	345	23	0	4.00	2	4	0	131	.824
Peter Ing	3	170	15	0	5.29	1	2	0	102	.853

Empty-net goals (do not count against a goaltender's average): Cheveldae 3, Essensa 3, Riendeau 1.
*Played with two or more NHL teams.

RESULTS

OCTOBER

5—At Dallas	L	4-6
8—At Anaheim	W	7-2
9—At Los Angeles	L	3-10
13—St. Louis	L	2-5
15—At Toronto	L	3-6
16—Toronto	L	1-2
18—At Buffalo	W	6-4
21—Winnipeg	W	6-2
23—At Chicago	L	2-4
25—Dallas	L	3-5
27—Los Angeles	W	8-3
30—At Quebec	W	5-3

NOVEMBER

2—Boston	W	6-1
4—Toronto	T	*3-3
6—Edmonton	L	2-4
13—At Pittsburgh	W	7-3
17—At Winnipeg	L	1-2
20—At New Jersey	W	*4-3
21—At St. Louis	T	*2-2
23—At San Jose	L	4-6
24—At Vancouver	W	*5-4
27—Dallas	W	10-4
28—At N.Y. Islanders	W	4-1

DECEMBER

1—At Hartford	L	3-5
3—Ottawa	W	8-1
5—At Winnipeg	L	4-6
6—Winnipeg	W	6-2
9—St. Louis	W	3-2
11—San Jose	W	5-3
14—Anaheim	W	5-2
17—N.Y. Rangers	W	6-4
18—At Montreal	L	1-8
21—Chicago	W	5-1
23—At Philadelphia	W	3-1
27—At Dallas	W	6-0
31—Los Angeles	T	*4-4

JANUARY

4—At St. Louis	T	*4-4
6—At San Jose	W	10-3
8—At Los Angeles	W	6-3
10—At Anaheim	W	6-4
12—Tampa Bay	L	2-4
14—Dallas	W	9-3
15—At Boston	W	3-2
17—Tampa Bay†	W	6-3
19—Anaheim	T	*4-4
25—Chicago	L	0-5
27—At Chicago	W	*4-3
29—Winnipeg	W	7-1
30—At Washington	L	3-6

FEBRUARY

2—At Tampa Bay	W	3-1
4—Pittsburgh	L	3-6
5—At Toronto	W	4-3
8—Vancouver	L	3-6
11—Philadelphia	W	6-3
12—At St. Louis	W	*5-4
15—At Toronto	L	*4-5
16—Florida	W	7-3
18—Edmonton	W	5-1
20—At Florida	W	*4-3
23—New Jersey	L	2-7
24—Hartford‡	W	3-0
26—San Jose	W	2-0

MARCH

1—Calgary	W	5-2
4—Toronto	L	*5-6
6—Buffalo	L	2-3
7—At N.Y. Rangers	W	6-3
9—At Calgary	W	5-1
11—At Edmonton	L	2-4
15—Vancouver	W	5-2
17—N.Y. Islanders	L	1-3
19—At Winnipeg	L	2-4
22—Chicago	W	3-1
23—At Ottawa	L	4-5
25—Washington	T	*2-2
27—At Chicago	W	3-1
29—Hartford	W	6-2
31—Quebec	L	2-4

APRIL

2—Calgary	T	*3-3
3—St. Louis	T	*3-3
5—At Vancouver	W	8-3
9—At Calgary	L	2-4
10—At Edmonton	L	3-4
13—Montreal	W	9-0
14—At Dallas	L	3-4

*Denotes overtime game.
†At Minneapolis.
‡At Cleveland.

EDMONTON OILERS
WESTERN CONFERENCE/PACIFIC DIVISION

1994-95 SCHEDULE

☐ Home games shaded.
* — All-Star Game at San Jose Arena.
† — At Saskatoon, Sask.
D — Day game.

OCTOBER
SUN	MON	TUE	WED	THU	FRI	SAT
						1
2 VAN	3	4	5 ANA	6	7 WIN	8
9 CHI	10	11	12 CAL	13	14	15 VAN
16 ANA	17	18	19 ANA	20	21 BOS	22
23 D DAL	24	25 QUE	26 MON	27	28 TOR	29
30 WAS	31					

NOVEMBER
SUN	MON	TUE	WED	THU	FRI	SAT
		1	2 FLA	3	4 CAL	5
6	7	8 WAS	9	10	11 FLA	12 TB
13	14 WIN	15	16 VAN	17	18 CAL	19
20 SJ	21	22	23 LA	24	25 CHI	26 CAL
27	28	29	30 WIN			

DECEMBER
SUN	MON	TUE	WED	THU	FRI	SAT
				1	2	3 D NJ
4 NYR	5	6 NYI	7	8 BOS	9	10 HAR
11	12	13 TOR	14	15	16	17 NYR
18 STL	19	20 SJ	21	22 LA	23	24
25	26	27 SJ	28	29	30 MON	31

JANUARY
SUN	MON	TUE	WED	THU	FRI	SAT
1	2† WIN	3	4	5	6	7 QUE
8	9 DAL	10	11 TB	12	13	14 VAN
15 BUF	16	17 LA	18	19	20	21*
22	23 CAL	24	25 CHI	26 STL	27	28 D DET
29	30 DET	31				

FEBRUARY
SUN	MON	TUE	WED	THU	FRI	SAT
			1 HAR	2	3 TOR	4
5 D ANA	6 LA	7	8 CHI	9	10 WIN	11
12 D ANA	13	14	15 DET	16	17	18 D PHI
19	20 STL	21	22 DAL	23	24	25 PHI
26	27	28 CAL				

MARCH
SUN	MON	TUE	WED	THU	FRI	SAT
			1 VAN	2	3 PIT	4
5 D DET	6	7	8 SJ	9 VAN	10	11
12 OTT	13	14 STL	15	16	17 NYI	18
19	20† TOR	21 NJ	22	23 DAL	24	25
26 OTT	27 TOR	28	29 BUF	30	31 LA	

APRIL
SUN	MON	TUE	WED	THU	FRI	SAT
						1
2	3 LA	4	5 ANA	6	7 SJ	8
9 SJ	10	11	12	13	14	15

1994-95 SEASON

CLUB DIRECTORY

Owner/governor
Peter Pocklington
Alternate governor
Glen Sather
General counsels
Lorne Ruzicka
Gary Frohlich
President/general manager
Glen Sather
Coach
George Burnett
Assistant coaches
To be announced
Exec. V.P./assistant general manager
Bruce MacGregor
Vice president, finance
Werner Baum
Executive secretary
Betsy Freedman
Director of public relations
Bill Tuele
Coord. of publications & statistics
Steve Knowles

Director of player personnel/chief scout
Barry Fraser
Hockey operations
Kevin Prendergast
Scouting staff
Ace Bailey
Ed Chadwick
Lorne Davis
Harry Howell
Curly Reeves
Jan Slepicka
Brad Smith
Athletic trainer
Barrie Stafford
Assistant trainer
Lyle Kulchisky
Athletic trainer/therapist
Ken Lowe
Massage therapist
Stewart Poirier
Team physicians
Dr. David C. Reid
Dr. Boris Boyko

DRAFT CHOICES

Rd.—Player	H/W	Overall	Pos.	Last team
1—Jason Bonsignore.....	6-4/208	4	C	Niagara Falls (OHL)
1—Ryan Smyth	6-1/183	6	LW	Moose Jaw (WHL)
2—Mike Watt.................	6-2/210	32	LW	Stratford (Jr. B)
3—Corey Neilson...........	6-4/207	53	D	North Bay (OHL)
3—Brad Symes...............	6-1/210	60	D	Portland (WHL)
4—Adam Copeland.........	6-2/184	79	RW	Burlington (Jr. B)
4—Jussi Tarvainen........	6-2/187	95	C	Kalpa Kuopio, Finland
5—Jon Gaskins	6-3/205	110	D	Dubuque (Jr. A)
6—Terry Marchant	6-0/206	136	LW	Niagara (Jr. A)
7—Curtis Sheptak..........	6-3/190	160	LW	Olds (Tier II, Jr. A)
7—Dmitri Shulga	6-2/189	162	RW	Tivali Minsk, CIS
7—Chris Wickenheiser ..	6-1/178	179	G	Red Deer (WHL)
8—Rob Guinn.................	6-1/210	185	D	Newmarket (OHL)
8—Jason Reid	6-3/196	188	D	St. Andrew's
9—Jeremy Jablonski	6-0/180	214	G	Victoria (WHL)
11—Ladislav Benysek	6-1/185	266	D	HC Olomouc, Czech.

MISCELLANEOUS DATA

Home ice (capacity)
Northlands Coliseum (17,503)
Address
Edmonton, Alta. T5B 4M9
Business phone
403-474-8561

Rink dimensions
200 feet by 85 feet
Club colors
Blue, orange and white

TRAINING CAMP ROSTER

No.	FORWARDS	Ht./Wt.	Place	BORN Date	NHL exp.	1993-94 clubs
7	Jason Arnott (C)	6-3/195	Collingworth, Ont.	10-11-74	1	Edmonton
	Jason Bonsignore (C)	6-4/208	Rochester, N.Y.	4-15-76	0	Newmarket (OHL), Niagara Falls (OHL), U.S. national team (Int'l)
16	Kelly Buchberger	6-2/210	Langenburg, Sask.	12-12-66	8	Edmonton
	Jozef Cierny (LW)	6-2/185	Zvolen, Czechoslovakia	5-13-74	1	Cape Breton (AHL), Edmonton
8	Zdeno Ciger (LW)	6-1/190	Martin, Czechoslovakia	10-19-69	4	Edmonton
9	Shayne Corson (LW/C)	6-1/200	Barrie, Ont.	8-13-66	9	Edmonton
29	Louie DeBrusk (LW)	6-2/215	Cambridge, Ont.	3-19-71	3	Edmonton
18	Kirk Maltby (RW)	6-0/180	Guelph, Ont.	12-22-72	1	Edmonton
36	Todd Marchant (C/LW)	6-0/190	Buffalo, N.Y.	8-12-73	1	U.S. national team (Int'l), U.S. Olympic Team (Int'l), Binghamton (AHL), New York Rangers, Edmonton, Cape Breton (AHL)
37	Dean McAmmond (C)	5-11/185	Grand Cache, Alta.	6-15-73	2	Edmonton, Cape Breton (AHL)
28	Roman Oksiuta (RW)	6-3/229	Murmansk, U.S.S.R.	8-21-70	1	Edmonton, Cape Breton (AHL)
	David Oliver (RW)	5-11/185	Sechelt, B.C.	4-17-71	0	University of Michigan (CCHA)
33	Scott Pearson (LW)	6-1/205	Cornwall, Ont.	12-19-69	6	Edmonton
12	Steve Rice (RW)	6-0/215	Waterloo, Ont.	5-26-71	4	Edmonton
	Ryan Smyth (LW)	6-1/185	Banff, Alta.	2-21-76	0	Moose Jaw (WHL)
25	Mike Stapleton (C/RW)	5-10/185	Sarnia, Ont.	5-5-66	7	Pittsburgh, Edmonton
17	Scott Thornton (C)	6-2/200	London, Ont.	1-9-71	4	Edmonton, Cape Breton (AHL)
23	Vladimir Vujtek (C)	6-1/190	O. Severomoravsky, Czech.	2-17-72	3	Edmonton
	David Vyborny (C)	5-10/174	Jihlava, Czechoslovakia	1-22-75	0	Sparta Praha (Czech Republic)
39	Doug Weight (C)	5-11/191	Warren, Mich.	1-21-71	4	Edmonton
19	Tyler Wright (C)	5-11/185	Canora, Sask.	4-6-73	2	Cape Breton (AHL), Edmonton
	DEFENSEMEN					
35	Adam Bennett	6-4/206	Georgetown, Ont.	3-30-71	3	Cape Breton (AHL), Edmonton
	Scott Ferguson	6-1/195	Camrose, Alta.	1-6-73	0	Kamloops (WHL)
6	Ian Herbers	6-4/225	Jasper, Alta.	7-18-67	1	Edmonton, Cape Breton (AHL)
21	Igor Kravchuk	6-1/200	Ufa, U.S.S.R.	9-13-66	3	Edmonton
32	Gord Mark	6-4/220	Edmonton, Alta.	9-10-64	3	Cape Breton (AHL), Edmonton
	Darcy Martini	6-4/220	Castlegar, B.C.	1-30-69	1	Cape Breton (AHL), Edmonton
20	Boris Mironov	6-3/220	Moscow, U.S.S.R.	3-21-72	1	Winnipeg, Edmonton
15	Fredrik Olausson	6-2/195	Vaxsjo, Sweden	10-5-66	8	Winnipeg, Edmonton
22	Luke Richardson	6-4/210	Ottawa	3-26-69	7	Edmonton
	Nick Stajduhar	6-2/1195	Kitchener, Ont.	12-6-74	0	London (OHL)
	GOALTENDERS					
31	Fred Brathwaite	5-7/170	Ottawa	11-24-72	1	Cape Breton (AHL), Edmonton
	Greg Louder	6-1/185	Concord, Ma.	11-16-71	0	Univ. of Notre Dame (CCHA)
	Steve Passmore	5-9/165	Thunder Bay, Ont.	1-29-73	0	Kamloops (WHL)
30	Bill Ranford	5-11/185	Brandon, Man.	12-14-66	9	Edmonton

1993-94 REVIEW

INDIVIDUAL STATISTICS

SCORING

	Games	G	A	Pts.	PIM	+/-	PPG	SHG	Shots	Shooting Pct.
Doug Weight	84	24	50	74	47	-22	4	1	188	12.8
Jason Arnott	78	33	35	68	104	1	10	0	194	17.0
Zdeno Ciger	84	22	35	57	8	-11	8	0	158	13.9
Shayne Corson	64	25	29	54	118	-8	11	0	171	14.6
Igor Kravchuk	81	12	38	50	16	-12	5	0	197	6.1
Scott Pearson	72	19	18	37	165	-4	3	0	160	11.9
Bob Beers*	66	10	27	37	74	-11	5	0	152	6.6
Steven Rice	63	17	15	32	36	-10	6	0	129	13.2
Fredrik Olausson*	55	9	19	28	20	-4	6	0	85	10.6
Ilya Byakin	44	8	20	28	30	-3	6	0	51	15.7
Dean McAmmond	45	6	21	27	16	12	2	0	52	11.5
Craig MacTavish*	66	16	10	26	80	-20	0	0	97	16.5
Kelly Buchberger	84	3	18	21	199	-20	0	0	93	3.2
Kirk Maltby	68	11	8	19	74	-2	0	1	89	12.4
Vladimir Vujtek	40	4	15	19	14	-7	1	0	66	6.1
Brent Grieve*	24	13	5	18	14	4	4	0	53	24.5
Dave Manson*	57	3	13	16	140	-4	0	0	144	2.1
Mike Stapleton*	23	5	9	14	28	-1	1	0	43	11.6
Scott Thornton	61	4	7	11	104	-15	0	0	65	6.2

	Games	G	A	Pts.	PIM	+/-	PPG	SHG	Shots	Shooting Pct.
Louie DeBrusk	48	4	6	10	185	-9	0	0	27	14.8
Adam Bennett	48	3	6	9	49	-8	1	0	57	5.3
Peter White	26	3	5	8	2	1	0	0	17	17.6
Shjon Podein	28	3	5	8	8	3	0	0	26	11.5
Luke Richardson	69	2	6	8	131	-13	0	0	92	2.2
Brad Werenka*	15	0	4	4	14	-1	0	0	11	0.0
Roman Oksiuta	10	1	2	3	4	-1	0	0	18	5.6
Geoff Smith*	21	0	3	3	12	-10	0	0	23	0.0
Chris Joseph*	10	1	1	2	28	-8	1	0	25	4.0
Boris Mironov*	14	0	2	2	14	-4	0	0	23	0.0
Ian Herbers	22	0	2	2	32	-6	0	0	16	0.0
Bill Ranford (goalie)	71	0	2	2	2	0	0	0	0	0.0
Todd Marchant*	3	0	1	1	2	-1	0	0	5	0.0
Gordon Mark	12	0	1	1	43	-2	0	0	8	0.0
Jozef Cierny	1	0	0	0	0	-1	0	0	0	0.0
Wayne Cowley (goalie)	1	0	0	0	0	0	0	0	0	0.0
Jeff Chychrun	2	0	0	0	0	1	0	0	2	0.0
Darcy Martini	2	0	0	0	0	-1	0	0	0	0.0
Bradley Zavisha	2	0	0	0	0	-2	0	0	1	0.0
Todd Elik*	4	0	0	0	6	0	0	0	5	0.0
Alexander Kerch	5	0	0	0	2	-8	0	0	4	0.0
Marc Laforge	5	0	0	0	21	-2	0	0	0	0.0
Tyler Wright	5	0	0	0	4	-3	0	0	2	0.0
Fred Brathwaite (goalie)	19	0	0	0	0	0	0	0	0	0.0

GOALTENDING

	Games	Min.	Goals	SO	Avg.	W	L	T	Shots	Sv. Pct.
Wayne Cowley	1	57	3	0	3.16	0	1	0	35	.914
Bill Ranford	71	4070	236	1	3.48	22	34	11	2325	.898
Fred Brathwaite	19	982	58	0	3.54	3	10	3	523	.889

Empty-net goals (do not count against a goaltender's average): Ranford 8.
*Played with two or more NHL teams.

RESULTS

OCTOBER

6—San Jose	W	3-2
8—N.Y. Islanders	W	5-1
11—At Vancouver	L	1-4
13—At Anaheim	L	3-4
14—At Los Angeles	T	*4-4
16—Vancouver	L	2-3
18—At Winnipeg	L	3-6
20—Calgary	L	3-5
22—Boston	L	1-3
24—Washington	L	*2-3
26—At San Jose	L	1-3
29—Buffalo	L	3-6
30—At Calgary	L	1-4

NOVEMBER

3—Ottawa	L	5-7
6—At St. Louis	L	*5-6
7—At Chicago	L	0-3
9—At Detroit	W	4-2
11—At Boston	L	1-5
13—At Hartford	T	*4-4
15—At Toronto	T	*5-5
17—At Montreal	L	1-3
20—Toronto	L	2-3
21—Anaheim	L	2-4
24—Chicago	L	1-3
27—Vancouver	W	2-1
29—Dallas	L	*5-6

DECEMBER

1—Philadelphia	W	3-1
5—At Dallas	L	3-4
7—At N.Y. Islanders	T	*4-4
8—At N.Y. Rangers	T	*1-1
11—At New Jersey	L	2-5
12—At Philadelphia	W	2-1
15—Vancouver	W	7-2
17—San Jose	W	4-2
19—St. Louis	L	1-4
21—At Vancouver	L	3-6
22—Calgary	W	7-3
27—Winnipeg	W	6-0
29—Montreal	W	6-3
30—At Calgary	L	1-7

JANUARY

2—San Jose	T	*4-4
7—Quebec	W	6-4
9—At Chicago	W	4-2
11—At Dallas	L	2-5
13—At St. Louis	L	4-6
15—At Pittsburgh	L	3-4
18—At Ottawa	T	*3-4
19—At Buffalo	T	*1-1
24—Vancouver†	L	*4-5
26—New Jersey	T	*3-3
28—St. Louis	L	2-3
29—Dallas	L	3-5

FEBRUARY

2—Los Angeles	W	6-4
4—Chicago	L	1-3
6—Winnipeg	W	5-2
7—At Calgary	L	3-4
9—Calgary	L	1-6
12—Hartford	L	2-5
13—Anaheim	L	3-6
15—At Washington	T	*2-2
18—At Detroit	L	1-5
19—At Toronto	L	2-3
23—Toronto	W	6-3
25—Los Angeles	T	*5-5
27—Tampa Bay	W	3-2

MARCH

1—At Vancouver	W	7-4
3—At San Jose	L	2-4
4—At Anaheim	L	1-4
9—Florida	L	3-5
11—Detroit	W	4-2
16—At Tampa Bay	T	*4-4
18—At Florida	T	*4-4
20—At Quebec	W	5-3
23—N.Y. Rangers	L	3-5
25—Los Angeles	L	*3-4
27—Pittsburgh	W	5-3
31—At Anaheim	W	*3-2

APRIL

2—At Los Angeles	W	5-3
3—Los Angeles‡	L	1-6
6—At Winnipeg	W	4-3
8—Anaheim	L	1-3
10—Detroit	W	4-3
13—At San Jose	T	*2-2
14—At Los Angeles	T	*2-2

*Denotes overtime game.
†At Saskatoon, Sask.
‡At Sacramento, Calif.

FLORIDA PANTHERS
EASTERN CONFERENCE/ATLANTIC DIVISION

1994-95 SCHEDULE

☐ — Home games shaded.
* — All-Star Game at San Jose Arena.
† — At Hamilton, Ont.
△ — At Denver.
D — Day game.

OCTOBER
SUN	MON	TUE	WED	THU	FRI	SAT
						1
2	3	4 PHI	5	6 STL	7	8 NYR
9	10 D BOS	11	12 HAR	13	14 DET	15
16 NJ	17	18	19 TOR	20	21 BUF	22 NYI
23	24	25 LA	26	27 BUF	28	29
30	31					

NOVEMBER
SUN	MON	TUE	WED	THU	FRI	SAT
		1	2 EDM	3	4	5 VAN
6 CAL	7	8	9 NYI	10	11 EDM	12
13 BOS	14	15	16	17 DET	18	19 WIN
20	21 QUE	22	23 MON	24	25	26 OTT
27 NYR	28	29	30 TB			

DECEMBER
SUN	MON	TUE	WED	THU	FRI	SAT
				1 SJ	2	3 CHI
4	5 TB	6	7	8	9 OTT	10 QUE
11 CHI	12	13 QUE	14	15 NJ	16	17 TOR
18	19	20 WAS	21	22 PIT	23	24
25	26	27 WAS	28	29 WAS	30 NJ	31

JANUARY
SUN	MON	TUE	WED	THU	FRI	SAT
1 NYR	D 2	3 VAN	4	5 PIT	6	7 STL
8	9 NYR	10	11 NYI	12 PHI	13	14 MON
15	16	17 NJ	18	19	20	21*
22	23 TB	24	25	26 CAL	27	28 D HAR
29	30 BOS	31 NYI				

FEBRUARY
SUN	MON	TUE	WED	THU	FRI	SAT
		1	2 MON	3	4 WAS
5 DAL	6	7 PIT	8	9 BUF	10	11 HAR
12 PIT	13	14	15 NYI	16	17 BUF	18
19 BOS	20	21	22	23 MON	24	25 OTT
26	27† MON	28 NYR				

MARCH
SUN	MON	TUE	WED	THU	FRI	SAT
			1	2 PHI	3	4 D NJ
5 ANA	6	7	8	9 QUE	10 WAS	11
12△ DET	13	14	15 WAS	16	17	18 PHI
19	20 LA	21 ANA	22	23 SJ	24	25
26 TB	D 27	28	29 HAR	30	31	

APRIL
SUN	MON	TUE	WED	THU	FRI	SAT
						1
2 TB	D 3	4	5 OTT	6	7 WIN	8
9 DAL	D 10	11	12	13	14	15

1994-95 SEASON

CLUB DIRECTORY

Owner
H. Wayne Huizenga
President
William A. Torrey
General manager
Bryan Murray
Vice president, business and marketing
Dean Jordan
Vice president, finance and administration
Jonathan Mariner
Consultant
Gary Green
Director of player personnel
John Chapman
Assistant to the general manager
Chuck Fletcher
Head coach
Roger Neilson
Assistant coaches
Craig Ramsay
Lindy Ruff

Goaltending coach
Bill Smith
Chief scout
Dennis Patterson
Eastern scout
Ron Harris
Director, public/media relations
Greg Bouris
Public/media relations associates
Kevin Dessart
Ron Colangelo
Director, promotions and special projects
Declan J. Bolger
Director, ticket and game day operations
Steve Dangerfield
Director, corporate sales and sponsorship
Kimberly Terranova
Director, merchandise
Ron Dennis
Athletic trainer
David Settlemeyer

DRAFT CHOICES

Rd.—Player	H/W	Overall	Pos.	Last team
1—Ed Jovanovski	6-2/205	1	D	Windsor (OHL)
2—Rhett Warrener	6-1/209	27	D	Saskatoon (WHL)
2—Jason Podollan	6-1/181	31	C	Spokane (WHL)
2—Ryan Johnson	6-1/180	36	C	Thunder Bay (Jr. A)
4—David Nemirovsky	6-2/176	84	RW	Ottawa (OHL)
5—Dave Geris	6-4/221	105	D	Windsor (OHL)
7—Matt O'Dette	6-4/205	157	D	Kitchener (OHL)
8—Jasson Boudrias.......	6-0/201	183	C	Laval (QMJHL)
10—Tero Lentera	6-0/185	235	LW	Espoo, Finland
11—Per Gustafsson	6-1/187	261	D	HV Jonkoping, Sweden

MISCELLANEOUS DATA

Home ice (capacity)
Miami Arena (14,515)
Address
100 North East Third Avenue
10th Floor
Fort Lauderdale, FL 33301

Business phone
305-768-1900
Rink dimensions
200 feet by 85 feet
Club colors
Red, navy blue and yellow-gold

TRAINING CAMP ROSTER

No.	FORWARDS	Ht./Wt.	Place	Born Date	NHL exp.	1993-94 clubs
14	Stu Barnes (C)	5-11/180	Edmonton, Alta.	12-25-70	3	Winnipeg, Florida
34	Len Barrie (C)	6-0/190	Kimberly, B.C.	6-4-69	3	Cincinnati (IHL), Florida
26	Jesse Belanger (C)	6-0/170	St. Georges Beauce, Que.	6-15-69	3	Florida
23	Jeff Daniels (LW)	6-1/200	Oshawa, Ont.	6-24-68	4	Pittsburgh, Florida
21	Tom Fitzgerald (RW/C)	6-1/195	Melrose, Mass.	8-28-68	6	Florida
24	Jeff Greenlaw (RW)	6-1/230	Toronto	2-28-68	6	Cincinnati (IHL), Florida
18	Mike Hough (LW)	6-1/192	Montreal	2-6-63	8	Florida
17	Jody Hull (RW)	6-2/200	Petrolia, Ont.	2-2-69	6	Florida
22	Bob Kudelski (RW)	6-1/199	Springfield, Mass.	3-3-64	7	Ottawa, Florida
38	Patrick Lebeau (LW)	5-10/173	St. Jerome, Que.	3-17-70	3	Cincinnati (IHL), Florida
	Jamie Linden (RW)	6-3/185	Medicine Hat, Alta.	7-19-72	0	Cincinnati (IHL)
11	Bill Lindsay (LW)	5-11/185	Big Fork, Mont.	5-17-71	3	Florida
19	Andrei Lomakin (LW)	5-10/175	Voskresensk, U.S.S.R.	4-3-64	3	Florida
10	Dave Lowry (LW)	6-1/195	Sudbury, Ont.	1-14-65	9	Florida
27	Scott Mellanby (RW)	6-1/205	Montreal	6-11-66	9	Florida
44	Rob Niedermayer (C)	6-2/200	Cassiar, B.C.	12-28-74	1	Florida
	Jason Podollan (RW/C)	6-1/181	Vernon, B.C.	2-18-76	0	Spokane (WHL)
20	Brian Skrudland (C)	6-0/196	Peace River, Alta.	7-31-63	9	Florida
	Steve Washburn (C)	6-1/178	Ottawa	4-10-75	0	Ottawa (OHL)
	DEFENSEMEN					
6	Peter Andersson	6-0/196	Orebro, Sweden	8-29-65	2	New York Rangers, Florida
	Chris Armstrong	6-0/184	Regina, Sask.	6-26-75	0	Moose Jaw (WHL), Cincinnati (IHL)
7	Brian Benning	6-0/195	Edmonton, Alta.	6-10-66	10	Florida
4	Keith Brown	6-1/192	Corner Brook, Nfld.	5-6-60	15	Florida
2	Joe Cirella	6-3/210	Hamilton, Ont.	5-9-63	13	Florida
52	Dallas Eakins	6-2/195	Dade City, Fla.	1-20-67	2	Cincinnati (IHL), Florida
	Ed Jovanovski	6-2/205	Windsor, Ont.	6-26-76	0	Windsor (OHL)
3	Paul Laus	6-1/212	Beamsville, Ont.	9-26-70	1	Florida
	Randy Moller	6-2/207	Red Deer, Alta.	8-23-63	13	Buffalo
5	Gord Murphy	6-2/195	Willowdale, Ont.	2-23-67	6	Florida
	Stephane Richer	5-11/190	Hull, Que.	4-28-66	2	Cincinnati (IHL), Florida
	Brent Severyn	6-2/210	Vegreville, Alta.	2-22-66	2	Florida
25	Geoff Smith	6-3/200	Edmonton, Alta.	3-7-69	5	Edmonton, Florida
	Rhett Warrener	6-1/209	Shaunavon, Sask.	1-27-76	0	Saskatoon (WHL)
	GOALTENDERS					
30	Mark Fitzpatrick	6-2/190	Toronto	11-13-68	6	Florida
	Pokey Reddick	5-8/170	Halifax, N.S.	10-6-64	6	Florida, Cincinnati (IHL)
34	John Vanbiesbrouck	5-8/172	Detroit	9-4-63	12	Florida

1993-94 REVIEW

INDIVIDUAL STATISTICS

SCORING

	Games	G	A	Pts.	PIM	+/-	PPG	SHG	Shots	Shooting Pct.
Scott Mellanby	80	30	30	60	149	0	17	0	204	14.7
Jesse Belanger	70	17	33	50	16	-4	11	0	104	16.3
Andrei Lomakin	76	19	28	47	26	1	3	0	139	13.7
Gord Murphy	84	14	29	43	71	-11	9	0	172	8.1
Brian Skrudland	79	15	25	40	136	13	0	2	110	13.6
Stu Barnes*	59	18	20	38	30	5	6	1	148	12.2
Dave Lowry	80	15	22	37	64	-4	3	0	122	12.3
Tom Fitzgerald	83	18	14	32	54	-3	0	3	144	12.5
Brian Benning	73	6	24	30	107	-7	2	0	112	5.4
Bob Kudelski*	44	14	15	29	10	-8	5	0	124	11.3
Mike Hough	78	6	23	29	62	3	0	1	106	5.7
Jody Hull	69	13	13	26	8	6	0	1	100	13.0
Rob Niedermayer	65	9	17	26	51	-11	3	0	67	13.4
Greg Hawgood*	33	2	14	16	9	8	0	0	55	3.6
Bill Lindsay	84	6	6	12	97	-2	0	0	90	6.7
Keith Brown	51	4	8	12	60	11	1	0	52	7.7
Scott Levins*	29	5	6	11	69	0	2	0	38	13.2
Brent Severyn	67	4	7	11	156	-1	1	0	93	4.3
Joe Cirella	63	1	9	10	99	8	0	0	63	1.6
Alexander Godynyuk*	26	0	10	10	35	5	0	0	43	0.0
Mike Foligno*	39	4	5	9	49	7	0	0	32	12.5
Randy Gilhen*	20	4	4	8	16	1	0	0	52	7.7
Evgeny Davydov*	21	2	6	8	8	-3	1	0	22	9.1

	Games	G	A	Pts.	PIM	+/-	PPG	SHG	Shots	Shooting Pct.
Geoff Smith*	56	1	5	6	38	-3	0	0	44	2.3
Paul Laus	39	2	0	2	109	9	0	0	15	13.3
Patrick Lebeau	4	1	1	2	4	0	1	0	4	25.0
Peter Andersson*	8	1	1	2	0	-5	0	0	11	9.1
Mark Fitzpatrick (goalie)	28	0	2	2	4	0	0	0	0	0.0
Jamie Leach	2	1	0	1	0	-2	0	0	2	50.0
Greg Smyth*	12	1	0	1	37	0	0	0	4	25.0
Stephane Richer	2	0	1	1	0	-1	0	0	3	0.0
Jeff Greenlaw	4	0	1	1	2	-1	0	0	6	0.0
Dallas Eakins	1	0	0	0	0	0	0	0	2	0.0
Doug Barrault	2	0	0	0	0	-2	0	0	2	0.0
Len Barrie	2	0	0	0	0	-2	0	0	0	0.0
Pokey Reddick (goalie)	2	0	0	0	0	0	0	0	0	0.0
Jeff Daniels*	7	0	0	0	0	0	0	0	6	0.0
John Vanbiesbrouck (goalie)	57	0	0	0	38	0	0	0	0	0.0

GOALTENDING

	Games	Min.	Goals	SO	Avg.	W	L	T	Shots	Sv. Pct.
John Vanbiesbrouck	57	3440	145	1	2.53	21	25	11	1912	.924
Mark Fitzpatrick	28	1603	73	1	2.73	12	8	6	844	.914
Pokey Reddick	2	80	8	0	6.00	0	1	0	45	.822

Empty-net goals (do not count against a goaltender's average): Vanbiesbrouck 4, Fitzpatrick 3.
*Played with two or more NHL teams.

RESULTS

OCTOBER

6—At Chicago	T	*4-4
7—At St. Louis	L	3-5
9—At Tampa Bay	W	2-0
12—Pittsburgh	L	1-2
14—Ottawa	W	5-4
17—Tampa Bay	T	*3-3
19—Los Angeles	T	*2-2
21—Toronto	L	*3-4
23—At New Jersey	L	1-2
26—Winnipeg	L	2-5
28—N.Y. Islanders	W	5-2
30—Tampa Bay	W	*2-1

NOVEMBER

2—Philadelphia	L	3-4
3—At Toronto	L	3-6
7—At Quebec	W	3-1
10—At Montreal	W	3-1
11—At Ottawa	W	5-4
14—Quebec	L	2-5
16—N.Y. Rangers	L	2-4
18—Chicago	L	2-3
20—Washington	W	4-3
23—Hartford	L	*1-2
26—At Boston	L	2-3
27—At Hartford	L	0-4

DECEMBER

2—Buffalo	W	*2-1
5—At San Jose	L	1-2
7—At Anaheim	W	3-2
8—At Los Angeles	W	6-5
10—At Winnipeg	W	5-2

12—At Dallas	T	*4-4
15—Montreal	T	*3-3
19—Boston	L	*1-2
22—N.Y. Rangers	W	3-2
26—Tampa Bay†	W	3-1
28—At Washington	T	*3-3
29—At Hartford	W	5-3

JANUARY

1—Anaheim	W	4-2
3—At N.Y. Rangers	L	2-3
7—At New Jersey	L	1-4
8—At Boston	T	*2-2
13—At Pittsburgh	T	*2-2
15—At Montreal	W	5-2
17—At N.Y. Islanders	W	2-1
19—Washington	W	5-1
24—Montreal	W	8-3
26—At Tampa Bay	T	*1-1
28—San Jose	T	*3-3
30—At Buffalo	W	3-2

FEBRUARY

1—At Pittsburgh	L	1-2
2—At Ottawa	W	4-1
4—Buffalo	L	2-7
6—Boston	W	3-0
10—At Philadelphia	L	*3-4
12—At N.Y. Islanders	W	4-3
13—Vancouver	W	2-1
16—At Detroit	L	3-7
18—At Buffalo	L	1-4
20—Detroit	L	*3-4
22—Winnipeg‡	W	3-2

24—Washington	L	1-2
26—At Washington	L	2-4
28—Pittsburgh	L	3-4

MARCH

2—New Jersey	L	2-3
4—Hartford	L	1-2
7—At Vancouver	W	2-1
9—At Edmonton	W	5-3
11—At Calgary	L	2-4
14—N.Y. Rangers	W	2-1
16—Calgary	W	2-1
18—Edmonton	T	*4-4
20—Philadelphia	W	5-3
21—New Jersey	T	*3-3
23—Toronto‡	T	*1-1
24—At Philadelphia	L	3-4
26—At N.Y. Islanders	W	3-1
28—Dallas	L	4-5
30—St. Louis	L	1-3

APRIL

2—Ottawa	T	*2-2
4—At N.Y. Rangers	L	2-3
5—At Quebec	T	*3-3
7—At Philadelphia	T	*3-3
10—New Jersey	T	*2-2
12—Quebec	L	2-5
14—N.Y. Islanders	W	4-1

*Denotes overtime game.
†At Orlando, Fla.
‡At Hamilton, Ont.

HARTFORD WHALERS
EASTERN CONFERENCE/NORTHEAST DIVISION

1994-95 SCHEDULE

Home games shaded.
* — All-Star Game at San Jose Arena.
† — At Denver.
Δ — At Phoenix.
D — Day game.

OCTOBER

SUN	MON	TUE	WED	THU	FRI	SAT
						1 PHI
2	3	4 TOR	5	6	7	8 QUE
9	10	11	12 FLA	13	14 BUF	15 NYR
16	17	18	19 OTT	20	21 WAS	22 WAS
23	24	25	26	27 QUE	28	29 WIN
30	31					

NOVEMBER

SUN	MON	TUE	WED	THU	FRI	SAT
		1 DET	2	3	4	5 PIT
6	7	8 MON	9 NYR	10	11	12 NYI
13 OTT	14	15	16 STL	17	18	19 NYI
20	21 MON	22	23 PHI	24	25	26 D ANA
27 TB	28	29 NYR	30			

DECEMBER

SUN	MON	TUE	WED	THU	FRI	SAT
				1 BOS	2	3 QUE
4 BOS	5	6	7 DET	8	9 BUF	10 EDM
11	12 CAL	13	14 OTT	15	16	17 WAS
18	19	20 NJ	21 DAL	22	23 BUF	24
25	26 BOS	27	28 PIT	29 QUE	30	31 OTT

JANUARY

SUN	MON	TUE	WED	THU	FRI	SAT
1	2	3	4 LA	5	6 VAN	7 BUF
8	9	10	11	12	13 PIT	14
15 CHI	16 DAL	17	18† DAL	19	20	21*
22	23 MON	24	25 OTT	26 PHI	27	28 D FLA
29 VAN	30	31				

FEBRUARY

SUN	MON	TUE	WED	THU	FRI	SAT
			1 EDM	2	3 CAL	4 WIN
5	6	7	8 SJ	9	10 TB	11 FLA
12	13 MON	14	15 MON	16	17	18 D PIT
19 D PIT	20	21	22 BOS	23	24 NYR	25 BUF
26	27	28 NYI				

MARCH

SUN	MON	TUE	WED	THU	FRI	SAT
			1 NJ	2	3	4 D CHI
5 BOS	6	7	8 PHI	9 STL	10	11
12 D SJ	13	14 LA	15 ANA	16	17	18Δ CHI
19	20	21	22 QUE	23	24	25 D NYI
26 D WAS	27	28	29 FLA	30	31 TB	

APRIL

SUN	MON	TUE	WED	THU	FRI	SAT
						1
2	3	4 NJ	5 D TOR	6	7	8 D NJ
9 D TB	10	11	12	13	14	15

1994-95 SEASON

CLUB DIRECTORY

Chief executive officer/governor
Peter Karmanos Jr.
General manager
Thomas Thewes
COO/president/general manager
Jim Rutherford
Vice president of hockey operations
Terry McDonnell
Director of hockey operations
Kevin Maxwell
Head coach
Paul Holmgren
Assistant coaches
Paul Gillis
Kevin McCarthy
Ted Nolan
Strength and conditioning coach
Doug McKenney
Goaltending instructor
Steve Weeks
Sr. V.P. of marketing and public relations
Russ Gregory

V.P. of finance and administration
Michael J. Amendola
V.P. of marketing and sales
Rick Francis
Director of public and media relations
John Forslund
Community relations director
Mary Lynn Gorman
Director of publications/chief statistician/archivist
Frank Polnaszek
Director of amateur hockey development
Mike Veisor
Scouts
Bruce Haralson
Claude Larose
Tom Rowe
Ken Schinkel
Medical trainer
Bud Gouveia
Equipment manager
Skip Cunningham

DRAFT CHOICES

Rd.—Player	H/W	Overall	Pos.	Last team
1—Jeff O'Neill	6-0/176	5	C	Guelph (OHL)
4—Hnat Domenichelli	5-11/173	83	C	Kamloops (WHL)
5—Ryan Risidore	6-4/192	109	D	Guelph (OHL)
8—Tom Buckley	6-1/204	187	C	St. Joseph H.S.
9—Ashlin Halfnight	6-0/185	213	D	Harvard University
9—Matt Ball	6-0/219	230	RW	Detroit (OHL)
10—Brian Regan	6-0/170	239	G	Westminster
11—Steve Nimigon	6-1/185	265	LW	Niagara Falls (OHL)

MISCELLANEOUS DATA

Home ice (capacity)
Hartford Civic Center (15,635)
Address
242 Trumbull Street
8th Floor
Hartford, CT 06103

Business phone
203-728-3366
Rink dimensions
200 feet by 85 feet
Club colors
Silver, blue, white and green

TRAINING CAMP ROSTER

No.	FORWARDS	Ht./Wt.	Place	BORN Date	NHL exp.	1993-94 clubs
	Rick Bennett (LW)	6-3/215	Springfield, Mass.	7-24-67	3	
	Jimmy Carson (C)	6-0/200	Southfield, Mich.	7-20-68	8	Los Angeles, Vancouver
21	Andrew Cassels (C)	6-0/192	Mississauga, Ont.	7-23-69	5	Hartford
32	Igor Chibirev (C)	6-0/170	Penza, U.S.S.R.	4-19-68	1	Springfield (AHL), Hartford
	Scott Daniels (LW)	6-3/200	Prince Albert, Sask.	9-19-69	1	Springfield (AHL)
	Ted Drury (C)	6-0/185	Boston	9-13-71	1	U.S. national team (Int'l), U.S. Olympic Team (Int'l), Calgary, Hartford
22	Mark Janssens (C/LW)	6-3/216	Surrey, B.C.	5-19-68	7	Hartford
38	Robert Kron (LW)	5-10/180	Brno, Czechoslovakia	2-27-67	4	Hartford
23	Jocelyn Lemieux (RW)	5-10/200	Mont-Laurier, Que.	11-18-67	8	Chicago, Hartford
	Andrei Nikolishin (LW)	5-11/189	Vorkuta, U.S.S.R.	3-25-73	0	Dynamo Moscow (CIS), Russian Olympic team (Int'l)
	Jeff O'Neill (C)	6-0/176	Richmond Hill, Ont.	2-23-76	0	Guelph (OHL)
39	Robert Petrovicky (C)	5-11/172	Kosice, Czechoslovakia	10-26-73	2	Hartford, Springfield (AHL), Slovakian Olympic team (Int'l)
28	Paul Ranheim (LW)	6-0/195	St. Louis	1-25-66	6	Calgary, Hartford
8	Geoff Sanderson (LW)	6-0/185	Hay River, N.W.T.	2-1-72	4	Hartford
52	Jim Sandlak (RW)	6-4/219	Kitchener, Ont.	12-12-66	9	Hartford
	Kevin Smyth (LW)	6-2/210	Banff, Alta.	11-22-73	1	Springfield (AHL), Hartford
	Jim Storm (LW)	6-2/200	Detroit	2-5-71	1	Michigan Tech (WCHA), U.S. national team (Int'l), Hartford
	Darren Turcotte (C)	6-0/178	Boston	3-2-68	6	New York Rangers, Hartford
16	Pat Verbeek (RW)	5-9/190	Sarnia, Ont.	5-24-64	12	Hartford
	DEFENSEMEN					
26	Jim Agnew	6-1/190	Deloraine, Man.	3-21-66	6	
6	Adam Burt	6-0/190	Detroit	1-15-69	6	Hartford
	Jeff Chychrun	6-4/215	Lasalle, Que.	5-3-66	8	Cape Breton (AHL), Edmonton
	Ted Crowley	6-2/190	Concord, Mass.	5-3-70	1	U.S. national team (Int'l), U.S. Olympic Team (Int'l), Hartford
5	Alexander Godynyuk	6-0/207	Kiev, U.S.S.R.	1-27-70	4	Florida, Hartford
4	Frantisek Kucera	6-2/205	Prague, Czechoslovakia	2-3-68	4	Chicago, Hartford
27	Bryan Marchment	6-1/198	Scarborough, Ont.	5-1-69	6	Chicago, Hartford
	Shayne McCosh	6-0/193	Oshawa, Ont.	1-27-74	0	Detroit (IHL)
10	Brad McCrimmon	5-11/197	Dodsland, Sask.	3-29-59	15	Hartford
	Chris Pronger	6-5/190	Dryden, Ont.	10-10-74	1	Hartford
45	John Stevens	6-1/195	Completon, N.B.	5-4-66	5	Springfield (AHL), Hartford
	Steve Yule	6-0/210	Gleichen, Alta.	5-27-72	0	Springfield (AHL)
	GOALTENDERS					
1	Sean Burke	6-4/210	Windsor, Ont.	1-29-67	6	Hartford
31	Mario Gosselin	5-8/160	Thetford Mines, Que.	6-15-63	9	Hartford, Springfield (AHL)
	Manny Legace	5-9/162	Toronto	2-4-73	0	Canadian national team (Int'l)

1993-94 REVIEW

INDIVIDUAL STATISTICS

SCORING

	Games	G	A	Pts.	PIM	+/-	PPG	SHG	Shots	Shooting Pct.
Pat Verbeek	84	37	38	75	177	-15	15	1	226	16.4
Geoff Sanderson	82	41	26	67	42	-13	15	1	266	15.4
Andrew Cassels	79	16	42	58	37	-21	8	1	126	12.7
Robert Kron	77	24	26	50	8	0	2	1	194	12.4
Michael Nylander*	58	11	33	44	24	-2	4	0	74	14.9
Zarley Zalapski*	56	7	30	37	56	-6	0	0	121	5.8
Chris Pronger	81	5	25	30	113	-3	2	0	174	2.9
Brian Propp	65	12	17	29	44	3	3	1	108	11.1
James Patrick*	47	8	20	28	32	-12	4	1	65	12.3
Adam Burt	63	1	17	18	75	-4	0	0	91	1.1
Randy Cunneyworth*	63	9	8	17	87	-2	0	1	121	7.4
Jim Storm	68	6	10	16	27	4	1	0	84	7.1
Igor Chibirev	37	4	11	15	2	7	0	0	30	13.3
Darren Turcotte*	19	2	11	13	4	-11	0	0	43	4.7
Alexander Godynyuk*	43	3	9	12	40	8	0	0	67	4.5
Mark Janssens	84	2	10	12	137	-13	0	0	52	3.8
Robert Petrovicky	33	6	5	11	39	-1	1	0	33	18.2
Bryan Marchment*	42	3	7	10	124	-12	0	1	74	4.1

	Games	G	A	Pts.	PIM	+/-	PPG	SHG	Shots	Shooting Pct.
Mark Greig*	31	4	5	9	31	-6	0	0	41	9.8
Jim Sandlak	27	6	2	8	32	6	2	0	32	18.8
Jocelyn Lemieux*	16	6	1	7	19	-8	0	0	22	27.3
Ted Drury*	16	1	5	6	10	-10	0	0	37	2.7
Brad McCrimmon	65	1	5	6	72	-7	0	0	39	2.6
Kevin Smyth	21	3	2	5	10	-1	0	0	8	37.5
Marc Potvin*	51	2	3	5	246	-5	0	0	25	8.0
Frantisek Kucera*	16	1	3	4	14	-12	1	0	32	3.1
Patrick Poulin*	9	2	1	3	11	-8	1	0	13	15.4
Ted Crowley	21	1	2	3	10	-1	1	0	28	3.6
Jim McKenzie*	26	1	2	3	67	-6	0	0	9	11.1
John Stevens	9	0	3	3	4	4	0	0	3	0.0
Paul Ranheim*	15	0	3	3	2	-11	0	0	21	0.0
Bob McGill*	30	0	3	3	41	-7	0	0	14	0.0
Eric Weinrich*	8	1	1	2	2	-5	1	0	10	10.0
Todd Harkins	28	1	0	1	49	-4	0	0	15	6.7
Dan Keczmer*	12	0	1	1	12	-6	0	0	12	0.0
Jeff Reese* (goalie)	19	0	1	1	0	0	0	0	0	0.0
Mike Lenarduzzi (goalie)	1	0	0	0	0	0	0	0	0	0.0
Mike Tomlak	1	0	0	0	0	0	0	0	2	0.0
Yvon Corriveau	3	0	0	0	0	0	0	0	0	0.0
Mario Gosselin (goalie)	7	0	0	0	0	0	0	0	0	0.0
Doug Houda*	7	0	0	0	23	-4	0	0	1	0.0
Allen Pedersen	7	0	0	0	9	-1	0	0	1	0.0
Nick Kypreos*	10	0	0	0	37	-8	0	0	5	0.0
Frank Pietrangelo (goalie)	19	0	0	0	2	0	0	0	0	0.0
Sean Burke (goalie)	47	0	0	0	16	0	0	0	0	0.0

GOALTENDING

	Games	Min.	Goals	SO	Avg.	W	L	T	Shots	Sv. Pct.
Mike Lenarduzzi	1	21	1	0	2.86	0	0	0	12	.917
Sean Burke	47	2750	137	2	2.99	17	24	5	1458	.906
Jeff Reese*	19	1086	56	1	3.09	5	9	3	524	.893
Frank Pietrangelo	19	984	59	0	3.60	5	11	1	473	.875
Mario Gosselin	7	239	21	0	5.27	0	4	0	107	.804

Empty-net goals (do not count against a goaltender's average): Burke 7, Reese 4, Gosselin 2, Pietrangelo 1.
*Played with two or more NHL teams.

RESULTS

OCTOBER
6—At Montreal	L	3-4
9—Philadelphia	L	2-5
10—At Buffalo	W	3-2
13—Montreal	W	4-3
14—At Chicago	W	6-2
16—At Pittsburgh	L	3-5
19—At Toronto	L	2-7
20—Quebec	L	2-5
23—Buffalo	T	*3-3
27—At Dallas	L	1-5
28—At St. Louis	L	1-2
30—N.Y. Rangers	L	1-4

NOVEMBER
1—St. Louis	L	2-4
3—Calgary	L	3-6
6—At N.Y. Islanders	L	3-5
10—Ottawa	W	*4-3
13—Edmonton	T	*4-4
17—Boston	L	2-4
18—At Philadelphia	L	3-6
20—San Jose	L	2-3
23—At Florida	W	*2-1
24—At Tampa Bay	L	1-4
27—Florida	W	4-0
29—At Ottawa	W	4-2

DECEMBER
1—Detroit	W	5-3
4—Pittsburgh	L	*6-7
7—At Washington	W	6-1
8—Vancouver	L	1-4
11—Buffalo	L	0-3
12—At Boston	T	*2-2
15—At N.Y. Rangers	L	2-5
18—Washington	W	4-1
22—New Jersey	W	6-3
23—At Ottawa	W	2-1
26—Ottawa	W	*3-2
28—At New Jersey	L	2-4
29—Florida	L	3-5

JANUARY
1—At N.Y. Islanders	W	4-3
2—Pittsburgh	W	7-2
5—Winnipeg	W	4-0
6—St. Louis†	L	1-2
8—N.Y. Islanders	W	6-0
12—At Los Angeles	L	4-6
14—At Anaheim	L	3-6
15—At San Jose	L	2-8
17—At Boston	L	3-5
19—Toronto	T	*3-3
24—Boston	L	1-2
26—Montreal	L	0-3
27—At Ottawa	T	*1-1
29—Quebec	L	2-3

FEBRUARY
1—At Quebec	W	2-1
2—At Montreal	L	2-9
4—At Winnipeg	T	*2-2
6—At Vancouver	W	4-2
11—At Calgary	L	1-4
12—At Edmonton	W	5-2
16—Buffalo	L	3-5

17—At Pittsburgh	L	4-6
19—N.Y. Rangers	W	4-2
24—Detroit†	L	0-3
26—New Jersey	T	*1-1
27—Washington	L	1-3

MARCH
2—Los Angeles	L	1-4
4—At Florida	W	2-1
5—At Tampa Bay	L	2-4
9—Tampa Bay	W	4-1
10—At New Jersey	L	0-4
12—Dallas	T	*2-2
13—Pittsburgh	L	2-3
16—At N.Y. Rangers	L	0-4
17—At Quebec	L	1-4
19—At Philadelphia	W	5-3
22—At Washington	L	1-4
25—At Buffalo	L	3-6
26—Anaheim	L	2-3
29—At Detroit	L	2-6
30—Chicago	W	*3-2

APRIL
2—Philadelphia	L	5-6
6—N.Y. Islanders	T	*3-3
7—At Quebec	L	2-5
10—Tampa Bay	W	6-4
11—Montreal	L	1-3
14—At Boston	W	3-2

*Denotes overtime game.
†At Cleveland.

LOS ANGELES KINGS
WESTERN CONFERENCE/PACIFIC DIVISION

1994-95 SCHEDULE

■ Home games shaded.
* — All-Star Game at San Jose Arena.
† — At Phoenix.
△ — At Las Vegas.
D — Day game.

OCTOBER

SUN	MON	TUE	WED	THU	FRI	SAT
						1 SJ
2	3	4	5 DET	6	7	8 CAL
9	10	11 SJ	12	13 VAN	14	15 BOS
16	17	18 NYI	19	20 NYR	21	22 PIT
23 CHI	24	25 FLA	26 TB	27	28 DET	29
30	31					

NOVEMBER

SUN	MON	TUE	WED	THU	FRI	SAT
		1 NYR	2	3	4 VAN	5
6 NJ	7	8 ANA	9	10 CAL	11	12 VAN
13	14	15 CHI	16	17 BUF	18	19
20	21	22 CAL	23 EDM	24	25	26 MON
27	28 OTT	29 QUE	30			

DECEMBER

SUN	MON	TUE	WED	THU	FRI	SAT
				1	2 BUF	3 TOR
4	5	6	7	8 WAS	9	10 TOR
11	12 VAN	13	14	15 PIT	16	17 NYI
18	19	20	21	22 EDM	23	24
25	26 ANA	27	28 ANA	29	30	31 D WIN

JANUARY

SUN	MON	TUE	WED	THU	FRI	SAT
1	2 DAL	3	4 HAR	5	6 WAS	7
8 CHI	9	10 STL	11	12 STL	13	14 DAL
15	16 CAL	17 EDM	18	19	20	21*
22	23 SJ	24 DAL	25	26 SJ	27	28 WIN
29	30	31† WIN				

FEBRUARY

SUN	MON	TUE	WED	THU	FRI	SAT
			1	2 STL	3	4 DET
5	6 EDM	7	8 NJ	9 DET	10	11 D BOS
12	13 PHI	14	15	16 QUE	17	18 OTT
19 ANA	20	21 ANA	22	23 PHI	24	25 CAL
26	27	28 TB				

MARCH

SUN	MON	TUE	WED	THU	FRI	SAT
			1	2△ STL	3	4 MON
5	6 DAL	7	8	9 TOR	10	11 WIN
12	13	14 HAR	15	16 STL	17	18 TOR
19	20 FLA	21	22	23 CHI	24	25 D SJ
26 SJ	D 27	28	29 VAN	30	31 EDM	

APRIL

SUN	MON	TUE	WED	THU	FRI	SAT
						1 WIN
2	3 EDM	4	5	6 VAN	7 CAL	8
9	D 10 ANA	11	12	13	14	15

1994-95 SEASON

CLUB DIRECTORY

Owners
Jeffrey Sudikoff
Joseph Cohen
Bruce McNall
Chairman of the board
Joseph Cohen
President
Bruce McNall
Assistant to the president
Rogatien Vachon
General manager
Sam McMaster
Executive vice president
Lester Wintz
Coach
Barry Melrose
Assistant coaches
Cap Raeder
John Perpich
Administrative assistant to general manager
John Wolf
Director of amateur scouting
Al Murray

Scouting staff
Serge Aubry
Gary Harker
Jan Lindegren
Vaclav Nedomansky
Don Perry
John Stanton
Vice president, finance
Michael Handelman, CPA
Vice president, marketing
Gregory McElroy
Vice president, public relations
Scott Carmichael
Director, media relations
Rick Minch
Trainers
Pete Demers
Peter Millar
Robert Zolg
Rick Garcia

DRAFT CHOICES

Rd.—Player	H/W	Overall	Pos.	Last team
1—James Storr	6-1/192	7	G	Owen Sound (OHL)
2—Matt Johnson	6-5/223	33	LW	Peterborough (OHL)
3—Vitali Yachmenev	5-9/180	59	RW	North Bay (OHL)
5—Chris Schmidt	6-3/193	111	C	Seattle (WHL)
7—Luc Gagne	6-1/185	163	RW	Sudbury (OHL)
8—Andrew Dale	6-1/196	189	C	Sudbury (OHL)
9—Jan Nemecek	6-1/194	215	D	HC Ceske Budejovice, Czech.
10—Sergei Shalani	5-7/154	241	LW	Spartak Moscow, CIS

MISCELLANEOUS DATA

Home ice (capacity)
The Great Western Forum (16,005)
Address
3900 West Manchester Blvd.
Inglewood, CA 90305
Business phone
310-419-3160

Rink dimensions
200 feet by 85 feet
Club colors
Black, white and silver

TRAINING CAMP ROSTER

No.	FORWARDS	Ht./Wt.	Place	Date	NHL exp.	1993-94 clubs
	Kevin Brown (RW)	6-1/212	Birmingham, England	5-11-74	0	Detroit (OHL), Belleville (OHL)
	Rob Brown (LW)	5-11/185	Kingston, Ont.	4-10-68	7	Kalamazoo (IHL), Dallas
15	Pat Conacher (LW/C)...	5-9/190	Edmonton, Alta.	5-1-59	12	Los Angeles
23	Phil Crowe (LW)	6-2/220	Red Deer, Alta.	4-14-70	1	Fort Wayne (IHL), Phoenix (IHL), Los Angeles
11	Mike Donnelly (LW)	5-11/185	Livonia, Mich.	10-10-63	8	Los Angeles
	John Druce (RW)	6-2/195	Peterborough, Ont.	2-23-66	6	Phoenix (IHL), Los Angeles
21	Tony Granato (RW).......	5-10/185	Downers Grove, Ill.	7-25-64	6	Los Angeles
99	Wayne Gretzky (C)	6-0/170	Brantford, Ont.	1-26-61	15	Los Angeles
	Matt Johnson (LW)	6-5/223	Pelham, Ont.	11-23-75	0	Peterborough (OHL)
17	Jari Kurri (C/RW)	6-1/195	Helsinki, Finland	5-18-60	13	Los Angeles
13	Robert Lang (C)...........	6-2/180	Teplice, Czechoslovakia	12-19-70	2	Phoenix (IHL), Los Angeles
28	Guy Leveque (C)...........	5-11/166	Kingston, Ont.	12-28-72	2	Los Angeles
	Brian McReynolds (C)...	6-1/192	Penetanguishene, Ont.	1-5-65	3	Phoenix (IHL), Los Angeles
	Yanic Perreault (C)	5-11/182	Sherbrooke, Que.	4-4-71	1	St. John's (AHL), Toronto
	Keith Redmond (LW).....	6-3/208	Richmond Hill, Ont.	10-25-72	1	Los Angeles, Phoenix (IHL)
10	Warren Rychel (LW).....	6-0/190	Tecumseh, Ont.	5-12-67	4	Los Angeles
	Jeff Shevalier (LW/C)...	5-11/180	Mississauga, Ont.	3-14-74	0	North Bay (OHL)
14	Gary Shuchuk (RW/C) .	5-10/185	Edmonton, Alta.	2-17-67	3	Los Angeles
	Rick Tocchet (RW).......	6-0/205	Scarborough, Ont.	4-9-64	10	Pittsburgh
	Kevin Todd (C)	5-10/180	Winnipeg, Man.	5-4-68	5	Chicago, Los Angeles
17	Dixon Ward (RW)	6-0/195	Edmonton, Alta.	9-23-68	2	Vancouver, Los Angeles
	Bob Wren (LW)	5-10/175	Preston, Ont.	9-16-74	0	Detroit (OHL)
	DEFENSEMEN					
4	Rob Blake....................	6-3/215	Simcoe, Ont.	12-10-69	5	Los Angeles
34	Donald Dufresne............	6-1/206	Quebec City	4-10-67	6	Tampa Bay, Los Angeles
	Justin Hocking	6-4/206	Stettler, Alta.	1-9-74	1	Medicine Hat (WHL), Phoenix (IHL), Los Angeles
22	Charlie Huddy...............	6-0/210	Oshawa, Ont.	6-2-59	14	Los Angeles
33	Marty McSorley.............	6-1/225	Hamilton, Ont.	5-18-63	11	Pittsburgh, Los Angeles
	Michel Petit..................	6-1/185	St. Malo, Que.	2-12-64	12	Calgary
25	Darryl Sydor	6-0/205	Edmonton, Alta.	5-13-72	3	Los Angeles
3	Brent Thompson............	6-2/175	Calgary, Alta.	1-9-71	3	Phoenix (IHL), Los Angeles
5	Timothy Watters	5-11/185	Kamloops, B.C.	7-25-59	13	Los Angeles
2	Alexei Zhitnik	5-11/180	Kiev, U.S.S.R.	10-10-72	2	Los Angeles
	GOALTENDERS					
	Sandy Allan	6-0/175	Nassau, Bahamas	1-22-74	0	North Bay (OHL)
32	Kelly Hrudey	5-10/189	Edmonton, Alta.	1-13-61	11	Los Angeles
35	Robb Stauber................	5-11/180	Duluth, Minn.	11-25-67	3	Los Angeles, Phoenix (IHL)
	Jamie Storr	6-2/192	Brampton, Ont.	12-28-75	0	Owen Sound (OHL), Canadian Olympic Team (Int'l)

1993-94 REVIEW

INDIVIDUAL STATISTICS

SCORING

	Games	G	A	Pts.	PIM	+/-	PPG	SHG	Shots	Shooting Pct.
Wayne Gretzky....................	81	38	†92	†130	20	-25	14	4	233	16.3
Luc Robitaille.....................	83	44	42	86	86	-20	24	0	267	16.5
Jari Kurri..........................	81	31	46	77	48	-24	14	4	198	15.7
Rob Blake..........................	84	20	48	68	137	-7	7	0	304	6.6
Alexei Zhitnik.....................	81	12	40	52	101	-11	11	0	227	5.3
Mike Donnelly.....................	81	21	21	42	34	2	4	2	177	11.9
Tomas Sandstrom*..............	51	17	24	41	59	-12	4	0	121	14.0
Darryl Sydor......................	84	8	27	35	94	-9	1	0	146	5.5
John Druce........................	55	14	17	31	50	16	1	1	104	13.5
Pat Conacher.....................	77	15	13	28	71	0	0	3	98	15.3
Shawn McEachern*..............	49	8	13	21	24	1	0	3	81	9.9
Tony Granato......................	50	7	14	21	150	-2	2	0	117	6.0
Warren Rychel.....................	80	10	9	19	322	-19	0	0	105	9.5
Robert Lang.......................	32	9	10	19	10	7	0	0	41	22.0
Charlie Huddy.....................	79	5	13	18	71	4	1	0	134	3.7
Jimmy Carson*...................	25	4	7	11	2	-2	1	0	47	8.5
Kevin Todd*.......................	12	3	8	11	8	-1	0	0	16	18.8
Marty McSorley*.................	18	4	6	10	55	-3	1	0	38	10.5
Tim Watters.......................	60	1	9	10	67	-11	0	1	38	2.6
Dixon Ward*......................	34	6	2	8	45	-8	2	0	44	13.6

	Games	G	A	Pts.	PIM	+/-	PPG	SHG	Shots	Shooting Pct.
Doug Houda*	54	2	6	8	165	-15	0	0	31	6.5
Dave Taylor	33	4	3	7	28	-1	0	1	39	10.3
Gary Shuchuk	56	3	4	7	30	-8	0	0	55	5.5
Dominic Lavoie	8	3	3	6	2	-2	2	0	21	14.3
Brian McReynolds	20	1	3	4	4	-2	0	0	10	10.0
Mark Hardy	16	0	3	3	27	-5	0	0	8	0.0
Dan Currie	5	1	1	2	0	-1	0	0	12	8.3
Jim Paek*	18	1	1	2	10	-1	0	0	11	9.1
Philip Crowe	31	0	2	2	77	4	0	0	5	0.0
Keith Redmond	12	1	0	1	20	-3	0	0	9	11.1
Brent Thompson	24	1	0	1	81	-1	0	0	9	11.1
Bob Jay	3	0	1	1	0	-2	0	0	2	0.0
Guy Leveque	5	0	1	1	2	1	0	0	3	0.0
Rob Murphy	8	0	1	1	22	-3	0	0	4	0.0
Kelly Hrudey (goalie)	64	0	1	1	6	0	0	0	0	0.0
David Goverde (goalie)	1	0	0	0	0	0	0	0	0	0.0
Justin Hocking	1	0	0	0	0	0	0	0	0	0.0
Marc Potvin*	3	0	0	0	26	-3	0	0	1	0.0
Rick Knickle (goalie)	4	0	0	0	0	0	0	0	0	0.0
Dave Thomlinson	7	0	0	0	21	-6	0	0	6	0.0
Donald Dufresne*	9	0	0	0	10	-5	0	0	7	0.0
Robb Stauber (goalie)	22	0	0	0	18	0	0	0	0	0.0

GOALTENDING

	Games	Min.	Goals	SO	Avg.	W	L	T	Shots	Sv. Pct.
Rick Knickle	4	174	9	0	3.10	1	2	0	71	.873
Robb Stauber	22	1144	65	1	3.41	4	11	5	706	.908
Kelly Hrudey	64	3713	228	1	3.68	22	31	7	2219	.897
David Goverde	1	60	7	0	7.00	0	1	0	37	.811

Empty-net goals (do not count against a goaltender's average): Hrudey 9, Knickle 2, Stauber 2.
*Played with two or more NHL teams.
†Led league.

RESULTS

OCTOBER
6—Vancouver	L	2-5
9—Detroit	W	10-3
10—San Jose	W	5-2
12—N.Y. Islanders	W	7-5
14—Edmonton	T	*4-4
16—Calgary	W	8-4
19—At Florida	T	*2-2
20—At Tampa Bay	W	4-3
22—At Washington	L	3-6
24—At N.Y. Rangers	L	2-3
26—At N.Y. Islanders	L	0-7
27—At Detroit	L	3-8
29—At Winnipeg	W	*4-3

NOVEMBER
3—New Jersey	W	3-2
6—Pittsburgh	W	8-3
9—At Calgary	L	2-3
10—At Vancouver	L	0-4
13—St. Louis	W	6-3
18—Toronto	L	2-3
20—At St. Louis	L	1-4
21—At Dallas	L	4-7
25—At Quebec	L	6-8
27—At Montreal	L	0-4
30—Winnipeg	L	6-8

DECEMBER
2—Anaheim	W	3-2
4—Tampa Bay	L	4-5
8—Florida	L	5-6
11—St. Louis	W	9-1
13—At Ottawa	L	2-5
14—At Pittsburgh	L	2-4
17—At Buffalo	L	0-2
18—At Toronto	L	1-4
20—At Calgary	W	*5-4
23—Dallas	L	1-2
26—At Anaheim	W	3-2
28—Vancouver	W	6-5
31—At Detroit	T	*4-4

JANUARY
1—At Toronto	W	7-4
4—Quebec	W	5-1
8—Detroit	L	3-6
11—At San Jose	T	*2-2
12—Hartford	W	6-4
15—At New Jersey	W	5-3
16—At Philadelphia	L	2-5
18—At Dallas	L	3-5
24—Calgary†	T	*3-3
25—Winnipeg	T	*4-4
27—N.Y. Rangers	L	*4-5
29—Anaheim	W	5-1
31—At Vancouver	L	1-3

FEBRUARY
2—At Edmonton	L	4-6
5—Calgary	L	*4-5
9—Chicago	W	4-2
11—At Anaheim	W	5-3
12—Washington	L	1-6
14—Boston	L	*2-3
18—Philadelphia	L	3-4
19—At San Jose	L	3-4
21—Toronto	L	4-6

23—Dallas	T	*0-0
25—At Edmonton	T	*5-5
26—At Calgary	L	2-4
28—Montreal	T	*3-3

MARCH
2—At Hartford	W	4-1
3—At Boston	L	4-6
6—At Chicago	T	*3-3
9—Chicago	L	0-4
12—Buffalo	L	3-5
15—Ottawa	W	7-0
16—At Anaheim	L	2-5
19—San Jose	W	2-1
20—At San Jose	T	*6-6
23—Vancouver	L	3-6
25—At Edmonton	W	*4-3
27—At Vancouver	L	3-4
30—Anaheim	L	2-5

APRIL
2—Edmonton	L	3-5
3—Edmonton‡	W	6-1
5—San Jose	L	1-2
7—At St. Louis	L	2-6
9—At Winnipeg	L	3-4
10—At Chicago	L	1-2
13—Calgary	W	6-4
14—Edmonton	T	*2-2

*Denotes overtime game.
†At Phoenix.
‡At Sacramento, Calif.

MONTREAL CANADIENS
EASTERN CONFERENCE/NORTHEAST DIVISION

1994-95 SCHEDULE

☐ Home games shaded.
* — All-Star Game at San Jose Arena.
† — At Phoenix.
∆ — At Hamilton, Ont.
D — Day games.

OCTOBER

SUN	MON	TUE	WED	THU	FRI	SAT
						1 BOS
2	3	4	5 WIN	6	7 BUF	8 BUF
9	10	11	12 NYI	13	14 WAS	15 PIT
16 CHI	17	18	19 DET	20	21	22 NYR
23 NJ	24	25	26 EDM	27 BOS	28	29 PIT
30	31					

NOVEMBER

SUN	MON	TUE	WED	THU	FRI	SAT
		1	2 TB	3	4	5 OTT
6	7	8 HAR	9	10 NJ	11	12 TOR
13	14	15	16 NYI	17 QUE	18	19 QUE
20	21 HAR	22	23 FLA	24	25	26 LA
27	28 WAS	29	30 STL			

DECEMBER

SUN	MON	TUE	WED	THU	FRI	SAT
				1 CHI	2	3 DET
4	5	6	7 CAL	8 PHI	9	10 PHI
11	12	13	14 BOS	15	16 BUF	17 OTT
18	19 TB	20	21 BUF	22	23 NYR	24
25	26	27 VAN	28	29	30 EDM	31 CAL

JANUARY

SUN	MON	TUE	WED	THU	FRI	SAT
1	2 ANA	3	4 SJ	5† QUE	6	7
8	9 OTT	10	11	12 QUE	13	14 FLA
15	16	17	18 ANA	19	20	21*
22	23 HAR	24	25	26	27	28 D NJ
29 D PHI	30	31				

FEBRUARY

SUN	MON	TUE	WED	THU	FRI	SAT
		1 TB	2 FLA	3	4 VAN	
5	6 SJ	7	8 OTT	9	10	11 PIT
12	13 HAR	14	15 HAR	16 NYR	17	18 STL
19	20 WAS	D 21	22	23 FLA	24	25 TOR
26	27† FLA	28				

MARCH

SUN	MON	TUE	WED	THU	FRI	SAT
			1 DAL	2	3	4 LA
5	6	7	8 WAS	9 NYI	10	11 NYR
12	13	14	15 WIN	16 BOS	17	18 DAL
19	20 PHI	21	22 BOS	23	24 PIT	25 BUF
26	27 TB	28	29	30 NYI	31	

APRIL

SUN	MON	TUE	WED	THU	FRI	SAT
						1 NJ
2	3 OTT	4	5 QUE	6 QUE	7	8 PIT
9	10	11	12	13	14	15

1994-95 SEASON

CLUB DIRECTORY

Chairman of the board, pres. and governor
Ronald Corey
V.P. hockey and managing director
Serge Savard
V.P., communications and marketing services
Bernard Brisset
Vice president, Forum operations
Aldo Giampaolo
Vice president, finance and administration
Fred Steer
Assistant to managing director
To be announced
Dir. of recruitment and asst. to managing dir.
Andre Boudrias
Coach
Jacques Demers
Assistant coaches
Francois Allaire
Jacques Laperriere
Steve Shutt

Goaltending instructor
Francois Allaire
Director of player development and scout
Claude Ruel
Chief scout
Doug Robinson
Director of communications
Donald Beauchamp
Director of team services
Michele Lapointe
Club physician
Dr. D.G. Kinnear
Athletic trainer
Gaetan Lefebvre
Equipment manager
Eddy Palchak
Assistants to the equipment manager
Pierre Gervais
Robert Boulanger
Pierre Ouellette

DRAFT CHOICES

Rd.—Player	H/W	Overall	Pos.	Last team
1—Brad Brown	6-3/218	18	D	North Bay (OHL)
2—Jose Theodore	5-10/178	44	G	St. Jean (QMJHL)
3—Chris Murray	6-1/205	54	RW	Kamloops (WHL)
3—Marko Kiprusoff	6-0/194	70	D	TPS Turku, CIS
3—Martin Belanger	6-0/206	74	D	Granby (QMJHL)
4—Arto Kuki	6-3/205	96	C	Espoo, Finland
5—Jimmy Drolet	6-1/174	122	D	St. Hyacinthe (QMJHL)
6—Joel Irving	6-3/190	148	C	Regina Midgets
7—Jessie Rezansoff	6-3/190	174	RW	Regina (WHL)
8—Peter Strom	6-0/178	200	LW	Vastra Frolunda, Sweden
9—Tomas Vokoun	5-11/180	226	G	HC Kladno, Czech.
10—Chris Aldous	6-2/175	252	D	Northwood Prep (N.Y.)
11—Ross Parsons	6-2/187	278	D	Regina (WHL)

MISCELLANEOUS DATA

Home ice (capacity)
Montreal Forum (17,959)
Address
2313 St. Catherine Street West
Montreal, Que. H3H 1N2
Business phone
514-932-2582

Rink dimensions
200 feet by 85 feet
Club colors
Red, white and blue

No.	FORWARDS	Ht./Wt.	BORN Place	Date	NHL exp.	1993-94 clubs
23	Brian Bellows (LW)	5-11/209	St. Catharines, Ont.	9-1-64	12	Montreal
35	Donald Brashear (LW)	6-3/214	Bedford, Ind.	1-7-72	1	Fredericton (AHL), Montreal
22	Benoit Brunet (LW)	5-11/193	Montreal	8-24-68	5	Montreal
	Valeri Bure (LW)	5-10/160	Moscow, U.S.S.R.	6-13-74	0	Spokane (WHL)
	Jim Campbell (C)	6-1/175	Worcester, Mass.	2-3-73	0	U.S. national team (Int'l), U.S. Olympic Team (Int'l), Fredericton (AHL)
21	Guy Carbonneau (C)	5-11/184	Sept Iles, Que.	3-18-60	13	Montreal
25	Vincent Damphousse	6-1/199	Montreal	12-17-67	8	Montreal
45	Gilbert Dionne (LW)	6-0/194	Drummondville, Que.	9-19-70	4	Montreal
15	Paul Dipietro (C)	5-9/181	Sault Ste. Marie, Ont.	9-8-70	3	Montreal
36	Gerry Fleming	6-5/240	Montreal	10-16-67	1	Fredericton (AHL), Montreal
12	Mike Keane (RW)	5-10/180	Winnipeg, Man.	5-29-67	6	Montreal
	Saku Koivu (C)	5-9/163	Turku, Finland	11-23-74	0	TPS Turku (Finland), Finland Olympic Team (Int'l)
17	John LeClair (C)	6-2/219	St. Albans, Vt.	7-5-69	4	Montreal
26	Gary Leeman (RW)	5-11/186	Toronto	2-19-64	12	Montreal, Fredericton (AHL)
11	Kirk Muller (LW)	6-0/205	Kingston, Ont.	2-8-66	10	Montreal
6	Oleg Petrov (RW)	5-9/166	Moscow, U.S.S.R.	4-18-71	2	Fredericton (AHL), Montreal
32	Mario Roberge (LW)	5-11/193	Quebec City	1-31-64	4	Montreal
31	Ed Ronan (RW)	6-0/197	Quincy, Mass.	3-21-68	3	Montreal
	Brian Savage (C)	6-2/191	Sudbury, Ont.	2-24-71	1	Canadian national team (Int'l), Canadian Olympic Team (Int'l), Fredericton (AHL), Montreal
	Pierre Sevigny (LW)	6-0/189	Trois-Rivieres, Que.	9-8-71	1	Montreal
18	Ron Wilson (C)	5-9/182	Toronto	5-13-56	14	Montreal
	DEFENSEMEN					
43	Patrice Brisebois	6-2/182	Montreal	1-27-71	4	Montreal
	Brad Brown	6-3/218	Mississauga, Ont.	12-27-75	0	North Bay (OHL)
48	J.J. Daigneault	5-11/199	Montreal	10-12-65	9	Montreal
28	Eric Desjardins	6-1/200	Rouyn, Que.	6-14-69	6	Montreal
	Bryan Fogarty	6-2/206	Montreal	6-11-69	5	Atlanta (IHL), Las Vegas (IHL), Kansas City (IHL), Montreal
	Marko Kiprusoff	6-0/194	Turku, Finland	6-6-72	0	TPS Turku (Finland)
24	Lyle Odelein	5-10/206	Quill Lake, Sask.	7-21-68	5	Montreal
34	Peter Popovic	6-5/241	Koping, Sweden	2-10-68	1	Montreal
	Yves Racine	6-0/200	Matane, Que.	2-7-69	5	Philadelphia
8	Mathieu Schneider	5-11/189	New York	6-12-69	6	Montreal
	Adam Wiesel	6-3/201	Holyoke, Mass.	1-25-75	0	Clarkson (ECAC)
	David Wilkie	6-2/202	Ellensburg, Wash.	5-30-74	0	Kamloops (WHL), Regina (WHL)
	GOALTENDERS					
	Les Kuntar	6-2/195	Buffalo, N.Y.	7-28-69	1	Fredericton (AHL), Montreal
	Marc Lamothe	6-2/186	New Liskeard, Ont.	2-27-74	0	Kingston (OHL)
37	Andre Racicot	5-11/176	Rouyn-Noranda, Que.	6-9-69	5	Montreal, Fredericton (AHL)
33	Patrick Roy	6-0/182	Quebec City	10-5-65	10	Montreal
1	Ron Tugnutt	5-11/155	Scarborough, Ont.	10-22-67	7	Anaheim, Montreal

1993-94 REVIEW

INDIVIDUAL STATISTICS

SCORING

	Games	G	A	Pts.	PIM	+/-	PPG	SHG	Shots	Shooting Pct.
Vincent Damphousse	84	40	51	91	75	0	13	0	274	14.6
Brian Bellows	77	33	38	71	36	9	13	0	251	13.1
Kirk Muller	76	23	34	57	96	-1	9	2	168	13.7
Matt Schneider	75	20	32	52	62	15	11	0	193	10.4
Mike Keane	80	16	30	46	119	6	6	2	129	12.4
Gilbert Dionne	74	19	26	45	31	-9	3	0	162	11.7
John LeClair	74	19	24	43	32	17	1	0	153	12.4
Lyle Odelein	79	11	29	40	276	8	6	0	116	9.5
Guy Carbonneau	79	14	24	38	48	16	0	1	120	11.7
Eric Desjardins	84	12	23	35	97	-1	6	1	193	6.2
Paul Dipietro	70	13	20	33	37	-2	2	0	115	11.3
Benoit Brunet	71	10	20	30	20	14	0	3	92	10.9
Oleg Petrov	55	12	15	27	2	7	1	0	107	11.2
Patrice Brisebois	53	2	21	23	63	5	1	0	71	2.8
Stephan Lebeau	34	9	7	16	8	1	4	0	61	14.8
Gary Leeman	31	4	11	15	17	5	0	0	53	7.5

	Games	G	A	Pts.	PIM	+/-	PPG	SHG	Shots	Shooting Pct.
Ed Ronan	61	6	8	14	42	3	0	0	49	12.2
Peter Popovic	47	2	12	14	26	10	1	0	58	3.4
J.J. Daigneault	68	2	12	14	73	16	0	0	61	3.3
Kevin Haller	68	4	9	13	118	3	0	0	72	5.6
Ron Wilson	48	2	10	12	12	-2	0	0	39	5.1
Pierre Sevigny	43	4	5	9	42	6	1	0	19	21.1
Donald Brashear	14	2	2	4	34	0	0	0	15	13.3
Christian Proulx	7	1	2	3	20	0	0	0	11	9.1
Bryan Fogarty	13	1	2	3	10	-4	0	0	22	4.5
Mario Roberge	28	1	2	3	55	-2	0	0	5	20.0
Brian Savage	3	1	0	1	0	0	0	0	3	33.3
Craig Ferguson	2	0	1	1	0	1	0	0	0	0.0
Rob Ramage*	6	0	1	1	2	-1	0	0	5	0.0
Patrick Roy (goalie)	68	0	1	1	30	0	0	0	0	0.0
Frederic Chabot* (goalie)	1	0	0	0	0	0	0	0	0	0.0
Lindsay Vallis	1	0	0	0	0	0	0	0	0	0.0
Turner Stevenson	2	0	0	0	2	-2	0	0	0	0.0
Gerry Fleming	5	0	0	0	25	-4	0	0	4	0.0
Les Kuntar (goalie)	6	0	0	0	2	0	0	0	0	0.0
Ron Tugnutt* (goalie)	8	0	0	0	0	0	0	0	0	0.0
Andre Racicot (goalie)	11	0	0	0	0	0	0	0	0	0.0
Ron Tugnutt	36	0	0	0	2	0	0	0	0	0.0

GOALTENDING

	Games	Min.	Goals	SO	Avg.	W	L	T	Shots	Sv. Pct.
Patrick Roy	68	3867	161	‡7	2.50	35	17	11	1956	.918
Les Kuntar	6	302	16	0	3.18	2	2	0	130	.877
Ron Tugnutt*	8	378	24	0	3.81	2	3	1	172	.860
Andre Racicot	11	500	37	0	4.44	2	6	2	246	.850
Frederic Chabot*	1	60	5	0	5.00	0	1	0	24	.792

Empty-net goals (do not count against a goaltender's average): Roy 4, Kuntar 1.
*Played with two or more NHL teams.
‡Tied for league lead.

RESULTS

OCTOBER

6—Hartford	W	4-3
7—At Pittsburgh	L	*1-2
9—Buffalo	W	7-4
11—At Boston	T	*1-1
13—At Hartford	L	3-4
16—Quebec	L	2-5
18—At Quebec	W	4-2
20—Dallas	W	5-2
23—Anaheim	W	4-1
26—At New Jersey	W	2-0
28—At N.Y. Rangers	T	*3-3
30—Toronto	W	5-2

NOVEMBER

3—Tampa Bay	W	1-0
6—Calgary	L	3-4
10—Florida	L	1-3
13—Ottawa	L	*2-3
15—At Ottawa	W	4-2
17—Edmonton	W	3-1
18—N.Y. Islanders†	L	1-5
20—Pittsburgh	T	*2-2
23—At N.Y. Rangers	L	*4-5
24—At Philadelphia	L	2-9
27—Los Angeles	W	4-0

DECEMBER

1—Ottawa	L	3-6
3—At Washington	T	*2-2
4—At Boston	W	8-1
6—Vancouver	W	*4-3
8—New Jersey	L	2-4
11—Washington	L	3-5

14—Tampa Bay‡	T	*1-1
15—At Florida	T	*3-3
18—Detroit	W	8-1
22—N.Y. Islanders	L	3-5
23—At Buffalo	L	0-5
27—At St. Louis	W	5-2
29—At Edmonton	L	3-6
31—At Calgary	W	5-2

JANUARY

2—At Vancouver	W	3-2
4—At San Jose	T	*2-2
5—Quebec§	W	4-0
8—N.Y. Rangers	W	3-2
10—Winnipeg	W	4-2
12—New Jersey	W	3-2
14—At N.Y. Islanders	L	2-5
15—Florida	L	2-5
17—Washington	W	3-1
19—Boston	T	*3-3
24—At Florida	L	3-8
26—At Hartford	W	3-0
29—Buffalo	L	2-3
30—Philadelphia	W	*5-4

FEBRUARY

2—Hartford	W	9-2
4—At Washington	W	4-0
5—At Ottawa	W	4-3
7—At Pittsburgh	W	4-1
9—N.Y. Rangers	W	*4-3
11—At Buffalo	L	1-5
12—Quebec	W	5-2
17—At Tampa Bay	L	3-5

19—Pittsburgh	W	4-1
21—At Philadelphia	L	7-8
23—San Jose	W	3-1
26—At Toronto	W	3-0
28—At Los Angeles	T	*3-3

MARCH

2—At Anaheim	W	5-2
6—At Dallas	T	*2-2
9—St. Louis	W	7-2
10—At Quebec	T	*4-4
12—Philadelphia	T	*4-4
14—Boston	W	5-4
16—Chicago	W	5-3
19—Quebec	W	5-2
23—At Winnipeg	L	1-3
24—At Chicago	T	*5-5
26—At Boston	L	3-6
28—Ottawa	W	3-2
29—At New Jersey	L	2-5

APRIL

1—At N.Y. Islanders	L	2-5
2—N.Y. Islanders	T	*3-3
6—Tampa Bay	L	1-3
8—At Buffalo	L	0-1
9—Pittsburgh	W	9-1
11—At Hartford	W	3-1
13—At Detroit	L	0-9

*Denotes overtime game.
†At Hamilton, Ont.
‡At Orlando, Fla.
§At Phoenix.

NEW JERSEY DEVILS
EASTERN CONFERENCE/ATLANTIC DIVISION

1994-95 SCHEDULE

Home games shaded.
* — All-Star Game at San Jose Arena.
† — At Denver.
Δ — At Halifax, N.S.
D — Day game.

OCTOBER

SUN	MON	TUE	WED	THU	FRI	SAT
						1 NYR
2	3	4	5	6 CHI	7	8 OTT
9	10	11	12 PHI	13	14	15 TB
16 FLA	17	18	19 WAS	20	21	22 D SJ
23	24 MON	25	26 CAL	27	28	29 VAN
30 WIN	31					

NOVEMBER

SUN	MON	TUE	WED	THU	FRI	SAT
		1 SJ	2	3	4 ANA	5
6 LA	7	8 PIT	9	10 MON	11	12 D BOS
13 D QUE	14	15	16 DAL	17	18 NYI	19 TB
20	21	22	23 OTT	24	25 D PHI	26 D DET
27	28	29	30			

DECEMBER

SUN	MON	TUE	WED	THU	FRI	SAT
				1	2 QUE	3 D EDM
4 STL	5	6	7 WIN	8	9 DET	10
11 PHI	12	13 OTT	14	15 FLA	16	17 DAL
18	19	20 HAR	21	22	23 OTT	24
25	26 BUF	27 BUF	28	29	30 FLA	31 WAS

JANUARY

SUN	MON	TUE	WED	THU	FRI	SAT
1	2	3	4 PIT	5	6	7 ANA
8	9† PIT	10	11 PHI	12	13 NYI	14
15 NYR	16	17 FLA	18 TB	19	20	21*
22	23	24	25 BUF	26 BOS	27	28 D MON
29	30	31 WAS				

FEBRUARY

SUN	MON	TUE	WED	THU	FRI	SAT
			1	2 BUF	3	4 D CHI
5 D QUE	6	7	8 LA	9	10 TOR	11
12Δ D WAS	13	14	15 STL	16	17 NYI	18 NYI
19	20	21 PIT	22	23 TB	24	25 D WAS
26 D WAS	27	28				

MARCH

SUN	MON	TUE	WED	THU	FRI	SAT
			1 HAR	2 BOS	3	4 D FLA
5	6 NYR	7 NYI	8	9	10	11 TOR
12	13	14 QUE	15 NYR	16	17	18 D TB
19 BOS	20	21 EDM	22	23 VAN	24 CAL	25
26	27	28	29	30 PHI	31	

APRIL

SUN	MON	TUE	WED	THU	FRI	SAT
						1 D MON
2	3	4 HAR	5 PIT	6	7	8 D HAR
9 NYR	10	11	12	13	14	15

1994-95 SEASON

CLUB DIRECTORY

Chairman
John J. McMullen
President and general manager
Louis A. Lamoriello
Executive vice president
Max McNab
Head coach
Jacques Lemaire
Assistant coach
Larry Robinson
Goaltending coach
Jacques Caron
Interim director, public and media relations
Mike Levine
Director of scouting
David Conte

Scouts
Claude Carrier
Marcel Pronovost
Milt Fisher
Ed Thomlinson
Dan Labraaten
Glen Dirk
Les Widdifield
Joe Mahoney
Ferny Flaman
Larry Perris
John Cunniff
Lou Reycroft
Bob Hoffmeyer
Jan Ludvig

DRAFT CHOICES

Rd.—Player	H/W	Overall	Pos.	Last team
1—Vadim Sharifjanov....	6-0/183	25	RW	Salavat Yulayev Ufa, CIS
2—Patrik Elias	6-0/176	51	LW	HC Kladno, Czech.
3—Sheldon Souray	6-2/210	71	D	Tri-City (WHL)
4—Zdenek Skorepa	6-0/187	103	LW	Chemopetrol (Czech Jrs.)
5—Christian Gosselin	6-4/206	129	D	St. Hyacinthe (QMJHL)
6—Ryan Smart	6-0/170	134	C	Meadville H.S.
6—Luciano Caravaggio .	5-11/173	155	G	Michigan Tech
7—Jeff Williams	6-0/175	181	C	Guelph (OHL)
8—Eric Bertrand	6-1/193	207	LW	Granby (QMJHL)
9—Steve Sullivan	5-9/155	233	C	Sault Ste. Marie (OHL)
10—Scott Swanjord	6-4/210	259	G	Waterloo (Jr. A)
11—Mike Hanson	6-1/185	269	C	Minot H.S.

MISCELLANEOUS DATA

Home ice (capacity)
Byrne Meadowlands Arena (19,040)
Address
P.O. Box 504
East Rutherford, N.J. 07073
Business phone
201-935-6050

Rink dimensions
200 feet by 85 feet
Club colors
Red, black and white

TRAINING CAMP ROSTER

No.	FORWARDS	Ht./Wt.	Place (BORN)	Date	NHL exp.	1993-94 clubs
	Sergei Brylin (C)	5-9/176	Moscow, U.S.S.R.	1-13-74	0	CSKA Moscow (CIS), Russian Penguins (IHL)
11	Bobby Carpenter (LW)	6-0/200	Beverly, Mass.	7-13-63	13	New Jersey
9	Tom Chorske (RW)	6-1/205	Minneapolis	9-18-66	5	New Jersey
28	Jim Dowd (C)	6-1/190	Brick, N.J.	12-25-68	3	New Jersey, Albany (AHL)
	David Emma (C)	5-11/180	Cranston, R.I.	1-14-69	2	New Jersey, Albany (AHL)
12	Bill Guerin (C/RW)	6-2/200	Wilbraham, Mass.	11-9-70	3	New Jersey
	Donevan Hextall (LW)	6-2/190	Wolseley, Sask.	2-24-72	0	Raleigh (ECHL), Albany (AHL)
16	Bobby Holik (RW)	6-3/220	Jihlava, Czechoslovakia	1-1-71	4	New Jersey
22	Claude Lemieux (RW)	6-1/215	Buckingham, Que.	7-16-65	11	New Jersey
15	John MacLean (RW)	6-0/200	Oshawa, Ont.	11-20-64	11	New Jersey
21	Randy McKay (RW)	6-1/205	Montreal	1-25-67	6	New Jersey
23	Corey Millen (C)	5-7/170	Cloquet, Minn.	4-29-64	5	New Jersey
17	Jason Miller (C)	6-1/195	Edmonton, Alta.	3-1-71	3	Albany (AHL)
	Denis Pederson (C)	6-2/190	Prince Albert, Sask.	9-10-75	0	Prince Albert (WHL)
	Scott Pellerin (LW)	5-11/180	Shediac, N.B.	1-9-70	2	New Jersey
	Mike Peluso (LW)	6-4/220	Hibbing, Minn.	11-8-65	5	New Jersey
	Stephane Richer (RW)	6-2/215	Buckingham, Que.	6-7-66	10	New Jersey
	Brian Rolston (C)	6-2/185	Flint, Mich.	2-21-73	0	U.S. national team (Int'l), U.S. Olympic Team (Int'l), Albany (AHL)
20	Alexander Semak (C)	5-10/185	Ufa, U.S.S.R.	2-11-66	3	New Jersey
	Brian Sullivan (LW)	6-4/195	South Windsor, Conn.	4-23-69	1	Albany (AHL)
25	Valeri Zelepukin (RW)	5-11/180	Voskresensk, U.S.S.R.	9-17-68	3	New Jersey
	DEFENSEMEN					
6	Tommy Albelin	6-1/190	Stockholm, Sweden	5-21-64	7	Albany (AHL), New Jersey
3	Ken Daneyko	6-0/210	Windsor, Ont.	4-17-64	11	New Jersey
23	Bruce Driver	6-0/185	Toronto	4-29-62	11	New Jersey
	Cale Hulse	6-3/210	Edmonton, Alta.	11-10-73	0	Albany (AHL)
	Dean Malkoc	6-3/200	Vancouver, B.C.	1-26-70	0	Albany (AHL)
	Jaroslav Modry	6-2/195	Ceske-Budejovice, Czech.	2-27-71	1	New Jersey, Albany (AHL)
27	Scott Niedermayer	6-0/200	Edmonton, Alta.	8-31-73	3	New Jersey
	Matt Ruchty	6-1/210	Kitchener, Ont.	11-27-69	0	Albany (AHL)
	Jason Smith	6-3/195	Calgary, Alta.	11-2-73	1	New Jersey, Albany (AHL), Erie (ECHL)
4	Scott Stevens	6-2/210	Kitchener, Ont.	4-1-64	12	New Jersey
	GOALTENDERS					
	Martin Brodeur	6-1/205	Montreal	5-6-72	2	New Jersey
	Mike Dunham	6-3/185	Johnson City, N.Y.	6-1-72	0	U.S. national team (Int'l), U.S. Olympic Team (Int'l), Albany (AHL)
	Corey Schwab	6-0/180	Battleford, Sask.	11-4-70	0	Albany (AHL)
31	Chris Terreri	5-8/160	Warwick, R.I.	11-15-64	7	New Jersey

1993-94 REVIEW

INDIVIDUAL STATISTICS

SCORING

	Games	G	A	Pts.	PIM	+/-	PPG	SHG	Shots	Shooting Pct.
Scott Stevens	83	18	60	78	112	†53	5	1	215	8.4
Stephane Richer	80	36	36	72	16	31	7	3	217	16.6
John MacLean	80	37	33	70	95	30	8	0	277	13.4
Valeri Zelepukin	82	26	31	57	70	36	8	0	155	16.8
Corey Millen	78	20	30	50	52	24	4	0	132	15.2
Bernie Nicholls	61	19	27	46	86	24	3	0	142	13.4
Scott Niedermayer	81	10	36	46	42	34	5	0	135	7.4
Bill Guerin	81	25	19	44	101	14	2	0	195	12.8
Claude Lemieux	79	18	26	44	86	13	5	0	181	9.9
Tom Chorske	76	21	20	41	32	14	1	1	131	16.0
Bobby Holik	70	13	20	33	72	28	2	0	130	10.0
Bob Carpenter	76	10	23	33	51	7	0	2	125	8.0
Bruce Driver	66	8	24	32	63	29	3	1	109	7.3
Alexander Semak	54	12	17	29	22	6	2	2	88	13.6
Randy McKay	78	12	15	27	244	24	0	0	77	15.6
Mike Peluso	69	4	16	20	238	19	0	0	44	9.1
Tommy Albelin	62	2	17	19	36	20	1	0	62	3.2
Jaroslav Modry	41	2	15	17	18	10	2	0	35	5.7
Jim Dowd	15	5	10	15	0	8	2	0	26	19.2

	Games	G	A	Pts.	PIM	+/-	PPG	SHG	Shots	Shooting Pct.
Viacheslav Fetisov	52	1	14	15	30	14	0	0	36	2.8
David Emma	15	5	5	10	2	0	1	0	24	20.8
Ken Daneyko	78	1	9	10	176	27	0	0	60	1.7
Jason Smith	41	0	5	5	43	7	0	0	47	0.0
Chris Terreri (goalie)	44	0	2	2	4	0	0	0	0	0.0
Ben Hankinson	13	1	0	1	23	0	0	0	14	7.1
Scott Pellerin	1	0	0	0	2	0	0	0	0	0.0
Peter Sidorkiewicz (goalie)	3	0	0	0	0	0	0	0	0	0.0
Martin Brodeur (goalie)	47	0	0	0	2	0	0	0	0	0.0

GOALTENDING

	Games	Min.	Goals	SO	Avg.	W	L	T	Shots	Sv. Pct.
Martin Brodeur	47	2625	105	3	2.40	27	11	8	1238	.915
Chris Terreri	44	2340	106	2	2.72	20	11	4	1141	.907
Peter Sidorkiewicz	3	130	6	0	2.77	0	3	0	55	.891

Empty-net goals (do not count against a goaltender's average): Terreri 2, Sidorkiewicz 1.
*Played with two or more NHL teams.
†Led league.

RESULTS

OCTOBER

6—Tampa Bay	W	2-1
8—At Washington	W	6-3
9—Washington	W	6-4
12—Winnipeg	W	7-4
16—At N.Y. Islanders	W	6-3
20—Anaheim	W	4-0
23—Florida	W	2-1
26—Montreal	L	0-2
30—Philadelphia	W	5-3
31—N.Y. Rangers†	L	1-4

NOVEMBER

3—At Los Angeles	L	2-3
5—At Anaheim	W	6-3
7—At San Jose	W	2-1
10—N.Y. Islanders	W	5-3
11—At Philadelphia	W	5-3
13—San Jose	L	2-4
17—Buffalo	W	4-0
18—At Ottawa	W	5-2
20—Detroit	L	*3-4
23—At Quebec	T	*1-1
24—At Buffalo	W	5-3
26—At St. Louis	T	*6-6
30—N.Y. Rangers	L	1-3

DECEMBER

2—At Pittsburgh	T	*2-2
4—Chicago	T	*2-2
5—At N.Y. Rangers	L	1-2
8—At Montreal	W	4-2
9—Quebec	L	2-3
11—Edmonton	W	5-2

14—At N.Y. Islanders	L	1-4
15—Boston	L	4-5
18—At Quebec	W	6-2
19—Philadelphia	W	4-2
22—At Hartford	L	3-6
23—Toronto	W	3-2
26—At N.Y. Rangers	L	3-8
28—Hartford	W	4-2

JANUARY

1—At Ottawa	W	7-1
4—N.Y. Islanders	W	6-3
7—Florida	W	4-1
9—Washington	L	0-4
12—At Montreal	L	2-3
14—At Washington	W	5-2
15—Los Angeles	L	3-5
19—At Winnipeg	W	4-0
24—At Dallas	W	6-2
26—At Edmonton	T	*3-3
28—At Calgary	T	*2-2
29—At Vancouver	L	3-6

FEBRUARY

2—Buffalo	L	2-3
4—Ottawa	W	5-2
5—Pittsburgh	W	7-3
10—Vancouver	W	7-3
12—At Boston	L	3-5
13—At Tampa Bay	T	*3-3
17—At Toronto	L	1-2
19—Tampa Bay	W	5-4
20—At Chicago	T	*1-1
23—At Detroit	W	7-2

24—N.Y. Rangers	L	1-3
26—At Hartford	T	*1-1
28—St. Louis	W	5-1

MARCH

2—At Florida	W	3-2
3—At Tampa Bay	W	*5-4
5—Calgary	W	6-3
7—Quebec	T	*2-2
10—Hartford	W	4-0
12—Boston	W	2-1
13—Dallas	W	4-0
15—At N.Y. Islanders	L	2-3
17—At Buffalo	W	6-1
19—At Boston	W	8-6
21—At Florida	T	*3-3
24—Tampa Bay	W	2-1
26—Philadelphia	W	7-2
27—Quebec‡	W	5-2
29—Montreal	W	5-2

APRIL

1—At Washington	L	1-2
2—N.Y. Rangers	L	2-4
6—At Pittsburgh	L	1-3
8—Pittsburgh	W	7-2
10—At Florida	T	*2-2
12—At Philadelphia	L	2-4
14—Ottawa	W	4-1

*Denotes overtime game.
†At Halifax, N.S.
‡At Minneapolis.

NEW YORK ISLANDERS
EASTERN CONFERENCE/ATLANTIC DIVISION

1994-95 SCHEDULE

Home games shaded.
* — All-Star Game at San Jose Arena.
† — At San Antonio.
△ — At Halifax, N.S.
D — Day game.

OCTOBER

SUN	MON	TUE	WED	THU	FRI	SAT
						1 TB
2	3	4	5	6	7 OTT	8 WAS
9	10	11	12 MON	13	14	15 DET
16	17	18 LA	19	20	21	22 FLA
23	24	25 VAN	26	27	28	29 CAL
30	31					

NOVEMBER

SUN	MON	TUE	WED	THU	FRI	SAT
		1 DAL	2 STL	3	4	5 TB
6	7 DAL	8	9 FLA	10	11 NYR	12 HAR
13	14	15	16 MON	17	18 NJ	19 HAR
20	21	22	23 TB	24	25	26 TOR
27 BUF	28	29 BOS	30			

DECEMBER

SUN	MON	TUE	WED	THU	FRI	SAT
				1 PHI	2	3 BUF
4	5	6 EDM	7	8 NYR	9	10 OTT
11	12	13† NYR	14 SJ	15	16	17 LA
18 ANA	19	20 CHI	21	22	23 QUE	24
25	26 WAS	27	28 OTT	29	30 PHI	31 PIT

JANUARY

SUN	MON	TUE	WED	THU	FRI	SAT
1	2	3 CHI	4	5 NYR	6	7 WAS
8	9△ BUF	10	11 FLA	12	13 NJ	14 PIT
15	16 PHI	D 17	18 QUE	19	20	21*
22	23	24 STL	25	26 WAS	27	28 TB
29	30 NYR	31 FLA				

FEBRUARY

SUN	MON	TUE	WED	THU	FRI	SAT
			1	2 PHI	3	4 D BOS
5	6	7 WIN	8	9	10	11 D SJ
12	13 TB	14	15 FLA	16	17 NJ	18 NJ
19	20 DET	21	22 BUF	23	24 TOR	25 PIT
26	27	28 HAR				

MARCH

SUN	MON	TUE	WED	THU	FRI	SAT
			1	2 WAS	3	4 NYR
5 OTT	6	7 NJ	8	9 MON	10	11 QUE
12	13	14 VAN	15	16	17 EDM	18
19 CAL	20	21	22	23 PHI	24	25 D HAR
26 D ANA	27	28 BOS	29	30 MON	31	

APRIL

SUN	MON	TUE	WED	THU	FRI	SAT
						1 D BUF
2 QUE	D 3	4 PIT	5	6 BOS	7	8
9 WIN	D 10	11	12	13	14	15

1994-95 SEASON

CLUB DIRECTORY

Co-chairmen
Robert Rosenthal
Stephen Walsh
Chief operating officer
Ralph Palleschi
Executive vice president
Paul Greenwood
Senior vice president & CFO
Arthur J. McCarthy
Vice president of hockey operations
Al Arbour
Consultant
John H. Krumpe
General counsel
William M. Skehan
General manager
Don Maloney
Assistant general manager
Darcy Regier
Coach
Lorne Henning
Assistant coaches
Rick Green
Ron Kennedy
Director of scouting
Gerry Ehman
Director of pro scouting
Ken Morrow
Scouts
Harry Boyd
Earl Ingarfield
Gord Lane
Bert Marshall
Mario Saraceno
Vice president/communications
Pat Calabria

Director of media relations
Ginger Killian
Media relations assistant
Eric Mirlis
Dir. of publications/media relations assoc.
Chris Botta
Director of community relations
Maureen Brady
Director of game events
Tim Beach
Dir. of amateur hoc. dev. & alumni relations
Bob Nystrom
Director of ticket sales
Jim Johnson
Director of administration
Joseph Dreyer
Controller
Ralph Sellitti
Athletic trainer
Ed Tyburski
Equipment manager
John Doolan
Assistant trainer
Jerry Iannarelli
Team orthopedists
Jeffery Minkoff, M.D.
Barry Simonson, M.D.
Team internists
Gerald Cordani, M.D.
Larry Smith, M.D.
Physical therapist
Steve Wirth
Team dentists
Bruce Michnick, D.D.S.
Jan Sherman, D.D.S.

DRAFT CHOICES

Rd.—Player	H/W	Overall	Pos.	Last team
1—Brett Lindros	6-4/215	9	RW	Kingston (OHL)
2—Jason Holland	6-2/190	38	D	Kamloops (WHL)
3—Jason Strudwick	6-3/210	63	D	Kamloops (WHL)
4—Brad Lukowich	6-0/170	90	D	Kamloops (WHL)
5—Mark McArthur	5-11/179	112	G	Guelph (OHL)
5—Albert O'Connell	6-0/188	116	LW	St. Sebastian's H.S. (Mass.)
6—Jason Stewart	5-11/185	142	D	Simley H.S.
8—Mike Loach	6-1/181	194	C	Windsor (OHL)
8—Peter Hogard	5-10/183	203	C	Vastra Frolunda, Sweden
9—Gord Walsh	6-1/186	220	LW	Kingston (OHL)
10—Kirk Dewaele	6-0/187	246	D	Lethbridge (WHL)
11—Dick Tarnstrom	6-0/183	272	D	AIK Solna, Sweden

MISCELLANEOUS DATA

Home ice (capacity)
Nassau Veterans Memorial Coliseum
(16,297)
Address
Uniondale, NY 11553
Business phone
516-794-4100

Rink dimensions
200 feet by 85 feet
Club colors
Blue, white and orange

TRAINING CAMP ROSTER

No.	FORWARDS	Ht./Wt.	BORN Place	Date	NHL exp.	1993-94 clubs
	Derek Armstrong (C)	5-11/180	Ottawa	4-23-73	0	Salt Lake City (IHL)
9	Dave Chyzowski (LW) ..	6-1/190	Edmonton, Alta.	7-11-71	4	Salt Lake City (IHL), New York Islanders
15	Brad Dalgarno (RW)	6-4/215	Vancouver, B.C.	8-8-67	8	New York Islanders
20	Ray Ferraro (C)	5-10/185	Trail, B.C.	8-23-64	10	New York Islanders
26	Patrick Flatley (RW)	6-2/200	Toronto	10-3-63	11	New York Islanders
39	Travis Green (C)...........	6-0/195	Creston, B.C.	12-20-70	2	New York Islanders
33	Benoit Hogue (LW)	5-10/190	Repentigny, Que.	10-28-66	7	New York Islanders
	Steve Junker (LW)	6-0/184	Castlegar, B.C.	6-26-72	2	Salt Lake City (IHL), New York Islanders
17	Yan Kaminsky (LW)......	6-1/176	Penza, U.S.S.R.	7-28-71	1	Moncton (AHL), Winnipeg, New York Islanders
27	Derek King (LW)	6-1/210	Hamilton, Ont.	2-11-67	8	New York Islanders
	Brett Lindros (RW)........	6-4/215	Toronto	12-2-75	0	Kingston (OHL), Canadian national team (Int'l)
	Troy Loney (LW)	6-3/210	Bow Island, Alta.	9-21-63	11	Anaheim
	Chris Marinucci (C)	6-0/175	Grand Rapids, Minn.	12-29-71	0	Minnesota-Duluth (WCHA)
18	Marty McInnis (C/LW) .	6-0/185	Weymouth, Mass.	6-2-70	3	New York Islanders
68	Zigmund Palffy (LW)	5-10/169	Skalica, Czechoslovakia	5-5-72	1	Salt Lake City (IHL), Slovakian Olympic team (Int'l), New York Islanders
34	Dan Plante (RW)	6-0/207	St. Louis	10-5-71	1	Salt Lake City (IHL), New York Islanders
38	Scott Scissons (C)	6-1/201	Saskatoon, Sask.	10-29-71	3	New York Islanders, Salt Lake City (IHL)
	Ron Sutter (C)	6-0/207	Viking, Alta.	12-2-63	12	St. Louis, Quebec
32	Steve Thomas (LW/RW) .	5-11/186	Stockport, England	7-15-63	10	New York Islanders
77	Pierre Turgeon (C)	6-1/203	Rouyn, Que.	8-29-69	7	New York Islanders
12	Mick Vukota (RW).........	6-2/215	Saskatoon, Sask.	9-14-66	7	New York Islanders
	DEFENSEMEN					
3	Dean Chynoweth	6-2/193	Saskatoon, Sask.	10-30-68	5	Salt Lake City (IHL), New York Islanders
	Jason Holland................	6-2/190	Morinville, Alta.	4-30-76	0	Kamloops (WHL)
11	Darius Kasparaitis........	5-11/190	Elektrenai, U.S.S.R.	10-16-72	2	New York Islanders
7	Scott Lachance	6-2/197	Charlottesville, Va.	10-22-72	3	New York Islanders
	Brad Lukowich	6-1/170	Surrey, B.C.	8-12-76	0	Kamloops (WHL)
2	Christopher Luongo	6-0/199	Detroit	3-17-67	3	Salt Lake City (IHL), New York Islanders
23	Vladimir Malakhov.........	6-3/220	Sverdlovsk, U.S.S.R.	8-30-68	2	New York Islanders
	Bryan McCabe................	6-1/200	St. Catherine's, Ont.	6-8-75	0	Spokane (WHL)
47	Rich Pilon......................	6-0/195	Saskatoon, Sask.	4-30-68	6	New York Islanders, Salt Lake City (IHL)
	Jason Strudwick	6-3/210	Edmonton, Alta.	7-17-75	0	Kamloops (WHL)
37	Dennis Vaske.................	6-2/211	Rockford, Ill.	10-11-67	4	New York Islanders
	GOALTENDERS					
72	Ron Hextall	6-3/192	Winnipeg, Man.	5-3-64	8	New York Islanders
	Milan Hnilicka	6-0/180	Kladno, Czechoslovakia	6-24-73	0	Salt Lake City (IHL), Richmond (ECHL)
29	Jamie McLennan............	6-0/189	Edmonton, Alta.	6-30-71	1	Salt Lake City (IHL), New York Islanders
	Tommy Salo...................	5-11/161	Surahammar, Sweden	2-1-71	0	Swedish Olympic Team (Int'l), Vasteras (Sweden)

1993-94 REVIEW

INDIVIDUAL STATISTICS

SCORING

	Games	G	A	Pts.	PIM	+/-	PPG	SHG	Shots	Shooting Pct.
Pierre Turgeon	69	38	56	94	18	14	10	4	254	15.0
Steve Thomas	78	42	33	75	139	-9	17	0	249	16.9
Derek King	78	30	40	70	59	18	10	0	171	17.5
Benoit Hogue	83	36	33	69	73	-7	9	5	218	16.5
Vladimir Malakhov	76	10	47	57	80	29	4	0	235	4.3
Marty McInnis	81	25	31	56	24	31	3	5	136	18.4
Ray Ferraro	82	21	32	53	83	1	5	0	136	15.4
Patrick Flatley	64	12	30	42	40	12	2	1	112	10.7
Travis Green	83	18	22	40	44	16	1	0	164	11.0
Tom Kurvers	66	9	31	40	47	7	5	0	141	6.4

	Games	G	A	Pts.	PIM	+/-	PPG	SHG	Shots	Shooting Pct.
Brad Dalgarno	73	11	19	30	62	14	3	0	97	11.3
Uwe Krupp	41	7	14	21	30	11	3	0	82	8.5
Dave Volek	32	5	9	14	10	0	2	0	56	8.9
Scott Lachance	74	3	11	14	70	-5	0	0	59	5.1
Dennis Vaske	65	2	11	13	76	21	0	0	71	2.8
Darius Kasparaitis	76	1	10	11	142	-6	0	0	81	1.2
Keith Acton*	71	2	7	9	50	-1	0	0	33	6.1
David Maley*	37	0	6	6	74	-6	0	0	19	0.0
Wayne McBean*	19	1	4	5	16	-13	0	0	33	3.0
Richard Pilon	28	1	4	5	75	-4	0	0	20	5.0
Mick Vukota	72	3	1	4	237	-5	0	0	26	11.5
Chris Luongo	17	1	3	4	13	-1	0	0	16	6.3
Dean Chynoweth	39	0	4	4	122	3	0	0	26	0.0
Yan Kaminsky*	23	2	1	3	4	4	0	0	23	8.7
Ron Hextall (goalie)	65	0	3	3	52	0	0	0	0	0.0
Claude Loiselle	17	1	1	2	49	-2	0	0	14	7.1
Dave Chyzowski	3	1	0	1	4	-1	0	0	4	25.0
Dan Plante	12	0	1	1	4	-2	0	0	9	0.0
Jamie McLennan (goalie)	22	0	1	1	6	0	0	0	0	0.0
Derek Armstrong	1	0	0	0	0	0	0	0	2	0.0
Scott Scissons	1	0	0	0	0	0	0	0	0	0.0
Brent Grieve*	3	0	0	0	7	0	0	0	1	0.0
Bob McGill*	3	0	0	0	5	0	0	0	0	0.0
Jason Simon	4	0	0	0	34	0	0	0	0	0.0
Steve Junker	5	0	0	0	0	0	0	0	2	0.0
Zigmund Palffy	5	0	0	0	0	-6	0	0	5	0.0
Tom Draper (goalie)	7	0	0	0	0	0	0	0	0	0.0
Joe Day	24	0	0	0	30	-7	0	0	16	0.0

GOALTENDING

	Games	Min.	Goals	SO	Avg.	W	L	T	Shots	Sv. Pct.
Jamie McLennan	22	1287	61	0	2.84	8	7	6	639	.905
Ron Hextall	65	3581	184	5	3.08	27	26	6	1801	.898
Tom Draper	7	227	16	0	4.23	1	3	0	118	.864

Empty-net goals (do not count against a goaltender's average): Hextall 3.
*Played with two or more NHL teams.

RESULTS

OCTOBER
5—At Calgary	L		1-2
8—At Edmonton	L		1-5
10—At Anaheim	W	*4-3	
12—At Los Angeles	L		5-7
16—New Jersey	L		3-6
19—Pittsburgh	L		2-3
22—At Philadelphia	L		3-4
23—Ottawa	T	*5-5	
26—Los Angeles	W		7-0
28—At Florida	L		2-5
29—At Tampa Bay	W		4-2

NOVEMBER
2—Vancouver	L		1-2
4—At Chicago	L		2-4
6—Hartford	W		5-3
9—Winnipeg	L		2-5
10—At New Jersey	L		3-5
13—Boston	L		2-5
17—At Ottawa	W		8-1
18—Montreal†	W		5-1
21—At Philadelphia	W	*5-4	
24—At Dallas	T	*2-2	
27—N.Y. Rangers	W		6-4
28—Detroit	L		1-4
30—Washington	W		6-4

DECEMBER
2—At Boston	L		3-7
3—Quebec	L		2-3
7—At Edmonton	T	*4-4	
11—Philadelphia	W		5-2
14—New Jersey	W		4-1
17—Toronto	W		6-2
19—At Pittsburgh	W		6-3
22—At Montreal	W		5-3
26—Buffalo	W	*4-3	
28—Anaheim	L		0-3
29—At Quebec	L		3-5

JANUARY
1—Hartford	L		3-4
4—At New Jersey	L		3-6
7—Calgary	W		6-2
8—At Hartford	L		0-6
10—At Ottawa	T	*3-3	
14—Montreal	W		5-2
15—Chicago	T	*5-5	
17—Florida	L		1-2
19—At Tampa Bay	L	*3-4	
26—At Toronto	L		3-4
28—Boston	L		0-3
29—At Boston	L		1-2

FEBRUARY
1—San Jose	W		5-4
2—At N.Y. Rangers	T	*4-4	
5—At Quebec	W		3-2
6—At Buffalo	L		1-4
8—Buffalo	W		3-1
10—At Pittsburgh	W		5-3
12—Florida	L		3-4
15—Tampa Bay	W		2-1
18—At Washington	L		1-3
19—Ottawa	W		4-0
21—Washington	W		4-0
24—At Philadelphia	L	*4-5	

(continued)
25—Philadelphia	W		2-0
27—Quebec	W		5-2

MARCH
1—St. Louis	W		4-2
4—At N.Y. Rangers	T	*3-3	
5—N.Y. Rangers	L		4-5
7—At Winnipeg	W		7-2
9—At Vancouver	L		4-5
10—At San Jose	L		3-4
12—At St. Louis	T	*5-5	
15—New Jersey	W		3-2
17—At Detroit	W		3-1
18—Buffalo‡	T	*2-2	
20—Pittsburgh	L		1-2
22—Tampa Bay	W	*5-4	
26—Florida	L		1-3
27—At Buffalo	L		1-4
29—At Washington	T	*2-2	

APRIL
1—Montreal	W		5-2
2—At Montreal	T	*3-3	
5—At Washington	W	*4-3	
6—At Hartford	T	*3-3	
8—Dallas	W		5-1
10—N.Y. Rangers	W		5-4
13—At Tampa Bay	W		2-0
14—At Florida	L		1-4

*Denotes overtime game.
†At Hamilton, Ont.
‡At Minneapolis.

NEW YORK RANGERS
EASTERN CONFERENCE/ATLANTIC DIVISION

1994-95 SCHEDULE

Home games shaded.
* — All-Star Game at San Jose Arena.
† — At Portland, Ore.
Δ — At Phoenix.
D — Day game.

OCTOBER

SUN	MON	TUE	WED	THU	FRI	SAT
						1 NJ
2	3 PIT	4	5	6 PHI	7	8 D FLA
9	10	11 TB	12	13 STL	14	15 HAR
16	17	18 QUE	19	20 LA	21	22 MON
23 SJ	24	25	26 DAL	27	28 CAL	29
30 VAN	31					

NOVEMBER

SUN	MON	TUE	WED	THU	FRI	SAT
		1 LA	2 ANA	3	4	5 SJ
6	7	8 HAR	9	10	11 NYI	12
13 WAS	14	15	16	17 PHI	18	19 OTT
20	21	22	23 PIT	24	25 WIN	26
27 FLA	28	29 HAR	30 BUF			

DECEMBER

SUN	MON	TUE	WED	THU	FRI	SAT
				1	2 ANA	3
4 EDM	5	6 PIT	7	8 NYI	9	10
11	12	13† NYI	14 VAN	15	16	17 EDM
18 CAL	19	20	21 BOS	22	23 MON	24
25	26 OTT	27 WAS	28	29	30 TB	31

JANUARY

SUN	MON	TUE	WED	THU	FRI	SAT
1 D FLA	2	3 STL	4	5 NYI	6	7 TB
8	9 FLA	10	11 PIT	12	13	14 WAS
15 NJ	16	17 DET	18	19	20	21°
22	23 QUE	24	25 BOS	26	27 TB	28 QUE
29	30 NYI	31				

FEBRUARY

SUN	MON	TUE	WED	THU	FRI	SAT
			1	2 CHI	3	4 OTT
5	6 WIN	7 BOS	8	9 PHI	10	11 TB
12	13	14	15 BUF	16 MON	17	18 TOR
19	20 D TOR	21	22	23	24 HAR	25
26 BUF	27	28 FLA				

MARCH

SUN	MON	TUE	WED	THU	FRI	SAT
			1	2	3 PHI	4 NYI
5	6 NJ	7	8 BUF	9	10	11 MON
12	13 PHI	14	*15 NJ	16	17	18 WAS
19	20	21 DAL	22	23Δ CAL	24	25
26	27	28 DET	29	30 QUE	31	

APRIL

SUN	MON	TUE	WED	THU	FRI	SAT
					1 D BOS	1 D
2 CHI	3 D	4	5 WAS	6	7 OTT	8
9 NJ	10 D	11	12	13	14	15

1994-95 SEASON

CLUB DIRECTORY

Governor, president and G.M.
Neil Smith
Vice president, general counsel
Ken Munoz
Vice president, finance
Jim Abry
Director of communications
Barry Watkins
Director of marketing
Kevin Kennedy
Director of administration
John Gentile
Alternate NHL governors
Neil Smith
Ken Munoz
Bob Gutkowski
Assistant G.M., player development
Larry Pleau
Coach
To be announced
Associate coaches
Colin Campbell
Dick Todd

Scouting staff
Darwin Bennett
Tony Feltrin
Herb Hammond
Martin Madden
Christer Rockstrom
Scouting manager
Bill Short
Manager of team operations
Matthew Loughran
Manager of communications
Kevin McDonald
Public relations assistant
John Rosasco
Team physician and orthopedic surgeon
Barton Nisonson, M.D.
Medical trainer
Dave Smith
Equipment trainer
Joe Murphy

DRAFT CHOICES

Rd.—Player	H/W	Overall	Pos.	Last team
1—Dan Cloutier	6-1/182	26	G	Sault Ste. Marie (OHL)
2—Rudolf Vercik	6-1/188	52	LW	Slovan Bratislava, Slovakia
3—Adam Smith	6-0/190	78	D	Tacoma (WHL)
4—Alexander Korobolin	6-2/189	100	D	Chelyabinsk, CIS
4—Sylvain Blouin	6-2/216	104	D	Laval (QMJHL)
5—Martin Etnier	6-1/178	130	D	Beauport (QMJHL)
6—Yuri Litvinov	5-10/176	135	C	Krylja Sovetov, CIS
6—David Brosseau	6-1/189	156	C	Shawinigan (QMJHL)
7—Alexei Lazarenko	5-11/176	182	LW	CSKA Moscow, CIS
8—Craig Anderson	6-1/171	208	D	Park Center H.S.
9—Vitali Yereneyev	5-10/167	209	G	Torpedo Kamenogorsk, CIS
9—Eric Boulton	6-0/201	234	LW	Oshawa (OHL)
10—Radoslav Kropac	6-0/187	260	LW	Slovan Bratislava, Slovakia
11—Jamie Butt	5-11/180	267	LW	Tacoma (WHL)
11—Kim Johnsson	6-1/169	286	D	Malmo, Sweden

MISCELLANEOUS DATA

Home ice (capacity)
Madison Square Garden (18,200)
Address
4 Pennsylvania Plaza
New York, NY 10001
Business phone
212-465-6000

Rink dimensions
200 feet by 85 feet
Club colors
Blue, red and white

TRAINING CAMP ROSTER

No.	FORWARDS	Ht./Wt.	Place	Born Date	NHL exp.	1993-94 clubs
	Glenn Anderson (RW)	6-1/190	Vancouver, B.C.	10-2-60	14	Toronto, New York Rangers
17	Greg Gilbert (LW)	6-1/190	Mississauga, Ont.	1-22-67	13	New York Rangers
9	Adam Graves (LW)	6-0/207	Toronto	4-12-68	7	New York Rangers
18	Mike Hartman (LW)	6-0/192	W. Bloomfield, Mich.	2-7-67	8	New York Rangers
15	Mike Hudson (C)	6-1/205	Guelph, Ont.	2-6-67	6	New York Rangers
26	Joey Kocur (RW)	6-0/205	Calgary, Alta.	12-21-64	10	New York Rangers
27	Alexei Kovalev (C)	6-0/200	Moscow, U.S.S.R.	2-24-73	2	New York Rangers
	Andrei Kudinov (C)	6-0/185	Chelyabinsk, CIS	6-28-70	0	
	Nick Kypreos (LW)	6-0/205	Toronto	6-4-66	5	Hartford, New York Rangers
	Daniel Lacroix (LW)	6-2/188	Montreal	3-11-69	1	New York Rangers, Binghamton (AHL)
28	Steve Larmer (RW)	5-11/185	Peterborough, Ont.	6-16-61	14	New York Rangers
	Stephane Matteau (LW)	6-3/200	Rouyn, Que.	9-2-69	4	Chicago, New York Rangers
11	Mark Messier (C)	6-1/205	Edmonton, Alta.	1-18-61	15	New York Rangers
	Petr Nedved (C)	6-3/185	Liberec, Czech.	12-9-71	4	Canadian national team (Int'l), Canadian Olympic Team (Int'l), St. Louis
13	Sergei Nemchinov (C)	6-0/200	Moscow, U.S.S.R.	1-14-64	3	New York Rangers
	Brian Noonan (RW)	6-1/200	Boston	5-29-65	7	Chicago, New York Rangers
12	Ed Olczyk (C)	6-1/205	Chicago	8-16-66	10	New York Rangers
	Jean-Yves Roy (RW)	5-10/185	Rosemere, Que.	2-17-69	0	Canadian national team (Int'l), Canadian Olympic Team (Int'l), Binghamton (AHL)
	Dimitri Starostenko	6-0/185	Minsk, U.S.S.R.	3-18-73	0	Binghamton (AHL)
	Niklas Sundstrom (LW)	5-11/183	Ornskoldsvik, Sweden	6-6-75	0	MoDo (Sweden)

DEFENSEMEN

No.		Ht./Wt.	Place	Date	NHL exp.	1993-94 clubs
23	Jeff Beukeboom	6-5/225	Ajax, Ont.	3-28-65	9	New York Rangers
	Sylvain Blouin	6-2/216	Montreal	5-21-74	0	Laval (QMJHL)
	Eric Cairns	6-6/217	Oakville, Ont.	6-27-74	0	Detroit (OHL)
25	Alexander Karpovtsev	6-1/205	Moscow	4-7-70	1	New York Rangers
2	Brian Leetch	5-11/195	Corpus Christi, Tex.	3-3-68	7	New York Rangers
4	Kevin Lowe	6-2/195	Lachute, Que.	4-15-59	15	New York Rangers
8	Joby Messier	6-0/193	Regina, Sask.	3-2-70	2	New York Rangers, Binghamton (AHL)
5	Mattias Norstrom	6-1/205	Stockholm, Sweden	1-2-72	1	New York Rangers, Binghamton (AHL)
	Barry Richter	6-2/203	Madison, Wis.	9-11-70	0	U.S. national team (Int'l), U.S. Olympic Team (Int'l), Binghamton (AHL)
	Michael Stewart	6-2/197	Calgary, Alta.	3-30-72	0	Binghamton (AHL)
24	Jay Wells	6-1/210	Paris, Ont.	5-18-59	15	New York Rangers
21	Sergei Zubov	6-0/195	Moscow, U.S.S.R.	7-22-70	2	New York Rangers, Binghamton (AHL)

GOALTENDERS

No.		Ht./Wt.	Place	Date	NHL exp.	1993-94 clubs
30	Glenn Healy	5-10/185	Pickering, Ont.	8-23-62	8	New York Rangers
	Corey Hirsch	5-10/160	Medicine Hat, Alta.	7-1-72	1	Canadian national team (Int'l), Canadian Olympic Team (Int'l), Binghamton (AHL)
35	Mike Richter	5-11/182	Philadelphia	9-22-66	6	New York Rangers

1993-94 REVIEW

INDIVIDUAL STATISTICS

SCORING

	Games	G	A	Pts.	PIM	+/-	PPG	SHG	Shots	Shooting Pct.
Sergei Zubov	78	12	77	89	39	20	9	0	222	5.4
Mark Messier	76	26	58	84	76	25	6	2	216	12.0
Adam Graves	84	52	27	79	127	27	20	4	291	17.9
Brian Leetch	84	23	56	79	67	28	17	1	328	7.0
Steve Larmer	68	21	39	60	41	14	6	4	146	14.4
Alexei Kovalev	76	23	33	56	154	18	7	0	184	12.5
Esa Tikkanen	83	22	32	54	114	5	5	3	257	8.6
Mike Gartner*	71	28	24	52	58	11	10	5	245	11.4
Sergei Nemchinov	76	22	27	49	36	13	4	0	144	15.3
Tony Amonte*	72	16	22	38	31	5	3	0	179	8.9
Kevin Lowe	71	5	14	19	70	4	0	0	50	10.0
Alexander Karpovtsev	67	3	15	18	58	12	1	0	78	3.8
Jeff Beukeboom	68	8	8	16	170	18	1	0	58	13.8

	Games	G	A	Pts.	PIM	+/-	PPG	SHG	Shots	Shooting Pct.
Greg Gilbert	76	4	11	15	29	-3	1	0	64	6.3
Mike Hudson	48	4	7	11	47	-5	0	0	48	8.3
Jay Wells	79	2	7	9	110	4	0	0	64	3.1
Ed Olczyk	37	3	5	8	28	-1	0	0	40	7.5
Nick Kypreos*	46	3	5	8	102	-8	0	0	29	10.3
Stephane Matteau*	12	4	3	7	2	5	1	0	22	18.2
Glenn Anderson*	12	4	2	6	12	1	2	0	22	18.2
Craig MacTavish*	12	4	2	6	11	6	1	0	25	16.0
Brian Noonan*	12	4	2	6	12	5	2	0	26	15.4
Darren Turcotte*	13	2	4	6	13	-2	0	0	17	11.8
Joey Kocur	71	2	1	3	129	-9	0	0	43	4.7
James Patrick*	6	0	3	3	2	1	0	0	6	0.0
Peter Andersson*	8	1	1	2	2	-3	0	1	10	10.0
Mike Hartman	35	1	1	2	70	-5	0	0	19	5.3
Joby Messier	4	0	2	2	0	-1	0	0	7	0.0
Mattias Norstrom	9	0	2	2	6	0	0	0	3	0.0
Glenn Healy (goalie)	29	0	2	2	2	0	0	0	0	0.0
Doug Lidster	34	0	2	2	33	-12	0	0	25	0.0
Phil Bourque*	16	0	1	1	8	-2	0	0	2	0.0
Todd Marchant*	1	0	0	0	0	-1	0	0	1	0.0
Jim Hiller	2	0	0	0	7	1	0	0	0	0.0
Dan Lacroix	4	0	0	0	0	0	0	0	0	0.0
Mike Richter (goalie)	68	0	0	0	2	0	0	0	0	0.0

GOALTENDING

	Games	Min.	Goals	SO	Avg.	W	L	T	Shots	Sv. Pct.
Mike Richter	68	3710	159	5	2.57	†42	12	6	1758	.910
Glenn Healy	29	1368	69	2	3.03	10	12	2	567	.878

Empty-net goals (do not count against a goaltender's average): Healy 2, Richter 1.
*Played with two or more NHL teams.
†Led league.

RESULTS

OCTOBER

5—Boston	L	3-4
7—Tampa Bay	W	5-4
9—At Pittsburgh	L	2-3
11—Washington	W	5-2
13—Quebec	W	6-4
15—At Buffalo	W	5-2
16—At Philadelphia	L	3-4
19—Anaheim	L	2-4
22—At Tampa Bay	L	1-4
24—Los Angeles	W	3-2
28—Montreal	T	*3-3
30—At Hartford	W	4-1
31—New Jersey†	W	4-1

NOVEMBER

3—Vancouver	W	6-3
6—At Quebec	W	4-2
8—Tampa Bay	W	6-3
10—Winnipeg	W	2-1
13—At Washington	W	2-0
14—San Jose	T	*3-3
16—At Florida	W	4-2
19—At Tampa Bay	W	5-3
23—Montreal	W	*5-4
24—At Ottawa	W	7-1
27—At N.Y. Islanders	L	4-6
28—Washington	W	3-1
30—At New Jersey	W	3-1

DECEMBER

4—At Toronto	W	4-3
5—New Jersey	W	2-1
8—Edmonton	T	*1-1
13—Buffalo	W	2-0
15—Hartford	W	5-2
17—At Detroit	L	4-6
19—Ottawa	W	6-3
22—At Florida	L	2-3
23—At Washington	W	1-0
26—New Jersey	W	8-3
29—At St. Louis	W	4-3
31—At Buffalo	L	1-4

JANUARY

3—Florida	W	3-2
5—Calgary	L	1-4
8—At Montreal	L	2-3
10—Tampa Bay	L	2-5
14—Philadelphia	W	5-2
16—At Chicago	W	5-1
18—St. Louis	W	4-1
25—At San Jose	W	8-3
27—At Los Angeles	W	*5-4
28—At Anaheim	L	2-3
31—Pittsburgh	W	5-3

FEBRUARY

2—N.Y. Islanders	T	*4-4
3—At Boston	W	3-0
7—Washington	L	1-4
9—At Montreal	L	*3-4
12—At Ottawa	W	*4-3
14—At Quebec	W	4-2
18—Ottawa	W	3-0
19—At Hartford	L	2-4
21—Pittsburgh	W	*4-3

MARCH

2—Quebec	W	5-2
4—N.Y. Islanders	T	*3-3
5—At N.Y. Islanders	W	5-4
7—Detroit	L	3-6
9—Washington†	W	7-5
10—At Boston	T	*2-2
12—At Pittsburgh	L	2-6
14—At Florida	L	1-2
16—Hartford	W	4-0
18—Chicago	L	3-7
22—At Calgary	T	*4-4
23—At Edmonton	W	5-3
25—At Vancouver	W	5-2
27—At Winnipeg	L	1-3
29—At Philadelphia	W	4-3

APRIL

1—Dallas	W	3-0
2—At New Jersey	W	4-2
4—Florida	W	3-2
8—Toronto	W	5-3
10—At N.Y. Islanders	L	4-5
12—Buffalo	W	3-2
14—Philadelphia	T	*2-2

23—Boston	L	3-6
24—At New Jersey	W	3-1
26—At Dallas	L	1-3
28—Philadelphia	W	4-1

*Denotes overtime game.
†At Halifax, N.S.

OTTAWA SENATORS
EASTERN CONFERENCE/NORTHEAST DIVISION

1994-95 SCHEDULE

- ▢ Home games shaded.
- * — All-Star Game at San Jose Arena.
- † — At Hamilton, Ont.
- △ — At Phoenix.
- D — Day game.

OCTOBER

SUN	MON	TUE	WED	THU	FRI	SAT
						1 WIN
2	3 BOS	4	5 WAS	6	7 NYI	8 NJ
9	10	11 TOR	12	13	14	15 DAL
16	17	18	19 HAR	20	21	22 D PHI
23 TB	24	25	26 PIT	27	28	29 DET
30	31					

NOVEMBER

SUN	MON	TUE	WED	THU	FRI	SAT
		1 PIT	2 PHI	3	4	5 MON
6	7 BOS	8	9	10 BUF	11	12 D QUE
13 HAR	14	15	16 PIT	17 PIT	18	19 NYR
20	21	22	23 NJ	24	25	26 FLA
27	28 LA	29	30 WAS			

DECEMBER

SUN	MON	TUE	WED	THU	FRI	SAT
				1	2	3 PHI
4 CAL	5	6	7 TB	8 FLA	9	10 NYI
11	12	13 HAR	14 HAR	15	16	17 MON
18	19 BUF	20	21 TB	22	23 NJ	24
25	26 NYR	27	28 NYI	29	30	31 HAR

JANUARY

SUN	MON	TUE	WED	THU	FRI	SAT
1	2 TOR	3	4	5 WIN	6	7 TOR
8	9 MON	10	11 BOS	12	13	14 PHI
15 ANA	16	17	18	19	20	21△
22	23 BUF	24	25 HAR	26	27 WAS	28 BUF
29	30	31				

FEBRUARY

SUN	MON	TUE	WED	THU	FRI	SAT
			1 SJ	2 BOS	3	4 NYR
5	6 VAN	7	8 MON	9	10	11 QUE
12	13	14	15 SJ	16	17 ANA	18 LA
19	20	21 CHI	22	23 QUE	24	25 FLA
26	27	28 CHI				

MARCH

SUN	MON	TUE	WED	THU	FRI	SAT
			1 DET	2	3	4 D BOS
5 NYI	6	7 STL	8	9△ CHI	10	11 VAN
12 EDM	13	14	15 CAL	16	17	18 D PIT
19 DAL	20	21 WAS	22 TB	23	24	25 QUE
26 EDM	27	28	29 STL	30	31	

APRIL

SUN	MON	TUE	WED	THU	FRI	SAT
						1
2 BUF	3 MON	4	5 FLA	6	7 NYR	8 QUE
9	10	11	12	13	14	15

1994-95 SEASON

CLUB DIRECTORY

Chairman, governor, and CEO
Rod Bryden
President, G.M., and alt. governor
Randy J. Sexton
Senior V.P., commercial operations and CFO
Bernie Ashe
Assistant general manager
Ray Shero
Head coach
Rick Bowness
Assistant coaches
E.J. MacGuire
Alain Vigneault
Director of hockey operations
Brian McKenna
Director of player personnel
John Ferguson

Athletic trainer
Conrad Lackten
Assistant trainer
John Gervais
Head equipment trainer
Ed Georgica
Administrative assistant
Allison Vaughan
Vice president of marketing
Jim Steel
Vice president of sales
Mark Bonneau
Director of media relations
Laurent Benoit
Media relations assistant
Dominick Saillant

DRAFT CHOICES

Rd.—Player	H/W	Overall	Pos.	Last team
1—Radek Bonk	6-3/215	3	C	Las Vegas (IHL)
2—Stanislav Neckar	6-1/196	29	D	HC Ceske Budejovice, Czech.
4—Bryan Masotta	6-2/195	81	G	Hotchkiss H.S. (N.Y.)
6—Mike Gaffney	6-0/202	131	D	St. Johns H.S.
6—Daniel Alfredsson	5-11/187	133	RW	Vastra Frolunda, Sweden
7—Doug Sproule	6-3/195	159	LW	Hotchkiss H.S. (N.Y.)
9—Frederic Cassivi	6-3/193	210	G	St. Hyacinthe (QMJHL)
9—Danny Dupont	6-3/221	211	D	Laval (QMJHL)
10—Stephen MacKinnon	6-4/200	237	D	Cushing Acad. (Mass.)
11—Antti Tormanen	6-1/198	274	RW	Jokerit, Finland

MISCELLANEOUS DATA

Home ice (capacity)
Ottawa Civic Centre (10,575)
Address
301 Moodie Drive
Nepean, Ont. K2H 9C4
Business phone
613-721-0115

Rink dimensions
200 feet by 85 feet
Club colors
Black, red and gold

No.	FORWARDS	Ht./Wt.	Place	BORN Date	NHL exp.	1993-94 clubs
15	Dave Archibald (C/LW)	6-1/210	Chilliwack, B.C.	4-14-69	5	Ottawa
	Claude Boivin (LW)	6-2/200	St. Foy, Que.	3-1-70	3	Hershey (AHL), Philadelphia, Ottawa
	Radek Bonk (C)	6-3/215	Kronov, Czechoslovakia	1-9-76	0	Las Vegas (IHL)
	Phil Bourque (LW)	6-1/196	Chelmsford, Mass.	6-8-62	10	New York Rangers, Ottawa
	Randy Cunneyworth	6-0/180	Etobicoke, Ont.	5-10-61	11	Chicago, Hartford
	Alexandre Daigle (C)	6-0/185	Montreal	2-7-75	1	Ottawa
	Evgeny Davydov (LW)	6-0/200	Chelyabinsk, U.S.S.R.	5-27-67	3	Florida, Ottawa
78	Pavol Demitra (LW)	6-0/184	Dubnica, Czech.	11-29-74	1	Ottawa, P.E.I. (AHL)
	Cosmo Dupaul (C)	6-0/185	Pointe Claire, Que.	4-11-75	0	Victoriaville (QMJHL)
	Pat Elynuik (RW)	6-0/185	Foam Lake, Sask.	10-30-67	7	Washington, Tampa Bay
	Bill Huard (LW)	6-1/215	Alland, Ont.	6-24-67	2	Ottawa
	Scott Levins (C/RW)	6-4/200	Portland, Ore.	1-30-70	2	Florida, Ottawa
8	Troy Mallette (LW)	6-2/210	Sudbury, Ont.	2-25-70	5	Ottawa
7	David McLlwain (C/RW)	6-0/185	Seaforth, Ont.	1-9-67	7	Ottawa
	Troy Murray (C)	6-1/195	Winnipeg, Man.	7-31-62	13	Chicago, Indianapolis (IHL), Ottawa
	Chad Penney (LW)	6-0/195	Labrador City, Nfld.	9-18-73	1	P.E.I. (AHL), Ottawa
	Sylvain Turgeon (LW)	6-0/200	Noranda, Que.	1-17-65	11	Ottawa
	Alexei Yashin (C)	6-3/215	Sverdlovsk, U.S.S.R.	11-5-73	1	Ottawa
	DEFENSEMEN					
	Radim Bicanek	6-1/195	U. Hradiste, Czech.	1-18-75	0	Belleville (OHL)
	Chris Dahlquist	6-1/195	Fridley, Minn.	12-14-62	9	Calgary
	Dimitri Filimonov	6-4/220	Perm, U.S.S.R.	10-14-71	1	Ottawa, P.E.I. (AHL)
	Corey Foster	6-3/204	Ottawa	10-27-69	2	Hershey (AHL)
	Sean Hill	6-0/195	Duluth, Minn.	2-14-70	4	Anaheim
	Kerry Huffman	6-1/200	Peterborough, Ont.	1-3-68	8	Quebec, Ottawa
	Steve Konroyd	6-1/195	Scarborough, Ont.	2-10-61	14	Detroit, Ottawa
35	Francois Leroux	6-6/225	St. Adele, Que.	4-18-70	6	Ottawa, P.E.I. (AHL)
22	Norm Maciver	5-11/180	Thunder Bay, Ont.	9-8-64	8	Ottawa
	Derek Mayer	6-0/185	Rossland, B.C.	5-21-67	1	Canadian national team (Int'l), Canadian Olympic Team (Int'l), Ottawa
	Jim Paek	6-1/195	Seoul, South Korea	4-7-67	4	Pittsburgh, Los Angeles
	Lance Pitlick	6-0/190	Fridley, Minn.	11-5-67	0	Hershey (AHL)
34	Darren Rumble	6-1/200	Barrie, Ont.	1-23-69	3	Ottawa, P.E.I. (AHL)
4	Brad Shaw	6-0/190	Cambridge, Ont.	4-28-64	9	Ottawa
29	Dennis Vial	6-1/218	Sault Ste. Marie, Ont.	4-10-69	4	Ottawa
	GOALTENDERS					
	Mike Bales	6-1/180	Saskatoon, Sask.	8-6-71	1	Providence (AHL)
1	Craig Billington	5-10/170	London, Ont.	9-11-66	6	Ottawa
30	Darrin Madeley	5-11/170	Holland Landing, Ont.	2-25-68	2	Ottawa, P.E.I. (AHL)

1993-94 REVIEW

INDIVIDUAL STATISTICS

SCORING

	Games	G	A	Pts.	PIM	+/-	PPG	SHG	Shots	Shooting Pct.
Alexei Yashin	83	30	49	79	22	-49	11	2	232	12.9
Alexandre Daigle	84	20	31	51	40	-45	4	0	168	11.9
Dave McLlwain	66	17	26	43	48	-40	1	1	115	14.8
Bob Kudelski*	42	26	15	41	14	-25	12	0	127	20.5
Mark Lamb*	66	11	18	29	56	-41	4	1	105	10.5
Sylvain Turgeon	47	11	15	26	52	-25	7	0	116	9.5
Troy Mallette	82	7	16	23	166	-33	0	0	100	7.0
Brad Shaw	66	4	19	23	59	-41	1	0	113	3.5
Norm Maciver	53	3	20	23	26	-26	0	0	88	3.4
Gord Dineen	77	0	21	21	89	-52	0	0	62	0.0
Andrew McBain	55	11	8	19	64	-41	8	0	91	12.1
David Archibald	33	10	8	18	14	-7	2	0	65	15.4
Vladimir Ruzicka	42	5	13	18	14	-21	4	0	64	7.8
Darren Rumble	70	6	9	15	116	-50	0	0	95	6.3
Brian Glynn*	48	2	13	15	41	-15	1	0	66	3.0
Evgeny Davydov*	40	5	7	12	38	-6	0	0	44	11.4
Kerry Huffman*	34	4	8	12	12	-30	2	1	68	5.9
Scott Levins*	33	3	5	8	93	-26	2	0	39	7.7
Dan Quinn	13	7	0	7	6	0	2	0	31	22.6
Brad Lauer	30	2	5	7	6	-15	0	1	45	4.4

	Games	G	A	Pts.	PIM	+/-	PPG	SHG	Shots	Shooting Pct.
Dennis Vial	55	2	5	7	214	-9	0	0	37	5.4
Jarmo Kekalainen	28	1	5	6	14	-8	0	0	18	5.6
Phil Bourque*	11	2	3	5	0	-2	0	2	19	10.5
Troy Murray*	15	2	3	5	4	1	0	1	14	14.3
Robert Burakowsky	23	2	3	5	6	-7	0	0	40	5.0
Dimitri Filimonov	30	1	4	5	18	-10	0	0	15	6.7
Derek Mayer	17	2	2	4	8	-16	1	0	29	6.9
Bill Huard	63	2	2	4	162	-19	0	0	24	8.3
Hank Lammens	27	1	2	3	22	-20	0	0	6	16.7
Darcy Loewen	44	0	3	3	52	-11	0	0	39	0.0
Pavol Demitra	12	1	1	2	4	-7	1	0	10	10.0
Steve Konroyd*	8	0	2	2	2	-4	0	0	9	0.0
Claude Boivin*	15	1	0	1	38	-6	0	0	6	16.7
Kent Paynter	9	0	1	1	8	-6	0	0	8	0.0
Francois Leroux	23	0	1	1	70	-4	0	0	8	0.0
Daniel Berthiaume (goalie)	1	0	0	0	0	0	0	0	0	0.0
Kevin MacDonald	1	0	0	0	2	0	0	0	0	0.0
Greg Pankewicz	3	0	0	0	2	-1	0	0	3	0.0
Chad Penney	3	0	0	0	2	-2	0	0	2	0.0
Mark Laforest (goalie)	5	0	0	0	0	0	0	0	0	0.0
Radek Hamr	7	0	0	0	0	-10	0	0	5	0.0
Andy Schneider	10	0	0	0	15	-6	0	0	4	0.0
Graeme Townshend	14	0	0	0	9	-7	0	0	5	0.0
Herb Raglan	29	0	0	0	52	-13	0	0	13	0.0
Darrin Madeley (goalie)	32	0	0	0	0	0	0	0	0	0.0
Craig Billington (goalie)	63	0	0	0	8	0	0	0	1	0.0

GOALTENDING

	Games	Min.	Goals	SO	Avg.	W	L	T	Shots	Sv. Pct.
Darrin Madeley	32	1583	115	0	4.36	3	18	5	868	.868
Craig Billington	63	3319	†254	0	4.59	11	†41	4	1801	.859
Mark Laforest	5	182	17	0	5.60	0	2	0	96	.823
Daniel Berthiaume	1	1	2	0	120.00	0	0	0	2	.000

Empty-net goals (do not count against a goaltender's average): Billington 6, Madeley 3.
*Played with two or more NHL teams.
†Led league.

RESULTS

OCTOBER
6—Quebec	T	*5-5	
9—At St. Louis	L	5-7	
14—At Florida	L	4-5	
16—At Tampa Bay	L	1-4	
21—Dallas	L	*5-6	
23—At N.Y. Islanders	T	*5-5	
25—Anaheim	W	4-1	
27—Philadelphia	L	2-5	
28—At Boston	L	2-6	
30—At Dallas	W	*5-4	

NOVEMBER
3—At Edmonton	W	7-5
5—At Winnipeg	W	*7-6
10—At Hartford	L	*3-4
11—Florida	L	4-5
13—At Montreal	W	*3-2
15—Montreal	L	2-4
17—N.Y. Islanders	L	1-8
18—New Jersey	L	2-5
22—Buffalo	L	2-5
24—N.Y. Rangers	L	1-7
26—At Buffalo	L	2-5
27—At Pittsburgh	T	*2-2
29—Hartford	L	2-4

DECEMBER
1—At Montreal	W	6-3
3—At Detroit	L	1-8
4—Washington	L	1-6
6—Calgary	L	1-6
8—Buffalo	L	1-3
9—Dallas†	L	1-6

11—At Quebec	L	2-5
13—Los Angeles	W	5-2
15—At Tampa Bay	L	3-4
17—At Washington	L	2-11
19—At N.Y. Rangers	L	3-6
21—Quebec	W	2-1
23—Hartford	L	1-2
26—At Hartford	L	*2-3
27—Boston	L	3-5
30—Tampa Bay	L	0-3

JANUARY
1—New Jersey	L	1-7
3—Pittsburgh	L	1-4
5—Vancouver	L	2-7
6—At Toronto	L	3-6
8—Winnipeg	L	2-3
10—N.Y. Islanders	T	*3-3
11—At Philadelphia	L	1-4
14—At Vancouver	T	*2-2
15—At Calgary	L	0-10
18—Edmonton	W	*4-3
25—At Pittsburgh	L	2-4
27—Hartford	T	*1-1
29—At Chicago	T	*3-3
31—Chicago	L	0-1

FEBRUARY
2—Florida	L	1-4
4—At New Jersey	L	2-5
5—Montreal	L	3-4
8—Philadelphia	T	*3-3
10—Tampa Bay	L	2-6

12—N.Y. Rangers	L	*3-4
18—At N.Y. Rangers	L	0-3
19—At N.Y. Islanders	L	0-4
24—San Jose	W	6-4
26—St. Louis	L	1-11
28—Toronto	L	1-4

MARCH
2—Buffalo	L	2-7
4—Winnipeg†	L	1-6
5—At Boston	L	1-6
8—At Quebec	L	2-5
10—At Philadelphia	L	2-8
13—At Anaheim	L	1-5
15—At Los Angeles	L	0-7
17—At San Jose	W	2-1
20—At Buffalo	L	2-6
23—Detroit	W	5-4
24—At Pittsburgh	L	1-5
28—At Montreal	L	2-3
30—Quebec	W	6-4

APRIL
2—At Florida	T	*2-2
6—Washington	W	6-5
7—At Boston	L	4-5
9—At Washington	L	4-8
11—Pittsburgh	L	0-4
13—Boston	L	0-8
14—At New Jersey	L	1-4

*Denotes overtime game.
†At Minneapolis.

PHILADELPHIA FLYERS
EASTERN CONFERENCE/ATLANTIC DIVISION

1994-95 SCHEDULE

Home games shaded.
* — All-Star Game at San Jose Arena.
† — At San Antonio.
∆ — At Halifax, N.S.
D — Day game.

OCTOBER
SUN	MON	TUE	WED	THU	FRI	SAT
						1 HAR
2	3	4 FLA	5	6 NYR	7	8 TB
9	10	11	12 NJ	13	14 WIN	15
16 CAL	17 VAN	18	19	20 QUE	21	22 D OTT
23	24	25	26	27 VAN	28	29 TOR
30	31					

NOVEMBER
SUN	MON	TUE	WED	THU	FRI	SAT
		1	2 OTT	3	4 BUF	5 BUF
6	7	8 QUE	9	10 WAS	11	12 WAS
13 DAL	14	15	16	17 NYR	18	19 PIT
20 DET	21	22	23 HAR	24	25 D NJ	26 D TB
27	28	29	30 DET			

DECEMBER
SUN	MON	TUE	WED	THU	FRI	SAT
				1 NYI	2	3 OTT
4	5	6	7	8 MON	9	10 MON
11 NJ	12	13	14	15 WIN	16	17 D QUE
18 CHI	19	20	21 QUE	22	23 WAS	24
25	26 TB	27 FLA	28	29	30 NYI	31 BUF

JANUARY
SUN	MON	TUE	WED	THU	FRI	SAT
1	2	3	4	5 BOS	6	7† PIT
8	9 ANA	10	11 NJ	12 FLA	13	14 OTT
15 NYI	16 D	17	18 WAS	19	20	21*
22	23 PIT	24	25	26 HAR	27	28 D BOS
29 D MON	30	31 CHI				

FEBRUARY
SUN	MON	TUE	WED	THU	FRI	SAT
			1	2 NYI	3	4 D BUF
5	6	7 TOR	8	9 NYR	10∆ WAS	11
12 LA	13	14	15	16 STL	17	18 D EDM
19 SJ	20 D	21	22 ANA	23 LA	24	25 EDM
26	27	28				

MARCH
SUN	MON	TUE	WED	THU	FRI	SAT
			1	2 FLA	3 NYR	4
5 SJ	6	7	8 HAR	9 CAL	10	11 TB
12	13 NYR	14	15 DAL	16	17	18 FLA
19	20 MON	21	22	23 NYI	24	25
26 PIT	27	28 PIT	29	30 NJ	31 WAS	

APRIL
SUN	MON	TUE	WED	THU	FRI	SAT
						1
2 D BOS	3	4 BOS	5	6 TB	7	8
9 STL	10	11	12	13	14	15

1994-95 SEASON

CLUB DIRECTORY

Chairman of the exec. committee/owner
Edward M. Snider
President and general manager
Bob Clarke
Chairman of the board emeritus
Joseph C. Scott
Executive vice president
Keith Allen
Chief operating officer
Ron Ryan
Assistant general manager
John Blackwell
Vice president, finance
Dan Clemmens
Coach
Terry Murray
Assistant coaches
Keith Acton
Tom Webster
Goaltending instructor
Bernie Parent
Phys. conditioning and rehabilitation coach
Pat Croce
Director of pro scouting
Bill Barber

Chief scout
Jerry Melnyk
Scouts
Inge Hammarstrom
Vaclav Slansky
Simon Nolet
Bill Dineen
Evgeny Zimin
Vice president, public relations
Mark Piazza
Ticket manager
Ceil Baker
Vice president, sales
Jack Betson
Director of team services
Joe Kadlec
Athletic therapist
Gary Smith
Trainers
Jim Evers
Harry Bricker
Orthopedic surgeon
Arthur Bartolozzi

DRAFT CHOICES

Rd. — Player	H/W	Overall	Pos.	Last team
3—Arten Anisimov	6-1/187	62	D	Itil Kazan, CIS
4—Adam Magarrell	6-3/178	88	D	Brandon (WHL)
4—Sebastien Vallee	6-4/180	101	LW	Victoriaville (QMJHL)
6—Alexander Selivanov	6-1/187	140	RW	Spartak Moscow, CIS
7—Colin Forbes	6-1/190	166	LW	Sherwood Park (Tier II)
8—Derek Diener	6-4/182	192	D	Lethbridge (WHL)
8—Raymond Giroux	6-0/160	202	D	Pomasson (Tier II)
9—Johan Hedberg	5-11/178	218	G	Leksand, Sweden
10—Andre Payette	6-1/182	244	C	Sault Ste. Marie (OHL)
11—Jan Lipiansky	6-1/183	270	RW	Slovan Bratislava, Slovakia

MISCELLANEOUS DATA

Home ice (capacity)
The Spectrum (17,380)
Address
Pattison Place
Philadelphia, PA 19148
Business phone
215-465-4500

Rink dimensions
200 feet by 85 feet
Club colors
Orange, white and black

TRAINING CAMP ROSTER

No.	FORWARDS	Ht./Wt.	Place	BORN Date	NHL exp.	1993-94 clubs
42	Josef Beranek (LW)	6-2/185	Litvinov, Czechoslovakia	10-25-69	3	Philadelphia
17	Rod Brind'Amour (C/LW)	6-1/198	Ottawa	8-9-70	6	Philadelphia
21	Dave Brown (RW)	6-5/222	Saskatoon, Sask.	10-12-62	12	Philadelphia
15	Al Conroy (RW)	5-8/170	Calgary, Alta.	1-17-66	3	Philadelphia
20	Rob DiMaio (C)	5-10/190	Calgary, Alta.	2-19-68	6	Philadelphia, Tampa Bay
11	Kevin Dineen (RW)	5-11/190	Quebec City	10-28-63	10	Philadelphia
	Yanick Dupre (LW)	6-0/195	Montreal	11-20-72	1	Hershey (AHL)
36	Andre Faust (C)	6-1/190	Joliette, Que.	10-7-69	2	Hershey (AHL), Philadelphia
18	Brent Fedyk (LW)	6-0/196	Yorkton, Sask.	3-8-67	7	Philadelphia
	Chris Herperger (LW)	6-0/195	Esterhazy, Sask.	2-24-74	0	Seattle (WHL)
	Patrik Juhlin (LW)	6-0/187	Huddinge, Sweden	4-24-70	0	Vasteras (Sweden), Swedish Olympic Team (Int'l)
22	Mark Lamb (C)	5-10/175	Swift Current, Sask.	8-3-64	9	Ottawa, Philadelphia
88	Eric Lindros (C)	6-4/229	London, Ont.	2-28-73	2	Philadelphia
	Craig MacTavish (C)	6-1/195	London, Ont.	8-15-58	15	Edmonton, New York Rangers
	Shjon Podein (LW)	6-2/200	Rochester, Minn.	3-5-68	2	Edmonton, Cape Breton (AHL)
8	Mark Recchi (RW)	5-10/185	Kamloops, B.C.	2-1-68	6	Philadelphia
19	Mikael Renberg (LW)	6-1/218	Pitea, Sweden	5-5-72	1	Philadelphia
	Alexander Selivanov	6-1/187	Moscow, U.S.S.R.	3-23-71	0	Spartak Moscow (CIS)
14	Dave Tippett (C/LW)	5-10/173	Moosomin, Sask.	8-25-61	11	Philadelphia
40	Chris Winnes (RW)	6-0/170	Ridgefield, Conn.	2-12-68	4	Hershey (AHL), Philadelphia

DEFENSEMEN

No.	DEFENSEMEN	Ht./Wt.	Place	BORN Date	NHL exp.	1993-94 clubs
	Vladislav Boulin	6-4/196	Penza, U.S.S.R.	5-18-72	0	Dynamo Moscow (CIS)
28	Jason Bowen	6-4/215	Courtenay, B.C.	11-11-73	2	Philadelphia
25	Jeff Finley	6-2/205	Edmonton, Alta.	4-14-67	6	Philadelphia
3	Garry Galley	6-0/204	Ottawa	4-16-63	10	Philadelphia
	Kevin Haller	6-2/183	Trochu, Alta.	12-5-70	5	Montreal
	Milos Holan	5-11/183	Bilovec, Czechoslovakia	4-22-71	1	Philadelphia, Hershey (AHL)
23	Stewart Malgunas	6-0/200	Prince George, B.C.	4-21-70	1	Philadelphia
27	Ryan McGill	6-2/205	Prince Albert, Sask.	2-28-69	3	Philadelphia
	Terran Sandwith	6-4/210	Edmonton, Alta.	4-17-72	0	Hershey (AHL)
	Chris Therien	6-4/230	Ottawa	12-14-71	0	Hershey (AHL)
	Bob Wilkie	6-2/220	Calgary, Alta.	2-11-69	2	Hershey (AHL), Philadelphia
2	Dimitri Yushkevich	5-11/208	Yaroslavl, U.S.S.R.	11-19-71	2	Philadelphia
26	Rob Zettler	6-3/200	Sept Iles, Que.	3-8-68	6	San Jose, Philadelphia

GOALTENDERS

No.	GOALTENDERS	Ht./Wt.	Place	BORN Date	NHL exp.	1993-94 clubs
	Scott LaGrand	6-1/170	Potsdam, N.Y.	2-11-70	0	Hershey (AHL)
	Neil Little	6-1/180	Medicine Hat, Alta.	12-18-71	0	Hershey (AHL)
33	Dominic Roussel	6-1/190	Hull, Que.	2-22-70	3	Philadelphia
30	Tommy Soderstrom	5-9/156	Stockholm, Sweden	7-17-69	2	Hershey (AHL), Philadelphia

1993-94 REVIEW

INDIVIDUAL STATISTICS

SCORING

	Games	G	A	Pts.	PIM	+/-	PPG	SHG	Shots	Shooting Pct.
Mark Recchi	84	40	67	107	46	-2	11	0	217	18.4
Eric Lindros	65	44	53	97	103	16	13	2	197	22.3
Rod Brind'Amour	84	35	62	97	85	-9	14	1	230	15.2
Mikael Renberg	83	38	44	82	36	8	9	0	195	19.5
Garry Galley	81	10	60	70	91	-11	5	1	186	5.4
Yves Racine	67	9	43	52	48	-11	5	1	142	6.3
Josef Beranek	80	28	21	49	85	-2	6	0	182	15.4
Kevin Dineen	71	19	23	42	113	-9	5	1	156	12.2
Brent Fedyk	72	20	18	38	74	-14	5	0	104	19.2
Dimitri Yushkevich	75	5	25	30	86	-8	1	0	136	3.7
Viacheslav Butsayev*	47	12	9	21	58	2	2	0	79	15.2
Pelle Eklund*	48	1	16	17	8	-1	0	0	49	2.0
Dave Tippett	73	4	11	15	38	-20	0	2	45	8.9
Greg Hawgood*	19	3	12	15	19	2	0	0	37	8.1
Andre Faust	37	8	5	13	10	-1	0	0	33	24.2
Jeff Finley	55	1	8	9	24	16	0	0	43	2.3
Rob DiMaio*	14	3	5	8	6	1	0	0	30	10.0
Allan Conroy	62	4	3	7	65	-12	0	1	40	10.0
Mark Lamb*	19	1	6	7	16	-3	0	0	19	5.3
Jason Bowen	56	1	5	6	87	12	0	0	50	2.0
Dave Brown	71	1	4	5	137	-12	0	0	16	6.3
Bob Wilkie	10	1	3	4	8	-2	0	0	10	10.0
Ryan McGill	50	1	3	4	112	-5	0	0	53	1.9

	Games	G	A	Pts.	PIM	+/-	PPG	SHG	Shots	Shooting Pct.
Stewart Malgunas	67	1	3	4	86	2	0	0	54	1.9
Rob Zettler*	33	0	4	4	69	-19	0	0	27	0.0
Jim Cummins*	22	1	2	3	71	0	0	0	17	5.9
Milos Holan	8	1	1	2	4	-4	1	0	26	3.8
Claude Boivin*	26	1	1	2	57	-11	0	0	11	9.1
Chris Winnes	4	0	2	2	0	1	0	0	4	0.0
Todd Hlushko	2	1	0	1	0	1	0	0	2	50.0
Rob Ramage*	15	0	1	1	14	-11	0	0	18	0.0
Dominic Roussel (goalie)	60	0	1	1	4	0	0	0	0	0.0
Aris Brimanis	1	0	0	0	0	-1	0	0	1	0.0
Claude Vilgrain	2	0	0	0	0	-1	0	0	0	0.0
Frederic Chabot* (goalie)	4	0	0	0	0	0	0	0	0	0.0
Dan Kordic	4	0	0	0	5	0	0	0	0	0.0
Tommy Soderstrom (goalie)	34	0	0	0	0	0	0	0	0	0.0

GOALTENDING

	Games	Min.	Goals	SO	Avg.	W	L	T	Shots	Sv. Pct.
Dominic Roussel	60	3285	183	1	3.34	29	20	5	1762	.896
Tommy Soderstrom	34	1736	116	2	4.01	6	18	4	851	.864
Frederic Chabot*	4	70	5	0	4.29	0	1	1	40	.875

Empty-net goals (do not count against a goaltender's average): Soderstrom 7, Roussel 3.
*Played with two or more NHL teams.

RESULTS

OCTOBER
5—Pittsburgh	W	4-3
9—At Hartford	W	5-2
10—Toronto	L	4-5
12—Buffalo	W	5-3
15—At Washington	W	3-0
16—N.Y. Rangers	W	4-3
22—N.Y. Islanders	W	4-3
23—Winnipeg	L	6-9
26—At Quebec	W	4-2
27—At Ottawa	L	5-2
30—At New Jersey	L	3-5
31—At Chicago	W	9-6

NOVEMBER
2—At Florida	W	4-3
4—Quebec	W	4-1
6—At Toronto	L	3-5
7—Vancouver	L	2-5
10—At Buffalo	W	5-3
11—New Jersey	L	3-5
13—Buffalo	L	2-7
16—At Pittsburgh	L	5-11
18—Hartford	W	6-3
20—At Boston	T	*5-5
21—N.Y. Islanders	L	*4-5
24—Montreal	W	9-2
26—Tampa Bay	W	3-0
27—At Tampa Bay	W	*4-3

DECEMBER
1—At Edmonton	L	1-3
2—At Vancouver	W	6-3
4—At Calgary	L	0-6
9—Washington	L	2-4
11—At N.Y. Islanders	L	2-5
12—Edmonton	L	1-2
16—Quebec	W	3-2
18—Chicago	T	*2-2
19—At New Jersey	L	2-4
21—Washington	L	1-4
23—Detroit	L	1-3
27—At Buffalo	W	2-0
28—At Pittsburgh	T	*4-4
31—Boston†	W	4-3

JANUARY
6—At Dallas	L	0-8
8—At Tampa Bay	L	2-4
11—Ottawa	W	4-1
13—Boston	W	6-2
14—At N.Y. Rangers	L	2-5
16—Los Angeles	W	5-2
19—St. Louis	W	8-3
25—At Quebec	L	4-6
29—Washington	L	2-4
30—At Montreal	L	*4-5

FEBRUARY
2—Washington‡	L	2-5
3—San Jose	L	*2-3
5—At Boston	L	0-4
8—At Ottawa	T	*3-3
10—Florida	W	*4-3
11—At Detroit	L	3-6
13—Pittsburgh	L	0-3
15—At San Jose	W	6-4
16—At Anaheim	L	3-6

(continued)
18—At Los Angeles	W	4-3
21—Montreal	W	8-7
24—N.Y. Islanders	W	*5-4
25—At N.Y. Islanders	L	0-2
28—At N.Y. Rangers	L	1-4

MARCH
4—At Washington	T	*3-3
6—At Tampa Bay	W	3-1
8—Dallas	L	*3-4
10—Ottawa	W	8-2
12—At Montreal	T	*4-4
13—Tampa Bay	T	*5-5
19—Hartford	L	3-5
20—At Florida	L	3-5
22—At St. Louis	L	6-3
24—Florida	W	4-3
26—At New Jersey	L	2-7
27—Anaheim	L	*2-3
29—N.Y. Rangers	L	3-4
31—Calgary	L	1-4

APRIL
2—At Hartford	W	6-5
4—At Winnipeg	T	*2-2
7—Florida	T	*3-3
10—Boston	L	3-4
12—New Jersey	W	4-2
14—At N.Y. Rangers	T	*2-2

*Denotes overtime game.
†At Minneapolis.
‡At Cleveland.

PITTSBURGH PENGUINS
EASTERN CONFERENCE/NORTHEAST DIVISION

1994-95 SCHEDULE

Home games shaded.
* — All-Star Game at San Jose Arena.
† — At San Antonio.
△ — At Denver.
D — Day game.

OCTOBER
SUN	MON	TUE	WED	THU	FRI	SAT
						1 CHI
2	3 NYR	4	5 BUF	6	7 WAS	8
9	10	11 QUE	12 WAS	13	14	15 MON
16	17	18 TB	19	20	21 DET	22 LA
23	24	25 DAL	26 OTT	27	28	29 MON
30	31					

NOVEMBER
SUN	MON	TUE	WED	THU	FRI	SAT
		1 OTT	2	3 BOS	4	5 HAR
6	7	8 NJ	9	10 DAL	11	12 STL
13	14	15	16 OTT	17 OTT	18	19 PHI
20	21 BOS	22	23 NYR	24	25 WAS	26 SJ
27	28	29 ANA	30			

DECEMBER
SUN	MON	TUE	WED	THU	FRI	SAT
				1 WAS	2	3 BOS
4	5	6 NYR	7 BUF	8	9	10 BUF
11	12	13 ANA	14	15 LA	16	17 SJ
18	19	20 DET	21	22 FLA	23 TB	24
25	26	27	28 HAR	29 BUF	30	31 NYI

JANUARY
SUN	MON	TUE	WED	THU	FRI	SAT
1	2	3	4 NJ	5 FLA	6	7† PHI
8	9△ NJ	10	11 NYR	12	13 HAR	14 NYI
15	16	17	18 BOS	19	20	21*
22	23 PHI	24	25	26	27 VAN	28 TOR
29	30	31				

FEBRUARY
SUN	MON	TUE	WED	THU	FRI	SAT
			1	2 WIN	3	4 TB
5	6	7 FLA	8	9 QUE	10	11 MON
12 FLA	13	14 EDM	15	16 CHI	17	18 D HAR
19 D HAR	20	21 NJ	22	23	24 STL	25 NYI
26	27	28 VAN				

MARCH
SUN	MON	TUE	WED	THU	FRI	SAT
			1	2 CAL	3 EDM	4
5	6 QUE	7	8	9 QUE	10	11 D CAL
12	13 WIN	14	15	16 TB	17	18 D OTT
19 D QUE	20	21 BUF	22	23	24 MON	25
26 PHI	27	28 PHI	29	30 BOS	31	

APRIL
SUN	MON	TUE	WED	THU	FRI	SAT
						1
2 TOR	D 3	4	5 NYI	6 NJ	7	8 MON
9	10	11	12	13	14	15

1994-95 SEASON

CLUB DIRECTORY

Owners
Howard Baldwin
Morris Belzberg
Thomas Ruta
Chairman of the board and governor
Howard Baldwin
Chief operating officer
Pittsburgh Sports Associates
Roy Mlakar
President
Jack Kelley
Executive V.P. and general manager
Craig Patrick
Head coach
Ed Johnston
Assistant coaches
Rick Kehoe
Bryan Trottier
Scouts
Mark Kelley
Greg Malone
Gilles Meloche
Les Binkley
John Gill
Charlie Hodge
Ralph Cox

Senior executive vice president
Bill Barnes
Executive V.P. and chief financial officer
Donn Patton
Executive V.P. PHA Sports Marketing LTD
Richard Chmura
V.P. public and community relations
Phil Langan
Controller
Kevin Hart
Director of public relations
Cindy Himes
Director of media relations
Harry Sanders
Assistant director of media relations
Steve Bovino
Director of ticket sales
Jeff Mercer
Trainer
Charles Thayer
Strength and conditioning coach
John Welday
Equipment manager
Steve Latin
Team physician
Dr. Charles Burke

DRAFT CHOICES

Rd.—Player	H/W	Overall	Pos.	Last team
1—Chris Wells	6-6/215	24	C	Seattle (WHL)
2—Richard Park	5-11/176	50	C	Belleville (OHL)
3—Sven Butenschon	6-5/201	57	D	Brandon (WHL)
3—Greg Crozier	6-3/180	73	LW	Lawrence Acad. (Mass.)
3—Alexei Krivchenkov	6-0/185	76	D	CSKA Moscow, CIS
4—Thomas O'Connor	6-2/190	102	D	Springfield (Jr. B)
5—Clint Johnson	6-2/200	128	LW	Duluth East H.S. (Minn.)
6—Valentin Morozov	5-11/176	154	C	CSKA Moscow, CIS
7—Serge Aubin	6-0/176	161	C	Granby (QMJHL)
7—Drew Palmer	6-3/209	180	D	Seattle (WHL)
8—Boris Zelenko	6-1/172	206	LW	CSKA Moscow, CIS
9—Jason Godbout	5-11/180	232	D	Hill Murray H.S. (Minn.)
10—Mikhail Kazakevich	6-1/187	258	LW	Torpedo Jaroslav, CIS
11—Brian Leitza	6-2/185	284	G	Sioux City (Jr. A)

MISCELLANEOUS DATA

Home ice (capacity)
Civic Arena (17,537)
Address
Gate No. 9
Pittsburgh, PA 15219
Business phone
412-642-1800

Rink dimensions
200 feet by 85 feet
Club colors
Black, gold and white

TRAINING CAMP ROSTER

No.	FORWARDS	Ht./Wt.	Place	Born Date	NHL exp.	1993-94 clubs
24	Doug Brown (RW)	5-10/185	Southborough, Mass.	6-12-64	8	Pittsburgh
	John Cullen (C)	5-10/187	Puslinch, Ont.	8-2-64	6	Toronto
	Joe Dziedzic (LW)	6-3/200	Minneapolis	12-18-71	0	University of Minnesota (WCHA)
	Brian Farrell (C)	5-11/182	Hartford, Conn.	4-16-72	0	Harvard University (ECAC)
10	Ron Francis (C)	6-2/200	Sault Ste. Marie, Ont.	3-1-63	13	Pittsburgh
68	Jaromir Jagr (RW)	6-2/208	Kladno, Czechoslovakia	2-15-72	4	Pittsburgh
66	Mario Lemieux (C)	6-4/210	Montreal	10-5-65	10	Pittsburgh
15	Shawn McEachern (C)	6-0/195	Waltham, Mass.	2-28-69	3	Los Angeles, Pittsburgh
33	Jim McKenzie (LW)	6-3/205	Gull Lake, Sask.	11-3-69	5	Hartford, Dallas, Pittsburgh
7	Joe Mullen (RW)	5-9/180	New York	2-26-57	14	Pittsburgh
	Markus Naslund (LW)	5-11/180	Harnosand, Sweden	7-30-73	1	Pittsburgh, Cleveland (IHL)
	Richard Park (C)	5-11/176	Seoul, South Korea	5-27-76	0	Belleville (OHL)
44	Ed Patterson (RW)	6-2/210	Delta, B.C.	11-14-72	1	Cleveland (IHL), Pittsburgh
	Domenic Pittis (C)	5-11/180	Calgary, Alta.	10-1-74	0	Lethbridge (WHL)
	Luc Robitaille (LW)	6-1/190	Montreal	2-17-66	8	Los Angeles
	Dave Roche (LW)	6-4/224	Lindsay, Ont.	6-13-75	0	Peterborough (OHL), Windsor (OHL)
17	Tomas Sandstrom (RW)	6-2/200	Jakobstad, Finland	9-4-64	10	Los Angeles, Pittsburgh
25	Kevin Stevens (LW)	6-3/217	Brockton, Mass.	4-15-65	7	Pittsburgh
82	Martin Straka (C)	5-10/180	Plzen, Czechoslovakia	9-3-72	2	Pittsburgh
	Chris Wells (C)	6-6/215	Calgary, Alta.	11-12-75	0	Seattle (WHL)
	DEFENSEMEN					
	Stefan Bergqvist	6-3/216	Leksand, Sweden	3-10-75	0	Leksand (Sweden)
	Paul Dyck	6-1/192	Steinbach, Man.	4-15-71	0	Cleveland (IHL)
20	Greg Hawgood	5-10/190	St. Albert, Alta.	8-10-68	7	Philadelphia, Florida, Pittsburgh
3	Grant Jennings	6-3/200	Hudson Bay, Sask.	5-5-65	7	Pittsburgh
	Ian Moran	5-11/170	Cleveland	8-24-72	0	U.S. national team (Int'l), Cleveland (IHL)
55	Larry Murphy	6-2/210	Scarborough, Ont.	3-8-61	14	Pittsburgh
	Patrick Neaton	6-0/180	Redford, Mich.	5-21-71	1	Cleveland (IHL), Pittsburgh
28	Kjell Samuelsson	6-6/233	Tyngsryd, Sweden	10-18-58	9	Pittsburgh
5	Ulf Samuelsson	6-1/195	Fagersta, Sweden	3-26-64	10	Pittsburgh
32	Peter Taglianetti	6-2/195	Framingham, Mass.	8-15-63	10	Pittsburgh
2	Chris Tamer	6-2/185	Dearborn, Mich.	11-17-70	1	Cleveland (IHL), Pittsburgh
	GOALTENDERS					
35	Tom Barrasso	6-3/211	Boston	3-31-65	11	Pittsburgh
	Phillippe DeRouville	6-2/180	Arthabaska, Que.	8-7-74	0	Verdun (QMJHL)
	Rob Dopson	6-0/200	Smith Falls, Ont.	8-21-67	1	Cleveland (IHL), Pittsburgh
	Patrick Lalime	6-2/165	St. Bonaventure, Que.	7-7-74	0	Shawinigan (QMJHL)
31	Ken Wregget	6-1/195	Brandon, Man.	3-25-64	11	Pittsburgh

1993-94 REVIEW

INDIVIDUAL STATISTICS

SCORING

	Games	G	A	Pts.	PIM	+/-	PPG	SHG	Shots	Shooting Pct.
Jaromir Jagr	80	32	67	99	61	15	9	0	298	10.7
Ron Francis	82	27	66	93	62	-3	8	0	216	12.5
Kevin Stevens	83	41	47	88	155	-24	21	0	284	14.4
Larry Murphy	84	17	56	73	44	10	7	0	236	7.2
Joe Mullen	84	38	32	70	41	9	6	2	231	16.5
Martin Straka	84	30	34	64	24	24	2	0	130	23.1
Doug Brown	77	18	37	55	18	19	2	0	152	11.8
Rick Tocchet	51	14	26	40	134	-15	5	1	150	9.3
Mario Lemieux	22	17	20	37	32	-2	7	0	92	18.5
Ulf Samuelsson	80	5	24	29	199	23	1	0	106	4.7
Shawn McEachern*	27	12	9	21	10	13	0	2	78	15.4
Marty McSorley*	47	3	18	21	139	-9	0	0	122	2.5
Tomas Sandstrom*	27	6	11	17	24	5	0	0	72	8.3
Bryan Trottier	41	4	11	15	36	-12	0	0	45	8.9
Peter Taglianetti	60	2	12	14	142	5	0	0	57	3.5
Kjell Samuelsson	59	5	8	13	118	18	1	0	57	8.8
Mike Stapleton*	58	7	4	11	18	-4	3	0	59	11.9
Markus Naslund	71	4	7	11	27	-3	1	0	80	5.0
Greg Brown	36	3	8	11	28	1	1	0	37	8.1
Jeff Daniels*	63	3	5	8	20	-1	0	0	46	6.5
Grant Jennings	61	2	4	6	126	-10	0	1	49	4.1

	Games	G	A	Pts.	PIM	+/-	PPG	SHG	Shots	Shooting Pct.
Ed Patterson	27	3	1	4	10	-5	0	0	15	20.0
Mike Ramsey	65	2	2	4	22	-4	0	0	31	6.5
Jim Paek*	41	0	4	4	8	-7	0	0	24	0.0
Greg Hawgood*	12	1	2	3	8	-1	1	0	20	5.0
Pat Neaton	9	1	1	2	12	3	1	0	11	9.1
Larry DePalma	7	1	0	1	5	1	0	0	2	50.0
Mike Needham*	25	1	0	1	2	0	0	0	6	16.7
Ken Wregget (goalie)	42	0	1	1	8	0	0	0	0	0.0
Tom Barrasso (goalie)	44	0	1	1	42	0	0	0	0	0.0
Rob Dopson (goalie)	2	0	0	0	0	0	0	0	0	0.0
Roberto Romano (goalie)	2	0	0	0	0	0	0	0	0	0.0
Greg Andrusak	3	0	0	0	2	-1	0	0	4	0.0
Justin Duberman	4	0	0	0	0	0	0	0	2	0.0
Ladislav Karabin	9	0	0	0	2	0	0	0	3	0.0
Jim McKenzie*	11	0	0	0	16	-5	0	0	6	0.0
Chris Tamer	12	0	0	0	9	3	0	0	10	0.0

GOALTENDING

	Games	Min.	Goals	SO	Avg.	W	L	T	Shots	Sv. Pct.
Roberto Romano	2	125	3	0	1.44	1	0	1	56	.946
Tom Barrasso	44	2482	139	2	3.36	22	15	5	1304	.893
Ken Wregget	42	2456	138	1	3.37	21	12	7	1291	.893
Rob Dopson	2	45	3	0	4.00	0	0	0	23	.870

Empty-net goals (do not count against a goaltender's average): Barrasso 2.
*Played with two or more NHL teams.

RESULTS

OCTOBER

5—At Philadelphia	L	3-4
7—Montreal	W	*2-1
9—N.Y. Rangers	W	3-2
10—At Quebec	L	4-7
12—At Florida	W	2-1
14—At Tampa Bay	L	2-3
16—Hartford	W	5-3
19—At N.Y. Islanders	W	3-2
22—At Buffalo	W	4-2
23—St. Louis	T	*3-3
28—Quebec	L	3-7
30—Chicago	W	4-3

NOVEMBER

2—At San Jose	T	*3-3
3—Buffalo†	W	6-2
6—At Los Angeles	L	3-8
7—At Anaheim	W	5-4
9—At St. Louis	T	*3-3
11—At Chicago	L	1-4
13—Detroit	L	3-7
16—Philadelphia	W	11-5
18—Washington	W	3-2
20—At Montreal	T	*2-2
24—Boston	W	7-3
26—At Washington	T	*4-4
27—Ottawa	T	*2-2

DECEMBER

2—New Jersey	T	*2-2
4—At Hartford	W	*7-6
8—At Dallas	L	2-3
11—At Tampa Bay	W	6-3
14—Los Angeles	W	4-2
16—Buffalo	W	2-1
19—N.Y. Islanders	L	3-6
21—Tampa Bay	W	8-3
23—At Boston	W	4-3
26—At Washington	L	3-7
28—Philadelphia	T	*4-4
31—Quebec	L	4-5

JANUARY

2—At Hartford	L	2-7
3—At Ottawa	W	4-1
7—At Buffalo	W	*4-3
8—Calgary	T	*2-2
11—Boston	W	*5-4
13—Florida	T	*2-2
15—Edmonton	W	4-3
18—At Quebec	L	3-6
25—Ottawa	W	4-2
27—Quebec	W	3-0
29—At Toronto	T	*4-4
31—At N.Y. Rangers	L	3-5

FEBRUARY

1—Florida	W	2-1
4—At Detroit	W	6-3
5—At New Jersey	L	3-7
7—Montreal	L	1-4
10—N.Y. Islanders	L	3-5
12—Dallas	L	3-9
13—At Philadelphia	W	3-0
15—Winnipeg	W	5-3
17—Hartford	W	6-4
19—At Montreal	L	1-4
21—At N.Y. Rangers	L	*3-4
24—Anaheim	T	*2-2
26—Buffalo	W	4-3
28—At Florida	W	4-3

MARCH

4—At Buffalo	L	1-2
6—At Winnipeg	W	5-3
8—Boston	W	7-3
10—Toronto	L	2-4
12—N.Y. Rangers	W	6-2
13—At Hartford	W	3-2
15—Washington	L	*4-5
17—At Boston	W	4-2
19—Vancouver	W	5-4
20—At N.Y. Islanders	W	2-1
22—San Jose	T	*2-2
24—Ottawa	W	5-1
26—At Calgary	L	3-5
27—At Edmonton	L	3-5
30—At Vancouver	W	3-1

APRIL

3—Boston‡	W	6-2
4—Tampa Bay	W	2-1
6—New Jersey	W	3-1
8—At New Jersey	L	2-7
9—At Montreal	L	1-9
11—At Ottawa	W	4-0

*Denotes overtime game.
†At Sacramento, Calif.
‡At Cleveland.

QUEBEC NORDIQUES
EASTERN CONFERENCE/NORTHEAST DIVISION

1994-95 SCHEDULE

Home games shaded.
* — All-Star Game at San Jose Arena.
† — At Phoenix.
△ — At Saskatoon, Sask.
D — Day game.

OCTOBER

SUN	MON	TUE	WED	THU	FRI	SAT
						1 BUF
2	3	4 TB	5	6 BOS	7	8 HAR
9	10	11 PIT	12	13 TOR	14	15 CHI
16	17	18 NYR	19	20 PHI	21	22 DET
23 BUF	24	25 EDM	26	27 HAR	28	29 DAL
30	31					

NOVEMBER

SUN	MON	TUE	WED	THU	FRI	SAT
		1 TB	2	3	4	5 WAS
6	7	8 PHI	9	10 BOS	11	12 D OTT
13 NJ	D 14	15	16	17 MON	18	19 MON
20	21 FLA	22	23 DAL	24 STL	25	26 WAS
27	28	29 LA	30			

DECEMBER

SUN	MON	TUE	WED	THU	FRI	SAT
				1 NJ	2	3 HAR
4	5	6 CAL	7	8	9 TB	10 FLA
11	12	13 FLA	14	15 DET	16	17 D PHI
18 TB	D 19	20	21 PHI	22	23 NYI	24
25	26	27 TOR	28	29 HAR	30	31 VAN

JANUARY

SUN	MON	TUE	WED	THU	FRI	SAT
1	2	3	4	5† MON	6	7 EDM
8 CAL	9	10	11	12 MON	13	14 BOS
15	16	17 ANA	18 NYI	19	20	21*
22	23 NYR	24 WAS	25	26	27 BUF	28 NYR
29	30	31				

FEBRUARY

SUN	MON	TUE	WED	THU	FRI	SAT
			1	2 WAS	3	4 D SJ
5 NJ	D 6	7	8	9 PIT	10	11 OTT
12	13	14	15 ANA	16 LA	17	18 SJ
19	20△ VAN	21	22	23 OTT	24	25 BOS
26	27	28 BOS				

MARCH

SUN	MON	TUE	WED	THU	FRI	SAT
			1	2 WIN	3	4 BUF
5	6 PIT	7	8 FLA	9 PIT	10	11 NYI
12	13	14 NJ	15	16 WIN	17	18
19 PIT	D 20	21	22 HAR	23	24 BUF	25 OTT
26	27	28 STL	29	30 NYR	31 CHI	

APRIL

SUN	MON	TUE	WED	THU	FRI	SAT
						1
2 NYI	D 3	4	5 MON	6 MON	7	8 OTT
9	10	11	12	13	14	15

1994-95 SEASON

CLUB DIRECTORY

President and governor
Marcel Aubut
General manager
Pierre Lacroix
Assistant to the g.m./hockey operations
Sherry Bassin
Admin. asst. to the general manager
Francois Giguere
Head coach
Marc Crawford
Assistant coach
Jacques Martin
V.P./administration and finance
Jean Laflamme
Director of public relations
Jacques Labrie
Director of press relations
Jean Martineau
Coordinator of public relations
Nicole Bouchard
Scout/pro hockey and special assignment
Orval Tessier
Psysiotherapist
Jacques Lavergne

Trainers
Rene Lacasse
Jacques Rene Lavigueur
Jean-Rene Lavigueur
Scouts
Herb Boxer
Shannon Currie
Roland Duplessis
Paul Gagnon
Yvon Gendron
Jan Janda
Frank Jay
Bengt Lundholm
Brian MacDonald
Dave Mayville
Don McKenney
Frank Moberg
Lewis A. Mongelluzzo
Don Paarup
Dave Peterson
Normand Poisson
Richard Rothermel
Peter Sullivan

DRAFT CHOICES

Rd.—Player	H/W	Overall	Pos.	Last team
1—Wade Belak	6-4/213	12	D	Saskatoon (WHL)
1—Jeffrey Kealty	6-4/175	22	D	Catholic Mem. H.S. (Mass.)
2—Josef Marha	6-1/176	35	C	Dukla Jihlava, Czech.
3—Sebastien Bety	6-2/201	61	D	Drummondville (QMJHL)
3—Chris Drury	5-10/180	72	C	Fairfield Prep (Ct.)
4—Milan Hejduk	5-11/163	87	RW	HC Pardubice, Czech.
5—Tony Tuzzolino	6-2/180	113	RW	Michigan State
6—Nicholas Windsor	6-1/174	139	D	Cornwall (Tier II)
7—Calvin Elfring	6-0/150	165	D	Powell River (Tier II)
8—Jay Bertsch	6-2/208	191	RW	Spokane (WHL)
9—Tim Thomas	5-11/180	217	G	Univ. of Vermont (ECAC)
10—Chris Pittman	6-2/170	243	LW	Kitchener (OHL)
11—Steven Low	6-0/178	285	D	Sherbrooke (QMJHL)

MISCELLANEOUS DATA

Home ice (capacity)
Quebec Colisee (15,399)
Address
2205 Avenue du Colisee
Quebec, Que. G1L 4W7
Business phone
418-529-8441

Rink dimensions
200 feet by 85 feet
Club colors
Blue, white and red

TRAINING CAMP ROSTER

No.	FORWARDS	Ht./Wt.	Place BORN	Date	NHL exp.	1993-94 clubs
28	Bob Bassen (C)	5-10/180	Calgary, Alta.	5-6-65	9	St. Louis, Quebec
	Wendel Clark (LW)	5-10/194	Kelvington, Sask.	10-25-66	9	Toronto
	Rene Corbet (LW)	6-0/187	Victoriaville, Que.	6-25-73	1	Cornwall (AHL), Quebec
	Adam Deadmarsh (RW)	6-0/195	Trail, B.C.	5-10-75	0	Portland (WHL)
	Peter Forsberg (C)	5-11/190	Ornskoldsvik, Sweden	7-20-73	0	Swedish Olympic Team (Int'l), MoDo (Sweden)
34	Iain Fraser (C)	5-10/175	Scarborough, Ont.	8-10-69	2	Quebec, Canadian national team (Int'l)
31	Valeri Kamensky (LW)	6-2/198	Voskresensk, U.S.S.R.	4-18-66	3	Quebec
51	Andrei Kovalenko (RW)	5-10/200	Gorky, U.S.S.R.	7-7-70	2	Quebec
47	Claude Lapointe (C)	5-9/181	Ville Emard, Que.	10-11-68	4	Quebec
	Chris Lindberg (LW)	6-1/185	Fort Francis, Ont.	4-16-67	3	Quebec, Cornwall (AHL)
11	Owen Nolan (RW)	6-1/201	Belfast, N. Ireland	2-12-72	4	Quebec
	Dwayne Norris (RW)	5-10/175	St. John's, Nfld.	1-8-70	1	Canadian national team (Int'l), Canadian Olympic Team (Int'l), Quebec, Cornwall (AHL)
9	Mike Ricci (C)	6-0/190	Scarborough, Ont.	10-27-71	4	Quebec
25	Martin Rucinsky (LW)	6-0/190	Most, Czechoslovakia	3-11-71	3	Quebec
19	Joe Sakic (C)	5-11/185	Burnaby, B.C.	7-7-69	6	Quebec
15	Reggie Savage (RW)	5-10/192	Montreal	5-1-70	3	Quebec, Cornwall (AHL)
12	Chris Simon (LW)	6-3/219	Wawa, Ont.	1-30-72	2	Quebec
	Ed Ward (RW)	6-3/205	Edmonton, Alta.	11-10-69	1	Cornwall (AHL), Quebec
	Landon Wilson (RW)	6-2/202	St. Louis	3-15-75	0	Univ. of North Dakota (WCHA)
48	Scott Young (RW)	6-0/190	Clinton, Mass.	10-1-67	6	Quebec
	DEFENSEMEN					
29	Steven Finn	6-0/191	Laval, Que.	8-20-66	9	Quebec
52	Adam Foote	6-1/202	Toronto	7-10-71	3	Quebec
5	Alexei Gusarov	6-3/185	Leningrad, U.S.S.R.	7-8-64	4	Quebec
59	David Karpa	6-1/202	Regina, Sask.	5-7-71	3	Quebec, Cornwall (AHL)
	Jon Klemm	6-3/200	Cranbrook, B.C.	1-6-70	2	Cornwall (AHL), Quebec
4	Uwe Krupp	6-6/235	Cologne, W. Germany	6-24-65	8	New York Islanders
	Janne Laukkanen	6-0/180	Lahti, Finland	3-19-70	0	HPK Hameenlinna (Finland), Finland Olympic Team (Int'l)
2	Sylvain Lefebvre	6-2/205	Richmond, Que.	10-14-67	5	Toronto
7	Curtis Leschyshyn	6-1/205	Thompson, Man.	9-21-69	6	Quebec
45	Mike McKee	6-3/203	Toronto	6-18-69	1	Cornwall (AHL), Quebec
36	Brad Werenka	6-2/205	Two Hills, Alta.	2-12-69	2	Cape Breton (AHL), Edmonton, Canadian national team (Int'l), Canadian Olympic Team (Int'l), Quebec
6	Craig Wolanin	6-3/205	Grosse Point, Mich.	7-27-67	9	Quebec
	GOALTENDERS					
32	Jacques Cloutier	5-7/168	Noranda, Que.	1-3-60	12	Quebec
35	Stephane Fiset	6-1/195	Montreal	6-17-70	5	Cornwall (AHL), Quebec
	Garth Snow	6-3/200	Wrentham, Mass.	7-28-69	1	U.S. national team (Int'l), U.S. Olympic Team (Int'l), Quebec, Cornwall (AHL)
	Jocelyn Thibault	5-11/170	Montreal	1-12-75	1	Cornwall (AHL), Quebec

1993-94 REVIEW

INDIVIDUAL STATISTICS

SCORING

	Games	G	A	Pts.	PIM	+/-	PPG	SHG	Shots	Shooting Pct.
Joe Sakic	84	28	64	92	18	-8	10	1	279	10.0
Mats Sundin	84	32	53	85	60	1	6	2	226	14.2
Valeri Kamensky	76	28	37	65	42	12	6	0	170	16.5
Mike Ricci	83	30	21	51	113	-9	13	3	138	21.7
Scott Young	76	26	25	51	14	-4	6	1	236	11.0
Iain Fraser	60	17	20	37	23	-5	2	0	109	15.6
Andrei Kovalenko	58	16	17	33	46	-5	5	0	92	17.4
Martin Rucinsky	60	9	23	32	58	4	4	0	96	9.4
Claude Lapointe	59	11	17	28	70	2	1	1	73	15.1
Alexei Gusarov	76	5	20	25	38	3	0	1	84	6.0
Ron Sutter*	37	9	13	22	44	3	4	0	66	13.6
Curtis Leschyshyn	72	5	17	22	65	-2	3	0	97	5.2
Bob Bassen*	37	11	8	19	55	-3	1	0	56	19.6
Dave Karpa	60	5	12	17	148	0	2	0	48	10.4

	Games	G	A	Pts.	PIM	+/-	PPG	SHG	Shots	Shooting Pct.
Steven Finn	80	4	13	17	159	-9	0	0	74	5.4
Craig Wolanin	63	6	10	16	80	16	0	0	78	7.7
Mike McKee	48	3	12	15	41	5	2	0	60	5.0
Chris Lindberg	37	6	8	14	12	-1	0	0	42	14.3
Martin Gelinas*	31	6	6	12	8	-2	0	0	53	11.3
Garth Butcher*	34	3	9	12	67	-1	0	1	29	10.3
Tommy Sjodin*	22	1	9	10	18	5	1	0	46	2.2
Chris Simon	37	4	4	8	132	-2	0	0	39	10.3
Adam Foote	45	2	6	8	67	3	0	0	42	4.8
Reggie Savage	17	3	4	7	16	3	1	0	25	12.0
Brad Werenka*	11	0	7	7	8	4	0	0	17	0.0
Kerry Huffman*	28	0	6	6	28	2	0	0	44	0.0
Paul MacDermid	44	2	3	5	35	-3	0	0	16	12.5
Owen Nolan	6	2	2	4	8	2	0	0	15	13.3
Tony Twist	49	0	4	4	101	-1	0	0	15	0.0
Stephane Fiset (goalie)	50	0	3	3	8	0	0	0	0	0.0
Dwayne Norris	4	1	1	2	4	1	0	0	7	14.3
Rene Corbet	9	1	1	2	0	1	0	0	14	7.1
Ed Ward	7	1	0	1	5	0	0	0	3	33.3
Mike Hurlbut	1	0	0	0	0	-1	0	0	1	0.0
Aaron Miller	1	0	0	0	0	-1	0	0	0	0.0
Paxton Schulte	1	0	0	0	2	0	0	0	0	0.0
Garth Snow (goalie)	5	0	0	0	0	0	0	0	0	0.0
Alain Cote	6	0	0	0	4	-2	0	0	4	0.0
Jon Klemm	7	0	0	0	4	-1	0	0	11	0.0
Jacques Cloutier (goalie)	14	0	0	0	2	0	0	0	0	0.0
Jocelyn Thibault (goalie)	29	0	0	0	2	0	0	0	0	0.0

GOALTENDING

	Games	Min.	Goals	SO	Avg.	W	L	T	Shots	Sv. Pct.
Jacques Cloutier	14	475	24	0	3.03	3	2	1	232	.897
Jocelyn Thibault	29	1504	83	0	3.31	8	13	3	768	.892
Stephane Fiset	50	2798	158	2	3.39	20	25	4	1434	.890
Garth Snow	5	279	16	0	3.44	3	2	0	127	.874

Empty-net goals (do not count against a goaltender's average): Fiset 7, Thibault 3, Cloutier 1.
*Played with two or more NHL teams.

RESULTS

OCTOBER
6—At Ottawa	T	*5-5
9—At Boston	L	3-7
10—Pittsburgh	W	7-4
13—At N.Y. Rangers	L	4-6
16—At Montreal	W	5-2
18—Montreal	L	2-4
20—At Hartford	W	5-2
21—At Chicago	L	2-3
23—Dallas	W	3-2
26—Philadelphia	L	2-4
28—At Pittsburgh	W	7-3
30—Detroit	L	3-5

NOVEMBER
2—Tampa Bay	W	8-2
4—At Philadelphia	L	1-4
6—N.Y. Rangers	L	2-4
7—Florida	L	1-3
9—At Washington	L	1-2
13—At Tampa Bay	L	3-4
14—At Florida	W	5-2
20—Winnipeg	T	*5-5
23—New Jersey	T	*1-1
25—Los Angeles	W	8-6
27—Buffalo	T	*2-2
30—Boston	L	2-5

DECEMBER
3—At N.Y. Islanders	W	3-2
4—Vancouver	W	3-1
7—Calgary	T	*4-4
9—At New Jersey	W	3-2
11—Ottawa	W	5-2
13—Washington	W	5-3
16—At Philadelphia	L	2-3
18—New Jersey	L	2-6
19—San Jose	W	7-5
21—At Ottawa	L	1-2
23—At Winnipeg	L	2-5
28—Tampa Bay	L	1-4
29—N.Y. Islanders	W	5-3
31—At Pittsburgh	W	5-4

JANUARY
2—At Dallas	W	6-4
4—At Los Angeles	L	1-5
5—Montreal†	L	0-4
7—At Edmonton	L	4-6
11—At Calgary	L	0-1
12—At Vancouver	L	3-4
15—Washington	L	0-4
18—Pittsburgh	W	6-3
25—Philadelphia	W	6-4
27—At Pittsburgh	L	0-3
29—At Hartford	W	3-2
31—At Boston	L	3-4

FEBRUARY
1—Hartford	L	1-2
3—At St. Louis	W	4-3
5—N.Y. Islanders	L	2-3
8—Boston	L	1-6
12—At Montreal	L	2-5
14—N.Y. Rangers	L	2-4
17—At San Jose	W	8-2
18—At Anaheim	W	1-0
21—At Buffalo	L	1-2

(continued)
24—St. Louis	W	6-0
26—Anaheim	L	3-6
27—At N.Y. Islanders	L	2-5

MARCH
2—At N.Y. Rangers	L	2-5
5—Toronto	W	4-1
7—At New Jersey	T	*2-2
8—Ottawa	W	5-2
10—Montreal	T	*4-4
12—At Washington	W	4-3
14—Chicago	W	5-1
17—Hartford	W	4-1
19—At Montreal	L	2-5
20—Edmonton	L	3-5
22—Boston	W	5-3
26—At Toronto	L	3-6
27—New Jersey‡	L	2-5
30—At Ottawa	L	4-6
31—At Detroit	W	4-2

APRIL
2—Buffalo	L	2-6
4—Buffalo	W	6-4
5—Florida	T	*3-3
7—Hartford	W	5-2
10—At Buffalo	L	1-4
12—At Florida	W	5-2
14—At Tampa Bay	L	2-5

*Denotes overtime game.
†At Phoenix.
‡At Minneapolis.

ST. LOUIS BLUES
WESTERN CONFERENCE/CENTRAL DIVISION

1994-95 SCHEDULE

- Home games shaded.
- * — All-Star Game at San Jose Arena.
- † — At Las Vegas.
- D — Day game.

OCTOBER
SUN	MON	TUE	WED	THU	FRI	SAT
						1 DET
2 CHI	3	4	5	6 FLA	7 TB	8
9	10	11 CHI	12	13 NYR	14	15 TOR
16 TB	17	18 SJ	19	20	21	22 TOR
23 VAN	24	25 WAS	26	27	28	29 SJ
30 ANA	31					

NOVEMBER
SUN	MON	TUE	WED	THU	FRI	SAT
		1	2 NYI	3	4	5 WIN
6	7	8 CAL	9	10 WIN	11	12 PIT
13 CHI	14	15	16 HAR	17 BOS	18	19 TOR
20	21	22	23 DET	24 QUE	25	26 DAL
27	28 WIN	29	30 MON			

DECEMBER
SUN	MON	TUE	WED	THU	FRI	SAT
				1	2	3
4 NJ	5	6	7 DAL	8	9	10 DAL
11 DET	12	13	14	15	16 VAN	17
18 EDM	19	20 CAL	21	22	23 VAN	24
25	26 DAL	27 CHI	28	29 SJ	30	31 DAL

JANUARY
SUN	MON	TUE	WED	THU	FRI	SAT
1	2 WAS	3 NYR	4	5	6	7 FLA
8 WIN	9	10 LA	11	12 LA	13	14 SJ
15	16	17 WIN	18	19	20	21*
22	23	24 NYI	25	26 EDM	27	28 CAL
29	30	31 ANA				

FEBRUARY
SUN	MON	TUE	WED	THU	FRI	SAT
			1	2 LA	3	4 DAL
5	6	7	8	9† ANA	10	11 CAL
12 DET	13	14	15 NJ	16 PHI	17	18 MON
19	20 EDM	21	22 TOR	23	24 PIT	25 CHI
26	27 TOR	28				

MARCH
SUN	MON	TUE	WED	THU	FRI	SAT
			1	2† LA	3	4 D WIN
5 CHI	6 D	7 OTT	8	9 HAR	10	11
12 BUF	13	14 EDM	15	16 LA	17	18
19 ANA	20 D	21 VAN	22	23 ANA	24	25
26 BOS	27	28 QUE	29 OTT	30	31 TOR	

APRIL
SUN	MON	TUE	WED	THU	FRI	SAT
						1
2 DET	3 D	4 BUF	5	6 DET	7	8
9 PHI	10 D	11	12	13	14	15

1994-95 SEASON

CLUB DIRECTORY

Board of directors
Michael F. Shanahan
Jud Perkins
Al Kerth
Jack Quinn
Ed Trusheim
Andy Craig
Horace Wilkins
Chairman of the board
Michael F. Shanahan
President
Jack J. Quinn
Executive vice president
Ronald Caron
General manager/head coach
Mike Keenan
Associate coach
Bob Berry
Assistant coach
Ted Sator
Vice president/director of sales
Bruce Affleck
V.P./dir. of player personnel and scouting/ assistant general manager
Ted Hampson

V.P./director of player development
Bob Plager
V.P./dir. of broadcast sales
Matt Hyland
V.P./dir. of finance and administration
Jerry Jasiek
V.P./dir. of marketing and P.R.
Susie Mathieu
Assistant director of scouting
Jack Evans
Western Canada/U.S. scout
Pat Ginnell
New England scout
Matt Keator
Assistant directors of public relations
Jeff Trammel
Mike Caruso
Trainers
Tom Nash
Ron Dubuque
Equipment managers
Frank Burns
Terry Roof

DRAFT CHOICES

Rd. — Player	H/W	Overall	Pos.	Last team
3—Stephane Roy	5-10/173	68	C	Val-d'Or (QMJHL)
4—Tyler Harlton	6-3/201	94	D	Vernon (Tier II, Jr. A)
5—Edwin Frylen	6-0/211	120	D	Vasteras, Sweden
7—Roman Vopat	6-3/216	172	C	Chemopetrol (Czech Jrs.)
8—Steve Noble	6-1/185	198	C	Stratford (Jr. B)
9—Marc Stephan	6-2/205	224	C	Tri-City (WHL)
10—Kevin Harper	6-2/170	250	D	Wexford (Jr. A)
11—Scott Fankhouser	6-1/195	276	G	Loomis-Chaffee H.S. (Pa.)

MISCELLANEOUS DATA

Home ice (capacity)
Kiel Center (18,500)
Address
1401 Clark
St. Louis, MO 63103
Business phone
314-622-2500

Rink dimensions
200 feet by 85 feet
Club colors
Blue, gold, red and white

TRAINING CAMP ROSTER

No.	FORWARDS	Ht./Wt.	Place	Born Date	NHL exp.	1993-94 clubs
36	Philippe Bozon (LW)	5-10/185	Chamonix, France	11-30-66	3	St. Louis
39	Kelly Chase (RW)	5-11/195	Porcupine Plain, Sask.	10-25-67	5	St. Louis
	Denis Chasse (RW)	6-2/200	Montreal	2-7-70	1	Cornwall (AHL), St. Louis
9	Denny Felsner (LW)	6-0/195	Warren, Mich.	4-29-70	3	Peoria (IHL), St. Louis
	Tony Hrkac (C)	5-11/185	Thunder Bay, Ont.	7-7-66	7	St. Louis, Peoria (IHL)
16	Brett Hull (RW)	5-10/200	Belleville, Ont.	8-9-64	9	St. Louis
15	Craig Janney (C)	6-1/190	Hartford, Conn.	9-26-67	7	St. Louis
	Craig Johnson (LW)	6-2/185	St. Paul, Minn.	3-18-72	0	U.S. national team (Int'l), U.S. Olympic Team (Int'l)
12	Vitali Karamnov (LW)	6-2/185	Moscow, U.S.S.R.	7-6-68	2	St. Louis, Peoria (IHL)
38	Igor Korolev (C)	6-1/190	Moscow, U.S.S.R.	9-6-70	2	St. Louis
	Ian Laperriere (C)	6-1/195	Montreal	1-19-74	1	Drummondville (QMJHL), St. Louis, Peoria (IHL)
17	Basil McRae (LW)	6-2/205	Beaverton, Ont.	1-5-61	13	St. Louis
37	Kevin Miehm (C)	6-2/195	Kitchener, Ont.	9-10-69	2	St. Louis, Peoria (IHL)
14	Kevin Miller (LW)	5-11/190	Lansing, Mich.	8-9-65	6	St. Louis
	Kurtis Miller (LW)	5-11/180	Bemidji, Minn.	6-1-70	0	Lake Superior State (CCHA)
	Jim Montgomery (C)	5-9/180	Montreal	6-30-69	1	St. Louis, Peoria (IHL)
25	Vitali Prokhorov (LW)	5-9/185	Moscow, U.S.S.R.	12-25-66	2	St. Louis, Peoria (IHL)
	David Roberts (LW)	6-0/185	Alameda, Calif.	5-28-70	1	U.S. national team (Int'l), U.S. Olympic Team (Int'l), Peoria (IHL), St. Louis
	Brendan Shanahan	6-3/215	Mimico, Ont.	1-23-69	7	St. Louis
26	Peter Stastny (C)	6-1/200	Bratislava, Czech.	9-18-56	14	Slovakian Olympic team (Int'l), Slovan Bratislava (Slovakia), St. Louis
	Esa Tikkanen (C)	6-1/200	Helsinki, Finland	1-25-65	10	New York Rangers
	Tony Twist (LW)	6-0/208	Sherwood Park, Alta.	5-9-68	5	Quebec
	DEFENSEMEN					
34	Murray Baron	6-3/215	Prince George, B.C.	6-1-67	5	St. Louis
	Jeff Batters	6-2/210	Victoria, B.C.	10-23-70	1	Peoria (IHL), St. Louis
28	Steve Duchesne	5-11/195	Sept-Illes, Que.	6-30-65	8	St. Louis
44	Terry Hollinger	6-1/200	Regina, Sask.	2-24-71	1	Peoria (IHL), St. Louis
41	Dan Laperriere	6-1/180	Laval, Que.	3-28-69	2	Peoria (IHL), St. Louis
	Doug Lidster	6-1/200	Kamloops, B.C.	10-18-60	11	New York Rangers
	Al MacInnis	6-2/196	Inverness, N.S.	7-11-63	13	Calgary
	Jason Marshall	6-2/195	Cranbrook, B.C.	2-22-71	1	Canadian national team (Int'l), Peoria (IHL)
	Jamie Rivers	6-0/180	Ottawa	3-16-75	0	Sudbury (OHL)
	Tom Tilley	6-0/190	Trenton, Ont.	3-28-65	4	St. Louis
4	Rick Zombo	6-1/195	Des Plaines, Ill.	5-8-63	10	St. Louis
	GOALTENDERS					
	Jon Casey	5-10/155	Grand Rapids, Minn.	8-29-62	9	Boston
30	Jim Hrivnak	6-2/195	Montreal	5-28-68	5	St. Louis
31	Curtis Joseph	5-10/182	Keswick, Ont.	4-29-67	5	St. Louis
	Geoff Sarjeant	5-9/180	Orillia, Ont.	11-30-69	0	Peoria (IHL)

1993-94 REVIEW

INDIVIDUAL STATISTICS

SCORING

	Games	G	A	Pts.	PIM	+/-	PPG	SHG	Shots	Shooting Pct.
Brendan Shanahan	81	52	50	102	211	-9	15	†7	†397	13.1
Brett Hull	81	57	40	97	38	-3	‡25	3	392	14.5
Craig Janney	69	16	68	84	24	-14	8	0	95	16.8
Jeff Brown*	63	13	47	60	46	-13	7	0	196	6.6
Kevin Miller	75	23	25	48	83	6	6	3	154	14.9
Steve Duchesne	36	12	19	31	14	1	8	0	115	10.4
Vitali Prokhorov	55	15	10	25	20	-6	3	0	85	17.6
Philippe Bozon	80	9	16	25	42	4	0	1	118	7.6
Phil Housley	26	7	15	22	12	-5	4	0	60	11.7
Vitali Karamnov	59	9	12	21	51	-3	2	0	66	13.6
Petr Nedved	19	6	14	20	8	2	2	0	63	9.5
Jim Montgomery	67	6	14	20	44	-1	0	0	67	9.0
Ron Sutter*	36	6	12	18	46	-1	1	0	42	14.3
Igor Korolev	73	6	10	16	40	-12	0	0	93	6.5
Peter Stastny	17	5	11	16	4	-2	2	0	30	16.7
Murray Baron	77	5	9	14	123	-14	0	0	73	6.8
Tony Hrkac	36	6	5	11	8	-11	1	1	43	14.0

	Games	G	A	Pts.	PIM	+/-	PPG	SHG	Shots	Shooting Pct.
Bret Hedican*	61	0	11	11	64	-8	0	0	78	0.0
Rick Zombo	74	2	8	10	85	-15	0	0	53	3.8
Bob Bassen*	46	2	7	9	44	-14	0	1	73	2.7
Doug Crossman	50	2	7	9	10	1	1	0	30	6.7
Tom Tilley	48	1	7	8	32	3	0	0	41	2.4
Kelly Chase	68	2	5	7	278	-5	0	0	57	3.5
Garth Butcher*	43	1	6	7	76	-6	0	1	37	2.7
Dave Mackey	30	2	3	5	56	-4	0	0	21	9.5
Nathan Lafayette*	38	2	3	5	14	-9	0	0	23	8.7
Daniel Laperriere	20	1	3	4	8	-1	1	0	20	5.0
Basil McRae	40	1	2	3	103	-7	0	0	23	4.3
Curtis Joseph (goalie)	71	0	3	3	4	0	0	0	0	0.0
Alexei Kasatonov*	8	0	2	2	19	5	0	0	6	0.0
Denny Felsner	6	1	0	1	2	-1	0	0	6	16.7
Denis Chasse	3	0	1	1	15	1	0	0	5	0.0
Kevin Miehm	14	0	1	1	4	-3	0	0	5	0.0
Jim Hrivnak (goalie)	23	0	1	1	2	0	0	0	0	0.0
Ian Laperriere	1	0	0	0	0	0	0	0	1	0.0
David Roberts	1	0	0	0	2	0	0	0	1	0.0
Terry Hollinger	2	0	0	0	0	1	0	0	0	0.0
Jeff Batters	6	0	0	0	7	1	0	0	1	0.0

GOALTENDING

	Games	Min.	Goals	SO	Avg.	W	L	T	Shots	Sv. Pct.
Curtis Joseph	71	4127	213	1	3.10	36	23	11	†2382	.911
Jim Hrivnak	23	970	69	0	4.27	4	10	0	563	.877

Empty-net goals (do not count against a goaltender's average): Hrivnak 1.
*Played with two or more NHL teams.
†Led league.
‡Tied for league lead.

RESULTS

OCTOBER

7—Florida	W	5-3
9—Ottawa	W	7-5
13—At Detroit	W	5-2
16—At Dallas	L	0-4
19—At San Jose	W	4-1
21—San Jose†	W	5-2
23—At Pittsburgh	T	*3-3
26—At Chicago	L	2-9
28—Hartford	W	2-1
30—At Boston	W	2-1

NOVEMBER

1—At Hartford	W	4-2
3—At Winnipeg	W	3-0
6—Edmonton	W	*6-5
9—Pittsburgh	T	*3-3
11—Toronto	W	3-2
13—At Los Angeles	L	3-6
16—At Vancouver	L	0-3
18—Calgary	T	*3-3
20—Los Angeles	W	4-1
21—Detroit	T	*2-2
24—At Washington	L	2-5
26—New Jersey	T	*6-6
28—Winnipeg	L	3-4

DECEMBER

1—At Toronto	L	2-4
2—Toronto	L	4-5
4—Dallas	W	4-3
7—Chicago	W	3-2
9—At Detroit	L	2-3
11—At Los Angeles	L	1-9

12—At Anaheim	L	*1-2
15—At San Jose	W	3-1
17—At Calgary	W	4-3
19—At Edmonton	W	4-1
23—Tampa Bay	W	7-4
26—Chicago	W	3-2
27—Montreal	L	2-5
29—N.Y. Rangers	L	3-4
31—At Winnipeg	L	1-2

JANUARY

2—Calgary	W	*4-3
4—Detroit	T	*4-4
6—At Hartford‡	W	2-1
8—Anaheim	L	3-5
9—At Dallas	L	1-2
13—Edmonton	W	6-4
15—Buffalo	W	2-1
18—At N.Y. Rangers	L	1-4
19—At Philadelphia	L	3-8
24—At Anaheim	W	*3-2
25—At Vancouver	T	*3-3
28—At Edmonton	W	3-2
29—At Calgary	W	5-3

FEBRUARY

1—Toronto	T	*4-4
3—Quebec	L	3-4
5—San Jose	W	4-3
8—Winnipeg	W	6-5
10—Washington	L	3-4
12—Detroit	L	*4-5
15—Vancouver	W	3-2
18—Boston	W	3-1

20—Anaheim	W	4-1
24—At Quebec	L	0-6
26—At Ottawa	W	11-1
28—At New Jersey	L	1-5

MARCH

1—At N.Y. Islanders	L	2-4
3—Vancouver	L	0-4
7—At Toronto	W	3-2
9—At Montreal	L	2-7
12—N.Y. Islanders	T	*5-5
16—At Winnipeg	L	0-4
18—At Toronto	L	2-4
20—At Chicago	W	*4-3
22—Philadelphia	L	3-6
23—At Buffalo	W	3-2
25—Dallas	W	5-3
27—San Jose	L	3-4
30—At Florida	W	3-1

APRIL

1—At Tampa Bay	L	3-4
3—At Detroit	T	*3-3
5—Chicago	W	5-1
7—Los Angeles	W	6-2
8—At Chicago	L	1-6
10—Dallas	T	*2-2
12—At Dallas	L	5-9
14—Winnipeg	W	3-1

*Denotes overtime game.
†At Sacramento, Calif.
‡At Cleveland.

SAN JOSE SHARKS
WESTERN CONFERENCE/PACIFIC DIVISION

1994-95 SCHEDULE

- ▨ Home games shaded.
- * — All-Star Game at San Jose Arena.
- † — At Portland, Ore.
- △ — At Phoenix.
- D — Day game.

OCTOBER

SUN	MON	TUE	WED	THU	FRI	SAT
						1 LA
2	3	4	5 VAN	6	7 DET	8
9 VAN	D 10	11 LA	12 BOS	13	14 CAL	15
16 WIN	17	18 STL	19	20 CHI	21	22 D NJ
23 NYR	24	25	26	27	28	29 STL
30	31					

NOVEMBER

SUN	MON	TUE	WED	THU	FRI	SAT
		1 NJ	2	3	4	5 NYR
6	7 VAN	8 VAN	9	10 ANA	11	12 BUF
13	14	15 CAL	16	17	18 DAL	19
20 EDM	21	22 CHI	23 ANA	24	25	26 PIT
27	28 DET	29	30			

DECEMBER

SUN	MON	TUE	WED	THU	FRI	SAT
				1 FLA	2 TB	3
4	5 DAL	6	7 TOR	8	9 ANA	10 WAS
11	12	13	14 NYI	15	16 ANA	17 PIT
18	19	20 EDM	21† VAN	22	23	24
25	26	27 EDM	28	29 STL	30	31 DET

JANUARY

SUN	MON	TUE	WED	THU	FRI	SAT
1 CHI	2	3	4 MON	5	6	7 D CAL
8	9	10	11 DAL	12	13	14 STL
15	16 VAN	17	18	19	20	21*
22	23 LA	24	25 WIN	26 LA	27	28 D DAL
29	30 TOR	31				

FEBRUARY

SUN	MON	TUE	WED	THU	FRI	SAT
			1 OTT	2	3	4 D QUE
5	6 MON	7	8 HAR	9 BOS	10	11 D NYI
12	13	14	15 OTT	16 VAN	17	18 QUE
19	20 PHI	21 D	22△ CAL	23	24 ANA	25
26 D TB	27	28 BUF				

MARCH

SUN	MON	TUE	WED	THU	FRI	SAT
			1 TOR	2	3	4 WAS
5 PHI	6	7	8 EDM	9	10 DET	11
12 HAR	D 13	14	15 TOR	16	17 CAL	18
19 WIN	D 20	21 CHI	22	23 FLA	24	25 D LA
26 LA	D 27	28 WIN	29	30	31 CAL	

APRIL

SUN	MON	TUE	WED	THU	FRI	SAT
						1
2 D ANA	3	4	5 CAL	6	7 D EDM	8
9 EDM	10	11	12	13	14	15

1994-95 SEASON

CLUB DIRECTORY

Co-owner & chairman
George Gund III
Co-owner
Gordon Gund
President & chief executive officer
Arthur L. Savage
Exec. V.P. & chief operating officer
Greg Jamison
Exec. V.P., development
Matt Levine
Exec. vice president, building operations
Frank Jirik
Vice president/dir. of hockey operations
Dean Lombardi
Vice president/dir. of player personnel
Chuck Grillo
Head coach
Kevin Constantine
Asst. coach & asst. to dir. of hoc. operations
Wayne Thomas
Assistant coaches
Drew Remenda
Vasily Tikhonov
Strength & conditioning coach
Steve Millard
Scouting coordinator
Joe Will
Executive assistant
Brenda Knight
Director of media relations
Tim Bryant

Assistant director of media relations
Ken Arnold
Media relations assistant
Paul Turner
Scouting staff
Ray Payne
Tim Burke
Sakari Pietila
Rob Grillo
Larry Ross
Pat Funk
Tim Gorski
Thomas Holm
Randy Joevanazzo
Konstantin Krylov
Jack Morganstern
Joe Rowley
Dan Summers
Bob Friedlander
Head trainer
Tom Woodcock
Equipment manager
Bob Crocker Jr.
Assistant equipment manager
Sergei Tchekmarev
Team physician
Dr. Arthur Ting
Director of ticket operations
Daniel DeBoer

DRAFT CHOICES

1—Jeff Friesen	6-0/183	11	LW	Regina (WHL)
2—Angel Nikolov	6-1/176	37	D	Chemopetrol (Czech Jrs.)
3—Alexei Yegorov	5-9/174	66	C	CSKA St. Petersburg, CIS
4—Vaclav Varada	6-0/198	89	RW	HC Vitkovice, Czech.
5—Brian Swanson	5-9/180	115	C	Omaha (Jr. A)
6—Alexander Korolyuk	5-9/165	141	RW	Krylja Sovetov, CIS
7—Sergei Gorbachev	6-0/183	167	RW	Dynamo Moscow, CIS
8—Eric Landry	5-11/186	193	RW	Guelph (OHL)
9—Yevgeny Nabokov	5-11/165	219	G	Tor. UST Kamenogorsk, CIS
10—Tomas Pisa	6-1/185	240	RW	HC Pardubice, Czech.
10—Aniket Dhadphale	6-3/195	245	LW	Marquette
11—David Beauregard	5-10/165	271	LW	St. Hyacinthe (QMJHL)

MISCELLANEOUS DATA

Home ice (capacity)
San Jose Arena (17,190)
Address
525 West Santa Clara Street
San Jose, CA 95113
Business phone
408-287-7070

Rink dimensions
200 feet by 85 feet
Club colors
Pacific teal, gray, black and white

TRAINING CAMP ROSTER

No.	FORWARDS	Ht./Wt.	BORN Place	BORN Date	NHL exp.	1993-94 clubs
13	Jamie Baker (C)	6-0/190	Nepean, Que.	8-31-66	5	San Jose
	Mark Beaufait (C)	5-9/165	Livonia, Mich.	5-13-70	1	U.S. national team (Int'l), U.S. Olympic Team (Int'l), Kansas City (IHL)
	Slava Butsayev (C)	6-2/200	Tolyatti, U.S.S.R.	6-13-70	2	Philadelphia, San Jose
	Jan Caloun (RW)	5-10/175	Usti-nad-Labem, Czech.	12-20-72	0	Chemopetrol Lit. (Czech Republic)
	Alexander Cherbayev (RW)	6-1/190	Voskresensk, U.S.S.R.	8-13-73	0	Kansas City (IHL)
33	Dale Craigwell (C)	5-10/180	Toronto	4-24-71	3	Kansas City (IHL), San Jose
	Ulf Dahlen (LW)	6-2/195	Ostersund, Sweden	1-12-67	7	Dallas, San Jose
	Shean Donovan (RW)	6-1/172	Timmins, Ont.	1-22-75	0	Ottawa (OHL)
	Gaetan Duchesne (LW)	5-11/200	Quebec City	7-11-62	13	San Jose
	Todd Elik (C)	6-2/195	Brampton, Ont.	4-15-66	5	Edmonton, San Jose
12	Bob Errey (LW)	5-10/183	Montreal	9-21-64	11	San Jose
17	Pat Falloon (RW)	5-11/190	Foxwarren, Man.	9-22-72	3	San Jose
	Jeff Friesen (LW)	6-0/183	Meadow Lake, Sask.	8-5-76	0	Regina (WHL)
	Johan Garpenlov (LW)	5-11/185	Stockholm, Sweden	3-21-68	4	San Jose
37	Rob Gaudreau (RW)	5-11/185	Cranston, R.I.	1-20-70	2	San Jose
	Viktor Kozlov (RW)	6-5/209	Togliatti, U.S.S.R.	2-14-75	0	Dynamo Moscow (CIS)
	Igor Larionov (C)	5-9/170	Voskresensk, U.S.S.R.	12-3-60	4	San Jose
	Sergei Makarov (RW)	5-11/185	Chelyabinsk, U.S.S.R.	6-19-58	5	San Jose
	Jamie Matthews (C)	6-1/208	Amherst, N.S.	5-25-73	0	Sudbury (OHL)
	Kip Miller (C)	5-11/160	Lansing, Mich.	6-11-69	3	San Jose, Kansas City (IHL)
	Andrei Nazarov (LW)	6-4/210	Chelyabinsk, U.S.S.R.	3-21-72	1	Kansas City (IHL), San Jose
36	Jeff Odgers (LW)	6-0/195	Spy Hill, Sask.	5-31-69	3	San Jose
	Jaroslav Otevrel (C)	6-3/200	Gottwaldov, Czech.	9-16-68	2	Kansas City (IHL), San Jose
14	Ray Whitney (C)	5-9/160	Edmonton, Alta.	5-8-72	3	San Jose

DEFENSEMEN

No.		Ht./Wt.	Place	Date	exp.	1993-94 clubs
44	Shawn Cronin	6-2/210	Flushing, Mich.	8-20-63	6	San Jose
	Vlastimil Kroupa	6-2/176	Most, Czechoslovakia	4-27-75	1	San Jose, Kansas City (IHL)
4	Jay More	6-1/200	Souris, Man.	1-12-69	5	San Jose, Kansas City (IHL)
8	Jeff Norton	6-2/190	Cambridge, Mass.	11-25-65	7	San Jose
	Sandis Ozolinsh	6-1/195	Riga, U.S.S.R.	8-3-72	2	San Jose
41	Tom Pederson	5-9/175	Bloomington, Minn.	1-14-70	2	Kansas City (IHL), San Jose
	Marcus Ragnarsson	6-1/200	Ostervala, Sweden	8-13-71	0	Djurgarden (Sweden)
	Mike Rathje	6-5/2205	Manville, Alta.	5-11-74	1	San Jose, Kansas City (IHL)
	Michal Sykora	6-4/210	Pardubice, Czech.	7-5-73	1	San Jose, Kansas City (IHL)

GOALTENDERS

No.		Ht./Wt.	Place	Date	exp.	1993-94 clubs
31	Wade Flaherty	6-0/170	Terreace, B.C.	1-11-68	2	Kansas City (IHL)
32	Arturs Irbe	5-7/180	Riga, U.S.S.R.	2-2-67	3	San Jose
29	Jimmy Waite	6-1/180	Sherbrooke, Que.	4-15-69	6	San Jose

1993-94 REVIEW

INDIVIDUAL STATISTICS

SCORING

	Games	G	A	Pts.	PIM	+/-	PPG	SHG	Shots	Shooting Pct.
Sergei Makarov	80	30	38	68	78	11	10	0	155	19.4
Todd Elik*	75	25	41	66	89	-3	9	0	180	13.9
Sandis Ozolinsh	81	26	38	64	24	16	4	0	157	16.6
Igor Larionov	60	18	38	56	40	20	3	2	72	25.0
Pat Falloon	83	22	31	53	18	-3	6	0	193	11.4
Johan Garpenlov	80	18	35	53	28	9	7	0	125	14.4
Ray Whitney	61	14	26	40	14	2	1	0	82	17.1
Jeff Norton	64	7	33	40	36	16	1	0	92	7.6
Rob Gaudreau	84	15	20	35	28	-10	6	0	151	9.9
Bob Errey	64	12	18	30	126	-11	5	0	89	13.5
Gaetan Duchesne	84	12	18	30	28	8	0	1	121	9.9
Tom Pederson	74	6	19	25	31	3	3	0	185	3.2
Jeff Odgers	81	13	8	21	222	-13	7	0	73	17.8
Jamie Baker	65	12	5	17	38	-2	0	0	68	17.6
Ulf Dahlen*	13	6	6	12	0	0	3	0	43	14.0
Mike Rathje	47	1	9	10	59	-9	1	0	30	3.3
Dale Craigwell	58	3	6	9	16	-13	0	1	35	8.6
Jay More	49	1	6	7	63	-5	0	0	38	2.6
Jaroslav Otevrel	9	3	2	5	2	-5	1	0	11	27.3
Michal Sykora	22	1	4	5	14	-4	0	0	22	4.5
Kip Miller	11	2	2	4	6	-1	0	0	21	9.5
Mike Sullivan*	26	2	2	4	4	-3	0	2	21	9.5

	Games	G	A	Pts.	PIM	+/-	PPG	SHG	Shots	Shooting Pct.
Vlastimil Kroupa	27	1	3	4	20	-6	0	0	16	6.3
Doug Zmolek*	68	0	4	4	122	-9	0	0	29	0.0
Rob Zettler*	42	0	3	3	65	-7	0	0	28	0.0
Viacheslav Butsayev*	12	0	2	2	10	-2	0	0	6	0.0
Mike Lalor*	23	0	2	2	8	-5	0	0	19	0.0
Shawn Cronin	34	0	2	2	76	2	0	0	14	0.0
Arturs Irbe (goalie)	74	0	2	2	16	0	0	0	0	0.0
Gary Emmons	3	1	0	1	0	-4	1	0	6	16.7
Jeff McLean	6	1	0	1	0	1	0	0	5	20.0
Dave Capuano	4	0	1	1	0	-5	0	0	5	0.0
Andrei Nazarov	1	0	0	0	0	0	0	0	0	0.0
David Bruce	2	0	0	0	0	-2	0	0	5	0.0
Jim Waite (goalie)	15	0	0	0	6	0	0	0	0	0.0
David Maley*	19	0	0	0	30	-1	0	0	4	0.0

GOALTENDING

	Games	Min.	Goals	SO	Avg.	W	L	T	Shots	Sv. Pct.
Arturs Irbe	†74	†4412	209	3	2.84	30	28	†16	2064	.899
Jim Waite	15	697	50	0	4.30	3	7	0	319	.843

Empty-net goals (do not count against a goaltender's average): Irbe 4, Waite 2.
*Played with two or more NHL teams.
†Led league.

RESULTS

OCTOBER

6—At Edmonton	L	2-3
7—At Calgary	L	2-6
10—At Los Angeles	L	2-5
14—Calgary	L	1-2
16—Boston	T	*1-1
19—St. Louis	L	1-4
21—St. Louis†	L	2-5
23—Vancouver	L	4-6
24—At Vancouver	L	*2-3
26—Edmonton	W	3-1
28—Anaheim	W	4-3
30—Washington	L	2-4
31—At Anaheim	W	*2-1

NOVEMBER

2—Pittsburgh	T	*3-3
5—Dallas	W	4-2
7—New Jersey	L	1-2
9—Toronto	T	*2-2
11—At Dallas	L	0-4
13—At New Jersey	W	4-2
14—At N.Y. Rangers	T	*3-3
16—At Washington	W	2-1
18—At Boston	L	1-3
20—At Hartford	W	3-2
21—At Buffalo	L	5-6
23—Detroit	W	6-4
26—At Anaheim	W	4-3
27—Anaheim	W	1-0

DECEMBER

3—Winnipeg	T	*3-3
5—Florida	W	2-1

7—Tampa Bay	L	1-3
11—At Detroit	L	3-5
12—At Chicago	L	1-2
15—St. Louis	L	1-3
17—At Edmonton	L	2-4
19—At Quebec	L	5-7
22—At Toronto	T	*2-2
23—At Chicago	L	3-5
28—Calgary	T	*3-3
31—At Vancouver	W	3-2

JANUARY

2—At Edmonton	T	*4-4
4—Montreal	T	*2-2
6—Detroit	T	3-10
11—Los Angeles	T	*2-2
12—At Anaheim	W	5-2
15—Hartford	W	8-2
17—Calgary	W	3-2
25—N.Y. Rangers	L	3-8
28—At Florida	T	*3-3
29—At Tampa Bay	W	2-1

FEBRUARY

1—At N.Y. Islanders	L	4-5
3—At Philadelphia	W	*3-2
5—At St. Louis	L	3-4
6—At Dallas	W	7-1
8—Chicago†	W	4-3
11—Chicago	W	4-3
13—Chicago	W	1-0
15—Philadelphia	L	4-6
17—Quebec	L	2-8

19—Los Angeles	W	4-3
21—Dallas	L	3-6
23—At Montreal	L	1-3
24—At Ottawa	L	4-6
26—At Detroit	L	0-2
28—At Winnipeg	T	*3-3

MARCH

3—Edmonton	W	4-2
6—Anaheim	W	6-0
8—Buffalo	T	*4-4
10—N.Y. Islanders	W	4-3
12—At Calgary	L	0-2
17—Ottawa	L	1-2
19—At Los Angeles	L	1-2
20—Los Angeles	T	*6-6
22—At Pittsburgh	T	*2-2
24—At Toronto	W	2-1
25—At Winnipeg	W	8-3
27—At St. Louis	W	4-3
29—Winnipeg	W	9-4
31—Toronto	W	5-3

APRIL

2—Vancouver	W	7-4
5—At Los Angeles	W	2-1
7—At Vancouver	L	2-3
8—At Calgary	L	2-5
10—Vancouver	W	3-1
13—Edmonton	T	*2-2

*Denotes overtime game.
†At Sacramento, Calif.

TAMPA BAY LIGHTNING
EASTERN CONFERENCE/ATLANTIC DIVISION

1994-95 SCHEDULE

- ▢ Home games shaded.
- * — All-Star Game at San Jose Arena.
- † — At Hamilton, Ont.
- △ — At Minneapolis.
- D — Day game.

OCTOBER

SUN	MON	TUE	WED	THU	FRI	SAT
						1 NYI
2	3	4 QUE	5	6	7 STL	8 PHI
9	10 NYR	11	12	13	14	15 NJ
16 STL	17	18 PIT	19	20 TOR	21	22
23 OTT	D 24	25	26 LA	27	28	29
30 CHI	31					

NOVEMBER

SUN	MON	TUE	WED	THU	FRI	SAT
		1 QUE	2 MON	3	4	5 NYI
6	7	8 BUF	9 TOR	10	11	12 EDM
13	14	15	16 DET	17	18 WIN	19 NJ
20	21	22	23 NYI	24	25	26 D PHI
27 HAR	28	29	30 FLA			

DECEMBER

SUN	MON	TUE	WED	THU	FRI	SAT
				1	2 SJ	3 WAS
4	5 FLA	6	7 OTT	8	9 QUE	10
11	12	13	14 BUF	15	16 CHI	17
18 QUE	D 19 MON	20	21 OTT	22	23 PIT	24
25	26 PHI	27	28	29	30 NYR	31

JANUARY

SUN	MON	TUE	WED	THU	FRI	SAT
1	2 BOS	D 3	4 VAN	5	6 DAL	7 NYR
8	9	10 CAL	11 EDM	12	13 VAN	14
15 WIN	16	17	18 NJ	19	20	21*
22	23 FLA	24	25 CAL	26	27 NYR	28 NYI
29	30	31				

FEBRUARY

SUN	MON	TUE	WED	THU	FRI	SAT
			1 MON	2 DAL	3	4 PIT
5	6† DET	7	8 WAS	9	10 HAR	11 NYR
12	13 NYI	14	15 WAS	16	17 BOS	18 BUF
19	20	21	22 DET	23 NJ	24	25
26 SJ	D 27	28 LA				

MARCH

SUN	MON	TUE	WED	THU	FRI	SAT
			1 ANA	2	3	4
5	6 ANA	7	8	9△ BOS	10	11 PHI
12	13 WAS	14	15	16 PIT	17	18 D NJ
19 BUF	D 20	21	22 OTT	23	24 BOS	25
26 FLA	D 27 MON	28	29 WAS	30	31 HAR	

APRIL

SUN	MON	TUE	WED	THU	FRI	SAT
						1
2 FLA	D 3	4	5	6 PHI	7	8 D BOS
9 HAR	D 10	11	12	13	14	15

1994-95 SEASON

CLUB DIRECTORY

Pres., Lightning Partners, Ltd.
Yoshio Nakamura
Governor
David LeFevre
Pres., general manager and alt. gov.
Phil Esposito
Executive V.P., treasurer and alt. gov.
Mel Lowell
Executive V.P., alternate governor
Chris Phillips
Counsel
Henry Paul
Director of hockey operations
Tony Esposito
Head coach
Terry Crisp
Assistant coaches
Wayne Cashman
Danny Gare
Chief financial officer
Mark Anderson
Accounting manager
Vincent Ascanio
Vice president, communications
Gerry Helper
Media relations manager
Barry Hanrahan

Director of team services
Carrie Esposito
Director of sales
Paul D'Aiuto
Director of merchandising
Kevin Murphy
Director of ticket operations
Jeff Morander
Special assignment scout
Don Murdoch
Scouting staff
Angelo Bumbacco
Jacques Campeau
Jake Goertzen
Doug Macauley
Richard Rose
Jonathan Sparrow
Luke Williams
Head trainer
Larry Ness
Assistant trainer
Bill Cronin
Equipment manager
Jocko Cayer

DRAFT CHOICES

Rd.—Player	H/W	Overall	Pos.	Last team
1—Jason Weimer	6-1/215	8	LW	Portland (WHL)
2—Colin Cloutier	6-3/224	34	C	Brandon (WHL)
3—Vadim Epanchintsev	5-9/165	55	C	Spartak Moscow, CIS
4—Dmitri Klevakin	5-11/163	86	RW	Spartak Moscow, CIS
6—Daniel Juden	6-3/195	137	C	Gov. Dummer H.S. (Mass.)
6—Bryce Salvador	6-1/194	138	D	Lethbridge (WHL)
7—Chris Maillet	6-5/188	164	D	Red Deer (WHL)
8—Alexei Baranov	6-1/174	190	C	Dynamo Moscow, CIS
9—Yuri Shirnov	5-11/172	216	C	Spartak Moscow, CIS
10—Shawn Gervais	6-0/190	242	C	Seattle (WHL)
11—Brian White	6-1/180	268	D	Arlington Catholic H.S.

MISCELLANEOUS DATA

Home ice (capacity)
Florida Suncoast Dome (26,000)
Address
501 East Kennedy Blvd.
Tampa, Fla. 33602
Business phone
813-229-2658

Rink dimensions
200 feet by 85 feet
Club colors
Black, blue, silver and white

TRAINING CAMP ROSTER

No.	FORWARDS	Ht./Wt.	Place (BORN)	Date	NHL exp.	1993-94 clubs
34	Mikael Andersson (RW)	5-11/185	Malmo, Sweden	5-10-66	9	Tampa Bay
19	Brian Bradley (C)	5-10/177	Kitchener, Ont.	1-21-65	9	Tampa Bay
28	Marc Bureau (C)	6-1/198	Trois-Rivieres, Que.	5-17-66	5	Tampa Bay
	Colin Cloutier (C)	6-3/224	Winnipeg, Man.	1-27-76	0	Brandon (WHL)
24	Danton Cole (RW)	5-11/185	Pontiac, Mich.	1-10-67	5	Tampa Bay
10	Adam Creighton (C)	6-5/210	Burlington, Ont.	6-2-65	11	Tampa Bay
12	Jim Cummins (LW)	6-2/205	Dearborn, Mich.	5-17-70	3	Philadelphia, Hershey (AHL), Atlanta (IHL), Tampa Bay
17	Gerard Gallant (LW)	5-10/190	Summerside, P.E.I.	9-2-63	10	Tampa Bay
	Aaron Gavey (C)	6-1/169	Sudbury, Ont.	2-22-74	0	Sault Ste. Marie (OHL)
77	Chris Gratton (C)	6-3/202	Brantford, Ont.	7-5-75	1	Tampa Bay
	Brent Gretzky (C)	5-10/160	Brantford, Ont.	2-20-72	1	Atlanta (IHL), Tampa Bay
85	Petr Klima (LW/RW)	6-0/190	Chaomutov, Czech.	12-23-64	9	Tampa Bay
	Bill McDougall (C)	6-0/180	Mississauga, Ont.	8-10-66	3	Tampa Bay, Atlanta (IHL)
	Brantt Myhres (LW)	6-3/195	Edmonton, Alta.	3-18-74	0	Atlanta (IHL), Lethbridge (WHL), Spokane (WHL)
8	Jason Ruff (LW)	6-2/200	Kelowna, B.C.	1-27-70	2	Atlanta (IHL), Tampa Bay
9	Denis Savard (C)	5-10/175	Pointe Gatineau, Que.	2-4-61	14	Tampa Bay
14	John Tucker (RW)	6-0/000	Windsor, Ont.	9-29-64	10	Tampa Bay
	Jason Wiemer (LW)	6-1/215	Kimberley, B.C.	4-14-76	0	Portland (WHL)
7	Rob Zamuner (LW/C) ...	6-2/210	Oakville, Ont.	9-17-69	3	Tampa Bay

No.	DEFENSEMEN	Ht./Wt.	Place	Date	NHL exp.	1993-94 clubs
	Drew Bannister	6-1/193	Belleville, Ont.	9-4-74	0	Sault Ste. Marie (OHL)
25	Marc Bergevin	6-1/197	Montreal	8-11-65	10	Tampa Bay
22	Shawn Chambers	6-2/200	Royal Oaks, Mich.	10-11-66	7	Tampa Bay
3	Eric Charron	6-3/195	Verdun, Que.	1-14-70	2	Tampa Bay, Atlanta (IHL)
39	Enrico Ciccone	6-4/200	Montreal	4-10-70	3	Washington, Portland (AHL), Tampa Bay
4	Cory Cross	6-5/215	Prince Albert, Sask.	1-3-71	1	Atlanta (IHL), Tampa Bay
44	Roman Hamrlik..............	6-2/189	Gottwaldov, Czech.	4-12-74	2	Tampa Bay
2	Chris Joseph................	6-2/210	Burnaby, B.C.	9-10-69	7	Edmonton, Tampa Bay
40	Chris LiPuma	6-0/183	Chicago	3-23-71	2	Tampa Bay
20	Rudy Poeschek..............	6-2/210	Terrace, B.C.	9-29-66	6	Tampa Bay

No.	GOALTENDERS	Ht./Wt.	Place	Date	NHL exp.	1993-94 clubs
30	Jean-Claude Bergeron...	5-9/181	Hauterive, Que.	10-14-68	3	Tampa Bay, Atlanta (IHL)
	Mike Greenlay..............	6-3/210	Calgary, Alta.	9-15-68	1	Atlanta (IHL)
93	Daren Puppa	6-3/205	Kirkland Lake, Ont.	3-23-65	9	Tampa Bay
1	Wendell Young	5-9/181	Halifax, N.S.	8-1-63	9	Tampa Bay, Atlanta (IHL)

1993-94 REVIEW

INDIVIDUAL STATISTICS

SCORING

	Games	G	A	Pts.	PIM	+/-	PPG	SHG	Shots	Shooting Pct.
Brian Bradley....................	78	24	40	64	56	-8	6	0	180	13.3
Petr Klima.......................	75	28	27	55	76	-15	10	0	167	16.8
Denis Savard....................	74	18	28	46	106	-1	2	1	181	9.9
Danton Cole.....................	81	20	23	43	32	7	8	1	149	13.4
Chris Gratton...................	84	13	29	42	123	-25	5	1	161	8.1
John Tucker.....................	66	17	23	40	28	9	2	0	126	13.5
Shawn Chambers...............	66	11	23	34	23	-6	6	1	142	7.7
Chris Joseph*..................	66	10	19	29	108	-13	7	0	154	6.5
Pat Elynuik*....................	63	12	14	26	64	-18	3	1	103	11.7
Mikael Andersson.............	76	13	12	25	23	8	1	1	136	9.6
Roman Hamrlik.................	64	3	18	21	135	-14	0	0	158	1.9
Adam Creighton................	53	10	10	20	37	-7	2	0	77	13.0
Marc Bergevin..................	83	1	15	16	87	-5	0	0	76	1.3
Rob DiMaio*....................	39	8	7	15	40	-5	2	0	51	15.7
Marc Bureau....................	75	8	7	15	30	-9	0	1	110	7.3
Gerard Gallant..................	51	4	9	13	74	-6	1	0	45	8.9
Rob Zamuner....................	59	6	6	12	42	-9	0	0	109	5.5
Joe Reekie*.....................	73	1	11	12	127	8	0	0	88	1.1
Tim Bergland*..................	51	6	5	11	6	-14	0	0	61	9.8
Rudy Poeschek.................	71	3	6	9	118	3	0	0	46	6.5
Donald Dufresne*..............	51	2	6	8	48	-2	0	0	49	4.1
Bill McDougall.................	22	3	3	6	8	-4	1	0	26	11.5
Bob Beers*......................	16	1	5	6	12	-11	1	0	35	2.9
Chris LiPuma	27	0	4	4	77	1	0	0	20	0.0

	Games	G	A	Pts.	PIM	+/-	PPG	SHG	Shots	Shooting Pct.
Jason Ruff	6	1	2	3	2	2	0	0	14	7.1
Brent Gretzky	10	1	2	3	2	0	0	0	14	7.1
Enrico Ciccone*	11	0	1	1	52	-2	0	0	10	0.0
Daren Puppa (goalie)	63	0	1	1	2	0	0	0	0	0.0
Jason Lafreniere	1	0	0	0	0	-1	0	0	2	0.0
J.C. Bergeron (goalie)	3	0	0	0	0	0	0	0	0	0.0
Eric Charron	4	0	0	0	2	0	0	0	1	0.0
Jim Cummins*	4	0	0	0	13	-1	0	0	3	0.0
Cory Cross	5	0	0	0	6	-3	0	0	5	0.0
Normand Rochefort	6	0	0	0	10	-1	0	0	4	0.0
Wendell Young (goalie)	9	0	0	0	4	0	0	0	0	0.0
Pat Jablonski (goalie)	15	0	0	0	0	0	0	0	0	0.0

GOALTENDING

	Games	Min.	Goals	SO	Avg.	W	L	T	Shots	Sv. Pct.
Wendell Young	9	480	20	1	2.50	2	3	1	211	.905
Daren Puppa	63	3653	165	4	2.71	22	33	6	1637	.899
J.C. Bergeron	3	134	7	0	3.13	1	1	1	69	.899
Pat Jablonski	15	834	54	0	3.88	5	6	3	374	.856

Empty-net goals (do not count against a goaltender's average): Puppa 4, Young 1.
*Played with two or more NHL teams.

RESULTS

OCTOBER
6—At New Jersey .... L 1-2
7—At N.Y. Rangers ...... L 4-5
9—Florida .... L 0-2
14—Pittsburgh .... W 3-2
16—Ottawa .... W 4-1
17—At Florida .... T *3-3
20—Los Angeles .... L 3-4
22—N.Y. Rangers .... W 4-1
23—Toronto .... L 0-2
27—Winnipeg .... L 3-4
29—N.Y. Islanders .... L 2-4
30—At Florida .... L *1-2

NOVEMBER
2—At Quebec............... L 2-8
3—At Montreal .... L 0-1
6—At Boston .... T *1-1
8—At N.Y. Rangers ...... L 3-6
11—Washington .... L 1-4
13—Quebec .... W 4-3
17—At Dallas .... L 3-4
19—N.Y. Rangers .... L 3-5
20—Chicago .... W 4-3
24—Hartford .... W 4-1
26—At Philadelphia ...... L 0-3
27—Philadelphia .... L *3-4

DECEMBER
1—Buffalo.................... L 0-3
4—At Los Angeles........ W 5-4
5—At Anaheim .... W 4-2
7—At San Jose .... W 3-1
11—Pittsburgh .... L 3-6

14—Montreal† .... T *1-1
15—Ottawa................... W 4-3
18—Boston .... L 3-5
19—At Buffalo .... T *3-3
21—At Pittsburgh .... L 3-8
23—At St. Louis .... L 4-7
26—Florida† .... L 1-3
28—At Quebec .... W 4-1
30—At Ottawa .... W 3-0

JANUARY
1—At Washington .... T *5-5
2—Anaheim† .... L 1-4
4—Toronto‡ .... W 1-0
8—Philadelphia .... W 4-2
10—At N.Y. Rangers ...... W 5-2
12—At Detroit............... W 4-2
13—At Chicago .... L 0-1
16—At Winnipeg .... W *3-2
17—Detroit§ .... L 3-6
19—N.Y. Islanders .... W *4-3
24—Buffalo† .... W 4-0
26—Florida .... T *1-1
29—San Jose................ L 1-2

FEBRUARY
2—Detroit .... L 1-3
5—At Washington .... L 3-6
7—At Toronto .... W 2-1
10—At Ottawa .... W 6-2
12—Vancouver.............. L 2-3
13—New Jersey .... T *3-3
15—At N.Y. Islanders ..... L 1-2
17—Montreal .... W 5-3

19—At New Jersey .... L 4-5
20—Boston .... T *2-2
24—At Calgary............... W 4-0
26—At Vancouver........... L 1-3
27—At Edmonton .... L 2-3

MARCH
1—At Washington .... W 4-3
3—New Jersey .... L *4-5
5—Hartford .... W 4-2
6—Philadelphia .... L 1-3
9—At Hartford .... L 1-4
13—At Philadelphia .... T *5-5
15—Calgary .... L 3-7
16—Edmonton .... T *4-4
20—Washington† .... L 0-3
22—At N.Y. Islanders ..... L *4-5
24—At New Jersey .... L 1-2
27—Dallas .... T *2-2
30—At Buffalo .... W *3-2

APRIL
1—St. Louis .... W 4-3
4—At Pittsburgh .... L 1-2
6—At Montreal .... W 3-1
9—At Boston .... W 3-0
10—At Hartford .... L 4-6
13—N.Y. Islanders .... L 0-2
14—Quebec .... W 5-2

*Denotes overtime game.
†At Orlando, Fla.
‡At Hamilton, Ont.
§At Minneapolis.

TORONTO MAPLE LEAFS
WESTERN CONFERENCE/CENTRAL DIVISION

1994-95 SCHEDULE

Home games shaded.
* — All-Star Game at San Jose Arena.
† — At Hamilton, Ont.
△ — At Saskatoon, Sask.
D — Day game.

OCTOBER

SUN	MON	TUE	WED	THU	FRI	SAT
						1 WAS
2	3	4 HAR	5	6	7	8 BOS
9	10 BUF	11 OTT	12	13 QUE	14	15 STL
16	17	18	19 FLA	20 TB	21	22 STL
23	24 CAL	25	26	27	28 EDM	29 PHI
30	31					

NOVEMBER

SUN	MON	TUE	WED	THU	FRI	SAT
		1	2 WIN	3	4 DET	5 DET
6	7	8	9 TB	10 CHI	11	12 MGN
13	14	15	16 WIN	17	18 WAS	19 STL
20	21 VAN	22	23 WIN	24	25	26 NYI
27	28 DAL	29	30 ANA			

DECEMBER

SUN	MON	TUE	WED	THU	FRI	SAT
				1	2	3 LA
4	5	6 VAN	7 SJ	8	9	10 LA
11 ANA	12	13 EDM	14	15 CAL	16	17 FLA
18	19 DAL	20	21 CHI	22	23	24
25	26	27 QUE	28	29 DAL	30	31 BOS

JANUARY

SUN	MON	TUE	WED	THU	FRI	SAT
1	2† OTT	3	4	5	6	7 OTT
8	9	10 WIN	11	12 CHI	13	14 DET
15	16	17 CHI	18 DET	19	20	21*
22	23	24	25 VAN	26	27 CHI	28 PIT
29	30 SJ	31				

FEBRUARY

SUN	MON	TUE	WED	THU	FRI	SAT
			1 VAN	2	3 EDM	4 CAL
5	6	7 PHI	8	9	10 NJ	11 BUF
12	13 DAL	14	15 CHI	16	17	18 NYR
19 NYR	20 D NYR	21	22 STL	23	24 NYI	25 MON
26	27 STL	28				

MARCH

SUN	MON	TUE	WED	THU	FRI	SAT
			1 SJ	2	3 DET	4 CAL
5	6	7	8	9 LA	10	11 NJ
12	13 DAL	14	15 SJ	16	17 ANA	18 LA
19	20△ EDM	21	22	23	24 WIN	25 WIN
26	27 EDM	28	29 DAL	30	31 STL	

APRIL

SUN	MON	TUE	WED	THU	FRI	SAT
						1
2 PIT	3 D	4	5 HAR	6 CHI	7	8 DET
9	10	11	12	13	14	15

1994-95 SEASON

CLUB DIRECTORY

Chairman of the board and CEO
Steve A. Stavro
President, COO and general manager
Cliff Fletcher
Secretary-treasurer
J. Donald Crump
Alternate governors
Cliff Fletcher
Brian P. Bellmore
Assistant general manager
Bill Watters
Special consultant to the president
Darryl Sittler
Dir. of bus. operations and communications
Bob Stellick
Controller
Ian Clarke
Head coach
Pat Burns
Assistant coaches
Mike Kitchen
Mike Murphy
Goaltending consultant
Rick Wamsley
Director of professional development
Floyd Smith
Director of pro scouting
Tom Watt
Director of marketing
Bill Cluff

Public relations coordinator
Pat Park
Box office manager
Donna Henderson
Scouts
George Armstrong
Anders Hedberg
Peter Johnson
Garth Malarchuk
Dan Marr
Dick Bouchard
Jack Gardiner
Bob Johnson
Ernie Gare
Doug Woods
Head athletic therapist
Chris Broadhurst
Athletic therapist
Brent Smith
Trainers
Brian Papineau
Jim Carey
Team doctors
Dr. Michael Clarfield
Dr. Darrell Olgilvie-Harris
Dr. Leith Douglas
Dr. Michael Easterbrook
Dr. Simon McGrail
Dr. Ernie Lewis

DRAFT CHOICES

Rd.—Player	H/W	Overall	Pos.	Last team
1—Eric Fichaud	5-11/160	16	G	Chicoutimi (QMJHL)
2—Sean Haggerty	6-1/186	48	LW	Detroit (OHL)
3—Fredrik Modin	6-3/202	64	LW	Sundsvall Timra, Sweden
5—Mark Deyell	5-9/150	126	C	Saskatoon (WHL)
6—Kam White	6-3/195	152	D	Newmarket (OHL)
7—Tommi Rajanaki	6-2/183	178	D	Assat Pori Jrs., Finland
8—Rob Butler	6-2/175	204	LW	Niagara (Jr. A)
10—Sergei Berezin	5-10/172	256	RW	Khimik, CIS
11—Doug Nolan	6-1/180	282	LW	Catholic Mem. H.S. (Mass.)

MISCELLANEOUS DATA

Home ice (capacity)
Maple Leaf Gardens
(15,842, including standees)
Address
60 Carlton Street
Toronto, Ont. M5B 1L1

Business phone
416-977-1641
Rink dimensions
200 feet by 85 feet
Club colors
Blue and white

TRAINING CAMP ROSTER

No.	FORWARDS	Ht./Wt.	Place	BORN Date	NHL exp.	1993-94 clubs
14	Dave Andreychuk (LW)	6-3/220	Hamilton, Ont.	9-29-63	12	Toronto
	Ken Baumgartner (LW)	6-1/205	Flin Flon, Man.	3-11-66	7	Toronto
10	Bill Berg (LW)	6-1/205	St. Catharines, Ont.	10-21-67	5	Toronto
16	Nikolai Borschevsky	5-9/180	Tomsk, U.S.S.R.	1-12-65	2	Toronto
	Brandon Convery (C)	6-1/182	Kingston, Ont.	2-4-74	0	Niagara Falls (OHL), Belleville (OHL)
	Mike Craig (RW)	6-1/180	London, Ont.	6-6-71	4	Dallas
32	Michael Eastwood	6-3/205	Cornwall, Ont.	7-1-67	3	Toronto
	Mike Gartner (RW)	6-0/187	Ottawa	10-29-59	15	New York Rangers, Toronto
93	Doug Gilmour (C)	5-11/172	Kingston, Ont.	6-25-63	11	Toronto
	Chris Govedaris (LW)	6-0/200	Toronto	2-2-70	4	St. John's (AHL), Toronto
	Darby Hendrickson (C)	6-0/185	Richfield, Minn.	8-28-72	1	U.S. national team (Int'l), U.S. Olympic Team (Int'l), St. John's (AHL), Toronto
	Tomas Kucharcik	6-2/200	Vlasim, Czechoslovakia	5-10-70	0	Skoda Plzen (Czech Republic)
	Alexei Kudashov (C)	6-0/180	Elekhrostal, U.S.S.R.	7-21-71	1	Toronto, St. John's (AHL), Russian Olympic team (Int'l)
41	Eric Lacroix (LW)	6-1/200	Montreal	7-15-71	1	St. John's (AHL), Toronto
18	Kent Manderville (LW)	6-3/207	Edmonton, Alta.	4-12-71	3	Toronto
36	Ken McRae (RW)	6-1/195	Finch, Ont.	4-23-68	7	St. John's (AHL), Toronto
	Zdenek Nedved (RW)	6-0/180	Lany, Czechoslovakia	3-3-75	0	Sudbury (OHL)
21	Mark Osborne (LW)	6-2/205	Toronto	8-13-61	13	Toronto
	Martin Prochazka (RW)	5-11/180	Slany, Czechoslovakia	3-3-72	0	HC Kladno (Czech Republic)
	Mike Ridley (C)	6-0/195	Winnipeg, Man.	7-8-63	9	Washington
	David Sacco (RW)	6-0/190	Medford, Mass.	7-31-70	1	U.S. national team (Int'l), U.S. Olympic Team (Int'l), Toronto
	Mats Sundin (RW)	6-4/204	Sollentuna, Sweden	2-13-71	4	Quebec
	Todd Warriner (LW/C)	6-1/182	Chatham, Ont.	1-3-74	0	Cornwall (AHL), Canadian Olympic Team (Int'l), Kitchener (OHL)
25	Peter Zezel (C)	5-11/205	Toronto	4-22-65	10	Toronto

No.	DEFENSEMEN	Ht./Wt.	Place	BORN Date	NHL exp.	1993-94 clubs
55	Drake Berehowsky	6-1/211	Toronto	1-3-72	4	Toronto, St. John's (AHL)
	Garth Butcher	6-0/204	Regina, Sask.	1-8-63	13	St. Louis, Quebec
4	Dave Ellett	6-2/200	Cleveland	3-30-64	10	Toronto
23	Todd Gill	6-0/185	Brockville, Ont.	11-9-65	10	Toronto
	Kenny Jonsson	6-3/195	Angelholm, Sweden	10-5-74	0	Rogle (Sweden), Swedish Olympic Team (Int'l)
34	Jamie Macoun	6-2/200	Newmarket, Ont.	8-17-61	12	Toronto
	Matt Martin	6-3/190	Hamden, Conn.	4-30-71	1	U.S. Olympic Team (Int'l), Toronto, U.S. national team (Int'l), St. John's (AHL)
15	Dmitri Mironov	6-2/214	Moscow, U.S.S.R.	12-25-65	3	Toronto
3	Bob Rouse	6-2/210	Surrey, B.C.	6-18-64	11	Toronto

No.	GOALTENDERS	Ht./Wt.	Place	BORN Date	NHL exp.	1993-94 clubs
	Eric Fichaud	5-11/160	Montreal	11-4-75	0	Chicoutimi (QMJHL)
	Pat Jablonski	6-0/178	Toledo, O.	6-20-67	5	Tampa Bay, St. John's (AHL)
29	Felix Potvin	6-0/180	Anjou, Que.	6-23-71	3	Toronto
	Damian Rhodes	6-0/175	St. Paul, Minn.	5-28-69	2	Toronto

1993-94 REVIEW

INDIVIDUAL STATISTICS

SCORING

	Games	G	A	Pts.	PIM	+/-	PPG	SHG	Shots	Shooting Pct.
Doug Gilmour	83	27	84	111	105	25	10	1	167	16.2
Dave Andreychuk	83	53	46	99	98	22	21	5	333	15.9
Wendel Clark	64	46	30	76	115	10	21	0	275	16.7
Dave Ellett	68	7	36	43	42	6	5	0	146	4.8
Dmitri Mironov	76	9	27	36	78	5	3	0	147	6.1
Glenn Anderson*	73	17	18	35	50	-6	5	0	127	13.4
Nikolai Borschevsky	45	14	20	34	10	6	7	0	105	13.3
John Cullen	53	13	17	30	67	-2	2	0	80	16.3
Rob Pearson	67	12	18	30	189	-6	1	0	119	10.1
Jamie Macoun	82	3	27	30	115	-5	1	0	122	2.5
Todd Gill	45	4	24	28	44	8	2	0	74	5.4
Mark Osborne	73	9	15	24	145	2	1	1	103	8.7
Bill Berg	83	8	11	19	93	-3	0	0	99	8.1
Mike Eastwood	54	8	10	18	28	2	1	0	41	19.5

	Games	G	A	Pts.	PIM	+/-	PPG	SHG	Shots	Shooting Pct.
Peter Zezel	41	8	8	16	19	5	0	0	47	17.0
Kent Manderville	67	7	9	16	63	5	0	0	81	8.6
Bob Rouse	63	5	11	16	101	8	1	1	77	6.5
Mike Gartner*	10	6	6	12	4	9	1	0	30	20.0
Mike Krushelnyski	54	5	6	11	28	-5	1	0	71	7.0
Sylvain Lefebvre	84	2	9	11	79	33	0	0	96	2.1
Drake Berehowsky	49	2	8	10	63	-3	2	0	29	6.9
Ken Baumgartner	64	4	4	8	185	-6	0	0	34	11.8
Yanic Perreault	13	3	3	6	0	1	2	0	24	12.5
Chris Govedaris	12	2	2	4	14	4	0	0	16	12.5
Mark Greig*	13	2	2	4	10	1	0	0	14	14.3
Felix Potvin (goalie)	66	0	4	4	4	0	0	0	0	0.0
Guy Larose*	10	1	2	3	10	-2	0	0	9	11.1
David Sacco	4	1	1	2	4	-2	1	0	4	25.0
Ken McRae	9	1	1	2	36	1	0	0	11	9.1
Alexei Kudashov	25	1	0	1	4	-3	0	0	24	4.2
Greg Smyth*	11	0	1	1	38	-2	0	0	3	0.0
Matt Martin	12	0	1	1	6	0	0	0	6	0.0
Patrik Augusta	2	0	0	0	0	0	0	0	3	0.0
Chris Snell	2	0	0	0	2	-1	0	0	4	0.0
Frank Bialowas	3	0	0	0	12	0	0	0	1	0.0
Eric Lacroix	3	0	0	0	2	0	0	0	3	0.0
Mike Foligno*	4	0	0	0	4	0	0	0	3	0.0
David Harlock	6	0	0	0	0	-2	0	0	2	0.0
Damian Rhodes (goalie)	22	0	0	0	2	0	0	0	0	0.0

GOALTENDING

	Games	Min.	Goals	SO	Avg.	W	L	T	Shots	Sv. Pct.
Damian Rhodes	22	1213	53	0	2.62	9	7	3	541	.902
Felix Potvin	66	3883	187	3	2.89	34	22	9	2010	.907

Empty-net goals (do not count against a goaltender's average): Potvin 3.
*Played with two or more NHL teams.

RESULTS

OCTOBER

7—Dallas	W	6-3
9—Chicago	W	2-1
10—At Philadelphia	W	5-4
13—Washington	W	7-1
15—Detroit	W	6-3
16—At Detroit	W	2-1
19—At Hartford	W	7-2
21—At Florida	W	*4-3
23—At Tampa Bay	W	2-0
28—At Chicago	W	4-2
30—At Montreal	L	2-5

NOVEMBER

1—At Dallas	T	*3-3
3—Florida	W	6-3
4—At Detroit	T	*3-3
6—Philadelphia	W	5-3
9—At San Jose	T	*2-2
11—At St. Louis	L	2-3
13—Chicago	L	2-3
15—Edmonton	T	*5-5
17—At Anaheim	W	4-3
18—At Los Angeles	W	3-2
20—At Edmonton	W	3-2
22—At Vancouver	W	5-2
24—At Calgary	L	3-5
27—Boston	W	4-2
29—Buffalo	L	0-3

DECEMBER

1—St. Louis	W	4-2
2—At St. Louis	W	5-4
4—N.Y. Rangers	L	3-4
8—Winnipeg	L	4-5
11—Calgary	W	3-1
12—At Winnipeg	T	*3-3
15—Anaheim	L	0-1
17—At N.Y. Islanders	L	2-6
18—Los Angeles	W	4-1
22—San Jose	T	*2-2
23—At New Jersey	L	2-3
27—At Chicago	L	2-5
29—At Dallas	L	0-4

JANUARY

1—Los Angeles	L	4-7
2—At Buffalo	T	*3-3
4—Tampa Bay†	L	0-1
6—Ottawa	W	6-3
8—Vancouver	W	5-3
10—At Boston	W	3-0
11—At Washington	W	2-1
13—Dallas	W	*4-3
15—At Winnipeg	W	5-1
18—Anaheim	T	*3-3
19—At Hartford	T	*3-3
26—N.Y. Islanders	W	4-3
29—Pittsburgh	T	*4-4

FEBRUARY

1—At St. Louis	T	*4-4
5—Detroit	L	3-4
7—Tampa Bay	L	1-2
11—At Winnipeg	W	3-1
12—At Calgary	L	2-3
15—Detroit	W	*5-4
17—New Jersey	W	2-1
19—Edmonton	W	3-2
21—At Los Angeles	W	6-4
23—At Edmonton	L	3-6
26—Montreal	L	0-3
28—At Ottawa	W	4-1

MARCH

4—At Detroit	W	*6-5
5—At Quebec	L	1-4
7—St. Louis	L	2-3
9—Dallas	W	4-2
10—At Pittsburgh	W	4-2
12—Winnipeg	W	3-1
16—Vancouver	L	1-4
18—St. Louis	W	4-2
20—Calgary	L	3-6
23—Florida†	T	*1-1
24—San Jose	L	1-2
26—Quebec	W	6-3
28—At Vancouver	L	*2-3
31—At San Jose	L	3-5

APRIL

2—At Anaheim	L	1-3
5—At Dallas	W	6-4
8—At N.Y. Rangers	L	3-5
10—Winnipeg	W	7-0
12—Chicago	L	3-4
14—At Chicago	W	6-4

*Denotes overtime game.
†At Hamilton, Ont.

VANCOUVER CANUCKS
WESTERN CONFERENCE/PACIFIC DIVISION

1994-95 SCHEDULE

☐ Home games shaded.
* — All-Star Game at San Jose Arena.
† — At Portland, Ore.
△ — At Saskatoon, Sask.
D — Day game.

OCTOBER
SUN	MON	TUE	WED	THU	FRI	SAT
						1 CAL
2 EDM	3	4	5 SJ	6	7 ANA	8
9 D 10 SJ		11	12 ANA	13 LA	14	15 EDM
16	17 PHI	18	19 BOS	20	21 DAL	22
23 STL	24	25 NYI	26	27 PHI	28	29 NJ
30 NYR	31					

NOVEMBER
SUN	MON	TUE	WED	THU	FRI	SAT
		1	2 WAS	3	4 LA	5 FLA
6	7 SJ	8 SJ	9	10	11 ANA	12 LA
13	14	15	16 EDM	17 ANA	18	19 CAL
20	21 TOR	22	23 WAS	24	25 BUF	26
27 BOS	D 28	29	30			

DECEMBER
SUN	MON	TUE	WED	THU	FRI	SAT
				1	2 DAL	3 WIN
4	5	6 TOR	7	8 CHI	9	10 WIN
11	12 LA	13	14 NYR	15	16 STL	17
18	19	20	21† SJ	22	23 STL	24
25	26	27 MON	28	29 CAL	30	31 BUF

JANUARY
SUN	MON	TUE	WED	THU	FRI	SAT
1	2	3 FLA	4 TB	5	6 HAR	7
8	9	10	11 CHI	12	13 TB	14 EDM
15	16 SJ	17	18 BUF	19	20	21*
22	23	24 DET	25 TOR	26	27 PIT	28
29	30 HAR	31				

FEBRUARY
SUN	MON	TUE	WED	THU	FRI	SAT
			1 TOR	2	3	4 MON
5	6 OTT	7 QUE	8	9 CHI	10	11 WIN
12	13	14	15	16 SJ	17	18
19	20△ QUE	21	22 WIN	23	24 DAL	25
26 ANA	D 27	28 PIT				

MARCH
SUN	MON	TUE	WED	THU	FRI	SAT
			1 EDM	2	3	4
5	6 DET	7	8	9 EDM	10	11 OTT
12	13	14 NYI	15	16 CHI	17 DET	18
19	20	21 STL	22	23 NJ	24	25 DET
26 CAL	27	28	29 LA	30	31 ANA	

APRIL
SUN	MON	TUE	WED	THU	FRI	SAT
						1
2 CAL	D 3	4 DAL	5	6 LA	7	8 CAL
9	10	11	12	13	14	15

1994-95 SEASON

CLUB DIRECTORY

Governor
Arthur R. Griffiths
President, general manager, head coach
Pat Quinn
V.P./Dir. of marketing and communications
Glen Ringdal
Vice president of finance and administration
Carlos Mascarenhas
Director of media and public relations
Steve Tambellini
Director of hockey operations
George McPhee
Director of player development
Mike Penny
Director of hockey information
Steve Frost
Public relations assistant
Veronica Bateman
Assistant coaches
Glen Hanlon
Rick Ley
Ron Smith
Stan Smyl
Strength coach
Peter Twist
Director of amateur scouting
Mike Penny
Director of pro scouting
Murray Oliver

Scouts
Mats Dahlbeg
Ron Delorme
Jim Eagle
Ross Mahoney
Jack McCartan
Al McDonald
Ray Miron
Jim Pavlenko
Noel Price
Ken Slater
Paul McIntosh
Ed McColgan
Scott Carter
Jack Birch
Thomas Gradin
Ticket manager
Denise McDonald
Medical trainer
Larry Ashley
Equipment trainers
Pat O'Neill
Darren Granger
Team doctors
Dr. Ross Davidson
Dr. Doug Clement
Team dentist
Dr. David Lawson

DRAFT CHOICES

Rd. — Player	H/W	Overall	Pos.	Last team
1 — Mattias Ohlund	6-3/209	13	D	Pitea, Sweden
2 — Robb Gordon	5-11/170	39	C	Powell River (Tier II)
2 — Dave Scatchard	6-2/185	42	C	Portland (WHL)
3 — Chad Allan	6-1/192	65	D	Saskatoon (WHL)
4 — Mike Dubinsky	6-1/181	92	RW	Brandon (WHL)
5 — Yanick Dube	5-8/162	117	C	Laval (QMJHL)
7 — Yuri Kuznetsov	5-11/176	169	C	Avangard CMSK, CIS
8 — Rob Trumbley	5-10/177	195	C	Moose Jaw (WHL)
9 — Bill Muckalt	5-11/175	221	C	Kelowna (Tier II, Jr. A)
10 — Tyson Nash	5-11/180	247	LW	Kamloops (WHL)
11 — Robert Longpre	6-2/175	273	C	Medicine Hat (WHL)

MISCELLANEOUS DATA

Home ice (capacity)
Pacific Coliseum (16,150)
Address
100 North Renfrew St.
Vancouver, B.C. V5K 3N7
Business phone
604-254-5141

Rink dimensions
200 feet by 85 feet
Club colors
White, black, red and gold

TRAINING CAMP ROSTER

No.	FORWARDS	Ht./Wt.	Place	BORN Date	NHL exp.	1993-94 clubs
8	Greg Adams (LW)	6-3/195	Nelson, B.C.	8-1-63	10	Vancouver
18	Shawn Antoski (LW/RW)	6-4/240	Brantford, Ont.	5-25-70	4	Vancouver
10	Pavel Bure (RW/LW)	5-10/189	Moscow, U.S.S.R.	3-31-71	3	Vancouver
20	Jose Charbonneau (RW)	6-0/195	Ferme-Neuve, Que.	11-21-66	4	Vancouver, Hamilton (AHL)
14	Geoff Courtnall (LW)	6-1/195	Victoria, B.C.	8-18-62	11	Vancouver
32	Murray Craven (C/LW)	6-2/185	Medicine Hat, Alta.	7-20-64	12	Vancouver
	Yannick Dube (C)	5-9/170	Gaspe, Que.	6-14-74	0	Laval (QMJHL)
	Martin Gelinas (LW)	5-11/195	Shawinigan, Que.	6-5-70	6	Quebec, Vancouver
	Rick Girard (C)	5-11/180	Edmonton, Alta.	5-1-74	0	Swift Current (WHL), Hamilton (AHL)
26	Tim Hunter (LW/RW)	6-2/202	Calgary, Alta.	9-10-60	13	Vancouver
	Dane Jackson (RW)	6-1/190	Winnipeg, Man.	5-17-70	1	Hamilton (AHL), Vancouver
	Dan Kesa (RW)	6-0/198	Vancouver, B.C.	11-23-71	1	Hamilton (AHL), Vancouver
	Nathan Lafayette (C)	6-1/195	New Westminster, B.C.	2-17-73	1	Peoria (IHL), St. Louis, Vancouver
16	Trevor Linden (C)	6-4/205	Medicine Hat, Alta.	4-11-70	6	Vancouver
	Jay Mazur (C)	6-2/205	Hamilton, Ont.	1-22-65	4	Hamilton (AHL)
15	John McIntyre (C/LW)	6-1/190	Ravenswood, Ont.	4-29-69	5	Vancouver
27	Sergio Momesso (LW)	6-3/215	Montreal	9-4-65	10	Vancouver
29	Gino Odjick (LW)	6-3/210	Maniwaki, Que.	9-7-70	4	Vancouver
33	Mike Peca (RW/C)	5-11/175	Toronto	3-26-74	1	Ottawa (OHL), Vancouver
7	Cliff Ronning (C)	5-8/170	Vancouver, B.C.	10-1-65	8	Vancouver
	Alex Stojanov (LW)	6-4/225	Windsor, Ont.	4-25-73	0	Hamilton (AHL)

No.	DEFENSEMEN	Ht./Wt.	Place	BORN Date	NHL exp.	1993-94 clubs
44	Dave Babych	6-2/215	Edmonton, Alta.	5-23-61	14	Vancouver
	Jeff Brown	6-1/204	Ottawa	4-30-66	9	St. Louis, Vancouver
	Jassen Cullimore	6-5/225	Simcoe, Ont.	12-4-72	0	Hamilton (AHL)
4	Gerald Diduck	6-2/207	Edmonton, Alta.	4-6-65	10	Vancouver
	Brian Glynn	6-4/220	Iserlohn, W. Germany	11-23-67	7	Ottawa, Vancouver
	Bret Hedican	6-2/195	St. Paul, Minn.	8-10-70	3	St. Louis, Vancouver
21	Jyrki Lumme	6-1/207	Tampere, Finland	7-16-66	6	Vancouver
5	Dana Murzyn	6-2/200	Regina, Sask.	12-9-66	9	Vancouver
2	John Namestnikov	5-11/190	Novgorod, U.S.S.R.	10-9-71	1	Vancouver
	Mattias Ohlund	6-3/209	Pitea, Sweden	9-9-76	0	Pitea (Sweden Div. II)
24	Jiri Slegr	6-1/205	Litvinov, Czechoslovakia	5-30-71	2	Vancouver
	Brent Tully	6-3/185	Peterborough, Ont.	3-26-74	0	Hamilton (AHL), Peterborough (OHL), Canadian national team (Int'l)

No.	GOALTENDERS	Ht./Wt.	Place	BORN Date	NHL exp.	1993-94 clubs
	Mike Fountain	6-1/176	Gravenhurst, Ont.	1-26-72	0	Hamilton (AHL)
1	Kirk McLean	6-0/180	Willowdale, Ont.	6-26-66	9	Vancouver
	Sonny Mignacca	5-8/175	Winnipeg, Man.	1-4-74	0	Medicine Hat (WHL)
35	Kay Whitmore	5-11/185	Sudbury, Ont.	4-10-67	6	Vancouver

1993-94 REVIEW

INDIVIDUAL STATISTICS

SCORING

	Games	G	A	Pts.	PIM	+/-	PPG	SHG	Shots	Shooting Pct.
Pavel Bure	76	†60	47	107	86	1	‡25	4	374	16.0
Geoff Courtnall	82	26	44	70	123	15	12	1	264	9.8
Cliff Ronning	76	25	43	68	42	7	10	0	197	12.7
Trevor Linden	84	32	29	61	73	6	10	2	234	13.7
Murray Craven	78	15	40	55	30	5	2	1	115	13.0
Jyrki Lumme	83	13	42	55	50	3	1	3	161	8.1
Jiri Slegr	78	5	33	38	86	0	1	0	160	3.1
Greg Adams	68	13	24	37	20	-1	5	1	139	9.4
Dave Babych	73	4	28	32	52	0	0	0	96	4.2
Gino Odjick	76	16	13	29	271	13	4	0	121	13.2
Sergio Momesso	68	14	13	27	149	-2	4	0	112	12.5
Dana Murzyn	80	6	14	20	109	4	0	1	79	7.6
Jimmy Carson*	34	7	10	17	22	-13	2	0	82	8.5
Martin Gelinas*	33	8	8	16	26	-6	3	0	54	14.8
Jose Charbonneau	30	7	7	14	49	-3	1	0	28	25.0
Gerald Diduck	55	1	10	11	72	2	0	0	50	2.0
Adrien Plavsic	47	1	9	10	6	-5	0	0	41	2.4
John McIntyre	62	3	6	9	38	-9	0	0	30	10.0
Dixon Ward*	33	6	1	7	37	-14	2	0	46	13.0

	Games	G	A	Pts.	PIM	+/-	PPG	SHG	Shots	Shooting Pct.
Tim Hunter	56	3	4	7	171	-7	0	1	41	7.3
Dane Jackson	12	5	1	6	9	3	0	0	18	27.8
Dan Kesa	19	2	4	6	18	-3	1	0	18	11.1
Jeff Brown*	11	1	5	6	10	2	0	0	41	2.4
Robert Dirk*	65	2	3	5	105	18	0	0	38	5.3
Yevgeny Namestnikov	17	0	5	5	10	-2	0	0	11	0.0
Neil Eisenhut	13	1	3	4	21	0	0	0	13	7.7
Kirk McLean (goalie)	52	0	4	4	2	0	0	0	0	0.0
Shawn Antoski	55	1	2	3	190	-11	0	0	25	4.0
Stephane Morin	5	1	1	2	6	0	0	0	6	16.7
Nathan Lafayette*	11	1	1	2	4	2	0	0	11	9.1
Bret Hedican*	8	0	1	1	0	1	0	0	10	0.0
Mike Peca	4	0	0	0	2	-1	0	0	5	0.0
Brian Glynn*	16	0	0	0	12	-4	0	0	5	0.0
Kay Whitmore (goalie)	32	0	0	0	6	0	0	0	0	0.0

GOALTENDING

	Games	Min.	Goals	SO	Avg.	W	L	T	Shots	Sv. Pct.
Kirk McLean	52	3128	156	3	2.99	23	26	3	1430	.891
Kay Whitmore	32	1921	113	0	3.53	18	14	0	848	.867

Empty-net goals (do not count against a goaltender's average): McLean 5, Whitmore 2.
*Played with two or more NHL teams.
†Led league.
‡Tied for league lead.

RESULTS

OCTOBER

6—At Los Angeles	W	5-2
9—Calgary	L	1-5
11—Edmonton	W	4-1
16—At Edmonton	W	3-2
19—Boston	W	5-4
21—At Calgary	W	6-3
23—At San Jose	W	6-4
24—San Jose	W	*3-2
27—Washington	L	2-4
30—Buffalo	L	3-6

NOVEMBER

2—At N.Y. Islanders	W	2-1
3—At N.Y. Rangers	L	3-6
5—At Washington	L	2-3
7—At Philadelphia	W	5-2
10—Los Angeles	W	4-0
13—At Calgary	L	3-4
14—Anaheim	W	3-2
16—St. Louis	W	3-0
19—Anaheim	L	3-6
22—Toronto	L	2-5
24—Detroit	L	*4-5
26—At Winnipeg	W	5-3
27—At Edmonton	L	1-2
29—Chicago	W	*2-1

DECEMBER

2—Philadelphia	L	3-6
4—At Quebec	L	1-3
6—At Montreal	L	*3-4
8—At Hartford	W	4-1
9—At Boston	W	*3-2

14—At Calgary	L	4-8
15—At Edmonton	L	2-7
17—Winnipeg	W	6-1
19—Dallas	L	1-3
21—Edmonton	W	6-3
23—Calgary†	W	4-3
28—At Los Angeles	L	5-6
31—San Jose	L	2-3

JANUARY

2—Montreal	L	2-3
5—At Ottawa	W	7-2
8—At Toronto	L	3-5
9—At Buffalo	L	3-5
12—Quebec	W	4-3
14—Ottawa	T	*2-2
16—At Anaheim	W	4-3
19—Calgary	L	3-4
24—Edmonton†	W	*5-4
25—St. Louis	T	*3-3
27—Dallas	L	*2-3
29—New Jersey	W	6-3
31—Los Angeles	W	3-1

FEBRUARY

2—Chicago	W	6-4
4—At Anaheim	L	0-3
6—Hartford	L	2-4
8—At Detroit	W	6-3
10—At New Jersey	L	3-7
12—At Tampa Bay	W	3-2
13—At Florida	L	1-2
15—At St. Louis	L	2-3

17—At Chicago	W	4-2
22—Calgary	T	*4-4
26—Tampa Bay	W	3-1

MARCH

1—Edmonton	L	4-7
3—At St. Louis	W	4-0
4—At Dallas	W	4-1
7—Florida	L	1-2
9—N.Y. Islanders	W	5-4
11—At Winnipeg	W	8-4
13—At Chicago	L	2-5
15—At Detroit	L	2-5
16—At Toronto	W	4-1
19—At Pittsburgh	L	4-5
20—At Dallas	L	*1-2
23—At Los Angeles	W	6-3
25—N.Y. Rangers	L	2-5
27—Los Angeles	W	4-3
28—Toronto	W	*3-2
30—Pittsburgh	L	1-3

APRIL

1—Winnipeg	W	5-1
2—At San Jose	L	4-7
5—Detroit	L	3-8
7—San Jose	W	3-2
9—Anaheim	L	1-3
10—At San Jose	L	1-3
13—At Anaheim	W	2-1

*Denotes overtime game.
†At Saskatoon, Sask.

WASHINGTON CAPITALS
EASTERN CONFERENCE/ATLANTIC DIVISION

1994-95 SCHEDULE

- ☐ Home games shaded.
- * — All-Star Game at San Jose Arena.
- † — At Halifax, N.S.
- D — Day game.

OCTOBER

SUN	MON	TUE	WED	THU	FRI	SAT
						1 TOR
2	3	4	5 OTT	6	7 PIT	8 NYI
9	10	11	12 PIT	13	14 MON	15 BUF
16	17	18	19 NJ	20	21 HAR	22 HAR
23	24	25 STL	26	27 WIN	28	29
30 EDM	31					

NOVEMBER

SUN	MON	TUE	WED	THU	FRI	SAT
		1 CAL	2 VAN	3	4	5 QUE
6	7	8 EDM	9	10 PHI	11	12 PHI
13 NYR	14	15 DAL	16	17	18 TOR	19 BOS
20	21	22	23 VAN	24	25 PIT	26 QUE
27	28 MON	29	30 OTT			

DECEMBER

SUN	MON	TUE	WED	THU	FRI	SAT
				1 PIT	2	3 TB
4	5	6	7 ANA	8 LA	9	10 SJ
11	12	13 WIN	14	15	16 BOS	17 HAR
18	19	20 FLA	21	22	23 PHI	24
25 NYI	26 NYR	27	28	29 FLA	30	31 NJ

JANUARY

SUN	MON	TUE	WED	THU	FRI	SAT
1	2 STL	3 D	3	4	5	6 NYI	7
8	9	10	11 BUF	12	13	14 NYR
15	16 BOS	17 D	18 PHI	19	20	21*
22	23	24 QUE	25	26 NYI	27 OTT	28
29 CHI	30	31 NJ				

FEBRUARY

SUN	MON	TUE	WED	THU	FRI	SAT
			1	2	3 QUE	4 FLA
5	6	7	8 TB	9	10† PHI	11
12† NJ	13	14	15 TB	16	17 DET	18 DET
19	20 MON	21 D	22	23 CHI	24	25 D NJ
26 NJ	27 D	28				

MARCH

SUN	MON	TUE	WED	THU	FRI	SAT
			1	2 NYI	3	4 SJ
5	6	7 CAL	8 MON	9	10 FLA	11
12 D BOS	13 TB	14	15 FLA	16	17	18 NYR
19	20	21 OTT	22	23	24	25 D ANA
26 D HAR	27	28	29 TB	30	31 PHI	

APRIL

SUN	MON	TUE	WED	THU	FRI	SAT
						1
2 DAL	3 D	4	5 NYR	6	7 BUF	8 BUF
9	10	11	12	13	14	15

1994-95 SEASON

CLUB DIRECTORY

Chairman and governor
Abe Pollin
President and alternate governor
Richard M. Patrick
Vice president and general manager
David Poile
Legal counselors and alternate governors
David M. Osnos
Peter O'Malley
Vice president/finance
Edmund Stelzer
Vice president/communications
Ed Quinlan
Communications manager
Dan Kaufman
Vice president/marketing
Lew Strudler
Assistant director of marketing
Debi Angus
Director of community relations
Yvon Labre
Director of promotions and advertising
Charles Copeland
Admin. assistant to communications
Julie Hensley

Admin. assistant to the general manager
Pat Young
Coach
Jim Schoenfeld
Assistant coach
Tod Button
Strength and conditioning coach
Frank Costello
Dir. of player personnel and recruitment
Jack Button
Scouts
Craig Channell
Gilles Cote
Fred Devereaux
Eje Johansson
Bud Quinn
Hugh Rogers
Bob Schmidt
Dan Sylvester
Niklas Wikegard
Darrell Young
Trainer
Stan Wong
Assistant trainer/head equipment manager
Doug Shearer

DRAFT CHOICES

Rd.—Player	H/W	Overall	Pos.	Last team
1—Nolan Baumgartner ..	6-1/187	10	D	Kamloops (WHL)
1—Alexander Kharlanov	5-11/183	15	C	CSKA Moscow, CIS
2—Scott Cherrey	6-1/199	41	LW	North Bay (OHL)
4—Matthew Herr	6-1/180	93	C	Hotchkiss H.S. (N.Y.)
5—Yanick Jean	6-1/198	119	D	Chemopetrol (Czech Jrs.)
6—Dmitri Mekeskin	6-1/174	145	D	Avangard CMSK, CIS
7—Daniel Reja	6-1/180	171	C	London (OHL)
8—Chris Patrick	6-5/200	197	LW	Kent School (Ct.)
9—John Tudhy	6-2/180	223	D	Kent School (Ct.)
10—Richard Zeonik	5-11/172	249	RW	Banska Bystrica, Slovakia
11—Sergei Tertyshny	6-0/187	275	D	Chelyabinsk, CIS

MISCELLANEOUS DATA

Home ice (capacity)
USAir Arena (18,130)
Address
Landover, MD 20785
Business phone
301-386-7000

Rink dimensions
200 feet by 85 feet
Club colors
Red, white and blue

TRAINING CAMP ROSTER

No. FORWARDS	Ht./Wt.	Place	Date	NHL exp.	1993-94 clubs
41 Jason Allison (C)	6-2/192	Toronto	5-29-75	1	London (OHL), Washington
27 Craig Berube (LW)	6-1/205	Calihoo, Alta.	12-17-65	8	Washington
12 Peter Bondra (RW)	6-0/200	Luck, U.S.S.R.	2-7-68	4	Washington
18 Randy Burridge (LW)	5-9/185	Fort Erie, Ont.	1-7-66	9	Washington
Kerry Clark (RW)	6-1/190	Kelvington, Sask.	8-21-68	0	Portland (AHL)
Martin Gendron (RW)	5-8/182	Valleyfield, Que.	2-15-74	0	Canadian national team (Int'l), Hull (QMJHL)
32 Dale Hunter (C)	5-10/198	Petrolia, Ont.	7-31-60	14	Washington
26 Keith Jones (RW)	6-2/190	Brantford, Ont.	11-8-68	2	Washington, Portland (AHL)
90 Joe Juneau (C)	6-0/196	Pont-Rouge, Que.	1-5-68	3	Boston, Washington
Kevin Kaminski (C)	5-9/170	Churchbridge, Sask.	3-13-69	4	Portland (AHL), Washington
8 Dimitri Khristich (LW)	6-2/195	Kiev, U.S.S.R.	7-23-69	4	Washington
22 Steve Konowalchuk (C)	6-0/180	Salt Lake City	11-11-72	3	Portland (AHL), Washington
21 Todd Krygier (LW)	5-11/180	Northville, Mich.	10-12-65	5	Washington
10 Kelly Miller (LW)	5-11/197	Lansing, Mich.	3-3-63	10	Washington
Jeff Nelson (C)	6-0/180	Prince Albert, Sask.	12-18-72	0	Portland (AHL)
14 Pat Peake (RW)	6-0/195	Detroit	5-28-73	1	Portland (AHL), Washington
Rob Pearson (RW)	6-3/200	Oshawa, Ont.	8-3-71	3	Toronto
20 Michal Pivonka (C)	6-2/198	Kladno, Czechoslovakia	1-28-66	8	Washington
9 Dave Poulin (C)	5-11/190	Mississauga, Ont.	12-17-58	12	Washington
Stefan Ustorf (C)	5-11/170	Kaufbeuren, W. Germany	1-3-74	0	German Olympic team (Int'l), Kaufbeuren (Germany)

DEFENSEMEN

Nolan Baumgartner	6-1/187	Calgary, Alta.	3-23-76	0	Kamloops (WHL)
Patrick Boileau	6-0/185	Montreal	2-22-75	0	Laval (QMJHL)
3 Sylvain Cote	5-11/185	Quebec City	1-19-66	10	Washington
Sergei Gonchar	6-2/212	Chelyabinsk, U.S.S.R.	4-13-74	0	Dynamo Moscow (CIS), Portland (AHL)
4 Kevin Hatcher	6-4/225	Detroit	9-9-66	10	Washington
6 Calle Johansson	5-11/205	Goteborg, Sweden	2-14-67	7	Washington
2 Jim Johnson	6-1/190	New Hope, Minn.	8-9-62	9	Dallas, Washington
Joe Reekie	6-3/215	Victoria, B.C.	2-22-65	9	Tampa Bay, Washington
28 John Slaney	6-0/185	St. John's, Nfld.	2-7-72	1	Portland (AHL), Washington
Brendan Witt	6-1/205	Humboldt, Sask.	2-20-75	0	Seattle (WHL)
25 Jason Woolley	6-0/185	Toronto	7-27-69	3	Portland (AHL), Washington

GOALTENDERS

33 Don Beaupre	5-10/172	Kitchener, Ont.	9-19-61	14	Washington
35 Byron Dafoe	5-11/175	Duncan, B.C.	2-25-71	2	Portland (AHL), Washington
37 Olaf Kolzig	6-3/205	Johannesburg, S. Africa	4-6-70	3	Portland (AHL), Washington
31 Rick Tabaracci	5-11/180	Toronto	1-2-69	5	Portland (AHL), Washington

1993-94 REVIEW

INDIVIDUAL STATISTICS

SCORING

	Games	G	A	Pts.	PIM	+/-	PPG	SHG	Shots	Shooting Pct.
Mike Ridley	81	26	44	70	24	15	10	2	144	18.1
Dimitri Khristich	83	29	29	58	73	-2	10	0	195	14.9
Sylvain Cote	84	16	35	51	66	30	3	2	212	7.5
Michal Pivonka	82	14	36	50	38	2	5	0	138	10.1
Al Iafrate*	67	10	35	45	143	10	4	0	252	4.0
Peter Bondra	69	24	19	43	40	22	4	0	200	12.0
Randy Burridge	78	25	17	42	73	-1	8	1	150	16.7
Calle Johansson	84	9	33	42	59	3	4	0	141	6.4
Kevin Hatcher	72	16	24	40	108	-13	6	0	217	7.4
Kelly Miller	84	14	25	39	32	8	0	1	138	10.1
Dale Hunter	52	9	29	38	131	-4	1	0	61	14.8
Keith Jones	68	16	19	35	149	4	5	0	97	16.5
Todd Krygier	66	12	18	30	60	-4	0	1	146	8.2
Pat Peake	49	11	18	29	39	1	3	0	91	12.1
Steve Konowalchuk	62	12	14	26	33	9	0	0	63	19.0
Dave Poulin	63	6	19	25	52	-1	0	1	64	9.4
John Slaney	47	7	9	16	27	3	3	0	70	10.0
Craig Berube	84	7	7	14	305	-4	0	0	48	14.6
Joe Juneau*	11	5	8	13	6	0	2	0	22	22.7
Alan May*	43	4	7	11	97	-2	0	0	33	12.1
Shawn Anderson	50	0	9	9	12	-1	0	0	31	0.0
Joe Reekie*	12	0	5	5	29	7	0	0	10	0.0

	Games	G	A	Pts.	PIM	+/-	PPG	SHG	Shots	Shooting Pct.
Kevin Kaminski	13	0	5	5	87	2	0	0	9	0.0
Jason Woolley	10	1	2	3	4	2	0	0	15	6.7
Pat Elynuik*	4	1	1	2	0	-3	1	0	8	12.5
Enrico Ciccone*	46	1	1	2	174	-2	0	0	23	4.3
Todd Nelson	2	1	0	1	2	1	1	0	1	100.0
Brian Curran	26	1	0	1	61	-2	0	0	11	9.1
Jason Allison	2	0	1	1	0	1	0	0	5	0.0
Don Beaupre (goalie)	53	0	1	1	16	0	0	0	0	0.0
Tim Bergland*	3	0	0	0	4	-1	0	0	4	0.0
Byron Dafoe (goalie)	5	0	0	0	0	0	0	0	0	0.0
Keith Acton*	6	0	0	0	21	-4	0	0	2	0.0
Olaf Kolzig (goalie)	7	0	0	0	0	0	0	0	0	0.0
Jim Johnson*	8	0	0	0	12	-1	0	0	5	0.0
Rick Tabaracci (goalie)	32	0	0	0	6	0	0	0	0	0.0

GOALTENDING

	Games	Min.	Goals	SO	Avg.	W	L	T	Shots	Sv. Pct.
Don Beaupre	53	2853	135	2	2.84	24	16	8	1122	.880
Rick Tabaracci	32	1770	91	2	3.08	13	14	2	817	.889
Byron Dafoe	5	230	13	0	3.39	2	2	0	101	.871
Olaf Kolzig	7	224	20	0	5.36	0	3	0	128	.844

Empty-net goals (do not count against a goaltender's average): Beaupre 3, Kolzig 1.
*Played with two or more NHL teams.

RESULTS

OCTOBER
6—At Winnipeg	L	4-6
8—New Jersey	L	3-6
9—At New Jersey	L	4-6
11—At N.Y. Rangers	L	2-5
13—At Toronto	L	1-7
15—Philadelphia	L	0-3
16—Buffalo	W	4-3
22—Los Angeles	W	6-3
24—At Edmonton	W	*3-2
25—At Calgary	L	*2-3
27—At Vancouver	W	4-2
29—At Anaheim	W	5-2
30—At San Jose	W	4-2

NOVEMBER
5—Vancouver	W	3-2
9—Quebec	W	2-1
11—At Tampa Bay	W	4-1
13—N.Y. Rangers	L	0-2
16—San Jose	L	1-2
18—At Pittsburgh	L	2-3
20—At Florida	L	3-4
24—St. Louis	W	5-2
26—Pittsburgh	T	*4-4
28—At N.Y. Rangers	L	1-3
30—At N.Y. Islanders	L	4-6

DECEMBER
3—Montreal	T	*2-2
4—At Ottawa	W	6-1
7—Hartford	L	1-6
9—At Philadelphia	W	4-2
11—At Montreal	W	5-3
13—At Quebec	L	3-5
17—Ottawa	W	11-2
18—At Hartford	L	1-4
21—At Philadelphia	W	4-1
23—N.Y. Rangers	L	0-1
26—Pittsburgh	W	7-3
28—Florida	T	*3-3
30—Anaheim	W	3-0

JANUARY
1—Tampa Bay	T	*5-5
2—At Boston	L	2-8
8—Chicago	W	4-1
9—At New Jersey	W	4-0
11—Toronto	L	1-2
14—New Jersey	L	2-5
15—At Quebec	W	4-0
17—At Montreal	L	1-3
19—At Florida	L	1-5
25—Boston	L	1-3
27—At Buffalo	L	2-7
29—At Philadelphia	W	4-2
30—Detroit	W	6-3

FEBRUARY
2—Philadelphia†	W	5-2
4—Montreal	L	0-4
5—Tampa Bay	W	6-3
7—At N.Y. Rangers	W	4-1
10—At St. Louis	W	4-3
12—At Los Angeles	W	6-1
15—Edmonton	T	*2-2
18—N.Y. Islanders	W	3-1
20—Buffalo	T	*3-3
21—At N.Y. Islanders	L	0-4
24—At Florida	W	2-1
26—Florida	W	4-2
27—At Hartford	W	3-1

MARCH
1—Tampa Bay	L	3-4
4—Philadelphia	T	*3-3
6—Calgary	T	*4-4
7—At Boston	L	3-6
9—N.Y. Rangers‡	L	5-7
12—Quebec	L	3-4
15—At Pittsburgh	L	*5-4
18—At Dallas	L	2-6
20—Tampa Bay§	W	3-0
22—Hartford	W	4-1
25—At Detroit	T	*2-2
27—Boston	L	4-6
29—N.Y. Islanders	T	*2-2
31—At Chicago	W	6-3

APRIL
1—New Jersey	W	2-1
3—Dallas	L	3-6
5—N.Y. Islanders	L	*3-4
6—At Ottawa	L	5-6
9—Ottawa	W	8-4
12—Winnipeg	W	4-3
14—At Buffalo	W	3-2

*Denotes overtime game.
†At Cleveland.
‡At Halifax, N.S.
§At Orlando, Fla.

WINNIPEG JETS
WESTERN CONFERENCE/CENTRAL DIVISION

1994-95 SCHEDULE

- ▢ Home games shaded.
- * — All-Star Game at San Jose Arena.
- † — At Saskatoon, Sask.
- Δ — At Phoenix.
- D — Day game.

OCTOBER

SUN	MON	TUE	WED	THU	FRI	SAT
						1 OTT
2	3	4	5 MON	6	7 EDM	8
9	10	11 DAL	12	13 CHI	14 PHI	15
16 SJ	17	18 CAL	19 DAL	20	21	22 CHI
23 ANA	24	25	26	27 WAS	28	29 HAR
30 NJ	31					

NOVEMBER

SUN	MON	TUE	WED	THU	FRI	SAT
		1	2 TOR	3	4 DAL	5 STL
6	7	8 DET	9	10 STL	11	12 CHI
13	14 EDM	15	16 TOR	17	18 TB	19 FLA
20	21	22	23 TOR	24	25 NYR	26
27	28 STL	29	30 EDM			

DECEMBER

SUN	MON	TUE	WED	THU	FRI	SAT
				1	2	3 VAN
4	5	6	7 NJ	8	9	10 VAN
11	12	13 WAS	14	15 PHI	16	17 D DET
18 DET	19	20	21 ANA	22	23	24
25	26	27 CAL	28	29 BOS	30	31 D LA

JANUARY

SUN	MON	TUE	WED	THU	FRI	SAT
1	2† EDM	3	4	5 OTT	6	7 DAL
8 STL	9	10 TOR	11	12 BOS	13 DET	14
15 TB	16	17 STL	18 CAL	19	20	21*
22	23	24	25 SJ	26	27 ANA	28 LA
29	30	31Δ LA				

FEBRUARY

SUN	MON	TUE	WED	THU	FRI	SAT
		1	2 PIT	3	4 HAR	
5	6 NYR	7 NYI	8	9	10 EDM	11 VAN
12	13	14	15 CAL	16	17 DAL	18
19 D CHI	20 BUF	21	22 VAN	23	24 DET	25
26	27	28				

MARCH

SUN	MON	TUE	WED	THU	FRI	SAT
			1	2 QUE	3	4 STL
5	6	7 CHI	8 DAL	9	10 BUF	11 LA
12	13 PIT	14	15 MON	16 QUE	17	18
19 D SJ	20	21	22 DET	23	24 TOR	25 TOR
26	27	28 SJ	29 ANA	30	31	

APRIL

SUN	MON	TUE	WED	THU	FRI	SAT
						1 LA
2	3	4	5 CHI	6	7 FLA	8
9 D NYI	10	11	12	13	14	15

1994-95 SEASON

CLUB DIRECTORY

President and governor
Barry L. Shenkarow
Alternate governor
Bill Davis
Vice president and general manager
Michael A. Smith
General manager and head coach
John Paddock
Asst. G.M./V.P of communications
Mike O'Hearn
Vice president of finance administration
Don Binda
Director of player development
Randy Carlyle
Associate coaches
Andy Murray
Zinetula Bilyaletdinov
Goaltending coach
Pete Peeters
Coordinator of coaching services
Glen Williamson
Director of scouting
Bill Lesuk

Assistant director of scouting
Joe Yannetti
Scouts
Tom Savage
Connie Broden
Sean Coady
Charlie Burroughs
Boris Yemeljanov
Larry Hornung
Vaughn Karpan
Director, hockey information
Igor Kuperman
Media/public relations
Richard Nairn
Athletic trainers
Gord Hart
Phil Walker
Equipment managers
Craig Heisinger
Mike Romani
Stan Wilson
Team physician
Dr. Brian Lukie

DRAFT CHOICES

Rd.—Player	H/W	Overall	Pos.	Last team
2—Deron Quint	6-1/182	30	D	Seattle (WHL)
3—Dorian Anneck	6-1/183	56	C	Victoria (WHL)
3—Tavis Hansen	6-1/180	58	C	Tacoma (WHL)
4—Steve Cheredaryk	6-2/197	82	D	Medicine Hat (WHL)
5—Craig Mills	5-11/174	108	RW	Belleville (OHL)
6—Steve Vezina	5-10/172	143	G	Beauport (QMJHL)
6—Chris Kibermanis	6-5/184	146	D	Red Deer (WHL)
8—Ramil Saifulin	6-1/187	186	C	Avangard CMSK, CIS
9—Henrik Shangs	5-11/174	212	G	Leksand, Sweden
10—Mike Mader	6-2/183	238	D	Loomis-Chaffee H.S. (Pa.)
11—Jason Issel	6-1/185	264	LW	Prince Albert (WHL)

MISCELLANEOUS DATA

Home ice (capacity)
Winnipeg Arena (15,393)
Address
15-1430 Maroons Road
Winnipeg, Man. R3G 0L5
Business phone
204-982-5387

Rink dimensions
200 feet by 85 feet
Club colors
Blue, red and white

TRAINING CAMP ROSTER

No.	FORWARDS	Ht./Wt.	BORN Place	Date	NHL exp.	1993-94 clubs
	Dorian Anneck (C)	6-1/183	Winnipeg, Man.	4-24-76	0	Victoria (WHL)
38	Luciano Borsato (C)	5-11/190	Richmond Hill, Ont.	1-7-66	4	Winnipeg
	Larry Courville (LW)	6-1/180	Timmins, Ont.	4-2-75	0	Newmarket (OHL), Moncton (AHL)
20	Tie Domi (RW)	5-10/200	Windsor, Ont.	11-1-69	5	Winnipeg
18	Dallas Drake (C)	6-0/180	Trail, B.C.	2-4-69	2	Detroit, Adirondack (AHL), Winnipeg
36	Mike Eagles (C)	5-10/190	Sussex, N.B.	3-7-63	10	Winnipeg
19	Nelson Emerson (C)	5-11/175	Hamilton, Ont.	8-17-67	4	Winnipeg
15	Randy Gilhen (C)	6-0/190	Zweibrucken, W. Germany	6-13-63	9	Florida, Winnipeg
60	Michal Grosek (LW)	6-2/183	Gottwaldov, Czech.	6-1-75	1	Moncton (AHL), Tacoma (WHL), Winnipeg
	Ravil Gusmanov (LW)	6-3/185	Nab. Chelny, U.S.S.R.	7-22-72	0	Traktor Chelyabinsk (CIS)
	Sheldon Kennedy (RW)	5-11/180	Brandon, Man.	6-15-69	5	Detroit
17	Kris King (LW)	5-11/210	Bracebridge, Ont.	2-18-66	7	Winnipeg
50	Rob Murray (C)	6-1/180	Toronto	4-4-67	5	Moncton (AHL), Winnipeg
21	Russ Romaniuk (LW)	6-0/185	Winnipeg, Man.	5-9-70	3	Canadian national team (Int'l), Moncton (AHL), Winnipeg
13	Teemu Selanne (RW)	6-0/181	Helsinki, Finland	7-3-70	2	Winnipeg
34	Darrin Shannon (LW)	6-2/200	Barrie, Ont.	12-8-69	6	Winnipeg
25	Thomas Steen (C)	5-11/185	Tocksmark, Sweden	6-8-60	13	Winnipeg
7	Keith Tkachuk (LW)	6-2/215	Melrose, Mass.	3-28-72	3	Winnipeg
10	Alexei Zhamnov (C)	6-1/187	Moscow, U.S.S.R.	10-1-70	2	Winnipeg
	DEFENSEMEN					
55	Arto Blomsten	6-3/198	Vaasa, Finland	3-16-65	1	Winnipeg, Moncton (AHL)
26	Dean Kennedy	6-2/212	Redvers, Sask.	1-18-63	11	Winnipeg
3	Dave Manson	6-2/210	Prince Albert, Sask.	1-27-67	8	Edmonton, Winnipeg
6	Wayne McBean	6-2/190	Calgary, Alta.	2-21-69	6	New York Islanders, Salt Lake City (IHL), Winnipeg
	Mike Muller	6-2/205	Minneapolis	9-18-71	0	Moncton (AHL)
27	Teppo Numminen	6-1/190	Tampere, Finland	7-3-68	6	Winnipeg
	Deron Quint	6-1/182	Dover, N.H.	3-12-76	0	Seattle (WHL)
4	Stephane Quintal	6-3/215	Boucherville, Que.	10-22-68	6	Winnipeg
28	Darryl Shannon	6-2/195	Barrie, Ont.	6-21-68	6	Moncton (AHL), Winnipeg
5	Igor Ulanov	6-2/202	Kraskokamsk, U.S.S.R.	10-1-69	3	Winnipeg
39	Mark Visheau	6-4/197	Burlington, Ont.	6-27-73	1	Moncton (AHL), Winnipeg
	Neil Wilkinson	6-3/190	Selkirk, Man.	8-15-67	5	Chicago
	GOALTENDERS					
30	Stephane Beauregard	5-11/190	Cowansville, Que.	1-10-68	5	Moncton (AHL), Winnipeg
29	Tim Cheveldae	5-10/195	Melville, Sask.	2-15-68	6	Detroit, Adirondack (AHL), Winnipeg
	Nikolai Khabibulin	6-1/176	Sverdlovsk, U.S.S.R.	1-13-73	0	CSKA Moscow (CIS), Russian Penguins (IHL)
	Scott Langkow	5-11/180	Edmonton, Alta.	4-21-75	0	Portland (WHL)
1	Mike O'Neill	5-7/160	Montreal	11-3-67	3	Moncton (AHL), Fort Wayne (IHL), Winnipeg

1993-94 REVIEW

INDIVIDUAL STATISTICS

SCORING

	Games	G	A	Pts.	PIM	+/-	PPG	SHG	Shots	Shooting Pct.
Keith Tkachuk	84	41	40	81	255	-12	22	3	218	18.8
Nelson Emerson	83	33	41	74	80	-38	4	5	282	11.7
Alexei Zhamnov	61	26	45	71	62	-20	7	0	196	13.3
Darrin Shannon	77	21	37	58	87	-18	9	0	124	16.9
Teemu Selanne	51	25	29	54	22	-23	11	0	191	13.1
Thomas Steen	76	19	32	51	32	-38	6	0	137	13.9
Boris Mironov*	65	7	22	29	96	-29	5	0	122	5.7
Paul Ysebaert*	60	9	18	27	18	-8	1	0	120	7.5
Stephane Quintal	81	8	18	26	119	-25	1	1	154	5.2
Teppo Numminen	57	5	18	23	28	-23	4	0	89	5.6
Tie Domi	81	8	11	19	†347	-8	0	0	98	8.2
Luciano Borsato	75	5	13	18	28	-11	1	1	65	7.7
Igor Ulanov	74	0	17	17	165	-11	0	0	46	0.0
Russ Romaniuk	24	4	8	12	6	-11	3	0	36	11.1
Mike Eagles	73	4	8	12	96	-20	0	1	53	7.5
Kris King	83	4	8	12	205	-22	0	0	86	4.7
Wayne McBean*	31	2	9	11	24	-21	2	0	81	2.5

	Games	G	A	Pts.	PIM	+/-	PPG	SHG	Shots	Shooting Pct.
Dean Kennedy	76	2	8	10	164	-22	0	0	38	5.3
Stu Barnes*	18	5	4	9	8	-1	2	0	24	20.8
John LeBlanc	17	6	2	8	2	-2	1	1	29	20.7
Dallas Drake*	15	3	5	8	12	-6	1	1	34	8.8
Fredrik Olausson*	18	2	5	7	10	-3	1	0	41	4.9
Sergei Bautin*	59	0	7	7	78	-13	0	0	39	0.0
Randy Gilhen*	40	3	3	6	34	-13	0	0	43	7.0
Dave Manson*	13	1	4	5	51	-10	1	0	36	2.8
Dave Tomlinson	31	1	3	4	24	-12	0	0	29	3.4
Darryl Shannon	20	0	4	4	18	-6	0	0	14	0.0
Arto Blomsten	18	0	2	2	6	-6	0	0	15	0.0
Michal Grosek	3	1	0	1	0	-1	0	0	4	25.0
Oleg Mikulchik	4	0	1	1	17	-2	0	0	3	0.0
Yan Kaminsky*	1	0	0	0	0	1	0	0	0	0.0
Mark Visheau	1	0	0	0	0	0	0	0	1	0.0
Andy Brickley	2	0	0	0	0	-2	0	0	0	0.0
Craig Fisher	4	0	0	0	2	-1	0	0	5	0.0
Kevin McClelland	6	0	0	0	19	0	0	0	1	0.0
Rob Murray	6	0	0	0	2	0	0	0	1	0.0
Harijs Vitolinsh	8	0	0	0	4	0	0	0	7	0.0
Stephane Beauregard (goalie)	13	0	0	0	0	0	0	0	0	0.0
Tim Cheveldae* (goalie)	14	0	0	0	2	0	0	0	0	0.0
Bryan Erickson	16	0	0	0	6	-7	0	0	8	0.0
Michael O'Neill (goalie)	17	0	0	0	0	0	0	0	0	0.0
Bob Essensa* (goalie)	56	0	0	0	6	0	0	0	0	0.0

GOALTENDING

	Games	Min.	Goals	SO	Avg.	W	L	T	Shots	Sv. Pct.
Bob Essensa*	56	3136	201	1	3.85	19	30	6	1714	.883
Tim Cheveldae*	14	788	52	1	3.96	5	8	1	485	.893
Michael O'Neill	17	738	51	0	4.15	0	9	1	382	.866
Stephane Beauregard	13	418	34	0	4.88	0	4	1	211	.839

Empty-net goals (do not count against a goaltender's average): Essensa 5, O'Neill 1.
*Played with two or more NHL teams.
†Led league.

RESULTS

OCTOBER

6—Washington	W	6-4	
9—At Dallas	T	*3-3	
10—At Chicago	L	*3-4	
12—At New Jersey	L	4-7	
16—Chicago	W	*1-0	
18—Edmonton	W	6-3	
21—At Detroit	L	2-6	
23—At Philadelphia	W	9-6	
26—At Florida	W	5-2	
27—At Tampa Bay	W	4-3	
29—Los Angeles	L	*3-4	
31—Calgary	L	3-4	

NOVEMBER

3—St. Louis	L	0-3
5—Ottawa	L	*6-7
7—At Dallas	T	*1-1
9—At N.Y. Islanders	W	5-2
10—At N.Y. Rangers	L	1-2
13—Dallas	L	2-3
15—At Calgary	L	2-7
17—Detroit	W	2-1
19—At Buffalo	L	0-6
20—At Quebec	T	*5-5
24—Anaheim	L	1-2
26—Vancouver	L	3-5
28—At St. Louis	W	4-3
30—At Los Angeles	W	8-6

DECEMBER

1—At Anaheim	L	2-5
3—At San Jose	T	*3-3
5—Detroit	W	6-4

6—At Detroit	L	2-6
8—At Toronto	W	5-4
10—Florida	L	2-5
12—Toronto	T	*3-3
17—At Vancouver	L	1-6
18—At Calgary	L	*4-5
20—Anaheim	L	5-7
23—Quebec	W	5-2
27—At Edmonton	L	0-6
29—Chicago	W	3-2
31—St. Louis	W	2-1

JANUARY

2—At Chicago	L	1-5
5—At Hartford	L	0-4
6—At Boston	L	4-5
8—At Ottawa	W	3-2
10—At Montreal	L	2-4
12—Buffalo	W	3-2
15—Toronto	L	1-5
16—Tampa Bay	L	*2-3
19—New Jersey	L	0-4
25—At Los Angeles	T	*4-4
26—At Anaheim	L	1-3
29—At Detroit	L	1-7

FEBRUARY

2—Dallas	L	3-7
4—Hartford	T	*2-2
6—At Edmonton	L	2-5
8—At St. Louis	L	5-6
9—At Dallas	L	2-4
11—Toronto	L	1-3
15—At Pittsburgh	L	3-5

18—Chicago	L	2-7
20—Calgary	L	2-5
22—Florida†	L	2-3
24—At Chicago	L	3-6
25—Boston	L	6-7
28—San Jose	T	*3-3

MARCH

2—Dallas	W	4-2
4—Ottawa‡	W	6-1
6—Pittsburgh	L	3-5
7—N.Y. Islanders	L	2-7
11—Vancouver	L	4-8
12—At Toronto	L	1-3
16—St. Louis	W	4-0
19—Detroit	W	4-2
23—Montreal	L	3-1
25—San Jose	L	3-8
27—N.Y. Rangers	W	3-1
29—At San Jose	L	4-9

APRIL

1—At Vancouver	L	1-5
4—Philadelphia	T	*2-2
6—Edmonton	L	3-4
9—Los Angeles	W	4-3
10—At Toronto	L	0-7
12—At Washington	L	3-4
14—At St. Louis	L	1-3

*Denotes overtime game.
†At Hamilton, Ont.
‡At Minneapolis.

SCHEDULE

DAY BY DAY

*Denotes afternoon game.

SATURDAY, OCTOBER 1
Chicago at Pittsburgh
Winnipeg at Ottawa
Boston at Montreal
Buffalo at Quebec
Tampa Bay at N.Y. Islanders
N.Y. Rangers at New Jersey
Hartford at Philadelphia
Washington at Toronto
St. Louis at Detroit
Anaheim at Dallas
Vancouver at Calgary
Los Angeles at San Jose

SUNDAY, OCTOBER 2
St. Louis at Chicago
Vancouver at Edmonton

MONDAY, OCTOBER 3
Boston at Ottawa
Pittsburgh at N.Y. Rangers

TUESDAY, OCTOBER 4
Quebec at Tampa Bay
Philadelphia at Florida
Hartford at Toronto
Calgary at Dallas

WEDNESDAY, OCTOBER 5
Buffalo at Pittsburgh
Washington at Ottawa
Montreal at Winnipeg
Anaheim at Edmonton
San Jose at Vancouver
Detroit at Los Angeles

THURSDAY, OCTOBER 6
Quebec at Boston
Philadelphia at N.Y. Rangers
St. Louis at Florida
New Jersey at Chicago

FRIDAY, OCTOBER 7
Montreal at Buffalo
Ottawa at N.Y. Islanders
Pittsburgh at Washington
St. Louis at Tampa Bay
Edmonton at Winnipeg
Anaheim at Vancouver
Detroit at San Jose

SATURDAY, OCTOBER 8
Toronto at Boston
Quebec at Hartford
Buffalo at Montreal
Ottawa at New Jersey
Tampa Bay at Philadelphia
N.Y. Islanders at Washington
N.Y. Rangers at Florida*
Chicago at Dallas
Calgary at Los Angeles

SUNDAY, OCTOBER 9
Edmonton at Chicago
Vancouver at San Jose*
Calgary at Anaheim

MONDAY, OCTOBER 10
Florida at Boston*
Toronto at Buffalo

TUESDAY, OCTOBER 11
Pittsburgh at Quebec
Tampa Bay at N.Y. Rangers
Ottawa at Toronto
Chicago at St. Louis
Winnipeg at Dallas
San Jose at Los Angeles

WEDNESDAY, OCTOBER 12
Florida at Hartford
Washington at Pittsburgh
N.Y. Islanders at Montreal
Philadelphia at New Jersey
Buffalo at Detroit
Calgary at Edmonton
Boston at San Jose
Vancouver at Anaheim

THURSDAY, OCTOBER 13
Quebec at Toronto
Winnipeg at Chicago
N.Y. Rangers at St. Louis
Vancouver at Los Angeles

FRIDAY, OCTOBER 14
Hartford at Buffalo
Montreal at Washington
Florida at Detroit
Philadelphia at Winnipeg
San Jose at Calgary
Boston at Anaheim

SATURDAY, OCTOBER 15
N.Y. Rangers at Hartford
Montreal at Pittsburgh
Chicago at Quebec
Detroit at N.Y. Islanders
Buffalo at Washington
New Jersey at Tampa Bay
St. Louis at Toronto
Ottawa at Dallas
Edmonton at Vancouver
Boston at Los Angeles

SUNDAY, OCTOBER 16
New Jersey at Florida
Tampa Bay at St. Louis
San Jose at Winnipeg
Philadelphia at Calgary

MONDAY, OCTOBER 17
Chicago at Montreal
Dallas at Detroit
Philadelphia at Vancouver
Edmonton at Anaheim

TUESDAY, OCTOBER 18
N.Y. Rangers at Quebec
Los Angeles at N.Y. Islanders
Pittsburgh at Tampa Bay
San Jose at St. Louis
Winnipeg at Calgary

WEDNESDAY, OCTOBER 19
Ottawa at Hartford
Washington at New Jersey
Toronto at Florida

Montreal at Detroit
Dallas at Winnipeg
Anaheim at Edmonton
Boston at Vancouver

THURSDAY, OCTOBER 20
Los Angeles at N.Y. Rangers
Quebec at Philadelphia
Toronto at Tampa Bay
San Jose at Chicago
Anaheim at Calgary

FRIDAY, OCTOBER 21
Florida at Buffalo
Hartford at Washington
Pittsburgh at Detroit
Vancouver at Dallas
Boston at Edmonton

SATURDAY, OCTOBER 22
Washington at Hartford
Los Angeles at Pittsburgh
N.Y. Rangers at Montreal
Detroit at Quebec
Florida at N.Y. Islanders
San Jose at New Jersey*
Ottawa at Philadelphia*
Toronto at St. Louis
Chicago at Winnipeg
Boston at Calgary

SUNDAY, OCTOBER 23
Quebec at Buffalo
Tampa Bay at Ottawa*
San Jose at N.Y. Rangers
Los Angeles at Chicago
Vancouver at St. Louis
Edmonton at Dallas*
Anaheim at Winnipeg

MONDAY, OCTOBER 24
Calgary at Toronto
New Jersey at Montreal

TUESDAY, OCTOBER 25
Dallas at Pittsburgh
Edmonton at Quebec
Vancouver at N.Y. Islanders
Los Angeles at Florida
Anaheim at Detroit
Washington at St. Louis

WEDNESDAY, OCTOBER 26
Pittsburgh at Ottawa
Edmonton at Montreal
Dallas at N.Y. Rangers
Calgary at New Jersey
Los Angeles at Tampa Bay

THURSDAY, OCTOBER 27
Montreal at Boston
Quebec at Hartford
Vancouver at Philadelphia
Buffalo at Florida
Anaheim at Chicago
Washington at Winnipeg

FRIDAY, OCTOBER 28
Calgary at N.Y. Rangers
Edmonton at Toronto
Los Angeles at Detroit

SATURDAY, OCTOBER 29

Buffalo at Boston
Winnipeg at Hartford
Detroit at Ottawa
Pittsburgh at Montreal
Dallas at Quebec
Calgary at N.Y. Islanders
Vancouver at New Jersey
Toronto at Philadelphia
St. Louis at San Jose

SUNDAY, OCTOBER 30

Vancouver at N.Y. Rangers
Winnipeg at New Jersey
Tampa Bay at Chicago
Washington at Edmonton
St. Louis at Anaheim

TUESDAY, NOVEMBER 1

Ottawa at Pittsburgh
Tampa Bay at Quebec
Hartford at Detroit
N.Y. Islanders at Dallas
Washington at Calgary
New Jersey at San Jose
N.Y. Rangers at Los Angeles

WEDNESDAY, NOVEMBER 2

Chicago at Buffalo
Philadelphia at Ottawa
Tampa Bay at Montreal
N.Y. Islanders at St. Louis
Toronto at Winnipeg
Florida at Edmonton
Washington at Vancouver
N.Y. Rangers at Anaheim

THURSDAY, NOVEMBER 3

Pittsburgh at Boston

FRIDAY, NOVEMBER 4

Philadelphia at Buffalo
Toronto at Detroit
Winnipeg at Dallas
Edmonton at Calgary
Los Angeles at Vancouver
New Jersey at Anaheim

SATURDAY, NOVEMBER 5

Chicago at Boston
Hartford at Pittsburgh
Montreal at Ottawa
Buffalo at Philadelphia
Quebec at Washington
N.Y. Islanders at Tampa Bay
Detroit at Toronto
Winnipeg at St. Louis
Florida at Vancouver
N.Y. Rangers at San Jose

SUNDAY, NOVEMBER 6

Dallas at Chicago
Florida at Calgary
New Jersey at Los Angeles

MONDAY, NOVEMBER 7

Boston at Ottawa
Dallas at N.Y. Islanders
San Jose at Vancouver

TUESDAY, NOVEMBER 8

Montreal at Hartford
New Jersey at Pittsburgh
Tampa Bay at Buffalo
Philadelphia at Quebec
Edmonton at Washington
Winnipeg at Detroit
St. Louis at Calgary

Vancouver at San Jose
Anaheim at Los Angeles

WEDNESDAY, NOVEMBER 9

Hartford at N.Y. Rangers
N.Y. Islanders at Florida
Tampa Bay at Toronto

THURSDAY, NOVEMBER 10

Quebec at Boston
Ottawa at Buffalo
Montreal at New Jersey
Washington at Philadelphia
Toronto at Chicago
Pittsburgh at Dallas
St. Louis at Winnipeg
Anaheim at San Jose
Calgary at Los Angeles

FRIDAY, NOVEMBER 11

N.Y. Islanders at N.Y. Rangers
Edmonton at Florida
Vancouver at Anaheim

SATURDAY, NOVEMBER 12

Ottawa at Quebec*
Hartford at N.Y. Islanders
Boston at New Jersey*
Philadelphia at Washington
Edmonton at Tampa Bay
Montreal at Toronto
Pittsburgh at St. Louis
Detroit at Dallas
Chicago at Winnipeg
Buffalo at San Jose
Vancouver at Los Angeles

SUNDAY, NOVEMBER 13

Hartford at Ottawa
New Jersey at Quebec*
Washington at N.Y. Rangers
Dallas at Philadelphia
Boston at Florida
St. Louis at Chicago
Calgary at Anaheim

MONDAY, NOVEMBER 14

Edmonton at Winnipeg

TUESDAY, NOVEMBER 15

Dallas at Washington
Calgary at San Jose
Chicago at Los Angeles
Buffalo at Anaheim

WEDNESDAY, NOVEMBER 16

St. Louis at Hartford
Pittsburgh at Ottawa
N.Y. Islanders at Montreal
Dallas at New Jersey
Detroit at Tampa Bay
Winnipeg at Toronto
Vancouver at Edmonton

THURSDAY, NOVEMBER 17

St. Louis at Boston
Ottawa at Pittsburgh
Montreal at Quebec
N.Y. Rangers at Philadelphia
Detroit at Florida
Anaheim at Vancouver
Buffalo at Los Angeles

FRIDAY, NOVEMBER 18

N.Y. Islanders at New Jersey
Toronto at Washington
Winnipeg at Tampa Bay
San Jose at Dallas
Calgary at Edmonton

SATURDAY, NOVEMBER 19

Washington at Boston
N.Y. Islanders at Hartford
N.Y. Rangers at Ottawa
Quebec at Montreal
Pittsburgh at Philadelphia
New Jersey at Tampa Bay
Winnipeg at Florida
St. Louis at Toronto
Calgary at Vancouver

SUNDAY, NOVEMBER 20

Detroit at Philadelphia
San Jose at Edmonton
Chicago at Anaheim

MONDAY, NOVEMBER 21

Pittsburgh at Boston
Hartford at Montreal
Florida at Quebec
Vancouver at Toronto
Buffalo at Dallas

TUESDAY, NOVEMBER 22

Los Angeles at Calgary
Chicago at San Jose

WEDNESDAY, NOVEMBER 23

Philadelphia at Hartford
N.Y. Rangers at Pittsburgh
Boston at Buffalo
New Jersey at Ottawa
Florida at Montreal
Tampa Bay at N.Y. Islanders
Vancouver at Washington
St. Louis at Detroit
Quebec at Dallas
Toronto at Winnipeg
Los Angeles at Edmonton
San Jose at Anaheim

THURSDAY, NOVEMBER 24

Quebec at St. Louis
Chicago at Calgary

FRIDAY, NOVEMBER 25

Anaheim at Boston*
Vancouver at Buffalo
New Jersey at Philadelphia*
Pittsburgh at Washington
N.Y. Rangers at Winnipeg
Chicago at Edmonton

SATURDAY, NOVEMBER 26

Anaheim at Hartford*
San Jose at Pittsburgh
Florida at Ottawa
Los Angeles at Montreal
Washington at Quebec
Toronto at N.Y. Islanders
Tampa Bay at Philadelphia*
New Jersey at Detroit*
St. Louis at Dallas
Calgary at Edmonton

SUNDAY, NOVEMBER 27

Vancouver at Boston*
Tampa Bay at Hartford
N.Y. Islanders at Buffalo
Florida at N.Y. Rangers

MONDAY, NOVEMBER 28

Los Angeles at Ottawa
Washington at Montreal
San Jose at Detroit
Winnipeg at St. Louis
Toronto at Dallas

TUESDAY, NOVEMBER 29

N.Y. Rangers at Hartford
Anaheim at Pittsburgh
Los Angeles at Quebec
Boston at N.Y. Islanders

WEDNESDAY, NOVEMBER 30

Washington at Ottawa
Buffalo at N.Y. Rangers
Florida at Tampa Bay
Anaheim at Toronto
Philadelphia at Detroit
Montreal at St. Louis
Winnipeg at Edmonton

THURSDAY, DECEMBER 1

Hartford at Boston
Washington at Pittsburgh
Quebec at New Jersey
N.Y. Islanders at Philadelphia
San Jose at Florida
Montreal at Chicago

FRIDAY, DECEMBER 2

Los Angeles at Buffalo
Anaheim at N.Y. Rangers
San Jose at Tampa Bay
Calgary at Detroit
Dallas at Vancouver

SATURDAY, DECEMBER 3

Boston at Pittsburgh
Philadelphia at Ottawa
Detroit at Montreal
Hartford at Quebec
Buffalo at N.Y. Islanders
Edmonton at New Jersey*
Tampa Bay at Washington
Chicago at Florida
Los Angeles at Toronto
Winnipeg at Vancouver

SUNDAY, DECEMBER 4

Boston at Hartford
Calgary at Ottawa
Edmonton at N.Y. Rangers
Anaheim at Chicago
New Jersey at St. Louis

MONDAY, DECEMBER 5

Tampa Bay at Florida
San Jose at Dallas

TUESDAY, DECEMBER 6

N.Y. Rangers at Pittsburgh
Calgary at Quebec
Edmonton at N.Y. Islanders
Boston at Detroit
Toronto at Vancouver

WEDNESDAY, DECEMBER 7

Detroit at Hartford
Pittsburgh at Buffalo
Calgary at Montreal
Ottawa at Tampa Bay
St. Louis at Dallas
New Jersey at Winnipeg
Toronto at San Jose
Washington at Anaheim

THURSDAY, DECEMBER 8

Edmonton at Boston
N.Y. Islanders at N.Y. Rangers
Montreal at Philadelphia
Ottawa at Florida
Vancouver at Chicago
Washington at Los Angeles

FRIDAY, DECEMBER 9

Hartford at Buffalo
Detroit at New Jersey
Quebec at Tampa Bay
Chicago at Dallas
Anaheim at San Jose

SATURDAY, DECEMBER 10

Calgary at Boston
Edmonton at Hartford
Buffalo at Pittsburgh
Philadelphia at Montreal
Ottawa at N.Y. Islanders
Quebec at Florida
Dallas at St. Louis
Vancouver at Winnipeg
Washington at San Jose
Toronto at Los Angeles

SUNDAY, DECEMBER 11

New Jersey at Philadelphia
Florida at Chicago
Detroit at St. Louis
Toronto at Anaheim

MONDAY, DECEMBER 12

Calgary at Hartford
Los Angeles at Vancouver

TUESDAY, DECEMBER 13

New Jersey at Ottawa
Florida at Quebec
N.Y. Rangers at N.Y. Islanders†
Winnipeg at Washington
Dallas at Detroit
Toronto at Edmonton
Pittsburgh at Anaheim
†Game played in Portland, Ore.

WEDNESDAY, DECEMBER 14

Ottawa at Hartford
Boston at Montreal
Buffalo at Tampa Bay
Dallas at Chicago
N.Y. Rangers at Vancouver
N.Y. Islanders at San Jose

THURSDAY, DECEMBER 15

Florida at New Jersey
Winnipeg at Philadelphia
Quebec at Detroit
Toronto at Calgary
Pittsburgh at Los Angeles

FRIDAY, DECEMBER 16

Montreal at Buffalo
Boston at Washington
Chicago at Tampa Bay
St. Louis at Vancouver
San Jose at Anaheim

SATURDAY, DECEMBER 17

Buffalo at Boston
Washington at Hartford
Ottawa at Montreal
Philadelphia at Quebec*
Florida at Toronto
Winnipeg at Detroit*
New Jersey at Dallas
N.Y. Rangers at Edmonton
Pittsburgh at San Jose
N.Y. Islanders at Los Angeles

SUNDAY, DECEMBER 18

Tampa Bay at Quebec*
Philadelphia at Chicago
Detroit at Winnipeg
N.Y. Rangers at Calgary

St. Louis at Edmonton
N.Y. Islanders at Anaheim

MONDAY, DECEMBER 19

Buffalo at Ottawa
Tampa Bay at Montreal
Dallas at Toronto

TUESDAY, DECEMBER 20

Detroit at Pittsburgh
Hartford at New Jersey
Washington at Florida
N.Y. Islanders at Chicago
St. Louis at Calgary
Edmonton at San Jose

WEDNESDAY, DECEMBER 21

Dallas at Hartford
Tampa Bay at Ottawa
Quebec at Philadelphia
Buffalo at Montreal
Boston at N.Y. Rangers
Chicago at Toronto
Anaheim at Winnipeg
Vancouver at San Jose†
†Game played in Portland, Ore.

THURSDAY, DECEMBER 22

Dallas at Boston
Pittsburgh at Florida
Anaheim at Calgary
Edmonton at Los Angeles

FRIDAY, DECEMBER 23

Hartford at Buffalo
Quebec at N.Y. Islanders
Montreal at N.Y. Rangers
Ottawa at New Jersey
Philadelphia at Washington
Pittsburgh at Tampa Bay
Chicago at Detroit
Vancouver at St. Louis

MONDAY, DECEMBER 26

Hartford at Boston
Washington at N.Y. Islanders
Ottawa at N.Y. Rangers
Buffalo at New Jersey
Philadelphia at Tampa Bay
Detroit at Chicago
St. Louis at Dallas
Los Angeles at Anaheim

TUESDAY, DECEMBER 27

New Jersey at Buffalo
Toronto at Quebec
N.Y. Rangers at Washington
Philadelphia at Florida
Chicago at St. Louis
Calgary at Winnipeg
San Jose at Edmonton
Montreal at Vancouver

WEDNESDAY, DECEMBER 28

Pittsburgh at Hartford
N.Y. Islanders at Ottawa
Dallas at Detroit
Anaheim at Los Angeles

THURSDAY, DECEMBER 29

Buffalo at Pittsburgh
Hartford at Quebec
Florida at Washington
Dallas at Toronto
San Jose at St. Louis
Boston at Winnipeg
Calgary at Vancouver

SCHEDULE

1994-95 NHL SEASON

SCHEDULE

— 85 —

FRIDAY, DECEMBER 30
Philadelphia at N.Y. Islanders
Florida at New Jersey
N.Y. Rangers at Tampa Bay
Montreal at Edmonton
Chicago at Anaheim

SATURDAY, DECEMBER 31
N.Y. Islanders at Pittsburgh
Philadelphia at Buffalo
Hartford at Ottawa
New Jersey at Washington
Boston at Toronto
San Jose at Detroit
Dallas at St. Louis
Los Angeles at Winnipeg*
Montreal at Calgary
Quebec at Vancouver

SUNDAY, JANUARY 1
N.Y. Rangers at Florida*
San Jose at Chicago

MONDAY, JANUARY 2
Tampa Bay at Boston*
Toronto at Ottawa†
St. Louis at Washington*
Los Angeles at Dallas
Winnipeg at Edmonton‡
Montreal at Anaheim*
†Game played in Hamilton, Ont.
‡Game played in Saskatoon, Sask.

TUESDAY, JANUARY 3
Chicago at N.Y. Islanders
St. Louis at N.Y. Rangers
Vancouver at Florida
Calgary at Detroit

WEDNESDAY, JANUARY 4
Los Angeles at Hartford
Pittsburgh at New Jersey
Vancouver at Tampa Bay
Montreal at San Jose

THURSDAY, JANUARY 5
Philadelphia at Boston
Florida at Pittsburgh
Montreal at Quebec†
N.Y. Rangers at N.Y. Islanders
Calgary at Chicago
Ottawa at Winnipeg
†Game played in Phoenix.

FRIDAY, JANUARY 6
Vancouver at Hartford
Anaheim at Buffalo
Los Angeles at Washington
Dallas at Tampa Bay
Chicago at Detroit

SATURDAY, JANUARY 7
Detroit at Boston
Buffalo at Hartford
Philadelphia at Pittsburgh†
Toronto at Ottawa
Washington at N.Y. Islanders
Anaheim at New Jersey
N.Y. Rangers at Tampa Bay
Florida at St. Louis
Winnipeg at Dallas
Quebec at Edmonton
Calgary at San Jose*
†Game played in San Antonio.

SUNDAY, JANUARY 8
Los Angeles at Chicago
Winnipeg at St. Louis
Quebec at Calgary

MONDAY, JANUARY 9
N.Y. Islanders at Buffalo†
Ottawa at Montreal
Florida at N.Y. Rangers
Pittsburgh at New Jersey‡
Anaheim at Philadelphia
Dallas at Edmonton
†Game played in Minneapolis.
‡Game played in Denver.

TUESDAY, JANUARY 10
Winnipeg at Toronto
Los Angeles at St. Louis
Tampa Bay at Calgary

WEDNESDAY, JANUARY 11
Washington at Buffalo
Boston at Ottawa
Florida at N.Y. Islanders
Pittsburgh at N.Y. Rangers
Philadelphia at New Jersey
Anaheim at Detroit
Tampa Bay at Edmonton
Chicago at Vancouver
Dallas at San Jose

THURSDAY, JANUARY 12
Winnipeg at Boston
Montreal at Quebec
Florida at Philadelphia
Anaheim at Toronto
Chicago at Calgary
St. Louis at Los Angeles

FRIDAY, JANUARY 13
Hartford at Pittsburgh
N.Y. Islanders at New Jersey
Winnipeg at Detroit
Buffalo at Calgary
Tampa Bay at Vancouver

SATURDAY, JANUARY 14
N.Y. Islanders at Pittsburgh
Florida at Montreal
Boston at Quebec
Ottawa at Philadelphia
N.Y. Rangers at Washington
Detroit at Toronto
Edmonton at Vancouver
St. Louis at San Jose
Dallas at Los Angeles

SUNDAY, JANUARY 15
Anaheim at Ottawa
New Jersey at N.Y. Rangers
Hartford at Chicago
Tampa Bay at Winnipeg
Buffalo at Edmonton

MONDAY, JANUARY 16
Washington at Boston*
Philadelphia at N.Y. Islanders*
Hartford at Dallas
Los Angeles at Calgary
Vancouver at San Jose

TUESDAY, JANUARY 17
Anaheim at Quebec
Detroit at N.Y. Rangers
New Jersey at Florida
Chicago at Toronto
St. Louis at Winnipeg
Los Angeles at Edmonton

WEDNESDAY, JANUARY 18
Pittsburgh at Boston
Anaheim at Montreal
Quebec at N.Y. Islanders

Washington at Philadelphia
New Jersey at Tampa Bay
Toronto at Detroit
Hartford at Dallas†
Winnipeg at Calgary
Buffalo at Vancouver
†Game played in Denver.

SATURDAY, JANUARY 21
All-Star Game at San Jose Arena.

MONDAY, JANUARY 23
Philadelphia at Pittsburgh
Ottawa at Buffalo
Hartford at Montreal
Quebec at N.Y. Rangers
Tampa Bay at Florida
Edmonton at Calgary
Los Angeles at San Jose

TUESDAY, JANUARY 24
Washington at Quebec
St. Louis at N.Y. Islanders
Vancouver at Detroit
Dallas at Los Angeles

WEDNESDAY, JANUARY 25
Ottawa at Hartford
New Jersey at Buffalo
Boston at N.Y. Rangers
Calgary at Tampa Bay
Vancouver at Toronto
Edmonton at Chicago
Winnipeg at San Jose
Dallas at Anaheim

THURSDAY, JANUARY 26
New Jersey at Boston
Washington at N.Y. Islanders
Hartford at Philadelphia
Calgary at Florida
Edmonton at St. Louis
San Jose at Los Angeles

FRIDAY, JANUARY 27
Vancouver at Pittsburgh
Quebec at Buffalo
Tampa Bay at N.Y. Rangers
Ottawa at Washington
Toronto at Chicago
Winnipeg at Anaheim

SATURDAY, JANUARY 28
Florida at Hartford*
Toronto at Pittsburgh
Buffalo at Ottawa
New Jersey at Montreal*
N.Y. Rangers at Quebec
Tampa Bay at N.Y. Islanders
Boston at Philadelphia*
Edmonton at Detroit*
Calgary at St. Louis
Dallas at San Jose*
Winnipeg at Los Angeles

SUNDAY, JANUARY 29
Philadelphia at Montreal*
Chicago at Washington*

MONDAY, JANUARY 30
Florida at Boston
N.Y. Islanders at N.Y. Rangers
San Jose at Toronto
Detroit at Edmonton
Hartford at Vancouver

TUESDAY, JANUARY 31
Washington at New Jersey
Chicago at Philadelphia

N.Y. Islanders at Florida
Anaheim at St. Louis
Los Angeles at Winnipeg†
†Game played in Phoenix.

WEDNESDAY, FEBRUARY 1
San Jose at Ottawa
Montreal at Tampa Bay
Detroit at Calgary
Hartford at Edmonton
Toronto at Vancouver

THURSDAY, FEBRUARY 2
Ottawa at Boston
Chicago at N.Y. Rangers
Buffalo at New Jersey
N.Y. Islanders at Philadelphia
Quebec at Washington
Montreal at Florida
Los Angeles at St. Louis
Tampa Bay at Dallas
Pittsburgh at Winnipeg

FRIDAY, FEBRUARY 3
Hartford at Calgary
Toronto at Edmonton
Detroit at Anaheim

SATURDAY, FEBRUARY 4
N.Y. Islanders at Boston*
Tampa Bay at Pittsburgh
N.Y. Rangers at Ottawa
Vancouver at Montreal
San Jose at Quebec*
Chicago at New Jersey*
Buffalo at Philadelphia*
Florida at Washington
Dallas at St. Louis
Hartford at Winnipeg
Toronto at Calgary
Detroit at Los Angeles

SUNDAY, FEBRUARY 5
New Jersey at Quebec*
Dallas at Florida
Edmonton at Anaheim*

MONDAY, FEBRUARY 6
Vancouver at Ottawa
San Jose at Montreal
Winnipeg at N.Y. Rangers
Tampa Bay at Detroit†
Edmonton at Los Angeles
†Game played in Hamilton, Ont.

TUESDAY, FEBRUARY 7
N.Y. Rangers at Boston
Florida at Pittsburgh
Dallas at Buffalo
Vancouver at Quebec
Winnipeg at N.Y. Islanders
Philadelphia at Toronto

WEDNESDAY, FEBRUARY 8
San Jose at Hartford
Montreal at Ottawa
Los Angeles at New Jersey
Washington at Tampa Bay
Chicago at Edmonton
Calgary at Anaheim

THURSDAY, FEBRUARY 9
San Jose at Boston
Quebec at Pittsburgh
Florida at Buffalo
N.Y. Rangers at Philadelphia
Los Angeles at Detroit
Anaheim at St. Louis†

Chicago at Vancouver
†Game played in Las Vegas.

FRIDAY, FEBRUARY 10
Toronto at New Jersey
Washington at Philadelphia†
Hartford at Tampa Bay
Calgary at Dallas
Winnipeg at Edmonton
†Game played in Halifax, N.S.

SATURDAY, FEBRUARY 11
Los Angeles at Boston*
Montreal at Pittsburgh
Ottawa at Quebec
San Jose at N.Y. Islanders*
N.Y. Rangers at Tampa Bay
Hartford at Florida
Buffalo at Toronto
Calgary at St. Louis
Detroit at Dallas
Winnipeg at Vancouver

SUNDAY, FEBRUARY 12
Boston at Buffalo
New Jersey at Washington*†
Pittsburgh at Florida
Detroit at St. Louis
Anaheim at Edmonton*
†Game played in Halifax, N.S.

MONDAY, FEBRUARY 13
Hartford at Montreal
Los Angeles at Philadelphia
N.Y. Islanders at Tampa Bay
Toronto at Dallas
Anaheim at Calgary

TUESDAY, FEBRUARY 14
Edmonton at Pittsburgh

WEDNESDAY, FEBRUARY 15
Montreal at Hartford
N.Y. Rangers at Buffalo
St. Louis at New Jersey
Tampa Bay at Washington
N.Y. Islanders at Florida
Chicago at Toronto
Edmonton at Detroit
Boston at Dallas
Calgary at Winnipeg
Ottawa at San Jose
Quebec at Anaheim

THURSDAY, FEBRUARY 16
Montreal at N.Y. Rangers
St. Louis at Philadelphia
Pittsburgh at Chicago
San Jose at Vancouver
Quebec at Los Angeles

FRIDAY, FEBRUARY 17
N.Y. Islanders at New Jersey
Boston at Tampa Bay
Buffalo at Florida
Washington at Detroit
Dallas at Winnipeg
Ottawa at Anaheim

SATURDAY, FEBRUARY 18
Pittsburgh at Hartford*
St. Louis at Montreal
New Jersey at N.Y. Islanders
Edmonton at Philadelphia*
Detroit at Washington
Buffalo at Tampa Bay
N.Y. Rangers at Toronto
Dallas at Calgary

Quebec at San Jose
Ottawa at Los Angeles

SUNDAY, FEBRUARY 19
Hartford at Pittsburgh*
Boston at Florida
Winnipeg at Chicago*
Los Angeles at Anaheim

MONDAY, FEBRUARY 20
Winnipeg at Buffalo
Toronto at N.Y. Rangers*
Montreal at Washington*
N.Y. Islanders at Detroit
Edmonton at St. Louis
Dallas at Calgary
Quebec at Vancouver†
Philadelphia at San Jose*
†Game played in Saskatoon, Sask.

TUESDAY, FEBRUARY 21
Pittsburgh at New Jersey
Ottawa at Chicago
Anaheim at Los Angeles

WEDNESDAY, FEBRUARY 22
Boston at Hartford
N.Y. Islanders at Buffalo
Tampa Bay at Detroit
Toronto at St. Louis
Vancouver at Winnipeg
San Jose at Calgary†
Dallas at Edmonton
Philadelphia at Anaheim
†Game played in Phoenix.

THURSDAY, FEBRUARY 23
Quebec at Ottawa
Tampa Bay at New Jersey
Montreal at Florida
Washington at Chicago
Philadelphia at Los Angeles

FRIDAY, FEBRUARY 24
St. Louis at Pittsburgh
Hartford at N.Y. Rangers
N.Y. Islanders at Toronto
Vancouver at Dallas
Detroit at Winnipeg
Anaheim at San Jose

SATURDAY, FEBRUARY 25
Buffalo at Hartford
Florida at Ottawa
Toronto at Montreal
Boston at Quebec
Pittsburgh at N.Y. Islanders
Washington at New Jersey*
Chicago at St. Louis
Philadelphia at Edmonton
Calgary at Los Angeles

SUNDAY, FEBRUARY 26
N.Y. Rangers at Buffalo
New Jersey at Washington*
Detroit at Chicago
Tampa Bay at San Jose*
Vancouver at Anaheim*

MONDAY, FEBRUARY 27
Florida at Montreal†
St. Louis at Toronto
†Game played in Hamilton, Ont.

TUESDAY, FEBRUARY 28
Quebec at Boston
San Jose at Buffalo
Chicago at Ottawa
Hartford at N.Y. Islanders

Florida at N.Y. Rangers
Edmonton at Calgary
Pittsburgh at Vancouver
Tampa Bay at Los Angeles

WEDNESDAY, MARCH 1

New Jersey at Hartford
San Jose at Toronto
Ottawa at Detroit
Montreal at Dallas
Vancouver at Edmonton
Tampa Bay at Anaheim

THURSDAY, MARCH 2

New Jersey at Boston
Florida at Philadelphia
N.Y. Islanders at Washington
Buffalo at Chicago
Quebec at Winnipeg
Pittsburgh at Calgary
St. Louis at Los Angeles†
†Game played in Las Vegas.

FRIDAY, MARCH 3

Philadelphia at N.Y. Rangers
Toronto at Detroit
Anaheim at Dallas
Pittsburgh at Edmonton

SATURDAY, MARCH 4

Ottawa at Boston*
Chicago at Hartford*
Buffalo at Quebec
N.Y. Rangers at N.Y. Islanders
Florida at New Jersey*
San Jose at Washington
Calgary at Toronto
St. Louis at Winnipeg*
Montreal at Los Angeles

SUNDAY, MARCH 5

Boston at Hartford
Calgary at Buffalo
N.Y. Islanders at Ottawa
San Jose at Philadelphia
Anaheim at Florida
St. Louis at Chicago*
Detroit at Edmonton*

MONDAY, MARCH 6

Pittsburgh at Quebec
New Jersey at N.Y. Rangers
Anaheim at Tampa Bay
Los Angeles at Dallas
Detroit at Vancouver

TUESDAY, MARCH 7

New Jersey at N.Y. Islanders
Calgary at Washington
Winnipeg at Chicago
Ottawa at St. Louis

WEDNESDAY, MARCH 8

Philadelphia at Hartford
Washington at Montreal
Buffalo at N.Y. Rangers
Quebec at Florida
Dallas at Winnipeg
Edmonton at San Jose

THURSDAY, MARCH 9

Quebec at Pittsburgh
Montreal at N.Y. Islanders
Calgary at Philadelphia
Boston at Tampa Bay†
Los Angeles at Toronto
Ottawa at Chicago‡
Hartford at St. Louis
Edmonton at Vancouver

Detroit at Anaheim
†Game played in Minneapolis.
‡Game played in Phoenix.

FRIDAY, MARCH 10

Florida at Washington
Buffalo at Winnipeg
Detroit at San Jose

SATURDAY, MARCH 11

Calgary at Pittsburgh*
N.Y. Rangers at Montreal
N.Y. Islanders at Quebec
Philadelphia at Tampa Bay
New Jersey at Toronto
Los Angeles at Winnipeg
Ottawa at Vancouver
Dallas at Anaheim†
†Game played in San Antonio.

SUNDAY, MARCH 12

Boston at Washington*
Detroit at Florida†
Calgary at Chicago*
Buffalo at St. Louis
Ottawa at Edmonton
Hartford at San Jose*
†Game played in Denver.

MONDAY, MARCH 13

Winnipeg at Pittsburgh
N.Y. Rangers at Philadelphia
Washington at Tampa Bay
Toronto at Dallas

TUESDAY, MARCH 14

Buffalo at Boston†
Quebec at New Jersey
Chicago at Detroit
St. Louis at Edmonton
N.Y. Islanders at Vancouver
Hartford at Los Angeles
†Game played in Hamilton, Ont.

WEDNESDAY, MARCH 15

Winnipeg at Montreal
New Jersey at N.Y. Rangers
Washington at Florida
Philadelphia at Dallas
Ottawa at Calgary
Toronto at San Jose
Hartford at Anaheim

THURSDAY, MARCH 16

Montreal at Boston
Tampa Bay at Pittsburgh
Detroit at Buffalo
Winnipeg at Quebec
Vancouver at Chicago
St. Louis at Los Angeles

FRIDAY, MARCH 17

Vancouver at Detroit
San Jose at Calgary
N.Y. Islanders at Edmonton
Toronto at Anaheim

SATURDAY, MARCH 18

Buffalo at Boston*
Chicago at Hartford†
Pittsburgh at Ottawa*
Dallas at Montreal
Tampa Bay at New Jersey*
N.Y. Rangers at Washington
Philadelphia at Florida
Toronto at Los Angeles
†Game played in Phoenix.

SUNDAY, MARCH 19

Tampa Bay at Buffalo*
Dallas at Ottawa
Pittsburgh at Quebec*
Boston at New Jersey
San Jose at Winnipeg*
N.Y. Islanders at Calgary
St. Louis at Anaheim*

MONDAY, MARCH 20

Montreal at Philadelphia
Edmonton at Toronto†
Florida at Los Angeles
†Game played in Saskatoon, Sask.

TUESDAY, MARCH 21

Pittsburgh at Buffalo
Ottawa at Washington
N.Y. Rangers at Dallas
Detroit at Calgary
New Jersey at Edmonton
St. Louis at Vancouver
Chicago at San Jose
Florida at Anaheim

WEDNESDAY, MARCH 22

Quebec at Hartford
Boston at Montreal
Ottawa at Tampa Bay
Detroit at Winnipeg

THURSDAY, MARCH 23

Philadelphia at N.Y. Islanders
Calgary at N.Y. Rangers†
Anaheim at St. Louis
Edmonton at Dallas
New Jersey at Vancouver
Florida at San Jose
Chicago at Los Angeles
†Game played in Phoenix.

FRIDAY, MARCH 24

Montreal at Pittsburgh
Quebec at Buffalo
Boston at Tampa Bay
Winnipeg at Toronto
New Jersey at Calgary

SATURDAY, MARCH 25

N.Y. Islanders at Hartford*
Buffalo at Montreal
Ottawa at Quebec
Anaheim at Washington*
Toronto at Winnipeg
Detroit at Vancouver
San Jose at Los Angeles*

SUNDAY, MARCH 26

Edmonton at Ottawa
Anaheim at N.Y. Islanders*
Pittsburgh at Philadelphia
Hartford at Washington*
Tampa Bay at Florida*
Dallas at Chicago*
Boston at St. Louis
Vancouver at Calgary
Los Angeles at San Jose*

MONDAY, MARCH 27

Montreal at Tampa Bay
Edmonton at Toronto
Chicago at Dallas

TUESDAY, MARCH 28

N.Y. Islanders at Boston
Philadelphia at Pittsburgh
St. Louis at Quebec
N.Y. Rangers at Detroit
Winnipeg at San Jose

WEDNESDAY, MARCH 29

Edmonton at Buffalo
St. Louis at Ottawa
Washington at Tampa Bay
Hartford at Florida
Dallas at Toronto
Detroit at Chicago
Los Angeles at Vancouver
Winnipeg at Anaheim

THURSDAY, MARCH 30

Boston at Pittsburgh
Montreal at N.Y. Islanders
Quebec at N.Y. Rangers
New Jersey at Philadelphia

FRIDAY, MARCH 31

Philadelphia at Washington
Hartford at Tampa Bay
Quebec at Chicago
Toronto at St. Louis
San Jose at Calgary
Los Angeles at Edmonton
Anaheim at Vancouver

SATURDAY, APRIL 1

N.Y. Rangers at Boston*
Buffalo at N.Y. Islanders*
Montreal at New Jersey
Detroit at Dallas*
Winnipeg at Los Angeles

SUNDAY, APRIL 2

Ottawa at Buffalo*

N.Y. Islanders at Quebec*
Boston at Philadelphia*
Florida at Tampa Bay*
Pittsburgh at Toronto*
St. Louis at Detroit*
N.Y. Rangers at Chicago*
Washington at Dallas*
Calgary at Vancouver*
San Jose at Anaheim*

MONDAY, APRIL 3

Montreal at Ottawa
Edmonton at Los Angeles

TUESDAY, APRIL 4

Philadelphia at Boston
St. Louis at Buffalo
Pittsburgh at N.Y. Islanders
Hartford at New Jersey
Dallas at Vancouver

WEDNESDAY, APRIL 5

Toronto at Hartford
New Jersey at Pittsburgh
Quebec at Montreal
Washington at N.Y. Rangers
Ottawa at Florida
Chicago at Winnipeg
Calgary at San Jose
Edmonton at Anaheim

THURSDAY, APRIL 6

Montreal at Quebec

Boston at N.Y. Islanders
Tampa Bay at Philadelphia
Toronto at Chicago
Detroit at St. Louis
Vancouver at Los Angeles

FRIDAY, APRIL 7

Washington at Buffalo
Ottawa at N.Y. Rangers
Florida at Winnipeg
Los Angeles at Calgary
Edmonton at San Jose
Dallas at Anaheim

SATURDAY, APRIL 8

Tampa Bay at Boston*
New Jersey at Hartford*
Quebec at Ottawa
Pittsburgh at Montreal
Buffalo at Washington
Detroit at Toronto
Vancouver at Calgary

SUNDAY, APRIL 9

Tampa Bay at Hartford*
N.Y. Rangers at New Jersey*
Boston at Chicago*
Philadelphia at St. Louis*
Florida at Dallas*
N.Y. Islanders at Winnipeg*
San Jose at Edmonton
Los Angeles at Anaheim*

1993-94 NHL REVIEW

Regular season

Stanley Cup playoffs

All-Star Game

Awards

Player drafts

REGULAR SEASON

FINAL STANDINGS

EASTERN CONFERENCE

NORTHEAST DIVISION

	G	W	L	T	Pts.	GF	GA	Home	Away	Div. Rec.
Pittsburgh Penguins	84	44	27	13	101	299	285	25- 9- 8	19-18- 5	21- 9- 2
Boston Bruins	84	42	29	13	97	289	252	20-14- 8	22-15- 5	14-13- 4
Montreal Canadiens	84	41	29	14	96	283	248	26-12- 4	15-17-10	17-10- 4
Buffalo Sabres	84	43	32	9	95	282	218	22-17- 3	21-15- 6	19- 9- 3
Quebec Nordiques	84	34	42	8	76	277	292	19-17- 6	15-25- 2	13-15- 3
Hartford Whalers	84	27	48	9	63	227	288	14-22- 6	13-26- 3	9-18- 3
Ottawa Senators	84	14	61	9	37	201	397	8-30- 4	6-31- 5	4-23- 3

ATLANTIC DIVISION

	G	W	L	T	Pts.	GF	GA	Home	Away	Div. Rec.
New York Rangers	84	52	24	8	112	299	231	28- 8- 6	24-16- 2	21- 8- 3
New Jersey Devils	84	47	25	12	106	306	220	29-11- 2	18-14-10	17-11- 3
Washington Capitals	84	39	35	10	88	277	263	17-16- 9	22-19- 1	13-15- 4
New York Islanders	84	36	36	12	84	282	264	23-15- 4	13-21- 8	14-13- 3
Florida Panthers	84	33	34	17	83	233	233	15-18- 9	18-16- 8	13-11- 6
Philadelphia Flyers	84	35	39	10	80	294	314	19-20- 3	16-19- 7	11-16- 4
Tampa Bay Lightning	84	30	43	11	71	224	251	14-22- 6	16-21- 5	5-20- 5

WESTERN CONFERENCE

CENTRAL DIVISION

	G	W	L	T	Pts.	GF	GA	Home	Away	Div. Rec.
Detroit Red Wings	84	46	30	8	100	356	275	23-13- 6	23-17- 2	13-13- 4
Toronto Maple Leafs	84	43	29	12	98	280	243	23-15- 4	20-14- 8	18- 8- 4
Dallas Stars	84	42	29	13	97	286	265	23-12- 7	19-17- 6	12-13- 5
St. Louis Blues	84	40	33	11	91	270	283	23-11- 8	17-22- 3	12-13- 5
Chicago Blackhawks	84	39	36	9	87	254	240	21-16- 5	18-20- 4	14-15- 1
Winnipeg Jets	84	24	51	9	57	245	344	15-23- 4	9-28- 5	10-17- 3

PACIFIC DIVISION

	G	W	L	T	Pts.	GF	GA	Home	Away	Div. Rec.
Calgary Flames	84	42	29	13	97	302	256	25-12- 5	17-17- 8	20- 8- 4
Vancouver Canucks	84	41	40	3	85	279	276	20-19- 3	21-21- 0	17-14- 1
San Jose Sharks	84	33	35	16	82	252	265	19-13-10	14-22- 6	14-11- 5
Mighty Ducks of Anaheim	84	33	46	5	71	229	251	14-26- 2	19-20- 3	11-18- 1
Los Angeles Kings	84	27	45	12	66	294	322	18-19- 5	9-26- 7	12-14- 6
Edmonton Oilers	84	25	45	14	64	261	305	17-22- 3	8-23-11	9-18- 5

INDIVIDUAL LEADERS

SCORING

TOP SCORERS

	Games	G	A	Pts.	PIM	+/-	PPG	SHG	Shots	Shooting Pct.
Wayne Gretzky, Los Angeles	81	38	*92	*130	20	-25	14	4	233	16.3
Sergei Fedorov, Detroit	82	56	64	120	34	48	13	4	337	16.6
Adam Oates, Boston	77	32	80	112	45	10	16	2	197	16.2
Doug Gilmour, Toronto	83	27	84	111	105	25	10	1	167	16.2
Pavel Bure, Vancouver	76	*60	47	107	86	1	*25	4	374	16.0
Jeremy Roenick, Chicago	84	46	61	107	125	21	24	5	281	16.4
Mark Recchi, Philadelphia	84	40	67	107	46	-2	11	0	217	18.4
Brendan Shanahan, St. Louis	81	52	50	102	211	-9	15	*7	*397	13.1
Dave Andreychuk, Toronto	83	53	46	99	98	22	21	5	333	15.9
Jaromir Jagr, Pittsburgh	80	32	67	99	61	15	9	0	298	10.7
Brett Hull, St. Louis	81	57	40	97	38	-3	*25	3	392	14.5
Eric Lindros, Philadelphia	65	44	53	97	103	16	13	2	197	22.3
Rod Brind'Amour, Philadelphia	84	35	62	97	85	-9	14	1	230	15.2
Pierre Turgeon, N.Y. Islanders	69	38	56	94	18	14	10	4	254	15.0
Ray Sheppard, Detroit	82	52	41	93	26	13	19	0	260	20.0
Mike Modano, Dallas	76	50	43	93	54	-8	18	0	281	17.8
Robert Reichel, Calgary	84	40	53	93	58	20	14	0	249	16.1
Ron Francis, Pittsburgh	82	27	66	93	62	-3	8	0	216	12.5
Joe Sakic, Quebec	84	28	64	92	18	-8	10	1	279	10.0

	Games	G	A	Pts.	PIM	+/-	PPG	SHG	Shots	Shooting Pct.
Vincent Damphousse, Montreal	84	40	51	91	75	0	13	0	274	14.6
Ray Bourque, Boston	72	20	71	91	58	26	10	3	386	5.2

The scoring leader is awarded the Art Ross Memorial Trophy.
*Indicates league-leading figure.

Games

Bob Kudelski, Ott./Fla.	86
Glenn Anderson, Tor./NYR	85
Mark Lamb, Ott./Phi.	85
Joe Reekie, T.B./Was.	85
Many tied with	84

Points

Wayne Gretzky, Los Angeles	130
Sergei Fedorov, Detroit	120
Adam Oates, Boston	112
Doug Gilmour, Toronto	111
Pavel Bure, Vancouver	107
Mark Recchi, Philadelphia	107
Jeremy Roenick, Chicago	107
Brendan Shanahan, St. Louis	102
Dave Andreychuk, Toronto	99
Jaromir Jagr, Pittsburgh	99

Points by a defenseman

Ray Bourque, Boston	91
Sergei Zubov, N.Y. Rangers	89
Al MacInnis, Calgary	82
Brian Leetch, N.Y. Rangers	79
Scott Stevens, New Jersey	78

Goals

Pavel Bure, Vancouver	60
Brett Hull, St. Louis	57
Sergei Fedorov, Detroit	56
Dave Andreychuk, Toronto	53
Adam Graves, N.Y. Rangers	52
Brendan Shanahan, St. Louis	52
Ray Sheppard, Detroit	52
Mike Modano, Dallas	50
Cam Neely, Boston	50
Wendel Clark, Toronto	46
Jeremy Roenick, Chicago	46

Assists

Wayne Gretzky, Los Angeles	92
Doug Gilmour, Toronto	84
Adam Oates, Boston	80
Sergei Zubov, N.Y. Rangers	77
Ray Bourque, Boston	71
Craig Janney, St. Louis	68
Jaromir Jagr, Pittsburgh	67
Mark Recchi, Philadelphia	67
Ron Francis, Pittsburgh	66
Joe Juneau, Bos./Was.	66

Power-play goals

Pavel Bure, Vancouver	25
Brett Hull, St. Louis	25
Luc Robitaille, Los Angeles	24

Jeremy Roenick, Chicago	24
Keith Tkachuk, Winnipeg	22

Shorthanded goals

Brendan Shanahan, St. Louis	7
Dave Andreychuk, Toronto	5
Nelson Emerson, Winnipeg	5
Mike Gartner, NYR/Tor.	5
Benoit Hogue, N.Y. Islanders	5
Shawn McEachern, L.A./Pit.	5
Marty McInnis, N.Y. Islanders	5
Wayne Presley, Buffalo	5
Jeremy Roenick, Chicago	5

Game-winning goals

Cam Neely, Boston	13
Vincent Damphousse, Montreal	10
Sergei Fedorov, Detroit	10
Pavel Bure, Vancouver	9
Eric Lindros, Philadelphia	9
Joe Mullen, Pittsburgh	9
Stephane Richer, New Jersey	9
Joe Sakic, Quebec	9

Game-tying goals

Ray Ferraro, N.Y. Islanders	3
Gord Murphy, Florida	3
Stephane Richer, New Jersey	3
Mike Ridley, Washington	3
Many tied with	2

Shots

Brendan Shanahan, St. Louis	397
Brett Hull, St. Louis	392
Ray Bourque, Boston	386
Pavel Bure, Vancouver	374
Sergei Fedorov, Detroit	337

Shooting percentage (84 shots minimum)

Cam Neely, Boston	27.0
Martin Straka, Pittsburgh	23.1
Eric Lindros, Philadelphia	22.3
Mike Ricci, Quebec	21.7
Gary Roberts, Calgary	20.3

Plus/minus

Scott Stevens, New Jersey	53
Sergei Fedorov, Detroit	48
Nicklas Lidstrom, Detroit	43
Frank Musil, Calgary	38
Gary Roberts, Calgary	37

Penalty minutes

Tie Domi, Winnipeg	347
Shane Churla, Dallas	333
Warren Rychel, Los Angeles	322

Craig Berube, Washington	305
Kelly Chase, St. Louis	278
Lyle Odelein, Montreal	276
Bob Probert, Detroit	275
Rob Ray, Buffalo	274
Todd Ewen, Anaheim	272
Marc Potvin, L.A./Har.	272

Consecutive-game point streaks

Dave Andreychuk, Toronto	16
Rod Brind'Amour, Philadelphia	13
Dave Gagner, Dallas	13
Adam Oates, Boston	13
Pierre Turgeon, N.Y. Islanders	13

Consecutive-game goal streaks

Josef Beranek, Philadelphia	8
Pavel Bure, Vancouver	8
Dave Andreychuk, Toronto	7
Wendel Clark, Toronto	7
Eric Lindros, Philadelphia	7

Consecutive-game assist streaks

Garry Galley, Philadelphia	11
Steve Yzerman, Detroit	11
Darrin Shannon, Winnipeg	10
Steve Yzerman, Detroit	9

Most games scoring three or more goals

Brendan Shanahan, St. Louis	4
Pavel Bure, Vancouver	3
Brett Hull, St. Louis	3
Cam Neely, Boston	3
Many tied with	2

Points by a rookie

Mikael Renberg, Philadelphia	82
Alexei Yashin, Ottawa	79
Jason Arnott, Edmonton	68
Derek Plante, Buffalo	56
Alexandre Daigle, Ottawa	51
Bryan Smolinski, Boston	51

Goals by a rookie

Mikael Renberg, Philadelphia	38
Jason Arnott, Edmonton	33
Bryan Smolinski, Boston	31
Alexei Yashin, Ottawa	30
Derek Plante, Buffalo	21

Assists by a rookie

Alexei Yashin, Ottawa	49
Mikael Renberg, Philadelphia	44
Jason Arnott, Edmonton	35
Derek Plante, Buffalo	35
Jesse Belanger, Florida	33

GOALTENDING

Games

Arturs Irbe, San Jose	74
Curtis Joseph, St. Louis	71
Bill Ranford, Edmonton	71
Ed Belfour, Chicago	70
Bob Essensa, Win./Det.	69

Minutes

Arturs Irbe, San Jose	4412
Curtis Joseph, St. Louis	4127
Bill Ranford, Edmonton	4070
Ed Belfour, Chicago	3998
Bob Essensa, Win./Det.	3914

Goals allowed

Craig Billington, Ottawa	254
Bill Ranford, Edmonton	236
Bob Essensa, Win./Det.	235
Kelly Hrudey, Los Angeles	228
Curtis Joseph, St. Louis	213

Shutouts

Ed Belfour, Chicago.............................. 7
Dominik Hasek, Buffalo.......................7
Patrick Roy, Montreal 7
Ron Hextall, N.Y. Islanders 5
Mike Richter, N.Y. Rangers.................5

Lowest goals-against average
(27 games played minimum)

Dominik Hasek, Buffalo.................. 1.95
Martin Brodeur, New Jersey 2.40
Patrick Roy, Montreal 2.50
John Vanbiesbrouck, Florida..........2.53
Mike Richter, N.Y. Rangers.............2.57

Highest goals-against average
(27 games played minimum)

Craig Billington, Ottawa..................4.59
Darrin Madeley, Ottawa 4.36
Tommy Soderstrom, Philadelphia .. 4.01
Kelly Hrudey, Los Angeles 3.68
Grant Fuhr, Buffalo 3.68

Games won

Mike Richter, N.Y. Rangers.............42
Ed Belfour, Chicago 37
Curtis Joseph, St. Louis.................36
Patrick Roy, Montreal 35
Felix Potvin, Toronto......................34

Best winning percentage
(27 games played minimum)

Mike Richter, NYR (42-12-6) .... .750
Chris Osgood, Det. (23-8-5).........708
Martin Brodeur, N.J. (27-11-8) ... .674
Patrick Roy, Mon. (35-17-11)....643
Jon Casey, Bos. (30-15-9) 639

Worst winning percentage
(27 games played minimum)

Darrin Madeley, Ott. (3-18-5)...... .212
Craig Billington, Ott. (11-41-4) ... .232
Tommy Soderstrom, Phi. (6-18-4) . .286
Bob Essensa, Win./Det. (23-37-8) .397
Jocelyn Thibault, Que. (8-13-3) .. .399

Games lost

Craig Billington, Ottawa....................41
Bob Essensa, Win./Det....................37
Bill Ranford, Edmonton 34
Darren Puppa, Tampa Bay................33
Kelly Hrudey, Los Angeles 31

Shots against

Curtis Joseph, St. Louis 2382
Bill Ranford, Edmonton 2325
Kelly Hrudey, Los Angeles 2219
Arturs Irbe, San Jose....................2064
Felix Potvin, Toronto....................2010

Saves

Curtis Joseph, St. Louis 2169
Bill Ranford, Edmonton 2089
Kelly Hrudey, Los Angeles 1991
Arturs Irbe, San Jose....................1855
Felix Potvin, Toronto....................1823

Highest save percentage
(27 games played minimum)

Dominik Hasek, Buffalo.................. .930
John Vanbiesbrouck, Florida........ .924
Patrick Roy, Montreal 918
Martin Brodeur, New Jersey .... .915
Mark Fitzpatrick, Florida .... .914

Lowest save percentage
(27 games played minimum)

Craig Billington, Ottawa...................859
Tommy Soderstrom, Philadelphia.. .864
Kay Whitmore, Vancouver........... .867
Darrin Madeley, Ottawa .... .8675
Glenn Healy, N.Y. Rangers .... .8683

STATISTICS OF PLAYERS WITH TWO OR MORE TEAMS

SCORING

	Games	G	A	Pts.	PIM	+/-	PPG	SHG	Shots	Shooting Pct.
Keith Acton, Washington	6	0	0	0	21	-4	0	0	2	0.0
Keith Acton, N.Y. Islanders	71	2	7	9	50	-1	0	0	33	6.1
Totals	77	2	7	9	71	-5	0	0	35	5.7
Tony Amonte, N.Y. Rangers	72	16	22	38	31	5	3	0	179	8.9
Tony Amonte, Chicago	7	1	3	4	6	-5	1	0	16	6.3
Totals	79	17	25	42	37	0	4	0	195	8.7
Glenn Anderson, Toronto	73	17	18	35	50	-6	5	0	127	13.4
Glenn Anderson, N.Y. Rangers	12	4	2	6	12	1	2	0	22	18.2
Totals	85	21	20	41	62	-5	7	0	149	14.1
Peter Andersson, N.Y. Rangers	8	1	1	2	2	-3	0	1	10	10.0
Peter Andersson, Florida	8	1	1	2	0	-5	0	0	11	9.1
Totals	16	2	2	4	2	-8	0	1	21	9.5
Stu Barnes, Winnipeg	18	5	4	9	8	-1	2	0	24	20.8
Stu Barnes, Florida	59	18	20	38	30	5	6	1	148	12.2
Totals	77	23	24	47	38	4	8	1	172	13.4
Bob Bassen, St. Louis	46	2	7	9	44	-14	0	1	73	2.7
Bob Bassen, Quebec	37	11	8	19	55	-3	1	0	56	19.6
Totals	83	13	15	28	99	-17	1	1	129	10.1
Sergei Bautin, Winnipeg	59	0	7	7	78	-13	0	0	39	0.0
Sergei Bautin, Detroit	1	0	0	0	0	1	0	0	0	0.0
Totals	60	0	7	7	78	-12	0	0	39	0.0
Bob Beers, Tampa Bay	16	1	5	6	12	-11	1	0	35	2.9
Bob Beers, Edmonton	66	10	27	37	74	-11	5	0	152	6.6
Totals	82	11	32	43	86	-22	6	0	187	5.9
Tim Bergland, Tampa Bay	51	6	5	11	6	-14	0	0	61	9.8
Tim Bergland, Washington	3	0	0	0	4	-1	0	0	4	0.0
Totals	54	6	5	11	10	-15	0	0	65	9.2
James Black, Dallas	13	2	3	5	2	-4	2	0	16	12.5
James Black, Buffalo	2	0	0	0	0	0	0	0	2	0.0
Totals	15	2	3	5	2	-4	2	0	18	11.1
Claude Boivin, Philadelphia	26	1	1	2	57	-11	0	0	11	9.1
Claude Boivin, Ottawa	15	1	0	1	38	-6	0	0	6	16.7
Totals	41	2	1	3	95	-17	0	0	17	11.8
Phil Bourque, N.Y. Rangers	16	0	1	1	8	-2	0	0	2	0.0
Phil Bourque, Ottawa	11	2	3	5	0	-2	0	2	19	10.5
Totals	27	2	4	6	8	-4	0	2	21	9.5
Jeff Brown, St. Louis	63	13	47	60	46	-13	7	0	196	6.6
Jeff Brown, Vancouver	11	1	5	6	10	2	0	0	41	2.4
Totals	74	14	52	66	56	-11	7	0	237	5.9

	Games	G	A	Pts.	PIM	+/-	PPG	SHG	Shots	Shooting Pct.
Garth Butcher, St. Louis	43	1	6	7	76	-6	0	1	37	2.7
Garth Butcher, Quebec	34	3	9	12	67	-1	0	1	29	10.3
Totals	77	4	15	19	143	-7	0	2	66	6.1
Viacheslav Butsayev, Philadelphia	47	12	9	21	58	2	2	0	79	15.2
Viacheslav Butsayev, San Jose	12	0	2	2	10	-2	0	0	6	0.0
Totals	59	12	11	23	68	0	2	0	85	14.1
Keith Carney, Buffalo	7	1	3	4	4	-1	0	0	6	16.7
Keith Carney, Chicago	30	3	5	8	35	15	0	0	31	9.7
Totals	37	4	8	12	39	14	0	0	37	10.8
Jimmy Carson, Los Angeles	25	4	7	11	2	-2	1	0	47	8.5
Jimmy Carson, Vancouver	34	7	10	17	22	-13	2	0	82	8.5
Totals	59	11	17	28	24	-15	3	0	129	8.5
Frederic Chabot, Montreal	1	0	0	0	0	0	0	0	0	0.0
Frederic Chabot, Philadelphia	4	0	0	0	0	0	0	0	0	0.0
Totals	5	0	0	0	0	0	0	0	0	0.0
Tim Cheveldae, Detroit	30	0	1	1	0	0	0	0	0	0.0
Tim Cheveldae, Winnipeg	14	0	0	0	2	0	0	0	0	0.0
Totals	44	0	1	1	2	0	0	0	0	0.0
Enrico Ciccone, Washington	46	1	1	2	174	-2	0	0	23	4.3
Enrico Ciccone, Tampa Bay	11	0	1	1	52	-2	0	0	10	0.0
Totals	57	1	2	3	226	-4	0	0	33	3.0
Jim Cummins, Philadelphia	22	1	2	3	71	0	0	0	17	5.9
Jim Cummins, Tampa Bay	4	0	0	0	13	-1	0	0	3	0.0
Totals	26	1	2	3	84	-1	0	0	20	5.0
Randy Cunneyworth, Hartford	63	9	8	17	87	-2	0	1	121	7.4
Randy Cunneyworth, Chicago	16	4	3	7	13	1	0	0	33	12.1
Totals	79	13	11	24	100	-1	0	1	154	8.4
Ulf Dahlen, Dallas	65	19	38	57	10	-1	12	0	147	12.9
Ulf Dahlen, San Jose	13	6	6	12	0	0	3	0	43	14.0
Totals	78	25	44	69	10	-1	15	0	190	13.2
Jeff Daniels, Pittsburgh	63	3	5	8	20	-1	0	0	46	6.5
Jeff Daniels, Florida	7	0	0	0	0	0	0	0	6	0.0
Totals	70	3	5	8	20	-1	0	0	52	5.8
Evgeny Davydov, Florida	21	2	6	8	8	-3	1	0	22	9.1
Evgeny Davydov, Ottawa	40	5	7	12	38	-6	0	0	44	11.4
Totals	61	7	13	20	46	-9	1	0	66	10.6
Rob DiMaio, Tampa Bay	39	8	7	15	40	-5	2	0	51	15.7
Rob DiMaio, Philadelphia	14	3	5	8	6	1	0	0	30	10.0
Totals	53	11	12	23	46	-4	2	0	81	13.6
Robert Dirk, Vancouver	65	2	3	5	105	18	0	0	38	5.3
Robert Dirk, Chicago	6	0	0	0	26	0	0	0	4	0.0
Totals	71	2	3	5	131	18	0	0	42	4.8
Gord Donnelly, Buffalo	7	0	0	0	31	1	0	0	2	0.0
Gord Donnelly, Dallas	18	0	1	1	66	-4	0	0	5	0.0
Totals	25	0	1	1	97	-3	0	0	7	0.0
Dallas Drake, Detroit	47	10	22	32	37	5	0	1	78	12.8
Dallas Drake, Winnipeg	15	3	5	8	12	-6	1	1	34	8.8
Totals	62	13	27	40	49	-1	1	2	112	11.6
Ted Drury, Calgary	34	5	7	12	26	-5	0	1	43	11.6
Ted Drury, Hartford	16	1	5	6	10	-10	0	0	37	2.7
Totals	50	6	12	18	36	-15	0	1	80	7.5
Donald Dufresne, Tampa Bay	51	2	6	8	48	-2	0	0	49	4.1
Donald Dufresne, Los Angeles	9	0	0	0	10	-5	0	0	7	0.0
Totals	60	2	6	8	58	-7	0	0	56	3.6
Pelle Eklund, Philadelphia	48	1	16	17	8	-1	0	0	49	2.0
Pelle Eklund, Dallas	5	2	1	3	2	-1	0	0	4	50.0
Totals	53	3	17	20	10	-2	0	0	53	5.7
Todd Elik, Edmonton	4	0	0	0	6	0	0	0	5	0.0
Todd Elik, San Jose	75	25	41	66	89	-3	9	0	180	13.9
Totals	79	25	41	66	95	-3	9	0	185	13.5
Pat Elynuik, Washington	4	1	1	2	0	-3	1	0	8	12.5
Pat Elynuik, Tampa Bay	63	12	14	26	64	-18	3	1	103	11.7
Totals	67	13	15	28	64	-21	4	1	111	11.7
Bob Essensa, Winnipeg	56	0	0	0	6	0	0	0	0	0.0
Bob Essensa, Detroit	13	0	2	2	0	0	0	0	0	0.0
Totals	69	0	2	2	6	0	0	0	0	0.0
Mike Foligno, Toronto	4	0	0	0	4	0	0	0	3	0.0
Mike Foligno, Florida	39	4	5	9	49	7	0	0	32	12.5
Totals	43	4	5	9	53	7	0	0	35	11.4
Mike Gartner, N.Y. Rangers	71	28	24	52	58	11	10	5	245	11.4
Mike Gartner, Toronto	10	6	6	12	4	9	1	0	30	20.0
Totals	81	34	30	64	62	20	11	5	275	12.4
Martin Gelinas, Quebec	31	6	6	12	8	-2	0	0	53	11.3
Martin Gelinas, Vancouver	33	8	8	16	26	-6	3	0	54	14.8
Totals	64	14	14	28	34	-8	3	0	107	13.1

	Games	G	A	Pts.	PIM	+/-	PPG	SHG	Shots	Shooting Pct.
Randy Gilhen, Florida	20	4	4	8	16	1	0	0	52	7.7
Randy Gilhen, Winnipeg	40	3	3	6	34	-13	0	0	43	7.0
Totals	60	7	7	14	50	-12	0	0	95	7.4
Brian Glynn, Ottawa	48	2	13	15	41	-15	1	0	66	3.0
Brian Glynn, Vancouver	16	0	0	0	12	-4	0	0	5	0.0
Totals	64	2	13	15	53	-19	1	0	71	2.8
Alexander Godynyuk, Florida	26	0	10	10	35	5	0	0	43	0.0
Alexander Godynyuk, Hartford	43	3	9	12	40	8	0	0	67	4.5
Totals	69	3	19	22	75	13	0	0	110	2.7
Mark Greig, Hartford	31	4	5	9	31	-6	0	0	41	9.8
Mark Greig, Toronto	13	2	2	4	10	1	0	0	14	14.3
Totals	44	6	7	13	41	-5	0	0	55	10.9
Brent Grieve, N.Y. Islanders	3	0	0	0	7	0	0	0	1	0.0
Brent Grieve, Edmonton	24	13	5	18	14	4	4	0	53	24.5
Totals	27	13	5	18	21	4	4	0	54	24.1
Greg Hawgood, Philadelphia	19	3	12	15	19	2	3	0	37	8.1
Greg Hawgood, Florida	33	2	14	16	9	8	0	0	55	3.6
Greg Hawgood, Pittsburgh	12	1	2	3	8	-1	1	0	20	5.0
Totals	64	6	28	34	36	9	4	0	112	5.4
Bret Hedican, St. Louis	61	0	11	11	64	-8	0	0	78	0.0
Bret Hedican, Vancouver	8	0	1	1	0	1	0	0	10	0.0
Totals	69	0	12	12	64	-7	0	0	88	0.0
Doug Houda, Hartford	7	0	0	0	23	-4	0	0	1	0.0
Doug Houda, Los Angeles	54	2	6	8	165	-15	0	0	31	6.5
Totals	61	2	6	8	188	-19	0	0	32	6.3
Kerry Huffman, Quebec	28	0	6	6	28	2	0	0	44	0.0
Kerry Huffman, Ottawa	34	4	8	12	12	-30	2	1	68	5.9
Totals	62	4	14	18	40	-28	2	1	112	3.6
Al Iafrate, Washington	67	10	35	45	143	10	4	0	252	4.0
Al Iafrate, Boston	12	5	8	13	20	6	2	0	47	10.6
Totals	79	15	43	58	163	16	6	0	299	5.0
Jim Johnson, Dallas	53	0	7	7	51	-6	0	0	44	0.0
Jim Johnson, Washington	8	0	0	0	12	-1	0	0	5	0.0
Totals	61	0	7	7	63	-7	0	0	49	0.0
Chris Joseph, Edmonton	10	1	1	2	28	-8	1	0	25	4.0
Chris Joseph, Tampa Bay	66	10	19	29	108	-13	7	0	154	6.5
Totals	76	11	20	31	136	-21	8	0	179	6.1
Joe Juneau, Boston	63	14	58	72	35	11	4	0	142	9.9
Joe Juneau, Washington	11	5	8	13	6	0	2	0	22	22.7
Totals	74	19	66	85	41	11	6	0	164	11.6
Yan Kaminsky, Winnipeg	1	0	0	0	0	1	0	0	0	0.0
Yan Kaminsky, N.Y. Islanders	23	2	1	3	4	4	0	0	23	8.7
Totals	24	2	1	3	4	5	0	0	23	8.7
Alexei Kasatonov, Anaheim	55	4	18	22	43	-8	1	0	81	4.9
Alexei Kasatonov, St. Louis	8	0	2	2	19	5	0	0	6	0.0
Totals	63	4	20	24	62	-3	1	0	87	4.6
Dan Keczmer, Hartford	12	0	1	1	12	-6	0	0	12	0.0
Dan Keczmer, Calgary	57	1	20	21	48	-2	0	0	104	1.0
Totals	69	1	21	22	60	-8	0	0	116	0.9
Steve Konroyd, Detroit	19	0	0	0	10	1	0	0	12	0.0
Steve Konroyd, Ottawa	8	0	2	2	2	-4	0	0	9	0.0
Totals	27	0	2	2	12	-3	0	0	21	0.0
Frantisek Kucera, Chicago	60	4	13	17	34	9	2	0	90	4.4
Frantisek Kucera, Hartford	16	1	3	4	14	-12	1	0	32	3.1
Totals	76	5	16	21	48	-3	3	0	122	4.1
Bob Kudelski, Ottawa	42	26	15	41	14	-25	12	0	127	20.5
Bob Kudelski, Florida	44	14	15	29	10	-8	5	0	124	11.3
Totals	†86	40	30	70	24	-33	17	0	251	15.9
Nick Kypreos, Hartford	10	0	0	0	37	-8	0	0	5	0.0
Nick Kypreos, N.Y. Rangers	46	3	5	8	102	-8	0	0	29	10.3
Totals	56	3	5	8	139	-16	0	0	34	8.8
Nathan Lafayette, St. Louis	38	2	3	5	14	-9	0	0	23	8.7
Nathan Lafayette, Vancouver	11	1	1	2	4	2	0	0	11	9.1
Totals	49	3	4	7	18	-7	0	0	34	8.8
Mike Lalor, San Jose	23	0	2	2	8	-5	0	0	19	0.0
Mike Lalor, Dallas	12	0	1	1	6	-5	0	0	3	0.0
Totals	35	0	3	3	14	-10	0	0	22	0.0
Mark Lamb, Ottawa	66	11	18	29	56	-41	4	1	105	10.5
Mark Lamb, Philadelphia	19	1	6	7	16	-3	0	0	19	5.3
Totals	85	12	24	36	72	-44	4	1	124	9.7
Guy Larose, Toronto	10	1	2	3	10	-2	0	0	9	11.1
Guy Larose, Calgary	7	0	1	1	4	-3	0	0	3	0.0
Totals	17	1	3	4	14	-5	0	0	12	8.3

	Games	G	A	Pts.	PIM	+/-	PPG	SHG	Shots	Shooting Pct.
Stephan Lebeau, Montreal	34	9	7	16	8	1	4	0	61	14.8
Stephan Lebeau, Anaheim	22	6	4	10	14	-5	2	0	37	16.2
Totals	56	15	11	26	22	-4	6	0	98	15.3
Jocelyn Lemieux, Chicago	66	12	8	20	63	5	0	0	129	9.3
Jocelyn Lemieux, Hartford	16	6	1	7	19	-8	0	0	22	27.3
Totals	82	18	9	27	82	-3	0	0	151	11.9
Scott Levins, Florida	29	5	6	11	69	0	2	0	38	13.2
Scott Levins, Ottawa	33	3	5	8	93	-26	2	0	39	7.7
Totals	62	8	11	19	162	-26	4	0	77	10.4
Craig MacTavish, Edmonton	66	16	10	26	80	-20	0	0	97	16.5
Craig MacTavish, N.Y. Rangers	12	4	2	6	11	6	1	0	25	16.0
Totals	78	20	12	32	91	-14	1	0	122	16.4
David Maley, San Jose	19	0	0	0	30	-1	0	0	4	0.0
David Maley, N.Y. Islanders	37	0	6	6	74	-6	0	0	19	0.0
Totals	56	0	6	6	104	-7	0	0	23	0.0
Dave Manson, Edmonton	57	3	13	16	140	-4	0	0	144	2.1
Dave Manson, Winnipeg	13	1	4	5	51	-10	1	0	36	2.8
Totals	70	4	17	21	191	-14	1	0	180	2.2
Todd Marchant, N.Y. Rangers	1	0	0	0	0	-1	0	0	1	0.0
Todd Marchant, Edmonton	3	0	1	1	2	-1	0	0	5	0.0
Totals	4	0	1	1	2	-2	0	0	6	0.0
Bryan Marchment, Chicago	13	1	4	5	42	-2	0	0	18	5.6
Bryan Marchment, Hartford	42	3	7	10	124	-12	0	1	74	4.1
Totals	55	4	11	15	166	-14	0	1	92	4.3
Stephane Matteau, Chicago	65	15	16	31	55	10	2	0	113	13.3
Stephane Matteau, N.Y. Rangers	12	4	3	7	2	5	1	0	22	18.2
Totals	77	19	19	38	57	15	3	0	135	14.1
Alan May, Washington	43	4	7	11	97	-2	0	0	33	12.1
Alan May, Dallas	8	1	0	1	18	-1	0	0	7	14.3
Totals	51	5	7	12	115	-3	0	0	40	12.5
Wayne McBean, N.Y. Islanders	19	1	4	5	16	-13	0	0	33	3.0
Wayne McBean, Winnipeg	31	2	9	11	24	-21	2	0	81	2.5
Totals	50	3	13	16	40	-34	2	0	114	2.6
Shawn McEachern, Los Angeles	49	8	13	21	24	1	0	3	81	9.9
Shawn McEachern, Pittsburgh	27	12	9	21	10	13	0	2	78	15.4
Totals	76	20	22	42	34	14	0	5	159	12.6
Bob McGill, N.Y. Islanders	3	0	0	0	5	0	0	0	0	0.0
Bob McGill, Hartford	30	0	3	3	41	-7	0	0	14	0.0
Totals	33	0	3	3	46	-7	0	0	14	0.0
Jim McKenzie, Hartford	26	1	2	3	67	-6	0	0	9	11.1
Jim McKenzie, Dallas	34	2	3	5	63	4	0	0	18	11.1
Jim McKenzie, Pittsburgh	11	0	0	0	16	-5	0	0	6	0.0
Totals	71	3	5	8	146	-7	0	0	33	9.1
Marty McSorley, Pittsburgh	47	3	18	21	139	-9	0	0	122	2.5
Marty McSorley, Los Angeles	18	4	6	10	55	-3	1	0	38	10.5
Totals	65	7	24	31	194	-12	1	0	160	4.4
Boris Mironov, Winnipeg	65	7	22	29	96	-29	5	0	122	5.7
Boris Mironov, Edmonton	14	0	2	2	14	-4	0	0	23	0.0
Totals	79	7	24	31	110	-33	5	0	145	4.8
Craig Muni, Chicago	9	0	4	4	4	3	0	0	6	0.0
Craig Muni, Buffalo	73	2	8	10	62	28	0	1	39	5.1
Totals	82	2	12	14	66	31	0	1	45	4.4
Troy Murray, Chicago	12	0	1	1	6	1	0	0	7	0.0
Troy Murray, Ottawa	15	2	3	5	4	1	0	1	14	14.3
Totals	27	2	4	6	10	2	0	1	21	9.5
Mike Needham, Pittsburgh	25	1	0	1	2	0	0	0	6	16.7
Mike Needham, Dallas	5	0	0	0	0	-2	0	0	3	0.0
Totals	30	1	0	1	2	-2	0	0	9	11.1
Brian Noonan, Chicago	64	14	21	35	57	2	8	0	134	10.4
Brian Noonan, N.Y. Rangers	12	4	2	6	12	5	2	0	26	15.4
Totals	76	18	23	41	69	7	10	0	160	11.3
Michael Nylander, Hartford	58	11	33	44	24	-2	4	0	74	14.9
Michael Nylander, Calgary	15	2	9	11	6	10	0	0	21	9.5
Totals	73	13	42	55	30	8	4	0	95	13.7
Fredrik Olausson, Winnipeg	18	2	5	7	10	-3	1	0	41	4.9
Fredrik Olausson, Edmonton	55	9	19	28	20	-4	6	0	85	10.6
Totals	73	11	24	35	30	-7	7	0	126	8.7
Jim Paek, Pittsburgh	41	0	4	4	8	-7	0	0	24	0.0
Jim Paek, Los Angeles	18	1	1	2	10	-1	0	0	11	9.1
Totals	59	1	5	6	18	-8	0	0	35	2.9
James Patrick, N.Y. Rangers	6	0	3	3	2	-1	0	0	6	0.0
James Patrick, Hartford	47	8	20	28	32	-12	4	1	65	12.3
James Patrick, Calgary	15	2	2	4	6	6	1	0	20	10.0
Totals	68	10	25	35	40	-5	5	1	91	11.0

	Games	G	A	Pts.	PIM	+/-	PPG	SHG	Shots	Shooting Pct.
Marc Potvin, Los Angeles	3	0	0	0	26	-3	0	0	1	0.0
Marc Potvin, Hartford	51	2	3	5	246	-5	0	0	25	8.0
Totals	54	2	3	5	272	-8	0	0	26	7.7
Patrick Poulin, Hartford	9	2	1	3	11	-8	1	0	13	15.4
Patrick Poulin, Chicago	58	12	13	25	40	0	1	0	83	14.5
Totals	67	14	14	28	51	-8	2	0	96	14.6
Rob Ramage, Montreal	6	0	1	1	2	-1	0	0	5	0.0
Rob Ramage, Philadelphia	15	0	1	1	14	-11	0	0	18	0.0
Totals	21	0	2	2	16	-12	0	0	23	0.0
Paul Ranheim, Calgary	67	10	14	24	20	-7	0	2	110	9.1
Paul Ranheim, Hartford	15	0	3	3	2	-11	0	0	21	0.0
Totals	82	10	17	27	22	-18	0	2	131	7.6
Joe Reekie, Tampa Bay	73	1	11	12	127	8	0	0	88	1.1
Joe Reekie, Washington	12	0	5	5	29	7	0	0	10	0.0
Totals	85	1	16	17	156	15	0	0	98	1.0
Jeff Reese, Calgary	1	0	0	0	0	0	0	0	0	0.0
Jeff Reese, Hartford	19	0	1	1	0	0	0	0	0	0.0
Totals	20	0	1	1	0	0	0	0	0	0.0
Vincent Riendeau, Detroit	8	0	0	0	0	0	0	0	0	0.0
Vincent Riendeau, Boston	18	0	1	1	0	0	0	0	0	0.0
Totals	26	0	1	1	0	0	0	0	0	0.0
Tomas Sandstrom, Los Angeles	51	17	24	41	59	-12	4	0	121	14.0
Tomas Sandstrom, Pittsburgh	27	6	11	17	24	5	0	0	72	8.3
Totals	78	23	35	58	83	-7	4	0	193	11.9
Tommy Sjodin, Dallas	7	0	2	2	4	-1	0	0	8	0.0
Tommy Sjodin, Quebec	22	1	9	10	18	5	1	0	46	2.2
Totals	29	1	11	12	22	4	1	0	54	1.9
Geoff Smith, Edmonton	21	0	3	3	12	-10	0	0	23	0.0
Geoff Smith, Florida	56	1	5	6	38	-3	0	0	44	2.3
Totals	77	1	8	9	50	-13	0	0	67	1.5
Greg Smyth, Florida	12	1	0	1	37	0	0	0	4	25.0
Greg Smyth, Toronto	11	0	1	1	38	-2	0	0	3	0.0
Greg Smyth, Chicago	38	0	0	0	108	-2	0	0	29	0.0
Totals	61	1	1	2	183	-4	0	0	36	2.8
Mike Stapleton, Pittsburgh	58	7	4	11	18	-4	3	0	59	11.9
Mike Stapleton, Edmonton	23	5	9	14	28	-1	1	0	43	11.6
Totals	81	12	13	25	46	-5	4	0	102	11.8
Mike Sullivan, San Jose	26	2	2	4	4	-3	0	2	21	9.5
Mike Sullivan, Calgary	19	2	3	5	6	2	0	0	27	7.4
Totals	45	4	5	9	10	-1	0	2	48	8.3
Gary Suter, Calgary	25	4	9	13	20	-3	2	1	51	7.8
Gary Suter, Chicago	16	2	3	5	18	-9	2	0	35	5.7
Totals	41	6	12	18	38	-12	4	1	86	7.0
Ron Sutter, St. Louis	36	6	12	18	46	-1	1	0	42	14.3
Ron Sutter, Quebec	37	9	13	22	44	3	4	0	66	13.6
Totals	73	15	25	40	90	2	5	0	108	13.9
Kevin Todd, Chicago	35	5	6	11	16	-2	1	0	49	10.2
Kevin Todd, Los Angeles	12	3	8	11	8	-1	3	0	16	18.8
Totals	47	8	14	22	24	-3	4	0	65	12.3
Ron Tugnutt, Anaheim	28	0	0	0	2	0	0	0	0	0.0
Ron Tugnutt, Montreal	8	0	0	0	0	0	0	0	0	0.0
Totals	36	0	0	0	2	0	0	0	0	0.0
Darren Turcotte, N.Y. Rangers	13	2	4	6	13	-2	0	0	17	11.8
Darren Turcotte, Hartford	19	2	11	13	4	-11	0	0	43	4.7
Totals	32	4	15	19	17	-13	0	0	60	6.7
Dixon Ward, Vancouver	33	6	1	7	37	-14	2	0	46	13.0
Dixon Ward, Los Angeles	34	6	2	8	45	-8	2	0	44	13.6
Totals	67	12	3	15	82	-22	4	0	90	13.3
Eric Weinrich, Hartford	8	1	1	2	2	-5	1	0	10	10.0
Eric Weinrich, Chicago	54	3	23	26	31	6	1	0	105	2.9
Totals	62	4	24	28	33	1	2	0	115	3.5
Brad Werenka, Edmonton	15	0	4	4	14	-1	0	0	11	0.0
Brad Werenka, Quebec	11	0	7	7	8	4	0	0	17	0.0
Totals	26	0	11	11	22	3	0	0	28	0.0
Paul Ysebaert, Winnipeg	60	9	18	27	18	-8	1	0	120	7.5
Paul Ysebaert, Chicago	11	5	3	8	8	1	2	0	31	16.1
Totals	71	14	21	35	26	-7	3	0	151	9.3
Zarley Zalapski, Hartford	56	7	30	37	56	-6	0	0	121	5.8
Zarley Zalapski, Calgary	13	3	7	10	18	0	1	0	35	8.6
Totals	69	10	37	47	74	-6	1	0	156	6.4
Rob Zettler, San Jose	42	0	3	3	65	-7	0	0	28	0.0
Rob Zettler, Philadelphia	33	0	4	4	69	-19	0	0	27	0.0
Totals	75	0	7	7	134	-26	0	0	55	0.0
Doug Zmolek, San Jose	68	0	4	4	122	-9	0	0	29	0.0
Doug Zmolek, Dallas	7	1	0	1	11	1	0	0	3	33.3
Totals	75	1	4	5	133	-8	0	0	32	3.1

GOALTENDING

	Games	Min.	Goals	SO	Avg.	W	L	T	Shots	Sv. Pct.
Frederic Chabot, Montreal	1	60	5	0	5.00	0	1	0	24	.792
Frederic Chabot, Philadelphia	4	70	5	0	4.29	0	1	1	40	.875
Totals	5	130	10	0	4.62	0	2	1	64	.844
Tim Cheveldae, Detroit	30	1572	91	1	3.47	16	9	1	727	.875
Tim Cheveldae, Winnipeg	14	788	52	1	3.96	5	8	1	485	.893
Totals	44	2360	143	2	3.64	21	17	2	1212	.882
Bob Essensa, Winnipeg	56	3136	201	1	3.85	19	30	6	1714	.883
Bob Essensa, Detroit	13	778	34	1	2.62	4	7	2	337	.899
Totals	69	3914	235	2	3.60	23	37	8	2051	.885
Jeff Reese, Calgary	1	13	1	0	4.62	0	0	0	5	.800
Jeff Reese, Hartford	19	1086	56	1	3.09	5	9	3	524	.893
Totals	20	1099	57	1	3.11	5	9	0	529	.892
Vincent Riendeau, Detroit	8	345	23	0	4.00	2	4	0	131	.824
Vincent Riendeau, Boston	18	976	50	1	3.07	7	6	1	415	.880
Totals	26	1321	73	1	3.32	9	10	1	546	.866
Ron Tugnutt, Anaheim	28	1520	76	1	3.00	10	15	1	828	.908
Ron Tugnutt, Montreal	8	378	24	0	3.81	2	3	1	172	.860
Totals	36	1898	100	1	3.16	12	18	2	1000	.900

†Led league.

MISCELLANEOUS

HAT TRICKS

(Players scoring three or more goals in a game)

Date	Player, Team	Opp.	Goals
10- 6-93	Teemu Selanne, Winnipeg	Was.	3
10- 7-93	Brendan Shanahan, St. Louis	Fla.	3
10- 9-93	Dominic Lavoie, Los Angeles	Det.	3
10- 9-93	Adam Oates, Boston	Que.	3
10-14-93	Pat Verbeek, Hartford	Chi.	3
10-15-93	Doug Gilmour, Toronto	Det.	3
10-16-93	Alexander Semak, New Jersey	NYI	3
10-18-93	Shawn Burr, Detroit	Buf.	3
10-19-93	Terry Yake, Anaheim	NYR	3
10-21-93	Kevin Miller, St. Louis	S.J.	3
10-22-93	Randy Burridge, Washington	L.A.	3
10-23-93	Keith Tkachuk, Winnipeg	Phi.	3
10-23-93	Sylvain Turgeon, Ottawa	NYI	3
10-23-93	Derek King, N.Y. Islanders	Ott.	3
10-30-93	Vincent Damphousse, Montreal	Tor.	3
10-31-93	Kevin Dineen, Philadelphia	Chi.	4
11- 3-93	Alexei Yashin, Ottawa	Edm.	3
11- 3-93	Joel Otto, Calgary	Har.	3
11- 4-93	Cam Neely, Boston	Cal.	3
11- 5-93	Bob Kudelski, Ottawa	Win.	3
11- 9-93	Alexei Zhamnov, Winnipeg	NYI	3
11-13-93	Mike Donnelly, Los Angeles	St.L.	3
11-15-93	Shayne Corson, Edmonton	Tor.	3
11-17-93	Pierre Turgeon, N.Y. Islanders	Ott.	3
11-19-93	Alexander Mogilny, Buffalo	Win.	3
11-24-93	Kevin Dineen, Philadelphia	Mon.	3
11-25-93	Luc Robitaille, Los Angeles	Que.	4
11-27-93	Steve Thomas, N.Y. Islanders	NYR	3
11-30-93	Alexei Zhamnov, Winnipeg	L.A.	3
11-30-93	Travis Green, N.Y. Islanders	Was.	3
12- 1-93	Dave Andreychuk, Toronto	St.L.	3
12- 1-93	Derek Plante, Buffalo	T.B.	3
12- 2-93	Viacheslav Butsayev, Philadelphia	Van.	3
12- 6-93	Gary Roberts, Calgary	Ott.	3
12- 7-93	Pat Verbeek, Hartford	Was.	3
12-14-93	Joe Nieuwendyk, Calgary	Van.	3
12-15-93	Glen Wesley, Boston	N.J.	3
12-18-93	Oleg Petrov, Montreal	Det.	3
12-19-93	Scott Young, Quebec	S.J.	3
12-19-93	Brett Hull, St. Louis	Edm.	3
12-23-93	Teemu Selanne, Winnipeg	Que.	3
12-26-93	Brendan Shanahan, St. Louis	Chi.	3
12-27-93	Guy Carbonneau, Montreal	St.L.	3
1- 1-94	Bernie Nicholls, New Jersey	Ott.	3
1- 2-94	Cam Neely, Boston	Was.	3

Date	Player, Team	Opp.	Goals
1- 2-94	Jocelyn Lemieux, Chicago	Win.	3
1- 6-94	Ray Sheppard, Detroit	S.J.	3
1- 6-94	Vyacheslav Kozlov, Detroit	S.J.	3
1-11-94	Kevin Stevens, Pittsburgh	Bos.	3
1-15-94	Igor Larionov, San Jose	Har.	3
1-15-94	Robert Reichel, Calgary	Ott.	3
1-19-94	Eric Lindros, Philadelphia	St.L.	3
1-24-94	Pavel Bure, Vancouver	Edm.	3
1-29-94	Ray Sheppard, Detroit	Win.	3
1-31-94	Mark Gartner, N.Y. Rangers	Pit.	3
2- 1-94	Patrick Flatley, N.Y. Islanders	S.J.	3
2- 1-94	Brett Hull, St. Louis	Tor.	3
2- 2-94	Adam Graves, N.Y. Rangers	NYI	3
2- 4-94	Vincent Damphousse, Montreal	Was.	3
2- 5-94	Peter Bondra, Washington	T.B.	5
2- 6-94	Rob Gaudreau, San Jose	Dal.	3
2- 8-94	Adam Oates, Boston	Que.	3
2-12-94	Cam Neely, Boston	N.J.	3
2-15-94	Mikael Renberg, Philadelphia	S.J.	3
2-17-94	Mike Ricci, Quebec	S.J.	5
2-21-94	Mike Modano, Dallas	S.J.	3
2-24-94	Jeremy Roenick, Chicago	Win.	4
2-25-94	Brent Grieve, Edmonton	L.A.	3
2-26-94	Brendan Shanahan, St. Louis	Ott.	3
2-28-94	Wendel Clark, Toronto	Ott.	3
3- 1-94	Sergei Fedorov, Detroit	Cal.	3
3- 4-94	Wendel Clark, Toronto	Det.	3
3- 7-94	Steve Duchesne, St. Louis	Tor.	3
3- 8-94	Martin Straka, Pittsburgh	Bos.	3
3- 9-94	Lyle Odelein, Montreal	St.L.	3
3- 9-94	Pierre Turgeon, N.Y. Islanders	Van.	3
3-11-94	Pavel Bure, Vancouver	Win.	3
3-15-94	Randy Burridge, Washington	Pit.	3
3-15-94	Gary Roberts, Calgary	T.B.	4
3-20-94	Robert Reichel, Calgary	Tor.	3
3-25-94	Brett Hull, St. Louis	Dal.	3
3-25-94	Igor Larionov, San Jose	Win.	3
3-27-94	Pavel Bure, Vancouver	L.A.	3
3-29-94	Sergei Makarov, San Jose	Win.	3
3-31-94	Theoren Fleury, Calgary	Phi.	3
4- 2-94	Ulf Dahlen, San Jose	Van.	3
4- 5-94	Dino Ciccarelli, Detroit	Van.	4
4- 9-94	Todd Krygier, Washington	Ott.	3
4-12-94	Dave Gagner, Dallas	St.L.	4
4-12-94	Brendan Shanahan, St. Louis	Dal.	3
4-13-94	John Druce, Los Angeles	Cal.	3

OVERTIME GOALS

Date	Player, Team	Opponent	Time	Final score
10- 7-93	Joe Mullen, Pittsburgh	Montreal	1:13	Pittsburgh 2, Montreal 1
10-10-93	Dirk Graham, Chicago	Winnipeg	4:50	Chicago 4, Winnipeg 3
10-10-93	Pierre Turgeon, N.Y. Islanders	Anaheim	2:43	N.Y. Islanders 4, Anaheim 3
10-16-93	Nelson Emerson, Winnipeg	Chicago	0:41	Winnipeg 1, Chicago 0
10-21-93	Brent Gilchrist, Dallas	Ottawa	1:56	Dallas 6, Ottawa 5
10-21-93	Rob Pearson, Toronto	Florida	2:17	Toronto 4, Florida 3
10-24-93	Kelly Miller, Washington	Edmonton	1:39	Washington 3, Edmonton 2
10-24-93	Geoff Courtnall, Vancouver	San Jose	0:28	Vancouver 3, San Jose 2
10-25-93	Ted Drury, Calgary	Washington	2:57	Calgary 3, Washington 2
10-29-93	Rob Blake, Los Angeles	Winnipeg	3:07	Los Angeles 4, Winnipeg 3
10-30-93	Dave Lowry, Florida	Tampa Bay	4:56	Florida 2, Tampa Bay 1
10-30-93	David Archibald, Ottawa	Dallas	4:40	Ottawa 5, Dallas 4
10-31-93	Tom Pederson, San Jose	Anaheim	1:47	San Jose 2, Anaheim 1
11- 5-93	Bob Kudelski, Ottawa	Winnipeg	1:33	Ottawa 7, Winnipeg 6
11- 6-93	Ron Sutter, St. Louis	Edmonton	0:15	St. Louis 6, Edmonton 5
11-10-93	Brian Propp, Hartford	Ottawa	0:20	Hartford 4, Ottawa 3
11-13-93	Dave McIlwain, Ottawa	Montreal	3:22	Ottawa 3, Montreal 2
11-20-93	Vyacheslav Kozlov, Detroit	New Jersey	0:29	Detroit 4, New Jersey 3
11-21-93	Pierre Turgeon, N.Y. Islanders	Philadelphia	0:24	N.Y. Islanders 5, Philadelphia 4
11-23-93	Robert Kron, Hartford	Florida	3:55	Hartford 2, Florida 1
11-24-93	Sergei Fedorov, Detroit	Vancouver	1:18	Detroit 5, Vancouver 4
11-27-93	Kevin Dineen, Philadelphia	Tampa Bay	0:34	Philadelphia 4, Tampa Bay 3
11-29-93	Dave Gagner, Dallas	Edmonton	2:26	Dallas 6, Edmonton 5
11-29-93	Dixon Ward, Vancouver	Chicago	0:15	Vancouver 2, Chicago 1
12- 2-93	Jesse Belanger, Florida	Buffalo	0:23	Florida 2, Buffalo 1
12- 4-93	Jaromir Jagr, Pittsburgh	Hartford	2:04	Pittsburgh 7, Hartford 6
12- 6-93	Gilbert Dionne, Montreal	Vancouver	3:21	Montreal 4, Vancouver 3
12- 9-93	Cliff Ronning, Vancouver	Boston	0:37	Vancouver 3, Boston 2
12-12-93	Jarrod Skalde, Anaheim	St. Louis	2:56	Anaheim 2, St. Louis 1
12-18-93	Ronnie Stern, Calgary	Winnipeg	2:32	Calgary 5, Winnipeg 4
12-19-93	Joe Juneau, Boston	Florida	1:55	Boston 2, Florida 1
12-20-93	Warren Rychel, Los Angeles	Calgary	4:59	Los Angeles 5, Calgary 4
12-22-93	Dean Evason, Dallas	Anaheim	3:20	Dallas 3, Anaheim 2
12-26-93	Geoff Sanderson, Hartford	Ottawa	4:10	Hartford 3, Ottawa 2
12-26-93	Benoit Hogue, N.Y. Islanders	Buffalo	2:28	N.Y. Islanders 4, Buffalo 3
1- 2-94	Craig Janney, St. Louis	Calgary	3:52	St. Louis 4, Calgary 3
1- 4-94	Dirk Graham, Chicago	Dallas	3:46	Chicago 2, Dallas 1
1- 7-94	Ron Francis, Pittsburgh	Buffalo	4:54	Pittsburgh 4, Buffalo 3
1-11-94	Kevin Stevens, Pittsburgh	Boston	4:09	Pittsburgh 5, Boston 4
1-13-94	Glenn Anderson, Toronto	Dallas	4:46	Toronto 4, Dallas 3
1-16-94	Mikael Andersson, Tampa Bay	Winnipeg	0:09	Tampa Bay 3, Winnipeg 2
1-18-94	Sylvain Turgeon, Ottawa	Edmonton	1:23	Ottawa 4, Edmonton 3
1-19-94	Chris Gratton, Tampa Bay	N.Y. Islanders	4:20	Tampa Bay 4, N.Y. Islanders 3
1-24-94	Pavel Bure, Vancouver	Edmonton	0:54	Vancouver 5, Edmonton 4
1-24-94	Kevin Miller, St. Louis	Anaheim	1:10	St. Louis 3, Anaheim 2
1-27-94	Ray Sheppard, Detroit	Chicago	0:51	Detroit 4, Chicago 3
1-27-94	Dave Gagner, Dallas	Vancouver	3:36	Dallas 3, Vancouver 2
1-27-94	Mark Messier, N.Y. Rangers	Los Angeles	4:58	N.Y. Rangers 5, Los Angeles 4
1-30-94	Guy Carbonneau, Montreal	Philadelphia	2:29	Montreal 5, Philadelphia 4
2- 3-94	Sergei Makarov, San Jose	Philadelphia	3:13	San Jose 4, Philadelphia 3
2- 5-94	Al MacInnis, Calgary	Los Angeles	4:22	Calgary 5, Los Angeles 4
2- 9-94	Eric Desjardins, Montreal	N.Y. Rangers	1:27	Montreal 4, N.Y. Rangers 3
2-10-94	Eric Lindros, Philadelphia	Florida	0:50	Philadelphia 4, Florida 3
2-12-94	Mike Gartner, N.Y. Rangers	Ottawa	2:37	N.Y. Rangers 4, Ottawa 3
2-12-94	Darren McCarty, Detroit	St. Louis	3:16	Detroit 5, St. Louis 4
2-14-94	Glen Murray, Boston	Los Angeles	4:03	Boston 3, Los Angeles 2
2-15-94	Wendel Clark, Toronto	Detroit	2:55	Toronto 5, Detroit 4
2-20-94	Sergei Fedorov, Detroit	Florida	4:26	Detroit 4, Florida 3
2-21-94	Tony Amonte, N.Y. Rangers	Pittsburgh	0:08	N.Y. Rangers 4, Pittsburgh 3
2-24-94	Rod Brind'Amour, Philadelphia	N.Y. Islanders	1:25	Philadelphia 5, N.Y. Islanders 4
3- 3-94	John MacLean, New Jersey	Tampa Bay	3:04	New Jersey 5, Tampa Bay 4
3- 4-94	Wendel Clark, Toronto	Detroit	0:53	Toronto 6, Detroit 5
3- 8-94	Neal Broten, Dallas	Philadelphia	2:43	Dallas 4, Philadelphia 3
3-15-94	Randy Burridge, Washington	Pittsburgh	0:40	Washington 5, Pittsburgh 4
3-20-94	Peter Stastny, St. Louis	Chicago	0:33	St. Louis 4, Chicago 3
3-20-94	Paul Broten, Dallas	Vancouver	0:13	Dallas 2, Vancouver 1
3-22-94	Vladimir Malakhov, N.Y. Islanders	Tampa Bay	3:59	N.Y. Islanders 5, Tampa Bay 4
3-25-94	Mike Donnelly, Los Angeles	Edmonton	2:24	Los Angeles 4, Edmonton 3
3-27-94	Garry Valk, Anaheim	Philadelphia	0:24	Anaheim 3, Philadelphia 2
3-28-94	Murray Craven, Vancouver	Toronto	3:57	Vancouver 3, Toronto 2
3-30-94	Andrew Cassels, Hartford	Chicago	3:15	Hartford 3, Chicago 2
3-30-94	Brian Bradley, Tampa Bay	Buffalo	3:52	Tampa Bay 3, Buffalo 2
3-31-94	Jason Arnott, Edmonton	Anaheim	1:44	Edmonton 3, Anaheim 2
4- 5-94	Benoit Hogue, N.Y. Islanders	Washington	3:34	N.Y. Islanders 4, Washington 3

PENALTY-SHOT INFORMATION

Date	Shooter	Goaltender	Scored	Final score
10- 5-93	Alexei Kovalev, N.Y. Rangers	Jon Casey, Boston	No	Boston 4, N.Y. Rangers 3
10- 6-93	Pavel Bure, Vancouver	Kelly Hrudey, Los Angeles	No	Vancouver 5, Los Angeles 2
10-15-93	Cam Neely, Boston	Ron Tugnutt, Anaheim	No	Boston 1, Anaheim 1
10-30-93	Bob Kudelski, Ottawa	Darcy Wakaluk, Dallas	Yes	Ottawa 5, Dallas 4
10-31-93	Paul Ranheim, Calgary	Bob Essensa, Winnipeg	Yes	Calgary 4, Winnipeg 3
11- 3-93	Philippe Bozon, St. Louis	Bob Essensa, Winnipeg	No	St. Louis 3, Winnipeg 0
11-20-93	Scott Pearson, Edmonton	Damian Rhodes, Toronto	No	Toronto 3, Edmonton 2
11-24-93	Wendel Clark, Toronto	Trevor Kidd, Calgary	Yes	Calgary 5, Toronto 3
11-25-93	Tony Granato, Los Angeles	Jocelyn Thibault, Quebec	No	Quebec 8, Los Angeles 6
12- 4-93	Andrei Kovalenko, Quebec	Kirk McLean, Vancouver	Yes	Quebec 3, Vancouver 1
12-17-93	Alexander Mogilny, Buffalo	Robb Stauber, Los Angeles	No	Buffalo 2, Los Angeles 0
12-17-93	Kevin Miller, St. Louis	Mike Vernon, Calgary	No	St. Louis 4, Calgary 3
12-27-93	Sergei Fedorov, Detroit	Andy Moog, Dallas	Yes	Detroit 6, Dallas 0
1-11-94	Randy Wood, Buffalo	Jeff Hackett, Chicago	Yes	Buffalo 5, Chicago 2
1-16-94	Steve Larmer, N.Y. Rangers	Ed Belfour, Chicago	Yes	N.Y. Rangers, Chicago 1
1-27-94	Brent Gilchrist, Dallas	Kirk McLean, Vancouver	No	Dallas 3, Vancouver 2
1-27-94	Tony Amonte, N.Y. Rangers	Kelly Hrudey, Los Angeles	No	N.Y. Rangers 5, Los Angeles 4
2- 4-94	Roman Oksiuta, Edmonton	Ed Belfour, Chicago	No	Chicago 3, Edmonton 1
2- 7-94	Robert Reichel, Calgary	Bill Ranford, Edmonton	Yes	Calgary 4, Edmonton 3
2-10-94	Wayne Presley, Buffalo	Vincent Riendeau, Boston	No	Buffalo 3, Boston 3
3- 4-94	Peter Zezel, Toronto	Chris Osgood, Detroit	No	Toronto 6, Detroit 5
3-19-94	Ray Bourque, Boston	Chris Terreri, New Jersey	Yes	New Jersey 8, Boston 6
3-22-94	Mark Howe, Detroit	Ed Belfour, Chicago	No	Detroit 3, Chicago 1
3-29-94	Sergei Makarov, San Jose	Tim Cheveldae, Winnipeg	Yes	San Jose 9, Winnipeg 4
4- 6-94	Andrew Cassels, Hartford	Ron Hextall, N.Y. Islanders	Yes	Hartford 3, N.Y. Islanders 3
4- 7-94	Mike Donnelly, Los Angeles	Curtis Joseph, St. Louis	No	St. Louis 6, Los Angeles 2
4-14-94	Zigmund Palffy, N.Y. Islanders	John Vanbiesbrouck, Florida	No	Florida 4, N.Y. Islanders 1

TEAM STREAKS

Most consecutive games won

Toronto, Oct. 7-28	10
New Jersey, Oct. 6-23	7
N.Y. Rangers, Oct. 30-Nov. 13	7
San Jose, Mar. 24-Apr. 5	7

Most consecutive home games won

Chicago, Nov. 4-Dec. 27	8
Detroit, Nov. 27-Dec. 21	8
Toronto, Oct. 7-Nov. 6	7
Montreal, Jan. 30-Mar. 9	7
New Jersey, Mar. 10-29	7

Most consecutive road games won

Dallas, Jan. 26-Feb. 21	7
N.Y. Rangers, Oct. 30-Nov. 24	6
Detroit, Jan. 6-27	6

Most consecutive games undefeated

N.Y. Rangers, Oct. 24-Nov. 24	14
Toronto, Jan. 6-Feb. 1	11
Montreal, Feb. 23-Mar. 19	11
Toronto, Oct. 7-28	10

Most consecutive home games undefeated

N.Y. Rangers, Oct. 24-Jan. 3	16
Montreal, Jan. 30-Apr. 2	13
St. Louis, Oct. 7-Nov. 26	11
Dallas, Nov. 1-Dec. 12	11
New Jersey, Feb. 28-Mar. 29	10

Most consecutive road games undefeated

Detroit, Dec. 23-Jan. 27	9
New Jersey, Nov. 5-Dec. 2	8
Dallas, Jan. 26-Feb. 23	8

TEAM OVERTIME GAMES

	OVERALL					HOME					AWAY				
Team	G	W	L	T	Pct.	G	W	L	T	Pct.	G	W	L	T	Pct.
Hartford	14	4	1	9	.607	10	3	1	6	.600	4	1	0	3	.625
Detroit	15	5	2	8	.600	7	0	1	6	.429	8	5	1	2	.750
Toronto	17	4	1	12	.588	6	2	0	4	.667	11	2	1	8	.545
N.Y. Rangers	12	3	1	8	.583	7	1	0	6	.571	5	2	1	2	.600
N.Y. Islanders	19	5	2	12	.579	6	2	0	4	.667	13	3	2	8	.538
Dallas	22	6	3	13	.568	10	1	2	7	.450	12	5	1	6	.667
St. Louis	17	4	2	11	.559	11	2	1	8	.545	6	2	1	3	.583
Pittsburgh	19	4	2	13	.553	11	2	1	8	.545	8	2	1	5	.563
Vancouver	12	5	4	3	.542	8	3	2	3	.563	4	2	2	0	.500
Calgary	18	3	2	13	.528	8	2	1	5	.563	10	1	1	8	.500
Montreal	19	3	2	14	.526	8	3	1	4	.625	11	0	1	10	.455
San Jose	19	2	1	16	.526	10	0	0	10	.500	9	2	1	6	.556
Los Angeles	18	3	3	12	.500	8	0	3	5	.313	10	3	0	7	.650
Ottawa	17	4	4	9	.500	7	1	2	4	.429	10	3	2	5	.550
Boston	17	2	2	13	.500	9	0	1	8	.444	8	2	1	5	.563
Washington	14	2	2	10	.500	10	0	1	9	.450	4	2	1	1	.625
New Jersey	14	1	1	12	.500	3	0	1	2	.333	11	1	0	10	.545
Quebec	8	0	0	8	.500	6	0	0	6	.500	2	0	0	2	.500
Tampa Bay	18	3	4	11	.472	9	1	2	6	.444	9	2	2	5	.500
Philadelphia	18	3	5	10	.444	9	2	4	3	.389	9	1	1	7	.500
Florida	24	2	5	17	.438	15	2	4	9	.433	9	0	1	8	.444
Chicago	16	2	5	9	.406	8	1	2	5	.438	8	1	3	4	.375
Edmonton	21	1	6	14	.381	7	0	4	3	.214	14	1	2	11	.464
Anaheim	12	2	5	5	.375	8	1	5	2	.250	4	1	0	3	.625
Winnipeg	15	1	5	9	.367	8	1	3	4	.375	7	0	2	5	.357
Buffalo	13	0	4	9	.346	5	0	2	3	.300	8	0	2	6	.375
Totals	214	74	74	140	1.000	214	30	44	140	.467	214	44	30	140	.533

STANLEY CUP PLAYOFFS

RESULTS

CONFERENCE QUARTERFINALS

EASTERN CONFERENCE

	W	L	Pts.	GF	GA
N.Y. Rangers	4	0	8	22	3
N.Y. Islanders	0	4	0	3	22

(N.Y. Rangers won Eastern Conference quarterfinals, 4-0)

Sun.	April 17—N.Y. Islanders 0, at N.Y. Rangers 6
Mon.	April 18—N.Y. Islanders 0, at N.Y. Rangers 6
Thur.	April 21—N.Y. Rangers 5, at N.Y. Islanders 1
Sun.	April 24—N.Y. Rangers 5, at N.Y. Islanders 2

	W	L	Pts.	GF	GA
Washington Capitals	4	2	8	20	12
Pittsburgh Penguins	2	4	4	12	20

(Washington won Eastern Conference quarterfinals, 4-2)

Sun.	April 17—Washington 5, at Pittsburgh 3
Tue.	April 19—Washington 1, at Pittsburgh 2
Thur.	April 21—Pittsburgh 0, at Washington 4
Sat.	April 23—Pittsburgh 1, at Washington 4
Mon.	April 25—Washington 2, at Pittsburgh 3
Wed.	April 27—Pittsburgh 3, at Washington 6

	W	L	Pts.	GF	GA
New Jersey Devils	4	3	8	14	14
Buffalo Sabres	3	4	6	14	14

(New Jersey won Eastern Conference quarterfinals, 4-3)

Sun.	April 17—Buffalo 2, at New Jersey 0
Tue.	April 19—Buffalo 1, at New Jersey 2
Thur.	April 21—New Jersey 2, at Buffalo 1
Sat.	April 23—New Jersey 3, at Buffalo 5
Mon.	April 25—Buffalo 3, at New Jersey 5
Wed.	April 27—New Jersey 0, at Buffalo 1 (a)
Fri.	April 29—Buffalo 1, at New Jersey 2

(a)—Dave Hannan scored at 5:43 (4 OT) for Buffalo.

	W	L	Pts.	GF	GA
Boston Bruins	4	3	8	22	20
Montreal Canadiens	3	4	6	20	22

(Boston won Eastern Conference quarterfinals, 4-3)

Sat.	April 16—Montreal 2, at Boston 3
Mon.	April 18—Montreal 3, at Boston 2
Thur.	April 21—Boston 6, at Montreal 3
Sat.	April 23—Boston 2, at Montreal 5
Mon.	April 25—Montreal 2, at Boston 1 (b)
Wed.	April 27—Boston 3, at Montreal 2
Fri.	April 29—Montreal 3, at Boston 5

(b)—Kirk Muller scored at 17:18 (OT) for Montreal.

WESTERN CONFERENCE

	W	L	Pts.	GF	GA
San Jose Sharks	4	3	8	21	27
Detroit Red Wings	3	4	6	27	21

(San Jose won Western Conference quarterfinals, 4-3)

Mon.	April 18—San Jose 5, at Detroit 4
Wed.	April 20—San Jose 0, at Detroit 4
Fri.	April 22—Detroit 3, at San Jose 2
Sat.	April 23—Detroit 3, at San Jose 4
Tue.	April 26—Detroit 4, at San Jose 6
Thur.	April 28—San Jose 1, at Detroit 7
Sat.	April 30—San Jose 3, at Detroit 2

	W	L	Pts.	GF	GA
Vancouver Canucks	4	3	8	23	20
Calgary Flames	3	4	6	20	23

(Vancouver won Western Conference quarterfinals, 4-3)

Mon.	April 18—Vancouver 5, at Calgary 0
Wed.	April 20—Vancouver 5, at Calgary 7
Fri.	April 22—Calgary 4, at Vancouver 2
Sun.	April 24—Calgary 3, at Vancouver 2
Tue.	April 26—Vancouver 2, at Calgary 1 (c)
Thur.	April 28—Calgary 2, at Vancouver 3 (d)
Sat.	April 30—Vancouver 4, at Calgary 3 (e)

(c)—Geoff Courtnall scored at 7:15 (OT) for Vancouver.
(d)—Trevor Linden scored at 16:43 (OT) for Vancouver.
(e)—Pavel Bure scored at 2:20 (2 OT) for Vancouver.

	W	L	Pts.	GF	GA
Toronto Maple Leafs	4	2	8	15	10
Chicago Blackhawks	2	4	4	10	15

(Toronto won Western Conference quarterfinals, 4-2)

Mon.	April 18—Chicago 1, at Toronto 5
Wed.	April 20—Chicago 0, at Toronto 1 (f)
Sat.	April 23—Toronto 4, at Chicago 5
Sun.	April 24—Toronto 3, at Chicago 4 (g)
Tue.	April 26—Chicago 0, at Toronto 1
Thur.	April 28—Toronto 1, at Chicago 0

(f)—Todd Gill scored at 2:15 (OT) for Toronto.
(g)—Jeremy Roenick scored at 1:23 (OT) for Chicago.

	W	L	Pts.	GF	GA
Dallas Stars	4	0	8	16	10
St. Louis Blues	0	4	0	10	16

(Dallas won Western Conference quarterfinals, 4-0)

Sun.	April 17—St. Louis 3, at Dallas 5
Wed.	April 20—St. Louis 2, at Dallas 4
Fri.	April 22—Dallas 5, at St. Louis 4 (h)
Sun.	April 24—Dallas 2, at St. Louis 1

(h)—Paul Cavallini scored at 8:34 (OT) for Dallas.

CONFERENCE SEMIFINALS

EASTERN CONFERENCE

	W	L	Pts.	GF	GA
N.Y. Rangers	4	1	8	20	12
Washington Capitals	1	4	2	12	20

(N.Y. Rangers won Eastern Conference semifinals, 4-1)

Sun.	May 1—Washington 3, at N.Y. Rangers 6
Tue.	May 3—Washington 2, at N.Y. Rangers 5
Thur.	May 5—N.Y. Rangers 3, at Washington 0
Sat.	May 7—N.Y. Rangers 2, Washington 4
Mon.	May 9—Washington 3, at N.Y. Rangers 4

	W	L	Pts.	GF	GA
New Jersey Devils	4	2	8	22	17
Boston Bruins	2	4	4	17	22

(New Jersey won Eastern Conference semifinals, 4-2)

Sun.	May 1—Boston 2, at New Jersey 1
Tue.	May 3—Boston 6, at New Jersey 5 (i)
Thur.	May 5—New Jersey 4, at Boston 2
Sat.	May 7—New Jersey 5, at Boston 4 (j)
Mon.	May 9—Boston 0, at New Jersey 2
Wed.	May 11—New Jersey 5, at Boston 3

(i)—Don Sweeney scored at 9:08 (OT) for Boston.
(j)—Stephane Richer scored at 14:19 (OT) for New Jersey.

WESTERN CONFERENCE

	W	L	Pts.	GF	GA
Toronto Maple Leafs	4	3	8	26	21
San Jose Sharks	3	4	6	21	26

(Toronto won Western Conference semifinals, 4-3)

Mon. May 2—San Jose 3, at Toronto 2
Wed. May 4—San Jose 1, at Toronto 5
Fri. May 6—Toronto 2, at San Jose 5
Sun. May 8—Toronto 8, at San Jose 3
Tue. May 10—Toronto 2, at San Jose 5
Thur. May 12—San Jose 2, at Toronto 3 (k)
Sat. May 14—San Jose 2, at Toronto 4
(k)—Mike Gartner scored at 8:53 (OT) for Toronto.

	W	L	Pts.	GF	GA
Vancouver Canucks	4	1	8	18	11
Dallas Stars	1	4	2	11	18

(Vancouver won Western Conference semifinals, 4-1)

Mon. May 2—Vancouver 6, at Dallas 4
Wed. May 4—Vancouver 3, at Dallas 0
Fri. May 6—Dallas 4, at Vancouver 3
Sun. May 8—Dallas 1, at Vancouver 2 (l)
Tue. May 10—Dallas 2, at Vancouver 4
(l)—Sergio Momesso scored at 11:01 (OT) for Vancouver.

CONFERENCE FINALS

EASTERN CONFERENCE

	W	L	Pts.	GF	GA
N.Y. Rangers	4	3	8	18	16
New Jersey Devils	3	4	6	16	18

(N.Y. Rangers won Eastern Conference finals, 4-3)

Sun. May 15—New Jersey 4, at N.Y. Rangers 3 (m)
Tue. May 17—New Jersey 0, at N.Y. Rangers 4
Thur. May 19—N.Y. Rangers 3, at New Jersey 2 (n)
Sat. May 21—N.Y. Rangers 1, at New Jersey 3
Mon. May 23—New Jersey 4, at N.Y. Rangers 1
Wed. May 25—N.Y. Rangers 4, at New Jersey 2
Fri. May 27—New Jersey 1, at N.Y. Rangers 2 (o)
(m)—Stephane Richer scored at 15:23 (2 OT) for New Jersey.
(n)—Stephane Matteau scored at 6:13 (2 OT) for N.Y. Rangers.
(o)—Stephane Matteau scored at 4:24 (2 OT) for N.Y. Rangers.

WESTERN CONFERENCE

	W	L	Pts.	GF	GA
Vancouver Canucks	4	1	8	16	9
Toronto Maple Leafs	1	4	2	9	16

(Vancouver won Western Conference finals, 4-1)

Mon. May 16—Vancouver 2, at Toronto 3 (p)
Wed. May 18—Vancouver 4, at Toronto 3
Fri. May 20—Toronto 0, at Vancouver 4
Sun. May 22—Toronto 0, at Vancouver 2
Tue. May 24—Toronto 3, at Vancouver 4 (q)
(p)—Peter Zezel scored at 16:55 (OT) for Toronto.
(q)—Greg Adams scored at 0:14 (2 OT) for Vancouver.

STANLEY CUP FINALS

	W	L	Pts.	GF	GA
N.Y. Rangers	4	3	8	21	19
Vancouver Canucks	3	4	6	19	21

(N.Y. Rangers won Stanley Cup championship, 4-3)

Tue. May 31—Vancouver 3, at N.Y. Rangers 2 (r)
Thur. June 2—Vancouver 1, at N.Y. Rangers 3

Sat. June 4—N.Y. Rangers 5, at Vancouver 1
Tue. June 7—N.Y. Rangers 4, at Vancouver 2
Thur. June 9—Vancouver 3, at N.Y. Rangers 6
Sat. June 11—N.Y. Rangers 1, at Vancouver 4
Tue. June 14—Vancouver 2, at N.Y. Rangers 3
(r)—Greg Adams scored at 19:26 (OT) for Vancouver.

GAME SUMMARIES, STANLEY CUP FINALS

GAME 1

AT NEW YORK, MAY 31

Vancouver 3, N.Y. Rangers 2 (OT)

Vancouver	0 0	2	1—3
N.Y. Rangers	1 0	1	0—2

FIRST PERIOD—1. New York, Larmer 6 (Kovalev, Leetch), 3:32. Penalties—Wells, New York (cross-checking), 1:47; Linden, Vancouver (tripping), 2:26; McIntyre, Vancouver (roughing), 8:05; Lowe, New York (roughing), 8:05; Craven, Vancouver (slashing), 10:35; Beukeboom, New York (interference), 15:54.

SECOND PERIOD—None. Penalties—Messier, New York (hooking), 0:20; Lidster, New York (tripping), 8:49; Courtnall, Vancouver (interference), 13:18; Momesso, Vancouver (goalie interference), 16:15; Beukeboom, New York (high-sticking), 19:34.

THIRD PERIOD—2. Vancouver, Hedican 1 (Adams, Lumme), 5:45. 3. New York, Kovalev 6 (Leetch, Zubov), 8:29. 4. Vancouver, Gelinas 5 (Ronning, Momesso), 19:00. Penalties—None.

OVERTIME—5. Vancouver, Adams 6 (Bure, Ronning), 19:28. Penalties—Momesso, Vancouver (roughing), 9:31; Gilbert, New York (roughing), 9:31.

Shots on goal—Vancouver 10-5-7-9—31; New York 15-9-13-17—54. Power-play opportunities—Vancouver 0 of 5; New York 0 of 4. Goalies—Vancouver, McLean 13-5 (54 shots-52 saves); New York, Richter, 12-5 (31-28). A—18,200. Referee—Terry Gregson. Linesmen—Randy Mitton, Ray Scapinello.

GAME 2

AT NEW YORK, JUNE 2

N.Y. Rangers 3, Vancouver 1

Vancouver	1	0	0—1
N.Y. Rangers	1	1	1—3

FIRST PERIOD—1. New York, Lidster 1, 6:22. 2. Vancouver, Momesso 3 (Ronning, Hedican), 14:04. Penalties—Craven, Vancouver (tripping), 2:03; Lidster, New York (interference), 7:44; Hunter, Vancouver (roughing), 10:21; Hunter, Vancouver (misconduct), 15:26; Anderson, New York (interference), 16:55.

SECOND PERIOD—3. New York, Anderson 2 (Messier), 11:42 (sh). Penalties—Brown, Vancouver (hooking), 4:27; Matteau, New York (hooking), 6:12; Graves, New York (tripping), 10:35; Antoski, Vancouver (roughing), 13:58; Tikkanen, New York (goalie interference), 17:08.

THIRD PERIOD—4. New York, Leetch 7, 19:56 (en). Penalties—Lidster, New York (interference), 1:43; Diduck, Vancouver (high-sticking), 4:32; Kovalev, New York (high-sticking), 4:32; Brown, Vancouver (roughing), 15:29; Gilbert, New York (roughing), 15:29.

Shots on goal—Vancouver 10-6-13—29; New York 14-13-13—40. Power-play opportunities—Vancouver 0 of 6; New York 0 of 4. Goalies—Vancouver, McLean, 13-6 (39 shots-37 saves); New York, Richter, 13-5 (29-28). A—18,200. Referee—Bill McCreary. Linesmen—Kevin Collins, Gerard Gauthier.

GAME 3

AT VANCOUVER, JUNE 4

N.Y. Rangers 5, Vancouver 1

N.Y. Rangers	2	1	2—5
Vancouver	1	0	0—1

FIRST PERIOD—1. Vancouver, Bure 14 (Linden, Adams), 1:03. 2. New York, Leetch 8, 13:39. 3. New York, Anderson 3 (Nemchinov, Beukeboom), 19:19. Penalties—Wells, New York (tripping), 2:54; Anderson, New York (roughing), 5:42; Hunter, Vancouver (charging), 5:42; Lumme, Vancouver (holding), 9:57; MacTavish, New York (holding), 15:40; Leetch, New York (tripping), 17:56; Lowe, New York (high-sticking), 18:12; Ronning, Vancouver (high-sticking), 18:12; Messier, New York (roughing), 18:12; Momesso, Vancouver (roughing), 18:12; Bure, Vancouver (major-game misconduct—high-sticking), 18:21.

SECOND PERIOD—4. New York, Leetch 9 (Tikkanen, Beukeboom), 18:32. Penalties—Lowe, New York (roughing), 5:34; Antoski, Vancouver (roughing), 16:28; Messier, New York (roughing), 16:28.

THIRD PERIOD—5. New York, Larmer 7, 0:25. 6. New York, Kovalev 7 (Graves, Messier), 13:03 (pp). Penalties—Tikkanen, New York (hooking), 3:13; Hedican, Vancouver (holding), 5:34; McIntyre, Vancouver (holding), 7:58; MacTavish, New York (holding), 9:46; Momesso, Vancouver (cross-checking), 11:42; Gelinas, Vancouver (roughing), 16:35; Antoski, Vancouver (double minor—cross-checking, roughing), 19:19.

Shots on goal—New York 9-10-6—25; Vancouver 11-5-9—25. Power-play opportunities—New York 1 of 7; Vancouver 0 of 6. Goalies—New York, Richter, 14-5 (25 shots-24 saves); Vancouver, McLean, 13-7 (25-20). A—16,150. Referee—Andy van Hellemond. Linesmen—Ray Scapinello, Randy Mitton.

GAME 4

AT VANCOUVER, JUNE 7

N.Y. Rangers 4, Vancouver 2

N.Y. Rangers	0	2	2—4
Vancouver	2	0	0—2

FIRST PERIOD—1. Vancouver, Linden 10 (Lumme, Brown), 13:25 (pp). 2. Vancouver, Ronning 5 (Bure, Craven), 16:19. Penalties—Courtnall, Vancouver (elbowing), 3:11; Beukeboom, New York (high-sticking), 6:35; Graves, New York (holding), 13:02; Messier, New York (major—boarding), 14:17; Linden, Vancouver (holding stick), 15:07; Courtnall, Vancouver (interference), 17:54; Tikkanen, New York (roughing), 18:45.

SECOND PERIOD—3. New York, Leetch 10 (MacTavish, Gilbert), 4:03. 4. New York, Zubov 5 (Messier, Leetch), 19:44 (pp). Penalties—Lidster, New York (holding), 1:13; Brown, Vancouver (tripping), 7:19; Lidster, New York (holding), 16:58; Adams, Vancouver (boarding), 18:55.

THIRD PERIOD—5. New York, Kovalev 8 (Leetch, Zubov), 15:05 (pp). 6. New York, Larmer 8 (Zubov, Leetch), 17:56. Penalties—New York bench, served by Kocur (too many men), 3:53; Lumme, Vancouver (holding), 4:48; Tikkanen, New York (roughing), 10:42; Diduck, Vancouver (roughing), 10:42; Messier, New York (slashing), 11:29; Gelinas, Vancouver (roughing), 14:31.

Shots on goal—New York 8-8-11—27; Vancouver 8-12-10—30. Missed penalty shot—Bure, Vancouver, 6:31 second. Power-play opportunities—New York 2 of 5; Vancouver 1 of 10. Goalies—New York, Richter, 15-5 (30 shots-28 saves); Vancouver, McLean, 13-8 (27-23). A—16,150. Referee—Terry Gregson. Linesmen—Kevin Collins, Gerard Gauthier.

GAME 5

AT NEW YORK, JUNE 9

Vancouver 6, N.Y. Rangers 3

Vancouver	0	1	5—6
N.Y. Rangers	0	0	3—3

FIRST PERIOD—None. Penalties—Hunter, Vancouver (elbowing), 0:49; Momesso, Vancouver (minor-major—slashing, fighting), 10:06; Ronning, Vancouver (roughing), 10:06; Beukeboom, New York (minor-major-game misconduct—instigator, fighting), 10:06; Wells, New York (high-sticking), 10:06; Matteau, New York (roughing), 10:06; Hunter, Vancouver (roughing), 13:02; Wells, New York (roughing), 13:02; Ronning, Vancouver (holding), 17:20; Larmer, New York (holding), 17:20; Nemchinov, New York (elbowing), 19:42.

SECOND PERIOD—1. Vancouver, Brown 4 (Ronning, Antoski), 8:10. Penalties—Courtnall, Vancouver (major—elbowing), 10:13; Messier, New York (hooking), 18:19.

THIRD PERIOD—2. Vancouver, Courtnall 6 (Lafayette, Hedican), 0:26. 3. Vancouver, Bure 15 (Craven), 2:48. 4. New York, Lidster 2 (Kovalev), 3:27. 5. New York, Larmer 9 (Matteau, Nemchinov), 6:20. 6. New York, Messier 11 (Anderson, Graves), 9:02. 7. Vancouver, Babych 3 (Bure), 9:31. 8. Vancouver, Courtnall 7 (Lafayette, Lumme), 12:20. 9. Vancouver, Bure 16 (Ronning, Hedican), 13:04. Penalty—Kocur, New York (slashing), 18:41.

Shots on goal—Vancouver 12-8-17—37; New York 10-13-15—38. Power-play opportunities—Vancouver 0 of 4; New York 0 of 2. Goalies—Vancouver, McLean 14-8 (38 shots-35 saves); New York, Richter, 15-6 (37-31). A—18,200. Referee—Andy van Hellemond. Linesmen—Randy Mitton, Ray Scapinello.

GAME 6

AT VANCOUVER, JUNE 11

Vancouver 4, N.Y. Rangers 1

N.Y. Rangers	0	1	0—1
Vancouver	1	1	2—4

FIRST PERIOD—1. Vancouver, Brown 5 (Linden), 9:42 (pp). Penalties—Beukeboom, New York (elbowing), 3:02; Leetch, New York (interference), 9:39.

SECOND PERIOD—2. Vancouver, Courtnall 8 (Lumme, Bure), 12:29. 3. New York, Kovalev 9 (Messier, Leetch), 14:42 (pp). Penalties—Momesso, Vancouver (interference), 2:26; Diduck, Vancouver (tripping), 7:27; McIntyre, Vancouver (goalie interference), 13:23.

THIRD PERIOD—4. Vancouver, Brown 6, 8:35. 5. Vancouver, Courtnall 9 (Lafayette, Diduck), 18:28. Penalties—None.

Shots on goal—New York 7-12-10—29; Vancouver 16-8-7—31. Power-play opportunities—New York 1 of 3; Vancouver 1 of 2. Goalies—New York, Richter, 15-7 (31 shots-27 saves); Vancouver, McLean, 15-8 (29-28). A—16,150. Referee—Bill McCreary. Linesmen—Kevin Collins, Gerard Gauthier.

GAME 7

AT NEW YORK, JUNE 14

N.Y. Rangers 3, Vancouver 2

Vancouver	0	1	1—2
N.Y. Rangers	2	1	0—3

FIRST PERIOD—1. New York, Leetch 11 (Zubov, Messier), 11:02. 2. New York, Graves 10 (Kovalev, Zubov), 14:45 (pp). Penalties—Lumme, Vancouver (cross-checking), 14:03; Hedican, Vancouver (roughing), 18:50; Tikkanen, New York (roughing), 18:50.

SECOND PERIOD—3. Vancouver, Linden 11 (Glynn, Bure), 5:21 (sh). 4. New York, Messier 12 (Graves, Noonan), 13:29 (pp). Penalties—Brown, Vancouver (interference), 4:39; Babych, Vancouver (tripping), 12:46; Messier, New York (hooking), 16:39.

THIRD PERIOD—5. Vancouver, Linden 12 (Courtnall, Ronning), 4:50 (pp). Penalties—Tikkanen, New York (hooking), 4:16; Linden, Vancouver (roughing), 10:55; MacTavish, New York (roughing), 10:55.

Shots on goal—Vancouver 9-12-9—30; New York 12-14-9—35. Power-play opportunities—Vancouver 1 of 2; New York 2 of 3. Goalies—Vancouver, McLean, 15-9 (35 shots-32 saves); New York, Richter, 16-7 (30-28). A—18,200. Referee—Terry Gregson. Linesmen—Kevin Collins, Ray Scapinello.

INDIVIDUAL LEADERS

Goals: Pavel Bure, Vancouver (16)
Assists: Brian Leetch, N.Y. Rangers (23)
Points: Brian Leetch, N.Y. Rangers (34)
Penalty minutes: Mike Peluso, New Jersey (64)
Goaltending average: Dominik Hasek, Buffalo (1.61)
Shutouts: Kirk McLean, Vancouver (4)
Mike Richter, N.Y. Rangers (4)

TOP SCORERS

	Games	G	A	Pts.	PIM
Brian Leetch, N.Y. Rangers.......	23	11	23	34	6
Pavel Bure, Vancouver.............	24	16	15	31	40
Mark Messier, N.Y. Rangers	23	12	18	30	33
Doug Gilmour, Toronto.............	18	6	22	28	42
Trevor Linden, Vancouver..........	24	12	13	25	18
Alexei Kovalev, N.Y. Rangers......	23	9	12	21	18
Geoff Courtnall, Vancouver	24	9	10	19	51
Sergei Zubov, N.Y. Rangers	22	5	14	19	0
Claude Lemieux, New Jersey	20	7	11	18	44
Igor Larionov, San Jose	14	5	13	18	10
Dave Ellett, Toronto	18	3	15	18	31

INDIVIDUAL STATISTICS

BOSTON BRUINS

(Lost Eastern Conference semifinals to New Jersey, 4-2)

SCORING

	Games	G	A	Pts.	PIM
Adam Oates	13	3	9	12	8
Ray Bourque	13	2	8	10	0
Bryan Smolinski	13	5	4	9	4
Glen Murray.................................	13	4	5	9	14
Jozef Stumpel...............................	13	1	7	8	4
Ted Donato	13	4	2	6	10
Glen Wesley	13	3	3	6	12
Mariusz Czerkawski....................	13	3	3	6	4
Stephen Heinze	13	2	3	5	7
Al Iafrate	13	3	1	4	6
Don Sweeney	12	2	1	3	4
Fred Knipscheer	12	2	1	3	6
Brent Hughes	13	2	1	3	27
Dave Reid	13	2	1	3	2
David Shaw	13	1	2	3	16
Cameron Stewart	8	0	3	3	7
Stephen Leach	5	0	1	1	2
Dan Marois	11	0	1	1	16
Gordie Roberts	12	0	1	1	8
Glen Featherstone	1	0	0	0	0
Vincent Riendeau (goalie)	2	0	0	0	0
Jamie Huscroft	4	0	0	0	9
Jon Casey (goalie)	11	0	0	0	0

GOALTENDERS

	Games	Min.	W	L	T	Goals	SO	Avg.
Jon Casey.................	11	698	5	6	0	34	0	2.92
Vincent Riendeau	2	120	1	1	0	8	0	4.00

BUFFALO SABRES

(Lost Eastern Conference quarterfinals to New Jersey, 4-3)

SCORING

	Games	G	A	Pts.	PIM
Dale Hawerchuk	7	0	7	7	4
Alexander Mogilny	7	4	2	6	6
Yuri Khmylev	7	3	1	4	8
Wayne Presley	7	2	1	3	14
Doug Bodger	7	0	3	3	6
Philippe Boucher	7	1	1	2	2
Randy Moller................................	7	0	2	2	8
Brad May	7	0	2	2	9
Richard Smehlik	7	0	2	2	10
Todd Simon	5	1	0	1	0
Dave Hannan	7	1	0	1	6
Rob Ray	7	1	0	1	43
Derek Plante	7	1	0	1	0
Jason Dawe	6	0	1	1	6
Donald Audette............................	7	0	1	1	6
Bob Sweeney	1	0	0	0	0

	Games	G	A	Pts.	PIM
Petr Svoboda	3	0	0	0	4
Matthew Barnaby	3	0	0	0	17
Ken Sutton	4	0	0	0	2
Randy Wood	6	0	0	0	0
Dominik Hasek (goalie)	7	0	0	0	2
Craig Muni	7	0	0	0	4

GOALTENDERS

	Games	Min.	W	L	T	Goals	SO	Avg.
Dominik Hasek	7	484	3	4	0	13	2	1.61

CALGARY FLAMES

(Lost Western Conference quarterfinals to Vancouver, 4-3)

SCORING

	Games	G	A	Pts.	PIM
Theoren Fleury	7	6	4	10	5
Al MacInnis	7	2	6	8	12
Gary Roberts	7	2	6	8	24
Robert Reichel	7	0	5	5	0
Joe Nieuwendyk	6	2	2	4	0
Wes Walz	7	2	2	4	2
German Titov	7	2	1	3	4
Zarley Zalapski............................	7	0	3	3	2
Ronnie Stern	7	2	0	2	12
Mike Sullivan	7	1	1	2	8
Kelly Kisio	7	0	2	2	8
Joel Otto	3	0	1	1	4
Frank Musil	7	0	1	1	4
James Patrick...............................	7	0	1	1	6
Chris Dahlquist	1	0	0	0	0
Dan Keczmer	3	0	0	0	4
Michael Nylander	3	0	0	0	0
Kevin Dahl....................................	6	0	0	0	4
Mike Vernon (goalie)	7	0	0	0	2
Trent Yawney	7	0	0	0	16
Paul Kruse	7	0	0	0	14
Sandy McCarthy............................	7	0	0	0	34

GOALTENDERS

	Games	Min.	W	L	T	Goals	SO	Avg.
Mike Vernon	7	466	3	4	0	23	0	2.96

CHICAGO BLACKHAWKS

(Lost Western Conference quarterfinals to Toronto, 4-2)

SCORING

	Games	G	A	Pts.	PIM
Jeremy Roenick	6	1	6	7	2
Tony Amonte	6	4	2	6	4
Gary Suter	6	3	2	5	6
Joe Murphy	6	1	3	4	25
Chris Chelios	6	1	1	2	8
Eric Weinrich	6	0	2	2	6

	Games	G	A	Pts.	PIM
Dirk Graham	6	0	1	1	4
Keith Carney	6	0	1	1	4
Dave Christian	1	0	0	0	0
Darin Kimble	1	0	0	0	5
Robert Dirk	2	0	0	0	15
Neil Wilkinson	4	0	0	0	0
Patrick Poulin	4	0	0	0	0
Ed Belfour (goalie)	6	0	0	0	2
Randy Cunneyworth	6	0	0	0	8
Christian Ruuttu	6	0	0	0	2
Greg Smyth	6	0	0	0	0
Rich Sutter	6	0	0	0	2
Brent Sutter	6	0	0	0	2
Paul Ysebaert	6	0	0	0	8
Steve Dubinsky	6	0	0	0	10
Jeff Shantz	6	0	0	0	6

GOALTENDERS

	Games	Min.	W	L	T	Goals	SO	Avg.
Ed Belfour	6	360	2	4	0	15	0	2.50

DALLAS STARS

(Lost Western Conference semifinals to Vancouver, 4-1)

SCORING

	Games	G	A	Pts.	PIM
Mike Modano	9	7	3	10	16
Paul Cavallini	9	1	8	9	4
Russ Courtnall	9	1	8	9	0
Dave Gagner	9	5	1	6	2
Brent Gilchrist	9	3	1	4	2
Shane Churla	9	1	3	4	35
Neal Broten	9	2	1	3	6
Mike McPhee	9	2	1	3	2
Trent Klatt	9	2	1	3	4
Grant Ledyard	9	1	2	3	6
Pelle Eklund	9	0	3	3	4
Craig Ludwig	9	0	3	3	8
Richard Matvichuk	7	1	1	2	12
Paul Broten	9	1	1	2	2
Dean Evason	9	0	2	2	12
Derian Hatcher	9	0	2	2	14
Dave Barr	3	0	1	1	4
Doug Zmolek	7	0	1	1	4
Alan May	1	0	0	0	0
Mike Craig	4	0	0	0	2
Andy Moog (goalie)	4	0	0	0	0
Mike Lalor	5	0	0	0	6
Darcy Wakaluk (goalie)	5	0	0	0	0

GOALTENDERS

	Games	Min.	W	L	T	Goals	SO	Avg.
Andy Moog	4	246	1	3	0	12	0	2.93
Darcy Wakaluk	5	307	4	1	0	15	0	2.93

DETROIT RED WINGS

(Lost Western Conference quarterfinals to San Jose, 4-3)

SCORING

	Games	G	A	Pts.	PIM
Sergei Fedorov	7	1	7	8	6
Dino Ciccarelli	7	5	2	7	14
Vyacheslav Kozlov	7	2	5	7	12
Paul Coffey	7	1	6	7	8
Nicklas Lidstrom	7	3	2	5	0
Steve Chiasson	7	2	3	5	2
Kris Draper	7	2	2	4	4
Greg Johnson	7	2	2	4	2
Darren McCarty	7	2	2	4	8
Steve Yzerman	3	1	3	4	0
Ray Sheppard	7	2	1	3	4
Sheldon Kennedy	7	1	2	3	0
Shawn Burr	7	2	0	2	6
Bob Probert	7	1	1	2	8
Keith Primeau	7	0	2	2	6

	Games	G	A	Pts.	PIM
Vlad. Konstantinov	7	0	2	2	4
Mark Howe	6	0	1	1	0
Bob Halkidis	1	0	0	0	2
Bob Essensa (goalie)	2	0	0	0	0
Martin Lapointe	4	0	0	0	6
Chris Osgood (goalie)	6	0	0	0	0
Terry Carkner	7	0	0	0	4

GOALTENDERS

	Games	Min.	W	L	T	Goals	SO	Avg.
Chris Osgood	6	307	3	2	0	12	1	2.35
Bob Essensa	2	109	0	2	0	9	0	4.95

MONTREAL CANADIENS

(Lost Eastern Conference quarterfinals to Boston, 4-3)

SCORING

	Games	G	A	Pts.	PIM
Kirk Muller	7	6	2	8	4
Paul Dipietro	7	2	4	6	2
Benoit Brunet	7	1	4	5	16
Mike Keane	6	3	1	4	4
Guy Carbonneau	7	1	3	4	4
Patrice Brisebois	7	0	4	4	6
John LeClair	7	2	1	3	8
Gilbert Dionne	5	1	2	3	0
Brian Bellows	6	1	2	3	2
Vincent Damphousse	7	1	2	3	8
Kevin Haller	7	1	1	2	19
Turner Stevenson	3	0	2	2	0
Brian Savage	3	0	2	2	0
Eric Desjardins	7	0	2	2	4
Ed Ronan	7	1	0	1	0
Pierre Sevigny	3	0	1	1	0
Peter Popovic	6	0	1	1	0
J.J. Daigneault	7	0	1	1	12
Gary Leeman	1	0	0	0	0
Matt Schneider	1	0	0	0	0
Ron Tugnutt (goalie)	1	0	0	0	0
Oleg Petrov	2	0	0	0	0
Donald Brashear	2	0	0	0	0
Ron Wilson	4	0	0	0	0
Patrick Roy (goalie)	6	0	0	0	0
Lyle Odelein	7	0	0	0	17

GOALTENDERS

	Games	Min.	W	L	T	Goals	SO	Avg.
Patrick Roy	6	375	3	3	0	16	0	2.56
Ron Tugnutt	1	59	0	1	0	5	0	5.08

NEW JERSEY DEVILS

(Lost Eastern Conference finals to N.Y. Rangers, 4-3)

SCORING

	Games	G	A	Pts.	PIM
Claude Lemieux	20	7	11	18	44
John MacLean	20	6	10	16	22
Bernie Nicholls	16	4	9	13	28
Stephane Richer	20	7	5	12	6
Scott Stevens	20	2	9	11	42
Bruce Driver	20	3	5	8	12
Jim Dowd	19	2	6	8	8
Bob Carpenter	20	1	7	8	20
Valeri Zelepukin	20	5	2	7	14
Tom Chorske	20	4	3	7	0
Tommy Albelin	20	2	5	7	14
Scott Niedermayer	20	2	2	4	8
Bill Guerin	17	2	1	3	35
Randy McKay	20	1	2	3	24
Bobby Holik	20	0	3	3	6
Ben Hankinson	2	1	0	1	4
Corey Millen	7	1	0	1	2
Viacheslav Fetisov	14	1	0	1	8
Mike Peluso	17	1	0	1	64
Martin Brodeur (goalie)	17	0	1	1	0

	Games	G	A	Pts.	PIM
Ken Daneyko	20	0	1	1	45
Alexander Semak	2	0	0	0	0
Chris Terreri (goalie)	4	0	0	0	4
Jason Smith	6	0	0	0	7

GOALTENDERS

	Games	Min.	W	L	T	Goals	SO	Avg.
Martin Brodeur	17	1171	8	9	0	38	1	1.95
Chris Terreri	4	200	3	0	0	9	0	2.70

NEW YORK ISLANDERS

(Lost Eastern Conference quarterfinals to N.Y. Rangers, 4-0)

SCORING

	Games	G	A	Pts.	PIM
Dan Plante	1	1	0	1	2
Ray Ferraro	4	1	0	1	6
Steve Thomas	4	1	0	1	8
Benoit Hogue	4	0	1	1	4
Brad Dalgarno	4	0	1	1	4
Derek King	4	0	1	1	0
Uwe Krupp	4	0	1	1	4
Pierre Turgeon	4	0	1	1	0
Dennis Vaske	4	0	1	1	2
Dean Chynoweth	2	0	0	0	2
Dave Chyzowski	2	0	0	0	0
Yan Kaminsky	2	0	0	0	4
Jamie McLennan (goalie)	2	0	0	0	0
Ron Hextall (goalie)	3	0	0	0	4
Tom Kurvers	3	0	0	0	2
Scott Lachance	3	0	0	0	0
David Maley	3	0	0	0	0
Keith Acton	4	0	0	0	8
Mick Vukota	4	0	0	0	17
Travis Green	4	0	0	0	2
Darius Kasparaitis	4	0	0	0	8
Vladimir Malakhov	4	0	0	0	6
Marty McInnis	4	0	0	0	0

GOALTENDERS

	Games	Min.	W	L	T	Goals	SO	Avg.
Jamie McLennan	2	82	0	1	0	6	0	4.39
Ron Hextall	3	158	0	3	0	16	0	6.08

NEW YORK RANGERS

(Winner of 1994 Stanley Cup)

SCORING

	Games	G	A	Pts.	PIM
Brian Leetch	23	11	23	34	6
Mark Messier	23	12	18	30	33
Alexei Kovalev	23	9	12	21	18
Sergei Zubov	22	5	14	19	0
Adam Graves	23	10	7	17	24
Steve Larmer	23	9	7	16	14
Brian Noonan	22	4	7	11	17
Stephane Matteau	23	6	3	9	20
Esa Tikkanen	23	4	4	8	34
Sergei Nemchinov	23	2	5	7	6
Glenn Anderson	23	3	3	6	42
Jeff Beukeboom	22	0	6	6	50
Craig MacTavish	23	1	4	5	22
Greg Gilbert	23	1	3	4	8
Alexander Karpovtsev	17	0	4	4	12
Doug Lidster	9	2	0	2	10
Joey Kocur	20	1	1	2	17
Kevin Lowe	22	1	0	1	20
Ed Olczyk	1	0	0	0	0
Glenn Healy (goalie)	2	0	0	0	0
Nick Kypreos	3	0	0	0	2
Mike Richter (goalie)	23	0	0	0	2
Jay Wells	23	0	0	0	20

GOALTENDERS

	Games	Min.	W	L	T	Goals	SO	Avg.
Glenn Healy	2	68	0	0	0	1	0	0.88
Mike Richter	23	1417	16	7	0	49	4	2.07

PITTSBURGH PENGUINS

(Lost Eastern Conf. quarterfinals to Washington Capitals, 4-2)

SCORING

	Games	G	A	Pts.	PIM
Mario Lemieux	6	4	3	7	2
Jaromir Jagr	6	2	4	6	16
Rick Tocchet	6	2	3	5	20
Larry Murphy	6	0	5	5	0
Kevin Stevens	6	1	1	2	10
Peter Taglianetti	5	0	2	2	16
Ron Francis	6	0	2	2	2
Joe Mullen	6	1	0	1	2
Shawn McEachern	6	1	0	1	2
Martin Straka	6	1	0	1	4
Greg Brown	6	0	1	1	2
Ulf Samuelsson	6	0	1	1	18
Larry DePalma	1	0	0	0	0
Greg Hawgood	1	0	0	0	0
Mike Ramsey	1	0	0	0	0
Bryan Trottier	2	0	0	0	0
Grant Jennings	3	0	0	0	2
Jim McKenzie	3	0	0	0	0
Chris Tamer	5	0	0	0	2
Tom Barrasso (goalie)	6	0	0	0	0
Doug Brown	6	0	0	0	2
Kjell Samuelsson	6	0	0	0	26
Tomas Sandstrom	6	0	0	0	4

GOALTENDERS

	Games	Min.	W	L	T	Goals	SO	Avg.
Tom Barrasso	6	356	2	4	0	17	0	2.87

ST. LOUIS BLUES

(Lost Western Conference quarterfinals to Dallas, 4-0)

SCORING

	Games	G	A	Pts.	PIM
Brendan Shanahan	4	2	5	7	4
Craig Janney	4	1	3	4	0
Phil Housley	4	2	1	3	4
Brett Hull	4	2	1	3	0
Alexei Kasatonov	4	2	0	2	2
Steve Duchesne	4	0	2	2	2
Kevin Miller	3	1	0	1	4
Kelly Chase	4	0	1	1	6
Petr Nedved	4	0	1	1	4
Tom Tilley	4	0	1	1	2
Dave Mackey	2	0	0	0	2
Basil McRae	2	0	0	0	12
Igor Korolev	2	0	0	0	0
David Roberts	3	0	0	0	12
Murray Baron	4	0	0	0	10
Philippe Bozon	4	0	0	0	4
Tony Hrkac	4	0	0	0	0
Curtis Joseph (goalie)	4	0	0	0	0
Peter Stastny	4	0	0	0	6
Rick Zombo	4	0	0	0	11
Vitali Prokhorov	4	0	0	0	0

GOALTENDERS

	Games	Min.	W	L	T	Goals	SO	Avg.
Curtis Joseph	4	246	0	4	0	15	0	3.66

SAN JOSE SHARKS

(Lost Western Conference semifinals to Toronto, 4-3)

SCORING

	Games	G	A	Pts.	PIM
Igor Larionov	14	5	13	18	10
Sergei Makarov	14	8	2	10	4

	Games	G	A	Pts.	PIM
Todd Elik	14	5	5	10	12
Johan Garpenlov	14	4	6	10	6
Sandis Ozolinsh	14	0	10	10	8
Ulf Dahlen	14	6	2	8	0
Tom Pederson	14	1	6	7	2
Jeff Norton	14	1	5	6	20
Jamie Baker	14	3	2	5	30
Bob Errey	14	3	2	5	10
Gaetan Duchesne	14	1	4	5	12
Ray Whitney	14	0	4	4	8
Pat Falloon	14	1	2	3	6
Vlastimil Kroupa	14	1	2	3	21
Rob Gaudreau	14	2	0	2	0
Jay More	13	0	2	2	32
Shawn Cronin	14	1	0	1	20
Mike Rathje	1	0	0	0	0
Jim Waite (goalie)	2	0	0	0	0
Jeff Odgers	11	0	0	0	11
Arturs Irbe (goalie)	14	0	0	0	6

GOALTENDERS

	Games	Min.	W	L	T	Goals	SO	Avg.
Arturs Irbe	14	806	7	7	0	50	0	3.72
Jim Waite	2	40	0	0	0	3	0	4.50

TORONTO MAPLE LEAFS

(Lost Western Conference finals to Vancouver, 4-1)

SCORING

	Games	G	A	Pts.	PIM
Doug Gilmour	18	6	22	28	42
Dave Ellett	18	3	15	18	31
Wendel Clark	18	9	7	16	24
Dmitri Mironov	18	6	9	15	6
Mike Gartner	18	5	6	11	14
Dave Andreychuk	18	5	5	10	16
Mark Osborne	18	4	2	6	52
Peter Zezel	18	2	4	6	8
Todd Gill	18	1	5	6	37
Mike Eastwood	18	3	2	5	12
Nikolai Borschevsky	15	2	2	4	4
Bill Berg	18	1	2	3	10
Sylvain Lefebvre	18	0	3	3	16
Bob Rouse	18	0	3	3	29
Jamie Macoun	18	1	1	2	12
Kent Manderville	12	1	0	1	4
Rob Pearson	14	1	0	1	32
Damian Rhodes (goalie)	1	0	0	0	0
Chris Govedaris	2	0	0	0	0
Darby Hendrickson	2	0	0	0	0
Eric Lacroix	2	0	0	0	0
John Cullen	3	0	0	0	0
Mike Krushelnyski	6	0	0	0	0
Ken McRae	6	0	0	0	4
Ken Baumgartner	10	0	0	0	18
Felix Potvin (goalie)	18	0	0	0	4

GOALTENDERS

	Games	Min.	W	L	T	Goals	SO	Avg.
Damian Rhodes	1	0	0	0	0	0	0	0.00
Felix Potvin	18	1124	9	9	0	46	3	2.46

VANCOUVER CANUCKS

(Lost Stanley Cup finals to N.Y. Rangers, 4-3)

SCORING

	Games	G	A	Pts.	PIM
Pavel Bure	24	16	15	31	40
Trevor Linden	24	12	13	25	18
Geoff Courtnall	24	9	10	19	51
Jeff Brown	24	6	9	15	37
Cliff Ronning	24	5	10	15	16
Greg Adams	23	6	8	14	2
Murray Craven	22	4	9	13	18
Jyrki Lumme	24	2	11	13	16
Martin Gelinas	24	5	4	9	14
Nathan Lafayette	20	2	7	9	4
Dave Babych	24	3	5	8	12
Gerald Diduck	24	1	7	8	22
Sergio Momesso	24	3	4	7	56
Bret Hedican	24	1	6	7	16
Brian Glynn	17	0	3	3	10
Jose Charbonneau	3	1	0	1	4
Jimmy Carson	2	0	1	1	0
Shawn Antoski	16	0	1	1	36
John McIntyre	24	0	1	1	16
Kirk McLean (goalie)	24	0	1	1	0
Dana Murzyn	7	0	0	0	4
Gino Odjick	10	0	0	0	18
Tim Hunter	24	0	0	0	26

GOALTENDERS

	Games	Min.	W	L	T	Goals	SO	Avg.
Kirk McLean	24	1544	15	9	0	59	4	2.29

WASHINGTON CAPITALS

(Lost Eastern Conference semifinals to N.Y. Rangers, 4-1)

SCORING

	Games	G	A	Pts.	PIM
Mike Ridley	11	4	6	10	6
Joe Juneau	11	4	5	9	6
Kelly Miller	11	2	7	9	0
Sylvain Cote	9	1	8	9	6
Michal Pivonka	7	4	4	8	4
Kevin Hatcher	11	3	4	7	37
Peter Bondra	9	2	4	6	4
Dimitri Khristich	11	2	3	5	10
Dave Poulin	11	2	2	4	19
Calle Johansson	6	1	3	4	4
Joe Reekie	11	2	1	3	29
Dale Hunter	7	0	3	3	14
Todd Krygier	5	2	0	2	10
John Slaney	11	1	1	2	2
Randy Burridge	11	0	2	2	12
Jason Woolley	4	1	0	1	4
Shawn Anderson	8	1	0	1	12
Pat Peake	8	0	1	1	8
Keith Jones	11	0	1	1	36
Steve Konowalchuk	11	0	1	1	10
Rick Tabaracci (goalie)	2	0	0	0	0
Byron Dafoe (goalie)	2	0	0	0	0
Todd Nelson	4	0	0	0	0
Don Beaupre (goalie)	8	0	0	0	2
Craig Berube	8	0	0	0	21

GOALTENDERS

	Games	Min.	W	L	T	Goals	SO	Avg.
Byron Dafoe	2	118	0	2	0	39	5	2.54
Don Beaupre	8	429	5	2	0	21	1	2.94
Rick Tabaracci	2	111	0	2	0	6	0	3.24

MISCELLANEOUS

HAT TRICKS

(Players scoring three or more goals in a game)

Date	Player, Team	Opp.	Goals	Date	Player, Team	Opp.	Goals
4-23-94	Tony Amonte, Chicago	Tor.	4	5- 6-94	Ulf Dahlen, San Jose	Tor.	3
4-24-94	Gary Suter, Chicago	Tor.	3	5-25-94	Mark Messier, N.Y. Rangers	N.J.	3

OVERTIME GOALS

Date	Player, Team	Opponent	Time	Final score
4-20-94	Todd Gill, Toronto	Chicago	2:15	Toronto 1, Chicago 0
4-22-94	Paul Cavallini, Dallas	St. Louis	8:34	Dallas 5, St. Louis 4
4-24-94	Jeremy Roenick, Chicago	Toronto	1:23	Chicago 4, Toronto 3
4-25-94	Kirk Muller, Montreal	Boston	17:18	Montreal 2, Boston 1
4-26-94	Geoff Courtnall, Vancouver	Calgary	7:15	Vancouver 2, Calgary 1
4-27-94	Dave Hannan, Buffalo	New Jersey	†5:43	Buffalo 1, New Jersey 0
4-28-94	Trevor Linden, Vancouver	Calgary	16:43	Vancouver 3, Calgary 2
4-30-94	Pavel Bure, Vancouver	Calgary	*2:20	Vancouver 4, Calgary 3
5- 3-94	Don Sweeney, Boston	New Jersey	9:08	Boston 6, New Jersey 5
5- 7-94	Stephane Richer, New Jersey	Boston	14:19	New Jersey 5, Boston 4
5- 8-94	Sergio Momesso, Vancouver	Dallas	11:01	Vancouver 2, Dallas 1
5-12-94	Mike Gartner, Toronto	San Jose	8:53	Toronto 3, San Jose 2
5-15-94	Stephane Richer, New Jersey	N.Y. Rangers	*15:23	New Jersey 4, N.Y. Rangers 3
5-16-94	Peter Zezel, Toronto	Vancouver	16:55	Toronto 3, Vancouver 2
5-19-94	Stephane Matteau, N.Y. Rangers	New Jersey	*6:13	N.Y. Rangers 3, New Jersey 2
5-24-94	Greg Adams, Vancouver	Toronto	*0:14	Vancouver 4, Toronto 3
5-27-94	Stephane Matteau, N.Y. Rangers	New Jersey	*4:24	N.Y. Rangers 2, New Jersey 1
5-31-94	Greg Adams, Vancouver	N.Y. Rangers	19:26	Vancouver 3, N.Y. Rangers 2

*Goal scored in second overtime.
†Goal scored in fourth overtime.

PENALTY-SHOT INFORMATION

Date	Shooter	Goaltender	Scored	Final score
6- 7-94	Pavel Bure, Vancouver	Mike Richter, N.Y. Rangers	No	N.Y. Rangers 4, Vancouver 2

ALL-STAR GAME

AT MADISON SQUARE GARDEN, NEW YORK, JANUARY 22, 1994

ROSTERS

EASTERN CONFERENCE

Coach: Jacques Demers
Associate coaches: Jacques Laperriere, Charles Thiffault

Forwards (Pos.)	Club
Brian Bradley (C)	Tampa Bay Lightning
Adam Graves (LW)	New York Rangers
Bob Kudelski (RW)	Florida Panthers
Eric Lindros (C)	Philadelphia Flyers
Mark Messier (C)	New York Rangers
Alexander Mogilny (RW)	Buffalo Sabres
Joe Mullen† (RW)	Pittsburgh Penguins
Adam Oates (C)	Boston Bruins
Mark Recchi (RW)	Philadelphia Flyers
Joe Sakic (C)	Quebec Nordiques
Geoff Sanderson (C)	Hartford Whalers
Pierre Turgeon (C)	New York Islanders
Alexei Yashin (C)	Ottawa Senators

Defensemen	
Ray Bourque	Boston Bruins
Garry Galley	Philadelphia Flyers
Al Iafrate	Washington Capitals
Brian Leetch	New York Rangers
Larry Murphy	Pittsburgh Penguins
Scott Stevens	New Jersey Devils

Goaltenders	
Mike Richter	New York Rangers
Patrick Roy	Montreal Canadiens
John Vanbiesbrouck	Florida Panthers

Note: Jaromir Jagr of Pittsburgh was injured but was not replaced on the roster.
†Senior category (in recognition of career accomplishments).

WESTERN CONFERENCE

Coach: Barry Melrose
Assistant coach: Cap Raeder

Forwards (Pos.)	Club
Dave Andreychuk (LW)	Toronto Maple Leafs
Pavel Bure (RW)	Vancouver Canucks
Shayne Corson (LW)	Edmonton Oilers
Russ Courtnall (RW)	Dallas Stars
Sergei Fedorov (C)	Detroit Red Wings
Doug Gilmour (C)	Toronto Maple Leafs
Wayne Gretzky (C)	Los Angeles Kings
Brett Hull (RW)	St. Louis Blues
Joe Nieuwendyk (C)	Calgary Flames
Jeremy Roenick (C)	Chicago Blackhawks
Teemu Selanne (RW)	Winnipeg Jets
Brendan Shanahan* (LW)	St. Louis Blues
Dave Taylor† (RW)	Los Angeles Kings

Defensemen	
Rob Blake	Los Angeles Kings
Chris Chelios	Chicago Blackhawks
Paul Coffey	Detroit Red Wings
Alexei Kasatonov	Mighty Ducks of Anaheim
Al MacInnis	Calgary Flames
Sandis Ozolinsh	San Jose Sharks

Goaltenders	
Arturs Irbe*	San Jose Sharks
Curtis Joseph	St. Louis Blues
Felix Potvin	Toronto Maple Leafs

*Replacement for injured teammate (Shanahan for Wendel Clark, Irbe for Mike Vernon).
†Senior category (in recognition of career accomplishments).

GAME SUMMARY

Eastern Conference 9, Western Conference 8

Western Conference	4	2	2—8
Eastern Conference	3	2	4—9

FIRST PERIOD—1. Western, Roenick 1 (Nieuwendyk, Blake), 7:31. 2. Eastern, Kudelski (Turgeon, Bourque), 9:46. 3. Western, Fedorov (Bure, Ozolinsh), 10:20. 4. Eastern, Lindros, 11:00. 5. Western, Shanahan (Gretzky, Hull), 13:21. 6. Eastern, Yashin (Sakic, Turgeon), 14:29. 7. Western, Andreychuk (MacInnis, Fedorov), 15:10. Penalties—None.

SECOND PERIOD—8. Eastern, S. Stevens (Oates, Sanderson), 10:57. 9. Western, Coffey (Andreychuk, Gilmour), 12:36. 10. Western, Ozolinsh (Taylor, Roenick), 14:39. 11. Eastern, Messier (Mullen, Graves), 15:05. Penalties—None.

THIRD PERIOD—12. Western, Ozolinsh (Bure), 0:55. 13. Eastern, Mullen (Graves, Messier), 1:28. 14. Western, Shanahan (Gretzky, Chelios), 7:40. 15. Eastern, Sakic (Turgeon, Stevens), 10:41. 16. Eastern, Kudelski (Messier), 13:59. 17. Eastern, Yashin (Sakic, Turgeon), 16:18. Penalties—None.

Shots on goal—Western 17-21-8—46; Eastern 19-18-19—56. Power-play opportunities—None. Goalies—Western, Potvin (19 shots-16 saves); Irbe (0:00 second, 18-16); Joseph (0:00 third, 19-16). Eastern, Roy (16-12); Richter (0:00 second, 21-19); Vanbiesbrouck (0:00 third, 8-5). A—18,200. Referee—Bill McCreary. Linesmen—Gord Broseker, Pat Dapuzzo.

AWARDS

THE SPORTING NEWS

ALL-STAR TEAMS

John Vanbiesbrouck, Florida	Goaltender	Dominik Hasek, Buffalo
Ray Bourque, Boston	Defense	Brian Leetch, N.Y. Rangers
Scott Stevens, New Jersey	Defense	Al MacInnis, Calgary
Adam Graves, N.Y. Rangers	Left wing	Dave Andreychuk, Toronto
Sergei Fedorov, Detroit	Center	Wayne Gretzky, Los Angeles
Cam Neely, Boston	Right wing	Pavel Bure, Vancouver

Note: THE SPORTING NEWS All-Star Team is selected by the NHL players.

AWARD WINNERS

Player of the Year: Sergei Fedorov, Detroit
Rookie of the Year: Jason Arnott, Edmonton

Coach of the Year: Jacques Lemaire, New Jersey
Executive of the Year: Bobby Clarke, Florida

Note: THE SPORTING NEWS player and rookie awards are selected by the NHL players, the coaches award by the NHL coaches and the executive award by NHL executives.

NATIONAL HOCKEY LEAGUE

ALL-STAR TEAMS

Dominik Hasek, Buffalo	Goaltender	John Vanbiesbrouck, Florida
Ray Bourque, Boston	Defense	Brian Leetch, N.Y. Rangers
Scott Stevens, New Jersey	Defense	Al MacInnis, Calgary
Brendan Shanahan, St. Louis	Left wing	Adam Graves, N.Y. Rangers
Sergei Fedorov, Detroit	Center	Wayne Gretzky, Los Angeles
Pavel Bure, Vancouver	Right wing	Cam Neely, Boston

AWARD WINNERS

Art Ross Trophy: Wayne Gretzky, Los Angeles
Hart Memorial Trophy: Sergei Fedorov, Detroit
James Norris Memorial Trophy: Ray Bourque, Boston
Vezina Trophy: Dominik Hasek, Buffalo
Bill Jennings Trophy: Dominik Hasek, Buffalo
                    Grant Fuhr, Buffalo
Calder Memorial Trophy: Martin Brodeur, New Jersey

Lady Byng Memorial Trophy: Wayne Gretzky, Los Angeles
Conn Smythe Trophy: Brian Leetch, N.Y. Rangers
Bill Masterton Memorial Trophy: Cam Neely, Boston
Frank J. Selke Trophy: Sergei Fedorov, Detroit
Jack Adams Award: Jacques Lemaire, New Jersey
King Clancy Trophy: Adam Graves, N.Y. Rangers

PLAYER DRAFTS

SUPPLEMENTAL DRAFT—JUNE 28, 1994

Pick	Team selecting	Name, Position, College
1.	Florida	Sean McCann, D, Harvard
2.	Anaheim	Steve Rucchin, C, Western Ontario
3.	Ottawa	Steven Guolla, LW, Michigan State
4.	Winnipeg	Randy Stevens, RW, Michigan Tech
5.	Hartford	Steve Martins, C, Harvard

Pick	Team selecting	Name, Position, College
6.	Edmonton	Chad Dameworth, D, Northern Michigan
7.	Los Angeles	Quinn Fair, D, Kent
8.	Tampa Bay	Francois Bouchard, D, Northeastern
9.	Quebec	Reid Simonton, D, Union
10.	Philadelphia	Kirk Nielsen, RW, Harvard

ENTRY DRAFT—JUNE 28-29, 1994

FIRST ROUND

No.—Selecting club	Player	Pos.	Previous team (league)
1—Florida	Ed Jovanovski	D	Windsor (OHL)
2—Anaheim	Oleg Tverdovsky	D	Krylja Sovetov, CIS
3—Ottawa	Radek Bonk	C	Las Vegas (IHL)
4—Edmonton (from Winnipeg)	Jason Bonsignore	C	Niagara Falls (OHL)
5—Hartford	Jeff O'Neill	C	Guelph (OHL)
6—Edmonton	Ryan Smyth	LW	Moose Jaw (WHL)
7—Los Angeles	James Storr	G	Owen Sound (OHL)
8—Tampa Bay	Jason Weimer	LW	Portland (WHL)
9—N.Y. Islanders (from Quebec)	Brett Lindros	RW	Kingston (OHL)
10—Was. (from Phi. through Que. and Tor.)	Nolan Baumgartner	D	Kamloops (WHL)
11—San Jose	Jeff Friesen	LW	Regina (WHL)
12—Quebec (from N.Y. Islanders)	Wade Belak	D	Saskatoon (WHL)
13—Vancouver	Mattias Ohlund	D	Pitea, Sweden
14—Chicago	Ethan Moreau	LW	Niagara Falls (OHL)
15—Washington	Alexander Kharlanov	C	CSKA Moscow, CIS
16—Toronto (from St.L. through Was.)	Eric Fichaud	G	Chicoutimi (QMJHL)
17—Buffalo	Wayne Primeau	C	Owen Sound (OHL)
18—Montreal	Brad Brown	D	North Bay (OHL)
19—Calgary	Chris Dingman	LW	Brandon (WHL)
20—Dallas	Jason Botterill	LW	University of Michigan (CCHA)
21—Boston	Evgeni Ryabchikov	G	Molot Perm, CIS
22—Quebec (from Toronto)	Jeffrey Kealty	D	Catholic Memorial HS (Mass.)
23—Detroit	Yan Golubovsky	D	CSKA Moscow, CIS
24—Pittsburgh	Chris Wells	C	Seattle (WHL)
25—New Jersey	Vadim Sharifjanov	RW	Salavat Yulayev Ufa, CIS
26—N.Y. Rangers	Dan Cloutier	G	Sault Ste. Marie (OHL)

SECOND ROUND

No.—Selecting club	Player	Pos.	Previous team (league)
27—Florida	Rhett Warrener	D	Saskatoon (WHL)
28—Anaheim	Johan Davidsson	C	Jonkoping, Sweden
29—Ottawa	Stanislav Neckar	D	HC Ceske Budejovice, Czech.
30—Winnipeg	Deron Quint	D	Seattle (WHL)
31—Florida (from Hartford)	Jason Podollan	C	Spokane (WHL)
32—Edmonton	Mike Watt	LW	Stratford (Jr. B)
33—Los Angeles	Matt Johnson	LW	Peterborough (OHL)
34—Tampa Bay	Colin Cloutier	C	Brandon (WHL)
35—Quebec	Josef Marha	C	Dukla Jihlava, Czech.
36—Florida (from Philadelphia)	Ryan Johnson	C	Thunder Bay (Jr. A)
37—San Jose	Angel Nikolov	D	Chemopetrol (Czech Jrs.)
38—N.Y. Islanders	Jason Holland	D	Kamloops (WHL)
39—Vancouver	Robb Gordon	C	Powell River (Tier II)
40—Chicago	Jean-Yves Leroux	LW	Beauport (QMJHL)
41—Washington	Scott Cherrey	LW	North Bay (OHL)
42—Vancouver (from St. Louis)	Dave Scatchard	C	Portland (WHL)
43—Buffalo	Curtis Brown	C	Moose Jaw (WHL)
44—Montreal	Jose Theodore	G	St. Jean (QMJHL)
45—Calgary	Dmitri Ryabykin	D	Dynamo Moscow, CIS
46—Dallas	Lee Jinman	C	North Bay (OHL)
47—Boston	Daniel Goneau	LW	Laval (QMJHL)
48—Toronto	Sean Haggerty	LW	Detroit (OHL)
49—Detroit	Mathieu Dandenault	RW	Sherbrooke (QMJHL)
50—Pittsburgh	Richard Park	C	Belleville (OHL)
51—New Jersey	Patrik Elias	LW	HC Kladno, Czech.
52—N.Y. Rangers	Rudolf Vercik	LW	Slovan Bratislava, Slovakia

THIRD ROUND

No.—Selecting club	Player	Pos.	Previous team (league)
53—Edmonton (from Florida)	Corey Neilson	D	North Bay (OHL)
54—Montreal (from Anaheim)	Chris Murray	RW	Kamloops (WHL)
55—Tampa Bay (from Ott. through Ana.)	Vadim Epanchintsev	C	Spartak Moscow, CIS
56—Winnipeg	Dorian Anneck	C	Victoria (WHL)
57—Pittsburgh (from Hartford)	Sven Butenschon	D	Brandon (WHL)
58—Winnipeg (from Edmonton)	Tavis Hansen	C	Tacoma (WHL)
59—Los Angeles	Vitali Yachmenev	RW	North Bay (OHL)
60—Edmonton (from Tampa Bay)	Brad Symes	D	Portland (WHL)
61—Quebec	Sebastien Bety	D	Drummondville (QMJHL)
62—Philadelphia	Arten Anisimov	D	Itil Kazan, CIS
63—N.Y. Islanders (from San Jose)	Jason Strudwick	D	Kamloops (WHL)
64—Toronto (from N.Y. Islanders)	Fredrik Modin	LW	Sundsvall Timra, Sweden
65—Vancouver	Chad Allan	D	Saskatoon (WHL)
66—San Jose (from Chicago)	Alexei Yegorov	C	CSKA St. Petersburg, CIS
67—Anaheim (from Was. through T.B.)	Craig Reichert	RW	Red Deer (WHL)
68—St. Louis	Stephane Roy	C	Val-d'Or (QMJHL)
69—Buffalo	Rumun Ndur	D	Guelph (OHL)
70—Montreal	Marko Kiprusoff	D	TPS Turku, CIS
71—New Jersey (from Calgary)	Sheldon Souray	D	Tri-City (WHL)
72—Quebec (from Dallas)	Chris Drury	C	Fairfield Prep (Ct.)
73—Pittsburgh (from Boston)	Greg Crozier	LW	Lawrence Academy (Mass.)
74—Montreal (from Toronto)	Martin Belanger	D	Granby (QMJHL)
75—Detroit	Sean Gillam	D	Spokane (WHL)
76—Pittsburgh	Alexei Krivchenkov	D	CSKA Moscow, CIS
77—Calgary (from New Jersey)	Chris Clark	RW	Springfield (Jr. B)
78—N.Y. Rangers	Adam Smith	D	Tacoma (WHL)

FOURTH ROUND

No.—Selecting club	Player	Pos.	Previous team (league)
79—Edmonton (from Fla. through Win.)	Adam Copeland	RW	Burlington (Jr. B)
80—Anaheim	Byron Briske	D	Red Deer (WHL)
81—Ottawa	Bryan Masotta	G	Hotchkiss H.S. (N.Y.)
82—Winnipeg	Steve Cheredaryk	D	Medicine Hat (WHL)
83—Hartford	Hnat Domenichelli	C	Kamloops (WHL)
84—Florida (from Edmonton)	David Nemirovsky	RW	Ottawa (OHL)
85—Chicago (from Los Angeles)	Steve McLaren	D	North Bay (OHL)
86—Tampa Bay	Dmitri Klevakin	RW	Spartak Moscow, CIS
87—Quebec	Milan Hejduk	RW	HC Pardubice, Czech.
88—Philadelphia	Adam Magarrell	D	Brandon (WHL)
89—San Jose	Vaclav Varada	RW	HC Vitkovice, Czech.
90—N.Y. Islanders	Brad Lukowich	D	Kamloops (WHL)
91—Calgary (from Van. through T.B. and N.J.)	Ryan Duthie	C	Spokane (WHL)
92—Vancouver (from Chicago)	Mike Dubinsky	RW	Brandon (WHL)
93—Washington	Matthew Herr	C	Hotchkiss H.S. (N.Y.)
94—St. Louis	Tyler Harlton	D	Vernon (Tier II, Jr. A)
95—Edmonton (from Buffalo)	Jussi Tarvainen	C	Kalpa Kuopio, Finland
96—Montreal	Arto Kuki	C	Espoo, Finland
97—Calgary	Johan Finnstrom	D	Rogle Angelholm, Sweden
98—Dallas	Jamie Wright	LW	Guelph (OHL)
99—Boston	Eric Nickulas	C	Cushing Academy (Mass.)
100—N.Y. Rangers (from Toronto)	Alexander Korobolin	D	Chelyabinsk, CIS
101—Philadelphia (from Detroit)	Sebastien Vallee	LW	Victoriaville (QMJHL)
102—Pittsburgh	Thomas O'Connor	D	Springfield (Jr. B)
103—New Jersey	Zdenek Skorepa	LW	Chemopetrol (Czech Jrs.)
104—N.Y. Rangers	Sylvain Blouin	D	Laval (QMJHL)

FIFTH ROUND

No.—Selecting club	Player	Pos.	Previous team (league)
105—Florida	Dave Geris	D	Windsor (OHL)
106—Anaheim	Pavel Trnka	D	Skoda Pizen, Czech.
107—Calgary (from Ott. through N.J.)	Nils Ekman	RW	Stockholm Hammarby, Sweden
108—Winnipeg	Craig Mills	RW	Belleville (OHL)
109—Hartford	Ryan Risidore	D	Guelph (OHL)
110—Edmonton	Jon Gaskins	D	Dubuque (Jr. A)
111—Los Angeles	Chris Schmidt	C	Seattle (WHL)
112—N.Y. Islanders (from Tampa Bay)	Mark McArthur	G	Guelph (OHL)
113—Quebec	Tony Tuzzolino	RW	Michigan State
114—Detroit (from Philadelphia)	Frederic Deschenes	G	Granby (QMJHL)
115—San Jose	Brian Swanson	C	Omaha (Jr. A)
116—N.Y. Islanders	Albert O'Connell	LW	St. Sebastian's H.S. (Mass.)

No.—Selecting club	Player	Pos.	Previous team (league)
117—Vancouver	Yanick Dube	C	Laval (QMJHL)
118—Chicago	Marc Dupuis	D	Belleville (OHL)
119—Washington	Yanick Jean	D	Chemopetrol (Czech Jrs.)
120—St. Louis	Edwin Frylen	D	Vasteras, Sweden
121—Buffalo	Sergei Klimentjev	D	Medicine Hat (WHL)
122—Montreal	Jimmy Drolet	D	St. Hyacinthe (QMJHL)
123—Calgary	Frank Appel	D	Dusseldorf, Germany
124—Dallas	Marty Turco	G	Cambridge (Jr. B)
125—Boston	Darren Wright	D	Prince Albert (WHL)
126—Toronto	Mark Deyell	C	Saskatoon (WHL)
127—Detroit	Doug Battaglia	LW	Brockville (Tier II, Jr. A)
128—Pittsburgh	Clint Johnson	LW	Duluth East H.S. (Minn.)
129—New Jersey	Christian Gosselin	D	St. Hyacinthe (QMJHL)
130—N.Y. Rangers	Martin Etnier	D	Beauport (QMJHL)

SIXTH ROUND

No.—Selecting club	Player	Pos.	Previous team (league)
131—Ottawa (from Florida)	Mike Gaffney	D	St. Johns H.S.
132—Anaheim	Jon Battaglia	RW	Caledon (Jr. A)
133—Ottawa	Daniel Alfredsson	RW	Vastra Frolunda (Sweden)
134—New Jersey (from Winnipeg)	Ryan Smart	C	Meadville H.S.
135—N.Y. Rangers (from Hartford)	Yuri Litvinov	C	Krylja Sovetov, CIS
136—Edmonton	Terry Marchant	LW	Niagara (Jr. A)
137—Tampa Bay (from Los Angeles)	Daniel Juden	C	Governor Dummer H.S. (Mass.)
138—Tampa Bay	Bryce Salvador	D	Lethbridge (WHL)
139—Quebec	Nicholas Windsor	D	Cornwall (Tier II)
140—Philadelphia	Alexander Selivanov	RW	Spartak Moscow, CIS
141—San Jose	Alexander Korolyuk	RW	Krylja Sovetov, CIS
142—N.Y. Islanders	Jason Stewart	D	Simley H.S.
143—Winnipeg (from Vancouver)	Steve Vezina	G	Beauport (QMJHL)
144—Chicago	Jim Ensom	C	North Bay (OHL)
145—Washington	Dmitri Mekeskin	D	Avangard CMSK, CIS
146—Winnipeg (from St. Louis)	Chris Kibermanis	D	Red Deer (WHL)
147—Buffalo	Cal Benazic	D	Medicine Hat (WHL)
148—Montreal	Joel Irving	C	Regina Midgets
149—Calgary	Patrik Haltia	G	Farjestad Grums, Sweden
150—Dallas	Yevgeny Petrochinin	D	Spartak Moscow, CIS
151—Boston	Andre Roy	LW	Chicoutimi (QMJHL)
152—Toronto	Kam White	D	Newmarket (OHL)
153—Detroit	Pavel Agarkov	RW	Krylja Sovetov, CIS
154—Pittsburgh	Valentin Morozov	C	CSKA Moscow, CIS
155—New Jersey	Luciano Caravaggio	G	Michigan Tech
156—N.Y. Rangers	David Brosseau	C	Shawinigan (QMJHL)

SEVENTH ROUND

No.—Selecting club	Player	Pos.	Previous team (league)
157—Florida	Matt O'Dette	D	Kitchener (OHL)
158—Anaheim	Mark Welsing	D	Wisconsin (Jr. A)
159—Ottawa	Doug Sproule	LW	Hotchkiss H.S. (N.Y.)
160—Edmonton (from Winnipeg)	Curtis Sheptak	LW	Olds (Tier II, Jr. A)
161—Pittsburgh (from Hartford)	Serge Aubin	C	Granby (QMJHL)
162—Edmonton	Dmitri Shulga	RW	Tivali Minsk, CIS
163—Los Angeles	Luc Gagne	RW	Sudbury (OHL)
164—Tampa Bay	Chris Maillet	D	Red Deer (WHL)
165—Quebec	Calvin Elfring	D	Powell River (Tier II)
166—Philadelphia	Colin Forbes	LW	Sherwood Park (Tier II)
167—San Jose	Sergei Gorbachev	RW	Dynamo Moscow, CIS
168—Buffalo (from N.Y. Islanders)	Steve Plouffe	G	Granby (QMJHL)
169—Vancouver	Yuri Kuznetsov	C	Avangard CMSK, CIS
170—Chicago	Tyler Prosofsky	C	Tacoma (WHL)
171—Washington	Daniel Reja	C	London (OHL)
172—St. Louis	Roman Vopat	C	Chemopetrol (Czech Jrs.)
173—Buffalo	Shane Hnidy	D	Prince Albert (WHL)
174—Montreal	Jessie Rezansoff	RW	Regina (WHL)
175—Calgary	Ladislav Kohn	RW	Swift Current (WHL)
176—Buffalo (from Dallas)	Steve Webb	RW	Peterborough (OHL)
177—Boston	Jeremy Schaefer	LW	Medicine Hat (WHL)
178—Toronto	Tommi Rajanaki	D	Assat Pori Jrs., Finland
179—Edmonton (from Detroit)	Chris Wickenheiser	G	Red Deer (WHL)
180—Pittsburgh	Drew Palmer	D	Seattle (WHL)
181—New Jersey	Jeff Williams	C	Guelph (OHL)
182—N.Y. Rangers	Alexei Lazarenko	LW	CSKA Moscow, CIS

EIGHTH ROUND

No.—Selecting club	Player	Pos.	Previous team (league)
183—Florida	Jasson Boudrias	C	Laval (QMJHL)
184—Anaheim	John Brad Englehart	LW	Kimball Union Academy (Mass.)
185—Edmonton (from Ottawa)	Rob Guinn	D	Newmarket (OHL)
186—Winnipeg	Ramil Saifulin	C	Avangard CMSK, CIS
187—Hartford	Tom Buckley	C	St. Joseph H.S.
188—Edmonton	Jason Reid	D	St. Andrew's
189—Los Angeles	Andrew Dale	C	Sudbury (OHL)
190—Tampa Bay	Alexei Baranov	C	Dynamo Moscow, CIS
191—Quebec	Jay Bertsch	RW	Spokane (WHL)
192—Philadelphia	Derek Diener	D	Lethbridge (WHL)
193—San Jose	Eric Landry	RW	Guelph (OHL)
194—N.Y. Islanders	Mike Loach	C	Windsor (OHL)
195—Vancouver	Rob Trumbley	C	Moose Jaw (WHL)
196—Chicago	Mike Josephson	LW	Kamloops (WHL)
197—Washington	Chris Patrick	LW	Kent School (Ct.)
198—St. Louis	Steve Noble	C	Stratford (Jr. B)
199—Buffalo	Bob Westerby	LW	Kamloops (WHL)
200—Montreal	Peter Strom	LW	Vastra Frolunda (Sweden)
201—Calgary	Keith McCambridge	D	Swift Current (WHL)
202—Philadelphia (from Dallas)	Raymond Giroux	D	Pomasson (Tier II)
203—N.Y. Islanders (from Boston)	Peter Hogard	C	Vastra Frolunda (Sweden)
204—Toronto	Rob Butler	LW	Niagara (Jr. A)
205—Detroit	Jason Elliot	G	Kimberley (Jr. A)
206—Pittsburgh	Boris Zelenko	LW	CSKA Moscow, CIS
207—New Jersey	Eric Bertrand	LW	Granby (QMJHL)
208—N.Y. Rangers	Craig Anderson	D	Park Center H.S.

NINTH ROUND

No.—Selecting club	Player	Pos.	Previous team (league)
209—N.Y. Rangers (from Florida)	Vitali Yereneyev	G	Torpedo UST Kamenogorsk, CIS
210—Ottawa (from Anaheim)	Frederic Cassivi	G	St. Hyacinthe (QMJHL)
211—Ottawa	Danny Dupont	D	Laval (QMJHL)
212—Winnipeg	Henrik Shangs	G	Leksand, Sweden
213—Hartford	Ashlin Halfnight	D	Harvard University
214—Edmonton	Jeremy Jablonski	G	Victoria (WHL)
215—Los Angeles	Jan Nemecek	D	HC Ceske Budejovice, Czech.
216—Tampa Bay	Yuri Shirnov	C	Spartak Moscow, CIS
217—Quebec	Tim Thomas	G	University of Vermont (ECAC)
218—Philadelphia	Johan Hedberg	G	Leksand, Sweden
219—San Jose	Yevgeny Nabokov	G	Torpedo UST Kamenogorsk, CIS
220—N.Y. Islanders	Gord Walsh	LW	Kingston (OHL)
221—Vancouver	Bill Muckalt	C	Kelowna (Tier II, Jr. A)
222—Chicago	Lubomir Jandera	D	Chemopetrol (Czech Jrs.)
223—Washington	John Tudhy	D	Kent School (Ct.)
224—St. Louis	Marc Stephan	C	Tri-City (WHL)
225—Buffalo	Craig Millar	D	Swift Current (WHL)
226—Montreal	Tomas Vokoun	G	HC Kladno, Czech.
227—Calgary	Jorgen Jonsson	C	Rogle, Sweden
228—Dallas	Marty Flichel	RW	Tacoma (WHL)
229—Boston	John Grahame	G	Sioux City (Jr. A)
230—Hartford (from Toronto)	Matt Ball	RW	Detroit (OHL)
231—Detroit	Jeff Mikesch	C	Michigan Tech
232—Pittsburgh	Jason Godbout	D	Hill Murray H.S. (Minn.)
233—New Jersey	Steve Sullivan	C	Sault Ste. Marie (OHL)
234—N.Y. Rangers	Eric Boulton	LW	Oshawa (OHL)

10TH ROUND

No.—Selecting club	Player	Pos.	Previous team (league)
235—Florida	Tero Lentera	LW	Espoo, Finland
236—Anaheim	Tommi Miettinen	C	Kalpa Kuopio, Finland
237—Ottawa	Stephen MacKinnon	D	Cushing Academy (Mass.)
238—Winnipeg	Mike Mader	D	Loomis-Chaffee H.S. (Pa.)
239—Hartford	Brian Regan	G	Westminster
240—San Jose (from Edmonton)	Tomas Pisa	RW	HC Pardubice, Czech.
241—Los Angeles	Sergei Shalani	LW	Spartak Moscow, CIS
242—Tampa Bay	Shawn Gervais	C	Seattle (WHL)
243—Quebec	Chris Pittman	LW	Kitchener (OHL)
244—Philadelphia	Andre Payette	C	Sault Ste. Marie (OHL)
245—San Jose	Aniket Dhadphale	LW	Marquette
246—N.Y. Islanders	Kirk Dewaele	D	Lethbridge (WHL)

No.—Selecting club	Player	Pos.	Previous team (league)
247—Vancouver	Tyson Nash	LW	Kamloops (WHL)
248—Chicago	Lars Weibel	G	Lugano, Switzerland
249—Washington	Richard Zeonik	RW	Banska Bystrica, Slovakia
250—St. Louis	Kevin Harper	D	Wexford (Jr. A)
251—Buffalo	Mark Polak	C	Medicine Hat (WHL)
252—Montreal	Chris Aldous	D	Northwood Prep (N.Y.)
253—Calgary	Mike Peluso	C	Omaha (Jr. A)
254—Dallas	Jimmy Roy	C	Thunder Bay (Jr. A)
255—Boston	Heil Savary	G	Hull (QMJHL)
256—Toronto	Sergei Berezin	RW	Khimik, CIS
257—Detroit	Tomas Holmstrom	RW	Boden, Sweden
258—Pittsburgh	Mikhail Kazakevich	LW	Torpedo Jaroslav, CIS
259—New Jersey	Scott Swanjord	G	Waterloo (Jr. A)
260—N.Y. Rangers	Radoslav Kropac	LW	Slovan Bratislava, Slovakia

11TH ROUND

No.—Selecting club	Player	Pos.	Previous team (league)
261—Florida	Per Gustafsson	D	HV Jonkoping, Sweden
262—Anaheim	Jeremy Stevenson	LW	Sault Ste. Marie (OHL)
263—Chicago (from Ottawa)	Rob Hara	RW	Belmont Hill H.S. (Mass.)
264—Winnipeg	Jason Issel	LW	Prince Albert (WHL)
265—Hartford	Steve Nimigon	LW	Niagara Falls (OHL)
266—Edmonton	Ladislav Benysek	D	HC Olomouc, Czech.
267—N.Y. Rangers (from Los Angeles)	Jamie Butt	LW	Tacoma (WHL)
268—Tampa Bay	Brian White	D	Arlington Catholic H.S.
269—New Jersey (from Quebec)	Mike Hanson	C	Minot H.S.
270—Philadelphia	Jan Lipiansky	RW	Slovan Bratislava, Slovakia
271—San Jose	David Beauregard	LW	St. Hyacinthe (QMJHL)
272—N.Y. Islanders	Dick Tarnstrom	D	AIK Solna, Sweden
273—Vancouver	Robert Longpre	C	Medicine Hat (WHL)
274—Ottawa (from Chicago)	Antti Tormanen	RW	Jokerit, Finland
275—Washington	Sergei Tertyshny	D	Chelyabinsk, CIS
276—St. Louis	Scott Fankhouser	G	Loomis-Chaffee H.S. (Pa.)
277—Buffalo	Shanye Wright	D	Owen Sound (OHL)
278—Montreal	Ross Parsons	D	Regina (WHL)
279—Calgary	Pavel Torgayev	LW	TPS Turku, CIS
280—Dallas	Chris Szysky	RW	Swift Current (WHL)
281—Boston	Andrei Yakhanov	D	Salavat Yulayev Ufa, CIS
282—Toronto	Doug Nolan	LW	Catholic Memorial HS (Mass.)
283—Detroit	Toivo Suursoo	LW	Krylja Sovetov, CIS
284—Pittsburgh	Brian Leitza	G	Sioux City (Jr. A)
285—Quebec (from New Jersey)	Steven Low	D	Sherbrooke (QMJHL)
286—N.Y. Rangers	Kim Johnsson	D	Malmo, Sweden

NHL HISTORY

Stanley Cup champions

All-Star Games

Records

Award winners

Team histories

STANLEY CUP CHAMPIONS

Season	Club	Coach
1917-18	Toronto Arenas	Dick Carroll
1919-20	Ottawa Senators	Pete Green
1920-21	Ottawa Senators	Pete Green
1921-22	Toronto St. Pats	Eddie Powers
1922-23	Ottawa Senators	Pete Green
1923-24	Montreal Canadiens	Leo Dandurand
1924-25	Victoria Cougars	Lester Patrick
1925-26	Montreal Maroons	Eddie Gerard
1926-27	Ottawa Senators	Dave Gill
1927-28	New York Rangers	Lester Patrick
1928-29	Boston Bruins	Cy Denneny
1929-30	Montreal Canadiens	Cecil Hart
1930-31	Montreal Canadiens	Cecil Hart
1931-32	Toronto Maple Leafs	Dick Irvin
1932-33	New York Rangers	Lester Patrick
1933-34	Chicago Black Hawks	Tommy Gorman
1934-35	Montreal Maroons	Tommy Gorman
1935-36	Detroit Red Wings	Jack Adams
1936-37	Detroit Red Wings	Jack Adams
1937-38	Chicago Black Hawks	Bill Stewart
1938-39	Boston Bruins	Art Ross
1939-40	New York Rangers	Frank Boucher
1940-41	Boston Bruins	Cooney Weiland
1941-42	Toronto Maple Leafs	Hap Day
1942-43	Detroit Red Wings	Jack Adams
1943-44	Montreal Canadiens	Dick Irvin
1944-45	Toronto Maple Leafs	Hap Day
1945-46	Montreal Canadiens	Dick Irvin
1946-47	Toronto Maple Leafs	Hap Day
1947-48	Toronto Maple Leafs	Hap Day
1948-49	Toronto Maple Leafs	Hap Day
1949-50	Detroit Red Wings	Tommy Ivan
1950-51	Toronto Maple Leafs	Joe Primeau
1951-52	Detroit Red Wings	Tommy Ivan
1952-53	Montreal Canadiens	Dick Irvin
1953-54	Detroit Red Wings	Tommy Ivan
1954-55	Detroit Red Wings	Jimmy Skinner
1955-56	Montreal Canadiens	Toe Blake
1956-57	Montreal Canadiens	Toe Blake
1957-58	Montreal Canadiens	Toe Blake
1958-59	Montreal Canadiens	Toe Blake
1959-60	Montreal Canadiens	Toe Blake
1960-61	Chicago Black Hawks	Rudy Pilous
1961-62	Toronto Maple Leafs	Punch Imlach
1962-63	Toronto Maple Leafs	Punch Imlach
1963-64	Toronto Maple Leafs	Punch Imlach
1964-65	Montreal Canadiens	Toe Blake
1965-66	Montreal Canadiens	Toe Blake
1966-67	Toronto Maple Leafs	Punch Imlach
1967-68	Montreal Canadiens	Toe Blake
1968-69	Montreal Canadiens	Claude Ruel
1969-70	Boston Bruins	Harry Sinden
1970-71	Montreal Canadiens	Al MacNeil
1971-72	Boston Bruins	Tom Johnson
1972-73	Montreal Canadiens	Scotty Bowman
1973-74	Philadelphia Flyers	Fred Shero
1974-75	Philadelphia Flyers	Fred Shero
1975-76	Montreal Canadiens	Scotty Bowman
1976-77	Montreal Canadiens	Scotty Bowman
1977-78	Montreal Canadiens	Scotty Bowman
1978-79	Montreal Canadiens	Scotty Bowman
1979-80	New York Islanders	Al Arbour
1980-81	New York Islanders	Al Arbour
1981-82	New York Islanders	Al Arbour
1982-83	New York Islanders	Al Arbour
1983-84	Edmonton Oilers	Glen Sather
1984-85	Edmonton Oilers	Glen Sather
1985-86	Montreal Canadiens	Jean Perron
1986-87	Edmonton Oilers	Glen Sather
1987-88	Edmonton Oilers	Glen Sather
1988-89	Calgary Flames	Terry Crisp
1989-90	Edmonton Oilers	John Muckler
1990-91	Pittsburgh Penguins	Bob Johnson
1991-92	Pittsburgh Penguins	Scotty Bowman
1992-93	Montreal Canadiens	Jacques Demers
1993-94	New York Rangers	Mike Keenan

NOTE: 1918-19 series between Montreal and Seattle cancelled after five games because of influenza epidemic.

ALL-STAR GAMES

RESULTS

Date	Site	Winning team, score	Losing team, score	Att.
2-14-34†	Maple Leaf Gardens, Toronto	Toronto Maple Leafs, 7	NHL All-Stars, 3	* 14,000
11-3-37‡	Montreal Forum	NHL All-Stars, 6	Montreal All-Stars§, 5	8,683
10-29-39★	Montreal Forum	NHL All-Stars, 5	Montreal Canadiens, 2	*6,000
10-13-47	Maple Leaf Gardens, Toronto	NHL All-Stars, 4	Toronto Maple Leafs, 3	14,169
11-3-48	Chicago Stadium	NHL All-Stars, 3	Toronto Maple Leafs, 1	12,794
10-10-49	Maple Leaf Gardens, Toronto	NHL All-Stars, 3	Toronto Maple Leafs, 1	13,541
10-8-50	Olympia Stadium, Detroit	Detroit Red Wings, 7	NHL All-Stars, 1	9,166
10-9-51	Maple Leaf Gardens, Toronto	First Team•, 2	Second Team•, 2	11,469
10-5-52	Olympia Stadium, Detroit	First Team•, 1	Second Team•, 1	10,680
10-3-53	Montreal Forum	NHL All-Stars, 3	Montreal Canadiens, 1	14,153
10-2-54	Olympia Stadium, Detroit	NHL All-Stars, 2	Detroit Red Wings, 2	10,689
10-2-55	Olympia Stadium, Detroit	Detroit Red Wings, 3	NHL All-Stars, 1	10,111
10-9-56	Montreal Forum	NHL All-Stars, 1	Montreal Canadiens, 1	13,095
10-5-57	Montreal Forum	NHL All-Stars, 5	Montreal Canadiens, 3	13,095
10-4-58	Montreal Forum	Montreal Canadiens, 6	NHL All-Stars, 3	13,989
10-3-59	Montreal Forum	Montreal Canadiens, 6	NHL All-Stars, 1	13,818
10-1-60	Montreal Forum	NHL All-Stars, 2	Montreal Canadiens, 1	13,949
10-7-61	Chicago Stadium	NHL All-Stars, 3	Chicago Blackhawks, 1	14,534
10-6-62	Maple Leaf Gardens, Toronto	Toronto Maple Leafs, 4	NHL All-Stars, 1	14,236
10-5-63	Maple Leaf Gardens, Toronto	NHL All-Stars, 3	Toronto Maple Leafs, 3	14,034
10-10-64	Maple Leaf Gardens, Toronto	NHL All-Stars, 3	Toronto Maple Leafs, 2	14,232
10-20-65	Montreal Forum	NHL All-Stars, 5	Montreal Canadiens, 2	14,284
1-18-67	Montreal Forum	Montreal Canadiens, 3	NHL All-Stars, 0	14,284
1-16-68	Maple Leaf Gardens, Toronto	Toronto Maple Leafs, 4	NHL All-Stars, 3	15,753
1-21-69	Montreal Forum	West Division, 3	East Division, 3	16,260
1-20-70	St. Louis Arena	East Division, 4	West Division, 1	16,587
1-19-71	Boston Garden	West Division, 2	East Division, 1	14,790
1-25-72	Met Sports Center, Bloomington, Minn.	East Division, 3	West Division, 2	15,423
1-30-73	Madison Square Garden, New York	East Division, 5	West Division, 4	16,986
1-29-74	Chicago Stadium	West Division, 6	East Division, 4	16,426
1-21-75	Montreal Forum	Wales Conference, 7	Campbell Conference, 1	16,080
1-20-76	The Spectrum, Philadelphia	Wales Conference, 7	Campbell Conference, 5	16,436
1-25-77	Pacific Coliseum, Vancouver	Wales Conference, 4	Campbell Conference, 3	15,607
1-24-78	Buffalo Memorial Auditorium	Wales Conference, 3	Campbell Conference, 2 (OT)	16,433
	1979 All-Star Game replaced by Challenge Cup series between Team NHL and Soviet Union			
2-5-80	Joe Louis Arena, Detroit	Wales Conference, 6	Campbell Conference, 3	21,002
2-10-81	The Forum, Los Angeles	Campbell Conference, 4	Wales Conference, 1	15,761
2-9-82	Capital Centre, Landover, Md.	Wales Conference, 4	Campbell Conference, 2	18,130
2-8-83	Nassau Coliseum, Long Island, N.Y.	Campbell Conference, 9	Wales Conference, 3	15,230
1-31-84	Meadowlands Arena, East Rutherford, N.J.	Wales Conference, 7	Campbell Conference, 6	18,939
2-12-85	Olympic Saddledome, Calgary	Wales Conference, 6	Campbell Conference, 4	16,683
2-4-86	Hartford Civic Center	Wales Conference, 4	Campbell Conference, 3 (OT)	15,126
	1987 All-Star Game replaced by Rendez-Vous '87 between Team NHL and Soviet Union			
2-9-88	St. Louis Arena	Wales Conference, 6	Campbell Conference, 5 (OT)	17,878
2-7-89	Northlands Coliseum, Edmonton	Campbell Conference, 9	Wales Conference, 5	17,503
1-21-90	Pittsburgh Civic Arena	Wales Conference, 12	Campbell Conference, 7	17,503
1-19-91	Chicago Stadium	Campbell Conference, 11	Wales Conference, 5	18,472
1-18-92	The Spectrum, Philadelphia	Campbell Conference, 10	Wales Conference, 6	17,380
2-6-93	Montreal Forum	Wales Conference, 16	Campbell Conference, 6	17,137
1-22-94	Madison Square Garden, New York	Eastern Conference, 9	Western Conference, 8	18,200

*Estimated figure.
†Benefit game for Toronto Maple Leafs left wing Ace Bailey, who suffered a career-ending skull injury earlier in the season.
‡Benefit game for the family of Montreal Canadiens center Howie Morenz, who died of a heart attack earlier in the year.
§Montreal All-Star roster made up of players from Montreal Canadiens and Maroons.
★Benefit game for the family of Montreal Canadiens defenseman Babe Siebert, who drowned earlier in the year.
•First Team roster supplemented by players from the four American clubs and Second Team roster supplemented by players from the two Canadian clubs.

MOST VALUABLE PLAYERS

Date	Player, All-Star Game team (regular-season team)	Date	Player, All-Star Game team (regular-season team)
10-6-62	Eddie Shack, Toronto Maple Leafs	1-20-70	Bobby Hull, East Div. (Chicago Blackhawks)
10-5-63	Frank Mahovlich, Toronto Maple Leafs	1-19-71	Bobby Hull, West Div. (Chicago Blackhawks)
10-10-64	Jean Beliveau, All-Stars (Montreal Canadiens)	1-25-72	Bobby Orr, East Division (Boston Bruins)
10-20-65	Gordie Howe, All-Stars (Detroit Red Wings)	1-30-73	Greg Polis, West Division (Pittsburgh Penguins)
1-18-67	Henri Richard, Montreal Canadiens	1-29-74	Garry Unger, West Division (St. Louis Blues)
1-16-68	Bruce Gamble, Toronto Maple Leafs	1-21-75	Syl Apps Jr., Wales Conf. (Pittsburgh Penguins)
1-21-69	Frank Mahovlich, East Div. (Detroit Red Wings)	1-20-76	Peter Mahovlich, Wales Conf. (Mon. Canadiens)

Date	Player, All-Star Game team (regular-season team)	Date	Player, All-Star Game team (regular-season team)
1-25-77	Rick Martin, Wales Conference (Buffalo Sabres)	2-4-86	Grant Fuhr, Campbell Conf. (Edmonton Oilers)
1-24-78	Billy Smith, Campbell Conf. (New York Islanders)	2-9-88	Mario Lemieux, Wales Conf. (Pittsburgh Penguins)
2-5-80	Reggie Leach, Campbell Conf. (Phila. Flyers)	2-7-89	Wayne Gretzky, Campbell Conf. (L.A. Kings)
2-10-81	Mike Liut, Campbell Conf. (St. Louis Blues)	1-21-90	Mario Lemieux, Wales Conf. (Pittsburgh Penguins)
2-9-82	Mike Bossy, Wales Conf. (New York Islanders)	1-19-91	Vincent Damphousse, Camp. Conf. (T. Maple Leafs)
2-8-83	Wayne Gretzky, Campbell Conf. (Edmonton Oilers)	1-18-92	Brett Hull, Campbell Conf. (St. Louis Blues)
1-31-84	Don Maloney, Wales Conf. (New York Rangers)	2-6-93	Mike Gartner, Wales Conf. (New York Rangers)
2-12-85	Mario Lemieux, Wales Conf. (Pittsburgh Penguin	1-22-94	Mike Richter, Eastern Conf. (New York Rangers)

RECORDS

REGULAR SEASON

INDIVIDUAL—CAREER

Most seasons
NHL: 26—Gordie Howe, Detroit Red Wings and Hartford Whalers, 1946-47 through 1970-71 and 1979-80.
CHL: 9—Richie Hansen, Fort Worth Texans, Salt Lake Golden Eagles, Wichita Wind, 1975-76 through 1983-84.
AHL: 20—Fred Glover, Indianapolis Caps, St. Louis Flyers, Cleveland Barons.
Willie Marshall, Pittsburgh Hornets, Rochester Americans, Hershey Bears, Providence Reds, Baltimore Clippers.
IHL: 18—Glenn Ramsay, Cincinnati Mohawks, Fort Wayne Komets, Troy Bruins, Toledo Blades, St. Paul Saints, Omaha Knights, Des Moines Oak Leafs, Toledo Hornets, Port Huron Flags, 1956-57 through 1973-74.

Most games played
NHL: 1,767—Gordie Howe, Detroit Red Wings and Hartford Whalers (26 seasons).
AHL: 1,205—Willie Marshall, Pittsburgh Hornets, Rochester Americans, Hershey Bears, Providence Reds, Baltimore Clippers (20 seasons).
IHL: 1,053—Glenn Ramsay, Cincinnati Mohawks, Fort Wayne Komets, Troy Bruins, Toledo Blades, St. Paul Saints, Omaha Knights, Des Moines Oak Leafs, Toledo Hornets, Port Huron Flags (18 seasons).
CHL: 575—Richie Hansen, Fort Worth Texans, Salt Lake Golden Eagles, Wichita Wind (9 seasons).
WHA: 551—Andre Lacroix, Philadelphia Blazers, New York Golden Blades, Jersey Knights, San Diego Mariners, Houston Aeros and New England Whalers (7 seasons).

Most goals
NHL: 803—Wayne Gretzky, Edmonton Oilers, Los Angeles Kings (15 seasons).
IHL: 526—Joe Kastelic, Fort Wayne Komets, Troy Burins, Louisville Rebels, Muskegon Zephyrs, Muskegon Mohawks (15 seasons).
AHL: 523—Willie Marshall, Pittsburgh Hornets, Rochester Americans, Hershey Bears, Providence Reds, Baltimore Clippers (20 seasons).
WHA: 316—Marc Tardif, Quebec Nordiques (6 seasons).
CHL: 204—Richie Hansen, Fort Worth Texans, Salt Lake Golden Eagles, Wichita Wind (9 seasons).

Most assists
NHL: 1,655—Wayne Gretzky, Edmonton Oilers, Los Angeles Kings (15 seasons).
AHL: 852—Willie Marshall, Pittsburgh Hornets, Hershey Bears, Rochester Americans, Providence Reds, Baltimore Clippers (20 seasons).
IHL: 826—Len Thornson, Huntington Hornets, Indianapolis Chiefs, Fort Wayne Komets (13 seasons).
WHA: 547—Andre Lacroix, Philadelphia Blazers, Jersey Knights, San Diego Mariners, Houston Aeros, New England Whalers (7 seasons).
CHL: 374—Richie Hansen, Fort Worth Texans, Salt Lake Golden Eagles, Wichita Wind (9 seasons).

Most points
NHL: 2,458—Wayne Gretzky, Edmonton Oilers, Los Angeles Kings (15 seasons).
AHL: 1,375—Willie Marshall, Pittsburgh Hornets, Hershey Bears, Rochester Americans, Providence Reds, Baltimore Clippers (20 seasons).
IHL: 1,252—Len Thornson, Huntington Hornets, Indianapolis Chiefs, Fort Wayne Komets (13 seasons).
WHA: 798—Andre Lacroix, Philadelphia Blazers, Jersey Knights, San Diego Mariners, Houston Aeros, New England Whalers (7 seasons).
CHL: 578—Richie Hansen, Fort Worth Texans, Salt Lake Golden Eagles, Wichita Wind (9 seasons).

Most penalty minutes
NHL: 3,966—Dave "Tiger" Williams, Toronto Maple Leafs, Vancouver Canucks, Detroit Red Wings, Los Angeles Kings, Hartford Whalers (13 seasons).
AHL: 2,402—Fred Glover, Indianapolis Caps, St. Louis Flyers, Cleveland Barons (20 seasons).
IHL: 2,175—Gord Malinoski, Dayton Gems, Saginaw Gears (9 seasons).
WHA: 962—Paul Baxter, Cleveland Crusaders, Quebec Nordiques (5 seasons).
CHL: 899—Brad Gassoff, Tulsa Oilers, Dallas Black Hawks (5 seasons).

Most shutouts
NHL: 103—Terry Sawchuk, Detroit Red Wings, Boston Bruins, Los Angeles Kings, New York Rangers, Toronto Maple Leafs (20 seasons).
AHL: 45—Johnny Bower, Cleveland Barons, Providence Reds (11 seasons).
IHL: 45—Glenn Ramsay, Cincinnati Mohawks, Fort Wayne Komets, Troy Bruins, Toledo Blades, St. Paul Saints, Omaha Knights, Des Moines Oak Leafs, Toledo Hornets, Port Huron Flags (18 seasons).
WHA: 16—Ernie Wakely, Winnipeg Jets, San Diego Mariners, Houston Aeros (6 seasons).
CHL: 12—Michel Dumas, Dallas Black Hawks (4 seasons).
Mike Veisor, Dallas Black Hawks (5 seasons).

INDIVIDUAL — SEASON

Most goals

- NHL: 92—Wayne Gretzky, Edmonton Oilers, 1981-82 season.
- WHA: 77—Bobby Hull, Winnipeg Jets, 1974-75 season.
- CHL: 77—Alain Caron, St. Louis Braves, 1963-64 season.
- IHL: 75—Dan Lecours, Milwaukee Admirals, 1982-83 season.
- AHL: 70—Stephan Lebeau, Sherbrooke Canadiens, 1988-89 season.

Most goals by a defenseman

- NHL: 48—Paul Coffey, Edmonton Oilers, 1985-86 season.
- IHL: 34—Roly McLenahan, Cincinnati Mohawks, 1955-56 season.
- CHL: 29—Dan Poulin, Nashville South Stars, 1981-82 season.
- AHL: 28—Greg Tebbutt, Baltimore Skipjacks, 1982-83 season.
- WHA: 24—Kevin Morrison, Jersey Knights, 1973-74 season.

Most assists

- NHL: 163—Wayne Gretzky, Edmonton Oilers, 1985-86 season.
- IHL: 109—John Cullen, Flint Spirits, 1987-88 season.
- WHA: 106—Andre Lacroix, San Diego Mariners, 1974-75 season.
- AHL: 89—George "Red" Sullivan, Hershey Bears, 1953-54 season.
- CHL: 81—Richie Hansen, Salt Lake Golden Eagles, 1981-82 season.

Most assists by a defenseman

- NHL: 102—Bobby Orr, Boston Bruins, 1970-71 season.
- IHL: 86—Gerry Glaude, Muskegon Zephyrs, 1962-63 season.
- WHA: 77—J. C. Tremblay, Quebec Nordiques, 1975-76 season.
- AHL: 62—Craig Levie, Nova Scotia Voyageurs, 1980-81 season.
  Shawn Evans, Nova Scotia Oilers, 1987-88 season.
- CHL: 61—Barclay Plager, Omaha Knights, 1963-64 season.

Most points

- NHL: 215—Wayne Gretzky, Edmonton Oilers, 1985-86 season.
- IHL: 157—John Cullen, Flint Spirits, 1987-88 season.
- WHA: 154—Marc Tardif, Quebec Nordiques, 1977-78 season.
- AHL: 138—Don Biggs, Binghamton Rangers, 1992-93 season.
- CHL: 125—Alain Caron, St. Louis Braves, 1963-64 season.

Most points by a defenseman

- NHL: 139—Bobby Orr, Boston Bruins, 1970-71 season.
- IHL: 101—Gerry Glaude, Muskegon Zephyrs, 1962-63 season.
- WHA: 89—J. C. Tremblay, Quebec Nordiques, 1972-73 and 1975-76 seasons.
- CHL: 85—Dan Poulin, Nashville South Stars, 1981-82 season.
- AHL: 84—Greg Tebbutt, Baltimore Skipjacks, 1982-83 season.

Most penalty minutes

- IHL: 648—Kevin Evans, Kalamazoo, 1986-87 season.
- NHL: 472—Dave Schultz, Philadelphia Flyers, 1974-75 season.
- AHL: 446—Robert Ray, Rochester Americans, 1988-89 season.
- CHL: 411—Randy Holt, Dallas Black Hawks, 1974-75 season.
- WHA: 365—Curt Brackenbury, Minnesota Fighting Saints and Quebec Nordiques, 1975-76 season.

Most shutouts

- NHL: 22—George Hainsworth, Montreal Canadiens, 1928-29 season.
- NHL: 15—(modern era) Tony Esposito, Chicago Black Hawks, 1969-70 season.
- IHL: 10—Charlie Hodge, Cincinnati Mohawks, 1953-54 season.
  Joe Daley, Winnipeg Jets, 1975-76 season.
- CHL: 9—Marcel Pelletier, St. Paul Rangers, 1963-64 season.
- AHL: 9—Gordie Bell, Buffalo Bisons, 1942-43 season.
- WHA: 5—Gerry Cheevers, Cleveland Crusaders, 1972-73 season.

Lowest goals against average

- NHL: 0.98—George Hainsworth, Montreal Canadiens, 1928-29 season.
- AHL: 1.79—Frank Brimsek, Providence Reds, 1937-38 season.
- IHL: 1.88—Glenn Ramsay, Cincinnati Mohawks, 1956-57 season.
- CHL: 2.16—Russ Gillow, Oklahoma City Blazers, 1967-68 season.
- WHA: 2.57—Don McLeod, Houston Aeros, 1973-74 season.

INDIVIDUAL — GAME

Most goals

- NHL: 7—Joe Malone, Quebec Bulldogs vs. Toronto St. Pats, January 31, 1920.

NHL: 6—(modern era) Syd Howe, Detroit Red Wings vs. N.Y. Rangers, Feb. 3, 1944.
Gordon "Red" Berenson, St. Louis Blues vs. Philadelphia, Nov. 7, 1968.
Darryl Sittler, Toronto Maple Leafs vs. Boston, Feb. 7, 1976.
CHL: 6—Jim Mayer, Dallas Black Hawks, February 23, 1979.
AHL: 6—Bob Heron, Pittsburgh Hornets, 1941-42.
Harry Pidhirny, Springfield Indians, 1953-54.
Camille Henry, Providence Reds, 1955-56.
Patrick Lebeau, Fredericton Canadiens, Feb. 1, 1991.
IHL: 6—Pierre Brillant, Indianapolis Chiefs, Feb. 18, 1959.
Bryan McLay, Muskegon Zephyrs, Mar. 8, 1961.
Elliott Chorley, St. Paul Saints, Jan. 17, 1962.
Joe Kastelic, Muskegon Zephyrs, Mar. 1, 1962.
Tom St. James, Flint Generals, Mar. 15, 1985.
WHA: 5—Ron Ward, New York Raiders vs. Ottawa, January 4, 1973.
Ron Climie, Edmonton Oilers vs. N.Y. Golden Blades, November 6, 1973.
Andre Hinse, Houston Aeros vs. Edmonton, Jan. 16, 1975.
Vaclav Nedomansky, Toronto Toros vs. Denver Spurs, Nov. 13, 1975.
Wayne Connelly, Minnesota Fighting Saints vs. Cincinnati Stingers, Nov. 27, 1975.
Ron Ward, Cleveland Crusaders vs. Toronto Toros, Nov. 30, 1975.
Real Cloutier, Quebec Nordiques fs. Phoenix Roadrunners, Oct. 26, 1976.

Most assists

AHL: 9—Art Stratton, Buffalo Bisons vs. Pittsburgh, Mar. 17, 1963.
IHL: 9—Jean-Paul Denis, St. Paul Saints, Jan. 17, 1962.
NHL: 7—Billy Taylor, Detroit Red Wings vs. Chicago, Mar. 16, 1947.
Wayne Gretzky, Edmonton Oilers vs. Washington, Feb. 15, 1980.
WHA: 7—Jim Harrison, Alberta Oilers vs. New York, January 30, 1973.
Jim Harrison, Cleveland Crusaders vs. Toronto, Nov. 30, 1975.
CHL: 6—Art Stratton, St. Louis Braves, 1966-67.
Ron Ward, Tulsa Oilers, 1967-68.
Bill Hogaboam, Omaha Knights, January 15, 1972.
Jim Wiley, Tulsa Oilers, 1974-75.

Most points

IHL: 11—Elliott Chorley, St. Paul Saints, Jan. 17, 1962.
Jean-Paul Denis, St. Paul Saints, Jan. 17, 1962.
NHL: 10—Darryl Sittler, Toronto Maple Leafs vs. Boston, Feb. 7, 1976.
WHA: 10—Jim Harrison, Alberta Oilers vs. New York, January 30, 1973.
AHL: 9—Art Stratton, Buffalo Bisons vs Pittsburgh, Mar. 17, 1963.
CHL: 8—Steve Vickers, Omaha Knights vs. Kansas City, Jan. 15, 1972.

Most penalty minutes

NHL: 67—Randy Holt, Los Angeles Kings vs. Philadelphia, March 11, 1979.
IHL: 63—Willie Trognitz, Dayton Gems, Oct. 29, 1977.
AHL: 54—Wally Weir, Rochester Americans vs. New Brunswick, Jan. 16, 1981.
CHL: 49—Gary Rissling, Birmingham Bulls vs. Salt Lake, Dec. 5, 1980.
WHA: 46—Dave Hanson, Birmingham Bulls vs. Indianapolis, Feb. 5, 1978.

STANLEY CUP PLAYOFFS

INDIVIDUAL—CAREER

Most years in playoffs: 20—Gordie Howe, Detroit, Hartford.
Larry Robinson, Montreal, Los Angeles.
Most consecutive years in playoffs: 20—Larry Robinson, Montreal, Los Angeles.
Most games: 227—Larry Robinson, Montreal, Los Angeles.
Most games by goaltender: 131—Billy Smith, N.Y. Islanders.
Most goals: 110—Wayne Gretzky, Edmonton, Los Angeles.
Most assists: 236—Wayne Gretzky, Edmonton, Los Angeles.
Most points: 346—Wayne Gretzky, Edmonton, Los Angeles.
Most penalty minutes: 581—Dale Hunter, Quebec, Washington.
Most shutouts: 14—Jacques Plante, Montreal, St. Louis.

INDIVIDUAL—SEASON

Most goals: 19—Reggie Leach, Philadelphia (1975-76).
Jari Kurri, Edmonton (1984-85).
Most goals by a defenseman: 12—Paul Coffey, Edmonton (1984-85).
Most assists: 31—Wayne Gretzky, Edmonton (1987-88).
Most assists by a defenseman: 25—Paul Coffey, Edmonton (1984-85).
Most points: 47—Wayne Gretzky, Edmonton (1984-85).
Most points by a defenseman: 37—Paul Coffey, Edmonton (1984-85).
Most penalty minutes: 141—Chris Nilan, Montreal (1985-86).

Most shutouts: 4—Clint Benedict, Montreal Maroons (1927-28).
Dave Kerr, N.Y. Rangers (1936-37).
Frank McCool, Toronto (1944-45).
Terry Sawchuk, Detroit (1951-52).
Bernie Parent, Philadelphia (1974-75).
Ken Dryden, Montreal (1976-77).
Most consecutive shutouts: 3—Frank McCool, Toronto (1944-45).

INDIVIDUAL—GAME

Most goals: 5—Maurice Richard, Montreal vs. Toronto, March 23, 1944.
Darryl Sittler, Toronto vs. Philadelphia, April 22, 1976.
Reggie Leach, Philadelphia vs. Boston, May 6, 1976.
Mario Lemieux, Pittsburgh vs. Philadelphia, April 25, 1989.
Most assists: 6—Mikko Leinonen, N.Y. Rangers vs. Philadelphia, April 8, 1982.
Wayne Gretzky, Edmonton vs. Los Angeles, April 9, 1987.
Most points: 8—Patrik Sundstrom, New Jersey vs. Washington, April 22, 1988.
Mario Lemieux, Pittsburgh vs. Philadelphia, April 25, 1989.

CLUB

Most Stanley Cup championships: 24—Montreal Canadiens.
Most consecutive Stanley Cup championships: 5—Montreal Canadiens.
Most final series apperances: 32—Montreal Canadiens.
Most years in playoffs: 69—Montreal Canadiens.
Most consecutive playoff appearances: 27—Boston Bruins.
Most consecutive playoff game victories: 12—Edmonton Oilers.
Most goals, one team, one game: 13—Edmonton vs. Los Angeles, April 9, 1987.
Most goals, one team, one period: 7—Montreal Canadiens vs. Toronto, March 30, 1944, 3rd period.

AWARD WINNERS

ART ROSS TROPHY
(Leading scorer)

Season	Player, Team	Pts.
1917-18	Joe Malone, Montreal	44
1918-19	Newsy Lalonde, Montreal	32
1919-20	Joe Malone, Quebec Bulldogs	45
1920-21	Newsy Lalonde, Montreal	41
1921-22	Punch Broadbelt, Ottawa	46
1922-23	Babe Dye, Toronto	37
1923-24	Cy Denneny, Ottawa	23
1924-25	Babe Dye, Toronto	44
1925-26	Nels Stewart, Montreal Maroons	42
1926-27	Bill Cook, N.Y. Rangers	37
1927-28	Howie Morenz, Montreal	51
1928-29	Ace Bailey, Toronto	32
1929-30	Cooney Weiland, Boston	73
1930-31	Howie Morenz, Montreal	51
1931-32	Harvey Jackson, Toronto	53
1932-33	Bill Cook, N.Y. Rangers	50
1933-34	Charlie Conacher, Toronto	52
1934-35	Charlie Conacher, Toronto	57
1935-36	Dave Schriner, N.Y. Americans	45
1936-37	Dave Schriner, N.Y. Americans	46
1937-38	Gordie Drillion, Toronto	52
1938-39	Toe Blake, Montreal	47
1939-40	Milt Schmidt, Boston	52
1940-41	Bill Cowley, Boston	62
1941-42	Bryan Hextall, N.Y. Rangers	56
1942-43	Doug Bentley, Chicago	73
1943-44	Herbie Cain, Boston	82
1944-45	Elmer Lach, Montreal	80
1945-46	Max Bentley, Chicago	61
1946-47	Max Bentley, Chicago	72
1947-48	Elmer Lach, Montreal	61
1948-49	Roy Conacher, Chicago	68
1949-50	Ted Lindsay, Detroit	78
1950-51	Gordie Howe, Detroit	86
1951-52	Gordie Howe, Detroit	86
1952-53	Gordie Howe, Detroit	95
1953-54	Gordie Howe, Detroit	81
1954-55	Bernie Geoffrion, Montreal	75
1955-56	Jean Beliveau, Montreal	88
1956-57	Gordie Howe, Detroit	89
1957-58	Dickie Moore, Montreal	84
1958-59	Dickie Moore, Montreal	96
1959-60	Bobby Hull, Chicago	81
1960-61	Bernie Geoffrion, Montreal	95
1961-62	Bobby Hull, Chicago	84
1962-63	Gordie Howe, Detroit	86
1963-64	Stan Mikita, Chicago	89
1964-65	Stan Mikita, Chicago	87
1965-66	Bobby Hull, Chicago	97
1966-67	Stan Mikita, Chicago	97
1967-68	Stan Mikita, Chicago	87
1968-69	Phil Esposito, Boston	126
1969-70	Bobby Orr, Boston	120
1970-71	Phil Esposito, Boston	152
1971-72	Phil Esposito, Boston	133
1972-73	Phil Esposito, Boston	130
1973-74	Phil Esposito, Boston	145
1974-75	Bobby Orr, Boston	135
1975-76	Guy Lafleur, Montreal	125
1976-77	Guy Lafleur, Montreal	136
1977-78	Guy Lafleur, Montreal	132
1978-79	Bryan Trottier, N.Y. Islanders	134
1979-80	Marcel Dionne, Los Angeles	137
1980-81	Wayne Gretzky, Edmonton	164
1981-82	Wayne Gretzky, Edmonton	212
1982-83	Wayne Gretzky, Edmonton	196
1983-84	Wayne Gretzky, Edmonton	205
1984-85	Wayne Gretzky, Edmonton	208
1985-86	Wayne Gretzky, Edmonton	215
1986-87	Wayne Gretzky, Edmonton	183
1987-88	Mario Lemieux, Pittsburgh	168
1988-89	Mario Lemieux, Pittsburgh	199
1989-90	Wayne Gretzky, Los Angeles	142
1990-91	Wayne Gretzky, Los Angeles	163
1991-92	Mario Lemieux, Pittsburgh	131
1992-93	Mario Lemieux, Pittsburgh	160
1993-94	Wayne Gretzky, Los Angeles	130

The award was originally known as the Leading Scorer Trophy. The present trophy, first given in 1947, was presented to the NHL by Art Ross, former manager-coach of the Boston Bruins. In event of a tie, the player with the most goals receives the award.

HART MEMORIAL TROPHY
(Most Valuable Player)

Season	Player, Team
1923-24	Frank Nighbor, Ottawa
1924-25	Billy Burch, Hamilton
1925-26	Nels Stewart, Montreal Maroons
1926-27	Herb Gardiner, Montreal
1927-28	Howie Morenz, Montreal
1928-29	Roy Worters, N.Y. Americans
1929-30	Nels Stewart, Montreal Maroons
1930-31	Howie Morenz, Montreal
1931-32	Howie Morenz, Montreal
1932-33	Eddie Shore, Boston
1933-34	Aurel Joliat, Montreal
1934-35	Eddie Shore, Boston
1935-36	Eddie Shore, Boston
1936-37	Babe Siebert, Montreal
1937-38	Eddie Shore, Boston
1938-39	Toe Blake, Montreal
1939-40	Ebbie Goodfellow, Detroit
1940-41	Bill Cowley, Boston
1941-42	Tom Anderson, N.Y. Americans
1942-43	Bill Cowley, Boston
1943-44	Babe Pratt, Toronto
1944-45	Elmer Lach, Montreal
1945-46	Max Bentley, Chicago
1946-47	Maurice Richard, Montreal
1947-48	Buddy O'Connor, N.Y. Rangers
1948-49	Sid Abel, Detroit
1949-50	Chuck Rayner, N.Y. Rangers
1950-51	Milt Schmidt, Boston
1951-52	Gordie Howe, Detroit
1952-53	Gordie Howe, Detroit
1953-54	Al Rollins, Chicago
1954-55	Ted Kennedy, Toronto
1955-56	Jean Beliveau, Montreal
1956-57	Gordie Howe, Detroit
1957-58	Gordie Howe, Detroit
1958-59	Andy Bathgate, N.Y. Rangers
1959-60	Gordie Howe, Detroit
1960-61	Bernie Geoffrion, Montreal
1961-62	Jacques Plante, Montreal
1962-63	Gordie Howe, Detroit
1963-64	Jean Beliveau, Montreal
1964-65	Bobby Hull, Chicago
1965-66	Bobby Hull, Chicago
1966-67	Stan Mikita, Chicago
1967-68	Stan Mikita, Chicago
1968-69	Phil Esposito, Boston
1969-70	Bobby Orr, Boston
1970-71	Bobby Orr, Boston
1971-72	Bobby Orr, Boston
1972-73	Bobby Clarke, Philadelphia
1973-74	Phil Esposito, Boston
1974-75	Bobby Clarke, Philadelphia
1975-76	Bobby Clarke, Philadelphia
1976-77	Guy Lafleur, Montreal
1977-78	Guy Lafleur, Montreal
1978-79	Bryan Trottier, N.Y. Islanders
1979-80	Wayne Gretzky, Edmonton
1980-81	Wayne Gretzky, Edmonton
1981-82	Wayne Gretzky, Edmonton
1982-83	Wayne Gretzky, Edmonton
1983-84	Wayne Gretzky, Edmonton
1984-85	Wayne Gretzky, Edmonton
1985-86	Wayne Gretzky, Edmonton
1986-87	Wayne Gretzky, Edmonton

Season	Player, Team
1987-88	Mario Lemieux, Pittsburgh
1988-89	Wayne Gretzky, Los Angeles
1989-90	Mark Messier, Edmonton
1990-91	Brett Hull, St. Louis
1991-92	Mark Messier, N.Y. Rangers
1992-93	Mario Lemieux, Pittsburgh
1993-94	Sergei Fedorov, Detroit

JAMES NORRIS MEMORIAL TROPHY

(Outstanding defenseman)

Season	Player, Team
1953-54	Red Kelly, Detroit
1954-55	Doug Harvey, Montreal
1955-56	Doug Harvey, Montreal
1956-57	Doug Harvey, Montreal
1957-58	Doug Harvey, Montreal
1958-59	Tom Johnson, Montreal
1959-60	Doug Harvey, Montreal
1960-61	Doug Harvey, Montreal
1961-62	Doug Harvey, N.Y. Rangers
1962-63	Pierre Pilote, Chicago
1963-64	Pierre Pilote, Chicago
1964-65	Pierre Pilote, Chicago
1965-66	Jacques Laperriere, Montreal
1966-67	Harry Howell, N.Y. Rangers
1967-68	Bobby Orr, Boston
1968-69	Bobby Orr, Boston
1969-70	Bobby Orr, Boston
1970-71	Bobby Orr, Boston
1971-72	Bobby Orr, Boston
1972-73	Bobby Orr, Boston
1973-74	Bobby Orr, Boston
1974-75	Bobby Orr, Boston
1975-76	Denis Potvin, N.Y. Islanders
1976-77	Larry Robinson, Montreal
1977-78	Denis Potvin, N.Y. Islanders
1978-79	Denis Potvin, N.Y. Islanders
1979-80	Larry Robinson, Montreal
1980-81	Randy Carlyle, Pittsburgh
1981-82	Doug Wilson, Chicago
1982-83	Rod Langway, Washington
1983-84	Rod Langway, Washington
1984-85	Paul Coffey, Edmonton
1985-86	Paul Coffey, Edmonton
1986-87	Ray Bourque, Boston
1987-88	Ray Bourque, Boston
1988-89	Chris Chelios, Montreal
1989-90	Ray Bourque, Boston
1990-91	Ray Bourque, Boston
1991-92	Brian Leetch, N.Y. Rangers
1992-93	Chris Chelios, Chicago
1993-94	Ray Bourque, Boston

VEZINA TROPHY

(Outstanding goaltender)

Season	Player, Team	GAA
1926-27	George Hainsworth, Montreal	1.52
1927-28	George Hainsworth, Montreal	1.09
1928-29	George Hainsworth, Montreal	0.98
1929-30	Tiny Thompson, Boston	2.23
1930-31	Roy Worters, N.Y. Americans	1.68
1931-32	Charlie Gardiner, Chicago	2.10
1932-33	Tiny Thompson, Boston	1.83
1933-34	Charlie Gardiner, Chicago	1.73
1934-35	Lorne Chabot, Chicago	1.83
1935-36	Tiny Thompson, Boston	1.71
1936-37	Normie Smith, Detroit	2.13
1937-38	Tiny Thompson, Boston	1.85
1938-39	Frank Brimsek, Boston	1.60
1939-40	Dave Kerr, N.Y. Rangers	1.60
1940-41	Turk Broda, Toronto	2.60
1941-42	Frank Brimsek, Boston	2.38
1942-43	Johnny Mowers, Detroit	2.48
1943-44	Bill Durnan, Montreal	2.18
1944-45	Bill Durnan, Montreal	2.42
1945-46	Bill Durnan, Montreal	2.60
1946-47	Bill Durnan, Montreal	2.30
1947-48	Turk Broda, Toronto	2.38

Season	Player, Team	GAA
1948-49	Bill Durnan, Montreal	2.10
1949-50	Bill Durnan, Montreal	2.20
1950-51	Al Rollins, Toronto	1.75
1951-52	Terry Sawchuk, Detroit	1.98
1952-53	Terry Sawchuk, Detroit	1.94
1953-54	Harry Lumley, Toronto	1.85
1954-55	Terry Sawchuk, Detroit	1.94
1955-56	Jacques Plante, Montreal	1.86
1956-57	Jacques Plante, Montreal	2.02
1957-58	Jacques Plante, Montreal	2.09
1958-59	Jacques Plante, Montreal	2.15
1959-60	Jacques Plante, Montreal	2.54
1960-61	Johnny Bower, Toronto	2.50
1961-62	Jacques Plante, Montreal	2.37
1962-63	Glenn Hall, Chicago	2.51
1963-64	Charlie Hodge, Montreal	2.26
1964-65	Terry Sawchuk, Toronto	2.56
	Johnny Bower, Toronto	2.38
1965-66	Lorne Worsley, Montreal	2.36
	Charlie Hodge, Montreal	2.58
1966-67	Glenn Hall, Chicago	2.38
	Denis DeJordy, Chicago	2.46
1967-68	Lorne Worsley, Montreal	1.98
	Rogatien Vachon, Montreal	2.48
1968-69	Glenn Hall, St. Louis	2.17
	Jacques Plante, St. Louis	1.96
1969-70	Tony Esposito, Chicago	2.17
1970-71	Ed Giacomin, N.Y. Rangers	2.15
	Gilles Villemure, N.Y. Rangers	2.29
1971-72	Tony Esposito, Chicago	1.76
	Gary Smith, Chicago	2.41
1972-73	Ken Dryden, Montreal	2.26
1973-74	Bernie Parent, Philadelphia	1.89
	Tony Esposito, Chicago	2.04
1974-75	Bernie Parent, Philadelphia	2.03
1975-76	Ken Dryden, Montreal	2.03
1976-77	Ken Dryden, Montreal	2.14
	Michel Larocque, Montreal	2.09
1977-78	Ken Dryden, Montreal	2.05
	Michel Larocque, Montreal	2.67
1978-79	Ken Dryden, Montreal	2.30
	Michel Larocque, Montreal	2.84
1979-80	Bob Sauve, Buffalo	2.36
	Don Edwards, Buffalo	2.57
1980-81	Richard Sevigny, Montreal	2.40
	Michel Larocque, Montreal	3.03
	Denis Herron, Montreal	3.50
1981-82	Billy Smith, N.Y. Islanders	2.97
1982-83	Pete Peeters, Boston	2.36
1983-84	Tom Barrasso, Buffalo	2.84
1984-85	Pelle Lindbergh, Philadelphia	3.02
1985-86	John Vanbiesbrouck, N.Y. Rangers	3.32
1986-87	Ron Hextall, Philadelphia	3.00
1987-88	Grant Fuhr, Edmonton	3.43
1988-89	Patrick Roy, Montreal	2.47
1989-90	Patrick Roy, Montreal	2.53
1990-91	Ed Belfour, Chicago	2.47
1991-92	Patrick Roy, Montreal	2.36
1992-93	Ed Belfour, Chicago	2.59
1993-94	Dominik Hasek, Buffalo	1.95

The award was formerly presented to the goaltender(s) having played a minimum of 25 games for the team with the fewest goals scored against. Beginning with the 1981-82 season, it was awarded to the outstanding goaltender.

BILL JENNINGS TROPHY

(Leading goaltender)

Season	Player, Team	GAA
1981-82	Denis Herron, Montreal	2.64
	Rick Wamsley, Montreal	2.75
1982-83	Roland Melanson, N.Y. Islanders	2.66
	Billy Smith, N.Y. Islanders	2.87
1983-84	Pat Riggin, Washington	2.66
	Al Jensen, Washington	2.91
1984-85	Tom Barrasso, Buffalo	2.66
	Bob Sauve, Buffalo	3.22
1985-86	Bob Froese, Philadelphia	2.55
	Darren Jensen, Philadelphia	3.68
1986-87	Brian Hayward, Montreal	2.81

Season	Player, Team	GAA
	Patrick Roy, Montreal	2.93
1987-88	Brian Hayward, Montreal	2.86
	Patrick Roy, Montreal	2.90
1988-89	Patrick Roy, Montreal	2.47
	Brian Hayward, Montreal	2.90
1989-90	Rejean Lemelin, Boston	2.81
	Andy Moog, Boston	2.89
1990-91	Ed Belfour, Chicago	2.47
1991-92	Patrick Roy, Montreal	2.36
1992-93	Ed Belfour, Chicago	2.59
1993-94	Dominik Hasek, Buffalo	1.95
	Grant Fuhr, Buffalo	3.68

The award is presented to the goaltender(s) having played a minimum of 25 games for the team with the fewest goals scored against.

CALDER MEMORIAL TROPHY
(Rookie of the year)

Season	Player, Team
1932-33	Carl Voss, Detroit
1933-34	Russ Blinco, Montreal Maroons
1934-35	Dave Schriner, N.Y. Americans
1935-36	Mike Karakas, Chicago
1936-37	Syl Apps, Toronto
1937-38	Cully Dahlstrom, Chicago
1938-39	Frank Brimsek, Boston
1939-40	Kilby Macdonald, N.Y. Rangers
1940-41	John Quilty, Montreal
1941-42	Grant Warwick, N.Y. Rangers
1942-43	Gaye Stewart, Toronto
1943-44	Gus Bodnar, Toronto
1944-45	Frank McCool, Toronto
1945-46	Edgar Laprade, N.Y. Rangers
1946-47	Howie Meeker, Toronto
1947-48	Jim McFadden, Detroit
1948-49	Pentti Lund, N.Y. Rangers
1949-50	Jack Gelineau, Boston
1950-51	Terry Sawchuk, Detroit
1951-52	Bernie Geoffrion, Montreal
1952-53	Lorne Worsley, N.Y. Rangers
1953-54	Camille Henry, N.Y. Rangers
1954-55	Ed Litzenberger, Chicago
1955-56	Glenn Hall, Detroit
1956-57	Larry Regan, Boston
1957-58	Frank Mahovlich, Toronto
1958-59	Ralph Backstrom, Montreal
1959-60	Bill Hay, Chicago
1960-61	Dave Keon, Toronto
1961-62	Bobby Rousseau, Montreal
1962-63	Kent Douglas, Toronto
1963-64	Jacques Laperriere, Montreal
1964-65	Roger Crozier, Detroit
1965-66	Brit Selby, Toronto
1966-67	Bobby Orr, Boston
1967-68	Derek Sanderson, Boston
1968-69	Danny Grant, Minnesota
1969-70	Tony Esposito, Chicago
1970-71	Gilbert Perreault, Buffalo
1971-72	Ken Dryden, Montreal
1972-73	Steve Vickers, N.Y. Rangers
1973-74	Denis Potvin, N.Y. Islanders
1974-75	Eric Vail, Atlanta
1975-76	Bryan Trottier, N.Y. Islanders
1976-77	Willi Plett, Atlanta
1977-78	Mike Bossy, N.Y. Islanders
1978-79	Bobby Smith, Minnesota
1979-80	Ray Bourque, Boston
1980-81	Peter Stastny, Quebec
1981-82	Dale Hawerchuk, Winnipeg
1982-83	Steve Larmer, Chicago
1983-84	Tom Barrasso, Buffalo
1984-85	Mario Lemieux, Pittsburgh
1985-86	Gary Suter, Calgary
1986-87	Luc Robitaille, Los Angeles
1987-88	Joe Nieuwendyk, Calgary
1988-89	Brian Leetch, N.Y. Rangers
1989-90	Sergei Makarov, Calgary
1990-91	Ed Belfour, Chicago
1991-92	Pavel Bure, Vancouver

Season	Player, Team
1992-93	Teemu Selanne, Winnipeg
1993-94	Martin Brodeur, New Jersey

The award was originally known as the Leading Rookie Award. It was renamed the Calder Trophy in 1936-37 and became the Calder Memorial Trophy in 1942-43, following the death of NHL President Frank Calder.

LADY BYNG MEMORIAL TROPHY
(Most gentlemanly player)

Season	Player, Team
1924-25	Frank Nighbor, Ottawa
1925-26	Frank Nighbor, Ottawa
1926-27	Billy Burch, N.Y. Americans
1927-28	Frank Boucher, N.Y. Rangers
1928-29	Frank Boucher, N.Y. Rangers
1929-30	Frank Boucher, N.Y. Rangers
1930-31	Frank Boucher, N.Y. Rangers
1931-32	Joe Primeau, Toronto
1932-33	Frank Boucher, N.Y. Rangers
1933-34	Frank Boucher, N.Y. Rangers
1934-35	Frank Boucher, N.Y. Rangers
1935-36	Doc Romnes, Chicago
1936-37	Marty Barry, Detroit
1937-38	Gordie Drillon, Toronto
1938-39	Clint Smith, N.Y. Rangers
1939-40	Bobby Bauer, Boston
1940-41	Bobby Bauer, Boston
1941-42	Syl Apps, Toronto
1942-43	Max Bentley, Chicago
1943-44	Clint Smith, Chicago
1944-45	Bill Mosienko, Chicago
1945-46	Toe Blake, Montreal
1946-47	Bobby Bauer, Boston
1947-48	Buddy O'Connor, N.Y. Rangers
1948-49	Bill Quackenbush, Detroit
1949-50	Edgar Laprade, N.Y. Rangers
1950-51	Red Kelly, Detroit
1951-52	Sid Smith, Toronto
1952-53	Red Kelly, Detroit
1953-54	Red Kelly, Detroit
1954-55	Sid Smith, Toronto
1955-56	Earl Reibel, Detroit
1956-57	Andy Hebenton, N.Y. Rangers
1957-58	Camille Henry, N.Y. Rangers
1958-59	Alex Delvecchio, Detroit
1959-60	Don McKenney, Boston
1960-61	Red Kelly, Toronto
1961-62	Dave Keon, Toronto
1962-63	Dave Keon, Toronto
1963-64	Ken Wharram, Chicago
1964-65	Bobby Hull, Chicago
1965-66	Alex Delvecchio, Detroit
1966-67	Stan Mikita, Chicago
1967-68	Stan Mikita, Chicago
1968-69	Alex Delvecchio, Detroit
1969-70	Phil Goyette, St. Louis
1970-71	John Bucyk, Boston
1971-72	Jean Ratelle, N.Y. Rangers
1972-73	Gilbert Perreault, Buffalo
1973-74	John Bucyk, Boston
1974-75	Marcel Dionne, Detroit
1975-76	Jean Ratelle, N.Y. R.-Boston
1976-77	Marcel Dionne, Los Angeles
1977-78	Butch Goring, Los Angeles
1978-79	Bob MacMillan, Atlanta
1979-80	Wayne Gretzky, Edmonton
1980-81	Butch Goring, N.Y. Islanders
1981-82	Rick Middleton, Boston
1982-83	Mike Bossy, N.Y. Islanders
1983-84	Mike Bossy, N.Y. Islanders
1984-85	Jari Kurri, Edmonton
1985-86	Mike Bossy, N.Y. Islanders
1986-87	Joe Mullen, Calgary
1987-88	Mats Naslund, Montreal
1988-89	Joe Mullen, Calgary
1989-90	Brett Hull, St. Louis
1990-91	Wayne Gretzky, Los Angeles
1991-92	Wayne Gretzky, Los Angeles
1992-93	Pierre Turgeon, N.Y. Islanders
1993-94	Wayne Gretzky, Los Angeles

The award was originally known as the Lady Byng Trophy. After winning the award seven times, Frank Boucher received permanent possession and a new trophy was donated to the NHL in 1936. After Lady Byng's death in 1949, the NHL changed the name to Lady Byng Memorial Trophy.

CONN SMYTHE TROPHY

(Playoff MVP)

Season	Player, Team
1964-65	Jean Beliveau, Montreal
1965-66	Roger Crozier, Detroit
1966-67	Dave Keon, Toronto
1967-68	Glenn Hall, St. Louis
1968-69	Serge Savard, Montreal
1969-70	Bobby Orr, Boston
1970-71	Ken Dryden, Montreal
1971-72	Bobby Orr, Boston
1972-73	Yvan Cournoyer, Montreal
1973-74	Bernie Parent, Philadelphia
1974-75	Bernie Parent, Philadelphia
1975-76	Reggie Leach, Philadelphia
1976-77	Guy Lafleur, Montreal
1977-78	Larry Robinson, Montreal
1978-79	Bob Gainey, Montreal
1979-80	Bryan Trottier, N.Y. Islanders
1980-81	Butch Goring, N.Y. Islanders
1981-82	Mike Bossy, N.Y. Islanders
1982-83	Billy Smith, N.Y. Islanders
1983-84	Mark Messier, Edmonton
1984-85	Wayne Gretzky, Edmonton
1985-86	Patrick Roy, Montreal
1986-87	Ron Hextall, Philadelphia
1987-88	Wayne Gretzky, Edmonton
1988-89	Al MacInnis, Calgary
1989-90	Bill Ranford, Edmonton
1990-91	Mario Lemieux, Pittsburgh
1991-92	Mario Lemieux, Pittsburgh
1992-93	Patrick Roy, Montreal
1993-94	Brian Leetch, N.Y. Rangers

BILL MASTERTON MEMORIAL TROPHY

(Sportsmanship—dedication to hockey)

Season	Player, Team
1967-68	Claude Provost, Montreal
1968-69	Ted Hampson, Oakland
1969-70	Pit Martin, Chicago
1970-71	Jean Ratelle, N.Y. Rangers
1971-72	Bobby Clarke, Philadelphia
1972-73	Lowell MacDonald, Pittsburgh
1973-74	Henri Richard, Montreal
1974-75	Don Luce, Buffalo
1975-76	Rod Gilbert, N.Y. Rangers
1976-77	Ed Westfall, N.Y. Islanders
1977-78	Butch Goring, Los Angeles
1978-79	Serge Savard, Montreal
1979-80	Al MacAdam, Minnesota
1980-81	Blake Dunlop, St. Louis
1981-82	Glenn Resch, Colorado
1982-83	Lanny McDonald, Calgary
1983-84	Brad Park, Detroit
1984-85	Anders Hedberg, N.Y. Rangers
1985-86	Charlie Simmer, Boston
1986-87	Doug Jarvis, Hartford
1987-88	Bob Bourne, Los Angeles
1988-89	Tim Kerr, Philadelphia
1989-90	Gord Kluzak, Boston
1990-91	Dave Taylor, Los Angeles
1991-92	Mark Fitzpatrick, N.Y. Islanders
1992-93	Mario Lemieux, Pittsburgh
1993-94	Cam Neely, Boston

Presented by the Professional Hockey Writers' Association to the player who best exemplifies the qualities of perseverance, sportsmanship and dedication to hockey.

FRANK J. SELKE TROPHY

(Best defensive forward)

Season	Player, Team
1977-78	Bob Gainey, Montreal
1978-79	Bob Gainey, Montreal
1979-80	Bob Gainey, Montreal
1980-81	Bob Gainey, Montreal
1981-82	Steve Kasper, Boston
1982-83	Bobby Clarke, Philadelphia
1983-84	Doug Jarvis, Washington
1984-85	Craig Ramsay, Buffalo
1985-86	Troy Murray, Chicago
1986-87	Dave Poulin, Philadelphia
1987-88	Guy Carbonneau, Montreal
1988-89	Guy Carbonneau, Montreal
1989-90	Rick Meagher, St. Louis
1990-91	Dirk Graham, Chicago
1991-92	Guy Carbonneau, Montreal
1992-93	Doug Gilmour, Toronto
1993-94	Sergei Fedorov, Detroit

JACK ADAMS AWARD

(Coach of the year)

Season	Coach, Team
1973-74	Fred Shero, Philadelphia
1974-75	Bob Pulford, Los Angeles
1975-76	Don Cherry, Boston
1976-77	Scotty Bowman, Montreal
1977-78	Bobby Kromm, Detroit
1978-79	Al Arbour, N.Y. Islanders
1979-80	Pat Quinn, Philadelphia
1980-81	Red Berenson, St. Louis
1981-82	Tom Watt, Winnipeg
1982-83	Orval Tessier, Chicago
1983-84	Bryan Murray, Washington
1984-85	Mike Keenan, Philadelphia
1985-86	Glen Sather, Edmonton
1986-87	Jacques Demers, Detroit
1987-88	Jacques Demers, Detroit
1988-89	Pat Burns, Montreal
1989-90	Bob Murdoch, Winnipeg
1990-91	Brian Sutter, St. Louis
1991-92	Pat Quinn, Vancouver
1992-93	Pat Burns, Toronto
1993-94	Jacques Lemaire, New Jersey

KING CLANCY TROPHY

(Humanitarian contributions)

Season	Player, Team
1987-88	Lanny McDonald, Calgary
1988-89	Bryan Trottier, N.Y. Islanders
1989-90	Kevin Lowe, Edmonton
1990-91	Dave Taylor, Los Angeles
1991-92	Ray Bourque, Boston
1992-93	Dave Poulin, Boston
1993-94	Adam Graves, N.Y. Rangers

TEAM HISTORIES

MIGHTY DUCKS OF ANAHEIM

YEAR-BY-YEAR RECORDS

Season	W	L	T	Pts.	Finish	W	L	Highest round	Coach
					REGULAR SEASON			PLAYOFFS	
1993-94	33	46	5	71	4th/Pacific	—	—		Ron Wilson

FIRST-ROUND ENTRY DRAFT CHOICES

Year   Player, Overall, Last Amateur Team (League)
1993—Paul Kariya, 4, University of Maine

Year   Player, Overall, Last Amateur Team (League)
1994—Oleg Tverdovsky, 2, Krylja Sovetov (Russia)

FRANCHISE LEADERS

Current players in boldface

FORWARDS/DEFENSEMEN

Games

Joe Sacco	84
Terry Yake	82
Randy Ladouceur	81
Bill Houlder	80
Shaun Van Allen	80
Tim Sweeney	78
Garry Valk	78
Bobby Dollas	77
Stu Grimson	77
Bob Corkum	76
Todd Ewen	76

Goals

Bob Corkum	23
Terry Yake	21
Joe Sacco	19
Garry Valk	18
Tim Sweeney	16
Bill Houlder	14
Troy Loney	13
Patrik Carnback	12
Peter Douris	12
Anatoli Semenov	11

Assists

Terry Yake	31
Bob Corkum	28
Tim Sweeney	27
Garry Valk	27
Bill Houlder	25
Shaun Van Allen	25
Peter Douris	22
Sean Hill	20
Anatoli Semenov	19
Alexei Kasatonov	18
Joe Sacco	18

Points

Terry Yake	52
Bob Corkum	51
Garry Valk	45
Tim Sweeney	43
Bill Houlder	39
Joe Sacco	37
Peter Douris	34
Shaun Van Allen	33
Anatoli Semenov	30
Sean Hill	27

Penalty minutes

Todd Ewen	272
Stu Grimson	199

Garry Valk	100
Troy Loney	88
Sean Hill	78
Randy Ladouceur	74
Shaun Van Allen	64
Joe Sacco	61
Bobby Dollas	55
Patrik Carnback	54

GOALTENDERS

Games

Guy Hebert	52
Ron Tugnutt	28
Mikhail Shtalenkov	10

Shutouts

Guy Hebert	2
Ron Tugnutt	1

Goals-against average
(1200 minutes minimum)

Guy Hebert	2.83
Ron Tugnutt	3.00

Wins

Guy Hebert	20
Ron Tugnutt	10
Mikhail Shtalenkov	3

BOSTON BRUINS

YEAR-BY-YEAR RECORDS

Season	W	L	T	Pts.	Finish	W	L	Highest round	Coach
					REGULAR SEASON			PLAYOFFS	
1924-25	6	24	0	12	6th	—	—		Art Ross
1925-26	17	15	4	38	4th	—	—		Art Ross
1926-27	21	20	3	45	2nd/American	*2	2	Stanley Cup finals	Art Ross
1927-28	20	13	11	51	1st/American	*0	1	Semifinals	Art Ross
1928-29	26	13	5	57	1st/American	5	0	Stanley Cup champ	Cy Denneny
1929-30	38	5	1	77	1st/American	3	3	Stanley Cup finals	Art Ross
1930-31	28	10	6	62	1st/American	2	3	Semifinals	Art Ross
1931-32	15	21	12	42	4th/American	—	—		Art Ross
1932-33	25	15	8	58	1st/American	2	3	Semifinals	Art Ross
1933-34	18	25	5	41	4th/American	—	—		Art Ross
1934-35	26	16	6	58	1st/American	1	3	Semifinals	Frank Patrick
1935-36	22	20	6	50	2nd/American	1	1	Quarterfinals	Frank Patrick
1936-37	23	18	7	53	2nd/American	1	2	Quarterfinals	Art Ross
1937-38	30	11	7	67	1st/American	0	3	Semifinals	Art Ross
1938-39	36	10	2	74	1st	8	4	Stanley Cup champ	Art Ross
1939-40	31	12	5	67	1st	2	4	Semifinals	Ralph (Cooney) Weiland
1940-41	27	8	13	67	1st	8	3	Stanley Cup champ	Ralph (Cooney) Weiland
1941-42	25	17	6	56	3rd	2	3	Semifinals	Art Ross
1942-43	24	17	9	57	2nd	4	5	Stanley Cup finals	Art Ross
1943-44	19	26	5	43	5th	—	—		Art Ross

Season	W	L	T	Pts.	Finish	W	L	Highest round	Coach
1944-45	16	30	4	36	4th	3	4	League semifinals	Art Ross
1945-46	24	18	8	56	2nd	5	5	Stanley Cup finals	Dit Clapper
1946-47	26	23	11	63	3rd	1	4	League semifinals	Dit Clapper
1947-48	23	24	13	59	3rd	1	4	League semifinals	Dit Clapper
1948-49	29	23	8	66	2nd	1	4	League semifinals	Dit Clapper
1949-50	22	32	16	60	5th	—	—		George Boucher
1950-51	22	30	18	62	4th	†1	4	League semifinals	Lynn Patrick
1951-52	25	29	16	66	4th	3	4	League semifinals	Lynn Patrick
1952-53	28	29	13	69	3rd	5	6	League semifinals	Lynn Patrick
1953-54	32	28	10	74	4th	0	4	League semifinals	Lynn Patrick
1954-55	23	26	21	67	4th	1	4	League semifinals	Lynn Patrick, Milt Schmidt
1955-56	23	34	13	59	5th	—	—		Milt Schmidt
1956-57	34	24	12	80	3rd	5	5	Stanley Cup finals	Milt Schmidt
1957-58	27	28	15	69	4th	6	6	Stanley Cup finals	Milt Schmidt
1958-59	32	29	9	73	2nd	3	4	League semifinals	Milt Schmidt
1959-60	28	34	8	64	5th	—	—		Milt Schmidt
1960-61	15	42	13	43	6th	—	—		Milt Schmidt
1961-62	15	47	8	38	6th	—	—		Phil Watson
1962-63	14	39	17	45	6th	—	—		Phil Watson, Milt Schmidt
1963-64	18	40	12	48	6th	—	—		Milt Schmidt
1964-65	21	43	6	48	6th	—	—		Milt Schmidt
1965-66	21	43	6	48	5th	—	—		Milt Schmidt
1966-67	17	43	10	44	6th	—	—		Harry Sinden
1967-68	37	27	10	84	3rd/East	0	4	Division semifinals	Harry Sinden
1968-69	42	18	16	100	2nd/East	6	4	Division finals	Harry Sinden
1969-70	40	17	19	99	2nd/East	12	2	Stanley Cup champ	Harry Sinden
1970-71	57	14	7	121	1st/East	3	4	Division semifinals	Tom Johnson
1971-72	54	13	11	119	1st/East	12	3	Stanley Cup champ	Tom Johnson
1972-73	51	22	5	107	2nd/East	1	4	Division semifinals	Tom Johnson, Bep Guidolin
1973-74	52	17	9	113	1st/East	10	6	Stanley Cup finals	Bep Guidolin
1974-75	40	26	14	94	2nd/Adams	1	2	Preliminaries	Don Cherry
1975-76	48	15	17	113	1st/Adams	5	7	Semifinals	Don Cherry
1976-77	49	23	8	106	1st/Adams	8	6	Stanley Cup finals	Don Cherry
1977-78	51	18	11	113	1st/Adams	10	5	Stanley Cup finals	Don Cherry
1978-79	43	23	14	100	1st/Adams	7	4	Semifinals	Don Cherry
1979-80	46	21	13	105	2nd/Adams	4	6	Quarterfinals	Fred Creighton, Harry Sinden
1980-81	37	30	13	87	2nd/Adams	0	3	Preliminaries	Gerry Cheevers
1981-82	43	27	10	96	2nd/Adams	6	5	Division finals	Gerry Cheevers
1982-83	50	20	10	110	1st/Adams	9	8	Conference finals	Gerry Cheevers
1983-84	49	25	6	104	1st/Adams	0	3	Division semifinals	Gerry Cheevers
1984-85	36	34	10	82	4th/Adams	2	3	Division semifinals	Gerry Cheevers, Harry Sinden
1985-86	37	31	12	86	3rd/Adams	0	3	Division semifinals	Butch Goring
1986-87	39	34	7	85	3rd/Adams	0	4	Division semifinals	Butch Goring, Terry O'Reilly
1987-88	44	30	6	94	2nd/Adams	12	6	Conference finals	Terry O'Reilly
1988-89	37	29	14	88	2nd/Adams	5	5	Division finals	Terry O'Reilly
1989-90	46	25	9	101	1st/Adams	13	8	Stanley Cup finals	Mike Milbury
1990-91	44	24	12	100	1st/Adams	10	9	Conference finals	Mike Milbury
1991-92	36	32	12	84	2nd/Adams	8	7	Conference finals	Rick Bowness
1992-93	51	26	7	109	1st/Adams	0	4	Division semifinals	Brian Sutter
1993-94	42	29	13	97	2nd/Northeast	6	7	Conference semifinals	Brian Sutter

*Won-lost record does not indicate tie(s) resulting from two-game, total-goals series that year (two-game, total-goals series were played from 1917-18 through 1935-36).
†Tied after one overtime (curfew law).

FIRST-ROUND ENTRY DRAFT CHOICES

Year	Player, Overall, Last Amateur Team (League)
1969—	Don Tannahill, 3, Niagara Falls (OHL)
	Frank Spring, 4, Edmonton (WCHL)
	Ivan Boldirev, 11, Oshawa (OHL)
1970—	Reggie Leach, 3, Flin Flon (WCHL)
	Rick MacLeish, 4, Peterborough (OHL)
	Ron Plumb, 9, Peterborough (OHL)
	Bob Stewart, 13, Oshawa (OHL)
1971—	Ron Jones, 6, Edmonton (WCHL)
	Terry O'Reilly, 14, Oshawa (OHL)
1972—	Mike Bloom, 16, St. Catharines (OHL)
1973—	Andre Savard, 6, Quebec (QMJHL)
1974—	Don Laraway, 18, Swift Current (WCHL)
1975—	Doug Halward, 14, Peterborough (OHL)
1976—	Clayton Pachal, 16, New Westminster (WCHL)
1977—	Dwight Foster, 16, Kitchener (OHL)
1978—	Al Secord, 16, Hamilton (OHL)
1979—	Ray Bourque, 8, Verdun (QMJHL)
	Brad McCrimmon, 15, Brandon (WHL)

Year	Player, Overall, Last Amateur Team (League)
1980—	Barry Pederson, 18, Victoria (WHL)
1981—	Norm Leveille, 14, Chicoutimi (QMJHL)
1982—	*Gord Kluzak, 1, Billings (WHL)
1983—	Nevin Markwart, 21, Regina (WHL)
1984—	Dave Pasin, 19, Prince Albert (WHL)
1985—	No first round selection
1986—	Craig Janney, 13, Boston College
1987—	Glen Wesley, 3, Portland (WHL)
	Stephane Quintal, 14, Granby (QMJHL)
1988—	Robert Cimetta, 18, Toronto (OHL)
1989—	Shayne Stevenson, 17, Kitchener (OHL)
1990—	Bryan Smolinski, 21, Michigan State University
1991—	Glen Murray, 18, Sudbury (OHL)
1992—	Dmitri Kvartalnov, 16, San Diego (IHL)
1993—	Kevyn Adams, 25, Miami of Ohio
1994—	Evgeni Riabchikov, 21, Molot-Perm (Russia)
	*Designates first player chosen in draft.

FRANCHISE LEADERS

Current players in boldface

FORWARDS/DEFENSEMEN

Games

John Bucyk	1436
Ray Bourque	1100
Wayne Cashman	1027
Terry O'Reilly	891
Rick Middleton	881
Don Marcotte	868
Dallas Smith	861
Dit Clapper	833
Milt Schmidt	776
Woody Dumart	771

Goals

John Bucyk	545
Phil Esposito	459
Rick Middleton	402
Ray Bourque	311
Cam Neely	291
Ken Hodge	289
Wayne Cashman	277
Bobby Orr	264
Peter McNab	263
Don Marcotte	230

Assists

Ray Bourque	877
John Bucyk	794
Bobby Orr	624

Phil Esposito	553
Wayne Cashman	516
Rick Middleton	496
Terry O'Reilly	402
Ken Hodge	385
Bill Cowley	346
Milt Schmidt	346

Points

John Bucyk	1339
Ray Bourque	1188
Phil Esposito	1012
Rick Middleton	898
Bobby Orr	888
Wayne Cashman	793
Ken Hodge	674
Terry O'Reilly	606
Peter McNab	587
Milt Schmidt	575

Penalty minutes

Terry O'Reilly	2095
Mike Milbury	1552
Keith Crowder	1261
Wayne Cashman	1041
Eddie Shore	1038
Ted Green	1029

GOALTENDERS

Games

Cecil Thompson	468
Frankie Brimsek	444

Eddie Johnston	443
Gerry Cheevers	416
Gilles Gilbert	277
Jim Henry	236

Shutouts

Cecil Thompson	74
Frankie Brimsek	35
Eddie Johnston	27
Gerry Cheevers	26
Jim Henry	24
Hal Winkler	19
Gilles Gilbert	16
Don Simmons	15

Goals-against average
(2400 minutes minimum)

Hal Winkler	1.56
Cecil Thompson	1.99
Charles Stewart	2.46
John Henderson	2.52
Terry Sawchuk	2.57
Frankie Brimsek	2.58
Jim Henry	2.58

Wins

Cecil Thompson	252
Frankie Brimsek	230
Gerry Cheevers	229
Eddie Johnston	182
Gilles Gilbert	155

BUFFALO SABRES

YEAR-BY-YEAR RECORDS

	REGULAR SEASON					PLAYOFFS			
Season	W	L	T	Pts.	Finish	W	L	Highest round	Coach
1970-71	24	39	15	63	5th/East	—	—		Punch Imlach
1971-72	16	43	19	51	6th/East	—	—		Punch Imlach, Joe Crozier
1972-73	37	27	14	88	4th/East	2	4	Division semifinals	Joe Crozier
1973-74	32	34	12	76	5th/East	—	—		Joe Crozier
1974-75	49	16	15	113	1st/Adams	10	7	Stanley Cup finals	Floyd Smith
1975-76	46	21	13	105	2nd/Adams	4	5	Quarterfinals	Floyd Smith
1976-77	48	24	8	104	2nd/Adams	2	4	Quarterfinals	Floyd Smith
1977-78	44	19	17	105	2nd/Adams	3	5	Quarterfinals	Marcel Pronovost
1978-79	36	28	16	88	2nd/Adams	1	2	Preliminaries	Marcel Pronovost, Bill Inglis
1979-80	47	17	16	110	1st/Adams	9	5	Semifinals	Scotty Bowman
1980-81	39	20	21	99	1st/Adams	4	4	Quarterfinals	Roger Neilson
1981-82	39	26	15	93	3rd/Adams	1	3	Division semifinals	Jim Roberts, Scotty Bowman
1982-83	38	29	13	89	3rd/Adams	6	4	Division finals	Scotty Bowman
1983-84	48	25	7	103	2nd/Adams	0	3	Division semifinals	Scotty Bowman
1984-85	38	28	14	90	3rd/Adams	2	3	Divison semifinals	Scotty Bowman
1985-86	37	37	6	80	5th/Adams	—	—		Jim Schoenfeld, Scotty Bowman
1986-87	28	44	8	64	5th/Adams	—	—		Scotty Bowman, Craig Ramsay Ted Sator
1987-88	37	32	11	85	3rd/Adams	2	4	Division semifinals	Ted Sator
1988-89	38	35	7	83	3rd/Adams	1	4	Division semifinals	Ted Sator
1989-90	45	27	8	98	2nd/Adams	2	4	Division semifinals	Rick Dudley
1990-91	31	30	19	81	3rd/Adams	2	4	Division semifinals	Rick Dudley
1991-92	31	37	12	74	3rd/Adams	3	4	Division semifinals	Rick Dudley, John Muckler
1992-93	38	36	10	86	4th/Adams	4	4	Division finals	John Muckler
1993-94	43	32	9	95	4th/Northeast	3	4	Conference quarterfinals	John Muckler

FIRST-ROUND ENTRY DRAFT CHOICES

Year   Player, Overall, Last Amateur Team (League)
1970—*Gilbert Perreault, 1, Montreal (OHL)
1971—Rick Martin, 5, Montreal (OHL)
1972—Jim Schoenfeld, 5, Niagara Falls (OHL)
1973—Morris Titanic, 12, Sudbury (OHL)
1974—Lee Fogolin, 11, Oshawa (OHL)

Year   Player, Overall, Last Amateur Team (League)
1975—Robert Sauve, 17, Laval (QMJHL)
1976—No first round selection
1977—Ric Seiling, 14, St. Catharines (OHL)
1978—Larry Playfair, 13, Portland (WHL)
1979—Mike Ramsey, 11, University of Minnesota

Year	Player, Overall, Last Amateur Team (League)
1980	Steve Patrick, 20, Brandon (WHL)
1981	Jiri Dudacek, 17, Kladno (Czechoslovakia)
1982	Phil Housley, 6, South St. Paul H.S. (Minn.)
	Paul Cyr, 9, Victoria (WHL)
	Dave Andreychuk, 16, Oshawa (OHL)
1983	Tom Barrasso, 5, Acton Boxboro H.S. (Mass.)
	Norm Lacombe, 10, Univ. of New Hampshire
	Adam Creighton, 11, Ottawa (OHL)
1984	Bo Andersson, 18, Vastra Frolunda (Sweden)
1985	Carl Johansson, 14, Vastra Frolunda (Sweden)

Year	Player, Overall, Last Amateur Team (League)
1986	Shawn Anderson, 5, Team Canada
1987	*Pierre Turgeon, 1, Granby (QMJHL)
1988	Joel Savage, 13, Victoria (WHL)
1989	Kevin Haller, 14, Regina (WHL)
1990	Brad May, 14, Niagara Falls (OHL)
1991	Philippe Boucher, 13, Granby (QMJHL)
1992	David Cooper, 11, Medicine Hat (WHL)
1993	No first round selection
1994	Wayne Primeau, 17, Owen Sound (OHL)

*Designates first player chosen in draft.

FRANCHISE LEADERS

Current players in boldface

FORWARDS/DEFENSEMEN

Games

Gilbert Perreault	1191
Craig Ramsay	1070
Mike Ramsey	911
Bill Hajt	854
Don Luce	766
Dave Andreychuk	763
Rick Martin	681
Ric Seiling	664
Mike Foligno	662
Lindy Ruff	608
Phil Housley	608

Goals

Gilbert Perreault	512
Rick Martin	382
Dave Andreychuk	348
Danny Gare	267
Craig Ramsay	252
Mike Foligno	247
Rene Robert	222
Don Luce	216
Alexander Mogilny	**192**
Phil Housley	178

Assists

Gilbert Perreault	814
Dave Andreychuk	423
Craig Ramsay	420
Phil Housley	380
Rene Robert	330
Rick Martin	313

Don Luce	310
Mike Foligno	264
Dale Hawerchuk	**264**
Mike Ramsey	256

Points

Gilbert Perreault	1326
Dave Andreychuk	710
Rick Martin	771
Criag Ramsay	672
Phil Housley	558
Rene Robert	552
Don Luce	526
Mike Foligno	511
Danny Gare	500
Alexander Mogilny	**397**

Penalty minutes

Mike Foligno	1450
Larry Playfair	1390
Rob Ray	**1286**
Lindy Ruff	1126
Jim Schoenfeld	1025
Mike Ramsey	924
Mike Hartman	890
Jerry Korab	870
Brad May	**722**
Danny Gare	686

GOALTENDERS

Games

Don Edwards	307
Tom Barrasso	266
Bob Sauve	246
Daren Puppa	215

Roger Crozier	202
Jacques Cloutier	144
Dave Dryden	120
Gerry Desjardins	116
Clint Malarchuk	102
Dominik Hasek	**86**

Shutouts

Don Edwards	14
Tom Barrasso	13
Roger Crozier	10
Dominik Hasek	**7**
Bob Sauve	7

Goals-against average
(2400 minutes minimum)

Dominik Hasek	2.31
Gerry Desjardins	2.81
Don Edwards	2.90
Dave Dryden	3.06
Bob Sauve	3.20
Roger Crozier	3.23
Tom Barrasso	3.28
Clint Malarchuk	3.40
Daren Puppa	3.41
Grant Fuhr	**3.58**

Wins

Don Edwards	156
Tom Barrasso	124
Bob Sauve	119
Daren Puppa	96
Roger Crozier	74
Gerry Desjardins	66

CALGARY FLAMES

YEAR-BY-YEAR RECORDS

	REGULAR SEASON					PLAYOFFS			
Season	W	L	T	Pts.	Finish	W	L	Highest round	Coach
1972-73*	25	38	15	65	7th/West	—	—		Bernie Geoffrion
1973-74*	30	34	14	74	4th/West	0	4	Division semifinals	Bernie Geoffrion
1974-75*	34	31	15	83	4th/Patrick	—	—		Bernie Geoffrion, Fred Creighton
1975-76*	35	33	12	82	3rd/Patrick	0	2	Preliminaries	Fred Creighton
1976-77*	34	34	12	80	3rd/Patrick	1	2	Preliminaries	Fred Creighton
1977-78*	34	27	19	87	3rd/Patrick	0	2	Preliminaries	Fred Creighton
1978-79*	41	31	8	90	4th/Patrick	0	2	Preliminaries	Fred Creighton
1979-80*	35	32	13	83	4th/Patrick	1	3	Preliminaries	Al MacNeil
1980-81	39	27	14	92	3rd/Patrick	9	7	Semifinals	Al MacNeil
1981-82	29	34	17	75	3rd/Smythe	0	3	Division semifinals	Al MacNeil
1982-83	32	34	14	78	2nd/Smythe	4	5	Division finals	Bob Johnson
1983-84	34	32	14	82	2nd/Smythe	6	5	Division finals	Bob Johnson
1984-85	41	27	12	94	3rd/Smythe	1	3	Division semifinals	Bob Johnson
1985-86	40	31	9	89	2nd/Smythe	12	10	Stanley Cup finals	Bob Johnson
1986-87	46	31	3	95	2nd/Smythe	2	4	Division semifinals	Bob Johnson
1987-88	48	23	9	105	1st/Smythe	4	5	Division finals	Terry Crisp
1988-89	54	17	9	117	1st/Smythe	16	6	Stanley Cup champ	Terry Crisp
1989-90	42	23	15	99	1st/Smythe	2	4	Division semifinals	Terry Crisp
1990-91	46	26	8	100	2nd/Smythe	3	4	Division semifinals	Doug Risebrough
1991-92	31	37	12	74	5th/Smythe	—	—		Doug Risebrough, Guy Charron

Season	W	L	T	Pts.	Finish	W	L	Highest round	Coach
			REGULAR SEASON					**PLAYOFFS**	
1992-93	43	30	11	97	2nd/Smythe	2	4	Division semifinals	Dave King
1993-94	42	29	13	97	1st/Pacific	3	4	Conference quarterfinals	Dave King

*Atlanta Flames.

FIRST-ROUND ENTRY DRAFT CHOICES

Year   Player, Overall, Last Amateur Team (League)
1972—Jacques Richard, 2, Quebec (QMJHL)
1973—Tom Lysiak, 2, Medicine Hat (WCHL)
        Vic Mercredi, 16, New Westminster (WCHL)
1974—No first round selection
1975—Richcard Mulhern, 8, Sherbrooke (QMJHL)
1976—Dave Shand, 8, Peterborough (OHL)
        Harold Phillpoff, 10, New Westminster (WCHL)
1977—No first round selection
1978—Brad Marsh, 11, London (OHL)
1979—Paul Reinhart, 12, Kitchener (OHL)
1980—Denis Cyr, 13, Montreal (OHL)
1981—Al MacInnis, 15, Kitchener (OHL)
1982—No first round selection

Year   Player, Overall, Last Amateur Team (League)
1983—Dan Quinn, 13, Belleville (OHL)
1984—Gary Roberts, 12, Ottawa (OHL)
1985—Chris Biotti, 17, Belmont Hill H.S. (Mass.)
1986—George Pelawa, 16, Bemidji H.S. (Minn.)
1987—Bryan Deasley, 19, University of Michigan
1988—Jason Muzzatti, 21, Michigan State University
1989—No first round selection
1990—Trevor Kidd, 11, Brandon (WHL)
1991—Niklas Sundblad, 19, AIK (Sweden)
1992—Cory Stillman, 6, Windsor (OHL)
1993—Jesper Mattsson, 18, Malmo (Sweden)
1994—Chris Dingman, 19, Brandon (WHL)

FRANCHISE LEADERS

Current players in boldface

FORWARDS/DEFENSEMEN
Games
Al MacInnis	803
Jim Peplinski	705
Joel Otto	683
Gary Suter	617
Jamie Macoun	586
Tim Hunter	545
Gary Roberts	542
Eric Vail	539
Joe Nieuwendyk	531
Paul Reinhart	517

Goals
Joe Nieuwendyk	293
Gary Roberts	233
Kent Nilsson	229
Lanny McDonald	215
Al MacInnis	213
Eric Vail	206
Theoren Fleury	203
Guy Chouinard	193
Hakan Loob	193
Joe Mullen	190

Assists
Al MacInnis	609
Gary Suter	437
Guy Chouinard	336
Paul Reinhart	335
Kent Nilsson	333
Tom Lysiak	276

Joe Nieuwendyk	273
Jim Peplinski	262
Theoren Fleury	259
Joel Otto	248

Points
Al MacInnis	822
Gary Suter	565
Joe Nieuwendyk	566
Kent Nilsson	562
Guy Chouinard	529
Theoren Fleury	462
Gary Roberts	459
Eric Vail	452
Paul Reinhart	444
Tom Lysiak	431

Penalty minutes
Tim Hunter	2405
Gary Roberts	1615
Jim Peplinski	1456
Joel Otto	1510
Willi Plett	1267
Al MacInnis	960
Gary Suter	874
Ronnie Stern	857
Theoren Fleury	746
Jamie Macoun	666

GOALTENDERS
Games
Mike Vernon	467
Dan Bouchard	398
Reggie Lemelin	324

Phil Myre	211
Pat Riggin	119
Don Edwards	114
Rick Wamsley	111

Shutouts
Dan Bouchard	20
Phil Myre	11
Mike Vernon	9
Reggie Lemelin	6
Pat Riggin	4
Rick Wamsley	4

Goals-against average
(2400 minutes minimum)
Dan Bouchard	3.03
Phil Myre	3.21
Rick Wamsley	3.21
Mike Vernon	3.28
Reggie Lemelin	3.67
Pat Riggin	3.88
Don Edwards	4.06

Wins
Mike Vernon	248
Dan Bouchard	170
Reggie Lemelin	144
Phil Myre	76
Rick Wamsley	53
Pat Riggin	50
Don Edwards	40

CHICAGO BLACKHAWKS

YEAR-BY-YEAR RECORDS

Season	W	L	T	Pts.	Finish	W	L	Highest round	Coach
			REGULAR SEASON					**PLAYOFFS**	
1926-27	19	22	3	41	3rd/American	*0	1	Quarterfinals	Pete Muldoon
1927-28	7	34	3	17	5th/American	—	—		Barney Stanley, Hugh Lehman
1928-29	7	29	8	22	5th/American	—	—		Herb Gardiner
1929-30	21	18	5	47	2nd/American	*0	1	Quarterfinals	Tom Schaughnessy, Bill Tobin
1930-31	24	17	3	51	2nd/American	*5	3	Stanley Cup finals	Dick Irvin
1931-32	18	19	11	47	2nd/American	1	1	Quarterfinals	Dick Irvin, Bill Tobin
1932-33	16	20	12	44	4th/American	—	—		Godfrey Matheson, Emil Iverson
1933-34	20	17	11	51	2nd/American	6	2	Stanley Cup champ	Tom Gorman

— 133 —

Season	W	L	T	Pts.	Finish	W	L	Highest round	Coach
					REGULAR SEASON			PLAYOFFS	
1934-35	26	17	5	57	2nd/American	*0	1	Quarterfinals	Clem Loughlin
1935-36	21	19	8	50	3rd/American	1	1	Quarterfinals	Clem Loughlin
1936-37	14	27	7	35	4th/American	—	—		Clem Loughlin
1937-38	14	25	9	37	3rd/American	7	3	Stanley Cup champ	Bill Stewart
1938-39	12	28	8	32	7th	—	—		Bill Stewart, Paul Thompson
1939-40	23	19	6	52	4th	0	2	Quarterfinals	Paul Thompson
1940-41	16	25	7	39	5th	2	3	Semifinals	Paul Thompson
1941-42	22	23	3	47	4th	1	2	Quarterfinals	Paul Thompson
1942-43	17	18	15	49	5th	—	—		Paul Thompson
1943-44	22	23	5	49	4th	4	5	Stanley Cup finals	Paul Thompson
1944-45	13	30	7	33	5th	—	—		Paul Thompson, John Gottselig
1945-46	23	20	7	53	3rd	0	4	League semifinals	John Gottselig
1946-47	19	37	4	42	6th	—	—		John Gottselig
1947-48	20	34	6	46	6th	—	—		John Gottselig, Charlie Conacher
1948-49	21	31	8	50	5th	—	—		Charlie Conacher
1949-50	22	38	10	54	6th	—	—		Charlie Conacher
1950-51	13	47	10	36	6th	—	—		Ebbie Goodfellow
1951-52	17	44	9	43	6th	—	—		Ebbie Goodfellow
1952-53	27	28	15	69	4th	3	4	League semifinals	Sid Abel
1953-54	12	51	7	31	6th	—	—		Sid Abel
1954-55	13	40	17	43	6th	—	—		Frank Eddolls
1955-56	19	39	12	50	6th	—	—		Dick Irvin
1956-57	16	39	15	47	6th	—	—		Tommy Ivan
1957-58	24	39	7	55	5th	—	—		Tommy Ivan, Rudy Pilous
1958-59	28	29	13	69	3rd	2	4	League semifinals	Rudy Pilous
1959-60	28	29	13	69	3rd	0	4	League semifinals	Rudy Pilous
1960-61	29	24	17	75	3rd	8	4	Stanley Cup champ	Rudy Pilous
1961-62	31	26	13	75	3rd	6	6	Stanley Cup finals	Rudy Pilous
1962-63	32	21	17	81	2nd	2	4	League semifinals	Rudy Pilous
1963-64	36	22	12	84	2nd	3	4	League semifinals	Billy Reay
1964-65	34	28	8	76	3rd	7	7	Stanley Cup finals	Billy Reay
1965-66	37	25	8	82	2nd	2	4	League semifinals	Billy Reay
1966-67	41	17	12	94	1st	2	4	League semifinals	Billy Reay
1967-68	32	26	16	80	4th/East	5	6	Division finals	Billy Reay
1968-69	34	33	9	77	6th/East	—	—		Billy Reay
1969-70	45	22	9	99	1st/East	4	4	Division finals	Billy Reay
1970-71	49	20	9	107	1st/West	11	7	Stanley Cup finals	Billy Reay
1971-72	46	17	15	107	1st/West	4	4	Division finals	Billy Reay
1972-73	42	27	9	93	1st/West	10	6	Stanley Cup finals	Billy Reay
1973-74	41	14	23	105	2nd/West	6	5	Division finals	Billy Reay
1974-75	37	35	8	82	3rd/Smythe	3	5	Quarterfinals	Billy Reay
1975-76	32	30	18	82	1st/Smythe	0	4	Quarterfinals	Billy Reay
1976-77	26	43	11	63	3rd/Smythe	0	2	Preliminaries	Billy Reay, Bill White
1977-78	32	29	19	83	1st/Smythe	0	4	Quarterfinals	Bob Pulford
1978-79	29	36	15	73	1st/Smythe	0	4	Quarterfinals	Bob Pulford
1979-80	34	27	19	87	1st/Smythe	3	4	Quarterfinals	Eddie Johnston
1980-81	31	33	16	78	2nd/Smythe	0	3	Preliminaries	Keith Magnuson
1981-82	30	38	12	72	4th/Norris	8	7	Conference finals	Keith Magnuson, Bob Pulford
1982-83	47	23	10	104	1st/Norris	7	6	Conference finals	Orval Tessier
1983-84	30	42	8	68	4th/Norris	2	3	Division semifinals	Orval Tessier
1984-85	38	35	7	83	2nd/Norris	9	6	Conference finals	Orval Tessier, Bob Pulford
1985-86	39	33	8	86	1st/Norris	0	3	Division semifinals	Bob Pulford
1986-87	29	37	14	72	3rd/Norris	0	4	Division semifinals	Bob Pulford
1987-88	30	41	9	69	3rd/Norris	1	4	Division semifinals	Bob Murdoch
1988-89	27	41	12	66	4th/Norris	9	7	Conference finals	Mike Keenan
1989-90	41	33	6	88	1st/Norris	10	10	Conference finals	Mike Keenan
1990-91	49	23	8	106	1st/Norris	2	4	Division semifinals	Mike Keenan
1991-92	36	29	15	87	2nd/Norris	12	6	Stanley Cup finals	Mike Keenan
1992-93	47	25	12	106	1st/Norris	0	4	Division semifinals	Darryl Sutter
1993-94	39	36	9	87	5th/Central	2	4	Conference quarterfinals	Darryl Sutter

*Won-lost record does not indicate tie(s) resulting from two-game, total-goals series that year (two-game, total-goals series were played from 1917-18 through 1935-36).

FIRST-ROUND ENTRY DRAFT CHOICES

Year   Player, Overall, Last Amateur Team (League)

1969—J.P. Bordeleau, 13, Montreal (OHL)
1970—Dan Maloney, 14, London (OHL)
1971—Dan Spring, 12, Edmonton (WCHL)
1972—Phil Russell, 13, Edmonton (WCHL)
1973—Darcy Rota, 13, Edmonton (WCHL)
1974—Grant Mulvey, 16, Calgary (WCHL)
1975—Greg Vaydik, 7, Medicine Hat (WCHL)

1976—Real Cloutier, 9, Quebec (WHA)
1977—Doug Wilson, 6, Ottawa (OHL)
1978—Tim Higgins, 10, Ottawa (OHL)
1979—Keith Brown, 7, Portland (WHL)
1980—Denis Savard, 3, Montreal (QMJHL)
       Jerome Dupont, 15, Toronto (OHL)
1981—Tony Tanti, 12, Oshawa (OHL)

Year	Player, Overall, Last Amateur Team (League)
1982—Ken Yaremchuk, 7, Portland (WHL)
1983—Bruce Cassidy, 18, Ottawa (OHL)
1984—Ed Olczyk, 3, U.S. Olympic Team
1985—Dave Manson, 11, Prince Albert (WHL)
1986—Everett Sanipass, 14, Verdun (QMJHL)
1987—Jimmy Waite, 8, Chicoutimi (QMJHL)
1988—Jeremy Roenick, 8, Thayer Academy (Mass.)

Year	Player, Overall, Last Amateur Team (League)
1989—Adam Bennett, 6, Sudbury (OHL)
1990—Karl Dykhuis, 16, Hull (QMJHL)
1991—Dean McAmmond, 22, Prince Albert (WHL)
1992—Sergei Krivokrasov, 12, Central Red Army (CIS)
1993—Eric Lecompte, 24, Hull (QMJHL)
1994—Ethan Moreau, 14, Niagara Falls (OHL)

FRANCHISE LEADERS

Current players in boldface

FORWARDS/DEFENSEMEN

Games

Stan Mikita	1394
Bobby Hull	1036
Eric Nesterenko	1013
Bob Murray	1008
Doug Wilson	938
Dennis Hull	904
Steve Larmer	891
Chico Maki	840
Pierre Pilote	821
Cliff Koroll	814
Keith Brown	812
Ken Wharram	766
Harold March	759
Pit Martin	740
Denis Savard	736

Goals

Bobby Hull	604
Stan Mikita	541
Steve Larmer	406
Denis Savard	351
Dennis Hull	298
Bill Mosienko	258
Ken Wharram	252

Pit Martin	243
Jeremy Roenick	**225**
Doug Wilson	225
Doug Bentley	217
Jim Pappin	216
Al Secord	213
Cliff Koroll	208
Eric Nesterenko	207

Assists

Stan Mikita	926
Denis Savard	662
Doug Wilson	554
Bobby Hull	549
Steve Larmer	517
Jeremy Roenick	**448**
Pierre Pilote	400
Pit Martin	384
Bob Murray	382
Dennis Hull	342
Doug Bentley	313
Chico Maki	292
Troy Murray	291
Bill Mosienko	288
Eric Nesterenko	288

Points

Stan Mikita	1467
Bobby Hull	1153

Denis Savard	1013
Steve Larmer	923
Doug Wilson	779
Dennis Hull	640
Pit Martin	627
Bill Mosienko	550
Ken Wharram	533
Doug Bentley	531
Bob Murray	514
Eric Nesterenko	495
Jeremy Roenick	**495**
Troy Murray	488
Pierre Pilote	477

GOALTENDERS

Shutouts

Tony Esposito	74
Glenn Hall	51
Chuck Gardiner	42
Mike Karakas	28
Ed Belfour	**23**
Al Rollins	17
Denis DeJordy	13
Murray Bannerman	8
Lorne Chabot	8
Paul Goodman	6
Hugh Lehman	6

CLEVELAND BARONS (DEFUNCT)

YEAR-BY-YEAR RECORDS

	REGULAR SEASON					PLAYOFFS			
Season	W	L	T	Pts.	Finish	W	L	Highest round	Coach
1967-68†	15	42	17	42	6th/West	—	—		Bert Olmstead, Gordie Fashoway
1968-69†	29	36	11	69	2nd/West	3	4	Division semifinals	Fred Glover
1969-70†	22	40	14	58	4th/West	0	4	Division semifinals	Fred Glover
1970-71‡	20	53	5	45	7th/West	—	—		Fred Glover
1971-72‡	21	39	18	60	6th/West	—	—		Fred Glover, Vic Stasiuk
1972-73‡	16	46	16	48	8th/West	—	—		Garry Young, Fred Glover
1973-74‡	13	55	10	36	8th/West	—	—		Fred Glover, Marsh Johnston
1974-75‡	19	48	13	51	4th/Adams	—	—		Marsh Johnston
1975-76‡	27	42	11	65	4th/Adams	—	—		Jack Evans
1976-77	25	42	13	63	4th/Adams	—	—		Jack Evans
1977-78*	22	45	13	57	4th/Adams	—	—		Jack Evans

*Team disbanded after 1977-78 season. Owners bought Minnesota franchise and a number of Cleveland players were awarded to North Stars; remaining Cleveland players were dispersed to other clubs in draft.
†Oakland Seals.
‡California Golden Seals.

FIRST-ROUND ENTRY DRAFT CHOICES

Year	Player, Overall, Last Amateur Team (League)
1969—Tony Featherstone, 7, Peterborough (OHA)
1970—Chris Oddleifson, 10 Winnipeg (WCHL)
1971—No first-round selection
1972—No first-round selection
1973—No first-round selection

Year	Player, Overall, Last Amateur Team (League)
1974—Rick Hampton, 3, St. Catharines (OHA)
	Ron Chipperfield, 17, Brandon (WCHL)
1975—Ralph Klassen, 3, Saskatoon (WCHL)
1976—Bjorn Johansson, 5, Orebro IK (Sweden)
1977—Mike Crombeen, 5, Kingston (OHA)

DALLAS STARS

YEAR-BY-YEAR RECORDS

		REGULAR SEASON					PLAYOFFS			
Season	W	L	T	Pts.	Finish	W	L	Highest round		Coach
1967-68*	27	32	15	69	4th/West	7	7	Division finals		Wren Blair
1968-69*	18	43	15	51	6th/West	—	—			Wren Blair, John Muckler
1969-70*	19	35	22	60	3rd/West	2	4	Division semifinals		Wren Blair, Charlie Burns
1970-71*	28	34	16	72	4th/West	6	6	Division finals		Jack Gordon
1971-72*	37	29	12	86	2nd/West	3	4	Division semifinals		Jack Gordon
1972-73*	37	30	11	85	3rd/West	2	4	Division semifinals		Jack Gordon
1973-74*	23	38	17	63	7th/West	—	—			Jack Gordon, Parker MacDonald
1974-75*	23	50	7	53	4th/Smythe	—	—			Jack Gordon, Charlie Burns
1975-76*	20	53	7	47	4th/Smythe	—	—			Ted Harris
1976-77*	23	39	18	64	2nd/Smythe	0	2	Preliminaries		Ted Harris
1977-78*	18	53	9	45	5th/Smythe	—	—			Ted Harris, Andre Beaulieu, Lou Nanne
1978-79*	28	40	12	68	4th/Adams	—	—			Harry Howell, Glen Sonmor
1979-80*	36	28	16	88	3rd/Adams	8	7	Semifinals		Glen Sonmor
1980-81*	35	28	17	87	3rd/Adams	12	7	Stanley Cup finals		Glen Sonmor
1981-82*	37	23	20	94	1st/Norris	1	3	Division semifinals		Glen Sonmor, Murray Oliver
1982-83*	40	24	16	96	2nd/Norris	4	5	Division finals		Glen Sonmor, Murray Oliver
1983-84*	39	31	10	88	1st/Norris	7	9	Conference finals		Bill Maloney
1984-85*	25	43	12	62	4th/Norris	5	4	Division finals		Bill Maloney, Glen Sonmor
1985-86*	38	33	9	85	2nd/Norris	2	3	Division semifinals		Lorne Henning
1986-87*	30	40	10	70	5th/Norris	—	—			Lorne Henning, Glen Sonmor
1987-88*	19	48	13	51	5th/Norris	—	—			Herb Brooks
1988-89*	27	37	16	70	3rd/Norris	1	4	Division semifinals		Pierre Page
1989-90*	36	40	4	76	4th/Norris	3	4	Division semifinals		Pierre Page
1990-91*	27	39	14	68	4th/Norris	14	9	Stanley Cup finals		Bob Gainey
1991-92*	32	42	6	70	4th/Norris	3	4	Division semifinals		Bob Gainey
1992-93*	36	38	10	82	5th/Norris	—	—			Bob Gainey
1993-94*	42	29	13	97	3rd/Central	5	4	Conference semifinals		Bob Gainey

*Minnesota North Stars.

FIRST-ROUND ENTRY DRAFT CHOICES

Year Player, Overall, Last Amateur Team (League)

1969—Dick Redmond, 5, St. Catharines (OHL)
     Dennis O'Brien, 14, St. Catharines (OHL)
1970—No first-round selection
1971—No first-round selection
1972—Jerry Byers, 12, Kitchener (OHL)
1973—No first-round selection
1974—Doug Hicks, 6, Flin Flon (WCHL)
1975—Brian Maxwell, 4, Medicine Hat (WCHL)
1976—Glen Sharpley, 3, Hull (QMJHL)
1977—Brad Maxwell, 7, New Westminster (WCHL)
1978—*Bobby Smith, 1, Ottawa (OHL)
1979—Craig Hartsburg, 6, Birmingham (WHA)
     Tom McCarthy, 10, Oshawa (OHL)
1980—Brad Palmer, 16, Victoria (WHL)
1981—Ron Meighan, 13, Niagara Falls (OHL)
1982—Brian Bellows, 2, Kitchener (OHL)

Year Player, Overall, Last Amateur Team (League)

1983—*Brian Lawton, 1, Mount St. Charles H.S. (R.I.)
1984—David Quinn, 13, Kent H.S. (Ct.)
1985—No first-round selection
1986—Warren Babe, 12, Lethbridge (WHL)
1987—Dave Archibald, 6, Portland (WHL)
1988—*Mike Modano, 1, Prince Albert (WHL)
1989—Doug Zmolek, 7, John Marshall H.S. (Minn.)
1990—Derian Hatcher, 8, North Bay (OHL)
1991—Richard Matvichuk, 8, Saskatoon (WHL)
1992—No first-round selection
1993—Todd Harvey, 9, Detroit (OHL)
1994—Jason Botterill, 20, Michigan (CCHA)

*Designates first player chosen in draft.

FRANCHISE LEADERS

Current players in boldface

FORWARDS/DEFENSEMEN

Games

Neal Broten	955
Curt Giles	760
Brian Bellows	753
Fred Barrett	730
Bill Goldsworthy	670
Lou Nanne	635
Tom Reid	615
Steve Payne	613
Dino Ciccarelli	602
J.P. Parise	588

Goals

Brian Bellows	342
Dino Ciccarelli	332
Bill Goldsworthy	267
Neal Broten	266
Steve Payne	228
Dave Gagner	219
Bobby Smith	185
Tim Young	178
Danny Grant	176
Mike Modano	173

Assists

Neal Broten	582
Brian Bellows	380
Bobby Smith	369
Dino Ciccarelli	319
Tim Young	316
Craig Hartsburg	315
Dave Gagner	246
J.P. Parise	242

Bill Goldsworthy	239
Steve Payne	238

Points

Neal Broten	796
Brian Bellows	722
Dino Ciccarelli	651
Bobby Smith	554
Bill Goldsworthy	506
Tim Young	494
Dave Gagner	466
Steve Payne	466
Craig Hartsburg	413
Mike Modano	402

Penalty minutes

Basil McRae	1567
Shane Churla	1527

Willi Plett	1137	Pete LoPresti	173	Cesare Maniago	3.17
Brad Maxwell	1031	Kari Takko	131	**Andy Moog**	**3.27**
Mark Tinordi	**1015**	Gump Worsley	107	Jon Casey	3.28
Dennis O'Brien	836			Gilles Gilbert	3.39
Gordie Roberts	832	**Shutouts**		Gary Edwards	3.44
Craig Hartsburg	818	Cesare Maniago	29	Gilles Meloche	3.51
Bob Rouse	735	Jon Casey	12	Don Beaupre	3.74
		Gilles Meloche	9	Kari Takko	3.87

GOALTENDERS

Games

	Pete LoPresti ... 5
	Darcy Wakaluk ... **5**
Cesare Maniago	420
Gilles Meloche	328
Jon Casey	325
Don Beaupre	316

Goals-against average
(2400 minutes minimum)

Gump Worsley	2.62
Darcy Wakaluk	**3.15**

Wins

Cesare Maniago	143
Gilles Meloche	141
Jon Casey	128
Don Beaupre	126
Pete LoPresti	43

DETROIT RED WINGS

YEAR-BY-YEAR RECORDS

	REGULAR SEASON					PLAYOFFS			
Season	W	L	T	Pts.	Finish	W	L	Highest round	Coach
1926-27†	12	28	4	28	5th/American	—	—		Art Duncan, Duke Keats
1927-28†	19	19	6	44	4th/American				Jack Adams
1928-29†	19	16	9	47	3rd/American	0	2	Quarterfinals	Jack Adams
1929-30†	14	24	6	34	4th/American	—	—		Jack Adams
1930-31‡	16	21	7	39	4th/American	—	—		Jack Adams
1931-32‡	18	20	10	46	3rd/American	*0	1	Quarterfinals	Jack Adams
1932-33	25	15	8	58	2nd/American	2	2	Semifinals	Jack Adams
1933-34	24	14	10	58	1st/American	4	5	Stanley Cup finals	Jack Adams
1934-35	19	22	7	45	4th/American	—	—		Jack Adams
1935-36	24	16	8	56	1st/American	6	1	Stanley Cup champ	Jack Adams
1936-37	25	14	9	59	1st/American	6	4	Stanley Cup champ	Jack Adams
1937-38	12	25	11	35	4th/American	—	—		Jack Adams
1938-39	18	24	6	42	5th	3	3	Semifinals	Jack Adams
1939-40	16	26	6	38	5th	2	3	Semifinals	Jack Adams
1940-41	21	16	11	53	3rd	4	5	Stanley Cup finals	Jack Adams
1941-42	19	25	4	42	5th	7	5	Stanley Cup finals	Jack Adams
1942-43	25	14	11	61	1st	8	2	Stanley Cup champ	Jack Adams
1943-44	26	18	6	58	2nd	1	4	League semifinals	Jack Adams
1944-45	31	14	5	67	2nd	7	7	Stanley Cup finals	Jack Adams
1945-46	20	20	10	50	4th	1	4	League semifinals	Jack Adams
1946-47	22	27	11	55	4th	1	4	League semifinals	Jack Adams
1947-48	30	18	12	72	2nd	4	6	Stanley Cup finals	Tommy Ivan
1948-49	34	19	7	75	1st	4	7	Stanley Cup finals	Tommy Ivan
1949-50	37	19	14	88	1st	8	6	Stanley Cup champ	Tommy Ivan
1950-51	44	13	13	101	1st	2	4	League semifinals	Tommy Ivan
1951-52	44	14	12	100	1st	8	0	Stanley Cup champ	Tommy Ivan
1952-53	36	16	18	90	1st	2	4	League semifinals	Tommy Ivan
1953-54	37	19	14	88	1st	8	4	Stanley Cup champ	Tommy Ivan
1954-55	42	17	11	95	1st	8	3	Stanley Cup champ	Jimmy Skinner
1955-56	30	24	16	76	2nd	5	5	Stanley Cup finals	Jimmy Skinner
1956-57	38	20	12	88	1st	1	4	League semifinals	Jimmy Skinner
1957-58	29	29	12	70	3rd	0	4	League semifinals	Jimmy Skinner, Sid Abel
1958-59	25	37	8	58	6th	—	—		Sid Abel
1959-60	26	29	15	67	4th	2	4	League semifinals	Sid Abel
1960-61	25	29	16	66	4th	6	5	Stanley Cup finals	Sid Abel
1961-62	23	33	14	60	5th	—	—		Sid Abel
1962-63	32	25	13	77	4th	5	6	Stanley Cup finals	Sid Abel
1963-64	30	29	11	71	4th	7	7	Stanley Cup finals	Sid Abel
1964-65	40	23	7	87	1st	3	4	League semifinals	Sid Abel
1965-66	31	27	12	74	4th	6	6	Stanley Cup finals	Sid Abel
1966-67	27	39	4	58	5th	—	—		Sid Abel
1967-68	27	35	12	66	6th/East	—	—		Bill Gadsby
1968-69	33	31	12	78	5th/East	—	—		Bill Gadsby
1969-70	40	21	15	95	3rd/East	0	4	Division semifinals	Bill Gadsby, Sid Abel
1970-71	22	45	11	55	7th/East	—	—		Ned Harkness, Doug Barkley
1971-72	33	35	10	76	5th/East	—	—		Doug Barkley, Johnny Wilson
1972-73	37	29	12	86	5th/East	—	—		Johnny Wilson
1973-74	29	39	10	68	6th/East	—	—		Ted Garvin, Alex Delvecchio
1974-75	23	45	12	58	4th/Norris	—	—		Alex Delvecchio
1975-76	26	44	10	62	4th/Norris	—	—		Ted Garvin, Alex Delvecchio
1976-77	16	55	9	41	5th/Norris	—	—		Alex Delvecchio, Larry Wilson
1977-78	32	34	14	78	2nd/Norris	3	4	Quarterfinals	Bobby Kromm
1978-79	23	41	16	62	5th/Norris	—	—		Bobby Kromm
1979-80	26	43	11	63	5th/Norris	—	—		Bobby Kromm, Ted Lindsay

Season	W	L	T	Pts.	Finish	W	L	Highest round	Coach
		REGULAR SEASON					**PLAYOFFS**		
1980-81	19	43	18	56	5th/Norris	—	—		Ted Lindsay, Wayne Maxner
1981-82	21	47	12	54	6th/Norris				Wayne Maxner, Billy Dea
1982-83	21	44	15	57	5th/Norris	—	—		Nick Polano
1983-84	31	42	7	69	3rd/Norris	1	3	Division semifinals	Nick Polano
1984-85	27	41	12	66	3rd/Norris	0	3	Division semifinals	Nick Polano
1985-86	17	57	6	40	5th/Norris	—	—		Harry Neale, Brad Park, Dan Belisle
1986-87	34	36	10	78	2nd/Norris	9	7	Conference finals	Jacques Demers
1987-88	41	28	11	93	1st/Norris	9	7	Conference finals	Jacques Demers
1988-89	34	34	12	80	1st/Norris	2	4	Division semifinals	Jacques Demers
1989-90	28	38	14	70	5th/Norris	—	—		Jacques Demers
1990-91	34	38	8	76	3rd/Norris	3	4	Division semifinals	Bryan Murray
1991-92	43	25	12	98	1st/Norris	4	7	Division finals	Bryan Murray
1992-93	47	28	9	103	2nd/Norris	3	4	Division semifinals	Bryan Murray
1993-94	46	30	8	100	1st/Central	3	4	Conference quarterfinals	Scotty Bowman

*Won-lost record does not indicate tie(s) resulting from two-game, total goals series that year (two-game, total-goals series were played from 1917-18 through 1935-36).

†Detroit Cougars.

‡Detroit Falcons.

FIRST-ROUND ENTRY DRAFT CHOICES

Year Player, Overall, Last Amateur Team (League)

1969—Jim Rutherford, 10, Hamilton (OHL)
1970—Serge Lajeunesse, 12, Montreal (OHL)
1971—Marcel Dionne, 2, St. Catharines (OHL)
1972—No first-round selection
1973—Terry Richardson, 11, New Westminster (WCHL)
1974—Bill Lochead, 9, Oshawa (OHL)
1975—Rick Lapointe, 5, Victoria (WCHL)
1976—Fred Williams, 4, Saskatoon (WCHL)
1977—*Dale McCourt, 1, St. Catharines (OHL)
1978—Willie Huber, 9, Hamilton (OHL)
   Brent Peterson, 12, Portland (WCHL)
1979—Mike Foligno, 3, Sudbury (OHL)
1980—Mike Blaisdell, 11, Regina (WHL)
1981—No first-round selection
1982—Murray Craven, 17, Medicine Hat (WHL)

1983—Steve Yzerman, 4, Peterborough (OHL)
1984—Shawn Burr, 7, Kitchener (OHL)
1985—Brent Fedyk, 8, Regina (WHL)
1986—*Joe Murphy, 1, Michigan State University
1987—Yves Racine, 11, Longueuil (QMJHL)
1988—Kory Kocur, 17, Saskatoon (WHL)
1989—Mike Sillinger, 11, Regina (WHL)
1990—Keith Primeau, 3, Niagara Falls (OHL)
1991—Martin Lapointe, 10, Laval (QMJHL)
1992—Curtis Bowen, 22, Ottawa (OHL)
1993—Anders Eriksson, 22, MoDo (Sweden)
1994—Yan Golbvovsky, 23, Dynamo Moscow (Russia)

*Designates first player chosen in draft.

FRANCHISE LEADERS

Current players in boldface

FORWARDS/DEFENSEMEN

Games

Gordie Howe	1687
Alex Delvecchio	1549
Marcel Pronovost	983
Norm Ullman	875
Ted Lindsay	862
Nick Libett	861
Red Kelly	846
Steve Yzerman	815
Syd Howe	793
Reed Larson	708

Goals

Gordie Howe	786
Steve Yzerman	469
Alex Delvecchio	456
Ted Lindsay	335
Norm Ullman	324
John Ogrodnick	259
Nick Libett	217
Gerard Gallant	207
Syd Howe	202
Reed Larson	188

Assists

Gordie Howe	1023
Alex Delvecchio	825
Steve Yzerman	653
Norm Ullman	434

Ted Lindsay	393
Reed Larson	382
Red Kelly	297
Sid Abel	279
John Ogrodnick	275
Gerard Gallant	260

Points

Gordie Howe	1809
Alex Delvecchio	1281
Steve Yzerman	1122
Norm Ullman	758
Ted Lindsay	728
Reed Larson	570
John Ogrodnick	534
Gerard Gallant	467
Nick Libett	467
Sid Abel	463

GOALTENDERS

Games

Terry Sawchuk	734
Harry Lumley	324
Jim Rutherford	314
Roger Crozier	310
Greg Stefan	299
Tim Cheveldae	264
Roy Edwards	221
Glen Hanlon	186
Norm Smith	178
John Mowers	152

Shutouts

Terry Sawchuk	85
Harry Lumley	26
Roger Crozier	20
Clarence Dolson	17
Glenn Hall	17
Harry Holmes	17
Norm Smith	17

Goals-against average
(2400 minutes minimum)

Clarence Dolson	2.06
Harry Holmes	2.11
Glenn Hall	2.14
Alex Connell	2.25
John Ross Roach	2.26
Norm Smith	2.34
Terry Sawchuk	2.46
John Mowers	2.63
Cecil Thompson	2.65
Harry Lumley	2.73

Wins

Terry Sawchuk	352
Harry Lumley	163
Roger Crozier	130
Tim Cheveldae	128
Greg Stefan	115
Jim Rutherford	97
Roy Edwards	95
Norm Smith	76

EDMONTON OILERS

YEAR-BY-YEAR RECORDS

	REGULAR SEASON					PLAYOFFS			
Season	W	L	T	Pts.	Finish	W	L	Highest round	Coach
1972-73*	38	37	3	79	5th	—	—		Ray Kinasewich
1973-74†	38	37	3	79	3rd	1	4	League quarterfinals	Brian Shaw
1974-75†	36	38	4	76	5th	—	—		Brian Shaw, Bill Hunter
1975-76†	27	49	5	59	4th	0	4	League quarterfinals	Clare Drake, Bill Hunter
1976-77†	34	43	4	72	4th	1	4	League quarterfinals	Bep Guidolin, Glen Sather
1977-78†	38	39	3	79	5th	1	4	League quarterfinals	Glen Sather
1978-79†	48	30	2	98	1st	6	7	Avco World Cup finals	Glen Sather
1979-80	28	39	13	69	4th/Smythe	0	3	Preliminaries	Glen Sather
1980-81	29	35	16	74	4th/Smythe	5	4	Quarterfinals	Glen Sather
1981-82	48	17	15	111	1st/Smythe	2	3	Division semifinals	Glen Sather
1982-83	47	21	12	106	1st/Smythe	11	5	Stanley Cup finals	Glen Sather
1983-84	57	18	5	119	1st/Smythe	15	4	Stanley Cup champ	Glen Sather
1984-85	49	20	11	109	1st/Smythe	15	3	Stanley Cup champ	Glen Sather
1985-86	56	17	7	119	1st/Smythe	6	4	Division finals	Glen Sather
1986-87	50	24	6	106	1st/Smythe	16	5	Stanley Cup champ	Glen Sather
1987-88	44	25	11	99	2nd/Smythe	16	2	Stanley Cup champ	Glen Sather
1988-89	38	34	8	84	3rd/Smythe	3	4	Division semifinals	Glen Sather
1989-90	38	28	14	90	2nd/Smythe	16	6	Stanley Cup champ	John Muckler
1990-91	37	37	6	80	3rd/Smythe	9	9	Conference finals	John Muckler
1991-92	36	34	10	82	3rd/Smythe	8	8	Conference finals	Ted Green
1992-93	26	50	8	60	5th/Smythe	—	—		Ted Green
1993-94	25	45	14	64	6th/Pacific	—	—		Ted Green, Glen Sather

*Alberta Oilers, members of World Hockey Association.
†Members of World Hockey Association.

FIRST-ROUND ENTRY DRAFT CHOICES

Year   Player, Overall, Last Amateur Team (League)
1979—Kevin Lowe, 21, Quebec (QMJHL)
1980—Paul Coffey, 6, Kitchener (OHL)
1981—Grant Fuhr, 8, Victoria (WHL)
1982—Jim Playfair, 20, Portland (WHL)
1983—Jeff Beukeboom, 19, Sault Ste. Marie (OHL)
1984—Selmar Odelein, 21, Regina (WHL)
1985—Scott Metcalfe, 20, Kingston (OHL)
1986—Kim Issel, 21, Prince Albert (WHL)
1987—Peter Soberlak, 21, Swift Current (WHL)
1988—Francois Leroux, 19, St. Jean (QMJHL)
1989—Jason Soules, 15, Niagara Falls (OHL)

Year   Player, Overall, Last Amateur Team (League)
1990—Scott Allison, 17, Prince Albert (WHL)
1991—Tyler Wright, 12, Swift Current (WHL)
      Martin Rucinsky, 20, Litvinov (Czech.)
1992—Joe Hulbig, 13, St. Sebastian H.S. (Mass.)
1993—Jason Arnott, 7, Oshawa (OHL)
      Nick Stajduhar, 16, London (OHL)
1994—Jason Bonsignore, 4, Niagara Falls (OHL)
      Ryan Smyth, 6, Moose Jaw (WHL)

NOTE: Edmonton chose Dave Dryden, Bengt Gustafsson and Ed Mio as priority selections before the 1979 expansion draft.

FRANCHISE LEADERS

Current players in boldface

FORWARDS/DEFENSEMEN
Games

Kevin Lowe	966
Mark Messier	851
Glenn Anderson	828
Jari Kurri	754
Craig MacTavish	701
Wayne Gretzky	696
Charlie Huddy	694
Dave Hunter	653
Lee Fogolin	586
Paul Coffey	532

Goals

Wayne Gretzky	583
Jari Kurri	474
Glenn Anderson	413
Mark Messier	392
Paul Coffey	209
Craig Simpson	185
Esa Tikkanen	178
Craig MacTavish	155
Dave Hunter	119
Petr Klima	118

Assists

Wayne Gretzky	1086
Mark Messier	642
Jari Kurri	569
Glenn Anderson	483
Paul Coffey	460
Kevin Lowe	295
Charlie Huddy	287
Esa Tikkanen	258
Craig Simpson	180
Craig MacTavish	176

Points

Wayne Gretzky	1669
Jari Kurri	1043
Mark Messier	1034
Glenn Anderson	896
Paul Coffey	669
Esa Tikkanen	436
Charlie Huddy	368
Kevin Lowe	368
Craig Simpson	365
Craig MacTavish	331

Penalty minutes

Kevin McClelland	1298
Kevin Lowe	1164

Kelly Buchberger	1132
Mark Messier	1122
Steve Smith	1080
Dave Semenko	976
Lee Fogolin	886
Dave Hunter	776
Glenn Anderson	771
Esa Tikkanen	759

GOALTENDERS
Games

Grant Fuhr	423
Bill Ranford	356
Andy Moog	235
Eddie Mio	77
Ron Low	67
Ron Tugnutt	29
Jim Corsi	26
Fred Brathwaite	19
Gary Edwards	15
Dave Dryden	14

Shutouts

Grant Fuhr	9
Bill Ranford	5

| Andy Moog | 4 |
| Eddie Mio | 1 |

Goals-against average
(2400 minutes minimum)

| Bill Ranford | 3.47 |
| Andy Moog | 3.61 |

Grant Fuhr	3.69
Eddie Mio	4.02
Ron Low	4.03

Wins

| Grant Fuhr | 226 |
| Andy Moog | 143 |

Bill Ranford	135
Ron Low	30
Eddie Mio	25
Ron Tugnutt	10
Jim Corsi	8

FLORIDA PANTHERS

YEAR-BY-YEAR RECORDS

	REGULAR SEASON					PLAYOFFS			
Season	W	L	T	Pts.	Finish	W	L	Highest round	Coach
1993-94	33	34	17	83	5th/Atlantic	—	—		Roger Neilson

FIRST-ROUND ENTRY DRAFT CHOICES

Year   Player, Overall, Last Amateur Team (League)
1993—Rob Niedermayer, 5, Medicine Hat (WHL)
1994—*Ed Jovanovski, 1, Windsor (OHL)
*Designates first player chosen in draft.

FRANCHISE LEADERS

Current players in boldface

FORWARDS/DEFENSEMEN

Games

Bill Lindsay	84
Gord Murphy	84
Tom Fitzgerald	83
Dave Lowry	80
Scott Mellanby	80
Brian Skrudland	79
Mike Hough	78
Andrei Lomakin	76
Brian Benning	73
Jesse Belanger	70

Goals

Scott Mellanby	30
Andrei Lomakin	19
Tom Fitzgerald	18
Stu Barnes	18
Jesse Belanger	17
Dave Lowry	15
Brian Skrudland	15
Gord Murphy	14
Bob Kudelski	14
Jody Hull	13

Assists

Jesse Belanger	33
Scott Mellanby	30
Gord Murphy	29
Andrei Lomakin	28
Brian Skrudland	25
Brian Benning	24
Mike Hough	23
Dave Lowry	22
Stu Barnes	20
Rob Niedermayer	17

Points

Scott Mellanby	60
Jesse Belanger	50
Andrei Lomakin	47
Gord Murphy	43
Brian Skrudland	40
Stu Barnes	38
Dave Lowry	37
Tom Fitzgerald	32
Brian Benning	30
Bob Kudelski	29
Mike Hough	29

Penalty minutes

| Brent Severyn | 156 |

Scott Mellanby	149
Brian Skrudland	136
Paul Laus	109
Brian Benning	107
Joe Cirella	99
Bill Lindsay	97
Gord Murphy	71
Scott Levins	69
Dave Lowry	64

GOALTENDERS

Games

John Vanbiesbrouck	57
Mark Fitzpatrick	28
Pokey Reddick	2

Shutouts

| Mark Fitzpatrick | 1 |
| John Vanbiesbrouck | 1 |

Goals-against average
(1200 minutes minimum)

| John Vanbiesbrouck | 2.53 |
| Mark Fitzpatrick | 2.73 |

Wins

| John Vanbiesbrouck | 21 |
| Mark Fitzpatrick | 12 |

HARTFORD WHALERS

YEAR-BY-YEAR RECORDS

	REGULAR SEASON					PLAYOFFS			
Season	W	L	T	Pts.	Finish	W	L	Highest round	Coach
1972-73*	46	30	2	94	1st	12	3	Avco World Cup champ	Jack Kelley
1973-74*	43	31	4	90	1st	3	4	League quarterfinals	Ron Ryan
1974-75*	43	30	5	91	1st	2	4	League quarterfinals	Ron Ryan, Jack Kelley
1975-76*	33	40	7	73	3rd	6	4	League semifinals	Jack Kelley, Don Blackburn, Harry Neale
1976-77*	35	40	6	76	4th	1	4	League quarterfinals	Harry Neale
1977-78*	44	31	5	93	2nd	8	6	Avco World Cup finals	Harry Neale
1978-79*	37	34	9	83	4th	5	5	League semifinals	Bill Dineen, Don Blackburn
1979-80	27	34	19	73	4th/Norris	0	3	Preliminaries	Don Blackburn
1980-81	21	41	18	60	4th/Norris	—	—		Don Blackburn, Larry Pleau
1981-82	21	41	18	60	5th/Adams	—	—		Larry Pleau
1982-83	19	54	7	45	5th/Adams	—	—		Larry Kish, Larry Pleau, John Cunniff
1983-84	28	42	10	66	5th/Adams	—	—		Jack Evans
1984-85	30	41	9	69	5th/Adams	—	—		Jack Evans
1985-86	40	36	4	84	4th/Adams	6	4	Division finals	Jack Evans

Season	W	L	T	Pts.	Finish	W	L	Highest round	Coach
1986-87	43	30	7	93	1st/Adams	2	4	Division semifinals	Jack Evans
1987-88	35	38	7	77	4th/Adams	2	4	Division semifinals	Jack Evans, Larry Pleau
1988-89	37	38	5	79	4th/Adams	0	4	Division semifinals	Larry Pleau
1989-90	38	33	9	85	4th/Adams	3	4	Division semifinals	Rick Ley
1990-91	31	38	11	73	4th/Adams	2	4	Division semifinals	Rick Ley
1991-92	26	41	13	65	4th/Adams	3	4	Division semifinals	Jim Roberts
1992-93	26	52	6	58	5th/Adams	—	—		Paul Holmgren
1993-94	27	48	9	63	6th/Northeast	—	—		Paul Holmgren, Pierre McGuire

*New England Whalers, members of World Hockey Association.

FIRST-ROUND ENTRY DRAFT CHOICES

Year   Player, Overall, Last Amateur Team (League)
1979—Ray Allison, 18, Brandon (WHL)
1980—Fred Arthur, 8, Cornwall (QMJHL)
1981—Ron Francis, 4, Sault Ste. Marie (OHL)
1982—Paul Lawless, 14, Windsor (OHL)
1983—Sylvain Turgeon, 2, Hull (QMJHL)
        David A. Jensen, 20, Lawrence Academy (Mass.)
1984—Sylvain Cote, 11, Quebec (QMJHL)
1985—Dana Murzyn, 5, Calgary (WHL)
1986—Scott Young, 11, Boston University
1987—Jody Hull, 18, Peterborough (OHL)

Year   Player, Overall, Last Amateur Team (League)
1988—Chris Govedaris, 11, Toronto (OHL)
1989—Robert Holik, 10, Jihlava (Czechoslovakia)
1990—Mark Greig, 15, Lethbridge (WHL)
1991—Patrick Poulin, 9, St. Hyacinthe (QMJHL)
1992—Robert Petrovicky, 9, Dukla Trencin (Czech.)
1993—Chris Pronger, 2, Peterborough (OHL)
1994—Jeff O'Neill, 5, Guelph (OHL)

NOTE: Hartford chose Jordy Douglas, John Garrett and Mark Howe as priority selections before the 1979 expansion draft.

FRANCHISE LEADERS

Current players in boldface

FORWARDS/DEFENSEMEN
Games
Ron Francis	714
Kevin Dineen	489
Dave Tippett	483
Ulf Samuelsson	463
Joel Quenneville	457
Randy Ladouceur	452
Ray Ferraro	442
Dean Evason	434
Pat Verbeek	**404**
Sylvain Cote	382
Paul MacDermid	373

Goals
Ron Francis	264
Blaine Stoughton	219
Kevin Dineen	214
Pat Verbeek	**185**
Sylvain Turgeon	178
Ray Ferraro	157
Ray Neufeld	106
Geoff Sanderson	**101**
Dean Evason	87
Mark Johnson	85
Mike Rogers	85

Assists
Ron Francis	557
Kevin Dineen	262
Pat Verbeek	**200**
Dave Babych	196

Ray Ferraro	194
Blaine Stoughton	158
Sylvain Turgeon	150
Dean Evason	148
Mark Howe	147
Ulf Samuelsson	144

Points
Ron Francis	821
Kevin Dineen	446
Pat Verbeek	**385**
Blaine Stoughton	377
Ray Ferraro	351
Sylvain Turgeon	328
Dave Babych	240
Dean Evason	235
Ray Neufeld	226
Mike Rogers	210
Mark Johnson	203

Penalty minutes
Torrie Robertson	1368
Ulf Samuelsson	1108
Pat Verbeek	**1101**
Kevin Dineen	1029
Randy Ladouceur	717
Paul MacDermid	706
Dean Evason	617
Ron Francis	540
Ed Kastelic	485
Chris Kotsopoulos	443

GOALTENDERS
Games
Mike Liut	252
Greg Millen	219

Peter Sidorkiewicz	178
John Garrett	122
Sean Burke	**97**
Steve Weeks	94
Kay Whitmore	75
Mike Veisor	69

Shutouts
Mike Liut	13
Peter Sidorkiewicz	8
Greg Millen	4
Steve Weeks	4
Sean Burke	**2**

Goals-against average
(2400 minutes minimum)
Peter Sidorkiewicz	3.33
Mike Liut	3.36
Sean Burke	**3.56**
Kay Whitmore	3.61
Steve Weeks	3.68
Greg Millen	4.25
John Garrett	4.28
Mike Veisor	4.87

Wins
Mike Liut	115
Peter Sidorkiewicz	71
Greg Millen	62
Steve Weeks	42
John Garrett	36
Sean Burke	**33**

LOS ANGELES KINGS

YEAR-BY-YEAR RECORDS

Season	W	L	T	Pts.	Finish	W	L	Highest round	Coach
1967-68	31	33	10	72	2nd/West	3	4	Division semifinals	Red Kelly
1968-69	24	42	10	58	4th/West	4	7	Division finals	Red Kelly
1969-70	14	52	10	38	6th/West	—	—		Hal Laycoe, Johnny Wilson
1970-71	25	40	13	63	5th/West	—	—		Larry Regan

Season	W	L	T	Pts.	Finish	W	L	Highest round	Coach
1971-72	20	49	9	49	7th/West	—	—		Larry Regan, Fred Glover
1972-73	31	36	11	73	6th/West	—	—		Bob Pulford
1973-74	33	33	12	78	3rd/West	1	4	Division semifinals	Bob Pulford
1974-75	42	17	21	105	2nd/Norris	1	2	Preliminaries	Bob Pulford
1975-76	38	33	9	85	2nd/Norris	5	4	Quarterfinals	Bob Pulford
1976-77	34	31	15	83	2nd/Norris	4	5	Quarterfinals	Bob Pulford
1977-78	31	34	15	77	3rd/Norris	0	2	Preliminaries	Ron Stewart
1978-79	34	34	12	80	3rd/Norris	0	2	Preliminaries	Bob Berry
1979-80	30	36	14	74	4th/Norris	1	3	Preliminaries	Bob Berry
1980-81	43	24	13	99	2nd/Norris	1	3	Preliminaries	Bob Berry
1981-82	24	41	15	63	4th/Smythe	4	6	Division finals	Parker MacDonald, Don Perry
1982-83	27	41	12	66	5th/Smythe	—	—		Don Perry
1983-84	23	44	13	59	5th/Smythe	—	—		Don Perry, Rogie Vachon, Roger Neilson
1984-85	34	32	14	82	4th/Smythe	0	3	Division semifinals	Pat Quinn
1985-86	23	49	8	54	5th/Smythe	—	—		Pat Quinn
1986-87	31	41	8	70	4th/Smythe	1	4	Division semifinals	Pat Quinn, Mike Murphy
1987-88	30	42	8	68	4th/Smythe	1	4	Division semifinals	Mike Murphy, Rogie Vachon, Robbie Ftorek
1988-89	42	31	7	91	2nd/Norris	4	7	Division finals	Robbie Ftorek
1989-90	34	39	7	75	4th/Smythe	4	6	Division finals	Tom Webster
1990-91	46	24	10	102	1st/Smythe	6	6	Division finals	Tom Webster
1991-92	35	31	14	84	2nd/Smythe	2	4	Division semifinals	Tom Webster
1992-93	39	35	10	88	3rd/Smythe	13	11	Stanley Cup finals	Barry Melrose
1993-94	27	45	12	66	5th/Pacific	—	—		Barry Melrose

FIRST-ROUND ENTRY DRAFT CHOICES

Year   Player, Overall, Last Amateur Team (League)

1969—No first-round selection
1970—No first-round selection
1971—No first-round selection
1972—No first-round selection
1973—No first-round selection
1974—No first-round selection
1975—Tim Young, 16, Ottawa (OHL)
1976—No first-round selection
1977—No first-round selection
1978—No first-round selection
1979—Jay Wells, 16, Kingston (OHL)
1980—Larry Murphy, 4, Peterborough (OHL)
     Jim Fox, 10, Ottawa (OHL)
1981—Doug Smith, 2, Ottawa (OHL)

1982—No first-round selection
1983—No first-round selection
1984—Craig Redmond, 6, Canadian Olympic Team
1985—Craig Duncanson, 9, Sudbury (OHL)
     Dan Gratton, 10, Oshawa (OHL)
1986—Jimmy Carson, 2, Verdun (QMJHL)
1987—Wayne McBean, 4, Medicine Hat (WHL)
1988—Martin Gelinas, 7, Hull (QMJHL)
1989—No first-round selection
1990—Darryl Sydor, 7, Kamloops (WHL)
1991—No first-round selection
1992—No first-round selection
1993—No first-round selection
1994—Jamie Storr, 7, Owen Sound (OHL)

FRANCHISE LEADERS

Current players in boldface

FORWARDS/DEFENSEMEN

Games

Dave Taylor	1111
Marcel Dionne	921
Butch Goring	736
Mike Murphy	673
Luc Robitaille	**640**
Mark Hardy	**616**
Jay Wells	604
Bernie Nicholls	602
Jim Fox	578
Bob Berry	539

Goals

Marcel Dionne	550
Dave Taylor	431
Luc Robitaille	**392**
Bernie Nicholls	327
Butch Goring	275
Charlie Simmer	222
Wayne Gretzky	**220**
Mike Murphy	194
Jim Fox	186
Bob Berry	159

Assists

Marcel Dionne	757
Dave Taylor	638
Wayne Gretzky	**569**
Bernie Nicholls	431
Luc Robitaille	**411**
Butch Goring	384
Jim Fox	292
Mike Murphy	262
Mark Hardy	**250**
Charlie Simmer	244

Points

Marcel Dionne	1307
Dave Taylor	1069
Luc Robitaille	**803**
Wayne Gretzky	**789**
Bernie Nicholls	758
Butch Goring	659
Jim Fox	478
Charlie Simmer	466
Mike Murphy	456
Bob Berry	350

Penalty minutes

Marty McSorley	**1615**
Dave Taylor	1589

Jay Wells	1446
Jay Miller	865
Mark Hardy	**858**

GOALTENDERS

Games

Rogie Vachon	389
Kelly Hrudey	**289**
Mario Lessard	240
Gary Edwards	155
Roland Melanson	119
Gerry Desjardins	103
Bob Janecyk	102
Dennis DeJordy	86

Shutouts

Rogie Vachon	32
Kelly Hrudey	**10**
Mario Lessard	9
Gerry Desjardins	7
Gary Edwards	7

Goals-against average
(2400 minutes minimum)

Rogie Vachon	2.86
Wayne Rutledge	3.34

Gary Edwards	3.39	Mario Lessard	3.74	Mario Lessard	92
Kelly Hrudey	**3.49**	**Robb Stauber**	**3.89**	Gary Edwards	54
Gerry Desjardins	3.52		Wins	Bob Janecyk	41
Daniel Berthiaume	3.54	Rogie Vachon	171	Roland Melanson	40
Dennis DeJordy	3.73	**Kelly Hrudey**	**124**	Glenn Healy	37

MONTREAL CANADIENS

YEAR-BY-YEAR RECORDS

	REGULAR SEASON					PLAYOFFS			
Season	W	L	T	Pts.	Finish	W	L	Highest round	Coach
1917-18	13	9	0	26	1st/3rd	1	1	Semifinals	George Kennedy
1918-19	10	8	0	20	1st/2nd	†*6	3	Stanley Cup finals	George Kennedy
1919-20	13	11	0	26	2nd/3rd	—	—		George Kennedy
1920-21	13	11	0	26	3rd/2nd	—	—		George Kennedy
1921-22	12	11	1	25	3rd	—	—		Leo Dandurand
1922-23	13	9	2	28	2nd	1	1	Quarterfinals	Leo Dandurand
1923-24	13	11	0	26	2nd	6	0	Stanley Cup champ	Leo Dandurand
1924-25	17	11	2	36	3rd	3	3	Stanley Cup finals	Leo Dandurand
1925-26	11	24	1	23	7th	—	—		Cecil Hart
1926-27	28	14	2	58	2nd/Canadian	*1	1	Semifinals	Cecil Hart
1927-28	26	11	7	59	1st/Canadian	*0	1	Semifinals	Cecil Hart
1928-29	22	7	15	59	1st/Canadian	0	3	Semifinals	Cecil Hart
1929-30	21	14	9	51	2nd/Canadian	*5	0	Stanley Cup champ	Cecil Hart
1930-31	26	10	8	60	1st/Canadian	6	4	Stanley Cup champ	Cecil Hart
1931-32	25	16	7	57	1st/Canadian	1	3	Semifinals	Cecil Hart
1932-33	18	25	5	41	3rd/Canadian	*0	1	Quarterfinals	Newsy Lalonde
1933-34	22	20	6	50	2nd/Canadian	*0	1	Quarterfinals	Newsy Lalonde
1934-35	19	23	6	44	3rd/Canadian	*0	1	Quarterfinals	Newsy Lalonde, Leo Dandurand
1935-36	11	26	11	33	4th/Canadian	—	—		Sylvio Mantha
1936-37	24	18	6	54	1st/Canadian	2	3	Semifinals	Cecil Hart
1937-38	18	17	13	49	3rd/Canadian	1	2	Quarterfinals	Cecil Hart
1938-39	15	24	9	39	6th	1	2	Quarterfinals	Cecil Hart, Jules Dugal
1939-40	10	33	5	25	7th	—	—		Pit Lepine
1940-41	16	26	6	38	6th	1	2	Quarterfinals	Dick Irvin
1941-42	18	27	3	39	6th	1	2	Quarterfinals	Dick Irvin
1942-43	19	19	12	50	4th	1	4	League semifinals	Dick Irvin
1943-44	38	5	7	83	1st	8	1	Stanley Cup champ	Dick Irvin
1944-45	38	8	4	80	1st	2	4	League semifinals	Dick Irvin
1945-46	28	17	5	61	1st	8	1	Stanley Cup champ	Dick Irvin
1946-47	34	16	10	78	1st	6	5	Stanley Cup finals	Dick Irvin
1947-48	20	29	11	51	5th	—	—		Dick Irvin
1948-49	28	23	9	65	3rd	3	4	League semifinals	Dick Irvin
1949-50	29	22	19	77	2nd	1	4	League semifinals	Dick Irvin
1950-51	25	30	15	65	3rd	5	6	Stanley Cup finals	Dick Irvin
1951-52	34	26	10	78	2nd	4	7	Stanley Cup finals	Dick Irvin
1952-53	28	23	19	75	2nd	8	4	Stanley Cup champ	Dick Irvin
1953-54	35	24	11	81	2nd	7	4	Stanley Cup finals	Dick Irvin
1954-55	41	18	11	93	2nd	7	5	Stanley Cup finals	Dick Irvin
1955-56	45	15	10	100	1st	8	2	Stanley Cup champ	Toe Blake
1956-57	35	23	12	82	2nd	8	2	Stanley Cup champ	Toe Blake
1957-58	43	17	10	96	1st	8	2	Stanley Cup champ	Toe Blake
1958-59	39	18	13	91	1st	8	3	Stanley Cup champ	Toe Blake
1959-60	40	18	12	92	1st	8	0	Stanley Cup champ	Toe Blake
1960-61	41	19	10	92	1st	2	4	League semifinals	Toe Blake
1961-62	42	14	14	98	1st	2	4	League semifinals	Toe Blake
1962-63	28	19	23	79	3rd	1	4	League semifinals	Toe Blake
1963-64	36	21	13	85	1st	3	4	League semifinals	Toe Blake
1964-65	36	23	11	83	2nd	8	5	Stanley Cup champ	Toe Blake
1965-66	41	21	8	90	1st	8	2	Stanley Cup champ	Toe Blake
1966-67	32	25	13	77	2nd	6	4	Stanley Cup finals	Toe Blake
1967-68	42	22	10	54	1st/East	12	1	Stanley Cup champ	Toe Blake
1968-69	46	19	11	103	1st/East	12	2	Stanley Cup champ	Claude Ruel
1969-70	38	22	16	92	5th/East	—	—		Claude Ruel
1970-71	42	23	13	97	3rd/East	12	8	Stanley Cup champ	Claude Ruel, Al MacNeil
1971-72	46	16	16	108	3rd/East	2	4	Division semifinals	Scotty Bowman
1972-73	52	10	16	120	1st/East	12	5	Stanley Cup champ	Scotty Bowman
1973-74	45	42	9	99	2nd/East	2	4	Division semifinals	Scotty Bowman
1974-75	47	14	19	113	1st/Norris	6	5	Semifinals	Scotty Bowman
1975-76	58	11	11	127	1st/Norris	12	1	Stanley Cup champ	Scotty Bowman
1976-77	60	8	12	132	1st/Norris	12	2	Stanley Cup champ	Scotty Bowman
1977-78	59	10	11	129	1st/Norris	12	3	Stanley Cup champ	Scotty Bowman
1978-79	52	17	11	115	1st/Norris	12	4	Stanley Cup champ	Scotty Bowman
1979-80	47	20	13	107	1st/Norris	6	4	Quarterfinals	Bernie Geoffrion, Claude Ruel

Season	W	L	T	Pts.	Finish	W	L	Highest round	Coach
					REGULAR SEASON			**PLAYOFFS**	
1980-81	45	22	13	103	1st/Norris	0	3	Preliminaries	Claude Ruel
1981-82	46	17	17	109	1st/Adams	2	3	Division semifinals	Bob Berry
1982-83	42	24	14	98	2nd/Adams	0	3	Division semifinals	Bob Berry
1983-84	35	40	5	75	4th/Adams	9	6	Conference finals	Bob Berry, Jacques Lemaire
1984-85	41	27	12	94	1st/Adams	6	6	Division finals	Jacques Lemaire
1985-86	40	33	7	87	2nd/Adams	15	5	Stanley Cup champ	Jean Perron
1986-87	41	29	10	92	2nd/Adams	10	7	Conference finals	Jean Perron
1987-88	45	22	13	103	1st/Adams	5	6	Division finals	Jean Perron
1988-89	53	18	9	115	1st/Adams	14	7	Stanley Cup finals	Pat Burns
1989-90	41	28	11	93	3rd/Adams	5	6	Division finals	Pat Burns
1990-91	39	30	11	89	2nd/Adams	7	6	Division finals	Pat Burns
1991-92	41	28	11	93	1st/Adams	4	7	Division finals	Pat Burns
1992-93	48	30	6	102	3rd/Adams	16	4	Stanley Cup champ	Jacques Demers
1993-94	41	29	14	96	3rd/Northeast	3	4	Conference quarterfinals	Jacques Demers

*Won-lost record does not indicate tie(s) resulting from two-game, total-goals series that year (two-game, total-goals series were played from 1917-18 through 1935-36).

†1918-19 series abandoned with no Cup holder due to influenza epidemic.

FIRST-ROUND ENTRY DRAFT CHOICES

Year Player, Overall, Last Amateur Team (League)

1969—*Rejean Houle, 1, Montreal (OHL)
  Marc Tardif, 2, Montreal (OHL)
1970—Ray Martiniuk, 5, Flin Flon (WCHL)
  Chuck Lefley, 6, Canadian Nationals
1971—*Guy Lafleur, 1, Quebec (QMJHL)
  Chuck Arnason, 7, Flin Flon (WCHL)
  Murray Wilson, 11, Ottawa (OHL)
1972—Steve Shutt, 4, Toronto (OHL)
  Michel Larocque, 6, Ottawa (OHL)
  Dave Gardner, 8, Toronto (OHL)
  John Van Boxmeer, 14, Guelph (SOJHL)
1973—Bob Gainey, 8, Peterborough (OHL)
1974—Cam Connor, 5, Flin Flon (WCHL)
  Doug Risebrough, 7, Kitchener (OHL)
  Rick Chartraw, 10, Kitchener (OHL)
  Mario Tremblay, 12, Montreal (OHL)
  Gord McTavish, 15, Sudbury (OHL)
1975—Robin Sadler, 9, Edmonton (WCHL)
  Pierre Mondou, 15, Montreal (QMJHL)
1976—Peter Lee, 12, Ottawa (OHL)
  Rod Schutt, 13, Sudbury (OHL)
  Bruce Baker, 18, Ottawa (OHL)
1977—Mark Napier, 10, Birmingham (WHA)
  Normand Dupont, 18, Montreal (QMJHL)

Year Player, Overall, Last Amateur Team (League)

1978—Danny Geoffrion, 8, Cornwall (QMJHL)
  Dave Hunter, 17, Sudbury (OHL)
1979—No first-round selection
1980—*Doug Wickenheiser, 1, Regina (WHL)
1981—Mark Hunter, 7, Brantford (OHL)
  Gilbert Delorme, 18, Chicoutimi (QMJHL)
  Jan Ingman, 19, Farjestads (Sweden)
1982—Alain Heroux, 19, Chicoutimi (QMJHL)
1983—Alfie Turcotte, 17, Portland (WHL)
1984—Petr Svoboda, 5, Czechoslovakia
  Shayne Corson, 8, Brantford (OHL)
1985—Jose Charbonneau, 12, Drummondville (QMJHL)
  Tom Chorske, 16, Minneapolis SW H.S. (Minn.)
1986—Mark Pederson, 15, Medicine Hat (WHL)
1987—Andrew Cassels, 17, Ottawa (OHL)
1988—Eric Charron, 20, Trois-Rivieres (QMJHL)
1989—Lindsay Vallis, 13, Seattle (WHL)
1990—Turner Stevenson, 12, Seattle (WHL)
1991—Brent Bilodeau, 17, Seattle (WHL)
1992—David Wilkie, 20, Kamloops (WHL)
1993—Saku Koivu, 21, TPS Turku (Finland)
1994—Brad Brown, 18, North Bay (OHL)

*Designates first player chosen in draft.

FRANCHISE LEADERS

Current players in boldface

FORWARDS/DEFENSEMEN

Games

Henri Richard	1256
Larry Robinson	1202
Bob Gainey	1160
Jean Beliveau	1125
Claude Provost	1005
Maurice Richard	978
Yvan Cournoyer	968
Guy Lafleur	961
Serge Savard	917
Guy Carbonneau	**912**

Goals

Maurice Richard	544
Guy Lafleur	518
Jean Beliveau	507
Yvan Cournoyer	428
Steve Shutt	408
Bernie Geoffrion	371
Jacques Lemaire	366

Henri Richard	358
Aurele Joliat	270
Mario Tremblay	258

Assists

Guy Lafleur	728
Jean Beliveau	712
Henri Richard	688
Larry Robinson	686
Jacques Lemaire	469
Yvan Cournoyer	435
Maurice Richard	421
Elmer Lach	408
Guy Lapointe	406
Bernie Geoffrion	388

Points

Guy Lafleur	1246
Jean Beliveau	1219
Henri Richard	1046
Maurice Richard	965
Larry Robinson	883
Yvan Cournoyer	863
Jacques Lemaire	835

Steve Shutt	776
Bernie Geoffrion	759
Elmer Lach	623

Penalty minutes

Chris Nilan	2248
Maurice Richard	1285
John Ferguson	1214
Mario Tremblay	1043
Doug Harvey	1042
Jean Beliveau	1029
Doug Risebrough	959
Lyle Odelein	**952**
Henri Richard	928
Tom Johnson	897

GOALTENDERS

Games

Jacques Plante	556
Patrick Roy	**486**
Ken Dryden	397
Bill Durnan	383
Georges Vezina	328

George Hainsworth..........................321	**Shutouts**	Patrick Roy 27
Gerry McNeil...................................276	George Hainsworth...........................74	Wilf Cude......................................22
Wilf Cude...249	Jacques Plante 58	Charlie Hodge 21
Charlie Hodge 236	Ken Dryden 46	Michel Larocque 17
Michel Larocque............................231	Bill Durnan 34	Gump Worsley 16
	Gerry McNeil 28	

MONTREAL MAROONS (DEFUNCT)

YEAR - BY - YEAR RECORDS

	REGULAR SEASON					PLAYOFFS			
Season	**W**	**L**	**T**	**Pts.**	**Finish**	**W**	**L**	**Highest round**	**Coach**
1924-25	9	19	2	20	5th	—	—		Eddie Gerard
1925-26	20	11	5	45	2nd	3	1	Stanley Cup champ	Eddie Gerard
1926-27	20	20	4	44	3rd/Canadian	*0	1	Quarterfinals	Eddie Gerard
1927-28	24	14	6	54	2nd/Canadian	*5	3	Stanley Cup finals	Eddie Gerard
1928-29	15	20	9	39	5th/Canadian	—	—		Eddie Gerard
1929-30	23	16	5	51	1st/Canadian	1	3	Semifinals	Dunc Munro
1930-31	20	18	6	46	3rd/Canadian	*0	2	Quarterfinals	Dunc Munro, George Boucher
1931-32	19	22	7	45	4th/Canadian	*1	1	Semifinals	Sprague Cleghorn
1932-33	22	20	6	50	2nd/Canadian	0	2	Quarterfinals	Eddie Gerard
1933-34	19	18	11	49	3rd/Canadian	*1	2	Semifinals	Eddie Gerard
1934-35	24	19	5	53	2nd/Canadian	*5	0	Stanley Cup champ	Tommy Gorman
1935-36	22	16	10	54	1st/Canadian	0	3	Semifinals	Tommy Gorman
1936-37	22	17	9	53	2nd/Canadian	2	3	Semifinals	Tommy Gorman
1937-38	12	30	6	30	4th/Canadian	—	—		King Clancy, Tommy Gorman

*Won-lost record does not indicate tie(s) resulting from two-game, total goals series that year (two-game, total-goals series were played from 1917-18 through 1935-36).

MONTREAL WANDERERS (DEFUNCT)

YEAR - BY - YEAR RECORDS

	REGULAR SEASON					PLAYOFFS			
Season	**W**	**L**	**T**	**Pts.**	**Finish**	**W**	**L**	**Highest round**	**Coach**
1917-18*	1	5	0	2	4th	—	—		Art Ross

*Franchise disbanded after Montreal Arena burned down. Montreal Canadiens and Toronto each counted one win for defaulted games with Wanderers.

NEW JERSEY DEVILS

YEAR - BY - YEAR RECORDS

	REGULAR SEASON					PLAYOFFS			
Season	**W**	**L**	**T**	**Pts.**	**Finish**	**W**	**L**	**Highest round**	**Coach**
1974-75*	15	54	11	41	5th/Smythe	—	—		Bep Guidolin
1975-76*	12	56	12	36	5th/Smythe	—	—		Bep Guidolin, Sid Abel, Eddie Bush
1976-77†	20	46	14	54	5th/Smythe	—	—		John Wilson
1977-78†	19	40	21	59	2nd/Smythe	0	2	Preliminaries	Pat Kelly
1978-79†	15	53	12	42	4th/Smythe	—	—		Pat Kelly, Bep Guidolin
1979-80†	19	48	13	51	6th/Smythe	—	—		Don Cherry
1980-81†	22	45	13	57	5th/Smythe	—	—		Billy MacMillan
1981-82†	18	49	13	49	5th/Smythe	—	—		Bert Marshall, Marshall Johnston
1982-83	17	49	14	48	5th/Patrick	—	—		Billy MacMillan
1983-84	17	56	7	41	5th/Patrick	—	—		Billy MacMillan, Tom McVie
1984-85	22	48	10	54	5th/Patrick	—	—		Doug Carpenter
1985-86	28	49	3	59	5th/Patrick	—	—		Doug Carpenter
1986-87	29	45	6	64	6th/Patrick	—	—		Doug Carpenter
1987-88	38	36	6	82	4th/Patrick	11	9	Conference finals	Doug Carpenter, Jim Schoenfeld
1988-89	27	41	12	66	5th/Patrick	—	—		Jim Schoenfeld
1989-90	37	34	9	83	2nd/Patrick	2	4	Division semifinals	Jim Schoenfeld, John Cunniff
1990-91	32	33	15	79	4th/Patrick	3	4	Division semifinals	John Cunniff, Tom McVie
1991-92	38	31	11	87	4th/Patrick	3	4	Division semifinals	Tom McVie
1992-93	40	37	7	87	4th/Patrick	1	4	Division semifinals	Herb Brooks
1993-94	47	25	12	106	2nd/Atlantic	11	9	Conference finals	Jacques Lemaire

*Kansas City Scouts.
†Colorado Rockies.

FIRST-ROUND ENTRY DRAFT CHOICES

Year	Player, Overall, Last Amateur Team (League)
1974—	Wilf Paiement, 2, St. Catharines (OHL)
1975—	Barry Dean, 2, Medicine Hat (WCHL)
1976—	Paul Gardner, 11, Oshawa (OHL)
1977—	Barry Beck, 2, New Westminster (WCHL)
1978—	Mike Gillis, 5, Kingston (OHL)
1979—	*Rob Ramage, 1, Birmingham (WHA)
1980—	Paul Gagne, 19, Windsor (OHL)
1981—	Joe Cirella, 5, Oshawa (OHL)
1982—	Rocky Trottier, 8, Billings (WHL)
	Ken Daneyko, 18, Seattle (WHL)
1983—	John MacLean, 6, Oshawa (OHL)
1984—	Kirk Muller, 2, Guelph (OHL)
1985—	Craig Wolanin, 3, Kitchener (OHL)

Year	Player, Overall, Last Amateur Team (League)
1986—	Neil Brady, 3, Medicine Hat (WHL)
1987—	Brendan Shanahan, 2, London (OHL)
1988—	Corey Foster, 12, Peterborough (OHL)
1989—	Bill Guerin, 5, Springfield (Mass.) Jr.
	Jason Miller, 18, Medicine Hat (WHL)
1990—	Martin Brodeur, 20, St. Hyacinthe (QMJHL)
1991—	Scott Niedermayer, 3, Kamloops (WHL)
	Brian Rolston, 11, Detroit Compuware Jr.
1992—	Jason Smith, 18, Regina (WHL)
1993—	Denis Pederson, 13, Prince Albert (WHL)
1994—	Vadim Sharifjanov, 25, Salavat (Russia)

*Designates first player chosen in draft.

FRANCHISE LEADERS

Current players in boldface

FORWARDS/DEFENSEMEN

Games
John MacLean	706
Ken Daneyko	691
Bruce Driver	661
Aaron Broten	641
Kirk Muller	556
Joe Cirella	503
Mike Kitchen	474
Pat Verbeek	463
Wilf Paiement	392
Gary Croteau	390

Goals
John MacLean	278
Kirk Muller	185
Pat Verbeek	170
Aaron Broten	162
Wilf Paiement	153
Claude Lemieux	119
Paul Gagne	106
Stephane Richer	103
Brendan Shanahan	96
Gary Croteau	92

Assists
Kirk Muller	335
Aaron Broten	307
Bruce Driver	304
John MacLean	281
Wilf Paiement	183
Patrik Sundstrom	160
Joe Cirella	159
Pat Verbeek	151
Mel Bridgman	148
Scott Stevens	147

Points
John MacLean	489
Kirk Muller	520
Aaron Broten	469
Bruce Driver	383
Wilf Paiement	336
Pat Verbeek	321
Patrik Sundstrom	246
Claude Lemieux	240
Mark Johnson	229
Mel Bridgman	224

Penalty minutes
Ken Daneyko	1706
John MacLean	982
Pat Verbeek	943

Joe Cirella	938
Randy McKay	696
David Maley	683
Kirk Muller	572
Wilf Paiement	558
Perry Anderson	553
Rob Ramage	529

GOALTENDERS

Games
Chico Resch	267
Chris Terreri	249
Sean Burke	162

Shutouts
Chris Terreri	6
Craig Billington	4
Sean Burke	4

Goals-against average
(2400 minutes minimum)
Martin Brodeur	2.46
Chris Terreri	3.21
Sean Burke	3.66

Wins
Chris Terreri	100
Chico Resch	67
Sean Burke	62

NEW YORK AMERICANS (DEFUNCT)

YEAR-BY-YEAR RECORDS

	REGULAR SEASON					PLAYOFFS			
Season	W	L	T	Pts.	Finish	W	L	Highest round	Coach
1919-20‡	4	20	0	8	4th	—	—		Mike Quinn
1920-21§	6	18	0	12	4th	—	—		Percy Thompson
1921-22§	7	17	0	14	4th	—	—		Percy Thompson
1922-23§	6	18	0	12	4th	—	—		Art Ross
1923-24§	9	15	0	18	4th	—	—		Percy Lesueur
1924-25§	19	10	1	39	1st	†—	—		Jimmy Gardner
1925-26	12	20	4	28	5th	—	—		Tommy Gorman
1926-27	17	25	2	36	4th/Canadian	—	—		Newsy Lalonde
1927-28	11	27	6	28	5th/Canadian	—	—		Wilf Green
1928-29	19	13	12	50	2nd/Canadian	*0	1	Semifinals	Tommy Gorman
1929-30	14	25	5	33	5th/Canadian	—	—		Lionel Conacher
1930-31	18	16	10	46	4th/Canadian	—	—		Eddie Gerard
1931-32	16	24	8	40	4th/Canadian	—	—		Eddie Gerard
1932-33	15	22	11	41	4th/Canadian	—	—		Joe Simpson
1933-34	15	23	10	40	4th/Canadian	—	—		Joe Simpson
1934-35	12	27	9	33	4th/Canadian	—	—		Joe Simpson
1935-36	16	25	7	39	3rd/Canadian	2	3	Semifinals	Red Dutton
1936-37	15	29	4	34	4th/Canadian	—	—		Red Dutton
1937-38	19	18	11	49	2nd/Canadian	3	3	Semifinals	Red Dutton
1938-39	17	21	10	44	4th	0	2	Quarterfinals	Red Dutton
1939-40	15	29	4	34	6th	1	2	Quarterfinals	Red Dutton

Season	REGULAR SEASON					PLAYOFFS			Coach
	W	L	T	Pts.	Finish	W	L	Highest round	
1940-41	8	29	11	27	7th	—	—		Red Dutton
1941-42*	16	29	3	35	7th	—	—		Red Dutton

*Won-lost record does not indicate tie(s) resulting from two-game, total goals series that year (two-game, total-goals series were played from 1917-18 through 1935-36).
 †Refused to participate in playoffs—held out for more compensation.
 ‡Quebec Bulldogs.
 §Hamilton Tigers.
 *Brooklyn Americans.

NEW YORK ISLANDERS

YEAR-BY-YEAR RECORDS

Season	REGULAR SEASON					PLAYOFFS			Coach
	W	L	T	Pts.	Finish	W	L	Highest round	
1972-73	12	60	6	30	8th/East	—	—		Phil Goyette, Earl Ingarfield
1973-74	19	41	18	56	8th/East	—	—		Al Arbour
1974-75	33	25	22	88	3rd/Patrick	9	8	Semifinals	Al Arbour
1975-76	42	21	17	101	2nd/Patrick	7	6	Semifinals	Al Arbour
1976-77	47	21	12	106	2nd/Patrick	8	4	Semifinals	Al Arbour
1977-78	48	17	15	111	1st/Patrick	3	4	Quarterfinals	Al Arbour
1978-79	51	15	14	116	1st/Patrick	6	4	Semifinals	Al Arbour
1979-80	39	28	13	91	2nd/Patrick	15	6	Stanley Cup champ	Al Arbour
1980-81	48	18	14	110	1st/Patrick	15	3	Stanley Cup champ	Al Arbour
1981-82	54	16	10	118	1st/Patrick	15	4	Stanley Cup champ	Al Arbour
1982-83	42	26	12	96	2nd/Patrick	15	5	Stanley Cup champ	Al Arbour
1983-84	50	26	4	104	1st/Patrick	12	9	Stanley Cup finals	Al Arbour
1984-85	40	34	6	86	3rd/Patrick	4	6	Division finals	Al Arbour
1985-86	39	29	12	90	3rd/Patrick	0	3	Division semifinals	Al Arbour
1986-87	35	33	12	82	3rd/Patrick	7	7	Division finals	Terry Simpson
1987-88	39	31	10	88	1st/Patrick	2	4	Division semifinals	Terry Simpson
1988-89	28	47	5	61	6th/Patrick	—	—		Terry Simpson, Al Arbour
1989-90	31	38	11	73	4th/Patrick	1	4	Division semifinals	Al Arbour
1990-91	25	45	10	60	6th/Patrick	—	—		Al Arbour
1991-92	34	35	11	79	5th/Patrick	—	—		Al Arbour
1992-93	40	37	7	87	3rd/Patrick	9	9	Conference finals	Al Arbour
1993-94	36	36	12	84	4th/Atlantic	0	4	Conference quarterfinals	Al Arbour

FIRST-ROUND ENTRY DRAFT CHOICES

Year	Player, Overall, Last Amateur Team (League)
1972	*Billy Harris, 1, Toronto (OHL)
1973	*Denis Potvin, 1, Ottawa (OHL)
1974	Clark Gillies, 4, Regina (WCHL)
1975	Pat Price, 11, Vancouver (WHA)
1976	Alex McKendry, 14, Sudbury (OHL)
1977	Mike Bossy, 15, Laval (QMJHL)
1978	Steve Tambellini, 15, Lethbridge (WCHL)
1979	Duane Sutter, 17, Lethbridge (WHL)
1980	Brent Sutter, 17, Red Deer (AJHL)
1981	Paul Boutilier, 21, Sherbrooke (QMJHL)
1982	Pat Flatley, 21, University of Wisconsin
1983	Pat LaFontaine, 3, Verdun (QMJHL)
	Gerald Diduck, 16, Lethbridge (WHL)
1984	Duncan MacPherson, 20, Saskatoon (WHL)

Year	Player, Overall, Last Amateur Team (League)
1985	Brad Dalgarno, 6, Hamilton (OHL)
	Derek King, 13, Sault Ste. Marie (OHL)
1986	Tom Fitzgerald, 17, Austin Prep (Mass.)
1987	Dean Chynoweth, 13, Medicine Hat (WHL)
1988	Kevin Cheveldayoff, 16, Brandon (WHL)
1989	Dave Chyzowski, 2, Kamloops (WHL)
1990	Scott Scissons, 6, Saskatoon (WHL)
1991	Scott Lachance, 4, Boston University
1992	Darius Kasparaitis, 5, Dynamo Moscow (CIS)
1993	Todd Bertuzzi, 23, Guelph (OHL)
1994	Brett Lindros, 9, Kingston (OHL)

*Designates first player chosen in draft.

FRANCHISE LEADERS

Current players in boldface

FORWARDS/DEFENSEMEN

Games

Bryan Trottier	1123
Denis Potvin	1080
Bob Nystrom	900
Clark Gillies	872
Bob Bourne	814
Mike Bossy	752
Brent Sutter	694
Billy Smith	675

Billy Harris	623
Stefan Persson	622

Goals

Mike Bossy	573
Bryan Trottier	500
Denis Potvin	310
Clark Gillies	304
Pat LaFontaine	287
Brent Sutter	287
Bob Bourne	238
Bob Nystrom	235

John Tonelli	206
Billy Harris	184

Assists

Bryan Trottier	853
Denis Potvin	742
Mike Bossy	553
Clark Gillies	359
John Tonelli	338
Brent Sutter	323
Stefan Persson	317
Bob Bourne	304
Pat LaFontaine	279
Bob Nystrom	278

Points

Bryan Trottier	1353
Mike Bossy	1126
Denis Potvin	1052
Clark Gillies	663
Brent Sutter	610
Pat LaFontaine	566
John Tonelli	544
Bob Bourne	542
Bob Nystrom	513
Billy Harris	443

Penalty minutes

Mick Vukota	**1593**
Garry Howatt	1466
Denis Potvin	1354
Bob Nystrom	1248
Clark Gillies	891
Duane Sutter	891

Rich Pilon	821
Bryan Trottier	798
Gerry Hart	783
Brent Sutter	761

GOALTENDERS
Games

Billy Smith	675
Chico Resch	282
Kelly Hrudey	241
Glenn Healy	176
Roland Melanson	136
Mark Fitzpatrick	129
Gerry Desjardins	80

Shutouts

Chico Resch	25
Billy Smith	22
Kelly Hrudey	6

Goals-against average
(2400 minutes minimum)

Chico Resch	2.56
Ron Hextall	**3.08**
Roland Melanson	3.14
Billy Smith	3.16
Mark Fitzpatrick	3.41
Glenn Healy	3.45
Kelly Hrudey	3.46

Wins

Billy Smith	304
Chico Resch	157
Kelly Hrudey	106
Roland Melanson	77
Glenn Healy	66
Mark Fitzpatrick	51
Ron Hextall	**27**
Gerry Desjardins	14

NEW YORK RANGERS

YEAR-BY-YEAR RECORDS

	REGULAR SEASON					PLAYOFFS			
Season	W	L	T	Pts.	Finish	W	L	Highest round	Coach
1926-27	25	13	6	56	1st/American	*0	1	Semifinals	Lester Patrick
1927-28	19	16	9	47	2nd/American	*5	3	Stanley Cup champ	Lester Patrick
1928-29	21	13	10	52	2nd/American	*3	2	Stanley Cup finals	Lester Patrick
1929-30	17	17	10	44	3rd/American	*1	2	Semifinals	Lester Patrick
1930-31	19	16	9	47	3rd/American	2	2	Semifinals	Lester Patrick
1931-32	23	17	8	54	1st/American	3	4	Stanley Cup finals	Lester Patrick
1932-33	23	17	8	54	3rd/American	*6	1	Stanley Cup champ	Lester Patrick
1933-34	21	19	8	50	3rd/American	*0	1	Quarterfinals	Lester Patrick
1934-35	22	20	6	50	3rd/American	*1	1	Semifinals	Lester Patrick
1935-36	19	17	12	50	4th/American	—	—		Lester Patrick
1936-37	19	20	9	47	3rd/American	6	3	Stanley Cup finals	Lester Patrick
1937-38	27	15	6	60	2nd/American	1	2	Quarterfinals	Lester Patrick
1938-39	26	16	6	58	2nd	3	4	Semifinals	Lester Patrick
1939-40	27	11	10	64	2nd	8	4	Stanley Cup champ	Frank Boucher
1940-41	21	19	8	50	4th	1	2	Quarterfinals	Frank Boucher
1941-42	29	17	2	60	1st	2	4	Semifinals	Frank Boucher
1942-43	11	31	8	30	6th	—	—		Frank Boucher
1943-44	6	39	5	17	6th	—	—		Frank Boucher
1944-45	11	29	10	32	6th	—	—		Frank Boucher
1945-46	13	28	9	35	6th	—	—		Frank Boucher
1946-47	22	32	6	50	5th	—	—		Frank Boucher
1947-48	21	26	13	55	4th	2	4	League semifinals	Frank Boucher
1948-49	18	31	11	47	6th	—	—		Frank Boucher, Lynn Patrick
1949-50	28	31	11	67	4th	7	5	Stanley Cup finals	Lynn Patrick
1950-51	20	29	21	61	5th	—	—		Neil Colville
1951-52	23	34	13	59	5th	—	—		Neil Colville, Bill Cook
1952-53	17	37	16	50	6th	—	—		Bill Cook
1953-54	29	31	10	68	5th	—	—		Frank Boucher, Muzz Patrick
1954-55	17	35	18	52	5th	—	—		Muzz Patrick
1955-56	32	28	10	74	3rd	1	4	League semifinals	Phil Watson
1956-57	26	30	14	66	4th	1	4	League semifinals	Phil Watson
1957-58	32	25	13	77	2nd	2	4	League semifinals	Phil Watson
1958-59	26	32	12	64	5th	—	—		Phil Watson
1959-60	17	38	15	49	6th	—	—		Phil Watson, Alf Pike
1960-61	22	38	10	54	5th	—	—		Alf Pike
1961-62	26	32	12	64	4th	2	4	League semifinals	Doug Harvey
1962-63	22	36	12	56	5th	—	—		Muzz Patrick, Red Sullivan
1963-64	22	38	10	54	5th	—	—		Red Sullivan
1964-65	20	38	12	52	5th	—	—		Red Sullivan
1965-66	18	41	11	47	6th	—	—		Red Sullivan, Emile Francis
1966-67	30	28	12	72	4th	0	4	League semifinals	Emile Francis
1967-68	39	23	12	90	2nd/East	2	4	Division semifinals	Emile Francis
1968-69	41	26	9	91	3rd/East	0	4	Division semifinals	Bernie Geoffrion, Emile Francis
1969-70	38	22	16	92	4th/East	2	4	Division semifinals	Emile Francis
1970-71	49	18	11	109	2nd/East	7	6	Division finals	Emile Francis
1971-72	48	17	13	109	2nd/East	10	6	Stanley Cup finals	Emile Francis
1972-73	47	23	8	102	3rd/East	5	5	Division finals	Emile Francis
1973-74	40	24	14	94	3rd/East	7	6	Division finals	Larry Popein, Emile Francis
1974-75	37	29	14	88	2nd/Patrick	1	2	Preliminaries	Emile Francis
1975-76	29	42	9	67	4th/Patrick	—	—		Ron Stewart, John Ferguson

Season	W	L	T	Pts.	Finish	W	L	Highest round	Coach
			REGULAR SEASON					PLAYOFFS	
1976-77	29	37	14	72	4th/Patrick	—	—		John Ferguson
1977-78	30	37	13	73	4th/Patrick	1	2	Preliminaries	Jean-Guy Talbot
1978-79	40	29	11	91	3rd/Patrick	11	7	Stanley Cup finals	Fred Shero
1979-80	38	32	10	86	3rd/Patrick	4	5	Quarterfinals	Fred Shero
1980-81	30	36	14	74	4th/Patrick	7	7	Semifinals	Fred Shero, Craig Patrick
1981-82	39	27	14	92	2nd/Patrick	5	5	Division finals	Herb Brooks
1982-83	35	35	10	80	4th/Patrick	5	4	Division finals	Herb Brooks
1983-84	42	29	9	93	4th/Patrick	2	3	Division semifinals	Herb Brooks
1984-85	26	44	10	62	4th/Patrick	0	3	Division semifinals	Herb Brooks, Craig Patrick
1985-86	36	38	6	78	4th/Patrick	8	8	Conference finals	Ted Sator
1986-87	34	38	8	76	4th/Patrick	2	4	Division semifinals	Ted Sator, Tom Webster, Phil Esposito
1987-88	36	34	10	82	4th/Patrick	—	—		Michel Bergeron
1988-89	37	35	8	82	3rd/Patrick	0	4	Division semifinals	Michel Bergeron, Phil Esposito
1989-90	36	31	13	85	1st/Patrick	5	5	Division finals	Roger Neilson
1990-91	36	31	13	85	2nd/Patrick	2	4	Division semifinals	Roger Neilson
1991-92	50	25	5	105	1st/Patrick	6	7	Division finals	Roger Neilson
1992-93	34	39	11	79	6th/Patrick	—	—		Roger Neilson, Ron Smith
1993-94	52	24	8	112	1st/Atlantic	16	7	Stanley Cup champ	Mike Keenan

*Won-lost record does not indicate tie(s) resulting from two-game, total-goals series that year (two-game, total-goals series were played from 1917-18 through 1935-36).

FIRST-ROUND ENTRY DRAFT CHOICES

Year   Player, Overall, Last Amateur Team (League)

1969—Andre Dupont, 8, Montreal (OHL)
　　　Pierre Jarry, 12, Ottawa (OHL)
1970—Normand Gratton, 11, Montreal (OHL)
1971—Steve Vickers, 10, Toronto (OHL)
　　　Steve Durbano, 13, Toronto (OHL)
1972—Albert Blanchard, 10, Kitchener (OHL)
　　　Bobby MacMillan, 15, St. Catharines (OHL)
1973—Rick Middleton, 14, Oshawa (OHL)
1974—Dave Maloney, 14, Kitchener (OHL)
1975—Wayne Dillon, 12, Toronto (WHA)
1976—Don Murdoch, 6, Medicine Hat (WCHL)
1977—Lucien DeBlois, 8, Sorel (QMJHL)
　　　Ron Duguay, 13, Sudbury (OHL)
1978—No first-round selection
1979—Doug Sulliman, 13, Kitchener (OHL)

Year   Player, Overall, Last Amateur Team (League)

1980—Jim Malone, 14, Toronto (OHL)
1981—James Patrick, 9, Prince Albert (AJHL)
1982—Chris Kontos, 15, Toronto (OHL)
1983—Dave Gagner, 12, Brantford (OHL)
1984—Terry Carkner, 14, Peterborough (OHL)
1985—Ulf Dahlen, 7, Ostersund (Sweden)
1986—Brian Leetch, 9, Avon Old Farms Prep (Ct.)
1987—Jayson More, 10, New Westminster (WCHL)
1988—No first-round selection
1989—Steven Rice, 20, Kitchener (OHL)
1990—Michael Stewart, 13, Michigan State University
1991—Alexei Kovalev, 15, Dynamo Moscow (USSR)
1992—Peter Ferraro, 24, Waterloo (USHL)
1993—Niklas Sundstrom, 8, Ornskoldsvik (Sweden)
1994—Dan Cloutier, 26, Sault Ste. Marie (OHL)

FRANCHISE LEADERS

Current players in boldface

FORWARDS/DEFENSEMEN

Games

Harry Howell	1160
Rod Gilbert	1065
Ron Greschner	982
Walt Tkaczuk	945
Jean Ratelle	862
Vic Hadfield	838
Jim Neilson	810
Andy Bathgate	719
Steve Vickers	698
Dean Prentice	666

Goals

Rod Gilbert	406
Jean Ratelle	336
Andy Bathgate	272
Vic Hadfield	262
Camille Henry	256
Steve Vickers	246
Bill Cook	228
Walt Tkaczuk	227
Don Maloney	195
Bryan Hextall	187

Assists

Rod Gilbert	615
Jean Ratelle	481
Andy Bathgate	457
Walt Tkaczuk	451

Ron Greschner	431
James Patrick	363
Brian Leetch	**343**
Steve Vickers	340
Vic Hadfield	310
Don Maloney	307
Brad Park	283

Points

Rod Gilbert	1021
Jean Ratelle	817
Andy Bathgate	729
Walt Tkaczuk	678
Ron Greschner	610
Steve Vickers	586
Vic Hadfield	572
Don Maloney	502
Camille Henry	478
James Patrick	467

Penalty minutes

Ron Greschner	1226
Harry Howell	1147
Don Maloney	1113
Vic Hadfield	1036
Nick Fotiu	970

GOALTENDERS

Games

Gump Worsley	583
Ed Giacomin	539
John Vanbiesbrouck	449

Chuck Rayner	377
Dave Kerr	324
John Davidson	222
Mike Richter	**215**
Gilles Villemure	184

Shutouts

Ed Giacomin	49
Dave Kerr	40
John Ross Roach	30
Chuck Rayner	24
Gump Worsley	24
Lorne Chabot	21

Goals-against average
(2400 minutes minimum)

Lorne Chabot	1.61
Dave Kerr	2.07
John Ross Roach	2.16
Andy Aitkenhead	2.42
Johnny Bower	2.62
Gilles Villemure	2.62
Ed Giacomin	2.73

Wins

Ed Giacomin	266
Gump Worsley	204
John Vanbiesbrouck	200
Dave Kerr	157
Chuck Rayner	123
Mike Richter	**111**
Gilles Villemure	96
John Davidson	93

OTTAWA SENATORS (FIRST CLUB—DEFUNCT)

YEAR-BY-YEAR RECORDS

	REGULAR SEASON					PLAYOFFS			
Season	W	L	T	Pts.	Finish	W	L	Highest round	Coach
1917-18	9	13	0	18	3rd	—	—		Eddie Gerard
1918-19	12	6	0	24	1st	1	4	Semifinals	Alf Smith
1919-20	19	5	0	38	1st	3	2	Stanley Cup champ	Pete Green
1920-21	14	10	0	28	2nd	*4	2	Stanley Cup champ	Pete Green
1921-22	14	8	2	30	1st	*0	1	Semifinals	Pete Green
1922-23	14	9	1	29	1st	6	2	Stanley Cup champ	Pete Green
1923-24	16	8	0	32	1st	0	2	Semifinals	Pete Green
1924-25	17	12	1	35	4th	—	—		Pete Green
1925-26	24	8	4	52	1st	*0	1	Semifinals	Pete Green
1926-27	30	10	4	64	1st/Canadian	*3	0	Stanley Cup champ	Dave Gill
1927-28	20	14	10	50	3rd/Canadian	0	2	Quarterfinals	Dave Gill
1928-29	14	17	13	41	4th/Canadian	—	—		Dave Gill
1929-30	21	15	8	50	3rd/Canadian	*0	1	Semifinals	Newsy Lalonde
1930-31	10	30	4	24	5th/Canadian	—	—		Newsy Lalonde
1931-32					Club suspended operations for one season.				
1932-33	11	27	10	32	5th/Canadian	—	—		Cy Denneny
1933-34	13	29	6	32	5th/Canadian	—	—		George Boucher
1934-35†	11	31	6	28	5th/Canadian	—	—		Eddie Gerard, George Boucher

*Won-lost record does not indicate tie(s) resulting from two-game, total goals series that year (two-game, total-goals series were played from 1917-18 through 1935-36).

†St. Louis Eagles.

OTTAWA SENATORS (SECOND CLUB)

YEAR-BY-YEAR RECORDS

	REGULAR SEASON					PLAYOFFS			
Season	W	L	T	Pts.	Finish	W	L	Highest round	Coach
1992-93	10	70	4	24	6th/Adams	—	—		Rick Bowness
1993-94	14	61	9	37	7th/Northeast	—	—		Rick Bowness

FIRST-ROUND ENTRY DRAFT CHOICES

Year   Player, Overall, Last Amateur Team (League)
1992—Alexei Yashin, 2, Dynamo Moscow (CIS)
1993—*Alexandre Daigle, 1, Victoriaville (QMJHL)

Year   Player, Overall, Last Amateur Team (League)
1994—Radek Bonk, 3, Las Vegas (IHL)
*Designates first player chosen in draft.

FRANCHISE LEADERS

Current players in boldface

FORWARDS/DEFENSEMEN

Games

Brad Shaw	147
Darren Rumble	139
Mark Lamb	137
Norm Maciver	133
Darcy Loewen	123
Sylvain Turgeon	119
Andrew McBain	114
Gord Dineen	109
Bob Kudelski	90
Alexandre Daigle	84

Goals

Bob Kudelski	47
Sylvain Turgeon	36
Alexei Yashin	30
Alexandre Daigle	20
Norm Maciver	20
David Archibald	19
Jamie Baker	19
Mark Lamb	18
Andrew McBain	18
Dave McLiwain	17

Assists

Norm Maciver	66

Brad Shaw	53
Alexei Yashin	49
Mark Lamb	37
Sylvain Turgeon	33
Alexandre Daigle	31
Jamie Baker	29
Bob Kudelski	29
Dave McLiwain	26
Gord Dineen	25

Points

Norm Maciver	86
Alexei Yashin	79
Bob Kudelski	76
Sylvain Turgeon	69
Brad Shaw	64
Mark Lamb	55
Alexandre Daigle	51
Jamie Baker	48
Dave McLiwain	43
Jody Hull	34

Penalty minutes

Mike Peluso	318
Dennis Vial	214
Darcy Loewen	197
Darren Rumble	177
Troy Mallette	166
Sylvain Turgeon	156

Bill Huard	162
Mark Lamb	120
Gord Dineen	119
Norm Maciver	110

GOALTENDERS

Games

Peter Sidorkiewicz	64
Craig Billington	63
Darrin Madeley	34
Daniel Berthiaume	26
Steve Weeks	7
Mark Laforest	5
Darrin Madeley	2

Shutouts
Never accomplished

Goals-against average
(1200 minutes minimum)

Daniel Berthiaume	4.39
Peter Sidorkiewicz	4.43
Darrin Madeley	4.48
Craig Billington	4.59

Wins

Craig Billington	11
Peter Sidorkiewicz	8
Darrin Madeley	3
Daniel Berthiaume	2

YEAR-BY-YEAR RECORDS

	REGULAR SEASON					PLAYOFFS			
Season	W	L	T	Pts.	Finish	W	L	Highest round	Coach
1967-68	31	32	11	73	1st/West	3	4	Division semifinals	Keith Allen
1968-69	20	35	21	61	3rd/West	0	4	Division semifinals	Keith Allen
1969-70	17	35	24	58	5th/West	—	—		Vic Stasiuk
1970-71	28	33	17	73	3rd/West	0	4	Division semifinals	Vic Stasiuk
1971-72	26	38	14	66	5th/West	—	—		Fred Shero
1972-73	37	30	11	85	2nd/West	5	6	Division finals	Fred Shero
1973-74	50	16	12	112	1st/West	12	5	Stanley Cup champ	Fred Shero
1974-75	51	18	11	113	1st/Patrick	12	5	Stanley Cup champ	Fred Shero
1975-76	51	13	16	118	1st/Patrick	8	8	Stanley Cup finals	Fred Shero
1976-77	48	16	16	112	1st/Patrick	4	6	Semifinals	Fred Shero
1977-78	45	20	15	105	2nd/Patrick	7	5	Semifinals	Fred Shero
1978-79	40	25	15	95	2nd/Patrick	3	5	Quarterfinals	Bob McCammon, Pat Quinn
1979-80	48	12	20	116	1st/Patrick	13	6	Stanley Cup finals	Pat Quinn
1980-81	41	24	15	97	2nd/Patrick	6	6	Quarterfinals	Pat Quinn
1981-82	38	31	11	87	3rd/Patrick	1	3	Division semifinals	Pat Quinn, Bob McCammon
1982-83	49	23	8	106	1st/Patrick	0	3	Division semifinals	Bob McCammon
1983-84	44	26	10	98	3rd/Patrick	0	3	Division semifinals	Bob McCammon
1984-85	53	20	7	113	1st/Patrick	12	7	Stanley Cup finals	Mike Keenan
1985-86	53	23	4	110	1st/Patrick	2	3	Division semifinals	Mike Keenan
1986-87	46	26	8	100	1st/Patrick	15	11	Stanley Cup finals	Mike Keenan
1987-88	38	33	9	85	2nd/Patrick	3	4	Division semifinals	Mike Keenan
1988-89	36	36	8	80	4th/Patrick	10	9	Conference finals	Paul Holmgren
1989-90	30	39	11	71	6th/Patrick	—	—		Paul Holmgren
1990-91	33	37	10	76	5th/Patrick	—	—		Paul Holmgren
1991-92	32	37	11	75	6th/Patrick	—	—		Paul Holmgren, Bill Dineen
1992-93	36	37	11	83	6th/Patrick	—	—		Bill Dineen
1993-94	35	39	10	80	6th/Atlantic	—	—		Terry Simpson

FIRST-ROUND ENTRY DRAFT CHOICES

Year Player, Overall, Last Amateur Team (League)

1969—Bob Currier, 6, Cornwall (QMJHL)
1970—No first-round selection
1971—Larry Wright, 8, Regina (WCHL)
   Pierre Plante, 9, Drummondville (QMJHL)
1972—Bill Barber, 7, Kitchener (OHL)
1973—No first-round selection
1974—No first-round selection
1975—*Mel Bridgeman, 1, Victoria (WCHL)
1976—Mark Suzor, 17, Kingston (OHL)
1977—Kevin McCarthy, 17, Winnipeg (WCHL)
1978—Behn Wilson, 6, Kingston (OHL)
   Ken Linseman, 7, Birmingham (WHA)
   Dan Lucas, 14, Sault Ste. Marie (OHL)
1979—Brian Propp, 14, Brandon (WHL)
1980—Mike Stothers, 21, Kingston (OHL)
1981—Steve Smith, 16, Sault Ste. Marie (OHL)

Year Player, Overall, Last Amateur Team (League)

1982—Ron Sutter, 4, Lethbridge (WHL)
1983—No first-round selection
1984—No first-round selection
1985—Glen Seabrooke, 21, Peterborough (OHL)
1986—Kerry Huffman, 20, Guelph (OHL)
1987—Darren Rumble, 20, Kitchener (OHL)
1988—Claude Boivin, 14, Drummondville (QMJHL)
1989—No first-round selection
1990—Mike Ricci, 4, Peterborough (OHL)
1991—Peter Forsberg, 6, Modo (Sweden)
1992—Ryan Sittler, 7, Nichols H.S. (N.Y.)
   Jason Bowen, 15, Tri-City (WHL)
1993—No first-round selection
1994—No first-round selection

*Designates first player chosen in draft.

FRANCHISE LEADERS

Current players in boldface

FORWARDS/DEFENSEMEN

Games

Bobby Clarke	1144
Bill Barber	903
Brian Propp	790
Joe Watson	746
Bob Kelly	741
Rick MacLeish	741
Gary Dornhoefer	725
Ed Van Impe	617
Jim Watson	613
Reggie Leach	606

Goals

Bill Barber	420
Brian Propp	369
Tim Kerr	363
Bobby Clarke	358
Rick MacLeish	328
Reggie Leach	306
Rick Tocchet	215
Gary Dornhoefer	202
Ilkka Sinisalo	199
Dave Poulin	161

Assists

Bobby Clarke	852
Brian Propp	480
Bill Barber	463
Rick MacLeish	369
Mark Howe	342
Pelle Eklund	334
Gary Dornhoefer	316
Tim Kerr	287
Murray Craven	272
Rick Tocchet	247

Points

Bobby Clarke	1210
Bill Barber	883
Brian Propp	849
Rick MacLeish	697
Tim Kerr	650
Gary Dornhoefer	518
Reggie Leach	514
Mark Howe	480
Rick Tocchet	462
Pelle Eklund	452

Penalty minutes

Rick Tocchet	1683
Paul Holmgren	1600
Andre Dupont	1505
Bobby Clarke	1453
Dave Schultz	1386
Dave Brown	1329

Bob Kelly	1285	Pelle Lindbergh	157	Wayne Stephenson	2.77
Gary Dornhoefer	1256	Bob Froese	144	Doug Favell	2.78
Glen Cochrane	1110			Pete Peeters	3.19

Shutouts

Bernie Parent 50
Doug Favell 16
Bob Froese 12
Wayne Stephenson 10

GOALTENDERS
Games

Bernie Parent 486
Ron Hextall 281
Doug Favell 215
Pete Peeters 179
Wayne Stephenson 165

Goals-against average
(2400 minutes minimum)

Bernie Parent 2.42
Bob Froese 2.74

Rick St. Croix 3.23
Ron Hextall 3.27
Pelle Lindbergh 3.30

Wins

Bernie Parent 232
Ron Hextall 130
Wayne Stephenson 93
Bob Froese 92
Pelle Lindbergh 87

PITTSBURGH PENGUINS

YEAR-BY-YEAR RECORDS

	REGULAR SEASON					PLAYOFFS			
Season	W	L	T	Pts.	Finish	W	L	Highest round	Coach
1967-68	27	34	13	67	5th/West	—	—		Red Sullivan
1968-69	20	45	11	51	5th/West	—	—		Red Sullivan
1969-70	26	38	12	64	2nd/West	6	4	Division finals	Red Kelly
1970-71	21	37	20	62	6th/West	—	—		Red Kelly
1971-72	26	38	14	66	4th/West	0	4	Division semifinals	Red Kelly
1972-73	32	37	9	73	5th/West	—	—		Red Kelly, Ken Schinkel
1973-74	28	41	9	65	5th/West	—	—		Ken Schinkel, Marc Boileau
1974-75	37	28	15	89	3rd/Norris	5	4	Quarterfinals	Marc Boileau
1975-76	35	33	12	82	3rd/Norris	1	2	Preliminaries	Marc Boileau, Ken Schinkel
1976-77	34	33	13	81	3rd/Norris	1	2	Preliminaries	Ken Schinkel
1977-78	25	37	18	68	4th/Norris	—	—		Johnny Wilson
1978-79	36	31	13	85	2nd/Norris	2	5	Quarterfinals	Johnny Wilson
1979-80	30	37	13	73	3rd/Norris	2	3	Preliminaries	Johnny Wilson
1980-81	30	37	13	73	3rd/Norris	2	3	Preliminaries	Eddie Johnston
1981-82	31	36	13	75	4th/Patrick	2	3	Division semifinals	Eddie Johnston
1982-83	18	53	9	45	6th/Patrick	—	—		Eddie Johnston
1983-84	16	58	6	38	6th/Patrick	—	—		Lou Angotti
1984-85	24	51	5	53	5th/Patrick	—	—		Bob Berry
1985-86	34	38	8	76	5th/Patrick	—	—		Bob Berry
1986-87	30	38	12	72	5th/Patrick	—	—		Bob Berry
1987-88	36	35	9	81	6th/Patrick	—	—		Pierre Creamer
1988-89	40	33	7	87	2nd/Patrick	7	4	Division finals	Gene Ubriaco
1989-90	32	40	8	72	5th/Patrick	—	—		Gene Ubriaco, Craig Patrick
1990-91	41	33	6	88	1st/Patrick	16	8	Stanley Cup champ	Bob Johnson
1991-92	39	32	9	87	3rd/Patrick	16	5	Stanley Cup champ	Scotty Bowman
1992-93	56	21	7	119	1st/Patrick	7	5	Division finals	Scotty Bowman
1993-94	44	27	13	101	1st/Northeast	2	4	Conference quarterfinals	Eddie Johnston

FIRST-ROUND ENTRY DRAFT CHOICES

Year Player, Overall, Last Amateur Team (League)
1969—No first-round selection
1970—Greg Polis, 7, Estevan (WCHL)
1971—No first-round selection
1972—No first-round selection
1973—Blaine Stoughton, 7, Flin Flon (WCHL)
1974—Pierre Larouche, 8, Sorel (QMJHL)
1975—Gord Laxton, 13, New Westminster (WCHL)
1976—Blair Chapman, 2, Saskatoon (WCHL)
1977—No first-round selection
1978—No first-round selection
1979—No first-round selection
1980—Mike Bullard, 9, Brantford (OHL)
1981—No first-round selection
1982—Rich Sutter, 10, Lethbridge (WHL)
1983—Bob Errey, 15, Peterborough (OHL)

Year Player, Overall, Last Amateur Team (League)
1984—*Mario Lemieux, 1, Laval (QMJHL)
        Doug Bodger, 9, Kamloops (WHL)
        Roger Belanger, 16, Kingston (OHL)
1985—Craig Simpson, 2, Michigan State University
1986—Zarley Zalapski, 4, Team Canada
1987—Chris Joseph, 5, Seattle (WHL)
1988—Darrin Shannon, 4, Windsor (OHL)
1989—Jamie Heward, 16, Regina (WHL)
1990—Jaromir Jagr, 5, Poldi Kladno (Czech.)
1991—Markus Naslund, 16, MoDo (Sweden)
1992—Martin Straka, 19, Skoda Plzen (Czech.)
1993—Stefan Bergqvist, 26, Leksand (Sweden)
1994—Chris Wells, 24, Seattle (WHL)

*Designates first player chosen in draft.

FRANCHISE LEADERS

Current players in boldface

FORWARDS/DEFENSEMEN
Games

Jean Pronovost 753
Rick Kehoe 722

Ron Stackhouse 621
Ron Schock 619
Mario Lemieux 599
Dave Burrows 573
Bob Errey 518
Troy Loney 532

Syl Apps 495
Greg Malone 495
Goals
Mario Lemieux 494
Jean Pronovost 316
Rick Kehoe 312

Kevin Stevens	236	Ron Schock	404	Wendell Young	101
Mike Bullard	186	Greg Malone	364	Gary Inness	100
Syl Apps	151	Mike Bullard	361		
Greg Malone	143	Ron Stackhouse	343		
Lowell MacDonald	140				
Bob Errey	132				
Joe Mullen	130				

Assists (left) / Penalty minutes (middle) / Shutouts (right)

Assists

Mario Lemieux	717
Syl Apps	349
Paul Coffey	332
Rick Kehoe	324
Jean Pronovost	287
Ron Schock	280
Ron Stackhouse	277
Kevin Stevens	264
Randy Carlyle	257
Greg Malone	221

Penalty minutes

Troy Loney	980
Rod Buskas	959
Kevin Stevens	917
Bryan Watson	871
Paul Baxter	851
Gary Rissling	832
Jay Caufield	714
Russ Anderson	684
Jim Johnson	658
Bob Errey	651

Shutouts

Les Binkley	11
Tom Barrasso	8
Denis Herron	6
Dunc Wilson	5

Goals-against average
(2400 minutes minimum)

Al Smith	3.07
Les Binkley	3.12
Jim Rutherford	3.14
Gary Inness	3.34
Ken Wregget	3.47
Dunc Wilson	3.53
Tom Barrasso	3.57
Michel Plasse	3.59
Gilles Meloche	3.65
Andy Brown	3.78

Points

Mario Lemieux	1211
Rick Kehoe	636
Jean Pronovost	603
Syl Apps	500
Kevin Stevens	500
Paul Coffey	440

GOALTENDERS

Games

Denis Herron	290
Tom Barrasso	280
Les Binkley	196
Michel Dion	151
Greg Millen	135
Roberto Romano	123
Jim Rutherford	115
Gilles Meloche	104

Wins

Tom Barrasso	142
Denis Herron	88
Les Binkley	58
Greg Millen	57
Roberto Romano	45
Jim Rutherford	44

PITTSBURGH PIRATES (DEFUNCT)

YEAR-BY-YEAR RECORDS

	REGULAR SEASON					PLAYOFFS			
Season	W	L	T	Pts.	Finish	W	L	Highest round	Coach
1925-26	19	16	1	39	3rd	—	—		Odie Cleghorn
1926-27	15	26	3	33	4th/American	—	—		Odie Cleghorn
1927-28	19	17	8	46	3rd/American	1	1	Quarterfinals	Odie Cleghorn
1928-29	9	27	8	26	4th/American	—	—		Odie Cleghorn
1929-30	5	36	3	13	5th/American	—	—		Frank Frederickson
1930-31*	4	36	4	12	5th/American	—	—		Cooper Smeaton

*Philadelphia Quakers.

QUEBEC NORDIQUES

YEAR-BY-YEAR RECORDS

	REGULAR SEASON					PLAYOFFS			
Season	W	L	T	Pts.	Finish	W	L	Highest round	Coach
1972-73*	33	40	5	71	5th	—	—		Maurice Richard, Maurice Filion
1973-74*	38	36	4	80	5th	—	—		Jacques Plante
1974-75*	46	32	0	92	1st	8	7	Avco World Cup finals	Jean-Guy Gendron
1975-76*	50	27	4	104	2nd	1	4	League quarterfinals	Jean-Guy Gendron
1976-77*	47	31	3	97	1st	12	5	Avco World Cup champ	Marc Boileau
1977-78*	40	37	3	83	4th	5	6	League semifinals	Marc Boileau
1978-79*	41	34	5	87	2nd	0	4	League semifinals	Jacques Demers
1979-80	25	44	11	61	5th/Adams	—	—		Jacques Demers
1980-81	30	32	18	78	4th/Adams	2	3	Preliminaries	Maurice Filion, Michel Bergeron
1981-82	33	31	16	82	4th/Adams	7	9	Conference finals	Michel Bergeron
1982-83	34	34	12	80	4th/Adams	1	3	Division semifinals	Michel Bergeron
1983-84	42	28	10	94	3rd/Adams	5	4	Division finals	Michel Bergeron
1984-85	41	30	9	91	2nd/Adams	9	9	Conference finals	Michel Bergeron
1985-86	43	31	6	92	1st/Adams	0	3	Division semifinals	Michel Bergeron
1986-87	31	39	10	72	4th/Adams	7	6	Division finals	Michel Bergeron
1987-88	32	43	5	69	5th/Adams	—	—		Andre Savard, Ron Lapointe
1988-89	27	46	7	61	5th/Adams	—	—		Ron Lapointe, Jean Perron
1989-90	12	61	7	31	5th/Adams	—	—		Michel Bergeron
1990-91	16	50	14	46	5th/Adams	—	—		Dave Chambers
1991-92	20	48	12	52	5th/Adams	—	—		Dave Chambers, Pierre Page
1992-93	47	27	10	104	2nd/Adams	2	4	Division semifinals	Pierre Page
1993-94	34	42	8	76	5th/Northeast	—	—		Pierre Page

*Members of World Hockey Association.

FIRST-ROUND ENTRY DRAFT CHOICES

Year   Player, Overall, Last Amateur Team (League)
1979—Michel Goulet, 20, Birmingham (WHA)
1980—No first-round selection
1981—Randy Moller, 11, Lethbridge (WHL)
1982—David Shaw, 13, Kitchener (OHL)
1983—No first-round selection
1984—Trevor Steinburg, 15, Guelph (OHL)
1985—Dave Latta, 15, Kitchener (OHL)
1986—Ken McRae, 18, Sudbury (OHL)
1987—Bryan Fogarty, 9, Kingston (OHL)
       Joe Sakic, 15, Swift Current (WHL)
1988—Curtis Leschyshyn, 3, Saskatoon (WHL)
       Daniel Dore, 5, Drummondville (QMJHL)
1989—*Mats Sundin, 1, Nacka (Sweden)

Year   Player, Overall, Last Amateur Team (League)
1990—*Owen Nolan, 1, Cornwall (OHL)
1991—*Eric Lindros, 1, Oshawa (OHL)
1992—Todd Warriner, 4, Windsor (OHL)
1993—Jocelyn Thibault, 10, Sherbrooke (QMJHL)
       Adam Deadmarsh, 14, Portland (WHL)
1994—Wade Belak, 12, Saskatoon (WHL)
       Jeffrey Kealty, 22, Catholic Memorial H.S.

*Designates first player chosen in draft.
NOTE: Quebec chose Paul Baxter, Richard Brodeur and Garry Lariviere as priority selections before the 1979 expansion draft.

FRANCHISE LEADERS

Current players in boldface

FORWARDS/DEFENSEMEN

Games

Michel Goulet	813
Peter Stastny	737
Alain Cote	696
Anton Stastny	650
Paul Gillis	576
Steven Finn	**566**
Dale Hunter	523
Randy Moller	508
Normand Rochefort	480
Joe Sakic	**462**

Goals

Michel Goulet	456
Peter Stastny	380
Anton Stastny	252
Joe Sakic	**216**
Dale Hunter	140
Mats Sundin	135
Real Cloutier	122
Marc Tardif	116
Alain Cote	103
Wilf Paiement	102

Assists

Peter Stastny	668
Michel Goulet	489
Anton Stastny	384
Joe Sakic	348
Dale Hunter	318
Mats Sundin	199
Alain Cote	190
Real Cloutier	162
Mario Marois	162
Paul Gillis	146

Points

Peter Stastny	1048
Michel Goulet	945
Anton Stastny	636
Joe Sakic	**564**
Dale Hunter	458
Mats Sundin	334
Alain Cote	293
Real Cloutier	284
Marc Tardif	244
Marian Stastny	241

Penalty minutes

Dale Hunter	1545
Steven Finn	**1447**
Paul Gillis	1351
Randy Moller	1002
Mario Marois	778
Peter Stastny	687
Gord Donnelly	668
Wilf Paiement	619
Michel Goulet	613
Wally Weir	535

GOALTENDERS

Games

Dan Bouchard	225
Mario Gosselin	192
Ron Tugnutt	150
Clint Malarchuk	140
Stephane Fiset	**119**
Michel Dion	62

Shutouts

Mario Gosselin	6
Dan Bouchard	5
Clint Malarchuk	5

Goals-against average
(2400 minutes minimum)

Ron Hextall	3.45
Dan Bouchard	3.59
Stephane Fiset	**3.61**
Clint Malarchuk	3.63
Mario Gosselin	3.67
Michel Dion	4.02
Ron Tugnutt	4.07

Wins

Dan Bouchard	107
Mario Gosselin	79
Clint Malarchuk	62
Stephane Fiset	**45**
Ron Tugnutt	35
Ron Hextall	29

ST. LOUIS BLUES

YEAR-BY-YEAR RECORDS

	REGULAR SEASON					PLAYOFFS			
Season	W	L	T	Pts.	Finish	W	L	Highest round	Coach
1967-68	27	31	16	70	3rd/West	8	10	Stanley Cup finals	Lynn Patrick, Scotty Bowman
1968-69	37	25	14	88	1st/West	8	4	Stanley Cup finals	Scotty Bowman
1969-70	37	27	12	86	1st/West	8	8	Stanley Cup finals	Scotty Bowman
1970-71	34	25	19	87	2nd/West	2	4	Division semifinals	Al Arbour, Scotty Bowman
1971-72	28	39	11	67	3rd/West	4	7	Division finals	Sid Abel, Bill McCreary, Al Arbour
1972-73	32	34	12	76	4th/West	1	4	Division semifinals	Al Arbour, Jean-Guy Talbot
1973-74	26	40	12	64	6th/West	—	—		Jean-Guy Talbot, Lou Angotti
1974-75	35	31	14	84	2nd/Smythe	0	2	Preliminaries	Lou Angotti, Lynn Patrick, Garry Young
1975-76	29	37	14	72	3rd/Smythe	1	2	Preliminaries	Garry Young, Lynn Patrick, Leo Boivin
1976-77	32	39	9	73	1st/Smythe	0	4	Quarterfinals	Emile Francis
1977-78	20	47	13	53	4th/Smythe	—	—		Leo Boivin, Barclay Plager
1978-79	18	50	12	48	3rd/Smythe	—	—		Barclay Plager
1979-80	34	34	12	80	2nd/Smythe	0	3	Preliminaries	Barclay Plager, Red Berenson
1980-81	45	18	17	107	1st/Smythe	5	6	Quarterfinals	Red Berenson
1981-82	32	40	8	72	3rd/Norris	5	5	Division finals	Red Berenson, Emile Francis
1982-83	25	40	15	65	4th/Norris	1	3	Division semifinals	Emile Francis, Barclay Plager
1983-84	32	41	7	71	2nd/Norris	6	5	Division finals	Jacques Demers
1984-85	37	31	12	86	1st/Norris	0	3	Division semifinals	Jacques Demers

	REGULAR SEASON					PLAYOFFS			
Season	W	L	T	Pts.	Finish	W	L	Highest round	Coach
1985-86	37	34	9	83	3rd/Norris	10	9	Conference finals	Jacques Demers
1986-87	32	33	15	79	1st/Norris	2	4	Division semifinals	Jacques Martin
1987-88	34	38	8	76	2nd/Norris	5	5	Division finals	Jacques Martin
1988-89	33	35	12	78	2nd/Norris	5	5	Division finals	Brian Sutter
1989-90	37	34	9	83	2nd/Norris	7	5	Division finals	Brian Sutter
1990-91	47	22	11	105	2nd/Norris	6	7	Division finals	Brian Sutter
1991-92	36	33	11	83	3rd/Norris	2	4	Division semifinals	Brian Sutter
1992-93	37	36	11	85	4th/Norris	7	4	Division finals	Bob Plager, Bob Berry
1993-94	40	33	11	91	4th/Central	0	4	Conference quarterfinals	Bob Berry

FIRST-ROUND ENTRY DRAFT CHOICES

Year   Player, Overall, Last Amateur Team (League)
1969—No first-round selection
1970—No first-round selection
1971—Gene Carr, 4, Flin Flon (WCHL)
1972—Wayne Merrick, 9, Ottawa (OHL)
1973—John Davidson, 5, Calgary (WCHL)
1974—No first-round selection
1975—No first-round selection
1976—Bernie Federko, 7, Saskatoon (WCHL)
1977—Scott Campbell, 9, London (OHL)
1978—Wayne Babych, 3, Portland (WCHL)
1979—Perry Turnbull, 2, Portland (WHL)
1980—Rik Wilson, 12, Kingston (OHL)
1981—Marty Ruff, 20, Lethbridge (WHL)

Year   Player, Overall, Last Amateur Team (League)
1982—No first-round selection
1983—No first-round selection
1984—No first-round selection
1985—No first-round selection
1986—Jocelyn Lemieux, 10, Laval (QMJHL)
1987—Keith Osborne, 12, North Bay (OHL)
1988—Rod Brind'Amour, 9, Notre Dame Academy (Sask.)
1989—Jason Marshall, 9, Vernon (B.C.) Tier II
1990—No first-round selection
1991—No first-round selection
1992—No first-round selection
1993—No first-round selection
1994—No first-round selection

FRANCHISE LEADERS

Current players in boldface

FORWARDS/DEFENSEMEN

Games
Bernie Federko	927
Brian Sutter	779
Garry Unger	662
Bob Plager	615
Barclay Plager	614
Larry Patey	603
Red Berenson	519
Brett Hull	483
Gary Sabourin	463
Jack Brownschidle	455

Goals
Brett Hull	386
Bernie Federko	352
Brian Sutter	303
Garry Unger	292
Red Berenson	172
Jorgen Pettersson	161
Wayne Babych	155
Joe Mullen	151
Doug Gilmour	149
Perry Turnbull	139

Assists
Bernie Federko	721
Brian Sutter	334
Garry Unger	283
Brett Hull	263
Red Berenson	240
Rob Ramage	229
Adam Oates	228

Doug Gilmour	205
Blake Dunlop	201
Wayne Babych	190

Points
Bernie Federko	1073
Brett Hull	649
Brian Sutter	636
Garry Unger	575
Red Berenson	412
Doug Gilmour	354
Wayne Babych	345
Joe Mullen	335
Jorgen Pettersson	332
Rob Ramage	296

Penalty minutes
Brian Sutter	1786
Barclay Plager	1115
Kelly Chase	1005
Rob Ramage	998
Bob Gassoff	866
Perry Turnbull	829
Bob Plager	760
Garry Unger	744
Herb Raglan	571
Brendan Shanahan	556

GOALTENDERS

Games
Mike Liut	347
Curtis Joseph	244
Greg Millen	209
Rick Wamsley	154
Glenn Hall	140

Ed Staniowski	137
Vincent Riendeau	122
Ernie Wakely	111
Eddie Johnston	108
Wayne Stephenson	87

Shutouts
Glenn Hall	16
Mike Liut	10
Jacques Plante	10
Ernie Wakely	8
Greg Millen	7

Goals-against average
(2400 minutes minimum)
Jacques Plante	2.07
Glenn Hall	2.43
Ernie Wakely	2.77
Jacques Caron	3.02
Curtis Joseph	3.07
Wayne Stephenson	3.12
Vincent Riendeau	3.34
Eddie Johnston	3.36
John Davidson	3.37
Rick Wamsley	3.41
Greg Millen	3.43

Wins
Mike Liut	151
Curtis Joseph	117
Greg Millen	85
Rick Wamsley	75
Glenn Hall	58
Vincent Riendeau	58

SAN JOSE SHARKS

YEAR-BY-YEAR RECORDS

	REGULAR SEASON					PLAYOFFS			
Season	W	L	T	Pts.	Finish	W	L	Highest round	Coach
1991-92	17	58	5	39	6th/Smythe	—	—		George Kingston
1992-93	11	71	2	24	6th/Smythe	—	—		George Kingston
1993-94	33	35	16	82	3rd/Pacific	7	7	Conference semifinals	Kevin Constantine

FIRST-ROUND ENTRY DRAFT CHOICES

Year   Player, Overall, Last Amateur Team (League)
1991—Pat Falloon, 2, Spokane (WHL)
1992—Mike Rathje, 3, Medicine Hat (WHL)
          Andrei Nazarov, 10, Dynamo Moscow (CIS)

Year   Player, Overall, Last Amateur Team (League)
1993—Viktor Kozlov, 6, Moscow (CIS)
1994—Jeff Friesen, 11, Regina (WHL)

FRANCHISE LEADERS

Current players in boldface

FORWARDS/DEFENSEMEN
Games
Jeff Odgers 208
Pat Falloon 203
Rob Zettler 196
Johan Garpenlov 171
Mike Sullivan 171
Jay More 168
Dean Evason 158
Doug Zmolek 152
Rob Gaudreau 143
Kelly Kisio 126

Goals
Pat Falloon 61
Johan Garpenlov 45
Rob Gaudreau 38
Kelly Kisio 37
Sandis Ozolinsh 33
Jeff Odgers 32
Sergei Makarov 30
Todd Elik 25
David Bruce 24
Dean Evason 23

Assists
Johan Garpenlov 85

Pat Falloon 79
Kelly Kisio 78
Sandis Ozolinsh 54
Todd Elik 41
Rob Gaudreau 40
Igor Larionov 38
Sergei Makarov 38
David Williams 36
Doug Wilson 36

Points
Pat Falloon 140
Johan Garpenlov 130
Kelly Kisio 115
Sandis Ozolinsh 87
Rob Gaudreau 78
Sergei Makarov 68
Todd Elik 66
Jeff Odgers 59
Dean Evason 57
Igor Larionov 56

Penalty minutes
Jeff Odgers 692
Doug Zmolek 351
Jay More 327
Link Gaetz 326
Rob Zettler 314
Dean Evason 231

Neil Wilkinson 203
Dave Maley 156
Kelly Kisio 144
Perry Anderson 143

GOALTENDERS
Games
Arturs Irbe 123
Jeff Hackett 78
Jarmo Myllys 27
Brian Hayward 25
Jimmy Waite 15
Wade Flaherty 4

Shutouts
Arturs Irbe 4

Goals-against average
(1200 minutes minimum)
Arturs Irbe 3.36
Jeff Hackett 4.51
Jarmo Myllys 5.02
Brian Hayward 5.39

Wins
Arturs Irbe 39
Jeff Hackett 13
Brian Hayward 3
Jarmo Myllys 3
Jimmy Waite 3

TAMPA BAY LIGHTNING

YEAR-BY-YEAR RECORDS

		REGULAR SEASON					PLAYOFFS			
Season	W	L	T	Pts.	Finish	W	L	Highest round		Coach
1992-93	23	54	7	53	6th/Norris	—	—			Terry Crisp
1993-94	30	43	11	71	7th/Atlantic	—	—			Terry Crisp

FIRST-ROUND ENTRY DRAFT CHOICES

Year   Player, Overall, Last Amateur Team (League)
1992—*Roman Hamrlik, 1, Zlin (Czech.)
1993—Chris Gratton, 3, Kingston (OHL)

Year   Player, Overall, Last Amateur Team (League)
1994—Jason Weimer, 8, Portland (WHL)
*Designates first player chosen in draft.

FRANCHISE LEADERS

Current players in boldface

FORWARDS/DEFENSEMEN
Games
Marc Bergevin 161
Brian Bradley 158
Mikael Andersson 153
Danton Cole 148
John Tucker 144
Rob Zamuner 143
Marc Bureau 138
Adam Creighton 136
Roman Hamrlik 131
Shawn Chambers 121

Goals
Brian Bradley 66
John Tucker 34

Danton Cole 32
Mikael Andersson 29
Adam Creighton 29
Petr Klima 28
Chris Kontos 27
Shawn Chambers 21
Rob Zamuner 21
Marc Bureau 18
Denis Savard 18

Assists
Brian Bradley 84
John Tucker 62
Shawn Chambers 52
Danton Cole 38
Rob Zamuner 34
Roman Hamrlik 33

Adam Creighton 30
Bob Beers 29
Marc Bureau 28
Marc Bergevin 27

Points
Brian Bradley 150
John Tucker 96
Shawn Chambers 73
Danton Cole 70
Adam Creighton 59
Petr Klima 55
Rob Zamuner 55
Mikael Andersson 52
Chris Kontos 51
Marc Bureau 46
Denis Savard 46

Penalty minutes	
Roman Hamrlik	206
Mike Hartman	154
Marc Bergevin	153
Peter Taglianetti	150
Brian Bradley	148
Adam Creighton	147
Marc Bureau	141
Rob Ramage	138
Joe Reekie	127
Chris Gratton	123

GOALTENDERS

Games

Darren Puppa	63
Pat Jablonski	58
Wendell Young	40
J.C. Bergeron	24
Dave Littman	1

Shutouts

Darren Puppa	4
Pat Jablonski	1
Wendell Young	1

Goals-against average
(1200 minutes minimum)

Darren Puppa	2.71
Wendell Young	3.39
J.C. Bergeron	3.61
Pat Jablonski	3.95

Wins

Darren Puppa	22
Pat Jablonski	13
J.C. Bergeron	9
Wendell Young	9

TORONTO MAPLE LEAFS

YEAR-BY-YEAR RECORDS

		REGULAR SEASON					PLAYOFFS		
Season	W	L	T	Pts.	Finish	W	L	Highest round	Coach
1917-18‡	13	9	0	26	2nd	4	3	Stanley Cup champ	Dick Carroll
1918-19‡	5	13	0	10	3rd	—	—		Dick Carroll
1919-20§	12	12	0	24	3rd	—	—		Frank Heffernan, Harry Sproule
1920-21§	15	9	0	30	1st	0	2	Semifinals	Dick Carroll
1921-22§	13	10	1	27	2nd	*4	2	Stanley Cup champ	Eddie Powers
1922-23§	13	10	1	27	3rd	—	—		Charlie Querrie, Jack Adams
1923-24§	10	14	0	20	3rd	—	—		Eddie Powers
1924-25§	19	11	0	38	2nd	0	2	Semifinals	Eddie Powers
1925-26§	12	21	3	27	6th	—	—		Eddie Powers
1926-27§	15	24	5	35	5th/Canadian	—	—		Conn Smythe
1927-28	18	18	8	44	4th/Canadian	—	—		Alex Roveril, Conn Smythe
1928-29	21	18	5	47	3rd/Canadian	2	2	Semifinals	Alex Roveril, Conn Smythe
1929-30	17	21	6	40	4th/Canadian	—	—		Alex Roveril, Conn Smythe
1930-31	22	13	9	53	2nd/Canadian	*0	1	Quarterfinals	Conn Smythe, Art Duncan
1931-32	23	18	7	53	2nd/Canadian	5	2	Stanley Cup champ	Art Duncan, Dick Irvin
1932-33	24	18	6	54	1st/Canadian	4	5	Stanley Cup finals	Dick Irvin
1933-34	26	13	9	61	1st/Canadian	2	3	Semifinals	Dick Irvin
1934-35	30	14	4	64	1st/Canadian	3	4	Stanley Cup finals	Dick Irvin
1935-36	23	19	6	52	2nd/Canadian	4	5	Stanley Cup finals	Dick Irvin
1936-37	22	21	5	49	3rd/Canadian	0	2	Quarterfinals	Dick Irvin
1937-38	24	15	9	57	1st/Canadian			Stanley Cup finals	Dick Irvin
1938-39	19	20	9	47	3rd	5	5	Stanley Cup finals	Dick Irvin
1939-40	25	17	6	56	3rd	6	4	Stanley Cup finals	Dick Irvin
1940-41	28	14	6	62	2nd	3	4	Semifinals	Hap Day
1941-42	27	18	3	57	2nd	8	5	Stanley Cup champ	Hap Day
1942-43	22	19	9	53	3rd	2	4	League semifinals	Hap Day
1943-44	23	23	4	50	3rd	1	4	League semifinals	Hap Day
1944-45	24	22	4	52	3rd	8	5	Stanley Cup champ	Hap Day
1945-46	19	24	7	45	5th	—	—		Hap Day
1946-47	31	19	10	72	2nd	8	3	Stanley Cup champ	Hap Day
1947-48	32	15	13	77	1st	8	1	Stanley Cup champ	Hap Day
1948-49	22	25	13	57	4th	8	1	Stanley Cup champ	Hap Day
1949-50	31	27	12	74	3rd	3	4	League semifinals	Hap Day
1950-51	41	16	13	95	2nd	†8	2	Stanley Cup champ	Joe Primeau
1951-52	29	25	16	74	3rd	0	4	League semifinals	Joe Primeau
1952-53	27	30	13	67	5th	—	—		Joe Primeau
1953-54	32	24	14	78	3rd	1	4	League semifinals	King Clancy
1954-55	24	24	22	70	3rd	0	4	League semifinals	King Clancy
1955-56	24	33	13	61	4th	1	4	League semifinals	King Clancy
1956-57	21	34	15	57	5th	—	—		Howie Meeker
1957-58	21	38	11	53	6th	—	—		Billy Reay
1958-59	27	32	11	65	4th	5	7	Stanley Cup finals	Billy Reay, Punch Imlach
1959-60	35	26	9	79	2nd	4	6	Stanley Cup finals	Punch Imlach
1960-61	39	19	12	90	2nd	1	4	League semifinals	Punch Imlach
1961-62	37	22	11	85	2nd	8	4	Stanely Cup champ	Punch Imlach
1962-63	35	23	12	82	1st	8	2	Stanely Cup champ	Punch Imlach
1963-64	33	25	12	78	3rd	8	6	Stanley Cup champ	Punch Imlach
1964-65	30	26	14	74	4th	2	4	League semifinals	Punch Imlach
1965-66	34	25	11	79	3rd	0	4	League semifinals	Punch Imlach
1966-67	32	27	11	75	3rd	8	4	Stanley Cup champ	Punch Imlach
1967-68	33	31	10	76	5th/East	—	—		Punch Imlach
1968-69	35	26	15	85	4th/East	0	4	Division semifinals	Punch Imlach
1969-70	29	34	13	71	6th/East	—	—		John McLellan
1970-71	37	33	8	82	4th/East	2	4	Division semifinals	John McLellan
1971-72	33	31	14	80	4th/East	1	4	Division semifinals	John McLellan
1972-73	27	41	10	64	6th/East	—	—		John McLellan

			REGULAR SEASON			PLAYOFFS		
Season	W	L	T	Pts.	Finish	W	L	Highest round	Coach
1973-74	35	27	16	86	4th/East	0	4	Division semifinals	Red Kelly
1974-75	31	33	16	78	3rd/Adams	2	5	Quarterfinals	Red Kelly
1975-76	34	31	15	83	3rd/Adams	5	5	Quarterfinals	Red Kelly
1976-77	33	32	15	81	3rd/Adams	4	5	Quarterfinals	Red Kelly
1977-78	41	29	10	92	3rd/Adams	4	2	Quarterfinals	Roger Neilson
1978-79	34	33	13	81	3rd/Adams	4	7	Quarterfinals	Roger Neilson
1979-80	35	40	5	75	4th/Adams	0	3	Preliminaries	Floyd Smith
1980-81	28	37	15	71	5th/Adams	0	3	Preliminaries	Punch Imlach, Joe Crozier
1981-82	20	44	16	56	5th/Norris	—	—		Mike Nykoluk
1982-83	28	40	12	68	3rd/Norris	1	3	Division semifinals	Mike Nykoluk
1983-84	26	45	9	61	5th/Norris	—	—		Mike Nykoluk
1984-85	20	52	8	48	5th/Norris	—	—		Dan Maloney
1985-86	25	48	7	57	4th/Norris	6	4	Division finals	Dan Maloney
1986-87	32	42	6	70	4th/Norris	7	6	Division finals	John Brophy
1987-88	21	49	10	52	4th/Norris	2	4	Division semifinals	John Brophy
1988-89	28	46	6	62	5th/Norris	—	—		John Brophy, George Armstrong
1989-90	38	38	4	80	3rd/Norris	1	4	Division semifinals	Doug Carpenter
1990-91	23	46	11	57	5th/Norris	—	—		Doug Carpenter, Tom Watt
1991-92	30	43	7	67	5th/Norris	—	—		Tom Watt
1992-93	44	29	11	99	3rd/Norris	11	10	Conference finals	Pat Burns
1993-94	43	29	12	98	2nd/Central	9	9	Conference finals	Pat Burns

*Won-lost record does not indicate tie(s) resulting from two-game, total-goals series that year (two-game, total-goals series were played from 1917-18 through 1935-36).
†Tied after one overtime (curfew law).
‡Toronto Arenas.
§Toronto St. Patricks (until April 14, 1927).

FIRST-ROUND ENTRY DRAFT CHOICES

Year Player, Overall, Last Amateur Team (League)
1969—Ernie Moser, 9, Estevan (WCHL)
1970—Darryl Sittler, 8, London (OHL)
1971—No first-round selection
1972—George Ferguson, 11, Toronto (OHL)
1973—Lanny McDonald, 4, Medicine Hat (WCHL)
    Bob Neely, 10, Peterborough (OHL)
    Ian Turnbull, 15, Ottawa (OHL)
1974—Jack Valiquette, 13, Sault Ste. Marie (OHL)
1975—Don Ashby, 6, Calgary (WCHL)
1976—No first-round selection
1977—John Anderson, 11, Toronto (OHA)
    Trevor Johansen, 12, Toronto (OHA)
1978—No first-round selection
1979—Laurie Boschman, 9, Brandon (WHL)
1980—No first-round selection
1981—Jim Benning, 6, Portland (WHL)
1982—Gary Nylund, 3, Portland (WHL)
1983—Russ Courtnall, 7, Victoria (WHL)

Year Player, Overall, Last Amateur Team (League)
1984—Al Iafrate, 4, U.S. Olympics/Belleville (OHL)
1985—*Wendel Clark, 1, Saskatoon (WHL)
1986—Vincent Damphousse, 6, Laval (QMJHL)
1987—Luke Richardson, 7, Peterborough (OHL)
1988—Scott Pearson, 6, Kingston (OHL)
1989—Scott Thornton, 3, Belleville (OHL)
    Rob Pearson, 12, Belleville (OHL)
    Steve Bancroft, 21, Belleville (OHL)
1990—Drake Berehowsky, 10, Kingston (OHL)
1991—No first-round selection
1992—Brandon Convery, 8, Sudbury (OHL)
    Grant Marshall, 23, Ottawa (OHL)
1993—Kenny Jonsson, 12, Rogle (Sweden)
    Landon Wilson, 19, Dubuque (USHL)
1994—Eric Fichaud, 16, Chicoutimi (QMJHL)

*Designates first player chosen in draft.

FRANCHISE LEADERS

Current players in boldface

FORWARDS/DEFENSEMEN
Games

George Armstrong	1187
Tim Horton	1185
Borje Salming	1099
Dave Keon	1062
Ron Ellis	1034
Bob Pulford	947
Darryl Sittler	844
Ron Stewart	838
Bob Baun	739
Frank Mahovlich	720

Goals

Darryl Sittler	389
Dave Keon	365
Ron Ellis	332
Rick Vaive	299
George Armstrong	296
Frank Mahovlich	296

Bob Pulford	251
Ted Kennedy	231
Lanny McDonald	219
Syl Apps	201

Assists

Borje Salming	620
Darryl Sittler	527
Dave Keon	493
George Armstrong	417
Tim Horton	349
Ted Kennedy	329
Bob Pulford	312
Ron Ellis	308
Norm Ullman	305
Ian Turnbull	302

Points

Darryl Sittler	916
Dave Keon	858
Borje Salming	768
George Armstrong	713
Ron Ellis	640

Frank Mahovlich	597
Bob Pulford	563
Ted Kennedy	560
Rick Vaive	537
Norm Ullman	471

Penalty minutes

Dave Williams	1670
Tim Horton	1389
Wendel Clark	1343
Borje Salming	1292
Red Horner	1264
Bob Baun	1155
Bob McGill	988
Rick Vaive	940
Carl Brewer	917
Jim Thomson	830

GOALTENDERS
Games

Turk Broda	629
Johnny Bower	472

Mike Palmateer	296
Harry Lumley	267
Lorne Chabot	214
Bruce Gamble	210
Ken Wregget	200

Shutouts

Turk Broda	62
Harry Lumley	34
Lorne Chabot	33
Johnny Bower	32

| George Hainsworth | 19 |

Goals-against average
(2400 minutes minimum)

John Ross Roach	2.00
Al Rollins	2.05
Lorne Chabot	2.20
Harry Lumley	2.21
George Hainsworth	2.26
Jacques Plante	2.46
Johnny Bower	2.51

Turk Broda	2.53
Bernie Parent	2.59
Don Simmons	2.71
Felix Potvin	**2.71**

Wins

Turk Broda	302
Johnny Bower	220
Mike Palmateer	129
Lorne Chabot	108
Harry Lumley	104

VANCOUVER CANUCKS

YEAR-BY-YEAR RECORDS

	REGULAR SEASON					PLAYOFFS			
Season	W	L	T	Pts.	Finish	W	L	Highest round	Coach
1970-71	24	46	8	56	6th/East	—	—		Hal Laycoe
1971-72	20	50	8	48	7th/East	—	—		Hal Laycoe
1972-73	22	47	9	53	7th/East	—	—		Vic Stasiuk
1973-74	24	43	11	59	7th/East	—	—		Bill McCreary, Phil Maloney
1974-75	38	32	10	86	1st/Smythe	1	4	Quarterfinals	Phil Maloney
1975-76	33	32	15	81	2nd/Smythe	0	2	Preliminaries	Phil Maloney
1976-77	25	42	13	63	4th/Smythe	—	—		Phil Maloney, Orland Kurtenbach
1977-78	20	43	17	57	3rd/Smythe	—	—		Orland Kurtenbach
1978-79	25	42	13	63	2nd/Smythe	1	2	Preliminaries	Harry Neale
1979-80	27	37	16	70	3rd/Smythe	1	3	Preliminaries	Harry Neale
1980-81	28	32	20	76	3rd/Smythe	0	3	Preliminaries	Harry Neale
1981-82	30	33	17	77	2nd/Smythe	11	6	Stanley Cup finals	Harry Neale, Roger Neilson
1982-83	30	35	15	75	3rd/Smythe	1	3	Division semifinals	Roger Neilson
1983-84	32	39	9	73	3rd/Smythe	1	3	Division semifinals	Roger Neilson, Harry Neale
1984-85	25	46	9	59	5th/Smythe	—	—		Bill Laforge, Harry Neale
1985-86	23	44	13	59	4th/Smythe	0	3	Division semifinals	Tom Watt
1986-87	29	43	8	66	5th/Smythe	—	—		Tom Watt
1987-88	25	46	9	59	5th/Smythe	—	—		Bob McCammon
1988-89	33	39	8	74	4th/Smythe	3	4	Division semifinals	Bob McCammon
1989-90	25	41	14	64	5th/Smythe	—	—		Bob McCammon
1990-91	28	43	9	65	4th/Smythe	2	4	Division semifinals	Bob McCammon, Pat Quinn
1991-92	42	26	12	96	1st/Smythe	6	7	Division finals	Pat Quinn
1992-93	46	29	9	101	1st/Smythe	6	6	Division finals	Pat Quinn
1993-94	41	40	3	85	2nd/Pacific	15	9	Stanley Cup finals	Pat Quinn

FIRST-ROUND ENTRY DRAFT CHOICES

Year — Player, Overall, Last Amateur Team (League)

1970—Dale Tallon, 2, Toronto (OHL)
1971—Jocelyn Guevremont, 3, Montreal (OHL)
1972—Don Lever, 3, Niagara Falls (OHL)
1973—Dennis Ververgaert, 3, London (OHL)
    Bob Dailey, 9, Toronto (OHL)
1974—No first-round selection
1975—Rick Blight, 10, Brandon (WCHL)
1976—No first-round selection
1977—Jere Gillis, 4, Sherbrooke (QMJHL)
1978—Bill Derlago, 4, Brandon (WCHL)
1979—Rick Vaive, 5, Birmingham (WHA)
1980—Rick Lanz, 7, Oshawa (OHL)
1981—Garth Butcher, 10, Regina (WHL)
1982—Michel Petit, 11, Sherbrooke (QMJHL)

1983—Cam Neely, 9, Portland (WHL)
1984—J.J. Daigneault, 10, Can. Ol./Longueuil (QMJHL)
1985—Jim Sandlak, 4, London (OHL)
1986—Dan Woodley, 7, Portland (WHL)
1987—No first-round selection
1988—Trevor Linden, 2, Medicine Hat (WHL)
1989—Jason Herter, 8, University of North Dakota
1990—Petr Nedved, 2, Seattle (WHL)
    Shawn Antoski, 18, North Bay (OHL)
1991—Alex Stojanov, 7, Hamilton (OHL)
1992—Libor Polasek, 21, TJ Vikovice (Czech.)
1993—Mike Wilson, 20, Sudbury (OHL)
1994—Mattias Ohlund, 13, Pitea Div. I (Sweden)

FRANCHISE LEADERS

Current players in boldface

FORWARDS/DEFENSEMEN

Games

Stan Smyl	896
Harold Snepsts	781
Dennis Kearns	677
Doug Lidster	666
Thomas Gradin	613

Goals

| Stan Smyl | 262 |

Tony Tanti	250
Thomas Gradin	197
Don Lever	186
Trevor Linden	**180**

Assists

Stan Smyl	411
Thomas Gradin	353
Dennis Kearns	290
Andre Boudrias	267
Doug Lidster	242

Points

Stan Smyl	673
Thomas Gradin	550
Tony Tanti	470
Don Lever	407
Andre Boudrias	388

Penalty minutes

Garth Butcher	1668
Stan Smyl	1556
Harold Snepsts	1446

Gino Odjick	1422
Tiger Williams	1314

GOALTENDERS
Games

Richard Brodeur	377
Kirk McLean	**358**
Gary Smith	208
Dunc Wilson	148
Glen Hanlon	137
Frank Caprice	102
Curt Ridley	96
Cesare Maniago	93
Gary Bromley	73
Steve Weeks	66

Shutouts

Kirk McLean	16
Gary Smith	11
Richard Brodeur	6
Glen Hanlon	5
Gary Bromley	3
Ken Lockett	2
Cesare Maniago	2
Dunc Wilson	2

Goals-against average
(2400 minutes minimum)

Kirk McLean	**3.27**
Kay Whitmore	**3.32**
Gary Smith	3.33
Steve Weeks	3.44
Glen Hanlon	3.56

Gary Bromley	3.63
Cesare Maniago	3.68
Curt Ridley	3.80
Richard Brodeur	3.87
Dunc Wilson	3.93

Wins

Kirk McLean	**151**
Richard Brodeur	126
Gary Smith	72
Glen Hanlon	43
Kay Whitmore	**36**
Frank Caprice	31
Cesare Maniago	27
Gary Bromley	25
Curt Ridley	25
Dunc Wilson	24

WASHINGTON CAPITALS

YEAR-BY-YEAR RECORDS

	REGULAR SEASON					PLAYOFFS			
Season	W	L	T	Pts.	Finish	W	L	Highest round	Coach
1974-75	8	67	5	21	5th/Norris	—	—		Jim Anderson, Red Sullivan Milt Schmidt
1975-76	11	59	10	32	5th/Norris	—	—		Milt Schmidt, Tom McVie
1976-77	24	42	14	62	4th/Norris	—	—		Tom McVie
1977-78	17	49	14	48	5th/Norris	—	—		Tom McVie
1978-79	24	41	15	63	4th/Norris	—	—		Dan Belisle
1979-80	27	40	13	67	5th/Patrick	—	—		Dan Belisle, Gary Green
1980-81	26	36	18	70	5th/Patrick	—	—		Gary Green
1981-82	26	41	13	65	5th/Patrick	—	—		Gary Green, Roger Crozier Bryan Murray
1982-83	39	25	16	94	3rd/Patrick	1	3	Division semifinals	Bryan Murray
1983-84	48	27	5	101	2nd/Patrick	4	4	Division finals	Bryan Murray
1984-85	46	25	9	101	2nd/Patrick	2	3	Division semifinals	Bryan Murray
1985-86	50	23	7	107	2nd/Patrick	5	4	Division finals	Bryan Murray
1986-87	38	32	10	86	2nd/Patrick	3	4	Division semifinals	Bryan Murray
1987-88	38	33	9	85	2nd/Patrick	7	7	Division finals	Bryan Murray
1988-89	41	29	10	92	1st/Patrick	2	4	Division semifinals	Bryan Murray
1989-90	36	38	6	78	3rd/Patrick	8	7	Conference finals	Bryan Murray, Terry Murray
1990-91	37	36	7	81	3rd/Patrick	5	6	Division finals	Terry Murray
1991-92	45	27	8	98	2nd/Patrick	3	4	Division semifinals	Terry Murray
1992-93	43	34	7	93	2nd/Patrick	2	4	Division semifinals	Terry Murray
1993-94	39	35	10	88	3rd/Atlantic	5	6	Conference semifinals	Terry Murray, Jim Schoenfeld

FIRST-ROUND ENTRY DRAFT CHOICES

Year Player, Overall, Last Amateur Team (League)

1974—*Greg Joly, 1, Regina (WCHL)
1975—Alex Forsyth, 18, Kingston (OHA)
1976—*Rick Green, 1, London (OHL)
      Greg Carroll, 15, Medicine Hat (WCHL)
1977—Robert Picard, 3, Montreal (QMJHL)
1978—Ryan Walter, 2, Seattle (WCHL)
      Tim Coulis, 18, Hamilton (OHL)
1979—Mike Gartner, 4, Cincinnati (WHA)
1980—Darren Veitch, 5, Regina (WHL)
1981—Bobby Carpenter, 3, St. John's H.S. (Mass.)
1982—Scott Stevens, 5, Kitchener (OHL)
1983—No first-round selection
1984—Kevin Hatcher, 17, North Bay (OHL)
1985—Yvon Corriveau, 19, Toronto (OHL)

Year Player, Overall, Last Amateur Team (League)

1986—Jeff Greenlaw, 19, Team Canada
1987—No first-round selection
1988—Reggie Savage, 15, Victoriaville (QMJHL)
1989—Olaf Kolzig, 19, Tri-City (WHL)
1990—John Slaney, 9, Cornwall (OHL)
1991—Pat Peake, 14, Detroit (OHL)
      Trevor Halverson, 21, North Bay (OHL)
1992—Sergei Gonchar, 14, Dynamo Moscow (CIS)
1993—Brendan Witt, 11, Seattle (WHL)
      Jason Allison, 17, London (OHL)
1994—Nolan Baumgartner, 10, Kamloops (WHL)
      Alexander Kharlamov, 15, CSKA Moscow (Russia)

*Designates first player chosen in draft.

FRANCHISE LEADERS

Current players in boldface

FORWARDS/DEFENSEMEN
Games

Mike Gartner	758
Rod Langway	726
Kevin Hatcher	**685**
Bengt Gustafsson	629

Kelly Miller	**603**
Scott Stevens	601
Bobby Gould	600
Mike Ridley	588
Michal Pivonka	**583**
Dale Hunter	**531**

Goals

Mike Gartner	397

Mike Ridley	218
Bengt Gustafsson	196
Dave Christian	193
Bob Carpenter	188
Dennis Maruk	182
Kevin Hatcher	**149**
Michal Pivonka	**140**
Dale Hunter	**138**

Bobby Gould	134	Dave Christian	417	Bernie Wolfe	120

Bobby Gould 134

Dave Christian 417	Bernie Wolfe 120
Bobby Carpenter 395	Clint Malarchuk 96

Assists

Mike Gartner 392	**Penalty minutes**
Bengt Gustafsson 359	
Scott Stevens 331	Scott Stevens 1630
Mike Ridley 329	**Dale Hunter** **1460**
Michal Pivonka **302**	Alan May 1092
Dale Hunter **281**	**Kevin Hatcher** **998**
Kevin Hatcher **277**	Mike Gartner 770
Larry Murphy 259	Yvon Labre 756
Dennis Maruk 249	Greg Adams 694
Dave Christian 224	Al Iafrate 616
	Gord Lane 614
Points	Lou Franceschetti 562

Goals-against average
(2400 minutes minimum)

Pat Riggin 3.02
Pete Peeters 3.06
Don Beaupre **3.05**
Bob Mason 3.16
Al Jensen 3.26

Points

Mike Gartner 789
Bengt Gustafsson 555
Mike Ridley 547
Michal Pivonka **442**
Dennis Maruk 431
Scott Stevens 429
Kevin Hatcher **426**
Dale Hunter **419**

GOALTENDERS

Games

Don Beaupre **269**
Al Jensen 173
Ron Low 145
Pat Riggin 143
Pete Peeters 139

Wins

Don Beaupre **128**
Al Jensen 94
Pete Peeters 70
Pat Riggin 67
Clint Malarchuk 40

Shutouts

Don Beaupre **12**
Al Jensen 8
Pete Peeters 7
Pat Riggin 6
Clint Malarchuk 5

WINNIPEG JETS

YEAR-BY-YEAR RECORDS

	REGULAR SEASON					PLAYOFFS			
Season	W	L	T	Pts.	Finish	W	L	Highest round	Coach
1972-73*	43	31	4	90	1st	9	5	Avco World Cup finals	Nick Mickoski, Bobby Hull
1973-74*	34	39	5	73	4th	0	4	League quarterfinals	Nick Mickoski, Bobby Hull
1974-75*	38	35	5	81	3rd	—	—		Rudy Pilous
1975-76*	52	27	2	106	1st	12	1	Avco World Cup champ	Bobby Kromm
1976-77*	46	32	2	94	2nd	11	9	Avco World Cup finals	Bobby Kromm
1977-78*	50	28	2	102	1st	8	1	Avco World Cup champ	Larry Hillman
1978-79*	39	35	6	84	3rd	8	2	Avco World Cup champ	Larry Hillman, Tom McVie
1979-80	20	49	11	51	5th/Smythe	—	—		Tom McVie
1980-81	9	57	14	32	6th/Smythe	—	—		Tom McVie, Bill Sutherland, Mike Smith
1981-82	33	33	14	80	2nd/Norris	1	3	Division semifinals	Tom Watt
1982-83	33	39	8	74	4th/Smythe	0	3	Division semifinals	Tom Watt
1983-84	31	38	11	73	3rd/Smythe	0	3	Division semifinals	Tom Watt, Barry Long
1984-85	43	27	10	96	2nd/Smythe	3	5	Division finals	Barry Long
1985-86	26	47	7	59	3rd/Smythe	0	3	Division semifinals	Barry Long, John Ferguson
1986-87	40	32	8	88	3rd/Smythe	4	6	Division finals	Dan Maloney
1987-88	33	36	11	77	3rd/Smythe	1	4	Division semifinals	Dan Maloney
1988-89	26	42	12	64	5th/Smythe	—	—		Dan Maloney, Rick Bowness
1989-90	37	32	11	85	3rd/Smythe	3	4	Division semifinals	Bob Murdoch
1990-91	26	43	11	63	5th/Smythe	—	—		Bob Murdoch
1991-92	33	32	15	81	4th/Smythe	3	4	Division semifinals	John Paddock
1992-93	40	37	7	87	4th/Smythe	2	4	Division semifinals	John Paddock
1993-94	24	51	9	57	6th/Central	—	—		John Paddock

*Members of World Hockey Association.

FIRST-ROUND ENTRY DRAFT CHOICES

Year Player, Overall, Last Amateur Team (League)
1979—Jimmy Mann, 19, Sherbrooke (QMJHL)
1980—David Babych, 2, Portland (WHL)
1981—*Dale Hawerchuk, 1, Cornwall (QMJHL)
1982—Jim Kyte, 12, Cornwall (OHL)
1983—Andrew McBain, 8, North Bay (OHL)
　　　Bobby Dollas, 14, Laval (QMJHL)
1984—No first-round selection
1985—Ryan Stewart, 18, Kamloops (WHL)
1986—Pat Elynuik, 8, Prince Albert (WHL)
1987—Bryan Marchment, 16, Belleville (OHL)
1988—Teemu Selanne, 10, Jokerit (Finland)

Year Player, Overall, Last Amateur Team (League)
1989—Stu Barnes, 4, Tri-City (WHL)
1990—Keith Tkachuk, 19, Malden Cath. H.S. (Mass.)
1991—Aaron Ward, 5, University of Michigan
1992—Sergei Bautin, 17, Dynamo Moscow (CIS)
1993—Mats Lindgren, 15, Skelleftea (Sweden)
1994—No first-round selection

*Designates first player chosen in draft.
　NOTE: Winnipeg chose Scott Campbell, Morris Lukowich
and Markus Mattsson as priority selections before the 1979
expansion draft.

FRANCHISE LEADERS

Current players in boldface

FORWARDS/DEFENSEMEN

Games
Thomas Steen	**919**
Dale Hawerchuk	713
Doug Smail	691
Randy Carlyle	564
Ron Wilson	536

Goals
Dale Hawerchuk	379
Thomas Steen	**259**
Paul MacLean	248
Doug Smail	189
Morris Lukowich	168

Assists
Dale Hawerchuk	550
Thomas Steen	**543**
Paul MacLean	270
Fredrik Olausson	249
Dave Babych	248

Points
Dale Hawerchuk	929
Thomas Steen	**802**
Paul MacLean	518
Doug Smail	397
Laurie Boschman	379

Penalty minutes
Laurie Boschman	1338
Jim Kyte	772
Tim Watters	760

Thomas Steen	**739**
Randy Carlyle	736

GOALTENDERS
Shutouts
Bob Essensa	14
Daniel Berthiaume	4
Markus Mattsson	3
Stephane Beauregard	2
Dan Bouchard	2
Doug Soetaert	2
Ed Staniowski	2

Wins
Bob Essensa	116
Brian Hayward	63
Daniel Berthiaume	50
Pokey Reddick	41

MINOR LEAGUES

American Hockey League

International Hockey League

East Coast Hockey League

Central Hockey League

Colonial Hockey League

AMERICAN HOCKEY LEAGUE

LEAGUE OFFICE

Chairman of the board
Jack Butterfield
President and treasurer
David Andrews
Vice president and general counsel
Macgregor Kilpatrick
Vice president, secretary
Gordon C. Anziano

Director of marketing
Maria D'Agostino
Statistician
Hellen Schoeder
Media relations
Steve Luce

Address
425 Union Street
West Springfield, MA 01089
Phone
413-781-2030
FAX
413-733-4767

TEAMS

ADIRONDACK RED WINGS

General manager
Ken Holland
Head coach
Newell Brown
Home ice
Glens Falls Civic Center
Address
1 Civic Center Plaza
Glens Falls, NY 12801
Seating capacity
4,806
Phone
518-798-0366
FAX
518-798-0816

ALBANY RIVER RATS

President
Doug Burch
Head coach
Robbie Ftorek
Home ice
Knickerbocker Arena
Address
51 South Pearl St.
Albany, NY 12207
Seating capacity
6,500
Phone
518-487-2244
FAX
518-487-2248

BINGHAMTON RANGERS

Managing partner
Tom Mitchell
Head coach
Al Hill
Home ice
Broome County Veterans
Memorial Arena
Address
One Stuart Street
Binghamton, NY 13901
Seating capacity
4,803
Phone
607-723-8937
FAX
607-724-6892

CAPE BRETON OILERS

General manager
To be announced
Head coach
George Burnett
Home ice
Centre 200
Address
P.O. Box 1510
Sydney, Nova Scotia B1T 6R7
Seating capacity
4,763
Phone
902-562-0780
FAX
902-562-1806

CORNWALL ACES

General manager and head coach
Jacques Martin
Home ice
Cornwall Civic Complex
Address
100 Water Street
Cornwall, Ont. K6H 6G4
Seating capacity
4,036
Phone
613-937-4132
FAX
613-933-9632

FREDERICTON CANADIENS

Director of operations
Wayne Gamble
Head coach
Paulin Bordeleau
Home ice
Aitken University Centre
Address
P.O. Box HABS
Fredericton, N.B. E3B 4Y2
Seating capacity
3,583
Phone
506-459-4227
FAX
506-457-4250

HERSHEY BEARS

General manager
Jay Feaster
Head coach
Jay Leach
Home ice
Hersheypark Arena
Address
P.O. Box 866
Hershey, PA 17033
Seating capacity
7,256
Phone
717-534-3380
FAX
717-534-3383

PORTLAND PIRATES

President
Godfrey Wood
Head coach
Barry Trotz
Home ice
Cumberland County Civic Center
Address
1 Civic Center Square
Portland, ME 04101
Seating capacity
6,736
Phone
207-828-4665
FAX
207-773-3278

PRINCE EDWARD ISLAND SENATORS

Director of operations
Gary Thompson
Head coach
To be announced
Home ice
Charlottetown Civic Centre
Address
P.O. Box 22093
Charlottetown, PEI C1A 9J2
Seating capacity
3,417
Phone
902-566-5450
FAX
902-566-5170

PROVIDENCE BRUINS

Chief executive officer
Ed Anderson
Head coach
To be announced
Home ice
Providence Civic Center
Address
1 LaSalle Square
Providence, RI 02903
Seating capacity
11,909
Phone
401-273-5000
FAX
401-273-5004

ROCHESTER AMERICANS

General manager
Joe Baumann
Head coach
John Van Boxmeer
Home ice
War Memorial Auditorium
Address
100 Exchange Street
Rochester, NY 14614
Seating capacity
6,973
Phone
716-454-5335
FAX
716-454-3954

SAINT JOHN FLAMES

General manager
Gord Thorne
Head coach
Bob Francis

Home ice
Harbour Station
Address
P.O. Box 4040, Station B
Saint John, NB E2M 5E6
Seating capacity
6,071
Phone
506-635-2637
FAX
506-663-4625

ST. JOHN'S MAPLE LEAFS

General manager
Glenn Stanford
Head coach
Marc Crawford
Home ice
St. John's Memorial Stadium
Address
6 Logy Bay Road
St. John's, Newfoundland A1A 1J3
Seating capacity
3,910
Phone
709-726-1010
FAX
709-726-1511

SPRINGFIELD FALCONS

President
Peter R. Cooney
Head coach
Paul Gillis
Home ice
Springfield Civic Center
Address
P.O. Box 3190
Springfield, MA 01110

Seating capacity
7,542
Phone
413-739-3344
FAX
413-739-3389

SYRACUSE CRUNCH

General manager
David Gregory
Head coach
Jack McIlhargey
Home ice
Onondaga County War Memorial
Address
800 S. State St.
Syracuse, NY 13202
Seating capacity
6,200
Phone
315-473-4444
FAX
315-473-4449

WORCESTER ICECATS

General manager and head coach
Jim Roberts
Home ice
Worcester Centrum
Address
33 Waldo St.
Worcester, MA 01608
Seating capacity
12,500
Phone
508-798-5400
FAX
508-799-5267

1993-94 REGULAR SEASON

FINAL STANDINGS

ATLANTIC DIVISION

Team	G	W	L	T	Pts.	GF	GA
St. John's	80	45	23	12	102	360	287
Saint John	80	37	33	10	84	304	305
Moncton	80	37	36	7	81	310	303
Cape Breton	80	32	35	13	77	316	339
Fredericton	80	31	42	7	69	294	296
Prince Edward Island	80	23	49	8	54	269	356

NORTHERN DIVISION

Team	G	W	L	T	Pts.	GF	GA
Adirondack	80	45	27	8	98	333	273
Portland	80	43	27	10	96	328	269
Albany	80	38	34	8	84	312	315
Springfield	80	29	38	13	71	309	327
Providence	80	28	39	13	69	283	319

SOUTHERN DIVISION

Team	G	W	L	T	Pts.	GF	GA
Hershey	80	38	31	11	87	306	298
Hamilton	80	36	37	7	79	302	305
Cornwall	80	33	36	11	77	294	295
Rochester	80	31	34	15	77	277	300
Binghamton	80	33	38	9	75	312	322

INDIVIDUAL LEADERS

Goals: Patrik Augusta, St. John's (53)
Assists: Tim Taylor, Adirondack (81)
Points: Tim Taylor, Adirondack (117)
Penalty minutes: John Badduke, Hamilton (356)
Goaltending average: Frederic Chabot, Hershey (2.80)
Shutouts: Mike Fountain, Hamilton (4)

	Games	G	A	Pts.
Mitch Lamoureux, Hershey	80	45	60	105
Mike Tomlak, Springfield	79	44	56	100
Mark Pederson, Adirondack	62	52	45	97
Patrik Augusta, St. John's	77	53	43	96
Chris Snell, St. John's	75	22	74	96
Jay Mazur, Hamilton	78	40	55	95
Tim Tookey, Hershey	66	32	57	89
Mark Freer, Saint John	77	33	53	86
Michel Picard, Portland	61	41	44	85
Todd Simon, Rochester	55	33	52	85
Steve Maltais, Adirondack	73	35	49	84
Cory Stillman, Saint John	79	35	48	83
Claude Vilgrain, Hershey	76	30	53	83
Bill H. Armstrong, Albany	74	32	50	82
Yvon Corriveau, Springfield	71	42	39	81

TOP SCORERS

	Games	G	A	Pts.
Tim Taylor, Adirondack	79	36	81	117
Rich Chernomaz, St. John's	78	45	65	110
Stephane Morin, Hamilton	69	38	71	109
Jeff Nelson, Portland	80	34	73	107
Yanic Perreault, St. John's	62	45	60	105

INDIVIDUAL STATISTICS

ADIRONDACK RED WINGS

SCORING

	Games	G	A	Pts.	PIM
Tim Taylor	79	36	81	117	86
Mark Pederson	62	52	45	97	37
Steve Maltais	73	35	49	84	79
Brett Harkins	80	22	47	69	23
Jason York	74	10	56	66	98
Joe Frederick	68	28	30	58	130
Michael Maurice	70	25	30	55	53
Mike Casselman	77	17	38	55	34
Martin Lapointe	28	25	21	46	47
Kris Draper	46	20	23	43	49
Craig Martin	76	15	24	39	297
Bob Boughner	72	8	14	22	292
Jamie Pushor	73	1	17	18	124
Aaron Ward	58	4	12	16	87
Dmitri Motkov	70	2	14	16	124
Barry Potomski	50	9	5	14	224
Lev Berdichevsky	26	6	8	14	14
Chris Bergeron	41	6	5	11	37
Gord Kruppke	54	2	9	11	210
Greg Johnson	3	2	4	6	0
Sergei Bautin	9	1	5	6	6
Bob Halkidis	15	0	6	6	46
Dave Flanagan	18	2	2	4	19
Alex Hicks	8	1	3	4	2
Dallas Drake	1	2	0	2	0
Darren Perkins	2	0	2	2	2
Serge Anglehart	31	0	2	2	87
Vincent Riendeau (goalie)	10	0	2	2	4
Sylvain Cloutier	2	0	2	2	0
Rick Judson	2	1	0	1	0
Tony Gruba	1	1	0	1	0
Vyacheslav Kozlov	3	0	1	1	15
Scott Cashman (goalie)	3	0	1	1	2
Kevin Hodson (goalie)	37	0	1	1	8
Chris Osgood (goalie)	4	0	0	0	0
Igor Malykhin	2	0	0	0	2
Tim Cheveldae (goalie)	2	0	0	0	0
Peter Ing (goalie)	7	0	0	0	0
Maxim Michailovsky (goalie)	5	0	0	0	0
Daniel Berthiaume (goalie)	11	0	0	0	2
Duane Derksen (goalie)	11	0	0	0	2

GOALTENDING

	Games	Min.	W	L	T	Goals	SO	Avg.
Kevin Hodson	37	2083	20	10	5	102	2	2.94
Vincent Riendeau	10	583	6	3	0	30	0	3.09
Chris Osgood	4	240	3	1	0	13	0	3.26
Tim Cheveldae	2	125	1	0	1	7	0	3.36
Scott Cashman	3	99	0	1	0	6	1	3.64
Peter Ing	7	425	3	3	1	26	1	3.67

	Games	Min.	W	L	T	Goals	SO	Avg.
Duane Derksen	11	600	4	6	0	37	0	3.70
Daniel Berthiaume	11	553	7	2	0	35	0	3.80
Maxim Michailovsky	5	127	1	1	1	12	0	5.68

ALBANY RIVER RATS

SCORING

	Games	G	A	Pts.	PIM
Bill H. Armstrong	74	32	50	82	188
Jeff Christian	76	34	43	77	227
Jason Miller	77	22	53	75	65
Scott Pellerin	73	28	46	74	84
Jim Dowd	58	26	37	63	76
Brian Sullivan	77	31	30	61	140
David Emma	56	26	29	55	53
Kevin Dean	70	9	33	42	92
Pascal Rheaume	55	17	18	35	43
Curt Regnier	34	12	20	32	4
Mike Bodnarchuk	45	12	20	32	54
Ben Hankinson	29	9	14	23	80
Bryan Helmer	65	4	19	23	79
Matt Ruchty	68	11	11	22	303
Cale Hulse	79	7	14	21	186
Roy Mitchell	42	3	12	15	43
Geordie Kinnear	59	3	12	15	197
Reid Simpson	37	9	5	14	135
Brian Rolston	17	5	5	10	8
Jason Smith	20	6	3	9	31
Dean Malkoc	79	0	9	9	296
Krzysztof Oliwa	33	2	4	6	151
Jaroslav Modry	19	1	5	6	25
Corey Schwab	51	0	3	3	38
Chris Gotziaman	3	1	1	2	0
Tommy Albelin	4	0	2	2	17
Chris Nelson	7	0	2	2	4
Lyle Wildgoose	2	1	0	1	0
Donevan Hextall	4	1	0	1	0
Dan Bylsma	3	0	1	1	2
Peter Sidorkiewicz	15	0	1	1	0
Chad Erickson	4	0	0	0	2
Mark Gowans	1	0	0	0	0
Kevin Riehl	1	0	0	0	0
Derek Linnell	2	0	0	0	0
Matt DelGuidice	5	0	0	0	0
Brian Langlot	1	0	0	0	0
Mike Dunham	5	0	0	0	0

GOALTENDING

	Games	Min.	W	L	T	Goals	SO	Avg.
Brian Langlot	1	10	0	0	0	0	0	0.00
Corey Schwab	51	3059	27	21	3	184	0	3.61
Matt DelGuidice	5	310	1	2	2	19	0	3.68
Peter Sidorkiewicz	15	908	6	7	2	60	0	3.97

	Games	Min.	W	L	T	Goals	SO	Avg.
Chad Erickson	4	184	2	1	0	13	0	4.25
Mike Dunham	5	305	2	2	1	26	0	5.12
Mark Gowans	1	59	0	1	0	6	0	6.14

BINGHAMTON RANGERS

SCORING

	Games	G	A	Pts.	PIM
Ken Hodge	79	22	56	78	51
Shawn McCosh	75	31	44	75	68
Eric Murano	75	35	37	72	36
Craig Duncanson	70	25	44	69	83
Jean-Yves Roy	65	41	24	65	33
Jim Hiller	67	27	34	61	61
Michael Stewart	79	8	42	50	75
Daniel Lacroix	59	20	23	43	278
Rob Kenny	63	27	14	41	90
Dean Kolstad	68	7	26	33	92
Darcy Werenka	53	5	22	27	10
Mike McLaughlin	56	11	13	24	33
Peter Fiorentino	68	7	15	22	220
Dimitri Starostenko	41	12	9	21	10
Fredrik Jax	31	5	16	21	14
Joby Messier	42	6	14	20	58
Brad Tiley	29	6	10	16	6
Mattias Norstrom	55	1	9	10	70
Ed Kastelic	44	3	6	9	119
Todd Marchant	8	2	7	9	6
Darren Langdon	54	2	7	9	327
Barry Richter	21	0	9	9	12
Bob Babcock	20	1	6	7	67
Andrei Kudinov	25	3	3	6	6
Bruce Bell	13	1	5	6	16
Roy Mitchell	11	1	3	4	18
Sergei Zubov	2	1	2	3	0
Boris Rousson (goalie)	62	0	2	2	12
Mike Vukonich	3	1	0	1	0
Paval Komarov	1	0	1	1	2
Mike Gilmore (goalie)	7	0	0	0	0
Jon Hillebrandt (goalie)	7	0	0	0	0
Eric Germain	3	0	0	0	6
Corey Hirsch (goalie)	10	0	0	0	0

GOALTENDING

	Games	Min.	W	L	T	Goals	SO	Avg.
Jon Hillebrandt	7	294	1	3	0	18	0	3.67
Corey Hirsch	10	611	5	4	1	38	0	3.73
Boris Rousson	62	3599	26	26	8	232	0	3.87
Mike Gilmore	7	338	1	5	0	25	0	4.43

CAPE BRETON OILERS

SCORING

	Games	G	A	Pts.	PIM
Peter White	45	21	49	70	12
Jim Nesich	65	23	42	65	126
Alexander Kerch	57	24	38	62	16
Josef Cierny	73	30	27	57	88
Darcy Martini	65	18	38	56	131
Roman Oksiuta	47	31	22	53	90
Ralph Intranuovo	66	21	31	52	39
Tyler Wright	65	14	27	41	160
Brad Zavisha	58	19	15	34	114
Scott Allison	75	19	14	33	202
Gord Mark	49	11	20	31	116
Martin Bakula	71	6	22	28	65
Juha Riihijarvi	57	10	15	25	37
Ian Herbers	53	7	16	23	122
Brad Werenka	25	6	17	23	19
Brent Grieve	20	10	11	21	14
Dean McAmmond	28	9	12	21	38
Jeff Chychrun	41	2	16	18	111
Peter Marek	27	7	8	15	12

	Games	G	A	Pts.	PIM
Ilya Byakin	12	2	9	11	8
Dennis Bonvie	63	1	10	11	278
Craig Fisher	16	5	5	10	11
Terry Virtue	26	4	6	10	10
John Van Kessel	37	2	7	9	154
Shjon Podein	5	4	4	8	4
Serge Roberge	51	3	5	8	130
Adam Bennett	7	2	5	7	7
Todd Marchant	3	1	4	5	2
Louie DeBrusk	5	3	1	4	58
Scott Thornton	2	1	1	2	31
Bruce Campbell	9	0	2	2	6
Link Gaetz	21	0	1	1	140
Troy Binnie	2	0	1	1	0
Andrew Verner (goalie)	38	0	1	1	4
John Johnson	1	0	0	0	0
Steve Gibson	3	0	0	0	2
Marc Laforge	14	0	0	0	91
Fred Brathwaite (goalie)	2	0	0	0	0
Neil Fewster	2	0	0	0	0
Wayne Cowley (goalie)	44	0	0	0	18
Greg DeVries	9	0	0	0	11

GOALTENDING

	Games	Min.	W	L	T	Goals	SO	Avg.
Fred Brathwaite	2	119	1	1	0	6	0	3.04
Wayne Cowley	44	2486	20	17	5	150	0	3.62
Andrew Verner	38	2261	11	17	8	175	0	4.64

CORNWALL ACES

SCORING

	Games	G	A	Pts.	PIM
Rene Corbet	68	37	40	77	56
Denis Chasse	48	27	39	66	194
Paul Willett	56	24	34	58	60
Niklas Andersson	42	18	34	52	8
Mike Hurlbut	77	13	33	46	100
Paul Brousseau	69	18	26	44	35
Alain Cote	67	10	34	44	80
Ed Ward	60	12	30	42	65
Reggie Savage	33	21	13	34	56
Paxton Schulte	56	15	15	30	102
Jon Klemm	66	4	26	30	78
Ryan Hughes	54	17	12	29	24
Chris Lindberg	23	14	13	27	28
Eric Veilleux	77	8	19	27	69
Martin Simard	57	10	10	20	152
Mike McKee	24	6	14	20	18
Rick Kowalsky	65	9	8	17	86
Mark Matier	67	1	16	17	100
Brad Turner	29	3	13	16	19
Sean Whyte	18	6	9	15	16
Jeff Parrott	52	4	11	15	37
Aaron Miller	64	4	10	14	49
Michel Mongeau	7	3	11	14	4
Dwayne Norris	9	2	9	11	0
Randy Velischek	18	1	6	7	17
Wade Klippstein	27	2	3	5	4
Phil Berger	2	2	1	3	0
Blair Scott	19	1	2	3	13
John Tanner (goalie)	38	0	2	2	13
Paul Krake (goalie)	28	0	2	2	4
John Young	2	1	0	1	0
Sebastien LaPlante	5	1	0	1	0
Garth Snow (goalie)	16	0	1	1	6
Patrick LaBrecque (goalie)	4	0	0	0	2
Brendan Creagh	1	0	0	0	0
Stephane Fiset (goalie)	1	0	0	0	0
Chris Valicevic	6	0	0	0	0
Jocelyn Thibault (goalie)	4	0	0	0	0
Dave Karpa	1	0	0	0	0
Ron Aubrey	4	0	0	0	19
Joey St. Aubin	12	0	0	0	0
Christian Matte	1	0	0	0	0

GOALTENDING

	Games	Min.	W	L	T	Goals	SO	Avg.
Jocelyn Thibault	4	240	4	0	0	9	1	2.25
Patrick LaBrecque	4	198	1	2	0	8	96	2.42
Garth Snow	16	927	6	5	3	51	0	3.30
John Tanner	38	2035	14	15	4	123	1	3.63
Stephane Fiset	1	60	0	1	0	4	0	4.00
Paul Krake	28	1383	8	13	4	96	0	4.17

FREDERICTON CANADIENS

SCORING

	Games	G	A	Pts.	PIM
Robert Guillet	78	38	40	78	48
Donald Brashear	62	38	28	66	250
Craig Ferguson	57	29	32	61	60
Craig Darby	66	23	33	56	51
Turner Stevenson	66	19	28	47	155
Marc Laniel	79	6	41	47	76
Lindsay Vallis	75	9	30	39	103
Mario Doyon	56	12	21	33	44
Oleg Petrov	23	8	20	28	18
Yves Sarault	60	13	14	27	72
Brian Savage	17	12	15	27	4
Gary Leeman	23	18	8	26	16
Charles Poulin	35	9	15	24	70
Jim Campbell	19	6	17	23	6
Gerry Fleming	46	6	16	22	188
Ryan Kuwabara	44	13	8	21	51
Kevin Darby	64	4	16	20	12
Mark Bavis	45	7	10	17	86
Dave Flanagan	34	11	4	15	13
Christian Proulx	70	2	12	14	183
Kevin O'Sullivan	62	2	11	13	73
Marquis Mathieu	22	4	6	10	28
Christian Lariviere	51	2	6	8	56
Brent Bilodeau	72	2	5	7	89
Timothy Chase	8	0	4	4	0
Tony Prpic	13	1	2	3	7
Sebastian Fortier	4	0	3	3	11
Craig Rivet	4	0	2	2	2
Martin Brochu (goalie)	32	0	2	2	0
Jason Downey	15	0	1	1	35
Les Kuntar (goalie)	34	0	1	1	12
Frederic Chabot (goalie)	3	0	0	0	0
Eric Raymond (goalie)	4	0	0	0	0
Yvan Corbin	6	0	0	0	2
Andre Racicot (goalie)	6	0	0	0	0
David Littman (goalie)	16	0	0	0	8

GOALTENDING

	Games	Min.	W	L	T	Goals	SO	Avg.
Eric Raymond	4	200	2	2	0	9	1	2.70
Martin Brochu	32	1506	10	11	3	76	2	3.03
Andre Racicot	6	293	1	4	0	16	0	3.28
Les Kuntar	34	1804	10	17	3	109	1	3.62
David Littman	16	872	8	7	0	63	0	4.33
Frederic Chabot	3	143	0	1	1	12	0	5.03

HAMILTON CANUCKS

SCORING

	Games	G	A	Pts.	PIM
Stephane Morin	69	38	71	109	48
Jay Mazur	78	40	55	95	40
Dan Kesa	53	37	33	70	33
Dane Jackson	60	25	35	60	75
Neil Eisenhut	60	17	36	53	30
Doug Torrel	75	18	26	44	43
Phil Von Stefenelli	80	10	31	41	89
Scott Walker	77	10	29	39	272
Dan Ratushny	62	8	31	39	22
Brian Loney	67	18	16	34	76
John Namestnikov	59	7	27	34	97
Jassen Cullimore	71	8	20	28	86
Rob Woodward	60	11	14	25	45

	Games	G	A	Pts.	PIM
Libor Polasek	76	11	12	23	40
Cam Danyluk	60	11	12	23	159
Daryl Filipek	68	5	17	22	27
Sandy Moger	29	9	8	17	41
Jason Christie	28	6	9	15	36
John Badduke	55	6	8	14	356
Troy Neumeier	44	1	7	8	21
Jose Charbonneau	7	3	2	5	8
Adrian Aucoin	13	1	2	3	19
Rick Girard	1	1	1	2	0
Brian Goudie	5	1	0	1	20
Rob Schriner	2	0	1	1	0
Alex Stojanov	4	0	1	1	5
Adrien Plavsic	2	0	0	0	0
Danny Gratton	2	0	0	0	12
Jodi Murphy	2	0	0	0	0
Serge Tkachenko (goalie)	2	0	0	0	0
Mike Fountain (goalie)	70	0	0	0	20
Brent Tully	1	0	0	0	0
Jason Fitzsimmons (goalie)	17	0	0	0	0

GOALTENDING

	Games	Min.	W	L	T	Goals	SO	Avg.
Mike Fountain	70	4006	34	28	6	241	4	3.61
Jason Fitzsimmons	17	709	2	8	0	49	0	4.15
Serge Tkachenko	2	125	0	1	1	9	0	4.32

HERSHEY BEARS

SCORING

	Games	G	A	Pts.	PIM
Mitch Lamoureux	80	45	60	105	92
Tim Tookey	66	32	57	89	43
Claude Vilgrain	76	30	53	83	45
Mike McHugh	80	27	43	70	58
Bob Wilkie	69	8	53	61	100
Corey Foster	66	21	37	58	96
Chris Winnes	70	29	21	50	20
Yanick Dupre	51	22	20	42	42
Vaclav Prospal	55	14	21	35	38
Milos Holan	27	7	22	29	16
Aris Brimanis	75	8	15	23	65
Denis Metlyuk	73	8	13	21	46
Clayton Norris	62	8	10	18	217
Tracy Egeland	57	7	11	18	266
Lance Pitlick	58	4	13	17	93
Toni Porkka	51	6	7	13	43
Andre Faust	13	6	7	13	10
Jim Cummins	17	6	6	12	70
Bob Woods	28	2	9	11	21
Terran Sandwith	62	3	5	8	169
Claude Boivin	4	1	6	7	6
Todd Hlushko	9	6	0	6	4
Scott Beattie	9	3	2	5	0
Dan Kordic	64	0	4	4	164
Eric Dandenault	14	2	1	3	49
Frederic Chabot (goalie)	28	0	3	3	4
Shawn Wheeler	8	1	1	2	22
Randy Skarda	4	0	2	2	0
Phil Soukoroff	4	0	2	2	0
Rob Leask	17	0	1	1	17
Cory Banika	2	0	0	0	2
Dave Lacouture	2	0	0	0	0
Yanick DeGrace (goalie)	3	0	0	0	0
Tommy Soderstrom (goalie)	9	0	0	0	2
Norm Foster (goalie)	17	0	0	0	0
Neil Little (goalie)	1	0	0	0	0
Chris Therien	6	0	0	0	2
Scott LaGrand (goalie)	40	0	0	0	4

GOALTENDING

	Games	Min.	W	L	T	Goals	SO	Avg.
Frederic Chabot	28	1464	13	5	6	63	2	2.58
Neil Little	1	19	0	0	0	1	0	3.23
Scott LaGrand	40	2033	16	13	3	117	2	3.45

	Games	Min.	W	L	T	Goals	SO	Avg.
Norm Foster	17	775	5	7	1	58	0	4.49
Tommy Soderstrom	9	462	3	4	1	37	0	4.81
Yanick DeGrace	3	98	1	0	0	11	0	6.74

MONCTON HAWKS

SCORING

	Games	G	A	Pts.	PIM
Ross Wilson	75	29	38	67	49
Harijs Vitolinsh	70	28	34	62	41
Craig Fisher	46	26	35	61	36
Andy Brickley	53	20	39	59	20
Rob Murray	69	25	32	57	280
John LeBlanc	41	25	26	51	38
Ken Gernander	71	22	25	47	12
Oleg Mikulchik	67	9	38	47	121
Dave Tomlinson	39	23	23	46	38
Arto Blomsten	44	6	27	33	25
Brian Straub	76	8	24	32	107
Dan Bylsma	50	12	16	28	25
Russ Romaniuk	18	16	8	24	24
Jan Kaminsky	33	9	13	22	6
Frank Kovacs	69	11	10	21	196
Todd Copeland	80	4	17	21	158
Milan Tichy	48	1	20	21	103
Wayne Doucet	54	10	9	19	174
Mike Muller	61	2	14	16	88
Darryl Shannon	37	1	10	11	62
Sergei Sorokin	11	2	8	10	4
Mark Visheau	48	4	5	9	58
Andrei Raisky	12	3	5	8	14
Kevin McClelland	39	3	5	8	233
John Fritsche	11	2	5	7	16
Derek Donald	7	4	1	5	0
Tony Wormiell	2	2	1	3	0
Michal Grosek	20	1	2	3	47
Mark Richards (goalie)	29	0	3	3	4
Larry Courville	8	2	0	2	37
Mike O'Neill (goalie)	12	0	1	1	0
Sean Gauthier (goalie)	13	0	1	1	0
Bryan Erickson	3	0	1	1	2
Brian Goudie	3	0	1	1	13
Stephane Beauregard (goalie)	37	0	1	1	12
Doug Smith	1	0	0	0	5
Todd Tretter	1	0	0	0	0
Denis LeBlanc	2	0	0	0	0
Joe Cook	3	0	0	0	0

GOALTENDING

	Games	Min.	W	L	T	Goals	SO	Avg.
Mike O'Neill	12	717	8	4	0	33	1	2.76
S. Beauregard	37	2083	18	11	6	121	1	3.49
Sean Gauthier	13	617	3	5	1	41	0	3.99
Mark Richards	29	1419	8	16	0	103	0	4.35

PORTLAND PIRATES

SCORING

	Games	G	A	Pts.	PIM
Jeff Nelson	80	34	73	107	92
Michel Picard	61	41	44	85	99
Randy Pearce	80	32	36	68	97
Kent Hulst	72	34	33	67	68
Chris Jensen	56	33	28	61	52
Mike Boback	68	16	43	59	50
Martin Jiranek	73	15	37	52	75
Todd Nelson	80	11	34	45	69
Jason Woolley	41	12	29	41	14
Steve Poapst	78	14	21	35	47
Kevin Kaminski	39	10	22	32	263
John Slaney	29	14	13	27	17
Chris Longo	69	6	19	25	69
Jeff Sirkka	76	6	18	24	113
Darren McAusland	61	6	16	22	17
Andrew Brunette	23	9	11	20	10

	Games	G	A	Pts.	PIM
Steve Konowalchuk	8	11	4	15	4
Kerry Clark	55	9	5	14	309
Keith Jones	6	5	7	12	4
Ken Klee	65	2	9	11	87
Eric Fenton	25	2	5	7	104
Brian Curran	46	1	6	7	247
Jim Mathieson	43	0	7	7	89
Pat Peake	4	0	5	5	2
Byron Dafoe (goalie)	47	0	5	5	4
Lorne Knauft	7	3	1	4	16
Kevin Kerr	4	2	0	2	2
Rick Tabaracci (goalie)	3	0	1	1	15
Dave Lacouture	4	0	1	1	0
Victor Gervais	3	0	1	1	0
Olaf Kolzig (goalie)	29	0	1	1	21
Todd Dutiaume	1	0	0	0	0
David Goverde (goalie)	1	0	0	0	0
Blair Atcheynum	2	0	0	0	0
Jason Gladney	2	0	0	0	0
Vince Guidotti	2	0	0	0	0
Mario Thyer	3	0	0	0	0
Enrico Ciccone	6	0	0	0	27
Mike Parson (goalie)	6	0	0	0	0
Ron Pascucci	6	0	0	0	20

GOALTENDING

	Games	Min.	W	L	T	Goals	SO	Avg.
Rick Tabaracci	3	177	3	0	0	8	0	2.72
Olaf Kolzig	29	1726	16	8	5	88	3	3.06
Mike Parson	6	212	0	2	1	11	0	3.12
Byron Dafoe	47	2662	24	16	4	148	1	3.34
David Goverde	1	60	0	1	0	4	0	4.01

PRINCE EDWARD ISLAND SENATORS

SCORING

	Games	G	A	Pts.	PIM
Robert Burakovsky	52	29	38	67	28
Greg Pankewicz	69	33	29	62	241
Andy Schneider	61	15	46	61	119
Jason Firth	61	15	46	61	66
Chad Penney	73	20	30	50	66
Pavol Demitra	41	18	23	41	8
Norm Batherson	67	14	23	37	85
Radek Hamr	69	10	26	36	44
Graeme Townshend	56	16	13	29	107
Claude Savoie	77	13	15	28	118
Dimitri Filimonov	48	10	16	26	14
Kent Paynter	63	6	20	26	125
Martin St. Amour	37	13	12	25	65
Jake Grimes	42	12	13	25	24
Andrew McBain	26	6	10	16	102
Craig Woodcroft	33	5	9	14	41
Jarmo Kekalainen	18	6	6	12	18
Hank Lammens	50	2	9	11	32
Francois Leroux	25	4	6	10	52
Chris Rowland	40	6	2	8	122
Carl Valimont	32	3	5	8	30
Barry McKinlay	17	2	5	7	6
Kevin MacDonald	40	2	4	6	245
Darcy Simon	45	1	5	6	263
Scott White	15	1	4	5	6
Randy Skarda	20	1	3	4	14
Alain Deeks	35	1	3	4	36
Darren Rumble	3	2	0	2	0
Jean Blouin	8	2	0	2	7
Mark LaForest (goalie)	43	0	2	2	38
Tony Cimellaro	19	1	0	1	30
Peter Allen	6	0	1	1	6
Brian Melanson	3	0	1	1	2
Pat Traverse	3	0	1	1	0
Patrick Charbonneau (goalie)	3	0	1	1	0
Mel Angelstad	1	0	0	0	5
Lennie MacAusland	1	0	0	0	2
Duane Dennis	2	0	0	0	0
Tomas Jelinek	2	0	0	0	0

	Games	G	A	Pts.	PIM
Daniel Guerard	3	0	0	0	17
Trent McCleary	4	0	0	0	6
Darrin Madeley (goalie)	6	0	0	0	0
J.F. Labbee (goalie)	7	0	0	0	0
Brad Treliving	7	0	0	0	14
Daniel Berthiaume (goalie)	30	0	0	0	2

GOALTENDING

	Games	Min.	W	L	T	Goals	SO	Avg.
J.F. Labbee	7	390	4	3	0	22	0	3.39
Patrick Charbonneau	3	180	2	1	0	11	0	3.67
Mark LaForest	43	2359	9	25	5	161	0	4.09
Daniel Berthiaume	30	1640	8	16	3	130	0	4.76
Darrin Madeley	6	270	0	4	0	26	0	5.77

PROVIDENCE BRUINS

SCORING

	Games	G	A	Pts.	PIM
Jon Morris	67	22	44	66	20
Sergei Zholtok	54	29	33	62	16
Ken Hammond	65	12	45	57	100
Dave Capuano	51	24	29	53	64
Grigori Panteleev	55	24	26	50	20
Tod Hartje	80	22	27	49	157
Fred Knipscheer	62	26	13	39	50
Andrew McKim	46	13	24	37	49
Dennis Holland	61	10	26	36	44
Jon Rohloff	55	12	23	35	59
Mark Major	61	17	9	26	176
Dmitri Kvartalnov	23	13	13	26	8
Dennis Smith	58	2	22	24	89
Denis Chervyakov	58	2	16	18	128
Jozef Stumpel	17	5	12	17	4
Jim Wiemer	35	5	12	17	81
John Carter	47	11	5	16	82
Darren Stolk	57	4	10	14	56
Jamie Huscroft	32	1	10	11	157
Howie Rosenblatt	19	6	4	10	59
Darren Banks	41	6	3	9	189
Jeff Lazaro	16	3	4	7	26
Mark Bavis	12	2	5	7	18
Brent Hughes	6	2	5	7	4
Bill Armstrong	66	0	7	7	200
Cam Stewart	14	3	2	5	5
Sergei Berdnikov	16	3	1	4	4
Roman Gorev	11	1	2	3	2
Mark Krys	23	1	2	3	32
Dan Marois	6	1	2	3	6
Mikhail Tatarinov	3	0	3	3	0
Martin St. Amour	12	0	3	3	22
Derek Eberle	17	0	3	3	20
Matt Robbins	9	1	1	2	6
David Littman (goalie)	25	0	2	2	2
Scott Lindsay	2	0	1	1	0
Scott Bailey (goalie)	7	0	1	1	0
Mike Bales (goalie)	33	0	1	1	8
John Blue (goalie)	24	0	1	1	41
Andrei Bashkirov	1	0	0	0	2
Joakim Persson (goalie)	1	0	0	0	0
Dominic Amodeo	3	0	0	0	2
Andrew Brunette	3	0	0	0	0
Scott Meehan	6	0	0	0	0
Kurt Seher	8	0	0	0	8

GOALTENDING

	Games	Min.	W	L	T	Goals	SO	Avg.
Joakim Persson	1	25	0	0	0	0	0	0.00
John Blue	24	1298	7	11	4	76	1	3.51
David Littman	25	1385	10	11	3	83	0	3.59
Scott Bailey	7	377	2	2	2	24	0	3.82
Mike Bales	33	1757	9	15	4	130	0	4.44

ROCHESTER AMERICANS

SCORING

	Games	G	A	Pts.	PIM
Todd Simon	55	33	52	85	79
Viktor Gordiouk	74	28	39	67	26
James Black	45	19	32	51	28
Doug Macdonald	63	25	19	44	46
Jason Young	68	17	26	43	84
Matthew Barnaby	42	10	32	42	153
Jody Gage	44	18	21	39	57
Mikhail Volkov	62	12	26	38	28
Jason Dawe	48	22	14	36	44
Brad Rubachuk	65	18	18	36	246
David Cooper	68	10	25	35	82
Philippe Boucher	31	10	22	32	51
Sergei Petrenko	38	16	15	31	8
Dean Melanson	80	1	21	22	138
Brett Marietti	38	6	14	20	63
Mark Krys	58	2	13	15	77
Mike Bavis	65	3	11	14	89
Scott Metcalfe	16	5	7	12	16
Sean O'Donnell	64	2	10	12	242
Denis Tsygurov	24	1	10	11	10
Derek Booth	45	2	8	10	82
Scott Thomas	11	4	5	9	0
Peter Ambroziak	22	3	4	7	53
Rick Lessard	8	1	2	3	2
Brad Pascall	35	2	0	2	33
Kelly Sorensen	4	1	0	1	4
Jim Maher	5	1	0	1	0
Chris Bright	9	1	0	1	6
Cory Banika	7	1	0	1	12
Richie Walcott	17	1	0	1	66
Rob Melanson	13	0	1	1	24
Markus Ketterer (goalie)	32	0	1	1	2
Alex Kuzminski	1	0	0	0	0
Dominic Maltais	1	0	0	0	0
Todd Flichel	2	0	0	0	0
Jamey Hicks	2	0	0	0	4
Davis Payne	2	0	0	0	5
John Young	2	0	0	0	0
Brian Blad	3	0	0	0	0
Mike Parson (goalie)	3	0	0	0	0
Grant Fuhr (goalie)	5	0	0	0	0
Christian Lalonde	5	0	0	0	6
Duane Derksen (goalie)	6	0	0	0	0
Greg Capson	10	0	0	0	29
Bill Pye (goalie)	19	0	0	0	16
Bill Horn (goalie)	25	0	0	0	0

GOALTENDING

	Games	Min.	W	L	T	Goals	SO	Avg.
Grant Fuhr	5	310	3	0	2	10	0	1.94
Bill Horn	25	1395	9	9	5	81	0	3.49
Duane Derksen	6	235	2	1	1	14	0	3.57
Markus Ketterer	32	1775	9	15	5	110	1	3.72
Mike Parson	3	176	1	2	0	12	0	4.10
Bill Pye	19	980	7	7	2	70	0	4.29

SAINT JOHN SAINTS

SCORING

	Games	G	A	Pts.	PIM
Mark Freer	77	33	53	86	45
Cory Stillman	79	35	48	83	52
Vesa Viitakoski	67	28	39	67	24
Mike Stevens	79	20	37	57	293
David St. Pierre	77	19	30	49	42
Kevin Wortman	72	17	32	49	32
Len Esau	75	12	36	48	129
David Struch	58	18	25	43	87
Dale Kushner	73	20	17	37	199
Niklas Sundblad	76	13	19	32	75
David Haas	37	11	17	28	108
Peter Ahola	66	9	19	28	59

	Games	G	A	Pts.	PIM
Todd Harkins	38	13	9	22	64
Guy Larose	15	11	11	22	20
Francois Groleau	73	8	14	22	49
Alex Nikolic	57	6	13	19	285
Kris Miller	58	2	17	19	38
Jamie O'Brien	52	6	11	17	41
Brad Miller	36	3	12	15	174
Wes Walz	15	6	6	12	14
Jeff Perry	42	8	3	11	97
Brad Schlegel	21	2	8	10	6
Scott Morrow	8	2	2	4	0
Jason Muzzatti (goalie)	51	0	4	4	24
Mike Sullivan	5	2	0	2	4
Gary Socha	3	0	1	1	0
Todd Baird (goalie)	1	0	0	0	0
Joel Bouchard	1	0	0	0	0
Scott Beattie	2	0	0	0	2
Kevin Dahl	2	0	0	0	0
Alan Leggett	3	0	0	0	5
Roland Melanson (goalie)	7	0	0	0	2
Andrei Trefilov (goalie)	28	0	0	0	22

GOALTENDING

	Games	Min.	W	L	T	Goals	SO	Avg.
Andrei Trefilov	28	1629	10	10	7	93	0	3.42
Jason Muzzatti	51	2939	26	21	3	183	2	3.74
Roland Melanson	7	270	1	2	0	20	0	4.44
Todd Baird	1	6	0	0	0	2	0	20.22

ST. JOHN'S MAPLE LEAFS

SCORING

	Games	G	A	Pts.	PIM
Rich Chernomaz	78	45	65	110	199
Yanic Perreault	62	45	60	105	38
Patrik Augusta	77	53	43	96	105
Chris Snell	75	22	74	96	92
Chris Govedaris	62	35	35	70	76
Ken McRae	65	23	41	64	200
Todd Gillingham	59	20	25	45	260
Grant Marshall	67	11	29	40	155
Eric Lacroix	59	17	22	39	69
Steffon Walby	63	15	22	37	79
Guy Larose	23	13	16	29	41
Dan Stiver	57	11	18	29	39
Alexi Kudashov	27	7	15	22	21
Paul Holden	75	6	14	20	101
Curtis Hunt	72	3	13	16	175
Drake Berehowsky	18	3	12	15	40
Ryan VandenBussche	44	4	10	14	124
Mark Greig	9	4	6	10	0
Frank Bialowas	69	2	8	10	352
Guy Lehoux	71	2	8	10	217
Andy Sullivan	16	3	6	9	4
Matt Mallgrave	15	2	4	6	16
Matt Martin	12	1	5	6	9
Darby Hendrickson	6	4	1	5	4
Thomas Kurcharcik	8	2	3	5	4
David Sacco	5	3	1	4	2
Terry Chitaroni	19	2	2	4	43
Marcel Cousineau (goalie)	37	0	4	4	6
David Harlock	10	0	3	3	2
Greg Walters	13	0	2	2	67
Jim Sprott	9	1	0	1	35
Olaf Kjenstad	7	1	0	1	2
Vince Guidotti	11	0	1	1	8
Bruce Racine (goalie)	37	0	1	1	6
Pat Jablonski (goalie)	16	0	1	1	0
Darren Colbourne	1	0	0	0	0
Rob McLean	1	0	0	0	5
Robin Bartel	2	0	0	0	0
Lou Crawford	3	0	0	0	0
Rob Butz	5	0	0	0	26

GOALTENDING

	Games	Min.	W	L	T	Goals	SO	Avg.
Pat Jablonski	16	963	12	3	1	49	1	3.05
Marcel Cousineau	37	2015	13	11	9	118	0	3.51
Bruce Racine	37	1875	20	9	2	116	0	3.71

SPRINGFIELD INDIANS

SCORING

	Games	G	A	Pts.	PIM
Mike Tomlak	79	44	56	100	53
Yvon Corriveau	71	42	39	81	53
Rob Cowie	78	17	57	74	124
Scott Humeniuk	71	15	42	57	91
Denis Chalifoux	44	14	38	52	24
Igor Chibirev	36	28	23	51	4
Kevin Smyth	42	22	27	49	72
Clayton Young	36	19	28	47	50
Blair Atcheynum	40	18	22	40	13
Jeff Bloemberg	78	8	28	36	36
Rick Bennett	67	9	19	28	82
Scott Morrow	30	12	15	27	28
Igor Alexandrov	69	10	16	26	37
Robert Petrovicky	30	16	8	24	39
Craig Lyons	46	7	14	21	16
Scott Daniels	52	9	11	20	185
Steve Yule	61	4	13	17	133
Trevor Stienburg	47	4	10	14	134
John Stevens	71	3	9	12	85
Mikael Nylander	4	0	9	9	0
Corey Beaulieu	69	0	8	8	257
Dan Stiver	9	1	6	7	0
Allen Pedersen	45	2	4	6	28
Mark Woolf	15	2	3	5	4
Mark Greig	4	0	4	4	21
Ryan VandenBussche	9	1	2	3	29
Todd Harkins	1	0	3	3	0
Jarrett Reid	6	2	0	2	2
Barry Nieckar	30	0	2	2	67
Danny Lorenz (goalie)	14	0	2	2	0
Dan Keczmer	7	0	1	1	4
Mike Lenarduzzi (goalie)	22	0	1	1	0
Frank Pietrangelo (goalie)	23	0	1	1	12
Matt DelGuidice (goalie)	1	0	0	0	0
Darryl Gilmour (goalie)	1	0	0	0	0
Martin Hamrlik	1	0	0	0	0
Mario Gosselin (goalie)	2	0	0	0	0
Jukka Suomalainen	2	0	0	0	6
Darren Perkins	3	0	0	0	2
Garth Premak	3	0	0	0	2
Alan Schuler	3	0	0	0	2
Steve Bogoyevac	4	0	0	0	2
Chris Bright	5	0	0	0	4
Bob McGill	5	0	0	0	24
George Maneluk (goalie)	31	0	0	0	2

GOALTENDING

	Games	Min.	W	L	T	Goals	SO	Avg.
Darryl Gilmour	1	59	0	0	1	2	0	2.04
Mario Gosselin	2	120	2	0	0	5	0	2.50
Matt DelGuidice	1	65	0	0	1	3	0	2.77
Frank Pietrangelo	23	1315	9	10	2	73	0	3.33
George Maneluk	31	1515	8	14	6	107	0	4.24
Danny Lorenz	14	802	5	7	1	59	0	4.42
Mike Lenarduzzi	22	984	5	7	2	73	0	4.45

PLAYERS WITH TWO OR MORE TEAMS

SCORING

	Games	G	A	Pts.	PIM
Blair Atcheynum, Portland	2	0	0	0	0
Blair Atcheynum, Springfield	40	18	22	40	13
Totals	42	18	22	40	13
Cory Banika, Hershey	2	0	0	0	2
Cory Banika, Rochester	7	1	0	1	12
Totals	9	1	0	1	14

	Games	G	A	Pts.	PIM
Mark Bavis, Providence	12	2	5	7	18
Mark Bavis, Fredericton	45	7	10	17	86
Totals	57	9	15	24	104
Scott Beattie, Saint John	2	0	0	0	2
Scott Beattie, Hershey	9	3	2	5	0
Totals	11	3	2	5	2
Daniel Berthiaume, P.E.I. (g)	30	0	0	0	2
Daniel Berthiaume, Ad. (g)	11	0	0	0	2
Totals	41	0	0	0	4
Chris Bright, Rochester	9	1	0	1	6
Chris Bright, Springfield	5	0	0	0	4
Totals	14	1	0	1	10
Andrew Brunette, Portland	23	9	11	20	10
Andrew Brunette, Providence	3	0	0	0	0
Totals	26	9	11	20	10
Dan Bylsma, Albany	3	0	1	1	2
Dan Bylsma, Moncton	50	12	16	28	25
Totals	53	12	17	29	27
Frederic Chabot, Fredericton (g)	3	0	0	0	0
Frederic Chabot, Hershey (g)	28	0	3	3	4
Totals	31	0	3	3	4
Matt DelGuidice, Albany (g)	5	0	0	0	0
Matt DelGuidice, Springfield (g)	1	0	0	0	0
Totals	6	0	0	0	0
Duane Derksen, Rochester (g)	6	0	0	0	0
Duane Derksen, Adirondack (g)	11	0	0	0	2
Totals	17	0	0	0	2
Craig Fisher, Cape Breton	16	5	5	10	11
Craig Fisher, Moncton	46	26	35	61	36
Totals	62	31	40	71	47
Dave Flanagan, Adirondack	18	2	2	4	19
Dave Flanagan, Fredericton	34	11	4	15	13
Totals	52	13	6	19	32
Mark Greig, Springfield	4	0	4	4	21
Mark Greig, St. John's	9	4	6	10	0
Totals	13	4	10	14	21
Vince Guidotti, Portland	2	0	0	0	0
Vince Guidotti, Rochester	20	2	8	10	8
Vince Guidotti, St. John's	11	0	1	1	8
Totals	33	2	9	11	16
Todd Harkins, Saint John	38	13	9	22	64
Todd Harkins, Springfield	1	0	3	3	0
Totals	39	13	12	25	64
Mark Krys, Providence	23	1	2	3	32
Mark Krys, Rochester	58	2	13	15	77
Totals	81	3	15	18	109
Dave Lacouture, Portland	4	0	1	1	0
Dave Lacouture, Springfield	1	0	0	0	0
Dave Lacouture, Hershey	2	0	0	0	0
Totals	7	0	1	1	0

	Games	G	A	Pts.	PIM
Guy Larose, St. John's	23	13	16	29	41
Guy Larose, Saint John	15	11	11	22	20
Totals	38	24	27	51	61
David Littman, Providence (g)	25	0	2	2	8
David Littman, Fredericton (g)	16	0	0	0	8
Totals	41	0	2	2	16
Roy Mitchell, Binghamton	11	1	3	4	18
Roy Mitchell, Albany	42	3	12	15	43
Totals	53	4	15	19	61
Scott Morrow, Springfield	30	12	15	27	28
Scott Morrow, Saint John	8	2	2	4	0
Totals	38	14	17	31	28
Mike Parson, Portland (g)	6	0	0	0	0
Mike Parson, Rochester (g)	3	0	0	0	0
Totals	9	0	0	0	0
Martin St. Amour, P.E.I.	37	13	12	25	65
Martin St. Amour, Providence	12	0	3	3	22
Totals	49	13	15	28	87
Randy Skarda, P.E.I.	20	1	3	4	14
Randy Skarda, Hershey	4	0	2	2	0
Totals	24	1	5	6	14
Dan Stiver, St. John's	57	11	18	29	39
Dan Stiver, Springfield	9	1	6	7	0
Totals	66	12	24	36	39
Ryan VandenBussche, St. John's	44	4	10	14	124
Ryan VandenBussche, Spr.	9	1	2	3	29
Totals	53	5	12	17	153
John Young, Rochester	2	0	0	0	0
John Young, Cornwall	2	1	0	1	0
Totals	4	1	0	1	0

GOALTENDING

	Games	Min.	W	L	T	Goals	SO	Avg.
D. Berthiaume, P.E.I.	30	1640	8	16	3	130	0	4.76
D. Berthiaume, Ad.	11	553	7	2	0	35	0	3.80
Totals	41	2193	15	18	3	165	0	4.51
F. Chabot, Fred.	3	143	0	1	1	12	0	5.03
F. Chabot, Her.	28	1464	13	5	6	63	2	2.58
Totals	31	1607	13	6	7	75	2	2.80
M. DelGuidice, Alb.	5	310	1	2	2	19	0	3.68
M. DelGuidice, Spr.	1	65	0	0	1	3	0	2.77
Totals	6	375	1	2	3	22	0	3.52
D. Derksen, Roch.	6	235	2	1	1	14	0	3.57
Duane Derksen, Ad.	11	600	4	6	0	37	0	3.70
Totals	17	835	6	7	1	51	0	3.66
David Littman, Prov.	25	1385	10	11	3	83	0	3.59
David Littman, Fred.	16	872	8	7	0	63	0	4.33
Totals	41	2258	18	18	3	146	0	3.88
Mike Parson, Port.	6	212	0	2	1	11	0	3.12
Mike Parson, Roch.	3	175	1	2	0	12	0	4.10
Totals	9	387	1	4	1	23	0	3.57

1994 CALDER CUP PLAYOFFS

RESULTS

DIVISION SEMIFINALS

Series "A"

	W	L	Pts.	GF	GA
St. John's	4	1	8	25	14
Cape Breton	1	4	2	14	25

(St. John's won series, 4-1)

Series "B"

	W	L	Pts.	GF	GA
Moncton	4	3	8	19	19
Saint John	3	4	6	19	19

(Moncton won series, 4-3)

Series "C"

	W	L	Pts.	GF	GA
Adirondack	4	2	8	25	22
Springfield	2	4	4	22	25

(Adirondack won series, 4-2)

Series "D"

	W	L	Pts.	GF	GA
Portland	4	1	8	22	11
Albany	1	4	2	11	22

(Portland won series, 4-1)

Series "E"

	W	L	Pts.	GF	GA
Hershey	4	0	8	18	11
Rochester	0	4	0	11	18

(Hershey won series, 4-0)

Series "F"

	W	L	Pts.	GF	GA
Cornwall	4	0	8	20	13
Hamilton	0	4	0	13	20

(Cornwall won series, 4-0)

DIVISION FINALS

Series "G"

	W	L	Pts.	GF	GA
Moncton	4	2	8	22	19
St. John's	2	4	4	19	22

(Moncton won series, 4-2)

Series "H"

	W	L	Pts.	GF	GA
Portland	4	2	8	20	20
Adirondack	2	4	4	20	20

(Portland won series, 4-2)

Series "J"

	W	L	Pts.	GF	GA
Cornwall	4	3	8	22	20
Hershey	3	4	8	20	22

(Cornwall won series, 4-3)

LEAGUE SEMIFINALS

Series "K"

	W	L	Pts.	GF	GA
Moncton	2	0	4	9	3
Cornwall	0	2	0	3	9

(Moncton won series, 2-0)

FINALS—FOR THE CALDER CUP

Series "L"

	W	L	Pts.	GF	GA
Portland	4	2	8	17	16
Moncton	2	4	4	16	17

(Portland won series, 4-2)

INDIVIDUAL LEADERS

Goals: Yanic Perreault, St. John's (12)
Assists: Andy Brickley, Moncton (19)
Points: Mike Boback, Portland (27)
Andy Brickley, Moncton (27)
Penalty minutes: Kevin Kaminski, Portland (91)
Goaltending average: Olaf Kolzig, Portland (2.55)
Shutouts: Stephane Beauregard, Moncton (2)

TOP SCORERS

	Games	G	A	Pts.
Mike Boback, Portland	17	10	17	27
Andy Brickley, Moncton	19	8	19	27
Craig Fisher, Moncton	21	11	11	22
Michel Picard, Portland	17	11	10	21
Ross Wilson, Moncton	21	10	9	19
Yanic Perreault, St. John's	11	12	6	18
Chris Jensen, Portland	16	6	10	16
Rich Chernomaz, St. John's	11	5	11	16
Steve Maltais, Adirondack	12	5	11	16
Chris Snell, St. John's	11	1	15	16

INDIVIDUAL STATISTICS

ADIRONDACK RED WINGS

(Lost division finals to Portland, 4-2)

SCORING

	Games	G	A	Pts.	PIM
Steve Maltais	12	5	11	16	14
Joe Frederick	12	11	4	15	22
Jason York	12	3	11	14	22
Michael Maurice	12	7	6	13	4
Tim Taylor	12	2	10	12	12
Mark Pederson	12	4	7	11	10
Aaron Ward	9	2	6	8	6
Mike Casselman	12	2	4	6	10
Brett Harkins	10	1	5	6	4
Craig Martin	12	2	2	4	63
Gord Kruppke	12	1	3	4	32
Greg Johnson	4	0	4	4	2
Lev Berdichevsky	7	2	1	3	4
Bob Boughner	10	1	1	2	18
Martin Lapointe	4	1	1	2	8
Barry Potomski	11	1	1	2	44
Alex Hicks	5	0	2	2	2
Dmitri Motkov	8	0	2	2	23
Chris Bergeron	1	0	0	0	0
Jason MacDonald	1	0	0	0	0
Dave Lemay	2	0	0	0	0
Kevin Hodson (goalie)	3	0	0	0	0
Daniel Berthiaume (goalie)	11	0	0	0	0
Jamie Pushor	12	0	0	0	22

GOALTENDING

	Games	Min.	W	L	T	Goals	SO	Avg.
Daniel Berthiaume	11	632	6	4	0	30	0	2.85
Kevin Hodson	3	89	0	2	0	10	0	6.77

ALBANY RIVER RATS

(Lost division semifinals to Portland, 4-1)

SCORING

	Games	G	A	Pts.	PIM
Ben Hankinson	5	3	1	4	6
Scott Pellerin	5	2	1	3	11
Jeff Christian	5	1	2	3	19
Brian Rolston	5	1	2	3	0
David Emma	5	1	2	3	8
Cale Hulse	5	0	3	3	11
Brian Sullivan	5	1	1	2	18
Reid Simpson	5	1	1	2	18
Jason Miller	5	1	1	2	4
Kevin Dean	5	0	2	2	7
Pascal Rheaume	5	0	1	1	0
Matt Ruchty	5	0	1	1	18
Mike Bodnarchuk	2	0	0	0	2
Roy Mitchell	3	0	0	0	0
Bryan Helmer	5	0	0	0	9
Geordie Kinnear	5	0	0	0	21
Dean Malkoc	5	0	0	0	21
Corey Schwab (goalie)	5	0	0	0	0

GOALTENDING

	Games	Min.	W	L	T	Goals	SO	Avg.
Corey Schwab	5	298	1	4	0	20	0	4.02

CAPE BRETON OILERS

(Lost division semifinals to St. John's, 4-1)

SCORING

	Games	G	A	Pts.	PIM
Brent Grieve	4	2	4	6	16
Peter White	5	2	3	5	2
Roman Oksiuta	4	2	2	4	22

	Games	G	A	Pts.	PIM
Darcy Martini	5	1	3	4	26
Ralph Intranuovo	4	1	2	3	2
Ian Herbers	5	0	3	3	12
Tyler Wright	5	2	0	2	11
Alexander Kerch	4	1	1	2	2
Todd Marchant	5	1	1	2	0
Jim Nesich	5	1	1	2	10
Josef Cierny	4	1	1	2	4
Gord Mark	5	0	2	2	6
Scott Allison	3	0	1	1	2
Martin Bakula	4	0	1	1	0
Greg DeVries	1	0	0	0	0
Serge Roberge	1	0	0	0	0
Andrew Verner (goalie)	1	0	0	0	0
Brad Zavisha	2	0	0	0	2
Dennis Bonvie	4	0	0	0	11
Wayne Cowley (goalie)	5	0	0	0	10
John Van Kessel	5	0	0	0	12
Terry Virtue	5	0	0	0	17

GOALTENDING

	Games	Min.	W	L	T	Goals	SO	Avg.
Wayne Cowley	5	258	1	4	0	20	0	4.66
Andrew Verner	1	40	0	0	0	4	0	6.00

CORNWALL ACES

(Lost league semifinals to Moncton, 2-0)

SCORING

	Games	G	A	Pts.	PIM
Chris Lindberg	13	11	3	14	10
Paul Willett	13	2	10	12	0
Brad Werenka	12	2	10	12	22
Dwayne Norris	13	7	4	11	17
Mike Hurlbut	13	3	7	10	12
Rene Corbet	13	7	2	9	18
Eric Veilleux	13	1	7	8	20
Ryan Hughes	13	2	4	6	6
Todd Warriner	10	1	4	5	4
Martin Simard	7	3	1	4	7
Dave Karpa	12	2	2	4	27
Ed Ward	12	1	3	4	14
Sean Whyte	9	1	2	3	2
Jon Klemm	13	1	2	3	6
Mike McKee	10	0	3	3	4
Brad Turner	4	1	1	2	4
Alain Cote	11	0	2	2	11
Aaron Miller	13	0	2	2	10
Paul Brousseau	1	0	0	0	0
Mark Matier	3	0	0	0	4
Garth Snow (goalie)	13	0	0	0	14

GOALTENDING

	Games	Min.	W	L	T	Goals	SO	Avg.
Garth Snow	13	790	8	5	0	42	0	3.19

HAMILTON CANUCKS

(Lost division semifinals to Cornwall, 4-0)

SCORING

	Games	G	A	Pts.	PIM
Stephane Morin	4	3	2	5	4
Neil Eisenhut	4	1	4	5	0
Dan Kesa	4	1	4	5	4
Dane Jackson	4	2	2	4	16
Jay Mazur	4	2	2	4	4
Adrian Aucoin	4	0	2	2	6
John Namestnikov	4	0	2	2	19
Daryl Filipek	1	1	0	1	0
Brent Tully	1	1	0	1	0
Cam Danyluk	2	1	0	1	0
Phil Von Stefenelli	4	1	0	1	2
Jassen Cullimore	3	0	1	1	2
John Badduke	4	0	1	1	18
Scott Walker	4	0	1	1	25

	Games	G	A	Pts.	PIM
Jason Fitzsimmons (goalie)	2	0	0	0	0
Rob Woodward	2	0	0	0	0
Mike Fountain (goalie)	3	0	0	0	0
Libor Polasek	3	0	0	0	0
Brian Loney	4	0	0	0	8
Dan Ratushny	4	0	0	0	4
Doug Torrel	4	0	0	0	2

GOALTENDING

	Games	Min.	W	L	T	Goals	SO	Avg.
Jason Fitzsimmons	2	98	0	2	0	6	0	3.67
Mike Fountain	3	146	0	2	0	12	0	4.92

HERSHEY BEARS

(Lost division finals to Cornwall, 4-3)

SCORING

	Games	G	A	Pts.	PIM
Tim Tookey	11	4	9	13	8
Mike McHugh	11	9	3	12	14
Andre Faust	10	4	3	7	26
Mitch Lamoureux	11	3	4	7	26
Corey Foster	9	2	5	7	10
Claude Vilgrain	11	1	6	7	2
Denis Metlyuk	11	4	2	6	4
Bob Woods	11	2	4	6	8
Aris Brimanis	11	2	3	5	12
Bob Wilkie	9	1	4	5	8
Chris Winnes	7	1	3	4	0
Yanick Dupre	8	1	3	4	2
Todd Hlushko	6	2	1	3	4
Dan Kordic	11	0	3	3	26
Clayton Norris	10	1	0	1	18
Lance Pitlick	11	1	0	1	11
Terran Sandwith	2	0	1	1	4
Toni Porkka	10	0	1	1	8
Vaclav Prospal	2	0	0	0	2
Tracy Egeland	4	0	0	0	2
Frederic Chabot (goalie)	11	0	0	0	2

GOALTENDING

	Games	Min.	W	L	T	Goals	SO	Avg.
Frederic Chabot	11	665	7	4	0	32	0	2.89

MONCTON HAWKS

(Lost league finals to Portland, 4-2)

SCORING

	Games	G	A	Pts.	PIM
Andy Brickley	19	8	19	27	4
Craig Fisher	21	11	11	22	28
Ross Wilson	21	10	9	19	18
Arto Blomsten	20	4	10	14	8
Dave Tomlinson	20	6	6	12	24
Oleg Mikulchik	21	2	10	12	18
Brian Straub	20	1	9	10	25
John LeBlanc	20	3	6	9	6
Russ Romaniuk	17	2	6	8	30
Darryl Shannon	20	1	7	8	32
Ken Gernander	19	6	1	7	0
Dan Bylsma	21	3	4	7	31
Milan Tichy	20	3	3	6	12
Rob Murray	21	2	3	5	60
Larry Courville	10	2	2	4	27
Harijs Vitolinsh	20	1	3	4	4
Wayne Doucet	3	1	0	1	14
Joe Cook	1	0	1	1	0
Todd Copeland	19	0	1	1	54
Kevin McClelland	1	0	0	0	2
Mark Richards (goalie)	1	0	0	0	0
Michal Grosek	2	0	0	0	0
Stephane Beauregard (goalie)	21	0	0	0	28

GOALTENDING

	Games	Min.	W	L	T	Goals	SO	Avg.
Mark Richards	1	9	0	0	0	0	0	0.00
S. Beauregard	21	1305	12	9	0	57	2	2.62

PORTLAND PIRATES

(Winner of 1994 Turner Cup playoffs)

SCORING

	Games	G	A	Pts.	PIM
Mike Boback	17	10	17	27	4
Michel Picard	17	11	10	21	22
Chris Jensen	16	6	10	16	22
Jeff Nelson	17	10	5	15	20
Kent Hulst	17	4	6	10	14
Kevin Kaminski	16	4	5	9	91
Jeff Sirkka	15	2	6	8	47
Martin Jiranek	13	2	4	6	2
Chris Longo	17	2	4	6	11
Todd Nelson	11	0	6	6	6
Randy Pearce	17	1	4	5	36
Lorne Knauft	7	2	2	4	14
Jason Woolley	9	2	2	4	4
Jason Allison	6	2	1	3	0
Ken Klee	17	1	2	3	14
Kevin Kerr	8	0	3	3	21
Steve Poapst	12	0	3	3	8
Andrew Brunette	2	0	1	1	0
Jim Mathieson	12	0	1	1	36
Brian Curran	15	0	1	1	59
Byron Dafoe (goalie)	1	0	0	0	0
Jason Gladney	2	0	0	0	0
Sergei Gonchar	2	0	0	0	0
Darren McAusland	2	0	0	0	0
Kerry Clark	5	0	0	0	26
Olaf Kolzig (goalie)	17	0	0	0	2

GOALTENDING

	Games	Min.	W	L	T	Goals	SO	Avg.
Olaf Kolzig	17	1035	12	5	0	44	0	2.55
Byron Dafoe	1	9	0	0	0	1	0	6.79

ROCHESTER AMERICANS

(Lost division semifinals to Hershey, 4-0)

SCORING

	Games	G	A	Pts.	PIM
James Black	4	2	3	5	0
Jason Young	4	2	2	4	8
Viktor Gordiouk	4	3	0	3	2
Brad Rubachuk	4	1	1	2	10
David Cooper	4	1	1	2	8
Doug Macdonald	3	0	2	2	0
Davis Payne	4	0	2	2	2
Mikhail Volkov	4	0	2	2	2
Scott Metcalfe	4	1	0	1	31
Denis Tsygurov	1	0	1	1	0
Mike Bavis	2	0	1	1	0
Len Barrie	3	0	1	1	0
Mark Krys	4	0	1	1	6
Dean Melanson	4	0	1	1	2
Sean O'Donnell	4	0	1	1	21
Greg Capson	1	0	0	0	2
Bill Horn (goalie)	1	0	0	0	0
Cory Banika	3	0	0	0	0
Brad Pascall	3	0	0	0	0
Markus Ketterer (goalie)	4	0	0	0	0
Rick Lessard	4	0	0	0	2

GOALTENDING

	Games	Min.	W	L	T	Goals	SO	Avg.
Markus Ketterer	4	199	0	3	0	13	0	3.92
Bill Horn	1	42	0	1	0	5	0	7.13

SAINT JOHN FLAMES

(Lost division semifinals to Moncton, 4-3)

SCORING

	Games	G	A	Pts.	PIM
Mark Freer	7	2	4	6	16
Cory Stillman	7	2	4	6	16
Kevin Wortman	7	1	5	6	16
Guy Larose	7	3	2	5	22
Len Esau	7	2	2	4	6
Mike Stevens	6	1	3	4	34
Dale Kushner	7	2	1	3	28
Scott Morrow	7	2	1	3	10
Vesa Viitakoski	5	1	2	3	2
Peter Ahola	6	1	2	3	12
Niklas Sundblad	4	1	1	2	2
David St. Pierre	5	0	2	2	0
Brad Miller	6	1	0	1	21
David Struch	7	0	1	1	4
Francois Groleau	7	0	1	1	2
Brad Schlegel	7	0	1	1	6
Joel Bouchard	2	0	0	0	0
Jamie O'Brien	4	0	0	0	0
Jeff Perry	4	0	0	0	4
Jason Muzzatti (goalie)	7	0	0	0	0

GOALTENDING

	Games	Min.	W	L	T	Goals	SO	Avg.
Jason Muzzatti	7	415	3	4	0	19	0	2.75

ST. JOHN'S MAPLE LEAFS

(Lost division finals to Moncton, 4-2)

SCORING

	Games	G	A	Pts.	PIM
Yanic Perreault	11	12	6	18	14
Rich Chernomaz	11	5	11	16	18
Chris Snell	11	1	15	16	10
Patrik Augusta	11	4	8	12	4
Chris Govedaris	11	6	5	11	22
Eric Lacroix	11	5	3	8	6
Thomas Kurcharcik	10	3	4	7	2
Mark Greig	11	4	2	6	26
Matt Martin	11	1	5	6	33
Grant Marshall	11	1	5	6	17
Paul Holden	11	0	4	4	18
Frank Bialowas	7	0	3	3	25
Darby Hendrickson	3	1	1	2	0
Guy Lehoux	9	1	1	2	8
Todd Gillingham	10	0	2	2	12
Steffon Walby	2	0	0	0	2
Curtis Hunt	6	0	0	0	16
Brandon Convery	1	0	0	0	0
Bruce Racine (goalie)	1	0	0	0	0
Janne Gronvall	9	0	0	0	2
David Harlock	9	0	0	0	6
Pat Jablonski (goalie)	11	0	0	0	0

GOALTENDING

	Games	Min.	W	L	T	Goals	SO	Avg.
Bruce Racine	1	20	0	0	0	0	0	0.00
Pat Jablonski	11	676	6	5	0	36	0	3.19

SPRINGFIELD INDIANS

(Lost division semifinals to Adirondack, 4-2)

SCORING

	Games	G	A	Pts.	PIM
Yvon Corriveau	6	7	3	10	20
Kevin Smyth	6	4	5	9	0
Rob Cowie	6	3	6	9	4
Mike Tomlak	4	2	5	7	4
Clayton Young	6	5	0	5	26
Steve Yule	5	0	4	4	8
Scott Humeniuk	6	0	3	3	8
Jeff Bloemberg	6	0	3	3	8

	Games	G	A	Pts.	PIM
Robert Petrovicky	4	0	2	2	4
Blair Atcheynum	6	0	2	2	0
Rick Bennett	6	1	0	1	31
Frank Pietrangelo (goalie)	6	0	1	1	2
Dan Stiver	6	0	1	1	2
Darren Perkins	3	0	1	1	4
Scott Daniels	6	0	1	1	53
Allen Pedersen	3	0	1	1	6
Bob Woods	1	0	0	0	0
Corey Beaulieu	3	0	0	0	12
John Stevens	3	0	0	0	0

	Games	G	A	Pts.	PIM
Ryan VandenBussche	5	0	0	0	16
Danny Lorenz (goalie)	2	0	0	0	0
Igor Alexandrov	1	0	0	0	0
Mark Woolf	2	0	0	0	0
Craig Lyons	2	0	0	0	0

GOALTENDING

	Games	Min.	W	L	T	Goals	SO	Avg.
Danny Lorenz	2	35	0	0	0	0	0	0.00
Frank Pietrangelo	6	324	2	4	0	23	0	4.26

1993-94 AWARD WINNERS

ALL-STAR TEAMS

First team	Pos.	Second team
Byron Dafoe, Portland	G	Mike Fountain, Hamilton
Chris Snell, St. John's	D	Rob Cowie, Springfield
Jason York, Adirondack	D	Bob Wilkie, Hershey
Tim Taylor, Adirondack	C	Stephane Morin, Hamilton
Mark Pederson, Ad.	LW	Michel Picard, Portland
Rich Chernomaz, St. John's	RW	Patrik Augusta, St. John's

TROPHY WINNERS

John B. Sollenberger Trophy: Tim Taylor, Adirondack
Les Cunningham Plaque: Rich Chernomaz, St. John's
Harry (Hap) Holmes Memorial Trophy: Byron Dafoe, Portland
Olaf Kolzig, Portland
Dudley (Red) Garrett Memorial Trophy: Rene Corbet, Cornwall
Eddie Shore Plaque: Chris Snell, St. John's
Fred Hunt Memorial Award: Jim Nesich, Cape Breton
Louis A.R. Pieri Memorial Award: Barry Trotz, Portland
Baz Bastien Trophy: Frederic Chabot, Hershey
Jack Butterfield Trophy: Olaf Kolzig, Portland

ALL-TIME AWARD WINNERS

JOHN B. SOLLENBERGER TROPHY

(Leading scorer)

Season	Player, Team
1936-37	Jack Markle, Syracuse
1937-38	Jack Markle, Syracuse
1938-39	Don Deacon, Pittsburgh
1939-40	Norm Locking, Syracuse
1940-41	Les Cunningham, Cleveland
1941-42	Pete Kelly, Springfield
1942-43	Wally Kilrea, Hershy
1943-44	Tommy Burlington, Cleveland
1944-45	Bob Gracie, Pittsburgh
	Bob Walton, Pittsburgh
1945-46	Les Douglas, Indianapolis
1946-47	Phil Hergesheimer, Philadelphia
1947-48	Carl Liscombe, Providence
1948-49	Sid Smith, Pittsburgh
1949-50	Les Douglas, Cleveland
1950-51	Ab DeMarco, Buffalo
1951-52	Ray Powell, Providence
1952-53	Eddie Olson, Cleveland
1953-54	George Sullivan, Hershey
1954-55	Eddie Olson, Cleveland
1955-56	Zellio Toppazzini, Providence
1956-57	Fred Glover, Cleveland
1957-58	Willie Marshall, Hershey
1958-59	Bill Hicke, Rochester
1959-60	Fred Glover, Cleveland
1960-61	Bill Sweeney, Springfield
1961-62	Bill Sweeney, Springfield
1962-63	Bill Sweeney, Springfield
1963-64	Gerry Ehman, Rochester
1964-65	Art Stratton, Buffalo
1965-66	Dick Gamble, Rochester
1966-67	Gordon Labossiere, Quebec
1967-68	Simon Nolet, Quebec
1968-69	Jeannot Gilbert, Hershey
1969-70	Jude Drouin, Montreal
1970-71	Fred Speck, Baltimore
1971-72	Don Blackburn, Providence
1972-73	Yvon Lambert, Nova Scotia
1973-74	Steve West, New Haven
1974-75	Doug Gibson, Rochester

Season	Player, Team
1975-76	Jean-Guy Gratton, Hershey
1976-77	Andre Peloffy, Springfield
1977-78	Gord Brooks, Philadelphia
	Rick Adduono, Rochester
1978-79	Bernie Johnston, Maine
1979-80	Norm Dube, Nova Scotia
1980-81	Mark Lofthouse, Hershey
1981-82	Mike Kasczyki, New Brunswick
1982-83	Ross Yates, Binghamton
1983-84	Claude Larose, Sherbrooke
1984-85	Paul Gardner, Binghamton
1985-86	Paul Gardner, Rochester
1986-87	Tim Tookey, Hershey
1987-88	Bruce Boudreau, Springfield
1988-89	Stephan Lebeau, Sherbrooke
1989-90	Paul Ysebaert, Utica
1990-91	Kevin Todd, Utica
1991-92	Shaun Van Allen, Cape Breton
1992-93	Don Biggs, Binghamton
1993-94	Tim Taylor, Adirondack

LES CUNNINGHAM PLAQUE

(Most Valuable Player)

Season	Player, Team
1947-48	Carl Liscombe, Providence
1948-49	Carl Liscombe, Providence
1949-50	Les Douglas, Cleveland
1950-51	Ab DeMarco, Buffalo
1951-52	Ray Powell, Providence
1952-53	Eddie Olson, Cleveland
1953-54	George "Red" Sullivan, Hershey
1954-55	Ross Lowe, Springfield
1955-56	Johnny Bower, Providence
1956-57	Johnny Bower, Providence
1957-58	Johnny Bower, Cleveland
1958-59	Bill Hicke, Rochester
	Rudy Migay, Rochester
1959-60	Fred Glover, Cleveland
1960-61	Phil Maloney, Buffalo
1961-62	Fred Glover, Cleveland
1962-63	Denis DeJordy, Buffalo
1963-64	Fred Glover, Cleveland

Season	Player, Team
1964-65	Art Stratton, Buffalo
1965-66	Dick Gamble, Rochester
1966-67	Mike Nykoluk, Hershey
1967-68	Dave Creighton, Providence
1968-69	Gilles Villemure, Buffalo
1969-70	Gilles Villemure, Buffalo
1970-71	Fred Speck, Baltimore
1971-72	Garry Peters, Boston
1972-73	Billy Inglis, Cincinnati
1973-74	Art Stratton, Rochester
1974-75	Doug Gibson, Rochester
1975-76	Ron Andruff, Nova Scotia
1976-77	Doug Gibson, Rochester
1977-78	Blake Dunlop, Maine
1978-79	Rocky Saganiuk, New Brunswick
1979-80	Norm Dube, Nova Scotia
1980-81	Pelle Lindbergh, Maine
1981-82	Mike Kasczyki, New Brunswick
1982-83	Ross Yates, Binghamton
1983-84	Mal Davis, Rochester
	Garry Lariviere, St. Catharines
1984-85	Paul Gardner, Binghamton
1985-86	Paul Gardner, Rochester
1986-87	Tim Tookey, Hershey
1987-88	Jody Gage, Rochester
1988-89	Stephan Lebeau, Sherbrooke
1989-90	Paul Ysebaert, Utica
1990-91	Kevin Todd, Utica
1991-92	John Anderson, Hew Haven
1992-93	Don Biggs, Binghamton
1993-94	Rich Chernomaz, St. John's

HARRY (HAP) HOLMES MEMORIAL TROPHY

(Outstanding goaltender)

Season	Player, Team
1936-37	Bert Gardiner, Philadelphia
1937-38	Frank Brimsek, Providence
1938-39	Alfie Moore, Hershey
1939-40	Moe Roberts, Cleveland
1940-41	Chuck Rayner, Springfield
1941-42	Bill Beveridge, Cleveland
1942-43	Gordie Bell, Buffalo
1943-44	Nick Damore, Hershey
1944-45	Yves Nadon, Buffalo
1945-46	Connie Dion, St. Louis-Buffalo
1946-47	Baz Bastien, Pittsburgh
1947-48	Baz Bastien, Pittsburgh
1948-49	Baz Bastien, Pittsburgh
1949-50	Gil Mayer, Pittsburgh
1950-51	Gil Mayer, Pittsburgh
1951-52	Johnny Bower, Cleveland
1952-53	Gil Mayer, Pittsburgh
1953-54	Jacques Plante, Buffalo
1954-55	Gil Mayer, Pittsburgh
1955-56	Gil Mayer, Pittsburgh
1956-57	Johnny Bower, Providence
1957-58	Johnny Bower, Cleveland
1958-59	Bob Perreault, Hershey
1959-60	Ed Chadwick, Rochester
1960-61	Marcel Paille, Springfield
1961-62	Marcel Paille, Springfield
1962-63	Denis DeJordy, Buffalo
1963-64	Roger Crozier, Pittsburgh
1964-65	Gerry Cheevers, Rochester
1965-66	Les Binkley, Cleveland
1966-67	Andre Gill, Hershey
1967-68	Bob Perreault, Rochester
1968-69	Gilles Villemure, Buffalo
1969-70	Gilles Villemure, Buffalo
1970-71	Gary Kurt, Cleveland
1971-72	Dan Bouchard, Boston
	Ross Brooks, Boston
1972-73	Michel Larocque, Nova Scotia
1973-74	Jim Shaw, Nova Scotia
	Dave Elenbaas, Nova Scotia

Season	Player, Team
1974-75	Ed Walsh, Nova Scotia
	Dave Elenbaas, Nova Scotia
1975-76	Dave Elenbaas, Nova Scotia
	Ed Walsh, Nova Scotia
1976-77	Ed Walsh, Nova Scotia
	Dave Elenbaas, Nova Scotia
1977-78	Bob Holland, Nova Scotia
	Maurice Barrette, Nova Scotia
1978-79	Pete Peeters, Maine
	Robbie Moore, Maine
1979-80	Rick St. Croix, Maine
	Robbie Moore, Maine
1980-81	Pelle Lindbergh, Maine
	Robbie Moore, Maine
1981-82	Bob Janecyk, New Brunswick
	Warren Skorodenski, New Brunswick
1982-83	Brian Ford, Fredericton
	Clint Malarchuk, Fredericton
1983-84	Brian Ford, Fredericton
1984-85	Jon Casey, Baltimore
1985-86	Sam St. Laurent, Maine
	Karl Friesen, Maine
1986-87	Vincent Riendeau, Sherbrooke
1987-88	Vincent Riendeau, Sherbrooke
	Jocelyn Perreault, Sherbrooke
1988-89	Randy Exelby, Sherbrooke
	Francois Gravel, Sherbrooke
1989-90	Jean Claude Bergeron, Sherbrooke
	Andre Racicot, Sherbrooke
1990-91	David Littman, Rochester
	Darcy Wakaluk, Rochester
1991-92	David Littman, Rochester
1992-93	Corey Hirsch, Binghamton
	Boris Rousson, Binghamton
1993-94	Byron Dafoe, Portland
	Olaf Kolzig, Portland

Beginning with the 1983-84 season, the award goes to the top goaltending team with each goaltender having played a minimum of 25 games for the team with the fewest goals against.

DUDLEY (RED) GARRETT MEMORIAL TROPHY

(Top rookie)

Season	Player, Team
1947-48	Bob Solinger, Cleveland
1948-49	Terry Sawchuk, Indianapolis
1949-50	Paul Meger, Buffalo
1950-51	Wally Hergesheimer, Cleveland
1951-52	Earl "Dutch" Reibel, Indianapolis
1952-53	Guyle Fielder, St. Louis
1953-54	Don Marshall, Buffalo
1954-55	Jimmy Anderson, Springfield
1955-56	Bruce Cline, Providence
1956-57	Boris "Bo" Elik, Cleveland
1957-58	Bill Sweeney, Providence
1958-59	Bill Hicke, Rochester
1959-60	Stan Baluik, Providence
1960-61	Ronald "Chico" Maki, Buffalo
1961-62	Les Binkley, Cleveland
1962-63	Doug Robinson, Buffalo
1963-64	Roger Crozier, Pittsburgh
1964-65	Ray Cullen, Buffalo
1965-66	Mike Walton, Rochester
1966-67	Bob Rivard, Quebec
1967-68	Gerry Desjardins, Cleveland
1968-69	Ron Ward, Rochester
1969-70	Jude Drouin, Montreal
1970-71	Fred Speck, Baltimore
1971-72	Terry Caffery, Cleveland
1972-73	Ron Anderson, Boston
1973-74	Rick Middleton, Providence
1974-75	Jerry Holland, Providence
1975-76	Greg Holst, Providence
	Pierre Mondou, Nova Scotia

Season	Player, Team
1976-77	Rod Schutt, Nova Scotia
1977-78	Norm Dupont, Nova Scotia
1978-79	Mike Meeker, Binghamton
1979-80	Darryl Sutter, New Brunswick
1980-81	Pelle Lindbergh, Maine
1981-82	Bob Sullivan, Binghamton
1982-83	Mitch Lamoureux, Baltimore
1983-84	Claude Verret, Rochester
1984-85	Steve Thomas, St. Catharines
1985-86	Ron Hextall, Hershey
1986-87	Brett Hull, Moncton
1987-88	Mike Richard, Binghamton
1988-89	Stephan Lebeau, Sherbrooke
1989-90	Donald Audette, Rochester
1990-91	Patrick Lebeau, Fredericton
1991-92	Felix Potvin, St. John's
1992-93	Corey Hirsch, Binghamton
1993-94	Rene Corbet, Cornwall

EDDIE SHORE PLAQUE

(Outstanding defenseman)

Season	Player, Team
1958-59	Steve Kraftcheck, Rochester
1959-60	Larry Hillman, Providence
1960-61	Bob McCord, Springfield
1961-62	Kent Douglas, Springfield
1962-63	Marc Reaume, Hershey
1963-64	Ted Harris, Cleveland
1964-65	Al Arbour, Rochester
1965-66	Jim Morrison, Quebec
1966-67	Bob McCord, Pittsburgh
1967-68	Bill Needham, Cleveland
1968-69	Bob Blackburn, Buffalo
1969-70	Noel Price, Springfield
1970-71	Marshall Johnston, Cleveland
1971-72	Noel Price, Nova Scotia
1972-73	Ray McKay, Cincinnati
1973-74	Gordon Smith, Springfield
1974-75	Joe Zanussi, Providence
1975-76	Noel Price, Nova Scotia
1976-77	Brian Engblom, Nova Scotia
1977-78	Terry Murray, Maine
1978-79	Terry Murray, Maine
1979-80	Rick Vasko, Adirondack
1980-81	Craig Levie, Nova Scotia
1981-82	Dave Farrish, New Brunswick
1982-83	Greg Tebbutt, Baltimore
1983-84	Garry Lariviere, St. Catharines
1984-85	Richie Dunn, Binghamton
1985-86	Jim Wiemer, New Haven
1986-87	Brad Shaw, Binghamton
1987-88	Dave Fenyves, Hershey
1988-89	Dave Fenyves, Hershey
1989-90	Eric Weinrich, Utica
1990-91	Norm Maciver, Cape Breton
1991-92	Greg Hawgood, Cape Breton
1992-93	Bobby Dollas, Adirondack
1993-94	Chris Snell, St. John's

FRED HUNT MEMORIAL AWARD

(Sportsmanship, determination and dedication)

Season	Player, Team
1977-78	Blake Dunlop, Maine
1978-79	Bernie Johnston, Maine
1979-80	Norm Dube, Nova Scotia
1980-81	Tony Cassolato, Hershey
1981-82	Mike Kasczyki, New Brunswick
1982-83	Ross Yates, Binghamton
1983-84	Claude Larose, Sherbrooke
1984-85	Paul Gardner, Binghamton
1985-86	Steve Tsujiura, Maine
1986-87	Glenn Merkosky, Adirondack

Season	Player, Team
1987-88	Bruce Boudreau, Springfield
1988-89	Murray Eaves, Adirondack
1989-90	Murray Eaves, Adirondack
1990-91	Glenn Merkosky, Adirondack
1991-92	John Anderson, New Haven
1992-93	Tim Tookey, Hershey
1993-94	Jim Nesich, Cape Breton

LOUIS A.R. PIERI MEMORIAL AWARD

(Top coach)

Season	Coach, Team
1967-68	Vic Stasiuk, Quebec
1968-69	Frank Mathers, Hershey
1969-70	Fred Shero, Buffalo
1970-71	Terry Reardon, Baltimore
1971-72	Al MacNeil, Nova Scotia
1972-73	Floyd Smith, Cincinnati
1973-74	Don Cherry, Rochester
1974-75	John Muckler, Providence
1975-76	Chuck Hamilton, Hershey
1976-77	Al MacNeil, Nova Scotia
1977-78	Bob McCammon, Maine
1978-79	Parker MacDonald, New Haven
1979-80	Doug Gibson, Hershey
1980-81	Bob McCammon, Maine
1981-82	Orval Tessier, New Brunswick
1982-83	Jacques Demers, Fredericton
1983-84	Gene Ubriaco, Baltimore
1984-85	Bill Dineen, Adirondack
1985-86	Bill Dineen, Adirondack
1986-87	Larry Pleau, Binghamton
1987-88	John Paddock, Hershey
	Mike Milbury, Maine
1988-89	Tom McVie, Utica
1989-90	Jimmy Roberts, Springfield
1990-91	Don Lever, Rochester
1991-92	Doug Carpenter, New Haven
1992-93	Marc Crawford, St. John's
1993-94	Barry Trotz, Portland

BAZ BASTIEN TROPHY

(Coaches pick as top goaltender)

Season	Player, Team
1983-84	Brian Ford, Fredericton
1984-85	Jon Casey, Baltimore
1985-86	Sam St. Laurent, Maine
1986-87	Mark Laforest, Adirondack
1987-88	Wendell Young, Hershey
1988-89	Randy Exelby, Sherbrooke
1989-90	Jean Claude Bergeron, Sherbrooke
1990-91	Mark Laforest, Binghamton
1991-92	Felix Potvin, St. John's
1992-93	Corey Hirsch, Binghamton
1993-94	Frederic Chabot, Hershey

JACK BUTTERFIELD TROPHY

(Calder Cup playoff MVP)

Season	Player, Team
1983-84	Bud Stefanski, Maine
1984-85	Brian Skrudland, Sherbrooke
1985-86	Tim Tookey, Hershey
1986-87	Dave Fenyves, Rochester
1987-88	Wendell Young, Hershey
1988-89	Sam St. Laurent, Adirondack
1989-90	Jeff Hackett, Springfield
1990-91	Kay Whitmore, Springfield
1991-92	Allan Bester, Adirondack
1992-93	Bill McDougall, Cape Breton
1993-94	Olaf Kolzig, Portland

ALL-TIME LEAGUE CHAMPIONS

Season	Regular-Season Champion Team	Coach	Playoff Champion Team	Coach
1936-37	E—Philadelphia	Herb Gardiner	Syracuse	Eddie Powers
	W—Syracuse	Eddie Powers		
1937-38	E—Providence	Bun Cook	Providence	Bun Cook
	W—Cleveland	Bill Cook		
1938-39	E—Philadelphia	Herb Gardiner	Cleveland	Bill Cook
	W—Hershey	Herb Mitchell		
1939-40	E—Providence	Bun Cook	Providence	Bun Cook
	W—Indianapolis	Herb Lewis		
1940-41	E—Providence	Bun Cook	Cleveland	Bill Cook
	W—Cleveland	Bill Cook		
1941-42	E—Springfield	Johnny Mitchell	Indianapolis	Herb Lewis
	W—Indianapolis	Herb Lewis		
1942-43	—Hershey	Cooney Weiland	Buffalo	Art Chapman
1943-44	E—Hershey	Cooney Weiland	Buffalo	Art Chapman
	W—Cleveland	Bun Cook		
1944-45	E—Buffalo	Art Chapman	Cleveland	Bun Cook
	W—Cleveland	Bun Cook		
1945-46	E—Buffalo	Frank Beisler	Buffalo	Frank Beisler
	W—Indianapolis	Earl Seibert		
1946-47	E—Hershey	Don Penniston	Hershey	Don Penniston
	W—Cleveland	Bun Cook		
1947-48	E—Providence	Terry Reardon	Cleveland	Bun Cook
	W—Cleveland	Bun Cook		
1948-49	E—Providence	Terry Reardon	Providence	Terry Reardon
	W—St. Louis	Ebbie Goodfellow		
1949-50	E—Buffalo	Roy Goldsworthy	Indianapolis	Ott Heller
	W—Cleveland	Bun Cook		
1950-51	E—Buffalo	Roy Goldsworthy	Cleveland	Bun Cook
	W—Cleveland	Bun Cook		
1951-52	E—Hershey	John Crawford	Pittsburgh	King Clancy
	W—Pittsburgh	King Clancy		
1952-53	—Cleveland	Bun Cook	Cleveland	Bun Cook
1953-54	—Buffalo	Frank Eddolls	Cleveland	Bun Cook
1954-55	—Pittsburgh	Howie Meeker	Pittsburgh	Howie Meeker
1955-56	—Providence	John Crawford	Providence	John Crawford
1956-57	—Providence	John Crawford	Cleveland	Jack Gordon
1957-58	—Hershey	Frank Mathers	Hershey	Frank Mathers
1958-59	—Buffalo	Bobby Kirk	Hershey	Frank Mathers
1959-60	—Springfield	Pat Egan	Springfield	Pat Egan
1960-61	—Springfield	Pat Egan	Springfield	Pat Egan
1961-62	E—Springfield	Pat Egan	Springfield	Pat Egan
	W—Cleveland	Jack Gordon		
1962-63	E—Providence	Fern Flaman	Buffalo	Billy Reay
	W—Buffalo	Billy Reay		
1963-64	E—Quebec	Floyd Curry	Cleveland	Fred Glover
	W—Pittsburgh	Vic Stasiuk		
1964-65	E—Quebec	Bernie Geoffrion	Rochester	Joe Crozier
	W—Rochester	Joe Crozier		
1965-66	E—Quebec	Bernie Geoffrion	Rochester	Joe Crozier
	W—Rochester	Joe Crozier		
1966-67	E—Hershey	Frank Mathers	Pittsburgh	Baz Bastien
	W—Pittsburgh	Baz Bastien		
1967-68	E—Hershey	Frank Mathers	Rochester	Joe Crozier
	W—Rochester	Joe Crozier		
1968-69	E—Hershey	Frank Mathers	Hershey	Frank Mathers
	W—Buffalo	Fred Shero		
1969-70	E—Montreal	Al MacNeil	Buffalo	Fred Shero
	W—Buffalo	Fred Shero		
1970-71	E—Providence	Larry Wilson	Springfield	John Wilson
	W—Baltimore	Terry Reardon		
1971-72	E—Boston	Armond Guidolin	Nova Scotia	Al MacNeil
	W—Baltimore	Terry Reardon		
1972-73	E—Nova Scotia	Al MacNeil	Cincinnati	Floyd Smith
	W—Cincinnati	Floyd Smith		
1973-74	N—Rochester	Don Cherry	Hershey	Chuck Hamilton
	S—Baltimore	Terry Reardon		
1974-75	N—Providence	John Muckler	Springfield	Ron Stewart
	S—Virginia	Doug Barkley		
1975-76	N—Nova Scotia	Al MacNeil	Nova Scotia	Al MacNeil
	S—Hershey	Chuck Hamilton		
1976-77	—Nova Scotia	Al MacNeil	Nova Scotia	Al MacNeil
1977-78	N—Maine	Bob McCammon	Maine	Bob McCammon
	S—Rochester	Duane Rupp		
1978-79	N—Maine	Bob McCammon	Maine	Bob McCammon
	S—New Haven	Parker MacDonald		
1979-80	N—New Brunswick	Joe Crozier-Lou Angotti	Hershey	Doug Gibson
	S—New Haven	Parker MacDonald		

REGULAR-SEASON CHAMPION

PLAYOFF CHAMPION

Season	Team	Coach	Team	Coach
1980-81	N—Maine	Bob McCammon	Adirondack	Tom Webster-J.P. LeBlanc
	S—Hershey	Bryan Murray		
1981-82	N—New Brunswick	Orval Tessier	New Brunswick	Orval Tessier
	S—Binghamton	Larry Kish		
1982-83	N—Fredericton	Jacques Demers	Rochester	Mike Keenan
	S—Rochester	Mike Keenan		
1983-84	N—Fredericton	Earl Jessiman	Maine	John Paddock
	S—Baltimore	Gene Ubriaco		
1984-85	N—Maine	Tom McVie-John Paddock	Sherbrooke	Pierre Creamer
	S—Binghamton	Larry Pleau		
1985-86	N—Adirondack	Bill Dineen	Adirondack	Bill Dineen
	S—Hershey	John Paddock		
1986-87	N—Sherbrooke	Pierre Creamer	Rochester	John Van Boxmeer
	S—Rochester	John Van Boxmeer*		
1987-88	N—Maine	Mike Milbury	Hershey	John Paddock
	S—Hershey	John Paddock		
1988-89	N—Sherbrooke	Jean Hamel	Adirondack	Bill Dineen
	S—Adirondack	Bill Dineen		
1989-90	N—Sherbrooke	Jean Hamel	Springfield	Jimmy Roberts
	S—Rochester	John Van Boxmeer		
1990-91	N—Springfield	Jimmy Roberts	Springfield	Jimmy Roberts
	S—Rochester	Don Lever		
1991-92	N—Springfield	Jay Leach	Adirondack	Barry Melrose
	S—Binghamton	Ron Smith		
	A—Fredericton	Paulin Bordeleau		
1992-93	N—Providence	Mike O'Connell	Cape Breton	George Burnett
	S—Binghamton	Ron Smith-Colin Campbell		
	A—St. John's	Marc Crawford		
1993-94	N—Adirondack	Newell Brown	Portland	Barry Trotz
	S—Hershey	Jay Leach		
	A—St. John's	Marc Crawford		

*Rochester awarded division championship based on season-series record.

INTERNATIONAL HOCKEY LEAGUE

LEAGUE OFFICE

Commissioner
Robert P. Ufer
Chairman of the board of governors
Russel A. Parker
Senior V.P. of hockey operations
N. Thomas Berry Jr.
Director of operations
Michael A. Meyers
Consultants
N.R. (Bud) Poile
Jack Riley

Vice president of marketing
Greg Elliott
Vice president of communications
Tim Bryant
Business office address
505 N. Woodward Ave., Suite 1500
Bloomfield Hills, MI 48304
Phone
810-258-0580
FAX
810-540-0884

Hockey operations address
3850 Priority Way, Suite 100
Indianapolis, IN 46240
Phone
317-573-3888
FAX
317-573-3880

TEAMS

ATLANTA KNIGHTS

General manager
Joe Bucchino
Coach
John Paris Jr.
Home ice
Omni Coliseum
Address
100 Techwood Drive
Atlanta, GA 30303
Seating capacity
14,919
Phone
404-525-5800
FAX
404-525-0044

CHICAGO WOLVES

General manager
Grant Mulvey
Head coach
To be announced
Home ice
Rosemont Horizon
Address
10550 Lunt Avenue
Rosemont, IL 60018
Seating capacity
17,000
Phone
708-390-0404
FAX
708-390-9792

CINCINNATI CYCLONES

General manager
Doug Kirchhofer
Head coach
To be announced
Home ice
Cincinnati Gardens
Address
2250 Seymour Avenue
Cincinnati, OH 45212
Seating capacity
10,326
Phone
513-531-7825

FAX
513-531-0209

CLEVELAND LUMBERJACKS

General manager
Larry Gordon
Coach
Rick Paterson
Home ice
Gateway Arena
Address
One Center Ice
200 Huron Road
Cleveland, OH 44113
Seating capacity
20,750
Phone
216-696-0909
FAX
616-696-3909

DENVER GRIZZLIES

General manager
David Elmore
Head coach
Butch Goring
Home ice
McNichols Sports Arena
Address
1635 Clay Street
Denver, CO 80204
Seating capacity
16,210
Phone
303-592-7825
FAX
303-592-7171

DETROIT VIPERS

General manager and head coach
Rick Dudley
Home ice
The Palace of Auburn Hills
Address
2 Championship Drive
Auburn Hills, MI 48326

Seating capacity
20,500
Phone
810-377-0100
FAX
810-377-2695

FORT WAYNE KOMETS

General manager
David Franke
Head coach
Bruce Boudreau
Home ice
War Memorial Coliseum
Address
4000 Parnell
Fort Wayne, IN 46805
Seating capacity
8,103
Phone
219-483-0011
FAX
219-483-3899

HOUSTON AEROS

General manager
Peter Dineen
Head coach
Terry Ruskowski
Home ice
The Summit
Address
24 Greenway Plaza, Suite 800
Houston, TX 77046
Seating capacity
15,242
Phone
713-621-2842
FAX
713-627-0397

INDIANAPOLIS ICE

General manager
Ray Compton
Coach
Duane Sutter

Home ice
Market Square Arena
Address
1202 East 38th Street
Indianapolis, IN 46205
Seating capacity
15,837
Phone
317-924-1234
FAX
317-924-1248

KALAMAZOO WINGS

General manager
Bill Inglis
Coach
Ken Hitchcock
Home ice
Wings Stadium
Address
3620 Van Rick Drive
Kalamazoo, MI 49002
Seating capacity
5,113
Phone
616-349-9772
FAX
616-345-6584

KANSAS CITY BLADES

Vice president and general manager
Doug Soetaert
Coach
Jim Wiley
Home ice
Kemper Arena
Address
1800 Genessee
Kansas City, MO 64102
Seating capacity
15,373
Phone
816-842-5233
FAX
816-842-5610

LAS VEGAS THUNDER

General manager
Bob Strumm

Head coach
Bob Strumm
Home ice
Thomas & Mack Center
Address
4505 S. Maryland Parkway
Las Vegas, NV 89170
Phone
702-798-7825
FAX
702-798-9464

MILWAUKEE ADMIRALS

General manager
Phil Wittliff
Head coach
Phil Wittliff
Home ice
Bradley Center
Address
1001 North Fourth Street
Milwaukee, WI 53203
Seating capacity
18,394
Phone
414-227-0550
FAX
414-227-0568

MINNESOTA MOOSE

Vice president of business operations
Ron Minegar
Head coach
Frank Serratore
Home ice
St. Paul Civic Center
Address
28 W. Sixth Street
St. Paul, MN 55102
Seating capacity
15,594
Phone
612-292-3333
FAX
612-221-0292

PEORIA RIVERMEN

General manager
Denis Cyr

Coach
Paul MacLean
Home ice
Peoria Civic Center
Address
201 S.W. Jefferson
Peoria, IL 61602
Seating capacity
9,479
Phone
309-676-1040
FAX
309-676-2488

PHOENIX ROADRUNNERS

General manager
Adam Keller
Coach
Rob Laird
Home ice
Veterans Coliseum
Address
1826 West McDowell Road
Phoenix, AZ 85007
Seating capacity
13,749
Phone
602-340-0001
FAX
602-340-0041

SAN DIEGO GULLS

General manager
Don Waddell
Coach
Walt Kyle
Home ice
San Diego Sports Arena
Address
3780 Hancock Street
Suite "G"
San Diego, CA 92110
Seating capacity
13,100
Phone
619-688-1800
FAX
619-688-1808

1993-94 REGULAR SEASON

FINAL STANDINGS

EASTERN CONFERENCE

ATLANTIC DIVISION

Team	G	W	L	Pts.	GF	GA
Kalamazoo	81	48	26 (7)	103	337	297
Fort Wayne	81	41	29 (11)	93	347	297
Cleveland	81	31	36 (14)	76	278	344

CENTRAL DIVISION

Team	G	W	L	Pts.	GF	GA
Peoria	81	51	24 (6)	108	327	294
Cincinnati	81	49	23 (9)	107	336	282
Indianapolis	81	28	46 (7)	63	257	329

WESTERN CONFERENCE

MIDWEST DIVISION

Team	G	W	L	Pts.	GF	GA
Atlanta	81	45	22 (14)	104	321	282
Milwaukee	81	40	24 (17)	97	338	302
Kansas City	81	40	31 (10)	90	326	327
Russian Penguins	13	2	9 (2)	6	35	64

PACIFIC DIVISION

Team	G	W	L	Pts.	GF	GA
Las Vegas	81	52	18 (11)	115	319	282
San Diego	81	42	28 (11)	95	311	302
Phoenix	81	40	36 (5)	85	313	309
Salt Lake	81	24	52 (5)	53	243	377

( )—Indicates overtime losses and are worth one point.

INDIVIDUAL LEADERS

Goals: Ken Quinney, Las Vegas (55)
Assists: Rob Brown, Kalamazoo (113)
Points: Rob Brown, Kalamazoo (155)
Penalty minutes: Jason Simon, Salt Lake (323)
Goaltending average: Geoff Sarjeant, Peoria (2.45)
Shutouts: Troy Gamble, Kalamazoo (2)
       Pokey Reddick, Cincinnati (2)
       Chris Rogles, Indianapolis (2)
       Geoff Sarjeant, Peoria (2)
       Peter Sidorkiewicz, Fort Wayne (2)

	Games	G	A	Pts.
Ken Quinney, Las Vegas	79	55	53	108
Brian Dobbin, Milwaukee	81	48	53	101
Jock Callander, Cleveland	81	31	70	101
Marc Fortier, Phoenix	81	39	61	100
Colin Chin, Fort Wayne	81	36	64	100
Dave Michayluk, Cleveland	81	48	51	99
Patrice Lefebvre, Las Vegas	76	31	67	98
Steve Larouche, Atlanta	80	43	53	96
Chris Tancill, Kalamazoo	60	41	54	95
Sylvain Couturier, Milwaukee	80	41	51	92
Kip Miller, Kansas City	71	38	54	92
Lonnie Loach, San Diego	74	42	49	91
Doug Evans, Peoria	76	27	63	90
Patrick Lebeau, Cincinnati	74	47	42	89
Don Biggs, Cincinnati	80	30	59	89
Radek Bonk, Las Vegas	76	42	45	87

TOP SCORERS

	Games	G	A	Pts.
Rob Brown, Kalamazoo	79	42	113	155
Len Barrie, Cincinnati	77	45	71	116
Stan Drulia, Atlanta	79	54	60	114

INDIVIDUAL STATISTICS

ATLANTA KNIGHTS

SCORING

	Games	G	A	Pts.	PIM
Stan Drulia	79	54	60	114	70
Steve Larouche	80	43	53	96	73
Jeff Madill	80	42	44	86	186
Devin Edgerton	64	17	42	59	27
Jason Ruff	71	24	25	49	122
Bill McDougall	48	17	30	47	141
Colin Miller	80	13	32	45	48
Brent Gretzky	54	17	23	40	30
Eric DuBois	80	13	26	39	174
Shawn Rivers	76	6	30	36	88
Jeff Buchanan	76	5	24	29	253
Eric Charron	66	5	18	23	144
Marc Tardif	65	9	13	22	154
Martin Tanguay	58	7	15	22	28
Larry DePalma	21	10	10	20	109
Cory Cross	70	4	14	18	72
Christian Campeau	65	8	9	17	74
Tim Bergland	19	6	7	13	6
Normand Rochefort	65	5	7	12	43
Chris LiPuma	42	2	10	12	254
Jim Cummins	7	4	5	9	14
Bryan Fogarty	8	1	5	6	4
J.C. Bergeron (goalie)	48	0	4	4	19
Mike Greenlay (goalie)	34	0	3	3	11
Nicholas Vachon	3	1	1	2	0
Timothy Chase	1	1	0	1	0
Scott Gordon (goalie)	5	0	1	1	0
Brantt Myhres	2	0	0	0	17
Wendell Young (goalie)	2	0	0	0	2
Steve Flomenhoft	4	0	0	0	0
Scott Boston	7	0	0	0	2

GOALTENDING

	Games	Min.	W	L	OTL	Goals	SO	Avg.
Wendell Young	2	120	2	0	0	6	0	3.00
J.C. Bergeron	48	2755	27	11	7	141	0	3.07
Scott Gordon	5	233	0	1	3	13	0	3.34
Mike Greenlay	34	1741	16	10	4	104	0	3.58

CINCINNATI CYCLONES

SCORING

	Games	G	A	Pts.	PIM
Len Barrie	77	45	71	116	246
Patrick Lebeau	74	47	42	89	90
Don Biggs	80	30	59	89	128
Doug Barrault	75	36	28	64	59
Daniel Gauthier	74	30	34	64	101
Stephane J.G. Richer	66	9	55	64	80

	Games	G	A	Pts.	PIM
Gord Hynes	80	15	43	58	50
Paul Lawless	71	30	27	57	112
Chris Cichocki	69	22	20	42	101
Ian Kidd	79	8	30	38	93
Jamie Leach	74	15	19	34	64
Jeff Greenlaw	55	14	15	29	85
Jeff Serowik	79	6	21	27	98
Dallas Eakins	80	1	18	19	143
Jaroslav Nedved	44	2	10	12	89
Brad Smyth	30	7	3	10	54
Rick Hayward	61	2	6	8	302
Jason Cirone	26	4	2	6	61
Jamie Linden	47	1	5	6	55
Darcy Norton	9	2	3	5	4
Marc LaBelle	37	2	1	3	133
Ray LeBlanc (goalie)	34	0	2	2	4
Pokey Reddick (goalie)	54	0	2	2	0
Chris Armstrong	1	0	0	0	0
Joe Flanagan	1	0	0	0	0
David Craievich	3	0	0	0	0
Sandy Galuppo (goalie)	4	0	0	0	0

GOALTENDING

	Games	Min.	W	L	OTL	Goals	SO	Avg.
Pokey Reddick	54	2894	31	12	6	147	2	3.05
Ray LeBlanc	34	1779	17	9	3	104	1	3.51
Sandy Galuppo	4	170	1	2	0	16	0	5.62

CLEVELAND LUMBERJACKS

SCORING

	Games	G	A	Pts.	PIM
Jock Callander	81	31	70	101	126
Dave Michayluk	81	48	51	99	92
Ed Patterson	55	21	32	53	73
Greg Andrusak	69	13	26	39	109
Ladislav Karabin	58	13	26	39	48
Todd Hawkins	76	19	14	33	115
Leonid Toropchenko	59	13	20	33	36
Victor Gervais	37	16	16	32	18
Patrick Neaton	71	8	24	32	78
Perry Ganchar	63	14	17	31	48
Jamie Black	71	12	16	28	36
Mike Dagenais	65	8	18	26	120
Jamie Heward	73	8	16	24	72
Justin Duberman	59	9	13	22	63
Ian Moran	33	5	13	18	39
Travis Thiessen	74	2	13	15	75
Steve Bancroft	33	2	12	14	58
Mark Karpen	17	6	5	11	0
Grant Block	48	5	6	11	24
Paul Dyck	60	1	10	11	57

	Games	G	A	Pts.	PIM
Petr Sykora	13	4	5	9	8
Mike Needham	6	4	3	7	7
Markus Naslund	5	1	6	7	4
Larry DePalma	9	4	1	5	49
George Zajankala	18	2	1	3	32
Chris Tamer	53	1	2	3	160
Rob Dopson (goalie)	32	0	3	3	4
Olie Sundstrom (goalie)	46	0	3	3	33
Greg Hagen	5	0	2	2	2
Roberto Romano (goalie)	11	0	0	0	0

GOALTENDING

	Games	Min.	W	L	OTL	Goals	SO	Avg.
Rob Dopson	32	1681	9	10	8	109	0	3.89
Olie Sundstrom	46	2521	20	19	4	172	0	4.09
Roberto Romano	11	642	2	7	2	45	1	4.20

FORT WAYNE KOMETS

SCORING

	Games	G	A	Pts.	PIM
Colin Chin	81	36	64	100	71
John Purves	69	38	48	86	29
Kelly Hurd	75	35	49	84	52
Lee Davidson	74	25	42	67	32
Vladimir Tsyplakov	63	31	32	63	51
Mitch Messier	69	33	27	60	77
Doug Wickenheiser	73	22	37	59	22
Dave Smith	65	22	22	44	196
Dan Lambert	62	10	27	37	138
Max Middendorf	36	16	20	36	43
Darin Smith	42	21	14	35	53
Guy Dupuis	73	9	26	35	70
Brian McKee	54	9	24	33	62
Ian Boyce	55	12	16	28	26
Igor Malykhin	61	2	20	22	63
Grant Richison	59	3	17	20	50
David Tretowicz	72	3	12	15	30
Carey Lucyk	64	1	13	14	61
Joel Savage	31	2	11	13	29
Steve Fletcher	47	4	6	10	277
Shayne Stevenson	22	3	5	8	116
Dave Gagnon (goalie)	19	0	3	3	2
Darryl Gilmore (goalie)	28	0	3	3	4
Mike O'Neill (goalie)	11	0	2	2	0
Kevin MacDonald	32	0	2	2	156
Phil Crowe	5	0	1	1	26
Mark Deazeley	1	0	0	0	2
Joe Hawley	2	0	0	0	2
Kord Cernich	3	0	0	0	4
Brett Seguin	6	0	0	0	4
Peter Sidorkiewicz (goalie)	11	0	0	0	0
Sean Gauthier (goalie)	22	0	0	0	8

GOALTENDING

	Games	Min.	W	L	OTL	Goals	SO	Avg.
Peter Sidorkiewicz	11	591	6	3	0	27	2	2.74
Dave Gagnon	19	1026	7	6	3	58	0	3.39
Sean Gauthier	22	1139	9	9	3	66	0	3.48
Darryl Gilmour	28	1439	15	7	2	85	0	3.54
Mike O'Neill	11	642	4	4	3	38	0	3.55

INDIANAPOLIS ICE

SCORING

	Games	G	A	Pts.	PIM
Rob Cimetta	79	26	54	80	178
Yves Heroux	74	28	30	58	113
Shawn Byram	77	23	24	47	170
Sergei Krivokrasov	53	19	26	45	145
Steve Dubinsky	54	15	25	40	63
Hugo Belanger	75	23	15	38	8
Karl Dykhuis	73	7	25	32	132
Kevin St. Jacques	49	5	23	28	91

	Games	G	A	Pts.	PIM
Rob Conn	51	16	11	27	46
Dave Christian	40	8	18	26	6
Zac Boyer	54	13	12	25	67
Jeff Ricciardi	75	3	20	23	307
Ivan Droppa	55	9	10	19	71
Bob Kellogg	68	6	13	19	63
Bobby House	42	10	8	18	51
Mike Speer	64	7	11	18	146
Dave Hakstol	79	5	12	17	150
Jeff Shantz	19	5	9	14	20
Keith Carney	28	0	14	14	20
Tony Horacek	29	6	7	13	63
Dino Grossi	58	6	1	7	39
Troy Murray	8	3	3	6	12
Kerry Toporowski	32	1	4	5	126
Joe Crowley	34	1	3	4	17
Dan Gravelle	9	1	1	2	0
Alexander Andrijevski	4	0	1	1	2
Christian Soucy (goalie)	46	0	1	1	4
Chris Rogles (goalie)	44	0	1	1	4
Roch Belley (goalie)	1	0	0	0	0
Ray LeBlanc (goalie)	2	0	0	0	0

GOALTENDING

	Games	Min.	W	L	OTL	Goals	SO	Avg.
Chris Rogles	44	2421	14	20	6	147	2	3.64
Christian Soucy	46	2302	14	25	1	159	1	4.14
Ray LeBlanc	2	112	0	1	0	8	0	4.25
Roch Belley	1	2	0	0	0	1	0	29.51

KALAMAZOO WINGS

SCORING

	Games	G	A	Pts.	PIM
Rob Brown	79	42	113	155	188
Chris Tancill	60	41	54	95	55
Derrick Smith	77	44	37	81	90
Jarkko Varvio	58	29	16	45	18
Tommy Sjodin	38	12	32	44	22
Jason Herter	68	14	28	42	92
Mike Kennedy	63	20	18	38	42
Mark Lawrence	64	17	20	37	90
Alexander Andrijevski	57	6	22	28	58
Scott Gruhl	30	15	12	27	85
Cal McGowan	49	9	18	27	48
Neil Brady	43	10	16	26	188
Richard Matvichuk	43	8	17	25	84
Glenn Mulvenna	55	13	9	22	18
Brad Berry	45	3	19	22	91
Collin Bauer	66	3	19	22	56
Mark Osiecki	65	4	14	18	45
Herb Raglan	29	6	11	17	112
Rob Robinson	67	3	12	15	32
Ken Priestlay	25	9	5	14	34
Jeff Bes	30	2	12	14	30
Travis Richards	19	2	10	12	20
Mike Reier	16	2	5	7	29
Dave Barr	4	3	2	5	5
Trent Klatt	6	3	2	5	4
Pat Murray	17	2	3	5	6
Jay Caufield	45	2	3	5	176
Roy Mitchell	13	0	4	4	21
Troy Gamble (goalie)	48	0	4	4	6
Joel Savage	4	2	1	3	0
Yves Heroux	3	0	2	2	4
Paul Jerrard	24	0	2	2	60
Craig Bonner	20	0	2	2	49
Mike Torchia (goalie)	43	0	1	1	4
Phil Huber	1	0	0	0	0
Jeff Stolp (goalie)	1	0	0	0	0
Jeff Levy (goalie)	2	0	0	0	0
Steve Lingren	2	0	0	0	0
John Brill	3	0	0	0	0
Steve Wilson	3	0	0	0	2
Reid Simpson	5	0	0	0	16

GOALTENDING

	Games	Min.	W	L	OTL	Goals	SO	Avg.
Jeff Stolp	1	8	0	0	0	0	0	0.00
Troy Gamble	48	2607	25	13	5	146	2	3.36
Mike Torchia	43	2168	23	12	2	133	0	3.68
Jeff Levy	2	59	0	1	0	4	0	4.06

KANSAS CITY BLADES

SCORING

	Games	G	A	Pts.	PIM
Kip Miller	71	38	54	92	51
Gary Emmons	63	20	49	69	28
David Bruce	72	40	24	64	115
Mikhail Kravets	63	14	44	58	171
Jeff McLean	69	27	30	57	44
Jaroslav Otevrel	62	20	33	53	46
Ed Courtenay	62	27	21	48	60
Andrei Nazarov	71	15	18	33	64
J.F. Quintin	41	14	19	33	117
Alex Cherbayev	43	17	15	32	100
Duane Joyce	43	9	23	32	40
Victor Ignatjev	67	1	24	25	123
Claudio Scremin	38	7	17	24	39
Mark Beaufait	21	12	9	21	18
Dody Wood	48	5	15	20	320
Andrei Buschan	60	5	13	18	68
Michal Sykora	47	5	11	16	30
Lee Leslie	43	8	7	15	21
Vlastimil Kroupa	39	3	12	15	12
Joe Cleary	20	1	11	12	20
Mike Colman	77	4	7	11	215
Fredrick Nilsson	13	2	7	9	2
Sean Gorman	56	2	6	8	54
Guy Gosselin	19	1	6	7	2
Mike Sullivan	6	3	3	6	0
Dale Craigwell	5	3	1	4	0
Tom Pederson	7	3	1	4	0
Stephan Tepper	23	1	3	4	52
Wade Flaherty (goalie)	60	0	4	4	16
Bryan Fogarty	3	2	1	3	2
Jon Morris	3	0	3	3	2
Mario Doyon	5	0	3	3	0
Troy Frederick	21	0	3	3	55
Mike Rathje	6	0	2	2	0
Jayson More	2	1	0	1	25
Dan Ryder (goalie)	3	0	1	1	0
Trevor Robins (goalie)	4	0	0	0	0
Corwin Saurdiff (goalie)	17	0	0	0	2

GOALTENDING

	Games	Min.	W	L	OTL	Goals	SO	Avg.
Wade Flaherty	60	3564	32	19	9	202	0	3.40
Corwin Saurdiff	17	946	6	9	1	74	0	4.69
Dan Ryder	3	139	1	1	0	11	0	4.73
Trevor Robins	4	199	1	2	0	21	0	6.32

LAS VEGAS THUNDER

SCORING

	Games	G	A	Pts.	PIM
Ken Quinney	79	55	53	108	52
Patrice Lefebvre	76	31	67	98	71
Radek Bonk	76	42	45	87	208
Mark Vermette	77	22	38	60	61
Marc Habscheid	59	14	40	54	49
Jeff Sharples	68	18	32	50	68
Jean-Marc Richard	59	15	33	48	44
Todd Richards	80	11	35	46	122
Brad Lauer	32	21	21	42	30
Bob Joyce	63	15	18	33	45
Bryan Fogarty	33	3	16	19	38
Jim Kyte	75	2	16	18	246
Steve Gotaas	39	4	13	17	43
Shawn Heaphy	37	10	5	15	45
Randy Smith	53	7	7	14	78

	Games	G	A	Pts.	PIM
Marc Rodgers	40	7	7	14	110
Brent Ashton	16	4	10	14	29
Rod Buskas	69	2	9	11	131
Lyndon Byers	31	3	5	8	176
Steve Jaques	49	3	5	8	192
Kirk Tomlinson	15	2	6	8	95
Jack Duffy	19	1	7	8	18
Jeff Reid	16	2	5	7	10
Brett Hauer	21	0	7	7	8
Scott Hollis	23	3	1	4	65
Dave Neilson	12	1	3	4	14
Clint Malarchuk (goalie)	55	0	3	3	28
Greg Spenrath	43	2	0	2	222
Frank Evans	12	0	2	2	19
Kerry Toporowski	13	1	0	1	129
Peter Ing (goalie)	30	0	1	1	2
Frederic Chabot (goalie)	2	0	0	0	0
Corrie D'Alessio (goalie)	1	0	0	0	0
Larry DePalma	1	0	0	0	17
Doug Searle	1	0	0	0	0
Wes McCauley	2	0	0	0	4

GOALTENDING

	Games	Min.	W	L	OTL	Goals	SO	Avg.
Corrie D'Alessio	1	35	1	0	0	1	0	1.70
Frederic Chabot	2	110	1	1	0	5	0	2.72
Clint Malarchuk	55	3076	34	10	7	172	1	3.35
Peter Ing	30	1627	16	7	4	91	0	3.36

MILWAUKEE ADMIRALS

SCORING

	Games	G	A	Pts.	PIM
Brian Dobbin	81	48	53	101	73
Sylvain Couturier	80	41	51	92	123
Gino Cavallini	78	43	35	78	64
Pat MacLeod	73	21	52	73	18
Steve Tuttle	78	27	44	71	34
Jason Lafreniere	52	14	47	61	16
Mike McNeill	78	21	25	46	40
Yuri Krivokhija	50	10	28	38	59
Alex Galchenyuk	33	12	24	36	20
Jergus Baca	67	6	29	35	119
Matt Hervey	27	6	17	23	51
Trevor Sim	32	7	13	20	10
Ken Sabourin	81	6	13	19	279
Randy Velischek	53	7	11	18	28
Steve Strunk	31	8	8	16	28
Dale Henry	49	5	11	16	104
Scott Gruhl	28	6	9	15	102
Ladislav Tresl	19	6	7	13	10
Scott Robinson	24	8	3	11	52
John Byce	28	7	4	11	10
Jim Johannson	28	4	7	11	15
Richard Zemlak	61	3	8	11	243
Jeff Larmer	25	2	9	11	14
Don Gibson	43	4	6	10	233
Paul Jerrard	28	6	3	9	58
Fabian Joseph	18	3	6	9	4
Kevin Grant	16	3	6	9	64
Carl Valimont	14	1	7	8	20
Larry Dyck (goalie)	41	0	3	3	2
Shaun Kane	6	1	0	1	4
Trevor Halverson	4	1	0	1	8
Bob Mason (goalie)	40	0	1	1	10
Miroslav Ihnacak	1	0	0	0	0
Dave Marcinyshyn	1	0	0	0	0
Rob Dumas	8	0	0	0	16
Duane Derksen (goalie)	9	0	0	0	2

GOALTENDING

	Games	Min.	W	L	OTL	Goals	SO	Avg.
Larry Dyck	41	2145	15	13	7	121	0	3.38
Duane Derksen	9	490	4	2	2	28	0	3.42
Bob Mason	40	2206	21	9	8	132	0	3.59

IHL

PEORIA RIVERMEN

SCORING

	Games	G	A	Pts.	PIM
Doug Evans	76	27	63	90	108
Tony Hrkac	45	30	51	81	25
Darren Veitch	76	21	54	75	16
Michel Mongeau	52	29	36	65	50
Ron Hoover	80	26	24	50	89
Daniel Laperriere	56	10	37	47	16
Richard Pion	73	13	32	45	96
Terry Hollinger	78	12	31	43	96
Kevin Evans	67	10	29	39	254
Brian Pellerin	79	14	24	38	225
Dave Mackey	49	14	21	35	132
Greg Paslawski	29	16	16	32	12
Butch Kaebel	59	16	9	25	31
Nathan Lafayette	27	13	11	24	20
Vitali Prokhorov	19	13	10	23	16
Rene Chapdelaine	80	8	9	17	100
Jim Montgomery	12	7	8	15	10
Derek Frenette	55	5	7	12	35
Steve Staios	38	3	9	12	42
Jeff Batters	59	3	9	12	175
Martin Hamrlik	47	1	11	12	61
Denny Felsner	6	8	3	11	14
David Roberts	10	4	6	10	4
Patrice Tardif	11	4	4	8	21
Doug Crossman	8	3	5	8	0
Kevin Miehm	11	2	3	5	0
Mark Bassen	16	2	2	4	12
Jason Marshall	20	1	1	2	72
Geoff Sarjeant (goalie)	41	0	2	2	24
Tim Bean	3	0	2	2	0
Guy Rouleau	6	0	2	2	0
Kyle Reeves	3	0	1	1	2
Vitali Karamnov	3	0	1	1	2
David Goverde (goalie)	5	0	1	1	0
Steve Wilson	1	0	0	0	0
Derek Donald	3	0	0	0	2
Bruce Gardiner	3	0	0	0	0
Scott Burfoot	4	0	0	0	0
Darwin McPherson	5	0	0	0	2
Pat Cavanagh	6	0	0	0	21
Nick Vitucci (goalie)	11	0	0	0	0
John Roderick	13	0	0	0	10
Parris Duffus (goalie)	36	0	0	0	6

GOALTENDING

	Games	Min.	W	L	OTL	Goals	SO	Avg.
Geoff Sarjeant	41	2275	25	9	2	93	2	2.45
David Goverde	5	299	4	1	0	13	0	2.61
Parris Duffus	36	1845	19	10	3	141	0	4.58
Nick Vitucci	11	422	3	4	1	35	0	4.98

PHOENIX ROADRUNNERS

SCORING

	Games	G	A	Pts.	PIM
Marc Fortier	81	39	61	100	96
Dan Currie	74	37	49	86	96
Rob Murphy	72	23	34	57	101
Dominic Lavoie	58	20	33	53	70
Jim Vesey	60	20	30	50	75
Brian McReynolds	51	14	33	47	65
Brian Chapman	78	6	35	41	280
Robert Lang	44	11	24	35	34
Darryl Williams	52	11	18	29	237
Tim Breslin	50	9	18	27	29
Guy Leveque	39	10	16	26	47
Dave Thomlinson	39	10	15	25	70
Brad Tiley	35	8	15	23	21
Bob Jay	65	7	15	22	54
Keith Redmond	43	8	10	18	196
Dean Hulett	43	8	7	15	76
Pat Murray	25	6	8	14	44
Eric Lavigne	62	3	11	14	168

	Games	G	A	Pts.	PIM
Stephane Charbonneau	32	7	6	13	43
Brent Thompson	26	1	11	12	118
David Haas	11	7	4	11	43
John Druce	8	5	6	11	9
Steve Strunk	12	3	8	11	18
Mike Vukonich	22	4	6	10	8
Daniel Shank	7	4	6	10	26
Jim Maher	46	2	8	10	45
Davis Payne	22	6	3	9	51
Mark Hardy	54	5	3	8	48
Kevin Kerr	12	2	4	6	9
Dave Stewart	25	2	3	5	53
Mike Bodnarchuk	8	3	1	4	6
Kevin Grant	33	0	3	3	110
Rick Knickle (goalie)	25	0	2	2	4
Pauli Jaks (goalie)	33	0	2	2	0
David Goverde (goalie)	30	0	1	1	4
Phil Crowe	2	0	0	0	0
Brandy Semchuk	2	0	0	0	6
Justin Hocking	3	0	0	0	15
Robb Stauber (goalie)	3	0	0	0	0

GOALTENDING

	Games	Min.	W	L	OTL	Goals	SO	Avg.
David Goverde	30	1716	15	13	1	93	0	3.25
Pauli Jaks	33	1712	16	13	1	101	0	3.54
Rick Knickle	25	1292	8	9	3	89	1	4.13
Robb Stauber	3	121	1	1	0	13	0	6.42

RUSSIAN PENGUINS

SCORING

	Games	G	A	Pts.	PIM
Andrei Vasiliev	13	10	6	16	4
Sergei Brylin	13	4	5	9	18
Valentin Morozov	11	3	5	8	2
Denis Vinokurov	13	3	3	6	12
Vladislav Yakovenko	6	0	6	6	10
Oleg Belov	11	3	2	5	10
Albert Leschev	12	2	3	5	4
Alexander Osadchi	11	0	5	5	24
Alexander Kharlamov	12	2	2	4	4
Vladimir Zhashkov	9	2	1	3	19
Mikhail Belobragin	7	1	2	3	2
Boris Zelenko	9	1	2	3	0
Roman Mozgunov	8	2	0	2	4
Andrei Yakovenko	3	1	1	2	2
Yuri Yeresko	6	0	2	2	16
Vasili Turkovski	6	0	2	2	11
Arthur Oktyabrev	10	0	2	2	12
Dmitri Gorenko	8	1	0	1	2
Sergei Selyanin	9	0	1	1	24
Sergei Reshetnikov	5	0	1	1	2
Alexei Ysaikin	6	0	1	1	10
Stanislav Shalnov	2	0	0	0	2
Sergei Zvyagin (goalie)	4	0	0	0	0
Ian Golubovski	8	0	0	0	23
Alexander Titov	9	0	0	0	8
Nikolai Khabibulin (goalie)	12	0	0	0	0

GOALTENDING

	Games	Min.	W	L	OTL	Goals	SO	Avg.
Nikolai Khabibulin	12	639	2	7	2	47	0	4.41
Sergei Zvyagin	4	140	0	2	0	14	0	6.00

SALT LAKE GOLDEN EAGLES

SCORING

	Games	G	A	Pts.	PIM
Sandy Smith	78	21	39	60	170
Derek Armstrong	76	23	35	58	61
Zigmund Palffy	57	25	32	57	83
Darryl Olsen	73	17	32	49	97
Chris Taylor	79	21	20	41	38
Dave Chyzowski	66	27	13	40	151

	Games	G	A	Pts.	PIM
Chris Luongo	51	9	31	40	54
Scott Scissons	72	10	26	36	123
Dave MacIntyre	71	9	27	36	69
Joe Day	33	16	10	26	153
Dan Plante	66	7	17	24	148
Steve Junker	71	9	14	23	36
Kevan Guy	62	4	17	21	45
Larry DePalma	34	4	12	16	125
Joni Lehto	60	3	13	16	34
Kimbi Daniels	25	6	9	15	8
Brent Grieve	22	9	5	14	30
Jason Simon	50	7	7	14	323
Tony Joseph	43	4	2	6	213
Wayne McBean	5	0	6	6	2
Kevin Cheveldayoff	73	0	4	4	216
Rick Lessard	31	1	2	3	110
Scott White	15	0	3	3	8
Danny Lorenz (goalie)	21	0	3	3	0
Wayne Doucet	8	2	0	2	33
Marc Laforge	43	2	2	2	242
Dean Chynoweth	5	0	1	1	33
Martin LaCroix	4	0	1	1	0
Phil Huber	1	0	1	1	2
Steve Jaques	3	0	1	1	4
Tom Draper (goalie)	35	0	1	1	24
Perry Anderson	2	0	0	0	21
Chris Foy	2	0	0	0	2
Richard Pilon	2	0	0	0	8
Steve Wilson	2	0	0	0	0
Brendan Flynn	4	0	0	0	0
Mike Lenarduzzi (goalie)	4	0	0	0	0
Milan Hnilicka (goalie)	9	0	0	0	0
Jamie McLennan (goalie)	24	0	0	0	20

GOALTENDING

	Games	Min.	W	L	OTL	Goals	SO	Avg.
Jamie McLennan	24	1320	8	12	2	80	0	3.64
Milan Hnilicka	9	381	5	1	0	25	0	3.93
Tom Draper	35	1929	7	23	3	140	0	4.35
Danny Lorenz	20	982	4	12	0	91	0	5.56
Mike Lenarduzzi	4	211	0	4	0	22	0	6.25

SAN DIEGO GULLS

SCORING

	Games	G	A	Pts.	PIM
Lonnie Loach	74	42	49	91	65
Hubie McDonough	69	31	48	79	61
Scott Arniel	79	34	43	77	121
Dale DeGray	80	20	50	70	163
Daniel Shank	63	27	36	63	273
Jarrod Skalde	57	25	38	63	79
John Anderson	72	24	24	48	32
Clark Donatelli	50	11	32	43	54
Greg Brown	42	8	25	33	26
Larry Floyd	52	10	20	30	45
Denny Lambert	79	13	14	27	314
Anatoli Fedotov	66	14	12	26	42
Robin Bawa	25	6	15	21	54
Don McSween	38	5	13	18	36
Scott McKay	58	10	6	16	35
Mark DeSantis	54	5	10	15	95
Myles O'Connor	39	1	13	14	117
Trevor Halverson	58	4	9	13	115
Scott Chartier	49	2	6	8	84
Barry Dreger	57	2	6	8	166
Peter Laviolette	17	3	4	7	20
David Williams	16	1	6	7	17
Jean Francois Jomphe	29	2	3	5	12
Dominic Lavoie	9	2	2	4	12
John Lilley	2	2	1	3	0
Dean Ewen	19	0	3	3	45
Fredrik Jax	5	1	1	2	2
Joel Savage	20	0	2	2	4
John Tanner (goalie)	13	0	1	1	4
Mikhail Shtalenkov (goalie)	28	0	1	1	0

	Games	G	A	Pts.	PIM
Allan Bester (goalie)	46	0	1	1	8
Antoine Mindjimba (goalie)	1	0	0	0	0
Gord Dineen	3	0	0	0	0
Lee Norwood	4	0	0	0	0
Kevin Grant	5	0	0	0	18

GOALTENDING

	Games	Min.	W	L	OTL	Goals	SO	Avg.
Antoine Mindjimba	1	60	0	0	1	3	0	3.00
Mikhail Shtalenkov	28	1616	15	11	2	93	0	3.45
John Tanner	13	629	5	3	2	37	0	3.53
Allan Bester	46	2543	22	14	6	150	1	3.54

PLAYERS WITH TWO OR MORE TEAMS

SCORING

	Games	G	A	Pts.	PIM
Alexander Andrijevski, Ind.	4	0	1	1	2
Alexander Andrijevski, Kal.	57	6	22	28	58
Totals	61	6	23	29	60
Phil Crowe, Fort Wayne	5	0	1	1	26
Phil Crowe, Phoenix	2	0	0	0	0
Totals	7	0	1	1	26
Larry DePalma, Atlanta	21	10	10	20	109
Larry DePalma, Salt Lake	34	4	12	16	125
Larry DePalma, Las Vegas	1	0	0	0	17
Larry DePalma, Cleveland	9	4	1	5	49
Totals	65	18	23	41	300
Bryan Fogarty, Atlanta	8	1	5	6	4
Bryan Fogarty, Las Vegas	33	3	16	19	38
Bryan Fogarty, Kansas City	3	2	1	3	2
Totals	44	6	22	28	44
David Goverde, Phoenix (g)	30	0	1	1	4
David Goverde, Peoria (g)	5	0	1	1	0
Totals	35	0	2	2	4
Kevin Grant, Phoenix	33	0	3	3	110
Kevin Grant, San Diego	5	0	0	0	18
Kevin Grant, Milwaukee	16	3	6	9	64
Totals	54	3	9	12	192
Scott Gruhl, Milwaukee	28	6	9	15	102
Scott Gruhl, Kalamazoo	30	15	12	27	85
Totals	58	21	21	42	187
Trevor Halverson, San Diego	58	4	9	13	115
Trevor Halverson	4	1	0	1	8
Totals	62	5	9	14	123
Yves Heroux, Kalamazoo	3	0	2	2	4
Yves Heroux, Indianapolis	74	28	30	58	113
Totals	77	28	32	60	117
Phil Huber, Salt Lake	1	0	1	1	2
Phil Huber, Kalamazoo	1	0	0	0	0
Totals	2	0	1	1	2
Steve Jaques, Las Vegas	49	3	5	8	192
Steve Jaques, Salt Lake	3	0	1	1	4
Totals	52	3	6	9	196
Paul Jerrard, Kalamazoo	24	0	2	2	60
Paul Jerrard, Milwaukee	28	6	3	9	58
Totals	52	6	5	11	118
Dominic Lavoie, Phoenix	58	20	33	53	70
Dominic Lavoie, San Diego	9	2	2	4	12
Totals	67	22	35	57	82
Ray LeBlanc, Indianapolis (g)	2	0	0	0	0
Ray LeBlanc, Cincinnati (g)	34	0	2	2	4
Totals	36	0	2	2	4
Pat Murray, Kalamazoo	17	2	3	5	6
Pat Murray, Phoenix	25	6	8	14	44
Totals	42	8	11	19	50
Joel Savage, Fort Wayne	31	2	11	13	29
Joel Savage, San Diego	20	0	2	2	4
Joel Savage, Kalamazoo	4	2	1	3	0
Totals	55	4	14	18	33
Daniel Shank, San Diego	63	27	36	63	273
Daniel Shank, Phoenix	7	4	6	10	26
Totals	70	31	42	73	299
Steve Strunk, Milwaukee	31	8	8	16	28
Steve Strunk, Phoenix	12	3	8	11	18
Totals	43	11	16	27	46

	Games	G	A	Pts.	PIM
Kerry Toporowski, Indianapolis .	32	1	4	5	126
Kerry Toporowski, Las Vegas.....	13	1	0	1	129
Totals......................................	45	2	4	6	255
Steve Wilson, Salt Lake	2	0	0	0	0
Steve Wilson, Peoria	1	0	0	0	0
Steve Wilson, Kalamazoo............	3	0	0	0	2
Totals......................................	6	0	0	0	2

GOALTENDING

	Games	Min.	W	L	OTL	Goals	SO	Avg.
David Goverde, Pho.	30	1716	15	13	1	93	0	3.25
David Goverde, Peo.	5	299	4	1	0	13	0	2.61
Totals	35	2015	19	14	1	106	0	3.16
Ray LeBlanc, Ind.	2	112	0	1	0	8	0	4.25
Ray LeBlanc, Cin.	34	1779	17	9	3	104	1	3.51
Totals	36	1890	17	10	3	112	1	3.55

1994 TURNER CUP PLAYOFFS

RESULTS

QUARTERFINALS

WESTERN CONFERENCE
Series "A"

	W	L	Pts.	GF	GA
San Diego..................................	4	1	8	20	14
Las Vegas.................................	1	4	2	14	20

(San Diego won series, 4-1)

Series "B"

	W	L	Pts.	GF	GA
Atlanta......................................	4	0	8	21	11
Milwaukee.................................	0	4	0	11	21

(Atlanta won series, 4-0)

EASTERN CONFERENCE
Series "C"

	W	L	Pts.	GF	GA
Fort Wayne................................	4	2	8	26	18
Peoria.......................................	2	4	4	18	26

(Fort Wayne won series, 4-2)

Series "D"

	W	L	Pts.	GF	GA
Cincinnati	4	1	8	21	10
Kalamazoo	1	4	2	10	21

(Cincinnati won series, 4-1)

SEMIFINALS

WESTERN CONFERENCE
Series "E"

	W	L	Pts.	GF	GA
Atlanta......................................	4	0	8	20	6
San Diego..................................	0	4	0	6	20

(Atlanta won series, 4-0)

EASTERN CONFERENCE
Series "F"

	W	L	Pts.	GF	GA
Fort Wayne................................	4	2	8	20	24
Cincinnati..................................	2	4	4	24	20

(Fort Wayne won series, 4-2)

TURNER CUP FINALS
Series "G"

	W	L	Pts.	GF	GA
Atlanta......................................	4	2	8	22	19
Fort Wayne................................	2	4	4	19	22

(Atlanta won series, 4-2)

INDIVIDUAL LEADERS

Goals: Steve Larouche, Atlanta (16)
Assists: Jason Ruff, Atlanta (17)
Points: Steve Larouche, Atlanta (26)
Penalty minutes: Rick Hayward, Cincinnati (99)
Goaltending average: Mike Greenlay, Atlanta (2.32)
Shutouts: Mike Greenlay, Atlanta (1)
      Pokey Reddick, Cincinnati (1)
      Peter Sidorkiewicz, Fort Wayne (1)
      Mike Torchia, Kalamazoo (1)

TOP SCORERS

	Games	G	A	Pts.
Steve Larouche, Atlanta	14	16	10	26
Stan Drulia, Atlanta	14	13	12	25
John Purves, Fort Wayne	18	10	14	24
Jason Ruff, Atlanta	14	6	17	23
Len Barrie, Cincinnati	11	8	13	21
Bill McDougall, Atlanta	14	12	7	19
Colin Chin, Fort Wayne	18	9	10	19
Don Biggs, Cincinnati........................	11	8	9	17
Lee Davidson, Fort Wayne.................	17	4	12	16
Jarrod Skalde, San Diego..................	9	3	12	15
Dan Lambert, Fort Wayne..................	18	3	12	15

INDIVIDUAL STATISTICS

ATLANTA KNIGHTS

(Winner of 1994 Turner Cup playoffs)

SCORING

	Games	G	A	Pts.	PIM
Steve Larouche..........................	14	16	10	26	16
Stan Drulia................................	14	13	12	25	8
Jason Ruff.................................	14	6	17	23	41
Bill McDougall	14	12	7	19	30
Devin Edgerton	13	1	6	7	4
Eric DuBois...............................	14	0	7	7	48
Jeff Madill	14	4	2	6	33
Colin Miller...............................	3	2	3	5	0
Eric Charron..............................	14	1	4	5	28
Shawn Rivers.............................	12	1	4	5	21
Martin Tanguay..........................	9	2	1	3	8
Cory Cross	9	1	2	3	14
Jim Cummins.............................	13	1	2	3	90
Brent Gretzky............................	14	1	1	2	2

	Games	G	A	Pts.	PIM
Chris LiPuma	11	1	1	2	28
Normand Rochefort	13	0	2	2	6
Christian Campeau	14	1	0	1	2
Jeff Buchanan	14	0	1	1	20
J.C. Bergeron (goalie)	2	0	0	0	0
Mike Greenlay (goalie)	13	0	0	0	2

GOALTENDING

	Games	Min.	W	L	OTL	Goals	SO	Avg.
Mike Greenlay	13	749	11	1	0	29	1	2.32
J.C. Bergeron	2	153	1	1	0	6	0	2.34

CINCINNATI CYCLONES

(Lost semifinals to Fort Wayne, 4-2)

SCORING

	Games	G	A	Pts.	PIM
Len Barrie	11	8	13	21	60
Don Biggs	11	8	9	17	29
Patrick Lebeau	11	4	8	12	14
Stephane J.G. Richer	11	2	9	11	26
Doug Barrault	9	8	2	10	0
Paul Lawless	11	4	4	8	4
Gord Hynes	11	2	6	8	24
Daniel Gauthier	10	2	3	5	14
Chris Cichocki	11	2	2	4	12
Jeff Greenlaw	11	2	2	4	28
Jaroslav Nedved	11	1	3	4	20
Chris Armstrong	10	1	3	4	2
Ian Kidd	8	0	3	3	10
Jamie Leach	11	1	0	1	4
Marc LaBelle	4	0	1	1	6
Jeff Serowik	7	0	1	1	8
Dallas Eakins	8	0	1	1	41
Rick Hayward	8	0	1	1	99
Jamie Linden	2	0	0	0	2
Ray LeBlanc (goalie)	5	0	0	0	0
Pokey Reddick (goalie)	10	0	0	0	2

GOALTENDING

	Games	Min.	W	L	OTL	Goals	SO	Avg.
Pokey Reddick	10	498	6	2	0	21	1	2.53
Ray LeBlanc	5	159	0	3	0	9	0	3.39

FORT WAYNE KOMETS

(Lost finals to Atlanta, 4-2)

SCORING

	Games	G	A	Pts.	PIM
John Purves	18	10	14	24	12
Colin Chin	18	9	10	19	24
Lee Davidson	17	4	12	16	10
Dan Lambert	18	3	12	15	20
Mitch Messier	14	8	6	14	14
Vladimir Tsyplakov	14	6	8	14	16
Darin Smith	18	7	5	12	37
Kelly Hurd	17	6	4	10	10
Ian Boyce	18	3	6	9	2
Dave Smith	18	2	6	8	68
Guy Dupuis	17	1	7	8	28
Doug Wickenheiser	14	2	2	4	4
Igor Malykhin	7	1	3	4	6
Kevin MacDonald	15	0	4	4	76
Max Middendorf	9	1	2	3	24
Carey Lucyk	18	1	2	3	10
Grant Richison	17	0	3	3	28
David Tretowicz	16	1	0	1	4
Peter Sidorkiewicz (goalie)	18	0	1	1	10
Darryl Gilmour (goalie)	3	0	0	0	0
Steve Fletcher	5	0	0	0	33

GOALTENDING

	Games	Min.	W	L	OTL	Goals	SO	Avg.
Peter Sidorkiewicz	18	1054	10	6	2	59	1	3.36
Darryl Gilmour	3	70	0	0	0	5	0	4.24

KALAMAZOO WINGS

(Lost quarterfinals to Cincinnati, 4-1)

SCORING

	Games	G	A	Pts.	PIM
Scott Gruhl	5	1	4	5	26
Rob Brown	5	1	3	4	6
Jason Herter	5	3	0	3	14
Ken Priestlay	5	2	1	3	2
Mike Kennedy	3	1	2	3	2
Travis Richards	4	1	1	2	0
Neil Brady	5	1	1	2	10
Chris Tancill	5	0	2	2	8
Collin Bauer	5	0	1	1	6
Alexander Andrijevski	1	0	0	0	2
Brad Berry	1	0	0	0	0
Craig Bonner	1	0	0	0	0
Jarkko Varvio	1	0	0	0	0
Troy Gamble (goalie)	2	0	0	0	0
Joel Savage	2	0	0	0	4
Jay Caufield	4	0	0	0	18
Cal McGowan	4	0	0	0	2
Glenn Mulvenna	4	0	0	0	0
Mike Torchia (goalie)	4	0	0	0	0
Mark Osiecki	5	0	0	0	5
Herb Raglan	5	0	0	0	32
Rob Robinson	5	0	0	0	2
Derrick Smith	5	0	0	0	18

GOALTENDING

	Games	Min.	W	L	OTL	Goals	SO	Avg.
Mike Torchia	4	221	1	2	1	14	1	3.80
Troy Gamble	2	80	0	1	0	7	0	5.25

LAS VEGAS THUNDER

(Lost quarterfinals to San Diego, 4-1)

SCORING

	Games	G	A	Pts.	PIM
Patrice Lefebvre	5	3	4	7	4
Ken Quinney	5	3	3	6	2
Todd Richards	5	1	4	5	18
Jeff Sharples	5	2	1	3	6
Bob Joyce	5	2	1	3	8
Radek Bonk	5	1	2	3	10
Jean-Marc Richard	5	0	3	3	0
Marc Habscheid	5	1	1	2	15
Marc Rodgers	4	0	2	2	17
Rod Buskas	5	0	2	2	2
Brad Lauer	4	1	0	1	2
Jim Kyte	4	0	1	1	51
Lyndon Byers	1	0	0	0	4
Brett Hauer	1	0	0	0	0
Jeff Reid	1	0	0	0	0
Peter Ing (goalie)	2	0	0	0	0
Kerry Toporowski	2	0	0	0	31
Steve Gotaas	4	0	0	0	20
Mark Vermette	4	0	0	0	2
Shawn Heaphy	5	0	0	0	6
Steve Jaques	5	0	0	0	28
Clint Malarchuk (goalie)	5	0	0	0	31

GOALTENDING

	Games	Min.	W	L	OTL	Goals	SO	Avg.
Clint Malarchuk	5	257	1	3	0	16	0	3.74
Peter Ing	2	40	0	1	0	4	0	5.87

MILWAUKEE ADMIRALS

(Lost quarterfinals to Atlanta, 4-0)

SCORING

	Games	G	A	Pts.	PIM
Gino Cavallini	4	3	4	7	6
Kevin Grant	4	0	4	4	20
John Byce	3	2	1	3	0
Pat MacLeod	3	1	2	3	0

	Games	G	A	Pts.	PIM
Sylvain Couturier	4	1	2	3	2
Jergus Baca	3	1	1	2	4
Alex Galchenyuk	3	1	1	2	0
Steve Tuttle	4	0	2	2	4
Brian Dobbin	4	1	0	1	4
Trevor Sim	4	1	0	1	0
Mike McNeill	4	0	1	1	6
Yuri Krivokhija	2	0	1	1	6
Jeff Larmer	1	0	0	0	0
Trevor Halverson	2	0	0	0	17
Paul Jerrard	2	0	0	0	8
Richard Zemlak	2	0	0	0	16
Larry Dyck (goalie)	3	0	0	0	2
Don Gibson	3	0	0	0	10
Bob Mason (goalie)	3	0	0	0	0
Fabian Joseph	4	0	0	0	0
Ken Sabourin	4	0	0	0	10
Randy Velischek	4	0	0	0	2

GOALTENDING

	Games	Min.	W	L	OTL	Goals	SO	Avg.
Bob Mason	3	141	0	0	1	9	0	3.83
Larry Dyck	3	120	0	3	0	11	0	5.47

PEORIA RIVERMEN

(Lost quarterfinals to Fort Wayne, 4-2)

SCORING

	Games	G	A	Pts.	PIM
Doug Evans	6	2	6	8	10
Greg Paslawski	6	3	3	6	0
Rene Chapdelaine	6	1	3	4	10
Ian Laperriere	5	1	3	4	2
Richard Pion	6	2	1	3	8
Tony Hrkac	1	1	2	3	0
Derek Frenette	3	1	2	3	6
Terry Hollinger	6	0	3	3	31
Patrice Tardif	4	2	0	2	4
Jason Marshall	3	2	0	2	2
Darren Veitch	6	1	1	2	0
Daniel Laperriere	6	0	2	2	2
Kevin Miehm	4	1	0	1	0
Butch Kaebel	6	1	0	1	0
Vitali Karamnov	1	0	1	1	0
Geoff Sarjeant (goalie)	4	0	1	1	2
Martin Hamrlik	6	0	1	1	2

	Games	G	A	Pts.	PIM
Ron Hoover	6	0	1	1	10
David Goverde (goalie)	1	0	0	0	0
Parris Duffus (goalie)	2	0	0	0	2
Kevin Evans	4	0	0	0	6
Brian Pellerin	5	0	0	0	16
Jeff Batters	6	0	0	0	18

GOALTENDING

	Games	Min.	W	L	OTL	Goals	SO	Avg.
Geoff Sarjeant	4	211	2	2	0	13	0	3.69
Parris Duffus	2	92	0	1	0	6	0	3.88
David Goverde	1	59	0	1	0	7	0	7.05

SAN DIEGO GULLS

(Lost semifinals to Atlanta, 4-0)

SCORING

	Games	G	A	Pts.	PIM
Jarrod Skalde	9	3	12	15	10
Lonnie Loach	9	4	10	14	6
Scott Arniel	7	6	3	9	24
Scott McKay	9	2	5	7	6
Hubie McDonough	8	0	7	7	6
Myles O'Connor	9	1	4	5	83
Peter Laviolette	9	3	0	3	6
Dale DeGray	9	2	1	3	8
John Anderson	4	1	1	2	8
Maxim Bets	9	0	2	2	0
Dean Ewen	3	1	0	1	8
Larry Floyd	8	1	0	1	5
Dominic Lavoie	8	1	0	1	20
Denny Lambert	6	1	0	1	45
Lee Norwood	8	0	1	1	11
Clark Donatelli	9	0	1	1	23
Anatoli Fedotov	8	0	1	1	6
Barry Dreger	1	0	0	0	2
Mike Maneluk	1	0	0	0	0
John Tanner (goalie)	3	0	0	0	0
Scott Chartier	4	0	0	0	6
Robin Bawa	6	0	0	0	52
Allan Bester (goalie)	8	0	0	0	2

GOALTENDING

	Games	Min.	W	L	OTL	Goals	SO	Avg.
John Tanner	3	118	0	1	0	5	0	2.53
Allan Bester	8	419	4	4	0	28	0	4.00

1993-94 AWARD WINNERS

ALL-STAR TEAMS

First team	Pos.	Second team
Geoff Sarjeant, Peoria	G	Wade Flaherty, K.C.
Pat MacLeod, Milwaukee	D	Todd Richards, Las Vegas
Jean-Marc Richard, L.V.	D	Stephane Richer, Cin.
Ken Quinney, Las Vegas	LW	Paul Lawless, Cincinnati
		Derrick Smith, Kalamazoo
Rob Brown, Kalamazoo	C	Len Barrie, Cincinnati
Stan Drulia, Atlanta	RW	Brian Dobbin, Milwaukee

TROPHY WINNERS

James Gatschene Memorial Trophy: Rob Brown, Kalamazoo
Leo P. Lamoureux Memorial Trophy: Rob Brown, Kalamazoo
James Norris Memorial Trophy: J.C. Bergeron, Atlanta
　　　　　　　　　　　　　　　　　　　　　Mike Greenlay, Atlanta
Governors Trophy: Darren Veitch, Peoria
Garry F. Longman Memorial Trophy: Radek Bonk, Las Vegas
Ken McKenzie Trophy: Chris Rogles, Indianapolis
Commissioner's Trophy: Bruce Boudreau, Fort Wayne
N.R. (Bud) Poile Trophy: Stan Drulia, Atlanta
Fred A. Huber Trophy: Las Vegas Thunder
Joseph Turner Memorial Cup Winner: Atlanta Knights

ALL-TIME AWARD WINNERS

JAMES GATSCHENE MEMORIAL TROPHY

(Most Valuable Player)

Season	Player, Team
1946-47	Herb Jones, Detroit Auto Club
1947-48	Lyle Dowell, Det. Bright's Goodyears
1948-49	Bob McFadden, Det. Jerry Lynch
1949-50	Dick Kowcinak, Sarnia
1950-51	John McGrath, Toledo

Season	Player, Team
1951-52	Ernie Dick, Chatham
1952-53	Donnie Marshall, Cincinnati
1953-54	No award given
1954-55	Phil Goyette, Cincinnati
1955-56	George Hayes, Grand Rapids
1956-57	Pierre Brillant, Indianapolis
1957-58	Pierre Brillant, Indianapolis
1958-59	Len Thornson, Fort Wayne

Season	Player, Team
1959-60	Billy Reichart, Minneapolis
1960-61	Len Thornson, Fort Wayne
1961-62	Len Thornson, Fort Wayne
1962-63	Len Thornson, Fort Wayne
	Eddie Lang, Fort Wayne
1963-64	Len Thornson, Fort Wayne
1964-65	Chick Chalmers, Toledo
1965-66	Gary Schall, Muskegon
1966-67	Len Thornson, Fort Wayne
1967-68	Len Thornson, Fort Wayne
	Don Westbrooke, Dayton
1968-69	Don Westbrooke, Dayton
1969-70	Cliff Pennington, Des Moines
1970-71	Lyle Carter, Muskegon
1971-72	Len Fontaine, Port Huron
1972-73	Gary Ford, Muskegon
1973-74	Pete Mara, Des Moines
1974-75	Gary Ford, Muskegon
1975-76	Len Fontaine, Port Huron
1976-77	Tom Mellor, Toledo
1977-78	Dan Bonar, Fort Wayne
1978-79	Terry McDougall, Fort Wayne
1979-80	Al Dumba, Fort Wayne
1980-81	Marcel Comeau, Saginaw
1981-82	Brent Jarrett, Kalamazoo
1982-83	Claude Noel, Toledo
1983-84	Darren Jensen, Fort Wayne
1984-85	Scott Gruhl, Muskegon
1985-86	Darrell May, Peoria
1986-87	Jeff Pyle, Saginaw
	Jock Callander, Muskegon
1987-88	John Cullen, Flint
1988-89	Dave Michayluk, Muskegon
1989-90	Michel Mongeau, Peoria
1990-91	David Bruce, Peoria
1991-92	Dmitri Kvartalnov, San Diego
1992-93	Tony Hrkac, Indianapolis
1993-94	Rob Brown, Kalamazoo

LEO P. LAMOUREUX MEMORIAL TROPHY

(Leading scorer)

Season	Player, Team
1946-47	Harry Marchand, Windsor
1947-48	Dick Kowcinak, Det. Auto Club
1948-49	Leo Richard, Toledo
1949-50	Dick Kowcinak, Sarnia
1950-51	Herve Parent, Grand Rapids
1951-52	George Parker, Grand Rapids
1952-53	Alex Irving, Milwaukee
1953-54	Don Hall, Johnstown
1954-55	Phil Goyette, Cincinnati
1955-56	Max Mekilok, Cincinnati
1956-57	Pierre Brillant, Indianapolis
1957-58	Warren Hynes, Cincinnati
1958-59	George Ranieri, Louisville
1959-60	Chick Chalmers, Louisville
1960-61	Ken Yackel, Minneapolis
1961-62	Len Thornson, Fort Wayne
1962-63	Moe Bartoli, Minneapolis
1963-64	Len Thornson, Fort Wayne
1964-65	Lloyd Maxfield, Port Huron
1965-66	Bob Rivard, Fort Wayne
1966-67	Len Thornson, Fort Wayne
1967-68	Gary Ford, Muskegon
1968-69	Don Westbrooke, Dayton
1969-70	Don Westbrooke, Dayton
1970-71	Darrel Knibbs, Muskegon
1971-72	Gary Ford, Muskegon
1972-73	Gary Ford, Muskegon
1973-74	Pete Mara, Des Moines
1974-75	Rick Bragnalo, Dayton
1975-76	Len Fontaine, Port Huron
1976-77	Jim Koleff, Flint
1977-78	Jim Johnston, Flint

Season	Player, Team
1978-79	Terry McDougall, Fort Wayne
1979-80	Al Dumba, Fort Wayne
1980-81	Marcel Comeau, Saginaw
1981-82	Brent Jarrett, Kalamazoo
1982-83	Dale Yakiwchuk, Milwaukee
1983-84	Wally Schreiber, Fort Wayne
1984-85	Scott MacLeod, Salt Lake
1985-86	Scott MacLeod, Salt Lake
1986-87	Jock Callander, Muskegon
	Jeff Pyle, Saginaw
1987-88	John Cullen, Flint
1988-89	Dave Michayluk, Muskegon
1989-90	Michel Mongeau, Peoria
1990-91	Lonnie Loach, Fort Wayne
1991-92	Dmitri Kvartalnov, San Diego
1992-93	Tony Hrkac, Indianapolis
1993-94	Rob Brown, Kalamazoo

The award was originally known as the George H. Wilkinson Trophy from 1946-47 through 1959-60.

JAMES NORRIS MEMORIAL TROPHY

(Outstanding goaltenders)

Season	Player, Team
1955-56	Bill Tibbs, Troy
1956-57	Glenn Ramsey, Cincinnati
1957-58	Glenn Ramsey, Cincinnati
1958-59	Don Rigazio, Louisville
1959-60	Rene Zanier, Fort Wayne
1960-61	Ray Mikulan, Minneapolis
1961-62	Glenn Ramsey, Omaha
1962-63	Glenn Ramsey, Omaha
1963-64	Glenn Ramsey, Toledo
1964-65	Chuck Adamson, Fort Wayne
1965-66	Bob Sneddon, Port Huron
1966-67	Glenn Ramsey, Toledo
1967-68	Tim Tabor, Muskegon
	Bob Perani, Muskegon
1968-69	Pat Rupp, Dayton
	John Adams, Dayton
1969-70	Gaye Cooley, Des Moines
	Bob Perreault, Des Moines
1970-71	Lyle Carter, Muskegon
1971-72	Glenn Resch, Muskegon
1972-73	Robbie Irons, Fort Wayne
	Don Atchison, Fort Wayne
1973-74	Bill Hughes, Muskegon
1974-75	Bob Volpe, Flint
	Merlin Jenner, Flint
1975-76	Don Cutts, Muskegon
1976-77	Terry Richardson, Kalamazoo
1977-78	Lorne Molleken, Saginaw
	Pierre Chagnon, Saginaw
1978-79	Gord Laxton, Grand Rapids
1979-80	Larry Lozinski, Kalamazoo
1980-81	Claude Legris, Kalamazoo
	Georges Gagnon, Kalamazoo
1981-82	Lorne Molleken, Toledo
	Dave Tardich, Toledo
1982-83	Lorne Molleken, Toledo
1983-84	Darren Jensen, Fort Wayne
1984-85	Rick Heinz, Peoria
1985-86	Rick St. Croix, Fort Wayne
	Pokey Reddick, Fort Wayne
1986-87	Alain Raymond, Fort Wayne
	Michel Dufour, Fort Wayne
1987-88	Steve Guenette, Muskegon
1988-89	Rick Knickle, Fort Wayne
1989-90	Jimmy Waite, Indianapolis
1990-91	Guy Hebert, Peoria
	Pat Jablonski, Peoria
1991-92	Arturs Irbe, Kansas City
	Wade Flaherty, Kansas City
1992-93	Rick Knickle, San Diego
	Clint Malarchuk, San Diego

MINOR LEAGUES

Season	Player, Team
1993-94	J.C. Bergeron, Atlanta
	Mike Greenlay, Atlanta

GOVERNORS TROPHY

(Outstanding defenseman)

Season	Player, Team
1964-65	Lionel Repka, Fort Wayne
1965-66	Bob Lemieux, Muskegon
1966-67	Larry Mavety, Port Huron
1967-68	Carl Brewer, Muskegon
1968-69	Al Breaule, Dayton
	Moe Benoit, Dayton
1969-70	John Gravel, Toledo
1970-71	Bob LaPage, Des Moines
1971-72	Rick Pagnutti, Fort Wayne
1972-73	Bob McCammon, Port Huron
1973-74	Dave Simpson, Dayton
1974-75	Murry Flegel, Muskegon
1975-76	Murry Flegel, Muskegon
1976-77	Tom Mellor, Toledo
1977-78	Michel LaChance, Milwaukee
1978-79	Guido Tenesi, Grand Rapids
1979-80	John Gibson, Saginaw
1980-81	Larry Goodenough, Saginaw
1981-82	Don Waddell, Saginaw
1982-83	Jim Burton, Fort Wayne
	Kevin Willison, Milwaukee
1983-84	Kevin Willison, Milwaukee
1984-85	Lee Norwood, Peoria
1985-86	Jim Burton, Fort Wayne
1986-87	Jim Burton, Fort Wayne
1987-88	Phil Bourque, Muskegon
1988-89	Randy Boyd, Milwaukee
1989-90	Brian Glynn, Salt Lake
1990-91	Brian McKee, Fort Wayne
1991-92	Jean-Marc Richard, Fort Wayne
1992-93	Bill Houlder, San Diego
1993-94	Darren Veitch, Peoria

GARRY F. LONGMAN MEMORIAL TROPHY

(Outstanding rookie)

Season	Player, Team
1961-62	Dave Richardson, Fort Wayne
1962-63	John Gravel, Omaha
1963-64	Don Westbrooke, Toledo
1964-65	Bob Thomas, Toledo
1965-66	Frank Golembrowsky, Port Huron
1966-67	Kerry Bond, Columbus
1967-68	Gary Ford, Muskegon
1968-69	Doug Volmar, Columbus
1969-70	Wayne Zuk, Toledo
1970-71	Corky Agar, Flint
	Herb Howdle, Dayton
1971-72	Glenn Resch, Muskegon
1972-73	Danny Gloor, Des Moines
1973-74	Frank DeMarco, Des Moines
1974-75	Rick Bragnalo, Dayton
1975-76	Sid Veysey, Fort Wayne
1976-77	Ron Zanussi, Fort Wayne
	Garth MacGuigan, Muskegon
1977-78	Dan Bonar, Fort Wayne
1978-79	Wes Jarvis, Port Huron
1979-80	Doug Robb, Milwaukee
1980-81	Scott Vanderburgh, Kalamazoo
1981-82	Scott Howson, Toledo
1982-83	Tony Fiore, Flint
1983-84	Darren Jensen, Fort Wayne

Season	Player, Team
1984-85	Gilles Thibaudeau, Flint
1965-66	Guy Benoit, Muskegon
1986-87	Michel Mongeau, Saginaw
1987-88	Ed Belfour, Saginaw
	John Cullen, Flint
1988-89	Paul Ranheim, Salt Lake
1989-90	Rob Murphy, Milwaukee
1990-91	Nelson Emerson, Peoria
1991-92	Dmitri Kvartalnov, Kansas City
1992-93	Mikhail Shtalenkov, Milwaukee
1993-94	Radek Bonk, Las Vegas

KEN McKENZIE TROPHY

(Outstanding American-born rookie)

Season	Player, Team
1977-78	Mike Eruzione, Toledo
1978-79	Jon Fontas, Saginaw
1979-80	Bob Janecyk, Fort Wayne
1980-81	Mike Labianca, Toledo
	Steve Janaszak, Fort Wayne
1981-82	Steve Salvucci, Saginaw
1982-83	Paul Fenton, Peoria
1983-84	Mike Krensing, Muskegon
1984-85	Bill Schafhauser, Kalamazoo
1985-86	Brian Noonan, Saginaw
1986-87	Ray LeBlanc, Flint
1987-88	Dan Woodley, Flint
1988-89	Paul Ranheim, Salt Lake
1989-90	Tim Sweeney, Salt Lake
1990-91	C.J. Young, Salt Lake
1991-92	Kevin Wortman, Salt Lake
1992-93	Mark Beaufait, Kansas City
1993-94	Chris Rogles, Indianapolis

COMMISSIONER'S TROPHY

(Coach of the year)

Season	Coach, Team
1984-85	Rick Ley, Muskegon
	Pat Kelly, Peoria
1985-86	Rob Laird, Fort Wayne
1986-87	Wayne Thomas, Salt Lake
1987-88	Rick Dudley, Flint
1988-89	B. J. MacDonald, Muskegon
	Phil Russell, Muskegon
1989-90	Darryl Sutter, Indianapolis
1990-91	Bob Plager, Peoria
1991-92	Kevin Constantine, Kansas City
1992-93	Al Sims, Fort Wayne
1993-94	Bruce Boudreau, Fort Wayne

N.R. (BUD) POILE TROPHY

(Playoff MVP)

Season	Player, Team
1984-85	Denis Cyr, Peoria
1985-86	Jock Callander, Muskegon
1986-87	Rick Heinz, Salt Lake
1987-88	Peter Lappin, Salt Lake
1988-89	Dave Michayluk, Muskegon
1989-90	Mike McNeill, Indianapolis
1990-91	Michel Mongeau, Peoria
1991-92	Ron Handy, Kansas City
1992-93	Pokey Reddick, Fort Wayne
1993-94	Stan Drulia, Atlanta

The award was originally known as the Turner Cup Playoff MVP from 1984-85 through 1988-89.

IHL

REGULAR-SEASON CHAMPION

PLAYOFF CHAMPION

Season	Team	Coach	Team	Coach
1945-46	No trophy awarded		Detroit Auto Club	Jack Ward
1946-47	Windsor Staffords	Jack Ward	Windsor Spitfires	Ebbie Goodfellow
1947-48	Windsor Hettche Spitfires	Dent-Goodfellow	Toledo Mercurys	Andy Mulligan
1948-49	Toledo Mercurys	Andy Mulligan	Windsor Hettche Spitfires	Jimmy Skinner
1949-50	Sarnia Sailors	Dick Kowcinak	Catham Maroons	Bob Stoddart
1950-51	Grand Rapids Rockets	Lou Trudell	Toledo Mercurys	Alex Wood
1951-52	Grand Rapids Rockets	Lou Trudell	Toledo Mercurys	Alex Wood
1952-53	Cincinnati Mohawks	Buddy O'Conner	Cincinnati Mohawks	Buddy O'Conner
1953-54	Cincinnati Mohawks	Roly McLenahan	Cincinnati Mohawks	Roly McLenahan
1954-55	Cincinnati Mohawks	Roly McLenahan	Cincinnati Mohawks	Roly McLenahan
1955-56	Cincinnati Mohawks	Roly McLenahan	Cincinnati Mohawks	Roly McLenahan
1956-57	Cincinnati Mohawks	Roly McLenahan	Cincinnati Mohawks	Roly McLenahan
1957-58	Cincinnati Mohawks	Bill Gould	Indiana. Chiefs	Leo Lamoureux
1958-59	Louisville Rebels	Leo Gasparini	Louisville Rebels	Leo Gasparini
1959-60	Fort Wayne Komets	Ken Ullyot	St. Paul Saints	Fred Shero
1960-61	Minneapolis Millers	Ken Yachel	St. Paul Saints	Fred Shero
1961-62	Muskegon Zephrys	Moose Lallo	Muskegon Zephrys	Moose Lallo
1962-63	Fort Wayne Komets	Ken Ullyot	Fort Wayne Komets	Ken Ullyot
1963-64	Toledo Blades	Moe Benoit	Toledo Blades	Moe Benoit
1964-65	Port Huron Flags	Lloyd Maxfield	Fort Wayne Komets	Eddie Long
1965-66	Muskegon Mohawks	Moose Lallo	Port Huron Flags	Lloyd Maxfield
1966-67	Dayton Gems	Warren Back	Toledo Blades	Terry Slater
1967-68	Muskegon Mohawks	Moose Lallo	Muskegon Mohawks	Moose Lallo
1968-69	Dayton Gems	Larry Wilson	Dayton Gems	Larry Wilson
1969-70	Muskegon Mohawks	Moose Lallo	Dayton Gems	Larry Wilson
1970-71	Muskegon Mohawks	Moose Lallo	Port Huron Flags	Ted Garvin
1971-72	Muskegon Mohawks	Moose Lallo	Port Huron Flags	Ted Garvin
1972-73	Fort Wayne Komets	Marc Boileau	Fort Wayne Komets	Marc Boileau
1973-74	Des Moines Capitals	Dan Belisle	Des Moines Capitals	Dan Belisle
1974-75	Muskegon Mohawks	Moose Lallo	Toledo Goaldiggers	Ted Garvin
1975-76	Dayton Gems	Ivan Prediger	Dayton Gems	Ivan Prediger
1976-77	Saginaw Gears	Don Perry	Saginaw Gears	Don Perry
1977-78	Fort Wayne Komets	Gregg Pilling	Toledo Goaldiggers	Ted Garvin
1978-79	Grand Rapids Owls	Moe Bartoli	Kalamazoo Wings	Bill Purcell
1979-80	Kalamazoo Wings	Doug McKay	Kalamazoo Wings	Doug McKay
1980-81	Kalamazoo Wings	Doug McKay	Saginaw Gears	Don Perry
1981-82	Toledo Goaldiggers	Bill Inglis	Toledo Goaldiggers	Bill Inglis
1982-83	Toledo Goaldiggers	Bill Inglis	Toledo Goaldiggers	Bill Inglis
1983-84	Fort Wayne Komets	Ron Ullyot	Flint Generals	Dennis Desrosiers
1984-85	Peoria Rivermen	Pat Kelly	Peoria Rivermen	Pat Kelly
1985-86	Fort Wayne Komets	Rob Laird	Muskegon Lumberjacks	Rick Ley
1986-87	Fort Wayne Komets	Rob Laird	Salt Lake Golden Eagles	Wayne Thomas
1987-88	Muskegon Lumberjacks	Rick Ley	Salt Lake Golden Eagles	Paul Baxter
1988-89	Muskegon Lumberjacks	B.J. MacDonald	Muskegon Lumberjacks	B.J. MacDonald
1989-90	Muskegon Lumberjacks	B.J. MacDonald	Indianapolis Ice	Darryl Sutter
1990-91	Peoria Rivermen	Bob Plager	Peoria Rivermen	Bob Plager
1991-92	Kansas City Blades	Kevin Constantine	Kansas City Blades	Kevin Constantine
1992-93	San Diego Gulls	Rick Dudley	Fort Wayne Komets	Al Sims
1993-94	Las Vegas Thunder	Butch Goring	Atlanta Knights	Gene Ubriaco

The IHL regular-season champion is awarded the Fred A. Huber Trophy and the playoff champion is awarded the Joseph Turner Memorial Cup.

The regular-season championship award was originally called the J.P. McGuire Trophy from 1946-47 through 1953-54.

MINOR LEAGUES

IHL

EAST COAST HOCKEY LEAGUE

LEAGUE OFFICE

President/commissioner
Patrick Kelly
Director of operations
Doug Price
Administrative secretary
June Kelly

Address
AA 520
Mart Office Building
800 Briar Creek Road
Charlotte, NC 28205

Phone
704-358-3658
FAX
704-358-3560

TEAMS

BIRMINGHAM BULLS

General manager
Art Clarkson
Head coach
Phil Roberto
Home ice
Birmingham-Jefferson Civic Center
Coliseum
Address
P.O. Box 1506
Birmingham, AL 35201
Seating capacity
1,506
Phone
205-458-8833
FAX
205-458-8489

CHARLOTTE CHECKERS

General manager
Carl Scheer
Head coach
John Marks
Home ice
Independence Arena
Address
200 E. Independence Blvd.
Charlotte, NC 28205
Seating capacity
9,559
Phone
704-342-4423
FAX
704-377-4595

COLUMBUS CHILL

General manager
David Paitson
Head coach
Moe Mantha
Home ice
Fairgrounds Coliseum
Address
7001 Dublin Park Drive
Dublin, OH 43017
Seating capacity
5,800
Phone
614-791-9999
FAX
614-791-9302

DAYTON BOMBERS

General manager
Arnold Johnson
Head coach
Jim Playfair
Home ice
Hara Arena
Address
P.O. Box 5952
Dayton, OH 45405-5952
Seating capacity
5,543
Phone
513-277-3765
FAX
513-278-3007

ERIE PANTHERS

General manager and head coach
Ron Hansis
Home ice
Erie Civic Center
Address
P.O. Box 6116
Erie, PA 16512
Seating capacity
5,374
Phone
814-455-3936
FAX
814-456-8287

GREENSBORO MONARCHS

General manager and head coach
Jeff Brubaker
Home ice
Greensboro War Memorial Coliseum
Address
P.O. Box 5447
Greensboro, NC 27435-0447
Seating capacity
22,000
Phone
910-852-6170
FAX
910-852-6259

HAMPTON ROADS ADMIRALS

General manager and head coach
John Brophy
Home ice
Norfolk Scope

Address
P.O. Box 299
Norfolk, VA 23501
Seating capacity
8,994
Phone
804-640-1212
FAX
804-640-8447

HUNTINGTON BLIZZARD

General manager
Bob Henry
Head coach
Paul Pickard
Home ice
Huntington Civic Center
Address
763 Third Avenue
Huntington, WV 25701
Seating capacity
5,500
Phone
304-697-7825
FAX
304-697-7832

JOHNSTOWN CHIEFS

General manager and head coach
Eddie Johnstone
Home ice
Cambria County War Memorial Arena
Address
326 Napoleon Street
Johnstown, PA 15901
Seating capacity
4,050
Phone
814-539-1799
FAX
814-536-1316

KNOXVILLE CHEROKEES

General manager
Tim Bernal
Head coach
Barry Smith
Home ice
Knoxville Civic Coliseum
Address
500 East Church St.
Knoxville, TN 37915
Seating capacity
5,668

Phone
615-546-6707
FAX
615-546-5521

NASHVILLE KNIGHTS

General manager
Greg Lutz
Head coach
To be announced
Home ice
Municipal Auditorium
Address
417 4th Avenue North
Nashville, TN 37201
Seating capacity
7,941
Phone
615-255-7825
FAX
615-255-0024

RALEIGH ICECAPS

President
Pete Bock
Head coach
To be announced
Home ice
Dorton Arena
Address
P.O. Box 33219
Raleigh, NC 27636
Seating capacity
5,700
Phone
919-755-1427
FAX
919-755-0899

RICHMOND RENEGADES

General manager
To be announced
Head coach
Roy Sommer
Home ice
Richmond Coliseum

Address
601 East Leigh Street
Richmond, VA 23219
Seating capacity
11,000
Phone
804-643-7825
FAX
804-649-0651

ROANOKE EXPRESS

General manager
Pierre Paiemont
Head coach
Frank Anzalone
Home ice
Roanoke Civic Center
Address
4502 Starkey Road S.W., Ste. 211
Roanoke, VA 24014
Seating capacity
8,372
Phone
703-989-4625
FAX
703-989-8681

SOUTH CAROLINA STRINGRAYS

General manager
Frank Milne
Head coach
Rick Vaive
Home ice
North Charleston Coliseum
Address
5001 Coliseum Drive
N. Charleston, SC 29418
Seating capacity
10,500
Phone
803-744-2248
FAX
803-744-2898

TALLAHASSEE TIGER SHARKS

General manager
Tim Mouser

Head coach
To be announced
Home ice
Tallahassee Leon County Civic Center
Address
505 West Pensacola Street
Tallahassee, FL 32302
Seating capacity
13,500
Phone
904-224-7700
FAX
904-222-6947

TOLEDO STORM

General manager
To be announced
Head coach
Greg Puhalski
Home ice
Toledo Sports Arena
Address
One Main Street
Toledo, OH 43605
Seating capacity
5,094
Phone
419-691-0200
FAX
419-698-8998

WHEELING THUNDERBIRDS

General manager
Larry Kish
Head coach
Doug Sauter
Home ice
Wheeling Civic Center
Address
P.O. Box 6563
Wheeling, WV 26003-0815
Seating capacity
5,406
Phone
304-234-4625
FAX
304-233-4846

1993-94 REGULAR SEASON

FINAL STANDINGS

EAST DIVISION

Team	G	W	L	Pts.	GF	GA
Hampton Roads	68	41	19 (8)	90	298	246
Raleigh	68	41	20 (7)	89	296	221
Greensboro	68	41	21 (6)	88	319	262
Charlotte	68	39	25 (4)	82	281	271
Roanoke	68	37	28 (3)	77	300	290
South Carolina	68	33	26 (9)	75	294	291
Richmond	68	34	29 (5)	73	286	293

( )—Indicates overtime losses and are worth one point.

NORTH DIVISION

Team	G	W	L	Pts.	GF	GA
Toledo	68	44	20 (4)	92	338	289
Columbus	68	41	20 (7)	89	344	285
Wheeling	68	38	23 (7)	83	327	289
Johnstown	68	37	27 (4)	78	323	308
Dayton	68	29	31 (8)	66	316	308
Erie	68	27	36 (5)	59	264	334

WEST DIVISION

Team	G	W	L	Pts.	GF	GA
Knoxville	68	44	18 (6)	94	325	246
Birmingham	68	44	20 (4)	92	340	268
Nashville	68	26	36 (6)	58	255	289
Huntsville	68	20	39 (9)	49	241	315
Louisville	68	16	44 (8)	40	236	356
Huntington	68	14	49 (5)	33	191	413

INDIVIDUAL LEADERS

Goals: Darren Colbourne, Richmond (69)
Assists: Phil Berger, Greensboro (83)
Points: Phil Berger, Greensboro (139)
Penalty minutes: Trevor Buchanan, Louisville (422)
Goaltending average: Matt DelGuidice, Raleigh (2.94)
Shutouts: Cory Cadden, Knoxville (2)
Paul Cohen, Roanoke (2)

TOP SCORERS

	Games	G	A	Pts.
Phil Berger, Greensboro	68	56	83	139
Joe Flanagan, Birmingham	62	54	72	126
Darren Colbourne, Richmond	68	69	35	104
Dan Gravelle, Greensboro	58	38	66	104

	Games	G	A	Pts.
John Young, Greensboro	66	35	69	104
Derek Donald, Dayton	62	51	51	102
Tom Nemeth, Dayton	66	16	82	98
Tony Szabo, Roanoke	68	42	54	96
Scott Burfoot, Huntsville	62	31	65	96
Sylvain Fleury, South Carolina	68	46	49	95
Guy Phillips, Richmond	53	43	50	93
Steve Flomenhoft, Knoxville	64	38	55	93
Darren Schwartz, Wheeling	67	54	38	92
Joe Cook, Columbus	64	26	65	91
Greg Puhalski, Toledo	49	22	68	90
Jeff Whittle, Erie	67	47	42	89
Matt Robbins, Charlotte	53	33	56	89
Sergei Kharin, Dayton	59	30	59	89
Brendan Flynn, Richmond	63	20	69	89

INDIVIDUAL STATISTICS

BIRMINGHAM BULLS

SCORING

	Games	G	A	Pts.	PIM
Joe Flanagan	62	54	72	126	96
Paul Marshall	68	13	67	80	100
David Craievich	64	18	58	76	218
Darcy Norton	58	26	45	71	128
Jay Schiavo	59	25	46	71	32
Tom Neziol	62	35	34	69	58
Jerome Bechard	68	26	32	58	345
Mark Beran	68	23	35	58	77
Brad Smyth	29	26	30	56	38
Jim Larkin	42	26	30	56	37
Jamie Cooke	52	24	23	47	55
Murray Duval	51	6	17	23	185
Bill Kovacs	22	10	11	21	51
Dan Fournel	49	10	11	21	197
J.A. Schneider	63	3	16	19	202
Todd Harris	57	2	15	17	93
Jon Duval	62	3	12	15	244
Jamie Linden	16	3	7	10	38
Jason Cirone	11	3	3	6	45
Rick Girhiny	15	2	1	3	10
Jaroslav Nedved	2	1	1	2	2
Brad Mullahy (goalie)	41	0	2	2	20
Ed Krayer	1	1	0	1	0
Jeff Stolp (goalie)	2	0	0	0	0
Sandy Galuppo (goalie)	30	0	0	0	2

GOALTENDING

	Games	Min.	W	L	OTL	Goals	SO	Avg.
Jeff Stolp	2	120	2	0	0	4	0	2.00
Brad Mullahy	41	2298	20	16	1	150	1	3.92
Sandy Galuppo	30	1700	22	4	3	111	1	3.92

CHARLOTTE CHECKERS

SCORING

	Games	G	A	Pts.	PIM
Matt Robbins	53	33	56	89	14
Sergei Berdnikov	48	48	39	87	69
Dominic Amodeo	55	25	49	74	51
Andrei Bashkirov	62	28	42	70	25
Scott Lindsay	62	20	22	42	64
Howie Rosenblatt	44	21	17	38	173
Scott MacNair	67	10	24	34	65
Derek Eberle	46	8	21	29	97
Derek Gauthier	52	12	15	27	118
Roman Gorev	45	10	17	27	11
Joe Cleary	34	6	21	27	78
Kurt Seher	51	6	21	27	54

	Games	G	A	Pts.	PIM
Jason Christie	27	10	14	24	55
Daniel Murphy	64	7	12	19	58
Scott Meehan	53	6	11	17	100
Kevin Kaiser	12	9	4	13	6
Doug Evans	45	4	9	13	58
Brent Bobyck	44	2	11	13	14
Brian Blad	43	0	8	8	104
Gairin Smith	17	5	2	7	77
Jeff Winstanley	19	0	7	7	32
Alexei Deev	10	3	3	6	0
Jason Clarke	11	2	2	4	100
Mario Deslisle	4	3	0	3	10
Todd Hunter (goalie)	31	0	3	3	10
Pat Curcio	3	1	0	1	0
Geoff Simpson	7	1	0	1	7
Neal Sorochan	1	0	1	1	0
David Murphy	2	0	1	1	2
Brad Treliving	6	0	1	1	12
Scott Bailey (goalie)	36	0	1	1	30
Jack Tootikian	1	0	0	0	0

GOALTENDING

	Games	Min.	W	L	OTL	Goals	SO	Avg.
Scott Bailey	36	2180	22	11	3	130	1	3.58
Todd Hunter	31	1800	17	12	1	127	0	4.23

COLUMBUS CHILL

SCORING

	Games	G	A	Pts.	PIM
Joe Cook	63	26	63	89	48
Jason Smart	63	29	50	79	141
Clayton Young	39	33	45	78	98
Mark Woolf	51	42	29	71	103
Mike Ross	64	34	35	69	32
Martin Mercier	66	33	28	61	54
Rob Schriner	65	29	31	60	45
Derek Clancey	45	16	42	58	34
Darwin McClelland	58	22	34	56	59
Jesse Cooper	67	10	40	50	66
David Pensa	58	20	17	37	28
Blair Atcheynum	16	15	12	27	10
Lance Brady	56	5	22	27	130
Bryan Gendron	40	7	11	18	201
Mark Kuntz	57	3	15	18	255
Joe Crowley	20	10	6	16	56
Mark Cipriano	22	2	11	13	136
Aaron Boh	10	1	9	10	31
John Sandell	48	1	6	7	72
Ted Beattie	20	1	5	6	33
Shawn Yakimishyn	7	1	4	5	25
Yvan Corbin	10	2	2	4	17

	Games	G	A	Pts.	PIM
Sergei Tkachenko (goalie)	35	0	4	4	4
John Badduke	7	0	3	3	60
Gord Pell	2	1	1	2	2
Steve Daniels	4	1	1	2	20
Troy Neumeier	2	0	2	2	2
Jerry Rosenheck	10	0	2	2	2
Clayton Gainer	1	0	0	0	0
Kelly Harris	1	0	0	0	2
Kurt Woolf	1	0	0	0	0
Ludis Schnore	1	0	0	0	0
Ken Weiss (goalie)	2	0	0	0	0
Brian Langlot (goalie)	3	0	0	0	0
Jim Slazyk (goalie)	16	0	0	0	0
Sergei Khramtsov (goalie)	22	0	0	0	0

GOALTENDING

	Games	Min.	W	L	OTL	Goals	SO	Avg.
Sergei Khramtsov	22	1171	13	6	2	69	1	3.53
Brian Langlot	3	159	1	1	0	10	0	3.76
Sergei Tkachenko	34	1884	18	7	4	129	1	4.11
Jim Slazyk	16	836	8	5	1	58	1	4.16
Ken Weiss	2	54	1	1	0	5	0	5.58

DAYTON BOMBERS

SCORING

	Games	G	A	Pts.	PIM
Derek Donald	62	51	51	102	98
Tom Nemeth	66	16	82	98	91
Sergei Kharin	59	30	59	89	56
Phil Huber	44	25	42	67	107
Dan O'Shea	66	36	30	66	60
Mike Reier	38	26	31	57	62
Jim Lessard	46	17	27	44	205
Steve Bogoyevac	30	14	25	39	16
Steve Wilson	60	13	26	39	134
John Brill	57	13	19	32	68
Jason Disiewich	57	19	11	30	61
Ray Edwards	51	14	10	24	167
Rob Hartnell	37	9	15	24	133
Jason Downey	35	2	22	24	176
Mike Vandenberghe	37	6	14	20	85
Kord Cernich	21	4	13	17	14
Butch Kaebel	14	7	7	14	23
Rhys Hollyman	18	3	4	7	18
Mike Heaney	11	0	7	7	36
S. Panfilenkov	12	2	3	5	8
Darwin McPherson	16	0	4	4	90
John Roderick	26	2	1	3	46
Benoit Paquet	7	0	3	3	4
Jeff Bes	2	2	0	2	12
Rick Girhiny	5	2	0	2	0
Guy Prince	14	1	1	2	14
Ondrej Kriz	13	0	2	2	6
Marc Savard	11	0	1	1	14
Adam Young	16	0	1	1	10
Jeff Levy (goalie)	31	0	1	1	48
Jeff Stolp (goalie)	35	0	1	1	21
Chris Puscian (goalie)	1	0	0	0	0
Rob Laurie (goalie)	2	0	0	0	2
Joey Mittelsteadt	2	0	0	0	12
Kevin Koopman (goalie)	3	0	0	0	2
Daryl Reaugh (goalie)	4	0	0	0	0
Neal Sorochan	5	0	0	0	2

GOALTENDING

	Games	Min.	W	L	OTL	Goals	SO	Avg.
Kevin Koopman	3	135	2	0	0	6	0	2.67
Jeff Stolp	35	2017	15	13	5	132	0	3.93
Jeff Levy	31	1672	10	13	3	125	0	4.48
Rob Laurie	2	120	1	1	0	9	0	4.50
Daryl Reaugh	4	160	1	3	0	17	0	6.38
Chris Puscian	1	28	0	1	0	5	0	10.54

ERIE PANTHERS

SCORING

	Games	G	A	Pts.	PIM
Jeff Whittle	67	47	42	89	126
Brian Shantz	54	25	43	68	58
Jason Smith	68	22	37	59	44
Casey Hungle	64	28	17	45	51
John DePourcq	28	14	29	43	4
John Vary	55	10	29	39	129
Brandy Semchuk	44	17	15	32	37
S. Charbonneau	23	22	8	30	130
Dan O'Rourke	64	9	21	30	296
Marc Savard	47	2	27	29	111
V. Polikarkin	26	9	16	25	10
Jeff Budai	54	6	13	19	114
Fredrik Jax	14	6	11	17	12
Jim Lessard	17	5	10	15	93
Chris Nelson	26	2	13	15	53
Eric Gregoire	64	1	13	14	70
Mark Franks	14	5	6	11	22
Keith Cyr	10	4	5	9	14
Mirsad Mujcin	21	4	5	9	128
Shayne Green	5	1	5	6	0
Mark Bultje	15	1	5	6	19
Reo Lajeunesse	6	2	3	5	2
Mark Strapon	23	0	5	5	64
Andrei Kozlov	17	0	4	4	95
Sergei Stas	2	1	2	3	4
Brian Sutton	11	1	2	3	29
Darren Cota	5	0	2	2	11
Robert Haddock	8	0	2	2	16
Dan Goldie	10	0	2	2	27
Mark Bernard (goalie)	48	0	2	2	25
Jason Clarke	3	1	0	1	57
Marcel Richard	1	0	1	1	0
Oleg Kovalaenko	6	0	1	1	4
Serge Labelle	18	0	1	1	93
Vern Guetens (goalie)	22	0	1	1	6
Mike Gilmore (goalie)	1	0	0	0	0
Chris Puscian (goalie)	1	0	0	0	0
Justin Cullen	2	0	0	0	0
Jon Hillebrandt (goalie)	3	0	0	0	0
Adam Hayes	4	0	0	0	0

GOALTENDING

	Games	Min.	W	L	OTL	Goals	SO	Avg.
Mike Gilmore	1	34	1	0	0	0	0	0.00
Jon Hillebrandt	3	190	2	0	1	8	1	2.53
Vern Guetens	21	1116	5	11	1	83	0	4.46
Mark Bernard	48	2788	19	25	3	235	0	5.06
Chris Puscian	1	6	0	0	0	1	0	10.23

GREENSBORO MONARCHS

SCORING

	Games	G	A	Pts.	PIM
Phil Berger	68	56	83	139	118
Dan Gravelle	58	38	66	104	73
John Young	66	35	69	104	67
Sebastien LaPlante	60	35	38	73	206
Chris Valicevic	59	14	38	52	73
Darryl Noren	26	16	23	39	41
Trevor Burgess	36	9	29	38	76
Todd Tretter	59	14	23	37	61
Brendan Creagh	61	20	16	36	112
Davis Payne	36	17	17	34	139
Dan Bylsma	25	14	16	30	52
Dean Zayonce	56	11	16	27	260
Scott White	27	3	21	24	65
Sverre Sears	63	6	17	23	158
Greg Capson	50	8	14	22	277
J.F. Jomphe	25	9	9	18	41
Savo Mitrovic	29	3	14	17	12
Chris Wolanin	35	4	10	14	68

	Games	G	A	Pts.	PIM
Trevor Senn	4	2	3	5	50
Chris Marshall	10	3	1	4	8
Glen Mears	25	1	3	4	29
Jamie Nicolls	16	0	4	4	44
Paul Willett	2	1	0	1	4
Patrick Labrecque (goalie)	29	0	1	1	54
John Devereaux	1	0	0	0	0
Scott Hanley	3	0	0	0	4
Don Borgeson	4	0	0	0	25
Wade Klippenstein	4	0	0	0	0
Todd Gordon	5	0	0	0	17
Stig Salomonsson (goalie)	6	0	0	0	4
Chris Jensen	18	0	0	0	31
Tom Newman (goalie)	39	0	0	0	0

GOALTENDING

	Games	Min.	W	L	OTL	Goals	SO	Avg.
Stig Salomonsson	6	337	3	1	1	17	1	3.03
Patrick Labrecque	29	1609	17	8	2	89	0	3.32
Tom Newman	39	2152	21	12	3	142	0	3.96

HAMPTON ROADS ADMIRALS

SCORING

	Games	G	A	Pts.	PIM
Rod Taylor	65	54	34	88	133
Brendan Curley	67	25	54	79	106
Victor Gervais	31	22	53	75	82
Shawn Wheeler	47	31	43	74	156
Shawn Snesar	67	12	44	56	151
Dennis McEwen	58	14	38	52	58
Daniel Chaput	68	10	36	46	95
Kelly Sorensen	57	18	27	45	116
Ron Pascucci	58	11	33	44	81
Kevin Malgunas	37	12	28	40	132
Vincent Faucher	31	12	24	36	34
Ralph Barahona	27	13	20	33	12
Andrew Brunette	20	12	18	30	32
Eric Fenton	24	12	16	28	39
Brian Goudie	55	8	11	19	306
Jason MacIntyre	55	10	8	18	195
Darren Perkins	49	8	10	18	144
Stephen Perkovic	47	5	9	14	113
Dave Shute	8	2	4	6	6
Mark Michaud (goalie)	65	0	5	5	31
Glenn Kulka	9	2	1	3	8
Richie Walcott	41	2	1	3	143
Jim Brown	1	2	0	2	0
Brian Martin	3	0	2	2	29
Bill Harrington	4	1	0	1	4
Ken Murchison	3	0	0	0	0
Rob Madia	4	0	0	0	4
Shamus Gregga (goalie)	11	0	0	0	0

GOALTENDING

	Games	Min.	W	L	OTL	Goals	SO	Avg.
Mark Michaud	65	3723	38	17	8	214	1	3.45
Shamus Gregga	10	394	3	2	0	24	0	3.65

HUNTINGTON BLIZZARD

SCORING

	Games	G	A	Pts.	PIM
Brad Harrison	67	18	41	59	239
Geoff Simpson	60	16	28	44	77
Gordie Frantti	41	19	20	39	171
Ray Alcindor	63	17	16	33	61
Malcom Cameron	68	9	20	29	50
Murray Garbutt	34	14	12	26	40
Jay Neal	43	11	15	26	53
Shayne Antoski	45	10	13	23	25
Doug Roberts	31	12	9	21	4
Jerad Bedner	66	8	11	19	115
Mark Franks	16	12	5	17	14

	Games	G	A	Pts.	PIM
Pete Mehalic	33	6	8	14	84
Jim McGroarty	13	5	8	13	4
Ray Gallagher	34	6	4	10	20
Dave Dimitri	37	5	5	10	24
Kevin Kaiser	9	3	6	9	0
Alexei Deev	12	3	6	9	2
John Craighead	9	4	2	6	44
Doug Stromback	23	2	4	6	30
Derrick D'Amore	22	1	4	5	14
Chris Hatch	23	1	4	5	4
Helmut Karel	3	3	1	4	6
Andy Borggard	13	2	2	4	2
Marshall Kronewitt	29	2	2	4	46
Tom Sprague	10	0	3	3	39
Mark Velucci	13	0	3	3	14
Ron Majic	21	0	3	3	161
Greg Bailey	52	0	3	3	257
Bob Clouston	7	1	1	2	6
Todd Huyber	17	0	2	2	15
Jim Mill (goalie)	23	0	2	2	0
Marcel Sakic	5	1	0	1	13
Todd Tretter	1	0	1	1	0
John Finstrom	5	0	1	1	0
Robert Haddock	2	0	0	0	17
Doug Melvin (goalie)	4	0	0	0	0
Chris French (goalie)	23	0	0	0	0
Greg Scott (goalie)	31	0	0	0	0

GOALTENDING

	Games	Min.	W	L	OTL	Goals	SO	Avg.
Doug Melvin	4	194	0	3	1	16	0	4.96
Greg Scott	31	1442	6	18	1	131	0	5.45
Chris French	23	1200	4	11	3	115	0	5.75
Jim Mill	23	1198	4	16	0	135	0	6.76

HUNTSVILLE BLAST

SCORING

	Games	G	A	Pts.	PIM
Scott Burfoot	62	31	65	96	80
Ken House	68	41	39	80	51
Joe Dragon	59	10	35	45	108
Craig Herr	68	20	23	43	108
Pat Cavanagh	48	18	24	42	350
Greg Geldart	58	12	28	40	33
Bob McKillop	31	15	23	38	24
Rhys Hollyman	47	11	21	32	79
Steve Beadle	42	7	18	25	67
Rob Madia	56	15	9	24	39
Tom O'Rourke	49	8	16	24	83
Chris Belanger	23	6	18	24	36
Mike Jorgensen	37	13	10	23	8
Conrade Thomas	46	11	12	23	39
David Burke	59	4	16	20	53
Clark Polglase	34	2	14	16	200
Don Burke	25	2	8	10	27
Pat Curcio	13	1	9	10	16
Mark Bultje	12	4	3	7	10
Mario Deslisle	23	2	2	4	19
Savo Mitrovic	6	1	3	4	14
Vic Posa	9	1	3	4	33
Todd Chin (goalie)	47	0	4	4	29
Kurt Walston	13	1	2	3	107
Ray DeSouza	7	1	1	2	31
Curt Krolak	10	1	1	2	10
Dan Fowler	4	1	0	1	8
John Roderick	8	1	0	1	22
Todd Humphrey	3	1	0	1	71
Rob McDougall	1	0	1	1	0
Chris Jensen	14	0	1	1	8
Tony Colandra	1	0	0	0	0
Guy Prince	1	0	0	0	2
Todd King (goalie)	2	0	0	0	0
Jim Slazyk (goalie)	2	0	0	0	0
Ken Weiss (goalie)	1	0	0	0	0
Jamie Stewart (goalie)	26	0	0	0	0

GOALTENDING

	Games	Min.	W	L	OTL	Goals	SO	Avg.
Todd Chin	47	2395	15	19	4	175	0	4.38
Jamie Stewart	26	1350	5	15	3	101	0	4.49
Jim Slazyk	2	78	0	1	0	6	0	4.64
Ken Weiss	7	308	0	4	1	25	0	4.87
Todd King	2	39	0	1	0	11	0	16.73

JOHNSTOWN CHIEFS

SCORING

	Games	G	A	Pts.	PIM
Ted Dent	67	30	54	84	161
Dennis Purdie	57	36	46	82	171
Matt Hoffman	58	33	40	73	85
Bob Woods	43	18	37	55	57
Gord Christian	45	29	25	54	95
Perry Florio	62	12	40	52	117
Jason Jennings	44	19	26	45	38
Bruce Coles	24	23	20	43	56
Jamie Adams	43	16	21	37	16
Chuck Wiegand	46	18	18	36	36
Rob Leask	52	11	25	36	137
Cory Banika	48	16	14	30	262
Campbell Blair	52	5	22	27	56
Martin D'Orsonnens	53	5	22	27	94
Tim Hanus	20	9	14	23	28
Francois Bourdeau	63	6	17	23	61
Jan Beran	18	10	6	16	15
Glen Lang	31	4	8	12	14
Phil Soukoroff	13	2	9	11	9
Rival Fullum	12	4	6	10	11
Yannick Frechette	15	5	3	8	57
Ben Wyzansky	9	1	7	8	8
Dusty McLellan	10	2	5	7	39
Randy Skarda	9	1	6	7	6
Jeff Grant	10	1	6	7	15
Kevin Quinn	26	1	5	6	128
Matt Yingst	6	2	3	5	10
Helmut Karel	6	1	4	5	31
John Bradley	36	0	3	3	55
Eric Dandenault	2	1	1	2	6
Shayne Antoski	3	0	2	2	2
Shawn Bourgeois	7	0	2	2	7
Stephen Sangermano	2	1	0	1	0
David Murphy	4	1	0	1	5
Rob Laurie (goalie)	35	0	1	1	6
Gord Law	2	0	0	0	2
Garry Gulash	3	0	0	0	60
Kyle Blacklock	8	0	0	0	10
Adam Thompson (goalie)	8	0	0	0	0
John Bradley (goalie)	36	0	0	0	0

GOALTENDING

	Games	Min.	W	L	OTL	Goals	SO	Avg.
Rob Laurie	34	1942	18	13	1	128	0	3.96
John Bradley	36	1834	16	13	2	143	1	4.68
Adam Thompson	8	333	3	1	1	28	0	5.05

KNOXVILLE CHEROKEES

SCORING

	Games	G	A	Pts.	PIM
Steve Flomenhoft	64	38	55	93	52
Nicholas Vachon	61	29	57	86	139
Scott Metcalfe	56	25	56	81	136
Mike Murray	68	32	45	77	36
Kim Maier	66	35	32	67	54
Jeff Reid	57	27	31	58	46
Carl LeBlanc	68	15	42	57	157
Bruno Villeneuve	48	27	29	56	65
Scott Boston	64	9	30	39	213
Scott Hollis	28	20	16	36	99
Marc Rodgers	27	12	18	30	83
Wes McCauley	56	2	28	30	134

	Games	G	A	Pts.	PIM
Jon Larson	51	10	19	29	66
Hayden O'Rear	61	7	20	27	83
Martin Tanguay	17	7	19	26	13
Frank Evans	38	6	17	23	217
Jack Duffy	33	6	15	21	73
Doug Searle	65	6	12	18	154
Timothy Chase	37	2	15	17	65
Devin Edgerton	6	5	10	15	2
Yvan Corbin	9	4	1	5	4
Cory Cadden (goalie)	40	0	5	5	10
Dave Larouche	5	1	3	4	2
Scott Gordon (goalie)	27	0	1	1	8
Kevin Butt (goalie)	1	0	0	0	2
Manon Rheaume (goalie)	4	0	0	0	0

GOALTENDING

	Games	Min.	W	L	OTL	Goals	SO	Avg.
Cory Cadden	40	2349	26	8	4	121	2	3.09
Scott Gordon	26	1518	15	10	1	98	0	3.87
Kevin Butt	1	60	1	0	0	4	0	4.00
Manon Rheaume	4	187	2	0	1	13	0	4.17

LOUISVILLE ICEHAWKS

SCORING

	Games	G	A	Pts.	PIM
Jamie Steer	68	32	48	80	49
Brian Cook	67	28	52	80	82
Greg Hagen	63	31	33	64	25
Trevor Buchanan	65	26	26	52	422
Sheldon Gorski	41	22	28	50	85
Ken Plaquin	65	9	35	44	72
George Zajankala	40	13	22	35	114
Jeff Sebastian	66	11	19	30	51
Glenn Clark	57	12	15	27	84
Rob Sumner	68	4	21	25	229
Mike Fiset	33	12	11	23	36
Ray Gallagher	33	4	17	21	24
Adam Hayes	35	10	10	20	39
Brad Treliving	37	2	17	19	185
Jim McGroarty	30	4	11	15	6
Jeff Grant	31	5	4	9	36
Bryan Miller	23	2	5	7	12
Mike Chighisola	9	2	3	5	13
Keith Harris	9	2	3	5	19
Mark Sorensen	20	2	3	5	19
Keith Carney	15	1	4	5	14
Jay Luknowsky	5	0	5	5	6
Ron Majic	8	0	3	3	74
Paul Ohman	15	0	3	3	23
Scott Kelsey	27	0	3	3	10
Brian Schoen (goalie)	11	0	2	2	6
Kevin Koopman (goalie)	20	0	2	2	22
Joel Eagan	21	0	2	2	49
Chris Clifford (goalie)	35	0	2	2	8
Damion DiGiulian	6	0	1	1	0
John Van Dale	1	0	0	0	2
Kelly Hiltgen	9	0	0	0	39
Rocco Trentadue (goalie)	10	0	0	0	6

GOALTENDING

	Games	Min.	W	L	OTL	Goals	SO	Avg.
Brian Schoen	11	576	3	7	0	43	0	4.48
Chris Clifford	35	1894	11	18	4	152	0	4.82
Kevin Koopman	20	1053	1	10	4	89	0	5.07
Rocco Trentadue	10	581	1	9	0	61	0	6.30

NASHVILLE KNIGHTS

SCORING

	Games	G	A	Pts.	PIM
Greg Burke	68	29	46	75	190
Stansilav Tkach	67	36	35	71	143
Tim Sullivan	65	33	33	66	141

	Games	G	A	Pts.	PIM
Dean Gerard	68	24	30	54	123
Rob Dumas	52	11	36	47	203
Scott Rogers	61	19	20	39	100
Mike DeCarle	45	10	29	39	86
Scott Matusovich	68	4	35	39	52
Brandon Coates	42	20	17	37	111
Mike Chighisola	28	12	15	27	126
Gerry Daley	30	12	13	25	20
Jamie Adams	17	8	11	19	6
Ben Wyzansky	49	2	13	15	59
Chris Wayland	65	2	13	15	68
Jason Courtemanch	46	6	6	12	140
Doug Roberts	28	5	7	12	2
Chuck Wiegand	13	5	2	7	4
Murray Garbutt	20	5	2	7	41
Andy Borggard	18	5	1	6	45
Jim Peters	6	2	2	4	19
Andrei Dylevsky	28	0	3	3	20
Stephen Corfmat	42	2	0	2	304
Jeff Rohlicek	4	1	1	2	24
Link Gaetz	24	1	1	2	261
Pasi Shalin	4	0	2	2	0
Tom Cole (goalie)	30	0	2	2	2
Paolo D'Ambrosi	8	1	0	1	4
Todd King (goalie)	12	0	1	1	2
Eddie Sabo	1	0	0	0	11
Manon Rheaume (goalie)	4	0	0	0	0
Steven Sullivan	5	0	0	0	31
Jamie Stewart (goalie)	14	0	0	0	4
Mike Parson (goalie)	16	0	0	0	2

GOALTENDING

	Games	Min.	W	L	OTL	Goals	SO	Avg.
Manon Rheaume	4	198	3	0	0	12	0	3.64
Tom Cole	29	1612	11	14	0	104	0	3.87
Mike Parson	16	904	8	6	1	61	1	4.05
Todd King	12	596	3	6	2	41	0	4.13
Jamie Stewart	14	805	1	10	3	60	0	4.47

RALEIGH ICECAPS

SCORING

	Games	G	A	Pts.	PIM
Lyle Wildgoose	68	40	46	86	56
Jim Powers	55	18	45	63	61
Donevan Hextall	61	13	49	62	55
Steve Mirabile	41	20	28	48	80
Rick Barkovich	36	18	28	46	35
Alan Leggett	61	10	34	44	87
Mike Lappin	27	18	19	37	10
Karl Johnston	48	14	23	37	84
Ralph Barahona	36	14	21	35	12
Derek Linnell	60	18	14	32	43
Bill Gall	35	12	20	32	8
Jeff Jablonski	20	11	20	31	13
Shaun Kane	49	9	20	29	79
Kevin Riehl	21	11	14	25	35
Dave Shute	27	10	13	23	21
Jeff Winstanley	23	4	9	13	45
Curt Regnier	7	6	5	11	10
Jeff Robison	57	3	8	11	106
Eric Roberts	19	7	3	10	2
Barry Nieckar	18	4	6	10	126
Bruce MacDonald	25	4	6	10	21
Kevin Malgunas	10	6	3	9	26
Jarrett Reid	10	3	6	9	8
Chris Nelson	22	3	5	8	49
Chic Pojar	25	3	5	8	17
Yannick Frechette	19	5	2	7	62
Joe McCarthy	28	2	4	6	10
Matt DelGuidice (goalie)	32	0	6	6	14
Glen Lang	11	5	0	5	2
Jamie Erb	10	3	1	4	8
Chris Marshall	7	2	1	3	2
Krzysztof Oliwa	15	0	2	2	65

	Games	G	A	Pts.	PIM
Martin D'Orsonnens	11	0	2	2	39
Chad Erickson (goalie)	32	0	1	1	10
Scott Asburn	1	0	0	0	0
Brian Clark	1	0	0	0	0
Jason Jennings	2	0	0	0	4
Todd Person	2	0	0	0	0
Chris Taylor	2	0	0	0	0
Brian Langlot (goalie)	4	0	0	0	0
Stan Reddick (goalie)	4	0	0	0	0

GOALTENDING

	Games	Min.	W	L	OTL	Goals	SO	Avg.
Stan Reddick	4	183	3	0	0	7	0	2.29
Matt DelGuidice	31	1878	18	9	4	92	1	2.94
Chad Erickson	32	1884	19	9	3	101	0	3.22
Brian Langlot	4	168	1	2	0	10	0	3.57

RICHMOND RENEGADES

SCORING

	Games	G	A	Pts.	PIM
Darren Colbourne	68	69	35	104	100
Guy Phillips	53	43	50	93	50
Brendan Flynn	63	20	69	89	76
Alan Schuler	68	8	59	67	44
Chris Foy	65	17	31	48	164
Steve Bogoyevac	32	16	20	36	16
Ken Blum	61	11	25	36	215
Colin Gregor	40	10	21	31	79
John Craighead	28	18	12	30	89
Rob MacInnis	27	9	18	27	75
Jason Renard	35	12	12	24	262
Oleg Santuryan	47	7	13	20	90
Eric Germain	56	3	16	19	192
Jim McGeough	26	10	8	18	10
Peter Allen	52	2	16	18	62
Rob Hartnell	29	4	11	15	87
Mike Vandenberghe	28	5	5	10	135
Jim Ballantine	25	5	3	8	8
Devin Derksen	63	3	3	6	118
Jeff Marshall	12	3	2	5	10
Roger Larche	8	2	3	5	41
Mike Heaney	5	0	5	5	8
Sean Cowan	20	0	5	5	52
Alex Zahan	27	2	2	4	49
Jon Gustafson (goalie)	34	0	3	3	6
Milan Hnilicka (goalie)	43	0	3	3	10
Mike May	3	2	0	2	2
Mark Kuntz	4	2	0	2	32
Grant Chorney	4	1	1	2	31
Kyle O'Brien	3	1	0	1	6
Jodi Murphy	3	0	1	1	0
Rocco Amonte	1	0	0	0	2
Bob Jones (goalie)	1	0	0	0	0
Travis Peterson	1	0	0	0	10
Bill Harrington	2	0	0	0	2
Jason Anderson	4	0	0	0	2

GOALTENDING

	Games	Min.	W	L	OTL	Goals	SO	Avg.
Milan Hnilicka	43	2299	18	16	5	155	0	4.05
Jon Gustafson	34	1674	15	11	0	122	1	4.37
Bob Jones	1	47	0	1	0	4	0	5.14

ROANOKE VALLEY RAMPAGE

SCORING

	Games	G	A	Pts.	PIM
Tony Szabo	68	42	54	96	84
Pat Ferschweiler	68	27	58	85	79
Oleg Yashin	68	38	45	83	55
Jeff Jestadt	67	43	21	64	69
Ilja Dubkov	68	25	39	64	88
Michael Smith	67	5	57	62	62

	Games	G	A	Pts.	PIM
Lev Berdichevsky	44	39	19	58	47
Will Averill	65	6	45	51	94
chris Potter	64	11	26	37	107
Roger Larche	37	9	20	29	135
Claude Barthe	65	6	17	23	108
Dave Morissette	45	8	10	18	278
Trevor Burgess	25	6	12	18	37
Gairin Smith	38	6	11	17	137
Conrade Thomas	16	7	5	12	29
Kyle Galloway	59	1	9	10	101
Gerry Daley	13	6	3	9	10
Reggie Brezeault	26	4	4	8	75
Hughes Bouchard	41	1	6	7	49
Dan Dorion	8	3	3	6	4
Keith Cyr	8	3	2	5	4
Stephan Tepper	9	2	2	4	33
Ladislav Svobado	6	1	2	3	14
Tom Holdeman	14	1	2	3	12
Gord Pell	3	0	2	2	0
Paul Ohman	3	0	1	1	0
Dan Ryder (goalie)	43	0	1	1	58
Andrei Mecir (goalie)	1	0	0	0	0
Oleg Santuryan	1	0	0	0	0
Brian Schoen (goalie)	6	0	0	0	2
Jim Mill (goalie)	13	0	0	0	0
Paul Cohen (goalie)	24	0	0	0	4

GOALTENDING

	Games	Min.	W	L	OTL	Goals	SO	Avg.
Andrei Mecir	1	18	0	1	0	1	0	3.28
Paul Cohen	24	1237	10	7	2	73	2	3.54
Dan Ryder	42	1947	22	13	0	129	0	3.98
Brian Schoen	6	279	1	4	0	23	0	4.94
Jim Mill	13	598	4	3	1	50	0	5.01

SOUTH CAROLINA STINGRAYS

SCORING

	Games	G	A	Pts.	PIM
Sylvain Fleury	68	46	49	95	36
Chris Bright	59	40	47	87	134
Gary Socha	64	23	37	60	60
Mark Green	65	25	29	54	54
Ken Thibodeau	62	24	30	54	35
Jason Winch	57	15	37	52	47
Trevor Smith	68	13	39	52	64
Scott Beattie	29	20	28	48	40
Tim Harris	60	13	35	48	137
Jim Sprott	46	8	25	33	221
Dan Wiebe	38	15	16	31	40
Daniel Ruoho	56	7	22	29	106
Andrei Iakovenko	42	4	25	29	141
Andy Bezeau	36	10	10	20	352
Eric Brule	18	7	11	18	14
Francis Kearney	61	7	10	17	31
Tim Breslin	9	3	3	6	4
Garth Premak	13	2	4	6	18
Brad Pascall	32	1	5	6	68
Tom Holdeman	6	4	1	5	2
Russ Herrington	14	2	2	4	16
Alexander Legault	8	2	0	2	10
Matt Mallgrave	4	1	0	1	6
Rick Lessard	5	1	0	1	10
Slava Iakovenko	20	1	0	1	20
Derek Booth	3	0	1	1	15
Adam Thompson (goalie)	5	0	1	1	0
Stephen Sagermano	2	0	0	0	0
Troy Mohns	9	0	0	0	14
Adam Young	10	0	0	0	0
Bill Pye (goalie)	28	0	0	0	14
Francis Ouellette (goalie)	41	0	0	0	14

GOALTENDING

	Games	Min.	W	L	OTL	Goals	SO	Avg.
Bill Pye	28	1578	15	10	2	95	1	3.61
Francis Ouellette	41	2336	16	15	7	166	0	4.26
Adam Thompson	5	209	2	1	0	17	0	4.88

TOLEDO STORM

SCORING

	Games	G	A	Pts.	PIM
Greg Puhalski	49	22	68	90	90
Rick Judson	61	39	49	88	16
Jeff Rohlicek	57	28	54	82	36
Alex Hicks	60	31	49	80	240
Mark Deazeley	57	41	36	77	231
Rick Corriveau	48	21	40	61	124
Darren Perkins	64	23	31	54	160
John Hendry	68	23	31	54	107
Mike Markovich	58	9	29	38	119
Mark McCreary	30	15	18	33	14
Chris Belanger	31	11	20	31	47
Kyle Reeves	33	12	13	25	75
Dennis Snedden	26	7	14	21	27
Chris Bergeron	18	10	10	20	26
Jay Neal	24	8	10	18	36
Andy Suhy	61	5	11	16	237
Sasha Lakovic	24	5	10	15	198
Iain Duncan	8	6	8	14	23
Pat Pylypuik	46	3	11	14	157
Barry Potomski	13	9	4	13	81
Marc Lyons	66	0	11	11	80
Bruce MacDonald	17	3	6	9	4
Steve Dykstra	11	3	5	8	37
Dave Gagnon (goalie)	20	0	3	3	25
Joe Cook	1	0	2	2	0
Alain Harvey (goalie)	13	0	2	2	0
Kurt Semandel	5	1	0	1	6
Ron Aubrey	1	0	0	0	2
Scott Shaw (goalie)	1	0	0	0	0
Erin Whitten (goalie)	4	0	0	0	0
Nick Vitucci (goalie)	28	0	0	0	6

GOALTENDING

	Games	Min.	W	L	OTL	Goals	SO	Avg.
Dave Gagnon	20	1122	13	5	0	65	1	3.48
Nick Vitucci	27	1532	15	6	4	93	0	3.64
Scott Shaw	1	63	1	0	0	4	0	3.81
Alain Harvey	13	672	9	2	0	56	0	5.00
Erin Whitten	4	150	2	0	0	20	0	8.01

WHEELING THUNDERBIRDS

SCORING

	Games	G	A	Pts.	PIM
Darren Schwartz	67	54	38	92	201
Tim Tisdale	58	31	57	88	76
Vadim Slivchenko	45	39	46	85	65
Tim Roberts	66	18	58	76	68
Jim Bermingham	68	29	46	75	102
Steve Gibson	55	29	30	59	47
Derek DeCosty	52	23	25	48	92
John Johnson	57	12	22	34	60
Cory Paterson	52	9	24	33	74
Terry Virtue	34	5	28	33	61
Tony Prpic	40	17	16	33	39
Brock Woods	64	10	22	32	225
Rival Fullum	50	13	17	30	35
Sebastian Fortier	62	6	22	28	36
Brent Pope	63	8	19	27	230
Marquis Mathieu	42	12	11	23	75
Peter Marek	14	7	13	20	27
John Van Kessel	17	1	8	9	119
Clayton Gainer	11	3	1	4	49
Brett Abel (goalie)	43	0	4	4	23
Kelly Chase	4	0	2	2	2
Steve Walker	9	1	0	1	2
Dion Darling	3	0	1	1	7
Bill Horn (goalie)	4	0	1	1	0
Sylvain LaPointe	15	0	1	1	16
Hiroyuki Miura	6	0	0	0	0
Eric Raymond (goalie)	31	0	0	0	4

GOALTENDING

	Games	Min.	W	L	OTL	Goals	SO	Avg.
Bill Horn	4	107	2	0		5	0	2.80
Eric Raymond	30	1660	14	9	6	99	0	3.58
Brett Abel	43	2359	22	14	1	177	1	4.50

PLAYERS WITH TWO OR MORE TEAMS

SCORING

	Games	G	A	Pts.	PIM
Jamie Adams, Johnstown	43	16	21	37	16
Jamie Adams, Nashville	17	8	11	19	6
Totals	60	24	32	56	22
Shayne Antoski, Johnstown	3	0	2	2	2
Shayne Antoski, Huntington	45	10	13	23	25
Totals	48	10	15	25	27
Ralph Barahona, Raleigh	36	14	21	35	12
Ralph Barahona, H.R.	27	13	20	33	12
Totals	63	27	41	68	24
Chris Belanger, Toledo	31	11	20	31	47
Chris Belanger, Huntsville	23	6	18	24	36
Totals	54	17	38	55	83
Steve Bogoyevac, Dayton	30	14	25	39	16
Steve Bogoyevac, Richmond	32	16	20	36	16
Totals	62	30	45	75	32
Andy Borggard, Nashville	18	5	1	6	45
Andy Borggard, Huntington	13	2	2	4	2
Totals	31	7	3	10	47
Mark Bultje, Huntsville	12	4	3	7	10
Mark Bultje, Erie	15	1	5	6	19
Totals	27	5	8	13	29
Trevor Burgess, Greensboro	36	9	29	38	76
Trevor Burgess, Roanoke	25	6	12	18	37
Totals	61	15	41	56	113
Mike Chighisola, Nashville	28	12	15	27	126
Mike Chighisola, Louisville	9	2	3	5	13
Totals	37	14	18	32	139
Jason Clarke, Charlotte	11	2	2	4	100
Jason Clarke, Erie	3	1	0	1	57
Totals	14	3	2	5	157
Joe Cook, Toledo	1	0	2	2	0
Joe Cook, Columbus	63	26	63	89	48
Totals	64	26	65	91	48
Yvan Corbin, Knoxville	9	4	1	5	4
Yvan Corbin , Columbus	10	2	2	4	17
Totals	19	6	3	9	21
John Craighead, Huntington	9	4	2	6	44
John Craighead, Richmond	28	18	12	30	89
Totals	37	22	14	36	133
Pat Curcio, Charlotte	3	1	0	1	0
Pat Curcio, Huntsville	13	1	9	10	16
Totals	16	2	9	11	16
Keith Cyr, Erie	10	4	5	9	14
Keith Cyr, Roanoke	8	3	2	5	4
Totals	18	7	7	14	18
Gerry Daley, Roanoke	13	6	3	9	10
Gerry Daley, Nashville	30	12	13	25	20
Totals	43	18	16	34	30
Alexei Deev, Charlotte	10	3	3	6	0
Alexei Deev, Huntington	12	3	6	9	2
Totals	22	6	9	15	2
Mario Deslisle, Charlotte	4	3	0	3	10
Mario Deslisle, Huntsville	23	2	2	4	19
Totals	27	5	2	7	29
Martin D'Orsonnens, Raleigh	11	0	2	2	39
Martin D'Orsonnens, Johnstown	53	5	22	27	94
Totals	64	5	24	29	133
Mark Franks, Erie	14	5	6	11	22
Mark Franks, Huntington	16	12	5	17	14
Totals	30	17	11	28	36
Yannick Frechette, Raleigh	19	5	2	7	62
Yannick Frechette, Johnstown	15	5	3	8	57
Totals	34	10	5	15	119
Rival Fullum, Johnstown	12	4	6	10	11
Rival Fullum, Wheeling	50	13	17	30	35
Totals	62	17	23	40	46

	Games	G	A	Pts.	PIM
Clayton Gainer, Wheeling	11	3	1	4	49
Clayton Gainer, Columbus	1	0	0	0	0
Totals	12	3	1	4	49
Ray Gallagher, Louisville	33	4	17	21	24
Ray Gallagher, Huntington	34	6	4	10	20
Totals	67	10	21	31	44
Murray Garbutt, Nashville	20	5	2	7	41
Murray Garbutt, Huntington	34	14	12	26	40
Totals	54	19	14	33	81
Rick Girhiny, Dayton	5	2	0	2	0
Rick Girhiny, Birmingham	15	2	1	3	10
Totals	20	4	1	5	10
Jeff Grant, Louisville	31	5	4	9	36
Jeff Grant, Johnstown	10	1	6	7	15
Totals	41	6	10	16	51
Robert Haddock, Erie	8	0	2	2	16
Robert Haddock, Huntington	2	0	0	0	17
Totals	10	0	2	2	33
Bill Harrington, Hampton Roads	4	1	0	1	4
Bill Harrington, Richmond	2	0	0	0	2
Totals	6	1	0	1	6
Rob Hartnell, Richmond	29	4	11	15	87
Rob Hartnell, Dayton	37	9	15	24	133
Totals	66	13	26	39	220
Adam Hayes, Erie	4	0	0	0	0
Adam Hayes, Louisville	35	10	10	20	39
Totals	39	10	10	20	39
Mike Heaney, Richmond	5	0	5	5	8
Mike Heaney, Dayton	11	0	7	7	36
Totals	16	0	12	12	44
Tom Holdeman, South Carolina	6	4	1	5	2
Tom Holdeman, Roanoke	14	1	2	3	12
Totals	20	5	3	8	14
Rhys Hollyman, Huntsville	47	11	21	32	79
Rhys Hollyman, Dayton	18	3	4	7	18
Totals	65	14	25	39	97
Jason Jennings, Raleigh	2	0	0	0	4
Jason Jennings, Johnstown	44	19	26	45	38
Totals	46	19	26	45	42
Chris Jensen, Greensboro	18	0	0	0	31
Chris Jensen, Huntsville	14	0	1	1	8
Totals	32	0	1	1	39
Kevin Kaiser, Charlotte	12	9	4	13	6
Kevin Kaiser, Huntington	9	3	6	9	0
Totals	21	12	10	22	6
Helmut Karel, Johnstown	6	1	4	5	31
Helmut Karel, Huntington	3	3	1	4	6
Totals	9	4	5	9	37
Todd King, Nashville (g)	12	0	1	1	2
Todd King, Huntsville (g)	2	0	0	0	0
Totals	14	0	1	1	2
Kevin Koopman, Lou. (g)	20	0	2	2	22
Kevin Koopman, Dayton (g)	3	0	0	0	2
Totals	23	0	2	2	24
Mark Kuntz, Richmond	4	2	0	2	32
Mark Kuntz, Columbus	57	3	15	18	255
Totals	61	5	15	20	287
Glen Lang, Raleigh	11	5	0	5	2
Glen Lang, Johnstown	31	4	8	12	14
Totals	42	9	8	17	16
Brian Langlot, Raleigh (g)	4	0	0	0	0
Brian Langlot, Columbus (g)	3	0	0	0	0
Totals	7	0	0	0	0
Roger Larche, Richmond	8	2	3	5	41
Roger Larche, Roanoke	37	9	20	29	135
Totals	45	11	23	34	176
Rob Laurie, Dayton (g)	2	0	0	0	2
Rob Laurie, Johnstown (g)	35	0	1	1	6
Totals	37	0	1	1	6
Jim Lessard, Erie	17	5	10	15	93
Jim Lessard, Dayton	46	17	27	44	205
Totals	63	22	37	59	298
Bruce MacDonald, Toledo	17	3	6	9	4
Bruce MacDonald, Raleigh	25	4	6	10	21
Totals	42	7	12	19	25

	Games	G	A	Pts.	PIM
Rob Madia, Hampton Roads	4	0	0	0	4
Rob Madia, Huntsville	56	15	9	24	39
Totals	60	15	9	24	43
Ron Majic, Louisville	8	0	3	3	74
Ron Majic, Huntington	21	0	3	3	161
Totals	29	0	6	6	235
Kevin Malgunas, H.R.	37	12	28	40	132
Kevin Malgunas, Raleigh	10	6	3	9	26
Totals	47	18	31	49	158
Chris Marshall, Greensboro	10	3	1	4	8
Chris Marshall, Raleigh	7	2	1	3	2
Totals	17	5	2	7	10
Jim McGroarty, Huntington	13	5	8	13	4
Jim McGroarty, Louisville	30	4	11	15	6
Totals	43	9	19	28	10
Jim Mill, Roanoke (g)	13	0	0	0	0
Jim Mill, Huntington (g)	23	0	2	2	0
Totals	36	0	2	2	0
Savo Mitrovic, Greensboro	29	3	14	17	12
Savo Mitrovic, Huntsville	6	1	3	4	14
Totals	35	4	17	21	26
David Murphy, Charlotte	2	0	1	1	2
David Murphy, Johnstown	4	1	0	1	5
Totals	6	1	1	2	7
Jay Neal, Huntington	43	11	15	26	53
Jay Neal, Toledo	24	8	10	18	36
Totals	67	19	25	44	89
Chris Nelson, Raleigh	22	3	5	8	49
Chris Nelson, Erie	26	2	13	15	53
Totals	48	5	18	23	102
Paul Ohman, Louisville	15	0	3	3	23
Paul Ohman, Roanoke	3	0	1	1	0
Totals	18	0	4	4	23
Gord Pell, Columbus	2	1	1	2	2
Gord Pell, Roanoke	3	0	2	2	0
Totals	5	1	3	4	2
Darren Perkins, H.R.	49	8	10	18	144
Darren Perkins, Toledo	64	23	31	54	160
Totals	113	31	41	72	304
Guy Prince, Dayton	14	1	1	2	14
Guy Prince, Huntsville	1	0	0	0	2
Totals	15	1	1	2	16
Chris Puscian, Dayton (g)	1	0	0	0	0
Chris Puscian, Erie (g)	1	0	0	0	0
Totals	2	0	0	0	0
Manon Rheaume, Knoxville (g)	4	0	0	0	0
Manon Rheaume, Nashville (g)	4	0	0	0	0
Totals	8	0	0	0	0
Doug Roberts, Huntington	31	12	9	21	4
Doug Roberts, Nashville	28	5	7	12	2
Totals	59	17	16	33	6
John Roderick, Dayton	26	2	1	3	46
John Roderick, Huntsville	8	1	0	1	22
Totals	34	3	1	4	68
Jeff Rohlicek, Toledo	57	28	54	82	36
Jeff Rohlicek, Nashville	4	1	1	2	24
Totals	61	29	55	84	60
Oleg Santuryan, Richmond	47	7	13	20	90
Oleg Santuryan, Roanoke	1	0	0	0	0
Totals	48	7	13	20	90
Marc Savard, Dayton	11	0	1	1	14
Marc Savard, Erie	47	2	27	29	111
Totals	58	2	28	30	125
Brian Schoen, Roanoke (g)	6	0	0	0	2
Brian Schoen, Louisville (g)	11	0	2	2	6
Totals	17	0	2	2	8
Dave Shute, Raleigh	27	10	13	23	21
Dave Shute, Hampton Roads	8	2	4	6	6
Totals	35	12	17	29	27
Geoff Simpson, Charlotte	7	1	0	1	7
Geoff Simpson, Huntington	60	16	28	44	77
Totals	67	17	28	45	84
Jim Slazyk, Columbus	16	0	0	0	0
Jim Slazyk, Hunts	2	0	0	0	0
Totals	18	0	0	0	0

	Games	G	A	Pts.	PIM
Gairin Smith, Charlotte	17	5	2	7	77
Gairin Smith, Roanoke	38	6	11	17	137
Totals	55	11	13	24	214
Neal Sorochan, Charlotte	1	0	1	1	0
Neal Sorochan, Dayton	5	0	0	0	2
Totals	6	0	1	1	2
Jamie Stewart, Hunts.	26	0	0	0	4
Jamie Stewart, Nash.	14	0	0	0	4
Totals	40	0	0	0	8
Jeff Stolp, Birmingham (g)	2	0	0	0	0
Jeff Stolp, Dayton (g)	35	0	1	1	21
Totals	37	0	1	1	21
Conrade Thomas, Roanoke	16	7	5	12	29
Conrade Thomas, Huntsville	46	11	12	23	39
Totals	62	18	17	35	68
Adam Thompson, John. (g)	8	0	0	0	0
Adam Thompson, S.C. (g)	5	0	1	1	0
Totals	13	0	1	1	0
Brad Treliving, Charlotte	6	0	1	1	12
Brad Treliving, Louisville	37	2	17	19	185
Totals	43	2	18	20	197
Todd Tretter, Huntington	1	0	1	1	0
Todd Tretter, Greensboro	59	14	23	37	61
Totals	60	14	24	38	61
Mike Vandenberghe, Richmond	28	5	5	10	135
Mike Vandenberghe, Dayton	37	6	14	20	85
Totals	65	11	19	30	220
Ken Weiss, Columbus (g)	2	0	0	0	0
Ken Weiss, Huntsville (g)	7	0	0	0	0
Totals	9	0	0	0	0
Chuck Wiegand, Johnstown	46	18	18	36	36
Chuck Wiegand, Nashville	13	5	2	7	4
Totals	59	23	20	43	40
Jeff Winstanley, Raleigh	23	4	9	13	45
Jeff Winstanley, Charlotte	19	0	7	7	32
Totals	42	4	16	20	77
Ben Wyzansky, Nashville	49	2	13	15	59
Ben Wyzansky, Johnstown	9	1	7	8	8
Totals	58	3	20	23	67
Adam Young, Dayton	16	0	1	1	10
Adam Young, South Carolina	10	0	0	0	6
Totals	26	0	1	1	16

GOALTENDING

	Games	Min.	W	L	OTL	Goals	SO	Avg.
Todd King, Nash.	12	596	3	6	2	41	0	4.13
Todd King, Hunts.	2	39	0	1	0	11	0	16.73
Totals	14	635	3	7	2	52	0	4.91
K. Koopman, Lou.	20	1053	1	10	4	89	0	5.07
K. Koopman, Day.	3	135	2	0	0	6	0	2.67
Totals	23	1188	3	10	4	95	0	4.80
Brian Langlot, Ral. .	4	168	1	2	0	10	0	3.57
Brian Langlot, Col. .	3	159	1	1	0	10	0	3.76
Totals	7	327	2	3	0	20	0	3.66
Rob Laurie, Day.	2	120	1	1	0	9	0	4.50
Rob Laurie, John.	34	1942	18	13	1	128	0	3.96
Totals	36	2062	19	14	1	137	0	3.99
Jim Mill, Roanoke	13	598	4	3	1	50	0	5.01
J. Mill, Hunting.	23	1198	4	16	0	135	0	6.76
Totals	36	1796	8	19	1	185	0	6.18
Chris Puscian, Erie.	1	6	0	1	0	1	0	10.23
Chris Puscian, Day.	1	28	0	1	0	5	0	10.54
Totals	2	34	0	1	0	6	0	10.49
M. Rheaume, Knox..	4	187	2	0	1	13	0	4.17
M. Rheaume, Nash.	4	198	3	0	0	12	0	3.64
Totals	8	385	5	0	1	25	0	3.90
Brian Schoen, Roa..	6	279	1	4	0	23	0	4.94
Brian Schoen, Lou..	11	576	3	7	0	43	0	4.48
Totals	17	855	4	11	0	66	0	4.63
Jim Slazyk, Col.	16	836	8	5	1	58	1	4.16
Jim Slazyk, Hunts...	2	78	0	1	0	6	0	4.64
Totals	18	914	8	6	1	64	1	4.20
J. Stewart, Hun.	26	1350	5	15	3	101	0	4.49
J. Stewart, Nash.	14	805	1	10	3	60	0	4.47
Totals	40	2155	6	25	6	161	0	4.48

	Games		G	A	Pts.	PIM
Jeff Stolp, Birm.	2	120	2	0	4	0	2.00
Jeff Stolp, Dayton ...	35	2017	15	13	5	132	0	3.93
Totals.................	37	2137	17	13	5	136	0	3.82
A. Thompson, John..	8	333	3	1	1	28	0	5.05
A. Thompson, S.C...	5	209	2	1	0	17	0	4.88
Totals.................	13	542	5	2	1	45	0	4.99

	Games		G	A	Pts.	PIM
Ken Weiss, Col.	2	54	1	1	0	5	0	5.58
Ken Weiss, Hunts. ...	7	308	0	4	1	25	0	4.87
Totals.................	9	362	1	5	1	30	0	4.97

1994 RILEY CUP PLAYOFFS
RESULTS

PRELIMINARY ROUND

Series "A"

	W	L	Pts.	GF	GA
Toledo	2	1	4	14	10
Dayton	1	2	2	10	14

(Toledo won series, 2-1)

Series "B"

	W	L	Pts.	GF	GA
Columbus	2	1	4	14	7
Johnstown	1	2	2	7	14

(Columbus won series, 2-1)

Series "C"

	W	L	Pts.	GF	GA
Louisville	2	1	4	15	12
Knoxville	1	2	2	12	15

(Louisville won series, 2-1)

Series "D"

	W	L	Pts.	GF	GA
Birmingham	2	1	4	20	10
Huntsville	1	2	2	10	20

(Birmingham won series, 2-1)

Series "E"

	W	L	Pts.	GF	GA
Wheeling	2	0	4	7	3
Nashville	0	2	0	3	7

(Wheeling won series, 2-0)

Series "F"

	W	L	Pts.	GF	GA
Hampton Roads	2	1	4	14	8
South Carolina	1	2	2	8	14

(Hampton Roads won series, 2-1)

Series "G"

	W	L	Pts.	GF	GA
Raleigh	2	0	4	12	4
Roanoke	0	2	0	4	12

(Raleigh won series, 2-0)

Series "H"

	W	L	Pts.	GF	GA
Greensboro	2	1	4	12	10
Charlotte	1	2	2	10	12

(Greensboro won series, 2-1)

QUARTERFINALS

Series "I"

	W	L	Pts.	GF	GA
Toledo	3	0	6	21	9
Columbus	0	3	0	9	21

(Toledo won series, 3-0)

Series "J"

	W	L	Pts.	GF	GA
Birmingham	3	0	6	16	6
Louisville	0	3	0	6	16

(Birmingham won series, 3-0)

Series "K"

	W	L	Pts.	GF	GA
Wheeling	3	1	6	17	13
Hampton Roads	1	3	2	13	17

(Wheeling won series, 3-1)

Series "L"

	W	L	Pts.	GF	GA
Raleigh	3	2	6	16	11
Greensboro	2	3	4	11	16

(Raleigh won series, 3-2)

SEMIFINALS

Series "M"

	W	L	Pts.	GF	GA
Toledo	3	0	6	16	5
Wheeling	0	3	0	5	16

(Toledo won series, 3-0)

Series "N"

	W	L	Pts.	GF	GA
Raleigh	3	1	6	18	19
Birmingham	1	3	2	19	18

(Raleigh won series, 3-1)

RILEY CUP FINALS

Series "O"

	W	L	Pts.	GF	GA
Toledo	4	1	8	24	17
Raleigh	1	4	2	17	24

(Toledo won series, 4-1)

INDIVIDUAL LEADERS

Goals: Mark Deazeley, Toledo (16)
Assists: Greg Puhalski, Toledo (19)
Points: Mark Deazeley, Toledo (26)
Penalty minutes: Jason Cirone, Birmingham (67)
Goaltending average: Dave Gagnon, Toledo (2.70)
Shutouts: Mark Michaud, Hampton Roads (1)
    Brian Schoen, Louisville (1)

TOP SCORERS

	Games	G	A	Pts.
Mark Deazeley, Toledo	14	16	10	26
Greg Puhalski, Toledo	14	6	19	25
Alex Hicks, Toledo	14	10	10	20
Rick Judson, Toledo	14	5	13	18
Rick Barkovich, Raleigh	16	8	9	17
Steve Mirabile, Raleigh	16	8	9	17
Iain Duncan, Toledo	14	6	11	17
Rick Corriveau, Toledo	14	3	14	17
Mike Lappin, Raleigh	16	9	7	16
Brad Smyth, Birmingham	10	8	8	16
Jason Cirone, Birmingham	10	8	8	16
Joe Flanagan, Birmingham	10	5	11	16

INDIVIDUAL STATISTICS

BIRMINGHAM BULLS
(Lost semifinals to Raleigh, 3- 1)

SCORING

	Games	G	A	Pts.	PIM
Jason Cirone	10	8	8	16	67
Brad Smyth	10	8	8	16	19
Joe Flanagan	10	5	11	16	0
David Craievich	10	5	10	15	14
Jay Schiavo	10	9	4	13	4
Tom Neziol	10	5	8	13	4
Jim Larkin	10	1	10	11	4
Murray Duval	10	1	8	9	28
Paul Marshall	10	1	8	9	24
Jerome Bechard	9	4	4	8	54
Jamie Cooke	10	1	4	5	8
Darcy Norton	10	3	1	4	27
Mark Beran	10	2	2	4	10
J.A. Schneider	10	0	2	2	40
Brad Mullahy (goalie)	2	0	1	1	2
Sandy Galuppo (goalie)	8	0	0	0	0

GOALTENDING

	Games	Min.	W	L	OTL	Goals	SO	Avg.
Sandy Galuppo	8	477	5	3	0	25	0	3.14
Brad Mullahy	2	120	1	1	0	9	0	4.50

CHARLOTTE CHECKERS
(Lost in first round to Greensboro, 2- 1)

SCORING

	Games	G	A	Pts.	PIM
Howie Rosenblatt	3	3	3	6	2
Derek Eberle	3	0	3	3	4
Jason Christie	3	1	1	2	2
Roman Gorev	3	1	1	2	2
Scott Lindsay	3	1	1	2	15
Andrei Bashkirov	3	1	0	1	0
Sergei Berdnikov	3	1	0	1	4
Scott MacNair	3	1	0	1	4
Scott Meehan	3	1	0	1	24
Dominic Amodeo	3	0	1	1	4
Matt Robbins	3	0	1	1	2
Todd Hunter	1	0	0	0	0
Scott Bailey (goalie)	3	0	0	0	2
Brian Blad	3	0	0	0	19
Doug Evans	3	0	0	0	6
Daniel Murphy	3	0	0	0	2
Kurt Seher	3	0	0	0	2

GOALTENDING

	Games	Min.	W	L	OTL	Goals	SO	Avg.
Scott Bailey	3	188	1	1	1	12	0	3.83

COLUMBUS CHILL
(Lost quarterfinals to Toledo, 3-0)

SCORING

	Games	G	A	Pts.	PIM
Jason Smart	6	3	4	7	10
Joe Cook	6	2	5	7	4
Mike Ross	6	5	1	6	2
Darwin McClelland	6	3	3	6	14
Derek Clancey	6	1	5	6	4
David Pensa	6	3	2	5	4
Rob Schriner	6	2	2	4	4
Aaron Boh	6	2	1	3	17
Martin Mercier	6	1	2	3	4
Mark Woolf	6	1	2	3	8
Lance Brady	6	0	2	2	10
Jesse Cooper	6	0	2	2	2
John Sandell	6	0	1	1	8
Shawn Yakimishyn	6	0	1	1	18
Mark Kuntz	6	0	0	0	0
Sergei Khramtsov (goalie)	4	0	0	0	0
Sergei Tkachenko (goalie)	4	0	0	0	2
Bryan Gendron	6	0	0	0	29

GOALTENDING

	Games	Min.	W	L	OTL	Goals	SO	Avg.
Sergei Khramtsov	4	177	1	2	0	12	0	4.07
Sergei Tkachenko	4	182	1	2	0	16	0	5.27

DAYTON BOMBERS
(Lost in first round to Toledo, 2- 1)

SCORING

	Games	G	A	Pts.	PIM
Dan O'Shea	3	2	2	4	8
Mike Reier	3	0	4	4	2
Kord Cernich	3	1	2	3	4
Sergei Kharin	3	2	0	2	4
Phil Huber	3	1	1	2	17
Tom Nemeth	3	1	1	2	6
Derek Donald	3	0	2	2	8
John Brill	3	1	0	1	4
Jim Lessard	3	0	1	1	2
Steve Wilson	3	1	0	1	2
Mike Vandenberghe	3	0	1	1	4
Kevin Koopman (goalie)	1	0	0	0	0
Jason Disiewich	3	0	0	0	12
Jason Downey	3	0	0	0	20
Rob Hartnell	3	0	0	0	4
Rhys Hollyman	3	0	0	0	4
Jeff Stolp (goalie)	3	0	0	0	2

GOALTENDING

	Games	Min.	W	L	OTL	Goals	SO	Avg.
Jeff Stolp	3	208	1	0	1	11	0	3.18
Kevin Koopman	1	6	0	1	0	3	0	28.50

GREENSBORO MONARCHS

(Lost quarterfinals to Raleigh, 3-2)

SCORING

	Games	G	A	Pts.	PIM
John Young	8	4	5	9	18
Phil Berger	8	3	5	8	12
Todd Tretter	8	3	4	7	4
Dan Gravelle	8	3	3	6	14
Scott White	8	1	5	6	8
Greg Capson	8	3	1	4	43
Darryl Noren	8	1	3	4	20
Davis Payne	8	2	1	3	27
Chris Wolanin	8	1	2	3	20
Trevor Senn	8	0	2	2	37
Chris Valicevic	8	0	2	2	6
J.F. Jomphe	1	1	0	1	0
Sverre Sears	7	1	0	1	4
Sebastien LaPlante	8	0	1	1	26
Patrick Labrecque (goalie)	1	0	0	0	0
Brendan Creagh	6	0	0	0	10
Tom Newman (goalie)	8	0	0	0	0
Dean Zayonce	8	0	0	0	14

GOALTENDING

	Games	Min.	W	L	OTL	Goals	SO	Avg.
Tom Newman	8	464	4	4	0	21	0	2.72
Patrick Labrecque	1	22	0	0	0	4	0	10.76

HAMPTON ROADS ADMIRALS

(Lost quarterfinals to Wheeling, 3-1)

SCORING

	Games	G	A	Pts.	PIM
Andrew Brunette	7	7	6	13	18
Jim Brown	7	6	7	13	4
Daniel Chaput	7	2	8	10	15
Ralph Barahona	7	3	5	8	4
Vincent Faucher	6	3	3	6	20
Rod Taylor	7	1	5	6	24
Brendan Curley	7	3	2	5	4
Brian Goudie	7	2	2	4	57
Ron Pascucci	7	0	4	4	14
Dave Shute	5	0	2	2	2
Dennis McEwen	7	0	2	2	10
Shawn Snesar	7	0	2	2	34
Kelly Sorensen	7	0	2	2	33
Mark Michaud (goalie)	7	0	1	1	0
Jason MacIntyre	5	0	0	0	13
Darren Perkins	7	0	0	0	33

GOALTENDING

	Games	Min.	W	L	OTL	Goals	SO	Avg.
Mark Michaud	7	420	3	3	1	25	0	3.57

HUNTSVILLE BLAST

(Lost in first round to Birmingham, 2-1)

SCORING

	Games	G	A	Pts.	PIM
Scott Burfoot	3	4	5	9	4
Ken House	3	2	2	4	0
Chris Belanger	3	0	3	3	26
Tom O'Rourke	3	0	3	3	7
Craig Herr	3	2	0	2	2
Pat Curcio	3	1	0	1	2
John Roderick	3	1	0	1	10
Todd Chin (goalie)	2	0	1	1	0
David Burke	3	0	1	1	0
Joe Dragon	3	0	1	1	29
Mike Jorgensen	3	0	1	1	4
Rob Madia	3	0	1	1	4
Rob Poma	3	0	1	1	2
Greg Geldart	3	0	0	0	2
Conrade Thomas	3	0	0	0	0
Ken Weiss (goalie)	3	0	0	0	0

GOALTENDING

	Games	Min.	W	L	OTL	Goals	SO	Avg.
Todd Chin	2	65	0	1	0	7	0	6.48
Ken Weiss	3	115	1	1	0	13	0	6.77

JOHNSTOWN CHIEFS

(Lost in first round to Columbus, 2-1)

SCORING

	Games	G	A	Pts.	PIM
Dennis Purdie	3	3	2	5	8
Bob Woods	3	1	3	4	4
Rob Leask	3	1	2	3	14
Martin D'Orsonnens	3	1	0	1	0
Francois Bourdeau	3	0	1	1	0
Bruce Coles	3	0	1	1	10
Perry Florio	3	0	1	1	42
Matt Hoffman	3	0	1	1	0
Jason Jennings	3	0	1	1	0
Ben Wyzansky	3	0	1	1	0
John Bradley (goalie)	1	0	0	0	0
Shawn Bourgeois	3	0	0	0	0
Gord Christian	3	0	0	0	4
Ted Dent	3	0	0	0	21
Yannick Frechette	3	0	0	0	5
Tim Hanus	3	0	0	0	6
Rob Laurie (goalie)	3	0	0	0	0

GOALTENDING

	Games	Min.	W	L	OTL	Goals	SO	Avg.
Rob Laurie	3	153	1	2	0	11	0	4.31
John Bradley	1	27	0	0	0	3	0	6.70

KNOXVILLE CHEROKEES

(Lost in first round to Louisville, 2-1)

SCORING

	Games	G	A	Pts.	PIM
Kim Maier	3	4	0	4	0
Scott Hollis	3	3	1	4	8
Mike Murray	3	1	3	4	2
Steve Flomenhoft	3	1	2	3	0
Frank Evans	3	0	3	3	11
Wes McCauley	3	0	3	3	0
Bruno Villeneuve	3	2	0	2	2
Jack Duffy	3	1	0	1	10
Dave Larouche	3	0	1	1	0
Carl LeBlanc	3	0	1	1	12
Scott Metcalfe	3	0	1	1	20
Doug Searle	3	0	1	1	4
Cory Cadden (goalie)	3	0	0	0	0
Hayden O'Rear	3	0	0	0	0
Jeff Rold	3	0	0	0	2
Nicholas Vachon	3	0	0	0	2

GOALTENDING

	Games	Min.	W	L	OTL	Goals	SO	Avg.
Cory Cadden	3	179	1	2	0	14	0	4.68

LOUISVILLE ICEHAWKS

(Lost quarterfinals to Birmingham, 3-0)

SCORING

	Games	G	A	Pts.	PIM
George Zajankala	6	3	6	9	33
Sheldon Gorski	6	1	7	8	4
Brian Cook	6	4	3	7	16
Trevor Buchanan	6	3	3	6	52
Ken Plaquin	6	2	4	6	6
Jim McGroarty	6	1	4	5	4
Jamie Steer	6	3	1	4	0
Glenn Clark	6	2	1	3	17
Mike Fiset	6	1	2	3	12
Rob Sumner	6	0	2	2	33
Greg Hagen	6	1	0	1	14

	Games	G	A	Pts.	PIM
Brad Treliving	6	0	1	1	47
Chris Clifford (goalie)	1	0	0	0	0
Kelly Hiltgen	3	0	0	0	0
Scott Kelsey	6	0	0	0	9
Brian Schoen (goalie)	6	0	0	0	2
Jeff Sebastian	6	0	0	0	8

GOALTENDING

	Games	Min.	W	L	OTL	Goals	SO	Avg.
Brian Schoen	6	351	2	4	0	27	1	4.62
Chris Clifford	1	8	0	0	0	1	0	7.17

NASHVILLE KNIGHTS

(Lost in first round to Wheeling, 2-0)

SCORING

	Games	G	A	Pts.	PIM
Brandon Coates	2	1	1	2	0
Rob Dumas	2	1	0	1	2
Jeff Rohlicek	2	1	0	1	2
Scott Rogers	1	0	1	1	5
Greg Burke	2	0	1	1	2
Dean Gerard	2	0	1	1	5
Tim Sullivan	2	0	1	1	7
Stephen Corfmat	1	0	0	0	0
Mike Parson (goalie)	1	0	0	0	0
Jamie Stewart (goalie)	1	0	0	0	0
Jamie Adams	2	0	0	0	2
Jason Courtemanch	2	0	0	0	10
Gerry Daley	2	0	0	0	0
Scott Matusovich	2	0	0	0	2
Jim Peters	2	0	0	0	4
Stansilav Tkach	2	0	0	0	5
Chris Wayland	2	0	0	0	7
Chuck Wiegand	2	0	0	0	0

GOALTENDING

	Games	Min.	W	L	OTL	Goals	SO	Avg.
Mike Parson	1	60	0	1	0	3	0	3.00
Jamie Stewart	1	59	0	1	0	3	0	3.03

RALEIGH ICECAPS

(Lost Riley Cup finals to Toledo, 4-1)

SCORING

	Games	G	A	Pts.	PIM
Rick Barkovich	16	8	9	17	40
Steve Mirabile	16	8	9	17	20
Mike Lappin	16	9	7	16	14
Curt Regnier	16	6	9	15	6
Alan Leggett	16	5	10	15	8
Bill Gall	16	1	13	14	10
Barry Nieckar	16	5	7	12	51
Jeff Jablonski	16	6	5	11	20
Jim Powers	16	5	5	10	18
Donevan Hextall	13	1	8	9	18
Shaun Kane	16	3	5	8	41
Lyle Wildgoose	7	1	7	8	8
Kevin Malgunas	14	2	4	6	41
Karl Johnston	12	2	3	5	4
Derek Linnell	16	1	1	2	10
Matt DelGuidice (goalie)	13	0	1	1	14
Ian Paskowski	3	0	0	0	0
Chad Erickson (goalie)	7	0	0	0	35
Krzysztof Oliwa	9	0	0	0	0

GOALTENDING

	Games	Min.	W	L	OTL	Goals	SO	Avg.
Matt DelGuidice	12	707	6	4	0	37	0	3.14
Chad Erickson	6	287	3	1	0	21	0	4.40

ROANOKE EXPRESS

(Lost in first round to Raleigh, 2-0)

SCORING

	Games	G	A	Pts.	PIM
Kyle Galloway	2	1	1	2	0
Gairin Smith	2	1	1	2	0
Roger Larche	2	0	2	2	2
Tevor Burgess	2	1	0	1	2
Tony Szabo	2	1	0	1	0
Keith Cyr	2	0	1	1	0
Pat Ferschweiler	2	0	1	1	2
Dave Morissette	2	0	1	1	4
Claude Barthe	2	0	0	0	4
Paul Cohen (goalie)	2	0	0	0	0
Ilja Dubkov	2	0	0	0	15
Jeff Jestadt	2	0	0	0	2
Chris Potter	2	0	0	0	2
Michael Smith	2	0	0	0	0
Oleg Yashin	2	0	0	0	4
Will Averill	2	0	0	0	0

GOALTENDING

	Games	Min.	W	L	OTL	Goals	SO	Avg.
Paul Cohen	2	120	0	2	0	12	0	6.00

SOUTH CAROLINA STINGRAYS

(Lost in first round to Hampton Roads, 2-1)

SCORING

	Games	G	A	Pts.	PIM
Chris Bright	3	2	2	4	10
Sylvain Fleury	3	2	1	3	2
Gary Socha	3	2	0	2	0
Eric Brule	3	1	1	2	8
Mark Green	3	1	1	2	2
Rick Lessard	3	0	2	2	14
Daniel Ruoho	3	0	2	2	2
Trevor Smith	3	0	2	2	0
Tim Harris	2	0	1	1	2
Ken Thibodeau	2	0	1	1	0
Brad Pascall	3	0	1	1	4
Jason Winch	3	0	1	1	0
Andy Bezeau	2	0	0	0	23
Matt Mallgrave	3	0	0	0	15
Bill Pye (goalie)	3	0	0	0	0
Jim Sprott	3	0	0	0	5
Dan Wiebe	3	0	0	0	0

GOALTENDING

	Games	Min.	W	L	OTL	Goals	SO	Avg.
Bill Pye	3	179	1	2	0	12	0	4.03

TOLEDO STORM

(Winner of Riley Cup playoffs)

SCORING

	Games	G	A	Pts.	PIM
Mark Deazeley	14	16	10	26	37
Greg Puhalski	14	6	19	25	26
Alex Hicks	14	10	10	20	56
Rick Judson	14	5	13	18	6
Iain Duncan	14	6	11	17	32
Rick Corriveau	14	3	14	17	20
John Hendry	14	9	6	15	26
Darren Perkins	14	4	8	12	46
Chris Bergeron	5	7	3	10	2
Jay Neal	14	4	4	8	20
Andy Suhy	14	3	4	7	28
Marc Lyons	14	1	2	3	14
Mike Markovich	12	1	2	2	12
Steve Dykstra	12	0	2	2	23
Norm Dezainde	6	0	1	1	6
Pat Pylypuik	8	0	1	1	2
Nick Vitucci	1	0	0	0	0
Dave Gagnon (goalie)	14	0	0	0	8

GOALTENDING

	Games	Min.	W	L	OTL	Goals	SO	Avg.
Dave Gagnon	14	910	12	1	0	41	0	2.70

WHEELING THUNDERBIRDS

(Lost semifinals to Toledo, 3-0)

SCORING

	Games	G	A	Pts.	PIM
Darren Schwartz	9	8	3	11	35
Jim Bermingham	8	3	5	8	10
Tim Roberts	9	1	6	7	10
Derek DeCosty	9	4	2	6	16
Tony Prpic	8	3	3	6	15
Tim Tisdale	9	1	5	6	19
John Johnson	9	2	3	5	8

	Games	G	A	Pts.	PIM
Cory Paterson	9	1	4	5	4
Terry Virtue	6	2	2	4	4
Vadim Slivchenko	6	1	3	4	2
Peter Marek	7	1	3	4	12
Steve Gibson	9	1	3	4	23
Marquis Mathieu	9	1	3	4	23
Brent Pope	9	0	2	2	32
Dion Darling	9	0	1	1	14
Brett Abel (goalie)	1	0	0	0	0
Eric Raymond (goalie)	9	0	0	0	2
Brock Woods	9	0	0	0	38

GOALTENDING

	Games	Min.	W	L	OTL	Goals	SO	Avg.
Eric Raymond	9	522	5	4	0	30	0	3.45
Brett Abel	1	20	0	0	0	2	0	6.00

1993-94 AWARD WINNERS

ALL-STAR TEAMS

First team	Pos.	Second team
Cory Cadden, Knoxville	G	Mark Michaud, H.R.
Joe Cook, Columbus	D	David Craievich, Birm.
Tom Nemeth, Dayton	D	Paul Marshall, Birmingham
Darren Schwartz, Wheeling	LW	Rick Judson, Toledo
Joe Flanagan, Birmingham	C	Dan Gravelle, Greensboro
Phil Berger, Greensboro	RW	Darren Colbourne, Rich.

Coach of the Year: Barry Smith, Knoxville

TROPHY WINNERS

Most Valuable Player: Joe Flanagan, Birmingham
Scoring leader: Phil Berger, Greensboro
Outstanding defenseman: Tom Nemeth, Dayton
Outstanding goaltender: Cory Cadden, Knoxville
Rookie of the Year: Dan Gravelle, Greensboro
Playoff MVP: Dave Gagnon, Toledo
Coach of the Year: Barry Smith, Knoxville

ALL-TIME AWARD WINNERS

MOST VALUABLE PLAYER

Season	Player, Team
1988-89	Daryl Harpe, Erie
1989-90	Bill McDougall, Erie
1990-91	Stan Drulia, Knoxville
1991-92	Phil Berger, Greensboro
1992-93	Trevor Jobe, Nashville
1993-94	Joe Flanagan, Birmingham

TOP SCORER

Season	Player, Team
1988-89	Daryl Harpe, Erie
1989-90	Bill McDougall, Erie
1990-91	Stan Drulia, Knoxville
1991-92	Phil Berger, Greensboro
1992-93	Trevor Jobe, Nashville
1993-94	Phil Berger, Greensboro

ROOKIE OF THE YEAR

Season	Player, Team
1988-89	Tom Sasso, Johnstown
1989-90	Bill McDougall, Erie
1990-91	Dan Gauthier, Knoxville
1991-92	Darren Colbourne, Dayton
1992-93	Joe Flanagan, Birmingham
1993-94	Dan Gravelle, Greensboro

TOP GOALTENDER

Season	Player, Team
1988-89	Scott Gordon, Johnstown
1989-90	Alain Raymond, Hampton Roads
1990-91	Dean Anderson, Knoxville
1991-92	Frederic Chabot, Winston-Salem
1992-93	Nick Vitucci, Hampton Roads
1992-93	Cory Cadden, Knoxville

PLAYOFF MVP

Season	Player, Team
1988-89	Nick Vitucci, Carolina
1989-90	Wade Flaherty, Greensboro
1990-91	Dave Gagnon, Hampton Roads
	Dave Flanagan, Hampton Roads
1991-92	Mark Bernard, Hampton Roads
1992-93	Rick Judson, Toledo
1993-94	Dave Gagnon, Toledo

COACH OF THE YEAR

Season	Coach, Team
1988-89	Ron Hansis, Erie
1989-90	Dave Allison, Virginia
1990-91	Don Jackson, Knoxville
1991-92	Doug Sauter, Winston-Salem
1992-93	Kurt Kleinendorst, Raleigh
1993-94	Barry Smith, Knoxville

TOP DEFENSEMAN

Season	Player, Team
1988-89	Kelly Szautner, Erie
1989-90	Bill Whitfield, Virginia
1990-91	Brett McDonald, Nashville
1991-92	Scott White, Greensboro
1992-93	Derek Booth, Toledo
1993-94	Tom Nemeth, Dayton

ALL-TIME LEAGUE CHAMPIONS

REGULAR-SEASON CHAMPION

Season	Team	Coach
1988-89—	Erie Panthers	Ron Hansis
1989-90—	Winston-Salem Thunderbirds	C. McSorley, J. Fraser
1990-91—	Knoxville Cherokees	Don Jackson
1991-92—	Toledo Storm	Chris McSorley
1992-93—	Wheeling Thunderbirds	Doug Sauter
1993-94—	Knoxville Cherokees	Barry Smith

PLAYOFF CHAMPION

Team	Coach
Carolina Thunderbirds	Brendon Watson
Greensboro Monarchs	Jeff Brubaker
Hampton Roads Admirals	John Brophy
Hampton Roads Admirals	John Brophy
Toledo Storm	Chris McSorley
Toledo Storm	Chris McSorley

The ECHL playoff champion is awarded the Bob Payne Trophy.

CENTRAL HOCKEY LEAGUE

LEAGUE OFFICE

President
Ray Miron
Commissioner
Monte Miron
Administrative director
Marilyn Stilley
Director of public relations
Jason Rothwell

Special projects coordinator
Doug Mitcho
Address
5840 S. Memorial Drive
Suite 302
Tulsa, OK 74145

Phone
918-664-8881
FAX
918-664-2215

TEAMS

DALLAS FREEZE

General manager
Marty Owens
Head coach
Ron Flockhart
Home ice
Fair Park Coliseum
Address
600 Tower North
2700 Stemmons Freeway
Dallas, TX 75207
Seating Capacity
7,500
Phone
214-631-7825
FAX
214-631-8090

FORT WORTH FIRE

General manager
Tom Weisenbach
Head coach
Steve Harrison
Home ice
Fort Worth/Tarrant County
Convention Center
Address
910 Houston Street, Suite 400
Fort Worth, TX 76102
Seating capacity
13,000
Phone
817-336-1992
FAX
817-336-1997

MEMPHIS RIVERKINGS

General manager
Jim Riggs
Head coach
Herb Boxer

Home ice
Mid-South Coliseum
Address
The Fairgrounds
Memphis, TN 38104
Seating capacity
12,000
Phone
901-278-9009
FAX
901-274-3209

OKLAHOMA CITY BLAZERS

General manager
Brad Lund
Head coach
Michael McEwen
Home ice
Myriad Convention Center
and State Fair Arena
Address
Sheraton-Century Mall
100 W. Main, Suite 172
Oklahoma City, OK 73102-9201
Seating capacity
12,500 and 8,900
Phone
405-235-7825
FAX
405-272-9875

SAN ANTONIO IGUANAS

General manager
Jim Goodman
Head coach
Bill Goldsworthy
Home ice
Freeman Coliseum
Address
110 Broadway, Suite 25
San Antonio, TX 78205

Seating Capacity
9,600
Phone
210-227-4449
FAX
210-227-4484

TULSA OILERS

General manager
Jeff D. Lund
Head coach
Garry Unger
Home ice
Tulsa Convention Center
Address
4528 S. Sheridan Road, Suite 212
Tulsa, OK 74145
Seating Capacity
6,900
Phone
918-663-5888
FAX
918-663-5977

WICHITA THUNDER

General manager
Bill Shuck
Head coach
Doug Shedden
Home ice
Kansas Coliseum
Address
410-A N. St. Francis
Wichita, KS 67202
Seating Capacity
9,600
Phone
316-264-4625
FAX
316-264-3037

1993-94 REGULAR SEASON

FINAL STANDINGS

Team	G	W	L		Pts.	GF	GA
Wichita	64	40	18	(6)	86	309	275
Tulsa	64	36	24	(4)	76	347	281
Oklahoma City	64	35	23	(6)	76	260	246
Dallas	64	31	25	(8)	70	304	309
Memphis	64	25	34	(5)	55	243	294
Fort Worth	64	25	37	(2)	52	253	311

( )—Indicates overtime losses and are worth one point.

INDIVIDUAL LEADERS

Goals: Paul Jackson, Wichita (71)
Assists: Doug Lawrence, Tulsa (93)
Points: Paul Jackson, Wichita (135)
Penalty minutes: Mick MacWilliam, Tulsa (326)
Goaltending average: Alan Perry, Oklahoma City (3.58)
Shutouts: Roydon Gunn, Memphis (2)

	Games	G	A	Pts.
Troy Binnie, Dallas	56	54	42	96
Brent Sapergia, Wichita	46	55	33	88
Frank LaScala, Dallas	64	45	41	86
Robert Wallwork, Memphis	64	43	40	83
Craig Coxe, Tulsa	64	26	57	83
Trent Pankewicz, Oklahoma City	61	30	46	76
Derek Crawford, Dallas	61	26	50	76
Wayne Anchikoski, Dallas	60	35	39	74
Dave Doucette, Tulsa	62	10	63	73
Dominic Maltais, Fort Worth	64	44	27	71
Sean Whyte, Tulsa	50	42	29	71
Guy Girouard, Oklahoma City	64	17	53	70
Shaun Clouston, Tulsa	64	27	38	65
Mike Jackson, Memphis	64	26	37	63

TOP SCORERS

	Games	G	A	Pts.
Paul Jackson, Wichita	59	71	64	135
Doug Lawrence, Tulsa	63	25	93	118
Luc Beausoleil, Tulsa	60	64	50	114
Ron Handy, Wichita	57	29	80	109
Carl Boudreau, Oklahoma City	64	40	67	107
Bob Berg, Wichita	64	43	58	101

INDIVIDUAL STATISTICS

DALLAS FREEZE

SCORING

	Games	G	A	Pts.	Pen.
Troy Binnie	56	54	42	96	96
Frank LaScala	64	45	41	86	116
Derek Crawford	61	26	50	76	171
Wayne Anchikoski	60	35	39	74	78
Jason Taylor	64	24	38	62	180
Dave Doucette	52	9	53	62	93
Brian Bruininks	61	7	39	46	151
Jim McGeough	28	21	16	37	24
Mark Holick	57	15	19	34	179
Joe Mittelsteadt	62	10	23	33	220
Jeff Beaudin	64	14	14	28	133
Jim Ballantine	35	18	8	26	16
Don Dwyer	39	7	13	20	33
Dean Schmyr	50	2	12	14	96
Sean Cowan	33	2	11	13	22
Jason White	20	5	4	9	31
John Vecchiarelli	6	4	3	7	14
Guy Prince	14	3	4	7	9
Joey McTamney	26	2	4	6	45
Robert Lewis	27	1	4	5	25
Antoine Mindjimba (goalie)	7	0	4	4	10
Greg MacEachern	5	0	1	1	4
Yannick Gosselin (goalie)	18	0	1	1	8
Erin Whitten (goalie)	4	0	0	0	0
Ryan Schmidt	6	0	0	0	9
Randy Jaycock (goalie)	12	0	0	0	0
Greg Smith (goalie)	33	0	0	0	16

GOALTENDING

	Games	Min.	W	L	OTL	Goals	SO	Avg.
Yannick Gosselin	18	931	9	5	1	61	0	3.93
Antoine Mindjimba	7	419	4	2	1	29	0	4.15
Randy Jaycock	10	546	5	4	0	42	0	4.61
Erin Whitten	4	111	1	1	0	9	0	4.85
Greg Smith	33	1860	12	13	6	157	0	5.06

FORT WORTH FIRE

SCORING

	Games	G	A	Pts.	Pen.
Dominic Maltais	64	44	27	71	88
Mike Sanderson	63	27	34	61	37
Chad Johnson	62	17	41	58	56
Sean Rowe	61	22	35	57	43
Alex Kholomeyev	53	21	21	42	76
Ty Eigner	62	10	26	36	74
Mike McCormick	63	20	15	35	73
Stephen Tepper	25	23	11	34	54
Jason Brousseau	36	16	17	33	47
Mike Chighisola	23	10	18	28	81

	Games	G	A	Pts.	Pen.
Eric Brule	37	9	17	26	98
Stephane Desjardins	37	7	16	23	58
Tom Mutch	17	3	11	14	8
Derby Bognar	19	2	12	14	6
Scott Zygulski	60	3	10	13	42
Peter Holmes	11	7	5	12	0
Ryan Leschasin	43	5	5	10	75
Troy Frederick	10	3	7	10	2
Ron Aubrey	23	2	6	8	96
Ray Desouza	29	0	8	8	102
Eric Ricard	12	0	6	6	14
Darren Srochenski	16	1	3	4	55
Rob Striar	8	0	4	4	34
Chris Jensen	9	0	2	2	11
Reginald Brezeault	3	1	0	1	0
Sean Gorman	6	0	1	1	14
Trevor Robins (goalie)	9	0	1	1	2
Patrick McGarry (goalie)	47	0	1	1	51
Robert Lewis	1	0	0	0	0
Bob Emond	2	0	0	0	7
Everett Caldwell	3	0	0	0	0
Bryan Schoen (goalie)	4	0	0	0	0
Ken Matlock	5	0	0	0	22
Corwin Saurdiff (goalie)	5	0	0	0	4
Mike O'Hara (goalie)	6	0	0	0	2
Todd Huyber	31	0	0	0	91

GOALTENDING

	Games	Min.	W	L	OTL	Goals	SO	Avg.
Bryan Schoen	4	211	2	1	0	14	0	3.98
Patrick McGarry	47	2691	19	22	2	194	0	4.33
Corwin Saurdiff	5	293	1	4	0	22	0	4.51
Trevor Robins	9	452	2	6	0	42	0	5.58
Mike O'Hara	6	215	1	4	0	28	0	7.81

MEMPHIS RIVERKINGS

SCORING

	Games	G	A	Pts.	Pen.
Robert Wallwork	64	43	40	83	83
Mike Jackson	64	26	37	63	90
Mark McGinn	64	26	30	56	18
David Moore	53	16	38	54	71
Glenn Painter	53	13	34	47	34
Andy Ross	55	18	21	39	56
Marcel Sakac	50	17	12	29	66
Tom Mutch	35	17	10	27	65
Peter D'Amario	40	12	14	26	18
Mike Roberts	61	4	22	26	52
Ryan Leschasin	16	7	5	12	16
Ladislav Tresl	16	8	14	22	48
Dennis Snedden	12	5	9	14	4

	Games	G	A	Pts.	Pen.
Kyle Haviland	59	2	11	13	151
Steve Shaunessy	46	5	6	11	221
Ken Venis	55	3	8	11	74
Jason Brousseau	16	4	7	11	2
Jamie Hearn	10	4	5	9	8
Scot Johnston	13	3	3	6	10
Roger Hunt	14	3	3	6	14
Brian Sutton	18	1	5	6	26
Bryan Miller	10	0	6	6	6
Guy Prince	9	3	1	4	0
Ray Desouza	6	0	4	4	6
Chad Seibel	10	0	4	4	25
Aaron Morrison	14	2	1	3	30
Scott Phillips	9	1	2	3	6
Todd Meehan	2	0	2	2	5
Gord Pell	1	0	0	0	0
Darren Hersh (goalie)	2	0	0	0	0
Rocco Amonte	5	0	0	0	2
Terry MacLean	5	0	0	0	4
Rob Kelley	7	0	0	0	0
Adam Thompson (goalie)	7	0	0	0	4
Antoine Mindjimba (goalie)	23	0	0	0	15
Roydon Gunn (goalie)	38	0	0	0	8

GOALTENDING

	Games	Min.	W	L	OTL	Goals	SO	Avg.
Roydon Gunn	38	2161	15	18	3	137	2	3.80
Antoine Mindjimba	23	1307	7	13	2	104	1	4.91
Darren Hersh	1	60	0	1	1	6	0	6.00
Adam Thompson	1	20	0	0	0	3	0	9.00

	Games	G	A	Pts.	Pen.
Chris Robertson	26	23	14	37	24
Tom Karalis	46	6	30	36	172
Mike Berger	58	15	19	34	134
Boyd Sutton	53	9	23	32	22
Jody Praznik	59	5	25	30	52
Mike MacWilliam	39	16	12	28	326
Chad Seibel	53	4	24	28	117
Bill Campbell	20	12	15	27	4
Dave Doucette	10	1	10	11	8
David Moore	10	2	2	4	14
Al Murphy	6	1	3	4	47
Greg MacEachern	12	0	3	3	8
Mark McCoy	2	0	1	1	2
Derby Bognar	4	0	1	1	4
Damion DeGiulian	4	0	1	1	0
Brian Shantz	4	0	1	1	0
Roger Hunt	10	0	1	1	23
Tony Martino (goalie)	48	0	1	1	69
Mike Kisler (goalie)	2	0	0	0	0
Adam Thompson (goalie)	2	0	0	0	0
Jamie Loewen (goalie)	4	0	0	0	0
Brian Flatt (goalie)	22	0	0	0	15

GOALTENDING

	Games	Min.	W	L	OTL	Goals	SO	Avg.
Tony Martino	48	2721	30	12	4	173	1	3.82
Adam Thompson	2	68	1	0	0	5	0	4.41
Brian Flatt	21	901	4	10	0	81	0	5.39
Jamie Loewen	4	148	1	2	0	16	0	6.50
Mike Kisler	2	14	0	0	0	2	0	8.40

OKLAHOMA CITY BLAZERS

SCORING

	Games	G	A	Pts.	Pen.
Carl Boudreau	64	40	67	107	93
Trent Pankewicz	61	30	46	76	154
Guy Girouard	64	17	53	70	89
Steve Simoni	63	34	27	61	53
Joe Burton	54	32	24	56	28
James Richmond	64	19	27	46	74
Jeff Massey	63	21	21	42	64
Chris Laganas	58	20	22	42	157
Derry Menard	61	9	30	39	98
Jim Solly	55	11	18	29	46
Bruce Shoebottom	43	4	11	15	236
Kent Anderson	64	3	11	14	80
Craig Johnson	48	5	5	10	230
Tim Gilligan	28	2	7	9	99
Evgeny Serko	33	3	5	8	60
Jules Jardine	21	2	4	6	31
Ilia Borisychev	21	3	2	5	16
George Dupont	4	4	0	4	27
Mike Ciolli	8	1	1	2	6
Mike Williams (goalie)	41	0	2	2	22
Kevin Brown	2	0	1	1	2
Alan Perry (goalie)	28	0	0	0	8

GOALTENDING

	Games	Min.	W	L	OTL	Goals	SO	Avg.
Alan Perry	28	1524	15	11	2	91	0	3.58
Mike Williams	41	2350	20	12	4	147	1	3.75

TULSA OILERS

SCORING

	Games	G	A	Pts.	Pen.
Doug Lawrence	63	25	93	118	199
Luc Beausoleil	60	64	50	114	110
Craig Coxe	64	26	57	83	236
Sean Shyte	50	42	29	71	93
Shaun Clouston	64	27	38	65	69
Taylor Hall	64	33	26	59	95
Stu Kulak	59	17	29	46	101
Sylvain Naud	24	19	22	41	71

WICHITA THUNDER

SCORING

	Games	G	A	Pts.	Pen.
Paul Jackson	59	71	64	135	215
Ron Handy	57	29	80	109	98
Bob Berg	64	43	58	101	141
Brent Sapergia	46	55	33	88	297
Steve Chelios	61	8	51	59	153
Jim Latos	63	19	34	53	227
Jack Williams	64	17	32	49	104
Greg Neish	55	15	21	36	325
Paul Dukovac	63	14	21	35	72
Rob Weingartner	50	16	17	33	150
Stephane Venne	47	6	20	26	224
Jamie Hearn	54	4	16	20	120
Darren Srochenski	50	4	9	13	140
Steve Shaunessy	11	1	5	6	42
Bryan Miller	17	1	5	6	14
Robert Desjardins (goalie)	57	0	6	6	6
Brian Wells	3	5	0	5	25
Tom Karalis	3	1	2	3	6
Roger Hunt	39	0	2	2	55
Yannick Gosselin (goalie)	8	0	1	1	17
Darcy Kaminski	10	0	1	1	6
John Laan	1	0	0	0	15
Mike Sullivan	2	0	0	0	0
Darren Hersh (goalie)	3	0	0	0	0
Greg Smith (goalie)	5	0	0	0	2
Steve Daniels	6	0	0	0	32
Mark Bourgeois	9	0	0	0	6

GOALTENDING

	Games	Min.	W	L	OTL	Goals	SO	Avg.
Robert Desjardins	56	3296	38	12	5	220	1	4.00
Yannick Gosselin	7	292	3	1	2	23	0	4.73
Darren Hersh	3	73	0	1	0	7	0	5.75
Greg Smith	5	210	1	2	0	21	0	6.01

PLAYERS WITH TWO OR MORE TEAMS

SCORING

	Games	G	A	Pts.	Pen.
Derby Bognar, Fort Worth	19	2	12	14	6

	Games	G	A	Pts.	Pen.
Derby Bognar, Tulsa	4	0	1	1	4
Totals	23	2	13	15	10
Jason Brousseau, Fort Worth	36	16	17	33	47
Jason Brousseau, Memphis	16	4	7	11	2
Totals	52	20	24	44	49
Ray Desouza, Fort Worth	29	0	8	8	102
Ray Desouza, Memphis	6	0	4	4	6
Totals	35	0	12	12	108
Dave Doucette, Dallas	52	9	53	62	93
Dave Doucette, Tulsa	10	1	10	11	8
Totals	62	10	63	73	101
Yannick Gosselin, Wichita (g)	8	0	1	1	17
Yannick Gosselin, Dallas (g)	18	0	1	1	8
Totals	26	0	2	2	25
Jamie Hearn, Wichita	54	4	16	20	120
Jamie Hearn, Memphis	10	4	5	9	8
Totals	64	8	21	29	128
Darren Hersh, Memphis (g)	2	0	0	0	0
Darren Hersh, Wichita (g)	3	0	0	0	0
Totals	5	0	0	0	0
Roger Hunt, Wichita	39	0	2	2	55
Roger Hunt, Memphis	14	3	3	6	14
Roger Hunt, Tulsa	10	0	1	1	23
Totals	63	3	6	9	92
Tom Karalis, Tulsa	46	6	30	36	172
Tom Karalis, Wichita	3	1	2	3	6
Totals	49	7	32	39	178
Ryan Leschasin, Fort Worth	43	5	5	10	75
Ryan Leschasin, Memphis	16	7	5	12	16
Totals	59	12	10	22	91
Robert Lewis, Dallas	27	1	4	5	25
Robert Lewis, Fort Worth	1	0	0	0	0
Totals	28	1	4	5	25
Greg MacEachern, Tulsa	12	0	3	3	8
Greg MacEachern, Dallas	5	0	1	1	4
Totals	17	0	4	4	12
Bryan Miller, Wichita	17	1	5	6	14
Bryan Miller, Memphis	10	0	6	6	6
Totals	27	1	11	12	20
Antoine Mindjimba, Mem. (g)	23	0	0	0	15
Antoine Mindjimba, Dallas (g)	7	0	4	4	10
Totals	30	0	4	4	25

	Games	G	A	Pts.	Pen.
David Moore, Memphis	53	16	38	54	71
David Moore, Tulsa	10	2	2	4	14
Totals	63	18	40	58	85
Tom Mutch, Memphis	35	17	10	27	65
Tom Mutch, Fort Worth	17	3	11	14	8
Totals	52	20	21	41	73
Guy Prince, Dallas	14	3	4	7	9
Guy Prince, Memphis	9	3	1	4	0
Totals	23	6	5	11	9
Chad Seibel, Tulsa	53	4	24	28	117
Chad Seibel, Memphis	10	0	4	4	25
Totals	63	4	28	32	142
Steve Shaunessy, Memphis	46	5	6	11	221
Steve Shaunessy, Wichita	11	1	5	6	42
Totals	57	6	11	17	263
Greg Smith, Dallas (g)	33	0	0	0	16
Greg Smith, Wichita (g)	5	0	0	0	2
Totals	38	0	0	0	18
Darren Srochenski, Wichita	50	4	9	13	140
Darren Srochenski, Fort Worth	16	1	3	4	55
Totals	66	5	12	17	195
Adam Thompson, Tulsa (g)	2	0	0	0	0
Adam Thompson, Memphis (g)	7	0	0	0	4
Totals	9	0	0	0	4

GOALTENDING

	Games	Min.	W	L	OTL	Goals	SO	Avg.
Y. Gosselin, Wich.	7	292	1	3	1	23	0	4.73
Y. Gosselin, Dal.	18	931	9	5	1	61	0	3.93
Totals	25	1223	10	8	1	84	0	4.12
D. Hersh, Mem.	1	60	0	1	0	6	0	6.00
D. Hersh, Wich.	3	73	0	1	0	7	0	5.75
Totals	4	133	0	2	0	13	0	5.86
A. Mindjimba, M.	23	1307	7	13	2	107	1	4.91
A. Mindjimba, Dal.	7	419	4	2	1	29	0	4.15
Totals	30	1726	11	15	3	136	1	4.73
Greg Smith, Dal.	33	1860	12	13	6	157	0	5.06
Greg Smith, Wich.	5	210	1	2	0	21	0	6.01
Totals	38	2070	13	15	6	178	0	5.16
A. Thompson, Mem.	1	20	0	0	0	3	0	9.00
A. Thompson, Tul.	2	68	1	0	0	5	0	4.41
Totals	3	88	1	0	0	8	0	5.46

1994 PLAYOFFS

RESULTS

SEMIFINALS

Series "A"

	W	L	Pts.	GF	GA
Wichita	4	3	8	38	29
Dallas	3	4	6	29	38

(Wichita won series, 4-3)

Series "B"

	W	L	Pts.	GF	GA
Tulsa	4	3	8	30	27
Oklahoma City	3	4	6	27	30

(Tulsa won series, 4-3)

FINALS

Series "C"

	W	L	Pts.	GF	GA
Wichita	4	0	8	28	13
Tulsa	0	4	0	13	28

(Wichita won series, 4-0)

INDIVIDUAL LEADERS

Goals: Brent Sapergia, Wichita (15)
Assists: Paul Jackson, Wichita (12)
　　　　　Brent Sapergia, Wichita (12)
Points: Brent Sapergia, Wichita (27)
Penalty minutes: Brent Sapergia, Wichita (112)
Goaltending average: Mike Williams, Oklahoma City (3.69)
Shutouts: None

	Games	G	A	Pts.
Ron Handy, Wichita	11	12	10	22
Bob Berg, Wichita	10	9	8	17
Doug Lawrence, Tulsa	11	3	11	14
Craig Coxe, Tulsa	11	4	9	13
Dave Doucette, Tulsa	11	2	11	13
Tom Karalis, Wichita	11	3	9	12
Chris Robertson, Tulsa	11	7	4	11
Mike Berger, Tulsa	11	7	4	11
Paul Dukovac, Wichita	11	0	11	11
Steve Chelios, Wichita	9	0	11	11

TOP SCORERS

	Games	G	A	Pts.
Brent Sapergia, Wichita	11	15	12	27
Paul Jackson, Wichita	11	11	12	23

INDIVIDUAL STATISTICS

DALLAS FREEZE
(Lost semifinals to Wichita, 4-3)

SCORING

	Games	G	A	Pts.	PIM
Frank LaScala	7	5	5	10	10
Troy Binnie	7	5	4	9	2
Wayne Anchikoski	7	6	2	8	8
Jim McGeough	7	3	5	8	8
Jason Taylor	7	2	4	6	64
Derek Crawford	7	1	4	5	27
Brian Bruininks	7	0	5	5	21
Jim Ballantine	7	4	0	4	6
Joe Mittelsteadt	7	1	3	4	49
Mark Holick	7	1	2	3	58
Sean Cowan	7	0	3	3	10
Dean Schmyr	7	0	3	3	35
Jeff Beaudin	7	1	1	2	58
Don Dwyer	6	0	2	2	9
Antoine Mindjimba (goalie)	7	0	2	2	8
Greg MacEachern	1	0	1	1	0
Yannick Gosselin (goalie)	1	0	0	0	0

GOALTENDERS

	Games	Min.	W	L	OTL	Goals	SO	Avg.
Antoine Mindjimba	7	393	3	4	0	34	0	5.19
Yannick Gosselin	1	24	0	0	0	3	0	7.43

OKLAHOMA CITY BLAZERS
(Lost semifinals to Tulsa, 4-3)

SCORING

	Games	G	A	Pts.	PIM
Carl Boudreau	7	9	4	9	14
George Dupont	7	4	4	8	48
Jeff Massey	7	3	5	8	2
Joe Burton	7	4	3	7	4
Chris Laganas	7	3	3	6	30
Guy Girouard	7	1	4	5	10
Steve Simoni	7	1	4	5	4
Kent Anderson	7	2	2	4	12
Jim Solly	7	2	2	4	0
Derry Menard	7	0	4	4	10
Trent Pankewicz	7	1	2	3	14
James Richmond	7	1	2	3	23
Tim Gilligan	7	0	3	3	20
Alan Perry (goalie)	1	0	0	0	10
Bruce Shoebottom	1	0	0	0	14
Craig Johnson	4	0	0	0	2
Mike Williams (goalie)	7	0	0	0	4

GOALTENDERS

	Games	Min.	W	L	OTL	Goals	SO	Avg.
Mike Williams	7	422	3	2	1	26	0	3.69
Alan Perry	1	13	0	1	0	4	0	19.02

TULSA OILERS
(Lost finals to Wichita, 4-0)

SCORING

	Games	G	A	Pts.	PIM
Doug Lawrence	11	3	11	14	52
Craig Coxe	11	4	9	13	38
Dave Doucette	11	2	11	13	6
Mike Berger	11	7	4	11	22
Chris Robertson	11	7	4	11	16
David Moore	11	5	5	10	41
Luc Beausoleil	7	4	4	8	20
Taylor Hall	11	3	5	8	14
Boyd Sutton	11	1	5	6	5
Mike MacWilliam	8	4	0	4	88
Jody Praznik	10	2	2	4	12
Shaun Clouston	11	1	3	4	21
Roger Hunt	9	0	1	1	26
Mark McCoy	9	0	1	1	6
Brian Flatt (goalie)	1	0	0	0	0
Stu Kulak	8	0	0	0	28
Tony Martino (goalie)	11	0	0	0	24

GOALTENDERS

	Games	Min.	W	L	OTL	Goals	SO	Avg.
Tony Martino	11	662	4	5	2	51	0	4.62
Brian Flatt	1	12	0	0	0	2	0	9.69

WICHITA THUNDER
(Winner of 1994 CHL playoffs)

SCORING

	Games	G	A	Pts.	PIM
Brent Sapergia	11	15	12	27	112
Paul Jackson	11	11	12	23	20
Ron Handy	11	12	10	22	12
Bob Berg	10	9	8	17	17
Tom Karalis	11	3	9	12	24
Paul Dukovac	11	0	11	11	14
Steve Chelios	9	0	11	11	18
Brian Wells	11	6	3	9	88
Jim Latos	11	4	5	9	27
Jack Williams	11	3	2	5	4
Stephane Venne	10	1	4	5	60
Rob Weingartner	11	1	4	5	49
Greg Neish	10	1	4	5	53
Steve Shaunessy	11	0	5	5	13
Robert Desjardins (goalie)	10	0	2	2	0
Greg Smith (goalie)	2	0	0	0	0
Darcy Kaminski	4	0	0	0	21

GOALTENDERS

	Games	Min.	W	L	OTL	Goals	SO	Avg.
Greg Smith	2	67	0	1	0	4	0	3.58
Robert Desjardins	10	590	8	2	0	38	0	3.86

1993-94 AWARD WINNERS

ALL-STAR TEAMS

First team	Pos.	Second team
Robert Desjardins, Wichita	G	Roydon Gunn, Memphis
Dave Doucette, Dal.-Tul.	D	David Moore, Tulsa
Guy Girouard, Okla. City	D	Brian Bruininks, Dallas
		Tom Karalis, Tulsa
Paul Jackson, Wichita	C	Ron Handy, Wichita
Doug Lawrence, Tulsa	LW	Bob Berg, Wichita
Robert Wallwork, Memphis	RW	Brent Sapergia, Wichita

TROPHY WINNERS

Most Valuable Player: Robert Desjardins, Wichita
Ken McKenzie Trophy: Paul Jackson, Wichita
John Voss Trophy: Alan Perry, Oklahoma City
Defenseman of the Year: Guy Girouard, Oklahoma City
Rookie of the Year: Chad Seibel, Memphis
President's Trophy: Ron Handy, Wichita
Commissioner's Trophy: Doug Shedden, Wichita

CENTRAL — MINOR LEAGUES — CENTRAL

ALL-TIME AWARD WINNERS

MOST VALUABLE PLAYER

Season	Player, Team
1992-93	Sylvain Fleury, Oklahoma City
1993-94	Robert Desjardins, Wichita

KEN McKENZIE TROPHY

(Leading Scorer)

Season	Player, Team
1992-93	Sylvain Fleury, Oklahoma City
1993-94	Paul Jackson, Wichita

JOHN VOSS TROPHY

(Outstanding goaltender)

Season	Player, Team
1992-93	Tony Martino, Tulsa
1993-94	Alan Perry, Oklahoma City

DEFENSEMAN OF THE YEAR

Season	Player, Team
1992-93	Dave Doucette, Dallas
1993-94	Guy Girouard, Oklahoma City

ROOKIE OF THE YEAR

Season	Player, Team
1992-93	Robert Desjardins, Wichita
1993-94	Chad Seibel, Memphis

PRESIDENT'S TROPHY

(Playoff MVP)

Season	Player, Team
1992-93	Tony Fiore, Tulsa
1993-94	Ron Handy, Wichita

COMMISSIONER'S TROPHY

(Coach of the year)

Season	Coach, Team
1992-93	Garry Unger, Tulsa
1993-94	Doug Shedden, Wichita

ALL-TIME LEAGUE CHAMPIONS

REGULAR-SEASON CHAMPION

Season	Team	Coach
1992-93	Oklahoma City Blazers	Michael McEwen
1993-94	Wichita Thunder	Doug Shedden

PLAYOFF CHAMPION

Team	Coach
Tulsa Oilers	Garry Unger
Wichita Thunder	Doug Shedden

COLONIAL HOCKEY LEAGUE

LEAGUE OFFICE

Commissioner
  Bob Myers
Director of operations
  Gord Stellick
Secretary
  Irene Puddester

Address
  P.O. Box 45
  Copetown, Ontario L0R 1J0

Phone
  905-627-2096
FAX
  905-627-2097

TEAMS

BRANTFORD SMOKE

General manager
  Rod Davidson
Head coach
  Ken Gratton
Home ice
  Brantford Civic Centre
Address
  69-79 Market Street, South
  Brantford, Ontario N3T 5R7
Seating Capacity
  3,300
Phone
  519-751-9467
FAX
  519-751-2366

DETROIT FALCONS

General manager and head coach
  Lou Franceschetti
Home ice
  Fraser Ice Arena
Address
  34400 Utica Road
  Fraser, MI 48026
Seating capacity
  3,000
Phone
  313-294-2488
FAX
  313-294-2358

FLINT GENERALS

General manager and head coach
  Peter Horachek
Home ice
  IMA Sports Arena
Address
  3501 Lapeer Road
  Flint, MI 48503
Seating capacity
  4,021
Phone
  313-742-9422

FAX
  313-742-5892

LONDON BLUES

President
  Doug Tarry
Head coach
  To be announced
Home ice
  London Gardens
Address
  1408 Wellington Road S.
  London, ONT N6E 2Z5
Seating capacity
  3,900
Phone
  519-681-0800
FAX
  519-681-7291

MUSKEGON FURY

General manager
  Tony Lisman
Head coach
  Steve Ludzik
Home ice
  L.C. Walker Arena
Address
  470 W. Western Avenue
  Muskegon, MI 49440
Seating capacity
  5,400
Phone
  616-726-5058
FAX
  616-726-0428

SAGINAW WHEELS

General manager/head coach
  Tom Barrett
Home ice
  Wendler Arena

Address
  400 Johnson Street
  Saginaw, MI 48607
Seating capacity
  4,727
Phone
  517-752-4200
FAX
  517-752-1960

THUNDER BAY SENATORS

President and general manager
  Gary Cook
Head coach
  Bill MacDonald
Home ice
  Fort William Gardens
Address
  80 Wilson Avenue
  901 Myles Street E.
  Thunder Bay, ONT P7C 1J9
Seating Capacity
  4,300
Phone
  807-623-7121
FAX
  807-622-3306

NOTE: In addition to the above-mentioned teams, a new franchise will play in Utica for the 1994-95 season. Additional information was not available at deadline.

1993-94 REGULAR SEASON

FINAL STANDINGS

EAST DIVISION

Team	G	W	L		Pts.	GF	GA
Thunder Bay	64	45	15	(4)	94	331	236
Brantford	64	28	26	(10)	66	308	348
St. Thomas	64	22	34	(8)	52	284	343
Utica	64	21	39	(4)	46	226	330

WEST DIVISION

Team	G	W	L		Pts.	GF	GA
Chatham	64	39	18	(7)	85	336	281
Muskegon	64	35	24	(5)	75	319	301
Detroit	64	34	25	(5)	73	296	275
Flint	64	32	23	(9)	73	328	314

( )—Indicates overtime losses and are worth one point.

INDIVIDUAL LEADERS

Goals: Kevin Kerr, Flint (57)
Assists: Paul Polillo, Brantford (99)
Points: Paul Polillo, Brantford (141)
Penalty minutes: Mel Angelstad, Thunder Bay (374)
Goaltending average: Jean-Francois Labbe, Thunder Bay (3.10)
Shutouts: Jean-Francois Labbe, Thunder Bay (2)

	Games	G	A	Pts.
Mark Turner, Muskegon	61	46	58	104
Greg Walters, Brantford	42	42	62	104
Dan Woodley, Muskegon	58	43	58	101
Terry Menard, Thunder Bay	61	41	60	101
Tim Bean, St. Thomas	62	40	55	95
Jim Ritchie, Chatham	55	41	44	85
Joel Gardner, Chatham	42	30	54	84
Kent Hawley, St.T.-Bran.	51	22	62	84
Gary Callaghan, St. Thomas	48	43	38	81
Jamey Hicks, Brantford	62	37	44	81
Brian Downey, Thunder Bay	61	30	51	81
Paul Kelly, Muskegon	57	34	44	78
Keith Whitmore, Flint	55	19	59	78
Mark Karpen, Muskegon	45	29	46	75

TOP SCORERS

	Games	G	A	Pts.
Paul Polillo, Brantford	64	42	99	141
Brian Sakic, Flint	64	39	86	125
Gerry St. Cyr, Thunder Bay	62	50	63	113
Kevin Kerr, Flint	45	57	55	112
John Vecchiarelli, Chatham	48	45	64	109
Brett Strot, Flint	53	36	71	107

INDIVIDUAL STATISTICS

BRANTFORD SMOKE

SCORING

	Games	G	A	Pts.	PIM
Paul Polillo	64	42	99	141	37
Greg Walters	42	42	62	104	88
Jamey Hicks	62	37	44	81	64
Bruce Bell	51	10	38	48	22
Kent Hawley	26	10	28	38	38
Dave Moylan	60	10	26	36	85
Andy Bezeau	22	18	16	34	240
John Batten	29	11	20	31	155
Chris Crombie	51	12	18	30	42
Lou Crawford	21	12	17	29	39
Paul Mitton	47	6	21	27	93
Greg White	32	10	14	24	6
Jason Clarke	24	8	13	21	264
Todd Francis	54	5	15	20	83
Danny Gratton	12	9	10	19	16
Alex Kuzminski	30	8	10	18	4
Cory Banika	8	7	9	16	30
Darin Smith	6	9	5	14	7
Wayne MacPhee	37	1	12	13	19
Paul Pahkevitch	14	7	5	12	4
Vince Guidotti	20	4	7	11	8
Jason Taylor	43	4	6	10	176
Greg Bignell	23	2	7	9	94
Everton Blackwin	15	4	2	6	2
Graeme Bonar	10	1	5	6	6
Tom Moulton	13	4	1	5	10
Gord Pell	8	1	4	5	5
Gary St. Pierre	5	1	3	4	4
Jim Sprott	12	1	3	4	55
Terry McCutcheon	2	3	0	3	2
Rock Isabel	5	2	1	3	18
Stephen Morden	17	0	3	3	35
Peter Richards (goalie)	43	0	3	3	32
John Copple	18	1	1	2	2
John Laan	19	0	2	2	37
John Badduke	1	1	0	1	2
George Finn	2	1	0	1	17
Jamie McKee	3	1	0	1	4
Brad Gratton	3	0	1	1	0
Mike Teeple	3	0	1	1	0
Chris MacDonald	4	0	1	1	6
Kevin Smith	6	0	1	1	0
Kyle Blacklock	9	0	1	1	0
Jeff Wilson (goalie)	9	0	1	1	2
Scott McIntyre	1	0	0	0	0
Brian Millar	1	0	0	0	0
Matt Ocello (goalie)	1	0	0	0	0
Joe Persia (goalie)	1	0	0	0	0
Darren Snyder	1	0	0	0	0
Peno Chiapetta	2	0	0	0	2
Sonny Romano (goalie)	2	0	0	0	0
Rob Springer	2	0	0	0	0
Chris Harvey (goalie)	4	0	0	0	2
Darcy Austin (goalie)	6	0	0	0	0
Les Sirota (goalie)	10	0	0	0	2
Joe Boute	11	0	0	0	75

GOALTENDING

	Games	Min.	W	L	OTL	Goals	SO	Avg.
Joe Persia	1	0	0	0	0	0	0	0.00
Jeff Wilson	9	514	5	3	0	34	1	3.97
Matt Ocello	1	20	0	0	0	3	0	9.00
Peter Richards	43	2355	17	17	7	198	0	5.04
Les Sirota	10	506	5	4	1	44	0	5.22
Chris Harvey	4	171	1	0	1	16	0	5.63
Sonny Romano	2	68	0	0	0	14	0	12.32
Darcy Austin	6	246	0	2	1	30	0	7.31

CHATHAM WHEELS

SCORING

	Games	G	A	Pts.	PIM
John Vecchiarelli	48	45	64	109	105
Jim Ritchie	55	41	44	85	140
Joel Gardner	42	30	54	84	50
Wayne Muir	62	29	41	70	269
Paul Sutcliffe	62	28	35	63	22
Rob Wilson	51	13	39	52	110
Jamie Allan	30	16	33	49	119
Marty Wells	49	21	24	45	28
Jason Stos	62	9	35	44	57
Dave Lorentz	35	14	26	40	24
Brett MacDonald	42	8	31	39	29
John East	58	10	22	32	95
Jamie Dabonovich	35	7	15	22	9
Derek Prue	46	13	7	20	18
Sasha Lakovic	13	11	7	18	61
Scott Garrow	15	5	12	17	6
Shane Bogden	19	3	8	11	40
Brad Barton	38	1	10	11	125
Mike Murray	32	4	5	9	22
Gary St. Pierre	17	2	7	9	20
Scott Wasson	12	3	5	8	2
Darryl Brunoro	21	3	4	7	33
Kevin Butt (goalie)	43	0	6	6	29
Oleg Santourian	9	1	4	5	0
Dan Williams	17	1	4	5	60
Niklas Barklund	6	3	1	4	9
Jason Hannigan	6	3	1	4	2
Richard Borgo	8	2	2	4	14
Mike Gruttaduria	42	3	0	3	77
Daniel Dore	4	1	2	3	13
Paul Cohen	12	0	2	2	26
Jason Hanson	1	0	1	1	0

	Games	G	A	Pts.	PIM
Alain Harvey (goalie)	3	0	1	1	2
Mark Cavallin (goalie)	4	0	1	1	0
Andrei Dylevsky	7	0	1	1	0
John Laan	3	0	0	0	18
Matt Ocello (goalie)	4	0	0	0	0
Darren Bell	6	0	0	0	0
Scott Humphrey (goalie)	7	0	0	0	0
Marc Brodeur	9	0	0	0	2
Ryan Van Steinburg	10	0	0	0	19

GOALTENDING

	Games	Min.	W	L	OTL	Goals	SO	Avg.
Scott Humphrey	7	338	2	1	2	18	1	3.20
Mark Cavallin	4	192	1	1	1	13	0	4.05
Matt Ocello	4	206	1	2	0	14	0	4.07
Alain Harvey	3	187	1	1	1	13	0	4.18
Paul Cohen	12	588	6	2	1	42	0	4.29
Kevin Butt	43	2376	28	11	2	173	0	4.37

DETROIT FALCONS

SCORING

	Games	G	A	Pts.	PIM
Andy Rymsha	48	24	38	62	48
Darryl Noren	27	18	39	57	22
Christian Lalonde	64	15	36	51	75
Dave DiVita	62	12	34	46	173
Sergei Makarov	47	16	27	43	26
Kimbi Daniels	23	11	28	39	42
Vladimir Antipin	59	11	24	35	57
Bill Robinson	37	18	15	33	42
Jaroslav Kunik	47	17	14	31	40
Andy MacVicar	26	17	13	30	8
Mike May	29	14	16	30	43
Angelo Russo	34	10	20	30	32
Niklas Barklund	41	12	14	26	62
Jason Simon	13	9	16	25	87
Chris MacKenzie	21	6	17	23	7
Rinat Khasanov	41	9	13	22	40
Garry Gulash	31	7	15	22	146
Steve Beadle	15	7	12	19	8
Savo Mitrovic	12	8	10	18	8
Lennie MacAusland	55	5	13	18	58
Bob McKillop	15	9	7	16	4
Jacques Mailhot	21	1	9	10	122
Wayne Menard	21	6	3	9	83
Yuri Krivokhija	13	3	6	9	41
Mark Velucci	42	4	4	8	79
Chris Marshall	7	3	3	6	4
Scott Beattie	3	2	4	6	2
Clark Polglase	10	2	4	6	42
Kenstatin Shafronov	4	3	2	5	0
Everton Blackwin	12	3	2	5	15
Glen Carvey	6	0	4	4	4
Corey Krug	4	2	1	3	0
Frank Gianfreddo	5	1	2	3	5
Shane Bogden	10	1	2	3	8
Aaron Asp	3	2	0	2	0
Lou Franceschetti	2	1	1	2	6
Michel Couvrette	6	1	1	2	0
Keith Wembert	2	0	2	2	0
Marshall Kronewitt	7	0	2	2	4
Darren Miciak	21	0	2	2	95
Mike Risdale (goalie)	34	0	2	2	0
Andrei Sokolov	3	0	1	1	5
Jamie Smith	2	0	0	0	2
Cam Yager (goalie)	3	0	0	0	0
Scott Cashman (goalie)	7	0	0	0	0
Mike Sullivan	11	0	0	0	16
Maxim Michailovsky (goalie)	26	0	0	0	4

GOALTENDING

	Games	Min.	W	L	OTL	Goals	SO	Avg.
M. Michailovsky	26	1495	14	8	3	87	0	3.49
Mike Risdale	34	1953	17	14	2	134	0	4.12

	Games	Min.	W	L	OTL	Goals	SO	Avg.
Scott Cashman	7	268	2	2	0	25	0	5.60
Cam Yager	3	161	1	1	0	19	0	7.08

FLINT GENERALS

SCORING

	Games	G	A	Pts.	PIM
Brian Sakic	64	39	86	125	30
Kevin Kerr	45	57	55	112	299
Brett Strot	53	36	71	107	37
Keith Whitmore	55	19	59	78	131
Lorne Knauft	51	20	36	56	180
Dominic Niro	60	19	26	45	70
Jim Duhart	62	18	24	42	211
Keith Cyr	43	14	26	40	43
Stephan Brochu	54	8	32	40	116
Larry Bernard	26	10	24	34	67
Marc Vachon	56	16	16	32	30
John Heasty	51	16	4	20	34
Kevin St. Jacques	10	5	13	18	2
Ken Spangler	45	2	15	17	256
Mike Vukonich	8	7	8	15	12
Dan Elsener	47	6	9	15	49
Dave Stewart	8	1	14	15	8
Chris O'Rourke	47	1	13	14	168
Brett Stickney	40	4	9	13	22
Todd Humphrey	13	7	5	12	101
Paul Pahkevitch	19	4	8	12	19
Chris Crombie	6	4	2	6	9
Keith Carney	23	0	9	9	10
Dave Haksymiu	19	3	4	7	2
Bobby House	4	3	3	6	0
Clint Collins	14	2	2	4	90
Dino Grossi	5	3	0	3	10
Norm Tobin	14	1	2	3	4
Tyler Pella	3	1	0	1	7
Carl Picconatto (goalie)	10	1	0	1	6
Robb Barban	3	0	1	1	12
Rock Isabel	10	0	1	1	43
Darcy Austin (goalie)	21	0	1	1	4
Mark Gowans (goalie)	37	0	1	1	2
Rob Watson (goalie)	1	0	0	0	0
Matt Zilinskas	1	0	0	0	0
Aaron Morrison	12	0	0	0	53

GOALTENDING

	Games	Min.	W	L	OTL	Goals	SO	Avg.
Mark Gowans	37	2138	21	9	6	145	0	4.07
Darcy Austin	21	1126	7	10	2	95	0	5.06
Carl Picconatto	10	582	4	4	1	61	0	6.29
Rob Watson	1	35	0	0	0	4	0	6.88

MUSKEGON FURY

SCORING

	Games	G	A	Pts.	PIM
Mark Turner	61	46	58	104	57
Dan Woodley	58	43	58	101	217
Paul Kelly	57	34	44	78	32
Mark Karpen	45	29	46	75	20
Brett Seguin	46	24	50	74	105
Justin Morrison	64	27	33	60	86
Joe Hawley	45	19	33	52	88
Joe Simon	63	14	25	39	69
Todd Charlesworth	37	8	30	38	33
Darrel Newman	62	5	28	33	88
Bob Jones	54	12	18	30	88
Doug Stromback	39	13	12	25	33
Kevin Barrett	61	11	14	25	307
Scott Feasby	62	7	17	24	156
Scott Campbell	34	2	15	17	40
Rob Melanson	44	2	8	10	184
Donny Martin	7	4	3	7	4
Roch Belley (goalie)	48	0	7	7	18
Jodi Murphy	36	4	1	5	150

	Games	G	A	Pts.	PIM
Grant Block	3	2	1	3	5
Shayne Stevenson	1	2	0	2	0
Roman Hubalek	8	1	1	2	0
Jari Pasanen	11	1	1	2	2
Jaan Luik	2	1	0	1	2
Jeff Napierala	3	0	1	1	2
Rick Guirhney	5	0	1	1	2
Scott Kelsey	10	0	1	1	8
Mark Roof (goalie)	1	0	0	0	0
Brian Rorabeck	1	0	0	0	0
Les Sirota (goalie)	1	0	0	0	0
Jim Slazyk (goalie)	1	0	0	0	0
Mark Taylor	1	0	0	0	0
Pryce Wood	1	0	0	0	0
Dan Brooks	2	0	0	0	0
Fred Monfils	2	0	0	0	0
Aaron Morrison	2	0	0	0	0
John Petroney	3	0	0	0	59
Brent Convery (goalie)	4	0	0	0	0
Steve Herniman	4	0	0	0	24
Chris French (goalie)	5	0	0	0	4
Carl Picconatto (goalie)	5	0	0	0	0
Earl Switzer	5	0	0	0	4
Darryl Gilmour (goalie)	14	0	0	0	2

GOALTENDING

	Games	Min.	W	L	OTL	Goals	SO	Avg.
Brent Convery	3	113	1	1	0	6	0	3.20
Roch Belley	48	2704	24	17	5	185	1	4.11
Darryl Gilmour	14	665	8	2	0	50	0	4.51
Carl Picconatto	5	110	1	0	0	9	1	4.89
Chris French	5	214	1	3	0	21	0	5.89
Mark Roof	1	58	0	1	0	8	0	8.23
Jim Slazyk	1	10	0	1	0	3	0	18.62
Les Sirota	1	9	0	0	0	3	0	20.49

ST. THOMAS WILDCATS

SCORING

	Games	G	A	Pts.	PIM
Tim Bean	62	40	55	95	38
Gary Callaghan	48	43	38	81	67
Donny Martin	50	24	28	52	199
Kent Hawley	25	12	34	46	14
Trevor Dam	28	16	28	44	19
Bernie Johns	60	7	33	40	6
Darin Smith	28	8	30	38	39
Gary Miller	62	7	30	37	100
John Batten	28	16	18	34	133
Todd Coopman	61	8	26	34	39
Derek MacNair	59	15	18	33	29
Jeff Pawluk	56	8	23	31	23
Matt Ripley	33	10	20	30	23
Alex Kuzminski	34	10	20	30	10
Jamie Allan	18	10	12	22	87
Bernie Cassell	27	11	8	19	19
Mike Teeple	21	3	12	15	21
Jason Hannigan	20	8	6	14	16
Kyle Blacklock	18	1	6	7	8
Shayne Stevenson	6	3	3	6	15
Bob Emond	34	3	3	6	121
Marc Vachon	6	2	4	6	0
Derek Prue	11	2	4	6	2
Jason Anderson	11	1	5	6	10
Ron Bertrand (goalie)	53	0	5	5	21
Dan Elsener	3	1	2	3	2
Jaroslav Kunik	10	1	2	3	2
Rob Pallante	22	1	2	3	18
Andy Bezeau	1	2	0	2	12
Norm Tobin	15	1	1	2	8
Paul Cohen (goalie)	13	0	2	2	12
Ange Guzzo	15	1	0	1	13
Leon Slavo	3	0	1	1	0
Chris Garofalo	4	0	1	1	2
Sonny Romano (goalie)	13	0	1	1	0

	Games	G	A	Pts.	PIM
Jason Clairmont	2	0	0	0	0
Mark Gorgi	2	0	0	0	2
Darren Naylor	2	0	0	0	0
Oleg Bratash (goalie)	6	0	0	0	0
Jamie Hayden	7	0	0	0	0
Jake Linklater	7	0	0	0	5
Andy Doxtator	9	0	0	0	10
Mike Sullivan	11	0	0	0	7
Jason Coles	13	0	0	0	14
Kyle Merkley	13	0	0	0	5

GOALTENDING

	Games	Min.	W	L	OTL	Goals	SO	Avg.
Oleg Bratash	6	323	2	2	1	24	0	4.46
Paul Cohen	13	600	3	5	1	50	0	5.00
Ron Bertrand	53	2537	16	23	5	215	0	5.09
Sonny Romano	13	408	1	4	1	43	0	6.32

THUNDER BAY SENATORS

SCORING

	Games	G	A	Pts.	PIM
Gerry St. Cyr	62	50	63	113	265
Terry Menard	61	41	60	101	111
Brian Downey	61	30	51	81	17
Todd Howarth	49	23	41	64	80
Barry McKinlay	40	14	43	57	53
Chris Hynnes	59	13	40	53	45
Richard Borgo	51	14	31	45	55
Trent McCleary	51	23	17	40	123
Ron Talakoski	43	19	20	39	31
Llew McWana	64	12	27	39	51
Jean Blouin	23	22	12	34	31
Bruce Ramsay	63	9	22	31	313
Don Osborne	59	7	23	30	16
Jason Firth	13	10	16	26	2
Brian Wells	27	7	16	23	89
Mel Angelstad	58	1	20	21	374
Tom Warden	23	6	9	15	75
Jamie Hayden	43	2	13	15	22
Jake Grimes	10	7	5	12	6
Vern Ray	42	4	7	11	45
Paul MacLean	17	5	5	10	0
Chris Rowland	14	4	6	10	13
Alain Deeks	22	1	5	6	16
Mike O'Leary	14	2	3	5	13
Norm Batherson	3	1	2	3	2
Rod Saarinen	5	0	1	1	2
Matt Weir	5	0	1	1	0
Tomi Hietala (goalie)	21	0	1	1	2
Alain Harvey (goalie)	2	0	0	0	0
Tim Levesque	2	0	0	0	23
Gilbert Quevillon	3	0	0	0	0
Jean-Francois Labbe (goalie)	52	0	0	0	4

GOALTENDING

	Games	Min.	W	L	OTL	Goals	SO	Avg.
Alain Harvey	2	89	1	0	0	3	0	2.02
J.-F. Labbe	52	2901	35	11	4	150	2	3.10
Tomi Hietala	21	888	9	4	0	78	0	5.27

UTICA BULLDOGS

SCORING

	Games	G	A	Pts.	PIM
Tim Fingerhut	58	24	34	58	53
Mike Tomlinson	63	24	31	55	148
Mikhail Zakharov	40	19	27	46	42
Matt Zilinskas	52	22	19	41	61
Andrew Dickson	39	11	30	41	26
Scott Allen	64	16	23	39	61
Matt Weir	57	8	28	36	33
Dan Sawyer	45	10	21	31	63
Angelo Russo	27	13	12	25	46
Craig Deblois	33	14	8	22	46

	Games	G	A	Pts.	PIM
Andy MacVicar	31	9	11	20	10
Andy Stewart	50	6	13	19	84
Mike Jorgensen	26	8	10	18	23
Alan Brown	37	1	13	14	11
Bill Whistle	20	7	2	9	24
Matt Ripley	14	6	2	8	0
Larry Bernard	10	3	5	8	21
Robert Haddock	21	1	7	8	48
Pat Manning	8	5	2	7	4
Ted Fauss	20	3	4	7	48
John Massoud	15	2	5	7	0
Glen Carvey	16	0	7	7	11
Chris O'Brien	19	0	7	7	18
Mike Murray	14	3	3	6	4
Joey McTamney	14	2	4	6	2
John Schierbaum	13	1	3	4	2
Rob Pallante	20	0	4	4	28
John Stringfellow	8	1	2	3	15
Troy Mohns	11	1	2	3	2
Scott Kelsey	12	1	2	3	2
Kevin Doherty	7	0	3	3	2
Glen Carvey	10	0	3	3	7
Jason Julian	21	0	3	3	76
Kevin MacKay	3	1	1	2	2
Richie Moore	5	1	1	2	29
Tony Calandra	7	0	2	2	2
Pat Szturm (goalie)	37	0	2	2	4
Danny O'Brien	4	1	0	1	17
Josh Murray	8	1	0	1	2
Rod Saarinen	2	0	1	1	14
Tom Roman	5	0	1	1	2
Adam Hooper	8	0	1	1	5
Ange Guzzo	17	0	1	1	48
Michel Couvrette	1	0	0	0	0
Mike Thomas	1	0	0	0	0
Grant Wood (goalie)	1	0	0	0	0
Mike O'Leary	2	0	0	0	0
John Petrone	2	0	0	0	2
Bruno Umbro	2	0	0	0	15
Jay Zeidel	2	0	0	0	0
Brian Fleury	3	0	0	0	0
Dave Wright	3	0	0	0	0
Darren Miciak	6	0	0	0	129
Keith Adams	16	0	0	0	15
Wayne Marion (goalie)	37	0	0	0	21

GOALTENDING

	Games	Min.	W	L	OTL	Goals	SO	Avg.
Wayne Marion	36	1953	13	17	2	159	0	4.89
Pat Szturm	36	1888	8	21	2	155	0	4.93
Grant Wood	1	10	0	1	0	4	0	23.68

PLAYERS WITH TWO OR MORE TEAMS

SCORING

	Games	G	A	Pts.	PIM
Jamie Allan, St. Thomas	18	10	12	22	87
Jamie Allan, Chatham	30	16	33	49	119
Totals	48	26	45	71	206
Darcy Austin, Brantford (g)	6	0	0	0	0
Darcy Austin, Flint (g)	21	0	1	1	4
Totals	27	0	1	1	4
Niklas Barklund, Detroit	41	12	14	26	62
Niklas Barklund, Chatham	6	3	1	4	9
Totals	47	15	15	30	71
John Batten, Brantford	29	11	20	31	155
John Batten, St. Thomas	28	16	18	34	133
Totals	57	27	38	65	288
Larry Bernard, Utica	10	3	5	8	21
Larry Bernard, Flint	26	10	24	34	67
Totals	36	13	29	42	88
Andy Bezeau, Brantford	22	18	16	34	240
Andy Bezeau, St. Thomas	1	2	0	2	12
Totals	23	20	16	36	252
Kyle Blacklock, Brantford	9	0	1	1	0

	Games	G	A	Pts.	PIM
Kyle Blacklock, St. Thomas	18	1	6	7	8
Totals	27	1	7	8	8
Everton Blackwin, Detroit	12	3	2	5	15
Everton Blackwin, Brantford	15	4	2	6	2
Totals	27	7	4	11	17
Shane Bogden, Chatham	19	3	8	11	40
Shane Bogden, Detroit	10	1	2	3	8
Totals	29	4	10	14	48
Richard Borgo, Thunder Bay	51	14	31	45	55
Richard Borgo, Chatham	8	2	2	4	14
Totals	59	16	33	49	69
Paul Cohen, Chatham (g)	12	0	2	2	26
Paul Cohen, St. Thomas (g)	13	0	2	2	12
Totals	25	0	4	4	38
Michel Couvrette, Utica	1	0	0	0	0
Michel Couvrette, Detroit	6	1	1	2	0
Totals	7	1	1	2	0
Chris Crombie, Brantford	51	12	18	30	42
Chris Crombie, Flint	6	4	2	6	9
Totals	57	16	20	36	51
Dan Elsener, Flint	47	6	9	15	49
Dan Elsener, St. Thomas	3	1	2	3	2
Totals	50	7	11	18	51
Ange Guzzo, Utica	17	0	1	1	48
Ange Guzzo, Muskegon	33	1	2	3	50
Ange Guzzo, St. Thomas	15	1	0	1	13
Totals	55	2	3	5	111
Jason Hannigan, Chatham	6	3	1	4	2
Jason Hannigan, St. Thomas	20	8	6	14	16
Totals	26	11	7	18	18
Alain Harvey, Chatham (g)	3	0	1	1	2
Alain Harvey, Thunder Bay (g)	2	0	0	0	0
Totals	5	0	1	1	2
Kent Hawley, St. Thomas	25	12	34	46	14
Kent Hawley, Brantford	26	10	28	38	38
Totals	51	22	62	84	52
Jamie Hayden, Thunder Bay	43	2	13	15	22
Jamie Hayden, St. Thomas	7	0	0	0	0
Totals	50	2	13	15	22
Rock Isabel, Flint	10	0	1	1	43
Rock Isabel, Brantford	5	2	1	3	18
Totals	15	2	2	4	61
Scott Kelsey, Utica	12	1	2	3	2
Scott Kelsey, Muskegon	10	0	1	1	8
Totals	22	1	3	4	10
Jaroslav Kunik, St. Thomas	10	1	2	3	2
Jaroslav Kunik, Detroit	47	17	14	31	40
Totals	57	18	16	34	42
Alex Kuzminski, Brantford	30	8	10	18	4
Alex Kuzminski, St. Thomas	34	10	20	30	10
Totals	64	18	30	48	14
John Laan, Chatham	3	0	0	0	18
John Laan, Utica	11	0	1	1	78
John Laan, Brantford	19	0	2	2	37
Totals	33	0	3	3	133
Andy MacVicar, Utica	31	9	11	20	10
Andy MacVicar, Detroit	26	17	13	30	8
Totals	57	26	24	50	18
Donny Martin, St. Thomas	50	24	28	52	199
Donny Martin, Muskegon	7	4	3	7	4
Totals	57	28	31	59	203
Darren Miciak, Utica	6	0	0	0	129
Darren Miciak, St. Thomas	7	0	0	0	61
Darren Miciak, Detroit	21	0	2	2	95
Totals	34	0	2	2	285
Aaron Morrison, Flint	12	0	0	0	53
Aaron Morrison, Muskegon	2	0	0	0	0
Totals	14	0	0	0	53
Mike Murray, Chatham	32	4	5	9	22
Mike Murray, Utica	14	3	3	6	4
Totals	46	7	8	15	26
Matt Ocello, Chatham (g)	4	0	0	0	0
Matt Ocello, Brantford (g)	1	0	0	0	0
Totals	5	0	0	0	0
Mike O'Leary, Utica	2	0	0	0	0

	Games	G	A	Pts.	PIM
Mike O'Leary, Thunder Bay	14	2	3	5	13
Totals	16	2	3	5	13
Paul Pahkevitch, Flint	19	4	8	12	19
Paul Pahkevitch, Brantford	14	7	5	12	4
Totals	33	11	13	24	23
Rob Pallante, St. Thomas	22	1	2	3	18
Rob Pallante, Utica	20	0	4	4	28
Totals	42	1	6	7	46
Carl Picconatto, Flint (g)	10	1	0	1	6
Carl Picconatto, Muskegon (g)	5	0	0	0	0
Totals	15	1	0	1	6
Derek Prue, Chatham	46	13	7	20	18
Derek Prue, Utica	2	0	0	0	0
Derek Prue, St. Thomas	11	2	4	6	2
Totals	59	15	11	26	20
Matt Ripley, Utica	14	6	2	8	0
Matt Ripley, St. Thomas	33	10	20	30	23
Totals	47	16	22	38	23
Sonny Romano, Brantford (g)	2	0	0	0	0
Sonny Romano, St. Thomas (g)	13	0	1	1	0
Totals	15	0	1	1	0
Angelo Russo, Detroit	34	10	20	30	32
Angelo Russo, Utica	27	13	12	25	46
Totals	61	23	32	55	78
Rod Saarinen, Thunder Bay	5	0	1	1	2
Rod Saarinen, Utica	2	0	1	1	14
Totals	7	0	2	2	16
Gary St. Pierre, Chatham	17	2	7	9	20
Gary St. Pierre, St. Thomas	34	7	20	27	80
Gary St. Pierre, Brantford	5	1	3	4	4
Totals	56	10	30	40	104
Les Sirota, Brantford (g)	10	0	0	0	2
Les Sirota, Muskegon (g)	1	0	0	0	0
Totals	11	0	0	0	2
Darin Smith, St. Thomas	28	8	30	38	39
Darin Smith, Brantford	6	9	5	14	7
Totals	34	17	35	52	46
Shayne Stevenson, Muskegon	1	2	0	2	0
Shayne Stevenson, St. Thomas	6	3	3	6	15
Totals	7	5	3	8	15
Mike Sullivan, St. Thomas	11	0	0	0	7
Mike Sullivan, Detroit	11	0	0	0	16
Totals	22	0	0	0	23

	Games	G	A	Pts.	PIM
Mike Teeple, St. Thomas	21	3	12	15	21
Mike Teeple, Brantford	3	0	1	1	0
Totals	24	3	13	16	21
Norm Tobin, St. Thomas	15	1	1	2	8
Norm Tobin, Detroit	22	1	7	8	8
Norm Tobin, Flint	14	1	2	3	4
Totals	51	3	10	13	20
Marc Vachon, Flint	56	16	16	32	30
Marc Vachon, St. Thomas	6	2	4	6	0
Totals	62	18	20	38	30
Matt Weir, Thunder Bay	5	0	1	1	0
Matt Weir, Utica	57	8	28	36	33
Totals	62	8	29	37	33
Matt Zilinskas, Flint	1	0	0	0	0
Matt Zilinskas, Brantford	1	1	1	2	2
Matt Zilinskas, Utica	52	22	19	41	61
Totals	54	23	20	43	63

GOALTENDING

	Games	Min.	W	L	OTL	Goals	SO	Avg.
Darcy Austin, Brant.	6	246	0	2	1	30	0	7.31
Darcy Austin, Flint.	21	1126	7	10	2	95	0	5.06
Totals	27	1372	7	12	3	125	0	5.47
Paul Cohen, Chat.	12	588	6	2	1	42	0	4.29
Paul Cohen, St.T.	13	600	3	5	1	50	0	5.00
Totals	25	1188	9	7	2	92	0	4.64
Alain Harvey, Chat.	3	187	1	1	1	13	0	4.18
Alain Harvey, T.B.	2	89	1	0	0	3	0	2.02
Totals	5	276	2	1	1	16	0	3.48
Matt Ocello, Chat.	4	206	1	2	0	14	0	4.07
Matt Ocello, Brant.	1	20	0	0	0	3	0	9.00
Totals	5	226	1	2	0	17	0	4.51
C. Picconatto, Flint	10	582	4	4	1	61	0	6.29
C. Picconatto, Mus.	5	110	1	0	0	9	1	4.89
Totals	15	692	5	4	1	70	1	6.07
S. Romano, St.T.	13	408	1	4	1	43	0	6.32
S. Romano, Brant.	2	68	0	0	0	14	0	12.32
Totals	15	476	1	4	1	57	0	7.19
Les Sirota, Brant.	10	506	5	4	1	44	0	5.22
Les Sirota, Mus.	1	9	0	0	0	3	0	20.49
Totals	11	515	5	4	1	47	0	5.49

1994 COLONIAL CUP PLAYOFFS

RESULTS

PRELIMINARY ROUND

Series "A"

	W	L	Pts.	GF	GA
Chatham	3	0	6	22	9
St. Thomas	0	3	0	9	22

(Chatham won series, 3-0)

Series "B"

	W	L	Pts.	GF	GA
Brantford	3	0	6	14	9
Muskegon	0	3	0	9	14

(Brantford won series, 3-0)

Series "C"

	W	L	Pts.	GF	GA
Flint	3	1	6	16	12
Detroit	1	3	2	12	16

(Flint won series, 3-1)

SEMIFINALS

Series "D"

	W	L	Pts.	GF	GA
Thunder Bay	4	0	8	27	11
Brantford	0	4	0	11	27

(Thunder Bay won series, 4-0)

Series "E"

	W	L	Pts.	GF	GA
Chatham	4	3	8	35	34
Flint	3	4	6	34	35

(Chatham won series, 4-3)

FINALS

Series "F"

	W	L	Pts.	GF	GA
Thunder Bay	4	1	8	24	10
Chatham	1	4	2	10	24

(Thunder Bay won series, 4-1)

INDIVIDUAL LEADERS

Goals: Richard Borgo, Chatham (11)
Assists: John Vecchiarelli, Chatham (18)
Points: John Vecchiarelli, Chatham (28)
Penalty minutes: Jamie Allan, Chatham (95)
Goaltending average: Jean-Francois Labbe, Thunder Bay (2.19)
Shutouts: Jean-Francois Labbe, Thunder Bay (2)

	Games	G	A	Pts.
Brett Strot, Flint	10	10	10	20
Joel Gardner, Chatham	15	8	12	20
Kevin St. Jacques, Flint	10	4	14	18
Marty Wells, Chatham	15	9	8	17
Terry Menard, Thunder Bay	9	7	9	16
Todd Howarth, Thunder Bay	9	7	8	15
Brett MacDonald, Chatham	14	6	9	15
Mike Vukonich, Flint	10	7	7	14
Brian Downey, Thunder Bay	9	3	11	14

TOP SCORERS

	Games	G	A	Pts.
John Vecchiarelli, Chatham	15	10	18	28
Richard Borgo, Chatham	15	11	10	21

INDIVIDUAL STATISTICS

BRANTFORD SMOKE

(Lost semifinals to Thunder Bay)

SCORING

	Games	G	A	Pts.	PIM
Jamey Hicks	7	5	5	10	2
Paul Polillo	7	1	9	10	6
Greg Walters	7	5	3	8	8
Kent Hawley	7	3	4	7	2
Gary St. Pierre	7	0	7	7	6
Brad Gratton	7	4	2	6	4
Lou Crawford	7	4	0	4	17
Cory Banika	7	0	3	3	63
Vince Guidotti	7	1	1	2	6
Paul Mitton	7	1	0	1	5
Tom Moulton	7	1	0	1	2
Jeff Wilson	2	0	1	1	0
Todd Francis	7	0	1	1	2
Wayne MacPhee	7	0	1	1	4
Dave Moylan	7	0	1	1	4
Jason Clarke	1	0	0	0	0
Jason Taylor	5	0	0	0	22
Peter Richards (goalie)	6	0	0	0	0

GOALTENDING

	Games	Min.	W	L	OTL	Goals	SO	Avg.
Peter Richards	6	338	3	3	0	25	1	4.43

CHATHAM WHEELS

(Lost finals to Thunder Bay, 4-1)

SCORING

	Games	G	A	Pts.	PIM
John Vecchiarelli	15	10	18	28	41
Richard Borgo	15	11	10	21	36
Joel Gardner	15	8	12	20	19
Marty Wells	15	9	8	17	11
Brett MacDonald	14	6	9	15	4
Rob Wilson	15	0	13	13	34
Jim Ritchie	10	5	6	11	27
Jamie Allan	15	3	7	10	95
Jason Stos	15	1	9	10	27
Wayne Muir	15	5	4	9	54
Scott Garrow	13	3	6	9	6
Paul Sutcliffe	11	3	1	4	2
Jamie Dabonovich	15	1	3	4	4
Brad Barton	15	0	4	4	41
John East	11	2	1	3	39
Kevin Butt (goalie)	15	0	2	2	10
Mark Cavallin (goalie)	2	0	0	0	0
Darryl Brunoro	3	0	0	0	5
Mike Gruttaduria	8	0	0	0	44
Dan Williams	9	0	0	0	6

GOALTENDING

	Games	Min.	W	L	OTL	Goals	SO	Avg.
Kevin Butt	15	888	8	4	2	60	0	4.05
Mark Cavallin	2	53	0	1	0	6	0	6.74

DETROIT FALCONS

(Lost preliminary round to Flint, 3-1)

SCORING

	Games	G	A	Pts.	PIM
Bob McKillop	3	4	1	5	12
Chris MacKenzie	3	1	3	4	0
Steve Beadle	3	1	2	3	0
Christian Lalonde	3	1	2	3	2
Savo Mitrovic	3	1	2	3	4
Dave DiVita	3	0	3	3	4
Andy MacVicar	3	2	0	2	0
Bill Robinson	3	1	1	2	6
Garry Gulash	1	0	2	2	0
Clark Polglass	3	1	0	1	46
Vladimir Antipin	3	0	1	1	2
Lennie MacAusland	3	0	1	1	4
Jacques Mailhot	3	0	1	1	49
Sergei Makarov	3	0	1	1	0
Chris Marshall	3	0	1	1	26
Wayne Menard	1	0	0	0	5
Darren Miciak	1	0	0	0	25
Maxim Michailovsky (goalie)	2	0	0	0	0
Mike Risdale	2	0	0	0	0
Jaroslav Kunik	3	0	0	0	2

GOALTENDING

	Games	Min.	W	L	OTL	Goals	SO	Avg.
Maxim Michailovsky	2	118	1	1	0	8	0	4.04

FLINT GENERALS

(Lost semifinals to Chatham, 4-3)

SCORING

	Games	G	A	Pts.	PIM
Brett Strot	10	10	10	20	2
Kevin St. Jacques	10	4	14	18	19
Mike Vukonich	10	7	7	14	12
Kevin Kerr	7	7	6	13	79
Brian Sakic	10	6	7	13	2
Keith Whitmore	10	4	7	11	4
Dave Stewart	10	1	10	11	39
Chris Crombie	10	3	5	8	55
Larry Bernard	10	4	2	6	28
Jim Duhart	9	1	4	5	70
Stephan Brochu	10	1	4	5	2
Lorne Knauft	6	0	5	5	47
Ken Spangler	9	1	3	4	78
Chris O'Rourke	10	0	2	2	56
John Heasty	8	1	0	1	2
Dominic Niro	10	1	0	1	18
Darcy Austin (goalie)	2	0	1	1	0
Mark Gowans (goalie)	9	0	1	1	0
Keith Carney	7	0	0	0	4

GOALTENDING

	Games	Min.	W	L	OTL	Goals	SO	Avg.
Darcy Austin	2	112	2	0	0	6	0	3.21
Mark Gowans	9	516	3	4	1	39	0	4.53

MUSKEGON FURY

(Lost preliminary round to Thunder Bay, 4-3)

SCORING

	Games	G	A	Pts.	PIM
Scott Campbell	3	2	2	4	14
Brett Seguin	3	1	3	4	8
Mark Karpen	3	1	1	2	0
Paul Kelly	3	1	1	2	22
Rob Melanson	3	1	1	2	6
Justin Morrison	3	1	1	2	12
Grant Block	3	0	2	2	0
Joe Simon	3	0	2	2	0
Bob Jones	1	1	0	1	0
Donny Martin	3	1	0	1	4
Kevin Barrett	3	0	1	1	8
Todd Charlesworth	3	0	1	1	0
Scott Feasby	3	0	1	1	5
Joe Hawley	1	0	0	0	0
Jodi Murphy	1	0	0	0	2
Dan Woodley	1	0	0	0	0
Mark Turner	2	0	0	0	0
Roch Belley (goalie)	3	0	0	0	0
Darrel Newman	3	0	0	0	2

GOALTENDING

	Games	Min.	W	L	OTL	Goals	SO	Avg.
Roch Belley	3	176	0	3	0	13	0	4.42

ST. THOMAS WILDCATS

(Lost preliminary round to Chatham, 3-0)

SCORING

	Games	G	A	Pts.	PIM
Gary Miller	3	1	3	4	15
Marc Vachon	3	3	0	3	0
John Batten	3	1	2	3	10
Dan Elsener	3	1	1	2	0
Jason Hannigan	3	1	1	2	0
Gary Callaghan	3	0	2	2	0
Shayne Stevenson	2	0	2	2	9
Derek MacNair	3	1	0	1	0
Jeff Pawluk	3	1	0	1	2
Tim Bean	2	0	1	1	8

	Games	G	A	Pts.	PIM
Matt Ripley	2	0	1	1	0
Todd Coopman	3	0	1	1	0
Bernie Johns	3	0	1	1	0
Alex Kuzminski	3	0	1	1	2
Oleg Bratash	1	0	0	0	0
Jamie Hayden	1	0	0	0	0
Ron Bertrand (goalie)	3	0	0	0	0
Trevor Dam	3	0	0	0	0
Derek Prue	3	0	0	0	0

GOALTENDING

	Games	Min.	W	L	OTL	Goals	SO	Avg.
Ron Bertrand	3	159	0	3	0	18	0	6.77

THUNDER BAY THUNDER HAWKS

(Winner of 1994 Colonial Hockey League playoffs)

SCORING

	Games	G	A	Pts.	PIM
Terry Menard	9	7	9	16	12
Todd Howarth	9	7	8	15	19
Brian Downey	9	3	11	14	2
Trent McCleary	9	2	11	13	15
Ron Talakoski	9	7	3	10	0
Llew McWana	9	5	5	10	2
Alain Deeks	9	3	6	9	13
Barry McKinlay	9	3	6	9	11
Gerry St. Cyr	9	4	4	8	23
Chris Hynnes	9	2	6	8	6
Don Osborne	9	1	5	6	0
Chris Rowland	9	3	2	5	31
Jean Blouin	7	0	4	4	11
Bruce Ramsay	8	1	2	3	45
Mel Angelstad	9	1	2	3	65
Vern Ray	9	1	2	3	6
Tom Warden	3	1	0	1	14
Alain Harvey (goalie)	1	0	1	1	0
Jean-Francois Labbe (goalie)	8	0	1	1	0

GOALTENDING

	Games	Min.	W	L	OTL	Goals	SO	Avg.
J.-F. Labbe	8	493	7	1	0	18	2	2.19
Alain Harvey	1	60	1	0	0	3	0	3.00

1993-94 AWARD WINNERS

ALL-STAR TEAMS

First team	Pos.	Second team
Jean-Francois Labbe, T.B.	G	Maxim Mikhailovsky, Det.
Barry McKinley, T. Bay	D	Keith Whitmore, Flint
Lorne Knauft, Flint	D	Victor Antipin, Detroit
Paul Polillo, Brantford	LW	Tim Bean, St. Thomas
John Vecchiarelli, Chatham	C	Greg Walters, Brantford
Kevin Kerr, Flint	RW	Gerry St. Cyr, Thunder Bay

Coach of the Year: Tom Barrett, Chatham

TROPHY WINNERS

Most Valuable Player: Kevin Kerr, Flint
Scoring leader: Paul Polillo, Brantford
Outstanding defenseman: Barry McKinlay, Thunder Bay
Outstanding defensive forward: Jamie Hicks, Brantford
Rookie of the Year: Jean-Francois Labbe, Thunder Bay
Most sportsmanlike player of the year: Paul Polillo, Brantford
Playoff MVP: Jean-Francois Labbe, Thunder Bay
Coach of the Year: Tom Barrett, Chatham

ALL-TIME AWARD WINNERS

MOST VALUABLE PLAYER

Season	Player, Team
1991-92	Terry McCutcheon, Brantford
1992-93	Jason Firth, Thunder Bay
1993-94	Kevin Kerr, Flint

SCORING LEADER

Season	Player, Team
1991-92	Tom Sasso, Flint
1992-93	Len Soccio, St. Thomas
1993-94	Paul Polillo, Brantford

ROOKIE OF THE YEAR

Season	Player, Team
1991-92	Kevin Butt, St. Thomas
1992-93	Jason Firth, Thunder Bay
1993-94	Jean-Francois Labbe, Thunder Bay

DEFENSEMAN OF THE YEAR

Season	Player, Team
1991-92	Tom Searle, Brantford
1992-93	Tom Searle, Brantford
1993-94	Barry McKinlay, Thunder Bay

BEST DEFENSIVE FORWARD

Season   Player, Team
1991-92—Tim Bean, St. Thomas
1992-93—Todd Howarth, Thunder Bay
1993-94—Jamie Hicks, Brantford

MOST SPORTSMANLIKE PLAYER

Season   Player, Team
1991-92—Tom Sasso, Flint
1992-93—Paul Polillo, Brantford
1993-94—Paul Polillo, Brantford

PLAYOFF MVP

Season   Player, Team
1991-92—Gary Callaghan, Thunder Bay
1992-93—Roland Melanson, Brantford
1993-94—Jean-Francois Labbe, Thunder Bay

COACH OF THE YEAR

Season   Coach, Team
1991-92—Peter Horachek, St. Thomas
1992-93—Bill McDonald, Thunder Bay
1993-94—Tom Barrett, Chatham

ALL-TIME LEAGUE CHAMPIONS

REGULAR-SEASON CHAMPION

Season	Team	Coach
1991-92—	Michigan Falcons	Terry Christensen
1992-93—	Brantford Smoke	Ken Mann & Ken Gratton
1993-94—	Thunder Bay Thunder Hawks	Bill McDonald

PLAYOFF CHAMPION

Team	Coach
Thunder Bay Thunder Hawks	Bill McDonald
Brantford Smoke	Ken Gratton
Thunder Bay Thunder Hawks	Bill McDonald

MAJOR JUNIOR LEAGUES

Canadian Hockey League

Ontario Hockey League

Quebec Major Junior Hockey League

Western Hockey League

CANADIAN HOCKEY LEAGUE

GENERAL INFORMATION

The Canadian Hockey League is an alliance of the three Major Junior leagues—Ontario Hockey League, Quebec Major Junior Hockey League and Western Hockey League. After the regular season, the three leagues compete in a round-robin tournament to decide the Memorial Cup championship. Originally awarded to the national Junior champion, the Memorial Cup later signified Junior A supremacy (after Junior hockey in Canada was divided into "A" and "B" classes). Beginning in 1971, when Junior A hockey was split into Major Junior and Tier II Junior A, the Memorial Cup was awarded to the Major Junior champion.

LEAGUE OFFICE

Address
305 Milner Ave.
Scarborough, Ont. M1B 3V4
Phone
416-298-3523
FAX
416-298-3187
President
Ed Chynoweth

Vice presidents
David E. Branch
Gilles Courteau
Director of information
Jim Price
Directors
Jim Rutherford
Marcel Robert
Rick Brodsky

Director of officiating
Richard Doerksen
Member leagues
Ontario Hockey League
Quebec Major Junior Hockey League
Western Hockey League

1994 MEMORIAL CUP

FINAL STANDINGS

Team (League)	W	L	Pts.	GF	GA
Kamloops (WHL)	4	0	8	20	8
Chicoutimi (QMJHL)	2	2	4	7	10
Laval (QMJHL)	2	2	4	16	18
North Bay (OHL)	0	3	0	6	13

RESULTS

SATURDAY, MAY 14

Laval 5, North Bay 4

SUNDAY, MAY 15

Kamloops 5, Laval 4
Chicoutimi 3, North Bay 1

TUESDAY, MAY 17

Kamloops 5, Chicoutimi 0

WEDNESDAY, MAY 18

Kamloops 5, North Bay 1

THURSDAY, MAY 19

Chicoutimi 2, Laval 0

SATURDAY, MAY 21

Laval 4, Chicoutimi 2

SUNDAY, MAY 22

Kamloops 5, Laval 3

TOP TOURNAMENT SCORERS

	Games	G	A	Pts.
Darcy Tucker, Kamloops	4	*6	3	*9
Alain Cote, Laval	5	2	*7	*9
Daniel Goneau, Laval	5	5	2	7
Yanick Dube, Laval	5	2	4	6
Marc Beaucage, Laval	5	3	2	5
Michael Gaul, Laval	5	2	3	5
Louis Dumont, Kamloops	4	1	4	5
Rod Stevens, Kamloops	4	2	2	4
Chris Murray, Kamloops	4	2	2	4
Hnat Domenichelli, Kamloops	4	2	2	4
Vitali Yachmenev, North Bay	3	1	3	4
Tyson Nash, Kamloops	4	1	3	4

*Indicates tournament leader.

1993-94 AWARD WINNERS

ALL-STAR TEAMS

First team	Pos.	Second team
Norm Maracle, Sask.	G	Emmanuel Fernandez, Laval
Steve Gosselin, Chicoutimi	D	Chris Armstrong, M.J.
Brendan Witt, Seattle	D	Jamie Rivers, Sudbury
Darcy Tucker, Kamloops	LW	Marty Murray, Brandon
Jason Allison, London	C	Yanick Dube, Laval
Lonny Bohonos, Portland	RW	Kevin Brown, Detroit

Coach of the Year: Bert Templeton, North Bay

TROPHY WINNERS

Player of the year: Jason Allison, London
Plus/minus award: Mark Wotton, Saskatoon
Rookie of the year: Vitali Yachmenev, North Bay
Defenseman of the year: Steve Gosselin, Chicoutimi
Goaltender of the year: Norm Maracle, Saskatoon
Scholastic player of the year: Patrick Boileau, Laval
Coach of the year: Bert Templeton, North Bay
Executive of the year: Bob Brown, Kamloops
Most sportsmanlike player of the year: Yanick Dube, Laval
Top draft prospect award: Jeff O'Neill, Guelph
Humanitarian award: Stephane Roy, Val-d'Or

HISTORY

ALL-TIME MEMORIAL CUP WINNERS

Season	Team	Season	Team	Season	Team
1918-19	Univ. of Toronto Schools	1944-45	Toronto St. Michael's	1969-70	Montreal Jr. Canadiens
1919-20	Toronto Canoe Club	1945-46	Winnipeg Monarchs	1970-71	Quebec Remparts
1920-21	Winnipeg Falcons	1946-47	Toronto St. Michael's	1971-72	Cornwall Royals
1921-22	Fort William War Veterans	1947-48	Port Arthur W. End Bruins	1972-73	Toronto Marlboros
1922-23	Univ. of Manitoba-Winnipeg	1948-49	Montreal Royals	1973-74	Regina Pats
1923-24	Owen Sound Greys	1949-50	Montreal Jr. Canadiens	1974-75	Toronto Marlboros
1924-25	Regina Pats	1950-51	Barrie Flyers	1975-76	Hamilton Fincups
1925-26	Calgary Canadians	1951-52	Guelph Biltmores	1976-77	New Westminster Bruins
1926-27	Owen Sound Greys	1952-53	Barrie Flyers	1977-78	New Westminster Bruins
1927-28	Regina Monarchs	1953-54	St. Catharines Tee Pees	1978-79	Peterborough Petes
1928-29	Toronto Marlboros	1954-55	Toronto Marlboros	1979-80	Cornwall Royals
1929-30	Regina Pats	1955-56	Toronto Marlboros	1980-81	Cornwall Royals
1930-31	Winnipeg Elmwoods	1956-57	Flin Flon Bombers	1981-82	Kitchener Rangers
1931-32	Sudbury Wolves	1957-58	Ottawa-Hull Jr. Canadiens	1982-83	Portland Winter Hawks
1932-33	Newmarket	1958-59	Winnipeg Braves	1983-84	Ottawa 67's
1933-34	Toronto St. Michael's	1959-60	St. Catharines Tee Pees	1984-85	Prince Albert Raiders
1934-35	Winnipeg Monarchs	1960-61	Tor. St. Michael's Majors	1985-86	Guelph Platers
1935-36	West Toronto Redmen	1961-62	Hamilton Red Wings	1986-87	Medicine Hat Tigers
1936-37	Winnipeg Monarchs	1962-63	Edmonton Oil Kings	1987-88	Medicine Hat Tigers
1937-38	St. Boniface Seals	1963-64	Toronto Marlboros	1988-89	Swift Current Broncos
1938-39	Oshawa Generals	1964-65	Niagara Falls Flyers	1989-90	Oshawa Generals
1939-40	Oshawa Generals	1965-66	Edmonton Oil Kings	1990-91	Spokane Chiefs
1940-41	Winnipeg Rangers	1966-67	Toronto Marlboros	1991-92	Kamloops Blazers
1941-42	Portage la Prairie	1967-68	Niagara Falls Flyers	1992-93	Sault Ste. Marie Greyhounds
1942-43	Winnipeg Rangers	1968-69	Montreal Jr. Canadiens	1993-94	Kamloops Blazers
1943-44	Oshawa Generals				

ALL-TIME AWARD WINNERS

PLAYER OF THE YEAR AWARD

Season	Player, Team
1974-75	Ed Staniowski, Regina
1975-76	Peter Lee, Ottawa
1976-77	Dale McCourt, Ste. Catharines
1977-78	Bobby Smith, Ottawa
1978-79	Pierre LaCroix, Trois-Rivieres
1979-80	Doug Wickenheiser, Regina
1980-81	Dale Hawerchuk, Cornwall
1981-82	Dave Simpson, London
1982-83	Pat LaFontaine, Verdun
1983-84	Mario Lemieux, Laval
1984-85	Dan Hodgson, Prince Albert
1985-86	Luc Robitaille, Hull
1986-87	Rob Brown, Kamloops
1987-88	Joe Sakic, Swift Current
1988-89	Bryan Fogarty, Niagara Falls
1989-90	Mike Ricci, Peterborough
1990-91	Eric Lindros, Oshawa
1991-92	Charles Poulin, St. Hyacinthe
1992-93	Pat Peake, Detroit
1993-94	Jason Allison, London

PLUS/MINUS AWARD

Season	Player, Team
1986-87	Rob Brown, Kamloops
1987-88	Marc Saumier, Hull
1988-89	Bryan Fogarty, Niagara Falls
1989-90	Len Barrie, Kamloops
1990-91	Eric Lindros, Oshawa
1991-92	Dean McAmmond, Prince Albert
1992-93	Chris Pronger, Peterborough
1993-94	Mark Wotton, Saskatoon

ROOKIE OF THE YEAR AWARD

Season	Player, Team
1987-88	Martin Gelinas, Hull
1988-89	Yanic Perreault, Trois-Rivieres

Season	Player, Team
1989-90	Petr Nedved, Seattle
1990-91	Philippe Boucher, Granby
1991-92	Alexandre Daigle, Victoriaville
1992-93	Jeff Freisen, Regina
1993-94	Vitali Yachmenev, North Bay

DEFENSEMAN OF THE YEAR AWARD

Season	Player, Team
1987-88	Greg Hawgood, Kamloops
1988-89	Bryan Fogarty, Niagara Falls
1989-90	John Slaney, Cornwall
1990-91	Patrice Brisebois, Drummondville
1991-92	Drake Berehowsky, North Bay
1992-93	Chris Pronger, Peterborough
1993-94	Steve Gosselin, Chicoutimi

GOALTENDER OF THE YEAR AWARD

Season	Player, Team
1987-88	Stephane Beauregard, St. Jean
1988-89	Stephane Fiset, Victoriaville
1989-90	Trevor Kidd, Brandon
1990-91	Felix Potvin, Chicoutimi
1991-92	Corey Hirsch, Kamloops
1992-93	Jocelyn Thibault, Sherbrooke
1993-94	Norm Maracle, Saskatoon

SCHOLASTIC PLAYER OF THE YEAR AWARD

Season	Player, Team
1987-88	Darrin Shannon, Windsor
1988-89	Jeff Nelson, Prince Albert
1989-90	Jeff Nelson, Prince Albert
1990-91	Scott Niedermayer, Kamloops
1991-92	Nathan LaFayette, Cornwall
1992-93	David Trofimenkoff, Lethbridge
1993-94	Patrick Boileau, Laval

COACH OF THE YEAR AWARD

Season	Coach, Team
1987-88	Alain Vigneault, Hull
1988-89	Joe McDonnell, Kitchener
1989-90	Ken Hitchcock, Kamloops
1990-91	Joe Canale, Chicoutimi
1991-92	Bryan Maxwell, Spokane
1992-93	Marcel Comeau, Tacoma
1993-94	Bert Templeton, North Bay

EXECUTIVE OF THE YEAR AWARD

Season	Executive, Team or League
1988-89	John Horman, QMJHL
1989-90	Russ Farwell, Seattle
1990-91	Sherwood Bassin, Sault Ste. Marie
1991-92	Bert Templeton, North Bay
1992-93	Jim Rutherford, Detroit
1993-94	Bob Brown, Kamloops

MOST SPORTSMANLIKE PLAYER OF THE YEAR AWARD

Season	Player, Team
1989-90	Andrew McKim, Hull
1990-91	Pat Falloon, Spokane
1991-92	Martin Gendron, St. Hyacinthe
1992-93	Rick Girard, Swift Current
1993-94	Yanick Dube, Laval

TOP DRAFT PROSPECT AWARD

Season	Player, Team
1990-91	Eric Lindros, Oshawa
1991-92	Todd Warriner, Windsor
1992-93	Alexandre Daigle, Victoriaville
1993-94	Jeff O'Neill, Guelph

HUMANITARIAN AWARD

Season	Player, Team
1992-93	Keli Corpse, Kingston
1993-94	Stephane Roy, Val-d'Or

ONTARIO HOCKEY LEAGUE

LEAGUE OFFICE

Commissioner
David E. Branch
Chairman of the board
Jim Rutherford
Director of administration
Herb Morell
Director of hockey operations
Ted Baker

Director of officiating
Ken Bodendistel
Director of central scouting
Jack Ferguson
Address
305 Milner Avenue
Suite 208
Scarborough, Ontario M1B 3V4

Phone
416-299-8700
FAX
416-299-8787

1993-94 REGULAR SEASON

FINAL STANDINGS

MATT LEYDEN DIVISION

Team	G	W	L	T	Pts.	GF	GA
North Bay	66	46	15	5	97	351	226
Ottawa	66	33	22	11	77	274	229
Sudbury	66	34	26	6	74	299	275
Belleville	66	32	28	6	70	303	264
Kingston	66	30	28	8	68	265	259
Oshawa	66	26	32	8	60	272	309
Peterborough	66	15	41	10	40	252	350
Newmarket	66	9	47	10	28	231	377

HAP EMMS DIVISION

Team	G	W	L	T	Pts.	GF	GA
Detroit	66	42	20	4	88	312	237
Sault Ste. Marie	66	35	24	7	77	319	268
Guelph	66	32	28	6	70	323	290
Owen Sound	66	34	30	2	70	303	284
Kitchener	66	32	30	4	68	286	316
London	66	32	30	4	68	293	279
Windsor	66	25	36	5	55	253	298
Niagara Falls	66	21	41	4	46	277	352

INDIVIDUAL LEADERS

Goals: Vitali Yachmenev, North Bay (61)
Assists: Jamie Rivers, Sudbury (89)
Points: Vitali Yachmenev, North Bay (113)
Penalty minutes: David Ling, Kingston (254)
Goaltending average: Sandy Allan, North Bay (3.27)
Shutouts: Dan Cloutier, Sault Ste. Marie (2)
Marc Lamothe, Kingston (2)
Jeff Salajko, Ottawa (2)
Derek Wilkinson, Belleville (2)

	Games	G	A	Pts.
Bill Bowler, Windsor	66	47	76	123
Jamie Rivers, Sudbury	65	32	89	121
Trevor Gallant, Kitchener	66	39	80	119
Dave Gilmore, London	61	48	69	117
Jason MacDonald, Owen Sound	66	55	61	116
Sylvain Cloutier, Guelph	66	45	71	116
Vitali Yachmenev, North Bay	66	61	52	113
Steve Sullivan, Sault Ste. Marie	63	51	62	113
Michael Peca, Ottawa	55	50	63	113
Mike Prokopec, Guelph	66	52	58	110
Bob Wren, Detroit	57	45	64	109
B.J. MacPherson, North Bay	59	42	65	107
Darryl Lafrance, Oshawa	61	45	61	106
Rod Hinks, Owen Sound	62	46	58	104
Stephane Yelle, Oshawa	66	35	69	104
Aaron Gavey, Sault Ste. Marie	60	42	60	102

TOP SCORERS

	Games	G	A	Pts.
Jason Allison, London	56	55	87	142
Kevin Brown, Detroit	57	54	81	135
Jeff O'Neill, Guelph	66	45	81	126
Keli Corpse, Kingston	63	42	84	126

INDIVIDUAL STATISTICS

BELLEVILLE BULLS

SCORING

	Games	G	A	Pts.	PIM
Paul McCallion	66	36	43	79	69
Kevin S. Brown	58	29	48	77	29
Richard Park	59	27	49	76	70
Brian Secord	66	29	40	69	56
Paul Rushforth	63	28	35	63	109
Dan Preston	58	11	37	48	64
Radim Bicanek	63	16	27	43	49
Jarret Reid	25	15	23	38	16
Doug Doull	62	13	24	37	143
Brandon Convery	23	16	19	35	22
Craig Mills	63	15	18	33	88
Mark Donahue	29	14	19	33	36
Corey Isen	58	12	21	33	136
Marc Dupuis	66	7	25	32	37

	Games	G	A	Pts.	PIM
Jeff Ambrosio	59	13	17	30	18
Steve Carter	65	4	15	19	55
Dan Godbout	66	0	15	15	45
Rob Boyko	39	4	10	14	43
Joe Coombs	22	4	8	12	14
Chris Skoryna	3	2	5	7	6
Travis Riggin	33	0	6	6	8
Steve Tracze	10	3	2	5	4
Derek Wilkinson (goalie)	56	0	5	5	9
Paul Dillon	14	2	2	4	0
Ian Keiller	40	1	3	4	111
Sean P. Brown	28	1	2	3	53
Geordie Maynard	10	1	1	2	22
Jeff Smith	5	0	2	2	0
Serge Dunphy	18	0	2	2	44
Kyle Blacklock	2	0	1	1	0
Jason Hughes	7	0	1	1	4

	Games	G	A	Pts.	PIM
Mark Gowan (goalie)	24	0	1	1	0
Jeff Dickson	2	0	0	0	2
Scott Taylor	2	0	0	0	0

GOALTENDING

	Games	Min.	W	L	T	Goals	SO	Avg.
Derek Wilkinson	56	2860	24	16	4	179	2	3.76
Mark Gowan	24	1141	8	12	2	79	0	4.15

DETROIT JR. RED WINGS

SCORING

	Games	G	A	Pts.	PIM
Kevin J. Brown	57	54	81	135	85
Bob Wren	57	45	64	109	81
Todd Harvey	49	34	51	85	75
Sean Haggerty	60	31	32	63	21
Bill McCauley	59	18	39	57	51
Pat Barton	46	22	29	51	48
Jeff Mitchell	59	25	18	43	99
Eric Cairns	59	7	35	42	204
Dale Junkin	23	13	17	30	6
Kevin Paden	38	10	19	29	54
Mike Harding	23	16	12	28	40
Mike Rucinski	66	2	26	28	58
Nic Beaudoin	63	9	18	27	32
Jamie Allison	40	2	22	24	69
Shayne McCosh	25	3	18	21	33
Rick Morton	39	2	12	14	79
Dan Pawlaczyk	50	7	5	12	16
Matt Ball	43	3	7	10	11
Jeremy Meehan	55	2	7	9	27
Duane Harmer	20	1	6	7	16
Gerry Skrypec	21	1	5	6	48
Brad Cook	49	0	6	6	24
Richard Ujvary	28	2	2	4	20
Rob Boyko	11	2	1	3	24
Dylan Seca	36	1	2	3	34
Robin LaCour	50	0	3	3	20
Ryan Middleton	35	0	2	2	25
Jason Saal (goalie)	45	0	2	2	8
Ryan O'Neill	8	0	1	1	22
Aaron Ellis (goalie)	27	0	1	1	10
Chris Mailloux (goalie)	1	0	0	0	0
Ryan Coristine	2	0	0	0	0
Mike Mayhew	2	0	0	0	0
Ed Kowalski	3	0	0	0	0
Gerry Lanigan	5	0	0	0	0

GOALTENDING

	Games	Min.	W	L	T	Goals	SO	Avg.
Jason Saal	45	2551	28	11	3	143	0	3.36
Aaron Ellis	27	1425	14	9	1	88	0	3.71
Chris Mailloux	1	20	0	0	0	2	0	6.00

GUELPH STORM

SCORING

	Games	G	A	Pts.	PIM
Jeff O'Neill	66	45	81	126	95
Sylvain Cloutier	66	45	71	116	127
Mike Prokopec	66	52	58	110	93
Chris Skoryna	58	34	57	91	41
Todd Bertuzzi	61	28	54	82	165
Rumun Ndur	61	6	33	39	176
Mike Rusk	48	8	26	34	59
Ken Belanger	55	11	22	33	185
Jamie Wright	65	17	15	32	34
Kayle Short	44	5	24	29	62
Jeff Williams	62	14	12	26	19
Todd Norman	57	11	12	23	14
Duane Harmer	41	7	16	23	29
Eric Landry	57	7	15	22	96
Pat Barton	23	9	12	21	28
Mike Pittman	61	8	8	16	33

	Games	G	A	Pts.	PIM
Viktor Reuta	43	7	8	15	12
Grant Pritchett	42	3	9	12	43
Regan Stocco	46	1	11	12	41
Ryan Risidore	51	2	9	11	39
Murray Hogg	54	2	5	7	61
Stephane Lefebvre	19	0	4	4	2
Jeff Cowan	17	1	0	1	5
Chris McMurtry	3	0	1	1	0
Gord Walsh	8	0	1	1	9
Mark McArthur (goalie)	51	0	1	1	14
Ivano Stocco	1	0	0	0	0
Andy Adams (goalie)	20	0	0	0	4

GOALTENDING

	Games	Min.	W	L	T	Goals	SO	Avg.
Mark McArthur	51	2936	25	18	5	201	0	4.11
Andy Adams	20	1066	7	10	1	83	0	4.67

KINGSTON FRONTENACS

SCORING

	Games	G	A	Pts.	PIM
Keli Corpse	63	42	84	126	55
Steve Parson	64	35	63	98	70
David Ling	61	37	40	77	254
Craig Rivet	61	12	52	64	100
Martin Sychra	59	29	32	61	32
Chad Kilger	66	17	35	52	23
Greg Kraemer	65	13	23	36	80
Gord Walsh	55	14	19	33	52
Trent Cull	50	2	30	32	147
Alexander Zhurik	59	7	23	30	92
Brian Scott	58	13	10	23	26
Duncan Fader	63	6	15	21	83
Mike Ware	30	9	7	16	32
Jason Disher	62	4	12	16	170
Cail MacLean	53	7	7	14	15
Trevor Doyle	53	2	12	14	246
Brett Lindros	15	4	6	10	94
Ken Boone	59	3	7	10	173
Jeff DaCosta	28	3	6	9	2
Joel Yates	10	4	4	8	31
Matt Kiereck	14	2	2	4	27
Marc Moro	43	0	3	3	81
Richard Raymond	4	0	2	2	2
Bill Maranduik	54	0	2	2	47
Tyler Moss (goalie)	13	0	1	1	0
Marc Lamothe (goalie)	48	0	1	1	2
Mike Lockwood	1	0	0	0	0
Cory Johnson	2	0	0	0	0
Chris Gowan	4	0	0	0	0
Wes Snell	4	0	0	0	0
Tim Keyes (goalie)	6	0	0	0	0
Greg Lovell (goalie)	6	0	0	0	0
Eric Rylands	16	0	0	0	39

GOALTENDING

	Games	Min.	W	L	T	Goals	SO	Avg.
Tyler Moss	13	795	6	4	3	42	1	3.17
Marc Lamothe	48	2828	23	20	5	177	2	3.76
Greg Lovell	6	221	1	2	0	15	0	4.07
Tim Keyes	6	171	0	2	0	16	0	5.61

KITCHENER RANGERS

SCORING

	Games	G	A	Pts.	PIM
Trevor Gallant	66	39	80	119	49
Jason Gladney	61	18	74	92	96
Tim Spitzig	62	48	38	86	111
Norm Dezainde	62	30	42	72	104
Wes Swinson	64	26	46	72	111
Eric Manlow	49	28	32	60	25
Gord Dickie	63	18	36	54	24
Mark Donahue	33	13	26	39	28

	Games	G	A	Pts.	PIM
Ryan Pawluk	59	12	15	27	73
Chris Phelps	30	7	19	26	39
Jason Morgan	65	6	15	21	16
Peter Brearley	57	9	10	19	37
Jason Hughes	48	2	17	19	130
Joe Coombs	27	9	7	16	8
Greg McLean	66	3	12	15	166
Sergei Olympiev	21	6	5	11	24
Andrew Taylor	62	1	8	9	60
James Boyd	31	3	5	8	39
Chris Pittman	52	4	2	6	34
Darren Schmidt	43	1	4	5	31
Jason Johnson	61	0	5	5	73
Matt O'Dette	46	1	3	4	107
Shane Leamon	12	2	1	3	7
Travis Riggin	29	0	2	2	9
David Belitski (goalie)	51	0	1	1	2
Derek Pajot	1	0	0	0	5
Jeff Lillie (goalie)	2	0	0	0	0
C.J. Denomme (goalie)	3	0	0	0	0
Darryl Whyte (goalie)	25	0	0	0	4

GOALTENDING

	Games	Min.	W	L	T	Goals	SO	Avg.
C.J. Denomme	3	144	1	2	0	9	0	3.75
Jeff Lillie	2	87	0	2	0	6	0	4.14
David Belitski	51	2655	25	15	3	190	0	4.29
Darryl Whyte	24	1103	6	11	1	101	0	5.49

LONDON KNIGHTS

SCORING

	Games	G	A	Pts.	PIM
Jason Allison	56	55	87	142	68
Dave Gilmore	61	48	69	117	67
Ryan Black	60	36	58	94	50
Nick Stajduhar	52	34	52	86	58
Chris Brassard	62	28	37	65	57
Chris Zanutto	61	8	32	40	51
Dan Reja	66	15	19	34	44
Gord Ross	56	11	19	30	187
Brodie Coffin	59	10	12	22	56
Daryl Rivers	47	3	17	20	74
Cory Evans	17	9	8	17	41
John Guirestante	29	3	12	15	29
Rob Frid	56	4	10	14	150
Don Margettie	42	6	6	12	55
Brian Stacey	59	2	10	12	100
Kevin Slota	59	6	3	9	61
Ryan Burgoyne	59	1	8	9	29
Ryan Appel	45	2	6	8	55
Sean Perry	22	3	4	7	15
Ben Walker	58	0	7	7	8
Brent Holdsworth	43	1	4	5	44
Ian Keiller	23	1	3	4	102
Roy Gray	49	0	4	4	42
Jordan Willis (goalie)	44	0	3	3	33
Justin Steinbach	13	1	1	2	4
Dan Stewart (goalie)	1	0	0	0	0
Art Sarun	6	0	0	0	0
Tim Bacik (goalie)	28	0	0	0	6

GOALTENDING

	Games	Min.	W	L	T	Goals	SO	Avg.
Jordan Willis	44	2428	20	19	2	158	1	3.90
Tim Bacik	28	1548	12	11	2	112	0	4.34
Dan Stewart	1	12	0	0	0	2	0	10.00

NEWMARKET ROYALS

SCORING

	Games	G	A	Pts.	PIM
Aaron Brand	65	19	45	64	55
Jim Brown	40	26	28	54	48
Paul Andrea	64	26	23	49	18

	Games	G	A	Pts.	PIM
Todd Walker	59	21	25	46	17
Matt Hogan	60	18	24	42	32
Larry Courville	39	20	19	39	134
Dennis Maxwell	41	12	24	36	113
Ryan Tocher	48	7	19	26	71
Jason Bonsignore	17	7	17	24	22
Alan Letang	58	3	21	24	30
Dave Lemay	26	4	19	23	98
Dustin McArthur	48	9	13	22	40
Kiley Hill	52	7	15	22	58
Brendan Yarema	55	11	4	15	69
Rob Massa	58	11	4	15	70
Paul McInnes	49	2	12	14	44
Geordie Maynard	39	4	8	12	87
Derek Grant	12	2	10	12	8
Rob Guinn	63	2	8	10	130
Gerry Skrypec	17	0	10	10	59
Jeremy Stevenson	9	2	4	6	27
Kameron White	44	0	5	5	125
Corey Bricknell	17	1	3	4	38
Luc Gagne	19	1	2	3	17
Kurt Walsh	35	1	2	3	23
Jamie Sokolsky	41	0	3	3	11
Adam Parks	20	2	0	2	13
Adrian Murray	9	0	2	2	11
Ken Carroll (goalie)	43	0	2	2	2
Mikhael Nemirovsky	6	1	1	2	2
Dale Greenwood	10	1	0	1	6
Chris Lizotte	2	0	1	1	0
Bill Bara	3	0	1	1	0
Shawn Loiselle	1	0	0	0	0
Trent Walford	1	0	0	0	4
Jason Fortier	3	0	0	0	5
Darryl Foster (goalie)	6	0	0	0	0
Brian Roche	7	0	0	0	10
Todd Laurin (goalie)	32	0	0	0	4

GOALTENDING

	Games	Min.	W	L	T	Goals	SO	Avg.
Ken Carroll	43	2144	6	24	7	192	0	5.37
Todd Laurin	32	1642	3	20	2	157	0	5.74
Darryl Foster	6	240	0	3	1	23	0	5.75

NIAGARA FALLS THUNDER

SCORING

	Games	G	A	Pts.	PIM
Ethan Moreau	59	44	54	98	100
Bogdan Savenko	62	42	49	91	22
Derek Grant	47	30	33	63	33
Jason Bonsignore	41	15	47	62	41
Brandon Convery	29	24	29	53	30
Jeff Johnstone	65	12	35	47	14
Dale Junkin	41	28	18	46	39
Neil Fewster	58	17	28	45	94
Greg deVries	64	5	40	45	135
Tom Moores	62	15	26	41	52
Derek Sylvester	61	4	15	19	83
Joel Yates	20	6	11	17	64
Dennis Maxwell	17	2	14	16	41
Corey Bricknell	44	1	15	16	90
Jason Reesor	61	3	12	15	31
Steve Nimigon	39	5	8	13	40
Ryan Tocher	13	5	6	11	30
Dave Lylyk	34	3	8	11	31
Gerry Skrypec	16	0	8	8	41
Mike Perna	40	3	4	7	97
Tim Thompson	28	0	7	7	19
Dale Greenwood	16	3	3	6	16
Paul McInnes	17	0	6	6	18
Dustin McArthur	18	2	3	5	25
Anatoli Filatov	4	3	1	4	0
Matthew Mayo	51	2	2	4	2
Yianni Ioannou	51	0	4	4	41
Dylan Seca	23	2	1	3	9

	Games	G	A	Pts.	PIM
Kirby Tokarski	20	0	3	3	2
Ryan Middleton	22	1	0	1	24
Kevin S. Brown	1	0	1	1	0
Domo Kovacevic (goalie)	9	0	1	1	4
Jim Hibbert (goalie)	34	0	1	1	2
Paul Carter	1	0	0	0	0
David Day	1	0	0	0	0
Jason Goldade	1	0	0	0	0
George Kontos	1	0	0	0	0
Chris Baxter	2	0	0	0	2
Lucas Miller	9	0	0	0	2
Devin Jonathan	10	0	0	0	16
Kelly Wayling	12	0	0	0	10
Matt Langsford (goalie)	15	0	0	0	2
Darryl Foster (goalie)	24	0	0	0	14

GOALTENDING

	Games	Min.	W	L	T	Goals	SO	Avg.
Jim Hibbert	34	1688	11	15	1	139	0	4.94
Darryl Foster	24	1163	7	12	1	99	0	5.11
Matt Langsford	15	743	3	10	0	68	0	5.49
Domo Kovacevic	9	403	0	4	2	37	0	5.51

NORTH BAY CENTENNIALS

SCORING

	Games	G	A	Pts.	PIM
Vitali Yachmenev	66	61	52	113	18
Jeff Shevalier	64	52	49	101	52
Lee Jinman	66	31	66	97	33
Bill Lang	58	22	51	73	118
Jason Campeau	63	31	39	70	22
Stefan Rivard	62	22	41	63	170
Michael Burman	61	13	50	63	46
Paul Doherty	43	13	29	42	63
Scott Cherrey	63	15	26	41	45
Corey Neilson	62	3	35	38	46
Jim Ensom	44	16	20	36	67
Brad Brown	66	8	24	32	196
B.J. MacPherson	15	9	21	30	36
Robert Dubois	40	9	21	30	24
Damien Bloye	50	15	14	29	24
Jeff Andrews	36	11	8	19	42
Steve McLaren	55	2	15	17	130
Denis Gaudet	37	6	7	13	10
Ryan Gillis	49	2	9	11	47
Rob Lave	42	2	8	10	32
Andy Delmore	45	2	7	9	33
Bob Thornton	31	2	5	7	10
Brian Stagg	14	1	4	5	9
Derek Lahnalampi	27	0	5	5	25
Dave Lylyk	6	2	2	4	2
John Guirestante	13	1	1	2	7
Scott Roche (goalie)	32	0	2	2	4
Rob Stark	14	0	0	0	32
Sandy Allan (goalie)	45	0	0	0	24

GOALTENDING

	Games	Min.	W	L	T	Goals	SO	Avg.
Sandy Allan	45	2404	31	10	1	131	1	3.27
Scott Roche	32	1587	15	5	4	93	0	3.52

OSHAWA GENERALS

SCORING

	Games	G	A	Pts.	PIM
Darryl Lafrance	61	45	61	106	17
Stephane Yelle	66	35	69	104	22
Sean Brown	56	41	38	79	145
B.J. MacPherson	44	33	44	77	76
Marc Savard	61	18	39	57	24
Stephane Soulliere	63	25	24	49	120
B.J. Johnston	66	20	24	44	22
Ryan Lindsay	63	7	24	31	51
David Froh	59	4	25	29	66

	Games	G	A	Pts.	PIM
Rob McQuat	56	3	24	27	189
Jason McQuat	54	7	12	19	139
Paul Doherty	14	1	14	15	17
Damon Hardy	58	5	8	13	100
Joe Cook	46	0	13	13	73
Andrew Power	36	4	8	12	50
Chris Hall	57	4	8	12	75
Brandon Gray	40	3	8	11	27
Kevin Vaughan	54	2	7	9	84
Eric Boulton	45	4	3	7	149
Jeff Andrews	17	2	4	6	20
Kelly Vipond	7	1	4	5	9
Jan Snopek	52	0	5	5	51
Darryl Moxam	17	2	2	4	21
Lucas Miller	15	0	4	4	6
Steve LeCoure	12	3	0	3	27
Todd Bradley	9	2	1	3	20
Robert Dubois	7	0	3	3	0
Jason Sproul	9	0	2	2	14
Dylan Taylor	3	1	0	1	0
Serge Dunphy	23	0	1	1	19
Ken Shepard (goalie)	45	0	1	1	26
Ryan Martin	1	0	0	0	0
Mike McDougall	1	0	0	0	0
Paul Porcaro	1	0	0	0	0
Colin March (goalie)	4	0	0	0	0
Keegan Dunn (goalie)	5	0	0	0	0
Frank Ivankovic (goalie)	8	0	0	0	0
Joel Gagnon (goalie)	23	0	0	0	8

GOALTENDING

	Games	Min.	W	L	T	Goals	SO	Avg.
Ken Shepard	45	2383	20	15	5	157	0	3.95
Colin March	4	158	0	2	0	11	0	4.18
Frank Ivankovic	8	253	1	2	0	21	0	4.98
Joel Gagnon	23	1089	4	11	3	100	0	5.51
Keegan Dunn	5	128	1	2	0	12	0	5.63

OTTAWA 67's

SCORING

	Games	G	A	Pts.	PIM
Michael Peca	55	50	63	113	101
Shean Donovan	62	35	49	84	63
Steve Washburn	65	30	50	80	88
Curt Bowen	52	25	37	62	98
Mark Edmundson	65	21	35	56	34
Dave Nemirovsky	64	21	31	52	18
Alyn McCauley	38	13	23	36	10
Chris Phelps	34	5	27	32	33
Michael Johnson	65	12	17	29	102
Mike Carr	58	10	17	27	66
John Argiropoulos	64	10	17	27	42
Fredrik Oduya	51	11	12	23	181
Jure Kovacevic	61	8	14	22	36
Cory Murphy	57	2	13	15	68
Rich Bronilla	62	4	9	13	48
Wade Simpson	38	3	9	12	41
Jason Brooks	52	5	6	11	41
Jason Meloche	58	1	10	11	107
Chris Coveny	45	3	7	10	60
Sergei Olympiev	20	3	5	8	4
Steve Jones	52	0	8	8	12
Kelly Wayling	14	1	2	3	10
Dan Gilpin	19	1	1	2	16
Joel Yates	15	0	2	2	15
C.J. Denomme (goalie)	35	0	2	2	2
Jeff Salajko (goalie)	37	0	2	2	15
Chad Thompson	6	0	1	1	5
Steve Tracze	1	0	0	0	0
Patrick Dubuc (goalie)	37	0	0	0	0

GOALTENDING

	Games	Min.	W	L	T	Goals	SO	Avg.
C.J. Denomme	35	1973	20	8	5	108	1	3.28
Jeff Salajko	37	2022	13	13	6	114	2	3.38
Patrick Dubuc	1	37	0	1	0	4	0	6.49

OWEN SOUND PLATERS

SCORING

	Games	G	A	Pts.	PIM
Jason MacDonald	66	55	61	116	177
Marian Kacir	66	23	64	87	26
Rod Hinks	50	40	44	84	79
Wayne Primeau	65	25	50	75	75
Jeff Kostuch	66	30	43	73	27
Dave Lemay	42	6	45	51	120
Luigi Calce	66	22	26	48	124
Willie Skilliter	66	16	30	46	23
Rob Schweyer	66	14	23	37	73
Jim Brown	22	18	17	35	24
Shayne Wright	64	11	24	35	95
Jason Campbell	65	19	11	30	20
Jeremy Rebek	60	4	18	22	51
Brian Medeiros	62	7	10	17	46
Joe Harris	44	4	10	14	59
Shane Kenny	54	4	9	13	138
Ryan Mougenel	53	3	8	11	30
Craig Binns	53	1	6	7	114
Mike Morrone	57	0	7	7	99
Jeff Smith	15	0	4	4	35
Mark Vilneff	11	0	3	3	15
Joe Cook	19	0	3	3	18
Scott Penton	20	1	0	1	6
Kirk Furey	10	0	1	1	2
Kevin Weekes (goalie)	34	0	1	1	4
Jamie Storr (goalie)	35	0	1	1	12
Derek Lahnalampi	16	0	0	0	17
Tom Stewart	1	0	0	0	5
Scott Vader	1	0	0	0	0
David Zunic	3	0	0	0	0
Ron Watts	4	0	0	0	0

GOALTENDING

	Games	Min.	W	L	T	Goals	SO	Avg.
Jamie Storr	35	2004	21	11	1	120	1	3.59
Kevin Weekes	34	1974	13	19	1	158	0	4.80

PETERBOROUGH PETES

SCORING

	Games	G	A	Pts.	PIM
Jamie Langenbrunner	62	33	58	91	53
Mike Harding	32	25	33	58	100
Mike Williams	63	25	27	52	39
Dan DelMonte	55	20	29	49	44
Rick Emmett	55	12	36	48	31
Brent Tully	37	17	26	43	81
Dave Roche	34	15	22	37	127
Matt Johnson	50	13	24	37	233
Tim Hill	62	18	16	34	72
Matt St. Germain	66	12	22	34	64
Steve Hogg	64	14	18	32	31
Kelvin Solari	60	10	20	30	99
Cameron Mann	49	8	17	25	18
Rob Giffin	50	12	12	24	57
Chad Grills	20	5	18	23	46
Pat Paone	45	3	13	16	56
Henrik Eppers	58	3	11	14	43
Adrian Murray	54	2	11	13	96
Ryan Nauss	61	2	6	8	34
Darryl Moxam	15	1	6	7	4
Rick Morton	14	1	4	5	45
Jonathan Murphy	61	1	4	5	54
Mark Vilneff	32	0	4	4	31
Quade Lightbody	44	0	4	4	38
Stephen Webb	2	0	1	1	9
Craig Stenhouse	7	0	1	1	4
Zac Bierk (goalie)	9	0	1	1	2
Scott Stephens	14	0	1	1	0
Ryan Douglas (goalie)	15	0	1	1	6
Mike Bullock	1	0	0	0	0
Andrew Currie (goalie)	1	0	0	0	0
Bob Davis	2	0	0	0	0
Cal Larmer	5	0	0	0	0
Jeff Walker	5	0	0	0	2
Martin Duris	8	0	0	0	2
Chad Lang (goalie)	48	0	0	0	29

GOALTENDING

	Games	Min.	W	L	T	Goals	SO	Avg.
Andrew Currie	1	60	0	1	0	4	0	4.00
Chad Lang	48	2732	11	27	7	225	0	4.94
Zac Bierk	9	423	0	4	2	37	0	5.25
Ryan Douglas	15	802	4	9	1	78	0	5.84

SAULT STE. MARIE GREYHOUNDS

SCORING

	Games	G	A	Pts.	PIM
Steve Sullivan	63	51	62	113	82
Aaron Gavey	60	42	60	102	116
Jeff Toms	64	52	45	97	19
Tom MacDonald	55	34	36	70	175
Drew Bannister	58	7	43	50	108
Wade Gibson	55	7	42	49	114
Joe VanVolsen	56	20	28	48	49
Andrew Clark	62	20	24	44	72
Brad Baber	57	11	32	43	82
Briane Thompson	60	5	36	41	136
Gary Roach	45	5	35	40	28
Jeremy Stevenson	48	18	19	37	183
Peter MacKellar	56	14	15	29	10
Chad Grills	34	6	16	22	69
Richard Uniacke	54	4	15	19	4
Sean Gagnon	42	4	12	16	147
Jeff Gies	38	4	6	10	15
Oliver Pastinsky	41	1	9	10	20
Rhett Trombley	17	3	4	7	37
Kiley Hill	7	2	3	5	13
Andre Payette	40	2	3	5	98
Neal Martin	19	0	4	4	4
Steve Zoryk	20	1	1	2	11
Corey Moylan	27	1	1	2	11
Craig Nelson	14	0	2	2	6
Steve Spina	17	1	0	1	2
Keith Cassidy	8	0	1	1	9
Scott King	33	0	1	1	11
Joey Clarke	4	0	0	0	5
Richard Vachon	6	0	0	0	0
Andrea Carpano (goalie)	11	0	0	0	11
Ryan Douglas (goalie)	13	0	0	0	2
Dan Cloutier (goalie)	55	0	0	0	15

GOALTENDING

	Games	Min.	W	L	T	Goals	SO	Avg.
Dan Cloutier	55	2934	28	14	6	174	2	3.56
Ryan Douglas	13	586	3	5	0	43	0	4.40
Andrea Carpano	11	479	4	5	1	45	0	5.64

SUDBURY WOLVES

SCORING

	Games	G	A	Pts.	PIM
Jamie Rivers	65	32	89	121	58
Zdenek Nedved	60	50	50	100	42
Jamie Matthews	46	34	63	97	24
Barrie Moore	65	36	49	85	69
Mike Yeo	65	34	32	66	53
Rory Fitzpatrick	65	12	34	46	112
Steve Potvin	65	12	32	44	65
Ryan Shanahan	58	9	20	29	118
Rick Bodkin	63	10	16	26	26
Mike Wilson	60	4	22	26	62
Gary Coupal	48	9	15	24	194
Joel Poirier	28	17	5	22	44
Andrew Dale	53	8	13	21	21
Rod Hinks	12	6	14	20	14

	Games	G	A	Pts.	PIM
Sean Venedam	47	6	14	20	15
Ilya Lysenko	42	2	9	11	16
Jeff Smith	19	3	7	10	8
Bob MacIsaac	62	1	8	9	151
Shawn Frappier	40	3	5	8	41
Neal Martin	21	2	6	8	6
Chris McMurtry	40	3	2	5	41
Luc Gagne	11	3	1	4	2
Colin Wilson	18	0	4	4	15
Jimmy Ratte	11	1	1	2	15
Kayle Short	5	0	2	2	15
Jeff Melnechuk (goalie)	18	0	2	2	0
Simon Sherry	31	0	2	2	63
Mark O'Donnell	2	1	0	1	0
Mark Giannetti	10	1	0	1	4
Reuben Castella	1	0	1	1	0
Matt Kiereck	12	0	1	1	8
Matt Mullin (goalie)	35	0	1	1	4
Jay McKee	51	0	1	1	51
Dave MacDonald (goalie)	1	0	0	0	0
Andrew Williamson	1	0	0	0	0
Steve LeCoure	2	0	0	0	2
Ryan Connolly	5	0	0	0	5
Shawn Silver (goalie)	22	0	0	0	2

GOALTENDING

	Games	Min.	W	L	T	Goals	SO	Avg.
Matt Mullin	35	2113	23	9	3	110	1	3.12
Jeff Melnechuk	18	726	4	4	2	60	0	4.96
Shawn Silver	22	1098	7	12	1	96	0	5.25
Dave MacDonald	1	60	0	1	0	6	0	6.00

WINDSOR SPITFIRES

SCORING

	Games	G	A	Pts.	PIM
Bill Bowler	66	47	76	123	39
Craig Lutes	60	40	42	82	66
Ed Jovanovski	62	15	35	50	221
Rob Shearer	66	17	25	42	46
Daryl Lavoie	61	7	32	39	132
Dave Roche	29	14	20	34	73
Cory Evans	30	14	17	31	80
Mike Martin	64	2	29	31	94
Vladimir Kretchine	45	13	12	25	27
Mike Loach	47	12	13	25	86
Brady Blain	65	10	14	24	19
Shayne McCosh	34	3	21	24	46
Stephen Webb	33	6	15	21	117
Colin Wilson	26	9	11	20	19
Kevin Paden	24	8	11	19	30
Akil Adams	31	8	11	19	45
Adam Young	45	8	9	17	105
Joel Poirier	13	6	8	14	20
Dan West	61	6	7	13	107
John Cooper	62	4	9	13	5
Cory Johnson	8	3	4	7	2
Dave Geris	63	0	6	6	121
David Pluck	33	1	2	3	18
David Green	57	0	2	2	24
Jason Coles	6	0	1	1	9
Matt Mullin (goalie)	21	0	1	1	11
Luke Clowes	44	0	1	1	57
Brian Jones	1	0	0	0	0
Brent Pye	2	0	0	0	0
Paul Beazley (goalie)	3	0	0	0	0
Shawn Silver (goalie)	18	0	0	0	7
Travis Scott (goalie)	45	0	0	0	4
Ryan Stewart	47	0	0	0	11

GOALTENDING

	Games	Min.	W	L	T	Goals	SO	Avg.
Matt Mullin	21	910	3	9	2	60	1	3.96
Travis Scott	45	2312	20	18	0	158	1	4.10
Shawn Silver	17	637	2	7	3	60	0	5.65
Paul Beazley	3	138	0	2	0	15	0	6.52

PLAYERS WITH TWO OR MORE TEAMS

SCORING

	Games	G	A	Pts.	PIM
Jeff Andrews, North Bay	36	11	8	19	42
Jeff Andrews, Oshawa	17	2	4	6	20
Totals	53	13	12	25	62
Pat Barton, Detroit	46	22	29	51	48
Pat Barton, Guelph	23	9	12	21	28
Totals	69	31	41	72	76
Jason Bonsignore, Newmarket	17	7	17	24	22
Jason Bonsignore, N.F.	41	15	47	62	41
Totals	58	22	64	86	63
Rob Boyko, Detroit	11	2	1	3	24
Rob Boyko, Belleville	39	4	10	14	43
Totals	50	6	11	17	67
Corey Bricknell, Newmarket	17	1	3	4	38
Corey Bricknell, Niagara Falls	44	1	15	16	90
Totals	61	2	18	20	128
Jim Brown, Owen Sound	22	18	17	35	24
Jim Brown, Newmarket	40	26	28	54	48
Totals	62	44	45	89	72
Kevin S. Brown, Niagara Falls	1	0	1	1	0
Kevin S. Brown, Belleville	58	29	48	77	29
Totals	59	29	49	78	29
Brandon Convery, Niagara Falls	29	24	29	53	30
Brandon Convery, Belleville	23	16	19	35	22
Totals	52	40	48	88	52
Joe Cook, Oshawa	46	0	13	13	73
Joe Cook, Owen Sound	19	0	3	3	18
Totals	65	0	16	16	91
Joe Coombs, Kitchener	27	9	7	16	8
Joe Coombs, Belleville	22	4	8	12	14
Totals	49	13	15	28	22
C.J. Denomme (g), Kitchener	3	0	0	0	0
C.J. Denomme (g), Ottawa	35	0	2	2	2
Totals	38	0	2	2	2
Paul Doherty, North Bay	43	13	29	42	63
Paul Doherty, Oshawa	14	1	14	15	17
Totals	57	14	43	57	80
Mark Donahue, Belleville	29	14	19	33	36
Mark Donahue, Kitchener	33	13	26	39	28
Totals	62	27	45	72	62
Ryan Douglas (g), Pet.	15	0	1	1	6
Ryan Douglas (g), S.S.M.	13	0	0	0	2
Totals	28	0	1	1	8
Robert Dubois, North Bay	40	9	21	30	24
Robert Dubois, Oshawa	7	0	3	3	0
Totals	47	9	24	33	24
Serge Dunphy, Oshawa	23	0	1	1	19
Serge Dunphy, Belleville	18	0	2	2	44
Totals	41	0	3	3	63
Cory Evans, London	17	9	8	17	41
Cory Evans, Windsor	30	14	17	31	80
Totals	47	23	25	48	121
Darryl Foster (g), Newmarket	6	0	0	0	0
Darryl Foster (g), Niagara Falls	24	0	0	0	14
Totals	30	0	0	0	14
Luc Gagne, Newmarket	19	1	2	3	17
Luc Gagne, Sudbury	11	3	1	4	2
Totals	30	4	3	7	19
Derek Grant, Newmarket	12	2	10	12	8
Derek Grant, Niagara Falls	47	30	33	63	33
Totals	59	32	43	75	41
Dale Greenwood, Niagara Falls	16	3	3	6	16
Dale Greenwood, Newmarket	10	1	0	1	6
Totals	16	4	3	7	22
Chad Grills, Peterborough	20	5	18	23	46
Chad Grills, Sault Ste. Marie	34	6	16	22	69
Totals	54	11	34	45	113
John Guirestante, London	29	3	12	15	29
John Guirestante, North Bay	13	1	1	2	7
Totals	42	4	13	17	36
Mike Harding, Peterborough	32	25	33	58	100
Mike Harding, Detroit	23	16	12	28	40
Totals	55	41	45	86	140

	Games	G	A	Pts.	PIM
Duane Harmer, Guelph	41	7	16	23	29
Duane Harmer, Detroit	20	1	6	7	16
Totals	61	8	22	30	45
Kiley Hill, Sault Ste. Marie	7	2	3	5	13
Kiley Hill, Newmarket	52	7	15	22	58
Totals	59	9	18	27	71
Rod Hinks, Sudbury	12	6	14	20	14
Rod Hinks, Owen Sound	50	40	44	84	79
Totals	62	46	58	104	93
Jason Hughes, Belleville	7	0	1	1	4
Jason Hughes, Kitchener	48	2	17	19	130
Totals	55	2	18	20	134
Cory Johnson, Kingston	2	0	0	0	0
Cory Johnson, Windsor	8	3	4	7	2
Totals	10	3	4	7	2
Dale Junkin, Niagara Falls	41	28	18	46	39
Dale Junkin, Detroit	23	13	17	30	6
Totals	64	41	35	76	45
Ian Keiller, Belleville	40	1	3	4	111
Ian Keiller, London	23	1	3	4	102
Totals	63	2	6	8	213
Matt Kiereck, Sudbury	12	0	1	1	8
Matt Kiereck, Kingston	14	2	2	4	27
Totals	26	2	3	5	35
Derek Lahnalampi, North Bay	27	0	5	5	25
Derek Lahnalampi, Owen Sound.	16	0	0	0	17
Totals	43	0	5	5	42
Steve LeCoure, Sudbury	2	0	0	0	2
Steve LeCoure, Oshawa	12	3	0	3	27
Totals	14	3	0	3	29
Dave Lemay, Newmarket	26	4	19	23	98
Dave Lemay, Owen Sound	42	6	45	51	120
Totals	68	10	64	74	218
Dave Lylyk, North Bay	6	2	2	4	2
Dave Lylyk, Niagara Falls	34	3	8	11	31
Totals	40	5	10	15	33
B.J. MacPherson, Oshawa	44	33	44	77	76
B.J. MacPherson, North Bay	15	9	21	30	36
Totals	59	42	65	107	112
Neal Martin, Sault Ste. Marie	19	0	4	4	4
Neal Martin, Sudbury	21	2	6	8	6
Totals	40	2	10	12	10
Dennis Maxwell, Niagara Falls	17	2	14	16	41
Dennis Maxwell, Newmarket	41	12	24	36	113
Totals	58	14	38	52	154
Geordie Maynard, Belleville	10	1	1	2	22
Geordie Maynard, Newmarket	39	4	8	12	87
Totals	49	5	9	14	109
Dustin McArthur, Niagara Falls	18	2	3	5	25
Dustin McArthur, Newmarket	48	9	13	22	40
Totals	66	11	16	27	65
Shayne McCosh, Windsor	34	3	21	24	46
Shayne McCosh, Detroit	25	3	18	21	33
Totals	59	6	39	45	79
Paul McInnes, Niagara Falls	17	0	6	6	18
Paul McInnes, Newmarket	49	2	12	14	44
Totals	66	2	18	20	62
Chris McMurtry, Guelph	3	0	1	1	0
Chris McMurtry, Sudbury	40	3	2	5	41
Totals	43	3	3	6	41
Ryan Middleton, Detroit	35	0	2	2	25
Ryan Middleton, Niagara Falls	22	1	0	1	24
Totals	57	1	2	3	49
Lucas Miller, Oshawa	15	0	4	4	6
Lucas Miller, Niagara Falls	9	0	0	0	2
Totals	24	0	4	4	8
Rick Morton, Detroit	39	2	12	14	79
Rick Morton, Peterborough	14	1	4	5	45
Totals	53	3	16	19	124
Darryl Moxam, Peterborough	15	1	6	7	4
Darryl Moxam, Oshawa	17	2	2	4	21
Totals	32	3	8	11	25
Matt Mullin (g), Windsor	21	0	1	1	11
Matt Mullin (g), Sudbury	35	0	1	1	4
Totals	56	0	2	2	15

	Games	G	A	Pts.	PIM
Adrian Murray, Newmarket	9	0	2	2	11
Adrian Murray, Peterborough	54	2	11	13	96
Totals	63	2	13	15	107
Sergei Olympiev, Ottawa	20	3	5	8	4
Sergei Olympiev, Kitchener	21	6	5	11	24
Totals	41	9	10	19	28
Kevin Paden, Detroit	38	10	19	29	54
Kevin Paden, Windsor	24	8	11	19	30
Totals	62	18	30	48	84
Chris Phelps, Kitchener	30	7	19	26	39
Chris Phelps, Ottawa	34	5	27	32	33
Totals	64	12	46	58	72
Joel Poirier, Sudbury	28	17	5	22	44
Joel Poirier, Windsor	13	6	8	14	20
Totals	41	23	13	36	64
Travis Riggin, Belleville	33	0	6	6	8
Travis Riggin, Kitchener	29	0	2	2	9
Totals	62	0	8	8	17
Dave Roche, Peterborough	34	15	22	37	127
Dave Roche, Windsor	29	14	20	34	73
Totals	63	29	42	71	200
Dylan Seca, Detroit	36	1	2	3	34
Dylan Seca, Niagara Falls	23	2	1	3	9
Totals	59	3	3	6	43
Kayle Short, Sudbury	5	0	2	2	15
Kayle Short, Guelph	44	5	24	29	62
Totals	49	5	26	31	77
Shawn Silver (g), Sudbury	22	0	0	0	2
Shawn Silver (g), Windsor	18	0	0	0	7
Totals	40	0	0	0	9
Chris Skoryna, Belleville	3	2	5	7	6
Chris Skoryna, Guelph	58	34	57	91	41
Totals	61	36	62	98	47
Gerry Skrypec, Newmarket	17	0	10	10	59
Gerry Skrypec, Niagara Falls	16	0	8	8	41
Gerry Skrypec, Detroit	21	1	5	6	48
Totals	54	1	23	24	148
Jeff Smith, Owen Sound	15	0	4	4	35
Jeff Smith, Sudbury	19	3	7	10	8
Jeff Smith, Belleville	5	0	2	2	0
Totals	39	3	13	16	43
Jeremy Stevenson, Newmarket	9	2	4	6	27
Jeremy Stevenson, S.S.M.	48	18	19	37	183
Totals	57	20	23	43	210
Ryan Tocher, Niagara Falls	13	5	6	11	30
Ryan Tocher, Newmarket	48	7	19	26	71
Totals	61	12	25	37	101
Steve Tracze, Ottawa	1	0	0	0	0
Steve Tracze, Belleville	10	3	2	5	4
Totals	11	3	2	5	4
Mark Vilneff, Owen Sound	11	0	3	3	15
Mark Vilneff, Peterborough	32	0	4	4	31
Totals	43	0	7	7	46
Gord Walsh, Guelph	8	0	1	1	9
Gord Walsh, Kingston	55	14	19	33	52
Totals	63	14	20	34	61
Kelly Wayling, Niagara Falls	12	0	0	0	10
Kelly Wayling, Ottawa	14	1	2	3	10
Totals	26	1	2	3	20
Stephen Webb, Windsor	33	6	15	21	117
Stephen Webb, Peterborough	2	0	1	1	9
Totals	35	6	16	22	126
Colin Wilson, Windsor	26	9	11	20	19
Colin Wilson, Sudbury	18	0	4	4	15
Totals	44	9	15	24	34
Joel Yates, Kingston	10	4	4	8	31
Joel Yates, Niagara Falls	20	6	11	17	64
Joel Yates, Ottawa	15	0	2	2	15
Totals	45	10	17	27	110

GOALTENDING

	Games	Min.	W	L	T	Goals	SO	Avg.
C.J. Denomme, Kit.	3	144	1	2	0	9	0	3.75
C.J. Denomme, Ott.	35	1973	20	8	5	108	1	3.28
Totals	38	2117	21	10	5	117	1	3.32

	Games	Min.	W	L	OTL	Goals	SO	Avg.
Darryl Foster, New..	6	240	0	3	1	23	0	5.75
Darryl Foster, N.F....	24	1163	7	12	1	99	0	5.11
Totals	30	1403	7	15	2	122	0	5.22
Matt Mullin, Wind....	21	910	3	9	2	60	1	3.96
Matt Mullin, Sud......	35	2113	23	9	3	110	1	3.12
Totals	56	3023	26	18	5	170	2	3.37

	Games	Min.	W	L	OTL	Goals	SO	Avg.
Ryan Douglas, Pet...	15	802	4	9	1	78	0	5.84
R. Douglas, S.S.M. ...	13	586	3	5	0	43	0	4.40
Totals	28	1388	7	14	1	121	0	5.23
Shawn Silver, Sud. .	22	1098	7	12	1	96	0	5.25
Shawn Silver, Wind. .	17	637	2	7	3	60	0	5.65
Totals	39	1735	9	19	4	156	0	5.39

1994 J. ROSS ROBERTSON CUP PLAYOFFS

RESULTS

LEYDEN DIVISION

QUARTERFINALS

Series "A"

	W	L	Pts.	GF	GA
Ottawa	4	3	8	32	23
Peterborough.................	3	4	6	23	32

(Ottawa won series, 4-3)

Series "B"

	W	L	Pts.	GF	GA
Sudbury	4	1	8	18	14
Oshawa	1	4	2	14	18

(Sudbury won series, 4-1)

Series "C"

	W	L	Pts.	GF	GA
Belleville........................	4	2	8	21	14
Kingston.........................	2	4	4	14	21

(Belleville won series, 4-2)

SEMIFINALS

Series "D"

	W	L	Pts.	GF	GA
North Bay........................	4	2	8	28	21
Belleville........................	2	4	4	21	28

(North Bay won series, 4-2)

Series "E"

	W	L	Pts.	GF	GA
Ottawa	4	1	8	25	18
Sudbury	1	4	2	18	25

(Ottawa won series, 4-1)

FINALS

Series "F"

	W	L	Pts.	GF	GA
North Bay........................	4	1	8	26	16
Ottawa	1	4	2	16	26

(North Bay won series, 4-1)

EMMS DIVISION

QUARTERFINALS

Series "A"

	W	L	Pts.	GF	GA
Sault Ste. Marie	4	0	8	16	7
Windsor	0	4	0	7	16

(Sault Ste. Marie won series, 4-0)

Series "B"

	W	L	Pts.	GF	GA
Guelph...........................	4	1	8	27	18
London...........................	1	4	2	18	27

(Guelph won series, 4-1)

Series "C"

	W	L	Pts.	GF	GA
Owen Sound....................	4	1	8	26	22
Kitchener	1	4	2	22	26

(Owen Sound won series, 4-1)

SEMIFINALS

Series "D"

	W	L	Pts.	GF	GA
Detroit...........................	4	0	8	22	15
Owen Sound....................	0	4	0	15	22

(Detroit won series, 4-0)

Series "E"

	W	L	Pts.	GF	GA
Sault Ste. Marie	4	0	8	21	15
Guelph...........................	0	4	0	15	21

(Sault Ste. Marie won series, 4-0)

FINALS

Series "F"

	W	L	Pts.	GF	GA
Detroit...........................	4	2	8	33	22
Sault Ste. Marie	2	4	4	22	33

(Detroit won series, 4-2)

J. ROSS ROBERTSON CUP FINALS

Series "G"

	W	L	Pts.	GF	GA
North Bay.....................	4	3	8	32	31
Detroit	3	4	6	31	32

(North Bay won series, 4-3)

INDIVIDUAL LEADERS

Goals: Lee Jinman, North Bay (18)
Assists: Kevin J. Brown, Detroit (26)
Points: Kevin J. Brown, Detroit (40)
Penalty minutes: Sean Gagnon, Sault Ste. Marie (52)
Goaltending average: Jeff Salajko, Ottawa (3.27)
Shutouts: Derek Wilkinson, Belleville (1)
Sandy Allan, North Bay (1)

TOP SCORERS

	Games	G	A	Pts.
Kevin J. Brown, Detroit	17	14	26	40
Lee Jinman, North Bay	18	18	19	37
Vitali Yachmenev, North Bay	18	13	19	32
B.J. MacPherson, North Bay	18	11	20	31
Bob Wren, Detroit	17	12	18	30
Michael Peca, Ottawa	17	7	22	29
Dale Junkin, Detroit	17	13	13	26
Steve Sullivan, Sault Ste. Marie	14	9	16	25
Mike Harding, Detroit	17	12	12	24
Steve Washburn, Ottawa	17	7	16	23

INDIVIDUAL STATISTICS

BELLEVILLE BULLS

(Lost Leyden Division semifinals to North Bay, 4-2)

SCORING

	Games	G	A	Pts.	PIM
Kevin S. Brown	12	6	10	16	10
Paul McCallion	12	7	8	15	6
Brandon Convery	12	4	10	14	13
Jarret Reid	12	5	7	12	6
Radim Bicanek	12	2	8	10	21
Paul Rushforth	12	6	3	9	8
Richard Park	12	3	5	8	18
Brian Secord	12	2	4	6	16
Marc Dupuis	12	2	3	5	6
Corey Isen	12	0	4	4	24
Dan Preston	12	0	4	4	19
Craig Mills	12	2	1	3	11
Doug Doull	8	1	1	2	23
Derek Wilkinson (goalie)	12	0	2	2	2
Joe Coombs	10	1	0	1	2
Jeff Ambrosio	11	1	0	1	6
Dan Godbout	12	0	1	1	10
Mark Gowan (goalie)	2	0	0	0	2
Rob Boyko	6	0	0	0	2
Steve Carter	7	0	0	0	2
Sean P. Brown	8	0	0	0	17
Serge Dunphy	10	0	0	0	20

GOALTENDING

	Games	Min.	W	L	T	Goals	SO	Avg.
Derek Wilkinson	12	700	6	6	0	39	1	3.34
Mark Gowan	2	20	0	0	0	2	0	6.00

DETROIT JR. RED WINGS

(Lost J. Ross Robertson Cup finals to North Bay, 4-3)

SCORING

	Games	G	A	Pts.	PIM
Kevin J. Brown	17	14	26	40	28
Bob Wren	17	12	18	30	20
Dale Junkin	17	13	13	26	6
Mike Harding	17	12	12	24	49
Todd Harvey	17	10	12	22	26
Sean Haggerty	17	9	10	19	11
Bill McCauley	16	4	7	11	25
Shayne McCosh	17	3	8	11	24
Jamie Allison	17	2	9	11	35
Jeff Mitchell	17	3	5	8	22
Duane Harmer	17	1	7	8	21
Mike Rucinski	17	0	7	7	15
Eric Cairns	17	0	4	4	46
Nic Beaudoin	17	1	2	3	13
Matt Ball	17	2	0	2	0
Gerry Skrypec	17	0	2	2	36
Robin LaCour	5	0	0	0	4
Jason Saal (goalie)	7	0	0	0	0
Aaron Ellis (goalie)	12	0	0	0	8
Jeremy Meehan	13	0	0	0	4
Dan Pawlaczyk	17	0	0	0	2

GOALTENDING

	Games	Min.	W	L	T	Goals	SO	Avg.
Aaron Ellis	12	694	6	6	0	46	0	3.98
Jason Saal	7	346	5	0	0	23	0	3.99

GUELPH STORM

(Lost Emms Division semifinals to Sault Ste. Marie, 4-0)

SCORING

	Games	G	A	Pts.	PIM
Mike Prokopec	9	12	4	16	17
Sylvain Cloutier	9	7	9	16	32
Chris Skoryna	9	3	12	15	10
Jeff O'Neill	9	2	11	13	31
Mike Rusk	9	2	9	11	12
Pat Barton	9	4	6	10	4
Todd Bertuzzi	9	2	6	8	30
Rumun Ndur	9	4	1	5	24
Ken Belanger	9	2	3	5	30
Jamie Wright	8	2	1	3	10
Jeff Williams	9	2	1	3	4
Grant Pritchett	9	0	3	3	8
Mark McArthur (goalie)	9	0	1	1	2
Regan Stocco	9	0	1	1	12
Viktor Reuta	1	0	0	0	0
Kayle Short	4	0	0	0	0
Murray Hogg	5	0	0	0	0
Eric Landry	9	0	0	0	10
Todd Norman	9	0	0	0	0
Mike Pittman	9	0	0	0	4
Ryan Risidore	9	0	0	0	12

GOALTENDING

	Games	Min.	W	L	T	Goals	SO	Avg.
Mark McArthur	9	561	4	5	0	38	0	4.06

KINGSTON FRONTENACS

(Lost Leyden Division quarterfinals to Belleville, 4-2)

SCORING

	Games	G	A	Pts.	PIM
Chad Kilger	6	7	2	9	8
Keli Corpse	6	1	7	8	2
David Ling	6	4	2	6	16
Steve Parson	2	0	3	3	0
Craig Rivet	6	0	3	3	6
Martin Sychra	6	0	3	3	7
Greg Kraemer	6	1	1	2	8
Mike Ware	6	0	2	2	6
Richard Raymond	4	1	0	1	0
Ken Boone	5	0	1	1	7
Trent Cull	6	0	1	1	6
Duncan Fader	6	0	1	1	6
Gord Walsh	6	0	1	1	4
Cail MacLean	1	0	0	0	0
Jeff DaCosta	3	0	0	0	2
Trevor Doyle	3	0	0	0	4
Brett Lindros	3	0	0	0	18

	Games	G	A	Pts.	PIM
Tyler Moss (goalie)	3	0	0	0	0
Jason Disher	4	0	0	0	5
Eric Rylands	5	0	0	0	5
Marc Lamothe (goalie)	6	0	0	0	0
Bill Maranduik	6	0	0	0	2
Brian Scott	6	0	0	0	8
Alexander Zhurik	6	0	0	0	4

GOALTENDING

	Games	Min.	W	L	T	Goals	SO	Avg.
Marc Lamothe	6	224	2	2	0	12	0	3.21
Tyler Moss	3	136	0	2	0	8	0	3.53

KITCHENER RANGERS

(Lost Emms Division quarterfinals to Owen Sound, 4-1)

SCORING

	Games	G	A	Pts.	PIM
Trevor Gallant	5	1	9	10	0
Tim Spitzig	5	7	2	9	8
Norm Dezainde	5	6	3	9	20
Jason Gladney	5	1	8	9	10
Wes Swinson	5	2	6	8	18
Ryan Pawluk	5	2	1	3	2
Greg McLean	5	1	2	3	10
Jason Hughes	5	1	1	2	12
Gord Dickie	5	0	2	2	2
Jason Morgan	5	1	0	1	2
Todd Warriner	1	0	1	1	0
Eric Manlow	3	0	1	1	4
Mark Donahue	5	0	1	1	6
Andrew Taylor	5	0	1	1	6
Chris Pittman	2	0	0	0	2
Darren Schmidt	4	0	0	0	0
David Belitski (goalie)	5	0	0	0	0
James Boyd	5	0	0	0	0
Jason Johnson	5	0	0	0	8
Sergei Olympiev	5	0	0	0	0
Travis Riggin	5	0	0	0	2

GOALTENDING

	Games	Min.	W	L	T	Goals	SO	Avg.
David Belitski	5	307	1	4	0	25	0	4.89

LONDON KNIGHTS

(Lost Emms Division quarterfinals to Guelph, 4-1)

SCORING

	Games	G	A	Pts.	PIM
Jason Allison	5	2	13	15	13
Ryan Black	5	5	8	13	8
Dave Gilmore	5	7	4	11	4
Chris Zanutto	5	0	3	3	14
Sean Perry	5	2	0	2	12
Gord Ross	5	1	1	2	20
Brian Stacey	5	0	2	2	16
Nick Stajduhar	5	0	2	2	8
Chris Brassard	5	1	0	1	8
Daryl Rivers	3	0	1	1	6
Rob Frid	5	0	1	1	6
Ryan Appel	1	0	0	0	0
Jordan Willis (goalie)	1	0	0	0	0
Don Margettie	3	0	0	0	2
Brodie Coffin	4	0	0	0	2
Roy Gray	4	0	0	0	2
Tim Bacik (goalie)	5	0	0	0	2
Ryan Burgoyne	5	0	0	0	0
Ian Keiller	5	0	0	0	24
Dan Reja	5	0	0	0	6
Kevin Slota	5	0	0	0	4
Ben Walker	5	0	0	0	0

GOALTENDING

	Games	Min.	W	L	T	Goals	SO	Avg.
Tim Bacik	5	292	1	4	0	25	0	5.14
Jordan Willis	1	8	0	0	0	1	0	7.50

NORTH BAY CENTENNIALS

(Winner of 1994 J. Ross Robertson Cup playoffs)

SCORING

	Games	G	A	Pts.	PIM
Lee Jinman	18	18	19	37	8
Vitali Yachmenev	18	13	19	32	12
B.J. MacPherson	18	11	20	31	24
Jeff Shevalier	17	8	14	22	18
Michael Burman	18	2	20	22	22
Bill Lang	18	9	12	21	43
Brad Brown	18	3	12	15	33
Jason Campeau	18	5	4	9	10
Jim Ensom	16	4	5	9	6
Stefan Rivard	18	3	6	9	36
Scott Cherrey	18	5	3	8	10
Corey Neilson	18	1	5	6	10
Damien Bloye	15	2	2	4	2
Steve McLaren	18	0	3	3	50
Brian Stagg	5	1	0	1	4
Denis Gaudet	18	1	0	1	2
Bob Thornton	2	0	0	0	0
Scott Roche (goalie)	5	0	0	0	0
Sandy Allan (goalie)	17	0	0	0	8
Andy Delmore	17	0	0	0	2
Ryan Gillis	18	0	0	0	8
Rob Lave	18	0	0	0	15

GOALTENDING

	Games	Min.	W	L	T	Goals	SO	Avg.
Scott Roche	5	191	2	1	0	9	0	2.83
Sandy Allan	17	912	10	5	0	58	1	3.82

OSHAWA GENERALS

(Lost Leyden Division quarterfinals to Sudbury, 4-1)

SCORING

	Games	G	A	Pts.	PIM
Darryl Lafrance	5	1	9	10	0
Stephane Yelle	5	1	7	8	2
Marc Savard	5	4	3	7	8
Sean Brown	5	2	1	3	6
Paul Doherty	5	2	1	3	10
Chris Hall	5	1	1	2	6
Ryan Lindsay	5	1	1	2	4
Damon Hardy	5	1	0	1	9
Rob McQuat	5	1	0	1	21
Brandon Gray	5	0	1	1	0
Stephane Soulliere	5	0	1	1	12
Jeff Andrews	1	0	0	0	0
Robert Dubois	1	0	0	0	2
Jason McQuat	4	0	0	0	6
Andrew Power	4	0	0	0	4
Eric Boulton	5	0	0	0	16
Todd Bradley	5	0	0	0	8
David Froh	5	0	0	0	4
B.J. Johnston	5	0	0	0	2
Kevin Vaughan	5	0	0	0	8
Ken Shepard (goalie)	6	0	0	0	0

GOALTENDING

	Games	Min.	W	L	T	Goals	SO	Avg.
Ken Shepard	5	309	1	4	0	18	0	3.50

OTTAWA 67's

(Lost Leyden Division finals to North Bay, 4-1)

SCORING

	Games	G	A	Pts.	PIM
Michael Peca	17	7	22	29	30
Steve Washburn	17	7	16	23	10
Shean Donovan	17	10	11	21	14
Curt Bowen	17	8	13	21	14
Dave Nemirovsky	17	10	10	20	2
Alyn McCauley	13	5	14	19	4
Chris Phelps	17	3	11	14	16
Michael Johnson	17	4	6	10	10

	Games	G	A	Pts.	PIM
Jure Kovacevic	16	3	5	8	10
Mark Edmundson	16	4	3	7	8
Mike Carr	17	2	4	6	13
Wade Simpson	17	3	2	5	22
John Argiropoulos	9	0	4	4	0
Cory Murphy	10	3	0	3	4
Jason Meloche	15	1	2	3	16
Jason Brooks	16	1	2	3	5
Fredrik Oduya	17	0	3	3	22
Joel Yates	9	1	0	1	4
Chris Coveny	10	1	0	1	4
Rich Bronilla	14	0	1	1	6
Steve Jones	8	0	0	0	0
Jeff Salajko (goalie)	9	0	0	0	0
C.J. Denomme (goalie)	13	0	0	0	0

GOALTENDING

	Games	Min.	W	L	T	Goals	SO	Avg.
Jeff Salajko	9	312	3	1	0	17	0	3.27
C.J. Denomme	13	780	6	7	0	48	0	3.69

OWEN SOUND PLATERS

(Lost Emms Division semifinals to Detroit, 4-0)

SCORING

	Games	G	A	Pts.	PIM
Jason MacDonald	9	7	11	18	36
Dave Lemay	9	2	15	17	35
Shayne Wright	9	1	10	11	4
Jeff Kostuch	8	6	4	10	6
Rod Hinks	9	5	4	9	19
Marian Kacir	9	5	4	9	2
Luigi Calce	9	3	4	7	20
Jason Campbell	9	3	4	7	2
Wayne Primeau	9	1	6	7	2
Willie Skilliter	9	5	0	5	6
Rob Schweyer	9	0	4	4	18
Brian Medeiros	9	3	0	3	2
Jeremy Rebek	9	0	2	2	2
Joe Harris	5	0	1	1	12
Craig Binns	9	0	1	1	16
Ryan Mougenel	9	0	1	1	7
Shane Kenny	2	0	0	0	6
Derek Lahnalampi	6	0	0	0	2
Mike Morrone	6	0	0	0	4
Joe Cook	9	0	0	0	8
Jamie Storr (goalie)	9	0	0	0	4

GOALTENDING

	Games	Min.	W	L	T	Goals	SO	Avg.
Jamie Storr	9	547	4	5	0	44	0	4.83

PETERBOROUGH PETES

(Lost Leyden Division quarterfinals to Ottawa, 4-3)

SCORING

	Games	G	A	Pts.	PIM
Jamie Langenbrunner	7	4	6	10	2
Brent Tully	7	5	3	8	12
Steve Hogg	7	2	5	7	4
Dan DelMonte	7	2	4	6	20
Mike Williams	7	2	4	6	6
Rick Emmett	6	1	3	4	6
Tim Hill	6	1	3	4	4
Matt St. Germain	7	3	0	3	8
Adrian Murray	7	0	3	3	6
Pat Paone	7	0	3	3	4
Stephen Webb	6	1	1	2	10
Cameron Mann	7	1	1	2	6
Rick Morton	7	1	1	2	20
Kelvin Solari	7	0	2	2	2
Chad Lang (goalie)	7	0	1	1	4
Mark Vilneff	7	0	1	1	6
Zac Bierk (goalie)	1	0	0	0	0
Scott Stephens	1	0	0	0	0
Quade Lightbody	4	0	0	0	0

	Games	G	A	Pts.	PIM
Henrik Eppers	5	0	0	0	0
Jonathan Murphy	7	0	0	0	0
Ryan Nauss	7	0	0	0	0

GOALTENDING

	Games	Min.	W	L	T	Goals	SO	Avg.
Chad Lang	7	391	3	4	0	24	0	3.68
Zac Bierk	1	33	0	0	0	7	0	12.73

SAULT STE. MARIE GREYHOUNDS

(Lost Emms Division finals to Detroit, 4-2)

SCORING

	Games	G	A	Pts.	PIM
Steve Sullivan	14	9	16	25	22
Aaron Gavey	14	11	10	21	22
Gary Roach	14	1	17	18	16
Joe VanVolsen	14	6	11	17	20
Jeff Toms	14	11	4	15	2
Drew Bannister	14	6	9	15	20
Wade Gibson	14	1	12	13	16
Tom MacDonald	14	3	7	10	38
Brad Baber	14	4	5	9	29
Peter MacKellar	14	5	0	5	6
Briane Thompson	14	0	3	3	27
Sean Gagnon	14	1	1	2	52
Jeremy Stevenson	14	1	1	2	23
Chad Grills	14	0	2	2	28
Ryan Douglas (goalie)	1	0	1	1	0
Andrew Clark	13	0	1	1	0
Dan Cloutier (goalie)	14	0	1	1	0
Oliver Pastinsky	14	0	1	1	5
Jeff Gies	1	0	0	0	0
Rhett Trombley	14	0	0	0	17
Richard Uniacke	14	0	0	0	0

GOALTENDING

	Games	Min.	W	L	T	Goals	SO	Avg.
Ryan Douglas	1	40	0	0	0	2	0	3.00
Dan Cloutier	14	833	10	4	0	52	0	3.75

SUDBURY WOLVES

(Lost Leyden Division semifinals to Ottawa, 4-1)

SCORING

	Games	G	A	Pts.	PIM
Zdenek Nedved	10	7	8	15	10
Mike Yeo	10	8	4	12	4
Jamie Matthews	10	6	6	12	4
Jamie Rivers	10	1	9	10	14
Barrie Moore	10	3	5	8	14
Rory Fitzpatrick	10	2	5	7	10
Steve Potvin	10	2	4	6	10
Gary Coupal	10	1	5	6	13
Sean Venedam	10	3	2	5	6
Mike Wilson	9	1	3	4	8
Andrew Dale	9	0	3	3	4
Ryan Shanahan	10	2	0	2	15
Rick Bodkin	10	0	2	2	13
Bob MacIsaac	10	0	2	2	32
Colin Wilson	9	0	1	1	10
Neal Martin	10	0	1	1	5
Ilya Lysenko	1	0	0	0	0
Jeff Melnechuk (goalie)	1	0	0	0	0
Jimmy Ratte	2	0	0	0	0
Jay McKee	3	0	0	0	0
Simon Sherry	7	0	0	0	0
Shawn Frappier	10	0	0	0	8
Matt Mullin (goalie)	10	0	0	0	0

GOALTENDING

	Games	Min.	W	L	T	Goals	SO	Avg.
Matt Mullin	10	646	5	5	0	38	0	3.53
Jeff Melnechuk	1	16	0	0	0	1	0	3.75

WINDSOR SPITFIRES

(Lost Emms Division quarterfinals to Sault Ste. Marie, 4-0)

SCORING

	Games	G	A	Pts.	PIM
Bill Bowler	4	2	2	4	8
Vladimir Kretchine	4	2	1	3	0
Cory Evans	4	1	2	3	12
Mike Martin	4	1	2	3	4
Dave Roche	4	1	1	2	15
Daryl Lavoie	4	0	2	2	12
Rob Shearer	4	0	2	2	6
Kevin Paden	4	0	1	1	4
Luke Clowes	2	0	0	0	0
David Green	2	0	0	0	0
John Cooper	3	0	0	0	0
Dave Geris	3	0	0	0	6
David Pluck	3	0	0	0	0
Dan West	3	0	0	0	0
Akil Adams	4	0	0	0	10
Brady Blain	4	0	0	0	0
Ed Jovanovski	4	0	0	0	15
Mike Loach	4	0	0	0	9
Craig Lutes	4	0	0	0	0
Travis Scott (goalie)	4	0	0	0	0
Adam Young	4	0	0	0	7

GOALTENDING

	Games	Min.	W	L	T	Goals	SO	Avg.
Travis Scott	4	240	0	4	0	16	0	4.00

1993-94 AWARD WINNERS

ALL-STAR TEAMS

First team	Pos.	Second team
Jamie Storr, Owen Sound	G	Matt Mullin, Sudbury
Jamie Rivers, Sudbury	D	Drew Bannister, S.S.M.
Nick Stajduhar, London	D	Ed Jovanovski, Windsor
Jeff Shevalier, North Bay	LW	Bob Wren, Detroit
Jason Allison, London	C	Keli Corpse, Kingston
Kevin J. Brown, Detroit	RW	Jason MacDonald, O.S.

Coach of the Year: Bert Templeton, North Bay

TROPHY WINNERS

Red Tilson Trophy: Jason Allison, London
Eddie Powers Memorial Trophy: Jason Allison, London
Dave Pinkney Trophy: Sandy Allan, North Bay
Scott Roche, North Bay
Max Kaminsky Trophy: Jamie Rivers, Sudbury
William Hanley Trophy: Jason Allison, London
Emms Family Award: Vitali Yachmenev, North Bay
Matt Leyden Trophy: Bert Templeton, North Bay
Jim Mahon Memorial Trophy: Kevin J. Brown, Detroit
F.W. Dinty Moore Trophy: Scott Roche, North Bay
Leo Lalonde Memorial Trophy: B.J. MacPherson
Hamilton Spectator Trophy: North Bay Centennials
J. Ross Robertson Cup: North Bay Centennials

ALL-TIME AWARD WINNERS

RED TILSON TROPHY

(Outstanding player)

Season	Player, Team
1944-45	Doug McMurdy, St. Catharines
1945-46	Tod Sloan, St. Michael's
1946-47	Ed Sanford, St. Michael's
1947-48	George Armstrong, Stratford
1948-49	Gil Mayer, Barrie
1949-50	George Armstrong, Marlboros
1950-51	Glenn Hall, Windsor
1951-52	Bill Harrington, Kitchener
1952-53	Bob Attersley, Oshawa
1953-54	Brian Cullen, St. Catharines
1954-55	Hank Ciesla, St. Catharines
1955-56	Ron Howell, Guelph
1956-57	Frank Mahovlich, St. Michael's
1957-58	Murray Oliver, Hamilton
1958-59	Stan Mikita, St. Catharines
1959-60	Wayne Connelly, Peterborough
1960-61	Rod Gilbert, Guelph
1961-62	Pit Martin, Hamilton
1962-63	Wayne Maxner, Niagara Falls
1963-64	Yvan Cournoyer, Montreal
1964-65	Andre Lacroix, Peterborough
1965-66	Andre Lacroix, Peterborough
1966-67	Mickey Redmond, Peterborough
1967-68	Walt Tkaczuk, Kitchener
1968-69	Rejean Houle, Montreal
1969-70	Gilbert Perreault, Montreal
1970-71	Dave Gardner, Marlboros
1971-72	Don Lever, Niagara Falls
1972-73	Rick Middleton, Oshawa
1973-74	Jack Valiquette, Sault Ste. Marie
1974-75	Dennis Maruk, London
1975-76	Peter Lee, Ottawa
1976-77	Dale McCourt, St. Catharines
1977-78	Bobby Smith, Ottawa
1978-79	Mike Foligno, Sudbury
1979-80	Jim Fox, Ottawa
1980-81	Ernie Godden, Windsor

Season	Player, Team
1981-82	Dave Simpson, London
1982-83	Doug Gilmour, Cornwall
1983-84	John Tucker, Kitchener
1984-85	Wayne Groulx, Sault Ste. Marie
1985-86	Ray Sheppard, Cornwall
1986-87	Scott McCrory, Oshawa
1987-88	Andrew Cassels, Ottawa
1988-89	Bryan Fogarty, Niagara Falls
1989-90	Mike Ricci, Peterborough
1990-91	Eric Lindros, Oshawa
1991-92	Todd Simon, Niagara Falls
1992-93	Pat Peake, Detroit
1993-94	Jason Allison, London

EDDIE POWERS MEMORIAL TROPHY

(Scoring champion)

Season	Player, Team
1933-34	J. Groboski, Oshawa
1934-35	J. Good, Toronto Lions
1935-36	John O'Flaherty, West Toronto
1936-37	Billy Taylor, Oshawa
1937-38	Hank Goldup, Tor. Marlboros
1938-39	Billy Taylor, Oshawa
1939-40	Jud McAtee, Oshawa
1940-41	Gaye Stewart, Tor. Marlboros
1941-42	Bob Wiest, Brantford
1942-43	Norman "Red" Tilson, Oshawa
1943-44	Ken Smith, Oshawa
1944-45	Leo Gravelle, St. Michael's
1945-46	Tod Sloan, St. Michael's
1946-47	Fleming Mackell, St. Michael's
1947-48	George Armstrong, Stratford
1948-49	Bert Giesebrecht, Windsor
1949-50	Earl Reibel, Windsor
1950-51	Lou Jankowski, Oshawa
1951-52	Ken Laufman, Guelph
1952-53	Jim McBurney, Galt
1953-54	Brian Cullen, St. Catharines
1954-55	Hank Ciesla, St. Catharines

Season	Player, Team
1955-56	Stan Baliuk, Kitchener
1956-57	Bill Sweeney, Guelph
1957-58	John McKenzie, St. Catharines
1958-59	Stan Mikita, St. Catharines
1959-60	Chico Maki, St. Catharines
1960-61	Rod Gilbert, Guelph
1961-62	Andre Boudrias, Montreal
1962-63	Wayne Maxner, Niagara Falls
1963-64	Andre Boudrias, Montreal
1964-65	Ken Hodge, St. Catharines
1965-66	Andre Lacroix, Peterborough
1966-67	Derek Sanderson, Niagara Falls
1967-68	Tom Webster, Niagara Falls
1968-69	Rejean Houle, Montreal
1969-70	Marcel Dionne, St. Catharines
1970-71	Marcel Dionne, St. Catharines
1971-72	Bill Harris, Toronto
1972-73	Blake Dunlop, Ottawa
1973-74	Jack Valiquette, Sault Ste. Marie
	Rick Adduono, St. Catharines
1974-75	Bruce Boudreau, Toronto
1975-76	Mike Kaszycki, Sault Ste. Marie
1976-77	Dwight Foster, Kitchener
1977-78	Bobby Smith, Ottawa
1978-79	Mike Foligno, Sudbury
1979-80	Jim Fox, Ottawa
1980-81	John Goodwin, Sault Ste. Marie
1981-82	Dave Simpson, London
1982-83	Doug Gilmour, Cornwall
1983-84	Tim Salmon, Kingston
1984-85	Dave MacLean, Belleville
1985-86	Ray Sheppard, Cornwall
1986-87	Scott McCrory, Oshawa
1987-88	Andrew Cassels, Ottawa
1988-89	Bryan Fogarty, Niagara Falls
1989-90	Keith Primeau, Niagara Falls
1990-91	Eric Lindros, Oshawa
1991-92	Todd Simon, Niagara Falls
1992-93	Andrew Brunette, Owen Sound
1993-94	Jason Allison, London

DAVE PINKNEY TROPHY

(Top team goaltending)

Season	Player, Team
1948-49	Gil Mayer, Barrie
1949-50	Don Lockhart, Marlboros
1950-51	Don Lockhart, Marlboros
	Lorne Howes, Barrie
1951-52	Don Head, Marlboros
1952-53	John Henderson, Marlboros
1953-54	Dennis Riggin, Hamilton
1954-55	John Albani, Marlboros
1955-56	Jim Crockett, Marlboros
1956-57	Len Broderick, Marlboros
1957-58	Len Broderick, Marlboros
1958-59	Jacques Caron, Peterborough
1959-60	Gerry Cheevers, St. Michael's
1960-61	Bud Blom, Hamilton
1961-62	George Holmes, Montreal
1962-63	Chuck Goddard, Peterborough
1963-64	Bernie Parent, Niagara Falls
1964-65	Bernie Parent, Niagara Falls
1965-66	Ted Quimet, Montreal
1966-67	Peter MacDuffe, St. Catharines
1967-68	Bruce Mullet, Montreal
1968-69	Wayne Wood, Montreal
1969-70	John Garrett, Peterborough
1970-71	John Garrett, Peterborough
1971-72	Michel Larocque, Ottawa
1972-73	Mike Palmateer, Toronto
1973-74	Don Edwards, Kitchener
1974-75	Greg Millen, Peterborough
1975-76	Jim Bedard, Sudbury
1976-77	Pat Riggin, London
1977-78	Al Jensen, Hamilton
1978-79	Nick Ricci, Niagara Falls
1979-80	Rick LaFerriere, Peterborough
1980-81	Jim Ralph, Ottawa
1981-82	Marc D'Amour, Sault Ste. Marie

Season	Player, Team
1982-83	Peter Sidorkiewicz, Oshawa
	Jeff Hogg, Oshawa
1983-84	Darren Pang, Ottawa
	Greg Coram, Ottawa
1984-85	Scott Mosey, Sault Ste. Marie
	Marty Abrams, Sault Ste. Marie
1985-86	Kay Whitmore, Peterborough
	Ron Tugnutt, Peterborough
1986-87	Sean Evoy, Oshawa
	Jeff Hackett, Oshawa
1987-88	Todd Bojcun, Peterborough
	John Tanner, Peterborough
1988-89	Todd Bojcun, Peterborough
	John Tanner, Peterborough
1989-90	Jeff Wilson, Peterborough
	Sean Gauthier, Kingston
1990-91	Kevin Hodson, Sault Ste. Marie
	Mike Lenarduzzi, Sault Ste. Marie
1991-92	Kevin Hodson, Sault Ste. Marie
1992-93	Chad Lang, Peterborough
	Ryan Douglas, Peterborough
1993-94	Sandy Allan, North Bay
	Scott Roche, North Bay

MAX KAMINSKY TROPHY

(Outstanding defenseman)

Season	Player, Team
1969-70	Ron Plumb, Peterborough
1970-71	Jocelyn Guevremont, Montreal
1971-72	Denis Potvin, Ottawa
1972-73	Denis Potvin, Ottawa
1973-74	Jim Turkiewicz, Peterborough
1974-75	Mike O'Connell, Kingston
1975-76	Rick Green, London
1976-77	Craig Hartsburg, S. Ste. Marie
1977-78	Brad Marsh, London
	Rob Ramage, London
1978-79	Greg Theberge, Peterborough
1979-80	Larry Murphy, Peterborough
1980-81	Steve Smith, Sault Ste. Marie
1981-82	Ron Meighan, Niagara Falls
1982-83	Allan MacInnis, Kitchener
1983-84	Brad Shaw, Ottawa
1984-85	Bob Halkidis, London
1985-86	Terry Carkner, Peterborough
	Jeff Brown, Sudbury
1986-87	Kerry Huffman, Guelph
1987-88	Darryl Shannon, Windsor
1988-89	Bryan Fogarty, Niagara Falls
1989-90	John Slaney, Cornwall
1990-91	Chris Snell, Ottawa
1991-92	Drake Berehowsky, North Bay
1992-93	Chris Pronger, Peterborough
1993-94	Jamie Rivers, Sudbury

WILLIAM HANLEY TROPHY

(Most gentlemanly)

Season	Player, Team
1960-61	Bruce Draper, St. Michael's
1961-62	Lowell MacDonald, Hamilton
1962-63	Paul Henderson, Hamilton
1963-64	Fred Stanfield, St. Catharines
1964-65	Jimmy Peters, Hamilton
1965-66	Andre Lacroix, Peterborough
1966-67	Mickey Redmond, Peterborough
1967-68	Tom Webster, Niagara Falls
1968-69	Rejean Houle, Montreal
1969-74	No award presented
1974-75	Doug Jarvis, Peterborough
1975-76	Dale McCourt, Hamilton
1976-77	Dale McCourt, St. Catharines
1977-78	Waynbe Gretzky, S.S. Marie
1978-79	Sean Simpson, Ottawa
1979-80	Sean Simpson, Ottawa
1980-81	John Goodwin, Sault Ste. Marie
1981-82	Dave Simpson, London
1982-83	Kirk Muller, Guelph
1983-84	Kevin Conway, Kingston

Season	Player, Team
1984-85	Scott Tottle, Peterborough
1985-86	Jason Lafreniere, Belleville
1986-87	Scott McCrory, Oshawa
	Keith Gretzky, Hamilton
1987-88	Andrew Cassels, Ottawa
1988-89	Kevin Miehm, Oshawa
1989-90	Mike Ricci, Peterborough
1990-91	Dale Craigwell, Oshawa
1991-92	John Spoltore, North Bay
1992-93	Pat Peake, Detroit
1993-94	Jason Allison, London

EMMS FAMILY AWARD

(Rookie of the year)

Season	Player, Team
1972-73	Dennis Maruk, London
1973-74	Jack Valiquette, Sault Ste. Marie
1974-75	Danny Shearer, Hamilton
1975-76	John Travella, Sault Ste. Marie
1976-77	Yvan Joly, Ottawa
1977-78	Wayne Gretzky, S.S. Marie
1978-79	John Goodwin, Sault Ste. Marie
1979-80	Bruce Dowie, Toronto
1980-81	Tony Tanti, Oshawa
1981-82	Pat Verbeek, Sudbury
1982-83	Bruce Cassidy, Ottawa
1983-84	Shawn Burr, Kitchener
1984-85	Derek King, Sault Ste. Marie
1985-86	Lonnie Loach, Guelph
1986-87	Andrew Cassels, Ottawa
1987-88	Rick Corriveau, London
1988-89	Owen Nolan, Cornwall
1989-90	Chris Longo, Peterborough
1990-91	Cory Stillman, Windsor
1991-92	Chris Gratton, Kingston
1992-93	Jeff O'Neill, Guelph
1993-94	Vitali Yachmenev, North Bay

MATT LEYDEN TROPHY

(Coach of the year)

Season	Coach, Team
1971-72	Gus Bodnar, Oshawa
1972-73	George Armstrong, Toronto
1973-74	Jack Bownass, Kingston
1974-75	Bert Templeton, Hamilton
1975-76	Jerry Toppazzini, Sudbury
1976-77	Bill Long, London
1977-78	Bill White, Oshawa
1978-79	Gary Green, Peterborough
1979-80	Dave Chambers, Toronto
1980-81	Brian Kilrea, Ottawa
1981-82	Brian Kilrea, Ottawa
1982-83	Terry Crisp, Sault Ste. Marie
1983-84	Tom Barrett, Kitchener
1984-85	Terry Crisp, Sault Ste. Marie
1985-86	Jacques Martin, Guelph
1986-87	Paul Theriault, Oshawa
1987-88	Dick Todd, Peterborough
1988-89	Joe McDonnell, Kitchener
1989-90	Larry Mavety, Kingston
1990-91	George Burnett, Niagara Falls
1991-92	George Burnett, Niagara Falls
1992-93	Gary Agnew, London
1993-94	Bert Templeton, North Bay

JIM MAHON MEMORIAL TROPHY

(Top scoring right wing)

Season	Player, Team
1971-72	Bill Harris, Toronto
1972-73	Dennis Ververgaert, London
1973-74	Dave Gorman, St. Catharines
1974-75	Mark Napier, Toronto
1975-76	Peter Lee, Ottawa
1976-77	John Anderson, Toronto
1977-78	Dino Ciccarelli, London
1978-79	Mike Foligno, Sudbury
1979-80	Jim Fox, Ottawa
1980-81	Tony Tanti, Oshawa
1981-82	Tony Tanti, Oshawa
1982-83	Ian MacInnis, Cornwall
1983-84	Wayne Presley, Kitchener
1984-85	Dave MacLean, Belleville
1985-86	Ray Sheppard, Cornwall
1986-87	Ron Goodall, Kitchener
1987-88	Sean Williams, Oshawa
1988-89	Stan Drulia, Niagara Falls
1989-90	Owen Nolan, Cornwall
1990-91	Rob Pearson, Oshawa
1991-92	Darren McCarty, Belleville
1992-93	Kevin J. Brown, Detroit
1993-94	Kevin J. Brown, Detroit

F.W. DINTY MOORE TROPHY

(Lowest average by a rookie goalie)

Season	Player, Team
1975-76	Mark Locken, Hamilton
1976-77	Barry Heard, London
1977-78	Ken Ellacott, Peterborough
1978-79	Nick Ricci, Niagara Falls
1979-80	Mike Vezina, Ottawa
1980-81	John Vanbiesbrouck, Sault Ste. Marie
1981-82	Shawn Kilroy, Peterborough
1982-83	Dan Burrows, Belleville
1983-84	Jerry Iuliano, Sault Ste. Marie
1984-85	Ron Tugnutt, Peterborough
1985-86	Paul Henriques, Belleville
1986-87	Jeff Hackett, Oshawa
1987-88	Todd Bojcun, Peterborough
1988-89	Jeff Wilson, Kingston
1989-90	Sean Basilio, London
1990-91	Kevin Hodson, Sault Ste. Marie
1991-92	Sandy Allan, North Bay
1992-93	Ken Shepard, Oshawa
1993-94	Scott Roche, North Bay

LEO LALONDE MEMORIAL TROPHY

(Overage player of the year)

Season	Player, Team
1983-84	Don McLaren, Ottawa
1984-85	Dunc MacIntyre, Belleville
1985-86	Steve Guenette, Guelph
1986-87	Mike Richard, Toronto
1987-88	Len Soccio, North Bay
1988-89	Stan Drulia, Niagara Falls
1989-90	Iain Fraser, Oshawa
1990-91	Joey St. Aubin, Kitchener
1991-92	John Spoltore, North Bay
1992-93	Scott Hollis, Oshawa
1993-94	B.J. MacPherson, North Bay

REGULAR-SEASON CHAMPION	PLAYOFF CHAMPION
Season Team	**Team**
1933-34—No trophy awarded	St. Michael's College
1934-35—No trophy awarded	Kitchener
1935-36—No trophy awarded	West Toronto Redmen
1936-37—No trophy awarded	St. Michael's College
1937-38—No trophy awarded	Oshawa Generals
1938-39—No trophy awarded	Oshawa Generals
1939-40—No trophy awarded	Oshawa Generals
1940-41—No trophy awarded	Oshawa Generals
1941-42—No trophy awarded	Oshawa Generals
1942-43—No trophy awarded	Oshawa Generals
1943-44—No trophy awarded	Oshawa Generals
1944-45—No trophy awarded	St. Michael's College
1945-46—No trophy awarded	St. Michael's College
1946-47—No trophy awarded	St. Michael's College
1947-48—No trophy awarded	Barrie Flyers
1948-49—No trophy awarded	Barrie Flyers
1949-50—No trophy awarded	Guelph Biltmores
1950-51—No trophy awarded	Barrie Flyers
1951-52—No trophy awarded	Guelph Biltmores
1952-53—No trophy awarded	Barrie Flyers
1953-54—No trophy awarded	St. Catharines Tee Pees
1954-55—No trophy awarded	Toronto Marlboros
1955-56—No trophy awarded	Toronto Marlboros
1956-57—No trophy awarded	Guelph Biltmores
1957-58—St. Catharines Tee Pees	Toronto Marlboros
1958-59—St. Catharines Tee Pees	Peterborough TPTs
1959-60—Toronto Marlboros	St. Catharines Tee Pees
1960-61—Guelph Royals	St. Michael's College
1961-62—Montreal Jr. Canadiens	Hamilton Red Wings
1962-63—Niagara Falls Flyers	Niagara Falls Flyers
1963-64—Toronto Marlboros	Toronto Marlboros
1964-65—Niagara Falls Flyers	Niagara Falls Flyers
1965-66—Peterborough Petes	Oshawa Generals
1966-67—Kitchener Rangers	Toronto Marlboros
1967-68—Kitchener Rangers	Niagara Falls Flyers
1968-69—Montreal Jr. Canadiens	Montreal Jr. Canadiens
1969-70—Montreal Jr. Canadiens	Montreal Jr. Canadiens
1970-71—Peterborough Petes	St. Catharines Black Hawks
1971-72—Toronto Marlboros	Peterborough Petes
1972-73—Toronto Marlboros	Toronto Marlboros
1973-74—Kitchener Rangers	St. Catharines Black Hawks
1974-75—Toronto Marlboros	Toronto Marlboros
1975-76—Sudbury Wolves	Hamilton Steelhawks
1976-77—St. Catharines Fincups	Ottawa 67's
1977-78—Ottawa 67's	Peterborough Petes
1978-79—Peterborough Petes	Peterborough Petes
1979-80—Peterborough Petes	Peterborough Petes
1980-81—Sault St. Marie Greyhounds	Kitchener Rangers
1981-82—Ottawa 67's	Kitchener Rangers
1982-83—Sault Ste. Marie Greyhounds	Oshawa Generals
1983-84—Kitchener Rangers	Ottawa 67's
1984-85—Sault Ste. Marie Greyhounds	Sault Ste. Marie Greyhounds
1985-86—Peterborough Petes	Guelph Platers
1986-87—Oshawa Generals	Oshawa Generals
1987-88—Windsor Compuware Spitfires	Windsor Compuware Spitfires
1988-89—Kitchener Rangers	Peterborough Petes
1989-90—Oshawa Generals	Oshawa Generals
1990-91—Oshawa Generals	Sault Ste. Marie Greyhounds
1991-92—Peterborough Petes	Sault Ste. Marie Greyhounds
1992-93—Peterborough Petes	Peterborough Petes
1993-94—North Bay Centennials	North Bay Centennials

The OHL regular-season champion is awarded the Hamilton Spectator Trophy and the playoff champion is awarded the J. Ross Robertson Cup.

QUEBEC MAJOR JUNIOR HOCKEY LEAGUE

LEAGUE OFFICE

President and executive director
Gilles Courteau
Statistician
Richard Blouin

Communications assistants
Yves Desrosiers
Manon Gagnon
Administrative assistant
Claire Lussier

Address
255 Roland-Therien Blvd.
Suite 101
Longueuil, Quebec
Phone
514-442-3590

1993-94 REGULAR SEASON

FINAL STANDINGS

ROBERT LE BEL DIVISION

Team	G	W	L	T	Pts.	GF	GA
Laval	72	49	22	1	99	346	247
Verdun	72	41	29	2	84	278	242
Hull	72	38	31	3	79	310	304
St. Hyacinthe	72	35	30	7	77	297	290
St. Jean	72	29	37	6	64	264	265
Granby	72	30	40	2	62	297	309
Val-d'Or	72	17	54	1	35	254	397

FRANK DILIO DIVISION

Team	G	W	L	T	Pts.	GF	GA
Chicoutimi	72	43	24	5	91	340	254
Sherbrooke	72	41	29	2	84	317	247
Beauport	72	36	30	6	78	298	287
Shawinigan	72	36	31	5	77	316	313
Drummondville	72	31	35	6	68	289	308
Victoriaville	72	17	51	4	38	261	404

INDIVIDUAL LEADERS

Goals: Yanick Dube, Laval (66)
Assists: Danny Beauregard, Chicoutimi (82)
Patrick Carignan, Shawinigan (82)
Hugo Proulx, Hull (82)
Points: Yanick Dube, Laval (141)
Penalty minutes: Sylvain Blouin, Laval (492)
Goaltending average: Philippe De Rouville, Verdun (3.06)
Shutouts: Emmanuel Fernandez, Laval (5)

	Games	G	A	Pts.
Danny Beauregard, Chicoutimi	61	39	82	121
Ian Laperriere, Drummondville	62	41	72	113
Patrick Carignan, Shawinigan	70	31	82	113
Samuel Groleau, St. Jean	69	37	73	110
Eric Daze, Beauport	66	59	48	107
Alexei Lojkin, Chicoutimi	66	40	67	107
Robin Bouchard, Shawinigan	70	52	54	106
Steve Gosselin, Chicoutimi	68	29	77	106
Steve Brule, St. Jean	66	41	64	105
Patrick Deraspe, Beauport	70	49	53	102
Jean-Martin Morin, Victoriaville	70	40	62	102
Marc Beaucage, Laval	63	41	60	101
Christian Matte, Granby	59	50	47	97
Alain Cote, Laval	64	31	63	94
Stefan Simoes, Verdun	73	36	57	93

TOP SCORERS

	Games	G	A	Pts.
Yanick Dube, Laval	64	66	75	141
Hugo Proulx, Hull	72	47	82	129
Michel St. Jacques, Chicoutimi	62	58	68	126
Dave Tremblay, Shawinigan	71	50	76	126
Jocelyn Langlois, Verdun	72	43	80	123

INDIVIDUAL STATISTICS

BEAUPORT HARFANGS

SCORING

	Games	G	A	Pts.	PIM
Eric Daze	66	59	48	107	31
Patrick Deraspe	70	49	53	102	107
Joey Deliva	56	29	54	83	52
Ian McIntyre	71	23	53	76	129
Eric Montreuil	67	31	40	71	122
Herve Lapointe	71	11	42	53	169
Patrice Paquin	45	22	24	46	188
Jean-Yves Leroux	45	14	25	39	43
Dimitri Goubar	46	22	10	32	37
Marc Chouinard	62	11	19	30	23
Martin Ethier	61	4	19	23	53
Dominic Grand'maison	42	4	15	19	229
Stephane Madore	71	1	14	15	187
Claude St. Cyr	72	5	9	14	15
Keith Cassidy	30	2	11	13	51
Eric Moreau	27	1	12	13	30
Vitali Kozel	58	2	10	12	51

	Games	G	A	Pts.	PIM
Patrick Cote	48	2	4	6	230
Mario Cormier	48	1	5	6	131
Jean-Luc Grand-Pierre	46	1	4	5	27
Michel Boulay	1	0	0	0	0
Jean-Francois Tremblay	3	0	0	0	0
Stephane Menard (goalie)	41	—	—	—	2
Steve Vezina (goalie)	46	—	—	—	2

GOALTENDING

	Games	Min.	W	L	T	Goals	SO	Avg.
Stephane Menard	41	2034	17	15	2	123	2	3.63
Steve Vezina	46	2380	19	15	4	156	0	3.93

CHICOUTIMI SAGUENEENS

SCORING

	Games	G	A	Pts.	PIM
Michel St. Jacques	62	58	68	126	86
Danny Beauregard	61	39	82	121	66

	Games	G	A	Pts.	PIM
Alexei Lojkin	66	40	67	107	68
Steve Gosselin	68	29	77	106	155
Allan Sirois	70	32	37	69	142
Christian Caron	69	26	29	55	132
Yanick Jean	65	11	30	41	177
Andre Roy	65	10	21	31	277
Dominic Savard	62	13	17	30	34
Patrick Lacombe	65	1	28	29	275
Alain Nasreddine	60	3	24	27	218
Yann Vaillancourt	72	9	14	23	44
Jerome Boivin	72	9	12	21	88
Daniel Laflamme	48	5	16	21	46
Steve Dulac	34	9	8	17	18
Michel Lebouthillier	62	4	9	13	4
Sebastien Berube	52	3	9	12	160
Daniel Bienvenue	42	2	7	9	4
Patrick Desjardins	61	1	7	8	27
Pascal Gagnon	52	3	3	6	150
Eric Fichaud (goalie)	63	—	—	—	18
Sebastien Dupuis (goalie)	21	—	—	—	4
Frederic Allain (goalie)	8	—	—	—	0

GOALTENDING

	Games	Min.	W	L	T	Goals	SO	Avg.
Eric Fichaud	63	3493	37	21	3	192	4	3.30
Sebastien Dupuis	21	812	4	5	2	56	0	4.14
Frederic Alain	8	260	2	1	0	20	0	4.62

DRUMMONDVILLE VOLTIGEURS

SCORING

	Games	G	A	Pts.	PIM
Ian Laperriere	62	41	72	113	150
Stephane Larocque	59	37	51	88	113
Eric Plante	67	41	40	81	67
Alexandre Duchesne	53	38	36	74	109
Stephane St. Amour	46	19	33	52	32
Vincent Tremblay	46	14	37	51	38
Raymond Delarosbil	71	9	33	42	75
Luc Decelles	64	19	20	39	27
Mathieu Sunderland	60	19	13	32	118
Martin Latulippe	67	4	24	28	121
Steve Tardif	71	5	16	21	117
Patrick Livernoche	64	9	9	18	102
Paolo De Rubertis	68	8	9	17	149
Rock Isabel	40	9	6	15	264
Christian Marcoux	51	4	11	15	29
Patrice Charbonneau	49	2	11	13	45
Francois Sasseville	66	4	7	11	65
Sebastien Bety	67	3	8	11	164
Denis Gauthier	60	0	7	7	176
Emmanuel Labranche	55	1	5	6	121
Pascal Gagnon	16	1	2	3	0
Nicolas Savage	48	1	2	3	85
Stephane Routhier (goalie)	52	—	—	—	22
Yannick Gagnon	30				8

GOALTENDING

	Games	Min.	W	L	T	Goals	SO	Avg.
Stephane Routhier	52	2783	26	19	2	180	0	3.88
Yannick Gagnon	30	1501	5	14	4	111	0	4.44

GRANBY BISONS

SCORING

	Games	G	A	Pts.	PIM
Christian Matte	59	50	47	97	103
Serge Aubin	63	42	32	74	80
Dave Boudreault	71	32	34	66	178
Francois Gagnon	70	27	39	66	134
Jean Roberge	58	22	41	63	82
Bruno Gladu	72	22	31	53	16
Maxime Blouin	55	18	26	44	14
Martin Belanger	63	8	32	40	49
Dave Douville	68	14	24	38	10

	Games	G	A	Pts.	PIM
Xavier Delisle	46	11	22	33	25
Patrick Lamoureux	56	8	25	33	146
Martin Woods	58	8	20	28	222
Eric Bertrand	60	11	15	26	151
L. Philippe Sevigny	69	4	21	25	92
Hugues Gervais	56	7	8	15	158
Dave Savard	64	4	10	14	78
Martin Corbeil	39	6	7	13	12
Samy Nasreddine	67	3	10	13	48
Martin Beauchamp	32	2	11	13	66
Yannick Perron	45	6	5	11	88
Frederic Bouchard	45	1	9	10	67
Stephane Leblanc	25	3	3	6	0
Brian Stewart	33	2	2	4	22
Eric Hebert	13	1	2	3	10
Steve Plouffe (goalie)	46	—	—	—	10
Frederic Deschenes (goalie)	35	—	—	—	2

GOALTENDING

	Games	Min.	W	L	T	Goals	SO	Avg.
Steve Plouffe	46	2492	16	25	1	172	1	4.14
Frederic Deschenes	35	1861	14	15	1	132	0	4.26

HULL OLYMPIQUES

SCORING

	Games	G	A	Pts.	PIM
Hugo Proulx	72	47	82	129	61
Eric Lecompte	62	39	49	88	171
Sebastien Bordeleau	60	26	57	83	147
Martin Gendron	37	39	36	75	18
Claude Jutras	65	31	37	68	350
Jamie Bird	70	9	41	50	95
Eric Cloutier	64	16	25	41	321
Harold Hersh	69	16	21	37	80
Michael MacKay	70	16	21	37	38
Pierre-Francois Lalonde	36	11	26	37	20
Claude Filion	69	11	25	36	300
Carl Charland	65	15	19	34	223
Shane Doiron	71	12	22	34	78
Richard Safarik	65	7	14	21	24
Jeffrey Viitanen	70	7	9	16	124
Stephane Poulin	49	0	6	6	58
Roddie MacKenzie	52	2	2	4	62
Lars Bruggemann	58	1	3	4	93
Matt Young	44	0	3	3	62
Iannique Renaud	48	1	0	1	155
Carl Prud'homme	1	0	0	0	0
Francois Cloutier	7	0	0	0	2
Marc Legault (goalie)	39	—	—	—	29
Neil Savary (goalie)	32	—	—	—	6

GOALTENDING

	Games	Min.	W	L	T	Goals	SO	Avg.
Marc Legault	39	2276	23	14	2	148	0	3.90
Neil Savary	32	1708	15	14	0	118	2	4.15

LAVAL TITANS

SCORING

	Games	G	A	Pts.	PIM
Yanick Dube	64	66	75	141	30
Marc Beaucage	63	41	60	101	69
Alain Cote	64	31	63	94	90
Daniel Goneau	68	29	57	86	81
Frederic Chartier	72	28	54	82	141
Brant Blackned	63	31	48	79	151
Patrick Boileau	64	13	57	70	56
Jason Boudrias	61	17	25	42	62
Sylvain Blouin	62	18	22	40	492
J. Francois Brunelle	58	10	21	31	52
Jeff Loder	65	12	17	29	28
Michael Gaul	22	10	17	27	24
Benoit Gratton	51	9	14	23	70
Jason Bermingham	60	8	13	21	35

	Games	G	A	Pts.	PIM
Francois Pilon	66	3	16	19	74
Francis Bouillon	68	3	15	18	129
Frederic Jobin	67	4	11	15	150
Jeff Mercer	29	5	8	13	49
David Haynes	61	4	7	11	177
Dany Dupont	48	1	2	3	219
Robert Corbin	0	0	0	0	0
Philippe Trudeau	7	0	0	0	4
Emmanuel Fernandez (goalie)	51	—	—	—	12
Martin Villeneuve (goalie)	27	—	—	—	2
Francois Leblanc (goalie)	4	—	—	—	2

GOALTENDING

	Games	Min.	W	L	T	Goals	SO	Avg.
Francois Leblanc	4	239	3	1	0	9	1	2.26
E. Fernandez	51	2776	29	14	1	143	5	3.09
Martin Villeneuve	27	1318	15	6	0	88	0	4.01

ST. HYACINTHE LASERS

SCORING

	Games	G	A	Pts.	PIM
Normand Paquet	60	31	57	88	74
Eric Gauvin	64	44	41	85	72
Eric Landry	69	42	34	76	128
David Beauregard	59	21	35	56	23
Jimmy Drolet	72	10	46	56	93
Yannick Hubert	68	23	29	52	30
Gabriel Cote	69	19	31	50	97
Nicolas Maheux	45	19	29	48	6
Jean-Francois Tremblay	71	21	22	43	171
Sylvain Ducharme	57	14	28	42	135
David Desnoyers	70	7	32	39	244
Remy Boudreau	69	8	24	32	12
Richard Lacasse	56	5	15	20	78
Marc Sigouin	66	8	10	18	74
Hugo Veilleux	53	8	9	17	34
Yannick Turcotte	53	8	7	15	18
Martin Trudel	64	3	12	15	36
Patrick Lampron	51	2	12	14	109
Pascal Ouellet	45	3	8	11	33
Hugo Bertrand	67	1	10	11	198
Christian Gosselin	12	3	2	5	16
Yannick Plante	20	0	3	3	13
Jimmy Dostie	10	0	2	2	57
Frederic Delage	0	0	0	0	0
Jean-Francois Lachance	2	0	0	0	0
Frederick Beaubien (goalie)	47	—	—	—	6
Frederic Cassivi (goalie)	35	—	—	—	4
Frederic Parent (goalie)	6	—	—	—	0

GOALTENDING

	Games	Min.	W	L	T	Goals	SO	Avg.
Frederick Beaubien	47	2663	19	19	5	168	1	3.79
Frederic Cassivi	35	1751	15	13	3	127	1	4.35
Frederic Parent	6	258	2	2	0	23	0	5.35

ST. JEAN LYNX

SCORING

	Games	G	A	Pts.	PIM
Samuel Groleau	69	37	73	110	40
Steve Brule	66	41	64	105	46
Jimmy Provencher	64	33	29	62	82
Patrick Traverse	66	15	37	52	30
Denis Beauchamp	72	7	39	46	136
Nathan Morin	49	15	22	37	225
Rocco Anoia	63	13	22	35	41
Martin Rozon	45	7	28	35	24
Francois Archambault	70	16	18	34	39
Eric Houde	71	16	16	32	14
Jason Doig	63	8	17	25	65
Bruno Lajeunesse	48	7	18	25	25
Alex Richard	68	10	13	23	80
Georges Laraque	70	11	11	22	142

	Games	G	A	Pts.	PIM
Brian Casey	67	4	18	22	32
Jan Melichercik	48	5	14	19	2
Patrick Charbonneau	62	7	7	14	42
Frederic Barbeau	65	6	8	14	84
Dereck Michaud	59	6	4	10	19
Rony Valenti	40	5	5	10	90
Joel Theriault	57	3	0	3	63
Eric Bellemare	2	0	0	0	0
Pierre Gauthier	14	0	0	0	14
Jose Theodore (goalie)	57	—	—	—	10
Martin Rodrigue (goalie)	24	—	—	—	4

GOALTENDING

	Games	Min.	W	L	T	Goals	SO	Avg.
Martin Rodrigue	24	1153	9	8	0	65	0	3.38
Jose Theodore	57	3225	20	29	6	194	0	3.61

SHAWINIGAN CATARACTES

SCORING

	Games	G	A	Pts.	PIM
Dave Tremblay	71	50	76	126	10
Patrick Carignan	70	31	82	113	46
Robin Bouchard	70	52	54	106	238
Alain Savage	63	50	27	77	129
Carl Paradis	67	25	32	57	55
Simon Roy	64	10	46	56	30
David Brosseau	65	27	26	53	62
Jean-Francois Laroche	43	12	30	42	35
David Grenier	67	13	27	40	115
Yanick Evola	70	11	27	38	57
Martin Lepage	66	6	28	34	119
Benoit Larose	61	2	21	23	120
Stephane Robidas	67	3	18	21	33
Sylvain Brisson	63	1	20	21	102
Guy Loranger	67	6	11	17	44
Eric Ladouceur	40	5	7	12	30
Evan Levi	54	5	6	11	9
Steeve Finn	69	5	4	9	116
Sergei Polichouk	52	1	5	6	100
Jean-Francois Bessette	52	0	5	5	85
Patrick Lalime (goalie)	48	—	—	—	2
Sylvain Daigle (goalie)	31	—	—	—	8

GOALTENDING

	Games	Min.	W	L	T	Goals	SO	Avg.
Sylvain Daigle	31	1645	14	11	3	113	0	4.12
Patrick Lalime	48	2733	22	20	2	192	1	4.22

SHERBROOKE FAUCONS

SCORING

	Games	G	A	Pts.	PIM
Hugo Turcotte	63	35	54	89	43
Carl Fleury	59	28	45	73	81
Christian Dube	72	31	41	72	22
Etienne Beaudry	67	32	25	57	52
Pascal Trepanier	48	16	41	57	67
Stephane Julien	67	13	43	56	111
Dave Belliveau	58	16	38	54	67
Mathieu Dandenault	67	17	36	53	67
Louis Bernard	65	10	31	41	107
Yan St. Pierre	61	20	20	40	67
Francois Rivard	65	11	21	32	28
Pascal Bernier	68	12	18	30	72
Martin Lamarche	53	10	20	30	121
Denis Lamoureux	56	15	14	29	10
Eric Messier	67	4	24	28	69
J. Francois Boutin	40	7	13	20	21
Charles Paquette	63	5	14	19	165
Steven Low	68	4	14	18	154
Daniel Villeneuve	62	5	10	15	98
Mirko Langlois	17	4	7	11	20
Lachlan Coombe	47	1	5	6	15
Sebastien Pelletier	13	1	2	3	17

	Games	G	A	Pts.	PIM
Simon Provencher	18	1	0	1	39
Bruce Richardson	3	0	1	1	0
Hugo Hamelin (goalie)	52	—	—	—	6
Luc Belanger (goalie)	29	—	—	—	0

GOALTENDING

	Games	Min.	W	L	T	Goals	SO	Avg.
Luc Belanger	29	1488	16	7	0	80	3	3.23
Hugo Hamelin	52	2786	25	19	2	152	3	3.27

VAL-D'OR FOREURS

SCORING

	Games	G	A	Pts.	PIM
Ian Laterreur	68	27	31	58	29
Patrick Cassin	61	21	37	58	31
Patrick Grise	68	24	30	54	33
Stephane Roy	72	25	28	53	116
Francois Paquette	63	18	35	53	32
Nicolas Brousseau	53	23	16	39	126
Yannik Gaucher	49	16	17	33	75
Eric Sylvestre	71	7	20	27	71
Martin Belair	69	2	25	27	29
Thierry Mayer	62	10	14	24	269
Jeremy Caissie	24	7	17	24	28
Louis Bedard	60	8	15	23	285
Jason Dumont	25	9	11	20	10
Nicolas Morency	57	9	11	20	65
Francois Fortin	67	9	10	19	53
Daniel Germain	39	5	12	17	68
Carl Blondin	43	7	7	14	34
Nicolas Thibeault	43	4	8	12	27
Craig Copeland	33	4	6	10	41
Jocelyn Charbonneau	54	2	6	8	31
Mario Cormier	35	4	3	7	24
Marquis Gregoire	60	1	5	6	75
Steeve Leblanc	9	1	1	2	9
Pierre Frechette	24	0	2	2	45
Sylvain Rodrigue (goalie)	42	—	—	—	10
Francis Larivee (goalie)	36	—	—	—	62
Michel Lincourt (goalie)	6	—	—	—	0

GOALTENDING

	Games	Min.	W	L	T	Goals	SO	Avg.
Sylvain Rodrigue	42	2205	10	27	0	184	0	5.01
Francis Larivee	36	1706	5	20	1	162	0	5.70
Michel Lincourt	6	215	0	4	0	29	0	8.09

VERDUN COLLEGE-FRANCAIS

SCORING

	Games	G	A	Pts.	PIM
Jocelyn Langlois	72	43	80	123	53
Stefan Simoes	73	36	57	93	84
Francois Leroux	61	40	38	78	100
Joel Bouchard	60	15	55	70	62

	Games	G	A	Pts.	PIM
Daniel Guerard	53	31	34	65	169
Martin Chouinard	64	22	35	57	60
Pierre Gendron	70	15	31	46	113
Christian Laflamme	72	4	34	38	85
Jean-Francois Robert	64	15	20	35	74
Jonathan Delisle	61	16	17	33	130
Shin Larsson	48	5	16	21	12
Michel Vincent	57	10	9	19	36
Bobby Cunningham	54	9	10	19	24
Eddy Gervais	41	2	17	19	49
Samuel Lacroix	61	6	9	15	24
Derek Gosselin	70	2	9	11	132
Pascal Chiasson	48	0	11	11	138
Jason Groleau	67	0	11	11	99
Mathieu Carpentier	27	3	6	9	20
Martin Poitras	46	0	3	3	42
Marc Draiville	18	0	0	0	6
Philippe DeRouville (goalie)	51	—	—	—	0
J. Sebastien Giguere (goalie)	25	—	—	—	27

GOALTENDING

	Games	Min.	W	L	T	Goals	SO	Avg.
Philippe DeRouville	51	2845	28	22	0	145	1	3.06
J. Sebastien Giguere	25	1234	13	5	2	66	0	3.21

VICTORIAVILLE TIGRES

SCORING

	Games	G	A	Pts.	PIM
Jean-Martin Morin	70	40	62	102	67
David Lessard	68	38	37	75	110
Cosmo DuPaul	66	26	46	72	32
Carl Poirier	69	22	29	51	39
Maxime Roux	72	19	28	47	59
Dany Larochelle	67	12	32	44	38
Mario Dumoulin	70	15	28	43	208
Christian Labontc	43	19	21	40	86
Sebastien Vallee	72	17	22	39	22
Philippe Gelineau	70	13	26	39	103
Dominic Fafard	72	6	32	38	70
Eric Alarie	70	8	29	37	43
L.P. Charbonneau	53	5	15	20	367
Philippe Vezina	59	7	10	17	14
Alexandre Laporte	56	3	9	12	68
Dominic Marleau	67	2	10	12	45
Mathieu Raby	67	3	7	10	264
Pierre Morin	38	2	6	8	56
Benoit Larose	65	0	5	5	69
Pascal Levesque	38	2	2	4	4
Patrick Charbonneau	56	—	—	—	26
Bobby Rochon	18	—	—	—	0

GOALTENDING

	Games	Min.	W	L	T	Goals	SO	Avg.
P. Charbonneau	56	2948	11	34	2	261	0	5.31
Bobby Rochon	18	744	4	8	0	70	0	5.65

1994 PRESIDENT CUP PLAYOFFS

RESULTS

QUARTERFINALS

NOTE: QMJHL playoff teams played round-robin tournaments in the early rounds to determine semifinalist teams.

	W	L	Pts.	GF	GA
Laval	4	0	8	19	7
Beauport	0	4	0	7	19

(Laval won series, 4-0)

SEMIFINALS

	W	L	Pts.	GF	GA
Chicoutimi	4	3	8	29	26
Hull	3	4	6	26	29

(Chicoutimi won series, 4-3)

FINALS

	W	L	Pts.	GF	GA
Chicoutimi	4	2	8	21	22
Laval	2	4	4	22	21

(Chicoutimi won series, 4-2)

INDIVIDUAL LEADERS

Goals: Martin Gendron, Hull (21)
Assists: Alexei Lojkin, Chicoutimi (34)
Points: Danny Beauregard, Chicoutimi (43)
      Alexei Lojkin, Chicoutimi (43)
Penalty minutes: Sylvain Blouin, Laval (177)
Goaltending average: Emmanuel Fernandez, Laval (2.63)
Shutouts: Emmanuel Fernandez, Laval (1)
      Eric Fichaud, Chicoutimi (1)
      Marc Legault, Hull (1)

TOP SCORERS

	Games	G	A	Pts.
Danny Beauregard, Chicoutimi	27	16	27	43
Alexei Lojkin, Chicoutimi	27	9	34	43
Hugo Proulx, Hull..............................	20	17	24	41
Marc Beaucage, Laval	21	18	22	40
Martin Gendron, Hull	20	21	17	38
Michel St. Jacques, Chicoutimi	27	20	18	38
Steve Gosselin, Chicoutimi	26	7	24	31
Yanick Dub, Laval	21	12	18	30
Alain Cote, Laval	21	14	15	29
Daniel Goneau, Laval	19	8	21	29

INDIVIDUAL STATISTICS

NOTE: Only goaltenders with 120 or more minutes are listed in playoff statistics.

BEAUPORT HARFANGS

(Lost semifinals to Laval, 4-0)

SCORING

	Games	G	A	Pts.	PIM
Eric Daze....................................	15	16	8	24	2
Joey Deliva	15	7	12	19	10
Patrick Deraspe.........................	15	5	11	16	11
Ian McIntyre	12	3	11	14	27
Jean-Yves Leroux	15	7	6	13	33
Eric Montreuil	15	4	8	12	39
Herve Lapointe	14	4	7	11	16
Eric Moreau	14	1	9	10	16
Patrice Paquin	15	1	7	8	39
Dimitri Goubar	15	3	4	7	2
Marc Chouinard...........................	13	2	5	7	2
Dominic Grand'maison	15	3	3	6	63
Vitali Kozel	11	3	1	4	2
Martin Ethier	15	0	3	3	32
Keith Cassidy	15	0	3	3	10
Stephane Madore	15	0	2	2	27
Patrick Cote	12	1	0	1	61
Jean-Luc Grand-Pierre	1	0	0	0	0
Jean-Francois Tremblay.............	1	0	0	0	0
Mario Cormier	12	0	0	0	6
Claude St. Cyr	15	0	0	0	0
Stephane Menard (goalie)	9	—	—	—	0
Steve Vezina (goalie)	10	—	—	—	0

GOALTENDING

	Games	Min.	W	L	T	Goals	SO	Avg.
Steve Vezina...........	10	430	5	4	0	22	0	3.07
Stephane Menard	9	406	2	3	0	30	0	4.43

CHICOUTIMI SAGUENEENS

(Winner of 1994 President Cup playoffs)

SCORING

	Games	G	A	Pts.	PIM
Danny Beauregard	27	16	27	43	34
Alexei Lojkin	27	9	34	43	15
Michel St. Jacques	27	20	18	38	34
Steve Gosselin	26	7	24	31	24
Yanick Jean...............................	27	8	12	20	82
Christian Caron	27	10	9	19	59
Allan Sirois	27	5	14	19	29
Jerome Boivin	27	8	7	15	32
Steve Dulac	26	8	5	13	25
Dominic Savard	27	5	8	13	11
Alain Nasreddine	26	2	10	12	118
Andre Roy	25	3	6	9	94
Patrick Lacombe	27	2	6	8	112
Pascal Gagnon	27	2	5	7	49
Yann Vaillancourt	27	3	3	6	21
Daniel Laflamme........................	12	0	5	5	35

	Games	G	A	Pts.	PIM
Sebastien Berube	27	0	3	3	77
Patrick Desjardins......................	19	0	0	0	5
Michel Lebouthillier....................	26	0	0	0	2
Eric Fichaud (goalie)	26	—	—	—	8

GOALTENDING

	Games	Min.	W	L	T	Goals	SO	Avg.
Eric Fichaud............	26	1560	16	10	0	86	1	3.31

DRUMMONDVILLE VOLTIGEURS

SCORING

	Games	G	A	Pts.	PIM
Vincent Tremblay	9	6	7	13	8
Eric Plante	10	6	7	13	26
Stephane St. Amour	8	5	8	13	4
Stephane Larocque	10	3	8	11	17
Ian Laperriere	9	4	6	10	35
Martin Latulippe	10	2	6	8	17
Raymond Delarosbil	10	1	7	8	23
Alexandre Duchesne	7	3	0	3	8
Denis Gauthier	9	2	2	2	41
Paolo De Rubertis	8	0	2	2	16
Patrice Charbonneau	10	0	2	2	30
Patrick Livernoche	10	1	0	1	11
Francois Sasseville	10	1	0	1	8
Steve Tardif	10	0	1	1	19
Pascal Gagnon	1	0	0	0	0
Nicolas Savage	2	0	0	0	7
Luc Decelles	4	0	0	0	0
Mathieu Sunderland	5	0	0	0	19
Rock Isabel	8	0	0	0	40
Christian Marcoux	9	0	0	0	14
Sebastien Bety	10	0	0	0	17
Emmanuel Labranche.................	10	0	0	0	23
Yannick Gagnon (goalie)	9	—	—	—	12

GOALTENDING

	Games	Min.	W	L	T	Goals	SO	Avg.
Yannick Gagnon......	9	546	3	6	0	34	0	3.74

GRANBY BISONS

SCORING

	Games	G	A	Pts.	PIM
Christian Matte..........................	7	5	5	10	12
Bruno Gladu	7	5	4	9	5
Dave Boudreault........................	7	2	6	8	30
Dave Douville	7	1	5	6	4
Serge Aubin	7	2	3	5	8
Frederic Bouchard	7	1	3	4	8
Martin Woods	3	1	2	3	17
Hugues Gervais	7	1	2	3	12
Patrick Lamoureux......................	7	0	3	3	18
Xavier Delisle	7	2	0	2	0
Jean Roberge	7	2	0	2	26
Maxime Blouin	5	1	1	2	2

	Games	G	A	Pts.	PIM
Samy Nasreddine	7	0	2	2	4
Eric Bertrand	6	1	0	1	18
L. Philippe Sevigny	6	1	0	1	53
Martin Belanger	7	0	1	1	28
Francois Gagnon	7	0	1	1	18
Yannick Perron	2	0	0	0	17
Frederic Deschenes (goalie)	7	—	—	—	2

GOALTENDING

	Games	Min.	W	L	T	Goals	SO	Avg.
Frederic Deschenes	7	372	3	4	0	27	0	4.35

HULL OLYMPIQUES

(Lost semifinals to Chicoutimi, 4-3)

SCORING

	Games	G	A	Pts.	PIM
Hugo Proulx	20	17	24	41	18
Martin Gendron	20	21	17	38	8
Claude Jutras	18	11	14	25	79
Eric Lecompte	20	10	10	20	68
Sebastien Bordeleau	17	6	14	20	26
Pierre-Francois Lalonde	20	5	13	18	49
Jamie Bird	20	3	8	11	36
Harold Hersh	20	4	4	8	31
Claude Filion	20	3	5	8	86
Shane Doiron	20	1	7	8	33
Michael MacKay	20	1	6	7	12
Carl Charland	19	3	3	6	38
Eric Cloutier	20	1	5	6	126
Jeffrey Viitanen	19	1	4	5	31
Richard Safarik	19	1	3	4	2
Matt Young	20	0	4	4	18
Carl Prud'homme	1	0	0	0	0
Lars Bruggemann	6	0	0	0	0
Roddie MacKenzie	7	0	0	0	4
Stephane Poulin	15	0	0	0	2
Iannique Renaud	18	0	0	0	54
Neil Savary (goalie)	6	—	—	—	0
Marc Legault (goalie)	19	—	—	—	19

GOALTENDING

	Games	Min.	W	L	T	Goals	SO	Avg.
Marc Legault	19	1060	11	7	0	72	1	4.08
Neil Savary	6	158	0	2	0	14	0	5.32

LAVAL TITANS

(Lost finals to Chicoutimi, 4-2)

SCORING

	Games	G	A	Pts.	PIM
Marc Beaucage	21	18	22	40	55
Yanick Dube	21	12	18	30	8
Alain Cote	21	14	15	29	18
Daniel Goneau	19	8	21	29	45
Michael Gaul	21	5	15	20	14
Sylvain Blouin	21	4	13	17	177
Brant Blackned	20	7	9	16	34
Jason Boudrias	21	5	9	14	10
Jeff Mercer	21	7	4	11	68
Frederic Chartier	19	5	6	11	32
Francis Bouillon	19	2	9	11	48
David Haynes	20	2	9	11	56
Patrick Boileau	21	1	7	8	24
Francois Pilon	20	1	5	6	40
J. Francois Brunelle	21	2	3	5	6
Jeff Loder	18	2	1	3	8
Benoit Gratton	20	2	1	3	19
Frederic Jobin	21	2	1	3	40
Jason Bermingham	5	0	0	0	4
Dany Dupont	8	0	0	0	9
Martin Villeneuve (goalie)	3	—	—	—	0
Emmanuel Fernandez (goalie)	19	—	—	—	22

GOALTENDING

	Games	Min.	W	L	T	Goals	SO	Avg.
E. Fernandez	19	1116	14	5	0	49	1	2.63
Martin Villeneuve	3	150	0	2	0	10	0	4.00

ST. HYACINTHE LASERS

SCORING

	Games	G	A	Pts.	PIM
Normand Paquet	7	6	3	9	4
David Beauregard	7	4	5	9	4
Eric Gauvin	6	1	7	8	31
Jimmy Drolet	7	1	7	8	10
David Desnoyers	7	2	5	7	40
Eric Landry	7	4	2	6	13
Nicolas Maheux	6	2	3	5	15
Remy Boudreau	7	1	4	5	2
Jean-Francois Tremblay	5	2	2	4	19
Sylvain Ducharme	6	2	2	4	19
Hugo Bertrand	7	2	1	3	54
Yannick Hubert	7	0	3	3	6
Martin Trudel	6	2	0	2	4
Patrick Lampron	5	1	1	2	30
Yannick Turcotte	7	1	1	2	4
Hugo Veilleux	6	0	1	1	6
Gabriel Cote	7	0	1	1	10
Richard Lacasse	3	0	0	0	14
Yannick Plante	4	0	0	0	2
Marc Sigouin	7	0	0	0	9
Frederick Beaubien (goalie)	7	—	—	—	2

GOALTENDING

	Games	Min.	W	L	T	Goals	SO	Avg.
Frederick Beaubien	7	411	3	4	0	33	0	4.82

ST. JEAN LYNX

SCORING

	Games	G	A	Pts.	PIM
Bruno Lajeunesse	5	2	2	4	6
Patrick Traverse	5	0	4	4	4
Martin Rozon	5	2	1	3	2
Steve Brule	5	2	1	3	0
Samuel Groleau	5	2	0	2	4
Jimmy Provencher	5	1	1	2	6
Eric Houde	5	1	1	2	4
Denis Beauchamp	5	1	1	2	15
Jason Doig	5	0	2	2	2
Alex Richard	5	1	0	1	2
Dereck Michaud	3	0	1	1	0
Brian Casey	5	0	1	1	2
Jan Melichercik	5	0	1	1	0
Joel Theriault	5	0	1	1	0
Rocco Anoia	1	0	0	0	2
Nathan Morin	2	0	0	0	20
Georges Laraque	4	0	0	0	7
Rony Valenti	5	0	0	0	2
Frederic Barbeau	5	0	0	0	2
Francois Archambault	5	0	0	0	2
Jose Theodore (goalie)	5	—	—	—	2

GOALTENDING

	Games	Min.	W	L	T	Goals	SO	Avg.
Jose Theodore	5	296	1	4	0	18	0	3.65

SHAWINIGAN CATARACTES

SCORING

	Games	G	A	Pts.	PIM
Patrick Carignan	5	4	8	12	2
Dave Tremblay	5	5	5	10	2
Alain Savage	5	2	5	7	8
Robin Bouchard	5	3	3	6	20
Jean-Francois Laroche	5	2	3	5	2
Simon Roy	5	1	4	5	6
David Brosseau	5	3	0	3	2

MAJOR JUNIOR LEAGUES

	Games	G	A	Pts.	PIM
Yanick Evola	5	1	2	3	6
Carl Paradis	4	0	3	3	4
David Grenier	5	1	1	2	8
Guy Loranger	5	1	0	1	0
Jean-Francois Bessette	5	0	1	1	13
Martin Lepage	5	0	1	1	21
Sylvain Brisson	5	0	1	1	0
Benoit Larose	5	0	1	1	21
Stephane Robidas	1	0	0	0	0
Evan Levi	1	0	0	0	0
Steeve Finn	3	0	0	0	2
Eric Ladouceur	5	0	0	0	0
Sergei Polichouk	5	0	0	0	10
Patrick Lalime (goalie)	5	—	—	—	0

GOALTENDING

	Games	Min.	W	L	T	Goals	SO	Avg.
Patrick Lalime	5	223	1	3	0	25	0	6.73

SHERBROOKE FAUCONS

SCORING

	Games	G	A	Pts.	PIM
Carl Fleury	12	9	10	19	11
Mathieu Dandenault	12	4	10	14	12
Hugo Turcotte	9	3	8	11	4
Etienne Beaudry	12	5	5	10	4
Stephane Julien	12	2	7	9	6
Pascal Trepanier	12	1	8	9	14
Eric Messier	12	1	7	8	14
J. Francois Boutin	12	4	3	7	6
Dave Belliveau	12	3	4	7	0
Christian Dube	11	3	2	5	8
Yan St. Pierre	12	3	2	5	11
Pascal Bernier	12	2	2	4	11
Martin Lamarche	10	2	1	3	44
Louis Bernard	12	1	2	3	10
Francois Rivard	10	0	3	3	10
Steven Low	11	1	1	2	16
Charles Paquette	8	0	2	2	15
Mirko Langlois	2	0	0	0	0
Daniel Villeneuve	4	0	0	0	0
Lachlan Coombe	5	0	0	0	4
Hugo Hamelin (goalie)	3	—	—	—	0
Luc Belanger (goalie)	10	—	—	—	0

GOALTENDING

	Games	Min.	W	L	T	Goals	SO	Avg.
Luc Belanger	10	557	5	4	0	26	0	2.80
Hugo Hamelin	3	160	2	1	0	11	0	4.13

VERDUN COLLEGE-FRANCAIS

SCORING

	Games	G	A	Pts.	PIM
Daniel Guerard	4	3	1	4	4

	Games	G	A	Pts.	PIM
Jocelyn Langlois	4	1	2	3	13
Christian Laflamme	4	0	3	3	4
Martin Chouinard	3	1	1	2	2
Eddy Gervais	4	0	2	2	2
Joel Bouchard	4	1	0	1	6
Stefan Simoes	4	1	0	1	6
Francois Leroux	4	0	1	1	8
Jonathan Delisle	4	0	1	1	14
Pierre Gendron	4	0	1	1	12
Jean-Francois Robert	4	0	1	1	11
Derek Gosselin	4	0	1	1	10
Marc Draiville	1	0	0	0	17
Martin Poitras	2	0	0	0	0
Bobby Cunningham	3	0	0	0	0
Michel Vincent	3	0	0	0	0
Jason Groleau	4	0	0	0	9
Samuel Lacroix	4	0	0	0	5
Pascal Chiasson	4	0	0	0	22
Mathieu Carpentier	4	0	0	0	4
Philippe DeRouville (goalie)	4	—	—	—	0

GOALTENDING

	Games	Min.	W	L	T	Goals	SO	Avg.
Philippe DeRouville	4	210	0	4	0	14	0	4.00

VICTORIAVILLE TIGRES

SCORING

	Games	G	A	Pts.	PIM
Jean-Martin Morin	5	4	1	5	0
Cosmo DuPaul	5	2	2	4	6
Mario Dumoulin	5	0	3	3	13
L.P. Charbonneau	5	2	0	2	41
David Lessard	5	1	1	2	15
Eric Alarie	5	1	1	2	15
Philippe Gelineau	5	0	2	2	8
Carl Poirier	5	1	0	1	5
Alexandre Laporte	5	1	0	1	2
Maxime Roux	3	0	1	1	27
Pascal Levesque	4	0	1	1	0
Dominic Marleau	5	0	1	1	4
Philippe Vezina	5	0	1	1	8
Dominic Fafard	5	0	1	1	6
Dany Larochelle	5	0	1	1	4
Sebastien Vallee	1	0	0	0	0
Benoit Larose	5	0	0	0	2
Pierre Morin	5	0	0	0	11
Mathieu Raby	5	0	0	0	22
Patrick Charbonneau (goalie)	5	—	—	—	2

GOALTENDING

	Games	Min.	W	L	T	Goals	SO	Avg.
Patrick Charbonneau	5	212	1	4	0	24	0	6.79

1993-94 AWARD WINNERS

ALL-STAR TEAMS

First team	Pos.	Second team
Emmanuel Fernandez, Laval	G	Philippe DeRouville, Verdun
Joel Bouchard, Verdun	D	Stephane Julien, Sherbrooke
Steve Gosselin	D	Eric Messier, Sherbrooke
Michel St. Jacques, Chi.	LW	Francois Leroux, Verdun
Yanick Dube, Laval	C	Danny Beauregard, Chi.
Eric Daze, Beauport	RW	Christian Matte, Granby

Coach of the Year: Michel Therrien, Laval

TROPHY WINNERS

Frank Selke Trophy: Yanick Dube, Laval
Michel Bergeron Trophy: Christian Dube, Sherbrooke
Raymond Lagace Trophy: Jimmy Drolet, St. Hyacinthe
Jean Beliveau Trophy: Yanick Dube, Laval
Michel Briere Trophy: Emmanuel Fernandez, Laval
Marcel Robert Trophy: Patrick Boileau, Laval
Mike Bossy Trophy: Eric Fichaud, Chicoutimi
Emile "Butch" Bouchard Trophy: Steve Gosselin, Chicoutimi
Jacques Plante Trophy: Philippe DeRouville, Verdun
Guy Lafleur Trophy: Eric Fichaud, Chicoutimi
Robert LeBel Trophy: College Francais de Verdun
John Rougeau Trophy: Laval Titans
President Cup: Chicoutimi Sagueneens

FRANK SELKE TROPHY

(Most gentlemanly player)

Season	Player, Team
1970-71	Norm Dube, Sherbrooke
1971-72	Gerry Teeple, Cornwall
1972-73	Claude Larose, Drummondville
1973-74	Gary MacGregor, Cornwall
1974-75	Jean-Luc Phaneuf, Montreal
1975-76	Norm Dupont, Montreal
1976-77	Mike Bossy, Laval
1977-78	Kevin Reeves, Montreal
1978-79	Ray Bourque, Verdun
	Jean-Francois Sauve, Trois-Rivieres
1979-80	Jean-Francois Sauve, Trois-Rivieres
1980-81	Claude Verret, Trois-Rivieres
1981-82	Claude Verret, Trois-Rivieres
1982-83	Pat LaFontaine, Verdun
1983-84	Jerome Carrier, Verdun
1984-85	Patrick Emond, Chicoutimi
1985-86	Jimmy Carson, Verdun
1986-87	Luc Beausoleil, Laval
1987-88	Stephan Lebeau, Shawinigan
1988-89	Steve Cadieux, Shawinigan
1989-90	Andrew McKim, Hull
1990-91	Yanic Perreault, Trois-Rivieres
1991-92	Martin Gendron, St. Hyacinthe
1992-93	Martin Gendron, St. Hyacinthe
1993-94	Yanick Dube, Laval

MICHEL BERGERON TROPHY

(Top rookie forward)

Season	Player, Team
1969-70	Serge Martel, Verdun
1970-71	Bob Murphy, Cornwall
1971-72	Bob Murray, Cornwall
1972-73	Pierre Larouche, Sorel
1973-74	Mike Bossy, Laval
1974-75	Dennis Pomerleau, Hull
1975-76	Jean-Marc Bonamie, Shawinigan
1976-77	Rick Vaive, Sherbrooke
1977-78	Norm Rochefort, Trois-Rivieres
	Denis Savard, Montreal
1978-79	Alan Grenier, Laval
1979-80	Dale Hawerchuk, Cornwall
1980-81	Claude Verret, Trois-Rivieres
1981-82	Sylvain Turgeon, Hull
1982-83	Pat LaFontaine, Verdun
1983-84	Stephane Richer, Granby
1984-85	Jimmy Carson, Verdun
1985-86	Pierre Turgeon, Granby
1986-87	Rob Murphy, Laval
1987-88	Martin Gelinas, Hull
1988-89	Yanic Perreault, Trois-Rivieres
1989-90	Martin Lapointe, Laval
1990-91	Rene Corbet, Drummondville
1991-92	Alexandre Daigle, Victoriaville
1992-93	Steve Brule, St. Jean
1993-94	Christian Dube, Sherbrooke

Prior to 1980-81 season, award was given to QMJHL rookie of the year.

RAYMOND LAGACE TROPHY

(Top rookie defenseman or goaltender)

Season	Player, Team
1980-81	Billy Campbell, Montreal
1981-82	Michel Petit, Sherbrooke
1982-83	Bobby Dollas, Laval
1983-84	James Gasseau, Drummondville
1984-85	Robert Desjardins, Shawinigan

Season	Player, Team
1985-86	Stephane Guerard, Shawinigan
1986-87	Jimmy Waite, Chicoutimi
1987-88	Stephane Beauregard, St. Jean
1988-89	Karl Dykhuis, Hull
1989-90	Francois Groleau, Shawinigan
1990-91	Philippe Boucher, Granby
1991-92	Philippe DeRouville, Longueuil
1992-93	Stephane Routhier, Drummondville
1993-94	Jimmy Drolet, St. Hyacinthe

JEAN BELIVEAU TROPHY

(Scoring leader)

Season	Player, Team
1969-70	Luc Simard, Trois-Rivieres
1970-71	Guy Lafleur, Quebec
1971-72	Jacques Richard, Quebec
1972-73	Andre Savard, Quebec
1973-74	Pierre Larouche, Sorel
1974-75	Norm Dupont, Montreal
1975-76	Richard Dalpe, Trois-Rivieres
	Sylvain Locas, Chicoutimi
1976-77	Jean Savard, Quebec
1977-78	Ron Carter, Sherbrooke
1978-79	Jean-Francois Sauve, Trois-Rivieres
1979-80	Jean-Francois Sauve, Trois-Rivieres
1980-81	Dale Hawerchuk, Cornwall
1981-82	Claude Verret, Trois-Rivieres
1982-83	Pat LaFontaine, Verdun
1983-84	Mario Lemieux, Laval
1984-85	Guy Rouleau, Longueuil
1985-86	Guy Rouleau, Hull
1986-87	Marc Fortier, Chicoutimi
1987-88	Patrice Lefebvre, Shawinigan
1988-89	Stephane Morin, Chicoutimi
1989-90	Patrick Lebeau, Victoriaville
1990-91	Yanic Perreault, Trois-Rivieres
1991-92	Patrick Poulin, St. Hyacinthe
1992-93	Rene Corbet, Drummondville
1993-94	Yanick Dube, Laval

MICHEL BRIERE TROPHY

(Most Valuable Player)

Season	Player, Team
1972-73	Andre Savard, Quebec
1973-74	Gary MacGregor, Cornwall
1974-75	Mario Viens, Cornwall
1975-76	Peter Marsh, Sherbrooke
1976-77	Lucien DeBlois, Sorel
1977-78	Kevin Reeves, Montreal
1978-79	Pierre Lacroix, Trois-Rivieres
1979-80	Denis Savard, Montreal
1980-81	Dale Hawerchuk, Cornwall
1981-82	John Chabot, Sherbrooke
1982-83	Pat LaFontaine, Verdun
1983-84	Mario Lemieux, Laval
1984-85	Daniel Berthiaune, Chicoutimi
1985-86	Guy Rouleau, Hull
1986-87	Robert Desjardins, Longueuil
1987-88	Marc Saumier, Hull
1988-89	Stephane Morin, Chicoutimi
1989-90	Andrew McKim, Hull
1990-91	Yanic Perreault, Trois-Rivieres
1991-92	Charles Poulin, St. Hyacinthe
1992-93	Jocelyn Thibault, Sherbrooke
1993-94	Emmanuel Fernandez, Laval

MARCEL ROBERT TROPHY

(Top scholastic/athletic performer)

Season	Player, Team
1981-82	Jacques Sylvestre, Granby
1982-83	Claude Gosselin, Quebec
1983-84	Gilbert Paiement, Chicoutimi
1984-85	Claude Gosselin, Longueuil
1985-86	Bernard Morin, Laval
1986-87	Patrice Tremblay, Chicoutimi
1987-88	Stephane Beauregard, St. Jean
1988-89	Daniel Lacroix, Granby
1989-90	Yanic Perreault, Trois-Rivieres
1990-91	Benoit Larose, Laval
1991-92	Simon Toupin, Beauport
1992-93	Jocelyn Thibault, Sherbrooke
1993-94	Patrick Boileau, Laval

MIKE BOSSY TROPHY

(Top pro prospect)

Season	Player, Team
1980-81	Dale Hawerchuk, Cornwall
1981-82	Michel Petit, Sherbrooke
1982-83	Pat LaFontaine, Verdun
	Sylvain Turgeon, Hull
1983-84	Mario Lemieux, Laval
1984-85	Jose Charbonneau, Drummondville
1985-86	Jimmy Carson, Verdun
1986-87	Pierre Turgeon, Granby
1987-88	Daniel Dore, Drummondville
1988-89	Patrice Brisebois, Laval
1989-90	Karl Dykhuis, Hull
1990-91	Philippe Boucher, Granby
1991-92	Paul Brousseau, Hull
1992-93	Alexandre Daigle, Victoriaville
1993-94	Eric Fichaud, Chicoutimi

Originally known as Association of Journalism of Hockey Trophy from 1980-81 through 1982-83.

EMILE "BUTCH" BOUCHARD TROPHY

(Top defenseman)

Season	Player, Team
1975-76	Jean Gagnon, Quebec
1976-77	Robert Picard, Montreal
1977-78	Mark Hardy, Montreal
1978-79	Ray Bourque, Verdun
1979-80	Gaston Therrien, Quebec
1980-81	Fred Boimistruck, Cornwall
1981-82	Paul Andre Boutilier, Sherbrooke
1982-83	J.J. Daigneault, Longueuil
1983-84	Billy Campbell, Verdun
1984-85	Yves Beaudoin, Shawinigan
1985-86	Sylvain Cote, Hull
1986-87	Jean Marc Richard, Chicoutimi
1987-88	Eric Desjardins, Granby
1988-89	Yves Racine, Victoriaville
1989-90	Claude Barthe, Victoriaville
1990-91	Patrice Brisebois, Drummondville
1991-92	Francois Groleau, Shawinigan
1992-93	Benoit Larose, Laval
1993-94	Steve Gosselin, Chicoutimi

JACQUES PLANTE TROPHY

(Top goaltender)

Season	Player, Team
1969-70	Michael Deguise, Sorel

Season	Player, Team
1970-71	Reynald Fortier, Quebec
1971-72	Richard Brodeur, Cornwall
1972-73	Pierre Perusee, Quebec
1973-74	Claude Legris, Sorel
1974-75	Nick Sanza, Sherbrooke
1975-76	Tim Bernhardt, Cornwall
1976-77	Tim Bernhardt, Cornwall
1977-78	Tim Bernhardt, Cornwall
1978-79	Jacques Cloutier, Trois-Rivieres
1979-80	Corrado Micalef, Sherbrooke
1980-81	Michel Dufour, Sorel
1981-82	Jeff Barratt, Montreal
1982-83	Tony Haladuick, Laval
1983-84	Tony Haladuick, Laval
1984-85	Daniel Berthiaume, Chicoutimi
1985-86	Robert Desjardins, Hull
1986-87	Robert Desjardins, Longueuil
1987-88	Stephane Beauregard, St. Jean
1988-89	Stephane Fiset, Victoriaville
1989-90	Pierre Gagnon, Victoriaville
1990-91	Felix Potvin, Chicoutimi
1991-92	Jean-Francois Labbe, Trois-Rivieres
1992-93	Jocelyn Thibault, Sherbrooke
1993-94	Philippe DeRouville, Verdun

GUY LAFLEUR TROPHY

(Playoff MVP)

Season	Player, Team
1977-78	Richard David, Trois-Rivieres
1978-79	Jean-Francois Sauve, Trois-Rivieres
1979-80	Dale Hawerchuk, Cornwall
1980-81	Alain Lemieux, Trois-Rivieres
1981-82	Michel Morissette, Sherbrooke
1982-83	Pat LaFontaine, Verdun
1983-84	Mario Lemieux, Laval
1984-85	Claude Lemieux, Verdun
1985-86	Sylvain Cote, Hull
	Luc Robitaille, Hull
1986-87	Marc Saumier, Longueuil
1987-88	Marc Saumier, Hull
1988-89	Donald Audette, Laval
1989-90	Denis Chalifoux, Laval
1990-91	Felix Potvin, Chicoutimi
1991-92	Robert Guillet, Longueuil
1992-93	Emmanuel Fernandez, Laval
1993-94	Eric Fichaud, Chicoutimi

ROBERT LeBEL TROPHY

(Best team defensive average)

Season	Team
1977-78	Trois-Rivieres Draveurs
1978-79	Trois-Rivieres Draveurs
1979-80	Sherbrooke Beavers
1980-81	Sorel Black Hawks
1981-82	Montreal Juniors
1982-83	Shawinigan Cataracts
1983-84	Shawinigan Cataracts
1984-85	Shawinigan Cataracts
1985-86	Hull Olympiques
1986-78	Longueuil Chevaliers
1987-88	St. Jean Castors
1988-89	Hull Olympiques
1989-90	Victoriaville Tigres
1990-91	Chicoutimi Sagueneens
1991-92	Trois-Rivieres Draveurs
1992-93	Sherbrooke Faucons
1993-94	College Francais de Verdun

REGULAR-SEASON CHAMPION   PLAYOFF CHAMPION

Season	Team	Team
1969-70	Quebec Remparts	Quebec Remparts
1970-71	Quebec Remparts	Quebec Remparts
1971-72	Cornwall Royals	Cornwall Royals
1972-73	Quebec Remparts	Quebec Remparts
1973-74	Sorel Black Hawks	Quebec Remparts
1974-75	Sherbrooke Beavers	Sherbrooke Beavers
1975-76	Sherbrooke Beavers	Quebec Remparts
1976-77	Quebec Remparts	Sherbrooke Beavers
1977-78	Trois-Rivieres Draveurs	Trois-Rivieres Draveurs
1978-79	Trois-Rivieres Draveurs	Trois-Rivieres Draveurs
1979-80	Sherbrooke Beavers	Cornwall Royals
1980-81	Cornwall Royals	Cornwall Royals
1981-82	Sherbrooke Beavers	Sherbrooke Beavers
1982-83	Laval Voisins	Verdun Juniors
1983-84	Laval Voisins	Laval Voisins
1984-85	Shawinigan Cataracts	Verdun Junior Canadiens
1985-86	Hull Olympiques	Hull Olympiques
1986-87	Granby Bisons	Longueuil Chevaliers
1987-88	Hull Olympiques	Hull Olympiques
1988-89	Trois-Rivieres Draveurs	Laval Titans
1989-90	Victoriaville Tigres	Laval Titans
1990-91	Chicoutimi Sagueneens	Chicoutimi Sagueneens
1991-92	Longueuil College Francais	Longueuil College Francais
1992-93	Sherbrooke Faucons	Laval Titans
1993-94	Laval Titans	Chicoutimi Sagueneens

The QMJHL regular-season champion is awarded the John Rougeau Trophy and the playoff champion is awarded the Presidents Cup.

The John Rougeau Trophy was originally called the Governors Trophy from 1969-70 through 1982-83.

WESTERN HOCKEY LEAGUE

LEAGUE OFFICE

Note: League was known as Canadian Major Junior Hockey League in 1966-67 and Western Canadian Hockey League from 1967-68 through 1976-77.

Address
Suite 521, 10333 Southport Road SW
Calgary, Alberta T2W 3X6
Phone
403-253-8113

President
Ed Chynoweth
Vice president
Richard Doerksen

Executive assistant
Norman Dueck
Statistician
Stu Judge

1993-94 REGULAR SEASON

FINAL STANDINGS

EAST DIVISION

Team	G	W	L	T	Pts.	GF	GA
Saskatoon	72	49	22	1	99	326	229
Brandon	72	42	25	5	89	291	251
Lethbridge	72	35	32	5	75	306	317
Swift Current	72	35	33	4	74	284	258
Medicine Hat	72	33	33	6	72	263	264
Red Deer	72	35	36	1	71	310	304
Regina	72	34	36	2	70	308	341
Prince Albert	72	31	37	4	66	326	321
Moose Jaw	72	21	48	3	45	269	361

WEST DIVISION

Team	G	W	L	T	Pts.	GF	GA
Kamloops	72	50	16	6	106	381	225
Portland	72	49	22	1	99	392	260
Tacoma	72	33	34	5	71	303	301
Seattle	72	32	37	3	67	283	312
Spokane	72	31	37	4	66	324	320
Tri-City	72	19	48	5	43	272	373
Victoria	72	18	51	3	39	222	393

INDIVIDUAL LEADERS

Goals: Lonny Bohonos, Portland (62)
Assists: Lonny Bohonos, Portland (90)
Points: Lonny Bohonos, Portland (152)
Penalty minutes: David Jesiolowski, Spo.-Leth. (373)
Goaltending average: Steve Passmore, Kamloops (2.74)
Shutouts: Ian Gordon, Swift Current (6)

	Games	G	A	Pts.
Stacy Roest, Medicine Hat	72	48	72	120
Craig Reichert, Red Deer	72	52	67	119
Jeff Friesen, Regina	66	51	67	118
Maxim Bets, Spokane	63	46	70	116
Marty Murray, Brandon	64	43	71	114
Van Burgess, Prince Albert	69	44	67	111
Rod Stevens, Kamloops	62	51	58	109
Colin Foley, Portland	72	42	65	107
Ryan Smyth, Moose Jaw	72	50	55	105
Jarrett Deuling, Kamloops	70	44	59	103
Valeri Bure, Spokane	59	40	62	102
Karry Biette, Regina	71	40	61	101
Adam Deadmarsh, Portland	65	43	56	99
Denis Pederson, Prince Albert	71	53	45	98

TOP SCORERS

	Games	G	A	Pts.
Lonny Bohonos, Portland	70	62	90	152
Darcy Tucker, Kamloops	66	52	88	140
Domenic Pittis, Lethbridge	72	58	69	127
Ryan Duthie, Spokane	71	57	69	126
Allan Egeland, Tacoma	70	47	76	123
John Varga, Tacoma	65	60	62	122

INDIVIDUAL STATISTICS

BRANDON WHEAT KINGS

SCORING

	Games	G	A	Pts.	PIM
Marty Murray	64	43	71	114	33
Mike Maneluk	63	50	47	97	112
Darren Ritchie	54	45	40	85	19
Chris Johnston	68	27	51	78	149
Mark Kilesar	59	29	37	66	131
Chris Dingman	45	21	20	41	77
Wade Redden	64	4	35	39	98
Bobby Brown	71	18	19	37	138
Colin Cloutier	30	10	13	23	102
Mike Dubinsky	20	9	13	22	23
Sven Butenschon	70	3	19	22	51
Chris Low	69	8	12	20	23
Scott Laluk	68	2	18	20	48
Justin Kurtz	63	3	13	16	37
Mark Dutiaume	55	4	7	11	43
Dean Kletzel	44	4	6	10	59
Dwayne Gylwoychuk	55	1	8	9	93

	Games	G	A	Pts.	PIM
Jeff Staples	37	0	7	7	126
Jeff Hoad	5	2	3	5	0
Sean McFatridge	7	2	3	5	17
Paul Bailley	60	0	5	5	16
Adam Magarrell	40	2	1	3	69
Pete Mehallic	5	1	2	3	13
Scott Hlady	3	1	1	2	4
Joel Korenko	40	0	2	2	87
Byron Penstock (goalie)	58	0	2	2	10
Peter Schaefer	2	1	0	1	0
Chad Knippel	10	1	0	1	28
Jeff Temple	3	0	1	1	2
Ladislav Kohn	2	0	0	0	0
Kelly Smart	2	0	0	0	0
Darren Vanoene	2	0	0	0	7
Craig Hordal (goalie)	17	0	0	0	2

GOALTENDING

	Games	Min.	W	L	T	Goals	SO	Avg.
Byron Penstock	58	3447	35	18	4	182	2	3.17
Craig Hordal	17	927	7	7	1	63	0	4.08

KAMLOOPS BLAZERS

SCORING

	Games	G	A	Pts.	PIM
Darcy Tucker	66	52	88	140	143
Rod Stevens	62	51	58	109	31
Jarrett Deuling	70	44	59	103	171
Hnat Domenichelli	69	27	40	67	31
Tyson Nash	65	20	36	56	135
Nolan Baumgartner	69	13	42	55	109
Ryan Huska	69	23	31	54	66
Scott Ferguson	68	5	49	54	180
Shane Doan	52	24	24	48	88
Aaron Keller	58	6	38	44	8
Louis Dumont	34	18	20	38	33
Chris Murray	59	14	16	30	260
Jason Holland	59	14	15	29	80
David Wilkie	27	11	18	29	18
Jarome Iginla	48	6	23	29	33
Bob Maudie	65	11	13	24	29
Mike Josephson	48	11	12	23	114
Scott Loucks	23	5	13	18	48
Brad Lukowich	42	5	11	16	166
Bob Westerby	50	6	9	15	218
Jason Strudwick	61	6	8	14	118
Mike Krooshoop	60	3	9	12	207
Greg Hart	48	5	4	9	16
Steve Passmore (goalie)	36	0	4	4	26
Rod Branch (goalie)	44	0	2	2	18
Jarrett Bousquet	2	1	0	1	18
Dion Hagan	1	0	0	0	0
Shawn McNeil	1	0	0	0	0
Craig Swanson	1	0	0	0	0
Jason Becker	2	0	0	0	0
Cam Severson	2	0	0	0	0
Sean Matile (goalie)	3	0	0	0	0

GOALTENDING

	Games	Min.	W	L	T	Goals	SO	Avg.
Steve Passmore	36	1927	22	9	2	88	1	2.74
Rod Branch	44	2311	28	6	2	125	2	3.25
Sean Matile	3	161	0	1	2	9	0	3.35

LETHBRIDGE HURRICANES

SCORING

	Games	G	A	Pts.	PIM
Domenic Pittis	72	58	69	127	93
Shane Peacock	70	27	65	92	92
Mark Szoke	72	42	48	90	151
Ivan Vologjaninov	65	37	53	90	28
Todd Maclsaac	61	20	30	50	113
Jason Widmer	64	11	31	42	191
Aaron Zarowny	72	21	19	40	50
Scott Townsend	32	18	18	36	10
Ryan Smith	63	5	31	36	131
Lee Sorochan	46	5	27	32	123
Brantt Myhres	34	10	21	31	103
Brad Mehalko	62	9	9	18	48
Bryce Salvador	61	4	14	18	36
Byron Ritchie	44	4	11	15	44
Scott Grieco	54	8	5	13	45
Maurice Meagher	39	5	8	13	101
Derek Wood	59	4	8	12	108
Chad Gans	21	2	7	9	16
Derek Deiner	62	1	8	9	64
David Jesiolowski	29	3	5	8	146
Brad Zimmer	10	2	6	8	6
Jesse Wilson	6	3	4	7	6
Jay Bertsch	36	1	6	7	61
Kirk DeWaele	53	0	7	7	35
Randy Perry	59	3	3	6	19
Stan Matwijiw (goalie)	39	0	3	3	12
Larry McMorran	23	2	0	2	4
Jeff Jubenville	5	1	1	2	7
Slade Stephenson	8	0	2	2	17

	Games	G	A	Pts.	PIM
David Trofimenkoff (goalie)	42	0	2	2	6
Cadrin Smart	5	0	1	1	6
Travis Brigley	1	0	0	0	0
Jamie Liedl	1	0	0	0	0
Shawn Stickel (goalie)	1	0	0	0	0
Cam Morris (goalie)	2	0	0	0	0

GOALTENDING

	Games	Min.	W	L	T	Goals	SO	Avg.
Stan Matwijiw	39	2090	16	14	4	135	1	3.88
David Trofimenkoff	42	2176	18	18	1	169	1	4.66
Cam Morris	2	51	0	0	0	5	0	5.88
Shawn Stickel	1	60	1	0	0	6	0	6.00

MEDICINE HAT TIGERS

SCORING

	Games	G	A	Pts.	PIM
Stacy Roest	72	48	72	120	48
Lorne Toews	72	41	30	71	185
Ryan Petz	70	34	25	59	39
Mark Polak	70	20	26	46	48
Josh Green	63	22	22	44	43
Sergei Klimentiev	72	16	26	42	165
Henry Kuster	67	14	27	41	26
Steve Cheredaryk	72	3	35	38	151
Brad Wilson	71	13	23	36	80
Justin Hocking	68	7	26	33	236
Marc Hussey	41	6	24	30	90
Aaron Boh	28	4	15	19	99
Cal Benazic	64	2	15	17	157
Jeremy Thompson	61	8	8	16	243
Shawn Stone	41	4	9	13	24
Jeremy Schaefer	65	4	9	13	155
Kyuin Shim	14	6	4	10	2
Tim Keith	42	3	5	8	22
Robert Longpre	50	2	5	7	27
Dwayne Ripley	43	1	4	5	14
Rocky Thompson	68	1	4	5	166
Rob Sekura	51	2	1	3	45
Sonny Mignacca (goalie)	60	0	3	3	20
Trevor Wasyluk	1	1	1	2	0
Stacey Fritz	8	1	1	2	0
Lee Hamilton	5	0	1	1	2
Jay Fitzpatrick	6	0	1	1	11
Paxton Schafer (goalie)	19	0	1	1	0
Greg Cowie	1	0	0	0	0
Mark McCoy	1	0	0	0	0
Donovan Nunweiler (goalie)	1	0	0	0	0
Scott Bellefontaine (goalie)	2	0	0	0	0
Calvin Crowe	2	0	0	0	21
Kevin Kuntz	2	0	0	0	0
Jeremy Gizen	3	0	0	0	0

GOALTENDING

	Games	Min.	W	L	T	Goals	SO	Avg.
Donovan Nunweiler	1	27	0	0	0	1	0	2.22
Sonny Mignacca	60	3361	26	23	5	183	2	3.27
Paxton Schafer	19	909	6	9	1	67	0	4.42
Scott Bellefontaine	2	102	1	1	0	8	0	4.71

MOOSE JAW WARRIORS

SCORING

	Games	G	A	Pts.	PIM
Ryan Smyth	72	50	55	105	88
Jeff Hoad	55	36	41	77	100
Chris Armstrong	64	13	55	68	54
Curtis Brown	72	27	38	65	82
Todd Dutiaume	66	22	33	55	65
Rob Trumbley	61	15	24	39	342
Lance Burns	63	15	21	36	115
Grady Manson	49	13	19	32	76
Kevin Pozzo	40	7	20	27	71
Neil Johnston	30	13	13	26	65

MAJOR JUNIOR LEAGUES

	Games	G	A	Pts.	PIM
Chris Brandt	71	5	18	23	62
Jeff Dewar	37	9	11	20	46
Brad Toporowski	70	3	17	20	116
Scott Ducharmie	61	12	7	19	96
Matt Higgins	64	6	10	16	10
Chad Reich	59	7	8	15	102
Bob Graham	66	3	12	15	64
Dion Darling	23	4	6	10	96
Milt Mastad	41	2	8	10	74
Marc Hussey	17	4	5	9	33
Derek Shuel	56	1	3	4	110
Ryan Van Steinburg	14	1	2	3	67
Steve O'Rourke	12	0	3	3	11
Travis Stevenson	25	0	3	3	52
Jarrod Daniel (goalie)	21	0	2	2	10
Rob Wilson	48	0	2	2	71
Darren Stevenson	30	1	0	1	45
Russ West	6	0	1	1	0
Jody Lehman (goalie)	49	0	1	1	23
Rod Gorrill	2	0	0	0	0
Derek Ernest	5	0	0	0	0
Kevin McKay	6	0	0	0	2
Tyler Love (goalie)	12	0	0	0	4

GOALTENDING

	Games	Min.	W	L	T	Goals	SO	Avg.
Jarrod Daniel	21	1104	8	10	0	75	0	4.08
Jody Lehman	49	2663	11	31	3	215	0	4.84
Tyler Love	12	602	2	7	0	62	0	6.18

PORTLAND WINTER HAWKS

SCORING

	Games	G	A	Pts.	PIM
Lonny Bohonos	70	62	90	152	80
Colin Foley	72	42	65	107	67
Adam Deadmarsh	65	43	56	99	212
Layne Roland	72	50	46	96	89
Jason Wiemer	72	45	51	96	236
Scott Nichol	65	40	53	93	144
Brandon Smith	72	19	63	82	47
Jason McBain	63	15	51	66	86
Nolan Pratt	72	4	32	36	105
Shannon Briske	67	16	15	31	81
Dave Cammock	52	12	18	30	171
Dmitri Markovsky	57	9	17	26	22
Brad Symes	71	7	15	22	170
Shawn Collins	33	2	19	21	51
Mike Williamson	68	2	19	21	157
Dave Scatchard	47	9	11	20	46
Brad Isbister	64	7	10	17	45
Matt Davidson	59	4	12	16	18
Brad Swanson	33	1	4	5	20
Brett Fizzell	46	0	5	5	111
Mike Little	35	3	1	4	10
Jake Deadmarsh	12	0	1	1	11
Mike Arbulic	23	0	1	1	35
Scott Langkow (goalie)	39	0	1	1	13
David Pirnak (goalie)	2	0	0	0	0
Ryan Bast	6	0	0	0	4
Jarrod Daniel (goalie)	8	0	0	0	0
Scott Rideout (goalie)	26	0	0	0	6

GOALTENDING

	Games	Min.	W	L	T	Goals	SO	Avg.
Jarrod Daniel	8	488	6	2	0	24	1	2.95
Scott Langkow	39	2302	27	9	1	121	2	3.15
Scott Rideout	26	1449	14	11	0	99	0	4.10
David Pirnak	2	120	2	0	0	9	0	4.50

PRINCE ALBERT RAIDERS

SCORING

	Games	G	A	Pts.	PIM
Van Burgess	69	44	67	111	92

	Games	G	A	Pts.	PIM
Denis Pederson	71	53	45	98	157
Shayne Toporowski	68	37	45	82	183
Jeff Gorman	72	26	39	65	63
Steve Kelly	65	19	42	61	106
Brad Church	71	33	20	53	197
Paul Healey	63	23	26	49	70
Jeff Lank	72	9	38	47	62
Merv Haney	44	19	26	45	16
Jason Issel	61	12	24	36	62
Shane Hnidy	69	7	26	33	113
Shane Zulyniak	72	10	22	32	130
Mike McGhan	51	9	22	31	142
Brian Kostur	30	7	11	18	6
Russell Hogue	49	5	8	13	19
David Van Drunnen	63	3	10	13	95
Ryan Bast	47	2	8	10	139
Rodney Bowers	51	3	4	7	17
Mitch Shawara	55	3	3	6	185
Greg Harvey	54	0	5	5	201
Darren Wright	56	0	5	5	151
Jay Fitzpatrick	14	1	3	4	46
Dean Whitney (goalie)	18	0	2	2	8
Joaquin Gage (goalie)	53	0	2	2	19
Cory Donaldson	7	1	0	1	17
Charles Keshane	1	0	0	0	0
Phillip Lavallee (goalie)	1	0	0	0	0
Stan Matwijiw (goalie)	1	0	0	0	0
Kaleb Toth	2	0	0	0	0
Kendall Sidoruk (goalie)	6	0	0	0	0
Rob Lenz	15	0	0	0	12

GOALTENDING

	Games	Min.	W	L	T	Goals	SO	Avg.
Stan Matwijiw	1	60	1	0	0	3	0	3.00
Phillip Lavallee	1	20	0	0	0	1	0	3.00
Joaquin Gage	53	3041	24	25	3	212	1	4.18
Dean Whitney	18	974	6	7	1	71	1	4.37
Kendall Sidoruk	6	282	0	5	0	31	0	6.60

RED DEER REBELS

SCORING

	Games	G	A	Pts.	PIM
Craig Reichert	72	52	67	119	153
Darren Van Impe	58	20	64	84	125
Brad Zimmer	56	28	33	61	21
Curtis Cardinal	69	24	34	58	32
Tyler Quiring	44	21	34	55	46
Eddy Marchant	69	21	34	55	159
Sean Selmser	71	25	25	50	201
Neil Johnston	43	17	23	40	53
Pete LeBoutillier	66	19	20	39	300
Ken Richardson	67	17	16	33	205
Jonathon Zukiwsky	58	12	15	27	9
Byron Briske	61	6	21	27	174
Mike Barrie	19	11	14	25	53
Mark Toljanich	70	6	13	19	72
Terry Lindgren	62	4	14	18	226
Mike McBain	58	4	13	17	41
Berkley Pennock	66	7	8	15	52
Dale Donaldson	55	6	9	15	41
Peter Vandermeer	54	4	9	13	170
Sean Halifax	40	1	8	9	82
Chris Kibermanis	49	1	5	6	57
Vaclav Slansky	13	4	1	5	4
Jason Clague (goalie)	54	0	5	5	20
Chris Wickenheiser (goalie)	29	0	2	2	6
Craig Bilik	1	0	0	0	0
Darby Walker	1	0	0	0	0
Liam Weir	1	0	0	0	0
Tony Vlastelic	4	0	0	0	0
Dave Greenway	10	0	0	0	5
Chris Maillet	52	0	0	0	102

GOALTENDING

	Games	Min.	W	L	T	Goals	SO	Avg.
Jason Clague............	54	2985	24	23	1	218	2	4.38
Chris Wickenheiser .	29	1356	11	13	0	114	0	5.04

REGINA PATS

SCORING

	Games	G	A	Pts.	PIM
Jeff Friesen	66	51	67	118	48
Karry Biette	71	40	61	101	87
Cory Dosdall	69	28	50	78	242
Jeff Petruic	70	31	29	60	115
Louis Dumont	35	26	33	59	45
Nathan Dempsey	56	14	36	50	100
David Wilkie.................................	29	27	21	48	16
Rhett Gordon	60	19	28	47	14
Randy Toye	44	8	24	32	79
Scott Loucks................................	30	9	21	30	48
Dion Zukiwsky	72	9	19	28	118
Russell Hewson	22	8	12	20	24
Russ Gronick	34	7	11	18	46
Jesse Rezansoff..........................	69	6	9	15	56
Jeff Helperl.................................	67	4	11	15	254
Steve Dowhy	14	6	8	14	10
Ryan Phillips...............................	16	5	7	12	2
Perry Johnson	67	2	8	10	16
Vernon Beardy.............................	41	3	5	8	22
Rob Herring	41	2	5	7	40
Judd Casper	68	1	6	7	24
Ross Parsons..............................	68	1	5	6	47
Chris Zulyniak.............................	29	0	4	4	52
Jeromie Kufflick...........................	67	0	4	4	53
Shawn Collins	29	1	2	3	44
Mike Walker (goalie)	56	0	3	3	2
Chad Mercier (goalie)	31	0	2	2	6
Cadrin Smart	2	0	1	1	0
Russ West	5	0	1	1	10
Joey Bouvier	6	0	1	1	6
Brandon Coates...........................	9	0	1	1	18
Don Dunnigan	2	0	0	0	0
Darby Walker	2	0	0	0	11
Chad Wilchinsky	2	0	0	0	2
Tom Johnston..............................	4	0	0	0	0

GOALTENDING

	Games	Min.	W	L	T	Goals	SO	Avg.
Mike Walker	56	2961	27	19	2	207	1	4.19
Chad Mercier	31	1390	7	17	0	128	0	5.53

SASKATOON BLADES

SCORING

	Games	G	A	Pts.	PIM
Andy MacIntyre...........................	72	54	35	89	58
Derek Tibbatts	69	32	47	79	18
Paul Buczkowski..........................	71	30	48	78	71
Trevor Hanas	69	32	45	77	136
Frank Banham	65	28	39	67	99
Ivan Salon..................................	71	29	27	56	34
Mark Deyell.................................	66	17	36	53	52
Clarke Wilm	70	18	32	50	181
Mark Wotton................................	65	12	34	46	108
Andrew Kemper............................	71	7	25	32	144
Shane Calder	37	11	19	30	98
Todd Simpson..............................	51	7	19	26	175
Rhett Warrener	61	7	19	26	131
Chad Allan	70	6	16	22	123
Kirby Law	66	9	11	20	39
Jason Duda	72	5	14	19	22
Brian Kostur	23	8	9	17	2
Wade Belak	69	4	13	17	226
Trevor Ethier	65	6	4	10	67
Brent Sopel	11	2	2	4	2
Mike Gray	28	1	3	4	79
Mark Raiter	6	1	1	2	29

	Games	G	A	Pts.	PIM
Norman Maracle (goalie)	56	0	2	2	4
Don Larner..................................	2	0	1	1	5
Rob Douglas................................	6	0	1	1	2
Mike O'Grady...............................	13	0	1	1	29
Devon Hanson (goalie)	19	0	1	1	9
Terry Friesen (goalie)	1	0	0	0	0
Jesse Lacelle	1	0	0	0	0
Daryl Yuzik (goalie)	1	0	0	0	0
Chris McAllister	2	0	0	0	5
Darren Smadis (goalie)	3	0	0	0	0
Marty Zdan	4	0	0	0	0

GOALTENDING

	Games	Min.	W	L	T	Goals	SO	Avg.
Daryl Yuzik	1	20	0	0	0	0	0	0.00
Norman Maracle......	56	3219	41	13	1	148	2	2.76
Devon Hanson	19	920	8	7	0	54	2	3.52
Darren Smadis	3	173	0	2	0	17	0	5.90
Terry Friesen	1	19	0	0	0	2	0	6.32

SEATTLE THUNDERBIRDS

SCORING

	Games	G	A	Pts.	PIM
Chris Herperger	71	44	51	95	110
Chris Wells.................................	69	30	44	74	150
Olaf Kjenstad..............................	54	30	36	66	102
Regan Mueller	58	21	36	57	53
Paul Vincent...............................	66	27	26	53	57
Mike Barrie	48	24	28	52	119
Deron Quint	63	15	29	44	47
Brendan Witt	56	8	31	39	235
Darrel Sandback..........................	66	20	15	35	177
Troy Hyatt	60	6	25	31	27
Chris Schmidt	68	7	17	24	26
Alexandre Matvichuk....................	48	9	12	21	45
Shawn Gervais	70	2	18	20	32
Brett Duncan	66	5	10	15	283
Tyler Quiring...............................	17	5	8	13	28
Jason Kroffat	10	4	4	8	2
Travis Stevenson	30	3	5	8	32
Kevin Mylander	24	2	6	8	43
Jeff Dewar	28	6	1	7	18
A.J. Kelham................................	14	3	4	7	15
David Carson	62	4	1	5	21
Larry McMorran	12	2	3	5	11
Drew Palmer	67	0	5	5	154
Milt Mastad	29	1	3	4	59
Lloyd Shaw	47	0	4	4	107
Rob Tallas (goalie)	51	0	4	4	6
Jeff Peddigrew	53	3	0	3	18
Craig Mittleholt...........................	4	2	1	3	0
Kevin Lee (goalie)	1	0	0	0	0
Geoff Morris	2	0	0	0	0
Jim Burcar	5	0	0	0	14
Pavel Kablin	5	0	0	0	0
Darcy Smith	14	0	0	0	16
Doug Bonner (goalie)	29	0	0	0	8

GOALTENDING

	Games	Min.	W	L	T	Goals	SO	Avg.
Rob Tallas	51	2849	23	21	3	188	0	3.96
Doug Bonner	29	1481	9	15	0	111	1	4.50
Kevin Lee.................	1	35	0	1	0	7	0	12.00

SPOKANE CHIEFS

SCORING

	Games	G	A	Pts.	PIM
Ryan Duthie	71	57	69	126	111
Maxim Bets	63	46	70	116	111
Valeri Bure	59	40	62	102	48
Bryan McCabe	64	22	62	84	218
Jason Podollan	69	29	37	66	108
Scott Townsend	42	24	28	52	12

	Games	G	A	Pts.	PIM
Jeremy Stasiuk	59	12	25	37	84
Brantt Myhres	27	10	22	32	139
Kevin Sawyer	60	10	15	25	350
Darren Sinclair	66	9	15	24	54
Sean Gillam	70	7	17	24	106
Derek Descoteau	48	9	13	22	90
Craig Geekie	66	5	16	21	83
Joe Cardarelli	51	7	11	18	9
Dmitri Leonov	55	8	6	14	31
Hugh Hamilton	64	5	9	14	70
Randy Favaro	48	5	8	13	36
Kevin Pozzo	17	3	7	10	23
Jay Bertsch	29	5	4	9	87
David Jesiolowski	40	2	7	9	227
Dion Darling	45	1	8	9	190
John Cirjak	44	2	5	7	22
Trevor Shoaf	61	2	4	6	47
Kevin Popp	43	0	4	4	126
Darren Perkins	8	2	1	3	34
Barry Becker (goalie)	55	0	3	3	16
Trent Whitfield	5	1	1	2	0
Tyler Romanchuk	3	0	2	2	8
Ryan Hawes	5	1	0	1	2
Darren Smadis (goalie)	20	0	1	1	6
Ryan Young	1	0	0	0	0
Shawn Byrne	3	0	0	0	4
Ryan Berry	4	0	0	0	0
David Lemanowicz (goalie)	6	0	0	0	0
Beau Riedel (goalie)	7	0	0	0	0

GOALTENDING

	Games	Min.	W	L	T	Goals	SO	Avg.
Beau Riedel	7	206	0	1	0	14	0	4.08
Barry Becker	55	2928	22	27	2	206	0	4.22
Darren Smadis	20	996	8	7	2	73	0	4.40
David Lemanowicz	6	256	1	2	0	21	0	4.92

SWIFT CURRENT BRONCOS

SCORING

	Games	G	A	Pts.	PIM
Rick Girard	58	40	49	89	43
Ashley Buckberger	67	42	45	87	42
Todd Holt	56	40	47	87	59
Ladislav Kohn	69	33	35	68	68
Tyler Willis	71	19	26	45	263
Jarrett Bousquet	67	9	34	43	98
Jason Becker	60	9	33	42	28
Kevin Powell	56	22	18	40	61
Russell Hewson	48	15	25	40	31
Brad Larsen	64	15	18	33	37
Jason Horvath	60	7	22	29	155
Chad Kalmakoff	69	6	17	23	47
Bill Hooson	39	3	14	17	53
Chris Szysky	60	6	10	16	82
Jeff Kirwan	41	7	5	12	4
Ryan Brown	72	2	10	12	173
Craig Millar	66	2	9	11	53
Keith McCambridge	71	0	10	10	179
Ian Gordon (goalie)	65	0	7	7	4
John Kachur	20	2	3	5	0
Vernon Beardy	23	2	3	5	12
Regan Mueller	7	0	5	5	2
Cory Donaldson	15	1	3	4	6
Darren McLean	25	0	3	3	59
Craig Mittleholt	4	1	1	2	2
Chris Angione	6	1	1	2	0
Vinnie Jonasson	3	0	1	1	0
Shane Belter	6	0	1	1	11
Aaron MacDonald (goalie)	18	0	1	1	0
Ted Wood	2	0	0	0	0
Chris Low	3	0	0	0	2
Don Larner	4	0	0	0	0
Jaret Sledz	11	0	0	0	4
Jeremy Robinson	42	0	0	0	17

GOALTENDING

	Games	Min.	W	L	T	Goals	SO	Avg.
Ian Gordon	65	3657	29	27	4	204	6	3.35
Aaron MacDonald	18	710	6	6	0	48	0	4.06

TACOMA ROCKETS

SCORING

	Games	G	A	Pts.	PIM
Allan Egeland	70	47	76	123	204
John Varga	65	60	62	122	122
Marty Flichel	72	27	48	75	69
Alexandre Alexeev	64	12	48	60	106
Tavis Hansen	71	23	31	54	122
Burt Henderson	72	9	42	51	62
Trever Fraser	64	19	31	50	171
Michal Grosek	30	25	20	45	106
Tyler Prosofsky	70	20	22	42	132
Adam Smith	66	4	19	23	119
Dallas Thompson	67	14	7	21	112
Jamie Butt	64	8	13	21	214
Jason Deleurme	63	6	13	19	90
Mike Piersol	70	6	13	19	74
Kory Mullin	59	3	11	14	86
Kyle McLaren	62	1	9	10	53
Drew Schoneck	9	4	4	8	20
Ryan Phillips	27	2	6	8	17
Dennis Pinfold	55	2	6	8	219
Jeff Jubenville	21	4	2	6	40
Cory Stock	22	3	1	4	44
Barkley Swenson	14	2	2	4	20
Trevor Cairns	67	2	2	4	255
Jeff Calvert (goalie)	47	0	2	2	16
Doug Johnson	1	0	0	0	0
Chad Knippel	1	0	0	0	2
Bobby Rowland	2	0	0	0	0
Trevor Lornson	5	0	0	0	24
Toby Weishaar	6	0	0	0	0
Lada Hampeis	10	0	0	0	2
Todd MacDonald (goalie)	29	0	0	0	6

GOALTENDING

	Games	Min.	W	L	T	Goals	SO	Avg.
Jeff Calvert	47	2777	20	24	3	184	2	3.98
Todd MacDonald	29	1606	13	10	2	109	1	4.07

TRI-CITY AMERICANS

SCORING

	Games	G	A	Pts.	PIM
Daymond Langkow	61	40	43	83	174
Chad Cabana	67	27	33	60	201
Brent Ascroft	71	26	29	55	47
B.J. Young	54	19	24	43	66
Mark Hurley	65	14	28	42	31
Drew Schoneck	54	8	29	37	65
Terry Ryan	61	16	17	33	176
Steve Dowhy	41	19	12	31	34
Jesse Wilson	25	8	23	31	15
Marc Stephan	59	7	20	27	102
Geoff Lynch	69	11	15	26	24
Dean Tiltgen	35	8	15	23	26
Pete Mehallic	30	6	17	23	75
Kyuin Shim	42	10	12	22	33
Cory Johnson	42	12	9	21	21
Fran Defrenza	44	8	13	21	101
Ryan Marsh	66	8	9	17	170
Adam Rettschlag	13	3	7	10	21
Aaron Boh	27	3	7	10	97
Marc Hussey	16	3	6	9	26
Sheldon Souray	42	3	6	9	122
Jason Renard	22	3	4	7	97
Jonathon Shockey	51	0	7	7	71
Todd Simpson	12	2	3	5	32
Cadrin Smart	22	1	4	5	29
Kory Mullin	6	0	5	5	11

	Games	G	A	Pts.	PIM
Graeme Harder	28	0	5	5	53
Mark Raiter	8	1	3	4	11
Duane Hoppe	35	1	3	4	22
Slade Stephenson	20	0	4	4	45
Jeff Hoad	2	2	1	3	4
Mark Dutiaume	3	2	0	2	0
Justin Guy	27	1	1	2	15
Gary Lebsack	9	0	2	2	46
Bill Tibbetts	9	0	2	2	39
Boyd Olson	2	0	1	1	0
Bryce Goebel	8	0	1	1	8
Chad Cammock	23	0	1	1	149
Lance Leslie (goalie)	41	0	1	1	12
Darren Rattray	2	0	0	0	0
Craig Stahl	2	0	0	0	0
Ray Schultz	3	0	0	0	11
David Pirnak (goalie)	11	0	0	0	0
David Brumby (goalie)	28	0	0	0	6

GOALTENDING

	Games	Min.	W	L	T	Goals	SO	Avg.
David Pirnak	11	586	2	6	1	46	0	4.71
Lance Leslie	41	2273	10	26	2	189	2	4.99
David Brumby	28	1518	7	16	2	132	0	5.22

VICTORIA COUGARS

SCORING

	Games	G	A	Pts.	PIM
Alex Vasilevskii	69	34	51	85	78
Dorian Anneck	71	26	53	79	30
Rob Butz	72	24	24	48	161
Chris Petersen	71	14	30	44	53
Mike LeClerc	68	29	11	40	112
Peter Cox	69	16	24	40	125
Steve Lingren	58	14	21	35	118
Alexander Boikov	70	4	31	35	250
Dean Tiltgen	29	9	14	23	24
Andrew Laming	68	13	8	21	137
Cadrin Smart	45	3	18	21	36
Randy Chadney	72	8	11	19	43
Martin Hohenberger	61	3	13	16	28
Matt Van Horlick	65	6	7	13	204
Randy Toye	22	5	7	12	29
Graeme Harder	39	3	6	9	79
Derek Stevely	70	2	6	8	95
Clayton Catellier	70	1	6	7	249
Brad Hammerback	32	3	3	6	84
Mark Barrie	60	3	2	5	69
Ross Harris	5	1	4	5	2
Kelly Harris	15	1	4	5	63
Rhett Trombley	21	0	3	3	67
Dale Masson (goalie)	57	0	2	2	21
Adam Rettschlag	3	0	1	1	4
Spencer Bettenson	5	0	1	1	0
Jeremy Jablonski (goalie)	17	0	1	1	0
David Benard	23	0	1	1	20
James Reimer	3	0	0	0	0
Chris Mason (goalie)	5	0	0	0	2
Roland Monilaws	7	0	0	0	10
Corey Laniuk	8	0	0	0	14

GOALTENDING

	Games	Min.	W	L	T	Goals	SO	Avg.
Dale Masson	57	3362	15	38	2	281	0	5.01
Jeremy Jablonski	17	773	2	9	1	81	0	6.29
Chris Mason	5	237	1	4	0	27	0	6.84

PLAYERS WITH TWO OR MORE TEAMS

SCORING

	Games	G	A	Pts.	PIM
Mike Barrie, Red Deer	19	11	14	25	53
Mike Barrie, Seattle	48	24	28	52	119
Totals	67	35	42	77	172

	Games	G	A	Pts.	PIM
Ryan Bast, Portland	6	0	0	0	4
Ryan Bast, Prince Albert	47	2	8	10	139
Totals	53	2	8	10	143
Vernon Beardy, Regina	41	3	5	8	22
Vernon Beardy, Swift Current	23	2	3	5	12
Totals	64	5	8	13	34
Jason Becker, Kamloops	2	0	0	0	0
Jason Becker, Swift Current	60	9	33	42	28
Totals	62	9	33	42	28
Jay Bertsch, Lethbridge	36	1	6	7	61
Jay Bertsch, Spokane	29	5	4	9	87
Totals	65	6	10	16	148
Aaron Boh, Medicine Hat	28	4	15	19	99
Aaron Boh, Tri-City	27	3	7	10	97
Totals	55	7	22	29	196
Jarrett Bousquet, Kamloops	2	1	0	1	18
Jarrett Bousquet, Swift Current	67	9	34	43	98
Totals	69	10	34	44	116
Shawn Collins, Portland	33	2	19	21	51
Shawn Collins, Regina	29	1	2	3	44
Totals	62	3	21	24	95
Jarrod Daniel, Moose Jaw	21	0	2	2	10
Jarrod Daniel, Portland	8	0	0	0	0
Totals	29	0	2	2	10
Dion Darling, Spokane	45	1	8	9	190
Dion Darling, Moose Jaw	23	4	6	10	96
Totals	68	5	14	19	286
Jeff Dewar, Seattle	28	6	1	7	18
Jeff Dewar, Moose Jaw	37	9	11	20	46
Totals	65	15	12	27	64
Cory Donaldson, Prince Albert	7	1	0	1	17
Cory Donaldson, Swift Current	15	1	3	4	6
Totals	22	2	3	5	23
Steve Dowhy, Tri-City	41	19	12	31	34
Steve Dowhy, Regina	14	6	8	14	10
Totals	55	25	20	45	44
Louis Dumont, Regina	35	26	33	59	45
Louis Dumont, Kamloops	34	18	20	38	33
Totals	69	44	53	97	78
Mark Dutiaume, Tri-City	3	2	0	2	0
Mark Dutiaume, Brandon	55	4	7	11	43
Totals	58	6	7	13	43
Jay Fitzpatrick, Prince Albert	14	1	3	4	46
Jay Fitzpatrick, Medicine Hat	6	0	1	1	11
Totals	20	1	4	5	57
Graeme Harder, Tri-City	28	0	5	5	53
Graeme Harder, Victoria	39	3	6	9	79
Totals	67	3	11	14	132
Russell Hewson, Swift Current	48	15	25	40	31
Russell Hewson, Regina	22	8	12	20	24
Totals	70	23	37	60	55
Jeff Hoad, Brandon	5	2	3	5	0
Jeff Hoad, Tri-City	2	2	1	3	4
Jeff Hoad, Moose Jaw	55	36	41	77	100
Totals	62	40	45	85	104
Marc Hussey, Moose Jaw	17	4	5	9	33
Marc Hussey, Tri-City	16	3	6	9	26
Marc Hussey, Medicine Hat	41	6	24	30	90
Totals	74	13	35	48	149
David Jesiolowski, Spokane	40	2	7	9	227
David Jesiolowski, Lethbridge	29	3	5	8	146
Totals	69	5	12	17	373
Neil Johnston, Moose Jaw	30	13	13	26	65
Neil Johnston, Red Deer	43	17	23	40	53
Totals	73	30	36	66	118
Jeff Jubenville, Lethbridge	5	1	1	2	7
Jeff Jubenville, Tacoma	21	4	2	6	40
Totals	26	5	3	8	47
Chad Knippel, Tacoma	1	0	0	0	2
Chad Knippel, Brandon	10	1	0	1	28
Totals	11	1	0	1	30
Ladislav Kohn, Brandon	2	0	0	0	0
Ladislav Kohn, Swift Current	69	33	35	68	68
Totals	71	33	35	68	68

MAJOR JUNIOR LEAGUES

	Games	G	A	Pts.	PIM
Brian Kostur, Prince Albert	30	7	11	18	6
Brian Kostur, Saskatoon	23	8	9	17	2
Totals	53	15	20	35	8
Don Larner, Swift Current	4	0	0	0	0
Don Larner, Saskatoon	2	0	1	1	5
Totals	6	0	1	1	5
Scott Loucks, Kamloops	23	5	13	18	48
Scott Loucks, Regina	30	9	21	30	48
Totals	53	14	34	48	96
Chris Low, Swift Current	3	0	0	0	2
Chris Low, Brandon	69	8	12	20	23
Totals	72	8	12	20	25
Milt Mastad, Seattle	29	1	3	4	59
Milt Mastad, Moose Jaw	41	2	8	10	74
Totals	70	3	11	14	133
Stan Matwijiw, Prince Albert	1	0	0	0	0
Stan Matwijiw, Lethbridge	39	0	3	3	12
Totals	40	0	3	3	12
Larry McMorran, Seattle	12	2	3	5	11
Larry McMorran, Lethbridge	23	2	0	2	4
Totals	35	4	3	7	15
Pete Mehallic, Brandon	5	1	2	3	13
Pete Mehallic, Tri-City	30	6	17	23	75
Totals	35	7	19	26	88
Craig Mittleholt, Swift Current	4	1	1	2	2
Craig Mittleholt, Seattle	4	2	1	3	0
Totals	8	3	2	5	2
Regan Mueller, Swift Current	7	0	5	5	2
Regan Mueller, Seattle	58	21	36	57	53
Totals	65	21	41	62	55
Kory Mullin, Tri-City	6	0	5	5	11
Kory Mullin, Tacoma	59	3	11	14	86
Totals	65	3	16	19	97
Brantt Myhres, Lethbridge	34	10	21	31	103
Brantt Myhres, Spokane	27	10	22	32	139
Totals	61	20	43	63	242
Ryan Phillips, Tacoma	27	2	6	8	17
Ryan Phillips, Regina	16	5	7	12	2
Totals	43	7	13	20	19
David Pirnak, Tri-City	11	0	0	0	0
David Pirnak, Portland	2	0	0	0	0
Totals	13	0	0	0	0
Kevin Pozzo, Moose Jaw	40	7	20	27	71
Kevin Pozzo, Spokane	17	3	7	10	23
Totals	57	10	27	37	94
Tyler Quiring, Seattle	17	5	8	13	28
Tyler Quiring, Red Deer	44	21	34	55	46
Totals	61	26	42	68	74
Mark Raiter, Saskatoon	6	1	1	2	29
Mark Raiter, Tri-City	8	1	3	4	11
Totals	14	2	4	6	40
Adam Rettschlag, Tri-City	13	3	7	10	21
Adam Rettschlag, Victoria	3	0	1	1	4
Totals	16	3	8	11	25
Drew Schoneck, Tacoma	9	4	4	8	20
Drew Schoneck, Tri-City	54	8	29	37	65
Totals	63	12	33	45	85
Kyuin Shim, Tri-City	42	10	12	22	33
Kyuin Shim, Medicine Hat	14	6	4	10	2
Totals	56	16	16	32	35

	Games	G	A	Pts.	PIM
Todd Simpson, Tri-City	12	2	3	5	32
Todd Simpson, Saskatoon	51	7	19	26	175
Totals	63	9	22	31	207
Darren Smadis, Saskatoon	3	0	0	0	0
Darren Smadis, Spokane	20	0	1	1	6
Totals	23	0	1	1	6
Cadrin Smart, Lethbridge	5	0	1	1	6
Cadrin Smart, Victoria	45	3	18	21	36
Cadrin Smart, Regina	2	0	1	1	0
Cadrin Smart, Tri-City	22	1	4	5	29
Totals	74	4	24	28	71
Slade Stephenson, Lethbridge	8	0	2	2	17
Slade Stephenson, Tri-City	20	0	4	4	45
Totals	28	0	6	6	62
Travis Stevenson, Moose Jaw	25	0	3	3	52
Travis Stevenson, Seattle	30	3	5	8	32
Totals	55	3	8	11	84
Dean Tiltgen, Victoria	29	9	14	23	24
Dean Tiltgen, Tri-City	35	8	15	23	26
Totals	64	17	29	46	50
Scott Townsend, Spokane	42	24	28	52	12
Scott Townsend, Lethbridge	32	18	18	36	10
Totals	74	42	46	88	22
Randy Toye, Regina	44	8	24	32	79
Randy Toye, Victoria	22	5	7	12	29
Totals	66	13	31	44	108
Darby Walker, Red Deer	1	0	0	0	0
Darby Walker, Regina	2	0	0	0	11
Totals	3	0	0	0	11
Russ West, Regina	5	0	1	1	10
Russ West, Moose Jaw	6	0	1	1	0
Totals	11	0	2	2	10
David Wilkie, Kamloops	27	11	18	29	18
David Wilkie, Regina	29	27	21	48	16
Totals	56	38	39	77	34
Jesse Wilson, Tri-City	25	8	23	31	15
Jesse Wilson, Lethbridge	6	3	4	7	6
Totals	31	11	27	38	21
Brad Zimmer, Lethbridge	10	2	6	8	6
Brad Zimmer, Red Deer	56	28	33	61	21
Totals	66	30	39	69	27

GOALTENDING

	Games	Min.	W	L	T	Goals	SO	Avg.
Jarrod Daniel, M.J.	21	1104	8	10	0	75	0	4.08
Jarrod Daniel, Por.	8	488	6	2	0	24	1	2.95
Totals	29	1592	14	12	0	99	1	3.73
Stan Matwijiw, P.A.	1	60	1	0	0	3	0	3.00
Stan Matwijiw, Leth.	39	2090	16	14	4	135	1	3.88
Totals	40	2150	17	14	4	138	1	3.85
David Pirnak, T.C.	11	586	2	6	1	46	0	4.71
David Pirnak, Por.	2	120	2	0	0	9	0	4.50
Totals	13	706	4	6	1	55	0	4.67
D. Smadis, Sask.	3	173	0	2	0	17	0	5.90
D. Smadis, Spo.	20	996	8	7	2	73	0	4.40
Totals	23	1169	8	9	2	90	0	4.62

1994 PLAYOFFS

RESULTS

EAST DIVISION QUARTERFINALS

Series "A"

	W	L	Pts.	GF	GA
Brandon	3	1	6	20	11
Regina	1	3	2	11	20

(Brandon won series, 3-1)

Series "B"

	W	L	Pts.	GF	GA
Lethbridge	3	1	6	17	12
Red Deer	1	3	2	12	17

(Lethbridge won series, 3-1)

Series "C"

	W	L	Pts.	GF	GA
Swift Current	3	0	6	17	4
Medicine Hat	0	3	0	4	17

(Swift Current won series, 3-0)

WEST DIVISION QUARTERFINALS

Series "D"

	W	L	Pts.	GF	GA
Tacoma	3	1	6	18	10
Tri-City	1	3	2	10	18

(Tacoma won series, 3-1)

Series "E"

	W	L	Pts.	GF	GA
Seattle	3	0	6	23	14

(Seattle won series, 3-0)

EAST DIVISION SEMIFINALS

Series "F"

	W	L	Pts.	GF	GA
Saskatoon	4	0	8	17	8
Swift Current	0	4	0	8	17

(Saskatonn won series, 4-0)

Series "G"

	W	L	Pts.	GF	GA
Brandon	4	1	8	20	20
Lethbridge	1	4	2	20	20

(Brandon won series, 4-1)

WEST DIVISION SEMIFINALS

Series "H"

	W	L	Pts.	GF	GA
Kamloops	4	2	8	28	25
Seattle	2	4	4	25	28

(Kamloops won series, 4-2)

Series "I"

	W	L	Pts.	GF	GA
Portland	4	0	8	22	8
Tacoma	0	4	0	8	22

(Portland won series, 4-0)

EAST DIVISION FINALS

Series "J"

	W	L	Pts.	GF	GA
Saskatoon	4	1	8	18	16
Brandon	1	4	2	16	18

(Saskatoon won series, 4-1)

WEST DIVISION FINALS

Series "K"

	W	L	Pts.	GF	GA
Kamloops	4	2	8	26	22
Portland	2	4	4	22	26

(Kamloops won series, 4-2)

FINALS

Series "L"

	W	L	Pts.	GF	GA
Kamloops	4	3	8	30	19
Saskatoon	3	4	6	19	30

(Kamloops won series, 4-3)

INDIVIDUAL LEADERS

Goals: Jarrett Deuling, Kamloops (13)
Assists: Darcy Tucker, Kamloops (18)
Points: Darcy Tucker, Kamloops (27)
Penalty minutes: Bob Westerby, Kamloops (64)
Goaltending average: Ian Gordon, Swift Current (3.01)
Shutouts: Ian Gordon, Swift Current (1)
Norm Maracle, Saskatoon (1)
Stan Matwijiw, Lethbridge (1)

TOP SCORERS

	Games	G	A	Pts.
Darcy Tucker, Kamloops	19	9	18	27
Chris Herperger, Seattle	9	12	10	22
Hnat Domenichelli, Kamloops	19	10	12	22
Jarrett Deuling, Kamloops	18	13	8	21
Rod Stevens, Kamloops	19	9	12	21
Marty Murray, Brandon	14	6	14	20
Darren Ritchie, Brandon	14	9	10	19
Lonny Bohonos, Portland	10	8	11	19
Frank Banham, Saskatoon	16	8	11	19
Chris Johnston, Brandon	14	7	12	19

INDIVIDUAL STATISTICS

BRANDON WHEAT KINGS

(Lost East Division finals to Saskatoon, 4-1)

SCORING

	Games	G	A	Pts.	PIM
Marty Murray	14	6	14	20	14
Darren Ritchie	14	9	10	19	8
Chris Johnston	14	7	12	19	22
Mike Maneluk	13	11	3	14	23
Mark Kolesar	14	8	3	11	48
Chris Dingman	13	1	7	8	39
Colin Cloutier	11	2	5	7	23
Scott Laluk	14	1	6	7	8
Dean Kletzel	14	2	4	6	20
Wade Redden	14	2	4	6	10
Bobby Brown	14	5	0	5	12
Justin Kurtz	14	1	3	4	24
Chris Low	14	1	1	2	2
Sean McFatridge	3	0	2	2	12
Mark Dutiaume	12	0	2	2	6
Dwayne Gylwoychuk	12	0	2	2	22
Adam Magarrell	13	0	2	2	32
Byron Penstock (goalie)	14	0	2	2	9
Kelly Smart	2	0	0	0	0
Sven Butenschon	4	0	0	0	6
Joel Korenko	13	0	0	0	9
Paul Bailley	14	0	0	0	0

GOALTENDING

	Games	Min.	W	L	T	Goals	SO	Avg.
Byron Penstock	14	869	8	6	0	49	0	3.38

— 261 —

KAMLOOPS BLAZERS

(Winner of 1994 playoffs)

SCORING

	Games	G	A	Pts.	PIM
Darcy Tucker	19	9	18	27	43
Hnat Domenichelli	19	10	12	22	0
Jarrett Deuling	18	13	8	21	43
Rod Stevens	19	9	12	21	10
Nolan Baumgartner	19	3	14	17	33
Scott Ferguson	19	5	11	16	48
Aaron Keller	19	3	12	15	6
Ryan Huska	19	9	5	14	23
Louis Dumont	13	8	5	13	12
Mike Josephson	19	1	10	11	8
Jarome Iginla	19	3	6	9	10
Tyson Nash	16	3	4	7	12
Chris Murray	15	4	2	6	107
Jason Holland	18	2	3	5	4
Bob Westerby	19	1	4	5	64
Jason Strudwick	19	0	4	4	24
Bob Maudie	19	1	1	2	2
Mike Krooshoop	9	0	1	1	6
Brad Lukowich	16	0	1	1	35
Steve Passmore (goalie)	17	0	1	1	11
Dion Hagan	1	0	0	0	0
Rod Branch (goalie)	2	0	0	0	0
Greg Hart	8	0	0	0	2

GOALTENDING

	Games	Min.	W	L	T	Goals	SO	Avg.
Steve Passmore	18	1099	11	7	0	60	0	3.28
Rod Branch	2	72	1	0	0	4	0	3.33

LETHBRIDGE HURRICANES

(Lost East Division semifinals to Brandon, 4-1)

SCORING

	Games	G	A	Pts.	PIM
Domenic Pittis	8	4	11	15	16
Shane Peacock	9	3	9	12	6
Scott Townsend	9	5	6	11	4
Ivan Vologjaninov	9	3	7	10	2
Mark Szoke	9	2	8	10	8
Chad Gans	9	5	4	9	8
Jason Widmer	9	3	5	8	34
Lee Sorochan	9	4	3	7	16
Todd MacIsaac	9	4	2	6	8
Aaron Zarowny	9	1	4	5	15
Scott Grieco	9	1	2	3	7
David Jesiolowski	9	1	1	2	24
Derek Wood	9	1	0	1	13
Randy Perry	7	0	1	1	2
Stan Matwijiw (goalie)	9	0	1	1	0
Brad Mehalko	9	0	1	1	9
Bryce Salvador	9	0	1	1	2
David Trofimenkoff (goalie)	1	0	0	0	0
Derek Deiner	3	0	0	0	7
Larry McMorran	3	0	0	0	0
Byron Ritchie	6	0	0	0	14
Kirk DeWaele	9	0	0	0	5

GOALTENDING

	Games	Min.	W	L	T	Goals	SO	Avg.
David Trofimenkoff	1	20	0	0	0	0	0	0.00
Stan Matwijiw	9	529	4	5	0	31	1	3.52

MEDICINE HAT TIGERS

(Lost East Division quarterfinals to Swift Current, 3-0)

SCORING

	Games	G	A	Pts.	PIM
Lorne Toews	3	2	0	2	12
Robert Longpre	3	1	0	1	0
Stacy Roest	3	1	0	1	4
Steve Cheredaryk	3	0	1	1	9

	Games	G	A	Pts.	PIM
Marc Hussey	3	0	1	1	4
Mark Polak	3	0	1	1	2
Brad Wilson	3	0	1	1	0
Dwayne Ripley	1	0	0	0	0
Jeremy Schaefer	2	0	0	0	2
Cal Benazic	3	0	0	0	15
Josh Green	3	0	0	0	4
Justin Hocking	3	0	0	0	6
Tim Keith	3	0	0	0	0
Sergei Klimentiev	3	0	0	0	4
Henry Kuster	3	0	0	0	2
Sonny Mignacca (goalie)	3	0	0	0	4
Ryan Petz	3	0	0	0	0
Kyuin Shim	3	0	0	0	0
Jeremy Thompson	3	0	0	0	4
Rocky Thompson	3	0	0	0	2

GOALTENDING

	Games	Min.	W	L	T	Goals	SO	Avg.
Sonny Mignacca	3	180	0	3	0	17	0	5.67

PORTLAND WINTER HAWKS

(Lost West Division finals to Kamloops, 4-2)

SCORING

	Games	G	A	Pts.	PIM
Lonny Bohonos	10	8	11	19	13
Adam Deadmarsh	10	9	8	17	33
Colin Foley	10	6	6	12	6
Brandon Smith	10	2	10	12	8
Scott Nichol	10	3	8	11	16
Jason McBain	10	2	7	9	14
Dave Cammock	10	4	4	8	35
Jason Wiemer	10	4	4	8	32
Layne Roland	10	2	4	6	24
Dave Scatchard	10	2	1	3	4
Brad Swanson	8	1	2	3	2
Nolan Pratt	10	1	2	3	14
Brett Fizzell	8	0	2	2	10
Brad Isbister	10	0	2	2	0
Mike Williamson	10	0	2	2	41
Shannon Briske	10	0	1	1	28
Dmitri Markovsky	3	0	0	0	0
Mike Little	4	0	0	0	0
Brad Symes	7	0	0	0	21
Matt Davidson	10	0	0	0	4
Scott Langkow (goalie)	10	0	0	0	6

GOALTENDING

	Games	Min.	W	L	T	Goals	SO	Avg.
Scott Langkow	10	600	6	4	0	34	0	3.40

RED DEER REBELS

(Lost East Division quarterfinals to Lethbridge, 3-1)

SCORING

	Games	G	A	Pts.	PIM
Darren Van Impe	4	2	4	6	6
Craig Reichert	4	2	2	4	8
Ken Richardson	4	3	0	3	26
Brad Zimmer	4	1	2	3	2
Eddy Marchant	4	0	3	3	9
Tyler Quiring	4	1	1	2	9
Jonathon Zukiwsky	4	0	2	2	0
Jason Clague (goalie)	4	1	0	1	0
Neil Johnston	4	1	0	1	8
Sean Selmser	4	1	0	1	14
Pete LeBoutillier	2	0	1	1	4
Mark Toljanich	4	0	1	1	10
Chris Maillet	1	0	0	0	5
Curtis Cardinal	2	0	0	0	2
Sean Halifax	3	0	0	0	0
Dale Donaldson	4	0	0	0	7
Chris Kibermanis	4	0	0	0	7
Terry Lindgren	4	0	0	0	4

	Games	G	A	Pts.	PIM
Mike McBain	4	0	0	0	0
Berkley Pennock	4	0	0	0	0
Peter Vandermeer	4	0	0	0	20

GOALTENDING

	Games	Min.	W	L	T	Goals	SO	Avg.
Jason Clague	4	240	1	3	0	17	0	4.25

REGINA PATS

(Lost East Division quarterfinals to Brandon, 3-1)

SCORING

	Games	G	A	Pts.	PIM
Jeff Friesen	4	3	2	5	2
David Wilkie	4	1	4	5	4
Jeff Petruic	4	3	1	4	5
Karry Biette	4	1	3	4	15
Steve Dowhy	4	1	3	4	4
Russell Hewson	4	1	2	3	2
Cory Dosdall	4	0	3	3	12
Scott Loucks	4	1	0	1	4
Joey Bouvier	2	0	1	1	0
Jeff Helperl	4	0	1	1	12
Dion Zukiwsky	4	0	1	1	17
Chad Mercier (goalie)	1	0	0	0	0
Judd Casper	2	0	0	0	9
Shawn Collins	4	0	0	0	6
Nathan Dempsey	4	0	0	0	4
Rhett Gordon	4	0	0	0	7
Perry Johnson	4	0	0	0	2
Jeromie Kufflick	4	0	0	0	5
Ross Parsons	4	0	0	0	0
Jesse Rezansoff	4	0	0	0	5
Mike Walker (goalie)	4	0	0	0	5

GOALTENDING

	Games	Min.	W	L	T	Goals	SO	Avg.
Mike Walker	4	197	1	3	0	14	0	4.26
Chad Mercier	1	43	0	0	0	4	0	5.58

SASKATOON BLADES

(Lost WHL finals to Kamloops, 4-2)

SCORING

	Games	G	A	Pts.	PIM
Frank Banham	16	8	11	19	36
Derek Tibbatts	16	8	7	15	4
Mark Wotton	16	3	12	15	32
Jason Duda	16	7	7	14	10
Andy MacIntyre	16	6	6	12	16
Trevor Hanas	16	4	6	10	28
Paul Buczkowski	16	3	6	9	23
Clarke Wilm	16	0	9	9	19
Shane Calder	16	4	4	8	30
Mark Deyell	16	5	2	7	20
Todd Simpson	16	1	5	6	42
Rhett Warrener	16	0	5	5	33
Wade Belak	16	2	2	4	43
Ivan Salon	13	2	1	3	6
Norman Maracle (goalie)	16	0	3	3	0
Chad Allan	16	1	1	2	21
Andrew Kemper	16	0	1	1	29
Devon Hanson (goalie)	3	0	0	0	2
Brian Kostur	4	0	0	0	0
Trevor Ethier	15	0	0	0	10
Kirby Law	16	0	0	0	6

GOALTENDING

	Games	Min.	W	L	T	Goals	SO	Avg.
Norman Maracle	16	939	11	5	0	48	1	3.07
Devon Hanson	3	49	0	0	0	4	0	4.90

SEATTLE THUNDERBIRDS

(Lost West Division semifinals to Kamloops, 4-2)

SCORING

	Games	G	A	Pts.	PIM
Chris Herperger	9	12	10	22	12
Regan Mueller	9	5	12	17	6
Deron Quint	9	4	12	16	8
Olaf Kjenstad	9	4	9	13	16
Chris Wells	9	6	5	11	23
Brendan Witt	9	3	8	11	23
Mike Barrie	9	5	3	8	14
Darrel Sandback	9	3	4	7	11
Chris Schmidt	9	3	1	4	2
Paul Vincent	8	1	3	4	8
Brett Duncan	9	0	3	3	18
Troy Hyatt	9	1	1	2	4
Jeff Peddigrew	9	1	1	2	4
Travis Stevenson	9	0	2	2	4
Shawn Gervais	8	0	1	1	0
Alexandre Matvichuk	1	0	0	0	4
David Carson	2	0	0	0	0
Lloyd Shaw	8	0	0	0	23
Jason Kroffat	9	0	0	0	0
Drew Palmer	9	0	0	0	16
Rob Tallas (goalie)	9	0	0	0	4

GOALTENDING

	Games	Min.	W	L	T	Goals	SO	Avg.
Rob Tallas	9	567	5	4	0	40	0	4.23

SPOKANE CHIEFS

(Lost West Division quarterfinals to Seattle, 3-0)

SCORING

	Games	G	A	Pts.	PIM
Valeri Bure	3	5	3	8	2
Ryan Duthie	3	3	5	8	11
Brantt Myhres	3	1	4	5	7
Bryan McCabe	3	0	4	4	4
Jason Podollan	3	3	0	3	2
Maxim Bets	3	1	1	2	12
Derek Descoteau	3	1	0	1	0
Kevin Pozzo	3	0	1	1	4
Kevin Sawyer	3	0	1	1	6
Dmitri Leonov	1	0	0	0	0
Darren Smadis (goalie)	1	0	0	0	0
Joe Cardarelli	2	0	0	0	0
Randy Favaro	2	0	0	0	0
Kevin Popp	2	0	0	0	0
Trevor Shoaf	2	0	0	0	0
Barry Becker (goalie)	3	0	0	0	0
Jay Bertsch	3	0	0	0	16
John Cirjak	3	0	0	0	2
Craig Geekie	3	0	0	0	2
Sean Gillam	3	0	0	0	6
Hugh Hamilton	3	0	0	0	0
Darren Sinclair	3	0	0	0	0

GOALTENDING

	Games	Min.	W	L	T	Goals	SO	Avg.
Barry Becker	3	160	0	2	0	17	0	6.38
Darren Smadis	1	25	0	1	0	4	0	9.60

SWIFT CURRENT

(Lost East Division semifinals to Saskatoon, 4-0)

SCORING

	Games	G	A	Pts.	PIM
Todd Holt	7	11	7	18	8
Ladislav Kohn	7	5	4	9	8
Rick Girard	7	1	8	9	6
Kevin Powell	7	3	2	5	6
Bill Hooson	4	1	2	3	16
Jason Becker	7	1	2	3	6
Brad Larsen	7	1	2	3	4
Craig Millar	7	0	3	3	4
Jarrett Bousquet	7	1	1	2	8
Chad Kalmakoff	7	0	2	2	2

MAJOR JUNIOR LEAGUES

	Games	G	A	Pts.	PIM
Vernon Beardy	7	1	0	1	0
John Kachur	6	0	1	1	0
Ashley Buckberger	7	0	1	1	6
Ian Gordon (goalie)	7	0	1	1	0
Jason Horvath	7	0	1	1	8
Jeff Kirwan	7	0	1	1	0
Chris Szysky	7	0	1	1	12
Aaron MacDonald (goalie)	1	0	0	0	0
Tyler Willis	1	0	0	0	0
Chris Angione	3	0	0	0	2
Ryan Brown	7	0	0	0	6
Keith McCambridge	7	0	0	0	4

GOALTENDING

	Games	Min.	W	L	T	Goals	SO	Avg.
Ian Gordon	7	419	3	4	0	21	1	3.01
Aaron MacDonald	1	1	0	0	0	0	0	0.00

TACOMA ROCKETS

(Lost West Division semifinals to Portland, 4-0)

SCORING

	Games	G	A	Pts.	PIM
John Varga	8	2	8	10	14
Allan Egeland	8	5	3	8	26
Trever Fraser	7	5	1	6	14
Kyle McLaren	6	1	4	5	6
Marty Flichel	8	1	4	5	13
Alexandre Alexeev	8	0	5	5	9
Michal Grosek	7	2	2	4	30
Jamie Butt	8	1	3	4	18
Tavis Hansen	8	1	3	4	17
Burt Henderson	8	2	1	3	11
Jason Deleurme	6	2	0	2	7
Mike Piersol	8	1	1	2	8
Tyler Prosofsky	8	1	1	2	23
Dennis Pinfold	8	1	0	1	19
Dallas Thompson	8	1	0	1	18
Toby Weishaar	5	0	0	0	0
Trevor Cairns	8	0	0	0	27

	Games	G	A	Pts.	PIM
Jeff Calvert (goalie)	8	0	0	0	8
Kory Mullin	8	0	0	0	0
Adam Smith	8	0	0	0	10

GOALTENDING

	Games	Min.	W	L	T	Goals	SO	Avg.
Jeff Calvert	8	480	3	5	0	32	0	4.00

TRI-CITY AMERICANS

(Lost West Division quarterfinals to Tacoma, 3-1)

SCORING

	Games	G	A	Pts.	PIM
Brent Ascroft	4	1	4	5	5
Daymond Langkow	4	2	2	4	15
Drew Schoneck	4	0	3	3	13
Chad Cabana	4	2	0	2	24
B.J. Young	2	1	1	2	2
Pete Mehallic	4	1	1	2	14
Dean Tiltgen	4	1	1	2	12
Cory Johnson	4	0	2	2	4
Fran Defrenza	2	1	0	1	9
Mark Hurley	4	1	0	1	9
Terry Ryan	4	0	1	1	25
Cadrin Smart	4	0	1	1	0
Marc Stephan	4	0	1	1	8
David Brumby (goalie)	2	0	0	0	0
Chad Cammock	2	0	0	0	16
Lance Leslie (goalie)	2	0	0	0	0
Jonathon Shockey	3	0	0	0	6
Justin Guy	4	0	0	0	2
Duane Hoppe	4	0	0	0	11
Geoff Lynch	4	0	0	0	0
Ryan Marsh	4	0	0	0	11

GOALTENDING

	Games	Min.	W	L	T	Goals	SO	Avg.
David Brumby	2	120	1	1	0	9	0	4.50
Lance Leslie	2	120	0	2	0	9	0	4.50

1993-94 AWARD WINNERS

ALL-STAR TEAMS

EAST DIVISION

First team	Pos.	Second team
Norm Maracle, Saskatoon	G	Sonny Mignacca, Med. Hat
Chris Armstrong, M.J.	D	Nathan Dempsey, Regina
Darren Van Impe, Red Deer	D	Justin Hocking, Med. Hat
		Mark Wotton, Saskatoon
Rick Girard, S.C.	F	Andy MacIntyre, Sask.
Marty Murray, Brandon	F	Denis Pederson, P.A.
Stacy Roest, Med. Hat	F	Domenic Pittis, Lethbridge

WEST DIVISION

First team	Pos.	Second team
Steve Passmore, Kamloops	G	Scott Langkow, Portland
Bryan McCabe, Spokane	D	Alexandre Alexeev, Tac.
Brendan Witt, Seattle	D	Scott Ferguson, Kamloops
		Brandon Smith, Portland
Lonny Bohonos, Portland	F	Valeri Bure, Spokane
Ryan Duthie, Spokane	F	Allan Egeland, Tacoma
Darcy Tucker, Kamloops	F	John Varga, Tacoma

TROPHY WINNERS

Four Broncos Memorial Trophy: Sonny Mignacca, Medicine Hat
Bob Clarke Trophy: Lonny Bohonos, Portland
Jim Piggott Memorial Trophy: Wade Redden, Brandon
Brad Hornung Trophy: Lonny Bohonos, Portland
Bill Hunter Trophy: Brendan Witt, Seattle
Del Wilson Trophy: Norm Maracle, Saskatoon
Player of the Year: Sonny Mignacca, Medicine Hat
Dunc McCallum Memorial Trophy: Lorne Molleken, Saskatoon
Scott Munro Memorial Trophy: Kamloops Blazers
President's Cup: Kamloops Blazers

WHL

FOUR BRONCOS MEMORIAL TROPHY

(Most valuable player—selected by coaches)

Season	Player, Team
1966-67	Gerry Pinder, Saskatoon
1967-68	Jim Harrison, Estevan
1968-69	Bobby Clarke, Flin Flon
1969-70	Reggie Leach, Flin Flon
1970-71	Ed Dyck, Calgary
1971-72	John Davidson, Calgary
1972-73	Dennis Sobchuk, Regina
1973-74	Ron Chipperfield, Brandon
1974-75	Bryan Trottier, Lethbridge
1975-76	Bernie Federko, Saskatoon
1976-77	Barry Beck, New Westminster
1977-78	Ryan Walter, Seattle
1978-79	Perry Turnbull, Portland
1979-80	Doug Wickenheiser, Regina
1980-81	Steve Tsujiura, Medicine Hat
1981-82	Mike Vernon, Calgary
1982-83	Mike Vernon, Calgary
1983-84	Ray Ferraro, Brandon
1984-85	Cliff Ronning, New Westminster
1985-86	Emanuel Viveiros, Prince Albert (East Div.)
	Rob Brown, Kamloops (West Division)
1986-87	Joe Sakic, Swift Current (East Division)
	Rob Brown, Kamloops (West Division)
1987-88	Joe Sakic, Swift Current
1988-89	Stu Barnes, Tri-City
1989-90	Glen Goodall, Seattle
1990-91	Ray Whitney, Spokane
1991-92	Steve Konowalchuk, Portland
1992-93	Jason Krywulak, Swift Current
1993-94	Sonny Mignacca, Medicine Hat

BOB CLARKE TROPHY

(Top scorer)

Season	Player, Team
1966-67	Gerry Pinder, Saskatoon
1967-68	Bobby Clarke, Flin Flon
1968-69	Bobby Clarke, Flin Flon
1969-70	Reggie Leach, Flin Flon
1970-71	Chuck Arnason, Flin Flon
1971-72	Tom Lysiak, Medicine Hat
1972-73	Tom Lysiak, Medicine Hat
1973-74	Ron Chipperfield, Brandon
1974-75	Mel Bridgman, Victoria
1975-76	Bernie Federko, Saskatoon
1976-77	Bill Derlago, Brandon
1977-78	Brian Propp, Brandon
1978-79	Brian Propp, Brandon
1979-80	Doug Wickenheiser, Regina
1980-81	Brian Varga, Regina
1981-82	Jack Callander, Regina
1982-83	Dale Derkatch, Regina
1983-84	Ray Ferraro, Brandon
1984-85	Cliff Ronning, New Westminster
1985-86	Rob Brown, Kamloops
1986-87	Rob Brown, Kamloops
1987-88	Joe Sakic, Swift Current
	Theo Fleury, Moose Jaw
1988-89	Dennis Holland, Portland
1989-90	Len Barrie, Kamloops
1990-91	Ray Whitney, Spokane
1991-92	Kevin St. Jacques, Lethbridge
1992-93	Jason Krywulak, Swift Current
1993-94	Lonny Bohonos, Portland

The award was originally known as the Bob Brownridge Memorial Trophy

JIM PIGGOTT MEMORIAL TROPHY

(Rookie of the year)

Season	Player, Team
1966-67	Ron Garwasiuk, Regina
1967-68	Ron Fairbrother, Saskatoon
1968-69	Ron Williams, Edmonton
1969-70	Gene Carr, Flin Flon
1970-71	Stan Weir, Medicine Hat
1971-72	Dennis Sobchuk, Regina
1972-73	Rick Blight, Brandon
1973-74	Cam Connor, Flin Flon
1974-75	Don Murdoch, Medicine Hat
1975-76	Steve Tambellini, Lethbridge
1976-77	Brian Propp, Brandon
1977-78	John Orgrodnick, New Westminster
	Keith Brown, Portland
1978-79	Kelly Kisio, Calgary
1979-80	Grant Fuhr, Victoria
1980-81	Dave Michayluk, Regina
1981-82	Dale Derkatch, Regina
1982-83	Dan Hodgson, Prince Albert
1983-84	Cliff Ronning, New Westminster
1984-85	Mark Mackay, Moose Jaw
1985-86	Neil Brady, Medicine Hat (East Division)
	Ron Shudra, Kamloops, (West Division)
	Dave Waldie, Portland (West Division)
1986-87	Joe Sakic, Swift Current (East Division)
	Dennis Holland, Portland (West Division)
1987-88	Stu Barnes, New Westminster
1988-89	Wes Walz, Lethbridge
1989-90	Petr Nedved, Seattle
1990-91	Donevan Hextall, Prince Albert
1991-92	Ashley Buckberger, Swift Current
1992-93	Jeff Friesen, Regina
1993-94	Wade Redden, Brandon

The award was originally known as the Stewart "Butch" Paul Memorial Trophy.

BRAD HORNUNG TROPHY

(Most sportsmanlike player)

Season	Player, Team
1966-67	Morris Stefaniw, Estevan
1967-68	Bernie Blanchette, Saskatoon
1968-69	Bob Liddington, Calgary
1969-70	Randy Rota, Calgary
1970-71	Lorne Henning, Estevan
1971-72	Ron Chipperfield, Brandon
1972-73	Ron Chipperfield, Brandon
1973-74	Mike Rogers, Calgary
1974-75	Danny Arndt, Saskatoon
1975-76	Blair Chapman, Saskatoon
1976-77	Steve Tambellini, Lethbridge
1977-78	Steve Tambellini, Lethbridge
1978-79	Errol Rausse, Seattle
1979-80	Steve Tsujiura, Medicine Hat
1980-81	Steve Tsujiura, Medicine Hat
1981-82	Mike Moller, Lethbridge
1982-83	Darren Boyko, Winnipeg
1983-84	Mark Lamb, Medicine Hat
1984-85	Cliff Ronning, New Westminster
1985-86	Randy Smith, Saskatoon (East Division)
	Ken Morrison, Kamloops (West Division)
1986-87	Len Nielsen, Regina (East Division)
	Dave Archibald, Portland (West Division)
1987-88	Craig Endean, Regina
1988-89	Blair Atcheynum, Moose Jaw
1989-90	Bryan Bosch, Lethbridge
1990-91	Pat Falloon, Spokane
1991-92	Steve Junker, Spokane
1992-93	Rick Girard, Swift Current

MAJOR JUNIOR LEAGUES

WHL

Season   Player, Team
1993-94—Lonny Bohonos, Portland
    The award was originally known as the Frank Boucher Memorial Trophy for most gentlemanly player.

BILL HUNTER TROPHY
(Top defenseman)

Season   Player, Team
1966-67—Barry Gibbs, Estevan
1967-68—Gerry Hart, Flin Flon
1968-69—Dale Hoganson, Estevan
1969-70—Jim Hargreaves, Winnipeg
1970-71—Ron Jones, Edmonton
1971-72—Jim Watson, Calgary
1972-73—George Pesut, Saskatoon
1973-74—Pat Price, Saskatoon
1974-75—Rick LaPointe, Victoria
1975-76—Kevin McCarthy, Winnipeg
1976-77—Barry Beck, New Westminster
1977-78—Brad McCrimmon, Brandon
1978-79—Keith Brown, Portland
1979-80—David Babych, Portland
1980-81—Jim Benning, Portland
1981-82—Gary Nylund, Portland
1982-83—Gary Leeman, Regina
1983-84—Bob Rouse, Lethbridge
1984-85—Wendel Clark, Saskatoon
1985-86—Emanuel Viveiros, Prince Albert (East Division)
              Glen Wesley, Portland (West Division)
1986-87—Wayne McBean, Medicine Hat (East Division)
              Glen Wesley, Portland (West Division)
1987-88—Greg Hawgood, Kamloops
1988-89—Dan Lambert, Swift Current
1989-90—Kevin Haller, Regina
1990-91—Darryl Sydor, Kamloops
1991-92—Richard Matvichuk, Saskatoon
1992-93—Jason Smith, Regina
1993-94—Brendan Witt, Seattle

DEL WILSON TROPHY
(Top goaltender)

Season   Player, Team
1966-67—Ken Brown, Moose Jaw
1967-68—Chris Worthy, Flin Flon
1968-69—Ray Martyniuk, Flin Flon
1969-70—Ray Martyniuk, Flin Flon
1970-71—Ed Dyck, Calgary
1971-72—John Davidson, Calgary
1972-73—Ed Humphreys, Saskatoon
1973-74—Garth Malarchuk, Calgary
1974-75—Bill Oleschuk, Saskatoon
1975-76—Carey Walker, New Westminster
1976-77—Glen Hanlon, Brandon
1977-78—Bart Hunter, Portland
1978-79—Rick Knickle, Brandon
1979-80—Kevin Eastman, Victoria
1980-81—Grant Fuhr, Victoria
1981-82—Mike Vernon, Calgary
1982-83—Mike Vernon, Calgary
1983-84—Ken Wregget, Lethbridge
1984-85—Troy Gamble, Medicine Hat
1985-86—Mark Fitzpatrick, Medicine Hat
1986-87—Kenton Rein, Prince Albert (East Division)
              Dean Cook, Kamloops (West Division)

Season   Player, Team
1987-88—Troy Gamble, Spokane
1988-89—Danny Lorenz, Seattle
1989-90—Trevor Kidd, Brandon
1990-91—Jamie McLennan, Lethbridge
1991-92—Corey Hirsch, Kamloops
1992-93—Trevor Wilson, Brandon
1993-94—Norm Maracle, Saskatoon

PLAYER OF THE YEAR
(Selected by fans and media)

Season   Player, Team
1974-75—Ed Staniowski, Regina
1975-76—Bernie Federko, Saskatoon
1976-77—Kevin McCarthy, Winnipeg
1977-78—Ryan Walter, Seattle
1978-79—Brian Propp, Brandon
1979-80—Doug Wickenheiser, Regina
1980-81—Barry Pederson, Victoria
1981-82—Mike Vernon, Calgary
1982-83—Dean Evason, Kamloops
1983-84—Ray Ferraro, Brandon
1984-85—Dan Hodgson, Prince Albert
1985-86—Emanuel Viveiros, Prince Albert
1986-87—Rob Brown, Kamloops
1987-88—Joe Sakic, Swift Current
1988-89—Dennis Holland, Portland
1989-90—Wes Walz, Lethbridge
1990-91—Ray Whitney, Spokane
1991-92—Corey Hirsch, Kamloops
1992-93—Jason Krywulak, Swift Current
1993-94—Sonny Mignacca, Medicine Hat

DUNC McCALLUM MEMORIAL TROPHY
(Coach of the year)

Season   Coach, Team
1968-69—Scotty Munro, Calgary
1969-70—Pat Ginnell, Flin Flon
1970-71—Pat Ginnell, Flin Flon
1971-72—Earl Ingarfield, Regina
1972-73—Pat Ginnell, Flin Flon
1973-74—Stan Dunn, Swift Current
1974-75—Pat Ginnell, Victoria
1975-76—Ernie McLean, New Westminster
1976-77—Dunc McCallum, Brandon
1977-78—Jack Shupe, Victoria
              Dave King, Billings
1978-79—Dunc McCallum, Brandon
1979-80—Doug Sauter, Calgary
1980-81—Ken Hodge, Portland
1981-82—Jack Sangster, Seattle
1982-83—Darryl Lubiniecki, Saskatoon
1983-84—Terry Simpson, Prince Albert
1984-85—Doug Sauter, Medicine Hat
1985-86—Terry Simpson, Prince Albert
1986-87—Ken Hitchcock, Kam. (W. Division)
              Graham James, S. Curr. (E. Div.)
1987-88—Marcel Comeau, Saskatoon
1988-89—Ron Kennedy, Medicine Hat
1989-90—Ken Hitchcock, Kamloops
1990-91—Tom Renney, Kamloops
1991-92—Bryan Maxwell, Spokane
1992-93—Marcel Comeau, Tacoma
1993-94—Lorne Molleken, Saskatoon

REGULAR-SEASON CHAMPION

PLAYOFF CHAMPION

Season	Team	Team
1966-67	Edmonton Oil Kings	Moose Jaw Canucks
1967-68	Flin Flon Bombers	Estevan Bruins
1968-69	Flin Flon Bombers	Flin Flon Bombers
1969-70	Flin Flon Bombers	Flin Flon Bombers
1970-71	Edmonton Oil Kings	Edmonton Oil Kings
1971-72	Calgary Centennials	Edmonton Oil Kings
1972-73	Saskatoon Blades	Medicine Hat Tigers
1973-74	Regina Pats	Regina Pats
1974-75	Victoria Cougars	New Westminster Bruins
1975-76	New Westminster Bruins	New Westminster Bruins
1976-77	New Westminster Bruins	New Westminster Bruins
1977-78	Brandon Wheat Kings	New Westminster Bruins
1978-79	Brandon Wheat Kings	Brandon Wheat Kings
1979-80	Portland Winter Hawks	Regina Pats
1980-81	Victoria Cougars	Victoria Cougars
1981-82	Lethbridge Broncos	Portland Winter Hawks
1982-83	Saskatoon Blades	Lethbridge Broncos
1983-84	Kamloops Junior Oilers	Kamloops Junior Oilers
1984-85	Prince Albert Raiders	Prince Albert Raiders
1985-86	Medicine Hat Tigers	Kamloops Blazers
1986-87	Kamloops Blazers	Medicine Hat Tigers
1987-88	Saskatoon Blades	Medicine Hat Tigers
1988-89	Swift Current Broncos	Swift Current Broncos
1989-90	Kamloops Blazers	Kamloops Blazers
1990-91	Kamloops Blazers	Spokane Chiefs
1991-92	Kamloops Blazers	Kamloops Blazers
1992-93	Swift Current Broncos	Swift Current Broncos
1993-94	Kamloops Blazers	Kamloops Blazers

The WHL regular-season champion is awarded the Scott Munro Memorial Trophy and the playoff champion is awarded the President's Cup.

COLLEGE HOCKEY

NCAA Division I

Central Collegiate Hockey Association

Eastern College Athletic Conference

Hockey East

Western Collegiate Hockey Association

Independents

Canadian Interuniversity Athletic Union

Canadian Colleges

NCAA DIVISION I

1993-94 SEASON

NCAA TOURNAMENT

EAST REGIONAL
(Albany, N.Y.)
Wisconsin 6, Western Michigan 3
New Hampshire 2, Rensselaer 0
Boston University 4, Wisconsin 1
Harvard 7, New Hampshire 1

WEST REGIONAL
(East Lansing, Mich.)
Lake Superior State 6, Northeastern 5 (OT)
Lowell 4, Michigan State 3
Lake Superior State 5, Michigan 4 (OT)
Minnesota 2, Lowell 1 (2 OT)

SEMIFINAL SERIES
(St. Paul, Minn.)
Lake Superior State 3, Harvard 2 (OT)
Boston University 4, Minnesota 1

CHAMPIONSHIP GAME
(St. Paul, Minn.)
Lake Superior State 9, Boston University 1

ALL-TOURNAMENT TEAM

Player	Pos.	College
Blaine Lacher	G	Lake Superior State
Keith Aldridge	D	Lake Superior State
Steven Barnes	D	Lake Superior State
Clayton Beddoes	F	Lake Superior State
Mike Pomichter	F	Boston University
Sean Tallaire	F	Lake Superior State

NCAA Most Valuable Player: Sean Tallaire, Lake Superior State.

ALL-AMERICA TEAMS

EAST

First team	Pos.	Second team
Wayne Roloson, Lowell	G	Jamie Ram, Michigan Tech
Sean McCann, Harvard	D	John Gruden, Ferris State
Brian Mueller, Clarkson	D	Shawn Reid, Colorado Col.
Craig Conroy, Clarkson	F	Chris Marinucci, Min.-Duluth
Steve Martins, Harvard	F	David Oliver, Michigan
Mike Pomichter, Boston U.	F	Brian Wiseman, Michigan

WEST

First team	Pos.	Second team
J.P. McKersie, Boston U.	G	Steve Shields, Michigan
Rich Brennan, Boston U.	D	Chris McAlpine, Minnesota
Derek Maguire, Harvard	D	Jeff Wells, Bowling Green St.
Shane Henry, Lowell	F	Clayton Beddoes, L. Sup. St.
Jacques Joubert, Boston U.	F	Dean Fedorchuk, Alaska-Fair.
Chad Quenneville, Prov.	F	Steve Guolla, Michigan St.

HISTORY

TOURNAMENT CHAMPIONS

Year	Champion	Coach	Score	Runner-up	Most outstanding player
1948	Michigan	Vic Heyliger	8-4	Dartmouth	Joe Riley, F, Dartmouth
1949	Boston College	John Kelley	4-3	Dartmouth	Dick Desmond, G, Dartmouth
1950	Colorado College	Cheddy Thompson	13-4	Boston University	Ralph Bevins, G, Boston University
1951	Michigan	Vic Heyliger	7-1	Brown	Ed Whiston, G, Brown
1952	Michigan	Vic Heyliger	4-1	Colorado College	Kenneth Kinsley, G, Colorado College
1953	Michigan	Vic Heyliger	7-3	Minnesota	John Matchefts, F, Michigan
1954	Rensselaer	Ned Harkness	5-4*	Minnesota	Abbie Moore, F, Rensselaer
1955	Michigan	Vic Heyliger	5-3	Colorado College	Philip Hilton, D, Colorado College
1956	Michigan	Vic Heyliger	7-5	Michigan Tech	Lorne Howes, G, Michigan
1957	Colorado College	Thomas Bedecki	13-6	Michigan	Bob McCusker, F, Colorado College
1958	Denver	Murray Armstrong	6-2	North Dakota	Murray Massier, F, Denver
1959	North Dakota	Bob May	4-3*	Michigan State	Reg Morelli, F, North Dakota
1960	Denver	Murray Armstrong	5-3	Michigan Tech	Bob Marquis, F, Boston University
					Barry Urbanski, G, Boston University
					Louis Angotti, F, Michigan Tech
1961	Denver	Murray Armstrong	12-2	St. Lawrence	Bill Masterton, F, Denver
1962	Michigan Tech	John MacInnes	7-1	Clarkson	Louis Angotti, F, Michigan Tech
1963	North Dakota	Barney Thorndycraft	6-5	Denver	Al McLean, F, North Dakota
1964	Michigan	Allen Renfrew	6-3	Denver	Bob Gray, G, Michigan
1965	Michigan Tech	John MacInnes	8-2	Boston College	Gary Milroy, F, Michigan Tech
1966	Michigan State	Amo Bessone	6-1	Clarkson	Gaye Cooley, G, Michigan State
1967	Cornell	Ned Harkness	4-1	Boston University	Walt Stanowski, D, Cornell
1968	Denver	Murray Armstrong	4-0	North Dakota	Gerry Powers, G, Denver
1969	Denver	Murray Armstrong	4-3	Cornell	Keith Magnuson, D, Denver
1970	Cornell	Ned Harkness	6-4	Clarkson	Daniel Lodboa, D, Cornell
1971	Boston University	Jack Kelley	4-2	Minnesota	Dan Brady, G, Boston University
1972	Boston University	Jack Kelley	4-0	Cornell	Tim Regan, G, Boston University
1973	Wisconsin	Bob Johnson	4-2	Vacated	Dean Talafous, F, Wisconsin
1974	Minnesota	Herb Brooks	4-2	Michigan Tech	Brad Shelstad, G, Minnesota
1975	Michigan Tech	John MacInnes	6-1	Minnesota	Jim Warden, G, Michigan Tech
1976	Minnesota	Herb Brooks	6-4	Michigan Tech	Tom Vanelli, F, Minnesota

Year	Champion	Coach	Score	Runner-up	Most outstanding player
1977	Wisconsin	Bob Johnson	6-5*	Michigan	Julian Baretta, G, Wisconsin
1978	Boston University	Jack Parker	5-3	Boston College	Jack O'Callahan, D, Boston University
1979	Minnesota	Herb Brooks	4-3	North Dakota	Steve Janaszak, G, Minnesota
1980	North Dakota	John Gasparini	5-2	Northern Michigan	Doug Smail, F, North Dakota
1981	Wisconsin	Bob Johnson	6-3	Minnesota	Marc Behrend, G, Wisconsin
1982	North Dakota	John Gasparini	5-2	Wisconsin	Phil Sykes, F, North Dakota
1983	Wisconsin	Jeff Sauer	6-2	Harvard	Marc Behrend, G, Wisconsin
1984	Bowling Green State	Jerry York	5-4*	Minnesota-Duluth	Gary Kruzich, G, Bowling Green State
1985	Rensselaer	Mike Addesa	2-1	Providence	Chris Terreri, G, Providence
1986	Michigan State	Ron Mason	6-5	Harvard	Mike Donnelly, F, Michigan State
1987	North Dakota	John Gasparini	5-3	Michigan State	Tony Hrkac, F, North Dakota
1988	Lake Superior State	Frank Anzalone	4-3*	St. Lawrence	Bruce Hoffort, G, Lake Superior State
1989	Harvard	Bill Cleary	4-3*	Minnesota	Ted Donato, F, Harvard
1990	Wisconsin	Jeff Sauer	7-3	Colgate	Chris Tancill, F, Wisconsin
1991	Northern Michigan	Rick Comley	8-7*	Boston University	Scott Beattie, F, Northern Michigan
1992	Lake Superior State	Jeff Jackson	5-3	Wisconsin	Paul Constantin, F, Lake Superior State
1993	Maine	Shawn Walsh	5-4	Lake Superior State	Jim Montgomery, F, Maine
1994	Lake Superior State	Jeff Jackson	9-1	Boston University	Sean Tallaire, F, Lake Superior State

*Overtime.

ALL-TIME TOURNAMENT RECORDS

	Visits	W	L	GF	GA	Pct.	Finished 1st	2nd
Colgate	1	3	1	10	11	.750	0	1
Michigan	17	25	12	214	137	.676	7	2
‡Wisconsin	15	28	13	171	124	.683	5	3
North Dakota	13	22	11	132	102	.667	5	2
Denver	11	17	9	121	73	.654	5	2
#Lake Superior State	8	18	9	130	89	.667	3	1
*Northeastern	3	3	3	30	30	.500	0	0
Michigan Tech	10	13	9	118	85	.591	3	4
†Michigan State	14	22	17	165	144	.564	2	2
Maine	6	12	9	89	86	.571	1	0
#Rensselaer Polytechnic Institute	7	8	7	52	52	.533	2	0
Minnesota	19	24	21	231	210	.533	3	6
Northern Michigan	6	8	7	65	65	.533	1	1
Boston University	20	26	25	210	217	.510	3	4
Merrimack	1	2	2	14	16	.500	0	0
Yale	1	1	1	7	5	.500	0	0
Cornell	9	9	10	66	71	.474	2	2
Minnesota-Duluth	4	5	6	43	41	.455	0	1
Providence	6	9	11	71	73	.450	0	1
Dartmouth	5	4	5	38	37	.444	0	2
Clarkson	12	11	15	84	111	.423	0	3
*Bowling Green State	9	8	12	66	88	.400	1	0
Colorado College	9	6	10	76	84	.375	2	2
†Harvard	16	14	24	143	166	.368	1	2
Boston College	18	13	27	141	105	.325	1	2
Alaska-Anchorage	3	2	5	22	39	.286	0	0
Brown	4	2	5	31	45	.286	0	1
St. Lawrence	12	5	21	76	123	.192	0	2
New Hampshire	6	3	10	40	67	.231	0	0
‡Lowell	2	1	2	10	16	.333	0	0
Miami of Ohio	1	0	1	1	3	.000	0	0
St. Cloud State	1	0	2	5	10	.000	0	0
Vermont	1	0	2	2	10	.000	0	0
Western Michigan	2	0	3	7	17	.000	0	0

(Denver also participated in 1973 tournament but its record was voided by the NCAA in 1977 upon discovery of violations by the University. The team had finished second in '73.)

*Bowling Green State and Northeastern played to a 2-2 tie in 1981-82.
†Harvard and Michigan State played to a 3-3 tie in 1982-83.
#Lake Superior State and RPI played to a 3-3 tie in 1984-85.
‡Wisconsin and Lowell played to a 4-4 tie in 1987-88.
Hobey Baker Memorial Trophy (Top college hockey player in U.S.): Chris Marinucci, Minnesota-Duluth.

HOBEY BAKER AWARD WINNERS

(Top college hockey player in United States)

Year	Player, College
1981	Neal Broten, Minnesota
1982	George McPhee, Bowling Green St.
1983	Mark Fusco, Harvard
1984	Tom Kurvers, Minnesota-Duluth
1985	Bill Watson, Minnesota-Duluth
1986	Scott Fusco, Harvard
1987	Tony Hrkac, North Dakota
1988	Robb Stauber, Minnesota
1989	Lane MacDonald, Harvard
1990	Kip Miller, Michigan State
1991	David Emma, Boston College
1992	Scott Pellerin, Maine
1993	Paul Kariya, Maine
1994	Chris Marinucci, Min.-Duluth

CENTRAL COLLEGIATE HOCKEY ASSOCIATION

1993-94 SEASON

FINAL STANDINGS

Team	G	W	L	T	Pts.	GF	GA
Michigan (33-7-1)...	30	24	5	1	49	146	80
L. Sup. St. (31-10-4)..	30	18	8	4	40	129	69
Mich. St. (23-13-5)..	30	17	8	5	39	115	87
W. Mich. (24-13-3)...	30	18	10	2	38	117	101
Mia. of Ohio (21-16-1)	30	17	12	1	35	112	94
Bowl. Green (19-17-2)	30	15	13	2	32	114	105
Ferris St. (13-24-1)..	30	12	17	1	25	110	122
Notre Dame (11-22-5)	30	9	16	5	23	85	121
Ill.-Chi. (10-27-2).....	30	8	20	2	18	101	144
Ohio State (7-23-5)..	30	6	19	5	17	81	124
Kent (11-26-2)	30	6	22	2	14	109	172
A'ka F'banks (24-13-1)				Affiliate (8-7-0 vs. CCHA teams)			

Overall record in parentheses.

PLAYOFF RESULTS

FIRST ROUND

Miami of Ohio 5, Alaska-Fairbanks 3
Alaska-Fairbanks 6, Miami of Ohio 1
Miami of Ohio 4, Alaska-Fairbanks 3
(Miami of Ohio won series, 2-1)

Western Michigan 6, Notre Dame 3
Western Michigan 7, Notre Dame 1
(Western Michigan won series, 2-0)

Lake Superior State 5, Ohio State 0
Lake Superior State 8, Ohio State 0
(Lake Superior State won series, 2-0)

Illinois-Chicago 4, Michigan State 3
Michigan State 2, Illinois-Chicago 1 (OT)
Michigan State 8, Illinois-Chicago 3
(Michigan State won series, 2-1)

Michigan 5, Kent 4 (OT)
Michigan 10, Kent 3
(Michigan won series, 2-0)

Bowling Green State 3, Ferris State 0
Bowling Green State 3, Ferris State 2 (OT)
(Bowling Green State won series, 2-0)

QUARTERFINALS

Western Michigan 4, Miami of Ohio 3
Michigan State 3, Bowling Green State 2 (OT)

SEMIFINALS

Michigan 6, Western Michigan 4
Lake Superior State 4, Michigan State 0

CHAMPIONSHIP GAME

Michigan 3, Lake Superior State 0

ALL-STAR TEAMS

First team	Pos.	Second team
Steve Shields, Michigan	G	Mike Buzak, Mich. State
John Gruden, Ferris State	D	Bobby Marshall, Miami
Jeff Wells, Bowling Green	D	Keith Aldridge, L.S.S.
David Oliver, Michigan	F	Steve Guolla, Mich. State
Brian Wiseman, Michigan	F	Mike Knuble, Michigan
Anson Carter, Mich. State	F	Clayton Beddoes, L.S.S.

AWARD WINNERS

Player of the year: David Oliver, Michigan
Rookie of the year: Brendan Morrison, Michigan
Coach of the year: Red Berenson, Michigan
Leading scorers: Dean Fedorchuk, Alaska-Fairbanks
Tavis MacMillan, Alaska-Fairbanks
Playoff MVP: Mike Stone, Michigan

INDIVIDUAL STATISTICS

ALASKA-FAIRBANKS (AFFILIATE)
SCORING

	Pos.	Class	Games	G	A	Pts.	PIM
Dean Fedorchuk	F	Sr.	38	42	32	74	88
Tavis MacMillan	F	Sr.	38	42	32	74	66
Don Lester	D	Sr.	38	19	41	60	32
Jason Eckel	F	Jr.	36	25	28	53	29
Warren Carter........	F	Jr.	38	11	29	40	22
Corey Spring	F	Jr.	38	19	18	37	34
Dallas Ferguson	D	So.	37	6	31	37	18
Trent Schachle	F	So.	38	18	18	36	30
Pat Williams	F	Fr.	37	8	25	33	20
Greg Milles	F	So.	33	16	11	27	32
Lorne Kanigan	F	Sr.	32	7	19	26	66
Cody Bowtell..........	F	Fr.	31	3	10	13	2
Kirk Patton	D	Jr.	35	3	9	12	55
Glenn Odishaw.......	D	Sr.	37	3	8	11	33
Rob Phillips...........	F	Fr.	29	3	4	7	10
Mark Cotter............	D	Jr.	32	2	5	7	18
Fred Scott	F	So.	20	3	3	6	8
Chris Hodges	D	Fr.	18	3	3	6	24
Scott Keyes	F	Sr.	18	2	4	6	14
Dima Kulmanovsky.	F	Jr.	8	3	2	5	4
Kevin Oakenfold	F	So.	15	3	1	4	36
Marcel Aubin	D	Jr.	27	0	3	3	50
Derek Norton..........	F	Fr.	4	1	1	2	12
Kyle Armstrong	F	Fr.	1	0	0	0	0
Ryan Olier	F	Fr.	1	0	0	0	0
Chris Carney..........	D	Jr.	1	0	0	0	0
Bond Sutton	G	So.	2	0	0	0	0
Bob Schwark	D	So.	4	0	0	0	14
Larry Moberg........	G	So.	18	0	0	0	4
Brian Fish	G	Jr.	26	0	0	0	12

GOALTENDING

	Games	Min.	W	L	T	Goals	SO	Avg.
Brian Fish..................	26	1354	13	8	1	82	1	3.63
Larry Moberg	18	898	11	5	0	65	1	4.34
Bond Sutton..............	2	40	0	0	0	3	0	4.50

BOWLING GREEN STATE
SCORING

	Pos.	Class	Games	G	A	Pts.	PIM
Brian Holzinger	F	Jr.	38	22	15	37	24
Jeff Wells	D	Sr.	38	8	29	37	40
Sean Pronger	F	Sr.	38	17	17	34	38
Curtis Fry...............	F	Fr.	38	16	18	34	79
Todd Reirden	D	Sr.	38	7	23	30	56
Jason Clark............	F	So.	37	10	18	28	39
Tom Glantz.............	F	Jr.	29	8	14	22	22
Jason Helbing	F	So.	29	10	11	21	14
Kevin Lune	F	Jr.	29	10	10	20	24
Mike Johnson	F	Fr.	38	6	14	20	18

	Pos.	Class	Games	G	A	Pts.	PIM
Jeff Herman	F	So.	29	7	11	18	20
Kelly Perrault.........	D	Fr.	38	5	12	17	36
Mike Hall	F	So.	34	7	8	15	14
Jamie Williams	F	So.	38	5	10	15	28
Chad Ackerman	D	So.	37	4	8	12	28
Brandon Carper	D	Jr.	36	3	9	12	62
Brett Punchard......	F	Fr.	27	1	8	9	6
Jeff Elvin................	F	Fr.	32	3	4	7	8
Todd Kelman..........	D	Fr.	18	0	2	2	12
Matt Eldred	D	Fr.	25	0	2	2	44
Bob Petrie	G	Fr.	31	0	2	2	2
Kevin Seguin..........	F	Fr.	6	0	1	1	4
Noel Crawford........	G	So.	1	0	0	0	0
A.J. Plaskey...........	F	Sr.	2	0	0	0	2
Glen Mears.............	D	Sr.	4	0	0	0	2
Will Clarke	G	Jr.	11	0	0	0	2

GOALTENDING

	Games	Min.	W	L	T	Goals	SO	Avg.
Noel Crawford	1	2	0	0	0	0	0	0.00
Bob Petrie	31	1765	16	12	2	91	2	3.09
Will Clarke..............	11	549	3	5	0	39	0	4.26

FERRIS STATE
SCORING

	Pos.	Class	Games	G	A	Pts.	PIM
Tim Christian	F	Jr.	38	21	22	43	26
John Gruden	D	Sr.	38	11	25	36	52
Doug Smith	F	Sr.	29	20	13	33	32
Val Passarelli.........	F	So.	38	12	13	25	52
Robb McIntyre	F	Jr.	32	6	17	23	84
Derek Crimin	F	Fr.	38	12	9	21	34
Mike Kolenda	F	Jr.	37	8	11	19	68
Keith Sergott........	D	So.	36	4	15	19	32
Andy Roach	D	Fr.	32	4	15	19	18
John Duff	F	So.	25	10	7	17	40
Dwight Parrish	D	So.	38	1	15	16	60
Scot Bell	F	So.	32	7	8	15	42
Colin Dodunski.......	D	Jr.	26	2	8	10	52
Gary Kitching.........	F	Jr.	18	4	5	9	18
Phil Sturock	F	Fr.	36	3	5	8	10
Greg Paine	F	So.	32	3	5	8	12
Gordy Hunt	F	Fr.	37	2	3	5	42
Brad Burnham	F	Jr.	10	2	3	5	18
Dusty Anderson.....	F	Fr.	34	0	3	3	22
J. Sotropa..............	D/F	Jr.	29	1	1	2	18
Luke Harvey	F	Jr.	33	0	1	1	22
Craig Lisko.............	G	Sr.	33	0	1	1	4
J.J. Bamberger	F	So.	2	0	0	0	0
Rich Nagy	G	Jr.	5	0	0	0	0
Seth Appert............	G	So.	6	0	0	0	0

GOALTENDING

	Games	Min.	W	L	T	Goals	SO	Avg.
Craig Lisko	33	1904	12	17	1	115	0	3.62
Seth Appert	6	185	1	3	0	15	0	4.86
Rich Nagy	5	210	4	0	0	21	0	6.00

ILLINOIS-CHICAGO
SCORING

	Pos.	Class	Games	G	A	Pts.	PIM
Derek Knorr	F	Jr.	35	23	16	39	88
Chris MacDonald...	F	Jr.	37	11	24	35	34
Mike Peron	F	Fr.	36	19	13	32	102
Mark Zdan	F	Sr.	37	12	17	29	46
Mike Dennis	D	Sr.	39	8	19	27	50
Shannon Finn	D/F	Jr.	39	5	22	27	42
Rob Hutson	F	So.	21	9	7	16	44
Todd Finner	F	Sr.	35	3	13	16	78
Alan Dunbar	F	Fr.	36	9	5	14	124
Brian Thibodeau....	F	So.	36	6	8	14	56
Bob Gohde.............	D	Jr.	39	3	7	10	42
Matt Brenner	D	So.	35	2	8	10	24
Trevor Mathias......	F	So.	30	5	4	9	26
Rob Mottau	D	Jr.	34	3	6	9	32

	Pos.	Class	Games	G	A	Pts.	PIM
Jeff Blum................	D	Jr.	30	2	6	8	50
Matt McElwee........	F	Fr.	34	4	2	6	34
Matt Hanaman	F	Fr.	19	5	0	5	18
Marc Genest	F	So.	22	2	3	5	24
Connor Kerr	F	Fr.	20	2	2	4	4
Rick Lacroix	F/D	Jr.	30	0	4	4	6
Marty McMillan	D/F	So.	21	0	4	4	40
Ryan Walls.............	F	Fr.	25	1	2	3	4
Shaun Summerville.	F	Fr.	9	1	1	2	6
Sean Carter	G	Fr.	2	0	0	0	0
Jeff Featherstone ..	G	Sr.	20	0	0	0	0
Paul Spencer..........	G	Fr.	27	0	0	0	0

GOALTENDING

	Games	Min.	W	L	T	Goals	SO	Avg.
Paul Spencer	27	1391	9	16	1	101	0	4.36
Jeff Featherstone	20	934	5	11	1	75	0	4.82
Sean Carter	2	26	0	0	0	5	0	11.55

KENT
SCORING

	Pos.	Class	Games	G	A	Pts.	PIM
Claude Morin	F	Jr.	39	17	39	56	36
Dean Sylvester	F	Jr.	39	22	24	46	28
David Dartsch........	F	So.	39	15	20	35	68
Mark Kotary...........	F	Fr.	38	19	11	30	28
Bob Krosky	F	Sr.	39	13	15	28	104
Kevin McPherson ..	F	Sr.	35	10	15	25	40
Sam Thornbury	F	Sr.	39	9	16	25	36
Quinn Fair	D	So.	39	11	13	24	92
Jim Mitchell	F	So.	39	7	14	21	82
Steve Sabo	D	Fr.	36	3	15	18	64
Erik Raygor............	F	Fr.	38	9	3	12	64
Colin Muldoon........	D	Fr.	39	5	5	10	12
Lane Gunderson	D	Jr.	35	1	9	10	16
Marc Drouin	F	So.	29	3	6	9	20
Steve McLean	F	Sr.	18	3	3	6	8
Bob Mainhardt.......	F	Fr.	28	2	3	5	84
Jason Pain	F	Fr.	19	1	3	4	16
Jason Watt	D	Jr.	34	0	4	4	8
Evan Sylvester	F	Fr.	19	0	2	2	2
Roger Mischke	D	Sr.	33	0	2	2	122
Jason Ricci	D	Fr.	8	0	1	1	4
Sebastien Bilodeau	D	Fr.	19	0	1	1	0
Mario Lacasse	G	Jr.	15	0	0	0	0
Scott Shaw	G	Sr.	29	0	0	0	8

GOALTENDING

	Games	Min.	W	L	T	Goals	SO	Avg.
Mario Lacasse.........	15	726	5	7	0	64	0	5.29
Scott Shaw	29	1635	6	19	2	152	0	5.58

LAKE SUPERIOR STATE
SCORING

	Pos.	Class	Games	G	A	Pts.	PIM
Sean Tallaire.........	F	So.	45	23	32	55	22
Clayton Beddoes	F	Sr.	44	23	31	54	56
Wayne Strachan....	F	Jr.	45	24	23	47	74
Kurt Miller	F	Sr.	40	19	23	42	58
Rob Valicevic.........	F	Jr.	45	18	20	38	46
Mike Morin	F	Jr.	44	12	25	37	75
Gerald Tallaire	F	Fr.	35	11	23	34	28
Keith Aldridge	D	So.	45	10	24	34	86
Steven Barnes	D	Sr.	39	7	24	31	34
Jay Ness	F	Sr.	45	10	17	27	12
Jason Trzcinski	F	So.	43	12	6	18	32
Mike Matteucci......	D	So.	45	6	11	17	64
Brad Willner	D	Jr.	45	2	13	15	42
Matt Alvey	F	Fr.	41	6	8	14	16
Dan Angelelli	F	Fr.	44	4	8	12	66
Darren Wetherill ...	D	Sr.	44	1	8	9	92
Scott McCabe	F	Fr.	18	3	5	8	14
Danny Galarneau ..	F	Fr.	35	4	3	7	28
Gino Pulente...........	D	Fr.	21	2	3	5	4
Josh Bilben	D	Fr.	22	0	3	3	14

	Pos.	Class	Games	G	A	Pts.	PIM
Paul Sass	G	Fr.	11	0	3	3	0
Brian Felsner	F	Fr.	6	1	1	2	6
Blaine Lacher	G	Jr.	30	0	2	2	28
Ryan Sharpe	D	Fr.	8	0	1	1	8
Mike Koiranen	F	Fr.	10	0	1	1	8
Sean Kulick	G	Fr.	8	0	0	0	0

GOALTENDING

	Games	Min.	W	L	T	Goals	SO	Avg.
Blaine Lacher	30	1785	20	5	4	59	6	1.98
Sean Kulick	8	413	4	2	0	18	1	2.62
Paul Sass	11	539	7	3	0	25	0	2.78

MIAMI OF OHIO
SCORING

	Pos.	Class	Games	G	A	Pts.	PIM
Kevyn Adams	F	So.	36	15	28	43	24
Shawn Penn	F	Sr.	38	20	9	29	48
Enrico Blasi	F	Sr.	38	13	15	28	18
Marc Boxer	F	Jr.	36	7	21	28	18
Bobby Marshall	D	Sr.	38	3	24	27	76
Matt Oates	F	Jr.	33	14	12	26	60
Andrew Miller	F	Jr.	37	12	13	25	14
Dan Carter	F	Jr.	35	9	13	22	40
Jason Mallon	F	Jr.	35	9	8	17	28
Andrew Backen	D	So.	36	4	12	16	48
Barry Schutte	F	Fr.	34	9	6	15	40
Trent Eigner	D	Sr.	32	3	8	11	33
Stephen Rohr	F	Sr.	36	1	10	11	20
Dan Daikawa	D	Jr.	37	6	3	9	30
Pat Hanley	D/F	Fr.	37	4	4	8	76
Tom White	F	Fr.	31	1	6	7	26
Jeff Reid	D	Fr.	25	0	7	7	4
Rene Vonlanthen	F	Sr.	24	5	0	5	22
Justin Krall	D	So.	38	1	4	5	32
Bob Clouston	F	Fr.	10	1	4	5	2
Richard Shulmistra	G	Sr.	27	0	1	1	2
Eustace King	G	So.	1	0	0	0	0
Derek Block	F	Jr.	2	0	0	0	2
Jared Echternach	F	Fr.	5	0	0	0	0
Jason Crane	F	Jr.	11	0	0	0	4
K. Deschambeault	G	So.	15	0	0	0	2

GOALTENDING

	Games	Min.	W	L	T	Goals	SO	Avg.
Richard Shulmistra	27	1521	13	12	1	74	0	2.92
Kevin Deschambeault	15	740	8	4	0	39	0	3.16
Eustace King	1	12	0	0	0	1	0	4.97

MICHIGAN
SCORING

	Pos.	Class	Games	G	A	Pts.	PIM
Brian Wiseman	F	Sr.	40	19	50	69	44
David Oliver	F	Jr.	41	28	40	68	16
Mike Knuble	F	Jr.	41	32	26	58	71
Brendan Morrison	F	Fr.	38	20	28	48	24
Mike Stone	F	Sr.	41	14	27	41	22
Jason Botterill	F	Fr.	37	21	19	40	94
Kevin Hilton	F	So.	39	11	12	23	16
Mike Legg	F	Fr.	37	10	13	23	20
Warren Luhning	F	Fr.	38	13	6	19	83
Ryan Sittler	F	So.	26	9	9	18	14
John Madden	F	Fr.	36	6	11	17	14
Harold Schock	D	Jr.	41	3	14	17	42
Steven Halko	D	So.	41	2	13	15	32
Rick Willis	F	Jr.	40	8	5	13	83
Tim Hogan	D	Jr.	37	2	10	12	36
Anton Fedorov	F	Jr.	12	1	6	7	6
Blake Sloan	D	Fr.	38	2	4	6	48
John Arnold	F	So.	9	2	4	6	8
Steve Shields	G	Sr.	36	0	6	6	18
Chris Frescoln	D	Jr.	21	1	3	4	38
Peter Bourke	D	Fr.	24	0	4	4	16
Alan Sinclair	D	Jr.	18	0	4	4	14

	Pos.	Class	Games	G	A	Pts.	PIM
Ron Sacka	F	Jr.	17	1	2	3	10
Mark Sakala	D	Jr.	25	0	3	3	18
Al Loges	G	Jr.	5	0	1	1	2
Drew Denzin	D	So.	1	0	0	0	0
Chris Gordon	G	Sr.	11	0	0	0	0

GOALTENDING

	Games	Min.	W	L	T	Goals	SO	Avg.
Al Loges	5	80	0	0	0	3	0	2.25
Steve Shields	36	1961	28	6	1	87	2	2.66
Chris Gordon	11	422	5	1	0	19	0	2.70

MICHIGAN STATE
SCORING

	Pos.	Class	Games	G	A	Pts.	PIM
Steve Guolla	F	Jr.	41	23	46	69	16
Anson Carter	F	So.	39	30	24	54	36
Rem Murray	F	Jr.	41	16	38	54	18
Steve Suk	F	Jr.	41	12	28	40	14
Kelly Harper	F	Sr.	41	14	18	32	26
Steve Ferranti	F	Fr.	38	6	14	20	20
Nicolas Perreault	D	Sr.	40	6	10	16	109
Chris Smith	D	So.	33	6	10	16	32
Bart Turner	D	Sr.	41	5	11	16	40
Michael Burkett	F	Sr.	41	7	7	14	48
Scott Worden	F	Sr.	40	4	7	11	30
Chris Slater	D	So.	27	3	8	11	14
Brian Clifford	F	So.	35	6	4	10	22
Tony Tuzzolino	F	Fr.	38	4	3	7	50
John Wiegand	F	Fr.	34	4	3	7	40
Bart Vanstaalduinen	D	So.	41	0	7	7	60
Chris Sullivan	D	So.	31	2	4	6	24
Brian Crane	F	Fr.	21	3	1	4	10
Matt Albers	F	Jr.	20	3	0	3	22
Ryan Fleming	D	So.	13	1	2	3	4
Steve Norton	D	Sr.	23	0	3	3	36
Mike Buzak	G	Jr.	39	0	3	3	4
Eric Kruse	G	Jr.	6	0	1	1	2
Mike Ware	F	So.	19	0	1	1	14

GOALTENDING

	Games	Min.	W	L	T	Goals	SO	Avg.
Mike Buzak	39	2297	21	12	5	104	2	2.72
Eric Kruse	6	210	2	1	0	18	0	5.14

NOTRE DAME
SCORING

	Pos.	Class	Games	G	A	Pts.	PIM
Jamie Ling	F	So.	38	13	26	39	51
Matt Osiecki	D	Sr.	38	8	18	26	28
Tim Harberts	F	Fr.	36	10	12	22	19
Brent Lamppa	F	Jr.	37	10	7	17	24
Brett Bruininks	F	So.	38	9	7	16	76
Terry Lorenz	F	Fr.	38	10	5	15	42
Ben Nelsen	D	Fr.	37	7	8	15	30
Jay Matushak	F	So.	37	7	5	12	8
Brian McCarthy	F	Fr.	38	6	6	12	30
Jamie Morshead	F	So.	23	5	7	12	52
Jeremy Coe	D	So.	34	4	8	12	72
Troy Cusey	F	Jr.	31	3	9	12	44
Garry Gruber	D	So.	37	2	10	12	42
John Rushin	F	Jr.	36	3	6	9	60
Chris Bales	F	So.	26	3	6	9	14
Carey Nemeth	F	Jr.	32	3	4	7	30
Davide Dal Grande	D	So.	32	2	4	6	20
Bryan Welch	D	Fr.	34	3	2	5	72
Jeff Hasselman	F	Jr.	16	0	5	5	16
Sean McAlister	F	Fr.	14	3	0	3	12
Matt Bieck	D	So.	16	2	1	3	20
Ryan Thornton	F	Fr.	11	0	2	2	20
Greg Louder	G	Sr.	28	0	2	2	2
Patrick Bellmore	F	Fr.	3	0	1	1	0
Brent Lothrop	G	Sr.	14	0	1	1	0
Rob Bolton	D	So.	1	0	0	0	0
Wade Salzman	G	So.	10	0	0	0	2

GOALTENDING

	Games	Min.	W	L	T	Goals	SO	Avg.
Wade Salzman	10	452	2	3	1	30	0	3.98
Greg Louder	28	1333	7	13	4	93	0	4.19
Brent Lothrop	14	523	2	6	0	39	0	4.47

OHIO STATE

SCORING

	Pos.	Class	Games	G	A	Pts.	PIM
Steve Richards	F	Jr.	35	10	21	31	81
Ron White	F	Sr.	35	19	8	27	16
Joe Sellers	F	So.	33	8	12	20	21
Tim Green	D	Sr.	35	4	16	20	68
Sean Sutton	F	So.	35	5	12	17	16
Chad Power	F	Fr.	33	9	7	16	61
Sacha Guilbault	F	Jr.	34	6	8	14	30
Jeff Winter	D	So.	35	1	11	12	64
Craig Paterson	D	So.	35	3	8	11	114
Adam Smith	F	Jr.	33	5	5	10	25
Bryan Reidel	F	Sr.	34	6	3	9	60
Pierre Dufour	F	Fr.	30	2	7	9	8
Randy Holmes	F	So.	32	2	6	8	10
Steve Brent	F	Fr.	35	2	5	7	195
Bill Rathwell	F	So.	35	5	0	5	12
Rob Peters	F/D	Sr.	28	1	4	5	59
Gary Hirst	D	So.	29	0	2	2	8
Sandy Fraser	D	Jr.	32	0	2	2	38
Brian Keller	D	Fr.	14	0	1	1	4
Derek Nicolson	D	Fr.	15	0	1	1	0
Kurt Brown	G	So.	16	0	0	0	18
Tom Askey	G	So.	27	0	0	0	0

GOALTENDING

	Games	Min.	W	L	T	Goals	SO	Avg.
Kurt Brown	16	640	4	4	1	39	0	3.66
Tom Askey	27	1488	3	19	4	103	1	4.15

WESTERN MICHIGAN

SCORING

	Pos.	Class	Games	G	A	Pts.	PIM
Colin Ward	F	Sr.	40	31	19	50	66
Jamal Mayers	F	So.	40	17	32	49	40
Chris Brooks	F	So.	32	12	37	49	22
Jeremy Brown	F	So.	40	16	16	32	46
Ryan D'Arcy	F	Jr.	36	8	22	30	28
Brent Brekke	D	Sr.	39	4	25	29	76
Brian Gallentine	F	Jr.	40	14	14	28	70
Derek Innanen	F	So.	39	16	11	27	136
Derek Schooley	D	So.	40	4	23	27	60
Mike Whitton	F	Jr.	34	15	3	18	107
Mikhail Lapin	D	So.	35	6	9	15	68
Darren Maloney	D	Fr.	40	4	8	12	22
Matt Cressman	F	Fr.	40	4	8	12	34
Peter Wilkinson	F	Jr.	33	6	5	11	40
Tony Code	F	Fr.	34	3	5	8	10
Shawn Zimmerman	F	Fr.	35	2	5	7	24
Brendan Kenny	D	Fr.	39	1	6	7	44
Justin Cardwell	F	Fr.	32	2	3	5	44
Brian Renfrew	G	Jr.	20	0	2	2	2
Jim Holman	D	So.	28	0	2	2	4
Mark Jodoin	F	Fr.	3	0	1	1	6
David Agnew	D	Fr.	6	0	1	1	4
Tom Carriere	D/F	So.	7	0	1	1	0
Craig Brown	G	Sr.	24	0	0	0	10

GOALTENDING

	Games	Min.	W	L	T	Goals	SO	Avg.
Craig Brown	24	1324	14	5	2	63	1	2.86
Brian Renfrew	20	1089	10	8	1	65	1	3.58

EASTERN COLLEGE ATHLETIC CONFERENCE

1993-94 SEASON

FINAL STANDINGS

Team	G	W	L	T	Pts.	GF	GA
Harvard (24-4-4)	22	16	2	4	35	107	60
Clarkson (20-9-5)	22	13	5	4	30	92	67
R.P.I. (21-10-5)	22	12	6	4	28	99	75
Brown (15-12-5)	22	12	7	3	27	91	73
Vermont (15-12-6)..	22	10	6	6	26	88	75
Union (15-11-4)	22	10	9	3	23	83	89
Colgate (13-17-2) ..	22	10	10	2	22	97	90
Cornell (8-17-5)	22	7	10	5	19	73	89
Princeton (10-15-3) .	22	7	12	3	17	64	80
St. Law. (10-21-0)..	22	8	14	0	16	74	95
Yale (5-21-1)	22	5	16	1	11	58	102
Dartmouth (5-21-1) ..	22	4	17	1	9	80	111

Overall record in parentheses.

PLAYOFF RESULTS

PRELIMINARIES
Colgate 4, St. Lawrence 3
Cornell 5, Princeton 4 (OT)

Vermont 8, Brown 5
Brown 3, Vermont 2
Brown 3, Vermont 2
(Brown won series, 2-1)

QUARTERFINALS
Harvard 6, Cornell 4
Harvard 5, Cornell 3
(Harvard won series, 2-0)

Clarkson 7, Colgate 6
Clarkson 5, Colgate 2
(Clarkson won series, 2-0)

Union 4, Rensselaer 3
Rensselaer 5, Union 1
Rensselaer 8, Union 3
(Rensselaer won series, 2-1)

SEMIFINALS
Harvard 5, Brown 1
Rensselaer 6, Clarkson 2

CONSOLATION GAME
Clarkson 6, Brown 2

CHAMPIONSHIP GAME
Harvard 3, Rensselaer 0

ALL-STAR TEAMS

First team	Pos.	Second team
Geoff Finch, Brown	G	Jason Currie, Clarkson
Sean McCann, Harvard	D	Derek Maguire, Harvard
Brian Mueller, Clarkson	D	Sean O'Brien, Princeton
Craig Conroy, Clarkson	F	Bruce Gardiner, Colgate
Brian Farrell, Harvard	F	Chris Kaban, Brown
Steve Martins, Harvard	F	Ron Pasco, Rensselaer

AWARD WINNERS

Player of the year: Steve Martins, Harvard
Rookie of the year: Eric Perrin, Vermont
Coach of the year: Bruce Delventhal, Union
Leading scorer: Steve Martins, Harvard
Playoff MVP: Sean McCann, Harvard

INDIVIDUAL STATISTICS

BROWN
SCORING

	Pos.	Class	Games	G	A	Pts.	PIM
Kelly Jones.............	F	Sr.	31	12	24	36	56
Ryan Mulhern	F	So.	27	18	17	35	48
Brian Jardine	F	So.	31	7	28	35	36
Chris Kaban	F	Sr.	32	19	14	33	92
Mark Fabbro	F	Sr.	29	6	20	26	48
Eric Trach.............	F	Jr.	32	11	13	24	20
Tony Martino	F	Jr.	29	7	9	16	6
Steve Kathol	F	So.	30	7	8	15	14
Mike Flynn	F	Fr.	30	5	10	15	40
Mike Traggio.........	D	Jr.	32	3	12	15	90
Marty Clapton........	F	Fr.	19	3	8	11	8
Ron Smitko............	D	So.	32	2	9	11	22
Mark Shaughnessy.	D	Sr.	31	4	5	9	17
Patrick Thompson...	D	Jr.	32	3	4	7	34
Brendan Whittet	D	Sr.	25	2	4	6	16
Scott Humber	F	So.	11	3	2	5	6
Mike Noble	F	Fr.	26	1	4	5	20
Bill McKay	D	Fr.	21	2	2	4	42
Kim Hannah	F	Jr.	15	1	2	3	2
Robert Merrill.........	F	Fr.	14	0	1	1	2
Charlie Humber	D	So.	16	0	1	1	6
Scott Bradford	F	Fr.	21	0	1	1	16
Geoff Finch...........	G	Sr.	25	0	1	1	2
James Mooney	D	So.	1	0	0	0	2
Sean Murdoch	F	Sr.	1	0	0	0	0
Jeff Reschny	F	Jr.	4	0	0	0	4
Mike Parsons.........	G	So.	9	0	0	0	0

GOALTENDING

	Games	Min.	W	L	T	Goals	SO	Avg.
Geoff Finch	25	1453	13	9	3	78	0	3.22
Mike Parsons...........	9	502	2	4	1	36	0	4.30

CLARKSON
SCORING

	Pos.	Class	Games	G	A	Pts.	PIM
Craig Conroy..........	F	Sr.	34	26	39	65	48
Brian Mueller	D	Jr.	34	17	39	56	58
Marko Tuomainen .	F	Jr.	34	23	28	51	60
Patrice Robitaille ...	F	Jr.	30	16	29	45	16
Steve Palmer..........	F	So.	34	17	24	41	32
Jean-Francois Houle	F	Fr.	34	6	19	25	18
Todd White	F	Fr.	33	10	11	21	28
David Seitz.............	F	So.	32	3	14	17	18
Ed Henrich	D	Sr.	34	3	12	15	26
Chris de Ruiter	F	So.	32	4	9	13	42
Kevin Murphy	F	So.	30	2	10	12	31
Chris Lipsett	F	So.	34	8	3	11	28
Adam Wiesel..........	D	Fr.	33	3	7	10	28
Shawn Fotheringham	F	Sr.	33	3	5	8	52
Matt Pagnutti.........	D	Fr.	31	2	2	4	28
Josh Bartell...........	D	So.	30	1	2	3	42
Phil LeCavalier	D	Fr.	30	1	2	3	24
Jason Currie	G	Sr.	33	1	2	3	2
Patrick Theriault	D	Sr.	31	1	0	1	12
Chris Cameron	D	Fr.	3	0	1	1	2
Jerry Rosenheck.....	F	Jr.	19	0	1	1	4
Jason LaBarge	D	Fr.	1	0	0	0	0
Jeremy Lopata........	F	Fr.	1	0	0	0	0
Gregg Malicke........	G	Fr.	7	0	0	0	0

GOALTENDING

	Games	Min.	W	L	T	Goals	SO	Avg.
Jason Currie	33	1893	18	9	5	96	0	3.04
Gregg Malicke	7	172	2	0	0	17	0	5.94

COLGATE

SCORING

	Pos.	Class	Games	G	A	Pts.	PIM
Bruce Gardiner	F	Sr.	33	23	23	46	70
Mike Harder	F	Fr.	33	21	25	46	14
Ron Fogarty	F	Jr.	33	13	29	42	36
Chris DeProfio	F	So.	33	12	24	36	68
Earl Cronan...........	F	So.	32	14	18	32	78
Dan Gardner	F	Sr.	33	9	20	29	10
Rod Pamenter	D	So.	28	7	17	24	32
Brent Wilde	F	Sr.	29	9	12	21	47
Sam Raffoul	F	Sr.	30	10	8	18	57
Scott Steeves........	F	Fr.	27	6	7	13	20
Jason Craig..........	D	Jr.	32	2	9	11	26
Matt Garzone	D	Jr.	33	3	7	10	10
Jack McIntosh	D	Fr.	24	3	5	8	20
Steve DuBarry	F	Fr.	26	3	3	6	10
Nigel Creightney	D	Jr.	29	2	4	6	20
Greg Lewis	F	So.	27	1	5	6	42
Dave Debusschere.	F	Fr.	4	1	3	4	0
Rob Metz	F	Sr.	26	1	2	3	10
John Dance	D	Fr.	24	0	3	3	8
Clayton McCaffrey	F	Jr.	24	2	0	2	24
J.P. Paquin..........	D	So.	6	1	1	2	2
Todd Murphy	D	Fr.	11	1	1	2	2
Dan Gibson	D	Sr.	14	0	1	1	9
Jason Gates	G	Jr.	21	0	1	1	2
Shawn Murray	G	Sr.	3	0	0	0	0
Matt Weder	G	So.	13	0	0	0	2

GOALTENDING

	Games	Min.	W	L	T	Goals	SO	Avg.
Jason Gates.............	21	1145	7	12	1	82	1	4.30
Shawn Murray.........	3	126	1	2	0	9	0	4.30

CORNELL

SCORING

	Pos.	Class	Games	G	A	Pts.	PIM
Geoff Bumstead	F	Sr.	30	15	20	35	22
Mike Sancimino	F	So.	28	12	18	30	42
Jake Karam	F	Jr.	30	10	16	26	20
Vincent Auger........	F	Fr.	29	11	13	24	31
P.C. Drouin	F	So.	21	6	14	20	30
Brad Chartrand	F	So.	30	4	14	18	46
Mark Scollan	F	So.	23	5	11	16	11
Steve Wilson	D	Fr.	30	3	12	15	42
Geoff Lopatka	F	So.	30	8	5	13	48
Shaun Hannah.......	F	Sr.	26	5	6	11	18
Jamie Papp	F	Fr.	21	6	4	10	8
Chad Wilson	D	Fr.	26	1	9	10	22
Dan Dufresne........	D	So.	29	1	6	7	80
Tony Bargin	F	Fr.	16	3	3	6	20
Blair Ettles	D	Jr.	17	0	5	5	12
Andre Doll	F	So.	16	2	2	4	6
Tim Shean	D	So.	15	0	4	4	4
Jason Weber	F	So.	10	3	0	3	2
Jason Kendall	D	Fr.	24	0	3	3	36
Joel McArter	F	So.	12	1	1	2	4
Matt Cooney	F	Fr.	12	0	2	2	42
Christian Felli	D	Jr.	27	0	2	2	12
Tyler McManus	F	Jr.	11	1	0	1	8
Jiri Kloboucek	F	Jr.	8	0	1	1	10
Jason Zubkus	D	Fr.	10	0	1	1	4
John DeHart	F	So.	7	0	1	1	0
Andy Bandurski.....	G	Jr.	19	0	0	0	0
Eddy Skazyk	G	So.	22	0	0	0	2

GOALTENDING

	Games	Min.	W	L	T	Goals	SO	Avg.
Andy Bandurski	19	882	3	8	3	55	0	3.74
Eddy Skazyk	23	954	5	9	2	68	0	4.28

DARTMOUTH

SCORING

	Pos.	Class	Games	G	A	Pts.	PIM
Scott Fraser	F	Sr.	24	17	13	30	26

	Pos.	Class	Games	G	A	Pts.	PIM
Dion Del Monte	F	Jr.	25	11	18	29	38
Mike Stacchi	F	Jr.	27	14	7	21	48
Tony DelCarmine...	F	Sr.	27	4	14	18	66
Owen Hughes.........	F	Fr.	27	3	15	18	38
Tom Ruzzo...........	F	Fr.	27	7	9	16	22
Pat Turcotte..........	F	Jr.	20	9	6	15	8
Brent Retter	F	Fr.	26	7	7	14	20
Trevor Dodman......	D	Jr.	27	3	9	12	22
Darren Wercinski ..	F	Jr.	24	5	6	11	23
Dax Burkhart	D	So.	27	1	10	11	32
Dan Bloom	D	So.	25	3	7	10	24
Matt Collins	F	Sr.	27	4	5	9	27
Derek Geary	F	Sr.	26	3	6	9	16
Mike Loga	D	Sr.	26	1	6	7	72
Scott Dolesh	F	So.	13	1	3	4	16
Alex Dumas	D	Fr.	12	0	3	3	2
Yanick Roussin	D	Jr.	16	0	3	3	8
Bill Kelleher...........	F	So.	4	1	0	1	2
Erik Stien	F	So.	3	0	1	1	0
Mike Richardson....	F	Sr.	4	0	1	1	2
Dan Williams	F	Jr.	19	0	1	1	4
Ben Butters...........	D	Fr.	20	0	1	1	28
Mike Bracco..........	G	So.	23	0	1	1	2
Matt Wilson	F	Jr.	4	0	0	0	6
Ben Heller	G	Fr.	7	0	0	0	2

GOALTENDING

	Games	Min.	W	L	T	Goals	SO	Avg.
Mike Bracco	23	1294	4	17	1	99	0	4.59
Ben Heller	7	330	1	4	0	37	0	6.73

HARVARD

SCORING

	Pos.	Class	Games	G	A	Pts.	PIM
Steve Martins	F	Jr.	32	25	35	60	93
Chris Baird	F	Sr.	32	6	38	44	18
Brian Farrell	F	So.	33	29	14	43	47
Sean McCann........	D	Sr.	33	22	17	39	82
Derek Maguire	D	Sr.	31	6	32	38	14
Cory Gustafson	F	Jr.	31	22	10	32	28
Ben Coughlin	F	Jr.	33	12	17	29	30
Lou Body	D	So.	33	1	21	22	18
Kirk Nielsen	F	So.	32	6	9	15	41
Joe Craigen	F	Fr.	33	5	10	15	14
Tom Holmes	F	So.	32	5	9	14	26
Jason Karmanos ...	F	So.	30	5	7	12	26
Perry Cohagan	F	Jr.	30	3	8	11	44
Ashlin Halfnight	D	Fr.	30	2	8	10	24
Ian Kennish	F	Sr.	29	2	5	7	6
Peter McLaughlin..	D	So.	33	0	7	7	32
Bryan Lonsinger ...	D	Jr.	33	1	5	6	14
Stuart Swenson.....	F	Fr.	19	1	4	5	16
Marco Ferrari	D	Fr.	15	0	2	2	14
Keith McLean	F	Jr.	2	1	0	1	0
Ethan Philpott......	F	Fr.	8	1	0	1	8
Tripp Tracy	G	So.	17	0	1	1	2
Sean Wenham......	D	Sr.	2	0	0	0	4
Geb Marret	D	So.	5	0	0	0	0
Aaron Israel	G	So.	18	0	0	0	4

GOALTENDING

	Games	Min.	W	L	T	Goals	SO	Avg.
Aaron Israel.............	18	1046	12	2	2	40	2	2.30
Tripp Tracy	17	978	12	3	2	49	1	3.01

PRINCETON

SCORING

	Pos.	Class	Games	G	A	Pts.	PIM
J.P. O'Connor	F	So.	28	13	11	24	24
Ian Sharp	F	Jr.	28	9	13	22	38
Sean O'Brien	D	Sr.	28	8	14	22	36
Jonathan Kelley.....	F	So.	28	6	13	19	41
Mervin Kopeck	F	Jr.	28	4	13	17	10
Mike Bois	F	Fr.	26	6	10	16	10

	Pos.	Class	Games	G	A	Pts.	PIM
Jean Verdon...........	F	Fr.	27	5	9	14	24
Miro Pasic..............	F	Sr.	25	5	7	12	16
Joey Pelle..............	F	Fr.	19	2	10	12	10
Dan Brown..............	D	So.	27	2	10	12	32
Ethan Early............	F	Jr.	25	5	6	11	18
John Fust...............	F	Sr.	15	5	5	10	10
Tony Ranaldi..........	F	Fr.	20	4	6	10	6
Corey Rhodes.........	F	Jr.	24	4	4	8	20
Keith O'Brien.........	F	Fr.	17	2	4	6	14
Gavin Colquhoun ...	D	Jr.	25	2	3	5	72
Jason Smith...........	D	So.	16	1	4	5	56
Scott Almon............	D	Jr.	22	1	4	5	8
David Scowby..........	F	Jr.	24	1	4	5	20
Hartmann Schoebel	F	Jr.	15	1	3	4	12
Barrington Miller ...	D/F	So.	19	1	1	2	6
Brent Flahr............	D	So.	12	0	1	1	12
James Konte..........	G	So.	28	0	1	1	6
Tom Tucker	F	Jr.	3	0	0	0	6
Rod Yorke..............	G	Jr.	4	0	0	0	0

GOALTENDING

	Games	Min.	W	L	T	Goals	SO	Avg.
James Konte............	28	1634	10	13	3	92	0	3.38
Rod Yorke	4	84	0	2	0	8	0	5.70

RENSSELAER POLYTECHNIC INSTITUTE
SCORING

	Pos.	Class	Games	G	A	Pts.	PIM
Ron Pasco..............	F	Sr.	35	17	40	57	82
Bryan Richardson .	F	So.	36	23	29	52	46
Craig Hamelin........	F	Jr.	36	19	29	48	18
Wayne Clarke	F	Jr.	36	22	17	39	24
Jeff Brick...............	F	Jr.	36	19	13	32	48
Kelly Askew	F	Jr.	35	13	19	32	104
Tim Regan..............	F	So.	35	12	19	31	62
Xavier Majic...........	F	So.	35	13	17	30	48
Brad Layzell...........	D	Sr.	34	2	19	21	58
Jeff Gabriel............	F	So.	36	9	10	19	22
Patrick Rochon.......	D	So.	34	3	15	18	44
Eric Perardi...........	F	Jr.	36	5	9	14	60
Adam Bartell..........	D	Jr.	33	3	11	14	32
Jeff Matthews........	F	Jr.	34	3	10	13	34
Cam Cuthbert.........	D	Sr.	35	3	10	13	62
Jeff O'Connor.........	F	So.	32	4	4	8	24
Chris Kiley.............	D	So.	31	0	8	8	12
Jon Pirrong............	D	So.	32	1	5	6	16
Chris Maye.............	F	Jr.	16	1	2	3	2
Neil Little..............	G	Sr.	33	0	1	1	4
Tim Carvel.............	G	Sr.	1	0	0	0	0
Mike Rolanti...........	D	Fr.	6	0	0	0	23
Mike Tamburro	G	So.	7	0	0	0	2

GOALTENDING

	Games	Min.	W	L	T	Goals	SO	Avg.
Tim Carvel	1	5	0	0	0	0	0	0.00
Mike Tamburro........	7	335	2	1	0	10	0	1.79
Neil Little	33	1920	19	10	4	102	0	3.19

ST. LAWRENCE
SCORING

	Pos.	Class	Games	G	A	Pts.	PIM
Burke Murphy........	F	So.	30	20	17	37	42
Spencer Meany......	F	Sr.	31	14	15	29	62
Brian McCarthy	F	Jr.	28	12	14	26	32
Mike Allain............	F	Sr.	30	7	18	25	58
Mike McCourt	D	Sr.	30	5	20	25	38
Scott Stevens.........	F	Fr.	29	6	13	19	19
Troy Creuer............	D	Fr.	30	5	10	15	22
Kris Laamanen........	F	Fr.	24	0	14	14	8
Ryan Cassidy.........	F	Fr.	23	2	11	13	18
Tom Perry	D	So.	29	4	8	12	32
Jeff Kungle............	D	So.	15	4	6	10	10
Ken Ruddock..........	D	Fr.	30	6	2	8	54
Joel Prpic	F	Fr.	31	2	5	7	88

	Pos.	Class	Games	G	A	Pts.	PIM
Scott Murphy	F	Fr.	22	1	6	7	18
Cade Blackburn	F	Jr.	26	4	2	6	12
Mark McGeough	F	Sr.	29	1	5	6	32
Brian Kapeller........	F	Jr.	28	0	5	5	54
Dan Skene.............	F	Jr.	25	4	0	4	24
Tom Cullen.............	D	Fr.	23	1	2	3	32
Bren Genga............	F	So.	3	1	0	1	0
Brian LaVack..........	D	Fr.	4	0	1	1	0
Chris Dashney	D	So.	23	0	1	1	12
Paul Spagnoletti	G	Sr.	23	0	1	1	2
Patrick Dennehy	F	So.	6	0	0	0	0
Jon Bracco.............	G	Fr.	12	0	0	0	0

GOALTENDING

	Games	Min.	W	L	T	Goals	SO	Avg.
Jon Bracco..............	12	565	4	4	0	34	0	3.61
Paul Spagnoletti	23	1299	6	17	0	97	0	4.48

UNION
SCORING

	Pos.	Class	Games	G	A	Pts.	PIM
Chris Ford	F	Fr.	29	20	15	35	26
Troy Stevens..........	F	Fr.	30	6	28	34	24
Jeff Jiampetti.........	F	Sr.	29	16	13	29	32
Chris Albert............	F	Jr.	30	11	18	29	40
Russell Monteith.....	F	Fr.	27	10	17	27	22
Reid Simonton........	D	So.	30	4	20	24	74
Cory Holbrough	F	Jr.	29	8	14	22	40
Jon Sincinski..........	F	Fr.	30	10	10	20	12
Scott Boyd	D	So.	27	6	9	15	40
Jay Prentice	F	Fr.	30	3	12	15	2
Andrew Will	D	Fr.	29	2	11	13	32
Chad Thompson	F	So.	28	5	6	11	48
Dean Goulet	D	Jr.	26	2	9	11	23
Bill Moody	F	Jr.	26	4	4	8	14
Pat O'Flaherty	F	Fr.	19	3	3	6	22
Shane Holunga	D	So.	23	1	5	6	16
Ryan Donovan	F	Fr.	21	2	2	4	14
Brad Kukko	F	So.	4	1	3	4	0
Chris Hancock	F	So.	22	0	3	3	45
Greg Buchanan.......	D	Fr.	14	1	1	2	20
Luigi Villa	G	Jr.	12	0	1	1	0
Mike Gallant	G	Jr.	22	0	1	1	2
Keith Darby............	F	Jr.	2	0	0	0	0
Seabrook Satterlund	D	Fr.	3	0	0	0	0
Jamie Antoine........	F	Fr.	11	0	0	0	4
Craig Reckin	F	Fr.	17	0	0	0	8

GOALTENDING

	Games	Min.	W	L	T	Goals	SO	Avg.
Mike Gallant	22	1231	10	9	2	77	0	3.75
Luigi Villa	12	596	5	2	2	40	0	4.03

VERMONT
SCORING

	Pos.	Class	Games	G	A	Pts.	PIM
Martin St. Louis	F	Fr.	33	15	36	51	24
Eric Perrin	F	Fr.	32	24	21	45	34
Dominique Ducharme	F	Jr.	33	12	31	43	26
Nicolas Perrault.....	F	Sr.	31	20	21	41	24
Rob Pattison	F	Jr.	32	8	19	27	14
Dale Patterson	F	So.	28	6	15	21	18
Matt Johnson..........	F	So.	33	4	13	17	18
Eric Hallman	D	Fr.	32	2	10	12	56
Bill Lincoln	F	Jr.	28	6	4	10	28
Phil Eboli	F	So.	25	5	5	10	20
Brian Leddy	F	Jr.	31	5	4	9	34
Corey Machanic	D	Sr.	19	2	6	8	24
Mike Larkin	D	Jr.	32	4	3	7	68
Travis Lehouiller ...	F	Sr.	28	3	4	7	33
Jason Williams	D	Jr.	33	3	3	6	32
Eric Lavoie	F	So.	23	2	3	5	2
Jonathan Sorg	D	Fr.	31	1	3	4	20
Tom Quinn	D	Jr.	16	0	4	4	6

	Pos.	Class	Games	G	A	Pts.	PIM
Steve McKell	D	So.	33	0	4	4	32
J.C. Ruid	F	Fr.	19	3	0	3	18
Keith Festa	F	Jr.	6	1	1	2	4
Pavel Navrat	D	Fr.	11	1	1	2	12
Tim Thomas	G	Fr.	33	0	2	2	14
Tom Vukota	G	Jr.	3	0	0	0	0
Jon Miyamoto	G	Jr.	4	0	0	0	0

GOALTENDING

	Games	Min.	W	L	T	Goals	SO	Avg.
Tim Thomas	33	1863	15	11	6	95	1	3.06
Tom Vukota	3	73	0	1	0	8	0	6.55
Jon Miyamoto	4	70	0	0	0	9	0	7.70

YALE
SCORING

	Pos.	Class	Games	G	A	Pts.	PIM
Andy Weidenbach .	F	Jr.	24	12	13	25	50
Martin Leroux	F	Sr.	26	6	18	24	27
Zoran Kozic	F	Jr.	26	10	8	18	26
John Emmons	F	So.	24	5	12	17	76
Jason Cipolla	F	Jr.	23	7	8	15	40
Dan Nyberg	D	Jr.	27	5	7	12	12
Dan Brierly	D	So.	27	3	7	10	58
Jeff Sorem	F	So.	24	2	7	9	14
Keith Carpenter	F	So.	21	5	3	8	8

	Pos.	Class	Games	G	A	Pts.	PIM
Michael Yoshino	F	So.	14	2	6	8	8
Steve Lombardi......	F	Jr.	19	4	2	6	16
Brendan Doyle	F	So.	25	1	5	6	20
Chris Barbanti	F	Jr.	18	2	3	5	10
James Mackey	D	Sr.	23	1	4	5	46
Yvan Champagne ..	F	Fr.	6	3	1	4	8
Richard Giroux	D	Jr.	23	2	2	4	30
Sani Silvennoinen..	D	Fr.	14	2	1	3	2
Curtis Millen	D	So.	10	0	3	3	4
David Cochran.......	D	Sr.	21	0	3	3	12
Mike Cullinane.......	D	Sr.	22	1	1	2	6
Louie Loucks	F	Fr.	5	0	1	1	0
Josh Rabjohns	F	Fr.	16	0	1	1	18
Prescott Logan	D	So.	20	0	1	1	8
Art Chipman	F	Fr.	2	0	0	0	2
Sean Owen	F/D	Fr.	2	0	0	0	0
Dan Choquette	G	Fr.	3	0	0	0	0
Todd Carricato	F	Sr.	4	0	0	0	0
Mike Kamatovic.....	G	Sr.	7	0	0	0	0
Todd Sullivan.........	G	Jr.	23	0	0	0	2

GOALTENDING

	Games	Min.	W	L	T	Goals	SO	Avg.
Todd Sullivan	23	1257	4	15	1	88	0	4.20
Dan Choquette.........	3	128	1	1	0	12	0	5.64
Mike Kamatovic	7	258	0	6	0	32	0	7.45

1993-94 SEASON

FINAL STANDINGS

Team	G	W	L	T	Pts.	GF	GA
Boston U. (34-7-0) ...	24	21	3	0	42	195	113
Lowell (25-10-5)	24	14	6	4	32	169	121
New Hamp. (25-12-3)	24	13	9	2	28	159	137
N'eastern (20-12-7) ..	24	10	8	6	26	162	159
Providence (14-19-3)	24	9	13	2	20	120	149
Boston Col. (15-16-5)	24	7	12	5	19	145	133
Merrimack (16-19-2)	24	8	14	2	18	126	152
Maine (6-29-1)	24	3	20	1	7	142	130
Mass. (20-9-0)	Affiliate (0-2-0 vs. Hockey East teams)						

Overall record in parentheses.

PLAYOFF RESULTS

QUARTERFINALS

Boston University 8, Maine 5
Boston University 4, Maine 3
 (Boston University won series, 2-0)

Lowell 7, Merrimack 1
Lowell 3, Merrimack 0
 (Lowell won series, 2-0)

New Hampshire 4, Boston College 1
New Hampshire 6, Boston College 5 (2 OT)
 (New Hampshire won series, 2-0)

Northeastern 4, Providence 3
Northeastern 2, Providence 1 (OT)
 (Northeastern won series, 2-0)

SEMIFINALS

Boston University 5, Northeastern 2
Lowell 4, New Hampshire 2

CONSOLATION GAME

New Hampshire 4, Northeastern 4 (OT)

CHAMPIONSHIP GAME

Boston University 3, Lowell 2

ALL-STAR TEAMS

First team	Pos.	Second team
Dwayne Roloson, Lowell	G	Derek Herlofsky, Boston U.
Rich Brennan, Boston U.	D	Scott Malone, New Hamp.
Francois Bouchard, NE	D	Michael Spalla, Boston C.
Shane Henry, Lowell	F	J.F. Aube, Northeastern
Jacques Joubert, Boston U.	F	Greg Bullock, Lowell
Mike Taylor, Northeastern	F	Mike Latendresse, Maine

AWARD WINNERS

Player of the year: Dwayne Roloson, Lowell
Rookie of the year: Greg Bullock, Lowell
Coach of the year: Bruce Crowder, Lowell
Leading scorer: Greg Bullock, Lowell
Playoff MVP: Dwayne Roloson, Lowell

INDIVIDUAL STATISTICS

BOSTON COLLEGE

SCORING

	Pos.	Class	Games	G	A	Pts.	PIM
Ryan Haggerty	F	Jr.	36	17	23	40	16
Michael Spalla	D	Sr.	36	3	34	37	14
John Joyce..............	F	Sr.	36	16	18	34	40
David Hymovitz	F	So.	36	18	14	32	18
Jack Callahan........	F	Sr.	36	14	16	30	35
Don Chase.............	F	So.	35	14	13	27	58
Jerry Buckley	F	Jr.	36	13	10	23	74
Brian Callahan.......	F	Fr.	36	11	11	22	58
Rob Canavan	F	Jr.	30	7	14	21	28
Rob Laferriere........	F	Jr.	34	7	14	21	58
Jeff Connolly	F	Fr.	22	8	10	18	20
Tom Ashe..............	D	So.	35	3	11	14	68
Joe Harney	D	Fr.	31	1	11	12	34
Mike McCarthy	F	Jr.	35	3	6	9	6
Peter Masters	D	Fr.	32	1	5	6	44
Greg Callahan	D	So.	24	3	2	5	65
Clifton McHale	F	So.	30	2	3	5	2
Greg Taylor...........	G	Fr.	35	0	4	4	6
David Wainwright .	D	Fr.	36	2	1	3	38
Toby Harris...........	F	Fr.	12	1	1	2	4
Jim Krayer	F	Jr.	17	1	0	1	0
Brad Carlson.........	D	Fr.	14	0	1	1	6
Josh Singewald	G	Jr.	7	0	0	0	0
Ryan Taylor	D	Fr.	7	0	0	0	6

GOALTENDING

	Games	Min.	W	L	T	Goals	SO	Avg.
Greg Taylor	35	2090	14	15	5	121	0	3.47
Josh Singewald	6	149	1	1	0	10	0	4.03

BOSTON UNIVERSITY

SCORING

	Pos.	Class	Games	G	A	Pts.	PIM
Mike Pomichter......	F	Jr.	40	28	26	54	37
Jacques Joubert	F	Jr.	41	20	24	44	82
Jay Pandolfo..........	F	So.	37	17	25	42	27
Steve Thornton......	F	Jr.	41	13	26	39	26
Rich Brennan	D	Jr.	41	8	27	35	82
Mike Prendergast ..	F	Jr.	39	15	18	33	52
Bob Lachance........	F	So.	32	13	19	32	42
Doug Friedman	F	Sr.	41	9	23	32	110
Shawn Bates.........	F	Fr.	41	10	19	29	24
Kevin O'Sullivan	D	Sr.	32	5	18	23	25
Jon Jenkins...........	F	Jr.	38	12	9	21	27
Dan Donato...........	D	Sr.	36	4	17	21	58
Jon Pratt	F	Sr.	32	11	8	19	66
Mike Grier	F	Fr.	39	9	9	18	58
Kaj Linna	D	Jr.	34	4	13	17	26
Ken Rausch...........	F	Jr.	31	6	9	15	4
Jon Coleman	D	Fr.	29	1	14	15	26
Shane Johnson	D	Fr.	37	1	8	9	34
Billy Pierce...........	F	Fr.	31	4	4	8	28
Doug Wood	D	So.	33	3	2	5	57
Stephen Foster	D	Sr.	10	1	4	5	25
J.P. McKersie	G	Jr.	24	0	2	2	11
Matt Wright	F	Fr.	3	1	0	1	5
Shawn Ferullo........	G	Fr.	1	0	0	0	0
Chris Bise.............	G	Fr.	2	0	0	0	0
Derek Herlofsky	G	Jr.	20	0	0	0	0

GOALTENDING

	Games	Min.	W	L	T	Goals	SO	Avg.
Derek Herlofsky	20	1056	15	3	0	44	4	2.50
J.P. McKersie	24	1325	19	4	0	64	0	2.90
Chris Bise	1	11	0	0	0	3	0	15.93
Shawn Ferullo	1	3	0	0	0	1	0	21.95

LOWELL

SCORING

	Pos.	Class	Games	G	A	Pts.	PIM
Greg Bullock	F	Fr.	38	24	35	59	52
Shane Henry	F	Sr.	38	11	37	48	24

	Pos.	Class	Games	G	A	Pts.	PIM
Ian Hebert	F	Sr.	39	18	29	47	22
Christian Sbrocca .	F	So.	40	14	24	38	80
Normand Bazin	F	Sr.	39	20	15	35	48
Mike Murray	F	Sr.	35	17	11	28	92
Kerry Angus	D	Sr.	40	10	16	26	30
Ed Campbell	D	Fr.	40	8	16	24	114
Jeff Daw	F	So.	40	6	12	18	12
Neil Donovan	F	Fr.	36	7	10	17	51
Aaron Kriss	D	Jr.	34	5	10	15	48
Eric Brown	F	Jr.	33	8	5	13	18
Dave Barozzino	D	So.	34	4	5	9	91
David Mayes	D	So.	35	2	7	9	35
Bill Riga	F	So.	26	3	5	8	12
Jon Mahoney	F	So.	32	1	7	8	36
Travis Tucker	D	Sr.	30	1	6	7	83
Brendan Concannon	F	So.	30	4	1	5	8
Ryan Sandholm	F	Fr.	20	3	2	5	4
Paul Botto	D	Jr.	27	1	3	4	36
Ryan Golden	F	Fr.	14	0	3	3	12
Marc Salsman	F	Fr.	16	2	0	2	10
Jason Cormier	D	Fr.	4	0	1	1	0
Dwayne Roloson	G	Sr.	40	0	1	1	14
Craig Lindsay	G	Fr.	8	0	0	0	2

GOALTENDING

	Games	Min.	W	L	T	Goals	SO	Avg.
Dwayne Roloson	40	2305	23	10	7	106	2	2.76
Craig Lindsay	8	162	0	0	0	13	0	4.82

MAINE
SCORING

	Pos.	Class	Games	G	A	Pts.	PIM
Mike Latendresse ..	F	Jr.	33	20	19	39	43
Patrice Tardif	F	Sr.	34	18	15	33	42
Cal Ingraham	F	Sr.	24	12	17	29	20
Justin Tomberlin ..	F	Sr.	32	11	17	28	10
Dan Shermerhorn ..	F	Fr.	35	10	15	25	24
Reg Cardinal	F	So.	36	9	16	25	34
Paul Kariya	F	So.	12	8	16	24	4
Dave MacIssac	D	Jr.	31	4	20	24	22
Tim Lovell	F	Fr.	36	7	13	20	20
Wayne Conlan	F	Jr.	29	7	9	16	26
Brad Purdie	F	So.	36	6	8	14	20
Lee Saunders	D	Sr.	27	0	12	12	32
Barry Clukey	F	Fr.	28	7	3	10	26
Peter Ferraro	F	So.	4	3	6	9	16
Jacque Rodrigue	D	Jr.	14	2	7	9	18
Marcel Pineau	F	Fr.	19	5	3	8	16
Trevor Roenick	F	Fr.	32	4	3	7	18
Jason Weinrich	D	Sr.	18	3	4	7	30
Jason Mansoff	D	Fr.	28	1	6	7	24
Chuck Texeira	F	Sr.	26	1	4	5	58
Tony Frenette	F	Fr.	12	0	5	5	6
Brad Mahoney	F	Fr.	18	2	2	4	22
Leo Wlasow	D	Fr.	28	2	2	4	29
Andy Silverman	D	Jr.	35	0	3	3	80
Blair Allison	G	Fr.	28	0	2	2	4
Chris Ferraro	F	So.	4	0	1	1	8
Greg Hirsch	G	So.	1	0	0	0	0
John St. Pierre	F	Fr.	1	0	0	0	2
Mike Ray	F	Fr.	3	0	0	0	2
Jeff Tory	D	So.	3	0	0	0	4
Jason Dekker	D/F	Fr.	11	0	0	0	6
Blair Marsh	G	So.	18	0	0	0	2

GOALTENDING

	Games	Min.	W	L	T	Goals	SO	Avg.
Blair Allison	28	1387	11	8	3	78	1	3.37
Blair Marsh	18	777	6	7	1	50	0	3.86
Greg Hirsch	1	11	0	0	0	1	0	5.53

MASSACHUSETTS (AFFILIATE)
SCORING

	Pos.	Class	Games	G	A	Pts.	PIM
Rob Bonnean	F	Fr.	29	26	21	47	28
Warren Norris	F	Fr.	29	20	27	47	12

	Pos.	Class	Games	G	A	Pts.	PIM
Blair Wagar	F	Fr.	29	20	17	37	4
Dennis Wright	F	Fr.	28	11	26	37	48
Mike Evans	F	Fr.	27	19	12	31	38
Tom Perry	F	Fr.	25	16	15	31	18
Blair Manning	F	Fr.	27	8	23	31	24
Armand Latulippe..	D/F	Fr.	29	13	14	27	14
Jaynen Rissling	D	Fr.	19	7	15	22	22
Steve Corradi	F	Sr.	29	9	12	21	32
Tom Sheehan	F	Fr.	26	8	9	17	24
Tony Giusto	D	Fr.	29	2	15	17	62
Tiger Holland	D	Fr.	27	1	12	13	40
Jason Smith	F	Fr.	29	6	6	12	4
Rich Alger	D	Fr.	27	2	9	11	14
Dale Hooper	D	Fr.	14	1	9	10	18
Bill Condon	D	Fr.	26	1	9	10	45
Brett Pearlstein	F	Fr.	9	2	6	8	4
Gerry Cahill	F	Fr.	28	2	6	8	16
Brian Corcoran	D	Fr.	15	1	7	8	24
Judd Smith	F	Fr.	11	0	4	4	4
Jim Heffernan	D	Fr.	8	1	1	2	2
Rich Moriarty	G	Fr.	12	0	2	2	4
Dave Kilduff	G	Fr.	20	0	2	2	2

GOALTENDING

	Games	Min.	W	L	T	Goals	SO	Avg.
Dave Kilduff	20	1088	14	4	0	52	2	2.87
Rich Moriarty	13	653	6	5	0	41	2	3.77

MERRIMACK
SCORING

	Pos.	Class	Games	G	A	Pts.	PIM
Rob Atkinson	F	Sr.	37	17	24	41	30
Cooper Naylor	F	Sr.	37	12	26	38	42
Matt Adams	F	Jr.	37	14	19	33	40
Dan Hodge	D	Jr.	37	9	22	31	72
Tom Johnson	F	Fr.	37	11	14	25	20
Jim Gibson	F	Sr.	35	12	9	21	51
Claudio Peca	F	Fr.	36	10	11	21	40
Mark Goble	F	Jr.	37	9	11	20	22
Mark Comforth	D	Jr.	37	5	13	18	58
Daryl Krauss	F	Fr.	34	5	9	14	18
Rob Beck	F	Fr.	36	5	5	10	38
John Jakopin	D	Fr.	36	2	8	10	64
Chris Ross	D/F	Jr.	34	5	4	9	24
Ryan Mailhiot	F	So.	23	4	5	9	8
Quentin Fendelet ...	F	Sr.	37	1	5	6	12
Dean Capuano	D	Fr.	19	0	6	6	20
Tom Costa	D	So.	34	2	3	5	106
Eric Weichselbaumer	F	Fr.	16	1	4	5	4
Steve McKenna	D	Fr.	37	1	2	3	74
Ziggy Marszalek	F	Fr.	13	0	2	2	10
Martin Legault	G	Fr.	34	0	2	2	2
Karl Infanger	D	Fr.	15	1	0	1	10
Chris Davis	F	Jr.	1	0	0	0	0
Matt Gallo	F	Fr.	1	0	0	0	0
Matt Poska	G	Sr.	4	0	0	0	0
Eric Thibeault	G	Fr.	9	0	0	0	0

GOALTENDING

	Games	Min.	W	L	T	Goals	SO	Avg.
Martin Legault	34	1942	12	20	2	122	1	3.77
Eric Thibeault	9	260	2	1	0	24	0	5.54
Matt Poska	4	26	0	0	0	3	0	6.92

NEW HAMPSHIRE
SCORING

	Pos.	Class	Games	G	A	Pts.	PIM
Eric Flinton	F	Jr.	40	16	25	41	36
Nick Poole	F	Jr.	35	10	28	38	22
Jason Dexter	F	Sr.	40	16	18	34	22
Eric Boguniecki	F	Fr.	40	17	16	33	66
Rob Donovan	F	Sr.	36	14	19	33	52
Glenn Stewart	F	Sr.	40	14	18	32	82
Mike Sullivan	F	So.	40	13	14	27	30
Eric Royal	F	Jr.	24	9	14	23	24

	Pos.	Class	Games	G	A	Pts.	PIM
Ted Russell	D	Jr.	40	4	19	23	64
Tom Nolan	F	Fr.	35	10	12	22	38
Scott Malone	D	Jr.	40	14	6	20	162
Bob Chebator	F	Sr.	40	4	8	12	50
Kent Schmidtke	D	Jr.	40	0	12	12	20
Tom O'Brien	F	So.	38	4	7	11	28
Steve Pleau	D	So.	33	2	9	11	18
Tim Murray	D	Fr.	40	3	5	8	18
Dean Woodman	D	Fr.	38	4	3	7	24
Bryan Muir	D	So.	40	0	4	4	48
Brian Putnam	F	Fr.	12	3	0	3	0
Pat Norton	F	So.	16	1	1	2	4
Mike Heinke	G	Jr.	22	0	2	2	0
Jeff Lenz	F	So.	7	1	0	1	0
Mike McCready	D	Fr.	1	0	0	0	0
Corey Cash	F	So.	5	0	0	0	0
Trent Cavicchi	G	So.	25	0	0	0	0

GOALTENDING

	Games	Min.	W	L	T	Goals	SO	Avg.
Trent Cavicchi	25	1324	14	7	1	65	1	2.95
Mike Heinke	22	1116	11	5	2	67	1	3.60

NORTHEASTERN
SCORING

	Pos.	Class	Games	G	A	Pts.	PIM
Mike Taylor	F	Sr.	38	11	35	46	22
Jordon Shields	F	So.	37	15	29	44	32
J.F. Aube	F	Jr.	37	28	15	43	10
Tom O'Connor	F	Sr.	39	15	19	34	32
Francois Bouchard	D	Jr.	39	15	15	30	34
Danny McGillis	D	So.	38	4	25	29	82
Dan Lupo	F	So.	39	12	12	24	60
Jason Melong	F	Jr.	35	13	10	23	30
Hart Webb	F	Fr.	32	6	17	23	28
Eric Petersen	F	Fr.	39	7	12	19	24
Mike Collett	F	So.	35	5	14	19	38
Darryl MacNair	D	Jr.	37	7	10	17	54
David Penney	F	Fr.	36	5	9	14	18
Tom Parlon	F	Jr.	39	7	4	11	28
Brad Klyn	D	Fr.	22	2	5	7	12
Tomas Persson	F	So.	32	2	5	7	6
Rick Schuhwerk	D	Fr.	37	2	5	7	6
Jason Kelly	D	Jr.	30	1	3	4	52
Jeff Vaughan	D	Fr.	13	3	0	3	8
Craig Carmody	F	Jr.	7	1	1	2	0
Steve Phillips	F	Jr.	4	1	0	1	0

	Pos.	Class	Games	G	A	Pts.	PIM
Geoff Lucas	F	Jr.	22	0	1	1	8
Kevin Noke	G	Fr.	1	0	0	0	0
Justin Kummerer	D	So.	4	0	0	0	2
Mike Veisor	G	So.	15	0	0	0	2
Todd Reynolds	G	Jr.	27	0	0	0	15

GOALTENDING

	Games	Min.	W	L	T	Goals	SO	Avg.
Todd Reynolds	27	1566	12	9	5	97	0	3.72
Mike Veisor	15	775	7	3	2	55	0	4.26
Kevin Noke	1	60	0	1	0	7	0	7.00

PROVIDENCE
SCORING

	Pos.	Class	Games	G	A	Pts.	PIM
Chad Quenneville	F	Jr.	35	22	18	40	24
Brady Kramer	F	Jr.	36	12	26	38	50
David Green	F	Fr.	32	10	16	26	10
Russ Guzior	F	Fr.	34	9	13	22	8
George Breen	F	Jr.	32	8	14	22	22
Brian Ridolfi	F	Sr.	34	10	8	18	57
Dennis Burke	F	So.	34	8	10	18	28
Ian Paskowski	D	Sr.	35	5	10	15	43
Jon LaVarre	F	Jr.	27	7	7	14	10
Travis Dillabough	F	Fr.	33	4	8	12	42
Dennis Sousa	D	So.	35	1	10	11	40
Joe Hulbig	F	So.	28	6	4	10	36
Erik Peterson	F	Sr.	34	5	5	10	44
Justin Gould	D	So.	35	3	7	10	28
David Ruhly	F	Fr.	21	2	8	10	26
Jay Kenney	D	So.	21	2	7	9	8
Scott Balboni	D	So.	32	2	3	5	65
Stefan Brannare	D	Fr.	19	2	2	4	23
Hal Gill	D	Fr.	31	1	2	3	26
Eric Sundquist	D	So.	16	1	1	2	40
Trevor Hanson	F	So.	8	0	1	1	8
Chris Lamoriello	F	Sr.	16	0	1	1	8
Jon Rowe	D	So.	21	0	1	1	12
Dan Dennis	G	Fr.	20	0	0	0	5
Bob Bell	G	So.	22	0	0	0	7

GOALTENDING

	Games	Min.	W	L	T	Goals	SO	Avg.
Bob Bell	22	1137	6	11	2	68	2	3.59
Dan Dennis	19	971	5	10	1	74	0	4.57

WESTERN COLLEGIATE HOCKEY ASSOCIATION

1993-94 SEASON

FINAL STANDINGS

Team	G	W	L	T	Pts.	GF	GA
Colorado C. (23-11-5)	32	18	9	5	41	135	126
Minnesota (24-12-4)	32	18	10	4	40	111	109
Wisconsin (25-14-1)	32	19	12	1	39	128	103
St. Cloud St. (21-13-4)	32	16	12	4	36	127	111
N. Mich. (22-16-1)	32	17	14	1	35	129	120
A'ka Anch. (15-19-2) .	32	14	16	2	30	110	109
M.-Duluth (14-21-3) .	32	12	17	3	27	125	131
N. Dakota (11-23-4) ..	32	11	17	4	26	101	131
Denver (15-20-3)	32	11	18	3	25	116	130
Mich. Tech (13-27-5)	32	8	19	5	21	93	105

Overall record in parentheses.

PLAYOFF RESULTS

FIRST ROUND

Michigan Tech 3, Colorado College 2
Colorado College 3, Michigan Tech 0
Michigan Tech 3, Colorado College 2 (OT)
(Michigan Tech won series, 2-1)

Minnesota 8, Denver 5
Minnesota 6, Denver 3
(Minnesota won series, 2-0)

Wisconsin 6, North Dakota 1
Wisconsin 4, North Dakota 2
(Wisconsin won series, 2-0)

St. Cloud State 3, Minnesota-Duluth 0
St. Cloud State 8, Minnesota-Duluth 5
(St. Cloud State won series, 2-0)

Northern Michigan 5, Alaska-Anchorage 2
Northern Michigan 5, Alaska-Anchorage 1
(Northern Michigan won series, 2-0)

SECOND ROUND

Michigan Tech 5, Northern Michigan 1

SEMIFINALS

St. Cloud State 3, Wisconsin 2 (OT)
Minnesota 6, Michigan Tech 1

CONSOLATION GAME

Wisconsin 8, Michigan Tech 3

CHAMPIONSHIP GAME

Minnesota 3, St. Cloud State 2 (OT)

ALL-STAR TEAMS

First team	Pos.	Second team
Jamie Ram, Mich. Tech	G	Lee Schill, Alaska-Anch.
Shawn Reid, Colorado Col.	D	Kent Fearns, Colorado Col.
Chris McAlpine, Minnesota	D	Kelly Hultgren, St. Cloud St.
Chris Marinucci, Min.-Dul.	F	Andrew Shier, Wisconsin
Kelly Fairchild, Wisconsin	F	Jeff Nielsen, Minnesota
Jay McNeill, Colorado Col.	F	Mike Harding, N. Michigan

AWARD WINNERS

Most Valuable Player: Chris Marinucci, Minnesota-Duluth
Rookie of the year: Landon Wilson, North Dakota
Coach of the year: Don Lucia, Colorado College
Leading scorer: Chris Marinucci, Minnesota-Duluth
Playoff MVP: Chris McAlpine, Minnesota

INDIVIDUAL STATISTICS

ALASKA-ANCHORAGE

SCORING

	Pos.	Class	Games	G	A	Pts.	PIM
Keith Morris	F	Sr.	36	16	18	34	66
Mark Stitt	F	Jr.	36	15	17	32	62
Paul Williams	F	Jr.	36	13	16	29	14
Cotton Gore	F	Jr.	33	13	12	25	40
Mitch Kean	F	Sr.	36	12	13	25	20
Jason White	D	So.	36	5	15	20	46
Troy Norcross	F	Jr.	36	10	9	19	55
Jack Kowal	F	So.	36	7	12	19	52
Todd Bethard	D	Fr.	36	4	14	18	24
Garnet Deschamps .	F	Sr.	29	5	9	14	30
Petri Tuomisto	D	Jr.	36	3	10	13	76
Mika Rautakallio ...	F	Fr.	30	6	5	11	12
Jeremy Mylymok ...	D	So.	33	2	9	11	91
Glen Thornborough .	F	So.	33	4	5	9	46
Trent Leggett	F	Jr.	16	1	6	7	22
Todd Skoglund	F	Jr.	24	1	6	7	60
David Vallieres	F	Fr.	33	0	7	7	57
Brandon Carlson ...	F	So.	17	3	3	6	18
Darren Meek	D	So.	35	2	1	3	75
Randy Muise	F	Jr.	6	1	1	2	19
Kelly Melton	D	So.	21	0	2	2	10
Chris Kerr	D	Fr.	13	0	1	1	6
Chris Davis	G	Fr.	9	0	0	0	8
Lee Schill	G	Jr.	32	0	0	0	0

GOALTENDING

	Games	Min.	W	L	T	Goals	SO	Avg.
Lee Schill	32	1787	13	15	2	103	0	3.46
Chris Davis	9	390	2	4	0	27	0	4.15

COLORADO COLLEGE

SCORING

	Pos.	Class	Games	G	A	Pts.	PIM
Jay McNeill	F	So.	37	25	19	44	30
Peter Geronazzo	F	Jr.	36	19	19	38	56
Jody Jaraczewski..	F	Sr.	36	16	22	38	30
R.J. Enga	F	Jr.	39	15	23	38	49
Colin Schmidt	F	So.	38	14	21	35	49
Chad Remackel	F	So.	39	10	21	31	52
Kent Fearns	D	Jr.	39	11	19	30	62
Shawn Reid	D	Sr.	39	7	20	27	28
Steve Nelson	F	Sr.	38	14	9	23	26
Ryan Reynard	F	Jr.	38	9	10	19	54
Eric Rud	D	Fr.	39	3	13	16	14
Jim Paradise	F	Sr.	39	9	5	14	24
Chad Hartnell.........	F	Fr.	39	3	11	14	26
David Paxton	D	Jr.	38	2	12	14	53
Jason Christopherson	F	So.	33	2	10	12	41
Bob Needham..........	D	Fr.	38	0	8	8	34
Rob Shypitka	F	Jr.	39	3	4	7	12
Ryan Bach	G	So.	30	0	2	2	0
David Tucker	F	Sr.	21	1	0	1	4

	Pos.	Class	Games	G	A	Pts.	PIM
Steve Metzger	F	So.	5	0	1	1	0
John Steiner..........	D	Jr.	25	0	1	1	38
Paul Frank	G	Jr.	1	0	0	0	0
Andy Olds..............	F	Fr.	1	0	0	0	0
Judd Lambert	G	Fr.	11	0	0	0	0

GOALTENDING

	Games	Min.	W	L	T	Goals	SO	Avg.
Paul Frank..............	1	20	0	0	0	0	0	0.00
Judd Lambert	11	620	6	4	0	33	0	3.19
Ryan Bach	30	1733	17	7	5	105	0	3.63

DENVER
SCORING

	Pos.	Class	Games	G	A	Pts.	PIM
Jason Elders	F	Jr.	38	26	18	44	21
Angelo Ricci............	F	Jr.	38	13	29	42	58
Ian DeCorby	D	Sr.	38	10	28	38	52
Erik Andersson	F	So.	38	10	20	30	42
Chris Kenady	F	Jr.	37	14	11	25	125
Brian Konowalchuk	F	Sr.	34	9	15	24	26
Mike Naylor............	F	Jr.	37	9	14	23	39
Antti Laaksonen	F	Fr.	36	12	9	21	38
Kelly Hollingshead.	D	So.	37	4	15	19	87
Brent Cary	F	So.	15	6	12	18	4
Petri Gunther	F	Fr.	32	9	6	15	12
Craig McMillan	D	Jr.	38	4	8	12	45
John McLean	D	Jr.	38	5	6	11	48
Sean Ortiz	F	Jr.	38	4	4	8	18
Kelly Hrycun	F	Fr.	19	3	5	8	2
Mark Luger	D	Sr.	22	2	4	6	36
Mike Corbett	D	Fr.	17	0	5	5	2
Paul Koch	D	Jr.	17	2	2	4	22
Dave Klasnick........	F	So.	36	2	1	3	12
Corey Carlson	F	Sr.	10	1	1	2	27
Travis Smith	D	Fr.	18	0	2	2	14
Garrett Buzan	F	So.	20	0	2	2	13
Charlie Host	F	Fr.	22	1	0	1	4
Sinuhe Wallinheimo	G	So.	23	0	1	1	2
Chris Burns............	G	So.	3	0	0	0	0
Mike Rotsch	F	Fr.	10	0	0	0	4
Jim Mullin	G	Fr.	18	0	0	0	2

GOALTENDING

	Games	Min.	W	L	T	Goals	SO	Avg.
Sinuhe Wallinheimo	23	1238	10	12	1	81	0	3.93
Jim Mullin	18	873	4	6	2	58	0	3.98
Chris Burns	3	178	1	2	0	13	0	4.39

MICHIGAN TECH
SCORING

	Pos.	Class	Games	G	A	Pts.	PIM
Pat Mikesch	F	So.	45	14	36	50	118
Brent Peterson.......	F	Jr.	43	25	21	46	30
Randy Stevens.......	F	Jr.	42	21	12	33	42
Layne LeBel	F/D	Sr.	45	9	23	32	79
Jason Wright	D	So.	45	2	17	19	58
Martin Machacek ...	F	So.	35	11	6	17	52
Mike Figliomeni	F	So.	40	8	8	16	34
Kyle Peterson	F	Fr.	45	5	9	14	82
Jason Hanchuk.......	D	So.	43	1	13	14	82
Jeff Mikesch	F	Fr.	41	9	4	13	80
Justin Peca	F	Jr.	40	8	3	11	56
Mitch Lane.............	F	So.	40	7	4	11	36
Kirby Perrault	D	Sr.	44	3	8	11	120
Liam Garvey	D	Jr.	40	1	10	11	70
Kyle Ferguson	F	So.	36	4	5	9	63
Travis Seale	F	Jr.	19	4	3	7	14
Eric Jensen	D	Fr.	42	2	5	7	48
John Kisil	F	Fr.	39	1	5	6	22
Jeff Hill	D	Sr.	45	0	5	5	105
Jamie Ram	G	Sr.	39	0	2	2	10
Jay Storm	F	Sr.	3	0	0	0	2
Luciano Caravaggio	G	Fr.	13	0	0	0	15
Brian Hunter	D	Fr.	19	0	0	0	26

GOALTENDING

	Games	Min.	W	L	T	Goals	SO	Avg.
Jamie Ram..............	39	2192	12	20	5	117	1	3.20
Luciano Caravaggio	13	538	1	7	0	37	1	4.13

MINNESOTA
SCORING

	Pos.	Class	Games	G	A	Pts.	PIM
Jeff Nielsen	F	Sr.	41	29	16	45	94
Brian Bonin	F	So.	42	24	20	44	14
Justin McHugh	F	Jr.	42	15	20	35	59
Tony Bianchi	F	Sr.	36	8	27	35	16
Chris McAlpine	D	Sr.	36	12	18	30	121
Danny Trebil	D	So.	42	1	21	22	24
Dan Woog	F	Fr.	38	5	14	19	57
Bobby Dustin	F	So.	39	10	7	17	36
Joe Dziedzic	F	Sr.	18	7	10	17	48
Andy Brink	F	So.	40	7	10	17	8
Dave Larson	D	So.	31	6	11	17	75
Eric Means	D	Sr.	36	5	11	16	32
Charlie Wasley	D	So.	36	1	14	15	29
Steve Magnusson ..	F	Jr.	16	2	12	14	16
Nick Checco	F	Fr.	41	7	5	12	28
Jed Fiebelkorn	F	Jr.	39	5	6	11	65
Brian LaFleur.........	D	Fr.	40	0	9	9	12
Greg Zwakman	D	So.	42	2	6	8	36
Dan Hendrickson	F	Fr.	39	3	2	5	60
Jesse Bertogliat	F	So.	17	2	2	4	16
Jeff Moen	G	So.	20	0	1	1	0
Steve Green	G	Fr.	1	0	0	0	0
Jim Hillman	F	Fr.	6	0	0	0	8
Mike McAlpine	D	So.	7	0	0	0	0
Brent Godbout........	F	Fr.	12	0	0	0	6
John Hillman	F	Fr.	20	0	0	0	46
Jeff Callinan	G	Jr.	26	0	0	0	0

GOALTENDING

	Games	Min.	W	L	T	Goals	SO	Avg.
Steve Green	1	8	0	0	0	0	0	0.00
Jeff Callinan	26	1491	14	5	3	80	0	3.22
Jeff Moen................	20	1083	11	8	1	60	0	3.33

MINNESOTA-DULUTH
SCORING

	Pos.	Class	Games	G	A	Pts.	PIM
Chris Marinucci	F	Sr.	38	30	31	61	65
Brad Federenko	F	Jr.	36	13	23	36	25
Rusty Fitzgerald	F	Jr.	37	11	25	36	59
Rod Aldoff	D	Jr.	38	4	25	29	88
Brett Larson	D	Jr.	38	14	14	28	40
Brian Caruso..........	F	Sr.	37	11	10	21	61
Chris Sittlow	F	Jr.	36	5	14	19	60
Corey Osmak	F	Sr.	34	11	7	18	78
Kraig Karakas	F	Sr.	36	7	11	18	52
Rod Miller	D	Sr.	38	5	12	17	119
Joe Ciccarello	F	So.	38	3	10	13	28
Jeff Romfo	F	So.	38	7	4	11	16
Rick Mrozik	D	Fr.	38	2	9	11	38
Greg Hanson	D	So.	27	3	6	9	40
Adam Roy	F	Fr.	20	2	6	8	18
Jason Garatti	D	Fr.	34	3	4	7	10
Joe Tamminen	F	Jr.	19	2	4	6	22
Chet Culic	F	Jr.	23	2	4	6	24
Sergei Petrov	F	Fr.	28	2	4	6	25
Derek Locker	F	Fr.	16	1	4	5	10
Dan Jablonic	F	Jr.	15	2	0	2	2
David Buck	D	Fr.	12	0	2	2	14
Taras Lendzyk	G	So.	32	0	1	1	0
Marc Christian.......	F	Jr.	1	0	0	0	0
Niklas Axelsson	G	Jr.	2	0	0	0	0
Aaron Novak	F	Fr.	3	0	0	0	2
Jerome Butler	G	Jr.	7	0	0	0	0

GOALTENDING

	Games	Min.	W	L	T	Goals	SO	Avg.
Taras Landzyk	32	1917	13	17	2	123	0	3.85
Jerome Butler	7	328	1	4	1	27	0	4.95
Niklas Axelsson.......	2	49	0	0	0	7	0	8.52

NORTH DAKOTA
SCORING

	Pos.	Class	Games	G	A	Pts.	PIM
Landon Wilson......	F	Fr.	35	18	15	33	147
Marty Schriner	F	Sr.	37	11	22	33	129
Nick Naumenko	D	So.	32	4	22	26	22
Dean Grillo	F	So.	38	11	14	25	14
Brad Bombardir	D	Sr.	38	5	17	22	38
Kevin McKinnon	F	Sr.	38	13	7	20	24
Kevin Hoogsteen....	F	Fr.	35	8	12	20	20
Teeder Wynne.......	F	So.	25	8	10	18	35
Darcy Mitani	F	So.	34	4	12	16	49
Dane Litke	D	Fr.	34	0	14	14	6
Sean Beswick	F	So.	33	8	4	12	28
Chris Gotziaman	F	Sr.	33	8	4	12	29
Keith Murphy	F	So.	36	7	4	11	29
Brian Zierke	F	Fr.	24	3	6	9	96
Scott Kirton	F	Jr.	27	3	6	9	49
Mark Pivetz	D	Fr.	36	2	5	7	95
Corey Johnson.......	F	So.	36	3	3	6	33
Brett Hryniuk	F	Jr.	24	2	3	5	39
Darren Bear	D	Jr.	27	0	5	5	24
Jarrod Olson	D	Jr.	28	1	3	4	24
Kevin Rappana	D	So.	28	0	2	2	63
Toby Kvalevog	G	Fr.	32	0	2	2	6
Joby Bond	F	Sr.	1	0	0	0	2
Todd Jones	G	Sr.	3	0	0	0	0
Jeff Lembke	G	Jr.	3	0	0	0	0
Akil Adams	D	So.	4	0	0	0	14
Kevin Powell	F	So.	6	0	0	0	0

GOALTENDING

	Games	Min.	W	L	T	Goals	SO	Avg.
Toby Kvalevog	32	1813	11	17	3	120	0	3.97
Jeff Lembke............	3	140	0	2	0	10	0	4.29
Kevin Powell	6	225	0	2	1	19	0	5.07
Todd Jones	3	121	0	2	0	13	0	6.47

NORTHERN MICHIGAN
SCORING

	Pos.	Class	Games	G	A	Pts.	PIM
Mike Harding	F	Jr.	38	24	25	49	66
Dean Seymour	F	Fr.	39	12	29	41	14
Kory Karlander	F	So.	39	20	20	40	40
Jason Hehr.............	D/F	Jr.	39	11	26	37	56
Scott Green	F	Sr.	39	10	24	34	12
Steve Carpenter.....	D	Sr.	33	11	19	30	123
Greg Hadden	F	Jr.	28	9	20	29	85
Karson Kaebel	F	So.	36	7	20	27	90
Brent Riplinger.......	F	Jr.	34	13	13	26	33
Bryan Ganz	F	Sr.	25	10	6	16	65
Garett MacDonald .	D	Sr.	35	2	14	16	98
Darcy Dallas	D	Fr.	31	2	11	13	68
Shayne Tomlinson..	D	Fr.	38	2	9	11	74
Bill MacGillivray	F	Jr.	39	6	4	10	57
Don McCusker	F	So.	33	5	4	9	20
Scott Smith	F	Sr.	24	2	7	9	12
Steve Woog	F	Sr.	38	6	2	8	66
Trevor Janicki	D	Fr.	26	1	3	4	26
Chad Dameworth...	D	Jr.	36	0	4	4	26
Justin George	F	Jr.	9	3	0	3	18
Mike Hillock	D	Fr.	20	0	2	2	20
Brian Barker	F	Fr.	14	1	0	1	6
Patrik Hansson......	F	Fr.	2	0	0	0	0
Dieter Kochan	G	Fr.	20	0	0	0	0
Paul Taylor	G	So.	25	0	0	0	24

GOALTENDING

	Games	Min.	W	L	T	Goals	SO	Avg.
Dieter Kochan.........	20	984	9	7	0	57	0	3.47
Paul Taylor.............	25	1355	13	9	1	79	0	3.50

ST. CLOUD STATE
SCORING

	Pos.	Class	Games	G	A	Pts.	PIM
Kelly Hultgren........	D	Jr.	35	14	23	37	79
Marc Gagnon	F	Jr.	37	22	13	35	32
Bill Lund	F	Jr.	38	11	24	35	95
Brett Lievers	F	Jr.	32	16	16	32	2
Dave Holum	F	Jr.	37	17	14	31	66
Eric Johnson	F	Jr.	33	9	21	30	16
Tony Gruba	F	Sr.	38	10	17	27	106
Sandy Gasseau	F	Jr.	37	13	10	23	48
Gino Santerre.........	D	Jr.	38	7	16	23	30
Taj Melson	D	So.	38	4	18	22	45
Dave Paradise	F	Fr.	38	14	4	18	66
Kelly Rieder	F	So.	38	4	14	18	17
Jeff Schmidt...........	F	Jr.	34	7	5	12	37
Jay Geisbauer	F	So.	38	4	8	12	50
Dan Reimann	D	So.	36	1	10	11	61
Adam Rodak	F	Fr.	33	2	6	8	45
Chris Markstrom ...	F	Jr.	16	3	2	5	4
P.J. Lepler	D	So.	35	1	4	5	48
Mike O'Connell.......	F	Fr.	30	1	3	4	8
Mike Maristuen	F	Fr.	7	0	1	1	0
Randy Best	D	Fr.	15	0	1	1	24
Grant Sjerven	G	Sr.	31	0	1	1	41
Neil Cooper............	G	So.	12	0	0	0	15

GOALTENDING

	Games	Min.	W	L	T	Goals	SO	Avg.
Grant Sjerven	31	1786	16	10	3	93	0	3.12
Neil Cooper	12	508	5	3	1	30	0	3.54

WISCONSIN
SCORING

	Pos.	Class	Games	G	A	Pts.	PIM
Kelly Fairchild	F	Jr.	42	20	44	64	81
Andrew Shier	F	Sr.	42	17	45	62	76
Blaine Moore..........	F	Sr.	37	21	20	41	104
Jason Zent	F	Sr.	42	20	21	41	120
Ulvis Katlaps	D	Sr.	42	5	25	30	18
Jamie Spencer	F	Jr.	34	15	13	28	36
Chris Tucker	F	Sr.	42	9	19	28	32
Max Williams	F	So.	42	13	12	25	35
Brian Rafalski	D	Jr.	37	6	17	23	26
Mark Strobel	D	Jr.	41	7	12	19	57
Mickey Elick	D	So.	42	7	12	19	54
Mike Strobel	F	Jr.	41	6	12	18	72
Rob Granato...........	F	Sr.	40	8	7	15	16
Maco Balkovec	D	Jr.	39	4	10	14	74
Mike Doers	F	Sr.	41	4	8	12	39
Matt Buss	F	Sr.	36	5	4	9	62
Chris Tok	D	Jr.	41	2	5	7	97
Shawn Carter	F	Jr.	16	2	2	4	24
Jim Carey	G	So.	39	0	3	3	6
Scott Sanderson ...	F	So.	15	1	0	1	2
Dan Tompkins	F	Fr.	18	1	0	1	31
Troy Howard..........	F	So.	18	0	1	1	8
Jeff Sanderson	D	Sr.	3	0	0	0	2
Tim Krug	D	So.	5	0	0	0	0
Kirk Daubenspeck ..	G	Fr.	7	0	0	0	0

GOALTENDING

	Games	Min.	W	L	T	Goals	SO	Avg.
Jim Carey	39	2247	24	13	1	114	1	3.04
Kirk Daubenspeck ...	7	280	2	2	0	19	0	4.07

INDEPENDENTS

1993-94 SEASON

FINAL STANDINGS

	W	L	T	GF	GA	Pct.
Air Force	15	16	1	121	139	.484
Army	14	16	0	123	121	.467

INDIVIDUAL STATISTICS

AIR FORCE
SCORING

	Pos.	Class	Games	G	A	Pts.	PIM
Beau Bilek	D	Jr.	32	9	33	42	34
Andy Veneri	F	Jr.	32	21	20	41	66
John Decker	F	Jr.	32	17	20	37	53
Mark DeGironimo	F	So.	32	14	22	36	30
Greg Dumont	F	Fr.	30	17	10	27	45
Dan McAlister	F	Jr.	30	7	10	17	42
Tony Retka	D	Sr.	29	2	13	15	46
Paul Northon	F	Jr.	29	3	6	9	34
George Kriz	F	Jr.	22	2	7	9	8
Todd Lafortune	F	Fr.	25	6	2	8	10
Erik Brown	F	Jr.	30	4	4	8	40
Doug Smalley	D	Sr.	31	2	6	8	22
Joe Javorski	F	Jr.	31	4	3	7	28
Chris Mitchell	F	So.	28	3	3	6	20
Justin Scott	D	Fr.	25	2	4	6	32
Patrick Ryan	D	So.	29	2	4	6	4
Dan Leone	D	So.	28	2	3	5	18
Stephen Maturo	F	Fr.	26	1	3	4	6
Derek Sellnow	F	Fr.	2	2	0	2	0
John Sullivan	F	Jr.	6	1	0	1	4
David Michaud	D	So.	4	0	1	1	4
Brian Mulligan	F	Fr.	5	0	1	1	16
Peter Sandness	F/D	Fr.	8	0	1	1	4
John Giusto	D	So.	17	0	1	1	28
John Rimstad	D	Fr.	1	0	0	0	0
Jim Tuomi	F/D	Jr.	2	0	0	0	0
Kevin Magaletta	F	Jr.	3	0	0	0	0
Curt Wilcox	F	Fr.	8	0	0	0	11
Mike Benson	G	Jr.	13	0	0	0	0
Pat Kielb	G	Fr.	22	0	0	0	0

GOALTENDING

	Games	Min.	W	L	T	Goals	SO	Avg.
Pat Kielb	22	1239	12	8	1	73	2	3.54
Mike Benson	13	689	3	8	0	65	0	5.66

ARMY
SCORING

	Pos.	Class	Games	G	A	Pts.	PIM
Ian Winer	So.	F	23	16	16	32	28
Frank Fede	Fr.	F	29	10	17	27	16
Mike Landers	Sr.	D	29	8	14	22	24
Dave Pilarski	Sr.	F	27	7	13	20	20
Sean Hennessy	Jr.	D	30	4	15	19	37
Tony DiCarlo	Fr.	F	29	11	7	18	46
Justin Lambert	Jr.	F	28	10	8	18	28
Bill Morrison	Fr.	F	25	6	12	18	22
Troy Eigner	Jr.	F	21	5	13	18	10
Joe Sharrock	Fr.	F	24	4	11	15	20
Mark Stachelski	Jr.	F	28	8	6	14	54
Leif Hansen	Fr.	D	30	7	6	13	30
Mike Mansell	So.	D	19	2	9	11	24
John Compton	Sr.	D	28	0	10	10	60
Marc Dorrer	So.	F	11	3	6	9	6
Ted Doyle	Jr.	F	5	2	7	9	0
Craig Fellman	Jr.	F	23	5	3	8	29
Tom Deveans	Fr.	F	20	3	5	8	24
Brett Funck	Sr.	D	24	2	6	8	26
Chris Perron	Fr.	F	15	2	4	6	14
Mike Opdenaker	Fr.	D	21	1	5	6	14
Tim Hocking	Jr.	F	8	3	2	5	2
Eric Leetch	Jr.	F	4	1	3	4	4
Robie MacLaughlin	Jr.	F	9	1	2	3	31
Jason Dickie	So.	D	14	0	3	3	13
Milt Smith	Sr.	F	10	2	0	2	12
Ron Adimey	Jr.	G	13	0	1	1	14
Randy Erickson	Jr.	G	1	0	0	0	0
Sam Pearson	Sr.	G	1	0	0	0	0
Mike Gunning	So.	F	2	0	0	0	2
Brian Bolio	Jr.	G	22	0	0	0	4

GOALTENDING

	Games	Min.	W	L	T	Goals	SO	Avg.
Randy Erickson	1	2	0	0	0	0	0	0.00
Brian Bolio	22	1140	11	7	0	72	1	3.79
Ron Adimey	13	644	3	9	0	48	0	4.47
Sam Pearson	1	12	0	0	0	1	0	5.01

CANADIAN INTERUNIVERSITY ATHLETIC UNION

GENERAL INFORMATION

The Canadian Interuniversity Athletic Union is an alliance of three Canadian college leagues—the Atlantic Universities Athletic Association, Canada West University Athletic Association and Ontario Universities Athletic Association. After the regular season, the three leagues compete in an elimination tournament to decide the CIAU national champion. The award and trophy winners are based on regular-season play.

1994 NATIONAL CHAMPIONSHIPS

PLAYOFF STANDINGS

Team (League)	W	L	Pts.	GF	GA
Lethbridge (CWUAA)	2	0	4	14	8
U. of Guelph (OUAA)	1	1	2	8	10
Western Ontario (OUAA)	0	1	0	5	6
Acadia (AUAA)	0	1	0	6	9

RESULTS

SEMIFINALS

FRIDAY, MARCH 11

Lethbridge 9, Acadia 6
Guelph 6, W. Ontario 5 (2 OT)

FINAL

SUNDAY, MARCH 13

Lethbridge 5, Guelph 2

1993-94 AWARD WINNERS

ALL-STAR TEAMS

Pos.	Player
G	Trevor Kruger, Lethbridge
	Sean Basilio, Western Ontario
D	Kevin Knopp, Acadia
	Hardy Sauter, Regina
	Garth Joy, St. Thomas
	Dan Brown, Queen's
F	Duane Dennis, Acadia
	Steve Rucchin, Western Ontario
	John Spoltore, Wilfrid Laurier
	Todd Goodwin, Alberta
	Craig Teeple, St. Mary's
	Joey St. Aubin, Ottawa

TROPHY WINNERS

Player of the year: Duane Dennis, Acadia
Rookie of the year: Jarret Zukiwsky, Lethbridge
Scholastic player of the year: Craig Donaldson, Western Ontario
Coach of the year: Wayne Gowing, Wilfrid Laurier

TOP SCORERS

	Games	G	A	Pts.
Duane Dennis, Acadia	26	35	39	74
Craig Teeple, St. Mary's	26	19	46	65
Jarret Zukiwsky, Lethbridge	28	32	31	63
Trevor Ellerman, Lethbridge	28	22	40	62
John Spoltore, Laurier	24	20	38	58
Dale McTavish, St. Francis Xavier	25	29	24	53
Simon Olivier, Brandon	28	25	27	52
Steve Kluczkowski, St. Mary's	26	21	30	51
Greg Suchan, Calgary	28	21	29	50
Brian Purdy, Saskatchewan	28	13	37	50

CANADIAN COLLEGES

ATLANTIC UNIVERSITIES ATHLETIC ASSOCIATION, 1993-94 SEASON

FINAL STANDINGS

KELLY DIVISION

Team	G	W	L	T	Pts.	GF	GA
Dalhousie University..	26	19	3	4	42	152	87
Acadia University......	26	19	4	3	41	179	100
St. Francis Xavier U. ..	26	13	11	2	28	121	109
St. Mary's University .	26	12	11	3	27	117	136
U. Col. of Cape Breton.	26	6	18	2	14	110	168

MAC ADAM DIVISION

Team	G	W	L	T	Pts.	GF	GA
U. of New Brunswick ..	26	16	9	1	33	132	89
St. Thomas University	26	14	11	1	29	118	115
Univ. de Moncton.......	26	10	11	5	25	126	125
U. of P. Edward Island	26	5	17	4	14	113	163
Mount Allison Univ....	26	2	21	3	7	90	166

PLAYOFF RESULTS

KELLY DIVISION SEMIFINALS

Dalhousie 5, St. Mary's 4 (OT)
Dalhousie 5, St. Mary's 1

Acadia 7, St.F.X. 3

Acadia 5, St.F.X. 1

MAC ADAM DIVISION SEMIFINALS

Moncton 2, St. Thomas 1 (OT)
St. Thomas 2, Moncton 1 (OT)
Moncton 5, St. Thomas 4 (OT)

New Brunswick 3, P.E.I. 1
New Brunswick 6, P.E.I. 0

KELLY DIVISION FINALS

Acadia 12, Dalhousie 2
Acadia 9, Dalhousie 3

MAC ADAM DIVISION FINALS

Moncton 5, New Brunswick 4
New Brunswick 4, Moncton 3
New Brunswick 8, Moncton 4

LEAGUE FINALS

Acadia 5, New Brunswick 3
Acadia 7, New Brunswick 3

ALL-STAR TEAMS

Kelly Division	Pos.	MacAdam Division
Denis Sproxton, Acadia	G	Mark Cavallan, Mt. Allison
Kevin Knopp, Acadia	D	Garth Joy, St. Thomas
Kevin Meisner, Dalhousie	D	Kelly Reed, New Brunswick
Duane Dennis, Acadia	F	Jean Imbeau, Moncton
Dale McTavish, St.F.X.	F	Mark Rupnow, N. Brunswick
Craig Teeple, St. Mary's	F	Kevin White, P.E.I.

AWARD WINNERS

Most Valuable Player: Duane Dennis, Acadia
Rookie of the year: Derek Cormier, New Brunswick
Coach of the year: Darrell Young, Dalhousie
Leading scorer: Duane Dennis, Acadia

INDIVIDUAL LEADERS

Goals: Duane Dennis, Acadia (35)
Assists: Craig Teeple, St. Mary's (46)
Points: Duane Dennis, Acadia (74)
Penalty minutes: Mike Dawson, Acadia (155)
Goaltending average: Greg Reid, New Brunswick (2.74)

TOP SCORERS

	Games	G	A	Pts.
Duane Dennis, Acadia........................	26	35	39	74
Craig Teeple, St. Mary's.....................	26	19	46	65
Dale McTavish, St. Francis Xavier	25	29	24	53
Steve Kluczkowski, St. Mary's	26	21	30	51
Jerrett DeFazzio, St. Mary's	26	24	25	49
Joe Suk, Dalhousie	25	10	38	48
Todd Sparks, New Brunswick...........	26	14	33	47
Ken MacDermid, Dalhousie................	25	24	22	46
Derek Cormier, New Brunswick........	26	29	17	46
Kevin White, Prince Edward Island ...	24	18	26	44

CANADA WEST UNIVERSITY ATHLETIC ASSOCIATION, 1993-94 SEASON

FINAL STANDINGS

Team	G	W	L	T	Pts.	GF	GA
Leth. (28-9-3)..........	28	19	7	2	40	143	94
Calgary (23-11-6)....	28	17	7	4	38	138	113
Alberta (23-10-7)....	28	15	6	7	37	122	99
Regina (23-11-1).....	28	16	11	1	33	125	97
Manitoba (19-16-5) .	28	11	12	5	27	108	115
Brit. Col. (8-21-4)....	28	7	17	4	18	101	150
Sask. (11-24-2).......	28	7	19	2	16	113	153
Brandon (13-21-6)..	28	5	18	5	15	120	149

PLAYOFF RESULTS

SEMIFINALS

Regina 5, Lethbridge 4
Lethbridge 2, Regina 1 (2 OT)
Lethbridge 4, Regina 3 (2 OT)
Calgary 3, Alberta 1
Calgary 5, Alberta 2

FINALS

Lethbridge 2, Calgary 1 (OT)
Calgary 3, Lethbridge 2
Lethbridge 2, Calgary 1

ALL-STAR TEAMS

First team	Pos.	Second team
Trevor Kruger, Leth.	G	Craig Lumbard, Regina
Jamie Pegg, Calgary	D	Colin Baustad, Lethbridge
Hardy Sauter, Regina	D	Brad Woods, Manitoba
Trevor Ellerman, Leth.	F	Tracey Katelnikoff, Calgary
Todd Goodwin, Alberta	F	Brian Purdy, Saskatchewan
Rob Harvey, Regina	F	Jarret Zukiwsky, Lethbridge

AWARD WINNERS

Most Valuable Player: Trevor Kruger, Lethbridge
Rookie of the year: Jarret Zukiwsky, Lethbridge
Most gentlemanly player: Trevor Ellerman, Lethbridge
Coach of the year: Mike Babcock, Lethbridge
Leading scorer: Jarret Zukiwsky, Lethbridge

INDIVIDUAL LEADERS

Goals: Jarret Zukiwsky, Lethbridge (32)
Assists: Trevor Ellerman, Lethbridge (40)
Points: Jarret Zukiwsky, Lethbridge (63)
Penalty minutes: Marty Craigdallie, British Columbia (142)
Goaltending average: Trevor Kruger, Lethbridge (3.02)
Shutouts: Scott Ironside, Alberta (1)
Trevor Kruger, Lethbridge (1)
Craig Lumbard, Regina (1)

TOP SCORERS

	Games	G	A	Pts.
Jarret Zukiwsky, Lethbridge	28	32	31	63
Trevor Ellerman, Lethbridge	28	22	40	62
Simon Olivier, Brandon	28	25	27	52
Greg Suchan, Calgary	28	21	29	50
Brian Purdy, Saskatchewan	28	13	37	50
Sean Krakiwsky, Calgary	26	24	25	49
Derek Picklyk, Manitoba	28	16	33	49
Alan Patterson, Brandon	28	21	26	47
Tracey Katelnikoff, Calgary	28	17	28	45
Jason Krywulak, Calgary	28	21	22	43
Dean Richards, British Columbia	28	19	24	43
Blake Knox, British Columbia	21	15	28	43

ONTARIO UNIVERSITIES ATHLETIC ASSOCIATION. 1993-94 SEASON

FINAL STANDINGS

FAR EAST DIVISION

Team	G	W	L	T	Pts.	GF	GA
University of Ottawa	24	16	5	3	35	111	68
Que. at Trois-Rivieres	24	16	6	2	34	137	73
Concordia University	24	15	8	1	31	112	76
McGill University	24	13	10	1	27	97	75

MID EAST DIVISION

Team	G	W	L	T	Pts.	GF	GA
University of Guelph	26	15	10	1	31	120	99
Queen's University	26	7	18	1	15	75	107
University of Toronto	26	6	17	3	15	88	138
Royal Military College	26	2	24	0	4	64	187

MID WEST DIVISION

Team	G	W	L	T	Pts.	GF	GA
Brock University	26	13	12	1	27	116	95
York University	26	10	15	1	21	94	111
Laurentian University	26	10	16	0	20	106	123
Ryerson Poly. Inst.	26	4	20	2	10	103	189

FAR WEST DIVISION

Team	G	W	L	T	Pts.	GF	GA
U. of Western Ontario	24	22	1	1	45	122	63
Wilfrid Laurier Univ.	24	20	3	1	41	128	70
University of Waterloo	24	12	10	2	26	115	98
University of Windsor	24	8	14	2	18	83	99

PLAYOFF RESULTS

DIVISIONAL SEMIFINALS
Trois-Rivieres 6, Concordia 1
York 4, Laurentian 3
Toronto 4, Queen's 1
Laurier 5, Waterloo 2

Brock 3, York 2
York 4, Brock 3
York 2, Brock 0
W. Ontario 6, Laurier 5 (3 OT)
Western Ontario 5, Laurier 4

DIVISIONAL FINALS
Trois-Rivieres 5, Ottawa 2
Trois-Rivieres 5, Ottawa 3
Guelph 5, Toronto 2
Guelph 5, Toronto 4 (OT)

LEAGUE SEMIFINALS
Western Ontario 2, York 1
Guelph 3, Trois-Rivieres 2

LEAGUE FINALS
Guelph 2, Western 1

ALL-STAR TEAMS

EAST DIVISION

First team	Pos.	Second team
Francois Gravel, UQTR	G	Patrick Jeanson, McGill
Dan Brown, Queen's	D	Paul O'Hagan, Guelph
Derek Potts, Concordia	D	Martin Roy, Ottawa
Joey St. Aubin, Ottawa	F	Guy Boucher, McGill
Alain Tardif, Ottawa	F	Patrick Genest, UQTR
Alain Vogin, UQTR	F	Todd Wetzel, Guelph

WEST DIVISION

First team	Pos.	Second team
Sean Basilio, W. Ont.	G	Steve Thorpe, Windsor
Rob Radobenko, York	D	Brian Grieve, W. Ontario
John Wynne, Waterloo	D	Bob Shelp, Laurier
Jamie Caruso, Ryerson	F	Darren Macoretta, Brock
Steve Rucchin, W. Ontario	F	Dave Matsos, W. Ontario
John Spoltore, Laurier	F	Jason Mervyn, Waterloo

AWARD WINNERS

East Division Most Valuable Player: Alain Tardif, Ottawa
West Division Most Valuable Player: Steve Rucchin, W. Ontario
East Division rookie of the year: Todd Wetzel, Guelph
West Division rookie of the year: Dave Matsos, Western Ontario
East Division most gentlemanly player: Eric Ross, Guelph
West Division most gentlemanly player: Dwayne Brunet, Windsor
East Division coach of the year: Jean Pronovost, McGill
West Division coach of the year: Wayne Gowing, Laurier
Leading scorer: John Spoltore, Laurier

INDIVIDUAL LEADERS

Goals: Eric Ross, Guelph (27)
Assists: John Spoltore, Laurier (38)
Points: John Spoltore, Laurier (58)
Penalty minutes: Eric Rochette, Concordia (98)
Goaltending average: Sean Basilio, Western Ontario (2.48)

TOP SCORERS

	Games	G	A	Pts.
John Spoltore, Laurier	24	20	38	58
Jamie Caruso, Ryerson	24	18	27	45
Joey St. Aubin, Ottawa	24	21	21	42
Darren Macoretta, Brock	25	13	28	41
Todd Wetzel, Guelph	26	19	22	41
Dan Haylow, Guelph	25	13	27	40
Eric Ross, Guelph	26	27	12	39
Jason Mervyn, Waterloo	24	19	19	38
Ian Richardson, Ryerson	26	10	28	38
Alain Vogin, Trois-Rivieres	22	10	27	37
Guy Boucher, McGill	24	17	20	37

INDEX OF TEAMS

INDEX OF TEAMS

HOCKEY REGISTER

Players

NHL head coaches

EXPLANATION OF AWARDS

NHL AWARDS: Alka-Seltzer Plus Award: plus/minus leader. **Art Ross Trophy:** leading scorer. **Bill Masterton Memorial Trophy:** perseverance, sportsmanship and dedication to hockey. **Bud Light/NHL Man of the Year:** service to community; called Budweiser/NHL Man of the Year prior to 1990-91. **Budweiser/NHL Man of the Year:** service to community; renamed Bud Light/NHL Man of the Year in 1990-91. **Calder Memorial Trophy:** rookie of the year. **Conn Smythe Trophy:** most valuable player in playoffs. **Dodge Performance of the Year Award:** most outstanding achievement or single-game performance. **Dodge Performer of the Year Award:** most outstanding performer in regular season. **Dodge Ram Tough Award:** highest combined total of power-play, shorthanded, game-winning and game-tying goals. **Emery Edge Award:** plus/minus leader; awarded from 1982-83 through 1987-88. **Frank J. Selke Trophy:** best defensive forward. **Hart Memorial Trophy:** most valuable player. **Jack Adams Award:** coach of the year. **James Norris Memorial Trophy:** outstanding defenseman. **King Clancy Memorial Trophy:** humanitarian contributions. **Lady Byng Memorial Trophy:** most gentlemanly player. **Lester B. Pearson Award:** outstanding player as selected by NHL Players' Association. **Lester Patrick Trophy:** outstanding service to hockey in U.S. **Trico Goaltender Award:** best save percentage. **Vezina Trophy:** best goaltender; awarded to goalkeeper(s) having played minimum of 25 games for team with fewest goals scored against prior to 1981-82. **William M. Jennings Trophy:** goalkeeper(s) having played minimum of 25 games for team with fewest goals scored against.

MINOR LEAGUE AWARDS: Baz Bastien Trophy: top goaltender (AHL). **Bobby Orr Trophy:** best defenseman (CHL); awarded prior to 1984-85. **Bob Gassoff Award:** most improved defenseman (CHL); awarded prior to 1984-85. **Commissioner's Trophy:** coach of the year (IHL). **Dudley (Red) Garrett Memorial Trophy:** rookie of the year (AHL). **Eddie Shore Plaque:** outstanding defenseman (AHL). **Fred Hunt Memorial Award:** sportsmanship, determination and dedication (AHL). **Garry F. Longman Memorial Trophy:** outstanding rookie (IHL). **Governors Trophy:** outstanding defenseman (IHL). **Harry (Hap) Holmes Memorial Trophy:** goaltender(s) having played minimum of 25 games for team with fewest goals scored against (AHL); awarded to outstanding goaltender prior to 1983-84. **Jack Butterfield Trophy:** Calder Cup playoffs MVP (AHL). **Jake Milford Trophy:** coach of the year (CHL); awarded prior to 1984-85. **James Gatschene Memorial Trophy:** most valuable player (IHL). **James Norris Memorial Trophy:** outstanding goaltender (IHL). **John B. Sollenberger Trophy:** leading scorer (AHL); originally called Wally Kilrea Trophy, later changed to Carl Liscombe Trophy until summer of 1955. **Ken McKenzie Trophy:** outstanding U.S.-born rookie (IHL). **Ken McKenzie Trophy:** top rookie (CHL); awarded to scoring leader from 1992-93. **Leo P. Lamoureux Memorial Trophy:** leading scorer (IHL); originally called George H. Wilkinson Trophy from 1946-47 through 1959-60. **Les Cunningham Plaque:** most valuable player (AHL). **Louis A.R. Pieri Memorial Award:** top coach (AHL). **Max McNab Trophy:** playoff MVP (CHL); awarded prior to 1984-85. **N.R. (Bud) Poile Trophy:** playoff MVP (IHL); originally called Turner Cup Playoff MVP from 1984-85 through 1988-89. **Phil Esposito Trophy:** leading scorer (CHL); awarded prior to 1984-85. **Terry Sawchuk Trophy:** top goaltenders (CHL); awarded prior to 1984-85. **Tommy Ivan Trophy:** most valuable player (CHL); awarded prior to 1984-85. **Turner Cup Playoff MVP:** playoff MVP (IHL); renamed N.R. (Bud) Poile Trophy in 1989-90.

MAJOR JUNIOR LEAGUE AWARDS: Association of Journalists for Major Junior League Hockey Trophy: top pro prospect (QMJHL); renamed Michael Bossy Trophy in 1983-84. **Bill Hunter Trophy:** top defenseman (WHL); called Top Defenseman Trophy prior to 1987-88 season. **Bob Brownridge Memorial Trophy:** top scorer (WHL); later renamed Bob Clarke Trophy. **Bobby Smith Trophy:** scholastic player of the year (OHL). **Bob Clarke Trophy:** top scorer (WHL); originally called Bob Brownridge Memorial Trophy. **Brad Hornung Trophy:** most sportsmanlike player (WHL); called Frank Boucher Memorial Trophy for most gentlemanly player prior to 1987-88 season. **Dave Pinkney Trophy:** top team goaltending (OHL). **Del Wilson Trophy:** top goaltender (WHL); called Top Goaltender Trophy prior to 1987-88 season. **Des Instructeurs Trophy:** rookie of the year (QMJHL); awarded to top rookie forward since 1981-82 season; renamed Michel Bergeron Trophy in 1985-86. **Dunc McCallum Memorial Trophy:** coach of the year (WHL). **Eddie Powers Memorial Trophy:** scoring champion (OHL). **Emile (Butch) Bouchard Trophy:** best defenseman (QMJHL). **Emms Family Award:** rookie of the year (OHL). **Four Broncos Memorial Trophy:** most valuable player as selected by coaches (WHL); called Most Valuable Player Trophy prior to 1987-88 season. **Frank Boucher Memorial Trophy:** most gentlemanly player (WHL); renamed Brad Hornung Trophy during 1987-88 season. **Frank J. Selke Trophy:** most gentlemanly player (QMJHL). **F.W. (Dinty) Moore Trophy:** rookie goalie with best goals-against average (OHL). **George Parsons Trophy:** sportsmanship in Memorial Cup (Can.HL). **Guy Lafleur Trophy:** most valuable player during playoffs (QMJHL). **Hap Emms Memorial Trophy:** outstanding goaltender in Memorial Cup (Can.HL). **Jacques Plante Trophy:** best goaltender (QMJHL). **Jean Beliveau Trophy:** leading point scorer (QMJHL). **Jim Mahon Memorial Trophy:** top-scoring right winger (OHL). **Jim Piggott Memorial Trophy:** rookie of the year (WHL); originally called Stewart (Butch) Paul Memorial Trophy. **Leo Lalonde Memorial Trophy:** overage player of the year (OHL). **Marcel Robert Trophy:** top scholastic/athletic performer (QMJHL). **Matt Leyden Trophy:** coach of the year (OHL). **Max Kaminsky Trophy:** outstanding defenseman (OHL); awarded to most gentlemanly player prior to 1969-70. **Michael Bossy Trophy:** top pro prospect (QMJHL); originally called Association of Journalists for Major Junior League Hockey Trophy from 1980-81 through 1982-83. **Michel Bergeron Trophy:** top rookie forward (QMJHL); awarded to rookie of the year prior to 1980-81 season. **Michel Briere Trophy:** most valuable player (QMJHL). **Most Valuable Player Trophy:** most valuable player (WHL); renamed Four Broncos Memorial Trophy during 1987-88 season. **Raymond Lagace Trophy:** top rookie defenseman or goaltender (QMJHL). **Red Tilson Trophy:** outstanding player (OHL). **Shell Cup:** awarded to offensive player of the year and defensive player of the year (QMJHL). **Stafford Smythe Memorial Trophy:** most valuable player of Memorial Cup (Can.HL). **Stewart (Butch) Paul Memorial Trophy:** rookie of the year (WHL); renamed Jim Piggott Memorial Trophy during 1987-88 season. **Top Defenseman Trophy:** top defenseman (WHL); renamed Bill Hunter Trophy during 1987-88 season. **Top Goaltender Trophy:** top goaltender (WHL); renamed Del Wilson Trophy during 1987-88 season. **William Hanley Trophy:** most gentlemanly player (OHL).

COLLEGE AWARDS: Hobey Baker Memorial Trophy: top college hockey player in U.S. **Senator Joseph A. Sullivan Trophy:** outstanding player in Canadian Interuniversity Athletic Union.

OTHER AWARDS: Golden Puck Award: Sweden's Player of the Year. **Golden Stick Award:** Europe's top player. **Izvestia Trophy:** leading scorer (Soviet Union).

EXPLANATION OF FOOTNOTES AND ABBREVIATIONS

*   Led league.
†   Tied for league lead.
‡   Overtime loss.
. . . Statistic unavailable, unofficial or mathematically impossible to calculate.
— Statistic inapplicable.

POSITIONS: C: center. **D:** defenseman. **G:** goaltender. **LW:** left winger. **RW:** right winger.

STATISTICS: A: assists. **Avg.:** goals-against average. **G:** goals. **GA:** goals against. **Gms.:** games. **L:** losses. **Min.:** minutes. **PIM.:** penalties in minutes. **Pts:** points. **SO:** shutouts. **T:** ties. **W:** wins.

LEAGUES: AAHL: All American Hockey League. **ACHL:** Atlantic Coast Hockey League. **AHL:** American Hockey League. **AJHL:** Alberta Junior Hockey League. **AMHL:** Alberta Minor Hockey League. **AUAA:** Atlantic Universities Athletic Association. **BCJHL:** British Columbia Junior Hockey League. **CAHL:** Central Alberta Hockey League. **CAJHL:** Central Alberta Junior Hockey League. **Can. College:** Canadian College. **Can.HL:** Canadian Hockey League. **CCHA:** Central Collegiate Hockey Association. **CHL:** Central Hockey League. **CIS:** Commonwealth of Independent States. **CJHL:** Central Junior A Hockey League. **COJHL:** Central Ontario Junior Hockey League. **CPHL:** Central Professional Hockey League. **CWUAA:** Canada West University Athletic Association. **Conn. H.S.:** Connecticut High School. **Czech.:** Czechoslovakia. **Czech. Rep.:** Czechoslovakia Republic. **ECAC:** Eastern College Athletic Conference. **ECAC-II:** Eastern College Athletic Conference, Division II. **ECHL:** East Coast Hockey League. **EHL:** Eastern Hockey League. **Fin.:** Finland. **Ger.:** Germany. **GWHC:** Great Western Hockey Conference. **Hoc. East:** Hockey East. **IHL:** International Hockey League. **III. H.S.:** Illinois High School. **Indiana H.S.:** Indiana High School. **Int'l:** International. **KIJHL:** Kootenay International Junior Hockey League. **Mass. H.S.:** Massachusetts High School. **Md. H.S.:** Maryland High School. **Met. Bos.:** Metro Boston. **Mich. H.S.:** Michigan High School. **Minn. H.S.:** Minnesota High School. **MJHL:** Manitoba Junior Hockey League. **MTHL:** Metro Toronto Hockey League. **NAHL:** North American Hockey League. **NAJHL:** North American Junior Hockey League. **N.B. H.S.:** New Brunswick High School. **NCAA-II:** National Collegiate Athletic Association, Division II. **N.D. H.S.:** North Dakota High School. **NEJHL:** New England Junior Hockey League. **NHL:** National Hockey League. **N.H. H.S.:** New Hampshire High School. **N.J. H.S.:** New Jersey High School. **Nia. D. Jr. C:** Niagara District Junior C. **NSJHL:** Nova Scotia Junior Hockey League. **N.S.Jr.A:** Nova Scotia Junior A. **N.Y. H.S.:** New York High School. **NYMJHL:** New York Major Junior Hockey League. **NYOHL:** North York Ontario Hockey League. **ODHA:** Ottawa & District Hockey Association. **OHA:** Ontario Hockey Association. **OHA Jr. A:** Ontario Hockey Association Junior A. **OHA Mjr. Jr. A:** Ontario Hockey Association Major Junior A. **OHA Senior:** Ontario Hockey Association Senior. **OHL:** Ontario Hockey League. **O.H.S.:** Ohio High School. **OJHA:** Ontario Junior Hockey Association. **OJHL:** Ontario Junior Hockey League. **OMJHL:** Ontario Major Junior Hockey League. **OPJHL:** Ontario Provincial Junior Hockey League. **OUAA:** Ontario Universities Athletic Association. **PCJHL:** Peace Caribou Junior Hockey League. **PEIHA:** Prince Edward Island Hockey Association. **PEIJHL:** Prince Edward Island Junior Hockey League. **Penn. H.S.:** Pennsylvania High School. **QMJHL:** Quebec Major Junior Hockey League. **R.I. H.S.:** Rhode Island High School. **SAJHL:** Southern Alberta Junior Hockey League. **SJHL:** Saskatchewan Junior Hockey League. **Sask. H.S.:** Saskatchewan High School. **SOJHL:** Southern Ontario Junior Hockey League. **Swed. Jr.:** Sweden Junior. **Switz.:** Switzerland. **TBAHA:** Thunder Bay Amateur Hockey Association. **TBJHL:** Thunder Bay Junior Hockey League. **USHL:** United States Hockey League. **USHS:** United States High School. **USSR:** Union of Soviet Socialist Republics. **Vt. H.S.:** Vermont High School. **W. Germany, W. Ger.:** West Germany. **WCHA:** Western Collegiate Hockey Association. **WCHL:** Western Canada Hockey League. **WHA:** World Hockey Association. **WHL:** Western Hockey League. **Wisc. H.S.:** Wisconsin High School. **Yukon Sr.:** Yukon Senior.

Included in the Hockey Register are every player who appeared in an NHL game in 1993-94, top prospects, other players listed on NHL rosters and the NHL head coaches.

PLAYERS

AALTO, ANTTI
C, MIGHTY DUCKS

PERSONAL: Born March 4, 1975, in Lappeenranta, Finland. . . . 6-2/185. . . . Shoots left. . . . Name pronounced AN-tee AL-toh.

TRANSACTIONS/CAREER NOTES: Selected by Mighty Ducks of Anaheim in sixth round (sixth Mighty Ducks pick, 134th overall) of NHL entry draft (June 26, 1993).

			REGULAR SEASON					PLAYOFFS			
Season Team	League	Gms.	G	A	Pts.	PIM	Gms.	G	A	Pts.	PIM
91-92—SaiPa Jr.	Finland	19	10	10	20	38	—	—	—	—	—
—SaiPa	Finland	20	6	6	12	20	—	—	—	—	—
92-93—SaiPa	Finland	23	6	8	14	14	—	—	—	—	—
—TPS Jr.	Finland	14	6	8	14	18	—	—	—	—	—
—TPS Turku	Finland	1	0	0	0	0	—	—	—	—	—
93-94—TPS Turku	Finland	33	5	9	14	16	10	1	1	2	4

ACTON, KEITH
C

PERSONAL: Born April 15, 1958, in Newmarket, Ont. . . . 5-8/170. . . . Shoots left. . . . Full name: Keith Edward Acton.

TRANSACTIONS/CAREER NOTES: Selected by Montreal Canadiens in sixth round (eighth Canadiens pick, 103rd overall) of NHL entry draft (June 15, 1978). . . . Traded by Canadiens with RW Mark Napier and third-round pick in 1984 draft (C Ken Hodge) to Minnesota North Stars for C Bobby Smith (October 28, 1983). . . . Injured left wrist (April 20, 1984). . . . Traded by North Stars to Edmonton Oilers for D Moe Mantha (January 22, 1988). . . . Broke nose (December 14, 1988). . . . Traded by Oilers with sixth-round pick in 1991 draft (D Dimitri Yushkevich) to Philadelphia Flyers for RW Dave Brown (February 7, 1989). . . . Traded by Flyers with G Pete Peeters to Winnipeg Jets for future considerations (September 28, 1989). . . . Traded by Jets with G Pete Peeters to Flyers for fifth-round pick (C Juha Ylonen) in 1991 draft (October 3, 1989); Jets did not have to surrender future considerations in a previous deal for Shawn Cronin (the NHL fined both Flyers and Jets $10,000 for violating a league by-law against loaning players to another team). . . . Underwent elbow surgery (September 1990). . . . Sprained knee (October 1990); missed three games. . . . Fractured wrist (November 27, 1991); missed 26 games. . . . Signed as free agent by Washington Capitals (July 27, 1993). . . . Claimed on waivers by New York Islanders (October 22, 1993). . . . Named assistant coach of Philadelphia Flyers (July 12, 1994).

HONORS: Named to AHL All-Star second team (1979-80). . . . Played in NHL All-Star Game (1982).

MISCELLANEOUS: Member of Stanley Cup championship team (1988).

			REGULAR SEASON					PLAYOFFS			
Season Team	League	Gms.	G	A	Pts.	PIM	Gms.	G	A	Pts.	PIM
74-75—Wexford Jr. B	MTHL	43	23	29	52	46	—	—	—	—	—
75-76—Peterborough	OHA Mj. Jr. A	35	9	17	26	30	—	—	—	—	—
76-77—Peterborough	OMJHL	65	52	69	121	93	4	1	4	5	6
77-78—Peterborough	OMJHL	68	42	86	128	52	21	10	8	18	16
78-79—Nova Scotia	AHL	79	15	26	41	22	10	4	2	6	4
79-80—Nova Scotia	AHL	75	45	53	98	38	6	1	2	3	8
—Montreal	NHL	2	0	1	1	0	—	—	—	—	—
80-81—Montreal	NHL	61	15	24	39	74	2	0	0	0	6
81-82—Montreal	NHL	78	36	52	88	88	5	0	4	4	16
82-83—Montreal	NHL	78	24	26	50	63	3	0	0	0	0
83-84—Montreal	NHL	9	3	7	10	4	—	—	—	—	—
—Minnesota	NHL	62	17	38	55	60	15	4	7	11	12
84-85—Minnesota	NHL	78	20	38	58	90	9	4	4	8	6
85-86—Minnesota	NHL	79	26	32	58	100	5	0	3	3	6
86-87—Minnesota	NHL	78	16	29	45	56	—	—	—	—	—
87-88—Minnesota	NHL	46	8	11	19	74	—	—	—	—	—
—Edmonton	NHL	26	3	6	9	21	7	2	0	2	16
88-89—Edmonton	NHL	46	11	15	26	47	—	—	—	—	—
—Philadelphia	NHL	25	3	10	13	64	16	2	3	5	18
89-90—Philadelphia	NHL	69	13	14	27	80	—	—	—	—	—
90-91—Philadelphia	NHL	76	14	23	37	131	—	—	—	—	—
91-92—Philadelphia	NHL	50	7	10	17	98	—	—	—	—	—
92-93—Philadelphia	NHL	83	8	15	23	51	—	—	—	—	—
93-94—Washington	NHL	6	0	0	0	21	—	—	—	—	—
—New York Islanders	NHL	71	2	7	9	50	4	0	0	0	8
NHL totals		1023	226	358	584	1172	66	12	21	33	88

ADAMS, GREG
LW, CANUCKS

PERSONAL: Born August 1, 1963, in Nelson, B.C. . . . 6-3/195. . . . Shoots left.

COLLEGE: Northern Arizona.

TRANSACTIONS/CAREER NOTES: Signed as free agent by New Jersey Devils (June 25, 1984). . . . Tore tendon in right wrist (April 1986). . . . Traded by Devils with G Kirk McLean to Vancouver Canucks for C Patrik Sundstrom, fourth-round pick in 1988 draft (LW Matt Ruchty) and the option to flip second-round picks in 1988 draft; Devils exercised option and selected LW Jeff Christian and Canucks selected D Leif Rohlin (September 10, 1987). . . . Fractured ankle (February 1989). . . . Fractured cheekbone (January 4, 1990); missed 12 games. . . . Sprained left knee (October 17, 1990); missed 12 games. . . . Sprained forearm, wrist and abdomen (February 27, 1991). . . . Suffered concussion (October 8, 1991); missed one game. . . . Suffered charley horse (January 16, 1993); missed nine games. . . . Suffered charley horse (February 15, 1993); missed 22 games. . . . Suffered stress fracture in hand requiring minor surgery (December 14, 1993); missed 14 games. . . . Bruised foot (February 22, 1994); missed one game.

HONORS: Played in NHL All-Star Game (1988).

Season Team	League	REGULAR SEASON					PLAYOFFS				
		Gms.	G	A	Pts.	PIM	Gms.	G	A	Pts.	PIM
80-81—Kelowna	BCJHL	47	40	50	90	16	—	—	—	—	—
81-82—Kelowna	BCJHL	45	31	42	73	24	—	—	—	—	—
82-83—Northern Arizona Univ.	Indep.	29	14	21	35	46	—	—	—	—	—
83-84—Northern Arizona Univ.	Indep.	47	40	50	90	16	—	—	—	—	—
84-85—Maine	AHL	41	15	20	35	12	11	3	4	7	0
—New Jersey	NHL	36	12	9	21	14	—	—	—	—	—
85-86—New Jersey	NHL	78	35	42	77	30	—	—	—	—	—
86-87—New Jersey	NHL	72	20	27	47	19	—	—	—	—	—
87-88—Vancouver	NHL	80	36	40	76	30	—	—	—	—	—
88-89—Vancouver	NHL	61	19	14	33	24	7	2	3	5	2
89-90—Vancouver	NHL	65	30	20	50	18	—	—	—	—	—
90-91—Vancouver	NHL	55	21	24	45	10	5	0	0	0	2
91-92—Vancouver	NHL	76	30	27	57	26	6	0	2	2	4
92-93—Vancouver	NHL	53	25	31	56	14	12	7	6	13	6
93-94—Vancouver	NHL	68	13	24	37	20	23	6	8	14	2
NHL totals		644	241	258	499	205	53	15	19	34	16

ADAMS, KEVYN
C, BRUINS

PERSONAL: Born October 8, 1974, in Washington, D.C. . . . . 6-1/182. . . . Shoots right.
COLLEGE: Miami of Ohio.
TRANSACTIONS/CAREER NOTES: Selected by Boston Bruins in first round (first Bruins pick, 25th overall) of NHL entry draft (June 26, 1993).

Season Team	League	REGULAR SEASON					PLAYOFFS				
		Gms.	G	A	Pts.	PIM	Gms.	G	A	Pts.	PIM
90-91—Niagara	NAJHL	55	17	20	37	24	—	—	—	—	—
91-92—Niagara	NAJHL	40	25	33	58	51	—	—	—	—	—
92-93—Miami of Ohio	CCHA	41	17	16	33	18	—	—	—	—	—
93-94—Miami of Ohio	CCHA	36	15	28	43	24	—	—	—	—	—

AGARKOV, PAVEL
RW, RED WINGS

PERSONAL: Born April 23, 1975, in Moscow, U.S.S.R. . . . . 5-11/167. . . . Shoots left.
TRANSACTIONS/CAREER NOTES: Selected by Detroit Red Wings in sixth round (sixth Red Wings pick, 153rd overall) of NHL entry draft (June 29, 1994).

Season Team	League	REGULAR SEASON					PLAYOFFS				
		Gms.	G	A	Pts.	PIM	Gms.	G	A	Pts.	PIM
93-94—Soviet Wings	CIS	27	2	0	2	12	—	—	—	—	—

AGNEW, JIM
D, WHALERS

PERSONAL: Born March 21, 1966, in Deloraine, Man. . . . . 6-1/190. . . . Shoots left.
TRANSACTIONS/CAREER NOTES: Selected by Vancouver Canucks as underage junior in eighth round (10th Canucks pick, 157th overall) of NHL entry draft (June 9, 1984). . . . Tore knee ligaments (March 18, 1990). . . . Sprained left knee ligaments (November 19, 1990); missed 19 games. . . . Resprained left knee ligaments (January 6, 1991). . . . Signed as free agent by Hartford Whalers (June 29, 1992). . . . Pulled groin (November 15, 1992); missed eight games. . . . Sprained knee (December 9, 1992); missed 13 games. . . . Reinjured knee (January 21, 1993) and underwent knee surgery (January 25, 1993); missed remainder of 1992-93 season and entire 1993-94 season.
HONORS: Named to WHL (West) All-Star first team (1985-86). . . . Named to IHL All-Star second team (1989-90).

Season Team	League	REGULAR SEASON					PLAYOFFS				
		Gms.	G	A	Pts.	PIM	Gms.	G	A	Pts.	PIM
82-83—Brandon	WHL	14	1	1	2	9	—	—	—	—	—
83-84—Brandon	WHL	71	6	17	23	107	12	0	1	1	39
84-85—Brandon	WHL	19	3	15	18	82	—	—	—	—	—
—Portland	WHL	44	5	24	29	223	6	0	2	2	44
85-86—Portland	WHL	70	6	30	36	386	9	0	1	1	48
86-87—Vancouver	NHL	4	0	0	0	0	—	—	—	—	—
—Fredericton	AHL	67	0	5	5	261	—	—	—	—	—
87-88—Vancouver	NHL	10	0	1	1	16	—	—	—	—	—
—Fredericton	AHL	63	2	8	10	188	14	0	2	2	43
88-89—Milwaukee	IHL	47	2	10	12	181	11	0	2	2	34
89-90—Milwaukee	IHL	51	4	10	14	238	—	—	—	—	—
—Vancouver	NHL	7	0	0	0	36	—	—	—	—	—
90-91—Vancouver	NHL	20	0	0	0	81	—	—	—	—	—
—Milwaukee	IHL	3	0	0	0	33	—	—	—	—	—
91-92—Vancouver	NHL	24	0	0	0	56	4	0	0	0	6
92-93—Hartford	NHL	16	0	0	0	68	—	—	—	—	—
—Springfield	AHL	1	0	1	1	2	—	—	—	—	—
93-94—Hartford	NHL					Did not play—injured.					
NHL totals		81	0	1	1	257	4	0	0	0	6

AHOLA, PETER
D, FLAMES

PERSONAL: Born May 14, 1968, in Espoo, Finland. . . . 6-3/205. . . . Shoots left. . . . Full name: Peter Kristian Ahola. . . . Name pronounced AH-hoh-luh.
COLLEGE: Boston University.
TRANSACTIONS/CAREER NOTES: Signed as free agent by Los Angeles Kings (April 5, 1991). . . . Traded by Kings to Pittsburgh Penguins for D Jeff Chychrun (November 6, 1992). . . . Traded by Penguins to San Jose Sharks for future considerations (February 26, 1993). . . . Traded by Sharks to Tampa Bay Lightning for C Dave Capuano (June 19,

1993).... Traded by Lightning to Calgary Flames for future considerations (October 5, 1993).
HONORS: Named to Hockey East All-Rookie team (1989-90).... Named to NCAA All-America East second team (1990-91).

			REGULAR SEASON					PLAYOFFS				
Season	Team	League	Gms.	G	A	Pts.	PIM	Gms.	G	A	Pts.	PIM
89-90	Boston University	Hockey East	43	3	20	23	65	—	—	—	—	—
90-91	Boston University	Hockey East	39	12	24	36	88	—	—	—	—	—
91-92	Los Angeles	NHL	71	7	12	19	101	6	0	0	0	2
	Phoenix	IHL	7	3	3	6	34	—	—	—	—	—
92-93	Los Angeles	NHL	8	1	1	2	6	—	—	—	—	—
	Pittsburgh	NHL	22	0	1	1	14	—	—	—	—	—
	Cleveland	IHL	9	1	0	1	4	—	—	—	—	—
	San Jose	NHL	20	2	3	5	16	—	—	—	—	—
93-94	Saint John	AHL	66	9	19	28	59	6	1	2	3	12
	Calgary	NHL	2	0	0	0	0	—	—	—	—	—
	NHL totals		123	10	17	27	137	6	0	0	0	2

AIVAZOFF, MICAH
C/LW, RED WINGS

PERSONAL: Born May 4, 1969, in Powell River, B.C.... 6-0/185.... Shoots left.... Name pronounced MIGH-kuh A-vuh-zahf.
TRANSACTIONS/CAREER NOTES: Selected by Los Angeles Kings in sixth round (sixth Kings pick, 109th overall) of NHL entry draft (June 11, 1988).... Signed as free agent by Detroit Red Wings (July 2, 1991).

			REGULAR SEASON					PLAYOFFS				
Season	Team	League	Gms.	G	A	Pts.	PIM	Gms.	G	A	Pts.	PIM
85-86	Victoria	WHL	27	3	4	7	25	—	—	—	—	—
86-87	Victoria	WHL	72	18	39	57	112	5	1	0	1	2
87-88	Victoria	WHL	69	26	57	83	79	8	3	4	7	14
88-89	Victoria	WHL	70	35	65	100	136	8	5	7	12	2
89-90	New Haven	AHL	77	20	39	59	71	—	—	—	—	—
90-91	New Haven	AHL	79	11	29	40	84	—	—	—	—	—
91-92	Adirondack	AHL	61	9	20	29	50	†19	2	8	10	25
92-93	Adirondack	AHL	79	32	53	85	100	11	8	6	14	10
93-94	Detroit	NHL	59	4	4	8	38	—	—	—	—	—
	NHL totals		59	4	4	8	38	—	—	—	—	—

ALBELIN, TOMMY
D, DEVILS

PERSONAL: Born May 21, 1964, in Stockholm, Sweden.... 6-1/190.... Shoots left.... Name pronounced AL-buh-LEEN.
TRANSACTIONS/CAREER NOTES: Selected by Quebec Nordiques in eighth round (seventh Nordiques pick, 152nd overall) of NHL entry draft (June 8, 1983).... Traded by Nordiques to New Jersey Devils for fourth-round pick (LW Niclas Andersson) in 1989 draft (December 12, 1988).... Injured right knee (March 2, 1990); missed four games.... Injured groin (November 21, 1992); missed two games.... Suffered from urinary infection (1993-94 season); missed nine games.
HONORS: Named to Swedish League All-Star team (1986-87).

			REGULAR SEASON					PLAYOFFS				
Season	Team	League	Gms.	G	A	Pts.	PIM	Gms.	G	A	Pts.	PIM
82-83	Djurgarden	Sweden	17	2	5	7	4	6	1	0	1	2
83-84	Djurgarden	Sweden	37	9	8	17	36	4	0	1	1	2
84-85	Djurgarden	Sweden	32	9	8	17	22	8	2	1	3	4
85-86	Djurgarden	Sweden	35	4	8	12	26	—	—	—	—	—
86-87	Djurgarden	Sweden	33	7	5	12	49	2	0	0	0	0
87-88	Quebec	NHL	60	3	23	26	47	—	—	—	—	—
88-89	Halifax	AHL	8	2	5	7	4	—	—	—	—	—
	Quebec	NHL	14	2	4	6	27	—	—	—	—	—
	New Jersey	NHL	46	7	24	31	40	—	—	—	—	—
89-90	New Jersey	NHL	68	6	23	29	63	—	—	—	—	—
90-91	Utica	AHL	14	4	2	6	10	—	—	—	—	—
	New Jersey	NHL	47	2	12	14	44	3	0	1	1	2
91-92	New Jersey	NHL	19	0	4	4	4	1	1	1	2	0
	Utica	AHL	11	4	6	10	4	—	—	—	—	—
92-93	New Jersey	NHL	36	1	5	6	14	5	2	0	2	0
93-94	Albany	AHL	4	0	2	2	17	—	—	—	—	—
	New Jersey	NHL	62	2	17	19	36	20	2	5	7	14
	NHL totals		352	23	112	135	275	29	5	7	12	16

ALEXEYEV, ALEXANDER
D, JETS

PERSONAL: Born March 23, 1974, in Kiev, U.S.S.R.... 5-11/198.... Shoots left.... Name pronounced al-ihk-SAY-ehf.
TRANSACTIONS/CAREER NOTES: Selected by Winnipeg Jets in sixth round (fifth Jets pick, 132nd overall) of NHL entry draft (June 20, 1992).
HONORS: Named to WHL (West) All-Star second team (1993-94).

			REGULAR SEASON					PLAYOFFS				
Season	Team	League	Gms.	G	A	Pts.	PIM	Gms.	G	A	Pts.	PIM
90-91	Sokol Kiev	USSR	5	0	0	0	2	—	—	—	—	—
91-92	Sokol Kiev	CIS	25	1	5	6	22	—	—	—	—	—

Season Team	League	REGULAR SEASON					PLAYOFFS				
		Gms.	G	A	Pts.	PIM	Gms.	G	A	Pts.	PIM
92-93—Tacoma	WHL	44	3	33	36	67	7	2	7	9	4
93-94—Tacoma	WHL	64	12	48	60	106	8	0	5	5	9

ALFREDSSON, DANIEL
C/RW, SENATORS

PERSONAL: Born December 11, 1972, in Grums, Sweden. .... 5-11/187. .... Shoots right.
TRANSACTIONS/CAREER NOTES: Selected by Ottawa Senators in sixth round (fifth Senators pick, 133rd overall) of NHL entry draft (June 29, 1994).

Season Team	League	REGULAR SEASON					PLAYOFFS				
		Gms.	G	A	Pts.	PIM	Gms.	G	A	Pts.	PIM
91-92—Molndal Hockey	Swed. Dv.II	32	12	8	20	43	—	—	—	—	—
92-93—Vastra Frolunda.............	Sweden	20	1	5	6	8	—	—	—	—	—
93-94—Vastra Frolunda.............	Sweden	39	20	10	30	18	4	1	1	2	0

ALLAN, CHAD
D, CANUCKS

PERSONAL: Born July 12, 1976, in Davidson, Sask. .... 6-1/192. .... Shoots left.
HIGH SCHOOL: Marion Graham (Regina, Sask.).
TRANSACTIONS/CAREER NOTES: Selected by Vancouver Canucks in third round (fourth Canucks pick, 65th overall) of NHL entry draft (June 29, 1994).

Season Team	League	REGULAR SEASON					PLAYOFFS				
		Gms.	G	A	Pts.	PIM	Gms.	G	A	Pts.	PIM
91-92—Saskatoon	WHL	1	0	0	0	2	—	—	—	—	—
92-93—Saskatoon	WHL	69	2	10	12	67	9	0	0	0	25
93-94—Saskatoon	WHL	70	6	16	22	123	16	1	1	2	21

ALLAN, SANDY
G, KINGS

PERSONAL: Born January 22, 1974, in Nassau, Bahamas. .... 6-0/175. .... Catches left.
HIGH SCHOOL: Chippewa Secondary School (North Bay, Ont.).
TRANSACTIONS/CAREER NOTES: Selected by Los Angeles Kings in third round (second Kings pick, 63rd overall) of NHL entry draft (June 20, 1992).
HONORS: Won F.W. (Dinty) Moore Trophy (1991-92). .... Shared Dave Pinkney Trophy with Scott Roche (1993-94).

Season Team	League	REGULAR SEASON								PLAYOFFS						
		Gms.	Min.	W	L	T	GA	SO	Avg.	Gms.	Min.	W	L	GA	SO	Avg.
91-92—North Bay	OHL	34	1747	18	5	4	112	0	3.85	3	18	0	0	2	0	6.67
92-93—North Bay	OHL	39	1835	8	19	4	133	0	4.35	4	180	0	3	10	0	3.33
93-94—North Bay	OHL	45	2404	*31	10	1	131	1	*3.27	*17	*912	†10	5	57	0	3.75

ALLISON, JAMIE
D, FLAMES

PERSONAL: Born May 13, 1975, in Lindsay, Ont. .... 6-1/190. .... Shoots left.
TRANSACTIONS/CAREER NOTES: Selected by Calgary Flames in second round (second Flames pick, 44th overall) of NHL entry draft (June 26, 1993).

Season Team	League	REGULAR SEASON					PLAYOFFS				
		Gms.	G	A	Pts.	PIM	Gms.	G	A	Pts.	PIM
90-91—Waterloo Jr. B	OHA	45	3	8	11	91	—	—	—	—	—
91-92—Windsor	OHL	59	4	8	12	52	4	1	1	2	2
92-93—Detroit	OHL	61	0	13	13	64	15	2	5	7	23
93-94—Detroit	OHL	40	2	22	24	69	17	2	9	11	35

ALLISON, JASON
C, CAPITALS

PERSONAL: Born May 29, 1975, in Toronto. .... 6-2/192. .... Shoots right.
TRANSACTIONS/CAREER NOTES: Selected by Washington Capitals in first round (second Capitals pick, 17th overall) of NHL entry draft (June 26, 1993).
HONORS: Won Can.HL Player of the Year Award (1993-94). .... Won Can.HL Top Scorer Award (1993-94). .... Won Red Tilson Trophy (1993-94). .... Won William Hanley Trophy (1993-94). .... Won Eddie Powers Memorial Trophy (1993-94). .... Named to Can.HL All-Star first team (1993-94). .... Named to OHL All-Star first team (1993-94).

Season Team	League	REGULAR SEASON					PLAYOFFS				
		Gms.	G	A	Pts.	PIM	Gms.	G	A	Pts.	PIM
91-92—London	OHL	65	11	18	29	15	7	0	0	0	0
92-93—London	OHL	66	42	76	118	50	12	7	13	20	8
93-94—London	OHL	56	*55	87	*142	68	5	2	13	15	13
—Washington	NHL	2	0	1	1	0	—	—	—	—	—
NHL totals....................................		2	0	1	1	0					

ALLISON, SCOTT
LW, OILERS

PERSONAL: Born April 22, 1972, in St. Boniface, Man. .... 6-4/194. .... Shoots left.
TRANSACTIONS/CAREER NOTES: Selected by Edmonton Oilers in first round (first Oilers pick, 17th overall) of NHL entry draft (June 16, 1990).

Season Team	League	REGULAR SEASON					PLAYOFFS				
		Gms.	G	A	Pts.	PIM	Gms.	G	A	Pts.	PIM
88-89—Prince Albert.....................	WHL	51	6	9	15	37	3	0	0	0	0
89-90—Prince Albert.....................	WHL	66	22	16	38	73	11	1	4	5	8
90-91—Prince Albert.....................	WHL	37	0	6	6	44	—	—	—	—	—
—Portland	WHL	44	5	17	22	105	—	—	—	—	—

A

Season Team	League	REGULAR SEASON					PLAYOFFS				
		Gms.	G	A	Pts.	PIM	Gms.	G	A	Pts.	PIM
91-92—Moose Jaw	WHL	72	37	45	82	238	3	1	1	2	25
92-93—Cape Breton	AHL	49	3	5	8	34	—	—	—	—	—
—Wheeling	ECHL	6	3	3	6	8	—	—	—	—	—
93-94—Cape Breton	AHL	75	19	14	33	202	3	0	1	1	2

ALVEY, MATT
C, BRUINS

PERSONAL: Born May 15, 1975, in Troy, N.Y.... 6-2/210.... Shoots right.
TRANSACTIONS/CAREER NOTES: Selected by Boston Bruins in second round (second Bruins pick, 51st overall) of NHL entry draft (June 26, 1993).

Season Team	League	REGULAR SEASON					PLAYOFFS				
		Gms.	G	A	Pts.	PIM	Gms.	G	A	Pts.	PIM
90-91—Springfield Jr. B	NEJHL	...	12	20	32	...	—	—	—	—	—
91-92—Springfield Jr. B	NEJHL	32	22	35	57	34	—	—	—	—	—
92-93—Springfield Jr. B	NEJHL	38	22	37	59	85	—	—	—	—	—
93-94—Lake Superior State	CCHA	41	6	8	14	16	—	—	—	—	—

AMBROZIAK, PETER
LW, SABRES

PERSONAL: Born September 15, 1971, in Toronto.... 6-0/191.... Shoots left.... Name pronounced am-BROH-zee-ak.
TRANSACTIONS/CAREER NOTES: Selected by Buffalo Sabres in fourth round (fourth Sabres pick, 72nd overall) of NHL entry draft (June 22, 1991).

Season Team	League	REGULAR SEASON					PLAYOFFS				
		Gms.	G	A	Pts.	PIM	Gms.	G	A	Pts.	PIM
88-89—Ottawa	OHL	50	8	15	23	11	12	1	2	3	2
89-90—Ottawa	OHL	60	13	19	32	37	4	0	0	0	2
90-91—Ottawa	OHL	62	30	32	62	56	17	15	9	24	24
91-92—Rochester	AHL	2	0	1	1	0	—	—	—	—	—
—Ottawa	OHL	49	32	49	81	50	11	3	7	10	33
92-93—Rochester	AHL	50	8	10	18	37	12	4	3	7	16
93-94—Rochester	AHL	22	3	4	7	53	—	—	—	—	—

AMONTE, TONY
RW, BLACKHAWKS

PERSONAL: Born August 2, 1970, in Weymouth, Mass.... 6-0/186.... Shoots left.... Full name: Anthony Lewis Amonte.... Name pronounced ah-MAHN-tee.
HIGH SCHOOL: Thayer Academy (Braintree, Mass.).
COLLEGE: Boston University.
TRANSACTIONS/CAREER NOTES: Selected by New York Rangers in fourth round (third Rangers pick, 68th overall) of NHL entry draft (June 11, 1988).... Separated shoulder (December 29, 1990).... Traded by Rangers with rights to LW Matt Oates to Chicago Blackhawks for LW Stephane Matteau and RW Brian Noonan (March 21, 1994).... Pulled groin (1993-94); missed three games.
HONORS: Named to Hockey East All-Rookie team (1989-90).... Named to NCAA All-Tournament team (1990-91).... Named to Hockey East All-Star second team (1990-91).... Named NHL Rookie of the Year by THE SPORTING NEWS (1991-92).... Named to NHL All-Rookie team (1991-92).

Season Team	League	REGULAR SEASON					PLAYOFFS				
		Gms.	G	A	Pts.	PIM	Gms.	G	A	Pts.	PIM
86-87—Thayer Academy	Mass. H.S.	...	25	32	57	...	—	—	—	—	—
87-88—Thayer Academy	Mass. H.S.	...	30	38	68	...	—	—	—	—	—
88-89—Team USA Juniors	Int'l	7	1	3	4	...	—	—	—	—	—
89-90—Boston University	Hockey East	41	25	33	58	52	—	—	—	—	—
90-91—Boston University	Hockey East	38	31	37	68	82	—	—	—	—	—
—New York Rangers	NHL	—	—	—	—	—	2	0	2	2	2
91-92—New York Rangers	NHL	79	35	34	69	55	13	3	6	9	2
92-93—New York Rangers	NHL	83	33	43	76	49	—	—	—	—	—
93-94—New York Rangers	NHL	72	16	22	38	31	—	—	—	—	—
—Chicago	NHL	7	1	3	4	6	6	4	2	6	4
NHL totals		241	85	102	187	141	21	7	10	17	8

ANDERSON, GLENN
RW, RANGERS

PERSONAL: Born October 2, 1960, in Vancouver.... 6-1/190.... Shoots left.... Full name: Glenn Chris Anderson.
COLLEGE: Denver.
TRANSACTIONS/CAREER NOTES: Selected by Edmonton Oilers in fourth round (third Oilers pick, 69th overall) of NHL entry draft (August 9, 1979).... Underwent knee surgery to remove bone chips (November 1980).... Underwent nose surgery to correct breathing problem (spring 1982).... Suspended eight games by NHL for fighting (December 13, 1985).... Pulled side muscle (November 1988).... Fined $500 for deliberately breaking the cheekbone of RW Tomas Sandstrom (February 28, 1990).... Missed first four games of 1990-91 season due to contract dispute (October 1990).... Injured thigh (March 5, 1991); missed two games.... Traded by Oilers with G Grant Fuhr and LW Craig Berube to Toronto Maple Leafs for LW Vincent Damphousse, D Luke Richardson, G Peter Ing, C Scott Thornton and future considerations (September 19, 1991).... Sprained knee (December 3, 1992); missed four games.... Injured knee (February 3, 1993); missed one game.... Traded by Maple Leafs with rights to Scott Malone and fourth-round pick in 1994 draft (D Alexander Korobolin) to New York Rangers for RW Mike Gartner (March 21, 1994).
HONORS: Played in NHL All-Star Game (1984-1986 and 1988).
RECORDS: Shares NHL single-game playoff record for most points in one period—4 (April 6, 1988).
MISCELLANEOUS: Member of Stanley Cup championship teams (1984, 1985, 1987, 1988, 1990 and 1994).

Season	Team	League	REGULAR SEASON Gms.	G	A	Pts.	PIM	PLAYOFFS Gms.	G	A	Pts.	PIM
77-78—Bellingham Jr. A	BCJHL	58	61	64	125	96	—	—	—	—	—
—New Westminster	WCHL	1	0	1	1	2	—	—	—	—	—
78-79—Seattle	WHL	2	0	1	1	0	—	—	—	—	—
—University of Denver	WCHA	40	26	29	55	58	—	—	—	—	—
79-80—Canadian Olympic Team ..	Int'l	49	21	21	42	46	—	—	—	—	—
—Seattle	WHL	7	5	5	10	4	—	—	—	—	—
80-81—Edmonton	NHL	58	30	23	53	24	9	5	7	12	12
81-82—Edmonton	NHL	80	38	67	105	71	5	2	5	7	8
82-83—Edmonton	NHL	72	48	56	104	70	16	10	10	20	32
83-84—Edmonton	NHL	80	54	45	99	65	19	6	11	17	33
84-85—Edmonton	NHL	80	42	39	81	69	18	10	16	26	38
85-86—Edmonton	NHL	72	54	48	102	90	10	8	3	11	14
86-87—Edmonton	NHL	80	35	38	73	65	21	14	13	27	59
87-88—Edmonton	NHL	80	38	50	88	58	19	9	16	25	49
88-89—Edmonton	NHL	79	16	48	64	93	7	1	2	3	8
89-90—Edmonton	NHL	73	34	38	72	107	22	10	12	22	20
90-91—Edmonton	NHL	74	24	31	55	59	18	6	7	13	41
91-92—Toronto	NHL	72	24	33	57	100	—	—	—	—	—
92-93—Toronto	NHL	76	22	43	65	117	21	7	11	18	31
93-94—Toronto	NHL	73	17	18	35	50	—	—	—	—	—
—New York Rangers	NHL	12	4	2	6	12	23	3	3	6	42
NHL totals................		1061	480	579	1059	1050	208	91	116	207	387

ANDERSON, SHAWN
D/LW, CAPITALS

PERSONAL: Born February 7, 1968, in Montreal.... 6-1/200.... Shoots left.
COLLEGE: Maine.

TRANSACTIONS/CAREER NOTES: Selected by Buffalo Sabres as underage player in first round (first Sabres pick, fifth overall) of NHL entry draft (June 21, 1986).... Sprained knee (October 1986).... Separated shoulder (March 3, 1987).... Reseparated shoulder (March 28, 1987).... Injured ankle (October 1987).... Injured ankle (December 1987).... Bruised knee (February 1988).... Traded by Sabres to Washington Capitals for D Bill Houlder (September 30, 1990).... Claimed by Quebec Nordiques in 1990 NHL waiver draft for $60,000 waiver price (October 2, 1990).... Traded by Nordiques to Winnipeg Jets for RW Sergei Kharin (October 22, 1991). ... Traded by Jets to Capitals for future considerations (October 23, 1991).... Suffered back spasms (February 20, 1993); missed six games.... Bruised hand (November 24, 1993); missed seven games.... Pulled abdominal muscle (March 29, 1994); missed three games.... Bruised ankle (April 12, 1994); missed one game.

Season	Team	League	REGULAR SEASON Gms.	G	A	Pts.	PIM	PLAYOFFS Gms.	G	A	Pts.	PIM
85-86—University of Maine	Hockey East	16	5	8	13	22	—	—	—	—	—
—Canadian national team ...	Int'l	33	2	6	8	16	—	—	—	—	—
86-87—Rochester	AHL	15	2	5	7	11	—	—	—	—	—
—Buffalo	NHL	41	2	11	13	23	—	—	—	—	—
87-88—Buffalo	NHL	23	1	2	3	17	—	—	—	—	—
—Rochester	AHL	22	5	16	21	19	6	0	0	0	0
88-89—Rochester	AHL	31	5	14	19	24	—	—	—	—	—
—Buffalo	NHL	33	2	10	12	18	5	0	1	1	4
89-90—Rochester	AHL	39	2	16	18	41	9	1	0	1	8
—Buffalo	NHL	16	1	3	4	8	—	—	—	—	—
90-91—Quebec	NHL	31	3	10	13	21	—	—	—	—	—
—Halifax	AHL	4	0	1	1	2	—	—	—	—	—
91-92—PEV Weiswasser..............	Germany	38	7	15	22	83	—	—	—	—	—
92-93—Baltimore....................	AHL	10	1	5	6	8	—	—	—	—	—
—Washington	NHL	60	2	6	8	18	6	0	0	0	0
93-94—Washington	NHL	50	0	9	9	12	8	1	0	1	12
NHL totals................		254	11	51	62	117	19	1	1	2	16

ANDERSSON, MIKAEL
RW, LIGHTNING

PERSONAL: Born May 10, 1966, in Malmo, Sweden. ... 5-11/185. ... Shoots left. ... Full name: Bo Mikael Andersson.... Name pronounced mih-KEHL AN-duhr-suhn.

TRANSACTIONS/CAREER NOTES: Selected by Buffalo Sabres in first round (first Sabres pick, 18th overall) of NHL entry draft (June 9, 1984).... Sprained ankle (March 3, 1987); missed three weeks.... Twisted ankle (March 1988).... Sprained neck and shoulder (December 1988).... Selected by Hartford Whalers in 1989 NHL waiver draft (October 2, 1989).... Bruised left knee (December 13, 1989).... Reinjured knee (February 9, 1990).... Pulled right hamstring (March 8, 1990).... Reinjured hamstring (March 17, 1990).... Reinjured hamstring (April 1990).... Underwent surgery to left knee (May 14, 1990).... Suffered from the flu (October 4, 1990); missed two games.... Pulled groin (January 1991).... Injured toe (October 26, 1991); missed one game.... Injured groin (December 17, 1991); missed three games.... Suffered chip fracture to foot (April 12, 1992).... Signed as free agent by Tampa Bay Lightning (July 8, 1992).... Suffered back spasms (November 21, 1992); missed four games.... Injured left rotator cuff (October 27, 1993); missed three games.

Season	Team	League	REGULAR SEASON Gms.	G	A	Pts.	PIM	PLAYOFFS Gms.	G	A	Pts.	PIM
83-84—Vastra Frolunda..............	Sweden	12	0	2	2	6	—	—	—	—	—
84-85—Vastra Frolunda..............	Sweden	32	16	11	27	18	6	3	2	5	2
85-86—Rochester	AHL	20	10	4	14	6	—	—	—	—	—
—Buffalo..............................	NHL	32	1	9	10	4	—	—	—	—	—

Season	Team	League	REGULAR SEASON					PLAYOFFS				
			Gms.	G	A	Pts.	PIM	Gms.	G	A	Pts.	PIM
86-87—Rochester		AHL	42	6	20	26	14	9	1	2	3	2
—Buffalo		NHL	16	0	3	3	0	—	—	—	—	—
87-88—Rochester		AHL	35	12	24	36	16	—	—	—	—	—
—Buffalo		NHL	37	3	20	23	10	1	1	0	1	0
88-89—Buffalo		NHL	14	0	1	1	4	—	—	—	—	—
—Rochester		AHL	56	18	33	51	12	—	—	—	—	—
89-90—Hartford		NHL	50	13	24	37	6	5	0	3	3	2
90-91—Hartford		NHL	41	4	7	11	8	—	—	—	—	—
—Springfield		AHL	26	7	22	29	10	18	†10	8	18	12
91-92—Hartford		NHL	74	18	29	47	14	7	0	2	2	6
92-93—Tampa Bay		NHL	77	16	11	27	14	—	—	—	—	—
93-94—Tampa Bay		NHL	76	13	12	25	23	—	—	—	—	—
NHL totals			417	68	116	184	83	13	1	5	6	8

ANDERSSON, NICLAS
LW

PERSONAL: Born May 20, 1971, in Kunglav, Sweden. . . . 5-9/175. . . . Shoots left.

TRANSACTIONS/CAREER NOTES: Selected by Quebec Nordiques in fourth round (fifth Nordiques pick, 68th overall) of NHL entry draft (June 17, 1989).

Season	Team	League	REGULAR SEASON					PLAYOFFS				
			Gms.	G	A	Pts.	PIM	Gms.	G	A	Pts.	PIM
87-88—Frolunda		Sweden	15	5	5	10	. . .	—	—	—	—	—
88-89—Frolunda		Sweden	30	13	24	37	. . .	—	—	—	—	—
89-90—Frolunda		Sweden	38	10	21	31	14	—	—	—	—	—
90-91—Frolunda		Sweden	22	6	10	16	16	—	—	—	—	—
91-92—Halifax		AHL	57	8	26	34	41	—	—	—	—	—
92-93—Halifax		AHL	76	32	50	82	42	—	—	—	—	—
—Quebec		NHL	3	0	1	1	2	—	—	—	—	—
93-94—Cornwall		AHL	42	18	34	52	8	—	—	—	—	—
NHL totals			3	0	1	1	2					

ANDERSSON, PETER
D, PANTHERS

PERSONAL: Born August 29, 1965, in Orebro, Sweden. . . . 6-0/196. . . . Shoots left.

TRANSACTIONS/CAREER NOTES: Selected by New York Rangers in fourth round (fifth Rangers pick, 73rd overall) of NHL entry draft (June 8, 1983). . . . Separated shoulder (October 24, 1992); missed five games. . . . Traded by Rangers to Florida Panthers for ninth-round pick (G Vitali Yeremenev) in 1994 draft (March 21, 1994).

HONORS: Named to Swedish League All-Star team (1991-92).

Season	Team	League	REGULAR SEASON					PLAYOFFS				
			Gms.	G	A	Pts.	PIM	Gms.	G	A	Pts.	PIM
83-84—Farjestad		Sweden	36	4	7	11	22	—	—	—	—	—
84-85—Farjestad		Sweden	35	5	12	17	24	—	—	—	—	—
85-86—Farjestad		Sweden	34	6	10	16	18	—	—	—	—	—
86-87—Farjestad		Sweden	32	9	8	17	32	—	—	—	—	—
87-88—Farjestad		Sweden	38	14	20	34	44	—	—	—	—	—
—Swedish Olympic Team		Int'l	8	2	2	4	4	—	—	—	—	—
88-89—Farjestad		Sweden	33	6	17	23	44	—	—	—	—	—
89-90—Malmo		Sweden-II				Statistics unavailable.						
90-91—Malmo		Sweden	34	9	17	26	26	—	—	—	—	—
91-92—Malmo		Sweden	40	12	20	32	18	—	—	—	—	—
—Swedish Olympic Team		Int'l	8	0	1	1	4	—	—	—	—	—
92-93—New York Rangers		NHL	31	4	11	15	18	—	—	—	—	—
—Binghamton		AHL	27	11	22	33	16	—	—	—	—	—
93-94—New York Rangers		NHL	8	1	1	2	2	—	—	—	—	—
—Florida		NHL	8	1	1	2	0	—	—	—	—	—
NHL totals			47	6	13	19	20					

ANDERSSON-JUNKKA, JONAS
D, PENGUINS

PERSONAL: Born May 4, 1975, in Kiruna, Sweden. . . . 6-2/165. . . . Shoots right.

TRANSACTIONS/CAREER NOTES: Selected by Pittsburgh Penguins in fourth round (fourth Penguins pick, 104th overall) of NHL entry draft (June 26, 1993).

Season	Team	League	REGULAR SEASON					PLAYOFFS				
			Gms.	G	A	Pts.	PIM	Gms.	G	A	Pts.	PIM
91-92—Kiruna		Swed. Dv.II	1	0	0	0	0	—	—	—	—	—
92-93—Kiruna		Swed. Dv.II	30	3	7	10	32	—	—	—	—	—
93-94—Kiruna		Swed. Dv.II	32	6	10	16	84	—	—	—	—	—

ANDREYCHUK, DAVE
LW, MAPLE LEAFS

PERSONAL: Born September 29, 1963, in Hamilton, Ont. . . . 6-3/220. . . . Shoots right. . . . Name pronounced AN-druh-chuhk.

TRANSACTIONS/CAREER NOTES: Selected by Buffalo Sabres as underage junior in first round (third Sabres pick, 16th overall) of NHL entry draft (June 9, 1982).

... Sprained knee (March 1983).... Fractured collarbone (March 1985).... Twisted knee (September 1985).... Injured right knee (September 1986).... Strained medial collateral ligaments in left knee (November 27, 1988).... Broke left thumb (February 18, 1990).... Suspended two off-days and fined $500 by NHL for cross-checking (November 16, 1992).... Traded by Sabres with G Daren Puppa and first-round pick in 1993 draft (D Kenny Jonsson) to Toronto Maple Leafs for G Grant Fuhr and conditional pick in 1995 draft (February 2, 1993).... Injured knee (December 27, 1993); missed one game.

HONORS: Played in NHL All-Star Game (1990 and 1994).... Named to THE SPORTING NEWS All-Star second team (1993-94).
MISCELLANEOUS: Played with Team Canada in World Junior Championships (1982-83).
STATISTICAL NOTES: Led NHL with 32 power-play goals in 1992-93.

Season	Team	League	REGULAR SEASON Gms.	G	A	Pts.	PIM	PLAYOFFS Gms.	G	A	Pts.	PIM
80-81	Oshawa	OMJHL	67	22	22	44	80	10	3	2	5	20
81-82	Oshawa	OHL	67	58	43	101	71	3	1	4	5	16
82-83	Oshawa	OHL	14	8	24	32	6	—	—	—	—	—
	Buffalo	NHL	43	14	23	37	16	4	1	0	1	4
83-84	Buffalo	NHL	78	38	42	80	42	2	0	1	1	2
84-85	Buffalo	NHL	64	31	30	61	54	5	4	2	6	4
85-86	Buffalo	NHL	80	36	51	87	61	—	—	—	—	—
86-87	Buffalo	NHL	77	25	48	73	46	—	—	—	—	—
87-88	Buffalo	NHL	80	30	48	78	112	6	2	4	6	0
88-89	Buffalo	NHL	56	28	24	52	40	5	0	3	3	0
89-90	Buffalo	NHL	73	40	42	82	42	6	2	5	7	2
90-91	Buffalo	NHL	80	36	33	69	32	6	2	2	4	8
91-92	Buffalo	NHL	80	41	50	91	71	7	1	3	4	12
92-93	Buffalo	NHL	52	29	32	61	48	—	—	—	—	—
	Toronto	NHL	31	25	13	38	8	21	12	7	19	35
93-94	Toronto	NHL	83	53	46	99	98	18	5	5	10	16
NHL totals			877	426	482	908	670	80	29	32	61	83

ANDRIJEVSKI, ALEXANDER
RW, BLACKHAWKS

PERSONAL: Born August 10, 1968, in Minsk, U.S.S.R. ... 6-5/211. ... Shoots right. ... Name pronounced ahn-dray-EHV-skee.
TRANSACTIONS/CAREER NOTES: Selected by Chicago Blackhawks in 10th round (13th Blackhawks pick, 220th overall) of NHL entry draft (June 22, 1991).

Season	Team	League	REGULAR SEASON Gms.	G	A	Pts.	PIM	PLAYOFFS Gms.	G	A	Pts.	PIM
90-91	Dynamo Moscow	USSR	44	9	7	16	28	—	—	—	—	—
91-92	Dynamo Moscow	CIS	28	8	6	14	16	—	—	—	—	—
92-93	Indianapolis	IHL	66	26	25	51	59	4	2	3	5	10
	Chicago	NHL	1	0	0	0	0	—	—	—	—	—
93-94	Indianapolis	IHL	4	0	1	1	2	—	—	—	—	—
	Kalamazoo	IHL	57	6	22	28	58	1	0	0	0	2
NHL totals			1	0	0	0	0					

ANDRUSAK, GREG
D, PENGUINS

PERSONAL: Born November 14, 1969, in Cranbrook, B.C. ... 6-1/195. ... Shoots right. ... Full name: Greg Frederick Andrusak. ... Name pronounced AN-druh-sak.
COLLEGE: Minnesota-Duluth.
TRANSACTIONS/CAREER NOTES: Selected by Pittsburgh Penguins in fifth round (fifth Penguins pick, 88th overall) of NHL entry draft (June 11, 1988).
HONORS: Named to WCHA All-Star first team (1991-92).

Season	Team	League	REGULAR SEASON Gms.	G	A	Pts.	PIM	PLAYOFFS Gms.	G	A	Pts.	PIM
86-87	Kelowna	BCJHL	45	10	24	34	95	—	—	—	—	—
87-88	Minnesota-Duluth	WCHA	37	4	5	9	42	—	—	—	—	—
88-89	Minnesota-Duluth	WCHA	35	4	8	12	74	—	—	—	—	—
	Canadian national team	Int'l	2	0	0	0	0	—	—	—	—	—
89-90	Minnesota-Duluth	WCHA	35	5	29	34	74	—	—	—	—	—
90-91	Canadian national team	Int'l	53	4	11	15	34	—	—	—	—	—
91-92	Minnesota-Duluth	WCHA	36	7	27	34	125	—	—	—	—	—
92-93	Cleveland	IHL	55	3	22	25	78	2	0	0	0	2
	Muskegon	Col.HL	2	0	3	3	7	—	—	—	—	—
93-94	Cleveland	IHL	69	13	26	39	109	—	—	—	—	—
	Pittsburgh	NHL	3	0	0	0	2	—	—	—	—	—
NHL totals			3	0	0	0	2					

ANGLEHART, SERGE
D

PERSONAL: Born April 18, 1970, in Hull, Que. ... 6-2/200. ... Shoots right. ... Name pronounced AN-guhl-HAHR.
TRANSACTIONS/CAREER NOTES: Selected by Detroit Red Wings as underage junior in second round (second Red Wings pick, 38th overall) of NHL entry draft (June 11, 1988).... Suspended one game by QMJHL for being aggressor in fight (March 26, 1989).... Traded by Drummondville Voltigeurs with LW Claude Boivin and fifth-round draft pick to Laval Titans for D Luc Doucet, D Brad MacIsaac and second- and third-round draft picks (February 15, 1990).

Season Team	League	Gms.	G	A	Pts.	PIM	Gms.	G	A	Pts.	PIM
			REGULAR SEASON					PLAYOFFS			
87-88—Drummondville	QMJHL	44	1	8	9	122	17	0	3	3	19
88-89—Drummondville	QMJHL	39	6	15	21	89	3	0	0	0	37
—Adirondack	AHL	—	—	—	—	—	2	0	0	0	0
89-90—Laval	QMJHL	48	2	19	21	131	10	1	6	7	69
90-91—Adirondack	AHL	52	3	8	11	113	—	—	—	—	—
91-92—Adirondack	AHL	16	0	1	1	43	—	—	—	—	—
92-93—Adirondack	AHL	3	0	0	0	4	—	—	—	—	—
—Fort Wayne	IHL	2	0	0	0	2	—	—	—	—	—
93-94—Adirondack	AHL	31	0	2	2	87	—	—	—	—	—

ANISIMOV, ARTEM
D, FLYERS

PERSONAL: Born July 27, 1976, in Kazan, U.S.S.R. . . . 6-1/187. . . . Shoots left.
TRANSACTIONS/CAREER NOTES: Selected by Philadelphia Flyers in third round (first Flyers pick, 62nd overall) of NHL entry draft (June 29, 1994).

Season Team	League	Gms.	G	A	Pts.	PIM	Gms.	G	A	Pts.	PIM
			REGULAR SEASON					PLAYOFFS			
93-94—Itil Kazan	CIS	38	0	1	1	12	5	0	0	0	0

ANNECK, DORIAN
C, JETS

PERSONAL: Born April 24, 1976, in Winnipeg, Man. . . . 6-1/183. . . . Shoots left.
TRANSACTIONS/CAREER NOTES: Selected by Winnipeg Jets in third round (second Jets pick, 56th overall) of NHL entry draft (June 29, 1994).

Season Team	League	Gms.	G	A	Pts.	PIM	Gms.	G	A	Pts.	PIM
			REGULAR SEASON					PLAYOFFS			
92-93—Victoria	WHL	63	5	6	11	19	—	—	—	—	—
93-94—Victoria	WHL	71	26	53	79	30	—	—	—	—	—

ANTOSKI, SHAWN
LW/RW, CANUCKS

PERSONAL: Born May 25, 1970, in Brantford, Ont. . . . 6-4/240. . . . Shoots left. . . . Name pronounced an-TAH-skee.
TRANSACTIONS/CAREER NOTES: Injured knee ligament (December 1988). . . . Separated shoulder (March 1989). . . . Selected by Vancouver Canucks in first round (second Canucks pick, 18th overall) of NHL entry draft (June 17, 1989). . . . Suffered sore back (December 1991). . . . Fractured knuckle (December 15, 1993); missed eight games. . . . Sprained thumb (January 19, 1994); missed three games. . . . Suffered sore hand (April 1, 1994); missed three games.

Season Team	League	Gms.	G	A	Pts.	PIM	Gms.	G	A	Pts.	PIM
			REGULAR SEASON					PLAYOFFS			
87-88—North Bay	OHL	52	3	4	7	163	—	—	—	—	—
88-89—North Bay	OHL	57	6	21	27	201	9	5	3	8	24
89-90—North Bay	OHL	59	25	31	56	201	5	1	2	3	17
90-91—Milwaukee	IHL	62	17	7	24	330	5	1	2	3	10
—Vancouver	NHL	2	0	0	0	0	—	—	—	—	—
91-92—Milwaukee	IHL	52	17	16	33	346	5	2	0	2	20
—Vancouver	NHL	4	0	0	0	29	—	—	—	—	—
92-93—Hamilton	AHL	41	3	4	7	172	—	—	—	—	—
—Vancouver	NHL	2	0	0	0	0	—	—	—	—	—
93-94—Vancouver	NHL	55	1	2	3	190	16	0	1	1	36
NHL totals		63	1	2	3	219	16	0	1	1	36

APPEL, FRANK
D, FLAMES

PERSONAL: Born May 12, 1976, in Dusseldorf, West Germany. . . . 6-4/207. . . . Shoots left.
TRANSACTIONS/CAREER NOTES: Selected by Calgary Flames in fifth round (seventh Flames pick, 123rd overall) of NHL entry draft (June 29, 1994).

Season Team	League	Gms.	G	A	Pts.	PIM	Gms.	G	A	Pts.	PIM
			REGULAR SEASON					PLAYOFFS			
93-94—Dusseldorf	Germany	4	0	0	0	4	—	—	—	—	—

ARCHIBALD, DAVE
C/LW, SENATORS

PERSONAL: Born April 14, 1969, in Chilliwack, B.C. . . . 6-1/210. . . . Shoots left. . . . Full name: David John Archibald.
TRANSACTIONS/CAREER NOTES: Underwent shoulder surgery (January 1984). . . . Lacerated hand (October 1986). . . . Selected as underage junior by Minnesota North Stars in first round (first North Stars pick, sixth overall) of NHL entry draft (June 13, 1987). . . . Injured shoulder (September 1987). . . . Suffered sore back (February 1989). . . . Traded by North Stars to New York Rangers for D Jayson More (November 1, 1989). . . . Traded by Rangers to Ottawa Senators for fifth-round pick (traded to Los Angeles Kings who selected G Frederick Beaubien) in 1993 draft (November 6, 1992). . . . Injured back (January 8, 1993); missed 26 games. . . . Injured groin (March 25, 1993); missed one game. . . . Injured shoulder (November 13, 1993); missed 14 games. . . . Injured groin (January 14, 1994); missed remainder of season.

Season Team	League	Gms.	G	A	Pts.	PIM	Gms.	G	A	Pts.	PIM
			REGULAR SEASON					PLAYOFFS			
84-85—Portland	WHL	47	7	11	18	10	3	0	2	2	0
85-86—Portland	WHL	70	29	35	64	56	15	6	7	13	11
86-87—Portland	WHL	65	50	57	107	40	20	10	18	28	11
87-88—Minnesota	NHL	78	13	20	33	26	—	—	—	—	—

Season	Team	League	REGULAR SEASON Gms.	G	A	Pts.	PIM	PLAYOFFS Gms.	G	A	Pts.	PIM
88-89—Minnesota		NHL	72	14	19	33	14	5	0	1	1	0
89-90—Minnesota		NHL	12	1	5	6	6	—	—	—	—	—
—New York Rangers		NHL	19	2	3	5	6	—	—	—	—	—
—Flint		IHL	41	14	38	52	16	4	3	2	5	0
90-91—Canadian national team		Int'l	29	19	12	31	20	—	—	—	—	—
91-92—Canadian national team		Int'l	58	20	43	63	62	—	—	—	—	—
—Canadian Olympic Team		Int'l	8	7	1	8	18	—	—	—	—	—
—Bolzon		Italy	12	12	12	24	16	—	—	—	—	—
92-93—Binghamton		AHL	8	6	3	9	10	—	—	—	—	—
—Ottawa		NHL	44	9	6	15	32	—	—	—	—	—
93-94—Ottawa		NHL	33	10	8	18	14	—	—	—	—	—
NHL totals			258	49	61	110	98	5	0	1	1	0

ARMSTRONG, BILL
LW, DEVILS

PERSONAL: Born June 25, 1966, in London, Ont. . . . 6-2/195. . . . Shoots left. . . . Full name: William Harold Armstrong.
COLLEGE: Western Michigan.
TRANSACTIONS/CAREER NOTES: Signed as free agent by Philadelphia Flyers (May 16, 1989). . . . Signed as free agent by New Jersey Devils (March 21, 1993).

Season	Team	League	REGULAR SEASON Gms.	G	A	Pts.	PIM	PLAYOFFS Gms.	G	A	Pts.	PIM
86-87—Western Michigan Univ.		CCHA	43	13	20	33	86	—	—	—	—	—
87-88—Western Michigan Univ.		CCHA	41	22	17	39	88	—	—	—	—	—
88-89—Western Michigan Univ.		CCHA	40	23	19	42	97	—	—	—	—	—
89-90—Hershey		AHL	58	10	6	16	99	—	—	—	—	—
90-91—Philadelphia		NHL	1	0	1	1	0	—	—	—	—	—
—Hershey		AHL	70	36	27	63	150	6	2	8	10	19
91-92—Hershey		AHL	64	26	22	48	185	6	2	2	4	6
92-93—Cincinnati		IHL	42	14	11	25	99	—	—	—	—	—
—Utica		AHL	32	18	21	39	60	—	—	—	—	—
93-94—Albany		AHL	74	32	50	82	188	—	—	—	—	—
NHL totals			1	0	1	1	0					

ARMSTRONG, BILL
D, BRUINS

PERSONAL: Born May 18, 1970, in Richmond Hill, Ont. . . . 6-5/220. . . . Shoots left.
TRANSACTIONS/CAREER NOTES: Selected by Philadelphia Flyers in third round (fifth Flyers pick, 46th overall) of NHL entry draft (June 16, 1990). . . . Signed as free agent by Boston Bruins (June 23, 1993).

Season	Team	League	REGULAR SEASON Gms.	G	A	Pts.	PIM	PLAYOFFS Gms.	G	A	Pts.	PIM
86-87—Barrie Jr. B		OHA	45	1	11	12	45	—	—	—	—	—
87-88—Toronto		OHL	64	1	10	11	99	—	—	—	—	—
88-89—Toronto		OHL	64	1	16	17	82	—	—	—	—	—
89-90—Dukes of Hamilton		OHL	18	0	2	2	38	—	—	—	—	—
—Niagara Falls		OHL	4	0	1	1	17	—	—	—	—	—
—Oshawa		OHL	41	2	8	10	115	17	0	7	7	39
90-91—Hershey		AHL	56	1	9	10	117	1	0	0	0	0
91-92—Hershey		AHL	†80	2	14	16	159	3	0	0	0	2
92-93—Hershey		AHL	80	2	10	12	205	—	—	—	—	—
93-94—Providence		AHL	66	0	7	7	200	—	—	—	—	—

ARMSTRONG, CHRIS
D, PANTHERS

PERSONAL: Born June 26, 1975, in Regina, Sask. . . . 6-0/184. . . . Shoots left.
HIGH SCHOOL: Vanier Collegiate (Moose Jaw, Sask.).
TRANSACTIONS/CAREER NOTES: Selected by Florida Panthers in third round (third Panthers pick, 57th overall) of NHL entry draft (June 26, 1993).
HONORS: Named to Can.HL All-Star second team (1993-94). . . . Named to WHL (East) All-Star first team (1993-94).

Season	Team	League	REGULAR SEASON Gms.	G	A	Pts.	PIM	PLAYOFFS Gms.	G	A	Pts.	PIM
91-92—Moose Jaw		WHL	43	2	7	9	19	4	0	0	0	0
92-93—Moose Jaw		WHL	67	9	35	44	104	—	—	—	—	—
93-94—Moose Jaw		WHL	64	13	55	68	54	—	—	—	—	—
—Cincinnati		IHL	1	0	0	0	0	10	1	3	4	2

ARMSTRONG, DEREK
C, ISLANDERS

PERSONAL: Born April 23, 1973, in Ottawa. . . . 5-11/180. . . . Shoots right.
HIGH SCHOOL: Lo-Ellen Park Secondary School (Sudbury, Ont.).
TRANSACTIONS/CAREER NOTES: Selected by New York Islanders in sixth round (fifth Islanders pick, 128th overall) of NHL entry draft (June 20, 1992).

Season	Team	League	REGULAR SEASON Gms.	G	A	Pts.	PIM	PLAYOFFS Gms.	G	A	Pts.	PIM
89-90—Hawkesbury		COJHL	48	8	10	18	30	—	—	—	—	—
90-91—Sudbury		OHL	2	0	2	2	0	—	—	—	—	—
—Hawkesbury		COJHL	54	27	45	72	49	—	—	—	—	—

Season Team	League	REGULAR SEASON Gms.	G	A	Pts.	PIM	PLAYOFFS Gms.	G	A	Pts.	PIM
91-92—Sudbury	OHL	66	31	54	85	22	9	2	2	4	2
92-93—Sudbury	OHL	66	44	62	106	56	14	9	10	19	26
93-94—Salt Lake City	IHL	76	23	35	58	61	—	—	—	—	—

ARNIEL, SCOTT
LW/C

PERSONAL: Born September 17, 1962, in Kingston, Ont. . . . 6-1/188. . . . Shoots left.
TRANSACTIONS/CAREER NOTES: Selected by Winnipeg Jets as underage junior in second round (second Jets pick, 22nd overall) of NHL entry draft (June 10, 1981). . . . Traded by Jets to Buffalo Sabres for LW Gilles Hamel (June 21, 1986). . . . Bruised abdominal muscle (March 1988). . . . Suffered concussion (April 9, 1990). . . . Traded by Sabres with D Phil Housley, RW Jeff Parker and first-round pick in 1990 draft (C Keith Tkachuk) to Jets for C Dale Hawerchuk, first-round pick in 1990 draft (LW Brad May) and future considerations (June 16, 1990); RW Greg Paslawski sent to Sabres to complete deal (February 5, 1991). . . . Traded by Jets to Boston Bruins for future considerations (November 22, 1991). . . . Strained shoulder (December 1, 1991); missed four games. . . . Fractured right thumb (January 1992). . . . Signed as free agent by San Diego Gulls (October 7, 1992).

Season Team	League	REGULAR SEASON Gms.	G	A	Pts.	PIM	PLAYOFFS Gms.	G	A	Pts.	PIM
79-80—Cornwall	QMJHL	61	22	28	50	51	—	—	—	—	—
80-81—Cornwall	QMJHL	68	52	71	123	102	19	14	19	33	24
81-82—Cornwall	OHL	24	18	26	44	43	—	—	—	—	—
—Winnipeg	NHL	17	1	8	9	14	3	0	0	0	0
82-83—Winnipeg	NHL	75	13	5	18	46	2	0	0	0	0
83-84—Winnipeg	NHL	80	21	35	56	68	2	0	0	0	5
84-85—Winnipeg	NHL	79	22	22	44	81	8	1	2	3	9
85-86—Winnipeg	NHL	80	18	25	43	40	3	0	0	0	12
86-87—Buffalo	NHL	63	11	14	25	59	—	—	—	—	—
87-88—Buffalo	NHL	73	17	23	40	61	6	0	1	1	5
88-89—Buffalo	NHL	80	18	23	41	46	5	1	0	1	4
89-90—Buffalo	NHL	79	18	14	32	77	5	0	1	1	4
90-91—Winnipeg	NHL	75	5	17	22	87	—	—	—	—	—
91-92—New Haven	AHL	11	3	3	6	10	—	—	—	—	—
—Boston	NHL	29	5	3	8	20	—	—	—	—	—
—Maine	AHL	14	4	4	8	8	—	—	—	—	—
92-93—San Diego	IHL	79	35	48	83	116	14	6	5	11	16
93-94—San Diego	IHL	79	34	43	77	121	7	6	3	9	24
NHL totals		730	149	189	338	599	34	3	3	6	39

ARNOTT, JASON
C, OILERS

PERSONAL: Born October 11, 1974, in Collingworth, Ont. . . . 6-3/195. . . . Shoots right.
HIGH SCHOOL: Henry Street (Whitby, Ont.).
TRANSACTIONS/CAREER NOTES: Selected by Edmonton Oilers in first round (first Oilers pick, seventh overall) of NHL entry draft (June 26, 1993). . . . Suffered from tonsillitis (November 3, 1993); missed one game. . . . Suffered from bruised sternum (November 27, 1993); missed one game. . . . Suffered from back sprain (December 7, 1993); missed one game. . . . Underwent appendectomy (December 28, 1993); missed three games.
HONORS: Named NHL Rookie of the Year by THE SPORTING NEWS (1993-94). . . . Named to NHL All-Rookie team (1993-94).

Season Team	League	REGULAR SEASON Gms.	G	A	Pts.	PIM	PLAYOFFS Gms.	G	A	Pts.	PIM
90-91—Lindsay Jr. B	OHA	42	17	44	61	10	—	—	—	—	—
91-92—Oshawa	OHL	57	9	15	24	12	—	—	—	—	—
92-93—Oshawa	OHL	56	41	57	98	74	13	9	9	18	20
93-94—Edmonton	NHL	78	33	35	68	104	—	—	—	—	—
NHL totals		78	33	35	68	104					

ASKEY, TOM
G, MIGHTY DUCKS

PERSONAL: Born October 4, 1974, in Kenmore, N.Y. . . . 6-2/185. . . . Catches left.
COLLEGE: Ohio State.
TRANSACTIONS/CAREER NOTES: Selected by Mighty Ducks of Anaheim in eighth round (eighth Ducks pick, 186th overall) of NHL entry draft (June 26, 1993).

Season Team	League	REGULAR SEASON Gms.	Min.	W	L	T	GA	SO	Avg.	PLAYOFFS Gms.	Min.	W	L	GA	SO	Avg.
92-93—Ohio State	CCHA	25	1235	2	19	0	125	0	6.07	—	—	—	—	—	—	—
93-94—Ohio State	CCHA	27	1488	3	19	4	103	0	4.15	—	—	—	—	—	—	—

ASTLEY, MARK
D, SABRES

PERSONAL: Born March 30, 1969, in Calgary. . . . 5-11/185. . . . Shoots left. . . . Name pronounced AST-lee.
COLLEGE: Lake Superior State (Mich.).
TRANSACTIONS/CAREER NOTES: Selected by Buffalo Sabres in 10th round (ninth Sabres pick, 194th overall) of NHL entry draft (June 17, 1989). . . . Hospitalized with strep pneumonia (March 14, 1990). . . . Loaned by Sabres to Canadian Olympic Team (October 15, 1993).
HONORS: Named to CCHA All-Star second team (1990-91). . . . Named to NCAA All-America West first team (1991-92). . . . Named to CCHA All-Star first team (1991-92). . . . Named to NCAA All-Tournament team (1991-92).
MISCELLANEOUS: Member of silver-medal-winning Canadian Olympic team (1994).

Season	Team	League	REGULAR SEASON					PLAYOFFS				
			Gms.	G	A	Pts.	PIM	Gms.	G	A	Pts.	PIM
87-88—Calgary Canucks		AJHL	52	25	37	62	106	—	—	—	—	—
88-89—Lake Superior State		CCHA	42	3	12	15	26	—	—	—	—	—
89-90—Lake Superior State		CCHA	43	7	25	32	74	—	—	—	—	—
90-91—Lake Superior State		CCHA	45	19	27	46	50	—	—	—	—	—
91-92—Lake Superior State		CCHA	43	12	37	49	65	—	—	—	—	—
92-93—Lugano		Switzerland	30	10	12	22	57	—	—	—	—	—
—Canadian national team		Int'l	22	4	14	18	14	—	—	—	—	—
93-94—Buffalo		NHL	1	0	0	0	0	—	—	—	—	—
—Canadian national team		Int'l	21	4	9	13	10	—	—	—	—	—
—Canadian Olympic Team		Int'l	8	0	1	1	4	—	—	—	—	—
NHL totals			1	0	0	0	0					

ATCHEYNUM, BLAIR
RW

PERSONAL: Born April 20, 1969, in Estevan, Sask. . . . 6-2/190. . . . Shoots right. . . . Name pronounced ATCH-uh-num.
TRANSACTIONS/CAREER NOTES: Selected by Swift Current Broncos in special compensation draft to replace players injured and killed in a December 30, 1986 bus crash (February 1987). . . . Traded by Broncos to Moose Jaw Warriors for D Tim Logan (February 1987). . . . Selected by Hartford Whalers in third round (second Whalers pick, 52nd overall) of NHL entry draft (June 17, 1989). . . . Suffered concussion (January 12, 1991). . . . Selected by Ottawa Senators in NHL expansion draft (June 18, 1992).
HONORS: Won Brad Hornung Trophy (1988-89). . . . Named to WHL (East) All-Star first team (1988-89).

Season	Team	League	REGULAR SEASON					PLAYOFFS				
			Gms.	G	A	Pts.	PIM	Gms.	G	A	Pts.	PIM
85-86—North Battleford		SJHL	35	25	20	45	50	—	—	—	—	—
86-87—Saskatoon		WHL	21	0	4	4	4	—	—	—	—	—
—Swift Current		WHL	5	2	1	3	0	—	—	—	—	—
—Moose Jaw		WHL	12	3	0	3	2	—	—	—	—	—
87-88—Moose Jaw		WHL	60	32	16	48	52	—	—	—	—	—
88-89—Moose Jaw		WHL	71	70	68	138	70	7	2	5	7	13
89-90—Binghamton		AHL	78	20	21	41	45	—	—	—	—	—
90-91—Springfield		AHL	72	25	27	52	42	13	0	6	6	6
91-92—Springfield		AHL	62	16	21	37	64	6	1	1	2	2
92-93—New Haven		AHL	51	16	18	34	47	—	—	—	—	—
—Ottawa		NHL	4	0	1	1	0	—	—	—	—	—
93-94—Columbus		ECHL	16	15	12	27	10	—	—	—	—	—
—Portland		AHL	2	0	0	0	0	—	—	—	—	—
—Springfield		AHL	40	18	22	40	13	6	0	2	2	0
NHL totals			4	0	1	1	0					

AUCOIN, ADRIAN
D, CANUCKS

PERSONAL: Born July 3, 1973, in London, Ont. . . . 6-1/194. . . . Shoots right.
COLLEGE: Boston University.
TRANSACTIONS/CAREER NOTES: Selected by Vancouver Canucks in fifth round (seventh Canucks pick, 117th overall) of NHL entry draft (June 20, 1992).
MISCELLANEOUS: Member of silver-medal-winning Canadian Olympic team (1994).

Season	Team	League	REGULAR SEASON					PLAYOFFS				
			Gms.	G	A	Pts.	PIM	Gms.	G	A	Pts.	PIM
91-92—Boston University		Hockey East	33	2	10	12	62	—	—	—	—	—
92-93—Canadian national team		Int'l	42	8	10	18	71	—	—	—	—	—
93-94—Canadian national team		Int'l	63	5	12	17	82	—	—	—	—	—
—Canadian Olympic Team		Int'l	4	0	0	0	2	—	—	—	—	—
—Hamilton		AHL	13	1	2	3	19	4	0	2	2	6

AUDETTE, DONALD
RW, SABRES

PERSONAL: Born September 23, 1969, in Laval, Que. . . . 5-8/175. . . . Shoots right. . . . Name pronounced aw-DEHT.
TRANSACTIONS/CAREER NOTES: Selected by Buffalo Sabres in ninth round (eighth Sabres pick, 183rd overall) of NHL entry draft (June 17, 1989). . . . Broke left hand (February 11, 1990); missed seven games. . . . Bruised thigh (September 1990). . . . Bruised thigh (October 1990); missed five games. . . . Tore left knee ligaments (November 16, 1990). . . . Underwent surgery to left knee (December 10, 1990). . . . Sprained ankle (December 14, 1991); missed eight games. . . . Injured knee (March 31, 1992). . . . Underwent knee surgery prior to 1992-93 season; missed first 22 games of season.
HONORS: Won Guy Lafleur Trophy (1988-89). . . . Named to QMJHL All-Star first team (1988-89). . . . Won Dudley (Red) Garrett Memorial Trophy (1989-90). . . . Named to AHL All-Star first team (1989-90).

Season	Team	League	REGULAR SEASON					PLAYOFFS				
			Gms.	G	A	Pts.	PIM	Gms.	G	A	Pts.	PIM
86-87—Laval		QMJHL	66	17	22	39	36	14	2	6	8	10
87-88—Laval		QMJHL	63	48	61	109	56	14	7	12	19	20
88-89—Laval		QMJHL	70	76	85	161	123	17	*17	12	29	43
89-90—Rochester		AHL	70	42	46	88	78	15	9	8	17	29
—Buffalo		NHL	—	—	—	—	—	2	0	0	0	0
90-91—Rochester		AHL	5	4	0	4	2	—	—	—	—	—
—Buffalo		NHL	8	4	3	7	4	—	—	—	—	—
91-92—Buffalo		NHL	63	31	17	48	75	—	—	—	—	—

		REGULAR SEASON					PLAYOFFS				
92-93—Buffalo	NHL	44	12	7	19	51	8	2	2	4	6
—Rochester	AHL	6	8	4	12	10	—	—	—	—	—
93-94—Buffalo	NHL	77	29	30	59	41	7	0	1	1	6
NHL totals		192	76	57	133	171	17	2	3	5	12

AUGUSTA, PATRIK
RW, MAPLE LEAFS

PERSONAL: Born November 13, 1969, in Jihlava, Czechoslovakia. . . . 5-10/170. . . . Shoots left. . . . Name pronounced pa-TREEK ah-GOOS-tuh.
TRANSACTIONS/CAREER NOTES: Selected by Toronto Maple Leafs in seventh round (eighth Maple Leafs pick, 149th overall) of NHL entry draft (June 20, 1992).
HONORS: Named to AHL All-Star second team (1993-94).

Season Team	League	REGULAR SEASON					PLAYOFFS				
		Gms.	G	A	Pts.	PIM	Gms.	G	A	Pts.	PIM
89-90—Dukla Jihlava	Czech.	46	12	12	24	...	—	—	—	—	—
90-91—Dukla Jihlava	Czech.	49	20	22	42	18	—	—	—	—	—
91-92—Dukla Jihlava	Czech.	34	15	11	26	...	—	—	—	—	—
—Czech. Olympic Team	Int'l	8	3	2	5	...	—	—	—	—	—
92-93—St. John's	AHL	75	32	45	77	74	8	3	3	6	23
93-94—St. John's	AHL	77	*53	43	96	105	11	4	8	12	4
—Toronto	NHL	2	0	0	0	0	—	—	—	—	—
NHL totals		2	0	0	0	0					

BABYCH, DAVE
D, CANUCKS

PERSONAL: Born May 23, 1961, in Edmonton. . . . 6-2/215. . . . Shoots left. . . . Full name: David Michael Babych. . . . Name pronounced BA-bihch. . . . Brother of Wayne Babych, right winger for four NHL teams (1978-79 through 1986-87).
TRANSACTIONS/CAREER NOTES: Selected by Winnipeg Jets as underage junior in first round (first Jets pick, second overall) of NHL entry draft (June 11, 1980). . . . Separated shoulder (March 1984). . . . Suffered back spasms (December 1984). . . . Traded by Jets to Hartford Whalers for RW Ray Neufeld (November 21, 1985). . . . Injured hip (January 1987); missed 12 games. . . . Lacerated right hand (March 16, 1989); missed six games. . . . Bruised neck (March 1990). . . . Underwent surgery to right wrist (October 29, 1990); missed 44 games. . . . Broke right thumb (February 8, 1991); missed remainder of season. . . . Selected by Minnesota North Stars in NHL expansion draft (May 30, 1991). . . . Traded by North Stars to Vancouver Canucks for D Craig Ludwig as part of a three-club deal in which Canucks sent D Tom Kurvers to Islanders for Ludwig (June 22, 1991). . . . Suffered sore back (November 3, 1991); missed one game. . . . Suffered hernia (September 22, 1992); missed 22 games. . . . Sprained knee (December 7, 1992); missed 12 games. . . . Suffered from the flu (March 20, 1993); missed one game. . . . Suffered facial lacerations (April 4, 1993); missed three games. . . . Suffered facial lacerations (December 15, 1993); missed two games. . . . Bruised foot (February 13, 1994); missed one game.
HONORS: Won AJHL Top Defenseman Trophy (1977-78). . . . Won AJHL Rookie of the Year Trophy (1977-78). . . . Named to AJHL All-Star first team (1977-78). . . . Won Top Defenseman Trophy (1979-80). . . . Named to WHL All-Star first team (1979-80). . . . Played in NHL All-Star Game (1983 and 1984).

Season Team	League	REGULAR SEASON					PLAYOFFS				
		Gms.	G	A	Pts.	PIM	Gms.	G	A	Pts.	PIM
77-78—Portland	WCHL	6	1	3	4	4	—	—	—	—	—
—Fort Saskatchewan	AJHL	56	31	69	100	37	—	—	—	—	—
78-79—Portland	WHL	67	20	59	79	63	25	7	22	29	22
79-80—Portland	WHL	50	22	60	82	71	8	1	10	11	2
80-81—Winnipeg	NHL	69	6	38	44	90	—	—	—	—	—
81-82—Winnipeg	NHL	79	19	49	68	92	4	1	2	3	29
82-83—Winnipeg	NHL	79	13	61	74	56	3	0	0	0	0
83-84—Winnipeg	NHL	66	18	39	57	62	3	1	1	2	0
84-85—Winnipeg	NHL	78	13	49	62	78	8	2	7	9	6
85-86—Winnipeg	NHL	19	4	12	16	14	—	—	—	—	—
—Hartford	NHL	62	10	43	53	36	8	1	3	4	14
86-87—Hartford	NHL	66	8	33	41	44	6	1	1	2	14
87-88—Hartford	NHL	71	14	36	50	54	6	3	2	5	2
88-89—Hartford	NHL	70	6	41	47	54	4	1	5	6	2
89-90—Hartford	NHL	72	6	37	43	62	7	1	2	3	0
90-91—Hartford	NHL	8	0	6	6	4	—	—	—	—	—
91-92—Vancouver	NHL	75	5	24	29	63	13	2	6	8	10
92-93—Vancouver	NHL	43	3	16	19	44	12	2	5	7	6
93-94—Vancouver	NHL	73	4	28	32	52	24	3	5	8	12
NHL totals		930	129	512	641	805	98	18	39	57	95

BACA, JERGUS
D

PERSONAL: Born April 1, 1965, in Liptovsky Mikulas, Czechoslovakia. . . . 6-2/215. . . . Shoots left.
TRANSACTIONS/CAREER NOTES: Selected by Hartford Whalers in seventh round (sixth Whalers pick, 141st overall) of NHL entry draft (June 16, 1990). . . . Bruised shoulder (October 1990). . . . Signed as free agent by Milwaukee Admirals (September 10, 1993).
HONORS: Named Czechoslovakian League Rookie of the Year (1987-88). . . . Named to Czechoslovakian League All-Star team (1988-89 and 1989-90).

Season Team	League	REGULAR SEASON					PLAYOFFS				
		Gms.	G	A	Pts.	PIM	Gms.	G	A	Pts.	PIM
89-90—Kosice	Czech.	47	9	16	25	...	—	—	—	—	—
90-91—Hartford	NHL	9	0	2	2	14	—	—	—	—	—
—Springfield	AHL	57	6	23	29	89	18	3	13	16	18

Season Team	League	REGULAR SEASON Gms.	G	A	Pts.	PIM	PLAYOFFS Gms.	G	A	Pts.	PIM
91-92—Springfield	AHL	64	6	20	26	88	11	0	6	6	20
—Hartford	NHL	1	0	0	0	0	—	—	—	—	—
92-93—Milwaukee	IHL	73	9	29	38	108	6	0	3	3	2
93-94—Milwaukee	IHL	67	6	29	35	119	3	1	1	2	4
—Slovakian Olympic team	Int'l	8	1	2	3	10	—	—	—	—	—
NHL totals		10	0	2	2	14					

BAILEY, SCOTT
G, BRUINS

PERSONAL: Born May 2, 1972, in Calgary.... 5-11/185.... Catches left.
TRANSACTIONS/CAREER NOTES: Selected by Boston Bruins in fifth round (third Bruins pick, 112th overall) of NHL entry draft (June 20, 1992).
HONORS: Won WHL (West) Rookie of the Year Award (1990-91).... Named to WHL (West) All-Star second team (1990-91 and 1991-92).

Season Team	League	REGULAR SEASON Gms.	Min.	W	L	T	GA	SO	Avg.	PLAYOFFS Gms.	Min.	W	L	GA	SO	Avg.
88-89—Moose Jaw	WHL	2	34	...	...	...	7	0	12.35	—	—	—	—	—	—	—
89-90—							Did not play.									
90-91—Spokane	WHL	46	2537	33	11	0	157	4	3.71	—	—	—	—	—	—	—
91-92—Spokane	WHL	65	3748	34	23	5	206	1	3.30	10	605	5	5	43	0	4.26
92-93—Johnstown	ECHL	36	1750	13	15	‡3	112	1	3.84	—	—	—	—	—	—	—
93-94—Charlotte	ECHL	36	2180	22	11	3	130	1	3.58	3	188	1	2	12	0	3.83
—Providence	AHL	7	377	2	2	2	24	0	3.82	—	—	—	—	—	—	—

BAKER, JAMIE
C, SHARKS

PERSONAL: Born August 31, 1966, in Nepean, Ont.... 6-0/190.... Shoots left.... Full name: James Paul Baker.
HIGH SCHOOL: J.S. Woodsworth (Nepean, Ont.).
COLLEGE: St. Lawrence (N.Y.).
TRANSACTIONS/CAREER NOTES: Selected by Quebec Nordiques in NHL supplemental draft (June 10, 1988).... Broke left ankle (December 30, 1988).... Sprained ankle (January 9, 1992); missed two games.... Signed as free agent by Ottawa Senators (September 2, 1992).... Sprained ankle (December 15, 1992); missed six games.... Bruised foot (February 22, 1993); missed one game.... Signed as free agent by San Jose Sharks (August 18, 1993).... Suffered slight groin pull (October 16, 1993); missed 10 games.

Season Team	League	REGULAR SEASON Gms.	G	A	Pts.	PIM	PLAYOFFS Gms.	G	A	Pts.	PIM
85-86—St. Lawrence University	ECAC	31	9	16	25	52	—	—	—	—	—
86-87—St. Lawrence University	ECAC	32	8	24	32	59	—	—	—	—	—
87-88—St. Lawrence University	ECAC	38	26	28	54	44	—	—	—	—	—
88-89—St. Lawrence University	ECAC	13	11	16	27	16	—	—	—	—	—
89-90—Quebec	NHL	1	0	0	0	0	—	—	—	—	—
—Halifax	AHL	74	17	43	60	47	6	0	0	0	7
90-91—Quebec	NHL	18	2	0	2	8	—	—	—	—	—
—Halifax	AHL	50	14	22	36	85	—	—	—	—	—
91-92—Halifax	AHL	9	5	0	5	12	—	—	—	—	—
—Quebec	NHL	52	7	10	17	32	—	—	—	—	—
92-93—Ottawa	NHL	76	19	29	48	54	—	—	—	—	—
93-94—San Jose	NHL	65	12	5	17	38	14	3	2	5	30
NHL totals		212	40	44	84	132	14	3	2	5	30

BALES, MIKE
G, SENATORS

PERSONAL: Born August 6, 1971, in Saskatoon, Sask.... 6-1/180.... Catches left.... Full name: Michael Raymond Bales.
COLLEGE: Ohio State.
TRANSACTIONS/CAREER NOTES: Selected by Boston Bruins in fifth round (fourth Bruins pick, 105th overall) of NHL entry draft (June 16, 1990).... Signed as free agent by Ottawa Senators (July 4, 1994).

Season Team	League	REGULAR SEASON Gms.	Min.	W	L	T	GA	SO	Avg.	PLAYOFFS Gms.	Min.	W	L	GA	SO	Avg.
88-89—Estevan	SJHL	44	2412	...	...	...	197	1	4.90	—	—	—	—	—	—	—
89-90—Ohio State	CCHA	21	1117	6	13	2	95	0	5.10	—	—	—	—	—	—	—
90-91—Ohio State	CCHA	*39	*2180	11	24	3	*184	0	5.06	—	—	—	—	—	—	—
91-92—Ohio State	CCHA	36	2061	11	20	5	*180	...	5.24	—	—	—	—	—	—	—
92-93—Providence	AHL	44	2363	22	17	0	166	1	4.21	2	118	0	2	8	0	4.07
—Boston	NHL	1	25	0	0	0	1	0	2.40	—	—	—	—	—	—	—
93-94—Providence	AHL	33	1757	9	15	4	130	0	4.44	—	—	—	—	—	—	—
NHL totals		1	25	0	0	0	1	0	2.40							

BANCROFT, STEVE
D, PENGUINS

PERSONAL: Born October 6, 1970, in Toronto.... 6-1/214.... Shoots left.
TRANSACTIONS/CAREER NOTES: Underwent surgery to left shoulder (April 1989).... Selected by Toronto Maple Leafs in first round (third Maple Leafs pick, 21st overall) of NHL entry draft (June 17, 1989).... Traded by Maple Leafs to Boston Bruins for LW Rob Cimetta (November 9, 1990).... Traded by Bruins with 11th-round pick in 1993 draft (traded to Winnipeg who selected LW Russell Hewson) to Chicago Blackhawks for 11th-round pick in 1992 draft (LW Yevgeny Pavlov) and 12th-round pick in 1993 draft (January 8, 1992).... Traded by Blackhawks with undisclosed pick in 1993 draft to Winnipeg Jets for C Troy Mur-

B

ray (February 21, 1993); Jets received 11th-round pick in 1993 draft (LW Russell Hewson) to complete deal. . . . Selected by Florida Panthers in NHL expansion draft (June 24, 1993). . . . Signed as free agent by Pittsburgh Penguins (August 2, 1993).

Season Team	League	REGULAR SEASON					PLAYOFFS				
		Gms.	G	A	Pts.	PIM	Gms.	G	A	Pts.	PIM
86-87—St. Catharines Jr. B.	OHA	11	5	8	13	20	—	—	—	—	—
87-88—Belleville	OHL	56	1	8	9	42	—	—	—	—	—
88-89—Belleville	OHL	66	7	30	37	99	5	0	2	2	10
89-90—Belleville	OHL	53	10	33	43	135	11	3	9	12	38
90-91—Newmarket	AHL	9	0	3	3	22	—	—	—	—	—
—Maine	AHL	53	2	12	14	46	2	0	0	0	2
91-92—Maine	AHL	26	1	3	4	45	—	—	—	—	—
—Indianapolis	IHL	36	8	23	31	49	—	—	—	—	—
92-93—Indianapolis	IHL	53	10	35	45	138	—	—	—	—	—
—Chicago	NHL	1	0	0	0	0	—	—	—	—	—
—Moncton	AHL	21	3	13	16	16	5	0	0	0	16
93-94—Cleveland	IHL	33	2	12	14	58	—	—	—	—	—
NHL totals		1	0	0	0	0					

BANKS, DARREN
LW, BRUINS

PERSONAL: Born March 18, 1966, in Toronto. . . . 6-2/215. . . . Shoots left. . . . Full name: Darren Alexander Banks.
COLLEGE: Brock University (Ont.).
TRANSACTIONS/CAREER NOTES: Signed as free agent by Calgary Flames (December 12, 1990). . . . Signed as free agent by Boston Bruins (July 16, 1992).

Season Team	League	REGULAR SEASON					PLAYOFFS				
		Gms.	G	A	Pts.	PIM	Gms.	G	A	Pts.	PIM
86-87—Brock University	OUAA	24	5	3	8	82	—	—	—	—	—
87-88—Brock University	OUAA	26	10	11	21	110	—	—	—	—	—
88-89—Brock University	OUAA	26	19	14	33	88	—	—	—	—	—
89-90—Salt Lake City	IHL	6	0	0	0	11	1	0	0	0	10
—Fort Wayne	IHL	2	0	1	1	0	—	—	—	—	—
—Knoxville	ECHL	52	25	22	47	258	—	—	—	—	—
90-91—Salt Lake City	IHL	56	9	7	16	286	3	0	1	1	6
91-92—Salt Lake City	IHL	55	5	5	10	303	—	—	—	—	—
92-93—Providence	AHL	43	9	5	14	199	1	0	0	0	0
—Boston	NHL	16	2	1	3	64	—	—	—	—	—
93-94—Providence	AHL	41	6	3	9	189	—	—	—	—	—
—Boston	NHL	4	0	1	1	9	—	—	—	—	—
NHL totals		20	2	2	4	73					

BANNISTER, DREW
D, LIGHTNING

PERSONAL: Born September 4, 1974, in Belleville, Ont. . . . 6-1/193. . . . Shoots right.
HIGH SCHOOL: Bawating Collegiate School (Sault Ste. Marie, Ont.).
TRANSACTIONS/CAREER NOTES: Selected by Tampa Bay Lightning in second round (second Lightning pick, 26th overall) of NHL entry draft (June 20, 1992).
HONORS: Named to Memorial Cup All-Star team (1991-92). . . . Named to OHL All-Star second team (1993-94).

Season Team	League	REGULAR SEASON					PLAYOFFS				
		Gms.	G	A	Pts.	PIM	Gms.	G	A	Pts.	PIM
90-91—Sault Ste. Marie	OHL	41	2	8	10	51	4	0	0	0	0
91-92—Sault Ste. Marie	OHL	64	4	21	25	122	16	3	10	13	36
92-93—Sault Ste. Marie	OHL	59	5	28	33	114	18	2	7	9	12
93-94—Sault Ste. Marie	OHL	58	7	43	50	108	14	6	9	15	20

BARNABY, MATTHEW
LW, SABRES

PERSONAL: Born May 4, 1973, in Ottawa. . . . 6-0/170. . . . Shoots right.
TRANSACTIONS/CAREER NOTES: Selected by Buffalo Sabres in fourth round (fifth Sabres pick, 83rd overall) of NHL entry draft (June 20, 1992).

Season Team	League	REGULAR SEASON					PLAYOFFS				
		Gms.	G	A	Pts.	PIM	Gms.	G	A	Pts.	PIM
90-91—Beauport	QMJHL	52	9	5	14	262	—	—	—	—	—
91-92—Beauport	QMJHL	63	29	37	66	*476	—	—	—	—	—
92-93—Victoriaville	QMJHL	65	44	67	111	*448	6	2	4	6	44
—Buffalo	NHL	2	1	0	1	10	1	0	1	1	4
93-94—Buffalo	NHL	35	2	4	6	106	3	0	0	0	17
—Rochester	AHL	42	10	32	42	153	—	—	—	—	—
NHL totals		37	3	4	7	116	4	0	1	1	21

BARNES, STU
C, PANTHERS

PERSONAL: Born December 25, 1970, in Edmonton. . . . 5-11/180. . . . Shoots right.
TRANSACTIONS/CAREER NOTES: Selected by Winnipeg Jets in first round (first Jets pick, fourth overall) of NHL entry draft (June 17, 1989). . . . Traded by Jets to Florida Panthers for C Randy Gilhen (November 26, 1993). . . . Strained left calf (January 1, 1994); missed one game.
HONORS: Won Jim Piggott Memorial Trophy (1987-88). . . . Named to WHL All-Star second team (1987-88). . . . Won Four Broncos Memorial Trophy (1988-89). . . . Named to WHL All-Star first team (1988-89).

Season	Team	League	REGULAR SEASON Gms.	G	A	Pts.	PIM	PLAYOFFS Gms.	G	A	Pts.	PIM
86-87	St. Albert	AJHL	57	43	32	75	80	—	—	—	—	—
87-88	New Westminster	WHL	71	37	64	101	88	5	2	3	5	6
88-89	Tri-City	WHL	70	59	82	141	117	7	6	5	11	10
89-90	Tri-City	WHL	63	52	92	144	165	7	1	5	6	26
90-91	Canadian national team	Int'l	53	22	27	49	68	—	—	—	—	—
91-92	Winnipeg	NHL	46	8	9	17	26	—	—	—	—	—
	Moncton	AHL	30	13	19	32	10	11	3	9	12	6
92-93	Moncton	AHL	42	23	31	54	58	—	—	—	—	—
	Winnipeg	NHL	38	12	10	22	10	6	1	3	4	2
93-94	Winnipeg	NHL	18	5	4	9	8	—	—	—	—	—
	Florida	NHL	59	18	20	38	30	—	—	—	—	—
NHL totals			161	43	43	86	74	6	1	3	4	2

B

BARON, MURRAY
D, BLUES

PERSONAL: Born June 1, 1967, in Prince George, B.C.... 6-3/215.... Shoots left. **HIGH SCHOOL:** Kamloops (B.C.). **COLLEGE:** North Dakota.
TRANSACTIONS/CAREER NOTES: Selected by Philadelphia Flyers as underage player in eighth round (seventh Flyers pick, 167th overall) of NHL entry draft (June 21, 1986).... Separated left shoulder (October 5, 1989).... Underwent surgery to have bone spur removed from foot (April 1990).... Traded by Flyers with C Ron Sutter to St. Louis Blues for C Rod Brind'Amour and C Dan Quinn (September 22, 1991).... Injured shoulder (December 3, 1991); missed seven games.... Broke foot (March 22, 1993); missed remainder of regular season.... Injured groin (December 1, 1993); missed three games.... Injured groin (December 11, 1993); missed three games.... Injured knee (March 7, 1994); missed one game.

Season	Team	League	REGULAR SEASON Gms.	G	A	Pts.	PIM	PLAYOFFS Gms.	G	A	Pts.	PIM
84-85	Vernon	BCJHL	37	5	9	14	93	—	—	—	—	—
85-86	Vernon	BCJHL	49	15	32	47	176	7	1	2	3	13
86-87	Univ. of North Dakota	WCHA	41	4	10	14	62	—	—	—	—	—
87-88	Univ. of North Dakota	WCHA	41	1	10	11	95	—	—	—	—	—
88-89	Univ. of North Dakota	WCHA	40	2	6	8	92	—	—	—	—	—
	Hershey	AHL	9	0	3	3	8	—	—	—	—	—
89-90	Hershey	AHL	50	0	10	10	101	—	—	—	—	—
	Philadelphia	NHL	16	2	2	4	12	—	—	—	—	—
90-91	Hershey	AHL	6	2	3	5	0	—	—	—	—	—
	Philadelphia	NHL	67	8	8	16	74	—	—	—	—	—
91-92	St. Louis	NHL	67	3	8	11	94	2	0	0	0	2
92-93	St. Louis	NHL	53	2	2	4	59	11	0	0	0	12
93-94	St. Louis	NHL	77	5	9	14	123	4	0	0	0	10
NHL totals			280	20	29	49	362	17	0	0	0	24

BARR, DAVE
RW, STARS

PERSONAL: Born November 30, 1960, in Edmonton.... 6-1/195.... Shoots right.... Full name: David Angus Barr.
TRANSACTIONS/CAREER NOTES: Signed as free agent by Boston Bruins (September 28, 1981).... Traded by Bruins to New York Rangers for C/RW Dave Silk (October 5, 1983).... Traded by Rangers with third-round pick in 1984 draft (G Alan Perry) and cash to St. Louis Blues for C Larry Patey and rights to RW Bob Brooke (March 5, 1984).... Sprained knee (March 19, 1986).... Traded by Blues to Hartford Whalers for D Tim Bothwell (October 21, 1986).... Traded by Whalers to Detroit Red Wings for D Randy Ladouceur (January 12, 1987).... Separated right shoulder (November 1987).... Broke right foot (December 1987).... Broke right ankle (March 14, 1991).... Sent to New Jersey Devils with RW Randy McKay as compensation for Red Wings signing free agent RW Troy Crowder (September 9, 1991).... Separated left shoulder (September 21, 1991); missed first nine games of season.... Lacerated tendon and artery in wrist (February 21, 1992); missed final 21 games of season.... Suffered from the flu (January 9, 1993); missed three games. ... Suffered sore foot (March 29, 1993); missed two games.... Signed as free agent by Dallas Stars (August 27, 1993).... Underwent arthroscopic elbow surgery (October 2, 1993); missed 13 games.

Season	Team	League	REGULAR SEASON Gms.	G	A	Pts.	PIM	PLAYOFFS Gms.	G	A	Pts.	PIM
77-78	Pincher Creek	AJHL	60	16	32	48	53	—	—	—	—	—
78-79	Edmonton	WHL	72	16	19	35	61	—	—	—	—	—
79-80	Lethbridge	WHL	60	16	38	54	47	—	—	—	—	—
80-81	Lethbridge	WHL	72	26	62	88	106	10	4	10	14	4
81-82	Erie	AHL	76	18	48	66	29	—	—	—	—	—
	Boston	NHL	2	0	0	0	0	5	1	0	1	0
82-83	Baltimore	AHL	72	27	51	78	67	—	—	—	—	—
	Boston	NHL	10	1	1	2	7	10	0	0	0	2
83-84	New York Rangers	NHL	6	0	0	0	2	—	—	—	—	—
	Tulsa	CHL	50	28	37	65	24	—	—	—	—	—
	St. Louis	NHL	1	0	0	0	0	5	0	1	1	15
84-85	St. Louis	NHL	75	16	18	34	32	2	0	0	0	2
85-86	St. Louis	NHL	72	13	38	51	70	11	1	1	2	14
86-87	St. Louis	NHL	2	0	0	0	0	—	—	—	—	—
	Hartford	NHL	30	2	4	6	19	—	—	—	—	—
	Detroit	NHL	37	13	13	26	49	13	1	0	1	14
87-88	Detroit	NHL	51	14	26	40	58	16	5	7	12	22

Season	Team	League	REGULAR SEASON					PLAYOFFS				
			Gms.	G	A	Pts.	PIM	Gms.	G	A	Pts.	PIM
88-89—Detroit	NHL		73	27	32	59	69	6	3	1	4	6
89-90—Detroit	NHL		62	10	25	35	45	—	—	—	—	—
—Adirondack	AHL		9	1	14	15	17	—	—	—	—	—
90-91—Detroit	NHL		70	18	22	40	55	—	—	—	—	—
91-92—New Jersey	NHL		41	6	12	18	32	—	—	—	—	—
—Utica	AHL		1	0	0	0	7	—	—	—	—	—
92-93—New Jersey	NHL		62	6	8	14	61	5	1	0	1	6
93-94—Dallas	NHL		20	2	5	7	21	3	0	1	1	4
—Kalamazoo	IHL		4	3	2	5	5	—	—	—	—	—
NHL totals			614	128	204	332	520	76	12	11	23	85

BARRASSO, TOM
G, PENGUINS

PERSONAL: Born March 31, 1965, in Boston.... 6-3/211.... Catches right.... Name pronounced buh-RAH-soh.

HIGH SCHOOL: Acton (Mass.)-Boxborough.

TRANSACTIONS/CAREER NOTES: Selected by Buffalo Sabres in first round (first Sabres pick, fifth overall) of NHL entry draft (June 8, 1983).... Suffered chip fracture of ankle (November 1987).... Pulled groin (April 9, 1988).... Traded by Sabres with third-round pick in 1990 draft (RW Joe Dziedzic) to Pittsburgh Penguins for D Doug Bodger and LW Darrin Shannon (November 12, 1988).... Pulled groin muscle (January 17, 1989).... Injured shoulder (March 1989).... Underwent surgery to right wrist (October 30, 1989); missed 21 games.... Pulled groin (February 1990). ... Granted leave of absence to be with daughter as she underwent cancer treatment in Los Angeles (February 9, 1990).... Rejoined the Penguins (March 19, 1990).... Bruised right hand (October 29, 1991); missed two games.... Bruised right ankle (December 26, 1991); missed three games.... Suffered back spasms (March 1992); missed three games.... Suffered from chicken pox (January 14, 1993); missed nine games.... Strained groin (October 7, 1993); missed four games.... Injured hip (November 18, 1993); missed 12 games.

HONORS: Won Vezina Trophy (1983-84).... Won Calder Memorial Trophy (1983-84).... Named to THE SPORTING NEWS All-Star second team (1983-84, 1984-85 and 1987-88).... Named to NHL All-Star first team (1983-84).... Named to NHL All-Rookie team (1983-84).... Shared William M. Jennings Trophy with Bob Sauve (1984-85).... Named to NHL All-Star second team (1984-85 and 1992-93).... Played in NHL All-Star Game (1985).... Named to THE SPORTING NEWS All-Star first team (1992-93).

RECORDS: Shares NHL single-season playoff record for most wins by a goaltender—16 (1991-92); most consecutive wins by a goaltender—11 (1992).

MISCELLANEOUS: Member of U.S. National Junior Team (1983).... Member of Stanley Cup championship teams (1991 and 1992).

Season	Team	League	REGULAR SEASON								PLAYOFFS						
			Gms.	Min.	W	L	T	GA	SO	Avg.	Gms.	Min.	W	L	GA	SO	Avg.
81-82—Acton-Boxborough HS	Mass. HS		23	1035	...	...	...	32	7	1.86	—	—	—	—	—	—	—
82-83—Acton-Boxborough HS	Mass. HS		23	1035	...	...	...	17	10	0.99	—	—	—	—	—	—	—
83-84—Buffalo	NHL		42	2475	26	12	3	117	2	2.84	3	139	0	2	8	0	3.45
84-85—Rochester	AHL		5	267	3	1	1	6	1	1.35	—	—	—	—	—	—	—
—Buffalo	NHL		54	3248	25	18	10	144	*5	*2.66	5	300	2	3	22	0	4.40
85-86—Buffalo	NHL		60	*3561	29	24	5	214	2	3.61	—	—	—	—	—	—	—
86-87—Buffalo	NHL		46	2501	17	23	2	152	2	3.65	—	—	—	—	—	—	—
87-88—Buffalo	NHL		54	3133	25	18	8	173	2	3.31	4	224	1	3	16	0	4.29
88-89—Buffalo	NHL		10	545	2	7	0	45	0	4.95	—	—	—	—	—	—	—
—Pittsburgh	NHL		44	2406	18	15	7	162	0	4.04	11	631	7	4	40	0	3.80
89-90—Pittsburgh	NHL		24	1294	7	12	3	101	0	4.68	—	—	—	—	—	—	—
90-91—Pittsburgh	NHL		48	2754	27	16	3	165	1	3.59	20	1175	12	7	51	†1	*2.60
91-92—Pittsburgh	NHL		57	3329	25	22	9	196	1	3.53	*21	*1233	*16	5	*58	1	2.82
92-93—Pittsburgh	NHL		63	3702	*43	14	5	186	4	3.01	12	722	7	5	35	2	2.91
93-94—Pittsburgh	NHL		44	2482	22	15	5	139	2	3.36	6	356	2	4	17	0	2.87
NHL totals			546	31430	266	196	60	1794	21	3.42	82	4780	47	33	247	4	3.10

BARRAULT, DOUGLAS
RW, PANTHERS

PERSONAL: Born April 21, 1970, in Golden, B.C.... 6-2/200.... Shoots right. ... Name pronounced buh-ROH.

TRANSACTIONS/CAREER NOTES: Selected by Minnesota North Stars in eighth round (eighth North Stars pick, 155th overall) of NHL entry draft (June 16, 1990).... Selected by Florida Panthers in NHL expansion draft (June 24, 1993).

HONORS: Named to WHL (West) All-Star second team (1990-91).

Season	Team	League	REGULAR SEASON					PLAYOFFS				
			Gms.	G	A	Pts.	PIM	Gms.	G	A	Pts.	PIM
88-89—Lethbridge	WHL		57	14	13	27	34	—	—	—	—	—
89-90—Lethbridge	WHL		54	14	16	30	36	19	7	3	10	0
90-91—Lethbridge	WHL		4	2	2	4	16	—	—	—	—	—
—Seattle	WHL		61	42	42	84	69	6	5	3	8	4
91-92—Kalamazoo	IHL		60	5	14	19	26	—	—	—	—	—
92-93—Kalamazoo	IHL		78	32	34	66	74	—	—	—	—	—
—Minnesota	NHL		2	0	0	0	0	—	—	—	—	—
93-94—Cincinnati	IHL		75	36	28	64	59	9	8	2	10	0
—Florida	NHL		2	0	0	0	0	—	—	—	—	—
NHL totals			4	0	0	0	2					

BARRIE, LEN
C, PANTHERS

PERSONAL: Born June 4, 1969, in Kimberley, B.C. . . . 6-0/190. . . . Shoots right.
TRANSACTIONS/CAREER NOTES: Selected by Edmonton Oilers in sixth round (seventh Oilers pick, 124th overall) of NHL entry draft (June 11, 1988). . . . Broke finger (March 1989). . . . Traded by Victoria Cougars to Kamloops Blazers for RW Mark Cipriano (August 1989). . . . Signed as free agent by Philadelphia Flyers (February 8, 1990). . . . Signed as free agent by Florida Panthers (July 20, 1993).
HONORS: Won CHL Plus/Minus Award (1989-90). . . . Won Bob Clarke Trophy (1989-90). . . . Named to WHL (West) All-Star first team (1989-90). . . . Named to IHL All-Star second team (1993-94).

			REGULAR SEASON					PLAYOFFS			
Season Team	League	Gms.	G	A	Pts.	PIM	Gms.	G	A	Pts.	PIM
85-86—Calgary Spurs	AJHL	23	7	14	21	86	—	—	—	—	—
—Calgary	WHL	32	3	0	3	18	—	—	—	—	—
86-87—Calgary	WHL	34	13	13	26	81	—	—	—	—	—
—Victoria	WHL	34	7	6	13	92	5	0	1	1	15
87-88—Victoria	WHL	70	37	49	86	192	8	2	0	2	29
88-89—Victoria	WHL	67	39	48	87	157	7	5	2	7	23
89-90—Philadelphia	NHL	1	0	0	0	0	—	—	—	—	—
—Kamloops	WHL	70	*85	*100	*185	108	17	†14	23	†37	24
90-91—Hershey	AHL	63	26	32	58	60	7	4	0	4	12
91-92—Hershey	AHL	75	42	43	85	78	3	0	2	2	32
92-93—Hershey	AHL	61	31	45	76	162	—	—	—	—	—
—Philadelphia	NHL	8	2	2	4	9	—	—	—	—	—
93-94—Cincinnati	IHL	77	45	71	116	246	11	8	13	21	60
—Florida	NHL	2	0	0	0	0	—	—	—	—	—
NHL totals		11	2	2	4	9					

BASSEN, BOB
C, NORDIQUES

PERSONAL: Born May 6, 1965, in Calgary. . . . 5-10/180. . . . Shoots left. . . . Name pronounced BA-suhn. . . . Son of Hank Bassen, goalie, Chicago Blackhawks, Detroit Red Wings and Pittsburgh Penguins (1954-55 through 1967-68).
HIGH SCHOOL: Sir Winston Churchill (Calgary).
TRANSACTIONS/CAREER NOTES: Signed as free agent by New York Islanders (October 19, 1984). . . . Injured knee (October 12, 1985). . . . Traded by Islanders with D Steve Konroyd to Chicago Blackhawks for D Gary Nylund and D Marc Bergevin (November 25, 1988). . . . Selected by St. Louis Blues in 1990 waiver draft for $25,000 (October 2, 1990). . . . Broke right foot (December 4, 1992); missed 22 games. . . . Broke finger (January 28, 1993); missed nine games. . . . Traded by Blues with C Ron Sutter and D Garth Butcher to Quebec Nordiques for D Steve Duchesne and RW Denis Chasse (January 23, 1994). . . . Lacerated left eye (March 30, 1994); missed one game.
HONORS: Named to WHL (East) All-Star first team (1984-85). . . . Named to IHL All-Star first team (1989-90).

			REGULAR SEASON					PLAYOFFS			
Season Team	League	Gms.	G	A	Pts.	PIM	Gms.	G	A	Pts.	PIM
82-83—Medicine Hat	WHL	4	3	2	5	0	3	0	0	0	4
83-84—Medicine Hat	WHL	72	29	29	58	93	14	5	11	16	12
84-85—Medicine Hat	WHL	65	32	50	82	143	10	2	8	10	39
85-86—New York Islanders	NHL	11	2	1	3	6	3	0	1	1	0
—Springfield	AHL	54	13	21	34	111	—	—	—	—	—
86-87—New York Islanders	NHL	77	7	10	17	89	14	1	2	3	21
87-88—New York Islanders	NHL	77	6	16	22	99	6	0	1	1	23
88-89—New York Islanders	NHL	19	1	4	5	21	—	—	—	—	—
—Chicago	NHL	49	4	12	16	62	10	1	1	2	34
89-90—Indianapolis	IHL	73	22	32	54	179	12	3	8	11	33
—Chicago	NHL	6	1	1	2	8	—	—	—	—	—
90-91—St. Louis	NHL	79	16	18	34	183	13	1	3	4	24
91-92—St. Louis	NHL	79	7	25	32	167	6	0	2	2	4
92-93—St. Louis	NHL	53	9	10	19	63	11	0	0	0	10
93-94—St. Louis	NHL	46	2	7	9	44	—	—	—	—	—
—Quebec	NHL	37	11	8	19	55	—	—	—	—	—
NHL totals		533	66	112	178	797	63	3	10	13	116

BATES, SHAWN
C, BRUINS

PERSONAL: Born April 3, 1975, in Melrose, Mass. . . . 5-11/170. . . . Shoots right.
HIGH SCHOOL: Medford (Mass.).
COLLEGE: Boston University.
TRANSACTIONS/CAREER NOTES: Selected by Boston Bruins in fourth round (fourth Bruins pick, 103rd overall) of NHL entry draft (June 26, 1993).
HONORS: Named to Hockey East All-Rookie team (1993-94).

			REGULAR SEASON					PLAYOFFS			
Season Team	League	Gms.	G	A	Pts.	PIM	Gms.	G	A	Pts.	PIM
90-91—Medford H.S.	Mass. H.S.	22	18	43	61	6	—	—	—	—	—
91-92—Medford H.S.	Mass. H.S.	22	38	41	79	10	—	—	—	—	—
92-93—Medford H.S.	Mass. H.S.	25	49	46	95	20	—	—	—	—	—
93-94—Boston University	Hockey East	41	10	19	29	24	—	—	—	—	—

BATTAGLIA, DOUG
LW, RED WINGS

PERSONAL: Born October 26, 1975, in Newmarket, Ont. . . . 6-0/185. . . . Shoots left.
TRANSACTIONS/CAREER NOTES: Selected by Detroit Red Wings in fifth round (fifth Red Wings pick, 127th overall) of NHL entry draft (June 29, 1994).

Season Team	League	REGULAR SEASON					PLAYOFFS				
		Gms.	G	A	Pts.	PIM	Gms.	G	A	Pts.	PIM
93-94—Brockville	COJHL	47	35	39	74	212	—	—	—	—	—

BATTAGLIA, JON
LW, MIGHTY DUCKS

PERSONAL: Born December 13, 1975, in Chicago. . . . 6-2/185. . . . Shoots left. **TRANSACTIONS/CAREER NOTES:** Selected by Mighty Ducks of Anaheim in sixth round (sixth Mighty Ducks pick, 132nd overall) of NHL entry draft (June 29, 1994).

Season Team	League	REGULAR SEASON					PLAYOFFS				
		Gms.	G	A	Pts.	PIM	Gms.	G	A	Pts.	PIM
93-94—Caledon	Jr. A	44	15	33	48	104	—	—	—	—	—

BATTERS, JEFF
D, BLUES

PERSONAL: Born October 23, 1970, in Victoria, B.C. . . . 6-2/210. . . . Shoots right. . . . Full name: Jeffrey William Batters. **COLLEGE:** Alaska-Anchorage. **TRANSACTIONS/CAREER NOTES:** Selected by St. Louis Blues in seventh round (seventh Blues pick, 135th overall) of NHL entry draft (June 17, 1989).

Season Team	League	REGULAR SEASON					PLAYOFFS				
		Gms.	G	A	Pts.	PIM	Gms.	G	A	Pts.	PIM
88-89—Alaska-Anchorage	Indep.	33	8	14	22	123	—	—	—	—	—
89-90—Alaska-Anchorage	Indep.	34	6	9	15	102	—	—	—	—	—
90-91—Alaska-Anchorage	Indep.	39	16	14	30	90	—	—	—	—	—
91-92—Alaska-Anchorage	Indep.	34	6	17	23	86	—	—	—	—	—
92-93—Peoria	IHL	74	5	18	23	113	4	0	0	0	10
93-94—Peoria	IHL	59	3	9	12	175	6	0	0	0	18
—St. Louis	NHL	6	0	0	0	7	—	—	—	—	—
NHL totals		6	0	0	0	7					

BAUER, COLLIN
D, STARS

PERSONAL: Born September 6, 1970, in Edmonton. . . . 6-2/185. . . . Shoots left. **TRANSACTIONS/CAREER NOTES:** Selected by Edmonton Oilers in third round (fourth Oilers pick, 61st overall) of NHL entry draft (June 11, 1988). . . . Fractured three vertebrae and a rib (November 11, 1990). . . . Traded by Oilers to Minnesota North Stars for future consideration (August 4, 1992). . . . North Stars franchise moved from Minnesota to Dallas and renamed Stars for 1993-94 season. **HONORS:** Named to WHL (East) All-Star team (1988-89).

Season Team	League	REGULAR SEASON					PLAYOFFS				
		Gms.	G	A	Pts.	PIM	Gms.	G	A	Pts.	PIM
86-87—Saskatoon	WHL	61	1	25	26	37	11	0	6	6	10
87-88—Saskatoon	WHL	70	9	53	62	66	10	2	5	7	16
88-89—Saskatoon	WHL	61	17	62	79	71	8	1	8	9	8
89-90—Saskatoon	WHL	29	4	25	29	49	10	1	8	9	14
90-91—Cape Breton	AHL	40	4	14	18	18	4	1	1	2	4
91-92—Cape Breton	AHL	55	7	15	22	36	3	0	0	0	7
92-93—Kalamazoo	IHL	32	4	14	18	31	—	—	—	—	—
93-94—Kalamazoo	IHL	66	3	19	22	56	5	0	1	1	6

BAUMGARTNER, KEN
D/LW, MAPLE LEAFS

PERSONAL: Born March 11, 1966, in Flin Flon, Man. . . . 6-1/205. . . . Shoots left. . . . Full name: Ken James Baumgartner. **TRANSACTIONS/CAREER NOTES:** Selected by Buffalo Sabres as underage junior in 12th round (12th Sabres pick, 245th overall) of NHL entry draft (June 15, 1985). . . . Traded by Sabres with D Larry Playfair and RW Sean McKenna to Los Angeles Kings for D Brian Engblom and C Doug Smith (January 29, 1986). . . . Traded by Kings with C Hubie McDonough to New York Islanders for RW Mikko Makela (November 29, 1989). . . . Suspended one game by NHL for fighting (April 5, 1990). . . . Fractured right orbital bone (December 19, 1991); missed 14 games. . . . Traded by Islanders with C Dave McLlwain to Toronto Maple Leafs for C Claude Loiselle and RW Daniel Marois (March 10, 1992). . . . Broke bone in wrist (February 28, 1994); missed remainder of season.

Season Team	League	REGULAR SEASON					PLAYOFFS				
		Gms.	G	A	Pts.	PIM	Gms.	G	A	Pts.	PIM
83-84—Prince Albert	WHL	57	1	6	7	203	—	—	—	—	—
84-85—Prince Albert	WHL	60	3	9	12	252	13	1	3	4	*89
85-86—Prince Albert	WHL	70	4	23	27	277	20	3	9	12	112
86-87—Chur	Switzerland					Statistics unavailable.					
—New Haven	AHL	13	0	3	3	99	6	0	0	0	60
87-88—Los Angeles	NHL	30	2	3	5	189	5	0	1	1	28
—New Haven	AHL	48	1	5	6	181	—	—	—	—	—
88-89—Los Angeles	NHL	49	1	3	4	286	5	0	0	0	8
—New Haven	AHL	10	1	3	4	26	—	—	—	—	—
89-90—Los Angeles	NHL	12	1	0	1	28	—	—	—	—	—
—New York Islanders	NHL	53	0	5	5	194	4	0	0	0	27
90-91—New York Islanders	NHL	78	1	6	7	282	—	—	—	—	—
91-92—New York Islanders	NHL	44	0	1	1	202	—	—	—	—	—
—Toronto	NHL	11	0	0	0	23	—	—	—	—	—
92-93—Toronto	NHL	63	1	0	1	155	7	1	0	1	0
93-94—Toronto	NHL	64	4	4	8	185	10	0	0	0	18
NHL totals		404	10	22	32	1544	31	1	1	2	81

BAUMGARTNER, NOLAN
D, CAPITALS

PERSONAL: Born March 23, 1976, in Calgary. . . . 6-1/187. . . . Shoots right.
HIGH SCHOOL: Norkam Secondary (Kamloops, B.C.).
TRANSACTIONS/CAREER NOTES: Selected by Washington Capitals in first round (first Capitals pick, 10th overall) of NHL entry draft (June 28, 1994).
HONORS: Named to Memorial Cup All-Star team (1993-94).

			REGULAR SEASON					PLAYOFFS			
Season Team	League	Gms.	G	A	Pts.	PIM	Gms.	G	A	Pts.	PIM
92-93—Kamloops	WHL	43	0	5	5	30	11	1	1	2	0
93-94—Kamloops	WHL	69	13	42	55	109	19	3	14	17	33

BAUTIN, SERGEI
D, RED WINGS

PERSONAL: Born March 11, 1967, in Murmansk, U.S.S.R. . . . 6-3/218. . . . Shoots left. . . . Name pronounced ba-OO-tihn.
TRANSACTIONS/CAREER NOTES: Selected by Winnipeg Jets in first round (first Jets pick, 17th overall) of NHL entry draft (June 20, 1992). . . . Injured hip (December 29, 1993); missed one game. . . . Reinjured hip (January 2, 1993); missed two games. . . . Fractured foot (February 28, 1993); missed nine games. . . . Bruised foot (October 6, 1993); missed three games. . . . Traded by Jets with G Bob Essensa to Detroit Red Wings for G Tim Cheveldae and LW Dallas Drake (March 8, 1994).

			REGULAR SEASON					PLAYOFFS			
Season Team	League	Gms.	G	A	Pts.	PIM	Gms.	G	A	Pts.	PIM
90-91—Dynamo Moscow	USSR	33	2	0	2	28	—	—	—	—	—
91-92—Dynamo Moscow	CIS	37	1	3	4	88	—	—	—	—	—
—Unified Olympic Team	Int'l	8	0	0	0	6	—	—	—	—	—
92-93—Winnipeg	NHL	71	5	18	23	96	6	0	0	0	2
93-94—Winnipeg	NHL	59	0	7	7	78	—	—	—	—	—
—Detroit	NHL	1	0	0	0	0	—	—	—	—	—
—Adirondack	AHL	9	1	5	6	6	—	—	—	—	—
NHL totals		131	5	25	30	174	6	0	0	0	2

BAVIS, MARK
C, RANGERS

PERSONAL: Born March 13, 1970, in Roslindale, Mass. . . . 6-0/175. . . . Shoots left. . . . Full name: Mark Lawrence Bavis. . . . Name pronounced BAY-vihz.
HIGH SCHOOL: Catholic Memorial (Boston), then Cushing Academy (Ashburnham, Mass.).
COLLEGE: Boston University.
TRANSACTIONS/CAREER NOTES: Selected by New York Rangers in ninth round (10th Rangers pick, 181st overall) of NHL entry draft (June 17, 1989).

			REGULAR SEASON					PLAYOFFS			
Season Team	League	Gms.	G	A	Pts.	PIM	Gms.	G	A	Pts.	PIM
87-88—Catholic Memorial H.S.	Mass. H.S.	19	16	26	42	...	—	—	—	—	—
88-89—Cushing Academy	Mass. H.S.	29	27	31	58	18	—	—	—	—	—
89-90—Boston University	Hockey East	44	6	5	11	50	—	—	—	—	—
90-91—Boston University	Hockey East	40	5	18	23	47	—	—	—	—	—
91-92—Boston University	Hockey East	35	9	18	27	30	—	—	—	—	—
92-93—Boston University	Hockey East	40	14	10	24	58	—	—	—	—	—
93-94—Providence	AHL	12	2	5	7	18	—	—	—	—	—
—Fredericton	AHL	45	7	10	17	86	—	—	—	—	—

BAWA, ROBIN
RW, MIGHTY DUCKS

PERSONAL: Born March 26, 1966, in Chemainus, B.C. . . . 6-2/215. . . . Shoots right. . . . Name pronounced BAH-wah.
TRANSACTIONS/CAREER NOTES: Signed as free agent by Washington Capitals (May 22, 1987). . . . Traded by Capitals to Vancouver Canucks for future considerations (August 1, 1991). . . . Traded by Canucks to San Jose Sharks for D Rick Lessard (December 15, 1992). . . . Suffered from the flu (January 30, 1993); missed three games. . . . Injured ankle (April 9, 1993); missed one game. . . . Selected by Mighty Ducks of Anaheim in NHL expansion draft (June 24, 1993). . . . Pulled groin (October 12, 1993); missed four games.
HONORS: Named to WHL (West) All-Star first team (1986-87).

			REGULAR SEASON					PLAYOFFS			
Season Team	League	Gms.	G	A	Pts.	PIM	Gms.	G	A	Pts.	PIM
82-83—Kamloops	WHL	66	10	24	34	17	7	1	2	3	0
83-84—Kamloops	WHL	64	16	28	44	40	13	4	2	6	4
84-85—New Westminster	WHL	26	4	6	10	20	—	—	—	—	—
—Kamloops	WHL	26	2	13	15	25	15	4	9	13	14
85-86—Kamloops	WHL	63	29	43	72	78	16	5	13	18	4
86-87—Kamloops	WHL	62	57	56	113	91	13	6	7	13	22
87-88—Fort Wayne	IHL	55	12	27	39	239	6	1	3	4	24
88-89—Baltimore	AHL	75	23	24	47	205	—	—	—	—	—
89-90—Baltimore	AHL	61	7	18	25	189	11	1	2	3	49
—Washington	NHL	5	1	0	1	6	—	—	—	—	—
90-91—Fort Wayne	IHL	72	21	26	47	381	18	4	4	8	87
91-92—Milwaukee	IHL	70	27	14	41	238	5	2	2	4	8
—Vancouver	NHL	2	0	0	0	0	1	0	0	0	0
92-93—Hamilton	AHL	23	3	4	7	58	—	—	—	—	—
—Kansas City	IHL	5	2	0	2	20	—	—	—	—	—
—San Jose	NHL	42	5	0	5	47	—	—	—	—	—

Season Team	League	Gms.	G	A	Pts.	PIM	Gms.	G	A	Pts.	PIM
93-94—Anaheim	NHL	12	0	1	1	7	—	—	—	—	—
—San Diego	IHL	25	6	15	21	54	6	0	0	0	52
NHL totals		61	6	1	7	60	1	0	0	0	0

BEAUBIEN, FREDERICK
G, KINGS

PERSONAL: Born April 1, 1975, in Levis, Que.... 6-1/204.... Catches left.
TRANSACTIONS/CAREER NOTES: Selected by Los Angeles Kings in fifth round (fourth Kings pick, 105th overall) of NHL entry draft (June 26, 1993).

Season Team	League	Gms.	Min.	W	L	T	GA	SO	Avg.	Gms.	Min.	W	L	GA	SO	Avg.
92-93—St. Hyacinthe	QMJHL	33	1702	8	16	3	133	0	4.69	—	—	—	—	—	—	—
93-94—St. Hyacinthe	QMJHL	47	2663	19	19	5	168	1	3.79	7	411	3	4	33	0	4.82

BEAUFAIT, MARK
C, SHARKS

PERSONAL: Born May 13, 1970, in Livonia, Mich.... 5-9/165.... Shoots right.... Name pronounced boh-FAY.
COLLEGE: Northern Michigan.
TRANSACTIONS/CAREER NOTES: Selected by San Jose Sharks in NHL supplemental draft (June 21, 1991).
HONORS: Won Ken McKenzie Trophy (1992-93).

Season Team	League	Gms.	G	A	Pts.	PIM	Gms.	G	A	Pts.	PIM
88-89—Northern Michigan Univ...	WCHA	11	2	1	3	2	—	—	—	—	—
89-90—Northern Michigan Univ...	WCHA	34	10	14	24	12	—	—	—	—	—
90-91—Northern Michigan Univ...	WCHA	47	19	30	49	18	—	—	—	—	—
91-92—Northern Michigan Univ...	WCHA	41	31	50	81	47	—	—	—	—	—
92-93—Kansas City	IHL	66	19	40	59	22	9	1	1	2	8
—San Jose	NHL	5	1	0	1	0	—	—	—	—	—
93-94—U.S. national team	Int'l	51	22	29	51	36	—	—	—	—	—
—U.S. Olympic Team	Int'l	8	1	4	5	2	—	—	—	—	—
—Kansas City	IHL	21	12	9	21	18	—	—	—	—	—
NHL totals		5	1	0	1	0					

BEAUPRE, DON
G, CAPITALS

PERSONAL: Born September 19, 1961, in Kitchener, Ont.... 5-10/172.... Catches left.... Full name: Donald William Beaupre.... Name pronounced boh-PRAY.
TRANSACTIONS/CAREER NOTES: Selected by Minnesota North Stars as underage junior in second round (second North Stars pick, 37th overall) of NHL entry draft (June 11, 1980).... Bruised ribs (October 1981).... Sprained knee (February 1985).... Pulled groin muscle (December 1987).... Traded by North Stars to Washington Capitals for rights to D Claudio Scremin (November 1, 1988).... Injured ligaments in right thumb (January 31, 1990); missed nine games.... Pulled left groin (October 30, 1990); missed 12 games.... Pulled muscle (November 5, 1992); missed three games.... Pulled groin (January 2, 1993); missed two games.
HONORS: Named to OMJHL All-Star first team (1979-80).... Played in NHL All-Star Game (1981 and 1992).

Season Team	League	Gms.	Min.	W	L	T	GA	SO	Avg.	Gms.	Min.	W	L	GA	SO	Avg.
78-79—Sudbury	OMJHL	54	3248	...	...	...	*259	2	4.78	10	600	...	...	44	...	4.40
79-80—Sudbury	OMJHL	59	3447	28	29	2	248	0	4.32	9	552	5	4	38	0	4.13
80-81—Minnesota	NHL	44	2585	18	14	11	138	0	3.20	6	360	4	2	26	0	4.33
81-82—Nashville	CHL	5	299	2	3	0	25	0	5.02	—	—	—	—	—	—	—
—Minnesota	NHL	29	1634	11	8	9	101	0	3.71	2	60	0	1	4	0	4.00
82-83—Birmingham	CHL	10	599	8	2	0	31	0	3.11	—	—	—	—	—	—	—
—Minnesota	NHL	36	2011	19	10	5	120	0	3.58	4	245	2	2	20	0	4.90
83-84—Salt Lake City	CHL	7	419	2	5	0	30	0	4.30	—	—	—	—	—	—	—
—Minnesota	NHL	33	1791	16	13	2	123	0	4.12	13	782	6	7	40	1	3.07
84-85—Minnesota	NHL	31	1770	10	17	3	109	1	3.69	4	184	1	1	12	0	3.91
85-86—Minnesota	NHL	52	3073	25	20	6	182	1	3.55	5	300	2	3	17	0	3.40
86-87—Minnesota	NHL	47	2622	17	20	6	174	1	3.98	—	—	—	—	—	—	—
87-88—Minnesota	NHL	43	2288	10	22	3	161	0	4.22	—	—	—	—	—	—	—
88-89—Minnesota	NHL	1	59	0	1	0	3	0	3.05	—	—	—	—	—	—	—
—Kalamazoo	IHL	3	179	1	2	‡0	9	0	3.02	—	—	—	—	—	—	—
—Baltimore	AHL	30	1715	14	12	2	102	0	3.57	—	—	—	—	—	—	—
—Washington	NHL	11	578	5	4	0	28	1	2.91	—	—	—	—	—	—	—
89-90—Washington	NHL	48	2793	23	18	5	150	2	3.22	8	401	4	3	18	0	2.69
90-91—Baltimore	AHL	2	120	2	0	0	3	0	1.50	—	—	—	—	—	—	—
—Washington	NHL	45	2572	20	18	3	113	*5	2.64	11	624	5	5	29	†1	2.79
91-92—Baltimore	AHL	3	184	1	1	1	10	0	3.26	—	—	—	—	—	—	—
—Washington	NHL	54	3108	29	17	6	166	1	3.20	7	419	3	4	22	0	3.15
92-93—Washington	NHL	58	3282	27	23	5	181	1	3.31	2	119	1	1	9	0	4.54
93-94—Washington	NHL	53	2853	24	16	8	135	2	2.84	8	429	5	2	21	1	2.94
NHL totals		585	33019	254	221	72	1884	15	3.42	70	3923	33	31	218	3	3.33

BEAUREGARD, STEPHANE

G, JETS

PERSONAL: Born January 10, 1968, in Cowansville, Que.... 5-11/190. ... Catches right.... Name pronounced BOH-ree-gahrd.

TRANSACTIONS/CAREER NOTES: Selected by Winnipeg Jets in third round (third Jets pick, 52nd overall) of NHL entry draft (June 11, 1988).... Suffered hip flexor (October 29, 1991); missed four games.... Traded by Jets to Buffalo Sabres for C Christian Ruuttu and future considerations (June 15, 1992).... Traded by Sabres with future considerations to Chicago Blackhawks for G Dominik Hasek (August 7, 1992).... Traded by Blackhawks to Jets for C Christian Ruuttu and future considerations (August 10, 1992). ... Traded by Jets to Philadelphia Flyers for third-round pick in 1993 draft and fifth-round pick in 1994 draft (October 1, 1992).... Traded by Flyers to Jets for third-round pick in 1993 draft and future considerations (February 8, 1993); trade nullified by NHL, citing league bylaw that prohibits trading player within month of waiver draft and reacquiring him later in season (February 9, 1993).... Traded by Flyers to Jets for fourth-round pick in 1993 draft and fifth-round pick in 1994 draft (June 11, 1993).... Suffered from the flu (October 26, 1993); missed two games.

HONORS: Won Jacques Plante Trophy (1987-88).... Won Raymond Lagace Trophy (1987-88).... Won Marcel Robert Trophy (1987-88).... Named to QMJHL All-Star first team (1987-88).

					REGULAR SEASON							PLAYOFFS					
Season Team	League	Gms.	Min.	W	L	T	GA	SO	Avg.	Gms.	Min.	W	L	GA	SO	Avg.
86-87—St. Jean	QMJHL	13	785	6	7	0	58	0	4.43	5	260	1	3	26	0	6.00
87-88—St. Jean	QMJHL	*66	*3766	38	20	3	229	2	*3.65	7	423	3	4	34	0	4.82
88-89—Moncton	AHL	15	824	4	8	2	62	0	4.51	—	—	—	—	—	—	—
—Fort Wayne	IHL	16	830	9	5	‡0	43	0	3.11	9	484	4	4	21	*1	*2.60
89-90—Fort Wayne	IHL	33	1949	20	8	‡3	115	1	3.54	—	—	—	—	—	—	—
—Winnipeg	NHL	19	1079	7	8	3	59	0	3.28	4	238	1	3	12	0	3.03
90-91—Winnipeg	NHL	16	836	3	10	1	55	0	3.95	—	—	—	—	—	—	—
—Moncton	AHL	9	504	3	4	1	20	1	2.38	1	60	1	0	1	0	1.00
—Fort Wayne	IHL	32	1761	14	13	‡2	109	0	3.71	*19	*1158	10	9	57	2	2.95
91-92—Winnipeg	NHL	26	1267	6	8	6	61	2	2.89	—	—	—	—	—	—	—
92-93—Philadelphia	NHL	16	802	3	9	0	59	0	4.41	—	—	—	—	—	—	—
—Hershey	AHL	13	794	5	5	3	48	0	3.63	—	—	—	—	—	—	—
93-94—Winnipeg	NHL	13	418	0	4	1	34	0	4.88	—	—	—	—	—	—	—
—Moncton	AHL	37	2083	18	11	6	121	1	3.49	21	*1304	†12	*9	58	*2	2.62
NHL totals		90	4402	19	39	11	268	2	3.65	4	238	1	3	12	0	3.03

BEDDOES, CLAYTON

C, BRUINS

PERSONAL: Born November 10, 1970, in Bentley, Alta.... 5-10/180.... Shoots left.

HIGH SCHOOL: Bentley (Alta.).

COLLEGE: Lake Superior State (Mich.).

TRANSACTIONS/CAREER NOTES: Signed as free agent by Boston Bruins (May 24, 1994).

HONORS: Named to NCAA All-America second team (1993-94).... Named to CCHA All-Star second team (1993-94).

			REGULAR SEASON				PLAYOFFS				
Season Team	League	Gms.	G	A	Pts.	PIM	Gms.	G	A	Pts.	PIM
90-91—Lake Superior State	CCHA	45	14	28	42	26	—	—	—	—	—
91-92—Lake Superior State	CCHA	42	16	28	44	26	—	—	—	—	—
92-93—Lake Superior State	CCHA	45	18	40	58	32	—	—	—	—	—
93-94—Lake Superior State	CCHA	44	23	31	54	56	—	—	—	—	—

BEERS, BOB

D, OILERS

PERSONAL: Born May 20, 1967, in Pittsburgh.... 6-2/200.... Shoots right.

COLLEGE: Northern Arizona, then Maine.

TRANSACTIONS/CAREER NOTES: Selected by Boston Bruins in 11th round (10th Bruins pick, 220th overall) of NHL entry draft (June 15, 1985).... Broke right leg (May 9, 1990).... Underwent surgery to remove pin from right hip (December 10, 1990); missed four games.... Suffered tendinitis in right hip (January 6, 1991).... Traded by Bruins to Tampa Bay Lightning for D Stephane Richer (October 28, 1992).... Traded by Lightning to Edmonton Oilers for D Chris Joseph (November 12, 1993).

HONORS: Named to NCAA All-America East second team (1988-89).... Named to Hockey East All-Star second team (1988-89).

			REGULAR SEASON				PLAYOFFS				
Season Team	League	Gms.	G	A	Pts.	PIM	Gms.	G	A	Pts.	PIM
85-86—Northern Arizona Univ.	Indep.	28	11	39	50	96	—	—	—	—	—
86-87—University of Maine	Hockey East	38	0	13	13	46	—	—	—	—	—
87-88—University of Maine	Hockey East	41	3	11	14	72	—	—	—	—	—
88-89—University of Maine	Hockey East	44	10	27	37	53	—	—	—	—	—
89-90—Maine	AHL	74	7	36	43	63	—	—	—	—	—
—Boston	NHL	3	0	1	1	6	14	1	1	2	18
90-91—Maine	AHL	36	2	16	18	21	—	—	—	—	—
—Boston	NHL	16	0	1	1	10	6	0	0	0	4
91-92—Boston	NHL	31	0	5	5	29	1	0	0	0	0
—Maine	AHL	33	6	23	29	24	—	—	—	—	—
92-93—Providence	AHL	6	1	2	3	10	—	—	—	—	—
—Tampa Bay	NHL	64	12	24	36	70	—	—	—	—	—
—Atlanta	IHL	1	0	0	0	0	—	—	—	—	—
93-94—Tampa Bay	NHL	16	1	5	6	12	—	—	—	—	—
—Edmonton	NHL	66	10	27	37	74	—	—	—	—	—
NHL totals		196	23	63	86	201	21	1	1	2	22

BELAK, WADE

D, NORDIQUES

PERSONAL: Born July 3, 1976, in North Battleford, Sask.... 6-4/213.... Shoots right.
HIGH SCHOOL: North Battleford (Sask.) Comprehensive.
TRANSACTIONS/CAREER NOTES: Selected by Quebec Nordiques in first round (first Nordiques pick, 12th overall) of NHL entry draft (June 28, 1994).

			REGULAR SEASON					PLAYOFFS				
Season Team	League	Gms.	G	A	Pts.	PIM	Gms.	G	A	Pts.	PIM
91-92—North Battleford	SJHL	57	6	20	26	186	—	—	—	—	—
92-93—North Battleford	SJHL	32	3	13	16	142	—	—	—	—	—
93-94—Saskatoon	WHL	69	4	13	17	226	16	2	2	4	43

BELANGER, JESSE

C, PANTHERS

PERSONAL: Born June 15, 1969, in St. Georges Beauce, Que.... 6-0/170.... Shoots right.... Name pronounced buh-LAHN-zhay.
TRANSACTIONS/CAREER NOTES: Signed as free agent by Montreal Canadiens (October 3, 1990).... Selected by Florida Panthers in NHL expansion draft (June 24, 1993).... Strained right Achilles tendon (October 12, 1993); missed one game.... Broke bone in left hand (February 13, 1994); missed 12 games.
MISCELLANEOUS: Member of Stanley Cup championship team (1993).

			REGULAR SEASON					PLAYOFFS				
Season Team	League	Gms.	G	A	Pts.	PIM	Gms.	G	A	Pts.	PIM
87-88—Granby	QMJHL	69	33	43	76	10	5	3	3	6	0
88-89—Granby	QMJHL	67	40	63	103	26	4	0	5	5	0
89-90—Granby	QMJHL	67	53	54	107	53	—	—	—	—	—
90-91—Fredericton	AHL	75	40	58	98	30	6	2	4	6	0
91-92—Fredericton	AHL	65	30	41	71	26	7	3	3	6	2
—Montreal	NHL	4	0	0	0	0	—	—	—	—	—
92-93—Fredericton	AHL	39	19	32	51	24	—	—	—	—	—
—Montreal	NHL	19	4	2	6	4	9	0	1	1	0
93-94—Florida	NHL	70	17	33	50	16	—	—	—	—	—
NHL totals		93	21	35	56	20	9	0	1	1	0

BELANGER, MARTIN

D, CANADIENS

PERSONAL: Born February 3, 1976, in La Salle, Que.... 6-0/206.... Shoots right.... Name pronounced Mahr-TAN Bay-lahn-ZHAY.
TRANSACTIONS/CAREER NOTES: Selected by Montreal Canadiens in third round (fifth Canadiens pick, 74th overall) of NHL entry draft (June 29, 1994).

			REGULAR SEASON					PLAYOFFS				
Season Team	League	Gms.	G	A	Pts.	PIM	Gms.	G	A	Pts.	PIM
92-93—Granby	QMJHL	49	2	19	21	24	—	—	—	—	—
93-94—Granby	QMJHL	63	8	32	40	49	7	0	1	1	28

BELFOUR, ED

G, BLACKHAWKS

PERSONAL: Born April 21, 1965, in Carman, Man.... 5-11/182.... Catches left.
COLLEGE: North Dakota.
TRANSACTIONS/CAREER NOTES: Signed as free agent by Chicago Blackhawks (June 18, 1987).... Strained hip muscle (1993-94 season); missed four games.
HONORS: Named top goaltender in Manitoba Junior Hockey League (1985-86).... Named to NCAA All-America West second team (1986-87).... Named to NCAA All-Tournament team (1986-87).... Named to WCHA All-Star first team (1986-87).... Shared Garry F. Longman Memorial Trophy with John Cullen (1987-88).... Named to IHL All-Star first team (1987-88).... Named Rookie of the Year by THE SPORTING NEWS (1990-91).... Won Vezina Trophy (1990-91 and 1992-93).... Won Calder Memorial Trophy (1990-91).... Won William M. Jennings Trophy (1990-91 and 1992-93).... Won Trico Goaltender Award (1990-91).... Named to THE SPORTING NEWS All-Star first team (1990-91).... Named to NHL All-Star first team (1990-91 and 1992-93).... Named to NHL All-Rookie team (1990-91).... Played in NHL All-Star Game (1992 and 1993). ...Named to THE SPORTING NEWS All-Star second team (1992-93).
RECORDS: Shares NHL single-season playoff record for most consecutive wins by goaltender—11 (1992).

			REGULAR SEASON							PLAYOFFS						
Season Team	League	Gms.	Min.	W	L	T	GA	SO	Avg.	Gms.	Min.	W	L	GA	SO	Avg.
85-86—Winkler	MJHL	48	2880	...	...	...	124	1	2.58	—	—	—	—	—	—	—
86-87—Univ. of North Dakota	WCHA	34	2049	29	4	0	81	3	2.37	—	—	—	—	—	—	—
87-88—Saginaw	IHL	61	*3446	32	25	‡0	183	3	3.19	9	561	4	5	33	0	3.53
88-89—Chicago	NHL	23	1148	4	12	3	74	0	3.87	—	—	—	—	—	—	—
—Saginaw	IHL	29	1760	12	10	‡0	92	0	3.14	5	298	2	3	14	0	2.82
89-90—Can. national team	Int'l	33	1808	...	...	...	93	...	3.09	—	—	—	—	—	—	—
—Chicago	NHL	—	—	—	—	—	—	—	—	9	409	4	2	17	0	2.49
90-91—Chicago	NHL	*74	*4127	*43	19	7	170	4	*2.47	6	295	2	4	20	0	4.07
91-92—Chicago	NHL	52	2928	21	18	10	132	†5	2.70	18	949	12	4	39	1	*2.47
92-93—Chicago	NHL	*71	*4106	41	18	11	177	*7	2.59	4	249	0	4	13	0	3.13
93-94—Chicago	NHL	70	3998	37	24	6	178	†7	2.67	6	360	2	4	15	0	2.50
NHL totals		290	16307	146	91	37	731	23	2.69	43	2262	20	18	104	1	2.76

BELLOWS, BRIAN

LW, CANADIENS

PERSONAL: Born September 1, 1964, in St. Catharines, Ont.... 5-11/209.... Shoots right.
TRANSACTIONS/CAREER NOTES: Separated shoulder (November 1981); coached Kitchener Rangers for two games while recovering (became the youngest coach in OHL history at 17 years old).... Selected by Minnesota North Stars as underage junior in first round (first North Stars pick, second

overall) of NHL entry draft (June 9, 1982).... Suffered tendinitis in elbow (October 1984).... Injured wrist (October 1986); missed 13 games.... Strained abdominal muscles (February 1989); missed 20 games.... Bruised left knee (September 1990). ... Strained hip and groin (December 18, 1990).... Traded by North Stars to Montreal Canadiens for RW Russ Courtnall (August 31, 1992).... Injured neck (December 3, 1992); missed two games.... Injured rib cage (November 20, 1993); missed seven games.

HONORS: Named to Memorial Cup All-Star team (1980-81).... Won George Parsons Trophy (1981-82).... Named to OHL All-Star first team (1981-82).... Played in NHL All-Star Game (1984, 1988 and 1992).... Named to THE SPORTING NEWS All-Star second team (1989-90).... Named to NHL All-Star second team (1989-90).

MISCELLANEOUS: Member of Stanley Cup championship team (1993).

			REGULAR SEASON					PLAYOFFS			
Season Team	League	Gms.	G	A	Pts.	PIM	Gms.	G	A	Pts.	PIM
80-81—Kitchener	OMJHL	66	49	67	116	23	16	14	13	27	13
81-82—Kitchener	OHL	47	45	52	97	23	15	16	13	29	11
82-83—Minnesota	NHL	78	35	30	65	27	9	5	4	9	18
83-84—Minnesota	NHL	78	41	42	83	66	16	2	12	14	6
84-85—Minnesota	NHL	78	26	36	62	72	9	2	4	6	9
85-86—Minnesota	NHL	77	31	48	79	46	5	5	0	5	16
86-87—Minnesota	NHL	65	26	27	53	34	—	—	—	—	—
87-88—Minnesota	NHL	77	40	41	81	81	—	—	—	—	—
88-89—Minnesota	NHL	60	23	27	50	55	5	2	3	5	8
89-90—Minnesota	NHL	80	55	44	99	72	7	4	3	7	10
90-91—Minnesota	NHL	80	35	40	75	43	23	10	19	29	30
91-92—Minnesota	NHL	80	30	45	75	41	7	4	4	8	14
92-93—Montreal	NHL	82	40	48	88	44	18	6	9	15	18
93-94—Montreal	NHL	77	33	38	71	36	6	1	2	3	2
NHL totals		912	415	466	881	617	105	41	60	101	131

BENAZIC, CAL
D, SABRES

PERSONAL: Born September 29, 1975, in Mackenzie, B.C.... 6-3/187.... Name pronounced ben-A-chick.
COLLEGE: Medicine Hat (Alta.).
TRANSACTIONS/CAREER NOTES: Selected by Buffalo Sabres in sixth round (fifth Sabres pick, 147th overall) of NHL entry draft (June 29, 1994).

			REGULAR SEASON					PLAYOFFS			
Season Team	League	Gms.	G	A	Pts.	PIM	Gms.	G	A	Pts.	PIM
91-92—Surrey	BCJHL	27	0	1	1	20	—	—	—	—	—
92-93—Surrey	BCJHL	60	5	37	42	210	—	—	—	—	—
93-94—Medicine Hat	WHL	64	2	15	17	157	3	0	0	0	15

BENNETT, ADAM
D, OILERS

PERSONAL: Born March 30, 1971, in Georgetown, Ont.... 6-4/206.... Shoots right.
TRANSACTIONS/CAREER NOTES: Separated both shoulders (1987-88).... Selected by Chicago Blackhawks in first round (first Blackhawks pick, sixth overall) of NHL entry draft (June 17, 1989).... Traded by Blackhawks to Edmonton Oilers for C Kevin Todd (October 7, 1993).... Suffered foot infection (December 12, 1993); missed three games.... Injured knee (March 23, 1994); missed remainder of season.
HONORS: Named to OHL All-Star second team (1990-91).

			REGULAR SEASON					PLAYOFFS			
Season Team	League	Gms.	G	A	Pts.	PIM	Gms.	G	A	Pts.	PIM
86-87—Georgetown Jr. B	OHA	1	0	0	0	0	—	—	—	—	—
87-88—Georgetown Jr. B	OHA	32	9	31	40	63	—	—	—	—	—
88-89—Sudbury	OHL	66	7	22	29	133	—	—	—	—	—
89-90—Sudbury	OHL	65	18	43	61	116	7	1	2	3	23
90-91—Sudbury	OHL	54	21	29	50	123	5	1	2	3	11
—Indianapolis	IHL	3	0	1	1	12	2	0	0	0	0
91-92—Indianapolis	IHL	59	4	10	14	89	—	—	—	—	—
—Chicago	NHL	5	0	0	0	12	—	—	—	—	—
92-93—Indianapolis	IHL	39	8	16	24	69	2	0	0	0	2
—Chicago	NHL	16	0	2	2	8	—	—	—	—	—
93-94—Cape Breton	AHL	7	2	5	7	7	—	—	—	—	—
—Edmonton	NHL	48	3	6	9	49	—	—	—	—	—
NHL totals		69	3	8	11	69					

BENNETT, RICK
LW, WHALERS

PERSONAL: Born July 24, 1967, in Springfield, Mass.... 6-3/215.... Shoots left.... Full name: Eric John Bennett.
HIGH SCHOOL: Wilbraham (Mass.) and Monson Academy.
COLLEGE: Providence.
TRANSACTIONS/CAREER NOTES: Selected by Minnesota North Stars in third round (fourth North Stars pick, 54th overall) of NHL entry draft (June 21, 1986).... Rights traded by North Stars with C Brian Lawton and LW Igor Liba to New York Rangers for D Mark Tinordi, D Paul Jerrard, C Mike Sullivan, RW Brett Barnett and Los Angeles Kings third-round pick (C Murray Garbutt) in 1989 draft (October 11, 1988).... Underwent surgery to left knee (January 24, 1990).... Signed as free agent by Hartford Whalers (August 1993).
HONORS: Named to Hockey East All-Freshman team (1986-87).... Named to NCAA All-America East second team (1988-89). ... Named to Hockey East All-Star second team (1989-90).

			REGULAR SEASON					PLAYOFFS			
Season Team	League	Gms.	G	A	Pts.	PIM	Gms.	G	A	Pts.	PIM
85-86—Wilbraham Monson Acad.	Mass. H.S.	20	30	39	69	25	—	—	—	—	—
86-87—Providence College	Hockey East	32	15	12	27	34	—	—	—	—	—

Season Team	League	REGULAR SEASON					PLAYOFFS				
		Gms.	G	A	Pts.	PIM	Gms.	G	A	Pts.	PIM
87-88—Providence College	Hockey East	33	9	16	25	70	—	—	—	—	—
88-89—Providence College	Hockey East	32	14	32	46	74	—	—	—	—	—
89-90—Providence College	Hockey East	31	12	24	36	74	—	—	—	—	—
—New York Rangers	NHL	6	1	0	1	5	—	—	—	—	—
90-91—Binghamton	AHL	71	27	32	59	206	10	2	1	3	27
—New York Rangers	NHL	6	0	0	0	6	—	—	—	—	—
91-92—Binghamton	AHL	76	15	22	37	114	11	0	1	1	23
—New York Rangers	NHL	3	0	1	1	2	—	—	—	—	—
92-93—Binghamton	AHL	76	15	22	37	114	10	0	0	0	30
93-94—Springfield	AHL	67	9	19	28	82	6	1	0	1	31
NHL totals..............		15	1	1	2	13					

BENNING, BRIAN
D, PANTHERS

PERSONAL: Born June 10, 1966, in Edmonton.... 6-0/195.... Shoots left.... Full name: Brian Anthony Benning.... Brother of Jim Benning, defenseman, Toronto Maple Leafs and Vancouver Canucks (1981-82 through 1989-90).
HIGH SCHOOL: St. Joseph (Edmonton).

TRANSACTIONS/CAREER NOTES: Cracked bone in right wrist (December 1983); missed 38 games.... Selected by St. Louis Blues as underage junior in second round (first Blues pick, 26th overall) of NHL entry draft (June 9, 1984).... Broke right leg (December 28, 1984).... Traded by Blues to Los Angeles Kings for third-round pick (RW Kyle Reeves) in 1991 draft (November 10, 1989).... Underwent appendectomy (March 6, 1990); missed three weeks.... Suspended three games by NHL for cross-checking (September 28, 1990).... Suffered back spasms (December 1990).... Injured groin (October 22, 1991); missed three games.... Traded by Kings with D Jeff Chychrun and first-round pick (LW Jason Bowen) in 1992 draft to Pittsburgh Penguins for D Paul Coffey (February 19, 1992).... Traded by Penguins with RW Mark Recchi and first-round pick in 1992 draft (LW Jason Bowen) previously acquired from Kings to Philadelphia Flyers for RW Rick Tocchet, D Kjell Samuelsson, G Ken Wregget and third-round pick (RW Sergei Zholtok) in 1992 draft (February 19, 1992).... Strained back (October 26, 1992); missed three games.... Traded by Flyers to Edmonton Oilers for C Josef Beranek and D Greg Hawgood (January 16, 1993).... Strained groin (January 23, 1993); missed five games.... Strained wrist (February 23, 1993); missed three games.... Signed as free agent by Florida Panthers (July 15, 1993).... Bruised left shoulder (October 12, 1993); missed five games.... Suspended four games by NHL for slashing (November 16, 1993).

Season Team	League	REGULAR SEASON					PLAYOFFS				
		Gms.	G	A	Pts.	PIM	Gms.	G	A	Pts.	PIM
83-84—Portland	WHL	38	6	41	47	108	—	—	—	—	—
84-85—Kamloops	WHL	17	3	18	21	26	—	—	—	—	—
—St. Louis	NHL	4	0	2	2	0	—	—	—	—	—
85-86—Canadian national team ...	Int'l	60	6	13	19	43	—	—	—	—	—
—St. Louis	NHL	—	—	—	—	—	6	1	2	3	13
86-87—St. Louis	NHL	78	13	36	49	110	6	0	4	4	9
87-88—St. Louis	NHL	77	8	29	37	107	10	1	6	7	25
88-89—St. Louis	NHL	66	8	26	34	102	7	1	1	2	11
89-90—St. Louis	NHL	7	1	1	2	2	—	—	—	—	—
—Los Angeles....................	NHL	48	5	18	23	104	7	0	2	2	10
90-91—Los Angeles....................	NHL	61	7	24	31	127	12	0	5	5	6
91-92—Los Angeles....................	NHL	53	2	30	32	99	—	—	—	—	—
—Philadelphia....................	NHL	22	2	12	14	35	—	—	—	—	—
92-93—Philadelphia....................	NHL	37	9	17	26	93	—	—	—	—	—
—Edmonton........................	NHL	18	1	7	8	59	—	—	—	—	—
93-94—Florida...........................	NHL	73	6	24	30	107	—	—	—	—	—
NHL totals.........................		544	62	226	288	945	48	3	20	23	74

BERANEK, JOSEF
LW, FLYERS

PERSONAL: Born October 25, 1969, in Litvinov, Czechoslovakia. ... 6-2/185. ... Shoots left.... Name pronounced JOH-sehf buh-RAH-nehk.
TRANSACTIONS/CAREER NOTES: Selected by Edmonton Oilers in fourth round (third Oilers pick, 78th overall) of NHL entry draft (June 17, 1989).... Traded by Oilers with D Greg Hawgood to Philadelphia Flyers for D Brian Benning (January 16, 1993).... Bruised left shoulder (January 30, 1994); missed three games.

Season Team	League	REGULAR SEASON					PLAYOFFS				
		Gms.	G	A	Pts.	PIM	Gms.	G	A	Pts.	PIM
87-88—CHZ Litvinov	Czech.	14	7	4	11	12	—	—	—	—	—
88-89—CHZ Litvinov	Czech.	32	18	10	28	47	—	—	—	—	—
—Czechoslovakia Jr.	Czech.	5	2	7	9	2	—	—	—	—	—
89-90—Dukla Trencin	Czech.	49	16	21	37	...	—	—	—	—	—
90-91—CHZ Litvinov	Czech.	50	27	27	54	98	—	—	—	—	—
91-92—Edmonton........................	NHL	58	12	16	28	18	12	2	1	3	0
92-93—Edmonton........................	NHL	26	2	6	8	28	—	—	—	—	—
—Cape Breton	AHL	6	1	2	3	8	—	—	—	—	—
—Philadelphia....................	NHL	40	13	12	25	50	—	—	—	—	—
93-94—Philadelphia....................	NHL	80	28	21	49	85	—	—	—	—	—
NHL totals.........................		204	55	55	110	181	12	2	1	3	0

BEREHOWSKY, DRAKE
D, MAPLE LEAFS

PERSONAL: Born January 3, 1972, in Toronto.... 6-1/211.... Shoots right.... Name pronounced BAIR-uh-HOW-skee.
TRANSACTIONS/CAREER NOTES: Injured knees and underwent reconstructive surgery (October 13, 1989); missed remainder of season. ... Selected by

Toronto Maple Leafs in first round (first Maple Leafs pick, 10th overall) of NHL entry draft (June 16, 1990)....Sprained knee (April 15, 1993); missed remainder of season....Underwent off-season knee surgery; missed four games.
HONORS: Won Can.HL Defenseman of the Year Award (1991-92)....Won Max Kaminsky Trophy (1991-92)....Named to Can.HL All-Star first team (1991-92)....Named to OHL All-Star first team (1991-92).

			REGULAR SEASON					PLAYOFFS			
Season Team	League	Gms.	G	A	Pts.	PIM	Gms.	G	A	Pts.	PIM
87-88—Barrie Jr. B	OHA	40	10	36	46	81	—	—	—	—	—
88-89—Kingston	OHL	63	7	39	46	85	—	—	—	—	—
89-90—Kingston	OHL	9	3	11	14	28	—	—	—	—	—
90-91—Toronto	NHL	8	0	1	1	25	—	—	—	—	—
—Kingston	OHL	13	5	13	18	28	—	—	—	—	—
—North Bay	OHL	26	7	23	30	51	10	2	7	9	21
91-92—North Bay	OHL	62	19	63	82	147	21	7	24	31	22
—Toronto	NHL	1	0	0	0	0	—	—	—	—	—
—St. John's	AHL	—	—	—	—	—	6	0	5	5	21
92-93—Toronto	NHL	41	4	15	19	61	—	—	—	—	—
—St. John's	AHL	28	10	17	27	38	—	—	—	—	—
93-94—Toronto	NHL	49	2	8	10	63	—	—	—	—	—
—St. John's	AHL	18	3	12	15	40	—	—	—	—	—
NHL totals		99	6	24	30	149					

BERG, BILL
LW, MAPLE LEAFS

PERSONAL: Born October 21, 1967, in St. Catharines, Ont....6-1/205....Shoots left....Brother of Bob Berg, left winger.
TRANSACTIONS/CAREER NOTES: Broke ankle (March 1985)....Selected by New York Islanders as underage junior in third round (third Islanders pick, 59th overall) of NHL entry draft (June 21, 1986)....Injured knee (October 1986)....Separated shoulder (May 1990)....Fractured left foot (November 9, 1991); missed 12 games....Claimed on waivers by Toronto Maple Leafs (December 3, 1992)....Injured hip flexor (November 18, 1993); missed one game.
MISCELLANEOUS: Moved from defense to left wing (1990).

			REGULAR SEASON					PLAYOFFS			
Season Team	League	Gms.	G	A	Pts.	PIM	Gms.	G	A	Pts.	PIM
84-85—Grimsby Jr. B	OHA	42	10	22	32	153	—	—	—	—	—
85-86—Toronto	OHL	64	3	35	38	143	4	0	0	0	19
86-87—Toronto	OHL	57	3	15	18	138	—	—	—	—	—
—Springfield	AHL	4	1	1	2	4	—	—	—	—	—
87-88—Springfield	AHL	76	6	26	32	148	—	—	—	—	—
—Peoria	IHL	5	0	1	1	8	7	0	3	3	31
88-89—New York Islanders	NHL	7	1	2	3	10	—	—	—	—	—
—Springfield	AHL	69	17	32	49	122	—	—	—	—	—
89-90—Springfield	AHL	74	12	42	54	74	15	5	12	17	35
90-91—New York Islanders	NHL	78	9	14	23	67	—	—	—	—	—
91-92—New York Islanders	NHL	47	5	9	14	28	—	—	—	—	—
—Capital District	AHL	3	0	2	2	16	—	—	—	—	—
92-93—New York Islanders	NHL	22	6	3	9	49	—	—	—	—	—
—Toronto	NHL	58	7	8	15	54	21	1	1	2	18
93-94—Toronto	NHL	83	8	11	19	93	18	1	2	3	10
NHL totals		295	36	47	83	301	39	2	3	5	28

BERG, BOB
LW

PERSONAL: Born July 2, 1970, in Beamsville, Ont....6-1/195....Shoots left....Brother of Bill Berg, left winger, Toronto Maple Leafs.
TRANSACTIONS/CAREER NOTES: Selected by Los Angeles Kings in third round (third Kings pick, 49th overall) of NHL entry draft (June 16, 1990)....Traded by Niagara Falls Thunder to Sudbury Wolves for sixth-round draft pick (January 10, 1991).
HONORS: Named to OHL All-Star first team (1989-90)....Named to CHL All-Star second team (1993-94).

			REGULAR SEASON					PLAYOFFS			
Season Team	League	Gms.	G	A	Pts.	PIM	Gms.	G	A	Pts.	PIM
85-86—Grimsby Jr. B	OHA	40	22	12	34	73	—	—	—	—	—
86-87—Grimsby Jr. B	OHA	36	13	16	29	115	—	—	—	—	—
87-88—Belleville	OHL	61	15	27	42	59	—	—	—	—	—
88-89—Belleville	OHL	66	33	51	84	88	5	1	3	4	8
89-90—Belleville	OHL	66	48	49	97	124	8	2	2	4	14
90-91—Niagara Falls	OHL	12	8	4	12	11	—	—	—	—	—
—Sudbury	OHL	23	12	15	27	34	5	2	1	3	6
—New Haven	AHL	19	0	1	1	8	—	—	—	—	—
91-92—Phoenix	IHL	24	2	8	10	18	—	—	—	—	—
—Richmond	ECHL	37	19	14	33	65	6	2	1	3	0
92-93—Phoenix	IHL	1	0	0	0	0	—	—	—	—	—
—Muskegon	Col.HL	49	19	24	43	87	6	1	1	2	5
93-94—Wichita	CHL	64	43	58	101	141	10	9	8	17	17

BERGERON, JEAN-CLAUDE
G, LIGHTNING

PERSONAL: Born October 14, 1968, in Hauterive, Que....5-9/181....Catches left.
TRANSACTIONS/CAREER NOTES: Selected by Montreal Canadiens in fifth round (sixth Canadiens pick, 104th overall of NHL entry draft

(June 11, 1988).... Traded by Canadiens to Tampa Bay Lightning for G Frederic Chabot (June 18, 1992).
HONORS: Won Aldege (Baz) Bastien Trophy (1989-90).... Shared Harry (Hap) Holmes Memorial Trophy with Andre Racicot (1989-90).... Named to AHL All-Star first team (1989-90).... Shared James Norris Memorial Trophy with Mike Greenlay (1993-94).

			REGULAR SEASON							PLAYOFFS					
Season Team	League	Gms.	Min.	W	L	T	GA	SO	Avg.	Gms.	Min.	W	L	GA	SO	Avg.
85-86—Shawinigan	QMJHL	33	1796	...	...	...	156	0	5.21	—	—	—	—	—	—	—
86-87—Verdun	QMJHL	52	2991	...	...	...	*306	0	6.14	—	—	—	—	—	—	—
87-88—Verdun	QMJHL	49	2715	13	31	3	*265	0	5.86	—	—	—	—	—	—	—
88-89—Verdun	QMJHL	44	2417	8	34	1	199	0	4.94	—	—	—	—	—	—	—
—Sherbrooke	AHL	5	302	4	1	0	18	0	3.58	—	—	—	—	—	—	—
89-90—Sherbrooke	AHL	40	2254	21	8	7	103	2	*2.74	9	497	6	2	28	0	3.38
90-91—Montreal	NHL	19	941	7	6	2	59	0	3.76	—	—	—	—	—	—	—
—Fredericton	AHL	18	1083	12	6	0	59	1	3.27	10	546	5	5	32	0	3.52
91-92—Fredericton	AHL	13	791	5	7	1	57	0	4.32	—	—	—	—	—	—	—
—Peoria	IHL	27	1632	14	9	‡3	96	1	3.53	6	352	3	3	24	0	4.09
92-93—Atlanta	IHL	31	1722	21	7	‡0	92	1	3.21	6	368	3	3	19	0	3.10
—Tampa Bay	NHL	21	1163	8	10	1	71	0	3.66	—	—	—	—	—	—	—
93-94—Tampa Bay	NHL	3	134	1	1	1	7	0	3.13	—	—	—	—	—	—	—
—Atlanta	IHL	48	2755	27	11	‡7	141	0	3.07	2	153	1	1	6	0	2.35
NHL totals		43	2238	16	17	4	137	0	3.67							

BERGEVIN, MARC
D, LIGHTNING

PERSONAL: Born August 11, 1965, in Montreal.... 6-1/197.... Shoots left.... Name pronounced BUHR-zhuh-van.
TRANSACTIONS/CAREER NOTES: Selected by Chicago Blackhawks as underage junior in third round (third Blackhawks pick, 59th overall) of NHL entry draft (June 8, 1983)....
Sprained neck (March 18, 1987).... Traded by Blackhawks with D Gary Nylund to New York Islanders for D Steve Konroyd and C Bob Bassen (November 25, 1988).... Bruised ribs (November 25, 1989).... Broke hand (May 1990).... Traded by Islanders to Hartford Whalers for future considerations; Islanders later received fifth-round pick (C Ryan Duthie) in 1992 draft (October 31, 1990).... Signed as free agent by Tampa Bay Lightning (July 9, 1992).... Injured foot (March 18, 1993); missed one game.... Bruised back (November 19, 1993); missed one game.

			REGULAR SEASON					PLAYOFFS			
Season Team	League	Gms.	G	A	Pts.	PIM	Gms.	G	A	Pts.	PIM
82-83—Chicoutimi	QMJHL	64	3	27	30	113	—	—	—	—	—
83-84—Chicoutimi	QMJHL	70	10	35	45	125	—	—	—	—	—
—Springfield	AHL	7	0	1	1	2	—	—	—	—	—
84-85—Chicago	NHL	60	0	6	6	54	6	0	3	3	2
—Springfield	AHL	—	—	—	—	—	4	0	0	0	0
85-86—Chicago	NHL	71	7	7	14	60	3	0	0	0	0
86-87—Chicago	NHL	66	4	10	14	66	3	1	0	1	2
87-88—Chicago	NHL	58	1	6	7	85	—	—	—	—	—
—Saginaw	IHL	10	2	7	9	20	—	—	—	—	—
88-89—Chicago	NHL	11	0	0	0	18	—	—	—	—	—
—New York Islanders	NHL	58	2	13	15	62	—	—	—	—	—
89-90—New York Islanders	NHL	18	0	4	4	30	—	—	—	—	—
—Springfield	AHL	47	7	16	23	66	17	2	11	13	16
90-91—Hartford	NHL	4	0	0	0	4	—	—	—	—	—
—Capital District	AHL	7	0	5	5	6	—	—	—	—	—
—Springfield	AHL	58	4	23	27	85	18	0	7	7	26
91-92—Hartford	NHL	75	7	17	24	64	5	0	0	0	2
92-93—Tampa Bay	NHL	78	2	12	14	66	—	—	—	—	—
93-94—Tampa Bay	NHL	83	1	15	16	87	—	—	—	—	—
NHL totals		582	24	90	114	596	17	1	3	4	6

BERGLAND, TIM
RW, CAPITALS

PERSONAL: Born January 11, 1965, in Crookston, Minn.... 6-3/194.... Shoots right.... Full name: Timothy Daniel Bergland.
HIGH SCHOOL: Lincoln (Thief River Falls, Minn.).
COLLEGE: Minnesota.
TRANSACTIONS/CAREER NOTES: Selected by Washington Capitals as underage junior in fourth round (first Capitals pick, 75th overall) of NHL entry draft (June 8, 1983).... Selected by Tampa Bay Lightning in NHL expansion draft (June 18, 1992).... Claimed on waivers by Washington Capitals (March 17, 1994).

			REGULAR SEASON					PLAYOFFS			
Season Team	League	Gms.	G	A	Pts.	PIM	Gms.	G	A	Pts.	PIM
82-83—Lincoln High School	Minn. H.S.	20	26	22	48	...	—	—	—	—	—
83-84—University of Minnesota	WCHA	24	4	11	15	4	—	—	—	—	—
84-85—University of Minnesota	WCHA	46	7	12	19	16	—	—	—	—	—
85-86—University of Minnesota	WCHA	48	11	16	27	26	—	—	—	—	—
86-87—University of Minnesota	WCHA	49	18	17	35	48	—	—	—	—	—
87-88—Fort Wayne	IHL	13	2	1	3	9	—	—	—	—	—
—Binghamton	AHL	63	21	26	47	31	4	0	0	0	0
88-89—Baltimore	AHL	78	24	29	53	39	—	—	—	—	—
89-90—Baltimore	AHL	47	12	19	31	55	—	—	—	—	—
—Washington	NHL	32	2	5	7	31	15	1	1	2	10

Season	Team	League	REGULAR SEASON					PLAYOFFS				
			Gms.	G	A	Pts.	PIM	Gms.	G	A	Pts.	PIM
90-91—Washington		NHL	47	5	9	14	21	11	1	1	2	12
—Baltimore		AHL	15	8	9	17	16	—	—	—	—	—
91-92—Washington		NHL	22	1	4	5	2	—	—	—	—	—
—Baltimore		AHL	11	6	10	16	5	—	—	—	—	—
92-93—Atlanta		IHL	49	18	21	39	26	9	3	3	6	10
—Tampa Bay		NHL	27	3	3	6	11	—	—	—	—	—
93-94—Atlanta		IHL	19	6	7	13	6	—	—	—	—	—
—Tampa Bay		NHL	51	6	5	11	6	—	—	—	—	—
—Washington		NHL	3	0	0	0	4	—	—	—	—	—
NHL totals			182	17	26	43	75	26	2	2	4	22

BERGQVIST, STEFAN
D, PENGUINS

PERSONAL: Born March 10, 1975, in Leksand, Sweden. . . . 6-3/216. . . . Shoots left. . . . Brother of Jonas Bergqvist, right winger, Calgary Flames (1989-90).
TRANSACTIONS/CAREER NOTES: Selected by Pittsburgh Penguins in first round (first Penguins pick, 26th overall) of NHL entry draft (June 26, 1993).

Season	Team	League	REGULAR SEASON					PLAYOFFS				
			Gms.	G	A	Pts.	PIM	Gms.	G	A	Pts.	PIM
92-93—Leksand		Sweden	15	0	0	0	6	—	—	—	—	—
93-94—Leksand		Sweden	6	0	0	0	0	—	—	—	—	—

BERNARD, LOUIS
D, CANADIENS

PERSONAL: Born July 10, 1974, in Victoriaville, Que. . . . 6-1/203. . . . Shoots right.
TRANSACTIONS/CAREER NOTES: Selected by Montreal Canadiens in fourth round (fifth Canadiens pick, 82nd overall) of NHL entry draft (June 20, 1992).

Season	Team	League	REGULAR SEASON					PLAYOFFS				
			Gms.	G	A	Pts.	PIM	Gms.	G	A	Pts.	PIM
91-92—Drummondville		QMJHL	70	8	24	32	59	4	0	1	1	4
92-93—Drummondville		QMJHL	68	8	38	46	78	10	0	4	4	14
93-94—Sherbrooke		QMJHL	65	10	31	41	107	12	1	2	3	10

BERRY, BRAD
D, STARS

PERSONAL: Born April 1, 1965, in Bashaw, Alta. . . . 6-2/190. . . . Shoots left.
COLLEGE: North Dakota.
TRANSACTIONS/CAREER NOTES: Selected by Winnipeg Jets in second round (third Jets pick, 29th overall) of NHL entry draft (June 8, 1983). . . . Signed as free agent by Minnesota North Stars (October 14, 1991). . . . Strained lower back (December 31, 1992); missed two games. . . . Sprained knee (March 21, 1993); missed four games. . . . North Stars franchise moved from Minnesota to Dallas and renamed Stars for 1993-94 season. . . . Suffered mild concussion (October 20, 1993); missed two games.

Season	Team	League	REGULAR SEASON					PLAYOFFS				
			Gms.	G	A	Pts.	PIM	Gms.	G	A	Pts.	PIM
83-84—North Dakota		WCHA	32	2	7	9	8	—	—	—	—	—
84-85—North Dakota		WCHA	40	4	26	30	26	—	—	—	—	—
85-86—North Dakota		WCHA	40	6	29	35	26	—	—	—	—	—
—Winnipeg		NHL	13	1	0	1	10	3	0	0	0	0
86-87—Winnipeg		NHL	52	2	8	10	60	7	0	1	1	14
87-88—Winnipeg		NHL	48	0	6	6	75	—	—	—	—	—
—Moncton		AHL	10	1	3	4	14	—	—	—	—	—
88-89—Winnipeg		NHL	38	0	9	9	45	—	—	—	—	—
—Moncton		AHL	38	3	16	19	39	—	—	—	—	—
89-90—Winnipeg		NHL	12	1	2	3	6	1	0	0	0	0
—Moncton		AHL	38	1	9	10	58	—	—	—	—	—
90-91—Brynas		Sweden	38	3	1	4	38	—	—	—	—	—
91-92—Kalamazoo		IHL	65	5	18	23	90	5	2	0	2	6
—Minnesota		NHL	7	0	0	0	6	2	0	0	0	2
92-93—Minnesota		NHL	63	0	3	3	109	—	—	—	—	—
93-94—Dallas		NHL	8	0	0	0	12	—	—	—	—	—
—Kalamazoo		IHL	45	3	19	22	91	1	0	0	0	0
NHL totals			241	4	28	32	323	13	0	1	1	16

BERTHIAUME, DANIEL
G

PERSONAL: Born January 26, 1966, in Longueuil, Que. . . . 5-9/160. . . . Catches left. . . . Name pronounced bairt-YOHM.
TRANSACTIONS/CAREER NOTES: Traded by Drummondville Voltigeurs to Chicoutimi Saguéneens for RW Simon Massie (October 1984). . . . Selected by Winnipeg Jets as underage junior in third round (third Jets pick, 60th overall) of NHL entry draft (June 15, 1985). . . . Pulled chest muscle (March 1, 1988). . . . Suspended by Jets for failing to report to Moncton (October 4, 1988); suspension lifted (October 11, 1988). . . . Suspended by Moncton (November 4, 1988); suspension lifted (November 29, 1988). . . . Injured shoulder and suspended eight games by AHL for altercation (December 17, 1988). . . . Traded by Jets to Minnesota North Stars for future considerations (January 22, 1990). . . . Injured knee (February 13, 1990); missed 13 games. . . . Traded by North Stars to Los Angeles Kings for LW Craig Duncanson (September 6, 1990). . . . Suffered concussion (December 5, 1991); missed two games. . . . Traded by Kings to Boston Bruins for future considerations (January 20, 1992). . . . Traded by Bruins to Jets for LW Doug Evans (June 10, 1992). . . . Signed as free agent by Ottawa Senators (December 16, 1992). . . . Traded by Senators to Detroit Red Wings for D Steve Konroyd (March 21, 1994).

HONORS: Won Michel Briere Trophy (1984-85).... Won Jacques Plante Trophy (1984-85).

			REGULAR SEASON								PLAYOFFS						
Season	Team	League	Gms.	Min.	W	L	T	GA	SO	Avg.	Gms.	Min.	W	L	GA	SO	Avg.
83-84—Drummondville	QMJHL	28	1562	...	...	...	131	0	5.03	—	—	—	—	—	—	—
84-85—Drummondville/Chicoutimi	QMJHL	*59	*3347	40	11	2	215	†2	3.85	†14	770	8	6	*51	0	3.97
85-86—Chicoutimi	QMJHL	*66	*3718	34	29	3	*286	1	4.62	9	580	4	5	36	0	3.72
—Winnipeg	NHL	—	—	—	—	—	—	—	—	1	68	0	1	4	0	3.53
86-87—Sherbrooke	AHL	7	420	4	3	0	23	0	3.29	—	—	—	—	—	—	—
—Winnipeg	NHL	31	1758	18	7	3	93	1	3.17	8	439	4	4	21	0	2.87
87-88—Winnipeg	NHL	56	3010	22	19	7	176	2	3.51	5	300	1	4	25	0	5.00
88-89—Winnipeg	NHL	9	443	0	8	0	44	0	5.96	—	—	—	—	—	—	—
—Moncton	AHL	21	1083	6	9	2	76	0	4.21	3	180	1	2	11	0	3.67
89-90—Winnipeg	NHL	24	1387	10	11	3	86	1	3.72	—	—	—	—	—	—	—
—Minnesota	NHL	5	240	1	3	0	14	0	3.50	—	—	—	—	—	—	—
90-91—Los Angeles	NHL	37	2119	20	11	4	117	1	3.31	—	—	—	—	—	—	—
91-92—Los Angeles	NHL	19	979	7	10	1	66	0	4.04	—	—	—	—	—	—	—
—Boston	NHL	8	399	1	4	2	21	0	3.16	—	—	—	—	—	—	—
92-93—Ottawa	NHL	25	1326	2	17	1	95	0	4.30	—	—	—	—	—	—	—
93-94—Prince Edward Island	AHL	30	1640	8	16	3	130	0	4.76	—	—	—	—	—	—	—
—Ottawa	NHL	1	1	0	0	0	2	0	120.00	—	—	—	—	—	—	—
—Adirondack	AHL	11	553	7	2	0	35	0	3.80	11	632	6	4	30	0	2.85
NHL totals		215	11662	81	90	21	714	5	3.67	14	807	5	9	50	0	3.72

BERTUZZI, TODD
C/RW, ISLANDERS

PERSONAL: Born February 2, 1975, in Sudbury, Ont.... 6-3/227.... Shoots left.
HIGH SCHOOL: Bishop MacDonnell (Guelph, Ont.).
TRANSACTIONS/CAREER NOTES: Selected by New York Islanders in first round (first Islanders pick, 23rd overall) of NHL entry draft (June 26, 1993).

			REGULAR SEASON					PLAYOFFS				
Season	Team	League	Gms.	G	A	Pts.	PIM	Gms.	G	A	Pts.	PIM
91-92—Guelph	OHL	47	7	14	21	145	—	—	—	—	—
92-93—Guelph	OHL	60	27	31	58	168	5	2	2	4	6
93-94—Guelph	OHL	61	28	54	82	165	9	2	6	8	30

BERUBE, CRAIG
LW, CAPITALS

PERSONAL: Born December 17, 1965, in Calihoo, Alta.... 6-1/205.... Shoots left.... Name pronounced buh-ROO-bee.
TRANSACTIONS/CAREER NOTES: Signed as free agent by Philadelphia Flyers (March 19, 1986).
... Sprained left knee (March 1988).... Traded by Flyers with RW Scott Mellanby and C Craig Fisher to Edmonton Oilers for RW Dave Brown, D Corey Foster and the NHL rights to RW Jari Kurri (May 30, 1991)....
Traded by Oilers with G Grant Fuhr and RW/LW Glenn Anderson to Toronto Maple Leafs for LW Vincent Damphousse, D Luke Richardson, G Peter Ing, C Scott Thornton and future considerations (September 19, 1991).... Traded by Maple Leafs with D Alexander Godynyuk, RW Gary Leeman, D Michel Petit and G Jeff Reese to Calgary Flames for C Doug Gilmour, D Jamie Macoun, LW Kent Manderville, D Ric Nattress and G Rick Wamsley (January 2, 1992).... Traded by Flames to Washington Capitals for fifth-round pick (C Darryl LaFrance) in 1993 draft (June 26, 1993).

			REGULAR SEASON					PLAYOFFS				
Season	Team	League	Gms.	G	A	Pts.	PIM	Gms.	G	A	Pts.	PIM
82-83—Williams Lake	PCJHL	33	9	24	33	99	—	—	—	—	—
—Kamloops	WHL	4	0	0	0	0	—	—	—	—	—
83-84—New Westminster	WHL	70	11	20	31	104	8	1	2	3	5
84-85—New Westminster	WHL	70	25	44	69	191	10	3	2	5	4
85-86—Kamloops	WHL	32	17	14	31	119	—	—	—	—	—
—Medicine Hat	WHL	34	14	16	30	95	25	7	8	15	102
86-87—Hershey	AHL	63	7	17	24	325	—	—	—	—	—
—Philadelphia	NHL	7	0	0	0	57	5	0	0	0	17
87-88—Hershey	AHL	31	5	9	14	119	—	—	—	—	—
—Philadelphia	NHL	27	3	2	5	108	—	—	—	—	—
88-89—Hershey	AHL	7	0	2	2	19	—	—	—	—	—
—Philadelphia	NHL	53	1	1	2	199	16	0	0	0	56
89-90—Philadelphia	NHL	74	4	14	18	291	—	—	—	—	—
90-91—Philadelphia	NHL	74	8	9	17	293	—	—	—	—	—
91-92—Toronto	NHL	40	5	7	12	109	—	—	—	—	—
—Calgary	NHL	36	1	4	5	155	—	—	—	—	—
92-93—Calgary	NHL	77	4	8	12	209	6	0	1	1	21
93-94—Washington	NHL	84	7	7	14	305	8	0	0	0	21
NHL totals		472	33	52	85	1726	35	0	1	1	115

BES, JEFF
C, STARS

PERSONAL: Born July 31, 1973, in Tillsonburg, Ont.... 6-0/185.... Shoots left.
HIGH SCHOOL: Bishop MacDonnell (Guelph, Ont.).
TRANSACTIONS/CAREER NOTES: Selected by Minnesota North Stars in third round (second North Stars pick, 58th overall) of NHL entry draft (June 20, 1992).... North Stars franchise moved from Minnesota to Dallas and renamed Stars for 1993-94 season.

			REGULAR SEASON					PLAYOFFS				
Season	Team	League	Gms.	G	A	Pts.	PIM	Gms.	G	A	Pts.	PIM
87-88—Woodstock Jr. C	OHA	33	19	10	29	16	—	—	—	—	—
88-89—St. Mary's Jr. B	OHA	37	8	22	30	37	—	—	—	—	—

Season	Team	League	REGULAR SEASON					PLAYOFFS				
			Gms.	G	A	Pts.	PIM	Gms.	G	A	Pts.	PIM
89-90	St. Mary's Jr. B	OHA	39	25	37	62	127	—	—	—	—	—
90-91	Dukes of Hamilton	OHL	66	23	47	70	53	4	1	4	5	4
91-92	Guelph	OHL	62	40	62	102	123	—	—	—	—	—
92-93	Guelph	OHL	59	48	67	115	128	5	3	5	8	4
	Kalamazoo	IHL	3	1	3	4	6	—	—	—	—	—
93-94	Dayton	ECHL	2	2	0	2	12	—	—	—	—	—
	Kalamazoo	IHL	30	2	12	14	30	—	—	—	—	—

BESTER, ALLAN

G, MIGHTY DUCKS

PERSONAL: Born March 26, 1964, in Hamilton, Ont.... 5-7/155.... Catches left.
TRANSACTIONS/CAREER NOTES: Selected by Toronto Maple Leafs as underage junior in third round (third Maple Leafs pick, 48th overall) of NHL entry draft (June 8, 1983).... Sprained left knee ligaments (February 1988); missed 14 games.... Suffered phlebitis in right leg (January 1989).... Stretched knee ligaments (April 1989).... Suffered from bone spurs in right heel (October 1989).... Underwent surgery for calcium deposits on his heels (October 1990).... Traded by Maple Leafs to Detroit Red Wings for sixth-round pick (C Alexander Kuzminsky) in 1991 draft (March 5, 1991).... Signed as free agent by Mighty Ducks of Anaheim (September 7, 1993).
HONORS: Named to OHL All-Star first team (1982-83).... Won Jack Butterfield Trophy (1991-92).

Season	Team	League	REGULAR SEASON							PLAYOFFS						
			Gms.	Min.	W	L	T	GA	SO	Avg.	Gms.	Min.	W	L	GA SO	Avg.
81-82	Brantford	OHL	19	970	4	11	0	68	0	4.21	—	—	—	—	— —	—
82-83	Brantford	OHL	56	3210	29	21	3	188	0	3.51	8	480	3	3	20 †1	*2.50
83-84	Brantford	OHL	23	1271	12	9	1	71	1	3.35	1	60	0	1	5 0	5.00
	Toronto	NHL	32	1848	11	16	4	134	0	4.35	—	—	—	—	— —	—
84-85	St. Catharines	AHL	30	1669	9	18	1	133	0	4.78	—	—	—	—	— —	—
	Toronto	NHL	15	767	3	9	1	54	1	4.22	—	—	—	—	— —	—
85-86	St. Catharines	AHL	50	2855	23	23	3	173	1	3.64	11	637	7	3	27 0	2.54
	Toronto	NHL	1	20	0	0	0	2	0	6.00	—	—	—	—	— —	—
86-87	Newmarket	AHL	3	190	1	0	0	6	0	1.89	—	—	—	—	— —	—
	Toronto	NHL	36	1808	10	14	3	110	2	3.65	1	39	0	0	1 0	1.54
87-88	Toronto	NHL	30	1607	8	12	5	102	2	3.81	5	253	2	3	21 0	4.98
88-89	Toronto	NHL	43	2460	17	20	2	156	2	3.80	—	—	—	—	— —	—
89-90	Newmarket	AHL	5	264	2	1	1	18	0	4.09	—	—	—	—	— —	—
	Toronto	NHL	42	2206	20	16	0	165	0	4.49	—	—	—	—	— —	—
90-91	Toronto	NHL	6	247	0	4	0	18	0	4.37	—	—	—	—	— —	—
	Detroit	NHL	3	178	0	3	0	13	0	4.38	1	20	0	0	1 0	3.00
	Newmarket	AHL	19	1157	7	8	4	58	1	3.01	—	—	—	—	— —	—
91-92	Detroit	NHL	1	31	0	0	0	2	0	3.87	—	—	—	—	— —	—
	Adirondack	AHL	22	1268	13	8	0	78	0	3.69	†19	1174	*14	5	50 1	2.56
92-93	Adirondack	AHL	41	2268	16	15	5	133	1	3.52	10	633	7	3	26 †1	2.46
93-94	San Diego	IHL	46	2543	22	14	‡6	150	1	3.54	8	419	4	4	28 0	4.01
NHL totals			209	11172	69	94	16	756	7	4.06	7	312	2	3	23 0	4.42

BETS, MAXIM

LW, MIGHTY DUCKS

PERSONAL: Born January 31, 1974, in Chelyabinsk, U.S.S.R.... 6-1/185.... Shoots left.... Name pronounced MAKS-eem BEHTS.
TRANSACTIONS/CAREER NOTES: Selected by St. Louis Blues in second round (first Blues pick, 37th overall) of NHL entry draft (June 26, 1993).... Traded by Blues with sixth-round draft pick in 1995 draft to Anaheim Mighty Ducks for D Alexei Kasatonov (March 21, 1994).
HONORS: Named to Can.HL All-Rookie team (1992-93).

Season	Team	League	REGULAR SEASON					PLAYOFFS				
			Gms.	G	A	Pts.	PIM	Gms.	G	A	Pts.	PIM
90-91	Traktor Juniors	CIS	60	71	37	108	...	—	—	—	—	—
91-92	Traktor Chelyabinsk	CIS	25	1	1	2	8	—	—	—	—	—
92-93	Spokane	WHL	54	49	57	106	130	9	5	6	11	20
93-94	Spokane	WHL	63	46	70	116	111	3	1	1	2	12
	Anaheim	NHL	3	0	0	0	0	—	—	—	—	—
	San Diego	IHL	—	—	—	—	—	9	0	2	2	0
NHL totals			3	0	0	0	0					

BETY, SEBASTIEN

D, NORDIQUES

PERSONAL: Born May 6, 1976, in St.-Bernard Beauce, Que.... 6-2/201.... Shoots left.... Name pronounced Say-bast-yehn BETTY.
TRANSACTIONS/CAREER NOTES: Selected by Quebec Nordiques in third round (fourth Nordiques pick, 61st overall) of NHL entry draft (June 29, 1994).

Season	Team	League	REGULAR SEASON					PLAYOFFS				
			Gms.	G	A	Pts.	PIM	Gms.	G	A	Pts.	PIM
92-93	Drummondville	QMJHL	70	1	21	22	126	10	1	2	3	24
93-94	Drummondville	QMJHL	67	3	8	11	164	10	0	0	0	17

BEUKEBOOM, JEFF

D, RANGERS

PERSONAL: Born March 28, 1965, in Ajax, Ont.... 6-5/225.... Shoots right.... Name pronounced BOO-kuh-BOOM.... Nephew of Ed Kea, defenseman, Atlanta Flames and St. Louis Blues (1973-74 through 1982-83); and cousin of Joe Nieuwendyk, center, Calgary Flames.

TRANSACTIONS/CAREER NOTES: Selected by Edmonton Oilers as underage junior in first round (first Oilers pick, 19th overall) of NHL entry draft (June 8, 1983). . . . Injured knee (December 1984). . . . Lacerated knuckle (October 24, 1987). . . . Suspended 10 games by NHL for leaving the bench (October 2, 1988). . . . Sprained right knee (January 1989). . . . Suffered hairline fracture of ankle (February 22, 1991); missed two games. . . . Traded by Oilers to New York Rangers for D David Shaw (November 12, 1991), completing deal in which Oilers traded C Mark Messier with future considerations to Rangers for C Bernie Nicholls, LW Louie DeBrusk, RW Steven Rice and future considerations (October 4, 1991). . . . Strained back (March 16, 1992); missed one game. . . . Injured knee (December 21, 1992); missed one game. . . . Bruised ankle (February 1, 1993); missed one game. . . . Suspended one game by NHL for hitting from behind (May 25, 1994).
HONORS: Named to OHL All-Star first team (1984-85).
MISCELLANEOUS: Member of Stanley Cup championship teams (1987, 1988, 1990 and 1994).

Season	Team	League	REGULAR SEASON					PLAYOFFS				
			Gms.	G	A	Pts.	PIM	Gms.	G	A	Pts.	PIM
81-82	Newmarket	OPJHL	49	5	30	35	218	—	—	—	—	—
82-83	Sault Ste. Marie	OHL	70	0	25	25	143	16	1	14	15	46
83-84	Sault Ste. Marie	OHL	61	6	30	36	178	16	1	7	8	43
84-85	Sault Ste. Marie	OHL	37	4	20	24	85	16	4	6	10	47
85-86	Nova Scotia	AHL	77	9	20	29	175	—	—	—	—	—
	Edmonton	NHL	—	—	—	—	—	1	0	0	0	4
86-87	Nova Scotia	AHL	14	1	7	8	35	—	—	—	—	—
	Edmonton	NHL	44	3	8	11	124	—	—	—	—	—
87-88	Edmonton	NHL	73	5	20	25	201	7	0	0	0	16
88-89	Cape Breton	AHL	8	0	4	4	36	—	—	—	—	—
	Edmonton	NHL	36	0	5	5	94	1	0	0	0	2
89-90	Edmonton	NHL	46	1	12	13	86	2	0	0	0	0
90-91	Edmonton	NHL	67	3	7	10	150	18	1	3	4	28
91-92	Edmonton	NHL	18	0	5	5	78	—	—	—	—	—
	New York Rangers	NHL	56	1	10	11	122	13	2	3	5	*47
92-93	New York Rangers	NHL	82	2	17	19	153	—	—	—	—	—
93-94	New York Rangers	NHL	68	8	8	16	170	22	0	6	6	50
NHL totals			490	23	92	115	1178	64	3	12	15	147

BIALOWAS, FRANK
D, MAPLE LEAFS

PERSONAL: Born July 11, 1969, in Winnipeg. . . . 5-11/220. . . . Shoots left. . . . Name pronounced bigh-uh-LOH-uhz.
TRANSACTIONS/CAREER NOTES: Signed as free agent by Toronto Maple Leafs (December 1992).

Season	Team	League	REGULAR SEASON					PLAYOFFS				
			Gms.	G	A	Pts.	PIM	Gms.	G	A	Pts.	PIM
92-93	Richmond	ECHL	60	3	18	21	261	1	0	0	0	2
	St. John's	AHL	7	1	0	1	28	1	0	0	0	0
93-94	St. John's	AHL	69	2	8	10	352	7	0	3	3	25
	Toronto	NHL	3	0	0	0	12	—	—	—	—	—
NHL totals			3	0	0	0	12					

BICANEK, RADIM
D, SENATORS

PERSONAL: Born January 18, 1975, in Uherske Hradiste, Czechoslovakia. . . . 6-1/195. . . . Shoots left.
TRANSACTIONS/CAREER NOTES: Selected by Ottawa Senators in second round (second Senators pick, 27th overall) of NHL entry draft (June 26, 1993).

Season	Team	League	REGULAR SEASON					PLAYOFFS				
			Gms.	G	A	Pts.	PIM	Gms.	G	A	Pts.	PIM
92-93	Jihlava	Czech.	43	2	3	5	. . .	—	—	—	—	—
93-94	Belleville	OHL	63	16	27	43	49	12	2	8	10	21

BIGGS, DON
C

PERSONAL: Born April 7, 1965, in Mississauga, Ont. . . . 5-8/180. . . . Shoots right.
TRANSACTIONS/CAREER NOTES: Injured knee ligaments (April 1982). . . . Selected by Minnesota North Stars as underage junior in eighth round (ninth North Stars pick, 156th overall) of NHL entry draft (June 8, 1983). . . . Traded by North Stars with RW Gord Sherven to Edmonton Oilers for C Marc Habscheid, D Emanuel Viveiros and LW Don Barber (December 20, 1985). . . . Signed as free agent by Philadelphia Flyers (July 17, 1987). . . . Suspended five games by AHL for biting (December 16, 1989). . . . Signed to play with Olten, Switzerland (May 1990). . . . Claimed on waivers by Rochester Americans after signing contract with Hershey Bears upon returning from Switzerland (November 1, 1990). . . . Suspended three games by AHL for physically abusing linesman (February 1, 1991). . . . Traded by Flyers to New York Rangers for future considerations (August 8, 1991). . . . Signed as free agent by Cincinnati Cyclones (July 12, 1993).
HONORS: Won Les Cunningham Plaque (1992-93). . . . Won John B. Sollenberger Trophy (1992-93). . . . Named to AHL All-Star first team (1992-93).

Season	Team	League	REGULAR SEASON					PLAYOFFS				
			Gms.	G	A	Pts.	PIM	Gms.	G	A	Pts.	PIM
82-83	Oshawa	OHL	70	22	53	75	145	16	3	6	9	17
83-84	Oshawa	OHL	58	31	60	91	149	7	4	4	8	18
84-85	Oshawa	OHL	60	48	69	117	105	5	3	4	7	6
	Springfield	AHL	6	0	3	3	0	2	1	0	1	0
	Minnesota	NHL	1	0	0	0	0	—	—	—	—	—
85-86	Springfield	AHL	28	15	16	31	46	—	—	—	—	—
	Nova Scotia	AHL	47	6	23	29	36	—	—	—	—	—
86-87	Nova Scotia	AHL	80	22	25	47	165	5	1	2	3	4
87-88	Hershey	AHL	77	38	41	79	151	12	5	†11	†16	22

Season	Team	League	REGULAR SEASON					PLAYOFFS				
			Gms.	G	A	Pts.	PIM	Gms.	G	A	Pts.	PIM
88-89—Hershey		AHL	76	36	67	103	158	11	5	9	14	30
89-90—Philadelphia		NHL	11	2	0	2	8	—	—	—	—	—
—Hershey		AHL	66	39	53	92	125	—	—	—	—	—
90-91—Olten		Switzerland					Statistics unavailable.					
—Rochester		AHL	65	31	57	88	115	15	9	*14	*23	14
91-92—Binghamton		AHL	74	32	50	82	122	11	3	7	10	8
92-93—Binghamton		AHL	78	54	*84	*138	112	14	3	9	12	32
93-94—Cincinnati		IHL	80	30	59	89	128	11	8	9	17	29
NHL totals			12	2	0	2	8					

BILLINGTON, CRAIG
G, SENATORS

PERSONAL: Born September 11, 1966, in London, Ont. . . . 5-10/170. . . . Catches left.

TRANSACTIONS/CAREER NOTES: Selected by New Jersey Devils as underage junior in second round (second Devils pick, 23rd overall) of NHL entry draft (June 9, 1984). . . . Suffered from mononucleosis (July 1984). . . . Injured hamstring (February 15, 1992); missed two games. . . . Strained knee (March 11, 1992); missed six games. . . . Underwent arthroscopic knee surgery (April 13, 1992). . . . Suffered from sore throat (March 27, 1993); missed one game. . . . Traded by Devils with C/LW Troy Mallette and fourth-round pick in 1993 draft (C Cosmo Dupaul) to Ottawa Senators for G Peter Sidorkiewicz and future considerations (June 20, 1993); Senators sent LW Mike Peluso to Devils to complete deal (June 26, 1993).

HONORS: Won Bobby Smith Trophy (1984-85). . . . Named to OHL All-Star first team (1984-85). . . . Played in NHL All-Star Game (1993).

Season	Team	League	REGULAR SEASON							PLAYOFFS						
			Gms.	Min.	W	L	T	GA	SO	Avg.	Gms.	Min.	W	L	GA	SO	Avg.
82-83—London Diamonds		OPJHL	23	1338	...	...	...	76	0	3.41	—	—	—	—	—	—	—
83-84—Belleville		OHL	44	2335	20	19	0	162	1	4.16	1	30	0	0	3	0	6.00
84-85—Belleville		OHL	47	2544	26	19	0	180	1	4.25	14	761	7	5	47	†1	3.71
85-86—Belleville		OHL	3	180	2	1	0	11	0	3.67	†20	1133	9	6	*68	0	3.60
—New Jersey		NHL	18	902	4	9	1	77	0	5.12	—	—	—	—	—	—	—
86-87—Maine		AHL	20	1151	9	8	2	70	0	3.65	—	—	—	—	—	—	—
—New Jersey		NHL	22	1114	4	13	2	89	0	4.79	—	—	—	—	—	—	—
87-88—Utica		AHL	*59	*3404	22	27	8	*208	1	3.67	—	—	—	—	—	—	—
88-89—New Jersey		NHL	3	140	1	1	0	11	0	4.71	—	—	—	—	—	—	—
—Utica		AHL	41	2432	17	18	6	150	2	3.70	4	219	1	3	18	0	4.93
89-90—Utica		AHL	38	2087	20	13	1	138	2	3.97	—	—	—	—	—	—	—
90-91—Can. national team		Int'l	34	1879	17	14	2	110	2	3.51	—	—	—	—	—	—	—
91-92—New Jersey		NHL	26	1363	13	7	1	69	2	3.04	—	—	—	—	—	—	—
92-93—New Jersey		NHL	42	2389	21	16	4	146	2	3.67	2	78	0	1	5	0	3.85
93-94—Ottawa		NHL	63	3319	11	*41	4	*254	0	4.59	—	—	—	—	—	—	—
NHL totals			174	9227	54	87	12	646	4	4.20	2	78	0	1	5	0	3.85

BILODEAU, BRENT
D, CANADIENS

PERSONAL: Born March 27, 1973, in Dallas. . . . 6-4/215. . . . Shoots left. . . . Name pronounced BIHL-uh-DOH.

TRANSACTIONS/CAREER NOTES: Selected by Montreal Canadiens in first round (first Canadiens pick, 17th overall) of NHL entry draft (June 22, 1991).

HONORS: Named to WHL (East) All-Star second team (1991-92 and 1992-93).

Season	Team	League	REGULAR SEASON					PLAYOFFS				
			Gms.	G	A	Pts.	PIM	Gms.	G	A	Pts.	PIM
88-89—St. Albert		AJHL	55	8	17	25	167	—	—	—	—	—
89-90—Seattle		WHL	68	14	29	43	170	13	3	5	8	31
90-91—Seattle		WHL	55	7	18	25	145	6	1	0	1	12
91-92—Seattle		WHL	7	1	2	3	43	—	—	—	—	—
—Swift Current		WHL	56	10	47	57	118	8	2	3	5	11
92-93—Swift Current		WHL	59	11	57	68	77	17	5	14	19	18
93-94—Fredericton		AHL	72	2	5	7	89	—	—	—	—	—

BLACK, JAMES
C, SABRES

PERSONAL: Born August 15, 1969, in Regina, Sask. . . . 5-11/185. . . . Shoots left.

TRANSACTIONS/CAREER NOTES: Selected by Hartford Whalers in fifth round (fourth Whalers pick, 94th overall) of NHL entry draft (June 17, 1989). . . . Traded by Whalers to Minnesota North Stars for C Mark Janssens (September 3, 1992). . . . North Stars franchise moved from Minnesota to Dallas and renamed Stars for 1993-94 season. . . . Traded by Stars with seventh-round pick in 1994 draft (RW Steve Webb) to Buffalo Sabres for RW Gord Donnelly (December 15, 1993). . . . Suffered forehead laceration (October 27, 1993); missed five games.

Season	Team	League	REGULAR SEASON					PLAYOFFS				
			Gms.	G	A	Pts.	PIM	Gms.	G	A	Pts.	PIM
87-88—Portland		WHL	72	30	50	80	50	—	—	—	—	—
88-89—Portland		WHL	71	45	51	96	57	19	13	6	19	28
89-90—Hartford		NHL	1	0	0	0	0	—	—	—	—	—
—Binghamton		AHL	80	37	35	72	34	—	—	—	—	—
90-91—Hartford		NHL	1	0	0	0	0	—	—	—	—	—
—Springfield		AHL	79	35	61	96	34	18	9	9	18	6

Season Team	League	REGULAR SEASON					PLAYOFFS				
		Gms.	G	A	Pts.	PIM	Gms.	G	A	Pts.	PIM
91-92—Springfield	AHL	47	15	25	40	33	10	3	2	5	18
—Hartford	NHL	30	4	6	10	10	—	—	—	—	—
92-93—Minnesota	NHL	10	2	1	3	4	—	—	—	—	—
—Kalamazoo	IHL	63	25	45	70	40	—	—	—	—	—
93-94—Dallas	NHL	13	2	3	5	2	—	—	—	—	—
—Buffalo	NHL	2	0	0	0	0	—	—	—	—	—
—Rochester	AHL	45	19	32	51	28	4	2	3	5	0
NHL totals		57	8	10	18	16					

BLACK, RYAN
LW, DEVILS

PERSONAL: Born October 25, 1973, in Guelph, Ont. . . . 6-1/180. . . . Shoots left.
HIGH SCHOOL: Thomas A. Stewart (Peterborough, Ont.).
TRANSACTIONS/CAREER NOTES: Selected by New Jersey Devils in fifth round (sixth Devils pick, 114th overall) of NHL entry draft (June 20, 1992).

Season Team	League	REGULAR SEASON					PLAYOFFS				
		Gms.	G	A	Pts.	PIM	Gms.	G	A	Pts.	PIM
88-89—New Hamburg Jr. C	OHA	23	3	3	6	24	—	—	—	—	—
89-90—Elmira Jr. B	OHA	33	19	21	40	94	—	—	—	—	—
—Waterloo Jr. B	OHA	15	5	4	9	37	—	—	—	—	—
90-91—Peterborough	OHL	59	7	16	23	41	4	0	1	1	0
91-92—Peterborough	OHL	66	18	33	51	57	7	1	1	2	11
92-93—Peterborough	OHL	66	30	41	71	41	20	7	4	11	28
93-94—London	OHL	60	36	58	94	50	5	5	8	13	8

BLAKE, ROB
D, KINGS

PERSONAL: Born December 10, 1969, in Simcoe, Ont. . . . 6-3/215. . . . Shoots right. . . . Full name: Robert Bowlby Blake.
COLLEGE: Bowling Green State.
TRANSACTIONS/CAREER NOTES: Dislocated shoulder (April 1987). . . . Selected by Los Angeles Kings in fourth round (fourth Kings pick, 70th overall) of NHL entry draft (June 11, 1988). . . . Sprained knee (April 1990). . . . Injured knee (February 12, 1991); missed two games. . . . Injured shoulder (October 8, 1991); missed 11 games. . . . Sprained knee ligaments (November 28, 1991); missed six games. . . . Suffered from the flu (January 23, 1992); missed one game. . . . Suffered from the flu (February 13, 1992); missed one game. . . . Strained shoulder (March 14, 1992); missed four games. . . . Broke rib (December 19, 1992); missed three games. . . . Suffered lower back contusion (April 3, 1993); missed final five games of regular season and one playoff game.
HONORS: Named to CCHA All-Star second team (1988-89). . . . Named to NCAA All-America West first team (1989-90). . . . Named to CCHA All-Star first team (1989-90). . . . Named to NHL All-Rookie team (1990-91). . . . Played in NHL All-Star Game (1994).

Season Team	League	REGULAR SEASON					PLAYOFFS				
		Gms.	G	A	Pts.	PIM	Gms.	G	A	Pts.	PIM
86-87—Stratford Jr. B	OHA	31	11	20	31	115	—	—	—	—	—
87-88—Bowling Green State	CCHA	36	5	8	13	72	—	—	—	—	—
88-89—Bowling Green State	CCHA	46	11	21	32	140	—	—	—	—	—
89-90—Bowling Green State	CCHA	42	23	36	59	140	—	—	—	—	—
—Los Angeles	NHL	4	0	0	0	4	8	1	3	4	4
90-91—Los Angeles	NHL	75	12	34	46	125	12	1	4	5	26
91-92—Los Angeles	NHL	57	7	13	20	102	6	2	1	3	12
92-93—Los Angeles	NHL	76	16	43	59	152	23	4	6	10	46
93-94—Los Angeles	NHL	84	20	48	68	137	—	—	—	—	—
NHL totals		296	55	138	193	520	49	8	14	22	88

BLOEMBERG, JEFF
D, WHALERS

PERSONAL: Born January 31, 1968, in Listowel, Ont. . . . 6-2/205. . . . Shoots right. . . . Name pronounced BLOOM-buhrg.
TRANSACTIONS/CAREER NOTES: Selected by New York Rangers as underage junior in fifth round (fifth Rangers pick, 93rd overall) of NHL entry draft (June 21, 1986). . . . Selected by Tampa Bay Lightning in NHL expansion draft (June 18, 1992). . . . Traded by Lightning to Edmonton Oilers for future considerations (September 25, 1992). . . . Signed as free agent by Hartford Whalers (August 1993).
HONORS: Named to AHL All-Star second team (1990-91).

Season Team	League	REGULAR SEASON					PLAYOFFS				
		Gms.	G	A	Pts.	PIM	Gms.	G	A	Pts.	PIM
84-85—Listowel Jr. B	OHA	31	7	14	21	73	—	—	—	—	—
85-86—North Bay	OHL	60	2	11	13	76	8	1	2	3	9
86-87—North Bay	OHL	60	5	13	18	91	21	1	6	7	13
87-88—North Bay	OHL	46	9	26	35	60	—	—	—	—	—
—Colorado	IHL	5	0	0	0	0	11	1	0	1	8
88-89—New York Rangers	NHL	9	0	0	0	0	—	—	—	—	—
—Denver	IHL	64	7	22	29	55	1	0	0	0	0
89-90—Flint	IHL	44	7	21	28	24	—	—	—	—	—
—New York Rangers	NHL	28	3	3	6	25	7	0	3	3	5
90-91—Binghamton	AHL	77	16	46	62	28	10	0	6	6	10
91-92—Binghamton	AHL	66	6	41	47	22	11	1	10	11	10
—New York Rangers	NHL	3	0	1	1	0	—	—	—	—	—
92-93—Cape Breton	AHL	76	6	45	51	34	16	5	10	15	10

Season Team	League	REGULAR SEASON					PLAYOFFS				
		Gms.	G	A	Pts.	PIM	Gms.	G	A	Pts.	PIM
93-94—Springfield	AHL	78	8	28	36	36	6	0	3	3	8
NHL totals		40	3	4	7	25	7	0	3	3	5

BLOMSTEN, ARTO
D, JETS

PERSONAL: Born March 16, 1965, in Vaasa, Finland.... 6-3/198.... Shoots left.
TRANSACTIONS/CAREER NOTES: Selected by Winnipeg Jets in 11th round (11th Jets pick, 239th overall) of NHL entry draft (June 21,1986).... Strained groin (October 29, 1993); missed two games.

Season Team	League	REGULAR SEASON					PLAYOFFS				
		Gms.	G	A	Pts.	PIM	Gms.	G	A	Pts.	PIM
83-84—Djurgarden	Sweden	3	0	0	0	4	—	—	—	—	—
84-85—Djurgarden	Sweden	19	3	1	4	22	8	0	0	0	8
85-86—Djurgarden	Sweden	8	0	3	3	6	—	—	—	—	—
86-87—Djurgarden	Sweden	29	2	4	6	28	—	—	—	—	—
87-88—Djurgarden	Sweden	39	12	6	18	36	2	1	0	1	0
88-89—Djurgarden	Sweden	40	10	9	19	38	—	—	—	—	—
89-90—Djurgarden	Sweden	36	5	21	26	28	8	4	1	5	6
90-91—Djurgarden	Sweden	38	2	9	11	42	—	—	—	—	—
91-92—Djurgarden	Sweden	39	6	8	14	34	10	2	0	2	8
92-93—Djurgarden	Sweden	40	4	16	20	52	—	—	—	—	—
93-94—Winnipeg	NHL	18	0	2	2	6	—	—	—	—	—
—Moncton	AHL	44	6	27	33	25	20	4	10	14	8
NHL totals		18	0	2	2	6					

BLOUIN, SYLVAIN
D, RANGERS

PERSONAL: Born May 21, 1974, in Montreal.... 6-2/216.... Shoots left.
TRANSACTIONS/CAREER NOTES: Selected by New York Rangers in fourth round (fifth Rangers pick, 104th overall) of NHL entry draft (June 29, 1994).

Season Team	League	REGULAR SEASON					PLAYOFFS				
		Gms.	G	A	Pts.	PIM	Gms.	G	A	Pts.	PIM
91-92—Laval	QMJHL	28	0	0	0	23	9	0	0	0	35
92-93—Laval	QMJHL	68	0	10	10	373	13	1	0	1	*66
93-94—Laval	QMJHL	62	18	22	40	*492	21	4	13	17	*177

BLUE, JOHN
G, BRUINS

PERSONAL: Born February 9, 1966, in Huntington Beach, Calif.... 5-10/185.... Catches left.
COLLEGE: Minnesota.
TRANSACTIONS/CAREER NOTES: Selected by Winnipeg Jets in 10th round (ninth Jets pick, 197th overall) of NHL entry draft (June 21, 1986).... Traded by Jets to Minnesota North Stars for seventh-round pick (C Markus Akerbloom) in 1988 draft (March 7, 1988).... Signed as free agent by Boston Bruins (August 1, 1991).
HONORS: Named to WCHA All-Star second team (1984-85).... Named to WCHA All-Star first team (1985-86).

Season Team	League	REGULAR SEASON							PLAYOFFS						
		Gms.	Min.	W	L	T	GA	SO	Avg.	Gms.	Min.	W	L	GA	SO	Avg.
83-84—Des Moines	USHL	15	753	...	...	...	63	...	5.02	—	—	—	—	—	—	—
84-85—Univ. of Minnesota	WCHA	34	1964	23	10	0	111	2	3.39	—	—	—	—	—	—	—
85-86—Univ. of Minnesota	WCHA	29	1588	20	6	0	80	3	3.02	—	—	—	—	—	—	—
86-87—Univ. of Minnesota	WCHA	33	1889	21	9	1	99	3	3.14	—	—	—	—	—	—	—
87-88—Kalamazoo	IHL	15	847	3	8	‡4	65	0	4.60	1	40	0	1	6	0	9.00
—U.S. national team	Int'l	13	588	3	4	1	33	0	3.37	—	—	—	—	—	—	—
—U.S. Olympic Team	Int'l							Did not play.								
88-89—Kalamazoo	IHL	17	970	8	6	‡0	69	0	4.27	—	—	—	—	—	—	—
—Virginia	ECHL	10	570	...	...	...	38	0	4.00	—	—	—	—	—	—	—
89-90—Kalamazoo	IHL	4	232	2	1	‡1	18	0	4.66	—	—	—	—	—	—	—
—Phoenix	IHL	19	986	5	10	‡3	93	0	5.66	—	—	—	—	—	—	—
—Knoxville	ECHL	19	1000	6	10	‡1	85	0	5.10	—	—	—	—	—	—	—
90-91—Maine	AHL	10	545	3	4	2	22	0	2.42	1	40	0	1	7	0	10.50
—Kalamazoo	IHL	1	64	1	0	‡0	2	0	1.88	—	—	—	—	—	—	—
—Albany	IHL	19	1077	11	6	‡0	71	0	3.96	—	—	—	—	—	—	—
—Peoria	IHL	4	240	4	0	‡0	12	0	3.00	—	—	—	—	—	—	—
—Knoxville	ECHL	3	149	1	1	‡0	13	0	5.23	—	—	—	—	—	—	—
91-92—Maine	AHL	43	2168	11	*23	6	165	1	4.57	—	—	—	—	—	—	—
92-93—Providence	AHL	19	1159	14	4	1	67	0	3.47	—	—	—	—	—	—	—
—Boston	NHL	23	1322	9	8	4	64	1	2.90	2	96	0	1	5	0	3.13
93-94—Boston	NHL	18	944	5	8	3	47	0	2.99	—	—	—	—	—	—	—
—Providence	AHL	24	1298	7	11	4	76	1	3.51	—	—	—	—	—	—	—
NHL totals		41	2266	14	16	7	111	1	2.94	2	96	0	1	5	0	3.13

BOBACK, MIKE
C, CAPITALS

PERSONAL: Born August 13, 1970, in Mt. Clemens, Mich. ... 5-11/180. ... Shoots right. ... Name pronounced BOH-BAK.
COLLEGE: Providence.
TRANSACTIONS/CAREER NOTES: Selected by Washington Capitals in 10th round (12th Capitals pick, 198th overall) of NHL entry draft (June 16, 1990).
HONORS: Named to Hockey East All-Star first team (1989-90 and 1991-92).

B

Season Team	League	REGULAR SEASON					PLAYOFFS				
		Gms.	G	A	Pts.	PIM	Gms.	G	A	Pts.	PIM
88-89—Providence College	Hockey East	29	19	19	38	24	—	—	—	—	—
89-90—Providence College	Hockey East	31	13	29	42	28	—	—	—	—	—
90-91—Providence College	Hockey East	26	15	24	39	6	—	—	—	—	—
91-92—Providence College	Hockey East	36	24	*48	*72	34	—	—	—	—	—
92-93—Baltimore	AHL	69	11	68	79	14	5	3	3	6	6
93-94—Portland	AHL	68	16	43	59	50	17	10	17	*27	4

BODGER, DOUG
D, SABRES

PERSONAL: Born June 18, 1966, in Chemainus, B.C.... 6-2/213.... Shoots left.... Name pronounced BAH-juhr.

TRANSACTIONS/CAREER NOTES: Selected by Pittsburgh Penguins as underage junior in first round (second Penguins pick, ninth overall) of NHL entry draft (June 9, 1984).... Underwent surgery to remove bone chip on left foot (April 1985).... Sprained knee (December 1987).... Strained left knee (October 1988).... Traded by Penguins with LW Darrin Shannon to Buffalo Sabres for G Tom Barrasso and third-round pick (RW Joe Dziedzic) in 1990 draft (November 12, 1988).... Sprained left knee (October 1989); missed eight games.... Injured shoulder (December 28, 1990); missed four games.... Separated left shoulder (February 17, 1991); missed 18 games.... Reinjured left shoulder (March 30, 1991).... Injured eye (February 11, 1992); missed seven games.... Suffered sore back (December 2, 1993); missed four games.

HONORS: Named to WHL All-Star second team (1982-83).... Named to WHL (West) All-Star first team (1983-84).

Season Team	League	REGULAR SEASON					PLAYOFFS				
		Gms.	G	A	Pts.	PIM	Gms.	G	A	Pts.	PIM
82-83—Kamloops	WHL	72	26	66	92	98	7	0	5	5	2
83-84—Kamloops	WHL	70	21	77	98	90	17	2	15	17	12
84-85—Pittsburgh	NHL	65	5	26	31	67	—	—	—	—	—
85-86—Pittsburgh	NHL	79	4	33	37	63	—	—	—	—	—
86-87—Pittsburgh	NHL	76	11	38	49	52	—	—	—	—	—
87-88—Pittsburgh	NHL	69	14	31	45	103	—	—	—	—	—
88-89—Pittsburgh	NHL	10	1	4	5	7	—	—	—	—	—
—Buffalo	NHL	61	7	40	47	52	5	1	1	2	11
89-90—Buffalo	NHL	71	12	36	48	64	6	1	5	6	6
90-91—Buffalo	NHL	58	5	23	28	54	4	0	1	1	0
91-92—Buffalo	NHL	73	11	35	46	108	7	2	1	3	2
92-93—Buffalo	NHL	81	9	45	54	87	8	2	3	5	0
93-94—Buffalo	NHL	75	7	32	39	76	7	0	3	3	6
NHL totals		718	86	343	429	733	37	6	14	20	25

BODNARCHUK, MIKE
RW, DEVILS

PERSONAL: Born March 26, 1970, in Bramalea, Ont.... 6-1/175.... Shoots right.... Name pronounced bahd-NAHR-chuhk.

TRANSACTIONS/CAREER NOTES: Selected by New Jersey Devils in fourth round (sixth Devils pick, 64th overall) of NHL entry draft (June 16, 1990).

HONORS: Named to OHL All-Star second team (1989-90).

Season Team	League	REGULAR SEASON					PLAYOFFS				
		Gms.	G	A	Pts.	PIM	Gms.	G	A	Pts.	PIM
86-87—Bramalea	MTHL	34	12	8	20	33	—	—	—	—	—
87-88—Kingston	OHL	63	12	20	32	12	—	—	—	—	—
88-89—Kingston	OHL	63	22	38	60	30	—	—	—	—	—
89-90—Kingston	OHL	66	40	59	99	31	7	2	4	6	4
90-91—Utica	AHL	69	23	32	55	28	—	—	—	—	—
91-92—Utica	AHL	76	21	19	40	36	4	0	2	2	0
92-93—Utica	AHL	21	6	10	16	4	4	2	0	2	4
—Cincinnati	IHL	47	15	18	33	65	—	—	—	—	—
93-94—Phoenix	IHL	8	3	1	4	6	—	—	—	—	—
—Albany	AHL	45	12	20	32	54	2	0	0	0	2

BOILEAU, PATRICK
D, CAPITALS

PERSONAL: Born February 22, 1975, in Montreal.... 6-0/185.... Shoots right.... Name pronounced BOY-loh.

HIGH SCHOOL: CEGEP Lionel-Groulx (Que.).

TRANSACTIONS/CAREER NOTES: Selected by Washington Capitals in third round (third Capitals pick, 69th overall) of NHL entry draft (June 26, 1993).

HONORS: Named to Can.HL All-Rookie team (1992-93).... Won Marcel Robert Trophy (1993-94).... Won Can.HL Scholastic Player of the Year Award (1993-94).

Season Team	League	REGULAR SEASON					PLAYOFFS				
		Gms.	G	A	Pts.	PIM	Gms.	G	A	Pts.	PIM
92-93—Laval	QMJHL	69	4	19	23	73	13	1	2	3	10
93-94—Laval	QMJHL	64	13	57	70	56	21	1	7	8	24

BOIVIN, CLAUDE
LW, SENATORS

PERSONAL: Born March 1, 1970, in St. Foy, Que.... 6-2/200.... Shoots left.... Name pronounced BOY-vihn.

TRANSACTIONS/CAREER NOTES: Selected by Philadelphia Flyers in first round (first Flyers pick, 14th overall) of NHL entry draft (June 11, 1988).... Traded by Drummondville Voltigeurs with D Serge Anglehart and fifth-round draft pick to Laval Titans for D Luc Doucet, D Brad MacIsaac and second- and third-round draft picks (February 15, 1990).... Separated shoulder and bruised chest (October 6, 1992); missed first five games of season. . . . Tore ligaments in left knee (January 2, 1993) and underwent reconstructive knee surgery (January 18, 1993); missed remainder of season. . . . Lacerated left elbow (October 30, 1993). . . . Underwent arthroscopic knee surgery (November 18, 1993); missed 18 games. . . . Traded by Flyers with G Kirk Daubenspeck to Ottawa Senators for C Mark Lamb (March 5, 1994).

			REGULAR SEASON					PLAYOFFS				
Season	Team	League	Gms.	G	A	Pts.	PIM	Gms.	G	A	Pts.	PIM
87-88—Drummondville		QMJHL	63	23	26	49	233	17	5	3	8	74
88-89—Drummondville		QMJHL	63	20	36	56	218	4	0	2	2	27
89-90—Laval		QMJHL	59	24	51	75	309	13	7	13	20	59
90-91—Hershey		AHL	65	13	32	45	159	7	1	5	6	28
91-92—Hershey		AHL	20	4	5	9	96	—	—	—	—	—
—Philadelphia		NHL	58	5	13	18	187	—	—	—	—	—
92-93—Philadelphia		NHL	30	5	4	9	76	—	—	—	—	—
93-94—Hershey		AHL	4	1	6	7	6	—	—	—	—	—
—Philadelphia		NHL	26	1	1	2	57	—	—	—	—	—
—Ottawa		NHL	15	1	0	1	38	—	—	—	—	—
NHL totals			129	12	18	30	358					

BONDRA, PETER
RW, CAPITALS

PERSONAL: Born February 7, 1968, in Luck, U.S.S.R. . . . 6-0/200. . . . Shoots left. . . . Name pronounced BAHN-druh.
TRANSACTIONS/CAREER NOTES: Selected by Washington Capitals in eighth round (ninth Capitals pick, 156th overall) of NHL entry draft (June 16, 1990). . . . Dislocated left shoulder (January 17, 1991). . . . Suffered recurring shoulder problems (February 13, 1991); missed 13 games. . . . Suffered throat injury (April 4, 1993); missed one game. . . . Broke left hand (November 26, 1993); missed 12 games.
HONORS: Played in NHL All-Star Game (1993).

			REGULAR SEASON					PLAYOFFS				
Season	Team	League	Gms.	G	A	Pts.	PIM	Gms.	G	A	Pts.	PIM
88-89—Kosice		Czech.	40	30	10	40	20	—	—	—	—	—
89-90—Kosice		Czech.	42	29	17	46	...	—	—	—	—	—
90-91—Washington		NHL	54	12	16	28	47	4	0	1	1	2
91-92—Washington		NHL	71	28	28	56	42	7	6	2	8	4
92-93—Washington		NHL	83	37	48	85	70	6	0	6	6	0
93-94—Washington		NHL	69	24	19	43	40	9	2	4	6	4
NHL totals			277	101	111	212	199	26	8	13	21	10

BONK, RADEK
C, SENATORS

PERSONAL: Born January 9, 1976, in Kronov, Czechoslovakia. . . . 6-3/215. . . . Shoots left. . . . Name pronounced RA-dihk Bahnk.
TRANSACTIONS/CAREER NOTES: Selected by Ottawa Senators in first round (first Senators pick, third overall) of NHL entry draft (June 28, 1994).
HONORS: Won Garry F. Longman Memorial Trophy (1993-94).

			REGULAR SEASON					PLAYOFFS				
Season	Team	League	Gms.	G	A	Pts.	PIM	Gms.	G	A	Pts.	PIM
90-91—Opava		Czech.	35	47	42	89	25	—	—	—	—	—
91-92—ZPS Zlin		Czech.	30	5	5	10	10	—	—	—	—	—
92-93—ZPS Zlin		Czech.	30	5	5	10	10	—	—	—	—	—
93-94—Las Vegas		IHL	76	42	45	87	208	5	1	2	3	10

BONSIGNORE, JASON
C, OILERS

PERSONAL: Born April 15, 1976, in Rochester, N.Y. . . . 6-4/208. . . . Shoots right. . . . Name pronounced BAHN-sih-nyohr.
TRANSACTIONS/CAREER NOTES: Selected by Edmonton Oilers in first round (first Oilers pick, fourth overall) of NHL entry draft (June 28, 1994).

			REGULAR SEASON					PLAYOFFS				
Season	Team	League	Gms.	G	A	Pts.	PIM	Gms.	G	A	Pts.	PIM
92-93—Newmarket		OHL	66	22	20	42	6	—	—	—	—	—
93-94—Newmarket		OHL	17	7	17	24	22	—	—	—	—	—
—Niagara Falls		OHL	41	15	47	62	41	—	—	—	—	—
—U.S. national team		Int'l	5	0	2	2	0	—	—	—	—	—

BORDELEAU, SEBASTIEN
C, CANADIENS

PERSONAL: Born February 15, 1975, in Vancouver. . . . 5-10/176. . . . Shoots right. . . . Name pronounced BOHR-duh-loh. . . . Son of Paulin Bordeleau, coach, Fredericton Canadiens of American Hockey League.
TRANSACTIONS/CAREER NOTES: Selected by Montreal Canadiens in third round (third Canadiens pick, 73rd overall) of NHL entry draft (June 26, 1993).

			REGULAR SEASON					PLAYOFFS				
Season	Team	League	Gms.	G	A	Pts.	PIM	Gms.	G	A	Pts.	PIM
91-92—Hull		QMJHL	62	26	32	58	91	5	0	3	3	23
92-93—Hull		QMJHL	60	18	39	57	95	10	3	8	11	20
93-94—Hull		QMJHL	60	26	57	83	147	17	6	14	20	26

BORSATO, LUCIANO
C, JETS

PERSONAL: Born January 7, 1966, in Richmond Hill, Ont. . . . 5-11/190. . . . Shoots right. . . . Name pronounced LOO-chee-AH-noh bohr-SAH-toh.
COLLEGE: Clarkson (N.Y.).
TRANSACTIONS/CAREER NOTES: Selected by Winnipeg Jets as underage junior in seventh round (seventh Jets pick, 135th overall) of NHL entry draft (June 9, 1984). . . . Suffered back spasms (October 28,

1992); missed three games. . . . Fractured finger (November 19, 1992); missed eight games. . . . Suffered back spasms (January 17, 1993); missed six games. . . . Suffered back spasms (February 28, 1994); missed three games.
HONORS: Named to NCAA All-America East second team (1987-88). . . . Named to ECAC All-Star second team (1987-88).

			REGULAR SEASON					PLAYOFFS			
Season Team	League	Gms.	G	A	Pts.	PIM	Gms.	G	A	Pts.	PIM
83-84—Bramalea	MTHL	37	20	36	56	59	—	—	—	—	—
84-85—Clarkson	ECAC	33	15	17	32	37	—	—	—	—	—
85-86—Clarkson	ECAC	32	17	20	37	50	—	—	—	—	—
86-87—Clarkson	ECAC	31	16	*41	57	55	—	—	—	—	—
87-88—Clarkson	ECAC	33	15	29	44	38	—	—	—	—	—
—Moncton	AHL	3	1	1	2	0	—	—	—	—	—
88-89—Tappara	Finland	44	31	36	67	69	7	0	3	3	4
—Moncton	AHL	6	2	5	7	4	—	—	—	—	—
89-90—Moncton	AHL	1	1	0	1	0	—	—	—	—	—
90-91—Moncton	AHL	41	14	24	38	40	9	3	7	10	22
—Winnipeg	NHL	1	0	1	1	2	—	—	—	—	—
91-92—Moncton	AHL	14	2	7	9	39	—	—	—	—	—
—Winnipeg	NHL	56	15	21	36	45	1	0	0	0	0
92-93—Winnipeg	NHL	67	15	20	35	38	6	1	0	1	4
93-94—Winnipeg	NHL	75	5	13	18	28	—	—	—	—	—
NHL totals		199	35	55	90	113	7	1	0	1	4

BORSCHEVSKY, NIKOLAI
RW, MAPLE LEAFS

PERSONAL: Born January 12, 1965, in Tomsk, U.S.S.R. . . . 5-9/180. . . . Shoots left. . . . Name pronounced bohr-SHEHV-skee.
TRANSACTIONS/CAREER NOTES: Selected by Toronto Maple Leafs in fourth round (third Maple Leafs pick, 77th overall) of NHL entry draft (June 20, 1992). . . . Bruised buttock (November 7, 1992); missed one game. . . . Strained neck (December 31, 1992); missed three games. . . . Strained back (March 9, 1993); missed one game. . . . Broke orbital bone (April 19, 1993); missed first five playoff games. . . . Suffered ruptured spleen (November 3, 1993); missed 22 games. . . . Separated shoulder (February 28, 1994); missed 14 games.
HONORS: Named CIS Player of the Year (1991-92).

			REGULAR SEASON					PLAYOFFS			
Season Team	League	Gms.	G	A	Pts.	PIM	Gms.	G	A	Pts.	PIM
83-84—Dynamo Moscow	USSR	34	4	5	9	4	—	—	—	—	—
84-85—Dynamo Moscow	USSR	34	5	9	14	6	—	—	—	—	—
85-86—Dynamo Moscow	USSR	31	6	4	10	4	—	—	—	—	—
86-87—Dynamo Moscow	USSR	28	1	4	5	8	—	—	—	—	—
87-88—Dynamo Moscow	USSR	37	11	7	18	6	—	—	—	—	—
88-89—Dynamo Moscow	USSR	43	7	8	15	18	—	—	—	—	—
89-90—Spartak Moscow	USSR	48	17	25	42	8	—	—	—	—	—
90-91—Spartak Moscow	USSR	45	19	16	35	16	—	—	—	—	—
91-92—Spartak Moscow	CIS	40	25	14	39	16	—	—	—	—	—
—Unified Olympic Team	Int'l	8	7	2	9	0	—	—	—	—	—
92-93—Toronto	NHL	78	34	40	74	28	16	2	7	9	0
93-94—Toronto	NHL	45	14	20	34	10	15	2	2	4	4
NHL totals		123	48	60	108	38	31	4	9	13	4

BOTTERILL, JASON
LW, STARS

PERSONAL: Born May 19, 1976, in Edmonton. . . . 6-3/205. . . . Shoots left.
COLLEGE: Michigan.
TRANSACTIONS/CAREER NOTES: Selected by Dallas Stars in first round (first Stars pick, 20th overall) of NHL entry draft (June 28, 1994).
HONORS: Named to CCHA All-Rookie team (1993-94).

			REGULAR SEASON					PLAYOFFS			
Season Team	League	Gms.	G	A	Pts.	PIM	Gms.	G	A	Pts.	PIM
92-93—St. Paul	USHL	22	22	26	48	...	—	—	—	—	—
93-94—University of Michigan	CCHA	37	21	19	40	94	—	—	—	—	—

BOUCHARD, JOEL
D, FLAMES

PERSONAL: Born January 23, 1974, in Montreal. . . . 6-0/185. . . . Shoots left.
TRANSACTIONS/CAREER NOTES: Selected by Calgary Flames in sixth round (sixth Flames pick, 129th overall) of NHL entry draft (June 20, 1992).
HONORS: Named to QMJHL All-Star first team (1993-94).

			REGULAR SEASON					PLAYOFFS			
Season Team	League	Gms.	G	A	Pts.	PIM	Gms.	G	A	Pts.	PIM
90-91—Longueuil	QMJHL	53	3	19	22	34	8	0	1	1	11
91-92—Verdun	QMJHL	70	9	37	46	55	19	1	7	8	20
92-93—Verdun	QMJHL	60	10	49	59	126	4	0	2	2	4
93-94—Verdun	QMJHL	60	15	55	70	62	4	1	0	1	6
—Saint John	AHL	1	0	0	0	0	2	0	0	0	0

BOUCHER, PHILIPPE
D, SABRES

PERSONAL: Born March 24, 1973, in St. Apollnaire, Que. . . . 6-2/188. . . . Shoots right. . . . Name pronounced boo-SHAY.
TRANSACTIONS/CAREER NOTES: Selected by Buffalo Sabres in first round (first Sabres pick, 13th overall) of NHL entry draft (June 22, 1991).
HONORS: Won Can.HL Rookie of the Year Award (1990-91). . . . Won Raymond Lagace Trophy (1990-91). . . . Won QMJHL Top Draft Prospect Award (1990-91). . . . Named to QMJHL All-Star second team (1990-91 and 1991-92).

Season Team	League	REGULAR SEASON					PLAYOFFS				
		Gms.	G	A	Pts.	PIM	Gms.	G	A	Pts.	PIM
90-91—Granby	QMJHL	69	21	46	67	92	—	—	—	—	—
91-92—Granby	QMJHL	49	22	37	59	47	—	—	—	—	—
—Laval	QMJHL	16	7	11	18	36	10	5	6	11	8
92-93—Laval	QMJHL	16	12	15	27	37	13	6	15	21	12
—Rochester	AHL	5	4	3	7	8	3	0	1	1	2
—Buffalo	NHL	18	0	4	4	14	—	—	—	—	—
93-94—Buffalo	NHL	38	6	8	14	29	7	1	1	2	2
—Rochester	AHL	31	10	22	32	51	—	—	—	—	—
NHL totals		56	6	12	18	43	7	1	1	2	2

BOUDRIAS, JASON
C, PANTHERS

PERSONAL: Born February 16, 1976, in Val d'Or, Que. . . . 6-0/201. . . . Shoots right.
TRANSACTIONS/CAREER NOTES: Selected by Florida Panthers in eighth round (eighth Panthers pick, 183rd overall) of NHL entry draft (June 29, 1994).

Season Team	League	REGULAR SEASON					PLAYOFFS				
		Gms.	G	A	Pts.	PIM	Gms.	G	A	Pts.	PIM
91-92—Gloucester	Tier II Jr. A	55	46	37	83	35	—	—	—	—	—
92-93—Laval	QMJHL	66	15	26	41	41	13	0	0	0	2
93-94—Laval	QMJHL	61	17	25	42	62	21	5	9	14	10

BOUGHNER, BOB
D, RED WINGS

PERSONAL: Born March 8, 1971, in Windsor, Ont. . . . 5-11/201. . . . Shoots right. . . . Name pronounced BOOG-nuhr.
TRANSACTIONS/CAREER NOTES: Selected by Detroit Red Wings in second round (second Red Wings pick, 32nd overall) of NHL entry draft (June 17, 1989).

Season Team	League	REGULAR SEASON					PLAYOFFS				
		Gms.	G	A	Pts.	PIM	Gms.	G	A	Pts.	PIM
87-88—St. Mary's Jr. B	OHA	36	4	18	22	177	—	—	—	—	—
88-89—Sault Ste. Marie	OHL	64	6	15	21	182	—	—	—	—	—
89-90—Sault Ste. Marie	OHL	49	7	23	30	122	—	—	—	—	—
90-91—Sault Ste. Marie	OHL	64	13	33	46	156	14	2	9	11	35
91-92—Adirondack	AHL	1	0	0	0	7	—	—	—	—	—
—Toledo	ECHL	28	3	10	13	79	5	2	0	2	15
92-93—Adirondack	AHL	69	1	16	17	190	—	—	—	—	—
93-94—Adirondack	AHL	72	8	14	22	292	10	1	1	2	18

BOULIN, VLADISLAV
D, FLYERS

PERSONAL: Born May 18, 1972, in Penza, U.S.S.R. . . . 6-4/196. . . . Shoots right. . . . Name pronounced BOO-leen.
TRANSACTIONS/CAREER NOTES: Selected by Philadelphia Flyers in fifth round (fourth Flyers pick, 103rd overall) of NHL entry draft (June 20, 1992).

Season Team	League	REGULAR SEASON					PLAYOFFS				
		Gms.	G	A	Pts.	PIM	Gms.	G	A	Pts.	PIM
90-91—Dizelist Penza	USSR Div. II	68	. . .	. . .	. . .	. . .	—	—	—	—	—
91-92—Dizelist Penza	CIS Div. II				Statistics unavailable.						
92-93—Dynamo Moscow	CIS	32	2	1	3	55	4	0	0	0	2
93-94—Dynamo Moscow	CIS	43	4	2	6	36	7	0	1	1	16

BOURQUE, PHIL
LW, SENATORS

PERSONAL: Born June 8, 1962, in Chelmsford, Mass. . . . 6-1/196. . . . Shoots left. . . . Full name: Phillippe Richard Bourque. . . . Name pronounced BOHRK.
TRANSACTIONS/CAREER NOTES: Signed as free agent by Pittsburgh Penguins (October 4, 1982). . . . Suffered back spasms (November 1989). . . . Sprained wrist (December 1990). . . . Suffered inflammation of left elbow (November 15, 1991); missed two games. . . . Strained back (December 18, 1991); missed three games. . . . Fractured left foot (January 10, 1992); missed nine games. . . . Reinjured foot (February 9, 1992); missed four games. . . . Signed as free agent by New York Rangers (August 31, 1992). . . . Suffered concussion (December 11, 1992); missed two games. . . . Sprained left knee (February 3, 1993); missed six games. . . . Bruised ankle (April 8, 1993); missed four games. . . . Traded by Rangers to Ottawa Senators for future considerations (March 21, 1994).
HONORS: Won Governors Trophy (1987-88). . . . Named to IHL All-Star first team (1987-88).
MISCELLANEOUS: Member of Stanley Cup championship teams (1991 and 1992).

Season Team	League	REGULAR SEASON					PLAYOFFS				
		Gms.	G	A	Pts.	PIM	Gms.	G	A	Pts.	PIM
80-81—Kingston	OMJHL	47	4	4	8	46	6	0	0	0	10
81-82—Kingston	OHL	67	11	40	51	111	4	0	0	0	0
82-83—Baltimore	AHL	65	1	15	16	93	—	—	—	—	—
83-84—Baltimore	AHL	58	5	17	22	96	—	—	—	—	—
—Pittsburgh	NHL	5	0	1	1	12	—	—	—	—	—
84-85—Baltimore	AHL	79	6	15	21	164	13	2	5	7	23
85-86—Pittsburgh	NHL	4	0	0	0	2	—	—	—	—	—
—Baltimore	AHL	74	8	18	26	226	—	—	—	—	—
86-87—Pittsburgh	NHL	22	2	3	5	32	—	—	—	—	—
—Baltimore	AHL	49	15	16	31	183	—	—	—	—	—
87-88—Muskegon	IHL	52	16	36	52	66	6	1	2	3	16
—Pittsburgh	NHL	21	4	12	16	20	—	—	—	—	—
88-89—Pittsburgh	NHL	80	17	26	43	97	11	4	1	5	66

Season Team	League	REGULAR SEASON					PLAYOFFS				
		Gms.	G	A	Pts.	PIM	Gms.	G	A	Pts.	PIM
89-90—Pittsburgh	NHL	76	22	17	39	108	—	—	—	—	—
90-91—Pittsburgh	NHL	78	20	14	34	106	24	6	7	13	16
91-92—Pittsburgh	NHL	58	10	16	26	58	†21	3	4	7	25
92-93—New York Rangers	NHL	55	6	14	20	39	—	—	—	—	—
93-94—New York Rangers	NHL	16	0	1	1	8	—	—	—	—	—
—Ottawa	NHL	11	2	3	5	0	—	—	—	—	—
NHL totals		426	83	107	190	482	56	13	12	25	107

BOURQUE, RAY
D, BRUINS

PERSONAL: Born December 28, 1960, in Montreal.... 5-11/210.... Shoots left.... Full name: Raymond Jean Bourque.... Name pronounced BOHRK.

TRANSACTIONS/CAREER NOTES: Selected by Boston Bruins in first round (first Bruins pick, eighth overall) of NHL entry draft (August 9, 1979).... Broke jaw (November 11, 1980).... Injured left shoulder (October 1981).... Fractured left wrist (April 21, 1982).... Refractured left wrist and fractured left forearm (summer 1982).... Broke bone over left eye (October 1982).... Sprained left knee ligaments (December 10, 1988).... Bruised hip (April 7, 1990).... Bruised right shoulder (October 17, 1990); missed four games.... Fractured finger (May 5, 1992); missed remainder of playoffs.... Injured back (December 19, 1992); missed two games.... Injured ankle (January 21, 1993); missed three games.... Injured knee (March 22, 1994); missed 11 games.

HONORS: Named to QMJHL All-Star first team (1977-78 and 1978-79).... Won Frank J. Selke Trophy (1978-79).... Won Emile (Butch) Bouchard Trophy (1978-79).... Named NHL Rookie of the Year by THE SPORTING NEWS (1979-80).... Won Calder Memorial Trophy (1979-80).... Named to NHL All-Star first team (1979-80, 1981-82, 1983-84, 1984-85, 1986-87, 1987-88 and 1989-90 through 1993-94).... Named to THE SPORTING NEWS All-Star second team (1980-81, 1982-83, 1985-86 and 1988-89).... Named to NHL All-Star second team (1980-81, 1982-83, 1985-86 and 1988-89).... Played in NHL All-Star Game (1981-1986 and 1988-1994).... Named to THE SPORTING NEWS All-Star first team (1981-82, 1983-84, 1984-85, 1986-87, 1987-88 and 1989-90 through 1993-94).... Won James Norris Memorial Trophy (1986-87, 1987-88, 1989-90, 1990-91 and 1993-94).... Won King Clancy Memorial Trophy (1991-92).

Season Team	League	REGULAR SEASON					PLAYOFFS				
		Gms.	G	A	Pts.	PIM	Gms.	G	A	Pts.	PIM
76-77—Sorel	QMJHL	69	12	36	48	61	—	—	—	—	—
77-78—Verdun	QMJHL	72	22	57	79	90	4	2	1	3	0
78-79—Verdun	QMJHL	63	22	71	93	44	11	3	16	19	18
79-80—Boston	NHL	80	17	48	65	73	10	2	9	11	27
80-81—Boston	NHL	67	27	29	56	96	3	0	1	1	2
81-82—Boston	NHL	65	17	49	66	51	9	1	5	6	16
82-83—Boston	NHL	65	22	51	73	20	17	8	15	23	10
83-84—Boston	NHL	78	31	65	96	57	3	0	2	2	0
84-85—Boston	NHL	73	20	66	86	53	5	0	3	3	4
85-86—Boston	NHL	74	19	57	76	68	3	0	0	0	0
86-87—Boston	NHL	78	23	72	95	36	4	1	2	3	0
87-88—Boston	NHL	78	17	64	81	72	23	3	18	21	26
88-89—Boston	NHL	60	18	43	61	52	10	0	4	4	6
89-90—Boston	NHL	76	19	65	84	50	17	5	12	17	16
90-91—Boston	NHL	76	21	73	94	75	19	7	18	25	12
91-92—Boston	NHL	80	21	60	81	56	12	3	6	9	12
92-93—Boston	NHL	78	19	63	82	40	4	1	0	1	2
93-94—Boston	NHL	72	20	71	91	58	13	2	8	10	0
NHL totals		1100	311	876	1187	857	152	33	103	136	133

BOWEN, CURT
LW, RED WINGS

PERSONAL: Born March 24, 1974, in Kenora, Ont.... 6-1/190.... Shoots left.

HIGH SCHOOL: Ridgemont (Ottawa).

TRANSACTIONS/CAREER NOTES: Selected by Detroit Red Wings in first round (first Red Wings pick, 22nd overall) of NHL entry draft (June 20, 1992).

Season Team	League	REGULAR SEASON					PLAYOFFS				
		Gms.	G	A	Pts.	PIM	Gms.	G	A	Pts.	PIM
90-91—Ottawa	OHL	42	12	14	26	31	—	—	—	—	—
91-92—Ottawa	OHL	65	31	45	76	94	11	3	7	10	11
92-93—Ottawa	OHL	21	9	19	28	51	—	—	—	—	—
93-94—Ottawa	OHL	52	25	37	62	98	17	8	13	21	14

BOWEN, JASON
D, FLYERS

PERSONAL: Born November 11, 1973, in Courtenay, B.C.... 6-4/215.... Shoots left.

TRANSACTIONS/CAREER NOTES: Selected by Philadelphia Flyers in first round (second Flyers pick, 15th overall) of NHL entry draft (June 20, 1992).... Suffered from hyphema in left eye (November 18, 1993); missed eight games.... Separated left shoulder (January 30, 1994); missed 14 games.

Season Team	League	REGULAR SEASON					PLAYOFFS				
		Gms.	G	A	Pts.	PIM	Gms.	G	A	Pts.	PIM
89-90—Tri-City	WHL	61	8	5	13	129	7	0	3	3	4
90-91—Tri-City	WHL	60	7	13	20	252	6	2	2	4	18
91-92—Tri-City	WHL	19	5	3	8	135	5	0	1	1	42
92-93—Tri-City	WHL	62	10	12	22	219	3	1	1	2	18
—Philadelphia	NHL	7	1	0	1	2	—	—	—	—	—
93-94—Philadelphia	NHL	56	1	5	6	87	—	—	—	—	—
NHL totals		63	2	5	7	89					

BOYER, ZAC
RW, BLACKHAWKS

PERSONAL: Born October 25, 1971, in Inuvik, N.W.T. . . . . 6-1/185. . . . Shoots right.
TRANSACTIONS/CAREER NOTES: Selected by Chicago Blackhawks in fourth round (sixth Blackhawks pick, 88th overall) of NHL entry draft (June 22, 1991).

			REGULAR SEASON					PLAYOFFS			
Season	Team	League	Gms.	G	A	Pts.	PIM	Gms.	G	A	Pts.	PIM
87-88—St. Albert		AJHL	55	16	31	47	258	—	—	—	—	—
88-89—Kamloops		WHL	42	10	17	27	22	16	9	8	17	10
89-90—Kamloops		WHL	71	24	47	71	63	17	4	4	8	8
90-91—Kamloops		WHL	64	45	60	105	58	12	6	10	16	8
91-92—Kamloops		WHL	70	40	69	109	90	17	9	*20	*29	16
92-93—Indianapolis		IHL	59	7	14	21	26	—	—	—	—	—
93-94—Indianapolis		IHL	54	13	12	25	67	—	—	—	—	—

BOZON, PHILIPPE
LW, BLUES

PERSONAL: Born November 30, 1966, in Chamonix, France. . . . 5-10/185. . . . Shoots left. . . . Name pronounced fih-LEEP BOH-zohn.
TRANSACTIONS/CAREER NOTES: Signed as free agent by St. Louis Blues (September 29, 1985). . . . On Blues inactive list while in France preparing for 1992 Olympics (1987-88 through 1990-91). . . . Returned to Blues (February 27, 1992). . . . Suffered from mononucleosis (January 30, 1993); missed 21 games. . . . Suffered facial injury (October 16, 1993); missed one game. . . . Injured stomach (January 13, 1994); missed one game. . . . Suffered concussion (April 1, 1994); missed two games.
HONORS: Named to QMJHL All-Star second team (1985-86).

			REGULAR SEASON					PLAYOFFS			
Season	Team	League	Gms.	G	A	Pts.	PIM	Gms.	G	A	Pts.	PIM
84-85—St. Jean		QMJHL	67	32	50	82	82	3	1	0	1	0
85-86—St. Jean		QMJHL	65	59	52	111	72	10	10	6	16	16
—Peoria		IHL	—	—	—	—	—	5	1	0	1	0
86-87—Peoria		IHL	28	4	11	15	17	—	—	—	—	—
—St. Jean		QMJHL	25	20	21	41	75	8	5	5	10	30
87-88—Mont-Blanc		France	18	11	15	26	34	10	15	6	21	6
—French Olympic Team		Int'l	6	3	2	5	0	—	—	—	—	—
88-89—Mont-Blanc		France	18	11	18	29	18	11	11	17	28	38
89-90—French national team		Int'l						Statistics unavailable.				
—Grenoble		France	36	45	38	83	34	6	4	3	7	2
90-91—Grenoble		France	26	22	16	38	16	10	7	8	15	8
91-92—Chamonix		France	10	12	8	20	20	—	—	—	—	—
—French Olympic Team		Int'l	7	3	2	5	4	—	—	—	—	—
—St. Louis		NHL	9	1	3	4	4	6	1	0	1	27
92-93—St. Louis		NHL	54	6	6	12	55	9	1	0	1	0
—Peoria		IHL	4	3	2	5	2	—	—	—	—	—
93-94—St. Louis		NHL	80	9	16	25	42	4	0	0	0	4
NHL totals			**143**	**16**	**25**	**41**	**101**	**19**	**2**	**0**	**2**	**31**

BRADLEY, BRIAN
C, LIGHTNING

PERSONAL: Born January 21, 1965, in Kitchener, Ont. . . . 5-10/177. . . . Shoots right. . . . Full name: Brian Walter Richard Bradley.
TRANSACTIONS/CAREER NOTES: Selected by Calgary Flames as underage junior in third round (second Flames pick, 51st overall) of NHL entry draft (June 8, 1983). . . . Traded by Flames with RW Peter Bakovic and future considerations (D Kevan Guy) to Vancouver Canucks for C Craig Coxe (March 6, 1988). . . . Bruised knee (January 1989). . . . Broke thumb knuckle (February 1, 1990); missed seven games. . . . Traded by Canucks to Toronto Maple Leafs for D Tom Kurvers (January 12, 1991). . . . Sprained ankle (November 10, 1991); missed six games. . . . Suffered back spasms (December 10, 1991); missed two games. . . . Selected by Tampa Bay Lightning in NHL expansion draft (June 18, 1992). . . . Suffered injury (October 6, 1993); missed three games. . . . Injured shoulder (October 22, 1993); missed one game. . . . Suffered from the flu (January 4, 1994); missed one game.
HONORS: Played in NHL All-Star Game (1993 and 1994).

			REGULAR SEASON					PLAYOFFS			
Season	Team	League	Gms.	G	A	Pts.	PIM	Gms.	G	A	Pts.	PIM
81-82—London		OHL	62	34	44	78	34	—	—	—	—	—
82-83—London		OHL	67	37	82	119	37	3	1	0	1	0
83-84—London		OHL	49	40	60	100	24	4	2	4	6	0
84-85—London		OHL	32	27	49	76	22	8	5	10	15	4
85-86—Calgary		NHL	5	0	1	1	0	1	0	0	0	0
—Moncton		AHL	59	23	42	65	40	10	6	9	15	4
86-87—Moncton		AHL	20	12	16	28	8	—	—	—	—	—
—Calgary		NHL	40	10	18	28	16	—	—	—	—	—
87-88—Canadian national team		Int'l	47	18	19	37	42	—	—	—	—	—
—Canadian Olympic Team		Int'l	7	0	4	4	0	—	—	—	—	—
—Vancouver		NHL	11	3	5	8	6	—	—	—	—	—
88-89—Vancouver		NHL	71	18	27	45	42	7	3	4	7	10
89-90—Vancouver		NHL	67	19	29	48	65	—	—	—	—	—
90-91—Vancouver		NHL	44	11	20	31	42	—	—	—	—	—
—Toronto		NHL	26	0	11	11	20	—	—	—	—	—
91-92—Toronto		NHL	59	10	21	31	48	—	—	—	—	—
92-93—Tampa Bay		NHL	80	42	44	86	92	—	—	—	—	—
93-94—Tampa Bay		NHL	78	24	40	64	56	—	—	—	—	—
NHL totals			**481**	**137**	**216**	**353**	**387**	**8**	**3**	**4**	**7**	**10**

B

BRADY, NEIL
C, STARS

PERSONAL: Born April 12, 1968, in Montreal. . . . 6-2/200. . . . Shoots left. . . . Full name: Neil Patrick Brady.
HIGH SCHOOL: Medicine Hat (Alta.).
TRANSACTIONS/CAREER NOTES: Selected by New Jersey Devils as underage junior in first round (first Devils pick, third overall) of NHL entry draft (June 21, 1986). . . . Traded by Devils to Ottawa Senators for future considerations (September 3, 1992). . . . Injured ankle (February 17, 1993); missed two games. . . . Suffered from the flu (February 23, 1993); missed two games. . . . Injured knee (March 4, 1993); missed one game. . . . Signed as free agent by Dallas Stars for 1993-94 season.
HONORS: Won WHL (East) Stewart (Butch) Paul Memorial Trophy (1985-86).

			REGULAR SEASON					PLAYOFFS				
Season	Team	League	Gms.	G	A	Pts.	PIM	Gms.	G	A	Pts.	PIM
84-85—Medicine Hat		WHL	—	—	—	—	—	3	0	0	0	2
85-86—Medicine Hat		WHL	72	21	60	81	104	21	9	11	20	23
86-87—Medicine Hat		WHL	57	19	64	83	126	18	1	4	5	25
87-88—Medicine Hat		WHL	61	16	35	51	110	15	0	3	3	19
88-89—Utica		AHL	75	16	21	37	56	4	0	3	3	0
89-90—New Jersey		NHL	19	1	4	5	13	—	—	—	—	—
—Utica		AHL	38	10	13	23	21	5	0	1	1	10
90-91—New Jersey		NHL	3	0	0	0	0	—	—	—	—	—
—Utica		AHL	77	33	63	96	91	—	—	—	—	—
91-92—Utica		AHL	33	12	30	42	28	—	—	—	—	—
—New Jersey		NHL	7	1	0	1	4	—	—	—	—	—
92-93—Ottawa		NHL	55	7	17	24	57	—	—	—	—	—
—New Haven		AHL	8	6	3	9	2	—	—	—	—	—
93-94—Kalamazoo		IHL	43	10	16	26	188	5	1	1	2	10
—Dallas		NHL	5	0	1	1	21	—	—	—	—	—
NHL totals			89	9	22	31	95					

BRASHEAR, DONALD
LW, CANADIENS

PERSONAL: Born January 7, 1972, in Bedford, Ind. . . . 6-3/214. . . . Shoots left.
TRANSACTIONS/CAREER NOTES: Signed as free agent by Montreal Canadiens (July 28, 1992). . . . Bruised knee (November 23, 1993); missed one game.

			REGULAR SEASON					PLAYOFFS				
Season	Team	League	Gms.	G	A	Pts.	PIM	Gms.	G	A	Pts.	PIM
89-90—Longueuil		QMJHL	64	12	14	26	169	7	0	0	0	11
90-91—Longueuil		QMJHL	68	12	26	38	195	8	0	3	3	33
91-92—Verdun		QMJHL	65	18	24	42	283	18	4	2	6	98
92-93—Fredericton		AHL	76	11	3	14	261	5	0	0	0	8
93-94—Fredericton		AHL	62	38	28	66	250	—	—	—	—	—
—Montreal		NHL	14	2	2	4	34	2	0	0	0	0
NHL totals			14	2	2	4	34	2	0	0	0	0

BRATHWAITE, FRED
G, OILERS

PERSONAL: Born November 24, 1972, in Ottawa. . . . 5-7/170. . . . Catches left. . . . Name pronounced BRATH-wayt.
TRANSACTIONS/CAREER NOTES: Signed as free agent by Las Vegas Thunder (August 18, 1993). . . . Signed as free agent by Edmonton Oilers for 1993-94 season.

			REGULAR SEASON							PLAYOFFS						
Season	Team	League	Gms.	Min.	W	L	T	GA	SO	Avg.	Gms.	Min.	W	L	GA	SO	Avg.
91-92—Oshawa		OHL	24	1248	12	7	2	81	0	3.89	—	—	—	—	—	—	—
—London		OHL	23	1325	15	6	2	61	4	2.76	10	615	5	5	36	0	3.51
92-93—Detroit		OHL	37	2192	23	10	4	134	0	3.67	15	858	9	6	48	1	3.36
93-94—Cape Breton		AHL	2	119	1	1	0	6	0	3.03	—	—	—	—	—	—	—
—Edmonton		NHL	19	982	3	10	3	58	0	3.54	—	—	—	—	—	—	—
NHL totals			19	982	3	10	3	58	0	3.54							

BREEN, GEORGE
RW, OILERS

PERSONAL: Born August 3, 1973, in Webster, Mass. . . . 6-2/200. . . . Shoots right. . . . Full name: George Bernard Breen.
HIGH SCHOOL: Shrewsbury (Mass.), then Cushing Academy (Ashburnham, Mass.).
COLLEGE: Providence.
TRANSACTIONS/CAREER NOTES: Selected by Edmonton Oilers in third round (third Oilers pick, 56th overall) of NHL entry draft (June 22, 1991).

			REGULAR SEASON					PLAYOFFS				
Season	Team	League	Gms.	G	A	Pts.	PIM	Gms.	G	A	Pts.	PIM
87-88—Shrewsbury H.S.		Mass. H.S.	20	11	9	20	. . .	—	—	—	—	—
88-89—Shrewsbury H.S.		Mass. H.S.	20	32	9	41	. . .	—	—	—	—	—
89-90—Cushing Academy		Mass. H.S.	20	9	8	17	. . .	—	—	—	—	—
90-91—Cushing Academy		Mass. H.S.	23	21	39	60	. . .	—	—	—	—	—
91-92—Providence College		Hockey East	36	8	4	12	24	—	—	—	—	—
92-93—Providence College		Hockey East	31	11	7	18	45	—	—	—	—	—
93-94—Providence College		Hockey East	32	8	14	22	22	—	—	—	—	—

BRENNAN, RICH
D, NORDIQUES

PERSONAL: Born November 26, 1972, in Schenectady, N.Y. . . . 6-2/200. . . . Shoots right.
HIGH SCHOOL: Albany (N.Y.) Academy, then Tabor Academy (Marion, Mass.).
COLLEGE: Boston University.
TRANSACTIONS/CAREER NOTES: Selected by Quebec Nordiques in third round (third Nordiques pick, 56th overall) of NHL entry draft (June 22, 1991).

Season Team	League	REGULAR SEASON					PLAYOFFS				
		Gms.	G	A	Pts.	PIM	Gms.	G	A	Pts.	PIM
88-89—Albany Academy	N.Y. H.S.	25	17	30	47	57	—	—	—	—	—
89-90—Tabor Academy	N.Y. H.S.	33	12	14	26	68	—	—	—	—	—
90-91—Tabor Academy	N.Y. H.S.	34	13	37	50	91	—	—	—	—	—
91-92—Boston University	Hockey East	31	4	13	17	54	—	—	—	—	—
92-93—Boston University	Hockey East	40	9	11	20	68	—	—	—	—	—
93-94—Boston University	Hockey East	41	8	27	35	82	—	—	—	—	—

BRICKLEY, ANDY
LW, ISLANDERS

PERSONAL: Born August 9, 1961, in Melrose, Mass.... 5-11/200.... Shoots left.
COLLEGE: New Hampshire.
TRANSACTIONS/CAREER NOTES: Selected by Philadelphia Flyers in 10th round (10th Flyers pick, 210th overall) of NHL entry draft (June 11, 1980).... Traded by Flyers with C Ron Flockhart, C/LW Mark Taylor and first-round pick in 1984 draft (RW/C Roger Belanger) to Pittsburgh Penguins for RW Rich Sutter and second-round (D Greg Smyth) and third-round (LW David McLay) picks in 1984 draft (October 23, 1983).... Strained ankle (December 1983).... Released by Penguins (August 1985).... Signed as free agent by Maine Mariners (September 1985).... Suffered tendinitis in shoulder (December 1985).... Signed as free agent by New Jersey Devils (July 8, 1986).... Injured foot (September 1987).... Selected by Boston Bruins in 1988 waiver draft for $12,500 (October 3, 1988). ... Strained groin (December 1988).... Sprained right ankle (September 24, 1989); missed nine games.... Tore right groin muscle (January 27, 1990); missed eight games.... Underwent surgery to right thigh (July 17, 1990).... Separated shoulder (March 1991).... Injured shoulder (November 16, 1991); missed 38 games.... Signed as free agent by Winnipeg Jets (November 14, 1992).... Suffered quad contusion (January 2, 1993); missed one game.... Suffered back spasms (March 6, 1993); missed five games.... Signed as free agent by New York Islanders (August 2, 1994).
HONORS: Named to NCAA All-America East team (1981-82).... Named to ECAC All-Star first team (1981-82).... Named to AHL All-Star second team (1982-83).

Season Team	League	REGULAR SEASON					PLAYOFFS				
		Gms.	G	A	Pts.	PIM	Gms.	G	A	Pts.	PIM
79-80—Univ. of New Hampshire	ECAC	27	15	17	32	8	—	—	—	—	—
80-81—Univ. of New Hampshire	ECAC	31	27	25	52	16	—	—	—	—	—
81-82—Univ. of New Hampshire	ECAC	35	26	27	53	6	—	—	—	—	—
82-83—Philadelphia	NHL	3	1	1	2	0	—	—	—	—	—
—Maine	AHL	76	29	54	83	10	17	9	5	14	0
83-84—Springfield	AHL	7	1	5	6	2	—	—	—	—	—
—Pittsburgh	NHL	50	18	20	38	9	—	—	—	—	—
—Baltimore	AHL	4	0	5	5	2	—	—	—	—	—
84-85—Baltimore	AHL	31	13	14	27	8	15	†10	8	18	0
—Pittsburgh	NHL	45	7	15	22	10	—	—	—	—	—
85-86—Maine	AHL	60	26	34	60	20	5	0	4	4	0
86-87—New Jersey	NHL	51	11	12	23	8	—	—	—	—	—
87-88—Utica	AHL	9	5	8	13	4	—	—	—	—	—
—New Jersey	NHL	45	8	14	22	14	4	0	1	1	4
88-89—Boston	NHL	71	13	22	35	20	10	0	2	2	0
89-90—Boston	NHL	43	12	28	40	8	2	0	0	0	0
90-91—Maine	AHL	17	8	17	25	2	1	0	0	0	0
—Boston	NHL	40	2	9	11	8	—	—	—	—	—
91-92—Maine	AHL	14	5	15	20	2	—	—	—	—	—
—Boston	NHL	23	10	17	27	2	—	—	—	—	—
92-93—Moncton	AHL	38	15	36	51	10	5	4	2	6	0
—Winnipeg	NHL	12	0	2	2	2	1	1	1	2	0
93-94—Moncton	AHL	53	20	39	59	20	19	8	* 19	*27	4
—Winnipeg	NHL	2	0	0	0	0	—	—	—	—	—
NHL totals		385	82	140	222	81	17	1	4	5	4

BRIGHT, CHRIS
C, WHALERS

PERSONAL: Born October 14, 1970, in Guelph, Ont.... 6-0/187.... Shoots left.
TRANSACTIONS/CAREER NOTES: Selected by Hartford Whalers in fourth round (fourth Whalers pick, 78th overall) of NHL entry draft (June 16, 1990).

Season Team	League	REGULAR SEASON					PLAYOFFS				
		Gms.	G	A	Pts.	PIM	Gms.	G	A	Pts.	PIM
87-88—Moose Jaw	WHL	20	2	2	4	10	—	—	—	—	—
88-89—Moose Jaw	WHL	71	18	27	45	61	7	2	0	2	6
89-90—Moose Jaw	WHL	72	36	38	74	107	—	—	—	—	—
90-91—Springfield	AHL	37	3	4	7	32	—	—	—	—	—
91-92—Springfield	AHL	8	1	0	1	6	—	—	—	—	—
—Louisville	ECHL	46	17	39	56	61	13	9	8	17	18
92-93—Louisville	ECHL	63	30	38	68	159	—	—	—	—	—
93-94—Rochester	AHL	9	1	0	1	6	—	—	—	—	—
—Springfield	AHL	5	0	0	0	4	—	—	—	—	—
—South Carolina	ECHL	59	40	47	87	134	3	2	2	4	10

BRIMANIS, ARIS
D, FLYERS

PERSONAL: Born March 14, 1972, in Cleveland. ... 6-3/195. ... Shoots right. ... Full name: Aris Aldis Brimanis.... Name pronounced AIR-ihz brih-MAN-ihz.
HIGH SCHOOL: Culver (Ind.) Military Academy.
COLLEGE: Bowling Green State.

TRANSACTIONS/CAREER NOTES: Selected by Philadelphia Flyers in fourth round (third Flyers pick, 86th overall) of NHL entry draft (June 22, 1991).

			REGULAR SEASON					PLAYOFFS				
Season	Team	League	Gms.	G	A	Pts.	PIM	Gms.	G	A	Pts.	PIM
88-89	Culver Military Academy..	Indiana H.S.	38	10	13	23	...	—	—	—	—	—
89-90	Culver Military Academy..	Indiana H.S.	37	15	10	25	...	—	—	—	—	—
90-91	Bowling Green State	CCHA	38	3	6	9	42	—	—	—	—	—
91-92	Bowling Green State	CCHA	32	2	9	11	38	—	—	—	—	—
92-93	Brandon	WHL	71	8	50	58	110	4	2	1	3	12
93-94	Hershey	AHL	75	8	15	23	65	11	2	3	5	12
	—Philadelphia	NHL	1	0	0	0	0	—	—	—	—	—
	NHL totals		1	0	0	0	0					

BRIND'AMOUR, ROD
C/LW, FLYERS

PERSONAL: Born August 9, 1970, in Ottawa.... 6-1/198.... Shoots left.... Full name: Rod Jean Brind'Amour.... Name pronounced BRIHND-uh-MOHR.
COLLEGE: Michigan State.
TRANSACTIONS/CAREER NOTES: Broke wrist (November 1985).... Selected by St. Louis Blues in first round (first Blues pick, ninth overall) of NHL entry draft (June 11, 1988).... Traded by Blues with C Dan Quinn to Philadelphia Flyers for C Ron Sutter and D Murray Baron (September 22, 1991).... Lacerated elbow (November 19, 1992); missed two games.... Bruised right hand (February 20, 1993); missed one game.
HONORS: Named CCHA Rookie of the Year (1988-89).... Named to CCHA All-Rookie team (1988-89).... Named to NHL All-Rookie team (1989-90).... Played in NHL All-Star Game (1992).

			REGULAR SEASON					PLAYOFFS				
Season	Team	League	Gms.	G	A	Pts.	PIM	Gms.	G	A	Pts.	PIM
87-88	Notre Dame	SJHL	56	46	61	107	136	—	—	—	—	—
88-89	Michigan State	CCHA	42	27	32	59	63	—	—	—	—	—
	—St. Louis	NHL	—	—	—	—	—	5	2	0	2	4
89-90	St. Louis	NHL	79	26	35	61	46	12	5	8	13	6
90-91	St. Louis	NHL	78	17	32	49	93	13	2	5	7	10
91-92	Philadelphia	NHL	80	33	44	77	100	—	—	—	—	—
92-93	Philadelphia	NHL	81	37	49	86	89	—	—	—	—	—
93-94	Philadelphia	NHL	84	35	62	97	85	—	—	—	—	—
	NHL totals		402	148	222	370	413	30	9	13	22	20

BRISEBOIS, PATRICE
D, CANADIENS

PERSONAL: Born January 27, 1971, in Montreal.... 6-2/182.... Shoots right.... Name pronounced pa-TREEZ BREES-bwah.
TRANSACTIONS/CAREER NOTES: Underwent surgery on fractured right thumb (February 1988).... Tore ligaments in left knee (March 1988).... Broke left thumb (August 1988).... Selected by Montreal Canadiens in second round (second Canadiens pick, 30th overall) of NHL entry draft (June 17, 1989).... Traded by Laval Titans with LW Allen Kerr to Drummondville Voltigeurs for second- and third-round picks in 1990 QMJHL draft (May 26, 1990).... Sprained right ankle (October 10, 1992); missed two games.... Suffered charley horse (December 16, 1992); missed two games.... Injured knee (October 30, 1993); missed 10 games.... Suffered hairline fracture of ankle (December 1, 1993); missed 14 games.... Sprained ankle (February 21, 1994); missed seven games.
HONORS: Won QMJHL top draft prospect award (1988-89).... Named to QMJHL All-Star second team (1989-90).... Won Can.HL Defenseman of the Year Award (1990-91).... Won Emile (Butch) Bouchard Trophy (1990-91).... Named to QMJHL All-Star first team (1990-91).... Named to Memorial Cup All-Star team (1990-91).
MISCELLANEOUS: Member of Stanley Cup championship team (1993).

			REGULAR SEASON					PLAYOFFS				
Season	Team	League	Gms.	G	A	Pts.	PIM	Gms.	G	A	Pts.	PIM
87-88	Laval	QMJHL	48	10	34	44	95	6	0	2	2	2
88-89	Laval	QMJHL	50	20	45	65	95	17	8	14	22	45
89-90	Laval	QMJHL	56	18	70	88	108	13	7	9	16	26
90-91	Montreal	NHL	10	0	2	2	4	—	—	—	—	—
	—Drummondville	QMJHL	54	17	44	61	72	14	6	18	24	49
91-92	Fredericton	AHL	53	12	27	39	51	—	—	—	—	—
	—Montreal	NHL	26	2	8	10	20	11	2	4	6	6
92-93	Montreal	NHL	70	10	21	31	79	20	0	4	4	18
93-94	Montreal	NHL	53	2	21	23	63	7	0	4	4	6
	NHL totals		159	14	52	66	166	38	2	12	14	30

BRISKE, BYRON
D, MIGHTY DUCKS

PERSONAL: Born January 23, 1976, in Jansen, Sask.... 6-3/194.... Shoots right.... Name pronounced BRIH-skee.
HIGH SCHOOL: Lindsay Thurber (Red Deer, Alta.).
TRANSACTIONS/CAREER NOTES: Selected by Mighty Ducks of Anaheim in fourth round (fourth Mighty Ducks pick, 80th overall) of NHL entry draft (June 29, 1994).

			REGULAR SEASON					PLAYOFFS				
Season	Team	League	Gms.	G	A	Pts.	PIM	Gms.	G	A	Pts.	PIM
91-92	Victoria	WHL	1	0	0	0	0	—	—	—	—	—
92-93	Victoria	WHL	66	1	10	11	110	—	—	—	—	—
93-94	Red Deer	WHL	61	6	21	27	174	—	—	—	—	—

BROCHU, MARTIN
G, CANADIENS

PERSONAL: Born March 10, 1973, in Anjou, Quebec.... 5-11/195.... Catches left.... Name pronounced MAHR-tai broh-SHOO.
TRANSACTIONS/CAREER NOTES: Signed as free agent by Montreal Canadiens (September 22, 1992).

— 336 —

Season Team	League	REGULAR SEASON								PLAYOFFS						
		Gms.	Min.	W	L	T	GA	SO	Avg.	Gms.	Min.	W	L	GA	SO	Avg.
91-92—Granby	QMJHL	52	2772	15	29	2	218	0	4.72	—	—	—	—	—	—	—
92-93—Hull	QMJHL	29	1453	9	15	1	137	0	5.66	2	69	0	1	7	0	6.09
93-94—Fredericton	AHL	32	1506	10	11	3	76	2	3.03	—	—	—	—	—	—	—

BRODEUR, MARTIN
G, DEVILS

PERSONAL: Born May 6, 1972, in Montreal. . . . 6-1/205. . . . Catches left. . . . Name pronounced MAHR-tihn broh-DOOR.
TRANSACTIONS/CAREER NOTES: Suffered pinched nerve in elbow and slight concussion (March 9, 1990). . . . Selected by New Jersey Devils in first round (first Devils pick, 20th overall) of NHL entry draft (June 16, 1990). . . . Strained knee (February 24, 1994).
HONORS: Named to QMJHL All-Star second team (1991-92). . . . Won Calder Memorial Trophy (1993-94). . . . Named to NHL All-Rookie team (1993-94).

Season Team	League	REGULAR SEASON								PLAYOFFS						
		Gms.	Min.	W	L	T	GA	SO	Avg.	Gms.	Min.	W	L	GA	SO	Avg.
89-90—St. Hyacinthe	QMJHL	42	2333	23	13	2	156	0	4.01	12	678	5	7	46	0	4.07
90-91—St. Hyacinthe	QMJHL	52	2946	22	24	4	162	2	3.30	4	232	0	4	16	0	4.14
91-92—St. Hyacinthe	QMJHL	48	2846	27	16	4	161	2	3.39	5	317	2	3	14	0	2.65
—New Jersey	NHL	4	179	2	1	0	10	0	3.35	1	32	0	1	3	0	5.63
92-93—Utica	AHL	32	1952	14	13	5	131	0	4.03	4	258	1	3	18	0	4.19
93-94—New Jersey	NHL	47	2625	27	11	8	105	3	2.40	17	1171	8	†9	38	1	1.95
NHL totals		51	2804	29	12	8	115	3	2.46	18	1203	8	10	41	1	2.04

BROSSEAU, DAVID
C, RANGERS

PERSONAL: Born January 16, 1976, in Montreal. . . . 6-2/189. . . . Shoots right.
TRANSACTIONS/CAREER NOTES: Selected by New York Rangers in sixth round (eighth Rangers pick, 156th overall) of NHL entry draft (June 29, 1994).

Season Team	League	REGULAR SEASON					PLAYOFFS				
		Gms.	G	A	Pts.	PIM	Gms.	G	A	Pts.	PIM
92-93—Shawinigan	QMJHL	56	5	4	9	28	—	—	—	—	—
93-94—Shawinigan	QMJHL	65	27	26	53	62	5	3	0	3	2

BROTEN, NEAL
C, STARS

PERSONAL: Born November 29, 1959, in Roseau, Minn. . . . 5-9/170. . . . Shoots left. . . . Full name: Neal LaMoy Broten. . . . Name pronounced BRAH-tuhn. . . . Brother of Aaron Broten, center/left winger for six NHL teams (1980-81 through 1991-92); and brother of Paul Broten, right winger, Dallas Stars.
HIGH SCHOOL: Roseau (Minn.).
COLLEGE: Minnesota.
TRANSACTIONS/CAREER NOTES: Selected by Minnesota North Stars in second round (third North Stars pick, 42nd overall) of NHL entry draft (August 9, 1979). . . . Fractured ankle (December 26, 1981). . . . Dislocated shoulder (October 30, 1986). . . . Tore shoulder ligaments (March 1987). . . . Separated shoulder (November 1987). . . . Underwent reconstructive shoulder surgery (February 1988). . . . Suffered sterno-clavicular sprain (February 14, 1989). . . . Strained groin (December 18, 1990). . . . North Stars franchise moved from Minnesota to Dallas and renamed Stars for 1993-94 season. . . . Pulled hip muscle (October 9, 1993); missed two games.
HONORS: Won WCHA Rookie of the Year Award (1978-79). . . . Won Hobey Baker Memorial Trophy (1980-81). . . . Named to NCAA All-America West team (1980-81). . . . Named to WCHA All-Star first team (1980-81). . . . Named to NCAA All-Tournament team (1980-81). . . . Played in NHL All-Star Game (1983 and 1986).
MISCELLANEOUS: Member of gold-medal-winning U.S. Olympic team (1980).

Season Team	League	REGULAR SEASON					PLAYOFFS				
		Gms.	G	A	Pts.	PIM	Gms.	G	A	Pts.	PIM
78-79—University of Minnesota	WCHA	40	21	50	71	18	—	—	—	—	—
79-80—U.S. national team	Int'l	55	25	30	55	20	—	—	—	—	—
—U.S. Olympic Team	Int'l	7	2	1	3	2	—	—	—	—	—
80-81—University of Minnesota	WCHA	36	17	54	71	56	—	—	—	—	—
—Minnesota	NHL	3	2	0	2	12	19	1	7	8	9
81-82—Minnesota	NHL	73	38	60	98	42	4	0	2	2	0
82-83—Minnesota	NHL	79	32	45	77	43	9	1	6	7	10
83-84—Minnesota	NHL	76	28	61	89	43	16	5	5	10	4
84-85—Minnesota	NHL	80	19	37	56	39	9	2	5	7	10
85-86—Minnesota	NHL	80	29	76	105	47	5	3	2	5	2
86-87—Minnesota	NHL	46	18	35	53	35	—	—	—	—	—
87-88—Minnesota	NHL	54	9	30	39	32	—	—	—	—	—
88-89—Minnesota	NHL	68	18	38	56	57	5	2	2	4	4
89-90—Minnesota	NHL	80	23	62	85	45	7	2	2	4	18
90-91—Minnesota	NHL	79	13	56	69	26	23	9	13	22	6
91-92—Minnesota	NHL	76	8	26	34	16	7	1	5	6	2
92-93—Minnesota	NHL	82	12	21	33	22	—	—	—	—	—
93-94—Dallas	NHL	79	17	35	52	62	9	2	1	3	6
NHL totals		955	266	582	848	521	113	28	50	78	71

BROTEN, PAUL
RW, STARS

PERSONAL: Born October 27, 1965, in Roseau, Minn. . . . 5-11/190. . . . Shoots right. . . . Name pronounced BRAH-tuhn. . . . Brother of Aaron Broten, center/left winger for six NHL teams (1980-81 through 1991-92); and brother of Neal Broten, center, Dallas Stars.
HIGH SCHOOL: Roseau (Minn.).

COLLEGE: Minnesota.
TRANSACTIONS/CAREER NOTES: Selected by New York Rangers in fourth round (third Rangers pick, 77th overall) of NHL entry draft (June 9, 1984).... Pulled thigh muscle (September 1990).... Selected by Dallas Stars in NHL waiver draft (October 2, 1993).

Season Team	League	Gms.	G	A	Pts.	PIM	Gms.	G	A	Pts.	PIM
			REGULAR SEASON					**PLAYOFFS**			
83-84—Roseau H.S.	Minn. H.S.	26	26	29	55	4	—	—	—	—	—
84-85—University of Minnesota	WCHA	44	8	8	16	26	—	—	—	—	—
85-86—University of Minnesota	WCHA	38	6	16	22	24	—	—	—	—	—
86-87—University of Minnesota	WCHA	48	17	22	39	52	—	—	—	—	—
87-88—University of Minnesota	WCHA	62	19	26	45	54	—	—	—	—	—
88-89—Denver	IHL	77	28	31	59	133	4	0	2	2	6
89-90—Flint	IHL	28	17	9	26	55	—	—	—	—	—
—New York Rangers	NHL	32	5	3	8	26	6	1	1	2	2
90-91—New York Rangers	NHL	28	4	6	10	18	5	0	0	0	2
—Binghamton	AHL	8	2	2	4	4	—	—	—	—	—
91-92—New York Rangers	NHL	74	13	15	28	102	13	1	2	3	10
92-93—New York Rangers	NHL	60	5	9	14	48	—	—	—	—	—
93-94—Dallas	NHL	64	12	12	24	30	9	1	1	2	2
NHL totals		258	39	45	84	224	33	3	4	7	16

BROUSSEAU, PAUL
RW, NORDIQUES

PERSONAL: Born September 18, 1973, in Montreal.... 6-1/203.... Shoots right.... Name pronounced broo-SOH.
COLLEGE: Heritage College (Fla.).
TRANSACTIONS/CAREER NOTES: Selected by Quebec Nordiques in second round (second Nordiques pick, 28th overall) of NHL entry draft (June 20, 1992).
HONORS: Won QMJHL Top Draft Prospect Award (1991-92).

Season Team	League	Gms.	G	A	Pts.	PIM	Gms.	G	A	Pts.	PIM
			REGULAR SEASON					**PLAYOFFS**			
89-90—Chicoutimi	QMJHL	57	17	24	41	32	7	0	3	3	0
90-91—Trois-Rivieres	QMJHL	67	30	66	96	48	6	3	2	5	2
91-92—Hull	QMJHL	57	35	61	96	54	6	3	5	8	10
92-93—Hull	QMJHL	59	27	48	75	49	10	7	8	15	6
93-94—Cornwall	AHL	69	18	26	44	35	1	0	0	0	0

BROWN, BRAD
D, CANADIENS

PERSONAL: Born December 27, 1975, in Mississauga, Ont.... 6-3/218.... Shoots right.
HIGH SCHOOL: Chippewa (North Bay, Ont.).
TRANSACTIONS/CAREER NOTES: Selected by Montreal Canadiens in first round (first Canadiens pick, 18th overall) of NHL entry draft (June 28, 1994).

Season Team	League	Gms.	G	A	Pts.	PIM	Gms.	G	A	Pts.	PIM
			REGULAR SEASON					**PLAYOFFS**			
91-92—North Bay	OHL	49	2	9	11	170	18	0	6	6	43
92-93—North Bay	OHL	61	4	9	13	228	2	0	2	2	13
93-94—North Bay	OHL	66	8	24	32	196	18	3	12	15	33

BROWN, CURTIS
C, SABRES

PERSONAL: Born February 12, 1976, in Unity, Sask.... 6-0/182.... Shoots left.
TRANSACTIONS/CAREER NOTES: Selected by Buffalo Sabres in second round (second Sabres pick, 43rd overall) of NHL entry draft (June 28, 1994).

Season Team	League	Gms.	G	A	Pts.	PIM	Gms.	G	A	Pts.	PIM
			REGULAR SEASON					**PLAYOFFS**			
92-93—Moose Jaw	WHL	71	13	16	29	30	—	—	—	—	—
93-94—Moose Jaw	WHL	72	27	38	65	82	—	—	—	—	—

BROWN, DAVE
RW, FLYERS

PERSONAL: Born October 12, 1962, in Saskatoon, Sask.... 6-5/222.... Shoots right.
TRANSACTIONS/CAREER NOTES: Selected by Philadelphia Flyers in seventh round (seventh Flyers pick, 140th overall) of NHL entry draft (June 9, 1982).... Bruised shoulder (March 1985). ... Suspended five games by NHL for stick-swinging incident (March 1987).... Suspended 15 games by NHL for crosschecking (October 16, 1987).... Bruised left hand and wrist (January 1988).... Traded by Flyers to Edmonton Oilers for C Keith Acton and future considerations (February 7, 1989).... Suffered facial laceration (March 3, 1989).... Sprained hand (March 1989).... Traded by Oilers with D Corey Foster and the NHL rights to RW Jari Kurri to Flyers for RW Scott Mellanby, LW Craig Berube and C Craig Fisher (May 30, 1991).... Injured shoulder (January 28, 1992); missed 10 games.
MISCELLANEOUS: Member of Stanley Cup championship team (1990).

Season Team	League	Gms.	G	A	Pts.	PIM	Gms.	G	A	Pts.	PIM
			REGULAR SEASON					**PLAYOFFS**			
80-81—Spokane Flyers	WHL	9	2	2	4	21	—	—	—	—	—
81-82—Saskatoon	WHL	62	11	33	44	344	5	1	0	1	4
82-83—Maine	AHL	71	8	6	14	*418	16	0	0	0	*107
—Philadelphia	NHL	2	0	0	0	5	—	—	—	—	—
83-84—Philadelphia	NHL	19	1	5	6	98	2	0	0	0	12
—Springfield	AHL	59	17	14	31	150	—	—	—	—	—
84-85—Philadelphia	NHL	57	3	6	9	165	11	0	0	0	59

Season Team	League	REGULAR SEASON Gms.	G	A	Pts.	PIM	PLAYOFFS Gms.	G	A	Pts.	PIM
85-86—Philadelphia	NHL	76	10	7	17	277	5	0	0	0	16
86-87—Philadelphia	NHL	62	7	3	10	274	26	1	2	3	59
87-88—Philadelphia	NHL	47	12	5	17	114	7	1	0	1	27
88-89—Philadelphia	NHL	50	0	3	3	100	—	—	—	—	—
—Edmonton	NHL	22	0	2	2	56	7	0	0	0	6
89-90—Edmonton	NHL	60	0	6	6	145	3	0	0	0	0
90-91—Edmonton	NHL	58	3	4	7	160	16	0	1	1	30
91-92—Philadelphia	NHL	70	4	2	6	81	—	—	—	—	—
92-93—Philadelphia	NHL	70	0	2	2	78	—	—	—	—	—
93-94—Philadelphia	NHL	71	1	4	5	137	—	—	—	—	—
NHL totals		**664**	**41**	**49**	**90**	**1690**	**77**	**2**	**3**	**5**	**209**

BROWN, DOUG
RW, PENGUINS

PERSONAL: Born June 12, 1964, in Southborough, Mass. . . . 5-10/185. . . . Shoots right. . . . Full name: Douglas Allen Brown. . . . Brother of Greg Brown, defenseman, Pittsburgh Penguins. **HIGH SCHOOL:** St. Mark's (Southborough, Mass.). **COLLEGE:** Boston College.
TRANSACTIONS/CAREER NOTES: Signed as free agent by New Jersey Devils (August 6, 1986). . . . Broke nose (October 1988). . . . Injured back (November 25, 1989). . . . Bruised right foot (February 13, 1991). . . . Suspended by Devils for refusing to report to Utica (November 20, 1992). . . . Reinstated by Devils (November 30, 1992). . . . Signed as free agent by Pittsburgh Penguins (September 29, 1993). . . . Injured leg (March 26, 1994); missed seven games.
HONORS: Named to NCAA All-America East second team (1984-85 and 1985-86). . . . Named to Hockey East All-Star second team (1984-85 and 1985-86).

Season Team	League	REGULAR SEASON Gms.	G	A	Pts.	PIM	PLAYOFFS Gms.	G	A	Pts.	PIM
82-83—Boston College	ECAC	22	9	8	17	0	—	—	—	—	—
83-84—Boston College	ECAC	38	11	10	21	6	—	—	—	—	—
84-85—Boston College	Hockey East	45	37	31	68	10	—	—	—	—	—
85-86—Boston College	Hockey East	38	16	40	56	16	—	—	—	—	—
86-87—Maine	AHL	73	24	34	58	15	—	—	—	—	—
—New Jersey	NHL	4	0	1	1	0	—	—	—	—	—
87-88—New Jersey	NHL	70	14	11	25	20	19	5	1	6	6
—Utica	AHL	2	0	2	2	2	—	—	—	—	—
88-89—New Jersey	NHL	63	15	10	25	15	—	—	—	—	—
—Utica	AHL	4	1	4	5	0	—	—	—	—	—
89-90—New Jersey	NHL	69	14	20	34	16	6	0	1	1	2
90-91—New Jersey	NHL	58	14	16	30	4	7	2	2	4	2
91-92—New Jersey	NHL	71	11	17	28	27	—	—	—	—	—
92-93—New Jersey	NHL	15	0	5	5	2	—	—	—	—	—
—Utica	AHL	25	11	17	28	8	—	—	—	—	—
93-94—Pittsburgh	NHL	77	18	37	55	18	6	0	0	0	2
NHL totals		**427**	**86**	**117**	**203**	**102**	**38**	**7**	**4**	**11**	**12**

BROWN, GREG
D, PENGUINS

PERSONAL: Born March 7, 1968, in Hartford, Conn. . . . 6-0/185. . . . Shoots right. . . . Full name: Gregory Curtis Brown. . . . Brother of Doug Brown, right winger, Pittsburgh Penguins. **HIGH SCHOOL:** St. Mark's (Southborough, Mass.). **COLLEGE:** Boston College.
TRANSACTIONS/CAREER NOTES: Selected by Buffalo Sabres in second round (second Sabres pick, 26th overall) of NHL entry draft (June 21, 1986). . . . Signed as free agent by Pittsburgh Penguins (September 30, 1993).
HONORS: Named to Hockey East All-Freshman team (1986-87). . . . Named Hockey East Player of the Year (1988-89 and 1989-90). . . . Named to NCAA All-America East first team (1988-89 and 1989-90). . . . Named to Hockey East All-Star first team (1988-89 and 1989-90).

Season Team	League	REGULAR SEASON Gms.	G	A	Pts.	PIM	PLAYOFFS Gms.	G	A	Pts.	PIM
84-85—St. Marks H.S.	Mass. H.S.	24	16	24	40	12	—	—	—	—	—
85-86—St. Marks H.S.	Mass. H.S.	19	22	28	50	30	—	—	—	—	—
86-87—Boston College	Hockey East	37	10	27	37	22	—	—	—	—	—
87-88—U.S. Olympic Team	Int'l	6	0	4	4	2	—	—	—	—	—
88-89—Boston College	Hockey East	40	9	34	43	24	—	—	—	—	—
89-90—Boston College	Hockey East	42	5	35	40	42	—	—	—	—	—
90-91—Buffalo	NHL	39	1	2	3	35	—	—	—	—	—
—Rochester	AHL	31	6	17	23	16	14	1	4	5	8
91-92—Rochester	AHL	56	8	30	38	25	16	1	5	6	4
—U.S. national team	Int'l	8	0	0	0	5	—	—	—	—	—
—U.S. Olympic Team	Int'l	7	0	0	0	2	—	—	—	—	—
92-93—Rochester	AHL	61	11	38	49	46	16	3	8	11	14
—Buffalo	NHL	10	0	1	1	6	—	—	—	—	—
93-94—San Diego	IHL	42	8	25	33	26	—	—	—	—	—
—Pittsburgh	NHL	36	3	8	11	28	6	0	1	1	4
NHL totals		**85**	**4**	**11**	**15**	**69**	**6**	**0**	**1**	**1**	**4**

BROWN, JEFF

D, CANUCKS

PERSONAL: Born April 30, 1966, in Ottawa.... 6-1/204.... Shoots right.... Full name: Jeff Randall Brown.
HIGH SCHOOL: Sudbury (Ont.).
TRANSACTIONS/CAREER NOTES: Selected by Quebec Nordiques as underage junior in second round (second Nordiques pick, 36th overall) of NHL entry draft (June 9, 1984).... Traded by Nordiques to St. Louis Blues for G Greg Millen and C Tony Hrkac (December 13, 1989).... Broke left ankle (February 14, 1991); missed 13 games.... Broke foot (January 14, 1993); missed 11 games.... Suffered from sore foot (February 11, 1993); missed two games.... Injured hand and foot (October 30, 1993); missed three games.... Broke thumb (January 15, 1994); missed six games.... Traded by Blues with D Brett Hedican and C Nathan LaFayette to Vancouver Canucks for C Craig Janney (March 21, 1994).
HONORS: Shared Max Kaminsky Trophy with Terry Carkner (1985-86).... Named to OHL All-Star first team (1985-86).

Season	Team	League	REGULAR SEASON					PLAYOFFS				
			Gms.	G	A	Pts.	PIM	Gms.	G	A	Pts.	PIM
81-82	Hawkesbury	COJHL	49	12	47	59	72	—	—	—	—	—
82-83	Sudbury	OHL	65	9	37	46	39	—	—	—	—	—
83-84	Sudbury	OHL	68	17	60	77	39	—	—	—	—	—
84-85	Sudbury	OHL	56	16	48	64	26	—	—	—	—	—
85-86	Sudbury	OHL	45	22	28	50	24	4	0	2	2	11
	Quebec	NHL	8	3	2	5	6	1	0	0	0	0
	Fredericton	AHL	—	—	—	—	—	1	0	1	1	0
86-87	Fredericton	AHL	26	2	14	16	16	—	—	—	—	—
	Quebec	NHL	44	7	22	29	16	13	3	3	6	2
87-88	Quebec	NHL	78	16	36	52	64	—	—	—	—	—
88-89	Quebec	NHL	78	21	47	68	62	—	—	—	—	—
89-90	Quebec	NHL	29	6	10	16	18	—	—	—	—	—
	St. Louis	NHL	48	10	28	38	37	12	2	10	12	4
90-91	St. Louis	NHL	67	12	47	59	39	13	3	9	12	6
91-92	St. Louis	NHL	80	20	39	59	38	6	2	1	3	2
92-93	St. Louis	NHL	71	25	53	78	58	11	3	8	11	6
93-94	St. Louis	NHL	63	13	47	60	46	—	—	—	—	—
	Vancouver	NHL	11	1	5	6	10	24	6	9	15	37
NHL totals			**577**	**134**	**336**	**470**	**394**	**80**	**19**	**40**	**59**	**57**

BROWN, KEITH

D, PANTHERS

PERSONAL: Born May 6, 1960, in Corner Brook, Nfld.... 6-1/192.... Shoots right.... Full name: Keith Jeffrey Brown.
TRANSACTIONS/CAREER NOTES: Selected by Chicago Blackhawks as underage junior in first round (first Blackhawks pick, seventh overall) of NHL entry draft (August 9, 1979).... Tore ligaments in right knee (December 23, 1981).... Separated right shoulder (January 26, 1983).... Strained leg (January 1985).... Broke finger (October 1985); missed 10 games.... Tore ligaments and damaged cartilage in left knee (October 1987).... Bruised shoulder (January 1990).... Bruised ribs (February 25, 1990); missed 10 games.... Bruised elbow (April 1990).... Strained shoulder (September 1990).... Bruised ribs (November 1990).... Separated left shoulder (December 16, 1990); missed 30 games.... Strained chest muscle (March 1991).... Injured eye (October 10, 1991); missed one game.... Pulled groin (November 7, 1991); missed two games.... Reinjured groin (November 19, 1991); missed two games.... Reinjured groin (December 1991); missed three games.... Sprained right ankle (January 27, 1992); missed 14 games.... Underwent left shoulder surgery (September 27, 1992); missed first 47 games of 1992-93 season.... Pulled groin (March 25, 1993); missed two games.... Traded by Blackhawks to Florida Panthers for RW Darin Kimble (September 30, 1993).... Injured neck (October 21, 1993); missed four games.... Suffered from sore right knee (November 13, 1993); missed two games.... Suffered from sore right knee (November 18, 1993); missed two games.... Underwent right knee surgery (November 28, 1993); missed 15 games.... Strained groin (February 16, 1994); missed three games.... Restrained groin (February 23, 1994); missed six games.
HONORS: Shared WCHL Rookie of the Year Award with John Ogrodnick (1977-78).... Named to WCHL All-Star second team (1977-78).... Won Top Defenseman Trophy (1978-79).... Named to WHL All-Star first team (1978-79).

Season	Team	League	REGULAR SEASON					PLAYOFFS				
			Gms.	G	A	Pts.	PIM	Gms.	G	A	Pts.	PIM
76-77	Fort Saskatchewan	AJHL	59	14	61	75	14	—	—	—	—	—
	Portland	WCHL	2	0	0	0	0	—	—	—	—	—
77-78	Portland	WCHL	72	11	53	64	51	8	0	3	3	2
78-79	Portland	WHL	70	11	85	96	75	25	3	*30	33	21
79-80	Chicago	NHL	76	2	18	20	27	6	0	0	0	4
80-81	Chicago	NHL	80	9	34	43	80	3	0	2	2	2
81-82	Chicago	NHL	33	4	20	24	26	4	0	2	2	5
82-83	Chicago	NHL	50	4	27	31	20	7	0	0	0	11
83-84	Chicago	NHL	74	10	25	35	94	5	0	1	1	10
84-85	Chicago	NHL	56	1	22	23	55	11	2	7	9	31
85-86	Chicago	NHL	70	11	29	40	87	3	0	1	1	9
86-87	Chicago	NHL	73	4	23	27	86	4	0	1	1	6
87-88	Chicago	NHL	24	3	6	9	45	5	0	2	2	10
88-89	Chicago	NHL	74	2	16	18	84	13	1	3	4	25
89-90	Chicago	NHL	67	5	20	25	87	18	0	4	4	43
90-91	Chicago	NHL	45	1	10	11	55	6	1	0	1	8
91-92	Chicago	NHL	57	6	10	16	69	14	0	8	8	18
92-93	Chicago	NHL	33	2	6	8	39	4	0	1	1	2
93-94	Florida	NHL	51	4	8	12	60	—	—	—	—	—
NHL totals			**863**	**68**	**274**	**342**	**914**	**103**	**4**	**32**	**36**	**184**

BROWN, KEVIN
RW, KINGS

PERSONAL: Born May 11, 1974, in Birmingham, England.... 6-1/212.... Shoots right.
HIGH SCHOOL: Quinte Secondary School (Belleville, Ont.).
TRANSACTIONS/CAREER NOTES: Selected by Los Angeles Kings in fourth round (third Kings pick, 87th overall) of NHL entry draft (June 20, 1992).
HONORS: Won Jim Mahon Memorial Trophy (1992-93 and 1993-94).... Named to OHL All-Star second team (1992-93).... Named to OHL All-Star first team (1993-94).... Named to Can.HL All-Star second team (1993-94).

			REGULAR SEASON					PLAYOFFS				
Season	Team	League	Gms.	G	A	Pts.	PIM	Gms.	G	A	Pts.	PIM
89-90—Georgetown Jr. B		OHA	31	3	8	11	59	—	—	—	—	—
90-91—Waterloo Jr. B		OHA	46	25	33	58	116	—	—	—	—	—
91-92—Belleville		OHL	66	24	24	48	52	5	1	4	5	8
92-93—Belleville		OHL	6	2	5	7	4	—	—	—	—	—
—Detroit		OHL	56	48	86	134	76	15	10	18	28	18
93-94—Detroit		OHL	57	54	81	135	85	17	14	*26	*40	28

BROWN, ROB
LW, KINGS

PERSONAL: Born April 10, 1968, in Kingston, Ont.... 5-11/185.... Shoots left.
TRANSACTIONS/CAREER NOTES: Selected by Pittsburgh Penguins as underage junior in fourth round (fourth Penguins pick, 67th overall) of NHL entry draft (June 21, 1986).... Separated right shoulder (February 12, 1989); missed 12 games.... Traded by Penguins to Hartford Whalers for RW Scott Young (December 21, 1990).... Injured Adam's apple (April 5, 1991); missed one playoff game.... Traded by Whalers to Chicago Blackhawks for D Steve Konroyd (January 24, 1992).... Signed as free agent by Dallas Stars (August 6, 1993).... Signed as free agent by Los Angeles Kings (June 1994).
HONORS: Won WHL (West) Most Valuable Player Trophy (1985-86 and 1986-87).... Won Bob Brownridge Memorial Trophy (1985-86).... Named to WHL (West) All-Star first team (1985-86 and 1986-87).... Won Can.HL Player of the Year Award (1986-87).... Won Can.HL Plus/Minus Award (1986-87).... Won WHL (West) Bob Brownridge Memorial Trophy (1986-87).... Won WHL Player of the Year Award (1986-87).... Played in NHL All-Star Game (1989).... Won James Gatschene Memorial Trophy (1993-94).... Won Leo P. Lamoureux Memorial Trophy (1993-94).... Named to IHL All-Star first team (1993-94).

			REGULAR SEASON					PLAYOFFS				
Season	Team	League	Gms.	G	A	Pts.	PIM	Gms.	G	A	Pts.	PIM
83-84—Kamloops		WHL	50	16	42	58	80	15	1	2	3	17
84-85—Kamloops		WHL	60	29	50	79	95	15	8	8	16	28
85-86—Kamloops		WHL	69	58	*115	*173	171	16	*18	*28	*46	14
86-87—Kamloops		WHL	63	*76	*136	*212	101	5	6	5	11	6
87-88—Pittsburgh		NHL	51	24	20	44	56	—	—	—	—	—
88-89—Pittsburgh		NHL	68	49	66	115	118	11	5	3	8	22
89-90—Pittsburgh		NHL	80	33	47	80	102	—	—	—	—	—
90-91—Pittsburgh		NHL	25	6	10	16	31	—	—	—	—	—
—Hartford		NHL	44	18	24	42	101	5	1	0	1	7
91-92—Hartford		NHL	42	16	15	31	39	—	—	—	—	—
—Chicago		NHL	25	5	11	16	34	8	2	4	6	4
92-93—Chicago		NHL	15	1	6	7	33	—	—	—	—	—
—Indianapolis		IHL	19	14	19	33	32	2	0	1	1	2
93-94—Kalamazoo		IHL	79	42	*113	*155	188	5	1	3	4	6
—Dallas		NHL	1	0	0	0	0	—	—	—	—	—
NHL totals			351	152	199	351	514	24	8	7	15	33

BROWN, RYAN
D, LIGHTNING

PERSONAL: Born September 19, 1974, in Boyle, Alta.... 6-3/215.... Shoots right.
TRANSACTIONS/CAREER NOTES: Selected by Tampa Bay Lightning in fifth round (fifth Lightning pick, 107th overall) of NHL entry draft (June 26, 1993).

91-92—Seattle		WHL	60	1	1	2	230	14	0	2	2	38
92-93—Seattle		WHL	19	0	1	1	70	—	—	—	—	—
—Swift Current		WHL	47	1	4	5	104	17	0	2	2	18
93-94—Swift Current		WHL	72	2	10	12	173	7	0	0	0	6

BRUCE, DAVID
LW, SHARKS

PERSONAL: Born October 7, 1964, in Thunder Bay, Ont.... 5-11/190.... Shoots right.
TRANSACTIONS/CAREER NOTES: Selected by Vancouver Canucks as underage junior in second round (second Canucks pick, 30th overall) of NHL entry draft (June 8, 1983).... Suffered from mononucleosis (November 1987).... Bruised foot (March 1988).... Tore cartilage near thumb on left hand and underwent surgery (March 1989).... Signed as free agent by St. Louis Blues (July 23, 1990).... Selected by San Jose Sharks in NHL expansion draft (May 30, 1991).... Tore abdominal muscle (March 19, 1992).... Strained groin (November 7, 1992).... Restrained groin (December 23, 1992); missed 33 games.... Restrained groin (March 11, 1993); missed remainder of season.
HONORS: Named to IHL All-Star first team (1989-90 and 1990-91).... Won James Gatschene Memorial Trophy (1990-91).

			REGULAR SEASON					PLAYOFFS				
Season	Team	League	Gms.	G	A	Pts.	PIM	Gms.	G	A	Pts.	PIM
81-82—Thunder Bay		TBJHL	35	27	31	58	74	—	—	—	—	—
82-83—Kitchener		OHL	67	36	35	71	199	12	7	9	16	27
83-84—Kitchener		OHL	62	52	40	92	203	10	5	8	13	20
84-85—Fredericton		AHL	56	14	11	25	104	5	0	0	0	37

— 341 —

B

Season Team	League		REGULAR SEASON						PLAYOFFS			
		Gms.	G	A	Pts.	PIM	Gms.	G	A	Pts.	PIM
85-86—Fredericton	AHL	66	25	16	41	151	2	0	1	1	12
—Vancouver	NHL	12	0	1	1	14	1	0	0	0	0
86-87—Fredericton	AHL	17	7	6	13	73	—	—	—	—	—
—Vancouver	NHL	50	9	7	16	109	—	—	—	—	—
87-88—Fredericton	AHL	30	27	18	45	115	—	—	—	—	—
—Vancouver	NHL	28	7	3	10	57	—	—	—	—	—
88-89—Vancouver	NHL	53	7	7	14	65	—	—	—	—	—
89-90—Milwaukee	IHL	68	40	35	75	148	6	5	3	8	0
90-91—St. Louis	NHL	12	1	2	3	14	2	0	0	0	2
—Peoria	IHL	60	*64	52	116	78	18	*18	11	*29	40
91-92—Kansas City	IHL	7	5	5	10	6	—	—	—	—	—
—San Jose	NHL	60	22	16	38	46	—	—	—	—	—
92-93—San Jose	NHL	17	2	3	5	33	—	—	—	—	—
93-94—San Jose	NHL	2	0	0	0	0	—	—	—	—	—
—Kansas City	IHL	72	40	24	64	115	—	—	—	—	—
NHL totals		234	48	39	87	338	3	0	0	0	2

BRULE, STEVE
C, DEVILS

PERSONAL: Born January 15, 1975, in Montreal.... 5-11/185.... Shoots right.... Name pronounced broo-LAY.

TRANSACTIONS/CAREER NOTES: Selected by New Jersey Devils in sixth round (sixth Devils pick, 143rd overall) of NHL entry draft (June 26, 1993).

HONORS: Won Michel Bergeron Trophy (1992-93).... Named to QMJHL All-Rookie team (1992-93).

Season Team	League		REGULAR SEASON						PLAYOFFS			
		Gms.	G	A	Pts.	PIM	Gms.	G	A	Pts.	PIM
92-93—St. Jean	QMJHL	70	33	47	80	46	4	0	0	0	9
93-94—St. Jean	QMJHL	66	41	64	105	46	5	2	1	3	0

BRUNET, BENOIT
LW, CANADIENS

PERSONAL: Born August 24, 1968, in Montreal.... 5-11/193.... Shoots left.... Name pronounced BEHN-wah broo-nay.

TRANSACTIONS/CAREER NOTES: Selected by Montreal Canadiens as underage junior in second round (second Canadiens pick, 27th overall) of NHL entry draft (June 21, 1986).... Injured ankle (September 1987).... Tore left knee ligaments (September 24, 1990); missed 24 games.... Fractured ankle (December 4, 1991).... Sprained left knee (November 21, 1992); missed 10 games.... Fractured thumb (January 22, 1993); missed 14 games.... Bruised knee (November 17, 1993); missed four games.... Suffered mild concussion (February 2, 1994); missed six games.... Suffered sore throat (April 8, 1994); missed three games.

HONORS: Named to QMJHL All-Star second team (1986-87).... Named to AHL All-Star first team (1988-89).

MISCELLANEOUS: Member of Stanley Cup championship team (1993).

Season Team	League		REGULAR SEASON						PLAYOFFS			
		Gms.	G	A	Pts.	PIM	Gms.	G	A	Pts.	PIM
85-86—Hull	QMJHL	71	33	37	70	81	—	—	—	—	—
86-87—Hull	QMJHL	60	43	67	110	105	6	7	5	12	8
87-88—Hull	QMJHL	62	54	89	143	131	10	3	10	13	11
88-89—Montreal	NHL	2	0	1	1	0	—	—	—	—	—
—Sherbrooke	AHL	73	41	*76	117	95	6	2	0	2	4
89-90—Sherbrooke	AHL	72	32	35	67	82	12	8	7	15	20
90-91—Fredericton	AHL	24	13	18	31	16	6	5	6	11	2
—Montreal	NHL	17	1	3	4	0	—	—	—	—	—
91-92—Fredericton	AHL	6	7	9	16	27	—	—	—	—	—
—Montreal	NHL	18	4	6	10	14	—	—	—	—	—
92-93—Montreal	NHL	47	10	15	25	19	20	2	8	10	8
93-94—Montreal	NHL	71	10	20	30	20	7	1	4	5	16
NHL totals		155	25	45	70	53	27	3	12	15	24

BRYLIN, SERGEI
C, DEVILS

PERSONAL: Born January 13, 1974, in Moscow, U.S.S.R.... 5-9/176.... Shoots left.

TRANSACTIONS/CAREER NOTES: Selected by New Jersey Devils in second round (second Devils pick, 42nd overall) of NHL entry draft (June 20, 1992).

Season Team	League		REGULAR SEASON						PLAYOFFS			
		Gms.	G	A	Pts.	PIM	Gms.	G	A	Pts.	PIM
91-92—CSKA Moscow	CIS	44	1	6	7	4	—	—	—	—	—
92-93—CSKA Moscow	CIS	42	5	4	9	36	—	—	—	—	—
93-94—CSKA Moscow	CIS	39	4	6	10	36	3	0	1	1	0
—Russian Penguins	IHL	13	4	5	9	18	—	—	—	—	—

BUCHANAN, JEFF
D, LIGHTNING

PERSONAL: Born May 23, 1971, in Swift Current, Sask.... 5-10/165.... Shoots right.

TRANSACTIONS/CAREER NOTES: Signed as free agent by Tampa Bay Lightning (August 13, 1992).

Season Team	League		REGULAR SEASON						PLAYOFFS			
		Gms.	G	A	Pts.	PIM	Gms.	G	A	Pts.	PIM
89-90—Saskatoon	WHL	66	7	12	19	96	9	0	2	2	2
90-91—Saskatoon	WHL	69	10	26	36	123	—	—	—	—	—

Season Team	League	REGULAR SEASON Gms.	G	A	Pts.	PIM	PLAYOFFS Gms.	G	A	Pts.	PIM
91-92—Saskatoon	WHL	72	17	37	54	143	—	—	—	—	—
92-93—Atlanta	IHL	68	4	18	22	282	9	0	0	0	26
93-94—Atlanta	IHL	76	5	24	29	253	14	0	1	1	20

BUCHBERGER, KELLY
RW/LW, OILERS

PERSONAL: Born December 12, 1966, in Langenburg, Sask. . . . 6-2/210. . . . Shoots left. . . . Full name: Kelly Michael Buchberger. . . . Name pronounced BUK-buhr-guhr.
HIGH SCHOOL: Langenburg (Sask.).
TRANSACTIONS/CAREER NOTES: Selected by Edmonton Oilers as underage junior in ninth round (eighth Oilers pick, 188th overall) of NHL entry draft (June 15, 1985). . . . Suspended six games by AHL for leaving bench to fight (March 30, 1988). . . . Fractured right ankle (March 1989). . . . Dislocated left shoulder (March 13, 1990). . . . Reinjured shoulder (May 4, 1990). . . . Strained shoulder (April 7, 1993); missed one game.
MISCELLANEOUS: Member of Stanley Cup championship teams (1987 and 1990).

Season Team	League	REGULAR SEASON Gms.	G	A	Pts.	PIM	PLAYOFFS Gms.	G	A	Pts.	PIM
83-84—Melville	SAJHL	60	14	11	25	139	—	—	—	—	—
84-85—Moose Jaw	WHL	51	12	17	29	114	—	—	—	—	—
85-86—Moose Jaw	WHL	72	14	22	36	206	13	11	4	15	37
86-87—Nova Scotia	AHL	70	12	20	32	257	5	0	1	1	23
—Edmonton	NHL	—	—	—	—	—	3	0	1	1	5
87-88—Edmonton	NHL	19	1	0	1	81	—	—	—	—	—
—Nova Scotia	AHL	49	21	23	44	206	2	0	0	0	11
88-89—Edmonton	NHL	66	5	9	14	234	—	—	—	—	—
89-90—Edmonton	NHL	55	2	6	8	168	19	0	5	5	13
90-91—Edmonton	NHL	64	3	1	4	160	12	2	1	3	25
91-92—Edmonton	NHL	79	20	24	44	157	16	1	4	5	32
92-93—Edmonton	NHL	83	12	18	30	133	—	—	—	—	—
93-94—Edmonton	NHL	84	3	18	21	199	—	—	—	—	—
NHL totals		**450**	**46**	**76**	**122**	**1132**	**50**	**3**	**11**	**14**	**75**

BUCKBERGER, ASHLEY
RW, NORDIQUES

PERSONAL: Born February 19, 1975, in Esterhazy, Sask. . . . 6-2/200. . . . Shoots right.
HIGH SCHOOL: Swift Current (Sask.) Comprehensive.
TRANSACTIONS/CAREER NOTES: Selected by Quebec Nordiques in second round (third Nordiques pick, 49th overall) of NHL entry draft (June 26, 1993).
HONORS: Won Jim Piggott Memorial Trophy (1991-92).

Season Team	League	REGULAR SEASON Gms.	G	A	Pts.	PIM	PLAYOFFS Gms.	G	A	Pts.	PIM
90-91—Swift Current	WHL	10	2	3	5	0	3	0	0	0	0
91-92—Swift Current	WHL	67	23	22	45	38	8	2	1	3	2
92-93—Swift Current	WHL	72	23	44	67	41	17	6	7	13	6
93-94—Swift Current	WHL	67	42	45	87	42	7	0	1	1	6

BUDAYEV, ALEXEI
C, JETS

PERSONAL: Born April 24, 1975, in Elektrostal, U.S.S.R. . . . 6-2/183. . . . Shoots right.
TRANSACTIONS/CAREER NOTES: Selected by Winnipeg Jets in second round (third Jets pick, 43rd overall) of NHL entry draft (June 26, 1993).

Season Team	League	REGULAR SEASON Gms.	G	A	Pts.	PIM	PLAYOFFS Gms.	G	A	Pts.	PIM
92-93—Kristall Elektrostal	CIS Div. II				Statistics unavailable.		—	—	—	—	—
93-94—Kristall Elektrostal	CIS Div. II	46	6	5	11	26	—	—	—	—	—

BURAKOVSKY, ROBERT
RW, SENATORS

PERSONAL: Born November 24, 1966, in Malmo, Sweden. . . . 5-10/178. . . . Shoots right. . . . Name pronounced boo-ruh-KAHV-skee.
TRANSACTIONS/CAREER NOTES: Selected by New York Rangers in 11th round (11th Rangers pick, 217th overall) of NHL entry draft (June 15, 1985). . . . Traded by Rangers to Ottawa Senators for future considerations (May 7, 1993).

Season Team	League	REGULAR SEASON Gms.	G	A	Pts.	PIM	PLAYOFFS Gms.	G	A	Pts.	PIM
85-86—Leksand	Sweden	19	4	3	7	4	—	—	—	—	—
86-87—Leksand	Sweden	36	21	15	36	26	—	—	—	—	—
87-88—Leksand	Sweden	36	10	11	21	10	—	—	—	—	—
88-89—Leksand	Sweden	40	23	20	43	44	10	6	7	13	4
89-90—AIK	Sweden	37	27	29	56	32	3	0	2	2	12
90-91—AIK	Sweden	30	8	15	23	26	—	—	—	—	—
91-92—Malmo	Sweden	40	19	22	41	42	9	5	0	5	4
92-93—Malmo	Sweden	32	8	10	18	40	6	4	4	8	9
93-94—Ottawa	NHL	23	2	3	5	6	—	—	—	—	—
—Prince Edward Island	AHL	52	29	38	67	28	—	—	—	—	—
NHL totals		**23**	**2**	**3**	**5**	**6**					

BURE, PAVEL

RW/LW, CANUCKS

PERSONAL: Born March 31, 1971, in Moscow, U.S.S.R. . . . 5-10/189. . . . Shoots left. . . . Name pronounced PA-vihl BUHR-ay. . . . Brother of Valeri Bure, left winger in Montreal Canadiens system.
TRANSACTIONS/CAREER NOTES: Selected by Vancouver Canucks in sixth round (fourth Canucks pick, 113th overall) of NHL entry draft (June 17, 1989). . . . Strained groin (October 24, 1993); missed eight games. . . . Fined $500 by NHL for hitting another player with flagrant elbow (May 6, 1994).
HONORS: Named Soviet League Rookie of the Year (1988-89). . . . Won Calder Memorial Trophy (1991-92). . . . Named to THE SPORTING NEWS All-Star second team (1993-94). . . . Played in NHL All-Star Game (1993 and 1994). . . . Named to NHL All-Star first team (1993-94).

Season Team	League	REGULAR SEASON					PLAYOFFS				
		Gms.	G	A	Pts.	PIM	Gms.	G	A	Pts.	PIM
87-88—CSKA Moscow	USSR	5	1	1	2	0	—	—	—	—	—
88-89—CSKA Moscow	USSR	32	17	9	26	8	—	—	—	—	—
89-90—CSKA Moscow	USSR	46	14	11	25	22	—	—	—	—	—
90-91—CSKA Moscow	USSR	46	35	12	47	24	—	—	—	—	—
91-92—Vancouver	NHL	65	34	26	60	30	13	6	4	10	14
92-93—Vancouver	NHL	83	60	50	110	69	12	5	7	12	8
93-94—Vancouver	NHL	76	*60	47	107	86	24	*16	15	31	40
NHL totals		224	154	123	277	185	49	27	26	53	62

BURE, VALERI

LW, CANADIENS

PERSONAL: Born June 13, 1974, in Moscow, U.S.S.R. . . . 5-10/160. . . . Shoots right. . . . Name pronounced BUHR-ay. . . . Brother of Pavel Bure, right winger/left winger, Vancouver Canucks.
TRANSACTIONS/CAREER NOTES: Selected by Montreal Canadiens in second round (second Canadiens pick, 33rd overall) of NHL entry draft (June 20, 1992).
HONORS: Named to WHL (West) All-Star first team (1992-93). . . . Named to WHL (West) All-Star second team (1993-94).

Season Team	League	REGULAR SEASON					PLAYOFFS				
		Gms.	G	A	Pts.	PIM	Gms.	G	A	Pts.	PIM
90-91—CSKA Moscow	USSR	3	0	0	0	0	—	—	—	—	—
91-92—Spokane	WHL	53	27	22	49	78	10	11	6	17	10
92-93—Spokane	WHL	66	68	79	147	49	9	6	11	17	14
93-94—Spokane	WHL	59	40	62	102	48	3	5	3	8	2

BUREAU, MARC

C, LIGHTNING

PERSONAL: Born May 17, 1966, in Trois-Rivieres, Que. . . . 6-1/198. . . . Shoots right. . . . Name pronounced BYOOR-oh.
TRANSACTIONS/CAREER NOTES: Traded by Chicoutimi Sagueneens with C Stephane Roy, Lee Duhemee, Sylvain Demers and D Rene L'Ecuyer to Granby Bisons for LW Greg Choules and C Stephane Richer (January 1985). . . . Signed as free agent by Calgary Flames (May 16, 1987). . . . Suffered eye contusion (March 25, 1990); missed final two weeks of season. . . . Traded by Flames to Minnesota North Stars for third-round pick (RW Sandy McCarthy) in 1991 draft (March 5, 1991). . . . Injured shoulder (January 13, 1992); missed four games. . . . Separated shoulder (February 15, 1992); missed five games. . . . Separated shoulder (March 1, 1992); missed eight games. . . . Claimed on waivers by Tampa Bay Lightning (October 16, 1992). . . . Bruised shoulder (November 17, 1992); missed six games. . . . Bruised right knee (April 3, 1993); missed remainder of season.
HONORS: Named to IHL All-Star second team (1989-90 and 1990-91).

Season Team	League	REGULAR SEASON					PLAYOFFS				
		Gms.	G	A	Pts.	PIM	Gms.	G	A	Pts.	PIM
83-84—Chicoutimi	QMJHL	56	6	16	22	14	—	—	—	—	—
84-85—Granby	QMJHL	68	50	70	120	29	—	—	—	—	—
85-86—Chicoutimi	QMJHL	63	36	62	98	69	9	3	7	10	10
86-87—Longueuil	QMJHL	66	54	58	112	68	20	17	20	37	12
87-88—Salt Lake City	IHL	69	7	20	27	86	7	0	3	3	8
88-89—Salt Lake City	IHL	76	28	36	64	119	14	7	5	12	31
89-90—Salt Lake City	IHL	67	43	48	91	173	11	4	8	12	0
—Calgary	NHL	5	0	0	0	4	—	—	—	—	—
90-91—Calgary	NHL	5	0	0	0	2	—	—	—	—	—
—Salt Lake City	IHL	54	40	48	88	101	—	—	—	—	—
—Minnesota	NHL	9	0	6	6	4	23	3	2	5	20
91-92—Minnesota	NHL	46	6	4	10	50	5	0	0	0	14
—Kalamazoo	IHL	7	2	8	10	2	—	—	—	—	—
92-93—Tampa Bay	NHL	63	10	21	31	111	—	—	—	—	—
93-94—Tampa Bay	NHL	75	8	7	15	30	—	—	—	—	—
NHL totals		203	24	38	62	201	28	3	2	5	34

BURKE, SEAN

G, WHALERS

PERSONAL: Born January 29, 1967, in Windsor, Ont. . . . 6-4/210. . . . Catches left.
TRANSACTIONS/CAREER NOTES: Selected by New Jersey Devils as underage junior in second round (second Devils pick, 24th overall) of NHL entry draft (June 15, 1985). . . . Injured groin (December 1988). . . . Underwent arthroscopic surgery to right knee (September 5, 1989). . . . Traded by Devils with D Eric Weinrich to Hartford Whalers for RW Bobby Holik, second-round pick in 1993 draft (LW Jay Pandolfo) and future considerations (August 28, 1992). . . . Sprained ankle (December 27, 1992); missed seven games. . . . Suffered back spasms (March 13, 1993); missed remainder of season. . . . Pulled hamstring (September 29, 1993); missed 7 games. . . . Reinjured hamstring (October 27, 1993); missed 14 games. . . . Suffered back spasms (December 23, 1993); missed one game.
HONORS: Played in NHL All-Star Game (1989).
MISCELLANEOUS: Member of silver-medal-winning Canadian Olympic team (1992).

Season	Team	League	REGULAR SEASON Gms.	Min.	W	L	T	GA	SO	Avg.	PLAYOFFS Gms.	Min.	W	L	GA	SO	Avg.
83-84	St. Michael's H.S.	MTHL	25	1482	...	...	...	120	0	4.86	—	—	—	—	—	—	—
84-85	Toronto	OHL	49	2987	25	21	3	211	0	4.24	5	266	1	3	25	0	5.64
85-86	Toronto	OHL	47	2840	16	27	3	†233	0	4.92	4	238	0	4	24	0	6.05
	—Can. national team	Int'l	5	284	...	...	...	22	0	4.65	—	—	—	—	—	—	—
86-87	Can. national team	Int'l	46	2670	...	...	...	138	0	3.10	—	—	—	—	—	—	—
87-88	Can. national team	Int'l	37	1962	19	9	2	92	1	2.81	—	—	—	—	—	—	—
	—Can. Olympic Team	Int'l	4	238	1	2	1	12	0	3.03	—	—	—	—	—	—	—
	—New Jersey	NHL	13	689	10	1	0	35	1	3.05	17	1001	9	8	*57	†1	3.42
88-89	New Jersey	NHL	62	3590	22	31	9	†230	3	3.84	—	—	—	—	—	—	—
89-90	New Jersey	NHL	52	2914	22	22	6	175	0	3.60	2	125	0	2	8	0	3.84
90-91	New Jersey	NHL	35	1870	8	12	8	112	0	3.59	—	—	—	—	—	—	—
91-92	Can. national team	Int'l	31	1721	18	6	4	75	1	2.61	—	—	—	—	—	—	—
	—Can. Olympic Team	Int'l	7	429	5	2	0	17	0	2.38	—	—	—	—	—	—	—
	—San Diego	IHL	7	424	4	2	‡1	17	0	2.41	3	160	0	3	13	0	4.88
92-93	Hartford	NHL	50	2656	16	27	3	184	0	4.16	—	—	—	—	—	—	—
93-94	Hartford	NHL	47	2750	17	24	5	137	2	2.99	—	—	—	—	—	—	—
NHL totals			259	14469	95	117	31	873	6	3.62	19	1126	9	10	65	1	3.46

BURR, SHAWN

LW, RED WINGS

PERSONAL: Born July 1, 1966, in Sarnia, Ont. . . . 6-1/195. . . . Shoots left.
TRANSACTIONS/CAREER NOTES: Selected by Detroit Red Wings as underage junior in first round (first Red Wings pick, seventh overall) of NHL entry draft (June 9, 1984). . . . Separated left shoulder (May 1988). . . . Suffered lower back spasms (October 20, 1992); missed three games. . . . Surgery on wrist (December 8, 1993); missed 18 games. . . . Injured leg (January 25, 1994); missed seven games.
HONORS: Won Emms Family Award (1983-84). . . . Named to OHL All-Star second team (1985-86).

Season	Team	League	REGULAR SEASON Gms.	G	A	Pts.	PIM	PLAYOFFS Gms.	G	A	Pts.	PIM
83-84	Kitchener	OHL	68	41	44	85	50	16	5	12	17	22
84-85	Kitchener	OHL	38	24	42	66	50	4	3	3	6	2
	—Detroit	NHL	9	0	0	0	2	—	—	—	—	—
	—Adirondack	AHL	4	0	0	0	2	—	—	—	—	—
85-86	Kitchener	OHL	59	60	67	127	104	5	2	3	5	8
	—Adirondack	AHL	3	2	2	4	2	17	5	7	12	32
	—Detroit	NHL	5	1	0	1	4	—	—	—	—	—
86-87	Detroit	NHL	80	22	25	47	107	16	7	2	9	20
87-88	Detroit	NHL	78	17	23	40	97	9	3	1	4	14
88-89	Detroit	NHL	79	19	27	46	78	6	1	2	3	6
89-90	Adirondack	AHL	3	4	2	6	2	—	—	—	—	—
	—Detroit	NHL	76	24	32	56	82	—	—	—	—	—
90-91	Detroit	NHL	80	20	30	50	112	7	0	4	4	15
91-92	Detroit	NHL	79	19	32	51	118	11	1	5	6	10
92-93	Detroit	NHL	80	10	25	35	74	7	2	1	3	2
93-94	Detroit	NHL	51	10	12	22	31	7	2	0	2	6
NHL totals			617	142	206	348	705	63	16	15	31	73

BURRIDGE, RANDY

LW, CAPITALS

PERSONAL: Born January 7, 1966, in Fort Erie, Ont. . . . 5-9/185. . . . Shoots left. . . . Name pronounced BUHR-ihdj.
TRANSACTIONS/CAREER NOTES: Selected by Boston Bruins in eighth round (seventh Bruins pick, 157th overall) of NHL entry draft (June 15, 1985). . . . Strained groin (March 1, 1986). . . . Suspended by AHL during playoffs (April 1987). . . . Sprained medial collateral ligament in left knee (February 6, 1990); missed 18 games. . . . Tore right knee ligaments (February 7, 1991). . . . Underwent surgery to right knee (February 13, 1991). . . . Traded by Bruins to Washington Capitals for RW Stephen Leach (June 21, 1991). . . . Partially tore left knee ligament (March 1, 1992); missed 14 games. . . . Underwent knee surgery (September 5, 1992); missed first 71 games of season. . . . Strained groin (October 6, 1993); missed three games.
HONORS: Played in NHL All-Star Game (1992).

Season	Team	League	REGULAR SEASON Gms.	G	A	Pts.	PIM	PLAYOFFS Gms.	G	A	Pts.	PIM
82-83	Fort Erie Jr. B	OHA	42	32	56	88	32	—	—	—	—	—
83-84	Peterborough	OHL	55	6	7	13	44	8	3	2	5	7
84-85	Peterborough	OHL	66	49	57	106	88	17	9	16	25	18
85-86	Peterborough	OHL	17	15	11	26	23	3	1	3	4	2
	—Boston	NHL	52	17	25	42	28	3	0	4	4	12
	—Moncton	AHL	—	—	—	—	—	3	0	2	2	2
86-87	Moncton	AHL	47	26	41	67	139	3	1	2	3	30
	—Boston	NHL	23	1	4	5	16	2	1	0	1	2
87-88	Boston	NHL	79	27	28	55	105	23	2	10	12	16
88-89	Boston	NHL	80	31	30	61	39	10	5	2	7	8
89-90	Boston	NHL	63	17	15	32	47	21	4	11	15	14
90-91	Boston	NHL	62	15	13	28	40	19	0	3	3	39
91-92	Washington	NHL	66	23	44	67	50	2	0	1	1	0
92-93	Baltimore	AHL	2	0	1	1	2	—	—	—	—	—
	—Washington	NHL	4	0	0	0	0	4	1	0	1	0
93-94	Washington	NHL	78	25	17	42	73	11	0	2	2	12
NHL totals			507	156	176	332	398	95	13	33	46	103

BURT, ADAM
D, WHALERS

PERSONAL: Born January 15, 1969, in Detroit.... 6-0/190.... Shoots left.
TRANSACTIONS/CAREER NOTES: Suffered broken jaw (December 1985).... Selected by Hartford Whalers as underage junior in second round (second Whalers pick, 39th overall) of NHL entry draft (June 13, 1987).... Separated left shoulder (September 13, 1988).... Bruised hip (December 1989).... Dislocated left shoulder (January 19, 1989).... Tore medial collateral ligaments in right knee (February 16, 1991); missed remainder of season.... Sprained left wrist (January 11, 1992); missed six games.... Broke bone in right foot (January 25, 1993); missed 13 games.... Sprained shoulder (February 27, 1994); missed remainder of season.
HONORS: Named to OHL All-Star second team (1987-88).

			REGULAR SEASON					PLAYOFFS				
Season	Team	League	Gms.	G	A	Pts.	PIM	Gms.	G	A	Pts.	PIM
85-86	North Bay	OHL	49	0	11	11	81	10	0	0	0	24
86-87	North Bay	OHL	57	4	27	31	138	24	1	6	7	68
87-88	North Bay	OHL	66	17	54	71	176	2	0	3	3	6
	Binghamton	AHL	—	—	—	—	—	2	1	1	2	0
88-89	North Bay	OHL	23	4	11	15	45	12	2	12	14	12
	Team USA Juniors	Int'l	7	1	6	7	...	—	—	—	—	—
	Binghamton	AHL	5	0	2	2	13	—	—	—	—	—
	Hartford	NHL	5	0	0	0	6	—	—	—	—	—
89-90	Hartford	NHL	63	4	8	12	105	2	0	0	0	0
90-91	Springfield	AHL	9	1	3	4	22	—	—	—	—	—
	Hartford	NHL	42	2	7	9	63	—	—	—	—	—
91-92	Hartford	NHL	66	9	15	24	93	2	0	0	0	0
92-93	Hartford	NHL	65	6	14	20	116	—	—	—	—	—
93-94	Hartford	NHL	63	1	17	18	75	—	—	—	—	—
	NHL totals		304	22	61	83	458	4	0	0	0	0

BUSCHAN, ANDREI
D, SHARKS

PERSONAL: Born August 21, 1970, in Kharkov, U.S.S.R.... 6-2/200.... Shoots left. ... Name pronounced boo-SHAHN.
TRANSACTIONS/CAREER NOTES: Selected by San Jose Sharks in fifth round (sixth Sharks pick, 106th overall) of NHL entry draft (June 26, 1993).

			REGULAR SEASON					PLAYOFFS				
Season	Team	League	Gms.	G	A	Pts.	PIM	Gms.	G	A	Pts.	PIM
88-89	Dynamo Kharkov	USSR	2	0	0	0	0	—	—	—	—	—
89-90	Dynamo Kharkov	USSR	21	0	0	0	10	—	—	—	—	—
90-91	Dynamo Kharkov	USSR Div. II	62	0	3	3	14	—	—	—	—	—
91-92	Dynamo Kharkov	CIS Div. II				Statistics unavailable.						
92-93	Sokol-Eskulap Kiev	CIS	41	8	5	13	16	3	0	0	0	4
93-94	Kansas City	IHL	60	5	13	18	68	—	—	—	—	—

BUSKAS, ROD
D

PERSONAL: Born January 7, 1961, in Wetaskiwin, Alta.... 6-1/206.... Shoots right.... Full name: Rod Dale Buskas.... Name pronounced BUZ-kuhz.
TRANSACTIONS/CAREER NOTES: Selected by Pittsburgh Penguins in sixth round (fifth Penguins pick, 112th overall) of NHL entry draft (June 10, 1981).... Injured shoulder (February 1985). ... Injured shoulder (November 1986).... Traded by Penguins to Vancouver Canucks for sixth-round pick (D Ian Moran) in 1990 draft (October 24, 1989).... Broke ankle (December 13, 1989); missed 29 games.... Traded by Canucks with RW Tony Tanti and C Barry Pederson to Penguins for C Dan Quinn, RW Andrew McBain and C Dave Capuano (January 8, 1990).... Selected by Los Angeles Kings in NHL waiver draft for $10,000 (October 1, 1990).... Strained chest muscle (December 20, 1990).... Injured foot (January 22, 1991).... Traded by Kings to Chicago Blackhawks for D Chris Norton (October 28, 1991). ... Bruised left foot (February 22, 1992); missed 14 games.... Loaned to Salt Lake City Golden Eagles (January 11, 1993).... Signed as free agent by Las Vegas Thunder (August 31, 1993).

			REGULAR SEASON					PLAYOFFS				
Season	Team	League	Gms.	G	A	Pts.	PIM	Gms.	G	A	Pts.	PIM
78-79	Red Deer	AJHL	37	13	22	35	63	—	—	—	—	—
	Billings	WHL	1	0	0	0	0	—	—	—	—	—
	Medicine Hat	WHL	35	1	12	13	60	—	—	—	—	—
79-80	Medicine Hat	WHL	72	7	40	47	284	—	—	—	—	—
80-81	Medicine Hat	WHL	72	14	46	60	164	5	1	1	2	8
81-82	Erie	AHL	69	1	18	19	78	—	—	—	—	—
82-83	Muskegon	IHL	1	0	0	0	9	—	—	—	—	—
	Baltimore	AHL	31	2	8	10	45	—	—	—	—	—
	Pittsburgh	NHL	41	2	2	4	102	—	—	—	—	—
83-84	Baltimore	AHL	33	2	12	14	100	10	1	3	4	22
	Pittsburgh	NHL	47	2	4	6	60	—	—	—	—	—
84-85	Pittsburgh	NHL	69	2	7	9	191	—	—	—	—	—
85-86	Pittsburgh	NHL	72	2	7	9	159	—	—	—	—	—
86-87	Pittsburgh	NHL	68	3	15	18	123	—	—	—	—	—
87-88	Pittsburgh	NHL	76	4	8	12	206	—	—	—	—	—
88-89	Pittsburgh	NHL	52	1	5	6	105	10	0	0	0	23
89-90	Vancouver	NHL	17	0	3	3	36	—	—	—	—	—
	Pittsburgh	NHL	6	0	0	0	13	—	—	—	—	—
90-91	Los Angeles	NHL	57	3	8	11	182	2	0	2	2	22
91-92	Los Angeles	NHL	5	0	0	0	11	—	—	—	—	—
	Chicago	NHL	42	0	4	4	80	6	0	1	1	0

Season	Team	League	Gms.	G	A	Pts.	PIM	Gms.	G	A	Pts.	PIM
92-93—Chicago	NHL	4	0	0	0	26	—	—	—	—	—
—Indianapolis	IHL	15	0	3	3	40	—	—	—	—	—
—Salt Lake City	IHL	31	0	2	2	52	—	—	—	—	—
93-94—Las Vegas	IHL	69	2	9	11	131	5	0	2	2	2
NHL totals		556	19	63	82	1294	18	0	3	3	45

BUTCHER, GARTH

D, MAPLE LEAFS

PERSONAL: Born January 8, 1963, in Regina, Sask.... 6-0/204.... Shoots right.
HIGH SCHOOL: Thom (Regina, Sask.).
TRANSACTIONS/CAREER NOTES: Selected by Vancouver Canucks as underage junior in first round (first Canucks pick, 10th overall) of NHL entry draft (June 10, 1981).... Separated shoulder (October 1984).... Traded by Canucks with C Dan Quinn to St. Louis Blues for LW Geoff Courtnall, D Robert Dirk, C Cliff Ronning, LW Sergio Momesso and fifth-round pick (RW Brian Loney) in 1992 draft (March 5, 1991).... Fractured bone in left foot (March 7, 1992); missed final 12 games of season.... Bruised foot (December 26, 1993); missed two games.... Traded by Blues with C Bob Bassen and C Ron Sutter to Quebec Nordiques for D Steve Duchesne and RW Denis Chasse (January 23, 1994).... Bruised thigh (March 10, 1994); missed two games.... Traded by Nordiques with C Mats Sundin, LW Todd Warriner and first-round pick (traded to Washington Capitals who selected D Nolan Baumgartner) in 1994 draft to Toronto Maple Leafs for LW Wendel Clark, D Sylvain Lefebvre, RW Landon Wilson and first-round pick (D Jeffrey Kealty) in 1994 draft (June 28, 1994).
HONORS: Named to WHL All-Star first team (1980-81 and 1981-82).... Played in NHL All-Star Game (1993).

Season	Team	League	Gms.	G	A	Pts.	PIM	Gms.	G	A	Pts.	PIM
79-80—Regina Tier II	SJHL	51	15	31	46	236	—	—	—	—	—
—Regina	WHL	13	0	4	4	20	9	0	0	0	45
80-81—Regina	WHL	69	9	77	86	230	11	5	17	22	60
81-82—Regina	WHL	65	24	68	92	318	19	3	17	20	95
—Vancouver	NHL	5	0	0	0	9	1	0	0	0	0
82-83—Kamloops	WHL	5	4	2	6	4	6	4	8	12	16
—Vancouver	NHL	55	1	13	14	104	3	1	0	1	2
83-84—Fredericton	AHL	25	4	13	17	43	6	0	2	2	19
—Vancouver	NHL	28	2	0	2	34	—	—	—	—	—
84-85—Vancouver	NHL	75	3	9	12	152	—	—	—	—	—
—Fredericton	AHL	3	1	0	1	11	—	—	—	—	—
85-86—Vancouver	NHL	70	4	7	11	188	3	0	0	0	0
86-87—Vancouver	NHL	70	5	15	20	207	—	—	—	—	—
87-88—Vancouver	NHL	80	6	17	23	285	—	—	—	—	—
88-89—Vancouver	NHL	78	0	20	20	227	7	1	1	2	22
89-90—Vancouver	NHL	80	6	14	20	205	—	—	—	—	—
90-91—Vancouver	NHL	69	6	12	18	257	—	—	—	—	—
—St. Louis	NHL	13	0	4	4	32	13	2	1	3	54
91-92—St. Louis	NHL	68	5	15	20	189	5	1	2	3	16
92-93—St. Louis	NHL	84	5	10	15	211	11	1	1	2	20
93-94—St. Louis	NHL	43	1	6	7	76	—	—	—	—	—
—Quebec	NHL	34	3	9	12	67	—	—	—	—	—
NHL totals		852	47	151	198	2243	43	6	5	11	114

BUTENSCHON, SVEN

D, PENGUINS

PERSONAL: Born March 22, 1976, in Itzehoe, West Germany.... 6-5/201.... Shoots left.... Name pronounced boot-en-SHOWN.
HIGH SCHOOL: Crocus Plains (Brandon, Man.).
TRANSACTIONS/CAREER NOTES: Selected by Pittsburgh Penguins in third round (third Penguins pick, 57th overall) of NHL entry draft (June 29, 1994).

Season	Team	League	Gms.	G	A	Pts.	PIM	Gms.	G	A	Pts.	PIM
93-94—Brandon	WHL	70	3	19	22	51	4	0	0	0	6

BUTSAYEV, SLAVA

C, SHARKS

PERSONAL: Born June 13, 1970, in Tolyatti, U.S.S.R.... 6-2/200.... Shoots left.... Name pronounced boot-SIGH-yehf.
TRANSACTIONS/CAREER NOTES: Selected by Philadelphia Flyers in sixth round (10th Flyers pick, 109th overall) of NHL entry draft (June 16, 1990).... Traded by Flyers to San Jose Sharks for D Rob Zettler (February 1, 1994).

Season	Team	League	Gms.	G	A	Pts.	PIM	Gms.	G	A	Pts.	PIM
89-90—CSKA Moscow	USSR	48	13	4	17	30	—	—	—	—	—
90-91—CSKA Moscow	USSR	46	14	9	23	32	—	—	—	—	—
91-92—CSKA Moscow	USSR	36	12	13	25	26	—	—	—	—	—
—Unified Olympic Team	Int'l	8	1	1	2	4	—	—	—	—	—
92-93—CSKA Moscow	CIS	5	3	4	7	6	—	—	—	—	—
—Philadelphia	NHL	52	2	14	16	61	—	—	—	—	—
—Hershey	AHL	24	8	10	18	51	—	—	—	—	—
93-94—Philadelphia	NHL	47	12	9	21	58	—	—	—	—	—
—San Jose	NHL	12	0	2	2	10	—	—	—	—	—
NHL totals		111	14	25	39	129	—	—	—	—	—

B

BYAKIN, ILYA
D, OILERS

PERSONAL: Born February 2, 1963, in Sverdlovsk, U.S.S.R. . . . 5-9/185. . . . Shoots left.
TRANSACTIONS/CAREER NOTES: Selected by Edmonton Oilers in 11th round (11th Oilers pick, 267th overall) of NHL entry draft (June 26, 1993). . . . Sprained knee (November 13, 1993); missed two games. . . . Sprained left wrist (January 7, 1994); missed four games.

			REGULAR SEASON					PLAYOFFS			
Season Team	League	Gms.	G	A	Pts.	PIM	Gms.	G	A	Pts.	PIM
83-84—Spartak Moscow	USSR	44	9	12	21	26	—	—	—	—	—
84-85—Spartak Moscow	USSR	46	7	11	18	56	—	—	—	—	—
85-86—Spartak Moscow	USSR	34	8	7	15	41	—	—	—	—	—
86-87—Avtomobilist Sverdlovsk	USSR				Did not play.						
87-88—Avtomobilist Sverdlovsk	USSR	30	10	10	20	37	—	—	—	—	—
88-89—Avtomobilist Sverdlovsk	USSR	40	11	9	20	53	—	—	—	—	—
89-90—Avtomobilist Sverdlovsk	USSR	27	14	7	21	20	—	—	—	—	—
90-91—CSKA Moscow	USSR	29	4	7	11	20	—	—	—	—	—
91-92—Rapperswill	Switzerland	36	27	40	67	36	—	—	—	—	—
92-93—Landshut	Germany	44	12	19	31	43	—	—	—	—	—
93-94—Cape Breton	AHL	12	2	9	11	8	—	—	—	—	—
—Edmonton	NHL	44	8	20	28	30	—	—	—	—	—
NHL totals		44	8	20	28	30					

BYRAM, SHAWN
LW, BLACKHAWKS

PERSONAL: Born September 12, 1968, in Neepawa, Man. . . . 6-2/204. . . . Shoots left.
TRANSACTIONS/CAREER NOTES: Selected by New York Islanders as underage junior in fourth round (fourth Islanders pick, 80th overall) of NHL entry draft (June 21, 1986). . . . Signed as free agent by Chicago Blackhawks (August 2, 1991).

			REGULAR SEASON					PLAYOFFS			
Season Team	League	Gms.	G	A	Pts.	PIM	Gms.	G	A	Pts.	PIM
85-86—Regina	WHL	46	7	6	13	45	9	0	1	1	11
86-87—Prince Albert	WHL	67	19	21	40	147	7	1	1	2	10
87-88—Prince Albert	WHL	61	23	28	51	178	10	5	2	7	27
88-89—Springfield	AHL	45	5	11	16	195	—	—	—	—	—
—Indianapolis	IHL	1	0	0	0	2	—	—	—	—	—
89-90—Springfield	AHL	31	4	4	8	30	—	—	—	—	—
—Johnstown	ECHL	8	5	5	10	35	—	—	—	—	—
90-91—Capital District	AHL	62	28	35	63	162	—	—	—	—	—
—New York Islanders	NHL	4	0	0	0	14	—	—	—	—	—
91-92—Indianapolis	IHL	69	18	21	39	154	—	—	—	—	—
—Chicago	NHL	1	0	0	0	0	—	—	—	—	—
92-93—Indianapolis	IHL	41	2	13	15	123	5	1	2	3	8
93-94—Indianapolis	IHL	77	23	24	47	170	—	—	—	—	—
NHL totals		5	0	0	0	14					

CABANA, CHAD
LW, PANTHERS

PERSONAL: Born October 1, 1974, in Bonnyville, Alta. . . . 6-1/200. . . . Shoots left. . . . Name pronounced kuh-BA-nuh.
HIGH SCHOOL: Kamiakin.
TRANSACTIONS/CAREER NOTES: Selected by Florida Panthers in 11th round (11th Panthers pick, 213th overall) of NHL entry draft (June 26, 1993).

			REGULAR SEASON					PLAYOFFS			
Season Team	League	Gms.	G	A	Pts.	PIM	Gms.	G	A	Pts.	PIM
90-91—Bonnyville	Jr. B	45	35	40	75	90	—	—	—	—	—
91-92—Tri-City	WHL	57	5	8	13	145	4	0	1	1	21
92-93—Tri-City	WHL	68	19	23	42	104	4	1	0	1	10
93-94—Tri-City	WHL	67	27	33	60	201	4	2	0	2	24

CAIRNS, ERIC
D, RANGERS

PERSONAL: Born June 27, 1974, in Oakville, Ont. . . . 6-6/217. . . . Shoots left.
TRANSACTIONS/CAREER NOTES: Selected by New York Rangers in third round (third Rangers pick, 72nd overall) of NHL entry draft (June 20, 1992).

			REGULAR SEASON					PLAYOFFS			
Season Team	League	Gms.	G	A	Pts.	PIM	Gms.	G	A	Pts.	PIM
90-91—Burlington Jr. B	OHA	37	5	16	21	120	—	—	—	—	—
91-92—Detroit	OHL	64	1	11	12	237	7	0	0	0	31
92-93—Detroit	OHL	64	3	13	16	194	15	0	3	3	24
93-94—Detroit	OHL	59	7	35	42	204	17	0	4	4	46

CALLANDER, JOCK
C/RW

PERSONAL: Born April 23, 1961, in Regina, Sask. . . . 6-1/188. . . . Shoots right. . . . Brother of Drew Callander, center, Philadelphia Flyers and Vancouver Canucks (1976-77 through 1979-80).
TRANSACTIONS/CAREER NOTES: Signed as free agent by St. Louis Blues (September 28, 1981). . . . Signed as free agent by Pittsburgh Penguins (July 31, 1987). . . . Underwent knee surgery (October 1990). . . . Tore knee ligaments (January 19, 1991). . . . Signed as free agent by Tampa Bay Lightning (July 29, 1992). . . . Signed as free agent by Cleveland Lumberjacks (August 12, 1993).
HONORS: Won Bob Brownridge Memorial Trophy (1981-82). . . . Named Turner Cup Playoff Most Valuable Player (1985-86). . . . Shared James Gatschene Memorial Trophy with Jeff Pyle (1986-87). . . . Shared Leo P. Lamoureux Memorial Trophy with

Jeff Pyle (1986-87).... Named to IHL All-Star first team (1986-87 and 1991-92).
MISCELLANEOUS: Member of Stanley Cup championship team (1992).

Season	Team	League	REGULAR SEASON Gms.	G	A	Pts.	PIM	PLAYOFFS Gms.	G	A	Pts.	PIM
78-79	—Regina	WHL	19	3	2	5	0	—	—	—	—	—
	—Regina Blues	SJHL	42	44	42	86	24	—	—	—	—	—
79-80	—Regina	WHL	39	9	11	20	25	18	8	5	13	0
80-81	—Regina	WHL	72	67	86	153	37	11	6	7	13	14
81-82	—Regina	WHL	71	79	111	*190	59	20	13	*26	39	37
82-83	—Salt Lake City	IHL	68	20	27	47	26	6	0	1	1	9
83-84	—Montana	CHL	72	27	32	59	69	—	—	—	—	—
	—Toledo	IHL	2	0	0	0	0	—	—	—	—	—
84-85	—Muskegon	IHL	82	39	68	107	86	17	8	13	21	33
85-86	—Muskegon	IHL	82	39	72	111	121	14	*12	11	*23	12
86-87	—Muskegon	IHL	82	54	82	†136	110	15	13	7	20	23
87-88	—Muskegon	IHL	31	20	36	56	49	6	2	3	5	25
	—Pittsburgh	NHL	41	11	16	27	45	—	—	—	—	—
88-89	—Muskegon	IHL	48	25	39	64	40	7	5	5	10	30
	—Pittsburgh	NHL	30	6	5	11	20	10	2	5	7	10
89-90	—Muskegon	IHL	46	29	49	78	118	15	6	†14	20	54
	—Pittsburgh	NHL	30	4	7	11	49	—	—	—	—	—
90-91	—Muskegon	IHL	30	14	20	34	102	—	—	—	—	—
91-92	—Muskegon	IHL	81	42	70	112	160	10	4	10	14	13
	—Pittsburgh	NHL	—	—	—	—	—	12	1	3	4	2
92-93	—Atlanta	IHL	69	34	50	84	172	9	†7	5	12	25
	—Tampa Bay	NHL	8	1	1	2	2	—	—	—	—	—
93-94	—Cleveland	IHL	81	31	70	101	126	—	—	—	—	—
NHL totals			109	22	29	51	116	22	3	8	11	12

C

CALOUN, JAN
RW, SHARKS

PERSONAL: Born December 20, 1972, in Usti-nad-Labem, Czechoslovakia. ... 5-10/175. ... Shoots right.
TRANSACTIONS/CAREER NOTES: Selected by San Jose Sharks in fourth round (fourth Sharks pick, 75th overall) of NHL entry draft (June 20, 1992).

Season	Team	League	REGULAR SEASON Gms.	G	A	Pts.	PIM	PLAYOFFS Gms.	G	A	Pts.	PIM
90-91	—CHZ Litvinov	Czech.	50	28	19	47	12	—	—	—	—	—
91-92	—Chemopetrol Litvinov	Czech.	46	39	13	52	...	—	—	—	—	—
92-93	—Chemopetrol Litvinov	Czech.	47	45	22	67	...	—	—	—	—	—
93-94	—Chemopetrol Litvinov	Czech Rep.	41	25	17	42	...	4	2	0	2	...

CAMPBELL, JIM
C, CANADIENS

PERSONAL: Born February 3, 1973, in Worcester, Mass.... 6-1/175.... Shoots right.
HIGH SCHOOL: Lawrence Academy (Groton, Mass.), then Northwood School (Lake Placid, N.Y.).
TRANSACTIONS/CAREER NOTES: Selected by Montreal Canadiens in second round (second Canadiens pick, 28th overall) of NHL entry draft (June 22, 1991).... Loaned by Canadiens to U.S. Olympic Team (September 26, 1993).

Season	Team	League	REGULAR SEASON Gms.	G	A	Pts.	PIM	PLAYOFFS Gms.	G	A	Pts.	PIM
88-89	—Lawrence Academy	Mass. H.S.	12	12	8	20	6	—	—	—	—	—
89-90	—Lawrence Academy	Mass. H.S.	8	14	7	21	8	—	—	—	—	—
90-91	—Northwood School	N.Y. H.S.	26	36	47	83	36	—	—	—	—	—
91-92	—Hull	QMJHL	64	41	44	85	51	6	7	3	10	8
92-93	—Hull	QMJHL	50	42	29	71	66	8	11	4	15	43
93-94	—U.S. national team	Int'l	56	24	33	57	59	—	—	—	—	—
	—U.S. Olympic Team	Int'l	8	0	0	0	6	—	—	—	—	—
	—Fredericton	AHL	19	6	17	23	6	—	—	—	—	—

CAPUANO, DAVE
LW/C, BRUINS

PERSONAL: Born July 27, 1968, in Warwick, R.I.... 6-2/190.... Shoots left.... Full name: David Alan Capuano.... Name pronounced kap-yoo-AH-noh.... Brother of Jack Capuano, defenseman, Toronto Maple Leafs, Vancouver Canucks and Boston Bruins (1989-90 through 1991-92).
HIGH SCHOOL: Mount St. Charles Academy (Woonsocket, R.I.).
COLLEGE: Maine.
TRANSACTIONS/CAREER NOTES: Selected by Pittsburgh Penguins in second round (second Penguins pick, 25th overall) of NHL entry draft (June 21, 1986).... Broke hand (August 1986).... Traded by Penguins with C Dan Quinn and RW Andrew McBain to Vancouver Canucks for RW Tony Tanti, C Barry Pederson and D Rod Buskas (January 8, 1990).... Injured knee (November 27, 1990). ... Underwent arthroscopic knee surgery (January 25, 1991); missed 14 games. ... Traded by Canucks with fourth-round pick in 1994 draft (traded to New Jersey Devils) to Tampa Bay Lightning for C Anatoli Semenov (November 3, 1992).... Traded by Lightning to San Jose Sharks for D Peter Ahola (June 19, 1993).... Traded by Sharks to Boston Bruins for future considerations (November 5, 1993).
HONORS: Named to Hockey East All-Freshman team (1986-87).... Named to NCAA All-America East first team (1987-88 and 1988-89).... Named to NCAA All-Tournament team (1987-88).... Named to Hockey East All-Star first team (1987-88 and 1988-89).

Season	Team	League	Gms.	G	A	Pts.	PIM	Gms.	G	A	Pts.	PIM
84-85	Mount St. Charles H.S.	R.I.H.S.	...	41	38	79	...	—	—	—	—	—
85-86	Mount St. Charles H.S.	R.I.H.S.	22	39	48	87	20	—	—	—	—	—
86-87	University of Maine	Hockey East	38	18	41	59	14	—	—	—	—	—
87-88	University of Maine	Hockey East	42	34	51	85	51	—	—	—	—	—
88-89	University of Maine	Hockey East	41	37	30	67	38	—	—	—	—	—
89-90	Muskegon	IHL	27	15	15	30	22	—	—	—	—	—
	Pittsburgh	NHL	6	0	0	0	2	—	—	—	—	—
	Vancouver	NHL	27	3	5	8	10	—	—	—	—	—
	Milwaukee	IHL	2	0	4	4	0	6	1	5	6	0
90-91	Vancouver	NHL	61	13	31	44	42	6	1	1	2	5
91-92	Milwaukee	IHL	9	2	6	8	8	—	—	—	—	—
92-93	Hamilton	AHL	4	0	1	1	0	—	—	—	—	—
	Atlanta	IHL	58	19	40	59	50	8	2	2	4	9
	Tampa Bay	NHL	6	1	1	2	2	—	—	—	—	—
93-94	San Jose	NHL	4	0	1	1	0	—	—	—	—	—
	Providence	AHL	51	24	29	53	64	—	—	—	—	—
	NHL totals		104	17	38	55	56	6	1	1	2	5

CARAVAGGIO, LUCIANO
G, DEVILS

PERSONAL: Born October 3, 1975, in Toronto. ... 5-11/173. ... Catches left. ... Full name: Luciano Anthony Caravaggio.
HIGH SCHOOL: Don Bosco (Weston, Ont.).
COLLEGE: Michigan Tech.
TRANSACTIONS/CAREER NOTES: Selected by New Jersey Devils in sixth round (seventh Devils pick, 155th overall) of NHL entry draft (June 29, 1994).

Season	Team	League	Gms.	Min.	W	L	T	GA	SO	Avg.	Gms.	Min.	W	L	GA	SO	Avg.
93-94	Michigan Tech	WCHA	13	537	1	7	0	37	1	4.13	—	—	—	—	—	—	—

CARBONNEAU, GUY
C, CANADIENS

PERSONAL: Born March 18, 1960, in Sept-Iles, Que. ... 5-11/184. ... Shoots right. ... Name pronounced GEE KAHR-buh-noh.
TRANSACTIONS/CAREER NOTES: Selected by Montreal Canadiens as underage junior in third round (fourth Canadiens pick, 44th overall) of NHL entry draft (August 9, 1979). ... Strained right knee ligaments (October 7, 1989); missed nine games. ... Broke nose (October 28, 1989). ... Suffered concussion (October 8, 1990). ... Fractured rib (January 13, 1992); missed six games. ... Injured elbow (March 2, 1992); missed one game. ... Suffered right knee tendinitis (October 1, 1992); missed five games. ... Broke finger (November 14, 1992); missed three games. ... Suffered knee tendinitis (February 4, 1993); missed 15 games. ... Suffered from the flu (February 11, 1994); missed one game.
HONORS: Named to QMJHL All-Star second team (1979-80). ... Won Frank J. Selke Trophy (1987-88, 1988-89 and 1991-92).
MISCELLANEOUS: Member of Stanley Cup championship teams (1986 and 1993).

Season	Team	League	Gms.	G	A	Pts.	PIM	Gms.	G	A	Pts.	PIM
76-77	Chicoutimi	QMJHL	59	9	20	29	8	4	1	0	1	0
77-78	Chicoutimi	QMJHL	70	28	55	83	60	—	—	—	—	—
78-79	Chicoutimi	QMJHL	72	62	79	141	47	4	2	1	3	4
79-80	Chicoutimi	QMJHL	72	72	110	182	66	12	9	15	24	28
	Nova Scotia	AHL	—	—	—	—	—	2	1	1	2	2
80-81	Montreal	NHL	2	0	1	1	0	—	—	—	—	—
	Nova Scotia	AHL	78	35	53	88	87	6	1	3	4	9
81-82	Nova Scotia	AHL	77	27	67	94	124	9	2	7	9	8
82-83	Montreal	NHL	77	18	29	47	68	3	0	0	0	2
83-84	Montreal	NHL	78	24	30	54	75	15	4	3	7	12
84-85	Montreal	NHL	79	23	34	57	43	12	4	3	7	8
85-86	Montreal	NHL	80	20	36	56	57	20	7	5	12	35
86-87	Montreal	NHL	79	18	27	45	68	17	3	8	11	20
87-88	Montreal	NHL	80	17	21	38	61	11	0	4	4	2
88-89	Montreal	NHL	79	26	30	56	44	21	4	5	9	10
89-90	Montreal	NHL	68	19	36	55	37	11	2	3	5	6
90-91	Montreal	NHL	78	20	24	44	63	13	1	5	6	10
91-92	Montreal	NHL	72	18	21	39	39	11	1	1	2	6
92-93	Montreal	NHL	61	4	13	17	20	20	3	3	6	10
93-94	Montreal	NHL	79	14	24	38	48	7	1	3	4	4
	NHL totals		912	221	326	547	623	161	30	43	73	125

CAREY, JIM
G, CAPITALS

PERSONAL: Born May 31, 1974, in Dorchester, Mass. ... 6-2/190. ... Catches left. ... Brother of Paul Carey, first baseman, Baltimore Orioles organization.
HIGH SCHOOL: Catholic Memorial (Boston).
COLLEGE: Wisconsin.
TRANSACTIONS/CAREER NOTES: Selected by Washington Capitals in second round (second Capitals pick, 32nd overall) of NHL entry draft (June 20, 1992).
HONORS: Won WCHA Rookie of the Year Award (1992-93). ... Named to WCHA All-Star second team (1992-93). ... Named to WCHA All-Rookie team (1992-93).

Season Team	League	REGULAR SEASON								PLAYOFFS						
		Gms.	Min.	W	L	T	GA	SO	Avg.	Gms.	Min.	W	L	GA	SO	Avg.
89-90—Catholic Memorial H.S..	Mass. HS	12	...	12	0	0	...	...	...	—	—	—	—	—	—	—
90-91—Catholic Memorial H.S..	Mass. HS	14	...	13	0	0	...	6	...	—	—	—	—	—	—	—
91-92—Catholic Memorial H.S..	Mass. HS	21	1108	19	2	0	29	6	1.57	—	—	—	—	—	—	—
92-93—Univ. of Wisconsin	WCHA	26	1525	15	8	1	78	1	3.07	—	—	—	—	—	—	—
93-94—Univ. of Wisconsin	WCHA	39	*2247	*24	13	1	114	1	*3.04	—	—	—	—	—	—	—

CARKNER, TERRY
D, RED WINGS

PERSONAL: Born March 7, 1966, in Smith Falls, Ont.... 6-3/212.... Shoots left.
TRANSACTIONS/CAREER NOTES: Selected by New York Rangers as underage junior in first round (first Rangers pick, 14th overall) of NHL entry draft (June 9, 1984).... Traded by Rangers with LW Jeff Jackson to Quebec Nordiques for LW John Ogrodnick and D David Shaw (September 30, 1987).... Suspended 10 games by NHL for leaving bench during fight (January 24, 1988).... Traded by Nordiques to Philadelphia Flyers for D Greg Smyth and third-round pick (G John Tanner) in 1989 draft (July 25, 1988).... Underwent surgery to left knee (September 23, 1989); missed 15 games.... Bruised ankle (March 1990).... Bruised foot (November 23, 1991); missed two games.... Bruised wrist (November 19, 1992); missed one game.... Traded by Flyers to Detroit Red Wings for D Yves Racine and fourth-round pick (LW Sebastien Vallee) in 1994 draft (October 5, 1993).... Injured left shoulder (March 19, 1994); missed 11 games.
HONORS: Named to OHL All-Star second team (1984-85).... Shared Max Kaminsky Trophy with Jeff Brown (1985-86).... Named to OHL All-Star first team (1985-86).

Season Team	League	REGULAR SEASON					PLAYOFFS				
		Gms.	G	A	Pts.	PIM	Gms.	G	A	Pts.	PIM
82-83—Brockville	COJHL	47	8	32	40	94	—	—	—	—	—
83-84—Peterborough	OHL	66	4	21	25	91	8	0	6	6	13
84-85—Peterborough	OHL	64	14	47	61	125	17	2	10	12	11
85-86—Peterborough	OHL	54	12	32	44	106	16	1	7	8	17
86-87—New Haven	AHL	12	2	6	8	56	3	1	0	1	0
—New York Rangers	NHL	52	2	13	15	120	1	0	0	0	0
87-88—Quebec	NHL	63	3	24	27	159	—	—	—	—	—
88-89—Philadelphia	NHL	78	11	32	43	149	19	1	5	6	28
89-90—Philadelphia	NHL	63	4	18	22	167	—	—	—	—	—
90-91—Philadelphia	NHL	79	7	25	32	204	—	—	—	—	—
91-92—Philadelphia	NHL	73	4	12	16	195	—	—	—	—	—
92-93—Philadelphia	NHL	83	3	16	19	150	—	—	—	—	—
93-94—Detroit	NHL	68	1	6	7	130	7	0	0	0	4
NHL totals		559	35	146	181	1274	27	1	5	6	32

CARNBACK, PATRIK
LW, MIGHTY DUCKS

PERSONAL: Born February 1, 1968, in Goteborg, Sweden.... 6-0/187.... Shoots left.
TRANSACTIONS/CAREER NOTES: Selected by Montreal Canadiens in sixth round (seventh Canadiens pick, 125th overall) of NHL entry draft (June 11, 1988).... Traded by Canadiens with RW Todd Ewen to Mighty Ducks of Anaheim for third-round pick (RW Chris Murray) in 1994 draft (August 10, 1993).... Strained groin (December 20, 1993); missed five games.
HONORS: Named Swedish League Rookie of the Year (1989-90).

Season Team	League	REGULAR SEASON					PLAYOFFS				
		Gms.	G	A	Pts.	PIM	Gms.	G	A	Pts.	PIM
86-87—Vastra Frolunda	Swed. Dv.II	28	3	1	4	4	—	—	—	—	—
87-88—Vastra Frolunda	Swed. Dv.II	33	16	19	35	10	11	4	5	9	8
88-89—Vastra Frolunda	Swed. Dv.II	53	39	36	75	52	—	—	—	—	—
89-90—Vastra Frolunda	Sweden	40	26	27	53	34	—	—	—	—	—
90-91—Vastra Frolunda	Sweden	22	10	9	19	46	28	15	24	39	24
91-92—Vastra Frolunda	Sweden	33	17	24	41	32	3	1	5	6	20
—Swedish Olympic Team	Int'l	7	1	1	2	2	—	—	—	—	—
92-93—Fredericton	AHL	45	20	37	57	45	5	0	3	3	14
—Montreal	NHL	6	0	0	0	2	—	—	—	—	—
93-94—Anaheim	NHL	73	12	11	23	54	—	—	—	—	—
NHL totals		79	12	11	23	56					

CARNEY, KEITH
D, BLACKHAWKS

PERSONAL: Born February 3, 1970, in Pawtucket, R.I.... 6-2/205.... Shoots left.... Full name: Keith Edward Carney.
COLLEGE: Maine.
TRANSACTIONS/CAREER NOTES: Selected by Buffalo Sabres in fourth round (third Sabres pick, 76th overall) of NHL entry draft (June 11, 1988).... Traded by Sabres to Chicago Blackhawks for D Craig Muni (October 27, 1993).
HONORS: Named to Hockey East All-Rookie team (1988-89).... Named to NCAA All-America East second team (1989-90).... Named to Hockey East All-Star second team (1989-90).... Named to NCAA All-America East first team (1990-91).... Named to Hockey East All-Star first team (1990-91).

Season Team	League	REGULAR SEASON					PLAYOFFS				
		Gms.	G	A	Pts.	PIM	Gms.	G	A	Pts.	PIM
88-89—University of Maine	Hockey East	40	4	22	26	24	—	—	—	—	—
89-90—University of Maine	Hockey East	41	3	41	44	43	—	—	—	—	—
90-91—University of Maine	Hockey East	40	7	49	56	38	—	—	—	—	—
91-92—U.S. national team	Int'l	49	2	17	19	16	—	—	—	—	—
—Rochester	AHL	24	1	10	11	2	2	0	2	2	0
—Buffalo	NHL	14	1	2	3	18	7	0	3	3	0

Season Team	League	Gms.	G	A	Pts.	PIM	Gms.	G	A	Pts.	PIM
			REGULAR SEASON					PLAYOFFS			
92-93—Buffalo	NHL	30	2	4	6	55	8	0	3	3	6
—Rochester	AHL	41	5	21	26	32	—	—	—	—	—
93-94—Louisville	ECHL	15	1	4	5	14	—	—	—	—	—
—Buffalo	NHL	7	1	3	4	4	—	—	—	—	—
—Indianapolis	IHL	28	0	14	14	20	—	—	—	—	—
—Chicago	NHL	30	3	5	8	35	6	0	1	1	4
NHL totals		81	7	14	21	112	21	0	7	7	10

CARPENTER, BOBBY
LW, DEVILS

PERSONAL: Born July 13, 1963, in Beverly, Mass.... 6-0/200.... Shoots left. **HIGH SCHOOL:** St. John's Prep (Danvers, Mass.).
TRANSACTIONS/CAREER NOTES: Selected by Washington Capitals as underage junior in first round (first Capitals pick, third overall) of NHL entry draft (June 10, 1981). ... Traded by Capitals with second-round pick in 1989 draft (RW Jason Prosofsky) to New York Rangers for C Mike Ridley, C Kelly Miller and RW Bobby Crawford (January 1, 1987).... Traded by Rangers with D Tom Laidlaw to Los Angeles Kings for C Marcel Dionne, C Jeff Crossman and third-round pick in 1989 draft (March 10, 1987).... Tore rotator cuff (January 1988). ... Broke right thumb and wrist (December 31, 1988).... Traded by Kings to Boston Bruins for C Steve Kasper and LW Jay Miller (January 23, 1989).... Tore ligaments of right wrist (April 1989).... Injured left knee (October 1990).... Suffered multiple fracture of left kneecap (December 8, 1990); missed remainder of season.... Injured left wrist and suffered stiffness in knee (April 5, 1991).... Strained calf (March 19, 1992).... Signed as free agent by Capitals (June 30, 1992).... Signed as free agent by New Jersey Devils (September 30, 1993).
HONORS: Played in NHL All-Star Game (1985).

Season Team	League	Gms.	G	A	Pts.	PIM	Gms.	G	A	Pts.	PIM
			REGULAR SEASON					PLAYOFFS			
79-80—St. John's Prep School	Mass. H.S.	...	28	37	65	...	—	—	—	—	—
80-81—St. John's Prep School	Mass. H.S.	...	14	24	38	...	—	—	—	—	—
81-82—Washington	NHL	80	32	35	67	69	—	—	—	—	—
82-83—Washington	NHL	80	32	37	69	64	4	1	0	1	2
83-84—Washington	NHL	80	28	40	68	51	8	2	1	3	25
84-85—Washington	NHL	80	53	42	95	87	5	1	4	5	8
85-86—Washington	NHL	80	27	29	56	105	9	5	4	9	12
86-87—Washington	NHL	22	5	7	12	21	—	—	—	—	—
—New York Rangers	NHL	28	2	8	10	20	—	—	—	—	—
—Los Angeles	NHL	10	2	3	5	6	5	1	2	3	2
87-88—Los Angeles	NHL	71	19	33	52	84	5	1	1	2	0
88-89—Los Angeles	NHL	39	11	15	26	16	—	—	—	—	—
—Boston	NHL	18	5	9	14	10	8	1	1	2	4
89-90—Boston	NHL	80	25	31	56	97	21	4	6	10	39
90-91—Boston	NHL	29	8	8	16	22	1	0	1	1	2
91-92—Boston	NHL	60	25	23	48	46	8	0	1	1	6
92-93—Washington	NHL	68	11	17	28	65	6	1	4	5	6
93-94—New Jersey	NHL	76	10	23	33	51	20	1	7	8	20
NHL totals		901	295	360	655	814	100	18	32	50	126

CARSON, JIMMY
C, WHALERS

PERSONAL: Born July 20, 1968, in Southfield, Mich.... 6-0/200.... Shoots right.
TRANSACTIONS/CAREER NOTES: Selected by Los Angeles Kings as underage junior in first round (first Kings pick, second overall) of NHL entry draft (June 21, 1986).... Traded by Kings with LW Martin Gelinas and first-round picks in 1989 (traded to New Jersey), 1991 (LW Martin Rucinsky) and 1993 (D Nick Stajduhar) drafts and cash to Edmonton Oilers for C Wayne Gretzky, RW/D Marty McSorley and LW/C Mike Krushelnyski (August 9, 1988).... Bruised right knee (September 27, 1989).... Traded by Oilers with C Kevin McClelland and fifth-round pick in 1991 draft (traded to Montreal Canadiens who selected D Brad Layzell) to Detroit Red Wings for C/RW Joe Murphy, C/LW Adam Graves, LW Petr Klima and D Jeff Sharples (November 2, 1989).... Injured right knee ligaments (February 3, 1990); missed 14 games.... Suffered from tonsillitis and mononucleosis (March 1990).... Suffered sore left shoulder (November 1990).... Strained right knee (January 11, 1991); missed 15 games.... Underwent surgery to left shoulder ligaments (April 25, 1991).... Traded by Red Wings with RW Marc Potvin and C Gary Shuchuk to Kings for D Paul Coffey, RW Jim Hiller and C/LW Sylvain Couturier (January 29, 1993).... Suffered throat infection (November 6, 1993); missed three games.... Traded by Kings to Vancouver Canucks for LW Dixon Ward and future considerations (January 8, 1994).... Signed as free agent by Hartford Whalers (July 13, 1994).
HONORS: Won Frank J. Selke Trophy (1985-86).... Won QMJHL Top Draft Prospect Award (1985-86).... Named to QMJHL All-Star second team (1985-86).... Named to NHL All-Rookie team (1986-87).... Played in NHL All-Star Game (1989).

Season Team	League	Gms.	G	A	Pts.	PIM	Gms.	G	A	Pts.	PIM
			REGULAR SEASON					PLAYOFFS			
84-85—Verdun	QMJHL	68	44	72	116	16	—	—	—	—	—
85-86—Verdun	QMJHL	69	70	83	153	46	5	2	6	8	0
86-87—Los Angeles	NHL	80	37	42	79	22	5	1	2	3	6
87-88—Los Angeles	NHL	80	55	52	107	45	5	5	3	8	4
88-89—Edmonton	NHL	80	49	51	100	36	7	2	1	3	6
89-90—Edmonton	NHL	4	1	2	3	0	—	—	—	—	—
—Detroit	NHL	44	20	16	36	8	—	—	—	—	—
90-91—Detroit	NHL	64	21	25	46	28	7	2	1	3	4
91-92—Detroit	NHL	80	34	35	69	30	11	2	3	5	0
92-93—Detroit	NHL	52	25	26	51	18	—	—	—	—	—
—Los Angeles	NHL	34	12	10	22	14	18	5	4	9	2

Season Team	League	REGULAR SEASON					PLAYOFFS				
		Gms.	G	A	Pts.	PIM	Gms.	G	A	Pts.	PIM
93-94—Los Angeles	NHL	25	4	7	11	2	—	—	—	—	—
—Vancouver	NHL	34	7	10	17	22	2	0	1	1	0
NHL totals		577	265	276	541	225	55	17	15	32	22

CARTER, JOHN
LW

PERSONAL: Born May 3, 1963, in Woburn, Mass.... 5-10/175.... Shoots left.
COLLEGE: Rensselaer Polytechnic Institute (N.Y.).
TRANSACTIONS/CAREER NOTES: Sprained knee (February 1986).... Signed as free agent by Boston Bruins (March 1986).... Bruised knee (March 1987).... Bruised knee (February 1988).... Suffered from the flu (October 31, 1990); missed two weeks.... Suffered concussion (December 1, 1990).... Signed as free agent by San Jose Sharks (August 22, 1991).
HONORS: Named to ECAC All-Star second team (1983-84).... Named to NCAA All-America East second team (1984-85).... Named to ECAC All-Star first team (1984-85).

Season Team	League	REGULAR SEASON					PLAYOFFS				
		Gms.	G	A	Pts.	PIM	Gms.	G	A	Pts.	PIM
82-83—R.P.I.	ECAC	29	16	22	38	33	—	—	—	—	—
83-84—R.P.I.	ECAC	38	35	39	74	52	—	—	—	—	—
84-85—R.P.I.	ECAC	37	43	29	72	52	—	—	—	—	—
85-86—R.P.I.	ECAC	27	23	18	41	68	—	—	—	—	—
—Boston	NHL	3	0	0	0	0	—	—	—	—	—
86-87—Moncton	AHL	58	25	30	55	60	6	2	3	5	5
—Boston	NHL	8	0	1	1	0	—	—	—	—	—
87-88—Boston	NHL	4	0	1	1	2	—	—	—	—	—
—Maine	AHL	76	38	38	76	145	10	4	4	8	44
88-89—Maine	AHL	24	13	6	19	12	—	—	—	—	—
—Boston	NHL	44	12	10	22	24	10	1	2	3	6
89-90—Maine	AHL	2	2	2	4	2	—	—	—	—	—
—Boston	NHL	76	17	22	39	26	21	6	3	9	45
90-91—Boston	NHL	50	4	7	11	68	—	—	—	—	—
—Maine	AHL	16	5	9	14	16	1	0	0	0	10
91-92—Kansas City	IHL	42	11	15	26	116	15	6	9	15	18
—San Jose	NHL	4	0	0	0	0	—	—	—	—	—
92-93—San Jose	NHL	55	7	9	16	81	—	—	—	—	—
—Kansas City	IHL	9	4	2	6	14	—	—	—	—	—
93-94—Providence	AHL	47	11	5	16	82	—	—	—	—	—
NHL totals		244	40	50	90	201	31	7	5	12	51

CASEY, JON
G, BLUES

PERSONAL: Born August 29, 1962, in Grand Rapids, Minn.... 5-10/155.... Catches left.
HIGH SCHOOL: Grand Rapids (Minn.).
COLLEGE: North Dakota.
TRANSACTIONS/CAREER NOTES: Signed as free agent by Minnesota North Stars (April 1, 1984).... North Stars franchise moved from Minnesota to Dallas and renamed Stars for 1993-94 season.... Traded by Stars to Boston Bruins for G Andy Moog (June 25, 1993) to complete deal in which Bruins sent D Gord Murphy to Stars for future considerations (June 20, 1993).... Signed as free agent by St. Louis Blues (June 30, 1993).
HONORS: Named to WCHL All-Star first team (1981-82 and 1983-84).... Won Harry (Hap) Holmes Memorial Trophy (1984-85).... Won Aldege (Baz) Bastien Trophy (1984-85).... Named to AHL All-Star first team (1984-85).... Played in NHL All-Star Game (1993).

Season Team	League	REGULAR SEASON							PLAYOFFS						
		Gms.	Min.	W	L	T	GA	SO	Avg.	Gms.	Min.	W	L	GA SO	Avg.
80-81—Univ. of North Dakota	WCHA	6	300	3	1	0	19	0	3.80	—	—	—	—	— —	—
81-82—Univ. of North Dakota	WCHA	18	1038	15	3	0	48	1	2.77	—	—	—	—	— —	—
82-83—Univ. of North Dakota	WCHA	17	1020	9	6	2	42	0	2.47	—	—	—	—	— —	—
83-84—Univ. of North Dakota	WCHA	37	2180	25	10	2	115	2	3.17	—	—	—	—	— —	—
—Minnesota	NHL	2	84	1	0	0	6	0	4.29	—	—	—	—	— —	—
84-85—Baltimore	AHL	46	2646	30	11	4	116	†4	*2.63	13	689	8	3	38 0	3.31
85-86—Springfield	AHL	9	464	4	3	1	30	0	3.88	—	—	—	—	— —	—
—Minnesota	NHL	26	1402	11	11	1	91	0	3.89	—	—	—	—	— —	—
86-87—Indianapolis	CHL	31	1794	14	15	0	133	0	4.45	—	—	—	—	— —	—
—Springfield	AHL	13	770	1	8	0	56	0	4.36	—	—	—	—	— —	—
87-88—Kalamazoo	IHL	42	2541	24	13	‡5	154	2	3.64	7	382	3	3	26 0	4.08
—Minnesota	NHL	14	663	1	7	4	41	0	3.71	—	—	—	—	— —	—
88-89—Minnesota	NHL	55	2961	18	17	12	151	1	3.06	4	211	1	3	16 0	4.55
89-90—Minnesota	NHL	61	3407	*31	22	4	183	3	3.22	7	415	3	4	21 1	3.04
90-91—Minnesota	NHL	55	3185	21	20	11	158	3	2.98	*23	*1205	*14	7	*61 †1	3.04
91-92—Minnesota	NHL	52	2911	19	23	5	165	2	3.40	7	437	3	4	22 0	3.02
—Kalamazoo	IHL	4	250	2	1	‡1	11	0	2.64	—	—	—	—	— —	—
92-93—Minnesota	NHL	60	3476	26	26	5	193	3	3.33	—	—	—	—	— —	—
93-94—Boston	NHL	57	3192	30	15	9	153	4	2.88	11	698	5	6	34 0	2.92
NHL totals		382	21281	158	141	51	1141	16	3.22	52	2966	26	24	154 2	3.12

CASSELS, ANDREW
C, WHALERS

PERSONAL: Born July 23, 1969, in Mississauga, Ont.... 6-0/192.... Shoots left.... Name pronounced KAS-uhls.
TRANSACTIONS/CAREER NOTES: Broke wrist (January 1986).... Selected by Montreal Canadiens as underage junior in first round (first Canadiens pick, 17th overall)

— 353 —

of NHL entry draft (June 13, 1987).... Sprained left knee ligaments (September 1988).... Separated right shoulder (November 22, 1989); missed 10 games.... Traded by Canadiens to Hartford Whalers for second-round pick (RW Valeri Bure) in 1992 draft (September 17, 1991).... Bruised kneecap (December 4, 1993); missed one game.... Suffered facial injury (March 13, 1994); missed four games.

HONORS: Won Emms Family Award (1986-87).... Won Red Tilson Trophy (1987-88).... Won Eddie Powers Memorial Trophy (1987-88).... Won William Hanley Trophy (1987-88).... Named to OHL All-Star first team (1987-88 and 1988-89).

			REGULAR SEASON					PLAYOFFS			
Season	Team	League	Gms.	G	A	Pts.	PIM	Gms.	G	A	Pts.	PIM
85-86—Bramalea Jr. B	OHA	33	18	25	43	26	—	—	—	—	—
86-87—Ottawa	OHL	66	26	66	92	28	11	5	9	14	7
87-88—Ottawa	OHL	61	48	*103	*151	39	16	8	*24	†32	13
88-89—Ottawa	OHL	56	37	97	134	66	12	5	10	15	10
89-90—Sherbrooke	AHL	55	22	45	67	25	12	2	11	13	6
—Montreal	NHL	6	2	0	2	2	—	—	—	—	—
90-91—Montreal	NHL	54	6	19	25	20	8	0	2	2	2
91-92—Hartford	NHL	67	11	30	41	18	7	2	4	6	6
92-93—Hartford	NHL	84	21	64	85	62	—	—	—	—	—
93-94—Hartford	NHL	79	16	42	58	37	—	—	—	—	—
NHL totals		290	56	155	211	139	15	2	6	8	8

CAUFIELD, JAY
RW

PERSONAL: Born July 17, 1965, in Philadelphia.... 6-4/230.... Shoots right.
COLLEGE: North Dakota.
TRANSACTIONS/CAREER NOTES: Signed as free agent by New York Rangers (October 8, 1985).... Injured knee (October 1986).... Traded by Rangers with C Dave Gagner to Minnesota North Stars for D Jari Gronstrand and D Paul Boutilier (October 8, 1987).... Selected by Pittsburgh Penguins in NHL waiver draft for $40,000 (October 3, 1988).... Injured ankle and suffered blood poisoning (October 1988).... Pinched nerve in neck (December 1988).... Dislocated finger on right hand and underwent surgery (February 2, 1990); missed 18 games.... Suffered back spasms during preseason (September 1991); missed first eight games of season.... Suspended eight off-days and fined $500 by NHL for fighting (February 26, 1993).... Signed as free agent by Kalamazoo Wings for 1993-94 season.
MISCELLANEOUS: Member of Stanley Cup championship teams (1991 and 1992).

			REGULAR SEASON					PLAYOFFS			
Season	Team	League	Gms.	G	A	Pts.	PIM	Gms.	G	A	Pts.	PIM
84-85—Univ. of North Dakota	WCHA	1	0	0	0	0	—	—	—	—	—
85-86—New Haven	AHL	42	2	3	5	40	1	0	0	0	0
—Toledo	IHL	30	5	3	8	54	—	—	—	—	—
86-87—New Haven	AHL	13	0	0	0	43	—	—	—	—	—
—Flint	IHL	14	4	3	7	59	—	—	—	—	—
—New York Rangers	NHL	13	2	1	3	45	3	0	0	0	12
87-88—Kalamazoo	IHL	65	5	10	15	273	6	0	1	1	47
—Minnesota	NHL	1	0	0	0	0	—	—	—	—	—
88-89—Pittsburgh	NHL	58	1	4	5	285	9	0	0	0	28
89-90—Pittsburgh	NHL	37	1	2	3	123	—	—	—	—	—
90-91—Muskegon	IHL	3	1	0	1	18	—	—	—	—	—
—Pittsburgh	NHL	23	1	1	2	71	—	—	—	—	—
91-92—Pittsburgh	NHL	50	0	0	0	175	5	0	0	0	2
92-93—Pittsburgh	NHL	26	0	0	0	60	—	—	—	—	—
93-94—Kalamazoo	IHL	45	2	3	5	176	4	0	0	0	18
NHL totals		208	5	8	13	759	17	0	0	0	42

CAVALLINI, GINO
LW

PERSONAL: Born November 24, 1962, in Toronto.... 6-2/215.... Shoots left.... Full name: Gino John Cavallini.... Name pronounced KAV-uh-LEE-nee.... Brother of Paul Cavallini, defenseman, Dallas Stars.
COLLEGE: Bowling Green State.
TRANSACTIONS/CAREER NOTES: Signed as free agent by Calgary Flames (July 1984).... Traded by Flames with LW Eddy Beers and D Charles Bourgeois to St. Louis Blues for D Terry Johnson, RW Joe Mullen and D Rik Wilson (February 1, 1986).... Broke right hand (January 1988); missed 16 games.... Strained left knee (February 1989).... Claimed on waivers by Quebec Nordiques (February 27, 1992).... Sprained left knee (February 12, 1993); missed 13 games.... Signed as free agent by Milwaukee Admirals (September 14, 1993).

			REGULAR SEASON					PLAYOFFS			
Season	Team	League	Gms.	G	A	Pts.	PIM	Gms.	G	A	Pts.	PIM
81-82—Toronto St. Mikes	OJHL	37	27	56	83	...	—	—	—	—	—
82-83—Bowling Green State	CCHA	40	8	16	24	52	—	—	—	—	—
83-84—Bowling Green State	CCHA	43	25	23	48	16	—	—	—	—	—
84-85—Moncton	AHL	51	29	19	48	28	—	—	—	—	—
—Calgary	NHL	27	6	10	16	14	3	0	0	0	4
85-86—Moncton	AHL	4	3	2	5	7	—	—	—	—	—
—Calgary	NHL	27	7	7	14	26	—	—	—	—	—
—St. Louis	NHL	30	6	5	11	36	17	4	5	9	10
86-87—St. Louis	NHL	80	18	26	44	54	6	3	1	4	2
87-88—St. Louis	NHL	64	15	17	32	62	10	5	5	10	19
88-89—St. Louis	NHL	74	20	23	43	79	9	0	2	2	17
89-90—St. Louis	NHL	80	15	15	30	77	12	1	3	4	2
90-91—St. Louis	NHL	78	8	27	35	81	13	1	3	4	2

Season	Team	League	REGULAR SEASON					PLAYOFFS				
			Gms.	G	A	Pts.	PIM	Gms.	G	A	Pts.	PIM
91-92—St. Louis	NHL	48	9	7	16	40	—	—	—	—	—
—Quebec	NHL	18	1	7	8	4	—	—	—	—	—
92-93—Quebec	NHL	67	9	15	24	34	4	0	0	0	0
93-94—Milwaukee	IHL	78	43	35	78	64	4	3	4	7	6
NHL totals		593	114	159	273	507	74	14	19	33	56

CAVALLINI, PAUL
D, STARS

PERSONAL: Born October 13, 1965, in Toronto. . . . 6-1/202. . . . Shoots left. . . . Full name: Paul Edward Cavallini. . . . Name pronounced KAV-uh-LEE-nee. . . . Brother of Gino Cavallini, left winger, Calgary Flames, St. Louis Blues and Quebec Nordiques (1984-85 through 1992-93).

HIGH SCHOOL: Henry Carr (Rexdale, Ont.).
COLLEGE: Providence.
TRANSACTIONS/CAREER NOTES: Selected by Washington Capitals as underage junior in 10th round (ninth Capitals pick, 205th overall) of NHL entry draft (June 9, 1984). . . . Traded by Capitals to St. Louis Blues for second-round pick (D Wade Bartley) in 1988 draft (December 1987). . . . Broke hand (December 11, 1987). . . . Injured neck (December 11, 1988). . . . Dislocated left shoulder (February 25, 1989). . . . Lost tip of left index finger (December 22, 1990); missed 13 games. . . . Strained knee ligament (October 20, 1991); missed 13 games. . . . Traded by Blues to Capitals for C Kevin Miller (November 1, 1992). . . . Missed one game due to personal reasons (March 16, 1993). . . . Traded by Capitals to Dallas Stars for future considerations (June 20, 1993); Stars sent D Enrico Ciccone to Capitals to complete deal (June 25, 1993). . . . Fractured eye (January 16, 1994); missed five games.
HONORS: Named to Hockey East All-Freshman team (1984-85). . . . Won Alka-Seltzer Plus Award (1989-90). . . . Played in NHL All-Star Game (1990).

C

Season	Team	League	REGULAR SEASON					PLAYOFFS				
			Gms.	G	A	Pts.	PIM	Gms.	G	A	Pts.	PIM
83-84—Henry Carr H.S.	MTHL	54	20	41	61	190	—	—	—	—	—
84-85—Providence College	Hockey East	45	5	14	19	64	—	—	—	—	—
85-86—Canadian national team	Int'l	52	1	11	12	95	—	—	—	—	—
—Binghamton	AHL	15	3	4	7	20	6	0	2	2	56
86-87—Binghamton	AHL	66	12	24	36	188	13	2	7	9	35
—Washington	NHL	6	0	2	2	8	—	—	—	—	—
87-88—Washington	NHL	24	2	3	5	66	—	—	—	—	—
—St. Louis	NHL	48	4	7	11	86	10	1	6	7	26
88-89—St. Louis	NHL	65	4	20	24	128	10	2	2	4	14
89-90—St. Louis	NHL	80	8	39	47	106	12	2	3	5	20
90-91—St. Louis	NHL	67	10	25	35	89	13	2	3	5	20
91-92—St. Louis	NHL	66	10	25	35	95	4	0	1	1	6
92-93—St. Louis	NHL	11	1	4	5	10	—	—	—	—	—
—Washington	NHL	71	5	8	13	46	6	0	2	2	18
93-94—Dallas	NHL	74	11	33	44	82	9	1	8	9	4
NHL totals		512	55	166	221	716	64	8	25	33	108

CHABOT, FREDERIC
G, FLYERS

PERSONAL: Born February 12, 1968, in Hebertville, Que. . . . 5-11/175. . . . Catches right. . . . Name pronounced shuh-BAHT.
TRANSACTIONS/CAREER NOTES: Selected by New Jersey Devils in 10th round (10th Devils pick, 192nd overall) of NHL entry draft (June 21, 1986). . . . Signed as free agent by Montreal Canadiens (January 16, 1990). . . . Selected by Tampa Bay Lightning in NHL expansion draft (June 18, 1992). . . . Traded by Lightning to Canadiens for G Jean-Claude Bergeron (June 18, 1992). . . . Traded by Canadiens to Philadelphia Flyers for future considerations (February 21, 1994).
HONORS: Named to Memorial Cup All-Star team (1981-82). . . . Named to WHL (East) All-Star first team (1988-89). . . . Won Aldege (Baz) Bastien Trophy (1993-94).
STATISTICAL NOTES: Member of Stanley Cup championship team (1993).

Season	Team	League	REGULAR SEASON								PLAYOFFS						
			Gms.	Min.	W	L	T	GA	SO	Avg.	Gms.	Min.	W	L	GA	SO	Avg.
86-87—Drummondville	QMJHL	*62	*3508	31	29	0	293	1	5.01	8	481	2	6	40	0	4.99
87-88—Drummondville	QMJHL	58	3276	27	24	4	237	1	4.34	*16	1019	10	6	56	†1	*3.30
88-89—Moose Jaw	WHL	26	1385	...	...	...	114	1	4.94	—	—	—	—	—	—	—
—Prince Albert	WHL	28	1572	...	...	...	88	1	3.36	4	199	1	1	16	0	4.82
89-90—Fort Wayne	IHL	23	1208	6	13	‡3	87	1	4.32	—	—	—	—	—	—	—
—Sherbrooke	AHL	2	119	1	1	0	8	0	4.03	—	—	—	—	—	—	—
90-91—Montreal	NHL	3	108	0	0	1	6	0	3.33	—	—	—	—	—	—	—
—Fredericton	AHL	35	1800	9	15	5	122	0	4.07	—	—	—	—	—	—	—
91-92—Winston-Salem	ECHL	25	1449	15	7	‡2	71	0	*2.94	—	—	—	—	—	—	—
—Fredericton	AHL	30	1761	17	9	4	79	2	*2.69	7	457	3	4	20	0	2.63
92-93—Fredericton	AHL	45	2544	22	17	4	141	0	3.33	4	261	1	3	16	0	3.68
—Montreal	NHL	1	40	0	0	0	1	0	1.50	—	—	—	—	—	—	—
93-94—Fredericton	AHL	3	143	0	1	1	12	0	5.03	—	—	—	—	—	—	—
—Las Vegas	IHL	2	110	1	1	‡1	5	0	2.73	—	—	—	—	—	—	—
—Montreal	NHL	1	60	0	1	0	5	0	5.00	—	—	—	—	—	—	—
—Hershey	AHL	31	1607	13	6	7	75	2	*2.80	11	665	7	4	32	0	2.89
—Philadelphia	NHL	4	70	0	1	1	5	0	4.29	—	—	—	—	—	—	—
NHL totals		9	278	0	2	2	17	0	3.67							

CHAMBERS, SHAWN

D, LIGHTNING

PERSONAL: Born October 11, 1966, in Royal Oak, Mich. . . . 6-2/200. . . . Shoots left. . . . Full name: Shawn Randall Chambers.
COLLEGE: Alaska-Fairbanks.
TRANSACTIONS/CAREER NOTES: Selected by Minnesota North Stars in NHL supplemental draft (June 13, 1987). . . . Dislocated shoulder (February 1988). . . . Separated right shoulder (September 1988). . . . Injured left knee (September 11, 1990); missed first 11 games of season. . . . Fractured left kneecap (December 5, 1990); missed three months. . . . Underwent surgery to left knee to remove piece of loose cartilage (May 1991). . . . Traded by North Stars to Washington Capitals for C Trent Klatt and LW Steve Maltais (June 21, 1991). . . . Suffered sore knee (October 1991); missed first 47 games of season. . . . Reinjured knee (January 26, 1992); missed remainder of season. . . . Underwent arthroscopic knee surgery (February 4, 1992). . . . Selected by Tampa Bay Lightning in NHL expansion draft (June 18, 1992). . . . Underwent arthroscopic knee surgery (October 9, 1992); missed 14 games. . . . Underwent arthroscopic knee surgery (October 21, 1993); missed 14 games. . . . Injured shoulder (November 13, 1993); missed two games. . . . Suffered facial cuts (January 2, 1994); missed one game.

Season	Team	League	REGULAR SEASON					PLAYOFFS				
			Gms.	G	A	Pts.	PIM	Gms.	G	A	Pts.	PIM
85-86	Alaska-Fairbanks	GWHC	25	15	21	36	34	—	—	—	—	—
86-87	Alaska-Fairbanks	GWHC	17	11	19	30	. . .	—	—	—	—	—
	—Seattle	WHL	28	8	25	33	58	—	—	—	—	—
	—Fort Wayne	IHL	12	2	6	8	0	10	1	4	5	5
87-88	Minnesota	NHL	19	1	7	8	21	—	—	—	—	—
	—Kalamazoo	IHL	19	1	6	7	22	—	—	—	—	—
88-89	Minnesota	NHL	72	5	19	24	80	3	0	2	2	0
89-90	Minnesota	NHL	78	8	18	26	81	7	2	1	3	0
90-91	Minnesota	NHL	29	1	3	4	24	23	0	7	7	16
	—Kalamazoo	IHL	3	1	1	2	0	—	—	—	—	—
91-92	Baltimore	AHL	5	2	3	5	9	—	—	—	—	—
	—Washington	NHL	2	0	0	0	2	—	—	—	—	—
92-93	Atlanta	IHL	6	0	2	2	18	—	—	—	—	—
	—Tampa Bay	NHL	55	10	29	39	36	—	—	—	—	—
93-94	Tampa Bay	NHL	66	11	23	34	23	—	—	—	—	—
NHL totals			**321**	**36**	**99**	**135**	**267**	**33**	**2**	**10**	**12**	**16**

CHAPDELAINE, RENE

D

PERSONAL: Born September 27, 1966, in Weyburn, Sask. . . . 6-1/195. . . . Shoots right. . . . Full name: Rene Ronald Chapdelaine. . . . Name pronounced SHAP-duh-LAYN.
COLLEGE: Lake Superior State (Mich.).
TRANSACTIONS/CAREER NOTES: Selected by Los Angeles Kings in eighth round (seventh Kings pick, 149th overall) of NHL entry draft (June 21, 1986).

Season	Team	League	REGULAR SEASON					PLAYOFFS				
			Gms.	G	A	Pts.	PIM	Gms.	G	A	Pts.	PIM
84-85	Weyburn	SJHL	61	3	17	20	. . .	—	—	—	—	—
85-86	Lake Superior State	CCHA	40	2	7	9	24	—	—	—	—	—
86-87	Lake Superior State	CCHA	28	1	5	6	51	—	—	—	—	—
87-88	Lake Superior State	CCHA	35	1	9	10	44	—	—	—	—	—
88-89	Lake Superior State	CCHA	46	4	9	13	52	—	—	—	—	—
89-90	New Haven	AHL	41	0	1	1	35	—	—	—	—	—
90-91	Phoenix	IHL	17	0	2	2	10	11	0	0	0	8
	—New Haven	AHL	65	3	11	14	49	—	—	—	—	—
	—Los Angeles	NHL	3	0	1	1	10	—	—	—	—	—
91-92	Los Angeles	NHL	16	0	1	1	10	—	—	—	—	—
	—Phoenix	IHL	62	4	22	26	87	—	—	—	—	—
	—New Haven	AHL	—	—	—	—	—	4	0	2	2	0
92-93	Phoenix	IHL	44	1	17	18	54	—	—	—	—	—
	—Los Angeles	NHL	13	0	0	0	12	—	—	—	—	—
	—San Diego	IHL	9	1	1	2	8	14	0	1	1	27
93-94	Peoria	IHL	80	8	9	17	100	6	1	3	4	10
NHL totals			**32**	**0**	**2**	**2**	**32**					

CHARBONNEAU, JOSE

RW, CANUCKS

PERSONAL: Born November 21, 1966, in Ferme-Neuve, Que. . . . 6-0/195. . . . Shoots right. . . . Name pronounced JOH-see SHAHR-buh-noh.
TRANSACTIONS/CAREER NOTES: Selected by Montreal Canadiens as underage junior in first round (first Canadiens pick, 12th overall) of NHL entry draft (June 21, 1986). . . . Traded by Canadiens to Vancouver Canucks for C Dan Woodley (January 25, 1989). . . . Separated right shoulder (November 1984). . . . Reinjured shoulder (December 1984). . . . Injured shoulder (January 1985). . . . Suffered back spasms (December 6, 1993); missed 24 games. . . . Sprained knee (February 6, 1994); missed eight games.

Season	Team	League	REGULAR SEASON					PLAYOFFS				
			Gms.	G	A	Pts.	PIM	Gms.	G	A	Pts.	PIM
83-84	Drummondville	QMJHL	65	31	59	90	110	—	—	—	—	—
84-85	Drummondville	QMJHL	46	34	40	74	91	12	5	10	15	20
85-86	Drummondville	QMJHL	57	44	45	89	158	23	16	20	36	40
86-87	Sherbrooke	AHL	72	14	27	41	94	16	5	12	17	17
87-88	Montreal	NHL	16	0	2	2	6	8	0	0	0	4
	—Sherbrooke	AHL	55	30	35	65	108	—	—	—	—	—

Season	Team	League	REGULAR SEASON					PLAYOFFS				
			Gms.	G	A	Pts.	PIM	Gms.	G	A	Pts.	PIM
88-89—Montreal	NHL	9	1	3	4	6	—	—	—	—	—
—Sherbrooke	AHL	33	13	15	28	95	—	—	—	—	—
—Vancouver	NHL	13	0	1	1	6	—	—	—	—	—
—Milwaukee	IHL	13	8	5	13	46	10	3	2	5	23
89-90—Milwaukee	IHL	65	23	38	61	137	5	0	1	1	8
90-91—Canadian national team	Int'l	56	22	29	51	54	—	—	—	—	—
91-92—Canadian national team	Int'l			Statistics unavailable.							
92-93—Vancouver	NHL			Did not play.							
93-94—Vancouver	NHL	30	7	7	14	49	3	1	0	1	4
—Hamilton	AHL	7	3	2	5	8	—	—	—	—	—
NHL totals		68	8	13	21	67	11	1	0	1	8

CHARBONNEAU, PATRICK
G, SENATORS

PERSONAL: Born July 22, 1975, in St. Jean-sur-Richelie, Que. . . . 5-11/205. . . . Catches left.

TRANSACTIONS/CAREER NOTES: Selected by Ottawa Senators in third round (third Senators pick, 53rd overall) of NHL entry draft (June 26, 1993).

Season	Team	League	REGULAR SEASON								PLAYOFFS						
			Gms.	Min.	W	L	T	GA	SO	Avg.	Gms.	Min.	W	L	GA	SO	Avg.
91-92—Victoriaville	QMJHL	37	1943	9	23	2	163	0	5.03	—	—	—	—	—	—	—
92-93—Victoriaville	QMJHL	59	3121	35	22	0	216	0	4.15	2	92	1	0	4	0	2.61
93-94—Prince Edward Island	AHL	3	180	2	1	0	11	0	3.67	—	—	—	—	—	—	—
—Victoriaville	QMJHL	56	2948	11	34	2	261	0	5.31	5	212	1	4	24	0	6.79

C

CHARRON, ERIC
D, LIGHTNING

PERSONAL: Born January 14, 1970, in Verdun, Que. . . . 6-3/195. . . . Shoots left.

TRANSACTIONS/CAREER NOTES: Selected by Montreal Canadiens in first round (first Canadiens pick, 20th overall) of NHL entry draft (June 11, 1988). . . . Traded by Canadiens with D Alain Cote and future considerations to Tampa Bay Lightning for D Rob Ramage (March 20, 1993); Canadiens sent D Donald Dufresne to Lightning to complete deal (June 18, 1993).

Season	Team	League	REGULAR SEASON					PLAYOFFS				
			Gms.	G	A	Pts.	PIM	Gms.	G	A	Pts.	PIM
87-88—Trois-Rivieres	QMJHL	67	3	13	16	135	—	—	—	—	—
88-89—Sherbrooke	AHL	1	0	0	0	0	—	—	—	—	—
—Verdun	QMJHL	67	4	31	35	177	—	—	—	—	—
89-90—St. Hyacinthe	QMJHL	68	13	38	51	152	11	3	4	7	67
—Sherbrooke	AHL	—	—	—	—	—	2	0	0	0	0
90-91—Fredericton	AHL	71	1	11	12	108	2	1	0	1	29
91-92—Fredericton	AHL	59	2	11	13	98	6	1	0	1	4
92-93—Fredericton	AHL	54	3	13	16	93	—	—	—	—	—
—Montreal	NHL	3	0	0	0	2	—	—	—	—	—
—Atlanta	IHL	11	0	2	2	12	3	0	1	1	6
93-94—Tampa Bay	NHL	4	0	0	0	2	—	—	—	—	—
—Atlanta	IHL	66	5	18	23	144	14	1	4	5	28
NHL totals		7	0	0	0	4	—	—	—	—	—

CHARTIER, SCOTT
D, MIGHTY DUCKS

PERSONAL: Born January 19, 1972, in St. Lazare, Man. . . . 6-1/200. . . . Shoots right. . . . Name pronounced SHAHR-tee-yayr.

TRANSACTIONS/CAREER NOTES: Signed as free agent by Mighty Ducks of Anaheim (July 30, 1993).

Season	Team	League	REGULAR SEASON					PLAYOFFS				
			Gms.	G	A	Pts.	PIM	Gms.	G	A	Pts.	PIM
91-92—Kelowna	BCJHL	55	13	33	46	—	—	—	—	—	—
92-93—Western Michigan Univ.	CCHA	38	6	22	28	84	—	—	—	—	—
93-94—San Diego	IHL	49	2	6	8	84	4	0	0	0	6

CHASE, DON
C, CANADIENS

PERSONAL: Born March 17, 1974, in Springfield, Mass. . . . 5-11/190. . . . Shoots right.

TRANSACTIONS/CAREER NOTES: Selected by Montreal Canadiens in fifth round (seventh Canadiens pick, 116th overall) of NHL entry draft (June 20, 1992).

Season	Team	League	REGULAR SEASON					PLAYOFFS				
			Gms.	G	A	Pts.	PIM	Gms.	G	A	Pts.	PIM
91-92—Springfield Jr. B	NEJHL	49	69	75	144	80	—	—	—	—	—
92-93—Boston College	Hockey East	38	7	5	12	48	—	—	—	—	—
93-94—Boston College	Hockey East	35	14	13	27	58	—	—	—	—	—

CHASE, KELLY
RW, BLUES

PERSONAL: Born October 25, 1967, in Porcupine Plain, Sask. . . . 5-11/195. . . . Shoots right. . . . Full name: Kelly Wayne Chase.

HIGH SCHOOL: Porcupine Plain (Sask.).

TRANSACTIONS/CAREER NOTES: Signed as free agent by St. Louis Blues (May 24, 1988). . . . Bruised right foot (January 1990). . . . Suffered back spasms (March 1990). . . . Suspended 10 games by NHL for fighting

(March 18, 1991). . . . Injured knee (December 11, 1991); missed two games. . . . Sprained left wrist (January 14, 1992); missed three games. . . . Bruised thigh (February 2, 1992); missed five games. . . . Injured hand (February 23, 1992); missed four games. . . . Pulled groin (October 26, 1992); missed six games. . . . Injured wrist (January 9, 1993); missed five games. . . . Bruised lower leg (March 30, 1993); missed last six games of season. . . . Suffered from the flu (December 4, 1993); missed one game. . . . Injured leg (January 2, 1994); missed four games. . . . Injured elbow (January 28, 1994); missed three games. . . . Pulled groin (March 24, 1994); missed three games. . . . Injured hand (April 5, 1994); missed one game.

Season Team	League	REGULAR SEASON					PLAYOFFS				
		Gms.	G	A	Pts.	PIM	Gms.	G	A	Pts.	PIM
85-86—Saskatoon	WHL	57	7	18	25	172	10	3	4	7	37
86-87—Saskatoon	WHL	68	17	29	46	285	11	2	8	10	37
87-88—Saskatoon	WHL	70	21	34	55	*343	9	3	5	8	32
88-89—Peoria	IHL	38	14	7	21	278	—	—	—	—	—
89-90—Peoria	IHL	10	1	2	3	76	—	—	—	—	—
—St. Louis	NHL	43	1	3	4	244	9	1	0	1	46
90-91—Peoria	IHL	61	20	34	54	406	10	4	3	7	61
—St. Louis	NHL	2	1	0	1	15	6	0	0	0	18
91-92—St. Louis	NHL	46	1	2	3	264	1	0	0	0	7
92-93—St. Louis	NHL	49	2	5	7	204	—	—	—	—	—
93-94—St. Louis	NHL	68	2	5	7	278	4	0	1	1	6
NHL totals		208	7	15	22	1005	20	1	1	2	77

CHASSE, DENIS
RW, BLUES

PERSONAL: Born February 7, 1970, in Montreal. . . . 6-2/200. . . . Shoots right. . . . Name pronounced shah-SAY.

TRANSACTIONS/CAREER NOTES: Signed as free agent by Quebec Nordiques (May 14, 1991). . . . Traded by Nordiques with D Steve Duchesne to St. Louis Blues for C Ron Sutter, C Bob Bassen and D Garth Butcher (January 23, 1994). . . . Injured neck (January 29, 1993); missed remainder of season. . . . Underwent neck surgery (March 9, 1994); missed remainder of season.

Season Team	League	REGULAR SEASON					PLAYOFFS				
		Gms.	G	A	Pts.	PIM	Gms.	G	A	Pts.	PIM
87-88—St. Jean	QMJHL	13	0	1	1	2	1	0	0	0	0
88-89—Verdun	QMJHL	38	12	12	24	61	—	—	—	—	—
—Drummondville	QMJHL	30	15	16	31	77	3	0	2	2	28
89-90—Drummondville	QMJHL	34	14	29	43	85	—	—	—	—	—
—Chicoutimi	QMJHL	33	19	27	46	105	7	7	4	11	50
90-91—Drummondville	QMJHL	62	47	54	101	246	13	9	11	20	56
91-92—Halifax	AHL	73	26	35	61	254	—	—	—	—	—
92-93—Halifax	AHL	75	35	41	76	242	—	—	—	—	—
93-94—Cornwall	AHL	48	27	39	66	194	—	—	—	—	—
—St. Louis	NHL	3	0	1	1	15	—	—	—	—	—
NHL totals		3	0	1	1	15					

CHEBATURKIN, VLADIMIR
D, ISLANDERS

PERSONAL: Born April 23, 1975, in Tyumen, U.S.S.R. . . . 6-2/189. . . . Shoots left. . . . Name pronounced CHEH-buh-TURK-in.

TRANSACTIONS/CAREER NOTES: Selected by New York Islanders in third round (third Islanders pick, 66th overall) of NHL entry draft (June 26, 1993).

Season Team	League	REGULAR SEASON					PLAYOFFS				
		Gms.	G	A	Pts.	PIM	Gms.	G	A	Pts.	PIM
92-93—Kristall Elektrostal	CIS Div. II				Statistics unavailable.						
93-94—Kristall Elektrostal	CIS Div. II	42	4	4	8	38	—	—	—	—	—

CHELIOS, CHRIS
D, BLACKHAWKS

PERSONAL: Born January 25, 1962, in Chicago. . . . 6-1/186. . . . Shoots right. . . . Name pronounced CHEHL-ee-ohz.

COLLEGE: Wisconsin.

TRANSACTIONS/CAREER NOTES: Selected by Montreal Canadiens as underage junior in second round (fifth Canadiens pick, 40th overall) of NHL entry draft (June 10, 1981). . . . Sprained right ankle (January 1985). . . . Injured left knee (April 1985). . . . Sprained knee (December 19, 1985). . . . Reinjured knee (January 20, 1986). . . . Suffered back spasms (October 1986). . . . Broke finger on left hand (December 1987). . . . Bruised tailbone (February 7, 1988). . . . Strained left knee ligaments (February 1990). . . . Underwent surgery to repair torn abdominal muscle (April 30, 1990). . . . Traded by Canadiens with second-round pick in 1991 draft (C Michael Pomichter) to Chicago Blackhawks for C Denis Savard (June 29, 1990). . . . Lacerated left temple (February 9, 1991). . . . Suspended four games by NHL (October 15, 1993). . . . Suspended four games without pay and fined $500 by NHL for eye-scratching incident (February 5, 1994).

HONORS: Named to NCAA All-Tournament team (1982-83). . . . Named to WCHA All-Star second team (1982-83). . . . Named to NHL All-Rookie team (1984-85). . . . Played in NHL All-Star Game (1985 and 1990-1994). . . . Won James Norris Memorial Trophy (1988-89 and 1992-93). . . . Named to THE SPORTING NEWS All-Star first team (1988-89 and 1992-93). . . . Named to NHL All-Star first team (1988-89 and 1992-93). . . . Named to THE SPORTING NEWS All-Star second team (1990-91 and 1991-92). . . . Named to NHL All-Star second team (1990-91).

MISCELLANEOUS: Member of Stanley Cup championship team (1986).

Season Team	League	REGULAR SEASON					PLAYOFFS				
		Gms.	G	A	Pts.	PIM	Gms.	G	A	Pts.	PIM
79-80—Moose Jaw	SJHL	53	12	31	43	118	—	—	—	—	—
80-81—Moose Jaw	SJHL	54	23	64	87	175	—	—	—	—	—

Season Team	League	REGULAR SEASON					PLAYOFFS				
		Gms.	G	A	Pts.	PIM	Gms.	G	A	Pts.	PIM
81-82—University of Wisconsin ...	WCHA	43	6	43	49	50	—	—	—	—	—
82-83—University of Wisconsin ...	WCHA	45	16	32	48	62	—	—	—	—	—
83-84—U.S. national team	Int'l	60	14	35	49	58	—	—	—	—	—
—U.S. Olympic Team	Int'l	6	0	3	3	8	—	—	—	—	—
—Montreal	NHL	12	0	2	2	12	15	1	9	10	17
84-85—Montreal	NHL	74	9	55	64	87	9	2	8	10	17
85-86—Montreal	NHL	41	8	26	34	67	20	2	9	11	49
86-87—Montreal	NHL	71	11	33	44	124	17	4	9	13	38
87-88—Montreal	NHL	71	20	41	61	172	11	3	1	4	29
88-89—Montreal	NHL	80	15	58	73	185	21	4	15	19	28
89-90—Montreal	NHL	53	9	22	31	136	5	0	1	1	8
90-91—Chicago	NHL	77	12	52	64	192	6	1	7	8	46
91-92—Chicago	NHL	80	9	47	56	245	18	6	15	21	37
92-93—Chicago	NHL	84	15	58	73	282	4	0	2	2	14
93-94—Chicago	NHL	76	16	44	60	212	6	1	1	2	8
NHL totals...............................		719	124	438	562	1714	132	24	77	101	291

CHERBAYEV, ALEXANDER
LW, SHARKS

PERSONAL: Born August 13, 1973, in Voskresensk, U.S.S.R. .... 6-1/190.... Shoots left.... Name pronounced chuhr-BIGH-ehv.
TRANSACTIONS/CAREER NOTES: Selected by San Jose Sharks in third round (third Sharks pick, 51st overall) of NHL entry draft (June 20, 1992).

Season Team	League	REGULAR SEASON					PLAYOFFS				
		Gms.	G	A	Pts.	PIM	Gms.	G	A	Pts.	PIM
90-91—Khimik Voskresensk........	USSR	16	2	2	4	0	—	—	—	—	—
91-92—Khimik Voskresensk........	CIS	38	3	3	6	14	—	—	—	—	—
92-93—Khimik Voskresensk........	CIS	33	18	9	27	74	2	1	0	1	0
93-94—Kansas City.....................	IHL	43	17	15	32	100	—	—	—	—	—

CHEREDARYK, STEVE
D, JETS

PERSONAL: Born November 20, 1975, in Calgary.... 6-3/197.... Shoots left.... Name pronounced share-a-derek.
HIGH SCHOOL: Medicine Hat (Alta.).
TRANSACTIONS/CAREER NOTES: Selected by Winnipeg Jets in fourth round (fourth Jets pick, 82nd overall) of NHL entry draft (June 29, 1994).

Season Team	League	REGULAR SEASON					PLAYOFFS				
		Gms.	G	A	Pts.	PIM	Gms.	G	A	Pts.	PIM
92-93—Medicine Hat..................	WHL	67	1	9	10	88	10	0	1	1	16
93-94—Medicine Hat..................	WHL	72	3	35	38	151	3	0	1	1	9

CHERNOMAZ, RICHARD
RW, MAPLE LEAFS

PERSONAL: Born September 1, 1963, in Selkirk, Man.... 5-8/185.... Shoots right.... Name pronounced CHUHT-noh-maz.
TRANSACTIONS/CAREER NOTES: Selected by Colorado Rockies as underage junior in second round (third Rockies pick, 26th overall) of NHL entry draft (June 10, 1981).... Suffered recurring pain caused by separated shoulder; missed parts of 1981-82 season.... Injured knee ligaments (January 1983).... Sprained left knee and underwent arthroscopic surgery (November 27, 1984).... Signed as free agent by Calgary Flames (August 4, 1987).... Underwent surgery to remove ligament from right knee (November 1989); missed 13 games.... Signed as free agent by Toronto Maple Leafs (August 3, 1993).
HONORS: Named to WHL All-Star first team (1982-83).... Named to IHL All-Star second team (1987-88 and 1990-91).... Won Les Cunningham Plaque (1993-94).... Named to AHL All-Star first team (1993-94).

Season Team	League	REGULAR SEASON					PLAYOFFS				
		Gms.	G	A	Pts.	PIM	Gms.	G	A	Pts.	PIM
79-80—Saskatoon	SJHL	51	33	37	70	75	—	—	—	—	—
—Saskatoon	WHL	25	9	10	19	33	15	11	15	26	38
80-81—Victoria...........................	WHL	72	49	64	113	92	15	11	15	26	38
81-82—Victoria...........................	WHL	49	36	62	98	69	4	1	2	3	13
—Colorado	NHL	2	0	0	0	0	—	—	—	—	—
82-83—Victoria...........................	WHL	64	71	53	124	113	12	10	5	15	18
83-84—Maine..............................	AHL	69	17	29	46	39	2	0	1	1	0
—New Jersey......................	NHL	7	2	1	3	2	—	—	—	—	—
84-85—Maine..............................	AHL	64	17	34	51	64	10	2	2	4	4
—New Jersey......................	NHL	3	0	2	2	2	—	—	—	—	—
85-86—Maine..............................	AHL	78	21	28	49	82	5	0	0	0	2
86-87—Maine..............................	AHL	58	35	27	62	65	—	—	—	—	—
—New Jersey......................	NHL	25	6	4	10	8	—	—	—	—	—
87-88—Calgary............................	NHL	2	1	0	1	0	—	—	—	—	—
—Salt Lake City..................	IHL	73	48	47	95	122	18	4	14	18	30
88-89—Calgary............................	NHL	1	0	0	0	0	—	—	—	—	—
—Salt Lake City..................	IHL	81	33	68	101	122	14	7	5	12	47
89-90—Salt Lake City..................	IHL	65	39	35	74	170	11	6	6	12	32
90-91—Salt Lake City..................	IHL	81	39	58	97	213	4	3	1	4	8

Season Team	League	REGULAR SEASON					PLAYOFFS				
		Gms.	G	A	Pts.	PIM	Gms.	G	A	Pts.	PIM
91-92—Salt Lake City	IHL	66	20	40	60	201	5	1	2	3	10
—Calgary	NHL	11	0	0	0	6	—	—	—	—	—
92-93—Salt Lake City	IHL	76	26	48	74	172	—	—	—	—	—
93-94—St. John's	AHL	78	45	65	110	199	11	5	11	16	18
NHL totals		51	9	7	16	18					

CHERREY, SCOTT
LW, CAPITALS

PERSONAL: Born May 27, 1976, in Drayton, Ont. . . . 6-1/199. . . . Shoots left.
HIGH SCHOOL: Chippewa (North Bay, Ont.).
TRANSACTIONS/CAREER NOTES: Selected by Washington Capitals in second round (third Capitals pick, 41st overall) of NHL entry draft (June 28, 1994).

Season Team	League	REGULAR SEASON					PLAYOFFS				
		Gms.	G	A	Pts.	PIM	Gms.	G	A	Pts.	PIM
92-93—Listowel Jr. B	OHA	46	17	10	27	63	—	—	—	—	—
93-94—North Bay	OHL	63	15	26	41	45	18	5	3	8	10

CHERVYAKOV, DENIS
D, BRUINS

PERSONAL: Born April 20, 1970, in St. Petersburg, U.S.S.R. . . . 6-0/185. . . . Shoots left. . . . Name pronounced CHAIR-vuh-kahf.
TRANSACTIONS/CAREER NOTES: Selected by Boston Bruins in 11th round (ninth Bruins pick, 256th overall) of NHL entry draft (June 20, 1992). . . . Loaned to Atlanta Knights (February 26, 1993). . . . Returned to Providence Bruins (March 2, 1993).

Season Team	League	REGULAR SEASON					PLAYOFFS				
		Gms.	G	A	Pts.	PIM	Gms.	G	A	Pts.	PIM
88-89—CSKA Moscow	USSR	4	1	2	3	. . .	—	—	—	—	—
89-90—CSKA Moscow	USSR	40	4	9	13	16	—	—	—	—	—
90-91—CSKA Moscow	USSR	60	5	14	19	34	—	—	—	—	—
91-92—Riga	CIS	48	4	6	10	46	—	—	—	—	—
92-93—Boston	NHL	2	0	0	0	2	—	—	—	—	—
—Providence	AHL	48	4	12	16	99	—	—	—	—	—
—Atlanta	IHL	1	0	0	0	0	—	—	—	—	—
93-94—Providence	AHL	58	2	16	18	128	—	—	—	—	—
NHL totals		2	0	0	0	2					

CHEVELDAE, TIM
G, JETS

PERSONAL: Born February 15, 1968, in Melville, Sask. . . . 5-10/195. . . . Catches left. . . . Name pronounced SHEH-vehl-day.
TRANSACTIONS/CAREER NOTES: Selected by Detroit Red Wings as underage junior in fourth round (fourth Red Wings pick, 64th overall) of NHL entry draft (June 21, 1986). . . . Sprained right knee (October 5, 1993); missed 16 games. . . . Traded by Red Wings with LW Dallas Drake to Winnipeg Jets for G Bob Essensa and D Sergei Bautin (March 8, 1994).
HONORS: Named to WHL (East) All-Star first team (1987-88). . . . Played in NHL All-Star Game (1992).

Season Team	League	REGULAR SEASON								PLAYOFFS						
		Gms.	Min.	W	L	T	GA	SO	Avg.	Gms.	Min.	W	L	GA	SO	Avg.
84-85—Melville	SAJHL	23	1167	. . .	. . .	. . .	98	0	5.04	—						
85-86—Saskatoon	WHL	36	2030	21	10	3	165	0	4.88	8	480	6	2	29	0	3.63
86-87—Saskatoon	WHL	33	1909	20	11	0	133	2	4.18	5	308	4	1	20	0	3.90
87-88—Saskatoon	WHL	66	3798	44	19	3	235	1	3.71	6	364	4	2	27	0	4.45
88-89—Detroit	NHL	2	122	0	2	0	9	0	4.43	—						
—Adirondack	AHL	30	1694	20	8	0	98	1	3.47	2	99	1	0	9	0	5.45
89-90—Adirondack	AHL	31	1848	17	8	6	116	0	3.77	—						
—Detroit	NHL	28	1600	10	9	8	101	0	3.79	—						
90-91—Detroit	NHL	65	3615	30	26	5	*214	2	3.55	7	398	3	4	22	0	3.32
91-92—Detroit	NHL	*72	*4236	†38	23	9	226	2	3.20	11	597	3	7	25	†2	2.51
92-93—Detroit	NHL	67	3880	34	24	7	210	4	3.25	7	423	3	4	24	0	3.40
93-94—Detroit	NHL	30	1572	16	9	1	91	1	3.47	—						
—Adirondack	AHL	2	125	1	0	1	7	0	3.36	—						
—Winnipeg	NHL	14	788	5	8	1	52	1	3.96	—						
NHL totals		278	15813	133	101	31	903	10	3.43	25	1418	9	15	71	2	3.00

CHEVELDAYOFF, KEVIN
D, ISLANDERS

PERSONAL: Born February 4, 1970, in Saskatoon, Sask. . . . 6-0/202. . . . Shoots right. . . . Name pronounced sheh-vehl-DAY-ahf.
TRANSACTIONS/CAREER NOTES: Selected by New York Islanders in first round (first Islanders pick, 16th overall) of NHL entry draft (June 11, 1988). . . . Underwent reconstructive surgery to left knee (January 6, 1989); missed remainder of season and part of 1989-90 season.

Season Team	League	REGULAR SEASON					PLAYOFFS				
		Gms.	G	A	Pts.	PIM	Gms.	G	A	Pts.	PIM
86-87—Brandon	WHL	70	0	16	16	259	—	—	—	—	—
87-88—Brandon	WHL	71	3	29	32	265	4	0	2	2	20
88-89—Brandon	WHL	40	4	12	16	135	—	—	—	—	—
89-90—Brandon	WHL	33	5	12	17	56	—	—	—	—	—
—Springfield	AHL	4	0	0	0	0	—	—	—	—	—

Season Team	League	REGULAR SEASON					PLAYOFFS				
		Gms.	G	A	Pts.	PIM	Gms.	G	A	Pts.	PIM
90-91—Capital District	AHL	76	0	14	14	203	—	—	—	—	—
91-92—Capital District	AHL	44	0	4	4	110	7	0	0	0	22
92-93—Capital District	AHL	79	3	8	11	113	4	0	1	1	8
93-94—Salt Lake City	IHL	73	0	4	4	216	—	—	—	—	—

CHIASSON, STEVE
D, FLAMES

PERSONAL: Born April 14, 1967, in Barrie, Ont. . . . 6-1/205. . . . Shoots left. . . . Name pronounced CHAY-sahn.
TRANSACTIONS/CAREER NOTES: Selected by Detroit Red Wings as underage junior in third round (third Red Wings pick, 50th overall) of NHL entry draft (June 15, 1985). . . . Injured hand (October 1985). . . . Separated right shoulder (February 1988). . . . Injured foot (May 1988). . . . Injured groin (October 1988). . . . Bruised ribs (January 1989). . . . Injured ankle (February 1990). . . . Injured knee (November 29, 1990); missed three games. . . . Broke right ankle (January 2, 1991). . . . Reinjured right ankle (February 19, 1991); missed 26 games. . . . Reinjured right ankle (March 9, 1991). . . . Injured ankle (October 22, 1991); missed 14 games. . . . Bruised thigh (October 25, 1992); missed three games. . . . Pulled hamstring (January 21, 1993); missed one game. . . . Suffered injuries (April 2, 1994); missed two games. . . . Traded by Red Wings to Calgary Flames for G Mike Vernon (June 29, 1994).
HONORS: Won Stafford Smythe Memorial Trophy (1985-86). . . . Named to Memorial Cup All-Star team (1985-86). . . . Played in NHL All-Star Game (1993).

Season Team	League	REGULAR SEASON					PLAYOFFS				
		Gms.	G	A	Pts.	PIM	Gms.	G	A	Pts.	PIM
83-84—Guelph	OHL	55	1	9	10	112	—	—	—	—	—
84-85—Guelph	OHL	61	8	22	30	139	—	—	—	—	—
85-86—Guelph	OHL	54	12	29	41	126	18	10	10	20	37
86-87—Detroit	NHL	45	1	4	5	73	2	0	0	0	19
87-88—Adirondack	AHL	23	6	11	17	58	—	—	—	—	—
—Detroit	NHL	29	2	9	11	57	9	2	2	4	31
88-89—Detroit	NHL	65	12	35	47	149	5	2	1	3	6
89-90—Detroit	NHL	67	14	28	42	114	—	—	—	—	—
90-91—Detroit	NHL	42	3	17	20	80	5	3	1	4	19
91-92—Detroit	NHL	62	10	24	34	136	11	1	5	6	12
92-93—Detroit	NHL	79	12	50	62	155	7	2	2	4	19
93-94—Detroit	NHL	82	13	33	46	122	7	2	3	5	2
NHL totals		471	67	200	267	886	46	12	14	26	108

CHIBIREV, IGOR
C, WHALERS

PERSONAL: Born April 19, 1968, in Penza, U.S.S.R. . . . 6-0/170. . . . Shoots left. . . . Name pronounced EE-gohr CHEE-bihr-ehv.
TRANSACTIONS/CAREER NOTES: Selected by Hartford Whalers in 11th round (eighth Whalers pick, 266th overall) of NHL entry draft (June 26, 1993).

Season Team	League	REGULAR SEASON					PLAYOFFS				
		Gms.	G	A	Pts.	PIM	Gms.	G	A	Pts.	PIM
87-88—CSKA Moscow	USSR	29	5	1	6	8	—	—	—	—	—
88-89—CSKA Moscow	USSR	34	7	9	16	16	—	—	—	—	—
89-90—CSKA Moscow	USSR				Did not play.						
90-91—CSKA Moscow	USSR				Did not play.						
91-92—CSKA Moscow	USSR	30	16	16	32	12	—	—	—	—	—
92-93—Fort Wayne	IHL	60	33	36	69	2	12	7	13	20	2
93-94—Springfield	AHL	36	28	23	51	4	—	—	—	—	—
—Hartford	NHL	37	4	11	15	2	—	—	—	—	—
NHL totals		37	4	11	15	2	—	—	—	—	—

CHIN, COLIN
C

PERSONAL: Born August 28, 1961, in Fort Wayne, Ind. . . . 5-8/165. . . . Shoots left.
COLLEGE: Illinois-Chicago.
TRANSACTIONS/CAREER NOTES: Signed as free agent by Pittsburgh Penguins (October 1985).

Season Team	League	REGULAR SEASON					PLAYOFFS				
		Gms.	G	A	Pts.	PIM	Gms.	G	A	Pts.	PIM
83-84—Illinois-Chicago	CCHA	35	11	25	36	14	—	—	—	—	—
84-85—Illinois-Chicago	CCHA	38	23	42	65	22	—	—	—	—	—
85-86—Baltimore	AHL	78	17	28	45	38	—	—	—	—	—
86-87—Fort Wayne	IHL	75	33	42	75	35	9	3	1	4	12
87-88—Fort Wayne	IHL	75	31	35	66	60	6	4	0	4	4
88-89—Fort Wayne	IHL	76	21	35	56	71	11	5	4	9	8
89-90—Fort Wayne	IHL	74	21	38	59	79	2	0	2	2	2
90-91—Fort Wayne	IHL	65	18	35	53	69	17	6	6	12	25
91-92—Fort Wayne	IHL	73	35	55	90	64	7	3	6	9	8
92-93—Fort Wayne	IHL	69	30	51	81	44	8	5	2	7	10
93-94—Fort Wayne	IHL	81	36	64	100	71	18	9	10	19	24

CHITARONI, TERRY
C, MAPLE LEAFS

PERSONAL: Born December 9, 1972, in Haileybury, Ont. . . . 5-11/200. . . . Shoots right. . . . Name pronounced CHIH-tuh-ROH-nee.
TRANSACTIONS/CAREER NOTES: Selected by Toronto Maple Leafs in fourth round (second Maple Leafs pick, 69th overall) of NHL entry draft (June 22, 1991).

Season Team	League	REGULAR SEASON					PLAYOFFS				
		Gms.	G	A	Pts.	PIM	Gms.	G	A	Pts.	PIM
88-89—Sudbury	OHL	58	17	23	40	103	—	—	—	—	—
89-90—Sudbury	OHL	65	21	47	68	173	7	4	1	5	15
90-91—Sudbury	OHL	61	28	43	71	162	5	1	1	2	18
91-92—Sudbury	OHL	51	31	47	78	119	11	7	5	12	39
—St. John's	AHL	—	—	—	—	—	2	0	1	1	5
92-93—St. John's	AHL	30	4	7	11	107	—	—	—	—	—
—Baltimore	AHL	16	2	1	3	14	—	—	—	—	—
93-94—St. John's	AHL	19	2	2	4	43	—	—	—	—	—

CHORSKE, TOM
RW, DEVILS

PERSONAL: Born September 18, 1966, in Minneapolis.... 6-1/205.... Shoots right.... Name pronounced CHOR-skee.
HIGH SCHOOL: Southwest (Minneapolis).
COLLEGE: Minnesota.
TRANSACTIONS/CAREER NOTES: Selected by Montreal Canadiens in first round (second Canadiens pick, 16th overall) of NHL entry draft (June 15, 1985).... Separated shoulder (November 18, 1988); missed 11 games.... Suffered hip pointer (October 26, 1989).... Sprained right shoulder (March 14, 1991).... Traded by Canadiens with RW Stephane Richer to New Jersey Devils for LW Kirk Muller and G Roland Melanson (September 20, 1991).... Suffered charley horse (January 14, 1993); missed two games.... Injured elbow (April 14, 1994); missed one game.
HONORS: Named to WCHA All-Star first team (1988-89).

C

Season Team	League	REGULAR SEASON					PLAYOFFS				
		Gms.	G	A	Pts.	PIM	Gms.	G	A	Pts.	PIM
84-85—Minn. Southwest H.S.	Minn. H.S.	23	44	26	70	...	—	—	—	—	—
85-86—University of Minnesota	WCHA	39	6	4	10	6	—	—	—	—	—
86-87—University of Minnesota	WCHA	47	20	22	42	20	—	—	—	—	—
87-88—U.S. national team	Int'l	36	9	16	25	24	—	—	—	—	—
88-89—University of Minnesota	WCHA	37	25	24	49	28	—	—	—	—	—
89-90—Montreal	NHL	14	3	1	4	2	—	—	—	—	—
—Sherbrooke	AHL	59	22	24	46	54	12	4	4	8	8
90-91—Montreal	NHL	57	9	11	20	32	—	—	—	—	—
91-92—New Jersey	NHL	76	19	17	36	32	7	0	3	3	4
92-93—New Jersey	NHL	50	7	12	19	25	1	0	0	0	0
—Utica	AHL	6	1	4	5	2	—	—	—	—	—
93-94—New Jersey	NHL	76	21	20	41	32	20	4	3	7	0
NHL totals		273	59	61	120	123	28	4	6	10	4

CHRISTIAN, DAVE
RW

PERSONAL: Born May 12, 1959, in Warroad, Minn.... 5-11/195.... Shoots right.... Son of Bill Christian and nephew of Roger Christian, members of 1960 gold-medal-winning U.S. Olympic team and 1964 U.S. Olympic team; and nephew of Gordon Christian, member of 1956 U.S. Olympic team.
COLLEGE: North Dakota.
TRANSACTIONS/CAREER NOTES: Selected by Winnipeg Jets in second round (second Jets pick, 40th overall) of NHL entry draft (August 9, 1979).... Tore shoulder muscles (December 1982); missed 25 games.... Traded by Jets to Washington Capitals for first-round pick (D Bobby Dollas) in 1983 draft (June 8, 1983).... Traded by Capitals to Boston Bruins for LW Bob Joyce (December 13, 1989).... Signed as free agent by St. Louis Blues; Bruins tried to block the signing, claiming Christian was not a free agent. Blues and Bruins later arranged trade in which Boston received D Glen Featherstone and LW Dave Thomlinson for Christian, third-round (LW Vitali Prokhorov) and seventh-round (C Lance Burns) picks in 1992 draft (July 30, 1991).... Bruised ribs (January 16, 1992); missed one game.... Selected by Chicago Blackhawks in NHL waiver draft (October 4, 1992).
HONORS: Played in NHL All-Star Game (1991).
MISCELLANEOUS: Member of gold-medal-winning U.S. Olympic team (1980).

Season Team	League	REGULAR SEASON					PLAYOFFS				
		Gms.	G	A	Pts.	PIM	Gms.	G	A	Pts.	PIM
77-78—Univ. of North Dakota	WCHA	38	8	16	24	14	—	—	—	—	—
78-79—Univ. of North Dakota	WCHA	40	22	24	46	22	—	—	—	—	—
79-80—U.S. national team	Int'l	59	10	20	30	26	—	—	—	—	—
—U.S. Olympic Team	Int'l	7	0	8	8	6	—	—	—	—	—
—Winnipeg	NHL	15	8	10	18	2	—	—	—	—	—
80-81—Winnipeg	NHL	80	28	43	71	22	—	—	—	—	—
81-82—Winnipeg	NHL	80	25	51	76	28	4	0	1	1	2
82-83—Winnipeg	NHL	55	18	26	44	23	3	0	0	0	0
83-84—Washington	NHL	80	29	52	81	28	8	5	4	9	5
84-85—Washington	NHL	80	26	43	69	14	5	1	1	2	0
85-86—Washington	NHL	80	41	42	83	15	9	4	4	8	0
86-87—Washington	NHL	76	23	27	50	8	7	1	3	4	6
87-88—Washington	NHL	80	37	21	58	26	14	5	6	11	6
88-89—Washington	NHL	80	34	31	65	12	6	1	1	2	0
89-90—Washington	NHL	28	3	8	11	4	—	—	—	—	—
—Boston	NHL	50	12	17	29	8	21	4	1	5	4
90-91—Boston	NHL	78	32	21	53	41	19	8	4	12	4
91-92—St. Louis	NHL	78	20	24	44	41	4	3	0	3	0
92-93—Chicago	NHL	60	4	14	18	12	1	0	0	0	0

Season Team	League	REGULAR SEASON					PLAYOFFS				
		Gms.	G	A	Pts.	PIM	Gms.	G	A	Pts.	PIM
93-94—Chicago	NHL	9	0	3	3	0	1	0	0	0	0
—Indianapolis	IHL	40	8	18	26	6	—	—	—	—	—
NHL totals		1009	340	433	773	284	102	32	25	57	27

CHRISTIAN, JEFF
LW, PENGUINS

PERSONAL: Born July 30, 1970, in Burlington, Ont. . . . 6-1/196. . . . Shoots left.
TRANSACTIONS/CAREER NOTES: Selected by New Jersey Devils in second round (second Devils pick, 23rd overall) of NHL entry draft (June 11, 1988). . . . Traded by London Knights to Owen Sound Platers for C Todd Hlushko and D David Noseworthy (November 27, 1989). . . . Suspended three games by OHL for high-sticking (March 28, 1990). . . . Signed as free agent by Pittsburgh Penguins (August 2, 1994).

Season Team	League	REGULAR SEASON					PLAYOFFS				
		Gms.	G	A	Pts.	PIM	Gms.	G	A	Pts.	PIM
86-87—Dundas Jr. C	OHA	29	20	34	54	42	—	—	—	—	—
87-88—London	OHL	64	15	29	44	154	9	1	5	6	27
88-89—London	OHL	60	27	30	57	221	20	3	4	7	56
89-90—London	OHL	18	14	7	21	64	—	—	—	—	—
—Owen Sound	OHL	37	19	26	45	145	10	6	7	13	43
90-91—Utica	AHL	80	24	42	66	165	—	—	—	—	—
91-92—Utica	AHL	76	27	24	51	198	4	0	0	0	16
—New Jersey	NHL	2	0	0	0	2	—	—	—	—	—
92-93—Utica	AHL	22	4	6	10	39	—	—	—	—	—
—Cincinnati	IHL	36	5	12	17	113	—	—	—	—	—
—Hamilton	AHL	11	2	5	7	35	—	—	—	—	—
93-94—Albany	AHL	76	34	43	77	227	5	1	2	3	19
NHL totals		2	0	0	0	2					

CHURLA, SHANE
RW, STARS

PERSONAL: Born June 24, 1965, in Fernie, B.C. . . . 6-1/200. . . . Shoots right. . . . Name pronounced CHUR-luh.
TRANSACTIONS/CAREER NOTES: Selected by Hartford Whalers in sixth round (fourth Whalers pick, 110th overall) of NHL entry draft (June 15, 1985). . . . Pulled stomach muscles (October 1985). . . . Suspended three games by AHL (October 5, 1986). . . . Traded by Whalers with D Dana Murzyn to Calgary Flames for D Neil Sheehy, C Carey Wilson and the rights to LW Lane MacDonald (January 3, 1988). . . . Traded by Flames with C Perry Berezan to Minnesota North Stars for LW Brian MacLellan and fourth-round pick (C Robert Reichel) in 1989 draft (March 4, 1989). . . . Broke wrist (April 2, 1989). . . . Bruised right hand (November 1989). . . . Suspended 10 games by NHL for fighting (December 28, 1989). . . . Underwent surgery to wrist (April 1990). . . . Tore rib cartilage (November 17, 1990); missed five games. . . . Separated shoulder (December 11, 1990); missed seven games. . . . Separated right shoulder (January 17, 1991); missed 23 games. . . . Selected by San Jose Sharks in dispersal draft of North Stars roster (May 30, 1991). . . . Traded by Sharks to North Stars for C Kelly Kisio (June 3, 1991). . . . Suffered back spasms (January 30, 1992); missed five games. . . . Injured shoulder (March 19, 1992); missed five games. . . . Injured shoulder (December 1, 1992); missed one game. . . . Injured shoulder (December 22, 1992); missed two games. . . . Strained neck (February 28, 1993); missed two games. . . . Suspended three games by NHL during 1992-93 season for game misconduct penalties. . . . North Stars franchise moved from Minnesota to Dallas and renamed Stars for 1993-94 season. . . . Pulled groin (October 23, 1993); missed two games. . . . Pulled leg muscle (November 24, 1993); missed nine games. . . . Strained bicep muscle (January 9, 1994); missed one game. . . . Bruised hip (April 10, 1994); missed one game.

Season Team	League	REGULAR SEASON					PLAYOFFS				
		Gms.	G	A	Pts.	PIM	Gms.	G	A	Pts.	PIM
83-84—Medicine Hat	WHL	48	3	7	10	115	14	1	5	6	41
84-85—Medicine Hat	WHL	70	14	20	34	*370	9	1	0	1	55
85-86—Binghamton	AHL	52	4	10	14	306	3	0	0	0	22
86-87—Binghamton	AHL	24	1	5	6	249	—	—	—	—	—
—Hartford	NHL	20	0	1	1	78	2	0	0	0	42
87-88—Binghamton	AHL	25	5	8	13	168	—	—	—	—	—
—Hartford	NHL	2	0	0	0	14	—	—	—	—	—
—Calgary	NHL	29	1	5	6	132	7	0	1	1	17
88-89—Calgary	NHL	5	0	0	0	25	—	—	—	—	—
—Salt Lake City	IHL	32	3	13	16	278	—	—	—	—	—
—Minnesota	NHL	13	1	0	1	54	7	0	0	0	44
89-90—Minnesota	NHL	53	2	3	5	292	22	2	1	3	90
90-91—Minnesota	NHL	40	2	2	4	286	—	—	—	—	—
91-92—Minnesota	NHL	57	4	1	5	278	—	—	—	—	—
92-93—Minnesota	NHL	73	5	16	21	286	9	1	3	4	35
93-94—Dallas	NHL	69	6	7	13	333	47	3	5	8	228
NHL totals		361	21	35	56	1778					

CHYCHRUN, JEFF
D, WHALERS

PERSONAL: Born May 3, 1966, in La Salle, Que. . . . 6-4/215. . . . Shoots right. . . . Name pronounced CHIHK-ruhn.
TRANSACTIONS/CAREER NOTES: Selected by Philadelphia Flyers as underage junior in second round (second Flyers pick, 37th overall) of NHL entry draft (June 9, 1984). . . . Suffered viral infection (November 1989). . . . Suffered concussion (October 11, 1990); missed three games. . . . Suffered concussion (October 23, 1990); missed three games. . . . Fractured navicular bone in left wrist and underwent surgery (November 23, 1990); missed 41 games. . . . Traded by Flyers with rights to RW Jari Kurri to Los Angeles Kings for D Steve Duchesne, C Steve Kasper and fourth-round pick (D Aris Brimanis) in 1991 draft (May 30, 1991). . . . Underwent wrist surgery (summer 1991);

missed 25 games. . . . Traded by Kings with D Brian Benning and first-round pick in 1992 draft (LW Jason Bowen) to Pittsburgh Penguins for D Paul Coffey (February 19, 1992). . . . Suspended by Penguins after he missed team flight (October 29, 1992). . . . Reinstated by Penguins (November 3, 1992). . . . Traded by Penguins to Los Angeles Kings for D Peter Ahola (November 6, 1992). . . . Traded by Kings to Edmonton Oilers for future considerations (November 2, 1993). . . . Signed as free agent by Hartford Whalers (1994).

MISCELLANEOUS: Member of Stanley Cup championship team (1992).

Season Team	League	REGULAR SEASON					PLAYOFFS				
		Gms.	G	A	Pts.	PIM	Gms.	G	A	Pts.	PIM
83-84—Kingston	OHL	83	1	13	14	137	—	—	—	—	—
84-85—Kingston	OHL	58	4	10	14	206	—	—	—	—	—
85-86—Kingston	OHL	61	4	21	25	127	10	2	1	3	17
—Kalamazoo	IHL	—	—	—	—	—	3	1	0	1	0
—Hershey	AHL	—	—	—	—	—	4	0	1	1	9
86-87—Hershey	AHL	74	1	17	18	239	4	0	0	0	10
—Philadelphia	NHL	1	0	0	0	4	—	—	—	—	—
87-88—Philadelphia	NHL	3	0	0	0	4	—	—	—	—	—
—Hershey	AHL	55	0	5	5	210	12	0	2	2	44
88-89—Philadelphia	NHL	80	1	4	5	245	19	0	2	2	65
89-90—Philadelphia	NHL	79	2	7	9	250	—	—	—	—	—
90-91—Philadelphia	NHL	36	0	6	6	105	—	—	—	—	—
91-92—Phoenix	IHL	3	0	0	0	6	—	—	—	—	—
—Los Angeles	NHL	26	0	3	3	76	—	—	—	—	—
—Pittsburgh	NHL	17	0	1	1	35	—	—	—	—	—
92-93—Pittsburgh	NHL	1	0	0	0	2	—	—	—	—	—
—Los Angeles	NHL	17	0	1	1	23	—	—	—	—	—
—Phoenix	IHL	11	2	0	2	44	—	—	—	—	—
93-94—Cape Breton	AHL	41	2	16	18	111	—	—	—	—	—
—Edmonton	NHL	2	0	0	0	0	—	—	—	—	—
NHL totals		262	3	22	25	744	19	0	2	2	65

CHYNOWETH, DEAN
D, ISLANDERS

PERSONAL: Born October 30, 1968, in Saskatoon, Sask. . . . 6-2/193. . . . Shoots right. . . . Name pronounced shih-NOWTH. . . . Son of Ed Chynoweth, president of the Western Hockey League.

TRANSACTIONS/CAREER NOTES: Broke hand (September 1985). . . . Broke hand (April 1986). . . . Broke hand (October 1986). . . . Fractured rib and punctured lung (April 1987). . . . Selected by New York Islanders as underage junior in first round (first Islanders pick, 13th overall) of NHL entry draft (June 13, 1987). . . . Injured left eye (October 27, 1988); missed two months. . . . Developed Osgood-Schlatter disease, an abnormal relationship between the muscles and the growing bones (December 1988); missed remainder of season. . . . Injured ankle (October 31, 1989). . . . Sprained ligaments in right thumb (November 1989). . . . Strained shoulder (February 24, 1994); missed one game. . . . Strained groin (March 15, 1994); missed 10 games.

HONORS: Named to Memorial Cup All-Star team (1987-88).

Season Team	League	REGULAR SEASON					PLAYOFFS				
		Gms.	G	A	Pts.	PIM	Gms.	G	A	Pts.	PIM
85-86—Medicine Hat	WHL	69	3	12	15	208	17	3	2	5	52
86-87—Medicine Hat	WHL	67	3	18	21	285	13	4	2	6	28
87-88—Medicine Hat	WHL	64	1	21	22	274	16	0	6	6	*87
88-89—New York Islanders	NHL	6	0	0	0	48	—	—	—	—	—
89-90—New York Islanders	NHL	20	0	2	2	39	—	—	—	—	—
—Springfield	AHL	40	0	7	7	98	17	0	4	4	36
90-91—New York Islanders	NHL	25	1	1	2	59	—	—	—	—	—
—Capital District	AHL	44	1	5	6	176	—	—	—	—	—
91-92—Capital District	AHL	43	4	6	10	164	6	1	1	2	39
—New York Islanders	NHL	11	1	0	1	23	—	—	—	—	—
92-93—Capital District	AHL	52	3	10	13	197	4	0	1	1	9
93-94—Salt Lake City	IHL	5	0	1	1	33	—	—	—	—	—
—New York Islanders	NHL	39	0	4	4	122	2	0	0	0	2
NHL totals		101	2	7	9	291	2	0	0	0	2

CHYZOWSKI, DAVE
LW, ISLANDERS

PERSONAL: Born July 11, 1971, in Edmonton. . . . 6-1/190. . . . Shoots left. . . . Name pronounced chih-ZOW-skee.

TRANSACTIONS/CAREER NOTES: Selected by New York Islanders in first round (first Islanders pick, second overall) of NHL entry draft (June 17, 1989).

HONORS: Named to WHL (West) All-Star first team (1988-89).

Season Team	League	REGULAR SEASON					PLAYOFFS				
		Gms.	G	A	Pts.	PIM	Gms.	G	A	Pts.	PIM
87-88—Kamloops	WHL	66	16	17	33	117	18	2	4	6	26
88-89—Kamloops	WHL	68	56	48	104	139	16	15	13	28	32
89-90—Kamloops	WHL	4	5	2	7	17	17	11	6	17	46
—Springfield	AHL	4	0	0	0	7	—	—	—	—	—
—New York Islanders	NHL	34	8	6	14	45	—	—	—	—	—
90-91—Capital District	AHL	7	3	6	9	22	—	—	—	—	—
—New York Islanders	NHL	56	5	9	14	61	—	—	—	—	—
91-92—New York Islanders	NHL	12	1	1	2	17	—	—	—	—	—
—Capital District	AHL	55	15	18	33	121	6	1	1	2	23

Season Team	League	REGULAR SEASON					PLAYOFFS				
		Gms.	G	A	Pts.	PIM	Gms.	G	A	Pts.	PIM
92-93—Capital District	AHL	66	15	21	36	177	3	2	0	2	0
93-94—Salt Lake City	IHL	66	27	13	40	151	—	—	—	—	—
—New York Islanders	NHL	3	1	0	1	4	2	0	0	0	0
NHL totals		105	15	16	31	127	2	0	0	0	0

CIAVAGLIA, PETER
C, SABRES

PERSONAL: Born July 15, 1969, in Albany, N.Y. . . . 5-10/173. . . . Shoots left. . . . Full name: Peter Anthony Ciavaglia. . . . Name pronounced sa-VAG-lia.
COLLEGE: Harvard.
TRANSACTIONS/CAREER NOTES: Selected by Calgary Flames in seventh round (eighth Flames pick, 145th overall) of NHL entry draft (June 13, 1987). . . . Signed as free agent by Buffalo Sabres (August 1990). . . . Suffered stiff neck (February 14, 1993); missed two games.
HONORS: Named to ECAC All-Star second team (1988-89). . . . Named to NCAA All-America East second team (1990-91). . . . Named ECAC Player of Year (1990-91). . . . Named to ECAC All-Star first team (1990-91).

Season Team	League	REGULAR SEASON					PLAYOFFS				
		Gms.	G	A	Pts.	PIM	Gms.	G	A	Pts.	PIM
86-87—Nichols/Wheatfield Jr. B.	NY Jr. B	...	53	84	137	...	—	—	—	—	—
87-88—Harvard University	ECAC	30	10	23	33	16	—	—	—	—	—
88-89—Harvard University	ECAC	34	15	48	63	36	—	—	—	—	—
89-90—Harvard University	ECAC	28	17	18	35	22	—	—	—	—	—
90-91—Harvard University	ECAC	28	24	39	63	4	—	—	—	—	—
91-92—Rochester	AHL	77	37	61	98	16	6	2	5	7	6
—Buffalo	NHL	2	0	0	0	0	—	—	—	—	—
92-93—Rochester	AHL	64	35	67	102	32	17	9	16	25	12
—Buffalo	NHL	3	0	0	0	0	—	—	—	—	—
93-94—Leksand	Sweden	39	14	18	32	34	4	1	2	3	0
—U.S. national team	Int'l	18	2	9	11	6	—	—	—	—	—
—U.S. Olympic Team	Int'l	8	2	4	6	0	—	—	—	—	—
NHL totals		5	0	0	0	0					

CICCARELLI, DINO
RW, RED WINGS

PERSONAL: Born February 8, 1960, in Sarnia, Ont. . . . 5-10/175. . . . Shoots right. . . . Name pronounced Sih-sah-REHL-ee.
TRANSACTIONS/CAREER NOTES: Fractured midshaft of right femur (spring 1978). . . . Signed as free agent by Minnesota North Stars (September 1979). . . . Injured shoulder (November 1984). . . . Broke right wrist (December 1984). . . . Suspended three games by NHL for making contact with linesman (October 5, 1987). . . . Suspended 10 games by NHL for stick-swinging incident (January 6, 1988). . . . Suspended by North Stars for failure to report to training camp (September 10, 1988). . . . Traded by North Stars with D Bob Rouse to Washington Capitals for RW Mike Gartner and D Larry Murphy (March 7, 1989). . . . Suffered concussion (March 8, 1989). . . . Sprained left knee (April 23, 1990). . . . Fractured right hand (October 20, 1990); missed 21 games. . . . Injured groin (March 24, 1991); missed five games. . . . Injured eye (December 4, 1991); missed one game. . . . Traded by Capitals to Detroit Red Wings for RW Kevin Miller (June 20, 1992). . . . Suffered from the flu (January 30, 1993); missed two games. . . . Injured foot (January 15, 1994); missed 17 games.
HONORS: Won Jim Mahon Memorial Trophy (1977-78). . . . Named to OMJHL All-Star second team (1977-78). . . . Played in NHL All-Star Game (1982, 1983 and 1989).
RECORDS: Holds NHL single-season playoff record for most points by rookie—21; and most goals by rookie—14 (1981). . . . Shares NHL single-season playoff record for most power-play goals in one game—3 (April 29, 1993).

Season Team	League	REGULAR SEASON					PLAYOFFS				
		Gms.	G	A	Pts.	PIM	Gms.	G	A	Pts.	PIM
76-77—London	OMJHL	66	39	43	82	45	—	—	—	—	—
77-78—London	OMJHL	68	*72	70	142	49	9	6	10	16	6
78-79—London	OMJHL	30	8	11	19	25	7	3	5	8	0
79-80—London	OMJHL	62	50	53	103	72	5	2	6	8	15
—Oklahoma City	CHL	6	3	2	5	0	—	—	—	—	—
80-81—Oklahoma City	CHL	48	32	25	57	45	—	—	—	—	—
—Minnesota	NHL	32	18	12	30	29	19	14	7	21	25
81-82—Minnesota	NHL	76	55	51	106	138	4	3	1	4	2
82-83—Minnesota	NHL	77	37	38	75	94	9	4	6	10	11
83-84—Minnesota	NHL	79	38	33	71	58	16	4	5	9	27
84-85—Minnesota	NHL	51	15	17	32	41	9	3	3	6	8
85-86—Minnesota	NHL	75	44	45	89	51	5	0	1	1	6
86-87—Minnesota	NHL	80	52	51	103	88	—	—	—	—	—
87-88—Minnesota	NHL	67	41	45	86	79	—	—	—	—	—
88-89—Minnesota	NHL	65	32	27	59	64	—	—	—	—	—
—Washington	NHL	11	12	3	15	12	6	3	3	6	12
89-90—Washington	NHL	80	41	38	79	122	8	8	3	11	6
90-91—Washington	NHL	54	21	18	39	76	11	5	4	9	22
91-92—Washington	NHL	78	38	38	76	78	7	5	4	9	14
92-93—Detroit	NHL	82	41	56	97	81	7	4	2	6	16
93-94—Detroit	NHL	66	28	29	57	73	7	5	2	7	14
NHL totals		973	513	501	1014	1084	108	58	41	99	163

CICCONE, ENRICO
D, LIGHTNING

PERSONAL: Born April 10, 1970, in Montreal. . . . 6-4/200. . . . Shoots left. . . . Name pronounced CHIH-koh-nee.
TRANSACTIONS/CAREER NOTES: Selected by Minnesota North Stars in fifth round (fifth North Stars pick, 92nd overall) of NHL entry draft (June 16, 1990). . . . North Stars

franchise moved from Minnesota to Dallas and renamed Stars for 1993-94 season. . . . Traded by Stars to Washington Capitals (June 25, 1993) to complete deal in which Capitals sent D Paul Cavallini to Stars for future considerations (June 20, 1993). . . . Suffered pulled groin (January 25, 1994); missed seven games. . . . Traded by Capitals with third-round pick in 1994 draft (traded to Mighty Ducks of Anaheim who selected RW Craig Reichert) and conditional draft pick to Tampa Bay Lightning for D Joe Reekie (March 21, 1994).

Season Team	League		REGULAR SEASON					PLAYOFFS			
		Gms.	G	A	Pts.	PIM	Gms.	G	A	Pts.	PIM
87-88—Shawinigan	QMJHL	61	2	12	14	324	—	—	—	—	—
88-89—Shawinigan/T-Rivieres	QMJHL	58	7	19	26	289	—	—	—	—	—
89-90—Trois-Rivieres	QMJHL	40	4	24	28	227	3	0	0	0	15
90-91—Kalamazoo	IHL	57	4	9	13	384	4	0	1	1	32
91-92—Kalamazoo	IHL	53	4	16	20	406	10	0	1	1	58
—Minnesota	NHL	11	0	0	0	48	—	—	—	—	—
92-93—Minnesota	NHL	31	0	1	1	115	—	—	—	—	—
—Kalamazoo	IHL	13	1	3	4	50	—	—	—	—	—
—Hamilton	AHL	6	1	3	4	44	—	—	—	—	—
93-94—Washington	NHL	46	1	1	2	174	—	—	—	—	—
—Portland	AHL	6	0	0	0	27	—	—	—	—	—
—Tampa Bay	NHL	11	0	1	1	52	—	—	—	—	—
NHL totals		99	1	3	4	389					

C

CIERNY, JOZEF
LW, OILERS

PERSONAL: Born May 13, 1974, in Zvolen, Czechoslovakia. . . . 6-2/185. . . . Shoots left. . . . Name pronounced JOH-sehf CHUHR-nee.
TRANSACTIONS/CAREER NOTES: Selected by Buffalo Sabres in second round (second Sabres pick, 35th overall) of NHL entry draft (June 20, 1992). . . . Traded by Sabres with undisclosed draft pick to Edmonton Oilers for LW Craig Simpson (September 1, 1993).

Season Team	League		REGULAR SEASON					PLAYOFFS			
		Gms.	G	A	Pts.	PIM	Gms.	G	A	Pts.	PIM
91-92—Zvolen	Czech.	26	10	3	13	8	—	—	—	—	—
92-93—Rochester	AHL	54	27	27	54	36	—	—	—	—	—
93-94—Cape Breton	AHL	73	30	27	57	88	4	1	1	2	4
—Edmonton	NHL	1	0	0	0	0	—	—	—	—	—
NHL totals		1	0	0	0	0					

CIGER, ZDENO
LW, OILERS

PERSONAL: Born October 19, 1969, in Martin, Czechoslovakia. . . . 6-1/190. . . . Shoots left. . . . Name pronounced zuh-DAY-noh SEE-guhr.
TRANSACTIONS/CAREER NOTES: Selected by New Jersey Devils in third round (third Devils pick, 54th overall) of NHL entry draft (June 11, 1988). . . . Bruised left shoulder (October 6, 1990). . . . Injured elbow (January 24, 1991). . . . Fractured right wrist (September 24, 1991); missed first 59 games of season. . . . Traded by Devils with C Kevin Todd to Edmonton Oilers for C Bernie Nicholls (January 13, 1993).
HONORS: Named Czechoslovakian League Rookie of the Year (1988-89).

Season Team	League		REGULAR SEASON					PLAYOFFS			
		Gms.	G	A	Pts.	PIM	Gms.	G	A	Pts.	PIM
88-89—Dukla Trencin	Czech.	32	15	21	36	18	—	—	—	—	—
89-90—Dukla Trencin	Czech.	53	18	28	46	...	—	—	—	—	—
90-91—New Jersey	NHL	45	8	17	25	8	6	0	2	2	4
—Utica	AHL	8	5	4	9	2	—	—	—	—	—
91-92—New Jersey	NHL	20	6	5	11	10	7	2	4	6	0
92-93—New Jersey	NHL	27	4	8	12	2	—	—	—	—	—
—Edmonton	NHL	37	9	15	24	6	—	—	—	—	—
93-94—Edmonton	NHL	84	22	35	57	8	—	—	—	—	—
NHL totals		213	49	80	129	34	13	2	6	8	4

CIMETTA, ROB
LW, BLACKHAWKS

PERSONAL: Born February 15, 1970, in Toronto. . . . 6-0/190. . . . Shoots left. . . . Name pronounced sih-MEH-tuh.
TRANSACTIONS/CAREER NOTES: Fractured wrist (October 1986). . . . Selected by Boston Bruins in first round (first Bruins pick, 18th overall) of NHL entry draft (June 11, 1988). . . . Traded by Bruins to Toronto Maple Leafs for D Steve Bancroft (November 9, 1990). . . . Bruised bicep (March 16, 1991). . . . Pulled groin (December 11, 1991); missed eight games. . . . Signed as free agent by Chicago Blackhawks (September 8, 1993).
HONORS: Named to OHL All-Star first team (1988-89).

Season Team	League		REGULAR SEASON					PLAYOFFS			
		Gms.	G	A	Pts.	PIM	Gms.	G	A	Pts.	PIM
86-87—Toronto	OHL	66	21	35	56	65	—	—	—	—	—
87-88—Toronto	OHL	64	34	42	76	90	4	2	2	4	7
88-89—Toronto	OHL	50	*55	47	102	89	6	3	3	6	0
—Boston	NHL	7	2	0	2	0	1	0	0	0	15
89-90—Boston	NHL	47	8	9	17	33	—	—	—	—	—
—Maine	AHL	9	3	2	5	13	—	—	—	—	—
90-91—Toronto	NHL	25	2	4	6	21	—	—	—	—	—
—Newmarket	AHL	29	16	18	34	24	—	—	—	—	—
91-92—Toronto	NHL	24	4	3	7	12	—	—	—	—	—
—St. John's	AHL	19	4	13	17	23	10	3	7	10	24

Season Team	League	Gms.	G	A	Pts.	PIM	Gms.	G	A	Pts.	PIM
92-93—St. John's	AHL	76	28	57	85	125	9	2	10	12	32
93-94—Indianapolis	IHL	79	26	54	80	178	—	—	—	—	—
NHL totals		103	16	16	32	66	1	0	0	0	15

CIRELLA, JOE
D, PANTHERS

PERSONAL: Born May 9, 1963, in Hamilton, Ont. . . . 6-3/210. . . . Shoots right. . . . Name pronounced sih-REHL-uh.

TRANSACTIONS/CAREER NOTES: Selected by Colorado Rockies as underage junior in first round (first Rockies pick, fifth overall) of NHL entry draft (June 10, 1981). . . . Injured left knee (November 26, 1985). . . . Traded by New Jersey Devils to Quebec Nordiques for C Walt Poddubny (June 17, 1989). . . . Broke right foot (January 18, 1990). . . . Strained lower back (February 28, 1990). . . . Injured knee (October 21, 1990). . . . Traded by Nordiques to New York Rangers for C Aaron Broten and fifth-round pick (LW Bill Lindsay) in 1991 draft (January 17, 1991). . . . Strained lower back (October 4, 1991); missed 10 games. . . . Selected by Florida Panthers in NHL expansion draft (June 24, 1993). . . . Fractured right cheekbone (November 23, 1993); missed three games. . . . Underwent right eye surgery (December 18, 1993); missed 12 games. . . . Broke nose (February 4, 1994); missed four games.

HONORS: Named to OHL All-Star first team (1982-83). . . . Named to Memorial Cup All-Star team (1982-83). . . . Played in NHL All-Star Game (1984).

Season Team	League	Gms.	G	A	Pts.	PIM	Gms.	G	A	Pts.	PIM
80-81—Oshawa	OMJHL	56	5	31	36	220	11	0	2	2	41
81-82—Oshawa	OHL	3	0	1	1	10	11	7	10	17	32
—Colorado	NHL	65	7	12	19	52	—	—	—	—	—
82-83—Oshawa	OHL	56	13	55	68	110	17	4	16	20	37
—New Jersey	NHL	2	0	1	1	4	—	—	—	—	—
83-84—New Jersey	NHL	79	11	33	44	137	—	—	—	—	—
84-85—New Jersey	NHL	66	6	18	24	143	—	—	—	—	—
85-86—New Jersey	NHL	66	6	23	29	147	—	—	—	—	—
86-87—New Jersey	NHL	65	9	22	31	111	—	—	—	—	—
87-88—New Jersey	NHL	80	8	31	39	191	19	0	7	7	49
88-89—New Jersey	NHL	80	3	19	22	155	—	—	—	—	—
89-90—Quebec	NHL	56	4	14	18	67	—	—	—	—	—
90-91—Quebec	NHL	39	2	10	12	59	—	—	—	—	—
—New York Rangers	NHL	19	1	0	1	52	6	0	2	2	26
91-92—New York Rangers	NHL	67	3	12	15	121	13	0	4	4	23
92-93—New York Rangers	NHL	55	3	6	9	85	—	—	—	—	—
93-94—Florida	NHL	63	1	9	10	99	—	—	—	—	—
NHL totals		802	64	210	274	1423	38	0	13	13	98

CLARK, CHRIS
RW, FLAMES

PERSONAL: Born March 8, 1976, in South Windsor, Conn. . . . 6-0/180. . . . Shoots right.

TRANSACTIONS/CAREER NOTES: Selected by Calgary Flames in third round (third Flames pick, 77th overall) of NHL entry draft (June 29, 1994).

Season Team	League	Gms.	G	A	Pts.	PIM	Gms.	G	A	Pts.	PIM
93-94—Springfield Jr. B	NEJHL	35	31	26	57	185	—	—	—	—	—

CLARK, KERRY
RW, CAPITALS

PERSONAL: Born August 21, 1968, in Kelvington, Sask. . . . 6-1/190. . . . Shoots right. . . . Brother of Wendel Clark, left winger, Quebec Nordiques.

TRANSACTIONS/CAREER NOTES: Selected by New York Islanders as underage junior in 10th round (12th Islanders pick, 206th overall) of NHL entry draft (June 21, 1986). . . . Broke ankle (1986-87). . . . Suspended six games by AHL for fighting (October 15, 1988). . . . Signed as free agent by Calgary Flames (July 23, 1990). . . . Signed as free agent by Portland Pirates (July 1993).

Season Team	League	Gms.	G	A	Pts.	PIM	Gms.	G	A	Pts.	PIM
84-85—Regina	WHL	36	1	1	2	66	—	—	—	—	—
85-86—Regina	WHL	23	4	4	8	58	—	—	—	—	—
—Saskatoon	WHL	39	5	8	13	104	13	2	2	4	33
86-87—Saskatoon	WHL	54	12	10	22	229	8	0	1	1	23
87-88—Saskatoon	WHL	67	15	11	26	241	10	2	2	4	16
88-89—Springfield	AHL	63	7	7	14	264	—	—	—	—	—
—Indianapolis	IHL	3	0	1	1	12	—	—	—	—	—
89-90—Phoenix	IHL	38	4	8	12	262	—	—	—	—	—
—Springfield	AHL	21	0	1	1	73	—	—	—	—	—
90-91—Salt Lake City	IHL	62	14	14	28	372	4	1	1	2	12
91-92—Salt Lake City	IHL	74	12	14	26	266	5	1	0	1	34
92-93—Salt Lake City	IHL	64	14	15	29	255	—	—	—	—	—
93-94—Portland	AHL	55	9	5	14	309	5	0	0	0	26

CLARK, WENDEL
LW, NORDIQUES

PERSONAL: Born October 25, 1966, in Kelvington, Sask. . . . 5-10/194. . . . Shoots left. . . . Brother of Kerry Clark, right winger in Washington Capitals system.

TRANSACTIONS/CAREER NOTES: Selected by Toronto Maple Leafs as underage junior in first round (first Maple Leafs pick, first overall) of NHL entry draft (June 15, 1985). . . . Suf-

fered from virus (November 1985).... Broke right foot (November 26, 1985); missed 14 games.... Suffered back spasms (November 1987); missed 23 games.... Suffered tendinitis in right shoulder (October 1987).... Reinjured back (February 1988); missed 90 regular season games (March 1, 1989).... Suffered recurrence of back problems (October 1989).... Bruised muscle above left knee (November 4, 1989); missed seven games.... Tore ligament of right knee (January 26, 1990); missed 29 games.... Separated left shoulder (December 18, 1990).... Pulled rib cage muscle (February 6, 1991); missed 12 games.... Partially tore knee ligaments (October 7, 1991); missed 12 games.... Strained knee ligaments (November 6, 1991); missed 24 games.... Injured groin (October 24, 1992); missed four games.... Strained rib muscle (January 17, 1993); missed 13 games.... Strained knee (October 13, 1993); missed two games.... Bruised foot (December 22, 1993); missed 17 games. ... Traded by Maple Leafs with D Sylvain Lefebvre, RW Landon Wilson and first-round pick in 1994 draft (D Jeffrey Kealty) to Quebec Nordiques for C Mats Sundin, D Garth Butcher, LW Todd Warriner and first-round pick (traded to Washington Capitals who selected D Nolan Baumgartner) in 1994 draft (June 28, 1994).
HONORS: Won Top Defenseman Trophy (1984-85).... Named to WHL (East) All-Star first team (1984-85).... Named NHL Rookie of the Year by THE SPORTING NEWS (1985-86).... Named to NHL All-Rookie team (1985-86).... Played in NHL All-Star Game (1986).

Season Team	League		REGULAR SEASON						PLAYOFFS			
		Gms.	G	A	Pts.	PIM	Gms.	G	A	Pts.	PIM
83-84—Saskatoon	WHL	72	23	45	68	225	—	—	—	—	—
84-85—Saskatoon	WHL	64	32	55	87	253	3	3	3	6	7
85-86—Toronto	NHL	66	34	11	45	227	10	5	1	6	47
86-87—Toronto	NHL	80	37	23	60	271	13	6	5	11	38
87-88—Toronto	NHL	28	12	11	23	80	—	—	—	—	—
88-89—Toronto	NHL	15	7	4	11	66	—	—	—	—	—
89-90—Toronto	NHL	38	18	8	26	116	5	1	1	2	19
90-91—Toronto	NHL	63	18	16	34	152	—	—	—	—	—
91-92—Toronto	NHL	43	19	21	40	123	—	—	—	—	—
92-93—Toronto	NHL	66	17	22	39	193	21	10	10	20	51
93-94—Toronto	NHL	64	46	30	76	115	18	9	7	16	24
NHL totals		463	208	146	354	1343	67	31	24	55	179

CLOUTIER, COLIN
C, LIGHTNING

PERSONAL: Born January 27, 1976, in Winnipeg.... 6-3/224.... Shoots left.... Name pronounced CLOO-tee-yay.
HIGH SCHOOL: Crocus Plains (Brandon, Man.).
TRANSACTIONS/CAREER NOTES: Selected by Tampa Bay Lightning in second round (second Lightning pick, 34th overall) of NHL entry draft (June 28, 1994).

Season Team	League		REGULAR SEASON						PLAYOFFS			
		Gms.	G	A	Pts.	PIM	Gms.	G	A	Pts.	PIM
91-92—St. Boniface	MJHL	42	7	15	22	113	—	—	—	—	—
92-93—Brandon	WHL	60	11	15	26	138	4	0	0	0	18
93-94—Brandon	WHL	30	10	13	23	102	11	2	5	7	23

CLOUTIER, DAN
G, RANGERS

PERSONAL: Born April 22, 1976, in Mont-Laurier, Que.... 6-1/182.... Catches left.... Name pronounced CLOO-tee-yay.... Brother of Sylvain Cloutier, center in Detroit Red Wings system.
HIGH SCHOOL: Notre-Dame-des-Grands-Lacs (Sault Ste. Marie, Ont.).
TRANSACTIONS/CAREER NOTES: Selected by New York Rangers in first round (first Rangers pick, 26th overall) of NHL entry draft (June 28, 1994).

Season Team	League		REGULAR SEASON							PLAYOFFS					
		Gms.	Min.	W	L	T	GA	SO	Avg.	Gms.	Min.	W	L	GA	SO	Avg.
91-92—St. Thomas	Jr. B	14	823	...	...	...	80	1	5.83	—	—	—	—	—	—	—
92-93—Sault Ste. Marie	OHL	12	572	4	6	0	44	0	4.62	4	231	1	2	12	0	3.12
93-94—Sault Ste. Marie	OHL	55	2934	28	14	6	174	†2	3.56	14	833	†10	4	52	0	3.75

CLOUTIER, JACQUES
G, NORDIQUES

PERSONAL: Born January 3, 1960, in Noranda, Que.... 5-7/168.... Catches left. ... Name pronounced KLOO-chay.
TRANSACTIONS/CAREER NOTES: Selected by Buffalo Sabres as underage junior in third round (fourth Sabres pick, 55th overall) of NHL entry draft (August 9, 1979).... Broke collarbone (January 1982).... Tore ligaments in knee (December 1984); missed remainder of season; spent the year as an assistant coach with Rochester Americans.... Traded by Sabres to Chicago Blackhawks for future considerations; Steve Ludzik and draft pick later sent to Sabres to complete deal (September 1989).... Pulled groin (December 11, 1989); missed six games.... Strained left knee (March 25, 1990).... Traded by Blackhawks to Quebec Nordiques for LW Tony McKegney (January 29, 1991).... Sprained left ankle (December 16, 1992); missed 24 games.... Pulled neck muscle (December 19, 1993); missed six games.... Suffered from stomach virus (March 21, 1994), missed one game.
HONORS: Won Jacques Plante Trophy (1978-79).... Named to QMJHL All-Star first team (1978-79).

Season Team	League		REGULAR SEASON							PLAYOFFS					
		Gms.	Min.	W	L	T	GA	SO	Avg.	Gms.	Min.	W	L	GA	SO	Avg.
76-77—Trois-Rivieres	QMJHL	24	1109	...	...	...	93	0	5.03	—	—	—	—	—	—	—
77-78—Trois-Rivieres	QMJHL	*71	*4134	...	...	...	240	*4	3.48	13	779	...	...	40	1	3.08
78-79—Trois-Rivieres	QMJHL	*72	*4168	...	...	...	218	†3	*3.14	13	780	...	...	36	0	2.77
79-80—Trois-Rivieres	QMJHL	55	3222	27	20	7	231	†2	4.30	7	420	3	4	33	0	4.71
80-81—Rochester	AHL	*61	*3478	27	27	6	*209	1	3.61	—	—	—	—	—	—	—
81-82—Rochester	AHL	23	1366	14	7	2	64	0	2.81	—	—	—	—	—	—	—
—Buffalo	NHL	7	311	5	1	0	13	0	2.51	—	—	—	—	—	—	—

Season	Team	League	REGULAR SEASON								PLAYOFFS						
			Gms.	Min.	W	L	T	GA	SO	Avg.	Gms.	Min.	W	L	GA	SO	Avg.
82-83	Buffalo	NHL	25	1390	10	7	6	81	0	3.50	—	—	—	—	—	—	—
	Rochester	AHL	13	634	7	3	1	42	0	3.97	16	992	12	4	47	0	2.84
83-84	Rochester	AHL	*51	*2841	26	22	1	172	1	3.63	*18	*1145	9	9	*68	0	3.56
84-85	Rochester	AHL	14	803	10	2	1	36	0	2.69	—	—	—	—	—	—	—
	Buffalo	NHL	1	65	0	0	1	4	0	3.69	—	—	—	—	—	—	—
85-86	Rochester	AHL	14	835	10	2	2	38	1	2.73	—	—	—	—	—	—	—
	Buffalo	NHL	15	872	5	9	1	49	0	3.37	—	—	—	—	—	—	—
86-87	Buffalo	NHL	40	2167	11	19	5	137	0	3.79	—	—	—	—	—	—	—
87-88	Buffalo	NHL	20	851	4	8	2	67	0	4.72	—	—	—	—	—	—	—
88-89	Buffalo	NHL	36	1786	15	14	0	108	0	3.63	4	238	1	3	10	1	2.52
	Rochester	AHL	11	527	2	7	0	41	0	4.67	—	—	—	—	—	—	—
89-90	Chicago	NHL	43	2178	18	15	2	112	2	3.09	4	175	0	2	8	0	2.74
90-91	Chicago	NHL	10	403	2	3	0	24	0	3.57	—	—	—	—	—	—	—
	Quebec	NHL	15	829	3	8	2	61	0	4.41	—	—	—	—	—	—	—
91-92	Quebec	NHL	26	1345	6	14	3	88	0	3.93	—	—	—	—	—	—	—
92-93	Quebec	NHL	3	154	0	2	1	10	0	3.90	—	—	—	—	—	—	—
93-94	Quebec	NHL	14	475	3	2	1	24	0	3.03	—	—	—	—	—	—	—
NHL totals			255	12826	82	102	24	778	3	3.64	8	413	1	5	18	1	2.62

CLOUTIER, SYLVAIN

C, RED WINGS

PERSONAL: Born February 13, 1974, in Mont-Laurier, Que.... 6-0/195.... Shoots left.... Name pronounced CLOO-tee-yay.... Brother of Dan Cloutier, center in New York Rangers system.
HIGH SCHOOL: Bishop MacDonnell (Guelph, Ont.).
TRANSACTIONS/CAREER NOTES: Selected by Detroit Red Wings in third round (third Red Wings pick, 70th overall) of NHL entry draft (June 20, 1992).

Season	Team	League	REGULAR SEASON					PLAYOFFS				
			Gms.	G	A	Pts.	PIM	Gms.	G	A	Pts.	PIM
91-92	Guelph	OHL	62	35	31	66	74	—	—	—	—	—
92-93	Guelph	OHL	44	26	29	55	78	5	0	5	5	14
93-94	Guelph	OHL	66	45	71	116	127	9	7	9	16	32
	Adirondack	AHL	2	0	2	2	2	—	—	—	—	—

COFFEY, PAUL

D, RED WINGS

PERSONAL: Born June 1, 1961, in Weston, Ont.... 6-1/195.... Shoots left.... Full name: Paul Douglas Coffey.
TRANSACTIONS/CAREER NOTES: Selected by Edmonton Oilers in first round (first Oilers pick, sixth overall) of NHL entry draft (June 11, 1980).... Suffered recurring back spasms (December 1986); missed 10 games.... Traded by Oilers with LW Dave Hunter and RW Wayne Van Dorp to Pittsburgh Penguins for C Craig Simpson, C Dave Hannan, D Moe Mantha and D Chris Joseph (November 24, 1987).... Tore knee cartilage (December 1987).... Bruised right shoulder (November 16, 1988).... Broke finger (May 1990).... Injured back (February 27, 1991).... Injured hip muscle (March 9, 1991).... Scratched left eye cornea (April 9, 1991).... Broke jaw (April 1991).... Pulled hip muscle (February 3, 1992); missed three games.... Traded by Penguins to Los Angeles Kings for D Brian Benning, D Jeff Chychrun and first-round pick (LW Jason Bowen) in 1992 draft (February 19, 1992).... Suffered back spasms (March 3, 1992); missed three games.... Fractured wrist (March 17, 1992); missed five games.... Traded by Kings with RW Jim Hiller and C/LW Sylain Couturier to Detroit Red Wings for C Jimmy Carson, RW Marc Potvin and C Gary Shuchuk (January 29, 1993).... Injured groin (March 18, 1993); missed one game.... Injured groin and left knee (October 18, 1993); missed four games.
HONORS: Named to OMJHL All-Star second team (1979-80).... Named to NHL All-Star second team (1980-81 through 1983-84 and 1989-90).... Named to THE SPORTING NEWS All-Star second team (1981-82 through 1983-84, 1986-87 and 1989-90).... Played in NHL All-Star Game (1982-1986 and 1988-1994).... Won James Norris Memorial Trophy (1984-85 and 1985-86).... Named to THE SPORTING NEWS All-Star first team (1984-85, 1985-86 and 1988-89).... Named to NHL All-Star first team (1984-85, 1985-86 and 1988-89).
RECORDS: Holds NHL career records for most goals by a defenseman—330; most assists by a defenseman—871; and most points by a defenseman—1,201.... Holds NHL single-season record for most goals by a defenseman—48 (1985-86).... Shares NHL single-game record for most points by a defenseman—8; and most assists by a defenseman—6 (March 14, 1986). ... Holds NHL record for most consecutive games scoring points by a defenseman—28 (1985-86).... Holds NHL single-season playoff records for most goals by a defenseman—12; assists by a defenseman—25; and points by a defenseman—37 (1985).... Holds NHL single-game playoff record for most points by a defenseman—6 (May 14, 1985).
MISCELLANEOUS: Member of Stanley Cup championship teams (1984, 1985, 1987 and 1991).

Season	Team	League	REGULAR SEASON					PLAYOFFS				
			Gms.	G	A	Pts.	PIM	Gms.	G	A	Pts.	PIM
77-78	Kingston	OMJHL	8	2	2	4	11	—	—	—	—	—
	North York	MTHL	50	14	33	47	64	—	—	—	—	—
78-79	Sault Ste. Marie	OMJHL	68	17	72	89	99	—	—	—	—	—
79-80	Sault Ste. Marie	OMJHL	23	10	21	31	63	—	—	—	—	—
	Kitchener	OMJHL	52	19	52	71	130	—	—	—	—	—
80-81	Edmonton	NHL	74	9	23	32	130	9	4	3	7	22
81-82	Edmonton	NHL	80	29	60	89	106	5	1	1	2	6
82-83	Edmonton	NHL	80	29	67	96	87	16	7	7	14	14
83-84	Edmonton	NHL	80	40	86	126	104	19	8	14	22	21
84-85	Edmonton	NHL	80	37	84	121	97	18	12	25	37	44
85-86	Edmonton	NHL	79	48	90	138	120	10	1	9	10	30
86-87	Edmonton	NHL	59	17	50	67	49	17	3	8	11	30

Season Team	League	REGULAR SEASON					PLAYOFFS				
		Gms.	G	A	Pts.	PIM	Gms.	G	A	Pts.	PIM
87-88—Pittsburgh	NHL	46	15	52	67	93	—	—	—	—	—
88-89—Pittsburgh	NHL	75	30	83	113	195	11	2	13	15	31
89-90—Pittsburgh	NHL	80	29	74	103	95	—	—	—	—	—
90-91—Pittsburgh	NHL	76	24	69	93	128	12	2	9	11	6
91-92—Pittsburgh	NHL	54	10	54	64	62	—	—	—	—	—
—Los Angeles	NHL	10	1	4	5	25	6	4	3	7	2
92-93—Los Angeles	NHL	50	8	49	57	50	—	—	—	—	—
—Detroit	NHL	30	4	26	30	27	7	2	9	11	2
93-94—Detroit	NHL	80	14	63	77	106	7	1	6	7	8
NHL totals		1033	344	934	1278	1474	137	47	107	154	216

COLE, DANTON
RW, LIGHTNING

PERSONAL: Born January 10, 1967, in Pontiac, Mich. . . . 5-11/185. . . . Shoots right. . . . Full name: Danton Edward Cole.
COLLEGE: Michigan State.
TRANSACTIONS/CAREER NOTES: Selected by Winnipeg Jets in sixth round (sixth Jets pick, 123rd overall) of NHL entry draft (June 15, 1985). . . . Strained knee (January 26, 1992); missed 11 games. . . . Traded by Jets to Tampa Bay Lightning for future considerations (June 19, 1992). . . . Tore ligament in left knee (December 15, 1992); missed 10 games. . . . Injured groin (October 23, 1993); missed one game. . . . Suffered cut to mouth (October 30, 1993); missed one game.

Season Team	League	REGULAR SEASON					PLAYOFFS				
		Gms.	G	A	Pts.	PIM	Gms.	G	A	Pts.	PIM
84-85—Aurora	OHA	41	51	44	95	91	—	—	—	—	—
85-86—Michigan State	CCHA	43	11	10	21	22	—	—	—	—	—
86-87—Michigan State	CCHA	44	9	15	24	16	—	—	—	—	—
87-88—Michigan State	CCHA	46	20	36	56	38	—	—	—	—	—
88-89—Michigan State	CCHA	47	29	33	62	46	—	—	—	—	—
89-90—Winnipeg	NHL	2	1	1	2	0	—	—	—	—	—
—Moncton	AHL	80	31	42	73	18	—	—	—	—	—
90-91—Winnipeg	NHL	66	13	11	24	24	—	—	—	—	—
—Moncton	AHL	3	1	1	2	0	—	—	—	—	—
91-92—Winnipeg	NHL	52	7	5	12	32	—	—	—	—	—
92-93—Tampa Bay	NHL	67	12	15	27	23	—	—	—	—	—
—Atlanta	IHL	1	1	0	1	2	—	—	—	—	—
93-94—Tampa Bay	NHL	81	20	23	43	32	—	—	—	—	—
NHL totals		268	53	55	108	111					

COLEMAN, JONATHAN
D, RED WINGS

PERSONAL: Born March 9, 1975, in Boston. . . . 6-2/195. . . . Shoots left.
HIGH SCHOOL: Phillips Academy (Andover, Mass.).
TRANSACTIONS/CAREER NOTES: Selected by Detroit Red Wings in second round (second Red Wings pick, 48th overall) of NHL entry draft (June 26, 1993).

Season Team	League	REGULAR SEASON					PLAYOFFS				
		Gms.	G	A	Pts.	PIM	Gms.	G	A	Pts.	PIM
89-90—Phillips Andover Acad.	Mass. H.S.	24	8	20	28	10	—	—	—	—	—
90-91—Phillips Andover Acad.	Mass. H.S.	24	11	25	36	18	—	—	—	—	—
91-92—Phillips Andover Acad.	Mass. H.S.	24	12	29	41	26	—	—	—	—	—
92-93—Phillips Andover Acad.	Mass. H.S.	23	14	33	47	72	—	—	—	—	—
93-94—Boston University	Hockey East	29	1	14	15	26	—	—	—	—	—

CONACHER, PAT
LW/C, KINGS

PERSONAL: Born May 1, 1959, in Edmonton. . . . 5-9/190. . . . Shoots left. . . . Full name: Patrick John Conacher. . . . Name pronounced KON-a-KER.
TRANSACTIONS/CAREER NOTES: Selected by New York Rangers in fourth round (third Rangers pick, 76th overall) of NHL entry draft (August 9, 1979). . . . Fractured left ankle (September 21, 1980); missed entire 1980-81 season. . . . Injured shoulder (November 1982). . . . Signed as free agent by Edmonton Oilers (October 4, 1983). . . . Injured groin (December 1984). . . . Signed as free agent by New Jersey Devils (August 14, 1985). . . . Sprained back (February 1988). . . . Bruised left shoulder (December 1988). . . . Underwent major reconstructive surgery to left shoulder (April 7, 1989). . . . Lacerated face and lost two teeth (October 13, 1989). . . . Sprained left knee (April 9, 1990). . . . Strained left knee (September 22, 1990). . . . Suffered ulcer problems (February 1991). . . . Injured groin (October 24, 1991); missed two games. . . . Injured groin (December 1991). . . . Underwent hernia surgery (January 9, 1992); missed 34 games. . . . Traded by Devils to Los Angeles Kings for future considerations (September 3, 1992). . . . Strained lower back (November 21, 1992); missed four games.
MISCELLANEOUS: Member of Stanley Cup championship team (1984).

Season Team	League	REGULAR SEASON					PLAYOFFS				
		Gms.	G	A	Pts.	PIM	Gms.	G	A	Pts.	PIM
77-78—Billings	WCHL	72	31	44	75	105	20	15	14	29	22
78-79—Billings	WHL	39	25	37	62	50	—	—	—	—	—
—Saskatoon	WHL	33	15	32	47	37	—	—	—	—	—
79-80—New York Rangers	NHL	17	0	5	5	4	3	0	1	1	2
—New Haven	AHL	53	11	14	25	43	7	1	1	2	4
80-81—New York Rangers	NHL			Did not play—injured.							
81-82—Springfield	AHL	77	23	22	45	38	—	—	—	—	—

— 370 —

Season	Team	League	REGULAR SEASON Gms.	G	A	Pts.	PIM	PLAYOFFS Gms.	G	A	Pts.	PIM
82-83—Tulsa	CHL		63	29	28	57	44	—	—	—	—	—
—New York Rangers	NHL		5	0	1	1	4	—	—	—	—	—
83-84—Moncton	AHL		28	7	16	23	30	—	—	—	—	—
—Edmonton	NHL		45	2	8	10	31	3	1	0	1	2
84-85—Nova Scotia	AHL		68	20	45	65	44	6	3	2	5	0
85-86—New Jersey	NHL		2	0	2	2	2	—	—	—	—	—
—Maine	AHL		69	15	30	45	83	5	1	1	2	11
86-87—Maine	AHL		56	12	14	26	47	—	—	—	—	—
87-88—Utica	AHL		47	14	33	47	32	—	—	—	—	—
—New Jersey	NHL		24	2	5	7	12	17	2	2	4	14
88-89—New Jersey	NHL		55	7	5	12	14	—	—	—	—	—
89-90—Utica	AHL		57	13	36	49	53	—	—	—	—	—
—New Jersey	NHL		19	3	3	6	4	5	1	0	1	10
90-91—Utica	AHL		4	0	1	1	6	—	—	—	—	—
—New Jersey	NHL		49	5	11	16	27	7	0	2	2	2
91-92—New Jersey	NHL		44	7	3	10	16	7	1	1	2	4
92-93—Los Angeles	NHL		81	9	8	17	20	24	6	4	10	6
93-94—Los Angeles	NHL		77	15	13	28	71	—	—	—	—	—
NHL totals			418	50	64	114	205	66	11	10	21	40

CONNOLLY, JEFF
C, CANUCKS

PERSONAL: Born February 1, 1974, in Worcester, Mass. . . . 6-0/185. . . . Shoots right.
HIGH SCHOOL: Milton (Mass.) Academy, then St. Sebastian's Country Day School (Needham, Mass.).
TRANSACTIONS/CAREER NOTES: Selected by Vancouver Canucks in third round (fourth Canucks pick, 69th overall) of NHL entry draft (June 20, 1992).

Season	Team	League	REGULAR SEASON Gms.	G	A	Pts.	PIM	PLAYOFFS Gms.	G	A	Pts.	PIM
89-90—Milton Academy	Mass. H.S.		21	14	18	32	...	—	—	—	—	—
90-91—Milton Academy	Mass. H.S.		23	28	19	47	...	—	—	—	—	—
91-92—St. Sebastian's	Mass. H.S.		28	31	35	66	...	—	—	—	—	—
92-93—St. Sebastian's	Mass. H.S.		24	17	34	51	...	—	—	—	—	—
93-94—Boston College	Hockey East		22	8	10	18	20	—	—	—	—	—

CONROY, AL
RW, FLYERS

PERSONAL: Born January 17, 1966, in Calgary. . . . 5-8/170. . . . Shoots right.
TRANSACTIONS/CAREER NOTES: Signed as free agent by Detroit Red Wings (August 1989). . . . Signed as free agent by Philadelphia Flyers (August 21, 1991).
HONORS: Named to WHL (East) All-Star first team (1985-86).

Season	Team	League	REGULAR SEASON Gms.	G	A	Pts.	PIM	PLAYOFFS Gms.	G	A	Pts.	PIM
86-87—Rapperswill	Switzerland		...	30	32	62	...	—	—	—	—	—
—Rochester	AHL		13	4	4	8	40	13	1	3	4	50
87-88—Varese	Italy		36	25	39	64	...	—	—	—	—	—
—Adirondack	AHL		13	5	8	13	20	11	1	3	4	41
88-89—Dortmund	Germany		46	53	78	131	...	—	—	—	—	—
89-90—Adirondack	AHL		77	23	33	56	147	5	0	0	0	20
90-91—Adirondack	AHL		80	26	39	65	172	2	1	1	2	0
91-92—Hershey	AHL		47	17	28	45	90	6	4	2	6	12
—Philadelphia	NHL		31	2	9	11	74	—	—	—	—	—
92-93—Hershey	AHL		60	28	32	60	130	—	—	—	—	—
—Philadelphia	NHL		21	3	2	5	17	—	—	—	—	—
93-94—Philadelphia	NHL		62	4	3	7	65	—	—	—	—	—
NHL totals			114	9	14	23	156	—	—	—	—	—

CONVERY, BRANDON
C, MAPLE LEAFS

PERSONAL: Born February 4, 1974, in Kingston, Ont. . . . 6-1/182. . . . Shoots right.
HIGH SCHOOL: Lasalle Secondary School (Sudbury, Ont.).
TRANSACTIONS/CAREER NOTES: Selected by Toronto Maple Leafs in first round (first Maple Leafs pick, eighth overall) of NHL entry draft (June 20, 1992).
HONORS: Won OHL Top Prospect Award (1991-92).

Season	Team	League	REGULAR SEASON Gms.	G	A	Pts.	PIM	PLAYOFFS Gms.	G	A	Pts.	PIM
89-90—Kingston Jr. B	OHA		42	13	25	38	4	—	—	—	—	—
90-91—Sudbury	OHL		56	26	22	48	18	5	1	1	2	2
91-92—Sudbury	OHL		44	40	27	67	44	5	3	2	5	4
92-93—Niagara Falls	OHL		51	38	39	77	24	4	1	3	4	4
—Sudbury	OHL		7	7	9	16	6	—	—	—	—	—
—St. John's	AHL		3	0	0	0	0	5	0	1	1	0
93-94—Niagara Falls	OHL		29	24	29	53	30	—	—	—	—	—
—Belleville	OHL		23	16	19	35	22	12	4	10	14	13

COOPER, DAVID
D, SABRES

PERSONAL: Born November 2, 1973, in Ottawa.... 6-1/190.... Shoots left.
HIGH SCHOOL: Medicine Hat (Alta.).
TRANSACTIONS/CAREER NOTES: Selected by Buffalo Sabres in first round (first Sabres pick, 11th overall) of NHL entry draft (June 20, 1992).
HONORS: Won WHL Top Prospect Award (1991-92).... Named to WHL (East) All-Star first team (1991-92).

Season Team	League	REGULAR SEASON					PLAYOFFS				
		Gms.	G	A	Pts.	PIM	Gms.	G	A	Pts.	PIM
89-90—Medicine Hat	WHL	61	4	11	15	65	3	0	2	2	2
90-91—Medicine Hat	WHL	64	12	31	43	66	11	1	3	4	23
91-92—Medicine Hat	WHL	72	17	47	64	176	4	1	4	5	8
92-93—Medicine Hat	WHL	63	15	50	65	88	10	2	2	4	32
—Rochester	AHL	0	0	0	0	0	2	0	0	0	2
93-94—Rochester	AHL	68	10	25	35	82	4	1	1	2	2

COPELAND, ADAM
RW, OILERS

PERSONAL: Born June 5, 1976, in Burlington, Ont.... 6-2/184.... Shoots right.
TRANSACTIONS/CAREER NOTES: Selected by Edmonton Oilers in fourth round (sixth Oilers pick, 79th overall) of NHL entry draft (June 29, 1994).

Season Team	League	REGULAR SEASON					PLAYOFFS				
		Gms.	G	A	Pts.	PIM	Gms.	G	A	Pts.	PIM
93-94—Burlington Jr. B	OHA	39	28	44	72	55	—	—	—	—	—

COPELAND, TODD
D, SABRES

PERSONAL: Born May 18, 1968, in Ridgewood, N.J.... 6-2/210.... Shoots left.... Full name: John Todd Copeland.
HIGH SCHOOL: Belmont (Mass.) Hill.
COLLEGE: Michigan.
TRANSACTIONS/CAREER NOTES: Injured knee (February 1986).... Selected by New Jersey Devils in second round (second Devils pick, 24th overall) of NHL entry draft (June 21, 1986).... Signed as free agent by Winnipeg Jets (August 1993).... Signed as free agent by Buffalo Sabres (July 7, 1994).

Season Team	League	REGULAR SEASON					PLAYOFFS				
		Gms.	G	A	Pts.	PIM	Gms.	G	A	Pts.	PIM
84-85—Belmont Hill H.S.	Mass. H.S.	23	8	25	33	18	—	—	—	—	—
85-86—Belmont Hill H.S.	Mass. H.S.	19	4	19	23	19	—	—	—	—	—
86-87—University of Michigan	CCHA	34	2	10	12	57	—	—	—	—	—
87-88—University of Michigan	CCHA	41	3	10	13	58	—	—	—	—	—
88-89—University of Michigan	CCHA	39	5	14	19	102	—	—	—	—	—
89-90—University of Michigan	CCHA	34	6	16	22	62	—	—	—	—	—
90-91—Utica	AHL	79	6	24	30	53	—	—	—	—	—
91-92—Utica	AHL	80	4	23	27	96	4	2	2	4	2
92-93—Utica	AHL	16	3	2	5	10	—	—	—	—	—
—Cincinnati	IHL	37	0	3	3	47	—	—	—	—	—
—Moncton	AHL	16	1	4	5	16	5	1	3	4	2
93-94—Moncton	AHL	80	4	17	21	158	19	0	1	1	54

CORBET, RENE
LW, NORDIQUES

PERSONAL: Born June 25, 1973, in Victoriaville, Que.... 6-0/187.... Shoots left.... Name pronounced ruh-NAY kohr-BAY.
TRANSACTIONS/CAREER NOTES: Selected by Quebec Nordiques in second round (second Nordiques pick, 24th overall) of NHL entry draft (June 22, 1991).
HONORS: Won Michel Bergeron Trophy (1990-91).... Named to QMJHL All-Rookie team (1990-91).... Won Jean Beliveau Trophy (1992-93).... Named to Can.HL All-Star first team (1992-93).... Named to QMJHL All-Star first team (1992-93). ... Won Dudley (Red) Garrett Memorial Trophy (1993-94).

Season Team	League	REGULAR SEASON					PLAYOFFS				
		Gms.	G	A	Pts.	PIM	Gms.	G	A	Pts.	PIM
90-91—Drummondville	QMJHL	45	25	40	65	34	14	11	6	17	15
91-92—Drummondville	QMJHL	56	46	50	96	90	4	1	2	3	17
92-93—Drummondville	QMJHL	63	*79	69	*148	143	10	7	13	20	16
93-94—Cornwall	AHL	68	37	40	77	56	13	7	2	9	18
—Quebec	NHL	9	1	1	2	0	—	—	—	—	—
NHL totals		9	1	1	2	0					

CORKUM, BOB
C/RW, MIGHTY DUCKS

PERSONAL: Born December 18, 1967, in Salisbury, Mass.... 6-2/212.... Shoots right.... Full name: Robert Freeman Corkum.
HIGH SCHOOL: Triton Regional (Byfield, Mass.).
COLLEGE: Maine.
TRANSACTIONS/CAREER NOTES: Selected by Buffalo Sabres in third round (third Sabres pick, 47th overall) of NHL entry draft (June 21, 1986).... Injured hip (March 19, 1992).... Selected by Mighty Ducks of Anaheim in NHL expansion draft (June 24, 1993).... Ruptured ankle tendon (March 27, 1994); missed remainder of season.

Season Team	League	REGULAR SEASON					PLAYOFFS				
		Gms.	G	A	Pts.	PIM	Gms.	G	A	Pts.	PIM
84-85—Triton Regional H.S.	Mass. H.S.	18	35	36	71	...	—	—	—	—	—
85-86—University of Maine	Hockey East	39	7	16	23	53	—	—	—	—	—
86-87—University of Maine	Hockey East	35	18	11	29	24	—	—	—	—	—

Season	Team	League	REGULAR SEASON					PLAYOFFS				
			Gms.	G	A	Pts.	PIM	Gms.	G	A	Pts.	PIM
87-88—University of Maine	Hockey East	40	14	18	32	64	—	—	—	—	—
88-89—University of Maine	Hockey East	45	17	31	48	64	—	—	—	—	—
89-90—Rochester	AHL	43	8	11	19	45	12	2	5	7	16
—Buffalo	NHL	8	2	0	2	4	5	1	0	1	4
90-91—Rochester	AHL	69	13	21	34	77	15	4	4	8	4
91-92—Rochester	AHL	52	16	12	28	47	8	0	6	6	8
—Buffalo	NHL	20	2	4	6	21	4	1	0	1	0
92-93—Buffalo	NHL	68	6	4	10	38	5	0	0	0	2
93-94—Anaheim	NHL	76	23	28	51	18	—	—	—	—	—
NHL totals		172	33	36	69	81	14	2	0	2	6

CORPSE, KELI
C, CANADIENS

PERSONAL: Born May 14, 1974, in London, Ont. . . . 5-11/174. . . . Shoots left. . . . Name pronounced KAL-ee KOHRPS.
HIGH SCHOOL: Loyalist Collegiate (Kingston, Ont.).
TRANSACTIONS/CAREER NOTES: Selected by Montreal Canadiens in second round (third Canadiens pick, 44th overall) of NHL entry draft (June 20, 1992).
HONORS: Won Can.HL Humanitarian Award (1992-93). . . . Named to OHL All-Star second team (1993-94).

Season	Team	League	REGULAR SEASON					PLAYOFFS				
			Gms.	G	A	Pts.	PIM	Gms.	G	A	Pts.	PIM
89-90—London Jr. B	OHA	39	26	31	57	10	—	—	—	—	—
90-91—Kingston	OHL	58	18	33	51	34	—	—	—	—	—
91-92—Kingston	OHL	65	31	52	83	20	—	—	—	—	—
92-93—Kingston	OHL	54	32	75	107	45	16	9	20	29	10
—Canadian national team	Int'l	1	0	0	0	2	—	—	—	—	—
93-94—Kingston	OHL	63	42	84	126	55	6	1	7	8	2

CORRIVEAU, YVON
LW, WHALERS

PERSONAL: Born February 8, 1967, in Welland, Ont. . . . 6-1/195. . . . Shoots left. . . . Name pronounced IGH-vihn KOHR-ih-voh. . . . Brother of Rick Corriveau, defenseman in Washington Capitals system.
TRANSACTIONS/CAREER NOTES: Injured shoulder (March 1985). . . . Selected by Washington Capitals as underage junior in first round (first Capitals pick, 19th overall) of NHL entry draft (June 15, 1985). . . . Bruised thigh (November 1988). . . . Traded by Capitals to Hartford Whalers for G Mike Liut (March 5, 1990). . . . Bruised foot (October 1990). . . . Traded by Whalers to Washington Capitals (August 20, 1992) to complete deal in which Whalers sent RW Mark Hunter to Capitals for LW Nick Kypreos (June 15, 1992). . . . Selected by San Jose Sharks in NHL waiver draft (October 4, 1992). . . . Strained back (October 26, 1992); missed 11 games. . . . Strained back (November 21, 1992); missed 16 games. . . . Traded by Sharks to Hartford Whalers (January 21, 1993) to complete deal in which Whalers sent LW Michel Picard to Sharks for future considerations (October 9, 1992).

Season	Team	League	REGULAR SEASON					PLAYOFFS				
			Gms.	G	A	Pts.	PIM	Gms.	G	A	Pts.	PIM
83-84—Welland Jr. B	OHA	36	16	21	37	51	—	—	—	—	—
84-85—Toronto	OHL	59	23	28	51	65	3	0	0	0	5
85-86—Toronto	OHL	59	54	36	90	75	4	1	1	2	0
—Washington	NHL	2	0	0	0	0	4	0	3	3	2
86-87—Toronto	OHL	23	14	19	33	23	—	—	—	—	—
—Binghamton	AHL	7	0	0	0	2	8	0	1	1	0
—Washington	NHL	17	1	1	2	24	—	—	—	—	—
87-88—Binghamton	AHL	35	15	14	29	64	—	—	—	—	—
—Washington	NHL	44	10	9	19	84	13	1	2	3	30
88-89—Baltimore	AHL	33	16	23	39	65	—	—	—	—	—
—Washington	NHL	33	3	2	5	62	1	0	0	0	0
89-90—Washington	NHL	50	9	6	15	50	—	—	—	—	—
—Hartford	NHL	13	4	1	5	22	4	1	0	1	0
90-91—Hartford	NHL	23	1	1	2	18	—	—	—	—	—
—Springfield	AHL	44	17	25	42	10	18	†10	6	16	31
91-92—Hartford	NHL	38	12	8	20	36	7	3	2	5	18
—Springfield	AHL	39	26	15	41	40	—	—	—	—	—
92-93—San Jose	NHL	20	3	7	10	0	—	—	—	—	—
—Hartford	NHL	37	5	5	10	14	—	—	—	—	—
93-94—Hartford	NHL	3	0	0	0	0	—	—	—	—	—
—Springfield	AHL	71	42	39	81	53	6	7	3	10	20
NHL totals		280	48	40	88	310	29	5	7	12	50

CORSON, SHAYNE
LW/C, OILERS

PERSONAL: Born August 13, 1966, in Barrie, Ont. . . . 6-1/200. . . . Shoots left.
TRANSACTIONS/CAREER NOTES: Selected by Montreal Canadiens in first round (second Canadiens pick, eighth overall) of NHL entry draft (June 9, 1984). . . . Broke jaw (January 24, 1987). . . . Strained ligament in right knee (September 1987). . . . Injured groin (March 1988). . . . Injured knee (April 1988). . . . Injured knee (April 1989). . . . Bruised left shoulder (October 29, 1989). . . . Broke toe on right foot (December 1989). . . . Suffered hip pointer (November 10, 1990); missed seven games. . . . Pulled groin (February 11, 1991). . . . Traded by Canadiens with LW Vladimir Vujtek and C Brent Gilchrist to Edmonton Oilers for LW Vincent Damphousse and fourth-round pick (D Adam Wiesel) in 1993 draft (August 27, 1992). . . . Fractured fibula (February 18, 1994); missed 12 games. . . . Injured leg (March 23, 1994); missed remainder of season.
HONORS: Played in NHL All-Star Game (1990 and 1994).

Season Team	League	REGULAR SEASON					PLAYOFFS				
		Gms.	G	A	Pts.	PIM	Gms.	G	A	Pts.	PIM
82-83—Barrie	COJHL	23	13	29	42	87	—	—	—	—	—
83-84—Brantford	OHL	66	25	46	71	165	6	4	1	5	26
84-85—Hamilton	OHL	54	27	63	90	154	11	3	7	10	19
85-86—Hamilton	OHL	47	41	57	98	153	—	—	—	—	—
—Montreal	NHL	3	0	0	0	2	—	—	—	—	—
86-87—Montreal	NHL	55	12	11	23	144	17	6	5	11	30
87-88—Montreal	NHL	71	12	27	39	152	3	1	0	1	12
88-89—Montreal	NHL	80	26	24	50	193	21	4	5	9	65
89-90—Montreal	NHL	76	31	44	75	144	11	2	8	10	20
90-91—Montreal	NHL	71	23	24	47	138	13	9	6	15	36
91-92—Montreal	NHL	64	17	36	53	118	10	2	5	7	15
92-93—Edmonton	NHL	80	16	31	47	209	—	—	—	—	—
93-94—Edmonton	NHL	64	25	29	54	118	—	—	—	—	—
NHL totals		564	162	226	388	1218	75	24	29	53	178

COTE, ALAIN

D, NORDIQUES

PERSONAL: Born April 14, 1967, in Montmagny, Que.... 6-0/207.... Shoots right.... Full name: Alain Gabriel Cote.... Name pronounced al-LAI KOH-tay.... Brother of Sylvain Cote, defenseman, Washington Capitals.

TRANSACTIONS/CAREER NOTES: Selected by Boston Bruins as underage junior in second round (first Bruins pick, 31st overall) of NHL entry draft (June 15, 1985).... Traded by Bruins to Washington Capitals for RW Bobby Gould (September 27, 1989).... Traded by Capitals to Montreal Canadiens for D Marc Deschamps (June 23, 1990).... Injured eye (March 30, 1991).... Traded by Canadiens with D Eric Charron and future considerations to Tampa Bay Lightning for D Rob Ramage (March 20, 1993); Canadiens sent D Donald Dufresne to Lightning to complete deal (June 18, 1993).... Signed as free agent by Quebec Nordiques (July 3, 1993).

Season Team	League	REGULAR SEASON					PLAYOFFS				
		Gms.	G	A	Pts.	PIM	Gms.	G	A	Pts.	PIM
83-84—Quebec	QMJHL	60	3	17	20	40	—	—	—	—	—
84-85—Quebec	QMJHL	68	9	25	34	173	—	—	—	—	—
85-86—Granby	QMJHL	22	4	12	16	48	—	—	—	—	—
—Moncton	AHL	3	0	0	0	0	—	—	—	—	—
—Boston	NHL	32	0	6	6	14	—	—	—	—	—
86-87—Granby	QMJHL	43	7	24	31	185	4	0	3	3	2
—Boston	NHL	3	0	0	0	0	—	—	—	—	—
87-88—Boston	NHL	2	0	0	0	0	—	—	—	—	—
—Maine	AHL	69	9	34	43	108	9	2	4	6	19
88-89—Maine	AHL	37	5	16	21	111	—	—	—	—	—
—Boston	NHL	31	2	3	5	51	—	—	—	—	—
89-90—Washington	NHL	2	0	0	0	7	—	—	—	—	—
—Baltimore	AHL	57	5	19	24	161	3	0	0	0	9
90-91—Montreal	NHL	28	0	6	6	26	11	0	2	2	26
—Fredericton	AHL	49	8	19	27	110	—	—	—	—	—
91-92—Montreal	NHL	13	0	3	3	22	—	—	—	—	—
—Fredericton	AHL	20	1	10	11	24	7	0	1	1	4
92-93—Fredericton	AHL	61	10	17	27	83	—	—	—	—	—
—Tampa Bay	NHL	2	0	0	0	0	—	—	—	—	—
—Atlanta	IHL	8	1	0	1	0	1	0	0	0	0
93-94—Cornwall	AHL	67	10	34	44	80	11	0	2	2	11
—Quebec	NHL	6	0	0	0	4	—	—	—	—	—
NHL totals		119	2	18	20	124	11	0	2	2	26

COTE, SYLVAIN

D, CAPITALS

PERSONAL: Born January 19, 1966, in Quebec City.... 5-11/185.... Shoots right.... Name pronounced KOH-tay.... Brother of Alain Cote, defenseman, Quebec Nordiques.

TRANSACTIONS/CAREER NOTES: Selected by Hartford Whalers as underage junior in first round (first Whalers pick, 11th overall) of NHL entry draft (June 9, 1984).... Broke toe on left foot (October 28, 1989).... Sprained left knee (December 1989).... Fractured right foot (January 22, 1990).... Traded by Whalers to Washington Capitals for second-round pick (LW Andrei Nikolishin) in 1992 draft (September 8, 1991).... Broke wrist (September 25, 1992); missed six games.... Suffered hip pointer (January 7, 1993); missed one game.

HONORS: Named to QMJHL All-Star second team (1983-84).... Won Emile (Butch) Bouchard Trophy (1985-86).... Shared Guy Lafleur Trophy with Luc Robitaille (1985-86).... Named to QMJHL All-Star first team (1985-86).

Season Team	League	REGULAR SEASON					PLAYOFFS				
		Gms.	G	A	Pts.	PIM	Gms.	G	A	Pts.	PIM
82-83—Quebec	QMJHL	66	10	24	34	50	—	—	—	—	—
83-84—Quebec	QMJHL	66	15	50	65	89	5	1	1	2	0
84-85—Hartford	NHL	67	3	9	12	17	—	—	—	—	—
85-86—Hartford	NHL	2	0	0	0	0	—	—	—	—	—
—Hull	QMJHL	26	10	33	43	14	13	6	*28	34	22
86-87—Binghamton	AHL	12	2	4	6	0	—	—	—	—	—
—Hartford	NHL	67	2	8	10	20	2	0	2	2	2
87-88—Hartford	NHL	67	7	21	28	30	6	1	1	2	4
88-89—Hartford	NHL	78	8	9	17	49	3	0	1	1	4
89-90—Hartford	NHL	28	4	2	6	14	5	0	0	0	0

Season Team	League	REGULAR SEASON					PLAYOFFS				
		Gms.	G	A	Pts.	PIM	Gms.	G	A	Pts.	PIM
90-91—Hartford	NHL	73	7	12	19	17	6	0	2	2	2
91-92—Washington	NHL	78	11	29	40	31	7	1	2	3	4
92-93—Washington	NHL	77	21	29	50	34	6	1	1	2	4
93-94—Washington	NHL	84	16	35	51	66	9	1	8	9	6
NHL totals		621	79	154	233	278	44	4	17	21	26

COURTENAY, ED
RW, SHARKS

PERSONAL: Born February 2, 1968, in Verdun, Que. . . . 6-4/215. . . . Shoots right.
TRANSACTIONS/CAREER NOTES: Signed as free agent by Minnesota North Stars (October 1, 1989). . . . Selected by San Jose Sharks in NHL dispersal draft (May 30, 1991). . . . Injured wrist (October 18, 1991); missed four games. . . . Injured back prior to 1992-93 season; missed first two games of season. . . . Sprained shoulder (October 23, 1992); missed four games.

Season Team	League	REGULAR SEASON					PLAYOFFS				
		Gms.	G	A	Pts.	PIM	Gms.	G	A	Pts.	PIM
87-88—Granby	QMJHL	54	37	34	71	19	5	1	1	2	2
88-89—Granby	QMJHL	68	59	55	114	68	4	1	1	2	22
—Kalamazoo	IHL	1	0	0	0	0	1	0	0	0	2
89-90—Kalamazoo	IHL	57	25	28	53	16	3	0	0	0	0
90-91—Kalamazoo	IHL	76	35	36	71	37	8	2	3	5	12
91-92—Kansas City	IHL	36	14	12	26	46	15	8	9	17	15
—San Jose	NHL	5	0	0	0	0	—	—	—	—	—
92-93—San Jose	NHL	39	7	13	20	10	—	—	—	—	—
—Kansas City	IHL	32	15	11	26	25	—	—	—	—	—
93-94—Kansas City	IHL	62	27	21	48	60	—	—	—	—	—
NHL totals		44	7	13	20	10					

COURTNALL, GEOFF
LW, CANUCKS

PERSONAL: Born August 18, 1962, in Victoria, B.C. . . . 6-1/195. . . . Shoots left. . . . Brother of Russ Courtnall, right winger, Dallas Stars.
TRANSACTIONS/CAREER NOTES: Signed as free agent by Boston Bruins (September 1983). . . . Traded by Bruins with G Bill Ranford to Edmonton Oilers for G Andy Moog (March 8, 1988). . . . Traded by Oilers to Washington Capitals for C Greg Adams (July 22, 1988). . . . Traded by Capitals to St. Louis Blues for C Peter Zezel and D Mike Lalor (July 13, 1990). . . . Traded by Blues with D Robert Dirk, C Cliff Ronning, LW Sergio Momesso and fifth-round pick in 1992 draft (RW Brian Loney) to Vancouver Canucks for C Dan Quinn and D Garth Butcher (March 5, 1991). . . . Lacerated foot (February 28, 1992) and suffered from chronic fatigue (March 1992); missed nine games. . . . Suspended two games by NHL (November 14, 1993).
MISCELLANEOUS: Member of Stanley Cup championship team (1988).

Season Team	League	REGULAR SEASON					PLAYOFFS				
		Gms.	G	A	Pts.	PIM	Gms.	G	A	Pts.	PIM
80-81—Victoria	WHL	11	3	5	8	6	15	2	1	3	7
81-82—Victoria	WHL	72	35	57	92	100	4	1	0	1	2
83-84—Victoria	WHL	71	41	73	114	186	12	6	7	13	42
—Hershey	AHL	74	14	12	26	51	—	—	—	—	—
—Boston	NHL	5	0	0	0	0	—	—	—	—	—
84-85—Hershey	AHL	9	8	4	12	4	—	—	—	—	—
—Boston	NHL	64	12	16	28	82	5	0	2	2	7
85-86—Moncton	AHL	12	8	8	16	6	—	—	—	—	—
—Boston	NHL	64	21	16	37	61	3	0	0	0	2
86-87—Boston	NHL	65	13	23	36	117	1	0	0	0	0
87-88—Boston	NHL	62	32	26	58	108	—	—	—	—	—
—Edmonton	NHL	12	4	4	8	15	19	0	3	3	23
88-89—Washington	NHL	79	42	38	80	112	6	2	5	7	12
89-90—Washington	NHL	80	35	39	74	104	15	4	9	13	32
90-91—St. Louis	NHL	66	27	30	57	56	—	—	—	—	—
—Vancouver	NHL	11	6	2	8	8	6	3	5	8	4
91-92—Vancouver	NHL	70	23	34	57	116	12	6	8	14	20
92-93—Vancouver	NHL	84	31	46	77	167	12	4	10	14	12
93-94—Vancouver	NHL	82	26	44	70	123	24	9	10	19	51
NHL totals		744	272	318	590	1069	103	28	52	80	163

COURTNALL, RUSS
RW, STARS

PERSONAL: Born June 3, 1965, in Victoria, B.C. . . . 5-11/185. . . . Shoots right. . . . Brother of Geoff Courtnall, left winger, Vancouver Canucks.
TRANSACTIONS/CAREER NOTES: Selected by Toronto Maple Leafs as underage junior in first round (first Maple Leafs pick, seventh overall) of NHL entry draft (June 8, 1983). . . . Bruised knee (November 1987). . . . Suffered from virus (February 1988). . . . Suffered back spasms (March 1988). . . . Traded by Maple Leafs to Montreal Canadiens for RW John Kordic and sixth-round pick (RW Michael Doers) in 1989 draft (November 7, 1988). . . . Pulled muscle in right shoulder (October 8, 1991); missed 41 games. . . . Injured hand (January 15, 1992); missed 12 games. . . . Traded by Canadiens to Minnesota North Stars for LW Brian Bellows (August 31, 1992). . . . North Stars franchise moved from Minnesota to Dallas and renamed Stars for 1993-94 season.
HONORS: Played in NHL All-Star Game (1994).

Season Team	League	REGULAR SEASON					PLAYOFFS				
		Gms.	G	A	Pts.	PIM	Gms.	G	A	Pts.	PIM
82-83—Victoria	WHL	60	36	61	97	33	12	11	7	18	6
83-84—Victoria	WHL	32	29	37	66	63	—	—	—	—	—

Season	Team	League	REGULAR SEASON					PLAYOFFS				
			Gms.	G	A	Pts.	PIM	Gms.	G	A	Pts.	PIM
	—Canadian Olympic Team ..	Int'l	16	4	7	11	10	—	—	—	—	—
	—Toronto	NHL	14	3	9	12	6	—	—	—	—	—
84-85	—Toronto	NHL	69	12	10	22	44	—	—	—	—	—
85-86	—Toronto	NHL	73	22	38	60	52	10	3	6	9	8
86-87	—Toronto	NHL	79	29	44	73	90	13	3	4	7	11
87-88	—Toronto	NHL	65	23	26	49	47	6	2	1	3	0
88-89	—Toronto	NHL	9	1	1	2	4	—	—	—	—	—
	—Montreal	NHL	64	22	17	39	15	21	8	5	13	18
89-90	—Montreal	NHL	80	27	32	59	27	11	5	1	6	10
90-91	—Montreal	NHL	79	26	50	76	29	13	8	3	11	7
91-92	—Montreal	NHL	27	7	14	21	6	10	1	1	2	4
92-93	—Minnesota	NHL	84	36	43	79	49	—	—	—	—	—
93-94	—Dallas	NHL	84	23	57	80	59	9	1	8	9	0
NHL totals			727	231	341	572	428	93	31	29	60	58

COURVILLE, LARRY
LW, JETS

PERSONAL: Born April 2, 1975, in Timmins, Ont. . . . 6-1/180. . . . Shoots left.
HIGH SCHOOL: Huron Heights Secondary School (Newmarket, Ont.).
TRANSACTIONS/CAREER NOTES: Selected by Winnipeg Jets in fifth round (sixth Jets pick, 119th overall) of NHL entry draft (June 26, 1993).

Season	Team	League	REGULAR SEASON					PLAYOFFS				
			Gms.	G	A	Pts.	PIM	Gms.	G	A	Pts.	PIM
90-91	—Waterloo	USHL	48	20	18	38	144	—	—	—	—	—
91-92	—Cornwall	OHL	60	8	12	20	80	6	0	0	0	8
92-93	—Newmarket	OHL	64	21	18	39	181	7	0	6	6	14
93-94	—Newmarket	OHL	39	20	19	39	134	—	—	—	—	—
	—Moncton	AHL	8	2	0	2	37	10	2	2	4	27

COUSINEAU, MARCEL
G, BRUINS

PERSONAL: Born April 30, 1973, in Delson, Que. . . . 5-10/175. . . . Catches left. . . . Name pronounced KOO-sih-noh.
TRANSACTIONS/CAREER NOTES: Selected by Boston Bruins in third round (third Bruins pick, 62nd overall) of NHL entry draft (June 22, 1991).
HONORS: Named to QMJHL All-Rookie team (1990-91).

Season	Team	League	REGULAR SEASON							PLAYOFFS						
			Gms.	Min.	W	L	T	GA	SO	Avg.	Gms.	Min.	W	L	GA	SO	Avg.
90-91	—Beauport	QMJHL	49	2739	13	29	3	196	1	4.29	—	—	—	—	—	—	—
91-92	—Beauport	QMJHL	*67	*3673	26	*32	5	*241	0	3.94	—	—	—	—	—	—	—
92-93	—Drummondville	QMJHL	60	3298	20	32	2	225	0	4.09	9	498	3	6	37	1	4.46
93-94	—St. John's	AHL	37	2015	13	11	9	118	0	3.51	—	—	—	—	—	—	—

COUTURIER, SYLVAIN
C/LW, RED WINGS

PERSONAL: Born April 23, 1968, in Greenfield Park, Que. . . . 6-2/205. . . . Shoots left. . . . Name pronounced SIHL-vai koh-TOOR-ee-yay.
TRANSACTIONS/CAREER NOTES: Selected by Los Angeles Kings as underage junior in fourth round (third Kings pick, 65th overall) of NHL entry draft (June 21, 1986). . . . Broke jaw (October 1989). . . . Traded by Kings with D Paul Coffey and RW Jim Hiller to Detroit Red Wings for C Jimmy Carson, RW Marc Potvin and C Gary Shuchuk (January 29, 1993). . . . Loaned to Fort Wayne Komets (May 13, 1993).

Season	Team	League	REGULAR SEASON					PLAYOFFS				
			Gms.	G	A	Pts.	PIM	Gms.	G	A	Pts.	PIM
85-86	—Laval	QMJHL	68	21	37	58	64	14	1	7	8	28
86-87	—Laval	QMJHL	67	39	51	90	77	13	12	14	26	19
87-88	—Laval	QMJHL	67	70	67	137	115	—	—	—	—	—
88-89	—Los Angeles	NHL	16	1	3	4	2	—	—	—	—	—
	—New Haven	AHL	44	18	20	38	33	10	2	2	4	11
89-90	—New Haven	AHL	50	9	8	17	47	—	—	—	—	—
90-91	—Los Angeles	NHL	3	0	1	1	0	—	—	—	—	—
	—Phoenix	IHL	66	50	37	87	49	10	8	2	10	10
91-92	—Los Angeles	NHL	14	3	1	4	2	—	—	—	—	—
	—Phoenix	IHL	39	19	20	39	68	—	—	—	—	—
92-93	—Phoenix	IHL	38	23	16	39	63	—	—	—	—	—
	—Adirondack	AHL	29	17	17	34	12	11	3	5	8	10
	—Fort Wayne	IHL	—	—	—	—	—	4	2	3	5	2
93-94	—Milwaukee	IHL	80	41	51	92	123	4	1	2	3	2
NHL totals			33	4	5	9	4					

COWLEY, WAYNE
G, OILERS

PERSONAL: Born December 4, 1964, in Scarborough, Ont. . . . 6-0/185. . . . Catches left. . . . Full name: Wayne Robert Cowley.
COLLEGE: Colgate.
TRANSACTIONS/CAREER NOTES: Dislocated left shoulder (December 19, 1987). . . . Signed as free agent by Calgary Flames (May 1, 1988). . . . Signed as free agent by Cape Breton Oilers (March 4, 1992).
HONORS: Named to ECAC All-Star second team (1986-87). . . . Named to ECHL All-Star second team (1990-91).

Season	Team	League	Gms.	Min.	W	L	T	GA	SO	Avg.	Gms.	Min.	W	L	GA	SO	Avg.
				REGULAR SEASON								**PLAYOFFS**					
85-86	Colgate University	ECAC	7	313	2	2	0	23	1	4.41	—	—	—	—	—	—	—
86-87	Colgate University	ECAC	31	1805	21	8	1	106	0	3.52	—	—	—	—	—	—	—
87-88	Colgate University	ECAC	20	1162	11	7	1	58	0	2.99	—	—	—	—	—	—	—
88-89	Salt Lake City	IHL	29	1423	17	7	‡1	94	0	3.96	2	69	1	0	6	0	5.22
89-90	Salt Lake City	IHL	36	2009	15	12	‡5	124	1	3.70	3	118	0	0	6	0	3.05
90-91	Salt Lake City	IHL	7	377	3	4	‡0	23	1	3.66	—	—	—	—	—	—	—
	—Cincinnati	ECHL	30	1680	19	9	‡2	108	1	3.86	4	249	...	...	13	*1	3.13
91-92	Raleigh	ECHL	38	2213	16	18	‡2	137	1	3.71	—	—	—	—	—	—	—
	—Cape Breton	AHL	11	644	6	5	0	42	0	3.91	1	61	0	1	3	0	2.95
92-93	Cape Breton	AHL	42	2334	14	17	6	152	1	3.91	16	1014	*14	2	47	†1	2.78
	—Wheeling	ECHL	1	60	1	0	‡0	3	0	3.00	—	—	—	—	—	—	—
93-94	Cape Breton	AHL	44	2486	20	17	5	150	0	3.62	5	258	1	4	20	0	4.65
	—Edmonton	NHL	1	57	0	1	0	3	0	3.16	—	—	—	—	—	—	—
NHL totals			1	57	0	1	0	3	0	3.16	—	—	—	—	—	—	—

CRAIG, MIKE
RW, STARS

PERSONAL: Born June 6, 1971, in London, Ont.... 6-1/180.... Shoots right.
TRANSACTIONS/CAREER NOTES: Selected by Minnesota North Stars in second round (second North Stars pick, 28th overall) of NHL entry draft (June 17, 1989).... Broke fibula (January 28, 1990). ... Broke right wrist (February 4, 1991); missed 17 games.... Sprained knee (February 25, 1993); missed 12 games.... North Stars franchise moved from Minnesota to Dallas and renamed Stars for 1993-94 season.

Season	Team	League	Gms.	G	A	Pts.	PIM	Gms.	G	A	Pts.	PIM
				REGULAR SEASON					**PLAYOFFS**			
86-87	Woodstock Jr. C.	OHA	32	29	19	48	64	—	—	—	—	—
87-88	Oshawa	OHL	61	6	10	16	39	7	7	0	7	11
88-89	Oshawa	OHL	63	36	36	72	34	6	3	1	4	6
89-90	Oshawa	OHL	43	36	40	76	85	17	10	16	26	46
90-91	Minnesota	NHL	39	8	4	12	32	10	1	1	2	20
91-92	Minnesota	NHL	67	15	16	31	155	4	1	0	1	7
92-93	Minnesota	NHL	70	15	23	38	106	—	—	—	—	—
93-94	Dallas	NHL	72	13	24	37	139	4	0	0	0	2
NHL totals			248	51	67	118	432	18	2	1	3	29

CRAIGWELL, DALE
C, SHARKS

PERSONAL: Born April 24, 1971, in Toronto.... 5-10/180.... Shoots left.
COLLEGE: Toronto.
TRANSACTIONS/CAREER NOTES: Selected by San Jose Sharks in 10th round (11th Sharks pick, 199th overall) of NHL entry draft (June 22, 1991).... Strained back (October 1992); missed two games.... Strained back (November 1, 1992); missed 10 games.... Injured groin (November 18, 1993); missed three games.
HONORS: Won William Hanley Trophy (1990-91).

Season	Team	League	Gms.	G	A	Pts.	PIM	Gms.	G	A	Pts.	PIM
				REGULAR SEASON					**PLAYOFFS**			
88-89	Oshawa	OHL	55	9	14	23	15	6	0	0	0	0
89-90	Oshawa	OHL	64	22	41	63	39	17	7	7	14	11
90-91	Oshawa	OHL	56	27	68	95	34	16	7	16	23	9
91-92	Kansas City	IHL	48	6	19	25	29	12	4	7	11	4
	—San Jose	NHL	32	5	11	16	8	—	—	—	—	—
92-93	San Jose	NHL	8	3	1	4	4	—	—	—	—	—
	—Kansas City	IHL	60	15	38	53	24	12	†7	5	12	2
93-94	Kansas City	IHL	5	3	1	4	0	—	—	—	—	—
	—San Jose	NHL	58	3	6	9	16	—	—	—	—	—
NHL totals			98	11	18	29	28					

CRAVEN, MURRAY
C/LW, CANUCKS

PERSONAL: Born July 20, 1964, in Medicine Hat, Alta.... 6-2/185.... Shoots left.
TRANSACTIONS/CAREER NOTES: Selected by Detroit Red Wings as underage junior in first round (first Red Wings pick, 17th overall) of NHL entry draft (June 9, 1982).... Injured left knee cartilage (January 15, 1983).... Traded by Red Wings with LW/C Joe Paterson to Philadelphia Flyers for C Darryl Sittler (October 1984).... Broke foot (April 16, 1987).... Hyperextended right knee and lacerated eye (November 1988).... Bruised right foot (January 1989).... Fractured left wrist (February 24, 1989). ... Fractured right wrist (April 5, 1989).... Suffered back spasms (February 1990).... Injured rotator cuff (March 24, 1990).... Traded by Flyers with fourth-round pick in 1992 draft (LW Kevin Smyth) to Hartford Whalers for RW Kevin Dineen (November 13, 1991).... Injured groin (January 21, 1992).... Traded by Whalers with fifth-round pick in 1993 draft to Vancouver Canucks for LW Robert Kron, third-round pick in 1993 draft (D Marek Malik) and future considerations (March 22, 1993); Canucks sent RW Jim Sandlak to complete deal (May 17, 1993).... Injured hip (November 2, 1993); missed three games.... Strained groin (November 14, 1993); missed two games.

Season	Team	League	Gms.	G	A	Pts.	PIM	Gms.	G	A	Pts.	PIM
				REGULAR SEASON					**PLAYOFFS**			
80-81	Medicine Hat	WHL	69	5	10	15	18	5	0	0	0	2
81-82	Medicine Hat	WHL	72	35	46	81	49	—	—	—	—	—
82-83	Medicine Hat	WHL	28	17	29	46	35	—	—	—	—	—
	—Detroit	NHL	31	4	7	11	6	—	—	—	—	—

Season Team	League	REGULAR SEASON					PLAYOFFS				
		Gms.	G	A	Pts.	PIM	Gms.	G	A	Pts.	PIM
83-84—Medicine Hat	WHL	48	38	56	94	53	4	5	3	8	4
—Detroit	NHL	15	0	4	4	6	—	—	—	—	—
84-85—Philadelphia	NHL	80	26	35	61	30	19	4	6	10	11
85-86—Philadelphia	NHL	78	21	33	54	34	5	0	3	3	4
86-87—Philadelphia	NHL	77	19	30	49	38	12	3	1	4	9
87-88—Philadelphia	NHL	72	30	46	76	58	7	2	5	7	4
88-89—Philadelphia	NHL	51	9	28	37	52	1	0	0	0	0
89-90—Philadelphia	NHL	76	25	50	75	42	—	—	—	—	—
90-91—Philadelphia	NHL	77	19	47	66	53	—	—	—	—	—
91-92—Philadelphia	NHL	12	3	3	6	8	—	—	—	—	—
—Hartford	NHL	61	24	30	54	38	7	3	3	6	6
92-93—Hartford	NHL	67	25	42	67	20	—	—	—	—	—
—Vancouver	NHL	10	0	10	10	12	12	4	6	10	4
93-94—Vancouver	NHL	78	15	40	55	30	22	4	9	13	18
NHL totals		785	220	405	625	427	85	20	33	53	56

CREIGHTON, ADAM
C, LIGHTNING

PERSONAL: Born June 2, 1965, in Burlington, Ont. . . . 6-5/210. . . . Shoots left. . . . Son of Dave Creighton, center with four NHL teams (1948-49 through 1959-60). **TRANSACTIONS/CAREER NOTES:** Selected by Buffalo Sabres in first round (third Sabres pick, 11th overall) of NHL entry draft (June 8, 1983). . . . Underwent knee surgery (January 1988). . . . Sprained knee (September 1988). . . . Traded by Sabres to Chicago Blackhawks for RW Rick Vaive (December 2, 1988). . . . Suspended five games by NHL for stick-swinging incident in preseason game (September 30, 1990). . . . Sprained right hand (February 10, 1991). . . . Traded by Blackhawks with LW Steve Thomas to New York Islanders for C Brent Sutter and RW Brad Lauer (October 25, 1991). . . . Selected by Tampa Bay Lightning in NHL waiver draft (October 4, 1992). . . . Sprained right knee ligaments (October 7, 1993); missed 14 games. . . . Reinjured right knee (November 11, 1993); missed eight games. . . . Injured groin (December 19, 1993); missed three games.
HONORS: Won Stafford Smythe Memorial Cup (May 1984). . . . Named to Memorial Cup All-Star team (1983-84).

Season Team	League	REGULAR SEASON					PLAYOFFS				
		Gms.	G	A	Pts.	PIM	Gms.	G	A	Pts.	PIM
81-82—Ottawa	OHL	60	14	27	41	73	17	7	1	8	40
82-83—Ottawa	OHL	68	44	46	90	88	9	0	2	2	12
83-84—Ottawa	OHL	56	42	49	91	79	13	16	11	27	28
—Buffalo	NHL	7	2	2	4	4	—	—	—	—	—
84-85—Ottawa	OHL	10	4	14	18	23	5	6	2	8	11
—Rochester	AHL	6	5	3	8	2	5	2	1	3	20
—Buffalo	NHL	30	2	8	10	33	—	—	—	—	—
85-86—Rochester	AHL	32	17	21	38	27	—	—	—	—	—
—Buffalo	NHL	20	1	1	2	2	—	—	—	—	—
86-87—Buffalo	NHL	56	18	22	40	26	—	—	—	—	—
87-88—Buffalo	NHL	36	10	17	27	87	—	—	—	—	—
88-89—Buffalo	NHL	24	7	10	17	44	—	—	—	—	—
—Chicago	NHL	43	15	14	29	92	15	5	6	11	44
89-90—Chicago	NHL	80	34	36	70	224	20	3	6	9	59
90-91—Chicago	NHL	72	22	29	51	135	6	0	1	1	10
91-92—Chicago	NHL	11	6	6	12	16	—	—	—	—	—
—New York Islanders	NHL	66	15	9	24	102	—	—	—	—	—
92-93—Tampa Bay	NHL	83	19	20	39	110	—	—	—	—	—
93-94—Tampa Bay	NHL	53	10	10	20	37	—	—	—	—	—
NHL totals		581	161	184	345	912	41	8	13	21	113

CRONIN, SHAWN
D, SHARKS

PERSONAL: Born August 20, 1963, in Flushing, Mich. . . . 6-2/210. . . . Shoots left. . . . Full name: Shawn Patrick Cronin.
COLLEGE: Illinois-Chicago.
TRANSACTIONS/CAREER NOTES: Signed as free agent by Hartford Whalers (March 1986). . . . Signed as free agent by Washington Capitals (June 6, 1988). . . . Signed as free agent by Philadelphia Flyers (June 13, 1989). . . . Traded by Flyers to Winnipeg Jets for future considerations (July 21, 1989); future considerations later canceled. . . . Bruised hand (February 1990). . . . Bruised foot (October 27, 1991); missed three games. . . . Injured ribs (December 23, 1991). . . . Traded by Jets to Quebec Nordiques for D Danny Lambert (August 25, 1992). . . . Selected by Flyers in NHL waiver draft (October 4, 1992). . . . Sprained left knee (April 12, 1993); missed remainder of season. . . . Traded by Flyers to San Jose Sharks for future considerations (August 5, 1993). . . . Sprained knee (January 17, 1994); missed 12 games. . . . Suffered split finger (March 24, 1994); missed three games.

Season Team	League	REGULAR SEASON					PLAYOFFS				
		Gms.	G	A	Pts.	PIM	Gms.	G	A	Pts.	PIM
82-83—Illinois-Chicago	CCHA	36	1	5	6	52	—	—	—	—	—
83-84—Illinois-Chicago	CCHA	32	0	4	4	41	—	—	—	—	—
84-85—Illinois-Chicago	CCHA	31	2	6	8	52	—	—	—	—	—
85-86—Illinois-Chicago	CCHA	38	3	8	11	70	—	—	—	—	—
86-87—Binghamton	AHL	12	0	1	1	60	10	0	0	0	41
—Salt Lake City	IHL	53	8	16	24	118	—	—	—	—	—
87-88—Binghamton	AHL	66	3	8	11	212	4	0	0	0	15
88-89—Washington	NHL	1	0	0	0	0	—	—	—	—	—
—Baltimore	AHL	75	3	9	12	267	—	—	—	—	—

Season Team	League	Gms.	G	A	Pts.	PIM	Gms.	G	A	Pts.	PIM
89-90—Winnipeg	NHL	61	0	4	4	243	5	0	0	0	7
90-91—Winnipeg	NHL	67	1	5	6	189	—	—	—	—	—
91-92—Winnipeg	NHL	65	0	4	4	271	4	0	0	0	6
92-93—Philadelphia	NHL	35	2	1	3	37	—	—	—	—	—
—Hershey	AHL	7	0	1	1	12	—	—	—	—	—
93-94—San Jose	NHL	34	0	2	2	76	14	1	0	1	20
NHL totals		263	3	16	19	816	23	1	0	1	33

CROSS, CORY
D, LIGHTNING

PERSONAL: Born January 3, 1971, in Prince Albert, Sask. . . . 6-5/215. . . . Shoots left. . . . Full name: Cory James Cross.
HIGH SCHOOL: Lloydminister (Alta.) Comprehensive.
COLLEGE: Alberta.
TRANSACTIONS/CAREER NOTES: Selected by Tampa Bay Lightning in NHL supplemental draft (June 19, 1992).
HONORS: Named to CWUAA All-Star second team (1992-93).

Season Team	League	Gms.	G	A	Pts.	PIM	Gms.	G	A	Pts.	PIM
90-91—University of Alberta	CWUAA	20	2	5	7	16	—	—	—	—	—
91-92—University of Alberta	CWUAA	39	3	10	13	76	—	—	—	—	—
92-93—Atlanta	IHL	7	0	1	1	2	4	0	0	0	6
93-94—Atlanta	IHL	70	4	14	18	72	9	1	2	3	14
—Tampa Bay	NHL	5	0	0	0	6	—	—	—	—	—
NHL totals		5	0	0	0	6					

CROSSMAN, DOUG
D

PERSONAL: Born June 30, 1960, in Peterborough, Ont. . . . 6-2/190. . . . Shoots left.
TRANSACTIONS/CAREER NOTES: Selected by Chicago Blackhawks as underage junior in sixth round (sixth Blackhawks pick, 112th overall) of NHL entry draft (August 9, 1979). . . . Injured thumb (February 1983). . . . Traded by Blackhawks with second-round pick in 1984 draft (RW Scott Mellanby) to Philadelphia Flyers for D Behn Wilson (June 8, 1983). . . . Traded by Flyers to Los Angeles Kings for D Jay Wells (September 29, 1988). . . . Traded by Kings to New York Islanders (May 23, 1989) to complete deal in which Islanders sent G Kelly Hrudey to Kings for G Mark Fitzpatrick, D Wayne McBean and future considerations (February 22, 1989). . . . Injured foot (November 6, 1990). . . . Traded by Islanders to Hartford Whalers for C Ray Ferraro (November 13, 1990). . . . Injured leg (February 12, 1991). . . . Traded by Whalers to Detroit Red Wings for D Doug Houda (February 20, 1991). . . . Traded by Red Wings with D Dennis Vial to Quebec Nordiques for cash (June 15, 1992). . . . Selected by Tampa Bay Lightning in NHL expansion draft (June 18, 1992). . . . Traded by Lightning with LW Basil McRae to St. Louis Blues for LW Jason Ruff, sixth-round pick in 1996 draft and third-round pick in 1995 draft (January 28, 1993). . . . Injured toe (December 29, 1993); missed one game. . . . Injured knee (January 13, 1994); missed one game.
HONORS: Named to OMJHL All-Star first team (1979-80).

Season Team	League	Gms.	G	A	Pts.	PIM	Gms.	G	A	Pts.	PIM
76-77—London	OMJHL	1	0	0	0	0	—	—	—	—	—
77-78—Ottawa	OMJHL	65	4	17	21	17	—	—	—	—	—
78-79—Ottawa	OMJHL	67	12	51	63	63	4	1	3	4	0
79-80—Ottawa	OMJHL	66	20	96	116	48	11	7	6	13	19
80-81—Chicago	NHL	9	0	2	2	2	—	—	—	—	—
—New Brunswick	AHL	70	13	43	56	90	13	5	6	11	36
81-82—Chicago	NHL	70	12	28	40	24	11	0	3	3	4
82-83—Chicago	NHL	80	13	40	53	46	13	3	7	10	6
83-84—Philadelphia	NHL	78	7	28	35	63	3	0	0	0	0
84-85—Philadelphia	NHL	80	4	33	37	65	19	4	6	10	38
85-86—Philadelphia	NHL	80	6	37	43	55	5	0	1	1	4
86-87—Philadelphia	NHL	78	9	31	40	29	26	4	14	18	31
87-88—Philadelphia	NHL	76	9	29	38	43	7	1	1	2	8
88-89—New Haven	AHL	3	0	0	0	0	—	—	—	—	—
—Los Angeles	NHL	74	10	15	25	53	2	0	1	1	2
89-90—New York Islanders	NHL	80	15	44	59	54	5	0	1	1	6
90-91—New York Islanders	NHL	16	1	6	7	12	—	—	—	—	—
—Hartford	NHL	41	4	19	23	19	—	—	—	—	—
—Detroit	NHL	17	3	4	7	17	6	0	5	5	6
91-92—Detroit	NHL	26	0	8	8	14	—	—	—	—	—
92-93—Tampa Bay	NHL	40	8	21	29	18	—	—	—	—	—
—St. Louis	NHL	19	2	7	9	10	—	—	—	—	—
93-94—St. Louis	NHL	50	2	7	9	10	—	—	—	—	—
—Peoria	IHL	8	3	5	8	0	—	—	—	—	—
NHL totals		914	105	359	464	534	97	12	39	51	105

CROWE, PHIL
LW, KINGS

PERSONAL: Born April 14, 1970, in Red Deer, Alta. . . . 6-2/220. . . . Shoots left.
TRANSACTIONS/CAREER NOTES: Signed as free agent by Phoenix Roadrunners (1993).

Season Team	League	Gms.	G	A	Pts.	PIM	Gms.	G	A	Pts.	PIM
93-94—Fort Wayne	IHL	5	0	1	1	26	—	—	—	—	—

— 379 —

Season	Team	League	REGULAR SEASON					PLAYOFFS				
			Gms.	G	A	Pts.	PIM	Gms.	G	A	Pts.	PIM
	—Phoenix	IHL	2	0	0	0	0	—	—	—	—	—
	—Los Angeles	NHL	31	0	2	2	77	—	—	—	—	—
NHL totals			31	0	2	2	77					

CROWLEY, TED

D, WHALERS

PERSONAL: Born May 3, 1970, in Concord, Mass. . . . 6-2/190. . . . Shoots right.
COLLEGE: Boston College.
TRANSACTIONS/CAREER NOTES: Selected by Toronto Maple Leafs in fourth round (fourth Maple Leafs pick, 69th overall) of NHL entry draft (June 11, 1988). . . . Traded by Maple Leafs to Hartford Whalers for LW Mark Greig and sixth-round pick in 1995 draft (January 25, 1994).

Season	Team	League	REGULAR SEASON					PLAYOFFS				
			Gms.	G	A	Pts.	PIM	Gms.	G	A	Pts.	PIM
89-90	—Boston College	Hockey East	39	7	24	31	34	—	—	—	—	—
90-91	—Boston College	Hockey East	39	12	24	36	61	—	—	—	—	—
91-92	—U.S. national team	Int'l	42	6	7	13	65	—	—	—	—	—
	—St. John's	AHL	29	5	4	9	33	10	3	1	4	11
92-93	—St. John's	AHL	79	19	38	57	41	9	2	2	4	4
93-94	—U.S. national team	Int'l	48	9	13	22	80	—	—	—	—	—
	—U.S. Olympic Team	Int'l	8	0	2	2	8	—	—	—	—	—
	—Hartford	NHL	21	1	2	3	10	—	—	—	—	—
NHL totals			21	1	2	3	10					

CROZIER, GREG

LW, PENGUINS

PERSONAL: Born July 6, 1976, in Williamsville, N.Y. . . . 6-4/200. . . . Shoots left. . . . Son of Joe Crozier, scout, Buffalo Sabres.
HIGH SCHOOL: Lawrence Academy (Groton, Mass.).
TRANSACTIONS/CAREER NOTES: Selected by Pittsburgh Penguins in third round (fourth Penguins pick, 73rd overall) of NHL entry draft (June 29, 1994).

Season	Team	League	REGULAR SEASON					PLAYOFFS				
			Gms.	G	A	Pts.	PIM	Gms.	G	A	Pts.	PIM
90-91	—Amherst	Mass. H.S.	41	52	34	86	...	—	—	—	—	—
91-92	—Amherst	Mass. H.S.	46	61	47	108	47	—	—	—	—	—
92-93	—Lawrence Academy	Mass. H.S.	21	22	13	35	9	—	—	—	—	—
93-94	—Lawrence Academy	Mass. H.S.	18	22	26	48	10	—	—	—	—	—

CULLEN, JOHN

C

PERSONAL: Born August 2, 1964, in Puslinch, Ont. . . . 5-10/187. . . . Shoots right. . . . Full name: Barry John Cullen. . . . Son of Barry Cullen, right winger, Toronto Maple Leafs and Detroit Red Wings (1955-56 through 1959-64).
COLLEGE: Boston University.
TRANSACTIONS/CAREER NOTES: Selected by Buffalo Sabres in NHL supplemental draft (September 17, 1986). . . . Signed as free agent by Pittsburgh Penguins (July 1988). . . . Suffered from hepatitis (October 1989); missed seven games. . . . Pulled stomach muscle (November 17, 1990). . . . Traded by Penguins with D Zarley Zalapski and RW Jeff Parker to Whalers for C Ron Francis, D Ulf Samuelsson and D Grant Jennings (March 4, 1991). . . . Missed first three games of 1991-92 season due to contract dispute. . . . Traded by Whalers to Toronto Maple Leafs for second-round pick in 1993 or 1994 draft (November 24, 1992). . . . Suffered herniated disc in neck (March 2, 1993); missed 16 games. . . . Sprained ankle (January 26, 1994); missed 21 games.
HONORS: Named ECAC Rookie of the Year (1983-84). . . . Named to Hockey East All-Star first team (1984-85 and 1985-86). . . . Named to NCAA All-America East second team (1985-86). . . . Named to Hockey East All-Star second team (1986-87). . . . Won James Gatschene Memorial Trophy (1987-88). . . . Won Leo P. Lamoureux Memorial Trophy (1987-88). . . . Shared Garry F. Longman Memorial Trophy with Ed Belfour (1987-88). . . . Named to IHL All-Star first team (1987-88). . . . Played in NHL All-Star Game (1991 and 1992).

Season	Team	League	REGULAR SEASON					PLAYOFFS				
			Gms.	G	A	Pts.	PIM	Gms.	G	A	Pts.	PIM
83-84	—Boston University	ECAC	40	23	33	56	28	—	—	—	—	—
84-85	—Boston University	Hockey East	41	27	32	59	46	—	—	—	—	—
85-86	—Boston University	Hockey East	43	25	49	74	54	—	—	—	—	—
86-87	—Boston University	Hockey East	36	23	29	52	35	—	—	—	—	—
87-88	—Flint	IHL	81	48	*109	*157	113	16	11	†15	26	16
88-89	—Pittsburgh	NHL	79	12	37	49	112	11	3	6	9	28
89-90	—Pittsburgh	NHL	72	32	60	92	138	—	—	—	—	—
90-91	—Pittsburgh	NHL	65	31	63	94	83	—	—	—	—	—
	—Hartford	NHL	13	8	8	16	18	6	2	7	9	10
91-92	—Hartford	NHL	77	26	51	77	141	7	2	1	3	12
92-93	—Hartford	NHL	19	5	4	9	58	—	—	—	—	—
	—Toronto	NHL	47	13	28	41	53	12	2	3	5	0
93-94	—Toronto	NHL	53	13	17	30	67	3	0	0	0	0
NHL totals			425	140	268	408	670	39	9	17	26	50

CULLIMORE, JASSEN

D, CANUCKS

PERSONAL: Born December 4, 1972, in Simcoe, Ont. . . . 6-5/225. . . . Shoots left. . . . Name pronounced KUHL-ih-MOHR.
TRANSACTIONS/CAREER NOTES: Selected by Vancouver Canucks in second round (second Canucks pick, 29th overall) of NHL entry draft (June 22, 1991).
HONORS: Named to OHL All-Star second team (1991-92).

Season Team	League	REGULAR SEASON					PLAYOFFS				
		Gms.	G	A	Pts.	PIM	Gms.	G	A	Pts.	PIM
88-89—Peterborough	OHL	20	2	1	3	6	—	—	—	—	—
89-90—Peterborough	OHL	59	2	6	8	61	11	0	2	2	8
90-91—Peterborough	OHL	62	8	16	24	74	4	1	0	1	7
91-92—Peterborough	OHL	54	9	37	46	65	10	3	6	9	8
92-93—Hamilton	AHL	56	5	7	12	60	—	—	—	—	—
93-94—Hamilton	AHL	71	8	20	28	86	3	0	1	1	2

CUMMINS, JIM
LW, LIGHTNING

PERSONAL: Born May 17, 1970, in Dearborn, Mich. . . . 6-2/205. . . . Shoots right. . . . Full name: James Stephen Cummins.
COLLEGE: Michigan State.
TRANSACTIONS/CAREER NOTES: Selected by New York Rangers in fourth round (fifth Rangers pick, 67th overall) of NHL entry draft (June 17, 1989). . . . Traded by Rangers with C Kevin Miller and D Dennis Vial to Detroit Red Wings for RW Joe Kocur and D Per Djoos (March 5, 1991). . . . Suspended 11 games by NHL for leaving penalty box to join fight (January 23, 1993). . . . Traded by Red Wings with fourth-round pick in 1993 draft (traded to Boston who selected D Charles Paquette) to Philadelphia Flyers for rights to C Greg Johnson and future considerations (June 20, 1993). . . . Suffered slightly separated shoulder. . . . Traded by Flyers with fourth-round pick in 1995 draft to Tampa Bay Lightning for C Rob DiMaio (March 18, 1994).

Season Team	League	REGULAR SEASON					PLAYOFFS				
		Gms.	G	A	Pts.	PIM	Gms.	G	A	Pts.	PIM
87-88—Detroit Compuware	NAJHL	31	11	15	26	146	—	—	—	—	—
88-89—Michigan State	CCHA	36	3	9	12	100	—	—	—	—	—
89-90—Michigan State	CCHA	41	8	7	15	94	—	—	—	—	—
90-91—Michigan State	CCHA	34	9	6	15	110	—	—	—	—	—
91-92—Adirondack	AHL	65	7	13	20	338	5	0	0	0	19
—Detroit	NHL	1	0	0	0	7	—	—	—	—	—
92-93—Adirondack	AHL	43	16	4	20	179	9	3	1	4	4
—Detroit	NHL	7	1	1	2	58	—	—	—	—	—
93-94—Philadelphia	NHL	22	1	2	3	71	—	—	—	—	—
—Hershey	AHL	17	6	6	12	70	—	—	—	—	—
—Atlanta	IHL	7	4	5	9	14	13	1	2	3	90
—Tampa Bay	NHL	4	0	0	0	13	—	—	—	—	—
NHL totals		34	2	3	5	149					

CUNNEYWORTH, RANDY
LW, SENATORS

PERSONAL: Born May 10, 1961, in Etobicoke, Ont. . . . 6-0/180. . . . Shoots left. . . . Full name: Randolph William Cunneyworth.
TRANSACTIONS/CAREER NOTES: Selected by Buffalo Sabres as underage junior in eighth round (ninth Sabres pick, 167th overall) of NHL entry draft (June 11, 1980). . . . Attended Pittsburgh Penguins training camp as unsigned free agent (summer 1985); Sabres then traded his equalization rights with RW Mike Moller to Penguins for future considerations (October 4, 1985); Penguins sent RW Pat Hughes to Sabres to complete deal (October 1985). . . . Suspended three games by NHL (January 1988). . . . Suspended five games by NHL (January 1988). . . . Fractured right foot (January 24, 1989). . . . Traded by Penguins with G Richard Tabaracci and RW Dave McLlwain to Winnipeg Jets for RW Andrew McBain, D Jim Kyte and LW Randy Gilhen (June 17, 1989). . . . Broke bone in right foot (October 1989). . . . Traded by Jets to Hartford Whalers for C Paul MacDermid (December 13, 1989). . . . Broke tibia bone in left leg (November 28, 1990); missed 38 games. . . . Strained lower back (December 1991); missed one game. . . . Strained ankle (December 21, 1991); missed two games. . . . Strained left ankle (January 16, 1992); missed three games. . . . Reinjured ankle (February 1, 1992); missed six games. . . . Bruised ribs (November 15, 1992); missed four games. . . . Suffered neck spasms (December 31, 1992); missed three games. . . . Traded by Hartford with D Gary Suter and undisclosed draft pick to Chicago Blackhawks for D Frantisek Kucera and LW Jocelyn Lemieux (March 11, 1994). . . . Signed as free agent by Ottawa Senators (June 30, 1994).

Season Team	League	REGULAR SEASON					PLAYOFFS				
		Gms.	G	A	Pts.	PIM	Gms.	G	A	Pts.	PIM
79-80—Ottawa	OMJHL	63	16	25	41	145	11	0	1	1	13
80-81—Ottawa	OMJHL	67	54	74	128	240	15	5	8	13	35
—Rochester	AHL	1	0	1	1	2	—	—	—	—	—
—Buffalo	NHL	1	0	0	0	2	—	—	—	—	—
81-82—Rochester	AHL	57	12	15	27	86	9	4	0	4	30
—Buffalo	NHL	20	2	4	6	47	—	—	—	—	—
82-83—Rochester	AHL	78	23	33	56	111	16	4	4	8	35
83-84—Rochester	AHL	54	18	17	35	85	17	5	5	10	55
84-85—Rochester	AHL	72	30	38	68	148	5	2	1	3	16
85-86—Pittsburgh	NHL	75	15	30	45	74	—	—	—	—	—
86-87—Pittsburgh	NHL	79	26	27	53	142	—	—	—	—	—
87-88—Pittsburgh	NHL	71	35	39	74	141	—	—	—	—	—
88-89—Pittsburgh	NHL	70	25	19	44	156	11	3	5	8	26
89-90—Winnipeg	NHL	28	5	6	11	34	—	—	—	—	—
—Hartford	NHL	43	9	9	18	41	4	0	0	0	2
90-91—Springfield	AHL	2	0	0	0	5	—	—	—	—	—
—Hartford	NHL	32	9	5	14	49	1	0	0	0	0
91-92—Hartford	NHL	39	7	10	17	71	7	3	0	3	9
92-93—Hartford	NHL	39	5	4	9	63	—	—	—	—	—
93-94—Hartford	NHL	63	9	8	17	87	—	—	—	—	—
—Chicago	NHL	16	4	3	7	13	6	0	0	0	8
NHL totals		576	151	164	315	920	29	6	5	11	45

C

CURRAN, BRIAN

D

PERSONAL: Born November 5, 1963, in Toronto.... 6-4/220.... Shoots left.
TRANSACTIONS/CAREER NOTES: Underwent appendectomy (November 1981).... Selected by Boston Bruins as underage junior in second round (second Bruins pick, 22nd overall) of NHL entry draft (June 9, 1982).... Broke ankle (September 1982).... Bruised thigh (November 1984).... Broke leg (February 1, 1986).... Signed as free agent by New York Islanders (August 1986); Bruins awarded D Paul Boutilier as compensation.... Fractured jaw (January 12, 1988).... Traded by Islanders to Toronto Maple Leafs for sixth-round pick (RW Pavel Gross) in 1988 draft (March 1988).... Pulled pelvic muscle (November 1988).... Bruised spine (December 1, 1988).... Dislocated right wrist (February 25, 1989).... Bruised left wrist (November 1990).... Traded by Maple Leafs with LW Lou Franceschetti to Buffalo Sabres for RW Mike Foligno and eighth-round pick (C Thomas Kucharcik) in 1991 draft (December 17, 1990).... Injured shoulder (December 28, 1990); missed four games.... Signed as free agent by Edmonton Oilers (October 27, 1992).... Signed as free agent by Portland Pirates (July 1993).

			REGULAR SEASON					PLAYOFFS				
Season Team	League	Gms.	G	A	Pts.	PIM	Gms.	G	A	Pts.	PIM
80-81—Portland	WHL	51	2	16	18	132	14	1	7	8	63
81-82—Portland	WHL	59	2	28	30	275	7	0	1	1	13
82-83—Portland	WHL	56	1	30	31	187	14	1	3	4	57
83-84—Hershey	AHL	23	0	2	2	94	—	—	—	—	—
—Boston	NHL	16	1	1	2	57	3	0	0	0	7
84-85—Hershey	AHL	4	0	0	0	19	—	—	—	—	—
—Boston	NHL	56	0	1	1	158	—	—	—	—	—
85-86—Boston	NHL	43	2	5	7	192	2	0	0	0	4
86-87—New York Islanders	NHL	68	0	10	10	356	8	0	0	0	51
87-88—Springfield	AHL	8	1	0	1	43	—	—	—	—	—
—New York Islanders	NHL	22	0	1	1	68	—	—	—	—	—
—Toronto	NHL	7	0	1	1	19	6	0	0	0	41
88-89—Toronto	NHL	47	1	4	5	185	—	—	—	—	—
89-90—Toronto	NHL	72	2	9	11	301	5	0	1	1	19
90-91—Toronto	NHL	4	0	0	0	7	—	—	—	—	—
—Buffalo	NHL	17	0	1	1	43	—	—	—	—	—
—Newmarket	AHL	6	0	1	1	32	—	—	—	—	—
—Rochester	AHL	10	0	0	0	36	—	—	—	—	—
91-92—Buffalo	NHL	3	0	0	0	14	—	—	—	—	—
—Rochester	AHL	36	0	3	3	122	—	—	—	—	—
92-93—Cape Breton	AHL	61	2	24	26	223	12	0	3	3	12
93-94—Portland	AHL	46	1	6	7	247	15	0	1	1	59
—Washington	NHL	26	1	0	1	61	—	—	—	—	—
NHL totals		381	7	33	40	1461	24	0	1	1	122

CURRIE, DAN

LW, KINGS

PERSONAL: Born March 15, 1968, in Burlington, Ont.... 6-2/195.... Shoots left.... Full name: Daniel Robert Currie.
TRANSACTIONS/CAREER NOTES: Selected by Edmonton Oilers as underage junior in fourth round (fourth Oilers pick, 84th overall) of NHL entry draft (June 21, 1986).... Signed as free agent by Phoenix Roadrunners (July 16, 1993).
HONORS: Named to OHL All-Star first team (1987-88).... Named to AHL All-Star second team (1991-92).... Named to AHL All-Star first team (1992-93).

			REGULAR SEASON					PLAYOFFS				
Season Team	League	Gms.	G	A	Pts.	PIM	Gms.	G	A	Pts.	PIM
85-86—Sault Ste. Marie	OHL	66	21	22	43	37	—	—	—	—	—
86-87—Sault Ste. Marie	OHL	66	31	52	83	53	4	2	1	3	2
87-88—Sault Ste. Marie	OHL	57	50	59	109	53	6	3	9	12	4
—Nova Scotia	AHL	3	4	2	6	0	5	4	3	7	0
88-89—Cape Breton	AHL	77	29	36	65	29	—	—	—	—	—
89-90—Cape Breton	AHL	77	36	40	76	28	—	—	—	—	—
90-91—Cape Breton	AHL	71	47	45	92	51	4	3	1	4	8
—Edmonton	NHL	5	0	0	0	0	—	—	—	—	—
91-92—Cape Breton	AHL	66	*50	42	92	39	5	4	5	9	4
—Edmonton	NHL	7	1	0	1	0	—	—	—	—	—
92-93—Cape Breton	AHL	75	57	41	98	73	16	7	4	11	31
—Edmonton	NHL	5	0	0	0	4	—	—	—	—	—
93-94—Los Angeles	NHL	5	1	1	2	0	—	—	—	—	—
—Phoenix	IHL	74	37	49	86	96	—	—	—	—	—
NHL totals		22	2	1	3	4					

CZERKAWSKI, MARIUSZ

RW, BRUINS

PERSONAL: Born April 13, 1972, in Radomski, Poland.... 5-11/185.... Shoots right.... Name pronounced chehr-KAWV-skee.
TRANSACTIONS/CAREER NOTES: Selected by Boston Bruins (fifth Bruins pick, 106th overall) of NHL entry draft (June 22, 1991).

			REGULAR SEASON					PLAYOFFS				
Season Team	League	Gms.	G	A	Pts.	PIM	Gms.	G	A	Pts.	PIM
90-91—GKS Tychy	Poland	24	25	15	40	...	—	—	—	—	—
91-92—Djurgarden	Sweden	39	8	5	13	4	3	0	0	0	2
—Polish Olympic Team	Int'l	5	0	1	1	4	—	—	—	—	—
92-93—Hammarby	Swed. Dv.II	32	39	30	69	74	—	—	—	—	—

Season Team	League	Gms.	G	A	Pts.	PIM	Gms.	G	A	Pts.	PIM
93-94—Djurgarden	Sweden	39	13	21	34	20	—	—	—	—	—
—Boston	NHL	4	2	1	3	0	13	3	3	6	4
NHL totals		4	2	1	3	0	13	3	3	6	4

DAFOE, BYRON
G, CAPITALS

PERSONAL: Born February 25, 1971, in Duncan, B.C. . . . 5-11/175. . . . Catches left. . . . Full name: Byron Jaromir Dafoe.
TRANSACTIONS/CAREER NOTES: Selected by Washington Capitals in second round (second Capitals pick, 35th overall) of NHL entry draft (June 17, 1989). . . . Underwent emergency appendectomy (December 1989).
HONORS: Shared Harry (Hap) Holmes Memorial Trophy with Olaf Kolzig (1993-94). . . . Named to AHL All-Star first team (1993-94).

Season Team	League	Gms.	Min.	W	L	T	GA	SO	Avg.	Gms.	Min.	W	L	GA	SO	Avg.
87-88—Juan de Fuca	BCJHL	32	1716	...	...	...	129	0	4.51	—	—	—	—	—	—	—
88-89—Portland	WHL	59	3279	29	24	3	*291	1	5.32	*18	*1091	10	8	*81	*1	4.45
89-90—Portland	WHL	40	2265	14	21	3	193	0	5.11	—	—	—	—	—	—	—
90-91—Portland	WHL	8	414	1	5	1	41	0	5.94	—	—	—	—	—	—	—
—Prince Albert	WHL	32	1839	13	12	4	124	0	4.05	—	—	—	—	—	—	—
91-92—New Haven	AHL	7	364	3	2	1	22	0	3.63	—	—	—	—	—	—	—
—Baltimore	AHL	33	1847	12	16	4	119	0	3.87	—	—	—	—	—	—	—
—Hampton Roads	ECHL	10	562	6	4	‡0	26	1	2.78	—	—	—	—	—	—	—
92-93—Baltimore	AHL	48	2617	16	*20	7	191	1	4.38	5	241	2	3	22	0	5.48
—Washington	NHL	1	1	0	0	0	0	0	0.00	—	—	—	—	—	—	—
93-94—Portland	AHL	47	2662	24	16	4	148	1	3.34	1	9	0	0	1	0	6.67
—Washington	NHL	5	230	2	2	0	13	0	3.39	2	118	0	2	5	0	2.54
NHL totals		6	231	2	2	0	13	0	3.38	2	118	0	2	5	0	2.54

DAGENAIS, MIKE
D, PENGUINS

PERSONAL: Born July 22, 1969, in Ottawa. . . . 6-3/200. . . . Shoots left. . . . Name pronounced DA-zhuh-NAY.
TRANSACTIONS/CAREER NOTES: Selected by Chicago Blackhawks in third round (fourth Blackhawks pick, 60th overall) of NHL entry draft (June 13, 1987). . . . Traded by Blackhawks to Quebec Nordiques for D Ryan McGill (September 26, 1991). . . . Signed as free agent by Pittsburgh Penguins (August 26, 1993).

Season Team	League	Gms.	G	A	Pts.	PIM	Gms.	G	A	Pts.	PIM
85-86—Peterborough	OHL	45	1	3	4	40	—	—	—	—	—
86-87—Peterborough	OHL	56	1	17	18	66	12	4	1	5	20
87-88—Peterborough	OHL	66	11	23	34	125	12	1	1	2	31
88-89—Peterborough	OHL	62	14	23	37	122	13	3	3	6	12
89-90—Peterborough	OHL	44	14	26	40	74	12	4	1	5	18
90-91—Indianapolis	IHL	76	13	14	27	115	4	0	0	0	4
91-92—Halifax	AHL	69	11	21	32	143	—	—	—	—	—
92-93—Cincinnati	IHL	69	14	22	36	128	—	—	—	—	—
93-94—Cleveland	IHL	65	8	18	26	120	—	—	—	—	—

DAHL, KEVIN
D, FLAMES

PERSONAL: Born December 30, 1968, in Regina, Sask. . . . 5-11/190. . . . Shoots right.
COLLEGE: Bowling Green State.
TRANSACTIONS/CAREER NOTES: Selected by Montreal Canadiens in 11th round (12th Canadiens pick, 230th overall) of NHL entry draft (June 11, 1988). . . . Signed as free agent by Calgary Flames (August 1, 1991). . . . Suffered charley horse (November 2, 1992); missed two games. . . . Injured heel (November 28, 1992); missed one game. . . . Strained left knee (December 15, 1992); missed 18 games. . . . Fractured left foot (April 9, 1993); missed one game. . . . Separated left shoulder (November 6, 1993); missed nine games. . . . Strained left shoulder (December 7, 1993); missed 30 games.

Season Team	League	Gms.	G	A	Pts.	PIM	Gms.	G	A	Pts.	PIM
87-88—Bowling Green State	CCHA	44	2	23	25	78	—	—	—	—	—
88-89—Bowling Green State	CCHA	46	9	26	35	51	—	—	—	—	—
89-90—Bowling Green State	CCHA	43	8	22	30	74	—	—	—	—	—
90-91—Fredericton	AHL	32	1	15	16	45	9	0	1	1	11
—Winston-Salem	ECHL	36	7	17	24	58	—	—	—	—	—
91-92—Canadian national team	Int'l	45	2	15	17	44	—	—	—	—	—
—Canadian Olympic Team	Int'l	8	2	0	2	6	—	—	—	—	—
—Salt Lake City	IHL	13	0	2	2	12	5	0	0	0	13
92-93—Calgary	NHL	61	2	9	11	56	6	0	2	2	8
93-94—Calgary	NHL	33	0	3	3	23	6	0	0	0	4
—Saint John	AHL	2	0	0	0	0	—	—	—	—	—
NHL totals		94	2	12	14	79	12	0	2	2	12

DAHLEN, ULF
LW, SHARKS

PERSONAL: Born January 12, 1967, in Ostersund, Sweden. . . . 6-2/195. . . . Shoots right. . . . Name pronounced DAH-lihn.
TRANSACTIONS/CAREER NOTES: Selected by New York Rangers in first round (first Rangers pick, seventh overall) of NHL entry draft (June 15, 1985). . . . Bruised shin (November 1987). . . .

CD

Bruised left shoulder (November 1988).... Separated right shoulder (January 1989).... Traded by Rangers with fourth-round pick in 1990 draft (C Cal McGowan) and future considerations to Minnesota North Stars for RW Mike Gartner (March 6, 1990).... North Stars franchise moved from Minnesota to Dallas and renamed Stars for 1993-94 season.... Traded by Stars with future considerations to San Jose Sharks for D Mike Lalor and D Doug Zmolek (March 19, 1994).

			REGULAR SEASON					PLAYOFFS			
Season Team	League	Gms.	G	A	Pts.	PIM	Gms.	G	A	Pts.	PIM
83-84—Ostersund	Sweden	36	15	11	26	10	—	—	—	—	—
84-85—Ostersund	Sweden	36	33	26	59	20	—	—	—	—	—
85-86—Bjorkloven	Sweden	22	4	3	7	8	—	—	—	—	—
86-87—Bjorkloven	Sweden	31	9	12	21	20	6	6	2	8	4
87-88—New York Rangers	NHL	70	29	23	52	26	—	—	—	—	—
—Colorado	IHL	2	2	2	4	0	—	—	—	—	—
88-89—New York Rangers	NHL	56	24	19	43	50	4	0	0	0	0
89-90—New York Rangers	NHL	63	18	18	36	30	—	—	—	—	—
—Minnesota	NHL	13	2	4	6	0	7	1	4	5	2
90-91—Minnesota	NHL	66	21	18	39	6	15	2	6	8	4
91-92—Minnesota	NHL	79	36	30	66	10	7	0	3	3	2
92-93—Minnesota	NHL	83	35	39	74	6	—	—	—	—	—
93-94—Dallas	NHL	65	19	38	57	10	—	—	—	—	—
—San Jose	NHL	13	6	6	12	0	14	6	2	8	0
NHL totals		508	190	195	385	138	47	9	15	24	8

DAHLQUIST, CHRIS
D, SENATORS

PERSONAL: Born December 14, 1962, in Fridley, Minn.... 6-1/195.... Shoots left. ... Name pronounced DAHL-KWIHST.
COLLEGE: Lake Superior State (Mich.).
TRANSACTIONS/CAREER NOTES: Signed as free agent by Pittsburgh Penguins (May 1985).... Traded by Penguins with Jim Johnson to Minnesota North Stars for D Peter Taglianetti and D Larry Murphy (December 11, 1990).... Broke left wrist (January 1991).... Selected by Calgary Flames in NHL waiver draft (October 4, 1992). ... Bruised ribs (November 11, 1992); missed five games.... Suffered charley horse (February 26, 1993); missed two games. ... Signed as free agent by Ottawa Senators (July 4, 1994).

			REGULAR SEASON					PLAYOFFS			
Season Team	League	Gms.	G	A	Pts.	PIM	Gms.	G	A	Pts.	PIM
81-82—Lake Superior State	CCHA	39	4	10	14	18	—	—	—	—	—
82-83—Lake Superior State	CCHA	35	0	12	12	63	—	—	—	—	—
83-84—Lake Superior State	CCHA	40	4	19	23	76	—	—	—	—	—
84-85—Lake Superior State	CCHA	44	4	15	19	112	—	—	—	—	—
85-86—Baltimore	AHL	65	4	21	25	64	—	—	—	—	—
—Pittsburgh	NHL	5	1	2	3	2	—	—	—	—	—
86-87—Baltimore	AHL	51	1	16	17	50	—	—	—	—	—
—Pittsburgh	NHL	19	0	1	1	20	—	—	—	—	—
87-88—Pittsburgh	NHL	44	3	6	9	69	—	—	—	—	—
88-89—Pittsburgh	NHL	43	1	5	6	42	2	0	0	0	0
—Muskegon	IHL	10	3	6	9	14	—	—	—	—	—
89-90—Muskegon	IHL	6	1	1	2	8	—	—	—	—	—
—Pittsburgh	NHL	62	4	10	14	56	—	—	—	—	—
90-91—Pittsburgh	NHL	22	1	2	3	30	—	—	—	—	—
—Minnesota	NHL	42	2	6	8	33	23	1	6	7	20
91-92—Minnesota	NHL	74	1	13	14	68	7	0	0	0	6
92-93—Calgary	NHL	74	3	7	10	66	6	3	1	4	4
93-94—Calgary	NHL	77	1	11	12	52	1	0	0	0	0
NHL totals		462	17	63	80	438	39	4	7	11	30

DAIGLE, ALEXANDRE
C, SENATORS

PERSONAL: Born February 7, 1975, in Montreal.... 6-0/185.... Shoots left.... Name pronounced DAYG.
TRANSACTIONS/CAREER NOTES: Selected by Ottawa Senators in first round (first Senators pick, first overall) of NHL entry draft (June 26, 1993).
HONORS: Won Can.HL Rookie of the Year Award (1991-92).... Named QMJHL Rookie of the Year (1991-92).... Named to Can.HL All-Rookie team (1991-92).... Won Michel Bergeron Trophy (1991-92).... Named to the QMJHL All-Star second team (1991-92).... Won Can.HL Top Draft Prospect Award (1992-93).... Won QMJHL Top Draft Prospect Award (1992-93).... Named to QMJHL All-Star first team (1992-93).

			REGULAR SEASON					PLAYOFFS			
Season Team	League	Gms.	G	A	Pts.	PIM	Gms.	G	A	Pts.	PIM
91-92—Victoriaville	QMJHL	66	35	75	110	63	—	—	—	—	—
92-93—Victoriaville	QMJHL	53	45	92	137	85	6	5	6	11	4
93-94—Ottawa	NHL	84	20	31	51	40	—	—	—	—	—
NHL totals		84	20	31	51	40					

DAIGNEAULT, J.J.
D, CANADIENS

PERSONAL: Born October 12, 1965, in Montreal. ... 5-11/199. ... Shoots left. ... Name pronounced DAYN-yoh.
TRANSACTIONS/CAREER NOTES: Underwent knee surgery (March 1984).... Selected by Vancouver Canucks as underage junior in first round (first Canucks pick, 10th overall) of NHL entry draft (June 1984).... Broke finger (March 19, 1986).... Traded by Canucks with second-round pick in 1986 draft (C Kent Hawley) and fifth-round pick in 1987 draft to Philadelphia Flyers for RW Rich Sutter, D Dave Richter and

third-round pick (D Don Gibson) in 1986 draft (June 1986).... Sprained ankle (April 12, 1987).... Traded by Flyers to Montreal Canadiens for D Scott Sandelin (November 1988).... Bruised shoulder (December 1990).... Suffered left hip pointer (March 16, 1991).... Injured knee (April 7, 1991).... Bruised left knee (November 28, 1992); missed one game.... Injured shoulder (December 23, 1992); missed two games.... Sprained right ankle (March 1, 1993); missed 11 games.... Suffered injury (December 22, 1993); missed one game.... Suspended three games and fined $500 by NHL for elbowing (January 7, 1994).... Sprained wrist (January 10, 1994); missed six games.... Suffered sore back (March 1, 1994); missed one game.

HONORS: Won Emile (Butch) Bouchard Trophy (1982-83).... Named to QMJHL All-Star first team (1982-83).

MISCELLANEOUS: Member of Stanley Cup championship team (1993).

			REGULAR SEASON					PLAYOFFS				
Season	Team	League	Gms.	G	A	Pts.	PIM	Gms.	G	A	Pts.	PIM
81-82	Laval	QMJHL	64	4	25	29	41	18	1	3	4	2
82-83	Longueuil	QMJHL	70	26	58	84	58	15	4	11	15	35
83-84	Canadian Olympic Team	Int'l	62	6	15	21	40	—	—	—	—	—
	Longueuil	QMJHL	10	2	11	13	6	14	3	13	16	30
84-85	Vancouver	NHL	67	4	23	27	69	—	—	—	—	—
85-86	Vancouver	NHL	64	5	23	28	45	3	0	2	2	0
86-87	Philadelphia	NHL	77	6	16	22	56	9	1	0	1	0
87-88	Philadelphia	NHL	28	2	2	4	12	—	—	—	—	—
	Hershey	AHL	10	1	5	6	8	—	—	—	—	—
88-89	Hershey	AHL	12	0	10	10	13	—	—	—	—	—
	Sherbrooke	AHL	63	10	33	43	48	6	1	3	4	2
89-90	Sherbrooke	AHL	28	8	19	27	18	—	—	—	—	—
	Montreal	NHL	36	2	10	12	14	9	0	0	0	2
90-91	Montreal	NHL	51	3	16	19	31	5	0	1	1	0
91-92	Montreal	NHL	79	4	14	18	36	11	0	3	3	4
92-93	Montreal	NHL	66	8	10	18	57	20	1	3	4	22
93-94	Montreal	NHL	68	2	12	14	73	7	0	1	1	12
NHL totals			536	36	126	162	393	64	2	10	12	40

DALGARNO, BRAD
RW, ISLANDERS

PERSONAL: Born August 8, 1967, in Vancouver.... 6-4/215.... Shoots right.

TRANSACTIONS/CAREER NOTES: Selected by New York Islanders as underage junior in first round (first Islanders pick, sixth overall) of NHL entry draft (June 15, 1985).... Suffered concussion (November 1988).... Fractured orbital bone of left eye (February 21, 1989).... Sat out season in retirement (1989-90).... Bruised kidney (December 9, 1990); missed four games.... Lacerated jaw (January 13, 1991); missed three games.... Sprained left shoulder (November 27, 1991); missed four games.... Reinjured left shoulder (December 11, 1991); missed seven games.... Fractured left wrist (January 12, 1992); missed final 37 games of season.... Underwent shoulder surgery (April 1, 1992).... Bruised shoulder (February 3, 1993); missed one game.... Strained hip flexor (November 9, 1993); missed 10 games.

			REGULAR SEASON					PLAYOFFS				
Season	Team	League	Gms.	G	A	Pts.	PIM	Gms.	G	A	Pts.	PIM
83-84	Markham	MTHL	40	17	11	28	59	—	—	—	—	—
84-85	Hamilton	OHL	66	23	30	53	86	—	—	—	—	—
85-86	Hamilton	OHL	54	22	43	65	79	—	—	—	—	—
	New York Islanders	NHL	2	1	0	1	0	—	—	—	—	—
86-87	Hamilton	OHL	60	27	32	59	100	—	—	—	—	—
	New York Islanders	NHL	—	—	—	—	—	1	0	1	1	0
87-88	New York Islanders	NHL	38	2	8	10	58	4	0	0	0	19
	Springfield	AHL	39	13	11	24	76	—	—	—	—	—
88-89	New York Islanders	NHL	55	11	10	21	86	—	—	—	—	—
89-90	—					Did not play—retired.						
90-91	New York Islanders	NHL	41	3	12	15	24	—	—	—	—	—
	Capital District	AHL	27	6	14	20	26	—	—	—	—	—
91-92	Capital District	AHL	14	7	8	15	34	—	—	—	—	—
	New York Islanders	NHL	15	2	1	3	12	—	—	—	—	—
92-93	Capital District	AHL	19	10	4	14	16	—	—	—	—	—
	New York Islanders	NHL	57	15	17	32	62	18	2	2	4	14
93-94	New York Islanders	NHL	73	11	19	30	62	4	0	1	1	4
NHL totals			281	45	67	112	304	27	2	4	6	37

DAMPHOUSSE, VINCENT
LW, CANADIENS

PERSONAL: Born December 17, 1967, in Montreal.... 6-1/199.... Shoots left.... Name pronounced dahm-FOOZ.

TRANSACTIONS/CAREER NOTES: Selected by Toronto Maple Leafs as underage junior in first round (first Maple Leafs pick, sixth overall) of NHL entry draft (June 21, 1986).... Traded by Maple Leafs with D Luke Richardson, G Peter Ing, C Scott Thornton and future considerations to Edmonton Oilers for G Grant Fuhr, LW/RW Glenn Anderson and LW Craig Berube (September 19, 1991).... Traded by Oilers with fourth-round pick in 1993 draft (D Adam Wiesel) to Montreal Canadiens for LW Shayne Corson, LW Vladimir Vutek and C Brent Gilchrist (August 27, 1992).

HONORS: Named to QMJHL All-Star second team (1985-86).... Played in NHL All-Star Game (1991 and 1992).... Named All-Star Game Most Valuable Player (1991).

RECORDS: Shares NHL All-Star single-game record for most goals—4 (1991).

MISCELLANEOUS: Member of Stanley Cup championship team (1993).

			REGULAR SEASON					PLAYOFFS				
Season	Team	League	Gms.	G	A	Pts.	PIM	Gms.	G	A	Pts.	PIM
83-84	Laval	QMJHL	66	29	36	65	25	—	—	—	—	—
84-85	Laval	QMJHL	68	35	68	103	62	—	—	—	—	—

Season	Team	League	Gms.	G	A	Pts.	PIM	Gms.	G	A	Pts.	PIM
			REGULAR SEASON					PLAYOFFS				
85-86	Laval	QMJHL	69	45	110	155	70	14	9	27	36	12
86-87	Toronto	NHL	80	21	25	46	26	12	1	5	6	8
87-88	Toronto	NHL	75	12	36	48	40	6	0	1	1	10
88-89	Toronto	NHL	80	26	42	68	75	—	—	—	—	—
89-90	Toronto	NHL	80	33	61	94	56	5	0	2	2	2
90-91	Toronto	NHL	79	26	47	73	65	—	—	—	—	—
91-92	Edmonton	NHL	80	38	51	89	53	16	6	8	14	8
92-93	Montreal	NHL	84	39	58	97	98	20	11	12	23	16
93-94	Montreal	NHL	84	40	51	91	75	7	1	2	3	8
	NHL totals		642	235	371	606	488	66	19	30	49	52

DANDENAULT, MATHIEU
RW, RED WINGS

PERSONAL: Born February 3, 1976, in Magog, Que. . . . 6-0/174. . . . Shoots right. . . . Name pronounced Dan-dehn-OH. . . . Cousin of Eric Dandenault, defenseman in Philadelphia Flyers system.
HIGH SCHOOL: CEGEP de Sherbrooke (Que.).

TRANSACTIONS/CAREER NOTES: Selected by Detroit Red Wings in second round (second Red Wings pick, 49th overall) of NHL entry draft (June 28, 1994).

Season	Team	League	Gms.	G	A	Pts.	PIM	Gms.	G	A	Pts.	PIM
			REGULAR SEASON					PLAYOFFS				
91-92	Gloucester	OPJHL	6	3	4	7	0	—	—	—	—	—
92-93	Gloucester	OPJHL	55	11	26	37	64	—	—	—	—	—
93-94	Sherbrooke	QMJHL	67	17	36	53	67	12	4	10	14	12

DANEYKO, KEN
D, DEVILS

PERSONAL: Born April 17, 1964, in Windsor, Ont. . . . 6-0/210. . . . Shoots left. . . . Name pronounced DAN-ee-LOH.
TRANSACTIONS/CAREER NOTES: Selected by Seattle Breakers from Spokane Flyers in WHL dispersal draft (December 1981). . . . Selected by New Jersey Devils as underage junior in first round (second Devils pick, 18th overall) of NHL entry draft (June 1982). . . . Fractured right fibula (November 2, 1983). . . . Suspended one game and fined $500 by NHL for playing in West Germany without permission (October 1985). . . . Injured wrist (February 25, 1987). . . . Broke nose (February 24, 1988). . . . Injured shoulder (March 29, 1994); missed six games.

Season	Team	League	Gms.	G	A	Pts.	PIM	Gms.	G	A	Pts.	PIM
			REGULAR SEASON					PLAYOFFS				
80-81	Spokane Flyers	WHL	62	6	13	19	140	4	0	0	0	6
81-82	Spokane Flyers	WHL	26	1	11	12	147	—	—	—	—	—
	Seattle	WHL	38	1	22	23	151	14	1	9	10	49
82-83	Seattle	WHL	69	17	43	60	150	4	1	3	4	14
83-84	Kamloops	WHL	19	6	28	34	52	17	4	9	13	28
	New Jersey	NHL	11	1	4	5	17	—	—	—	—	—
84-85	New Jersey	NHL	1	0	0	0	10	—	—	—	—	—
	Maine	AHL	80	4	9	13	206	11	1	3	4	36
85-86	Maine	AHL	21	3	2	5	75	—	—	—	—	—
	New Jersey	NHL	44	0	10	10	100	—	—	—	—	—
86-87	New Jersey	NHL	79	2	12	14	183	—	—	—	—	—
87-88	New Jersey	NHL	80	5	7	12	239	20	1	6	7	83
88-89	New Jersey	NHL	80	5	5	10	283	—	—	—	—	—
89-90	New Jersey	NHL	74	6	15	21	216	6	2	0	2	21
90-91	New Jersey	NHL	80	4	16	20	249	7	0	1	1	10
91-92	New Jersey	NHL	80	1	7	8	170	7	0	3	3	16
92-93	New Jersey	NHL	84	2	11	13	236	5	0	0	0	8
93-94	New Jersey	NHL	78	1	9	10	176	20	0	1	1	45
	NHL totals		691	27	96	123	1879	65	3	11	14	183

DANIELS, JEFF
LW, PANTHERS

PERSONAL: Born June 24, 1968, in Oshawa, Ont. . . . 6-1/200. . . . Shoots left.
TRANSACTIONS/CAREER NOTES: Selected by Pittsburgh Penguins as underage junior in sixth round (sixth Penguins pick, 109th overall) of NHL entry draft (June 21, 1986). . . . Traded by Penguins to Florida Panthers for D Greg Hawgood (March 19, 1994).
MISCELLANEOUS: Member of Stanley Cup championship team (1992).

Season	Team	League	Gms.	G	A	Pts.	PIM	Gms.	G	A	Pts.	PIM
			REGULAR SEASON					PLAYOFFS				
84-85	Oshawa	OHL	59	7	11	18	16	—	—	—	—	—
85-86	Oshawa	OHL	62	13	19	32	23	6	0	1	1	0
86-87	Oshawa	OHL	54	14	9	23	22	15	3	2	5	5
87-88	Oshawa	OHL	64	29	39	68	59	4	2	3	5	0
88-89	Muskegon	IHL	58	21	21	42	58	11	3	5	8	11
89-90	Muskegon	IHL	80	30	47	77	39	6	1	1	2	7
90-91	Pittsburgh	NHL	11	0	2	2	2	—	—	—	—	—
	Muskegon	IHL	62	23	29	52	18	5	1	3	4	2
91-92	Pittsburgh	NHL	2	0	0	0	0	—	—	—	—	—
	Muskegon	IHL	44	19	16	35	38	10	5	4	9	9
92-93	Pittsburgh	NHL	58	5	4	9	14	12	3	2	5	0
	Cleveland	IHL	3	2	1	3	0	—	—	—	—	—

Season	Team	League	REGULAR SEASON					PLAYOFFS				
			Gms.	G	A	Pts.	PIM	Gms.	G	A	Pts.	PIM
93-94—Pittsburgh		NHL	63	3	5	8	20	—	—	—	—	—
—Florida		NHL	7	0	0	0	0	—	—	—	—	—
NHL totals			141	8	11	19	36	12	3	2	5	0

DANIELS, SCOTT
LW, WHALERS

PERSONAL: Born September 19, 1969, in Prince Albert, Sask. . . . 6-3/200. . . . Shoots left.
TRANSACTIONS/CAREER NOTES: Selected by Hartford Whalers in seventh round (sixth Whalers pick, 136th overall) of NHL entry draft (June 17, 1989).

Season	Team	League	REGULAR SEASON					PLAYOFFS				
			Gms.	G	A	Pts.	PIM	Gms.	G	A	Pts.	PIM
86-87—Kamloops		WHL	43	6	4	10	68	—	—	—	—	—
—New Westminster		WHL	19	4	7	11	30	—	—	—	—	—
87-88—New Westminster		WHL	37	6	11	17	157	—	—	—	—	—
—Regina		WHL	19	2	3	5	83	—	—	—	—	—
88-89—Regina		WHL	64	21	26	47	241	—	—	—	—	—
89-90—Regina		WHL	52	28	31	59	171	—	—	—	—	—
90-91—Springfield		AHL	40	2	6	8	121	—	—	—	—	—
—Louisville		ECHL	9	5	3	8	34	1	0	2	2	0
91-92—Springfield		AHL	54	7	15	22	213	10	0	0	0	32
92-93—Hartford		NHL	1	0	0	0	19	—	—	—	—	—
—Springfield		AHL	60	11	12	23	181	12	2	7	9	12
93-94—Springfield		AHL	52	9	11	20	185	6	0	1	1	53
NHL totals			1	0	0	0	19					

DARBY, CRAIG
C, CANADIENS

PERSONAL: Born September 26, 1972, in Oneida, N.Y. . . . 6-3/180. . . . Shoots right.
HIGH SCHOOL: Albany (N.Y.) Academy.
COLLEGE: Providence.
TRANSACTIONS/CAREER NOTES: Selected by Montreal Canadiens in second round (third Canadiens pick, 43rd overall) of NHL entry draft (June 22, 1991).
HONORS: Named Hockey East co-Rookie of the Year with Ian Moran (1991-92). . . . Named to Hockey East All-Rookie team (1991-92).

Season	Team	League	REGULAR SEASON					PLAYOFFS				
			Gms.	G	A	Pts.	PIM	Gms.	G	A	Pts.	PIM
89-90—Albany Academy		N.Y. H.S.	29	32	53	85	...	—	—	—	—	—
90-91—Albany Academy		N.Y. H.S.	...	33	61	94	...	—	—	—	—	—
91-92—Providence College		Hockey East	35	17	24	41	47	—	—	—	—	—
92-93—Providence College		Hockey East	35	11	21	32	62	—	—	—	—	—
93-94—Fredericton		AHL	66	23	33	56	51	—	—	—	—	—

DAVIDSSON, JOHAN
C, MIGHTY DUCKS

PERSONAL: Born January 6, 1976, in Jonkoping, Sweden. . . . 5-11/170. . . . Shoots left.
TRANSACTIONS/CAREER NOTES: Selected by Mighty Ducks of Anaheim in second round (second Mighty Ducks pick, 28th overall) of NHL entry draft (June 28, 1994).

Season	Team	League	REGULAR SEASON					PLAYOFFS				
			Gms.	G	A	Pts.	PIM	Gms.	G	A	Pts.	PIM
92-93—HV 71 Jonkoping		Sweden	8	1	0	1	0	—	—	—	—	—
93-94—HV 71 Jonkoping		Sweden	38	2	5	7	4	—	—	—	—	—

DAVYDOV, EVGENY
LW, SENATORS

PERSONAL: Born May 27, 1967, in Chelyabinsk, U.S.S.R. . . . 6-0/200. . . . Shoots right. . . . Name pronounced yehv-GEH-nee DAY-vuh-dahf.
TRANSACTIONS/CAREER NOTES: Selected by Winnipeg Jets in 12th round (14th Jets pick, 235th overall) of NHL entry draft (June 17, 1989). . . . Traded by Jets with future draft pick to Florida Panthers for future draft pick (September 30, 1993). . . . Suffered from the flu (November 10, 1993); missed one game. . . . Suffered from the flu (December 27, 1993); missed one game. . . . Traded by Panthers with C Scott Levins and sixth-round pick in 1994 draft (D Mike Gaffney) to Ottawa Senators for RW Bob Kudelski (January 6, 1994). . . . Injured wrist (April 14, 1994); missed one game.
MISCELLANEOUS: Member of gold-medal-winning Unified Olympic team (1992).

Season	Team	League	REGULAR SEASON					PLAYOFFS				
			Gms.	G	A	Pts.	PIM	Gms.	G	A	Pts.	PIM
84-85—Chelyabinsk		USSR	5	1	0	1	2	—	—	—	—	—
85-86—Chelyabinsk		USSR	39	11	5	16	22	—	—	—	—	—
86-87—CSKA Moscow		USSR	32	11	2	13	8	—	—	—	—	—
87-88—CSKA Moscow		USSR	44	16	7	23	18	—	—	—	—	—
88-89—CSKA Moscow		USSR	35	9	7	16	4	—	—	—	—	—
89-90—CSKA Moscow		USSR	44	17	6	23	16	—	—	—	—	—
90-91—CSKA Moscow		USSR	44	10	10	20	26	—	—	—	—	—
91-92—CSKA Moscow		CIS	27	13	12	25	14	—	—	—	—	—
—Unified Olympic Team		Int'l	8	3	3	6	2	—	—	—	—	—
—Winnipeg		NHL	12	4	3	7	8	7	2	2	4	2

Season Team	League	REGULAR SEASON					PLAYOFFS				
		Gms.	G	A	Pts.	PIM	Gms.	G	A	Pts.	PIM
92-93—Winnipeg	NHL	79	28	21	49	66	4	0	0	0	0
93-94—Florida	NHL	21	2	6	8	8	—	—	—	—	—
—Ottawa	NHL	40	5	7	12	38	—	—	—	—	—
NHL totals		152	39	37	76	120	11	2	2	4	2

DAWE, JASON
RW, SABRES

PERSONAL: Born May 29, 1973, in North York, Ont. . . . 5-10/195. . . . Shoots left. . . . Name pronounced DAW.
TRANSACTIONS/CAREER NOTES: Tore ankle ligaments (September 1989). . . . Selected by Buffalo Sabres in second round (second Sabres pick, 35th overall) of NHL entry draft (June 22, 1991).
HONORS: Won George Parsons Trophy (1992-93). . . . Named to Can.HL All-Star second team (1992-93). . . . Named to OHL All-Star first team (1992-93).

Season Team	League	REGULAR SEASON					PLAYOFFS				
		Gms.	G	A	Pts.	PIM	Gms.	G	A	Pts.	PIM
89-90—Peterborough	OHL	50	15	18	33	19	12	4	7	11	4
90-91—Peterborough	OHL	66	43	27	70	43	4	3	1	4	0
91-92—Peterborough	OHL	66	53	55	108	55	4	5	0	5	0
92-93—Peterborough	OHL	59	58	68	126	80	21	18	33	51	18
—Rochester	AHL	0	0	0	0	0	3	1	0	1	0
93-94—Rochester	AHL	48	22	14	36	44	—	—	—	—	—
—Buffalo	NHL	32	6	7	13	12	6	0	1	1	6
NHL totals		32	6	7	13	12	6	0	1	1	6

DAY, JOE
C

PERSONAL: Born May 11, 1968, in Chicago. . . . 5-11/180. . . . Shoots left. . . . Full name: Joseph Christopher Day.
COLLEGE: St. Lawrence (N.Y.).
TRANSACTIONS/CAREER NOTES: Selected by Hartford Whalers in ninth round (eighth Whalers pick, 186th overall) of NHL entry draft (June 13, 1987). . . . Fractured right foot (April 4, 1992); missed playoffs. . . . Signed as free agent by New York Islanders (August 24, 1993). . . . Signed as free agent by Detroit Vipers (July 18, 1994).
HONORS: Named to ECAC All-Star second team (1989-90).

Season Team	League	REGULAR SEASON					PLAYOFFS				
		Gms.	G	A	Pts.	PIM	Gms.	G	A	Pts.	PIM
85-86—Chicago Minor Hawks	Ill.	30	23	18	41	69	—	—	—	—	—
86-87—St. Lawrence University	ECAC	33	9	11	20	25	—	—	—	—	—
87-88—St. Lawrence University	ECAC	33	23	17	40	40	—	—	—	—	—
88-89—St. Lawrence University	ECAC	36	21	27	48	44	—	—	—	—	—
89-90—St. Lawrence University	ECAC	30	18	26	44	24	—	—	—	—	—
90-91—Springfield	AHL	75	24	29	53	82	18	5	5	10	27
91-92—Springfield	AHL	50	33	25	58	92	—	—	—	—	—
—Hartford	NHL	24	0	3	3	10	—	—	—	—	—
92-93—Springfield	AHL	33	15	20	35	118	15	0	8	8	40
—Hartford	NHL	24	1	7	8	47	—	—	—	—	—
93-94—Salt Lake City	IHL	33	16	10	26	153	—	—	—	—	—
—New York Islanders	NHL	24	0	0	0	30	—	—	—	—	—
NHL totals		72	1	10	11	87					

DAZE, ERIC
LW, BLACKHAWKS

PERSONAL: Born July 2, 1975, in Montreal. . . . 6-4/202. . . . Shoots left.
TRANSACTIONS/CAREER NOTES: Selected by Chicago Blackhawks in fourth round (fifth Blackhawks pick, 90th overall) of NHL entry draft (June 26, 1993).
HONORS: Named to QMJHL All-Star first team (1993-94).

Season Team	League	REGULAR SEASON					PLAYOFFS				
		Gms.	G	A	Pts.	PIM	Gms.	G	A	Pts.	PIM
92-93—Beauport	QMJHL	68	19	36	55	24	—	—	—	—	—
93-94—Beauport	QMJHL	66	59	48	107	31	15	16	8	24	2

DEADMARSH, ADAM
RW, NORDIQUES

PERSONAL: Born May 10, 1975, in Trail, B.C. . . . 6-0/195. . . . Shoots right.
HIGH SCHOOL: Lakeridge (Fruitvale, B.C.).
TRANSACTIONS/CAREER NOTES: Selected by Quebec Nordiques in first round (second Nordiques pick, 14th overall) of NHL entry draft (June 26, 1993).

Season Team	League	REGULAR SEASON					PLAYOFFS				
		Gms.	G	A	Pts.	PIM	Gms.	G	A	Pts.	PIM
91-92—Portland	WHL	68	30	30	60	81	6	3	3	6	13
92-93—Portland	WHL	58	33	36	69	126	16	7	8	15	29
93-94—Portland	WHL	65	43	56	99	212	10	9	8	17	33

DeBRUSK, LOUIE
LW, OILERS

PERSONAL: Born March 19, 1971, in Cambridge, Ont. . . . 6-2/215. . . . Shoots left. . . . Full name: Dennis Louis DeBrusk. . . . Name pronounced duh-BRUHSK.
HIGH SCHOOL: Saugeen (Port Elgin, Ont.).
TRANSACTIONS/CAREER NOTES: Selected by New York Rangers in third round (fourth Rangers pick, 49th overall) of NHL entry draft (June 17, 1989). . . . Traded by Rangers with C Bernie Nicholls, RW Steven Rice

and future considerations to Edmonton Oilers for C Mark Messier and future considerations (October 4, 1991); Rangers traded D David Shaw to Oilers for D Jeff Beukeboom to complete the deal (November 12, 1991).... Separated shoulder (January 28, 1992); missed four games.... Strained groin (January 1993); missed five games.... Strained abdominal muscle (January 1993); missed 11 games.

Season	Team	League	REGULAR SEASON					PLAYOFFS				
			Gms.	G	A	Pts.	PIM	Gms.	G	A	Pts.	PIM
87-88	Stratford Jr. B	OHA	43	13	14	27	205	—	—	—	—	—
88-89	London	OHL	59	11	11	22	149	19	1	1	2	43
89-90	London	OHL	61	21	19	40	198	6	2	2	4	24
90-91	London	OHL	61	31	33	64	*223	7	2	2	4	14
	Binghamton	AHL	2	0	0	0	7	2	0	0	0	9
91-92	Edmonton	NHL	25	2	1	3	124	—	—	—	—	—
	Cape Breton	AHL	28	2	2	4	73	—	—	—	—	—
92-93	Edmonton	NHL	51	8	2	10	205	—	—	—	—	—
93-94	Edmonton	NHL	48	4	6	10	185	—	—	—	—	—
	Cape Breton	AHL	5	3	1	4	58	—	—	—	—	—
NHL totals			124	14	9	23	514					

DeGRAY, DALE

D

PERSONAL: Born September 3, 1963, in Oshawa, Ont. ... 6-0/206. ... Shoots right. ... Full name: Dale Edward DeGray.

TRANSACTIONS/CAREER NOTES: Selected by Calgary Flames as underage junior in eighth round (seventh Flames pick, 162nd overall) of NHL entry draft (June 10, 1981). ... Traded by Flames to Toronto Maple Leafs for future considerations (September 1987). ... Separated left shoulder (January 1988); missed 15 games. ... Selected by Los Angeles Kings in 1988 NHL waiver draft for $12,500 (October 3, 1988). ... Sprained knee (October 1988). ... Suffered concussion (December 1988). ... Traded by Kings to Buffalo Sabres for D Bob Halkidis (November 24, 1989). ... Signed as free agent by San Diego Gulls (August 27, 1992).

HONORS: Named to AHL All-Star second team (1984-85). ... Named to IHL All-Star second team (1992-93).

Season	Team	League	REGULAR SEASON					PLAYOFFS				
			Gms.	G	A	Pts.	PIM	Gms.	G	A	Pts.	PIM
79-80	Oshawa Jr. B	ODHA	42	14	14	28	34	—	—	—	—	—
	Oshawa	OMJHL	1	0	0	0	2	—	—	—	—	—
80-81	Oshawa	OMJHL	61	11	10	21	93	8	1	1	2	19
81-82	Oshawa	OHL	66	11	22	33	162	12	3	4	7	49
82-83	Oshawa	OHL	69	20	30	50	149	17	7	7	14	36
83-84	Colorado	CHL	67	16	14	30	67	6	1	1	2	2
84-85	Moncton	AHL	77	24	37	61	63	—	—	—	—	—
85-86	Moncton	AHL	76	10	31	41	128	6	0	1	1	0
	Calgary	NHL	1	0	0	0	0	—	—	—	—	—
86-87	Moncton	AHL	45	10	22	32	57	5	2	1	3	19
	Calgary	NHL	27	6	7	13	29	—	—	—	—	—
87-88	Toronto	NHL	56	6	18	24	63	5	0	1	1	16
	Newmarket	AHL	8	2	10	12	8	—	—	—	—	—
88-89	Los Angeles	NHL	63	6	22	28	97	8	1	2	3	12
89-90	New Haven	AHL	16	2	10	12	38	—	—	—	—	—
	Rochester	AHL	50	6	25	31	118	17	5	6	11	59
	Buffalo	NHL	6	0	0	0	6	—	—	—	—	—
90-91	Rochester	AHL	64	9	25	34	121	15	3	4	7	*76
91-92	Alleghe	Italy	27	6	24	30	46	—	—	—	—	—
92-93	San Diego	IHL	79	18	64	82	181	14	3	11	14	77
93-94	San Diego	IHL	80	20	50	70	163	9	2	1	3	8
NHL totals			153	18	47	65	195	13	1	3	4	28

DEMITRA, PAVOL

LW, SENATORS

PERSONAL: Born November 29, 1974, in Dubnica, Czechoslovakia. ... 6-0/184. ... Shoots left.

TRANSACTIONS/CAREER NOTES: Selected by Ottawa Senators in ninth round (ninth Senators pick, 227th overall) of NHL entry draft (June 26, 1993). ... Broke ankle (October 14, 1993); missed 23 games.

Season	Team	League	REGULAR SEASON					PLAYOFFS				
			Gms.	G	A	Pts.	PIM	Gms.	G	A	Pts.	PIM
91-92	Sparta Dubnica	Czech Dv.II	28	13	10	23	12	—	—	—	—	—
92-93	Dukla Trencin	Czech.	46	11	17	28	0	—	—	—	—	—
93-94	Ottawa	NHL	12	1	1	2	4	—	—	—	—	—
	Prince Edward Island	AHL	41	18	23	41	8	—	—	—	—	—
NHL totals			12	1	1	2	4					

DePALMA, LARRY

LW, PENGUINS

PERSONAL: Born October 27, 1965, in Trenton, Mich. ... 5-11/200. ... Shoots left.

TRANSACTIONS/CAREER NOTES: Signed as free agent by Minnesota North Stars (March 1986). ... Injured wrist (October 1987). ... Sprained ankle ligaments (February 1989). ... Signed as free agent by San Jose Sharks (August 30, 1991). ... Injured back (December 18, 1992); missed nine games. ... Signed as free agent by New York Islanders (December 1, 1993). ... Claimed on waivers by Pittsburgh Penguins (March 9, 1994).

HONORS: Named to WHL All-Star second team (1985-86).

Season	Team	League	Gms.	G	A	Pts.	PIM	Gms.	G	A	Pts.	PIM
84-85—New Westminster	WHL	65	14	16	30	87	10	1	1	2	25
85-86—Saskatoon	WHL	65	61	51	112	232	13	7	9	16	58
—Minnesota	NHL	1	0	0	0	0	—	—	—	—	—
86-87—Springfield	AHL	9	2	2	4	82	—	—	—	—	—
—Minnesota	NHL	56	9	6	15	219	—	—	—	—	—
87-88—Baltimore	AHL	16	8	10	18	121	—	—	—	—	—
—Kalamazoo	IHL	22	6	11	17	215	—	—	—	—	—
—Minnesota	NHL	7	1	1	2	15	—	—	—	—	—
88-89—Minnesota	NHL	43	5	7	12	102	2	0	0	0	6
89-90—Kalamazoo	IHL	36	7	14	21	218	4	1	1	2	32
90-91—Kalamazoo	IHL	55	27	32	59	160	11	5	4	9	25
—Minnesota	NHL	14	3	0	3	26	—	—	—	—	—
91-92—Kansas City	IHL	62	28	29	57	188	15	7	13	20	34
92-93—Kansas City	IHL	30	11	11	22	83	10	1	4	5	20
—San Jose	NHL	20	2	6	8	41	—	—	—	—	—
93-94—Atlanta	IHL	21	10	10	20	109	—	—	—	—	—
—Salt Lake City	IHL	34	4	12	16	125	—	—	—	—	—
—Las Vegas	IHL	1	0	0	0	17	—	—	—	—	—
—Cleveland	IHL	9	4	1	5	49	—	—	—	—	—
—Pittsburgh	NHL	7	1	0	1	5	1	0	0	0	0
NHL totals		148	21	20	41	408	3	0	0	0	6

DeROUVILLE, PHILLIPPE
G, PENGUINS

PERSONAL: Born August 7, 1974, in Arthabaska, Que. . . . 6-2/180. . . . Catches left.

TRANSACTIONS/CAREER NOTES: Selected by Pittsburgh Penguins in fifth round (fifth Penguins pick, 115th overall) of NHL entry draft (June 20, 1992).

HONORS: Won Raymond Lagace Trophy (1991-92). . . . Named to QMJHL All-Star second team (1992-93). . . . Won Jacques Plante Trophy (1993-94). . . . Named to QMJHL All-Star second team (1993-94).

Season	Team	League	Gms.	Min.	W	L	T	GA	SO	Avg.	Gms.	Min.	W	L	GA	SO	Avg.
90-91—Longueuil	QMJHL	20	1030	13	6	0	50	0	2.91	—	—	—	—	—	—	—
91-92—Longueuil	QMJHL	34	1854	20	6	3	99	2	3.20	11	593	†7	2	28	†1	2.83
92-93—Verdun	QMJHL	*61	*3491	30	27	2	210	1	3.61	4	257	0	4	18	0	4.20
93-94—Verdun	QMJHL	51	2845	28	22	0	145	1	*3.06	4	210	0	4	14	0	4.00

DeSANTIS, MARK
D, MIGHTY DUCKS

PERSONAL: Born August 2, 1972, in Brampton, Ont. . . . 6-0/205. . . . Shoots right.

TRANSACTIONS/CAREER NOTES: Signed as free agent by Mighty Ducks of Anaheim (August 2, 1993).

Season	Team	League	Gms.	G	A	Pts.	PIM	Gms.	G	A	Pts.	PIM
89-90—Newmarket	OHL	59	3	17	20	79	—	—	—	—	—
90-91—Newmarket	OHL	41	7	15	22	78	—	—	—	—	—
91-92—Newmarket	OHL	66	10	45	55	105	—	—	—	—	—
92-93—Newmarket	OHL	66	19	70	89	131	7	3	11	14	14
93-94—San Diego	IHL	54	5	10	15	95	—	—	—	—	—

DESCHENES, FREDERIC
G, RED WINGS

PERSONAL: Born January 12, 1976, in Quebec. . . . 5-9/164. . . . Catches left.

TRANSACTIONS/CAREER NOTES: Selected by Detroit Red Wings in fifth round (fourth Red Wings pick, 114th overall) of NHL entry draft (June 29, 1994).

Season	Team	League	Gms.	Min.	W	L	T	GA	SO	Avg.	Gms.	Min.	W	L	GA	SO	Avg.
93-94—Granby	QMJHL	35	1861	14	15	1	132	0	4.26	7	372	3	4	27	0	4.35

DESJARDINS, ERIC
D, CANADIENS

PERSONAL: Born June 14, 1969, in Rouyn, Que. . . . 6-1/200. . . . Shoots right. . . . Name pronounced deh-ZHAHR-dai.

TRANSACTIONS/CAREER NOTES: Selected by Montreal Canadiens as underage junior in second round (third Canadiens pick, 38th overall) of NHL entry draft (June 13, 1987). . . . Suffered from the flu (January 1989). . . . Pulled groin (November 2, 1989); missed seven games. . . . Sprained left ankle (January 26, 1991); missed 16 games. . . . Fractured right thumb (December 8, 1991); missed two games.

HONORS: Named to QMJHL All-Star second team (1986-87). . . . Won Emile (Butch) Bouchard Trophy (1987-88). . . . Named to QMJHL All-Star first team (1987-88). . . . Played in NHL All-Star Game (1992).

RECORDS: Shares NHL single-game playoff record for most goals by defensemen—3 (June 3, 1993).

MISCELLANEOUS: Member of Stanley Cup championship team (1993).

Season	Team	League	Gms.	G	A	Pts.	PIM	Gms.	G	A	Pts.	PIM
86-87—Granby	QMJHL	66	14	24	38	75	8	3	2	5	10
87-88—Granby	QMJHL	62	18	49	67	138	5	0	3	3	10
—Sherbrooke	AHL	3	0	0	0	6	4	0	2	2	2

Season Team	League	REGULAR SEASON					PLAYOFFS				
		Gms.	G	A	Pts.	PIM	Gms.	G	A	Pts.	PIM
88-89—Montreal	NHL	36	2	12	14	26	14	1	1	2	6
89-90—Montreal	NHL	55	3	13	16	51	6	0	0	0	10
90-91—Montreal	NHL	62	7	18	25	27	13	1	4	5	8
91-92—Montreal	NHL	77	6	32	38	50	11	3	3	6	4
92-93—Montreal	NHL	82	13	32	45	98	20	4	10	14	23
93-94—Montreal	NHL	84	12	23	35	97	7	0	2	2	4
NHL totals		396	43	130	173	349	71	9	20	29	55

DEULING, JARRETT
LW, ISLANDERS

PERSONAL: Born March 4, 1974, in Vernon, B.C. . . . 6-0/198. . . . Shoots left. . . . Name pronounced DOO-lihng.
HIGH SCHOOL: Norkam Secondary (Kamloops, B.C.).
TRANSACTIONS/CAREER NOTES: Selected by New York Islanders in third round (second Islanders pick, 56th overall) of NHL entry draft (June 20, 1992).
HONORS: Named WHL Playoff Most Valuable Player (1991-92).

Season Team	League	REGULAR SEASON					PLAYOFFS				
		Gms.	G	A	Pts.	PIM	Gms.	G	A	Pts.	PIM
90-91—Kamloops	WHL	48	4	12	16	43	12	5	2	7	7
91-92—Kamloops	WHL	68	28	24	52	79	17	10	6	16	18
92-93—Kamloops	WHL	68	31	32	63	93	13	6	7	13	14
93-94—Kamloops	WHL	70	44	59	103	171	18	*13	8	21	43

DEYELL, MARK
C, MAPLE LEAFS

PERSONAL: Born March 26, 1976, in Regina, Sask. . . . 5-9/160. . . . Shoots right.
TRANSACTIONS/CAREER NOTES: Selected by Toronto Maple Leafs in fifth round (fourth Maple Leafs pick, 126th overall) of NHL entry draft (June 29, 1994).

Season Team	League	REGULAR SEASON					PLAYOFFS				
		Gms.	G	A	Pts.	PIM	Gms.	G	A	Pts.	PIM
93-94—Saskatoon	WHL	66	17	36	53	52	16	5	2	7	20

DIDUCK, GERALD
D, CANUCKS

PERSONAL: Born April 6, 1965, in Edmonton. . . . 6-2/207. . . . Shoots right. . . . Name pronounced DIH-duhk.
TRANSACTIONS/CAREER NOTES: Selected by New York Islanders as underage junior in first round (second Islanders pick, 16th overall) of NHL entry draft (June 8, 1983). . . . Fractured left foot (November 1987). . . . Fractured right hand (November 1988). . . . Injured knee (January 1989). . . . Traded by Islanders to Montreal Canadiens for D Craig Ludwig (September 4, 1990). . . . Traded by Canadiens to Vancouver Canucks for fourth-round pick (LW Vladimir Vujtek) in 1991 draft (January 12, 1991). . . . Bruised knee (March 16, 1991). . . . Strained groin (January 4, 1993); missed three games. . . . Suffered stress fracture in ankle (January 1, 1994); missed 14 games. . . . Bruised foot (February 17, 1994); missed six games. . . . Suffered eye contusion (March 31, 1994); missed five games.

Season Team	League	REGULAR SEASON					PLAYOFFS				
		Gms.	G	A	Pts.	PIM	Gms.	G	A	Pts.	PIM
81-82—Lethbridge	WHL	71	1	15	16	81	12	0	3	3	27
82-83—Lethbridge	WHL	67	8	16	24	151	20	3	12	15	49
83-84—Lethbridge	WHL	65	10	24	34	133	5	1	4	5	27
—Indianapolis	IHL	—	—	—	—	—	10	1	6	7	19
84-85—New York Islanders	NHL	65	2	8	10	80	—	—	—	—	—
85-86—New York Islanders	NHL	10	1	2	3	2	—	—	—	—	—
—Springfield	AHL	61	6	14	20	175	—	—	—	—	—
86-87—Springfield	AHL	45	6	8	14	120	—	—	—	—	—
—New York Islanders	NHL	30	2	3	5	67	14	0	1	1	35
87-88—New York Islanders	NHL	68	7	12	19	113	6	1	0	1	42
88-89—New York Islanders	NHL	65	11	21	32	155	—	—	—	—	—
89-90—New York Islanders	NHL	76	3	17	20	163	5	0	0	0	12
90-91—Montreal	NHL	32	1	2	3	39	—	—	—	—	—
—Vancouver	NHL	31	3	7	10	66	6	1	0	1	11
91-92—Vancouver	NHL	77	6	21	27	229	5	0	0	0	10
92-93—Vancouver	NHL	80	6	14	20	171	12	4	2	6	12
93-94—Vancouver	NHL	55	1	10	11	72	24	1	7	8	22
NHL totals		589	43	117	160	1157	72	7	10	17	144

DiMAIO, ROB
C, FLYERS

PERSONAL: Born February 19, 1968, in Calgary. . . . 5-10/190. . . . Shoots right. . . . Name pronounced duh-MIGH-oh.
TRANSACTIONS/CAREER NOTES: Traded by Kamloops Blazers with LW Dave Mackey and C Kalvin Knibbs to Medicine Hat Tigers for LW Doug Pickel and LW Sean Pass (December 1985). . . . Selected by New York Islanders in sixth round (sixth Islanders pick, 118th overall) of NHL entry draft (June 13, 1987). . . . Suspended two games by WHL for leaving bench during fight (January 28, 1988). . . . Bruised left hand (February 1989). . . . Sprained clavicle (November 1989). . . . Sprained wrist (February 20, 1992); missed four games. . . . Reinjured wrist (February 29, 1992); missed final 17 games of season. . . . Underwent surgery to repair torn ligaments in wrist (March 11, 1992). . . . Selected by Tampa Bay Lightning in NHL expansion draft (June 18, 1992). . . . Bruised wrist (November 28, 1992); missed four games. . . . Sprained ankle (February 14, 1993); missed nine games. . . . Reinjured right ankle (March 20, 1993); missed three games. . . . Reinjured right ankle (April 1, 1993); missed remainder of season. . . . Broke left leg (October 16, 1993); missed 27 games. . . . Traded by Lightning to Philadelphia Flyers for RW Jim Cummins and fourth-round pick in 1995 draft (March 18, 1994).

Won Stafford Smythe Memorial Trophy (1987-88).... Named to Memorial Cup All-Star team (1987-88).

Season Team	League	REGULAR SEASON					PLAYOFFS				
		Gms.	G	A	Pts.	PIM	Gms.	G	A	Pts.	PIM
84-85—Kamloops	WHL	55	9	18	27	29	—	—	—	—	—
85-86—Kamloops	WHL	6	1	0	1	0	—	—	—	—	—
—Medicine Hat	WHL	55	20	30	50	82	—	—	—	—	—
86-87—Medicine Hat	WHL	70	27	43	70	130	20	7	11	18	46
87-88—Medicine Hat	WHL	54	47	43	90	120	14	12	19	†31	59
88-89—New York Islanders	NHL	16	1	0	1	30	—	—	—	—	—
—Springfield	AHL	40	13	18	31	67	—	—	—	—	—
89-90—New York Islanders	NHL	7	0	0	0	2	1	1	0	1	4
—Springfield	AHL	54	25	27	52	69	16	4	7	11	45
90-91—New York Islanders	NHL	1	0	0	0	0	—	—	—	—	—
—Capital District	AHL	12	3	4	7	22	—	—	—	—	—
91-92—New York Islanders	NHL	50	5	2	7	43	—	—	—	—	—
92-93—Tampa Bay	NHL	54	9	15	24	62	—	—	—	—	—
93-94—Tampa Bay	NHL	39	8	7	15	40	—	—	—	—	—
—Philadelphia	NHL	14	3	5	8	6	—	—	—	—	—
NHL totals		181	26	29	55	183	1	1	0	1	4

DINEEN, GORD
D, ISLANDERS

PERSONAL: Born September 21, 1962, in Quebec City.... 6-0/195.... Shoots right.... Son of Bill Dineen, right winger, Detroit Red Wings and Chicago Blackhawks (1953-54 through 1957-58) and former head coach, Philadelphia Flyers (1992-93); brother of Kevin Dineen, right winger, Flyers; and brother of Peter Dineen, defenseman, Los Angeles Kings and Red Wings (1986-87 and 1989-90).

HIGH SCHOOL: St. Micheal (Toronto).

TRANSACTIONS/CAREER NOTES: Selected by New York Islanders as underage junior in second round (second Islanders pick, 42nd overall) of NHL entry draft (June 10, 1981).... Bruised ribs (January 15, 1985).... Sprained left ankle (February 1988).... Traded by Islanders with future considerations to Minnesota North Stars for D Chris Pryor (March 1988).... Traded by North Stars with LW Scott Bjugstad to Pittsburgh Penguins for D Ville Siren and C Steve Gotaas (December 17, 1988).... Signed as free agent by Ottawa Senators (August 31, 1992).... Loaned to San Diego Gulls prior to 1992-93 season.... Returned to Senators (January 20, 1993).... Signed as free agent by New York Islanders (August 2, 1994).

HONORS: Won Bobby Orr Trophy (1982-83).... Won Bob Gassoff Award (1982-83).... Named to CHL All-Star first team (1982-83).... Named to IHL All-Star first team (1991-92).

Season Team	League	REGULAR SEASON					PLAYOFFS				
		Gms.	G	A	Pts.	PIM	Gms.	G	A	Pts.	PIM
79-80—St. Michael's Jr. B	ODHA	42	15	35	50	103	—	—	—	—	—
80-81—Sault Ste. Marie	OMJHL	68	4	26	30	158	19	1	7	8	58
81-82—Sault Ste. Marie	OHL	68	9	45	54	185	13	1	2	3	52
82-83—Indianapolis	CHL	73	10	47	57	78	13	2	10	12	29
—New York Islanders	NHL	2	0	0	0	4	—	—	—	—	—
83-84—Indianapolis	CHL	26	4	13	17	63	—	—	—	—	—
—New York Islanders	NHL	43	1	11	12	32	9	1	1	2	28
84-85—Springfield	AHL	25	1	8	9	46	—	—	—	—	—
—New York Islanders	NHL	48	1	12	13	89	10	0	0	0	26
85-86—New York Islanders	NHL	57	1	8	9	81	3	0	0	0	2
—Springfield	AHL	11	2	3	5	20	—	—	—	—	—
86-87—New York Islanders	NHL	71	4	10	14	110	7	0	4	4	4
87-88—New York Islanders	NHL	57	4	12	16	62	—	—	—	—	—
—Minnesota	NHL	13	1	1	2	21	—	—	—	—	—
88-89—Kalamazoo	IHL	25	2	6	8	49	—	—	—	—	—
—Minnesota	NHL	2	0	1	1	2	—	—	—	—	—
—Pittsburgh	NHL	38	1	2	3	42	11	0	2	2	8
89-90—Pittsburgh	NHL	69	1	8	9	125	—	—	—	—	—
90-91—Muskegon	IHL	40	1	14	15	57	5	0	2	2	0
—Pittsburgh	NHL	9	0	0	0	6	—	—	—	—	—
91-92—Muskegon	IHL	79	8	37	45	83	14	2	4	6	33
—Pittsburgh	NHL	1	0	0	0	0	—	—	—	—	—
92-93—San Diego	IHL	41	6	23	29	36	—	—	—	—	—
—Ottawa	NHL	32	2	4	6	30	—	—	—	—	—
93-94—Ottawa	NHL	77	0	21	21	89	—	—	—	—	—
—San Diego	IHL	3	0	0	0	2	—	—	—	—	—
NHL totals		519	16	90	106	693	40	1	7	8	68

DINEEN, KEVIN
RW, FLYERS

PERSONAL: Born October 28, 1963, in Quebec City.... 5-11/190.... Shoots right.... Son of Bill Dineen, right winger with Detroit Red Wings and Chicago Blackhawks (1953-54 through 1957-58) and former head coach, Philadelphia Flyers (1992-93); brother of Gord Dineen, defenseman with four NHL teams (1982-83 through 1993-94); and brother of Peter Dineen, defenseman, Los Angeles Kings and Red Wings (1986-87 and 1989-90).

COLLEGE: Denver.

TRANSACTIONS/CAREER NOTES: Selected by Hartford Whalers as underage junior in third round (third Whalers pick, 56th overall) of NHL entry draft (June 9, 1982).... Sprained left shoulder (October 24, 1985); missed nine games.... Broke knuckle (January 12, 1986); missed seven games.... Sprained knee (February 14, 1986).... Suffered shoulder tendinitis (September 1988).... Underwent surgery to right knee cartilage (August 1, 1990).... Suffered hip pointer (November 28, 1990).... Hospitalized due to complications caused by Crohn's disease (January 1, 1991); missed eight games. . . . Injured groin (March 1991). . . . Traded by Whalers to Philadelphia Flyers for C/LW Murray Craven and fourth-round pick (LW Kevin Smyth) in 1992 draft (November 13, 1991). . . . Sprained wrist (February 4, 1992); missed one game. . . . Strained right rotator cuff (December 3, 1992); missed one game. . . . Suffered injury (October 9, 1993); missed one game. . . . Bruised right shoulder (November 13, 1993); missed two games. . . . Suffered recurrence of Chron's Disease (February 10, 1994); missed five games. . . . Separated shoulder (March 8, 1994); missed three games.

HONORS: Named to THE SPORTING NEWS All-Star second team (1986-87). . . . Played in NHL All-Star Game (1988 and 1989). . . . Named Bud Light/NHL Man of the Year (1990-91).

			REGULAR SEASON					PLAYOFFS				
Season Team	League	Gms.	G	A	Pts.	PIM	Gms.	G	A	Pts.	PIM
80-81—St. Michael's Jr. B............	ODHA	40	15	28	43	167	—	—	—	—	—
81-82—University of Denver.......	WCHA	38	12	22	34	105	—	—	—	—	—
82-83—University of Denver.......	WCHA	36	16	13	29	108	—	—	—	—	—
83-84—Canadian Olympic Team ..	Int'l				Statistics unavailable.						
84-85—Binghamton	AHL	25	15	8	23	41	—	—	—	—	—
—Hartford...........................	NHL	57	25	16	41	120	—	—	—	—	—
85-86—Hartford.........................	NHL	57	33	35	68	124	10	6	7	13	18
86-87—Hartford.........................	NHL	78	40	39	79	110	6	2	1	3	31
87-88—Hartford.........................	NHL	74	25	25	50	219	6	4	4	8	8
88-89—Hartford.........................	NHL	79	45	44	89	167	4	1	0	1	10
89-90—Hartford.........................	NHL	67	25	41	66	164	6	3	2	5	18
90-91—Hartford.........................	NHL	61	17	30	47	104	6	1	0	1	16
91-92—Hartford.........................	NHL	16	4	2	6	23	—	—	—	—	—
—Philadelphia...................	NHL	64	26	30	56	130	—	—	—	—	—
92-93—Philadelphia...................	NHL	83	35	28	63	201	—	—	—	—	—
93-94—Philadelphia...................	NHL	71	19	23	42	113	—	—	—	—	—
NHL totals................................		707	294	313	607	1475	38	17	14	31	101

DINGMAN, CHRIS
LW, FLAMES

PERSONAL: Born July 6, 1976, in Edmonton. . . . 6-4/225. . . . Shoots left.
HIGH SCHOOL: Crocus Plains (Brandon, Man.).
TRANSACTIONS/CAREER NOTES: Selected by Calgary Flames in first round (first Flames pick, 19th overall) of NHL entry draft (June 28, 1994).

			REGULAR SEASON					PLAYOFFS				
Season Team	League	Gms.	G	A	Pts.	PIM	Gms.	G	A	Pts.	PIM
92-93—Brandon..........................	WHL	50	10	17	27	64	4	0	0	0	0
93-94—Brandon..........................	WHL	45	21	20	41	77	13	1	7	8	39

DIONNE, GILBERT
LW, CANADIENS

PERSONAL: Born September 19, 1970, in Drummondville, Que. . . . 6-0/194. . . . Shoots left. . . . Name pronounced ZHIHL-bair dee-AHN. . . . Brother of Marcel Dionne, Hall of Fame center, Detroit Red Wings, Los Angeles Kings and New York Rangers (1971-72 through 1988-89).

TRANSACTIONS/CAREER NOTES: Selected by Montreal Canadiens in fourth round (fifth Canadiens pick, 81st overall) of NHL entry draft (June 16, 1990). . . . Injured hand (December 3, 1992); missed one game. . . . Pulled groin (December 18, 1993); missed eight games.
HONORS: Named to NHL All-Rookie team (1991-92).
MISCELLANEOUS: Member of Stanley Cup championship team (1993).

			REGULAR SEASON					PLAYOFFS				
Season Team	League	Gms.	G	A	Pts.	PIM	Gms.	G	A	Pts.	PIM
87-88—Niagara Falls Jr. B...........	OHA	38	36	48	84	60	—	—	—	—	—
88-89—Kitchener........................	OHL	66	11	33	44	13	5	1	1	2	4
89-90—Kitchener........................	OHL	64	48	57	105	85	17	13	10	23	22
90-91—Fredericton	AHL	77	40	47	87	62	9	6	5	11	8
—Montreal	NHL	2	0	0	0	0	—	—	—	—	—
91-92—Fredericton	AHL	29	19	27	46	20	—	—	—	—	—
—Montreal	NHL	39	21	13	34	10	11	3	4	7	10
92-93—Montreal	NHL	75	20	28	48	63	20	6	6	12	20
—Fredericton	AHL	3	4	3	7	0	—	—	—	—	—
93-94—Montreal	NHL	74	19	26	45	31	5	1	2	3	0
NHL totals................................		190	60	67	127	104	36	10	12	22	30

DIPIETRO, PAUL
C, CANADIENS

PERSONAL: Born September 8, 1970, in Sault Ste. Marie, Ont. . . . 5-9/181. . . . Shoots right. . . . Name pronounced dee-pee-AY-troh.
TRANSACTIONS/CAREER NOTES: Selected by Montreal Canadiens in fifth round (sixth Canadiens pick, 102nd overall) of NHL entry draft (June 16, 1990). . . . Strained hip flexor (February 12, 1992). . . . Bruised thumb (November 24, 1993). . . . Suffered contusion (January 4, 1994); missed two games. . . . Separated shoulder (January 15, 1994); missed six games.
MISCELLANEOUS: Member of Stanley Cup championship team (1993).

			REGULAR SEASON					PLAYOFFS				
Season Team	League	Gms.	G	A	Pts.	PIM	Gms.	G	A	Pts.	PIM
86-87—Sudbury...........................	OHL	49	5	11	16	13	—	—	—	—	—
87-88—Sudbury...........................	OHL	63	25	42	67	27	—	—	—	—	—
88-89—Sudbury...........................	OHL	57	31	48	79	27	—	—	—	—	—

D

Season Team	League	REGULAR SEASON					PLAYOFFS				
		Gms.	G	A	Pts.	PIM	Gms.	G	A	Pts.	PIM
89-90—Sudbury	OHL	66	56	63	119	57	7	3	6	9	7
90-91—Fredericton	AHL	78	39	31	70	38	9	5	6	11	2
91-92—Fredericton	AHL	43	26	31	57	52	7	3	4	7	8
—Montreal	NHL	33	4	6	10	25	—	—	—	—	—
92-93—Fredericton	AHL	26	8	16	24	16	—	—	—	—	—
—Montreal	NHL	29	4	13	17	14	17	8	5	13	8
93-94—Montreal	NHL	70	13	20	33	37	7	2	4	6	2
NHL totals		132	21	39	60	76	24	10	9	19	10

DIRK, ROBERT

D, MIGHTY DUCKS

PERSONAL: Born August 20, 1966, in Regina, Sask. . . . 6-4/218. . . . Shoots left.
TRANSACTIONS/CAREER NOTES: Selected by St. Louis Blues as underage junior in third round (fourth Blues pick, 53rd overall) of NHL entry draft (June 9, 1984). . . . Traded by Blues with LW Geoff Courtnall, C Cliff Ronning, LW Sergio Momesso and fifth-round pick in 1992 draft (RW Brian Loney) to Vancouver Canucks for C Dan Quinn and D Garth Butcher (March 5, 1991). . . . Sprained ankle (November 26, 1991); missed three games. . . . Sprained knee (February 1, 1992); missed four games. . . . Bruised ribs (March 6, 1993); missed four games. . . . Injured shoulder (September 22, 1992); missed two games. . . . Pulled groin (February 12, 1993); missed six games. . . . Traded by Canucks to Chicago Blackhawks for fourth-round pick in 1994 draft (March 21, 1994). . . . Suffered from sore shoulder (1994); missed four games. . . . Traded by Blackhawks to Mighty Ducks of Anaheim for fourth-round pick in 1995 draft (July 12, 1994).
HONORS: Named to WHL All-Star second team (1985-86).

Season Team	League	REGULAR SEASON					PLAYOFFS				
		Gms.	G	A	Pts.	PIM	Gms.	G	A	Pts.	PIM
82-83—Regina	WHL	1	0	0	0	0	—	—	—	—	—
—Kelowna	BCJHL	40	8	23	31	87	—	—	—	—	—
83-84—Regina	WHL	62	2	10	12	64	23	1	12	13	24
84-85—Regina	WHL	69	10	34	44	97	8	0	0	0	4
85-86—Regina	WHL	72	19	60	79	140	10	3	5	8	8
86-87—Peoria	IHL	76	5	17	22	155	—	—	—	—	—
87-88—St. Louis	NHL	7	0	1	1	16	6	0	1	1	2
—Peoria	IHL	54	4	21	25	126	—	—	—	—	—
88-89—St. Louis	NHL	9	0	1	1	11	—	—	—	—	—
—Peoria	IHL	22	0	2	2	54	—	—	—	—	—
89-90—Peoria	IHL	24	1	2	3	79	3	0	0	0	0
—St. Louis	NHL	37	1	1	2	128	9	0	1	1	2
90-91—Peoria	IHL	3	0	0	0	2	—	—	—	—	—
—St. Louis	NHL	41	1	3	4	100	—	—	—	—	—
—Vancouver	NHL	11	1	0	1	20	6	0	0	0	13
91-92—Vancouver	NHL	72	2	7	9	126	13	0	0	0	20
92-93—Vancouver	NHL	69	4	8	12	150	9	0	0	0	6
93-94—Vancouver	NHL	65	2	3	5	105	—	—	—	—	—
—Chicago	NHL	6	0	0	0	26	2	0	0	0	15
NHL totals		317	11	24	35	682	45	0	2	2	58

DOBBIN, BRIAN

RW

PERSONAL: Born August 18, 1966, in Petrolia, Ont. . . . 6-1/205. . . . Shoots right.
TRANSACTIONS/CAREER NOTES: Selected by Philadelphia Flyers as underage junior in fifth round (sixth Flyers pick, 100th overall) of NHL entry draft (June 9, 1984). . . . Damaged ligament in right knee (September 1986). . . . Traded by Flyers with D Gord Murphy and third-round pick in 1992 draft (LW Sergei Zholtok) to Boston Bruins for D Garry Galley, C Wes Walz and future considerations (January 2, 1992). . . . Strained lower back (February 1, 1992).
HONORS: Named to AHL All-Star first team (1988-89). . . . Named to AHL All-Star second team (1989-90). . . . Named to IHL All-Star second team (1993-94).

Season Team	League	REGULAR SEASON					PLAYOFFS				
		Gms.	G	A	Pts.	PIM	Gms.	G	A	Pts.	PIM
81-82—Mooretown Jr. C	OHA	38	31	24	55	50	—	—	—	—	—
82-83—Kingston	OHL	69	16	39	55	35	—	—	—	—	—
83-84—London	OHL	70	30	40	70	70	—	—	—	—	—
84-85—London	OHL	53	42	57	99	63	8	7	4	11	2
85-86—London	OHL	59	38	55	93	113	5	2	1	3	9
—Hershey	AHL	2	1	0	1	0	18	5	5	10	21
86-87—Hershey	AHL	52	26	35	61	66	5	4	2	6	15
—Philadelphia	NHL	12	2	1	3	14	—	—	—	—	—
87-88—Hershey	AHL	54	36	47	83	58	12	7	8	15	15
—Philadelphia	NHL	21	3	5	8	6	—	—	—	—	—
88-89—Philadelphia	NHL	14	0	1	1	8	2	0	0	0	17
—Hershey	AHL	59	43	48	91	61	11	7	6	13	12
89-90—Hershey	AHL	68	38	47	85	58	—	—	—	—	—
—Philadelphia	NHL	9	1	1	2	11	—	—	—	—	—
90-91—Hershey	AHL	80	33	43	76	82	7	1	2	3	7
91-92—New Haven	AHL	33	16	21	37	20	—	—	—	—	—
—Maine	AHL	33	21	15	36	14	—	—	—	—	—
—Boston	NHL	7	1	0	1	22	—	—	—	—	—

Season Team	League	REGULAR SEASON					PLAYOFFS				
		Gms.	G	A	Pts.	PIM	Gms.	G	A	Pts.	PIM
92-93—Milwaukee	IHL	80	39	45	84	50	6	4	3	7	6
93-94—Milwaukee	IHL	81	48	53	101	73	4	1	0	1	4
NHL totals		63	7	8	15	61	2	0	0	0	17

DOLLAS, BOBBY
D, MIGHTY DUCKS

PERSONAL: Born January 31, 1965, in Montreal. . . . 6-2/212. . . . Shoots left.
TRANSACTIONS/CAREER NOTES: Selected by Winnipeg Jets as underage junior in first round (second Jets pick, 14th overall) of NHL entry draft (June 8, 1983). . . . Traded by Jets to Quebec Nordiques for RW Stu Kulak (December 17, 1987). . . . Signed as free agent by Detroit Red Wings (October 18, 1990). . . . Suffered from the flu (December 15, 1990); missed two games. . . . Injured leg (January 9, 1991). . . . Strained abdomen (November 7, 1991); missed 15 games. . . . Selected by Mighty Ducks of Anaheim in NHL expansion draft (June 24, 1993). . . . Sprained left thumb (October 1, 1993); missed five games.
HONORS: Won Raymond Lagace Trophy (1982-83). . . . Named to QMJHL All-Star second team (1982-83). . . . Won Eddie Shore Plaque (1992-93). . . . Named to AHL All-Star first team (1992-93).

Season Team	League	REGULAR SEASON					PLAYOFFS				
		Gms.	G	A	Pts.	PIM	Gms.	G	A	Pts.	PIM
82-83—Laval	QMJHL	63	16	45	61	144	11	5	5	10	23
83-84—Laval	QMJHL	54	12	33	45	80	14	1	8	9	23
—Winnipeg	NHL	1	0	0	0	0	—	—	—	—	—
84-85—Winnipeg	NHL	9	0	0	0	0	—	—	—	—	—
—Sherbrooke	AHL	8	1	3	4	4	17	3	6	9	17
85-86—Sherbrooke	AHL	25	4	7	11	29	—	—	—	—	—
—Winnipeg	NHL	46	0	5	5	66	3	0	0	0	2
86-87—Sherbrooke	AHL	75	6	18	24	87	16	2	4	6	13
87-88—Quebec	NHL	9	0	0	0	2	—	—	—	—	—
—Moncton	AHL	26	4	10	14	20	—	—	—	—	—
—Fredericton	AHL	33	4	8	12	27	15	2	2	4	24
88-89—Halifax	AHL	57	5	19	24	65	4	1	0	1	14
—Quebec	NHL	16	0	3	3	16	—	—	—	—	—
89-90—Canadian national team	Int'l	68	8	29	37	60	—	—	—	—	—
90-91—Detroit	NHL	56	3	5	8	20	7	1	0	1	13
91-92—Detroit	NHL	27	3	1	4	20	2	0	1	1	0
—Adirondack	AHL	19	1	6	7	33	18	7	4	11	22
92-93—Adirondack	AHL	64	7	36	43	54	11	3	8	11	8
—Detroit	NHL	6	0	0	0	2	—	—	—	—	—
93-94—Anaheim	NHL	77	9	11	20	55	—	—	—	—	—
NHL totals		247	15	25	40	181	12	1	1	2	15

DOMENICHELLI, HNAT
C/LW, WHALERS

PERSONAL: Born February 17, 1976, in Edmonton. . . . 6-0/173. . . . Shoots left. . . . Name pronounced NAT dom-en-i-CHELLY.
TRANSACTIONS/CAREER NOTES: Selected by Hartford Whalers in fourth round (second Whalers pick, 83rd overall) of NHL entry draft (June 29, 1994).

Season Team	League	REGULAR SEASON					PLAYOFFS				
		Gms.	G	A	Pts.	PIM	Gms.	G	A	Pts.	PIM
92-93—Kamloops	WHL	45	12	8	20	15	11	1	1	2	2
93-94—Kamloops	WHL	69	27	40	67	31	19	10	12	22	0

DOMI, TIE
RW, JETS

PERSONAL: Born November 1, 1969, in Windsor, Ont. . . . 5-10/200. . . . Shoots right. . . . Name pronounced DOH-mee.
TRANSACTIONS/CAREER NOTES: Suspended indefinitely by OHL for leaving the bench during fight (November 2, 1986). . . . Selected by Toronto Maple Leafs in second round (second Maple Leafs pick, 27th overall) of NHL entry draft (June 11, 1988). . . . Traded by Maple Leafs with G Mark Laforest to New York Rangers for RW Greg Johnston (June 28, 1990). . . . Suspended six games by AHL for pre-game fighting (November 25, 1990). . . . Sprained right knee (March 11, 1992); missed eight games. . . . Traded by Rangers with LW Kris King to Winnipeg Jets for C Ed Olczyk (December 28, 1992). . . . Fined $500 by NHL for premeditated fight (January 4, 1993). . . . Sprained knee (January 25, 1994); missed three games.

Season Team	League	REGULAR SEASON					PLAYOFFS				
		Gms.	G	A	Pts.	PIM	Gms.	G	A	Pts.	PIM
85-86—Windsor Jr. B	OHA	32	8	17	25	346	—	—	—	—	—
86-87—Peterborough	OHL	18	1	1	2	79	—	—	—	—	—
87-88—Peterborough	OHL	60	22	21	43	*292	12	3	9	12	24
88-89—Peterborough	OHL	43	14	16	30	175	17	10	9	19	*70
89-90—Newmarket	AHL	57	14	11	25	285	—	—	—	—	—
—Toronto	NHL	2	0	0	0	42	—	—	—	—	—
90-91—New York Rangers	NHL	28	1	0	1	185	—	—	—	—	—
—Binghamton	AHL	25	11	6	17	219	7	3	2	5	16
91-92—New York Rangers	NHL	42	2	4	6	246	6	1	1	2	32
92-93—New York Rangers	NHL	12	2	0	2	95	—	—	—	—	—
—Winnipeg	NHL	49	3	10	13	249	6	1	0	1	23
93-94—Winnipeg	NHL	81	8	11	19	*347	—	—	—	—	—
NHL totals		214	16	25	41	1164	12	2	1	3	55

D

DONATO, TED
C, BRUINS

PERSONAL: Born April 28, 1968, in Dedham, Mass. . . . 5-10/170. . . . Shoots left. . . . Full name: Edward Paul Donato. . . . Name pronounced duh-NAH-toh.
HIGH SCHOOL: Catholic Memorial (Boston).
COLLEGE: Harvard.
TRANSACTIONS/CAREER NOTES: Selected by Boston Bruins in sixth round (sixth Bruins pick, 98th overall) of NHL entry draft (June 13, 1987). . . . Broke collarbone (November 18, 1989).
HONORS: Named NCAA Tournament Most Valuable Player (1988-89). . . . Named to NCAA All-Tournament team (1988-89). . . . Named to ECAC All-Star first team (1990-91).

Season Team	League	REGULAR SEASON Gms.	G	A	Pts.	PIM	PLAYOFFS Gms.	G	A	Pts.	PIM
86-87—Catholic Memorial H.S.	Mass. H.S.	22	29	34	63	30	—	—	—	—	—
87-88—Harvard University	ECAC	28	12	14	26	24	—	—	—	—	—
88-89—Harvard University	ECAC	34	14	37	51	30	—	—	—	—	—
89-90—Harvard University	ECAC	16	5	6	11	34	—	—	—	—	—
90-91—Harvard University	ECAC	28	19	37	56	26	—	—	—	—	—
91-92—U.S. national team	Int'l	52	11	22	33	24	—	—	—	—	—
—U.S. Olympic Team	Int'l	8	4	3	7	8	—	—	—	—	—
—Boston	NHL	10	1	2	3	8	15	3	4	7	4
92-93—Boston	NHL	82	15	20	35	61	4	0	1	1	0
93-94—Boston	NHL	84	22	32	54	59	13	4	2	6	10
NHL totals		**176**	**38**	**54**	**92**	**128**	**32**	**7**	**7**	**14**	**14**

DONNELLY, GORD
D/RW, STARS

PERSONAL: Born April 5, 1962, in Montreal. . . . 6-1/202. . . . Shoots right.
TRANSACTIONS/CAREER NOTES: Selected by St. Louis Blues in third round (third Blues pick, 62nd overall) of NHL entry draft (June 10, 1981). . . . Sent by Blues along with D Claude Julien to Quebec Nordiques as compensation for Blues signing coach Jacques Demers (August 1983). . . . Suspended five games by NHL for kneeing (October 29, 1987). . . . Suspended five games and fined $100 by NHL for pre-game fighting (February 26, 1988). . . . Suspended 10 games by NHL for hitting with stick (March 27, 1988); missed final four games of 1987-88 season and first six games of 1988-89 season. . . . Traded by Nordiques to Winnipeg Jets for D Mario Marois (December 6, 1988). . . . Fined $500 by NHL for kicking (April 12, 1990). . . . Traded by Jets with RW Dave McIlwain, fifth-round pick in 1992 draft (LW Yuri Khmylev) and future considerations to Buffalo Sabres for LW Darrin Shannon, LW Mike Hartman and D Dean Kennedy (October 11, 1991). . . . Traded by Sabres to Dallas Stars for LW James Black and seventh-round pick (RW Steve Webb) in 1994 draft (December 15, 1993).

Season Team	League	REGULAR SEASON Gms.	G	A	Pts.	PIM	PLAYOFFS Gms.	G	A	Pts.	PIM
78-79—Laval	QMJHL	71	1	14	15	79	—	—	—	—	—
79-80—Laval	QMJHL	44	5	10	15	47	—	—	—	—	—
—Chicoutimi	QMJHL	24	1	5	6	64	—	—	—	—	—
80-81—Sherbrooke	QMJHL	67	15	23	38	252	14	1	2	3	35
81-82—Sherbrooke	QMJHL	60	8	41	49	250	22	2	7	9	*106
82-83—Salt Lake City	IHL	67	3	12	15	222	6	1	1	2	8
83-84—Fredericton	AHL	30	2	3	5	146	7	1	1	2	43
—Quebec	NHL	38	0	5	5	60	—	—	—	—	—
84-85—Fredericton	AHL	42	1	5	6	134	6	0	1	1	25
—Quebec	NHL	22	0	0	0	33	—	—	—	—	—
85-86—Fredericton	AHL	37	3	5	8	103	5	0	0	0	33
—Quebec	NHL	36	2	2	4	85	1	0	0	0	0
86-87—Quebec	NHL	38	0	2	2	143	13	0	0	0	53
87-88—Quebec	NHL	63	4	3	7	301	—	—	—	—	—
88-89—Quebec	NHL	16	4	0	4	46	—	—	—	—	—
—Winnipeg	NHL	57	6	10	16	228	—	—	—	—	—
89-90—Winnipeg	NHL	55	3	3	6	222	6	0	1	1	8
90-91—Winnipeg	NHL	57	3	4	7	265	—	—	—	—	—
91-92—Winnipeg	NHL	4	0	0	0	11	—	—	—	—	—
—Buffalo	NHL	67	2	3	5	305	6	0	1	1	0
92-93—Buffalo	NHL	60	3	8	11	221	—	—	—	—	—
93-94—Buffalo	NHL	7	0	0	0	31	—	—	—	—	—
—Dallas	NHL	18	0	1	1	66	—	—	—	—	—
NHL totals		**538**	**27**	**41**	**68**	**2017**	**26**	**0**	**2**	**2**	**61**

DONNELLY, MIKE
LW, KINGS

PERSONAL: Born October 10, 1963, in Livonia, Mich. . . . 5-11/185. . . . Shoots left. . . . Full name: Michael Chene Donnelly.
HIGH SCHOOL: Franklin (Livonia, Mich.).
COLLEGE: Michigan State.
TRANSACTIONS/CAREER NOTES: Signed as free agent by New York Rangers (August 1986). . . . Dislocated and fractured right index finger (November 1987). . . . Traded by Rangers with fifth-round pick in 1988 draft (RW Alexander Mogilny) to Buffalo Sabres for LW Paul Cyr and 10th-round pick (C Eric Fenton) in 1988 draft (December 1987). . . . Traded by Sabres to Los Angeles Kings for LW Mikko Makela (October 1, 1990).
HONORS: Named NCAA Tournament Most Valuable Player (1985-86). . . . Named to NCAA All-America West first team (1985-86). . . . Named to NCAA All-Tournament team (1985-86). . . . Named to CCHA All-Star first team (1985-86).

Season Team	League	REGULAR SEASON Gms.	G	A	Pts.	PIM	PLAYOFFS Gms.	G	A	Pts.	PIM
82-83—Michigan State	CCHA	24	7	13	20	8	—	—	—	—	—
83-84—Michigan State	CCHA	44	18	14	32	40	—	—	—	—	—

Season	Team	League	REGULAR SEASON Gms.	G	A	Pts.	PIM	PLAYOFFS Gms.	G	A	Pts.	PIM
84-85—Michigan State		CCHA	44	26	21	47	48	—	—	—	—	—
85-86—Michigan State		CCHA	44	*59	38	97	65	—	—	—	—	—
86-87—New York Rangers		NHL	5	1	1	2	0	—	—	—	—	—
—New Haven		AHL	58	27	34	61	52	7	2	0	2	9
87-88—Colorado		IHL	8	7	11	18	15	—	—	—	—	—
—New York Rangers		NHL	17	2	2	4	8	—	—	—	—	—
—Buffalo		NHL	40	6	8	14	44	—	—	—	—	—
88-89—Buffalo		NHL	22	4	6	10	10	—	—	—	—	—
—Rochester		AHL	53	32	37	69	53	—	—	—	—	—
89-90—Rochester		AHL	68	43	55	98	71	16	*12	7	19	9
—Buffalo		NHL	12	1	2	3	8	—	—	—	—	—
90-91—Los Angeles		NHL	53	7	5	12	41	12	5	4	9	6
—New Haven		AHL	18	10	6	16	2	—	—	—	—	—
91-92—Los Angeles		NHL	80	29	16	45	20	6	1	0	1	4
92-93—Los Angeles		NHL	84	29	40	69	45	24	6	7	13	14
93-94—Los Angeles		NHL	81	21	21	42	34	—	—	—	—	—
NHL totals			394	100	101	201	210	42	12	11	23	24

DONOVAN, SHEAN
RW, SHARKS

PERSONAL: Born January 22, 1975, in Timmins, Ont. . . . 6-1/172. . . . Shoots right. . . . Name pronounced SHAWN DAHN-ih-vihn.

TRANSACTIONS/CAREER NOTES: Selected by San Jose Sharks in second round (second Sharks pick, 28th overall) of NHL entry draft (June 26, 1993).

Season	Team	League	REGULAR SEASON Gms.	G	A	Pts.	PIM	PLAYOFFS Gms.	G	A	Pts.	PIM
91-92—Ottawa		OHL	58	11	8	19	14	11	1	0	1	5
92-93—Ottawa		OHL	66	29	23	52	33	—	—	—	—	—
93-94—Ottawa		OHL	62	35	49	84	63	17	10	11	21	14

DOPSON, ROB
G, PENGUINS

PERSONAL: Born August 21, 1967, in Smith Falls, Ont. . . . 6-0/200. . . . Catches left.

COLLEGE: Wilfrid Laurier (Ont.).

TRANSACTIONS/CAREER NOTES: Signed as free agent by Pittsburgh Penguins (July 15, 1991).

HONORS: Won CIAU Championship MVP (1989-90).

Season	Team	League	REGULAR SEASON Gms.	Min.	W	L	T	GA	SO	Avg.	PLAYOFFS Gms.	Min.	W	L	GA	SO	Avg.
89-90—Wilfrid Laurier Univ.		OUAA	22	1319	...	...	...	57	0	2.59	—	—	—	—	—	—	—
90-91—Muskegon		IHL	24	1243	...	...	...	90	0	4.34	—	—	—	—	—	—	—
91-92—Muskegon		IHL	29	1655	13	12	‡2	90	4	3.26	12	697	8	4	40	0	3.44
92-93—Cleveland		IHL	50	2825	26	15	‡0	167	1	3.55	4	203	0	4	20	0	5.91
93-94—Cleveland		IHL	32	1681	9	10	‡8	109	0	3.89	—	—	—	—	—	—	—
—Pittsburgh		NHL	2	45	0	0	0	3	0	4.00	—	—	—	—	—	—	—
NHL totals			2	45	0	0	0	3	0	4.00							

DOURIS, PETER
RW, MIGHTY DUCKS

PERSONAL: Born February 19, 1966, in Toronto. . . . 6-1/195. . . . Shoots right. . . . Name pronounced DOOR-ihz.

COLLEGE: New Hampshire.

TRANSACTIONS/CAREER NOTES: Selected by Winnipeg Jets in second round (first Jets pick, 30th overall) of NHL entry draft (June 9, 1984). . . . Traded by Jets to St. Louis Blues for LW/D Kent Carlson and 12th-round pick (RW Sergei Kharin) in 1989 draft (September 29, 1988). . . . Signed as free agent by Boston Bruins (September 1989). . . . Injured ankle (December 1990). . . . Strained hip flexor (November 1991); missed three games. . . . Signed as free agent by Mighty Ducks of Anaheim (July 22, 1993). . . . Sprained left knee (September 16, 1993); missed eight games.

Season	Team	League	REGULAR SEASON Gms.	G	A	Pts.	PIM	PLAYOFFS Gms.	G	A	Pts.	PIM
83-84—Univ. of New Hampshire		ECAC	37	19	15	34	14	—	—	—	—	—
84-85—Univ. of New Hampshire		Hockey East	42	27	24	51	34	—	—	—	—	—
85-86—Canadian national team		Int'l	33	16	7	23	18	—	—	—	—	—
—Winnipeg		NHL	11	0	0	0	0	—	—	—	—	—
86-87—Sherbrooke		AHL	62	14	28	42	24	17	7	*15	†22	16
—Winnipeg		NHL	6	0	0	0	0	—	—	—	—	—
87-88—Moncton		AHL	73	42	37	79	53	—	—	—	—	—
—Winnipeg		NHL	4	0	2	2	0	1	0	0	0	0
88-89—Peoria		IHL	81	28	41	69	32	4	1	2	3	0
89-90—Maine		AHL	38	17	20	37	14	—	—	—	—	—
—Boston		NHL	36	5	6	11	15	8	0	1	1	8
90-91—Maine		AHL	35	16	15	31	9	7	0	1	1	6
—Boston		NHL	39	5	2	7	9	2	3	0	3	2
91-92—Boston		NHL	54	10	13	23	10	7	2	3	5	0
—Maine		AHL	12	4	3	7	2	—	—	—	—	—
92-93—Providence		AHL	50	29	26	55	12	—	—	—	—	—
—Boston		NHL	19	4	4	8	4	4	1	0	1	0
93-94—Anaheim		NHL	74	12	22	34	21	—	—	—	—	—
NHL totals			243	36	49	85	59	22	6	4	10	10

DOWD, JIM
C, DEVILS

PERSONAL: Born December 25, 1968, in Brick, N.J.... 6-1/190.... Shoots right.
HIGH SCHOOL: Brick Township (N.J.).
COLLEGE: Lake Superior State (Mich.).
TRANSACTIONS/CAREER NOTES: Selected by New Jersey Devils in eighth round (seventh Devils pick, 149th overall) of NHL entry draft (June 13, 1987).
HONORS: Named to NCAA All-America West second team (1989-90).... Named to CCHA All-Star second team (1989-90).... Named CCHA Player of the Year (1990-91).... Named to NCAA All-America West first team (1990-91).... Named to CCHA All-Star first team (1990-91).

Season	Team	League	REGULAR SEASON					PLAYOFFS				
			Gms.	G	A	Pts.	PIM	Gms.	G	A	Pts.	PIM
85-86	Brick Township H.S.	N.J. H.S.	...	47	51	98	...	—	—	—	—	—
86-87	Brick Township H.S.	N.J. H.S.	24	22	33	55	...	—	—	—	—	—
87-88	Lake Superior State	CCHA	45	18	27	45	16	—	—	—	—	—
88-89	Lake Superior State	CCHA	46	24	35	59	40	—	—	—	—	—
89-90	Lake Superior State	CCHA	46	25	67	92	30	—	—	—	—	—
90-91	Lake Superior State	CCHA	44	24	54	78	53	—	—	—	—	—
91-92	Utica	AHL	78	17	42	59	47	4	2	2	4	4
	New Jersey	NHL	1	0	0	0	0	—	—	—	—	—
92-93	Utica	AHL	78	27	45	72	62	5	1	7	8	10
	New Jersey	NHL	1	0	0	0	0	—	—	—	—	—
93-94	New Jersey	NHL	15	5	10	15	0	19	2	6	8	8
	Albany	AHL	58	26	37	63	76	—	—	—	—	—
NHL totals			17	5	10	15	0	19	2	6	8	8

DOYLE, TREVOR
D, PANTHERS

PERSONAL: Born January 1, 1974, in Ottawa.... 6-3/204.... Shoots right.
TRANSACTIONS/CAREER NOTES: Selected by Florida Panthers in seventh round (ninth Panthers pick, 161st overall) of NHL entry draft (June 26, 1993).

Season	Team	League	REGULAR SEASON					PLAYOFFS				
			Gms.	G	A	Pts.	PIM	Gms.	G	A	Pts.	PIM
91-92	Kingston	OHL	26	0	1	1	19	—	—	—	—	—
92-93	Kingston	OHL	62	1	8	9	148	16	2	3	5	25
93-94	Kingston	OHL	53	2	12	14	246	3	0	0	0	4

DRAKE, DALLAS
C, JETS

PERSONAL: Born February 4, 1969, in Trail, B.C.... 6-0/180.... Shoots left.... Full name: Dallas James Drake.
COLLEGE: Northern Michigan.
TRANSACTIONS/CAREER NOTES: Selected by Detroit Red Wings in sixth round (sixth Red Wings pick, 116th overall) of NHL entry draft (June 17, 1989).... Suffered left leg contusion (November 27, 1992); missed three games.... Suffered back spasms (December 28, 1992); missed one game.... Bruised kneecap (January 23, 1993); missed three games.... Suffered concussion (February 13, 1993); missed one game.... Injured right wrist (October 16, 1993); missed three games.... Injured tendon in right hand (December 14, 1993); missed 16 games.... Traded by Detroit Red Wings with G Tim Cheveldae to Winnipeg Jets for G Bob Essensa and D Sergei Bautin (March 8, 1994).
HONORS: Won WCHA Player of the Year Award (1991-92).... Named to NCAA All-America West first team (1991-92).... Named to WCHA All-Star first team (1991-92).

Season	Team	League	REGULAR SEASON					PLAYOFFS				
			Gms.	G	A	Pts.	PIM	Gms.	G	A	Pts.	PIM
84-85	Rossland	KIJHL	30	13	37	50	...	—	—	—	—	—
85-86	Rossland	KIJHL	41	53	73	126	...	—	—	—	—	—
86-87	Rossland	KIJHL	40	55	80	135	...	—	—	—	—	—
87-88	Vernon	BCJHL	47	39	85	124	50	11	9	17	26	30
88-89	Northern Michigan Univ.	WCHA	45	18	24	42	26	—	—	—	—	—
89-90	Northern Michigan Univ.	WCHA	36	13	24	37	42	—	—	—	—	—
90-91	Northern Michigan Univ.	WCHA	44	22	36	58	89	—	—	—	—	—
91-92	Northern Michigan Univ.	WCHA	40	*39	44	83	58	—	—	—	—	—
92-93	Detroit	NHL	72	18	26	44	93	7	3	3	6	6
93-94	Detroit	NHL	47	10	22	32	37	—	—	—	—	—
	Adirondack	AHL	1	2	0	2	0	—	—	—	—	—
	Winnipeg	NHL	15	3	5	8	12	—	—	—	—	—
NHL totals			134	31	53	84	142	7	3	3	6	6

DRAPER, KRIS
C/LW, RED WINGS

PERSONAL: Born May 24, 1971, in Toronto.... 5-11/190.... Shoots left.... Full name: Kris Bruce Draper.
TRANSACTIONS/CAREER NOTES: Selected by Winnipeg Jets in third round (fourth Jets pick, 62nd overall) of NHL entry draft (June 17, 1989).... Traded by Jets to Detroit Red Wings for future considerations (June 30, 1993).

Season	Team	League	REGULAR SEASON					PLAYOFFS				
			Gms.	G	A	Pts.	PIM	Gms.	G	A	Pts.	PIM
88-89	Canadian national team	Int'l	60	11	15	26	16	—	—	—	—	—
89-90	Canadian national team	Int'l	61	12	22	34	44	—	—	—	—	—
90-91	Winnipeg	NHL	3	1	0	1	5	—	—	—	—	—
	Moncton	AHL	7	2	1	3	2	—	—	—	—	—
	Ottawa	OHL	39	19	42	61	35	17	8	11	19	20

Season	Team	League	Gms.	G	A	Pts.	PIM	Gms.	G	A	Pts.	PIM
91-92—Moncton	AHL	61	11	18	29	113	4	0	1	1	6
—Winnipeg	NHL	10	2	0	2	2	2	0	0	0	0
92-93—Winnipeg	NHL	7	0	0	0	2	—	—	—	—	—
—Moncton	AHL	67	12	23	35	40	5	2	2	4	18
93-94—Adirondack	AHL	46	20	23	43	49	—	—	—	—	—
—Detroit	NHL	39	5	8	13	31	7	2	2	4	4
NHL totals		59	8	8	16	40	9	2	2	4	4

DRAPER, TOM
G, ISLANDERS

PERSONAL: Born November 20, 1966, in Outremont, Que. . . . 5-11/185. . . . Catches left. . . . Full name: Thomas Edward Draper.
COLLEGE: Vermont.
TRANSACTIONS/CAREER NOTES: Selected by Winnipeg Jets in eight round (eighth Jets pick, 165th overall) of NHL entry draft (June 15, 1985). . . . Traded by Jets to St. Louis Blues for future considerations (February 28, 1991); C Jim Vesey sent to Jets by Blues to complete deal (May 24, 1991). . . . Traded by Blues to Jets for future considerations (May 24, 1991). . . . Traded by Jets to Buffalo Sabres for future considerations; Jets later received seventh-round pick in 1992 draft (D Artur Oktyabrev) to complete deal (June 22, 1991). . . . Traded by Sabres to New York Islanders for seventh-round pick (G Steve Plouffe) in 1994 draft (September 30, 1993).
HONORS: Named to ECAC All-Star first team (1985-86). . . . Named to AHL All-Star second team (1988-89).

Season	Team	League	Gms.	Min.	W	L	T	GA	SO	Avg.	Gms.	Min.	W	L	GA	SO	Avg.
83-84—University of Vermont	ECAC	20	1205	8	12	0	82	0	4.08	—	—	—	—	—	—	—
84-85—University of Vermont	ECAC	24	1316	5	17	0	90	0	4.10	—	—	—	—	—	—	—
85-86—University of Vermont	ECAC	29	1697	15	12	1	87	1	3.08	—	—	—	—	—	—	—
86-87—University of Vermont	ECAC	29	1662	16	13	0	96	2	3.47	—	—	—	—	—	—	—
87-88—Tappara	Finland	28	1619	16	3	9	87	0	3.22	—	—	—	—	—	—	—
88-89—Moncton	AHL	54	2962	27	17	5	171	2	3.46	7	419	5	2	24	0	3.44
—Winnipeg	NHL	2	120	1	1	0	12	0	6.00	—	—	—	—	—	—	—
89-90—Moncton	AHL	51	2844	20	24	3	167	1	3.52	—	—	—	—	—	—	—
—Winnipeg	NHL	6	359	2	4	0	26	0	4.35	—	—	—	—	—	—	—
90-91—Fort Wayne	IHL	10	564	5	3	‡1	32	0	3.40	—	—	—	—	—	—	—
—Moncton	AHL	30	1779	15	13	2	95	1	3.20	—	—	—	—	—	—	—
—Peoria	IHL	10	584	6	3	‡1	36	0	3.70	4	214	2	1	10	0	2.80
91-92—Rochester	AHL	9	531	3	3	2	28	0	3.16	—	—	—	—	—	—	—
—Buffalo	NHL	26	1403	10	9	5	75	1	3.21	7	433	3	4	19	1	2.63
92-93—Buffalo	NHL	11	664	5	6	0	41	0	3.70	—	—	—	—	—	—	—
—Rochester	AHL	5	303	3	2	0	22	0	4.36	—	—	—	—	—	—	—
93-94—New York Islanders	NHL	7	227	1	3	0	16	0	4.23	—	—	—	—	—	—	—
—Salt Lake City	IHL	35	1929	7	23	‡3	140	0	4.35	—	—	—	—	—	—	—
NHL totals		52	2773	19	23	5	170	1	3.68	7	433	3	4	19	1	2.63

DRIVER, BRUCE
D, DEVILS

PERSONAL: Born April 29, 1962, in Toronto. . . . 6-0/185. . . . Shoots left. . . . Full name: Bruce Douglas Driver.
COLLEGE: Wisconsin.
TRANSACTIONS/CAREER NOTES: Selected by Colorado Rockies as underage junior in sixth round (sixth Rockies pick, 108th overall) of NHL entry draft (June 10, 1981). . . . Rockies franchise moved from Colorado to New Jersey and renamed Devils for 1982-83 season. . . . Underwent surgery to left knee (February 1985). . . . Reinjured knee (April 2, 1985). . . . Bruised shoulder (March 9, 1986). . . . Sprained ankle (February 1988). . . . Broke right leg in three places (December 7, 1988). . . . Broke rib (January 8, 1991); missed three games. . . . Reinjured rib (January 22, 1991); missed four games. . . . Injured shoulder (December 5, 1993); missed 14 games.
HONORS: Named to NCAA All-America West team (1981-82). . . . Named to NCAA All-Tournament team (1981-82). . . . Named to WCHA All-Star first team (1981-82). . . . Named to WCHA All-Star second team (1982-83).

Season	Team	League	Gms.	G	A	Pts.	PIM	Gms.	G	A	Pts.	PIM
79-80—Royal York Royals	OPJHL	43	13	57	70	102	—	—	—	—	—
80-81—University of Wisconsin	WCHA	42	5	15	20	42	—	—	—	—	—
81-82—University of Wisconsin	WCHA	46	7	37	44	84	—	—	—	—	—
82-83—University of Wisconsin	WCHA	39	16	34	50	50	—	—	—	—	—
83-84—Canadian Olympic Team	Int'l	61	11	17	28	44	—	—	—	—	—
—Maine	AHL	12	2	6	8	15	16	0	10	10	8
—New Jersey	NHL	4	0	2	2	0	—	—	—	—	—
84-85—New Jersey	NHL	67	9	23	32	36	—	—	—	—	—
85-86—Maine	AHL	15	4	7	11	16	—	—	—	—	—
—New Jersey	NHL	40	3	15	18	32	—	—	—	—	—
86-87—New Jersey	NHL	74	6	28	34	36	—	—	—	—	—
87-88—New Jersey	NHL	74	15	40	55	68	20	3	7	10	14
88-89—New Jersey	NHL	27	1	15	16	24	—	—	—	—	—
89-90—New Jersey	NHL	75	7	46	53	63	6	1	5	6	6
90-91—New Jersey	NHL	73	9	36	45	62	7	1	2	3	12
91-92—New Jersey	NHL	78	7	35	42	66	7	0	4	4	2
92-93—New Jersey	NHL	83	14	40	54	66	5	1	3	4	4
93-94—New Jersey	NHL	66	8	24	32	63	20	3	5	8	12
NHL totals		661	79	304	383	516	65	9	26	35	50

DROLET, JIMMY
D, CANADIENS

PERSONAL: Born February 19, 1976, in Vanier, Que.... 6-0/168.... Shoots left.... Name pronounced Droh-LAY.

TRANSACTIONS/CAREER NOTES: Selected by Montreal Canadiens in fifth round (seventh Canadiens pick, 122nd overall) of NHL entry draft (June 29, 1994).

HONORS: Won Raymond Lagace Trophy (1993-94).... Named to QMJHL All-Rookie team (1993-94).

Season Team	League	REGULAR SEASON					PLAYOFFS				
		Gms.	G	A	Pts.	PIM	Gms.	G	A	Pts.	PIM
93-94—St. Hyacinthe	QMJHL	72	10	46	56	93	7	1	7	8	10

DROPPA, IVAN
D, BLACKHAWKS

PERSONAL: Born February 1, 1972, in Liptovsky Mikulas, Czechoslovakia.... 6-2/209.... Shoots left.... Name pronounced IGH-vihn DROH-puh.

TRANSACTIONS/CAREER NOTES: Selected by Chicago Blackhawks in second round (second Blackhawks pick, 37th overall) of NHL entry draft (June 16, 1990).

Season Team	League	REGULAR SEASON					PLAYOFFS				
		Gms.	G	A	Pts.	PIM	Gms.	G	A	Pts.	PIM
89-90—Liptovsky Mikulas	Czech.				Statistics unavailable.						
90-91—VSZ Kosice	Czech.	49	1	7	8	12	—	—	—	—	—
91-92—VSZ Kosice	Czech.	43	4	9	13	...	—	—	—	—	—
92-93—Indianapolis	IHL	77	14	29	43	92	5	0	1	1	2
93-94—Indianapolis	IHL	55	9	10	19	71	—	—	—	—	—
—Chicago	NHL	12	0	1	1	12	—	—	—	—	—
NHL totals		12	0	1	1	12	—	—	—	—	—

DRUCE, JOHN
RW, KINGS

PERSONAL: Born February 23, 1966, in Peterborough, Ont.... 6-2/195.... Shoots right.... Name pronounced DROOZ.

TRANSACTIONS/CAREER NOTES: Broke collarbone (October 1983).... Tore ligaments in ankle (December 1984).... Selected by Washington Capitals in second round (second Capitals pick, 40th overall) of NHL entry draft (June 15, 1985).... Tore thumb ligaments (October 1985).... Fractured wrist (October 18, 1992); missed 18 games.... Traded by Capitals to Winnipeg Jets with conditional pick in 1993 draft for RW Pat Elynuik (October 1, 1992).... Signed as free agent by Los Angeles Kings (August 2, 1993).

Season Team	League	REGULAR SEASON					PLAYOFFS				
		Gms.	G	A	Pts.	PIM	Gms.	G	A	Pts.	PIM
83-84—Peterborough Jr. B	OHA	40	15	18	33	69	—	—	—	—	—
84-85—Peterborough	OHL	54	12	14	26	90	17	6	2	8	21
85-86—Peterborough	OHL	49	22	24	46	84	16	0	5	5	34
86-87—Binghamton	AHL	7	13	9	22	131	12	0	3	3	28
87-88—Binghamton	AHL	68	32	29	61	82	1	0	0	0	0
88-89—Washington	NHL	48	8	7	15	62	1	0	0	0	0
—Baltimore	AHL	16	2	11	13	10	—	—	—	—	—
89-90—Washington	NHL	45	8	3	11	52	15	14	3	17	23
—Baltimore	AHL	26	15	16	31	38	—	—	—	—	—
90-91—Washington	NHL	80	22	36	58	46	11	1	1	2	7
91-92—Washington	NHL	67	19	18	37	39	7	1	0	1	2
92-93—Winnipeg	NHL	50	6	14	20	37	2	0	0	0	0
93-94—Phoenix	IHL	8	5	6	11	9	—	—	—	—	—
—Los Angeles	NHL	55	14	17	31	50	—	—	—	—	—
NHL totals		345	77	95	172	286	36	16	4	20	32

DRULIA, STAN
RW, LIGHTNING

PERSONAL: Born January 5, 1968, in Elmira, N.Y.... 5-11/190.... Shoots right.... Name pronounced DROOL-yuh.

TRANSACTIONS/CAREER NOTES: Selected by Pittsburgh Penguins as underage junior in 11th round (11th Penguins pick, 214th overall) of NHL entry draft (June 21, 1986).... Signed as free agent by Edmonton Oilers (May 1989).... Signed as free agent by Tampa Bay Lightning (September 1, 1992).

HONORS: Won Jim Mahon Memorial Trophy (1988-89).... Won Leo Lalonde Memorial Trophy (1988-89).... Named to OHL All-Star first team (1988-89).... Won ECHL Most Valuable Player Award (1990-91).... Won ECHL Top Scorer Award (1990-91).... Named to ECHL All-Star first team (1990-91).... Named to AHL All-Star second team (1991-92).... Named to IHL All-Star first team (1993-94).

Season Team	League	REGULAR SEASON					PLAYOFFS				
		Gms.	G	A	Pts.	PIM	Gms.	G	A	Pts.	PIM
84-85—Belleville	OHL	63	24	31	55	33	—	—	—	—	—
85-86—Belleville	OHL	66	43	37	80	73	—	—	—	—	—
86-87—Hamilton	OHL	55	27	51	78	26	—	—	—	—	—
87-88—Hamilton	OHL	65	52	69	121	44	14	8	16	24	12
88-89—Niagara Falls	OHL	47	52	93	145	59	17	11	*26	37	18
—Maine	AHL	3	1	1	2	0	—	—	—	—	—
89-90—Cape Breton	AHL	31	5	7	12	2	—	—	—	—	—
—Phoenix	IHL	16	6	3	9	2	—	—	—	—	—
90-91—Knoxville	ECHL	64	*63	77	*140	39	3	3	2	5	4
91-92—New Haven	AHL	77	49	53	102	46	5	2	4	6	4
92-93—Tampa Bay	NHL	24	2	1	3	10	—	—	—	—	—
—Atlanta	IHL	47	28	26	54	38	3	2	3	5	4
93-94—Atlanta	IHL	79	54	60	114	70	14	13	12	25	8
NHL totals		24	2	1	3	10					

DRURY, CHRIS
C, NORDIQUES

PERSONAL: Born August 20, 1976, in Trumbull, Conn.... 5-10/180.... Shoots right.
TRANSACTIONS/CAREER NOTES: Selected by Quebec Nordiques in third round (fifth Nordiques pick, 72nd overall) of NHL entry draft (June 29, 1994).

		REGULAR SEASON					PLAYOFFS				
Season Team	League	Gms.	G	A	Pts.	PIM	Gms.	G	A	Pts.	PIM
93-94—Fairfield College Prep	Conn. H.S.	24	37	18	55	...	—	—	—	—	—

DRURY, TED
C, WHALERS

PERSONAL: Born September 13, 1971, in Boston.... 6-0/185.... Shoots left.... Full name: Theodore Evans Drury.... Name pronounced DROO-ree.
HIGH SCHOOL: Fairfield (Conn.) College Prep School.
COLLEGE: Harvard.
TRANSACTIONS/CAREER NOTES: Broke ankle (January 1988).... Selected by Calgary Flames in second round (second Flames pick, 42nd overall) of NHL entry draft (June 17, 1989).... Fractured kneecap (December 22, 1993); missed 15 games.... Traded by Flames with D Gary Suter and LW Paul Ranheim to Hartford Whalers for C Mikael Nylander, D Zarley Zalapski and D James Patrick (March 10, 1994).
HONORS: Named ECAC Player of the Year (1992-93).... Named to NCAA All-America East first team (1992-93).... Named to ECAC All-Star first team (1992-93).

		REGULAR SEASON					PLAYOFFS				
Season Team	League	Gms.	G	A	Pts.	PIM	Gms.	G	A	Pts.	PIM
87-88—Fairfield College Prep	Conn. H.S.	...	21	28	49	...	—	—	—	—	—
88-89—Fairfield College Prep	Conn. H.S.	...	35	31	66	...	—	—	—	—	—
89-90—Harvard University	ECAC	17	9	13	22	10	—	—	—	—	—
90-91—Harvard University	ECAC	26	18	18	36	22	—	—	—	—	—
91-92—U.S. national team	Int'l	53	11	23	34	30	—	—	—	—	—
—U.S. Olympic Team	Int'l	7	1	1	2	0	—	—	—	—	—
92-93—Harvard University	ECAC	31	22	41	*63	26	—	—	—	—	—
93-94—Calgary	NHL	34	5	7	12	26	—	—	—	—	—
—U.S. national team	Int'l	11	1	4	5	11	—	—	—	—	—
—U.S. Olympic Team	Int'l	7	1	2	3	2	—	—	—	—	—
—Hartford.....................	NHL	16	1	5	6	10	—	—	—	—	—
NHL totals...		**50**	**6**	**12**	**18**	**36**					

DUBE, YANNICK
C, CANUCKS

PERSONAL: Born June 14, 1974, in Gaspe, Que.... 5-9/170.... Shoots right.
TRANSACTIONS/CAREER NOTES: Selected by Vancouver Canucks in fifth round (sixth Canucks pick, 117th overall) of NHL entry draft (June 29, 1994).
HONORS: Won Can.HL Most Sportsmanlike Player of the Year Award (1993-94).... Won George Parsons Trophy (1993-94).... Won Jean Beliveau Trophy (1993-94).... Won Frank J. Selke Trophy (1993-94).... Named to Can.HL All-Star second team (1993-94).... Named to QMJHL All-Star first team (1993-94).

		REGULAR SEASON					PLAYOFFS				
Season Team	League	Gms.	G	A	Pts.	PIM	Gms.	G	A	Pts.	PIM
91-92—Laval	QMJHL	65	14	19	33	8	10	0	2	2	2
92-93—Laval	QMJHL	68	45	38	83	25	13	6	7	13	6
93-94—Laval	QMJHL	64	*66	75	*141	30	21	12	18	30	8

DUBERMAN, JUSTIN
RW, PENGUINS

PERSONAL: Born March 23, 1970, in New Haven, Conn.... 6-1/185.... Shoots right.... Name pronounced DOO-buhr-muhn.
COLLEGE: North Dakota.
TRANSACTIONS/CAREER NOTES: Selected by Montreal Canadiens in 11th round (11th Canadiens pick, 230th overall) of 1989 NHL entry draft (June 17, 1989).... Signed as free agent by Pittsburgh Penguins (October 1, 1992).

		REGULAR SEASON					PLAYOFFS				
Season Team	League	Gms.	G	A	Pts.	PIM	Gms.	G	A	Pts.	PIM
88-89—North Dakota	WCHA	33	3	1	4	30	—	—	—	—	—
89-90—North Dakota	WCHA	42	10	9	19	50	—	—	—	—	—
90-91—North Dakota	WCHA	42	19	18	37	68	—	—	—	—	—
91-92—North Dakota	WCHA	39	17	27	44	90	—	—	—	—	—
92-93—Cleveland	IHL	77	29	42	71	69	4	0	0	0	12
93-94—Cleveland	IHL	59	9	13	22	63	—	—	—	—	—
—Pittsburgh	NHL	4	0	0	0	0	—	—	—	—	—
NHL totals..		**4**	**0**	**0**	**0**	**0**					

DUBINSKY, MIKE
RW, CANUCKS

PERSONAL: Born August 26, 1976, in Edmonton.... 6-2/185.... Shoots right.... Name pronounced doo-BIHN-skee.
TRANSACTIONS/CAREER NOTES: Selected by Vancouver Canucks in fourth round (fifth Canucks pick, 92nd overall) of NHL entry draft (June 29, 1994).

		REGULAR SEASON					PLAYOFFS				
Season Team	League	Gms.	G	A	Pts.	PIM	Gms.	G	A	Pts.	PIM
92-93—Brandon..........................	WHL	64	10	25	35	44	3	0	0	0	0
93-94—Brandon..........................	WHL	20	9	13	22	23	—	—	—	—	—

DUBINSKY, STEVE
C, BLACKHAWKS

PERSONAL: Born July 9, 1970, in Montreal.... 6-0/190.... Shoots left.... Name pronounced doo-BIHN-skee.
TRANSACTIONS/CAREER NOTES: Selected by Chicago Blackhawks in 11th round (11th Blackhawks pick, 226th overall) of NHL entry draft (June 16, 1990).

Season Team	League	REGULAR SEASON					PLAYOFFS				
		Gms.	G	A	Pts.	PIM	Gms.	G	A	Pts.	PIM
89-90—Clarkson	ECAC	35	7	10	17	24	—	—	—	—	—
90-91—Clarkson	ECAC	38	15	23	38	26	—	—	—	—	—
91-92—Clarkson	ECAC	33	21	34	55	40	—	—	—	—	—
92-93—Clarkson	ECAC	35	18	26	44	58	—	—	—	—	—
93-94—Chicago	NHL	27	2	6	8	16	6	0	0	0	10
—Indianapolis	IHL	54	15	25	40	63	—	—	—	—	—
NHL totals		27	2	6	8	16	6	0	0	0	10

DuBOIS, ERIC
D, LIGHTNING

PERSONAL: Born May 10, 1970, in Moncton, N.B. . . . . 6-0/195. . . . Shoots right.
TRANSACTIONS/CAREER NOTES: Selected by Quebec Nordiques in fourth round (sixth Nordiques pick, 76th overall) of NHL entry draft (June 17, 1989). . . . Signed as free agent by Atlanta Knights (July 2, 1993).
HONORS: Named to QMJHL All-Star first team (1988-89).

Season Team	League	REGULAR SEASON					PLAYOFFS				
		Gms.	G	A	Pts.	PIM	Gms.	G	A	Pts.	PIM
86-87—Laval	QMJHL	61	1	17	18	29	—	—	—	—	—
87-88—Laval	QMJHL	69	8	32	40	132	14	1	7	8	12
88-89—Laval	QMJHL	68	15	44	59	126	17	1	11	12	55
89-90—Laval	QMJHL	66	9	36	45	153	13	3	8	11	29
90-91—Laval	QMJHL	57	15	45	60	122	13	3	5	8	29
91-92—New Haven	AHL	1	0	0	0	2	—	—	—	—	—
—Halifax	AHL	14	0	0	0	8	—	—	—	—	—
—Greensboro	ECHL	36	7	17	24	62	11	4	4	8	40
92-93—Greensboro	ECHL	25	5	20	25	70	—	—	—	—	—
—Atlanta	IHL	43	3	9	12	44	9	0	0	0	10
93-94—Atlanta	IHL	80	13	26	39	174	14	0	7	7	48

DUCHESNE, GAETAN
LW, SHARKS

PERSONAL: Born July 11, 1962, in Quebec City. . . . 5-11/200. . . . Shoots left. . . . Name pronounced gay-TAN doo-SHAYN.
TRANSACTIONS/CAREER NOTES: Selected by Washington Capitals in eighth round (eighth Capitals pick, 152nd overall) of NHL entry draft (June 10, 1981). . . . Bruised right ankle (December 30, 1981). . . . Broke finger (October 11, 1984). . . . Traded by Capitals with C Alan Haworth and first-round pick in 1987 draft (C Joe Sakic) to Quebec Nordiques for C Dale Hunter and G Clint Malarchuk (June 1987). . . . Sprained left knee (January 26, 1988). . . . Sprained left shoulder (November 1988). . . . Traded by Nordiques to Minnesota North Stars for C Kevin Kaminski (June 18, 1989). . . . Sprained right knee (November 11, 1989); missed eight games. . . . North Stars franchise moved from Minnesota to Dallas and renamed Stars for 1993-94 season. . . . Traded by Stars to San Jose Sharks for sixth-round pick in 1993 draft (June 20, 1993).

Season Team	League	REGULAR SEASON					PLAYOFFS				
		Gms.	G	A	Pts.	PIM	Gms.	G	A	Pts.	PIM
79-80—Quebec	QMJHL	46	9	28	37	22	5	0	2	2	9
80-81—Quebec	QMJHL	72	27	45	72	63	7	1	4	5	6
81-82—Washington	NHL	74	9	14	23	46	—	—	—	—	—
82-83—Hershey	AHL	1	1	0	1	0	—	—	—	—	—
—Washington	NHL	77	18	19	37	52	4	1	1	2	4
83-84—Washington	NHL	79	17	19	36	29	8	2	1	3	2
84-85—Washington	NHL	67	15	23	38	32	5	0	1	1	7
85-86—Washington	NHL	80	11	28	39	39	9	4	3	7	12
86-87—Washington	NHL	74	17	35	52	53	7	3	0	3	14
87-88—Quebec	NHL	80	24	23	47	83	—	—	—	—	—
88-89—Quebec	NHL	70	8	21	29	56	—	—	—	—	—
89-90—Minnesota	NHL	72	12	8	20	33	7	0	0	0	6
90-91—Minnesota	NHL	68	9	9	18	18	23	2	3	5	34
91-92—Minnesota	NHL	73	8	15	23	102	7	1	0	1	6
92-93—Minnesota	NHL	84	16	13	29	30	—	—	—	—	—
93-94—San Jose	NHL	84	12	18	30	28	14	1	4	5	12
NHL totals		982	176	245	421	601	84	14	13	27	97

DUCHESNE, STEVE
D, BLUES

PERSONAL: Born June 30, 1965, in Sept-Iles, Que. . . . 5-11/195. . . . Shoots left. . . . Name pronounced doo-SHAYN.
TRANSACTIONS/CAREER NOTES: Signed as free agent by Los Angeles Kings (October 1, 1984). . . . Strained left knee (January 26, 1988). . . . Separated left shoulder (November 1988). . . . Traded by Kings with C Steve Kasper and fourth-round pick in 1991 draft (D Aris Brimanis) to Philadelphia Flyers for D Jeff Chychrun and rights to RW Jari Kurri (May 30, 1991). . . . Traded by Flyers with G Ron Hextall, C Mike Ricci, C Peter Forsberg, D Kerry Huffman, first-round pick in 1993 draft (G Jocelyn Thibault), cash and future considerations to Quebec Nordiques for C Eric Lindros (June 20, 1992); Flyers sent LW Chris Simon and first-round pick in 1994 draft (traded to Toronto Maple Leafs) to Nordiques to complete deal (July 21, 1992). . . . Suffered a concussion (January 2, 1993); missed one game. . . . Suffered from the flu (March 20, 1993); missed one game. . . . Refused to report to Nordiques in 1993-94 due to contract dispute. . . . Traded by Nordiques with RW Denis Chasse to St. Louis Blues for C Ron Sutter, C Bob Bassen and D Garth Butcher (January 23, 1994). . . . Injured back (March 30, 1994); missed one game.
HONORS: Named to QMJHL All-Star first team (1984-85). . . . Named to NHL All-Rookie team (1986-87). . . . Played in NHL All-Star Game (1989, 1990 and 1993).

Season Team	League	REGULAR SEASON					PLAYOFFS				
		Gms.	G	A	Pts.	PIM	Gms.	G	A	Pts.	PIM
83-84—Drummondville	QMJHL	67	1	34	35	79	—	—	—	—	—
84-85—Drummondville	QMJHL	65	22	54	76	94	5	4	7	11	8
85-86—New Haven	AHL	75	14	35	49	76	5	0	2	2	9
86-87—Los Angeles	NHL	75	13	25	38	74	5	2	2	4	4
87-88—Los Angeles	NHL	71	16	39	55	109	5	1	3	4	14
88-89—Los Angeles	NHL	79	25	50	75	92	11	4	4	8	12
89-90—Los Angeles	NHL	79	20	42	62	36	10	2	9	11	6
90-91—Los Angeles	NHL	78	21	41	62	66	12	4	8	12	8
91-92—Philadelphia	NHL	78	18	38	56	86	—	—	—	—	—
92-93—Quebec	NHL	82	20	62	82	57	6	0	5	5	6
93-94—St. Louis	NHL	36	12	19	31	14	4	0	2	2	2
NHL totals		578	145	316	461	534	53	13	33	46	52

DUFFUS, PARRIS
G, BLUES

PERSONAL: Born January 27, 1970, in Denver.... 6-2/192.... Catches left.... Name pronounced PAIR-ihz DOO-fihz.
COLLEGE: Cornell.
TRANSACTIONS/CAREER NOTES: Selected by St. Louis Blues in ninth round (sixth Blues pick, 180th overall) of NHL entry draft (June 16, 1990).
HONORS: Named to NCAA All-America East first team (1991-92).... Named to ECAC All-Star second team (1991-92).

Season Team	League	REGULAR SEASON							PLAYOFFS						
		Gms.	Min.	W	L	T	GA	SO	Avg.	Gms.	Min.	W	L	GA	SO	Avg.
88-89—Melfort	SJHL	39	2207	5	28	3	227	1	6.17	—	—	—	—	—	—	—
89-90—Melfort	SJHL	51	2828	17	26	3	226	2	4.79	—	—	—	—	—	—	—
90-91—Cornell University	ECAC	4	37	0	0	0	3	0	4.86	—	—	—	—	—	—	—
91-92—Cornell University	ECAC	28	1677	14	11	3	74	1	2.65	—	—	—	—	—	—	—
92-93—Hampton Roads	ECHL	4	245	3	1	‡0	13	0	3.18	—	—	—	—	—	—	—
—Peoria	IHL	37	2149	16	15	‡0	142	0	3.96	1	59	0	1	5	0	5.08
93-94—Peoria	IHL	36	1845	19	10	‡3	141	0	4.59	2	92	0	1	6	0	3.91

DUFRESNE, DONALD
D, KINGS

PERSONAL: Born April 10, 1967, in Quebec City.... 6-1/206.... Shoots left.... Name pronounced DOH-nal doo-FRAYN.
TRANSACTIONS/CAREER NOTES: Suffered from pneumonia (November 1984).... Selected by Montreal Canadiens in sixth round (eighth Canadiens pick, 117th overall) of NHL entry draft (June 15, 1985).... Dislocated shoulder (January 8, 1988).... Sprained ankle (February 1989). ... Separated shoulder (October 5, 1989); missed 15 games.... Reinjured shoulder (December 9, 1989).... Tore ligaments in right knee (December 9, 1991); missed 15 games.... Sprained knee (February 20, 1993); missed three games.... Strained rib cage muscles (March 3, 1993); missed three games.... Traded by Canadiens to Tampa Bay Lightning (June 18, 1993) to complete deal in which Canadiens sent D Eric Charron, D Alain Cote and future considerations to Lightning for D Rob Ramage (March 20, 1993).... Suffered knee ligament sprain (January 26, 1994); missed eight games.... Reinjured knee (February 17, 1994); missed seven games.... Traded by Lightning to Los Angeles Kings for sixth-round pick (C Daniel Juden) in 1994 draft (March 19, 1994).
HONORS: Named to QMJHL All-Star second team (1985-86 and 1986-87).
MISCELLANEOUS: Member of Stanley Cup championship team (1993).

Season Team	League	REGULAR SEASON					PLAYOFFS				
		Gms.	G	A	Pts.	PIM	Gms.	G	A	Pts.	PIM
83-84—Trois-Rivieres	QMJHL	67	7	12	19	97	—	—	—	—	—
84-85—Trois-Rivieres	QMJHL	65	5	30	35	112	7	1	3	4	12
85-86—Trois-Rivieres	QMJHL	63	8	32	40	160	1	0	0	0	0
86-87—Longueuil	QMJHL	67	5	29	34	97	20	1	8	9	38
87-88—Sherbrooke	AHL	47	1	8	9	107	6	1	1	2	34
88-89—Montreal	NHL	13	0	1	1	43	6	1	1	2	4
—Sherbrooke	AHL	47	0	12	12	170	—	—	—	—	—
89-90—Montreal	NHL	18	0	4	4	23	10	0	1	1	18
—Sherbrooke	AHL	38	2	11	13	104	0	0	0	0	0
90-91—Fredericton	AHL	10	1	4	5	35	1	0	0	0	0
—Montreal	NHL	53	2	13	15	55	10	0	1	1	21
91-92—Montreal	NHL	3	0	0	0	2	—	—	—	—	—
—Fredericton	AHL	31	8	12	20	60	7	0	0	0	10
92-93—Montreal	NHL	32	1	2	3	32	2	0	0	0	0
93-94—Tampa Bay	NHL	51	2	6	8	48	—	—	—	—	—
—Los Angeles	NHL	9	0	0	0	10	—	—	—	—	—
NHL totals		179	5	26	31	213	28	1	3	4	43

DUNCANSON, CRAIG
LW, RANGERS

PERSONAL: Born March 17, 1967, in Sudbury, Ont.... 6-0/190.... Shoots left.... Full name: Craig Murray Duncanson.
TRANSACTIONS/CAREER NOTES: Tore knee ligaments (September 1984).... Selected by Los Angeles Kings as underage junior in first round (first Kings pick, ninth overall) of NHL entry draft (June 15, 1985).... Suffered deep leg bruise (November 23, 1986).... Traded by Kings to Minnesota North Stars for G Daniel Berthiaume (September 6, 1990).... Traded by North Stars to Winnipeg Jets for C Brian Hunt (September 6, 1990).... Traded by Jets with LW Brent Hughes and C Simon Wheeldon to Washington Capitals for LW Bob Joyce, D Kent Paynter and C Tyler Larter (May 21, 1991).... Loaned to Jets organization (February 26, 1992).... Signed as free agent by New York Rangers (September 4, 1992).

Season	Team	League	REGULAR SEASON					PLAYOFFS				
			Gms.	G	A	Pts.	PIM	Gms.	G	A	Pts.	PIM
82-83—St. Michael's Jr. B	ODHA	32	14	19	33	68	—	—	—	—	—
83-84—Sudbury	OHL	62	38	38	76	178	—	—	—	—	—
84-85—Sudbury	OHL	53	35	28	63	129	—	—	—	—	—
85-86—Sudbury	OHL	21	12	17	29	55	—	—	—	—	—
—Cornwall	OHL	40	31	50	81	135	6	4	7	11	2
—Los Angeles	NHL	2	0	1	1	0	—	—	—	—	—
—New Haven	AHL	—	—	—	—	—	2	0	0	0	5
86-87—Cornwall	OHL	52	22	45	67	88	5	4	3	7	20
—Los Angeles	NHL	2	0	0	0	24	—	—	—	—	—
87-88—New Haven	AHL	57	15	25	40	170	—	—	—	—	—
—Los Angeles	NHL	9	0	0	0	12	—	—	—	—	—
88-89—New Haven	AHL	69	25	39	64	200	17	4	8	12	60
—Los Angeles	NHL	5	0	0	0	0	—	—	—	—	—
89-90—Los Angeles	NHL	10	3	2	5	9	—	—	—	—	—
—New Haven	AHL	51	17	30	47	152	—	—	—	—	—
90-91—Moncton	AHL	58	16	34	50	107	9	3	11	14	31
—Winnipeg	NHL	7	2	0	2	16	—	—	—	—	—
91-92—Baltimore	AHL	46	20	26	46	98	—	—	—	—	—
—Moncton	AHL	19	12	9	21	6	11	6	4	10	10
92-93—Binghamton	AHL	69	35	59	94	126	14	7	5	12	9
—New York Rangers	NHL	3	0	1	1	0	—	—	—	—	—
93-94—Binghamton	AHL	70	25	44	69	83	—	—	—	—	—
NHL totals		38	5	4	9	61					

DUNHAM, MIKE
G, DEVILS

PERSONAL: Born June 1, 1972, in Johnson City, N.Y. . . . . 6-3/185. . . . Catches left. . . . Full name: Michael Francis Dunham.
HIGH SCHOOL: Canterbury (New Milford, Conn.).
COLLEGE: Maine.
TRANSACTIONS/CAREER NOTES: Selected by New Jersey Devils in third round (fourth Devils pick, 53rd overall) of NHL entry draft (June 16, 1990).
HONORS: Named to NCAA All-America East first team (1992-93). . . . Named to Hockey East All-Star first team (1992-93).

Season	Team	League	REGULAR SEASON							PLAYOFFS						
			Gms.	Min.	W	L	T	GA	SO	Avg.	Gms.	Min.	W	L	GA	SO	Avg.
88-89—Canterbury School	Conn. HS	25	...	...	...	...	63	2	...	—	—	—	—	—	—	—
89-90—Canterbury School	Conn. HS	32	1558	...	...	...	55	...	2.12	—	—	—	—	—	—	—
90-91—University of Maine	Hoc. East	23	1275	14	5	2	63	2	*2.96	—	—	—	—	—	—	—
91-92—University of Maine	Hoc. East	7	382	6	0	0	14	1	2.20	—	—	—	—	—	—	—
—U.S. national team	Int'l	3	157	0	1	1	10	0	3.82	—	—	—	—	—	—	—
—U.S. Olympic Team	Int'l				Did not play.					—	—	—	—	—	—	—
92-93—University of Maine	Hoc. East	25	1429	21	1	1	63	...	2.65	—	—	—	—	—	—	—
93-94—U.S. national team	Int'l	33	1983	...	...	...	125	...	3.78	—	—	—	—	—	—	—
—U.S. Olympic Team	Int'l	3	179	...	...	...	15	0	5.03	—	—	—	—	—	—	—
—Albany	AHL	5	305	2	2	1	26	0	5.11	—	—	—	—	—	—	—

DUPAUL, COSMO
C, SENATORS

PERSONAL: Born April 11, 1975, in Pointe-Claire, Que. . . . 6-0/185. . . . Shoots left.
TRANSACTIONS/CAREER NOTES: Selected by Ottawa Senators in fourth round (fourth Senators pick, 91st overall) of NHL entry draft (June 26, 1993).

Season	Team	League	REGULAR SEASON					PLAYOFFS				
			Gms.	G	A	Pts.	PIM	Gms.	G	A	Pts.	PIM
92-93—Victoriaville	QMJHL	67	23	35	58	16	6	1	3	4	2
93-94—Victoriaville	QMJHL	66	26	46	72	32	5	2	2	4	6

DUPRE, YANICK
LW, FLYERS

PERSONAL: Born November 20, 1972, in Montreal. . . . 6-0/195. . . . Shoots left. . . . Name pronounced YAH-nihk doo-PRAY.
TRANSACTIONS/CAREER NOTES: Pulled ankle ligament (September 1989). . . . Traded by Chicoutimi Sagueneens with D Guy Lehoux and RW Eric Meloche to Drummondville Voltigeurs for RW Daniel Dore, RW Denis Chasse and D Pierre-Paul Landry (December 19, 1989). . . . Injured knee ligament (October 1990). . . . Selected by Philadelphia Flyers in third round (second Flyers pick, 50th overall) of NHL entry draft (June 22, 1991).

Season	Team	League	REGULAR SEASON					PLAYOFFS				
			Gms.	G	A	Pts.	PIM	Gms.	G	A	Pts.	PIM
89-90—Chicoutimi	QMJHL	24	5	9	14	27	—	—	—	—	—
—Drummondville	QMJHL	30	10	10	20	32	—	—	—	—	—
90-91—Drummondville	QMJHL	58	29	38	67	87	11	8	5	13	33
91-92—Philadelphia	NHL	1	0	0	0	0	—	—	—	—	—
—Drummondville	QMJHL	28	19	17	36	48	—	—	—	—	—
—Verdun	QMJHL	12	7	14	21	21	19	9	9	18	20
92-93—Hershey	AHL	63	13	24	37	22	—	—	—	—	—
93-94—Hershey	AHL	51	22	20	42	42	8	1	3	4	2
NHL totals		1	0	0	0	0					

DUPUIS, MARC
D, BLACKHAWKS

PERSONAL: Born April 22, 1976, in Cornwall, Ont. . . . 5-11/176. . . . Shoots left.
TRANSACTIONS/CAREER NOTES: Selected by Chicago Blackhawks in fifth round (fourth Blackhawks pick, 118th overall) of NHL entry draft (June 29, 1994).

		REGULAR SEASON					PLAYOFFS				
Season Team	League	Gms.	G	A	Pts.	PIM	Gms.	G	A	Pts.	PIM
92-93—Belleville	OHL	64	2	10	12	34	7	0	5	5	10
93-94—Belleville	OHL	66	7	25	32	37	12	2	3	5	6

DUTHIE, RYAN
C, FLAMES

PERSONAL: Born September 2, 1974, in Strathmore, Alta. . . . 5-10/180. . . . Shoots right. . . . Name pronounced DOO-THEE.
HIGH SCHOOL: Joel E. Ferris (Spokane, Wash.).
TRANSACTIONS/CAREER NOTES: Selected by New York Islanders in fifth round (fourth Islanders pick, 105th overall) of NHL entry draft (June 20, 1992). . . . Returned to the draft pool by Islanders and selected by Calgary Flames in fourth round (fourth Flames pick, 91st overall) of NHL entry draft (June 29, 1994).
HONORS: Named to WHL (West) All-Star first team (1993-94).

		REGULAR SEASON					PLAYOFFS				
Season Team	League	Gms.	G	A	Pts.	PIM	Gms.	G	A	Pts.	PIM
91-92—Spokane	WHL	67	23	37	60	119	10	5	10	15	18
92-93—Spokane	WHL	60	26	58	84	122	9	7	2	9	8
93-94—Spokane	WHL	71	57	69	126	111	3	3	5	8	11

DYCK, PAUL
D, PENGUINS

PERSONAL: Born April 15, 1971, in Steinbach, Man. . . . 6-1/192. . . . Shoots left. . . . Name pronounced DIHK.
TRANSACTIONS/CAREER NOTES: Selected by Pittsburgh Penguins in 11th round (11th Penguins pick, 236th overall) of NHL entry draft (June 22, 1991).

		REGULAR SEASON					PLAYOFFS				
Season Team	League	Gms.	G	A	Pts.	PIM	Gms.	G	A	Pts.	PIM
89-90—Moose Jaw	WHL	72	5	10	15	86	—	—	—	—	—
90-91—Moose Jaw	WHL	72	12	41	53	63	8	0	7	7	17
91-92—Muskegon	IHL	73	6	21	27	40	14	1	3	4	4
92-93—Cleveland	IHL	69	6	21	27	69	1	0	0	0	0
93-94—Cleveland	IHL	60	1	10	11	57	—	—	—	—	—

DYKHUIS, KARL
D, BLACKHAWKS

PERSONAL: Born July 8, 1972, in Sept-Iles, Que. . . . 6-3/195. . . . Shoots left. . . . Name pronounced DIGH-kowz.
TRANSACTIONS/CAREER NOTES: Selected by Chicago Blackhawks in first round (first Blackhawks pick, 16th overall) of NHL entry draft (June 16, 1990). . . . QMJHL rights traded by Hull Olympiques to College Francais for first- and sixth-round draft picks (January 10, 1991).
HONORS: Won Raymond Lagace Trophy (1988-89). . . . Won QMJHL Top Draft Prospect Award (1989-90). . . . Named to QMJHL All-Star first team (1989-90).

		REGULAR SEASON					PLAYOFFS				
Season Team	League	Gms.	G	A	Pts.	PIM	Gms.	G	A	Pts.	PIM
88-89—Hull	QMJHL	63	2	29	31	59	9	1	9	10	6
89-90—Hull	QMJHL	69	10	45	55	119	11	2	5	7	2
90-91—Longueuil	QMJHL	3	1	4	5	6	—	—	—	—	—
—Canadian national team	Int'l				Statistics unavailable.						
91-92—Longueuil	QMJHL	29	5	19	24	55	17	0	12	12	14
—Chicago	NHL	6	1	3	4	4	—	—	—	—	—
92-93—Indianapolis	IHL	59	5	18	23	76	5	1	1	2	8
—Chicago	NHL	12	0	5	5	0	—	—	—	—	—
93-94—Indianapolis	IHL	73	7	25	32	132	—	—	—	—	—
NHL totals		18	1	8	9	4					

DZIEDZIC, JOE
LW, PENGUINS

PERSONAL: Born December 18, 1971, in Minneapolis. . . . 6-3/200. . . . Shoots left. . . . Full name: Joseph Walter Dziedzic.
HIGH SCHOOL: Edison (Minneapolis).
COLLEGE: Minnesota.
TRANSACTIONS/CAREER NOTES: Selected by Pittsburgh Penguins in third round (second Penguins pick, 61st overall) of NHL entry draft (June 16, 1990).

		REGULAR SEASON					PLAYOFFS				
Season Team	League	Gms.	G	A	Pts.	PIM	Gms.	G	A	Pts.	PIM
88-89—Minneapolis Edison H.S.	Minn. H.S.	25	47	27	74	...	—	—	—	—	—
89-90—Minneapolis Edison H.S.	Minn. H.S.	17	29	19	48	...	—	—	—	—	—
90-91—University of Minnesota	WCHA	20	6	4	10	26	—	—	—	—	—
91-92—University of Minnesota	WCHA	37	9	10	19	68	—	—	—	—	—
92-93—University of Minnesota	WCHA	41	11	14	25	62	—	—	—	—	—
93-94—University of Minnesota	WCHA	18	7	10	17	48	—	—	—	—	—

EAGLES, MIKE
C, JETS

PERSONAL: Born March 7, 1963, in Sussex, N.B. . . . 5-10/190. . . . Shoots left. . . . Full name: Michael Bryant Eagles.
TRANSACTIONS/CAREER NOTES: Selected by Quebec Nordiques as underage junior in sixth round (fifth Nordiques pick, 116th overall) of NHL entry draft (June 10, 1981). . . . Broke hand (Octo-

ber 1984).... Injured ribs (February 21, 1986).... Traded by Nordiques to Chicago Blackhawks for G Bob Mason (July 1988). ... Broke left hand (February 1989).... Bruised kidney (January 15, 1990); missed eight games.... Traded by Blackhawks to Winnipeg Jets for fourth-round pick (D Igor Kravchuk) in 1991 draft (December 14, 1990).... Fractured thumb (February 17, 1992); missed 14 games.... Suffered concussion (November 30, 1993); missed one game.... Strained shoulder (March 7, 1994); missed one game.... Bruised kidneys (March 27, 1994); missed remainder of season.

Season Team	League	REGULAR SEASON					PLAYOFFS				
		Gms.	G	A	Pts.	PIM	Gms.	G	A	Pts.	PIM
79-80—Melville	SJHL	55	46	30	76	77	—	—	—	—	—
80-81—Kitchener	OMJHL	56	11	27	38	64	18	4	2	6	36
81-82—Kitchener	OHL	62	26	40	66	148	15	3	11	14	27
82-83—Kitchener	OHL	58	26	36	62	133	12	5	7	12	27
—Quebec	NHL	2	0	0	0	2	—	—	—	—	—
83-84—Fredericton	AHL	68	13	29	42	85	4	0	0	0	5
84-85—Fredericton	AHL	36	4	20	24	80	3	0	0	0	2
85-86—Quebec	NHL	73	11	12	23	49	3	0	0	0	2
86-87—Quebec	NHL	73	13	19	32	55	4	1	0	1	10
87-88—Quebec	NHL	76	10	10	20	74	—	—	—	—	—
88-89—Chicago	NHL	47	5	11	16	44	—	—	—	—	—
89-90—Indianapolis	IHL	24	11	13	24	47	13	*10	10	20	34
—Chicago	NHL	23	1	2	3	34	—	—	—	—	—
90-91—Indianapolis	IHL	25	15	14	29	47	—	—	—	—	—
—Winnipeg	NHL	44	0	9	9	79	—	—	—	—	—
91-92—Winnipeg	NHL	65	7	10	17	118	7	0	0	0	8
92-93—Winnipeg	NHL	84	8	18	26	131	5	0	1	1	6
93-94—Winnipeg	NHL	73	4	8	12	96	—	—	—	—	—
NHL totals		**560**	**59**	**99**	**158**	**682**	**19**	**1**	**1**	**2**	**26**

EAKINS, DALLAS
D, PANTHERS

PERSONAL: Born January 20, 1967, in Dade City, Fla.... 6-2/195.... Shoots left.... Name pronounced EE-kihns.
TRANSACTIONS/CAREER NOTES: Selected by Washington Capitals as underage junior in 10th round (11th Capitals pick, 208th overall) of NHL entry draft (June 15, 1985).... Injured back (October 1988).... Signed as free agent by Winnipeg Jets (September 1989).... Signed as free agent by Florida Panthers (July 14, 1993).

Season Team	League	REGULAR SEASON					PLAYOFFS				
		Gms.	G	A	Pts.	PIM	Gms.	G	A	Pts.	PIM
84-85—Peterborough	OHL	48	0	8	8	96	7	0	0	0	18
85-86—Peterborough	OHL	60	6	16	22	134	16	0	1	1	30
86-87—Peterborough	OHL	54	3	11	14	145	12	1	4	5	37
87-88—Peterborough	OHL	64	11	27	38	129	12	3	12	15	16
88-89—Baltimore	AHL	62	0	10	10	139	—	—	—	—	—
89-90—Moncton	AHL	75	2	11	13	189	—	—	—	—	—
90-91—Moncton	AHL	75	1	12	13	132	9	0	1	1	44
91-92—Moncton	AHL	67	3	13	16	136	11	2	1	3	16
92-93—Moncton	AHL	55	4	6	10	132	—	—	—	—	—
—Winnipeg	NHL	14	0	2	2	38	—	—	—	—	—
93-94—Cincinnati	IHL	80	1	18	19	143	8	0	1	1	41
—Florida	NHL	1	0	0	0	0	—	—	—	—	—
NHL totals		**15**	**0**	**2**	**2**	**38**					

EASTWOOD, MICHAEL
C/RW, MAPLE LEAFS

PERSONAL: Born July 1, 1967, in Cornwall, Ont.... 6-3/205.... Shoots right.
COLLEGE: Western Michigan.
TRANSACTIONS/CAREER NOTES: Selected by Toronto Maple Leafs in fifth round (fifth Maple Leafs pick, 91st overall) of NHL entry draft (June 13, 1987).
HONORS: Named to CCHA All-Star second team (1990-91).

Season Team	League	REGULAR SEASON					PLAYOFFS				
		Gms.	G	A	Pts.	PIM	Gms.	G	A	Pts.	PIM
86-87—Pembroke	COJHL			Statistics unavailable.							
87-88—Western Michigan Univ.	CCHA	42	5	8	13	14	—	—	—	—	—
88-89—Western Michigan Univ.	CCHA	40	10	13	23	87	—	—	—	—	—
89-90—Western Michigan Univ.	CCHA	40	25	27	52	36	—	—	—	—	—
90-91—Western Michigan Univ.	CCHA	42	29	32	61	84	—	—	—	—	—
91-92—St. John's	AHL	61	18	25	43	28	16	9	10	19	16
—Toronto	NHL	9	0	2	2	4	—	—	—	—	—
92-93—St. John's	AHL	60	24	35	59	32	—	—	—	—	—
—Toronto	NHL	12	1	6	7	21	10	1	2	3	8
93-94—Toronto	NHL	54	8	10	18	28	18	3	2	5	12
NHL totals		**75**	**9**	**18**	**27**	**53**	**28**	**4**	**4**	**8**	**20**

EGELAND, ALLAN
C, LIGHTNING

PERSONAL: Born January 31, 1973, in Lethbridge, Alta.... 6-0/184.... Shoots left.... Name pronounced EHG-luhnd.
TRANSACTIONS/CAREER NOTES: Selected by Tampa Bay Lightning in third round (third Lightning pick, 55th overall) of NHL entry draft (June 26, 1993).
HONORS: Named to WHL (West) All-Star first team (1992-93).... Named to WHL (West) All-Star second team (1993-94).

Season Team	League	REGULAR SEASON Gms.	G	A	Pts.	PIM	PLAYOFFS Gms.	G	A	Pts.	PIM
90-91—Lethbridge	WHL	67	2	16	18	57	9	0	0	0	0
91-92—Tacoma	WHL	72	35	39	74	115	4	0	1	1	18
92-93—Tacoma	WHL	71	56	57	113	119	7	9	7	16	18
93-94—Tacoma	WHL	70	47	76	123	204	8	5	3	8	26

EGELAND, TRACY
RW, FLYERS

PERSONAL: Born August 20, 1970, in Lethbridge, Alta. . . . 6-1/180. . . . Shoots right. . . . Name pronounced EHG-luhnd.

TRANSACTIONS/CAREER NOTES: Injured elbow (November 1986); missed two weeks. . . . Traded by Swift Current Broncos to Medicine Hat Tigers for C Travis Kellin (August 1988). . . . Selected by Chicago Blackhawks in seventh round (fifth Blackhawks pick, 132nd overall) of NHL entry draft (June 17, 1989). . . . Signed as free agent by Philadelphia Flyers (August 4, 1993).

Season Team	League	REGULAR SEASON Gms.	G	A	Pts.	PIM	PLAYOFFS Gms.	G	A	Pts.	PIM
86-87—Swift Current	WHL	48	3	2	5	20	—	—	—	—	—
87-88—Swift Current	WHL	63	10	22	32	34	—	—	—	—	—
88-89—Medicine Hat	WHL	42	11	12	23	64	—	—	—	—	—
—Prince Albert	WHL	24	17	10	27	24	4	0	1	1	13
89-90—Prince Albert	WHL	61	39	26	65	160	13	7	10	17	26
90-91—Indianapolis	IHL	79	17	22	39	205	7	2	1	3	21
91-92—Indianapolis	IHL	66	20	11	31	214	—	—	—	—	—
92-93—Indianapolis	IHL	43	11	14	25	122	—	—	—	—	—
93-94—Hershey	AHL	57	7	11	18	266	4	0	0	0	2

EISENHUT, NEIL
C, FLAMES

PERSONAL: Born February 9, 1967, in Osoyoos, B.C. . . . 6-1/190. . . . Shoots left. . . . Name pronounced IGHS-ihn-huht.

COLLEGE: North Dakota.

TRANSACTIONS/CAREER NOTES: Selected by Vancouver Canucks in 12th round (11th Canucks pick, 233rd overall) of NHL entry draft (June 13, 1987). . . . Signed as free agent by Calgary Flames (June 27, 1994).

Season Team	League	REGULAR SEASON Gms.	G	A	Pts.	PIM	PLAYOFFS Gms.	G	A	Pts.	PIM
86-87—Langley Eagles	BCJHL	43	41	34	75	...	—	—	—	—	—
87-88—North Dakota	WCHA	42	12	20	32	14	—	—	—	—	—
88-89—North Dakota	WCHA	41	22	16	38	26	—	—	—	—	—
89-90—North Dakota	WCHA	45	22	32	54	46	—	—	—	—	—
90-91—North Dakota	WCHA	20	9	15	24	10	—	—	—	—	—
91-92—Milwaukee	IHL	76	13	23	36	26	2	1	2	3	0
92-93—Hamilton	AHL	72	22	40	62	41	—	—	—	—	—
93-94—Hamilton	AHL	60	17	36	53	30	4	1	4	5	0
—Vancouver	NHL	13	1	3	4	21	—	—	—	—	—
NHL totals		13	1	3	4	21					

EKLUND, PELLE
LW, STARS

PERSONAL: Born March 22, 1963, in Stockholm, Sweden. . . . 5-10/175. . . . Shoots left. . . . Name pronounced EHK-luhnd.

TRANSACTIONS/CAREER NOTES: Selected by Philadelphia Flyers in eighth round (seventh Flyers pick, 161st overall) of NHL entry draft (June 8, 1983). . . . Bruised hip (March 1988). . . . Strained left knee (October 1989). . . . Bruised right knee (November 24, 1989). . . . Strained hip flexor and stomach muscles (January 31, 1991); missed five games. . . . Bruised shoulder (November 20, 1991); missed one game. . . . Sprained knee (January 12, 1992); missed eight games. . . . Reinjured knee (February 6, 1992); missed five games. . . . Reinjured knee (February 27, 1992); missed three games. . . . Sprained knee (March 1992); missed final six games of season. . . . Underwent arthroscopic knee surgery (April 14, 1992). . . . Broke right foot (October 1, 1992); missed first 22 games of season. . . . Suffered hip flexor (December 30, 1992); missed two games. . . . Suffered cut over left eye (February 18, 1993); missed one game. . . . Bruised thigh (March 30, 1993); missed three games. . . . Traded by Philadelphia Flyers to Dallas Stars for future considerations (March 21, 1994). . . . Suffered bilateral hernia (March 20, 1994); missed six games. . . . Suffered from stomach pain due to bilateral hernia (April 10, 1994); missed one game.

HONORS: Won Golden Puck Award (1983-84). . . . Named to Swedish League All-Star team (1983-84).

RECORDS: Holds NHL playoff record for fastest goal from the start of a period—six seconds (April 25, 1989).

MISCELLANEOUS: Member of bronze-medal-winning Swedish Olympic team (1984). . . . Named Sweden's Athlete of the Year (1984).

Season Team	League	REGULAR SEASON Gms.	G	A	Pts.	PIM	PLAYOFFS Gms.	G	A	Pts.	PIM
81-82—Stockholm AIK	Sweden	23	2	3	5	2	—	—	—	—	—
82-83—Stockholm AIK	Sweden	34	13	17	30	14	3	1	4	5	2
83-84—Stockholm AIK	Sweden	35	9	18	27	24	6	6	7	13	2
—Swedish Olympic Team	Int'l	7	2	6	8	0	—	—	—	—	—
84-85—Stockholm AIK	Sweden	35	16	33	49	10	—	—	—	—	—
85-86—Philadelphia	NHL	70	15	51	66	12	5	0	2	2	0
86-87—Philadelphia	NHL	72	14	41	55	2	26	7	20	27	2
87-88—Philadelphia	NHL	71	10	32	42	12	7	0	3	3	0
88-89—Philadelphia	NHL	79	18	51	69	23	19	3	8	11	2
89-90—Philadelphia	NHL	70	23	39	62	16	—	—	—	—	—
90-91—Philadelphia	NHL	73	19	50	69	14	—	—	—	—	—

E

Season Team	League	REGULAR SEASON					PLAYOFFS				
		Gms.	G	A	Pts.	PIM	Gms.	G	A	Pts.	PIM
91-92—Philadelphia	NHL	51	7	16	23	4	—	—	—	—	—
92-93—Philadelphia	NHL	55	11	38	49	16	—	—	—	—	—
93-94—Philadelphia	NHL	48	1	16	17	8	—	—	—	—	—
—Dallas	NHL	5	2	1	3	2	9	0	3	3	4
NHL totals		594	120	335	455	109	66	10	36	46	8

EKMAN, NILS
LW, FLAMES

PERSONAL: Born March 11, 1976, in Stockholm, Sweden. . . . 5-11/ 167. . . . Shoots left.
TRANSACTIONS/CAREER NOTES: Selected by Calgary Flames in fifth round (sixth Flames pick, 107th overall) of NHL entry draft (June 29, 1994).

Season Team	League	REGULAR SEASON					PLAYOFFS				
		Gms.	G	A	Pts.	PIM	Gms.	G	A	Pts.	PIM
93-94—Hammarby	Swed. Dv.II	18	7	2	9	4	—	—	—	—	—

ELIAS, PATRIK
LW, DEVILS

PERSONAL: Born April 13, 1976, in Trebic, Czechoslovakia. . . . 6-0/ 176. . . . Shoots left.
TRANSACTIONS/CAREER NOTES: Selected by New Jersey Devils in second round (second Devils pick, 51st overall) of NHL entry draft (June 28, 1994).

Season Team	League	REGULAR SEASON					PLAYOFFS				
		Gms.	G	A	Pts.	PIM	Gms.	G	A	Pts.	PIM
92-93—Poldi Kladno	Czech.	2	0	0	0	0	—	—	—	—	—
93-94—HC Kladno	Czech Rep.	15	1	2	3	...	11	2	2	4	0
—Czech Republic Olympic	Int'l	5	2	5	7	...	—	—	—	—	—

ELIK, TODD
C, SHARKS

PERSONAL: Born April 15, 1966, in Brampton, Ont. . . . 6-2/ 195. . . . Shoots left. . . . Name pronounced EHL-ihk.
COLLEGE: Regina (Sask.).
TRANSACTIONS/CAREER NOTES: Signed as free agent by New York Rangers (February 26, 1988). . . . Traded by Rangers with LW Igor Liba, D Michael Boyce and future considerations to Los Angeles Kings for D Dean Kennedy and D Denis Larocque (December 12, 1988). . . . Suffered lacerations near right eye (January 1991). . . . Injured thigh (February 26, 1991); missed one game. . . . Traded by Kings to Minnesota North Stars for D Charlie Huddy, LW Randy Gilhen, RW Jim Thomson and fourth-round pick (D Alexei Zhitnik) in 1991 draft (June 22, 1991). . . . Broke foot (November 14, 1992); missed five games. . . . Suffered head injury (January 23, 1993); missed six games. . . . Traded by North Stars to Edmonton Oilers for C Brent Gilchrist (March 5, 1993). . . . Injured shoulder (April 6, 1993); missed remainder of season. . . . Claimed on waivers by San Jose Sharks (October 26, 1993).
HONORS: Named to CWUAA All-Star second team (1986-87).

Season Team	League	REGULAR SEASON					PLAYOFFS				
		Gms.	G	A	Pts.	PIM	Gms.	G	A	Pts.	PIM
83-84—Kingston	OHL	64	5	16	21	17	—	—	—	—	—
84-85—Kingston	OHL	34	14	11	25	6	—	—	—	—	—
—North Bay	OHL	23	4	6	10	2	4	2	0	2	0
85-86—North Bay	OHL	40	12	34	46	20	10	7	6	13	0
86-87—University of Regina	CWUAA	27	26	34	60	137	—	—	—	—	—
87-88—Denver	IHL	81	44	56	100	83	12	8	12	20	9
88-89—Denver	IHL	28	20	15	35	22	—	—	—	—	—
—New Haven	AHL	43	11	25	36	31	17	10	12	22	44
89-90—Los Angeles	NHL	48	10	23	33	41	10	3	9	12	10
—New Haven	AHL	32	20	23	43	42	—	—	—	—	—
90-91—Los Angeles	NHL	74	21	37	58	58	12	2	7	9	6
91-92—Minnesota	NHL	62	14	32	46	125	5	1	1	2	2
92-93—Minnesota	NHL	46	13	18	31	48	—	—	—	—	—
—Edmonton	NHL	14	1	9	10	8	—	—	—	—	—
93-94—Edmonton	NHL	4	0	0	0	6	—	—	—	—	—
—San Jose	NHL	75	25	41	66	89	14	5	5	10	12
NHL totals		323	84	160	244	375	41	11	22	33	30

ELLETT, DAVE
D, MAPLE LEAFS

PERSONAL: Born March 30, 1964, in Cleveland. . . . 6-2/200. . . . Shoots left.
COLLEGE: Bowling Green State.
TRANSACTIONS/CAREER NOTES: Selected by Winnipeg Jets as underage junior in fourth round (third Jets pick, 75th overall) of NHL entry draft (June 9, 1982). . . . Bruised thigh (March 6, 1988); missed 10 games. . . . Sprained ankle (November 16, 1988). . . . Traded by Jets with C Paul Fenton to Toronto Maple Leafs for C Ed Olczyk and LW Mark Osborne (November 10, 1990). . . . Separated shoulder (March 2, 1993); missed 14 games. . . . Suffered rib strain (December 11, 1993); missed 10 games. . . . Separated shoulder (March 31, 1994); missed remainder of season.
HONORS: Named to NCAA All-Tournament team (1983-84). . . . Named to CCHA All-Star second team (1983-84). . . . Played in NHL All-Star Game (1989 and 1992).

Season Team	League	REGULAR SEASON					PLAYOFFS				
		Gms.	G	A	Pts.	PIM	Gms.	G	A	Pts.	PIM
81-82—Ottawa	COJHL	50	9	35	44	...	—	—	—	—	—
82-83—Bowling Green State	CCHA	40	4	13	17	34	—	—	—	—	—
83-84—Bowling Green State	CCHA	43	15	39	54	9	—	—	—	—	—

Season Team	League	REGULAR SEASON					PLAYOFFS				
		Gms.	G	A	Pts.	PIM	Gms.	G	A	Pts.	PIM
84-85—Winnipeg	NHL	80	11	27	38	85	8	1	5	6	4
85-86—Winnipeg	NHL	80	15	31	46	96	3	0	1	1	0
86-87—Winnipeg	NHL	78	13	31	44	53	10	0	8	8	2
87-88—Winnipeg	NHL	68	13	45	58	106	5	1	2	3	10
88-89—Winnipeg	NHL	75	22	34	56	62	—	—	—	—	—
89-90—Winnipeg	NHL	77	17	29	46	96	7	2	0	2	6
90-91—Winnipeg	NHL	17	4	7	11	6	—	—	—	—	—
—Toronto	NHL	60	8	30	38	69	—	—	—	—	—
91-92—Toronto	NHL	79	18	33	51	95	—	—	—	—	—
92-93—Toronto	NHL	70	6	34	40	46	21	4	8	12	8
93-94—Toronto	NHL	68	7	36	43	42	18	3	15	18	31
NHL totals		752	134	337	471	756	72	11	39	50	61

ELYNUIK, PAT
RW, SENATORS

PERSONAL: Born October 30, 1967, in Foam Lake, Sask. . . . 6-0/185. . . . Shoots right. . . . Full name: Pat Gerald Elynuik. . . . Name pronounced EHL-ih-nuhk.
TRANSACTIONS/CAREER NOTES: Selected by Winnipeg Jets as underage junior in first round (first Jets pick, eighth overall) of NHL entry draft (June 21, 1986). . . . Separated left shoulder (March 7, 1989). . . . Strained groin (December 14, 1991); missed six games. . . . Sprained knee (February 2, 1992); missed three games. . . . Injured eye (March 17, 1992); missed five games. . . . Traded by Jets to Washington Capitals for RW John Druce and conditional pick in 1993 draft (October 1, 1992). . . . Traded by Capitals to Tampa Bay Lightning for fifth-round pick in 1995 draft (October 22, 1993). . . . Signed as free agent by Ottawa Senators (June 21, 1994).
HONORS: Named to WHL (East) All-Star first team (1985-86 and 1986-87).

Season Team	League	REGULAR SEASON					PLAYOFFS				
		Gms.	G	A	Pts.	PIM	Gms.	G	A	Pts.	PIM
84-85—Prince Albert	WHL	70	23	20	43	54	13	9	3	12	7
85-86—Prince Albert	WHL	68	53	53	106	62	20	7	9	16	17
86-87—Prince Albert	WHL	64	51	62	113	40	8	5	5	10	12
87-88—Winnipeg	NHL	13	1	3	4	12	—	—	—	—	—
—Moncton	AHL	30	11	18	29	35	—	—	—	—	—
88-89—Winnipeg	NHL	56	26	25	51	29	—	—	—	—	—
—Moncton	AHL	7	8	2	10	2	—	—	—	—	—
89-90—Winnipeg	NHL	80	32	42	74	83	7	2	4	6	2
90-91—Winnipeg	NHL	80	31	34	65	73	—	—	—	—	—
91-92—Winnipeg	NHL	60	25	25	50	65	7	2	2	4	4
92-93—Washington	NHL	80	22	35	57	66	6	2	3	5	19
93-94—Washington	NHL	4	1	1	2	0	—	—	—	—	—
—Tampa Bay	NHL	63	12	14	26	64	—	—	—	—	—
NHL totals		436	150	179	329	392	20	6	9	15	25

EMERSON, NELSON
C, JETS

PERSONAL: Born August 17, 1967, in Hamilton, Ont. . . . 5-11/175. . . . Shoots right. . . . Full name: Nelson Donald Emerson.
COLLEGE: Bowling Green State.
TRANSACTIONS/CAREER NOTES: Selected by St. Louis Blues in third round (second Blues pick, 44th overall) of NHL entry draft (June 15, 1985). . . . Fractured bone under his eye (December 28, 1991). . . . Injured leg (April 3, 1993); missed one game. . . . Traded by Blues with D Stephane Quintal to Winnipeg Jets for D Phil Housley (September 24, 1993). . . . Sprained neck (January 25, 1994); missed one game.
HONORS: Named CCHA Rookie of the Year (1986-87). . . . Named to NCAA All-America West second team (1987-88). . . . Named to CCHA All-Star first team (1987-88 and 1989-90). . . . Named to NCAA All-America West first team (1989-90). . . . Named to CCHA All-Star second team (1988-89). . . . Won Garry F. Longman Memorial Trophy (1990-91). . . . Named to IHL All-Star first team (1990-91).

Season Team	League	REGULAR SEASON					PLAYOFFS				
		Gms.	G	A	Pts.	PIM	Gms.	G	A	Pts.	PIM
84-85—Stratford Jr. B	OHA	40	23	38	61	70	—	—	—	—	—
85-86—Stratford Jr. B	OHA	39	54	58	112	91	—	—	—	—	—
86-87—Bowling Green State	CCHA	45	26	35	61	28	—	—	—	—	—
87-88—Bowling Green State	CCHA	45	34	49	83	54	—	—	—	—	—
88-89—Bowling Green State	CCHA	44	22	46	68	46	—	—	—	—	—
89-90—Bowling Green State	CCHA	44	30	52	82	42	—	—	—	—	—
—Peoria	IHL	3	1	1	2	0	—	—	—	—	—
90-91—St. Louis	NHL	4	0	3	3	2	—	—	—	—	—
—Peoria	IHL	73	36	79	115	91	17	9	12	21	16
91-92—St. Louis	NHL	79	23	36	59	66	6	3	3	6	21
92-93—St. Louis	NHL	82	22	51	73	62	11	1	6	7	6
93-94—Winnipeg	NHL	83	33	41	74	80	—	—	—	—	—
NHL totals		248	78	131	209	210	17	4	9	13	27

EMMA, DAVID
C, DEVILS

PERSONAL: Born January 14, 1969, in Cranston, R.I. . . . 5-11/180. . . . Shoots left. . . . Full name: David Anaclethe Emma.
HIGH SCHOOL: Bishop Hendricken (Warwick, R.I.).
COLLEGE: Boston College.

E

TRANSACTIONS/CAREER NOTES: Selected by New Jersey Devils in sixth round (sixth Devils pick, 110th overall) of NHL entry draft (June 17, 1989).
HONORS: Named to Hockey East All-Freshman team (1987-88).... Named to Hockey East All-Star second team (1988-89). ... Named to Hockey East All-Star first team (1989-90 and 1990-91).... Won Hobey Baker Memorial Trophy (1990-91).... Named Hockey East Player of the Year (1990-91).... Named to NCAA All-America East first team (1989-90 and 1990-91).

Season Team	League	REGULAR SEASON					PLAYOFFS				
		Gms.	G	A	Pts.	PIM	Gms.	G	A	Pts.	PIM
87-88—Boston College	Hockey East	30	19	16	35	30	—	—	—	—	—
88-89—Boston College	Hockey East	36	20	31	51	36	—	—	—	—	—
89-90—Boston College	Hockey East	42	38	34	*72	46	—	—	—	—	—
90-91—Boston College	Hockey East	39	35	46	81	44	—	—	—	—	—
91-92—U.S. national team	Int'l	55	15	16	31	32	—	—	—	—	—
—U.S. Olympic Team	Int'l	6	0	1	1	6	—	—	—	—	—
—Utica	AHL	15	4	7	11	12	4	1	1	2	2
92-93—Utica	AHL	61	21	40	61	47	5	2	1	3	6
—New Jersey	NHL	2	0	0	0	0	—	—	—	—	—
93-94—New Jersey	NHL	15	5	5	10	2	—	—	—	—	—
—Albany	AHL	56	26	29	55	53	5	1	2	3	8
NHL totals		17	5	5	10	2					

EMMONS, GARY
C

PERSONAL: Born December 30, 1963, in Winnipeg.... 5-9/170.... Shoots right.
COLLEGE: Northern Michigan.
TRANSACTIONS/CAREER NOTES: Selected by New York Rangers in NHL supplemental draft (September 17, 1986).... Signed as free agent by Edmonton Oilers (July 27, 1987).... Signed as free agent by Minnesota North Stars (July 11, 1989).... Signed as free agent by San Jose Sharks (October 18, 1993).... Suffered hip flexor (October 24, 1993); missed four games.
HONORS: Named CCHA co-Rookie of the Year with Bill Shibicky (1983-84).... Named to WCHA All-Star first team (1985-86 and 1986-87).... Named to NCAA All-America West second team (1986-87).... Named to WCHA All-Star second team (1986-87).

Season Team	League	REGULAR SEASON					PLAYOFFS				
		Gms.	G	A	Pts.	PIM	Gms.	G	A	Pts.	PIM
83-84—Northern Michigan Univ.	CCHA	40	28	21	49	42	—	—	—	—	—
84-85—Northern Michigan Univ.	WCHA	40	25	28	53	22	—	—	—	—	—
85-86—Northern Michigan Univ.	WCHA	36	45	30	75	34	—	—	—	—	—
86-87—Northern Michigan Univ.	WCHA	35	32	34	66	59	—	—	—	—	—
87-88—Milwaukee	IHL	13	3	4	7	4	—	—	—	—	—
—Nova Scotia	AHL	59	18	27	45	22	—	—	—	—	—
88-89—Canadian national team	Int'l	49	16	26	42	42	—	—	—	—	—
89-90—Kalamazoo	IHL	81	41	59	100	38	—	—	—	—	—
90-91—Kalamazoo	IHL	62	25	33	58	26	11	5	8	13	6
91-92—Kansas City	IHL	80	29	54	83	60	15	6	13	19	8
92-93—Kansas City	IHL	80	37	44	81	80	12	†7	6	13	8
93-94—Kansas City	IHL	63	20	49	69	28	—	—	—	—	—
—San Jose	NHL	3	1	0	1	0	—	—	—	—	—
NHL totals		3	1	0	1	0					

ENSOM, JIM
C, BLACKHAWKS

PERSONAL: Born August 24, 1976, in Oshawa, Ont.... 6-3/191.... Shoots left.
HIGH SCHOOL: Chippewa (North Bay, Ont.).
TRANSACTIONS/CAREER NOTES: Selected by Chicago Blackhawks in sixth round (fifth Blackhawks pick, 144th overall) of NHL entry draft (June 29, 1994).

Season Team	League	REGULAR SEASON					PLAYOFFS				
		Gms.	G	A	Pts.	PIM	Gms.	G	A	Pts.	PIM
91-92—Muskoka	Tier II Jr. A	40	19	33	52	92	—	—	—	—	—
92-93—North Bay	OHL	65	7	17	24	70	5	1	0	1	7
93-94—North Bay	OHL	44	16	20	36	67	16	4	5	9	6

ERICKSON, BRYAN
RW, JETS

PERSONAL: Born March 7, 1960, in Roseau, Minn.... 5-9/170.... Shoots right.... Full name: Bryan Lee Erickson.
COLLEGE: Minnesota.
TRANSACTIONS/CAREER NOTES: Fractured wrist (January 1983).... Signed as free agent by Washington Capitals (April 5, 1983).... Broke thumb (October 1984).... Traded by Capitals to Los Angeles Kings for D Bruce Shoebottom (October 31, 1985).... Injured left knee cartilage (October 23, 1986).... Traded by Kings to Pittsburgh Penguins for C Chris Kontos and sixth-round pick (C Micah Aivazoff) in 1989 draft (February 5, 1988).... Separated shoulder (March 1988).... Signed as free agent by Winnipeg Jets (March 2, 1990).... Strained abdomen (October 12, 1991); missed 11 games.... Restrained abdomen (December 1991); missed remainder of season.... Underwent off-season abdominal surgery (1992); missed 23 games.... Suffered back spasms (January 23, 1993); missed five games.... Suffered back spasms (October 31, 1993); missed one game.... Strained groin (December 22, 1993); missed 12 games.
HONORS: Named to WCHA All-Star second team (1981-82).... Named to WCHA All-Star first team (1982-83).

Season Team	League	REGULAR SEASON					PLAYOFFS				
		Gms.	G	A	Pts.	PIM	Gms.	G	A	Pts.	PIM
79-80—University of Minnesota	WCHA	23	10	15	25	14	—	—	—	—	—
80-81—University of Minnesota	WCHA	44	39	47	86	30	—	—	—	—	—
81-82—University of Minnesota	WCHA	35	25	20	45	20	—	—	—	—	—

Season	Team	League	REGULAR SEASON					PLAYOFFS				
			Gms.	G	A	Pts.	PIM	Gms.	G	A	Pts.	PIM
82-83—	University of Minnesota ...	WCHA	42	35	47	82	30	—	—	—	—	—
	—Hershey	AHL	1	0	1	1	0	3	3	0	3	0
83-84—	Hershey	AHL	31	16	12	28	11	—	—	—	—	—
	—Washington	NHL	45	12	17	29	16	8	2	3	5	7
84-85—	Binghamton	AHL	13	6	11	17	8	—	—	—	—	—
	—Washington	NHL	57	15	13	28	23	—	—	—	—	—
85-86—	Binghamton	AHL	7	5	3	8	2	—	—	—	—	—
	—New Haven	AHL	14	8	3	11	11	—	—	—	—	—
	—Los Angeles	NHL	55	20	23	43	36	—	—	—	—	—
86-87—	Los Angeles	NHL	68	20	30	50	26	3	1	1	2	0
87-88—	Los Angeles	NHL	42	6	15	21	20	—	—	—	—	—
	—Pittsburgh	NHL	11	1	4	5	0	—	—	—	—	—
	—New Haven	AHL	3	0	0	0	0	—	—	—	—	—
88-89—							Did not play.					
89-90—	Moncton	AHL	13	4	7	11	4	—	—	—	—	—
90-91—	Winnipeg	NHL	6	0	7	7	0	—	—	—	—	—
	—Moncton	AHL	36	18	14	32	16	—	—	—	—	—
91-92—	Winnipeg	NHL	10	2	4	6	0	—	—	—	—	—
92-93—	Moncton	AHL	2	1	1	2	4	—	—	—	—	—
	—Winnipeg	NHL	41	4	12	16	14	3	0	0	0	0
93-94—	Winnipeg	NHL	16	0	0	0	6	—	—	—	—	—
	—Moncton	AHL	3	0	1	1	2	—	—	—	—	—
NHL totals			351	80	125	205	141	14	3	4	7	7

ERIKSSON, ANDERS
D, RED WINGS

PERSONAL: Born January 9, 1975, in Bollnas, Sweden.... 6-3/218.... Shoots left.
TRANSACTIONS/CAREER NOTES: Selected by Detroit Red Wings in first round (first Red Wings pick, 22nd overall) of NHL entry draft (June 26, 1993).

Season	Team	League	REGULAR SEASON					PLAYOFFS				
			Gms.	G	A	Pts.	PIM	Gms.	G	A	Pts.	PIM
92-93—	MoDo	Sweden	20	0	2	2	2	—	—	—	—	—
93-94—	MoDo	Sweden	38	2	8	10	42	11	0	0	0	8

ERREY, BOB
LW, SHARKS

PERSONAL: Born September 21, 1964, in Montreal. ... 5-10/183. ... Shoots left. ... Name pronounced AIR-ee.
TRANSACTIONS/CAREER NOTES: Selected by Pittsburgh Penguins as underage junior in first round (first Penguins pick, 15th overall) of NHL entry draft (June 8, 1983).... Sprained right knee (March 18, 1987).... Broke right wrist (October 1987).... Injured shoulder (May 9, 1992).... Sprained ankle (September 29, 1992).... Bruised tailbone (February 27, 1993); missed two games.... Traded by Penguins to Buffalo Sabres for D Mike Ramsey (March 22, 1993). ... Sprained ankle (April 4, 1993); missed four games. ... Injured hip (April 18, 1993); missed two games.... Signed as free agent by San Jose Sharks (August 17, 1993).... Suffered rib injury (October 10, 1993); missed three games.... Suffered from the flu (October 26, 1993); missed three games.... Suspended two games by NHL for checking from behind (December 31, 1993). ... Suffered hyperextended knee (February 1, 1994); missed two games. ... Sprained knee (March 22, 1994); missed five games.
HONORS: Named to OHL All-Star first team (1982-83).
MISCELLANEOUS: Member of Stanley Cup championship teams (1991 and 1992).

Season	Team	League	REGULAR SEASON					PLAYOFFS				
			Gms.	G	A	Pts.	PIM	Gms.	G	A	Pts.	PIM
81-82—	Peterborough	OHL	68	29	31	60	39	9	3	1	4	9
82-83—	Peterborough	OHL	67	53	47	100	74	4	1	3	4	7
83-84—	Pittsburgh	NHL	65	9	13	22	29	—	—	—	—	—
84-85—	Baltimore	AHL	59	17	24	41	14	8	3	4	7	11
	—Pittsburgh	NHL	16	0	2	2	7	—	—	—	—	—
85-86—	Baltimore	AHL	18	8	7	15	28	—	—	—	—	—
	—Pittsburgh	NHL	37	11	6	17	8	—	—	—	—	—
86-87—	Pittsburgh	NHL	72	16	18	34	46	—	—	—	—	—
87-88—	Pittsburgh	NHL	17	3	6	9	18	—	—	—	—	—
88-89—	Pittsburgh	NHL	76	26	32	58	124	11	1	2	3	12
89-90—	Pittsburgh	NHL	78	20	19	39	109	—	—	—	—	—
90-91—	Pittsburgh	NHL	79	20	22	42	115	24	5	2	7	29
91-92—	Pittsburgh	NHL	78	19	16	35	119	14	3	0	3	10
92-93—	Pittsburgh	NHL	54	8	6	14	76	—	—	—	—	—
	—Buffalo	NHL	8	1	3	4	4	4	0	1	1	10
93-94—	San Jose	NHL	64	12	18	30	126	14	3	2	5	10
NHL totals			644	145	161	306	781	67	12	7	19	71

ESAU, LEN
D, FLAMES

PERSONAL: Born March 16, 1968, in Meadow Lake, Sask.... 6-3/190.... Shoots right.... Full name: Leonard Roy Esau.... Name pronounced EE-saw.
COLLEGE: St. Cloud (Minn.) State.
TRANSACTIONS/CAREER NOTES: Selected by Toronto Maple Leafs in fifth round (fifth Maple Leafs pick, 86th overall) of NHL entry draft (June 11, 1988).... Traded by Maple Leafs to Quebec Nordiques for C Ken McRae (July 21, 1992).... Signed as free agent by Calgary Flames (September 6, 1993).

Season Team	League	REGULAR SEASON					PLAYOFFS				
		Gms.	G	A	Pts.	PIM	Gms.	G	A	Pts.	PIM
86-87—Humboldt	SJHL	57	4	26	30	278	—	—	—	—	—
87-88—Humboldt	SJHL	57	16	37	53	229	—	—	—	—	—
88-89—St. Cloud State	WCHA	35	12	27	39	69	—	—	—	—	—
89-90—St. Cloud State	WCHA	29	8	11	19	83	—	—	—	—	—
90-91—Newmarket	AHL	75	4	14	18	28	—	—	—	—	—
91-92—St. John's	AHL	78	9	29	38	68	13	0	2	2	14
—Toronto	NHL	2	0	0	0	0	—	—	—	—	—
92-93—Halifax	AHL	75	11	31	42	19	—	—	—	—	—
—Quebec	NHL	4	0	1	1	2	—	—	—	—	—
93-94—Saint John	AHL	75	12	36	48	129	7	2	2	4	6
—Calgary	NHL	6	0	3	3	7	—	—	—	—	—
NHL totals		12	0	4	4	9					

ESSENSA, BOB
G, RED WINGS

PERSONAL: Born January 14, 1965, in Toronto.... 6-0/180.... Catches left.... Full name: Robert Earle Essensa.... Name pronounced EH-sehn-suh.
HIGH SCHOOL: Henry Carr (Rexdale, Ont.).
COLLEGE: Michigan State.
TRANSACTIONS/CAREER NOTES: Selected by Winnipeg Jets in fourth round (fifth Jets pick, 69th overall) of NHL entry draft (June 8, 1983).... Suffered severe lacerations to both hands and wrist (February 1985).... Injured groin (September 1990); missed three weeks.... Sprained knee (October 12, 1991); missed four games.... Injured left hamstring (December 8, 1991); missed four games.... Sprained knee (March 6, 1992); missed seven games.... Strained knee (March 6, 1993); missed two games. ... Traded by Jets with D Sergei Bautin to Detroit Red Wings for G Tim Cheveldae and LW Dallas Drake (March 8, 1994).
HONORS: Named to CCHA All-Star first team (1984-85).... Named to CCHA All-Star second team (1985-86).... Named to NHL All-Rookie team (1989-90).

Season Team	League	REGULAR SEASON							PLAYOFFS						
		Gms.	Min.	W	L	T	GA	SO	Avg.	Gms.	Min.	W	L	GA	SO	Avg.
81-82—Henry Carr H.S.	MTHL	17	948	...	...	...	79	...	5.00	—	—	—	—	—	—	—
82-83—Henry Carr H.S.	MTHL	31	1840	...	...	...	98	2	3.20	—	—	—	—	—	—	—
83-84—Michigan State	CCHA	17	947	11	4	0	44	2	2.79	—	—	—	—	—	—	—
84-85—Michigan State	CCHA	18	1059	15	2	0	29	2	1.64	—	—	—	—	—	—	—
85-86—Michigan State	CCHA	23	1333	17	4	1	74	1	3.33	—	—	—	—	—	—	—
86-87—Michigan State	CCHA	25	1383	19	3	1	64	*2	*2.78	—	—	—	—	—	—	—
87-88—Moncton	AHL	27	1287	7	11	1	100	1	4.66	—	—	—	—	—	—	—
88-89—Winnipeg	NHL	20	1102	6	8	3	68	1	3.70	—	—	—	—	—	—	—
—Fort Wayne	IHL	22	1287	14	7	‡0	70	0	3.26	—	—	—	—	—	—	—
89-90—Moncton	AHL	6	358	3	3	0	15	0	2.51	—	—	—	—	—	—	—
—Winnipeg	NHL	36	2035	18	9	5	107	1	3.15	4	206	2	1	12	0	3.50
90-91—Moncton	AHL	2	125	1	0	1	6	0	2.88	—	—	—	—	—	—	—
—Winnipeg	NHL	55	2916	19	24	6	153	4	3.15	—	—	—	—	—	—	—
91-92—Winnipeg	NHL	47	2627	21	17	6	126	†5	2.88	1	33	0	0	3	0	5.45
92-93—Winnipeg	NHL	67	3855	33	26	6	227	2	3.53	6	367	2	4	20	0	3.27
93-94—Winnipeg	NHL	56	3136	19	30	6	201	1	3.85	—	—	—	—	—	—	—
—Detroit	NHL	13	778	4	7	2	34	1	2.62	2	109	0	2	9	0	4.95
NHL totals		294	16449	120	121	34	916	15	3.34	13	715	4	7	44	0	3.69

ETHIER, MARTIN
D, RANGERS

PERSONAL: Born September 3, 1976, in Ste.-Eustache, Que.... 6-1/178.... Shoots right.
HIGH SCHOOL: Francois-Xavier Garneau CEGEP (Que.).
TRANSACTIONS/CAREER NOTES: Selected by New York Rangers in fifth round (sixth Rangers pick, 130th overall) of NHL entry draft (June 29, 1994).

Season Team	League	REGULAR SEASON					PLAYOFFS				
		Gms.	G	A	Pts.	PIM	Gms.	G	A	Pts.	PIM
93-94—Beauport	QMJHL	61	4	19	23	53	15	0	3	3	32

EVANS, DOUG
LW

PERSONAL: Born June 2, 1963, in Peterborough, Ont.... 5-9/185.... Shoots left.... Full name: Doug Thomas Evans.
TRANSACTIONS/CAREER NOTES: Signed as free agent by St. Louis Blues (June 10, 1985).... Separated left shoulder (September 1987).... Traded by Blues to Winnipeg Jets for C Ron Wilson (January 22, 1990).... Loaned to Peoria Rivermen (November 9, 1991); returned (December 15, 1991).... Traded by Jets to Boston Bruins for G Daniel Berthiaume (June 10, 1992).... Selected by Philadelphia Flyers in NHL waiver draft (October 4, 1992).... Broke right foot (March 13, 1993); missed remainder of season.... Signed as free agent by Rivermen (August 2, 1993).
HONORS: Named to IHL All-Star first team (1985-86).

Season Team	League	REGULAR SEASON					PLAYOFFS				
		Gms.	G	A	Pts.	PIM	Gms.	G	A	Pts.	PIM
80-81—Peterborough	OMJHL	51	9	24	33	139	—	—	—	—	—
81-82—Peterborough	OHL	56	17	49	66	176	9	0	2	2	41
82-83—Peterborough	OHL	65	31	55	86	165	4	0	3	3	23
83-84—Peterborough	OHL	61	45	79	124	98	8	4	12	16	26
84-85—Peoria	IHL	81	36	61	97	189	20	18	14	32	†88
85-86—St. Louis	NHL	13	1	0	1	2	—	—	—	—	—
—Peoria	IHL	69	46	51	97	179	10	4	6	10	32

E

Season Team	League	REGULAR SEASON					PLAYOFFS				
		Gms.	G	A	Pts.	PIM	Gms.	G	A	Pts.	PIM
86-87—Peoria	IHL	18	10	15	25	39	—	—	—	—	—
—St. Louis	NHL	53	3	13	16	91	5	0	0	0	10
87-88—Peoria	IHL	11	4	16	20	64	—	—	—	—	—
—St. Louis	NHL	41	5	7	12	49	2	0	0	0	0
88-89—St. Louis	NHL	53	7	12	19	81	7	1	2	3	16
89-90—Peoria	IHL	42	19	28	47	128	—	—	—	—	—
—St. Louis	NHL	3	0	0	0	0	—	—	—	—	—
—Winnipeg	NHL	27	10	8	18	33	7	2	2	4	10
90-91—Winnipeg	NHL	70	7	27	34	108	—	—	—	—	—
91-92—Winnipeg	NHL	30	7	7	14	68	1	0	0	0	2
—Peoria	IHL	16	5	14	19	38	—	—	—	—	—
—Moncton	AHL	10	7	8	15	10	—	—	—	—	—
92-93—Philadelphia	NHL	65	8	13	21	70	—	—	—	—	—
93-94—Peoria	IHL	76	27	63	90	108	6	2	6	8	10
NHL totals		355	48	87	135	502	22	3	4	7	38

EVANS, KEVIN
LW

PERSONAL: Born July 10, 1965, in Peterborough, Ont. . . . 5-11/185. . . . Shoots left. . . . Full name: Kevin Robert Evans.

TRANSACTIONS/CAREER NOTES: Signed as free agent by Minnesota North Stars (August 8, 1988). . . . Suspended three games and fined $100 by IHL for fighting (December 28, 1988). . . . Severed five tendons and an artery (February 24, 1989). . . . Suspended one game and fined $300 by IHL for fighting (November 25, 1989). . . . Underwent reconstructive knee surgery (December 1990). . . . Selected by San Jose Sharks in NHL dispersal draft (May 30, 1991). . . . Signed as free agent by North Stars (July 17, 1992). . . . North Stars franchise moved from Minnesota to Dallas and renamed Stars for 1993-94 season. . . . Signed as free agent by Peoria Rivermen (September 7, 1993).

Season Team	League	REGULAR SEASON					PLAYOFFS				
		Gms.	G	A	Pts.	PIM	Gms.	G	A	Pts.	PIM
83-84—Peterborough Jr. B	OHA	39	17	34	51	210	—	—	—	—	—
84-85—London	OHL	52	3	7	10	148	—	—	—	—	—
85-86—Victoria	WHL	66	16	39	55	*441	—	—	—	—	—
—Kalamazoo	IHL	11	3	5	8	97	6	3	0	3	56
86-87—Kalamazoo	IHL	73	19	31	50	*648	—	—	—	—	—
87-88—Kalamazoo	IHL	54	9	28	37	404	5	1	1	2	46
88-89—Kalamazoo	IHL	54	22	32	54	328	—	—	—	—	—
89-90—Kalamazoo	IHL	76	30	54	84	346	—	—	—	—	—
90-91—Minnesota	NHL	4	0	0	0	19	—	—	—	—	—
—Kalamazoo	IHL	16	10	12	22	70	—	—	—	—	—
91-92—San Jose	NHL	5	0	1	1	25	—	—	—	—	—
—Kansas City	IHL	66	10	39	49	342	14	2	13	15	70
92-93—Kalamazoo	IHL	49	7	24	31	283	—	—	—	—	—
93-94—Peoria	IHL	67	10	29	39	254	4	0	0	0	6
NHL totals		9	0	1	1	44					

EVASON, DEAN
C, STARS

PERSONAL: Born August 22, 1964, in Flin Flon, Man. . . . 5-10/180. . . . Shoots right. . . . Name pronounced EH-vih-suhn.

TRANSACTIONS/CAREER NOTES: Selected by Kamloops Junior Oilers in WHL dispersal draft of players of Spokane Flyers (December 1981). . . . Selected by Washington Capitals as under-age junior in fifth round (third Capitals pick, 89th overall) of NHL entry draft (June 9, 1982). . . . Traded by Capitals with G Peter Sidorkiewicz to Hartford Whalers for LW David A. Jensen (March 1985). . . . Strained left ankle ligaments (December 14, 1988). . . . Traded by Whalers to San Jose Sharks for D Dan Keczmer (October 2, 1991). . . . Pulled abdominal muscles (January 27, 1992); missed two games. . . . Traded by Sharks to Dallas Stars for sixth-round pick (LW Petri Varis) in 1993 draft (June 26, 1993).

HONORS: Won WHL Player of the Year Award (1982-83). . . . Named to WHL (West) All-Star first team (1983-84).

Season Team	League	REGULAR SEASON					PLAYOFFS				
		Gms.	G	A	Pts.	PIM	Gms.	G	A	Pts.	PIM
80-81—Spokane Flyers	WHL	3	1	1	2	0	—	—	—	—	—
81-82—Kamloops	WHL	70	29	69	98	112	4	2	1	3	0
82-83—Kamloops	WHL	70	71	93	164	102	7	5	7	12	18
83-84—Kamloops	WHL	57	49	88	137	89	17	†21	20	41	33
—Washington	NHL	2	0	0	0	2	—	—	—	—	—
84-85—Binghamton	AHL	65	27	49	76	38	8	3	5	8	9
—Washington	NHL	15	3	4	7	2	—	—	—	—	—
—Hartford	NHL	2	0	0	0	0	—	—	—	—	—
85-86—Binghamton	AHL	26	9	17	26	29	—	—	—	—	—
—Hartford	NHL	55	20	28	48	65	10	1	4	5	10
86-87—Hartford	NHL	80	22	37	59	67	5	3	2	5	35
87-88—Hartford	NHL	77	10	18	28	115	6	1	1	2	2
88-89—Hartford	NHL	67	11	17	28	60	4	1	2	3	10
89-90—Hartford	NHL	78	18	25	43	138	7	2	2	4	22
90-91—Hartford	NHL	75	6	23	29	170	6	0	4	4	29
91-92—San Jose	NHL	74	11	15	26	99	—	—	—	—	—

E

Season Team	League	REGULAR SEASON					PLAYOFFS				
		Gms.	G	A	Pts.	PIM	Gms.	G	A	Pts.	PIM
92-93—San Jose	NHL	84	12	19	31	132	—	—	—	—	—
93-94—Dallas	NHL	80	11	33	44	66	9	0	2	2	12
NHL totals		689	124	219	343	916	47	8	17	25	120

EWEN, DEAN
LW, MIGHTY DUCKS

PERSONAL: Born February 28, 1969, in St. Albert, Alta.... 6-2/225.... Shoots left. **TRANSACTIONS/CAREER NOTES:** Selected by New York Islanders in third round (third Islanders pick, 55th overall) of NHL entry draft (June 13, 1987).... Missed entire 1992-93 season due to knee injury.... Signed as free agent by Mighty Ducks of Anaheim (January 21, 1994).

Season Team	League	REGULAR SEASON					PLAYOFFS				
		Gms.	G	A	Pts.	PIM	Gms.	G	A	Pts.	PIM
88-89—Spokane	WHL	5	0	0	0	5	—	—	—	—	—
—Seattle	WHL	56	22	30	52	254	—	—	—	—	—
89-90—Springfield	AHL	34	0	7	7	...	—	—	—	—	—
90-91—Capital District	AHL					Did not play.					
91-92—Capital District	AHL	41	5	8	13	106	—	—	—	—	—
92-93—						Did not play—injured.					
93-94—San Diego	IHL	19	0	3	3	45	—	—	—	—	—

EWEN, TODD
RW, MIGHTY DUCKS

PERSONAL: Born March 22, 1966, in Saskatoon, Sask.... 6-2/220.... Shoots right.... Name pronounced YOO-ihn. **TRANSACTIONS/CAREER NOTES:** Selected by Edmonton Oilers as underage junior in eighth round (eighth Oilers pick, 168th overall) of NHL entry draft (June 9, 1984).... Traded by Oilers to St. Louis Blues for D Shawn Evans (October 15, 1986).... Sprained ankle (October 1987).... Suspended one game by NHL for third game misconduct of season (January 1988).... Pulled groin (October 1988).... Tore right eye muscle (December 1988).... Pulled left hamstring and bruised shoulder (February 1989).... Suspended 10 games by NHL for coming off bench to instigate fight during playoff game (April 18, 1989); missed three playoff games and first seven games of 1989-90 season. ... Broke right hand (October 28, 1989).... Traded by Blues to Montreal Canadiens for the return of a draft pick dealt to Montreal for D Mike Lalor (December 12, 1989).... Strained knee ligaments and underwent surgery (November 19, 1990); missed 24 games.... Fractured right hand at home (February 14, 1991); missed remainder of season.... Separated shoulder (February 12, 1992); missed two games.... Injured hand (January 10, 1993); missed two games.... Pulled muscle in back (February 20, 1993); missed three games.... Traded by Canadiens with C Patrik Carnback to Mighty Ducks of Anaheim for third-round pick (RW Chris Murray) in 1994 draft (August 10, 1993).... Broke nose (October 19, 1993); missed one game.... Sprained shoulder (April 2, 1994); missed five games. **MISCELLANEOUS:** Member of Stanley Cup championship team (1993).

Season Team	League	REGULAR SEASON					PLAYOFFS				
		Gms.	G	A	Pts.	PIM	Gms.	G	A	Pts.	PIM
82-83—Vernon	BCJHL	42	20	23	43	195	—	—	—	—	—
—Kamloops	WHL	3	0	0	0	2	2	0	0	0	0
83-84—New Westminster	WHL	68	11	13	24	176	7	2	1	3	15
84-85—New Westminster	WHL	56	11	20	31	304	10	1	8	9	60
85-86—New Westminster	WHL	60	28	24	52	289	—	—	—	—	—
—Maine	AHL	—	—	—	—	—	3	0	0	0	7
86-87—Peoria	IHL	16	3	3	6	110	—	—	—	—	—
—St. Louis	NHL	23	2	0	2	84	4	0	0	0	23
87-88—St. Louis	NHL	64	4	2	6	227	6	0	0	0	21
88-89—St. Louis	NHL	34	4	5	9	171	2	0	0	0	21
89-90—Peoria	IHL	2	0	0	0	12	—	—	—	—	—
—St. Louis	NHL	3	0	0	0	11	—	—	—	—	—
—Montreal	NHL	41	4	6	10	158	10	0	0	0	4
90-91—Montreal	NHL	28	3	2	5	128	—	—	—	—	—
91-92—Montreal	NHL	46	1	2	3	130	3	0	0	0	18
92-93—Montreal	NHL	75	5	9	14	193	1	0	0	0	0
93-94—Anaheim	NHL	76	9	9	18	272	—	—	—	—	—
NHL totals		390	32	35	67	1374	26	0	0	0	87

FALLOON, PAT
RW, SHARKS

PERSONAL: Born September 22, 1972, in Foxwarren, Man.... 5-11/190.... Shoots right. **TRANSACTIONS/CAREER NOTES:** WHL rights traded with future considerations by Regina Pats to Spokane Chiefs for RW Jamie Heward (October 1987).... Tore right knee cartilage and underwent surgery (July 24, 1990).... Selected by San Jose Sharks in first round (first Sharks pick, second overall) of NHL entry draft (June 22, 1991).... Bruised shoulder (November 19, 1992); missed one game.... Dislocated right shoulder (January 10, 1993) and underwent arthroscopic surgery (January 15, 1993); missed remainder of season. **HONORS:** Named WHL (West) Division Rookie of the Year (1988-89).... Named to WHL All-Star second team (1988-89).... Won WHL (West) Division Most Sportsmanlike Player Award (1989-90).... Named to WHL (West) All-Star first team (1989-90 and 1990-91).... Won Can.HL Most Sportsmanlike Player of the Year Award (1990-91).... Won Brad Hornung Trophy (1990-91).... Won Stafford Smythe Memorial Trophy (1990-91).... Named to Memorial Cup All-Star team (1990-91).

Season Team	League	REGULAR SEASON					PLAYOFFS				
		Gms.	G	A	Pts.	PIM	Gms.	G	A	Pts.	PIM
88-89—Spokane	WHL	72	22	56	78	41	5	5	8	13	4
89-90—Spokane	WHL	71	60	64	124	48	6	5	8	13	4

Season Team	League	REGULAR SEASON					PLAYOFFS				
		Gms.	G	A	Pts.	PIM	Gms.	G	A	Pts.	PIM
90-91—Spokane	WHL	61	64	74	138	33	15	10	14	24	10
91-92—San Jose	NHL	79	25	34	59	16	—	—	—	—	—
92-93—San Jose	NHL	41	14	14	28	12	—	—	—	—	—
93-94—San Jose	NHL	83	22	31	53	18	14	1	2	3	6
NHL totals		203	61	79	140	46	14	1	2	3	6

FARRELL, BRIAN
C, PENGUINS

PERSONAL: Born April 16, 1972, in Hartford, Conn. . . . 5-11/182. . . . Shoots left. . . . Full name: Brian Patrick Farrell.
HIGH SCHOOL: Avon (Conn.) Old Farms School for Boys.
COLLEGE: Harvard.
TRANSACTIONS/CAREER NOTES: Selected by Pittsburgh Penguins in fifth round (fourth Penguins pick, 89th overall) of NHL entry draft (June 16, 1990).
HONORS: Named to ECAC All-Star first team (1993-94).

Season Team	League	REGULAR SEASON					PLAYOFFS				
		Gms.	G	A	Pts.	PIM	Gms.	G	A	Pts.	PIM
88-89—Avon Old Farms H.S.	Conn. H.S.	27	13	24	37	...	—	—	—	—	—
89-90—Avon Old Farms H.S.	Conn. H.S.	24	22	23	45	...	—	—	—	—	—
90-91—Harvard University	ECAC	29	3	8	11	16	—	—	—	—	—
91-92—Harvard University	ECAC	9	5	3	8	8	—	—	—	—	—
92-93—Harvard University	ECAC	31	10	23	33	33	—	—	—	—	—
93-94—Harvard University	ECAC	33	29	14	43	47	—	—	—	—	—

FAUST, ANDRE
C, FLYERS

PERSONAL: Born October 7, 1969, in Joliette, Que. . . . 6-1/190. . . . Shoots left.
COLLEGE: Princeton.
TRANSACTIONS/CAREER NOTES: Selected by New Jersey Devils in ninth round (eighth Devils pick, 173rd overall) of NHL entry draft (June 17, 1989). . . . Signed as free agent by Philadelphia Flyers (October 14, 1992).
HONORS: Named to ECAC All-Star second team (1989-90 and 1991-92).

Season Team	League	REGULAR SEASON					PLAYOFFS				
		Gms.	G	A	Pts.	PIM	Gms.	G	A	Pts.	PIM
88-89—Princeton University	ECAC	27	15	24	39	28	—	—	—	—	—
89-90—Princeton University	ECAC	22	9	28	37	20	—	—	—	—	—
90-91—Princeton University	ECAC	26	15	22	37	51	—	—	—	—	—
91-92—Princeton University	ECAC	27	14	21	35	38	—	—	—	—	—
92-93—Hershey	AHL	62	26	25	51	71	—	—	—	—	—
—Philadelphia	NHL	10	2	2	4	4	—	—	—	—	—
93-94—Hershey	AHL	13	6	7	13	10	10	4	3	7	26
—Philadelphia	NHL	37	8	5	13	10	—	—	—	—	—
NHL totals		47	10	7	17	14					

FEARNS, KENT
D, WHALERS

PERSONAL: Born September 13, 1972, in Langley, B.C. . . . 6-0/180. . . . Shoots left.
COLLEGE: Colorado College.
TRANSACTIONS/CAREER NOTES: Selected by Hartford Whalers in NHL supplemental draft (June 25, 1993).
HONORS: Named to WCHA All-Star second team (1993-94).

Season Team	League	REGULAR SEASON					PLAYOFFS				
		Gms.	G	A	Pts.	PIM	Gms.	G	A	Pts.	PIM
92-93—Colorado College	WCHA	33	7	15	22	78	—	—	—	—	—
93-94—Colorado College	WCHA	39	11	19	30	62	—	—	—	—	—

FEATHERSTONE, GLEN
D, BRUINS

PERSONAL: Born July 8, 1968, in Toronto. . . . 6-4/215. . . . Shoots left.
TRANSACTIONS/CAREER NOTES: Selected by St. Louis Blues as underage junior in fourth round (fourth Blues pick, 73rd overall) of NHL entry draft (June 21, 1986). . . . Suffered sore back (March 7, 1991); missed two games. . . . Signed as free agent by Boston Bruins (July 25, 1991); Bruins and Blues later arranged a trade in which Bruins received Featherstone and LW Dave Thomlinson for RW Dave Christian, third-round (LW Vitali Prokhorov) and seventh-round (C Lance Burns) picks in 1992 draft. . . . Suffered hip pointer (October 5, 1991); missed three games. . . . Strained back (November 1991); missed remainder of season. . . . Underwent back surgery (November 15, 1991). . . . Injured groin (December 31, 1992); missed seven games. . . . Injured knee and thigh (March 1, 1993); missed remainder of season. . . . Injured shoulder (November 18, 1993); missed five games. . . . Suffered sore shoulder (January 24, 1994); missed four games. . . . Injured knee (February 12, 1994); missed four games. . . . Reinjured knee (March 8, 1994); missed two games. . . . Suffered from the flu (April 1, 1994); missed one game.

Season Team	League	REGULAR SEASON					PLAYOFFS				
		Gms.	G	A	Pts.	PIM	Gms.	G	A	Pts.	PIM
85-86—Windsor	OHL	49	0	6	6	135	14	1	1	2	23
86-87—Windsor	OHL	47	6	11	17	154	14	2	6	8	19
87-88—Windsor	OHL	53	7	27	34	201	12	6	9	15	47
88-89—Peoria	IHL	37	5	19	24	97	—	—	—	—	—
—St. Louis	NHL	18	0	2	2	22	6	0	0	0	25

Season Team	League	REGULAR SEASON					PLAYOFFS				
		Gms.	G	A	Pts.	PIM	Gms.	G	A	Pts.	PIM
89-90—Peoria	IHL	15	1	4	5	43	—	—	—	—	—
—St. Louis	NHL	58	0	12	12	145	12	0	2	2	47
90-91—St. Louis	NHL	68	5	15	20	204	9	0	0	0	31
91-92—Boston	NHL	7	1	0	1	20	—	—	—	—	—
92-93—Providence	AHL	8	3	4	7	60	—	—	—	—	—
—Boston	NHL	34	5	5	10	102	—	—	—	—	—
93-94—Boston	NHL	58	1	8	9	152	1	0	0	0	0
NHL totals		243	12	42	54	645	28	0	2	2	103

FEDOROV, SERGEI
C, RED WINGS

PERSONAL: Born December 13, 1969, in Minsk, U.S.S.R. . . . 6-1/191. . . . Shoots left. . . . Name pronounced FEH-duh-rahf.

TRANSACTIONS/CAREER NOTES: Selected by Detroit Red Wings in fourth round (fourth Red Wings pick, 74th overall) of NHL entry draft (June 17, 1989). . . . Bruised left shoulder (October 1990). . . . Reinjured left shoulder (January 16, 1991). . . . Sprained left shoulder (November 27, 1992); missed seven games. . . . Suffered from the flu (January 30, 1993); missed two games. . . . Suffered charley horse (February 11, 1993); missed one game. . . . Suffered concussion (April 5, 1994); missed two games. . . . Suspended four games without pay and fined $500 by NHL for improper conduct in playoff game (May 17, 1994).

HONORS: Named to NHL All-Rookie team (1990-91). . . . Played in NHL All-Star Game (1992 and 1994). . . . Named NHL Player of the Year by THE SPORTING NEWS (1993-94). . . . Named to THE SPORTING NEWS All-Star first team (1993-94). . . . Won Hart Memorial Trophy (1993-94). . . . Won Frank J. Selke Trophy (1993-94). . . . Won Lester B. Pearson Award (1993-94). . . . Named to NHL All-Star first team (1993-94).

Season Team	League	REGULAR SEASON					PLAYOFFS				
		Gms.	G	A	Pts.	PIM	Gms.	G	A	Pts.	PIM
85-86—Dynamo Minsk	USSR	15	6	1	7	10	—	—	—	—	—
86-87—CSKA Moscow	USSR	29	6	6	12	12	—	—	—	—	—
87-88—CSKA Moscow	USSR	48	7	9	16	20	—	—	—	—	—
88-89—CSKA Moscow	USSR	44	9	8	17	35	—	—	—	—	—
89-90—CSKA Moscow	USSR	48	19	10	29	20	—	—	—	—	—
90-91—Detroit	NHL	77	31	48	79	66	7	1	5	6	4
91-92—Detroit	NHL	80	32	54	86	72	11	5	5	10	8
92-93—Detroit	NHL	73	34	53	87	72	7	3	6	9	23
93-94—Detroit	NHL	82	56	64	120	34	7	1	7	8	6
NHL totals		312	153	219	372	244	32	10	23	33	41

FEDOTOV, ANATOLI
D, MIGHTY DUCKS

PERSONAL: Born May 11, 1966, in Saratov, U.S.S.R. . . . 5-11/178. . . . Shoots left. . . . Name pronounced An-uh-TOH-lee FEH-duh-tahf.

TRANSACTIONS/CAREER NOTES: Signed as free agent by Winnipeg Jets (July 4, 1991). . . . Selected by Mighty Ducks of Anaheim in 10th round (10th Mighty Ducks pick, 238th overall) in NHL entry draft (June 26, 1993).

Season Team	League	REGULAR SEASON					PLAYOFFS				
		Gms.	G	A	Pts.	PIM	Gms.	G	A	Pts.	PIM
85-86—Dynamo Moscow	USSR	35	0	2	2	10	—	—	—	—	—
86-87—Dynamo Moscow	USSR	18	3	2	5	12	—	—	—	—	—
87-88—Dynamo Moscow	USSR	48	2	3	5	38	—	—	—	—	—
88-89—Dynamo Moscow	USSR	40	2	1	3	24	—	—	—	—	—
89-90—Dynamo Moscow	USSR	41	2	4	6	22	—	—	—	—	—
90-91—Dynamo Moscow	USSR				Did not play.						
91-92—Dynamo Moscow	CIS	11	1	0	1	8	—	—	—	—	—
92-93—Moncton	AHL	76	10	37	47	99	2	0	0	0	0
—Winnipeg	NHL	1	0	2	2	0	—	—	—	—	—
93-94—San Diego	IHL	66	14	12	26	42	8	0	1	1	6
—Anaheim	NHL	3	0	0	0	0	—	—	—	—	—
NHL totals		4	0	2	2	0					

FEDYK, BRENT
LW, FLYERS

PERSONAL: Born March 8, 1967, in Yorkton, Sask. . . . 6-0/196. . . . Shoots right. . . . Name pronounced FEH-dihk.

TRANSACTIONS/CAREER NOTES: Selected by Detroit Red Wings as underage junior in first round (first Red Wings pick, eighth overall) of NHL entry draft (June 15, 1985). . . . Strained hip in training camp (September 1985); missed three weeks. . . . Traded by Regina Pats with RW Ken McIntyre, LW Grant Kazuik, D Gerald Bzdel and the WHL rights to LW Kevin Kowalchuk to Seattle Thunderbirds for RW Craig Endean, C Ray Savard, Grant Chorney, C Erin Ginnell and WHL rights to LW Frank Kovacs (November 1986). . . . Traded by Thunderbirds to Portland Winter Hawks for future considerations (February 1987). . . . Injured knee (December 22, 1990); missed one game. . . . Suffered deep shin bruise (January 26, 1991); missed five games. . . . Suffered concussion (March 1991). . . . Traded by Red Wings to Philadelphia Flyers for fourth-round pick (later traded to Boston who selected D Charles Paquette) in 1993 draft (October 1, 1992). . . . Strained right shoulder (December 11, 1992); missed three games. . . . Fractured thumb (January 31, 1993); missed one game. . . . Sprained left ankle (March 1993); missed one game. . . . Fractured toe (April 6, 1993); missed remainder of season. . . . Strained left wrist (February 24, 1994); missed three games. . . . Suspended one game by NHL for second stick-related game misconduct (March 24, 1994).

HONORS: Named to WHL All-Star second team (1985-86).

Season	Team	League	REGULAR SEASON Gms.	G	A	Pts.	PIM	PLAYOFFS Gms.	G	A	Pts.	PIM
82-83	—Regina	WHL	1	0	0	0	0	—	—	—	—	—
83-84	—Regina	WHL	63	15	28	43	30	23	8	7	15	6
84-85	—Regina	WHL	66	35	35	70	48	8	5	4	9	0
85-86	—Regina	WHL	50	43	34	77	47	5	0	1	1	0
86-87	—Regina	WHL	12	9	6	15	9	—	—	—	—	—
	—Seattle	WHL	13	5	11	16	9	—	—	—	—	—
	—Portland	WHL	11	5	4	9	6	14	5	6	11	0
87-88	—Detroit	NHL	2	0	1	1	2	—	—	—	—	—
	—Adirondack	AHL	34	9	11	20	22	5	0	2	2	6
88-89	—Detroit	NHL	5	2	0	2	0	—	—	—	—	—
	—Adirondack	AHL	66	40	28	68	33	15	7	8	15	23
89-90	—Detroit	NHL	27	1	4	5	6	—	—	—	—	—
	—Adirondack	AHL	33	14	15	29	24	6	2	1	3	4
90-91	—Detroit	NHL	67	16	19	35	38	6	1	0	1	2
91-92	—Adirondack	AHL	1	0	2	2	0	—	—	—	—	—
	—Detroit	NHL	61	5	8	13	42	1	0	0	0	2
92-93	—Philadelphia	NHL	74	21	38	59	48	—	—	—	—	—
93-94	—Philadelphia	NHL	72	20	18	38	74	—	—	—	—	—
NHL totals			308	65	88	153	210	7	1	0	1	4

FELSNER, DENNY
LW, BLUES

PERSONAL: Born April 29, 1970, in Warren, Mich. . . . 6-0/195. . . . Shoots left. . . . Full name: Denny Walter Felsner. **COLLEGE:** Michigan. **TRANSACTIONS/CAREER NOTES:** Selected by St. Louis Blues in third round (third Blues pick, 55th overall) of NHL entry draft (June 17, 1989). . . . Injured knee (December 29, 1989). . . . Broke ankle during off-season; missed four games. . . . Suffered sore ankle (January 25, 1994); missed seven games. . . . Suffered sore ankle (February 20, 1994). **HONORS:** Named to CCHA All-Rookie team (1988-89). . . . Named to NCAA All-America West second team (1990-91). . . . Named to CCHA All-Star first team (1990-91 and 1991-92). . . . Named to NCAA All-America West first team (1991-92).

Season	Team	League	REGULAR SEASON Gms.	G	A	Pts.	PIM	PLAYOFFS Gms.	G	A	Pts.	PIM
86-87	—Detroit Falcons	NAJHL	37	22	33	55	18	—	—	—	—	—
87-88	—Detroit Junior Red Wings	NAJHL	39	35	43	78	46	—	—	—	—	—
88-89	—University of Michigan	CCHA	39	30	19	49	22	—	—	—	—	—
89-90	—University of Michigan	CCHA	33	27	16	43	24	—	—	—	—	—
90-91	—University of Michigan	CCHA	46	40	35	75	58	—	—	—	—	—
91-92	—University of Michigan	CCHA	44	42	*52	*94	48	—	—	—	—	—
	—St. Louis	NHL	3	0	1	1	0	1	0	0	0	0
92-93	—Peoria	IHL	29	14	21	35	8	—	—	—	—	—
	—St. Louis	NHL	6	0	3	3	2	9	2	3	5	2
93-94	—Peoria	IHL	6	8	3	11	14	—	—	—	—	—
	—St. Louis	NHL	6	1	0	1	2	—	—	—	—	—
NHL totals			15	1	4	5	4	10	2	3	5	2

FERGUSON, CRAIG
RW, CANADIENS

PERSONAL: Born April 8, 1970, in Castro Valley, Calif. . . . 6-0/185. . . . Shoots left. **COLLEGE:** Yale. **TRANSACTIONS/CAREER NOTES:** Selected by Montreal Canadiens in seventh round (seventh Canadiens pick, 146th overall) of NHL entry draft (June 22, 1991).

Season	Team	League	REGULAR SEASON Gms.	G	A	Pts.	PIM	PLAYOFFS Gms.	G	A	Pts.	PIM
88-89	—Yale University	ECAC	24	11	6	17	20	—	—	—	—	—
89-90	—Yale University	ECAC	35	6	15	21	38	—	—	—	—	—
90-91	—Yale University	ECAC	29	11	10	21	34	—	—	—	—	—
91-92	—Yale University	ECAC	27	9	16	25	28	—	—	—	—	—
92-93	—Wheeling	ECHL	9	6	5	11	24	—	—	—	—	—
	—Fredericton	AHL	55	15	13	28	20	5	0	1	1	2
93-94	—Fredericton	AHL	57	29	32	61	60	—	—	—	—	—
	—Montreal	NHL	2	0	1	1	0	—	—	—	—	—
NHL totals			2	0	1	1	0					

FERGUSON, SCOTT
D, OILERS

PERSONAL: Born January 6, 1973, in Camrose, Alta. . . . 6-1/195. . . . Shoots left. **TRANSACTIONS/CAREER NOTES:** Signed as free agent by Edmonton Oilers (June 2, 1994).

Season	Team	League	REGULAR SEASON Gms.	G	A	Pts.	PIM	PLAYOFFS Gms.	G	A	Pts.	PIM
90-91	—Kamloops	WHL	4	0	0	0	0	—	—	—	—	—
91-92	—Kamloops	WHL	62	4	10	14	148	12	0	2	2	21
92-93	—Kamloops	WHL	71	4	19	23	206	13	0	2	2	24
93-94	—Kamloops	WHL	68	5	49	54	180	19	5	11	16	48

F

FERNANDEZ, EMMANUEL
G, STARS

PERSONAL: Born August 27, 1974, in Etobicoke, Ont. . . . 6-0/173. . . . Catches left. . . . Nephew of Jacques Lemaire, center, Montreal Canadiens (1967-68 through 1978-79) and current head coach, New Jersey Devils.

TRANSACTIONS/CAREER NOTES: Selected by Quebec Nordiques in third round (fourth Nordiques pick, 52nd overall) of NHL entry draft (June 20, 1992). . . . Traded by Nordiques to Dallas Stars for D Tommy Sjodin and undisclosed draft pick (February 13, 1994).

HONORS: Won Guy Lafleur Trophy (1992-93). . . . Won Michel Briere Trophy (1993-94). . . . Named to Can.HL All-Star second team (1993-94). . . . Named to QMJHL All-Star first team (1993-94).

								REGULAR SEASON						PLAYOFFS					
Season	Team	League	Gms.	Min.	W	L	T	GA	SO	Avg.	Gms.	Min.	W	L	GA	SO	Avg.
91-92	Laval	QMJHL	31	1593	14	13	2	99	1	3.73	9	468	3	5	†39	0	5.00
92-93	Laval	QMJHL	43	2348	26	14	2	141	1	3.60	13	818	12	1	42	0	3.08
93-94	Laval	QMJHL	51	2776	29	14	1	143	*5	3.09	19	1116	14	5	49	†1	*2.63

FERNER, MARK
D, MIGHTY DUCKS

PERSONAL: Born September 5, 1965, in Regina, Sask. . . . 6-0/193. . . . Shoots left.

TRANSACTIONS/CAREER NOTES: Selected by Buffalo Sabres in 10th round (12th Sabres pick, 194th overall) of NHL entry draft (June 8, 1983). . . . Broke foot (March 1986). . . . Traded by Sabres to Washington Capitals for C Scott McCrory (June 1, 1989). . . . Traded by Capitals to Toronto Maple Leafs for future considerations (February 27, 1992). . . . Signed as free agent by Ottawa Senators (August 6, 1992). . . . Loaned to San Diego Gulls (February 17, 1993). . . . Selected by Mighty Ducks of Anaheim in NHL expansion draft (June 24, 1993). . . . Strained groin (November 13, 1993); missed five games. . . . Suffered deep contusion (November 26, 1993); missed three games. . . . Suffered deep contusion to left thigh (December 14, 1993); missed two games.

HONORS: Named to WHL (West) All-Star first team (1984-85). . . . Named to AHL All-Star second team (1990-91).

				REGULAR SEASON					PLAYOFFS			
Season	Team	League	Gms.	G	A	Pts.	PIM	Gms.	G	A	Pts.	PIM
82-83	Kamloops	WHL	69	6	15	21	81	7	0	0	0	7
83-84	Kamloops	WHL	72	9	30	39	162	14	1	8	9	20
84-85	Kamloops	WHL	69	15	39	54	91	15	4	9	13	21
85-86	Rochester	AHL	63	3	14	17	87	—	—	—	—	—
86-87	Buffalo	NHL	13	0	3	3	9	—	—	—	—	—
	Rochester	AHL	54	0	12	12	157	—	—	—	—	—
87-88	Rochester	AHL	69	1	25	26	165	7	1	4	5	31
88-89	Buffalo	NHL	2	0	0	0	2	—	—	—	—	—
	Rochester	AHL	55	0	18	18	97	—	—	—	—	—
89-90	Washington	NHL	2	0	0	0	0	—	—	—	—	—
	Baltimore	AHL	74	7	28	35	76	11	1	2	3	21
90-91	Baltimore	AHL	61	14	40	54	38	6	1	4	5	24
	Washington	NHL	7	0	1	1	4	—	—	—	—	—
91-92	Baltimore	AHL	57	7	38	45	67	—	—	—	—	—
	St. John's	AHL	15	1	8	9	6	14	2	14	16	39
92-93	New Haven	AHL	34	5	7	12	69	—	—	—	—	—
	San Diego	IHL	26	0	15	15	34	11	1	2	3	8
93-94	Anaheim	NHL	50	3	5	8	30	—	—	—	—	—
NHL totals			**74**	**3**	**9**	**12**	**45**					

FERRARO, CHRIS
RW, RANGERS

PERSONAL: Born January 24, 1973, in Port Jefferson, N.Y. . . . 5-10/175. . . . Shoots right. . . . Twin brother of Peter Ferraro, center in New York Rangers system.

COLLEGE: Maine.

TRANSACTIONS/CAREER NOTES: Selected by New York Rangers in fourth round (fourth Rangers pick, 85th overall) of NHL entry draft (June 20, 1992).

HONORS: Named to Hockey East Rookie All-Star team (1992-93).

				REGULAR SEASON					PLAYOFFS			
Season	Team	League	Gms.	G	A	Pts.	PIM	Gms.	G	A	Pts.	PIM
90-91	Dubuque	USHL	45	53	44	97	. . .	—	—	—	—	—
91-92	Waterloo	USHL	38	49	50	99	106	—	—	—	—	—
92-93	University of Maine	Hockey East	39	25	26	51	46	—	—	—	—	—
93-94	U.S. national team	Int'l	48	8	34	42	58	—	—	—	—	—
	University of Maine	Hockey East	4	0	1	1	8	—	—	—	—	—

FERRARO, PETER
C, RANGERS

PERSONAL: Born January 24, 1973, in Port Jefferson, N.Y. . . . 5-10/175. . . . Shoots right. . . . Twin brother of Chris Ferraro, right winger in New York Rangers system.

COLLEGE: Maine.

TRANSACTIONS/CAREER NOTES: Selected by New York Rangers in first round (first Rangers pick, 24th overall) of NHL entry draft (June 20, 1992).

				REGULAR SEASON					PLAYOFFS			
Season	Team	League	Gms.	G	A	Pts.	PIM	Gms.	G	A	Pts.	PIM
90-91	Dubuque	USHL	29	21	31	52	83	—	—	—	—	—
91-92	Waterloo	USHL	42	48	53	101	168	—	—	—	—	—
92-93	University of Maine	Hockey East	36	18	32	50	106	—	—	—	—	—
93-94	U.S. national team	Int'l	59	28	39	67	48	—	—	—	—	—
	U.S. Olympic Team	Int'l	8	6	0	6	6	—	—	—	—	—
	University of Maine	Hockey East	4	3	6	9	16	—	—	—	—	—

FERRARO, RAY

C, ISLANDERS

PERSONAL: Born August 23, 1964, in Trail, B.C. . . . 5-10/185. . . . Shoots left. . . . Name pronounced fuh-RAH-roh.
TRANSACTIONS/CAREER NOTES: Selected by Hartford Whalers as underage junior in fifth round (fifth Whalers pick, 88th overall) of NHL entry draft (June 9, 1982). . . . Traded by Whalers to New York Islanders for D Doug Crossman (November 13, 1990). . . . Fractured right fibula (December 10, 1992); missed 36 games. . . . Suffered from the flu (March 25, 1993); missed one game.
HONORS: Won Four Broncos Memorial Trophy (1983-84). . . . Won Bob Brownridge Memorial Trophy (1983-84). . . . Won WHL Player of the Year Award (1983-84). . . . Named to WHL (East) All-Star first team (1983-84). . . . Played in NHL All-Star Game (1992).

			REGULAR SEASON					PLAYOFFS				
Season	Team	League	Gms.	G	A	Pts.	PIM	Gms.	G	A	Pts.	PIM
81-82	Penticton	BCJHL	48	65	70	135	50	—	—	—	—	—
82-83	Portland	WHL	50	41	49	90	39	14	14	10	24	13
83-84	Brandon	WHL	72	*108	84	*192	84	11	13	15	28	20
84-85	Binghamton	AHL	37	20	13	33	29	—	—	—	—	—
	Hartford	NHL	44	11	17	28	40	—	—	—	—	—
85-86	Hartford	NHL	76	30	47	77	57	10	3	6	9	4
86-87	Hartford	NHL	80	27	32	59	42	6	1	1	2	8
87-88	Hartford	NHL	68	21	29	50	81	6	1	1	2	6
88-89	Hartford	NHL	80	41	35	76	86	4	2	0	2	4
89-90	Hartford	NHL	79	25	29	54	109	7	0	3	3	2
90-91	Hartford	NHL	15	2	5	7	18	—	—	—	—	—
	New York Islanders	NHL	61	19	16	35	52	—	—	—	—	—
91-92	New York Islanders	NHL	80	40	40	80	92	—	—	—	—	—
92-93	New York Islanders	NHL	46	14	13	27	40	18	13	7	20	18
	Capital District	AHL	1	0	2	2	2	—	—	—	—	—
93-94	New York Islanders	NHL	82	21	32	53	83	4	1	0	1	6
NHL totals			711	251	295	546	700	55	21	18	39	48

FETISOV, SLAVA

D, DEVILS

PERSONAL: Born May 20, 1958, in Moscow, U.S.S.R. . . . 6-1/215. . . . Shoots left. . . . Name pronounced SLAH-vuh fuh-TEE-sahf.
TRANSACTIONS/CAREER NOTES: Selected by Montreal Canadiens in 12th round (14th Canadiens pick, 201st overall) of NHL entry draft (June 15, 1978). . . . Selected by New Jersey Devils in eighth round (sixth Devils pick, 150th overall) of NHL entry draft (June 8, 1983). . . . Tore cartilage in left knee (November 22, 1989); missed six games. . . . Suffered bronchial pneumonia and hospitalized twice (November 28, 1990); missed 10 games. . . . Suffered from the flu (October 14, 1992); missed one game. . . . Sprained knee (November 30, 1993); missed four games.
HONORS: Named to Soviet League All-Star team (1977-78 and 1981-82 through 1987-88). . . . Won Soviet Player of the Year Award (1981-82 and 1985-86). . . . Won Golden Stick Award (1983-84, 1987-88 and 1988-89).
MISCELLANEOUS: Member of silver-medal-winning (1980) and gold-medal-winning U.S.S.R. Olympic teams (1984 and 1988).

			REGULAR SEASON					PLAYOFFS				
Season	Team	League	Gms.	G	A	Pts.	PIM	Gms.	G	A	Pts.	PIM
76-77	CSKA Moscow	USSR	28	3	4	7	14	—	—	—	—	—
77-78	CSKA Moscow	USSR	35	9	18	27	46	—	—	—	—	—
78-79	CSKA Moscow	USSR	29	10	19	29	40	—	—	—	—	—
79-80	CSKA Moscow	USSR	37	10	14	24	46	—	—	—	—	—
	Soviet Olympic Team	Int'l	7	5	4	9	10	—	—	—	—	—
80-81	CSKA Moscow	USSR	48	13	16	29	44	—	—	—	—	—
81-82	CSKA Moscow	USSR	46	15	26	41	20	—	—	—	—	—
82-83	CSKA Moscow	USSR	43	6	17	23	46	—	—	—	—	—
83-84	CSKA Moscow	USSR	44	19	30	49	38	—	—	—	—	—
	Soviet Olympic Team	Int'l	7	3	8	11	8	—	—	—	—	—
84-85	CSKA Moscow	USSR	20	13	12	25	6	—	—	—	—	—
85-86	CSKA Moscow	USSR	40	15	19	34	12	—	—	—	—	—
86-87	CSKA Moscow	USSR	39	13	20	33	18	—	—	—	—	—
87-88	CSKA Moscow	USSR	46	18	17	35	26	—	—	—	—	—
	Soviet Olympic Team	Int'l	8	4	9	13	6	—	—	—	—	—
88-89	CSKA Moscow	USSR	23	9	8	17	18	—	—	—	—	—
89-90	New Jersey	NHL	72	8	34	42	52	6	0	2	2	10
90-91	New Jersey	NHL	67	3	16	19	62	7	0	0	0	17
	Utica	AHL	1	1	1	2	0	—	—	—	—	—
91-92	New Jersey	NHL	70	3	23	26	108	6	0	3	3	8
92-93	New Jersey	NHL	76	4	23	27	158	5	0	2	2	4
93-94	New Jersey	NHL	52	1	14	15	30	14	1	0	1	8
NHL totals			337	19	110	129	410	38	1	7	8	47

FICHAUD, ERIC

G, MAPLE LEAFS

PERSONAL: Born November 4, 1975, in Montreal. . . . 5-11/160. . . . Catches left. . . . Name pronounced Ay-RIHK Fee-SHOH.
HIGH SCHOOL: CEGEP de Chicoutimi (Que.).
TRANSACTIONS/CAREER NOTES: Selected by Toronto Maple Leafs in first round (first Maple Leafs pick, 16th overall) of NHL entry draft (June 28, 1994).
HONORS: Named to Memorial Cup All-Star team (1993-94). . . . Won Hap Emms Memorial Trophy (1993-94). . . . Won QMJHL Top Draft Prospect Award (1993-94). . . . Won Guy Lafleur Award (1993-94).

Season Team	League	Gms.	Min.	W	L	T	GA	SO	Avg.	Gms.	Min.	W	L	GA	SO	Avg.
92-93—Chicoutimi	QMJHL	43	2040	18	13	1	149	0	4.38	—	—	—	—	—	—	—
93-94—Chicoutimi	QMJHL	63	3493	37	21	3	192	4	3.30	26	1560	16	10	86	†1	3.31

FILIMONOV, DIMITRI
D, SENATORS

PERSONAL: Born October 14, 1971, in Perm, U.S.S.R.... 6-4/220.... Shoots right. ... Name pronounced fih-lih-MAH-nahf.

TRANSACTIONS/CAREER NOTES: Selected by Winnipeg Jets in third round (second Jets pick, 49th overall) of NHL entry draft (June 22, 1991).... Traded by Jets to Ottawa Senators for fourth-round pick in 1993 draft (D Ruslan Batyrshin) and future considerations (March 15, 1993).

Season Team	League	Gms.	G	A	Pts.	PIM	Gms.	G	A	Pts.	PIM
90-91—Dynamo Moscow	USSR	45	4	6	10	12	—	—	—	—	—
91-92—Dynamo Moscow	CIS	38	3	2	5	12	—	—	—	—	—
92-93—Dynamo Moscow	CIS	42	2	3	5	30	—	—	—	—	—
93-94—Ottawa	NHL	30	1	4	5	18	—	—	—	—	—
—Prince Edward Island	AHL	48	10	16	26	14	—	—	—	—	—
NHL totals		30	1	4	5	18					

FINLEY, JEFF
D, FLYERS

PERSONAL: Born April 14, 1967, in Edmonton.... 6-2/205.... Shoots left.

TRANSACTIONS/CAREER NOTES: Selected by New York Islanders as underage junior in third round (fourth Islanders pick, 55th overall) of NHL entry draft (June 15, 1985).... Suffered swollen left knee (September 1988).... Traded by Islanders to Ottawa Senators for D Chris Luongo (June 30, 1993).... Signed as free agent by Philadelphia Flyers (August 2, 1993).

Season Team	League	Gms.	G	A	Pts.	PIM	Gms.	G	A	Pts.	PIM
83-84—Portland	WHL	5	0	0	0	0	5	0	1	1	4
—Summerland	BCJHL	49	0	21	21	14	—	—	—	—	—
84-85—Portland	WHL	69	6	44	50	57	6	1	2	3	2
85-86—Portland	WHL	70	11	59	70	83	15	1	7	8	16
86-87—Portland	WHL	72	13	53	66	113	20	1	†21	22	27
87-88—Springfield	AHL	52	5	18	23	50	—	—	—	—	—
—New York Islanders	NHL	10	0	5	5	15	1	0	0	0	2
88-89—New York Islanders	NHL	4	0	0	0	6	—	—	—	—	—
—Springfield	AHL	65	3	16	19	55	—	—	—	—	—
89-90—New York Islanders	NHL	11	0	1	1	0	5	0	2	2	2
—Springfield	AHL	57	1	15	16	41	13	1	4	5	23
90-91—Capital District	AHL	67	10	34	44	34	—	—	—	—	—
—New York Islanders	NHL	11	0	0	0	4	—	—	—	—	—
91-92—Capital District	AHL	20	1	9	10	6	—	—	—	—	—
—New York Islanders	NHL	51	1	10	11	26	—	—	—	—	—
92-93—Capital District	AHL	61	6	29	35	34	4	0	1	1	0
93-94—Philadelphia	NHL	55	1	8	9	24	—	—	—	—	—
NHL totals		142	2	24	26	75	6	0	2	2	4

FINN, SHANNON
D, FLYERS

PERSONAL: Born January 25, 1972, in Toronto.... 6-2/190.... Shoots left.

COLLEGE: Illinois-Chicago.

TRANSACTIONS/CAREER NOTES: Selected by Philadelphia Flyers in NHL supplemental draft (June 25, 1993).

Season Team	League	Gms.	G	A	Pts.	PIM	Gms.	G	A	Pts.	PIM
91-92—Illinois-Chicago	CCHA	36	6	14	20	80	—	—	—	—	—
92-93—Illinois-Chicago	CCHA	36	6	13	19	48	—	—	—	—	—
93-94—Illinois-Chicago	CCHA	39	5	22	27	42	—	—	—	—	—

FINN, STEVEN
D, NORDIQUES

PERSONAL: Born August 20, 1966, in Laval, Que.... 6-0/191.... Shoots left.

TRANSACTIONS/CAREER NOTES: Selected by Quebec Nordiques as underage junior in third round (third Nordiques pick, 57th overall) of NHL entry draft (June 9, 1984).... Separated left shoulder (January 31, 1990).... Lacerated right index finger (October 25, 1990); missed five games. ...Sprained wrist (November 25, 1991); missed six games.... Sprained right wrist (February 15, 1992); missed seven games. ... Injured eye (January 22, 1993); missed one game.... Bruised left arm (March 8, 1993); missed one game.... Suffered from stomach virus (December 17, 1993); missed one game.

HONORS: Named to QMJHL All-Star first team (1983-84).... Named to QMJHL All-Star second team (1984-85).

Season Team	League	Gms.	G	A	Pts.	PIM	Gms.	G	A	Pts.	PIM
82-83—Laval	QMJHL	69	7	30	37	108	6	0	2	2	6
83-84—Laval	QMJHL	68	7	39	46	159	14	1	6	7	27
84-85—Laval	QMJHL	61	20	33	53	169	—	—	—	—	—
—Fredericton	AHL	4	0	0	0	14	6	1	1	2	4
85-86—Laval	QMJHL	29	4	15	19	111	14	6	16	22	57
—Quebec	NHL	17	0	1	1	28	—	—	—	—	—

F

Season Team	League	REGULAR SEASON					PLAYOFFS				
		Gms.	G	A	Pts.	PIM	Gms.	G	A	Pts.	PIM
86-87—Fredericton	AHL	38	7	19	26	73	—	—	—	—	—
—Quebec	NHL	36	2	5	7	40	13	0	2	2	29
87-88—Quebec	NHL	75	3	7	10	198	—	—	—	—	—
88-89—Quebec	NHL	77	2	6	8	235	—	—	—	—	—
89-90—Quebec	NHL	64	3	9	12	208	—	—	—	—	—
90-91—Quebec	NHL	71	6	13	19	228	—	—	—	—	—
91-92—Quebec	NHL	65	4	7	11	194	—	—	—	—	—
92-93—Quebec	NHL	80	5	9	14	160	6	0	1	1	8
93-94—Quebec	NHL	80	4	13	17	159	—	—	—	—	—
NHL totals		565	29	70	99	1450	19	0	3	3	37

FINNSTROM, JOHAN
D, FLAMES

PERSONAL: Born March 27, 1976, in Broby, Sweden.... 6-3/205.... Shoots left. **TRANSACTIONS/CAREER NOTES:** Selected by Calgary Flames in fourth round (fifth Flames pick, 97th overall) of NHL entry draft (June 29, 1994).

Season Team	League	REGULAR SEASON					PLAYOFFS				
		Gms.	G	A	Pts.	PIM	Gms.	G	A	Pts.	PIM
93-94—Rogle	Sweden	7	1	1	2	2	—	—	—	—	—

FIORENTINO, PETER
D, RANGERS

PERSONAL: Born December 22, 1968, in Niagara Falls, Ont.... 6-1/205.... Shoots right.... Name pronounced fyohr-ihn-TEE-noh. **TRANSACTIONS/CAREER NOTES:** Selected by New York Rangers in 11th round (11th Rangers pick, 215th overall) of NHL entry draft (June 11, 1988).... Suspended three games (October 19, 1990).... Tore tendon in left ring finger (March 1991).

Season Team	League	REGULAR SEASON					PLAYOFFS				
		Gms.	G	A	Pts.	PIM	Gms.	G	A	Pts.	PIM
84-85—Niagara Falls Jr. B	OHA	38	7	10	17	149	—	—	—	—	—
85-86—Sault Ste. Marie	OHL	58	1	6	7	87	—	—	—	—	—
86-87—Sault Ste. Marie	OHL	64	1	12	13	187	4	2	1	3	5
87-88—Sault Ste. Marie	OHL	65	5	27	32	252	6	2	2	4	21
88-89—Sault Ste. Marie	OHL	55	5	24	29	220	—	—	—	—	—
—Denver	IHL	10	0	0	0	39	4	0	0	0	24
89-90—Flint	IHL	64	2	7	9	302	—	—	—	—	—
90-91—Binghamton	AHL	55	2	11	13	361	1	0	0	0	0
91-92—Binghamton	AHL	70	2	11	13	340	5	0	1	1	24
—New York Rangers	NHL	1	0	0	0	0	—	—	—	—	—
92-93—Binghamton	AHL	64	9	5	14	286	13	0	3	3	22
93-94—Binghamton	AHL	68	7	15	22	220	—	—	—	—	—
NHL totals		1	0	0	0	0					

FISET, STEPHANE
G, NORDIQUES

PERSONAL: Born June 17, 1970, in Montreal.... 6-1/195.... Catches left.... Name pronounced fih-SEHT. **TRANSACTIONS/CAREER NOTES:** Selected by Quebec Nordiques in second round (third Nordiques pick, 24th overall) of NHL entry draft (June 13, 1987).... Underwent shoulder surgery (May 1989).... Twisted knee (December 9, 1990).... Sprained left knee (January 14, 1992); missed 12 games.... Suffered slipped disc (November 4, 1993); missed 18 games. **HONORS:** Won Can.HL Goaltender of the Year Award (1988-89).... Won Jacques Plante Trophy (1988-89).... Named to QMJHL All-Star first team (1988-89).

Season Team	League	REGULAR SEASON							PLAYOFFS						
		Gms.	Min.	W	L	T	GA	SO	Avg.	Gms.	Min.	W	L	GA	SO	Avg.
87-88—Victoriaville	QMJHL	40	2221	14	17	4	146	1	3.94	2	163	0	2	10	0	3.68
88-89—Victoriaville	QMJHL	43	2401	25	14	0	138	1	*3.45	12	711	9	2	33	0	*2.78
89-90—Victoriaville	QMJHL	24	1383	14	6	3	63	1	2.73	*14	*790	7	6	*49	0	3.72
—Quebec	NHL	6	342	0	5	1	34	0	5.96	—	—	—	—	—	—	—
90-91—Quebec	NHL	3	186	0	2	1	12	0	3.87	—	—	—	—	—	—	—
—Halifax	AHL	36	1902	10	15	8	131	0	4.13	—	—	—	—	—	—	—
91-92—Halifax	AHL	29	1675	8	14	6	110	†3	3.94	—	—	—	—	—	—	—
—Quebec	NHL	23	1133	7	10	2	71	1	3.76	—	—	—	—	—	—	—
92-93—Quebec	NHL	37	1939	18	9	4	110	0	3.40	1	21	0	0	1	0	2.86
—Halifax	AHL	3	180	2	1	0	11	0	3.67	—	—	—	—	—	—	—
93-94—Cornwall	AHL	1	60	0	1	0	4	0	4.00	—	—	—	—	—	—	—
—Quebec	NHL	50	2798	20	25	4	158	2	3.39	—	—	—	—	—	—	—
NHL totals		119	6398	45	51	12	385	3	3.61	1	21	0	0	1	0	2.86

FISHER, CRAIG
C, BLACKHAWKS

PERSONAL: Born June 30, 1970, in Oshawa, Ont.... 6-3/180.... Shoots left.... Full name: Craig Francis Fisher. **COLLEGE:** Miami of Ohio. **TRANSACTIONS/CAREER NOTES:** Suffered concussion (October 1987).... Selected by Philadelphia Flyers in third round (third Flyers pick, 56th overall) of NHL entry draft (June 11, 1988).... Traded by Flyers with RW Scott Mellanby and LW Craig Berube to Edmonton Oilers for RW Dave Brown, D Corey Foster and the NHL rights to RW Jari Kurri (May 30, 1991).... Traded by Oilers to Winnipeg Jets for future considerations (December 9, 1993).... Signed as free

agent by Chicago Blackhawks (June 23, 1994).
HONORS: Named to CCHA All-Rookie team (1988-89).... Named to CCHA All-Star first team (1989-90).

			REGULAR SEASON					PLAYOFFS				
Season Team	League	Gms.	G	A	Pts.	PIM	Gms.	G	A	Pts.	PIM
86-87—Oshawa Jr. B	OHA	34	22	26	48	18	—	—	—	—	—
87-88—Oshawa Jr. B	OHA	36	42	34	76	48	—	—	—	—	—
88-89—Miami of Ohio	CCHA	37	22	20	42	37	—	—	—	—	—
89-90—Miami of Ohio	CCHA	39	37	29	66	38	—	—	—	—	—
—Philadelphia	NHL	2	0	0	0	0	—	—	—	—	—
90-91—Hershey	AHL	77	43	36	79	46	7	5	3	8	2
—Philadelphia	NHL	2	0	0	0	0	—	—	—	—	—
91-92—Cape Breton	AHL	60	20	25	45	28	1	0	0	0	0
92-93—Cape Breton	AHL	75	32	29	61	74	1	0	0	0	2
93-94—Cape Breton	AHL	16	5	5	10	11	—	—	—	—	—
—Moncton	AHL	46	26	35	61	36	21	11	11	22	28
—Winnipeg	NHL	4	0	0	0	2	—	—	—	—	—
NHL totals		8	0	0	0	2					

FITZGERALD, RUSTY
C, PENGUINS

PERSONAL: Born October 4, 1972, in Minneapolis.... 6-1/185.... Shoots left.
HIGH SCHOOL: William M. Kelley (Silver Bay, Minn.), then Silver Bay (Minn.), then East (Duluth, Minn.).
COLLEGE: Minnesota-Duluth.

TRANSACTIONS/CAREER NOTES: Selected by Pittsburgh Penguins in second round (second Penguins pick, 38th overall) of NHL entry draft (June 22, 1991).

			REGULAR SEASON					PLAYOFFS				
Season Team	League	Gms.	G	A	Pts.	PIM	Gms.	G	A	Pts.	PIM
87-88—William M. Kelley H.S.	Minn. H.S.	20	19	26	45	18	—	—	—	—	—
88-89—William M. Kelley H.S.	Minn. H.S.	22	24	25	49	26	—	—	—	—	—
89-90—William M. Kelley H.S.	Minn. H.S.	21	25	26	51	24	—	—	—	—	—
—Northland Jr. B	Minn.	20	11	5	16	12	—	—	—	—	—
—Silver Bay H.S.	Minn. H.S.	21	25	26	51	24	—	—	—	—	—
90-91—Duluth East High School	Minn. H.S.	15	14	11	25	...	—	—	—	—	—
91-92—Minnesota-Duluth	WCHA	37	9	11	20	40	—	—	—	—	—
92-93—Minnesota-Duluth	WCHA	39	24	23	47	58	—	—	—	—	—
93-94—Minnesota-Duluth	WCHA	37	11	25	36	59	—	—	—	—	—

FITZGERALD, TOM
RW/C, PANTHERS

PERSONAL: Born August 28, 1968, in Melrose, Mass.... 6-1/195.... Shoots right....
Full name: Thomas James Fitzgerald.
HIGH SCHOOL: Austin Prep (Reading, Mass.).
COLLEGE: Providence.

TRANSACTIONS/CAREER NOTES: Selected by New York Islanders in first round (first Islanders pick, 17th overall) of NHL entry draft (June 21, 1986).... Bruised left knee (November 7, 1990).... Strained abdominal muscle (October 22, 1991); missed 16 games.... Tore rib cage muscle (October 24, 1992); missed four games.... Selected by Florida Panthers in NHL expansion draft (June 24, 1993).... Sore hip (March 18, 1994); missed one game.
RECORDS: Shares NHL single-game playoff record for most shorthanded goals—2 (May 8, 1993).

			REGULAR SEASON					PLAYOFFS				
Season Team	League	Gms.	G	A	Pts.	PIM	Gms.	G	A	Pts.	PIM
84-85—Austin Prep.	Mass. H.S.	18	20	21	41	...	—	—	—	—	—
85-86—Austin Prep.	Mass. H.S.	24	35	38	73	...	—	—	—	—	—
86-87—Providence College	Hockey East	15	2	0	2	2	—	—	—	—	—
87-88—Providence College	Hockey East	36	19	15	34	50	—	—	—	—	—
88-89—Springfield	AHL	61	24	18	42	43	—	—	—	—	—
—New York Islanders	NHL	23	3	5	8	10	—	—	—	—	—
89-90—Springfield	AHL	53	30	23	53	32	14	2	9	11	13
—New York Islanders	NHL	19	2	5	7	4	4	1	0	1	4
90-91—New York Islanders	NHL	41	5	5	10	24	—	—	—	—	—
—Capital District	AHL	27	7	7	14	50	—	—	—	—	—
91-92—New York Islanders	NHL	45	6	11	17	28	—	—	—	—	—
—Capital District	AHL	4	1	1	2	4	—	—	—	—	—
92-93—New York Islanders	NHL	77	9	18	27	34	18	2	5	7	18
93-94—Florida	NHL	83	18	14	32	54	—	—	—	—	—
NHL totals		288	43	58	101	154	22	3	5	8	22

FITZPATRICK, MARK
G, PANTHERS

PERSONAL: Born November 13, 1968, in Toronto.... 6-2/190.... Catches left.
TRANSACTIONS/CAREER NOTES: Injured knee (February 1987).... Selected by Los Angeles Kings as underage junior in second round (second Kings pick, 27th overall) of NHL entry draft (June 13, 1987).... Traded by Kings with D Wayne McBean and future considerations to New York Islanders for G Kelly Hrudey (February 22, 1989); Kings sent D Doug Crossman to Islanders to complete the deal (May 23, 1989).... Developed Eosinophilic Myalgia Syndrome (EMS) after a reaction to L-Trytophan, an ingredient in a vitamin supplement (September 1990); returned to play (March 1991).... Suffered recurrence of EMS and underwent biopsy on right thigh (October 22, 1991); missed 10 games.... Strained abdominal muscle (December 15, 1992); missed five games.... Traded by Islanders with first-round pick in 1993 draft (C Adam Deadmarsh) to Quebec Nordiques for G Ron Hextall and first-round pick (C/RW Todd Bertuzzi) in 1993 draft (June 20, 1993).... Selected by Florida Panthers in NHL expansion draft (June 24, 1993).... Suspended two games without pay and fined $500 by NHL for high-sticking incident (February 16, 1994).

HONORS: Won Top Goaltender Trophy (1985-86).... Named to WHL All-Star second team (1985-86 and 1987-88).... Named to Memorial Cup All-Star team (1986-87 and 1987-88).... Won Bill Masterton Memorial Trophy (1991-92).

				REGULAR SEASON							PLAYOFFS						
Season	Team	League	Gms.	Min.	W	L	T	GA	SO	Avg.	Gms.	Min.	W	L	GA	SO	Avg.
83-84	Revelstoke	BCJHL	21	1019	...	...	...	90	0	5.30	—	—	—	—	—	—	—
84-85	Medicine Hat	WHL	3	180	...	...	...	9	0	3.00	—	—	—	—	—	—	—
85-86	Medicine Hat	WHL	41	2074	26	6	1	99	1	*2.86	*19	986	12	5	*58	0	3.53
86-87	Medicine Hat	WHL	50	2844	31	11	4	159	*4	3.35	*20	*1224	12	8	71	†1	3.48
87-88	Medicine Hat	WHL	63	3600	36	15	6	194	†2	*3.23	16	959	12	4	52	†1	*3.25
88-89	New Haven	AHL	18	980	10	5	1	54	1	3.31	—	—	—	—	—	—	—
	Los Angeles	NHL	17	957	6	7	3	64	0	4.01	—	—	—	—	—	—	—
	New York Islanders	NHL	11	627	3	5	2	41	0	3.92	—	—	—	—	—	—	—
89-90	New York Islanders	NHL	47	2653	19	19	5	150	3	3.39	4	152	0	2	13	0	5.13
90-91	Capital District	AHL	12	734	3	7	2	47	0	3.84	—	—	—	—	—	—	—
	New York Islanders	NHL	2	120	1	1	0	6	0	3.00	—	—	—	—	—	—	—
91-92	Capital District	AHL	14	782	6	5	1	39	0	2.99	—	—	—	—	—	—	—
	New York Islanders	NHL	30	1743	11	13	5	93	0	3.20	—	—	—	—	—	—	—
92-93	New York Islanders	NHL	39	2253	17	15	5	130	0	3.46	3	77	0	1	4	0	3.12
	Capital District	AHL	5	284	1	3	1	18	0	3.80	—	—	—	—	—	—	—
93-94	Florida	NHL	28	1603	12	8	6	73	1	2.73	—	—	—	—	—	—	—
	NHL totals		174	9956	69	68	26	557	4	3.36	7	229	0	3	17	0	4.45

FITZPATRICK, RORY
D, CANADIENS

PERSONAL: Born January 11, 1975, in Rochester, N.Y.... 6-1/190.... Shoots right.
TRANSACTIONS/CAREER NOTES: Selected by Montreal Canadiens in second round (second Canadiens pick, 47th overall) of NHL entry draft (June 26, 1993).
HONORS: Named to OHL All-Rookie team (1992-93).

				REGULAR SEASON				PLAYOFFS				
Season	Team	League	Gms.	G	A	Pts.	PIM	Gms.	G	A	Pts.	PIM
90-91	Rochester Jr. B	OHA	40	0	5	5	...	—	—	—	—	—
91-92	Rochester Jr. B	OHA	28	8	28	36	141	—	—	—	—	—
92-93	Sudbury	OHL	58	4	20	24	68	14	0	0	0	17
93-94	Sudbury	OHL	65	12	34	46	112	10	2	5	7	10

FITZSIMMONS, JASON
G, CANUCKS

PERSONAL: Born June 3, 1971, in Regina, Sask.... 5-11/185.... Catches left.
TRANSACTIONS/CAREER NOTES: Selected by Vancouver Canucks in 11th round (10th Canucks pick, 227th overall) of NHL entry draft (June 22, 1991).

				REGULAR SEASON							PLAYOFFS						
Season	Team	League	Gms.	Min.	W	L	T	GA	SO	Avg.	Gms.	Min.	W	L	GA	SO	Avg.
89-90	Moose Jaw	WHL	28	1392	10	10	1	90	0	3.88	—	—	—	—	—	—	—
90-91	Moose Jaw	WHL	44	2170	15	23	2	179	0	4.95	8	481	4	4	27	0	3.37
91-92	Moose Jaw	WHL	60	3286	29	28	1	222	0	4.05	4	186	0	4	27	0	8.71
92-93	Columbus	ECHL	23	1340	10	9	‡3	91	0	4.07	—	—	—	—	—	—	—
	Hamilton	AHL	14	788	5	8	1	53	0	4.04	—	—	—	—	—	—	—
93-94	Hamilton	AHL	17	709	2	8	0	49	0	4.15	2	98	0	2	6	0	3.67

FLAHERTY, WADE
G, SHARKS

PERSONAL: Born January 11, 1968, in Terreace, B.C.... 6-0/170.... Catches right.
TRANSACTIONS/CAREER NOTES: Selected by Buffalo Sabres in ninth round (10th Sabres pick, 181st overall) of NHL entry draft (June 11, 1988).... Signed as free agent by San Jose Sharks (September 3, 1991).
HONORS: Named to WHL All-Star second team (1987-88).... Won ECHL Playoff Most Valuable Player Award (1989-90).... Shared James Norris Memorial Trophy with Arturs Irbe (1991-92).... Named to IHL All-Star second team (1992-93 and 1993-94).

				REGULAR SEASON							PLAYOFFS						
Season	Team	League	Gms.	Min.	W	L	T	GA	SO	Avg.	Gms.	Min.	W	L	GA	SO	Avg.
84-85	Kelowna Wings	WHL	1	55	0	0	0	5	0	5.45	—	—	—	—	—	—	—
85-86	Seattle	WHL	9	271	1	3	0	36	0	7.97	—	—	—	—	—	—	—
	Spokane	WHL	5	161	0	3	0	21	0	7.83	—	—	—	—	—	—	—
86-87	Nanaimo	BCJHL	15	830	...	...	...	53	0	3.83	—	—	—	—	—	—	—
	Victoria	WHL	3	127	0	2	0	16	0	7.56	—	—	—	—	—	—	—
87-88	Victoria	WHL	36	2052	20	15	0	135	0	3.95	5	300	2	3	18	0	3.60
88-89	Victoria	WHL	42	2408	21	19	0	180	0	4.49	8	480	3	5	35	0	4.38
89-90	Kalamazoo	IHL	1	13	0	0	‡0	0	0	0.00	—	—	—	—	—	—	—
	Greensboro	ECHL	27	1308	12	10	‡0	96	...	4.40	†9	567	8	1	21	0	*2.22
90-91	Kansas City	IHL	†56	2990	16	31	‡4	*224	0	4.49	1	1	0	0	0	0	0.00
91-92	Kansas City	IHL	43	2603	26	14	‡3	140	1	3.23	1	1	0	0	0	0	0.00
	San Jose	NHL	3	178	0	3	0	13	0	4.38	—	—	—	—	—	—	—
92-93	Kansas City	IHL	61	*3642	*34	19	‡0	*195	2	3.21	12	*733	6	*5	†34	*1	2.78
	San Jose	NHL	1	60	0	1	0	5	0	5.00	—	—	—	—	—	—	—
93-94	Kansas City	IHL	60	*3564	32	19	‡9	202	0	3.40	—	—	—	—	—	—	—
	NHL totals		4	238	0	4	0	18	0	4.54							

F

FLATLEY, PATRICK

RW, ISLANDERS

PERSONAL: Born October 3, 1963, in Toronto. . . . 6-2/200. . . . Shoots right. . . . Full name: Patrick William Flatley.
HIGH SCHOOL: Henry Carr (Rexdale, Ont.).
COLLEGE: Wisconsin.

TRANSACTIONS/CAREER NOTES: Selected by New York Islanders as underage junior in first round (first Islanders pick, 21st overall) of NHL entry draft (June 9, 1982). . . . Broke bone in left hand (April 1985). . . . Strained left knee ligaments (February 4, 1987). . . . Separated right shoulder (November 1987). . . . Injured right knee (January 1988). . . . Underwent reconstructive knee surgery (February 1988). . . . Injured right knee (December 1988). . . . Suffered sore right ankle (February 1989). . . . Re-injured right knee (March 1989). . . . Bruised right ankle (October 1989). . . . Pulled groin muscle (February 13, 1990). . . . Re-injured groin (March 2, 1990); missed six games. . . . Sprained right knee (October 13, 1990). . . . Bruised left knee (November 30, 1990). . . . Fractured finger on left hand (February 16, 1991). . . . Fractured right thumb (December 19, 1991); missed 42 games. . . . Broke ribs (January 5, 1993); missed four games. . . . Broke jaw (October 22, 1993); missed eight games. . . . Suffered sore foot (January 8, 1994); missed one game. . . . Pulled abdominal muscle (March 27, 1994); missed 10 games.
HONORS: Named to NCAA All-America West team (1982-83). . . . Named to NCAA All-Tournament team (1982-83). . . . Named to WCHA All-Star first team (1982-83).

			REGULAR SEASON					PLAYOFFS				
Season Team	League	Gms.	G	A	Pts.	PIM	Gms.	G	A	Pts.	PIM
80-81—Henry Carr H.S.	MTHL	42	30	61	91	122	—	—	—	—	—
81-82—University of Wisconsin	WCHA	33	17	20	37	65	—	—	—	—	—
82-83—University of Wisconsin	WCHA	43	25	44	69	76	—	—	—	—	—
83-84—Canadian Olympic Team	Int'l	57	33	17	50	136	—	—	—	—	—
—New York Islanders	NHL	16	2	7	9	6	21	9	6	15	14
84-85—New York Islanders	NHL	78	20	31	51	106	4	1	0	1	6
85-86—New York Islanders	NHL	73	18	34	52	66	3	0	0	0	21
86-87—New York Islanders	NHL	63	16	35	51	81	11	3	2	5	6
87-88—New York Islanders	NHL	40	9	15	24	28	—	—	—	—	—
88-89—New York Islanders	NHL	41	10	15	25	31	—	—	—	—	—
—Springfield	AHL	2	1	1	2	2	—	—	—	—	—
89-90—New York Islanders	NHL	62	17	32	49	101	5	3	0	3	2
90-91—New York Islanders	NHL	56	20	25	45	74	—	—	—	—	—
91-92—New York Islanders	NHL	38	8	28	36	31	—	—	—	—	—
92-93—New York Islanders	NHL	80	13	47	60	63	15	2	7	9	12
93-94—New York Islanders	NHL	64	12	30	42	40	—	—	—	—	—
NHL totals		611	145	299	444	627	59	18	15	33	61

FLEMING, GERRY

D, CANADIENS

PERSONAL: Born October 16, 1967, in Montreal. . . . 6-5/240. . . . Shoots left.
COLLEGE: Prince Edward Island.
TRANSACTIONS/CAREER NOTES: Signed as free agent by Montreal Canadiens (February 17, 1992).

			REGULAR SEASON					PLAYOFFS				
Season Team	League	Gms.	G	A	Pts.	PIM	Gms.	G	A	Pts.	PIM
89-90—Fredericton	AHL	24	12	18	30	83	—	3	6	9	—
90-91—Prince Edward Island U.	AUAA				Statistics unavailable.						
91-92—Charlottetown	Sr.				Statistics unavailable.						
—Fredericton	AHL	37	4	6	10	133	1	0	0	0	7
92-93—Fredericton	AHL	64	9	17	26	262	5	1	2	3	14
93-94—Fredericton	AHL	46	6	16	22	188	—	—	—	—	—
—Montreal	NHL	5	0	0	0	25	—	—	—	—	—
NHL totals		5	0	0	0	25					

FLEURY, THEO

C/RW, FLAMES

PERSONAL: Born June 29, 1968, in Oxbow, Sask. . . . 5-6/160. . . . Shoots right. . . . Name pronounced FLUH-ree.
TRANSACTIONS/CAREER NOTES: Selected by Calgary Flames in eighth round (ninth Flames pick, 166th overall) of NHL entry draft (June 13, 1987).
HONORS: Named to WHL (East) All-Star first team (1986-87). . . . Shared Bob Clarke Trophy with Joe Sakic (1987-88). . . . Named to WHL All-Star second team (1987-88). . . . Shared Alka-Seltzer Plus Award with Marty McSorley (1990-91). . . . Played in NHL All-Star Game (1991 and 1992).
RECORDS: Holds NHL single-game record for highest plus-minus rating—9 (February 10, 1993).
MISCELLANEOUS: Member of Stanley Cup championship team (1989).

			REGULAR SEASON					PLAYOFFS				
Season Team	League	Gms.	G	A	Pts.	PIM	Gms.	G	A	Pts.	PIM
84-85—Moose Jaw	WHL	71	29	46	75	82	—	—	—	—	—
85-86—Moose Jaw	WHL	72	43	65	108	124	—	—	—	—	—
86-87—Moose Jaw	WHL	66	61	68	129	110	9	7	9	16	34
87-88—Moose Jaw	WHL	65	68	92	†160	235	—	—	—	—	—
—Salt Lake City	IHL	2	3	4	7	7	8	11	5	16	16
88-89—Salt Lake City	IHL	40	37	37	74	81	—	—	—	—	—
—Calgary	NHL	36	14	20	34	46	22	5	6	11	24
89-90—Calgary	NHL	80	31	35	66	157	6	2	3	5	10
90-91—Calgary	NHL	79	51	53	104	136	7	2	5	7	14
91-92—Calgary	NHL	80	33	40	73	133	—	—	—	—	—
92-93—Calgary	NHL	83	34	66	100	88	6	5	7	12	27
93-94—Calgary	NHL	83	40	45	85	186	7	6	4	10	5
NHL totals		441	203	259	462	746	48	20	25	45	80

FLINTON, ERIC
LW, SENATORS

PERSONAL: Born February 2, 1972, in Will Lake, B.C. . . . . 6-2/200. . . . Shoots left.
COLLEGE: New Hampshire.
TRANSACTIONS/CAREER NOTES: Selected by Ottawa Senators in NHL supplemental draft (June 25, 1993).

			REGULAR SEASON					PLAYOFFS				
Season Team	League	Gms.	G	A	Pts.	PIM	Gms.	G	A	Pts.	PIM
92-93—Univ. of New Hampshire ...	Hockey East	37	18	18	36	14	—	—	—	—	—
93-94—Univ. of New Hampshire ...	Hockey East	40	16	25	41	36	—	—	—	—	—

FOGARTY, BRYAN
D, CANADIENS

PERSONAL: Born June 11, 1969, in Montreal. . . . 6-2/206. . . . Shoots left.
TRANSACTIONS/CAREER NOTES: Selected by Quebec Nordiques as underage junior in first round (first Nordiques pick, ninth overall) of NHL entry draft (June 13, 1987). . . . Traded by Kingston Raiders to Niagara Falls Thunder for D Garth Joy, LW Jason Simon, Kevin Lune and fourth-round pick in 1989 draft (August 1988). . . . Underwent appendectomy (September 1989). . . . Underwent substance-abuse treatment (February 1991); missed one month. . . . Left Nordiques to report to halfway house (March 28, 1991). . . . Suffered from the flu (November 30, 1991); missed five games. . . . Traded by Nordiques to Pittsburgh Penguins for rights to RW Scott Young (March 10, 1992). . . . Suspended by Penguins for leaving Cleveland Lumberjacks without approval (January 22, 1993). . . . Reinstated by Penguins (March 16, 1993). . . . Suffered from amygdalitis, throat condition, (April 6, 1993); missed four games. . . . Signed as free agent by Tampa Bay Lightning (September 1, 1993). . . . Traded by Las Vegas Thunder to Kansas City Blades for future considerations (February 12, 1994). . . . Signed as free agent by Montreal Canadiens (February 26, 1994).
HONORS: Named to OHL All-Star first team (1986-87 and 1988-89). . . . Won Can.HL Player of the Year Award (1988-89). . . . Won Can.HL Defenseman of the Year Award (1988-89). . . . Won Can.HL Plus/Minus Award (1988-89). . . . Won Red Tilson Trophy (1988-89). . . . Won Eddie Powers Memorial Trophy (1988-89). . . . Won Max Kaminsky Trophy (1988-89).

			REGULAR SEASON					PLAYOFFS				
Season Team	League	Gms.	G	A	Pts.	PIM	Gms.	G	A	Pts.	PIM
84-85—Aurora	OHA	66	18	39	57	180	—	—	—	—	—
85-86—Kingston	OHL	47	2	19	21	14	10	1	3	4	4
86-87—Kingston	OHL	56	20	50	70	46	12	2	3	5	5
87-88—Kingston	OHL	48	11	36	47	50	—	—	—	—	—
88-89—Niagara Falls	OHL	60	47	*108	*155	88	17	10	22	32	36
89-90—Quebec	NHL	45	4	10	14	31	—	—	—	—	—
—Halifax	AHL	22	5	14	19	6	6	4	2	6	0
90-91—Halifax	AHL	5	0	2	2	0	—	—	—	—	—
—Quebec	NHL	45	9	22	31	24	—	—	—	—	—
91-92—Quebec	NHL	20	3	12	15	16	—	—	—	—	—
—Halifax	AHL	2	0	0	0	2	—	—	—	—	—
—New Haven	AHL	4	0	1	1	6	—	—	—	—	—
—Muskegon	IHL	8	2	4	6	30	—	—	—	—	—
92-93—Pittsburgh	NHL	12	0	4	4	4	—	—	—	—	—
—Cleveland	IHL	15	2	5	7	8	3	0	1	1	17
93-94—Atlanta	IHL	8	1	5	6	4	—	—	—	—	—
—Las Vegas	IHL	33	3	16	19	38	—	—	—	—	—
—Kansas City	IHL	3	2	1	3	2	—	—	—	—	—
—Montreal	NHL	13	1	2	3	10	—	—	—	—	—
NHL totals		135	17	50	67	85					

FOLIGNO, MIKE
RW, PANTHERS

PERSONAL: Born January 29, 1959, in Sudbury, Ont. . . . 6-2/200. . . . Shoots right. . . . Full name: Mike Anthony Foligno. . . . Name pronounced foh-LEE-noh.
TRANSACTIONS/CAREER NOTES: Selected by Detroit Red Wings in first round (first Red Wings pick, third overall) of NHL entry draft (August 9, 1979). . . . Traded by Red Wings with C Dale McCourt, C Brent Peterson and future considerations to Buffalo Sabres for G Bob Sauve, D Jim Schoenfeld and LW/C Derek Smith (December 2, 1981). . . . Injured tailbone (October 31, 1982). . . . Injured shoulder (February 12, 1983). . . . Bruised kidney (December 7, 1986). . . . Suffered back spasms (February 1988). . . . Pulled rib cartilage (January 14, 1989). . . . Fractured left thumb (February 18, 1990). . . . Traded by Sabres with eighth-round pick in 1991 draft (C Thomas Kucharcik) to Toronto Maple Leafs for D Brian Curran and LW Lou Franceschetti (December 17, 1990). . . . Tore medial collateral ligament in the left knee (December 18, 1990); missed seven games. . . . Fractured tibia (December 21, 1991); missed remainder of season. . . . Traded by Maple Leafs to Florida Panthers for future considerations (November 5, 1993). . . . Suspended three games by NHL for headbutting (November 16, 1993). . . . Bruised hip (February 10, 1994); missed 12 games.
HONORS: Won Red Tilson Trophy (1978-79). . . . Won Eddie Powers Memorial Trophy (1978-79). . . . Won Jim Mahon Memorial Trophy (1978-79). . . . Named to OMJHL All-Star first team (1978-79).

			REGULAR SEASON					PLAYOFFS				
Season Team	League	Gms.	G	A	Pts.	PIM	Gms.	G	A	Pts.	PIM
75-76—Sudbury	OHA Mj. Jr. A	57	22	14	36	45	—	—	—	—	—
76-77—Sudbury	OMJHL	66	31	44	75	62	—	—	—	—	—
77-78—Sudbury	OMJHL	67	47	39	86	112	—	—	—	—	—
78-79—Sudbury	OMJHL	68	65	85	*150	98	10	5	5	10	14
79-80—Detroit	NHL	80	36	35	71	109	—	—	—	—	—
80-81—Detroit	NHL	80	28	35	63	210	—	—	—	—	—
81-82—Detroit	NHL	26	13	13	26	28	—	—	—	—	—
—Buffalo	NHL	56	20	31	51	149	4	2	0	2	9
82-83—Buffalo	NHL	66	22	25	47	135	10	2	3	5	39
83-84—Buffalo	NHL	70	32	31	63	151	3	2	1	3	19

— 425 —

Season Team	League	REGULAR SEASON Gms.	G	A	Pts.	PIM	PLAYOFFS Gms.	G	A	Pts.	PIM
84-85—Buffalo	NHL	77	27	29	56	154	5	1	3	4	12
85-86—Buffalo	NHL	79	41	39	80	168	—	—	—	—	—
86-87—Buffalo	NHL	75	30	29	59	176	—	—	—	—	—
87-88—Buffalo	NHL	74	29	28	57	220	6	3	2	5	31
88-89—Buffalo	NHL	75	27	22	49	156	5	3	1	4	21
89-90—Buffalo	NHL	61	15	25	40	99	6	0	1	1	12
90-91—Buffalo	NHL	31	4	5	9	42	—	—	—	—	—
—Toronto	NHL	37	8	7	15	65	—	—	—	—	—
91-92—Toronto	NHL	33	6	8	14	50	—	—	—	—	—
92-93—Toronto	NHL	55	13	5	18	84	18	2	6	8	42
93-94—Toronto	NHL	4	0	0	0	4	—	—	—	—	—
—Florida	NHL	39	4	5	9	49	—	—	—	—	—
NHL totals		1018	355	372	727	2049	57	15	17	32	185

FOOTE, ADAM
D, NORDIQUES

PERSONAL: Born July 10, 1971, in Toronto.... 6-1/202.... Shoots right.... Full name: Adam David Vernon Foote.

TRANSACTIONS/CAREER NOTES: Selected by Quebec Nordiques in second round (second Nordiques pick, 22nd overall) of NHL entry draft (June 17, 1989).... Fractured right thumb (February 1992); missed remainder of season.... Injured knee (October 21, 1992); missed one game.... Suffered from the flu (January 28, 1993); missed two games.... Injured groin (January 18, 1994); missed eight games.... Suffered herniated disc (February 11, 1994); underwent surgery and missed remainder of season.

HONORS: Named to OHL All-Star first team (1990-91).

Season Team	League	REGULAR SEASON Gms.	G	A	Pts.	PIM	PLAYOFFS Gms.	G	A	Pts.	PIM
88-89—Sault Ste. Marie	OHL	66	7	32	39	120	—	—	—	—	—
89-90—Sault Ste. Marie	OHL	61	12	43	55	199	—	—	—	—	—
90-91—Sault Ste. Marie	OHL	59	18	51	69	93	14	5	12	17	28
91-92—Quebec	NHL	46	2	5	7	44	—	—	—	—	—
—Halifax	AHL	6	0	1	1	2	—	—	—	—	—
92-93—Quebec	NHL	81	4	12	16	168	6	0	1	1	2
93-94—Quebec	NHL	45	2	6	8	67	—	—	—	—	—
NHL totals		172	8	23	31	279	6	0	1	1	2

FORSBERG, PETER
C, NORDIQUES

PERSONAL: Born July 20, 1973, in Ornskoldsvik, Sweden.... 5-11/190.... Shoots left.

TRANSACTIONS/CAREER NOTES: Selected by Philadelphia Flyers in first round (first Flyers pick, sixth overall) of NHL entry draft (June 22, 1991).... Traded by Flyers with G Ron Hextall, C Mike Ricci, D Steve Duchesne, D Kerry Huffman, first-round pick in 1993 draft (G Jocelyn Thibault), cash and future considerations to Quebec Nordiques for C Eric Lindros (June 20, 1992); Flyers sent LW Chris Simon and first-round pick in 1994 draft (traded to Toronto Maple Leafs) to Nordiques to complete deal (July 21, 1992).

HONORS: Named to Swedish League All-Star team (1991-92).... Named Swedish League Player of the Year (1993-94).

MISCELLANEOUS: Member of gold-medal-winning Swedish Olympic team (1994).

Season Team	League	REGULAR SEASON Gms.	G	A	Pts.	PIM	PLAYOFFS Gms.	G	A	Pts.	PIM
89-90—MoDo	Sweden Jr.	30	15	12	27	42	—	—	—	—	—
90-91—MoDo	Sweden	23	7	10	17	22	—	—	—	—	—
91-92—MoDo	Sweden	39	9	19	28	78	—	—	—	—	—
92-93—MoDo	Sweden	39	23	24	47	92	3	4	1	5	0
93-94—MoDo	Sweden	39	18	26	44	82	11	9	7	16	14
—Swedish Olympic Team	Int'l	8	2	6	8	6	—	—	—	—	—

FORTIER, MARC
C, KINGS

PERSONAL: Born February 26, 1966, in Sherbrooke, Que.... 6-0/192.... Shoots right.... Name pronounced FOHRT-yay.

TRANSACTIONS/CAREER NOTES: Signed as free agent by Quebec Nordiques (February 3, 1987).... Injured groin (February 18, 1992).... Signed as free agent by Ottawa Senators (October 1, 1992).... Traded by Senators with RW Jim Thomson to Los Angeles Kings for RW Bob Kudelski and C Shawn McCosh (December 20, 1992).

HONORS: Won Jean Beliveau Trophy (1986-87).... Named to QMJHL All-Star first team (1986-87).

Season Team	League	REGULAR SEASON Gms.	G	A	Pts.	PIM	PLAYOFFS Gms.	G	A	Pts.	PIM
84-85—Chicoutimi	QMJHL	68	35	63	98	114	14	8	4	12	16
85-86—Chicoutimi	QMJHL	71	47	86	133	49	9	2	14	16	12
86-87—Chicoutimi	QMJHL	65	66	*135	*201	39	19	11	*40	*51	20
87-88—Quebec	NHL	27	4	10	14	12	—	—	—	—	—
—Fredericton	AHL	50	26	36	62	48	—	—	—	—	—
88-89—Quebec	NHL	57	20	19	39	45	—	—	—	—	—
—Halifax	AHL	16	11	11	22	14	—	—	—	—	—
89-90—Halifax	AHL	15	5	6	11	6	—	—	—	—	—
—Quebec	NHL	59	13	17	30	28	—	—	—	—	—
90-91—Halifax	AHL	58	24	32	56	85	—	—	—	—	—
—Quebec	NHL	14	0	4	4	6	—	—	—	—	—

Season	Team	League	REGULAR SEASON Gms.	G	A	Pts.	PIM	PLAYOFFS Gms.	G	A	Pts.	PIM
91-92	—Halifax	AHL	16	9	16	25	44	—	—	—	—	—
	—Quebec	NHL	39	5	9	14	33	—	—	—	—	—
92-93	—Ottawa	NHL	10	0	1	1	6	—	—	—	—	—
	—New Haven	AHL	16	9	15	24	42	—	—	—	—	—
	—Los Angeles	NHL	6	0	0	0	5	—	—	—	—	—
	—Phoenix	IHL	17	4	9	13	34	—	—	—	—	—
93-94	—Phoenix	IHL	81	39	61	100	96	—	—	—	—	—
NHL totals			212	42	60	102	135					

FOSTER, COREY
D, SENATORS

PERSONAL: Born October 27, 1969, in Ottawa. . . . 6-3/204. . . . Shoots left.
TRANSACTIONS/CAREER NOTES: Selected by New Jersey Devils in first round (first Devils pick, 12th overall) of NHL entry draft (June 11, 1988). . . . Traded by Devils to Edmonton Oilers for first-round pick (C Jason Miller) in 1989 draft (June 17, 1989). . . . Traded by Oilers with RW Dave Brown and rights to RW Jari Kurri to Philadelphia Flyers for RW Scott Mellanby, LW Craig Berube and C Craig Fisher (May 30, 1991). . . . Fractured collarbone during preseason (September 1991); missed 14 games. . . . Signed as free agent by Ottawa Senators (June 20, 1994).

Season	Team	League	REGULAR SEASON Gms.	G	A	Pts.	PIM	PLAYOFFS Gms.	G	A	Pts.	PIM
86-87	—Peterborough	OHL	30	3	4	7	4	1	0	0	0	0
87-88	—Peterborough	OHL	66	13	31	44	58	11	5	9	14	13
88-89	—Peterborough	OHL	55	14	42	56	42	17	1	17	18	12
	—New Jersey	NHL	2	0	0	0	0	—	—	—	—	—
89-90	—Cape Breton	AHL	54	7	17	24	32	1	0	0	0	0
90-91	—Cape Breton	AHL	67	14	11	25	51	4	2	4	6	4
91-92	—Philadelphia	NHL	25	3	4	7	20	—	—	—	—	—
	—Hershey	AHL	19	5	9	14	26	6	1	1	2	5
92-93	—Hershey	AHL	80	9	25	34	102	—	—	—	—	—
93-94	—Hershey	AHL	66	21	37	58	96	—	—	—	—	—
NHL totals			27	3	4	7	20					

FOUNTAIN, MIKE
G, CANUCKS

PERSONAL: Born January 26, 1972, in Gravenhurst, Ont. . . . 6-1/176. . . . Catches left.
COLLEGE: Trent (Ont.).
TRANSACTIONS/CAREER NOTES: Selected by Vancouver Canucks in second round (third Canucks pick, 45th overall) of NHL entry draft (June 20, 1992).
HONORS: Named to Can.HL All-Star second team (1991-92). . . . Named to OHL All-Star first team (1991-92). . . . Named to AHL All-Star second team (1993-94).

Season	Team	League	REGULAR SEASON Gms.	Min.	W	L	T	GA	SO	Avg.	PLAYOFFS Gms.	Min.	W	L	GA	SO	Avg.
88-89	—Huntsville Jr. C.	OHA	22	1306	...	...	...	82	0	3.77	—	—	—	—	—	—	—
89-90	—Chatham Jr. B	OHA	21	1249	...	...	...	76	0	3.65	—	—	—	—	—	—	—
90-91	—Sault Ste. Marie	OHL	7	380	5	2	0	19	0	3.00	—	—	—	—	—	—	—
	—Oshawa	OHL	30	1483	17	5	1	84	0	3.40	8	292	1	4	26	0	5.34
91-92	—Oshawa	OHL	40	2260	18	13	6	149	1	3.96	7	428	3	4	26	0	3.64
92-93	—Canadien national team	Int'l	13	...	7	5	1	37	1	2.98	—	—	—	—	—	—	—
	—Hamilton	AHL	12	618	2	8	0	46	0	4.47	—	—	—	—	—	—	—
93-94	—Hamilton	AHL	*70	*4005	*34	28	6	241	*4	3.61	3	146	0	2	12	0	4.93

FRANCIS, RON
C, PENGUINS

PERSONAL: Born March 1, 1963, in Sault Ste. Marie, Ont. . . . 6-2/200. . . . Shoots left. . . . Cousin of Mike Liut, goaltender, St. Louis Blues, Hartford Whalers and Washington Capitals (1979-80 through 1991-92) and Cincinnati Stingers of WHA (1977-78 and 1978-79).
TRANSACTIONS/CAREER NOTES: Selected by Hartford Whalers as underage junior in first round (first Whalers pick, fourth overall) of NHL entry draft (June 10, 1981). . . . Injured eye (January 27, 1982); missed three weeks. . . . Strained ligaments in right knee (November 30, 1983). . . . Broke left ankle (January 18, 1986); missed 27 games. . . . Broke left index finger (January 28, 1989); missed 11 games. . . . Broke nose (November 24, 1990). . . . Traded by Whalers with D Ulf Samuelsson and D Grant Jennings to Pittsburgh Penguins for C John Cullen, D Zarley Zalapski and RW Jeff Parker (March 4, 1991).
HONORS: Played in NHL All-Star Game (1983, 1985 and 1990).
MISCELLANEOUS: Member of Stanley Cup championship teams (1991 and 1992).

Season	Team	League	REGULAR SEASON Gms.	G	A	Pts.	PIM	PLAYOFFS Gms.	G	A	Pts.	PIM
80-81	—Sault Ste. Marie	OMJHL	64	26	43	69	33	19	7	8	15	34
81-82	—Sault Ste. Marie	OHL	25	18	30	48	46	—	—	—	—	—
	—Hartford	NHL	59	25	43	68	51	—	—	—	—	—
82-83	—Hartford	NHL	79	31	59	90	60	—	—	—	—	—
83-84	—Hartford	NHL	72	23	60	83	45	—	—	—	—	—
84-85	—Hartford	NHL	80	24	57	81	66	—	—	—	—	—
85-86	—Hartford	NHL	53	24	53	77	24	10	1	2	3	4
86-87	—Hartford	NHL	75	30	63	93	45	6	2	2	4	6
87-88	—Hartford	NHL	80	25	50	75	89	6	2	5	7	2
88-89	—Hartford	NHL	69	29	48	77	36	4	0	2	2	0
89-90	—Hartford	NHL	80	32	69	101	73	7	3	3	6	8

F

FRASER, IAIN
C, NORDIQUES

Season	Team	League	REGULAR SEASON					PLAYOFFS				
		Gms.	G	A	Pts.	PIM	Gms.	G	A	Pts.	PIM
90-91—Hartford	NHL	67	21	55	76	51	—	—	—	—	—
—Pittsburgh	NHL	14	2	9	11	21	24	7	10	17	24
91-92—Pittsburgh	NHL	70	21	33	54	30	21	8	*19	27	6
92-93—Pittsburgh	NHL	84	24	76	100	68	12	6	11	17	19
93-94—Pittsburgh	NHL	82	27	66	93	62	6	0	2	2	6
NHL totals		964	338	741	1079	721	96	29	56	85	75

PERSONAL: Born August 10, 1969, in Scarborough, Ont. . . . 5-10/175. . . . Shoots left. **TRANSACTIONS/CAREER NOTES:** Selected by New York Islanders in 12th round (14th Islanders pick, 233rd overall) of NHL entry draft (June 17, 1989). . . . Signed as free agent by Quebec Nordiques (August 3, 1993). . . . Suffered mouth injury (October 15, 1993); missed one game. . . . Suffered from the flu (November 22, 1993); missed one game. . . . Bruised left foot (December 28, 1993); missed three games. . . . Bruised right knee (January 26, 1994); missed one game. . . . Injured back (February 21, 1994); missed six games. **HONORS:** Won Leo LaLonde Memorial Trophy (1989-90). . . . Won Stafford Smythe Memorial Trophy (1989-90). . . . Named to Memorial Cup All-Star team (1989-90). . . . Named to AHL All-Star second team (1992-93).

Season	Team	League	REGULAR SEASON					PLAYOFFS				
			Gms.	G	A	Pts.	PIM	Gms.	G	A	Pts.	PIM
86-87—Oshawa Jr. B	OHA	31	18	22	40	119	—	—	—	—	—
87-88—Oshawa	OHL	16	4	4	8	22	6	2	3	5	2
88-89—Oshawa	OHL	62	33	57	90	87	6	2	8	10	12
89-90—Oshawa	OHL	56	40	65	105	75	17	10	*22	32	8
90-91—Richmond	ECHL	3	1	1	2	0	—	—	—	—	—
—Capital District	AHL	32	5	13	18	16	—	—	—	—	—
91-92—Capital District	AHL	45	9	11	20	24	—	—	—	—	—
92-93—Capital District	AHL	74	41	69	110	16	4	0	1	1	0
—New York Islanders	NHL	7	2	2	4	2	—	—	—	—	—
93-94—Quebec	NHL	60	17	20	37	23	—	—	—	—	—
—Canadian national team	Int'l	4	0	1	1	4	—	—	—	—	—
NHL totals		67	19	22	41	25					

FREER, MARK
C, FLAMES

PERSONAL: Born July 14, 1968, in Peterborough, Ont. . . . 5-10/180. . . . Shoots left. . . . Name pronounced FREER. **HIGH SCHOOL:** Crestwood (Peterborough, Ont.). **TRANSACTIONS/CAREER NOTES:** Signed as free agent by Philadelphia Flyers (September 1986). . . . Selected by Ottawa Senators in NHL expansion draft (June 18, 1992). . . . Suffered charley horse (October 24, 1992); missed 14 games. . . . Signed as free agent by Calgary Flames (August 10, 1993).

Season	Team	League	REGULAR SEASON					PLAYOFFS				
			Gms.	G	A	Pts.	PIM	Gms.	G	A	Pts.	PIM
85-86—Peterborough	OHL	65	16	28	44	24	14	3	4	7	13
86-87—Peterborough	OHL	65	39	43	82	44	12	2	6	8	5
—Philadelphia	NHL	1	0	1	1	0	—	—	—	—	—
87-88—Philadelphia	NHL	1	0	0	0	0	—	—	—	—	—
—Peterborough	OHL	63	38	71	109	63	12	5	12	17	4
88-89—Philadelphia	NHL	5	0	1	1	0	—	—	—	—	—
—Hershey	AHL	75	30	49	79	77	12	4	6	10	2
89-90—Hershey	AHL	65	28	36	64	31	—	—	—	—	—
90-91—Hershey	AHL	77	18	44	62	45	7	1	3	4	17
91-92—Hershey	AHL	31	13	11	24	38	6	0	3	3	2
—Philadelphia	NHL	50	6	7	13	18	—	—	—	—	—
92-93—Ottawa	NHL	63	10	14	24	39	—	—	—	—	—
93-94—Saint John	AHL	77	33	53	86	45	7	2	4	6	16
—Calgary	NHL	2	0	0	0	4	—	—	—	—	—
NHL totals		122	16	23	39	61					

FRIESEN, JEFF
LW, SHARKS

PERSONAL: Born August 5, 1976, in Meadow Lake, Sask. . . . 6-0/183. . . . Shoots left. **HIGH SCHOOL:** Robert Usher (Regina, Sask.). **TRANSACTIONS/CAREER NOTES:** Selected by San Jose Sharks in first round (first Sharks pick, 11th overall) of NHL entry draft (June 28, 1994). **HONORS:** Won Can.HL Rookie of the Year (1992-93). . . . Won Jim Piggott Memorial Trophy (1992-92).

Season	Team	League	REGULAR SEASON					PLAYOFFS				
			Gms.	G	A	Pts.	PIM	Gms.	G	A	Pts.	PIM
91-92—Regina	WHL	4	3	1	4	2	—	—	—	—	—
92-93—Regina	WHL	70	45	38	83	23	13	7	10	17	8
93-94—Regina	WHL	66	51	67	118	48	4	3	2	5	2

FRYLEN, EDVIN
D, BLUES

PERSONAL: Born December 23, 1975, in Jarfalla, Sweden. . . . 6-0/211. . . . Shoots left. **TRANSACTIONS/CAREER NOTES:** Selected by St. Louis Blues in fifth round (third Blues pick, 120th overall) of NHL entry draft (June 29, 1994).

Season	Team	League	REGULAR SEASON					PLAYOFFS				
			Gms.	G	A	Pts.	PIM	Gms.	G	A	Pts.	PIM
91-92—Vasteras	Sweden	2	0	0	0	0	—	—	—	—	—
92-93—Vasteras	Sweden	29	0	2	2	14	3	0	0	0	0
93-94—Vasteras	Sweden	32	1	0	1	26	—	—	—	—	—

FUHR, GRANT
G, SABRES

PERSONAL: Born September 28, 1962, in Spruce Grove, Alta. . . . 5-9/190. . . . Catches right. . . . Name pronounced FYOOR.

TRANSACTIONS/CAREER NOTES: Selected by Edmonton Oilers in first round (first Oilers pick, eighth overall) of NHL entry draft (June 10, 1981). . . . Suffered partial separation of right shoulder (December 1981). . . . Strained left knee ligaments and underwent surgery (December 13, 1983). . . . Separated shoulder (February 1985). . . . Bruised left shoulder (November 3, 1985); missed 10 games. . . . Bruised left shoulder (November 1987). . . . Injured right knee (November 1987). . . . Suffered cervical neck strain (January 18, 1989). . . . Underwent appendectomy (September 14, 1989); missed first six games of season. . . . Underwent reconstructive surgery to left shoulder (December 27, 1989). . . . Tore adhesions in left shoulder (March 13, 1990). . . . Suspended six months by NHL for admitting to using drugs earlier in career (September 27, 1990). . . . Traded by Oilers with RW/LW Glenn Anderson and LW Craig Berube to Toronto Maple Leafs for LW Vincent Damphousse, D Luke Richardson, G Peter Ing, C Scott Thornton and future considerations (September 19, 1991). . . . Sprained thumb (October 17, 1991); missed two games. . . . Pulled groin (November 12, 1991); missed three games. . . . Sprained knee (February 11, 1992); missed four games. . . . Sprained knee (October 20, 1992); missed 10 games. . . . Strained shoulder (December 5, 1992); missed three games. . . . Bruised shoulder muscle (January 17, 1993); missed four games. . . . Traded by Maple Leafs with conditional pick in 1995 draft to Buffalo Sabres for LW Dave Andreychuk, G Daren Puppa and first-round pick (D Kenny Jonsson) in 1993 draft (February 2, 1993). . . . Injured knee (November 24, 1993); missed 24 games.

HONORS: Won Stewart (Butch) Paul Memorial Trophy (1979-80). . . . Named to WHL All-Star first team (1979-80 and 1980-81). . . . Won Top Goaltender Trophy (1980-81). . . . Named to THE SPORTING NEWS All-Star second team (1981-82 and 1985-86). . . . Named to NHL All-Star second team (1981-82). . . . Played in NHL All-Star Game (1982, 1984-1986, 1988 and 1989). . . . Named NHL All-Star Game Most Valuable Player (1986). . . . Named to THE SPORTING NEWS All-Star first team (1987-88). . . . Won Venzina Trophy (1987-88). . . . Named to NHL All-Star first team (1987-88). . . . Shared William M. Jennings Trophy with Dominik Hasek (1993-94).

RECORDS: Holds NHL single-season record for most points by a goaltender—14 (1983-84); and most games by a goaltender—75 (1987-88). . . . Shares NHL single-season playoff record for most wins by a goaltender—16 (1987-88).

MISCELLANEOUS: Member of Stanley Cup championship teams (1984, 1985, 1987, 1988 and 1990).

						REGULAR SEASON							PLAYOFFS					
Season Team	League	Gms.	Min.	W	L	T	GA	SO	Avg.	Gms.	Min.	W	L	GA	SO	Avg.
79-80—Victoria	WHL	43	2488	30	12	0	130	2	3.14	8	465	5	3	22	0	2.84
80-81—Victoria	WHL	59	*3448	48	9	1	160	†4	*2.78	15	899	12	3	45	1	3.00
81-82—Edmonton	NHL	48	2847	28	5	14	157	0	3.31	5	309	2	3	26	0	5.05
82-83—Moncton	AHL	10	604	4	5	1	40	0	3.97	—	—	—	—	—	—	—
—Edmonton	NHL	32	1803	13	12	5	129	0	4.29	1	11	0	0	0	0	0.00
83-84—Edmonton	NHL	45	2625	30	10	4	171	1	3.91	16	883	11	4	44	1	2.99
84-85—Edmonton	NHL	46	2559	26	8	7	165	1	3.87	†18	*1064	*15	3	55	0	3.10
85-86—Edmonton	NHL	40	2184	29	8	0	143	0	3.93	9	541	5	4	28	0	3.11
86-87—Edmonton	NHL	44	2388	22	13	3	137	0	3.44	19	1148	14	5	47	0	2.46
87-88—Edmonton	NHL	*75	*4304	40	24	9	*246	†4	3.43	*19	*1136	*16	2	55	0	2.90
88-89—Edmonton	NHL	59	3341	23	26	6	213	1	3.83	7	417	3	4	24	1	3.45
89-90—Cape Breton	AHL	2	120	2	0	0	6	0	3.00	—	—	—	—	—	—	—
—Edmonton	NHL	21	1081	9	7	3	70	1	3.89	—	—	—	—	—	—	—
90-91—Cape Breton	AHL	4	240	2	2	0	17	0	4.25	—	—	—	—	—	—	—
—Edmonton	NHL	13	778	6	4	3	39	1	3.01	17	1019	8	7	51	0	3.00
91-92—Toronto	NHL	65	3774	25	*33	5	*230	2	3.66	—	—	—	—	—	—	—
92-93—Toronto	NHL	29	1665	13	9	4	87	1	3.14	—	—	—	—	—	—	—
—Buffalo	NHL	29	1694	11	15	2	98	0	3.47	8	474	3	4	27	1	3.42
93-94—Buffalo	NHL	32	1726	13	12	3	106	2	3.68	—	—	—	—	—	—	—
—Rochester	AHL	5	310	3	0	2	10	0	1.94	—	—	—	—	—	—	—
NHL totals		578	32769	288	186	68	1991	14	3.65	119	7002	77	36	357	3	3.06

GAETZ, LINK
LW, OILERS

PERSONAL: Born October 2, 1968, in Vancouver. . . . 6-2/223. . . . Shoots left. . . . Name pronounced GAYTZ.

TRANSACTIONS/CAREER NOTES: Suspended indefinitely by Spokane Chiefs (April 12, 1988). . . . Selected by Minnesota North Stars in second round (second North Stars pick, 40th overall) of NHL entry draft (June 11, 1988). . . . Suspended four games by IHL for high-sticking (January 23, 1989). . . . Suspended by North Stars for not reporting to Kansas City Blades (November 9, 1990). . . . Suspended by Blades for off-ice incident (February 5, 1991). . . . Entered in-patient alcohol abuse program (February 19, 1991). . . . Selected by San Jose Sharks in NHL dispersal draft (May 30, 1991). . . . Injured hand (October 5, 1991); missed four games. . . . Sprained knee (November 2, 1991); missed four games. . . . Suffered injuries from auto accident (April 2, 1992); missed first 62 games of 1992-93 season. . . . Traded by Sharks to Edmonton Oilers for conditional 10th-round pick in 1994 draft (September 10, 1993).

FG

			REGULAR SEASON					PLAYOFFS			
Season Team	League	Gms.	G	A	Pts.	PIM	Gms.	G	A	Pts.	PIM
85-86—Quesnel	PCJHL	15	0	7	7	4	—	—	—	—	—
86-87—New Westminster	WHL	44	2	7	9	52	—	—	—	—	—
—Merritt	BCJHL	7	4	2	6	27	—	—	—	—	—
—Delta	BCJHL	23	9	12	21	53	—	—	—	—	—
87-88—Spokane	WHL	59	9	20	29	313	10	2	2	4	70
88-89—Minnesota	NHL	12	0	2	2	53	—	—	—	—	—
—Kalamazoo	IHL	37	3	4	7	192	5	0	0	0	56
89-90—Kalamazoo	IHL	61	5	16	21	318	9	2	2	4	59
—Minnesota	NHL	5	0	0	0	33	—	—	—	—	—
90-91—Kalamazoo	IHL	9	0	1	1	44	—	—	—	—	—
—Kansas City	IHL	18	1	10	11	178	—	—	—	—	—
91-92—San Jose	NHL	48	6	6	12	326	—	—	—	—	—

Season	Team	League	REGULAR SEASON Gms.	G	A	Pts.	PIM	PLAYOFFS Gms.	G	A	Pts.	PIM
92-93—Nashville	ECHL	3	1	0	1	10	—	—	—	—	—	
—Kansas City	IHL	2	0	0	0	14	—	—	—	—	—	
93-94—Nashville	ECHL	24	1	1	2	261	—	—	—	—	—	
—Cape Breton	AHL	21	0	1	1	140	—	—	—	—	—	
NHL totals			65	6	8	14	412	—	—	—	—	—

GAFFNEY, MIKE
D. SENATORS

PERSONAL: Born June 19, 1976, in Worcester, Mass. . . . 6-1/195. . . . Shoots right.
HIGH SCHOOL: St. John's Prep (Danvers, Mass.).
TRANSACTIONS/CAREER NOTES: Selected by Ottawa Senators in sixth round (fourth Senators pick, 131st overall) of NHL entry draft (June 29, 1994).

Season	Team	League	REGULAR SEASON Gms.	G	A	Pts.	PIM	PLAYOFFS Gms.	G	A	Pts.	PIM
91-92—St. John's Prep	Mass. H.S.	24	4	13	17	14	—	—	—	—	—	
92-93—St. John's Prep	Mass. H.S.	24	6	19	25	10	—	—	—	—	—	
93-94—St. John's Prep	Mass. H.S.	20	6	16	22	...	—	—	—	—	—	

GAGE, JOAQUIN
G, OILERS

PERSONAL: Born October 19, 1973, in Vancouver. . . . 6-0/200. . . . Catches left. . . . Name pronounced wah-KEEN GAYJ.
COLLEGE: Portland (Ore.) Community College.
TRANSACTIONS/CAREER NOTES: Selected by Edmonton Oilers in fifth round (sixth Oilers pick, 109th overall) of NHL entry draft (June 20, 1992).

Season	Team	League	REGULAR SEASON Gms.	Min.	W	L	T	GA	SO	Avg.	PLAYOFFS Gms.	Min.	W	L	GA	SO	Avg.
90-91—Bellingham Jr. A	BCJHL	16	751	...	...	...	64	0	5.11	—	—	—	—	—	—	—
—Portland	WHL	3	180	0	3	0	17	0	5.67	—	—	—	—	—	—	—
91-92—Portland	WHL	63	3635	27	30	4	269	2	4.44	6	366	2	4	28	0	4.59
92-93—Portland	WHL	38	2302	21	16	1	153	2	3.99	8	427	5	2	30	0	4.22
93-94—Prince Albert	WHL	53	3041	24	25	3	212	1	4.18	—	—	—	—	—	—	—

GAGNER, DAVE
C, STARS

PERSONAL: Born December 11, 1964, in Chatham, Ont. . . . 5-10/180. . . . Shoots left. . . . Name pronounced GAN-yay.
TRANSACTIONS/CAREER NOTES: Selected by New York Rangers as underage junior in first round (first Rangers pick, 12th overall) of NHL entry draft (June 8, 1983). . . . Fractured ankle (February 5, 1986). . . . Underwent emergency appendectomy (December 1986). . . . Traded by Rangers with RW Jay Caufield to Minnesota North Stars for D Jari Gronstrand and D Paul Boutilier (October 8, 1987). . . . Broke kneecap (March 31, 1989). . . . Underwent surgery to left knee cartilage (November 11, 1990). . . . Underwent arthroscopic knee surgery (December 18, 1991); missed one game. . . . Hyperextended knee (March 17, 1992); missed one game. . . . North Stars franchise moved from Minnesota to Dallas and renamed Stars for 1993-94 season. . . . Separated shoulder (November 1, 1993); missed seven games.
HONORS: Won Bobby Smith Trophy (1982-83). . . . Named to OHL All-Star second team (1982-83). . . . Played in NHL All-Star Game (1991).
RECORDS: Shares NHL single-game playoff record for most points in one period—4 (April 8, 1991, first period.).

Season	Team	League	REGULAR SEASON Gms.	G	A	Pts.	PIM	PLAYOFFS Gms.	G	A	Pts.	PIM
81-82—Brantford	OHL	68	30	46	76	31	11	3	6	9	6
82-83—Brantford	OHL	70	55	66	121	57	8	5	5	10	4
83-84—Canadian Olympic Team	Int'l	50	19	18	37	26	—	—	—	—	—
—Brantford	OHL	12	7	13	20	4	6	0	4	4	6
84-85—New Haven	AHL	38	13	20	33	23	—	—	—	—	—
—New York Rangers	NHL	38	6	6	12	16	—	—	—	—	—
85-86—New York Rangers	NHL	32	4	6	10	19	—	—	—	—	—
—New Haven	AHL	16	10	11	21	11	4	1	2	3	2
86-87—New York Rangers	NHL	10	1	4	5	12	—	—	—	—	—
—New Haven	AHL	56	22	41	63	50	7	1	5	6	18
87-88—Kalamazoo	IHL	14	16	10	26	26	—	—	—	—	—
—Minnesota	NHL	51	8	11	19	55	—	—	—	—	—
88-89—Minnesota	NHL	75	35	43	78	104	—	—	—	—	—
—Kalamazoo	IHL	1	0	1	1	4	—	—	—	—	—
89-90—Minnesota	NHL	79	40	38	78	54	7	2	3	5	16
90-91—Minnesota	NHL	73	40	42	82	114	23	12	15	27	28
91-92—Minnesota	NHL	78	31	40	71	107	7	2	4	6	8
92-93—Minnesota	NHL	84	33	43	76	143	—	—	—	—	—
93-94—Dallas	NHL	76	32	29	61	83	9	5	1	6	2
NHL totals			596	230	262	492	707	46	21	23	44	54

GAGNON, DAVE
G, RED WINGS

PERSONAL: Born October 31, 1967, in Windsor, Ont. . . . 6-0/185. . . . Catches left. . . . Full name: David Anthony Gagnon. . . . Name pronounced GAN-yahn.
COLLEGE: Colgate.
TRANSACTIONS/CAREER NOTES: Signed as free agent by Detroit Red Wings (June 11, 1990).
. . . Injured hamstring (December 1, 1991).
HONORS: Named ECAC Player of the Year (1989-90). . . . Named to NCAA All-America East first team (1989-90). . . . Named to

ECAC All-Star first team (1989-90).... Named to ECAC All-Tournament team (1989-90).... Won ECHL Playoff Most Valuable Player Award (1990-91).

			REGULAR SEASON								PLAYOFFS						
Season	Team	League	Gms.	Min.	W	L	T	GA	SO	Avg.	Gms.	Min.	W	L	GA	SO	Avg.
87-88—Colgate University	ECAC	13	743	6	4	2	43	1	3.47	—	—	—	—	—	—	—	
88-89—Colgate University	ECAC	28	1622	17	9	2	102	0	3.77	—	—	—	—	—	—	—	
89-90—Colgate University	ECAC	33	1986	28	3	1	93	0	2.81	—	—	—	—	—	—	—	
90-91—Detroit	NHL	2	35	0	1	0	6	0	10.29	—	—	—	—	—	—	—	
—Adirondack	AHL	24	1356	7	8	5	94	0	4.16	—	—	—	—	—	—	—	
—Hampton Roads	ECHL	10	606	7	1	‡2	26	2	2.57	11	696	*10	1	27	0	*2.33	
91-92—Toledo	ECHL	7	354	4	2	‡0	18	0	3.05	—	—	—	—	—	—	—	
—Fort Wayne	IHL	2	125	2	0	‡0	7	0	3.36	—	—	—	—	—	—	—	
92-93—Fort Wayne	IHL	31	1771	15	11	‡0	116	0	3.93	1	6	0	0	0	0	0.00	
—Adirondack	AHL	1	60	0	1	0	5	0	5.00	—	—	—	—	—	—	—	
93-94—Toledo	ECHL	20	1122	13	5	‡0	65	1	3.48	*14	*910	*12	2	41	0	*2.70	
—Fort Wayne	IHL	19	1026	7	6	‡3	58	0	3.39	—	—	—	—	—	—	—	
NHL totals		2	35	0	1	0	6	0	10.29								

GAGNON, JOEL
G, MIGHTY DUCKS

PERSONAL: Born March 14, 1975, in Hearst, Ont.... 6-0/194.... Catches left.... Name pronounced GAN-yahn.
TRANSACTIONS/CAREER NOTES: Selected by Mighty Ducks of Anaheim in fourth round (fourth Mighty Ducks pick, 82nd overall) of NHL entry draft (June 26, 1993).

			REGULAR SEASON								PLAYOFFS						
Season	Team	League	Gms.	Min.	W	L	T	GA	SO	Avg.	Gms.	Min.	W	L	GA	SO	Avg.
92-93—Oshawa	OHL	48	2248	19	19	1	159	0	4.24	7	285	3	0	21	0	4.42	
93-94—Oshawa	OHL	23	1089	4	11	3	100	0	5.51	—	—	—	—	—	—	—	

GALANOV, MAXIM
D, RANGERS

PERSONAL: Born March 13, 1974, in Krasnoyarsk, U.S.S.R.... 6-1/167.... Shoots left.
TRANSACTIONS/CAREER NOTES: Selected by New York Rangers in third round (third Rangers pick, 61st overall) of NHL entry draft (June 26, 1993).

			REGULAR SEASON				PLAYOFFS			
Season	Team	League	Gms.	G	A	Pts.	PIM	Gms.	G	A	Pts.	PIM
92-93—Lada Togliatti	CIS	41	4	2	6	12	10	1	1	2	12
93-94—Lada Togliatti	CIS	7	1	0	1	4	12	1	0	1	8

GALLANT, GERARD
LW, LIGHTNING

PERSONAL: Born September 2, 1963, in Summerside, P.E.I.... 5-10/190.... Shoots left.... Name pronounced guh-LAHNT.
TRANSACTIONS/CAREER NOTES: Selected by Detroit Red Wings in sixth round (fourth Red Wings pick, 107th overall) of NHL entry draft (June 10, 1981).... Broke jaw (December 11, 1985); missed 25 games.... Fined $500 by NHL for stick-swinging incident (April 8, 1989).... Suspended five games by NHL for slashing (October 7, 1989).... Suspended three games by NHL for hitting linesman (January 13, 1990).... Suffered sore back (November 1990); missed eight games.... Suffered back spasms (December 1990); missed 18 games.... Underwent surgery to remove bone spur in back (March 14, 1991); missed remainder of season.... Injured hand (February 1992); missed five games.... Strained back (March 20, 1992); missed five games.... Injured hip (December 15, 1992); missed three games.... Suffered from the flu (January 17, 1993); missed one game.... Signed as free agent by Tampa Bay Lightning (July 21, 1993).... Sprained back (November 17, 1993); missed four games.... Sprained back (April 1, 1994); missed six games.
HONORS: Named to NHL All-Star second team (1988-89).

			REGULAR SEASON				PLAYOFFS			
Season	Team	League	Gms.	G	A	Pts.	PIM	Gms.	G	A	Pts.	PIM
79-80—Summerside	PEIHA	45	60	55	115	90	—	—	—	—	—
80-81—Sherbrooke	QMJHL	68	41	60	101	220	14	6	13	19	46
81-82—Sherbrooke	QMJHL	58	34	58	92	260	22	14	24	38	84
82-83—St. Jean	QMJHL	33	28	25	53	139	—	—	—	—	—
—Verdun	QMJHL	29	26	49	75	105	15	†14	19	33	*84
83-84—Adirondack	AHL	77	31	33	64	195	7	1	3	4	34
84-85—Adirondack	AHL	46	18	29	47	131	—	—	—	—	—
—Detroit	NHL	32	6	12	18	66	3	0	0	0	11
85-86—Detroit	NHL	52	20	19	39	106	—	—	—	—	—
86-87—Detroit	NHL	80	38	34	72	216	16	8	6	14	43
87-88—Detroit	NHL	73	34	39	73	242	16	6	9	15	55
88-89—Detroit	NHL	76	39	54	93	230	6	1	2	3	40
89-90—Detroit	NHL	69	36	44	80	254	—	—	—	—	—
90-91—Detroit	NHL	45	10	16	26	111	—	—	—	—	—
91-92—Detroit	NHL	69	14	22	36	187	11	2	2	4	25
92-93—Detroit	NHL	67	10	20	30	188	6	1	2	3	4
93-94—Tampa Bay	NHL	51	4	9	13	74	—	—	—	—	—
NHL totals		614	211	269	480	1674	58	18	21	39	178

GALLEY, GARRY
D, FLYERS

PERSONAL: Born April 16, 1963, in Ottawa.... 6-0/204.... Shoots left.
COLLEGE: Bowling Green State.
TRANSACTIONS/CAREER NOTES: Selected by Los Angeles Kings in fifth round (fourth Kings pick, 100th overall) of NHL entry draft (June 8, 1983).... Injured knee (December 8,

G

1985).... Traded by Kings to Washington Capitals for G Al Jensen (February 14, 1987).... Signed as free agent by Boston Bruins; third-round pick in 1989 draft awarded to Capitals as compensation (July 8, 1988).... Sprained left shoulder (September 30, 1989); missed first nine games of season.... Suffered lacerations to cheek, both lips and part of neck (October 6, 1990).... Dislocated right shoulder (December 22, 1990).... Bruised left kneecap (March 23, 1991); missed two games. ... Pulled hamstring (April 17, 1991); missed three playoff games.... Traded by Bruins with C Wes Walz and future considerations to Philadelphia Flyers for D Gord Murphy, RW Brian Dobbin and third-round pick (LW Sergei Zholtok) in 1992 draft (January 2, 1992).... Bruised ribs (January 9, 1992); missed one game.... Fractured foot (March 3, 1992); missed two games.... Bruised jaw (February 24, 1993); missed one game.... Strained shoulder (March 6, 1994); missed three games.
HONORS: Named to CCHA All-Star first team (1982-83 and 1983-84).... Named to NCAA All-Tournament team (1983-84). ... Played in NHL All-Star Game (1991 and 1994).

Season Team	League	REGULAR SEASON					PLAYOFFS				
		Gms.	G	A	Pts.	PIM	Gms.	G	A	Pts.	PIM
81-82—Bowling Green State	CCHA	42	3	36	39	48	—	—	—	—	—
82-83—Bowling Green State	CCHA	40	17	29	46	40	—	—	—	—	—
83-84—Bowling Green State	CCHA	44	15	52	67	61	—	—	—	—	—
84-85—Los Angeles	NHL	78	8	30	38	82	3	1	0	1	2
85-86—Los Angeles	NHL	49	9	13	22	46	—	—	—	—	—
—New Haven	AHL	4	2	6	8	6	—	—	—	—	—
86-87—Los Angeles	NHL	30	5	11	16	57	—	—	—	—	—
—Washington	NHL	18	1	10	11	10	2	0	0	0	0
87-88—Washington	NHL	58	7	23	30	44	13	2	4	6	13
88-89—Boston	NHL	78	8	21	29	80	9	0	1	1	33
89-90—Boston	NHL	71	8	27	35	75	21	3	3	6	34
90-91—Boston	NHL	70	6	21	27	84	16	1	5	6	17
91-92—Boston	NHL	38	2	12	14	83	—	—	—	—	—
—Philadelphia	NHL	39	3	15	18	34	—	—	—	—	—
92-93—Philadelphia	NHL	83	13	49	62	115	—	—	—	—	—
93-94—Philadelphia	NHL	81	10	60	70	91	—	—	—	—	—
NHL totals		693	80	292	372	801	64	7	13	20	99

GAMBLE, TROY
G, STARS

PERSONAL: Born April 7, 1967, in New Glasgow, N.S.... 5-11/195.... Catches left.
TRANSACTIONS/CAREER NOTES: Selected by Vancouver Canucks as underage junior in second round (second Canucks pick, 25th overall) of NHL entry draft (June 15, 1985).... Traded by Medicine Hat Tigers with D Kevin Ekdahl to Spokane Chiefs for D Keith Van Rooyen, RW Kirby Lindal and RW Rocky Dundas (December 1986).... Signed as free agent by Dallas Stars (August 27, 1993).
HONORS: Won Top Goaltender Trophy (1984-85).... Named to WHL All-Star first team (1984-85 and 1987-88).... Won Del Wilson Trophy (1987-88).

Season Team	League	REGULAR SEASON							PLAYOFFS						
		Gms.	Min.	W	L	T	GA	SO	Avg.	Gms.	Min.	W	L	GA SO	Avg.
83-84—Hobbema	AJHL	22	1102	...	...	...	90	0	4.90	—					
84-85—Medicine Hat	WHL	37	2095	27	6	2	100	*3	*2.86	2	120	1	1	9 0	4.50
85-86—Medicine Hat	WHL	45	2264	28	11	0	142	0	3.76	11	530	5	4	31 0	3.51
86-87—Medicine Hat	WHL	11	646	7	3	0	46	0	4.27	—					
—Spokane	WHL	38	2157	17	17	1	163	0	4.53	5	298	0	5	35 0	7.05
—Vancouver	NHL	1	60	0	1	0	4	0	4.00	—					
87-88—Spokane	WHL	*67	*3824	35	26	1	235	0	3.69	15	875	7	8	56 †1	3.84
88-89—Vancouver	NHL	5	302	2	3	0	12	0	2.38	—					
—Milwaukee	IHL	42	2198	23	9	‡0	138	0	3.77	11	640	5	5	35 0	3.28
89-90—Milwaukee	IHL	*56	3033	22	21	‡4	*213	2	4.21	—					
90-91—Vancouver	NHL	47	2433	16	16	6	140	1	3.45	4	249	1	3	16 0	3.86
91-92—Vancouver	NHL	19	1009	4	9	3	73	0	4.34	—					
—Milwaukee	IHL	9	521	2	4	‡2	31	0	3.57	—					
92-93—Hamilton	AHL	14	769	1	10	2	62	0	4.84	—					
—Cincinnati	IHL	33	1762	11	18	‡0	134	0	4.56	—					
93-94—Kalamazoo	IHL	48	2607	25	13	‡5	146	†2	3.36	2	80	0	1	7 0	5.25
NHL totals		72	3804	22	29	9	229	1	3.61	4	249	1	3	16 0	3.86

GARPENLOV, JOHAN
LW, SHARKS

PERSONAL: Born March 21, 1968, in Stockholm, Sweden.... 5-11/185.... Shoots left.... Name pronounced YOH-hahn GAHR-pehn-LAHV.
TRANSACTIONS/CAREER NOTES: Selected by Detroit Red Wings in fifth round (fifth Red Wings pick, 85th overall) of NHL entry draft (June 9, 1984).... Traded by Red Wings to San Jose Sharks for D Bob McGill and eighth-round pick (G C.J. Denomme) in 1992 draft (March 10, 1992).... Strained back (October 20, 1992); missed three games.... Suffered from the flu (March 25, 1993); missed one game.... Injured thigh (October 10, 1993); missed one game.

Season Team	League	REGULAR SEASON					PLAYOFFS				
		Gms.	G	A	Pts.	PIM	Gms.	G	A	Pts.	PIM
86-87—Djurgarden	Sweden	29	5	8	13	20	—	—	—	—	—
87-88—Djurgarden	Sweden	30	7	10	17	12	—	—	—	—	—
88-89—Djurgarden	Sweden	36	12	19	31	20	—	—	—	—	—
89-90—Djurgarden	Sweden	39	20	13	33	36	8	2	4	6	4
90-91—Detroit	NHL	71	18	22	40	18	6	0	1	1	4
91-92—Detroit	NHL	16	1	1	2	4	—	—	—	—	—
—Adirondack	AHL	9	3	3	6	6	—	—	—	—	—
—San Jose	NHL	12	5	6	11	4	—	—	—	—	—

Season	Team	League	REGULAR SEASON					PLAYOFFS				
			Gms.	G	A	Pts.	PIM	Gms.	G	A	Pts.	PIM
92-93—San Jose		NHL	79	22	44	66	56	—	—	—	—	—
93-94—San Jose		NHL	80	18	35	53	28	14	4	6	10	6
NHL totals			258	64	108	172	110	20	4	7	11	10

GARTNER, MIKE
RW, MAPLE LEAFS

PERSONAL: Born October 29, 1959, in Ottawa.... 6-0/187.... Shoots right.... Full name: Michael Alfred Gartner.

TRANSACTIONS/CAREER NOTES: Signed as underage junior by Cincinnati Stingers (August 1978).... Selected by Washington Capitals in first round (first Capitals pick, fourth overall) of NHL entry draft (August 9, 1979).... Injured eye (February 1983).... Underwent arthroscopic surgery to repair torn cartilage in left knee (March 1986).... Sprained right knee (November 1988).... Traded by Capitals with D Larry Murphy to Minnesota North Stars for RW Dino Ciccarelli and D Bob Rouse (March 7, 1989).... Underwent surgery to repair cartilage in left knee (April 14, 1989).... Traded by North Stars to New York Rangers for C Ulf Dahlen, fourth-round pick in 1990 draft (C Cal McGowan) and future considerations (March 6, 1990).... Underwent arthroscopic surgery to repair elbow (January 27, 1994); missed one game.... Traded by Rangers to Toronto Maple Leafs for RW Glenn Anderson, rights to D Scott Malone and fourth-round pick (D Alexander Korobolin) in 1994 draft (March 21, 1994).

HONORS: Won Emms Family Award (1976-77).... Named to OMJHL All-Star first team (1977-78).... Played in NHL All-Star Game (1980, 1985, 1986, 1988, 1990 and 1993).... Named All-Star Game Most Valuable Player (1993).

RECORDS: Holds NHL career record for most consecutive 30-goal seasons—15 (1979-80 through 1993-94).... Shares NHL career record for most 30-or-more goal seasons—15.... Holds NHL All-Star Game records for the fastest two goals from start of game—3:37 (1993); fastest two goals from the start of period—3:37 (1993).... Shares NHL All-Star Game record for most goals—4 (1991).

Season	Team	League	REGULAR SEASON					PLAYOFFS				
			Gms.	G	A	Pts.	PIM	Gms.	G	A	Pts.	PIM
75-76—St. Catharines		OHA Mj. Jr. A	3	1	3	4	0	—	—	—	—	—
76-77—Niagara Falls		OMJHL	62	33	42	75	125	—	—	—	—	—
77-78—Niagara Falls		OMJHL	64	41	49	90	56	—	—	—	—	—
78-79—Cincinnati		WHA	78	27	25	52	123	3	0	2	2	2
79-80—Washington		NHL	77	36	32	68	66	—	—	—	—	—
80-81—Washington		NHL	80	48	46	94	100	—	—	—	—	—
81-82—Washington		NHL	80	35	45	80	121	—	—	—	—	—
82-83—Washington		NHL	73	38	38	76	54	4	0	0	0	4
83-84—Washington		NHL	80	40	45	85	90	8	3	7	10	16
84-85—Washington		NHL	80	50	52	102	71	5	4	3	7	9
85-86—Washington		NHL	74	35	40	75	63	9	2	10	12	4
86-87—Washington		NHL	78	41	32	73	61	7	4	3	7	14
87-88—Washington		NHL	80	48	33	81	73	14	3	4	7	14
88-89—Washington		NHL	56	26	29	55	71	—	—	—	—	—
—Minnesota		NHL	13	7	7	14	2	5	0	0	0	0
89-90—Minnesota		NHL	67	34	36	70	32	—	—	—	—	—
—New York Rangers		NHL	12	11	5	16	6	10	5	3	8	12
90-91—New York Rangers		NHL	79	49	20	69	53	6	1	1	2	0
91-92—New York Rangers		NHL	76	40	41	81	55	13	8	8	16	4
92-93—New York Rangers		NHL	84	45	23	68	59	—	—	—	—	—
93-94—New York Rangers		NHL	71	28	24	52	58	—	—	—	—	—
—Toronto		NHL	10	6	6	12	4	18	5	6	11	14
WHA totals			78	27	25	52	123	3	0	2	2	2
NHL totals			1170	617	554	1171	1039	99	35	45	80	91

GASKINS, JON
D, OILERS

PERSONAL: Born January 11, 1976, in Pekin, Ill.... 6-3/205.... Shoots left.
TRANSACTIONS/CAREER NOTES: Selected by Edmonton Oilers in fifth round (eighth Oilers pick, 110th overall) of NHL entry draft (June 29, 1994).

Season	Team	League	REGULAR SEASON					PLAYOFFS				
			Gms.	G	A	Pts.	PIM	Gms.	G	A	Pts.	PIM
91-92—Orillia		Junior B	48	1	10	11	42	—	—	—	—	—
92-93—Dubuque		USHL	25	6	9	15	20	—	—	—	—	—
93-94—Dubuque		USHL	30	6	13	19	52	—	—	—	—	—

GAUDREAU, ROB
RW, SHARKS

PERSONAL: Born January 20, 1970, in Cranston, R.I.... 5-11/185.... Shoots right.... Full name: Robert Rene Gaudreau.... Name pronounced GUH-droh.
HIGH SCHOOL: Bishop Hendricken (Warwick, R.I.).
COLLEGE: Providence.
TRANSACTIONS/CAREER NOTES: Separated shoulder (February 1987).... Selected by Pittsburgh Penguins in ninth round (eighth Penguins pick, 127th overall) of NHL entry draft (June 11, 1988).... Traded by Penguins to Minnesota North Stars for C Richard Zemlak (November 1, 1988).... Selected by San Jose Sharks in NHL dispersal draft (May 30, 1991).... Bruised hand (March 21, 1993); missed one game.
HONORS: Named Hockey East co-Rookie of the Year with Scott Pellerin (1988-89).... Named to Hockey East All-Rookie team (1988-89).... Named to Hockey East All-Star second team (1990-91).... Named to NCAA All-America East second team (1991-92).... Named to Hockey East All-Star first team (1991-92).

Season	Team	League	REGULAR SEASON					PLAYOFFS				
			Gms.	G	A	Pts.	PIM	Gms.	G	A	Pts.	PIM
86-87—Bishop Hendricken		R.I.H.S.	33	41	39	80	...	—	—	—	—	—
87-88—Bishop Hendricken		R.I.H.S.	...	52	60	112	...	—	—	—	—	—

Season Team	League	REGULAR SEASON					PLAYOFFS				
		Gms.	G	A	Pts.	Pen.	Gms.	G	A	Pts.	Pen.
88-89—Providence College	Hockey East	42	28	29	57	32	—	—	—	—	—
89-90—Providence College	Hockey East	32	20	18	38	12	—	—	—	—	—
90-91—Providence College	Hockey East	36	34	27	61	20	—	—	—	—	—
91-92—Providence College	Hockey East	36	21	34	55	22	—	—	—	—	—
92-93—Kansas City	IHL	19	8	6	14	6	—	—	—	—	—
—San Jose	NHL	59	23	20	43	18	—	—	—	—	—
93-94—San Jose	NHL	84	15	20	35	28	14	2	0	2	0
NHL totals		143	38	40	78	46	14	2	0	2	0

GAUTHIER, DANIEL

C, BLACKHAWKS

PERSONAL: Born May 17, 1970, in Charlemagne, Que. . . . 6-2/ 192. . . . Shoots left.
TRANSACTIONS/CAREER NOTES: Selected by Pittsburgh Penguins in third round (third Penguins pick, 62nd overall) of NHL entry draft (June 11, 1988). . . . Left Victoriaville (January 2, 1990); returned (January 16, 1990). . . . Signed as free agent by Florida Panthers (July 27, 1993). . . . Signed as free agent by Chicago Blackhawks (June 23, 1994).
HONORS: Won ECHL Rookie of the Year Award (1990-91). . . . Named to ECHL All-Star first team (1990-91).

Season Team	League	REGULAR SEASON					PLAYOFFS				
		Gms.	G	A	Pts.	PIM	Gms.	G	A	Pts.	PIM
86-87—Longueuil	QMJHL	64	23	22	45	23	18	4	5	9	15
87-88—Victoriaville	QMJHL	66	43	47	90	53	5	2	1	3	0
88-89—Victoriaville	QMJHL	64	41	75	116	84	16	12	17	29	30
89-90—Victoriaville	QMJHL	62	45	69	114	32	16	8	*19	27	16
90-91—Albany	IHL	1	1	0	1	0	—	—	—	—	—
—Knoxville	ECHL	61	41	*93	134	40	2	0	4	4	4
91-92—Muskegon	IHL	68	19	18	37	28	9	3	6	9	8
92-93—Cleveland	IHL	80	40	66	106	88	4	2	2	4	14
93-94—Cincinnati	IHL	74	30	34	64	101	10	2	3	5	14

GAUTHIER, SEAN

G, JETS

PERSONAL: Born March 28, 1971, in Sudbury, Ont. . . . 5-11/202. . . . Catches left. . . . Name pronounced GO-chay.
TRANSACTIONS/CAREER NOTES: Selected by Winnipeg Jets in ninth round (seventh Jets pick, 181st overall) of NHL entry draft (June 22, 1991).
HONORS: Shared Dave Pinkney Trophy with Jeff Wilson (1992-93).

Season Team	League	REGULAR SEASON							PLAYOFFS					
		Gms.	Min.	W	L	T	GA	SO	Avg.	Gms.	Min.	W	L	GA	SO	Avg.
90-91—Kingston	OHL	*59	3200	16	36	3	282	0	5.29	—	—					—
91-92—Fort Wayne	IHL	18	978	10	4	‡2	59	1	3.62	2	48	0	0	7	0	8.75
—Moncton	AHL	25	1415	8	10	5	88	1	3.73	2	26	0	0	2	0	4.62
92-93—Moncton	AHL	38	2196	10	16	9	145	0	3.96	2	75	0	1	6	0	4.80
93-94—Moncton	AHL	13	617	3	5	1	41	0	3.99	—	—					—
—Fort Wayne	IHL	22	1139	9	9	‡3	66	0	3.48	—	—					—

GAVEY, AARON

C, LIGHTNING

PERSONAL: Born February 22, 1974, in Sudbury, Ont. . . . 6-1/ 169. . . . Shoots left.
TRANSACTIONS/CAREER NOTES: Selected by Tampa Bay Lightning in fourth round (fourth Lightning pick, 74th overall) of NHL entry draft (June 20, 1992).

Season Team	League	REGULAR SEASON					PLAYOFFS				
		Gms.	G	A	Pts.	PIM	Gms.	G	A	Pts.	PIM
90-91—Peterborough Jr. B	OHA	42	26	30	56	68	—	—	—	—	—
91-92—Sault Ste. Marie	OHL	48	7	11	18	27	19	5	1	6	10
92-93—Sault Ste. Marie	OHL	62	45	39	84	114	18	5	9	14	36
93-94—Sault Ste. Marie	OHL	60	42	60	102	116	14	11	10	21	22

GELINAS, MARTIN

LW, CANUCKS

G

PERSONAL: Born June 5, 1970, in Shawinigan, Que. . . . 5-11/ 195. . . . Shoots left. . . . Name pronounced MAHR-ta ZHEHL-ih-nuh.
HIGH SCHOOL: Polyvalente Val- Maurice (Shawinigan, Que.).
TRANSACTIONS/CAREER NOTES: Broke left clavicle (November 1983). . . . Suffered hairline fracture of clavicle (July 1986). . . . Selected by Los Angeles Kings in first round (first Kings pick, seventh overall) of NHL entry draft (June 11, 1988). . . . Traded by Kings with C Jimmy Carson, first-round picks in 1989 (traded to New Jersey Devils), 1991 (LW Martin Rucinsky) and 1993 (D Nick Stajduhar) drafts and cash to Edmonton Oilers for C Wayne Gretzky, RW/D Marty McSorley and LW/C Mike Krushelnyski (August 9, 1988). . . . Suspended five games (March 9, 1990). . . . Underwent shoulder surgery (June 1990). . . . Traded by Oilers with sixth-round pick in 1993 draft (C Nicholas Checco) to Quebec Nordiques for LW Scott Pearson (June 20, 1993). . . . Injured thigh (October 20, 1993); missed one game. . . . Separated left shoulder (November 25, 1993); missed 10 games. . . . Claimed on waivers by Vancouver Canucks (January 15, 1994). . . . Suffered charley horse (March 27, 1994); missed six games.
HONORS: Won Can.HL Rookie of the Year Award (1987-88). . . . Won Michel Bergeron Trophy (1987-88). . . . Named to QMJHL All-Star first team (1987-88).
MISCELLANEOUS: Member of Stanley Cup championship team (1990).

Season Team	League	REGULAR SEASON					PLAYOFFS				
		Gms.	G	A	Pts.	PIM	Gms.	G	A	Pts.	PIM
87-88—Hull	QMJHL	65	63	68	131	74	17	15	18	33	32
88-89—Edmonton	NHL	6	1	2	3	0	—	—	—	—	—

Season Team	League	REGULAR SEASON					PLAYOFFS				
		Gms.	G	A	Pts.	Pen.	Gms.	G	A	Pts.	Pen.
—Hull	QMJHL	41	38	39	77	31	9	5	4	9	14
89-90—Edmonton	NHL	46	17	8	25	30	20	2	3	5	6
90-91—Edmonton	NHL	73	20	20	40	34	18	3	6	9	25
91-92—Edmonton	NHL	68	11	18	29	62	15	1	3	4	10
92-93—Edmonton	NHL	65	11	12	23	30	—	—	—	—	—
93-94—Quebec	NHL	31	6	6	12	8	—	—	—	—	—
—Vancouver	NHL	33	8	8	16	26	24	5	4	9	14
NHL totals		322	74	74	148	190	77	11	16	27	55

GENDRON, MARTIN
RW, CAPITALS

PERSONAL: Born February 15, 1974, in Valleyfield, Que. . . . 5-8/182. . . . Shoots right. . . . Name pronounced MAHR-ta ZHEHN-drahn.

TRANSACTIONS/CAREER NOTES: Selected by Washington Capitals in third round (fourth Capitals pick, 71st overall) of NHL entry draft (June 20, 1992).

HONORS: Named to QMJHL All-Rookie team (1990-91). . . . Won Can.HL Most Sportsmanlike Player of the Year Award (1991-92). . . . Won Shell Cup (1991-92). . . . Won Frank J. Selke Trophy (1991-92 and 1992-93). . . . Named to QMJHL All-Star first team (1991-92). . . . Named to Can.HL All-Star first team (1992-93). . . . Named to QMJHL All-Star second team (1992-93).

Season Team	League	REGULAR SEASON					PLAYOFFS				
		Gms.	G	A	Pts.	PIM	Gms.	G	A	Pts.	PIM
90-91—St. Hyacinthe	QMJHL	55	34	23	57	33	4	1	2	3	0
91-92—St. Hyacinthe	QMJHL	69	*71	66	137	45	6	7	4	11	14
92-93—St. Hyacinthe	QMJHL	63	73	61	134	44	—	—	—	—	—
—Baltimore	AHL	10	1	2	3	2	3	0	0	0	0
93-94—Canadian national team	Int'l	19	4	5	9	2	—	—	—	—	—
—Hull	QMJHL	37	39	36	75	18	20	*21	17	38	8

GERIS, DAVE
D, PANTHERS

PERSONAL: Born June 7, 1976, in North Bay, Ont. . . . 6-5/221. . . . Shoots left. . . . Name pronounced JUR-is.

HIGH SCHOOL: W.F. Herman (Windsor, Ont.).

TRANSACTIONS/CAREER NOTES: Selected by Florida Panthers in fifth round (sixth Panthers pick, 105th overall) of NHL entry draft (June 29, 1994).

Season Team	League	REGULAR SEASON					PLAYOFFS				
		Gms.	G	A	Pts.	PIM	Gms.	G	A	Pts.	PIM
93-94—Windsor	OHL	63	0	6	6	121	3	0	0	0	6

GERNANDER, KEN
LW, JETS

PERSONAL: Born June 30, 1969, in Grand Rapids, Minn. . . . 5-10/175. . . . Shoots left. . . . Full name: Kenneth Robert Gernander. . . . Name pronounced juhr-NAN-duhr.

HIGH SCHOOL: Greenway (Coleraine, Minn.).

COLLEGE: Minnesota.

TRANSACTIONS/CAREER NOTES: Selected by Winnipeg Jets in fifth round (fourth Jets pick, 96th overall) of NHL entry draft (June 13, 1987).

Season Team	League	REGULAR SEASON					PLAYOFFS				
		Gms.	G	A	Pts.	PIM	Gms.	G	A	Pts.	PIM
85-86—Greenway H.S.	Minn. H.S.	23	14	23	37	...	—	—	—	—	—
86-87—Greenway H.S.	Minn. H.S.	26	35	34	69	...	—	—	—	—	—
87-88—University of Minnesota	WCHA	44	14	14	28	14	—	—	—	—	—
88-89—University of Minnesota	WCHA	44	9	11	20	2	—	—	—	—	—
89-90—University of Minnesota	WCHA	44	32	17	49	24	—	—	—	—	—
90-91—University of Minnesota	WCHA	44	23	20	43	24	—	—	—	—	—
91-92—Moncton	AHL	43	8	18	26	9	8	1	1	2	2
—Fort Wayne	IHL	13	7	6	13	2	—	—	—	—	—
92-93—Moncton	AHL	71	18	29	47	20	5	1	4	5	0
93-94—Moncton	AHL	71	22	25	47	12	19	6	1	7	0

GIBSON, STEVE
LW, OILERS

PERSONAL: Born September 10, 1972, in Listowel, Ont. . . . 6-0/204. . . . Shoots left.

TRANSACTIONS/CAREER NOTES: Selected by Edmonton Oilers in seventh round (seventh Oilers pick, 157th overall) of NHL entry draft (June 20, 1992).

Season Team	League	REGULAR SEASON					PLAYOFFS				
		Gms.	G	A	Pts.	PIM	Gms.	G	A	Pts.	PIM
89-90—Windsor	OHL	35	6	8	14	24	—	—	—	—	—
90-91—Windsor	OHL	62	15	18	33	37	—	—	—	—	—
91-92—Windsor	OHL	63	49	40	89	41	—	—	—	—	—
92-93—Windsor	OHL	60	48	52	100	44	—	—	—	—	—
—Johnstown	ECHL	—	—	—	—	—	3	0	1	1	2
93-94—Wheeling	ECHL	55	29	30	59	47	9	1	3	4	23
—Cape Breton	AHL	3	0	0	0	2	—	—	—	—	—

GILBERT, GREG
LW, RANGERS

PERSONAL: Born January 22, 1967, in Mississauga, Ont. . . . 6-1/190. . . . Shoots left. . . . Full name: Gregory Scott Gilbert.

TRANSACTIONS/CAREER NOTES: Sprained ankle (December 1979). . . . Selected by New York Islanders as underage junior in fourth round (fifth Islanders pick, 80th overall) of NHL entry

G

draft (June 11, 1980).... Stretched ligaments in left ankle (September 1984).... Injured ligaments in knee and underwent arthroscopic surgery then major reconstructive surgery (February 27, 1985).... Broke jaw (October 11, 1986); missed 10 games.... Bruised thigh (December 7, 1986).... Bruised hip (February 1987).... Separated right shoulder (March 1987). ... Bruised right knee (February 20, 1988).... Injured left foot (April 1988).... Suffered back spasms and injured left shoulder (February 1989).... Traded by Islanders to Chicago Blackhawks for fifth-round pick (RW Steve Young) in 1989 draft (March 7, 1989).... Broke foot (March 1989).... Strained abdominal muscle during practice (March 8, 1990).... Bruised left shoulder (September 28, 1990); missed first eight games of season.... Hyperextended left knee (April 1991).... Pulled lateral muscle (November 13, 1991); missed two games.... Fractured ankle (February 16, 1992).... Slightly strained left knee (April 4, 1992).... Suspended three off-days and fined $500 by NHL for fighting (February 26, 1993).... Suffered from the flu (March 5, 1993); missed two games.... Signed as free agent by New York Rangers (July 29, 1993).... Suffered injury (January 14, 1994); missed two games.... Sprained right knee (January 25, 1994); missed six games.
MISCELLANEOUS: Member of Stanley Cup championship teams (1982, 1983 and 1990).

			REGULAR SEASON					PLAYOFFS				
Season	Team	League	Gms.	G	A	Pts.	PIM	Gms.	G	A	Pts.	PIM
79-80—Toronto		OMJHL	68	10	11	21	35	—	—	—	—	—
80-81—Toronto		OMJHL	64	30	37	67	73	5	2	6	8	16
81-82—Toronto		OHL	65	41	67	108	119	10	4	12	16	23
—New York Islanders		NHL	1	1	0	1	0	4	1	1	2	2
82-83—Indianapolis		CHL	24	11	16	27	23	—	—	—	—	—
—New York Islanders		NHL	45	8	11	19	30	10	1	0	1	14
83-84—New York Islanders		NHL	79	31	35	66	59	21	5	7	12	39
84-85—New York Islanders		NHL	58	13	25	38	36	—	—	—	—	—
85-86—Springfield		AHL	2	0	0	0	2	—	—	—	—	—
—New York Islanders		NHL	60	9	19	28	82	2	0	0	0	9
86-87—New York Islanders		NHL	51	6	7	13	26	10	2	2	4	6
87-88—New York Islanders		NHL	76	17	28	45	46	4	0	0	0	6
88-89—New York Islanders		NHL	55	8	13	21	45	—	—	—	—	—
—Chicago		NHL	4	0	0	0	0	15	1	5	6	20
89-90—Chicago		NHL	70	12	25	37	54	19	5	8	13	34
90-91—Chicago		NHL	72	10	15	25	58	5	0	1	1	2
91-92—Chicago		NHL	50	7	5	12	35	10	1	3	4	16
92-93—Chicago		NHL	77	13	19	32	57	3	0	0	0	0
93-94—New York Rangers		NHL	76	4	11	15	29	23	1	3	4	8
NHL totals			774	139	213	352	557	126	17	30	47	156

GILCHRIST, BRENT
LW, STARS

PERSONAL: Born April 3, 1967, in Moose Jaw, Sask.... 5-11/185.... Shoots left.
TRANSACTIONS/CAREER NOTES: Strained medial collateral ligament (January 1985). ... Selected by Montreal Canadiens as underage junior in sixth round (sixth Canadiens pick, 79th overall) of NHL entry draft (June 15, 1985).... Injured knee (January 1987).... Broke right index finger (November 17, 1990); missed 19 games.... Separated left shoulder (February 6, 1991); missed two games.... Reinjured left shoulder (February 13, 1991); missed five games.... Traded by Canadiens with LW Shayne Corson and LW Vladimir Vujtek to Edmonton Oilers for LW Vincent Damphousse and fourth-round pick (D Adam Wiesel) in 1993 draft (August 27, 1992).... Suffered concussion (October 1992); missed two games.... Fractured nose (December 21, 1992); missed two games.... Traded by Oilers to Minnesota North Stars for C Todd Elik (March 5, 1993).... Separated shoulder (March 18, 1993); missed remainder of season.... North Stars franchise moved from Minnesota to Dallas and renamed Stars for 1993-94 season.... Strained shoulder (October 27, 1993); missed four games.... Pulled groin (November 21, 1993); missed four games.

			REGULAR SEASON					PLAYOFFS				
Season	Team	League	Gms.	G	A	Pts.	PIM	Gms.	G	A	Pts.	PIM
83-84—Kelowna Wings		WHL	69	16	11	27	16	—	—	—	—	—
84-85—Kelowna Wings		WHL	51	35	38	73	58	6	5	2	7	8
85-86—Spokane		WHL	52	45	45	90	57	9	6	7	13	19
86-87—Spokane		WHL	46	45	55	100	71	5	2	7	9	6
—Sherbrooke		AHL	—	—	—	—	—	10	2	7	9	2
87-88—Sherbrooke		AHL	77	26	48	74	83	6	1	3	4	6
88-89—Montreal		NHL	49	8	16	24	16	9	1	1	2	10
—Sherbrooke		AHL	7	6	5	11	7	—	—	—	—	—
89-90—Montreal		NHL	57	9	15	24	28	8	2	0	2	6
90-91—Montreal		NHL	51	6	9	15	10	13	5	3	8	6
91-92—Montreal		NHL	79	23	27	50	57	11	2	4	6	6
92-93—Edmonton		NHL	60	10	10	20	47	—	—	—	—	—
—Minnesota		NHL	8	0	1	1	2	—	—	—	—	—
93-94—Dallas		NHL	76	17	14	31	31	9	3	1	4	2
NHL totals			380	73	92	165	191	50	13	9	22	26

GILHEN, RANDY
C, JETS

PERSONAL: Born June 13, 1963, in Zweibrucken, West Germany.... 6-0/190.... Shoots left. ... Name pronounced GIHL-ihn.
TRANSACTIONS/CAREER NOTES: Selected by Hartford Whalers as underage junior in sixth round (sixth Whalers pick, 109th overall) of NHL entry draft (June 9, 1982).... Signed as free agent by Winnipeg Jets (August 1985).... Separated shoulder (November 16, 1988).... Traded by Jets with RW Andrew McBain and D Jim Kyte to Pittsburgh Penguins for C/LW Randy Cunneyworth, G Richard Tabaracci and RW Dave McIlwain (June 17, 1989).... Sprained knee (November 2, 1989).... Selected by Minnesota North Stars in NHL expansion draft (May 30, 1991).... Traded by North Stars with D Charlie Huddy, RW Jim Thomson and fourth-round pick in 1991 draft (D Alexei Zhitnik) to Los Angeles Kings for C Todd Elik (June 22, 1991).... Traded by Kings to New York Rangers for C Corey Millen

G

(December 23, 1991).... Sprained right knee (January 30, 1993); missed seven games.... Traded by Rangers to Tampa Bay Lightning for LW Mike Hartman (March 22, 1993).... Selected by Florida Panthers in NHL expansion draft (June 24, 1993). ... Traded by Panthers to Jets for C Stu Barnes (November 26, 1993).... Underwent elbow surgery (January 16, 1994); missed four games.... Dislocated shoulder (March 7, 1994); missed 15 games.

MISCELLANEOUS: Member of Stanley Cup championship team (1991).

Season Team	League	REGULAR SEASON					PLAYOFFS				
		Gms.	G	A	Pts.	PIM	Gms.	G	A	Pts.	PIM
79-80—Saskatoon	SJHL	55	18	34	52	112	—	—	—	—	—
—Saskatoon	WHL	9	2	2	4	20	—	—	—	—	—
80-81—Saskatoon	WHL	68	10	5	15	154	—	—	—	—	—
81-82—Winnipeg	WHL	61	41	37	78	87	—	—	—	—	—
82-83—Winnipeg	WHL	71	57	44	101	84	3	2	2	4	0
—Hartford	NHL	2	0	1	1	0	—	—	—	—	—
—Binghamton	AHL	—	—	—	—	—	5	2	0	2	2
83-84—Binghamton	AHL	73	8	12	20	72	—	—	—	—	—
84-85—Salt Lake City	IHL	57	20	20	40	28	—	—	—	—	—
—Binghamton	AHL	18	3	3	6	9	8	4	1	5	16
85-86—Fort Wayne	IHL	82	44	40	84	48	15	10	8	18	6
86-87—Winnipeg	NHL	2	0	0	0	0	—	—	—	—	—
—Sherbrooke	AHL	75	36	29	65	44	17	7	13	20	10
87-88—Winnipeg	NHL	13	3	2	5	15	4	1	0	1	10
—Moncton	AHL	68	40	47	87	51	—	—	—	—	—
88-89—Winnipeg	NHL	64	5	3	8	38	—	—	—	—	—
89-90—Pittsburgh	NHL	61	5	11	16	54	—	—	—	—	—
90-91—Pittsburgh	NHL	72	15	10	25	51	16	1	0	1	14
91-92—Los Angeles	NHL	33	3	6	9	14	—	—	—	—	—
—New York Rangers	NHL	40	7	7	14	14	13	1	2	3	2
92-93—New York Rangers	NHL	33	3	2	5	8	—	—	—	—	—
—Tampa Bay	NHL	11	0	2	2	6	—	—	—	—	—
93-94—Florida	NHL	20	4	4	8	16	—	—	—	—	—
—Winnipeg	NHL	40	3	3	6	34	—	—	—	—	—
NHL totals		391	48	51	99	250	33	3	2	5	26

GILL, TODD

D, MAPLE LEAFS

PERSONAL: Born November 9, 1965, in Brockville, Ont.... 6-0/185.... Shoots left. **TRANSACTIONS/CAREER NOTES:** Selected by Toronto Maple Leafs as underage junior in second round (second Maple Leafs pick, 25th overall) of NHL entry draft (June 9, 1984).... Broke bone in right foot (October 1987).... Bruised shoulder (March 1989).... Fractured finger (October 15, 1991); missed three games.... Strained back (February 8, 1992); missed three games.... Injured back; missed first two games of 1992-93 season.... Suffered foot contusion (November 14, 1992); missed 11 games.... Strained groin (November 1, 1993); missed 26 games.... Suffered back spasms (February 24, 1994); missed 13 games.

Season Team	League	REGULAR SEASON					PLAYOFFS				
		Gms.	G	A	Pts.	PIM	Gms.	G	A	Pts.	PIM
82-83—Windsor	OHL	70	12	24	36	108	3	0	0	0	11
83-84—Windsor	OHL	68	9	48	57	184	3	1	1	2	10
84-85—Toronto	NHL	10	1	0	1	13	—	—	—	—	—
—Windsor	OHL	53	17	40	57	148	4	0	1	1	14
85-86—St. Catharines	AHL	58	8	25	33	90	10	1	6	7	17
—Toronto	NHL	15	1	2	3	28	1	0	0	0	0
86-87—Newmarket	AHL	11	1	8	9	33	—	—	—	—	—
—Toronto	NHL	61	4	27	31	92	13	2	2	4	42
87-88—Newmarket	AHL	2	0	1	1	2	—	—	—	—	—
—Toronto	NHL	65	8	17	25	131	6	1	3	4	20
88-89—Toronto	NHL	59	11	14	25	72	—	—	—	—	—
89-90—Toronto	NHL	48	1	14	15	92	5	0	3	3	16
90-91—Toronto	NHL	72	2	22	24	113	—	—	—	—	—
91-92—Toronto	NHL	74	2	15	17	91	—	—	—	—	—
92-93—Toronto	NHL	69	11	32	43	66	21	1	10	11	26
93-94—Toronto	NHL	45	4	24	28	44	18	1	5	6	37
NHL totals		518	45	167	212	742	64	5	23	28	141

GILLAM, SEAN

D, RED WINGS

PERSONAL: Born May 7, 1976, in Lethbridge, Alta.... 6-2/187.... Shoots right. **HIGH SCHOOL:** Spokane (Wash.). **TRANSACTIONS/CAREER NOTES:** Selected by Detroit Red Wings in third round (third Red Wings pick, 75th overall) of NHL entry draft (June 29, 1994).

Season Team	League	REGULAR SEASON					PLAYOFFS				
		Gms.	G	A	Pts.	PIM	Gms.	G	A	Pts.	PIM
92-93—Spokane	WHL	70	6	27	33	121	10	0	2	2	10
93-94—Spokane	WHL	70	7	17	24	106	3	0	0	0	6

GILMORE, MIKE

G, RANGERS

PERSONAL: Born March 11, 1968, in Detroit.... 5-10/173.... Catches left. **COLLEGE:** Michigan State. **TRANSACTIONS/CAREER NOTES:** Selected by New York Rangers in NHL supplemental draft (June 15, 1990).

G

Season Team	League	Gms.	Min.	W	L	T	GA	SO	Avg.	Gms.	Min.	W	L	GA	SO	Avg.
88-89—Michigan State............	CCHA	3	74	1	0	0	5	0	4.05	—	—	—	—	—	—	—
89-90—Michigan State............	CCHA	12	638	9	1	0	29	0	2.73	—	—	—	—	—	—	—
90-91—Michigan State............	CCHA	22	1218	9	8	3	54	*2	2.66	—	—	—	—	—	—	—
91-92—Michigan State............	CCHA	36	2011	16	10	7	103	2	3.07	—	—	—	—	—	—	—
92-93—Erie	ECHL	31	1762	19	8	‡1	134	0	4.56	5	300	2	3	24	0	4.80
93-94—Erie	ECHL	1	34	1	0	0	0	0	0.00	—	—	—	—	—	—	—
—Binghamton	AHL	7	338	1	5	0	25	0	4.43	—	—	—	—	—	—	—

GILMOUR, DOUG
C, MAPLE LEAFS

PERSONAL: Born June 25, 1963, in Kingston, Ont.... 5-11/172.... Shoots left.
TRANSACTIONS/CAREER NOTES: Selected by St. Louis Blues as underage junior in seventh round (fourth Blues pick, 134th overall) of NHL entry draft (June 9, 1982).... Sprained ankle (October 7, 1985); missed four games.... Suffered concussion (January 1988).... Bruised shoulder (March 1988).... Traded by Blues with RW Mark Hunter, LW Steve Bozek and D/RW Michael Dark to Calgary Flames for C Mike Bullard, C Craig Coxe and D Tim Corkery (September 5, 1988).... Suffered abscessed jaw (March 1989); missed six games.... Broke bone in right foot (August 12, 1989).... Traded by Flames with D Ric Nattress, D Jamie Macoun, LW Kent Manderville and G Rick Wamsley to Toronto Maple Leafs for LW Craig Berube, D Alexander Godynyuk, LW Gary Leeman, D Michel Petit and G Jeff Reese (January 2, 1992).... Suspended eight off-days and fined $500 by NHL for slashing (November 27, 1992).... Suspended one preseason game and fined $500 by NHL for headbutting (September 26, 1993).
HONORS: Won Red Tilson Trophy (1982-83).... Won Eddie Powers Memorial Trophy (1982-83).... Named to OHL All-Star first team (1982-83).... Won Frank J. Selke Trophy (1992-93).... Named to THE SPORTING NEWS All-Star second team (1992-93).... Played in NHL All-Star Game (1993 and 1994).
MISCELLANEOUS: Member of Stanley Cup championship team (1989).

Season Team	League	Gms.	G	A	Pts.	PIM	Gms.	G	A	Pts.	PIM
80-81—Cornwall	QMJHL	51	12	23	35	35	—	—	—	—	—
81-82—Cornwall	OHL	67	46	*73	119	42	5	6	9	15	2
82-83—Cornwall	OHL	68	*70	*107	*177	62	8	8	10	18	16
83-84—St. Louis	NHL	80	25	28	53	57	11	2	9	11	10
84-85—St. Louis	NHL	78	21	36	57	49	3	1	1	2	2
85-86—St. Louis	NHL	74	25	28	53	41	19	9	12	†21	25
86-87—St. Louis	NHL	80	42	63	105	58	6	2	2	4	16
87-88—St. Louis	NHL	72	36	50	86	59	10	3	14	17	18
88-89—Calgary	NHL	72	26	59	85	44	22	11	11	22	20
89-90—Calgary	NHL	78	24	67	91	54	6	3	1	4	8
90-91—Calgary	NHL	78	20	61	81	144	7	1	1	2	0
91-92—Calgary	NHL	38	11	27	38	46	—	—	—	—	—
—Toronto	NHL	40	15	34	49	32	—	—	—	—	—
92-93—Toronto	NHL	83	32	95	127	100	21	10	25	35	30
93-94—Toronto	NHL	83	27	84	111	105	18	6	22	28	42
NHL totals................................		856	304	632	936	789	123	48	98	146	171

GIRARD, RICK
C, CANUCKS

PERSONAL: Born May 1, 1974, in Edmonton.... 5-11/180.... Shoots left.
TRANSACTIONS/CAREER NOTES: Selected by Vancouver Canucks in second round (second Canucks pick, 46th overall) of NHL entry draft (June 26, 1992).
HONORS: Won Brad Hornung Trophy (1992-93).... Won Can.HL Most Sportsmanlike Player of the Year Award (1992-93).... Named to WHL (East) All-Star first team (1992-93).... Named to WHL (East) All-Star first team (1993-94).

Season Team	League	Gms.	G	A	Pts.	PIM	Gms.	G	A	Pts.	PIM
91-92—Swift Current..................	WHL	45	14	17	31	6	8	2	0	2	2
92-93—Swift Current..................	WHL	72	71	70	141	25	17	9	17	26	10
93-94—Swift Current..................	WHL	58	40	49	89	43	7	1	8	9	6
—Hamilton.........................	AHL	1	1	1	2	0	—	—	—	—	—

G

GLYNN, BRIAN
D, CANUCKS

PERSONAL: Born November 23, 1967, in Iserlohn, West Germany.... 6-4/220.... Shoots left. ... Full name: Brian Thomas Glynn.
TRANSACTIONS/CAREER NOTES: Selected by Calgary Flames in second round (second Flames pick, 37th overall) of NHL entry draft (June 21, 1986).... Traded by Flames to Minnesota North Stars for D Frantisek Musil (October 26, 1990).... Traded by North Stars to Edmonton Oilers for D David Shaw (January 21, 1992).... Injured knee (March 15, 1992); missed seven games.... Injured knee (November 4, 1992); missed two games. ... Traded by Oilers to Ottawa Senators for eighth-round pick (D Rob Guinn) in 1994 draft (September 14, 1993).... Claimed on waivers by Vancouver Canucks (February 5, 1994).
HONORS: Won Governors Trophy (1989-90).... Named to IHL All-Star first team (1989-90).

Season Team	League	Gms.	G	A	Pts.	PIM	Gms.	G	A	Pts.	PIM
84-85—Saskatoon	SJHL	12	1	0	1	2	3	0	0	0	0
85-86—Saskatoon	WHL	66	7	25	32	131	13	0	3	3	30
86-87—Saskatoon	WHL	44	2	26	28	163	11	1	3	4	19
87-88—Calgary...........................	NHL	67	5	14	19	87	1	0	0	0	0

Season Team	League	REGULAR SEASON Gms.	G	A	Pts.	Pen.	PLAYOFFS Gms.	G	A	Pts.	Pen.
88-89—Salt Lake City	IHL	31	3	10	13	105	14	3	7	10	31
—Calgary	NHL	9	0	1	1	19	—	—	—	—	—
89-90—Calgary	NHL	1	0	0	0	0	—	—	—	—	—
—Salt Lake City	IHL	80	17	44	61	164	—	—	—	—	—
90-91—Salt Lake City	IHL	8	1	3	4	18	—	—	—	—	—
—Minnesota	NHL	66	8	11	19	83	23	2	6	8	18
91-92—Minnesota	NHL	37	2	12	14	24	—	—	—	—	—
—Edmonton	NHL	25	2	6	8	6	16	4	1	5	12
92-93—Edmonton	NHL	64	4	12	16	60	—	—	—	—	—
93-94—Ottawa	NHL	48	2	13	15	41	—	—	—	—	—
—Vancouver	NHL	16	0	0	0	12	17	0	3	3	10
NHL totals		333	23	69	92	332	57	6	10	16	40

GODYNYUK, ALEXANDER
D, WHALERS

PERSONAL: Born January 27, 1970, in Kiev, U.S.S.R. ... 6-0/207. ... Shoots left. ... Name pronounced goh-DIHN-yuhk.
TRANSACTIONS/CAREER NOTES: Selected by Toronto Maple Leafs in sixth round (fifth Maple Leafs pick, 115th overall) of NHL entry draft (June 16, 1990). ... Traded by Maple Leafs with LW Craig Berube, RW Gary Leeman, D Michel Petit and G Jeff Reese to Calgary Flames for C Doug Gilmour, D Jamie Macoun, LW Kent Manderville, D Ric Nattress and G Rick Wamsley (January 2, 1992). ... Injured shoulder (February 23, 1993); missed one game. ... Selected by Florida Panthers in NHL expansion draft (June 24, 1993). ... Strained stomach muscle (November 14, 1993); missed two games. ... Traded by Panthers to Hartford Whalers for D Jim McKenzie (December 16, 1993). ... Bruised knee (December 28, 1993); missed one game. ... Injured knee (March 25, 1994); missed remainder of season.

Season Team	League	REGULAR SEASON Gms.	G	A	Pts.	PIM	PLAYOFFS Gms.	G	A	Pts.	PIM
89-90—Sokol Kiev	USSR	38	3	2	5	31	—	—	—	—	—
90-91—Sokol Kiev	USSR	19	3	1	4	20	—	—	—	—	—
—Toronto	NHL	18	0	3	3	16	—	—	—	—	—
—Newmarket	AHL	11	0	1	1	29	—	—	—	—	—
91-92—Toronto	NHL	31	3	6	9	59	—	—	—	—	—
—Calgary	NHL	6	0	1	1	4	—	—	—	—	—
—Salt Lake City	IHL	17	2	1	3	24	—	—	—	—	—
92-93—Calgary	NHL	27	3	4	7	19	—	—	—	—	—
93-94—Florida	NHL	26	0	10	10	35	—	—	—	—	—
—Hartford	NHL	43	3	9	12	40	—	—	—	—	—
NHL totals		151	9	33	42	173	—	—	—	—	—

GOLUBOVSKY, YAN
D, RED WINGS

PERSONAL: Born March 9, 1976, in Novosibirsk, U.S.S.R. ... 6-3/185. ... Shoots right.
TRANSACTIONS/CAREER NOTES: Selected by Detroit Red Wings in first round (first Red Wings pick, 23rd overall) of NHL entry draft (June 28, 1994).

Season Team	League	REGULAR SEASON Gms.	G	A	Pts.	PIM	PLAYOFFS Gms.	G	A	Pts.	PIM
93-94—Dynamo-2 Moscow	CIS Div. III				Statistics unavailable.						
—Russian Penguins	IHL	8	0	0	0	23	—	—	—	—	—

GONCHAR, SERGEI
D, CAPITALS

PERSONAL: Born April 13, 1974, in Chelyabinsk, U.S.S.R. ... 6-2/212. ... Shoots left.
TRANSACTIONS/CAREER NOTES: Selected by Washington Capitals in first round (first Capitals pick, 14th overall) of NHL entry draft (June 20, 1992).

Season Team	League	REGULAR SEASON Gms.	G	A	Pts.	PIM	PLAYOFFS Gms.	G	A	Pts.	PIM
90-91—Mechel Chelyabinsk	USSR	2	0	0	0	0	—	—	—	—	—
91-92—Traktor Chelyabinsk	CIS	31	1	0	1	6	—	—	—	—	—
92-93—Dynamo Moscow	CIS	31	1	3	4	70	10	0	0	0	12
93-94—Dynamo Moscow	CIS	44	4	5	9	36	10	0	3	3	14
—Portland	AHL	—	—	—	—	—	2	0	0	0	0

GONEAU, DANIEL
LW, BRUINS

PERSONAL: Born January 16, 1976, in Lachine, Que. ... 6-1/196. ... Shoots left. ... Name pronounced Dan-YEL Gahn-OH.
TRANSACTIONS/CAREER NOTES: Selected by Boston Bruins in second round (second Bruins pick, 47th overall) of NHL entry draft (June 28, 1994).

Season Team	League	REGULAR SEASON Gms.	G	A	Pts.	PIM	PLAYOFFS Gms.	G	A	Pts.	PIM
92-93—Laval	QMJHL	62	16	25	41	44	13	0	4	4	4
93-94—Laval	QMJHL	68	29	57	86	81	19	8	21	29	45

GORDIOUK, VIKTOR
RW, SABRES

PERSONAL: Born April 11, 1970, in Moscow, U.S.S.R. ... 5-10/176. ... Shoots right. ... Name pronounced GOHR-dee-yuhk.
TRANSACTIONS/CAREER NOTES: Selected by Buffalo Sabres in seventh round (sixth Sabres pick, 142nd overall) of NHL entry draft (June 16, 1990).

G

Season	Team	League	Gms.	G	A	Pts.	PIM	Gms.	G	A	Pts.	PIM
89-90—Soviet Wings		USSR	48	11	4	15	24	—	—	—	—	—
90-91—Soviet Wings		USSR	46	12	10	22	22	—	—	—	—	—
91-92—Soviet Wings		CIS	42	16	7	23	24	—	—	—	—	—
92-93—Buffalo		NHL	16	3	6	9	0	—	—	—	—	—
—Rochester		AHL	35	11	14	25	8	17	9	9	18	4
93-94—Rochester		AHL	74	28	39	67	26	4	3	0	3	2
NHL totals			16	3	6	9	0					

GORDON, ROB
C, CANUCKS

PERSONAL: Born January 13, 1976, in Surrey, B.C. . . . 5-11/170. . . . Shoots right.
TRANSACTIONS/CAREER NOTES: Selected by Vancouver Canucks in second round (second Canucks pick, 39th overall) of NHL entry draft (June 28, 1994).

Season	Team	League	Gms.	G	A	Pts.	PIM	Gms.	G	A	Pts.	PIM
92-93—Powell River		BCJHL	60	55	38	93	76	—	—	—	—	—
93-94—Powell River		BCJHL	60	69	89	158	141	—	—	—	—	—

GOSSELIN, CHRISTIAN
D, DEVILS

PERSONAL: Born August 21, 1976, in St. Redempteur, Que. . . . 6-4/206. . . . Shoots left.
TRANSACTIONS/CAREER NOTES: Selected by New Jersey Devils in fifth round (fifth Devils pick, 129th overall) of NHL entry draft (June 29, 1994).

Season	Team	League	Gms.	G	A	Pts.	PIM	Gms.	G	A	Pts.	PIM
93-94—St. Hyacinthe		QMJHL	12	3	2	5	16	—	—	—	—	—

GOSSELIN, MARIO
G, WHALERS

PERSONAL: Born June 15, 1963, in Thetford Mines, Que. . . . 5-8/160. . . . Catches left. . . . Name pronounced GAHZ-uh-lai.
TRANSACTIONS/CAREER NOTES: Selected by Quebec Nordiques as underage junior in third round (third Nordiques pick, 55th overall) of NHL entry draft (June 9, 1982). . . . Injured knee (March 8, 1984); missed remainder of season. . . . Suffered from the flu (January 16, 1986); missed one game. . . . Signed as free agent by Los Angeles Kings (June 1989). . . . Suffered from the flu (October 1989). . . . Signed as free agent by Hartford Whalers (September 4, 1991). . . . Injured back (April 13, 1993); missed final two games of regular season. . . . Underwent knee surgery (November 29, 1993); missed remainder of season.
HONORS: Named to QMJHL All-Star second team (1981-82). . . . Named to QMJHL All-Star first team (1982-83). . . . Played in NHL All-Star Game (1986).

Season	Team	League	Gms.	Min.	W	L	T	GA	SO	Avg.	Gms.	Min.	W	L	GA	SO	Avg.
80-81—Shawinigan		QMJHL	21	907	4	9	0	75	0	4.96	1	20	0	0	2	0	6.00
81-82—Shawinigan		QMJHL	*60	*3404	...	...	...	230	0	4.05	14	788	...	...	58	0	4.42
82-83—Shawinigan		QMJHL	46	2556	32	9	1	133	*3	*3.12	8	457	5	3	29	0	3.81
83-84—Can. Olympic Team		Int'l	36	2007	...	...	...	126	0	3.77	—	—	—	—	—	—	—
—Quebec		NHL	3	148	2	0	0	3	1	1.22	—	—	—	—	—	—	—
84-85—Quebec		NHL	35	1960	19	10	3	109	1	3.34	17	1059	9	8	54	0	3.06
85-86—Fredericton		AHL	5	304	2	2	1	15	0	2.96	—	—	—	—	—	—	—
—Quebec		NHL	31	1726	14	14	1	111	2	3.86	1	40	0	1	5	0	7.50
86-87—Quebec		NHL	30	1625	13	11	1	86	0	3.18	11	654	7	4	37	0	3.39
87-88—Quebec		NHL	54	3002	20	28	4	189	2	3.78	—	—	—	—	—	—	—
88-89—Quebec		NHL	39	2064	11	19	3	146	0	4.24	—	—	—	—	—	—	—
—Halifax		AHL	3	183	3	0	0	9	0	2.95	—	—	—	—	—	—	—
89-90—Los Angeles		NHL	26	1226	7	11	1	79	0	3.87	3	63	0	2	3	0	2.86
90-91—Phoenix		IHL	46	2673	24	15	‡4	172	1	3.86	11	670	7	4	*43	0	3.85
91-92—Springfield		AHL	47	2606	28	11	5	142	0	3.27	6	319	1	4	18	0	3.39
92-93—Springfield		AHL	23	1345	8	7	7	75	0	3.35	—	—	—	—	—	—	—
—Hartford		NHL	16	867	5	9	1	57	0	3.94	—	—	—	—	—	—	—
93-94—Springfield		AHL	2	120	2	0	0	5	0	2.50	—	—	—	—	—	—	—
—Hartford		NHL	7	239	0	4	0	21	0	5.27	—	—	—	—	—	—	—
NHL totals			241	12857	91	106	14	801	6	3.74	32	1816	16	15	99	0	3.27

GOTZIAMAN, CHRIS
RW, DEVILS

PERSONAL: Born November 29, 1971, in Roseau, Minn. . . . 6-2/190. . . . Shoots right.
HIGH SCHOOL: Roseau (Minn.).
COLLEGE: North Dakota.
TRANSACTIONS/CAREER NOTES: Underwent surgery to knee cartilage (February 1988). . . . Selected by New Jersey Devils in second round (third Devils pick, 29th overall) of NHL entry draft (June 16, 1990). . . . Broke right wrist (December 1990).

Season	Team	League	Gms.	G	A	Pts.	PIM	Gms.	G	A	Pts.	PIM
88-89—Roseau H.S.		Minn. H.S.	25	13	18	31	...	—	—	—	—	—
89-90—Roseau H.S.		Minn. H.S.	28	34	31	65	...	—	—	—	—	—
90-91—Univ. of North Dakota		WCHA	40	11	8	19	26	—	—	—	—	—
91-92—Univ. of North Dakota		WCHA	38	9	6	15	47	—	—	—	—	—

G

Season Team	League	REGULAR SEASON					PLAYOFFS				
		Gms.	G	A	Pts.	Pen.	Gms.	G	A	Pts.	Pen.
92-93—Univ. of North Dakota	WCHA	35	10	10	20	50	—	—	—	—	—
93-94—Univ. of North Dakota	WCHA	33	8	4	12	29	—	—	—	—	—
—Albany	AHL	3	1	1	2	0	—	—	—	—	—

GOULET, MICHEL
LW, BLACKHAWKS

PERSONAL: Born April 21, 1960, in Peribonqua, Que. ... 6-1/195. ... Shoots left. ... Name pronounced goo-LAY.

TRANSACTIONS/CAREER NOTES: Signed as underage junior by Birmingham Bulls (July 1978). ... Selected by Quebec Nordiques in first round (first Nordiques pick, 20th overall) of NHL entry draft (August 9, 1979). ... Fractured thumb (January 2, 1985). ... Suspended by Nordiques after leaving training camp to renegotiate contract (September 1985). ... Broke finger on right hand (October 13, 1986). ... Strained ligaments in left knee (October 6, 1988). ... Underwent surgery to finger (May 1989). ... Sprained right ankle (October 28, 1989); missed nine games. ... Traded by Nordiques with G Greg Millen and sixth-round pick in 1991 draft (LW Kevin St. Jacques) to Chicago Blackhawks for LW Everett Sanipass, LW Dan Vincelette and D Mario Doyon (March 5, 1990). ... Bruised ribs and stretched rib cartilage (March 11, 1990). ... Bruised right ankle (November 1990). ... Sprained right knee (March 30, 1991); missed playoffs. ... Pulled groin (March 31, 1992). ... Pulled groin (December 8, 1992); missed nine games. ... Suffered from back spasms (1993-94 season); missed four games. ... Suffered concussion (March 16, 1994).

HONORS: Named to QMJHL All-Star second team (1977-78). ... Named to THE SPORTING NEWS All-Star second team (1982-83 and 1987-88). ... Named to NHL All-Star second team (1982-83 and 1987-88). ... Named to THE SPORTING NEWS All-Star first team (1983-84 through 1986-87). ... Named to NHL All-Star first team (1983-84, 1985-86, and 1986-87). ... Played in NHL All-Star Game (1983-1986 and 1988).

Season Team	League	REGULAR SEASON					PLAYOFFS				
		Gms.	G	A	Pts.	PIM	Gms.	G	A	Pts.	PIM
76-77—Quebec	QMJHL	37	17	18	35	9	14	3	8	11	19
77-78—Quebec	QMJHL	72	73	62	135	109	1	0	1	1	0
78-79—Birmingham	WHA	78	28	30	58	64	—	—	—	—	—
79-80—Quebec	NHL	77	22	32	54	48	—	—	—	—	—
80-81—Quebec	NHL	76	32	39	71	45	4	3	4	7	7
81-82—Quebec	NHL	80	42	42	84	48	16	8	5	13	6
82-83—Quebec	NHL	80	57	48	105	51	4	0	0	0	6
83-84—Quebec	NHL	75	56	65	121	76	9	2	4	6	17
84-85—Quebec	NHL	69	55	40	95	55	17	11	10	21	17
85-86—Quebec	NHL	75	53	50	103	64	3	1	2	3	10
86-87—Quebec	NHL	75	49	47	96	61	13	9	5	14	35
87-88—Quebec	NHL	80	48	58	106	56	—	—	—	—	—
88-89—Quebec	NHL	69	26	38	64	67	—	—	—	—	—
89-90—Quebec	NHL	57	16	29	45	42	—	—	—	—	—
—Chicago	NHL	8	4	1	5	9	14	4	2	6	6
90-91—Chicago	NHL	74	27	38	65	65	—	—	—	—	—
91-92—Chicago	NHL	75	22	41	63	69	9	3	4	7	6
92-93—Chicago	NHL	63	23	21	44	43	3	0	1	1	0
93-94—Chicago	NHL	56	16	14	30	26	—	—	—	—	—
WHA totals..		78	28	30	58	64					
NHL totals..		1125	803	1655	2458	467	180	110	236	346	64

GOVEDARIS, CHRIS
LW, MAPLE LEAFS

PERSONAL: Born February 2, 1970, in Toronto. ... 6-0/200. ... Shoots left. ... Name pronounced goh-vih-DAIR-ihz.

TRANSACTIONS/CAREER NOTES: Suspended two games by OHL (October 1986). ... Selected by Hartford Whalers in first round (first Whalers pick, 11th overall) of NHL entry draft (June 11, 1988). ... Suspended 15 games by OHL for shattering stick across another player's hip (January 22, 1989). ... Bruised right leg (January 23, 1991); missed five games. ... Suspended by Whalers for failure to report to AHL game (October 31, 1991); reinstated (January 3, 1992). ... Signed as free agent by Toronto Maple Leafs (September 7, 1993).

Season Team	League	REGULAR SEASON					PLAYOFFS				
		Gms.	G	A	Pts.	PIM	Gms.	G	A	Pts.	PIM
85-86—Toronto Young Nationals .	MTHL	38	35	50	85	...	—	—	—	—	—
86-87—Toronto............................	OHL	64	36	28	64	148	—	—	—	—	—
87-88—Toronto............................	OHL	62	42	38	80	118	4	2	1	3	10
88-89—Toronto............................	OHL	49	41	38	79	117	6	2	3	5	0
89-90—Hartford............................	NHL	12	0	1	1	6	2	0	0	0	2
—Binghamton	AHL	14	3	3	6	4	—	—	—	—	—
—Dukes of Hamilton	OHL	23	11	21	32	53	—	—	—	—	—
90-91—Hartford............................	NHL	14	1	3	4	4	—	—	—	—	—
—Springfield........................	AHL	56	26	36	62	133	9	2	5	7	36
91-92—Springfield........................	AHL	43	14	25	39	55	11	3	2	5	25
92-93—Springfield........................	AHL	65	31	24	55	58	15	7	4	11	18
—Hartford............................	NHL	7	1	0	1	0	—	—	—	—	—
93-94—St. John's	AHL	62	35	35	70	76	11	6	5	11	22
—Toronto............................	NHL	12	2	2	4	14	2	0	0	0	0
NHL totals..		45	4	6	10	24	4	0	0	0	2

GOVERDE, DAVID
G, KINGS

PERSONAL: Born April 9, 1970, in Toronto. ... 6-0/210. ... Catches right. ... Name pronounced goh-VUHR-dee.

TRANSACTIONS/CAREER NOTES: Selected by Los Angeles Kings in fifth round (fifth Kings pick, 91st overall) of NHL entry draft (June 16, 1990).

Season	Team	League	Gms.	Min.	W	L	T	GA	SO	Avg.	Gms.	Min.	W	L	GA	SO	Avg.
87-88—Windsor	OHL	10	471	...	...	...	28	0	3.57	—	—	—	—	—	—	—
88-89—Windsor	OHL	5	221	...	...	...	24	0	6.52	—	—	—	—	—	—	—
—Sudbury	OHL	39	2189	...	...	...	156	0	4.28	—	—	—	—	—	—	—
89-90—Sudbury	OHL	52	2941	28	12	7	182	0	3.71	7	394	3	3	25	0	3.81
90-91—Phoenix	IHL	40	2007	11	19	‡5	137	1	4.10	—	—	—	—	—	—	—
91-92—Phoenix	IHL	35	1951	11	19	‡3	129	1	3.97	—	—	—	—	—	—	—
—Los Angeles	NHL	2	120	1	1	0	9	0	4.50	—	—	—	—	—	—	—
—New Haven	AHL	5	248	1	3	0	17	0	4.11	—	—	—	—	—	—	—
92-93—Phoenix	IHL	46	2569	18	21	‡0	173	1	4.04	—	—	—	—	—	—	—
—Los Angeles	NHL	2	98	0	2	0	13	0	7.96	—	—	—	—	—	—	—
93-94—Los Angeles	NHL	1	60	0	1	0	7	0	7.00	—	—	—	—	—	—	—
—Portland	AHL	1	60	0	1	0	4	0	4.00	—	—	—	—	—	—	—
—Phoenix	IHL	30	1716	15	13	‡1	93	2	3.25	—	—	—	—	—	—	—
—Peoria	IHL	5	299	4	1	‡0	13	0	2.61	1	59	0	1	7	0	7.12
NHL totals		5	278	1	4	0	29	0	6.26							

GRAHAM, DIRK
LW/RW, BLACKHAWKS

PERSONAL: Born July 29, 1959, in Regina, Sask. . . . 5-11/198. . . . Shoots right. . . . Full name: Dirk Milton Graham.

TRANSACTIONS/CAREER NOTES: Selected by Vancouver Canucks in fifth round (fifth Canucks pick, 89th overall) of NHL entry draft (August 9, 1979). . . . Signed as free agent by Minnesota North Stars (August 17, 1983). . . . Sprained wrist (November 1987); missed seven games. . . . Traded by North Stars to Chicago Blackhawks for LW Curt Fraser (January 4, 1988). . . . Fined $500 by NHL for fighting (December 28, 1989). . . . Fractured left kneecap (March 17, 1990); missed six weeks. . . . Underwent surgery to left knee (May 1990). . . . Separated shoulder (February 18, 1994); missed 17 games.

HONORS: Named to WHL All-Star second team (1978-79). . . . Named to IHL All-Star second team (1980-81). . . . Named to IHL All-Star first team (1982-83). . . . Named to CHL All-Star first team (1983-84). . . . Won Frank J. Selke Trophy (1990-91).

Season	Team	League	Gms.	G	A	Pts.	PIM	Gms.	G	A	Pts.	PIM
75-76—Regina Blues	SJHL	54	36	32	68	82	—	—	—	—	—
—Regina	WCHL	2	0	0	0	0	6	1	1	2	5
76-77—Regina	WCHL	65	37	28	65	66	—	—	—	—	—
77-78—Regina	WCHL	72	49	61	110	87	13	15	19	34	37
78-79—Regina	WHL	71	48	60	108	252	—	—	—	—	—
79-80—Dallas	CHL	62	17	15	32	96	—	—	—	—	—
80-81—Fort Wayne	IHL	6	1	2	3	12	—	—	—	—	—
—Toledo	IHL	61	40	45	85	88	—	—	—	—	—
81-82—Toledo	IHL	72	49	56	105	68	13	10	11	21	8
82-83—Toledo	IHL	78	70	55	125	86	11	13	7	†20	30
83-84—Minnesota	NHL	6	1	1	2	0	1	0	0	0	2
—Salt Lake City	CHL	57	37	57	94	72	5	3	8	11	2
84-85—Springfield	AHL	37	20	28	48	41	—	—	—	—	—
—Minnesota	NHL	36	12	11	23	23	9	0	4	4	7
85-86—Minnesota	NHL	80	22	33	55	87	5	3	1	4	2
86-87—Minnesota	NHL	76	25	29	54	142	—	—	—	—	—
87-88—Minnesota	NHL	28	7	5	12	39	—	—	—	—	—
—Chicago	NHL	42	17	19	36	32	4	1	2	3	4
88-89—Chicago	NHL	80	33	45	78	89	16	2	4	6	38
89-90—Chicago	NHL	73	22	32	54	102	5	1	5	6	2
90-91—Chicago	NHL	80	24	21	45	88	6	1	2	3	17
91-92—Chicago	NHL	80	17	30	47	89	18	7	5	12	8
92-93—Chicago	NHL	84	20	17	37	139	4	0	0	0	0
93-94—Chicago	NHL	67	15	18	33	45	6	0	1	1	4
NHL totals		732	215	261	476	875	74	15	24	39	84

GRANATO, TONY
RW, KINGS

PERSONAL: Born July 25, 1964, in Downers Grove, Ill. . . . 5-10/185. . . . Shoots right. . . . Full name: Anthony Lewis Granato.

HIGH SCHOOL: Northwood School (Lake Placid, N.Y.).

COLLEGE: Wisconsin.

TRANSACTIONS/CAREER NOTES: Selected by New York Rangers in sixth round (fifth Rangers pick, 120th overall) of NHL entry draft (June 9, 1982). . . . Bruised foot (February 1989). . . . Traded by Rangers with RW Tomas Sandstrom to Los Angeles Kings for C Bernie Nicholls (January 20, 1990). . . . Pulled groin (January 25, 1990); missed 12 games. . . . Injured knee (March 20, 1990). . . . Tore rib cartilage (December 18, 1990); missed 10 games. . . . Strained back (October 6, 1992); missed three games. . . . Strained back (December 4, 1993); missed one game. . . . Strained lower back (December 13, 1993); missed nine games. . . . Suspended 15 games without pay and fined $500 by NHL for slashing incident (February 16, 1994). . . . Strained back (April 3, 1994); missed remainder of season.

HONORS: Named to NCAA All-America West second team (1984-85 and 1986-87). . . . Named to WCHA All-Star second team (1986-87). . . . Named to NHL All-Rookie team (1988-89).

Season	Team	League	Gms.	G	A	Pts.	PIM	Gms.	G	A	Pts.	PIM
81-82—Northwood School	N.Y. H.S.				Statistics unavailable.						
82-83—Northwood School	N.Y. H.S.				Statistics unavailable.						
83-84—University of Wisconsin	WCHA	35	14	17	31	48	—	—	—	—	—

Season Team	League	REGULAR SEASON					PLAYOFFS				
		Gms.	G	A	Pts.	Pen.	Gms.	G	A	Pts.	Pen.
84-85—University of Wisconsin ...	WCHA	42	33	34	67	94	—	—	—	—	—
85-86—University of Wisconsin ...	WCHA	32	25	24	49	36	—	—	—	—	—
86-87—University of Wisconsin ...	WCHA	42	28	45	73	64	—	—	—	—	—
87-88—U.S. national team	Int'l	49	40	31	71	55	—	—	—	—	—
—U.S. Olympic Team	Int'l	6	1	7	8	4	—	—	—	—	—
—Denver	IHL	22	13	14	27	36	8	9	4	13	16
88-89—New York Rangers	NHL	78	36	27	63	140	4	1	1	2	21
89-90—New York Rangers	NHL	37	7	18	25	77	—	—	—	—	—
—Los Angeles......................	NHL	19	5	6	11	45	10	5	4	9	12
90-91—Los Angeles......................	NHL	68	30	34	64	154	12	1	4	5	28
91-92—Los Angeles......................	NHL	80	39	29	68	187	6	1	5	6	10
92-93—Los Angeles......................	NHL	81	37	45	82	171	24	6	11	17	50
93-94—Los Angeles......................	NHL	50	7	14	21	150	—	—	—	—	—
NHL totals...............		413	161	173	334	924	56	14	25	39	121

GRANT, KEVIN
D, KINGS

PERSONAL: Born January 9, 1969, in Toronto.... 6-3/210.... Shoots right.
TRANSACTIONS/CAREER NOTES: Injured knee ligaments (February 1, 1987).... Selected by Calgary Flames as underage junior in second round (third Flames pick, 40th overall) of NHL entry draft (June 13, 1987).... Traded by Kitchener Rangers with C Sean Stansfield and fourth-round pick in 1989 draft (traded to Sault Ste. Marie Greyhounds) and fourth-round pick in 1990 draft to Sudbury Wolves for RW Pierre Gagnon, D John Uniac and seventh-round pick (Jamie Israel) in 1989 draft (November 1988).... Traded by Salt Lake City Golden Eagles to Phoenix Roadrunners for D Paul Holden (October 16, 1992).

Season Team	League	REGULAR SEASON					PLAYOFFS				
		Gms.	G	A	Pts.	PIM	Gms.	G	A	Pts.	PIM
85-86—Kitchener........................	OHL	63	2	15	17	204	5	0	1	1	11
86-87—Kitchener........................	OHL	52	5	18	23	125	4	0	1	1	16
87-88—Kitchener........................	OHL	48	3	20	23	138	4	0	1	1	4
88-89—Sudbury........................	OHL	60	9	41	50	186	—	—	—	—	—
—Salt Lake City..................	IHL	3	0	1	1	5	3	0	0	0	12
89-90—Salt Lake City..................	IHL	78	7	17	24	117	11	0	2	2	22
90-91—Salt Lake City..................	IHL	63	6	19	25	200	3	0	0	0	8
91-92—Salt Lake City..................	IHL	73	7	16	23	181	—	—	—	—	—
92-93—Salt Lake City..................	IHL	1	0	0	0	2	—	—	—	—	—
—Phoenix	IHL	49	4	17	21	119	—	—	—	—	—
—Cincinnati	IHL	2	0	0	0	2	—	—	—	—	—
93-94—Phoenix	IHL	33	0	3	3	110	—	—	—	—	—
—San Diego....................	IHL	5	0	0	0	18	—	—	—	—	—
—Milwaukee...................	IHL	16	3	6	9	64	4	0	4	4	20

GRATTON, CHRIS
C, LIGHTNING

PERSONAL: Born July 5, 1975, in Brantford, Ont.... 6-3/202.... Shoots left.
HIGH SCHOOL: Loyalist Collegiate (Brantford, Ont.).
TRANSACTIONS/CAREER NOTES: Selected by Tampa Bay Lightning in first round (first Lightning pick, third overall) of NHL entry draft (June 26, 1993).
HONORS: Won Emms Family Award (1991-92).... Named to OHL Rookie All-Star team (1991-92).... Won OHL Top Draft Prospect Award (1992-93).

Season Team	League	REGULAR SEASON					PLAYOFFS				
		Gms.	G	A	Pts.	PIM	Gms.	G	A	Pts.	PIM
90-91—Brantford Jr. B	OHA	31	30	30	60	28	—	—	—	—	—
91-92—Kingston	OHL	62	27	39	66	35	—	—	—	—	—
92-93—Kingston	OHL	58	55	54	109	125	16	11	18	29	42
93-94—Tampa Bay	NHL	84	13	29	42	123	—	—	—	—	—
NHL totals................		84	13	29	42	123					

GRAVES, ADAM
LW, RANGERS

PERSONAL: Born April 12, 1968, in Toronto.... 6-0/207.... Shoots left.
TRANSACTIONS/CAREER NOTES: Bruised shoulder (February 1986).... Selected by Detroit Red Wings as underage junior in second round (second Red Wings pick, 22nd overall) of NHL entry draft (June 21, 1986).... Traded by Red Wings with C/RW Joe Murphy, LW Petr Klima and D Jeff Sharples to Edmonton Oilers for C Jimmy Carson, C Kevin McClelland and fifth-round pick (later traded to Montreal Canadiens who selected D Brad Layzell) in 1991 draft (November 2, 1989).... Signed as free agent by New York Rangers (September 2, 1991); Oilers received C/LW Troy Mallette as compensation (September 9, 1991).
HONORS: Won King Clancy Memorial Trophy (1993-94).... Named to THE SPORTING NEWS All-Star first team (1993-94).... Named to NHL All-Star second team (1993-94).... Played in NHL All-Star Game (1994).
MISCELLANEOUS: Member of Stanley Cup championship teams (1990 and 1994).

Season Team	League	REGULAR SEASON					PLAYOFFS				
		Gms.	G	A	Pts.	PIM	Gms.	G	A	Pts.	PIM
84-85—King City Jr. B	OHA	25	23	33	56	29	—	—	—	—	—
85-86—Windsor	OHL	62	27	37	64	35	16	5	11	16	10
86-87—Windsor	OHL	66	45	55	100	70	14	9	8	17	32
—Adirondack	AHL	—	—	—	—	—	5	0	1	1	0
87-88—Detroit	NHL	9	0	1	1	8	—	—	—	—	—
—Windsor	OHL	37	28	†32	60	107	12	14	18	32	16

G

Season Team	League	REGULAR SEASON					PLAYOFFS				
		Gms.	G	A	Pts.	Pen.	Gms.	G	A	Pts.	Pen.
88-89—Detroit	NHL	56	7	5	12	60	5	0	0	0	4
—Adirondack	AHL	14	10	11	21	28	14	11	7	18	17
89-90—Detroit	NHL	13	0	1	1	13	—	—	—	—	—
—Edmonton	NHL	63	9	12	21	123	22	5	6	11	17
90-91—Edmonton	NHL	76	7	18	25	127	18	2	4	6	22
91-92—New York Rangers	NHL	80	26	33	59	139	10	5	3	8	22
92-93—New York Rangers	NHL	84	36	29	65	148	—	—	—	—	—
93-94—New York Rangers	NHL	84	52	27	79	127	23	10	7	17	24
NHL totals		465	137	126	263	745	78	22	20	42	89

GREEN, TRAVIS
C, ISLANDERS

PERSONAL: Born December 20, 1970, in Creston, B.C. . . . 6-0/195. . . . Shoots right.
TRANSACTIONS/CAREER NOTES: Selected by New York Islanders in second round (second Islanders pick, 23rd overall) of NHL entry draft (June 17, 1989). . . . Traded by Spokane Chiefs to Medicine Hat Tigers for RW Mark Woolf, D/LW Chris Lafreniere and C Frank Esposito (January 26, 1990).

Season Team	League	REGULAR SEASON					PLAYOFFS				
		Gms.	G	A	Pts.	PIM	Gms.	G	A	Pts.	PIM
85-86—Castlegar	KIJHL	35	30	40	70	41	—	—	—	—	—
86-87—Spokane	WHL	64	8	17	25	27	3	0	0	0	0
87-88—Spokane	WHL	72	33	53	86	42	15	10	10	20	13
88-89—Spokane	WHL	72	51	51	102	79	—	—	—	—	—
89-90—Spokane	WHL	50	45	44	89	80	—	—	—	—	—
—Medicine Hat	WHL	25	15	24	39	19	3	0	0	0	2
90-91—Capital District	AHL	73	21	34	55	26	—	—	—	—	—
91-92—Capital District	AHL	71	23	27	50	10	7	0	4	4	21
92-93—Capital District	AHL	20	12	11	23	39	—	—	—	—	—
—New York Islanders	NHL	61	7	18	25	43	12	3	1	4	6
93-94—New York Islanders	NHL	83	18	22	40	44	4	0	0	0	2
NHL totals		144	25	40	65	87	16	3	1	4	8

GREENLAW, JEFF
RW, PANTHERS

PERSONAL: Born February 28, 1968, in Toronto. . . . 6-1/230. . . . Shoots left. . . . Full name: Jeff Carl Greenlaw.
TRANSACTIONS/CAREER NOTES: Selected by Washington Capitals in first round (first Capitals pick, 19th overall) of NHL entry draft (June 21, 1986). . . . Suffered stress fracture of vertebrae (April 1987). . . . Suffered deep bruise in right leg (September 1989); missed 65 games. . . . Signed as free agent by Florida Panthers (July 14, 1993).

Season Team	League	REGULAR SEASON					PLAYOFFS				
		Gms.	G	A	Pts.	PIM	Gms.	G	A	Pts.	PIM
84-85—St. Catharines Jr. B	OHA	33	21	29	50	141	—	—	—	—	—
85-86—Canadian national team	Int'l	57	3	16	19	81	—	—	—	—	—
86-87—Washington	NHL	22	0	3	3	44	—	—	—	—	—
—Binghamton	AHL	4	0	2	2	0	—	—	—	—	—
87-88—Binghamton	AHL	56	8	7	15	142	1	0	0	0	2
—Washington	NHL	—	—	—	—	—	1	0	0	0	19
88-89—Baltimore	AHL	55	12	15	27	115	—	—	—	—	—
89-90—Baltimore	AHL	10	3	2	5	26	7	1	0	1	13
90-91—Baltimore	AHL	50	17	17	34	93	3	1	1	2	2
—Washington	NHL	10	2	0	2	10	1	0	0	0	2
91-92—Baltimore	AHL	37	6	8	14	57	—	—	—	—	—
—Washington	NHL	5	0	1	1	34	—	—	—	—	—
92-93—Baltimore	AHL	49	12	14	26	66	7	3	1	4	0
—Washington	NHL	16	1	1	2	18	—	—	—	—	—
93-94—Cincinnati	IHL	55	14	15	29	85	11	2	2	4	28
—Florida	NHL	4	0	1	1	2	—	—	—	—	—
NHL totals		57	3	6	9	108	2	0	0	0	21

G

GREENLAY, MIKE
G, LIGHTNING

PERSONAL: Born September 15, 1968, in Calgary. . . . 6-3/210. . . . Catches left. . . . Full name: Michael Ronald Greenlay.
COLLEGE: Lake Superior State (Mich.).
TRANSACTIONS/CAREER NOTES: Selected by Edmonton Oilers in ninth round (ninth Oilers pick, 189th overall) of NHL entry draft (June 21, 1986). . . . Loaned to Knoxville Cherokees (December 2, 1991); returned (January 6, 1992). . . . Loaned to Knoxville Cherokees (January 1992); returned (February 13, 1992). . . . Signed as free agent by Tampa Bay Lightning (July 29, 1992).
HONORS: Named to Memorial Cup All-Star team (1988-89). . . . Shared James Norris Memorial Trophy with Jean-Claude Bergeron (1993-94).

Season Team	League	REGULAR SEASON								PLAYOFFS					
		Gms.	Min.	W	L	T	GA	SO	Avg.	Gms.	Min.	W	L	GA	SO	Avg.
86-87—Lake Superior State	CCHA	17	744	7	5	0	44	0	3.55	—	—	—	—	—	—	—
87-88—Lake Superior State	CCHA	19	1023	10	3	3	57	0	3.34	—	—	—	—	—	—	—
88-89—Lake Superior State	CCHA	2	85	1	1	0	6	0	4.24	—	—	—	—	—	—	—
—Saskatoon	WHL	20	1128	10	8	1	86	0	4.57	6	174	2	0	16	0	5.52

Season	Team	League	REGULAR SEASON								PLAYOFFS						
			Gms.	Min.	W	L	T	GA	SO	Avg.	Gms.	Min.	W	L	GA	SO	Avg.
89-90—Cape Breton		AHL	46	2595	19	18	5	146	2	3.38	5	306	1	3	26	0	5.10
—Edmonton		NHL	2	20	0	0	0	4	0	12.00	—	—	—	—	—	—	—
90-91—Knoxville		ECHL	29	1725	17	9	‡2	108	2	3.76	—	—	—	—	—	—	—
—Cape Breton		AHL	11	493	5	2	0	33	0	4.02	—	—	—	—	—	—	—
91-92—Cape Breton		AHL	3	144	1	1	1	12	0	5.00	—	—	—	—	—	—	—
—Knoxville		ECHL	27	1415	8	12	‡2	113	1	4.79	—	—	—	—	—	—	—
92-93—Louisville		ECHL	27	1437	12	11	‡2	96	1	4.01	—	—	—	—	—	—	—
—Atlanta		IHL	12	637	5	3	‡2	40	0	3.77	—	—	—	—	—	—	—
93-94—Atlanta		IHL	34	1741	16	10	‡4	104	0	3.58	13	749	*11	1	29	†1	*2.32
NHL totals			2	20	0	0	0	4	0	12.00							

GREIG, MARK
RW, MAPLE LEAFS

PERSONAL: Born January 25, 1970, in High River, Alta. . . . 5-11/190. . . . Shoots right. . . . Name pronounced GRAYG.

TRANSACTIONS/CAREER NOTES: Selected by Hartford Whalers in first round (first Whalers pick, 15th overall) of NHL entry draft (June 16, 1990). . . . Injured right knee (April 11, 1993); missed final three games of regular season. . . . Traded by Whalers with sixth-round pick in 1995 draft to Toronto Maple Leafs for D Ted Crowley (January 25, 1994). . . . Suffered hip flexor strain (February 21, 1994); missed one game.

HONORS: Named to WHL (East) All-Star first team (1989-90).

Season	Team	League	REGULAR SEASON					PLAYOFFS				
			Gms.	G	A	Pts.	PIM	Gms.	G	A	Pts.	PIM
86-87—Calgary		WHL	5	0	0	0	0	—	—	—	—	—
87-88—Lethbridge		WHL	65	9	18	27	38	—	—	—	—	—
88-89—Lethbridge		WHL	71	36	72	108	113	8	5	5	10	16
89-90—Lethbridge		WHL	65	55	80	135	149	18	11	21	32	35
90-91—Hartford		NHL	4	0	0	0	0	—	—	—	—	—
—Springfield		AHL	73	32	55	87	73	17	2	6	8	22
91-92—Hartford		NHL	17	0	5	5	6	—	—	—	—	—
—Springfield		AHL	50	20	27	47	38	9	1	1	2	20
92-93—Hartford		NHL	22	1	7	8	27	—	—	—	—	—
—Springfield		AHL	55	20	38	58	86	—	—	—	—	—
93-94—Hartford		NHL	31	4	5	9	31	—	—	—	—	—
—Springfield		AHL	4	0	4	4	21	—	—	—	—	—
—Toronto		NHL	13	2	2	4	10	—	—	—	—	—
—St. John's		AHL	9	4	6	10	0	11	4	2	6	26
NHL totals			87	7	19	26	74					

GRETZKY, BRENT
C, LIGHTNING

PERSONAL: Born February 20, 1972, in Brantford, Ont. . . . 5-10/160. . . . Shoots left. . . . Brother of Wayne Gretzky, center, Los Angeles Kings.

HIGH SCHOOL: Quinte Secondary School (Belleville, Ont.).

TRANSACTIONS/CAREER NOTES: Selected by Tampa Bay Lightning in third round (third Lightning pick, 49th overall) of NHL entry draft (June 20, 1992).

Season	Team	League	REGULAR SEASON					PLAYOFFS				
			Gms.	G	A	Pts.	PIM	Gms.	G	A	Pts.	PIM
87-88—Brantford Jr. B		OHA	14	4	11	15	2	—	—	—	—	—
88-89—Brantford Jr. B		OHA	40	29	47	76	57	—	—	—	—	—
89-90—Belleville		OHL	40	29	47	76	57	11	0	0	0	2
90-91—Belleville		OHL	66	26	56	82	25	6	3	3	6	2
91-92—Belleville		OHL	62	43	78	121	37	—	—	—	—	—
92-93—Atlanta		IHL	77	20	34	54	84	9	3	2	5	8
93-94—Atlanta		IHL	54	17	23	40	30	14	1	1	2	4
—Tampa Bay		NHL	10	1	2	3	2	—	—	—	—	—
NHL totals			10	1	2	3	2					

GRETZKY, WAYNE
C, KINGS

PERSONAL: Born January 26, 1961, in Brantford, Ont. . . . 6-0/170. . . . Shoots left. . . . Full name: Wayne Douglas Gretzky. . . . Brother of Brent Gretzky, center in Tampa Bay Lightning system.

TRANSACTIONS/CAREER NOTES: Signed as underage junior by Indianapolis Racers to multi-year contract (May 1978). . . . Traded by Racers with LW Peter Driscoll and G Ed Mio to Edmonton Oilers for cash and future considerations (November 1978). . . . Bruised right shoulder (January 28, 1984). . . . Underwent surgery on left ankle to remove benign growth (June 1984). . . . Twisted right knee (December 30, 1987). . . . Suffered corneal abrasion to left eye (February 19, 1988); missed three games. . . . Traded by Oilers with RW/D Marty McSorley and LW/C Mike Krushelnyski to Los Angeles Kings for C Jimmy Carson, LW Martin Gelinas, first-round picks in 1989 (traded to New Jersey), 1991 (LW Martin Rucinsky) and 1993 (D Nick Stajduhar) drafts and cash (August 9, 1988). . . . Injured groin (March 17, 1990). . . . Strained lower back (March 22, 1990); missed five regular-season games and two playoff games. . . . Missed five games due to personal reasons (October 1991). . . . Sprained knee (February 25, 1992); missed one game. . . . Suffered herniated thoracic disc; missed first 39 games of 1992-93 season. . . . Sprained left knee (April 9, 1994).

HONORS: Won William Hanley Trophy (1977-78). . . . Won Emms Family Award (1977-78). . . . Named to OMJHL All-Star second team (1977-78). . . . Named WHA Rookie of the Year by THE SPORTING NEWS (1978-79). . . . Won WHA Rookie of the Year Award (1978-79). . . . Named to WHA All-Star second team (1978-79). . . . Won Hart Memorial Trophy (1979-80 through 1986-87 and 1988-89). . . . Won Lady Byng Memorial Trophy (1979-80, 1990-91, 1991-92 and 1993-94). . . . Named to THE SPORTING NEWS All-Star second team (1979-80, 1987-88, 1988-89, 1991-92 and 1993-94). . . . Named to NHL All-

Star second team (1979-80, 1987-88 through 1989-90 and 1993-94).... Named NHL Player of Year by THE SPORTING NEWS (1980-81 through 1986-87).... Won Art Ross Memorial Trophy (1980-81 through 1986-87, 1989-90, 1990-91 and 1993-94).... Named to THE SPORTING NEWS All-Star first team (1980-81 through 1986-87 and 1990-91) ... Named to NHL All-Star first team (1980-81 through 1986-87 and 1990-91).... Played in NHL All-Star Game (1980-1986 and 1988-1994).... Named Man of the Year by THE SPORTING NEWS (1981).... Won Lester B. Pearson Award (1981-82 through 1984-85 and 1986-87).... Won Emery Edge Award (1983-84, 1984-85 and 1986-87).... Named All-Star Game Most Valuable Player (1983 and 1989).... Named Canadian Athlete of the Year (1985).... Won Conn Smythe Trophy (1984-85 and 1987-88).... Won Dodge Performer of the Year Award (1984-85 through 1986-87).... Won Dodge Performance of the Year Award (1988-89).... Won Lester Patrick Trophy (1993-94).

RECORDS: Holds NHL career records for points—2,458; goals—803; assists—1,655; overtime assists—11; points by a center—2,458; goals by a center—803; assists by a center—1,655; most points including playoffs—2,804; most goals including playoffs—913; most assists including playoffs—1,891; most games with three or more goals—48; most 40-or-more goal seasons—12; most consecutive 40-or-more goal seasons—12 (1979-80 through 1990-91); most 60-or-more goal seasons—5; most consecutive 60-or-more goal seasons—4 (1981-82 through 1984-85); most 100-or-more point seasons—14; most consecutive 100-or-more point seasons—13 (1979-80 through 1991-92); highest assist-per-game average—1.471; and highest points-per-game average—2.185.... Shares NHL career records for most 50-or-more goal seasons—9; and most 60-or-more goal seasons—5.... Holds NHL single-season records for most goals—92 (1981-82); assists—163 (1985-86); points—215 (1985-86); games with three or more goals—10 (1981-82 and 1983-84); highest goals-per-game average—1.18 (1983-84); highest assists-per-game average—2.04 (1985-86); and highest points-per-game average—2.77 (1983-84); most points including playoffs—255 (1984-85); most goals including playoffs—100 (1983-84); most assists including playoffs—174 (1985-86); most points by a center—215 (1985-86); most goals by a center—92 (1981-82); most assists by a center—163 (1985-86); most goals, 50 games from start of season—61 (1981-82 and 1983-84).... Shares NHL single-game records for most assists—7 (February 15, 1980; December 11, 1985; and February 14, 1986); most assists for road game—7 (December 11, 1985); most goals in one period—4 (February 18, 1981).... Holds NHL records for most consecutive games scoring points—51 (October 5, 1983 through January 28, 1984); longest point-scoring streak from start of season—51 (1983-84); and most consecutive games with an assist—23 (1990-91); most assists in game by rookie—7 (February 15, 1980).... Holds NHL career playoff records for most points—346; most goals—110; most assists—236; and most games with three-or-more goals—8. ... Shares NHL career playoff record for most game-winning goals—21. ... Holds NHL single-season playoff records for most assists—31 (1988); and most points—47 (1985). ... Shares NHL single-season playoff record for most shorthanded goals—3 (1983).... Holds NHL final-series playoff records for most assists—10 (1988); and most points—13 (1988).... Shares NHL single-series playoff record for most assists—14 (1985).... Shares NHL single-game playoff records for most assists—6 (April 9, 1987); most shorthanded goals—2 (April 6, 1983); most assists in one period—3 (done five times); and most points in one period—4 (April 12, 1987).... Holds NHL career All-Star Game record for most goals—12.... Holds NHL All-Star Game records for most goals in one period—4 (1983); and most points in one period—4 (1983).... Shares NHL All-Star Game record for most goals—4 (February 8, 1983).

MISCELLANEOUS: Member of Stanley Cup championship teams (1984, 1985, 1987 and 1988).

			REGULAR SEASON					PLAYOFFS			
Season	Team	League	Gms.	G	A	Pts.	PIM	Gms.	G	A	Pts.	PIM
76-77—Peterborough		OMJHL	3	0	3	3	0	—	—	—	—	—
77-78—Sault Ste. Marie		OMJHL	64	70	112	182	14	13	6	20	26	0
78-79—Indianapolis		WHA	8	3	3	6	0	—	—	—	—	—
—Edmonton		WHA	72	43	61	104	19	13	†10	10	*20	2
79-80—Edmonton		NHL	79	51	*86	†137	21	3	2	1	3	0
80-81—Edmonton		NHL	80	55	*109	*164	28	9	7	14	21	4
81-82—Edmonton		NHL	80	*92	*120	*212	26	5	5	7	12	8
82-83—Edmonton		NHL	80	*71	*125	*196	59	16	12	*26	*38	4
83-84—Edmonton		NHL	74	*87	*118	*205	39	19	13	*22	*35	12
84-85—Edmonton		NHL	80	*73	*135	*208	52	18	17	*30	*47	4
85-86—Edmonton		NHL	80	52	*163	*215	46	10	8	11	19	2
86-87—Edmonton		NHL	79	*62	*121	*183	28	21	5	*29	*34	6
87-88—Edmonton		NHL	64	40	*109	149	24	19	12	*31	*43	16
88-89—Los Angeles		NHL	78	54	†114	168	26	11	5	17	22	0
89-90—Los Angeles		NHL	73	40	*102	*142	42	7	3	7	10	0
90-91—Los Angeles		NHL	78	41	*122	*163	16	12	4	11	15	2
91-92—Los Angeles		NHL	74	31	*90	121	34	6	2	5	7	2
92-93—Los Angeles		NHL	45	16	49	65	6	24	15	25	40	4
93-94—Los Angeles		NHL	81	38	*92	*130	20	—	—	—	—	—
WHA totals			80	46	64	110	19	13	10	10	20	2
NHL totals			1125	803	1655	2458	467	180	110	236	346	64

G

GRIEVE, BRENT
LW, BLACKHAWKS

PERSONAL: Born May 9, 1969, in Oshawa, Ont. ... 6-1/205. ... Shoots left. ... Name pronounced GREEV.

TRANSACTIONS/CAREER NOTES: Selected by New York Islanders in fourth round (fourth Islanders pick, 65th overall) of NHL entry draft (June 17, 1989).... Traded by Islanders to Edmonton Oilers for D Marc Laforge (December 15, 1993).... Signed as free agent by Chicago Blackhawks (July 7, 1994).

			REGULAR SEASON					PLAYOFFS			
Season	Team	League	Gms.	G	A	Pts.	PIM	Gms.	G	A	Pts.	PIM
86-87—Oshawa		OHL	60	9	19	28	102	24	3	8	11	22
87-88—Oshawa		OHL	56	19	20	39	122	7	0	1	1	8
88-89—Oshawa		OHL	49	34	33	67	105	6	4	3	7	4
89-90—Oshawa		OHL	62	46	47	93	125	17	10	10	20	26
90-91—Kansas City		IHL	5	2	2	4	2	—	—	—	—	—
—Capital District		AHL	61	14	13	27	80	—	—	—	—	—
91-92—Capital District		AHL	74	34	32	66	84	7	3	1	4	16
92-93—Capital District		AHL	79	34	28	62	122	4	1	1	2	10

Season	Team	League	Gms.	G	A	Pts.	Pen.	Gms.	G	A	Pts.	Pen.
93-94—Salt Lake City		IHL	22	9	5	14	30	—	—	—	—	—
—New York Islanders		NHL	3	0	0	0	7	—	—	—	—	—
—Cape Breton		AHL	20	10	11	21	14	4	2	4	6	16
—Edmonton		NHL	24	13	5	18	14	—	—	—	—	—
NHL totals			27	13	5	18	21					

GRIMES, JAKE
C, SENATORS

PERSONAL: Born September 13, 1972, in Montreal.... 6-1/196.... Shoots left.... Full name: Jake Stephen Grimes.

TRANSACTIONS/CAREER NOTES: Selected by Ottawa Senators in 10th round (10th Senators pick, 217th overall) of NHL entry draft (June 20, 1992).

				REGULAR SEASON					PLAYOFFS			
Season	Team	League	Gms.	G	A	Pts.	PIM	Gms.	G	A	Pts.	PIM
89-90—Belleville		OHA	66	9	12	21	11	—	—	—	—	—
90-91—Belleville		OHA	66	31	41	72	16	—	—	—	—	—
91-92—Belleville		OHA	66	44	69	113	18	—	—	—	—	—
92-93—New Haven		AHL	76	18	20	38	30	—	—	—	—	—
93-94—Thunder Bay		Col.HL	10	7	5	12	6	—	—	—	—	—
—Prince Edward Island		AHL	42	12	13	25	24	—	—	—	—	—

GRIMSON, STU
LW, MIGHTY DUCKS

PERSONAL: Born May 20, 1965, in Kamloops, B.C.... 6-5/227.... Shoots left.
COLLEGE: Manitoba.

TRANSACTIONS/CAREER NOTES: Fractured forearm (February 1983).... Selected by Detroit Red Wings in 10th round (11th Red Wings pick, 186th overall) of NHL entry draft (June 8, 1983).... Did not sign with Detroit and returned to entry draft pool (May 1985).... Selected by Calgary Flames in seventh round (eighth Flames pick, 143rd overall) of NHL entry draft (June 15, 1985).... Broke cheekbone (January 9, 1990).... Claimed on waivers by Chicago Blackhawks (October 1, 1990).... Injured eye (February 3, 1993).... Selected by Mighty Ducks of Anaheim in NHL expansion draft (June 24, 1993).... Lacerated hand (January 16, 1994); missed one game.... Lacerated hand (March 9, 1994); missed one game.... Lacerated hand (March 26, 1994); missed five games.

				REGULAR SEASON					PLAYOFFS			
Season	Team	League	Gms.	G	A	Pts.	PIM	Gms.	G	A	Pts.	PIM
82-83—Regina		WHL	48	0	1	1	144	5	0	0	0	14
83-84—Regina		WHL	63	8	8	16	131	21	0	1	1	29
84-85—Regina		WHL	71	24	32	56	248	8	1	2	3	14
85-86—University of Manitoba		CWUAA	12	7	4	11	113	3	1	1	2	20
86-87—University of Manitoba		CWUAA	29	8	8	16	67	14	4	2	6	28
87-88—Salt Lake City		IHL	38	9	5	14	268	—	—	—	—	—
88-89—Calgary		NHL	1	0	0	0	5	—	—	—	—	—
—Salt Lake City		IHL	72	9	18	27	*397	15	2	3	5	*86
89-90—Salt Lake City		IHL	62	8	8	16	319	4	0	0	0	8
—Calgary		NHL	3	0	0	0	17	—	—	—	—	—
90-91—Chicago		NHL	35	0	1	1	183	5	0	0	0	46
91-92—Chicago		NHL	54	2	2	4	234	14	0	1	1	10
—Indianapolis		IHL	5	1	1	2	17	—	—	—	—	—
92-93—Chicago		NHL	78	1	1	2	193	2	0	0	0	4
93-94—Anaheim		NHL	77	1	5	6	199	—	—	—	—	—
NHL totals			248	4	9	13	831	21	0	1	1	60

GROLEAU, FRANCOIS
D, FLAMES

PERSONAL: Born January 23, 1973, in Longueuil, Que.... 6-0/195.... Shoots left.... Name pronounced GROH-loh.

TRANSACTIONS/CAREER NOTES: Selected by Calgary Flames in second round (second Flames pick, 41st overall) of NHL entry draft (June 22, 1991).

HONORS: Won Raymond Lagace Trophy (1989-90).... Named to QMJHL All-Star second team (1989-90).... Won Emile (Butch) Bouchard Trophy (1991-92).... Named to QMJHL All-Star first team (1991-92).

				REGULAR SEASON					PLAYOFFS			
Season	Team	League	Gms.	G	A	Pts.	PIM	Gms.	G	A	Pts.	PIM
89-90—Shawinigan		QMJHL	60	11	54	65	80	6	0	1	1	12
90-91—Shawinigan		QMJHL	70	9	60	69	70	6	0	3	3	2
91-92—Shawinigan		QMJHL	65	8	70	78	74	10	5	15	20	8
92-93—St. Jean		QMJHL	48	7	38	45	66	4	0	1	1	14
93-94—Saint John		AHL	73	8	14	22	49	7	0	1	1	2

GRONMAN, TUOMAS
D, NORDIQUES

PERSONAL: Born March 22, 1974, in Vitasaari, Finland.... 6-2/193.... Shoots left.

TRANSACTIONS/CAREER NOTES: Selected by Quebec Nordiques in second round (third Nordiques pick, 29th overall) of NHL entry draft (June 20, 1992).

				REGULAR SEASON					PLAYOFFS			
Season	Team	League	Gms.	G	A	Pts.	PIM	Gms.	G	A	Pts.	PIM
90-91—Rauman Lukko		Finland	40	15	20	35	60	—	—	—	—	—
91-92—Tacoma		WHL	61	5	18	23	102	4	0	1	1	2

G

Season	Team	League	REGULAR SEASON					PLAYOFFS				
			Gms.	G	A	Pts.	Pen.	Gms.	G	A	Pts.	Pen.
	—Finland national Jr. team .	Int'l	7	1	0	1	10	—	—	—	—	—
92-93	—Rauman Lukko.................	Finland	45	2	11	13	46	—	—	—	—	—
93-94	—Lukko	Finland	44	4	12	16	40	9	0	1	1	14

GROSEK, MICHAL
LW, JETS

PERSONAL: Born June 1, 1975, in Gottwaldov, Czechoslovakia. . . . 6-2/ 183. . . . Shoots right.
TRANSACTIONS/CAREER NOTES: Selected by Winnipeg Jets in sixth round (seventh Jets pick, 145th overall) of NHL entry draft (June 26, 1993).

Season	Team	League	REGULAR SEASON					PLAYOFFS				
			Gms.	G	A	Pts.	PIM	Gms.	G	A	Pts.	PIM
92-93	—ZPS Zlin..........................	Czech.	17	1	3	4	0	—	—	—	—	—
93-94	—Moncton	AHL	20	1	2	3	47	2	0	0	0	0
	—Tacoma	WHL	30	25	20	45	106	7	2	2	4	30
	—Winnipeg	NHL	3	1	0	1	0	—	—	—	—	—
NHL totals.................................			**3**	**1**	**0**	**1**	**0**					

GRUDEN, JOHN
D, BRUINS

PERSONAL: Born April 6, 1970, in Hastings, Minn. . . . 6-0/ 180. . . . Shoots left.
COLLEGE: Ferris State.
TRANSACTIONS/CAREER NOTES: Selected by Boston Bruins in seventh round (seventh Bruins pick, 168th overall) of NHL entry draft (June 16, 1990).
HONORS: Named to NCAA All-America first team (1993-94).

Season	Team	League	REGULAR SEASON					PLAYOFFS				
			Gms.	G	A	Pts.	PIM	Gms.	G	A	Pts.	PIM
90-91	—Ferris State	CCHA	37	4	11	15	27	—	—	—	—	—
91-92	—Ferris State	CCHA	37	9	14	23	24	—	—	—	—	—
92-93	—Ferris State	CCHA	41	16	14	30	58	—	—	—	—	—
93-94	—Ferris State	CCHA	38	11	25	36	52	—	—	—	—	—
	—Boston	NHL	7	0	1	1	2	—	—	—	—	—
NHL totals.................................			**7**	**0**	**1**	**1**	**2**					

GRUHL, SCOTT
LW/D

PERSONAL: Born September 13, 1959, in Port Colborne, Ont. . . . 6-0/200. . . . Shoots left. . . . Full name: Scott Kenneth Gruhl.
COLLEGE: Northeastern.
TRANSACTIONS/CAREER NOTES: Signed as free agent by Los Angeles Kings (September 1980). . . . Signed as free agent by Pittsburgh Penguins (December 14, 1987). . . . Fractured left hand (March 1988). . . . Broke two bones in wrist (September 1990). . . . Claimed by Fort Wayne Komets on IHL waivers from Muskegon Lumberjacks (December 3, 1990).
HONORS: Named to IHL All-Star second team (1979-80, 1985-86 and 1991-92). . . . Named to IHL All-Star first team (1983-84 and 1984-85). . . . Won James Gatschene Memorial Trophy (1984-85).

Season	Team	League	REGULAR SEASON					PLAYOFFS				
			Gms.	G	A	Pts.	PIM	Gms.	G	A	Pts.	PIM
76-77	—Northeastern University...	Hockey East	17	6	4	10	. . .	—	—	—	—	—
77-78	—Northeastern University...	Hockey East	28	21	38	59	46	—	—	—	—	—
78-79	—Sudbury..........................	OMJHL	68	35	49	84	78	10	5	7	12	15
79-80	—Binghamton	AHL	4	1	0	1	6	—	—	—	—	—
	—Saginaw	IHL	75	53	40	93	100	7	2	6	8	16
80-81	—Houston	CHL	4	0	0	0	0	—	—	—	—	—
	—Saginaw	IHL	77	56	34	90	87	13	*11	8	*19	12
81-82	—New Haven......................	AHL	73	28	41	69	107	4	0	4	4	2
	—Los Angeles....................	NHL	7	2	1	3	2	—	—	—	—	—
82-83	—New Haven......................	AHL	68	25	38	63	114	12	3	3	6	22
	—Los Angeles....................	NHL	7	0	2	2	4	—	—	—	—	—
83-84	—Muskegon........................	IHL	56	40	56	96	49	—	—	—	—	—
84-85	—Muskegon........................	IHL	82	62	64	126	102	17	7	*16	23	25
85-86	—Muskegon........................	IHL	82	*59	50	109	178	14	7	†13	20	22
86-87	—Muskegon........................	IHL	67	34	39	73	157	15	5	7	12	54
87-88	—Pittsburgh	NHL	6	1	0	1	0	—	—	—	—	—
	—Muskegon........................	IHL	55	28	47	75	115	6	5	1	6	12
88-89	—Muskegon........................	IHL	79	37	55	92	163	14	8	11	19	37
89-90	—Muskegon........................	IHL	80	41	51	92	206	15	8	6	14	26
90-91	—Fort Wayne	IHL	59	23	47	70	109	19	4	6	10	39
91-92	—Fort Wayne	IHL	78	44	61	105	196	6	2	2	4	48
92-93	—Fort Wayne	IHL	73	34	47	81	290	12	4	11	15	14
93-94	—Milwaukee	IHL	28	6	9	15	102	—	—	—	—	—
	—Kalamazoo	IHL	30	15	12	27	85	5	1	4	5	26
NHL totals.................................			**20**	**3**	**3**	**6**	**6**					

GUERARD, DANIEL
RW, SENATORS

PERSONAL: Born April 9, 1974, in La Salle, Que. . . . 6-4/215. . . . Shoots right. . . . Name pronounced gair-AHR.
TRANSACTIONS/CAREER NOTES: Selected by Ottawa Senators in fifth round (fifth Senators pick, 98th overall) of NHL entry draft (June 20, 1992).

G

Season Team	League	REGULAR SEASON					PLAYOFFS				
		Gms.	G	A	Pts.	PIM	Gms.	G	A	Pts.	PIM
91-92—Victoriaville	QMJHL	31	5	16	21	66	—	—	—	—	—
92-93—Verdun	QMJHL	58	31	26	57	131	4	1	1	2	17
—New Haven	AHL	2	2	1	3	0	—	—	—	—	—
93-94—Verdun	QMJHL	53	31	34	65	169	4	3	1	4	4
—Prince Edward Island	AHL	3	0	0	0	17	—	—	—	—	—

GUERIN, BILL
C/RW, DEVILS

PERSONAL: Born November 9, 1970, in Wilbraham, Mass. . . . 6-2/200. . . . Shoots right. . . . Full name: William Robert Guerin. . . . Name pronounced GAIR-ihn.
COLLEGE: Boston College.
TRANSACTIONS/CAREER NOTES: Selected by New Jersey Devils in first round (first Devils pick, fifth overall) of NHL entry draft (June 17, 1989). . . . Suffered from the flu (February 1992); missed three games. . . . Suffered from sore leg (March 19, 1994); missed two games.

Season Team	League	REGULAR SEASON					PLAYOFFS				
		Gms.	G	A	Pts.	PIM	Gms.	G	A	Pts.	PIM
85-86—Springfield Jr. B	NEJHL	48	26	19	45	71	—	—	—	—	—
86-87—Springfield Jr. B	NEJHL	32	34	20	54	40	—	—	—	—	—
87-88—Springfield Jr. B	NEJHL	38	31	44	75	146	—	—	—	—	—
88-89—Springfield Jr. B	NEJHL	31	32	37	69	90	—	—	—	—	—
89-90—Boston College	Hockey East	39	14	11	25	64	—	—	—	—	—
90-91—Boston College	Hockey East	38	26	19	45	102	—	—	—	—	—
91-92—U.S. national team	Int'l	46	12	15	27	67	—	—	—	—	—
—Utica	AHL	22	13	10	23	6	4	1	3	4	14
—New Jersey	NHL	5	0	1	1	9	6	3	0	3	4
92-93—New Jersey	NHL	65	14	20	34	63	5	1	1	2	4
—Utica	AHL	18	10	7	17	47	—	—	—	—	—
93-94—New Jersey	NHL	81	25	19	44	101	17	2	1	3	35
NHL totals		151	39	40	79	173	28	6	2	8	43

GUILLET, ROBERT
RW, CANADIENS

PERSONAL: Born February 22, 1972, in Montreal. . . . 5-11/189. . . . Shoots right.
TRANSACTIONS/CAREER NOTES: Selected by Montreal Canadiens in third round (fourth Canadiens pick, 60th overall) of NHL entry draft (June 16, 1990).
HONORS: Named to QMJHL All-Star first team (1990-91). . . . Won Guy Lafleur Trophy (1991-92). . . . Named to QMJHL All-Star second team (1991-92).

Season Team	League	REGULAR SEASON					PLAYOFFS				
		Gms.	G	A	Pts.	PIM	Gms.	G	A	Pts.	PIM
89-90—Longueuil	QMJHL	69	32	40	72	132	7	2	1	3	16
90-91—Longueuil	QMJHL	69	55	32	87	96	8	4	7	11	27
91-92—Longueuil	QMJHL	67	56	62	118	104	19	†14	11	*25	26
92-93—Fredericton	AHL	42	16	15	31	38	1	0	0	0	0
—Wheeling	ECHL	15	16	14	30	8	—	—	—	—	—
93-94—Fredericton	AHL	78	38	40	78	48	—	—	—	—	—

GUSAROV, ALEXEI
D, NORDIQUES

PERSONAL: Born July 8, 1964, in Leningrad, U.S.S.R. . . . 6-3/185. . . . Shoots left. . . . Name pronounced goo-SAH-rahf.
TRANSACTIONS/CAREER NOTES: Selected by Quebec Nordiques in 11th round (11th Nordiques pick, 213th overall) in the NHL entry draft (June 11, 1988). . . . Suffered hairline fracture of left ankle (December 15, 1990); missed seven games. . . . Hyperextended right knee (February 28, 1991). . . . Fractured finger (October 13, 1991); missed four games. . . . Suffered from the flu (February 9, 1993); missed two games. . . . Suffered concussion (March 31, 1993); missed two games. . . . Bruised left thumb (November 13, 1993); missed one game. . . . Suffered from the flu (January 11, 1994); missed two games. . . . Suffered from sinusitis (March 30, 1994); missed two games.
MISCELLANEOUS: Member of gold-medal-winning U.S.S.R. Olympic team (1988).

Season Team	League	REGULAR SEASON					PLAYOFFS				
		Gms.	G	A	Pts.	PIM	Gms.	G	A	Pts.	PIM
81-82—Leningrad SKA	USSR	20	1	2	3	16	—	—	—	—	—
82-83—Leningrad SKA	USSR	42	2	1	3	32	—	—	—	—	—
83-84—Leningrad SKA	USSR	43	2	3	5	32	—	—	—	—	—
84-85—CSKA Moscow	USSR	36	3	2	5	26	—	—	—	—	—
85-86—CSKA Moscow	USSR	40	3	5	8	30	—	—	—	—	—
86-87—CSKA Moscow	USSR	38	4	7	11	24	—	—	—	—	—
87-88—CSKA Moscow	USSR	39	3	2	5	28	—	—	—	—	—
88-89—CSKA Moscow	USSR	42	5	4	9	37	—	—	—	—	—
89-90—CSKA Moscow	USSR	42	4	7	11	42	—	—	—	—	—
90-91—CSKA Moscow	USSR	15	0	0	0	12	—	—	—	—	—
—Quebec	NHL	36	3	9	12	12	—	—	—	—	—
—Halifax	AHL	2	0	3	3	2	—	—	—	—	—
91-92—Quebec	NHL	68	5	18	23	22	—	—	—	—	—
—Halifax	AHL	3	0	0	0	0	—	—	—	—	—
92-93—Quebec	NHL	79	8	22	30	57	5	0	1	1	0
93-94—Quebec	NHL	76	5	20	25	38	—	—	—	—	—
NHL totals		259	21	69	90	129	5	0	1	1	0

G

GUSMANOV, RAVIL
LW, JETS

PERSONAL: Born July 22, 1972, in Naberezhnye Chelny, U.S.S.R. . . . . 6-3/185. . . . . Shoots left.
TRANSACTIONS/CAREER NOTES: Selected by Winnipeg Jets in fourth round (fifth Jets pick, 93rd overall) of NHL entry draft (June 26, 1993).

			REGULAR SEASON					PLAYOFFS			
Season	Team	League	Gms.	G	A	Pts.	PIM	Gms.	G	A	Pts.	PIM
90-91—Traktor Chelyabinsk........	USSR	15	0	0	0	10	—	—	—	—	—
91-92—Traktor Chelyabinsk........	CIS	38	4	4	8	20	—	—	—	—	—
92-93—Traktor Chelyabinsk........	CIS	39	15	8	23	30	8	4	0	4	2
93-94—Traktor Chelyabinsk........	CIS	43	18	9	27	51	6	4	3	7	10

GUY, KEVAN
D, ISLANDERS

PERSONAL: Born July 16, 1965, in Edmonton. . . . 6-3/205. . . . Shoots right.
TRANSACTIONS/CAREER NOTES: Selected by Calgary Flames as underage junior in fourth round (fifth Flames pick, 71st overall) of NHL entry draft (June 8, 1983). . . . Traded by Flames to Vancouver Canucks to complete March 1988 deal in which Flames sent C Brian Bradley and RW Peter Bakovic to Canucks for C Craig Coxe (June 1988). . . . Fractured bone in right foot (February 18, 1990); missed 10 games. . . . Traded by Canucks with RW Ronnie Stern and option to switch fourth-round picks in 1992 draft to Flames for D Dana Murzyn; Calgary did not exercise option (March 5, 1991). . . . Pulled hamstring (December 2, 1991). . . . Signed as free agent by New York Islanders (September 18, 1993).

			REGULAR SEASON					PLAYOFFS			
Season	Team	League	Gms.	G	A	Pts.	PIM	Gms.	G	A	Pts.	PIM
82-83—Medicine Hat	WHL	69	7	20	27	89	5	0	3	3	16
83-84—Medicine Hat	WHL	72	15	42	57	117	14	3	4	7	14
84-85—Medicine Hat	WHL	31	7	17	24	46	10	1	2	3	2
85-86—Moncton	AHL	73	4	20	24	56	10	0	2	2	6
86-87—Moncton	AHL	46	2	10	12	38	—	—	—	—	—
—Calgary	NHL	24	0	4	4	19	4	0	1	1	23
87-88—Calgary	NHL	11	0	3	3	8	—	—	—	—	—
—Salt Lake City	IHL	61	6	30	36	49	19	1	6	7	26
88-89—Vancouver	NHL	45	2	2	4	34	1	0	0	0	0
89-90—Milwaukee	IHL	29	2	11	13	33	—	—	—	—	—
—Vancouver	NHL	30	2	5	7	32	—	—	—	—	—
90-91—Vancouver	NHL	39	1	6	7	39	—	—	—	—	—
—Calgary	NHL	4	0	0	0	4	—	—	—	—	—
91-92—Salt Lake City	IHL	60	3	14	17	89	5	0	1	1	4
—Calgary	NHL	3	0	0	0	2	—	—	—	—	—
92-93—Salt Lake City	IHL	33	1	9	10	50	—	—	—	—	—
93-94—Salt Lake City	IHL	62	4	17	21	45	—	—	—	—	—
NHL totals.........................		**156**	**5**	**20**	**25**	**138**	**5**	**0**	**1**	**1**	**23**

HAAS, DAVID
LW, FLAMES

PERSONAL: Born July 23, 1968, in Toronto. . . . 6-2/196. . . . Shoots left. . . . Full name: David John Haas. . . . Name pronounced HAHS.
TRANSACTIONS/CAREER NOTES: Selected by Edmonton Oilers as underage junior in fifth round (fifth Oilers pick, 105th overall) of NHL entry draft (June 21, 1986). . . . Traded by London Knights with C Kelly Cain and D Ed Kister to Kitchener Rangers for RW Peter Lisy, D Ian Pound, D Steve Marcolini and C Greg Hankkio (October 1986). . . . Loaned to New Haven Nighthawks (December 4, 1991). . . . Signed as free agent by Calgary Flames (August 10, 1993). . . . Suffered hip pointer (January 2, 1994); missed 11 games.
HONORS: Named to OHL All-Star second team (1987-88).

			REGULAR SEASON					PLAYOFFS			
Season	Team	League	Gms.	G	A	Pts.	PIM	Gms.	G	A	Pts.	PIM
85-86—London	OHL	62	4	13	17	91	5	0	1	1	0
86-87—London	OHL	5	1	0	1	5	—	—	—	—	—
—Kitchener........................	OHL	4	0	1	1	4	—	—	—	—	—
—Belleville........................	OHL	55	10	13	23	86	6	3	0	3	13
87-88—Belleville........................	OHL	5	1	1	2	9	—	—	—	—	—
—Windsor.........................	OHL	58	59	46	105	237	11	9	11	20	50
88-89—Cape Breton	AHL	61	9	9	18	325	—	—	—	—	—
89-90—Cape Breton	AHL	53	6	12	18	230	4	2	2	4	15
90-91—Cape Breton	AHL	60	24	23	47	137	3	0	2	2	12
—Edmonton.......................	NHL	5	1	0	1	0	—	—	—	—	—
91-92—Cape Breton	AHL	16	3	7	10	32	—	—	—	—	—
—New Haven.....................	AHL	50	13	23	36	97	5	3	0	3	13
92-93—Cape Breton	AHL	73	22	56	78	121	16	11	13	24	36
93-94—Saint John	AHL	37	11	17	28	108	—	—	—	—	—
—Calgary	NHL	2	1	1	2	7	—	—	—	—	—
—Phoenix	IHL	11	7	4	11	43	—	—	—	—	—
NHL totals.........................		**7**	**2**	**1**	**3**	**7**					

HACKETT, JEFF
G, BLACKHAWKS

GH

PERSONAL: Born June 1, 1968, in London, Ont. . . . 6-1/185. . . . Catches left.
TRANSACTIONS/CAREER NOTES: Selected by New York Islanders as underage junior in second round (second Islanders pick, 34th overall) of NHL entry draft (June 13, 1987). . . . Strained groin (May 13, 1990). . . . Selected by San Jose Sharks in NHL expansion draft (May 30, 1991). . . . Injured groin and hamstring (December 3, 1991); missed nine games. . . . Injured knee (March 23, 1992). . . . Injured groin (October 30, 1992); missed 12 games. . . . Suffered from the flu (February 20, 1993); missed five games. . . . Traded by

Sharks to Chicago Blackhawks for third-round pick (C Alexei Yegorov) in 1994 draft (July 13, 1993).
HONORS: Won F.W. (Dinty) Moore Trophy (1986-87).... Shared Dave Pinkney Trophy with Sean Evoy (1986-87).... Won Jack Butterfield Trophy (1989-90).

						REGULAR SEASON							PLAYOFFS					
Season	Team	League	Gms.	Min.	W	L	T	GA	SO	Avg.	Gms.	Min.	W	L	GA	SO	Avg.
85-86	London Jr. B	OHA	19	1150	...	...	...	66	0	3.44	—	—					—
86-87	Oshawa	OHL	31	1672	18	9	2	85	2	3.05	15	895	8	7	40	0	2.68
87-88	Oshawa	OHL	53	3165	30	21	2	205	0	3.89	7	438	3	4	31	0	4.25
88-89	New York Islanders	NHL	13	662	4	7	0	39	0	3.53	—	—	—	—	—	—	—
	Springfield	AHL	29	1677	12	14	2	116	0	4.15	—	—	—	—	—	—	—
89-90	Springfield	AHL	54	3045	24	25	3	187	1	3.68	†17	934	10	5	*60	0	3.85
90-91	New York Islanders	NHL	30	1508	5	18	1	91	0	3.62	—	—	—	—	—	—	—
91-92	San Jose	NHL	42	2314	11	27	1	148	0	3.84	—	—	—	—	—	—	—
92-93	San Jose	NHL	36	2000	2	30	1	176	0	5.28	—	—	—	—	—	—	—
93-94	Chicago	NHL	22	1084	2	12	3	62	0	3.43	—	—	—	—	—	—	—
NHL totals			143	7568	24	94	6	516	0	4.09							

HAGGERTY, SEAN
LW, MAPLE LEAFS

PERSONAL: Born February 11, 1976, in Greenwich, Conn.... 6-1/186.... Shoots left.
TRANSACTIONS/CAREER NOTES: Selected by Toronto Maple Leafs in second round (second Maple Leafs pick, 48th overall) of NHL entry draft (June 28, 1994).
HONORS: Named to OHL All-Rookie team (1993-94).

				REGULAR SEASON					PLAYOFFS			
Season	Team	League	Gms.	G	A	Pts.	PIM	Gms.	G	A	Pts.	PIM
90-91	Westminster Prep	USHS (E)	25	20	22	42	...	—	—	—	—	—
91-92	Westminster Prep	USHS (E)	25	24	36	64	...	—	—	—	—	—
92-93	Boston	NEJHL	72	70	111	181	80	—	—	—	—	—
93-94	Detroit	OHL	60	31	32	63	21	17	8	10	18	11

HAKANSSON, MIKAEL
C, MAPLE LEAFS

PERSONAL: Born March 31, 1974, in Stockholm, Sweden.... 6-1/196.... Shoots left.
TRANSACTIONS/CAREER NOTES: Selected by Toronto Maple Leafs in sixth round (seventh Maple Leafs pick, 125th overall) of NHL entry draft (June 20, 1992).

				REGULAR SEASON					PLAYOFFS			
Season	Team	League	Gms.	G	A	Pts.	PIM	Gms.	G	A	Pts.	PIM
90-91	Nacka	Sweden	27	2	5	7	6	—	—	—	—	—
91-92	Nacka	Sweden	29	3	15	18	24	—	—	—	—	—
92-93	Djurgarden	Sweden	40	0	1	1	6	6	0	0	0	0
93-94	Djurgarden	Sweden	37	3	3	6	12	6	0	0	0	0

HALKIDIS, BOB
D, RED WINGS

PERSONAL: Born March 5, 1966, in Toronto.... 5-11/200.... Shoots left.... Name pronounced hal-KEE-duhz.
TRANSACTIONS/CAREER NOTES: Broke ankle (September 1982).... Reinjured ankle (November 1982); missed two weeks.... Selected by Buffalo Sabres as underage junior in fourth round (fourth Sabres pick, 81st overall) of NHL entry draft (June 9, 1984).... Dislocated right shoulder (December 4, 1985); missed 15 games.... Suspended six games by AHL for fighting (October 23, 1987).... Injured ankle (December 1987).... Injured shoulder (December 1988).... Traded by Sabres to Los Angeles Kings for D Dale DeGray (November 24, 1989).... Underwent surgery to left shoulder (May 1990).... Underwent surgery to left shoulder (October 16, 1990).... Signed as free agent by Toronto Maple Leafs (July 24, 1991).... Pulled groin (November 21, 1991); missed three games.... Signed as free agent by Detroit Red Wings (September 2, 1993).... Torn left medial collateral ligament (December 21, 1993); missed 18 games.
HONORS: Won Max Kaminsky Trophy (1984-85).... Named to OHL All-Star first team (1984-85).

				REGULAR SEASON					PLAYOFFS			
Season	Team	League	Gms.	G	A	Pts.	PIM	Gms.	G	A	Pts.	PIM
82-83	London	OHL	37	3	12	15	52	—	—	—	—	—
83-84	London	OHL	51	9	22	31	123	8	0	2	2	27
84-85	London	OHL	62	14	50	64	154	8	3	6	9	22
	Buffalo	NHL	—	—	—	—	—	4	0	0	0	19
85-86	Buffalo	NHL	37	1	9	10	115	—	—	—	—	—
86-87	Buffalo	NHL	6	1	1	2	19	—	—	—	—	—
	Rochester	AHL	59	1	8	9	144	8	0	0	0	43
87-88	Rochester	AHL	15	2	5	7	50	—	—	—	—	—
	Buffalo	NHL	30	0	3	3	115	4	0	0	0	22
88-89	Buffalo	NHL	16	0	1	1	66	—	—	—	—	—
	Rochester	AHL	16	0	6	6	64	—	—	—	—	—
89-90	Rochester	AHL	18	1	13	14	70	—	—	—	—	—
	Los Angeles	NHL	20	0	4	4	56	—	—	—	—	—
	New Haven	AHL	30	3	17	20	67	—	—	—	—	—
90-91	Phoenix	IHL	4	1	5	6	6	—	—	—	—	—
	New Haven	AHL	7	1	3	4	10	—	—	—	—	—
	Los Angeles	NHL	34	1	3	4	133	3	0	0	0	0
91-92	Toronto	NHL	46	3	3	6	145	—	—	—	—	—
92-93	St. John's	AHL	29	2	13	15	61	—	—	—	—	—
	Milwaukee	IHL	26	0	9	9	79	5	0	1	1	27
93-94	Adirondack	AHL	15	0	6	6	46	—	—	—	—	—
	Detroit	NHL	28	1	4	5	93	1	0	0	0	2
NHL totals			217	7	28	35	742	12	0	0	0	43

H

HALLER, KEVIN
D, FLYERS

PERSONAL: Born December 5, 1970, in Trochu, Alta.... 6-2/183.... Shoots left.
TRANSACTIONS/CAREER NOTES: Broke leg (October 1986).... Broke leg (May 1987).... Selected by Buffalo Sabres in first round (first Sabres pick, 14th overall) of NHL entry draft (June 17, 1989).... Separated shoulder (May 7, 1991); missed seven games.... Traded by Sabres to Montreal Canadiens for D Petr Svoboda (March 10, 1992).... Suspended four games and fined $500 by NHL for slashing (November 2, 1993).... Traded by Canadiens to Philadelphia Flyers for D Yves Racine (June 29, 1994).
HONORS: Won Bill Hunter Trophy (1989-90).... Named to WHL (East) All-Star first team (1989-90).
MISCELLANEOUS: Member of Stanley Cup championship team (1993).

			REGULAR SEASON					PLAYOFFS				
Season	Team	League	Gms.	G	A	Pts.	PIM	Gms.	G	A	Pts.	PIM
87-88—Olds		AJHL	54	13	31	44	58	—	—	—	—	—
88-89—Regina		WHL	72	10	31	41	99	—	—	—	—	—
89-90—Regina		WHL	58	16	37	53	93	11	2	9	11	16
—Buffalo		NHL	2	0	0	0	0	—	—	—	—	—
90-91—Rochester		AHL	52	2	8	10	53	10	2	1	3	6
—Buffalo		NHL	21	1	8	9	20	6	1	4	5	10
91-92—Buffalo		NHL	58	6	15	21	75	—	—	—	—	—
—Rochester		AHL	4	0	0	0	18	—	—	—	—	—
—Montreal		NHL	8	2	2	4	17	9	0	0	0	6
92-93—Montreal		NHL	73	11	14	25	117	17	1	6	7	16
93-94—Montreal		NHL	68	4	9	13	118	7	1	1	2	19
NHL totals			230	24	48	72	347	39	3	11	14	51

HALTIA, PATRIK
G, FLAMES

PERSONAL: Born June 29, 1973, in Karlstad, Sweden.... 6-1/176.... Catches left.
TRANSACTIONS/CAREER NOTES: Selected by Calgary Flames in the sixth round (eighth Flames pick, 149th overall) of NHL entry draft (June 29, 1994).

			REGULAR SEASON							PLAYOFFS						
Season	Team	League	Gms.	Min.	W	L	T	GA	SO	Avg.	Gms.	Min.	W	L	GA	SO	Avg.
93-94—Grums		Swed. Dv.II					Statistics unavailable.										

HAMMOND, KEN
D

PERSONAL: Born August 23, 1963, in London, Ont.... 6-1/190.... Shoots left.... Full name: Kenneth Paul Hammond.
HIGH SCHOOL: Saunders (London, Ont.).
COLLEGE: Rensselaer Polytechnic Institute (N.Y.).
TRANSACTIONS/CAREER NOTES: Selected by Los Angeles Kings in eighth round (eighth Kings pick, 147th overall) of NHL entry draft (June 8, 1983).... Sprained knee (March 13, 1988).... Selected by Edmonton Oilers in NHL waiver draft for $30,000 (October 3, 1988).... Claimed on waivers by New York Rangers when the Oilers attempted to assign him to Cape Breton (November 1, 1988).... Traded by Rangers to Toronto Maple Leafs for LW Chris McRae (February 19, 1989).... Suffered back spasms (March 1989).... Sold by Maple Leafs to Boston Bruins (August 20, 1990).... Signed as free agent by San Jose Sharks (August 9, 1991).... Pulled groin (January 23, 1992); missed five games.... Fractured hand (February 21, 1992); missed seven games.... Traded by Sharks to Vancouver Canucks for eighth-round pick in 1992 draft (traded to Detroit Red Wings who selected G C.J. Denomme) (March 9, 1992).... Underwent surgery to hand (March 1992).... Selected by Ottawa Senators in NHL expansion draft (June 18, 1992).... Signed as free agent by Kansas City Blades (July 8, 1994).
HONORS: Named to NCAA All-America East first team (1984-85).... Named to NCAA All-Tournament team (1984-85).... Named to ECAC All-Star first team (1984-85).

			REGULAR SEASON					PLAYOFFS				
Season	Team	League	Gms.	G	A	Pts.	PIM	Gms.	G	A	Pts.	PIM
81-82—R.P.I.		ECAC	29	2	3	5	54	—	—	—	—	—
82-83—R.P.I.		ECAC	28	4	13	17	54	—	—	—	—	—
83-84—R.P.I.		ECAC	34	5	11	16	72	—	—	—	—	—
84-85—R.P.I.		ECAC	38	11	28	39	90	—	—	—	—	—
—Los Angeles		NHL	3	1	0	1	0	3	0	0	0	4
85-86—New Haven		AHL	67	4	12	16	96	4	0	0	0	7
—Los Angeles		NHL	3	0	1	1	2	—	—	—	—	—
86-87—New Haven		AHL	66	1	15	16	76	6	0	1	1	21
—Los Angeles		NHL	10	0	2	2	11	—	—	—	—	—
87-88—New Haven		AHL	26	3	8	11	27	—	—	—	—	—
—Los Angeles		NHL	46	7	9	16	69	2	0	0	0	4
88-89—Edmonton		NHL	5	0	1	1	8	—	—	—	—	—
—New York Rangers		NHL	3	0	0	0	0	—	—	—	—	—
—Toronto		NHL	14	0	2	2	12	—	—	—	—	—
—Denver		IHL	38	5	18	23	24	—	—	—	—	—
89-90—Newmarket		AHL	75	9	45	54	106	—	—	—	—	—
90-91—Boston		NHL	1	0	1	1	2	8	0	0	0	10
—Maine		AHL	80	10	41	51	159	2	0	1	1	16
91-92—San Jose		NHL	46	5	10	15	82	—	—	—	—	—
—Vancouver		NHL	—	—	—	—	—	2	0	0	0	6
92-93—Ottawa		NHL	62	4	4	8	104	—	—	—	—	—
—New Haven		AHL	4	0	1	1	4	—	—	—	—	—
93-94—Providence		AHL	65	12	45	57	100	—	—	—	—	—
NHL totals			193	18	29	47	290	15	0	0	0	24

HAMR, RADEK
D, SENATORS

PERSONAL: Born June 15, 1974, in Prague, Czechoslovakia. . . . 5-11/175. . . . Shoots left. . . . Name pronounced RA-dehk HAM-uhr.
TRANSACTIONS/CAREER NOTES: Selected by Ottawa Senators in fourth round (fourth Senators pick, 73rd overall) of NHL entry draft (June 20, 1992).

			REGULAR SEASON				PLAYOFFS				
Season Team	League	Gms.	G	A	Pts.	PIM	Gms.	G	A	Pts.	PIM
91-92—Sparta Prague	Czech.	3	0	0	0	0	—	—	—	—	—
92-93—New Haven	AHL	59	4	21	25	18	—	—	—	—	—
—Ottawa	NHL	4	0	0	0	0	—	—	—	—	—
93-94—Prince Edward Island	AHL	69	10	26	36	44	—	—	—	—	—
—Ottawa	NHL	7	0	0	0	0	—	—	—	—	—
NHL totals		11	0	0	0	0					

HAMRLIK, MARTIN
D, BLUES

PERSONAL: Born May 6, 1973, in Zlin, Czechoslovakia. . . . 5-11/176. . . . Shoots right. . . . Name pronounced HAM-uhr-lihk. . . . Brother of Roman Hamrlik, defenseman, Tampa Bay Lightning.
TRANSACTIONS/CAREER NOTES: Selected by Hartford Whalers in second round (second Whalers pick, 31st overall) of NHL entry draft (June 22, 1991). . . . Suffered from Lyme disease (October 1991); missed remainder of season. . . . Traded by Whalers to St. Louis Blues for future considerations (November 13, 1993).

			REGULAR SEASON				PLAYOFFS				
Season Team	League	Gms.	G	A	Pts.	PIM	Gms.	G	A	Pts.	PIM
89-90—TJ Zlin	Czech.	12	2	0	2	...	—	—	—	—	—
90-91—TJ Zlin	Czech.	50	8	14	22	44	—	—	—	—	—
91-92—ZPS Zlin	Czech.	4	0	2	2	...	—	—	—	—	—
92-93—Ottawa	OHL	26	4	11	15	41	—	—	—	—	—
—Springfield	AHL	8	1	3	4	16	—	—	—	—	—
93-94—Peoria	IHL	47	1	11	12	61	6	0	1	1	2
—Springfield	AHL	1	0	0	0	0	—	—	—	—	—

HAMRLIK, ROMAN
D, LIGHTNING

PERSONAL: Born April 12, 1974, in Gottwaldov, Czechoslovakia. . . . 6-2/189. . . . Shoots left. . . . Name pronounced ROH-muhn HAM-uhr-lihk. . . . Brother of Martin Hamrlik, defenseman in St. Louis Blues system.
TRANSACTIONS/CAREER NOTES: Selected by Tampa Bay Lightning in first round (first Lightning pick, first overall) of NHL entry draft (June 20, 1992). . . . Bruised shoulder (November 3, 1993); missed six games. . . . Bruised shoulder (March 1, 1994); missed seven games.

			REGULAR SEASON				PLAYOFFS				
Season Team	League	Gms.	G	A	Pts.	PIM	Gms.	G	A	Pts.	PIM
90-91—TJ Zlin	Czech.	14	2	2	4	18	—	—	—	—	—
91-92—ZPS Zlin	Czech.	34	5	5	10	34	—	—	—	—	—
92-93—Tampa Bay	NHL	67	6	15	21	71	—	—	—	—	—
—Atlanta	IHL	2	1	1	2	2	—	—	—	—	—
93-94—Tampa Bay	NHL	64	3	18	21	135	—	—	—	—	—
NHL totals		131	9	33	42	206					

HANKINSON, BEN
RW, DEVILS

PERSONAL: Born January 5, 1969, in Edina, Minn. . . . 6-2/215. . . . Shoots right. . . . Full name: Benjamin John Hankinson.
HIGH SCHOOL: Edina (Minn.).
COLLEGE: Minnesota.
TRANSACTIONS/CAREER NOTES: Selected by New Jersey Devils in sixth round (fifth Devils pick, 107th overall) of NHL entry draft (June 13, 1987).
HONORS: Named to WCHA All-Star first team (1989-90).

			REGULAR SEASON				PLAYOFFS				
Season Team	League	Gms.	G	A	Pts.	PIM	Gms.	G	A	Pts.	PIM
85-86—Edina High School	Minn. H.S.	...	9	21	30	...	—	—	—	—	—
86-87—Edina High School	Minn. H.S.	26	14	20	34	...	—	—	—	—	—
87-88—University of Minnesota	WCHA	24	4	7	11	36	—	—	—	—	—
88-89—University of Minnesota	WCHA	43	7	11	18	115	—	—	—	—	—
89-90—University of Minnesota	WCHA	46	25	41	66	34	—	—	—	—	—
90-91—University of Minnesota	WCHA	43	19	21	40	133	—	—	—	—	—
91-92—Utica	AHL	77	17	16	33	186	4	3	1	4	2
92-93—Utica	AHL	75	35	27	62	145	5	2	2	4	6
—New Jersey	NHL	4	2	1	3	9	—	—	—	—	—
93-94—New Jersey	NHL	13	1	0	1	23	2	1	0	1	4
—Albany	AHL	29	9	14	23	80	5	3	1	4	6
NHL totals		17	3	1	4	32	2	1	0	1	4

HANNAN, DAVE
C, SABRES

PERSONAL: Born November 26, 1961, in Sudbury, Ont. . . . 5-10/185. . . . Shoots left.
TRANSACTIONS/CAREER NOTES: Bruised shoulder; missed part of 1980-81 season. . . . Selected by Pittsburgh Penguins in 10th round (ninth Penguins pick, 196th overall) of NHL entry draft (June 10, 1981). . . . Injured knee and underwent surgery (January 9, 1987). . . . Traded by Penguins with C Craig Simpson, D Chris Joseph and D Moe Mantha to Edmonton Oilers for D Paul Coffey, LW Dave

H

Hunter and RW Wayne Van Dorp (November 24, 1987)....Selected by Penguins in NHL waiver draft (October 3, 1988); LW Dave Hunter was awarded to Oilers as compensation....Suffered hip pointer (October 1988)....Sprained knee (March 1989)....Selected by Toronto Maple Leafs in NHL waiver draft for $7,500 (October 2, 1989)....Injured left knee ligaments (November 22, 1989)....Underwent surgery to left knee (December 18, 1989); missed 23 games....Traded by Maple Leafs to Buffalo Sabres for fifth-round pick (RW Chris Deruiter) in 1992 draft (March 10, 1992)....Injured shoulder (April 12, 1992). ...Broke toe (January 19, 1993); missed three games.

MISCELLANEOUS: Member of Stanley Cup championship team (1988)....Member of silver-medal-winning Canadian Olympic team (1992).

			REGULAR SEASON					PLAYOFFS			
Season Team	League	Gms.	G	A	Pts.	PIM	Gms.	G	A	Pts.	PIM
77-78—Windsor	OMJHL	68	14	16	30	43	—	—	—	—	—
78-79—Sault Ste. Marie	OMJHL	26	7	8	15	13	—	—	—	—	—
79-80—Sault Ste. Marie	OMJHL	28	11	10	21	31	—	—	—	—	—
—Brantford	OMJHL	25	5	10	15	26	—	—	—	—	—
80-81—Brantford	OMJHL	56	46	35	81	155	6	2	4	6	20
81-82—Erie	AHL	76	33	37	70	129	—	—	—	—	—
—Pittsburgh	NHL	1	0	0	0	0	—	—	—	—	—
82-83—Baltimore	AHL	5	2	2	4	13	—	—	—	—	—
—Pittsburgh	NHL	74	11	22	33	127	—	—	—	—	—
83-84—Baltimore	AHL	47	18	24	42	98	10	2	6	8	27
—Pittsburgh	NHL	24	2	3	5	33	—	—	—	—	—
84-85—Baltimore	AHL	49	20	25	45	91	—	—	—	—	—
—Pittsburgh	NHL	30	6	7	13	43	—	—	—	—	—
85-86—Pittsburgh	NHL	75	17	18	35	91	—	—	—	—	—
86-87—Pittsburgh	NHL	58	10	15	25	56	—	—	—	—	—
87-88—Pittsburgh	NHL	21	4	3	7	23	—	—	—	—	—
—Edmonton	NHL	51	9	11	20	43	12	1	1	2	8
88-89—Pittsburgh	NHL	72	10	20	30	157	8	0	1	1	4
89-90—Toronto	NHL	39	6	9	15	55	3	1	0	1	4
90-91—Toronto	NHL	74	11	23	34	82	—	—	—	—	—
91-92—Toronto	NHL	35	2	2	4	16	—	—	—	—	—
—Canadian national team	Int'l	3	0	0	0	2	—	—	—	—	—
—Canadian Olympic Team	Int'l	8	3	5	8	8	—	—	—	—	—
—Buffalo	NHL	12	2	4	6	48	7	2	0	2	2
92-93—Buffalo	NHL	55	5	15	20	43	8	1	1	2	18
93-94—Buffalo	NHL	83	6	15	21	53	7	1	0	1	6
NHL totals		704	101	167	268	870	45	6	3	9	42

HANSEN, TRAVIS
C, JETS

PERSONAL: Born June 17, 1975, in Prince Albert, Sask....6-1/180....Shoots right.
TRANSACTIONS/CAREER NOTES: Selected by Winnipeg Jets in third round (third Jets pick, 58th overall) of NHL entry draft (June 29, 1994).

			REGULAR SEASON					PLAYOFFS			
Season Team	League	Gms.	G	A	Pts.	PIM	Gms.	G	A	Pts.	PIM
93-94—Tacoma	WHL	71	23	31	54	122	8	1	3	4	17

HARBERTS, TIM
C, PENGUINS

PERSONAL: Born May 20, 1975, in Edina, Minn....6-1/185....Shoots right.
HIGH SCHOOL: Wayzata (Plymouth, Minn.).
COLLEGE: Notre Dame.
TRANSACTIONS/CAREER NOTES: Selected by Pittsburgh Penguins in ninth round (ninth Penguins pick, 234th overall) of NHL entry draft (June 26, 1993).

			REGULAR SEASON					PLAYOFFS			
Season Team	League	Gms.	G	A	Pts.	PIM	Gms.	G	A	Pts.	PIM
90-91—Wayzata H.S.	Minn. H.S.	25	9	20	29	14	—	—	—	—	—
91-92—Wayzata H.S.	Minn. H.S.	21	19	23	42	18	—	—	—	—	—
92-93—Wayzata H.S.	Minn. H.S.	23	24	18	42	22	—	—	—	—	—
93-94—Univ. of Notre Dame	CCHA	36	10	12	22	19	—	—	—	—	—

HARDY, MARK
D, KINGS

PERSONAL: Born February 1, 1959, in Semaden, Switzerland....5-11/195....Shoots left.... Full name: Mark Lea Hardy.
TRANSACTIONS/CAREER NOTES: Selected by Los Angeles Kings in second round (third Kings pick, 30th overall) of NHL entry draft (August 9, 1979)....Underwent surgery to left wrist (October 1985); missed 25 games....Suffered viral infection (January 1988)....Traded by Kings to New York Rangers for RW Ron Duguay (February 23, 1988)....Traded by Rangers to Minnesota North Stars for future draft considerations (LW Louie DeBrusk) (June 13, 1988)....Injured wrist (October 19, 1988)....Traded by North Stars to Rangers for LW Larry Bernard and fifth-round pick (D Rhys Hollyman) in 1989 draft (December 10, 1988)....Sprained wrist (March 1989).... Sprained right ankle (March 3, 1990); missed 13 regular-season games and two playoff games....Reinjured ankle (April 9, 1990); missed remainder of playoffs....Suspended five games by NHL for stick-swinging (November 16, 1990)....Strained back (November 4, 1991); missed four games....Separated shoulder (December 31, 1991); missed 24 games....Traded by Rangers with fifth-round pick in 1993 draft (G Frederick Beaubien) to Los Angeles Kings for C John McIntyre (March 22, 1993).
HONORS: Won Emile (Butch) Bouchard Trophy (1977-78)....Named to QMJHL All-Star first team (1977-78).

H

			REGULAR SEASON					PLAYOFFS				
Season	Team	League	Gms.	G	A	Pts.	PIM	Gms.	G	A	Pts.	PIM
75-76—Montreal		QMJHL	64	6	17	23	44	—	—	—	—	—
76-77—Montreal		QMJHL	72	20	40	60	137	12	4	8	12	14
77-78—Montreal		QMJHL	72	25	57	82	150	13	3	10	13	22
78-79—Montreal		QMJHL	67	18	52	70	117	11	5	8	13	40
79-80—Binghamton		AHL	56	3	13	16	32	—	—	—	—	—
—Los Angeles		NHL	15	0	1	1	10	4	1	1	2	9
80-81—Los Angeles		NHL	77	5	20	25	77	4	1	2	3	4
81-82—Los Angeles		NHL	77	6	39	45	130	10	1	2	3	9
82-83—Los Angeles		NHL	74	5	34	39	101	—	—	—	—	—
83-84—Los Angeles		NHL	79	8	41	49	122	—	—	—	—	—
84-85—Los Angeles		NHL	78	14	39	53	97	3	0	1	1	2
85-86—Los Angeles		NHL	55	6	21	27	71	—	—	—	—	—
86-87—Los Angeles		NHL	73	3	27	30	120	5	1	2	3	10
87-88—Los Angeles		NHL	61	6	22	28	99	—	—	—	—	—
—New York Rangers		NHL	19	2	2	4	31	—	—	—	—	—
88-89—Minnesota		NHL	15	2	4	6	26	—	—	—	—	—
—New York Rangers		NHL	45	2	12	14	45	4	0	1	1	31
89-90—New York Rangers		NHL	54	0	15	15	94	3	0	1	1	2
90-91—New York Rangers		NHL	70	1	5	6	89	6	0	1	1	30
91-92—New York Rangers		NHL	52	1	8	9	65	13	0	3	3	31
92-93—New York Rangers		NHL	44	1	10	11	85	—	—	—	—	—
—Los Angeles		NHL	11	0	3	3	4	15	1	2	3	30
93-94—Los Angeles		NHL	16	0	3	3	27	—	—	—	—	—
—Phoenix		IHL	54	5	3	8	48	—	—	—	—	—
NHL totals			915	62	306	368	1293	67	5	16	21	158

HARKINS, BRETT
LW/C, RED WINGS

PERSONAL: Born July 2, 1970, in North Ridgefield, O. . . . 6-1/170. . . . Shoots left. . . . Full name: Brett Alan Harkins. . . . Brother of Todd Harkins, center, Hartford Whalers.
COLLEGE: Bowling Green State.
TRANSACTIONS/CAREER NOTES: Selected by New York Islanders in seventh round (ninth Islanders pick, 133rd overall) of NHL entry draft (June 17, 1989). . . . Signed as free agent by Adirondack Red Wings (1993).
HONORS: Named to CCHA All-Rookie team (1989-90).

			REGULAR SEASON					PLAYOFFS				
Season	Team	League	Gms.	G	A	Pts.	PIM	Gms.	G	A	Pts.	PIM
87-88—Brockville		COJHL	55	21	55	76	36	—	—	—	—	—
88-89—Detroit Compuware		NAJHL	38	23	46	69	94	—	—	—	—	—
89-90—Bowling Green State		CCHA	41	11	43	54	45	—	—	—	—	—
90-91—Bowling Green State		CCHA	40	22	38	60	30	—	—	—	—	—
91-92—Bowling Green State		CCHA	34	8	39	47	32	—	—	—	—	—
92-93—Bowling Green State		CCHA	35	19	28	47	28	—	—	—	—	—
93-94—Adirondack		AHL	80	22	47	69	23	10	1	5	6	4

HARKINS, TODD
RW, WHALERS

PERSONAL: Born October 8, 1968, in Cleveland. . . . 6-3/210. . . . Shoots right. . . . Full name: Todd Michael Harkins. . . . Brother of Brett Harkins, left winger/center in Detroit Red Wings system.
COLLEGE: Miami of Ohio.
TRANSACTIONS/CAREER NOTES: Selected by Calgary Flames in second round (second Flames pick, 42nd overall) of NHL entry draft (June 11, 1988). . . . Traded by Flames to Hartford Whalers for LW Scott Morrow (January 24, 1994). . . . Fined $500 by Whalers for involvement in bar brawl (April 1, 1994). . . . Suffered from the flu (April 2, 1994); missed two games.

			REGULAR SEASON					PLAYOFFS				
Season	Team	League	Gms.	G	A	Pts.	PIM	Gms.	G	A	Pts.	PIM
86-87—Aurora Jr. B		OHA	40	19	29	48	102	—	—	—	—	—
87-88—Miami of Ohio		CCHA	34	9	7	16	133	—	—	—	—	—
88-89—Miami of Ohio		CCHA	36	8	7	15	77	—	—	—	—	—
89-90—Miami of Ohio		CCHA	40	27	17	44	78	—	—	—	—	—
90-91—Salt Lake City		IHL	79	15	27	42	113	3	0	0	0	2
91-92—Salt Lake City		IHL	72	32	30	62	67	5	1	1	2	6
—Calgary		NHL	5	0	0	0	7	—	—	—	—	—
92-93—Salt Lake City		IHL	53	13	21	34	90	—	—	—	—	—
—Calgary		NHL	15	2	3	5	22	—	—	—	—	—
93-94—Saint John		AHL	38	13	9	22	64	—	—	—	—	—
—Springfield		AHL	1	0	3	3	0	—	—	—	—	—
—Hartford		NHL	28	1	0	1	49	—	—	—	—	—
NHL totals			48	3	3	6	78					

HARLOCK, DAVID
D, MAPLE LEAFS

PERSONAL: Born March 16, 1971, in Toronto. . . . 6-2/195. . . . Shoots left. . . . Full name: David Alan Harlock.
COLLEGE: Michigan.
TRANSACTIONS/CAREER NOTES: Injured knee (October 1988). . . . Selected by New Jersey Devils in second round (second Devils pick, 24th overall) of NHL entry draft (June 16, 1990). . . . Signed as free agent by Toronto Maple Leafs (August 20, 1993). . . . Loaned by Maple Leafs to Canadian Olympic Team (October 3, 1993).
MISCELLANEOUS: Member of silver-medal-winning Canadian Olympic team (1994).

H

Season Team	League	REGULAR SEASON					PLAYOFFS				
		Gms.	G	A	Pts.	PIM	Gms.	G	A	Pts.	PIM
86-87—Toronto Red Wings	MTHL	86	17	55	72	60	—	—	—	—	—
87-88—Toronto Red Wings	MTHL	70	16	56	72	100	—	—	—	—	—
88-89—St. Michael's Jr. B	ODHA	25	4	15	19	34	—	—	—	—	—
89-90—University of Michigan	CCHA	42	2	13	15	44	—	—	—	—	—
90-91—University of Michigan	CCHA	39	2	8	10	70	—	—	—	—	—
91-92—University of Michigan	CCHA	44	1	6	7	80	—	—	—	—	—
92-93—University of Michigan	CCHA	38	3	9	12	58	—	—	—	—	—
93-94—Canadian national team	Int'l	49	0	3	3	36	—	—	—	—	—
—Canadian Olympic Team	Int'l	8	0	0	0	8	—	—	—	—	—
—Toronto	NHL	6	0	0	0	0	—	—	—	—	—
—St. John's	AHL	10	0	3	3	2	9	0	0	0	6
NHL totals		6	0	0	0	0					

HARLTON, TYLER
D, BLUES

PERSONAL: Born January 11, 1976, in Regina, Sask. . . . 6-3/201. . . . Shoots left.
TRANSACTIONS/CAREER NOTES: Selected by St. Louis Blues in fourth round (second Blues pick, 94th overall) of NHL entry draft (June 29, 1994).

Season Team	League	REGULAR SEASON					PLAYOFFS				
		Gms.	G	A	Pts.	PIM	Gms.	G	A	Pts.	PIM
93-94—Vernon	BCJHL	60	3	18	21	102	—	—	—	—	—

HARTJE, TOD
RW

PERSONAL: Born February 27, 1968, in Anoka, Minn. . . . 6-1/200. . . . Shoots left. . . . Full name: Tod Dale Hartje. . . . Name pronounced HAHRT-jee.
HIGH SCHOOL: Anoka (Minn.).
COLLEGE: Harvard.
TRANSACTIONS/CAREER NOTES: Selected by Winnipeg Jets in seventh round (seventh Jets pick, 142nd overall) of NHL entry draft (June 13, 1987). . . . Assigned to Sokol Kiev for 1990-91 season (April 9, 1990).

Season Team	League	REGULAR SEASON					PLAYOFFS				
		Gms.	G	A	Pts.	PIM	Gms.	G	A	Pts.	PIM
85-86—Anoka H.S.	Minn. H.S.	22	25	34	59	. . .	—	—	—	—	—
86-87—Harvard University	ECAC	34	3	9	12	36	—	—	—	—	—
87-88—Harvard University	ECAC	32	5	17	22	40	—	—	—	—	—
88-89—Harvard University	ECAC	33	4	17	21	40	—	—	—	—	—
89-90—Harvard University	ECAC	28	6	10	16	29	—	—	—	—	—
90-91—Sokol Kiev	USSR	32	2	4	6	18	—	—	—	—	—
—Fort Wayne	IHL	1	1	0	1	2	—	—	—	—	—
91-92—Moncton	AHL	38	9	9	18	35	—	—	—	—	—
92-93—Moncton	AHL	29	3	7	10	2	—	—	—	—	—
—Fort Wayne	IHL	5	1	2	3	6	—	—	—	—	—
—Providence	AHL	29	2	14	16	32	4	1	0	1	20
93-94—Providence	AHL	80	22	27	49	157	—	—	—	—	—

HARTMAN, MIKE
LW, RANGERS

PERSONAL: Born February 7, 1967, in West Bloomfield, Mich. . . . 6-0/192. . . . Shoots left. . . . Full name: Michael Jay Hartman.
TRANSACTIONS/CAREER NOTES: Selected by Buffalo Sabres in seventh round (eighth Sabres pick, 131st overall) of NHL entry draft (June 21, 1986). . . . Suffered sore back (January 1989). . . . Sprained right ankle (December 1, 1989); missed five games. . . . Reinjured right ankle (December 29, 1989); missed five games. . . . Injured ankle (March 10, 1990). . . . Injured elbow (November 3, 1990); missed seven games. . . . Traded by Sabres with LW Darrin Shannon and D Dean Kennedy to Winnipeg Jets for RW Dave McLlwain, D Gordon Donnelly, fifth-round pick in 1992 draft (LW Yuri Khmylev) and future considerations (October 11, 1991). . . . Suffered from the flu (December 1991); missed one game. . . . Selected by Tampa Bay Lightning in NHL expansion draft (June 18, 1992). . . . Cut forearm (October 20, 1992); missed four games. . . . Bruised ribs (December 5, 1992); missed three games. . . . Traded by Lightning to New York Rangers for C Randy Gilhen (March 22, 1993). . . . Suffered injury (November 10, 1993); missed two games.
MISCELLANEOUS: Member of Stanley Cup championship team (1994).

Season Team	League	REGULAR SEASON					PLAYOFFS				
		Gms.	G	A	Pts.	PIM	Gms.	G	A	Pts.	PIM
84-85—Belleville	OHL	49	13	12	25	119	—	—	—	—	—
85-86—Belleville	OHL	4	2	1	3	5	—	—	—	—	—
—North Bay	OHL	53	19	16	35	205	10	2	4	6	34
86-87—North Bay	OHL	32	15	24	39	144	19	7	8	15	88
—Buffalo	NHL	17	3	3	6	69	—	—	—	—	—
87-88—Rochester	AHL	57	13	14	27	283	4	1	0	1	22
—Buffalo	NHL	18	3	1	4	90	6	0	0	0	35
88-89—Buffalo	NHL	70	8	9	17	316	5	0	0	0	34
89-90—Buffalo	NHL	60	11	10	21	211	6	0	0	0	18
90-91—Buffalo	NHL	60	9	3	12	204	2	0	0	0	17
91-92—Winnipeg	NHL	75	4	4	8	264	2	0	0	0	2
92-93—Tampa Bay	NHL	58	4	4	8	154	—	—	—	—	—
—New York Rangers	NHL	3	0	0	0	6	—	—	—	—	—
93-94—New York Rangers	NHL	35	1	1	2	70	—	—	—	—	—
NHL totals		396	43	35	78	1384	21	0	0	0	106

HARVEY, TODD
C, STARS

PERSONAL: Born February 17, 1975, in Hamilton, Ont. . . . 5-11/190. . . . Shoots right.
TRANSACTIONS/CAREER NOTES: Selected by Dallas Stars in first round (first Stars pick, ninth overall) of NHL entry draft (June 26, 1993).
HONORS: Named to Can.HL All-Rookie team (1991-92). . . . Named to OHL Rookie All-Star team (1991-92).

			REGULAR SEASON					PLAYOFFS				
Season Team	League	Gms.	G	A	Pts.	PIM	Gms.	G	A	Pts.	PIM
89-90—Cambridge Jr. B	OHA	41	35	27	62	213	—	—	—	—	—
90-91—Cambridge Jr. B	OHA	35	32	39	71	174	—	—	—	—	—
91-92—Detroit	OHL	58	21	43	64	141	7	3	5	8	32
92-93—Detroit	OHL	55	50	50	100	83	15	9	12	21	39
93-94—Detroit	OHL	49	34	51	85	75	17	10	12	22	26

HASEK, DOMINIK
G, SABRES

PERSONAL: Born January 29, 1965, in Pardubice, Czechoslovakia. . . . 5-11/168. . . . Catches left. . . . Name pronounced HAH-shihk.
TRANSACTIONS/CAREER NOTES: Selected by Chicago Blackhawks in 10th round (11th Blackhawks pick, 199th overall) of NHL entry draft (June 8, 1983). . . . Traded by Blackhawks to Buffalo Sabres for G Stephane Beauregard and future considerations (August 7, 1992). . . . Injured groin (November 25, 1992); missed three games. . . . Pulled stomach muscle (January 6, 1993); missed six games.
HONORS: Named Czechoslovakian League Player of the Year (1986-87, 1988-89 and 1989-90). . . . Named to Czechoslovakian League All-Star team (1988-89 and 1989-90). . . . Named to IHL All-Star first team (1990-91). . . . Named to NHL All-Rookie team (1991-92). . . . Won Vezina Trophy (1993-94). . . . Shared William M. Jennings Trophy with Grant Fuhr (1993-94). . . . Named to THE SPORTING NEWS All-Star second team (1993-94). . . . Named to NHL All-Star first team (1993-94).

			REGULAR SEASON							PLAYOFFS						
Season Team	League	Gms.	Min.	W	L	T	GA	SO	Avg.	Gms.	Min.	W	L	GA	SO	Avg.
81-82—Pardubice	Czech.	12	661	...	...	...	34	0	3.09	—	—	—	—	—	—	—
82-83—Pardubice	Czech.	42	2358	...	...	...	105	0	2.67	—	—	—	—	—	—	—
83-84—Pardubice	Czech.	40	2304	...	...	...	108	0	2.81	—	—	—	—	—	—	—
84-85—Pardubice	Czech.	42	2419	...	...	...	131	0	3.25	—	—	—	—	—	—	—
85-86—Pardubice	Czech.	45	2689	...	...	...	138	0	3.08	—	—	—	—	—	—	—
86-87—Pardubice	Czech.	23	2515	...	...	...	103	0	2.46	—	—	—	—	—	—	—
87-88—Pardubice	Czech.	31	2265	...	...	...	98	0	2.60	—	—	—	—	—	—	—
—Czech. Olympic Team	Int'l	8	217	...	...	...	18	...	4.98	—	—	—	—	—	—	—
88-89—Pardubice	Czech.	42	2507	...	...	...	114	0	2.73	—	—	—	—	—	—	—
89-90—Dukla Jihlava	Czech.	40	2251	...	...	...	80	0	2.13	—	—	—	—	—	—	—
90-91—Chicago	NHL	5	195	3	0	1	8	0	2.46	3	69	0	0	3	0	2.61
—Indianapolis	IHL	33	1903	20	11	‡4	80	*5	*2.52	1	60	1	0	3	0	3.00
91-92—Indianapolis	IHL	20	1162	7	10	‡3	69	1	3.56	—	—	—	—	—	—	—
—Chicago	NHL	20	1014	10	4	1	44	1	2.60	3	158	0	2	8	0	3.04
92-93—Buffalo	NHL	28	1429	11	10	4	75	0	3.15	1	45	1	0	1	0	1.33
93-94—Buffalo	NHL	58	3358	30	20	6	109	†7	*1.95	7	484	3	4	13	2	*1.61
NHL totals		111	5996	54	34	12	236	8	2.36	14	756	4	6	25	2	1.98

HATCHER, DERIAN
D, STARS

PERSONAL: Born June 4, 1972, in Sterling Heights, Mich. . . . 6-5/225. . . . Shoots left. . . . Brother of Kevin Hatcher, defenseman, Washington Capitals.
TRANSACTIONS/CAREER NOTES: Underwent knee surgery (January 1989). . . . Selected by Minnesota North Stars in first round (first North Stars pick, eighth overall) of NHL entry draft (June 16, 1990). . . . Suspended 10 games by NHL (December 1991). . . . Fractured ankle in off-ice incident (January 19, 1992); missed 21 games. . . . Sprained knee (January 6, 1993); missed 14 games. . . . Suspended one game by NHL for game misconduct penalties (March 9, 1993). . . . North Stars franchise moved from Minnesota to Dallas and renamed Stars for 1993-94 season.

			REGULAR SEASON					PLAYOFFS				
Season Team	League	Gms.	G	A	Pts.	PIM	Gms.	G	A	Pts.	PIM
88-89—Detroit G.P.D.	MNHL	51	19	35	54	100	—	—	—	—	—
89-90—North Bay	OHL	64	14	38	52	81	5	2	3	5	8
90-91—North Bay	OHL	64	13	50	63	163	10	2	10	12	28
91-92—Minnesota	NHL	43	8	4	12	88	5	0	2	2	8
92-93—Minnesota	NHL	67	4	15	19	178	—	—	—	—	—
—Kalamazoo	IHL	2	1	2	3	21	—	—	—	—	—
93-94—Dallas	NHL	83	12	19	31	211	9	0	2	2	14
NHL totals		193	24	38	62	477	14	0	4	4	22

HATCHER, KEVIN
D, CAPITALS

PERSONAL: Born September 9, 1966, in Detroit. . . . 6-4/225. . . . Shoots right. . . . Full name: Kevin John Hatcher. . . . Brother of Derian Hatcher, defenseman, Dallas Stars.
TRANSACTIONS/CAREER NOTES: Selected by Washington Capitals as underage junior in first round (first Capitals pick, 17th overall) of NHL entry draft (June 9, 1984). . . . Tore cartilage in left knee (October 1987). . . . Pulled groin (January 1989). . . . Fractured two metatarsal bones in left foot (February 5, 1989); missed 15 games. . . . Sprained left knee (April 27, 1990). . . . Did not attend Capitals training camp due to contract dispute (September 1990). . . . Injured right knee (November 10, 1990). . . . Suspended one game by NHL for game misconduct penalties (February 2, 1993). . . . Fractured right hand (December 23, 1993); missed 10 games. . . . Suffered from the flu (March 29, 1994); missed one game. . . . Pulled thigh (April 9, 1994); missed one game.
HONORS: Named to OHL All-Star second team (1984-85). . . . Played in NHL All-Star Game (1990 through 1992).

H

Season Team	League	REGULAR SEASON Gms.	G	A	Pts.	PIM	PLAYOFFS Gms.	G	A	Pts.	PIM
83-84—North Bay	OHL	67	10	39	49	61	4	2	2	4	11
84-85—North Bay	OHL	58	26	37	63	75	8	5	8	13	9
—Washington	NHL	2	1	0	1	0	1	0	0	0	0
85-86—Washington	NHL	79	9	10	19	119	9	1	1	2	19
86-87—Washington	NHL	78	8	16	24	144	7	1	0	1	20
87-88—Washington	NHL	71	14	27	41	137	14	5	7	12	55
88-89—Washington	NHL	62	13	27	40	101	6	1	4	5	20
89-90—Washington	NHL	80	13	41	54	102	11	0	8	8	32
90-91—Washington	NHL	79	24	50	74	69	11	3	3	6	8
91-92—Washington	NHL	79	17	37	54	105	7	2	4	6	19
92-93—Washington	NHL	83	34	45	79	114	6	0	1	1	14
93-94—Washington	NHL	72	16	24	40	108	11	3	4	7	37
NHL totals		685	149	277	426	999	83	16	32	48	224

HAUER, BRETT
D

PERSONAL: Born July 11, 1971, in Edina, Minn. . . . 6-2/180. . . . Shoots right. . . . Full name: Brett Timothy Hauer. . . . Cousin of Don Jackson, defenseman, Minnesota North Stars, Edmonton Oilers and New York Rangers (1977-78 through 1986-87).
HIGH SCHOOL: Richfield (Minn.).
COLLEGE: Minnesota-Duluth.
TRANSACTIONS/CAREER NOTES: Selected by Vancouver Canucks in fourth round (third Canucks pick, 71st overall) of NHL entry draft (June 17, 1989). . . . Separated shoulder (December 1990). . . . Signed as free agent by Las Vegas Thunder (February 15, 1994).
HONORS: Named WCHA Student-Athlete of the Year (1992-93). . . . Named to NCAA All-America West first team (1992-93). . . . Named to WCHA All-Star first team (1992-93).

Season Team	League	REGULAR SEASON Gms.	G	A	Pts.	PIM	PLAYOFFS Gms.	G	A	Pts.	PIM
87-88—Richfield H.S.	Minn. H.S.	24	3	3	6	...	—	—	—	—	—
88-89—Richfield H.S.	Minn. H.S.	24	8	15	23	70	—	—	—	—	—
89-90—Minnesota-Duluth	WCHA	37	2	6	8	44	—	—	—	—	—
90-91—Minnesota-Duluth	WCHA	30	1	7	8	54	—	—	—	—	—
91-92—Minnesota-Duluth	WCHA	33	8	14	22	40	—	—	—	—	—
92-93—Minnesota-Duluth	WCHA	40	10	46	56	54	—	—	—	—	—
93-94—U.S. national team	Int'l	57	6	14	20	88	—	—	—	—	—
—U.S. Olympic Team	Int'l	8	0	0	0	10	—	—	—	—	—
—Las Vegas	IHL	21	0	7	7	8	1	0	0	0	0

HAWERCHUK, DALE
C, SABRES

PERSONAL: Born April 4, 1963, in Toronto. . . . 5-11/190. . . . Shoots left. . . . Name pronounced HOW-uhr-CHUHK.
TRANSACTIONS/CAREER NOTES: Selected by Winnipeg Jets as underage junior in first round (first Jets pick, first overall) of NHL entry draft (June 10, 1981). . . . Broke rib (April 13, 1985). . . . Fractured cheekbone (February 1, 1989). . . . Traded by Jets with first-round pick in 1990 draft (LW Brad May) to Buffalo Sabres for D Phil Housley, LW Scott Arniel, RW Jeff Parker and first-round pick (C Keith Tkachuk) in 1990 draft (June 16, 1990). . . . Injured hip (March 8, 1992); missed one game. . . . Sprained right knee (February 12, 1993); missed three games.
HONORS: Won Instructeurs Trophy (1979-80). . . . Won Guy Lafleur Trophy (1979-80). . . . Named to Memorial Cup All-Star team (1979-80 and 1980-81). . . . Won Can.HL Player of the Year Award (1980-81). . . . Won Michel Briere Trophy (1980-81). . . . Won Jean Beliveau Trophy (1980-81). . . . Won Association of Journalists for Major Junior League Hockey Trophy (1980-81). . . . Won CCM Trophy (1980-81). . . . Named to QMJHL All-Star first team (1980-81). . . . Named NHL Rookie of the Year by THE SPORTING NEWS (1981-82). . . . Won Calder Memorial Trophy (1981-82). . . . Played in NHL All-Star Game (1982, 1985, 1986 and 1988). . . . Named to THE SPORTING NEWS All-Star second team (1984-85). . . . Named to NHL All-Star second team (1984-85).
RECORDS: Holds NHL single-game record for most assists in one period—5 (March 6, 1984).
STATISTICAL NOTES: Youngest player in NHL history to have 100-point season (18 years, 351 days).

Season Team	League	REGULAR SEASON Gms.	G	A	Pts.	PIM	PLAYOFFS Gms.	G	A	Pts.	PIM
79-80—Cornwall	QMJHL	72	37	66	103	21	18	20	25	45	0
80-81—Cornwall	QMJHL	72	*81	*102	*183	69	19	15	20	35	8
81-82—Winnipeg	NHL	80	45	58	103	47	4	1	7	8	5
82-83—Winnipeg	NHL	79	40	51	91	31	3	1	4	5	8
83-84—Winnipeg	NHL	80	37	65	102	73	3	1	1	2	0
84-85—Winnipeg	NHL	80	53	77	130	74	3	2	1	3	4
85-86—Winnipeg	NHL	80	46	59	105	44	3	0	3	3	0
86-87—Winnipeg	NHL	80	47	53	100	54	10	5	8	13	4
87-88—Winnipeg	NHL	80	44	77	121	59	5	3	4	7	16
88-89—Winnipeg	NHL	75	41	55	96	28	—	—	—	—	—
89-90—Winnipeg	NHL	79	26	55	81	60	7	3	5	8	2
90-91—Buffalo	NHL	80	31	58	89	32	6	2	4	6	10
91-92—Buffalo	NHL	77	23	75	98	27	7	2	5	7	0
92-93—Buffalo	NHL	81	16	80	96	52	8	5	9	14	2
93-94—Buffalo	NHL	81	35	51	86	91	7	0	7	7	4
NHL totals		1032	484	814	1298	672	66	25	58	83	55

H

HAWGOOD, GREG

D, PENGUINS

PERSONAL: Born August 10, 1968, in St. Albert, Alta. . . . 5-10/190. . . . Shoots left. . . . Full name: Gregory William Hawgood. **TRANSACTIONS/CAREER NOTES:** Selected by Boston Bruins as underage junior in 10th round (ninth Bruins pick, 202nd overall) of NHL entry draft (June 21, 1986). . . . Announced that he would play in Italy for 1990-91 season (July 1990). . . . Traded by Bruins to Edmonton Oilers for C Vladimir Ruzicka (October 22, 1990). . . . Traded by Oilers with C Josef Beranek to Philadelphia Flyers for D Brian Benning (January 16, 1993). . . . Traded by Flyers to Florida Panthers for future considerations (November 28, 1993). . . . Bruised left thumb (January 13, 1994); missed seven games. . . . Traded by Panthers to Pittsburgh Penguins for LW Jeff Daniels (March 19, 1994).
HONORS: Named to WHL (West) All-Star first team (1985-86 through 1987-88). . . . Won Can.HL Defenseman of the Year Award (1987-88). . . . Won Bill Hunter Trophy (1987-88). . . . Won Eddie Shore Plaque (1991-92). . . . Named to AHL All-Star first team (1991-92).

			REGULAR SEASON					PLAYOFFS			
Season Team	League	Gms.	G	A	Pts.	PIM	Gms.	G	A	Pts.	PIM
83-84—Kamloops	WHL	49	10	23	33	39	—	—	—	—	—
84-85—Kamloops	WHL	66	25	40	65	72	—	—	—	—	—
85-86—Kamloops	WHL	71	34	85	119	86	16	9	22	31	16
86-87—Kamloops	WHL	61	30	93	123	139	—	—	—	—	—
87-88—Boston	NHL	1	0	0	0	0	3	1	0	1	0
—Kamloops	WHL	63	48	85	133	142	16	10	16	26	33
88-89—Boston	NHL	56	16	24	40	84	10	0	2	2	2
—Maine	AHL	21	2	9	11	41	—	—	—	—	—
89-90—Boston	NHL	77	11	27	38	76	15	1	3	4	12
90-91—Asiago	Italy	2	...	...	0	...	—	—	—	—	—
—Maine	AHL	5	0	1	1	13	—	—	—	—	—
—Cape Breton	AHL	55	10	32	42	73	4	0	3	3	23
—Edmonton	NHL	6	0	1	1	6	—	—	—	—	—
91-92—Cape Breton	AHL	56	20	55	75	26	3	2	2	4	0
—Edmonton	NHL	20	2	11	13	22	13	0	3	3	23
92-93—Edmonton	NHL	29	5	13	18	35	—	—	—	—	—
—Philadelphia	NHL	40	6	22	28	39	—	—	—	—	—
93-94—Philadelphia	NHL	19	3	12	15	19	—	—	—	—	—
—Florida	NHL	33	2	14	16	9	—	—	—	—	—
—Pittsburgh	NHL	12	1	2	3	8	1	0	0	0	0
NHL totals		293	46	126	172	298	42	2	8	10	37

HAWKINS, TODD

RW, MAPLE LEAFS

PERSONAL: Born August 2, 1966, in Kingston, Ont. . . . 6-1/195. . . . Shoots right. **TRANSACTIONS/CAREER NOTES:** Selected by Vancouver Canucks in 11th round (10th Canucks pick, 217th overall) of NHL entry draft (June 21, 1986). . . . Suspended two games by OHL (October 1, 1986). . . . Bruised hand (September 1988). . . . Traded by Canucks to Toronto Maple Leafs for D Brian Blad (January 22, 1991).
HONORS: Named to OHL All-Star second team (1986-87).

			REGULAR SEASON					PLAYOFFS			
Season Team	League	Gms.	G	A	Pts.	PIM	Gms.	G	A	Pts.	PIM
84-85—Belleville	OHL	58	7	16	23	117	12	1	0	1	10
85-86—Belleville	OHL	60	14	13	27	172	24	9	7	16	60
86-87—Belleville	OHL	60	47	40	87	187	6	3	5	8	16
87-88—Flint	IHL	50	13	13	26	337	16	3	5	8	*174
—Fredericton	AHL	2	0	0	0	11	—	—	—	—	—
88-89—Vancouver	NHL	4	0	0	0	9	—	—	—	—	—
—Milwaukee	IHL	63	12	14	26	307	9	1	0	1	33
89-90—Vancouver	NHL	4	0	0	0	6	—	—	—	—	—
—Milwaukee	IHL	61	23	17	40	273	5	4	1	5	19
90-91—Milwaukee	IHL	39	9	11	20	134	—	—	—	—	—
—Newmarket	AHL	22	2	5	7	66	—	—	—	—	—
91-92—St. John's	AHL	66	30	27	57	139	7	1	0	1	10
—Toronto	NHL	2	0	0	0	0	—	—	—	—	—
92-93—St. John's	AHL	72	21	41	62	103	9	1	3	4	10
93-94—Cleveland	IHL	76	19	14	33	115	—	—	—	—	—
NHL totals		10	0	0	0	15					

HAYWARD, RICK

D

PERSONAL: Born February 25, 1966, in Toledo, O. . . . 6-0/200. . . . Shoots left. **TRANSACTIONS/CAREER NOTES:** Selected by Montreal Canadiens in eighth round (ninth Canadiens pick, 162nd overall) of NHL entry draft (June 21, 1986). . . . Traded by Canadiens to Calgary Flames for RW Martin Nicoletti (February 20, 1988). . . . Suspended six games by IHL for abusing an official (October 12, 1988). . . . Signed as free agent by Los Angeles Kings (August 1990). . . . Signed as free agent by New York Islanders (July 25, 1991). . . . Signed as free agent by Winnipeg Jets (July 30, 1992). . . . Traded by Jets to New York Islanders for future considerations (February 22, 1993). . . . Signed as free agent by Florida Panthers (September 7, 1993). . . . Signed as free agent by Cleveland Lumberjacks (June 24, 1994).

			REGULAR SEASON					PLAYOFFS			
Season Team	League	Gms.	G	A	Pts.	PIM	Gms.	G	A	Pts.	PIM
84-85—Hull	QMJHL	56	7	27	34	367	—	—	—	—	—
85-86—Hull	QMJHL	59	3	40	43	354	15	2	11	13	*98
86-87—Sherbrooke	AHL	43	2	3	5	153	3	0	1	1	15

H

Season Team	League	REGULAR SEASON					PLAYOFFS				
		Gms.	G	A	Pts.	Pen.	Gms.	G	A	Pts.	Pen.
87-88—Sherbrooke	AHL	22	1	5	6	91	—	—	—	—	—
—Saginaw	IHL	24	3	4	7	129	—	—	—	—	—
—Salt Lake City	IHL	17	1	3	4	124	13	0	1	1	120
88-89—Salt Lake City	IHL	72	4	20	24	313	10	4	3	7	42
89-90—Salt Lake City	IHL	58	5	13	18	*419	—	—	—	—	—
90-91—Los Angeles	NHL	4	0	0	0	5	—	—	—	—	—
—Phoenix	IHL	60	9	13	22	369	7	1	2	3	44
91-92—Capital District	AHL	27	3	8	11	139	7	0	0	0	58
92-93—Moncton	AHL	47	1	3	4	231	4	1	1	2	27
—Capital District	AHL	19	0	1	1	80	—	—	—	—	—
93-94—Cincinnati	IHL	61	2	6	8	302	8	0	1	1	*99
NHL totals		4	0	0	0	5					

HEALY, GLENN
G, RANGERS

PERSONAL: Born August 23, 1962, in Pickering, Ont. . . . 5- 10/ 185. . . . Catches left.
COLLEGE: Western Michigan.
TRANSACTIONS/CAREER NOTES: Signed as free agent by Los Angeles Kings (June 13, 1985). . . . Signed as free agent by New York Islanders (August 16, 1989); Kings awarded fourth-round pick in 1990 draft as compensation. . . . Strained left ankle ligaments (October 13, 1990); missed eight games. . . . Fractured right index finger (November 10, 1991); missed five games. . . . Fractured right thumb (January 3, 1992); missed 10 games. . . . Severed tip of finger in practice and underwent reconstructive surgery (March 2, 1992); missed 13 games. . . . Suffered from tendinitis in right wrist (January 9, 1993); missed four games. . . . Selected by Mighty Ducks of Anaheim in NHL expansion draft (June 24, 1993). . . . Selected by Tampa Bay Lightning in Phase II of NHL expansion draft (June 25, 1993). . . . Traded by Lightning to New York Rangers for third-round pick in 1993 draft (June 25, 1993).
HONORS: Named to NCAA All-America West second team (1984-85). . . . Named to CCHA All-Star second team (1984-85).
MISCELLANEOUS: Member of Stanley Cup championship team (1994).

Season Team	League	REGULAR SEASON								PLAYOFFS						
		Gms.	Min.	W	L	T	GA	SO	Avg.	Gms.	Min.	W	L	GA	SO	Avg.
81-82—Western Michigan U.	CCHA	27	1569	7	19	1	116	0	4.44	—	—	—	—	—	—	—
82-83—Western Michigan U.	CCHA	30	1733	8	19	2	116	0	4.02	—	—	—	—	—	—	—
83-84—Western Michigan U.	CCHA	38	2242	19	16	3	146	0	3.91	—	—	—	—	—	—	—
84-85—Western Michigan U.	CCHA	37	2172	21	14	2	118	. . .	3.26	—	—	—	—	—	—	—
85-86—Toledo	IHL	7	402	. . .	. . .	‡. . .	28	0	4.18	—	—	—	—	—	—	—
—New Haven	AHL	43	2410	21	15	4	160	0	3.98	2	119	0	2	11	0	5.55
—Los Angeles	NHL	1	51	0	0	0	6	0	7.06	—	—	—	—	—	—	—
86-87—New Haven	AHL	47	2828	21	15	0	173	1	3.67	7	427	3	4	19	0	2.67
87-88—Los Angeles	NHL	34	1869	12	18	1	135	1	4.33	4	240	1	3	20	0	5.00
88-89—Los Angeles	NHL	48	2699	25	19	2	192	0	4.27	3	97	0	1	6	0	3.71
89-90—New York Islanders	NHL	39	2197	12	19	6	128	2	3.50	4	166	1	2	9	0	3.25
90-91—New York Islanders	NHL	53	2999	18	24	9	166	0	3.32	—	—	—	—	—	—	—
91-92—New York Islanders	NHL	37	1960	14	16	4	124	1	3.80	—	—	—	—	—	—	—
92-93—New York Islanders	NHL	47	2655	22	20	2	146	1	3.30	18	1109	9	8	59	0	3.19
93-94—New York Rangers	NHL	29	1368	10	12	2	69	2	3.03	2	68	0	1	1	0	0.88
NHL totals		288	15798	113	128	26	966	7	3.67	31	1680	11	14	95	0	3.39

HEBERT, GUY
G, MIGHTY DUCKS

PERSONAL: Born January 7, 1967, in Troy, N.Y. . . . 5-11/ 185. . . . Catches left. . . . Full name: Guy Andrew Hebert. . . . Name pronounced GEE ay-BAIR.
HIGH SCHOOL: LaSalle Institute (Troy, N.Y.).
COLLEGE: Hamilton (N.Y.).
TRANSACTIONS/CAREER NOTES: Selected by St. Louis Blues in eighth round (eighth Blues choice, 159th overall) of NHL entry draft (June 13, 1987). . . . Selected by Mighty Ducks of Anaheim in NHL expansion draft (June 24, 1993).
HONORS: Shared James Norris Memorial Trophy with Pat Jablonski (1990-91). . . . Named to IHL All-Star second team (1990-91).

Season Team	League	REGULAR SEASON								PLAYOFFS						
		Gms.	Min.	W	L	T	GA	SO	Avg.	Gms.	Min.	W	L	GA	SO	Avg.
86-87—Hamilton College	Div. II	18	1070	12	5	0	40	0	2.24	—	—	—	—	—	—	—
87-88—Hamilton College	Div. II	8	450	5	3	0	19	0	2.53	—	—	—	—	—	—	—
88-89—Hamilton College	Div. II	25	1453	18	7	0	62	0	2.56	—	—	—	—	—	—	—
89-90—Peoria	IHL	30	1706	7	13	‡7	124	1	4.36	2	76	0	1	5	0	3.95
90-91—Peoria	IHL	36	2093	24	10	‡1	100	2	*2.87	8	458	3	4	32	0	4.19
91-92—Peoria	IHL	29	1731	20	9	‡0	98	0	3.40	4	239	3	1	9	0	*2.26
—St. Louis	NHL	13	738	5	5	1	36	0	2.93	—	—	—	—	—	—	—
92-93—St. Louis	NHL	24	1210	8	8	2	74	1	3.67	1	2	0	0	0	0	0.00
93-94—Anaheim	NHL	52	2991	20	27	3	141	2	2.83	—	—	—	—	—	—	—
NHL totals		89	4939	33	40	6	251	3	3.05	1	2	0	0	0		0

HEDICAN, BRET
D, CANUCKS

PERSONAL: Born August 10, 1970, in St. Paul, Minn. . . . 6-2/ 195. . . . Shoots left. . . . Full name: Bret Michael Hedican. . . . Name pronounced HEH-dih-kihn.
HIGH SCHOOL: North St. Paul (Minn.).
COLLEGE: St. Cloud (Minn.) State.
TRANSACTIONS/CAREER NOTES: Selected by St. Louis Blues in 10th round (10th Blues pick, 198th overall) of NHL entry draft (June 11, 1988). . . . Sprained knee ligaments (September 27, 1992); missed first 15 games of season. . . . Injured shoulder

(October 24, 1993); missed three games. . . . Injured groin (January 18, 1994); missed six games. . . . Traded by Blues with D Jeff Brown and C Nathan LaFayette to Vancouver Canucks for C Craig Janney (March 21, 1994). . . . Strained groin (March 27, 1994); missed three games.
HONORS: Named to WCHA All-Star first team (1990-91).

			REGULAR SEASON					PLAYOFFS			
Season Team	League	Gms.	G	A	Pts.	PIM	Gms.	G	A	Pts.	PIM
88-89—St. Cloud State	WCHA	28	5	3	8	28	—	—	—	—	—
89-90—St. Cloud State	WCHA	36	4	17	21	37	—	—	—	—	—
90-91—St. Cloud State	WCHA	41	18	30	48	52	—	—	—	—	—
91-92—U.S. national team	Int'l	54	1	8	9	59	—	—	—	—	—
—U.S. Olympic Team	Int'l	8	0	0	0	4	—	—	—	—	—
—St. Louis	NHL	4	1	0	1	0	5	0	0	0	0
92-93—Peoria	IHL	19	0	8	8	10	—	—	—	—	—
—St. Louis	NHL	42	0	8	8	30	10	0	0	0	14
93-94—St. Louis	NHL	61	0	11	11	64	—	—	—	—	—
—Vancouver	NHL	8	0	1	1	0	24	1	6	7	16
NHL totals		115	1	20	21	94	39	1	6	7	30

HEINZE, STEVE
RW, BRUINS

PERSONAL: Born January 30, 1970, in Lawrence, Mass. . . . 5-11/180. . . . Shoots right. . . . Full name: Stephen Herbert Heinze. . . . Name pronounced HIGHNS.
HIGH SCHOOL: Lawrence Academy (Groton, Mass.).
COLLEGE: Boston College.
TRANSACTIONS/CAREER NOTES: Selected by Boston Bruins in second round (second Bruins pick, 60th overall) of NHL entry draft (June 11, 1988). . . . Injured shoulder (May 1, 1992). . . . Injured shoulder (March 20, 1993); missed 11 games. . . . Injured knee (February 18, 1994); missed five games. . . . Reinjured knee (March 26, 1994); missed two games.
HONORS: Named to Hockey East All-Rookie team (1988-89). . . . Named to NCAA All-America East first team (1989-90). . . . Named to Hockey East All-Star first team (1989-90).

			REGULAR SEASON					PLAYOFFS			
Season Team	League	Gms.	G	A	Pts.	PIM	Gms.	G	A	Pts.	PIM
86-87—Lawrence Academy	Mass. H.S.	23	26	24	50	. . .	—	—	—	—	—
87-88—Lawrence Academy	Mass. H.S.	23	30	25	55	. . .	—	—	—	—	—
88-89—Boston College	Hockey East	36	26	23	49	26	—	—	—	—	—
89-90—Boston College	Hockey East	40	27	36	63	41	—	—	—	—	—
90-91—Boston College	Hockey East	35	21	26	47	35	—	—	—	—	—
91-92—U.S. national team	Int'l	49	18	15	33	38	—	—	—	—	—
—U.S. Olympic Team	Int'l	8	1	3	4	8	—	—	—	—	—
—Boston	NHL	14	3	4	7	6	7	0	3	3	17
92-93—Boston	NHL	73	18	13	31	24	4	1	1	2	2
93-94—Boston	NHL	77	10	11	21	32	13	2	3	5	7
NHL totals		164	31	28	59	62	24	3	7	10	26

HEJDUK, MILAN
RW, NORDIQUES

PERSONAL: Born February 14, 1976, in Usti-nad-Labem, Czechoslovakia. . . . 5-11/163. . . . Shoots right.
TRANSACTIONS/CAREER NOTES: Selected by Quebec Nordiques in fourth round (sixth Nordiques pick, 72nd overall) of NHL entry draft (June 29, 1994).
HONORS: Named Czechoslovokian League Rookie of the Year (1993-94).

			REGULAR SEASON					PLAYOFFS			
Season Team	League	Gms.	G	A	Pts.	PIM	Gms.	G	A	Pts.	PIM
93-94—HC Pardubice	Czech Rep.	22	6	3	9	. . .	10	5	1	6	0

HELENIUS, SAMI
D, FLAMES

PERSONAL: Born January 22, 1974, in Helsinki, Finland. . . . 6-5/220. . . . Shoots left.
TRANSACTIONS/CAREER NOTES: Selected by Calgary Flames in fifth round (fifth Flames pick, 102nd overall) of NHL entry draft (June 20, 1992).

			REGULAR SEASON					PLAYOFFS			
Season Team	League	Gms.	G	A	Pts.	PIM	Gms.	G	A	Pts.	PIM
91-92—Jokerit Helsinki Jrs.	Finland				Statistics unavailable.		—	—	—	—	—
92-93—Vantaa HT	Finland Dv.II	21	3	2	5	60	—	—	—	—	—
—Jokerit Helsinki Jrs.	Finland	1	0	0	0	0	—	—	—	—	—
93-94—Reipas Lahti	Finland	37	2	3	5	46	—	—	—	—	—

HENDRICKSON, DARBY
C, MAPLE LEAFS

PERSONAL: Born August 28, 1972, in Richfield, Minn. . . . 6-0/185. . . . Shoots left.
HIGH SCHOOL: Richfield (Minn.).
COLLEGE: Minnesota.
TRANSACTIONS/CAREER NOTES: Selected by Toronto Maple Leafs in fourth round (third Maple Leafs pick, 73rd overall) of NHL entry draft (June 16, 1990).
HONORS: Won WCHA Rookie of the Year Award (1991-92). . . . Named to WCHA All-Rookie team (1991-92).

			REGULAR SEASON					PLAYOFFS			
Season Team	League	Gms.	G	A	Pts.	PIM	Gms.	G	A	Pts.	PIM
87-88—Richfield H.S.	Minn. H.S.	22	12	9	21	10	—	—	—	—	—
88-89—Richfield H.S.	Minn. H.S.	22	22	20	42	12	—	—	—	—	—

H

Season Team	League	REGULAR SEASON					PLAYOFFS				
		Gms.	G	A	Pts.	Pen.	Gms.	G	A	Pts.	Pen.
89-90—Richfield H.S.	Minn. H.S.	24	23	27	50	49	—	—	—	—	—
90-91—Richfield H.S.	Minn. H.S.	27	32	29	61	...	—	—	—	—	—
91-92—University of Minnesota	WCHA	44	25	30	55	63	—	—	—	—	—
92-93—University of Minnesota	WCHA	31	12	15	27	35	—	—	—	—	—
93-94—U.S. national team	Int'l	59	12	16	28	30	—	—	—	—	—
—U.S. Olympic Team	Int'l	8	0	0	0	6	—	—	—	—	—
—St. John's	AHL	6	4	1	5	4	3	1	1	2	0
—Toronto	NHL	—	—	—	—	—	2	0	0	0	0
NHL totals							2	0	0	0	0

HERBERS, IAN
D, OILERS

PERSONAL: Born July 18, 1967, in Jasper, Alta. ... 6-4/225. ... Shoots left.
COLLEGE: Alberta.
TRANSACTIONS/CAREER NOTES: Signed as free agent by Edmonton Oilers (September 9, 1992).
HONORS: Named to CWUAA All-Star second team (1989-90). ... Named to CIAU All-Canadian team (1990-91 and 1991-92). ... Named to CWUAA All-Star first team (1990-91 and 1991-92). ... Won Spectrum-Randy Gregg Award (1991-92). ... Won Mervyn Red Dutton Trophy (1991-92).

Season Team	League	REGULAR SEASON					PLAYOFFS				
		Gms.	G	A	Pts.	PIM	Gms.	G	A	Pts.	PIM
88-89—University of Alberta	CWUAA	47	4	22	26	137	—	—	—	—	—
89-90—University of Alberta	CWUAA	45	5	31	36	83	—	—	—	—	—
90-91—University of Alberta	CWUAA	45	6	24	30	87	—	—	—	—	—
91-92—University of Alberta	CWUAA	43	14	34	48	86	—	—	—	—	—
92-93—Cape Breton	AHL	77	7	15	22	129	10	0	1	1	16
93-94—Edmonton	NHL	22	0	2	2	32	—	—	—	—	—
—Cape Breton	AHL	53	7	16	23	122	5	0	3	3	12
NHL totals		22	0	2	2	32					

HEROUX, YVES
RW

PERSONAL: Born April 27, 1965, in Terrebonne, Que. ... 6-0/200. ... Shoots right. ... Name pronounced EEV hair-OO.
TRANSACTIONS/CAREER NOTES: Suffered foot infection (December 1981). ... Selected by Quebec Nordiques in second round (first Nordiques pick, 32nd overall) of NHL entry draft (June 8, 1983). ... Signed as free agent by St. Louis Blues (March 13, 1990). ... Signed as free agent by Minnesota North Stars (August 5, 1992). ... North Stars franchise moved from Minnesota to Dallas and renamed Stars for 1993-94 season.

Season Team	League	REGULAR SEASON					PLAYOFFS				
		Gms.	G	A	Pts.	PIM	Gms.	G	A	Pts.	PIM
82-83—Chicoutimi	QMJHL	70	41	40	81	44	5	0	4	4	8
83-84—Chicoutimi	QMJHL	56	28	25	53	67	—	—	—	—	—
—Fredericton	AHL	4	0	0	0	0	—	—	—	—	—
84-85—Chicoutimi	QMJHL	66	42	54	96	123	14	5	8	13	16
85-86—Fredericton	AHL	31	12	10	22	42	2	0	1	1	7
—Muskegon	IHL	42	14	8	22	41	—	—	—	—	—
86-87—Fredericton	AHL	37	8	6	14	13	—	—	—	—	—
—Quebec	NHL	1	0	0	0	0	—	—	—	—	—
—Muskegon	IHL	25	6	8	14	31	2	0	0	0	0
87-88—Baltimore	AHL	5	0	2	2	2	—	—	—	—	—
88-89—Flint	IHL	82	43	42	85	98	—	—	—	—	—
89-90—Peoria	IHL	14	3	2	5	4	5	2	2	4	0
90-91—Albany	IHL	45	22	18	40	46	—	—	—	—	—
—Peoria	IHL	33	16	8	24	26	17	4	4	8	16
91-92—Peoria	IHL	80	41	36	77	72	8	5	1	6	6
92-93—Kalamazoo	IHL	80	38	30	68	86	—	—	—	—	—
93-94—Kalamazoo	IHL	3	0	2	2	4	—	—	—	—	—
—Indianapolis	IHL	74	28	30	58	113	—	—	—	—	—
NHL totals		1	0	0	0	0					

HERPERGER, CHRIS
LW, FLYERS

PERSONAL: Born February 24, 1974, in Esterhazy, Sask. ... 6-0/195. ... Shoots left.
TRANSACTIONS/CAREER NOTES: Signed by Philadelphia Flyers in 10th round (223rd overall) of NHL entry draft (June 20, 1992).

Season Team	League	REGULAR SEASON					PLAYOFFS				
		Gms.	G	A	Pts.	PIM	Gms.	G	A	Pts.	PIM
90-91—Swift Current	WHL	10	0	1	1	5	—	—	—	—	—
91-92—Swift Current	WHL	72	14	19	33	44	8	0	1	1	9
92-93—Seattle	WHL	66	29	18	47	61	5	1	1	2	6
93-94—Seattle	WHL	71	44	51	95	110	9	12	10	22	12

H

HERR, MATT
C, CAPITALS

PERSONAL: Born May 26, 1976, in New Windsor, N.Y. ... 6-1/180. ... Shoots left.
TRANSACTIONS/CAREER NOTES: Selected by Washington Capitals in fourth round (fourth Capitals pick, 93rd overall) of NHL entry draft (June 29, 1994).

Season Team	League	Gms.	G	A	Pts.	PIM	Gms.	G	A	Pts.	PIM
		REGULAR SEASON					PLAYOFFS				
90-91—Hotchkiss	N.Y. H.S.	26	9	5	14	...	—	—	—	—	—
91-92—Hotchkiss	N.Y. H.S.	25	17	16	33	...	—	—	—	—	—
92-93—Hotchkiss	N.Y. H.S.	26	51	32	83	...	—	—	—	—	—
93-94—Hotchkiss	N.Y. H.S.	20	28	19	47	...	—	—	—	—	—

HERTER, JASON
D, STARS

PERSONAL: Born October 2, 1970, in Hafford, Sask.... 6-1/190.... Shoots right. **COLLEGE:** North Dakota.
TRANSACTIONS/CAREER NOTES: Strained shoulder (September 1988).... Selected by Vancouver Canucks in first round (first Canucks pick, eighth overall) of NHL entry draft (June 17, 1989).... Signed as free agent by Dallas Stars (August 5, 1993).
HONORS: Named to WCHA All-Star second team (1989-90 and 1990-91).

Season Team	League	Gms.	G	A	Pts.	PIM	Gms.	G	A	Pts.	PIM
		REGULAR SEASON					PLAYOFFS				
87-88—Notre Dame	SJHL	54	5	33	38	152	—	—	—	—	—
88-89—Univ. of North Dakota	WCHA	41	8	24	32	62	—	—	—	—	—
89-90—Univ. of North Dakota	WCHA	38	11	39	50	40	—	—	—	—	—
90-91—Univ. of North Dakota	WCHA	39	11	26	37	52	—	—	—	—	—
91-92—Milwaukee	IHL	56	7	18	25	34	1	0	0	0	2
92-93—Hamilton	AHL	70	7	16	23	68	—	—	—	—	—
93-94—Kalamazoo	IHL	68	14	28	42	92	5	3	0	3	14

HERVEY, MATT
D, LIGHTNING

PERSONAL: Born May 16, 1966, in Whittier, Calif.... 5-11/205.... Shoots right.
TRANSACTIONS/CAREER NOTES: Suspended six games by WHL for stick-swinging incident (November 1986).... Signed as free agent by Winnipeg Jets (October 1987).... Signed as free agent by Boston Bruins (August 15, 1991).... Suffered sore back (March 23, 1992).... Traded by Bruins with C Ken Hodge to Tampa Bay Lightning for RW Darin Kimble and future considerations (September 4, 1992).

Season Team	League	Gms.	G	A	Pts.	PIM	Gms.	G	A	Pts.	PIM
		REGULAR SEASON					PLAYOFFS				
83-84—Victoria	WHL	67	4	19	23	89	—	—	—	—	—
84-85—Victoria	WHL	14	1	3	4	17	—	—	—	—	—
—Lethbridge	WHL	54	3	9	12	88	—	—	—	—	—
85-86—Lethbridge	WHL	60	9	17	26	110	—	—	—	—	—
86-87—Seattle	WHL	9	4	5	9	59	—	—	—	—	—
—Richmond	BCJHL	17	4	21	25	99	11	3	10	13	22
87-88—Moncton	AHL	69	9	20	29	265	—	—	—	—	—
88-89—Moncton	AHL	73	8	28	36	295	10	1	2	3	42
—Winnipeg	NHL	2	0	0	0	4	—	—	—	—	—
89-90—Moncton	AHL	47	3	13	16	168	—	—	—	—	—
90-91—Moncton	AHL	71	4	28	32	132	7	0	1	1	23
91-92—Boston	NHL	16	0	1	1	55	5	0	0	0	6
—Maine	AHL	36	1	7	8	47	—	—	—	—	—
92-93—Atlanta	IHL	49	12	19	31	122	9	0	4	4	19
—Tampa Bay	NHL	17	0	4	4	38	—	—	—	—	—
93-94—Milwaukee	IHL	27	6	17	23	51	—	—	—	—	—
NHL totals		35	0	5	5	97	5	0	0	0	6

HEWARD, JAMIE
D, PENGUINS

PERSONAL: Born March 30, 1971, in Regina, Sask.... 6-2/198.... Shoots right.
TRANSACTIONS/CAREER NOTES: Traded by Spokane Chiefs to Regina Pats for RW Pat Falloon and future considerations (October 1987).... Broke jaw (November 1988).... Selected by Pittsburgh Penguins in first round (first Penguins pick, 16th overall) of NHL entry draft (June 17, 1989).... Suffered from mononucleosis (September 1989).
HONORS: Named to WHL (East) All-Star first team (1990-91).

Season Team	League	Gms.	G	A	Pts.	PIM	Gms.	G	A	Pts.	PIM
		REGULAR SEASON					PLAYOFFS				
87-88—Regina	WHL	68	10	17	27	17	4	1	1	2	2
88-89—Regina	WHL	52	31	28	59	29	—	—	—	—	—
89-90—Regina	WHL	72	14	44	58	42	11	2	2	4	10
90-91—Regina	WHL	71	23	61	84	41	8	2	9	11	6
91-92—Muskegon	IHL	54	6	21	27	37	14	1	4	5	4
92-93—Cleveland	IHL	58	9	18	27	64	—	—	—	—	—
93-94—Cleveland	IHL	73	8	16	24	72	—	—	—	—	—

HEXTALL, DONEVAN
LW, DEVILS

PERSONAL: Born February 24, 1972, in Wolseley, Sask.... 6-2/190.... Shoots left.
TRANSACTIONS/CAREER NOTES: Selected by New Jersey Devils in second round (third Devils pick, 33rd overall) of NHL entry draft (June 22, 1991).
HONORS: Won Jim Piggott Memorial Trophy (1990-91).... Named to WHL (East) All-Star second team (1991-92).

H

Season Team	League	REGULAR SEASON					PLAYOFFS				
		Gms.	G	A	Pts.	PIM	Gms.	G	A	Pts.	PIM
89-90—Prince Albert	WHL	7	1	2	3	4	—	—	—	—	—
—Weyburn	SJHL	63	23	45	68	127	—	—	—	—	—
90-91—Prince Albert	WHL	70	30	59	89	55	3	1	3	4	0
91-92—Prince Albert	WHL	71	33	71	104	105	10	3	6	9	10
92-93—Utica	AHL	51	11	11	22	12	2	1	0	1	0
93-94—Raleigh	ECHL	61	13	49	62	55	13	1	8	9	18
—Albany	AHL	4	1	0	1	0	—	—	—	—	—

HEXTALL, RON
G, ISLANDERS

PERSONAL: Born May 3, 1964, in Winnipeg. . . . 6-3/192. . . . Catches left.
TRANSACTIONS/CAREER NOTES: Selected by Philadelphia Flyers as underage junior in sixth round (sixth Flyers pick, 119th overall) of NHL entry draft (June 9, 1982). . . . Suspended eight games by NHL for slashing (May 1987). . . . Pulled hamstring (March 7, 1989). . . . Suspended first 12 games of 1989-90 season by NHL for attacking opposing player in final playoff game (May 11, 1989). . . . Did not attend training camp due to a contract dispute (September 1989). . . . Pulled groin (November 4, 1989). . . . Pulled hamstring (November 15, 1989). . . . Tore right groin muscle (December 13, 1989); missed 29 games. . . . Injured left groin (March 8, 1990). . . . Pulled groin (October 11, 1990); missed five games. . . . Sprained left knee medial collateral ligament (October 27, 1990); missed five weeks. . . . Tore groin muscle (March 12, 1991); missed nine games. . . . Suffered from the flu (November 14, 1991); missed one game. . . . Developed shoulder tendinitis (November 27, 1991); missed nine games. . . . Traded by Flyers with C Mike Ricci, C Peter Forsberg, D Steve Duchesne, D Kerry Huffman, first-round pick in 1993 draft (G Jocelyn Thibault), cash and future considerations to Quebec Nordiques for C Eric Lindros (June 20, 1992); Flyers sent LW Chris Simon and first-round pick in 1994 draft (traded to Toronto Maple Leafs) to Nordiques to complete deal (July 21, 1992). . . . Strained muscle in left thigh (February 20, 1993); missed 14 games. . . . Traded by Nordiques with first-round pick in 1993 draft to New York Islanders for G Mark Fitzpatrick and first-round pick (C Adam Deadmarsh) in 1993 draft (June 20, 1993).
HONORS: Won Dudley (Red) Garrett Memorial Trophy (1985-86). . . . Named to AHL All-Star first team (1985-86). . . . Named NHL Rookie of the Year by THE SPORTING NEWS (1986-87). . . . Won Vezina Trophy (1986-87). . . . Won Conn Smythe Trophy (1986-87). . . . Named to THE SPORTING NEWS All-Star second team (1986-87). . . . Named to NHL All-Star first team (1986-87). . . . Named to NHL All-Rookie team (1986-87). . . . Played in NHL All-Star Game (1988).
STATISTICAL NOTES: Scored a goal into a Washington empty net, becoming the first goalie to score a goal in Stanley Cup play (April 11, 1989).

Season Team	League	REGULAR SEASON								PLAYOFFS						
		Gms.	Min.	W	L	T	GA	SO	Avg.	Gms.	Min.	W	L	GA	SO	Avg.
80-81—Melville	SJHL	42	2127	..	..	..	254	0	7.17	—						
81-82—Brandon	WHL	30	1398	12	11	0	133	0	5.71	3	103	0	2	16	0	9.32
82-83—Brandon	WHL	44	2589	13	30	0	249	0	5.77	—						
83-84—Brandon	WHL	46	2670	29	13	2	190	0	4.27	10	592	5	5	37	0	3.75
84-85—Kalamazoo	IHL	19	1103	6	11	†1	80	0	4.35	—						
—Hershey	AHL	11	555	4	6	0	34	0	3.68	—						
85-86—Hershey	AHL	*53	*3061	30	19	2	174	*5	3.41	13	780	5	7	42	*1	3.23
86-87—Philadelphia	NHL	*66	*3799	37	21	6	190	1	3.00	*26	*1540	15	11	*71	†2	2.77
87-88—Philadelphia	NHL	62	3561	30	22	7	208	0	3.50	7	379	2	4	30	0	4.75
88-89—Philadelphia	NHL	64	3756	30	28	6	202	0	3.23	15	886	8	7	49	0	3.32
89-90—Philadelphia	NHL	8	419	4	2	1	29	0	4.15	—						
—Hershey	AHL	1	49	1	0	0	3	0	3.67	—						
90-91—Philadelphia	NHL	36	2035	13	16	5	106	0	3.13	—						
91-92—Philadelphia	NHL	45	2668	16	21	6	151	3	3.40	—						
92-93—Quebec	NHL	54	2988	29	16	5	172	0	3.45	6	372	2	4	18	0	2.90
93-94—New York Islanders	NHL	65	3581	27	26	6	184	5	3.08	3	158	0	3	16	0	6.08
NHL totals		400	22807	186	152	42	1242	9	3.27	57	3335	27	29	184	2	3.31

HILL, SEAN
D, SENATORS

PERSONAL: Born February 14, 1970, in Duluth, Minn. . . . 6-0/195. . . . Shoots right. . . . Full name: Sean Ronald Hill.
COLLEGE: Wisconsin.
TRANSACTIONS/CAREER NOTES: Selected by Montreal Canadiens in eighth round (ninth Canadiens pick, 167th overall) of NHL entry draft (June 11, 1988). . . . Injured knee (December 29, 1990). . . . Suspended two games by WCHA for elbowing (January 18, 1991). . . . Suffered abdominal strain (October 13, 1992); missed 14 games. . . . Selected by Mighty Ducks of Anaheim in NHL expansion draft (June 24, 1993). . . . Sprained shoulder (January 6, 1994); missed nine games. . . . Traded by Mighty Ducks with ninth-round pick in 1994 draft (G Frederic Cassivi) to Ottawa Senators for third-round pick (traded to Tampa Bay Lightning who selected C Vadim Yepanchintsev) in 1994 draft (June 29, 1994).
HONORS: Named to WCHA All-Star second team (1989-90 and 1990-91). . . . Named to NCAA All-America West second team (1990-91).
MISCELLANEOUS: Member of Stanley Cup championship team (1993).

Season Team	League	REGULAR SEASON					PLAYOFFS				
		Gms.	G	A	Pts.	PIM	Gms.	G	A	Pts.	PIM
88-89—University of Wisconsin	WCHA	45	2	23	25	69	—	—	—	—	—
89-90—University of Wisconsin	WCHA	42	14	39	53	78	—	—	—	—	—
90-91—University of Wisconsin	WCHA	37	19	32	51	122	—	—	—	—	—
—Fredericton	AHL	—	—	—	—	—	3	0	2	2	2
—Montreal	NHL	—	—	—	—	—	1	0	0	0	0
91-92—Fredericton	AHL	42	7	20	27	65	7	1	3	4	6
—U.S. national team	Int'l	12	4	3	7	16	—	—	—	—	—
—U.S. Olympic Team	Int'l	8	2	0	2	6	—	—	—	—	—
—Montreal	NHL	—	—	—	—	—	4	1	0	1	2

H

Season Team	League	REGULAR SEASON					PLAYOFFS				
		Gms.	G	A	Pts.	Pen.	Gms.	G	A	Pts.	Pen.
92-93—Montreal	NHL	31	2	6	8	54	3	0	0	0	4
—Fredericton	AHL	6	1	3	4	10	—	—	—	—	—
93-94—Anaheim	NHL	68	7	20	27	78	—	—	—	—	—
NHL totals		99	9	26	35	132	8	1	0	1	6

HILLER, JIM
RW, RANGERS

PERSONAL: Born May 15, 1969, in Port Alberni, B.C.... 6-0/190.... Shoots right.
COLLEGE: Northern Michigan.
TRANSACTIONS/CAREER NOTES: Selected by Los Angeles Kings in 10th round (10th Kings pick, 207th overall) of NHL entry draft (June 10, 1989).... Strained back (November 21, 1992); missed four games.... Traded by Kings with D Paul Coffey and C/LW Sylvain Couturier to Detroit Red Wings for C Jimmy Carson, RW Marc Potvin and C Gary Shuchuk (January 29, 1993).... Separated shoulder (March 18, 1993); missed four games.... Claimed on waivers by New York Rangers (October 12, 1993).
HONORS: Named to NCAA All-America West second team (1991-92).... Named to WCHA All-Star second team (1991-92).

Season Team	League	REGULAR SEASON					PLAYOFFS				
		Gms.	G	A	Pts.	PIM	Gms.	G	A	Pts.	PIM
89-90—Northern Michigan Univ...	WCHA	39	23	33	56	52	—	—	—	—	—
90-91—Northern Michigan Univ...	WCHA	43	22	41	63	59	—	—	—	—	—
91-92—Northern Michigan Univ...	WCHA	39	28	52	80	115	—	—	—	—	—
92-93—Los Angeles	NHL	40	6	6	12	90	—	—	—	—	—
—Phoenix	IHL	3	0	2	2	2	—	—	—	—	—
—Detroit	NHL	21	2	6	8	19	2	0	0	0	4
93-94—Binghamton	AHL	67	27	34	61	61	—	—	—	—	—
—New York Rangers	NHL	2	0	0	0	7	—	—	—	—	—
NHL totals		63	8	12	20	116	2	0	0	0	4

HILTON, KEVIN
C, RED WINGS

PERSONAL: Born January 12, 1975, in Trenton, Mich.... 5-11/170.... Shoots left.
COLLEGE: Michigan.
TRANSACTIONS/CAREER NOTES: Selected by Detroit Red Wings in third round (third Red Wings pick, 74th overall) of NHL entry draft (June 26, 1993).

Season Team	League	REGULAR SEASON					PLAYOFFS				
		Gms.	G	A	Pts.	PIM	Gms.	G	A	Pts.	PIM
91-92—Detroit Compuware	NAJHL	39	35	42	77	42	—	—	—	—	—
92-93—University of Michigan	CCHA	38	16	15	31	8	—	—	—	—	—
93-94—University of Michigan	CCHA	39	11	12	23	16	—	—	—	—	—

HIRSCH, COREY
G, RANGERS

PERSONAL: Born July 1, 1972, in Medicine Hat, Alta.... 5-10/160.... Catches left.
TRANSACTIONS/CAREER NOTES: Selected by New York Rangers in eighth round (seventh Rangers pick, 169th overall) in NHL entry draft (June 22, 1991).... Loaned by Rangers to Canadian Olympic Team (October 1, 1993).... Returned to Rangers (March 8, 1994).
HONORS: Named to WHL (West) All-Star second team (1989-90).... Won Can.HL Goaltender of the Year Award (1991-92). ... Won Hap Emms Memorial Trophy (1991-92)... Won Del Wilson Trophy (1991-92).... Won WHL Player of the Year Award (1991-92).... Named to Can.HL All-Star first team (1991-92).... Named to Memorial Cup All-Star team (1991-92). ... Named to WHL (West) All-Star first team (1991-92).... Won Aldege (Baz) Bastien Trophy (1992-93).... Won Dudley (Red) Garrett Memorial Trophy (1992-93).... Shared Harry (Hap) Holmes Memorial Trophy with Boris Rousson (1992-93). ... Named to AHL All-Star first team (1992-93).
MISCELLANEOUS: Member of silver-medal-winning Canadian Olympic team (1994).

Season Team	League	REGULAR SEASON							PLAYOFFS					
		Gms.	Min.	W	L	T	GA	SO	Avg.	Gms.	Min.	W	L	GA	SO	Avg.
88-89—Kamloops	WHL	32	1516	11	12	2	106	2	4.20	5	245	3	2	19	0	4.65
89-90—Kamloops	WHL	63	3608	48	13	0	230	3	3.82	17	1043	14	3	60	0	3.45
90-91—Kamloops	WHL	38	1970	26	7	1	100	3	3.05	11	623	5	6	42	0	4.04
91-92—Kamloops	WHL	48	2732	35	10	2	124	*5	*2.72	*16	*954	*11	5	35	*2	*2.20
92-93—Binghamton	AHL	46	2692	*35	4	5	125	1	*2.79	14	831	7	7	46	0	3.32
—New York Rangers	NHL	4	224	1	2	1	14	0	3.75	—	—	—	—	—	—	—
93-94—Can. national team	Int'l	45	2653	24	17	3	124	0	2.80	—	—	—	—	—	—	—
—Can. Olympic Team	Int'l	8	495	5	2	1	18	0	2.18	—	—	—	—	—	—	—
—Binghamton	AHL	10	611	5	4	1	38	0	3.73	—	—	—	—	—	—	—
NHL totals		4	224	1	2	1	14	0	3.75							

HLUSHKO, TODD
LW, FLAMES

PERSONAL: Born February 7, 1970, in Toronto.... 5-11/185.... Shoots left.
TRANSACTIONS/CAREER NOTES: Selected by Washington Capitals in 14th round (14th Capitals pick, 240th overall) in NHL entry draft (June 16, 1990).... Signed as free agent by Philadelphia Flyers (March 6, 1994).... Signed as free agent by Calgary Flames (June 27, 1994).

Season Team	League	REGULAR SEASON					PLAYOFFS				
		Gms.	G	A	Pts.	PIM	Gms.	G	A	Pts.	PIM
88-89—Guelph	OHL	66	28	18	46	71	7	5	3	8	18
89-90—London	OHL	65	36	34	70	70	6	2	4	6	10
90-91—Baltimore	AHL	66	9	14	23	55	—	—	—	—	—
91-92—Baltimore	AHL	74	16	35	51	113	—	—	—	—	—

H

Season Team	League	REGULAR SEASON					PLAYOFFS				
		Gms.	G	A	Pts.	Pen.	Gms.	G	A	Pts.	Pen.
92-93—Canadian national team ...	Int'l	58	22	26	48	10	—	—	—	—	—
93-94—Canadian national team ...	Int'l	63	27	6	33	67	—	—	—	—	—
—Canadian Olympic Team ..	Int'l	8	5	0	5	6	—	—	—	—	—
—Philadelphia	NHL	2	1	0	1	0	—	—	—	—	—
—Hershey	AHL	9	6	0	6	4	6	2	1	3	4
NHL totals...		2	1	0	1	0					

HNILICKA, MILAN

G, ISLANDERS

PERSONAL: Born June 24, 1973, in Kladno, Czechoslovakia. ... 6-0/180. ... Catches left. ... Name pronounced MEE-lahn nun-LEECH-kuh.
TRANSACTIONS/CAREER NOTES: Selected by New York Islanders in fourth round (fourth Islanders pick, 70th overall) of NHL entry draft (June 22, 1991).

Season Team	League	REGULAR SEASON								PLAYOFFS						
		Gms.	Min.	W	L	T	GA	SO	Avg.	Gms.	Min.	W	L	GA	SO	Avg.
90-91—Poldi Kladno	Czech.	35	2122	...	...	...	98	...	2.77	—	—	—	—	—	—	—
91-92—Poldi Kladno	Czech.	30	1788	...	...	...	107	...	3.59	—	—	—	—	—	—	—
92-93—Swift Current...............	WHL	65	3679	*46	12	2	206	2	3.36	17	1017	12	5	54	*2	3.19
93-94—Richmond	ECHL	43	2299	18	16	‡5	155	0	4.05	—	—	—	—	—	—	—

HOCKING, JUSTIN

D, KINGS

PERSONAL: Born January 9, 1974, in Stettler, Alta. ... 6-4/206. ... Shoots right.
COLLEGE: Spokane (Wash.) Falls Community College.
TRANSACTIONS/CAREER NOTES: Selected by Los Angeles Kings in second round (first Kings pick, 39th overall) of NHL entry draft (June 20, 1992).
HONORS: Named to WHL (East) All-Star second team (1993-94).

Season Team	League	REGULAR SEASON					PLAYOFFS				
		Gms.	G	A	Pts.	PIM	Gms.	G	A	Pts.	PIM
90-91—Fort Saskatchewan	AJHL	38	4	6	10	84	—	—	—	—	—
91-92—Spokane	WHL	71	4	6	10	309	10	0	3	3	28
92-93—Spokane	WHL	16	0	1	1	75	—	—	—	—	—
—Medicine Hat......................	WHL	54	1	9	10	119	10	0	1	1	75
93-94—Medicine Hat..................	WHL	68	7	26	33	236	3	0	0	0	6
—Phoenix	IHL	3	0	0	0	15	—	—	—	—	—
—Los Angeles......................	NHL	1	0	0	0	0	—	—	—	—	—
NHL totals...		1	0	0	0	0					

HODGE, KEN

C

PERSONAL: Born April 13, 1966, in Windsor, Ont. ... 6-1/200. ... Shoots left. ... Full name: Kenneth David Hodge Jr. ... Son of Ken Hodge, right winger, Chicago Blackhawks, Boston Bruins and New York Rangers (1965-66 through 1977-78).
HIGH SCHOOL: St. John's Prep School (Danvers, Mass.).
COLLEGE: Boston College.
TRANSACTIONS/CAREER NOTES: Selected by Minnesota North Stars in third round (second North Stars pick, 46th overall) of NHL entry draft (June 9, 1984). ... Injured shoulders (November 1987). ... Reinjured shoulders (November 1987). ... Traded by North Stars to Boston Bruins for future considerations; North Stars later received fourth-round pick in 1992 draft (RW Jere Lehtinen) to complete deal (August 21, 1990). ... Sprained knee (October 27, 1991); missed nine games. ... Traded by Bruins with D Matt Hervey to Tampa Bay Lightning for RW Darin Kimble and future considerations (September 4, 1992). ... Cut upper lip (October 24, 1992); missed three games. ... Signed as free agent by San Diego Gulls (February 9, 1993). ... Signed as free agent by New York Rangers (September 2, 1993).
HONORS: Named Hockey East Freshman of the Year (1984-85). ... Named to Hockey East All-Freshman team (1984-85). ... Named to NHL All-Rookie team (1990-91).

Season Team	League	REGULAR SEASON					PLAYOFFS				
		Gms.	G	A	Pts.	PIM	Gms.	G	A	Pts.	PIM
83-84—St. John's Prep School......	Mass. H.S.	22	25	38	63	...	—	—	—	—	—
84-85—Boston College	Hockey East	41	20	44	64	28	—	—	—	—	—
85-86—Boston College	Hockey East	21	11	17	28	16	—	—	—	—	—
86-87—Boston College	Hockey East	37	29	33	62	30	—	—	—	—	—
87-88—Kalamazoo	IHL	70	15	35	50	24	—	—	—	—	—
88-89—Minnesota	NHL	5	1	1	2	0	—	—	—	—	—
—Kalamazoo	IHL	72	26	45	71	34	6	1	5	6	16
89-90—Kalamazoo	IHL	68	33	53	86	19	10	5	13	18	2
90-91—Maine	AHL	8	7	10	17	2	—	—	—	—	—
—Boston	NHL	70	30	29	59	20	15	4	6	10	6
91-92—Boston	NHL	42	6	11	17	10	—	—	—	—	—
—Maine	AHL	19	6	11	17	4	—	—	—	—	—
92-93—Tampa Bay	NHL	25	2	7	9	2	—	—	—	—	—
—Atlanta	IHL	16	10	17	27	0	—	—	—	—	—
—San Diego	IHL	30	11	24	35	16	14	4	6	10	6
93-94—Binghamton	AHL	79	22	56	78	51	—	—	—	—	—
NHL totals..		142	39	48	87	32	15	4	6	10	6

HODSON, KEVIN

G, RED WINGS

PERSONAL: Born March 27, 1972, in Winnipeg. ... 6-0/182. ... Catches left.
TRANSACTIONS/CAREER NOTES: Signed as free agent by Detroit Red Wings (May 3, 1993).

Season Team	League	Gms.	Min.	W	L	T	GA	SO	Avg.	Gms.	Min.	W	L	GA	SO	Avg.
90-91—S.S. Marie	OHL	30	1638	18	11	0	88	2	3.22	10	600	*9	1	28	0	2.80
91-92—S.S. Marie	OHL	50	2722	28	12	4	151	0	3.33	18	1116	12	6	59	1	3.17
92-93—S.S. Marie	OHL	26	1470	18	5	2	76	1	*3.10	8	448	8	0	17	0	2.28
93-94—Adirondack	AHL	37	2083	20	10	5	102	2	2.94	3	89	0	2	10	0	6.74

HOGAN, TIM
D, BLACKHAWKS

PERSONAL: Born January 7, 1974, in Oshawa, Ont.... 6-2/180.... Shoots right.
COLLEGE: Michigan.
TRANSACTIONS/CAREER NOTES: Selected by Chicago Blackhawks in fifth round (fifth Blackhawks pick, 113th overall) of NHL entry draft (June 20, 1992).

Season Team	League	Gms.	G	A	Pts.	PIM	Gms.	G	A	Pts.	PIM
90-91—Wexford Jr. B	MTHL	33	5	19	24	46	—	—	—	—	—
91-92—University of Michigan	CCHA	34	2	8	10	34	—	—	—	—	—
92-93—University of Michigan	CCHA	22	4	1	5	24	—	—	—	—	—
93-94—University of Michigan	CCHA	37	2	10	12	36	—	—	—	—	—

HOGUE, BENOIT
LW, ISLANDERS

PERSONAL: Born October 28, 1966, in Repentigny, Que.... 5-10/190.... Shoots left.... Name pronounced behn-WAH HOHG.
TRANSACTIONS/CAREER NOTES: Selected by Buffalo Sabres as underage junior in second round (second Sabres pick, 35th overall) of NHL entry draft (June 15, 1985).... Suspended six games by AHL for fighting (October 1987).... Suffered sore back (March 1988).... Broke left cheekbone (October 11, 1989); missed 20 games.... Sprained left ankle (March 14, 1990).... Traded by Sabres with C Pierre Turgeon, D Uwe Krupp and C Dave McLlwain to New York Islanders for C Pat LaFontaine, LW Randy Wood, D Randy Hillier and future considerations; Sabres later received fourth-round pick (D Dean Melanson) in 1992 draft (October 25, 1991).... Suffered stiff neck (December 7, 1992); missed five games.... Suffered sore hand and foot (January 14, 1993); missed three games.... Sprained knee ligament (March 14, 1993); missed six games.

Season Team	League	Gms.	G	A	Pts.	PIM	Gms.	G	A	Pts.	PIM
83-84—St. Jean	QMJHL	59	14	11	25	42	—	—	—	—	—
84-85—St. Jean	QMJHL	63	46	44	90	92	—	—	—	—	—
85-86—St. Jean	QMJHL	65	54	54	108	115	9	6	4	10	26
86-87—Rochester	AHL	52	14	20	34	52	12	5	4	9	8
87-88—Buffalo	NHL	3	1	1	2	0	—	—	—	—	—
—Rochester	AHL	62	24	31	55	141	7	6	1	7	46
88-89—Buffalo	NHL	69	14	30	44	120	5	0	0	0	17
89-90—Buffalo	NHL	45	11	7	18	79	3	0	0	0	10
90-91—Buffalo	NHL	76	19	28	47	76	5	3	1	4	10
91-92—Buffalo	NHL	3	0	1	1	0	—	—	—	—	—
—New York Islanders	NHL	72	30	45	75	67	—	—	—	—	—
92-93—New York Islanders	NHL	70	33	42	75	108	18	6	6	12	31
93-94—New York Islanders	NHL	83	36	33	69	73	4	0	1	1	4
NHL totals		421	144	187	331	523	35	9	8	17	72

HOLAN, MILOS
D, FLYERS

PERSONAL: Born April 22, 1971, in Bilovec, Czechoslovakia.... 5-11/183.... Shoots left.... Name pronounced MEE-lohz HOH-lihn.
TRANSACTIONS/CAREER NOTES: Selected by Philadelphia Flyers in third round (third Flyers pick, 77th overall) of NHL entry draft (June 26, 1993).

Season Team	League	Gms.	G	A	Pts.	PIM	Gms.	G	A	Pts.	PIM
88-89—TJ Vitkovice	Czech.	7	0	0	0	0	—	—	—	—	—
89-90—TJ Vitkovice	Czech.	50	8	8	16	...	—	—	—	—	—
90-91—Dukla Trencin	Czech.	53	6	13	19	...	—	—	—	—	—
91-92—Dukla Trencin	Czech.	51	13	22	35	32	—	—	—	—	—
92-93—TJ Vitkovice	Czech.	53	35	33	68	...	—	—	—	—	—
93-94—Philadelphia	NHL	8	1	1	2	4	—	—	—	—	—
—Hershey	AHL	27	7	22	29	16	—	—	—	—	—
NHL totals		8	1	1	2	4					

HOLDEN, PAUL
D, MAPLE LEAFS

PERSONAL: Born March 15, 1970, in Kitchener, Ont.... 6-3/210.... Shoots left.
TRANSACTIONS/CAREER NOTES: Selected by Los Angeles Kings in second round (second Kings pick, 28th overall) of NHL entry draft (June 11, 1988).... Traded by Phoenix Roadrunners to Salt Lake City Golden Eagles for D Kevin Grant (October 16, 1992).... Traded by Calgary Flames with LW Todd Gillingham to Toronto Maple Leafs for LW Jeff Perry and D Brad Miller (September 2, 1993).
HONORS: Named to OHL All-Star second team (1989-90).

Season Team	League	Gms.	G	A	Pts.	PIM	Gms.	G	A	Pts.	PIM
86-87—St. Thomas Jr. B	OHA	23	5	11	16	112	—	—	—	—	—
87-88—London	OHL	65	8	12	20	87	12	1	1	2	10
88-89—London	OHL	54	11	21	32	90	20	1	3	4	17

H

Season Team	League	REGULAR SEASON					PLAYOFFS				
		Gms.	G	A	Pts.	Pen.	Gms.	G	A	Pts.	Pen.
89-90—London	OHL	61	11	31	42	78	6	1	1	2	7
—New Haven	AHL	2	1	1	2	2	—	—	—	—	—
90-91—New Haven	AHL	59	2	8	10	23	—	—	—	—	—
91-92—Phoenix	IHL	47	3	3	6	63	—	—	—	—	—
92-93—Phoenix	IHL	3	0	0	0	6	—	—	—	—	—
—Salt Lake City	IHL	63	5	8	13	86	—	—	—	—	—
93-94—St. John's	AHL	75	6	14	20	101	11	0	4	4	18

HOLIK, BOBBY
RW, DEVILS

PERSONAL: Born January 1, 1971, in Jihlava, Czechoslovakia.... 6-3/220.... Shoots right.... Name pronounced hoh-LEEK.
TRANSACTIONS/CAREER NOTES: Selected by Hartford Whalers in first round (first Whalers pick, 10th overall) of NHL entry draft (June 17, 1989).... Broke right thumb (February 1990).... Traded by Whalers with second-round pick in 1993 draft (LW Jay Pandolfo) and future considerations to New Jersey Devils for G Sean Burke and D Eric Weinrich (August 28, 1992).... Fractured right thumb (January 22, 1993); missed 22 games.... Bruised left shoulder (December 8, 1993); missed 11 games.

Season Team	League	REGULAR SEASON					PLAYOFFS				
		Gms.	G	A	Pts.	PIM	Gms.	G	A	Pts.	PIM
87-88—Dukla Jihlava	Czech.	31	5	9	14	...	—	—	—	—	—
88-89—Dukla Jihlava	Czech.	24	7	10	17	...	—	—	—	—	—
89-90—Dukla Jihlava	Czech.	31	12	18	30	...	—	—	—	—	—
90-91—Hartford	NHL	78	21	22	43	113	6	0	0	0	7
91-92—Hartford	NHL	76	21	24	45	44	7	0	1	1	6
92-93—Utica	AHL	1	0	0	0	2	—	—	—	—	—
—New Jersey	NHL	61	20	19	39	76	5	1	1	2	6
93-94—New Jersey	NHL	70	13	20	33	72	20	0	3	3	6
NHL totals		285	75	85	160	305	38	1	5	6	25

HOLLAND, JASON
D, ISLANDERS

PERSONAL: Born April 30, 1976, in Morinville, Alta.... 6-2/190.... Shoots right.
HIGH SCHOOL: Norkam (Kamloops, B.C.).
TRANSACTIONS/CAREER NOTES: Selected by New York Islanders in second round (second Islanders pick, 38th overall) of NHL entry draft (June 28, 1994).

Season Team	League	REGULAR SEASON					PLAYOFFS				
		Gms.	G	A	Pts.	PIM	Gms.	G	A	Pts.	PIM
92-93—Kamloops	WHL	4	0	0	0	2	—	—	—	—	—
93-94—Kamloops	WHL	59	14	15	29	80	18	2	3	5	4

HOLLINGER, TERRY
D, BLUES

PERSONAL: Born February 24, 1971, in Regina, Sask.... 6-1/200.... Shoots left.
TRANSACTIONS/CAREER NOTES: Selected by St. Louis Blues in sixth round (sixth Blues pick, 153rd overall) of NHL entry draft (June 22, 1991).

Season Team	League	REGULAR SEASON					PLAYOFFS				
		Gms.	G	A	Pts.	PIM	Gms.	G	A	Pts.	PIM
87-88—Regina	WHL	7	1	1	2	4	—	—	—	—	—
88-89—Regina	WHL	65	2	27	29	49	—	—	—	—	—
89-90—Regina	WHL	70	14	43	57	40	11	1	3	4	10
90-91—Regina	WHL	8	1	6	7	6	—	—	—	—	—
—Lethbridge	WHL	62	9	32	41	113	16	3	14	17	22
91-92—Lethbridge	WHL	65	23	62	85	155	5	1	2	3	13
—Peoria	IHL	1	0	2	2	0	5	0	1	1	0
92-93—Peoria	IHL	72	2	28	30	67	4	1	1	2	0
93-94—Peoria	IHL	78	12	31	43	96	6	0	3	3	31
—St. Louis	NHL	2	0	0	0	0	—	—	—	—	—
NHL totals		2	0	0	0	0					

HOOVER, RON
C

PERSONAL: Born October 28, 1966, in Oakville, Ont.... 6-1/190.... Shoots left.... Full name: Ronald Kenneth Hoover.
COLLEGE: Western Michigan.
TRANSACTIONS/CAREER NOTES: Selected by Hartford Whalers in eighth round (seventh Whalers pick, 158th overall) of NHL entry draft (June 21, 1986).... Signed as free agent by Boston Bruins (September 1, 1989).... Injured right eye (February 2, 1991); missed two weeks.... Signed as free agent by St. Louis Blues (July 23, 1991).
HONORS: Named to CCHA All-Star second team (1987-88).

Season Team	League	REGULAR SEASON					PLAYOFFS				
		Gms.	G	A	Pts.	PIM	Gms.	G	A	Pts.	PIM
85-86—Western Michigan Univ.	CCHA	43	10	23	33	36	—	—	—	—	—
86-87—Western Michigan Univ.	CCHA	34	7	10	17	22	—	—	—	—	—
87-88—Western Michigan Univ.	CCHA	42	39	23	62	40	—	—	—	—	—
88-89—Western Michigan Univ.	CCHA	42	32	27	59	66	—	—	—	—	—
89-90—Boston	NHL	2	0	0	0	0	—	—	—	—	—
—Maine	AHL	75	28	26	54	57	—	—	—	—	—
90-91—Maine	AHL	62	28	16	44	40	—	—	—	—	—
—Boston	NHL	15	4	0	4	31	8	0	0	0	18

H

Season Team	League	REGULAR SEASON Gms.	G	A	Pts.	Pen.	PLAYOFFS Gms.	G	A	Pts.	Pen.
91-92—Peoria	IHL	71	27	34	61	30	10	4	4	8	4
—St. Louis	NHL	1	0	0	0	0	—	—	—	—	—
92-93—Peoria	IHL	58	17	13	30	28	4	1	1	2	2
93-94—Peoria	IHL	80	26	24	50	89	6	0	1	1	10
NHL totals		18	4	0	4	31	8	0	0	0	18

HORACEK, TONY
LW, BLACKHAWKS

PERSONAL: Born February 3, 1967, in Vancouver. . . . 6-4/215. . . . Shoots left. . . . Name pronounced HOHR-uh-CHECK.
TRANSACTIONS/CAREER NOTES: Selected by Philadelphia Flyers as underage junior in seventh round (eighth Flyers pick, 147th overall) of NHL entry draft (June 15, 1985). . . . Suspended one game by WHL for swinging stick at fans (November 1, 1987). . . . Suspended eight games by WHL for fighting (November 27, 1987). . . . Suffered broken knuckle (December 1989). . . . Injured left eye (March 19, 1991); missed six games. . . . Traded by Flyers to Chicago Blackhawks for D Ryan McGill (February 7, 1992). . . . Suffered hip pointer (February 25, 1992); missed nine games.

Season Team	League	REGULAR SEASON Gms.	G	A	Pts.	PIM	PLAYOFFS Gms.	G	A	Pts.	PIM
84-85—Kelowna Wings	WHL	67	9	18	27	114	6	0	1	1	11
85-86—Spokane	WHL	64	19	28	47	129	9	4	5	9	29
86-87—Spokane	WHL	64	23	37	60	177	5	1	3	4	18
—Hershey	AHL	1	0	0	0	0	1	0	0	0	0
87-88—Hershey	AHL	1	0	0	0	0	—	—	—	—	—
—Spokane	WHL	24	17	23	40	63	—	—	—	—	—
—Kamloops	WHL	26	14	17	31	51	18	6	4	10	73
88-89—Hershey	AHL	10	0	0	0	38	—	—	—	—	—
—Indianapolis	IHL	43	11	13	24	138	—	—	—	—	—
89-90—Philadelphia	NHL	48	5	5	10	117	—	—	—	—	—
—Hershey	AHL	12	0	5	5	25	—	—	—	—	—
90-91—Hershey	AHL	19	5	3	8	35	4	2	0	2	14
—Philadelphia	NHL	34	3	6	9	49	—	—	—	—	—
91-92—Philadelphia	NHL	34	1	3	4	51	—	—	—	—	—
—Chicago	NHL	12	1	4	5	21	2	1	0	1	2
92-93—Indianapolis	IHL	6	1	1	2	28	5	3	2	5	18
93-94—Indianapolis	IHL	29	6	7	13	63	—	—	—	—	—
—Chicago	NHL	7	0	0	0	53	—	—	—	—	—
NHL totals		135	10	18	28	291	2	1	0	1	2

HOUDA, DOUG
D, SABRES

PERSONAL: Born June 3, 1966, in Blairmore, Alta. . . . 6-2/190. . . . Shoots right. . . . Name pronounced HOO-duh.
TRANSACTIONS/CAREER NOTES: Selected by Detroit Red Wings as underage junior in second round (second Red Wings pick, 28th overall) of NHL entry draft (June 9, 1984). . . . Fractured left cheekbone (September 23, 1988). . . . Injured knee and underwent surgery (November 21, 1989). . . . Traded by Red Wings to Hartford Whalers for D Doug Crossman (February 20, 1991). . . . Separated shoulder (February 28, 1994); missed three games. . . . Strained shoulder (March 15, 1994); missed two games. . . . Traded by Whalers to Los Angeles Kings for RW Marc Potvin (November 3, 1993). . . . Traded by Kings to Buffalo Sabres for D Sean O'Donnell (July 26, 1994).
HONORS: Named to WHL All-Star second team (1984-85). . . . Named to AHL All-Star first team (1987-88).

Season Team	League	REGULAR SEASON Gms.	G	A	Pts.	PIM	PLAYOFFS Gms.	G	A	Pts.	PIM
81-82—Calgary	WHL	3	0	0	0	0	—	—	—	—	—
82-83—Calgary	WHL	71	5	23	28	99	16	1	3	4	44
83-84—Calgary	WHL	69	6	30	36	195	4	0	0	0	7
84-85—Calgary	WHL	65	20	54	74	182	8	3	4	7	29
—Kalamazoo	IHL	—	—	—	—	—	7	0	2	2	10
85-86—Calgary	WHL	16	4	10	14	60	—	—	—	—	—
—Medicine Hat	WHL	35	9	23	32	80	25	4	19	23	64
—Detroit	NHL	6	0	0	0	4	—	—	—	—	—
86-87—Adirondack	AHL	77	6	23	29	142	11	1	8	9	50
87-88—Detroit	NHL	11	1	1	2	10	—	—	—	—	—
—Adirondack	AHL	71	10	32	42	169	11	0	3	3	44
88-89—Adirondack	AHL	7	0	3	3	8	—	—	—	—	—
—Detroit	NHL	57	2	11	13	67	6	0	1	1	0
89-90—Detroit	NHL	73	2	9	11	127	—	—	—	—	—
90-91—Adirondack	AHL	38	9	17	26	67	—	—	—	—	—
—Detroit	NHL	22	0	4	4	43	—	—	—	—	—
—Hartford	NHL	19	1	2	3	41	6	0	0	0	8
91-92—Hartford	NHL	56	3	6	9	125	6	0	2	2	13
92-93—Hartford	NHL	60	2	6	8	167	—	—	—	—	—
93-94—Hartford	NHL	7	0	0	0	23	—	—	—	—	—
—Los Angeles	NHL	54	2	6	8	165	—	—	—	—	—
NHL totals		365	13	45	58	772	18	0	3	3	21

H

HOUGH, MIKE

LW, PANTHERS

PERSONAL: Born February 6, 1963, in Montreal. . . . 6-1/192. . . . Shoots left. . . . Name pronounced HUHF.

TRANSACTIONS/CAREER NOTES: Selected by Quebec Nordiques as underage junior in ninth round (seventh Nordiques pick, 181st overall) of NHL entry draft (June 9, 1982). . . . Sprained left shoulder and developed tendinitis (November 5, 1989); missed 14 games. . . . Broke right thumb (January 23, 1990); missed 12 games. . . . Injured back (November 8, 1990); missed nine games. . . . Separated left shoulder (January 15, 1991); missed three games. . . . Suffered concussion (February 10, 1991). . . . Injured knee (December 28, 1991); missed three games. . . . Fractured left thumb (February 15, 1992); missed 14 games. . . . Suffered concussion in preseason (October 1992); missed first two games of season. . . . Sprained right shoulder (April 6, 1993); missed four games. . . . Traded by Nordiques to Washington Capitals for RW Paul MacDermid and RW Reggie Savage (June 20, 1993). . . . Selected by Florida Panthers in NHL expansion draft (June 24, 1993). . . . Hyperextended left knee (October 30, 1993); missed five games.

Season	Team	League	REGULAR SEASON Gms.	G	A	Pts.	PIM	PLAYOFFS Gms.	G	A	Pts.	PIM
80-81	Dixie	OPJHL	24	15	20	35	84	—	—	—	—	—
81-82	Kitchener	OHL	58	14	34	48	172	14	1	5	6	16
82-83	Kitchener	OHL	61	17	27	44	156	12	5	4	9	30
83-84	Fredericton	AHL	69	11	16	27	142	1	0	0	0	7
84-85	Fredericton	AHL	76	21	27	48	49	6	1	1	2	2
85-86	Fredericton	AHL	74	21	33	54	68	6	0	3	3	8
86-87	Quebec	NHL	56	6	8	14	79	9	0	3	3	26
	Fredericton	AHL	10	1	3	4	20	—	—	—	—	—
87-88	Fredericton	AHL	46	16	25	41	133	15	4	8	12	55
	Quebec	NHL	17	3	2	5	2	—	—	—	—	—
88-89	Halifax	AHL	22	11	10	21	87	—	—	—	—	—
	Quebec	NHL	46	9	10	19	39	—	—	—	—	—
89-90	Quebec	NHL	43	13	13	26	84	—	—	—	—	—
90-91	Quebec	NHL	63	13	20	33	111	—	—	—	—	—
91-92	Quebec	NHL	61	16	22	38	77	—	—	—	—	—
92-93	Quebec	NHL	77	8	22	30	69	6	0	1	1	2
93-94	Florida	NHL	78	6	23	29	62	—	—	—	—	—
NHL totals			**441**	**74**	**120**	**194**	**523**	**15**	**0**	**4**	**4**	**28**

HOULDER, BILL

D, MIGHTY DUCKS

PERSONAL: Born March 11, 1967, in Thunder Bay, Ont. . . . 6-3/218. . . . Shoots left.

TRANSACTIONS/CAREER NOTES: Selected by Washington Capitals as underage junior in fourth round (fourth Capitals pick, 82nd overall) of NHL entry draft (June 15, 1985). . . . Pulled groin (January 1989). . . . Traded by Capitals to Buffalo Sabres for D Shawn Anderson (September 30, 1990). . . . Selected by Mighty Ducks of Anaheim in NHL expansion draft (June 24, 1993).

HONORS: Named to AHL All-Star first team (1990-91). . . . Won Governors Trophy (1992-93). . . . Named to IHL All-Star first team (1992-93).

Season	Team	League	REGULAR SEASON Gms.	G	A	Pts.	PIM	PLAYOFFS Gms.	G	A	Pts.	PIM
83-84	Thunder Bay Beavers	TBAHA	23	4	18	22	37	—	—	—	—	—
84-85	North Bay	OHL	66	4	20	24	37	8	0	0	0	2
85-86	North Bay	OHL	59	5	30	35	97	10	1	6	7	12
86-87	North Bay	OHL	62	17	51	68	68	22	4	19	23	20
87-88	Washington	NHL	30	1	2	3	10	—	—	—	—	—
	Fort Wayne	IHL	43	10	14	24	32	—	—	—	—	—
88-89	Baltimore	AHL	65	10	36	46	50	—	—	—	—	—
	Washington	NHL	8	0	3	3	4	—	—	—	—	—
89-90	Baltimore	AHL	26	3	7	10	12	7	0	2	2	4
	Washington	NHL	41	1	11	12	28	—	—	—	—	—
90-91	Rochester	AHL	69	13	53	66	28	15	5	13	18	4
	Buffalo	NHL	7	0	2	2	4	—	—	—	—	—
91-92	Rochester	AHL	42	8	26	34	16	16	5	6	11	4
	Buffalo	NHL	10	1	0	1	8	—	—	—	—	—
92-93	San Diego	IHL	64	24	48	72	39	—	—	—	—	—
	Buffalo	NHL	15	3	5	8	6	8	0	2	2	4
93-94	Anaheim	NHL	80	14	25	39	40	—	—	—	—	—
NHL totals			**191**	**20**	**48**	**68**	**100**	**8**	**0**	**2**	**2**	**4**

HOULE, JEAN-FRANCOIS

LW, CANADIENS

PERSONAL: Born January 14, 1975, in La Salle, Que. . . . 5-8/145. . . . Shoots left. . . . Son of Rejean Houle, left winger/right winger, Montreal Canadiens (1969-70 through 1972-73 and 1976-77 through 1982-83) and Quebec Nordiques of WHA (1973-74 through 1975-76).

HIGH SCHOOL: Northwood (Lake Placid, N.Y.).

TRANSACTIONS/CAREER NOTES: Selected by Montreal Canadiens in fourth round (fifth Canadiens pick, 99th overall) of NHL entry draft (June 26, 1993).

Season	Team	League	REGULAR SEASON Gms.	G	A	Pts.	PIM	PLAYOFFS Gms.	G	A	Pts.	PIM
92-93	Northwood School	N.Y. H.S.	28	37	45	82	0	—	—	—	—	—
93-94	Clarkson	ECAC	34	6	19	25	18	—	—	—	—	—

HOUSLEY, PHIL
D, FLAMES

PERSONAL: Born March 9, 1964, in St. Paul, Minn. . . . 5-10/185. . . . Shoots left.
HIGH SCHOOL: South St. Paul (Minn.).
TRANSACTIONS/CAREER NOTES: Selected by Buffalo Sabres as underage player in first round (first Sabres pick, sixth overall) of NHL entry draft (June 9, 1982). . . . Bruised shoulder (January 1984). . . . Suspended three games by NHL (October 1984). . . . Injured back (November 1987). . . . Bruised back (January 12, 1989). . . . Suffered hip pointer and bruised back (March 18, 1989). . . . Pulled shoulder ligaments while playing at World Cup Tournament (April 1989). . . . Traded by Sabres with LW Scott Arniel, RW Jeff Parker and first-round pick (C Keith Tkachuk) in 1990 draft to Winnipeg Jets for C Dale Hawerchuk and first-round pick (LW Brad May) in 1990 draft (June 16, 1990). . . . Strained abdomen (February 1992); missed five games. . . . Strained groin (October 31, 1992); missed two games. . . . Sprained wrist (January 19, 1992); missed two games. . . . Traded by Jets to St. Louis Blues for RW Nelson Emerson and D Stephane Quintal (September 24, 1993). . . . Suffered back spasms (October 26, 1993); missed five games. . . . Suffered sore back (November 18, 1993). . . . Underwent back surgery (January 4, 1994); missed 53 games. . . . Traded by Blues with second-round pick in 1996 and 1997 drafts to Calgary Flames for free-agent rights to D Al MacInnis and fourth-round pick in 1997 draft (July 4, 1994).
HONORS: Named to NHL All-Rookie team (1982-83). . . . Played in NHL All-Star Game (1984 and 1989-1993). . . . Named to THE SPORTING NEWS All-Star second team (1991-92). . . . Named to NHL All-Star second team (1991-92).
MISCELLANEOUS: Member of Team U.S.A. at World Junior Championships (1982). . . . Member of Team U.S.A. at World Cup Tournament (1982).

			REGULAR SEASON					PLAYOFFS			
Season Team	League	Gms.	G	A	Pts.	PIM	Gms.	G	A	Pts.	PIM
80-81—St. Paul	USHL	6	7	7	14	6	—	—	—	—	—
81-82—South St. Paul H.S.	Minn. H.S.	22	31	34	65	18	—	—	—	—	—
82-83—Buffalo	NHL	77	19	47	66	39	10	3	4	7	2
83-84—Buffalo	NHL	75	31	46	77	33	3	0	0	0	6
84-85—Buffalo	NHL	73	16	53	69	28	5	3	2	5	2
85-86—Buffalo	NHL	79	15	47	62	54	—	—	—	—	—
86-87—Buffalo	NHL	78	21	46	67	57	—	—	—	—	—
87-88—Buffalo	NHL	74	29	37	66	96	6	2	4	6	6
88-89—Buffalo	NHL	72	26	44	70	47	5	1	3	4	2
89-90—Buffalo	NHL	80	21	60	81	32	6	1	4	5	4
90-91—Winnipeg	NHL	78	23	53	76	24	—	—	—	—	—
91-92—Winnipeg	NHL	74	23	63	86	92	7	1	4	5	0
92-93—Winnipeg	NHL	80	18	79	97	52	6	0	7	7	2
93-94—St. Louis	NHL	26	7	15	22	12	4	2	1	3	4
NHL totals		866	249	590	839	566	52	13	29	42	28

HOWE, MARK
D, RED WINGS

PERSONAL: Born May 28, 1955, in Detroit. . . . 5-11/185. . . . Shoots left. . . . Full name: Mark Steven Howe. . . . Son of Gordie Howe, Hall of Fame right winger, Detroit Red Wings and Hartford Whalers (1946-47 through 1970-71 and 1979-80) and Houston Aeros and New England Whalers of WHA (1973-74 through 1978-79); and brother of Marty Howe, defenseman, Hartford Whalers and Boston Bruins (1979-80 through 1984-85) and Houston Aeros and New England Whalers of WHA (1973-74 through 1978-79).
TRANSACTIONS/CAREER NOTES: Signed by Houston Aeros (June 1972). . . . Traded by London Knights to Toronto Marlboros for D Larry Goodenough and C Dennis Maruk (August 1972). . . . Underwent corrective knee surgery; missed most of 1971-72 season. . . . Selected by Boston Bruins from Marlboros in second round (second Bruins pick, 25th overall) of amateur draft (May 28, 1974). . . . Separated shoulder; missed part of 1976-77 season. . . . Signed as free agent by New England Whalers (June 1977). . . . Injured ribs; missed part of 1977-78 season. . . . Selected by Boston Bruins in NHL reclaim draft, but remained Hartford Whalers property as a priority selection for the expansion draft (June 9, 1979). . . . Suffered five-inch puncture wound to upper thigh (December 27, 1980). . . . Traded by Whalers with third-round pick in 1983 draft to Philadelphia Flyers for C Ken Linseman, C Greg Adams and first-round (LW David A. Jensen) and third-round picks in 1983 draft (August 19, 1982). . . . Injured shoulder (February 1984). . . . Bruised collarbone (January 1985). . . . Suffered back spasms (January 1987). . . . Broke rib and vertebrae (September 1987). . . . Strained back (March 1988). . . . Bruised right foot (October 1988). . . . Pulled groin muscle (December 1988). . . . Sprained left knee cruciate ligament (February 1989); missed eight games. . . . Reinjured left knee (February 27, 1989). . . . Injured groin (December 22, 1989). . . . Injured back (January 27, 1990). . . . Injured back (November 3, 1990); missed four games. . . . Reinjured back (November 25, 1990). . . . Underwent surgery for herniated disk (January 18, 1991); missed 54 games. . . . Aggravated back injury (October 4, 1991); missed seven games. . . . Fractured thumb (November 23, 1991); missed 24 games. . . . Signed as free agent by Detroit Red Wings (July 8, 1992). . . . Injured back (November 28, 1992); missed three games. . . . Injured rib (December 28, 1992); missed three games. . . . Injured back (January 17, 1993); missed two games. . . . Sprained neck (March 18, 1993); missed eight games. . . . Sprained left knee (October 5, 1993); missed four games. . . . Suffered back spasms (December 5, 1993); missed two games. . . . Strained back (January 6, 1994); missed 22 games.
HONORS: Won Most Valuable Player and Outstanding Forward Awards (1970-71). . . . Named to SOJHL All-Star first team (1970-71). . . . Won WHA Rookie of the Year Award (1973-74). . . . Named to WHA All-Star second team (1973-74 and 1976-77). . . . Named to WHA All-Star first team (1978-79). . . . Named to THE SPORTING NEWS All-Star second team (1979-80). . . . Played in NHL All-Star Game (1981, 1983, 1986 and 1988). . . . Named to THE SPORTING NEWS All-Star first team (1982-83, 1985-86 and 1986-87). . . . Named to NHL All-Star first team (1982-83, 1985-86 and 1986-87). . . . Won Emery Edge Award (1985-86).

			REGULAR SEASON					PLAYOFFS			
Season Team	League	Gms.	G	A	Pts.	PIM	Gms.	G	A	Pts.	PIM
70-71—Detroit Junior Red Wings	SOJHL	44	37	*70	*107	...	—	—	—	—	—
71-72—Detroit Junior Red Wings	SOJHL	9	5	9	14	...	—	—	—	—	—
—U.S. Olympic Team	Int'l				Statistics unavailable.						
72-73—Toronto	OHA Mj. Jr. A	60	38	66	104	27	—	—	—	—	—
73-74—Houston	WHA	76	38	41	79	20	14	9	10	19	4
74-75—Houston	WHA	74	36	40	76	30	13	†10	12	*22	0

H

Season Team	League	REGULAR SEASON					PLAYOFFS				
		Gms.	G	A	Pts.	Pen.	Gms.	G	A	Pts.	Pen.
75-76—Houston	WHA	72	39	37	76	38	†17	6	10	16	18
76-77—Houston	WHA	57	23	52	75	46	10	4	10	14	2
77-78—New England	WHA	70	30	61	91	32	14	8	7	15	18
78-79—New England	WHA	77	42	65	107	32	6	4	2	6	6
79-80—Hartford	NHL	74	24	56	80	20	3	1	2	3	2
80-81—Hartford	NHL	63	19	46	65	54	—	—	—	—	—
81-82—Hartford	NHL	76	8	45	53	18	—	—	—	—	—
82-83—Philadelphia	NHL	76	20	47	67	18	3	0	2	2	4
83-84—Philadelphia	NHL	71	19	34	53	44	3	0	0	0	2
84-85—Philadelphia	NHL	73	18	39	57	31	19	3	8	11	6
85-86—Philadelphia	NHL	77	24	58	82	36	5	0	4	4	0
86-87—Philadelphia	NHL	69	15	43	58	37	26	2	10	12	4
87-88—Philadelphia	NHL	75	19	43	62	62	7	3	6	9	4
88-89—Philadelphia	NHL	52	9	29	38	45	19	0	15	15	10
89-90—Philadelphia	NHL	40	7	21	28	24	—	—	—	—	—
90-91—Philadelphia	NHL	19	0	10	10	8	—	—	—	—	—
91-92—Philadelphia	NHL	42	7	18	25	18	—	—	—	—	—
92-93—Detroit	NHL	60	3	31	34	22	7	1	3	4	2
93-94—Detroit	NHL	44	4	20	24	8	6	0	1	1	0
WHA totals		426	208	296	504	198	74	41	51	92	48
NHL totals		911	196	540	736	445	98	10	51	61	34

HRIVNAK, JIM

G, BLUES

PERSONAL: Born May 28, 1968, in Montreal.... 6-2/195.... Catches left.... Full name: James Richard Hrivnak.... Name pronounced RIHV-nak.

COLLEGE: Merrimack (Mass.).

TRANSACTIONS/CAREER NOTES: Selected by Washington Capitals in third round (fourth Capitals pick, 61st overall) of NHL entry draft (June 21, 1986).... Traded by Capitals with future considerations to Winnipeg Jets for G Rick Tabaracci (March 22, 1993).... Traded by Jets to St. Louis Blues for sixth-round pick (D Chris Kibermanis) in 1994 draft (July 29, 1993).

HONORS: Named to AHL All-Star second team (1989-90).

Season Team	League	REGULAR SEASON								PLAYOFFS						
		Gms.	Min.	W	L	T	GA	SO	Avg.	Gms.	Min.	W	L	GA	SO	Avg.
85-86—Merrimack College	ECAC-II	21	1230	12	6	2	75	0	3.66	—	—	—	—	—	—	—
86-87—Merrimack College	ECAC-II	34	1618	27	7	0	58	3	2.15	—	—	—	—	—	—	—
87-88—Merrimack College	ECAC-II	37	2119	31	6	0	84	4	2.38	—	—	—	—	—	—	—
88-89—Merrimack College	ECAC-II	22	1295	...	...	...	52	4	2.41	—	—	—	—	—	—	—
—Baltimore	AHL	10	502	1	8	0	55	0	6.57	—	—	—	—	—	—	—
89-90—Washington	NHL	11	609	5	5	0	36	0	3.55	—	—	—	—	—	—	—
—Baltimore	AHL	47	2722	24	19	2	139	*4	3.06	6	360	4	2	19	*1	3.17
90-91—Washington	NHL	9	432	4	2	1	26	0	3.61	—	—	—	—	—	—	—
—Baltimore	AHL	42	2481	20	16	6	134	1	3.24	6	324	2	3	21	0	3.89
91-92—Washington	NHL	12	605	6	3	0	35	0	3.47	—	—	—	—	—	—	—
—Baltimore	AHL	22	1303	10	8	3	73	0	3.36	—	—	—	—	—	—	—
92-93—Washington	NHL	27	1421	13	9	2	83	0	3.50	—	—	—	—	—	—	—
—Winnipeg	NHL	3	180	2	1	0	13	0	4.33	—	—	—	—	—	—	—
93-94—St. Louis	NHL	23	970	4	10	0	69	0	4.27	—	—	—	—	—	—	—
NHL totals		85	4217	34	30	3	262	0	3.73							

HRKAC, TONY

C, BLUES

PERSONAL: Born July 7, 1966, in Thunder Bay, Ont.... 5-11/185.... Shoots left.... Name pronounced HUHR-kihz.

COLLEGE: North Dakota.

TRANSACTIONS/CAREER NOTES: Selected by St. Louis Blues as underage junior in second round (second Blues pick, 32nd overall) of NHL entry draft (June 9, 1984).... Suspended six games for disciplinary reasons (January 1985).... Bruised left leg (January 1987).... Sprained shoulder (January 12, 1988).... Lacerated ankle (March 1988).... Bruised left shoulder (November 28, 1989).... Traded by Blues with G Greg Millen to Quebec Nordiques for D Jeff Brown (December 13, 1989).... Traded by Nordiques to San Jose Sharks for RW Greg Paslawski (May 30, 1991).... Injured wrist during preseason (September 1991); missed first 27 games of season.... Traded by Sharks to Chicago Blackhawks for conditional pick in 1993 draft (February 7, 1992).... Signed as free agent by Blues (July 30, 1993).

HONORS: Won Hobey Baker Memorial Trophy (1986-87).... Won WCHA Most Valuable Player Award (1986-87).... Named NCAA Tournament Most Valuable Player (1986-87).... Named to NCAA All-America West first team (1986-87).... Named to WCHA All-Star first team (1986-87).... Named to NCAA All-Tournament team (1986-87).... Won James Gatschene Memorial Trophy (1992-93).... Won Leo P. Lamoureux Memorial Trophy (1992-93).... Named to IHL All-Star first team (1992-93).

Season Team	League	REGULAR SEASON					PLAYOFFS				
		Gms.	G	A	Pts.	PIM	Gms.	G	A	Pts.	PIM
83-84—Orillia	OHA	42	*52	54	*106	20	—	—	—	—	—
84-85—Univ. of North Dakota	WCHA	36	18	36	54	16	—	—	—	—	—
85-86—Canadian national team	Int'l	62	19	30	49	36	—	—	—	—	—
86-87—Univ. of North Dakota	WCHA	48	46	*70	*116	48	—	—	—	—	—
—St. Louis	NHL	—	—	—	—	—	3	0	0	0	0
87-88—St. Louis	NHL	67	11	37	48	22	10	6	1	7	4
88-89—St. Louis	NHL	70	17	28	45	8	4	1	1	2	0
89-90—St. Louis	NHL	28	5	12	17	8					

Season	Team	League	REGULAR SEASON Gms.	G	A	Pts.	Pen.	PLAYOFFS Gms.	G	A	Pts.	Pen.
	—Quebec	NHL	22	4	8	12	2	—	—	—	—	—
	—Halifax	AHL	20	12	21	33	4	6	5	9	14	4
90-91	—Halifax	AHL	3	4	1	5	2	—	—	—	—	—
	—Quebec	NHL	70	16	32	48	16	—	—	—	—	—
91-92	—San Jose	NHL	22	2	10	12	4	—	—	—	—	—
	—Chicago	NHL	18	1	2	3	6	3	0	0	0	2
92-93	—Indianapolis	IHL	80	45	*87	*132	70	5	0	2	2	2
93-94	—St. Louis	NHL	36	6	5	11	8	4	0	0	0	0
	—Peoria	IHL	45	30	51	81	25	1	1	2	3	0
NHL totals			333	62	134	196	74	24	7	2	9	6

HRUDEY, KELLY

G, KINGS

PERSONAL: Born January 13, 1961, in Edmonton. . . . 5-10/189. . . . Catches left. . . . Full name: Kelly Stephen Hrudey. . . . Name pronounced ROO-dee.

TRANSACTIONS/CAREER NOTES: Selected by New York Islanders as underage junior in second round (second Islanders pick, 38th overall) of NHL entry draft (June 11, 1980). . . . Traded by Islanders to Los Angeles Kings for D Wayne McBean, G Mark Fitzpatrick and future considerations (February 27, 1989); Kings sent D Doug Crossman to Islanders to complete deal (May 23, 1989). . . . Suffered from the flu (April 1989). . . . Suffered from mononucleosis (February 1990); missed 14 games. . . . Bruised ribs (April 20, 1990). . . . Suffered from the flu (March 11, 1993); missed one game. . . . Suffered from the flu (March 26, 1993); missed one game.

HONORS: Named to WHL All-Star second team (1980-81). . . . Shared Terry Sawchuk Trophy with Robert Holland (1981-82 and 1982-83). . . . Won Max McNab Trophy (1981-82). . . . Named to CHL All-Star first team (1981-82 and 1982-83). . . . Won Tommy Ivan Trophy (1982-83).

Season	Team	League	REGULAR SEASON Gms.	Min.	W	L	T	GA	SO	Avg.	PLAYOFFS Gms.	Min.	W	L	GA	SO	Avg.
78-79	—Medicine Hat	WHL	57	3093	12	34	7	*318	0	6.17	—	—	—	—	—	—	—
79-80	—Medicine Hat	WHL	57	3049	25	23	4	212	1	4.17	13	638	6	6	48	0	4.51
80-81	—Medicine Hat	WHL	55	3023	32	19	1	200	†4	3.97	4	244	...	...	17	0	4.18
	—Indianapolis	CHL	—	—	—	—	—	—	—	—	2	135	...	...	8	0	3.56
81-82	—Indianapolis	CHL	51	3033	27	19	4	149	1	*2.95	13	842	11	2	34	*1	*2.42
82-83	—Indianapolis	CHL	47	2744	26	17	1	139	2	3.04	10	†637	*7	3	28	0	*2.64
83-84	—Indianapolis	CHL	6	370	3	2	1	21	0	3.41	—	—	—	—	—	—	—
	—New York Islanders	NHL	12	535	7	2	0	28	0	3.14	—	—	—	—	—	—	—
84-85	—New York Islanders	NHL	41	2335	19	17	3	141	2	3.62	5	281	1	3	8	0	1.71
85-86	—New York Islanders	NHL	45	2563	19	15	8	137	1	3.21	2	120	0	2	6	0	3.00
86-87	—New York Islanders	NHL	46	2634	21	15	7	145	0	3.30	14	842	7	7	38	0	2.71
87-88	—New York Islanders	NHL	47	2751	22	17	5	153	3	3.34	6	381	2	4	23	0	3.62
88-89	—New York Islanders	NHL	50	2800	18	24	3	183	0	3.92	—	—	—	—	—	—	—
	—Los Angeles	NHL	16	974	10	4	2	47	1	2.90	10	566	4	6	35	0	3.71
89-90	—Los Angeles	NHL	52	2860	22	21	6	194	2	4.07	9	539	4	4	39	0	4.34
90-91	—Los Angeles	NHL	47	2730	26	13	6	132	3	2.90	12	798	6	6	37	0	2.78
91-92	—Los Angeles	NHL	60	3509	26	17	*13	197	1	3.37	6	355	2	4	22	0	3.72
92-93	—Los Angeles	NHL	50	2718	18	21	6	175	2	3.86	20	1261	10	10	74	0	3.52
93-94	—Los Angeles	NHL	64	3713	22	31	7	228	1	3.68	—	—	—	—	—	—	—
NHL totals			530	30122	230	197	66	1760	16	3.51	84	5143	36	46	282	0	3.29

HUARD, BILL

LW, SENATORS

PERSONAL: Born June 24, 1967, in Alland, Ont. . . . 6-1/215. . . . Shoots left. . . . Name pronounced HYOO-ahrd.

TRANSACTIONS/CAREER NOTES: Signed as free agent by New Jersey Devils (October 1, 1989). . . . Signed as free agent by Boston Bruins (December 4, 1992). . . . Signed as free agent by Ottawa Senators (July 20, 1993). . . . Injured hip (December 9, 1993); missed three games. . . . Strained back (February 23, 1994); missed nine games.

Season	Team	League	REGULAR SEASON Gms.	G	A	Pts.	PIM	PLAYOFFS Gms.	G	A	Pts.	PIM
88-89	—Carolina	ECHL	40	27	21	48	177	10	7	2	9	70
89-90	—Utica	AHL	27	1	7	8	67	5	0	1	1	33
	—Nashville	ECHL	34	24	27	51	212	—	—	—	—	—
90-91	—Utica	AHL	72	11	16	27	359	—	—	—	—	—
91-92	—Utica	AHL	62	9	11	20	233	4	1	1	2	4
92-93	—Providence	AHL	72	18	19	37	302	6	3	0	3	9
	—Boston	NHL	2	0	0	0	0	—	—	—	—	—
93-94	—Ottawa	NHL	63	2	2	4	162	—	—	—	—	—
NHL totals			65	2	2	4	162					

HUDDY, CHARLIE

D, KINGS

PERSONAL: Born June 2, 1959, in Oshawa, Ont. . . . 6-0/210. . . . Shoots left. . . . Full name: Charles William Huddy. . . . Name pronounced HUH-dee.

TRANSACTIONS/CAREER NOTES: Signed as free agent by Edmonton Oilers (September 14, 1979). . . . Injured shoulder (November 10, 1980). . . . Suffered back spasms (February 1986); missed three games. . . . Broke finger (April 1986). . . . Suffered hematoma of left thigh and underwent surgery (May 7, 1988); missed six playoff games. . . . Strained hamstring (January 2, 1989). . . . Sprained right ankle (December 22, 1990); missed 17 games. . . . Broke left toe (February 16, 1991); missed nine games. . . . Twisted back (March 1991). . . . Selected by Minnesota North Stars in NHL expansion draft (May 30, 1991). . . . Traded by North Stars with LW Randy Gilhen, RW Jim Thomson and fourth-round pick (D Alexei Zhitnik) in 1991 draft to Los Angeles Kings for C Todd Elik (June 22, 1991). . . . Injured groin (October 10, 1991); missed seven games. . . . Strained groin (November 7, 1991); missed five games. . . . Suffered

chest contusion (February 1, 1992); missed seven games. . . . Suffered chest contusion (March 3, 1992); missed five games. . . . Suffered from the flu (January 14, 1993); missed one game. . . . Strained groin (October 27, 1993); missed five games.
HONORS: Won Emery Edge Award (1982-83).
MISCELLANEOUS: Member of Stanley Cup championship teams (1984, 1985, 1987, 1988 and 1990).

Season Team	League	REGULAR SEASON					PLAYOFFS				
		Gms.	G	A	Pts.	PIM	Gms.	G	A	Pts.	PIM
77-78—Oshawa	OMJHL	59	17	18	35	81	6	2	1	3	10
78-79—Oshawa	OMJHL	64	20	38	58	108	5	3	4	7	12
79-80—Houston	CHL	79	14	34	48	46	6	1	0	1	2
80-81—Edmonton	NHL	12	2	5	7	6	—	—	—	—	—
—Wichita	CHL	47	8	36	44	71	17	3	11	14	10
81-82—Wichita	CHL	32	7	19	26	51	—	—	—	—	—
—Edmonton	NHL	41	4	11	15	46	5	1	2	3	14
82-83—Edmonton	NHL	76	20	37	57	58	15	1	6	7	10
83-84—Edmonton	NHL	75	8	34	42	43	12	1	9	10	8
84-85—Edmonton	NHL	80	7	44	51	46	18	3	17	20	17
85-86—Edmonton	NHL	76	6	35	41	55	7	0	2	2	0
86-87—Edmonton	NHL	58	4	15	19	35	21	1	7	8	21
87-88—Edmonton	NHL	77	13	28	41	71	13	4	5	9	10
88-89—Edmonton	NHL	76	11	33	44	52	7	2	0	2	4
89-90—Edmonton	NHL	70	1	23	24	56	22	0	6	6	11
90-91—Edmonton	NHL	53	5	22	27	32	18	3	7	10	10
91-92—Los Angeles	NHL	56	4	19	23	43	6	1	1	2	10
92-93—Los Angeles	NHL	82	2	25	27	64	23	1	4	5	12
93-94—Los Angeles	NHL	79	5	13	18	71	—	—	—	—	—
NHL totals		911	92	344	436	678	167	18	66	84	127

HUDSON, MIKE
C, RANGERS

PERSONAL: Born February 6, 1967, in Guelph, Ont. . . . 6-1/205. . . . Shoots left.
TRANSACTIONS/CAREER NOTES: Traded by Hamilton Steelhawks with D Keith Vanrooyen to Sudbury Wolves for C Brad Belland (October 1985). . . . Selected by Chicago Blackhawks as underage junior in seventh round (sixth Blackhawks pick, 140th overall) of NHL entry draft (June 21, 1986). . . . Lacerated right hand (December 21, 1989); missed 12 games. . . . Suffered elbow tendinitis (September 1990). . . . Underwent elbow surgery (May 1991). . . . Suffered viral infection (December 20, 1992); missed 21 games. . . . Traded by Blackhawks to Edmonton Oilers for D Craig Muni (March 22, 1993). . . . Suffered nerve disorder in left shoulder (March 1993); missed two games. . . . Fractured left hand (October 9, 1993); missed 16 games. . . . Selected by New York Rangers in 1993 waiver draft (October 3, 1993). . . . Suspended one game for high-sticking incident (March 13, 1994). . . . Suspended 10 games and fined $500 by NHL for hitting another player with a two-handed swing (March 16, 1994). . . .
MISCELLANEOUS: Member of Stanley Cup championship team (1994).

Season Team	League	REGULAR SEASON					PLAYOFFS				
		Gms.	G	A	Pts.	PIM	Gms.	G	A	Pts.	PIM
84-85—Hamilton	OHL	50	10	12	22	13	—	—	—	—	—
85-86—Hamilton	OHL	7	3	2	5	4	—	—	—	—	—
—Sudbury	OHL	59	35	42	77	20	4	2	5	7	7
86-87—Sudbury	OHL	63	40	57	97	18	—	—	—	—	—
87-88—Saginaw	IHL	75	18	30	48	44	10	2	3	5	20
88-89—Chicago	NHL	41	7	16	23	20	10	1	2	3	18
—Saginaw	IHL	30	15	17	32	10	—	—	—	—	—
89-90—Chicago	NHL	49	9	12	21	56	4	0	0	0	2
90-91—Chicago	NHL	55	7	9	16	62	6	0	2	2	8
—Indianapolis	IHL	3	1	2	3	0	—	—	—	—	—
91-92—Chicago	NHL	76	14	15	29	92	16	3	5	8	26
92-93—Chicago	NHL	36	1	6	7	44	—	—	—	—	—
—Edmonton	NHL	5	0	1	1	2	—	—	—	—	—
93-94—New York Rangers	NHL	48	4	7	11	47	—	—	—	—	—
NHL totals		310	42	66	108	323	36	4	9	13	54

HUFFMAN, KERRY
D, SENATORS

PERSONAL: Born January 3, 1968, in Peterborough, Ont. . . . 6-1/200. . . . Shoots left. . . . Brother-in-law of Mike Posavad, defenseman, St. Louis Blues (1985-86 and 1986-87).
TRANSACTIONS/CAREER NOTES: Selected by Philadelphia Flyers as underage junior in first round (first Flyers pick, 20th overall) of NHL entry draft (June 21, 1986). . . . Sprained ankle (November 1987). . . . Suffered calcium deposits in thigh (January 1988); missed 22 games. . . . Bruised right knee (March 15, 1990). . . . Suspended by Flyers after leaving team in dispute over ice time (November 16, 1990). . . . Returned to Flyers (December 10, 1990). . . . Suffered from tonsillitis (October 1991); missed one game. . . . Traded by Flyers with G Ron Hextall, C Mike Ricci, C Peter Forsberg, D Steve Duchesne, first-round pick in 1993 draft (G Jocelyn Thibault), cash and future considerations to Quebec Nordiques for C Eric Lindros (June 20, 1992); Flyers sent LW Chris Simon and first-round pick in 1994 draft (traded to Toronto Maple Leafs) to Nordiques to complete deal (July 21, 1992). . . . Broke ribs (October 17, 1992); missed three games. . . . Injured shoulder (November 28, 1992); missed 14 games. . . . Fractured finger (March 8, 1993); missed 10 games. . . . Claimed on waivers by Ottawa Senators (January 15, 1994). . . . Suffered back spasms (March 23, 1994); missed two games.
HONORS: Won Max Kaminsky Trophy (1986-87). . . . Named to OHL All-Star first team (1986-87).

Season Team	League	REGULAR SEASON					PLAYOFFS				
		Gms.	G	A	Pts.	PIM	Gms.	G	A	Pts.	PIM
84-85—Peterborough Jr. B	OHA	24	2	5	7	53	—	—	—	—	—
85-86—Guelph	OHL	56	3	24	27	35	20	1	10	11	10
86-87—Guelph	OHL	44	4	31	35	20	5	0	2	2	8

— 474 —

H

Season Team	League	Gms.	G	A	Pts.	Pen.	Gms.	G	A	Pts.	Pen.
				REGULAR SEASON					PLAYOFFS		
—Hershey	AHL	3	0	1	1	0	4	0	0	0	0
—Philadelphia	NHL	9	0	0	0	2	—	—	—	—	—
87-88—Philadelphia	NHL	52	6	17	23	34	2	0	0	0	0
88-89—Hershey	AHL	29	2	13	15	16	—	—	—	—	—
—Philadelphia	NHL	29	0	11	11	31	—	—	—	—	—
89-90—Philadelphia	NHL	43	1	12	13	34	—	—	—	—	—
90-91—Hershey	AHL	45	5	29	34	20	7	1	2	3	0
—Philadelphia	NHL	10	1	2	3	10	—	—	—	—	—
91-92—Philadelphia	NHL	60	14	18	32	41	—	—	—	—	—
92-93—Quebec	NHL	52	4	18	22	54	3	0	0	0	0
93-94—Quebec	NHL	28	0	6	6	28	—	—	—	—	—
—Ottawa	NHL	34	4	8	12	12	—	—	—	—	—
NHL totals		317	30	92	122	246	5	0	0	0	0

HUGHES, BRENT
LW, BRUINS

PERSONAL: Born April 5, 1966, in New Westminster, B.C. . . . 5-11/180. . . . Shoots left. . . . Full name: Brent Allen Hughes.
TRANSACTIONS/CAREER NOTES: Traded by New Westminster Bruins to Victoria Cougars for future considerations (October 1986). . . . Signed as free agent by Winnipeg Jets (July 1987). . . . Traded by Jets with LW Craig Duncanson and C Simon Wheeldon to Washington Capitals for LW Bob Joyce, D Kent Paynter and C Tyler Larter (May 21, 1991). . . . Traded by Capitals with future considerations to Boston Bruins for RW John Byce and D Dennis Smith (February 24, 1992). . . . Separated shoulder (November 28, 1992); missed 11 games.
HONORS: Named to WHL (West) All-Star first team (1986-87).

Season Team	League	Gms.	G	A	Pts.	PIM	Gms.	G	A	Pts.	PIM
				REGULAR SEASON					PLAYOFFS		
83-84—New Westminster	WHL	67	21	18	39	133	9	2	2	4	27
84-85—New Westminster	WHL	64	25	32	57	135	11	2	1	3	37
85-86—New Westminster	WHL	71	28	52	80	180	—	—	—	—	—
86-87—New Westminster	WHL	8	5	4	9	22	—	—	—	—	—
—Victoria	WHL	61	38	61	99	146	5	4	1	5	8
87-88—Moncton	AHL	77	13	19	32	206	—	—	—	—	—
88-89—Winnipeg	NHL	28	3	2	5	82	—	—	—	—	—
—Moncton	AHL	54	34	34	68	286	10	9	4	13	40
89-90—Moncton	AHL	65	31	29	60	277	—	—	—	—	—
—Winnipeg	NHL	11	1	2	3	33	—	—	—	—	—
90-91—Moncton	AHL	63	21	22	43	144	3	0	0	0	7
91-92—Baltimore	AHL	55	25	29	54	190	—	—	—	—	—
—Maine	AHL	12	6	4	10	34	—	—	—	—	—
—Boston	NHL	8	1	1	2	38	10	2	0	2	20
92-93—Boston	NHL	62	5	4	9	191	1	0	0	0	2
93-94—Providence	AHL	6	2	5	7	4	—	—	—	—	—
—Boston	NHL	77	13	11	24	143	13	2	1	3	27
NHL totals		186	23	20	43	487	24	4	1	5	49

HUGHES, RYAN
C, NORDIQUES

PERSONAL: Born January 17, 1972, in Montreal. . . . 6-2/196. . . . Shoots left. . . . Full name: Ryan Laine Hughes.
COLLEGE: Cornell.
TRANSACTIONS/CAREER NOTES: Selected by Quebec Nordiques in second round (second Nordiques pick, 22nd overall) of NHL entry draft (June 16, 1990).

Season Team	League	Gms.	G	A	Pts.	PIM	Gms.	G	A	Pts.	PIM
				REGULAR SEASON					PLAYOFFS		
89-90—Cornell University	ECAC	28	7	16	23	35	—	—	—	—	—
90-91—Cornell University	ECAC	32	18	34	52	28	—	—	—	—	—
—Victoria	WHL	1	0	1	1	2	—	—	—	—	—
91-92—Cornell University	ECAC	27	8	13	21	36	—	—	—	—	—
92-93—Cornell University	ECAC	26	8	14	22	30	—	—	—	—	—
93-94—Cornwall	AHL	54	17	12	29	24	13	2	4	6	6

HULBIG, JOE
LW, OILERS

PERSONAL: Born September 29, 1973, in Wrentham, Mass. . . . 6-3/215. . . . Shoots left.
HIGH SCHOOL: St. Sebastian's Country Day (Needham, Mass.).
COLLEGE: Providence.
TRANSACTIONS/CAREER NOTES: Selected by Edmonton Oilers in first round (first Oilers pick, 13th overall) of NHL entry draft (June 20, 1992).

Season Team	League	Gms.	G	A	Pts.	PIM	Gms.	G	A	Pts.	PIM
				REGULAR SEASON					PLAYOFFS		
90-91—St. Sebastian's	Mass. H.S.	...	23	19	42	...	—	—	—	—	—
91-92—St. Sebastian's	Mass. H.S.	17	19	24	43	30	—	—	—	—	—
92-93—Providence College	Hockey East	26	3	13	16	22	—	—	—	—	—
93-94—Providence College	Hockey East	28	6	4	10	36	—	—	—	—	—

HULL, BRETT
RW, BLUES

PERSONAL: Born August 9, 1964, in Belleville, Ont. . . . 5-10/200. . . . Shoots right. . . . Son of Bobby Hull, Hall of Fame left winger, Chicago Blackhawks, Winnipeg Jets and Hartford Whalers (1957-58 through 1971-72 and 1979-80) and Winnipeg Jets of WHA (1972-73 through 1978-79); and nephew of Dennis Hull, left winger, Blackhawks and Detroit Red Wings (1964-65

through 1977-78).
COLLEGE: Minnesota-Duluth.
TRANSACTIONS/CAREER NOTES: Selected by Calgary Flames in sixth round (sixth Flames pick, 117th overall) of NHL entry draft (June 9, 1984).... Traded by Flames with LW Steve Bozek to St. Louis Blues for D Rob Ramage and G Rick Wamsley (March 7, 1988).... Sprained left ankle (January 15, 1991); missed two regular-season games and All-Star Game.... Suffered back spasms (March 12, 1992); missed seven games.... Suffered sore wrist (March 20, 1993); missed four games.... Suffered abdominal injury (October 7, 1993); missed three games.
HONORS: Won WCHA Freshman of the Year Award (1984-85).... Named to WCHA All-Star first team (1985-86).... Won Dudley (Red) Garrett Memorial Trophy (1986-87).... Named to AHL All-Star first team (1986-87).... Won Lady Byng Memorial Trophy (1989-90).... Won Dodge Ram Tough Award (1989-90 and 1990-91).... Named to THE SPORTING NEWS All-Star first team (1989-90 through 1991-92).... Named to NHL All-Star first team (1989-90 through 1991-92).... Played in NHL All-Star Game (1989, 1990, 1992-1994).... Named NHL Player of the Year by THE SPORTING NEWS (1990-91).... Won Hart Memorial Trophy (1990-91).... Won Lester B. Pearson Award (1990-91).... Won Pro Set NHL Player of the Year Award (1990-91).... Named All-Star Game Most Valuable Player (1992).
RECORDS: Holds NHL single-season record for most goals by a right winger—86 (1990-91).
MISCELLANEOUS: Shares distinction with Bobby Hull of being the first father-son duo to win the same NHL trophy (both the Lady Byng Memorial and Hart Memorial trophies).
STATISTICAL NOTES: Became the first son of an NHL 50-goal scorer to score 50 goals in one season (1989-90).

Season Team	League	Gms.	REGULAR SEASON G	A	Pts.	PIM	Gms.	PLAYOFFS G	A	Pts.	PIM
82-83—Penticton	BCJHL	50	48	56	104	27	—	—	—	—	—
83-84—Penticton	BCJHL	56	*105	83	*188	20	—	—	—	—	—
84-85—Minnesota-Duluth	WCHA	48	32	28	60	24	—	—	—	—	—
85-86—Minnesota-Duluth	WCHA	42	*52	32	84	46	—	—	—	—	—
—Calgary	NHL	—	—	—	—	—	2	0	0	0	0
86-87—Moncton	AHL	67	50	42	92	16	3	2	2	4	2
—Calgary	NHL	5	1	0	1	0	4	2	1	3	0
87-88—Calgary	NHL	52	26	24	50	12	—	—	—	—	—
—St. Louis	NHL	13	6	8	14	4	10	7	2	9	4
88-89—St. Louis	NHL	78	41	43	84	33	10	5	5	10	6
89-90—St. Louis	NHL	80	*72	41	113	24	12	13	8	21	17
90-91—St. Louis	NHL	78	*86	45	131	22	13	11	8	19	4
91-92—St. Louis	NHL	73	*70	39	109	48	6	4	4	8	4
92-93—St. Louis	NHL	80	54	47	101	41	11	8	5	13	2
93-94—St. Louis	NHL	81	57	40	97	38	4	2	1	3	0
NHL totals		540	413	287	700	222	72	52	34	86	37

HULL, JODY
RW, PANTHERS

PERSONAL: Born February 2, 1969, in Petrolia, Ont.... 6-2/200.... Shoots right.
HIGH SCHOOL: Thomas A. Stewart (Peterborough, Ont.).
TRANSACTIONS/CAREER NOTES: Strained ankle ligaments (September 1986).... Pulled groin (February 1987).... Selected by Hartford Whalers as underage junior in first round (first Whalers pick, 18th overall) of NHL entry draft (June 13, 1987).... Pulled hamstring (March 1989).... Traded by Whalers to New York Rangers for C Carey Wilson and third-round pick (C Mikael Nylander) in 1991 draft (July 9, 1990).... Sprained muscle in right hand (October 6, 1990).... Bruised left big toe (November 19, 1990); missed six games.... Injured knee (March 13, 1991).... Traded by Rangers to Ottawa Senators for future considerations (July 28, 1992).... Injured groin (December 7, 1992); missed three games.... Suffered concussion (January 10, 1993); missed one game.... Sprained ankle (January 19, 1993); missed eight games.... Sprained left ankle (April 1, 1993); missed two games.... Signed as free agent by Florida Panthers (August 10, 1993).... Bruised right shoulder (February 1, 1994); missed one game.... Separated right shoulder (March 4, 1994); missed three games.... Separated right shoulder (March 18, 1994); missed six games.
HONORS: Named to OHL All-Star second team (1987-88).

Season Team	League	Gms.	REGULAR SEASON G	A	Pts.	PIM	Gms.	PLAYOFFS G	A	Pts.	PIM
84-85—Cambridge Jr. B	OHA	38	13	17	30	39	—	—	—	—	—
85-86—Peterborough	OHL	61	20	22	42	29	16	1	5	6	4
86-87—Peterborough	OHL	49	18	34	52	22	12	4	9	13	14
87-88—Peterborough	OHL	60	50	44	94	33	12	10	8	18	8
88-89—Hartford	NHL	60	16	18	34	10	1	0	0	0	2
89-90—Binghamton	AHL	21	7	10	17	6	—	—	—	—	—
—Hartford	NHL	38	7	10	17	21	5	0	1	1	2
90-91—New York Rangers	NHL	47	5	8	13	10	—	—	—	—	—
91-92—New York Rangers	NHL	3	0	0	0	2	—	—	—	—	—
—Binghamton	AHL	69	34	31	65	28	11	5	2	7	4
92-93—Ottawa	NHL	69	13	21	34	14	—	—	—	—	—
93-94—Florida	NHL	69	13	13	26	8	—	—	—	—	—
NHL totals		286	54	70	124	65	6	0	1	1	4

HULSE, CALE
D, DEVILS

PERSONAL: Born November 10, 1973, in Edmonton.... 6-3/210.... Shoots right.... Name pronounced HUHLS.
COLLEGE: Portland.
TRANSACTIONS/CAREER NOTES: Selected by New Jersey Devils in third round (third Devils pick, 66th overall) of NHL entry draft (June 20, 1992).

Season Team	League	Gms.	REGULAR SEASON G	A	Pts.	PIM	Gms.	PLAYOFFS G	A	Pts.	PIM
90-91—Calgary Royals	AJHL	49	3	23	26	220	—	—	—	—	—
91-92—Portland	WHL	70	4	18	22	250	6	0	2	2	27

Season	Team	League	REGULAR SEASON					PLAYOFFS				
			Gms.	G	A	Pts.	Pen.	Gms.	G	A	Pts.	Pen.
92-93—Portland		WHL	72	10	26	36	284	16	4	4	8	*65
93-94—Albany		AHL	79	7	14	21	186	5	0	3	3	11

HUMENIUK, SCOTT
LW, WHALERS

PERSONAL: Born September 10, 1969, in Saskatoon, Sask. . . . 6-0/190. . . . Shoots left. . . . Name pronounced HYOO-mih-nuhk.
TRANSACTIONS/CAREER NOTES: Suspended five games by WHL and fined $500 for leaving bench during fight (November 1987). . . . Traded by Spokane Chiefs to Moose Jaw Warriors for the WHL rights to D Scott Chartier (September 1988). . . . Signed as free agent by Hartford Whalers (March 22, 1990).
HONORS: Named to WHL All-Star second team (1989-90).

Season	Team	League	REGULAR SEASON					PLAYOFFS				
			Gms.	G	A	Pts.	PIM	Gms.	G	A	Pts.	PIM
86-87—Spokane		WHL	10	2	0	2	2	1	0	0	0	0
87-88—Spokane		WHL	58	6	20	26	154	8	1	0	1	19
88-89—Moose Jaw		WHL	56	18	39	57	159	7	5	0	5	32
89-90—Binghamton		AHL	4	0	1	1	11	—	—	—	—	—
—Moose Jaw		WHL	71	23	47	70	141	—	—	—	—	—
90-91—Springfield		AHL	57	6	17	23	69	14	2	2	4	18
91-92—Springfield		AHL	28	2	3	5	27	—	—	—	—	—
—Louisville		ECHL	26	7	21	28	93	13	1	11	12	33
92-93—Springfield		AHL	16	0	3	3	28	14	1	3	4	8
93-94—Springfield		AHL	71	15	42	57	91	6	0	3	3	8

HUNTER, DALE
C, CAPITALS

PERSONAL: Born July 31, 1960, in Petrolia, Ont. . . . 5-10/198. . . . Shoots left. . . . Full name: Dale Robert Hunter. . . . Brother of Mark Hunter, right winger for four NHL teams (1981-82 through 1992-93); and brother of Dave Hunter, left winger, Edmonton Oilers of WHA (1978-79); and Edmonton Oilers, Pittsburgh Penguins and Winnipeg Jets (1979-80 through 1988-89).
TRANSACTIONS/CAREER NOTES: Selected by Quebec Nordiques as underage junior in second round (second Nordiques pick, 41st overall) of NHL entry draft (August 9, 1979). . . . Suspended three games by NHL (March 1984). . . . Suffered hand infection (April 21, 1985). . . . Broke lower fibula of left leg (November 25, 1986). . . . Traded by Nordiques with G Clint Malarchuk to Washington Capitals for C Alan Haworth, LW Gaetan Duchesne and first-round pick (C Joe Sakic) in 1987 draft (June 13, 1987). . . . Broke thumb (September 1988). . . . Suspended four games by NHL for elbowing D Gord Murphy (February 10, 1991). . . . Suspended for first 21 games of 1993-94 season by NHL for blindside check on player (May 4, 1993). . . . Injured medial collateral knee ligament (November 26, 1993); missed 10 games.
RECORDS: Holds NHL career playoff record for most penalty minutes—613.

Season	Team	League	REGULAR SEASON					PLAYOFFS				
			Gms.	G	A	Pts.	PIM	Gms.	G	A	Pts.	PIM
77-78—Kitchener		OMJHL	68	22	42	64	115	—	—	—	—	—
78-79—Sudbury		OMJHL	59	42	68	110	188	10	4	12	16	47
79-80—Sudbury		OMJHL	61	34	51	85	189	9	6	9	15	45
80-81—Quebec		NHL	80	19	44	63	226	5	4	2	6	34
81-82—Quebec		NHL	80	22	50	72	272	16	3	7	10	52
82-83—Quebec		NHL	80	17	46	63	206	4	2	1	3	24
83-84—Quebec		NHL	77	24	55	79	232	9	2	3	5	41
84-85—Quebec		NHL	80	20	52	72	209	17	4	6	10	*97
85-86—Quebec		NHL	80	28	42	70	265	3	0	0	0	15
86-87—Quebec		NHL	46	10	29	39	135	13	1	7	8	56
87-88—Washington		NHL	79	22	37	59	240	14	7	5	12	98
88-89—Washington		NHL	80	20	37	57	219	6	0	4	4	29
89-90—Washington		NHL	80	23	39	62	233	15	4	8	12	61
90-91—Washington		NHL	76	16	30	46	234	11	1	9	10	41
91-92—Washington		NHL	80	28	50	78	205	7	1	4	5	16
92-93—Washington		NHL	84	20	59	79	198	6	7	1	8	35
93-94—Washington		NHL	52	9	29	38	131	7	0	3	3	14
NHL totals			1054	278	599	877	3005	133	36	60	96	613

HUNTER, TIM
LW/RW, CANUCKS

PERSONAL: Born September 10, 1960, in Calgary. . . . 6-2/202. . . . Shoots right. . . . Full name: Timothy Robert Hunter.
TRANSACTIONS/CAREER NOTES: Selected by Atlanta Flames in third round (fourth Flames pick, 54th overall) of NHL entry draft (August 9, 1979). . . . Flames franchise moved to Calgary (May 21, 1980). . . . Bruised hand (October 1987). . . . Injured right eye (October 17, 1988). . . . Suspended 10 games and fined $500 by NHL for leaving bench to fight (November 1, 1989). . . . Tore shoulder muscles (October 6, 1990); missed four games. . . . Reinjured shoulder (October 18, 1990); missed 21 games. . . . Reinjured shoulder (December 2, 1990); missed 20 games. . . . Suffered back spasms (October 1991); missed one game. . . . Fractured left ankle (December 8, 1991); missed 39 games. . . . Selected by Tampa Bay Lightning in NHL expansion draft (June 18, 1992). . . . Traded by Lightning to Quebec Nordiques for future considerations (June 22, 1992); Nordiques sent RW Martin Simard to Lightning to complete deal (September 14, 1992). . . . Bruised knee (December 29, 1992); missed one game. . . . Suffered back spasms (January 28, 1993); missed three games. . . . Claimed on waivers by Vancouver Canucks (February 12, 1993). . . . Sprained knee (November 2, 1993); missed 14 games. . . . Suffered back spasms (March 3, 1994); missed seven games. . . . Suspended three games by NHL for wrestling with linesman (March 26, 1994).
MISCELLANEOUS: Member of Stanley Cup championship team (1989).

H

Season	Team	League		REGULAR SEASON					PLAYOFFS			
			Gms.	G	A	Pts.	PIM	Gms.	G	A	Pts.	PIM
77-78—Kamloops		BCJHL	51	9	28	37	266	—	—	—	—	—
—Seattle		WCHL	3	1	2	3	4	—	—	—	—	—
78-79—Seattle		WHL	70	8	41	49	300	—	—	—	—	—
79-80—Seattle		WHL	72	14	53	67	311	12	1	2	3	41
80-81—Birmingham		CHL	58	3	5	8	*236	—	—	—	—	—
—Nova Scotia		AHL	17	0	0	0	62	6	0	1	1	45
81-82—Oklahoma City		CHL	55	4	12	16	222	—	—	—	—	—
—Calgary		NHL	2	0	0	0	9	—	—	—	—	—
82-83—Calgary		NHL	16	1	0	1	54	9	1	0	1	*70
—Colorado		CHL	46	5	12	17	225	—	—	—	—	—
83-84—Calgary		NHL	43	4	4	8	130	7	0	0	0	21
84-85—Calgary		NHL	71	11	11	22	259	4	0	0	0	24
85-86—Calgary		NHL	66	8	7	15	291	19	0	3	3	108
86-87—Calgary		NHL	73	6	15	21	361	6	0	0	0	51
87-88—Calgary		NHL	68	8	5	13	337	9	4	0	4	32
88-89—Calgary		NHL	75	3	9	12	*375	19	0	4	4	32
89-90—Calgary		NHL	67	2	3	5	279	6	0	0	0	4
90-91—Calgary		NHL	34	5	2	7	143	7	0	0	0	10
91-92—Calgary		NHL	30	1	3	4	167	—	—	—	—	—
92-93—Quebec		NHL	48	5	3	8	94	—	—	—	—	—
—Vancouver		NHL	26	0	4	4	99	11	0	0	0	26
93-94—Vancouver		NHL	56	3	4	7	171	24	0	0	0	26
NHL totals			675	57	70	127	2769	121	5	7	12	404

HURD, KELLY

RW

PERSONAL: Born May 13, 1968, in Castlegar, B.C. . . . 5-11/185. . . . Shoots right.
COLLEGE: Michigan Tech.
TRANSACTIONS/CAREER NOTES: Selected by Detroit Red Wings in seventh round (sixth Red Wings pick, 143rd overall) of NHL entry draft (June 11, 1988).
HONORS: Named to WCHA All-Star second team (1990-91).

Season	Team	League		REGULAR SEASON					PLAYOFFS			
			Gms.	G	A	Pts.	PIM	Gms.	G	A	Pts.	PIM
86-87—Kelowna		BCJHL	50	40	53	93	121	—	—	—	—	—
87-88—Michigan Tech		WCHA	41	18	22	40	34	—	—	—	—	—
88-89—Michigan Tech		WCHA	42	18	14	32	36	—	—	—	—	—
89-90—Michigan Tech		WCHA	37	12	13	25	50	—	—	—	—	—
90-91—Michigan Tech		WCHA	35	29	22	51	44	—	—	—	—	—
91-92—Adirondack		AHL	35	9	7	16	16	8	1	4	5	2
—Fort Wayne		IHL	30	13	9	22	12	3	3	0	3	9
92-93—Fort Wayne		IHL	71	23	31	54	81	10	4	5	9	12
93-94—Fort Wayne		IHL	75	35	49	84	52	17	6	4	10	10

HURLBUT, MIKE

D, NORDIQUES

PERSONAL: Born July 10, 1966, in Massensa, N.Y. . . . 6-2/200. . . . Shoots left. . . . Full name: Michael Ray Hurlbut.
COLLEGE: St. Lawrence (N.Y.).
TRANSACTIONS/CAREER NOTES: Selected by New York Rangers in NHL supplemental draft (June 10, 1988). . . . Sprained left knee (January 25, 1993); missed 13 games. . . . Traded by Rangers to Quebec Nordiques for D Alexander Karpovtsev (September 9, 1993).
HONORS: Named to NCAA All-America East first team (1988-89). . . . Named to ECAC All-Star first team (1988-89).

Season	Team	League		REGULAR SEASON					PLAYOFFS			
			Gms.	G	A	Pts.	PIM	Gms.	G	A	Pts.	PIM
85-86—St. Lawrence University		ECAC	25	2	10	12	40	—	—	—	—	—
86-87—St. Lawrence University		ECAC	35	8	15	23	44	—	—	—	—	—
87-88—St. Lawrence University		ECAC	38	6	12	18	18	—	—	—	—	—
88-89—St. Lawrence University		ECAC	36	8	25	33	30	—	—	—	—	—
—Flint		IHL	8	0	2	2	13	4	1	2	3	2
89-90—Flint		IHL	74	3	34	37	38	3	0	1	1	2
90-91—Binghamton		AHL	33	2	11	13	27	3	0	1	1	0
—San Diego		IHL	2	1	0	1	0	—	—	—	—	—
91-92—Binghamton		AHL	79	16	39	55	64	11	2	7	9	8
92-93—Binghamton		AHL	46	11	25	36	46	14	2	5	7	12
—New York Rangers		NHL	23	1	8	9	16	—	—	—	—	—
93-94—Cornwall		AHL	77	13	33	46	100	13	3	7	10	12
—Quebec		NHL	1	0	0	0	0	—	—	—	—	—
NHL totals			24	1	8	9	16					

HUSCROFT, JAMIE

D, BRUINS

PERSONAL: Born January 9, 1967, in Creston, B.C. . . . 6-2/200. . . . Shoots right.
TRANSACTIONS/CAREER NOTES: Selected by New Jersey Devils as underage junior in ninth round (ninth Devils pick, 171st overall) of NHL entry draft (June 15, 1985). . . . Fractured arm (October 1986); missed eight weeks. . . . Traded by Seattle Thunderbirds to Medicine Hat Tigers for C Mike Schwengler (February 1987). . . . Fractured right wrist (October 1988). . . . Injured groin (December 1988). . . . Broke foot (January 1989); missed 19 games. . . . Signed as free agent by Boston Bruins (July 16, 1992).

Season Team	League	REGULAR SEASON					PLAYOFFS				
		Gms.	G	A	Pts.	PIM	Gms.	G	A	Pts.	PIM
83-84—Portland	WHL	63	0	12	12	77	5	0	0	0	15
84-85—Seattle	WHL	69	3	13	16	273	—	—	—	—	—
85-86—Seattle	WHL	66	6	20	26	394	5	0	1	1	18
86-87—Seattle	WHL	21	1	18	19	99	20	0	3	3	0
—Medicine Hat	WHL	35	4	21	25	170	20	0	3	3	*125
87-88—Flint	IHL	3	1	0	1	2	16	0	1	1	110
—Utica	AHL	71	5	7	12	316	—	—	—	—	—
88-89—Utica	AHL	41	2	10	12	215	5	0	0	0	40
—New Jersey	NHL	15	0	2	2	51	—	—	—	—	—
89-90—New Jersey	NHL	42	2	3	5	149	5	0	0	0	16
—Utica	AHL	22	3	6	9	122	—	—	—	—	—
90-91—New Jersey	NHL	8	0	1	1	27	3	0	0	0	6
—Utica	AHL	59	3	15	18	339	—	—	—	—	—
91-92—Utica	AHL	50	4	7	11	224	—	—	—	—	—
92-93—Providence	AHL	69	2	15	17	257	2	0	1	1	6
93-94—Providence	AHL	32	1	10	11	157	—	—	—	—	—
—Boston	NHL	36	0	1	1	144	4	0	0	0	9
NHL totals		101	2	7	9	371	12	0	0	0	31

HUSKA, RYAN
LW, BLACKHAWKS

PERSONAL: Born July 2, 1975, in Cranbrook, B.C.... 6-2/194.... Shoots left. **HIGH SCHOOL:** Norkam Secondary (Kamloops, B.C.). **TRANSACTIONS/CAREER NOTES:** Selected by Chicago Blackhawks in third round (fourth Blackhawks pick, 76th overall) of NHL entry draft (June 26, 1993).

Season Team	League	REGULAR SEASON					PLAYOFFS				
		Gms.	G	A	Pts.	PIM	Gms.	G	A	Pts.	PIM
91-92—Kamloops	WHL	44	4	5	9	23	6	0	1	1	0
92-93—Kamloops	WHL	68	17	15	32	50	13	2	6	8	4
93-94—Kamloops	WHL	69	23	31	54	66	19	9	5	14	23

HUSSEY, MARC
D, PENGUINS

PERSONAL: Born January 22, 1974, in Chatham, N.B.... 6-4/185.... Shoots right. **HIGH SCHOOL:** Vanier Collegiate (Moose Jaw, Sask.). **TRANSACTIONS/CAREER NOTES:** Selected by Pittsburgh Penguins in second round (second Penguins pick, 43rd overall) of NHL entry draft (June 20, 1992).

Season Team	League	REGULAR SEASON					PLAYOFFS				
		Gms.	G	A	Pts.	PIM	Gms.	G	A	Pts.	PIM
90-91—Moose Jaw	WHL	68	5	8	13	67	8	2	2	4	7
91-92—Moose Jaw	WHL	72	7	27	34	203	4	1	1	2	0
92-93—Moose Jaw	WHL	68	12	28	40	121	—	—	—	—	—
93-94—Moose Jaw	WHL	17	4	5	9	33	—	—	—	—	—
—Tri-City	WHL	16	3	6	9	26	—	—	—	—	—
—Medicine Hat	WHL	41	6	24	30	90	3	0	1	1	4

HYNES, GORD
D, PANTHERS

PERSONAL: Born July 22, 1966, in Montreal.... 6-1/170.... Shoots left. **TRANSACTIONS/CAREER NOTES:** Selected by Boston Bruins in sixth round (fifth Bruins pick, 115th overall) of NHL entry draft (June 15, 1985).... Signed as free agent by Philadelphia Flyers (August 25, 1992).... Selected by Florida Panthers in NHL expansion draft (June 24, 1993). **MISCELLANEOUS:** Member of silver-medal-winning Canadian Olympic team (1992).

Season Team	League	REGULAR SEASON					PLAYOFFS				
		Gms.	G	A	Pts.	PIM	Gms.	G	A	Pts.	PIM
83-84—Medicine Hat	WHL	72	5	14	19	39	14	0	0	0	0
84-85—Medicine Hat	WHL	70	18	45	63	61	10	6	9	15	17
85-86—Medicine Hat	WHL	58	22	39	61	45	25	8	15	23	32
86-87—Moncton	AHL	69	2	19	21	21	4	0	0	0	2
87-88—Maine	AHL	69	5	30	35	65	7	1	3	4	4
88-89—Canadian national team	Int'l	61	8	38	46	44	—	—	—	—	—
89-90—Canadian national team	Int'l	12	3	1	4	4	—	—	—	—	—
—Varese	Italy	29	13	36	49	16	3	3	3	6	0
90-91—Canadian national team	Int'l	57	12	30	42	62	—	—	—	—	—
91-92—Canadian national team	Int'l	48	12	22	34	50	—	—	—	—	—
—Canadian Olympic Team	Int'l	8	3	3	6	6	—	—	—	—	—
—Boston	NHL	15	0	5	5	6	12	1	2	3	6
92-93—Philadelphia	NHL	37	3	4	7	16	—	—	—	—	—
—Hershey	AHL	9	1	3	4	4	—	—	—	—	—
93-94—Cincinnati	IHL	80	15	43	58	50	11	2	6	8	24
NHL totals		52	3	9	12	22	12	1	2	3	6

IAFRATE, AL
D, BRUINS

PERSONAL: Born March 21, 1966, in Dearborn, Mich.... 6-3/220.... Shoots left.... Full name: Al Anthony Iafrate.... Name pronounced IGH-uh-FRAY-tee. **TRANSACTIONS/CAREER NOTES:** Selected by Toronto Maple Leafs as underage junior in first round (first Maple Leafs pick, fourth overall) of NHL entry draft (June 9, 1984).... Bruised knee (February 1985).... Broke nose (October 2, 1985); missed five games.... Strained neck (January 29, 1986); missed six games. ... Suffered stiff back (January 1988).... Broke back (October 22, 1988).... Lacerated hand (December 9, 1988).... Tore right knee ligament (March 24, 1990).... Underwent knee surgery (April 9, 1990).... Traded by Maple Leafs to Washington Capitals for D Bob Rouse and C Peter Zezel (January 16, 1991).... Took a leave of absence due to mental exhaustion (March 30, 1991).... Injured eye (February 19, 1992); missed one game.... Pulled hamstring (April 10, 1993); missed three games. ... Sprained right knee (December 21, 1993); missed four games.... Suffered sore right knee (January 2, 1994); missed one game.... Traded by Capitals to Boston Bruins for LW Joe Juneau (March 21, 1994).

HONORS: Played in NHL All-Star Game (1988, 1990, 1993 and 1994).... Named to THE SPORTING NEWS All-Star second team (1992-93).... Named to NHL All-Star second team (1992-93).

RECORDS: Shares NHL single-game playoff record for most goals by a defenseman—3 (April 26, 1993).

Season Team	League	REGULAR SEASON Gms.	G	A	Pts.	PIM	PLAYOFFS Gms.	G	A	Pts.	PIM
83-84—U.S. national team	Int'l	55	4	17	21	26	—	—	—	—	—
—U.S. Olympic Team	Int'l	6	0	0	0	2	—	—	—	—	—
—Belleville	OHL	10	2	4	6	2	3	0	1	1	2
84-85—Toronto	NHL	68	5	16	21	51	—	—	—	—	—
85-86—Toronto	NHL	65	8	25	33	40	10	0	3	3	4
86-87—Toronto	NHL	80	9	21	30	55	13	1	3	4	11
87-88—Toronto	NHL	77	22	30	52	80	6	3	4	7	6
88-89—Toronto	NHL	65	13	20	33	72	—	—	—	—	—
89-90—Toronto	NHL	75	21	42	63	135	—	—	—	—	—
90-91—Toronto	NHL	42	3	15	18	113	—	—	—	—	—
—Washington	NHL	30	6	8	14	124	10	1	3	4	22
91-92—Washington	NHL	78	17	34	51	180	7	4	2	6	14
92-93—Washington	NHL	81	25	41	66	169	6	6	0	6	4
93-94—Washington	NHL	67	10	35	45	143	—	—	—	—	—
—Boston	NHL	12	5	8	13	20	13	3	1	4	6
NHL totals		**740**	**144**	**295**	**439**	**1182**	**65**	**18**	**16**	**34**	**67**

IMES, CHRIS
D, PANTHERS

PERSONAL: Born August 27, 1972, in Birchdale, Mich.... 5-11/195.... Shoots right.... Name pronounced IGHMS.

COLLEGE: Maine.

TRANSACTIONS/CAREER NOTES: Selected by Florida Panthers in NHL supplemental draft (June 25, 1993).

HONORS: Named to NCAA All-America East first team (1992-93).... Named to NCAA All-Tournament team (1992-93).... Named to Hockey East All-Star first team (1992-93).

Season Team	League	REGULAR SEASON Gms.	G	A	Pts.	PIM	PLAYOFFS Gms.	G	A	Pts.	PIM
90-91—University of Maine	Hockey East	37	6	8	14	16	—	—	—	—	—
91-92—University of Maine	Hockey East	31	4	19	23	22	—	—	—	—	—
92-93—University of Maine	Hockey East	45	12	23	35	24	—	—	—	—	—
93-94—U.S. national team	Int'l	58	6	10	16	12	—	—	—	—	—
—U.S. Olympic Team	Int'l	8	0	0	0	2	—	—	—	—	—

ING, PETER
G, RED WINGS

PERSONAL: Born April 28, 1969, in Toronto.... 6-2/165.... Catches left.

TRANSACTIONS/CAREER NOTES: Selected by Toronto Maple Leafs in third round (third Maple Leafs pick, 48th overall) of NHL entry draft (June 11, 1988).... Traded by Maple Leafs with LW Vincent Damphousse, D Luke Richardson, C Scott Thornton and future considerations to Edmonton Oilers for G Grant Fuhr, RW/LW Glenn Anderson and LW Craig Berube (September 19, 1991).... Signed as free agent by Detroit Falcons (January 8, 1993).... Signed as free agent by San Diego Gulls (January 20, 1993).... Signed as free agent by Las Vegas Thunder (August 18, 1993).... Traded by Oilers to Detroit Red Wings for future considerations (August 31, 1993).

Season Team	League	REGULAR SEASON Gms.	Min.	W	L	T	GA	SO	Avg.	PLAYOFFS Gms.	Min.	W	L	GA	SO	Avg.
86-87—Windsor	OHL	28	1615	13	11	3	105	0	3.90	5	161	4	0	9	0	3.35
87-88—Windsor	OHL	43	2422	30	7	1	125	2	3.10	3	225	2	0	7	0	1.87
88-89—Windsor	OHL	19	1043	7	7	3	76	1	4.37	—	—	—	—	—	—	—
—London	OHL	32	1848	18	11	2	104	†2	3.38	*21	*1093	11	9	*82	0	4.50
89-90—Toronto	NHL	3	182	0	2	1	18	0	5.93	—	—	—	—	—	—	—
—Newmarket	AHL	48	2829	16	19	2	184	1	3.90	—	—	—	—	—	—	—
90-91—Toronto	NHL	56	3126	16	†29	8	200	1	3.84	—	—	—	—	—	—	—
91-92—Edmonton	NHL	12	463	3	4	0	33	0	4.28	—	—	—	—	—	—	—
—Cape Breton	AHL	24	1411	9	10	4	92	0	3.91	1	60	0	1	9	0	9.00
92-93—Detroit	Col.HL	3	136	2	1	‡0	6	0	2.65	—	—	—	—	—	—	—
—San Diego	IHL	17	882	11	4	‡0	53	0	3.61	4	183	2	2	13	0	4.26
93-94—Las Vegas	IHL	30	1627	16	7	‡4	91	0	3.36	2	40	0	1	4	0	6.00
—Adirondack	AHL	7	425	3	3	1	26	1	3.67	—	—	—	—	—	—	—
—Detroit	NHL	3	170	1	2	0	15	0	5.29	—	—	—	—	—	—	—
NHL totals		**74**	**3941**	**20**	**37**	**9**	**266**	**1**	**4.05**							

INTRANUOVO, RALPH
C, OILERS

PERSONAL: Born December 11, 1973, in Scarborough, Ont.... 5-8/185.... Shoots left.... Name pronounced ihn-trah-NOO-voh.

TRANSACTIONS/CAREER NOTES: Selected by Edmonton Oilers in fourth round (fifth Oilers pick, 96th overall) of NHL entry draft (June 20, 1992).

			REGULAR SEASON					PLAYOFFS				
Season Team	League	Gms.	G	A	Pts.	PIM	Gms.	G	A	Pts.	PIM
90-91—Sault Ste. Marie	OHL	63	25	42	67	22	14	7	13	20	17
91-92—Sault Ste. Marie	OHL	65	50	63	113	44	18	10	14	24	12
92-93—Sault Ste. Marie	OHL	54	31	47	78	61	18	10	16	26	30
93-94—Cape Breton	AHL	66	21	31	52	39	4	1	2	3	2

IRBE, ARTURS
G, SHARKS

PERSONAL: Born February 2, 1967, in Riga, U.S.S.R. . . . . 5-7/180. . . . Catches left. . . . Name pronounced AHR-tuhrs UHR-bay.
TRANSACTIONS/CAREER NOTES: Selected by Minnesota North Stars in 10th round (11th North Stars pick, 196th overall) of NHL entry draft (June 17, 1989). . . . Selected by San Jose Sharks in NHL dispersal draft (May 30, 1991). . . . Sprained knee (November 27, 1992); missed 19 games.
HONORS: Named Soviet League Rookie of the Year (1987-88). . . . Shared James Norris Memorial Trophy with Wade Flaherty (1991-92). . . . Named to IHL All-Star first team (1991-92). . . . Played in NHL All-Star Game (1994).
RECORDS: Holds NHL single-season record for most minutes played by goaltender—4,412 (1993-94).

			REGULAR SEASON							PLAYOFFS					
Season Team	League	Gms.	Min.	W	L	T	GA	SO	Avg.	Gms.	Min.	W	L	GA	SO	Avg.
86-87—Dynamo Riga................	USSR	2	27	...	...	...	1	0	2.22	—	—	—	—	—	—	—
87-88—Dynamo Riga................	USSR	34	1870	...	...	...	84	0	2.70	—	—	—	—	—	—	—
88-89—Dynamo Riga................	USSR	41	2460	...	...	...	117	0	2.85	—	—	—	—	—	—	—
89-90—Dynamo Riga................	USSR	48	2880	...	...	...	116	0	2.42	—	—	—	—	—	—	—
90-91—Dynamo Riga................	USSR	46	2713	...	...	...	133	0	2.94	—	—	—	—	—	—	—
91-92—Kansas City................	IHL	32	1955	24	7	‡1	80	0	*2.46	15	914	12	3	44	0	2.89
—San Jose......................	NHL	13	645	2	6	3	48	0	4.47	—	—	—	—	—	—	—
92-93—Kansas City................	IHL	6	364	3	3	‡0	20	0	3.30	—	—	—	—	—	—	—
—San Jose......................	NHL	36	2074	7	26	0	142	1	4.11	—	—	—	—	—	—	—
93-94—San Jose....................	NHL	*74	*4412	30	28	*16	209	3	2.84	14	806	7	7	50	0	3.72
NHL totals...........		123	7131	39	60	19	399	4	3.36	14	806	7	7	50	0	3.72

JABLONSKI, PAT
G, MAPLE LEAFS

PERSONAL: Born June 20, 1967, in Toledo, O. . . . 6-0/178. . . . Catches right.
TRANSACTIONS/CAREER NOTES: Selected by St. Louis Blues in seventh round (sixth Blues pick, 138th overall) of NHL entry draft (June 15, 1985). . . . Pulled groin (December 7, 1991); missed 26 games. . . . Traded by Blues with D Rob Robinson, RW Darin Kimble and RW Steve Tuttle to Tampa Bay Lightning for future considerations (June 19, 1992). . . . Traded by Lightning to Toronto Maple Leafs for future considerations (February 21, 1994).
HONORS: Shared James Norris Memorial Trophy with Guy Hebert (1990-91).

			REGULAR SEASON							PLAYOFFS					
Season Team	League	Gms.	Min.	W	L	T	GA	SO	Avg.	Gms.	Min.	W	L	GA	SO	Avg.
84-85—Detroit Compuware......	NAJHL	29	1483	...	...	...	95	0	3.84	—	—	—	—	—	—	—
85-86—Windsor......................	OHL	29	1600	6	16	4	119	1	4.46	6	263	0	3	20	0	4.56
86-87—Windsor......................	OHL	41	2328	22	14	2	128	†3	3.30	12	710	8	4	38	0	3.21
87-88—Windsor......................	OHL	18	994	14	3	0	48	2	*2.90	9	537	8	0	28	0	3.13
—Peoria..........................	IHL	5	285	2	2	‡1	17	0	3.58	—	—	—	—	—	—	—
88-89—Peoria........................	IHL	35	2051	11	20	‡3	163	1	4.77	3	130	0	2	13	0	6.00
89-90—St. Louis....................	NHL	4	208	0	3	0	17	0	4.90	—	—	—	—	—	—	—
—Peoria..........................	IHL	36	2043	14	17	‡4	165	0	4.85	4	223	1	3	19	0	5.11
90-91—St. Louis....................	NHL	8	492	2	3	3	25	0	3.05	3	90	0	0	5	0	3.33
—Peoria..........................	IHL	29	1738	23	3	‡2	87	0	3.00	10	532	7	2	23	0	*2.59
91-92—St. Louis....................	NHL	10	468	3	6	0	38	0	4.87	—	—	—	—	—	—	—
—Peoria..........................	IHL	8	493	6	1	‡1	29	1	3.53	—	—	—	—	—	—	—
92-93—Tampa Bay..................	NHL	43	2268	8	24	4	150	1	3.97	—	—	—	—	—	—	—
93-94—Tampa Bay..................	NHL	15	834	5	6	3	54	0	3.88	—	—	—	—	—	—	—
—St. John's......................	AHL	16	963	12	3	1	49	1	3.05	—	—	—	—	—	—	—
NHL totals...........		80	4270	18	42	10	284	1	3.99	3	90	0	0	5	0	3.33

JACKSON, DANE
RW, CANUCKS

PERSONAL: Born May 17, 1970, in Winnipeg. . . . 6-1/190. . . . Shoots right.
COLLEGE: North Dakota.
TRANSACTIONS/CAREER NOTES: Selected by Vancouver Canucks in third round (third Canucks pick, 44th overall) of NHL entry draft (June 11, 1988). . . . Suffered shoulder contusion (January 9, 1994); missed two games.

			REGULAR SEASON					PLAYOFFS				
Season Team	League	Gms.	G	A	Pts.	PIM	Gms.	G	A	Pts.	PIM
87-88—Vernon......................	BCJHL	50	28	32	60	99	13	7	10	17	49
88-89—Univ. of North Dakota.......	WCHA	30	4	5	9	33	—	—	—	—	—
89-90—Univ. of North Dakota.......	WCHA	44	15	11	26	56	—	—	—	—	—
90-91—Univ. of North Dakota.......	WCHA	37	17	9	26	79	—	—	—	—	—
91-92—Univ. of North Dakota.......	WCHA	39	23	19	42	81	—	—	—	—	—
92-93—Hamilton....................	AHL	68	23	20	43	59	—	—	—	—	—
93-94—Hamilton....................	AHL	60	25	35	60	75	4	2	2	4	16
—Vancouver......................	NHL	12	5	1	6	9	—	—	—	—	—
NHL totals.............................		12	5	1	6	9					

JAGR, JAROMIR
RW, PENGUINS

PERSONAL: Born February 15, 1972, in Kladno, Czechoslovakia. . . . 6-2/208. . . . Shoots left. . . . Name pronounced YAH-guhr.
TRANSACTIONS/CAREER NOTES: Selected by Pittsburgh Penguins in first round (first Penguins pick, fifth overall) of NHL entry draft (June 16, 1990). . . . Separated shoulder (February 23, 1993); missed three games. . . . Strained groin (January 21, 1994); missed four games.
HONORS: Named to Czechoslovakian League All-Star team (1989-90). . . . Named to NHL All-Rookie team (1990-91). . . . Played in NHL All-Star Game (1992 and 1993).
MISCELLANEOUS: Member of Stanley Cup championship teams (1991 and 1992).

			REGULAR SEASON					PLAYOFFS				
Season Team	League	Gms.	G	A	Pts.	PIM	Gms.	G	A	Pts.	PIM
88-89—Poldi Kladno	Czech.	39	8	10	18	. . .	—	—	—	—	—
89-90—Poldi Kladno	Czech.	51	30	30	60	. . .	—	—	—	—	—
90-91—Pittsburgh	NHL	80	27	30	57	42	24	3	10	13	6
91-92—Pittsburgh	NHL	70	32	37	69	34	†21	11	13	24	6
92-93—Pittsburgh	NHL	81	34	60	94	61	12	5	4	9	23
93-94—Pittsburgh	NHL	80	32	67	99	61	6	2	4	6	16
NHL totals		311	125	194	319	198	63	21	31	52	51

JAKOPIN, JOHN
LW, RED WINGS

PERSONAL: Born July 2, 1975, in Cranbrook, B.C. . . . 6-2/194. . . . Shoots left.
HIGH SCHOOL: St. Michael's (Victoria, B.C.).
COLLEGE: Merrimack (Mass.).
TRANSACTIONS/CAREER NOTES: Selected by Detroit Red Wings in fourth round (fourth Red Wings pick, 97th overall) of NHL entry draft (June 26, 1993).
HONORS: Named to Hockey East All-Rookie team (1993-94).

			REGULAR SEASON					PLAYOFFS				
Season Team	League	Gms.	G	A	Pts.	PIM	Gms.	G	A	Pts.	PIM
92-93—St. Michael's H.S.	Jr. A	45	9	21	30	42	—	—	—	—	—
93-94—Merrimack College	Hockey East	36	2	8	10	64	—	—	—	—	—

JAKS, PAULI
G, KINGS

PERSONAL: Born January 25, 1972, in Schaffhausen, Switzerland. . . . 6-0/194. . . . Catches left. . . . Name pronounced PAWL-ee YAKS.
TRANSACTIONS/CAREER NOTES: Selected by Los Angeles Kings in fifth round (fourth Kings pick, 108th overall) of NHL entry draft (June 22, 1991).

			REGULAR SEASON							PLAYOFFS					
Season Team	League	Gms.	Min.	W	L	T	GA	SO	Avg.	Gms.	Min.	W	L	GA SO	Avg.
90-91—Ambri Piotta	Switz.	22	1247	. . .	. . .	. . .	100	0	4.81	—	—	—	—	—	—
91-92—Ambri Piotta	Switz.	33	1890	25	7	1	97	2	2.93	—	—	—	—	—	—
92-93—Ambri Piotta	Switz.	29	. . .	. . .	. . .	. . .	92	. . .	3.17	—	—	—	—	—	—
93-94—Phoenix	IHL	33	1712	16	13	‡1	101	0	3.54	—	—	—	—	—	—

JANNEY, CRAIG
C, BLUES

PERSONAL: Born September 26, 1967, in Hartford, Conn. . . . 6-1/190. . . . Shoots left. . . . Full name: Craig Harlan Janney.
HIGH SCHOOL: Deerfield (Mass.) Academy.
COLLEGE: Boston College.
TRANSACTIONS/CAREER NOTES: Broke collarbone (December 1985). . . . Selected by Boston Bruins in first round (first Bruins pick, 13th overall) of NHL entry draft (June 21, 1986). . . . Suffered from mononucleosis (December 1986). . . . Pulled right groin (December 1988); missed seven games. . . . Tore right groin muscle (October 26, 1989); missed 21 games. . . . Strained left shoulder (April 5, 1990). . . . Sprained left shoulder (December 13, 1990). . . . Sprained right ankle (March 30, 1991). . . . Traded by Bruins with D Stephane Quintal to St. Louis Blues for C Adam Oates (February 7, 1992). . . . Suffered leg laceration (December 1, 1993); missed one game. . . . Strained knee (February 20, 1994); missed 11 games. . . . Awarded to Vancouver Canucks with second-round pick in 1994 draft (C Dave Scatchard) as compensation for Blues signing free agent C Petr Nedved (March 14, 1994). . . . Traded by Canucks to Blues for D Jeff Brown, D Bret Hedican, and C Nathan LaFayette (March 21, 1994).
HONORS: Named to NCAA All-America East first team (1986-87). . . . Named to Hockey East All-Star first team (1986-87).

			REGULAR SEASON					PLAYOFFS				
Season Team	League	Gms.	G	A	Pts.	PIM	Gms.	G	A	Pts.	PIM
84-85—Deerfield Academy	Mass. H.S.	17	33	35	68	6	—	—	—	—	—
85-86—Boston College	Hockey East	34	13	14	27	8	—	—	—	—	—
86-87—Boston College	Hockey East	37	28	*55	*83	6	—	—	—	—	—
87-88—U.S. national team	Int'l	52	26	44	70	6	—	—	—	—	—
—U.S. Olympic Team	Int'l	5	3	1	4	2	—	—	—	—	—
—Boston	NHL	15	7	9	16	0	23	6	10	16	11
88-89—Boston	NHL	62	16	46	62	12	10	4	9	13	21
89-90—Boston	NHL	55	24	38	62	4	18	3	19	22	2
90-91—Boston	NHL	77	26	66	92	8	18	4	18	22	11
91-92—Boston	NHL	53	12	39	51	20	—	—	—	—	—
—St. Louis	NHL	25	6	30	36	2	6	0	6	6	0
92-93—St. Louis	NHL	84	24	82	106	12	11	2	9	11	0
93-94—St. Louis	NHL	69	16	68	84	24	4	1	3	4	0
NHL totals		440	131	378	509	82	90	20	74	94	45

JANSSENS, MARK
C/LW, WHALERS

PERSONAL: Born May 19, 1968, in Surrey, B.C. . . . 6-3/216. . . . Shoots left.
TRANSACTIONS/CAREER NOTES: Selected by New York Rangers as underage junior in fourth round (fourth Rangers pick, 72nd overall) of NHL entry draft (June 21, 1986). . . . Fractured skull and suffered cerebral concussion (December 10, 1988). . . . Trad-

ed by Rangers to Minnesota North Stars for C Mario Thyer and third-round pick (D Maxim Galanov) in 1993 draft (March 10, 1992).... Traded by North Stars to Hartford Whalers for C James Black (September 3, 1992).... Separated shoulder (December 26, 1992); missed five games.... Fined $500 by Whalers for involvement in bar brawl (April 1, 1994).

			REGULAR SEASON					PLAYOFFS			
Season	Team	League	Gms.	G	A	Pts.	PIM	Gms.	G	A	Pts.	PIM
84-85—Regina		WHL	70	8	22	30	51	5	1	1	2	0
85-86—Regina		WHL	71	25	38	63	146	9	0	2	2	17
86-87—Regina		WHL	68	24	38	62	209	3	0	1	1	14
87-88—Regina		WHL	71	39	51	90	202	4	3	4	7	6
—New York Rangers		NHL	1	0	0	0	0	—	—	—	—	—
—Colorado		IHL	6	2	2	4	24	12	3	2	5	20
88-89—New York Rangers		NHL	5	0	0	0	0	—	—	—	—	—
—Denver		IHL	38	19	19	38	104	4	3	0	3	18
89-90—New York Rangers		NHL	80	5	8	13	161	9	2	1	3	10
90-91—New York Rangers		NHL	67	9	7	16	172	6	3	0	3	6
91-92—New York Rangers		NHL	4	0	0	0	5	—	—	—	—	—
—Binghamton		AHL	55	10	23	33	109	—	—	—	—	—
—Minnesota		NHL	3	0	0	0	0	—	—	—	—	—
—Kalamazoo		IHL	2	0	0	0	2	11	1	2	3	22
92-93—Hartford		NHL	76	12	17	29	237	—	—	—	—	—
93-94—Hartford		NHL	84	2	10	12	137	—	—	—	—	—
NHL totals			320	28	42	70	712	15	5	1	6	16

JAY, BOB
D

PERSONAL: Born November 18, 1965, in Burlington, Mass.... 5-11/190.... Shoots right.
TRANSACTIONS/CAREER NOTES: Signed as free agent by Los Angeles Kings (July 16, 1993).... Signed as free agent by Detroit Vipers (July 5, 1994).

			REGULAR SEASON					PLAYOFFS			
Season	Team	League	Gms.	G	A	Pts.	PIM	Gms.	G	A	Pts.	PIM
90-91—Fort Wayne		IHL	40	1	8	9	24	14	0	3	3	16
91-92—Fort Wayne		IHL	76	1	19	20	119	7	0	2	2	4
92-93—Fort Wayne		IHL	78	5	21	26	100	8	0	2	2	14
93-94—Los Angeles		NHL	3	0	1	1	0	—	—	—	—	—
—Phoenix		IHL	65	7	15	22	54	—	—	—	—	—
NHL totals			3	0	1	1	0					

JEAN, YANICK
D, CAPITALS

PERSONAL: Born November 26, 1975, in Alma, Que.... 6-1/198.... Shoots left.... Name pronounced Yan-ihck Zhawn.
HIGH SCHOOL: CEGEP de Chicoutimi (Que.).
TRANSACTIONS/CAREER NOTES: Selected by Washington Capitals in fifth round (fifth Capitals pick, 119th overall) of NHL entry draft (June 29, 1994).

			REGULAR SEASON					PLAYOFFS			
Season	Team	League	Gms.	G	A	Pts.	PIM	Gms.	G	A	Pts.	PIM
92-93—Chicoutimi		QMJHL	50	2	2	4	40	3	0	0	0	0
93-94—Chicoutimi		QMJHL	65	11	30	41	177	27	8	12	20	82

JENNINGS, GRANT
D, PENGUINS

PERSONAL: Born May 5, 1965, in Hudson Bay, Sask.... 6-3/200.... Shoots left.
TRANSACTIONS/CAREER NOTES: Injured shoulder (1984-85) ... Signed as free agent by Washington Capitals (June 25, 1985).... Injured knee (October 1986).... Traded by Capitals with RW Ed Kastelic to Hartford Whalers for D Neil Sheehy and RW Mike Millar (July 6, 1988).... Broke left hand (October 6, 1988).... Bruised right foot (October 1988).... Sprained left shoulder (December 1988).... Underwent surgery to left shoulder (April 14, 1989).... Sprained left knee (February 7, 1990). ... Twisted knee (March 14, 1990).... Strained left ankle (September 1990).... Bruised shoulder (December 1, 1990); missed six games.... Injured shoulder (February 13, 1991).... Traded by Whalers with C Ron Francis and D Ulf Samuelsson to Pittsburgh Penguins for C John Cullen, D Zarley Zalapski and RW Jeff Parker (March 4, 1991).... Separated left shoulder (March 1991).... Bruised hand (February 15, 1992); missed seven games.... Bruised right hand (March 15, 1992); missed one game.... Bruised left foot (March 11, 1993); missed one game.... Injured groin (December 11, 1993); missed two games. ... Sprained knee (December 28, 1993); missed 14 games.... Bruised shoulder (January 31, 1994); missed one game.... Injured hand (March 8, 1994); missed one game.
MISCELLANEOUS: Member of Stanley Cup championship teams (1991 and 1992).

			REGULAR SEASON					PLAYOFFS			
Season	Team	League	Gms.	G	A	Pts.	PIM	Gms.	G	A	Pts.	PIM
83-84—Saskatoon		WHL	64	5	13	18	102	—	—	—	—	—
84-85—Saskatoon		WHL	47	10	24	34	134	2	1	0	1	2
85-86—Binghamton		AHL	51	0	4	4	109	—	—	—	—	—
86-87—Fort Wayne		IHL	3	0	0	0	0	—	—	—	—	—
—Binghamton		AHL	47	1	5	6	125	13	0	2	2	17
87-88—Binghamton		AHL	56	2	12	14	195	3	1	0	1	15
—Washington		NHL	—	—	—	—	—	1	0	0	0	0
88-89—Hartford		NHL	55	3	10	13	159	4	1	0	1	17
—Binghamton		AHL	2	0	0	0	2	—	—	—	—	—
89-90—Hartford		NHL	64	3	6	9	171	7	0	0	0	13

Season Team	League	REGULAR SEASON					PLAYOFFS				
		Gms.	G	A	Pts.	Pen.	Gms.	G	A	Pts.	Pen.
90-91—Hartford	NHL	44	1	4	5	82	—	—	—	—	—
—Pittsburgh	NHL	13	1	3	4	26	13	1	1	2	16
91-92—Pittsburgh	NHL	53	4	5	9	104	10	0	0	0	12
92-93—Pittsburgh	NHL	58	0	5	5	65	12	0	0	0	8
93-94—Pittsburgh	NHL	61	2	4	6	126	3	0	0	0	2
NHL totals		348	14	37	51	733	50	2	1	3	68

JINMAN, LEE
C, STARS

PERSONAL: Born January 10, 1976, in Scarborough, Ont. . . . 5-10/155. . . . Shoots right. **HIGH SCHOOL:** Chippewa (North Bay, Ont.). **TRANSACTIONS/CAREER NOTES:** Selected by Dallas Stars in second round (second Stars pick, 46th overall) of NHL entry draft (June 28, 1994). **HONORS:** Named to Can.HL All-Rookie team (1993-94). . . . Named to OHL All-Rookie team (1993-94).

Season Team	League	REGULAR SEASON					PLAYOFFS				
		Gms.	G	A	Pts.	PIM	Gms.	G	A	Pts.	PIM
92-93—Wexford	Jr. A	4	1	2	3	0	—	—	—	—	—
93-94—North Bay	OHL	66	31	66	97	33	18	*18	19	37	8

JOHANSSON, CALLE
D, CAPITALS

PERSONAL: Born February 14, 1967, in Goteborg, Sweden. . . . 5-11/205. . . . Shoots left. . . . Name pronounced KAL-ee yoh-HAHN-sehn. **TRANSACTIONS/CAREER NOTES:** Selected by Buffalo Sabres in first round (first Sabres pick, 14th overall) of NHL entry draft (June 15, 1985). . . . Dislocated thumb (October 9, 1988). . . . Traded by Sabres with second-round pick in 1989 draft (G Byron Dafoe) to Washington Capitals for D Grant Ledyard, G Clint Malarchuk and sixth-round pick in 1991 draft (March 6, 1989). . . . Injured back (October 7, 1989); missed 10 games. . . . Bruised ribs (January 9, 1993); missed seven games. **HONORS:** Named to NHL All-Rookie team (1987-88).

Season Team	League	REGULAR SEASON					PLAYOFFS				
		Gms.	G	A	Pts.	PIM	Gms.	G	A	Pts.	PIM
83-84—Vastra Frolunda	Sweden	34	5	10	15	20	—	—	—	—	—
84-85—Vastra Frolunda	Sweden	36	14	15	29	20	6	1	2	3	4
85-86—Bjorkloven	Sweden	17	1	1	2	14	—	—	—	—	—
86-87—Bjorkloven	Sweden	30	2	13	15	18	6	1	3	4	6
87-88—Buffalo	NHL	71	4	38	42	37	6	0	1	1	0
88-89—Buffalo	NHL	47	2	11	13	33	—	—	—	—	—
—Washington	NHL	12	1	7	8	4	6	1	2	3	0
89-90—Washington	NHL	70	8	31	39	25	15	1	6	7	4
90-91—Washington	NHL	80	11	41	52	23	10	2	7	9	8
91-92—Washington	NHL	80	14	42	56	49	7	0	5	5	4
92-93—Washington	NHL	77	7	38	45	56	6	0	5	5	4
93-94—Washington	NHL	84	9	33	42	59	6	1	3	4	4
NHL totals		521	56	241	297	286	56	5	29	34	24

JOHANSSON, ROGER
D, FLAMES

PERSONAL: Born April 17, 1967, in Ljungby, Sweden. . . . 6-3/190. . . . Shoots left. . . . Name pronounced joh-HAN-suhn. **TRANSACTIONS/CAREER NOTES:** Selected by Calgary Flames in fourth round (fifth Flames pick, 80th overall) of NHL entry draft (June 15, 1985). . . . Suffered intestinal infection (November 24, 1990); missed 11 games. . . . Suffered infected elbow (December 12, 1992); missed two games. **MISCELLANEOUS:** Member of gold-medal-winning Swedish Olympic team (1994).

Season Team	League	REGULAR SEASON					PLAYOFFS				
		Gms.	G	A	Pts.	PIM	Gms.	G	A	Pts.	PIM
83-84—Troja Sr.	Sweden	8	2	1	3	8	—	—	—	—	—
84-85—Troja Sr.	Sweden	30	1	10	11	28	—	—	—	—	—
85-86—Troja Sr.	Sweden	32	5	16	21	42	—	—	—	—	—
86-87—Farjestad	Sweden	31	6	11	17	22	7	1	1	2	8
87-88—Farjestad	Sweden	24	3	11	14	20	—	—	—	—	—
88-89—Farjestad	Sweden	40	5	15	20	36	—	—	—	—	—
89-90—Calgary	NHL	35	0	5	5	48	—	—	—	—	—
90-91—Calgary	NHL	38	4	13	17	47	—	—	—	—	—
91-92—Leksand	Sweden	22	3	9	12	42	—	—	—	—	—
92-93—Calgary	NHL	77	4	16	20	62	5	0	1	1	2
93-94—Leksand	Sweden	38	6	15	21	56	4	0	1	1	0
—Swedish Olympic Team	Int'l	8	2	0	2	8	—	—	—	—	—
NHL totals		150	8	34	42	157	5	0	1	1	2

JOHNSON, CLINT
LW, PENGUINS

PERSONAL: Born April 7, 1976, in Duluth, Minn. . . . 6-2/200. . . . Shoots left. **TRANSACTIONS/CAREER NOTES:** Selected by Pittsburgh Penguins in fifth round (seventh Penguins pick, 128th overall) of NHL entry draft (June 29, 1994).

Season Team	League	REGULAR SEASON					PLAYOFFS				
		Gms.	G	A	Pts.	PIM	Gms.	G	A	Pts.	PIM
91-92—Duluth East High School	Minn. H.S.	24	11	8	19	16	—	—	—	—	—
92-93—Duluth East High School	Minn. H.S.	23	15	14	29	24	—	—	—	—	—
93-94—Duluth East High School	Minn. H.S.	28	30	31	61	0	—	—	—	—	—

JOHNSON, CRAIG
LW, BLUES

PERSONAL: Born March 18, 1972, in St. Paul, Minn. . . . 6-2/185. . . . Shoots left.
HIGH SCHOOL: Hill-Murray (St. Paul, Minn.).
COLLEGE: Minnesota.
TRANSACTIONS/CAREER NOTES: Suffered stress fracture of vertebrae (February 1987). . . . Selected by St. Louis Blues in second round (first Blues pick, 33rd overall) of NHL entry draft (June 16, 1990). . . . Separated shoulder (December 1990).
HONORS: Named to WCHA All-Rookie Team (1990-91).

			REGULAR SEASON					PLAYOFFS			
Season Team	League	Gms.	G	A	Pts.	PIM	Gms.	G	A	Pts.	PIM
87-88—Hill Murray H.S.	Minn. H.S.	28	14	20	34	4	—	—	—	—	—
88-89—Hill Murray H.S.	Minn. H.S.	24	22	30	52	10	—	—	—	—	—
89-90—Hill Murray H.S.	Minn. H.S.	23	15	36	51	...	—	—	—	—	—
90-91—University of Minnesota ...	WCHA	33	13	18	31	34	—	—	—	—	—
91-92—University of Minnesota ...	WCHA	44	19	39	58	70	—	—	—	—	—
92-93—University of Minnesota ...	WCHA	42	22	24	46	70	—	—	—	—	—
93-94—U.S. national team	Int'l	54	25	26	51	64	—	—	—	—	—
—U.S. Olympic Team	Int'l	8	0	4	4	4	—	—	—	—	—

JOHNSON, GREG
C, RED WINGS

PERSONAL: Born March 16, 1971, in Thunder Bay, Ont. . . . 5-10/174. . . . Shoots left. . . . Brother of Ryan Johnson, center in Florida Panthers system.
COLLEGE: North Dakota.
TRANSACTIONS/CAREER NOTES: Selected by Philadelphia Flyers in second round (first Flyers pick, 33rd overall) of NHL entry draft (June 17, 1989). . . . Separated right shoulder (November 24, 1990). . . . Rights traded by Flyers with future considerations to Detroit Red Wings for RW Jim Cummins and fourth-round pick (traded to Boston who selected D Charles Paquette) in 1993 draft (June 20, 1993). . . . Loaned to Canadian Olympic Team (January 19, 1994). . . . Returned to Red Wings (March 1, 1994).
HONORS: Named to USHL All-Star first team (1988-89). . . . Named Canadian Junior A Player of the Year (1989). . . . Named to Centennial Cup All-Star first team (1989). . . . Named to NCAA All-America West first team (1990-91 and 1992-93). . . . Named to WCHA All-Star first team (1990-91 through 1992-93). . . . Named to NCAA West All-America second team (1991-92).
MISCELLANEOUS: Member of silver-medal-winning Canadian Olympic team (1994).

			REGULAR SEASON					PLAYOFFS			
Season Team	League	Gms.	G	A	Pts.	PIM	Gms.	G	A	Pts.	PIM
88-89—Thunder Bay Jrs.	USHL	47	32	64	96	4	12	5	13	18	0
89-90—Univ. of North Dakota	WCHA	44	17	38	55	11	—	—	—	—	—
90-91—Univ. of North Dakota	WCHA	38	18	*61	79	6	—	—	—	—	—
91-92—Univ. of North Dakota	WCHA	39	20	54	74	8	—	—	—	—	—
92-93—Canadian national team ...	Int'l	23	6	14	20	2	—	—	—	—	—
—Univ. of North Dakota	WCHA	34	19	45	64	18	—	—	—	—	—
93-94—Detroit	NHL	52	6	11	17	22	7	2	2	4	2
—Canadian national team ...	Int'l	14	2	9	11	4	—	—	—	—	—
—Canadian Olympic Team ..	Int'l	8	0	3	3	0	—	—	—	—	—
—Adirondack	AHL	3	2	4	6	0	4	0	4	4	2
NHL totals...		52	6	11	17	22	7	2	2	4	2

JOHNSON, JIM
D, CAPITALS

PERSONAL: Born August 9, 1962, in New Hope, Minn. . . . 6-1/190. . . . Shoots left. . . . Full name: James Erik Johnson.
HIGH SCHOOL: Cooper (New Hope, Minn.).
COLLEGE: Minnesota-Duluth.
TRANSACTIONS/CAREER NOTES: Signed as free agent by Pittsburgh Penguins (June 9, 1985). . . . Tore cartilage in right knee (January 1988). . . . Suffered back pain (October 1990). . . . Injured neck (November 12, 1990); missed three games. . . . Traded by Penguins with D Chris Dahlquist to Minnesota North Stars for D Peter Taglianetti and D Larry Murphy (December 11, 1990). . . . Sprained back (February 12, 1991); missed two games. . . . Bruised hip (April 1991). . . . Injured groin (December 7, 1991); missed five games. . . . Strained hamstring (March 10, 1992); missed two games. . . . Lacerated face (November 14, 1992); missed two games. . . . Broke finger (January 3, 1993); missed one game. . . . Sprained knee (April 14, 1993); missed final two games of season. . . . North Stars franchise moved from Minnesota to Dallas and renamed Stars for 1993-94 season. . . . Sprained knee (October 23, 1993); missed three games. . . . Injured neck (January 18, 1994); missed 14 games. . . . Traded by Stars to Washington Capitals for LW Alan May and seventh-round pick in 1995 draft (March 21, 1994). . . . Tore medial collateral knee ligament (April 5, 1994); missed remainder of season.

			REGULAR SEASON					PLAYOFFS			
Season Team	League	Gms.	G	A	Pts.	PIM	Gms.	G	A	Pts.	PIM
81-82—Minnesota-Duluth	WCHA	40	0	10	10	62	—	—	—	—	—
82-83—Minnesota-Duluth	WCHA	44	3	18	21	118	—	—	—	—	—
83-84—Minnesota-Duluth	WCHA	43	3	13	16	116	—	—	—	—	—
84-85—Minnesota-Duluth	WCHA	47	7	29	36	49	—	—	—	—	—
85-86—Pittsburgh	NHL	80	3	26	29	115	—	—	—	—	—
86-87—Pittsburgh	NHL	80	5	25	30	116	—	—	—	—	—
87-88—Pittsburgh	NHL	55	1	12	13	87	—	—	—	—	—
88-89—Pittsburgh	NHL	76	2	14	16	163	11	0	5	5	44
89-90—Pittsburgh	NHL	75	3	13	16	154	—	—	—	—	—
90-91—Pittsburgh	NHL	24	0	5	5	23	—	—	—	—	—
—Minnesota	NHL	44	1	9	10	100	14	0	1	1	52
91-92—Minnesota	NHL	71	4	10	14	102	7	1	3	4	18
92-93—Minnesota	NHL	79	3	20	23	105	—	—	—	—	—

Season Team	League	REGULAR SEASON					PLAYOFFS				
		Gms.	G	A	Pts.	Pen.	Gms.	G	A	Pts.	Pen.
93-94—Dallas	NHL	53	0	7	7	51	—	—	—	—	—
—Washington	NHL	8	0	0	0	12	—	—	—	—	—
NHL totals		645	22	141	163	1028	32	1	9	10	114

JOHNSON, MATT
LW, KINGS

PERSONAL: Born November 23, 1975, in Pelham, Ont.... 6-5/223.... Shoots left.
TRANSACTIONS/CAREER NOTES: Selected by Los Angeles Kings in second round (second Kings pick, 33rd overall) of NHL entry draft (June 28, 1994).

Season Team	League	REGULAR SEASON					PLAYOFFS				
		Gms.	G	A	Pts.	PIM	Gms.	G	A	Pts.	PIM
91-92—Welland	Jr. B	38	6	19	25	214	—	—	—	—	—
92-93—Peterborough	OHL	66	8	17	25	211	16	1	1	2	54
93-94—Peterborough	OHL	50	13	24	37	233	—	—	—	—	—

JOHNSON, RYAN
C, PANTHERS

PERSONAL: Born June 14, 1976, in Thunder Bay, Ont. ... 6-2/180.... Shoots left. ... Brother of Greg Johnson, center, Detroit Red Wings.
TRANSACTIONS/CAREER NOTES: Selected by Florida Panthers in second round (fourth Panthers pick, 36th overall) of NHL entry draft (June 28, 1994).

Season Team	League	REGULAR SEASON					PLAYOFFS				
		Gms.	G	A	Pts.	PIM	Gms.	G	A	Pts.	PIM
93-94—Thunder Bay Jrs.	USHL	48	14	36	50	28	—	—	—	—	—

JOMPHE, JEAN-FRANCOIS
C, MIGHTY DUCKS

PERSONAL: Born December 28, 1972, in Harve St. Pierre, Que. ... 6-1/193.... Shoots left.... Name pronounced zhohm-PHEE.
TRANSACTIONS/CAREER NOTES: Signed as free agent by Mighty Ducks of Anaheim (September 7, 1993).

Season Team	League	REGULAR SEASON					PLAYOFFS				
		Gms.	G	A	Pts.	PIM	Gms.	G	A	Pts.	PIM
90-91—Shawinigan	QMJHL	42	17	22	39	14	6	2	1	3	2
91-92—Shawinigan	QMJHL	44	28	33	61	69	10	6	10	16	10
92-93—Sherbrooke	QMJHL	60	43	43	86	86	15	10	13	23	18
93-94—San Diego	IHL	29	2	3	5	12	—	—	—	—	—
—Greensboro	ECHL	25	9	9	18	41	1	1	0	1	0

JONES, KEITH
RW, CAPITALS

PERSONAL: Born November 8, 1968, in Brantford, Ont.... 6-2/190.... Shoots left.
COLLEGE: Western Michigan.
TRANSACTIONS/CAREER NOTES: Selected by Washington Capitals in seventh round (seventh Capitals pick, 141st overall) of NHL entry draft (June 11, 1988).... Suffered from the flu (January 21, 1993); missed two games.... Sprained wrist (January 25, 1994); missed six games.
HONORS: Named to CCHL All-Star first team (1991-92).

Season Team	League	REGULAR SEASON					PLAYOFFS				
		Gms.	G	A	Pts.	PIM	Gms.	G	A	Pts.	PIM
87-88—Niagara Falls	OHA	40	50	80	130	...	—	—	—	—	—
88-89—Western Michigan Univ.	CCHA	37	9	12	21	51	—	—	—	—	—
89-90—Western Michigan Univ.	CCHA	40	19	18	37	82	—	—	—	—	—
90-91—Western Michigan Univ.	CCHA	41	30	19	49	106	—	—	—	—	—
91-92—Western Michigan Univ.	CCHA	35	25	31	56	77	—	—	—	—	—
—Baltimore	AHL	6	2	4	6	0	—	—	—	—	—
92-93—Baltimore	AHL	8	7	3	10	4	—	—	—	—	—
—Washington	NHL	71	12	14	26	124	6	0	0	0	10
93-94—Washington	NHL	68	16	19	35	149	11	0	1	1	36
—Portland	AHL	6	5	7	12	4	—	—	—	—	—
NHL totals		139	28	33	61	273	17	0	1	1	46

JONSSON, KENNY
D, MAPLE LEAFS

PERSONAL: Born October 5, 1974, in Angelholm, Sweden.... 6-3/195.... Shoots left.
TRANSACTIONS/CAREER NOTES: Selected by Toronto Maple Leafs in first round (first Maple Leafs pick, 12th overall) of NHL entry draft (June 26, 1993).
HONORS: Named Swedish League Rookie of the Year (1992-93).

Season Team	League	REGULAR SEASON					PLAYOFFS				
		Gms.	G	A	Pts.	PIM	Gms.	G	A	Pts.	PIM
91-92—Rogle	Sweden	30	4	11	15	24	—	—	—	—	—
92-93—Rogle	Sweden	39	3	10	13	42	—	—	—	—	—
93-94—Rogle	Sweden	36	4	13	17	40	3	1	1	2	0
—Swedish Olympic Team	Int'l	3	1	0	1	0	—	—	—	—	—

JOSEPH, CHRIS
D, LIGHTNING

PERSONAL: Born September 10, 1969, in Burnaby, B.C.... 6-2/210.... Shoots right.... Full name: Robin Christopher Joseph.
HIGH SCHOOL: Alpha (Burnaby, B.C.).
TRANSACTIONS/CAREER NOTES: Selected by Pittsburgh Penguins in first round (first Penguins pick, fifth overall) of NHL entry draft (June 13, 1987).... Traded by Penguins with C Craig Simpson, C Dave Hannan and D

Moe Mantha to Edmonton Oilers for D Paul Coffey, LW Dave Hunter and RW Wayne Van Dorp (November 24, 1987). . . .
Strained knee ligaments (January 1989). . . . Traded by Oilers to Tampa Bay Lightning for D Bob Beers (November 12, 1993).

			REGULAR SEASON					PLAYOFFS				
Season	Team	League	Gms.	G	A	Pts.	PIM	Gms.	G	A	Pts.	PIM
85-86—	Seattle	WHL	72	4	8	12	50	5	0	3	3	12
86-87—	Seattle	WHL	67	13	45	58	155	—	—	—	—	—
87-88—	Pittsburgh	NHL	17	0	4	4	12	—	—	—	—	—
	—Edmonton	NHL	7	0	4	4	6	—	—	—	—	—
	—Nova Scotia	AHL	8	0	2	2	8	4	0	0	0	9
	—Seattle	WHL	23	5	14	19	49	—	—	—	—	—
88-89—	Cape Breton	AHL	5	1	1	2	18	—	—	—	—	—
	—Edmonton	NHL	44	4	5	9	54	—	—	—	—	—
89-90—	Edmonton	NHL	4	0	2	2	2	—	—	—	—	—
	—Cape Breton	AHL	61	10	20	30	69	6	2	1	3	4
90-91—	Edmonton	NHL	49	5	17	22	59	5	1	3	4	2
91-92—	Edmonton	NHL	7	0	0	0	8	5	0	2	2	8
	—Cape Breton	AHL	63	14	29	43	72	—	—	—	—	—
92-93—	Edmonton	NHL	33	2	10	12	48	—	—	—	—	—
93-94—	Edmonton	NHL	10	1	1	2	28	—	—	—	—	—
	—Tampa Bay	NHL	66	10	19	29	108	—	—	—	—	—
NHL totals			237	22	62	84	325	5	1	3	4	2

JOSEPH, CURTIS
G, BLUES

PERSONAL: Born April 29, 1967, in Keswick, Ont. . . . 5-10/182. . . . Catches left. . . . Full name: Curtis Shayne Joseph.
HIGH SCHOOL: Huron Heights (Newmarket, Ont.).
COLLEGE: Wisconsin.
TRANSACTIONS/CAREER NOTES: Signed as free agent by St. Louis Blues (June 16, 1989). . . . Dislocated left shoulder (April 11, 1990). . . . Underwent surgery to left shoulder (May 10, 1990). . . . Sprained right knee (February 26, 1991); missed remainder of season. . . . Injured ankle (March 12, 1992); missed seven games. . . . Suffered sore knee (January 2, 1993); missed three games. . . . Suffered from the flu (February 9, 1993); missed one game.
HONORS: Named OHA Most Valuable Player (1986-87). . . . Won WCHA Most Valuable Player Award (1988-89). . . . Won WCHA Rookie of the Year Award (1988-89). . . . Named to NCAA All-America West second team (1988-89). . . . Named to WCHA All-Star first team (1988-89). . . . Played in NHL All-Star Game (1994).

			REGULAR SEASON							PLAYOFFS					
Season	Team	League	Gms.	Min.	W	L	T	GA	SO	Avg.	Gms.	Min.	W	L	GA	SO	Avg.
86-87—	Richmond Hill	OHA					Statistics unavailable.								
87-88—	Notre Dame	SCMHL	36	2174	25	4	7	94	1	2.59	—	—	—	—	—	—	—
88-89—	Univ. of Wisconsin	WCHA	38	2267	21	11	5	94	1	2.49	—	—	—	—	—	—	—
89-90—	Peoria	IHL	23	1241	10	8	‡2	80	0	3.87	—	—	—	—	—	—	—
	—St. Louis	NHL	15	852	9	5	1	48	0	3.38	6	327	4	1	18	0	3.30
90-91—	St. Louis	NHL	30	1710	16	10	2	89	0	3.12	—	—	—	—	—	—	—
91-92—	St. Louis	NHL	60	3494	27	20	10	175	2	3.01	6	379	2	4	23	0	3.64
92-93—	St. Louis	NHL	68	3890	29	28	9	196	1	3.02	11	715	7	4	27	2	2.27
93-94—	St. Louis	NHL	71	4127	36	23	11	213	1	3.10	4	246	0	4	15	0	3.66
NHL totals			244	14073	117	86	33	721	4	3.07	27	1667	13	13	83	2	2.99

JOUBERT, JACQUES
C, STARS

PERSONAL: Born March 23, 1971, in South Bend, Ind. . . . 6-1/191. . . . Shoots left. . . . Name pronounced zhoh-BAIR.
COLLEGE: Boston University.
TRANSACTIONS/CAREER NOTES: Selected by Dallas Stars in NHL supplemental draft (June 25, 1993).
HONORS: Named to Hockey East All-Star first team (1993-94).

			REGULAR SEASON					PLAYOFFS				
Season	Team	League	Gms.	G	A	Pts.	PIM	Gms.	G	A	Pts.	PIM
92-93—	Boston University	Hockey East	40	17	18	35	54	—	—	—	—	—
93-94—	Boston University	Hockey East	41	20	24	44	82	—	—	—	—	—

JOVANOVSKI, ED
D, PANTHERS

PERSONAL: Born June 26, 1976, in Windsor, Ont. . . . 6-2/205. . . . Shoots left. . . . Name pronounced Zhoh-van-AHV-skee.
HIGH SCHOOL: Riverside Secondary (Windsor, Ont.).
TRANSACTIONS/CAREER NOTES: Selected by Florida Panthers in first round (first Panthers pick, first overall) of NHL entry draft (June 28, 1994).
HONORS: Named to Can.HL All-Rookie team (1993-94). . . . Named to OHL All-Star second team (1993-94). . . . Named to OHL All-Rookie team (1993-94).

			REGULAR SEASON					PLAYOFFS				
Season	Team	League	Gms.	G	A	Pts.	PIM	Gms.	G	A	Pts.	PIM
92-93—	Windsor	OHL Jr. B	48	7	46	53	88	—	—	—	—	—
93-94—	Windsor	OHL	62	15	35	50	221	4	0	0	0	15

JOYCE, DUANE
D

PERSONAL: Born May 5, 1965, in Pembroke, Mass. . . . 6-2/203. . . . Shoots right.
TRANSACTIONS/CAREER NOTES: Signed as free agent by San Jose Sharks (August 13, 1991). . . . Signed as free agent by Dallas Stars (December 1, 1993). . . . Released by Dallas Stars (December 9, 1993).

Season Team	League	REGULAR SEASON					PLAYOFFS				
		Gms.	G	A	Pts.	PIM	Gms.	G	A	Pts.	PIM
89-90—Kalamazoo	IHL	2	0	0	0	2	—	—	—	—	—
—Fort Wayne	IHL	66	10	26	36	53	—	—	—	—	—
—Muskegon	IHL	13	3	10	13	8	12	3	7	10	13
90-91—Kalamazoo	IHL	80	12	32	44	53	11	0	3	3	6
91-92—Kansas City	IHL	80	12	32	44	62	15	6	11	17	8
92-93—Kansas City	IHL	75	15	25	40	30	12	1	2	3	6
93-94—Dallas	NHL	3	0	0	0	0	—	—	—	—	—
—Kansas City	IHL	43	9	23	32	40	—	—	—	—	—
NHL totals		3	0	0	0	0					

JUDEN, DANIEL
RW, LIGHTNING

PERSONAL: Born April 17, 1976, in Beverly, Mass. . . . 6-3/190. . . . Shoots right. . . . Cousin of Jeff Juden, pitcher in Philadelphia Phillies system.
TRANSACTIONS/CAREER NOTES: Selected by Tampa Bay Lightning in sixth round (fifth Lightning pick, 137th overall) of NHL entry draft (June 29, 1994).

Season Team	League	REGULAR SEASON					PLAYOFFS				
		Gms.	G	A	Pts.	PIM	Gms.	G	A	Pts.	PIM
91-92—Governor Dummer	Mass. H.S.	25	9	11	20	2	—	—	—	—	—
92-93—Governor Dummer	Mass. H.S.	25	14	15	29	2	—	—	—	—	—
93-94—Governor Dummer	Mass. H.S.	30	20	28	48	8	—	—	—	—	—

JUHLIN, PATRIK
LW, FLYERS

PERSONAL: Born April 24, 1970, in Huddinge, Sweden. . . . 6-0/187. . . . Shoots left.
TRANSACTIONS/CAREER NOTES: Selected by Philadelphia Flyers in second round (second Flyers pick, 34th overall) of NHL entry draft (June 17, 1989).
MISCELLANEOUS: Member of gold-medal-winning Swedish Olympic team (1994).

Season Team	League	REGULAR SEASON					PLAYOFFS				
		Gms.	G	A	Pts.	PIM	Gms.	G	A	Pts.	PIM
87-88—Vasteras	Sweden	28	25	10	35	. . .	—	—	—	—	—
88-89—Vasteras	Sweden	30	29	13	42	. . .	—	—	—	—	—
89-90—Vasteras	Sweden	35	10	13	23	18	2	0	0	0	0
90-91—Vasteras	Sweden	40	13	9	22	24	—	—	—	—	—
91-92—Vasteras	Sweden	39	15	12	27	40	—	—	—	—	—
92-93—Vasteras	Sweden	34	14	12	26	22	3	0	1	1	0
93-94—Vasteras	Sweden	40	15	16	31	20	4	1	1	2	0
—Swedish Olympic Team	Int'l	8	7	1	8	16	—	—	—	—	—

JUNEAU, JOE
C, CAPITALS

PERSONAL: Born January 5, 1968, in Pont-Rouge, Que. . . . 6-0/196. . . . Shoots left. . . . Name pronounced ZHOH-ay ZHOO-noh.
COLLEGE: Rensselaer Polytechnic Institute (N.Y.).
TRANSACTIONS/CAREER NOTES: Selected by Boston Bruins in fourth round (third Bruins pick, 81st overall) of NHL entry draft (June 11, 1988). . . . Suffered ligament problem in back (November 1990). . . . Broke jaw (November 7, 1993); missed seven games. . . . Reinjured jaw (February 18, 1994); missed two games. . . . Traded by Boston to Washington Capitals for D Al Iafrate (March 21, 1994).
HONORS: Named to NCAA All-America East first team (1989-90). . . . Named to ECAC All-Star first team (1989-90). . . . Named to NCAA All-America East second team (1990-91). . . . Named to ECAC All-Star second team (1990-91). . . . Named to NHL All-Rookie team (1992-93).
RECORDS: Holds NHL single-season record for most assists by a left winger—70 (1992-93). . . . Shares NHL single-season record for most assists by a rookie—70 (1992-93).
MISCELLANEOUS: Member of silver-medal-winning Canadian Olympic team (1992).

Season Team	League	REGULAR SEASON					PLAYOFFS				
		Gms.	G	A	Pts.	PIM	Gms.	G	A	Pts.	PIM
87-88—R.P.I.	ECAC	31	16	29	45	18	—	—	—	—	—
88-89—R.P.I.	ECAC	30	12	23	35	40	—	—	—	—	—
89-90—R.P.I.	ECAC	34	18	*52	*70	31	—	—	—	—	—
90-91—R.P.I.	ECAC	29	23	40	63	70	—	—	—	—	—
91-92—Canadian national team	Int'l	60	20	49	69	35	—	—	—	—	—
—Canadian Olympic Team	Int'l	8	6	9	15	4	—	—	—	—	—
—Boston	NHL	14	5	14	19	4	15	4	8	12	21
92-93—Boston	NHL	84	32	70	102	33	4	2	4	6	6
93-94—Boston	NHL	63	14	58	72	35	—	—	—	—	—
—Washington	NHL	11	5	8	13	6	11	4	5	9	6
NHL totals		172	56	150	206	78	30	10	17	27	33

JUNKER, STEVE
LW, ISLANDERS

PERSONAL: Born June 26, 1972, in Castlegar, B.C. . . . 6-0/184. . . . Shoots left.
TRANSACTIONS/CAREER NOTES: Selected by New York Islanders in fifth round (fifth Islanders pick, 92nd overall) of NHL entry draft (June 22, 1991).

Season Team	League	REGULAR SEASON					PLAYOFFS				
		Gms.	G	A	Pts.	PIM	Gms.	G	A	Pts.	PIM
90-91—Spokane	WHL	71	39	38	77	86	15	5	13	18	6
91-92—Spokane	WHL	58	28	32	60	110	10	6	7	13	18

Season	Team	League	REGULAR SEASON					PLAYOFFS				
			Gms.	G	A	Pts.	Pen.	Gms.	G	A	Pts.	Pen.
92-93	—Capital District	AHL	79	16	31	47	20	4	0	0	0	0
	—New York Islanders	NHL	—	—	—	—	—	3	0	1	1	0
93-94	—Salt Lake City	IHL	71	9	14	23	36	—	—	—	—	—
	—New York Islanders	NHL	5	0	0	0	0	—	—	—	—	—
NHL totals			5	0	0	0	0	3	0	1	1	0

KACIR, MARIAN
RW, LIGHTNING

PERSONAL: Born September 29, 1974, in Hodonin, Czechoslovakia. . . . 6-1/183. . . . Shoots left. . . . Name pronounced kuh-SIHR.
TRANSACTIONS/CAREER NOTES: Selected by Tampa Bay Lightning in fourth round (fourth Lightning pick, 81st overall) of NHL entry draft (June 26, 1993).

Season	Team	League	REGULAR SEASON					PLAYOFFS				
			Gms.	G	A	Pts.	PIM	Gms.	G	A	Pts.	PIM
91-92	—Czechoslovakia Jr.	Czech.	6	6	4	10	2	8	3	5	8	4
92-93	—Owen Sound	OHL	56	20	36	56	8	8	3	5	8	4
93-94	—Owen Sound	OHL	66	23	64	87	26	9	5	4	9	2

KAMENSKY, VALERI
LW, NORDIQUES

PERSONAL: Born April 18, 1966, in Voskresensk, U.S.S.R. . . . 6-2/198. . . . Shoots right. . . . Name pronounced kuh-MEHN-skee.
TRANSACTIONS/CAREER NOTES: Selected by Quebec Nordiques in seventh round (eighth Nordiques pick, 129th overall) of NHL entry draft (June 11, 1988). . . . Fractured leg (October 1991); missed 57 games. . . . Broke left thumb (October 17, 1992); missed three games. . . . Broke right ankle (October 27, 1992); missed 47 games. . . . Bruised left foot (October 21, 1993); missed two games. . . . Bruised right foot (December 21, 1993); missed one game.
HONORS: Won Soviet Player of the Year Award (1990-91).
MISCELLANEOUS: Member of gold-medal-winning U.S.S.R. Olympic team (1988).

Season	Team	League	REGULAR SEASON					PLAYOFFS				
			Gms.	G	A	Pts.	PIM	Gms.	G	A	Pts.	PIM
82-83	—Khimik	USSR	5	0	0	0	0	—	—	—	—	—
83-84	—Khimik	USSR	20	2	2	4	6	—	—	—	—	—
84-85	—Khimik	USSR	45	9	3	12	24	—	—	—	—	—
85-86	—CSKA Moscow	USSR	40	15	9	24	8	—	—	—	—	—
86-87	—CSKA Moscow	USSR	37	13	8	21	16	—	—	—	—	—
87-88	—CSKA Moscow	USSR	51	26	20	46	40	—	—	—	—	—
	—Soviet Olympic Team	Int'l	8	4	2	6	4	—	—	—	—	—
88-89	—CSKA Moscow	USSR	40	18	10	28	30	—	—	—	—	—
89-90	—CSKA Moscow	USSR	45	19	18	37	38	—	—	—	—	—
90-91	—CSKA Moscow	USSR	46	20	26	46	66	—	—	—	—	—
91-92	—Quebec	NHL	23	7	14	21	14	6	0	1	1	6
92-93	—Quebec	NHL	32	15	22	37	14	—	—	—	—	—
93-94	—Quebec	NHL	76	28	37	65	42	—	—	—	—	—
NHL totals			131	50	73	123	70	6	0	1	1	6

KAMINSKI, KEVIN
C, CAPITALS

PERSONAL: Born March 13, 1969, in Churchbridge, Sask. . . . 5-9/170. . . . Shoots left.
TRANSACTIONS/CAREER NOTES: Selected by Minnesota North Stars as underage junior in third round (third North Stars pick, 48th overall) of NHL entry draft (June 13, 1987). . . . Suspended 12 games by WHL for cross-checking (November 4, 1987). . . . Traded by North Stars to Quebec Nordiques for LW Gaetan Duchesne (June 18, 1989). . . . Separated shoulder in training camp (September 1989). . . . Suspended two games by AHL for head-butting (January 26, 1990). . . . Signed as free agent by Portland Pirates (1993).

Season	Team	League	REGULAR SEASON					PLAYOFFS				
			Gms.	G	A	Pts.	PIM	Gms.	G	A	Pts.	PIM
84-85	—Saskatoon	WHL	5	0	1	1	17	—	—	—	—	—
85-86	—Saskatoon	WHL	4	1	1	2	35	11	5	6	11	45
86-87	—Saskatoon	WHL	67	26	44	70	235	11	5	6	11	45
87-88	—Saskatoon	WHL	55	38	61	99	247	10	5	7	12	37
88-89	—Saskatoon	WHL	52	25	43	68	199	8	4	9	13	25
	—Minnesota	NHL	1	0	0	0	0	—	—	—	—	—
89-90	—Quebec	NHL	1	0	0	0	0	—	—	—	—	—
	—Halifax	AHL	19	3	4	7	128	2	0	0	0	5
90-91	—Halifax	AHL	7	1	0	1	44	—	—	—	—	—
	—Fort Wayne	IHL	56	9	15	24	*455	19	4	2	6	*169
91-92	—Halifax	AHL	63	18	27	45	329	—	—	—	—	—
	—Quebec	NHL	5	0	0	0	45	—	—	—	—	—
92-93	—Halifax	AHL	79	27	37	64	*345	—	—	—	—	—
93-94	—Portland	AHL	39	10	22	32	263	16	4	5	9	*91
	—Washington	NHL	13	0	5	5	87	—	—	—	—	—
NHL totals			20	0	5	5	132					

KAMINSKY, YAN
LW, ISLANDERS

PERSONAL: Born July 28, 1971, in Penza, U.S.S.R. . . . 6-1/176. . . . Shoots left.
TRANSACTIONS/CAREER NOTES: Selected by Winnipeg Jets in fifth round (fourth Jets pick, 99th overall) of NHL entry draft (June 22, 1991). . . . Separated shoulder (January 6, 1994); missed six games. . . . Traded by Jets to New York Islanders for D Wayne McBean (February 1, 1994).

Season Team	League	REGULAR SEASON Gms.	G	A	Pts.	PIM	PLAYOFFS Gms.	G	A	Pts.	PIM
89-90—Dynamo Moscow	USSR	6	1	0	1	4	—	—	—	—	—
90-91—Dynamo Moscow	USSR	25	10	5	15	2	—	—	—	—	—
91-92—Dynamo Moscow	CIS	42	9	7	16	22	—	—	—	—	—
92-93—Dynamo Moscow	CIS	39	15	14	29	12	10	2	5	7	8
93-94—Moncton	AHL	33	9	13	22	6	—	—	—	—	—
—Winnipeg	NHL	1	0	0	0	0	—	—	—	—	—
—New York Islanders	NHL	23	2	1	3	4	2	0	0	0	4
NHL totals		24	2	1	3	4	2	0	0	0	4

KARABIN, LADISLAV
LW, PENGUINS

PERSONAL: Born February 16, 1970, in Bratislava, Czechoslovakia. . . . 6-1/189. . . . Shoots left.
TRANSACTIONS/CAREER NOTES: Selected by Pittsburgh Penguins in ninth round (ninth Penguins pick, 173rd overall) of NHL entry draft (June 16, 1990).

Season Team	League	REGULAR SEASON Gms.	G	A	Pts.	PIM	PLAYOFFS Gms.	G	A	Pts.	PIM
91-92—Bratislava	Czech.	24	4	8	12	. . .	—	—	—	—	—
92-93—Bratislava	Czech.	39	21	23	44	. . .	—	—	—	—	—
93-94—Cleveland	IHL	58	13	26	39	48	—	—	—	—	—
—Pittsburgh	NHL	9	0	0	0	2	—	—	—	—	—
NHL totals		9	0	0	0	2					

KARALAHTI, JERE
D, KINGS

PERSONAL: Born March 25, 1975, in Helsinki, Finland. . . . 6-2/185. . . . Shoots right.
TRANSACTIONS/CAREER NOTES: Selected by Los Angeles Kings in sixth round (seventh Kings pick, 146th overall) of NHL entry draft (June 26, 1993).

Season Team	League	REGULAR SEASON Gms.	G	A	Pts.	PIM	PLAYOFFS Gms.	G	A	Pts.	PIM
91-92—HIFK Juniors	Finland Jrs	30	12	5	17	36	—	—	—	—	—
92-93—HIFK Juniors	Finland Jrs	30	2	13	15	49	—	—	—	—	—
93-94—HIFK Helsinki	Finland	46	1	10	11	36	3	0	0	0	6

KARAMNOV, VITALI
LW, BLUES

PERSONAL: Born July 6, 1968, in Moscow, U.S.S.R. . . . 6-2/185. . . . Shoots left. . . . Name pronounced vee-TAL-ee kuh-RAHM-nahf.
TRANSACTIONS/CAREER NOTES: Selected by St. Louis Blues in third round (second Blues pick, 62nd overall) of NHL entry draft (June 20, 1992). . . . Pulled groin (October 15, 1992); missed 14 games. . . . Injured ankle (January 28, 1994); missed four games. . . . Reinjured ankle (February 5, 1994); missed five games. . . . Suffered from the flu (March 13, 1994); missed one game.

Season Team	League	REGULAR SEASON Gms.	G	A	Pts.	PIM	PLAYOFFS Gms.	G	A	Pts.	PIM
86-87—Dynamo Moscow	USSR	4	0	0	0	0	—	—	—	—	—
87-88—Dynamo Moscow	USSR	2	0	1	1	0	—	—	—	—	—
88-89—Dynamo Kharkov	USSR	23	4	1	5	19	—	—	—	—	—
89-90—Torpedo Yaroslavl	USSR	47	6	7	13	32	—	—	—	—	—
90-91—Torpedo Yaroslavl	USSR	45	14	7	21	30	—	—	—	—	—
91-92—Dynamo Moscow	CIS	40	13	19	32	25	—	—	—	—	—
92-93—St. Louis	NHL	7	0	1	1	0	—	—	—	—	—
—Peoria	IHL	23	8	12	20	47	—	—	—	—	—
93-94—St. Louis	NHL	59	9	12	21	51	—	—	—	—	—
—Peoria	IHL	3	0	1	1	2	1	0	1	1	0
NHL totals		66	9	13	22	51					

KARIYA, PAUL
LW, MIGHTY DUCKS

PERSONAL: Born October 16, 1974, in Vancouver. . . . 5-11/157. . . . Shoots left.
COLLEGE: Maine.
TRANSACTIONS/CAREER NOTES: Selected by Mighty Ducks of Anaheim in first round (first Mighty Ducks pick, fourth overall) of NHL entry draft (June 26, 1993).
HONORS: Won Hobey Baker Memorial Trophy (1992-93). . . . Named Hockey East Player of the Year (1992-93). . . . Named Hockey East Rookie of the Year (1992-93). . . . Named to NCAA All-America East first team (1992-93). . . . Named to NCAA All-Tournament team (1992-93). . . . Named to Hockey East All-Star first team (1992-93). . . . Named to Hockey East All-Rookie team (1992-93).
MISCELLANEOUS: Member of silver-medal-winning Canadian Olympic team (1994).

Season Team	League	REGULAR SEASON Gms.	G	A	Pts.	PIM	PLAYOFFS Gms.	G	A	Pts.	PIM
90-91—Penticton	BCJHL	54	45	67	112	8	—	—	—	—	—
91-92—Penticton	BCJHL	40	46	86	132	16	—	—	—	—	—
92-93—University of Maine	Hockey East	39	25	*75	*100	12	—	—	—	—	—
93-94—Canadian national team	Int'l	31	10	38	48	4	—	—	—	—	—
—Canadian Olympic Team	Int'l	8	3	4	7	2	—	—	—	—	—
—University of Maine	Hockey East	12	8	16	24	4	—	—	—	—	—

KARPA, DAVID
D, NORDIQUES

PERSONAL: Born May 7, 1971, in Regina, Sask. . . . 6-1/202. . . . Shoots right. . . . Full name: David James Karpa.
COLLEGE: Ferris State (Mich.).
TRANSACTIONS/CAREER NOTES: Selected by Quebec Nordiques in fourth round (fourth Nordiques pick, 68th overall) of NHL entry draft (June 22, 1991). . . . Broke right wrist (January 26, 1994); missed 18 games.

			REGULAR SEASON					PLAYOFFS				
Season Team	League	Gms.	G	A	Pts.	PIM		Gms.	G	A	Pts.	PIM
88-89—Notre Dame	SCMHL	...	16	37	53	—		—	—	—	—	—
89-90—Notre Dame	SCMHL	43	9	19	28	271		—	—	—	—	—
90-91—Ferris State	CCHA	41	6	19	25	109		—	—	—	—	—
91-92—Ferris State	CCHA	34	7	12	19	124		—	—	—	—	—
—Halifax	AHL	2	0	0	0	4		—	—	—	—	—
—Quebec	NHL	4	0	0	0	14		—	—	—	—	—
92-93—Halifax	AHL	71	4	27	31	167		—	—	—	—	—
—Quebec	NHL	12	0	1	1	13		3	0	0	0	0
93-94—Quebec	NHL	60	5	12	17	148		—	—	—	—	—
—Cornwall	AHL	1	0	0	0	0		12	2	2	4	27
NHL totals		76	5	13	18	175		3	0	0	0	0

KARPOV, VALERI
LW/RW, MIGHTY DUCKS

PERSONAL: Born August 5, 1971, in Chelyabinsk, U.S.S.R. . . . 5-10/176. . . . Shoots left. . . . Name pronounced VAL-uhr-ee KAHR-pahf.
TRANSACTIONS/CAREER NOTES: Selected by Mighty Ducks of Anaheim in third round (third Mighty Ducks pick, 56th overall) of NHL entry draft (June 26, 1993).
HONORS: Named to CIS All-Star team (1992-93 and 1993-94).

			REGULAR SEASON					PLAYOFFS				
Season Team	League	Gms.	G	A	Pts.	PIM		Gms.	G	A	Pts.	PIM
88-89—Traktor Chelyabinsk	USSR	5	0	0	0	0		—	—	—	—	—
89-90—Traktor Chelyabinsk	USSR	24	1	2	3	6		—	—	—	—	—
90-91—Traktor Chelyabinsk	USSR	25	8	4	12	15		—	—	—	—	—
91-92—Traktor Chelyabinsk	CIS	44	16	10	26	34		—	—	—	—	—
92-93—CSKA Moscow	CIS	9	2	6	8	0		—	—	—	—	—
—Traktor Chelyabinsk	CIS	38	12	21	33	6		8	0	1	1	10
93-94—Traktor Chelyabinsk	CIS	32	11	19	30	18		6	2	5	7	2
—Russian Olympic team	Int'l	8	3	1	4	2		—	—	—	—	—

KARPOVTSEV, ALEXANDER
D, RANGERS

PERSONAL: Born April 7, 1970, in Moscow, U.S.S.R. . . . 6-1/205. . . . Shoots left. . . . Name pronounced kahr-PAHV-tsehf.
TRANSACTIONS/CAREER NOTES: Selected by Quebec Nordiques in seventh round (seventh Nordiques pick, 158th overall) of NHL entry draft (June 16, 1990). . . . Traded by Nordiques to New York Rangers for D Mike Hurlbut (September 9, 1993). . . . Bruised buttocks (October 9, 1993); missed one game. . . . Bruised hip (November 3, 1993); missed six games. . . . Reinjured hip (November 23, 1993); missed one game. . . . Suffered facial injury (February 28, 1994); missed two games. . . . Suffered injury (March 14, 1994); missed two games.
MISCELLANEOUS: Member of Stanley Cup championship team (1994).

			REGULAR SEASON					PLAYOFFS				
Season Team	League	Gms.	G	A	Pts.	PIM		Gms.	G	A	Pts.	PIM
89-90—Dynamo Moscow	USSR	35	1	1	2	27		—	—	—	—	—
90-91—Dynamo Moscow	USSR	40	0	5	5	15		—	—	—	—	—
91-92—Dynamo Moscow	CIS	28	3	2	5	22		—	—	—	—	—
92-93—Dynamo Moscow	CIS	40	3	11	14	100		—	—	—	—	—
93-94—New York Rangers	NHL	67	3	15	18	58		17	0	4	4	12
NHL totals		67	3	15	18	58		17	0	4	4	12

KASATONOV, ALEXEI
D, BRUINS

PERSONAL: Born October 14, 1959, in Leningrad, U.S.S.R. . . . 6-1/215. . . . Shoots left. . . . Name pronounced uh-LEHK-see KAS-ih-TAH-nahf.
TRANSACTIONS/CAREER NOTES: Selected by New Jersey Devils in 12th round (ninth Devils pick, 225th overall) of NHL entry draft (June 8, 1983). . . . Broke toe on right foot (February 1990). . . . Suffered from hemorrhoids (December 1991); missed three games. . . . Injured left hand (October 6, 1992); missed three games. . . . Suffered from the flu (December 27, 1992); missed two games. . . . Selected by Mighty Ducks of Anaheim in NHL expansion draft (June 24, 1993). . . . Suffered from the flu (October 30, 1993); missed one game. . . . Bruised right foot (January 26, 1994); missed three games. . . . Suffered hairline fracture of right foot (February 20, 1994); missed 11 games with Mighty Ducks and first four games with St. Louis Blues. . . . Traded by Mighty Ducks to Blues for LW Maxim Bets and sixth-round pick in 1995 draft (March 21, 1994). . . . Signed as free agent by Boston Bruins (June 22, 1994).
HONORS: Named to Soviet League All-Star first team (1979-80 through 1987-88). . . . Played in NHL All-Star Game (1994).
MISCELLANEOUS: Member of silver-medal-winning U.S.S.R. Olympic team (1980) and gold-medal-winning U.S.S.R. Olympic team (1984 and 1988).

			REGULAR SEASON					PLAYOFFS				
Season Team	League	Gms.	G	A	Pts.	PIM		Gms.	G	A	Pts.	PIM
76-77—Leningrad SKA	USSR	7	0	0	0	0		—	—	—	—	—
77-78—Leningrad SKA	USSR	35	4	7	11	15		—	—	—	—	—
78-79—CSKA Moscow	USSR	40	5	14	19	30		—	—	—	—	—

K

Season Team	League	REGULAR SEASON					PLAYOFFS				
		Gms.	G	A	Pts.	Pen.	Gms.	G	A	Pts.	Pen.
79-80—CSKA Moscow	USSR	37	5	8	13	26	—	—	—	—	—
—Soviet Olympic Team	Int'l	7	2	5	7	8	—	—	—	—	—
80-81—CSKA Moscow	USSR	47	10	12	22	38	—	—	—	—	—
81-82—CSKA Moscow	USSR	46	12	27	39	45	—	—	—	—	—
82-83—CSKA Moscow	USSR	44	12	19	31	37	—	—	—	—	—
83-84—CSKA Moscow	USSR	39	12	24	36	20	—	—	—	—	—
—Soviet Olympic Team	Int'l	7	3	2	5	0	—	—	—	—	—
84-85—CSKA Moscow	USSR	40	18	18	36	26	—	—	—	—	—
85-86—CSKA Moscow	USSR	40	6	17	23	27	—	—	—	—	—
86-87—CSKA Moscow	USSR	40	13	17	30	16	—	—	—	—	—
87-88—CSKA Moscow	USSR	43	8	12	20	8	—	—	—	—	—
—Soviet Olympic Team	Int'l	7	2	6	8	0	—	—	—	—	—
88-89—CSKA Moscow	USSR	41	8	14	22	8	—	—	—	—	—
89-90—New Jersey	NHL	39	6	15	21	16	6	0	3	3	14
—Utica	AHL	3	0	2	2	7	—	—	—	—	—
90-91—New Jersey	NHL	78	10	31	41	76	7	1	3	4	8
91-92—New Jersey	NHL	76	12	28	40	70	7	1	1	2	12
92-93—New Jersey	NHL	64	3	14	17	57	4	0	0	0	0
93-94—Anaheim	NHL	55	4	18	22	43	—	—	—	—	—
—St. Louis	NHL	8	0	2	2	19	4	2	0	2	2
NHL totals		320	35	108	143	281	28	4	7	11	36

KASPARAITIS, DARIUS
D, ISLANDERS

PERSONAL: Born October 16, 1972, in Elektrenai, U.S.S.R. . . . 5-11/190. . . . Shoots left. . . . Name pronounced KAZ-puhr-IGH-tihz.
TRANSACTIONS/CAREER NOTES: Selected by New York Islanders in first round (first Islanders pick, fifth overall) of NHL entry draft (June 20, 1992). . . . Suffered back spasms (February 12, 1993); missed two games. . . . Strained back (April 15, 1993); missed one game. . . . Strained lower back (November 10, 1993); missed two games. . . . Jammed wrist (March 5, 1994); missed four games.
MISCELLANEOUS: Member of gold-medal-winning Unified Olympic team (1992).

Season Team	League	REGULAR SEASON					PLAYOFFS				
		Gms.	G	A	Pts.	PIM	Gms.	G	A	Pts.	PIM
89-90—Dynamo Moscow	USSR	1	0	0	0	0	—	—	—	—	—
90-91—Dynamo Moscow	USSR	17	0	1	1	10	—	—	—	—	—
91-92—Dynamo Moscow	CIS	31	2	10	12	14	—	—	—	—	—
—Unified Olympic Team	Int'l	8	0	2	2	2	—	—	—	—	—
92-93—Dynamo Moscow	CIS	7	1	3	4	8	—	—	—	—	—
—New York Islanders	NHL	79	4	17	21	166	18	0	5	5	31
93-94—New York Islanders	NHL	76	1	10	11	142	4	0	0	0	8
NHL totals		155	5	27	32	308	22	0	5	5	39

KEALTY, JEFF
D, NORDIQUES

PERSONAL: Born April 9, 1976, in Framingham, Mass. . . . 6-4/175. . . . Shoots left.
TRANSACTIONS/CAREER NOTES: Selected by Quebec Nordiques in first round (second Nordiques pick, 22nd overall) of NHL entry draft (June 28, 1994).

Season Team	League	REGULAR SEASON					PLAYOFFS				
		Gms.	G	A	Pts.	PIM	Gms.	G	A	Pts.	PIM
90-91—Catholic Memorial H.S.	Mass. H.S.	5	0	2	2	0	—	—	—	—	—
91-92—Catholic Memorial H.S.	Mass. H.S.	25	2	13	15	8	—	—	—	—	—
92-93—Catholic Memorial H.S.	Mass. H.S.	24	3	22	25	10	—	—	—	—	—
93-94—Catholic Memorial H.S.	Mass. H.S.	25	10	22	32	...	—	—	—	—	—

KEANE, MIKE
RW, CANADIENS

PERSONAL: Born May 29, 1967, in Winnipeg. . . . 5-10/180. . . . Shoots right.
TRANSACTIONS/CAREER NOTES: Signed as free agent by Montreal Canadiens (March 1987). . . . Separated right shoulder (December 21, 1988). . . . Lacerated left kneecap (October 31, 1990); missed seven games. . . . Injured neck (March 1991). . . . Sprained ankle (January 16, 1992); missed four games. . . . Resprained ankle (February 1, 1992); missed 10 games. . . . Bruised ankle (March 11, 1992); missed one game. . . . Suspended four off-days and fined $500 by NHL for swinging stick in preseason game (October 13, 1992). . . . Suffered wrist tendinitis (January 26, 1993); missed three games. . . . Suffered back spasms (February 12, 1993); missed two games. . . . Fractured toe (February 27, 1993); missed two games. . . . Suffered back spasms (October 16, 1993); missed one game. . . . Suffered back spasms (January 12, 1994); missed three games.
MISCELLANEOUS: Member of Stanley Cup championship team (1993).

Season Team	League	REGULAR SEASON					PLAYOFFS				
		Gms.	G	A	Pts.	PIM	Gms.	G	A	Pts.	PIM
83-84—Winnipeg	WHL	1	0	0	0	0	—	—	—	—	—
84-85—Moose Jaw	WHL	65	17	26	43	141	—	—	—	—	—
85-86—Moose Jaw	WHL	67	34	49	83	162	13	6	8	14	9
86-87—Moose Jaw	WHL	53	25	45	70	107	9	3	9	12	11
—Sherbrooke	AHL	—	—	—	—	—	9	2	2	4	16
87-88—Sherbrooke	AHL	78	25	43	68	70	6	1	1	2	18
88-89—Montreal	NHL	69	16	19	35	69	21	4	3	7	17
89-90—Montreal	NHL	74	9	15	24	78	11	0	1	1	8

Season	Team	League	REGULAR SEASON					PLAYOFFS				
			Gms.	G	A	Pts.	Pen.	Gms.	G	A	Pts.	Pen.
90-91—Montreal		NHL	73	13	23	36	50	12	3	2	5	6
91-92—Montreal		NHL	67	11	30	41	64	8	1	1	2	16
92-93—Montreal		NHL	77	15	45	60	95	19	2	13	15	6
93-94—Montreal		NHL	80	16	30	46	119	6	3	1	4	4
NHL totals			440	80	162	242	475	77	13	21	34	57

KECZMER, DAN
D, FLAMES

PERSONAL: Born May 25, 1968, in Mt. Clemens, Mich. . . . 6-1/190. . . . Shoots left. . . . Full name: Daniel Leonard Keczmer. . . . Name pronounced KEHS-muhr.
COLLEGE: Lake Superior State (Mich.).
TRANSACTIONS/CAREER NOTES: Selected by Minnesota North Stars in 10th round (11th North Stars pick, 201st overall) of NHL entry draft (June 21, 1986). . . . Injured shoulder (February 2, 1990). . . . Claimed by San Jose Sharks as part of ownership change with North Stars (October 1990). . . . Traded by Sharks to Hartford Whalers for C Dean Evason (October 2, 1991). . . . Released by U.S. National team prior to Olympics (January 1992). . . . Suffered right leg contusion (February 8, 1993); missed three games. . . . Traded by Whalers to Calgary Flames for G Jeff Reese and future considerations (November 19, 1993).
HONORS: Named to CCHA All-Star second team (1989-90).

Season	Team	League	REGULAR SEASON					PLAYOFFS				
			Gms.	G	A	Pts.	PIM	Gms.	G	A	Pts.	PIM
86-87—Lake Superior State		CCHA	38	3	5	8	28	—	—	—	—	—
87-88—Lake Superior State		CCHA	41	2	15	17	34	—	—	—	—	—
88-89—Lake Superior State		CCHA	46	3	26	29	70	—	—	—	—	—
89-90—Lake Superior State		CCHA	43	13	23	36	48	—	—	—	—	—
90-91—Minnesota		NHL	9	0	1	1	6	—	—	—	—	—
—Kalamazoo		IHL	60	4	20	24	60	9	1	2	3	10
91-92—U.S. national team		Int'l	51	3	11	14	56	—	—	—	—	—
—Springfield		AHL	18	3	4	7	10	4	0	0	0	6
—Hartford		NHL	1	0	0	0	0	—	—	—	—	—
92-93—Springfield		AHL	37	1	13	14	38	12	0	4	4	14
—Hartford		NHL	23	4	4	8	28	—	—	—	—	—
93-94—Hartford		NHL	12	0	1	1	12	—	—	—	—	—
—Springfield		AHL	7	0	1	1	4	—	—	—	—	—
—Calgary		NHL	57	1	20	21	48	3	0	0	0	4
NHL totals			102	5	26	31	94	3	0	0	0	4

KEKALAINEN, JARMO
LW, SENATORS

PERSONAL: Born July 3, 1966, in Tampere, Finland. . . . 6-0/190. . . . Shoots right. . . . Name pronounced kee-kih-LAY-nehn.
COLLEGE: Clarkson (N.Y.).
TRANSACTIONS/CAREER NOTES: Signed as free agent by Boston Bruins (May 3, 1989). . . . Underwent surgery on abdominal muscle (February 1990). . . . Underwent surgery on abdominal muscles (October 15, 1990). . . . Signed as free agent by Ottawa Senators (August 13, 1993). . . . Injured groin (December 31, 1993); missed nine games. . . . Loaned by Senators to Rapperswil (February 24, 1994).
HONORS: Named to ECAC All-Star second team (1988-89).

Season	Team	League	REGULAR SEASON					PLAYOFFS				
			Gms.	G	A	Pts.	PIM	Gms.	G	A	Pts.	PIM
87-88—Clarkson		ECAC	32	7	11	18	38	—	—	—	—	—
88-89—Clarkson		ECAC	31	19	25	44	47	—	—	—	—	—
89-90—Boston		NHL	11	2	2	4	8	—	—	—	—	—
—Maine		AHL	18	5	11	16	6	—	—	—	—	—
90-91—Maine		AHL	11	2	4	6	4	1	0	1	1	0
—Boston		NHL	16	2	1	3	6	—	—	—	—	—
91-92—Kalpa		Finland	24	2	8	10	24	—	—	—	—	—
92-93—Tappara		Finland	47	15	12	27	34	—	—	—	—	—
93-94—Prince Edward Island		AHL	18	6	6	12	18	—	—	—	—	—
—Ottawa		NHL	28	1	5	6	14	—	—	—	—	—
—Rapperswil		Switz. Div. II	Played in playoffs; statistics unavailable.									
NHL totals			55	5	8	13	28					

KELLOGG, ROBERT
D, BLACKHAWKS

PERSONAL: Born February 16, 1971, in Springfield, Mass. . . . 6-4/210. . . . Shoots left. . . . Full name: Robert Edward Kellogg.
HIGH SCHOOL: Cathedral (Springfield, Mass.).
COLLEGE: Northeastern.
TRANSACTIONS/CAREER NOTES: Selected by Chicago Blackhawks in third round (third Blackhawks pick, 48th overall) of NHL entry draft (June 17, 1989). . . . Suffered from mononucleosis (November 1990); missed 30 games.

Season	Team	League	REGULAR SEASON					PLAYOFFS				
			Gms.	G	A	Pts.	PIM	Gms.	G	A	Pts.	PIM
87-88—Springfield Jr. B		NEJHL	38	8	36	44	54	—	—	—	—	—
88-89—Springfield Jr. B		NEJHL	...	13	34	47	...	—	—	—	—	—
89-90—Northeastern University		Hockey East	36	3	12	15	30	—	—	—	—	—
90-91—Northeastern University		Hockey East	2	0	0	0	6	—	—	—	—	—
91-92—Northeastern University		Hockey East	27	2	3	5	34	—	—	—	—	—

Season Team	League	REGULAR SEASON					PLAYOFFS				
		Gms.	G	A	Pts.	Pen.	Gms.	G	A	Pts.	Pen.
92-93—Northeastern University...	Hockey East	35	5	15	20	44	—	—	—	—	—
93-94—Indianapolis	IHL	68	6	13	19	63	—	—	—	—	—

KENNEDY, DEAN
D, JETS

PERSONAL: Born January 18, 1963, in Redvers, Sask.... 6-2/212.... Shoots right.... Full name: Edward Dean Kennedy.

TRANSACTIONS/CAREER NOTES: Selected by Los Angeles Kings as underage junior in second round (second Kings pick, 39th overall) of NHL entry draft (June 10, 1981).... Suspended four games by NHL for off-ice altercation (February 18, 1983).... Injured knee; missed part of 1981-82 season.... Suffered hip pointer (March 1987).... Broke finger (November 1987).... Injured groin (March 1988).... Suffered concussion (November 10, 1988).... Traded by Kings with D Denis Larocque to New York Rangers for LW Igor Liba, C Todd Elik, D Michael Boyce and future considerations (December 12, 1988).... Traded by Rangers to Los Angeles Kings for fifth-round pick in 1990 draft (February 3, 1989).... Traded by Kings to Buffalo Sabres for fourth-round pick in 1990 draft (October 4, 1989).... Suffered hip pointer (January 31, 1991); missed nine games.... Broke jaw (April 5, 1991).... Traded by Sabres with LW Darrin Shannon and D Mike Hartman to Winnipeg Jets for RW Dave McLlwain, D Gordon Donnelly, fifth-round pick in 1992 draft (LW Yuri Khmylev) and future considerations (October 11, 1991).... Injured knee (November 20, 1991).... Suffered back spasms (December 21, 1992); missed two games.

Season Team	League	REGULAR SEASON					PLAYOFFS				
		Gms.	G	A	Pts.	PIM	Gms.	G	A	Pts.	PIM
79-80—Weyburn	SJHL	57	12	20	32	64	—	—	—	—	—
—Brandon	WHL	1	0	0	0	0	—	—	—	—	—
80-81—Brandon	WHL	71	3	29	32	157	5	0	2	2	7
81-82—Brandon	WHL	49	5	38	43	103	—	—	—	—	—
82-83—Brandon	WHL	14	2	15	17	22	—	—	—	—	—
—Los Angeles	NHL	55	0	12	12	97	—	—	—	—	—
—Saskatoon	WHL	—	—	—	—	—	4	0	3	3	0
83-84—New Haven	AHL	26	1	7	8	23	—	—	—	—	—
—Los Angeles	NHL	37	1	5	6	50	—	—	—	—	—
84-85—New Haven	AHL	76	3	14	17	104	—	—	—	—	—
85-86—Los Angeles	NHL	78	2	10	12	132	—	—	—	—	—
86-87—Los Angeles	NHL	66	6	14	20	91	5	0	2	2	10
87-88—Los Angeles	NHL	58	1	11	12	158	4	0	1	1	10
88-89—New York Rangers	NHL	16	0	1	1	40	—	—	—	—	—
—Los Angeles	NHL	51	3	10	13	63	11	0	2	2	8
89-90—Buffalo	NHL	80	2	12	14	53	6	1	1	2	12
90-91—Buffalo	NHL	64	4	8	12	119	2	0	1	1	17
91-92—Winnipeg	NHL	18	2	4	6	21	2	0	0	0	0
92-93—Winnipeg	NHL	78	1	7	8	105	6	0	0	0	2
93-94—Winnipeg	NHL	76	2	8	10	164	—	—	—	—	—
NHL totals...............................		677	24	102	126	1093	36	1	7	8	59

KENNEDY, SHELDON
RW, JETS

PERSONAL: Born June 15, 1969, in Brandon, Man.... 5-11/180.... Shoots right.

TRANSACTIONS/CAREER NOTES: Broke ankle (January 18, 1987); missed six weeks. ... Selected by Detroit Red Wings in fourth round (fifth Red Wings pick, 80th overall) of NHL entry draft (June 11, 1988).... Separated shoulder (December 5, 1989).... Injured thumb (March 2, 1990).... Took leave of absence to attend alcohol treatment program (March 21, 1990). ... Injured left arm in automobile accident (summer 1990); missed 48 games.... Suffered from tonsillitis (February 8, 1991); missed two games.... Suffered from food poisoning (February 19, 1991).... Sent to alcohol treatment center for evaluation (March 27, 1991).... Bruised ribs (November 27, 1993); missed two games.... Injured sternum (March 22, 1994); missed five games.... Traded by Red Wings to Winnipeg Jets for third-round pick in 1995 draft (May 25, 1994).

HONORS: Named to Memorial Cup All-Star team (1988-89).

Season Team	League	REGULAR SEASON					PLAYOFFS				
		Gms.	G	A	Pts.	PIM	Gms.	G	A	Pts.	PIM
86-87—Swift Current	WHL	49	23	41	64	64	4	0	3	3	4
87-88—Swift Current	WHL	59	53	64	117	45	10	8	9	17	12
88-89—Swift Current	WHL	51	58	48	106	92	—	—	—	—	—
89-90—Detroit	NHL	20	2	7	9	10	—	—	—	—	—
—Adirondack	AHL	26	11	15	26	35	—	—	—	—	—
90-91—Adirondack	AHL	11	1	3	4	8	—	—	—	—	—
—Detroit	NHL	7	1	0	1	12	—	—	—	—	—
91-92—Adirondack	AHL	46	25	24	49	56	16	5	9	14	12
—Detroit	NHL	27	3	8	11	24	—	—	—	—	—
92-93—Detroit	NHL	68	19	11	30	46	7	1	1	2	2
93-94—Detroit	NHL	61	6	7	13	30	7	1	2	3	0
NHL totals...............................		183	31	33	64	122	14	2	3	5	2

KENNEY, JAY
D, SENATORS

PERSONAL: Born September 21, 1973, in New York.... 6-2/190.... Shoots left.

COLLEGE: Providence.

TRANSACTIONS/CAREER NOTES: Selected by Ottawa Senators in eighth round (eighth Senators pick, 169th overall) of NHL entry draft (June 20, 1992).

K

Season Team	League	REGULAR SEASON					PLAYOFFS				
		Gms.	G	A	Pts.	PIM	Gms.	G	A	Pts.	PIM
91-92—Canterbury School..........	Conn. H.S.	35	7	36	43	0	—	—	—	—	—
92-93—Providence College	Hockey East	24	1	8	9	10	—	—	—	—	—
93-94—Providence College	Hockey East	21	2	7	9	8	—	—	—	—	—

KERCH, ALEXANDER
LW, OILERS

PERSONAL: Born March 16, 1967, in Arkhangelsk, U.S.S.R. .... 5-10/190. .... Shoots right.... Name pronounced KUHRCH.
TRANSACTIONS/CAREER NOTES: Selected by Edmonton Oilers in third round (fifth Oilers pick, 60th overall) of NHL entry draft (June 26, 1993).

Season Team	League	REGULAR SEASON					PLAYOFFS				
		Gms.	G	A	Pts.	PIM	Gms.	G	A	Pts.	PIM
84-85—Dynamo Riga...................	USSR	8	0	0	0	6	—	—	—	—	—
85-86—Dynamo Riga...................	USSR	23	5	2	7	16	—	—	—	—	—
86-87—Dynamo Riga...................	USSR	26	5	4	9	10	—	—	—	—	—
87-88—Dynamo Riga...................	USSR	50	14	4	18	28	—	—	—	—	—
88-89—Dynamo Riga...................	USSR	39	6	7	13	41	—	—	—	—	—
89-90—Dynamo Riga...................	USSR	46	9	11	20	22	—	—	—	—	—
90-91—Dynamo Riga...................	USSR	46	16	17	33	46	—	—	—	—	—
91-92—Riga...............................	CIS	42	23	14	37	28	—	—	—	—	—
92-93—Pardaugava Riga.............	CIS	42	23	14	37	28	2	1	2	3	12
93-94—Cape Breton	AHL	57	24	38	62	16	4	1	1	2	2
—Edmonton........................	NHL	5	0	0	0	2	—	—	—	—	—
NHL totals..................................		**5**	**0**	**0**	**0**	**2**					

KERR, KEVIN
RW

PERSONAL: Born September 18, 1967, in North Bay, Ont.... 5-10/190.... Shoots right.
TRANSACTIONS/CAREER NOTES: Selected by Buffalo Sabres as underage junior in third round (fourth Sabres pick, 56th overall) of NHL entry draft (June 21, 1986).... Suspended two games by AHL for striking linesman with stick during fight (October 28, 1988).... Suspended remainder of season by AHL for biting (March 11, 1989).... Signed as free agent by Flint Generals (September 10, 1993).
HONORS: Won Col.HL Most Valuable Player Award (1993-94).... Named to Col.HL All-Star first team (1993-94).

Season Team	League	REGULAR SEASON					PLAYOFFS				
		Gms.	G	A	Pts.	PIM	Gms.	G	A	Pts.	PIM
84-85—Windsor........................	OHL	57	5	16	21	189	—	—	—	—	—
85-86—Windsor........................	OHL	59	21	51	72	*266	16	6	8	14	55
86-87—Windsor........................	OHL	63	27	41	68	*264	14	3	8	11	45
87-88—Rochester......................	AHL	72	18	11	29	352	5	1	3	4	42
88-89—Rochester......................	AHL	66	20	18	38	306	—	—	—	—	—
89-90—Rochester......................	AHL	8	0	1	1	22	—	—	—	—	—
—Fort Wayne	IHL	43	11	16	27	219	5	0	1	1	3
—Phoenix	IHL	6	0	0	0	25	—	—	—	—	—
90-91—Fort Wayne	IHL	13	1	6	7	32	—	—	—	—	—
—Cincinnati........................	ECHL	36	25	34	59	228	4	0	6	6	23
91-92—Cincinnati......................	ECHL	37	27	18	45	203	9	4	9	13	64
—Utica	AHL	19	3	3	6	25	—	—	—	—	—
92-93—Birmingham...................	ECHL	39	30	34	64	217	—	—	—	—	—
—Cincinnati........................	IHL	39	18	23	41	93	—	—	—	—	—
93-94—Flint	Col.HL	45	*57	55	112	299	7	7	6	13	79
—Phoenix	IHL	12	2	4	6	9	—	—	—	—	—
—Portland	AHL	4	2	0	2	2	8	0	3	3	21

KESA, DAN
RW, CANUCKS

PERSONAL: Born November 23, 1971, in Vancouver. .... 6-0/198. .... Shoots right. ... Name pronounced KEH-suh.
TRANSACTIONS/CAREER NOTES: Selected by Vancouver Canucks in fifth round (fifth Canucks pick, 95th overall) of NHL entry draft (June 22, 1991).

Season Team	League	REGULAR SEASON					PLAYOFFS				
		Gms.	G	A	Pts.	PIM	Gms.	G	A	Pts.	PIM
90-91—Prince Albert..................	WHL	69	30	23	53	116	3	1	1	2	0
91-92—Prince Albert..................	WHL	62	46	51	97	201	10	9	10	19	27
92-93—Hamilton.......................	AHL	62	16	24	40	76	—	—	—	—	—
93-94—Hamilton.......................	AHL	53	37	33	70	33	4	1	4	5	4
—Vancouver......................	NHL	19	2	4	6	18	—	—	—	—	—
NHL totals..................................		**19**	**2**	**4**	**6**	**18**					

KETTERER, MARKUS
G, SABRES

PERSONAL: Born August 23, 1967, in Helsinki, Finland. .... 5-11/169. .... Catches left.
TRANSACTIONS/CAREER NOTES: Selected by Buffalo Sabres in fifth round (sixth Sabres pick, 107th overall) of NHL entry draft (June 20, 1992).

Season Team	League	REGULAR SEASON							PLAYOFFS					
		Gms.	Min.	W	L	T	GA	SO	Avg.	Gms.	Min.	W	L	GA	SO	Avg.
87-88—Jokerit	Finland	21	...	...	...	...	61	0	...	—	—	...	...	—	—	—
88-89—TPS Turku.....................	Finland	34	2021	...	...	...	95	2	2.82	3	139	...	...	6	0	2.59

Season Team	League	Gms.	Min.	W	L	T	GA	SO	Avg.	Gms.	Min.	W	L	GA	SO	Avg.
89-90—TPS Turku	Finland	29	1709	...	...	...	68	1	2.39	7	422	...	...	15	1	2.13
90-91—TPS Turku	Finland	36	2022	...	...	...	85	2	2.52	8	440	...	...	13	2	1.77
91-92—Finland Olympic Team..	Int'l	3	180	...	...	...	8	0	2.67	—	—	—	—	—	—	—
—Jokerit	Finland	37	2128	...	...	...	97	0	2.73	—	—	—	—	—	—	—
92-93—Jokerit	Finland	37	2064	...	...	...	96	...	2.79	2	130	...	...	11	...	5.08
93-94—Rochester	AHL	32	1775	9	15	5	110	1	3.72	4	199	0	3	13	0	3.92

KHABIBULIN, NIKOLAI
G, JETS

PERSONAL: Born January 13, 1973, in Sverdlovsk, U.S.S.R. . . . 6-1/176. . . . Catches left.
TRANSACTIONS/CAREER NOTES: Selected by Winnipeg Jets in ninth round (eighth Jets pick, 204th overall) of NHL entry draft (June 20, 1992).

Season Team	League	Gms.	Min.	W	L	T	GA	SO	Avg.	Gms.	Min.	W	L	GA	SO	Avg.
88-89—Avtomobilist Sverdlovsk	USSR	1	3	0	0	0	0	0	0.00	—	—	—	—	—	—	—
89-90—Avtomo. Sverdlovsk Jr.	USSR						Statistics unavailable.									
90-91—Sputnik Nizhny Tagil	USSR Dv.III						Statistics unavailable.									
91-92—CSKA Moscow	CIS	2	34	...	...	...	2	...	3.53	—	—	—	—	—	—	—
92-93—CSKA Moscow	CIS	13	491	...	...	...	27	...	3.30	—	—	—	—	—	—	—
93-94—CSKA Moscow	CIS	46	2625	...	...	...	116	...	2.65	3	193	...	...	11	...	3.42
—Russian Penguins	IHL	12	639	2	7	‡2	47	0	4.41	—	—	—	—	—	—	—

KHARLAMOV, ALEXANDER
LW, CAPITALS

PERSONAL: Born September 23, 1975, in Moscow, U.S.S.R. . . . 5-10/180. . . . Shoots left. . . . Name pronounced HAR-la-moff. . . . Son of Valery Kharlamov, left winger, CSKA Moscow and Soviet national team (1968-81).
TRANSACTIONS/CAREER NOTES: Selected by Washington Capitals in first round (second Capitals pick, 15th overall) of NHL entry draft (June 28, 1994).

Season Team	League	Gms.	G	A	Pts.	PIM	Gms.	G	A	Pts.	PIM
92-93—CSKA Moscow	CIS	42	8	4	12	12	—	—	—	—	—
93-94—CSKA Moscow	CIS	46	7	7	14	26	3	1	0	1	2
—Russian Penguins	IHL	12	2	2	4	4	—	—	—	—	—

KHMYLEV, YURI
LW, SABRES

PERSONAL: Born August 9, 1964, in Moscow, U.S.S.R. . . . 6-1/189. . . . Shoots right. . . . Name pronounced HIHM-ih-lehf.
TRANSACTIONS/CAREER NOTES: Selected by Buffalo Sabres in fifth round (seventh Sabres pick, 108th overall) of NHL entry draft (June 20, 1992). . . . Strained right shoulder (November 2, 1992); missed two games. . . . Strained neck (September 19, 1993); missed six games. . . . Suffered left fibula hairline fracture (March 27, 1994); missed six games.
MISCELLANEOUS: Member of gold-medal-winning Unified Olympic team (1992).

Season Team	League	Gms.	G	A	Pts.	PIM	Gms.	G	A	Pts.	PIM
81-82—Soviet Wings	USSR	8	2	2	4	2	—	—	—	—	—
82-83—Soviet Wings	USSR	51	9	7	16	14	—	—	—	—	—
83-84—Soviet Wings	USSR	43	7	8	15	10	—	—	—	—	—
84-85—Soviet Wings	USSR	30	11	4	15	24	—	—	—	—	—
85-86—Soviet Wings	USSR	40	24	9	33	22	—	—	—	—	—
86-87—Soviet Wings	USSR	40	15	15	30	48	—	—	—	—	—
87-88—Soviet Wings	USSR	48	21	8	29	46	—	—	—	—	—
88-89—Soviet Wings	USSR	44	16	18	34	38	—	—	—	—	—
89-90—Soviet Wings	USSR	44	14	13	27	30	—	—	—	—	—
90-91—Soviet Wings	USSR	45	25	14	39	26	—	—	—	—	—
91-92—Soviet Wings	CIS	42	19	17	36	20	—	—	—	—	—
—Unified Olympic Team	Int'l	8	4	6	10	...	—	—	—	—	—
92-93—Buffalo	NHL	68	20	19	39	28	8	4	3	7	4
93-94—Buffalo	NHL	72	27	31	58	49	7	3	1	4	8
NHL totals		140	47	50	97	77	15	7	4	11	12

KHRISTICH, DIMITRI
LW, CAPITALS

PERSONAL: Born July 23, 1969, in Kiev, U.S.S.R. . . . 6-2/195. . . . Shoots right. . . . Name pronounced KRIH-stihch.
TRANSACTIONS/CAREER NOTES: Selected by Washington Capitals in sixth round (sixth Capitals pick, 120th overall) of NHL entry draft (June 11, 1988). . . . Injured hip (February 16, 1990); missed six games. . . . Broke foot (October 3, 1992); missed 20 games.

Season Team	League	Gms.	G	A	Pts.	PIM	Gms.	G	A	Pts.	PIM
88-89—Sokol Kiev	USSR	42	17	8	25	15	—	—	—	—	—
89-90—Sokol Kiev	USSR	47	14	22	36	32	—	—	—	—	—
90-91—Sokol Kiev	USSR	28	10	12	22	20	—	—	—	—	—
—Baltimore	AHL	3	0	0	0	0	—	—	—	—	—
—Washington	NHL	40	13	14	27	21	11	1	3	4	6
91-92—Washington	NHL	80	36	37	73	35	7	3	2	5	15

Season Team	League	REGULAR SEASON					PLAYOFFS				
		Gms.	G	A	Pts.	Pen.	Gms.	G	A	Pts.	Pen.
92-93—Washington	NHL	64	31	35	66	28	6	2	5	7	2
93-94—Washington	NHL	83	29	29	58	73	11	2	3	5	10
NHL totals		267	109	115	224	157	35	8	13	21	33

KIBERMANIS, CHRIS
D, JETS

PERSONAL: Born March 24, 1976, in Calgary.... 6-6/184.... Shoots right. **HIGH SCHOOL:** Lindsay Thurber (Red Deer, Alta.). **TRANSACTIONS/CAREER NOTES:** Selected by Winnipeg Jets in sixth round (seventh Jets pick, 146th overall) of NHL entry draft (June 29, 1994).

Season Team	League	REGULAR SEASON					PLAYOFFS				
		Gms.	G	A	Pts.	PIM	Gms.	G	A	Pts.	PIM
93-94—Red Deer	WHL	49	1	5	6	57	4	0	0	0	7

KIDD, TREVOR
G, FLAMES

PERSONAL: Born March 29, 1972, in St. Boniface, Man.... 6-2/190.... Catches left. **TRANSACTIONS/CAREER NOTES:** Broke finger (December 1987).... Selected by Calgary Flames in first round (first Flames pick, 11th overall) of NHL entry draft (June 16, 1990).... Traded by Brandon Wheat Kings with D Bart Cote to Spokane Chiefs for RW Bobby House, C Marty Murray and G Don Blishen (January 21, 1991).... Sprained left ankle (October 18, 1993); missed one game.
HONORS: Won Del Wilson Trophy (1989-90).... Named to WHL (West) All-Star first team (1989-90).
MISCELLANEOUS: Member of silver-medal-winning Canadian Olympic team (1992).

Season Team	League	REGULAR SEASON							PLAYOFFS						
		Gms.	Min.	W	L	T	GA	SO	Avg.	Gms.	Min.	W	L	GA	SO	Avg.
88-89—Brandon	WHL	32	1509	...	...	...	102	0	4.06	—	—	—	—	—	—	—
89-90—Brandon	WHL	*63	*3676	24	32	2	254	2	4.15	—	—	—	—	—	—	—
90-91—Brandon	WHL	30	1730	10	19	1	117	0	4.06	—	—	—	—	—	—	—
—Spokane	WHL	14	749	8	3	0	44	0	3.52	15	926	*14	1	32	*2	*2.07
91-92—Can. national team	Int'l	28	1349	18	4	4	79	2	3.51	—	—	—	—	—	—	—
—Can. Olympic Team	Int'l	1	60	1	0	0	0	1	0.00	—	—	—	—	—	—	—
—Calgary	NHL	2	120	1	1	0	8	0	4.00	—	—	—	—	—	—	—
92-93—Salt Lake City	IHL	30	1696	10	16	‡0	111	1	3.93	—	—	—	—	—	—	—
93-94—Calgary	NHL	31	1614	13	7	6	85	0	3.16	—	—	—	—	—	—	—
NHL totals		33	1734	14	8	6	93	0	3.22							

KIMBLE, DARIN
RW, BLACKHAWKS

PERSONAL: Born November 22, 1968, in Lucky Lake, Sask.... 6-2/205.... Shoots right. **TRANSACTIONS/CAREER NOTES:** Traded by Brandon Wheat Kings with Kerry Angus to Prince Albert Raiders for C Graham Garden, C Ryan Stewart and Kim Rasmussen (September 1986).... Selected by Quebec Nordiques in fourth round (fifth Nordiques pick, 66th overall) of NHL entry draft (June 11, 1988).... Suspended eight games by NHL for slashing (March 23, 1989); missed final four games of 1988-89 season and first four games of 1989-90.... Sprained right wrist (September 1989).... Bruised ribs (November 5, 1989).... Pulled abdominal muscle (December 1990).... Bruised right hand (January 24, 1991).... Traded by Nordiques to St. Louis Blues for RW Herb Raglan, D Tony Twist and LW Andy Rymsha (February 4, 1991).... Broke nose (February 1992). ... Traded by Blues with D Rob Robinson, G Pat Jablonski and RW Steve Tuttle to Tampa Bay Lightning for future considerations (June 19, 1992).... Traded by Lightning with future considerations to Boston Bruins for C Ken Hodge and D Matt Hervey (September 4, 1992).... Signed as free agent by Florida Panthers (July 14, 1993).... Traded by Panthers to Chicago Blackhawks for LW Evgeny Davydov (September 30, 1993).

Season Team	League	REGULAR SEASON					PLAYOFFS				
		Gms.	G	A	Pts.	PIM	Gms.	G	A	Pts.	PIM
84-85—Swift Current Jr. A	SAJHL	59	28	32	60	264	—	—	—	—	—
—Calgary	WHL	—	—	—	—	—	1	0	0	0	0
85-86—Calgary	WHL	37	14	8	22	93	—	—	—	—	—
—New Westminster	WHL	11	1	1	2	22	—	—	—	—	—
—Brandon	WHL	15	1	6	7	39	—	—	—	—	—
86-87—Prince Albert	WHL	68	17	13	30	190	—	—	—	—	—
87-88—Prince Albert	WHL	67	35	36	71	307	10	3	2	5	4
88-89—Halifax	AHL	39	8	6	14	188	—	—	—	—	—
—Quebec	NHL	26	3	1	4	149	—	—	—	—	—
89-90—Quebec	NHL	44	5	5	10	185	—	—	—	—	—
—Halifax	AHL	18	6	6	12	37	6	1	1	2	61
90-91—Halifax	AHL	7	1	4	5	20	—	—	—	—	—
—Quebec	NHL	35	2	5	7	114	—	—	—	—	—
—St. Louis	NHL	26	1	1	2	128	13	0	0	0	38
91-92—St. Louis	NHL	46	1	3	4	166	5	0	0	0	7
92-93—Providence	AHL	12	1	4	5	34	—	—	—	—	—
—Boston	NHL	55	7	3	10	177	4	0	0	0	2
93-94—Chicago	NHL	65	4	2	6	133	1	0	0	0	5
NHL totals		297	23	20	43	1052	23	0	0	0	52

KING, DEREK
LW, ISLANDERS

PERSONAL: Born February 11, 1967, in Hamilton, Ont.... 6-1/210.... Shoots left. **TRANSACTIONS/CAREER NOTES:** Selected by New York Islanders as underage junior in first round (second Islanders pick, 13th overall) of NHL entry draft (June 15, 1985).... Sprained right knee (September 1985).... Fractured left wrist (December 12, 1987).... Separated shoulder (Novem-

Season Team	League	REGULAR SEASON					PLAYOFFS				
		Gms.	G	A	Pts.	PIM	Gms.	G	A	Pts.	PIM
83-84—Hamilton Jr. A.	OHA	37	10	14	24	142	—	—	—	—	—
84-85—Sault Ste. Marie	OHL	63	35	38	73	106	16	3	13	16	11
85-86—Sault Ste. Marie	OHL	25	12	17	29	33	—	—	—	—	—
—Oshawa	OHL	19	8	13	21	15	6	3	2	5	13
86-87—Oshawa	OHL	57	53	53	106	74	17	14	10	24	40
—New York Islanders	NHL	2	0	0	0	0	—	—	—	—	—
87-88—New York Islanders	NHL	55	12	24	36	30	5	0	2	2	2
—Springfield	AHL	10	7	6	13	6	—	—	—	—	—
88-89—Springfield	AHL	4	4	0	4	0	—	—	—	—	—
—New York Islanders	NHL	60	14	29	43	14	—	—	—	—	—
89-90—Springfield	AHL	21	11	12	23	33	—	—	—	—	—
—New York Islanders	NHL	46	13	27	40	20	4	0	0	0	4
90-91—New York Islanders	NHL	66	19	26	45	44	—	—	—	—	—
91-92—New York Islanders	NHL	80	40	38	78	46	—	—	—	—	—
92-93—New York Islanders	NHL	77	38	38	76	47	18	3	11	14	14
93-94—New York Islanders	NHL	78	30	40	70	59	4	0	1	1	0
NHL totals		464	166	222	388	260	31	3	14	17	20

KING, KRIS
LW, JETS

PERSONAL: Born February 18, 1966, in Bracebridge, Ont.... 5-11/210.... Shoots left.
TRANSACTIONS/CAREER NOTES: Selected by Washington Capitals as underage junior in fourth round (fourth Capitals pick, 80th overall) of NHL entry draft (June 9, 1984).... Signed as free agent by Detroit Red Wings (June 1987).... Traded by Red Wings to New York Rangers for LW Chris McRae and fifth-round pick (D Tony Burns) in 1990 draft (September 7, 1989).... Sprained knee (January 7, 1991); missed six games. ... Traded by Rangers with RW Tie Domi to Winnipeg Jets for C Ed Olczyk (December 28, 1992).

Season Team	League	REGULAR SEASON					PLAYOFFS				
		Gms.	G	A	Pts.	PIM	Gms.	G	A	Pts.	PIM
82-83—Gravenhurst	SOJHL	32	72	53	125	115	—	—	—	—	—
83-84—Peterborough	OHL	62	13	18	31	168	8	3	3	6	14
84-85—Peterborough	OHL	61	18	35	53	222	16	2	8	10	28
85-86—Peterborough	OHL	58	19	40	59	254	8	4	0	4	21
86-87—Peterborough	OHL	46	23	33	56	160	12	5	8	13	41
—Binghamton	AHL	7	0	0	0	18	—	—	—	—	—
87-88—Adirondack	AHL	78	21	32	53	337	10	4	4	8	53
—Detroit	NHL	3	1	0	1	2	—	—	—	—	—
88-89—Detroit	NHL	55	2	3	5	168	2	0	0	0	2
89-90—New York Rangers	NHL	68	6	7	13	286	10	0	1	1	38
90-91—New York Rangers	NHL	72	11	14	25	154	6	2	0	2	36
91-92—New York Rangers	NHL	79	10	9	19	224	13	4	1	5	14
92-93—New York Rangers	NHL	30	0	3	3	67	—	—	—	—	—
—Winnipeg	NHL	48	8	8	16	136	6	1	1	2	4
93-94—Winnipeg	NHL	83	4	8	12	205	—	—	—	—	—
NHL totals		438	42	52	94	1242	37	7	3	10	94

KING, STEVEN
RW, MIGHTY DUCKS

PERSONAL: Born July 22, 1969, in East Greenwich, R.I.... 6-0/195.... Shoots right.
COLLEGE: Brown.
TRANSACTIONS/CAREER NOTES: Selected by New York Rangers in NHL supplemental draft (June 21, 1991).... Selected by Mighty Ducks of Anaheim in NHL expansion draft (June 24, 1993). ... Sprained shoulder (January 1, 1994); missed six games.... Underwent reconstructive shoulder surgery (February 3, 1994); missed remainder of season.

Season Team	League	REGULAR SEASON					PLAYOFFS				
		Gms.	G	A	Pts.	PIM	Gms.	G	A	Pts.	PIM
87-88—Brown University	ECAC	24	10	5	15	30	—	—	—	—	—
88-89—Brown University	ECAC	26	8	5	13	73	—	—	—	—	—
89-90—Brown University	ECAC	27	19	8	27	53	—	—	—	—	—
90-91—Brown University	ECAC	27	19	15	34	76	—	—	—	—	—
91-92—Binghamton	AHL	66	27	15	42	56	10	2	0	2	14
92-93—Binghamton	AHL	53	35	33	68	100	14	7	9	16	26
—New York Rangers	NHL	24	7	5	12	16	—	—	—	—	—
93-94—Anaheim	NHL	36	8	3	11	44	—	—	—	—	—
NHL totals		60	15	8	23	60	—	—	—	—	—

KIPRUSOFF, MARKO
D, CANADIENS

PERSONAL: Born June 6, 1972, in Turku, Finland.... 6-0/194.... Shoots right.
TRANSACTIONS/CAREER NOTES: Selected by Montreal Canadiens in fourth round (fourth Canadiens pick, 70th overall) of NHL entry draft (June 29, 1994).
HONORS: Named to Finnish League All-Star team (1993-94).

Season Team	League	REGULAR SEASON Gms.	G	A	Pts.	PIM	PLAYOFFS Gms.	G	A	Pts.	PIM
90-91—TPS Turku	Finland	3	0	0	0	0	—	—	—	—	—
91-92—TPS Turku	Finland	23	0	2	2	0	—	—	—	—	—
—HPK Hameenlinna	Finland	3	0	0	0	0	—	—	—	—	—
92-93—TPS Turku	Finland	43	3	7	10	14	12	2	3	5	6
93-94—TPS Turku	Finland	48	5	19	24	8	11	0	6	6	4

KISIO, KELLY

C, FLAMES

PERSONAL: Born September 18, 1959, in Peace River, Alta. . . . 5-10/185. . . . Shoots right. . . . Name pronounced KIHZ-ee-oh.

HIGH SCHOOL: Lindsay Thurber (Red Deer, Alta.).

TRANSACTIONS/CAREER NOTES: Traded by Toledo Goaldiggers to Kalamazoo Wings for LW/C Jean Chouinard (February 1981). . . . Signed as free agent by Detroit Red Wings (February 1983). . . . Suspended five games by NHL for stick-swinging incident (February 1985). . . . Traded by Red Wings with RW Lane Lambert, D Jim Leavins and fifth-round pick in 1988 draft to New York Rangers for G Glen Hanlon, third-round picks in 1987 (C Dennis Holland) and 1988 (C Guy Dupuis) drafts (July 29, 1986). . . . Dislocated left shoulder (October 1986). . . . Underwent shoulder surgery (April 1987). . . . Bruised and twisted left knee (February 1988). . . . Fractured left hand (October 1988); missed five games. . . . Suffered back spasms (November 1988). . . . Bruised left thigh and suffered back spasms (November 9, 1989); missed 11 games. . . . Tore ligaments and suffered chip fracture of right ankle (October 6, 1990); missed 18 games. . . . Bruised thigh (December 7, 1990). . . . Injured groin (January 17, 1991). . . . Selected by Minnesota North Stars in NHL expansion draft (May 30, 1991). . . . Traded by North Stars to San Jose Sharks for RW Shane Churla (June 3, 1991). . . . Injured ankle (October 17, 1991); missed 18 games. . . . Strained abdominal muscle (February 4, 1992); missed two games. . . . Injured shoulder (March 19, 1992). . . . Suffered sore body (January 1993); missed one game. . . . Strained groin (February 22, 1993); missed four games. . . . Signed as free agent by Calgary Flames (August 18, 1993). . . . Fractured right kneecap (October 1, 1993); missed 18 games. . . . Fractured rib (January 2, 1994); missed 12 games. . . . Fractured cheekbone (March 11, 1994); missed three games.

HONORS: Named to AJHL All-Star first team (1977-78). . . . Played in NHL All-Star Game (1993).

Season Team	League	REGULAR SEASON Gms.	G	A	Pts.	PIM	PLAYOFFS Gms.	G	A	Pts.	PIM
76-77—Red Deer	AJHL	60	53	48	101	101	—	—	—	—	—
77-78—Red Deer	AJHL	58	74	68	142	66	—	—	—	—	—
78-79—Calgary	WHL	70	60	61	121	73	—	—	—	—	—
79-80—Calgary	WHL	71	65	73	138	64	—	—	—	—	—
80-81—Adirondack	AHL	41	10	14	24	43	—	—	—	—	—
—Kalamazoo	IHL	31	27	16	43	48	8	7	7	14	13
81-82—Dallas	CHL	78	*62	39	101	59	16	*12	†17	*29	38
82-83—Davos HC	Switzerland	...	49	38	87	...	—	—	—	—	—
—Detroit	NHL	15	4	3	7	0	—	—	—	—	—
83-84—Detroit	NHL	70	23	37	60	34	4	1	0	1	4
84-85—Detroit	NHL	75	20	41	61	56	3	0	2	2	2
85-86—Detroit	NHL	76	21	48	69	85	—	—	—	—	—
86-87—New York Rangers	NHL	70	24	40	64	73	4	0	1	1	2
87-88—New York Rangers	NHL	77	23	55	78	88	—	—	—	—	—
88-89—New York Rangers	NHL	70	26	36	62	91	4	0	0	0	9
89-90—New York Rangers	NHL	68	22	44	66	105	10	2	8	10	8
90-91—New York Rangers	NHL	51	15	20	35	58	—	—	—	—	—
91-92—San Jose	NHL	48	11	26	37	54	—	—	—	—	—
92-93—San Jose	NHL	78	26	52	78	90	—	—	—	—	—
93-94—Calgary	NHL	51	7	23	30	28	7	0	2	2	8
NHL totals		749	222	425	647	762	32	3	13	16	33

KLATT, TRENT

RW, STARS

PERSONAL: Born January 30, 1971, in Robbinsdale, Minn. . . . 6-1/205. . . . Shoots right. . . . Full name: Trent Thomas Klatt.

HIGH SCHOOL: Osseo (Minn.).

COLLEGE: Minnesota.

TRANSACTIONS/CAREER NOTES: Selected by Washington Capitals in fourth round (fifth Capitals pick, 82nd overall) of NHL entry draft (June 17, 1989). . . . Rights traded by Capitals with LW Steve Maltais to Minnesota North Stars for D Sean Chambers (June 21, 1991). . . . Injured finger (January 7, 1993); missed three games. . . . North Stars franchise moved from Minnesota to Dallas and renamed Stars for 1993-94 season. . . . Strained back (November 9, 1993); missed one game. . . . Sprained knee (November 11, 1993); missed two games. . . . Sprained knee (February 6, 1994); missed three games.

Season Team	League	REGULAR SEASON Gms.	G	A	Pts.	PIM	PLAYOFFS Gms.	G	A	Pts.	PIM
87-88—Ossea H.S.	Minn. H.S.	22	19	17	36	...	—	—	—	—	—
88-89—Ossea H.S.	Minn. H.S.	22	24	39	63	...	—	—	—	—	—
89-90—University of Minnesota	WCHA	38	22	14	36	16	—	—	—	—	—
90-91—University of Minnesota	WCHA	39	16	28	44	58	—	—	—	—	—
91-92—University of Minnesota	WCHA	44	30	36	66	78	—	—	—	—	—
—Minnesota	NHL	1	0	0	0	0	6	0	0	0	2
92-93—Kalamazoo	IHL	31	8	11	19	18	—	—	—	—	—
—Minnesota	NHL	47	4	19	23	38	—	—	—	—	—
93-94—Dallas	NHL	61	14	24	38	30	9	2	1	3	4
—Kalamazoo	IHL	6	3	2	5	4	—	—	—	—	—
NHL totals		109	18	43	61	68	15	2	1	3	6

K

KLEE, KEN
D, CAPITALS

PERSONAL: Born April 24, 1971, in Indianapolis. . . . 6-1/200. . . . Shoots right. . . . Full name: Kenneth William Klee.
HIGH SCHOOL: Rockhurst (Kansas City, Mo.).
COLLEGE: St. Michael's College (Vt.), then Bowling Green State.
TRANSACTIONS/CAREER NOTES: Selected by Washington Capitals in ninth round (11th Capitals pick, 177th overall) of NHL entry draft (June 16, 1990).

			REGULAR SEASON					PLAYOFFS			
Season Team	League	Gms.	G	A	Pts.	PIM	Gms.	G	A	Pts.	PIM
89-90—Bowling Green State	CCHA	39	0	5	5	52	—	—	—	—	—
90-91—Bowling Green State	CCHA	37	7	28	35	50	—	—	—	—	—
91-92—Bowling Green State	CCHA	10	0	1	1	14	—	—	—	—	—
92-93—Baltimore........................	AHL	77	4	14	18	68	7	0	1	1	15
93-94—Portland	AHL	65	2	9	11	87	17	1	2	3	14

KLEMM, JON
D, NORDIQUES

PERSONAL: Born January 6, 1970, in Cranbrook, B.C. . . . 6-3/200. . . . Shoots right. . . . Full name: Jonathan Darryl Klemm.
TRANSACTIONS/CAREER NOTES: Signed as free agent by Quebec Nordiques (May 1991).
HONORS: Named to WHL (West) All-Star second team (1990-91).

			REGULAR SEASON					PLAYOFFS			
Season Team	League	Gms.	G	A	Pts.	PIM	Gms.	G	A	Pts.	PIM
87-88—Seattle	WHL	68	6	7	13	24	—	—	—	—	—
88-89—Seattle	WHL	2	1	1	2	0	—	—	—	—	—
—Spokane	WHL	66	6	34	40	42	—	—	—	—	—
89-90—Spokane	WHL	66	3	28	31	100	6	1	1	2	5
90-91—Spokane	WHL	72	7	58	65	65	15	3	6	9	8
91-92—Halifax	AHL	70	6	13	19	40	—	—	—	—	—
—Quebec	NHL	4	0	1	1	0	—	—	—	—	—
92-93—Halifax	AHL	80	3	20	23	32	—	—	—	—	—
93-94—Cornwall	AHL	66	4	26	30	78	13	1	2	3	6
—Quebec	NHL	7	0	0	0	4	—	—	—	—	—
NHL totals............................		11	0	1	1	4					

KLEVAKIN, DMITRI
RW, LIGHTNING

PERSONAL: Born February 20, 1976, in Angarsk, U.S.S.R. . . . 5-11/163. . . . Shoots left.
TRANSACTIONS/CAREER NOTES: Selected by Tampa Bay Lightning in fourth round (fourth Lightning pick, 86th overall) of NHL entry draft (June 29, 1994).

			REGULAR SEASON					PLAYOFFS			
Season Team	League	Gms.	G	A	Pts.	PIM	Gms.	G	A	Pts.	PIM
92-93—Spartak Moscow	CIS	8	1	1	2	0	—	—	—	—	—
93-94—Spartak Moscow	CIS	42	6	3	9	6	4	1	0	1	0

KLIMA, PETR
LW/RW, LIGHTNING

PERSONAL: Born December 23, 1964, in Chaomutov, Czechoslovakia. . . . 6-0/190. . . . Shoots right. . . . Name pronounced KLEE-muh.
TRANSACTIONS/CAREER NOTES: Selected by Detroit Red Wings in fifth round (fifth Red Wings pick, 88th overall) of NHL entry draft (June 8, 1983). . . . Broke right thumb (May 1988). . . . Sprained right ankle (November 12, 1988). . . . Pulled groin (December 1988). . . . Injured back (February 1989). . . . Traded by Red Wings with C/RW Joe Murphy, C/LW Adam Graves and D Jeff Sharples to Edmonton Oilers for C Jimmy Carson, C Kevin McClelland and fifth-round pick (traded to Montreal Canadiens who selected D Brad Layzell) in 1991 draft (November 2, 1989). . . . Suspended four games by NHL for butt-ending player (October 25, 1990). . . . Pulled groin (March 15, 1991). . . . Scratched cornea in right eye (November 18, 1991); missed one game. . . . Strained groin (February 2, 1992); missed six games. . . . Strained left knee ligaments (October 14, 1992); missed six games. . . . Strained groin (January 7, 1993); missed eight games. . . . Traded by Oilers to Tampa Bay Lightning for future considerations (June 16, 1993). . . . Slightly separated shoulder (February 27, 1994); missed eight games.
MISCELLANEOUS: Member of Stanley Cup championship team (1990).

			REGULAR SEASON					PLAYOFFS			
Season Team	League	Gms.	G	A	Pts.	PIM	Gms.	G	A	Pts.	PIM
82-83—Czech. national team	Int'l	44	19	17	36	74	—	—	—	—	—
83-84—Dukla Jihlava	Czech.	41	20	16	36	46	—	—	—	—	—
—Czech. national team	Int'l	7	6	5	11	. . .	—	—	—	—	—
84-85—Dukla Jihlava	Czech.	35	23	22	45	. . .	—	—	—	—	—
85-86—Detroit	NHL	74	32	24	56	16	—	—	—	—	—
86-87—Detroit	NHL	77	30	23	53	42	13	1	2	3	4
87-88—Detroit	NHL	78	37	25	62	46	12	10	8	18	10
88-89—Adirondack	AHL	5	5	1	6	4	—	—	—	—	—
—Detroit	NHL	51	25	16	41	44	6	2	4	6	19
89-90—Detroit	NHL	13	5	5	10	6	—	—	—	—	—
—Edmonton	NHL	63	25	28	53	66	21	5	0	5	8
90-91—Edmonton	NHL	70	40	28	68	113	18	7	6	13	16
91-92—Edmonton	NHL	57	21	13	34	52	15	1	4	5	8
92-93—Edmonton	NHL	68	32	16	48	100	—	—	—	—	—
93-94—Tampa Bay	NHL	75	28	27	55	76	—	—	—	—	—
NHL totals............................		626	275	205	480	561	85	26	24	50	65

KLIMENTIEV, SERGEI

D, SABRES

PERSONAL: Born April 5, 1975, in Kiev, U.S.S.R. . . . 5-11/200. . . . Shoots left.
TRANSACTIONS/CAREER NOTES: Selected by Buffalo Sabres in fifth round (fourth Sabres pick, 121st overall) of NHL entry draft (June 29, 1994).

Season Team	League	REGULAR SEASON					PLAYOFFS				
		Gms.	G	A	Pts.	PIM	Gms.	G	A	Pts.	PIM
91-92—SVSM Kiev	CIS Div. III	42	4	15	19	...	—	—	—	—	—
92-93—Sokol-Eskulap Kiev	CIS	3	0	0	0	4	1	0	0	0	0
93-94—Medicine Hat	WHL	72	16	26	42	165	3	0	0	0	4

KLIMENTIEV, SERGEI

D, SABRES

PERSONAL: Born April 5, 1975, in Kiev, U.S.S.R. . . . 5-11/200. . . . Shoots left.
TRANSACTIONS/CAREER NOTES: Selected by Buffalo Sabres in fifth round (fourth Sabres pick, 121st overall) of NHL entry draft (June 29, 1994).

Season Team	League	REGULAR SEASON					PLAYOFFS				
		Gms.	G	A	Pts.	PIM	Gms.	G	A	Pts.	PIM
91-92—SVSM Kiev	CIS Div. III	42	4	15	19	...	—	—	—	—	—
92-93—Sokol-Eskulap Kiev	CIS	3	0	0	0	4	1	0	0	0	0
93-94—Medicine Hat	WHL	72	16	26	42	165	3	0	0	0	4

KNICKLE, RICK

G, KINGS

PERSONAL: Born February 26, 1960, in Chatham, N.B. . . . 5-10/175. . . . Catches left.
TRANSACTIONS/CAREER NOTES: Selected by Buffalo Sabres as underage junior in sixth round (seventh Buffalo pick, 116th overall) of NHL entry draft (August 9, 1979). . . . Sprained thumb (February 1981). . . . Signed as free agent by Montreal Canadiens (February 8, 1985). . . . Signed as free agent by Springfield Indians (1991). . . . Signed as free agent by Los Angeles Kings (February 15, 1993). . . . Suspended indefinitely by Phoenix Roadrunners for failing to report on temporary assignment to Fort Wayne Komets (January 25, 1994).
HONORS: Won Top Goaltender Trophy (1978-79). . . . Named to WHL All-Star first team (1978-79). . . . Named to EHL All-Star first team (1980-81). . . . Named to IHL All-Star second team (1983-84 and 1991-92). . . . Won James Norris Memorial Trophy (1988-89). . . . Named to IHL All-Star first team (1988-89). . . . Shared James Norris Memorial Trophy with Clint Malarchuk (1992-93). . . . Named to IHL All-Star first team (1992-93).

Season Team	League	REGULAR SEASON								PLAYOFFS						
		Gms.	Min.	W	L	T	GA	SO	Avg.	Gms.	Min.	W	L	GA	SO	Avg.
77-78—Brandon	WCHL	49	2806	34	5	7	182	0	3.89	8	450	..	..	36	0	4.80
78-79—Brandon	WHL	38	2240	26	3	8	118	1	*3.16	16	886	12	3	41	*1	*2.78
79-80—Brandon	WHL	33	1604	11	14	1	125	0	4.68	—	—	—	—	—	—	—
—Muskegon	IHL	16	829	..	..	..	51	0	3.69	3	156	..	..	17	0	6.54
80-81—Erie	AHL	43	2347	..	..	..	125	1	*3.20	*8	*446	..	..	14	0	*1.88
81-82—Rochester	AHL	31	1753	10	12	5	108	1	3.70	3	125	0	2	7	0	3.36
82-83—Flint	IHL	27	1638	..	..	..	92	†2	3.37	3	193	..	..	10	0	3.11
—Rochester	AHL	4	143	..	..	..	11	0	4.62	—	—	—	—	—	—	—
83-84—Flint	IHL	60	3518	32	21	‡5	203	3	3.46	8	480	8	0	24	0	*3.00
84-85—Sherbrooke	AHL	14	780	7	6	0	53	0	4.08	—	—	—	—	—	—	—
—Flint	IHL	36	2018	18	11	‡3	115	2	3.42	7	401	3	4	27	0	4.04
85-86—Saginaw	IHL	39	2235	16	15	‡0	135	2	3.62	3	193	2	1	12	0	3.73
86-87—Saginaw	IHL	26	1413	9	13	‡0	113	0	4.80	5	329	1	4	21	0	3.83
87-88—Flint	IHL	1	60	0	1	‡0	4	0	4.00	—	—	—	—	—	—	—
—Peoria	IHL	13	705	2	8	‡1	58	0	4.94	6	294	3	3	20	0	4.08
88-89—Fort Wayne	IHL	47	2719	22	16	‡0	141	1	3.11	4	173	1	2	15	0	5.20
89-90—Flint	IHL	55	2998	25	24	‡1	210	1	4.20	2	101	0	2	13	0	7.72
90-91—Springfield	AHL	9	509	6	0	2	28	0	3.30	—	—	—	—	—	—	—
91-92—San Diego	IHL	46	2686	*28	13	‡4	155	0	3.46	2	78	0	1	3	0	2.31
92-93—San Diego	IHL	41	2437	33	4	‡0	88	*4	*2.17	—	—	—	—	—	—	—
—Los Angeles	NHL	10	532	6	4	0	35	0	3.95	—	—	—	—	—	—	—
93-94—Los Angeles	NHL	4	174	1	2	0	9	0	3.10	—	—	—	—	—	—	—
—Phoenix	IHL	25	1292	8	9	‡3	89	1	4.13	—	—	—	—	—	—	—
NHL totals		14	706	7	6	0	44	0	3.74							

KNIPSCHEER, FRED

C, BRUINS

PERSONAL: Born September 3, 1969, in Fort Wayne, Ind. . . . 5-11/185. . . . Shoots left. . . . Name pronounced kuh-NIHP-sheer.
COLLEGE: St. Cloud (Minn.) State.
TRANSACTIONS/CAREER NOTES: Signed as free agent by Boston Bruins (April 30, 1993).

Season Team	League	REGULAR SEASON					PLAYOFFS				
		Gms.	G	A	Pts.	PIM	Gms.	G	A	Pts.	PIM
90-91—St. Cloud State	WCHA	40	9	10	19	57	—	—	—	—	—
91-92—St. Cloud State	WCHA	33	15	17	32	48	—	—	—	—	—
92-93—St. Cloud State	WCHA	36	34	26	60	68	—	—	—	—	—
93-94—Boston	NHL	11	3	2	5	14	12	2	1	3	6
—Providence	AHL	62	26	13	39	50	—	—	—	—	—
NHL totals		11	3	2	5	14	12	2	1	3	6

KNUBLE, MICHAEL

RW, RED WINGS

PERSONAL: Born July 4, 1972, in Toronto.... 6-3/200.... Shoots right.
HIGH SCHOOL: East Kentwood (Mich.).
COLLEGE: Michigan.
TRANSACTIONS/CAREER NOTES: Selected by Detroit Red Wings in fourth round (fourth Red Wings pick, 76th overall) of NHL entry draft (June 22, 1991).
HONORS: Named to CCHA All-Star first team (1993-94).

			REGULAR SEASON					PLAYOFFS				
Season Team	League	Gms.	G	A	Pts.	PIM	Gms.	G	A	Pts.	PIM
88-89—East Kentwood H.S.	Mich. H.S.	28	52	37	89	60	—	—	—	—	—
89-90—East Kentwood H.S.	Mich. H.S.	29	63	40	103	40	—	—	—	—	—
90-91—Kalamazoo	NAJHL	36	18	24	42	30	—	—	—	—	—
91-92—University of Michigan	CCHA	43	7	8	15	48	—	—	—	—	—
92-93—University of Michigan	CCHA	39	26	16	42	57	—	—	—	—	—
93-94—University of Michigan	CCHA	41	32	26	58	71	—	—	—	—	—

KOCHAN, DIETER

G, CANUCKS

PERSONAL: Born November 5, 1974, in Saskatoon, Sask.... 6-1/165.... Catches left.
TRANSACTIONS/CAREER NOTES: Selected by Vancouver Canucks in fourth round (third Canucks pick, 98th overall) of NHL entry draft (June 26, 1993).

			REGULAR SEASON							PLAYOFFS						
Season Team	League	Gms.	Min.	W	L	T	GA	SO	Avg.	Gms.	Min.	W	L	GA	SO	Avg.
91-92—Sioux City	USHL	23	1131	7	10	0	100	...	5.31	—	—	—	—	—	—	—
92-93—Kelowna	BCJHL	44	2582	34	8	0	137	1	*3.18	—	—	—	—	—	—	—
93-94—N. Michigan U.	WCHA	16	984	9	7	0	57	0	3.48	—	—	—	—	—	—	—

KOCUR, JOEY

RW, RANGERS

PERSONAL: Born December 21, 1964, in Calgary.... 6-0/205.... Shoots right.... Name pronounced KOH-suhr.... Cousin of Kory Kocur, right winger in Detroit Red Wings system.
TRANSACTIONS/CAREER NOTES: Stretched knee ligaments (December 1981).... Selected by Detroit Red Wings as underage junior in fifth round (sixth Red Wings pick, 88th overall) of NHL entry draft (June 8, 1983).... Lacerated right hand (January 1985).... Sprained thumb (December 11, 1985).... Strained ligaments (March 26, 1986).... Suffered sore right elbow (October 1987).... Strained sternum and collarbone (November 1987).... Injured shoulder (December 1987).... Separated shoulder (May 1988).... Injured knee (November 1988).... Injured back (February 1989).... Bruised right foot (February 16, 1990).... Strained right knee ligaments (March 1990).... Injured right hand and arm (December 1, 1990); missed three weeks.... Traded by Red Wings with D Per Djoos to New York Rangers for C Kevin Miller, D Dennis Vial and RW Jim Cummins (March 5, 1991).... Suspended four games by NHL for high-sticking (March 10, 1991).... Suspended additional four games by NHL for high-sticking during appeal of March 10 incident (March 14, 1991); missed final seven games of 1990-91 season and first game of 1991-92 season.... Underwent surgery to middle knuckle of right hand (May 10, 1991).... Injured hip flexor (October 1991); missed first five games of season.... Separated shoulder (January 28, 1992); missed 13 games.... Slightly sprained right knee (March 5, 1992); missed six games.... Sprained leg (November 21, 1992); missed one game.... Injured back (February 10, 1993); missed two games.... Injured back (February 20, 1993); missed two games.... Pulled groin (April 9, 1993); missed three games.... Bruised hand (January 28, 1994); missed three games.... Reinjured hand (February 9, 1994); missed four games.... Suffered back spasms (April 4, 1994); missed two games.
MISCELLANEOUS: Member of Stanley Cup championship team (1994).

			REGULAR SEASON					PLAYOFFS				
Season Team	League	Gms.	G	A	Pts.	PIM	Gms.	G	A	Pts.	PIM
80-81—Yorkton	SJHL	48	6	9	15	307	—	—	—	—	—
81-82—Yorkton	SJHL	47	20	21	41	199	—	—	—	—	—
82-83—Saskatoon	WHL	62	23	17	40	289	6	2	3	5	25
83-84—Saskatoon	WHL	69	40	41	81	258	—	—	—	—	—
84-85—Detroit	NHL	17	1	0	1	64	3	1	0	1	5
—Adirondack	AHL	47	12	7	19	171	—	—	—	—	—
85-86—Adirondack	AHL	9	6	2	8	34	—	—	—	—	—
—Detroit	NHL	59	9	6	15	*377	—	—	—	—	—
86-87—Detroit	NHL	77	9	9	18	276	16	2	3	5	71
87-88—Detroit	NHL	64	7	7	14	263	10	0	1	1	13
88-89—Detroit	NHL	60	9	9	18	213	3	0	1	1	6
89-90—Detroit	NHL	71	16	20	36	268	—	—	—	—	—
90-91—Detroit	NHL	52	5	4	9	253	—	—	—	—	—
—New York Rangers	NHL	5	0	0	0	36	6	0	2	2	21
91-92—New York Rangers	NHL	51	7	4	11	121	12	1	1	2	38
92-93—New York Rangers	NHL	65	3	6	9	131	—	—	—	—	—
93-94—New York Rangers	NHL	71	2	1	3	129	20	1	1	2	17
NHL totals................................		592	68	66	134	2131	70	5	9	14	171

KOIVU, SAKU

C, CANADIENS

PERSONAL: Born November 23, 1974, in Turku, Finland.... 5-9/163.... Shoots left.
TRANSACTIONS/CAREER NOTES: Selected by Montreal Canadiens in first round (first Canadiens pick, 21st overall) of NHL entry draft (June 26, 1993).
MISCELLANEOUS: Member of bronze-medal-winning Finnish Olympic team (1994).

			REGULAR SEASON					PLAYOFFS				
Season Team	League	Gms.	G	A	Pts.	PIM	Gms.	G	A	Pts.	PIM
91-92—TPS Jr..............................	Finland	42	30	37	67	63	—	—	—	—	—
92-93—TPS.................................	Finland	46	3	7	10	28	—	—	—	—	—
93-94—TPS Turku	Finland	47	23	30	53	42	11	4	8	12	16
—Finland Olympic Team......	Int'l	8	4	3	7	12	—	—	—	—	—

KOLSTAD, DEAN
D, RANGERS

PERSONAL: Born June 16, 1968, in Edmonton.... 6-6/228.... Shoots left.
TRANSACTIONS/CAREER NOTES: Selected by Minnesota North Stars as underage junior in second round (third North Stars pick, 33rd overall) of NHL entry draft (June 21, 1986). ... Selected by San Jose Sharks in NHL dispersal draft (May 30, 1991).... Signed as free agent by New York Rangers (September 1, 1993).
HONORS: Named to WHL All-Star first team (1986-87).... Named to IHL All-Star second team (1989-90).

Season Team	League	REGULAR SEASON Gms.	G	A	Pts.	PIM	PLAYOFFS Gms.	G	A	Pts.	PIM
84-85—Langley Eagles	BCJHL	25	3	11	14	61	—	—	—	—	—
—New Westminster	WHL	13	0	0	0	16	—	—	—	—	—
85-86—New Westminster	WHL	16	0	5	5	19	—	—	—	—	—
—Prince Albert	WHL	54	2	15	17	80	20	5	3	8	26
86-87—Prince Albert	WHL	72	17	37	54	112	8	1	5	6	8
87-88—Prince Albert	WHL	72	14	37	51	121	10	0	9	9	20
88-89—Minnesota	NHL	25	1	5	6	42	—	—	—	—	—
—Kalamazoo	IHL	51	10	23	33	91	6	1	0	1	23
89-90—Kalamazoo	IHL	77	10	40	50	172	10	3	4	7	14
90-91—Minnesota	NHL	5	0	0	0	15	—	—	—	—	—
—Kalamazoo	IHL	33	4	8	12	50	9	1	6	7	4
91-92—Kansas City	IHL	74	9	20	29	83	15	3	6	9	8
92-93—Kansas City	IHL	63	9	21	30	79	3	0	0	0	2
—San Jose	NHL	10	0	2	2	12	—	—	—	—	—
93-94—Binghamton	AHL	68	7	26	33	92	—	—	—	—	—
NHL totals		**40**	**1**	**7**	**8**	**69**					

KOLZIG, OLAF
G, CAPITALS

PERSONAL: Born April 6, 1970, in Johannesburg, South Africa.... 6-3/205.... Catches left.... Name pronounced OH-lahf KOHLT-zihg.
TRANSACTIONS/CAREER NOTES: Underwent surgery to right knee (November 1988).... Selected by Washington Capitals in first round (first Capitals pick, 19th overall) of NHL entry draft (June 17, 1989).... Loaned to Rochester Americans (October 2, 1992).... Dislocated kneecap (October 13, 1993); missed 14 games.
HONORS: Shared Harry (Hap) Holmes Memorial Trophy with Byron Dafoe (1993-94).... Won Jack Butterfield Trophy (1993-94).

Season Team	League	REGULAR SEASON Gms.	Min.	W	L	T	GA	SO	Avg.	PLAYOFFS Gms.	Min.	W	L	GA	SO	Avg.
87-88—New Westminster	WHL	15	650	6	5	0	48	1	4.43	—	—	—	—	—	—	—
88-89—Tri-City	WHL	30	1671	16	10	2	97	1	*3.48	—	—	—	—	—	—	—
89-90—Washington	NHL	2	120	0	2	0	12	0	6.00	—	—	—	—	—	—	—
—Tri-City	WHL	48	2504	27	27	3	187	1	4.48	6	318	4	0	27	0	5.09
90-91—Baltimore	AHL	26	1367	10	12	1	72	0	3.16	—	—	—	—	—	—	—
—Hampton Roads	ECHL	21	1248	11	9	†1	71	2	3.41	3	180	1	2	14	0	4.67
91-92—Baltimore	AHL	28	1503	5	17	2	105	1	4.19	—	—	—	—	—	—	—
—Hampton Roads	ECHL	14	847	11	3	‡0	41	0	2.90	—	—	—	—	—	—	—
92-93—Rochester	AHL	49	2737	25	16	4	168	0	3.68	17	*1040	9	*8	61	0	3.52
—Washington	NHL	1	20	0	0	0	2	0	6.00	—	—	—	—	—	—	—
93-94—Portland	AHL	29	1726	16	8	5	88	3	3.06	17	1035	†12	5	44	0	*2.55
—Washington	NHL	7	224	0	3	0	20	0	5.36	—	—	—	—	—	—	—
NHL totals		**10**	**364**	**0**	**5**	**0**	**34**	**0**	**5.60**							

KONOWALCHUK, STEVE
C, CAPITALS

PERSONAL: Born November 11, 1972, in Salt Lake City.... 6-0/180.... Shoots left.... Full name: Steven Reed Konowalchuk.... Name pronounced kahn-uh-WAHL-chuhk.
TRANSACTIONS/CAREER NOTES: Selected by Washington Capitals in third round (fifth Capitals pick, 58th overall) of NHL entry draft (June 22, 1991).
HONORS: Won Four Broncos Memorial Trophy (1991-92).... Named to Can.HL All-Star second team (1991-92).... Named to WHL (West) All-Star first team (1991-92).

Season Team	League	REGULAR SEASON Gms.	G	A	Pts.	PIM	PLAYOFFS Gms.	G	A	Pts.	PIM
90-91—Portland	WHL	72	43	49	92	78	—	—	—	—	—
91-92—Portland	WHL	64	51	53	104	95	6	3	6	9	12
—Baltimore	AHL	3	1	1	2	0	—	—	—	—	—
—Washington	NHL	1	0	0	0	0	—	—	—	—	—
92-93—Baltimore	AHL	37	18	28	46	74	—	—	—	—	—
—Washington	NHL	36	4	7	11	16	2	0	1	1	0
93-94—Portland	AHL	8	11	4	15	4	—	—	—	—	—
—Washington	NHL	62	12	14	26	33	11	0	1	1	10
NHL totals		**99**	**16**	**21**	**37**	**49**	**13**	**0**	**2**	**2**	**10**

KONROYD, STEVE
D, SENATORS

PERSONAL: Born February 10, 1961, in Scarborough, Ont.... 6-1/195.... Shoots left.... Full name: Stephen Mark Konroyd.
TRANSACTIONS/CAREER NOTES: Selected by Calgary Flames as underage junior in second round (fourth Flames pick, 39th overall) of NHL entry draft (June 11, 1980).... Dislo-

cated elbow (December 1984).... Pulled chest muscle (February 1986).... Traded by Flames with LW Richard Kromm to New York Islanders for LW/C John Tonelli (March 1986).... Bruised collarbone (December 1986).... Suspended four games by NHL for stick-swinging incident (January 1988).... Traded by Islanders with C Bob Bassen to Chicago Blackhawks for D Gary Nylund and D Marc Bergevin (November 25, 1988).... Bruised thigh (January 1990).... Suffered back spasms (February 10, 1991).... Broke knuckle on little finger of right hand (March 10, 1991); missed 18 days.... Traded by Blackhawks to Hartford Whalers for RW Rob Brown (January 24, 1992).... Traded by Whalers to Detroit Red Wings for sixth-round pick (traded back to Red Wings who selected RW Tim Spitzig) in 1993 draft (March 22, 1993).... Traded by Red Wings to Ottawa Senators for G Daniel Berthiaume (March 21, 1994).... Suffered back spasms (March 31, 1994); missed three games.
HONORS: Won Bobby Smith Trophy (1979-80).... Named to OMJHL All-Star second team (1980-81).

Season Team	League	REGULAR SEASON					PLAYOFFS				
		Gms.	G	A	Pts.	PIM	Gms.	G	A	Pts.	PIM
78-79—Oshawa	OMJHL	65	4	19	23	63	—	—	—	—	—
79-80—Oshawa	OMJHL	62	11	23	34	133	7	0	2	2	14
80-81—Calgary	NHL	4	0	0	0	4	—	—	—	—	—
—Oshawa	OMJHL	59	19	49	68	232	11	3	11	14	35
81-82—Oklahoma City	CHL	14	2	3	5	15	—	—	—	—	—
—Calgary	NHL	63	3	14	17	78	3	0	0	0	12
82-83—Calgary	NHL	79	4	13	17	73	9	2	1	3	18
83-84—Calgary	NHL	80	1	13	14	94	8	1	2	3	8
84-85—Calgary	NHL	64	3	23	26	73	4	1	4	5	2
85-86—Calgary	NHL	59	7	20	27	64	—	—	—	—	—
—New York Islanders	NHL	14	0	5	5	16	3	0	0	0	6
86-87—New York Islanders	NHL	72	5	16	21	70	14	1	4	5	10
87-88—New York Islanders	NHL	62	2	15	17	99	6	1	0	1	4
88-89—New York Islanders	NHL	21	1	5	6	2	—	—	—	—	—
—Chicago	NHL	57	5	7	12	40	16	2	0	2	10
89-90—Chicago	NHL	75	3	14	17	34	20	1	3	4	19
90-91—Chicago	NHL	70	0	12	12	40	6	1	0	1	8
91-92—Chicago	NHL	49	2	14	16	65	—	—	—	—	—
—Hartford	NHL	33	2	10	12	32	7	0	1	1	2
92-93—Hartford	NHL	59	3	11	14	63	—	—	—	—	—
—Detroit	NHL	6	0	1	1	4	1	0	0	0	0
93-94—Detroit	NHL	19	0	0	0	10	—	—	—	—	—
—Ottawa	NHL	8	0	2	2	2	—	—	—	—	—
NHL totals		894	41	195	236	863	97	10	15	25	99

KONSTANTINOV, VLADIMIR
D, RED WINGS

PERSONAL: Born March 19, 1967, in Murmansk, U.S.S.R.... 5-11/176. ... Shoots right. ... Name pronounced KAHN-stan-TEE-nahf.
TRANSACTIONS/CAREER NOTES: Selected by Detroit Red Wings in 11th round (12th Red Wings pick, 221st overall) of NHL entry draft (June 17, 1989).... Injured groin (December 3, 1992); missed two games.... Sprained knee (October 27, 1993); missed four games.
HONORS: Named to NHL All-Rookie team (1991-92).

Season Team	League	REGULAR SEASON					PLAYOFFS				
		Gms.	G	A	Pts.	PIM	Gms.	G	A	Pts.	PIM
84-85—CSKA Moscow	USSR	40	1	4	5	10	—	—	—	—	—
85-86—CSKA Moscow	USSR	26	4	3	7	12	—	—	—	—	—
86-87—CSKA Moscow	USSR	35	2	2	4	19	—	—	—	—	—
87-88—CSKA Moscow	USSR	50	3	6	9	32	—	—	—	—	—
88-89—CSKA Moscow	USSR	37	7	8	15	20	—	—	—	—	—
89-90—CSKA Moscow	USSR	47	14	13	27	44	—	—	—	—	—
90-91—CSKA Moscow	USSR	45	5	12	17	42	—	—	—	—	—
91-92—Detroit	NHL	79	8	26	34	172	11	0	1	1	16
92-93—Detroit	NHL	82	5	17	22	137	7	0	1	1	8
93-94—Detroit	NHL	80	12	21	33	138	7	0	2	2	4
NHL totals		241	25	64	89	447	25	0	4	4	28

KONTOS, CHRIS
C/LW, LIGHTNING

PERSONAL: Born December 10, 1963, in Toronto.... 6-1/195.... Shoots left.
TRANSACTIONS/CAREER NOTES: Traded by Sudbury Wolves to Toronto Marlboros for C Keith Knight (October 1981).... Selected by New York Rangers as underage junior in first round (first Rangers pick, 15th overall) of NHL entry draft (June 1982).... Suspended by Rangers after refusing to report to Tulsa Oilers (November 1983).... Reinstated by Rangers (January 1984).... Traded by Rangers to Pittsburgh Penguins for RW Ron Duguay (January 1987).... Traded by Penguins with sixth-round pick in 1988 draft (C Micah Aivazoff) to Los Angeles Kings for RW Bryan Erickson (February 5, 1988).... Signed as free agent by Tampa Bay Lightning (July 21, 1992).... Strained knee (March 12, 1993); missed remainder of season.... Signed by Canadian National Team (November 12, 1993).
RECORDS: Holds NHL single-series playoff record for most power-play goals—6 (1989).
MISCELLANEOUS: Member of silver-medal-winning Canadian Olympic team (1994).

Season Team	League	REGULAR SEASON					PLAYOFFS				
		Gms.	G	A	Pts.	PIM	Gms.	G	A	Pts.	PIM
79-80—North York Flames	OPJHL	42	39	55	94	37	—	—	—	—	—
80-81—Sudbury	OMJHL	56	17	27	44	36	—	—	—	—	—

Season	Team	League	REGULAR SEASON					PLAYOFFS				
			Gms.	G	A	Pts.	Pen.	Gms.	G	A	Pts.	Pen.
81-82—Sudbury		OHL	12	6	6	12	18	—	—	—	—	—
—Toronto		OHL	59	36	56	92	68	10	7	9	16	2
82-83—Toronto		OHL	28	21	33	54	23	—	—	—	—	—
—New York Rangers		NHL	44	8	7	15	33	—	—	—	—	—
83-84—New York Rangers		NHL	6	0	1	1	8	—	—	—	—	—
—Tulsa		CHL	21	5	13	18	8	—	—	—	—	—
84-85—New Haven		AHL	48	19	24	43	30	—	—	—	—	—
—New York Rangers		NHL	28	4	8	12	24	—	—	—	—	—
85-86—New Haven		AHL	21	8	15	23	12	5	4	2	6	4
86-87—New Haven		AHL	36	14	17	31	29	—	—	—	—	—
—Pittsburgh		NHL	31	8	9	17	6	—	—	—	—	—
87-88—Pittsburgh		NHL	36	1	7	8	12	—	—	—	—	—
—Los Angeles		NHL	6	2	10	12	2	4	1	0	1	4
—New Haven		AHL	16	8	16	24	4	—	—	—	—	—
—Muskegon		IHL	10	3	6	9	8	—	—	—	—	—
88-89—Kloten		Switzerland			Statistics unavailable.							
—Los Angeles		NHL	7	2	1	3	2	11	9	0	9	8
89-90—New Haven		AHL	42	10	20	30	25	—	—	—	—	—
—Los Angeles		NHL	6	2	2	4	4	5	1	0	1	0
90-91—Phoenix		IHL	69	26	36	62	19	11	9	12	21	0
91-92—Canadian national team		Int'l	25	10	10	20	16	—	—	—	—	—
92-93—Tampa Bay		NHL	66	27	24	51	12	—	—	—	—	—
93-94—Canadian national team		Int'l	43	19	17	36	14	—	—	—	—	—
—Canadian Olympic Team		Int'l	8	3	1	4	2	—	—	—	—	—
NHL totals			230	54	69	123	103	20	11	0	11	12

KORDIC, DAN
D, FLYERS

PERSONAL: Born April 18, 1971, in Edmonton.... 6-5/220.... Shoots left.... Name pronounced KOHR-dihk.... Brother of John Kordic, right winger for four NHL teams (1985-86 through 1991-92).

TRANSACTIONS/CAREER NOTES: Selected by Philadelphia Flyers in fifth round (eighth Flyers pick, 88th overall) of NHL entry draft (June 16, 1990).... Suffered from the flu (January 1992); missed five games.

Season	Team	League	REGULAR SEASON					PLAYOFFS				
			Gms.	G	A	Pts.	PIM	Gms.	G	A	Pts.	PIM
87-88—Medicine Hat		WHL	63	1	5	6	75	—	—	—	—	—
88-89—Medicine Hat		WHL	70	1	13	14	190	—	—	—	—	—
89-90—Medicine Hat		WHL	59	4	12	16	182	3	0	0	0	9
90-91—Medicine Hat		WHL	67	8	15	23	150	12	2	6	8	42
91-92—Philadelphia		NHL	46	1	3	4	126	—	—	—	—	—
92-93—Hershey		AHL	14	0	2	2	17	—	—	—	—	—
93-94—Hershey		AHL	64	0	4	4	164	11	0	3	3	26
—Philadelphia		NHL	4	0	0	0	5	—	—	—	—	—
NHL totals			50	1	3	4	131					

KOROBOLIN, ALEXANDER
D, RANGERS

PERSONAL: Born March 12, 1976, in Chelyabinsk, U.S.S.R.... 6-2/189.... Shoots left.

TRANSACTIONS/CAREER NOTES: Selected by New York Rangers in fourth round (fourth Rangers pick, 100th overall) of NHL entry draft (June 29, 1994).

Season	Team	League	REGULAR SEASON					PLAYOFFS				
			Gms.	G	A	Pts.	PIM	Gms.	G	A	Pts.	PIM
93-94—Mechel Chelyabinsk		CIS Div. II	32	0	0	0	30	—	—	—	—	—

KOROLEV, IGOR
C, BLUES

PERSONAL: Born September 6, 1970, in Moscow, U.S.S.R.... 6-1/190.... Shoots left.... Name pronounced EE-gohr KOHR-ih-lehv.

TRANSACTIONS/CAREER NOTES: Selected by St. Louis Blues in second round (first Blues pick, 38th overall) of NHL entry draft (June 20, 1992).... Suffered from the flu (March 3, 1994); missed one game.... Injured hip (March 12, 1994); missed three games.

Season	Team	League	REGULAR SEASON					PLAYOFFS				
			Gms.	G	A	Pts.	PIM	Gms.	G	A	Pts.	PIM
88-89—Dynamo Moscow		USSR	1	0	0	0	2	—	—	—	—	—
89-90—Dynamo Moscow		USSR	17	3	2	5	2	—	—	—	—	—
90-91—Dynamo Moscow		USSR	38	12	4	16	12	—	—	—	—	—
91-92—Dynamo Moscow		CIS	39	15	12	27	16	—	—	—	—	—
92-93—Dynamo Moscow		CIS	5	1	2	3	4	—	—	—	—	—
—St. Louis		NHL	74	4	23	27	20	3	0	0	0	0
93-94—St. Louis		NHL	73	6	10	16	40	2	0	0	0	0
NHL totals			147	10	33	43	60	5	0	0	0	0

KOROLYUK, ALEXANDER
RW, SHARKS

PERSONAL: Born January 15, 1976, in Moscow, U.S.S.R. . . . 5-9/165. . . . Shoots left.
TRANSACTIONS/CAREER NOTES: Selected by San Jose Sharks in sixth round (sixth Sharks pick, 141st overall) of NHL entry draft (June 29, 1994).

			REGULAR SEASON					PLAYOFFS			
Season Team	League	Gms.	G	A	Pts.	PIM	Gms.	G	A	Pts.	PIM
93-94—Soviet Wings	CIS	22	4	4	8	20	3	1	0	1	4

KOVACS, FRANK
LW, STARS

PERSONAL: Born June 3, 1971, in Regina, Sask. . . . 6-2/210. . . . Shoots left.
TRANSACTIONS/CAREER NOTES: WHL rights traded by Seattle Thunderbirds with RW Craig Endean, C Ray Savard and Grant Chorney to Regina Pats for RW Ken McIntyre, RW Brent Fedyk, LW Grant Kazuik, D Gerald Bzdel and rights to LW Kevin Kowalchuk (November 1986). . . . Selected by Minnesota North Stars in fourth round (fourth North Stars pick, 71st overall) of NHL entry draft (June 16, 1990). . . . North Stars franchise moved from Minnesota to Dallas and renamed Stars for 1993-94 season.
HONORS: Named to WHL (East) All-Star second team (1991-92).

			REGULAR SEASON					PLAYOFFS			
Season Team	League	Gms.	G	A	Pts.	PIM	Gms.	G	A	Pts.	PIM
87-88—Regina	WHL	70	10	8	18	48	4	0	1	1	4
88-89—Regina	WHL	70	16	27	43	90	—	—	—	—	—
89-90—Regina	WHL	71	26	32	58	165	11	4	4	8	10
90-91—Regina	WHL	72	50	51	101	148	8	10	3	13	15
91-92—Regina	WHL	69	46	45	91	274	—	—	—	—	—
92-93—Kalamazoo	IHL	1	0	0	0	2	—	—	—	—	—
93-94—Moncton	AHL	69	11	10	21	196	—	—	—	—	—

KOVALENKO, ANDREI
RW, NORDIQUES

PERSONAL: Born July 7, 1970, in Gorky, U.S.S.R. . . . 5-10/200. . . . Shoots left. . . . Name pronounced koh-vuh-LEHN-koh.
TRANSACTIONS/CAREER NOTES: Selected by Quebec Nordiques in eighth round (sixth Nordiques pick, 148th overall) of NHL entry draft (June 16, 1990). . . . Suffered tonsillitis (December 22, 1992); missed two games. . . . Suffered from the flu (March 15, 1993); missed one game. . . . Suffered concussion (November 4, 1993); missed five games. . . . Bruised ribs (January 11, 1994); missed two games. . . . Injured shoulder (January 25, 1994); missed 14 games. . . . Suffered from tonsillitis (April 3, 1994); missed two games.

			REGULAR SEASON					PLAYOFFS			
Season Team	League	Gms.	G	A	Pts.	PIM	Gms.	G	A	Pts.	PIM
89-90—CSKA Moscow	USSR	48	8	5	13	18	—	—	—	—	—
90-91—CSKA Moscow	USSR	45	13	8	21	26	—	—	—	—	—
91-92—CSKA Moscow	CIS	44	19	13	32	32	—	—	—	—	—
—Unified Olympic Team	Int'l	8	1	1	2	2	—	—	—	—	—
92-93—CSKA Moscow	CIS	3	3	1	4	4	—	—	—	—	—
—Quebec	NHL	81	27	41	68	57	4	1	0	1	2
93-94—Quebec	NHL	58	16	17	33	46	—	—	—	—	—
NHL totals		139	43	58	101	103	4	1	0	1	2

KOVALEV, ALEXEI
C, RANGERS

PERSONAL: Born February 24, 1973, in Moscow, U.S.S.R. . . . 6-0/200. . . . Shoots left. . . . Name pronounced KOH-vuh-lehf.
TRANSACTIONS/CAREER NOTES: Selected by New York Rangers in first round (first Rangers pick, 15th overall) of NHL entry draft (June 22, 1991). . . . Suffered back spasms (January 16, 1993); missed one game. . . . Suspended one game by NHL (November 10, 1993). . . . Suspended five games by NHL for tripping (November 30, 1993). . . . Suspended two games by NHL (February 12, 1994).
MISCELLANEOUS: Member of Stanley Cup championship team (1994).

			REGULAR SEASON					PLAYOFFS			
Season Team	League	Gms.	G	A	Pts.	PIM	Gms.	G	A	Pts.	PIM
89-90—Dynamo Moscow	USSR	1	0	0	0	0	—	—	—	—	—
90-91—Dynamo Moscow	USSR	18	1	2	3	4	—	—	—	—	—
91-92—Dynamo Moscow	CIS	33	16	9	25	20	—	—	—	—	—
—Unified Olympic Team	Int'l	8	1	2	3	14	—	—	—	—	—
92-93—New York Rangers	NHL	65	20	18	38	79	—	—	—	—	—
—Binghamton	AHL	13	13	11	24	35	9	3	5	8	14
93-94—New York Rangers	NHL	76	23	33	56	154	23	9	12	21	18
NHL totals		141	43	51	94	233	23	9	12	21	18

KOZLOV, SLAVA
LW, RED WINGS

PERSONAL: Born May 3, 1972, in Voskresensk, U.S.S.R. . . . 5-10/175. . . . Shoots left. . . . Name pronounced KAHS-lahf.
TRANSACTIONS/CAREER NOTES: Selected by Detroit Red Wings in third round (second Red Wings pick, 45th overall) of NHL entry draft (June 16, 1990).
HONORS: Named Soviet League Rookie of the Year (1989-90).

			REGULAR SEASON					PLAYOFFS			
Season Team	League	Gms.	G	A	Pts.	PIM	Gms.	G	A	Pts.	PIM
89-90—Khimik	USSR	45	14	12	26	38	—	—	—	—	—
90-91—Khimik	USSR	45	11	13	24	46	—	—	—	—	—

K

Season	Team	League	REGULAR SEASON Gms.	G	A	Pts.	Pen.	PLAYOFFS Gms.	G	A	Pts.	Pen.
91-92	CSKA Moscow	CIS	11	6	5	11	12	—	—	—	—	—
	Detroit	NHL	7	0	2	2	2	—	—	—	—	—
92-93	Detroit	NHL	17	4	1	5	14	4	0	2	2	2
	Adirondack	AHL	45	23	36	59	54	4	1	1	2	4
93-94	Detroit	NHL	77	34	39	73	50	7	2	5	7	12
	Adirondack	AHL	3	0	1	1	15	—	—	—	—	—
	NHL totals		101	38	42	80	66	11	2	7	9	14

KOZLOV, VIKTOR
RW, SHARKS

PERSONAL: Born February 14, 1975, in Togliatti, U.S.S.R. . . . 6-5/209. . . . Shoots right.
TRANSACTIONS/CAREER NOTES: Selected by San Jose Sharks in first round (first Sharks pick, sixth overall) of NHL entry draft (June 26, 1993).

Season	Team	League	REGULAR SEASON Gms.	G	A	Pts.	PIM	PLAYOFFS Gms.	G	A	Pts.	PIM
90-91	Lada Togliatti	USSR Div. II	2	2	0	2	0	—	—	—	—	—
91-92	Lada Togliatti	CIS	3	0	0	0	0	—	—	—	—	—
92-93	Dynamo Moscow	CIS	30	6	5	11	4	10	3	0	3	0
93-94	Dynamo Moscow	CIS	42	16	9	25	14	7	3	2	5	0

KRAKE, PAUL
G, NORDIQUES

PERSONAL: Born March 25, 1969, in Lloydminster, Alta. . . . 6-0/175. . . . Catches left. . . . Name pronounced KRAYK.
COLLEGE: Alaska-Anchorage.
TRANSACTIONS/CAREER NOTES: Selected by Quebec Nordiques in 10th round (10th Nordiques pick, 148th overall) of NHL entry draft (June 17, 1989).

Season	Team	League	REGULAR SEASON Gms.	Min.	W	L	T	GA	SO	Avg.	PLAYOFFS Gms.	Min.	W	L	GA	SO	Avg.
88-89	Alaska-Anchorage	Indep.	19	1111	...	...	...	75	0	4.05	—	—	—	—	—	—	—
89-90	Alaska-Anchorage	Indep.	18	937	8	6	2	58	0	3.71	—	—	—	—	—	—	—
90-91	Alaska-Anchorage	Indep.	37	2183	18	15	3	123	4	3.38	—	—	—	—	—	—	—
91-92	Alaska-Anchorage	Indep.	28	1647	19	8	0	94	0	3.42	—	—	—	—	—	—	—
92-93	Halifax	AHL	17	916	8	6	1	57	6	3.73	—	—	—	—	—	—	—
	Oklahoma City	CHL	17	1029	13	4	†0	60	0	3.50	—	—	—	—	—	—	—
93-94	Cornwall	AHL	28	1383	8	13	4	96	0	4.16	—	—	—	—	—	—	—

KRAVCHUK, IGOR
D, OILERS

PERSONAL: Born September 13, 1966, in Ufa, U.S.S.R. . . . 6-1/200. . . . Shoots left. . . . Name pronounced EE-gohr KRAV-chuhk.
TRANSACTIONS/CAREER NOTES: Selected by Chicago Blackhawks in fourth round (fifth Blackhawks pick, 71st overall) of NHL entry draft (June 22, 1991). . . . Sprained knee (October 25, 1992); missed four games. . . . Sprained left ankle (December 29, 1992); missed 18 games. . . . Traded by Blackhawks with C Dean McAmmond to Edmonton Oilers for RW Joe Murphy (February 25, 1993). . . . Sprained left knee (April 6, 1993); missed remainder of season. . . . Strained groin (November 15, 1993); missed three games.
MISCELLANEOUS: Member of gold-medal-winning U.S.S.R. Olympic team (1988) and gold-medal-winning Unified Olympic team (1992).

Season	Team	League	REGULAR SEASON Gms.	G	A	Pts.	PIM	PLAYOFFS Gms.	G	A	Pts.	PIM
90-91	CSKA Moscow	USSR	41	6	5	11	16	—	—	—	—	—
91-92	CSKA Moscow	CIS	30	3	7	10	2	—	—	—	—	—
	Unified Olympic Team	Int'l	8	3	2	5	...	—	—	—	—	—
	Chicago	NHL	18	1	8	9	4	18	2	6	8	8
92-93	Chicago	NHL	38	6	9	15	30	—	—	—	—	—
	Edmonton	NHL	17	4	8	12	2	—	—	—	—	—
93-94	Edmonton	NHL	81	12	38	50	16	—	—	—	—	—
	NHL totals		154	23	63	86	52	18	2	6	8	8

KRAVETS, MIKHAIL
LW, SHARKS

PERSONAL: Born November 12, 1963, in Leningrad, U.S.S.R. . . . 5-10/190. . . . Shoots left. . . . Name pronounced mihk-HAYL KRAV-ihtz.
TRANSACTIONS/CAREER NOTES: Selected by San Jose Sharks in 12th round (13th Sharks pick, 243rd overall) of NHL entry draft (June 22, 1991).

Season	Team	League	REGULAR SEASON Gms.	G	A	Pts.	PIM	PLAYOFFS Gms.	G	A	Pts.	PIM
88-89	SKA Leningrad	USSR	44	9	5	14	36	—	—	—	—	—
89-90	SKA Leningrad	USSR	43	8	18	26	20	—	—	—	—	—
90-91	SKA Leningrad	USSR	25	8	6	14	28	—	—	—	—	—
91-92	Kansas City	IHL	74	10	32	42	172	15	6	8	14	12
	San Jose	NHL	1	0	0	0	0	—	—	—	—	—
92-93	San Jose	NHL	1	0	0	0	0	—	—	—	—	—
	Kansas City	IHL	71	19	49	68	153	10	2	5	7	55
93-94	Kansas City	IHL	63	14	44	58	171	—	—	—	—	—
	NHL totals		2	0	0	0	0					

KRIVCHENKOV, ALEXEI
D, PENGUINS

PERSONAL: Born June 11, 1974, in Novosibirsk, U.S.S.R. . . . 6-0/185. . . . Shoots left.
TRANSACTIONS/CAREER NOTES: Selected by Pittsburgh Penguins in third round (fifth Penguins pick, 76th overall) of NHL entry draft (June 29, 1994).

			REGULAR SEASON					PLAYOFFS			
Season Team	League	Gms.	G	A	Pts.	PIM	Gms.	G	A	Pts.	PIM
93-94—Sibir Novosibirsk	CIS Div. II	37	1	3	4	48	—	—	—	—	—
—CSKA Moscow.................	CIS	4	0	0	0	2	3	0	0	0	0

KRIVOKRASOV, SERGEI
RW, BLACKHAWKS

PERSONAL: Born April 15, 1974, in Angarsk, U.S.S.R. . . . 5-11/175. . . . Shoots left. . . . Name pronounced SAIR-gay krih-vuh-KRA-sahf.
TRANSACTIONS/CAREER NOTES: Selected by Chicago Blackhawks in first round (first Blackhawks pick, 12th overall) of NHL entry draft (June 20, 1992).

			REGULAR SEASON					PLAYOFFS			
Season Team	League	Gms.	G	A	Pts.	PIM	Gms.	G	A	Pts.	PIM
90-91—CSKA Moscow.................	USSR	41	4	0	4	8	—	—	—	—	—
91-92—CSKA Moscow.................	CIS	42	10	8	18	35	—	—	—	—	—
92-93—Chicago	NHL	4	0	0	0	2	—	—	—	—	—
—Indianapolis	IHL	78	36	33	69	157	5	3	1	4	2
93-94—Indianapolis	IHL	53	19	26	45	145	—	—	—	—	—
—Chicago	NHL	9	1	0	1	4	—	—	—	—	—
NHL totals........................		**13**	**1**	**0**	**1**	**6**					

KRON, ROBERT
LW, WHALERS

PERSONAL: Born February 27, 1967, in Brno, Czechoslovakia. . . . 5-10/180. . . . Shoots right. . . . Name pronounced KRAHN.
TRANSACTIONS/CAREER NOTES: Selected by Vancouver Canucks in fourth round (fifth Canucks pick, 88th overall) of NHL entry draft (June 15, 1985). . . . Played entire season with a broken bone in left wrist (1990-91). . . . Underwent surgery to repair torn knee ligaments and wrist fracture (March 22, 1991). . . . Fractured ankle (January 28, 1992); missed 22 games. . . . Traded by Canucks with third-round pick in 1993 draft (D Marek Malik) and future considerations to Hartford Whalers for C/LW Murray Craven and fifth-round pick (D Scott Walker) in 1993 draft (March 22, 1993); Canucks sent RW Jim Sandlak to Whalers to complete deal (May 17, 1993). . . . Sprained shoulder (February 26, 1994); missed seven games.

			REGULAR SEASON					PLAYOFFS			
Season Team	League	Gms.	G	A	Pts.	PIM	Gms.	G	A	Pts.	PIM
86-87—Zetor Brno	Czech.	28	14	11	25	...	—	—	—	—	—
87-88—Zetor Brno	Czech.	32	12	6	18	...	—	—	—	—	—
88-89—Zetor Brno	Czech.	43	28	19	47	...	—	—	—	—	—
89-90—Dukla Trencin	Czech.	39	22	22	44	...	—	—	—	—	—
90-91—Vancouver........................	NHL	76	12	20	32	21	—	—	—	—	—
91-92—Vancouver........................	NHL	36	2	2	4	2	11	1	2	3	2
92-93—Vancouver........................	NHL	32	10	11	21	14	—	—	—	—	—
—Hartford...........................	NHL	13	4	2	6	4	—	—	—	—	—
93-94—Hartford...........................	NHL	77	24	26	50	8	—	—	—	—	—
NHL totals........................		**234**	**52**	**61**	**113**	**49**	**11**	**1**	**2**	**3**	**2**

KROUPA, VLASTIMIL
D, SHARKS

PERSONAL: Born April 27, 1975, in Most, Czechoslovakia. . . . 6-2/176. . . . Shoots left. . . . Name pronounced VLAS-tuh-meel KROO-pah.
TRANSACTIONS/CAREER NOTES: Selected by San Jose Sharks in second round (third Sharks pick, 45th overall) of NHL entry draft (June 26, 1993).

			REGULAR SEASON					PLAYOFFS			
Season Team	League	Gms.	G	A	Pts.	PIM	Gms.	G	A	Pts.	PIM
92-93—Chemopetrol Litvinov	Czech.	9	0	1	1	...	—	—	—	—	—
93-94—San Jose...........................	NHL	27	1	3	4	20	14	1	2	3	21
—Kansas City.....................	IHL	39	3	12	15	12	—	—	—	—	—
NHL totals........................		**27**	**1**	**3**	**4**	**20**	**14**	**1**	**2**	**3**	**21**

KRUPP, UWE
D, NORDIQUES

PERSONAL: Born June 24, 1965, in Cologne, West Germany. . . . 6-6/235. . . . Shoots right. . . . Name pronounced YOO-ay KROOP.
TRANSACTIONS/CAREER NOTES: Selected by Buffalo Sabres in 11th round (13th Sabres pick, 214th overall) of NHL entry draft (June 8, 1983). . . . Bruised hip (November 1987). . . . Injured head (April 1988). . . . Broke rib (January 6, 1989). . . . Banned from international competition for 18 months by IIHF after failing random substance test (April 20, 1990). . . . Suffered from cyst on foot (January 2, 1991); missed NHL All-Star Game. . . . Traded by Sabres with C Pierre Turgeon, RW Benoit Hogue and C Dave McLlwain to New York Islanders for C Pat LaFontaine, LW Randy Wood, D Randy Hillier and future considerations; Sabres received fourth-round pick (D Dean Melanson) in 1992 draft to complete deal (October 25, 1991). . . . Sprained left knee (December 28, 1991); missed five games. . . . Bruised thigh (February 7, 1992). . . . Suffered from the flu (March 2, 1993); missed one game. . . . Suffered sore shoulder (April 10, 1993); missed three games. . . . Broke toe (October 10, 1993); missed three games. . . . Fractured sinus bone (October 26, 1993); missed 17 games. . . . Suffered severely sprained hamstring (December 19, 1993); missed nine games. . . . Suffered from the flu, bruised jaw and sprained wrist (February 27, 1994); missed four games. . . . Sprained wrist (March 5, 1994); missed nine games. . . . Traded by Islanders with first-round pick in 1994 draft (D Wade Belak) to Quebec Nordiques for C Ron Sutter and first-round pick (RW Brett Lindros) in 1994 draft (June 28, 1994).
HONORS: Played in NHL All-Star Game (1991).

Season Team	League	REGULAR SEASON					PLAYOFFS				
		Gms.	G	A	Pts.	PIM	Gms.	G	A	Pts.	PIM
83-84—KEC	W. Germany	40	0	4	4	22	—	—	—	—	—
84-85—KEC	W. Germany	39	11	8	19	36	—	—	—	—	—
85-86—KEC	W. Germany	45	10	21	31	83	—	—	—	—	—
86-87—Rochester	AHL	42	3	19	22	50	17	1	11	12	16
—Buffalo	NHL	26	1	4	5	23	—	—	—	—	—
87-88—Buffalo	NHL	75	2	9	11	151	6	0	0	0	15
88-89—Buffalo	NHL	70	5	13	18	55	5	0	1	1	4
89-90—Buffalo	NHL	74	3	20	23	85	6	0	0	0	4
90-91—Buffalo	NHL	74	12	32	44	66	6	1	1	2	6
91-92—Buffalo	NHL	8	2	0	2	6	—	—	—	—	—
—New York Islanders	NHL	59	6	29	35	43	—	—	—	—	—
92-93—New York Islanders	NHL	80	9	29	38	67	18	1	5	6	12
93-94—New York Islanders	NHL	41	7	14	21	30	4	0	1	1	4
NHL totals		507	47	150	197	526	45	2	8	10	45

KRUPPKE, GORD

D, RED WINGS

PERSONAL: Born April 2, 1969, in Edmonton. . . . 6-1/200. . . . Shoots right. . . . Name pronounced KRUHP-kee.

TRANSACTIONS/CAREER NOTES: Underwent surgery to have spleen removed (December 1986). . . . Selected by Detroit Red Wings as underage junior in second round (second Red Wings pick, 32nd overall) of NHL entry draft (June 13, 1987). . . . Injured left knee ligaments (October 1987). . . . Suffered elbow contusion (December 2, 1992); missed one game.

HONORS: Named to WHL All-Star second team (1988-89).

Season Team	League	REGULAR SEASON					PLAYOFFS				
		Gms.	G	A	Pts.	PIM	Gms.	G	A	Pts.	PIM
85-86—Prince Albert	WHL	62	1	8	9	81	20	4	4	8	22
86-87—Prince Albert	WHL	49	2	10	12	129	8	0	0	0	9
87-88—Prince Albert	WHL	54	8	8	16	113	10	0	0	0	46
88-89—Prince Albert	WHL	62	6	26	32	254	3	0	0	0	11
89-90—Adirondack	AHL	59	2	12	14	103	—	—	—	—	—
90-91—Adirondack	AHL	45	1	8	9	153	—	—	—	—	—
—Detroit	NHL	4	0	0	0	0	—	—	—	—	—
91-92—Adirondack	AHL	65	3	9	12	208	16	0	1	1	52
92-93—Adirondack	AHL	41	2	12	14	197	9	1	2	3	20
—Detroit	NHL	10	0	0	0	20	—	—	—	—	—
93-94—Adirondack	AHL	54	2	9	11	210	12	1	3	4	32
—Detroit	NHL	9	0	0	0	12	—	—	—	—	—
NHL totals		23	0	0	0	32	—	—	—	—	—

KRUSE, PAUL

LW, FLAMES

PERSONAL: Born March 15, 1970, in Merritt, B.C. . . . 6-0/202. . . . Shoots left. . . . Name pronounced KROOS.

TRANSACTIONS/CAREER NOTES: Selected by Calgary Flames in fourth round (sixth Flames pick, 83rd overall) of NHL entry draft (June 16, 1990). . . . Injured eye (March 8, 1992); missed four games. . . . Suffered hip pointer (March 21, 1993); missed one game. . . . Broke toe on right foot (September 27, 1993); missed 12 games.

Season Team	League	REGULAR SEASON					PLAYOFFS				
		Gms.	G	A	Pts.	PIM	Gms.	G	A	Pts.	PIM
86-87—Merritt	BCJHL	35	8	15	23	120	—	—	—	—	—
87-88—Merritt	BCJHL	44	12	32	44	227	4	1	4	5	18
—Moose Jaw	WHL	1	0	0	0	0	—	—	—	—	—
88-89—Kamloops	WHL	68	8	15	23	209	—	—	—	—	—
89-90—Kamloops	WHL	67	22	23	45	291	17	3	5	8	†79
90-91—Salt Lake City	IHL	83	24	20	44	313	4	1	1	2	4
—Calgary	NHL	1	0	0	0	7	—	—	—	—	—
91-92—Salt Lake City	IHL	57	14	15	29	267	5	1	2	3	19
—Calgary	NHL	16	3	1	4	65	—	—	—	—	—
92-93—Salt Lake City	IHL	35	1	4	5	206	—	—	—	—	—
—Calgary	NHL	27	2	3	5	41	—	—	—	—	—
93-94—Calgary	NHL	68	3	8	11	185	7	0	0	0	14
NHL totals		112	8	12	20	298	7	0	0	0	14

KRUSHELNYSKI, MIKE

C/LW, RED WINGS

PERSONAL: Born April 27, 1960, in Montreal. . . . 6-2/200. . . . Shoots left. . . . Name pronounced KROO-shihl-NIH-skee.

TRANSACTIONS/CAREER NOTES: Started 1978-79 season at St. Louis University then returned to junior hockey. . . . Selected by Boston Bruins as underage junior in sixth round (seventh Bruins pick, 120th overall) of NHL entry draft (August 9, 1979). . . . Separated right shoulder (January 1984). . . . Traded by Bruins to Edmonton Oilers for C Ken Linseman (June 1984). . . . Sprained right knee (December 10, 1985); missed 17 games. . . . Twisted knee (February 14, 1986); missed nine games. . . . Suspended by Oilers for not reporting to training camp (September 1987). . . . Traded by Oilers with C Wayne Gretzky and RW/D Marty McSorley to Los Angeles Kings for C Jimmy Carson, LW Martin Gelinas, first-round picks in 1989 (traded to New Jersey), 1991 (LW Martin Rucinsky) and 1993 (D Nick Stajduhar) drafts and cash (August 9, 1988). . . . Fractured left wrist (October 5, 1989); missed 17 games.

... Traded by Kings to Toronto Maple Leafs for C John McIntyre (November 9, 1990).... Suffered back disc irritation (January 4, 1994); missed 17 games.... Signed as free agent by Detroit Red Wings (August 1, 1994).
HONORS: Played in NHL All-Star Game (1985).
MISCELLANEOUS: Member of Stanley Cup championship teams (1985, 1987 and 1988).

			REGULAR SEASON					PLAYOFFS				
Season	Team	League	Gms.	G	A	Pts.	PIM	Gms.	G	A	Pts.	PIM
78-79—Montreal	QMJHL	46	15	29	44	42	11	3	4	7	8
79-80—Montreal	QMJHL	72	39	61	100	78	6	2	3	5	2
80-81—Springfield	AHL	80	25	38	63	47	7	1	1	2	29
81-82—Erie	AHL	62	31	52	83	44	—	—	—	—	—
—Boston	NHL	17	3	3	6	2	1	0	0	0	2
82-83—Boston	NHL	79	23	42	65	43	17	8	6	14	12
83-84—Boston	NHL	66	25	20	45	55	2	0	0	0	0
84-85—Edmonton	NHL	80	43	45	88	60	18	5	8	13	22
85-86—Edmonton	NHL	54	16	24	40	22	10	4	5	9	16
86-87—Edmonton	NHL	80	16	35	51	67	21	3	4	7	18
87-88—Edmonton	NHL	76	20	27	47	64	19	4	6	10	12
88-89—Los Angeles	NHL	78	26	36	62	110	11	1	4	5	4
89-90—Los Angeles	NHL	63	16	25	41	50	10	1	3	4	12
90-91—Los Angeles	NHL	15	1	5	6	10	—	—	—	—	—
—Toronto	NHL	59	17	22	39	48	—	—	—	—	—
91-92—Toronto	NHL	72	9	15	24	72	—	—	—	—	—
92-93—Toronto	NHL	84	19	20	39	62	16	3	7	10	8
93-94—Toronto	NHL	54	5	6	11	28	6	0	0	0	0
NHL totals		877	239	325	564	693	131	29	43	72	106

KRYGIER, TODD
LW, CAPITALS

PERSONAL: Born October 12, 1965, in Northville, Mich.... 5-11/180.... Shoots left.... Full name: Todd Andrew Krygier.... Name pronounced KREE-guhr.
COLLEGE: Connecticut.
TRANSACTIONS/CAREER NOTES: Selected by Hartford Whalers in NHL supplemental draft (June 10, 1988).... Bruised heel (March 13, 1990).... Traded by Whalers to Washington Capitals for fourth-round pick (traded to Calgary Flames who selected D Jason Smith) in 1993 draft (October 3, 1991).... Separated right shoulder (December 28, 1993); missed seven games.

			REGULAR SEASON					PLAYOFFS				
Season	Team	League	Gms.	G	A	Pts.	PIM	Gms.	G	A	Pts.	PIM
84-85—University of Connecticut.	ECAC-II	14	14	11	25	12	—	—	—	—	—
85-86—University of Connecticut.	ECAC-II	32	29	27	56	46	—	—	—	—	—
86-87—University of Connecticut.	ECAC-II	28	24	24	48	44	—	—	—	—	—
87-88—University of Connecticut.	ECAC-II	27	32	39	71	38	—	—	—	—	—
—New Haven	AHL	13	1	5	6	34	—	—	—	—	—
88-89—Binghamton	AHL	76	26	42	68	77	—	—	—	—	—
89-90—Binghamton	AHL	12	1	9	10	16	—	—	—	—	—
—Hartford	NHL	58	18	12	30	52	7	2	1	3	4
90-91—Hartford	NHL	72	13	17	30	95	6	0	2	2	0
91-92—Washington	NHL	67	13	17	30	107	5	2	1	3	4
92-93—Washington	NHL	77	11	12	23	60	6	1	1	2	4
93-94—Washington	NHL	66	12	18	30	60	5	2	0	2	10
NHL totals		340	67	76	143	374	29	7	5	12	22

KUCERA, FRANTISEK
D, WHALERS

PERSONAL: Born February 3, 1968, in Prague, Czechoslovakia.... 6-2/205.... Shoots right.... Name pronounced koo-CHAIR-uh.
TRANSACTIONS/CAREER NOTES: Selected by Chicago Blackhawks in fourth round (third Blackhawks pick, 77th overall) of NHL entry draft (June 21, 1986).... Pulled groin (March 20, 1993); missed 11 games.... Pulled groin (1993-94 season); missed five games.... Traded by Blackhawks with LW Jocelyn Lemieux to Hartford Whalers for LW Randy Cunneyworth and D Gary Suter (March 11, 1994).

			REGULAR SEASON					PLAYOFFS				
Season	Team	League	Gms.	G	A	Pts.	PIM	Gms.	G	A	Pts.	PIM
85-86—Sparta Prague	Czech.	15	0	0	0	...	—	—	—	—	—
86-87—Sparta Prague	Czech.	33	7	2	9	...	—	—	—	—	—
87-88—Sparta Prague	Czech.	34	4	2	6	...	—	—	—	—	—
88-89—Dukla Jihlava	Czech.	45	10	9	19	...	—	—	—	—	—
89-90—Dukla Jihlava	Czech.	43	9	10	19	...	—	—	—	—	—
90-91—Chicago	NHL	40	2	12	14	32	—	—	—	—	—
—Indianapolis	IHL	35	8	19	27	23	7	0	1	1	15
91-92—Chicago	NHL	61	3	10	13	36	6	0	0	0	0
—Indianapolis	IHL	7	1	2	3	4	—	—	—	—	—
92-93—Chicago	NHL	71	5	14	19	59	—	—	—	—	—
93-94—Chicago	NHL	60	4	13	17	34	—	—	—	—	—
—Hartford	NHL	16	1	3	4	14	—	—	—	—	—
NHL totals		248	15	52	67	175	6	0	0	0	0

KUCHARCIK, TOMAS
C/RW, MAPLE LEAFS

PERSONAL: Born May 10, 1970, in Vlasim, Czechoslovakia. . . . 6-2/200. . . . Shoots left. . . . Name pronounced koo-HARH-chihk.
TRANSACTIONS/CAREER NOTES: Selected by Toronto Maple Leafs in eighth round (167th overall) of NHL entry draft (June 22, 1991).

			REGULAR SEASON					PLAYOFFS				
Season Team	League	Gms.	G	A	Pts.	PIM	Gms.	G	A	Pts.	PIM
90-91—Dukla Jihlava	Czech.	23	7	6	13	6	—	—	—	—	—
91-92—Dukla Jihlava	Czech.	37	13	17	30	...	—	—	—	—	—
92-93—Dukla Jihlava	Czech.	39	17	20	37	...	—	—	—	—	—
93-94—Skoda Plzen	Czech Rep.	32	10	10	20	...	5	2	6	8	0

KUDASHOV, ALEXEI
C, MAPLE LEAFS

PERSONAL: Born July 21, 1971, in Elektrostal, U.S.S.R. . . . 6-0/180. . . . Shoots right. . . . Name pronounced KOO-duh-SHAHF.
TRANSACTIONS/CAREER NOTES: Selected by Toronto Maple Leafs in fifth round (third Maple Leafs pick, 102nd overall) of NHL entry draft (June 22, 1991). . . . Loaned to Unified Olympic Team (February 1, 1994). . . . Returned to Maple Leafs (March 1, 1994).

			REGULAR SEASON					PLAYOFFS				
Season Team	League	Gms.	G	A	Pts.	PIM	Gms.	G	A	Pts.	PIM
90-91—Soviet Wings	USSR	45	9	5	14	10	—	—	—	—	—
91-92—Soviet Wings	CIS	36	8	16	24	12	—	—	—	—	—
92-93—Soviet Wings	CIS	41	8	20	28	24	7	1	3	4	4
93-94—Toronto	NHL	25	1	0	1	4	—	—	—	—	—
—St. John's	AHL	27	7	15	22	21	—	—	—	—	—
—Unified Olympic team	Int'l	8	1	2	3	4	—	—	—	—	—
NHL totals		25	1	0	1	4					

KUDELSKI, BOB
RW, PANTHERS

PERSONAL: Born March 3, 1964, in Springfield, Mass. . . . 6-1/199. . . . Shoots right. . . . Name pronounced kuh-DEHL-skee.
HIGH SCHOOL: Cathedral (Springfield, Mass.).
COLLEGE: Yale.
TRANSACTIONS/CAREER NOTES: Selected by Los Angeles Kings in NHL supplemental draft (September 17, 1986). . . . Broke knuckle on left hand (November 22, 1989); missed 15 games. . . . Strained medial collateral knee ligament (April 24, 1991). . . . Traded by Kings with C Shawn McCosh to Ottawa Senators for RW Jim Thomson and C Marc Fortier (December 20, 1992). . . . Traded by Senators to Florida Panthers for C Scott Levins, LW Evgeny Davydov and sixth-round pick (D Mike Gaffney) in 1994 draft (January 6, 1994).
HONORS: Named to ECAC All-Star first team (1986-87). . . . Played in NHL All-Star Game (1994).

			REGULAR SEASON					PLAYOFFS				
Season Team	League	Gms.	G	A	Pts.	PIM	Gms.	G	A	Pts.	PIM
83-84—Yale University	ECAC	21	14	12	26	12	—	—	—	—	—
84-85—Yale University	ECAC	32	21	23	44	38	—	—	—	—	—
85-86—Yale University	ECAC	31	18	23	41	48	—	—	—	—	—
86-87—Yale University	ECAC	30	25	22	47	34	—	—	—	—	—
87-88—New Haven	AHL	50	15	19	34	41	—	—	—	—	—
—Los Angeles	NHL	26	0	1	1	8	—	—	—	—	—
88-89—New Haven	AHL	60	32	19	51	43	17	8	5	13	12
—Los Angeles	NHL	14	1	3	4	17	—	—	—	—	—
89-90—Los Angeles	NHL	62	23	13	36	49	8	1	2	3	2
90-91—Los Angeles	NHL	72	23	13	36	46	8	3	2	5	2
91-92—Los Angeles	NHL	80	22	21	43	42	6	0	0	0	0
92-93—Los Angeles	NHL	15	3	3	6	8	—	—	—	—	—
—Ottawa	NHL	48	21	14	35	22	—	—	—	—	—
93-94—Ottawa	NHL	42	26	15	41	14	—	—	—	—	—
—Florida	NHL	44	14	15	29	10	—	—	—	—	—
NHL totals		403	133	98	231	216	22	4	4	8	4

KUDINOV, ANDREI
C, RANGERS

PERSONAL: Born June 28, 1970, in Chelyabinsk, U.S.S.R. . . . 6-0/185. . . . Shoots left. . . . Name pronounced koo-DEE-nahf.
TRANSACTIONS/CAREER NOTES: Selected by New York Rangers in 10th round (10th Rangers pick, 242nd overall) of NHL entry draft (June 26, 1993).

			REGULAR SEASON					PLAYOFFS				
Season Team	League	Gms.	G	A	Pts.	PIM	Gms.	G	A	Pts.	PIM
90-91—Chelyabinsk	USSR	24	2	3	5	20	—	—	—	—	—
91-92—Chelyabinsk	CIS	36	9	7	16	40	—	—	—	—	—
92-93—Chelyabinsk	CIS	41	13	23	36	50	8	0	1	1	6
93-94—Chelyabinsk	CIS	6	0	3	3	4	—	—	—	—	—

KUKI, ARTO
C, CANADIENS

PERSONAL: Born February 22, 1976, in Espoo, Finland. . . . 6-3/205. . . . Shoots left.
TRANSACTIONS/CAREER NOTES: Selected by Montreal Canadiens in fourth round (sixth Canadiens pick, 96th overall) of NHL entry draft (June 29, 1994).

			REGULAR SEASON					PLAYOFFS				
Season Team	League	Gms.	G	A	Pts.	PIM	Gms.	G	A	Pts.	PIM
93-94—Kiekko-Espoo	Finland	26	1	10	11	28	—	—	—	—	—

K

KUNTAR, LES

G, CANADIENS

PERSONAL: Born July 28, 1969, in Buffalo, N.Y.... 6-2/195.... Catches left.... Full name: Leslie Steven Kuntar.
HIGH SCHOOL: Nichols School (Buffalo, N.Y.).
COLLEGE: St. Lawrence (N.Y.).
TRANSACTIONS/CAREER NOTES: Selected by Montreal Canadiens in sixth round (sixth Canadiens pick, 122nd overall) of NHL entry draft (June 13, 1987).
HONORS: Named to NCAA All-America East first team (1990-91).... Named to ECAC All-Star first team (1990-91).

Season Team	League				REGULAR SEASON								PLAYOFFS				
		Gms.	Min.	W	L	T	GA	SO	Avg.	Gms.	Min.	W	L	GA	SO	Avg.
86-87—Nichols School	N.Y. H.S.	22	1585	...	...	...	56	3	2.12	—	—	—	—	—	—	—
87-88—St. Lawrence Univ.	ECAC	10	488	6	1	0	27	0	3.32	—	—	—	—	—	—	—
88-89—St. Lawrence Univ.	ECAC	14	786	11	2	0	31	0	2.37	—	—	—	—	—	—	—
89-90—St. Lawrence Univ.	ECAC	19	1076	7	11	1	76	1	4.24	—	—	—	—	—	—	—
90-91—St. Lawrence Univ.	ECAC	*33	*1794	*19	11	1	97	2	*3.24	—	—	—	—	—	—	—
91-92—Fredericton	AHL	11	638	7	3	0	26	0	2.45	—	—	—	—	—	—	—
—U.S. national team	Int'l	2	100	...	...	...	4	0	2.40	—	—	—	—	—	—	—
92-93—Fredericton	AHL	42	2315	16	14	7	130	0	3.37	1	64	0	1	6	0	5.63
93-94—Fredericton	AHL	34	1804	10	17	3	109	1	3.63	—	—	—	—	—	—	—
—Montreal	NHL	6	302	2	2	0	16	0	3.18	—	—	—	—	—	—	—
NHL totals		6	302	2	2	0	16	0	3.18							

KURRI, JARI

C/RW, KINGS

PERSONAL: Born May 18, 1960, in Helsinki, Finland.... 6-1/195.... Shoots right.... Name pronounced YAR-ee KUHR-ee.
TRANSACTIONS/CAREER NOTES: Selected by Edmonton Oilers in fourth round (third Oilers pick, 69th overall) of NHL entry draft (June 11, 1980).... Pulled groin (November 24, 1981).... Pulled groin muscle (January 1984); missed 16 games.... Sprained medial collateral ligament in left knee (February 12, 1989).... Signed two-year contract with Milan Devils of Italian Hockey League (July 30, 1990).... Injured knee (January 1991).... Rights traded by Oilers with RW Dave Brown and D Corey Foster to Philadelphia Flyers for RW Scott Mellanby, LW Craig Berube and C Craig Fisher (May 30, 1991).... Rights traded by Flyers to Los Angeles Kings for D Steve Duchesne, C Steve Kasper and fourth-round pick (D Aris Brimanis) in 1991 draft (May 30, 1991).... Sprained shoulder (November 12, 1991); missed three games.... Suffered from the flu (January 1992); missed two games.... Suffered knee contusion (November 6, 1993); missed two games.
HONORS: Named to NHL All-Star second team (1983-84, 1985-86 and 1988-89).... Played in NHL All-Star Game (1983, 1985, 1986, 1988-1990 and 1993).... Won Lady Byng Memorial Trophy (1984-85).... Named to THE SPORTING NEWS All-Star first team (1984-85).... Named to NHL All-Star first team (1984-85 and 1986-87).... Named to THE SPORTING NEWS All-Star second team (1985-86 and 1988-89).
RECORDS: Shares NHL career record for most overtime goals—7.... Holds NHL single-season playoff record for most three-or-more-goal games—4 (1985).... Shares NHL single-season playoff records for most goals—19 (1985); and most game-winning goals—5 (1987).... Holds NHL single-series playoff records for most goals—12 (1985); and most three-or-more-goal games—3 (1985).... Shares NHL single-game playoff records for most shorthanded goals—2 (April 24, 1983); most shorthanded goals in one period—2 (April 24, 1983); and most power-play goals—3 (April 9, 1987).
MISCELLANEOUS: Member of Stanley Cup championship teams (1984, 1985, 1987, 1988 and 1990).

Season Team	League		REGULAR SEASON					PLAYOFFS			
		Gms.	G	A	Pts.	PIM	Gms.	G	A	Pts.	PIM
77-78—Jokerit	Finland	29	2	9	11	12	—	—	—	—	—
78-79—Jokerit	Finland	33	16	14	30	12	—	—	—	—	—
79-80—Jokerit	Finland	33	23	16	39	22	6	7	2	9	13
—Finland Olympic Team	Int'l	7	2	1	3	6	—	—	—	—	—
80-81—Edmonton	NHL	75	32	43	75	40	9	5	7	12	4
81-82—Edmonton	NHL	71	32	54	86	32	5	2	5	7	10
82-83—Edmonton	NHL	80	45	59	104	22	16	8	15	23	8
83-84—Edmonton	NHL	64	52	61	113	14	19	*14	14	28	13
84-85—Edmonton	NHL	73	71	64	135	30	18	*19	12	31	6
85-86—Edmonton	NHL	78	*68	63	131	22	10	2	10	12	4
86-87—Edmonton	NHL	79	54	54	108	41	21	*15	10	25	20
87-88—Edmonton	NHL	80	43	53	96	30	19	*14	17	31	12
88-89—Edmonton	NHL	76	44	58	102	69	7	3	5	8	6
89-90—Edmonton	NHL	78	33	60	93	48	22	10	15	25	18
90-91—Milan	Italy	40	37	60	97	8	10	10	12	22	2
91-92—Los Angeles	NHL	73	23	37	60	24	4	1	2	3	4
92-93—Los Angeles	NHL	82	27	60	87	38	24	9	8	17	12
93-94—Los Angeles	NHL	81	31	46	77	48	—	—	—	—	—
NHL totals		990	555	712	1267	458	174	102	120	222	117

KURVERS, TOM

D, MIGHTY DUCKS

PERSONAL: Born September 14, 1962, in Minneapolis.... 6-1/197.... Shoots left.... Full name: Thomas James Kurvers.
COLLEGE: Minnesota-Duluth.
TRANSACTIONS/CAREER NOTES: Selected by Montreal Canadiens as underage player in seventh round (10th Canadiens pick, 145th overall) of NHL entry draft (June 10, 1981).... Suffered facial injuries (October 23, 1984); missed five games.... Traded by Canadiens to Buffalo Sabres for second-round pick (LW Martin St. Amour) in 1988 draft (November 18, 1986).... Traded by Sabres to New Jersey Devils for third-round pick (LW Andrew MacVicar) in 1988 draft (June 13, 1987).... Fractured left index finger (November 1987).... Pulled groin (February 1988).... Injured right thumb (May 1988).... Pulled groin (November 17, 1988).... Traded by Devils to Toronto Maple Leafs for first-round pick (D Scott

Niedermayer) in 1991 draft (October 16, 1989).... Injured knee (March 8, 1990).... Underwent arthroscopic knee surgery (November 15, 1990).... Traded by Maple Leafs to Canucks for C Brian Bradley (January 12, 1991).... Traded by Canucks to New York Islanders as part of three-way deal in which Minnesota North Stars sent D Dave Babych to Canucks and Islanders sent D Craig Ludwig to North Stars (June 22, 1991).... Fractured thumb (November 30, 1993); missed seven games.... Traded by Islanders to Mighty Ducks of Anaheim for LW Troy Loney (June 29, 1994).
HONORS: Won Hobey Baker Memorial Trophy (1983-84).... Named to NCAA All-America West team (1983-84).... Named to WCHA All-Star first team (1983-84).
MISCELLANEOUS: Member of Stanley Cup championship team (1986).

			REGULAR SEASON					PLAYOFFS			
Season Team	League	Gms.	G	A	Pts.	PIM	Gms.	G	A	Pts.	PIM
80-81—Minnesota-Duluth..........	WCHA	39	6	24	30	48	—	—	—	—	—
81-82—Minnesota-Duluth..........	WCHA	37	11	31	42	18	—	—	—	—	—
82-83—Minnesota-Duluth..........	WCHA	45	8	36	44	42	—	—	—	—	—
83-84—Minnesota-Duluth..........	WCHA	43	18	58	76	46	—	—	—	—	—
84-85—Montreal.........................	NHL	75	10	35	45	30	12	0	6	6	6
85-86—Montreal.........................	NHL	62	7	23	30	36	—	—	—	—	—
86-87—Montreal.........................	NHL	1	0	0	0	0	—	—	—	—	—
—Buffalo............................	NHL	55	6	17	23	24	—	—	—	—	—
87-88—New Jersey.....................	NHL	56	5	29	34	46	19	6	9	15	38
88-89—New Jersey.....................	NHL	74	16	50	66	38	—	—	—	—	—
89-90—New Jersey.....................	NHL	1	0	0	0	0	—	—	—	—	—
—Toronto...........................	NHL	70	15	37	52	29	5	0	3	3	4
90-91—Toronto...........................	NHL	19	0	3	3	8	—	—	—	—	—
—Vancouver.......................	NHL	32	4	23	27	20	6	2	2	4	12
91-92—New York Islanders..........	NHL	74	9	47	56	30	—	—	—	—	—
92-93—New York Islanders..........	NHL	52	8	30	38	38	12	0	2	2	6
—Capital District.................	AHL	7	3	4	7	8	—	—	—	—	—
93-94—New York Islanders..........	NHL	66	9	31	40	47	3	0	0	0	2
NHL totals.................................		637	89	325	414	346	57	8	22	30	68

KUSHNER, DALE
RW, FLAMES

PERSONAL: Born June 13, 1966, in Terrace, B.C.... 6-1/195.... Shoots left.... Name pronounced KUSH-nuhr.
TRANSACTIONS/CAREER NOTES: Signed as free agent by New York Islanders (March 1987). ... Suspended six games by AHL for leaving penalty box to fight (December 30, 1988).... Suspended eight games by AHL for leaving penalty box to fight (November 24, 1989).... Signed as free agent by Philadelphia Flyers (August 1, 1990).... Signed as free agent by Calgary Flames (September 6, 1993).
HONORS: Named to Memorial Cup All-Star team (1986-87).

			REGULAR SEASON					PLAYOFFS			
Season Team	League	Gms.	G	A	Pts.	PIM	Gms.	G	A	Pts.	PIM
83-84—Fort McMurray..................	AJHL	44	15	6	21	139	—	—	—	—	—
—Prince Albert....................	WHL	1	0	0	0	5	—	—	—	—	—
84-85—Prince Albert....................	WHL	2	0	0	0	2	—	—	—	—	—
—Moose Jaw	WHL	17	5	2	7	23	—	—	—	—	—
—Medicine Hat	WHL	48	23	17	40	173	10	3	3	6	18
85-86—Medicine Hat	WHL	66	25	19	44	218	25	0	5	5	*114
86-87—Medicine Hat	WHL	65	34	34	68	250	20	8	13	21	57
87-88—Springfield......................	AHL	68	13	23	36	201	—	—	—	—	—
88-89—Springfield......................	AHL	45	5	8	13	132	—	—	—	—	—
89-90—New York Islanders..........	NHL	2	0	0	0	2	—	—	—	—	—
—Springfield......................	AHL	45	14	11	25	163	7	2	3	5	61
90-91—Philadelphia.....................	NHL	63	7	11	18	195	—	—	—	—	—
—Hershey..........................	AHL	5	3	4	7	14	—	—	—	—	—
91-92—Hershey..........................	AHL	46	9	7	16	98	6	0	2	2	23
—Philadelphia....................	NHL	19	3	2	5	18	—	—	—	—	—
92-93—Hershey..........................	AHL	26	1	7	8	98	—	—	—	—	—
—Capital District.................	AHL	7	0	1	1	29	2	1	0	1	29
93-94—Saint John	AHL	73	20	17	37	199	7	2	1	3	28
NHL totals.................................		84	10	13	23	215					

KVARTALNOV, DMITRI
LW/RW, BRUINS

PERSONAL: Born March 25, 1966, in Voskresensk, U.S.S.R.... 5-11/180.... Shoots left.... Name pronounced Kah-vahr-TAHL-nahf.
TRANSACTIONS/CAREER NOTES: Selected by Boston Bruins in first round (first Bruins pick, 16th overall) of NHL entry draft (June 20, 1992).... Suffered from strep throat (November 1992); missed three games.... Injured knee (February 1993); missed four games.... Injured wrist (March 1993); missed one game.... Suffered asthma attack (April 1993); missed one game.
HONORS: Won James Gatschene Memorial Trophy (1991-92).... Won Leo P. Lamoureux Memorial Trophy (1991-92).... Won Garry F. Longman Memorial Trophy (1991-92).... Named to IHL All-Star first team (1991-92).

			REGULAR SEASON					PLAYOFFS			
Season Team	League	Gms.	G	A	Pts.	PIM	Gms.	G	A	Pts.	PIM
82-83—Khimik Voskresensk........	USSR	7	0	0	0	0	—	—	—	—	—
83-84—Khimik Voskresensk........	USSR	2	0	0	0	0	—	—	—	—	—
84-85—SKA MVO Kalinin	USSR				Statistics unavailable.						
85-86—SKA MVO Kalinin	USSR				Statistics unavailable.						

Season—Team	League	Gms.	G	A	Pts.	PIM	Gms.	G	A	Pts.	PIM
86-87—Khimik Voskresensk	USSR	40	11	6	17	28	—	—	—	—	—
87-88—Khimik Voskresensk	USSR	43	16	11	27	16	—	—	—	—	—
88-89—Khimik Voskresensk	USSR	44	20	12	32	18	—	—	—	—	—
89-90—Khimik Voskresensk	USSR	46	25	28	*53	33	—	—	—	—	—
90-91—Khimik Voskresensk	USSR	42	12	10	22	18	—	—	—	—	—
91-92—San Diego	IHL	77	*60	58	*118	16	4	2	0	2	2
92-93—Khimik Voskresensk	CIS	3	0	0	0	0	—	—	—	—	—
—Boston	NHL	73	30	42	72	16	4	0	0	0	0
93-94—Boston	NHL	39	12	7	19	10	—	—	—	—	—
—Providence	AHL	23	13	13	26	8	—	—	—	—	—
NHL totals		112	42	49	91	26	4	0	0	0	0

KYPREOS, NICK

LW, RANGERS

PERSONAL: Born June 4, 1966, in Toronto. . . . 6-0/205. . . . Shoots left. . . . Full name: Nicholas George Kypreos. . . . Name pronounced KIHP-ree-ohz.

TRANSACTIONS/CAREER NOTES: Signed as free agent by Philadelphia Flyers (September 30, 1984). . . . Underwent surgery to right knee (Summer 1988); missed first 52 games of 1988-89 season. . . . Selected by Washington Capitals in NHL waiver draft for $20,000 (October 2, 1989). . . . Underwent surgery to right knee (February 8, 1990). . . . Traded by Capitals to Hartford Whalers for RW Mark Hunter and future considerations (June 15, 1992); Whalers sent LW Yvon Corriveau to Capitals to complete deal (August 20, 1992). . . . Suspended two games by NHL for game misconduct penalties (February 3, 1993). . . . Injured abdominal muscle (April 3, 1993); missed remainder of season. . . . Traded by Whalers with RW Steve Larmer, D Barry Richter, and undisclosed draft pick to New York Rangers for D James Patrick and C Darren Turcotte (November 2, 1993). . . . Suspended five games and fined $500 by NHL for deliberately injuring player with late hit (November 2, 1993). . . . Underwent root canal surgery (April 1, 1994); missed one game.

HONORS: Named to OHL All-Star first team (1985-86). . . . Named to OHL All-Star second team (1986-87).

MISCELLANEOUS: Member of Stanley Cup championship team (1994).

		REGULAR SEASON					PLAYOFFS				
Season Team	League	Gms.	G	A	Pts.	PIM	Gms.	G	A	Pts.	PIM
83-84—North Bay	OHL	51	12	11	23	36	4	3	2	5	9
84-85—North Bay	OHL	64	41	36	77	71	8	2	2	4	15
85-86—North Bay	OHL	64	62	35	97	112	—	—	—	—	—
86-87—North Bay	OHL	46	49	41	90	54	24	11	5	16	78
—Hershey	AHL	10	0	1	1	4	—	—	—	—	—
87-88—Hershey	AHL	71	24	20	44	101	12	0	2	2	17
88-89—Hershey	AHL	28	12	15	27	19	12	4	5	9	11
89-90—Washington	NHL	31	5	4	9	82	7	1	0	1	15
—Baltimore	AHL	14	6	5	11	6	7	4	1	5	17
90-91—Washington	NHL	79	9	9	18	196	9	0	1	1	38
91-92—Washington	NHL	65	4	6	10	206	—	—	—	—	—
92-93—Hartford	NHL	75	17	10	27	325	—	—	—	—	—
93-94—Hartford	NHL	10	0	0	0	37	—	—	—	—	—
—New York Rangers	NHL	46	3	5	8	102	3	0	0	0	2
NHL totals		306	38	34	72	948	19	1	1	2	55

KYTE, JIM

D

PERSONAL: Born March 21, 1964, in Ottawa. . . . 6-5/220. . . . Shoots left.

TRANSACTIONS/CAREER NOTES: Broke left wrist (March 1980). . . . Selected by Winnipeg Jets as underage junior in first round (first Jets pick, 12th overall) of NHL entry draft (June 9, 1982). . . . Suffered stress fracture in lower back (February 1988). . . . Sprained shoulder (March 1989). . . . Traded by Jets with RW Andrew McBain and LW Randy Gilhen to Pittsburgh Penguins for C/LW Randy Cunneyworth, G Richard Tabaracci and RW Dave McLlwain (June 17, 1989). . . . Traded by Penguins to Calgary Flames for C Jiri Hrdina (December 13, 1990). . . . Fractured bone in left hand during preseason (September 1991). . . . Fractured right ankle (January 27, 1991); missed remainder of season. . . . Signed as free agent by Ottawa Senators (September 10, 1992).

		REGULAR SEASON					PLAYOFFS				
Season Team	League	Gms.	G	A	Pts.	PIM	Gms.	G	A	Pts.	PIM
80-81—Hawkesbury	COJHL	42	2	24	26	133	—	—	—	—	—
81-82—Cornwall	OHL	52	4	13	17	148	5	0	0	0	10
82-83—Cornwall	OHL	65	6	30	36	195	8	0	2	2	24
—Winnipeg	NHL	2	0	0	0	0	—	—	—	—	—
83-84—Winnipeg	NHL	58	1	2	3	55	3	0	0	0	11
84-85—Winnipeg	NHL	71	0	3	3	111	8	0	0	0	14
85-86—Winnipeg	NHL	71	1	3	4	126	3	0	0	0	12
86-87—Winnipeg	NHL	72	5	5	10	162	10	0	4	4	36
87-88—Winnipeg	NHL	51	1	3	4	128	—	—	—	—	—
88-89—Winnipeg	NHL	74	3	9	12	190	—	—	—	—	—
89-90—Pittsburgh	NHL	56	3	1	4	125	—	—	—	—	—
90-91—Muskegon	IHL	25	2	5	7	157	—	—	—	—	—
—Pittsburgh	NHL	1	0	0	0	2	—	—	—	—	—
—Calgary	NHL	42	0	9	9	153	7	0	0	0	7
91-92—Calgary	NHL	21	0	1	1	107	—	—	—	—	—
—Salt Lake City	IHL	6	0	1	1	9	—	—	—	—	—
92-93—New Haven	AHL	63	6	18	24	163	—	—	—	—	—
—Ottawa	NHL	4	0	1	1	4	—	—	—	—	—
93-94—Las Vegas	IHL	75	2	16	18	246	4	0	1	1	51
NHL totals		523	14	37	51	1163	31	0	4	4	80

LABBE, JEAN-FRANCOIS
G, SENATORS

PERSONAL: Born June 15, 1972, in Sherbrooke, Que. ... 5-9/170. ... Catches left.

TRANSACTIONS/CAREER NOTES: Signed as free agent by Ottawa Senators (1993).

HONORS: Named Col.HL Playoff Most Valuable Player (1993-94).

				REGULAR SEASON							PLAYOFFS					
Season	Team	League	Gms.	Min.	W	L	T	GA	SO	Avg.	Gms.	Min.	W	L	GA	SO	Avg.
89-90—Trois-Rivieres	QMJHL	28	1499	13	10	0	106	1	4.24	3	132	1	1	8	0	3.64
90-91—Trois-Rivieres	QMJHL	54	2870	35	14	0	158	5	3.30	5	230	1	4	19	0	4.96
91-92—Trois-Rivieres	QMJHL	48	2749	31	13	3	142	3	3.10	15	791	10	3	33	1	2.50
92-93—Hull	QMJHL	46	2701	25	16	2	155	2	3.44	10	518	6	3	24	1	2.78
93-94—Prince Edward Island	AHL	7	390	4	3	0	22	0	3.38	—	—	—	—	—	—	—
—Thunder Bay	Col.HL	52	*2900	*35	11	4	150	*2	3.10	8	493	7	1	18	*2	2.19

LACHANCE, BOB
RW, BLUES

PERSONAL: Born February 1, 1974, in North Hampton, Mass. ... 5-11/175. ... Shoots right.

COLLEGE: Boston University.

TRANSACTIONS/CAREER NOTES: Selected by St. Louis Blues in sixth round (fifth Blues pick, 134th overall) of NHL entry draft (June 20, 1992).

			REGULAR SEASON				PLAYOFFS			
Season	Team	League	Gms.	G	A	Pts.	PIM	Gms.	G	A	Pts.	PIM
91-92—Springfield Jr. B	NEJHL	46	40	98	138	87	—	—	—	—	—
92-93—Boston University	Hockey East	33	4	10	14	24	—	—	—	—	—
93-94—Boston University	Hockey East	32	13	19	32	42	—	—	—	—	—

LACHANCE, SCOTT
D, ISLANDERS

PERSONAL: Born October 22, 1972, in Charlottesville, Va. ... 6-2/197. ... Shoots left. ... Full name: Scott Joseph Lachance.

COLLEGE: Boston University.

TRANSACTIONS/CAREER NOTES: Selected by New York Islanders in first round (first Islanders pick, fourth overall) of NHL entry draft (June 22, 1991). ... Sprained wrist (April 13, 1993); missed remainder of season. ... Underwent wrist surgery (April 30, 1993). ... Suffered mild separation of right shoulder (October 8, 1993); missed four games.

HONORS: Named to Hockey East All-Rookie team (1990-91).

			REGULAR SEASON				PLAYOFFS			
Season	Team	League	Gms.	G	A	Pts.	PIM	Gms.	G	A	Pts.	PIM
88-89—Springfield Jr. B	NEJHL	36	8	28	36	20	—	—	—	—	—
89-90—Springfield Jr. B	NEJHL	34	25	41	66	62	—	—	—	—	—
90-91—Boston University	Hockey East	31	5	19	24	48	—	—	—	—	—
91-92—U.S. national team	Int'l	36	1	10	11	34	—	—	—	—	—
—U.S. Olympic Team	Int'l	8	0	1	1	6	—	—	—	—	—
—New York Islanders	NHL	17	1	4	5	9	—	—	—	—	—
92-93—New York Islanders	NHL	75	7	17	24	67	—	—	—	—	—
93-94—New York Islanders	NHL	74	3	11	14	70	3	0	0	0	0
NHL totals		166	11	32	43	146	3	0	0	0	0

LACHER, BLAINE
G, BRUINS

PERSONAL: Born September 5, 1970, in Medicine Hat, Alta. ... 6-1/205. ... Catches left.

COLLEGE: Lake Superior State.

TRANSACTIONS/CAREER NOTES: Signed as free agent by Boston Bruins (May 19, 1994).

				REGULAR SEASON							PLAYOFFS					
Season	Team	League	Gms.	Min.	W	L	T	GA	SO	Avg.	Gms.	Min.	W	L	GA	SO	Avg.
91-92—Lake Superior State	CCHA	10	413	5	3	0	23	...	3.34	—	—	—	—	—	—	—
92-93—Lake Superior State	CCHA	34	1915	24	5	3	86	...	2.69	—	—	—	—	—	—	—
93-94—Lake Superior State	CCHA	30	1785	20	5	4	59	0	1.98	—	—	—	—	—	—	—

LACROIX, DANIEL
LW, RANGERS

PERSONAL: Born March 11, 1969, in Montreal. ... 6-2/188. ... Shoots left. ... Name pronounced luh-KWAH.

TRANSACTIONS/CAREER NOTES: Selected as underage junior by New York Rangers in second round (second Rangers pick, 31st overall) of NHL entry draft (June 13, 1987).

HONORS: Won Marcel Robert Trophy (1988-89).

			REGULAR SEASON				PLAYOFFS			
Season	Team	League	Gms.	G	A	Pts.	PIM	Gms.	G	A	Pts.	PIM
86-87—Granby	QMJHL	54	9	16	25	311	8	1	2	3	22
87-88—Granby	QMJHL	58	24	50	74	468	5	0	4	4	12
88-89—Granby	QMJHL	70	45	49	94	320	4	1	1	2	57
—Denver	IHL	2	0	1	1	0	2	0	1	1	0
89-90—Flint	IHL	61	12	16	28	128	4	2	0	2	24
90-91—Binghamton	AHL	54	7	12	19	237	5	1	0	1	24
91-92—Binghamton	AHL	52	12	20	32	149	11	2	4	6	28
92-93—Binghamton	AHL	73	21	22	43	255	—	—	—	—	—
93-94—New York Rangers	NHL	4	0	0	0	0	—	—	—	—	—
—Binghamton	AHL	59	20	23	43	278	—	—	—	—	—
NHL totals		4	0	0	0	0					

L

LACROIX, ERIC

LW, MAPLE LEAFS

PERSONAL: Born July 15, 1971, in Montreal.... 6-1/200.... Shoots left.... Name pronounced luh-KWAH. **COLLEGE:** St. Lawrence (N.Y.). **TRANSACTIONS/CAREER NOTES:** Selected by Toronto Maple Leafs in seventh round (136th overall) of NHL entry draft (June 16, 1990).... Separated shoulder (November 27, 1993); missed eight games.

			REGULAR SEASON					PLAYOFFS				
Season Team	League	Gms.	G	A	Pts.	PIM	Gms.	G	A	Pts.	PIM
90-91—St. Lawrence University ...	ECAC	35	13	11	24	35	—	—	—	—	—
91-92—St. Lawrence University ...	ECAC	34	11	20	31	40	—	—	—	—	—
92-93—St. John's	AHL	76	15	19	34	59	9	5	3	8	4
93-94—St. John's	AHL	59	17	22	39	69	11	5	3	8	6
—Toronto	NHL	3	0	0	0	2	2	0	0	0	0
NHL totals		3	0	0	0	2	2	0	0	0	0

LADOUCEUR, RANDY

D, MIGHTY DUCKS

PERSONAL: Born June 30, 1960, in Brockville, Ont.... 6-2/220.... Shoots left.... Name pronounced LAD-uh-SOOR. **TRANSACTIONS/CAREER NOTES:** Signed as free agent by Detroit Red Wings (November 1, 1979).... Suffered back spasms (March 1986).... Traded by Red Wings to Hartford Whalers for C Dave Barr (January 12, 1987).... Sprained right knee (March 1990).... Sprained knee (January 10, 1991); missed 10 games.... Bruised knee (October 28, 1992); missed one game.... Suffered right elbow infection (December 8, 1992); missed three games.... Suffered right foot contusion (March 3, 1993); missed two games.... Selected by Mighty Ducks of Anaheim in NHL expansion draft (June 24, 1993).... Bruised right thigh (January 10, 1994); missed three games.

			REGULAR SEASON					PLAYOFFS				
Season Team	League	Gms.	G	A	Pts.	PIM	Gms.	G	A	Pts.	PIM
78-79—Brantford	OMJHL	64	3	17	20	141	—	—	—	—	—
79-80—Brantford	OMJHL	37	6	15	21	125	8	0	5	5	18
80-81—Kalamazoo	IHL	80	7	30	37	52	8	1	3	4	10
81-82—Adirondack	AHL	78	4	28	32	78	5	1	1	2	6
82-83—Adirondack	AHL	48	11	21	32	54	—	—	—	—	—
—Detroit	NHL	27	0	4	4	16	—	—	—	—	—
83-84—Adirondack	AHL	11	3	5	8	12	—	—	—	—	—
—Detroit	NHL	71	3	17	20	58	4	1	0	1	6
84-85—Detroit	NHL	80	3	27	30	108	3	1	0	1	0
85-86—Detroit	NHL	78	5	13	18	196	—	—	—	—	—
86-87—Detroit	NHL	34	3	6	9	70	—	—	—	—	—
—Hartford	NHL	36	2	3	5	51	6	0	2	2	12
87-88—Hartford	NHL	67	1	7	8	91	6	1	1	2	4
88-89—Hartford	NHL	75	2	5	7	95	1	0	0	0	10
89-90—Hartford	NHL	71	3	12	15	126	7	1	0	1	10
90-91—Hartford	NHL	67	1	3	4	118	6	1	4	5	6
91-92—Hartford	NHL	74	1	9	10	127	7	0	1	1	11
92-93—Hartford	NHL	62	2	4	6	109	—	—	—	—	—
93-94—Anaheim	NHL	81	1	9	10	74	—	—	—	—	—
NHL totals		823	27	119	146	1239	40	5	8	13	59

LaFAYETTE, NATHAN

C, CANUCKS

PERSONAL: Born February 17, 1973, in New Westminster, B.C.... 6-1/195.... Shoots right.... Name pronounced LAH-fay-eht. **TRANSACTIONS/CAREER NOTES:** Traded by Kingston Frontenacs with Joel Sandie to Cornwall Royals for D Rod Pasma and Shawn Caplice (January 6, 1991).... Selected by St. Louis Blues in third round (third Blues pick, 65th overall) of NHL entry draft (June 22, 1991).... Traded by Blues with D Jeff Brown and D Bret Hedican to Vancouver Canucks for C Craig Janney (March 21, 1994). **HONORS:** Won Can.HL Scholastic Player of the Year Award (1991-92).... Won Bobby Smith Trophy (1990-91 and 1991-92).

			REGULAR SEASON					PLAYOFFS				
Season Team	League	Gms.	G	A	Pts.	PIM	Gms.	G	A	Pts.	PIM
89-90—Kingston	OHL	53	6	8	14	14	7	0	1	1	0
90-91—Kingston	OHL	35	13	13	26	10	—	—	—	—	—
—Cornwall	OHL	28	16	22	38	25	—	—	—	—	—
91-92—Cornwall	OHL	66	28	45	73	26	6	2	5	7	16
92-93—Newmarket	OHL	58	49	38	87	26	7	4	6	10	19
93-94—Peoria	IHL	27	13	11	24	20	—	—	—	—	—
—St. Louis	NHL	38	2	3	5	14	—	—	—	—	—
—Vancouver	NHL	11	1	1	2	4	20	2	7	9	4
NHL totals		49	3	4	7	18	20	2	7	9	4

LaFONTAINE, PAT

C, SABRES

PERSONAL: Born February 22, 1965, in St. Louis.... 5-10/177.... Shoots right.... Name pronounced luh-FAHN-tayn. **TRANSACTIONS/CAREER NOTES:** Selected by New York Islanders as underage junior in first round (first Islanders pick, third overall) of NHL entry draft (June 8, 1983).... Damaged ligaments in left knee (August 16, 1984).... Suffered from mononucleosis (January 1985).... Separated right shoulder (January 25, 1986).... Bruised knee (March 1988).... Broke nose (October 7, 1988); played entire season with injury.... Sprained ligaments in right wrist (November 5, 1988).... Strained left hamstring (October 13, 1990); missed three games.... Traded by Islanders with LW Randy Wood, D Randy Hillier and future considerations to Buffalo Sabres for C Pierre Turgeon, RW Benoit Hogue, D Uwe Krupp and C Dave McLlwain; Sabres later received fourth-round pick (D Dean Melanson) in 1992 draft (October 25, 1991).... Fractured jaw (November 16, 1991); missed 13 games.... Injured knee (November 13, 1993); missed remainder of season.

HONORS: Won Can.HL Player of the Year Award (1982-83).... Won Michel Briere Trophy (1982-83).... Won Jean Beliveau Trophy (1982-83).... Won Frank J. Selke Trophy (1982-83).... Won Des Instructeurs Trophy (1982-83).... Won Guy Lafleur Trophy (1982-83).... Named to QMJHL All-Star first team (1982-83).... Played in NHL All-Star Game (1988-1991 and 1993).... Won Dodge Performer of the Year Award (1989-90).... Named to THE SPORTING NEWS All-Star second team (1989-90).... Named to NHL All-Star second team (1992-93).

RECORDS: Holds NHL playoff record for fastest two goals from the start of a period—35 seconds (May 19, 1984).

			REGULAR SEASON					PLAYOFFS				
Season	Team	League	Gms.	G	A	Pts.	PIM	Gms.	G	A	Pts.	PIM
82-83	Verdun	QMJHL	70	*104	*130	*234	10	15	11	*24	*35	4
83-84	U.S. national team	Int'l	58	56	55	111	22	—	—	—	—	—
	U.S. Olympic Team	Int'l	6	5	3	8	0	—	—	—	—	—
	New York Islanders	NHL	15	13	6	19	6	16	3	6	9	8
84-85	New York Islanders	NHL	67	19	35	54	32	9	1	2	3	4
85-86	New York Islanders	NHL	65	30	23	53	43	3	1	0	1	0
86-87	New York Islanders	NHL	80	38	32	70	70	14	5	7	12	10
87-88	New York Islanders	NHL	75	47	45	92	52	6	4	5	9	8
88-89	New York Islanders	NHL	79	45	43	88	26	—	—	—	—	—
89-90	New York Islanders	NHL	74	54	51	105	38	2	0	1	1	0
90-91	New York Islanders	NHL	75	41	44	85	42	—	—	—	—	—
91-92	Buffalo	NHL	57	46	47	93	98	7	8	3	11	4
92-93	Buffalo	NHL	84	53	95	148	63	7	2	10	12	0
93-94	Buffalo	NHL	16	5	13	18	2	—	—	—	—	—
NHL totals			687	391	434	825	472	64	24	34	58	34

LAFOREST, MARK

G

PERSONAL: Born July 10, 1962, in Welland, Ont.... 5-11/190.... Catches left.... Full name: Mark Andrew Laforest.

TRANSACTIONS/CAREER NOTES: Signed as free agent by Detroit Red Wings (September 1983).... Traded by Red Wings to Philadelphia Flyers for second-round pick (D Bob Wilkie) in 1987 draft (June 1987).... Sprained knee (March 16, 1989).... Traded by Flyers to Toronto Maple Leafs for sixth- and seventh-round picks in 1991 draft (September 8, 1989).... Twisted left ankle (January 11, 1990); missed five weeks.... Traded with by Maple Leafs with RW Tie Domi to New York Rangers for RW Greg Johnston (June 18, 1990).... Selected by Ottawa Senators in NHL expansion draft (June 18, 1992).

HONORS: Won Aldege (Baz) Bastien Trophy (1986-87 and 1990-91).... Named to AHL All-Star second team (1990-91).

			REGULAR SEASON							PLAYOFFS					
Season	Team	League	Gms.	Min.	W	L	T	GA	SO	Avg.	Gms.	Min.	W	L	GA	SO	Avg.
81-82	Niagara Falls	OHL	24	1365	10	13	1	105	1	4.62	5	300	1	2	19	0	3.80
82-83	North Bay	OHL	54	3140	34	17	1	195	0	3.73	8	474	4	4	31	0	3.92
83-84	Adirondack	AHL	7	351	3	3	1	29	0	4.96	—	—	—	—	—	—	—
	Kalamazoo	IHL	13	718	4	5	‡2	48	1	4.01	—	—	—	—	—	—	—
84-85	Mohawk Valley Stars	ACHL	8	420				60	0	8.57	—	—	—	—	—	—	—
	Adirondack	AHL	11	430	2	3	1	35	0	4.88	—	—	—	—	—	—	—
85-86	Adirondack	AHL	19	1142	13	5	1	57	0	2.99	*17	*1075	12	5	*58	0	3.24
	Detroit	NHL	28	1383	4	21	0	114	1	4.95	—	—	—	—	—	—	—
86-87	Adirondack	AHL	37	2229	23	8	0	105	3	2.83	—	—	—	—	—	—	—
	Detroit	NHL	5	219	2	1	0	12	0	3.29	—	—	—	—	—	—	—
87-88	Hershey	AHL	5	309	2	1	2	13	0	2.52	—	—	—	—	—	—	—
	Philadelphia	NHL	21	972	5	9	2	60	1	3.70	2	48	1	0	1	0	1.25
88-89	Philadelphia	NHL	17	933	5	7	2	64	0	4.12	—	—	—	—	—	—	—
	Hershey	AHL	3	185	2	0	0	9	0	2.92	12	744	7	5	27	1	*2.18
89-90	Toronto	NHL	27	1343	9	14	0	87	0	3.89	—	—	—	—	—	—	—
	Newmarket	AHL	10	604	6	4	0	33	1	3.28	—	—	—	—	—	—	—
90-91	Binghamton	AHL	45	2452	25	14	2	129	0	3.16	9	442	3	4	28	*1	3.80
91-92	Binghamton	AHL	43	2559	25	15	3	146	1	3.42	11	662	7	4	34	0	3.08
92-93	New Haven	AHL	30	1688	10	18	1	121	1	4.30	—	—	—	—	—	—	—
	Brantford	Col.HL	10	565	5	3	‡1	35	†1	3.72	—	—	—	—	—	—	—
93-94	Prince Edward Island	AHL	43	2359	9	25	5	161	0	4.09	—	—	—	—	—	—	—
	Ottawa	NHL	5	182	0	2	0	17	0	5.60	—	—	—	—	—	—	—
NHL totals			103	5032	25	54	4	354	2	4.22	2	48	1	0	1	0	1.25

LAFORGE, MARC

RW/D, ISLANDERS

PERSONAL: Born January 3, 1968, in Sudbury, Ont.... 6-2/210.... Shoots left.

TRANSACTIONS/CAREER NOTES: Selected by Hartford Whalers as underage junior in second round (second Whalers pick, 32nd overall) of NHL entry draft (June 21, 1986).... Suspended nine games by OHL (October 1986).... Suspended two years by OHL for attacking several members of opposing team in game-ending fight (November 6, 1987).... Suspended three games by AHL for head-butting (November 26, 1988).... Suspended six games for leaving bench to start fight (December 8, 1988).... Suspended by Whalers for refusing to report to Indianapolis (December 28, 1988).... Whalers lifted suspension when he reported to Indianapolis (January 19, 1989).... Suffered sore back (November 1989).... Suspended five games by AHL for head-butting (February 5, 1990).... Traded by Whalers to Edmonton Oilers for rights to D Cam Brauer (March 6, 1990).... Suspended 10 games by AHL for cross-checking and kneeing (December 3, 1990).... Suspended 10 games by AHL for cross-checking (January 13, 1991).... Suspended six games by AHL for leaving the bench to start fight (February 1991).... Suspended 10 games by NHL (September 26, 1991). . . . Suffered groin strain (October 29, 1993); missed three games. . . . Traded by Oilers to New York Islanders for LW Brent Grieve (December 15, 1993).

			REGULAR SEASON					PLAYOFFS				
Season Team	League	Gms.	G	A	Pts.	PIM	Gms.	G	A	Pts.	PIM
84-85—Kingston	OHL	57	1	5	6	214	—	—	—	—	—
85-86—Kingston	OHL	60	1	13	14	248	10	0	1	1	30
86-87—Kingston	OHL	53	2	10	12	224	12	1	0	1	79
—Binghamton	AHL	—	—	—	—	—	4	0	0	0	7
87-88—Sudbury	OHL	14	0	2	2	68	—	—	—	—	—
88-89—Indianapolis	IHL	14	0	2	2	138	—	—	—	—	—
—Binghamton	AHL	38	2	2	4	179	—	—	—	—	—
89-90—Hartford	NHL	9	0	0	0	43	—	—	—	—	—
—Binghamton	AHL	25	2	6	8	111	—	—	—	—	—
—Cape Breton	AHL	3	0	1	1	24	3	0	0	0	27
90-91—Cape Breton	AHL	49	1	7	8	217	—	—	—	—	—
91-92—Cape Breton	AHL	59	0	14	14	341	4	0	0	0	24
92-93—Cape Breton	AHL	77	1	12	13	208	15	1	2	3	*78
93-94—Cape Breton	AHL	14	0	0	0	91	—	—	—	—	—
—Salt Lake City	IHL	43	0	2	2	242	—	—	—	—	—
—Edmonton	NHL	5	0	0	0	21	—	—	—	—	—
NHL totals		14	0	0	0	64					

LaFRANCE, DARRYL
C, FLAMES

PERSONAL: Born March 20, 1974, in Sudbury, Ont. . . . 5-11/175. . . . Shoots right.
HIGH SCHOOL: Henry Street (Whitby, Ont.).
TRANSACTIONS/CAREER NOTES: Selected by Calgary Flames in fifth round (sixth Flames pick, 121st overall) of NHL entry draft (June 26, 1993).

			REGULAR SEASON					PLAYOFFS				
Season Team	League	Gms.	G	A	Pts.	PIM	Gms.	G	A	Pts.	PIM
91-92—Oshawa	OHL	48	12	20	32	24	7	0	1	1	2
92-93—Oshawa	OHL	66	35	51	86	24	13	8	8	16	0
93-94—Oshawa	OHL	61	45	61	106	17	5	1	9	10	0

LAFRENIERE, JASON
C, LIGHTNING

PERSONAL: Born December 6, 1966, in St. Catharines, Ont. . . . 5-11/185. . . . Shoots right. . . . Name pronounced LAH-frehn-YAIR.
TRANSACTIONS/CAREER NOTES: Selected by Quebec Nordiques as underage junior in second round (second Nordiques pick, 36th overall) of NHL entry draft (June 15, 1985). . . . Traded by Hamilton Steelhawks with RW Peter Choma, G Steve Norkaitis and D Lawrence Hinch to Belleville Bulls for D Shane Doyle, RW John Purves, LW Niels Jensen and D Brian Hoard (November 1985). . . . Traded by Nordiques with D Norman Rochefort to New York Rangers for C Walt Poddubny, D Bruce Bell, D Jari Gronstrand and fourth-round pick (D Eric DuBois) in 1989 draft (August 1, 1988). . . . Signed as free agent by Tampa Bay Lightning (July 29, 1992).
HONORS: Won William Hanley Trophy (1985-86). . . . Named to OHL All-Star first team (1985-86).

			REGULAR SEASON					PLAYOFFS				
Season Team	League	Gms.	G	A	Pts.	PIM	Gms.	G	A	Pts.	PIM
83-84—Brantford	OHL	70	24	57	81	4	6	2	4	6	2
84-85—Hamilton	OHL	59	26	69	95	10	17	12	16	28	0
85-86—Hamilton	OHL	14	12	10	22	2	—	—	—	—	—
—Belleville	OHL	48	37	73	110	2	23	10	22	32	6
86-87—Quebec	NHL	56	13	15	28	8	12	1	5	6	2
—Fredericton	AHL	11	3	11	14	0	—	—	—	—	—
87-88—Quebec	NHL	40	10	19	29	4	—	—	—	—	—
—Fredericton	AHL	32	12	19	31	38	—	—	—	—	—
88-89—New York Rangers	NHL	38	8	16	24	6	3	0	0	0	17
—Denver	IHL	24	10	19	29	17	—	—	—	—	—
89-90—Flint	IHL	41	9	25	34	34	—	—	—	—	—
—Phoenix	IHL	14	4	9	13	0	—	—	—	—	—
90-91—Canadian national team	Int'l	59	26	33	59	50	—	—	—	—	—
91-92—San Diego	IHL	5	1	2	3	2	—	—	—	—	—
—Landshut	Germany	23	7	22	29	16	—	—	—	—	—
92-93—Atlanta	IHL	63	23	47	70	34	9	3	4	7	22
—Tampa Bay	NHL	11	3	3	6	4	—	—	—	—	—
93-94—Milwaukee	IHL	52	14	47	61	16	—	—	—	—	—
—Tampa Bay	NHL	1	0	0	0	0	—	—	—	—	—
NHL totals		146	34	53	87	22	15	1	5	6	19

LaGRAND, SCOTT
G, FLYERS

PERSONAL: Born February 11, 1970, in Potsdam, N.Y. . . . 6-1/170. . . . Catches left.
HIGH SCHOOL: Hotchkiss (Lakeville, Conn.).
COLLEGE: Boston College.
TRANSACTIONS/CAREER NOTES: Selected by Philadelphia Flyers in fourth round (fifth Flyers pick, 77th overall) of NHL entry draft (June 11, 1988).
HONORS: Named to Hockey East All-Star first team (1990-91). . . . Named to NCAA All-America East second team (1991-92).

			REGULAR SEASON							PLAYOFFS					
Season Team	League	Gms.	Min.	W	L	T	GA	SO	Avg.	Gms.	Min.	W	L	GA SO	Avg.
86-87—Hotchkiss	N.Y. H.S.	17	1020	. . .	. . .	. . .	36	0	2.12	—	—	—	—	— —	—
87-88—Hotchkiss	N.Y. H.S.						Statistics unavailable.								

Season	Team	League	REGULAR SEASON Gms.	G	A	Pts.	Pen.	PLAYOFFS Gms.	G	A	Pts.	Pen.
88-89	Hotchkiss	N.Y. H.S.					Statistics unavailable.					
89-90	Boston College	Hoc. East	24	1268	17	4	0	57	0	2.70	7	377 5 1 17 0 2.71
90-91	Boston College	Hoc. East	23	1153	12	8	0	63	2	3.28	—	— — — — —
91-92	Boston College	Hoc. East	30	1750	11	16	2	108	1	3.70	—	— — — — —
92-93	Hershey	AHL	32	1854	8	17	4	145	0	4.69	—	— — — — —
93-94	Hershey	AHL	40	2033	16	13	3	117	2	3.45	—	— — — — —

LALIME, PATRICK
G, PENGUINS

PERSONAL: Born July 7, 1974, in St. Bonaventure, Que. . . . 6-2/165. . . . Catches left. . . . Name pronounced luh-LEEM.
TRANSACTIONS/CAREER NOTES: Selected by Pittsburgh Penguins in sixth round (sixth Penguins pick, 156th overall) of NHL entry draft (June 26, 1993).

Season	Team	League	REGULAR SEASON Gms.	Min.	W	L	T	GA	SO	Avg.	PLAYOFFS Gms.	Min.	W	L	GA	SO	Avg.
92-93	Shawinigan	QMJHL	44	2467	10	24	4	192	0	4.67	—	—	—	—	—	—	—
93-94	Shawinigan	QMJHL	48	2733	22	20	2	192	1	4.22	5	223	1	3	25	0	6.73

LALOR, MIKE
D, STARS

PERSONAL: Born March 8, 1963, in Fort Erie, Ont. . . . 6-0/200. . . . Shoots left. . . . Full name: John Michael Lalor. . . . Name pronounced LAH-luhr.
TRANSACTIONS/CAREER NOTES: Signed as free agent by Montreal Canadiens (September 1983). . . . Suffered from bursitis in right ankle (September 1987). . . . Suffered stress fracture of left ankle (November 1, 1988). . . . Traded by Canadiens to St. Louis Blues for option to flip first-round picks in 1990 draft and second- or third-round picks in 1991 draft; Canadiens exercised option (January 16, 1989). . . . Traded by Blues with C Peter Zezel to Washington Capitals for LW Geoff Courtnall (July 13, 1990). . . . Traded by Capitals to Winnipeg Jets for RW Paul MacDermid (March 2, 1992). . . . Broke finger (November 12, 1992); missed 13 games. . . . Strained neck (January 8, 1993); missed one game. . . . Suffered rib contusion (March 23, 1993); missed two games. . . . Strained knee ligaments (October 26, 1993); missed 22 games. . . . Traded by San Jose Sharks with D Doug Zmolek to Dallas Stars for LW Ulf Dahlen and future considerations (March 19, 1994).
MISCELLANEOUS: Member of Stanley Cup championship team (1986).

Season	Team	League	REGULAR SEASON Gms.	G	A	Pts.	PIM	PLAYOFFS Gms.	G	A	Pts.	PIM
81-82	Brantford	OHL	64	3	13	16	114	11	0	6	6	11
82-83	Brantford	OHL	65	10	30	40	113	6	1	3	4	20
83-84	Nova Scotia	AHL	67	5	11	16	80	12	0	2	2	13
84-85	Sherbrooke	AHL	79	9	23	32	114	17	3	5	8	36
85-86	Montreal	NHL	62	3	5	8	56	17	1	2	3	29
86-87	Montreal	NHL	57	0	10	10	47	13	2	1	3	29
87-88	Montreal	NHL	66	1	10	11	113	11	0	0	0	11
88-89	Montreal	NHL	12	1	4	5	15	—	—	—	—	—
	St. Louis	NHL	36	1	14	15	54	10	1	1	2	14
89-90	St. Louis	NHL	78	0	16	16	81	12	0	2	2	31
90-91	Washington	NHL	68	1	5	6	61	10	1	2	3	22
91-92	Washington	NHL	64	5	7	12	64	—	—	—	—	—
	Winnipeg	NHL	15	2	3	5	14	7	0	0	0	19
92-93	Winnipeg	NHL	64	1	8	9	76	4	0	2	2	4
93-94	San Jose	NHL	23	0	2	2	8	—	—	—	—	—
	Dallas	NHL	12	0	1	1	6	5	0	0	0	6
NHL totals			557	15	85	100	595	89	5	10	15	165

LAMB, MARK
C, FLYERS

PERSONAL: Born August 3, 1964, in Swift Current, Sask. . . . 5-10/175. . . . Shoots left.
HIGH SCHOOL: Swift Current (Sask.).
TRANSACTIONS/CAREER NOTES: Selected by Calgary Flames as underage junior in fourth round (fifth Flames pick, 72nd overall) of NHL entry draft (June 9, 1982). . . . Refused to dress for a game after Nanaimo Islanders released coach Les Calder (December 1982). . . . Traded by Islanders to Medicine Hat Tigers for Glen Kulka and G Daryl Reaugh (December 1982). . . . Signed as free agent by Detroit Red Wings (July 1, 1986). . . . Selected by Edmonton Oilers in NHL waiver draft (October 5, 1987). . . . Pinched nerve in neck (October 21, 1990). . . . Selected by Ottawa Senators in NHL expansion draft (June 18, 1992). . . . Suffered sore foot (October 24, 1992); missed two games. . . . Injured neck (December 17, 1992); missed 10 games. . . . Traded by Senators to Philadelphia Flyers for LW Claude Boivin and G Kirk Daubenspeck (March 5, 1994).
HONORS: Won Frank Boucher Memorial Trophy (1983-84). . . . Named to WHL (East) All-Star first team (1983-84).
MISCELLANEOUS: Member of Stanley Cup championship team (1990).

Season	Team	League	REGULAR SEASON Gms.	G	A	Pts.	PIM	PLAYOFFS Gms.	G	A	Pts.	PIM
80-81	Billings	WHL	24	1	8	9	12	—	—	—	—	—
81-82	Billings	WHL	72	45	56	101	46	5	4	6	10	4
82-83	Nanaimo	WHL	30	14	37	51	16	—	—	—	—	—
	Medicine Hat	WHL	46	22	43	65	33	5	3	2	5	4
	Colorado	CHL	—	—	—	—	—	6	0	2	2	0
83-84	Medicine Hat	WHL	72	59	77	136	30	14	12	11	23	6
84-85	Medicine Hat	WHL	—	—	—	—	—	6	3	2	5	2
	Moncton	AHL	80	23	49	72	53	—	—	—	—	—

Season Team	League	Gms.	G	A	Pts.	Pen.	Gms.	G	A	Pts.	Pen.
85-86—Calgary	NHL	1	0	0	0	0	—	—	—	—	—
—Moncton	AHL	79	26	50	76	51	10	2	6	8	17
86-87—Detroit	NHL	22	2	1	3	8	11	0	0	0	11
—Adirondack	AHL	49	14	36	50	45	—	—	—	—	—
87-88—Nova Scotia	AHL	69	27	61	88	45	5	0	5	5	6
—Edmonton	NHL	2	0	0	0	0	—	—	—	—	—
88-89—Cape Breton	AHL	54	33	49	82	29	—	—	—	—	—
—Edmonton	NHL	20	2	8	10	14	6	0	2	2	8
89-90—Edmonton	NHL	58	12	16	28	42	22	6	11	17	2
90-91—Edmonton	NHL	37	4	8	12	25	15	0	5	5	20
91-92—Edmonton	NHL	59	6	22	28	46	16	1	1	2	10
92-93—Ottawa	NHL	71	7	19	26	64	—	—	—	—	—
93-94—Ottawa	NHL	66	11	18	29	56	—	—	—	—	—
—Philadelphia	NHL	19	1	6	7	16	—	—	—	—	—
NHL totals		355	45	98	143	271	70	7	19	26	51

LAMBERT, DAN

D

PERSONAL: Born January 12, 1970, in St. Boniface, Man. . . . 5-8/177. . . . Shoots left. . . . Name pronounced lam-BAIR.

TRANSACTIONS/CAREER NOTES: Selected by Quebec Nordiques in sixth round (eighth Nordiques pick, 106th overall) of NHL entry draft (June 17, 1989). . . . Suffered facial paralysis (December 4, 1991); missed two games. . . . Traded by Nordiques to Winnipeg Jets for D Shawn Cronin (August 25, 1992).
HONORS: Won Bill Hunter Trophy (1988-89). . . . Named to WHL (East) All-Star first team (1988-89 and 1989-90). . . . Named to Memorial Cup All-Star team (1988-89).

Season Team	League	Gms.	G	A	Pts.	PIM	Gms.	G	A	Pts.	PIM
86-87—Swift Current	WHL	68	13	53	66	95	4	1	1	2	9
87-88—Swift Current	WHL	69	20	63	83	120	10	2	10	12	45
88-89—Swift Current	WHL	57	25	77	102	158	12	9	19	28	12
89-90—Swift Current	WHL	50	17	51	68	119	4	2	3	5	12
90-91—Fort Wayne	IHL	49	10	27	37	65	19	4	10	14	20
—Halifax	AHL	30	7	13	20	20	—	—	—	—	—
—Quebec	NHL	1	0	0	0	0	—	—	—	—	—
91-92—Halifax	AHL	47	3	28	31	33	—	—	—	—	—
—Quebec	NHL	28	6	9	15	22	—	—	—	—	—
92-93—Moncton	AHL	73	11	30	41	100	5	1	2	3	2
93-94—Fort Wayne	IHL	62	10	27	37	138	18	3	12	15	20
NHL totals		29	6	9	15	22					

LAMBERT, DENNY

LW, MIGHTY DUCKS

PERSONAL: Born January 7, 1970, in Wawa, Ont. . . . 5-11/200. . . . Shoots left.
TRANSACTIONS/CAREER NOTES: Signed as free agent by Mighty Ducks of Anaheim (August 16, 1993).

Season Team	League	Gms.	G	A	Pts.	PIM	Gms.	G	A	Pts.	PIM
90-91—S.S. Marie	OHL	59	28	39	67	169	14	7	9	16	48
91-92—San Diego	IHL	71	17	14	31	229	3	0	0	0	10
92-93—St. Thomas	Col.HL	5	2	6	8	9	—	—	—	—	—
—San Diego	IHL	56	18	12	30	277	14	1	1	2	44
93-94—San Diego	IHL	79	13	14	27	314	6	1	0	1	45

LAMMENS, HANK

D

PERSONAL: Born February 21, 1966, in Brockville, Ont. . . . 6-0/196. . . . Shoots left. . . . Full name: Hank Jacob Lammens.
COLLEGE: St. Lawrence (N.Y.).
TRANSACTIONS/CAREER NOTES: Broke wrist and separated shoulder (November 1984). . . . Selected by New York Islanders in 10th round (10th Islanders pick, 160th overall) of NHL entry draft (June 15, 1985). . . . Signed as free agent by Ottawa Senators (June 25, 1993).
HONORS: Named to NCAA All-America East second team (1986-87). . . . Named to ECAC All-Star second team (1986-87 and 1987-88).

Season Team	League	Gms.	G	A	Pts.	PIM	Gms.	G	A	Pts.	PIM
83-84—Brockville	COJHL	46	7	11	18	106	—	—	—	—	—
84-85—St. Lawrence University	ECAC	21	1	7	8	16	—	—	—	—	—
85-86—St. Lawrence University	ECAC	30	3	14	17	60	—	—	—	—	—
86-87—St. Lawrence University	ECAC	35	6	13	19	92	—	—	—	—	—
87-88—St. Lawrence University	ECAC	36	3	7	10	70	—	—	—	—	—
88-89—Springfield	AHL	69	1	13	14	55	—	—	—	—	—
89-90—Springfield	AHL	43	0	6	6	27	7	0	0	0	14
90-91—Kansas City	IHL	17	0	1	1	27	—	—	—	—	—
—Capital District	AHL	32	0	5	5	14	—	—	—	—	—
92-93—Canadian national team	Int'l	64	8	14	22	83	—	—	—	—	—
93-94—Prince Edward Island	AHL	50	2	9	11	32	—	—	—	—	—
—Ottawa	NHL	27	1	2	3	22	—	—	—	—	—
NHL totals		27	1	2	3	22					

LAMOTHE, MARC
G, CANADIENS

PERSONAL: Born February 27, 1974, in New Liskeard, Ont. . . . 6-2/186. . . . Catches left. . . . Name pronounced LAH-maht.
TRANSACTIONS/CAREER NOTES: Selected by Montreal Canadiens in fourth round (sixth Canadiens pick, 92nd overall) of NHL entry draft (June 20, 1992).

				REGULAR SEASON							PLAYOFFS					
Season Team	League	Gms.	Min.	W	L	T	GA	SO	Avg.	Gms.	Min.	W	L	GA	SO	Avg.
90-91—Ottawa	OHA Mj Jr.A	25	1220	...	...	...	82	1	4.03	—	—	—	—	—	—	—
91-92—Kingston	OHL	42	2378	10	25	2	189	1	4.77	—	—	—	—	—	—	—
92-93—Kingston	OHL	45	2489	23	12	6	162	†1	3.91	15	733	8	5	46	†1	3.77
93-94—Kingston	OHL	48	2828	23	20	5	177	†2	3.76	6	224	2	2	12	0	3.21

LANG, CHAD
G, STARS

PERSONAL: Born February 11, 1975, in Newmarket, Ont. . . . 5-10/188. . . . Catches left. . . . Cousin of Gerard Gallant, left winger, Tampa Bay Lightning.
TRANSACTIONS/CAREER NOTES: Selected by Dallas Stars in fourth round (third Stars pick, 87th overall) of NHL entry draft (June 26, 1993).
HONORS: Shared Dave Pinkney Trophy with Ryan Douglas (1992-93). . . . Named to OHL All-Star second team (1992-93).

				REGULAR SEASON							PLAYOFFS					
Season Team	League	Gms.	Min.	W	L	T	GA	SO	Avg.	Gms.	Min.	W	L	GA	SO	Avg.
90-91—Newmarket	Jr. B	34	1733	...	...	...	149	1	5.16	—	—	—	—	—	—	—
91-92—Peterborough	OHL	16	886	7	5	1	63	0	4.27	2	65	0	0	9	0	8.31
92-93—Peterborough	OHL	43	2554	*32	6	4	140	†1	3.29	*21	*1224	*12	*8	*74	†1	3.63
93-94—Peterborough	OHL	48	2732	11	27	7	225	0	4.94	7	391	3	4	24	0	3.68

LANG, ROBERT
C, KINGS

PERSONAL: Born December 19, 1970, in Teplice, Czechoslovakia. . . . 6-2/180. . . . Shoots right. . . . Name pronounced LUHNG.
TRANSACTIONS/CAREER NOTES: Selected by Los Angeles Kings in seventh round (sixth Kings pick, 133rd overall) of NHL entry draft (June 16, 1990). . . . Dislocated shoulder (April 3, 1994); missed remainder of season.

			REGULAR SEASON				PLAYOFFS				
Season Team	League	Gms.	G	A	Pts.	PIM	Gms.	G	A	Pts.	PIM
89-90—Litvinov	Czech.	39	11	10	21	20	—	—	—	—	—
90-91—Litvinov	Czech.	48	24	22	46	38	—	—	—	—	—
91-92—Litvinov	Czech.	43	12	31	43	34	—	—	—	—	—
—Czech. national team	Int'l	8	5	8	13	8	—	—	—	—	—
—Czech. Olympic Team	Int'l	8	5	8	13	8	—	—	—	—	—
92-93—Los Angeles	NHL	11	0	5	5	2	—	—	—	—	—
—Phoenix	IHL	38	9	21	30	20	—	—	—	—	—
93-94—Phoenix	IHL	44	11	24	35	34	—	—	—	—	—
—Los Angeles	NHL	32	9	10	19	10	—	—	—	—	—
NHL totals		43	9	15	24	12					

LANGENBRUNNER, JAMIE
C, STARS

PERSONAL: Born April 21, 1975, in Edmonton. . . . 5-11/170. . . . Shoots right. . . . Name pronounced LANG-ihn-BROO-nuhr.
HIGH SCHOOL: Cloquet (Minn.).
TRANSACTIONS/CAREER NOTES: Selected by Dallas Stars in second round (second Stars pick, 35th overall) of NHL entry draft (June 26, 1993).

			REGULAR SEASON				PLAYOFFS				
Season Team	League	Gms.	G	A	Pts.	PIM	Gms.	G	A	Pts.	PIM
90-91—Cloquet H.S.	Minn. H.S.	20	6	16	22	8	—	—	—	—	—
91-92—Cloquet H.S.	Minn. H.S.	23	16	23	39	24	—	—	—	—	—
92-93—Cloquet H.S.	Minn. H.S.	27	27	62	89	18	—	—	—	—	—
93-94—Peterborough	OHL	62	33	58	91	53	7	4	6	10	2

LANGKOW, SCOTT
G, JETS

PERSONAL: Born April 21, 1975, in Edmonton. . . . 5-11/180. . . . Catches left. . . . Name pronounced LANG-koh.
HIGH SCHOOL: Aloha (Beaverton, Ore.).
TRANSACTIONS/CAREER NOTES: Selected by Winnipeg Jets in second round (second Jets pick, 31st overall) of NHL entry draft (June 26, 1993).
HONORS: Named to WHL (West) All-Star second team (1993-94).

				REGULAR SEASON							PLAYOFFS					
Season Team	League	Gms.	Min.	W	L	T	GA	SO	Avg.	Gms.	Min.	W	L	GA	SO	Avg.
91-92—Portland	WHL	1	33	0	0	0	2	0	3.64	—	—	—	—	—	—	—
92-93—Portland	WHL	34	2064	24	8	2	119	2	3.46	9	535	6	3	31	0	3.48
93-94—Portland	WHL	39	2302	27	9	1	121	2	3.15	10	600	6	4	34	0	3.40

LAPERRIERE, DAN
D, BLUES

PERSONAL: Born March 28, 1969, in Laval, Que. . . . 6-1/180. . . . Shoots left. . . . Full name: Daniel Jacques Laperriere. . . . Name pronounced luh-PAIR-ee-YAIR. . . . Son of Jacques Laperriere, Hall of Fame defenseman, Montreal Canadiens (1962-63 through 1973-74) and current assistant coach, Canadiens.
COLLEGE: St. Lawrence (N.Y.).
TRANSACTIONS/CAREER NOTES: Selected by St. Louis Blues in fifth round (fourth Blues pick, 93rd overall) of NHL entry draft

(June 17, 1989).... Suffered from the flu (October 9, 1992); missed two games.
HONORS: Named to ECAC All-Star second team (1990-91).... Named ECAC Player of the Year (1991-92).... Named ECAC Playoff Most Valuable Player (1991-92).... Named to NCAA All-America East first team (1991-92).... Named to ECAC All-Star first team (1991-92).

Season Team	League	REGULAR SEASON					PLAYOFFS				
		Gms.	G	A	Pts.	PIM	Gms.	G	A	Pts.	PIM
88-89—St. Lawrence University...	ECAC	34	1	11	12	14	—	—	—	—	—
89-90—St. Lawrence University...	ECAC	29	6	19	25	16	—	—	—	—	—
90-91—St. Lawrence University...	ECAC	34	7	32	39	18	—	—	—	—	—
91-92—St. Lawrence University...	ECAC	32	8	*45	53	36	—	—	—	—	—
92-93—St. Louis	NHL	5	0	1	1	0	—	—	—	—	—
—Peoria	IHL	54	4	20	24	28	—	—	—	—	—
93-94—Peoria	IHL	56	10	37	47	16	6	0	2	2	2
—St. Louis	NHL	20	1	3	4	8	—	—	—	—	—
NHL totals		25	1	4	5	8					

LAPERRIERE, IAN
C, BLUES

PERSONAL: Born January 19, 1974, in Montreal.... 6-1/195.... Shoots right.... Name pronounced EE-ihn luh-PAIR-ee-YAIR.
TRANSACTIONS/CAREER NOTES: Selected by St. Louis Blues in seventh round (sixth Blues pick, 158th overall) of NHL entry draft (June 20, 1992).
HONORS: Named to QMJHL All-Star second team (1992-93).

Season Team	League	REGULAR SEASON					PLAYOFFS				
		Gms.	G	A	Pts.	PIM	Gms.	G	A	Pts.	PIM
90-91—Drummondville	QMJHL	65	19	29	48	117	—	—	—	—	—
91-92—Drummondville	QMJHL	70	28	49	77	160	—	—	—	—	—
92-93—Drummondville	QMJHL	60	44	†96	140	188	10	6	13	19	20
93-94—Drummondville	QMJHL	62	41	72	113	150	9	4	6	10	35
—St. Louis	NHL	1	0	0	0	0	—	—	—	—	—
—Peoria	IHL	—	—	—	—	—	5	1	3	4	2
NHL totals		1	0	0	0	0					

LAPIN, MIKHAIL
D, MAPLE LEAFS

PERSONAL: Born May 12, 1975, in Moscow, U.S.S.R.... 6-2/190.... Shoots left.
COLLEGE: Western Michigan.
TRANSACTIONS/CAREER NOTES: Selected by Toronto Maple Leafs in 11th round (eighth Maple Leafs pick, 279th overall) of NHL entry draft (June 26, 1993).

Season Team	League	REGULAR SEASON					PLAYOFFS				
		Gms.	G	A	Pts.	PIM	Gms.	G	A	Pts.	PIM
90-91—National Select-16	USSR	30	15	22	37	30	—	—	—	—	—
91-92—Thornhill	Jr. A	32	3	5	8	34	—	—	—	—	—
92-93—Western Michigan Univ.	CCHA	30	0	3	3	58	—	—	—	—	—
93-94—Western Michigan Univ.	CCHA	35	6	9	15	68	—	—	—	—	—

LAPOINTE, CLAUDE
C, NORDIQUES

PERSONAL: Born October 11, 1968, in Ville Emard, Que.... 5-9/181.... Shoots left.... Name pronounced KLOHD luh-pwah.
TRANSACTIONS/CAREER NOTES: Traded by Trois-Rivieres Draveurs with G Alain Dubeau and third-round pick in QMJHL draft (D Patrice Brisebois) to Laval Titans for D Raymond Saumier, LW Mike Gober, D Eric Gobeil and second-round pick (D Eric Charron) in QMJHL draft (May 1987). ... Selected by Quebec Nordiques in 12th round (12th Nordiques pick, 234th overall) of NHL entry draft (June 11, 1988).... Tore groin muscle (February 9, 1991).... Injured groin (October 23, 1991); missed one game.... Injured back in training camp (September 1992); missed five games.... Bruised hip (April 6, 1993); missed two games.... Sprained left knee (October 18, 1993); missed 13 games.... Sprained back (February 1, 1994); missed nine games.... Injured back (March 19, 1994); missed three games.

Season Team	League	REGULAR SEASON					PLAYOFFS				
		Gms.	G	A	Pts.	PIM	Gms.	G	A	Pts.	PIM
85-86—Trois-Rivieres	QMJHL	72	19	38	57	74	—	—	—	—	—
86-87—Trois-Rivieres	QMJHL	70	47	57	104	123	—	—	—	—	—
87-88—Laval	QMJHL	69	37	83	120	143	13	2	17	19	53
88-89—Laval	QMJHL	63	32	72	104	158	17	5	14	19	66
89-90—Halifax	AHL	63	18	19	37	51	6	1	1	2	34
90-91—Quebec	NHL	13	2	2	4	4	—	—	—	—	—
—Halifax	AHL	43	17	17	34	46	—	—	—	—	—
91-92—Quebec	NHL	78	13	20	33	86	—	—	—	—	—
92-93—Quebec	NHL	74	10	26	36	98	6	2	4	6	8
93-94—Quebec	NHL	59	11	17	28	70	—	—	—	—	—
NHL totals		224	36	65	101	258	6	2	4	6	8

LAPOINTE, MARTIN
RW, RED WINGS

PERSONAL: Born September 12, 1973, in Lachine, Que.... 5-11/200.... Shoots right.... Name pronounced MAHR-tai luh-POYNT.
TRANSACTIONS/CAREER NOTES: Selected by Detroit Red Wings in first round (first Red Wings pick, 10th overall) of NHL entry draft (June 22, 1991).... Fractured wrist (October 9, 1991); missed 22 games.

HONORS: Won Michel Bergeron Trophy (1989-90).... Named to QMJHL All-Star first team (1989-90 and 1992-93).... Named to QMJHL All-Star second team (1990-91).

			REGULAR SEASON					PLAYOFFS				
Season	Team	League	Gms.	G	A	Pts.	PIM	Gms.	G	A	Pts.	PIM
89-90—Laval		QMJHL	65	42	54	96	77	14	8	17	25	54
90-91—Laval		QMJHL	64	44	54	98	66	13	7	14	21	26
91-92—Detroit		NHL	4	0	1	1	5	3	0	1	1	4
—Laval		QMJHL	31	25	30	55	84	10	4	10	14	32
—Adirondack		AHL	—	—	—	—	—	8	2	2	4	4
92-93—Adirondack		AHL	8	1	2	3	9	—	—	—	—	—
—Detroit		NHL	3	0	0	0	0	—	—	—	—	—
—Laval		QMJHL	35	38	51	89	41	13	*13	*17	*30	22
93-94—Adirondack		AHL	28	25	21	46	47	4	1	1	2	8
—Detroit		NHL	50	8	8	16	55	4	0	0	0	6
NHL totals			57	8	9	17	60	7	0	1	1	10

LARIONOV, IGOR
C, SHARKS

PERSONAL: Born December 3, 1960, in Voskresensk, U.S.S.R.... 5-9/170.... Shoots left. ... Name pronounced EE-gohr lair-ee-AH-nahf.

TRANSACTIONS/CAREER NOTES: Selected by Vancouver Canucks in 11th round (11th Canucks pick, 214th overall) of NHL entry draft (June 15, 1985).... Injured groin (October 25, 1990); missed four games.... Sprained ankle (January 8, 1991).... Reinjured ankle (January 30, 1991); missed seven games.... Signed to play with Lugano of Switzerland (July 14, 1992).... Selected by San Jose Sharks in NHL waiver draft (October 4, 1992).... Injured shoulder (September 30, 1993); missed four games.... Reinjured shoulder (October 16, 1993); missed four games.... Suffered from the flu (November 7, 1993); missed two games.... Sprained knee (December 12, 1993); missed 10 games.... Suffered from respiratory infection (February 11, 1994); missed one game.... Suffered from the flu (February 26, 1994); missed two games.

HONORS: Named to Soviet League All-Star team (1982-83 and 1985-86 through 1987-88).... Won Soviet Player of the Year Award (1987-88).

MISCELLANEOUS: Member of gold-medal-winning U.S.S.R. Olympic teams (1984 and 1988).

			REGULAR SEASON					PLAYOFFS				
Season	Team	League	Gms.	G	A	Pts.	PIM	Gms.	G	A	Pts.	PIM
77-78—Khimik Voskresensk		USSR	6	3	0	3	4	—	—	—	—	—
78-79—Khimik Voskresensk		USSR	25	3	4	7	12	—	—	—	—	—
79-80—Khimik Voskresensk		USSR	42	11	7	18	24	—	—	—	—	—
80-81—Khimik Voskresensk		USSR	56	22	23	45	36	—	—	—	—	—
81-82—CSKA Moscow		USSR	46	31	22	53	6	—	—	—	—	—
82-83—CSKA Moscow		USSR	44	20	19	39	20	—	—	—	—	—
83-84—CSKA Moscow		USSR	43	15	26	41	30	—	—	—	—	—
—Soviet Olympic Team		Int'l	7	1	4	5	6	—	—	—	—	—
84-85—CSKA Moscow		USSR	40	18	28	46	20	—	—	—	—	—
85-86—CSKA Moscow		USSR	40	21	31	52	33	—	—	—	—	—
86-87—CSKA Moscow		USSR	39	20	26	46	34	—	—	—	—	—
87-88—CSKA Moscow		USSR	51	25	32	57	54	—	—	—	—	—
—Soviet Olympic Team		Int'l	8	4	9	13	4	—	—	—	—	—
88-89—CSKA Moscow		USSR	31	15	12	27	22	—	—	—	—	—
89-90—Vancouver		NHL	74	17	27	44	20	—	—	—	—	—
90-91—Vancouver		NHL	64	13	21	34	14	6	1	0	1	6
91-92—Vancouver		NHL	72	21	44	65	54	13	3	7	10	4
92-93—Lugano		Switzerland	24	10	19	29	44	—	—	—	—	—
93-94—San Jose		NHL	60	18	38	56	40	14	5	13	18	10
NHL totals			270	69	130	199	128	33	9	20	29	20

LARMER, STEVE
RW, RANGERS

PERSONAL: Born June 16, 1961, in Peterborough, Ont.... 5-11/185.... Shoots left.... Full name: Steve Donald Larmer.... Brother of Jeff Larmer, left winger, Colorado Rockies, New Jersey Devils and Chicago Blackhawks (1981-82 through 1985-86).

TRANSACTIONS/CAREER NOTES: Selected by Chicago Blackhawks as underage junior in sixth round (11th Blackhawks pick, 120th overall) of NHL entry draft (June 11, 1980).... Traded by Blackhawks with D Bryan Marchment to Hartford for LW Patrick Poulin and D Eric Weinrich (November 2, 1993).... Traded by Whalers with LW Nick Kypreos, D Barry Richter, and undisclosed pick in 1994 draft to New York Rangers for D James Patrick and C Darren Turcotte (November 2, 1993).... Broke right hand (January 5, 1994); missed three games.

HONORS: Named to OMJHL All-Star second team (1980-81).... Named to AHL All-Star second team (1981-82).... Named NHL Rookie of the Year by THE SPORTING NEWS (1982-83).... Won Calder Memorial Trophy (1982-83).... Named to NHL All-Rookie team (1982-83).... Played in NHL All-Star Game (1990 and 1991).

MISCELLANEOUS: Member of Stanley Cup championship team (1982-83).

			REGULAR SEASON					PLAYOFFS				
Season	Team	League	Gms.	G	A	Pts.	PIM	Gms.	G	A	Pts.	PIM
77-78—Peterborough		OMJHL	62	24	17	41	51	18	5	7	12	27
78-79—Niagara Falls		OMJHL	66	37	47	84	108	—	—	—	—	—
79-80—Niagara Falls		OMJHL	67	45	69	114	71	10	5	9	14	15
80-81—Niagara Falls		OMJHL	61	55	78	133	73	12	13	8	21	24
—Chicago		NHL	4	0	1	1	0	—	—	—	—	—
81-82—New Brunswick		AHL	74	38	44	82	46	15	6	6	12	0
—Chicago		NHL	3	0	0	0	0	—	—	—	—	—

Season Team	League	REGULAR SEASON					PLAYOFFS				
		Gms.	G	A	Pts.	Pen.	Gms.	G	A	Pts.	Pen.
82-83—Chicago	NHL	80	43	47	90	28	11	5	7	12	8
83-84—Chicago	NHL	80	35	40	75	34	5	2	2	4	7
84-85—Chicago	NHL	80	46	40	86	16	15	9	13	22	14
85-86—Chicago	NHL	80	31	45	76	47	3	0	3	3	4
86-87—Chicago	NHL	80	28	56	84	22	4	0	0	0	2
87-88—Chicago	NHL	80	41	48	89	42	5	1	6	7	0
88-89—Chicago	NHL	80	43	44	87	54	16	8	9	17	22
89-90—Chicago	NHL	80	31	59	90	40	20	7	15	22	8
90-91—Chicago	NHL	80	44	57	101	79	6	5	1	6	4
91-92—Chicago	NHL	80	29	45	74	65	18	8	7	15	6
92-93—Chicago	NHL	84	35	35	70	48	4	0	3	3	0
93-94—New York Rangers	NHL	68	21	39	60	41	23	9	7	16	14
NHL totals		959	427	556	983	516	130	54	73	127	89

LAROSE, BENOIT
D, RED WINGS

PERSONAL: Born May 31, 1973, in Ottawa. . . . 6-0/200. . . . Shoots left.
TRANSACTIONS/CAREER NOTES: Selected by Detroit Red Wings in fourth round (fifth Red Wings pick, 100th overall) of NHL entry draft (June 26, 1993).
HONORS: Named to QMJHL All-Star first team (1992-93).

Season Team	League	REGULAR SEASON					PLAYOFFS				
		Gms.	G	A	Pts.	PIM	Gms.	G	A	Pts.	PIM
92-93—Laval	QMJHL	63	16	62	78	218	8	1	6	7	10
93-94—Shawinigan	QMJHL	61	2	21	23	120	5	0	1	1	21

LAROSE, GUY
C/LW, FLAMES

PERSONAL: Born July 31, 1967, in Hull, Que. . . . 5-10/175. . . . Shoots left. . . . Name pronounced GEE luh-ROHS. . . . Son of Claude Larose, right winger, Montreal Canadiens, Minnesota North Stars and St. Louis Blues (1962-63 through 1977-78).
TRANSACTIONS/CAREER NOTES: Fractured third left metacarpal (February 22, 1985). . . . Selected by Buffalo Sabres as underage junior in 11th round (11th Sabres pick, 224th overall) of NHL entry draft (June 15, 1985). . . . Signed as free agent by Winnipeg Jets (July 21, 1987). . . . Traded by Jets to New York Rangers for D Rudy Poeschek (January 22, 1991). . . . Traded by Rangers to Toronto Maple Leafs for C/LW Mike Stevens (December 26, 1991). . . . Injured stomach before season (1992); missed first two games of season. . . . Claimed on waivers by Calgary Flames (January 1, 1994). . . . Bruised ribs (January 2, 1994); missed eight games.

Season Team	League	REGULAR SEASON					PLAYOFFS				
		Gms.	G	A	Pts.	PIM	Gms.	G	A	Pts.	PIM
83-84—Ottawa	COJHL	54	37	66	103	66	—	—	—	—	—
84-85—Guelph	OHL	58	30	30	60	63	—	—	—	—	—
85-86—Guelph	OHL	37	12	36	48	55	—	—	—	—	—
—Ottawa	OHL	28	19	25	44	63	—	—	—	—	—
86-87—Ottawa	OHL	66	28	49	77	77	11	2	8	10	27
87-88—Moncton	AHL	77	22	31	53	127	—	—	—	—	—
88-89—Winnipeg	NHL	3	0	1	1	6	—	—	—	—	—
—Moncton	AHL	72	32	27	59	176	10	4	4	8	37
89-90—Moncton	AHL	79	44	26	70	232	—	—	—	—	—
90-91—Moncton	AHL	35	14	10	24	60	—	—	—	—	—
—Binghamton	AHL	34	21	15	36	48	10	8	5	13	37
—Winnipeg	NHL	7	0	0	0	8	—	—	—	—	—
91-92—Binghamton	AHL	30	10	11	21	36	—	—	—	—	—
—St. John's	AHL	15	7	7	14	26	—	—	—	—	—
—Toronto	NHL	34	9	5	14	27	—	—	—	—	—
92-93—Toronto	NHL	9	0	0	0	8	—	—	—	—	—
—St. John's	AHL	5	0	1	1	8	9	5	2	7	6
93-94—St. John's	AHL	23	13	16	29	41	—	—	—	—	—
—Toronto	NHL	10	1	2	3	10	—	—	—	—	—
—Calgary	NHL	7	0	1	1	4	—	—	—	—	—
—Saint John	AHL	15	11	11	22	20	7	3	2	5	22
NHL totals		70	10	9	19	63					

LAROUCHE, STEVE
C, CANADIENS

PERSONAL: Born April 14, 1971, in Rouyn, Que. . . . 5-11/180. . . . Shoots right.
TRANSACTIONS/CAREER NOTES: Selected by Montreal Canadiens in second round (third Canadiens pick, 41st overall) of NHL entry draft (June 17, 1989). . . . Injured shoulder (October 8, 1989). . . . QMJHL rights traded by Trois-Rivieres Draveurs with C Sabastien Parent and sixth-round pick in 1990 QMJHL draft to Chicoutimi Sagueneens for Paul Brosseau and Jasmin Ouellet (May 26, 1990). . . . Tore left knee ligaments (October 5, 1990); missed two months. . . . Sent home by Chicoutimi coach Joe Canale for indifferent play (January 1991).
HONORS: Named to QMJHL All-Star second team (1989-90).

Season Team	League	REGULAR SEASON					PLAYOFFS				
		Gms.	G	A	Pts.	PIM	Gms.	G	A	Pts.	PIM
87-88—Trois-Rivieres	QMJHL	66	11	29	40	25	—	—	—	—	—
88-89—Trois-Rivieres	QMJHL	70	51	102	153	53	4	4	2	6	6
89-90—Trois-Rivieres	QMJHL	60	55	90	145	40	7	3	5	8	8
90-91—Chicoutimi	QMJHL	45	35	41	76	64	17	†13	*20	*33	20

Season Team	League	REGULAR SEASON					PLAYOFFS				
		Gms.	G	A	Pts.	Pen.	Gms.	G	A	Pts.	Pen.
91-92—Fredericton	AHL	74	21	35	56	41	7	1	0	1	0
92-93—Fredericton	AHL	77	27	65	92	52	5	2	5	7	6
93-94—Atlanta	IHL	80	43	53	96	73	14	*16	10	*26	16

LAUER, BRAD
LW

PERSONAL: Born October 27, 1966, in Humboldt, Sask. . . . 6-0/195. . . . Shoots left.
TRANSACTIONS/CAREER NOTES: Selected by New York Islanders as underage junior in second round (third Islanders pick, 34th overall) of NHL entry draft (June 15, 1985). . . . Fractured left kneecap (October 1988). . . . Reinjured left knee (March 1989). . . . Strained abdomen (February 1990). . . . Bruised right quadricep (April 1990). . . . Traded by Islanders with C Brent Sutter to Chicago Blackhawks for C Adam Creighton and LW Steve Thomas (October 25, 1991). . . . Signed as free agent by Las Vegas Thunder (July 19, 1993). . . . Signed as free agent by Ottawa Senators (January 1, 1994). . . . Injured hip flexor (March 13, 1994); missed three games. . . . Suspended by Las Vegas Thunder for failing to report from Ottawa Senators (March 26, 1994).
HONORS: Named to IHL All-Star first team (1992-93).

Season Team	League	REGULAR SEASON					PLAYOFFS				
		Gms.	G	A	Pts.	PIM	Gms.	G	A	Pts.	PIM
83-84—Regina	WHL	60	5	7	12	51	16	0	1	1	24
84-85—Regina	WHL	72	33	46	79	57	8	6	6	12	9
85-86—Regina	WHL	57	36	38	74	69	10	4	5	9	2
86-87—New York Islanders	NHL	61	7	14	21	65	6	2	0	2	4
87-88—New York Islanders	NHL	69	17	18	35	67	5	3	1	4	4
88-89—Springfield	AHL	8	1	5	6	0	—	—	—	—	—
—New York Islanders	NHL	14	3	2	5	2	—	—	—	—	—
89-90—New York Islanders	NHL	63	6	18	24	19	4	0	2	2	10
—Springfield	AHL	7	4	2	6	0	—	—	—	—	—
90-91—New York Islanders	NHL	44	4	8	12	45	—	—	—	—	—
—Capital District	AHL	11	5	11	16	14	—	—	—	—	—
91-92—New York Islanders	NHL	8	1	0	1	2	—	—	—	—	—
—Indianapolis	IHL	57	24	30	54	46	—	—	—	—	—
—Chicago	NHL	6	0	0	0	4	7	1	1	2	2
92-93—Indianapolis	IHL	62	*50	41	91	80	5	3	1	4	6
—Chicago	NHL	7	0	1	1	2	—	—	—	—	—
93-94—Ottawa	NHL	30	2	5	7	6	—	—	—	—	—
—Las Vegas	IHL	32	21	21	42	30	4	1	0	1	2
NHL totals		302	40	66	106	212	22	6	4	10	20

LAUKKANEN, JANNE
D, NORDIQUES

PERSONAL: Born March 19, 1970, in Lahti, Finland. . . . 6-0/180. . . . Shoots left.
TRANSACTIONS/CAREER NOTES: Selected by Quebec Nordiques in eighth round (eighth Nordiques pick, 156th overall) of NHL entry draft (June 22, 1991).
MISCELLANEOUS: Member of bronze-medal-winning Finnish Olympic team (1994).

Season Team	League	REGULAR SEASON					PLAYOFFS				
		Gms.	G	A	Pts.	PIM	Gms.	G	A	Pts.	PIM
89-90—Ilves Tampere	Finland	39	5	6	11	10	—	—	—	—	—
90-91—Reipas	Finland	44	8	14	22	56	—	—	—	—	—
91-92—Helsinki HPK	Finland	43	5	14	19	62	—	—	—	—	—
—Finland Olympic Team	Int'l	8	0	1	1	6	—	—	—	—	—
92-93—HPK Hameenlinna	Finland	47	8	21	29	76	12	1	4	5	10
93-94—HPK Hameenlinna	Finland	48	5	24	29	46	—	—	—	—	—
—Finland Olympic Team	Int'l	8	0	2	2	12	—	—	—	—	—

LAUS, PAUL
D, PANTHERS

PERSONAL: Born September 26, 1970, in Beamsville, Ont. . . . 6-1/212. . . . Shoots right. . . . Name pronounced LOWZ.
TRANSACTIONS/CAREER NOTES: Suffered inflamed knuckles (September 1988). . . . Suspended three playoff games by OHL for spearing (April 28, 1989). . . . Selected by Pittsburgh Penguins in second round (second Penguins pick, 37th overall) of NHL entry draft (June 17, 1989). . . . Selected by Florida Panthers in NHL expansion draft (June 24, 1993).

Season Team	League	REGULAR SEASON					PLAYOFFS				
		Gms.	G	A	Pts.	PIM	Gms.	G	A	Pts.	PIM
86-87—St. Catharines Jr. B	OHA	40	1	8	9	56	—	—	—	—	—
87-88—Hamilton	OHL	56	1	9	10	171	14	0	0	0	28
88-89—Niagara Falls	OHL	49	1	10	11	225	15	0	5	5	56
89-90—Niagara Falls	OHL	60	13	35	48	231	16	6	16	22	71
90-91—Muskegon	IHL	35	3	4	7	103	4	0	0	0	13
—Albany	IHL	7	0	0	0	7	—	—	—	—	—
—Knoxville	ECHL	20	6	12	18	83	—	—	—	—	—
91-92—Muskegon	IHL	75	0	21	21	248	14	2	5	7	70
92-93—Cleveland	IHL	76	8	18	26	427	4	1	0	1	27
93-94—Florida	NHL	39	2	0	2	109	—	—	—	—	—
NHL totals		39	2	0	2	109					

LAVIGNE, ERIC

D, KINGS

PERSONAL: Born November 14, 1972, in Victoriaville, Que. . . . 6-3/194. . . . Shoots left. . . . Name pronounced luh-VEEN.

TRANSACTIONS/CAREER NOTES: Selected by Washington Capitals in second round (third Capitals pick, 25th overall) of NHL entry draft (June 22, 1991). . . . Signed as free agent by Los Angeles Kings (September 1993).

			REGULAR SEASON					PLAYOFFS				
Season Team		League	Gms.	G	A	Pts.	PIM	Gms.	G	A	Pts.	PIM
89-90—Hull		QMJHL	69	7	11	18	203	11	0	0	0	32
90-91—Hull		QMJHL	66	11	11	22	153	4	0	1	1	16
91-92—Hull		QMJHL	46	4	17	21	101	6	0	0	0	32
92-93—Hull		QMJHL	59	7	20	27	221	10	2	4	6	47
93-94—Phoenix		IHL	62	3	11	14	168	—	—	—	—	—

LAVIOLETTE, PETER

D, BRUINS

PERSONAL: Born December 7, 1964, in Franklin, Mass. . . . 6-2/200. . . . Shoots left.

TRANSACTIONS/CAREER NOTES: Signed as free agent by New York Rangers (June 1987). . . . Signed as free agent by Boston Bruins (September 8, 1992).

			REGULAR SEASON					PLAYOFFS				
Season Team		League	Gms.	G	A	Pts.	PIM	Gms.	G	A	Pts.	PIM
86-87—Indianapolis		IHL	72	10	20	30	146	5	0	2	2	12
87-88—U.S. national team		Int'l	56	3	22	25	. . .	—	—	—	—	—
—U.S. Olympic Team		Int'l	5	0	2	2	4	—	—	—	—	—
—Colorado		IHL	19	2	5	7	27	9	3	5	8	7
88-89—Denver		IHL	57	6	19	25	120	3	0	0	0	4
—New York Rangers		NHL	12	0	0	0	6	—	—	—	—	—
89-90—Flint		IHL	62	6	18	24	82	4	0	0	0	4
90-91—Binghamton		AHL	65	12	24	36	72	10	2	7	9	30
91-92—Binghamton		AHL	50	4	10	14	50	11	2	7	9	9
92-93—Providence		AHL	74	13	42	55	64	6	0	4	4	10
93-94—U.S. national team		Int'l	56	10	25	35	63	—	—	—	—	—
—U.S. Olympic Team		Int'l	8	1	0	1	6	—	—	—	—	—
—San Diego		IHL	17	3	4	7	20	9	3	0	3	6
NHL totals			12	0	0	0	6					

LAVOIE, DOMINIC

D, KINGS

PERSONAL: Born November 21, 1967, in Montreal. . . . 6-2/205. . . . Shoots right. . . . Name pronounced lahv-WAH.

TRANSACTIONS/CAREER NOTES: Signed as free agent by St. Louis Blues (September 22, 1986). . . . Dislocated shoulder (January 1991). . . . Suffered hairline fracture to foot during preseason (September 1991); missed first seven games of season. . . . Selected by Ottawa Senators in NHL expansion draft (June 18, 1992). . . . Claimed on waivers by Boston Bruins (November 20, 1992). . . . Signed as free agent by Los Angeles Kings (July 16, 1993).

HONORS: Named to IHL All-Star first team (1990-91). . . . Named to IHL All-Star second team (1991-92).

			REGULAR SEASON					PLAYOFFS				
Season Team		League	Gms.	G	A	Pts.	PIM	Gms.	G	A	Pts.	PIM
84-85—St. Jean		QMJHL	30	1	1	2	10	—	—	—	—	—
85-86—St. Jean		QMJHL	70	12	37	49	99	10	2	3	5	20
86-87—St. Jean		QMJHL	64	12	42	54	97	8	2	7	9	2
87-88—Peoria		IHL	65	7	26	33	54	7	2	2	4	8
88-89—St. Louis		NHL	1	0	0	0	0	—	—	—	—	—
—Peoria		IHL	69	11	31	42	98	4	0	0	0	4
89-90—St. Louis		NHL	13	1	1	2	16	—	—	—	—	—
—Peoria		IHL	58	19	23	42	32	5	2	2	4	16
90-91—St. Louis		NHL	6	1	2	3	2	—	—	—	—	—
—Peoria		IHL	46	15	25	40	72	16	5	7	12	22
91-92—Peoria		IHL	58	20	32	52	87	10	3	4	7	12
—St. Louis		NHL	6	0	1	1	10	—	—	—	—	—
92-93—New Haven		AHL	14	2	7	9	14	—	—	—	—	—
—Ottawa		NHL	2	0	1	1	0	—	—	—	—	—
—Boston		NHL	2	0	0	0	2	—	—	—	—	—
—Providence		AHL	53	16	27	43	62	6	1	2	3	24
93-94—Los Angeles		NHL	8	3	3	6	2	—	—	—	—	—
—Phoenix		IHL	58	20	33	53	70	—	—	—	—	—
—San Diego		IHL	9	2	2	4	12	8	1	0	1	20
NHL totals			38	5	8	13	32					

LAZARO, JEFF

LW

PERSONAL: Born March 21, 1968, in Waltham, Mass. . . . 5-10/180. . . . Shoots left. . . . Full name: Jeffrey Adam Lazaro.

HIGH SCHOOL: Waltham (Mass.).

COLLEGE: New Hampshire.

TRANSACTIONS/CAREER NOTES: Signed as free agent by Boston Bruins (September 26, 1990). . . . Bruised back (February 9, 1991). . . . Suffered concussion (February 23, 1991). . . . Sprained knee (January 23, 1992); missed 14 games. . . . Sprained knee (March 11, 1992). . . . Selected by Ottawa Senators in NHL expansion draft (June 18, 1992). . . . Suffered right leg contusion (January 10, 1993); missed 14 games.

MISCELLANEOUS: Played defense prior to 1989-90 season.

Season Team	League	REGULAR SEASON					PLAYOFFS				
		Gms.	G	A	Pts.	PIM	Gms.	G	A	Pts.	PIM
86-87—Univ. of New Hampshire ...	Hockey East	38	7	14	21	38	—	—	—	—	—
87-88—Univ. of New Hampshire ...	Hockey East	30	4	13	17	48	—	—	—	—	—
88-89—Univ. of New Hampshire ...	Hockey East	31	8	14	22	38	—	—	—	—	—
89-90—Univ. of New Hampshire ...	Hockey East	39	16	19	35	34	—	—	—	—	—
90-91—Maine	AHL	26	8	11	19	18	—	—	—	—	—
—Boston	NHL	49	5	13	18	67	19	3	2	5	30
91-92—Boston	NHL	27	3	6	9	31	9	0	1	1	2
—Maine	AHL	21	8	4	12	32	—	—	—	—	—
92-93—Ottawa	NHL	26	6	4	10	16	—	—	—	—	—
—New Haven	AHL	27	12	13	25	49	—	—	—	—	—
93-94—U.S. national team	Int'l	43	18	25	43	57	—	—	—	—	—
—U.S. Olympic Team	Int'l	8	2	2	4	4	—	—	—	—	—
—Providence	AHL	16	3	4	7	26	—	—	—	—	—
NHL totals		102	14	23	37	114	28	3	3	6	32

LEACH, JAMIE
RW, PANTHERS

PERSONAL: Born August 25, 1969, in Winnipeg.... 6-1/205.... Shoots right.... Son of Reggie Leach, right winger for four NHL teams (1970-71 through 1982-83).
HIGH SCHOOL: Cherry Hill (N.J.) East.
TRANSACTIONS/CAREER NOTES: Injured hip (February 1986).... Selected by Pittsburgh Penguins as underage junior in third round (third Penguins pick, 47th overall) of NHL entry draft (June 13, 1987).... Tore left knee ligaments (September 30, 1990).... Claimed on waivers by Hartford Whalers (November 21, 1992).... Signed as free agent by Florida Panthers (August 31, 1993).
MISCELLANEOUS: Member of Stanley Cup championship team (1992).

Season Team	League	REGULAR SEASON					PLAYOFFS				
		Gms.	G	A	Pts.	PIM	Gms.	G	A	Pts.	PIM
84-85—Cherry Hill East H.S.	N.J. H.S.	60	48	51	99	68	—	—	—	—	—
85-86—New Westminster	WHL	58	8	7	15	20	—	—	—	—	—
86-87—Hamilton	OHL	64	12	19	31	67	—	—	—	—	—
87-88—Hamilton	OHL	64	24	19	43	79	14	6	7	13	12
88-89—Niagara Falls	OHL	58	45	62	107	47	17	9	11	20	25
89-90—Muskegon	IHL	72	22	36	58	39	15	9	4	13	14
—Pittsburgh	NHL	10	0	3	3	0	—	—	—	—	—
90-91—Pittsburgh	NHL	7	2	0	2	0	—	—	—	—	—
—Muskegon	IHL	43	33	22	55	26	—	—	—	—	—
91-92—Pittsburgh	NHL	38	5	4	9	8	—	—	—	—	—
—Muskegon	IHL	3	1	1	2	2	—	—	—	—	—
92-93—Pittsburgh	NHL	5	0	0	0	2	—	—	—	—	—
—Hartford	NHL	19	3	2	5	2	—	—	—	—	—
—Springfield	AHL	29	13	15	28	33	—	—	—	—	—
—Cleveland	IHL	9	5	3	8	2	4	1	2	3	0
93-94—Cincinnati	IHL	74	15	19	34	64	11	1	0	1	4
—Florida	NHL	2	1	0	1	0	—	—	—	—	—
NHL totals		81	11	9	20	12	—	—	—	—	—

LEACH, STEVE
RW, BRUINS

PERSONAL: Born January 16, 1966, in Cambridge, Mass.... 5-11/200.... Shoots right.
HIGH SCHOOL: Matignon (Cambridge, Mass.).
COLLEGE: New Hampshire.
TRANSACTIONS/CAREER NOTES: Selected by Washington Capitals in second round (second Capitals pick, 34th overall) of NHL entry draft (June 9, 1984).... Strained left knee (February 1989).... Injured thumb (March 1990).... Suffered concussion (October 10, 1990).... Separated right shoulder (February 2, 1991); missed four games.... Traded by Capitals to Boston Bruins for LW Randy Burridge (June 21, 1991).... Injured thigh (October 1992); missed one game.... Injured ribs (January 1993); missed four games.... Injured knee (January 8, 1994); missed 25 games.... Reinjured knee (March 7, 1994); missed 15 games.
HONORS: Named to Hockey East All-Freshman team (1984-85).

Season Team	League	REGULAR SEASON					PLAYOFFS				
		Gms.	G	A	Pts.	PIM	Gms.	G	A	Pts.	PIM
83-84—Matignon H.S.	Mass. H.S.	21	27	22	49	49	—	—	—	—	—
84-85—Univ. of New Hampshire ...	Hockey East	41	12	25	37	53	—	—	—	—	—
85-86—Univ. of New Hampshire ...	Hockey East	25	22	6	28	30	—	—	—	—	—
—Washington	NHL	11	1	1	2	2	6	0	1	1	0
86-87—Binghamton	AHL	54	18	21	39	39	13	3	1	4	6
—Washington	NHL	15	1	0	1	6	—	—	—	—	—
87-88—U.S. national team	Int'l	53	26	20	46	...	—	—	—	—	—
—U.S. Olympic Team	Int'l	6	1	2	3	0	—	—	—	—	—
—Washington	NHL	8	1	1	2	17	9	2	1	3	0
88-89—Washington	NHL	74	11	19	30	94	6	1	0	1	12
89-90—Washington	NHL	70	18	14	32	104	14	2	2	4	6
90-91—Washington	NHL	68	11	19	30	99	9	1	2	3	8
91-92—Boston	NHL	78	31	29	60	147	15	4	0	4	10
92-93—Boston	NHL	79	26	25	51	126	4	1	1	2	2
93-94—Boston	NHL	42	5	10	15	74	5	0	1	1	2
NHL totals		445	105	118	223	669	68	11	8	19	40

LEBEAU, PATRICK

LW, PANTHERS

PERSONAL: Born March 17, 1970, in St. Jerome, Que.... 5-10/173.... Shoots left.... Name pronounced luh-BOH.... Brother of Stephan Lebeau, center, Mighty Ducks of Anaheim.

TRANSACTIONS/CAREER NOTES: Traded by Shawinigan Cataractes with QMJHL rights to G Eric Metivier to St. Jean Castors for LW Steve Cadieux and D Pierre Cote (November 5, 1988).... Selected by Montreal Canadiens in eighth round (eighth Canadiens pick, 147th overall) of NHL entry draft (June 17, 1989).... Traded by St. Jean Lynx with D Francois Leroux and LW Jean Blouin to Victoriaville Tigres for RW Trevor Duhaime, second- and third-round picks in QMJHL draft and future considerations (February 15, 1990).... Traded by Canadiens to Calgary Flames for future considerations (October 6, 1992).... Signed as free agent by Florida Panthers (August 10, 1993).

HONORS: Won Jean Beliveau Trophy (1989-90).... Named to QMJHL All-Star first team (1989-90).... Won Dudley (Red) Garrett Memorial Trophy (1990-91).... Named to AHL All-Star second team (1990-91).

MISCELLANEOUS: Member of silver-medal-winning Canadian Olympic team (1992).

Season Team	League	REGULAR SEASON					PLAYOFFS				
		Gms.	G	A	Pts.	PIM	Gms.	G	A	Pts.	PIM
86-87—Shawinigan	QMJHL	66	26	52	78	90	13	2	6	8	17
87-88—Shawinigan	QMJHL	53	43	56	99	116	11	3	9	12	16
88-89—Shawinigan/St. Jean	QMJHL	66	62	87	149	89	4	4	3	7	6
89-90—St. Jean/Victoriaville	QMJHL	72	68	*106	*174	109	16	7	15	22	12
90-91—Montreal	NHL	2	1	1	2	0	—	—	—	—	—
—Fredericton	AHL	69	50	51	101	32	9	4	7	11	8
91-92—Fredericton	AHL	55	33	38	71	48	7	4	5	9	10
—Canadian national team	Int'l	7	4	1	5	6	—	—	—	—	—
—Canadian Olympic Team	Int'l	8	1	3	4	4	—	—	—	—	—
92-93—Salt Lake City	IHL	75	40	60	100	65	—	—	—	—	—
—Calgary	NHL	1	0	0	0	0	—	—	—	—	—
93-94—Cincinnati	IHL	74	47	42	89	90	11	4	8	12	14
—Florida	NHL	4	1	1	2	4	—	—	—	—	—
NHL totals		7	2	2	4	4					

LEBEAU, STEPHAN

C, MIGHTY DUCKS

PERSONAL: Born February 28, 1968, in Sherbrooke, Que.... 5-10/173.... Shoots right.... Name pronounced leh-BOH.... Brother of Patrick Lebeau, left winger for Montreal Canadiens and Calgary Flames (1990 to 1993).

TRANSACTIONS/CAREER NOTES: Signed as free agent by Montreal Canadiens (September 27, 1986).... Injured thigh (January 25, 1992); missed one game.... Injured ankle (February 26, 1993); missed four games.... Reinjured ankle (March 17, 1993); missed nine games.... Bruised foot (November 17, 1993); missed five games.... Injured ankle (December 1, 1993); missed five games.... Reinjured ankle (January 14, 1994); missed 14 games.... Traded by Canadiens to Mighty Ducks of Anaheim for G Ron Tugnutt (February 20, 1994).

HONORS: Named to QMJHL All-Star second team (1986-87 and 1987-88).... Won Frank J. Selke Trophy (1987-88).... Won Les Cunningham Plaque (1988-89).... Won John B. Sollenberger Trophy (1988-89).... Won Dudley (Red) Garrett Memorial Trophy (1988-89).... Named to AHL All-Star first team (1988-89).

MISCELLANEOUS: Member of Stanley Cup championship team (1993).

Season Team	League	REGULAR SEASON					PLAYOFFS				
		Gms.	G	A	Pts.	PIM	Gms.	G	A	Pts.	PIM
84-85—Shawinigan	QMJHL	66	41	38	79	18	9	4	5	9	4
85-86—Shawinigan	QMJHL	72	69	77	146	22	5	4	2	6	4
86-87—Shawinigan	QMJHL	65	*77	90	167	60	14	9	20	29	20
87-88—Shawinigan	QMJHL	67	*94	94	188	66	11	†17	9	26	10
—Sherbrooke	AHL	—	—	—	—	—	1	0	1	1	0
88-89—Sherbrooke	AHL	78	*70	64	*134	47	6	1	4	5	8
—Montreal	NHL	1	0	1	1	2	—	—	—	—	—
89-90—Montreal	NHL	57	15	20	35	11	2	3	0	3	0
90-91—Montreal	NHL	73	22	31	53	24	7	2	1	3	2
91-92—Montreal	NHL	77	27	31	58	14	8	1	3	4	4
92-93—Montreal	NHL	71	31	49	80	20	13	3	3	6	6
93-94—Montreal	NHL	34	9	7	16	8	—	—	—	—	—
—Anaheim	NHL	22	6	4	10	14	—	—	—	—	—
NHL totals		335	110	143	253	93	30	9	7	16	12

LeBLANC, JOHN

RW, JETS

PERSONAL: Born January 21, 1964, in Campbellton, N.B.... 6-1/190.... Shoots left.... Full name: John Glenn LeBlanc.

TRANSACTIONS/CAREER NOTES: Suffered ankle contusion (February 1992); missed three games.... Signed as free agent by Vancouver Canucks (April 12, 1986).... Traded by Canucks with fifth-round pick in 1989 draft (LW Peter White) to Edmonton Oilers for C Doug Smith and LW Greg C. Adams (March 7, 1989).... Traded by Oilers with 10th-round pick in 1992 draft (C Teemu Numminen) to Winnipeg Jets for fifth-round pick (C Ryan Haggerty) in 1991 draft (June 12, 1991).

HONORS: Won Senator Joseph A. Sullivan Trophy (1985-86).

Season Team	League	REGULAR SEASON					PLAYOFFS				
		Gms.	G	A	Pts.	PIM	Gms.	G	A	Pts.	PIM
83-84—Hull	QMJHL	69	39	35	74	32	—	—	—	—	—
84-85—New Brunswick	AHL	24	25	34	59	32	—	—	—	—	—
85-86—New Brunswick	AHL	24	38	28	66	35	—	—	—	—	—
86-87—Vancouver	NHL	2	1	0	1	0	—	—	—	—	—
—Fredericton	AHL	75	40	30	70	27	—	—	—	—	—

Season	Team	League	Gms.	G	A	Pts.	Pen.	Gms.	G	A	Pts.	Pen.
			REGULAR SEASON					PLAYOFFS				
87-88—Vancouver	NHL	41	12	10	22	18	—	—	—	—	—
—Fredericton	AHL	35	26	25	51	54	15	6	7	13	34
88-89—Milwaukee	IHL	61	39	31	70	42	—	—	—	—	—
—Edmonton	NHL	2	1	0	1	0	1	0	0	0	0
—Cape Breton	AHL	3	4	0	4	0	—	—	—	—	—
89-90—Cape Breton	AHL	77	*54	34	88	50	6	4	0	4	4
90-91—Cape Breton	AHL					Did not play.					
91-92—Moncton	AHL	56	31	22	53	24	10	3	2	5	8
—Winnipeg	NHL	16	6	1	7	6	—	—	—	—	—
92-93—Winnipeg	NHL	3	0	0	0	2	—	—	—	—	—
—Moncton	AHL	77	48	40	88	29	5	2	1	3	6
93-94—Moncton	AHL	41	25	26	51	38	20	3	6	9	6
—Winnipeg	NHL	17	6	2	8	2	—	—	—	—	—
NHL totals		81	26	13	39	28	1	0	0	0	0

LeBLANC, RAY
G, BLACKHAWKS

PERSONAL: Born October 24, 1964, in Fitchburg, Mass. . . . 5-10/170. . . . Catches right.
TRANSACTIONS/CAREER NOTES: Signed as free agent by Chicago Blackhawks (September 1989).
HONORS: Named to ACHL All-Star second team (1984-85). . . . Won ECHL Top Goaltender Award (1985-86). . . . Named to ACHL All-Star first team (1985-86). . . . Won Ken McKenzie Trophy (1986-87). . . . Named to IHL All-Star second team (1986-87).

Season	Team	League	Gms.	Min.	W	L	T	GA	SO	Avg.	Gms.	Min.	W	L	GA	SO	Avg.
			REGULAR SEASON								PLAYOFFS						
82-83—Dixie Flyers	OPJHL	30	1705	...	...	...	111	0	3.91	—	—	—	—	—	—	—
83-84—Kitchener	OHL	*54	2965	...	...	...	185	1	3.74	†16	914	...	...	*79	0	5.19
84-85—Pinebridge	ACHL	40	2178	...	...	...	150	0	4.13	—	—	—	—	—	—	—
85-86—Carolina	ECHL	*42	*2505	...	...	...	133	*3	*3.19	*11	*669	...	...	42	0	*3.77
86-87—Flint	IHL	64	3417	...	...	...	222	1	3.90	—	—	—	—	—	—	—
87-88—Flint	IHL	60	3269	27	19	‡8	*239	1	4.39	16	925	10	6	55	†1	3.57
88-89—Flint	IHL	15	852	5	9	‡0	67	0	4.72	—	—	—	—	—	—	—
—Saginaw	IHL	29	1655	19	7	‡2	99	0	3.59	1	59	0	1	3	0	3.05
—New Haven	AHL	1	20	0	0	0	3	0	9.00	—	—	—	—	—	—	—
89-90—Fort Wayne	IHL	15	680	3	3	‡3	44	0	3.88	3	139	0	2	11	0	4.75
—Indianapolis	IHL	23	1334	15	6	‡2	71	2	3.19	—	—	—	—	—	—	—
90-91—Fort Wayne	IHL	21	1072	10	8	‡0	69	0	3.86	—	—	—	—	—	—	—
—Indianapolis	IHL	3	145	2	0	‡0	8	0	3.31	—	—	—	—	—	—	—
91-92—Indianapolis	IHL	25	1468	14	9	‡2	84	2	3.43	—	—	—	—	—	—	—
—U.S. national team	Int'l	17	891	5	10	1	54	0	3.64	—	—	—	—	—	—	—
—U.S. Olympic Team	Int'l	8	463	5	2	1	17	2	2.20	—	—	—	—	—	—	—
—Chicago	NHL	1	60	1	0	0	1	0	1.00	—	—	—	—	—	—	—
92-93—Indianapolis	IHL	56	3201	23	22	‡0	206	0	3.86	5	276	1	3	23	0	5.00
93-94—Indianapolis	IHL	2	112	0	1	‡0	8	0	4.29	—	—	—	—	—	—	—
—Cincinnati	IHL	34	1779	17	9	‡3	104	1	3.51	5	159	0	3	9	0	3.40
NHL totals		1	60	1	0	0	1	0	1.00							

LeCLAIR, JOHN
C, CANADIENS

PERSONAL: Born July 5, 1969, in St. Albans, Vt. . . . 6-2/219. . . . Shoots left. . . . Full name: John Clark LeClair.
HIGH SCHOOL: Bellows Free Academy (St. Albans, Vt.).
COLLEGE: Vermont.
TRANSACTIONS/CAREER NOTES: Selected by Montreal Canadiens in second round (second Canadiens pick, 33rd overall) of NHL entry draft (June 13, 1987). . . . Injured thigh; missed 16 games during 1988-89 season. . . . Injured knee and underwent surgery (January 20, 1990); missed remainder of season. . . . Injured shoulder (January 15, 1992); missed four games. . . . Suffered charley horse (January 20, 1993); missed four games. . . . Sprained knee (October 2, 1993); missed eight games. . . . Bruised sternum (March 28, 1994); missed two games.
HONORS: Named to ECAC All-Star second team (1990-91).
MISCELLANEOUS: Member of Stanley Cup championship team (1993).

Season	Team	League	Gms.	G	A	Pts.	PIM	Gms.	G	A	Pts.	PIM
			REGULAR SEASON					PLAYOFFS				
85-86—Bellows Free Academy	Vt. H.S.	22	41	28	69	14	—	—	—	—	—
86-87—Bellows Free Academy	Vt. H.S.	23	44	40	84	25	—	—	—	—	—
87-88—University of Vermont	ECAC	31	12	22	34	62	—	—	—	—	—
88-89—University of Vermont	ECAC	19	9	12	21	40	—	—	—	—	—
89-90—University of Vermont	ECAC	10	10	6	16	38	—	—	—	—	—
90-91—University of Vermont	ECAC	33	25	20	45	58	—	—	—	—	—
—Montreal	NHL	10	2	5	7	2	3	0	0	0	0
91-92—Montreal	NHL	59	8	11	19	14	8	1	1	2	4
—Fredericton	AHL	8	7	7	14	10	2	0	0	0	4
92-93—Montreal	NHL	72	19	25	44	33	20	4	6	10	14
93-94—Montreal	NHL	74	19	24	43	32	7	2	1	3	8
NHL totals		215	48	65	113	81	38	7	8	15	26

LECOMPTE, ERIC
LW, BLACKHAWKS

PERSONAL: Born April 4, 1975, in Montreal.... 6-4/190.... Shoots left.
TRANSACTIONS/CAREER NOTES: Selected by Chicago Blackhawks in first round (first Blackhawks pick, 24th overall) of NHL entry draft (June 26, 1993).

			REGULAR SEASON					PLAYOFFS				
Season	Team	League	Gms.	G	A	Pts.	PIM	Gms.	G	A	Pts.	PIM
91-92—Hull		QMJHL	60	16	17	33	138	6	1	0	1	4
92-93—Hull		QMJHL	66	33	38	71	149	10	4	4	8	52
93-94—Hull		QMJHL	62	39	49	88	171	20	10	10	20	68

LEDYARD, GRANT
D, STARS

PERSONAL: Born November 19, 1961, in Winnipeg.... 6-2/195.... Shoots left.
TRANSACTIONS/CAREER NOTES: Signed as free agent by New York Rangers (July 7, 1982).... Injured hip (October 1984).... Traded by Rangers to Los Angeles Kings for LW Brian MacLellan and fourth-round pick in 1987 draft (C Michael Sullivan); Rangers also sent second-round pick in 1986 draft (D Neil Wilkinson) and fourth-round pick in 1987 draft (RW John Weisbrod) to Minnesota North Stars and the North Stars sent G Roland Melanson to the Kings to complete three-way deal (December 1986).... Sprained ankle (October 1987).... Traded by Kings to Washington Capitals for RW Craig Laughlin (February 9, 1988).... Traded by Capitals with G Clint Malarchuk and sixth-round pick in 1991 draft to Buffalo Sabres for D Calle Johansson and second-round pick (G Byron Dafoe) in 1989 draft (March 6, 1989).... Injured knee (February 12, 1991).... Injured shoulder (March 2, 1991).... Bruised ankle (March 14, 1992); missed four games.... Broke finger (October 28, 1992); missed 25 games.... Injured eye (March 7, 1993); missed three games.... Signed as free agent by Dallas Stars (August 13, 1993).
HONORS: Named Manitoba Junior Hockey League Most Valuable Player (1981-82).... Named to MJHL All-Star first team (1981-82).... Won Bob Gassoff Award (1983-84).... Won Max McNab Trophy (1983-84).

			REGULAR SEASON					PLAYOFFS				
Season	Team	League	Gms.	G	A	Pts.	PIM	Gms.	G	A	Pts.	PIM
79-80—Fort Garry		MJHL	49	13	24	37	90	—	—	—	—	—
80-81—Saskatoon		WHL	71	9	28	37	148	—	—	—	—	—
81-82—Fort Garry		MJHL	63	25	45	70	150	—	—	—	—	—
82-83—Tulsa		CHL	80	13	29	42	115	—	—	—	—	—
83-84—Tulsa		CHL	58	9	17	26	71	9	5	4	9	10
84-85—New Haven		AHL	36	6	20	26	18	—	—	—	—	—
—New York Rangers		NHL	42	8	12	20	53	3	0	2	2	4
85-86—New York Rangers		NHL	27	2	9	11	20	—	—	—	—	—
—Los Angeles		NHL	52	7	18	25	78	—	—	—	—	—
86-87—Los Angeles		NHL	67	14	23	37	93	5	0	0	0	10
87-88—New Haven		AHL	3	2	1	3	4	—	—	—	—	—
—Los Angeles		NHL	23	1	7	8	52	—	—	—	—	—
—Washington		NHL	21	4	3	7	14	14	1	0	1	30
88-89—Washington		NHL	61	3	11	14	43	—	—	—	—	—
—Buffalo		NHL	13	1	5	6	8	5	1	2	3	2
89-90—Buffalo		NHL	67	2	13	15	37	—	—	—	—	—
90-91—Buffalo		NHL	60	8	23	31	46	6	3	3	6	10
91-92—Buffalo		NHL	50	5	16	21	45	—	—	—	—	—
92-93—Buffalo		NHL	50	2	14	16	45	8	0	0	0	8
—Rochester		AHL	5	0	2	2	8	—	—	—	—	—
93-94—Dallas		NHL	84	9	37	46	42	9	1	2	3	6
NHL totals			**617**	**66**	**191**	**257**	**576**	**50**	**6**	**9**	**15**	**70**

LEEMAN, GARY
RW, CANADIENS

PERSONAL: Born February 19, 1964, in Toronto.... 5-11/186.... Shoots right.
TRANSACTIONS/CAREER NOTES: Selected by Toronto Maple Leafs as underage junior in second round (second Maple Leafs pick, 24th overall) of NHL entry draft (June 9, 1982).... Broke finger (January 1984).... Broke wrist (March 1984).... Separated shoulder (March 1985).... Cracked kneecap (April 14, 1987).... Cracked bone in right hand (April 1988).... Fractured bone behind left ear (October 22, 1988).... Injured back (January 1988).... Separated right shoulder (November 10, 1990); missed 21 games. ... Suffered back spasms (November 18, 1991); missed one game.... Traded by Maple Leafs with D Alexander Godynyuk, LW Craig Berube, D Michel Petit and G Jeff Reese to Calgary Flames for C Doug Gilmour, D Jamie Macoun, LW Kent Manderville, D Ric Nattress and G Rick Wamsley (January 2, 1992).... Bruised thigh (February 1992).... Sprained ankle (February 21, 1992); missed eight games.... Traded by Flames to Montreal Canadiens for C Brian Skrudland (January 28, 1993).... Bruised lower back (February 3, 1993); missed four games.... Injured ankle (April 2, 1993); missed five games.... Injured shoulder (January 12, 1994); missed two games.... Fractured forearm (April 11, 1994); missed remainder of season.
HONORS: Won Top Defenseman Trophy (1982-83).... Named to WHL All-Star first team (1982-83).... Played in NHL All-Star Game (1989).
MISCELLANEOUS: Member of Stanley Cup championship team (1993).

			REGULAR SEASON					PLAYOFFS				
Season	Team	League	Gms.	G	A	Pts.	PIM	Gms.	G	A	Pts.	PIM
81-82—Regina		WHL	72	19	41	60	112	3	2	2	4	0
82-83—Regina		WHL	63	24	62	86	88	5	1	5	6	4
—Toronto		NHL	—	—	—	—	—	2	0	0	0	0
83-84—Toronto		NHL	52	4	8	12	31	—	—	—	—	—
84-85—St. Catharines		AHL	7	2	2	4	11	—	—	—	—	—
—Toronto		NHL	53	5	26	31	72	—	—	—	—	—
85-86—St. Catharines		AHL	25	15	13	28	6	—	—	—	—	—
—Toronto		NHL	53	9	23	32	20	10	2	10	12	2
86-87—Toronto		NHL	80	21	31	52	66	5	0	1	1	14
87-88—Toronto		NHL	80	30	31	61	62	2	2	0	2	2

Season	Team	League	Gms.	G	A	Pts.	Pen.	Gms.	G	A	Pts.	Pen.
					REGULAR SEASON					**PLAYOFFS**		
88-89—Toronto		NHL	61	32	43	75	66	—	—	—	—	—
89-90—Toronto		NHL	80	51	44	95	63	5	3	3	6	16
90-91—Toronto		NHL	52	17	12	29	39	—	—	—	—	—
91-92—Toronto		NHL	34	7	13	20	44	—	—	—	—	—
—Calgary		NHL	29	2	7	9	27	—	—	—	—	—
92-93—Calgary		NHL	30	9	5	14	10	—	—	—	—	—
—Montreal		NHL	20	6	12	18	14	11	1	2	3	2
93-94—Montreal		NHL	31	4	11	15	17	1	0	0	0	0
—Fredericton		AHL	23	18	8	26	16	—	—	—	—	—
NHL totals			655	197	266	463	531	36	8	16	24	36

LEETCH, BRIAN
D, RANGERS

PERSONAL: Born March 3, 1968, in Corpus Christi, Tex. . . . 5-11/195. . . . Shoots left. . . . Full name: Brian Joseph Leetch.
HIGH SCHOOL: Avon (Conn.) Old Farms School for Boys.
COLLEGE: Boston College.
TRANSACTIONS/CAREER NOTES: Selected by New York Rangers in first round (first Rangers pick, ninth overall) of NHL entry draft (June 21, 1986). . . . Sprained ligaments in left knee at U.S. Olympic Festival (July 1987). . . . Fractured bone in left foot (December 1988). . . . Suffered hip pointer (March 15, 1989). . . . Fractured left ankle (March 14, 1990). . . . Injured ankle (November 21, 1992); missed one game. . . . Suffered stretched nerve in neck (December 17, 1992); missed 34 games. . . . Broke ankle (March 19, 1993) and underwent ankle surgery (March 31, 1993); missed remainder of season.
HONORS: Named Hockey East Player of the Year (1986-87). . . . Named Hockey East Rookie of the Year (1986-87). . . . Named to NCAA All-America East first team (1986-87). . . . Named to Hockey East All-Star first team (1986-87). . . . Named to Hockey East All-Freshman team (1986-87). . . . Named NHL Rookie of the Year by THE SPORTING NEWS (1988-89). . . . Won Calder Memorial Trophy (1988-89). . . . Named to NHL All-Rookie team (1988-89). . . . Named to THE SPORTING NEWS All-Star second team (1990-91 and 1993-94). . . . Named to NHL All-Star second team (1990-91 and 1993-94). . . . Played in NHL All-Star Game (1990-1992 and 1994). . . . Won James Norris Memorial Trophy (1991-92). . . . Named to THE SPORTING NEWS All-Star first team (1991-92). . . . Named to NHL All-Star first team (1991-92). . . . Won Conn Smythe Trophy (1993-1994).
RECORDS: Holds NHL single-season record for most goals by a rookie defenseman—23 (1988-89).
MISCELLANEOUS: Member of Stanley Cup championship team (1994).

Season	Team	League	Gms.	G	A	Pts.	PIM	Gms.	G	A	Pts.	PIM
					REGULAR SEASON					**PLAYOFFS**		
84-85—Avon Old Farms H.S.		Conn. H.S.	26	30	46	76	15	—	—	—	—	—
85-86—Avon Old Farms H.S.		Conn. H.S.	28	40	44	84	18	—	—	—	—	—
86-87—Boston College		Hockey East	37	9	38	47	10	—	—	—	—	—
87-88—U.S. national team		Int'l	60	13	61	74	38	—	—	—	—	—
—U.S. Olympic Team		Int'l	6	1	5	6	4	—	—	—	—	—
—New York Rangers		NHL	17	2	12	14	0	—	—	—	—	—
88-89—New York Rangers		NHL	68	23	48	71	50	4	3	2	5	2
89-90—New York Rangers		NHL	72	11	45	56	26	—	—	—	—	—
90-91—New York Rangers		NHL	80	16	72	88	42	6	1	3	4	0
91-92—New York Rangers		NHL	80	22	80	102	26	13	4	11	15	4
92-93—New York Rangers		NHL	36	6	30	36	26	—	—	—	—	—
93-94—New York Rangers		NHL	84	23	56	79	67	23	11	*23	*34	6
NHL totals			437	103	343	446	237	46	19	39	58	12

LEFEBVRE, SYLVAIN
D, NORDIQUES

PERSONAL: Born October 14, 1967, in Richmond, Que. . . . 6-2/205. . . . Shoots left. . . . Name pronounced luh-FAYV.
TRANSACTIONS/CAREER NOTES: Signed as free agent by Montreal Canadiens (September 24, 1986). . . . Traded by Canadiens to Toronto Maple Leafs for third-round pick (D Martin Belanger) in 1994 draft (August 20, 1992). . . . Traded by Maple Leafs with LW Wendel Clark, RW Landon Wilson and first-round pick in 1994 draft (D Jeffrey Kealty) to Quebec Nordiques for C Mats Sundin, D Garth Butcher, LW Todd Warriner and first-round pick (traded to Washington Capitals who selected D Nolan Baumgartner) in 1994 draft (June 28, 1994).
HONORS: Named to AHL All-Star second team (1988-89).

Season	Team	League	Gms.	G	A	Pts.	PIM	Gms.	G	A	Pts.	PIM
					REGULAR SEASON					**PLAYOFFS**		
84-85—Laval		QMJHL	66	7	5	12	31	—	—	—	—	—
85-86—Laval		QMJHL	71	8	17	25	48	14	1	0	1	25
86-87—Laval		QMJHL	70	10	36	46	44	15	1	6	7	12
87-88—Sherbrooke		AHL	79	3	24	27	73	6	2	3	5	4
88-89—Sherbrooke		AHL	77	15	32	47	119	6	1	3	4	4
89-90—Montreal		NHL	68	3	10	13	61	6	0	0	0	2
90-91—Montreal		NHL	63	5	18	23	30	11	1	0	1	6
91-92—Montreal		NHL	69	3	14	17	91	2	0	0	0	2
92-93—Toronto		NHL	81	2	12	14	90	21	3	3	6	20
93-94—Toronto		NHL	84	2	9	11	79	18	0	3	3	16
NHL totals			365	15	63	78	351	58	4	6	10	46

LEGACE, MANNY
G, WHALERS

PERSONAL: Born February 4, 1973, in Toronto. . . . 5-9/162. . . . Catches left.
HIGH SCHOOL: Stamford Collegiate (Niagara Falls, Ont.).
TRANSACTIONS/CAREER NOTES: Selected by Hartford Whalers in eighth round (fifth Whalers pick, 188th overall) of NHL entry draft (June 26, 1993).

HONORS: Named to Can.HL All-Star second team (1992-93).... Named to OHL All-Star first team (1992-93).
MISCELLANEOUS: Member of silver-medal-winning Canadian Olympic team (1994).

Season	Team	League	REGULAR SEASON							PLAYOFFS						
			Gms.	Min.	W	L	T	GA	SO	Avg.	Gms.	Min.	W	L	GA	SO	Avg.
90-91	Niagara Falls	OHL	30	1515	...	...	...	107	0	4.24	4	119	...	...	10	0	5.04
91-92	Niagara Falls	OHL	43	2384	...	...	...	143	0	3.60	14	791	...	...	56	0	4.25
92-93	Niagara Falls	OHL	†48	*2630	22	19	3	*170	0	3.88	4	240	0	4	18	0	4.50
93-94	Can. national team	Int'l	16	859	8	6	0	36	2	2.51	—	—	—	—	—	—	—

LEGG, MIKE
RW, DEVILS

PERSONAL: Born May 25, 1975, in London, Ont.... 5-11/164.... Shoots right.
HIGH SCHOOL: Westminster (London, Ont.).
COLLEGE: Michigan.
TRANSACTIONS/CAREER NOTES: Selected by New Jersey Devils in 11th round (11th Devils pick, 273rd overall) of NHL entry draft (June 26, 1993).

Season	Team	League	REGULAR SEASON					PLAYOFFS				
			Gms.	G	A	Pts.	PIM	Gms.	G	A	Pts.	PIM
90-91	Westminster H.S.	Ont. H.S.	31	25	35	60	10	—	—	—	—	—
91-92	London Jr. B	OHA	45	26	34	60	16	—	—	—	—	—
92-93	London Jr. B	OHA	52	49	55	104	32	—	—	—	—	—
93-94	University of Michigan	CCHA	37	10	13	23	20	—	—	—	—	—

LEHTINEN, JERE
RW, STARS

PERSONAL: Born June 24, 1973, in Espoo, Finland.... 6-0/180.... Shoots right.... Name pronounced YAIR-ee LEH-tih-nehn.
TRANSACTIONS/CAREER NOTES: Selected by Minnesota North Stars in fourth round (third North Stars pick, 88th overall) of NHL entry draft (June 20, 1992).... North Stars franchise moved from Minnesota to Dallas and renamed Stars for 1993-94 season.
MISCELLANEOUS: Member of bronze-medal-winning Finnish Olympic team (1994).

Season	Team	League	REGULAR SEASON					PLAYOFFS				
			Gms.	G	A	Pts.	PIM	Gms.	G	A	Pts.	PIM
90-91	Kiekko-Espoo	Finland	32	15	9	24	12	—	—	—	—	—
91-92	Kiekko-Espoo	Finland	43	32	17	49	6	—	—	—	—	—
92-93	Kiekko-Espoo	Finland	45	13	14	27	6	—	—	—	—	—
93-94	TPS Turku	Finland	42	19	20	39	6	11	11	2	13	2
	Finnish Olympic Team	Int'l	8	3	0	3	11	—	—	—	—	—

LEHTO, JONI
D, ISLANDERS

PERSONAL: Born July 15, 1970, in Turku, Finland.... 6-0/205.... Shoots left.... Name pronounced YAH-nee LEH-toh.
TRANSACTIONS/CAREER NOTES: Selected by New York Islanders in sixth round (fifth Islanders pick, 111th overall) of NHL entry draft (June 16, 1990).... Damaged ligaments in left knee (December 1990); while sidelined, served as an assistant coach for Ottawa 67's; became acting head coach on December 2 when head coach Brian Kilrea was ejected and suspended for the following two games; coached the team to a 2-1 record.
HONORS: Named to OHL All-Star second team (1989-90).

Season	Team	League	REGULAR SEASON					PLAYOFFS				
			Gms.	G	A	Pts.	PIM	Gms.	G	A	Pts.	PIM
87-88	TPS Turku	Finland	30	9	14	23	42	—	—	—	—	—
88-89	Ottawa	OHL	63	9	25	34	26	—	—	—	—	—
91-92	Richmond	ECHL	18	2	9	11	10	—	—	—	—	—
	Capital District	AHL	26	2	5	7	6	—	—	—	—	—
92-93	Capital District	AHL	57	4	13	17	33	3	1	1	2	0
93-94	Salt Lake City	IHL	60	3	13	16	34	—	—	—	—	—

LEMIEUX, CLAUDE
RW, DEVILS

PERSONAL: Born July 16, 1965, in Buckingham, Que.... 6-1/215.... Shoots right.... Name pronounced luh-MYOO.... Brother of Jocelyn Lemieux, right winger, Hartford Whalers.
TRANSACTIONS/CAREER NOTES: Selected by Montreal Canadiens as underage junior in second round (second Canadiens pick, 26th overall) of NHL entry draft (June 8, 1983).... Tore ankle ligaments (October 1987).... Fractured orbital bone above right eye (January 14, 1988).... Pulled groin (March 1989).... Underwent surgery to repair torn stomach muscle (November 1, 1989); missed 41 games.... Traded by Canadiens to New Jersey Devils for LW Sylvain Turgeon (September 4, 1990).... Suffered contusion of right eye retina (February 25, 1991).... Suffered sore back (November 27, 1991); missed four games.... Injured ankle (March 11, 1992); missed two games.... Suffered back spasms (October 24, 1992); missed three games.... Injured right elbow (March 21, 1993); missed one game.
HONORS: Named to QMJHL All-Star second team (1983-84).... Won Guy Lafleur Trophy (1984-85).... Named to QMJHL All-Star first team (1984-85).
MISCELLANEOUS: Member of Stanley Cup championship team (1986).

Season	Team	League	REGULAR SEASON					PLAYOFFS				
			Gms.	G	A	Pts.	PIM	Gms.	G	A	Pts.	PIM
82-83	Trois-Rivieres	QMJHL	62	28	38	66	187	4	1	0	1	30
83-84	Verdun	QMJHL	51	41	45	86	225	9	8	12	20	63
	Montreal	NHL	8	1	1	2	12	—	—	—	—	—
	Nova Scotia	AHL	—	—	—	—	—	2	1	0	1	0
84-85	Verdun	QMJHL	52	58	66	124	152	14	*23	17	*40	38
	Montreal	NHL	1	0	1	1	7	—	—	—	—	—

| | | REGULAR SEASON | | | | | PLAYOFFS | | | | |
Season Team	League	Gms.	G	A	Pts.	Pen.	Gms.	G	A	Pts.	Pen.
85-86—Sherbrooke	AHL	58	21	32	53	145	—	—	—	—	—
—Montreal	NHL	10	1	2	3	22	20	10	6	16	68
86-87—Montreal	NHL	76	27	26	53	156	17	4	9	13	41
87-88—Montreal	NHL	78	31	30	61	137	11	3	2	5	20
88-89—Montreal	NHL	69	29	22	51	136	18	4	3	7	58
89-90—Montreal	NHL	39	8	10	18	106	11	1	3	4	38
90-91—New Jersey	NHL	78	30	17	47	105	7	4	0	4	34
91-92—New Jersey	NHL	74	41	27	68	109	7	4	3	7	26
92-93—New Jersey	NHL	77	30	51	81	155	5	2	0	2	19
93-94—New Jersey	NHL	79	18	26	44	86	20	7	11	18	44
NHL totals		589	216	213	429	1031	116	39	37	76	348

LEMIEUX, JOCELYN
RW, WHALERS

PERSONAL: Born November 18, 1967, in Mont-Laurier, Que. ... 5-10/200. ... Shoots left. ... Brother of Claude Lemieux, right winger, New Jersey Devils.

TRANSACTIONS/CAREER NOTES: Selected by St. Louis Blues as underage junior in first round (first Blues pick, 10th overall) of NHL entry draft (June 21, 1986). ... Severed tendon in little finger of left hand (December 1986). ... Broke left leg and tore ligaments (January 1988). ... Traded by Blues with G Darrell May and second-round pick in 1989 draft (D Patrice Brisebois) to Montreal Canadiens for LW Sergio Momesso and G Vincent Riendeau (August 9, 1988). ... Traded by Canadiens to Chicago Blackhawks for third-round pick (D Charles Poulin) in 1990 draft (January 5, 1990). ... Suffered concussion and cracked orbital bone above right eye (February 26, 1991); missed a month. ... Traded by Blackhawks with D Frantisek Kucera to Hartford Whalers for LW Randy Cunneyworth and D Gary Suter (March 11, 1994).

HONORS: Named to QMJHL All-Star first team (1985-86).

| | | REGULAR SEASON | | | | | PLAYOFFS | | | | |
Season Team	League	Gms.	G	A	Pts.	PIM	Gms.	G	A	Pts.	PIM
84-85—Laval	QMJHL	68	13	19	32	92	—	—	—	—	—
85-86—Laval	QMJHL	71	57	68	125	131	14	9	15	24	37
86-87—St. Louis	NHL	53	10	8	18	94	5	0	1	1	6
87-88—Peoria	IHL	8	0	5	5	35	—	—	—	—	—
—St. Louis	NHL	23	1	0	1	42	5	0	0	0	0
88-89—Montreal	NHL	1	0	1	1	0	—	—	—	—	—
—Sherbrooke	AHL	73	25	28	53	134	4	3	1	4	6
89-90—Montreal	NHL	34	4	2	6	61	—	—	—	—	—
—Chicago	NHL	39	10	11	21	47	18	1	8	9	28
90-91—Chicago	NHL	67	6	7	13	119	4	0	0	0	0
91-92—Chicago	NHL	78	6	10	16	80	18	3	1	4	33
92-93—Chicago	NHL	81	10	21	31	111	4	1	0	1	2
93-94—Chicago	NHL	66	12	8	20	63	—	—	—	—	—
—Hartford	NHL	16	6	1	7	19	—	—	—	—	—
NHL totals		458	65	69	134	636	54	5	10	15	69

LEMIEUX, MARIO
C, PENGUINS

PERSONAL: Born October 5, 1965, in Montreal. ... 6-4/210. ... Shoots right. ... Name pronounced luh-MYOO. ... Brother of Alain Lemieux, center, St. Louis Blues, Quebec Nordiques and Pittsburgh Penguins (1981-82 through 1986-87).

TRANSACTIONS/CAREER NOTES: Selected by Pittsburgh Penguins as underage junior in first round (first Penguins pick, first overall) of NHL entry draft (June 9, 1984). ... Sprained left knee (September 1984). ... Reinjured knee (December 2, 1984). ... Sprained right knee (December 20, 1986). ... Bruised right shoulder (November 1987). ... Sprained right wrist (November 3, 1988). ... Suffered herniated disk (February 14, 1990); missed 21 games. ... Underwent surgery to remove part of herniated disk (July 11, 1990); missed first 50 games of season. ... Suffered back spasms (October 1991); missed three games. ... Suffered back spasms (January 4, 1992); missed three games. ... Injured back (January 29, 1992); missed six games. ... Suffered from the flu (February 1992); missed one game. ... Fractured bone in hand (May 5, 1992). ... Injured heel (December 1992); missed one game. ... Injured back (January 5, 1993); missed three games. ... Diagnosed with Hodgkin's Disease (January 12, 1993) and underwent radiation treatment (February 1-March 2); missed 20 games. ... Injured back; missed first 10 games of 1993-94 season. ... Injured back (October 28, 1993); missed one game. ... Injured back (November 2, 1993); missed one game. ... Suffered from the flu (November 9, 1993); missed one game. ... Injured back (November 11, 1993); missed 38 games. ... Injured back (February 13, 1994); missed two games. ... Injured back (February 19, 1994); missed two games. ... Injured back (March 12, 1994); missed four games. ... Fined $500 by NHL for charging at a referee (April 6, 1994).

HONORS: Named to QMJHL All-Star second team (1982-83). ... Won Can.HL Player of the Year Award (1983-84). ... Won Michel Briere Trophy (1983-84). ... Won Jean Beliveau Trophy (1983-84). ... Won Michael Bossy Trophy (1983-84). ... Won Guy Lafleur Trophy (1983-84). ... Named to QMJHL All-Star first team (1983-84). ... Named NHL Rookie of the Year by THE SPORTING NEWS (1984-85). ... Won Calder Memorial Trophy (1984-85). ... Named to NHL All-Rookie team (1984-85). ... Won Lester B. Pearson Award (1985-86, 1987-88 and 1992-93). ... Named to THE SPORTING NEWS All-Star second team (1985-86). ... Named to NHL All-Star second team (1985-86, 1986-87 and 1991-92). ... Played in NHL All-Star Game (1985, 1986, 1988-1990 and 1992). ... Named All-Star Game Most Valuable Player (1985, 1988 and 1990). ... Named NHL Player of the Year by THE SPORTING NEWS (1987-88, 1988-89 and 1992-93). ... Won Hart Memorial Trophy (1987-88 and 1992-93). ... Won Art Ross Memorial Trophy (1987-88, 1988-89, 1991-92 and 1992-93). ... Won Dodge Performance of the Year Award (1987-88). ... Won Dodge Performer of the Year Award (1987-88 and 1988-89). ... Named to THE SPORTING NEWS All-Star first team (1987-88, 1988-89 and 1992-93). ... Named to NHL All-Star first team (1987-88, 1988-89 and 1992-93). ... Won Dodge Ram Tough Award (1988-89). ... Won Conn Smythe Trophy (1990-91 and 1991-92). ... Won Pro Set NHL Player of the Year Award (1991-92). ... Won Bill Masterton Memorial Trophy (1992-93).

RECORDS: Holds NHL career records for highest goals-per-game average—.825; and most overtime points—14. ... Shares NHL

career record for most overtime goals—7.... Holds NHL single-season record for most shorthanded goals—13 (1988-89)....
Shares NHL single-game playoff records for most goals—5 (April 25, 1989);most single-season playoff game-winning
goals—5 (1992); most points—8 (April 25, 1989); most goals in one period—4 (April 25, 1989); and most points in one period—4 (April 25, 1989 and April 23, 1992).... Holds NHL All-Star single-game record for most points—6 (1988).... Shares
NHL All-Star single-game record for most goals—4 (1990).

MISCELLANEOUS: Member of Stanley Cup championship teams (1991 and 1992).

Season Team	League	REGULAR SEASON					PLAYOFFS				
		Gms.	G	A	Pts.	PIM	Gms.	G	A	Pts.	PIM
81-82—Laval	QMJHL	64	30	66	96	22	18	5	9	14	31
82-83—Laval	QMJHL	66	84	100	184	76	12	†14	18	32	18
83-84—Laval	QMJHL	70	*133	*149	*282	92	14	*29	*23	*52	29
84-85—Pittsburgh	NHL	73	43	57	100	54	—	—	—	—	—
85-86—Pittsburgh	NHL	79	48	93	141	43	—	—	—	—	—
86-87—Pittsburgh	NHL	63	54	53	107	57	—	—	—	—	—
87-88—Pittsburgh	NHL	77	*70	98	*168	92	—	—	—	—	—
88-89—Pittsburgh	NHL	76	*85	†114	*199	100	11	12	7	19	16
89-90—Pittsburgh	NHL	59	45	78	123	78	—	—	—	—	—
90-91—Pittsburgh	NHL	26	19	26	45	30	23	16	*28	*44	16
91-92—Pittsburgh	NHL	64	44	87	*131	94	15	*16	18	*34	2
92-93—Pittsburgh	NHL	60	69	91	*160	38	11	8	10	18	10
93-94—Pittsburgh	NHL	22	17	20	37	32	6	4	3	7	2
NHL totals		599	494	717	1211	618	66	56	66	122	46

LENARDUZZI, MIKE
G, WHALERS

PERSONAL: Born September 14, 1972, in Mississauga, Ont.... 6-1/168.... Catches
left.... Name pronounced lehn-ahr-DOO-zee.

TRANSACTIONS/CAREER NOTES: Traded by Oshawa 67's with RW Mike DeCoff, RW
Jason Denomme, second-round picks in 1990 (D Drew Bannister) and 1991 drafts
and cash to Sault Ste. Marie Greyhounds for C Eric Lindros (December 17, 1989).... Selected by Hartford Whalers in third
round (third Whalers pick, 57th overall) of NHL entry draft (June 16, 1990).

HONORS: Shared Dave Pinkney Trophy with Kevin Hodson (1990-91).

Season Team	League	REGULAR SEASON							PLAYOFFS						
		Gms.	Min.	W	L	T	GA	SO	Avg.	Gms.	Min.	W	L	GA SO	Avg.
88-89—Markham Jr. B	OHA	20	1149	...	... ...	...	111	0	5.80	—	—	—	—	— —	—
—Oshawa	OHL	6	166	...	... ...	...	9	0	3.25	—	—	—	—	— —	—
89-90—Oshawa	OHL	12	444	6	3	1	32	0	4.32	—	—	—	—	— —	—
—Sault Ste. Marie	OHL	20	1117	...	... ...	...	66	0	3.55	—	—	—	—	— —	—
90-91—Sault Ste. Marie	OHL	35	1966	19	8	3	107	0	3.27	5	268	3	1	13 *1	2.91
91-92—Sault Ste. Marie	OHL	9	486	5	3	0	33	0	4.07	—	—	—	—	— —	—
—Ottawa	OHL	18	986	5	12	1	60	1	3.65	—	—	—	—	— —	—
—Sudbury	OHL	22	1201	11	5	4	84	2	4.20	11	651	4	7	38 0	3.50
—Springfield	AHL	—	—	—	—	—	—	—	—	1	39	0	0	2 0	3.08
92-93—Springfield	AHL	36	1945	10	17	5	142	0	4.38	2	100	1	0	5 0	3.00
—Hartford	NHL	3	168	1	1	1	9	0	3.21	—	—	—	—	— —	—
93-94—Springfield	AHL	22	984	5	7	2	73	0	4.45	—	—	—	—	— —	—
—Hartford	NHL	1	21	0	0	0	1	0	2.86	—	—	—	—	— —	—
—Salt Lake City	IHL	4	211	0	4	‡0	22	0	6.26	—	—	—	—	— —	—
NHL totals		4	189	1	1	1	10	0	3.17						

LEROUX, FRANCOIS
D, SENATORS

PERSONAL: Born April 18, 1970, in St. Adele, Que.... 6-6/225.... Shoots left....
Name pronounced fran-SWAH-luh-ROO.

TRANSACTIONS/CAREER NOTES: Selected by Edmonton Oilers in first round (first Oil-
ers pick, 19th overall) of NHL entry draft (June 11, 1988).... Separated shoulder
(March 20, 1989).... Traded by St. Jean Lynx with LW Patrick Lebeau and LW Jean Blouin to Victoriaville Tigres for RW
Trevor Duhaime, second- and third-round draft picks and future considerations (February 15, 1990).... Tore left knee liga-
ments (March 18, 1990).... Underwent surgery to left knee (March 22, 1990).... Claimed on waivers by Ottawa Senators
(October 6, 1993).... Fractured left thumb (December 6, 1993); missed 16 games.

Season Team	League	REGULAR SEASON					PLAYOFFS				
		Gms.	G	A	Pts.	PIM	Gms.	G	A	Pts.	PIM
87-88—St. Jean	QMJHL	58	3	8	11	143	7	2	0	2	21
88-89—Edmonton	NHL	2	0	0	0	0	—	—	—	—	—
—St. Jean	QMJHL	57	8	34	42	185	—	—	—	—	—
89-90—Edmonton	NHL	3	0	1	1	0	—	—	—	—	—
—St. Jean/Victoriaville	QMJHL	54	4	33	37	160	—	—	—	—	—
90-91—Cape Breton	AHL	71	2	7	9	124	4	0	1	1	19
—Edmonton	NHL	1	0	2	2	0	—	—	—	—	—
91-92—Cape Breton	AHL	61	7	22	29	114	5	0	0	0	8
—Edmonton	NHL	4	0	0	0	7	—	—	—	—	—
92-93—Cape Breton	AHL	55	10	24	34	139	16	0	5	5	29
—Edmonton	NHL	1	0	0	0	4	—	—	—	—	—
93-94—Ottawa	NHL	23	0	1	1	70	—	—	—	—	—
—Prince Edward Island	AHL	25	4	6	10	52	—	—	—	—	—
NHL totals		34	0	4	4	81					

LEROUX, JEAN-YVES
LW, BLACKHAWKS

PERSONAL: Born June 24, 1976, in Montreal. . . . 6-2/193. . . . Shoots left. . . . Name pronounced Zhan-Eev Lair-OO.
TRANSACTIONS/CAREER NOTES: Selected by Chicago Blackhawks in second round (second Blackhawks pick, 40th overall) of NHL entry draft (June 28, 1994).

			REGULAR SEASON					PLAYOFFS				
Season Team	League	Gms.	G	A	Pts.	PIM	Gms.	G	A	Pts.	PIM
92-93—Beauport	QMJHL	62	20	25	45	33	—	—	—	—	—
93-94—Beauport	QMJHL	45	14	25	39	43	15	7	6	13	33

LESCHYSHYN, CURTIS
D, NORDIQUES

PERSONAL: Born September 21, 1969, in Thompson, Man. . . . 6-1/205. . . . Shoots left. . . . Full name: Curtis Michael Leschyshyn. . . . Name pronounced luh-SIH-shuhn.
TRANSACTIONS/CAREER NOTES: Selected by Quebec Nordiques in first round (first Nordiques pick, third overall) of NHL entry draft (June 11, 1988). . . . Separated shoulder (January 10, 1989). . . . Sprained left knee (November 1989). . . . Damaged knee ligaments (February 18, 1991) and underwent surgery (February 20, 1991); missed final 19 games of 1990-91 season and first 30 games of 1991-92 season. . . . Strained back (October 13, 1992); missed two games. . . . Strained right collar bone (December 30, 1994); missed two games. . . . Pulled thigh muscle (March 19, 1994); missed two games. . . . Injured groin (March 31, 1994); missed remainder of season.
HONORS: Named to WHL (East) All-Star first team (1987-88).

			REGULAR SEASON					PLAYOFFS				
Season Team	League	Gms.	G	A	Pts.	PIM	Gms.	G	A	Pts.	PIM
85-86—Saskatoon	WHL	1	0	0	0	0	—	—	—	—	—
86-87—Saskatoon	WHL	70	14	26	40	107	11	1	5	6	14
87-88—Saskatoon	WHL	56	14	41	55	86	10	2	5	7	16
88-89—Quebec	NHL	71	4	9	13	71	—	—	—	—	—
89-90—Quebec	NHL	68	2	6	8	44	—	—	—	—	—
90-91—Quebec	NHL	55	3	7	10	49	—	—	—	—	—
91-92—Quebec	NHL	42	5	12	17	42	—	—	—	—	—
—Halifax	AHL	6	0	2	2	4	—	—	—	—	—
92-93—Quebec	NHL	82	9	23	32	61	6	1	1	2	6
93-94—Quebec	NHL	72	5	17	22	65	—	—	—	—	—
NHL totals		390	28	74	102	332	6	1	1	2	6

LEVEQUE, GUY
C, KINGS

PERSONAL: Born December 28, 1972, in Kingston, Ont. . . . 5-11/166. . . . Shoots right. . . . Full name: Guy Scott Leveque. . . . Name pronounced luh-VEHK. . . . Cousin of Mike Murray, center, Philadelphia Flyers (1987-88).
TRANSACTIONS/CAREER NOTES: Selected by Los Angeles Kings in second round (first Kings pick, 42nd overall) of NHL entry draft (June 22, 1991).

			REGULAR SEASON					PLAYOFFS				
Season Team	League	Gms.	G	A	Pts.	PIM	Gms.	G	A	Pts.	PIM
89-90—Cornwall	OHL	62	10	15	25	30	3	0	0	0	4
90-91—Cornwall	OHL	66	41	56	97	34	—	—	—	—	—
91-92—Cornwall	OHL	37	23	36	59	40	6	3	5	8	2
92-93—Phoenix	IHL	56	27	30	57	71	—	—	—	—	—
—Los Angeles	NHL	12	2	1	3	19	—	—	—	—	—
93-94—Phoenix	IHL	39	10	16	26	47	—	—	—	—	—
—Los Angeles	NHL	5	0	1	1	2	—	—	—	—	—
NHL totals		17	2	2	4	21					

LEVINS, SCOTT
C/RW, SENATORS

PERSONAL: Born January 30, 1970, in Portland, Ore. . . . 6-4/200. . . . Shoots right. . . . Name pronounced LEH-vihns.
TRANSACTIONS/CAREER NOTES: Selected by Winnipeg Jets in fourth round (fourth Jets pick, 75th overall) of NHL entry draft (June 16, 1990). . . . Bruised shoulder (November 17, 1992); missed four games. . . . Selected by Florida Panthers in NHL expansion draft (June 24, 1993). . . . Fractured hip bone (October 17, 1993); missed eight games. . . . Traded by Panthers with LW Evgeny Davydov and sixth-round pick (D Mike Gaffney) in 1994 draft to Ottawa Senators for RW Bob Kudelski (January 6, 1994). . . . Injured eye (January 10, 1994); missed one game. . . . Injured left knee (February 12, 1994); missed one game. . . . Injured back (March 15, 1994); missed four games.
HONORS: Named to WHL All-Star second team (1989-90).

			REGULAR SEASON					PLAYOFFS				
Season Team	League	Gms.	G	A	Pts.	PIM	Gms.	G	A	Pts.	PIM
88-89—Penticton	BCJHL	50	27	58	85	154	—	—	—	—	—
89-90—Tri-City	WHL	71	25	37	62	132	6	2	3	5	18
90-91—Moncton	AHL	74	12	26	38	133	4	0	0	0	4
91-92—Moncton	AHL	69	15	18	33	271	11	3	4	7	30
92-93—Moncton	AHL	54	22	26	48	158	5	1	3	4	14
—Winnipeg	NHL	9	0	1	1	18	—	—	—	—	—
93-94—Florida	NHL	29	5	6	11	69	—	—	—	—	—
—Ottawa	NHL	33	3	5	8	93	—	—	—	—	—
NHL totals		71	8	12	20	180					

LEVY, JEFF
G, STARS

PERSONAL: Born December 9, 1970, in Omaha, Neb. . . . 6-0/180. . . . Catches left. . . . Name pronounced LEH-vee.
COLLEGE: New Hampshire.
TRANSACTIONS/CAREER NOTES: Selected by Minnesota North Stars In seventh round (seventh North

Stars pick, 134th overall) of NHL entry draft (June 16, 1990).... North Stars franchise moved from Minnesota to Dallas and renamed Stars for 1993-94 season.... Placed on 14-day injured reserve list by Dayton Bombers (February 18, 1994).
HONORS: Named Hockey East Rookie of the Year (1990-91).... Named to NCAA All-America East second team (1990-91)....
Named to Hockey East All-Star second team (1990-91).

Season Team	League		REGULAR SEASON								PLAYOFFS					
		Gms.	Min.	W	L	T	GA	SO	Avg.	Gms.	Min.	W	L	GA	SO	Avg.
89-90—Rochester	USHL	32	1823	24	7	0	97	3	3.19	—	—	—	—	—	—	—
90-91—U. of New Hampshire	Hoc. East	24	1490	15	7	2	80	0	3.22	—	—	—	—	—	—	—
91-92—U. of New Hampshire	Hoc. East	35	2030	20	13	2	111	...	3.28	—	—	—	—	—	—	—
92-93—Kalamazoo	IHL	28	1512	8	14	‡0	115	0	4.56	—	—	—	—	—	—	—
—Dayton	ECHL	1	65	0	0	‡1	3	0	2.77	2	139	0	2	9	0	3.88
93-94—Dayton	ECHL	31	1672	10	13	3	125	0	4.49	—	—	—	—	—	—	—
—Kalamazoo	IHL	1	59	0	1	0	4	0	4.07	—	—	—	—	—	—	—

LIDSTER, DOUG
D, BLUES

PERSONAL: Born October 18, 1960, in Kamloops, B.C.... 6-1/200.... Shoots right.... Full name: John Douglas Andrew Lidster.
COLLEGE: Colorado College.
TRANSACTIONS/CAREER NOTES: Selected by Vancouver Canucks in seventh round (sixth Canucks pick, 133rd overall) of NHL entry draft (June 11, 1980).... Strained left knee (January 1988).... Hyperextended elbow (October 1988).... Broke hand (November 13, 1988).... Fractured cheekbone (March 1989).... Separated shoulder (March 1, 1992); missed 13 games.... Sprained knee (December 13, 1992); missed nine games.... Suffered from the flu (February 24, 1993); missed one game.... Traded by Canucks to New York Rangers (June 25, 1993) to complete deal in which Rangers sent G John Vanbiesbrouck to Canucks for future considerations (June 20, 1993).... Traded by Rangers with LW Esa Tikkanen to St. Louis Blues for C Petr Nedved (July 24, 1994); trade arranged as compensation for Blues signing Coach Mike Keenan.
HONORS: Named to WCHA All-Star first team (1981-82 and 1982-83).... Named to NCAA All-America West team (1982-83).
MISCELLANEOUS: Member of Stanley Cup championship team (1994).

Season Team	League		REGULAR SEASON					PLAYOFFS			
		Gms.	G	A	Pts.	PIM	Gms.	G	A	Pts.	PIM
78-79—Kamloops	BCJHL	59	36	47	83	50	—	—	—	—	—
79-80—Colorado College	WCHA	39	18	25	43	52	—	—	—	—	—
80-81—Colorado College	WCHA	36	10	30	40	54	—	—	—	—	—
81-82—Colorado College	WCHA	36	13	22	35	32	—	—	—	—	—
82-83—Colorado College	WCHA	34	15	41	56	30	—	—	—	—	—
83-84—Canadian Olympic Team	Int'l	59	6	20	26	28	—	—	—	—	—
—Vancouver	NHL	8	0	0	0	4	2	0	1	1	0
84-85—Vancouver	NHL	78	6	24	30	55	—	—	—	—	—
85-86—Vancouver	NHL	78	12	16	28	56	3	0	1	1	2
86-87—Vancouver	NHL	80	12	51	63	40	—	—	—	—	—
87-88—Vancouver	NHL	64	4	32	36	105	—	—	—	—	—
88-89—Vancouver	NHL	63	5	17	22	78	7	1	1	2	9
89-90—Vancouver	NHL	80	8	28	36	36	—	—	—	—	—
90-91—Vancouver	NHL	78	6	32	38	77	6	0	2	2	6
91-92—Vancouver	NHL	66	6	23	29	39	11	1	2	3	11
92-93—Vancouver	NHL	71	6	19	25	36	12	0	3	3	8
93-94—New York Rangers	NHL	34	0	2	2	33	9	2	0	2	10
NHL totals		700	65	244	309	559	50	4	10	14	46

LIDSTROM, NICKLAS
D, RED WINGS

PERSONAL: Born April 28, 1970, in Vasteras, Sweden.... 6-2/180.... Shoots left.... Name pronounced LIHD-STRUHM.
TRANSACTIONS/CAREER NOTES: Selected by Detroit Red Wings in third round (third Red Wings pick, 53rd overall) of NHL entry draft (June 17, 1989).
HONORS: Named to Swedish League All-Star team (1990-91).... Named to NHL All-Rookie team (1991-92).

Season Team	League		REGULAR SEASON					PLAYOFFS			
		Gms.	G	A	Pts.	PIM	Gms.	G	A	Pts.	PIM
88-89—Vasteras	Sweden	19	0	2	2	4	—	—	—	—	—
89-90—Vasteras	Sweden	39	8	8	16	14	—	—	—	—	—
90-91—Vasteras	Sweden	20	2	12	14	14	—	—	—	—	—
91-92—Detroit	NHL	80	11	49	60	22	11	1	2	3	0
92-93—Detroit	NHL	84	7	34	41	28	7	1	0	1	0
93-94—Detroit	NHL	84	10	46	56	26	7	3	2	5	0
NHL totals		248	28	129	157	76	25	5	4	9	0

LILLEY, JOHN
RW, MIGHTY DUCKS

PERSONAL: Born August 3, 1972, in Wakefield, Mass.... 5-0/170.... Shoots right.
TRANSACTIONS/CAREER NOTES: Selected by Winnipeg Jets in eighth round (eighth Jets pick, 140th overall) of NHL entry draft (June 16, 1990).... Signed as free agent by Mighty Ducks of Anaheim (March 9, 1994).

Season Team	League		REGULAR SEASON					PLAYOFFS			
		Gms.	G	A	Pts.	PIM	Gms.	G	A	Pts.	PIM
91-92—Boston University	Hockey East	23	9	9	18	43	—	—	—	—	—
92-93—Boston University	Hockey East	4	0	1	1	13	—	—	—	—	—
—Seattle	WHL	45	22	28	50	55	5	1	3	4	9

Season Team	League	REGULAR SEASON					PLAYOFFS				
		Gms.	G	A	Pts.	Pen.	Gms.	G	A	Pts.	Pen.
93-94—U.S. national team	Int'l	58	27	23	50	117	—	—	—	—	—
—U.S. Olympic Team	Int'l	8	3	1	4	16	—	—	—	—	—
—San Diego	IHL	2	2	1	3	0	—	—	—	—	—
—Anaheim	NHL	13	1	6	7	8	—	—	—	—	—
NHL totals		13	1	6	7	8	—	—	—	—	—

LINDBERG, CHRIS
LW, NORDIQUES

PERSONAL: Born April 16, 1967, in Fort Frances, Ont.... 6-1/185.... Shoots left. **COLLEGE:** Minnesota-Duluth. **TRANSACTIONS/CAREER NOTES:** Signed as free agent by Hartford Whalers (March 17, 1989).... Signed as free agent by Calgary Flames (August 1991).... Selected by Ottawa Senators in NHL expansion draft (June 18, 1992).... Traded by Senators to Calgary Flames for D Mark Osiecki (June 23, 1992).... Injured knee (January 19, 1993); missed two games.... Signed as free agent by Quebec Nordiques (September 9, 1993).... Suffered from stomach virus (October 7, 1994); missed one game.... Injured hip (February 5, 1994); missed 13 games.
MISCELLANEOUS: Member of silver-medal-winning Canadian Olympic team (1992).

Season Team	League	REGULAR SEASON					PLAYOFFS				
		Gms.	G	A	Pts.	PIM	Gms.	G	A	Pts.	PIM
87-88—Minnesota-Duluth	WCHA	35	12	10	22	36	—	—	—	—	—
88-89—Minnesota-Duluth	WCHA	36	15	18	33	51	—	—	—	—	—
89-90—Binghamton	AHL	32	4	4	8	36	—	—	—	—	—
90-91—Canadian national team	Int'l	55	25	31	56	53	—	—	—	—	—
—Springfield	AHL	1	0	0	0	2	1	0	0	0	0
91-92—Canadian national team	Int'l	56	33	35	68	63	—	—	—	—	—
—Canadian Olympic Team	Int'l	8	1	4	5	4	—	—	—	—	—
—Calgary	NHL	17	2	5	7	17	—	—	—	—	—
92-93—Calgary	NHL	62	9	12	21	18	2	0	1	1	2
93-94—Quebec	NHL	37	6	8	14	12	—	—	—	—	—
—Cornwall	AHL	23	14	13	27	28	13	11	3	14	10
NHL totals		116	17	25	42	47	2	0	1	1	2

LINDEN, JAMIE
RW, PANTHERS

PERSONAL: Born July 19, 1972, in Medicine Hat, Alta.... 6-3/185.... Shoots right. **TRANSACTIONS/CAREER NOTES:** Signed as free agent by Florida Panthers (1993).

Season Team	League	REGULAR SEASON					PLAYOFFS				
		Gms.	G	A	Pts.	PIM	Gms.	G	A	Pts.	PIM
92-93—Medicine Hat	WHL	65	12	10	22	205	—	—	—	—	—
93-94—Cincinnati	IHL	47	1	5	6	55	2	0	0	0	2

LINDEN, TREVOR
C, CANUCKS

PERSONAL: Born April 11, 1970, in Medicine Hat, Alta.... 6-4/205.... Shoots right. **TRANSACTIONS/CAREER NOTES:** Selected by Vancouver Canucks in first round (first Canucks pick, second overall) of NHL entry draft (June 11, 1988).... Hyperextended elbow (October 1989).... Separated shoulder (March 17, 1990).
HONORS: Named to WHL All-Star second team (1987-88).... Named to Memorial Cup All-Star team (1987-88).... Named to NHL All-Rookie team (1988-89).... Played in NHL All-Star Game (1991 and 1992).

Season Team	League	REGULAR SEASON					PLAYOFFS				
		Gms.	G	A	Pts.	PIM	Gms.	G	A	Pts.	PIM
85-86—Medicine Hat	WHL	5	2	0	2	0	—	—	—	—	—
86-87—Medicine Hat	WHL	72	14	22	36	59	20	5	4	9	17
87-88—Medicine Hat	WHL	67	46	64	110	76	16	†13	12	25	19
88-89—Vancouver	NHL	80	30	29	59	41	7	3	4	7	8
89-90—Vancouver	NHL	73	21	30	51	43	—	—	—	—	—
90-91—Vancouver	NHL	80	33	37	70	65	6	0	7	7	2
91-92—Vancouver	NHL	80	31	44	75	101	13	4	8	12	6
92-93—Vancouver	NHL	84	33	39	72	64	12	5	8	13	16
93-94—Vancouver	NHL	84	32	29	61	73	24	12	13	25	18
NHL totals		481	180	208	388	387	62	24	40	64	50

LINDGREN, MATS
C, OILERS

PERSONAL: Born October 1, 1974, in Skelleftea, Sweden.... 6-1/190.... Shoots left. **HIGH SCHOOL:** Lindsay Thurber (Red Deer, Alta.). **TRANSACTIONS/CAREER NOTES:** Selected by Winnipeg Jets in first round (first Jets pick, 15th overall) of NHL entry draft (June 26, 1993).... Traded by Jets with D Boris Mironov and first-round (C Jason Bonsignore) and fourth-round (RW Adam Copeland) picks in 1994 draft to Edmonton Oilers for D Dave Manson and sixth-round pick in 1994 draft (March 15, 1994).
HONORS: Named Swedish League Rookie of the Year (1993-94).

Season Team	League	REGULAR SEASON					PLAYOFFS				
		Gms.	G	A	Pts.	PIM	Gms.	G	A	Pts.	PIM
90-91—Skelleftea	Swed. Dv.II	1	0	0	0	0	—	—	—	—	—
91-92—Skelleftea	Swed. Dv.II	29	14	8	22	14	—	—	—	—	—
92-93—Skelleftea	Swed. Dv.II	32	20	14	34	18	—	—	—	—	—
93-94—Farjestad	Sweden	22	11	6	17	26	—	—	—	—	—

LINDROS, BRETT
RW, ISLANDERS

PERSONAL: Born December 2, 1975, in Toronto. . . . 6-4/215. . . . Shoots right. . . . Name pronounced LIHND-rahz. . . . Brother of Eric Lindros, center, Philadelphia Flyers.
TRANSACTIONS/CAREER NOTES: Injured left knee (January 6, 1994). . . . Selected by New York Islanders in first round (first Islanders pick, ninth overall) of NHL entry draft (June 28, 1994).

			REGULAR SEASON					PLAYOFFS			
Season Team	League	Gms.	G	A	Pts.	PIM	Gms.	G	A	Pts.	PIM
91-92—St. Michaels Tier II	Jr. A	34	21	21	42	210	—	—	—	—	—
92-93—Kingston	OHL	31	11	11	22	162	—	—	—	—	—
—Canadian national team	Int'l	11	1	6	7	33	—	—	—	—	—
93-94—Kingston	OHL	15	4	6	10	94	3	0	0	0	18
—Canadian national team	Int'l	44	7	7	14	118	—	—	—	—	—

LINDROS, ERIC
C, FLYERS

PERSONAL: Born February 28, 1973, in London, Ont. . . . 6-4/229. . . . Shoots right. . . . Name pronounced LIHND-rahz. . . . Brother of Brett Lindros, right winger in New York Islanders system.
TRANSACTIONS/CAREER NOTES: Selected by Sault Ste. Marie Greyhounds in OHL priority draft; refused to report (August 30, 1989); played for Detroit Compuware. . . . Rights traded by Greyhounds to Oshawa Generals for RW Mike DeCoff, RW Jason Denomme, G Mike Lenarduzzi, second-round picks in 1991 and 1992 drafts and cash (December 17, 1989). . . . Suspended two games by OHL for fighting (February 7, 1990). . . . Selected by Quebec Nordiques in first round (first Nordiques pick, first overall) of NHL entry draft (June 22, 1991); refused to report. . . . Traded by Nordiques to Philadelphia Flyers for G Ron Hextall, C Mike Ricci, C Peter Forsberg, D Steve Duchesne, D Kerry Huffman, first-round pick in 1993 draft (G Jocelyn Thibault), cash and future considerations (June 20, 1992); Flyers sent LW Chris Simon and first-round pick in 1994 draft (traded to Toronto Maple Leafs) to Nordiques to complete deal (July 21, 1992). . . . Sprained medial collateral ligament (November 22, 1992); missed nine games. . . . Injured knee (December 29, 1992); missed two games. . . . Reinjured knee (January 10, 1993); missed 12 games. . . . Tore ligament in right knee (November 12, 1993); missed 14 games. . . . Suffered back spasms (March 6, 1994); missed one game. . . . Sprained shoulder (April 4, 1994); missed remainder of season.
HONORS: Named to Memorial Cup All-Star Team (1989-90). . . . Won Can.HL Player of the Year Award (1990-91). . . . Won Can.HL Plus/Minus Award (1990-91). . . . Won Can.HL Top Draft Prospect Award (1990-91). . . . Won Red Tilson Trophy (1990-91). . . . Won Eddie Powers Memorial Trophy (1990-91). . . . Named to OHL All-Star first team (1990-91). . . . Named to NHL All-Rookie team (1992-93). . . . Played in NHL All-Star Game (1994).
MISCELLANEOUS: Member of silver-medal-winning Canadian Olympic team (1992).

			REGULAR SEASON					PLAYOFFS			
Season Team	League	Gms.	G	A	Pts.	PIM	Gms.	G	A	Pts.	PIM
88-89—St. Michaels	MTHL	36	25	42	67	...	—	—	—	—	—
89-90—Detroit Compuware	NAJHL	14	25	27	52	...	—	—	—	—	—
—Oshawa	OHL	25	17	19	36	61	17	*18	18	36	*76
90-91—Oshawa	OHL	57	*71	78	*149	189	16	*18	20	*38	*93
91-92—Oshawa	OHL	13	9	22	31	54	—	—	—	—	—
—Canadian national team	Int'l	24	19	16	35	34	—	—	—	—	—
—Canadian Olympic Team	Int'l	8	5	6	11	6	—	—	—	—	—
92-93—Philadelphia	NHL	61	41	34	75	147	—	—	—	—	—
93-94—Philadelphia	NHL	65	44	53	97	103	—	—	—	—	—
NHL totals		126	85	87	172	250					

LINDSAY, BILL
LW, PANTHERS

PERSONAL: Born May 17, 1971, in Big Fork, Mont. . . . 5-11/185. . . . Shoots left. . . . Full name: William Hamilton Lindsay.
TRANSACTIONS/CAREER NOTES: Selected by Quebec Nordiques in fifth round (sixth Nordiques pick, 103rd overall) of NHL entry draft (June 22, 1991). . . . Separated right shoulder (December 26, 1992); missed four games. . . . Selected by Florida Panthers in NHL expansion draft (June 24, 1993).
HONORS: Named to WHL (West) All-Star second team (1991-92).

			REGULAR SEASON					PLAYOFFS			
Season Team	League	Gms.	G	A	Pts.	PIM	Gms.	G	A	Pts.	PIM
89-90—Tri-City	WHL	72	40	45	85	84	—	—	—	—	—
90-91—Tri-City	WHL	63	46	47	93	151	—	—	—	—	—
91-92—Tri-City	WHL	42	34	59	93	111	3	2	3	5	16
—Quebec	NHL	23	2	4	6	14	—	—	—	—	—
92-93—Quebec	NHL	44	4	9	13	16	—	—	—	—	—
—Halifax	AHL	20	11	13	24	18	—	—	—	—	—
93-94—Florida	NHL	84	6	6	12	97	—	—	—	—	—
NHL totals		151	12	19	31	127					

LiPUMA, CHRIS
D, LIGHTNING

PERSONAL: Born March 23, 1971, in Chicago. . . . 6-0/183. . . . Shoots left. . . . Name pronounced luh-POO-muh.
TRANSACTIONS/CAREER NOTES: Signed as free agent by Tampa Bay Lightning (August 24, 1992).

			REGULAR SEASON					PLAYOFFS			
Season Team	League	Gms.	G	A	Pts.	PIM	Gms.	G	A	Pts.	PIM
88-89—Kitchener	OHL	59	7	13	20	101	—	—	—	—	—
89-90—Kitchener	OHL	63	11	26	37	125	17	1	4	5	6
90-91—Kitchener	OHL	61	6	30	36	145	4	0	1	1	4
91-92—Kitchener	OHL	61	13	59	72	115	14	4	9	13	34

Season	Team	League	REGULAR SEASON Gms.	G	A	Pts.	Pen.	PLAYOFFS Gms.	G	A	Pts.	Pen.
92-93—Atlanta	IHL	66	4	14	18	379	9	1	1	2	35	
—Tampa Bay	NHL	15	0	5	5	34	—	—	—	—	—	
93-94—Tampa Bay	NHL	27	0	4	4	77	—	—	—	—	—	
—Atlanta	AHL	42	2	10	12	254	11	1	1	2	28	
NHL totals			42	0	9	9	111					

LITTLE, NEIL
G, FLYERS

PERSONAL: Born December 18, 1971, in Medicine Hat, Alta.... 6-1/180.... Catches left.
TRANSACTIONS/CAREER NOTES: Selected by Philadelphia Flyers in 11th round (10th Flyers pick, 226th overall) of NHL entry draft (June 22, 1993).
HONORS: Named SJHL Rookie of the Year (1989-90).... Named to SJHL All-Star first team (1989-90).... Named to ECAC All-Star first team (1992-93).

Season	Team	League	REGULAR SEASON Gms.	Min.	W	L	T	GA	SO	Avg.	PLAYOFFS Gms.	Min.	W	L	GA	SO	Avg.
89-90—Estevan	SJHL	46	2707	21	19	4	150	1	3.32	—	—	—	—	—	—	—	
90-91—R.P.I.	ECAC	18	1032	9	8	0	71	0	4.13	—	—	—	—	—	—	—	
91-92—R.P.I.	ECAC	28	1532	11	11	3	96	0	3.76	—	—	—	—	—	—	—	
92-93—R.P.I.	ECAC	31	1801	19	3	0	88	0	2.93	—	—	—	—	—	—	—	
93-94—R.P.I.	ECAC	27	1570	16	7	4	88	0	3.36	—	—	—	—	—	—	—	
—Hershey	AHL	1	19	0	0	0	1	0	3.16	—	—	—	—	—	—	—	

LITTMAN, DAVID
G

PERSONAL: Born June 13, 1967, in Cranston, R.I.... 6-0/183.... Catches left.
COLLEGE: Boston College.
TRANSACTIONS/CAREER NOTES: Selected by Buffalo Sabres in 11th round (12th Sabres pick, 211th overall) of NHL entry draft (June 13, 1987).... Separated shoulder (December 1989); missed six games.... Signed as free agent by Tampa Bay Lightning (August 27, 1992).... Signed as free agent by Boston Bruins (August 6, 1993).
HONORS: Named to Hockey East All-Star second team (1987-88).... Named to NCAA All-America East second team (1988-89).... Named to Hockey East All-Star first team (1988-89).... Shared Harry (Hap) Holmes Memorial Trophy with Darcy Wakaluk (1990-91).... Named to AHL All-Star first team (1990-91).... Won Harry (Hap) Holmes Memorial Trophy (1991-92).... Named to AHL All-Star second team (1991-92).

Season	Team	League	REGULAR SEASON Gms.	Min.	W	L	T	GA	SO	Avg.	PLAYOFFS Gms.	Min.	W	L	GA	SO	Avg.
85-86—Boston College	Hoc. East	9	442	4	0	1	22	1	2.99	—	—	—	—	—	—	—	
86-87—Boston College	Hoc. East	21	1182	15	5	0	68	0	3.45	—	—	—	—	—	—	—	
87-88—Boston College	Hoc. East	30	1726	11	16	2	116	0	4.03	—	—	—	—	—	—	—	
88-89—Boston College	Hoc. East	32	1945	19	9	4	107	0	3.30	—	—	—	—	—	—	—	
89-90—Rochester	AHL	14	681	5	6	1	37	0	3.26	1	33	......		4	0	7.27	
—Phoenix	IHL	18	1047	8	7	‡2	64	0	3.67	—	—	—	—	—	—	—	
90-91—Buffalo	NHL	1	36	0	0	0	3	0	5.00	—	—	—	—	—	—	—	
—Rochester	AHL	*56	*3155	*33	13	5	160	3	3.04	8	378	4	2	16	0	2.54	
91-92—Rochester	AHL	*61	*3558	*29	20	9	174	†3	2.93	15	879	8	†7	43	1	2.94	
—Buffalo	NHL	1	60	0	1	0	4	0	4.00	—	—	—	—	—	—	—	
92-93—Atlanta	IHL	44	2390	23	12	‡4	134	0	3.36	3	178	1	2	8	0	2.70	
—Tampa Bay	NHL	1	45	0	1	0	7	0	9.33	—	—	—	—	—	—	—	
93-94—Fredericton	AHL	16	872	8	7	0	63	0	4.33	—	—	—	—	—	—	—	
NHL totals			3	141	0	2	0	14	0	5.96							

LITVINOV, YURI
C, RANGERS

PERSONAL: Born April 11, 1976, in Donetsk, U.S.S.R.... 5-10/1176.... Shoots right.
TRANSACTIONS/CAREER NOTES: Selected by New York Rangers in sixth round (seventh Rangers pick, 135th overall) of NHL entry draft (June 29, 1994).

Season	Team	League	REGULAR SEASON Gms.	G	A	Pts.	PIM	PLAYOFFS Gms.	G	A	Pts.	PIM
93-94—Soviet Wings	CIS	42	5	6	11	34	—	—	—	—	—	

LOACH, LONNIE
LW, MIGHTY DUCKS

PERSONAL: Born April 14, 1968, in New Liskeard, Ont.... 5-10/181.... Shoots left.
TRANSACTIONS/CAREER NOTES: Selected by Chicago Blackhawks as underage junior in fifth round (fourth Blackhawks pick, 98th overall) of NHL entry draft (June 21, 1986).... Signed as free agent by Fort Wayne Komets (August 1990).... Signed as free agent by Detroit Red Wings (April 20, 1991).... Selected by Ottawa Senators in NHL expansion draft (June 18, 1992).... Claimed on waivers by Los Angeles Kings (October 21, 1992).... Fractured thumb (December 13, 1992); missed 11 games.... Selected by Mighty Ducks of Anaheim in NHL expansion draft (June 24, 1993).
HONORS: Won Emms Family Award (1985-86).... Won Leo P. Lamoureux Memorial Trophy (1990-91).... Named to IHL All-Star second team (1990-91).

Season	Team	League	REGULAR SEASON Gms.	G	A	Pts.	PIM	PLAYOFFS Gms.	G	A	Pts.	PIM
84-85—St. Mary's Jr. B	OHA	44	26	36	62	113	—	—	—	—	—	
85-86—Guelph	OHL	65	41	42	83	63	20	7	8	15	16	
86-87—Guelph	OHL	56	31	24	55	42	5	2	1	3	2	
87-88—Guelph	OHL	66	43	49	92	75	—	—	—	—	—	
88-89—Saginaw	IHL	32	7	6	13	27	—	—	—	—	—	
—Flint	IHL	41	22	26	48	30	—	—	—	—	—	

Season	Team	League	REGULAR SEASON					PLAYOFFS				
			Gms.	G	A	Pts.	Pen.	Gms.	G	A	Pts.	Pen.
89-90—Indianapolis		IHL	3	0	1	1	0	—	—	—	—	—
—Fort Wayne		IHL	54	15	33	48	40	5	4	2	6	15
90-91—Fort Wayne		IHL	81	55	76	*131	45	19	5	11	16	13
91-92—Adirondack		AHL	67	37	49	86	69	†19	*13	4	17	10
92-93—Ottawa		NHL	3	0	0	0	0	—	—	—	—	—
—Los Angeles		NHL	50	10	13	23	27	1	0	0	0	0
—Phoenix		IHL	4	2	3	5	10	—	—	—	—	—
93-94—San Diego		IHL	74	42	49	91	65	9	4	10	14	6
—Anaheim		NHL	3	0	0	0	2	—	—	—	—	—
NHL totals			56	10	13	23	29	1	0	0	0	0

LOEWEN, DARCY
LW

PERSONAL: Born February 26, 1969, in Calgary. . . . 5-10/185. . . . Shoots left. . . . Full name: Darcy Alan Loewen. . . . Name pronounced LOH-wihn.

HIGH SCHOOL: H.J. Cody (Sylvan Lake, Alta.).

TRANSACTIONS/CAREER NOTES: Selected by Buffalo Sabres in third round (second Sabres pick, 55th overall) of NHL entry draft (June 11, 1988). . . . Selected by Ottawa Senators in NHL expansion draft (June 18, 1992). . . . Lacerated forearm (April 3, 1993); missed one game. . . . Suffered charley horse (December 9, 1993); missed four games. . . . Injured left knee (December 23, 1993); missed 21 games. . . . Dislocated finger (March 5, 1994); missed seven games.

Season	Team	League	REGULAR SEASON					PLAYOFFS				
			Gms.	G	A	Pts.	PIM	Gms.	G	A	Pts.	PIM
85-86—Spokane		WHL	8	2	1	3	19	—	—	—	—	—
86-87—Spokane		WHL	68	15	25	40	129	5	0	0	0	0
87-88—Spokane		WHL	72	30	44	74	231	15	7	5	12	54
88-89—Spokane		WHL	60	31	27	58	194	—	—	—	—	—
—Canadian national team		Int'l	2	0	0	0	0	—	—	—	—	—
89-90—Rochester		AHL	50	7	11	18	193	5	1	0	1	6
—Buffalo		NHL	4	0	0	0	4	—	—	—	—	—
90-91—Buffalo		NHL	6	0	0	0	8	—	—	—	—	—
—Rochester		AHL	71	13	15	28	130	15	1	5	6	14
91-92—Buffalo		NHL	2	0	0	0	2	—	—	—	—	—
—Rochester		AHL	73	11	20	31	193	4	0	1	1	8
92-93—Ottawa		NHL	79	4	5	9	145	—	—	—	—	—
93-94—Ottawa		NHL	44	0	3	3	52	—	—	—	—	—
NHL totals			135	4	8	12	211	—	—	—	—	—

LOISELLE, CLAUDE
C, ISLANDERS

PERSONAL: Born May 29, 1963, in Ottawa. . . . 5-11/195. . . . Shoots left. . . . Name pronounced lwah-ZEHL.

TRANSACTIONS/CAREER NOTES: Selected as underage junior by Detroit Red Wings in second round (first Red Wings pick, 23rd overall) of NHL entry draft (June 10, 1981). . . . Suspended six games by NHL for stick-swinging incident (January 7, 1984). . . . Injured knee (December 17, 1985); missed 11 games. . . . Traded by Red Wings to New Jersey Devils for RW Tim Higgins (June 25, 1986). . . . Separated right shoulder (February 1988). . . . Traded by Devils with D Joe Cirella and eighth-round pick in 1990 draft (D Alexander Karpovtsev) to Quebec Nordiques for C Walt Poddubny and fourth-round pick (RW Mike Bodnarchuk) in 1990 draft (June 17, 1989). . . . Broke finger on left hand (February 1990). . . . Traded by Nordiques to Calgary Flames for LW Bryan Deasley (March 2, 1991); trade voided when Loiselle claimed on waivers by Toronto Maple Leafs (March 4, 1991). . . . Traded by Maple Leafs with RW Daniel Marois to New York Islanders for LW Ken Baumgartner and C Dave McIlwain (March 10, 1992). . . . Suffered sore shoulder (December 12, 1992); missed seven games. . . . Suffered concussion (January 9, 1993); missed one game. . . . Suffered back spasms (April 2, 1993); missed two games. . . . Suffered back spasms (October 26, 1993); missed two games. . . . Tore anterior cruciate knee ligament (November 24, 1993); missed remainder of season.

Season	Team	League	REGULAR SEASON					PLAYOFFS				
			Gms.	G	A	Pts.	PIM	Gms.	G	A	Pts.	PIM
79-80—Gloucester		OPJHL	50	21	38	59	26	—	—	—	—	—
80-81—Windsor		OMJHL	68	38	56	94	103	11	3	3	6	40
81-82—Windsor		OHL	68	36	73	109	192	9	2	10	12	42
—Detroit		NHL	4	1	0	1	2	—	—	—	—	—
82-83—Detroit		NHL	18	2	0	2	15	—	—	—	—	—
—Windsor		OHL	46	39	49	88	75	—	—	—	—	—
—Adirondack		AHL	6	1	7	8	0	6	2	4	6	0
83-84—Adirondack		AHL	29	13	16	29	59	—	—	—	—	—
—Detroit		NHL	28	4	6	10	32	—	—	—	—	—
84-85—Adirondack		AHL	47	22	29	51	24	—	—	—	—	—
—Detroit		NHL	30	8	1	9	45	3	0	2	2	0
85-86—Adirondack		AHL	21	15	11	26	32	16	5	10	15	38
—Detroit		NHL	48	7	15	22	142	—	—	—	—	—
86-87—New Jersey		NHL	75	16	24	40	137	—	—	—	—	—
87-88—New Jersey		NHL	68	17	18	35	121	20	4	6	10	50
88-89—New Jersey		NHL	74	7	14	21	209	—	—	—	—	—
89-90—Quebec		NHL	72	11	14	25	104	—	—	—	—	—
90-91—Quebec		NHL	59	5	10	15	86	—	—	—	—	—
—Toronto		NHL	7	1	1	2	2	—	—	—	—	—

Season Team	League	REGULAR SEASON					PLAYOFFS				
		Gms.	G	A	Pts.	Pen.	Gms.	G	A	Pts.	Pen.
91-92—Toronto	NHL	64	6	9	15	102	—	—	—	—	—
—New York Islanders	NHL	11	1	1	2	13	—	—	—	—	—
92-93—New York Islanders	NHL	41	5	3	8	90	18	0	3	3	10
93-94—New York Islanders	NHL	17	1	1	2	49	—	—	—	—	—
NHL totals		616	92	117	209	1149	41	4	11	15	60

LOMAKIN, ANDREI
LW, PANTHERS

PERSONAL: Born April 3, 1964, in Voskresensk, U.S.S.R. . . . . 5-10/175. . . . Shoots left. . . . Name pronounced AHN-dray loh-MAH-kihn. **TRANSACTIONS/CAREER NOTES:** Selected by Philadelphia Flyers in seventh round (sixth Flyers pick, 107th overall) of NHL entry draft (June 22, 1991). . . . Fractured thumb (January 23, 1992); missed 15 games. . . . Bruised ribs; missed first game of 1992-93 season. . . . Bruised right foot (November 27, 1992); missed one game. . . . Separated shoulder (February 14, 1993); missed 10 games. . . . Selected by Florida Panthers in NHL expansion draft (June 24, 1993). . . . Bruised tendon in right knee (October 14, 1993); missed one game. . . . Bruised left shoulder (October 28, 1993); missed six games.
MISCELLANEOUS: Member of gold-medal-winning U.S.S.R. Olympic team (1988).

Season Team	League	REGULAR SEASON					PLAYOFFS				
		Gms.	G	A	Pts.	PIM	Gms.	G	A	Pts.	PIM
81-82—Khimik Voskresensk	USSR	8	1	1	2	2	—	—	—	—	—
82-83—Khimik Voskresensk	USSR	56	15	8	23	32	—	—	—	—	—
83-84—Khimik Voskresensk	USSR	44	10	8	18	26	—	—	—	—	—
84-85—Khimik Voskresensk	USSR	52	13	10	23	24	—	—	—	—	—
86-87—Dynamo Moscow	USSR	40	15	14	29	30	—	—	—	—	—
87-88—Dynamo Moscow	USSR	45	10	15	25	24	—	—	—	—	—
88-89—Dynamo Moscow	USSR	44	9	16	25	22	—	—	—	—	—
89-90—Dynamo Moscow	USSR	48	11	15	26	36	—	—	—	—	—
90-91—Dynamo Moscow	USSR	45	16	17	33	22	—	—	—	—	—
91-92—Philadelphia	NHL	57	14	16	30	26	—	—	—	—	—
92-93—Philadelphia	NHL	51	8	12	20	34	—	—	—	—	—
93-94—Florida	NHL	76	19	28	47	26	—	—	—	—	—
NHL totals		184	41	56	97	86	—	—	—	—	—

LONEY, TROY
LW, ISLANDERS

PERSONAL: Born September 21, 1963, in Bow Island, Alta. . . . 6-3/210. . . . Shoots left. . . . Name pronounced LOH-nee. **TRANSACTIONS/CAREER NOTES:** Selected by Pittsburgh Penguins as underage junior in third round (third Penguins pick, 52nd overall) of NHL entry draft (June 9, 1982). . . . Suspended by AHL (December 1986). . . . Sprained right shoulder (January 17, 1987). . . . Underwent knee surgery (October 1987). . . . Suspended 10 games by NHL for leaving bench to fight (November 13, 1988). . . . Broke right hand (November 24, 1989); missed 12 games. . . . Underwent surgery to right knee (June 1990); missed first two months of season. . . . Bruised neck (November 8, 1992); missed two games. . . . Selected by Mighty Ducks of Anaheim in NHL expansion draft (June 24, 1993). . . . Bruised right knee (October 28, 1993); missed four games. . . . Underwent arthroscopic knee surgery (November 17, 1993); missed 17 games. . . . Traded by Mighty Ducks to New York Islanders for D Tom Kurvers (June 29, 1994).
MISCELLANEOUS: Member of Stanley Cup championship teams (1991 and 1992).

Season Team	League	REGULAR SEASON					PLAYOFFS				
		Gms.	G	A	Pts.	PIM	Gms.	G	A	Pts.	PIM
80-81—Lethbridge	WHL	71	18	13	31	100	9	2	3	5	14
81-82—Lethbridge	WHL	71	26	31	57	152	12	3	3	6	10
82-83—Lethbridge	WHL	72	33	34	67	156	20	10	7	17	43
83-84—Baltimore	AHL	63	18	13	31	147	10	0	2	2	19
—Pittsburgh	NHL	13	0	0	0	9	—	—	—	—	—
84-85—Baltimore	AHL	15	4	2	6	25	—	—	—	—	—
—Pittsburgh	NHL	46	10	8	18	59	—	—	—	—	—
85-86—Baltimore	AHL	33	12	11	23	84	—	—	—	—	—
—Pittsburgh	NHL	47	3	9	12	95	—	—	—	—	—
86-87—Baltimore	AHL	40	13	14	27	134	—	—	—	—	—
—Pittsburgh	NHL	23	8	7	15	22	—	—	—	—	—
87-88—Pittsburgh	NHL	65	5	13	18	151	—	—	—	—	—
88-89—Pittsburgh	NHL	69	10	6	16	165	11	1	3	4	24
89-90—Pittsburgh	NHL	67	11	16	27	168	—	—	—	—	—
90-91—Muskegon	IHL	2	0	0	0	5	—	—	—	—	—
—Pittsburgh	NHL	44	7	9	16	85	24	2	2	4	41
91-92—Pittsburgh	NHL	76	10	16	26	127	†21	4	5	9	32
92-93—Pittsburgh	NHL	82	5	16	21	99	10	1	4	5	0
93-94—Anaheim	NHL	62	13	6	19	88	—	—	—	—	—
NHL totals		594	82	106	188	1068	66	8	14	22	97

LONGO, CHRIS
RW, CAPITALS

PERSONAL: Born January 5, 1972, in Belleville, Ont. . . . 5-10/180. . . . Shoots right. . . . Full name: Chris Anthony Longo. **TRANSACTIONS/CAREER NOTES:** Selected by Washington Capitals in third round (third Capitals pick, 51st overall) of NHL entry draft (June 16, 1990).
HONORS: Won Emms Family Award (1989-90).

Season	Team	League	REGULAR SEASON					PLAYOFFS				
			Gms.	G	A	Pts.	PIM	Gms.	G	A	Pts.	PIM
87-88—Kingston Jr. A		MTHL	37	15	16	31	...	—	—	—	—	—
88-89—Kingston Jr. A		MTHL	40	28	29	57	54	—	—	—	—	—
89-90—Peterborough		OHL	66	33	42	75	48	11	2	3	5	14
90-91—Peterborough		OHL	64	30	38	68	68	4	1	0	1	9
91-92—Peterborough		OHL	25	5	14	19	16	10	5	6	11	16
92-93—Baltimore		AHL	74	7	18	25	52	7	0	1	1	0
93-94—Portland		AHL	69	6	19	25	69	17	2	4	6	11

LORENZ, DANNY
G, PANTHERS

PERSONAL: Born December 12, 1969, in Murrayville, B.C. . . . 5-10/183. . . . Catches left. . . . Name pronounced luh-REHNS.

TRANSACTIONS/CAREER NOTES: Selected by New York Islanders in third round (fourth Islanders pick, 58th overall) of NHL entry draft (June 11, 1988). . . . Loaned by Islanders to Springfield Indians (February 2, 1994). . . . Signed as free agent by Florida Panthers (1994).

HONORS: Won Del Wilson Trophy (1988-89). . . . Named to WHL (West) All-Star first team (1988-89 and 1989-90).

Season	Team	League	REGULAR SEASON							PLAYOFFS						
			Gms.	Min.	W	L	T	GA	SO	Avg.	Gms.	Min.	W	L	GA	SO	Avg.
86-87—Seattle		WHL	38	2103	12	21	2	199	0	5.68	—	—	—	—	—	—	—
87-88—Seattle		WHL	62	3302	20	37	2	*314	0	5.71	—	—	—	—	—	—	—
88-89—Seattle		WHL	*68	*4003	31	33	4	240	*3	3.60	—	—	—	—	—	—	—
—Springfield		AHL	4	210	2	1	0	12	0	3.43	—	—	—	—	—	—	—
89-90—Seattle		WHL	56	3226	37	15	2	221	0	4.11	13	751	6	7	40	0	*3.20
90-91—New York Islanders		NHL	2	80	0	1	0	5	0	3.75	—	—	—	—	—	—	—
—Capital District		AHL	17	940	5	9	2	70	0	4.47	—	—	—	—	—	—	—
—Richmond		ECHL	20	1020	6	9	‡2	75	0	4.41	—	—	—	—	—	—	—
91-92—Capital District		AHL	53	3050	22	22	7	*181	2	3.56	7	442	3	4	25	0	3.39
—New York Islanders		NHL	2	120	0	2	0	10	0	5.00	—	—	—	—	—	—	—
92-93—Capital District		AHL	44	2412	16	17	5	146	1	3.63	4	219	0	3	12	0	3.29
—New York Islanders		NHL	4	157	1	2	0	10	0	3.82	—	—	—	—	—	—	—
93-94—Salt Lake City		IHL	20	982	4	12	‡0	91	0	5.56	—	—	—	—	—	—	—
—Springfield		AHL	14	802	5	7	1	59	0	4.41	—	—	—	—	—	—	—
NHL totals			8	357	1	5	0	25	0	4.20							

LOUDER, GREG
G, OILERS

PERSONAL: Born November 16, 1971, in Concord, Mass. . . . 6-1/185. . . . Catches left.
COLLEGE: Notre Dame.

TRANSACTIONS/CAREER NOTES: Selected by Edmonton Oilers in fifth round (fifth Oilers pick, 101st overall) of NHL entry draft (June 16, 1990).

Season	Team	League	REGULAR SEASON							PLAYOFFS						
			Gms.	Min.	W	L	T	GA	SO	Avg.	Gms.	Min.	W	L	GA	SO	Avg.
90-91—Univ. of Notre Dame		CCHA	33	1958	16	5	2	134	1	4.11	—	—	—	—	—	—	—
91-92—Univ. of Notre Dame		CCHA	18	1055	5	13	0	88	0	5.00	—	—	—	—	—	—	—
92-93—Univ. of Notre Dame		CCHA	24	1177	4	16	1	95	0	4.84	—	—	—	—	—	—	—
93-94—Univ. of Notre Dame		CCHA	28	1333	7	13	4	93	0	4.19	—	—	—	—	—	—	—

LOWE, KEVIN
D, RANGERS

PERSONAL: Born April 15, 1959, in Lachute, Que. . . . 6-2/195. . . . Shoots left. . . . Full name: Kevin Hugh Lowe. . . . Name pronounced LOH. . . . Husband of Karen Percy, Canadian Olympic bronze-medal-winning downhill skier (1988).

TRANSACTIONS/CAREER NOTES: Selected by Edmonton Oilers in first round (first Oilers pick, 21st overall) of NHL entry draft (August 9, 1979). . . . Broke index finger (March 7, 1986); missed six games. . . . Broke left wrist (March 9, 1988). . . . Pulled rib muscle (September 1988). . . . Suffered concussion (October 14, 1988). . . . Suffered back spasms (April 8, 1990). . . . Bruised back (December 28, 1991); missed one game. . . . Strained rotator cuff (January 28, 1992); missed three games. . . . Restrained rotator cuff (February 5, 1992); missed 21 games. . . . Strained groin (April 12, 1992); missed playoffs. . . . Did not report to Oilers in 1992-93 season because of contract dispute; missed 30 games. . . . Traded by Oilers to New York Rangers for RW Roman Oksyuta and third-round pick in 1993 draft (December 11, 1992). . . . Suffered stiff neck (December 19, 1992); missed one game. . . . Suffered from the flu (December 23, 1992); missed one game. . . . Injured back (February 15, 1993); missed one game. . . . Injured back (February 24, 1993); missed one game. . . . Suspended three preseason games and fined $500 by NHL for high-sticking incident (September 28, 1993). . . . Bruised right foot (October 9, 1993); missed two games. . . . Bruised thigh (October 15, 1993); missed one game. . . . Suffered from the flu (December 31, 1993); missed one game. . . . Injured back (February 28, 1994); missed one game. . . . Reinjured back (March 10, 1994); missed one game. . . . Reinjured back (March 14, 1994); missed two games. . . . Sprained wrist (April 2, 1994); missed five games.

HONORS: Named to QMJHL All-Star second team (1977-78 and 1978-79). . . . Played in NHL All-Star Game (1984-1986, 1988 through 1990 and 1993). . . . Won King Clancy Memorial Trophy (1989-90). . . . Named Budweiser/NHL Man of the Year (1989-90).

MISCELLANEOUS: Member of Stanley Cup championship teams (1984, 1985, 1987, 1988, 1990 and 1994).

Season	Team	League	REGULAR SEASON					PLAYOFFS				
			Gms.	G	A	Pts.	PIM	Gms.	G	A	Pts.	PIM
76-77—Quebec		QMJHL	69	3	19	22	39	—	—	—	—	—
77-78—Quebec		QMJHL	64	13	52	65	86	4	1	2	3	6
78-79—Quebec		QMJHL	68	26	60	86	120	6	1	7	8	36
79-80—Edmonton		NHL	64	2	19	21	70	3	0	1	1	0
80-81—Edmonton		NHL	79	10	24	34	94	9	0	2	2	11

Season	Team	League	REGULAR SEASON					PLAYOFFS				
			Gms.	G	A	Pts.	Pen.	Gms.	G	A	Pts.	Pen.
81-82—Edmonton		NHL	80	9	31	40	63	5	0	3	3	0
82-83—Edmonton		NHL	80	6	34	40	43	16	1	8	9	10
83-84—Edmonton		NHL	80	4	42	46	59	19	3	7	10	16
84-85—Edmonton		NHL	80	4	22	26	104	16	0	5	5	8
85-86—Edmonton		NHL	74	2	16	18	90	10	1	3	4	15
86-87—Edmonton		NHL	77	8	29	37	94	21	2	4	6	22
87-88—Edmonton		NHL	70	9	15	24	89	19	0	2	2	26
88-89—Edmonton		NHL	76	7	18	25	98	7	1	2	3	4
89-90—Edmonton		NHL	78	7	26	33	140	20	0	2	2	10
90-91—Edmonton		NHL	73	3	13	16	113	14	1	1	2	14
91-92—Edmonton		NHL	55	2	8	10	107	11	0	3	3	16
92-93—New York Rangers		NHL	49	3	12	15	58	—	—	—	—	—
93-94—New York Rangers		NHL	71	5	14	19	70	22	1	0	1	20
NHL totals			1086	81	323	404	1292	192	10	43	53	172

LOWRY, DAVE
LW, PANTHERS

PERSONAL: Born January 14, 1965, in Sudbury, Ont.... 6-1/195.... Shoots left.
HIGH SCHOOL: Sir Wilfrid Laurier (London, Ont.).
TRANSACTIONS/CAREER NOTES: Underwent arthroscopic knee surgery (December 1982).... Selected as underage junior by Vancouver Canucks in sixth round (fourth Canucks pick, 110th overall) of NHL entry draft (June 8, 1983).... Traded by Canucks to St. Louis Blues for C Ernie Vargas (September 29, 1988). ... Injured groin (March 1990).... Sprained shoulder (October 1991); missed two games.... Injured knee (October 26, 1992); missed 26 games.... Selected by Florida Panthers in NHL expansion draft (June 24, 1993).... Fractured cheekbone (November 26, 1993); missed three games.... Injured knee (December 12, 1993); missed one game.
HONORS: Named to OHL All-Star first team (1984-85).

Season	Team	League	REGULAR SEASON					PLAYOFFS				
			Gms.	G	A	Pts.	PIM	Gms.	G	A	Pts.	PIM
82-83—London		OHL	42	11	16	27	48	3	0	0	0	14
83-84—London		OHL	66	29	47	76	125	8	6	6	12	41
84-85—London		OHL	61	60	60	120	94	8	6	5	11	10
85-86—Vancouver		NHL	73	10	8	18	143	3	0	0	0	0
86-87—Vancouver		NHL	70	8	10	18	176	—	—	—	—	—
87-88—Fredericton		AHL	46	18	27	45	59	14	7	3	10	72
—Vancouver		NHL	22	1	3	4	38	—	—	—	—	—
88-89—Peoria		IHL	58	31	35	66	45	—	—	—	—	—
—St. Louis		NHL	21	3	3	6	11	10	0	5	5	4
89-90—St. Louis		NHL	78	19	6	25	75	12	2	1	3	39
90-91—St. Louis		NHL	79	19	21	40	168	13	1	4	5	35
91-92—St. Louis		NHL	75	7	13	20	77	6	0	1	1	20
92-93—St. Louis		NHL	58	5	8	13	101	11	2	0	2	14
93-94—Florida		NHL	80	15	22	37	64	—	—	—	—	—
NHL totals			556	87	94	181	853	55	5	11	16	112

LUDWIG, CRAIG
D, STARS

PERSONAL: Born March 15, 1961, in Rhinelander, Wis.... 6-3/217.... Shoots left.... Full name: Craig Lee Ludwig.... Name pronounced LUHD-wihg.
COLLEGE: North Dakota.
TRANSACTIONS/CAREER NOTES: Selected by Montreal Canadiens in third round (fifth Canadiens pick, 61st overall) of NHL entry draft (June 11, 1980).... Fractured knuckle in left hand (October 1984).... Broke hand (December 2, 1985); missed nine games.... Broke right facial bone (January 1988); missed five games.... Suspended five games by NHL for elbowing (November 19, 1988).... Separated right shoulder (March 21, 1990).... Traded by Canadiens to New York Islanders for D Gerald Diduck (September 4, 1990).... Traded by Islanders to Minnesota North Stars as part of a three-way deal in which North Stars sent D Dave Babych to Vancouver Canucks and Canucks sent D Tom Kurvers to Islanders (June 22, 1991).... Injured foot (December 8, 1991); missed six games.... Injured foot (January 30, 1993); missed two games.... Pinched nerve in neck (March 18, 1993); missed two games.... North Stars franchise moved from Minnesota to Dallas and renamed Stars for 1993-94 season.
HONORS: Named to WCHA All-Star second team (1981-82).
MISCELLANEOUS: Member of Stanley Cup championship team (1986).

Season	Team	League	REGULAR SEASON					PLAYOFFS				
			Gms.	G	A	Pts.	PIM	Gms.	G	A	Pts.	PIM
79-80—Univ. of North Dakota		WCHA	33	1	8	9	32	—	—	—	—	—
80-81—Univ. of North Dakota		WCHA	34	4	8	12	48	—	—	—	—	—
81-82—Univ. of North Dakota		WCHA	47	5	26	31	70	—	—	—	—	—
82-83—Montreal		NHL	80	0	25	25	59	3	0	0	0	2
83-84—Montreal		NHL	80	7	18	25	52	15	0	3	3	23
84-85—Montreal		NHL	72	5	14	19	90	12	0	2	2	6
85-86—Montreal		NHL	69	2	4	6	63	20	0	1	1	48
86-87—Montreal		NHL	75	4	12	16	105	17	2	3	5	30
87-88—Montreal		NHL	74	4	10	14	69	11	1	1	2	6
88-89—Montreal		NHL	74	3	13	16	73	21	0	2	2	24
89-90—Montreal		NHL	73	1	15	16	108	11	0	1	1	16
90-91—New York Islanders		NHL	75	1	8	9	77	—	—	—	—	—
91-92—Minnesota		NHL	73	2	9	11	54	7	0	1	1	19

Season Team	League	REGULAR SEASON					PLAYOFFS				
		Gms.	G	A	Pts.	Pen.	Gms.	G	A	Pts.	Pen.
92-93—Minnesota	NHL	78	1	10	11	153	—	—	—	—	—
93-94—Dallas	NHL	84	1	13	14	123	9	0	3	3	8
NHL totals		907	31	151	182	1026	126	3	17	20	182

LUHNING, WARREN
RW, ISLANDERS

PERSONAL: Born July 3, 1975, in Edmonton. . . . 6-2/185. . . . Shoots right.
COLLEGE: Michigan.
TRANSACTIONS/CAREER NOTES: Selected by New York Islanders in fourth round (fourth Islanders pick, 92nd overall) of NHL entry draft (June 26, 1993).

Season Team	League	REGULAR SEASON					PLAYOFFS				
		Gms.	G	A	Pts.	PIM	Gms.	G	A	Pts.	PIM
92-93—Calgary Royals	AJHL	46	18	25	43	287	—	—	—	—	—
93-94—University of Michigan	CCHA	38	13	6	19	83	—	—	—	—	—

LUKOWICH, BRAD
D, ISLANDERS

PERSONAL: Born August 12, 1976, in Surrey, B.C. . . . 6-1/170. . . . Shoots left.
HIGH SCHOOL: Norkam Secondary (Kamloops, B.C.).
TRANSACTIONS/CAREER NOTES: Selected by New York Islanders in fourth round (fourth Islanders pick, 90th overall) of NHL entry draft (June 29, 1994).

Season Team	League	REGULAR SEASON					PLAYOFFS				
		Gms.	G	A	Pts.	PIM	Gms.	G	A	Pts.	PIM
92-93—Cranbook	Tier II Jr. A	54	21	41	62	162	—	—	—	—	—
—Kamloops	WHL	1	0	0	0	0	—	—	—	—	—
93-94—Kamloops	WHL	42	5	11	16	166	16	0	1	1	35

LUMME, JYRKI
D, CANUCKS

PERSONAL: Born July 16, 1966, in Tampere, Finland. . . . 6-1/207. . . . Shoots left. . . . Name pronounced LOO-mee.
TRANSACTIONS/CAREER NOTES: Selected by Montreal Canadiens in third round (third Canadiens pick, 57th overall) of NHL entry draft (June 21, 1986). . . . Strained left knee ligaments (December 1988). . . . Stretched knee ligaments (February 21, 1989). . . . Bruised right foot (November 1989). . . . Traded by Canadiens to Vancouver Canucks for second-round pick (C Craig Darby) in 1991 draft (March 6, 1990). . . . Lacerated eye (November 19, 1991); missed three games. . . . Sprained knee (January 19, 1993); missed nine games.
MISCELLANEOUS: Member of silver-medal-winning Finnish Olympic team (1988).

Season Team	League	REGULAR SEASON					PLAYOFFS				
		Gms.	G	A	Pts.	PIM	Gms.	G	A	Pts.	PIM
84-85—Koo Vee	Finland	30	6	4	10	44	—	—	—	—	—
85-86—Ilves Tampere	Finland	31	1	5	6	4	—	—	—	—	—
86-87—Ilves Tampere	Finland	43	12	12	24	52	4	0	1	1	0
87-88—Ilves Tampere	Finland	43	8	22	30	75	—	—	—	—	—
—Finland Olympic Team	Int'l	6	0	1	1	2	—	—	—	—	—
88-89—Montreal	NHL	21	1	3	4	10	—	—	—	—	—
—Sherbrooke	AHL	26	4	11	15	10	6	1	3	4	4
89-90—Montreal	NHL	54	1	19	20	41	—	—	—	—	—
—Vancouver	NHL	11	3	7	10	8	—	—	—	—	—
90-91—Vancouver	NHL	80	5	27	32	59	6	2	3	5	0
91-92—Vancouver	NHL	75	12	32	44	65	13	2	3	5	4
92-93—Vancouver	NHL	74	8	36	44	55	12	0	5	5	6
93-94—Vancouver	NHL	83	13	42	55	50	24	2	11	13	16
NHL totals		398	43	166	209	288	55	6	22	28	26

LUONGO, CHRISTOPHER
D, ISLANDERS

PERSONAL: Born March 17, 1967, in Detroit. . . . 6-0/199. . . . Shoots right. . . . Full name: Christopher John Luongo. . . . Name pronounced loo-WAHN-goh.
HIGH SCHOOL: Notre Dame (Harper Woods, Mich.).
COLLEGE: Michigan State.
TRANSACTIONS/CAREER NOTES: Selected by Detroit Red Wings in fifth round (fifth Red Wings pick, 92nd overall) of NHL entry draft (June 15, 1985). . . . Signed as free agent by Ottawa Senators (September 9, 1992). . . . Traded by Senators to New York Islanders for D Jeff Finley (June 30, 1993).
HONORS: Named to NCAA All-Tournament team (1986-87). . . . Named to CCHA All-Star second team (1988-89).

Season Team	League	REGULAR SEASON					PLAYOFFS				
		Gms.	G	A	Pts.	PIM	Gms.	G	A	Pts.	PIM
84-85—St. Clair Shores	NAJHL	41	2	25	27	. . .	—	—	—	—	—
85-86—Michigan State	CCHA	38	1	5	6	29	—	—	—	—	—
86-87—Michigan State	CCHA	27	4	16	20	38	—	—	—	—	—
87-88—Michigan State	CCHA	45	3	15	18	49	—	—	—	—	—
88-89—Michigan State	CCHA	47	4	21	25	42	—	—	—	—	—
89-90—Adirondack	AHL	53	9	14	23	37	3	0	0	0	0
—Phoenix	IHL	23	5	9	14	41	—	—	—	—	—
90-91—Detroit	NHL	4	0	1	1	4	—	—	—	—	—
—Adirondack	AHL	76	14	25	39	71	2	0	0	0	7
91-92—Adirondack	AHL	80	6	20	26	60	19	3	5	8	10

Season Team	League	Gms.	G	A	Pts.	Pen.	Gms.	G	A	Pts.	Pen.
92-93—Ottawa	NHL	76	3	9	12	68	—	—	—	—	—
—New Haven	AHL	7	0	2	2	2	—	—	—	—	—
93-94—Salt Lake City	IHL	51	9	31	40	54	—	—	—	—	—
—New York Islanders	NHL	17	1	3	4	13	—	—	—	—	—
NHL totals		97	4	13	17	85					

MacDERMID, PAUL
RW, NORDIQUES

PERSONAL: Born April 14, 1963, in Chesley, Ont.... 6-1/205.... Shoots right.
TRANSACTIONS/CAREER NOTES: Selected by Hartford Whalers as underage junior in third round (second Whalers pick, 61st overall) of NHL entry draft (June 10, 1981). ... Injured knee (December 1982).... Injured neck and shoulder (December 6, 1988).... Sprained right knee ligament (February 4, 1989).... Traded by Whalers to Winnipeg Jets for C/LW Randy Cunneyworth (December 13, 1989).... Suffered back spasms (November 3, 1990); missed six games.... Strained knee (December 1990).... Traded by Jets to Washington Capitals for D Mike Lalor (March 2, 1992).... Traded by Capitals with RW Reggie Savage to Quebec Nordiques for LW Mike Hough (June 20, 1993).... Sprained right ankle (October 14, 1993); missed nine games.... Suffered lumbar sprain (November 22, 1993); missed 21 games.... Suffered lumbar sprain (April 5, 1994); missed four games.

		REGULAR SEASON					PLAYOFFS				
Season Team	League	Gms.	G	A	Pts.	PIM	Gms.	G	A	Pts.	PIM
79-80—Port Elgin Junior C	OHA	30	23	20	43	87	—	—	—	—	—
80-81—Windsor	OMJHL	68	15	17	32	106	—	—	—	—	—
81-82—Windsor	OHL	65	26	45	71	179	9	6	4	10	17
—Hartford	NHL	3	1	0	1	2	—	—	—	—	—
82-83—Windsor	OHL	42	35	45	80	90	—	—	—	—	—
—Hartford	NHL	7	0	0	0	2	—	—	—	—	—
83-84—Hartford	NHL	3	0	1	1	0	—	—	—	—	—
—Binghamton	AHL	70	31	30	61	130	—	—	—	—	—
84-85—Binghamton	AHL	48	9	31	40	87	—	—	—	—	—
—Hartford	NHL	31	4	7	11	299	—	—	—	—	—
85-86—Hartford	NHL	74	13	10	23	160	10	2	1	3	20
86-87—Hartford	NHL	72	7	11	18	202	6	2	1	3	34
87-88—Hartford	NHL	80	20	15	35	139	6	0	5	5	14
88-89—Hartford	NHL	74	17	27	44	141	4	1	1	2	16
89-90—Hartford	NHL	29	6	12	18	69	—	—	—	—	—
—Winnipeg	NHL	44	7	10	17	100	7	0	2	2	8
90-91—Winnipeg	NHL	69	15	21	36	128	—	—	—	—	—
91-92—Winnipeg	NHL	59	10	11	21	151	—	—	—	—	—
—Washington	NHL	15	2	5	7	43	7	0	1	1	22
92-93—Washington	NHL	72	9	8	17	80	—	—	—	—	—
93-94—Quebec	NHL	44	2	3	5	35	—	—	—	—	—
NHL totals		676	113	141	254	1551	40	5	11	16	114

MacDONALD, DOUG
LW, SABRES

PERSONAL: Born February 8, 1969, in Port Moody, B.C.... 6-0/192.... Shoots left. ... Full name: Douglas Bruce MacDonald.
COLLEGE: Wisconsin.
TRANSACTIONS/CAREER NOTES: Selected by Buffalo Sabres in fourth round (third Sabres pick, 77th overall) of NHL entry draft (June 17, 1989).... Injured knee (December 29, 1990).

		REGULAR SEASON					PLAYOFFS				
Season Team	League	Gms.	G	A	Pts.	PIM	Gms.	G	A	Pts.	PIM
85-86—Langley Eagles	BCJHL	42	19	37	56	16	—	—	—	—	—
86-87—Delta	BCJHL	51	28	49	77	61	—	—	—	—	—
87-88—Delta	BCJHL	51	50	54	104	70	9	5	9	14	16
88-89—University of Wisconsin	WCHA	44	23	25	48	50	—	—	—	—	—
89-90—University of Wisconsin	WCHA	44	16	35	51	52	—	—	—	—	—
90-91—University of Wisconsin	WCHA	31	20	26	46	50	—	—	—	—	—
91-92—University of Wisconsin	WCHA	33	16	28	44	76	—	—	—	—	—
92-93—Rochester	AHL	64	25	33	58	58	7	0	2	2	4
—Buffalo	NHL	5	1	0	1	2	—	—	—	—	—
93-94—Rochester	AHL	63	25	19	44	46	4	1	1	2	8
—Buffalo	NHL	4	0	0	0	0	—	—	—	—	—
NHL totals		9	1	0	1	2					

MacDONALD, JASON
RW, RED WINGS

PERSONAL: Born April 1, 1974, in Charlottetown, P.E.I.... 6-0/195.... Shoots right.
HIGH SCHOOL: St. Mary's (Owen Sound, Ont.).
TRANSACTIONS/CAREER NOTES: Selected by Detroit Red Wings in sixth round (fifth Red Wings pick, 142nd overall) of NHL entry draft (June 20, 1992).
HONORS: Named to OHL All-Star second team (1993-94).

		REGULAR SEASON					PLAYOFFS				
Season Team	League	Gms.	G	A	Pts.	PIM	Gms.	G	A	Pts.	PIM
89-90—Charlottetown	PEIJHL	25	11	29	40	206	—	—	—	—	—
90-91—North Bay	OHL	57	12	15	27	126	10	3	3	6	15

LM

Season Team	League	REGULAR SEASON Gms.	G	A	Pts.	Pen.	PLAYOFFS Gms.	G	A	Pts.	Pen.
91-92—North Bay	OHL	17	5	8	13	50	—	—	—	—	—
—Owen Sound	OHL	42	17	19	36	129	5	0	2	2	8
92-93—Owen Sound	OHL	55	46	43	89	197	8	6	5	11	28
93-94—Owen Sound	OHL	66	55	61	116	177	9	7	11	18	36
—Adirondack	AHL	—	—	—	—	—	1	0	0	0	0

MacDONALD, KEVIN
D, SENATORS

PERSONAL: Born February 24, 1966, in Prescott, Ont.... 6-0/200.... Shoots left.
TRANSACTIONS/CAREER NOTES: Signed as free agent by Ottawa Senators (December 22, 1993).

Season Team	League	REGULAR SEASON Gms.	G	A	Pts.	PIM	PLAYOFFS Gms.	G	A	Pts.	PIM
92-93—Fort Wayne	IHL	65	4	9	13	283	11	0	0	0	21
—Phoenix	IHL	6	0	1	1	23	—	—	—	—	—
93-94—Fort Wayne	IHL	29	0	3	3	140	15	0	4	4	76
—Prince Edward Island	AHL	40	2	4	6	245	—	—	—	—	—
—Ottawa	NHL	1	0	0	0	2	—	—	—	—	—
NHL totals		1	0	0	0	2					

MacDONALD, TODD
G, PANTHERS

PERSONAL: Born July 5, 1975, in Charlottetown, P.E.I.... 6-0/155.... Catches left.
TRANSACTIONS/CAREER NOTES: Selected by Florida Panthers in fifth round (seventh Panthers pick, 109th overall) of NHL entry draft (June 26, 1993).

Season Team	League	REGULAR SEASON Gms.	Min.	W	L	T	GA	SO	Avg.	PLAYOFFS Gms.	Min.	W	L	GA	SO	Avg.
91-92—Kingston	OHA Mj Jr.A	28	1680	...	...	...	84	0	3.00	—	—	—	—	—	—	—
92-93—Tacoma	WHL	19	823	6	6	0	59	0	4.30	—	—	—	—	—	—	—
93-94—Tacoma	WHL	29	1606	13	10	2	109	1	4.07	—	—	—	—	—	—	—

MacINNIS, AL
D, BLUES

PERSONAL: Born July 11, 1963, in Inverness, N.S.... 6-2/196.... Shoots right.... Name pronounced muh-KIHN-ihz.
TRANSACTIONS/CAREER NOTES: Selected by Calgary Flames as underage junior in first round (first Flames pick, 15th overall) of NHL entry draft (June 10, 1981).... Twisted knee (February 1985).... Lacerated hand (March 23, 1986).... Stretched ligaments of knee (April 8, 1990).... Separated shoulder (November 21, 1991); missed eight games.... Dislocated left hip (November 12, 1992); missed 34 games.... Strained shoulder (December 22, 1993); missed one game.... Strained shoulder (January 2, 1994); missed four games.... Bruised knee (February 24, 1994); missed four games.... Traded by Flames with fourth-round pick in 1997 draft to St. Louis Blues for D Phil Housley and second-round pick in 1996 and 1997 drafts (July 4, 1994).
HONORS: Named to OHL All-Star first team (1981-82 and 1982-83).... Named to Memorial Cup All-Star team (1981-82).... Won Max Kaminsky Trophy (1982-83).... Played in NHL All-Star Game (1985, 1988, 1990 through 1992 and 1994).... Named to NHL All-Star second team (1986-87, 1988-89 and 1993-94).... Won Conn Smythe Trophy (1988-89).... Named to THE SPORTING NEWS All-Star first team (1989-90 and 1990-91).... Named to THE SPORTING NEWS All-Star second team (1993-94).... Named to NHL All-Star first team (1989-90 and 1990-91).
MISCELLANEOUS: Member of Stanley Cup championship team (1989).

Season Team	League	REGULAR SEASON Gms.	G	A	Pts.	PIM	PLAYOFFS Gms.	G	A	Pts.	PIM
79-80—Regina Blues	SJHL	59	20	28	48	110	—	—	—	—	—
80-81—Kitchener	OMJHL	47	11	28	39	59	18	4	12	16	20
81-82—Kitchener	OHL	59	25	50	75	145	15	5	10	15	44
—Calgary	NHL	2	0	0	0	0	—	—	—	—	—
82-83—Kitchener	OHL	51	38	46	84	67	8	3	8	11	9
—Calgary	NHL	14	1	3	4	9	—	—	—	—	—
83-84—Colorado	CHL	19	5	14	19	22	—	—	—	—	—
—Calgary	NHL	51	11	34	45	42	11	2	12	14	13
84-85—Calgary	NHL	67	14	52	66	75	4	1	2	3	8
85-86—Calgary	NHL	77	11	57	68	76	21	4	*15	19	30
86-87—Calgary	NHL	79	20	56	76	97	4	1	0	1	0
87-88—Calgary	NHL	80	25	58	83	114	7	3	6	9	18
88-89—Calgary	NHL	79	16	58	74	126	22	7	*24	*31	46
89-90—Calgary	NHL	79	28	62	90	82	6	2	3	5	8
90-91—Calgary	NHL	78	28	75	103	90	7	2	3	5	8
91-92—Calgary	NHL	72	20	57	77	83	—	—	—	—	—
92-93—Calgary	NHL	50	11	43	54	61	6	1	6	7	10
93-94—Calgary	NHL	75	28	54	82	95	7	2	6	8	12
NHL totals		803	213	609	822	950	95	25	77	102	153

MacINTYRE, ANDY
LW, BLACKHAWKS

PERSONAL: Born April 16, 1974, in Thunder Bay, Ont.... 6-2/195.... Shoots left.
HIGH SCHOOL: Marion Graham (Saskatoon, Sask.).
TRANSACTIONS/CAREER NOTES: Selected by Chicago Blackhawks in fourth round (fourth Blackhawks pick, 89th overall) of NHL entry draft (June 20, 1992).
HONORS: Named to WHL (East) All-Star second team (1993-94).

M

Season	Team	League	REGULAR SEASON					PLAYOFFS				
			Gms.	G	A	Pts.	PIM	Gms.	G	A	Pts.	PIM
89-90—Elk Valley		BCJHL	40	24	22	46	14	—	—	—	—	—
90-91—Seattle		WHL	71	16	13	29	52	6	0	0	0	2
91-92—Seattle		WHL	12	6	2	8	18	—	—	—	—	—
—Saskatoon		WHL	55	22	13	35	66	22	10	2	12	17
92-93—Saskatoon		WHL	72	35	29	64	82	9	3	2	5	2
93-94—Saskatoon		WHL	72	54	35	89	58	16	6	6	12	16

MACIVER, NORM

D, SENATORS

PERSONAL: Born September 8, 1964, in Thunder Bay, Ont.... 5-11/180.... Shoots left....
Full name: Norman Steven Maciver.
HIGH SCHOOL: Sir Winston Churchill (Thunder Bay, Ont.).
COLLEGE: Minnesota-Duluth.
TRANSACTIONS/CAREER NOTES: Signed as free agent by New York Rangers (September 8, 1986).... Dislocated right shoulder (March 1988).... Suffered hip pointer (November 1988).... Traded by Rangers with LW Don Maloney and C Brian Lawton to Hartford Whalers for C Carey Wilson and fifth-round pick (C Lubos Rob) in 1990 draft (December 26, 1988).... Traded by Whalers to Edmonton Oilers for D Jim Ennis (October 9, 1989).... Selected by Ottawa Senators in NHL waiver draft (October 4, 1992).... Suffered sore back (December 9, 1992); missed one game.... Injured back (January 19, 1993); missed one game.... Injured wrist (January 28, 1993); missed two games.... Suffered chest contusion (October 26, 1993) ; missed 10 games.... Injured left knee (January 13, 1994); missed three games.... Injured ankle (March 2, 1994); missed 15 games.... Broke leg (April 10, 1994); missed three games.
HONORS: Named to WCHA All-Star second team (1983-84).... Named to NCAA All-America West first team (1984-85 and 1985-86).... Named to WCHA All-Star first team (1984-85 and 1985-86).... Won Eddie Shore Plaque (1990-91).... Named to AHL All-Star first team (1990-91).

Season	Team	League	REGULAR SEASON					PLAYOFFS				
			Gms.	G	A	Pts.	PIM	Gms.	G	A	Pts.	PIM
82-83—Minnesota-Duluth		WCHA	45	1	26	27	40	6	0	2	2	2
83-84—Minnesota-Duluth		WCHA	31	13	28	41	28	8	1	10	11	8
84-85—Minnesota-Duluth		WCHA	47	14	47	61	63	10	3	3	6	6
85-86—Minnesota-Duluth		WCHA	42	11	51	62	36	4	2	3	5	2
86-87—New Haven		AHL	71	6	30	36	73	7	0	0	0	9
—New York Rangers		NHL	3	0	1	1	0	—	—	—	—	—
87-88—Colorado		IHL	27	6	20	26	22	—	—	—	—	—
—New York Rangers		NHL	37	9	15	24	14	—	—	—	—	—
88-89—New York Rangers		NHL	26	0	10	10	14	—	—	—	—	—
—Hartford		NHL	37	1	22	23	24	1	0	0	0	2
89-90—Binghamton		AHL	2	0	0	0	0	—	—	—	—	—
—Cape Breton		AHL	68	13	37	50	55	6	0	7	7	10
—Edmonton		NHL	1	0	0	0	0	—	—	—	—	—
90-91—Cape Breton		AHL	56	13	46	59	60	—	—	—	—	—
—Edmonton		NHL	21	2	5	7	14	18	0	4	4	8
91-92—Edmonton		NHL	57	6	34	40	38	13	1	2	3	10
92-93—Ottawa		NHL	80	17	46	63	84	—	—	—	—	—
93-94—Ottawa		NHL	53	3	20	23	26	—	—	—	—	—
NHL totals			315	38	153	191	214	32	1	6	7	20

MACKEY, DAVE

LW, BLUES

PERSONAL: Born July 24, 1966, in New Westminster, B.C.... 6-0/205.... Shoots left....
Name pronounced MAK-ee.
TRANSACTIONS/CAREER NOTES: Selected by Chicago Blackhawks as underage junior in 11th round (12th Blackhawks pick, 224th overall) of NHL entry draft (June 9, 1984).... Traded by Kamloops Blazers with C Rob DiMaio and C Kalvin Knibbs to Medicine Hat Tigers for LW Doug Pickel and LW Sean Pass (December 1986).... Selected by Minnesota North Stars in NHL waiver draft for $40,000 (October 2, 1989).... Tore right thumb ligaments (November 6, 1989); missed 10 games.... Suspended five games and fined $500 by NHL for fighting (December 28, 1989).... Sprained knee and ankle (January 24, 1990); missed 15 games.... Traded by North Stars to Vancouver Canucks for future considerations (September 6, 1990).... Signed as free agent by St. Louis Blues (July 1991).

Season	Team	League	REGULAR SEASON					PLAYOFFS				
			Gms.	G	A	Pts.	PIM	Gms.	G	A	Pts.	PIM
82-83—Victoria		WHL	69	16	16	32	53	12	1	1	2	4
83-84—Victoria		WHL	69	15	15	30	97	—	—	—	—	—
84-85—Victoria		WHL	16	5	6	11	45	—	—	—	—	—
—Portland		WHL	56	28	32	60	122	6	2	1	3	13
85-86—Kamloops		WHL	9	3	4	7	13	—	—	—	—	—
—Medicine Hat		WHL	60	25	32	57	167	25	6	3	9	72
86-87—Saginaw		IHL	81	26	49	75	173	10	5	6	11	22
87-88—Saginaw		IHL	62	29	22	51	211	10	3	7	10	44
—Chicago		NHL	23	1	3	4	71	—	—	—	—	—
88-89—Chicago		NHL	23	1	2	3	78	—	—	—	—	—
—Saginaw		IHL	57	22	23	45	223	—	—	—	—	—
89-90—Minnesota		NHL	16	2	0	2	28	—	—	—	—	—
90-91—Milwaukee		IHL	82	28	30	58	226	6	7	2	9	6
91-92—Peoria		IHL	35	20	17	37	90	—	—	—	—	—
—St. Louis		NHL	19	1	0	1	49	1	0	0	0	0
92-93—Peoria		IHL	42	24	22	46	112	4	1	0	1	22
—St. Louis		NHL	15	1	4	5	23	—	—	—	—	—

M

Season	Team	League	REGULAR SEASON Gms.	G	A	Pts.	Pen.	PLAYOFFS Gms.	G	A	Pts.	Pen.
93-94	—Peoria	IHL	49	14	21	35	132	—	—	—	—	—
	—St. Louis	NHL	30	2	3	5	56	2	0	0	0	2
	NHL totals		126	8	12	20	305	3	0	0	0	2

MacLEAN, JOHN
RW, DEVILS

PERSONAL: Born November 20, 1964, in Oshawa, Ont. . . . 6-0/200. . . . Shoots right. . . . Name pronounced muh-KLAYN.

TRANSACTIONS/CAREER NOTES: Selected by New Jersey Devils as underage junior in first round (first Devils pick, sixth overall) of NHL entry draft (June 8, 1983). . . . Bruised shoulder (November 1984). . . . Injured right knee (January 25, 1985). . . . Reinjured knee and underwent arthroscopic surgery (January 31, 1985). . . . Bruised ankle (November 2, 1986). . . . Sprained right elbow (December 1988). . . . Bruised ribs (March 1, 1989). . . . Suffered concussion and stomach contusions (October 1990). . . . Suffered concussion (December 11, 1990). . . . Tore ligament in right knee (September 30, 1991); missed entire 1991-92 season. . . . Underwent surgery to right knee (November 23, 1991). . . . Injured forearm (November 3, 1993); missed two games. . . . Lacerated eye (February 24, 1994); missed one game.

HONORS: Named to Memorial Cup All-Star team (1982-83). . . . Played in NHL All-Star Game (1989 and 1991).

Season	Team	League	REGULAR SEASON Gms.	G	A	Pts.	PIM	PLAYOFFS Gms.	G	A	Pts.	PIM
81-82	—Oshawa	OHL	67	17	22	39	197	12	3	6	9	63
82-83	—Oshawa	OHL	66	47	51	98	138	17	*18	20	†38	35
83-84	—New Jersey	NHL	23	1	0	1	10	—	—	—	—	—
	—Oshawa	OHL	30	23	36	59	58	7	2	5	7	18
84-85	—New Jersey	NHL	61	13	20	33	44	—	—	—	—	—
85-86	—New Jersey	NHL	74	21	36	57	112	—	—	—	—	—
86-87	—New Jersey	NHL	80	31	36	67	120	—	—	—	—	—
87-88	—New Jersey	NHL	76	23	16	39	145	20	7	11	18	60
88-89	—New Jersey	NHL	74	42	45	87	127	—	—	—	—	—
89-90	—New Jersey	NHL	80	41	38	79	80	6	4	1	5	12
90-91	—New Jersey	NHL	78	45	33	78	150	7	5	3	8	20
91-92	—New Jersey	NHL					Did not play—injured.					
92-93	—New Jersey	NHL	80	24	24	48	102	5	0	1	1	10
93-94	—New Jersey	NHL	80	37	33	70	95	20	6	10	16	22
	NHL totals		706	278	281	559	985	58	22	26	48	124

MacLEOD, PAT
D

PERSONAL: Born June 15, 1969, in Melfort, Sask. . . . 5-11/190. . . . Shoots left. . . . Name pronounced muh-KLOWD.

TRANSACTIONS/CAREER NOTES: Injured knee (March 1989). . . . Selected by Minnesota North Stars in fifth round (fifth North Stars pick, 87th overall) of NHL entry draft (June 17, 1989). . . . Selected by San Jose Sharks in NHL dispersal draft (May 30, 1991). . . . Sprained shoulder (December 30, 1992); missed 21 games. . . . Signed as free agent by Milwaukee Admirals (September 10, 1993).

HONORS: Named to WHL All-Star first team (1988-89). . . . Named to IHL All-Star second team (1991-92). . . . Named to IHL All-Star first team (1993-94).

Season	Team	League	REGULAR SEASON Gms.	G	A	Pts.	PIM	PLAYOFFS Gms.	G	A	Pts.	PIM
87-88	—Kamloops	WHL	50	13	33	46	27	18	2	7	9	6
88-89	—Kamloops	WHL	37	11	34	45	14	15	7	18	25	24
89-90	—Kalamazoo	IHL	82	9	38	47	27	10	1	6	7	2
90-91	—Kalamazoo	IHL	59	10	30	40	16	11	1	2	3	5
	—Minnesota	NHL	1	0	1	1	0	—	—	—	—	—
91-92	—San Jose	NHL	37	5	11	16	4	—	—	—	—	—
	—Kansas City	IHL	45	9	21	30	19	11	1	4	5	4
92-93	—San Jose	NHL	13	0	1	1	10	—	—	—	—	—
	—Kansas City	IHL	18	8	8	16	14	10	2	4	6	7
93-94	—Milwaukee	IHL	73	21	52	73	18	3	1	2	3	0
	NHL totals		51	5	13	18	14					

MACOUN, JAMIE
D, MAPLE LEAFS

PERSONAL: Born August 17, 1961, in Newmarket, Ont. . . . 6-2/200. . . . Shoots left. . . . Name pronounced muh-KOW-uhn.

COLLEGE: Ohio State.

TRANSACTIONS/CAREER NOTES: Signed as free agent by Calgary Flames (January 30, 1983). . . . Fractured cheekbone (December 26, 1984). . . . Suffered nerve damage to left arm in automobile accident (May 1987). . . . Suffered concussion (January 23, 1989). . . . Traded by Flames with C Doug Gilmour, LW Kent Manderville, D Ric Nattress and G Rick Wamsley to Toronto Maple Leafs for LW Craig Berube, D Alexander Godynyuk, LW Gary Leeman, D Michel Petit and G Jeff Reese (January 2, 1992). . . . Pulled groin (February 27, 1993); missed four games. . . . Suspended for one game for two stick-related game misconducts (March 9, 1994). . . . Suffered from the flu (March 10, 1994); missed one game.

HONORS: Named to NHL All-Rookie team (1983-84).

MISCELLANEOUS: Member of Stanley Cup championship team (1989).

Season	Team	League	REGULAR SEASON Gms.	G	A	Pts.	PIM	PLAYOFFS Gms.	G	A	Pts.	PIM
80-81	—Ohio State	CCHA	38	9	20	29	83	—	—	—	—	—
81-82	—Ohio State	CCHA	25	2	18	20	89	—	—	—	—	—

Season	Team	League	REGULAR SEASON					PLAYOFFS				
			Gms.	G	A	Pts.	Pen.	Gms.	G	A	Pts.	Pen.
82-83	Ohio State	CCHA	19	6	21	27	54	—	—	—	—	—
	Calgary	NHL	22	1	4	5	25	9	0	2	2	8
83-84	Calgary	NHL	72	9	23	32	97	11	1	0	1	0
84-85	Calgary	NHL	70	9	30	39	67	4	1	0	1	4
85-86	Calgary	NHL	77	11	21	32	81	22	1	6	7	23
86-87	Calgary	NHL	79	7	33	40	111	3	0	1	1	8
87-88	Calgary	NHL	Did not play—injured.									
88-89	Calgary	NHL	72	8	19	27	78	22	3	6	9	30
89-90	Calgary	NHL	78	8	27	35	70	6	0	3	3	10
90-91	Calgary	NHL	79	7	15	22	84	7	0	1	1	4
91-92	Calgary	NHL	37	2	12	14	53	—	—	—	—	—
	Toronto	NHL	39	3	13	16	18	—	—	—	—	—
92-93	Toronto	NHL	77	4	15	19	55	21	0	6	6	36
93-94	Toronto	NHL	82	3	27	30	115	18	1	1	2	12
NHL totals			784	72	239	311	854	123	7	26	33	135

MacTAVISH, CRAIG

C, FLYERS

PERSONAL: Born August 15, 1958, in London, Ont. . . . 6-1/195. . . . Shoots left.
HIGH SCHOOL: Westminster (London, Ont.).
COLLEGE: Lowell (Mass.).
TRANSACTIONS/CAREER NOTES: Selected by Boston Bruins in ninth round (ninth Bruins pick, 153rd overall) of NHL amateur draft (June 15, 1978). . . . Involved in automobile accident in which another driver was killed (January 25, 1984); pleaded guilty to vehicular homicide, driving while under the influence of alcohol and reckless driving and sentenced to a year in prison (May 1984); missed 1984-85 season. . . . Signed as free agent by Edmonton Oilers (February 1, 1985). . . . Strained lower back (January 1993); missed one game. . . . Suffered concussion (March 10, 1993); missed one game. . . . Strained wrist (October 18, 1993); missed one game. . . . Reinjured wrist (December 7, 1993); missed one game. . . . Suffered whiplash (December 15, 1993); missed four games. . . . Bruised foot (December 30, 1993); missed one game. . . . Traded by Oilers to New York Rangers for C Todd Marchant (March 21, 1994). . . . Signed as free agent by Philadelphia Flyers (July 6, 1994).
HONORS: Named ECAC Division II Rookie of the Year (1977-78). . . . Named to ECAC-II All-Star second team (1977-78). . . . Named ECAC Division II Player of the Year (1978-79). . . . Named to NCAA All-America East first team (1978-79). . . . Named to ECAC-II All-Star first team (1978-79).
MISCELLANEOUS: Does not wear a helmet. . . . Member of Stanley Cup championship teams (1987, 1988, 1990 and 1994).

Season	Team	League	REGULAR SEASON					PLAYOFFS				
			Gms.	G	A	Pts.	PIM	Gms.	G	A	Pts.	PIM
77-78	University of Lowell	ECAC-II	24	26	19	45	. . .	—	—	—	—	—
78-79	University of Lowell	ECAC-II	31	36	52	*88	. . .	—	—	—	—	—
79-80	Binghamton	AHL	34	17	15	32	20	—	—	—	—	—
	Boston	NHL	46	11	17	28	8	10	2	3	5	7
80-81	Boston	NHL	24	3	5	8	13	—	—	—	—	—
	Springfield	AHL	53	19	24	43	89	7	5	4	9	8
81-82	Erie	AHL	72	23	32	55	37	—	—	—	—	—
	Boston	NHL	2	0	1	1	0	—	—	—	—	—
82-83	Boston	NHL	75	10	20	30	18	17	3	1	4	18
83-84	Boston	NHL	70	20	23	43	35	1	0	0	0	0
84-85	Boston	NHL	Did not play.									
85-86	Edmonton	NHL	74	23	24	47	70	10	4	4	8	11
86-87	Edmonton	NHL	79	20	19	39	55	21	1	9	10	16
87-88	Edmonton	NHL	80	15	17	32	47	19	0	1	1	31
88-89	Edmonton	NHL	80	21	31	52	55	7	0	1	1	8
89-90	Edmonton	NHL	80	21	22	43	89	22	2	6	8	29
90-91	Edmonton	NHL	80	17	15	32	76	18	3	3	6	20
91-92	Edmonton	NHL	80	12	18	30	98	16	3	0	3	28
92-93	Edmonton	NHL	82	10	20	30	110	—	—	—	—	—
93-94	Edmonton	NHL	66	16	10	26	80	—	—	—	—	—
	New York Rangers	NHL	12	4	2	6	11	23	1	4	5	22
NHL totals			930	203	244	447	765	164	19	32	51	190

MADELEY, DARRIN

G, SENATORS

PERSONAL: Born February 25, 1968, in Holland Landing, Ont. . . . 5-11/170. . . . Catches left. . . . Name pronounced MAY-duh-lee.
HIGH SCHOOL: Aurora (Ont.).
COLLEGE: Lake Superior State (Mich.).
TRANSACTIONS/CAREER NOTES: Signed as free agent by Ottawa Senators (June 20, 1992). . . . Bruised back (November 15, 1993); missed two games.
HONORS: Named to CCHA All-Star second team (1989-90). . . . Named to NCAA All-America West first team (1990-91). . . . Named to CCHA All-Star first team (1990-91 and 1991-92). . . . Named NCAA Tournament Most Valuable Player (1991-92). . . . Named CCHA Playoff Most Valuable Player (1991-92). . . . Named to NCAA All-Tournament team (1991-92). . . . Named to AHL All-Star second team (1992-93).

Season	Team	League	REGULAR SEASON							PLAYOFFS						
			Gms.	Min.	W	L	T	GA	SO	Avg.	Gms.	Min.	W	L	GA	SO	Avg.
89-90	Lake Superior State	CCHA	30	1683	21	7	1	68	. . .	2.42	—	—	—	—	—	—	—
90-91	Lake Superior State	CCHA	36	2137	29	3	3	93	. . .	*2.61	—	—	—	—	—	—	—
91-92	Lake Superior State	CCHA	35	2144	25	6	4	74	. . .	2.07	—	—	—	—	—	—	—

M

Season Team	League	REGULAR SEASON							PLAYOFFS					
		Gms.	Min.	W	L	T	GA	SO	Avg.	Gms.	Min.	W	L	GA	SO	Avg.
92-93—New Haven	AHL	41	2295	10	16	9	127	0	3.32	—	—	—	—	—	—	—
—Ottawa	NHL	2	90	0	2	0	10	0	6.67	—	—	—	—	—	—	—
93-94—Ottawa	NHL	32	1583	3	18	5	115	0	4.36	—	—	—	—	—	—	—
—Prince Edward Island	AHL	6	270	0	4	0	26	0	5.78	—	—	—	—	—	—	—
NHL totals		34	1673	3	20	5	125	0	4.48	—	—	—	—	—	—	—

MADILL, JEFF
RW

PERSONAL: Born June 21, 1965, in Oshawa, Ont. . . . 5-11/212. . . . Shoots right. . . . Son of former NHL referee Greg Madill.
COLLEGE: Ohio State.
TRANSACTIONS/CAREER NOTES: Selected by New Jersey Devils in NHL supplemental draft (June 13, 1987). . . . Suspended three games by AHL for abusing an official (April 11, 1990). . . . Suspended by Utica Devils for being overweight (December 6, 1990). . . . Selected by San Jose Sharks in NHL expansion draft (May 30, 1991). . . . Signed as free agent by Cincinnati Cyclones (September 21, 1992). . . . Traded by Cyclones to Milwaukee Admirals for D Ian Kidd and D Shaun Kane (February 25, 1993).
HONORS: Named to AHL All-Star second team (1990-91). . . . Named to IHL All-Star second team (1992-93).

Season Team	League	REGULAR SEASON					PLAYOFFS				
		Gms.	G	A	Pts.	PIM	Gms.	G	A	Pts.	PIM
84-85—Ohio State	CCHA	12	5	6	11	18	—	—	—	—	—
85-86—Ohio State	CCHA	41	32	25	57	65	—	—	—	—	—
86-87—Ohio State	CCHA	43	38	32	70	139	—	—	—	—	—
87-88—Utica	AHL	58	18	15	33	127	—	—	—	—	—
88-89—Utica	AHL	69	23	25	48	225	4	1	0	1	35
89-90—Utica	AHL	74	43	26	69	233	4	1	2	3	33
90-91—New Jersey	NHL	14	4	0	4	46	7	0	2	2	8
—Utica	AHL	54	42	35	77	151	—	—	—	—	—
91-92—Kansas City	IHL	62	32	20	52	167	6	2	2	4	30
92-93—Cincinnati	IHL	58	36	17	53	175	—	—	—	—	—
—Milwaukee	IHL	23	13	6	19	53	4	3	0	3	9
93-94—Atlanta	IHL	80	42	44	86	186	14	4	2	6	33
NHL totals		14	4	0	4	46	7	0	2	2	8

MAGARRELL, ADAM
D, FLYERS

PERSONAL: Born February 1, 1976, in Dormain, Man. . . . 6-3/178. . . . Shoots left.
HIGH SCHOOL: Crocus Plains (Brandon, Man.).
TRANSACTIONS/CAREER NOTES: Selected by Philadelphia Flyers in fourth round (second Flyers pick, 88th overall) of NHL entry draft (June 29, 1994).

Season Team	League	REGULAR SEASON					PLAYOFFS				
		Gms.	G	A	Pts.	PIM	Gms.	G	A	Pts.	PIM
92-93—Brandon	WHL	8	0	0	0	0	—	—	—	—	—
93-94—Brandon	WHL	40	2	1	3	69	13	0	2	2	32

MAJOR, MARK
LW, BRUINS

PERSONAL: Born March 20, 1970, in Toronto. . . . 6-4/216. . . . Shoots left.
TRANSACTIONS/CAREER NOTES: Selected by Pittsburgh Penguins in second round (second Penguins pick, 25th overall) of NHL entry draft (June 11, 1988). . . . Broke hand (September 1989); missed training camp. . . . Signed as free agent by Boston Bruins (July 22, 1993).

Season Team	League	REGULAR SEASON					PLAYOFFS				
		Gms.	G	A	Pts.	PIM	Gms.	G	A	Pts.	PIM
87-88—North Bay	OHL	57	16	17	33	272	4	0	2	2	8
88-89—North Bay	OHL	11	3	2	5	58	—	—	—	—	—
—Kingston	OHL	53	22	29	51	193	—	—	—	—	—
89-90—Kingston	OHL	62	29	32	61	168	6	3	3	6	12
90-91—Muskegon	IHL	60	8	10	18	160	5	0	0	0	0
91-92—Muskegon	IHL	80	13	18	31	302	12	1	3	4	29
92-93—Cleveland	IHL	82	13	15	28	155	3	0	0	0	0
93-94—Providence	AHL	61	17	9	26	176	—	—	—	—	—

MAKAROV, SERGEI
RW, SHARKS

PERSONAL: Born June 19, 1958, in Chelyabinsk, U.S.S.R. . . . 5-11/185. . . . Shoots left. . . . Name pronounced SAIR-gay muh-kah-rahf.
TRANSACTIONS/CAREER NOTES: Selected by Calgary Flames in 12th round (14th Flames pick, 231st overall) of NHL entry draft (June 8, 1983). . . . Traded by Flames to Hartford Whalers for future considerations (June 20, 1993). . . . Traded by Whalers with first-round (RW Victor Kozlov), second-round (D Vlastimil Kroupa) and third-round (LW Ville Peltonen) picks in 1993 draft to San Jose Sharks for first-round pick (D Chris Pronger) in 1993 draft (June 26, 1993). . . . Bruised big toe (March 22, 1994); missed one game.
HONORS: Won Golden Stick Award (1979-80 and 1985-86). . . . Won Soviet Player of the Year Award (1979-80, 1984-85 and 1988-89). . . . Won Izvestia Trophy (1979-80 through 1981-82 and 1983-84 through 1988-89). . . . Named to Soviet League All-Star team (1978-79 and 1980-81 through 1987-88). . . . Won Calder Memorial Trophy (1989-90). . . . Named to NHL All-Rookie team (1989-90).
MISCELLANEOUS: Member of silver-medal-winning U.S.S.R. Olympic team (1980) and gold-medal-winning U.S.S.R. Olympic team (1984 and 1988).

Season	Team	League	REGULAR SEASON					PLAYOFFS				
			Gms.	G	A	Pts.	PIM	Gms.	G	A	Pts.	PIM
76-77	Traktor Chelyabinsk........	USSR	11	1	0	1	4	—	—	—	—	—
77-78	Traktor Chelyabinsk........	USSR	36	18	13	31	10	—	—	—	—	—
78-79	CSKA Moscow..................	USSR	44	18	21	39	12	—	—	—	—	—
79-80	CSKA Moscow..................	USSR	44	29	39	*68	16	—	—	—	—	—
	Soviet Olympic Team........	Int'l	7	5	6	11	2	—	—	—	—	—
80-81	CSKA Moscow..................	USSR	49	42	37	*79	22	—	—	—	—	—
81-82	CSKA Moscow..................	USSR	46	32	43	*75	18	—	—	—	—	—
82-83	CSKA Moscow..................	USSR	30	25	17	42	6	—	—	—	—	—
83-84	CSKA Moscow..................	USSR	44	36	37	*73	28	—	—	—	—	—
	Soviet Olympic Team........	Int'l	7	3	3	6	6	—	—	—	—	—
84-85	CSKA Moscow..................	USSR	40	26	39	*65	28	—	—	—	—	—
85-86	CSKA Moscow..................	USSR	40	30	32	*62	28	—	—	—	—	—
86-87	CSKA Moscow..................	USSR	40	21	32	*53	26	—	—	—	—	—
87-88	CSKA Moscow..................	USSR	51	23	45	*68	50	—	—	—	—	—
	Soviet Olympic Team........	Int'l	8	3	8	11	10	—	—	—	—	—
88-89	CSKA Moscow..................	USSR	44	21	33	*54	42	—	—	—	—	—
89-90	Calgary..........................	NHL	80	24	62	86	55	6	0	6	6	0
90-91	Calgary..........................	NHL	78	30	49	79	44	3	1	0	1	0
91-92	Calgary..........................	NHL	68	22	48	70	60	—	—	—	—	—
92-93	Calgary..........................	NHL	71	18	39	57	40	—	—	—	—	—
93-94	San Jose.........................	NHL	80	30	38	68	78	14	8	2	10	4
	NHL totals...............		377	124	236	360	277	23	9	8	17	4

MAKELA, MIKKO
LW, BRUINS

PERSONAL: Born February 28, 1965, in Tampere, Finland.... 6-2/200.... Shoots left.
TRANSACTIONS/CAREER NOTES: Selected by New York Islanders in fourth round (fifth Islanders pick, 65th overall) of 1983 entry draft (June 8, 1983).... Injured back (November 1, 1985); missed 15 games.... Suffered elbow infection (February 1988).... Traded by Islanders to Los Angeles Kings for D Ken Baumgartner and C Hubie McDonough (November 29, 1989).... Bruised shoulder (December 13, 1989).... Traded by Kings to Buffalo Sabres for LW Mike Donnelly (October 1, 1990).... Signed as free agent by Boston Bruins (May 25, 1994).
HONORS: Won Most Gentlemanly Player Trophy (1984-85).... Named to Finnish League All-Star first team (1984-85).

Season	Team	League	REGULAR SEASON					PLAYOFFS				
			Gms.	G	A	Pts.	PIM	Gms.	G	A	Pts.	PIM
83-84	Ilves Tampere	Finland	35	17	11	28	26	2	0	1	1	0
84-85	Ilves Tampere	Finland	36	*34	25	59	24	9	4	7	11	10
85-86	Springfield.....................	AHL	2	1	1	2	0	—	—	—	—	—
	New York Islanders..........	NHL	58	16	20	36	28	—	—	—	—	—
86-87	New York Islanders..........	NHL	80	24	33	57	24	11	2	4	6	8
87-88	New York Islanders..........	NHL	73	36	40	76	22	6	1	4	5	6
88-89	New York Islanders..........	NHL	76	17	28	45	22	—	—	—	—	—
89-90	New York Islanders..........	NHL	20	2	3	5	2	—	—	—	—	—
	Los Angeles....................	NHL	45	7	14	21	16	1	0	0	0	0
90-91	Buffalo...........................	NHL	60	15	7	22	25	—	—	—	—	—
91-92	TPS Turku.......................	Finland	44	25	45	70	38	3	2	3	5	0
	Finnish Olympic Team......	Int'l	5	3	3	6	...	—	—	—	—	—
92-93	TPS Turku.......................	Finland	38	17	24	44	22	11	4	8	12	0
93-94	Malmo...........................	Sweden	37	15	21	36	20	11	4	7	11	2
	Finnish Olympic Team......	Int'l	8	2	3	5	4	—	—	—	—	—
	NHL totals.......................		412	117	145	262	139	18	3	8	11	14

MALAKHOV, VLADIMIR
D, ISLANDERS

PERSONAL: Born August 30, 1968, in Sverdlovsk, U.S.S.R.... 6-3/220.... Shoots.... Name pronounced MAL-ih-kahf.
TRANSACTIONS/CAREER NOTES: Selected by New York Islanders in 10th round (12th Islanders pick, 191st overall) of NHL entry draft (June 17, 1989).... Suffered sore groin; missed first two games of 1992-93 season.... Injured right shoulder (January 16, 1993); missed eight games.... Sprained shoulder (March 14, 1993); missed five games.... Suffered concussion (December 7, 1993); missed one game.... Strained lower back (December 28, 1993); missed six games.
HONORS: Named to NHL All-Rookie team (1992-93).
MISCELLANEOUS: Member of gold-medal-winning Unified Olympic team (1992).

Season	Team	League	REGULAR SEASON					PLAYOFFS				
			Gms.	G	A	Pts.	PIM	Gms.	G	A	Pts.	PIM
86-87	Spartak Moscow..............	USSR	22	0	1	1	12	—	—	—	—	—
87-88	Spartak Moscow..............	USSR	28	2	2	4	26	—	—	—	—	—
88-89	CSKA Moscow.................	USSR	34	6	2	8	16	—	—	—	—	—
89-90	CSKA Moscow.................	USSR	48	2	10	12	34	—	—	—	—	—
90-91	CSKA Moscow.................	USSR	46	5	13	18	22	—	—	—	—	—
91-92	CSKA Moscow.................	USSR	40	1	9	10	12	—	—	—	—	—
	Unified Olympic Team.......	Int'l	8	3	0	3	4	—	—	—	—	—
92-93	Capital District................	AHL	3	2	1	3	11	—	—	—	—	—
	New York Islanders..........	NHL	64	14	38	52	59	17	3	6	9	12
93-94	New York Islanders..........	NHL	76	10	47	57	80	4	0	0	0	6
	NHL totals.......................		140	24	85	109	139	21	3	6	9	18

M

MALARCHUK, CLINT

G, SABRES

PERSONAL: Born May 1, 1961, in Grande Prairie, Alta. . . . 6-0/185. . . . Catches left. . . . Name pronounced muh-LAHR-chuhk.

TRANSACTIONS/CAREER NOTES: Selected by Quebec Nordiques in fourth round (third Nordiques pick, 74th overall) of NHL entry draft (June 11, 1981). . . . Traded by Nordiques with C Dale Hunter to Washington Capitals for C Alan Haworth, LW Gaetan Duchesne and first-round pick (C Joe Sakic) in 1987 draft (June 1987). . . . Traded by Capitals with D Grant Ledyard and sixth-round pick in 1991 draft to Buffalo Sabres for D Calle Johansson and second-round pick (G Byron Dafoe) in 1989 draft (March 6, 1989). . . . Severed jugular vein (March 22, 1989). . . . Strained neck and shoulder (January 23, 1991); missed 14 games. . . . Suffered from strep throat (November 2, 1991). . . . Suffered from medicine reaction (January 27, 1992); missed six games. . . . Loaned to San Diego Gulls (October 12, 1992).

HONORS: Shared Harry (Hap) Holmes Memorial Trophy with Brian Ford (1982-83). . . . Shared James Norris Memorial Trophy with Rick Knickle (1992-93).

Season Team	League	REGULAR SEASON								PLAYOFFS						
		Gms.	Min.	W	L	T	GA	SO	Avg.	Gms.	Min.	W	L	GA	SO	Avg.
78-79—Portland	WHL	2	120	...	...	...	4	0	2.00	—	—	—	—	—	—	—
79-80—Portland	WHL	37	1948	21	10	0	147	0	4.53	1	40	0	0	3	0	4.50
80-81—Portland	WHL	38	2235	28	8	0	142	3	3.81	4	307	0	0	21	0	4.10
81-82—Quebec	NHL	2	120	0	1	1	14	0	7.00	—	—	—	—	—	—	—
—Fredericton	AHL	51	2962	15	34	2	*253	0	5.12	—	—	—	—	—	—	—
82-83—Quebec	NHL	15	900	8	5	2	71	0	4.73	—	—	—	—	—	—	—
—Fredericton	AHL	25	1506	0	0	0	78	1	*3.11	—	—	—	—	—	—	—
83-84—Fredericton	AHL	11	663	5	5	1	40	0	3.62	—	—	—	—	—	—	—
—Quebec	NHL	23	1215	10	9	2	80	0	3.95	—	—	—	—	—	—	—
84-85—Fredericton	AHL	*56	*3347	26	25	4	*198	2	3.55	6	379	2	4	20	0	3.17
85-86—Quebec	NHL	46	2657	26	12	4	142	4	3.21	3	143	0	2	11	0	4.62
86-87—Quebec	NHL	54	3092	18	26	9	175	1	3.40	3	140	0	2	8	0	3.43
87-88—Washington	NHL	54	2926	24	20	4	154	†4	3.16	4	193	0	2	15	0	4.66
88-89—Washington	NHL	42	2428	16	18	7	141	1	3.48	1	59	0	1	5	0	5.08
—Buffalo	NHL	7	326	3	1	1	13	1	2.39	—	—	—	—	—	—	—
89-90—Buffalo	NHL	29	1596	14	11	2	89	0	3.35	—	—	—	—	—	—	—
90-91—Buffalo	NHL	37	2131	12	14	10	119	1	3.35	4	246	2	2	17	0	4.15
91-92—Buffalo	NHL	29	1639	10	13	3	102	0	3.73	—	—	—	—	—	—	—
—Rochester	AHL	2	120	2	0	0	3	1	1.50	—	—	—	—	—	—	—
92-93—San Diego	IHL	27	1516	17	3	‡0	72	3	2.85	†12	668	6	3	†34	0	3.05
93-94—Las Vegas	IHL	55	3076	*34	10	‡7	172	1	3.36	5	257	1	2	16	0	3.74
NHL totals		338	19030	141	130	45	1100	12	3.47	15	781	2	9	56	0	4.30

MALEY, DAVID

C, ISLANDERS

M

PERSONAL: Born April 24, 1963, in Beaver Dam, Wis. . . . 6-3/200. . . . Shoots left. . . . Full name: David Joseph Maley.

HIGH SCHOOL: Edina (Minn.).

COLLEGE: Wisconsin.

TRANSACTIONS/CAREER NOTES: Selected by Montreal Canadiens as underage player in second round (fourth Canadiens pick, 33rd overall) of NHL entry draft (June 9, 1982). . . . Suspended by AHL (May 1987). . . . Traded by Canadiens to New Jersey Devils for third-round pick (D Mathieu Schneider) in 1987 draft (June 13, 1987). . . . Injured back (December 1988). . . . Tore right knee cartilage (January 16, 1990). . . . Underwent surgery to right knee (January 24, 1990); missed eight games. . . . Injured left hand ligaments (September 22, 1990). . . . Sprained left ankle (November 28, 1990); missed 11 games. . . . Fractured left wrist (March 27, 1991). . . . Traded by Devils to Edmonton Oilers for LW Troy Mallette (January 12, 1991). . . . Twisted knee (March 4, 1992); missed 12 games. . . . Claimed on waivers by San Jose Sharks (January 1, 1993). . . . Suspended three games by NHL for physically abusing an official (April 4, 1993). . . . Signed as free agent by Sharks (August 25, 1993). . . . Traded by Sharks to New York Islanders for future considerations (January 24, 1994).

MISCELLANEOUS: Member of Stanley Cup championship team (1986).

Season Team	League	REGULAR SEASON					PLAYOFFS				
		Gms.	G	A	Pts.	PIM	Gms.	G	A	Pts.	PIM
81-82—Edina High School	Minn. H.S.	26	22	28	50	26	—	—	—	—	—
82-83—University of Wisconsin	WCHA	47	17	23	40	24	—	—	—	—	—
83-84—University of Wisconsin	WCHA	38	10	28	38	56	—	—	—	—	—
84-85—University of Wisconsin	WCHA	35	19	9	28	86	—	—	—	—	—
85-86—University of Wisconsin	WCHA	42	20	40	60	*135	—	—	—	—	—
—Montreal	NHL	3	0	0	0	0	7	1	3	4	2
86-87—Sherbrooke	AHL	11	1	5	6	25	12	7	7	14	10
—Montreal	NHL	48	6	12	18	55	—	—	—	—	—
87-88—Utica	AHL	9	5	3	8	40	—	—	—	—	—
—New Jersey	NHL	44	4	2	6	65	20	3	1	4	80
88-89—New Jersey	NHL	68	5	6	11	249	—	—	—	—	—
89-90—New Jersey	NHL	67	8	17	25	160	6	0	0	0	25
90-91—New Jersey	NHL	64	8	14	22	151	—	—	—	—	—
91-92—New Jersey	NHL	37	7	11	18	58	—	—	—	—	—
—Edmonton	NHL	23	3	6	9	46	10	1	1	2	4
92-93—Edmonton	NHL	13	1	1	2	29	—	—	—	—	—
—San Jose	NHL	43	1	6	7	126	—	—	—	—	—
93-94—San Jose	NHL	19	0	0	0	30	—	—	—	—	—
—New York Islanders	NHL	37	0	6	6	74	3	0	0	0	0
NHL totals		466	43	81	124	1043	46	5	5	10	111

MALGUNAS, STEWART
D, FLYERS

PERSONAL: Born April 21, 1970, in Prince George, B.C. . . . 6-0/200. . . . Shoots left.

TRANSACTIONS/CAREER NOTES: Selected by Detroit Red Wings in fourth round (third Red Wings pick, 66th overall) of NHL entry draft (June 16, 1990). . . . Injured knee (September 26, 1992); missed first 10 games of season. . . . Traded by Red Wings to Philadelphia Flyers for future considerations (September 8, 1993). . . . Sprained medial collateral ligament in left knee (February 5, 1994); missed 12 games.

HONORS: Named to WHL (West) All-Star first team (1989-90).

| | | | REGULAR SEASON | | | | | PLAYOFFS | | | | |
Season Team	League	Gms.	G	A	Pts.	PIM	Gms.	G	A	Pts.	PIM
87-88—Prince George	BCJHL	54	12	34	46	99	—	—	—	—	—
—New Westminster	WHL	6	0	0	0	0	—	—	—	—	—
88-89—Seattle	WHL	72	11	41	52	51	—	—	—	—	—
89-90—Seattle	WHL	63	15	48	63	116	13	2	9	11	32
90-91—Adirondack	AHL	78	5	19	24	70	2	0	0	0	4
91-92—Adirondack	AHL	69	4	28	32	82	18	2	6	8	28
92-93—Adirondack	AHL	45	3	12	15	39	11	3	3	6	8
93-94—Philadelphia	NHL	67	1	3	4	86	—	—	—	—	—
NHL totals		67	1	3	4	86					

MALIK, MAREK
D, WHALERS

PERSONAL: Born June 24, 1975, in Ostrava, Czechoslovakia. . . . 6-5/185. . . . Shoots left.

TRANSACTIONS/CAREER NOTES: Selected by Hartford Whalers in third round (second Whalers pick, 72nd overall) of NHL entry draft (June 26, 1993).

| | | | REGULAR SEASON | | | | | PLAYOFFS | | | | |
Season Team	League	Gms.	G	A	Pts.	PIM	Gms.	G	A	Pts.	PIM
91-92—TJ Vitkovice Jrs	Czech. Jrs.				Statistics unavailable.						
92-93—TJ Vitkovice	Czech.				Did not play.						
93-94—HC Vitkovice	Czech Rep.	38	3	3	6	...	3	0	1	1	0

MALKOC, DEAN
D, DEVILS

PERSONAL: Born January 26, 1970, in Vancouver. . . . 6-3/200. . . . Shoots left. . . . Name pronounced MAL-kahk.

TRANSACTIONS/CAREER NOTES: Selected by New Jersey Devils in fifth round (seventh Devils pick, 95th overall) of NHL entry draft (June 16, 1990). . . . Traded by Kamloops Blazers with LW Todd Esselmont to Swift Current Broncos for RW Eddie Patterson (October 17, 1990).

| | | | REGULAR SEASON | | | | | PLAYOFFS | | | | |
Season Team	League	Gms.	G	A	Pts.	PIM	Gms.	G	A	Pts.	PIM
87-88—Williams Lake	PCJHL	...	6	32	38	215	—	—	—	—	—
88-89—Powell River	BCJHL	55	10	32	42	370	—	—	—	—	—
89-90—Kamloops	WHL	48	3	18	21	209	17	0	3	3	56
90-91—Kamloops	WHL	8	1	4	5	47	—	—	—	—	—
—Swift Current	WHL	56	10	23	33	248	3	0	2	2	5
—Utica	AHL	1	0	0	0	0	—	—	—	—	—
91-92—Utica	AHL	66	1	11	12	274	4	0	2	2	6
92-93—Utica	AHL	73	5	19	24	255	5	0	1	1	8
93-94—Albany	AHL	79	0	9	9	296	5	0	0	0	21

MALLETTE, TROY
LW, SENATORS

PERSONAL: Born February 25, 1970, in Sudbury, Ont. . . . 6-2/210. . . . Shoots left. . . . Full name: Troy Matthew Mallette. . . . Name pronounced muh-LEHT.

TRANSACTIONS/CAREER NOTES: Selected by New York Rangers in second round (first Rangers pick, 22nd overall) of NHL entry draft (June 11, 1988). . . . Fined $500 by NHL for head-butting (March 19, 1990). . . . Sprained left knee ligaments (September 1990). . . . Fined $500 by NHL for attempting to injure another player (October 28, 1990). . . . Reinjured knee (October 29, 1990). . . . Injured shoulder (January 13, 1991). . . . Awarded to Edmonton Oilers as compensation for Rangers signing free agent C/LW Adam Graves (September 9, 1991). . . . Strained knee ligament (November 1991); missed two games. . . . Traded by Oilers to New Jersey Devils for LW David Maley (January 12, 1992). . . . Sprained right ankle (January 24, 1992); missed four games. . . . Pinched nerve in neck (January 2, 1993); missed one game. . . . Traded by Devils with G Craig Billington and fourth-round pick in 1993 draft (C Cosmo Dupaul) to Ottawa Senators for G Peter Sidorkiewicz and future considerations (June 20, 1993); Senators sent LW Mike Peluso to Devils to complete deal (June 26, 1993).

| | | | REGULAR SEASON | | | | | PLAYOFFS | | | | |
Season Team	League	Gms.	G	A	Pts.	PIM	Gms.	G	A	Pts.	PIM
86-87—Sault Ste. Marie	OHL	65	20	25	45	157	4	0	2	2	2
87-88—Sault Ste. Marie	OHL	62	18	30	48	186	6	1	3	4	12
88-89—Sault Ste. Marie	OHL	64	39	37	76	172	—	—	—	—	—
89-90—New York Rangers	NHL	79	13	16	29	305	10	2	2	4	81
90-91—New York Rangers	NHL	71	12	10	22	252	5	0	0	0	18
91-92—Edmonton	NHL	15	1	3	4	36	—	—	—	—	—
—New Jersey	NHL	17	3	4	7	43	—	—	—	—	—
92-93—New Jersey	NHL	34	4	3	7	56	—	—	—	—	—
—Utica	AHL	5	3	3	6	17	—	—	—	—	—
93-94—Ottawa	NHL	82	7	16	23	166	—	—	—	—	—
NHL totals		298	40	52	92	858	15	2	2	4	99

M

MALTAIS, STEVE

PERSONAL: Born January 25, 1969, in Arvida, Ont. . . . 6-2/210. . . . Shoots left. . . . Name pronounced MAHL-tay.

TRANSACTIONS/CAREER NOTES: Selected by Washington Capitals as underage junior in third round (second Capitals pick, 57th overall) of NHL entry draft (June 13, 1987). . . . Traded by Capitals with C Trent Klatt to Minnesota North Stars for D Shawn Chambers (June 21, 1991). . . . Traded by North Stars to Quebec Nordiques for C Kip Miller (March 8, 1992). . . . Selected by Tampa Bay Lightning in NHL expansion draft (June 18, 1992). . . . Traded by Lightning to Detroit Red Wings for D Dennis Vial (June 8, 1993).

HONORS: Name to OHL All-Star second team (1988-89).

			—REGULAR SEASON—					—PLAYOFFS—			
Season Team	League	Gms.	G	A	Pts.	PIM	Gms.	G	A	Pts.	PIM
85-86—Wexford Junior B	MTHL	33	35	19	54	38					
86-87—Cornwall	OHL	65	32	12	44	29	5	0	0	0	2
87-88—Cornwall	OHL	59	39	46	85	30	11	9	6	15	33
88-89—Cornwall	OHL	58	53	70	123	67	18	14	16	30	16
—Fort Wayne	IHL	—	—	—	—	—	4	2	1	3	0
89-90—Washington	NHL	8	0	0	0	2	1	0	0	0	0
—Baltimore	AHL	67	29	37	66	54	12	6	10	16	6
90-91—Baltimore	AHL	73	36	43	79	97	6	1	4	5	10
—Washington	NHL	7	0	0	0	2	—	—	—	—	—
91-92—Kalamazoo	IHL	48	25	31	56	51	—	—	—	—	—
—Minnesota	NHL	12	2	1	3	2	—	—	—	—	—
—Halifax	AHL	10	3	3	6	0	—	—	—	—	—
92-93—Atlanta	IHL	16	14	10	24	22	—	—	—	—	—
—Tampa Bay	NHL	63	7	13	20	35	—	—	—	—	—
93-94—Adirondack	AHL	73	35	49	84	79	12	5	11	16	14
—Detroit	NHL	4	0	1	1	0	—	—	—	—	—
NHL totals		94	9	15	24	41	1	0	0	0	0

MALTBY, KIRK

PERSONAL: Born December 22, 1972, in Guelph, Ont. . . . 6-0/180. . . . Shoots right.
COLLEGE: Georgian (Ont.).
TRANSACTIONS/CAREER NOTES: Selected by Edmonton Oilers in third round (fourth Oilers pick, 65th overall) of NHL entry draft (June 20, 1992). . . . Suffered chip fracture of ankle bone (February 2, 1994); missed 13 games.

			—REGULAR SEASON—					—PLAYOFFS—			
Season Team	League	Gms.	G	A	Pts.	PIM	Gms.	G	A	Pts.	PIM
88-89—Cambridge Junior B	OHA	48	28	18	46	138	—	—	—	—	—
89-90—Owen Sound	OHL	61	12	15	27	90	12	1	6	7	15
90-91—Owen Sound	OHL	66	34	32	66	100	—	—	—	—	—
91-92—Owen Sound	OHL	64	50	41	91	99	5	3	3	6	18
92-93—Cape Breton	AHL	73	22	23	45	130	16	3	3	6	45
93-94—Edmonton	NHL	68	11	8	19	74	—	—	—	—	—
NHL totals		68	11	8	19	74					

MANDERVILLE, KENT

PERSONAL: Born April 12, 1971, in Edmonton. . . . 6-3/207. . . . Shoots left. . . . Full name: Kent Stephen Manderville.
COLLEGE: Cornell.
TRANSACTIONS/CAREER NOTES: Selected by Calgary Flames in second round (first Flames pick, 24th overall) of NHL entry draft (June 17, 1989). . . . Traded by Flames with C Doug Gilmour, D Jamie Macoun, D Ric Nattress and G Rick Wamsley to Toronto Maple Leafs for LW Craig Berube, D Alexander Godynyuk, RW Gary Leeman, D Michel Petit and G Jeff Reese (Janaury 2, 1992). . . . Bruised hand (October 5, 1993); missed one game. . . . Suffered from the flu (December 17, 1993); missed two games.
HONORS: Named ECAC Rookie of the Year (1989-90). . . . Named to ECAC All-Rookie team (1989-90).
MISCELLANEOUS: Member of silver-medal-winning Canadian Olympic team (1992).

			—REGULAR SEASON—					—PLAYOFFS—			
Season Team	League	Gms.	G	A	Pts.	PIM	Gms.	G	A	Pts.	PIM
88-89—Notre Dame	SJHL	58	39	36	75	165	—	—	—	—	—
89-90—Cornell University	ECAC	26	11	15	26	28	—	—	—	—	—
90-91—Cornell University	ECAC	28	17	14	31	60	—	—	—	—	—
—Canadian national team	Int'l	3	1	2	3	0	—	—	—	—	—
91-92—Canadian national team	Int'l	63	16	23	39	75	—	—	—	—	—
—Canadian Olympic Team	Int'l	8	1	2	3	0	—	—	—	—	—
—Toronto	NHL	15	0	4	4	0	—	—	—	—	—
—St. John's	AHL	—	—	—	—	—	12	5	9	14	14
92-93—Toronto	NHL	18	1	1	2	17	18	1	0	1	8
—St. John's	AHL	56	19	28	47	86	2	0	2	2	0
93-94—Toronto	NHL	67	7	9	16	63	12	1	0	1	4
NHL totals		100	8	14	22	80	30	2	0	2	12

MANELUK, MIKE

PERSONAL: Born October 1, 1973, in Winnipeg. . . . 5-11/188. . . . Shoots right. . . . Name pronounced MAN-ih-luhk.
TRANSACTIONS/CAREER NOTES: Signed as free agent by Mighty Ducks of Anaheim (January 28, 1994).

Season Team	League	REGULAR SEASON					PLAYOFFS				
		Gms.	G	A	Pts.	PIM	Gms.	G	A	Pts.	PIM
89-90—St. Boniface	MJHL	45	29	41	70	199	—	—	—	—	—
91-92—Brandon	WHL	68	23	30	53	102	—	—	—	—	—
92-93—Brandon	WHL	72	36	51	87	75	4	2	1	3	2
93-94—Brandon	WHL	63	50	47	97	112	13	11	3	14	23
—San Diego	IHL	—	—	—	—	—	1	0	0	0	0

MANLOW, ERIC
C, BLACKHAWKS

PERSONAL: Born April 7, 1975, in Belleville, Ont. . . . 6-0/190. . . . Shoots left.
TRANSACTIONS/CAREER NOTES: Selected by Chicago Blackhawks in second round (second Blackhawks pick, 50th overall) of NHL entry draft (June 26, 1993).

Season Team	League	REGULAR SEASON					PLAYOFFS				
		Gms.	G	A	Pts.	PIM	Gms.	G	A	Pts.	PIM
91-92—Kitchener	OHL	59	12	20	32	17	14	2	5	7	8
92-93—Kitchener	OHL	53	26	21	47	31	4	0	1	1	2
93-94—Kitchener	OHL	49	28	32	60	25	3	0	1	1	4

MANSON, DAVE
D, JETS

PERSONAL: Born January 27, 1967, in Prince Albert, Sask. . . . 6-2/210. . . . Shoots left.
HIGH SCHOOL: Carleton (Prince Albert, Sask.).
TRANSACTIONS/CAREER NOTES: Selected by Chicago Blackhawks as underage junior in first round (first Blackhawks pick, 11th overall) of NHL entry draft (June 15, 1985). . . . Suspended three games by NHL for pushing linesman (October 8, 1989). . . . Bruised right thigh (December 8, 1989). . . . Suspended 13 games by NHL for abusing linesman and returning to ice to fight (December 23, 1989). . . . Suspended three games by NHL for biting (February 27, 1990). . . . Suspended four games by NHL for attempting to injure another player (October 20, 1990). . . . Traded by Blackhawks with third-round pick in 1992 draft (RW Kirk Maltby) to Edmonton Oilers for D Steve Smith (October 2, 1991). . . . Suspended five off-days and fined $500 by NHL for spearing (October 19, 1992). . . . Strained ligaments in left knee (December 7, 1992); missed one game. . . . Separated shoulder (October 22, 1993); missed 13 games. . . . Traded by Oilers with sixth-round pick in 1994 draft to Winnipeg Jets for C Mats Lindgren, D Boris Mironov and first-round (C Jason Bonsignore) and fourth-round (RW Adam Copeland) picks in 1994 draft (March 15, 1994).
HONORS: Named to WHL All-Star second team (1985-86). . . . Played in NHL All-Star Game (1989 and 1993).

Season Team	League	REGULAR SEASON					PLAYOFFS				
		Gms.	G	A	Pts.	PIM	Gms.	G	A	Pts.	PIM
83-84—Prince Albert	WHL	70	2	7	9	233	5	0	0	0	4
84-85—Prince Albert	WHL	72	8	30	38	247	13	1	0	1	34
85-86—Prince Albert	WHL	70	14	34	48	177	20	1	8	9	63
86-87—Chicago	NHL	63	1	8	9	146	3	0	0	0	10
87-88—Saginaw	IHL	6	0	3	3	37	—	—	—	—	—
—Chicago	NHL	54	1	6	7	185	5	0	0	0	27
88-89—Chicago	NHL	79	18	36	54	352	16	0	8	8	*84
89-90—Chicago	NHL	59	5	23	28	301	20	2	4	6	46
90-91—Chicago	NHL	75	14	15	29	191	6	0	1	1	36
91-92—Edmonton	NHL	79	15	32	47	220	16	3	9	12	44
92-93—Edmonton	NHL	83	15	30	45	210	—	—	—	—	—
93-94—Edmonton	NHL	57	3	13	16	140	—	—	—	—	—
—Winnipeg	NHL	13	1	4	5	51	—	—	—	—	—
NHL totals		562	73	167	240	1796	66	5	22	27	247

MARACLE, NORM
G, RED WINGS

PERSONAL: Born October 2, 1974, in Belleville, Ont. . . . 5-9/175. . . . Catches left.
HIGH SCHOOL: Marion Graham (Regina, Sask.).
TRANSACTIONS/CAREER NOTES: Selected by Detroit Red Wings in fifth round (sixth Red Wings pick, 126th overall) of NHL entry draft (June 26, 1993).
HONORS: Named to Can.HL All-Rookie team (1991-92). . . . Named to WHL (East) All-Star second team (1992-93). . . . Won Del Wilson Trophy (1993-94). . . . Won Can.HL Goaltender-of-the-Year Award (1993-94). . . . Named to Can.HL All-Star first team (1993-94). . . . Named to WHL (East) All-Star first team (1993-94).

Season Team	League	REGULAR SEASON								PLAYOFFS						
		Gms.	Min.	W	L	T	GA	SO	Avg.	Gms.	Min.	W	L	GA	SO	Avg.
91-92—Saskatoon	WHL	29	1529	13	6	3	87	1	3.41	15	860	9	5	37	0	2.58
92-93—Saskatoon	WHL	53	2939	27	18	3	160	1	3.27	9	569	4	5	33	0	3.48
93-94—Saskatoon	WHL	56	3219	*41	13	1	148	2	2.76	16	939	†11	5	48	†1	3.07

MARCHANT, TERRY
LW, OILERS

PERSONAL: Born February 24, 1976, in Buffalo, N.Y. . . . 6-2/205. . . . Shoots left. . . . Brother of Todd Marchant, center/left winger, Edmonton Oilers.
TRANSACTIONS/CAREER NOTES: Selected by Edmonton Oilers in sixth round (ninth Oilers pick, 136th overall) of NHL entry draft (June 29, 1994).

Season Team	League	REGULAR SEASON					PLAYOFFS				
		Gms.	G	A	Pts.	PIM	Gms.	G	A	Pts.	PIM
93-94—Niagara	NAJHL	42	27	40	67	43	—	—	—	—	—

MARCHANT, TODD
C/LW, OILERS

PERSONAL: Born August 12, 1973, in Buffalo, N.Y. . . . 6-0/190. . . . Shoots left. . . . Brother of Terry Marchant, left winger in Edmonton Oilers system.
COLLEGE: Clarkson (N.Y.).
TRANSACTIONS/CAREER NOTES: Selected by New York Rangers in seventh round

(eighth Rangers pick, 164th overall) of NHL entry draft (June 26, 1993).... Traded by Rangers to Edmonton Oilers for C Craig MacTavish (March 21, 1994).

Season Team	League	REGULAR SEASON					PLAYOFFS				
		Gms.	G	A	Pts.	PIM	Gms.	G	A	Pts.	PIM
91-92—Clarkson	ECAC	33	20	12	32	32	—	—	—	—	—
92-93—Clarkson	ECAC	33	18	28	46	38	—	—	—	—	—
93-94—U.S. national team	Int'l	59	28	39	67	48	—	—	—	—	—
—U.S. Olympic Team	Int'l	8	1	1	2	6	—	—	—	—	—
—Binghamton	AHL	8	2	7	9	6	—	—	—	—	—
—New York Rangers	NHL	1	0	0	0	0	—	—	—	—	—
—Edmonton	NHL	3	0	1	1	2	—	—	—	—	—
—Cape Breton	AHL	3	1	4	5	2	5	1	1	2	0
NHL totals		4	0	1	1	2					

MARCHMENT, BRYAN
D, WHALERS

PERSONAL: Born May 1, 1969, in Scarborough, Ont.... 6-1/198.... Shoots left. **TRANSACTIONS/CAREER NOTES:** Suspended three games by OHL (October 1, 1986).... Selected by Winnipeg Jets as underage junior in first round (first Jets pick, 16th overall) of NHL entry draft (June 13, 1987).... Suspended six games by AHL for fighting (December 10, 1989).... Sprained shoulder (March 1990).... Suffered back spasms (March 13, 1991).... Traded by Jets with D Chris Norton to Chicago Blackhawks for C Troy Murray and LW Warren Rychel (July 22, 1991).... Fractured cheekbone (December 12, 1991); missed 12 games.... Suspended one preseason game and fined $500 by NHL for headbutting (September 30, 1993).... Traded with RW Steve Larmer by Blackhawks to Hartford Whalers for LW Patrick Poulin and D Eric Weinrich (November 2, 1993).... Suspended two games and fined $500 by NHL for illegal check (December 21, 1993).... Sprained ankle (January 14, 1994); missed three games.... Sprained ankle (February 19, 1994); missed remainder of season.
HONORS: Named to OHL All-Star second team (1988-89).

Season Team	League	REGULAR SEASON					PLAYOFFS				
		Gms.	G	A	Pts.	PIM	Gms.	G	A	Pts.	PIM
84-85—Toronto Nationals	MTHL	...	14	35	49	229	—	—	—	—	—
85-86—Belleville	OHL	57	5	15	20	225	21	0	7	7	*83
86-87—Belleville	OHL	52	6	38	44	238	6	0	4	4	17
87-88—Belleville	OHL	56	7	51	58	200	6	1	3	4	19
88-89—Belleville	OHL	43	14	36	50	198	5	0	1	1	12
—Winnipeg	NHL	2	0	0	0	2	—	—	—	—	—
89-90—Winnipeg	NHL	7	0	2	2	28	—	—	—	—	—
—Moncton	AHL	56	4	19	23	217	—	—	—	—	—
90-91—Winnipeg	NHL	28	2	2	4	91	—	—	—	—	—
—Moncton	AHL	33	2	11	13	101	—	—	—	—	—
91-92—Chicago	NHL	58	5	10	15	168	16	1	0	1	36
92-93—Chicago	NHL	78	5	15	20	313	4	0	0	0	12
93-94—Chicago	NHL	13	1	4	5	42	—	—	—	—	—
—Hartford	NHL	42	3	7	10	124	—	—	—	—	—
NHL totals		228	16	40	56	768	20	1	0	1	48

MARHA, JOSEF
C, NORDIQUES

PERSONAL: Born June 2, 1976, in Havl. Brod, Czechoslovakia.... 6-0/176.... Shoots left.... Name pronounced mar-HA.
TRANSACTIONS/CAREER NOTES: Selected by Quebec Nordiques in second round (third Nordiques pick, 35th overall) of NHL entry draft (June 28, 1994).

Season Team	League	REGULAR SEASON					PLAYOFFS				
		Gms.	G	A	Pts.	PIM	Gms.	G	A	Pts.	PIM
91-92—Jihlava	Czech.	25	12	13	25	0	—	—	—	—	—
92-93—Dukla Jihlava	Czech.	7	2	2	4	4	—	—	—	—	—
93-94—Dukla Jihlava	Czech Rep.	41	7	2	9	...	3	0	1	1	0

MARINUCCI, CHRIS
C, ISLANDERS

PERSONAL: Born December 29, 1971, in Grand Rapids, Minn.... 6-0/175.... Shoots left.... Full name: Christopher Jon Marinucci.
HIGH SCHOOL: Grand Rapids (Minn.).
COLLEGE: Minnesota-Duluth.
TRANSACTIONS/CAREER NOTES: Selected by New York Islanders in fifth round (fourth Islanders pick, 90th overall) of NHL entry draft (June 16, 1990).
HONORS: Named to WCHA All-Star second team (1992-93).... Won Hobey Baker Memorial Trophy (1993-94).... Named WCHA Player of the Year (1993-94).... Named to WCHA All-Star first team (1993-94).

Season Team	League	REGULAR SEASON					PLAYOFFS				
		Gms.	G	A	Pts.	PIM	Gms.	G	A	Pts.	PIM
88-89—Grand Rapids H.S.	Minn. H.S.	25	24	18	42	...	—	—	—	—	—
89-90—Grand Rapids H.S.	Minn. H.S.	28	24	39	63	0	—	—	—	—	—
90-91—Minnesota-Duluth	WCHA	36	6	10	16	20	—	—	—	—	—
91-92—Minnesota-Duluth	WCHA	37	6	13	19	41	—	—	—	—	—
92-93—Minnesota-Duluth	WCHA	40	35	42	77	52	—	—	—	—	—
93-94—Minnesota-Duluth	WCHA	38	*30	31	61	65	—	—	—	—	—

M

MARK, GORD
D, OILERS

PERSONAL: Born September 10, 1964, in Edmonton.... 6-4/220.... Shoots right.
TRANSACTIONS/CAREER NOTES: Selected by New Jersey Devils in sixth round (fourth Devils pick, 108th overall) of NHL entry draft (June 8, 1983).... Retired from 1988-89 through 1991-92 seasons.... Broke kneecap (September 1992).... Signed as free agent by Edmonton Oilers (November 10, 1992).

			REGULAR SEASON					PLAYOFFS				
Season	Team	League	Gms.	G	A	Pts.	PIM	Gms.	G	A	Pts.	PIM
82-83—Kamloops		WHL	71	12	20	32	135	7	1	1	2	8
83-84—Kamloops		WHL	67	12	30	42	202	17	2	6	8	27
84-85—Kamloops		WHL	32	11	23	34	68	7	1	2	3	10
85-86—Maine		AHL	77	9	13	22	134	5	0	1	1	9
86-87—New Jersey		NHL	36	3	5	8	82	—	—	—	—	—
—Maine		AHL	29	4	10	14	66	—	—	—	—	—
87-88—New Jersey		NHL	19	0	2	2	27	—	—	—	—	—
—Utica		AHL	50	5	21	26	96	—	—	—	—	—
88-89—						Did not play—retired.						
89-90—						Did not play—retired.						
90-91—						Did not play—retired.						
91-92—						Did not play—retired.						
92-93—Cape Breton		AHL	60	3	21	24	78	16	1	7	8	20
93-94—Cape Breton		AHL	49	11	20	31	116	5	0	2	2	6
—Edmonton		NHL	12	0	1	1	43	—	—	—	—	—
NHL totals			67	3	8	11	152					

MAROIS, DANIEL
RW, BRUINS

PERSONAL: Born October 3, 1968, in Montreal.... 6-0/190.... Shoots right.
TRANSACTIONS/CAREER NOTES: Selected by Toronto Maple Leafs as underage junior in second round (second Maple Leafs pick, 28th overall) of NHL entry draft (June 13, 1987).... Suffered from the flu (January 1989).... Damaged ligaments in right knee and underwent surgery (April 2, 1989).... Bruised left shoulder (November 12, 1989); missed 11 games.... Injured wrist (October 25, 1991); missed two games.... Traded by Maple Leafs with C Claude Loiselle to New York Islanders for LW Ken Baumgartner and C Dave McLlwain (March 10, 1992).... Strained lower back (December 23, 1992); missed three games.... Strained lower back (March 7, 1993); missed five games.... Traded by Islanders to Boston Bruins for eighth-round pick (C Peter Hogardh) in 1994 draft (March 18, 1993).... Underwent back surgery (April 1, 1993).... Injured shoulder (October 22, 1993); missed 54 games.

			REGULAR SEASON					PLAYOFFS				
Season	Team	League	Gms.	G	A	Pts.	PIM	Gms.	G	A	Pts.	PIM
85-86—Verdun		QMJHL	58	42	35	77	110	5	4	2	6	6
86-87—Chicoutimi		QMJHL	40	22	26	48	143	16	7	14	21	25
87-88—Verdun		QMJHL	67	52	36	88	153	—	—	—	—	—
—Newmarket		AHL	8	4	4	8	4	—	—	—	—	—
—Toronto		NHL	—	—	—	—	—	3	1	0	1	0
88-89—Toronto		NHL	76	31	23	54	76	—	—	—	—	—
89-90—Toronto		NHL	68	39	37	76	82	5	2	2	4	12
90-91—Toronto		NHL	78	21	9	30	112	—	—	—	—	—
91-92—Toronto		NHL	63	15	11	26	76	—	—	—	—	—
—New York Islanders		NHL	12	2	5	7	18	—	—	—	—	—
92-93—New York Islanders		NHL	28	2	5	7	35	—	—	—	—	—
—Capital District		AHL	4	2	0	2	0	—	—	—	—	—
93-94—Boston		NHL	22	7	3	10	18	11	0	1	1	16
—Providence		AHL	6	1	2	3	6	—	—	—	—	—
NHL totals			347	117	93	210	417	19	3	3	6	28

MARSHALL, BOBBY
D, FLAMES

PERSONAL: Born April 11, 1972, in North York, Ont.... 6-1/190.... Shoots left.
COLLEGE: Miami of Ohio.
TRANSACTIONS/CAREER NOTES: Selected by Calgary Flames in sixth round (seventh Flames pick, 129th overall) of NHL entry draft (June 22, 1991).
HONORS: Named to NCAA All-America West second team (1992-93).... Named to CCHA All-Star first team (1992-93).

			REGULAR SEASON					PLAYOFFS				
Season	Team	League	Gms.	G	A	Pts.	PIM	Gms.	G	A	Pts.	PIM
90-91—Miami of Ohio		CCHA	37	3	15	18	44	—	—	—	—	—
91-92—Miami of Ohio		CCHA	40	5	20	25	48	—	—	—	—	—
92-93—Miami of Ohio		CCHA	40	2	43	45	40	—	—	—	—	—
93-94—Miami of Ohio		CCHA	38	3	24	27	76	—	—	—	—	—

MARSHALL, GRANT
RW, MAPLE LEAFS

PERSONAL: Born June 9, 1973, in Toronto.... 6-1/185.... Shoots right.
HIGH SCHOOL: Hillcrest (Thunder Bay, Ont.).
TRANSACTIONS/CAREER NOTES: Selected by Toronto Maple Leafs in first round (second Maple Leafs pick, 23rd overall) of NHL entry draft (June 20, 1992).

			REGULAR SEASON					PLAYOFFS				
Season	Team	League	Gms.	G	A	Pts.	PIM	Gms.	G	A	Pts.	PIM
90-91—Ottawa		OHL	26	6	11	17	25	1	0	0	0	0
91-92—Ottawa		OHL	61	32	51	83	132	11	6	11	17	11

M

Season Team	League	REGULAR SEASON					PLAYOFFS				
		Gms.	G	A	Pts.	Pen.	Gms.	G	A	Pts.	Pen.
92-93—Newmarket	OHL	31	12	25	37	85	7	4	7	11	20
—Ottawa	OHL	30	14	28	42	83	—	—	—	—	—
—St. John's	AHL	2	0	0	0	0	2	0	0	0	2
93-94—St. John's	AHL	67	11	29	40	155	11	1	5	6	17

MARSHALL, JASON
D, BLUES

PERSONAL: Born February 22, 1971, in Cranbrook, B.C. . . . 6-2/195. . . . Shoots right.
TRANSACTIONS/CAREER NOTES: WHL rights traded by Regina Pats with RW Devin Derksen to Tri-City Americans for RW Mark Cipriano (August 1988). . . . Selected by St. Louis Blues in first round (first Blues pick, ninth overall) of NHL entry draft (June 17, 1989).

Season Team	League	REGULAR SEASON					PLAYOFFS				
		Gms.	G	A	Pts.	PIM	Gms.	G	A	Pts.	PIM
87-88—Columbia Valley	KIJHL	40	4	28	32	150	—	—	—	—	—
88-89—Vernon	BCJHL	48	10	30	40	197	31	6	6	12	141
—Canadian national team	Int'l	2	0	1	1	0	—	—	—	—	—
89-90—Canadian national team	Int'l	72	1	11	12	57	—	—	—	—	—
90-91—Tri-City	WHL	59	10	34	44	236	7	1	2	3	20
—Peoria	IHL	—	—	—	—	—	18	0	1	1	48
91-92—Peoria	IHL	78	4	18	22	178	10	0	1	1	16
—St. Louis	NHL	2	1	0	1	4	—	—	—	—	—
92-93—Peoria	IHL	77	4	16	20	229	4	0	0	0	20
93-94—Peoria	IHL	20	1	1	2	72	3	2	0	2	2
—Canadian national team	Int'l	41	3	10	13	60	—	—	—	—	—
NHL totals		2	1	0	1	4					

MARTIN, CRAIG
RW, RED WINGS

PERSONAL: Born January 21, 1971, in Amherst, N.S. . . . 6-2/219. . . . Shoots right.
TRANSACTIONS/CAREER NOTES: Suspended by QMJHL for opening game of 1990-91 season for fighting in a playoff game (April 14, 1990). . . . Selected by Winnipeg Jets in fifth round (sixth Jets pick, 98th overall) of NHL entry draft (June 16, 1990). . . . Suspended by QMJHL for striking referee with stick (December 9, 1990). . . . Signed as free agent by Detroit Red Wings (July 28, 1993).

Season Team	League	REGULAR SEASON					PLAYOFFS				
		Gms.	G	A	Pts.	PIM	Gms.	G	A	Pts.	PIM
87-88—Hull	QMJHL	66	5	5	10	137	—	—	—	—	—
88-89—Hull	QMJHL	70	14	29	43	260	—	—	—	—	—
89-90—Hull	QMJHL	66	14	31	45	299	11	2	1	3	65
90-91—St. Hyacinthe	QMJHL	54	13	16	29	257	—	—	—	—	—
91-92—Fort Wayne	IHL	24	0	0	0	115	—	—	—	—	—
—Moncton	AHL	11	1	1	2	70	—	—	—	—	—
92-93—Moncton	AHL	64	5	13	18	198	5	0	1	1	22
93-94—Adirondack	AHL	76	15	24	39	297	12	2	2	4	63

MARTIN, MATT
D, MAPLE LEAFS

PERSONAL: Born April 30, 1971, in Hamden, Conn. . . . 6-3/190. . . . Shoots left.
HIGH SCHOOL: Avon (Conn.) Old Farms School for Boys.
COLLEGE: Maine.
TRANSACTIONS/CAREER NOTES: Selected by Toronto Maple Leafs in fourth round (fourth Maple Leaf pick, 66th overall) of 1989 NHL entry draft (June 17, 1989). . . . Loaned to U.S. Olympic Team (October 5, 1993). . . . Returned to Maple Leafs (October 19, 1993). . . . Loaned to U.S. Olympic Team (October 28, 1993). . . . Returned to Maple Leafs (November 3, 1993). . . . Loaned to U.S. Olympic Team (November 15, 1993). . . . Returned to Maple Leafs (March 1, 1994).

Season Team	League	REGULAR SEASON					PLAYOFFS				
		Gms.	G	A	Pts.	PIM	Gms.	G	A	Pts.	PIM
88-89—Avon Old Farms H.S.	Conn. H.S.	. . .	9	23	32	. . .	—	—	—	—	—
89-90—					Statistics unavailable.						
90-91—University of Maine	Hockey East	35	3	12	15	48	—	—	—	—	—
91-92—University of Maine	Hockey East	30	4	14	18	46	—	—	—	—	—
92-93—University of Maine	Hockey East	44	6	26	32	88	—	—	—	—	—
—St. John's	AHL	2	0	0	0	2	9	1	5	6	4
93-94—U.S. Olympic Team	Int'l	8	0	2	2	8	—	—	—	—	—
—Toronto	NHL	12	0	1	1	6	—	—	—	—	—
—U.S. national team	Int'l	39	7	8	15	127	—	—	—	—	—
—St. John's	AHL	12	1	5	6	9	11	1	5	6	33
NHL totals		12	0	1	1	6					

MARTINI, DARCY
D, OILERS

PERSONAL: Born January 30, 1969, in Castlegar, B.C. . . . 6-4/220. . . . Shoots left.
COLLEGE: Michigan Tech.
TRANSACTIONS/CAREER NOTES: Selected by Edmonton Oilers in eighth round (eighth Oilers pick, 162nd overall) of NHL entry draft (June 17, 1989).

Season Team	League	REGULAR SEASON					PLAYOFFS				
		Gms.	G	A	Pts.	PIM	Gms.	G	A	Pts.	PIM
84-85—Castlegar	KIJHL	38	4	17	21	58	—	—	—	—	—
85-86—Castlegar	KIJHL	38	8	28	36	180	—	—	—	—	—

Season Team	League	REGULAR SEASON					PLAYOFFS				
		Gms.	G	A	Pts.	Pen.	Gms.	G	A	Pts.	Pen.
86-87—Castlegar	KIJHL	40	12	53	65	260	—	—	—	—	—
87-88—Vernon	BCJHL	48	9	26	35	193	12	2	9	11	28
88-89—Michigan Tech	WCHA	37	1	2	3	107	—	—	—	—	—
89-90—Michigan Tech	WCHA	36	3	16	19	150	—	—	—	—	—
90-91—Michigan Tech	WCHA	34	10	13	23	*186	—	—	—	—	—
91-92—Michigan Tech	WCHA	17	5	13	18	58	—	—	—	—	—
92-93—Cape Breton	AHL	47	1	6	7	36	2	0	1	1	0
—Wheeling	ECHL	6	0	2	2	2	—	—	—	—	—
93-94—Cape Breton	AHL	65	18	38	56	131	5	1	3	4	26
—Edmonton	NHL	2	0	0	0	0	—	—	—	—	—
NHL totals		2	0	0	0	0					

MASOTTA, BRYAN
G, SENATORS

PERSONAL: Born May 30, 1975, in New Haven, Conn.... 6-2/195.... Catches left.
HIGH SCHOOL: Hotchkiss (New York)
TRANSACTIONS/CAREER NOTES: Selected by Ottawa Senators in fourth round (third Senators pick, 81st overall) of NHL entry draft (June 29, 1994).

Season Team	League	REGULAR SEASON							PLAYOFFS						
		Gms.	Min.	W	L	T	GA	SO	Avg.	Gms.	Min.	W	L	GA SO	Avg.
91-92—Taft		14	...	...	...	...	...	1	3.10	—	—	—	—	— —	—
92-93—Hotchkiss	N.Y. H.S.	29	...	...	...	...	...	8	2.00	—	—	—	—	— —	—
93-94—Hotchkiss	N.Y. H.S.	18	856	...	...	...	38	8	2.66	—	—	—	—	— —	—

MATTE, CHRISTIAN
RW, NORDIQUES

PERSONAL: Born January 20, 1975, in Hull, Que.... 5-11/166.... Shoots right.
TRANSACTIONS/CAREER NOTES: Selected by Quebec Nordiques in sixth round (eighth Nordiques pick, 153rd overall) of NHL entry draft (June 26, 1993).
HONORS: Named to QMJHL All-Star second team (1993-94).

Season Team	League	REGULAR SEASON					PLAYOFFS				
		Gms.	G	A	Pts.	PIM	Gms.	G	A	Pts.	PIM
92-93—Granby	QMJHL	68	17	36	53	56	—	—	—	—	—
93-94—Granby	QMJHL	59	50	47	97	103	7	5	5	10	12
—Cornwall	AHL	1	0	0	0	0	—	—	—	—	—

MATTEAU, STEPHANE
LW, RANGERS

PERSONAL: Born September 2, 1969, in Rouyn, Que.... 6-3/200.... Shoots left.... Name pronounced ma-TOH.
TRANSACTIONS/CAREER NOTES: Selected by Calgary Flames as underage junior in second round (second Flames pick, 25th overall) of NHL entry draft (June 13, 1987).... Bruised thigh (October 10, 1991); missed 43 games.... Traded by Flames to Chicago Blackhawks for D Trent Yawney (December 16, 1991).... Fractured left foot (January 27, 1992); missed 12 games.... Suffered tonsillitis (September 1992); missed first three games of season.... Pulled groin (December 17, 1993); missed three games.... Traded by Blackhawks with RW Brian Noonan to New York Rangers for RW Tony Amonte and rights to LW Matt Oates (March 21, 1994).
MISCELLANEOUS: Member of Stanley Cup championship team (1994).

Season Team	League	REGULAR SEASON					PLAYOFFS				
		Gms.	G	A	Pts.	PIM	Gms.	G	A	Pts.	PIM
85-86—Hull	QMJHL	60	6	8	14	19	4	0	0	0	0
86-87—Hull	QMJHL	69	27	48	75	113	8	3	7	10	8
87-88—Hull	QMJHL	57	17	40	57	179	18	5	14	19	84
88-89—Hull	QMJHL	59	44	45	89	202	9	8	6	14	30
—Salt Lake City	IHL	—	—	—	—	—	9	0	4	4	13
89-90—Salt Lake City	IHL	81	23	35	58	130	10	6	3	9	38
90-91—Calgary	NHL	78	15	19	34	93	5	0	1	1	0
91-92—Calgary	NHL	4	1	0	1	19	—	—	—	—	—
—Chicago	NHL	20	5	8	13	45	18	4	6	10	24
92-93—Chicago	NHL	79	15	18	33	98	3	0	1	1	2
93-94—Chicago	NHL	65	15	16	31	55					
—New York Rangers	NHL	12	4	3	7	2	23	6	3	9	20
NHL totals		258	55	64	119	312	49	10	11	21	46

MATTHEWS, JAMIE
C, SHARKS

PERSONAL: Born May 25, 1973, in Amherst, N.S.... 6-1/208.... Shoots right.
TRANSACTIONS/CAREER NOTES: Selected by Chicago Blackhawks in second round (third Blackhawks pick, 44th overall) of NHL entry draft (June 22, 1991).... Selected by San Jose Sharks in 11th round (13th Sharks pick, 262nd overall) of NHL entry draft (June 26, 1993).

Season Team	League	REGULAR SEASON					PLAYOFFS				
		Gms.	G	A	Pts.	PIM	Gms.	G	A	Pts.	PIM
88-89—Amherst Junior A	NSJHL	38	39	43	82	9	—	—	—	—	—
89-90—Sudbury	OHL	60	16	17	33	25	7	1	0	1	4
90-91—Sudbury	OHL	66	14	38	52	41	5	3	5	8	8
91-92—Sudbury	OHL	64	26	69	95	30	11	2	11	13	4
92-93—Sudbury	OHL	65	30	62	92	65	14	7	17	24	22
93-94—Sudbury	OHL	46	34	63	97	24	10	6	6	12	4

MATTSSON, JESPER
C, FLAMES

PERSONAL: Born May 13, 1975, in Malmo, Sweden. . . . 6-0/173. . . . Shoots right.
TRANSACTIONS/CAREER NOTES: Selected by Calgary Flames in first round (first Flames pick, 18th overall) of NHL entry draft (June 26, 1993).

			REGULAR SEASON					PLAYOFFS				
Season Team	League	Gms.	G	A	Pts.	PIM	Gms.	G	A	Pts.	PIM
91-92—Malmo	Sweden	24	0	1	1	2	—	—	—	—	—
92-93—Malmo	Sweden	40	9	8	17	14	—	—	—	—	—
93-94—Malmo	Sweden	40	3	6	9	14	9	1	2	3	2

MATVICHUK, RICHARD
D, STARS

PERSONAL: Born February 5, 1973, in Edmonton. . . . 6-2/190. . . . Shoots left. . . . Name pronounced MAT-vih-CHUHK.
TRANSACTIONS/CAREER NOTES: Selected by Minnesota North Stars in first round (first North Stars pick, eighth overall) of 1991 NHL entry draft (June 22, 1991). . . . Strained lower back (November 9, 1992); missed two games. . . . Sprained ankle (December 27, 1992); missed 10 games. . . . North Stars franchise moved from Minnesota to Dallas and renamed Stars for 1993-94 season. . . . Bruised shoulder (April 5, 1994); missed one game.
HONORS: Won Bill Hunter Trophy (1991-92). . . . Named to Can.HL All-Star second team (1991-92). . . . Named to WHL (East) All-Star first team (1991-92).

			REGULAR SEASON					PLAYOFFS				
Season Team	League	Gms.	G	A	Pts.	PIM	Gms.	G	A	Pts.	PIM
88-89—Fort Saskatchewan	AJHL	58	7	36	43	147	—	—	—	—	—
89-90—Saskatoon	WHL	56	8	24	32	126	10	2	8	10	16
90-91—Saskatoon	WHL	68	13	36	49	117	—	—	—	—	—
91-92—Saskatoon	WHL	58	14	40	54	126	22	1	9	10	61
92-93—Minnesota	NHL	53	2	3	5	26	—	—	—	—	—
—Kalamazoo	IHL	3	0	1	1	6	—	—	—	—	—
93-94—Kalamazoo	IHL	43	8	17	25	84	—	—	—	—	—
—Dallas	NHL	25	0	3	3	22	7	1	1	2	12
NHL totals		78	2	6	8	48	7	1	1	2	12

MAY, ALAN
RW, STARS

PERSONAL: Born January 14, 1965, in Swan Hills, Alta. . . . 6-1/200. . . . Shoots right. . . . Full name: Alan Randy May.
TRANSACTIONS/CAREER NOTES: Signed as free agent by Boston Bruins (September 1987). . . . Traded by Bruins to Edmonton Oilers for LW Moe Lemay (March 8, 1988). . . . Traded by Oilers with D Jim Wiemer to Los Angeles Kings for C Brian Wilks and D John English (March 7, 1989). . . . Traded by Kings to Washington Capitals for fifth-round pick (G Tom Newman) in 1989 draft (June 17, 1989). . . . Fractured knuckle on left hand (October 20, 1990). . . . Strained shoulder (December 8, 1990). . . . Underwent surgery to nose (March 1992); missed two games. . . . Traded by Capitals with seventh-round pick to Dallas Stars with future considerations for Jim Johnson (March 21, 1994). . . . Broke left hand (November 10, 1993); missed 12 games.
HONORS: Named to ACHL All-Star second team (1986-87).

			REGULAR SEASON					PLAYOFFS				
Season Team	League	Gms.	G	A	Pts.	PIM	Gms.	G	A	Pts.	PIM
84-85—Estevan	SAJHL	64	51	47	98	409	—	—	—	—	—
85-86—Medicine Hat	WHL	6	1	0	1	25	—	—	—	—	—
86-87—New Westminster	WHL	32	8	9	17	81	—	—	—	—	—
—Springfield	AHL	4	0	2	2	11	—	—	—	—	—
—Carolina	ECHL	42	23	14	37	310	5	2	2	4	57
87-88—Maine	AHL	61	14	11	25	357	—	—	—	—	—
—Boston	NHL	3	0	0	0	15	—	—	—	—	—
—Nova Scotia	AHL	12	4	1	5	54	4	0	0	0	51
88-89—Edmonton	NHL	3	1	0	1	7	—	—	—	—	—
—Cape Breton	AHL	50	12	13	25	214	—	—	—	—	—
—New Haven	AHL	12	2	8	10	99	16	6	3	9	*105
89-90—Washington	NHL	77	7	10	17	339	15	0	0	0	37
90-91—Washington	NHL	67	4	6	10	264	11	1	1	2	37
91-92—Washington	NHL	75	6	9	15	221	7	0	0	0	0
92-93—Washington	NHL	83	6	10	16	268	6	0	1	1	6
93-94—Washington	NHL	43	4	7	11	97	—	—	—	—	—
—Dallas	NHL	8	1	0	1	18	1	0	0	0	0
NHL totals		359	29	42	71	1229	40	1	2	3	80

MAY, BRAD
LW, SABRES

PERSONAL: Born November 29, 1971, in Toronto. . . . 6-0/200. . . . Shoots left.
TRANSACTIONS/CAREER NOTES: Selected by Buffalo Sabres in first round (first Sabres pick, 14th overall) of NHL entry draft (June 16, 1990). . . . Injured knee (August 1990). . . . Injured left knee ligaments (November 1990).
HONORS: Named to OHL All-Star second team (1989-90 and 1990-91).

			REGULAR SEASON					PLAYOFFS				
Season Team	League	Gms.	G	A	Pts.	PIM	Gms.	G	A	Pts.	PIM
87-88—Markham Jr. B	OHA	6	1	1	2	21	—	—	—	—	—
88-89—Niagara Falls	OHL	65	8	14	22	304	17	0	1	1	55
89-90—Niagara Falls	OHL	61	33	58	91	223	16	9	13	22	64
90-91—Niagara Falls	OHL	34	37	32	69	93	14	11	14	25	53

M

Season	Team	League	REGULAR SEASON					PLAYOFFS				
			Gms.	G	A	Pts.	Pen.	Gms.	G	A	Pts.	Pen.
91-92—Buffalo		NHL	69	11	6	17	309	7	1	4	5	2
92-93—Buffalo		NHL	82	13	13	26	242	8	1	1	2	14
93-94—Buffalo		NHL	84	18	27	45	171	7	0	2	2	9
NHL totals			235	42	46	88	722	22	2	7	9	25

MAYER, DEREK
D, SENATORS

PERSONAL: Born May 21, 1967, in Rossland, B.C.... 6-0/185.... Shoots right.
COLLEGE: Denver.
TRANSACTIONS/CAREER NOTES: Selected by Detroit Red Wings in third round (third Red Wings pick, 43rd overall) of NHL entry draft (June 21, 1986).... Dislocated shoulder (January 1986).... Separated shoulder (December 1987).... Signed as free agent by Ottawa Senators (March 7, 1994).
MISCELLANEOUS: Member of silver-medal-winning Canadian Olympic team (1994).

Season	Team	League	REGULAR SEASON					PLAYOFFS				
			Gms.	G	A	Pts.	PIM	Gms.	G	A	Pts.	PIM
84-85—Penticton		BCJHL	42	6	30	36	137	—	—	—	—	—
85-86—University of Denver		WCHA	44	2	7	9	42	—	—	—	—	—
86-87—University of Denver		WCHA	38	5	17	22	87	—	—	—	—	—
87-88—University of Denver		WCHA	34	5	16	21	82	—	—	—	—	—
88-89—Canadian national team		Int'l	58	3	13	16	81	—	—	—	—	—
89-90—Adirondack		AHL	62	4	26	30	56	5	0	6	6	4
90-91—San Diego		IHL	31	9	24	33	31	—	—	—	—	—
—Adirondack		AHL	21	4	9	13	20	2	0	1	1	0
91-92—Adirondack		AHL	25	4	11	15	31	—	—	—	—	—
—San Diego		IHL	30	7	16	23	47	4	0	0	0	20
92-93—Canadian national team		Int'l	64	12	28	40	108	—	—	—	—	—
93-94—Canadian national team		Int'l	57	5	17	22	79	—	—	—	—	—
—Canadian Olympic Team		Int'l	8	1	2	3	18	—	—	—	—	—
—Ottawa		NHL	17	2	2	4	8	—	—	—	—	—
NHL totals			17	2	2	4	8					

MAYERS, JAMAL
C, BLUES

PERSONAL: Born October 24, 1974, in Toronto.... 6-0/190.... Shoots right.... Name pronounced MAY-ohrs.
COLLEGE: Western Michigan.
TRANSACTIONS/CAREER NOTES: Selected by St. Louis Blues in fourth round (third Blues pick, 89th overall) of NHL entry draft (June 26, 1993).

Season	Team	League	REGULAR SEASON					PLAYOFFS				
			Gms.	G	A	Pts.	PIM	Gms.	G	A	Pts.	PIM
90-91—Thornhill		Jr. A	44	12	24	36	78	—	—	—	—	—
91-92—Thornhill		Jr. A	56	38	69	107	36	—	—	—	—	—
92-93—Western Michigan Univ.		CCHA	38	8	17	25	26	—	—	—	—	—
93-94—Western Michigan Univ.		CCHA	40	17	32	49	40	—	—	—	—	—

M

MAZUR, JAY
C, CANUCKS

PERSONAL: Born January 22, 1965, in Hamilton, Ont.... 6-2/205.... Shoots right.... Full name: Jay John Mazur.... Name pronounced MAY-zuhr.
HIGH SCHOOL: Breck (Minneapolis).
COLLEGE: Maine.
TRANSACTIONS/CAREER NOTES: Selected by Vancouver Canucks in 12th round (12th Canucks pick, 230th overall) of NHL entry draft (June 8, 1983).... Strained rib cartilage (October 12, 1990).... Injured right calf and underwent emergency surgery to relieve circulatory problem (February 21, 1991); missed 11 games.

Season	Team	League	REGULAR SEASON					PLAYOFFS				
			Gms.	G	A	Pts.	PIM	Gms.	G	A	Pts.	PIM
82-83—Breck H.S.		Minn. H.S.				Statistics unavailable.						
83-84—University of Maine		ECAC	34	14	9	23	14	—	—	—	—	—
84-85—University of Maine		Hockey East	31	0	6	6	20	—	—	—	—	—
85-86—University of Maine		Hockey East	35	5	7	12	18	—	—	—	—	—
86-87—University of Maine		Hockey East	39	16	10	26	61	—	—	—	—	—
87-88—Flint		IHL	43	17	11	28	36	—	—	—	—	—
—Fredericton		AHL	31	14	6	20	28	15	4	2	6	38
88-89—Milwaukee		IHL	73	33	31	64	86	11	6	5	11	2
—Vancouver		NHL	1	0	0	0	0	—	—	—	—	—
89-90—Milwaukee		IHL	70	20	27	47	63	6	3	0	3	6
—Vancouver		NHL	5	0	0	0	4	—	—	—	—	—
90-91—Milwaukee		IHL	7	2	3	5	21	—	—	—	—	—
—Vancouver		NHL	36	11	7	18	14	6	0	1	1	8
91-92—Milwaukee		IHL	56	17	20	37	49	5	2	3	5	0
—Vancouver		NHL	5	0	0	0	2	—	—	—	—	—
92-93—Hamilton		AHL	59	21	17	38	30	—	—	—	—	—
93-94—Hamilton		AHL	78	40	55	95	40	4	2	2	4	4
NHL totals			47	11	7	18	20	6	0	1	1	8

McAMMOND, DEAN
C, OILERS

PERSONAL: Born June 15, 1973, in Grand Cache, Alta. . . . 5-11/185. . . . Shoots left.
TRANSACTIONS/CAREER NOTES: Selected by Chicago Blackhawks in first round (first Blackhawks pick, 22nd overall) of NHL entry draft (June 22, 1991). . . . Traded by Blackhawks with D Igor Kravchuk to Edmonton Oilers for RW Joe Murphy (February 25, 1993).
HONORS: Won Can.HL Plus/Minus Award (1991-92).

			REGULAR SEASON					PLAYOFFS				
Season	Team	League	Gms.	G	A	Pts.	PIM	Gms.	G	A	Pts.	PIM
89-90—Prince Albert		WHL	53	11	11	22	49	14	2	3	5	18
90-91—Prince Albert		WHL	71	33	35	68	108	2	0	1	1	6
91-92—Prince Albert		WHL	63	37	54	91	189	10	12	11	23	26
—Chicago		NHL	5	0	2	2	0	3	0	0	0	2
92-93—Prince Albert		WHL	30	19	29	48	44	—	—	—	—	—
—Swift Current		WHL	18	10	13	23	29	17	*16	19	35	20
93-94—Edmonton		NHL	45	6	21	27	16	—	—	—	—	—
—Cape Breton		AHL	28	9	12	21	38	—	—	—	—	—
NHL totals			50	6	23	29	16	3	0	0	0	2

McARTHUR, MARK
G, ISLANDERS

PERSONAL: Born November 16, 1975, in East York, Ont. . . . 5-11/179. . . . Catches left.
HIGH SCHOOL: Bishop MacDonnell (Guelph, Ont.).
TRANSACTIONS/CAREER NOTES: Selected by New York Islanders in fifth round (fifth Islanders pick, 112th overall) of NHL entry draft (June 29, 1994).

			REGULAR SEASON							PLAYOFFS						
Season	Team	League	Gms.	Min.	W	L	T	GA	SO	Avg.	Gms.	Min.	W	L	GA	SO	Avg.
91-92—Petersborough		Jr.B	25	1198	...	...	...	98	0	4.91	—	—	—	—	—	—	—
93-94—Guelph		OHL	35	1853	14	14	3	180	0	5.83	—	—	—	—	—	—	—
93-94—Guelph		OHL	51	2936	25	18	5	201	0	4.11	9	561	4	5	38	0	4.06

McBAIN, ANDREW
RW

PERSONAL: Born January 18, 1965, in Toronto. . . . 6-1/205. . . . Shoots right. . . . Full name: Andrew Burton McBain.
HIGH SCHOOL: David and Mary Thomson (Scarborough, Ont.).
TRANSACTIONS/CAREER NOTES: Fractured cheekbone (November 1982). . . . Separated sterno clavicular joint (March 1983). . . . Selected by Winnipeg Jets as underage junior in first round (first Jets pick, eighth overall) of NHL entry draft (June 8, 1983). . . . Suffered from mononucleosis (April 25, 1985). . . . Injured knee (December 8, 1985). . . . Suspended four games by NHL for stick-swinging incident (March 1987). . . . Traded by Jets with D Jim Kyte and LW Randy Gilhen to Pittsburgh Penguins for C/LW Randy Cunneyworth, G Richard Tabaracci and RW Dave McLlwain (June 17, 1989). . . . Traded by Penguins with C Dan Quinn and C Dave Capuano to Vancouver Canucks for RW Tony Tanti, C Barry Pederson and D Rod Buskas (January 8, 1990). . . . Suffered sore ribs (February 1990). . . . Signed as free agent by Ottawa Senators (June 23, 1992). . . . Injured knee (December 17, 1992); missed 18 games. . . . Signed as free agent by Las Vegas Thunder (July 22, 1994).
HONORS: Named to OHL All-Star second team (1982-83).

			REGULAR SEASON					PLAYOFFS				
Season	Team	League	Gms.	G	A	Pts.	PIM	Gms.	G	A	Pts.	PIM
81-82—Niagara Falls		OHL	68	19	25	44	35	5	0	3	3	4
82-83—North Bay		OHL	67	33	87	120	61	8	2	6	8	17
83-84—Winnipeg		NHL	78	11	19	30	37	3	2	0	2	0
84-85—Winnipeg		NHL	77	7	15	22	45	7	1	0	1	0
85-86—Winnipeg		NHL	28	3	3	6	17	—	—	—	—	—
86-87—Winnipeg		NHL	71	11	21	32	106	9	0	2	2	10
87-88—Winnipeg		NHL	74	32	31	63	145	5	2	5	7	29
88-89—Winnipeg		NHL	80	37	40	77	71	—	—	—	—	—
89-90—Pittsburgh		NHL	41	5	9	14	51	—	—	—	—	—
—Vancouver		NHL	26	4	5	9	22	—	—	—	—	—
90-91—Vancouver		NHL	13	0	5	5	32	—	—	—	—	—
—Milwaukee		IHL	47	27	24	51	69	6	2	5	7	12
91-92—Milwaukee		IHL	65	24	54	78	132	5	1	2	3	10
—Vancouver		NHL	6	1	0	1	0	—	—	—	—	—
92-93—Ottawa		NHL	59	7	16	23	43	—	—	—	—	—
—New Haven		AHL	1	0	1	1	4	—	—	—	—	—
93-94—Prince Edward Island		AHL	26	6	10	16	102	—	—	—	—	—
—Ottawa		NHL	55	11	8	19	64	—	—	—	—	—
NHL totals			608	129	172	301	633	24	5	7	12	39

McBAIN, JASON
D, WHALERS

PERSONAL: Born April 12, 1974, in Ilion, N.Y. . . . 6-2/178. . . . Shoots right.
TRANSACTIONS/CAREER NOTES: Selected by Hartford Whalers in fourth round (fifth Whalers pick, 81st overall) of NHL entry draft (June 20, 1992).

			REGULAR SEASON					PLAYOFFS				
Season	Team	League	Gms.	G	A	Pts.	PIM	Gms.	G	A	Pts.	PIM
90-91—Lethbridge		WHL	52	2	7	9	39	1	0	0	0	0
91-92—Lethbridge		WHL	13	0	1	1	12	—	—	—	—	—
—Portland		WHL	54	9	23	32	95	6	1	0	1	13
92-93—Portland		WHL	71	9	35	44	76	16	2	12	14	14
93-94—Portland		WHL	63	15	51	66	86	10	2	7	9	14

M

McBEAN, WAYNE
D, JETS

PERSONAL: Born February 21, 1969, in Calgary.... 6-2/190.... Shoots left. **TRANSACTIONS/CAREER NOTES:** Selected by Los Angeles Kings as underage junior in first round (first Kings pick, fourth overall) of NHL entry draft (June 13, 1987).... Traded by Kings with G Mark Fitzpatrick and future considerations to New York Islanders for G Kelly Hrudey (February 22, 1989); the Islanders sent D Doug Crossman to Kings to complete the deal.... Injured left knee (December 23, 1991); missed final 47 games of season.... Underwent arthroscopic surgery to left knee (December 31, 1991). ... Sprained left wrist (October 12, 1993); missed five games.... Suffered from sore left knee (November 21, 1994); missed three games.... Traded by Islanders to Winnipeg Jets for RW Yan Kaminsky (February 1, 1994).
HONORS: Won Top Defenseman Trophy East (1986-87).... Named to WHL (East) All-Star first team (1986-87).... Named to Memorial Cup All-Star team (1986-87).

			REGULAR SEASON					PLAYOFFS				
Season Team	League	Gms.	G	A	Pts.	PIM	Gms.	G	A	Pts.	PIM
85-86—Medicine Hat	WHL	67	1	14	15	73	25	1	5	6	36
86-87—Medicine Hat	WHL	71	12	41	53	163	20	2	8	10	40
87-88—Los Angeles	NHL	27	0	1	1	26	—	—	—	—	—
—Medicine Hat	WHL	30	15	30	45	48	16	6	17	23	50
88-89—New Haven	AHL	7	1	1	2	2	—	—	—	—	—
—Los Angeles	NHL	33	0	5	5	23	—	—	—	—	—
—New York Islanders	NHL	19	0	1	1	12	—	—	—	—	—
89-90—Springfield	AHL	68	6	33	39	48	17	4	11	15	31
—New York Islanders	NHL	5	0	1	1	2	2	1	1	2	0
90-91—Capital District	AHL	22	9	9	18	19	—	—	—	—	—
—New York Islanders	NHL	52	5	14	19	47	—	—	—	—	—
91-92—New York Islanders	NHL	25	2	4	6	18	—	—	—	—	—
92-93—Capital District	AHL	20	1	9	10	35	3	0	1	1	9
93-94—New York Islanders	NHL	19	1	4	5	16	—	—	—	—	—
—Salt Lake City	IHL	5	0	6	6	2	—	—	—	—	—
—Winnipeg	NHL	31	2	9	11	24	—	—	—	—	—
NHL totals		211	10	39	49	168	2	1	1	2	0

McCABE, BRYAN
D, ISLANDERS

PERSONAL: Born June 8, 1975, in St. Catherines, Ont.... 6-1/200.... Shoots left. **HIGH SCHOOL:** Ferris (Calgary). **TRANSACTIONS/CAREER NOTES:** Selected by New York Islanders in second round (second Islanders pick, 40th overall) of NHL entry draft (June 26, 1993).
HONORS: Named to WHL (West) All-Star second team (1992-93).... Named to WHL (West) All-Star first team (1993-94).

			REGULAR SEASON					PLAYOFFS				
Season Team	League	Gms.	G	A	Pts.	PIM	Gms.	G	A	Pts.	PIM
91-92—Medicine Hat	WHL	66	6	24	30	157	4	0	0	0	6
92-93—Medicine Hat	WHL	14	0	13	13	83	—	—	—	—	—
—Spokane	WHL	46	3	44	47	134	10	1	5	6	28
93-94—Spokane	WHL	64	22	62	84	218	3	0	4	4	4

McCABE, SCOTT
D, DEVILS

PERSONAL: Born May 28, 1974, in St. Claire Shores, Mich.... 6-4/189.... Shoots left. **COLLEGE:** Lake Superior State (Mich.). **TRANSACTIONS/CAREER NOTES:** Selected by New Jersey Devils in fourth round (fifth Devils pick, 94th overall) of NHL entry draft (June 20, 1992).

			REGULAR SEASON					PLAYOFFS				
Season Team	League	Gms.	G	A	Pts.	PIM	Gms.	G	A	Pts.	PIM
93-94—Lake Superior State	CCHA	18	3	5	8	14	—	—	—	—	—

McCARTHY, BRIAN
C, SABRES

PERSONAL: Born December 6, 1971, in Salem, Mass.... 6-2/190.... Shoots left.... Full name: Brian Edward McCarthy. **HIGH SCHOOL:** Pingree (South Hamilton, Mass.). **COLLEGE:** Providence, then St. Lawrence (N.Y.).
TRANSACTIONS/CAREER NOTES: Selected by Buffalo Sabres in fourth round (second Sabres pick, 82nd overall) of NHL entry draft (June 16, 1990).

			REGULAR SEASON					PLAYOFFS				
Season Team	League	Gms.	G	A	Pts.	PIM	Gms.	G	A	Pts.	PIM
86-87—Pingree School	Mass. H.S.	20	15	16	31	...	—	—	—	—	—
87-88—Pingree School	Mass. H.S.	24	22	36	58	24	—	—	—	—	—
88-89—Pingree School	Mass. H.S.	26	37	43	80	24	—	—	—	—	—
89-90—Pingree School	Mass. H.S.	...	25	40	65	...	—	—	—	—	—
90-91—Providence College	Hockey East	33	7	6	13	33	—	—	—	—	—
91-92—St. Lawrence University	ECAC	Did not play—transfer student.									
92-93—St. Lawrence University	ECAC	18	7	5	12	44	—	—	—	—	—
93-94—St. Lawrence University	ECAC	28	12	14	26	32	—	—	—	—	—

McCARTHY, SANDY
RW, FLAMES

PERSONAL: Born June 15, 1972, in Toronto.... 6-3/225.... Shoots right. **TRANSACTIONS/CAREER NOTES:** Suspended one game by QMJHL for attempting to injure another player (October 2, 1989).... Suspended one playoff game by QMJHL for pre-game fight (March 19, 1990).... Selected by Calgary Flames in third round (third Flames pick, 52nd overall) of NHL entry draft (June 22, 1991).... Strained right shoulder (December 18,

M

1993); missed two games.... Strained shoulder (December 27, 1993); missed one game.

			REGULAR SEASON					PLAYOFFS			
Season Team	League	Gms.	G	A	Pts.	PIM	Gms.	G	A	Pts.	PIM
89-90—Laval	QMJHL	65	10	11	21	269	—	—	—	—	—
90-91—Laval	QMJHL	68	21	19	40	297	—	—	—	—	—
91-92—Laval	QMJHL	62	39	51	90	326	8	4	5	9	81
92-93—Salt Lake City	IHL	77	18	20	38	220	—	—	—	—	—
93-94—Calgary	NHL	79	5	5	10	173	7	0	0	0	34
NHL totals		79	5	5	10	173	7	0	0	0	34

McCARTY, DARREN
RW, RED WINGS

PERSONAL: Born April 1, 1972, in Burnaby, B.C.... 6-1/214.... Shoots right. **HIGH SCHOOL:** Quinte Secondary School (Belleville, Ont.). **TRANSACTIONS/CAREER NOTES:** Selected by Detroit Red Wings in second round (second Red Wings pick, 46th overall) of NHL entry draft (June 20, 1992).... Injured groin (January 29, 1994); missed five games.... Injured shoulder (March 23, 1994); missed five games. **HONORS:** Won Jim Mahon Memorial Trophy (1991-92).... Named to Can.HL All-Star first team (1991-92).... Named to OHL All-Star first team (1991-92).

			REGULAR SEASON					PLAYOFFS			
Season Team	League	Gms.	G	A	Pts.	PIM	Gms.	G	A	Pts.	PIM
88-89—Peterborough Jr. B	OHA	34	18	17	35	135	—	—	—	—	—
89-90—Belleville	OHL	63	12	15	27	142	11	1	1	2	21
90-91—Belleville	OHL	60	30	37	67	151	6	2	2	4	13
91-92—Belleville	OHL	65	*55	72	127	177	5	1	4	5	13
92-93—Adirondack	AHL	73	17	19	36	278	11	0	1	1	33
93-94—Detroit	NHL	67	9	17	26	181	7	2	2	4	8
NHL totals		67	9	17	26	181	7	2	2	4	8

McCAULEY, BILL
C, PANTHERS

PERSONAL: Born April 20, 1975, in Detroit.... 6-0/173.... Shoots left. **TRANSACTIONS/CAREER NOTES:** Selected by Florida Panthers in fourth round (sixth Panthers pick, 83rd overall) of NHL entry draft (June 26, 1993).

			REGULAR SEASON					PLAYOFFS			
Season Team	League	Gms.	G	A	Pts.	PIM	Gms.	G	A	Pts.	PIM
91-92—Detroit Junior Red Wings	NAJHL	38	25	35	60	64	—	—	—	—	—
92-93—Detroit	OHL	65	13	37	50	24	15	1	4	5	6
93-94—Detroit	OHL	59	18	39	57	51	16	4	7	11	25

McCLELLAND, KEVIN
RW, SABRES

PERSONAL: Born July 4, 1962, in Oshawa, Ont.... 6-2/205.... Shoots right.... Full name: Kevin William McClelland. **TRANSACTIONS/CAREER NOTES:** Selected by Hartford Whalers as underage junior in fourth round (fourth Whalers pick, 71st overall) of NHL entry draft (June 11, 1980).... Acquired by Pittsburgh Penguins with C/LW Pat Boutette as compensation for Whalers signing free agent G Greg Millen. Decision required by NHL Arbitrator Judge Joseph Kane when Hartford and Pittsburgh were unable to agree on compensation (July 1981).... Dislocated shoulder (September 21, 1981).... Dislocated shoulder and underwent surgery (January 24, 1983); missed remainder of season.... Traded by Penguins with sixth-round pick in 1984 draft (D Emanuel Viveiros) to Edmonton Oilers for C Tom Roulston (December 5, 1983).... Sprained left knee (January 1985).... Suspended three games by NHL for being first off bench during fight (December 10, 1986).... Sprained knee (November 1987).... Bruised right knee (February 1988).... Traded by Oilers with C Jimmy Carson and fifth-round pick in 1991 draft (traded to Montreal Canadiens who selected D Brad Layzell) to Detroit Red Wings for C/RW Joe Murphy, C/LW Adam Graves, LW Petr Klima and D Jeff Sharples (November 2, 1989).... Suffered sore left shoulder (September 1990).... Released by Red Wings (April 21, 1991).... Signed as free agent by Toronto Maple Leafs (September 2, 1991).... Traded by Maple Leafs to Winnipeg Jets for future considerations (August 12, 1993).... Traded by Jets to Buffalo Sabres for future considerations (July 7, 1994). **MISCELLANEOUS:** Member of Stanley Cup championship team (1984, 1985, 1987 and 1988).

			REGULAR SEASON					PLAYOFFS			
Season Team	League	Gms.	G	A	Pts.	PIM	Gms.	G	A	Pts.	PIM
79-80—Niagara Falls	OMJHL	67	14	14	28	71	—	—	—	—	—
80-81—Niagara Falls	OMJHL	68	36	72	108	184	12	8	13	21	42
81-82—Niagara Falls	OHL	46	36	47	83	184	—	—	—	—	—
—Pittsburgh	NHL	10	1	4	5	4	5	1	1	2	5
82-83—Pittsburgh	NHL	38	5	4	9	73	—	—	—	—	—
83-84—Baltimore	AHL	3	1	1	2	0	—	—	—	—	—
—Pittsburgh	NHL	24	2	4	6	62	—	—	—	—	—
—Edmonton	NHL	52	8	20	28	127	18	4	6	10	42
84-85—Edmonton	NHL	62	8	15	23	205	18	1	3	4	75
85-86—Edmonton	NHL	79	11	25	36	266	10	1	0	1	32
86-87—Edmonton	NHL	72	12	13	25	238	21	2	3	5	43
87-88—Edmonton	NHL	74	10	6	16	281	19	2	3	5	68
88-89—Edmonton	NHL	79	6	14	20	161	7	0	2	2	16
89-90—Edmonton	NHL	10	1	1	2	13	—	—	—	—	—
—Detroit	NHL	61	4	5	9	183	—	—	—	—	—
90-91—Adirondack	AHL	27	5	14	19	125	—	—	—	—	—
—Detroit	NHL	3	0	0	0	7	—	—	—	—	—

Season Team	League	REGULAR SEASON					PLAYOFFS				
		Gms.	G	A	Pts.	Pen.	Gms.	G	A	Pts.	Pen.
91-92—St. John's	AHL	34	7	15	22	199	5	0	1	1	9
—Toronto	NHL	18	0	1	1	33	—	—	—	—	—
92-93—St. John's	AHL	55	7	20	27	221	1	0	0	0	7
93-94—Moncton	AHL	39	3	5	8	233	1	0	0	0	2
—Winnipeg	NHL	6	0	0	0	19	—	—	—	—	—
NHL totals		588	68	112	180	1672	98	11	18	29	281

McCOSH, SHAWN
C, RANGERS

PERSONAL: Born June 5, 1969, in Oshawa, Ont. . . . 6-0/188. . . . Shoots right.
TRANSACTIONS/CAREER NOTES: Selected by Detroit Red Wings in fifth round (fifth Red Wings pick, 95th overall) of NHL entry draft (June 17, 1989). . . . Traded by Red Wings to Los Angeles Kings for eighth-round pick (D Justin Krall) in 1992 draft (August 15, 1990). . . . Traded by Kings with RW Bob Kudelski to Ottawa Senators for RW Jim Thomson and C Marc Fortier (December 20, 1992). . . . Signed as free agent by New York Rangers (August 17, 1993).

Season Team	League	REGULAR SEASON					PLAYOFFS				
		Gms.	G	A	Pts.	PIM	Gms.	G	A	Pts.	PIM
86-87—Hamilton	OHL	50	11	17	28	49	6	1	0	1	2
87-88—Hamilton	OHL	64	17	36	53	96	14	6	8	14	14
88-89—Niagara Falls	OHL	56	41	62	103	75	14	4	13	17	23
89-90—Niagara Falls	OHL	9	6	10	16	24	—	—	—	—	—
—Dukes of Hamilton	OHL	39	24	28	52	65	—	—	—	—	—
90-91—New Haven	AHL	66	16	21	37	104	—	—	—	—	—
91-92—Los Angeles	NHL	4	0	0	0	4	—	—	—	—	—
—Phoenix	IHL	71	21	32	53	118	—	—	—	—	—
—New Haven	AHL	—	—	—	—	—	5	0	1	1	0
92-93—Phoenix	IHL	22	9	8	17	36	—	—	—	—	—
—New Haven	AHL	46	22	32	54	54	—	—	—	—	—
93-94—Binghamton	AHL	75	31	44	75	68	—	—	—	—	—
NHL totals		4	0	0	0	4					

McCOSH, SHAYNE
D, WHALERS

PERSONAL: Born January 27, 1974, in Oshawa, Ont. . . . 6-0/193. . . . Shoots left.
TRANSACTIONS/CAREER NOTES: Signed as free agent by Hartford Whalers (October 5, 1992).

Season Team	League	REGULAR SEASON					PLAYOFFS				
		Gms.	G	A	Pts.	PIM	Gms.	G	A	Pts.	PIM
90-91—Kitchener	OHL	62	3	22	25	26	6	0	1	1	4
91-92—Kitchener	OHL	62	7	36	43	46	14	1	2	3	28
92-93—Windsor	OHL	68	12	60	72	81	—	—	—	—	—
93-94—Detroit	OHL	59	6	39	45	79	17	3	8	11	4

M

McCRIMMON, BRAD
D, WHALERS

PERSONAL: Born March 29, 1959, in Dodsland, Sask. . . . 5-11/197. . . . Shoots left. . . . Full name: Byron Brad McCrimmon.
TRANSACTIONS/CAREER NOTES: Selected by Boston Bruins in first round (second Bruins pick, 15th overall) of NHL entry draft (August 9, 1979). . . . Traded by Bruins to Philadelphia Flyers for G Pete Peeters (June 1982). . . . Broke bone in right hand (February 2, 1985); missed 13 games. . . . Separated left shoulder and underwent surgery (May 9, 1985). . . . Missed start of 1986-87 season due to contract dispute. . . . Traded by Flyers to Calgary Flames for third-round pick in 1988 draft (G Dominic Roussel) and first-round pick in 1989 draft (August 1987). . . . Suffered from skin rash (February 1989). . . . Fractured ankle (March 1989). . . . Traded by Flames to Detroit Red Wings for second-round pick (traded to New Jersey Devils who selected D David Harlock) for in 1990 draft (June 16, 1990). . . . Fractured right ankle (January 12, 1991); missed 16 games. . . . Suffered from the flu (October 24, 1992); missed one game. . . . Traded by Red Wings to Hartford Whalers for sixth-round pick in 1993 draft (June 1, 1993).
HONORS: Named to WCHL All-Star second team (1976-77). . . . Won Top Defenseman Trophy (1977-78). . . . Named to WCHL All-Star first team (1977-78). . . . Named to WHL All-Star first team (1978-79). . . . Named to Memorial Cup All-Star team (1978-79). . . . Won Emery Edge Award (1987-88). . . . Named to THE SPORTING NEWS All-Star second team (1987-88). . . . Named to NHL All-Star second team (1987-88). . . . Played in NHL All-Star Game (1988).
MISCELLANEOUS: Member of Stanley Cup championship team (1989).

Season Team	League	REGULAR SEASON					PLAYOFFS				
		Gms.	G	A	Pts.	PIM	Gms.	G	A	Pts.	PIM
76-77—Brandon	WCHL	72	18	66	84	96	—	—	—	—	—
77-78—Brandon	WCHL	65	19	78	97	245	8	2	11	13	20
78-79—Brandon	WHL	66	24	74	98	139	22	9	19	28	34
79-80—Boston	NHL	72	5	11	16	94	10	1	1	2	28
80-81—Boston	NHL	78	11	18	29	148	3	0	1	1	2
81-82—Boston	NHL	78	1	8	9	83	2	0	0	0	2
82-83—Philadelphia	NHL	79	4	21	25	61	3	0	0	0	4
83-84—Philadelphia	NHL	71	0	24	24	76	1	0	0	0	4
84-85—Philadelphia	NHL	66	8	25	33	81	11	2	1	3	15
85-86—Philadelphia	NHL	80	13	42	55	85	5	2	0	2	2
86-87—Philadelphia	NHL	71	10	29	39	52	26	3	5	8	30
87-88—Calgary	NHL	80	7	35	42	98	9	2	3	5	22
88-89—Calgary	NHL	72	5	17	22	96	22	0	3	3	30

Season Team	League	REGULAR SEASON					PLAYOFFS				
		Gms.	G	A	Pts.	Pen.	Gms.	G	A	Pts.	Pen.
89-90—Calgary	NHL	79	4	15	19	78	6	0	2	2	8
90-91—Detroit	NHL	64	0	13	13	81	7	1	1	2	21
91-92—Detroit	NHL	79	7	22	29	118	11	0	1	1	8
92-93—Detroit	NHL	60	1	14	15	71	—	—	—	—	—
93-94—Hartford	NHL	65	1	5	6	72	—	—	—	—	—
NHL totals		1094	77	299	376	1294	116	11	18	29	176

McDONOUGH, HUBIE
C

PERSONAL: Born July 8, 1963, in Manchester, N.H. . . . 5-9/180. . . . Shoots left.
HIGH SCHOOL: Memorial (Manchester, N.H.).
COLLEGE: St. Anselm (N.H.).
TRANSACTIONS/CAREER NOTES: Signed as free agent by Los Angeles Kings (October 1987). . . . Traded by Kings with D Ken Baumgartner to New York Islanders for RW Mikko Makela (November 29, 1989). . . . Injured knee (September 1990). . . . Fractured left thumb (October 22, 1991). . . . Traded by Islanders to San Jose Sharks for cash (August 31, 1992). . . . Loaned to San Diego Gulls (September 29, 1992). . . . Returned to Sharks (January 6, 1993). . . . Loaned to Gulls (March 20, 1993). . . . Signed as free agent by Gulls (August 11, 1993).
HONORS: Named to IHL All-Star second team (1992-93).

Season Team	League	REGULAR SEASON					PLAYOFFS				
		Gms.	G	A	Pts.	PIM	Gms.	G	A	Pts.	PIM
82-83—St. Anselm College	ECAC-II	27	24	21	45	12	—	—	—	—	—
83-84—St. Anselm College	ECAC-II	26	37	15	52	20	—	—	—	—	—
84-85—St. Anselm College	ECAC-II	26	41	30	71	48	—	—	—	—	—
85-86—St. Anselm College	ECAC-II	25	22	20	42	16	—	—	—	—	—
86-87—Flint	IHL	82	27	52	79	59	6	3	2	5	0
87-88—New Haven	AHL	78	30	29	59	43	—	—	—	—	—
88-89—New Haven	AHL	74	37	55	92	41	17	10	*21	*31	6
—Los Angeles	NHL	4	0	1	1	0	—	—	—	—	—
89-90—Los Angeles	NHL	22	3	4	7	10	—	—	—	—	—
—New York Islanders	NHL	54	18	11	29	26	5	1	0	1	4
90-91—Capital District	AHL	17	9	9	18	4	—	—	—	—	—
—New York Islanders	NHL	52	6	6	12	10	—	—	—	—	—
91-92—Capital District	AHL	21	11	18	29	14	—	—	—	—	—
—New York Islanders	NHL	33	7	2	9	15	—	—	—	—	—
92-93—San Diego	IHL	48	26	49	75	26	14	4	7	11	6
—San Jose	NHL	30	6	2	8	6	—	—	—	—	—
93-94—San Diego	IHL	69	31	48	79	61	8	0	7	7	6
NHL totals		195	40	26	66	67	5	1	0	1	4

M

McDOUGALL, BILL
C, LIGHTNING

PERSONAL: Born August 10, 1966, in Mississauga, Ont. . . . 6-0/180. . . . Shoots right. . . . Full name: William Henry McDougall.
TRANSACTIONS/CAREER NOTES: Signed as free agent by Detroit Red Wings (March 1990). . . . Traded by Red Wings to Edmonton Oilers for C Max Middendorf (February 22, 1992). . . . Signed as free agent by Tampa Bay Lightning (August 13, 1993). . . . Hyperextended left elbow (October 23, 1993); missed two games.
HONORS: Won ECHL Most Valuable Player Award (1989-90). . . . Won ECHL Rookie of the Year Award (1989-90). . . . Named to ECHL All-Star first team (1989-90). . . . Won Jack Butterfield Trophy (1992-93).

Season Team	League	REGULAR SEASON					PLAYOFFS				
		Gms.	G	A	Pts.	PIM	Gms.	G	A	Pts.	PIM
89-90—Erie	ECHL	57	*80	68	*148	226	7	5	5	10	20
—Adirondack	AHL	11	10	7	17	4	2	1	1	2	2
90-91—Detroit	NHL	2	0	1	1	0	1	0	0	0	0
—Adirondack	AHL	71	47	53	100	192	2	1	2	3	2
91-92—Adirondack	AHL	45	28	24	52	112	—	—	—	—	—
—Cape Breton	AHL	22	8	18	26	36	4	0	1	1	8
92-93—Cape Breton	AHL	71	42	46	88	161	16	*26	*26	*52	30
—Edmonton	NHL	4	2	1	3	4	—	—	—	—	—
93-94—Tampa Bay	NHL	22	3	3	6	8	—	—	—	—	—
—Atlanta	IHL	48	17	30	47	141	14	12	7	19	30
NHL totals		28	5	5	10	12	1	0	0	0	0

McEACHERN, SHAWN
C, PENGUINS

PERSONAL: Born February 28, 1969, in Waltham, Mass. . . . 6-0/195. . . . Shoots left. . . . Name pronounced muh-GEH-kruhn.
HIGH SCHOOL: Matignon (Cambridge, Mass.).
COLLEGE: Boston University.
TRANSACTIONS/CAREER NOTES: Selected by Pittsburgh Penguins in sixth round (sixth Penguins pick, 110th overall) of NHL entry draft (June 13, 1987). . . . Traded by Penguins to Los Angeles Kings for D Marty McSorley (August 27, 1993). . . . Traded by Kings to Penguins for D Marty McSorley and D Jim Paek (February 15, 1994).
HONORS: Named to Hockey East All-Star second team (1989-90). . . . Named Hockey East Playoff Most Valuable Player (1990-91). . . . Named to NCAA All-America East first team (1990-91). . . . Named to Hockey East All-Star first team (1990-91).
MISCELLANEOUS: Member of Stanley Cup championship team (1992).

Season Team	League	REGULAR SEASON Gms.	G	A	Pts.	PIM	PLAYOFFS Gms.	G	A	Pts.	PIM
85-86—Matignon H.S.	Mass. H.S.	20	32	20	52	...	—	—	—	—	—
86-87—Matignon H.S.	Mass. H.S.	16	29	28	57	...	—	—	—	—	—
87-88—Matignon H.S.	Mass. H.S.	...	52	40	92	...	—	—	—	—	—
88-89—Boston University	Hockey East	36	20	28	48	32	—	—	—	—	—
89-90—Boston University	Hockey East	43	25	31	56	78	—	—	—	—	—
90-91—Boston University	Hockey East	41	34	48	82	43	—	—	—	—	—
91-92—U.S. national team	Int'l	57	26	23	49	38	—	—	—	—	—
—U.S. Olympic Team	Int'l	8	1	0	1	10	—	—	—	—	—
—Pittsburgh	NHL	15	0	4	4	0	19	2	7	9	4
92-93—Pittsburgh	NHL	84	28	33	61	46	12	3	2	5	10
93-94—Los Angeles	NHL	49	8	13	21	24	—	—	—	—	—
—Pittsburgh	NHL	27	12	9	21	10	6	1	0	1	2
NHL totals		175	48	59	107	80	37	6	9	15	16

McGILL, BOB
D, WHALERS

PERSONAL: Born April 27, 1962, in Edmonton.... 6-1/193.... Shoots right.... Full name: Robert Paul McGill.

TRANSACTIONS/CAREER NOTES: Selected by Toronto Maple Leafs as underage junior in second round (second Maple Leafs pick, 26th overall) of NHL entry draft (June 11, 1980).... Suspended three games by NHL (January 1985).... Suspended seven games by NHL (March 1, 1986).... Injured ankle (October 1986). ... Traded by Maple Leafs with RW Rick Vaive and LW Steve Thomas to Chicago Blackhawks for LW Al Secord and RW Ed Olczyk (September 3, 1987).... Broke cheekbone (November 4, 1989).... Fined $500 by NHL for fighting (December 28, 1989). ... Bruised left foot (May 1990).... Broke right foot in preparation for training camp (August 30, 1990); missed six weeks.... Selected by San Jose Sharks in NHL expansion draft (May 30, 1991).... Traded by Sharks with eighth-round pick in 1992 draft (G C.J. Denomme) to Detroit Red Wings for LW Johan Garpenlov (March 10, 1992).... Selected by Tampa Bay Lightning in NHL expansion draft (June 18, 1992).... Claimed on waivers by Toronto Maple Leafs (September 7, 1992).... Sprained knee (November 19, 1992); missed 13 games.... Broke jaw (March 27, 1993); missed final nine regular season games and first eight playoff games.... Signed as free agent by New York Islanders (September 7, 1993).... Claimed on waivers by Hartford Whalers (November 3, 1993).

Season Team	League	REGULAR SEASON Gms.	G	A	Pts.	PIM	PLAYOFFS Gms.	G	A	Pts.	PIM
78-79—Abbotsford	BCJHL	46	3	20	23	242	—	—	—	—	—
79-80—Victoria	WHL	70	3	18	21	230	15	0	5	5	64
80-81—Victoria	WHL	66	5	36	41	295	11	1	5	6	67
81-82—Toronto	NHL	68	1	10	11	263	—	—	—	—	—
82-83—Toronto	NHL	30	0	0	0	146	—	—	—	—	—
—St. Catharines	AHL	32	2	5	7	95	—	—	—	—	—
83-84—Toronto	NHL	11	0	2	2	51	—	—	—	—	—
—St. Catharines	AHL	55	1	15	16	217	6	0	0	0	26
84-85—Toronto	NHL	72	0	5	5	250	—	—	—	—	—
85-86—Toronto	NHL	61	1	4	5	141	9	0	0	0	35
86-87—Toronto	NHL	56	1	4	5	103	3	0	0	0	0
87-88—Chicago	NHL	67	4	7	11	131	3	0	0	0	2
88-89—Chicago	NHL	68	0	4	4	155	16	0	0	0	33
89-90—Chicago	NHL	69	2	10	12	204	5	0	0	0	2
90-91—Chicago	NHL	77	4	5	9	151	5	0	0	0	2
91-92—San Jose	NHL	62	3	1	4	70	—	—	—	—	—
—Detroit	NHL	12	0	0	0	21	8	0	0	0	14
92-93—Toronto	NHL	19	1	0	1	34	—	—	—	—	—
93-94—New York Islanders	NHL	3	0	0	0	5	—	—	—	—	—
—Hartford	NHL	30	0	3	3	41	—	—	—	—	—
NHL totals		705	17	55	72	1766	49	0	0	0	88

McGILL, RYAN
D, FLYERS

PERSONAL: Born February 28, 1969, in Prince Albert, Sask.... 6-2/205.... Shoots right.

TRANSACTIONS/CAREER NOTES: Sprained ankle (January 1986).... Underwent knee surgery (July 1986).... Selected by Chicago Blackhawks as underage junior in second round (second Blackhawks pick, 29th overall) of NHL entry draft (June 13, 1987).... Traded by Swift Current Broncos to Medicine Hat Tigers for G Kelly Hitching (September 1987).... Traded by Blackhawks with C Mike McNeil to Quebec Nordiques for LW Dan Vincelette and C Paul Gillis (March 5, 1991).... Traded by Nordiques to Blackhawks for C Mike Dagenais (September 26, 1991).... Traded by Blackhawks to Philadelphia Flyers for LW Tony Horacek (February 7, 1992). ... Bruised left wrist (October 15, 1993); missed one game.... Sprained left wrist (December 7, 1993); missed eight games.

HONORS: Named to IHL All-Star second team (1990-91).

Season Team	League	REGULAR SEASON Gms.	G	A	Pts.	PIM	PLAYOFFS Gms.	G	A	Pts.	PIM
85-86—Lethbridge	WHL	64	5	10	15	171	10	0	1	1	9
86-87—Swift Current	WHL	71	12	36	48	226	4	1	0	1	9
87-88—Medicine Hat	WHL	67	5	30	35	224	15	7	3	10	47
88-89—Medicine Hat	WHL	57	26	45	71	172	3	0	2	2	15
—Saginaw	IHL	8	2	0	2	12	6	0	0	0	42
89-90—Indianapolis	IHL	77	11	17	28	215	14	2	2	4	29
90-91—Indianapolis	IHL	63	11	40	51	200	—	—	—	—	—
—Halifax	AHL	7	0	4	4	6	—	—	—	—	—

M

Season Team	League	REGULAR SEASON					PLAYOFFS				
		Gms.	G	A	Pts.	Pen.	Gms.	G	A	Pts.	Pen.
91-92—Indianapolis	IHL	40	7	19	26	170	—	—	—	—	—
—Chicago	NHL	9	0	2	2	20	—	—	—	—	—
—Hershey	AHL	17	3	5	8	67	6	1	1	2	4
92-93—Hershey	AHL	4	0	2	2	26	—	—	—	—	—
—Philadelphia	NHL	72	3	10	13	238	—	—	—	—	—
93-94—Philadelphia	NHL	50	1	3	4	112	—	—	—	—	—
NHL totals		131	4	15	19	370					

McGOWAN, CAL
C, STARS

PERSONAL: Born June 19, 1970, in Sidney, Neb. . . . 6-1/185. . . . Shoots left. . . . Name pronounced muh-GOW-uhn.

TRANSACTIONS/CAREER NOTES: Selected by Minnesota North Stars in fourth round (third North Stars pick, 70th overall) of NHL entry draft (June 16, 1990). . . . North Stars franchise moved from Minnesota to Dallas and renamed Stars for 1993-94 season.

HONORS: Named to WHL (West) All-Star first team (1990-91).

Season Team	League	REGULAR SEASON					PLAYOFFS				
		Gms.	G	A	Pts.	PIM	Gms.	G	A	Pts.	PIM
86-87—Merritt	BCJHL	50	18	30	48	60	—	—	—	—	—
87-88—Merritt	BCJHL	50	24	62	86	40	4	2	7	9	14
88-89—Kamloops	WHL	72	21	31	52	44	—	—	—	—	—
89-90—Kamloops	WHL	71	33	44	77	78	17	4	5	9	42
90-91—Kamloops	WHL	71	58	81	139	147	12	7	7	14	24
91-92—Kalamazoo	IHL	77	13	30	43	62	1	0	0	0	2
92-93—Kalamazoo	IHL	78	18	42	60	62	—	—	—	—	—
93-94—Kalamazoo	IHL	49	9	18	27	48	4	0	0	0	2

McHUGH, MIKE
LW, FLYERS

PERSONAL: Born August 16, 1965, in Bowdoin, Mass. . . . 5-10/190. . . . Shoots left.

COLLEGE: Maine.

TRANSACTIONS/CAREER NOTES: Selected by Minnesota North Stars in NHL supplemental draft (June 10, 1988). . . . Selected by San Jose Sharks in NHL dispersal draft (May 30, 1991). . . . Traded by Sharks to Hartford Whalers for LW Paul Fenton (October 18, 1991). . . . Signed as free agent by Hershey Bears (1993).

HONORS: Named Hockey East Player of the Year (1987-88). . . . Named to NCAA All-America East second team (1987-88). . . . Named to Hockey East All-Rookie team (1987-88).

Season Team	League	REGULAR SEASON					PLAYOFFS				
		Gms.	G	A	Pts.	PIM	Gms.	G	A	Pts.	PIM
84-85—University of Maine	Hockey East	25	9	8	17	9	—	—	—	—	—
85-86—University of Maine	Hockey East	38	9	10	19	24	—	—	—	—	—
86-87—University of Maine	Hockey East	42	21	29	50	40	—	—	—	—	—
87-88—University of Maine	Hockey East	44	29	37	66	90	—	—	—	—	—
88-89—Kalamazoo	IHL	70	17	29	46	89	6	3	1	4	17
—Minnesota	NHL	3	0	0	0	2	—	—	—	—	—
89-90—Kalamazoo	IHL	73	14	17	31	96	10	0	6	6	16
—Minnesota	NHL	3	0	0	0	0	—	—	—	—	—
90-91—Kalamazoo	IHL	69	27	38	65	82	11	3	8	11	6
—Minnesota	NHL	6	0	0	0	0	—	—	—	—	—
91-92—San Jose	NHL	8	1	0	1	14	—	—	—	—	—
—Springfield	AHL	70	23	31	54	51	11	4	7	11	25
92-93—Springfield	AHL	67	19	27	46	111	11	5	2	7	12
93-94—Hershey	AHL	80	27	43	70	58	11	9	3	12	14
NHL totals		20	1	0	1	16					

McINNIS, MARTY
C/LW, ISLANDERS

PERSONAL: Born June 2, 1970, in Weymouth, Mass. . . . 6-0/185. . . . Shoots right. . . . Full name: Martin Edward McInnis. . . . Name pronounced muh-KIH-nihz.

HIGH SCHOOL: Milton (Mass.) Academy.

COLLEGE: Boston College.

TRANSACTIONS/CAREER NOTES: Selected by New York Islanders in eighth round (10th Islanders pick, 163rd overall) of NHL entry draft (June 11, 1988). . . . Injured eye (March 9, 1993); missed two games. . . . Fractured patella (March 27, 1993); missed remainder of regular season and 14 playoff games.

Season Team	League	REGULAR SEASON					PLAYOFFS				
		Gms.	G	A	Pts.	PIM	Gms.	G	A	Pts.	PIM
86-87—Milton Academy	Mass. H.S.	. . .	21	19	40	. . .	—	—	—	—	—
87-88—Milton Academy	Mass. H.S.	. . .	26	25	51	. . .	—	—	—	—	—
88-89—Boston College	Hockey East	39	13	19	32	8	—	—	—	—	—
89-90—Boston College	Hockey East	41	24	29	53	43	—	—	—	—	—
90-91—Boston College	Hockey East	38	21	36	57	40	—	—	—	—	—
91-92—U.S. national team	Int'l	54	15	19	34	20	—	—	—	—	—
—U.S. Olympic Team	Int'l	8	5	2	7	4	—	—	—	—	—
—New York Islanders	NHL	15	3	5	8	0	—	—	—	—	—
92-93—New York Islanders	NHL	56	10	20	30	24	3	0	1	1	0
—Capital District	AHL	10	4	12	16	2	—	—	—	—	—
93-94—New York Islanders	NHL	81	25	31	56	24	4	0	0	0	0
NHL totals		152	38	56	94	48	7	0	1	1	0

McINTYRE, IAN
LW, NORDIQUES

PERSONAL: Born February 12, 1974, in Montreal. . . . 6-0/184. . . . Shoots left.
TRANSACTIONS/CAREER NOTES: Selected by Quebec Nordiques in fourth round (fifth Nordiques pick, 76th overall) of NHL entry draft (June 20, 1992).
HONORS: Named to Can.HL All-Rookie team (1991-92). . . . Named to QMJHL All-Rookie team (1991-92).

| | | | —REGULAR SEASON— | | | | —PLAYOFFS— | | | |
Season Team	League	Gms.	G	A	Pts.	PIM	Gms.	G	A	Pts.	PIM
91-92—Beauport	QMJHL	63	29	32	61	250	—	—	—	—	—
92-93—Beauport	QMJHL	44	14	18	32	115	—	—	—	—	—
93-94—Beauport	QMJHL	71	23	53	76	129	12	3	11	14	27

McINTYRE, JOHN
C/LW, CANUCKS

PERSONAL: Born April 29, 1969, in Ravenswood, Ont. . . . 6-1/190. . . . Shoots left.
TRANSACTIONS/CAREER NOTES: Broke ankle (November 1985). . . . Severed nerve in right leg (February 1987). . . . Selected by Toronto Maple Leafs as underage junior in third round (third Maple Leafs pick, 49th overall) of NHL entry draft (June 13, 1987). . . . Traded by Maple Leafs to Los Angeles Kings for LW/C Mike Krushelnyski (November 9, 1990). . . . Sprained left thumb (October 22, 1991); missed two games. . . . Broke nose (March 9, 1992); missed five games. . . . Traded by Kings to New York Rangers for D Mike Hardy and fifth-round pick (G Frederick Beaubien) in 1993 draft (March 22, 1993). . . . Claimed on waivers by Vancouver Canucks (October 3, 1993). . . . Suffered concussion (October 21, 1993); missed four games. . . . Fractured foot (November 5, 1993); missed 16 games.
HONORS: Won Bobby Smith Trophy (1986-87).

| | | | —REGULAR SEASON— | | | | —PLAYOFFS— | | | |
Season Team	League	Gms.	G	A	Pts.	PIM	Gms.	G	A	Pts.	PIM
84-85—Strathroy Junior B	OHA	48	21	23	44	49	—	—	—	—	—
85-86—Guelph	OHL	30	4	6	10	25	20	1	5	6	31
86-87—Guelph	OHL	47	8	22	30	95	—	—	—	—	—
87-88—Guelph	OHL	39	24	18	42	109	—	—	—	—	—
88-89—Guelph	OHL	52	30	26	56	129	7	5	4	9	25
—Newmarket	AHL	3	0	2	2	7	5	1	1	2	20
89-90—Newmarket	AHL	6	2	2	4	12	—	—	—	—	—
—Toronto	NHL	59	5	12	17	117	2	0	0	0	2
90-91—Toronto	NHL	13	0	3	3	25	—	—	—	—	—
—Los Angeles	NHL	56	8	5	13	115	12	0	1	1	24
91-92—Los Angeles	NHL	73	5	19	24	100	6	0	4	4	12
92-93—Los Angeles	NHL	49	2	5	7	80	—	—	—	—	—
—New York Rangers	NHL	11	1	0	1	4	—	—	—	—	—
93-94—Vancouver	NHL	62	3	6	9	38	24	0	1	1	16
NHL totals		323	24	50	74	479	44	0	6	6	54

McKAY, RANDY
RW, DEVILS

PERSONAL: Born January 25, 1967, in Montreal. . . . 6-1/205. . . . Shoots right. . . . Full name: Hugh Randall McKay.
COLLEGE: Michigan Tech.
TRANSACTIONS/CAREER NOTES: Selected by Detroit Red Wings in sixth round (sixth Red Wings pick, 113th overall) of NHL entry draft (June 15, 1985). . . . Injured knee (February 1989). . . . Lacerated forearm (February 23, 1991). . . . Sent by Red Wings with C Dave Barr to New Jersey Devils as compensation for Red Wings signing free agent RW Troy Crowder (September 9, 1991). . . . Sprained knee (January 16, 1993); missed nine games. . . . Bruised shoulder (November 3, 1993); missed three games. . . . Bruised shoulder (January 24, 1994); missed three games.

| | | | —REGULAR SEASON— | | | | —PLAYOFFS— | | | |
Season Team	League	Gms.	G	A	Pts.	PIM	Gms.	G	A	Pts.	PIM
84-85—Michigan Tech	WCHA	25	4	5	9	32	—	—	—	—	—
85-86—Michigan Tech	WCHA	40	12	22	34	46	—	—	—	—	—
86-87—Michigan Tech	WCHA	39	5	11	16	46	—	—	—	—	—
87-88—Michigan Tech	WCHA	41	17	24	41	70	—	—	—	—	—
—Adirondack	AHL	10	0	3	3	12	6	0	4	4	0
88-89—Adirondack	AHL	58	29	34	63	170	14	4	7	11	60
—Detroit	NHL	3	0	0	0	0	2	0	0	0	2
89-90—Detroit	NHL	33	3	6	9	51	—	—	—	—	—
—Adirondack	AHL	36	16	23	39	99	6	3	0	3	35
90-91—Detroit	NHL	47	1	7	8	183	5	0	1	1	41
91-92—New Jersey	NHL	80	17	16	33	246	7	1	3	4	10
92-93—New Jersey	NHL	73	11	11	22	206	5	0	0	0	16
93-94—New Jersey	NHL	78	12	15	27	244	20	1	2	3	24
NHL totals		314	44	55	99	930	39	2	6	8	93

McKAY, SCOTT
C, MIGHTY DUCKS

PERSONAL: Born January 26, 1972, in Burlington, Ont. . . . 5-11/200. . . . Shoots right.
TRANSACTIONS/CAREER NOTES: Signed as free agent by Mighty Ducks of Anaheim (August 2, 1993).

| | | | —REGULAR SEASON— | | | | —PLAYOFFS— | | | |
Season Team	League	Gms.	G	A	Pts.	PIM	Gms.	G	A	Pts.	PIM
89-90—London	OHL	59	20	29	49	37	5	1	1	2	12
90-91—London	OHL	62	29	40	69	29	7	4	2	6	6
91-92—London	OHL	64	30	45	75	97	10	3	8	11	8

M

Season	Team	League	Gms.	G	A	Pts.	Pen.	Gms.	G	A	Pts.	Pen.
92-93—London		OHL	63	38	57	95	49	12	1	14	15	6
93-94—San Diego		IHL	58	10	6	16	35	9	2	5	7	6
—Anaheim		NHL	1	0	0	0	0	—	—	—	—	—
NHL totals			1	0	0	0	0					

McKEE, MIKE
D, NORDIQUES

PERSONAL: Born June 18, 1969, in Toronto.... 6-3/203.... Shoots right.
COLLEGE: Princeton.
TRANSACTIONS/CAREER NOTES: Selected by Quebec Nordiques (first pick overall) in NHL supplemental draft (June 16, 1990).
HONORS: Named to ECAC All-Star second team (1989-90).

Season	Team	League	Gms.	G	A	Pts.	PIM	Gms.	G	A	Pts.	PIM
88-89—Princeton University		ECAC	16	2	1	3	14	—	—	—	—	—
89-90—Princeton University		ECAC	26	7	18	25	18	—	—	—	—	—
90-91—Princeton University		ECAC	15	1	4	5	16	—	—	—	—	—
91-92—Princeton University		ECAC	27	12	17	29	34	—	—	—	—	—
92-93—Halifax		AHL	32	6	7	13	25	—	—	—	—	—
—Greensboro		ECHL	7	1	3	4	6	—	—	—	—	—
93-94—Cornwall		AHL	24	6	14	20	18	10	0	3	3	4
—Quebec		NHL	48	3	12	15	41	—	—	—	—	—
NHL totals			48	3	12	15	41					

McKENZIE, JIM
LW, PENGUINS

PERSONAL: Born November 3, 1969, in Gull Lake, Sask.... 6-3/205.... Shoots left.
TRANSACTIONS/CAREER NOTES: Selected by Hartford Whalers in fourth round (third Whalers pick, 73rd overall) of NHL entry draft (June 17, 1989).... Injured elbow (January 31, 1992); missed two games.... Suffered hip flexor (November 11, 1992); missed three games. ... Suffered hip flexor (December 5, 1992); missed four games.... Suffered back spasms (January 24, 1993); missed three games.... Suspended two games by NHL for game misconduct penalties (April 3, 1993).... Suspended three games by NHL for game misconduct penalties (April 10, 1993).... Traded by Whalers to Florida Panthers for D Alexander Godynyuk (December 16, 1993).... Traded by Panthers to Dallas Stars for fourth-round pick in 1994 draft (December 16, 1993).... Traded by Stars to Pittsburgh Penguins for RW Mike Needham (March 21, 1994).... Broke toe (November 24, 1993); missed four games.

Season	Team	League	Gms.	G	A	Pts.	PIM	Gms.	G	A	Pts.	PIM
85-86—Moose Jaw		WHL	3	0	2	2	0	—	—	—	—	—
86-87—Moose Jaw		WHL	65	5	3	8	125	9	0	0	0	7
87-88—Moose Jaw		WHL	62	1	17	18	134	—	—	—	—	—
88-89—Victoria		WHL	67	15	27	42	176	8	1	4	5	30
89-90—Binghamton		AHL	56	4	12	16	149	—	—	—	—	—
—Hartford		NHL	5	0	0	0	4	—	—	—	—	—
90-91—Springfield		AHL	24	3	4	7	102	—	—	—	—	—
—Hartford		NHL	41	4	3	7	108	6	0	0	0	8
91-92—Hartford		NHL	67	5	1	6	87	—	—	—	—	—
92-93—Hartford		NHL	64	3	6	9	202	—	—	—	—	—
93-94—Hartford		NHL	26	1	2	3	67	—	—	—	—	—
—Dallas		NHL	34	2	3	5	63	—	—	—	—	—
—Pittsburgh		NHL	11	0	0	0	16	3	0	0	0	0
NHL totals			248	15	15	30	547	9	0	0	0	8

McKIM, ANDREW
C, BRUINS

PERSONAL: Born July 6, 1970, in St. Johns, N.B.... 5-7/170.... Shoots right.... Full name: Andrew Harry McKim.
TRANSACTIONS/CAREER NOTES: Traded by Verdun Jr. Canadiens with C Trevor Boland to Hull Olympiques for third-round pick (G Martin Brodeur) in 1989 QMJHL draft (May 26, 1989).... Signed as free agent by Calgary Flames (October 5, 1990).... Signed as free agent by Boston Bruins (July 16, 1992).... Broke jaw (January 2, 1993); missed 17 games.
HONORS: Won Can.HL Most Sportsmanlike Player of the Year Award (1989-90).... Won Frank J. Selke Trophy (1989-90).... Won Michel Briere Trophy (1989-90).... Named to QMJHL All-Star first team (1989-90).

Season	Team	League	Gms.	G	A	Pts.	PIM	Gms.	G	A	Pts.	PIM
86-87—Verdun		QMJHL	70	28	59	87	12	—	—	—	—	—
87-88—Verdun		QMJHL	62	27	32	59	27	—	—	—	—	—
88-89—Verdun		QMJHL	68	50	56	106	36	—	—	—	—	—
89-90—Hull		QMJHL	70	66	64	130	44	11	8	10	18	8
90-91—Salt Lake City		IHL	74	30	30	60	48	4	0	2	2	6
91-92—St. John's		AHL	79	43	50	93	79	16	11	12	23	4
92-93—Providence		AHL	61	23	46	69	64	6	2	2	4	0
—Boston		NHL	7	1	3	4	0	—	—	—	—	—
93-94—Providence		AHL	46	13	24	37	49	—	—	—	—	—
—Boston		NHL	29	0	1	1	4	—	—	—	—	—
NHL totals			36	1	4	5	4					

M

McLAREN, STEVE
D, BLACKHAWKS

PERSONAL: Born February 3, 1975, in Owen Sound, Ont.... 6-0/194.... Shoots left.
HIGH SCHOOL: Widdlifield (North Bay, Ont.).
TRANSACTIONS/CAREER NOTES: Selected by Chicago Blackhawks in fourth round (third Blackhawks pick, 85th overall) of NHL entry draft (June 29, 1994).

			REGULAR SEASON					PLAYOFFS				
Season Team	League	Gms.	G	A	Pts.	PIM	Gms.	G	A	Pts.	PIM
93-94—North Bay	OHL	55	2	15	17	130	18	0	3	3	50

McLAUGHLIN, MIKE
LW, RANGERS

PERSONAL: Born March 29, 1970, in Springfield, Mass.... 6-1/175.... Shoots left. ... Full name: Michael Sean McLaughlin.
HIGH SCHOOL: Choate Rosemary Hall (Wallingford, Conn.).
COLLEGE: Vermont.
TRANSACTIONS/CAREER NOTES: Selected by Buffalo Sabres in sixth round (seventh Sabres pick, 118th overall) of NHL entry draft (June 11, 1988).... Signed as free agent by New York Rangers (August 17, 1993).

			REGULAR SEASON					PLAYOFFS				
Season Team	League	Gms.	G	A	Pts.	PIM	Gms.	G	A	Pts.	PIM
86-87—Choate Rosemary Hall	Conn. H.S.	...	19	18	37	...	—	—	—	—	—
87-88—Choate Rosemary Hall	Conn. H.S.	...	17	18	35	...	—	—	—	—	—
88-89—University of Vermont	ECAC	32	5	6	11	12	—	—	—	—	—
89-90—University of Vermont	ECAC	29	11	12	23	37	—	—	—	—	—
90-91—University of Vermont	ECAC	32	12	14	26	26	—	—	—	—	—
91-92—University of Vermont	ECAC	30	9	9	18	34	—	—	—	—	—
92-93—Rochester	AHL	71	19	35	54	27	16	4	2	6	8
93-94—Binghamton	AHL	56	11	13	24	33	—	—	—	—	—

McLEAN, JEFF
C, SHARKS

PERSONAL: Born October 6, 1969, in Port Moody, B.C.... 5-10/185.... Shoots left.
COLLEGE: North Dakota.
TRANSACTIONS/CAREER NOTES: Selected by San Jose Sharks in NHL supplemental draft (June 22, 1991).

			REGULAR SEASON					PLAYOFFS				
Season Team	League	Gms.	G	A	Pts.	PIM	Gms.	G	A	Pts.	PIM
87-88—North Dakota	WCHA	37	0	3	3	14	—	—	—	—	—
88-89—New Westminster	BCJHL	60	70	91	161	128	—	—	—	—	—
89-90—North Dakota	WCHA	45	10	16	26	42	—	—	—	—	—
90-91—North Dakota	WCHA	42	19	26	45	22	—	—	—	—	—
91-92—North Dakota	WCHA	39	27	43	70	40	—	—	—	—	—
92-93—Kansas City	IHL	60	21	23	44	45	10	3	1	4	2
93-94—Kansas City	IHL	69	27	30	57	44	—	—	—	—	—
—San Jose	NHL	6	1	0	1	0	—	—	—	—	—
NHL totals		6	1	0	1	0					

McLEAN, KIRK
G, CANUCKS

PERSONAL: Born June 26, 1966, in Willowdale, Ont.... 6-0/180.... Catches left.
TRANSACTIONS/CAREER NOTES: Selected by New Jersey Devils as underage junior in sixth round (sixth Devils pick, 107th overall) of NHL entry draft (June 9, 1984).... Traded by Devils with C Greg Adams and second-round pick in 1988 draft to Vancouver Canucks for C Patrik Sundstrom, fourth-round pick in 1988 draft (LW Matt Ruchty) and second-round pick in 1988 draft (September 15, 1987).... Suffered tendinitis in left wrist (February 25, 1991).
HONORS: Played in NHL All-Star Game (1990 and 1992).... Named to THE SPORTING NEWS All-Star second team (1991-92). ... Named to NHL All-Star second team (1991-92).
RECORDS: Holds NHL single-season playoff record for most minutes played by a goaltender—1,544 (1994).

			REGULAR SEASON							PLAYOFFS					
Season Team	League	Gms.	Min.	W	L	T	GA	SO	Avg.	Gms.	Min.	W	L	GA	SO	Avg.
83-84—Oshawa	OHL	17	940	5	9	0	67	0	4.28	—	—	—	—	—	—	—
84-85—Oshawa	OHL	47	2581	23	17	2	143	1	*3.32	5	271	1	3	21	0	4.65
85-86—Oshawa	OHL	51	2830	24	21	2	169	1	3.58	4	201	1	2	18	0	5.37
—New Jersey	NHL	2	111	1	1	0	11	0	5.95	—	—	—	—	—	—	—
86-87—New Jersey	NHL	4	160	1	1	0	10	0	3.75	—	—	—	—	—	—	—
—Maine	AHL	45	2606	15	23	4	140	1	3.22	—	—	—	—	—	—	—
87-88—Vancouver	NHL	41	2380	11	27	3	147	1	3.71	—	—	—	—	—	—	—
88-89—Vancouver	NHL	42	2477	20	17	3	127	4	3.08	5	302	2	3	18	0	3.58
89-90—Vancouver	NHL	*63	*3739	21	30	10	*216	0	3.47	—	—	—	—	—	—	—
90-91—Vancouver	NHL	41	1969	10	22	3	131	0	3.99	2	123	1	1	7	0	3.41
91-92—Vancouver	NHL	65	3852	†38	17	9	176	†5	2.74	13	785	6	7	33	†2	2.52
92-93—Vancouver	NHL	54	3261	28	21	5	184	3	3.39	12	754	6	6	42	0	3.34
93-94—Vancouver	NHL	52	3128	23	26	3	156	3	2.99	24	*1544	15	†9	59	†4	2.29
NHL totals		364	21077	153	162	36	1158	16	3.30	56	3508	30	26	159	6	2.72

McLENNAN, JAMIE
G, ISLANDERS

PERSONAL: Born June 30, 1971, in Edmonton.... 6-0/189.... Catches left.
TRANSACTIONS/CAREER NOTES: Selected by New York Islanders in third round (third Islanders pick, 48th overall) of NHL entry draft (June 22, 1991).
HONORS: Won Del Wilson Trophy (1990-91).... Named to WHL (East) All-Star first team (1990-91).

M

Season	Team	League	Gms.	Min.	W	L	T	GA	SO	Avg.	Gms.	Min.	W	L	GA	SO	Avg.
					REGULAR SEASON								PLAYOFFS				
88-89—Spokane	WHL	11	578	...	...	...	63	0	6.54	—							
—Lethbridge	WHL	7	368	...	...	...	22	0	3.59	—							
89-90—Lethbridge	WHL	34	1690	20	4	2	110	1	3.91	13	677	6	5	44	0	3.90	
90-91—Lethbridge	WHL	56	3230	32	18	4	205	0	3.81	*16	*970	8	8	*56	0	3.46	
91-92—Capital District	AHL	18	952	4	10	2	60	1	3.78	—							
—Richmond	ECHL	32	1837	16	12	†2	114	0	3.72	—							
92-93—Capital District	AHL	38	2171	17	14	6	117	1	3.23	1	20	0	1	5	0	15.00	
93-94—Salt Lake City	IHL	24	1320	8	12	†2	80	0	3.64	—							
—New York Islanders	NHL	22	1287	8	7	6	61	0	2.84	2	82	0	1	6	0	4.39	
NHL totals		22	1287	8	7	6	61	0	2.84	2	82	0	1	6	0	4.39	

McLLWAIN, DAVID
C/RW, SENATORS

PERSONAL: Born January 9, 1967, in Seaforth, Ont.... 6-0/185.... Shoots right.... Name pronounced MAK-ihl-wayn.

TRANSACTIONS/CAREER NOTES: Traded by Kitchener Rangers with D John Keller and RW Todd Stromback to North Bay Centennials for RW Ron Sanko, RW Peter Lisy, Richard Hawkins and D Brett MacDonald (November 1985).... Selected by Pittsburgh Penguins as underage junior in ninth round (ninth Penguins pick, 172nd overall) of NHL entry draft (June 21, 1986).... Traded by Penguins with C/LW Randy Cunneyworth and G Richard Tabaracci to Winnipeg Jets for RW Andrew McBain, D Jim Kyte and LW Randy Gilhen (June 17, 1989).... Injured wrist (October 28, 1990).... Tore medial collateral ligament of right knee (December 3, 1990); missed 16 games.... Traded by Jets with D Gord Donnelly, fifth-round pick in 1992 draft (LW Yuri Khmylev) and future considerations to Buffalo Sabres for LW Darrin Shannon, LW Mike Hartman and D Dean Kennedy (October 11, 1991).... Traded by Sabres with C Pierre Turgeon, RW Benoit Hogue and D Uwe Krupp to New York Islanders for C Pat LaFontaine, LW Randy Wood, D Randy Hillier and future considerations; Sabres received fourth-round pick (D Dean Melanson) in 1992 draft to complete deal (October 25, 1991).... Traded by Islanders with LW Ken Baumgartner to Toronto Maple Leafs for C Claude Loiselle and RW Daniel Marois (March 10, 1992).... Selected by Ottawa Senators in 1993 waiver draft (October 3, 1993).... Separated left shoulder (December 30, 1993); missed 17 games.... Suffered charley horse (April 7, 1994); missed one game.
HONORS: Named to OHL All-Star second team (1986-87).

Season	Team	League	Gms.	G	A	Pts.	PIM	Gms.	G	A	Pts.	PIM
				REGULAR SEASON					PLAYOFFS			
84-85—Kitchener	OHL	61	13	21	34	29	—					
85-86—Kitchener	OHL	13	7	7	14	12	—					
—North Bay	OHL	51	30	28	58	25	10	4	4	8	2	
86-87—North Bay	OHL	60	46	73	119	35	24	7	18	25	40	
87-88—Muskegon	IHL	9	4	6	10	23	6	2	3	5	8	
—Pittsburgh	NHL	66	11	8	19	40	—					
88-89—Muskegon	IHL	46	37	35	72	51	7	8	2	10	6	
—Pittsburgh	NHL	24	1	2	3	4	3	0	1	1	0	
89-90—Winnipeg	NHL	80	25	26	51	60	7	0	1	1	2	
90-91—Winnipeg	NHL	60	14	11	25	46	—					
91-92—Winnipeg	NHL	3	1	1	2	2	—					
—Buffalo	NHL	5	0	0	0	2	—					
—New York Islanders	NHL	54	8	15	23	28	—					
—Toronto	NHL	11	1	2	3	4	—					
92-93—Toronto	NHL	66	14	4	18	30	4	0	0	0	0	
93-94—Ottawa	NHL	66	17	26	43	48	—					
NHL totals		435	92	95	187	264	14	0	2	2	2	

McNEILL, MIKE
RW

PERSONAL: Born July 22, 1966, in Winona, Minn.... 6-1/175.... Shoots right.
COLLEGE: Notre Dame.

TRANSACTIONS/CAREER NOTES: Selected by St. Louis Blues in NHL supplemental draft (June 10, 1988).... Signed as free agent by Chicago Blackhawks (September 1989).... Traded by Blackhawks with D Ryan McGill to Quebec Nordiques for LW Dan Vincelette and C Paul Gillis (March 5, 1991).... Separated shoulder (February 15, 1992).
HONORS: Won N.R. (Bud) Poile Trophy (1989-90).

Season	Team	League	Gms.	G	A	Pts.	PIM	Gms.	G	A	Pts.	PIM
				REGULAR SEASON					PLAYOFFS			
84-85—University of Notre Dame	Indep.	28	16	26	42	12	—					
85-86—University of Notre Dame	Indep.	34	18	29	47	32	—					
86-87—University of Notre Dame	Indep.	30	21	16	37	24	—					
87-88—University of Notre Dame	Indep.	32	28	44	72	12	—					
88-89—Fort Wayne	IHL	75	27	35	62	12	11	1	5	6	2	
—Moncton	AHL	1	0	0	0	0	—					
89-90—Indianapolis	IHL	74	17	24	41	15	14	6	4	10	21	
90-91—Indianapolis	IHL	33	16	9	25	19	—					
—Chicago	NHL	23	2	2	4	6	—					
—Quebec	NHL	14	2	5	7	4	—					
91-92—Quebec	NHL	26	1	4	5	8	—					
—Halifax	AHL	30	10	8	18	20	—					
92-93—Milwaukee	IHL	75	17	17	34	34	6	2	0	2	0	
93-94—Milwaukee	IHL	78	21	25	46	40	4	0	1	1	6	
NHL totals		63	5	11	16	18						

McPHEE, MIKE

LW, STARS

PERSONAL: Born February 14, 1960, in Sydney, N.S.... 6-1/205.... Shoots left.... Full name: Michael Joseph McPhee.

COLLEGE: Rensselaer Polytechnic Institute (N.Y.).

TRANSACTIONS/CAREER NOTES: Selected by Montreal Canadiens in sixth round (eighth Canadiens pick, 124th overall) of NHL entry draft (June 11, 1980).... Broke hand (September 1982).... Injured ankle (January 10, 1986); missed 10 games.... Broke little toe on left foot (February 1989).... Pulled muscle in rib cage (April 8, 1989).... Tore abdominal muscle (October 7, 1989); missed 13 games.... Injured groin, knee and thumb (November 13, 1990); missed 16 games.... Bruised thigh (February 26, 1992); missed one game.... Traded by Canadiens to Minnesota North Stars for fifth-round pick (D Jeff Lank) in 1993 draft (August 17, 1992).... North Stars franchise moved from Minnesota to Dallas and renamed Stars for 1993-94 season.... Strained back (December 9, 1993); missed three games.... Bruised knee (February 13, 1994); missed one game.

HONORS: Played in NHL All-Star Game (1989).

MISCELLANEOUS: Member of Stanley Cup championship team (1986).

			REGULAR SEASON					PLAYOFFS			
Season Team	League	Gms.	G	A	Pts.	PIM	Gms.	G	A	Pts.	PIM
78-79—R.P.I.	ECAC	26	14	19	33	16	—	—	—	—	—
79-80—R.P.I.	ECAC	27	15	21	36	22	—	—	—	—	—
80-81—R.P.I.	ECAC	29	28	18	46	22	—	—	—	—	—
81-82—R.P.I.	ECAC	6	0	3	3	4	—	—	—	—	—
82-83—Nova Scotia	AHL	42	10	15	25	29	7	1	1	2	14
83-84—Nova Scotia	AHL	67	22	33	55	101	—	—	—	—	—
—Montreal	NHL	14	5	2	7	41	15	1	0	1	31
84-85—Montreal	NHL	70	17	22	39	120	12	4	1	5	32
85-86—Montreal	NHL	70	19	21	40	69	20	3	4	7	45
86-87—Montreal	NHL	79	18	21	39	58	17	7	2	9	13
87-88—Montreal	NHL	77	23	20	43	53	11	4	3	7	8
88-89—Montreal	NHL	73	19	22	41	74	20	4	7	11	30
89-90—Montreal	NHL	56	23	18	41	47	9	1	1	2	16
90-91—Montreal	NHL	64	22	21	43	56	13	1	7	8	12
91-92—Montreal	NHL	78	16	15	31	63	8	1	1	2	4
92-93—Minnesota	NHL	84	18	22	40	44	—	—	—	—	—
93-94—Dallas	NHL	79	20	15	35	36	9	2	1	3	2
NHL totals		744	200	199	399	661	134	28	27	55	193

McRAE, BASIL

LW, BLUES

PERSONAL: Born January 5, 1961, in Beaverton, Ont.... 6-2/205.... Shoots left.... Full name: Basil Paul McRae.... Name pronounced BA-zihl muh-KRAY.... Brother of Chris McRae, left winger, Toronto Maple Leafs and Detroit Red Wings (1987-88 through 1989-90).

TRANSACTIONS/CAREER NOTES: Selected by Quebec Nordiques as underage junior in fifth round (third Nordiques pick, 87th overall) of NHL entry draft (June 11, 1980).... Traded by Nordiques to Toronto Maple Leafs for D Richard Turmel (August 12, 1983).... Signed as free agent by Detroit Red Wings (August 1985).... Traded by Red Wings with LW John Ogrodnick and RW Doug Shedden to Nordiques for LW Brent Ashton, RW Mark Kumpel and D Gilbert Delorme (January 17, 1987).... Signed as free agent by Minnesota North Stars (July 1987).... Strained right knee ligaments (October 10, 1989); missed nine games.... Suspended five games and fined $500 by NHL for fighting (December 28, 1989).... Strained abdominal muscle (October 1990).... Underwent abdominal surgery (November 29, 1990); missed 35 games.... Severed tendon (February 29, 1992); missed final 17 games of regular season.... Selected by Tampa Bay Lightning in NHL expansion draft (June 18, 1992).... Fractured bone in lower leg (October 11, 1992); missed 35 games.... Traded by Lightning with D Doug Crossman to St. Louis Blues for LW Jason Ruff, sixth-round pick in 1996 draft and third-round pick in 1995 draft (January 28, 1993).... Suffered allergic reaction (November 16, 1993); missed two games.... Pulled abdominal muscle (January 3, 1994); missed seven games.... Underwent abdominal surgery (February 10, 1994); missed 18 games.... Injured abdomen (March 22, 1994); missed three games.... Injured rib (April 1, 1994); missed remainder of season.

			REGULAR SEASON					PLAYOFFS			
Season Team	League	Gms.	G	A	Pts.	PIM	Gms.	G	A	Pts.	PIM
77-78—Seneca Junior B	OHA	36	21	38	59	80	—	—	—	—	—
78-79—London	OMJHL	66	13	28	41	79	—	—	—	—	—
79-80—London	OMJHL	67	23	35	58	116	5	0	0	0	18
80-81—London	OMJHL	65	29	23	52	266	—	—	—	—	—
81-82—Fredericton	AHL	47	11	15	26	175	—	—	—	—	—
—Quebec	NHL	20	4	3	7	69	9	1	0	1	34
82-83—Fredericton	AHL	53	22	19	41	146	12	1	5	6	75
—Quebec	NHL	22	1	1	2	59	—	—	—	—	—
83-84—Toronto	NHL	3	0	0	0	19	—	—	—	—	—
—St. Catharines	AHL	78	14	25	39	187	6	0	0	0	40
84-85—St. Catharines	AHL	72	30	25	55	186	—	—	—	—	—
—Toronto	NHL	1	0	0	0	0	—	—	—	—	—
85-86—Detroit	NHL	4	0	0	0	5	—	—	—	—	—
—Adirondack	AHL	69	22	30	52	259	17	5	4	9	101
86-87—Detroit	NHL	36	2	2	4	193	—	—	—	—	—
—Quebec	NHL	33	9	5	14	149	13	3	1	4	*99
87-88—Minnesota	NHL	80	5	11	16	382	—	—	—	—	—
88-89—Minnesota	NHL	78	12	19	31	365	5	0	0	0	58
89-90—Minnesota	NHL	66	9	17	26	*351	7	1	0	1	24
90-91—Minnesota	NHL	40	1	3	4	224	22	1	1	2	*94
91-92—Minnesota	NHL	59	5	8	13	245	—	—	—	—	—
92-93—Tampa Bay	NHL	14	2	3	5	71	—	—	—	—	—
—St. Louis	NHL	33	1	3	4	98	11	0	1	1	24

M

Season Team	League	REGULAR SEASON					PLAYOFFS				
		Gms.	G	A	Pts.	Pen.	Gms.	G	A	Pts.	Pen.
93-94—St. Louis	NHL	40	1	2	3	103	2	0	0	0	12
NHL totals		529	52	77	129	2333	69	6	3	9	345

McRAE, KEN
RW, MAPLE LEAFS

PERSONAL: Born April 23, 1968, in Finch, Ont. . . . 6-1/195. . . . Shoots right. . . . Full name: Kenneth Duncan McRae.

TRANSACTIONS/CAREER NOTES: Selected by Quebec Nordiques as underage junior in first round (first Nordiques pick, 18th overall) of NHL entry draft (June 21, 1986). . . . Traded by Sudbury Wolves with C Andy Paquette and D Ken Alexander to Hamilton Steelhawks for C Dan Hie, C Joe Simon, RW Steve Locke, C Shawn Heaphy and D Jordan Fois (December 1986). . . . Lacerated right elbow (December 26, 1989); missed seven games. . . . Bruised shoulder (March 10, 1990). . . . Traded by Nordiques to Toronto Maple Leafs for D Leonard Esau (July 21, 1992).

Season Team	League	REGULAR SEASON					PLAYOFFS				
		Gms.	G	A	Pts.	PIM	Gms.	G	A	Pts.	PIM
84-85—Hawkesbury	COJHL	51	38	50	88	77	—	—	—	—	—
85-86—Sudbury	OHL	66	25	40	65	127	4	2	1	3	12
86-87—Sudbury	OHL	21	12	15	27	40	—	—	—	—	—
—Hamilton	OHL	20	7	12	19	25	7	1	1	2	12
87-88—Fredericton	AHL	—	—	—	—	—	3	0	0	0	8
—Quebec	NHL	1	0	0	0	0	—	—	—	—	—
—Hamilton	OHL	62	30	55	85	158	14	13	9	22	35
88-89—Halifax	AHL	41	20	21	41	87	—	—	—	—	—
—Quebec	NHL	37	6	11	17	68	—	—	—	—	—
89-90—Quebec	NHL	66	7	8	15	191	—	—	—	—	—
90-91—Quebec	NHL	12	0	0	0	36	—	—	—	—	—
—Halifax	AHL	60	10	36	46	193	—	—	—	—	—
91-92—Halifax	AHL	52	30	41	71	184	—	—	—	—	—
—Quebec	NHL	10	0	1	1	31	—	—	—	—	—
92-93—St. John's	AHL	64	30	44	74	135	9	6	6	12	27
—Toronto	NHL	2	0	0	0	2	—	—	—	—	—
93-94—St. John's	AHL	65	23	41	64	200	—	—	—	—	—
—Toronto	NHL	9	1	1	2	36	6	0	0	0	4
NHL totals		137	14	21	35	364	6	0	0	0	4

McREYNOLDS, BRIAN
C, KINGS

PERSONAL: Born January 5, 1965, in Penetanguishene, Ont. . . . 6-1/192. . . . Shoots left.

COLLEGE: Michigan State.

TRANSACTIONS/CAREER NOTES: Selected by New York Rangers as underage junior in sixth round (sixth Rangers pick, 112th overall) of NHL entry draft (June 15, 1985). . . . Signed as free agent by Winnipeg Jets (July 1989). . . . Traded by Jets to Rangers for C Simon Wheeldon (July 10, 1990). . . . Signed as free agent by Los Angeles Kings (July 29, 1993).

Season Team	League	REGULAR SEASON					PLAYOFFS				
		Gms.	G	A	Pts.	PIM	Gms.	G	A	Pts.	PIM
84-85—Orillia	OHA	48	40	54	94	...	—	—	—	—	—
85-86—Michigan State	CCHA	45	14	24	38	78	—	—	—	—	—
86-87—Michigan State	CCHA	45	16	24	40	68	—	—	—	—	—
87-88—Michigan State	CCHA	43	10	24	34	50	—	—	—	—	—
88-89—Canadian national team ...	Int'l	58	5	25	30	59	—	—	—	—	—
89-90—Winnipeg	NHL	9	0	2	2	4	—	—	—	—	—
—Moncton	AHL	72	18	41	59	87	—	—	—	—	—
90-91—Binghamton	AHL	77	30	42	72	74	10	0	4	4	6
—New York Rangers	NHL	1	0	0	0	0	—	—	—	—	—
91-92—Binghamton	AHL	48	19	28	47	22	7	2	2	4	12
92-93—Binghamton	AHL	79	30	70	100	88	14	3	10	13	18
93-94—Phoenix	IHL	51	14	33	47	65	—	—	—	—	—
—Los Angeles	NHL	20	1	3	4	4	—	—	—	—	—
NHL totals		30	1	5	6	8	—	—	—	—	—

McSORLEY, MARTY
D/RW, KINGS

PERSONAL: Born May 18, 1963, in Hamilton, Ont. . . . 6-1/225. . . . Shoots right. . . . Full name: Martin James McSorley.

TRANSACTIONS/CAREER NOTES: Signed as free agent by Pittsburgh Penguins (April 1983). . . . Traded by Penguins with C Tim Hrynewich to Edmonton Oilers for G Gilles Meloche (August 1985). . . . Suspended by NHL for AHL incident (March 1987). . . . Sprained knee (November 1987). . . . Suspended three playoff games by NHL for spearing (April 23, 1988). . . . Traded by Oilers with C Wayne Gretzky and LW/C Mike Krushelnyski to Los Angeles Kings for C Jimmy Carson, LW Martin Gelinas, first-round picks in 1989 (traded to New Jersey), 1991 (LW Martin Rucinsky) and 1993 (D Nick Stajduhar) drafts and cash (August 9, 1988). . . . Injured shoulder (December 31, 1988). . . . Sprained knee (February 1989). . . . Suspended four games by NHL for game-misconduct penalties (1989-90). . . . Twisted right knee (October 14, 1990); missed four games. . . . Twisted ankle (February 9, 1991). . . . Suspended three games by NHL for striking another player with a gloved hand (March 2, 1991). . . . Suffered from throat virus (November 23, 1991); missed six games. . . . Sprained shoulder (February 19, 1992); missed three games. . . . Suspended six off-days and fined $500 by NHL for cross-checking (October 31, 1992). . . . Suspended one game by NHL for game misconduct penalties (November 27, 1992). . . . Traded by Kings to Pittsburgh Penguins for C Shawn McEachern (August 27, 1993). . . .

Sprained ankle (November 16, 1993); missed eight games. . . . Traded by Penguins with D Jim Paek to Los Angeles Kings for RW Thomas Sandstrom and C Shawn McEachern (February 15, 1993). . . . Suspended four games without pay and fined $500 for eye-gouging incident (February 23, 1994). . . . Sprained abdomen (April 7, 1994); missed remainder of season.
HONORS: Shared Alka-Seltzer Plus Award with Theoren Fleury (1990-91).
MISCELLANEOUS: Member of Stanley Cup championship teams (1987 and 1988).

			REGULAR SEASON					PLAYOFFS			
Season	Team	League	Gms.	G	A	Pts.	PIM	Gms.	G	A	Pts.	PIM
81-82	Belleville	OHL	58	6	13	19	234	—	—	—	—	—
82-83	Belleville	OHL	70	10	41	51	183	4	0	0	0	7
	Baltimore	AHL	2	0	0	0	22	—	—	—	—	—
83-84	Pittsburgh	NHL	72	2	7	9	224	—	—	—	—	—
84-85	Baltimore	AHL	58	6	24	30	154	14	0	7	7	47
	Pittsburgh	NHL	15	0	0	0	15	—	—	—	—	—
85-86	Edmonton	NHL	59	11	12	23	265	8	0	2	2	50
	Nova Scotia	AHL	9	2	4	6	34	—	—	—	—	—
86-87	Edmonton	NHL	41	2	4	6	159	21	4	3	7	65
	Nova Scotia	AHL	7	2	2	4	48	—	—	—	—	—
87-88	Edmonton	NHL	60	9	17	26	223	16	0	3	3	67
88-89	Los Angeles	NHL	66	10	17	27	350	11	0	2	2	33
89-90	Los Angeles	NHL	75	15	21	36	322	10	1	3	4	18
90-91	Los Angeles	NHL	61	7	32	39	221	12	0	0	0	58
91-92	Los Angeles	NHL	71	7	22	29	268	6	1	0	1	21
92-93	Los Angeles	NHL	81	15	26	41	*399	24	4	6	10	60
93-94	Pittsburgh	NHL	47	3	18	21	139	—	—	—	—	—
	Los Angeles	NHL	18	4	6	10	55	—	—	—	—	—
NHL totals			666	85	182	267	2640	108	10	19	29	372

McSWEEN, DON
D, MIGHTY DUCKS

PERSONAL: Born June 9, 1964, in Detroit. . . . 5-11/197. . . . Shoots left. . . . Full name: Donald Kennedy McSween.
COLLEGE: Michigan State.
TRANSACTIONS/CAREER NOTES: Selected by Buffalo Sabres in eighth round (10th Sabres pick, 154th overall) of NHL entry draft (June 8, 1983). . . . Signed as free agent by Detroit Red Wings (August 29, 1992). . . . Loaned to San Diego Gulls (October 6, 1992). . . . Signed as free agent by Mighty Ducks of Anaheim (January 12, 1994). . . . Suffered from chicken pox (March 7, 1994); missed seven games.
HONORS: Named to NCAA All-America West second team (1985-86 and 1986-87). . . . Named to NCAA All-Tournament team (1986-87). . . . Named to CCHA All-Star first team (1985-86 and 1986-87). . . . Named to AHL All-Star first team (1989-90).

			REGULAR SEASON					PLAYOFFS			
Season	Team	League	Gms.	G	A	Pts.	PIM	Gms.	G	A	Pts.	PIM
83-84	Michigan State	CCHA	46	10	26	36	30	—	—	—	—	—
84-85	Michigan State	CCHA	44	2	23	25	52	—	—	—	—	—
85-86	Michigan State	CCHA	45	9	29	38	18	—	—	—	—	—
86-87	Michigan State	CCHA	45	7	23	30	34	—	—	—	—	—
87-88	Rochester	AHL	63	9	29	38	108	6	0	1	1	15
	Buffalo	NHL	5	0	1	1	4	—	—	—	—	—
88-89	Rochester	AHL	66	7	22	29	45	—	—	—	—	—
89-90	Buffalo	NHL	4	0	0	0	6	—	—	—	—	—
	Rochester	AHL	70	16	43	59	43	17	3	10	13	12
90-91	Rochester	AHL	74	7	44	51	57	15	2	5	7	8
91-92	Rochester	AHL	75	6	32	38	60	16	5	6	11	18
92-93	San Diego	IHL	80	15	40	55	85	14	1	2	3	10
93-94	San Diego	IHL	38	5	13	18	36	—	—	—	—	—
	Anaheim	NHL	32	3	9	12	39	—	—	—	—	—
NHL totals			41	3	10	13	49					

MEKESHKIN, DMITRI
D, CAPITALS

PERSONAL: Born January 29, 1976, in Izhevsk, U.S.S.R. . . . 6-1/174. . . . Shoots left.
TRANSACTIONS/CAREER NOTES: Selected by Washington Capitals in sixth round (sixth Capitals pick, 145th overall) of NHL entry draft (June 29, 1994).

			REGULAR SEASON					PLAYOFFS			
Season	Team	League	Gms.	G	A	Pts.	PIM	Gms.	G	A	Pts.	PIM
93-94	Avangard Omsk	CIS	21	0	0	0	14	3	0	0	0	2

MELANSON, DEAN
D, SABRES

PERSONAL: Born November 19, 1973, in Antigonish, N.S. . . . 6-0/213. . . . Shoots right. . . . Name pronounced muh-LAHN-suhn.
TRANSACTIONS/CAREER NOTES: Selected by Buffalo Sabres in fourth round (fourth Sabres pick, 80th overall) of NHL entry draft (June 20, 1992).

			REGULAR SEASON					PLAYOFFS			
Season	Team	League	Gms.	G	A	Pts.	PIM	Gms.	G	A	Pts.	PIM
90-91	St. Hyacinthe	QMJHL	69	10	17	27	110	4	0	1	1	2
91-92	St. Hyacinthe	QMJHL	42	8	19	27	158	6	1	2	3	25
92-93	St. Hyacinthe	QMJHL	57	13	29	42	253	—	—	—	—	—
	Rochester	AHL	8	0	1	1	6	14	1	6	7	18
93-94	Rochester	AHL	80	1	21	22	138	4	0	1	1	2

MELLANBY, SCOTT

RW, PANTHERS

PERSONAL: Born June 11, 1966, in Montreal.... 6-1/205.... Shoots right.... Full name: Scott Edgar Mellanby.
HIGH SCHOOL: Henry Carr (Rexdale, Ont.).
COLLEGE: Wisconsin.

TRANSACTIONS/CAREER NOTES: Selected by Philadelphia Flyers as underage junior in second round (first Flyers pick, 27th overall) of NHL entry draft (June 9, 1984).... Lacerated right index finger (October 1987).... Severed nerve and damaged tendon in left forearm (August 1989); missed first 20 games of season.... Suffered viral infection (November 1989).... Traded by Flyers with LW Craig Berube and C Craig Fisher to Edmonton Oilers for RW Dave Brown, D Corey Foster and rights to RW Jari Kurri (May 30, 1991).... Injured shoulder (February 14, 1993); missed 15 games.... Selected by Florida Panthers in NHL expansion draft (June 24, 1993).... Fractured nose and lacerated face (February 1, 1994); missed four games.

			REGULAR SEASON					PLAYOFFS			
Season Team	League	Gms.	G	A	Pts.	PIM	Gms.	G	A	Pts.	PIM
83-84—Henry Carr H.S.	MTHL	39	37	37	74	97	—	—	—	—	—
84-85—University of Wisconsin	WCHA	40	14	24	38	60	—	—	—	—	—
85-86—University of Wisconsin	WCHA	32	21	23	44	89	—	—	—	—	—
—Philadelphia	NHL	2	0	0	0	0	—	—	—	—	—
86-87—Philadelphia	NHL	71	11	21	32	94	24	5	5	10	46
87-88—Philadelphia	NHL	75	25	26	51	185	7	0	1	1	16
88-89—Philadelphia	NHL	76	21	29	50	183	19	4	5	9	28
89-90—Philadelphia	NHL	57	6	17	23	77	—	—	—	—	—
90-91—Philadelphia	NHL	74	20	21	41	155	—	—	—	—	—
91-92—Edmonton	NHL	80	23	27	50	197	16	2	1	3	29
92-93—Edmonton	NHL	69	15	17	32	147	—	—	—	—	—
93-94—Florida	NHL	80	30	30	60	149	—	—	—	—	—
NHL totals		584	151	188	339	1187	66	11	12	23	119

MESSIER, JOBY

D, RANGERS

PERSONAL: Born March 2, 1970, in Regina, Sask.... 6-0/193.... Shoots right.... Full name: Marcus Cyril Messier.... Name pronounced MEHZ-yay.... Brother of Mitch Messier, center/right winger in Dallas Stars system; and cousin of Mark Messier, center, New York Rangers.

COLLEGE: Michigan State.
TRANSACTIONS/CAREER NOTES: Broke right arm (December 1984).... Broke right arm (September 1987).... Selected by New York Rangers in sixth round (seventh Rangers pick, 118th overall) of NHL entry draft (June 17, 1989).
HONORS: Named to NCAA All-America West first team (1991-92).... Named to CCHA All-Star first team (1991-92).
MISCELLANEOUS: Member of Stanley Cup championship team (1994).

			REGULAR SEASON					PLAYOFFS			
Season Team	League	Gms.	G	A	Pts.	PIM	Gms.	G	A	Pts.	PIM
87-88—Notre Dame	SJHL	53	9	22	31	208	—	—	—	—	—
88-89—Michigan State	CCHA	46	2	10	12	70	—	—	—	—	—
89-90—Michigan State	CCHA	42	1	11	12	58	—	—	—	—	—
90-91—Michigan State	CCHA	39	5	11	16	71	—	—	—	—	—
91-92—Michigan State	CCHA	44	13	16	29	85	—	—	—	—	—
92-93—Binghamton	AHL	60	5	16	21	63	14	1	1	2	6
—New York Rangers	NHL	11	0	0	0	6	—	—	—	—	—
93-94—New York Rangers	NHL	4	0	2	2	0	—	—	—	—	—
—Binghamton	AHL	42	6	14	20	58	—	—	—	—	—
NHL totals		15	0	2	2	6	—	—	—	—	—

MESSIER, MARK

C, RANGERS

PERSONAL: Born January 18, 1961, in Edmonton.... 6-1/205.... Shoots left.... Full name: Mark Douglas Messier.... Name pronounced MEHZ-yay.... Brother of Paul Messier, center, Colorado Rockies (1978-79); cousin of Mitch Messier, center/right winger in Dallas Stars system; cousin of Joby Messier, defenseman in New York Rangers system; and brother-in-law of John Blum, defenseman for four NHL teams (1982-83 through 1989-90).

TRANSACTIONS/CAREER NOTES: Given five-game trial by Indianapolis Racers (November 1978).... Signed as free agent by Cincinnati Stingers (January 1979).... Selected by Edmonton Oilers in third round (second Oilers pick, 48th overall) of NHL entry draft (August 9, 1979).... Injured ankle (November 7, 1981).... Chipped bone in wrist (March 1983).... Suspended six games by NHL for hitting another player with stick (January 18, 1984).... Sprained knee ligaments (November 1984).... Suspended 10 games by NHL for injuring another player (December 26, 1984).... Bruised left foot (December 3, 1985); missed 17 games.... Suspended and fined by Oilers after refusing to report to training camp (October 1987); missed three weeks of camp.... Suspended six games by NHL for injuring another player with stick (October 23, 1988).... Twisted left knee (January 28, 1989).... Strained right knee (February 3, 1989).... Bruised left knee (February 12, 1989).... Sprained left knee ligaments (October 16, 1990); missed 10 games.... Reinjured left knee (December 12, 1990); missed three games.... Reinjured knee (December 22, 1990); missed nine games.... Broke left thumb (February 11, 1991); missed eight games.... Missed one game due to contract dispute (October 1991).... Traded by Oilers with future considerations to New York Rangers for C Bernie Nicholls, LW Louie DeBrusk, RW Steven Rice and future considerations (October 4, 1991); Oilers traded D Jeff Beukeboom to Rangers for D David Shaw to complete deal (November 12, 1991).... Sprained ligament in wrist (January 19, 1993); missed six games.... Strained rib cage muscle (February 27, 1993); missed two games.... Strained rib cage muscle (March 11, 1993); missed one game.... Suspended three off-days and fined $500 by NHL for stick-swinging incident (March 18, 1993). ...Sprained wrist (December 22, 1993); missed six games.... Bruised thigh (March 16, 1994); missed two games.

HONORS: Named to THE SPORTING NEWS All-Star first team (1981-82, 1982-83, 1989-90 and 1991-92).... Named to NHL All-Star first team (1981-82, 1982-83, 1989-90 and 1991-92).... Played in NHL All-Star Game (1982-1984, 1986, 1988 through 1992 and 1994).... Won Conn Smythe Trophy (1983-84).... Named to NHL All-Star second team (1983-84).... Named to THE SPORTING NEWS All-Star second team (1986-87).... Named NHL Player of the Year by THE SPORTING NEWS (1989-90 and 1991-92).... Won Hart Memorial Trophy (1989-90 and 1991-92).... Won Lester B. Pearson Award (1989-90 and 1991-92).

RECORDS: Holds NHL career playoff record for most shorthanded goals—11. . . . Shares NHL single-game playoff record for most shorthanded goals—2 (April 21, 1992).

MISCELLANEOUS: Member of Stanley Cup championship teams (1984, 1985, 1987, 1988, 1990 and 1994).

Season Team	League	REGULAR SEASON Gms.	G	A	Pts.	PIM	PLAYOFFS Gms.	G	A	Pts.	PIM
76-77—Spruce Grove	AJHL	57	27	39	66	91	—	—	—	—	—
77-78—St. Albert	AJHL			Statistics unavailable.							
—Portland	WHL	—	—	—	—	—	7	4	1	5	2
78-79—Indianapolis	WHA	5	0	0	0	0	—	—	—	—	—
—Cincinnati	WHA	47	1	10	11	58	—	—	—	—	—
79-80—Houston	CHL	4	0	3	3	4	—	—	—	—	—
—Edmonton	NHL	75	12	21	33	120	3	1	2	3	2
80-81—Edmonton	NHL	72	23	40	63	102	9	2	5	7	13
81-82—Edmonton	NHL	78	50	38	88	119	5	1	2	3	8
82-83—Edmonton	NHL	77	48	58	106	72	15	15	6	21	14
83-84—Edmonton	NHL	73	37	64	101	165	19	8	18	26	19
84-85—Edmonton	NHL	55	23	31	54	57	18	12	13	25	12
85-86—Edmonton	NHL	63	35	49	84	68	10	4	6	10	18
86-87—Edmonton	NHL	77	37	70	107	73	21	12	16	28	16
87-88—Edmonton	NHL	77	37	74	111	103	19	11	23	34	29
88-89—Edmonton	NHL	72	33	61	94	130	7	1	11	12	8
89-90—Edmonton	NHL	79	45	84	129	79	22	9	*22	†31	20
90-91—Edmonton	NHL	53	12	52	64	34	18	4	11	15	16
91-92—New York Rangers	NHL	79	35	72	107	76	11	7	7	14	6
92-93—New York Rangers	NHL	75	25	66	91	72	—	—	—	—	—
93-94—New York Rangers	NHL	76	26	58	84	76	23	12	18	30	33
WHA totals		52	1	10	11	58					
NHL totals		1081	478	838	1316	1346	200	99	160	259	214

MESSIER, MITCH
C/RW, STARS

PERSONAL: Born August 21, 1965, in Regina, Sask. . . . 6-2/210. . . . Shoots right. . . . Full name: Mitch Ron Messier. . . . Brother of Joby Messier, defenseman in New York Rangers system; and cousin of Mark Messier, center, New York Rangers.
HIGH SCHOOL: Notre Dame (Sask.).

COLLEGE: Michigan State.

TRANSACTIONS/CAREER NOTES: Selected by Minnesota North Stars in third round (fourth North Stars pick, 56th overall) of NHL entry draft (June 8, 1983). . . . Bruised knee (November 1987). . . . North Stars franchise moved from Minnesota to Dallas and renamed Stars for 1993-94 season.

HONORS: Named to NCAA All-America East first team (1986-87). . . . Named to CCHA All-Star first team (1986-87).

Season Team	League	REGULAR SEASON Gms.	G	A	Pts.	PIM	PLAYOFFS Gms.	G	A	Pts.	PIM
81-82—Notre Dame H.S.	Sask. H.S.	26	8	20	28	. . .	—	—	—	—	—
82-83—Notre Dame H.S.	Sask. H.S.	60	108	73	181	160	—	—	—	—	—
83-84—Michigan State	CCHA	37	6	15	21	22	—	—	—	—	—
84-85—Michigan State	CCHA	42	12	21	33	46	—	—	—	—	—
85-86—Michigan State	CCHA	38	24	40	64	36	—	—	—	—	—
86-87—Michigan State	CCHA	45	44	48	92	89	—	—	—	—	—
87-88—Kalamazoo	IHL	69	29	37	66	42	4	2	1	3	0
—Minnesota	NHL	13	0	1	1	11	—	—	—	—	—
88-89—Minnesota	NHL	3	0	1	1	0	—	—	—	—	—
—Kalamazoo	IHL	67	34	46	80	71	6	4	3	7	0
89-90—Minnesota	NHL	2	0	0	0	0	—	—	—	—	—
—Kalamazoo	IHL	65	26	58	84	56	8	4	3	7	25
90-91—Minnesota	NHL	2	0	0	0	0	—	—	—	—	—
—Kalamazoo	IHL	73	30	46	76	34	11	4	8	12	2
91-92—Kalamazoo	IHL	77	43	33	76	42	12	3	3	6	25
92-93—Milwaukee	IHL	62	18	23	41	84	6	0	1	1	0
93-94—Fort Wayne	IHL	69	33	27	60	77	14	8	6	14	14
NHL totals		20	0	2	2	11					

METLYUK, DENIS
C, FLYERS

PERSONAL: Born January 30, 1972, in Togliatti, U.S.S.R. . . . 5-10/183. . . . Shoots left. . . . Name pronounced MEHT-lee-ook.
TRANSACTIONS/CAREER NOTES: Selected by Philadelphia Flyers in second round (third Flyers pick, 31st overall) of NHL entry draft (June 20, 1992).

Season Team	League	REGULAR SEASON Gms.	G	A	Pts.	PIM	PLAYOFFS Gms.	G	A	Pts.	PIM
90-91—Lada Togliatti	USSR	25	5	6	11	8	—	—	—	—	—
91-92—Lada Togliatti	CIS	26	0	1	1	6	—	—	—	—	—
92-93—Lada Togliatti	CIS	39	7	12	19	20	10	0	1	1	2
93-94—Hershey	AHL	73	8	13	21	46	11	4	2	6	4

MICHAYLUK, DAVE
LW, PENGUINS

PERSONAL: Born May 18, 1962, in Wakaw, Sask. . . . 5-10/185. . . . Shoots left.
TRANSACTIONS/CAREER NOTES: Selected by Philadelphia Flyers as underage junior in fourth round (fifth Flyers pick, 65th overall) of NHL entry draft (June 10, 1981). . . . Lacerated right arm (May 1989). . . . Signed as free agent by Pittsburgh Penguins

M

(May 24, 1989).
HONORS: Won Stewart (Butch) Paul Memorial Trophy (1980-81).... Named to WHL All-Star second team (1980-81 and 1981-82).... Named to IHL All-Star second team (1984-85, 1991-92 and 1992-93).... Named to IHL All-Star first team (1986-87 through 1989-90).... Won James Gatschene Memorial Trophy (1988-89).... Won Leo P. Lamoureux Memorial Trophy (1988-89).... Named Turner Cup Playoff Most Valuable Player (1988-89).
MISCELLANEOUS: Member of Stanley Cup championship team (1992).

Season Team	League	REGULAR SEASON					PLAYOFFS				
		Gms.	G	A	Pts.	PIM	Gms.	G	A	Pts.	PIM
79-80—Prince Albert	AJHL	60	46	67	113	49	—	—	—	—	—
80-81—Regina	WHL	72	62	71	133	39	11	5	12	17	8
81-82—Regina	WHL	72	62	111	173	128	12	16	24	*40	23
—Philadelphia	NHL	1	0	0	0	0	—	—	—	—	—
82-83—Philadelphia	NHL	13	2	6	8	8	—	—	—	—	—
—Maine	AHL	69	32	40	72	16	8	0	2	2	0
83-84—Springfield	AHL	79	18	44	62	37	4	0	0	0	2
84-85—Hershey	AHL	3	0	2	2	2	—	—	—	—	—
—Kalamazoo	IHL	82	*66	33	99	49	11	7	7	14	0
85-86—Nova Scotia	AHL	3	0	1	1	0	—	—	—	—	—
—Muskegon	IHL	77	52	52	104	73	14	6	9	15	12
86-87—Muskegon	IHL	82	47	53	100	69	15	2	14	16	8
87-88—Muskegon	IHL	81	*56	81	137	46	6	2	0	2	18
88-89—Muskegon	IHL	80	50	72	*122	84	13	†9	12	†21	24
89-90—Muskegon	IHL	79	*51	51	102	80	15	8	†14	*22	10
90-91—Muskegon	IHL	83	40	62	102	116	5	2	2	4	4
91-92—Muskegon	IHL	82	39	63	102	154	13	9	8	17	4
—Pittsburgh	NHL	—	—	—	—	—	7	1	1	2	0
92-93—Cleveland	IHL	82	47	65	112	104	4	1	2	3	4
93-94—Cleveland	IHL	81	48	51	99	92	—	—	—	—	—
NHL totals		14	2	6	8	8	7	1	1	2	0

MIDDENDORF, MAX
C

PERSONAL: Born August 18, 1967, in Syracuse, N.Y.... 6-4/210.... Shoots right.
TRANSACTIONS/CAREER NOTES: Selected by Quebec Nordiques as underage junior in third round (third Nordiques pick, 57th overall) of NHL entry draft (June 15, 1985). ... Dislocated thumb (February 1, 1987).... Suspended five games by AHL for stick-fighting (January 26, 1990).... Traded by Nordiques to Edmonton Oilers for ninth-round pick (D Brent Brekke) in 1991 draft (November 10, 1990).... Traded by Oilers to Detroit Red Wings for C Bill McDougall (February 22, 1992).... Traded by Fort Wayne Komets to San Diego Gulls (January 4, 1993) to complete deal involving RW Peter Hankinson (December 17, 1992).

Season Team	League	REGULAR SEASON					PLAYOFFS				
		Gms.	G	A	Pts.	PIM	Gms.	G	A	Pts.	PIM
84-85—Sudbury	OHL	63	16	28	44	106	—	—	—	—	—
85-86—Sudbury	OHL	61	40	42	82	71	4	4	2	6	11
86-87—Quebec	NHL	6	1	4	5	4	—	—	—	—	—
—Sudbury	OHL	31	31	29	60	7	—	—	—	—	—
—Kitchener	OHL	17	7	15	22	6	4	2	5	7	5
87-88—Fredericton	AHL	38	11	13	24	57	12	4	4	8	18
—Quebec	NHL	1	0	0	0	0	—	—	—	—	—
88-89—Halifax	AHL	72	41	39	80	85	4	1	2	3	6
89-90—Quebec	NHL	3	0	0	0	0	—	—	—	—	—
—Halifax	AHL	48	20	17	37	60	—	—	—	—	—
90-91—Fort Wayne	IHL	15	9	11	20	12	—	—	—	—	—
—Cape Breton	AHL	44	14	21	35	82	4	0	1	1	6
—Edmonton	NHL	3	1	0	1	2	—	—	—	—	—
91-92—Cape Breton	AHL	51	20	19	39	108	—	—	—	—	—
—Adirondack	AHL	6	3	5	8	12	5	0	1	1	16
92-93—Fort Wayne	IHL	24	9	13	22	8	—	—	—	—	—
—San Diego	IHL	30	15	11	26	25	8	1	2	3	8
93-94—Fort Wayne	IHL	36	16	20	36	43	9	1	2	3	24
NHL totals		13	2	4	6	6					

MIEHM, KEVIN
C, BLUES

PERSONAL: Born September 10, 1969, in Kitchener, Ont.... 6-2/195.... Shoots left.... Name pronounced MEE-yuhm.
TRANSACTIONS/CAREER NOTES: Selected by St. Louis Blues as underage junior in third round (second Blues pick, 54th overall) of NHL entry draft (June 13, 1987).... Suffered sore groin (October 7, 1993); missed two games.... Injured knee (October 28, 1993); missed six games.
HONORS: Won William Hanley Trophy (1988-89).

Season Team	League	REGULAR SEASON					PLAYOFFS				
		Gms.	G	A	Pts.	PIM	Gms.	G	A	Pts.	PIM
85-86—Kitchener Jr. B	OHA	1	0	0	0	0	—	—	—	—	—
86-87—Oshawa	OHL	61	12	27	39	19	26	1	8	9	12
87-88—Oshawa	OHL	52	16	36	52	30	7	2	5	7	0
88-89—Oshawa	OHL	63	43	79	122	19	6	6	6	12	0
—Peoria	IHL	3	1	1	2	0	4	0	2	2	0

Season Team	League	REGULAR SEASON					PLAYOFFS				
		Gms.	G	A	Pts.	Pen.	Gms.	G	A	Pts.	Pen.
89-90—Peoria	IHL	76	23	38	61	20	3	0	0	0	4
90-91—Peoria	IHL	73	25	39	64	14	16	5	7	12	2
91-92—Peoria	IHL	66	21	53	74	22	10	3	4	7	2
92-93—Peoria	IHL	30	12	33	45	13	4	0	1	1	2
—St. Louis	NHL	8	1	3	4	4	2	0	1	1	0
93-94—St. Louis	NHL	14	0	1	1	4	—	—	—	—	—
—Peoria	IHL	11	2	3	5	0	4	1	0	1	0
NHL totals		22	1	4	5	8	2	0	1	1	0

MIGNACCA, SONNY
G, CANUCKS

PERSONAL: Born January 4, 1974, in Winnipeg. . . . 5-8/175. . . . Catches left. . . . Name pronounced migh-NAH-kuh.

TRANSACTIONS/CAREER NOTES: Selected by Vancouver in ninth round (10th Canucks pick, 213th overall) of NHL entry draft (June 20, 1992).

HONORS: Named to WHL (East) All-Star second team (1991-92 and 1993-94). . . . Won Four Broncos Memorial Trophy (1993-94). . . . Named WHL Player of the Year (1993-94).

Season Team	League	REGULAR SEASON							PLAYOFFS						
		Gms.	Min.	W	L	T	GA	SO	Avg.	Gms.	Min.	W	L	GA	SO	Avg.
90-91—Medicine Hat	WHL	33	1743	17	9	2	121	0	4.17	1	13	0	0	2	0	9.23
91-92—Medicine Hat	WHL	56	3207	35	19	0	189	2	3.54	4	240	0	4	17	0	4.25
92-93—Medicine Hat	WHL	50	2724	18	25	2	210	1	4.63	10	605	5	5	36	0	3.57
93-94—Medicine Hat	WHL	60	3361	26	23	5	183	2	3.27	3	180	0	3	17	0	5.67

MIKULCHIK, OLEG
D, JETS

PERSONAL: Born June 27, 1964, in Minsk, U.S.S.R. . . . 6-2/200. . . . Shoots right. . . . Name pronounced OH-lehg mih-KOOL-chik.

TRANSACTIONS/CAREER NOTES: Signed as free agent by Winnipeg Jets (July 1992). . . . Sprained elbow (December 22, 1993); missed five games.

Season Team	League	REGULAR SEASON					PLAYOFFS				
		Gms.	G	A	Pts.	PIM	Gms.	G	A	Pts.	PIM
89-90—Dynamo Moscow	USSR	32	1	3	4	31	—	—	—	—	—
90-91—Dynamo Moscow	USSR	36	2	6	8	40	—	—	—	—	—
91-92—Khimik	CIS	15	3	2	5	20	—	—	—	—	—
—New Haven	AHL	30	3	3	6	63	—	—	—	—	—
92-93—Moncton	AHL	75	6	20	26	159	—	—	—	—	—
93-94—Moncton	AHL	67	9	38	47	121	21	2	10	12	18
—Winnipeg	NHL	4	0	1	1	17	—	—	—	—	—
NHL totals		4	0	1	1	17					

MILLEN, COREY
C, DEVILS

PERSONAL: Born April 29, 1964, in Cloquet, Minn. . . . 5-7/170. . . . Shoots right.

HIGH SCHOOL: Cloquet (Minn.).

COLLEGE: Minnesota.

TRANSACTIONS/CAREER NOTES: Selected by New York Rangers as underage player in third round (third Rangers pick, 57th overall) of NHL entry draft (June 9, 1982). . . . Injured knee and underwent surgery (November 1982). . . . Injured shoulder (October 1984). . . . Tested positive for a non-anabolic steroid in a random test at World Cup Tournament and was banned from play (April 1989). . . . Sprained left knee ligaments and underwent surgery (September 18, 1989); missed four months. . . . Underwent surgery to left knee (August 1990); missed four months. . . . Traded by Rangers to Los Angeles Kings for C Randy Gilhen (December 23, 1991). . . . Suffered shoulder contusion (February 29, 1992); missed one game. . . . Strained back (October 13, 1992); missed four games. . . . Strained groin (December 22, 1992); missed 38 games. . . . Traded by Kings to New Jersey Devils for fifth-round pick (G Jason Saal) in 1993 draft (June 26, 1993).

HONORS: Named to WCHA All-Star second team (1984-85 through 1986-87). . . . Named to NCAA All-America West second team (1985-86). . . . Named to NCAA All-Tournament team (1986-87).

Season Team	League	REGULAR SEASON					PLAYOFFS				
		Gms.	G	A	Pts.	PIM	Gms.	G	A	Pts.	PIM
81-82—Cloquet H.S.	Minn. H.S.	18	46	35	81	. . .	—	—	—	—	—
82-83—University of Minnesota	WCHA	21	14	15	29	18	—	—	—	—	—
83-84—U.S. national team	Int'l	45	15	11	26	10	—	—	—	—	—
—U.S. Olympic Team	Int'l	6	0	0	0	2	—	—	—	—	—
84-85—University of Minnesota	WCHA	38	28	36	64	60	—	—	—	—	—
85-86—University of Minnesota	WCHA	48	41	42	83	64	—	—	—	—	—
86-87—University of Minnesota	WCHA	42	36	29	65	62	—	—	—	—	—
87-88—U.S. Olympic Team	Int'l	51	46	45	91	. . .	—	—	—	—	—
88-89—Ambri Piotta	Switzerland	36	32	22	54	18	6	4	3	7	0
89-90—New York Rangers	NHL	4	0	0	0	2	—	—	—	—	—
—Flint	IHL	11	4	5	9	2	—	—	—	—	—
90-91—Binghamton	AHL	40	19	37	56	68	6	0	7	7	8
—New York Rangers	NHL	4	3	1	4	0	6	1	2	3	0
91-92—New York Rangers	NHL	11	1	4	5	10	—	—	—	—	—
—Binghamton	AHL	15	8	7	15	44	—	—	—	—	—
—Los Angeles	NHL	46	20	21	41	44	6	0	1	1	6
92-93—Los Angeles	NHL	42	23	16	39	42	23	2	4	6	12
93-94—New Jersey	NHL	78	20	30	50	52	7	1	0	1	2
NHL totals		185	67	72	139	150	42	4	7	11	20

M

MILLER, AARON
D, NORDIQUES

PERSONAL: Born August 11, 1971, in Buffalo, N.Y. . . . 6-3/197. . . . Shoots right. . . . Full name: Aaron Michael Miller.
COLLEGE: Vermont.
TRANSACTIONS/CAREER NOTES: Selected by New York Rangers in fifth round (sixth Rangers pick, 88th overall) of NHL entry draft (June 17, 1989). . . . Traded by Rangers with fifth-round pick in 1991 draft (LW Bill Lindsay) to Quebec Nordiques for D Joe Cirella (January 17, 1991).
HONORS: Named to ECAC All-Rookie team (1989-90). . . . Named to NCAA All-America East second team (1992-93). . . . Named to ECAC All-Star first team (1992-93).

			REGULAR SEASON					PLAYOFFS				
Season	Team	League	Gms.	G	A	Pts.	PIM	Gms.	G	A	Pts.	PIM
87-88—Niagara		NAJHL	30	4	9	13	2	—	—	—	—	—
88-89—Niagara		NAJHL	59	24	38	62	60	—	—	—	—	—
89-90—University of Vermont		ECAC	31	1	15	16	24	—	—	—	—	—
90-91—University of Vermont		ECAC	30	3	7	10	22	—	—	—	—	—
91-92—University of Vermont		ECAC	31	3	16	19	36	—	—	—	—	—
92-93—University of Vermont		ECAC	30	4	13	17	16	—	—	—	—	—
93-94—Cornwall		AHL	64	4	10	14	49	13	0	2	2	10
—Quebec		NHL	1	0	0	0	0	—	—	—	—	—
NHL totals			1	0	0	0	0					

MILLER, BRAD
D

PERSONAL: Born July 23, 1969, in Edmonton. . . . 6-4/226. . . . Shoots left.
TRANSACTIONS/CAREER NOTES: Selected by Buffalo Sabres as underage junior in second round (second Sabres pick, 22nd overall) of NHL entry draft (June 13, 1987). . . . Suspended three games by AHL for abusing an official (February 23, 1990). . . . Suspended nine games by AHL for abuse of officials and continuing to fight (April 11, 1990). . . . Selected by Ottawa Senators in NHL expansion draft (June 18, 1992). . . . Traded by Senators to Toronto Maple Leafs for ninth-round pick (Pavol Demitra) in 1993 draft (February 25, 1993). . . . Traded by Maple Leafs with LW Jeff Perry to Calgary Flames for LW Todd Gillingham and D Paul Holden (September 3, 1993).

			REGULAR SEASON					PLAYOFFS				
Season	Team	League	Gms.	G	A	Pts.	PIM	Gms.	G	A	Pts.	PIM
85-86—Regina		WHL	71	2	14	16	99	10	1	1	2	4
86-87—Regina		WHL	67	10	38	48	154	3	0	0	0	6
87-88—Regina		WHL	61	9	34	43	148	4	1	1	2	12
—Rochester		AHL	3	0	0	0	4	2	0	0	0	2
88-89—Buffalo		NHL	7	0	0	0	6	—	—	—	—	—
—Rochester		AHL	3	0	0	0	4	—	—	—	—	—
—Regina		WHL	34	8	18	26	95	—	—	—	—	—
89-90—Buffalo		NHL	1	0	0	0	0	—	—	—	—	—
—Rochester		AHL	60	2	10	12	273	8	1	0	1	52
90-91—Buffalo		NHL	13	0	0	0	67	—	—	—	—	—
—Rochester		AHL	49	0	9	9	248	12	0	4	4	67
91-92—Buffalo		NHL	42	1	4	5	192	—	—	—	—	—
—Rochester		AHL	27	0	4	4	113	11	0	0	0	61
92-93—Ottawa		NHL	11	0	0	0	42	—	—	—	—	—
—New Haven		AHL	41	1	9	10	138	—	—	—	—	—
—St. John's		AHL	20	0	3	3	61	8	0	2	2	10
93-94—Calgary		NHL	8	0	1	1	14	—	—	—	—	—
—Saint John		AHL	36	3	12	15	174	6	1	0	1	21
NHL totals			82	1	5	6	321					

MILLER, JASON
C, DEVILS

PERSONAL: Born March 1, 1971, in Edmonton. . . . 6-1/195. . . . Shoots left.
TRANSACTIONS/CAREER NOTES: Separated shoulder (May 1986). . . . Selected by New Jersey Devils in first round (second Devils pick, 18th overall) of NHL entry draft (June 17, 1989). . . . Suffered sore back (January 23, 1993); missed two games.
HONORS: Named to WHL (East) All-Star second team (1990-91).

			REGULAR SEASON					PLAYOFFS				
Season	Team	League	Gms.	G	A	Pts.	PIM	Gms.	G	A	Pts.	PIM
87-88—Medicine Hat		WHL	71	11	18	29	28	15	0	1	1	2
88-89—Medicine Hat		WHL	72	51	55	106	44	3	1	2	3	2
89-90—Medicine Hat		WHL	66	43	56	99	40	3	3	2	5	0
90-91—New Jersey		NHL	1	0	0	0	0	—	—	—	—	—
—Medicine Hat		WHL	66	60	76	136	31	12	9	10	19	8
91-92—Utica		AHL	71	23	32	55	31	4	1	3	4	0
—New Jersey		NHL	3	0	0	0	0	—	—	—	—	—
92-93—Utica		AHL	72	28	42	70	43	5	4	4	8	2
—New Jersey		NHL	2	0	0	0	0	—	—	—	—	—
93-94—Albany		AHL	77	22	53	75	65	5	1	1	2	4
NHL totals			6	0	0	0	0					

MILLER, KELLY
LW, CAPITALS

PERSONAL: Born March 3, 1963, in Lansing, Mich. . . . 5-11/197. . . . Shoots left. . . . Full name: Kelly David Miller. . . . Brother of Kevin Miller, right winger, St. Louis Blues; and brother of Kip Miller, center in San Jose Sharks system.
HIGH SCHOOL: Eastern (Lansing, Mich.).
COLLEGE: Michigan State.

Season Team	League	REGULAR SEASON					PLAYOFFS				
		Gms.	G	A	Pts.	PIM	Gms.	G	A	Pts.	PIM
81-82—Michigan State	CCHA	40	11	19	30	21	—	—	—	—	—
82-83—Michigan State	CCHA	36	16	19	35	12	—	—	—	—	—
83-84—Michigan State	CCHA	46	28	21	49	12	—	—	—	—	—
84-85—Michigan State	CCHA	43	27	23	50	21	—	—	—	—	—
—New York Rangers	NHL	5	0	2	2	2	3	0	0	0	2
85-86—New York Rangers	NHL	74	13	20	33	52	16	3	4	7	4
86-87—New York Rangers	NHL	38	6	14	20	22	—	—	—	—	—
—Washington	NHL	39	10	12	22	26	7	2	2	4	0
87-88—Washington	NHL	80	9	23	32	35	14	4	4	8	10
88-89—Washington	NHL	78	19	21	40	45	6	1	0	1	2
89-90—Washington	NHL	80	18	22	40	49	15	3	5	8	23
90-91—Washington	NHL	80	24	26	50	29	11	4	2	6	6
91-92—Washington	NHL	78	14	38	52	49	7	1	2	3	4
92-93—Washington	NHL	84	18	27	45	32	6	0	3	3	2
93-94—Washington	NHL	84	14	25	39	32	11	2	7	9	0
NHL totals		720	145	230	375	373	96	20	29	49	53

MILLER, KEVIN
LW, BLUES

PERSONAL: Born August 9, 1965, in Lansing, Mich.... 5-11/190.... Shoots right.... Full name: Kevin Bradley Miller.... Brother of Kelly Miller, left winger, Washington Capitals; and brother of Kip Miller, center in San Jose Sharks system.
HIGH SCHOOL: Eastern (Lansing, Mich.).
COLLEGE: Michigan State.
TRANSACTIONS/CAREER NOTES: Selected by New York Rangers in 10th round (10th Rangers pick, 202nd overall) of NHL entry draft (June 9, 1984).... Pulled groin (September 1990).... Sprained shoulder (December 1990).... Traded by Rangers with D Dennis Vial and RW Jim Cummings to Detroit Red Wings for RW Joe Kocur and D Per Djoos (March 5, 1991).... Traded by Red Wings to Washington Capitals for RW Dino Ciccarelli (June 20, 1992).... Traded by Capitals to St. Louis Blues for D Paul Cavallini (November 1, 1992).... Suffered sore knee (November 3, 1993); missed two games.... Injured knee (November 24, 1993); missed two games.... Injured hip (March 30, 1994); missed one game.... Suffered sore groin (April 8, 1994); missed three games.

Season Team	League	REGULAR SEASON					PLAYOFFS				
		Gms.	G	A	Pts.	PIM	Gms.	G	A	Pts.	PIM
84-85—Michigan State	CCHA	44	11	29	40	84	—	—	—	—	—
85-86—Michigan State	CCHA	45	19	52	71	112	—	—	—	—	—
86-87—Michigan State	CCHA	42	25	56	81	63	—	—	—	—	—
87-88—Michigan State	CCHA	9	6	3	9	18	—	—	—	—	—
—U.S. Olympic Team	Int'l	50	32	34	66	...	—	—	—	—	—
88-89—New York Rangers	NHL	24	3	5	8	2	—	—	—	—	—
—Denver	IHL	55	29	47	76	19	4	2	1	3	2
89-90—New York Rangers	NHL	16	0	5	5	2	1	0	0	0	0
—Flint	IHL	48	19	23	42	41	—	—	—	—	—
90-91—New York Rangers	NHL	63	17	27	44	63	—	—	—	—	—
—Detroit	NHL	11	5	2	7	4	7	3	2	5	20
91-92—Detroit	NHL	80	20	26	46	53	9	0	2	2	4
92-93—Washington	NHL	10	0	3	3	35	—	—	—	—	—
—St. Louis	NHL	72	24	22	46	65	10	0	3	3	11
93-94—St. Louis	NHL	75	23	25	48	83	3	1	0	1	4
NHL totals		351	92	115	207	307	30	4	7	11	39

MILLER, KIP
C, ISLANDERS

PERSONAL: Born June 11, 1969, in Lansing, Mich.... 5-11/160.... Shoots left.... Full name: Kip Charles Miller.... Brother of Kelly Miller, left winger, Washington Capitals; and brother of Kevin Miller, left winger, St. Louis Blues.
HIGH SCHOOL: Eastern (Lansing, Mich.).
COLLEGE: Michigan State.
TRANSACTIONS/CAREER NOTES: Selected by Quebec Nordiques in fourth round (fourth Nordiques pick, 72nd overall) of NHL entry draft (June 13, 1987).... Injured hand and forearm in off-ice accident (November 1987).... Traded by Nordiques to Minnesota North Stars for LW Steve Maltais (March 8, 1992).... North Stars franchise moved from Minnesota to Dallas and renamed Stars for 1993-94 season.... Signed as free agent by San Jose Sharks (August 10, 1993).... Signed as free agent by New York Islanders (August 2, 1994).
HONORS: Named to NCAA All-America West first team (1988-89 and 1989-90).... Named to CCHA All-Star first team (1988-89 and 1989-90).... Won Hobey Baker Memorial Trophy (1989-90).... Named CCHA Player of the Year (1989-90).

Season Team	League	REGULAR SEASON					PLAYOFFS				
		Gms.	G	A	Pts.	PIM	Gms.	G	A	Pts.	PIM
86-87—Michigan State	CCHA	45	22	19	41	96	—	—	—	—	—
87-88—Michigan State	CCHA	39	16	25	41	51	—	—	—	—	—
88-89—Michigan State	CCHA	47	32	45	77	94	—	—	—	—	—
89-90—Michigan State	CCHA	45	*48	53	*101	60	—	—	—	—	—

M

Season Team	League	REGULAR SEASON					PLAYOFFS				
		Gms.	G	A	Pts.	Pen.	Gms.	G	A	Pts.	Pen.
90-91—Quebec	NHL	15	4	3	7	7	—	—	—	—	—
—Halifax	AHL	66	36	33	69	40	—	—	—	—	—
91-92—Quebec	NHL	36	5	10	15	12	—	—	—	—	—
—Halifax	AHL	24	9	17	26	8	—	—	—	—	—
—Minnesota	NHL	3	1	2	3	2	—	—	—	—	—
—Kalamazoo	IHL	6	1	8	9	4	12	3	9	12	12
92-93—Kalamazoo	IHL	61	17	39	56	59	—	—	—	—	—
93-94—San Jose	NHL	11	2	2	4	6	—	—	—	—	—
—Kansas City	IHL	71	38	54	92	51	—	—	—	—	—
NHL totals		65	12	17	29	27					

MILLER, KURTIS
LW, BLUES

PERSONAL: Born June 1, 1970, in Bemidji, Minn. . . . 5-11/180. . . . Shoots left. . . . Full name: Kurtis Michael Miller.
HIGH SCHOOL: Greenway (Coleraine, Minn.).
COLLEGE: Lake Superior State (Mich.).
TRANSACTIONS/CAREER NOTES: Injured back (December 1986). . . . Injured back and shoulder (January 1989). . . . Suffered hip pointer (June 1989). . . . Selected by St. Louis Blues in sixth round (fourth Blues pick, 117th overall) of NHL entry draft (June 16, 1990).
HONORS: Named USHL Most Valuable Player (1989-90). . . . Won USHL Best Forward Trophy (1989-90). . . . Named to USHL All-Star first team (1989-90).

Season Team	League	REGULAR SEASON					PLAYOFFS				
		Gms.	G	A	Pts.	PIM	Gms.	G	A	Pts.	PIM
88-89—Rochester	USHL	48	28	21	49	50	—	—	—	—	—
89-90—Rochester	USHL	50	50	39	89	56	—	—	—	—	—
90-91—Lake Superior State	CCHA	45	10	12	22	48	—	—	—	—	—
91-92—Lake Superior State	CCHA	15	6	7	13	32	—	—	—	—	—
92-93—Lake Superior State	CCHA	26	9	14	23	24	—	—	—	—	—
93-94—Lake Superior State	CCHA	40	19	23	42	58	—	—	—	—	—

MILLS, CRAIG
RW, JETS

PERSONAL: Born August 27, 1976, in Toronto. . . . 6-0/174. . . . Shoots right.
TRANSACTIONS/CAREER NOTES: Selected by Winnipeg Jets in fifth round (fifth Jets pick, 108th overall) of NHL entry draft (June 29, 1994).

Season Team	League	REGULAR SEASON					PLAYOFFS				
		Gms.	G	A	Pts.	PIM	Gms.	G	A	Pts.	PIM
92-93—St. Michaels Tier II	Jr. A	44	8	12	20	51	—	—	—	—	—
93-94—Belleville	OHL	63	15	18	33	88	12	2	1	3	11

M

MIRONOV, BORIS
D, OILERS

PERSONAL: Born March 21, 1972, in Moscow, U.S.S.R. . . . 6-3/220. . . . Shoots right. . . . Name pronounced mih-RAH-nahf. . . . Brother of Dimitri Mironov, defenseman, Toronto Maple Leafs.
TRANSACTIONS/CAREER NOTES: Selected by Winnipeg Jets in second round (second Jets pick, 27th overall) of NHL entry draft (June 20, 1992). . . . Suffered back contusion (February 2, 1994); missed three games. . . . Traded by Jets with C Mats Lindgren and first-round (C Jason Bonsignore) and fourth-round (RW Adam Copeland) picks in 1994 draft to Edmonton Oilers for D Dave Mason and sixth-round pick in 1994 draft (March 15, 1994).
HONORS: Named to NHL All-Rookie team (1993-94).

Season Team	League	REGULAR SEASON					PLAYOFFS				
		Gms.	G	A	Pts.	PIM	Gms.	G	A	Pts.	PIM
88-89—CSKA Moscow	USSR	1	0	0	0	0	—	—	—	—	—
89-90—CSKA Moscow	USSR	7	0	0	0	0	—	—	—	—	—
90-91—CSKA Moscow	USSR	36	1	5	6	16	—	—	—	—	—
91-92—CSKA Moscow	CIS	36	2	1	3	22	—	—	—	—	—
92-93—CSKA Moscow	CIS	19	0	5	5	20	—	—	—	—	—
93-94—Winnipeg	NHL	65	7	22	29	96	—	—	—	—	—
—Edmonton	NHL	14	0	2	2	14	—	—	—	—	—
NHL totals		79	7	24	31	110					

MIRONOV, DMITRI
D, MAPLE LEAFS

PERSONAL: Born December 25, 1965, in Moscow, U.S.S.R. . . . 6-2/214. . . . Shoots right. . . . Name pronounced mih-RAH-nehf. . . . Brother of Boris Mironov, defenseman, Edmonton Oilers.
TRANSACTIONS/CAREER NOTES: Selected by Toronto Maple Leafs in eighth round (seventh Maple Leafs pick, 160th overall) of NHL entry draft (June 22, 1991). . . . Broke nose (March 23, 1992). . . . Suffered infected tooth (March 18, 1993); missed 10 games. . . . Suffered quad contusion (December 28, 1993); missed one game. . . . Lacerated lip (March 7, 1994); missed two games. . . . Suffered rib and muscle strain (April 2, 1994); missed remainder of season.
MISCELLANEOUS: Member of gold-medal-winning Unified Olympic team (1992).

Season Team	League	REGULAR SEASON					PLAYOFFS				
		Gms.	G	A	Pts.	PIM	Gms.	G	A	Pts.	PIM
90-91—Soviet Wings	USSR	44	16	12	28	22	—	—	—	—	—
91-92—Soviet Wings	USSR	30	11	16	27	44	—	—	—	—	—

Season	Team	League	Gms.	G	A	Pts.	Pen.	Gms.	G	A	Pts.	Pen.
	—Unified Olympic Team.......	Int'l	8	3	1	4	4	—	—	—	—	—
	—Toronto..........................	NHL	7	1	0	1	0	—	—	—	—	—
92-93	—Toronto..........................	NHL	59	7	24	31	40	14	1	2	3	2
93-94	—Toronto..........................	NHL	76	9	27	36	78	18	6	9	15	6
	NHL totals.................		142	17	51	68	118	32	7	11	18	8

MODANO, MIKE
RW/C, STARS

PERSONAL: Born June 7, 1970, in Livonia, Mich.... 6-3/190.... Shoots left.... Name pronounced muh-DAH-noh.
TRANSACTIONS/CAREER NOTES: Selected by Minnesota North Stars in first round (first North Stars pick, first overall) of NHL entry draft (June 11, 1988).... Fractured scaphoid bone in left wrist (January 24, 1989).... Broke nose (March 4, 1990).... Pulled groin (November 30, 1992); missed two games.... North Stars franchise moved from Minnesota to Dallas and renamed Stars for 1993-94 season.... Strained medial collateral knee ligament (January 6, 1994); missed six games.... Suffered concussion (February 26, 1994); missed two games.
HONORS: Named to WHL (East) All-Star first team (1988-89).... Named to NHL All-Rookie team (1989-90).... Played in NHL All-Star Game (1993).

Season	Team	League	Gms.	G	A	Pts.	PIM	Gms.	G	A	Pts.	PIM
86-87	—Prince Albert....................	WHL	70	32	30	62	96	8	1	4	5	4
87-88	—Prince Albert....................	WHL	65	47	80	127	80	9	7	11	18	18
88-89	—Prince Albert....................	WHL	41	39	66	105	74	—	—	—	—	—
	—Minnesota	NHL	—	—	—	—	—	2	0	0	0	0
89-90	—Minnesota	NHL	80	29	46	75	63	7	1	1	2	12
90-91	—Minnesota	NHL	79	28	36	64	65	23	8	12	20	16
91-92	—Minnesota	NHL	76	33	44	77	46	7	3	2	5	4
92-93	—Minnesota	NHL	82	33	60	93	83	—	—	—	—	—
93-94	—Dallas	NHL	76	50	43	93	54	9	7	3	10	16
	NHL totals......................................		393	173	229	402	311	48	19	18	37	48

MODIN, FREDRIK
LW, MAPLE LEAFS

PERSONAL: Born October 8, 1974, in Jonkoping, Sweden.... 6-3/202.... Shoots left.
TRANSACTIONS/CAREER NOTES: Selected by Toronto Maple Leafs in third round (third Maple Leafs pick, 64th overall) of NHL entry draft (June 29, 1994).

Season	Team	League	Gms.	G	A	Pts.	PIM	Gms.	G	A	Pts.	PIM
91-92	—Sundsvall Timra	Swed. Dv.II	11	1	0	1	0	—	—	—	—	—
92-93	—Sundsvall Timra	Swed. Dv.II	30	5	7	12	12	—	—	—	—	—
93-94	—Sundsvall Timra	Swed. Dv.II	30	16	15	31	36	—	—	—	—	—

MODRY, JAROSLAV
D, DEVILS

PERSONAL: Born February 27, 1971, in Ceske-Budejovice, Czechoslovakia.... 6-2/195.... Shoots left.... Name pronounced moh-DREE.
TRANSACTIONS/CAREER NOTES: Selected by New Jersey Devils in ninth round (10th Devils pick, 179th overall) of NHL entry draft (June 16, 1990).

Season	Team	League	Gms.	G	A	Pts.	PIM	Gms.	G	A	Pts.	PIM
88-89	—Budejovice........................	Czech.	28	0	1	1	...	—	—	—	—	—
89-90	—Budejovice........................	Czech.	41	2	2	4	...	—	—	—	—	—
90-91	—Dukla Trencin	Czech.	33	1	9	10	6	—	—	—	—	—
91-92	—Dukla Trencin	Czech.	18	0	4	4	...	—	—	—	—	—
	—Budejovice........................	Czech II	14	4	10	14	...	—	—	—	—	—
92-93	—Utica	AHL	80	7	35	42	62	5	0	2	2	2
93-94	—New Jersey.......................	NHL	41	2	15	17	18	—	—	—	—	—
	—Albany..............................	AHL	19	1	5	6	25	—	—	—	—	—
	NHL totals........................		41	2	15	17	18					

MOGILNY, ALEXANDER
RW, SABRES

PERSONAL: Born February 18, 1969, in Khabarovsk, U.S.S.R.... 5-11/187.... Shoots left.... Name pronounced moh-GIHL-nee.
TRANSACTIONS/CAREER NOTES: Selected by Buffalo Sabres in fifth round (fourth Sabres pick, 89th overall) of NHL entry draft (June 11, 1988).... Suffered from the flu (November 26, 1989).... Missed games due to fear of flying (January 22, 1990); spent remainder of season traveling on ground.... Separated shoulder (February 8, 1991); missed six games.... Suffered from the flu (November 1991); missed two games.... Suffered from the flu (December 18, 1991); missed one game.... Bruised shoulder (October 10, 1992); missed six games.... Broke fibula and tore ankle ligaments (May 6, 1993); missed remainder of 1992-93 playoffs and first nine games of 1993-94 season.... Suffered sore ankle (February 2, 1994); missed four games.... Suffered inflamed tendon in ankle (February 15, 1994); missed four games.
HONORS: Played in NHL All-Star Game (1992 through 1994).... Named to THE SPORTING NEWS All-Star second team (1992-93).... Named to NHL All-Star second team (1992-93).
RECORDS: Shares NHL record for fastest goal from start of a game—5 seconds (December 21, 1991).
MISCELLANEOUS: Member of gold-medal-winning U.S.S.R. Olympic team (1988).

M

Season Team	League	REGULAR SEASON					PLAYOFFS				
		Gms.	G	A	Pts.	PIM	Gms.	G	A	Pts.	PIM
86-87—CSKA Moscow	USSR	28	15	1	16	4	—	—	—	—	—
87-88—CSKA Moscow	USSR	39	12	8	20	20	—	—	—	—	—
88-89—CSKA Moscow	USSR	31	11	11	22	24	—	—	—	—	—
89-90—Buffalo	NHL	65	15	28	43	16	4	0	1	1	2
90-91—Buffalo	NHL	62	30	34	64	16	6	0	6	6	2
91-92—Buffalo	NHL	67	39	45	84	73	2	0	2	2	0
92-93—Buffalo	NHL	77	†76	51	127	40	7	7	3	10	6
93-94—Buffalo	NHL	66	32	47	79	22	7	4	2	6	6
NHL totals		337	192	205	397	167	26	11	14	25	16

MOLLER, RANDY

D, PANTHERS

PERSONAL: Born August 23, 1963, in Red Deer, Alta. . . . 6-2/207. . . . Shoots right. . . . Name pronounced MOH-luhr. . . . Brother of Mike Moller, right winger, Buffalo Sabres and Edmonton Oilers (1980-81 through 1986-87).

TRANSACTIONS/CAREER NOTES: Tore knee ligaments and underwent surgery (December 1980). . . . Selected by Quebec Nordiques in first round (first Nordiques pick, 11th overall) of NHL entry draft (June 10, 1981). . . . Broke hand (October 28, 1986). . . . Suffered lingering neck problem (November 1987). . . . Injured knee (January 1988). . . . Suffered back spasms (March 1988). . . . Separated shoulder (October 29, 1988). . . . Broke toe (September 1989). . . . Traded by Nordiques to New York Rangers for D Michel Petit (October 5, 1989). . . . Dislocated right shoulder (December 13, 1989). . . . Suffered back spasms (March 21, 1990); missed six games. . . . Dislocated left shoulder (November 7, 1990); missed 15 games. . . . Separated shoulder (January 22, 1992); missed four games. . . . Traded by Rangers to Buffalo Sabres for D Jay Wells (March 9, 1992). . . . Suffered knee ligament damage (November 11, 1992); missed 25 games. . . . Strained back muscle (January 17, 1993); missed 21 games. . . . Signed as free agent by Florida Panthers (July 12, 1994).

HONORS: Named to WHL All-Star second team (1981-82).

Season Team	League	REGULAR SEASON					PLAYOFFS				
		Gms.	G	A	Pts.	PIM	Gms.	G	A	Pts.	PIM
79-80—Red Deer	AJHL	56	3	34	37	253	—	—	—	—	—
80-81—Lethbridge	WHL	46	4	21	25	176	9	0	4	4	24
81-82—Lethbridge	WHL	60	20	55	75	249	12	4	6	10	65
—Quebec	NHL	—	—	—	—	—	1	0	0	0	2
82-83—Quebec	NHL	75	2	12	14	145	4	1	0	1	4
83-84—Quebec	NHL	74	4	14	18	147	9	1	0	1	45
84-85—Quebec	NHL	79	7	22	29	120	18	2	2	4	40
85-86—Quebec	NHL	69	5	18	23	141	3	0	0	0	26
86-87—Quebec	NHL	71	5	9	14	144	13	1	4	5	23
87-88—Quebec	NHL	66	3	22	25	169	—	—	—	—	—
88-89—Quebec	NHL	74	7	22	29	136	—	—	—	—	—
89-90—New York Rangers	NHL	60	1	12	13	139	10	1	6	7	32
90-91—New York Rangers	NHL	61	4	19	23	161	6	0	2	2	11
91-92—New York Rangers	NHL	43	2	7	9	78	—	—	—	—	—
—Binghamton	AHL	3	0	1	1	0	—	—	—	—	—
—Buffalo	NHL	13	1	2	3	59	7	0	0	0	8
92-93—Buffalo	NHL	35	2	7	9	83	—	—	—	—	—
—Rochester	AHL	3	1	0	1	10	—	—	—	—	—
93-94—Buffalo	NHL	78	2	11	13	154	7	0	2	2	8
NHL totals		798	45	177	222	1676	78	6	16	22	199

MOMESSO, SERGIO

LW, CANUCKS

PERSONAL: Born September 4, 1965, in Montreal. . . . 6-3/215. . . . Shoots left. . . . Name pronounced moh-MEH-soh.

TRANSACTIONS/CAREER NOTES: Selected by Montreal Canadiens as underage junior in second round (third Canadiens pick, 27th overall) of NHL entry draft (June 8, 1983). . . . Tore cruciate ligament in left knee and underwent surgery (December 5, 1985); missed remainder of season. . . . Tore ligaments, injured cartilage and fractured left knee (December 5, 1986). . . . Lacerated leg (February 1988). . . . Traded by Canadiens with G Vincent Riendeau to St. Louis Blues for LW Jocelyn Lemieux, G Darrell May and second-round pick (D Patrice Brisebois) in 1989 draft (August 9, 1988). . . . Fractured right ankle (November 12, 1988). . . . Traded by Blues with LW Geoff Courtnall, D Robert Dirk, C Cliff Ronning and fifth-round pick in 1992 draft (RW Brian Loney) to Vancouver Canucks for C Dan Quinn and D Garth Butcher (March 5, 1991). . . . Separated shoulder (December 3, 1991); missed 22 games. . . . Sprained knee (November 30, 1993); missed 11 games. . . . Suspended two games and fined $500 by NHL for stick-swinging incident (March 28, 1994).

HONORS: Named to QMJHL All-Star first team (1984-85).

Season Team	League	REGULAR SEASON					PLAYOFFS				
		Gms.	G	A	Pts.	PIM	Gms.	G	A	Pts.	PIM
82-83—Shawinigan	QMJHL	70	27	42	69	93	10	5	4	9	55
83-84—Nova Scotia	AHL	—	—	—	—	—	8	0	2	2	4
—Shawinigan	QMJHL	68	42	88	130	235	6	4	4	8	13
—Montreal	NHL	1	0	0	0	0	—	—	—	—	—
84-85—Shawinigan	QMJHL	64	56	90	146	216	8	7	8	15	17
85-86—Montreal	NHL	24	8	7	15	46	—	—	—	—	—
86-87—Montreal	NHL	59	14	17	31	96	11	1	3	4	31
—Sherbrooke	AHL	6	1	6	7	10	—	—	—	—	—
87-88—Montreal	NHL	53	7	14	21	101	6	0	2	2	16
88-89—St. Louis	NHL	53	9	17	26	139	10	2	5	7	24
89-90—St. Louis	NHL	79	24	32	56	199	12	3	2	5	63

Season	Team	League	Gms.	G	A	Pts.	Pen.	Gms.	G	A	Pts.	Pen.
90-91—St. Louis		NHL	59	10	18	28	131	—	—	—	—	—
—Vancouver		NHL	11	6	2	8	43	6	0	3	3	25
91-92—Vancouver		NHL	58	20	23	43	198	13	0	5	5	30
92-93—Vancouver		NHL	84	18	20	38	200	12	3	0	3	30
93-94—Vancouver		NHL	68	14	13	27	149	24	3	4	7	56
NHL totals			549	130	163	293	1302	94	12	24	36	275

MONGEAU, MICHEL
C

PERSONAL: Born February 9, 1965, in Nun's Island, Que.... 5-9/180.... Shoots left. ... Name pronounced mahn-ZHOW.
TRANSACTIONS/CAREER NOTES: Signed as free agent by St. Louis Blues (August 21, 1989).... Selected by Tampa Bay Lightning in NHL expansion draft (June 18, 1992).... Loaned to Milwaukee Admirals at beginning of 1992-93 season.... Traded by Lightning with RW Martin Simard and RW Steve Tuttle to Quebec Nordiques for RW Herb Raglan (February 12, 1993).
HONORS: Named to QMJHL All-Star second team (1985-86).... Won Garry F. Longman Memorial Trophy (1986-87).... Won James Gatschene Memorial Trophy (1989-90).... Won Leo P. Lamoureux Memorial Trophy (1989-90).... Named to IHL All-Star first team (1989-90).... Won N.R. (Bud) Poile Trophy (1990-91).... Named to IHL All-Star second team (1990-91).

Season	Team	League	Gms.	G	A	Pts.	PIM	Gms.	G	A	Pts.	PIM
83-84—Laval		QMJHL	60	45	49	94	30	—	—	—	—	—
84-85—Laval		QMJHL	67	60	84	144	56	—	—	—	—	—
85-86—Laval		QMJHL	72	71	109	180	45	—	—	—	—	—
86-87—Saginaw		IHL	76	42	53	95	34	10	3	6	9	10
87-88—Played in France		France	30	31	21	52	...	—	—	—	—	—
88-89—Flint		IHL	82	41	*76	117	57	—	—	—	—	—
89-90—St. Louis		NHL	7	1	5	6	2	2	0	1	1	0
—Peoria		IHL	73	39	*78	*117	53	5	3	4	7	6
90-91—St. Louis		NHL	7	1	1	2	0	—	—	—	—	—
—Peoria		IHL	73	41	65	106	114	19	10	*16	26	32
91-92—Peoria		IHL	32	21	34	55	77	10	5	14	19	8
—St. Louis		NHL	36	3	12	15	6	—	—	—	—	—
92-93—Milwaukee		IHL	45	24	41	65	69	4	1	4	5	4
—Tampa Bay		NHL	4	1	1	2	2	—	—	—	—	—
—Halifax		AHL	22	13	18	31	10	—	—	—	—	—
93-94—Cornwall		AHL	7	3	11	14	4	—	—	—	—	—
—Peoria		IHL	52	29	36	65	50	—	—	—	—	—
NHL totals			54	6	19	25	10	2	0	1	1	0

MONTGOMERY, JIM
C, BLUES

PERSONAL: Born June 30, 1969, in Montreal.... 5-9/180.... Shoots right.
COLLEGE: Maine.
TRANSACTIONS/CAREER NOTES: Signed as free agent by St. Louis Blues (June 2, 1993).... Suspended four games and fined $500 by NHL for high-sticking incident (October 4, 1993).
HONORS: Named to NCAA All-America East second team (1990-91 and 1992-93).... Named to Hockey East All-Star second team (1990-91 and 1991-92).... Named NCAA Tournament Most Valuable Player (1992-93).... Named Hockey East Playoff Most Valuable Player (1992-93).... Named to NCAA All-Tournament team (1992-93).... Named to Hockey East All-Star first team (1992-93).

Season	Team	League	Gms.	G	A	Pts.	PIM	Gms.	G	A	Pts.	PIM
89-90—University of Maine		Hockey East	45	26	34	60	35	—	—	—	—	—
90-91—University of Maine		Hockey East	43	24	57	81	44	—	—	—	—	—
91-92—University of Maine		Hockey East	37	21	44	65	46	—	—	—	—	—
92-93—University of Maine		Hockey East	45	32	63	95	40	—	—	—	—	—
93-94—St. Louis		NHL	67	6	14	20	44	—	—	—	—	—
—Peoria		IHL	12	7	8	15	10	—	—	—	—	—
NHL totals			67	6	14	20	44					

MOOG, ANDY
G, STARS

PERSONAL: Born February 18, 1960, in Penticton, B.C.... 5-8/170.... Catches left.... Full name: Donald Andrew Moog.... Name pronounced MOHG.
TRANSACTIONS/CAREER NOTES: Selected by Edmonton Oilers in seventh round (sixth Oilers pick, 132nd overall) of NHL entry draft (June 11, 1980).... Suffered viral infection (December 1983). ... Injured ligaments in both knees (March 1, 1985).... Traded by Oilers to Boston Bruins for LW Geoff Courtnall and G Bill Ranford (March 1988).... Hyperextended right knee (January 31, 1991); missed three weeks.... Injured back (January 1993); missed three games.... Injured hamstring (February 1993); missed four games.... Traded by Bruins to Dallas Stars for G Jon Casey (June 25, 1993) to complete deal in which Bruins sent D Gord Murphy to Stars for future considerations (June 20, 1993).... Strained groin (November 24, 1993); missed five games.
HONORS: Named to WHL All-Star second team (1979-80).... Named to CHL All-Star second team (1981-82).... Named to THE SPORTING NEWS All-Star second team (1982-83).... Played in NHL All-Star Game (1985, 1986 and 1991).... Shared William M. Jennings Trophy with Rejean Lemelin (1989-90).
MISCELLANEOUS: Member of Stanley Cup championship teams (1984, 1985 and 1987).

M

Season Team	League	REGULAR SEASON								PLAYOFFS						
		Gms.	Min.	W	L	T	GA	SO	Avg.	Gms.	Min.	W	L	GA	SO	Avg.
76-77—Kamloops	BCJHL	44	2735	...	... ...		173	0	*3.80	—	—	—	—	—	—	—
—Kamloops	WCHL	1	35	...	... ...		6	0	10.29	—	—	—	—	—	—	—
77-78—Penticton	BCJHL	39	2243	...	... ...		191	0	5.11	—	—	—	—	—	—	—
78-79—Billings	WHL	26	1306	13	5	4	90	*3	4.13	5	229	1	3	21	0	5.50
79-80—Billings	WHL	46	2435	23	14	1	149	1	3.67	3	190	2	1	10	0	3.16
80-81—Wichita	CHL	29	1602	14	13	1	89	0	3.33	5	300	3	2	16	0	3.20
—Edmonton	NHL	7	313	3	3	0	20	0	3.83	9	526	5	4	32	0	3.65
81-82—Edmonton	NHL	8	399	3	5	0	32	0	4.81	—	—	—	—	—	—	—
—Wichita	CHL	40	2391	23	13	3	119	1	2.99	7	434	3	4	23	0	3.18
82-83—Edmonton	NHL	50	2833	33	8	7	167	1	3.54	16	949	11	5	48	0	3.03
83-84—Edmonton	NHL	38	2212	27	8	1	139	1	3.77	7	263	4	0	12	0	2.74
84-85—Edmonton	NHL	39	2019	22	9	3	111	1	3.30	2	20	0	0	0	0	0.00
85-86—Edmonton	NHL	47	2664	27	9	7	164	1	3.69	1	60	1	0	1	0	1.00
86-87—Edmonton	NHL	46	2461	28	11	3	144	0	3.51	2	120	2	0	8	0	4.00
87-88—Can. national team	Int'l	27	1438	10	7	5	86	0	3.59	—	—	—	—	—	—	—
—Can. Olympic Team	Int'l	4	240	4	0	0	9	1	2.25	—	—	—	—	—	—	—
—Boston	NHL	6	360	4	2	0	17	1	2.83	7	354	1	4	25	0	4.24
88-89—Boston	NHL	41	2482	18	14	8	133	1	3.22	6	359	4	2	14	0	2.34
89-90—Boston	NHL	46	2536	24	10	7	122	3	2.89	20	1195	13	7	44	*2	*2.21
90-91—Boston	NHL	51	2844	25	13	9	136	4	2.87	19	1133	10	9	60	0	3.18
91-92—Boston	NHL	62	3640	28	22	9	196	1	3.23	15	866	8	7	46	1	3.19
92-93—Boston	NHL	55	3194	37	14	3	168	3	3.16	3	161	0	3	14	0	5.22
93-94—Dallas	NHL	55	3121	24	20	7	170	2	3.27	4	246	1	3	12	0	2.93
NHL totals		551	31078	303	148	64	1719	19	3.32	111	6252	60	44	316	3	3.03

MORAN, IAN

D, PENGUINS

PERSONAL: Born August 24, 1972, in Cleveland.... 5-11/170.... Shoots right. **HIGH SCHOOL:** Belmont Hill (Mass.).
COLLEGE: Boston College.
TRANSACTIONS/CAREER NOTES: Underwent knee surgery (June 1988).... Separated shoulder (March 1989).... Selected by Pittsburgh Penguins in sixth round (fifth Penguins pick, 107th overall) of NHL entry draft (June 16, 1990).
HONORS: Named Hockey East co-Rookie of the Year with Craig Darby (1991-92).... Named to Hockey East All-Rookie team (1991-92).

Season Team	League	REGULAR SEASON					PLAYOFFS				
		Gms.	G	A	Pts.	PIM	Gms.	G	A	Pts.	PIM
87-88—Belmont Hill H.S.	Mass. H.S.	25	3	13	16	15	—	—	—	—	—
88-89—Belmont Hill H.S.	Mass. H.S.	23	7	25	32	8	—	—	—	—	—
89-90—Belmont Hill H.S.	Mass. H.S.	...	10	36	46	0	—	—	—	—	—
90-91—Belmont Hill H.S.	Mass. H.S.	23	7	44	51	12	—	—	—	—	—
91-92—Boston College	Hockey East	30	2	16	18	44	—	—	—	—	—
92-93—Boston College	Hockey East	31	8	12	20	32	—	—	—	—	—
93-94—U.S. national team	Int'l	50	8	15	23	69	—	—	—	—	—
—Cleveland	IHL	33	5	13	18	39	—	—	—	—	—

MORE, JAY

D, SHARKS

PERSONAL: Born January 12, 1969, in Souris, Man.... 6-1/200.... Shoots right.
TRANSACTIONS/CAREER NOTES: Selected by New York Rangers as underage junior in first round (first Rangers pick, 10th overall) of NHL entry draft (June 13, 1987).... Traded by Rangers to Minnesota North Stars for C Dave Archibald (November 1, 1989).... Traded by North Stars to Montreal Canadiens for G Brian Hayward (November 7, 1990).... Selected by San Jose Sharks in NHL expansion draft (May 30, 1991).... Injured foot during preseason (September 1991); missed 16 games.... Injured knee (March 1992).... Pulled groin (December 9, 1992); missed four games.... Reaggravated groin injury (December 23, 1992); missed four games.... Suspended one game by NHL for accumulating three game misconduct penalties (January 27, 1993).... Strained hip (March 7, 1993); missed one game.... Suspended for last game of season and first game of 1993-94 season for accumulating four game misconduct penalties (April 11, 1993).... Fractured wrist (October 23, 1993); missed 25 games.
HONORS: Named to WHL (West) All-Star first team (1987-88).

Season Team	League	REGULAR SEASON					PLAYOFFS				
		Gms.	G	A	Pts.	PIM	Gms.	G	A	Pts.	PIM
84-85—Lethbridge	WHL	71	3	9	12	101	4	1	0	1	7
85-86—Lethbridge	WHL	61	7	18	25	155	9	0	2	2	36
86-87—New Westminster	WHL	64	8	29	37	217	—	—	—	—	—
87-88—New Westminster	WHL	70	13	47	60	270	5	0	2	2	26
88-89—Denver	IHL	62	7	15	22	138	3	0	1	1	26
—New York Rangers	NHL	1	0	0	0	0	—	—	—	—	—
89-90—Flint	IHL	9	1	5	6	41	—	—	—	—	—
—Kalamazoo	IHL	64	9	25	34	216	10	0	3	3	13
—Minnesota	NHL	5	0	0	0	16	—	—	—	—	—
90-91—Kalamazoo	IHL	10	0	5	5	46	—	—	—	—	—
—Fredericton	AHL	57	7	17	24	152	9	1	1	2	34
91-92—San Jose	NHL	46	4	13	17	85	—	—	—	—	—
—Kansas City	IHL	2	0	2	2	4	—	—	—	—	—
92-93—San Jose	NHL	73	5	6	11	179	—	—	—	—	—

Season Team	League	REGULAR SEASON					PLAYOFFS				
		Gms.	G	A	Pts.	Pen.	Gms.	G	A	Pts.	Pen.
93-94—San Jose	NHL	49	1	6	7	63	13	0	2	2	32
—Kansas City	IHL	2	1	0	1	25	—	—	—	—	—
NHL totals		174	10	25	35	343	13	0	2	2	32

MOREAU, ETHAN
LW, BLACKHAWKS

PERSONAL: Born September 22, 1975, in Orillia, Ont. . . . 6-2/205. . . . Shoots left. . . . Name pronounced MOHR-oh. **TRANSACTIONS/CAREER NOTES:** Selected by Chicago Blackhawks in first round (first Blackhawks pick, 14th overall) of NHL entry draft (June 28, 1994). **HONORS:** Won Bobby Smith Trophy (1993-94).

Season Team	League	REGULAR SEASON					PLAYOFFS				
		Gms.	G	A	Pts.	PIM	Gms.	G	A	Pts.	PIM
90-91—Orillia	OHA	42	17	22	39	26	—	—	—	—	—
91-92—Niagara Falls	OHL	62	20	35	55	39	17	4	6	10	4
92-93—Niagara Falls	OHL	65	32	41	73	69	4	0	3	3	4
93-94—Niagara Falls	OHL	59	44	54	98	100	—	—	—	—	—

MORIN, STEPHANE
C, CANUCKS

PERSONAL: Born March 27, 1969, in Montreal. . . . 6-0/175. . . . Shoots left. . . . Name pronounced moh-RAI. **TRANSACTIONS/CAREER NOTES:** Traded by Shawinigan Cataractes with second-round pick in QMJHL draft to Chicoutimi Sagueneens for D Daniel Bock (December 1987). . . . Selected by Quebec Nordiques in third round (third Nordiques pick, 43rd overall) of NHL entry draft (June 17, 1989). . . . Stretched right knee ligaments (January 8, 1991); missed six games. . . . Broke finger on right hand (February 20, 1991); missed eight games. . . . Sprained knee (October 12, 1991); missed nine games. . . . Signed as free agent by Vancouver Canucks (October 5, 1992). **HONORS:** Won Michel Briere Trophy (1988-89). . . . Won Jean Beliveau Trophy (1988-89). . . . Named to QMJHL All-Star first team (1988-89). . . . Named to AHL All-Star second team (1993-94).

Season Team	League	REGULAR SEASON					PLAYOFFS				
		Gms.	G	A	Pts.	PIM	Gms.	G	A	Pts.	PIM
86-87—Shawinigan	QMJHL	65	9	14	23	28	14	1	3	4	27
87-88—Shawinigan/Chicoutimi	QMJHL	68	38	45	83	18	6	3	8	11	2
88-89—Chicoutimi	QMJHL	70	77	*109	*186	71	—	—	—	—	—
89-90—Quebec	NHL	6	0	2	2	2	—	—	—	—	—
—Halifax	AHL	65	28	32	60	60	6	3	4	7	6
90-91—Halifax	AHL	17	8	14	22	18	—	—	—	—	—
—Quebec	NHL	48	13	27	40	30	—	—	—	—	—
91-92—Quebec	NHL	30	2	8	10	14	—	—	—	—	—
—Halifax	AHL	30	17	13	30	29	—	—	—	—	—
92-93—Hamilton	AHL	70	31	54	85	49	—	—	—	—	—
—Vancouver	NHL	1	0	1	1	0	—	—	—	—	—
93-94—Hamilton	AHL	69	38	71	109	48	4	3	2	5	4
—Vancouver	NHL	5	1	1	2	6	—	—	—	—	—
NHL totals		90	16	39	55	52					

MOROZOV, VALENTIN
C, PENGUINS

PERSONAL: Born June 1, 1975, in Moscow, U.S.S.R. . . . 5-11/176. . . . Shoots left. **TRANSACTIONS/CAREER NOTES:** Selected by Pittsburgh Penguins in sixth round (eighth Penguins pick, 154th overall) of NHL entry draft (June 29, 1994).

Season Team	League	REGULAR SEASON					PLAYOFFS				
		Gms.	G	A	Pts.	PIM	Gms.	G	A	Pts.	PIM
92-93—CSKA Moscow	CIS	17	0	0	0	6	—	—	—	—	—
93-94—CSKA Moscow	CIS	18	4	1	5	8	3	0	1	1	0

MORRIS, JON
C, BRUINS

PERSONAL: Born May 6, 1966, in Lowell, Mass. . . . 6-0/175. . . . Shoots right. **HIGH SCHOOL:** Chelmsford (North Chelmsford, Mass.). **COLLEGE:** Lowell (Mass.). **TRANSACTIONS/CAREER NOTES:** Selected by New Jersey Devils in fifth round (fifth Devils pick, 86th overall) of NHL entry draft (June 9, 1984). . . . Missed most of 1988-89 season while attending school. . . . Strained rib cage (October 7, 1990). . . . Claimed on waivers by San Jose Sharks (March 13, 1993). . . . Traded by Sharks to Boston Bruins for future considerations (October 29, 1993). **HONORS:** Named to Hockey East All-Freshman team (1984-85). . . . Named to NCAA All-America East second team (1986-87). . . . Named to Hockey East All-Star first team (1986-87).

Season Team	League	REGULAR SEASON					PLAYOFFS				
		Gms.	G	A	Pts.	PIM	Gms.	G	A	Pts.	PIM
83-84—Chelmsford H.S.	Mass. H.S.	24	31	50	81	...	—	—	—	—	—
84-85—University of Lowell	Hockey East	42	29	31	60	16	—	—	—	—	—
85-86—University of Lowell	Hockey East	39	25	31	56	52	—	—	—	—	—
86-87—University of Lowell	Hockey East	36	28	33	61	48	—	—	—	—	—
87-88—University of Lowell	Hockey East	37	15	39	54	39	—	—	—	—	—
88-89—New Jersey	NHL	4	0	2	2	0	—	—	—	—	—

M

Season Team	League	REGULAR SEASON					PLAYOFFS				
		Gms.	G	A	Pts.	Pen.	Gms.	G	A	Pts.	Pen.
89-90—Utica	AHL	49	27	37	64	6	—	—	—	—	—
—New Jersey	NHL	20	6	7	13	8	6	1	3	4	23
90-91—New Jersey	NHL	53	9	19	28	27	5	0	4	4	2
—Utica	AHL	6	4	2	6	5	—	—	—	—	—
91-92—New Jersey	NHL	7	1	2	3	6	—	—	—	—	—
—Utica	AHL	7	1	4	5	0	—	—	—	—	—
92-93—Utica	AHL	31	16	24	40	28	—	—	—	—	—
—Cincinnati	IHL	18	7	19	26	24	—	—	—	—	—
—New Jersey	NHL	2	0	0	0	0	—	—	—	—	—
—San Jose	NHL	13	0	3	3	6	—	—	—	—	—
93-94—Kansas City	IHL	3	0	3	3	2	—	—	—	—	—
—Providence	AHL	67	22	44	66	20	—	—	—	—	—
—Boston	NHL	4	0	0	0	0	—	—	—	—	—
NHL totals		103	16	33	49	47	11	1	7	8	25

MORRISON, BRENDAN
C, DEVILS

PERSONAL: Born August 12, 1975, in North Vancouver. . . . 5-11/170. . . . Shoots left.
COLLEGE: Michigan.
TRANSACTIONS/CAREER NOTES: Selected by New Jersey Devils in second round (third Devils pick, 39th overall) of NHL entry draft (June 26, 1993).
HONORS: Won CCHA Rookie-of-the-year award (1993-94). . . . Named to CCHA All-Rookie team (1993-94).

Season Team	League	REGULAR SEASON					PLAYOFFS				
		Gms.	G	A	Pts.	PIM	Gms.	G	A	Pts.	PIM
92-93—Penticton	BCJHL	56	35	59	94	45	—	—	—	—	—
93-94—University of Michigan	CCHA	38	20	28	48	24	—	—	—	—	—

MOSS, TYLER
G, LIGHTNING

PERSONAL: Born June 29, 1975, in Ottawa. . . . 6-0/168. . . . Catches right.
TRANSACTIONS/CAREER NOTES: Selected by Tampa Bay Lightning in second round (second Lightning pick, 29th overall) of NHL entry draft (June 26, 1993).
HONORS: Named to OHL All-Rookie team (1992-93).

Season Team	League	REGULAR SEASON							PLAYOFFS						
		Gms.	Min.	W	L	T	GA	SO	Avg.	Gms.	Min.	W	L	GA	SO	Avg.
91-92—Nepean	COJHL	26	1335	...	...	...	109	0	4.90	—	—	—	—	—	—	—
92-93—Kingston	OHL	31	1537	13	7	5	97	0	3.79	6	228	1	2	19	0	5.00
93-94—Kingston	OHL	13	795	6	4	3	42	1	3.17	3	136	0	2	8	0	3.53

MOTKOV, DIMITRI
D, RED WINGS

PERSONAL: Born February 23, 1971, in Moscow, U.S.S.R. . . . 6-3/190. . . . Shoots left. . . . Name pronounced MAHT-kahf.
TRANSACTIONS/CAREER NOTES: Selected by Detroit Red Wings in fifth round (fifth Red Wings pick, 98th overall) of NHL entry draft (June 22, 1991).

Season Team	League	REGULAR SEASON					PLAYOFFS				
		Gms.	G	A	Pts.	PIM	Gms.	G	A	Pts.	PIM
89-90—CSKA Moscow	USSR	30	0	1	1	30	—	—	—	—	—
90-91—CSKA Moscow	USSR	32	0	2	2	14	—	—	—	—	—
91-92—CSKA Moscow	CIS	36	0	2	2	53	—	—	—	—	—
92-93—Adirondack	AHL	41	3	7	10	30	—	—	—	—	—
93-94—Adirondack	AHL	70	2	14	16	124	8	0	2	2	23

MROZIK, RICK
D, STARS

PERSONAL: Born January 2, 1975, in Duluth, Minn. . . . 6-2/185. . . . Shoots left. . . . Name pronounced MROH-zihk.
HIGH SCHOOL: Cloquet (Minn.).
COLLEGE: Minnesota-Duluth.
TRANSACTIONS/CAREER NOTES: Selected by Dallas Stars in sixth round (fourth Stars pick, 136th overall) of NHL entry draft (June 26, 1993).

Season Team	League	REGULAR SEASON					PLAYOFFS				
		Gms.	G	A	Pts.	PIM	Gms.	G	A	Pts.	PIM
92-93—Cloquet H.S.	Minn. H.S.	28	9	38	47	12	—	—	—	—	—
93-94—Minnesota-Duluth	WCHA	38	2	9	11	38	—	—	—	—	—

MULLEN, BRIAN
RW, ISLANDERS

PERSONAL: Born March 16, 1962, in New York. . . . 5-10/185. . . . Shoots left. . . . Full name: Brian Patrick Mullen. . . . Brother of Joe Mullen, right winger, Pittsburgh Penguins.
COLLEGE: Wisconsin.
TRANSACTIONS/CAREER NOTES: Selected by Winnipeg Jets in seventh round (seventh Jets pick, 128th overall) of NHL entry draft (June 11, 1980). . . . Traded by Jets with 10th-round pick in 1987 draft (LW Brett Barnett) to New York Rangers for fifth-round pick in 1988 draft (LW Benoit Lebeau) and third-round pick (later traded to St. Louis Blues) in 1989 draft (June 8, 1987). . . . Bruised left knee (January 1988). . . . Traded by Rangers with future considerations to San Jose Sharks for RW/C Tim Kerr (May 30, 1991). . . . Sprained knee (January 3, 1992); missed six games. . . . Traded by Sharks to New York Islanders for rights to C Markus Thuresson (August 24, 1992). . . . Underwent open heart surgery to repair hole in heart (September 13, 1993); missed entire 1993-94 season.
HONORS: Played in NHL All-Star Game (1989).

Season	Team	League	REGULAR SEASON					PLAYOFFS				
			Gms.	G	A	Pts.	PIM	Gms.	G	A	Pts.	PIM
77-78—New York Westsiders		NYMJHL	33	21	36	57	38	—	—	—	—	—
78-79—New York Westsiders		NYMJHL				Statistics unavailable.						
79-80—New York Westsiders		NYMJHL				Statistics unavailable.						
80-81—University of Wisconsin ...		WCHA	38	11	13	24	28	—	—	—	—	—
81-82—University of Wisconsin ...		WCHA	33	20	17	37	10	—	—	—	—	—
82-83—Winnipeg		NHL	80	24	26	50	14	3	1	0	1	0
83-84—Winnipeg		NHL	75	21	41	62	28	3	0	3	3	6
84-85—Winnipeg		NHL	69	32	39	71	32	8	1	2	3	4
85-86—Winnipeg		NHL	79	28	34	62	38	3	1	2	3	6
86-87—Winnipeg		NHL	69	19	32	51	20	9	4	2	6	0
87-88—New York Rangers		NHL	74	25	29	54	42	—	—	—	—	—
88-89—New York Rangers		NHL	78	29	35	64	60	3	0	1	1	4
89-90—New York Rangers		NHL	76	27	41	68	42	10	2	2	4	8
90-91—New York Rangers		NHL	79	19	43	62	44	6	0	2	2	0
91-92—San Jose		NHL	72	18	28	46	66	—	—	—	—	—
92-93—New York Islanders..........		NHL	81	18	14	32	28	18	3	4	7	2
93-94—New York Islanders..........		NHL				Did not play—injured.						
NHL totals...			832	260	362	622	414	63	12	18	30	30

MULLEN, JOE

RW, PENGUINS

PERSONAL: Born February 26, 1957, in New York.... 5-9/180.... Shoots right.... Full name: Joseph Patrick Mullen.... Brother of Brian Mullen, right winger, New York Islanders.
COLLEGE: Boston College.
TRANSACTIONS/CAREER NOTES: Signed as free agent by St. Louis Blues (August 16, 1979).... Injured leg (October 18, 1982).... Tore ligaments in left knee and underwent surgery (January 29, 1983); missed remainder of season.... Traded by Blues with D Terry Johnson and D Rik Wilson to Calgary Flames for LW Eddy Beers, LW Gino Cavallini and D Charles Bourgeois (February 1, 1986).... Bruised knee (April 1988).... Suffered from the flu (April 1989).... Traded by Flames to Pittsburgh Penguins for second-round pick (D Nicolas Perreault) in 1990 draft (June 16, 1990).... Injured neck (January 22, 1991).... Underwent neck surgery for herniated disk (February 6, 1991); missed remainder of season.... Damaged ligament in knee (May 5, 1992); missed remainder of playoffs and first 11 games of 1992-93 season.
HONORS: Named NYMJHL Most Valuable Player (1974-75).... Named to NCAA All-America East first team (1977-78 and 1978-79).... Named to ECAC All-Star first team (1977-78 and 1978-79).... Won Ken McKenzie Trophy (1979-80).... Named to CHL All-Star second team (1979-80).... Won Tommy Ivan Trophy (1980-81).... Won Phil Esposito Trophy (1980-81).... Named to CHL All-Star first team (1980-81).... Won Lady Byng Memorial Trophy (1986-87 and 1988-89). ... Named to THE SPORTING NEWS All-Star first team (1988-89).... Named to NHL All-Star first team (1988-89).... Played in NHL All-Star Game (1989, 1990 and 1994).... Named to THE SPORTING NEWS All-Star second team (1991-92).
MISCELLANEOUS: Member of Stanley Cup championship teams (1989, 1991 and 1992).

Season	Team	League	REGULAR SEASON					PLAYOFFS				
			Gms.	G	A	Pts.	PIM	Gms.	G	A	Pts.	PIM
71-72—New York 14th Precinct....		NYMJHL	30	13	11	24	2	—	—	—	—	—
72-73—New York Westsiders		NYMJHL	40	14	28	42	8	—	—	—	—	—
73-74—New York Westsiders		NYMJHL	†42	71	49	120	41	7	9	9	18	0
74-75—New York Westsiders		NYMJHL	40	*110	72	*182	20	13	*24	13	*37	2
75-76—Boston College		ECAC	24	16	18	34	4	—	—	—	—	—
76-77—Boston College		ECAC	28	28	26	54	8	—	—	—	—	—
77-78—Boston College		ECAC	34	34	34	68	12	—	—	—	—	—
78-79—Boston College		ECAC	25	32	24	56	8	—	—	—	—	—
79-80—Salt Lake City...................		IHL	75	40	32	72	21	13	†9	11	20	0
—St. Louis		NHL	—	—	—	—	—	1	0	0	0	0
80-81—Salt Lake City...................		IHL	80	59	58	*117	8	17	11	9	20	0
81-82—Salt Lake City...................		IHL	27	21	27	48	12	—	—	—	—	—
—St. Louis		NHL	45	25	34	59	4	10	7	11	18	4
82-83—St. Louis		NHL	49	17	30	47	6	—	—	—	—	—
83-84—St. Louis		NHL	80	41	44	85	19	6	2	0	2	0
84-85—St. Louis		NHL	79	40	52	92	6	3	0	0	0	0
85-86—St. Louis		NHL	48	28	24	52	10	—	—	—	—	—
—Calgary		NHL	29	16	22	38	11	21	*12	7	19	4
86-87—Calgary		NHL	79	47	40	87	14	6	2	1	3	0
87-88—Calgary		NHL	80	40	44	84	30	7	2	4	6	10
88-89—Calgary		NHL	79	51	59	110	16	21	*16	8	24	4
89-90—Calgary		NHL	78	36	33	69	24	6	3	0	3	0
90-91—Pittsburgh		NHL	47	17	22	39	6	22	8	9	17	4
91-92—Pittsburgh		NHL	77	42	45	87	30	9	3	1	4	4
92-93—Pittsburgh		NHL	72	33	37	70	14	12	4	2	6	6
93-94—Pittsburgh		NHL	84	38	32	70	41	6	1	0	1	2
NHL totals...			926	471	518	989	231	130	60	43	103	38

MULLER, KIRK

LW, CANADIENS

PERSONAL: Born February 8, 1966, in Kingston, Ont.... 6-0/205.... Shoots left.
TRANSACTIONS/CAREER NOTES: Selected by New Jersey Devils as underage junior in first round (first Devils pick, second overall) of NHL entry draft (June 9, 1984).... Strained knee (January 13, 1986).... Fractured ribs (April 1986).... Traded by Devils with G Roland Melanson to Montreal Canadiens for RW Stephane Richer and RW Tom Chorske (September 1991).... Injured eye (January 21, 1992);

M

missed one game. ... Bruised ribs (November 7, 1992); missed one game. ... Sprained wrist (March 6, 1993); missed two games. ... Injured shoulder (October 11, 1993); missed eight games.
HONORS: Won William Hanley Trophy (1982-83). ... Played in NHL All-Star Game (1985, 1986, 1988, 1990, 1992 and 1993).
MISCELLANEOUS: Member of Stanley Cup championship team (1993).

Season Team	League	REGULAR SEASON					PLAYOFFS				
		Gms.	G	A	Pts.	PIM	Gms.	G	A	Pts.	PIM
80-81—Kingston	OMJHL	2	0	0	0	0	—	—	—	—	—
81-82—Kingston	OHL	67	12	39	51	27	4	5	1	6	4
82-83—Guelph	OHL	66	52	60	112	41	—	—	—	—	—
83-84—Canadian Olympic Team ..	Int'l	15	2	2	4	6	—	—	—	—	—
—Guelph	OHL	49	31	63	94	27	—	—	—	—	—
84-85—New Jersey	NHL	80	17	37	54	69	—	—	—	—	—
85-86—New Jersey	NHL	77	25	41	66	45	—	—	—	—	—
86-87—New Jersey	NHL	79	26	50	76	75	—	—	—	—	—
87-88—New Jersey	NHL	80	37	57	94	114	20	4	8	12	37
88-89—New Jersey	NHL	80	31	43	74	119	—	—	—	—	—
89-90—New Jersey	NHL	80	30	56	86	74	6	1	3	4	11
90-91—New Jersey	NHL	80	19	51	70	76	7	0	2	2	10
91-92—Montreal	NHL	78	36	41	77	86	11	4	3	7	31
92-93—Montreal	NHL	80	37	57	94	77	20	10	7	17	18
93-94—Montreal	NHL	76	23	34	57	96	7	6	2	8	4
NHL totals		790	281	467	748	831	71	25	25	50	111

MULLER, MIKE
D, JETS

PERSONAL: Born September 18, 1971, in Minneapolis. ... 6-2/205. ... Shoots left. ... Full name: Mike Todd Muller.
HIGH SCHOOL: Wayzata (Plymouth, Minn.).
COLLEGE: Minnesota.
TRANSACTIONS/CAREER NOTES: Selected by Winnipeg Jets in second round (second Jets pick, 35th overall) of NHL entry draft (June 16, 1990).

Season Team	League	REGULAR SEASON					PLAYOFFS				
		Gms.	G	A	Pts.	PIM	Gms.	G	A	Pts.	PIM
88-89—Wayzata H.S.	Minn. H.S.	24	10	11	21	56	—	—	—	—	—
89-90—Wayzata H.S.	Minn. H.S.	23	11	15	26	45	—	—	—	—	—
90-91—University of Minnesota ...	WCHA	33	4	4	8	44	—	—	—	—	—
91-92—University of Minnesota ...	WCHA	44	4	12	16	60	—	—	—	—	—
92-93—Dynamo Moscow	CIS	11	1	0	1	8	—	—	—	—	—
93-94—Moncton	AHL	61	2	14	16	88	—	—	—	—	—

MUNI, CRAIG
D, SABRES

PERSONAL: Born July 19, 1962, in Toronto. ... 6-3/200. ... Shoots left. ... Full name: Craig Douglas Muni. ... Name pronounced MYOO-ne.
TRANSACTIONS/CAREER NOTES: Selected by Toronto Maple Leafs as underage junior in second round (first Maple Leafs pick, 25th overall) of NHL entry draft (June 11, 1980). ... Tore left knee ligaments (September 1981). ... Broke ankle (January 1983). ... Signed as free agent by Edmonton Oilers (August 18, 1986). ... Traded by Oilers to Buffalo Sabres for cash (October 2, 1986). ... Traded by Sabres to Pittsburgh Penguins for future considerations (October 3, 1986). ... Traded by Penguins to Oilers to complete earlier trade for G Gilles Meloche (October 6, 1986). ... Bruised kidney (May 1987). ... Bruised ankle (January 1988). ... Bruised ankle (December 17, 1988). ... Strained right shoulder (January 1989). ... Broke little finger of right hand (January 27, 1990); missed eight games. ... Pinched nerve (January 15, 1992); missed 17 games. ... Injured knee (March 19, 1992); missed eight games. ... Suspended two games by NHL during playoffs for kneeing (May 22, 1992); missed final 1992 playoff game and first game of 1992-93 regular season. ... Suffered from the flu (December 1992); missed one game. ... Injured eye (February 18, 1993); missed two games. ... Traded by Oilers to Chicago Blackhawks for C Mike Hudson (March 22, 1993). ... Traded by Blackhawks to Buffalo Sabres for D Keith Carney (October 27, 1993).
MISCELLANEOUS: Member of Stanley Cup championship teams (1987, 1988 and 1990).

Season Team	League	REGULAR SEASON					PLAYOFFS				
		Gms.	G	A	Pts.	PIM	Gms.	G	A	Pts.	PIM
79-80—Kingston	OMJHL	66	6	28	34	114	—	—	—	—	—
80-81—Kingston	OMJHL	38	2	14	16	65	—	—	—	—	—
—Windsor	OMJHL	25	5	11	16	41	11	1	4	5	14
—New Brunswick	AHL	—	—	—	—	—	2	0	1	1	10
81-82—Toronto	NHL	3	0	0	0	2	—	—	—	—	—
—Windsor	OHL	49	5	32	37	92	9	2	3	5	16
—Cincinnati	CHL	—	—	—	—	—	3	0	2	2	2
82-83—Toronto	NHL	2	0	1	1	0	—	—	—	—	—
—St. Catharines	AHL	64	6	32	38	52	—	—	—	—	—
83-84—St. Catharines	AHL	64	4	16	20	79	7	0	1	1	0
84-85—St. Catharines	AHL	68	7	17	24	54	—	—	—	—	—
—Toronto	NHL	8	0	0	0	0	—	—	—	—	—
85-86—Toronto	NHL	6	0	1	1	4	—	—	—	—	—
—St. Catharines	AHL	73	3	34	37	91	13	0	5	5	16
86-87—Edmonton	NHL	79	7	22	29	85	14	0	2	2	17
87-88—Edmonton	NHL	72	4	15	19	77	19	0	4	4	31
88-89—Edmonton	NHL	69	5	13	18	71	7	0	3	3	8
89-90—Edmonton	NHL	71	5	12	17	81	22	0	3	3	16
90-91—Edmonton	NHL	76	1	9	10	77	18	0	3	3	20

M

Season	Team	League	Gms.	G	A	Pts.	Pen.	Gms.	G	A	Pts.	Pen.
					REGULAR SEASON					PLAYOFFS		
91-92—Edmonton		NHL	54	2	5	7	34	3	0	0	0	2
92-93—Edmonton		NHL	72	0	11	11	67	—	—	—	—	—
—Chicago		NHL	9	0	0	0	8	4	0	0	0	2
93-94—Chicago		NHL	9	0	4	4	4	—	—	—	—	—
—Buffalo		NHL	73	2	8	10	62	7	0	0	0	4
NHL totals			603	26	101	127	572	94	0	15	15	100

MURANO, ERIC
C

PERSONAL: Born May 4, 1967, in La Salle, Que. . . . 6-0/200. . . . Shoots right. . . . Name pronounced muh-RAH-noh.
COLLEGE: Denver.
TRANSACTIONS/CAREER NOTES: Selected by Vancouver Canucks in fifth round (fourth Canucks pick, 91st overall) of NHL entry draft (June 21, 1986). . . . Traded by Canucks to Washington Capitals for C Tim Taylor (January 29, 1993). . . . Signed as free agent by New York Rangers (August 20, 1993). . . . Signed as free agent by Cleveland Lumberjacks (June 14, 1994).
HONORS: Named to WCHA All-Star second team (1989-90).

Season	Team	League	Gms.	G	A	Pts.	PIM	Gms.	G	A	Pts.	PIM
					REGULAR SEASON					PLAYOFFS		
85-86—Calgary Canucks		AJHL	52	34	47	81	32	—	—	—	—	—
86-87—University of Denver		WCHA	31	5	7	12	12	—	—	—	—	—
87-88—University of Denver		WCHA	37	8	13	21	26	—	—	—	—	—
88-89—University of Denver		WCHA	42	13	16	29	52	—	—	—	—	—
89-90—University of Denver		WCHA	42	33	35	68	52	—	—	—	—	—
—Canadian national team		Int'l	6	1	0	1	4	—	—	—	—	—
90-91—Milwaukee		IHL	63	32	35	67	63	3	0	1	1	4
91-92—Milwaukee		IHL	80	35	48	83	61	5	3	4	7	0
92-93—Hamilton		AHL	42	25	24	49	10	—	—	—	—	—
—Baltimore		AHL	32	16	14	30	10	7	7	5	12	6
93-94—Binghamton		AHL	75	35	37	72	36	—	—	—	—	—

MURPHY, GORD
D, PANTHERS

PERSONAL: Born February 23, 1967, in Willowdale, Ont. . . . 6-2/195. . . . Shoots right.
TRANSACTIONS/CAREER NOTES: Injured clavicle (January 1985). . . . Selected by Philadelphia Flyers as underage junior in ninth round (10th Flyers pick, 189th overall) of NHL entry draft (June 15, 1985). . . . Injured left foot and suffered hip pointer (March 24, 1990). . . . Traded by Flyers with RW Brian Dobbin and third-round pick in 1992 draft (LW Sergei Zholtok) to Boston Bruins for D Garry Galley, C Wes Walz and future considerations (January 2, 1992). . . . Injured ankle (January 1993); missed 16 games. . . . Traded by Bruins to Dallas Stars for future considerations (June 20, 1993); Bruins sent G Andy Moog to Stars for G Jon Casey to complete deal (June 25, 1993). . . . Selected by Florida Panthers in NHL expansion draft (June 24, 1993).
HONORS: Named to Memorial Cup All-Star team (1986-87).

Season	Team	League	Gms.	G	A	Pts.	PIM	Gms.	G	A	Pts.	PIM
					REGULAR SEASON					PLAYOFFS		
83-84—Don Mills Flyers		MTHL	65	24	42	66	130	—	—	—	—	—
84-85—Oshawa		OHL	59	3	12	15	25	—	—	—	—	—
85-86—Oshawa		OHL	64	7	15	22	56	6	1	1	2	6
86-87—Oshawa		OHL	56	7	30	37	95	24	6	16	22	22
87-88—Hershey		AHL	62	8	20	28	44	12	0	8	8	12
88-89—Philadelphia		NHL	75	4	31	35	68	19	2	7	9	13
89-90—Philadelphia		NHL	75	14	27	41	95	—	—	—	—	—
90-91—Philadelphia		NHL	80	11	31	42	58	—	—	—	—	—
91-92—Philadelphia		NHL	31	2	8	10	33	—	—	—	—	—
—Boston		NHL	42	3	6	9	51	15	1	0	1	12
92-93—Boston		NHL	49	5	12	17	62	—	—	—	—	—
—Providence		AHL	2	1	3	4	2	—	—	—	—	—
93-94—Florida		NHL	84	14	29	43	71	—	—	—	—	—
NHL totals			436	53	144	197	438	34	3	7	10	25

MURPHY, JOE
RW, BLACKHAWKS

PERSONAL: Born October 16, 1967, in London, Ont. . . . 6-1/190. . . . Shoots left. . . . Full name: Joseph Patrick Murphy.
COLLEGE: Michigan State.
TRANSACTIONS/CAREER NOTES: Selected by Detroit Red Wings in first round (first Red Wings pick, first overall) of NHL entry draft (June 21, 1986). . . . Sprained right ankle (January 1988). . . . Traded by Red Wings with C/LW Adam Graves, LW Petr Klima and D Jeff Sharples to Edmonton Oilers for C Jimmy Carson, C Kevin McClelland and fifth-round pick (traded to Montreal Canadiens who selected D Brad Layzell) in 1991 draft (November 2, 1989). . . . Bruised both thighs (March 1990). . . . Did not report to Oilers in 1992-93 season because of contract dispute; missed 63 games. . . . Traded by Oilers to Chicago Blackhawks for D Igor Kravchuk and C Dean McAmmond (February 25, 1993).
HONORS: Named BCJHL Rookie of the Year (1984-85). . . . Named CCHA Rookie of the Year (1985-86).
MISCELLANEOUS: Member of Stanley Cup championship team (1990).

Season	Team	League	Gms.	G	A	Pts.	PIM	Gms.	G	A	Pts.	PIM
					REGULAR SEASON					PLAYOFFS		
84-85—Penticton		BCJHL	51	68	84	*152	92	—	—	—	—	—
85-86—Michigan State		CCHA	35	24	37	61	50	—	—	—	—	—
—Canadian national team		Int'l	8	3	3	6	2	—	—	—	—	—

M

Season	Team	League	REGULAR SEASON					PLAYOFFS				
			Gms.	G	A	Pts.	Pen.	Gms.	G	A	Pts.	Pen.
86-87—Adirondack		AHL	71	21	38	59	61	10	2	1	3	33
—Detroit		NHL	5	0	1	1	2	—	—	—	—	—
87-88—Adirondack		AHL	6	5	6	11	4	—	—	—	—	—
—Detroit		NHL	50	10	9	19	37	8	0	1	1	6
88-89—Detroit		NHL	26	1	7	8	28	—	—	—	—	—
—Adirondack		AHL	47	31	35	66	66	16	6	11	17	17
89-90—Detroit		NHL	9	3	1	4	4	—	—	—	—	—
—Edmonton		NHL	62	7	18	25	56	22	6	8	14	16
90-91—Edmonton		NHL	80	27	35	62	35	15	2	5	7	14
91-92—Edmonton		NHL	80	35	47	82	52	16	8	16	24	12
92-93—Chicago		NHL	19	7	10	17	18	4	0	0	0	8
93-94—Chicago		NHL	81	31	39	70	111	6	1	3	4	25
NHL totals			412	121	167	288	343	71	17	33	50	81

MURPHY, LARRY

D, PENGUINS

PERSONAL: Born March 8, 1961, in Scarborough, Ont.... 6-2/210.... Shoots right.... Full name: Lawrence Thomas Murphy.

TRANSACTIONS/CAREER NOTES: Selected by Los Angeles Kings as underage junior in first round (first Kings pick, fourth overall) of NHL entry draft (June 11, 1980).... Traded by Kings to Washington Capitals for D Brian Engblom and RW Ken Houston (October 18, 1983).... Injured foot (October 29, 1985).... Broke ankle (May 1988).... Traded by Capitals with RW Mike Gartner to Minnesota North Stars for RW Dino Ciccarelli and D Bob Rouse (March 7, 1989).... Traded by North Stars with D Peter Taglianetti to Pittsburgh Penguins for D Jim Johnson and D Chris Dahlquist (December 11, 1990).... Fractured right foot (February 22, 1991); played until March 5 then missed five games.... Suffered back spasms (March 28, 1993); missed one game.

HONORS: Won Max Kaminsky Trophy (1979-80).... Named to OMJHL All-Star first team (1979-80).... Named to Memorial Cup All-Star team (1979-80).... Named to THE SPORTING NEWS All-Star second team (1986-87 and 1992-93).... Named to NHL All-Star second team (1986-87 and 1992-93).... Played in NHL All-Star Game (1994).

RECORDS: Holds NHL rookie-season records for most points by a defenseman—76; and most assists by a defenseman—60 (1980-81).

MISCELLANEOUS: Member of Stanley Cup championship teams (1991 and 1992).

Season	Team	League	REGULAR SEASON					PLAYOFFS				
			Gms.	G	A	Pts.	PIM	Gms.	G	A	Pts.	PIM
78-79—Peterborough		OMJHL	66	6	21	27	82	19	1	9	10	42
79-80—Peterborough		OMJHL	68	21	68	89	88	14	4	13	17	20
80-81—Los Angeles		NHL	80	16	60	76	79	4	3	0	3	2
81-82—Los Angeles		NHL	79	22	44	66	95	10	2	8	10	12
82-83—Los Angeles		NHL	77	14	48	62	81	—	—	—	—	—
83-84—Los Angeles		NHL	6	0	3	3	0	—	—	—	—	—
—Washington		NHL	72	13	33	46	50	8	0	3	3	6
84-85—Washington		NHL	79	13	42	55	51	5	2	3	5	0
85-86—Washington		NHL	78	21	44	65	50	9	1	5	6	6
86-87—Washington		NHL	80	23	58	81	39	7	2	2	4	6
87-88—Washington		NHL	79	8	53	61	72	13	4	4	8	33
88-89—Washington		NHL	65	7	29	36	70	—	—	—	—	—
—Minnesota		NHL	13	4	6	10	12	5	0	2	2	8
89-90—Minnesota		NHL	77	10	58	68	44	7	1	2	3	31
90-91—Minnesota		NHL	31	4	11	15	38	—	—	—	—	—
—Pittsburgh		NHL	44	5	23	28	30	23	5	18	23	44
91-92—Pittsburgh		NHL	77	21	56	77	48	†21	6	10	16	19
92-93—Pittsburgh		NHL	83	22	63	85	73	12	2	11	13	10
93-94—Pittsburgh		NHL	84	17	56	73	44	6	0	5	5	0
NHL totals			1104	220	687	907	876	130	28	73	101	177

MURPHY, ROB

C, KINGS

PERSONAL: Born April 7, 1969, in Hull, Que.... 6-3/205.... Shoots left.
HIGH SCHOOL: Philemon Wright (Hull, Que.).
TRANSACTIONS/CAREER NOTES: Selected by Vancouver Canucks as underage junior in second round (first Canucks pick, 24th overall) of NHL entry draft (June 13, 1987).... Separated shoulder (November 13, 1988).... Sprained right knee (November 3, 1990).... Selected by Ottawa Senators in NHL expansion draft (June 18, 1992).... Signed as free agent by Los Angeles Kings (August 2, 1993).
HONORS: Won Michel Bergeron Trophy (1986-87).... Won Garry F. Longman Memorial Trophy (1989-90).

Season	Team	League	REGULAR SEASON					PLAYOFFS				
			Gms.	G	A	Pts.	PIM	Gms.	G	A	Pts.	PIM
86-87—Laval		QMJHL	70	35	54	89	86	14	3	4	7	15
87-88—Vancouver		NHL	5	0	0	0	2	—	—	—	—	—
—Laval		QMJHL	26	11	25	36	82	—	—	—	—	—
—Drummondville		QMJHL	33	16	28	44	41	17	4	15	19	45
88-89—Drummondville		QMJHL	26	13	25	38	16	4	1	3	4	20
—Vancouver		NHL	8	0	1	1	2	—	—	—	—	—
—Milwaukee		IHL	8	4	2	6	4	11	3	5	8	34
89-90—Milwaukee		IHL	64	24	47	71	87	6	2	6	8	12
—Vancouver		NHL	12	1	1	2	0	—	—	—	—	—
90-91—Vancouver		NHL	42	5	1	6	90	4	0	0	0	2
—Milwaukee		IHL	23	1	7	8	48	—	—	—	—	—

— 592 —

Season Team	League	Gms.	G	A	Pts.	Pen.	Gms.	G	A	Pts.	Pen.
91-92—Milwaukee	IHL	73	26	38	64	141	5	0	3	3	2
—Vancouver	NHL	6	0	1	1	6	—	—	—	—	—
92-93—Ottawa	NHL	44	3	7	10	30	—	—	—	—	—
—New Haven	AHL	26	8	12	20	28	—	—	—	—	—
93-94—Los Angeles	NHL	8	0	1	1	22	—	—	—	—	—
—Phoenix	IHL	72	23	34	57	101	—	—	—	—	—
NHL totals		125	9	12	21	152	4	0	0	0	2

MURRAY, CHRIS
RW, CANADIENS

PERSONAL: Born October 25, 1974, in Port Hardy, B.C. . . . 6-2/214. . . . Shoots right.
TRANSACTIONS/CAREER NOTES: Selected by Montreal Canadiens in third round (third Canadiens pick, 54th overall) of NHL entry draft (June 29, 1994).

		REGULAR SEASON					PLAYOFFS				
Season Team	League	Gms.	G	A	Pts.	PIM	Gms.	G	A	Pts.	PIM
90-91—Bellingham Jr. A	BCJHL	54	5	8	13	150	—	—	—	—	—
91-92—Kamloops	WHL	33	1	1	2	168	5	0	0	0	10
92-93—Kamloops	WHL	62	6	10	16	217	13	0	4	4	34
93-94—Kamloops	WHL	59	14	16	30	260	15	4	2	6	107

MURRAY, GLEN
RW, BRUINS

PERSONAL: Born November 1, 1972, in Halifax, N.S. . . . 6-2/200. . . . Shoots right.
TRANSACTIONS/CAREER NOTES: Selected by Boston Bruins in first round (first Bruins pick, 18th overall) of NHL entry draft (June 22, 1991). . . . Injured elbow (December 15, 1993); missed two games.

		REGULAR SEASON					PLAYOFFS				
Season Team	League	Gms.	G	A	Pts.	PIM	Gms.	G	A	Pts.	PIM
89-90—Sudbury	OHL	62	8	28	36	17	7	0	0	0	4
90-91—Sudbury	OHL	66	27	38	65	82	5	8	4	12	10
91-92—Sudbury	OHL	54	37	47	84	93	11	7	4	11	18
—Boston	NHL	5	3	1	4	0	15	4	2	6	10
92-93—Providence	AHL	48	30	26	56	42	6	1	4	5	4
—Boston	NHL	27	3	4	7	8	—	—	—	—	—
93-94—Boston	NHL	81	18	13	31	48	13	4	5	9	14
NHL totals		113	24	18	42	56	28	8	7	15	24

MURRAY, MARTY
C, FLAMES

PERSONAL: Born February 16, 1975, in Deloraine, Man. . . . 5-9/170. . . . Shoots left.
TRANSACTIONS/CAREER NOTES: Selected by Calgary Flames in fourth round (fifth Flames pick, 96th overall) of NHL entry draft (June 26, 1993).
HONORS: Named to Can.HL All-Star second team (1993-94). . . . Named to WHL (East) All-Star first team (1993-94).

		REGULAR SEASON					PLAYOFFS				
Season Team	League	Gms.	G	A	Pts.	PIM	Gms.	G	A	Pts.	PIM
91-92—Brandon	WHL	68	20	36	56	12	—	—	—	—	—
92-93—Brandon	WHL	67	29	65	94	50	4	1	3	4	0
93-94—Brandon	WHL	64	43	71	114	33	14	6	14	20	14

MURRAY, RAYMOND
LW/C, KINGS

PERSONAL: Born October 9, 1972, in Stratford, Ont. . . . 6-1/183. . . . Shoots left.
COLLEGE: Michigan State.
TRANSACTIONS/CAREER NOTES: Selected by Los Angeles Kings in sixth round (fifth Kings pick, 135th overall) of NHL entry draft (June 20, 1992).

		REGULAR SEASON					PLAYOFFS				
Season Team	League	Gms.	G	A	Pts.	PIM	Gms.	G	A	Pts.	PIM
90-91—Stratford Jr. B	OHA	48	39	59	98	22	—	—	—	—	—
91-92—Michigan State	CCHA	44	12	36	48	16	—	—	—	—	—
92-93—Michigan State	CCHA	40	22	35	57	24	—	—	—	—	—
93-94—Michigan State	CCHA	41	16	38	54	18	—	—	—	—	—

MURRAY, ROB
C, JETS

PERSONAL: Born April 4, 1967, in Toronto. . . . 6-1/180. . . . Shoots right.
TRANSACTIONS/CAREER NOTES: Selected by Washington Capitals as underage junior in third round (third Capitals pick, 61st overall) of NHL entry draft (June 15, 1985). . . . Suspended two games by OHL (November 2, 1986). . . . Injured right hip (December 21, 1989); missed 10 games. . . . Selected by Minnesota North Stars in NHL expansion draft (May 30, 1991). . . . Traded by North Stars with future considerations to Winnipeg Jets for seventh-round pick in 1991 draft (G Geoff Finch) and future considerations (May 30, 1991). . . . Strained groin (November 2, 1992); missed three games. . . . Suffered back spasms (December 15, 1992); missed six games.

		REGULAR SEASON					PLAYOFFS				
Season Team	League	Gms.	G	A	Pts.	PIM	Gms.	G	A	Pts.	PIM
83-84—Mississauga	OHA	35	18	36	54	32	—	—	—	—	—
84-85—Peterborough	OHL	63	12	9	21	155	17	2	7	9	45
85-86—Peterborough	OHL	52	14	18	32	125	16	1	2	3	50

M

Season Team	League	REGULAR SEASON Gms.	G	A	Pts.	Pen.	PLAYOFFS Gms.	G	A	Pts.	Pen.
86-87—Peterborough	OHL	62	17	37	54	204	3	1	4	5	8
87-88—Fort Wayne	IHL	80	12	21	33	139	6	0	2	2	16
88-89—Baltimore	AHL	80	11	23	34	235	—	—	—	—	—
89-90—Baltimore	AHL	23	5	4	9	63	—	—	—	—	—
—Washington	NHL	41	2	7	9	58	9	0	0	0	18
90-91—Baltimore	AHL	48	6	20	26	177	4	0	0	0	12
—Washington	NHL	17	0	3	3	19	—	—	—	—	—
91-92—Moncton	AHL	60	16	15	31	247	8	0	1	1	56
—Winnipeg	NHL	9	0	1	1	18	—	—	—	—	—
92-93—Moncton	AHL	56	16	21	37	147	3	0	0	0	6
—Winnipeg	NHL	10	1	0	1	6	—	—	—	—	—
93-94—Moncton	AHL	69	25	32	57	280	21	2	3	5	60
—Winnipeg	NHL	6	0	0	0	2	—	—	—	—	—
NHL totals		83	3	11	14	103	9	0	0	0	18

MURRAY, TROY
C, SENATORS

PERSONAL: Born July 31, 1962, in Winnipeg. . . . 6-1/195. . . . Shoots right. . . . Full name: Troy Norman Murray.
COLLEGE: North Dakota.
TRANSACTIONS/CAREER NOTES: Selected by Chicago Blackhawks in third round (sixth Blackhawks pick, 57th overall) of NHL entry draft (June 11, 1980). . . . Injured knee ligaments (November 1983). . . . Lacerated face (December 1988). . . . Injured right elbow and underwent surgery (December 26, 1989); missed 11 games. . . . Developed bursitis on right elbow and hospitalized (February 8, 1990). . . . Traded by Blackhawks with LW Warren Rychel to Winnipeg Jets for D Bryan Marchment and D Chris Norton (July 22, 1991). . . . Separated shoulder (October 23, 1991); missed four games. . . . Lacerated knee (December 14, 1991); missed three games. . . . Separated shoulder (October 7, 1992); missed five games. . . . Suffered hip pointer (November 10, 1992); missed two games. . . . Fractured foot (December 19, 1992); missed 22 games. . . . Traded by Jets to Chicago Blackhawks for D Steve Bancroft and undisclosed pick in 1993 draft (February 21, 1993). . . . Traded by Blackhawks to Ottawa Senators for future considerations (March 11, 1994).
HONORS: Won WCHA Freshman of the Year Award (1980-81). . . . Named to WCHA All-Star second team (1980-81 and 1981-82). . . . Won Frank J. Selke Trophy (1985-86).

Season Team	League	REGULAR SEASON Gms.	G	A	Pts.	PIM	PLAYOFFS Gms.	G	A	Pts.	PIM
79-80—St. Albert	AJHL	60	53	47	100	101	—	—	—	—	—
80-81—Univ. of North Dakota	WCHA	38	33	45	78	28	—	—	—	—	—
81-82—Univ. of North Dakota	WCHA	42	22	29	51	62	—	—	—	—	—
—Chicago	NHL	1	0	0	0	0	7	1	0	1	5
82-83—Chicago	NHL	54	8	8	16	27	2	0	0	0	0
83-84—Chicago	NHL	61	15	15	30	45	5	1	0	1	7
84-85—Chicago	NHL	80	26	40	66	82	15	5	14	19	24
85-86—Chicago	NHL	80	45	54	99	94	2	0	0	0	2
86-87—Chicago	NHL	77	28	43	71	59	4	0	0	0	5
87-88—Chicago	NHL	79	22	36	58	96	5	1	0	1	8
88-89—Chicago	NHL	79	21	30	51	113	16	3	6	9	25
89-90—Chicago	NHL	68	17	38	55	86	20	4	4	8	22
90-91—Chicago	NHL	75	14	23	37	74	6	0	1	1	12
91-92—Winnipeg	NHL	74	17	30	47	69	7	0	0	0	2
92-93—Winnipeg	NHL	29	3	4	7	34	—	—	—	—	—
—Chicago	NHL	22	1	3	4	25	4	0	0	0	2
93-94—Chicago	NHL	12	0	1	1	6	—	—	—	—	—
—Indianapolis	IHL	8	3	3	6	12	—	—	—	—	—
—Ottawa	NHL	15	2	3	5	4	—	—	—	—	—
NHL totals		806	219	328	547	814	93	15	25	40	114

MURZYN, DANA
D, CANUCKS

PERSONAL: Born December 9, 1966, in Regina, Sask. . . . 6-2/200. . . . Shoots left. . . . Name pronounced MUHR-zihn.
TRANSACTIONS/CAREER NOTES: Selected by Hartford Whalers as underage junior in first round (first Whalers pick, fifth overall) of NHL entry draft (June 15, 1985). . . . Traded by Whalers with RW Shane Churla to Calgary Flames for C Carey Wilson, D Neil Sheehy and LW Lane MacDonald (January 3, 1988). . . . Strained knee (March 13, 1989). . . . Pulled groin (February 4, 1990). . . . Bruised hip (October 25, 1990); missed 11 games. . . . Separated shoulder (December 1, 1990); missed 34 games. . . . Traded by Flames to Vancouver Canucks for RW Ron Stern, D Kevan Guy and option to switch fourth-round picks in 1992 draft; Flames did not exercise option (March 5, 1991). . . . Suffered from the flu (February 26, 1993); missed two games.
HONORS: Named to WHL (East) All-Star first team (1984-85). . . . Named to NHL All-Rookie team (1985-86).
MISCELLANEOUS: Member of Stanley Cup championship team (1989).

Season Team	League	REGULAR SEASON Gms.	G	A	Pts.	PIM	PLAYOFFS Gms.	G	A	Pts.	PIM
83-84—Calgary	WHL	65	11	20	31	135	2	0	0	0	0
84-85—Calgary	WHL	72	32	60	92	233	8	1	11	12	16
85-86—Hartford	NHL	78	3	23	26	125	4	0	0	0	10
86-87—Hartford	NHL	74	9	19	28	95	6	2	1	3	29
87-88—Hartford	NHL	33	1	6	7	45	—	—	—	—	—
—Calgary	NHL	41	6	5	11	94	5	2	0	2	13
88-89—Calgary	NHL	63	3	19	22	142	21	0	3	3	20

M

Season Team	League	REGULAR SEASON					PLAYOFFS				
		Gms.	G	A	Pts.	Pen.	Gms.	G	A	Pts.	Pen.
89-90—Calgary	NHL	78	7	13	20	140	6	2	2	4	2
90-91—Calgary	NHL	19	0	2	2	30	—	—	—	—	—
—Vancouver	NHL	10	1	0	1	8	6	0	1	1	8
91-92—Vancouver	NHL	70	3	11	14	147	1	0	0	0	15
92-93—Vancouver	NHL	79	5	11	16	196	12	3	2	5	18
93-94—Vancouver	NHL	80	6	14	20	109	7	0	0	0	4
NHL totals		625	44	123	167	1131	68	9	9	18	119

MUSIL, FRANK
D, FLAMES

PERSONAL: Born December 17, 1964, in Pardubice, Czechoslovakia. . . . 6-3/215. . . . Shoots left. . . . Name pronounced moo-SIHL.
TRANSACTIONS/CAREER NOTES: Selected by Minnesota North Stars in second round (third North Stars pick, 38th overall) of NHL entry draft (June 8, 1983). . . . Separated shoulder (December 9, 1986). . . . Fractured foot (December 17, 1988). . . . Suffered concussion (February 9, 1989). . . . Strained lower back muscles (February 18, 1989). . . . Suffered back spasms (November 2, 1989); missed 10 games. . . . Separated right shoulder (April 1990). . . . Traded by North Stars to Calgary Flames for D Brian Glynn (October 26, 1990). . . . Suffered back spasms (November 8, 1993); missed one game. . . . Strained neck (December 28, 1993); missed four games. . . . Hyperextended elbow (March 22, 1994); missed four games.

Season Team	League	REGULAR SEASON					PLAYOFFS				
		Gms.	G	A	Pts.	PIM	Gms.	G	A	Pts.	PIM
85-86—Dukla Jihlava	Czech.	35	3	7	10	85	—	—	—	—	—
86-87—Minnesota	NHL	72	2	9	11	148	—	—	—	—	—
87-88—Minnesota	NHL	80	9	8	17	213	—	—	—	—	—
88-89—Minnesota	NHL	55	1	19	20	54	5	1	1	2	4
89-90—Minnesota	NHL	56	2	8	10	109	4	0	0	0	14
90-91—Minnesota	NHL	8	0	2	2	23	—	—	—	—	—
—Calgary	NHL	67	7	14	21	160	7	0	0	0	10
91-92—Calgary	NHL	78	4	8	12	103	—	—	—	—	—
92-93—Calgary	NHL	80	6	10	16	131	6	1	1	2	7
93-94—Calgary	NHL	75	1	8	9	50	7	0	1	1	4
NHL totals		571	32	86	118	991	29	2	3	5	39

MUZZATTI, JASON
G, FLAMES

PERSONAL: Born February 3, 1970, in Toronto. . . . 6-1/190. . . . Catches left. . . . Full name: Jason Mark Muzzatti. . . . Name pronounced moo-ZAH-tee.
COLLEGE: Michigan State.
TRANSACTIONS/CAREER NOTES: Selected by Calgary Flames in first round (first Flames pick, 21st overall) of NHL entry draft (June 11, 1988). . . . Loaned to Indianapolis Ice (January 11, 1993). . . . Suffered from the flu (November 4, 1993); missed four games.
HONORS: Named to CCHA All-Star second team (1987-88). . . . Named to NCAA All-America West second team (1989-90). . . . Named to CCHA All-Star first team (1989-90). . . . Named to CCHA All-Tournament team (1989-90).

Season Team	League	REGULAR SEASON								PLAYOFFS						
		Gms.	Min.	W	L	T	GA	SO	Avg.	Gms.	Min.	W	L	GA	SO	Avg.
86-87—St. Mikes Jr. B	MTHL	20	1054	...	...	...	69	1	3.93	—	—	—	—	—	—	—
87-88—Michigan State	CCHA	33	1916	19	9	3	109	1	3.41	—	—	—	—	—	—	—
88-89—Michigan State	CCHA	42	2515	32	9	1	127	3	3.03	—	—	—	—	—	—	—
89-90—Michigan State	CCHA	33	1976	24	6	0	99	0	3.01	—	—	—	—	—	—	—
90-91—Michigan State	CCHA	22	1204	8	10	2	75	0	3.74	—	—	—	—	—	—	—
91-92—Salt Lake City	IHL	52	3033	24	22	‡5	167	2	3.30	4	247	1	3	18	0	4.37
92-93—Salt Lake City	IHL	13	747	5	6	‡0	52	0	4.18	—	—	—	—	—	—	—
—Can. national team	Int'l	16	880	6	9	0	53	0	3.61	—	—	—	—	—	—	—
—Indianapolis	IHL	12	707	5	6	‡0	48	0	4.07	—	—	—	—	—	—	—
93-94—Calgary	NHL	1	60	0	1	0	8	0	8.00	—	—	—	—	—	—	—
—Saint John	AHL	51	2939	26	21	3	183	2	3.74	7	415	3	4	19	0	2.75
NHL totals		1	60	0	1	0	8	0	8.00							

MYHRES, BRANTT
LW, LIGHTNING

PERSONAL: Born March 18, 1974, in Edmonton. . . . 6-3/195. . . . Shoots right. . . . Name pronounced MIGHRS.
HIGH SCHOOL: Sir Winston Churchill (Calgary).
TRANSACTIONS/CAREER NOTES: Selected by Tampa Bay Lightning in fifth round (fifth Lightning pick, 97th overall) of NHL entry draft (June 20, 1992).

Season Team	League	REGULAR SEASON					PLAYOFFS				
		Gms.	G	A	Pts.	PIM	Gms.	G	A	Pts.	PIM
90-91—Portland	WHL	59	2	7	9	125	—	—	—	—	—
91-92—Portland	WHL	4	0	2	2	22	—	—	—	—	—
—Lethbridge	WHL	53	4	11	15	359	5	0	0	0	36
92-93—Lethbridge	WHL	64	13	35	48	277	3	0	0	0	11
93-94—Atlanta	IHL	2	0	0	0	17	—	—	—	—	—
—Lethbridge	WHL	34	10	21	31	103	—	—	—	—	—
—Spokane	WHL	27	10	22	32	139	3	1	4	5	7

M

NAMESTNIKOV, JOHN
D, CANUCKS

PERSONAL: Born October 9, 1971, in Novgorod, U.S.S.R. .... 5-11/190. .... Shoots right. .... Name pronounced ehv-GEH-nee nuh-MEHZ-nih-kahf.
TRANSACTIONS/CAREER NOTES: Selected by Vancouver Canucks in sixth round (fifth Canucks pick, 117th overall) of NHL entry draft (June 22, 1991).

Season Team	League	REGULAR SEASON					PLAYOFFS				
		Gms.	G	A	Pts.	PIM	Gms.	G	A	Pts.	PIM
90-91—CSKA Moscow	USSR	45	1	2	3	47	—	—	—	—	—
91-92—CSKA Moscow	CIS	34	1	0	1	37	—	—	—	—	—
92-93—CSKA Moscow	CIS	42	5	5	10	68	—	—	—	—	—
93-94—Hamilton	AHL	59	7	27	34	97	4	0	2	2	19
—Vancouver	NHL	17	0	5	5	10	—	—	—	—	—
NHL totals		17	0	5	5	10					

NASLUND, MARKUS
LW, PENGUINS

PERSONAL: Born July 30, 1973, in Harnosand, Sweden. .... 5-11/180. .... Shoots left. .... Name pronounced NAZ-luhnd.
TRANSACTIONS/CAREER NOTES: Selected by Pittsburgh Penguins in first round (first Penguins pick, 16th overall) of NHL entry draft (June 22, 1991).

Season Team	League	REGULAR SEASON					PLAYOFFS				
		Gms.	G	A	Pts.	PIM	Gms.	G	A	Pts.	PIM
89-90—MoDo	Sweden Jr.	33	43	35	78	20	—	—	—	—	—
90-91—MoDo	Sweden	32	10	9	19	14	—	—	—	—	—
91-92—MoDo	Sweden	39	22	17	39	52	—	—	—	—	—
92-93—MoDo	Sweden	39	22	17	39	67	3	3	2	5	0
93-94—Pittsburgh	NHL	71	4	7	11	27	—	—	—	—	—
—Cleveland	IHL	5	1	6	7	4	—	—	—	—	—
NHL totals		71	4	7	11	27					

NAZAROV, ANDREI
LW, SHARKS

PERSONAL: Born March 21, 1972, in Chelyabinsk, U.S.S.R. .... 6-4/210. .... Shoots right. .... Name pronounced nuh-ZAH-rahf.
TRANSACTIONS/CAREER NOTES: Selected by San Jose Sharks in first round (second Sharks pick, 10th overall) of NHL entry draft (June 20, 1992).

Season Team	League	REGULAR SEASON					PLAYOFFS				
		Gms.	G	A	Pts.	PIM	Gms.	G	A	Pts.	PIM
90-91—Mechel Chelyabinsk	USSR	2	0	0	0	0	—	—	—	—	—
91-92—Dynamo Moscow	CIS	2	1	0	1	2	—	—	—	—	—
92-93—Dynamo Moscow	CIS	42	8	2	10	79	10	1	1	2	8
93-94—Kansas City	IHL	71	15	18	33	64	—	—	—	—	—
—San Jose	NHL	1	0	0	0	0	—	—	—	—	—
NHL totals		1	0	0	0	0					

NDUR, RUMUN
D, SABRES

PERSONAL: Born July 7, 1975, in Zaria, Nigeria. .... 6-2/200. .... Shoots left. .... Name pronounced ROO-muhn nih-DOOR.
HIGH SCHOOL: Bishop MacDonnell (Guelph, Ont.).
TRANSACTIONS/CAREER NOTES: Selected by Buffalo Sabres in third round (third Sabres pick, 69th overall) of NHL entry draft (June 29, 1994).

Season Team	League	REGULAR SEASON					PLAYOFFS				
		Gms.	G	A	Pts.	PIM	Gms.	G	A	Pts.	PIM
91-92—Clearwater	Jr. C	4	0	4	4	4	—	—	—	—	—
—Sarnia	Jr. B	30	2	5	7	46	—	—	—	—	—
92-93—Guelph	Jr. B	24	7	8	15	202	—	—	—	—	—
—Guelph	OHL	22	1	3	4	30	4	0	1	1	4
93-94—Guelph	OHL	61	6	33	39	176	9	4	1	5	24

NEATON, PATRICK
D, PENGUINS

PERSONAL: Born May 21, 1971, in Redford, Mich. .... 6-0/180. .... Shoots left.
COLLEGE: Michigan.
TRANSACTIONS/CAREER NOTES: Selected by Pittsburgh Penguins in seventh round (ninth Penguins pick, 145th overall) of NHL entry draft (June 16, 1990).
HONORS: Named to CCHA All-Star second team (1990-91). .... Named to CCHA All-Star first team (1992-93).

Season Team	League	REGULAR SEASON					PLAYOFFS				
		Gms.	G	A	Pts.	PIM	Gms.	G	A	Pts.	PIM
89-90—University of Michigan	CCHA	42	3	23	26	36	—	—	—	—	—
90-91—University of Michigan	CCHA	44	15	28	43	78	—	—	—	—	—
91-92—University of Michigan	CCHA	43	10	20	30	62	—	—	—	—	—
92-93—University of Michigan	CCHA	38	10	18	28	37	—	—	—	—	—
93-94—Cleveland	IHL	71	8	24	32	78	—	—	—	—	—
—Pittsburgh	NHL	9	1	1	2	12	—	—	—	—	—
NHL totals		9	1	1	2	12					

NECKAR, STANISLAV
D, SENATORS

PERSONAL: Born December 22, 1975, in Ceske Budejovice, Czechoslovakia. .... 6-1/196. .... Shoots left.
TRANSACTIONS/CAREER NOTES: Selected by Ottawa Senators in second round (second Senators pick, 29th overall) of NHL entry draft (June 28, 1994).

Season	Team	League	REGULAR SEASON Gms.	G	A	Pts.	PIM	PLAYOFFS Gms.	G	A	Pts.	PIM
91-92—Budejovice		Czech II	18	1	3	4	...	—	—	—	—	—
92-93—Motor Ceske-Budejovice..		Czech.	42	2	9	11	12	—	—	—	—	—
93-94—HC Ceske Budejovice		Czech Rep.	12	3	2	5	2	3	0	0	0	0

NEDVED, PETR
C, RANGERS

PERSONAL: Born December 9, 1971, in Liberec, Czechoslovakia.... 6-3/185.... Shoots left.... Name pronounced NEHD-VEHD.... Brother of Zdenek Nedved, right winger in Toronto Maple Leafs system.
TRANSACTIONS/CAREER NOTES: Defected from Czechoslovakia to Canada when Czechoslovakian midget team was playing in Calgary (January 1989).... WHL rights traded by Moose Jaw Warriors with D Brian Ilkuf to Seattle Thunderbirds for D Corey Beaulieu (February 3, 1989).... Selected by Vancouver Canucks in first round (first Canucks pick, second overall) of NHL entry draft (June 16, 1990).... Signed as free agent by St. Louis Blues (March 4, 1994); C Craig Janney and second-round pick in 1994 draft (C Dave Scatchard) awarded to Canucks as compensation (March 14, 1994).... Traded by Blues to New York Rangers for LW Esa Tikkanen and D Doug Lidster (July 24, 1994); trade arranged as compensation for Blues signing Coach Mike Keenan.
HONORS: Won Can.HL Rookie of the Year Award (1989-90).... Won Jim Piggott Memorial Trophy (1989-90).
MISCELLANEOUS: Member of silver-medal-winning Canadian Olympic team (1994).

Season	Team	League	REGULAR SEASON Gms.	G	A	Pts.	PIM	PLAYOFFS Gms.	G	A	Pts.	PIM
89-90—Seattle		WHL	71	65	80	145	80	11	4	9	13	2
90-91—Vancouver		NHL	61	10	6	16	20	6	0	1	1	0
91-92—Vancouver		NHL	77	15	22	37	36	10	1	4	5	16
92-93—Vancouver		NHL	84	38	33	71	96	12	2	3	5	2
93-94—Canadian national team		Int'l	25	24	13	37	22	—	—	—	—	—
—Canadian Olympic Team		Int'l	8	5	1	6	6	—	—	—	—	—
—St. Louis		NHL	19	6	14	20	8	4	0	1	1	4
NHL totals			241	69	75	144	160	32	3	9	12	22

NEDVED, ZDENEK
RW, MAPLE LEAFS

PERSONAL: Born March 3, 1975, in Lany, Czechoslovakia.... 6-0/180.... Shoots left.... Name pronounced NEHD-VEHD.... Brother of Petr Nedved, center, New York Rangers.
TRANSACTIONS/CAREER NOTES: Selected by Toronto Maple Leafs in fifth round (third Maple Leafs pick, 123rd overall) of NHL entry draft (June 26, 1993).

Season	Team	League	REGULAR SEASON Gms.	G	A	Pts.	PIM	PLAYOFFS Gms.	G	A	Pts.	PIM
91-92—PZ Kladno		Czech.	19	15	12	27	22	—	—	—	—	—
92-93—Sudbury		OHL	18	3	9	12	6	—	—	—	—	—
93-94—Sudbury		OHL	60	50	50	100	42	10	7	8	15	10

NEEDHAM, MIKE
RW, STARS

PERSONAL: Born April 4, 1970, in Calgary.... 5-10/185.... Shoots right.
TRANSACTIONS/CAREER NOTES: Selected by Pittsburgh Penguins in sixth round (seventh Penguins pick, 126th overall) of NHL entry draft (June 17, 1989).... Sprained left knee (October 8, 1992); missed one game.... Suffered back spasms (December 11, 1992); missed eight games.... Bruised left foot (February 25, 1993); missed one game.... Injured back (October 23, 1993); missed 27 games.... Traded by Penguins to Dallas Stars for LW Jim McKenzie (March 21, 1994).
HONORS: Shared Most Dedicated Player Trophy with Bob Calhoon (1985-86).... Named to WHL (West) All-Star first team (1989-90).
MISCELLANEOUS: Member of Stanley Cup championship team (1992).

Season	Team	League	REGULAR SEASON Gms.	G	A	Pts.	PIM	PLAYOFFS Gms.	G	A	Pts.	PIM
85-86—Fort Saskatchewan		AJHL	49	19	26	45	97	—	—	—	—	—
86-87—Fort Saskatchewan		AJHL				Statistics unavailable.						
—Kamloops		WHL	3	1	2	3	0	11	2	1	3	5
87-88—Kamloops		WHL	64	31	33	64	93	5	0	1	1	5
88-89—Kamloops		WHL	49	24	27	51	55	16	2	9	11	13
89-90—Kamloops		WHL	60	59	66	125	75	17	11	13	24	10
90-91—Muskegon		IHL	65	14	32	46	17	5	2	2	4	5
91-92—Muskegon		IHL	80	41	37	78	83	8	4	4	8	6
—Pittsburgh		NHL	—	—	—	—	—	5	1	0	1	2
92-93—Pittsburgh		NHL	56	8	5	13	14	9	1	0	1	2
—Cleveland		IHL	1	2	0	2	0	—	—	—	—	—
93-94—Pittsburgh		NHL	25	1	0	1	2	—	—	—	—	—
—Cleveland		IHL	6	4	3	7	7	—	—	—	—	—
—Dallas		NHL	5	0	0	0	0	—	—	—	—	—
NHL totals			86	9	5	14	16	14	2	0	2	4

NEELY, CAM
RW, BRUINS

PERSONAL: Born June 6, 1965, in Comox, B.C.... 6-1/210.... Shoots right.... Full name: Cameron Michael Neely.
TRANSACTIONS/CAREER NOTES: Selected by Vancouver Canucks as underage junior in first round (first Canucks pick, ninth overall) of NHL entry draft (June 8, 1983).... Dislocated kneecap (October 1984).... Traded by Canucks with first-round pick in 1987 draft (D Glen Wesley) to Boston Bruins for C Barry Pederson (June 6, 1986).... Slipped right kneecap (March 1988).... Fractured right thumb and inflamed right knee (December 1988). ... Suffered recurrence of right knee inflammation (March 1989).... Hyperextended knee (October 1989).... Pulled groin (March 1990).... Suspended five games by NHL for high-sticking (November 23, 1990).... Injured thigh (May 11, 1991);

missed first 38 games of 1991-92 season. . . . Suffered knee inflammation (January 1992). . . . Underwent knee surgery (February 3, 1992); missed remainder of season. . . . Underwent arthroscopic knee surgery (September 17, 1992); missed first 60 games of season. . . . Injured knee (March 1993); missed eight games. . . . Injured knee (April 1993); missed three games. . . . Reinjured knee (October 9, 1993); missed three games. . . . Injured groin (February 10, 1994); missed one game. . . . Injured knee (March 22, 1994); missed 12 games.

HONORS: Named to THE SPORTING NEWS All-Star first team (1987-88 and 1993-94). . . . Named to NHL All-Star second team (1987-88, 1989-90, 1990-91 and 1993-94). . . . Played in NHL All-Star Game (1988-1991). . . . Named to THE SPORTING NEWS All-Star second team (1989-90 and 1990-91). . . . Won Bill Masterton Memorial Trophy (1993-94).

RECORDS: Shares NHL single-season playoff record for most power-play goals—9 (1991).

Season Team	League	REGULAR SEASON					PLAYOFFS				
		Gms.	G	A	Pts.	PIM	Gms.	G	A	Pts.	PIM
82-83—Portland	WHL	72	56	64	120	130	14	9	11	20	17
83-84—Portland	WHL	19	8	18	26	29	—	—	—	—	—
—Vancouver	NHL	56	16	15	31	57	4	2	0	2	2
84-85—Vancouver	NHL	72	21	18	39	137	—	—	—	—	—
85-86—Vancouver	NHL	73	14	20	34	126	3	0	0	0	6
86-87—Boston	NHL	75	36	36	72	143	4	5	1	6	8
87-88—Boston	NHL	69	42	27	69	175	23	9	8	17	51
88-89—Boston	NHL	74	37	38	75	190	10	7	2	9	8
89-90—Boston	NHL	76	55	37	92	117	21	12	16	28	51
90-91—Boston	NHL	69	51	40	91	98	19	16	4	20	36
91-92—Boston	NHL	9	9	3	12	16	—	—	—	—	—
92-93—Boston	NHL	13	11	7	18	25	4	4	1	5	4
93-94—Boston	NHL	49	50	24	74	54	—	—	—	—	—
NHL totals		635	342	265	607	1138	88	55	32	87	166

NELSON, COREY
D, OILERS

PERSONAL: Born August 22, 1976, in Oromocto, N.B. . . . 6-5/207. . . . Shoots right.
TRANSACTIONS/CAREER NOTES: Selected by Edmonton Oilers in third round (fourth Oilers pick, 53rd overall) of NHL entry draft (June 29, 1994).
HONORS: Named to OHL All-Rookie team (1993-94).

Season Team	League	REGULAR SEASON					PLAYOFFS				
		Gms.	G	A	Pts.	PIM	Gms.	G	A	Pts.	PIM
93-94—North Bay	OHL	62	3	35	38	46	18	1	5	6	10

NELSON, CHRISTOPHER
D, DEVILS

PERSONAL: Born February 12, 1969, in Philadelphia. . . . 6-2/190. . . . Shoots right. . . . Full name: Christopher Viscount Nelson.
COLLEGE: Wisconsin.
TRANSACTIONS/CAREER NOTES: Selected by New Jersey Devils in fifth round (sixth Devils pick, 96th overall) of NHL entry draft (June 11, 1988).

Season Team	League	REGULAR SEASON					PLAYOFFS				
		Gms.	G	A	Pts.	PIM	Gms.	G	A	Pts.	PIM
87-88—Rochester	USHL	48	6	29	35	82	—	—	—	—	—
88-89—University of Wisconsin	WCHA	21	1	4	5	24	—	—	—	—	—
89-90—University of Wisconsin	WCHA	38	1	3	4	38	—	—	—	—	—
90-91—University of Wisconsin	WCHA	42	5	12	17	48	—	—	—	—	—
91-92—University of Wisconsin	WCHA	43	4	12	16	96	—	—	—	—	—
92-93—Utica	AHL	21	1	1	2	20	1	0	0	0	2
—Cincinnati	IHL	58	4	26	30	69	—	—	—	—	—
93-94—Albany	AHL	7	0	2	2	4	—	—	—	—	—
—Raleigh	ECHL	22	3	5	8	49	—	—	—	—	—
—Erie	ECHL	26	2	13	15	53	—	—	—	—	—

NELSON, JEFF
C, CAPITALS

PERSONAL: Born December 18, 1972, in Prince Albert, Sask. . . . 6-0/180. . . . Shoots left. . . . Full name: Jeffrey Arthur Nelson. . . . Brother of Todd Nelson, defenseman in Pittsburgh Penguins system.
TRANSACTIONS/CAREER NOTES: Selected by Washington Capitals in second round (fourth Capitals pick, 36th overall) of NHL entry draft (June 22, 1991).
HONORS: Won Can.HL Scholastic Player of the Year Award (1988-89 and 1989-90). . . . Named WHL Scholastic Player of the Year (1988-89 and 1989-90). . . . Named WHL (East) Player of the Year (1990-91). . . . Named to WHL All-Star second team (1990-91). . . . Named to WHL (East) All-Star second team (1991-92).

Season Team	League	REGULAR SEASON					PLAYOFFS				
		Gms.	G	A	Pts.	PIM	Gms.	G	A	Pts.	PIM
88-89—Prince Albert	WHL	71	30	57	87	74	4	0	3	3	4
89-90—Prince Albert	WHL	72	28	69	97	79	14	2	11	13	10
90-91—Prince Albert	WHL	72	46	74	120	58	3	1	1	2	4
91-92—Prince Albert	WHL	64	48	65	113	84	9	7	14	21	18
92-93—Baltimore	AHL	72	14	38	52	12	7	1	3	4	2
93-94—Portland	AHL	†80	34	73	107	92	17	10	5	15	20

NELSON, TODD
D, PENGUINS

PERSONAL: Born May 15, 1969, in Prince Albert, Sask. . . . 6-0/200. . . . Shoots left. . . . Brother of Jeff Nelson, center in Washington Capitals system.
TRANSACTIONS/CAREER NOTES: Dislocated right shoulder (October 1986). . . . Dislocated left shoulder (May 1987). . . . Selected by Pittsburgh Penguins in fourth round (fourth Penguins

pick, 79th overall) of NHL entry draft (June 17, 1989).
HONORS: Named to WHL All-Star second team (1988-89 and 1989-90).

			REGULAR SEASON					PLAYOFFS			
Season Team	League	Gms.	G	A	Pts.	PIM	Gms.	G	A	Pts.	PIM
85-86—Prince Albert	WHL	4	0	0	0	0	—	—	—	—	—
86-87—Prince Albert	WHL	35	1	6	7	10	4	0	0	0	0
87-88—Prince Albert	WHL	72	3	21	24	59	10	3	2	5	4
88-89—Prince Albert	WHL	72	14	45	59	72	4	1	3	4	4
89-90—Prince Albert	WHL	69	13	42	55	88	14	3	12	15	12
90-91—Muskegon	IHL	79	4	20	24	32	3	0	0	0	4
91-92—Muskegon	IHL	80	6	35	41	46	14	1	11	12	4
—Pittsburgh	NHL	1	0	0	0	0	—	—	—	—	—
92-93—Cleveland	IHL	76	7	35	42	115	4	0	2	2	4
93-94—Portland	AHL	80	11	34	45	69	11	0	6	6	6
—Washington	NHL	2	1	0	1	2	4	0	0	0	0
NHL totals		3	1	0	1	2	4	0	0	0	0

NEMCHINOV, SERGEI
C, RANGERS

PERSONAL: Born January 14, 1964, in Moscow, U.S.S.R. . . . 6-0/200. . . . Shoots left. . . . Name pronounced SAIR-gay nehm-CHEE-nahf.
TRANSACTIONS/CAREER NOTES: Selected by New York Rangers in 12th round (14th Rangers pick, 244th overall) of NHL entry draft (June 16, 1990). . . . Sprained knee (November 4, 1991); missed seven games. . . . Strained buttock (April 4, 1993); missed three games. . . . Suspended eight games and fined $500 by NHL for hitting another player (March 16, 1994).
MISCELLANEOUS: Member of Stanley Cup championship team (1994).

			REGULAR SEASON					PLAYOFFS			
Season Team	League	Gms.	G	A	Pts.	PIM	Gms.	G	A	Pts.	PIM
81-82—Soviet Wings	USSR	15	1	0	1	0	—	—	—	—	—
82-83—CSKA Moscow	USSR	11	0	0	0	2	—	—	—	—	—
83-84—CSKA Moscow	USSR	20	6	5	11	4	—	—	—	—	—
84-85—CSKA Moscow	USSR	31	2	4	6	4	—	—	—	—	—
85-86—Soviet Wings	USSR	39	7	12	19	28	—	—	—	—	—
86-87—Soviet Wings	USSR	40	13	9	22	24	—	—	—	—	—
87-88—Soviet Wings	USSR	48	17	11	28	26	—	—	—	—	—
88-89—Soviet Wings	USSR	43	15	14	29	28	—	—	—	—	—
89-90—Soviet Wings	USSR	48	17	16	33	34	—	—	—	—	—
90-91—Soviet Wings	USSR	46	21	24	45	30	—	—	—	—	—
91-92—New York Rangers	NHL	73	30	28	58	15	13	1	4	5	8
92-93—New York Rangers	NHL	81	23	31	54	34	—	—	—	—	—
93-94—New York Rangers	NHL	76	22	27	49	36	23	2	5	7	6
NHL totals		230	75	86	161	85	36	3	9	12	14

NEMIROVSKY, DAVID
RW, PANTHERS

PERSONAL: Born August 1, 1976, in Toronto. . . . 6-2/176. . . . Shoots right.
TRANSACTIONS/CAREER NOTES: Selected by Florida Panthers in fourth round (fifth Panthers pick, 84th overall) of NHL entry draft (June 29, 1994).

			REGULAR SEASON					PLAYOFFS			
Season Team	League	Gms.	G	A	Pts.	PIM	Gms.	G	A	Pts.	PIM
91-92—Pickering-Weston	Jr. A	38	27	23	50	70	—	—	—	—	—
92-93—Weston-North York	MTHL	40	19	23	42	27	—	—	—	—	—
93-94—Ottawa	OHL	64	21	31	52	18	17	10	10	20	2

NESICH, JIM
RW/C

PERSONAL: Born February 22, 1966, in Dearborn, Mich. . . . 5-11/160. . . . Shoots right.
TRANSACTIONS/CAREER NOTES: Selected by Montreal Canadiens in sixth round (eighth Canadiens pick, 116th overall) of NHL entry draft (June 9, 1984). . . . Broke ankle (December 10, 1989). . . . Traded by Canadiens to Minnesota North Stars for future considerations (August 9, 1991). . . . North Stars franchise moved from Minnesota to Dallas and renamed Stars for 1993-94 season.
HONORS: Won Fred T. Hunt Memorial Trophy (1993-94).

			REGULAR SEASON					PLAYOFFS			
Season Team	League	Gms.	G	A	Pts.	PIM	Gms.	G	A	Pts.	PIM
83-84—Verdun	QMJHL	70	22	24	46	35	10	11	5	16	2
84-85—Verdun	QMJHL	65	19	33	52	72	14	1	6	7	25
85-86—Verdun	QMJHL	71	26	55	81	114	5	0	0	0	8
—Sherbrooke	AHL	4	0	1	1	0	—	—	—	—	—
86-87—Verdun	QMJHL	62	20	50	70	133	—	—	—	—	—
87-88—Sherbrooke	AHL	53	4	10	14	51	4	1	2	3	20
88-89—Sherbrooke	AHL	74	12	34	46	112	6	1	2	3	10
89-90—Sherbrooke	AHL	62	21	31	52	79	12	2	†13	15	18
90-91—Fredericton	AHL	72	13	30	43	79	9	0	4	4	36
91-92—Kalamazoo	IHL	80	13	19	32	85	12	3	7	10	12
93-94—Cape Breton	AHL	65	23	42	65	126	5	1	1	2	10

NICHOLLS, BERNIE
C, BLACKHAWKS

PERSONAL: Born June 24, 1961, in Haliburton, Ont. . . . 6-0/185. . . . Shoots right. . . . Full name: Bernard Irvine Nicholls.
TRANSACTIONS/CAREER NOTES: Selected by Los Angeles Kings as underage junior in fourth round (fourth Kings pick, 73rd overall) of NHL entry draft (June 11, 1980). . . .

Partially tore medial colateral ligament in right knee (November 18, 1982).... Broke jaw (February 1984); missed two games. ... Fractured left index finger in three places (October 8, 1987).... Traded by Kings to New York Rangers for RW Tomas Sandstrom and LW Tony Granato (January 20, 1990)....Separated left shoulder (January 22, 1991); missed five games.... Suspended three games by NHL for stick-swinging incident (February 14, 1991).... Traded by Rangers with LW Louie DeBrusk, RW Steven Rice and future considerations to Edmonton Oilers for C Mark Messier and future considerations (October 4, 1991); Rangers traded D David Shaw to Oilers for D Jeff Beukeboom to complete the deal (November 12, 1991).... Did not report to Oilers to be with his wife for the birth of their child (October 4, 1991); missed 27 games.... Reported to Oilers (December 6, 1991).... Strained abdominal muscle (February 16, 1992); missed two games.... Suspended seven off-days and fined $500 by NHL for swinging stick in preseason game (October 13, 1992).... Traded by Oilers to New Jersey Devils for C Kevin Todd and LW Zdeno Ciger (January 13, 1993).... Fractured left foot (February 27, 1993); missed 13 games.... Sprained left knee (December 4, 1993); missed nine games.... Injured hand (April 10, 1994); missed one game.... Suspended one game by NHL for cross-check to neck (May 21, 1994).... Signed as free agent by Chicago Blackhawks (July 14, 1994).
HONORS: Played in NHL All-Star Game (1984, 1989 and 1990).

Season Team	League	REGULAR SEASON					PLAYOFFS				
		Gms.	G	A	Pts.	PIM	Gms.	G	A	Pts.	PIM
78-79—Kingston	OMJHL	2	0	1	1	0	—	—	—	—	—
79-80—Kingston	OMJHL	68	36	43	79	85	3	1	0	1	10
80-81—Kingston	OMJHL	65	63	89	152	109	14	8	10	18	17
81-82—New Haven	AHL	55	41	30	71	31	—	—	—	—	—
—Los Angeles	NHL	22	14	18	32	27	10	4	0	4	23
82-83—Los Angeles	NHL	71	28	22	50	124	—	—	—	—	—
83-84—Los Angeles	NHL	78	41	54	95	83	—	—	—	—	—
84-85—Los Angeles	NHL	80	46	54	100	76	3	1	1	2	9
85-86—Los Angeles	NHL	80	36	61	97	78	—	—	—	—	—
86-87—Los Angeles	NHL	80	33	48	81	101	5	2	5	7	6
87-88—Los Angeles	NHL	65	32	46	78	114	5	2	6	8	11
88-89—Los Angeles	NHL	79	70	80	150	96	11	7	9	16	12
89-90—Los Angeles	NHL	47	27	48	75	66	—	—	—	—	—
—New York Rangers	NHL	32	12	25	37	20	10	7	5	12	16
90-91—New York Rangers	NHL	71	25	48	73	96	5	4	3	7	8
91-92—New York Rangers	NHL	1	0	0	0	0	—	—	—	—	—
—Edmonton	NHL	49	20	29	49	60	16	8	11	19	25
92-93—Edmonton	NHL	46	8	32	40	40	—	—	—	—	—
—New Jersey	NHL	23	5	15	20	40	5	0	0	0	6
93-94—New Jersey	NHL	61	19	27	46	86	16	4	9	13	28
NHL totals		885	416	607	1023	1107	86	39	49	88	144

NICKULAS, ERIC
C, BRUINS

PERSONAL: Born March 25, 1975, in Cape Cod, Mass.... 5-11/190.... Shoots right.
TRANSACTIONS/CAREER NOTES: Selected by Boston Bruins in fourth round (third Bruins pick, 99th overall) of NHL entry draft (June 29, 1994).

Season Team	League	REGULAR SEASON					PLAYOFFS				
		Gms.	G	A	Pts.	PIM	Gms.	G	A	Pts.	PIM
91-92—Barnstable H.S.	Mass. Jr. A	24	30	25	55	...	—	—	—	—	—
92-93—Tabor Academy	N.Y. H.S.	28	25	25	50	...	—	—	—	—	—
93-94—Cushing Academy	Mass. H.S.	25	46	36	82	...	—	—	—	—	—

NIEDERMAYER, ROB
C, PANTHERS

PERSONAL: Born December 28, 1974, in Cassiar, B.C.... 6-2/200.... Shoots left. ... Name pronounced nee-duhr-MIGH-uhr.... Brother of Scott Niedermayer, defenseman, New Jersey Devils.
COLLEGE: Medicine Hat.
TRANSACTIONS/CAREER NOTES: Selected by Florida Panthers in first round (first Panthers pick, fifth overall) of NHL entry draft (June 26, 1993).... Separated right shoulder (November 18, 1993); missed 17 games.
HONORS: Won WHL Top Draft Prospect Award (1992-93).... Named to WHL (East) All-Star first team (1992-93).

Season Team	League	REGULAR SEASON					PLAYOFFS				
		Gms.	G	A	Pts.	PIM	Gms.	G	A	Pts.	PIM
90-91—Medicine Hat	WHL	71	24	26	50	8	12	3	7	10	2
91-92—Medicine Hat	WHL	71	32	46	78	77	4	2	3	5	2
92-93—Medicine Hat	WHL	52	43	34	77	67	—	—	—	—	—
93-94—Florida	NHL	65	9	17	26	51	—	—	—	—	—
NHL totals		65	9	17	26	51	—	—	—	—	—

NIEDERMAYER, SCOTT
D, DEVILS

PERSONAL: Born August 31, 1973, in Edmonton.... 6-0/200.... Shoots left. . .. Name pronounced NEE-duhr-MIGH-uhr.... Brother of Rob Niedermayer, center, Florida Panthers.
TRANSACTIONS/CAREER NOTES: Stretched left knee ligaments (March 12, 1991); missed nine games.... Selected by New Jersey Devils in first round (first Devils pick, third overall) of NHL entry draft (June 22, 1991).... Suffered sore back (December 9, 1992); missed four games.
HONORS: Won Can.HL Scholastic Player of the Year Award (1990-91).... Named WHL Scholastic Player of the Year (1990-91).... Named to WHL (West) All-Star first team (1990-91 and 1991-92).... Won Stafford Smythe Memorial Trophy (1991-92).... Named to Can.HL All-Star first team (1991-92).... Named to Memorial Cup All-Star team (1991-92).... Named to NHL All-Rookie team (1992-93).

Season Team	League	REGULAR SEASON					PLAYOFFS				
		Gms.	G	A	Pts.	PIM	Gms.	G	A	Pts.	PIM
89-90—Kamloops	WHL	64	14	55	69	64	17	2	14	16	35
90-91—Kamloops	WHL	57	26	56	82	52	—	—	—	—	—
91-92—New Jersey	NHL	4	0	1	1	2	—	—	—	—	—
—Kamloops	WHL	35	7	32	39	61	17	9	14	23	28
92-93—New Jersey	NHL	80	11	29	40	47	5	0	3	3	2
93-94—New Jersey	NHL	81	10	36	46	42	20	2	2	4	8
NHL totals		165	21	66	87	91	25	2	5	7	10

NIELSEN, JEFFREY
RW, RANGERS

PERSONAL: Born September 20, 1971, in Grand Rapids, Minn. . . . 6-0/170. . . . Shoots right. . . . Full name: Jeffrey Michael Nielsen.
HIGH SCHOOL: Grand Rapids (Minn.).
COLLEGE: Minnesota.
TRANSACTIONS/CAREER NOTES: Selected by New York Rangers in fourth round (fourth Rangers pick, 69th overall) of NHL entry draft (June 16, 1990).
HONORS: Named to WCHA All-Star second team (1993-94).

Season Team	League	REGULAR SEASON					PLAYOFFS				
		Gms.	G	A	Pts.	PIM	Gms.	G	A	Pts.	PIM
87-88—Grand Rapids H.S.	Minn. H.S.	21	9	11	20	14	—	—	—	—	—
88-89—Grand Rapids H.S.	Minn. H.S.	25	13	17	30	26	—	—	—	—	—
89-90—Grand Rapids H.S.	Minn. H.S.	28	32	25	57	. . .	—	—	—	—	—
90-91—University of Minnesota	WCHA	45	11	14	25	50	—	—	—	—	—
91-92—University of Minnesota	WCHA	44	15	15	30	74	—	—	—	—	—
92-93—University of Minnesota	WCHA	42	21	20	41	80	—	—	—	—	—
93-94—University of Minnesota	WCHA	41	29	16	45	94	—	—	—	—	—

NIEUWENDYK, JOE
C, FLAMES

PERSONAL: Born September 10, 1966, in Oshawa, Ont. . . . 6-1/195. . . . Shoots left. . . . Name pronounced NOO-ihn-DIGHK. . . . Cousin of Jeff Beukeboom, defenseman, New York Rangers.
COLLEGE: Cornell.
TRANSACTIONS/CAREER NOTES: Selected by Calgary Flames in second round (second Flames pick, 27th overall) of NHL entry draft (June 15, 1985). . . . Suffered concussion (November 1987). . . . Bruised ribs (May 25, 1989). . . . Tore anterior cruciate ligament of left knee (April 17, 1990). . . . Underwent arthroscopic knee surgery (September 28, 1991); missed 12 games. . . . Suffered from the flu (November 19, 1992); missed one game. . . . Strained right knee (March 26, 1993); missed four games. . . . Suffered from charley horse (November 13, 1993); missed three games. . . . Strained right knee ligaments (February 24, 1994); missed 17 games.
HONORS: Won Ivy League Rookie of the Year Trophy (1984-85). . . . Named to NCAA All-America East first team (1985-86 and 1986-87). . . . Named to ECAC All-Star first team (1985-86 and 1986-87). . . . Named ECAC Player of the Year (1986-87). . . . Named NHL Rookie of the Year by THE SPORTING NEWS (1987-88). . . . Won Calder Memorial Trophy (1987-88). . . . Won Dodge Ram Tough Award (1987-88). . . . Named to NHL All-Rookie team (1987-88). . . . Played in NHL All-Star Game (1988-1990 and 1994).
RECORDS: Shares NHL single-game record for most goals in one period—4 (January 11, 1989).
MISCELLANEOUS: Member of Stanley Cup championship team (1989).
STATISTICAL NOTES: Third player in NHL history to score 50 goals in each of his first two seasons.

Season Team	League	REGULAR SEASON					PLAYOFFS				
		Gms.	G	A	Pts.	PIM	Gms.	G	A	Pts.	PIM
83-84—Pickering Jr. B	MTHL	38	30	28	58	35	—	—	—	—	—
84-85—Cornell University	ECAC	29	21	24	45	30	—	—	—	—	—
85-86—Cornell University	ECAC	29	26	28	54	67	—	—	—	—	—
86-87—Cornell University	ECAC	23	26	26	52	26	—	—	—	—	—
—Calgary	NHL	9	5	1	6	0	6	2	2	4	0
87-88—Calgary	NHL	75	51	41	92	23	8	3	4	7	2
88-89—Calgary	NHL	77	51	31	82	40	22	10	4	14	10
89-90—Calgary	NHL	79	45	50	95	40	6	4	6	10	4
90-91—Calgary	NHL	79	45	40	85	36	7	4	1	5	10
91-92—Calgary	NHL	69	22	34	56	55	—	—	—	—	—
92-93—Calgary	NHL	79	38	37	75	52	6	3	6	9	10
93-94—Calgary	NHL	64	36	39	75	51	6	2	2	4	0
NHL totals		531	293	273	566	297	61	28	25	53	36

NIINIMAA, JANNE
D, FLYERS

PERSONAL: Born May 22, 1975, in Raahe, Finland. . . . 6-1/196. . . . Shoots left.
TRANSACTIONS/CAREER NOTES: Selected by Philadelphia Flyers in second round (first Flyers pick, 36th overall) of NHL entry draft (June 26, 1993).

Season Team	League	REGULAR SEASON					PLAYOFFS				
		Gms.	G	A	Pts.	PIM	Gms.	G	A	Pts.	PIM
91-92—Karpat Oulu	Finland Dv.II	41	2	11	13	49	—	—	—	—	—
92-93—Karpat Oulu	Finland Dv.II	29	2	3	5	14	—	—	—	—	—
—Karpat Jr.	Finland	10	3	9	12	16	—	—	—	—	—
93-94—Jokerit	Finland	45	3	8	11	24	12	1	1	2	4

NIKOLISHIN, ANDREI
LW, WHALERS

PERSONAL: Born March 25, 1973, in Vorkuta, U.S.S.R. . . . 5-11/189. . . . Shoots left.
TRANSACTIONS/CAREER NOTES: Selected by Hartford Whalers in second round (second Whalers pick, 47th overall) of NHL entry draft (June 20, 1992).

			REGULAR SEASON					PLAYOFFS			
Season	Team	League	Gms.	G	A	Pts.	PIM	Gms.	G	A	Pts.	PIM
90-91—Dynamo Moscow		USSR	2	0	0	0	0	—	—	—	—	—
91-92—Dynamo Moscow		CIS	18	1	0	1	4	—	—	—	—	—
92-93—Dynamo Moscow		CIS	42	5	7	12	30	10	2	1	3	8
93-94—Dynamo Moscow		CIS	41	8	12	20	30	9	1	3	4	4
—Russian Olympic team		Int'l	8	2	5	7	6	—	—	—	—	—

NIKOLOV, ANGEL
D, SHARKS

PERSONAL: Born November 18, 1975, in Most, Czechoslovakia.... 6-1/176.... Shoots left.

TRANSACTIONS/CAREER NOTES: Selected by San Jose Sharks in second round (second Sharks pick, 37th overall) of NHL entry draft (June 29, 1994).

			REGULAR SEASON					PLAYOFFS			
Season	Team	League	Gms.	G	A	Pts.	PIM	Gms.	G	A	Pts.	PIM
93-94—Chemopetrol Litvinov		Czech.	10	2	2	4	...	3	0	0	0	0

NILSSON, FREDRICK
C, SHARKS

PERSONAL: Born April 16, 1971, in Vasteras, Sweden.... 6-1/200.... Shoots left. ... Name pronounced NEEL-son.

TRANSACTIONS/CAREER NOTES: Selected by San Jose Sharks in sixth round (seventh Sharks pick, 111th overall) of NHL entry draft (June 22, 1991).

			REGULAR SEASON					PLAYOFFS			
Season	Team	League	Gms.	G	A	Pts.	PIM	Gms.	G	A	Pts.	PIM
89-90—Vasteras		Sweden	23	1	1	2	4	1	0	0	0	0
90-91—Vasteras		Sweden	35	13	7	20	20	—	—	—	—	—
91-92—Vasteras		Sweden	40	5	14	19	40	—	—	—	—	—
92-93—Vasteras		Sweden	40	14	15	29	69	1	1	1	2	0
93-94—Kansas City		IHL	13	2	7	9	2	—	—	—	—	—

NOLAN, OWEN
RW, NORDIQUES

PERSONAL: Born February 12, 1972, in Belfast, Northern Ireland.... 6-1/201.... Shoots right. TRANSACTIONS/CAREER NOTES: Separated shoulder (February 22, 1990); missed eight games. ... Selected by Quebec Nordiques in first round (first Nordiques pick, first overall) of NHL entry draft (June 16, 1990).... Suffered concussion, sore knee and sore back (October 1990). ... Suspended four off-days by NHL for cross-checking (December 7, 1992).... Bruised hand (March 2, 1993); missed three games.... Suffered shoulder contusion (March 15, 1993); eight games.... Injured right shoulder (October 19, 1993); missed 11 games.... Dislocated left shoulder (November 12, 1994); missed remainder of season.

HONORS: Won Emms Family Award (1988-89).... Won Jim Mahon Memorial Trophy (1989-90).... Named to OHL All-Star first team (1989-90).... Played in NHL All-Star Game (1992).

			REGULAR SEASON					PLAYOFFS			
Season	Team	League	Gms.	G	A	Pts.	PIM	Gms.	G	A	Pts.	PIM
88-89—Cornwall		OHL	62	34	25	59	213	18	5	11	16	41
89-90—Cornwall		OHL	58	51	59	110	240	6	7	5	12	26
90-91—Quebec		NHL	59	3	10	13	109	—	—	—	—	—
—Halifax		AHL	6	4	4	8	11	—	—	—	—	—
91-92—Quebec		NHL	75	42	31	73	183	—	—	—	—	—
92-93—Quebec		NHL	73	36	41	77	185	5	1	0	1	2
93-94—Quebec		NHL	6	2	2	4	8	—	—	—	—	—
NHL totals			213	83	84	167	485	5	1	0	1	2

NOONAN, BRIAN
RW, RANGERS

PERSONAL: Born May 29, 1965, in Boston.... 6-1/200.... Shoots right.

HIGH SCHOOL: Archbishop Williams (Braintree, Mass.).

TRANSACTIONS/CAREER NOTES: Selected by Chicago Blackhawks in ninth round (10th Blackhawks pick, 179th overall) of NHL entry draft (June 8, 1983).... Separated shoulder (April 3, 1988).... Refused to report to Indianapolis (October 18, 1990); returned home and suspended without pay by Blackhawks.... Suffered death in family (February 28, 1991); missed six games.... Damaged left knee ligaments (January 30, 1992); missed 12 games.... Bruised shoulder (October 31, 1992); missed four games.... Suspended one game by NHL for accumulating three game misconduct penalties (January 21, 1993).... Suffered from the flu (February 25, 1993); missed three games.... Traded by Blackhawks with LW Stephane Matteau to New York Rangers for RW Tony Amonte and rights to LW Matt Oates (March 21, 1994).

HONORS: Won Ken McKenzie Trophy (1985-86).... Named to IHL All-Star second team (1989-90).... Named to IHL All-Star first team (1990-91).

MISCELLANEOUS: Member of Stanley Cup championship team (1994).

			REGULAR SEASON					PLAYOFFS			
Season	Team	League	Gms.	G	A	Pts.	PIM	Gms.	G	A	Pts.	PIM
82-83—Archbishop Williams H.S.		Mass. H.S.	21	26	17	43	...	—	—	—	—	—
83-84—Archbishop Williams H.S.		Mass. H.S.	17	14	23	37	...	—	—	—	—	—
84-85—New Westminster		WHL	72	50	66	116	76	11	8	7	15	4
85-86—Saginaw		IHL	76	39	39	78	69	11	6	3	9	6
—Nova Scotia		AHL	2	0	0	0	0	—	—	—	—	—
86-87—Nova Scotia		AHL	70	25	26	51	30	5	3	1	4	4
87-88—Chicago		NHL	77	10	20	30	44	3	0	0	0	4

Season Team	League	REGULAR SEASON					PLAYOFFS				
		Gms.	G	A	Pts.	Pen.	Gms.	G	A	Pts.	Pen.
88-89—Chicago	NHL	45	4	12	16	28	1	0	0	0	0
—Saginaw	IHL	19	18	13	31	36	1	0	0	0	0
89-90—Chicago	NHL	8	0	2	2	6	—	—	—	—	—
—Indianapolis	IHL	56	40	36	76	85	14	6	9	15	20
90-91—Indianapolis	IHL	59	38	53	91	67	7	6	4	10	18
—Chicago	NHL	7	0	4	4	2	—	—	—	—	—
91-92—Chicago	NHL	65	19	12	31	81	18	6	9	15	30
92-93—Chicago	NHL	63	16	14	30	82	4	3	0	3	4
93-94—Chicago	NHL	64	14	21	35	57	—	—	—	—	—
—New York Rangers	NHL	12	4	2	6	12	22	4	7	11	17
NHL totals		341	67	87	154	312	26	9	9	18	38

NORRIS, CLAYTON
RW, FLYERS

PERSONAL: Born March 8, 1972, in Edmonton.... 6-2/200.... Shoots right.
TRANSACTIONS/CAREER NOTES: Selected by Philadelphia Flyers in sixth round (fifth Flyers pick, 116th overall) of NHL entry draft (June 22, 1991).
HONORS: Named to WHL (East) All-Star second team (1991-92).

Season Team	League	REGULAR SEASON					PLAYOFFS				
		Gms.	G	A	Pts.	PIM	Gms.	G	A	Pts.	PIM
88-89—Medicine Hat	WHL	66	4	9	13	122	3	0	0	0	2
89-90—Medicine Hat	WHL	72	13	18	31	176	3	0	0	0	15
90-91—Medicine Hat	WHL	71	26	27	53	165	12	5	4	9	41
91-92—Medicine Hat	WHL	69	26	39	65	300	2	0	0	0	9
92-93—Medicine Hat	WHL	41	21	16	37	128	10	3	2	5	14
—Hershey	AHL	4	0	0	0	5	—	—	—	—	—
—Roanoke	ECHL	4	0	0	0	0	—	—	—	—	—
93-94—Hershey	AHL	62	8	10	18	217	10	1	0	1	18

NORRIS, DWAYNE
RW, NORDIQUES

PERSONAL: Born January 8, 1970, in St. John's, Nfld.... 5-10/175.... Shoots right.... Full name: Dwayne Carl Norris.
COLLEGE: Michigan State.
TRANSACTIONS/CAREER NOTES: Selected by Quebec Nordiques in seventh round (fifth Nordiques pick, 127th overall) of NHL entry draft (June 16, 1990).
HONORS: Named CCHA Player of the Year (1991-92).... Named to NCAA All-America West first team (1991-92).... Named to CCHA All-Star first team (1991-92).
MISCELLANEOUS: Member of silver-medal-winning Canadian Olympic team (1994).

Season Team	League	REGULAR SEASON					PLAYOFFS				
		Gms.	G	A	Pts.	PIM	Gms.	G	A	Pts.	PIM
88-89—Michigan State	CCHA	47	16	23	39	40	—	—	—	—	—
89-90—Michigan State	CCHA	36	19	26	45	30	—	—	—	—	—
90-91—Michigan State	CCHA	40	26	25	51	60	—	—	—	—	—
91-92—Michigan State	CCHA	44	*44	39	83	62	—	—	—	—	—
92-93—Halifax	AHL	50	25	28	53	62	—	—	—	—	—
93-94—Canadian national team	Int'l	56	20	16	36	26	—	—	—	—	—
—Canadian Olympic Team	Int'l	8	2	2	4	4	—	—	—	—	—
—Quebec	NHL	4	1	1	2	4	—	—	—	—	—
—Cornwall	AHL	9	2	9	11	0	13	7	4	11	17
NHL totals		4	1	1	2	4					

NORSTROM, MATTIAS
D, RANGERS

PERSONAL: Born January 2, 1972, in Stockholm, Sweden.... 6-1/205.... Shoots left.... Name pronounced NOHR-struhm.
TRANSACTIONS/CAREER NOTES: Selected by New York Rangers in second round (second Rangers pick, 48th overall) of NHL entry draft (June 20, 1992).
MISCELLANEOUS: Member of Stanley Cup championship team (1994).

Season Team	League	REGULAR SEASON					PLAYOFFS				
		Gms.	G	A	Pts.	PIM	Gms.	G	A	Pts.	PIM
91-92—AIK Solna	Sweden	39	4	4	8	28	—	—	—	—	—
92-93—AIK Solna	Sweden	22	0	1	1	16	—	—	—	—	—
93-94—New York Rangers	NHL	9	0	2	2	6	—	—	—	—	—
—Binghamton	AHL	55	1	9	10	70	—	—	—	—	—
NHL totals		9	0	2	2	6					

NORTON, JEFF
D, SHARKS

PERSONAL: Born November 25, 1965, in Cambridge, Mass.... 6-2/190.... Shoots left.... Full name: Jeffrey Zaccari Norton.
HIGH SCHOOL: Cushing Academy (Ashburnham, Mass.).
COLLEGE: Michigan.
TRANSACTIONS/CAREER NOTES: Selected by New York Islanders in third round (third Islanders pick, 62nd overall) of NHL entry draft (June 9, 1984).... Bruised ribs (November 16, 1988).... Injured groin (February 1990).... Strained groin and abdominal muscles (March 2, 1990).... Suffered concussion (April 9, 1990).... Suspended eight games by NHL for intentionally injuring another player in preseason game (September 30, 1990).... Dislocated right shoulder (November 3, 1990); missed four games.... Reinjured shoulder (December 27, 1990); missed five games.... Reinjured shoulder and underwent surgery (February 23, 1991); missed remainder of season.... Suffered concussion (October 26, 1991); missed one game.

. . . Tore ligaments in left wrist (January 3, 1992); missed final 42 games of season. . . . Underwent surgery to left wrist (January 8, 1992). . . . Suffered hip flexor (October 23, 1992); missed five games. . . . Suffered sore shoulder (December 31, 1992); missed one game. . . . Pulled groin (February 25, 1993); missed two games. . . . Traded by Islanders to San Jose Sharks for third-round pick (D Jason Strudwick) in 1994 draft (June 20, 1993). . . . Sprained ankle (December 11, 1993); missed nine games. . . . Reinjured ankle (January 4, 1994); missed five games. . . . Sprained ankle (February 19, 1994); missed five games.
HONORS: Named to CCHA All-Star second team (1986-87).

Season Team	League	REGULAR SEASON					PLAYOFFS				
		Gms.	G	A	Pts.	PIM	Gms.	G	A	Pts.	PIM
83-84—Cushing Academy............	Mass. H.S.	21	22	33	55	...	—	—	—	—	—
84-85—University of Michigan	CCHA	37	8	16	24	103	—	—	—	—	—
85-86—University of Michigan	CCHA	37	15	30	45	99	—	—	—	—	—
86-87—University of Michigan	CCHA	39	12	37	49	92	—	—	—	—	—
87-88—U.S. national team	Int'l	57	7	25	32	...	—	—	—	—	—
—U.S. Olympic Team	Int'l	6	0	4	4	4	—	—	—	—	—
—New York Islanders..........	NHL	15	1	6	7	14	3	0	2	2	13
88-89—New York Islanders..........	NHL	69	1	30	31	74	—	—	—	—	—
89-90—New York Islanders..........	NHL	60	4	49	53	65	4	1	3	4	17
90-91—New York Islanders..........	NHL	44	3	25	28	16	—	—	—	—	—
91-92—New York Islanders..........	NHL	28	1	18	19	18	—	—	—	—	—
92-93—New York Islanders..........	NHL	66	12	38	50	45	10	1	1	2	4
93-94—San Jose......................	NHL	64	7	33	40	36	14	1	5	6	20
NHL totals.........		346	29	199	228	268	31	3	11	14	54

NORWOOD, LEE
D

PERSONAL: Born February 2, 1960, in Oakland, Calif. . . . 6-0/190. . . . Shoots left. . . . Full name: Lee Charles Norwood.
HIGH SCHOOL: Trenton (Mich.).
TRANSACTIONS/CAREER NOTES: Selected by Quebec Nordiques as underage junior in third round (third Nordiques pick, 62nd overall) of NHL entry draft (August 9, 1979). . . . Traded by Nordiques to Washington Capitals for C Tim Tookey and seventh-round pick (D Daniel Poudrier) in 1982 draft (January 1982). . . . Traded by Capitals to Toronto Maple Leafs for D Dave Shand (October 6, 1983). . . . Signed as free agent by St. Louis Blues (August 13, 1985). . . . Traded by Blues to Detroit Red Wings for D Larry Trader (August 7, 1986). . . . Pulled stomach muscle (February 1987). . . . Injured groin (October 1987). . . . Injured knee (December 1987). . . . Sprained ankle (November 1988). . . . Pulled hamstring (February 1989). . . . Suffered hip pointer (November 6, 1989); missed six games. . . . Sprained right wrist (March 15, 1990). . . . Traded by Red Wings with future considerations to New Jersey Devils for C Paul Ysebaert; Devils received fourth-round pick in 1992 draft (D Scott McCabe) to complete deal (November 27, 1990). . . . Separated left shoulder (January 3, 1991); missed six games. . . . Fractured cheekbone and underwent surgery (February 16, 1991); missed 19 games. . . . Underwent surgery to left shoulder (summer 1991). . . . Traded by Devils to Hartford Whalers for future considerations (October 3, 1991). . . . Traded by Whalers to Blues for future considerations (November 13, 1991). . . . Injured ankle (January 28, 1992); missed one game. . . . Broke ankle (January 22, 1993); missed remainder of regular season. . . . Released by Blues (June 30, 1993). . . . Signed as free agent by Calgary Flames (October 20, 1993). . . . Strained hip (December 5, 1993); missed 17 games.
HONORS: Won Governors Trophy (1984-85). . . . Named to IHL All-Star first team (1984-85).

Season Team	League	REGULAR SEASON					PLAYOFFS				
		Gms.	G	A	Pts.	PIM	Gms.	G	A	Pts.	PIM
77-78—Hull	QMJHL	51	3	17	20	83	—	—	—	—	—
78-79—Oshawa	OMJHL	61	23	38	61	171	5	2	2	4	17
79-80—Oshawa	OMJHL	60	13	39	52	143	6	2	7	9	15
80-81—Hershey	AHL	52	11	32	43	78	8	0	4	4	14
—Quebec	NHL	11	1	1	2	9	3	0	0	0	2
81-82—Fredericton	AHL	29	6	13	19	74	—	—	—	—	—
—Quebec	NHL	2	0	0	0	2	—	—	—	—	—
—Washington	NHL	26	7	10	17	125	—	—	—	—	—
82-83—Washington	NHL	8	0	1	1	14	—	—	—	—	—
—Hershey	AHL	67	12	36	48	90	5	0	1	1	2
83-84—St. Catharines	AHL	75	13	46	59	91	7	0	5	5	31
84-85—Peoria	IHL	80	17	60	77	229	18	1	11	12	62
85-86—St. Louis	NHL	71	5	24	29	134	19	2	7	9	64
86-87—Adirondack	AHL	3	0	3	3	0	—	—	—	—	—
—Detroit	NHL	57	6	21	27	163	16	1	6	7	31
87-88—Detroit	NHL	51	9	22	31	131	16	2	6	8	40
88-89—Detroit	NHL	66	10	32	42	100	6	1	2	3	16
89-90—Detroit	NHL	64	8	14	22	95	—	—	—	—	—
90-91—Detroit	NHL	21	3	7	10	50	—	—	—	—	—
—New Jersey	NHL	28	3	2	5	87	4	0	0	0	18
91-92—Hartford....................	NHL	6	0	0	0	16	—	—	—	—	—
—St. Louis	NHL	44	3	11	14	94	1	0	1	1	0
92-93—St. Louis	NHL	32	3	7	10	63	—	—	—	—	—
93-94—Calgary.....................	NHL	16	0	1	1	16	—	—	—	—	—
—San Diego	IHL	4	0	0	0	0	8	0	1	1	11
NHL totals.........		503	58	153	211	1099	65	6	22	28	171

NUMMINEN, TEPPO
D, JETS

PERSONAL: Born July 3, 1968, in Tampere, Finland. . . . 6-1/190. . . . Shoots right. . . . Full name: Teppo Kalevi Numminen. . . . Name pronounced TEH-poh NOO-mih-nehn.
TRANSACTIONS/CAREER NOTES: Selected by Winnipeg Jets in second round (second Jets pick, 29th overall) of NHL entry draft (June 21, 1986). . . . Separated shoulder

(March 5, 1989).... Broke thumb (April 14, 1990).... Fractured foot (January 28, 1993); missed 17 games.... Dislocated thumb (February 9, 1994); missed remainder of season.

MISCELLANEOUS: Member of silver-medal-winning Finnish Olympic team (1988).

			REGULAR SEASON					PLAYOFFS			
Season Team	League	Gms.	G	A	Pts.	PIM	Gms.	G	A	Pts.	PIM
84-85—Tappara	Finland	30	14	17	31	10	—	—	—	—	—
85-86—Tappara	Finland	39	2	4	6	6	8	0	0	0	0
86-87—Tappara	Finland	44	9	9	18	16	9	4	1	5	4
87-88—Tappara	Finland	44	10	10	20	29	10	6	6	12	6
—Finland Olympic Team	Int'l	6	1	4	5	0	—	—	—	—	—
88-89—Winnipeg	NHL	69	1	14	15	36	—	—	—	—	—
89-90—Winnipeg	NHL	79	11	32	43	20	7	1	2	3	10
90-91—Winnipeg	NHL	80	8	25	33	28	—	—	—	—	—
91-92—Winnipeg	NHL	80	5	34	39	32	7	0	0	0	0
92-93—Winnipeg	NHL	66	7	30	37	33	6	1	1	2	2
93-94—Winnipeg	NHL	57	5	18	23	28	—	—	—	—	—
NHL totals		431	37	153	190	177	20	2	3	5	12

NYLANDER, MICHAEL
C, FLAMES

PERSONAL: Born October 3, 1972, in Stockholm, Sweden.... 5-11/190.... Shoots left.... Name pronounced NEE-lan-duhr.
TRANSACTIONS/CAREER NOTES: Selected by Hartford Whalers in third round (fourth Whalers pick, 59th overall) of NHL entry draft (June 22, 1991)....
Broke jaw (January 23, 1993); missed 15 games.... Traded by Whalers with D Zarley Zalapski and D James Patrick to Calgary Flames for D Gary Suter, LW Paul Ranheim and C Ted Drury (March 10, 1994).
HONORS: Named Swedish League Rookie of the Year (1991-92).

			REGULAR SEASON					PLAYOFFS			
Season Team	League	Gms.	G	A	Pts.	PIM	Gms.	G	A	Pts.	PIM
89-90—Huddinge	Sweden	31	7	15	22	4	—	—	—	—	—
90-91—Huddinge	Sweden	33	14	20	34	10	—	—	—	—	—
91-92—AIK Solna	Sweden	40	11	17	28	30	—	—	—	—	—
—Swedish national Jr. team	Sweden	7	8	9	17	...	—	—	—	—	—
—Swedish national team	Int'l	6	0	1	1	0	—	—	—	—	—
92-93—Hartford	NHL	59	11	22	33	36	—	—	—	—	—
93-94—Hartford	NHL	58	11	33	44	24	—	—	—	—	—
—Springfield	AHL	4	0	9	9	0	—	—	—	—	—
—Calgary	NHL	15	2	9	11	6	3	0	0	0	0
NHL totals		132	24	64	88	66	3	0	0	0	0

OATES, ADAM
C, BRUINS

PERSONAL: Born August 27, 1962, in Weston, Ont.... 5-11/190.... Shoots right.... Name pronounced OHTZ.
COLLEGE: Rensselaer Polytechnic Institute (N.Y.).
TRANSACTIONS/CAREER NOTES: Signed as free agent by Detroit Red Wings (June 28, 1985)....
Pulled abdominal muscle (October 1987).... Suffered from chicken pox (November 1988).... Bruised thigh (December 1988).... Traded by Red Wings with RW Paul MacLean to St. Louis Blues for LW Tony McKegney and C Bernie Federko (June 15, 1989).... Tore rib and abdominal muscles (November 5, 1990); missed 18 games.... Traded by Blues to Boston Bruins for C Craig Janney and D Stephane Quintal (February 7, 1992).... Injured groin (January 6, 1994); missed seven games.
HONORS: Named to ECAC All-Star second team (1983-84).... Named to NCAA All-America East first team (1984-85).... Named to NCAA All-Tournament team (1984-85).... Named to ECAC All-Star first team (1984-85).... Named to THE SPORTING NEWS All-Star second team (1990-91).... Named to NHL All-Star second team (1990-91).... Played in NHL All-Star Game (1991 - 1994).
RECORDS: Holds NHL All-Star Game record for most assists in one period—4 (first period, 1993).

			REGULAR SEASON					PLAYOFFS			
Season Team	League	Gms.	G	A	Pts.	PIM	Gms.	G	A	Pts.	PIM
82-83—R.P.I.	ECAC	22	9	33	42	8	—	—	—	—	—
83-84—R.P.I.	ECAC	38	26	57	83	15	—	—	—	—	—
84-85—R.P.I.	ECAC	38	31	60	91	29	—	—	—	—	—
85-86—Adirondack	AHL	34	18	28	46	4	17	7	14	21	4
—Detroit	NHL	38	9	11	20	10	—	—	—	—	—
86-87—Detroit	NHL	76	15	32	47	21	16	4	7	11	6
87-88—Detroit	NHL	63	14	40	54	20	16	8	12	20	6
88-89—Detroit	NHL	69	16	62	78	14	6	0	8	8	2
89-90—St. Louis	NHL	80	23	79	102	30	12	2	12	14	4
90-91—St. Louis	NHL	61	25	90	115	29	13	7	13	20	10
91-92—St. Louis	NHL	54	10	59	69	12	—	—	—	—	—
—Boston	NHL	26	10	20	30	10	15	5	14	19	4
92-93—Boston	NHL	84	45	*97	142	32	4	0	9	9	4
93-94—Boston	NHL	77	32	80	112	45	13	3	9	12	8
NHL totals		628	199	570	769	223	95	29	84	113	44

O'CONNELL, ALBIE
LW, ISLANDERS

PERSONAL: Born May 20, 1976, in Cambridge, Mass.... 6-0/188.... Shoots left.
HIGH SCHOOL: St. Sebastian's Country Day (Needham, Mass.).
TRANSACTIONS/CAREER NOTES: Selected by New York Islanders in fifth round (sixth Islanders pick, 116th overall) of NHL entry draft (June 29, 1994).

NO

Season Team	League	REGULAR SEASON					PLAYOFFS				
		Gms.	G	A	Pts.	PIM	Gms.	G	A	Pts.	PIM
91-92—St. Sebastian's	Mass. H.S.	16	4	9	13	10	—	—	—	—	—
92-93—St. Sebastian's	Mass. H.S.	23	7	15	22	15	—	—	—	—	—
93-94—St. Sebastian's	Mass. H.S.	24	16	23	39	26	—	—	—	—	—

O'CONNOR, MYLES
D, MIGHTY DUCKS

PERSONAL: Born April 2, 1967, in Calgary.... 5-11/190.... Shoots left.... Full name: Myles Alexander O'Connor.
COLLEGE: Michigan.
TRANSACTIONS/CAREER NOTES: Selected by New Jersey Devils in third round (fourth Devils pick, 45th overall) of NHL entry draft (June 15, 1985).... Fractured ankle (February 18, 1991).... Signed as free agent by Mighty Ducks of Anaheim (July 22, 1993).... Strained groin (October 29, 1993).... Suffered from chicken pox (March 8, 1994); missed seven games.
HONORS: Named to NCAA All-America West first team (1988-89).... Named to CCHA All-Star first team (1988-89).

Season Team	League	REGULAR SEASON					PLAYOFFS				
		Gms.	G	A	Pts.	PIM	Gms.	G	A	Pts.	PIM
84-85—Notre Dame H.S.	Sask. H.S.	40	20	35	55	40	—	—	—	—	—
85-86—University of Michigan	CCHA	37	6	19	25	73	—	—	—	—	—
—Canadian national team	Int'l	8	0	0	0	0	—	—	—	—	—
86-87—University of Michigan	CCHA	39	15	30	45	111	—	—	—	—	—
87-88—University of Michigan	CCHA	40	9	25	34	78	—	—	—	—	—
88-89—University of Michigan	CCHA	40	3	31	34	91	—	—	—	—	—
—Utica	AHL	1	0	0	0	0	—	—	—	—	—
89-90—Utica	AHL	76	14	33	47	124	5	1	2	3	26
90-91—New Jersey	NHL	22	3	1	4	41	—	—	—	—	—
—Utica	AHL	33	6	17	23	62	—	—	—	—	—
91-92—Utica	AHL	66	9	39	48	184	—	—	—	—	—
—New Jersey	NHL	9	0	2	2	13	—	—	—	—	—
92-93—Utica	AHL	9	1	5	6	10	—	—	—	—	—
—New Jersey	NHL	7	0	0	0	9	—	—	—	—	—
93-94—Anaheim	NHL	5	0	1	1	6	—	—	—	—	—
—San Diego	IHL	39	1	13	14	117	9	1	4	5	83
NHL totals		43	3	4	7	69					

O'CONNOR, THOMAS
D, PENGUINS

PERSONAL: Born January 9, 1976, in Springfield, Mass.... 6-2/190.... Shoots left.
TRANSACTIONS/CAREER NOTES: Selected by Pittsburgh Penguins in fourth round (sixth Penguins pick, 102nd overall) of NHL entry draft (June 29, 1994).

Season Team	League	REGULAR SEASON					PLAYOFFS				
		Gms.	G	A	Pts.	PIM	Gms.	G	A	Pts.	PIM
91-92—Springfield Jr. B	NEJHL	40	1	12	13	12	—	—	—	—	—
92-93—Springfield Jr. B	NEJHL	42	11	19	30	40	—	—	—	—	—
93-94—Springfield Jr. B	EJHL	36	4	15	19	73	—	—	—	—	—

ODELEIN, LYLE
D, CANADIENS

PERSONAL: Born July 21, 1968, in Quill Lake, Sask.... 5-10/206.... Shoots right.... Name pronounced OH-duh-LIGHN.
TRANSACTIONS/CAREER NOTES: Selected by Montreal Canadiens as underage junior in seventh round (eighth Canadiens pick, 141st overall) of NHL entry draft (June 21, 1986).... Bruised right ankle (January 22, 1991); missed five games.... Twisted right ankle (February 9, 1991).... Suspended one game by NHL for game misconduct penalties (March 1, 1993).... Bruised shoulder (January 24, 1994); missed three games.
MISCELLANEOUS: Member of Stanley Cup championship team (1993).

Season Team	League	REGULAR SEASON					PLAYOFFS				
		Gms.	G	A	Pts.	PIM	Gms.	G	A	Pts.	PIM
85-86—Moose Jaw	WHL	67	9	37	46	117	13	1	6	7	34
86-87—Moose Jaw	WHL	59	9	50	59	70	9	2	5	7	26
87-88—Moose Jaw	WHL	63	15	43	58	166	—	—	—	—	—
88-89—Sherbrooke	AHL	33	3	4	7	120	3	0	2	2	5
—Peoria	IHL	36	2	8	10	116	—	—	—	—	—
89-90—Sherbrooke	AHL	68	7	24	31	265	12	6	5	11	79
—Montreal	NHL	8	0	2	2	33	—	—	—	—	—
90-91—Montreal	NHL	52	0	2	2	259	12	0	0	0	54
91-92—Montreal	NHL	71	1	7	8	212	7	0	0	0	11
92-93—Montreal	NHL	83	2	14	16	205	20	1	5	6	30
93-94—Montreal	NHL	79	11	29	40	276	7	0	0	0	17
NHL totals		293	14	54	68	985	46	1	5	6	112

ODGERS, JEFF
LW, SHARKS

PERSONAL: Born May 31, 1969, in Spy Hill, Sask.... 6-0/195.... Shoots right.... Name pronounced AHD-juhrs.
TRANSACTIONS/CAREER NOTES: Signed as free agent by San Jose Sharks (September 3, 1991).... Injured hand (December 21, 1991); missed four games.... Broke hand (November 5, 1992); missed 15 games.... Suspended one game by NHL for accumulating three game misconduct penalties (January 29, 1993).... Suspended two games by NHL for accumulating four game misconduct penalties (February 19, 1993).

Season Team	League		REGULAR SEASON					PLAYOFFS			
		Gms.	G	A	Pts.	PIM	Gms.	G	A	Pts.	PIM
86-87—Brandon	WHL	70	7	14	21	150	—	—	—	—	—
87-88—Brandon	WHL	70	17	18	35	202	4	1	1	2	14
88-89—Brandon	WHL	71	31	29	60	277	—	—	—	—	—
89-90—Brandon	WHL	64	37	28	65	209	—	—	—	—	—
90-91—Kansas City	IHL	77	12	19	31	*318	—	—	—	—	—
91-92—Kansas City	IHL	12	2	2	4	56	9	3	0	3	13
—San Jose	NHL	61	7	4	11	217	—	—	—	—	—
92-93—San Jose	NHL	66	12	15	27	253	—	—	—	—	—
93-94—San Jose	NHL	81	13	8	21	222	11	0	0	0	11
NHL totals		208	32	27	59	692	11	0	0	0	11

ODJICK, GINO
LW, CANUCKS

PERSONAL: Born September 7, 1970, in Maniwaki, Que.... 6-3/210.... Shoots left.... Name pronounced OH-jihk.
TRANSACTIONS/CAREER NOTES: Suspended five games by QMJHL for attempting to attack another player (May 1, 1989).... Suspended one game by QMJHL for fighting (March 19, 1990). ... Suspended one game by QMJHL for fighting (April 14, 1990).... Selected by Vancouver Canucks in fifth round (fifth Canucks pick, 86th overall) of NHL entry draft (June 16, 1990).... Broke cheekbone (February 27, 1991).... Suspended six games by NHL for stick foul (November 26, 1991).... Underwent arthroscopic knee surgery (February 11, 1993); missed five games.... Suspended one game by NHL for accumulating three game misconduct penalties (January 27, 1993).... Suspended one game by NHL for accumulating four game misconduct penalties (March 26, 1993).... Suspended two games by NHL for stick incident (April 8, 1993).... Separated shoulder (November 27, 1993); missed two games.

Season Team	League		REGULAR SEASON					PLAYOFFS			
		Gms.	G	A	Pts.	PIM	Gms.	G	A	Pts.	PIM
88-89—Laval	QMJHL	50	9	15	24	278	16	0	9	9	*129
89-90—Laval	QMJHL	51	12	26	38	280	13	6	5	11	*110
90-91—Milwaukee	IHL	17	7	3	10	102	—	—	—	—	—
—Vancouver	NHL	45	7	1	8	296	6	0	0	0	18
91-92—Vancouver	NHL	65	4	6	10	348	4	0	0	0	6
92-93—Vancouver	NHL	75	4	13	17	370	1	0	0	0	0
93-94—Vancouver	NHL	76	16	13	29	271	10	0	0	0	18
NHL totals		261	31	33	64	1285	21	0	0	0	42

OHLUND, MATTIAS
D, CANUCKS

PERSONAL: Born September 9, 1976, in Pitea, Sweden.... 6-3/209.... Shoots left.
TRANSACTIONS/CAREER NOTES: Selected by Vancouver Canucks in first round (first Canucks pick, 13th overall) of NHL entry draft (June 28, 1994).

Season Team	League		REGULAR SEASON					PLAYOFFS			
		Gms.	G	A	Pts.	PIM	Gms.	G	A	Pts.	PIM
92-93—Pitea	Swed. Dv.II	22	0	6	6	16	—	—	—	—	—
93-94—Pitea	Swed. Dv.II	28	7	10	17	62	—	—	—	—	—

OKSIUTA, ROMAN
RW, OILERS

PERSONAL: Born August 21, 1970, in Murmansk, U.S.S.R.... 6-3/229.... Shoots left. ... Name pronounced ohk-SOO-tah.
TRANSACTIONS/CAREER NOTES: Selected by New York Rangers in 10th round (11th Rangers pick, 202nd overall) of NHL entry draft (June 17, 1989).... Traded by Rangers with third-round draft pick in 1993 draft (RW Alexander Kerch) to Edmonton Oilers for D Kevin Lowe (December 11, 1992).

Season Team	League		REGULAR SEASON					PLAYOFFS			
		Gms.	G	A	Pts.	PIM	Gms.	G	A	Pts.	PIM
87-88—Khimik Voskresensk	USSR	11	1	0	1	4	—	—	—	—	—
88-89—Khimik Voskresensk	USSR	34	13	3	16	14	—	—	—	—	—
89-90—Khimik Voskresensk	USSR	37	13	6	19	16	—	—	—	—	—
90-91—Khimik Voskresensk	USSR	41	12	8	20	24	—	—	—	—	—
91-92—Khimik Voskresensk	CIS	42	24	20	*44	28	—	—	—	—	—
92-93—Cape Breton	AHL	43	26	25	51	22	16	9	19	28	12
93-94—Edmonton	NHL	10	1	2	3	4	—	—	—	—	—
—Cape Breton	AHL	47	31	22	53	90	4	2	2	4	22
NHL totals		10	1	2	3	4					

OLAUSSON, FREDRIK
D, OILERS

PERSONAL: Born October 5, 1966, in Vaxsjo, Sweden.... 6-2/195.... Shoots right.... Name pronounced OHL-uh-suhn.
TRANSACTIONS/CAREER NOTES: Selected by Winnipeg Jets in fourth round (fourth Jets pick, 81st overall) of NHL entry draft (June 15, 1985).... Dislocated shoulder (August 1987).... Underwent shoulder surgery (November 1987).... Signed five-year contract with Farjestads, Sweden (June 19, 1989); Farjestads agreed to allow Olausson to remain in Winnipeg.... Sprained knee (January 22, 1993); missed 11 games.... Lacerated ankle (November 8, 1993); missed two games.... Suffered from the flu (January 18, 1993); missed one game.... Sprained knee (January 23, 1993); missed 11 games.... Suffered from the flu (March 4, 1993); missed one game. ... Traded by Jets with seventh-round pick in 1994 draft (LW Curtis Sheptak) to Edmonton Oilers for third-round pick (C Travis Hansen) in 1994 draft (December 5, 1993).... Strained knee (January 11, 1994).
HONORS: Named to Swedish League All-Star team (1985-86).

— 607 —

O

Season Team	League	REGULAR SEASON					PLAYOFFS				
		Gms.	G	A	Pts.	PIM	Gms.	G	A	Pts.	PIM
83-84—Nybro	Sweden	28	8	14	22	32	—	—	—	—	—
84-85—Farjestad	Sweden	34	6	12	18	24	3	1	0	1	0
85-86—Farjestad	Sweden	33	5	12	17	14	8	3	2	5	6
86-87—Winnipeg	NHL	72	7	29	36	24	10	2	3	5	4
87-88—Winnipeg	NHL	38	5	10	15	18	5	1	1	2	0
88-89—Winnipeg	NHL	75	15	47	62	32	—	—	—	—	—
89-90—Winnipeg	NHL	77	9	46	55	32	7	0	2	2	2
90-91—Winnipeg	NHL	71	12	29	41	24	—	—	—	—	—
91-92—Winnipeg	NHL	77	20	42	62	34	7	1	5	6	4
92-93—Winnipeg	NHL	68	16	41	57	22	6	0	2	2	2
93-94—Winnipeg	NHL	18	2	5	7	10	—	—	—	—	—
—Edmonton	NHL	55	9	19	28	20	—	—	—	—	—
NHL totals		551	95	268	363	216	35	4	13	17	12

OLCZYK, ED
C, RANGERS

PERSONAL: Born August 16, 1966, in Chicago. . . . 6-1/205. . . . Shoots left. . . . Name pronounced OHL-chehk.

TRANSACTIONS/CAREER NOTES: Selected by Chicago Blackhawks in first round (first Blackhawks pick, third overall) of NHL entry draft (June 9, 1984). . . . Hyperextended knee (September 3, 1984). . . . Broke bone in left foot (December 16, 1984). . . . Traded by Blackhawks with LW Al Secord to Toronto Maple Leafs for RW Rick Vaive, LW Steve Thomas and D Bob McGill (September 1987). . . . Pinched nerve in left knee (January 3, 1990). . . . Traded by Maple Leafs with LW Mark Osborne to Winnipeg Jets for D Dave Ellett and LW Paul Fenton (November 10, 1990). . . . Dislocated elbow and sprained ankle (January 8, 1992); missed 15 games. . . . Sprained knee (November 24, 1992); missed nine games. . . . Traded by Jets to New York Rangers for LW Kris King and RW Tie Domi (December 28, 1992). . . . Fractured right thumb (January 31, 1994); missed 24 games.

MISCELLANEOUS: Member of Stanley Cup championship team (1994).

Season Team	League	REGULAR SEASON					PLAYOFFS				
		Gms.	G	A	Pts.	PIM	Gms.	G	A	Pts.	PIM
83-84—U.S. national team	Int'l	56	19	40	59	36	—	—	—	—	—
—U.S. Olympic Team	Int'l	6	2	6	8	0	—	—	—	—	—
84-85—Chicago	NHL	70	20	30	50	67	15	6	5	11	11
85-86—Chicago	NHL	79	29	50	79	47	3	0	0	0	0
86-87—Chicago	NHL	79	16	35	51	119	4	1	1	2	4
87-88—Toronto	NHL	80	42	33	75	55	6	5	4	9	2
88-89—Toronto	NHL	80	38	52	90	75	—	—	—	—	—
89-90—Toronto	NHL	79	32	56	88	78	5	1	2	3	14
90-91—Toronto	NHL	18	4	10	14	13	—	—	—	—	—
—Winnipeg	NHL	61	26	31	57	69	—	—	—	—	—
91-92—Winnipeg	NHL	64	32	33	65	67	6	2	1	3	4
92-93—Winnipeg	NHL	25	8	12	20	26	—	—	—	—	—
—New York Rangers	NHL	46	13	16	29	26	—	—	—	—	—
93-94—New York Rangers	NHL	37	3	5	8	28	1	0	0	0	0
NHL totals		718	263	363	626	670	40	15	13	28	35

OLIMPIYEV, SERGEI
LW, RANGERS

PERSONAL: Born January 12, 1975, in Minsk, U.S.S.R. . . . 5-10/172. . . . Shoots left.
TRANSACTIONS/CAREER NOTES: Selected by New York Rangers in fourth round (fourth Rangers pick, 86th overall) of NHL entry draft (June 26, 1993).

Season Team	League	REGULAR SEASON					PLAYOFFS				
		Gms.	G	A	Pts.	PIM	Gms.	G	A	Pts.	PIM
91-92—Traktor Lipetsk	CIS Div. III	20	0	0	0	2	—	—	—	—	—
92-93—Dynamo Minsk	CIS	6	1	0	1	2	—	—	—	—	—
93-94—Ottawa	OHL	20	3	5	8	4	—	—	—	—	—
—Kitchener	OHL	21	6	5	11	24	5	0	0	0	0

OLIVER, DAVID
RW, OILERS

PERSONAL: Born April 17, 1971, in Sechelt, B.C. . . . 5-11/185. . . . Shoots right.
COLLEGE: Michigan.
TRANSACTIONS/CAREER NOTES: Selected by Edmonton Oilers in seventh round (seventh Oilers pick, 144th overall) of NHL entry draft (June 22, 1991).
HONORS: Named to CCHA All-Star second team (1992-93). . . . Named CCHA Player of the Year (1993-94). . . . Named to NCAA All-America West first team (1993-94).

Season Team	League	REGULAR SEASON					PLAYOFFS				
		Gms.	G	A	Pts.	PIM	Gms.	G	A	Pts.	PIM
90-91—University of Michigan	CCHA	227	13	11	24	34	—	—	—	—	—
91-92—University of Michigan	CCHA	44	31	27	58	32	—	—	—	—	—
92-93—University of Michigan	CCHA	40	35	20	55	18	—	—	—	—	—
93-94—University of Michigan	CCHA	41	28	40	68	16	—	—	—	—	—

OLSEN, DARRYL
D

PERSONAL: Born October 7, 1966, in Calgary. . . . 6-0/180. . . . Shoots left.
COLLEGE: Northern Michigan.
TRANSACTIONS/CAREER NOTES: Selected by Calgary Flames in ninth round (10th Flames pick, 185th overall) of NHL entry draft (June 15, 1985). . . . Signed as free agent by Boston Bruins (July 16, 1992). . . . Signed as free agent by San Diego Gulls (February 26, 1993).

HONORS: Named to NCAA All-America West second team (1988-89).... Named to WCHA All-Star first team (1988-89).

			REGULAR SEASON					PLAYOFFS				
Season Team	League	Gms.	G	A	Pts.	PIM	Gms.	G	A	Pts.	PIM
84-85—St. Albert	AJHL	57	19	48	67	77	—	—	—	—	—
85-86—Northern Michigan Univ...	WCHA	37	5	20	25	46	—	—	—	—	—
86-87—Northern Michigan Univ...	WCHA	37	5	20	25	96	—	—	—	—	—
87-88—Northern Michigan Univ...	WCHA	35	11	20	31	59	—	—	—	—	—
88-89—Northern Michigan Univ...	WCHA	45	16	26	42	88	—	—	—	—	—
—Canadian national team ...	Int'l	3	1	0	1	4	—	—	—	—	—
89-90—Salt Lake City	IHL	72	16	50	66	90	11	3	6	9	2
90-91—Salt Lake City	IHL	76	15	40	55	89	4	1	5	6	2
91-92—Salt Lake City	IHL	59	7	33	40	80	5	2	1	3	4
—Calgary	NHL	1	0	0	0	0	—	—	—	—	—
92-93—Providence	AHL	50	7	27	34	38	—	—	—	—	—
—San Diego	IHL	21	2	8	10	26	10	1	3	4	30
93-94—Salt Lake City	IHL	73	17	32	49	97	—	—	—	—	—
NHL totals		1	0	0	0	0					

O'NEILL, JEFF
C, WHALERS

PERSONAL: Born February 23, 1976, in Richmond Hill, Ont.... 6-0/176.... Shoots right.
HIGH SCHOOL: Bishop MacDonnell (Guelph, Ont.).
TRANSACTIONS/CAREER NOTES: Selected by Hartford Whalers in first round (first Whalers pick, fifth overall) of NHL entry draft (June 28, 1994).
HONORS: Won Emms Family Award (1992-93).... Named to Can.HL All-Rookie team (1992-93).... Named to OHL All-Rookie team (1992-93).... Won Can.HL Top Draft Prospect Award (1993-94).

			REGULAR SEASON					PLAYOFFS				
Season Team	League	Gms.	G	A	Pts.	PIM	Gms.	G	A	Pts.	PIM
91-92—Thornhill	Tier II Jr. A	43	27	53	80	48	—	—	—	—	—
92-93—Guelph	OHL	65	32	47	79	88	5	2	2	4	6
93-94—Guelph	OHL	66	45	81	126	95	9	2	11	13	31

O'NEILL, MIKE
G, JETS

PERSONAL: Born November 3, 1967, in Montreal.... 5-7/160.... Catches left.... Full name: Michael Anthony O'Neill Jr.
COLLEGE: Yale.
TRANSACTIONS/CAREER NOTES: Selected by Winnipeg Jets in NHL supplemental draft (June 10, 1988).... Dislocated shoulder (April 8, 1991); missed remainder of playoffs.... Dislocated shoulder (February 1, 1993); missed two games.... Underwent shoulder surgery (February 12, 1993); missed remainder of season.... Injured knee (March 16, 1994); missed one game.
HONORS: Named to ECAC All-Star first team (1986-87 and 1988-89).... Named to NCAA All-America East first team (1988-89).

			REGULAR SEASON						PLAYOFFS					
Season Team	League	Gms.	Min.	W	L	T	GA	SO	Avg.	Gms.	Min.	W	L	GA	SO	Avg.
85-86—Yale University	ECAC	6	389	3	1	0	17	0	2.62	—	—	—	—	—	—	—
86-87—Yale University	ECAC	16	964	9	6	1	55	2	3.42	—	—	—	—	—	—	—
87-88—Yale University	ECAC	24	1385	6	17	0	101	0	4.38	—	—	—	—	—	—	—
88-89—Yale University	ECAC	25	1490	10	14	1	93	0	3.74	—	—	—	—	—	—	—
89-90—Tappara	Finland	41	2369	23	13	5	127	2	3.22	—	—	—	—	—	—	—
90-91—Fort Wayne	IHL	8	490	5	2	‡1	31	0	3.80	—	—	—	—	—	—	—
—Moncton	AHL	30	1613	13	7	6	84	0	3.12	8	435	3	4	29	0	4.00
91-92—Fort Wayne	IHL	33	1858	22	6	‡3	97	†4	3.13	—	—	—	—	—	—	—
—Moncton	AHL	32	1902	14	16	2	108	1	3.41	11	670	4	†7	43	1	3.85
—Winnipeg	NHL	1	13	0	0	0	1	0	4.62	—	—	—	—	—	—	—
92-93—Moncton	AHL	30	1649	13	10	4	88	1	3.20	—	—	—	—	—	—	—
—Winnipeg	NHL	2	73	0	0	1	6	0	4.93	—	—	—	—	—	—	—
93-94—Moncton	AHL	12	717	8	4	0	33	1	2.76	—	—	—	—	—	—	—
—Fort Wayne	IHL	11	642	4	4	‡3	38	0	3.55	—	—	—	—	—	—	—
—Winnipeg	NHL	17	738	0	9	1	51	0	4.15	—	—	—	—	—	—	—
NHL totals		20	824	0	9	2	58	0	4.22							

OSADCHY, ALEXANDER
D, SHARKS

PERSONAL: Born July 19, 1975, in Kharkov, U.S.S.R. ... 5-11/190. ... Shoots right.
TRANSACTIONS/CAREER NOTES: Selected by San Jose Sharks in fourth round (fifth Sharks pick, 80th overall) of NHL entry draft (June 26, 1993).

			REGULAR SEASON					PLAYOFFS				
Season Team	League	Gms.	G	A	Pts.	PIM	Gms.	G	A	Pts.	PIM
92-93—CSKA Moscow	CIS	37	0	1	1	60	—	—	—	—	—
93-94—CSKA Moscow	CIS	46	5	2	7	33	3	0	0	0	0
—Russian Penguins	IHL	11	0	5	5	24	—	—	—	—	—

OSBORNE, MARK
LW, MAPLE LEAFS

PERSONAL: Born August 13, 1961, in Toronto.... 6-2/205.... Shoots left.... Full name: Mark Anatole Osborne.
TRANSACTIONS/CAREER NOTES: Selected by Detroit Red Wings as underage junior in third round (second Red Wings pick, 46th overall) of NHL entry draft (June 11, 1980)....

Traded by Red Wings with D Willie Huber and RW Mike Blaisdell to New York Rangers for RW Ron Duguay, G Eddie Mio and RW Ed Johnstone (June 13, 1983).... Injured hip (October 1984).... Sprained ankle (February 12, 1986); missed 12 games.... Suffered laceration behind left knee (February 1987).... Traded by Rangers to Toronto Maple Leafs for third-round pick (C Rob Zamuner) in 1989 draft (March 5, 1987).... Separated left shoulder (April 1988).... Traded by Maple Leafs with C/RW Ed Olczyk to Winnipeg Jets for D Dave Ellett and C Paul Fenton (November 10, 1990).... Fractured left thumb and injured ligaments (December 3, 1990); missed 21 games.... Separated shoulder (October 29, 1991); missed three games.... Fractured ankle (January 1992); missed 14 games.... Traded by Jets to Maple Leafs for RW Lucien Deblois (March 10, 1992).... Sprained knee (March 28, 1993); missed seven games.... Strained rib muscle (November 24, 1993); missed eight games.

Season	Team	League	REGULAR SEASON					PLAYOFFS				
			Gms.	G	A	Pts.	PIM	Gms.	G	A	Pts.	PIM
78-79	Niagara Falls	OMJHL	62	17	25	42	53	—	—	—	—	—
79-80	Niagara Falls	OMJHL	52	10	33	43	104	10	2	1	3	23
80-81	Niagara Falls	OMJHL	54	39	41	80	140	12	11	10	21	20
	Adirondack	AHL	—	—	—	—	—	13	2	3	5	2
81-82	Detroit	NHL	80	26	41	67	61	—	—	—	—	—
82-83	Detroit	NHL	80	19	24	43	83	—	—	—	—	—
83-84	New York Rangers	NHL	73	23	28	51	88	5	0	1	1	7
84-85	New York Rangers	NHL	23	4	4	8	33	3	0	0	0	4
85-86	New York Rangers	NHL	62	16	24	40	80	15	2	3	5	26
86-87	New York Rangers	NHL	58	17	15	32	101	—	—	—	—	—
	Toronto	NHL	16	5	10	15	12	9	1	3	4	6
87-88	Toronto	NHL	79	23	37	60	102	6	1	3	4	16
88-89	Toronto	NHL	75	16	30	46	112	—	—	—	—	—
89-90	Toronto	NHL	78	23	50	73	91	5	2	3	5	12
90-91	Toronto	NHL	18	3	3	6	4	—	—	—	—	—
	Winnipeg	NHL	37	8	8	16	59	—	—	—	—	—
91-92	Winnipeg	NHL	43	4	12	16	65	—	—	—	—	—
	Toronto	NHL	11	3	1	4	8	—	—	—	—	—
92-93	Toronto	NHL	76	12	14	26	89	19	1	1	2	16
93-94	Toronto	NHL	73	9	15	24	145	18	4	2	6	52
NHL totals			882	211	316	527	1133	80	11	16	27	139

OSGOOD, CHRIS
G, RED WINGS

PERSONAL: Born November 26, 1972, in Peace River, Alta.... 5-10/160.... Catches left.
TRANSACTIONS/CAREER NOTES: Selected by Detroit Red Wings in third round (third Red Wings pick, 54th overall) of NHL entry draft (June 22, 1991).
HONORS: Named to WHL (East) All-Star second team (1990-91).

Season	Team	League	REGULAR SEASON							PLAYOFFS						
			Gms.	Min.	W	L	T	GA	SO	Avg.	Gms.	Min.	W	L	GA	SO	Avg.
89-90	Medicine Hat	WHL	57	3094	24	28	2	228	0	4.42	3	173	3	4	17	0	5.90
90-91	Medicine Hat	WHL	46	2630	23	18	3	173	2	3.95	12	714	7	5	42	0	3.53
91-92	Medicine Hat	WHL	15	819	10	3	0	44	0	3.22	—	—	—	—	—	—	—
	Brandon	WHL	16	890	3	10	1	60	1	4.04	—	—	—	—	—	—	—
	Seattle	WHL	21	1217	12	7	1	65	1	3.20	15	904	9	6	51	0	3.38
92-93	Adirondack	AHL	45	2438	19	19	2	159	0	3.91	1	59	0	1	2	0	2.03
93-94	Adirondack	AHL	4	240	3	1	0	13	0	3.25	—	—	—	—	—	—	—
	Detroit	NHL	41	2206	23	8	5	105	2	2.86	6	307	3	2	12	1	2.35
NHL totals			41	2206	23	8	5	105	2	2.86	6	307	3	2	12	1	2.35

OSIECKI, MARK
D, STARS

PERSONAL: Born July 23, 1968, in St. Paul, Minn.... 6-2/200.... Shoots right.... Full name: Mark Anthony Osiecki.... Name pronounced oh-SEE-kee.
COLLEGE: Wisconsin.
TRANSACTIONS/CAREER NOTES: Selected by Calgary Flames in ninth round (10th Flames pick, 187th overall) of NHL entry draft (June 13, 1987).... Traded by Flames to Ottawa Senators for LW Chris Lindberg (June 23, 1992).... Claimed on waivers by Winnipeg Jets (February 20, 1993).... Traded by Jets to Minnesota North Stars for ninth- and 10th-round picks in 1993 draft (March 20, 1993).... North Stars franchise moved from Minnesota to Dallas and renamed Stars for 1993-94 season.
HONORS: Named to NCAA All-Tournament team (1989-90).

Season	Team	League	REGULAR SEASON					PLAYOFFS				
			Gms.	G	A	Pts.	PIM	Gms.	G	A	Pts.	PIM
86-87	University of Wisconsin	WCHA	8	0	1	1	4	—	—	—	—	—
87-88	University of Wisconsin	WCHA	18	0	1	1	22	—	—	—	—	—
88-89	University of Wisconsin	WCHA	44	1	3	4	56	—	—	—	—	—
89-90	University of Wisconsin	WCHA	46	5	38	43	78	—	—	—	—	—
90-91	Salt Lake City	IHL	75	1	24	25	36	4	2	0	2	2
91-92	Calgary	NHL	50	2	7	9	24	—	—	—	—	—
	Salt Lake City	IHL	1	0	0	0	0	—	—	—	—	—
92-93	Ottawa	NHL	34	0	4	4	12	—	—	—	—	—
	New Haven	AHL	4	0	1	1	0	—	—	—	—	—
	Winnipeg	NHL	4	1	0	1	2	—	—	—	—	—
	Minnesota	NHL	5	0	0	0	5	—	—	—	—	—
93-94	Kalamazoo	IHL	65	4	14	18	45	5	0	0	0	5
NHL totals			93	3	11	14	43					

O'SULLIVAN, CHRIS
D, FLAMES

PERSONAL: Born May 15, 1974, in Dorchester, Mass.... 6-2/180.... Shoots left.
HIGH SCHOOL: Catholic Memorial (Boston).
COLLEGE: Boston University.
TRANSACTIONS/CAREER NOTES: Selected by Calgary Flames in second round (second Flames pick, 30th overall) of NHL entry draft (June 20, 1992).

			REGULAR SEASON					PLAYOFFS			
Season Team	League	Gms.	G	A	Pts.	PIM	Gms.	G	A	Pts.	PIM
91-92—Catholic Memorial H.S.	Mass. H.S.	26	26	23	49	65	—	—	—	—	—
92-93—Boston University	Hockey East	5	0	2	2	4	—	—	—	—	—
93-94—Boston University	Hockey East	32	5	18	23	25	—	—	—	—	—

OTEVREL, JAROSLAV
C, SHARKS

PERSONAL: Born September 16, 1968, in Gottwaldov, Czechoslovakia.... 6-3/200.... Shoots left.
TRANSACTIONS/CAREER NOTES: Selected by San Jose Sharks in seventh round (eighth Sharks pick, 133rd overall) of NHL entry draft (June 22, 1991).... Bruised thigh (January 26, 1993); missed four games.

			REGULAR SEASON					PLAYOFFS			
Season Team	League	Gms.	G	A	Pts.	PIM	Gms.	G	A	Pts.	PIM
87-88—TJ Gottwaldov.................	Czech.	32	4	7	11	18	—	—	—	—	—
88-89—TJ Zlin	Czech.	40	14	6	20	37	—	—	—	—	—
89-90—Dukla Trencin	Czech.	43	7	10	17	20	—	—	—	—	—
90-91—TJ Zlin	Czech.	49	24	26	50	105	—	—	—	—	—
91-92—ZPS Zlin	Czech.	40	14	15	29	...	—	—	—	—	—
92-93—Kansas City...................	IHL	62	17	27	44	58	6	1	4	5	4
—San Jose...................	NHL	7	0	2	2	0	—	—	—	—	—
93-94—Kansas City...................	IHL	62	20	33	53	46	—	—	—	—	—
—San Jose...................	NHL	9	3	2	5	2	—	—	—	—	—
NHL totals................		**16**	**3**	**4**	**7**	**2**					

OTTO, JOEL
C, FLAMES

PERSONAL: Born October 29, 1961, in Elk River, Minn.... 6-4/220.... Shoots right.... Full name: Joel Stuart Otto.
COLLEGE: Bemidji State (Minn.).
TRANSACTIONS/CAREER NOTES: Signed as free agent by Calgary Flames (September 11, 1984).... Tore cartilage in right knee (March 10, 1987).... Strained right knee ligaments (October 8, 1987).... Bruised ribs (November 1989).... Hospitalized after being crosschecked from behind (January 13, 1990).... Injured ankle (March 10, 1992); missed two games.... Suffered rib injury (January 5, 1993); missed eight games.... Bruised foot (February 2, 1993); missed one game.
MISCELLANEOUS: Member of Stanley Cup championship team (1989).

			REGULAR SEASON					PLAYOFFS			
Season Team	League	Gms.	G	A	Pts.	PIM	Gms.	G	A	Pts.	PIM
80-81—Bemidji State...................	NCAA-II	23	5	11	16	10	—	—	—	—	—
81-82—Bemidji State...................	NCAA-II	31	19	33	52	24	—	—	—	—	—
82-83—Bemidji State...................	NCAA-II	37	33	28	61	68	—	—	—	—	—
83-84—Bemidji State...................	NCAA-II	31	32	43	75	32	—	—	—	—	—
84-85—Moncton	AHL	56	27	36	63	89	—	—	—	—	—
—Calgary......................	NHL	17	4	8	12	30	3	2	1	3	10
85-86—Calgary......................	NHL	79	25	34	59	188	22	5	10	15	80
86-87—Calgary......................	NHL	68	19	31	50	185	2	0	2	2	6
87-88—Calgary......................	NHL	62	13	39	52	194	9	3	2	5	26
88-89—Calgary......................	NHL	72	23	30	53	213	22	6	13	19	46
89-90—Calgary......................	NHL	75	13	20	33	116	6	2	2	4	2
90-91—Calgary......................	NHL	76	19	20	39	183	7	1	2	3	8
91-92—Calgary......................	NHL	78	13	21	34	161	—	—	—	—	—
92-93—Calgary......................	NHL	75	19	33	52	150	6	4	2	6	4
93-94—Calgary......................	NHL	81	11	12	23	92	3	0	1	1	4
NHL totals................		**683**	**159**	**248**	**407**	**1512**	**80**	**23**	**35**	**58**	**186**

OZOLINSH, SANDIS
D, SHARKS

PERSONAL: Born August 3, 1972, in Riga, U.S.S.R.... 6-1/195.... Shoots left.... Name pronounced SAN-dihz OH-zoh-LIHNCH.
TRANSACTIONS/CAREER NOTES: Selected by San Jose Sharks in second round (third Sharks pick, 30th overall) of NHL entry draft (June 22, 1991).... Strained back (November 7, 1992); missed one game.... Tore knee ligaments (December 30, 1992) and underwent surgery to repair anterior cruciate ligament; missed remainder of season.... Injured knee (December 11, 1993); missed one game.
HONORS: Played in NHL All-Star Game (1994).

			REGULAR SEASON					PLAYOFFS			
Season Team	League	Gms.	G	A	Pts.	PIM	Gms.	G	A	Pts.	PIM
90-91—Dynamo Riga....................	USSR	44	0	3	3	49	—	—	—	—	—
91-92—Riga	CIS	30	5	0	5	42	—	—	—	—	—
—Kansas City....................	IHL	34	6	9	15	20	15	2	5	7	22
92-93—San Jose......................	NHL	37	7	16	23	40	—	—	—	—	—
93-94—San Jose......................	NHL	81	26	38	64	24	14	0	10	10	8
NHL totals................		**118**	**33**	**54**	**87**	**64**	**14**	**0**	**10**	**10**	**8**

PADEN, KEVIN
C/LW, OILERS

PERSONAL: Born February 12, 1975, in Woodhaven, Mich. . . . . 6-3/175. . . . Shoots left. . . . Name pronounced PAY-dehn.

TRANSACTIONS/CAREER NOTES: Selected by Edmonton Oilers in third round (fourth Oilers pick, 59th overall) of NHL entry draft (June 26, 1993).

			REGULAR SEASON					PLAYOFFS			
Season Team	League	Gms.	G	A	Pts.	PIM	Gms.	G	A	Pts.	PIM
92-93—Detroit	OHL	54	14	9	23	41	15	1	1	2	2
93-94—Detroit	OHL	38	10	19	29	54	—	—	—	—	—
—Windsor	OHL	24	0	11	11	30	4	0	1	1	4

PAEK, JIM
D, SENATORS

PERSONAL: Born April 7, 1967, in Seoul, South Korea. . . . 6-1/195. . . . Shoots left. . . . Name pronounced PAK.

TRANSACTIONS/CAREER NOTES: Selected by Pittsburgh Penguins as underage junior in ninth round (ninth Penguins pick, 170th overall) of NHL entry draft (June 15, 1985). . . . Suspended two games by OHL for being involved in bench-clearing incident (November 2, 1986). . . . Dislocated finger on left hand (January 10, 1992); missed 14 games. . . . Suspended three off-days and fined $500 by NHL for fighting (February 26, 1993). . . . Injured eye (September 26, 1993); missed 13 games. . . . Traded by Penguins to Los Angeles Kings for RW Tomas Sandstrom and C Shawn McEachern (February 15, 1994). . . . Traded by Kings to Ottawa Senators for future considerations (June 25, 1994).

MISCELLANEOUS: Member of Stanley Cup championship teams (1991 and 1992).

			REGULAR SEASON					PLAYOFFS			
Season Team	League	Gms.	G	A	Pts.	PIM	Gms.	G	A	Pts.	PIM
84-85—Oshawa	OHL	54	2	13	15	57	5	1	0	1	9
85-86—Oshawa	OHL	64	5	21	26	122	6	0	1	1	9
86-87—Oshawa	OHL	57	5	17	22	75	26	1	14	15	43
87-88—Muskegon	IHL	82	7	52	59	141	6	0	0	0	29
88-89—Muskegon	IHL	80	3	54	57	96	14	1	10	11	24
89-90—Muskegon	IHL	81	9	41	50	115	15	1	10	11	41
90-91—Canadian national team	Int'l	48	2	12	14	24	—	—	—	—	—
—Pittsburgh	NHL	3	0	0	0	9	8	1	0	1	2
91-92—Pittsburgh	NHL	49	1	7	8	36	19	0	4	4	6
92-93—Pittsburgh	NHL	77	3	15	18	64	—	—	—	—	—
93-94—Pittsburgh	NHL	41	0	4	4	8	—	—	—	—	—
—Los Angeles	NHL	18	1	1	2	10	—	—	—	—	—
NHL totals		188	5	27	32	127	27	1	4	5	8

PALFFY, ZIGMUND
LW, ISLANDERS

PERSONAL: Born May 5, 1972, in Skalica, Czechoslovakia. . . . 5-10/169. . . . Shoots left. . . . Name pronounced PAHL-fee.

TRANSACTIONS/CAREER NOTES: Selected by New York Islanders in second round (second Islanders pick, 26th overall) of NHL entry draft (June 22, 1991). . . . Loaned to Slovak Olympic Team (January 31, 1994).

HONORS: Named Czechoslovakian League Rookie of the Year (1990-91). . . . Named to Czechoslovakian League All-Star team (1991-92).

			REGULAR SEASON					PLAYOFFS			
Season Team	League	Gms.	G	A	Pts.	PIM	Gms.	G	A	Pts.	PIM
90-91—Nitra	Czech.	50	34	16	50	18	—	—	—	—	—
91-92—Dukla Trencin	Czech.	32	23	25	*48	...	—	—	—	—	—
92-93—Dukla Trencin	Czech.	43	38	41	79	...	—	—	—	—	—
93-94—Salt Lake City	IHL	57	25	32	57	83	—	—	—	—	—
—Slovakian Olympic team	Int'l	8	3	7	10	8	—	—	—	—	—
—New York Islanders	NHL	5	0	0	0	0	—	—	—	—	—
NHL totals		5	0	0	0	0					

PANDOLFO, JAY
LW, DEVILS

PERSONAL: Born December 27, 1974, in Winchester, Mass. . . . 6-1/195. . . . Shoots left.
HIGH SCHOOL: Burlington (Mass.).
COLLEGE: Boston University.
TRANSACTIONS/CAREER NOTES: Selected by New Jersey Devils in second round (second Devils pick, 32nd overall) of NHL entry draft (June 26, 1993).

			REGULAR SEASON					PLAYOFFS			
Season Team	League	Gms.	G	A	Pts.	PIM	Gms.	G	A	Pts.	PIM
90-91—Burlington H.S.	Mass. H.S.	20	19	27	46	10	—	—	—	—	—
91-92—Burlington H.S.	Mass. H.S.	20	35	34	69	14	—	—	—	—	—
92-93—Boston University	Hockey East	39	17	23	40	16	—	—	—	—	—
93-94—Boston University	Hockey East	37	17	25	42	27	—	—	—	—	—

PANKEWICZ, GREG
RW, SENATORS

PERSONAL: Born October 6, 1970, in Valley, Alta. . . . 6-0/189. . . . Shoots right.
TRANSACTIONS/CAREER NOTES: Signed as free agent by Ottawa Senators (May 27, 1993).

			REGULAR SEASON					PLAYOFFS			
Season Team	League	Gms.	G	A	Pts.	PIM	Gms.	G	A	Pts.	PIM
89-90—Regina	WHL	63	14	24	38	136	10	1	3	4	19
90-91—Regina	WHL	72	39	41	80	134	8	4	7	11	12
91-92—Knoxville	ECHL	59	41	39	80	214	—	—	—	—	—
92-93—New Haven	AHL	62	23	20	43	163	—	—	—	—	—

P

Season	Team	League	REGULAR SEASON					PLAYOFFS				
			Gms.	G	A	Pts.	Pen.	Gms.	G	A	Pts.	Pen.
93-94—Prince Edward Island		AHL	69	33	29	62	241	—	—	—	—	—
—Ottawa		NHL	3	0	0	0	2	—	—	—	—	—
NHL totals			3	0	0	0	2					

PANTELEEV, GRIGORI
LW/RW, BRUINS

PERSONAL: Born November 13, 1972, in Riga, U.S.S.R. . . . 5-9/194. . . . Shoots left. . . . Name pronounced grih-GOHR-ee PAN-tuh-lay-ehf.
TRANSACTIONS/CAREER NOTES: Selected by Boston Bruins in sixth round (fifth Bruins pick, 136th overall) of NHL entry draft (June 20, 1992).

Season	Team	League	REGULAR SEASON					PLAYOFFS				
			Gms.	G	A	Pts.	PIM	Gms.	G	A	Pts.	PIM
90-91—Dynamo Riga		USSR	23	4	1	5	4	—	—	—	—	—
91-92—Riga		CIS	26	4	8	12	4	—	—	—	—	—
92-93—Providence		AHL	39	17	30	47	22	3	0	0	0	10
—Boston		NHL	39	8	6	14	12	—	—	—	—	—
93-94—Providence		AHL	55	24	26	50	20	—	—	—	—	—
—Boston		NHL	10	0	0	0	0	—	—	—	—	—
NHL totals			49	8	6	14	12					

PAQUETTE, CHARLES
D, BRUINS

PERSONAL: Born June 17, 1975, in Lachute, Que. . . . 6-1/193. . . . Shoots left. . . . Name pronounced pa-KEHT.
TRANSACTIONS/CAREER NOTES: Selected by Boston Bruins in fourth round (third Bruins pick, 88th overall) of NHL entry draft (June 26, 1993).

Season	Team	League	REGULAR SEASON					PLAYOFFS				
			Gms.	G	A	Pts.	PIM	Gms.	G	A	Pts.	PIM
91-92—Trois-Rivieres		QMJHL	60	1	7	8	101	6	0	0	0	2
92-93—Sherbrooke		QMJHL	54	2	5	7	104	15	0	0	0	33
93-94—Sherbrooke		QMJHL	63	5	14	19	165	8	0	2	2	15

PARK, RICHARD
C, PENGUINS

PERSONAL: Born May 27, 1976, in Seoul, South Korea. . . . 5-11/176. . . . Shoots right.
TRANSACTIONS/CAREER NOTES: Selected by Pittsburgh Penguins in second round (second Penguins pick, 50th overall) of NHL entry draft (June 28, 1994).

Season	Team	League	REGULAR SEASON					PLAYOFFS				
			Gms.	G	A	Pts.	PIM	Gms.	G	A	Pts.	PIM
91-92—Williams Lake		PCJHL	76	49	58	107	91	—	—	—	—	—
92-93—Belleville		OHL	66	23	38	61	38	5	0	0	0	14
93-94—Belleville		OHL	59	27	49	76	70	12	3	5	8	18

PARKS, GREG
C, ISLANDERS

PERSONAL: Born March 25, 1967, in Edmonton. . . . 5-9/180. . . . Shoots right. . . . Full name: Gregory Roy Parks.
COLLEGE: Bowling Green State.
TRANSACTIONS/CAREER NOTES: Signed as free agent by Springfield Indians (September 1989). . . . Signed as free agent by New York Islanders (August 13, 1990). . . . Loaned to Canadian Olympic team (January 31, 1994).
HONORS: Named to NCAA All-America West first team (1988-89). . . . Named to CCHA All-Star first team (1988-89).
MISCELLANEOUS: Member of silver-medal-winning Canadian Olympic team (1994).

Season	Team	League	REGULAR SEASON					PLAYOFFS				
			Gms.	G	A	Pts.	PIM	Gms.	G	A	Pts.	PIM
84-85—St. Albert		AJHL	48	36	74	110	...	—	—	—	—	—
85-86—Bowling Green State		CCHA	41	16	26	42	43	—	—	—	—	—
86-87—Bowling Green State		CCHA	45	23	27	50	52	—	—	—	—	—
87-88—Bowling Green State		CCHA	45	30	44	74	86	—	—	—	—	—
88-89—Bowling Green State		CCHA	47	32	42	74	96	—	—	—	—	—
89-90—Springfield		AHL	49	22	32	54	30	18	9	†13	*22	22
—Johnstown		ECHL	8	5	9	14	7	—	—	—	—	—
90-91—Capital District		AHL	48	32	43	75	67	—	—	—	—	—
—New York Islanders		NHL	20	1	2	3	4	—	—	—	—	—
91-92—New York Islanders		NHL	1	0	0	0	2	—	—	—	—	—
—Capital District		AHL	70	36	57	93	84	7	5	8	13	4
92-93—Leksand		Sweden	39	21	19	40	66	1	0	0	0	4
—Canadian national team		Int'l	9	2	2	4	4	—	—	—	—	—
—New York Islanders		NHL	2	0	0	0	0	2	0	0	0	0
93-94—Leksand		Sweden	39	21	18	39	44	4	3	1	4	...
—Canadian national team		Int'l	21	2	3	5	122	—	—	—	—	—
—Canadian Olympic Team		Int'l	8	1	2	3	10	—	—	—	—	—
NHL totals			23	1	2	3	6	2	0	0	0	0

PARROTT, JEFF
D, NORDIQUES

PERSONAL: Born April 6, 1971, in The Pas, Man. . . . 6-1/195. . . . Shoots right.
COLLEGE: Minnesota-Duluth.
TRANSACTIONS/CAREER NOTES: Strained knee ligaments (November 1988). . . . Selected by Quebec Nordiques in sixth round (fourth Nordiques pick, 106th overall) of NHL entry draft (June 16, 1990).

P

Season Team	League	REGULAR SEASON					PLAYOFFS				
		Gms.	G	A	Pts.	PIM	Gms.	G	A	Pts.	PIM
88-89—Notre Dame	SJHL	51	6	18	24	143	—	—	—	—	—
89-90—Minnesota-Duluth	WCHA	35	1	6	7	64	—	—	—	—	—
90-91—Minnesota-Duluth	WCHA	39	2	8	10	65	—	—	—	—	—
91-92—Minnesota-Duluth	WCHA	33	1	8	9	78	—	—	—	—	—
92-93—Minnesota-Duluth	WCHA	39	4	13	17	116	—	—	—	—	—
93-94—Cornwall	AHL	52	4	11	15	37	—	—	—	—	—

PASLAWSKI, GREG

RW, FLAMES

PERSONAL: Born August 25, 1961, in Kindersley, Sask.... 5-11/190.... Shoots right. ... Full name: Gregory Stephen Paslawski.

TRANSACTIONS/CAREER NOTES: Signed as free agent by Montreal Canadiens (October 5, 1981).... Traded by Canadiens with C Doug Wickenheiser and D Gilbert Delorme to St. Louis Blues for LW Perry Turnbull (December 21, 1983).... Injured knee (February 20, 1986).... Injured knee (December 1986).... Pinched nerve in left leg (October 1987).... Underwent disk surgery (November 1987).... Traded by Blues with third-round pick in 1989 draft (C Kris Draper) to Winnipeg Jets for second-round pick (LW Denny Felsner) in 1989 draft (June 17, 1989).... Ruptured bicep muscle in right shoulder (December 13, 1990).... Pulled groin (January 21, 1991).... Traded by Jets to Buffalo Sabres to complete the C Dale Hawerchuk trade of June 1990 (February 4, 1991).... Selected by San Jose Sharks in NHL expansion draft (May 30, 1991).... Traded by Sharks to Quebec Nordiques for C Tony Hrkac (May 30, 1991).... Signed as free agent by Philadelphia Flyers (August 25, 1992).... Traded by Flyers to Calgary Flames for future considerations (March 18, 1993).... Strained left knee ligaments (November 9, 1993); missed 20 games.

Season Team	League	REGULAR SEASON					PLAYOFFS				
		Gms.	G	A	Pts.	PIM	Gms.	G	A	Pts.	PIM
80-81—Prince Albert	SJHL	59	55	60	115	106	—	—	—	—	—
81-82—Nova Scotia	AHL	43	15	11	26	31	—	—	—	—	—
82-83—Nova Scotia	AHL	75	46	42	88	32	6	1	3	4	8
83-84—Montreal	NHL	26	1	4	5	4	—	—	—	—	—
—St. Louis	NHL	34	8	6	14	17	9	1	0	1	2
84-85—St. Louis	NHL	72	22	20	42	21	3	0	0	0	2
85-86—St. Louis	NHL	56	22	11	33	18	17	10	7	17	13
86-87—St. Louis	NHL	76	29	35	64	27	6	1	1	2	4
87-88—St. Louis	NHL	17	2	1	3	4	3	1	1	2	2
88-89—St. Louis	NHL	75	26	26	52	18	9	2	1	3	2
89-90—Winnipeg	NHL	71	18	30	48	14	7	1	3	4	0
90-91—Winnipeg	NHL	43	9	10	19	10	—	—	—	—	—
—Buffalo	NHL	12	2	1	3	4	—	—	—	—	—
91-92—Quebec	NHL	80	28	17	45	18	—	—	—	—	—
92-93—Philadelphia	NHL	60	14	19	33	12	—	—	—	—	—
—Calgary	NHL	13	4	5	9	0	6	3	0	3	0
93-94—Calgary	NHL	15	2	0	2	2	—	—	—	—	—
—Peoria	IHL	29	16	16	32	12	6	3	3	6	0
NHL totals		650	187	185	372	169	60	19	13	32	25

PASSMORE, STEVE

G, OILERS

PERSONAL: Born January 29, 1973, in Thunder Bay, Ont.... 5-9/165.... Catches left.

TRANSACTIONS/CAREER NOTES: Selected by Quebec Nordiques in ninth round (10th Nordiques pick, 196th overall) of NHL entry draft (June 20, 1992).... Traded by Nordiques to Edmonton Oilers for D Brad Werenka (March 21, 1994).

HONORS: Named to WHL (West) All-Star first team (1992-93).

Season Team	League	REGULAR SEASON							PLAYOFFS					
		Gms.	Min.	W	L	T	GA	SO	Avg.	Gms.	Min.	W	L	GA	SO	Avg.
88-89—Tri-City	WHL	1	60	...	...	...	6	0	6.00	—	—	—	—	—	—	—
89-90—Tri-City	WHL	4	215	...	...	...	17	0	4.74	—	—	—	—	—	—	—
90-91—Victoria	WHL	35	1838	3	25	1	190	0	6.20	—	—	—	—	—	—	—
91-92—Victoria	WHL	*71	*4228	15	50	7	347	0	4.93	—	—	—	—	—	—	—
92-93—Victoria	WHL	43	2402	14	24	2	150	1	3.75	—	—	—	—	—	—	—
—Kamloops	WHL	25	1479	19	6	0	69	1	2.80	7	401	4	2	22	1	3.29
93-94—Kamloops	WHL	36	1927	22	9	2	88	1	*2.74	18	1099	11	7	60	0	3.28

PATRICK, JAMES

D, FLAMES

PERSONAL: Born June 14, 1963, in Winnipeg.... 6-2/200.... Shoots right.... Brother of Steve Patrick, right winger, Buffalo Sabres, New York Rangers and Quebec Nordiques (1980-81 through 1985-86).

COLLEGE: North Dakota.

TRANSACTIONS/CAREER NOTES: Selected by New York Rangers as underage junior in first round (first Rangers pick, ninth overall) of NHL entry draft (June 10, 1981).... Injured groin (October 1984).... Pinched nerve (December 15, 1985).... Strained left knee ligaments (March 1988).... Bruised shoulder and chest (December 1988).... Pulled groin (March 13, 1989).... Sprained shoulder (November 4, 1992); missed three games.... Bruised right shoulder (November 27, 1992); missed three games.... Sprained left knee (January 27, 1993); missed four games.... Suffered herniated disc (February 24, 1993); missed two games.... Suffered herniated disc (March 28, 1993); missed remainder of season... Traded by Rangers with C Darren Turcotte to Hartford Whalers for RW Steve Larmer, LW Nick Kypreos and undisclosed draft pick (November 2, 1993).... Suffered herniated disc (December 7, 1993); missed five games.... Traded by Whalers with C Mikael Nylander and D Zarley Zalapski to Calgary Flames for D Gary Suter, LW Paul Ranheim and C Ted Drury (March 10, 1994).

HONORS: Named SJHL Player of the Year (1980-81).... Named to SJHL All-Star first team (1980-81).... Won WCHA Rookie of the Year Award (1981-82).... Named to WCHA All-Star second team (1981-82).... Named to NCAA All-Tournament team (1981-82).... Named to NCAA All-America West team (1982-83).... Named to WCHA All-Star first team (1982-83).

P

Season Team	League	REGULAR SEASON					PLAYOFFS				
		Gms.	G	A	Pts.	PIM	Gms.	G	A	Pts.	PIM
80-81—Prince Albert....................	SJHL	59	21	61	82	162	4	1	6	7	0
81-82—Univ. of North Dakota......	WCHA	42	5	24	29	26	—	—	—	—	—
82-83—Univ. of North Dakota....	WCHA	36	12	36	48	29	—	—	—	—	—
83-84—Canadian Olympic Team ..	Int'l	63	7	24	31	52	—	—	—	—	—
—New York Rangers...........	NHL	12	1	7	8	2	5	0	3	3	2
84-85—New York Rangers........	NHL	75	8	28	36	71	3	0	0	0	4
85-86—New York Rangers........	NHL	75	14	29	43	88	16	1	5	6	34
86-87—New York Rangers........	NHL	78	10	45	55	62	6	1	2	3	2
87-88—New York Rangers........	NHL	70	17	45	62	52	—	—	—	—	—
88-89—New York Rangers........	NHL	68	11	36	47	41	4	0	1	1	2
89-90—New York Rangers........	NHL	73	14	43	57	50	10	3	8	11	0
90-91—New York Rangers........	NHL	74	10	49	59	58	6	0	0	0	6
91-92—New York Rangers........	NHL	80	14	57	71	54	13	0	7	7	12
92-93—New York Rangers........	NHL	60	5	21	26	61	—	—	—	—	—
93-94—New York Rangers........	NHL	6	0	3	3	2	—	—	—	—	—
—Hartford........................	NHL	47	8	20	28	32	—	—	—	—	—
—Calgary........................	NHL	15	2	2	4	6	7	0	1	1	6
NHL totals...................................		733	114	385	499	579	70	5	27	32	68

PATTERSON, ED
RW, PENGUINS

PERSONAL: Born November 14, 1972, in Delta, B.C.... 6-2/210.... Shoots right.
TRANSACTIONS/CAREER NOTES: Selected by Pittsburgh Penguins in seventh round (seventh Penguins pick, 148th overall) of NHL entry draft (June 22, 1991).

Season Team	League	REGULAR SEASON					PLAYOFFS				
		Gms.	G	A	Pts.	PIM	Gms.	G	A	Pts.	PIM
90-91—Swift Current....................	WHL	7	2	7	9	0	—	—	—	—	—
—Kamloops......................	WHL	55	14	33	47	134	5	0	0	0	7
91-92—Kamloops	WHL	38	19	25	44	120	1	0	0	0	0
92-93—Cleveland	IHL	63	4	16	20	131	3	1	1	2	2
93-94—Cleveland	IHL	55	21	32	53	73	—	—	—	—	—
—Pittsburgh	NHL	27	3	1	4	10	—	—	—	—	—
NHL totals...................................		27	3	1	4	10					

PAYNTER, KENT
D

PERSONAL: Born April 27, 1965, in Summerside, P.E.I.... 6-0/185.... Shoots left.... Full name: Kent Douglas Paynter.
HIGH SCHOOL: Three Oaks (Summerside, P.E.I.).
TRANSACTIONS/CAREER NOTES: Selected by Chicago Blackhawks as underage junior in eighth round (ninth Blackhawks pick, 159th overall) of NHL entry draft (June 8, 1983).... Signed as free agent by Washington Capitals (August 21, 1989).... Traded by Capitals with LW Bob Joyce and C Tyler Larter to Winnipeg Jets for LW Brent Hughes, LW Craig Duncanson and C Simon Wheeldon (May 21, 1991).... Selected by Ottawa Senators in NHL expansion draft (June 18, 1992).... Suffered charley horse (January 30, 1993); missed four games.

Season Team	League	REGULAR SEASON					PLAYOFFS				
		Gms.	G	A	Pts.	PIM	Gms.	G	A	Pts.	PIM
81-82—Western Capitals	PEIJHL	35	7	23	30	66	—	—	—	—	—
82-83—Kitchener..........................	OHL	65	4	11	15	97	12	1	0	1	20
83-84—Kitchener..........................	OHL	65	9	27	36	94	16	4	9	13	18
84-85—Kitchener..........................	OHL	58	7	28	35	93	4	2	1	3	4
85-86—Nova Scotia......................	AHL	23	1	2	3	36	—	—	—	—	—
—Saginaw	IHL	4	0	1	1	2	—	—	—	—	—
86-87—Nova Scotia......................	AHL	66	2	6	8	57	2	0	0	0	0
87-88—Saginaw	IHL	74	8	20	28	141	10	0	1	1	30
—Chicago	NHL	2	0	0	0	2	—	—	—	—	—
88-89—Chicago	NHL	1	0	0	0	2	—	—	—	—	—
—Saginaw	IHL	69	12	14	26	148	6	2	2	4	17
89-90—Washington	NHL	13	1	2	3	18	3	0	0	0	10
—Baltimore.......................	AHL	60	7	20	27	110	11	5	6	11	34
90-91—Baltimore.......................	AHL	43	10	17	27	64	6	2	1	3	8
—Washington	NHL	1	0	0	0	15	1	0	0	0	0
91-92—Moncton	AHL	62	3	30	33	71	11	2	6	8	25
—Winnipeg	NHL	5	0	0	0	4	—	—	—	—	—
92-93—New Haven	AHL	48	7	17	24	81	—	—	—	—	—
—Ottawa..........................	NHL	6	0	0	0	20	—	—	—	—	—
93-94—Ottawa............................	NHL	9	0	1	1	8	—	—	—	—	—
—Prince Edward Island	AHL	63	6	20	26	125	—	—	—	—	—
NHL totals...................................		37	1	3	4	69	4	0	0	0	10

PEAKE, PAT
RW, CAPITALS

PERSONAL: Born May 28, 1973, in Detroit.... 6-0/195.... Shoots right.... Full name: Patrick Michael Peake.
TRANSACTIONS/CAREER NOTES: Injured wrist (August 31, 1990).... Selected by Washington Capitals in first round (first Capitals pick, 14th overall) of NHL entry draft (June 22, 1991).... Suffered sore ankle (October 30, 1993); missed two games.... Suffered sore shoulder (December 23, 1993); missed six games.... Suffered from the flu (February 2, 1994); missed two games.... Bruised ribs (February 21, 1994); missed 14 games.

P

HONORS: Won Can.HL Player of the Year Award (1992-93).... Won Red Tilson Trophy (1992-93).... Won William Hanley Trophy (1992-93).... Named to Can.HL All-Star first team (1992-93).... Named to OHL All-Star first team (1992-93).

Season Team	League	REGULAR SEASON					PLAYOFFS				
		Gms.	G	A	Pts.	PIM	Gms.	G	A	Pts.	PIM
89-90—Detroit Compuware	NAJHL	40	36	37	73	57	—	—	—	—	—
90-91—Detroit	OHL	63	39	51	90	54	—	—	—	—	—
91-92—Detroit	OHL	53	41	52	93	44	7	8	9	17	10
—Baltimore	AHL	3	1	0	1	4	—	—	—	—	—
92-93—Detroit	OHL	46	58	78	136	64	2	1	3	4	2
93-94—Portland	AHL	4	0	5	5	2	—	—	—	—	—
—Washington	NHL	49	11	18	29	39	8	0	1	1	8
NHL totals		49	11	18	29	39	8	0	1	1	8

PEARSON, ROB
RW, CAPITALS

PERSONAL: Born August 3, 1971, in Oshawa, Ont.... 6-3/200.... Shoots right. **TRANSACTIONS/CAREER NOTES:** Broke wrist (November 18, 1988).... Selected by Toronto Maple Leafs in first round (second Maple Leafs pick, 12th overall) of NHL entry draft (June 17, 1989).... Dislocated right knee (August 15, 1989).... Suspended five games by OHL for checking from behind (February 7, 1990).... Broke collarbone (August 1990).... Traded by Belleville Bulls to Oshawa Generals for C Jarrod Skalde (November 18, 1990).... Partially tore knee ligament (October 23, 1993); missed 13 games.... Traded by Maple Leafs with first-round pick in 1994 draft (D Nolan Baumgartner) to Washington Capitals for C Mike Ridley and first-round pick (G Eric Fichaud) in 1994 draft (June 28, 1994). **HONORS:** Won Jim Mahon Memorial Trophy (1990-91).... Named to OHL All-Star first team (1990-91).

Season Team	League	REGULAR SEASON					PLAYOFFS				
		Gms.	G	A	Pts.	PIM	Gms.	G	A	Pts.	PIM
88-89—Belleville	OHL	26	8	12	20	51	—	—	—	—	—
89-90—Belleville	OHL	58	48	40	88	174	11	5	5	10	26
90-91—Belleville	OHL	10	6	3	9	27	—	—	—	—	—
—Oshawa	OHL	41	57	52	109	76	16	16	17	33	39
—Newmarket	AHL	3	0	0	0	29	—	—	—	—	—
91-92—Toronto	NHL	47	14	10	24	58	—	—	—	—	—
—St. John's	AHL	27	15	14	29	107	13	5	4	9	40
92-93—Toronto	NHL	78	23	14	37	211	14	2	2	4	31
93-94—Toronto	NHL	67	12	18	30	189	14	1	0	1	32
NHL totals		192	49	42	91	458	28	3	2	5	63

PEARSON, SCOTT
LW, OILERS

PERSONAL: Born December 19, 1969, in Cornwall, Ont.... 6-1/205.... Shoots left. **TRANSACTIONS/CAREER NOTES:** Underwent surgery to left wrist (May 1988).... Selected by Toronto Maple Leafs in first round (first Maple Leafs pick, sixth overall) of NHL entry draft (June 11, 1988).... Traded by Maple Leafs with second-round picks in 1991 (D Eric Lavigne) and 1992 drafts (D Tuomas Gronman) to Quebec Nordiques for C/LW Aaron Broten, D Michel Petit and RW Lucien Deblois (November 17, 1990).... Sprained left knee (September 27, 1992); missed first 22 games of season.... Traded by Nordiques to Edmonton Oilers for LW Martin Gelinas and sixth-round pick (C Nicholas Checco) in 1993 draft (June 20, 1993). ... Sprained medial collateral knee ligament (February 2, 1994); missed 11 games.

Season Team	League	REGULAR SEASON					PLAYOFFS				
		Gms.	G	A	Pts.	PIM	Gms.	G	A	Pts.	PIM
85-86—Kingston	OHL	63	16	23	39	56	—	—	—	—	—
86-87—Kingston	OHL	62	30	24	54	101	9	3	3	6	42
87-88—Kingston	OHL	46	26	32	58	118	—	—	—	—	—
88-89—Kingston	OHL	13	9	8	17	34	—	—	—	—	—
—Niagara Falls	OHL	32	26	34	60	90	17	14	10	24	53
—Toronto	NHL	9	0	1	1	2	—	—	—	—	—
89-90—Newmarket	AHL	18	12	11	23	64	—	—	—	—	—
—Toronto	NHL	41	5	10	15	90	2	2	0	2	10
90-91—Toronto	NHL	12	0	0	0	20	—	—	—	—	—
—Quebec	NHL	35	11	4	15	86	—	—	—	—	—
—Halifax	AHL	24	12	15	27	44	—	—	—	—	—
91-92—Quebec	NHL	10	1	2	3	14	—	—	—	—	—
—Halifax	AHL	5	2	1	3	4	—	—	—	—	—
92-93—Halifax	AHL	5	3	1	4	25	—	—	—	—	—
—Quebec	NHL	41	13	1	14	95	3	0	0	0	0
93-94—Edmonton	NHL	72	19	18	37	165	—	—	—	—	—
NHL totals		220	49	36	85	472	5	2	0	2	10

PECA, MIKE
RW/C, CANUCKS

PERSONAL: Born March 26, 1974, in Toronto.... 5-11/175.... Shoots right.... Name pronounced PEH-kuh. **HIGH SCHOOL:** LaSalle Secondary (Kinston, Ont.). **TRANSACTIONS/CAREER NOTES:** Selected by Vancouver Canucks in second round (second Canucks pick, 40th overall) of NHL entry draft (June 20, 1992).

Season Team	League	REGULAR SEASON					PLAYOFFS				
		Gms.	G	A	Pts.	PIM	Gms.	G	A	Pts.	PIM
90-91—Sudbury	OHL	62	14	27	41	24	5	1	0	1	7
91-92—Sudbury	OHL	39	16	34	50	61	—	—	—	—	—
—Ottawa	OHL	27	8	17	25	32	11	6	10	16	6

P

Season	Team	League	REGULAR SEASON Gms.	G	A	Pts.	Pen.	PLAYOFFS Gms.	G	A	Pts.	Pen.
92-93—Ottawa	OHL	55	38	64	102	80	—	—	—	—	—
—Hamilton	AHL	9	6	3	9	11	—	—	—	—	—
93-94—Ottawa	OHL	55	50	63	113	101	17	7	22	29	30
—Vancouver	NHL	4	0	0	0	2	—	—	—	—	—
NHL totals		4	0	0	0	2					

PEDERSEN, ALLEN
D, WHALERS

PERSONAL: Born January 13, 1965, in Edmonton. . . . 6-3/210. . . . Shoots left. . . . Name pronounced PEE-duhr-suhn.

TRANSACTIONS/CAREER NOTES: Selected by Boston Bruins as underage junior in fifth round (fifth Bruins pick, 102nd overall) of NHL entry draft (June 8, 1983). . . . Separated right shoulder (November 3, 1988). . . . Pulled abdominal muscle (December 1988). . . . Bruised hip (January 1990). . . . Selected by Minnesota North Stars in NHL expansion draft (May 30, 1991). . . . Suffered back spasms (October 28, 1991); missed nine games. . . . Tore abdominal muscles (February 17, 1992); missed 23 games. . . . Traded by North Stars to Hartford Whalers for future considerations (June 15, 1992). . . . Injured groin (February 17, 1993); missed six games.

Season	Team	League	REGULAR SEASON Gms.	G	A	Pts.	PIM	PLAYOFFS Gms.	G	A	Pts.	PIM
82-83—Medicine Hat	WHL	63	3	10	13	49	5	0	0	0	7
83-84—Medicine Hat	WHL	44	0	11	11	47	14	0	2	2	24
84-85—Medicine Hat	WHL	72	6	16	22	66	10	0	0	0	9
85-86—Moncton	AHL	59	1	8	9	39	3	0	0	0	0
86-87—Boston	NHL	79	1	11	12	71	4	0	0	0	4
87-88—Boston	NHL	78	0	6	6	90	21	0	0	0	34
88-89—Boston	NHL	51	0	6	6	69	10	0	0	0	2
89-90—Boston	NHL	68	1	2	3	71	21	0	0	0	41
90-91—Maine	AHL	15	0	6	6	18	2	0	1	1	2
—Boston	NHL	57	2	6	8	107	8	0	0	0	10
91-92—Minnesota	NHL	29	0	1	1	10	—	—	—	—	—
92-93—Hartford	NHL	59	1	4	5	60	—	—	—	—	—
93-94—Hartford	NHL	7	0	0	0	9	—	—	—	—	—
—Springfield	AHL	45	2	4	6	28	3	0	1	1	6
NHL totals		428	5	36	41	487	64	0	0	0	91

PEDERSON, DENIS
C, DEVILS

PERSONAL: Born September 10, 1975, in Prince Albert, Sask. . . . 6-2/190. . . . Shoots right.

HIGH SCHOOL: Carlton Comprehensive (Prince Albert, Sask.).

TRANSACTIONS/CAREER NOTES: Selected by New Jersey Devils in first round (first Devils pick, 13th overall) of NHL entry draft (June 26, 1993).

HONORS: Named to WHL All-Rookie team (1992-93). . . . Named to WHL (East) All-Star second team (1993-94).

Season	Team	League	REGULAR SEASON Gms.	G	A	Pts.	PIM	PLAYOFFS Gms.	G	A	Pts.	PIM
91-92—Prince Albert	WHL	10	0	0	0	6	7	0	1	1	13
92-93—Prince Albert	WHL	72	33	40	73	134	—	—	—	—	—
93-94—Prince Albert	WHL	71	53	45	98	157	—	—	—	—	—

PEDERSON, MARK
LW, RED WINGS

PERSONAL: Born January 14, 1968, in Prelate, Sask. . . . 6-2/196. . . . Shoots left. . . . Name pronounced PEE-duhr-suhn.

TRANSACTIONS/CAREER NOTES: Injured shoulder (March 1985). . . . Selected by Montreal Canadiens as underage junior in first round (first Canadiens pick, 15th overall) of NHL entry draft (June 21, 1986). . . . Traded by Canadiens to Philadelphia Flyers for second-round pick in 1991 draft (C Jim Campbell) and future considerations (March 5, 1991). . . . Dislocated shoulder (November 23, 1991); missed 10 games. . . . Traded by Flyers to San Jose Sharks for RW Dave Snuggerud (December 19, 1992). . . . Separated shoulder (January 5, 1993); missed 13 games. . . . Sprained knee (February 14, 1993); missed nine games. . . . Signed as free agent by Detroit Red Wings (August 24, 1993).

HONORS: Named to WHL (East) All-Star first team (1986-87). . . . Named to WHL All-Star second team (1987-88). . . . Named to AHL All-Star first team (1989-90 and 1993-94).

Season	Team	League	REGULAR SEASON Gms.	G	A	Pts.	PIM	PLAYOFFS Gms.	G	A	Pts.	PIM
84-85—Medicine Hat	WHL	71	42	40	82	63	10	3	2	5	0
85-86—Medicine Hat	WHL	72	46	60	106	46	25	12	6	18	25
86-87—Medicine Hat	WHL	69	56	46	102	58	20	†19	7	26	14
87-88—Medicine Hat	WHL	62	53	58	111	55	16	†13	6	19	16
88-89—Sherbrooke	AHL	75	43	38	81	53	6	7	5	12	4
89-90—Montreal	NHL	9	0	2	2	2	2	0	0	0	0
—Sherbrooke	AHL	72	53	42	95	60	11	10	8	18	19
90-91—Montreal	NHL	47	8	15	23	18	—	—	—	—	—
—Philadelphia	NHL	12	2	1	3	5	—	—	—	—	—
91-92—Philadelphia	NHL	58	15	25	40	22	—	—	—	—	—
92-93—Philadelphia	NHL	14	3	4	7	6	—	—	—	—	—
—San Jose	NHL	27	7	3	10	22	—	—	—	—	—
93-94—Adirondack	AHL	62	52	45	97	37	12	4	7	11	10
—Detroit	NHL	2	0	0	0	2	—	—	—	—	—
NHL totals		169	35	50	85	77	2	0	0	0	0

P

PEDERSON, TOM
D, SHARKS

PERSONAL: Born January 14, 1970, in Bloomington, Minn.... 5-9/175.... Shoots right.... Full name: Thomas Stuart Pederson.
HIGH SCHOOL: Thomas Jefferson (Bloomington, Minn.).
COLLEGE: Minnesota.
TRANSACTIONS/CAREER NOTES: Selected by Minnesota North Stars in 11th round (12th North Stars pick, 217th overall) of NHL entry draft (June 17, 1989).... Selected by San Jose Sharks in NHL dispersal draft (May 30, 1991).... Strained back (January 8, 1993); missed one game.... Injured shoulder (January 30, 1993); missed four games.... Strained groin (February 22, 1993); missed five games.

			REGULAR SEASON					PLAYOFFS			
Season Team	League	Gms.	G	A	Pts.	PIM	Gms.	G	A	Pts.	PIM
87-88—Jefferson H.S..................	Minn. H.S.	22	16	27	43	...	—	—	—	—	—
88-89—University of Minnesota ...	WCHA	42	5	24	29	46	—	—	—	—	—
89-90—University of Minnesota ...	WCHA	43	8	30	38	58	—	—	—	—	—
90-91—University of Minnesota ...	WCHA	36	12	20	32	46	—	—	—	—	—
91-92—U.S. national team	Int'l	44	3	11	14	41	—	—	—	—	—
—Kansas City....................	IHL	20	6	9	15	16	13	1	6	7	14
92-93—Kansas City....................	IHL	26	6	15	21	10	12	1	6	7	2
—San Jose........................	NHL	44	7	13	20	31	—	—	—	—	—
93-94—Kansas City....................	IHL	7	3	1	4	0	—	—	—	—	—
—San Jose........................	NHL	74	6	19	25	31	14	1	6	7	2
NHL totals........................		118	13	32	45	62	14	1	6	7	2

PELLERIN, BRIAN
RW

PERSONAL: Born February 20, 1970, in Hinton, Alta.... 5-10/172.... Shoots right.... Name pronounced PEHL-ih-rihn.
TRANSACTIONS/CAREER NOTES: Signed as free agent by St. Louis Blues (May 31, 1991). ... Signed as free agent by Houston Aeros (July 14, 1994).
HONORS: Named to WHL (East) All-Star first team (1990-91).

			REGULAR SEASON					PLAYOFFS			
Season Team	League	Gms.	G	A	Pts.	PIM	Gms.	G	A	Pts.	PIM
87-88—Prince Albert..................	WHL	62	6	2	8	113	10	0	0	0	17
88-89—Prince Albert..................	WHL	60	17	16	33	216	3	0	1	1	27
89-90—Prince Albert..................	WHL	53	6	15	21	175	10	1	3	4	26
90-91—Prince Albert..................	WHL	68	46	42	88	223	3	0	0	0	12
91-92—Peoria	IHL	70	7	16	23	231	10	1	2	3	49
92-93—Peoria	IHL	78	15	25	40	204	4	1	1	2	8
93-94—Peoria	IHL	79	14	24	38	225	5	0	0	0	16

PELLERIN, SCOTT
LW, DEVILS

PERSONAL: Born January 9, 1970, in Shediac, N.B.... 5-11/180.... Shoots left.... Full name: Jaque-Frederick Scott Pellerin.
COLLEGE: Maine.
TRANSACTIONS/CAREER NOTES: Selected by New Jersey Devils in third round (fourth Devils pick, 47th overall) of NHL entry draft (June 17, 1989).
HONORS: Named Hockey East co-Rookie of the Year with Rob Gaudreau (1988-89).... Named to Hockey East All-Rookie team (1988-89).... Won Hobey Baker Memorial Trophy (1991-92).... Named Hockey East Player of the Year (1991-92).... Named Hockey East Playoff Most Valuable Player (1991-92).... Named to NCAA All-America East first team (1991-92).... Named to Hockey East All-Star first team (1991-92).

			REGULAR SEASON					PLAYOFFS			
Season Team	League	Gms.	G	A	Pts.	PIM	Gms.	G	A	Pts.	PIM
87-88—Notre Dame	SJHL	57	37	49	86	139	—	—	—	—	—
88-89—University of Maine	Hockey East	45	29	33	62	92	—	—	—	—	—
89-90—University of Maine	Hockey East	42	22	34	56	68	—	—	—	—	—
90-91—University of Maine	Hockey East	43	23	25	48	60	—	—	—	—	—
91-92—University of Maine	Hockey East	37	†32	25	57	54	—	—	—	—	—
—Utica.............................	AHL	—	—	—	—	—	3	1	0	1	0
92-93—Utica.............................	AHL	27	15	18	33	33	2	0	1	1	0
—New Jersey....................	NHL	45	10	11	21	41	—	—	—	—	—
93-94—Albany...........................	AHL	73	28	46	74	84	5	2	1	3	11
—New Jersey....................	NHL	1	0	0	0	2	—	—	—	—	—
NHL totals........................		46	10	11	21	43	—	—	—	—	—

PELTONEN, VILLE
LW/RW, SHARKS

PERSONAL: Born May 24, 1973, in Vantaa, Finland.... 5-10/172.... Shoots left.
TRANSACTIONS/CAREER NOTES: Selected by San Jose Sharks in third round (fourth Sharks pick, 58th overall) of NHL entry draft (June 26, 1993).
MISCELLANEOUS: Member of bronze-medal-winning Finnish Olympic team (1994).

			REGULAR SEASON					PLAYOFFS			
Season Team	League	Gms.	G	A	Pts.	PIM	Gms.	G	A	Pts.	PIM
91-92—HIFK Helsinki	Finland	6	0	0	0	0	—	—	—	—	—
92-93—HIFK Helsinki	Finland	46	13	24	37	16	4	0	2	2	2
93-94—HIFK Helsinki	Finland	43	16	22	38	14	3	0	0	0	2
—Finnish Olympic Team......	Int'l	8	4	3	7	0	—	—	—	—	—

P

PELUSO, MIKE
LW, DEVILS

PERSONAL: Born November 8, 1965, in Hibbing, Minn. . . . 6-4/220. . . . Shoots left. . . . Full name: Michael David Peluso. . . . Name pronounced puh-LOO-soh.
HIGH SCHOOL: Greenway (Coleraine, Minn.).
COLLEGE: Alaska-Anchorage.
TRANSACTIONS/CAREER NOTES: Selected by New Jersey Devils in 10th round (10th Devils pick, 190th overall) of NHL entry draft (June 15, 1985). . . . Signed as free agent by Chicago Blackhawks (September 7, 1989). . . . Bruised jaw and cheek (November 8, 1990); missed five games. . . . Suspended 10 games by NHL for fighting (March 17, 1991). . . . Selected by Ottawa Senators in NHL expansion draft (June 18, 1992). . . . Suspended one game by NHL for accumulating three game misconduct penalties (February 1, 1993). . . . Pinched nerve in neck (March 27, 1993); missed two games. . . . Traded by Senators to Devils (June 26, 1993) to complete deal in which Devils sent G Craig Billington, C/LW Troy Mallette and fourth-round pick in 1993 draft (C Cosmo Dupaul) to Senators for G Peter Sidorkiewicz and future considerations (June 20, 1993). . . . Suffered concussion (December 18, 1993); missed two games. . . . Suspended one game by NHL for non-stick related game misconduct (January 7, 1994). . . . Suspended two games by NHL for non-stick related game misconduct (February 4, 1994). . . . Suspended three games by NHL for non-stick related game misconduct (March 7, 1994).

			REGULAR SEASON					PLAYOFFS				
Season Team	League	Gms.	G	A	Pts.	PIM	Gms.	G	A	Pts.	PIM
84-85—Stratford	OPJHL	52	11	45	56	114	—	—	—	—	—
85-86—Alaska-Anchorage	Indep.	32	2	11	13	59	—	—	—	—	—
86-87—Alaska-Anchorage	Indep.	30	5	21	26	68	—	—	—	—	—
87-88—Alaska-Anchorage	Indep.	35	4	33	37	76	—	—	—	—	—
88-89—Alaska-Anchorage	Indep.	33	10	27	37	75	—	—	—	—	—
89-90—Indianapolis	IHL	75	7	10	17	279	14	0	1	1	58
—Chicago	NHL	2	0	0	0	15	—	—	—	—	—
90-91—Indianapolis	IHL	6	2	1	3	21	5	0	2	2	40
—Chicago	NHL	53	6	1	7	320	3	0	0	0	2
91-92—Chicago	NHL	63	6	3	9	*408	17	1	2	3	8
—Indianapolis	IHL	4	0	1	1	15	—	—	—	—	—
92-93—Ottawa	NHL	81	15	10	25	318	—	—	—	—	—
93-94—New Jersey	NHL	69	4	16	20	238	17	1	0	1	*64
NHL totals		268	31	30	61	1299	37	2	2	4	74

PENNEY, CHAD
LW, SENATORS

PERSONAL: Born September 18, 1973, in Labrador City, Nfld. . . . 6-0/195. . . . Shoots left. . . . Full name: Chadwick Paul Penney.
HIGH SCHOOL: Chippewa Secondary (North Bay, Ont.).
TRANSACTIONS/CAREER NOTES: Selected by Ottawa Senators in second round (second Senators pick, 25th overall) of NHL entry draft (June 20 1992).

			REGULAR SEASON					PLAYOFFS				
Season Team	League	Gms.	G	A	Pts.	PIM	Gms.	G	A	Pts.	PIM
90-91—North Bay	OHL	66	33	34	67	56	10	2	6	8	12
91-92—North Bay	OHL	57	25	27	52	93	21	13	17	30	9
—Can. national Jr. team	Int'l	7	0	0	0	2	—	—	—	—	—
92-93—North Bay	OHL	18	8	7	15	19	—	—	—	—	—
—Sault Ste. Marie	OHL	48	29	44	73	67	18	7	10	17	18
93-94—Prince Edward Island	AHL	73	20	30	50	66	—	—	—	—	—
—Ottawa	NHL	3	0	0	0	2	—	—	—	—	—
NHL totals		3	0	0	0	2					

PENNEY, DAVID
LW, MIGHTY DUCKS

PERSONAL: Born May 16, 1974, in Easton, Mass. . . . 6-1/175. . . . Shoots left.
HIGH SCHOOL: Worcester (Mass.) Academy.
COLLEGE: Northeastern.
TRANSACTIONS/CAREER NOTES: Selected by Mighty Ducks of Anaheim in 11th round (11th Mighty Ducks pick, 264th overall) of NHL entry draft (June 26, 1993).

			REGULAR SEASON					PLAYOFFS				
Season Team	League	Gms.	G	A	Pts.	PIM	Gms.	G	A	Pts.	PIM
93-94—Northeastern University	Hockey East	36	5	9	14	18	—	—	—	—	—

PERREAULT, NICOLAS
D, FLAMES

PERSONAL: Born April 24, 1972, in Loretteville, Que. . . . 6-3/200. . . . Shoots left.
COLLEGE: Michigan State.
TRANSACTIONS/CAREER NOTES: Separated shoulder (April 1988). . . . Selected by Calgary Flames in second round (second Flames pick, 26th overall) of NHL entry draft (June 16, 1990).

			REGULAR SEASON					PLAYOFFS				
Season Team	League	Gms.	G	A	Pts.	PIM	Gms.	G	A	Pts.	PIM
89-90—Hawksbury Hawks	QJHL	46	22	34	56	188	—	—	—	—	—
90-91—Michigan State	CCHA	34	1	7	8	32	—	—	—	—	—
91-92—Michigan State	CCHA	44	12	11	23	77	—	—	—	—	—
92-93—Michigan State	CCHA	38	7	6	13	90	—	—	—	—	—
93-94—Michigan State	CCHA	40	6	10	16	109	—	—	—	—	—

PERREAULT, YANIC
C, KINGS

PERSONAL: Born April 4, 1971, in Sherbrooke, Que. . . . 5-11/182. . . . Shoots left. . . . Name pronounced puh-ROH.
TRANSACTIONS/CAREER NOTES: Selected by Toronto Maple Leafs in third round (first Maple Leafs pick, 47th overall) of NHL entry draft (June 22, 1991). . . . Signed as

P

free agent by Los Angeles Kings (July 14, 1994).
HONORS: Won Can.HL Rookie of the Year Award (1988-89).... Won Michel Bergeron Trophy (1988-89).... Won Marcel Robert Trophy (1989-90).... Won Michel Briere Trophy (1990-91).... Won Jean Beliveau Trophy (1990-91).... Won Frank J. Selke Trophy (1990-91).... Won Shell Cup (1990-91).... Named to QMJHL All-Star first team (1990-91).

Season Team	League	REGULAR SEASON					PLAYOFFS				
		Gms.	G	A	Pts.	PIM	Gms.	G	A	Pts.	PIM
88-89—Trois-Rivieres	QMJHL	70	53	55	108	48	—	—	—	—	—
89-90—Trois-Rivieres	QMJHL	63	51	63	114	75	7	6	5	11	19
90-91—Trois-Rivieres	QMJHL	67	*87	98	*185	103	6	4	7	11	6
91-92—St. John's	AHL	62	38	38	76	19	16	7	8	15	4
92-93—St. John's	AHL	79	49	46	95	56	9	4	5	9	2
93-94—St. John's	AHL	62	45	60	105	38	11	*12	6	18	14
—Toronto	NHL	13	3	3	6	0	—	—	—	—	—
NHL totals		13	3	3	6	0					

PERSSON, JOAKIM
G, BRUINS

PERSONAL: Born May 4, 1970, in Stockholm, Sweden.... 5-11/172.... Catches left.
TRANSACTIONS/CAREER NOTES: Selected by Boston Bruins in 10th round (10th Bruins pick, 259th overall) of NHL entry draft (June 26, 1993).

Season Team	League	REGULAR SEASON								PLAYOFFS						
		Gms.	Min.	W	L	T	GA	SO	Avg.	Gms.	Min.	W	L	GA	SO	Avg.
91-92—Hemmarby Stockholm	Sweden						Statistics unavailable.									
92-93—Hemmarby Stockholm	Sweden						Statistics unavailable.									
93-94—Hemmarby Stockholm	Sweden	23	...	...	...	...	59	...	2.57	—	—	—	—	—	—	—
—Providence	AHL	1	25	0	0	0	0	0	0.00	—	—	—	—	—	—	—

PETERSON, BRENT
LW, LIGHTNING

PERSONAL: Born July 20, 1972, in Calgary.... 6-3/195.... Shoots left.
COLLEGE: Michigan Tech.
TRANSACTIONS/CAREER NOTES: Selected by Tampa Bay Lightning in NHL supplemental draft (June 25, 1993).

Season Team	League	REGULAR SEASON					PLAYOFFS				
		Gms.	G	A	Pts.	PIM	Gms.	G	A	Pts.	PIM
92-93—Michigan Tech	WCHA	37	24	18	42	32	—	—	—	—	—
93-94—Michigan Tech	WCHA	43	25	21	46	30	—	—	—	—	—

PETIT, MICHEL
D, KINGS

PERSONAL: Born February 12, 1964, in St. Malo, Que.... 6-1/185.... Shoots right.... Name pronounced puh-TEE.
TRANSACTIONS/CAREER NOTES: Selected by Vancouver Canucks as underage junior in first round (first Canucks pick, 11th overall) of NHL entry draft (June 9, 1982).... Separated shoulder (March 1984).... Injured knee (February 1987).... Traded by Canucks to New York Rangers for D Willie Huber and D Larry Melnyk (November 1987).... Pulled groin (December 1987).... Fractured right collarbone (December 27, 1988); missed 11 games.... Traded by Rangers to Quebec Nordiques for D Randy Moller (October 5, 1989).... Traded by Nordiques with C/LW Aaron Broten and RW Lucien DeBlois to Toronto Maple Leafs for LW Scott Pearson and second-round picks in 1991 (D Eric Lavigne) and 1992 drafts (D Tuomas Gronman) (November 17, 1990).... Sprained knee (February 4, 1991); missed five games.... Sprained thumb (November 9, 1991); missed six games.... Traded by Maple Leafs with D Alexander Godynyuk, RW Gary Leeman, LW Craig Berube and G Jeff Reese to Calgary Flames for C Doug Gilmour, D Jamie Macoun, LW Kent Manderville, D Ric Nattress and G Rick Wamsley (January 2, 1992).... Suffered back spasms (March 3, 1992); missed four games.... Pulled groin; missed first four games of 1992-93 season.... Dislocated right shoulder (October 22, 1992); missed 29 games.... Suffered hip pointer (October 21, 1993); missed one game.... Suffered concussion (January 15, 1994); missed two games.... Pulled groin (February 2, 1994); missed four games.... Signed as free agent by Los Angeles Kings (June 1994).
HONORS: Won Raymond Lagace Trophy (1981-82).... Won Association of Journalists of Hockey Trophy (1981-82).... Named to QMJHL All-Star first team (1981-82 and 1982-83).

Season Team	League	REGULAR SEASON					PLAYOFFS				
		Gms.	G	A	Pts.	PIM	Gms.	G	A	Pts.	PIM
81-82—Sherbrooke	QMJHL	63	10	39	49	106	22	5	20	25	24
82-83—St. Jean	QMJHL	62	19	67	86	196	3	0	0	0	35
—Vancouver	NHL	2	0	0	0	0	—	—	—	—	—
83-84—Canadian Olympic Team	Int'l	19	3	10	13	58	—	—	—	—	—
—Vancouver	NHL	44	6	9	15	53	1	0	0	0	0
84-85—Vancouver	NHL	69	5	26	31	127	—	—	—	—	—
85-86—Fredericton	AHL	25	0	13	13	79	—	—	—	—	—
—Vancouver	NHL	32	1	6	7	27	—	—	—	—	—
86-87—Vancouver	NHL	69	12	13	25	131	—	—	—	—	—
87-88—Vancouver	NHL	10	0	3	3	35	—	—	—	—	—
—New York Rangers	NHL	64	9	24	33	223	—	—	—	—	—
88-89—New York Rangers	NHL	69	8	25	33	156	4	0	2	2	27
89-90—Quebec	NHL	63	12	24	36	215	—	—	—	—	—
90-91—Quebec	NHL	19	4	7	11	47	—	—	—	—	—
—Toronto	NHL	54	9	19	28	132	—	—	—	—	—
91-92—Toronto	NHL	34	1	13	14	85	—	—	—	—	—
—Calgary	NHL	36	3	10	13	79	—	—	—	—	—
92-93—Calgary	NHL	35	3	9	12	54	—	—	—	—	—
93-94—Calgary	NHL	63	2	21	23	110	—	—	—	—	—
NHL totals		663	75	209	284	1474	5	0	2	2	27

PETRENKO, SERGEI
LW, SABRES

PERSONAL: Born September 10, 1968, in Kharkov, U.S.S.R. . . . 5-11/167. . . . Shoots left.

TRANSACTIONS/CAREER NOTES: Selected by Buffalo Sabres in seventh round (fifth Sabres pick, 168th overall) of NHL entry draft (June 26, 1993).

			REGULAR SEASON					PLAYOFFS			
Season Team	League	Gms.	G	A	Pts.	PIM	Gms.	G	A	Pts.	PIM
90-91—Dynamo Moscow	USSR	43	14	13	27	10	—	—	—	—	—
91-92—Dynamo Moscow	CIS	31	9	10	19	10	—	—	—	—	—
—Unified Olympic Team	Int'l	8	3	2	5	0	—	—	—	—	—
92-93—Dynamo Moscow	CIS	41	12	11	23	. . .	—	—	—	—	—
93-94—Buffalo	NHL	14	0	4	4	0	—	—	—	—	—
—Rochester	AHL	38	16	15	31	8	—	—	—	—	—
NHL totals		14	0	4	4	0					

PETROCHININ, YEVGENY
D, STARS

PERSONAL: Born February 7, 1976, in Murmansk, U.S.S.R. . . . 5-9/165. . . . Shoots left.

TRANSACTIONS/CAREER NOTES: Selected by Dallas Stars in sixth round (fifth Stars pick, 150th overall) of NHL entry draft (June 29, 1994).

			REGULAR SEASON					PLAYOFFS			
Season Team	League	Gms.	G	A	Pts.	PIM	Gms.	G	A	Pts.	PIM
93-94—Spartak Moscow	CIS	2	0	0	0	. . .	—	—	—	—	—

PETROV, OLEG
RW, CANADIENS

PERSONAL: Born April 18, 1971, in Moscow, U.S.S.R. . . . 5-9/166. . . . Shoots left. . . . Name pronounced PAY-trahf.

TRANSACTIONS/CAREER NOTES: Selected by Montreal Canadiens in sixth round (ninth Canadiens pick, 127th overall) of NHL entry draft (June 22, 1991). . . . Suffered injury (January 5, 1994); missed one game. . . . Sprained ankle (April 6, 1994); missed three games.

HONORS: Named to NHL All-Rookie team (1993-94).

			REGULAR SEASON					PLAYOFFS			
Season Team	League	Gms.	G	A	Pts.	PIM	Gms.	G	A	Pts.	PIM
90-91—CSKA Moscow	USSR	43	7	4	11	8	—	—	—	—	—
91-92—CSKA Moscow	CIS	34	8	13	21	6	—	—	—	—	—
92-93—Montreal	NHL	9	2	1	3	10	1	0	0	0	0
—Fredericton	AHL	55	26	29	55	36	5	4	1	5	0
93-94—Fredericton	AHL	23	8	20	28	18	—	—	—	—	—
—Montreal	NHL	55	12	15	27	2	2	0	0	0	0
NHL totals		64	14	16	30	12	3	0	0	0	0

PETROVICKY, ROBERT
C, WHALERS

PERSONAL: Born October 26, 1973, in Kosice, Czechoslovakia. . . . 5-11/172. . . . Shoots left. . . . Name pronounced PEHT-roh-VEETS-kee.

TRANSACTIONS/CAREER NOTES: Selected by Hartford Whalers in first round (first Whalers pick, ninth overall) of NHL entry draft (June 20, 1992). . . . Sprained left ankle (February 28, 1993); missed five games. . . . Loaned to Slovakian Olympic Team (February 11, 1994). . . . Returned to Whalers (February 28, 1994).

HONORS: Named to Czechoslovakian League All-Star team (1991-92).

			REGULAR SEASON					PLAYOFFS			
Season Team	League	Gms.	G	A	Pts.	PIM	Gms.	G	A	Pts.	PIM
90-91—Dukla Trencin	Czech.	33	9	14	23	12	—	—	—	—	—
91-92—Dukla Trencin	Czech.	46	25	36	61	. . .	—	—	—	—	—
92-93—Hartford	NHL	42	3	6	9	45	—	—	—	—	—
—Springfield	AHL	16	5	3	8	39	15	5	6	11	14
93-94—Hartford	NHL	33	6	5	11	39	—	—	—	—	—
—Springfield	AHL	30	16	8	24	39	4	0	2	2	4
—Slovakian Olympic team	Int'l	8	1	6	7	18	—	—	—	—	—
NHL totals		75	9	11	20	84					

PICARD, MICHEL
LW, SENATORS

PERSONAL: Born November 7, 1969, in Beauport, Que. . . . 5-11/190. . . . Shoots left.

TRANSACTIONS/CAREER NOTES: Selected by Hartford Whalers in ninth round (eighth Whalers pick, 178th overall) of NHL entry draft (June 17, 1989). . . . Separated shoulder (November 14, 1991); missed seven games. . . . Traded by Whalers to San Jose Sharks for future considerations (October 9, 1992); Sharks sent LW Yvon Corriveau to Whalers to complete deal (January 21, 1993). . . . Signed as free agent by Portland Pirates (1993). . . . Signed as free agent by Ottawa Senators (June 23, 1994).

HONORS: Named to QMJHL All-Star second team (1988-89). . . . Named to AHL All-Star first team (1990-91). . . . Named to AHL All-Star second team (1993-94).

			REGULAR SEASON					PLAYOFFS			
Season Team	League	Gms.	G	A	Pts.	PIM	Gms.	G	A	Pts.	PIM
86-87—Trois-Rivieres	QMJHL	66	33	35	68	53	—	—	—	—	—
87-88—Trois-Rivieres	QMJHL	69	40	55	95	71	—	—	—	—	—
88-89—Trois-Rivieres	QMJHL	66	59	81	140	107	4	1	3	4	2
89-90—Binghamton	AHL	67	16	24	40	98	—	—	—	—	—

P

Season Team	League	REGULAR SEASON					PLAYOFFS				
		Gms.	G	A	Pts.	Pen.	Gms.	G	A	Pts.	Pen.
90-91—Hartford	NHL	5	1	0	1	2	—	—	—	—	—
—Springfield	AHL	77	*56	40	96	61	18	8	13	21	18
91-92—Hartford	NHL	25	3	5	8	6	—	—	—	—	—
—Springfield	AHL	40	21	17	38	44	11	2	0	2	34
92-93—Kansas City	IHL	33	7	10	17	51	12	3	2	5	20
—San Jose	NHL	25	4	0	4	24	—	—	—	—	—
93-94—Portland	AHL	61	41	44	85	99	17	11	10	21	22
NHL totals		55	8	5	13	32					

PIETRANGELO, FRANK
G, ISLANDERS

PERSONAL: Born December 17, 1964, in Niagara Falls, Ont. . . . 5-10/185. . . . Catches left. . . . Name pronounced PEE-tuhr-AN-juh-loh.
COLLEGE: Minnesota.
TRANSACTIONS/CAREER NOTES: Selected by Pittsburgh Penguins in fourth round (fourth Penguins pick, 63rd overall) of NHL entry draft (June 8, 1983). . . . Pulled groin (February 1989). . . . Pulled groin (February 3, 1991); missed eight games. . . . Injured back (November 9, 1991); missed four games. . . . Traded by Penguins to Hartford Whalers for conditional draft pick (March 10, 1992); arbitrator ruled that Penguins would receive third-round (D Sven Butenschon) and seventh-round (C Serge Aubin) picks in 1994 draft from Whalers (September 14, 1992). . . . Injured groin (October 17, 1992); missed one game. . . . Fractured kneecap (December 5, 1992); missed six games. . . . Suffered from the flu (February 15, 1993); missed one game. . . . Bruised ribs (March 3, 1993); missed nine games. . . . Reinjured bruised ribs (April 1, 1993); missed remainder of season. . . . Suffered hip flexor (November 17, 1993); missed one game . . . Injured back (November 24, 1993); missed five games. . . . Signed as free agent by New York Islanders (August 2, 1994).
MISCELLANEOUS: Member of Stanley Cup championship team (1991).

Season Team	League	REGULAR SEASON								PLAYOFFS						
		Gms.	Min.	W	L	T	GA	SO	Avg.	Gms.	Min.	W	L	GA	SO	Avg.
82-83—Univ. of Minnesota	WCHA	25	1348	15	6	1	80	1	3.56	—	—	—	—	—	—	—
83-84—Univ. of Minnesota	WCHA	20	1141	13	7	0	66	0	3.47	—	—	—	—	—	—	—
84-85—Univ. of Minnesota	WCHA	17	912	8	3	3	52	0	3.42	—	—	—	—	—	—	—
85-86—Univ. of Minnesota	WCHA	23	1284	15	7	0	76	0	3.55	—	—	—	—	—	—	—
86-87—Muskegon	IHL	35	2090	23	11	0	119	2	3.42	15	923	10	4	46	0	*2.99
87-88—Pittsburgh	NHL	21	1207	9	11	0	80	1	3.98	—	—	—	—	—	—	—
—Muskegon	IHL	15	868	11	3	‡1	43	2	2.97	—	—	—	—	—	—	—
88-89—Pittsburgh	NHL	15	669	5	3	0	45	0	4.04	—	—	—	—	—	—	—
—Muskegon	IHL	13	760	10	1	†0	38	1	3.00	9	566	8	1	29	0	3.07
89-90—Muskegon	IHL	12	691	9	2	†1	38	0	3.30	—	—	—	—	—	—	—
—Pittsburgh	NHL	21	1066	8	6	2	77	0	4.33	—	—	—	—	—	—	—
90-91—Pittsburgh	NHL	25	1311	10	11	1	86	0	3.94	5	288	4	1	15	†1	3.13
91-92—Pittsburgh	NHL	5	225	2	1	0	20	0	5.33	—	—	—	—	—	—	—
—Hartford	NHL	5	306	3	1	1	12	0	2.35	7	425	3	4	19	0	2.68
92-93—Hartford	NHL	30	1373	4	15	1	111	0	4.85	—	—	—	—	—	—	—
93-94—Hartford	NHL	19	984	5	11	1	59	0	3.60	—	—	—	—	—	—	—
—Springfield	AHL	23	1315	9	10	2	73	0	3.33	—	—	—	—	—	—	—
NHL totals		141	7141	46	59	6	490	1	4.12	12	713	7	5	34	1	2.86

PILON, RICH
D, ISLANDERS

PERSONAL: Born April 30, 1968, in Saskatoon, Sask. . . . 6-0/195. . . . Shoots left. . . . Name pronounced PEE-lahn.
TRANSACTIONS/CAREER NOTES: Selected by New York Islanders as underage junior in seventh round (ninth Islanders pick, 143rd overall) of NHL entry draft (June 21, 1986). . . . Injured right leg (December 1988). . . . Injured right eye (November 4, 1989); missed remainder of season. . . . Injured medial collateral ligament in left knee (February 23, 1991). . . . Suffered sore left shoulder (January 9, 1992); missed three games. . . . Lacerated finger (January 30, 1992); missed four games. . . . Bruised hand (October 31, 1992); missed two games. . . . Bruised hand (November 22, 1992); missed four games. . . . Sprained left knee (December 10, 1992); missed eight games. . . . Injured lower back (January 10, 1993); missed 11 games. . . . Injured left shoulder (November 13, 1993); missed seven games. . . . Reinjured left shoulder (December 3, 1993); missed 32 games. . . . Reinjured left shoulder (March 17, 1994); missed 14 games.
HONORS: Named to WHL All-Star second team (1987-88).

Season Team	League	REGULAR SEASON					PLAYOFFS				
		Gms.	G	A	Pts.	PIM	Gms.	G	A	Pts.	PIM
85-86—Prince Albert	WHL	6	0	0	0	0	—	—	—	—	—
86-87—Prince Albert	WHL	68	4	21	25	192	7	1	6	7	17
87-88—Prince Albert	WHL	65	13	34	47	177	9	0	6	6	38
88-89—New York Islanders	NHL	62	0	14	14	242	—	—	—	—	—
89-90—New York Islanders	NHL	14	0	2	2	31	—	—	—	—	—
90-91—New York Islanders	NHL	60	1	4	5	126	—	—	—	—	—
91-92—New York Islanders	NHL	65	1	6	7	183	—	—	—	—	—
92-93—New York Islanders	NHL	44	1	3	4	164	15	0	0	0	50
—Capital District	AHL	6	0	1	1	8	—	—	—	—	—
93-94—New York Islanders	NHL	28	1	4	5	75	—	—	—	—	—
—Salt Lake City	IHL	2	0	0	0	8	—	—	—	—	—
NHL totals		273	4	33	37	821	15	0	0	0	50

P

PITLICK, LANCE
D, SENATORS

PERSONAL: Born November 5, 1967, in Fridley, Minn. . . . 6-0/190. . . . Shoots right.
HIGH SCHOOL: Cooper (New Hope, Minn.).
COLLEGE: Minnesota.
TRANSACTIONS/CAREER NOTES: Selected by Minnesota North Stars in ninth round (10th

North Stars pick, 180th overall) of NHL entry draft (June 21, 1986). . . . Severely pulled lower abdominal muscles (December 1, 1989). . . . Underwent surgery to have tendons sewn onto his abdominal muscle for reinforcement (January 18, 1990). . . . Signed as free agent by Philadelphia Flyers (September 5, 1990). . . . Signed as free agent by Ottawa Senators (June 22, 1994).

			REGULAR SEASON					PLAYOFFS			
Season Team	League	Gms.	G	A	Pts.	PIM	Gms.	G	A	Pts.	PIM
84-85—Cooper H.S.	Minn. H.S.	23	8	4	12	...	—	—	—	—	—
85-86—Cooper H.S.	Minn. H.S.	21	17	8	25	...	—	—	—	—	—
86-87—University of Minnesota ...	WCHA	45	0	9	9	88	10	0	2	2	4
87-88—University of Minnesota ...	WCHA	38	3	9	12	76	8	1	1	2	14
88-89—University of Minnesota ...	WCHA	47	4	9	13	95	8	2	1	3	95
89-90—University of Minnesota ...	WCHA	14	3	2	5	26	—	—	—	—	—
90-91—Hershey	AHL	64	6	15	21	75	3	0	0	0	9
91-92—U.S. national team	Int'l	19	0	1	1	38	—	—	—	—	—
—Hershey	AHL	4	0	0	0	6	3	0	0	0	4
92-93—Hershey	AHL	53	5	10	15	77	—	—	—	—	—
93-94—Hershey	AHL	58	4	13	17	93	11	1	0	1	11

PITTIS, DOMENIC
C, PENGUINS

PERSONAL: Born October 1, 1974, in Calgary. . . . 5-11/180. . . . Shoots left. . . . Name pronounced PIH-tihz.
HIGH SCHOOL: Catholic Central (Lethbridge, Alta).
TRANSACTIONS/CAREER NOTES: Selected by Pittsburgh Penguins in second round (second Penguins pick, 52nd overall) of NHL entry draft (June 26, 1993).
HONORS: Named to WHL (East) All-Star second team (1993-94).

			REGULAR SEASON					PLAYOFFS			
Season Team	League	Gms.	G	A	Pts.	PIM	Gms.	G	A	Pts.	PIM
91-92—Lethbridge......................	WHL	65	6	17	23	48	5	0	2	2	4
92-93—Lethbridge......................	WHL	66	46	73	119	69	4	3	3	6	8
93-94—Lethbridge......................	WHL	72	58	69	127	93	8	4	11	15	16

PIVONKA, MICHAL
C, CAPITALS

PERSONAL: Born January 28, 1966, in Kladno, Czechoslovakia. . . . 6-2/198. . . . Shoots left. . . . Name pronounced puh-VAHN-kuh.
TRANSACTIONS/CAREER NOTES: Selected by Washington Capitals in third round (third Capitals pick, 59th overall) of NHL entry draft (June 9, 1984). . . . Strained ankle ligaments (March 1987). . . . Sprained right wrist (October 1987). . . . Sprained left ankle (March 1988). . . . Sprained left knee (March 9, 1990). . . . Pulled groin (October 10, 1992); missed three games. . . . Pulled groin (October 21, 1992); missed 12 games. . . . Suffered concussion (March 25, 1994); missed one game.

			REGULAR SEASON					PLAYOFFS			
Season Team	League	Gms.	G	A	Pts.	PIM	Gms.	G	A	Pts.	PIM
85-86—Dukla Jihlava	Czech.				Statistics unavailable.						
86-87—Washington	NHL	73	18	25	43	41	7	1	1	2	2
87-88—Washington	NHL	71	11	23	34	28	14	4	9	13	4
88-89—Baltimore........................	AHL	31	12	24	36	19	—	—	—	—	—
—Washington	NHL	52	8	19	27	30	6	3	1	4	10
89-90—Washington	NHL	77	25	39	64	54	11	0	2	2	6
90-91—Washington	NHL	79	20	50	70	34	11	2	3	5	8
91-92—Washington	NHL	80	23	57	80	47	7	1	5	6	13
92-93—Washington	NHL	69	21	53	74	66	6	0	2	2	0
93-94—Washington	NHL	82	14	36	50	38	7	4	4	8	4
NHL totals..............		583	140	302	442	338	69	15	27	42	47

PLANTE, DAN
RW, ISLANDERS

PERSONAL: Born October 5, 1971, in St. Louis. . . . 6-0/207. . . . Shoots right. . . . Full name: Daniel Leon Plante.
HIGH SCHOOL: Edina (Minn.).
COLLEGE: Wisconsin.
TRANSACTIONS/CAREER NOTES: Selected by New York Islanders in third round (third Islanders pick, 48th overall) of NHL entry draft (June 16, 1990).

			REGULAR SEASON					PLAYOFFS			
Season Team	League	Gms.	G	A	Pts.	PIM	Gms.	G	A	Pts.	PIM
88-89—Edina High School............	Minn. H.S.	27	10	26	36	12	—	—	—	—	—
89-90—Edina High School............	Minn. H.S.	24	8	18	26	...	—	—	—	—	—
90-91—University of Wisconsin ...	WCHA	33	1	2	3	54	—	—	—	—	—
91-92—University of Wisconsin ...	WCHA	40	15	16	31	113	—	—	—	—	—
92-93—University of Wisconsin ...	WCHA	42	26	31	57	142	—	—	—	—	—
93-94—Salt Lake City..................	IHL	66	7	17	24	148	—	—	—	—	—
—New York Islanders..........	NHL	12	0	1	1	4	1	1	0	1	2
NHL totals..............		12	0	1	1	4	1	1	0	1	2

PLANTE, DEREK
C, SABRES

PERSONAL: Born January 17, 1971, in Cloquet, Minn. . . . 5-11/160. . . . Shoots left. . . . Full name: Derek John Plante. . . . Name pronounced PLAHNT.
HIGH SCHOOL: Cloquet (Minn.).
COLLEGE: Minnesota-Duluth.

P

TRANSACTIONS/CAREER NOTES: Broke arm (March 1988).... Selected by Buffalo Sabres in eighth round (seventh Sabres pick, 161st overall) of NHL entry draft (June 17, 1989).... Injured collarbone (December 15, 1989).... Reinjured collarbone (January 20, 1990).... Bruised left shoulder (March 8, 1994); missed two games.

HONORS: Named WCHA Player of the Year (1992-93).... Named to NCAA All-America West first team (1992-93).... Named to WCHA All-Star first team (1992-93).

Season Team	League	REGULAR SEASON					PLAYOFFS				
		Gms.	G	A	Pts.	PIM	Gms.	G	A	Pts.	PIM
87-88—Cloquet H.S.	Minn. H.S.	23	16	25	41	...	—	—	—	—	—
88-89—Cloquet H.S.	Minn. H.S.	24	30	33	63	...	—	—	—	—	—
89-90—Minnesota-Duluth	WCHA	28	10	11	21	12	—	—	—	—	—
90-91—Minnesota-Duluth	WCHA	36	23	20	43	6	—	—	—	—	—
91-92—Minnesota-Duluth	WCHA	37	27	36	63	28	—	—	—	—	—
92-93—Minnesota-Duluth	WCHA	37	*36	*56	*92	30	—	—	—	—	—
93-94—U.S. national team	Int'l	2	...	1	1	...	—	—	—	—	—
—Buffalo	NHL	77	21	35	56	24	7	1	0	1	0
NHL totals		77	21	35	56	24	7	1	0	1	0

PLAVSIC, ADRIEN
D, CANUCKS

PERSONAL: Born January 13, 1970, in Montreal.... 6-1/200.... Shoots left.... Name pronounced PLAV-sihk.

COLLEGE: New Hampshire.

TRANSACTIONS/CAREER NOTES: Selected by St. Louis Blues in second round (second Blues pick, 30th overall) of NHL entry draft (June 11, 1988).... Suffered concussion (September 25, 1989).... Traded by Blues with first-round pick in 1990 draft (Shawn Antoski) and second-round pick in 1991 draft to Vancouver Canucks for RW Rich Sutter, D Harold Snepsts and second-round pick (Craig Johnson) in 1990 draft (March 6, 1990).... Sprained knee (November 9, 1990); missed 15 games.... Suffered from the flu (February 22, 1993); missed one game.... Suffered concussion (December 4, 1993); missed four games.

MISCELLANEOUS: Member of silver-medal-winning Canadian Olympic team (1992).

Season Team	League	REGULAR SEASON					PLAYOFFS				
		Gms.	G	A	Pts.	PIM	Gms.	G	A	Pts.	PIM
87-88—Univ. of New Hampshire	Hockey East	30	5	6	11	45	—	—	—	—	—
88-89—Canadian national team	Int'l	62	5	10	15	25	—	—	—	—	—
89-90—Peoria	IHL	51	7	14	21	87	—	—	—	—	—
—St. Louis	NHL	4	0	1	1	2	—	—	—	—	—
—Vancouver	NHL	11	3	2	5	8	—	—	—	—	—
—Milwaukee	IHL	3	1	2	3	14	6	1	3	4	6
90-91—Vancouver	NHL	48	2	10	12	62	—	—	—	—	—
91-92—Canadian national team	Int'l	38	6	9	15	29	—	—	—	—	—
—Canadian Olympic Team	Int'l	8	0	2	2	0	—	—	—	—	—
—Vancouver	NHL	16	1	9	10	14	13	1	7	8	4
92-93—Vancouver	NHL	57	6	21	27	53	—	—	—	—	—
93-94—Vancouver	NHL	47	1	9	10	6	—	—	—	—	—
—Hamilton	AHL	2	0	0	0	0	—	—	—	—	—
NHL totals		183	13	52	65	145	13	1	7	8	4

PODEIN, SHJON
LW, FLYERS

PERSONAL: Born March 5, 1968, in Rochester, Minn.... 6-2/200.... Shoots left.... Name pronounced SHAWN poh-DEEN.

COLLEGE: Minnesota-Duluth.

TRANSACTIONS/CAREER NOTES: Selected by Edmonton Oilers in eighth round (ninth Oilers pick, 166th overall) of NHL entry draft (June 11, 1988).... Injured knee (March 9, 1994); missed five games.... Signed as free agent by Philadelphia Flyers (July 27, 1994).

Season Team	League	REGULAR SEASON					PLAYOFFS				
		Gms.	G	A	Pts.	PIM	Gms.	G	A	Pts.	PIM
87-88—Minnesota-Duluth	WCHA	30	4	4	8	48	—	—	—	—	—
88-89—Minnesota-Duluth	WCHA	36	7	5	12	46	—	—	—	—	—
89-90—Minnesota-Duluth	WCHA	35	21	18	39	36	—	—	—	—	—
90-91—Cape Breton	AHL	63	14	15	29	65	4	0	0	0	5
91-92—Cape Breton	AHL	80	30	24	54	46	5	3	1	4	2
92-93—Cape Breton	AHL	38	18	21	39	32	9	2	2	4	29
—Edmonton	NHL	40	13	6	19	25	—	—	—	—	—
93-94—Edmonton	NHL	28	3	5	8	8	—	—	—	—	—
—Cape Breton	AHL	5	4	4	8	4	—	—	—	—	—
NHL totals		68	16	11	27	33					

PODOLLAN, JASON
RW/C, PANTHERS

PERSONAL: Born February 18, 1976, in Vernon, B.C.... 6-1/181.... Shoots right.

HIGH SCHOOL: University (Spokane, Wash.).

TRANSACTIONS/CAREER NOTES: Selected by Florida Panthers in second round (third Panthers pick, 31st overall) of NHL entry draft (June 28, 1994).

Season Team	League	REGULAR SEASON					PLAYOFFS				
		Gms.	G	A	Pts.	PIM	Gms.	G	A	Pts.	PIM
91-92—Penticton	Jr. A	59	20	26	46	66	—	—	—	—	—
—Spokane	WHL	2	0	0	0	2	10	3	1	4	16
92-93—Spokane	WHL	72	36	33	69	108	10	4	4	8	14
93-94—Spokane	WHL	69	29	37	66	108	3	3	0	3	2

P

POESCHEK, RUDY
D, LIGHTNING

PERSONAL: Born September 29, 1966, in Terrace, B.C. . . . 6-2/210. . . . Shoots right. . . . Full name: Rudolph Leopold Poeschek. . . . Name pronounced POH-shehk.
TRANSACTIONS/CAREER NOTES: Injured knee (December 1984). . . . Selected by New York Rangers as underage junior in 12th round (12th Rangers pick, 238th overall) of NHL entry draft (June 15, 1985). . . . Injured shoulder (November 1986). . . . Bruised right hand (February 1989). . . . Suspended six games by AHL for a pre-game fight (November 25, 1990). . . . Traded by Rangers to Winnipeg Jets for C Guy Larose (January 22, 1991). . . . Signed as free agent by Tampa Bay Lightning (August 13, 1993).

			REGULAR SEASON					PLAYOFFS				
Season Team	League	Gms.	G	A	Pts.	PIM	Gms.	G	A	Pts.	PIM
83-84—Kamloops	WHL	47	3	9	12	93	8	0	2	2	7
84-85—Kamloops	WHL	34	6	7	13	100	15	0	3	3	56
85-86—Kamloops	WHL	32	3	13	16	92	16	3	7	10	40
86-87—Kamloops	WHL	54	13	18	31	153	15	2	4	6	37
87-88—New York Rangers	NHL	1	0	0	0	2	—	—	—	—	—
—Colorado	IHL	82	7	31	38	210	12	2	2	4	31
88-89—Denver	IHL	2	0	0	0	6	—	—	—	—	—
—New York Rangers	NHL	52	0	2	2	199	—	—	—	—	—
89-90—Flint	IHL	38	8	13	21	109	4	0	0	0	16
—New York Rangers	NHL	15	0	0	0	55	—	—	—	—	—
90-91—Binghamton	AHL	38	1	3	4	162	—	—	—	—	—
—Moncton	AHL	23	2	4	6	67	9	1	1	2	41
—Winnipeg	NHL	1	0	0	0	5	—	—	—	—	—
91-92—Moncton	AHL	63	4	18	22	170	11	0	2	2	46
—Winnipeg	NHL	4	0	0	0	17	—	—	—	—	—
92-93—St. John's	AHL	78	7	24	31	189	9	0	4	4	13
93-94—Tampa Bay	NHL	71	3	6	9	118	—	—	—	—	—
NHL totals		144	3	8	11	396					

POLASEK, LIBOR
C, CANUCKS

PERSONAL: Born April 22, 1974, in Vitkovice, Czechoslovakia. . . . 6-3/198. . . . Shoots right. . . . Name pronounced LEE-bohr poh-LA-sihk.
TRANSACTIONS/CAREER NOTES: Selected by Vancouver Canucks in first round (first Canucks pick, 21st overall) of NHL entry draft (June 20, 1992).

			REGULAR SEASON					PLAYOFFS				
Season Team	League	Gms.	G	A	Pts.	PIM	Gms.	G	A	Pts.	PIM
91-92—TJ Vitkovice	Czech.	17	2	2	4	2	—	—	—	—	—
92-93—Hamilton	AHL	60	7	12	19	34	—	—	—	—	—
93-94—Hamilton	AHL	76	11	12	23	40	3	0	0	0	0

POMICHTER, MIKE
C, BLACKHAWKS

PERSONAL: Born September 10, 1973, in New Haven, Conn. . . . 6-1/200. . . . Shoots left.
HIGH SCHOOL: North Haven (Conn.).
COLLEGE: Boston University.
TRANSACTIONS/CAREER NOTES: Selected by Chicago Blackhawks in second round (second Blackhawks pick, 39th overall) of NHL entry draft (June 22, 1991).

			REGULAR SEASON					PLAYOFFS				
Season Team	League	Gms.	G	A	Pts.	PIM	Gms.	G	A	Pts.	PIM
88-89—North Haven H.S.	Conn. H.S.	22	52	22	74	. . .	—	—	—	—	—
89-90—Springfield Jr. B	NEJHL	39	37	31	68	8	—	—	—	—	—
90-91—Springfield Jr. B	NEJHL	38	61	64	125	22	—	—	—	—	—
91-92—Boston University	Hockey East	35	11	27	38	14	—	—	—	—	—
92-93—Boston University	Hockey East	30	16	14	30	23	—	—	—	—	—
93-94—Boston University	Hockey East	40	28	26	54	37	—	—	—	—	—

POPOVIC, PETER
D, CANADIENS

PERSONAL: Born February 10, 1968, in Koping, Sweden. . . . 6-5/241. . . . Shoots right. . . . Name pronounced PAH-poh-VIHK.
TRANSACTIONS/CAREER NOTES: Selected by Montreal Canadiens in fifth round (fifth Canadiens pick, 93rd overall) of NHL entry draft (June 11, 1988). . . . Injured knee (November 20, 1993); missed six games. . . . Bruised shoulder (December 22, 1993); missed seven games.

			REGULAR SEASON					PLAYOFFS				
Season Team	League	Gms.	G	A	Pts.	PIM	Gms.	G	A	Pts.	PIM
86-87—Vasteras	Sweden	24	1	2	3	10	—	—	—	—	—
87-88—Vasteras	Sweden	28	3	17	20	16	—	—	—	—	—
88-89—Vasteras	Sweden	22	1	4	5	32	—	—	—	—	—
89-90—Vasteras	Sweden	30	2	10	12	24	2	0	1	1	2
90-91—Vasteras	Sweden	40	3	2	5	62	4	0	0	0	4
91-92—Vasteras	Sweden	34	7	10	17	30	—	—	—	—	—
92-93—Vasteras	Sweden	39	6	12	18	46	3	0	1	1	2
93-94—Montreal	NHL	47	2	12	14	26	6	0	1	1	0
NHL totals		47	2	12	14	26	6	0	1	1	0

PORKKA, TONI
D, FLYERS

PERSONAL: Born February 4, 1970, in Rauma, Finland. . . . 6-2/190. . . . Shoots right. . . . Name pronounced POHR-kuh.
TRANSACTIONS/CAREER NOTES: Selected by Philadelphia Flyers in ninth round (12th Flyers pick, 172nd overall) of NHL entry draft (June 16, 1990).

P

Season	Team	League	REGULAR SEASON					PLAYOFFS				
			Gms.	G	A	Pts.	PIM	Gms.	G	A	Pts.	PIM
89-90—Lukko		Finland	41	0	3	3	18	—	—	—	—	—
90-91—Lukko		Finland	34	2	2	4	8	—	—	—	—	—
91-92—Hershey		AHL	64	3	5	8	34	—	—	—	—	—
92-93—Hershey		AHL	49	6	13	19	22	—	—	—	—	—
93-94—Hershey		AHL	51	6	7	13	43	10	0	1	1	8

POTVIN, FELIX

G, MAPLE LEAFS

PERSONAL: Born June 23, 1971, in Anjou, Que.... 6-0/180.... Catches left.... Name pronounced PAHT-vihn.

TRANSACTIONS/CAREER NOTES: Selected by Toronto Maple Leafs in second round (second Maple Leafs pick, 31st overall) of NHL entry draft (June 16, 1990).

HONORS: Named to QMJHL All-Star second team (1989-90).... Won Can.HL Goaltender of the Year Award (1990-91).... Won Hap Emms Memorial Trophy (1990-91).... Won Jacques Plante Trophy (1990-91).... Won Shell Cup (1990-91).... Won Guy Lafleur Trophy (1990-91).... Named to Memorial Cup All-Star team (1990-91).... Named to QMJHL All-Star first team (1990-91).... Won Aldege (Baz) Bastien Trophy (1991-92).... Won Dudley (Red) Garrett Memorial Trophy (1991-92).... Named to AHL All-Star first team (1991-92).... Named to NHL All-Rookie team (1992-93).... Played in NHL All-Star Game (1994).

Season	Team	League	REGULAR SEASON							PLAYOFFS						
			Gms.	Min.	W	L	T	GA	SO	Avg.	Gms.	Min.	W	L	GA	SO	Avg.
88-89—Chicoutimi		QMJHL	*65	*3489	25	31	1	*271	†2	4.66	—	—	—	—	—	—	—
89-90—Chicoutimi		QMJHL	*62	*3478	31	26	2	231	†2	3.99	—	—	—	—	—	—	—
90-91—Chicoutimi		QMJHL	54	3216	33	15	4	145	*6	†2.71	*16	*992	*11	5	46	0	*2.78
91-92—St. John's		AHL	35	2070	18	10	6	101	2	2.93	11	642	7	4	41	0	3.83
—Toronto		NHL	4	210	0	2	1	8	0	2.29	—	—	—	—	—	—	—
92-93—Toronto		NHL	48	2781	25	15	7	116	2	*2.50	21	1308	11	10	62	1	2.84
—St. John's		AHL	5	309	3	0	2	18	0	3.50	—	—	—	—	—	—	—
93-94—Toronto		NHL	66	3883	34	22	9	187	3	2.89	18	1124	9	†9	46	3	2.46
NHL totals			118	6874	59	39	17	311	5	2.71	39	2432	20	19	108	4	2.66

POTVIN, MARC

RW, BRUINS

PERSONAL: Born January 29, 1967, in Ottawa.... 6-1/215.... Shoots right.... Full name: Marc Richard Potvin.... Name pronounced PAHT-vihn.

COLLEGE: Bowling Green State.

TRANSACTIONS/CAREER NOTES: Selected by Detroit Red Wings in ninth round (ninth Red Wings pick, 169th overall) of NHL entry draft (June 21, 1986).... Traded by Red Wings with C Jimmy Carson and C Gary Shuchuk to Los Angeles Kings for D Paul Coffey, RW Jim Hiller and C/LW Sylvain Couturier (January 29, 1993).... Broke nose (February 18, 1993); missed one game.... Traded by Kings to Hartford Whalers for D Doug Houda (November 3, 1993).... Suffered from post-concussion syndrome (March 9, 1994); missed six games.... Fined $500 by Whalers for involvement in bar brawl (April 1, 1994).... Signed as free agent by Boston Bruins (June 28, 1994).

Season	Team	League	REGULAR SEASON					PLAYOFFS				
			Gms.	G	A	Pts.	PIM	Gms.	G	A	Pts.	PIM
85-86—Stratford		OPJHL	63	5	6	11	117	—	—	—	—	—
86-87—Bowling Green State		CCHA	43	5	15	20	74	—	—	—	—	—
87-88—Bowling Green State		CCHA	45	15	21	36	80	—	—	—	—	—
88-89—Bowling Green State		CCHA	46	23	12	35	63	—	—	—	—	—
89-90—Bowling Green State		CCHA	40	19	17	36	72	—	—	—	—	—
—Adirondack		AHL	5	2	1	3	9	4	0	1	1	23
90-91—Adirondack		AHL	63	9	13	22	†365	—	—	—	—	—
—Detroit		NHL	9	0	0	0	55	6	0	0	0	32
91-92—Adirondack		AHL	51	13	16	29	314	†19	5	4	9	57
—Detroit		NHL	5	1	0	1	52	1	0	0	0	0
92-93—Adirondack		AHL	37	8	12	20	109	—	—	—	—	—
—Los Angeles		NHL	20	0	1	1	61	1	0	0	0	0
93-94—Los Angeles		NHL	3	0	0	0	26	—	—	—	—	—
—Hartford		NHL	51	2	3	5	246	—	—	—	—	—
NHL totals			88	3	4	7	440	8	0	0	0	32

POULIN, DAVE

C, CAPITALS

PERSONAL: Born December 17, 1958, in Mississauga, Ont.... 5-11/190.... Shoots left.... Full name: David James Poulin.... Name pronounced POO-lihn.

COLLEGE: Notre Dame.

TRANSACTIONS/CAREER NOTES: Signed as free agent by Philadelphia Flyers (February 1983).... Pulled hamstring and groin muscle (November 1986).... Fractured rib (April 16, 1987).... Pulled groin (February 1988).... Separated shoulder (November 1988).... Sent home due to irregular heartbeat (December 15, 1988).... Bruised right hand (January 1989).... Fractured right ring finger (April 8, 1989).... Suffered multiple fracture of left thumb (May 1989).... Bruised abdomen (October 1989).... Broke left thumb (October 28, 1989).... Traded by Flyers to Boston Bruins for C Ken Linseman (January 16, 1990).... Stretched nerve in neck and left arm (April 21, 1990).... Pulled groin (October 15, 1990); missed 17 games.... Broke jaw (December 28, 1990); missed 14 games.... Broke right shoulder blade (February 2, 1991); missed 15 games.... Strained groin and abdomen (September 1991); missed first 61 games of season.... Underwent surgery to groin and abdomen (December 6, 1991).... Signed as free agent by Washington Capitals (August 3, 1993).... Underwent root canal (October 27, 1993); missed one game.... Suffered from asthma (January 25, 1994); missed five games.... Suffered from asthma (February 10, 1994); missed 12 games.

HONORS: Named to CCHA All-Star second team (1981-82).... Won Frank J. Selke Trophy (1986-87).... Played in NHL All-Star Game (1986 and 1988).... Won King Clancy Memorial Trophy (1992-93).

Season Team	League	REGULAR SEASON					PLAYOFFS				
		Gms.	G	A	Pts.	PIM	Gms.	G	A	Pts.	PIM
78-79—University of Notre Dame	WCHA	37	28	31	59	32	—	—	—	—	—
79-80—University of Notre Dame	WCHA	24	19	24	43	46	—	—	—	—	—
80-81—University of Notre Dame	WCHA	35	13	22	35	53	—	—	—	—	—
81-82—University of Notre Dame	WCHA	39	29	30	59	44	—	—	—	—	—
82-83—Rogle	Sweden	33	35	18	53	. . .	—	—	—	—	—
—Maine	AHL	16	7	9	16	2	—	—	—	—	—
—Philadelphia	NHL	2	2	0	2	2	3	1	3	4	9
83-84—Philadelphia	NHL	73	31	45	76	47	3	0	0	0	2
84-85—Philadelphia	NHL	73	30	44	74	59	11	3	5	8	6
85-86—Philadelphia	NHL	79	27	42	69	49	5	2	0	2	2
86-87—Philadelphia	NHL	75	25	45	70	53	15	3	3	6	14
87-88—Philadelphia	NHL	68	19	32	51	32	7	2	6	8	4
88-89—Philadelphia	NHL	69	18	17	35	49	19	6	5	11	16
89-90—Philadelphia	NHL	28	9	8	17	12	—	—	—	—	—
—Boston	NHL	32	6	19	25	12	18	8	5	13	8
90-91—Boston	NHL	31	8	12	20	25	16	0	9	9	20
91-92—Boston	NHL	18	4	4	8	18	15	3	3	6	22
92-93—Boston	NHL	84	16	33	49	62	4	1	1	2	10
93-94—Washington	NHL	63	6	19	25	52	11	2	2	4	19
NHL totals		695	201	320	521	472	127	31	42	73	132

POULIN, PATRICK
LW, BLACKHAWKS

PERSONAL: Born April 23, 1973, in Vanier, Que. . . . 6-1/208. . . . Shoots left. . . . Name pronounced POO-lai.

TRANSACTIONS/CAREER NOTES: Broke wrist (January 15, 1991). . . . Selected by Hartford Whalers in first round (first Whalers pick, ninth overall) of NHL entry draft (June 22, 1991). . . . Traded by Whalers with D Eric Weinrich to the Chicago Blackhawks for RW Steve Larmer and D Bryan Marchment (November 2, 1993).

HONORS: Won Jean Beliveau Trophy (1991-92). . . . Named to Can.HL All-Star first team (1991-92). . . . Named to QMJHL All-Star first team (1991-92).

Season Team	League	REGULAR SEASON					PLAYOFFS				
		Gms.	G	A	Pts.	PIM	Gms.	G	A	Pts.	PIM
89-90—St. Hyacinthe	QMJHL	60	25	26	51	55	12	1	9	10	5
90-91—St. Hyacinthe	QMJHL	56	32	38	70	82	4	0	2	2	23
91-92—St. Hyacinthe	QMJHL	56	52	86	*138	58	5	2	2	4	4
—Springfield	AHL	—	—	—	—	—	1	0	0	0	0
—Hartford	NHL	1	0	0	0	2	7	2	1	3	0
92-93—Hartford	NHL	81	20	31	51	37	—	—	—	—	—
93-94—Hartford	NHL	9	2	1	3	11	—	—	—	—	—
—Chicago	NHL	58	12	13	25	40	4	0	0	0	0
NHL totals		149	34	45	79	90	11	2	1	3	0

POZZO, KEVIN
D, SABRES

PERSONAL: Born October 10, 1974, in Calgary. . . . 6-1/176. . . . Shoots right. . . . Name pronounced POH-zoh.

HIGH SCHOOL: Vanier Collegiate (Moose Jaw, Sask.).

TRANSACTIONS/CAREER NOTES: Selected by Buffalo Sabres in sixth round (fourth Sabres pick, 142nd overall) of NHL entry draft (June 26, 1993).

Season Team	League	REGULAR SEASON					PLAYOFFS				
		Gms.	G	A	Pts.	PIM	Gms.	G	A	Pts.	PIM
92-93—Moose Jaw	WHL	72	10	29	39	95	—	—	—	—	—
93-94—Moose Jaw	WHL	40	7	20	27	71	—	—	—	—	—
—Spokane	WHL	17	3	7	10	23	3	0	1	1	4

PRATT, NOLAN
D, WHALERS

PERSONAL: Born August 14, 1975, in Fort McMurray, Alta. . . . 6-2/190. . . . Shoots left.

HIGH SCHOOL: Sunset (Beaverton, Ore.).

TRANSACTIONS/CAREER NOTES: Selected by Hartford Whalers in fifth round (fourth Whalers pick, 115th overall) of NHL entry draft (June 26, 1993).

Season Team	League	REGULAR SEASON					PLAYOFFS				
		Gms.	G	A	Pts.	PIM	Gms.	G	A	Pts.	PIM
91-92—Portland	WHL	22	2	9	11	13	6	1	3	4	12
92-93—Portland	WHL	70	4	19	23	97	16	2	7	9	31
93-94—Portland	WHL	72	4	32	36	105	10	1	2	3	14

PRESLEY, WAYNE
RW, SABRES

PERSONAL: Born March 23, 1965, in Dearborn, Mich. . . . 5-11/180. . . . Shoots right.

TRANSACTIONS/CAREER NOTES: Selected by Chicago Blackhawks as an underage junior in second round (second Blackhawks pick, 39th overall) of NHL entry draft (June 8, 1983). . . . Traded by Kitchener Rangers to Sault Ste. Marie Greyhounds for RW Shawn Tyers (January 1985). . . . Underwent surgery to repair ligaments and cartilage in right knee (November 1987); missed 36 games. . . . Dislocated shoulder (May 6, 1989). . . . Traded by Blackhawks to San Jose Sharks for third-round pick in 1993 draft (September 20, 1991). . . . Injured knee (November 17, 1991). . . . Injured hand (December 3, 1991); missed eight games. . . . Traded by Sharks to Buffalo Sabres for C Dave Snuggerud (March 9, 1992). . . . Bruised foot (October 8, 1992); missed one

P

game. . . . Injured knee (October 1993); missed four games.
HONORS: Won Jim Mahon Memorial Trophy (1983-84). . . . Named to OHL All-Star first team (1983-84).
RECORDS: Shares NHL single-season and single-series playoff records for most shorthanded goals—3 (1989).

			REGULAR SEASON					PLAYOFFS				
Season	Team	League	Gms.	G	A	Pts.	PIM	Gms.	G	A	Pts.	PIM
82-83—Kitchener		OHL	70	39	48	87	99	12	1	4	5	9
83-84—Kitchener		OHL	70	63	76	139	156	16	12	16	28	38
84-85—Kitchener		OHL	31	25	21	46	77	—	—	—	—	—
—Sault Ste. Marie		OHL	11	5	9	14	14	16	13	9	22	13
—Chicago		NHL	3	0	1	1	0	—	—	—	—	—
85-86—Nova Scotia		AHL	29	6	9	15	22	—	—	—	—	—
—Chicago		NHL	38	7	8	15	38	3	0	0	0	0
86-87—Chicago		NHL	80	32	29	61	114	4	1	0	1	9
87-88—Chicago		NHL	42	12	10	22	52	5	0	0	0	4
88-89—Chicago		NHL	72	21	19	40	100	14	7	5	12	18
89-90—Chicago		NHL	49	6	7	13	69	19	9	6	15	29
90-91—Chicago		NHL	71	15	19	34	122	6	0	1	1	38
91-92—San Jose		NHL	47	8	14	22	76	—	—	—	—	—
—Buffalo		NHL	12	2	2	4	57	7	3	3	6	14
92-93—Buffalo		NHL	79	15	17	32	96	8	1	0	1	6
93-94—Buffalo		NHL	65	17	8	25	103	7	2	1	3	14
NHL totals			558	135	134	269	827	73	23	16	39	132

PRIMEAU, KEITH
C/LW, RED WINGS

PERSONAL: Born November 24, 1971, in Toronto. . . . 6-4/220. . . . Shoots left. . . . Name pronounced PREE-moh. . . . Brother of Wayne Primeau, center, in Buffalo Sabres system.
TRANSACTIONS/CAREER NOTES: Selected by Detroit Red Wings in first round (first Red Wings pick, third overall) of NHL entry draft (June 16, 1990). . . . Suffered from the flu (January 13, 1993); missed two games. . . . Sprained right shoulder (February 9, 1993); missed one game. . . . Sprained right knee (March 2, 1993); missed two games. . . . Sprained right knee (April 1, 1993); missed four games.
HONORS: Won Eddie Powers Memorial Trophy (1989-90). . . . Named to OHL All-Star second team (1989-90).

			REGULAR SEASON					PLAYOFFS				
Season	Team	League	Gms.	G	A	Pts.	PIM	Gms.	G	A	Pts.	PIM
87-88—Hamilton		OHL	47	6	6	12	69	11	0	2	2	2
88-89—Niagara Falls		OHL	48	20	35	55	56	17	9	6	15	12
89-90—Niagara Falls		OHL	65	*57	70	*127	97	16	*16	17	*33	49
90-91—Detroit		NHL	58	3	12	15	106	5	1	1	2	25
—Adirondack		AHL	6	3	5	8	8	—	—	—	—	—
91-92—Detroit		NHL	35	6	10	16	83	11	0	0	0	14
—Adirondack		AHL	42	21	24	45	89	9	1	7	8	27
92-93—Detroit		NHL	73	15	17	32	152	7	0	2	2	26
93-94—Detroit		NHL	78	31	42	73	173	7	0	2	2	6
NHL totals			244	55	81	136	514	30	1	5	6	71

PRIMEAU, WAYNE
C, SABRES

PERSONAL: Born June 4, 1976, in Scarborough, Ont. . . . 6-3/193. . . . Shoots left. . . . Name pronounced PREE-moh. . . . Brother of Keith Primeau, center/left winger, Detroit Red Wings.
HIGH SCHOOL: St. Mary's (Owen Sound, Ont.).
TRANSACTIONS/CAREER NOTES: Selected by Buffalo Sabres in first round (first Sabres pick, 17th overall) of NHL entry draft (June 28, 1994).

			REGULAR SEASON					PLAYOFFS				
Season	Team	League	Gms.	G	A	Pts.	PIM	Gms.	G	A	Pts.	PIM
92-93—Owen Sound		OHL	66	10	27	37	110	8	1	4	5	0
93-94—Owen Sound		OHL	65	25	50	75	75	9	1	6	7	8

PROBERT, BOB
LW, BLACKHAWKS

PERSONAL: Born June 5, 1965, in Windsor, Ont. . . . 6-3/215. . . . Shoots left. . . . Name pronounced PROH-burt.
TRANSACTIONS/CAREER NOTES: Selected by Detroit Red Wings as underage junior in third round (third Red Wings pick, 46th overall) of NHL entry draft (June 8, 1983). . . . Entered in-patient alcohol abuse treatment center (July 22, 1986). . . . Suspended six games by NHL during the 1987-88 season for game misconduct penalties. . . . Suspended without pay by Red Wings for skipping practice and missing team buses, flights and curfews (September 23, 1988). . . . Reactivated by Red Wings (November 23, 1988). . . . Suspended three games by NHL for hitting another player (December 10, 1988). . . . Removed from team after showing up late for a game (January 26, 1989). . . . Reactivated by Red Wings (February 15, 1989). . . . Charged with smuggling cocaine into the United States (March 2, 1989). . . . Expelled from the NHL (March 4, 1989). . . . Reinstated by NHL (March 14, 1990). . . . Unable to play any games in Canada while appealing deportation order by U.S. Immigration Department during 1990-91 and 1991-92 seasons. . . . Fractured left wrist (December 1, 1990); missed 12 games. . . . Suspended one game by NHL for game misconduct penalties (February 9, 1993). . . . Bruised tailbone (November 20, 1993); missed eight games. . . . Suspended four games by NHL for stick-swinging incident (October 16, 1993). . . . Suspended two games and fined $500 by NHL for head-butting (April 7, 1994). . . . Signed as free agent by Chicago Blackhawks (July 23, 1994).
HONORS: Played in NHL All-Star Game (1988).

			REGULAR SEASON					PLAYOFFS				
Season	Team	League	Gms.	G	A	Pts.	PIM	Gms.	G	A	Pts.	PIM
82-83—Brantford		OHL	51	12	16	28	133	8	2	2	4	23
83-84—Brantford		OHL	65	35	38	73	189	6	0	3	3	16

Season	Team	League	Gms.	G	A	Pts.	Pen.	Gms.	G	A	Pts.	Pen.
			REGULAR SEASON					PLAYOFFS				
84-85—Hamilton		OHL	4	0	1	1	21	—	—	—	—	—
—Sault Ste. Marie		OHL	44	20	52	72	172	15	6	11	17	*60
85-86—Adirondack		AHL	32	12	15	27	152	10	2	3	5	68
—Detroit		NHL	44	8	13	21	186	—	—	—	—	—
86-87—Detroit		NHL	63	13	11	24	221	16	3	4	7	63
—Adirondack		AHL	7	1	4	5	15	—	—	—	—	—
87-88—Detroit		NHL	74	29	33	62	*398	16	8	13	21	51
88-89—Detroit		NHL	25	4	2	6	106	—	—	—	—	—
89-90—Detroit		NHL	4	3	0	3	21	—	—	—	—	—
90-91—Detroit		NHL	55	16	23	39	315	6	1	2	3	50
91-92—Detroit		NHL	63	20	24	44	276	11	1	6	7	28
92-93—Detroit		NHL	80	14	29	43	292	7	0	3	3	10
93-94—Detroit		NHL	66	7	10	17	275	7	1	1	2	8
NHL totals			474	114	145	259	2090	63	14	29	43	210

PROCHAZKA, MARTIN
RW, MAPLE LEAFS

PERSONAL: Born March 3, 1972, in Slany, Czechoslovakia. . . . 5-11/180. . . . Shoots right. . . . Name pronounced pro-HAHS-kah.
TRANSACTIONS/CAREER NOTES: Selected by Toronto Maple Leafs in seventh round (eighth Maple Leafs pick, 135th overall) of NHL entry draft (June 22, 1991).

Season	Team	League	Gms.	G	A	Pts.	PIM	Gms.	G	A	Pts.	PIM
			REGULAR SEASON					PLAYOFFS				
89-90—Kladno		Czech.	49	18	12	30	. . .	—	—	—	—	—
90-91—Kladno		Czech.	50	19	10	29	21	—	—	—	—	—
91-92—Dukla Jihlava		Czech.	44	18	11	29	2	—	—	—	—	—
92-93—Kladno		Czech.	46	26	12	38	38	—	—	—	—	—
93-94—HC Kladno		Czech Rep.	43	24	16	40	. . .	2	2	0	2	0

PROKHOROV, VITALI
LW, BLUES

PERSONAL: Born December 25, 1966, in Moscow, U.S.S.R. . . . 5-9/185. . . . Shoots left. . . . Name pronounced vee-TAL-ee PROH-kuh-RAHF.
TRANSACTIONS/CAREER NOTES: Selected by St. Louis Blues in third round (third Blues pick, 64th overall) of NHL entry draft (June 20, 1992). . . . Injured shoulder (November 10, 1992); missed two games. . . . Injured shoulder (December 17, 1992); missed 14 games. . . . Reinjured shoulder (February 10, 1993); missed remainder of season. . . . Broke toe (October 9, 1993); missed six games.
MISCELLANEOUS: Member of gold-medal-winning Unified Olympic team (1992).

Season	Team	League	Gms.	G	A	Pts.	PIM	Gms.	G	A	Pts.	PIM
			REGULAR SEASON					PLAYOFFS				
83-84—Spartak Moscow		USSR	5	0	0	0	0	—	—	—	—	—
84-85—Spartak Moscow		USSR	31	1	1	2	10	—	—	—	—	—
85-86—Spartak Moscow		USSR	29	3	9	12	4	—	—	—	—	—
86-87—Spartak Moscow		USSR	27	1	6	7	2	—	—	—	—	—
87-88—Spartak Moscow		USSR	19	5	0	5	4	—	—	—	—	—
88-89—Spartak Moscow		USSR	37	11	5	16	10	—	—	—	—	—
89-90—Spartak Moscow		USSR	43	13	8	21	35	—	—	—	—	—
90-91—Spartak Moscow		USSR	43	21	10	31	29	—	—	—	—	—
91-92—Spartak Moscow		CIS	38	13	19	32	68	—	—	—	—	—
—Unified Olympic Team		Int'l	8	2	4	6	6	—	—	—	—	—
92-93—St. Louis		NHL	26	4	1	5	15	—	—	—	—	—
93-94—St. Louis		NHL	55	15	10	25	20	4	0	0	0	0
—Peoria		IHL	19	13	10	23	16	—	—	—	—	—
NHL totals			81	19	11	30	35	4	0	0	0	0

PRONGER, CHRIS
D, WHALERS

PERSONAL: Born October 10, 1974, in Dryden, Ont. . . . 6-5/190. . . . Shoots left. . . . Brother of Sean Pronger, center in Vancouver Canucks system.
COLLEGE: Trent (Ont.).
TRANSACTIONS/CAREER NOTES: Selected by Hartford Whalers in first round (first Whalers pick, second overall) of NHL entry draft (June 26, 1993). . . . Bruised left wrist (March 29, 1994); missed three games. . . . Fined $500 by Whalers for involvement in bar brawl (April 1, 1994).
HONORS: Named to Can.HL All-Rookie team (1991-92). . . . Named to OHL Rookie All-Star team (1991-92). . . . Won Can.HL Plus/Minus Award (1992-93). . . . Won Can.HL Top Defenseman Award (1992-93). . . . Won Max Kaminsky Award (1992-93). . . . Named to Can.HL All-Star first team (1992-93). . . . Named to OHL All-Star first team (1992-93). . . . Named to NHL All-Rookie team (1993-94).

Season	Team	League	Gms.	G	A	Pts.	PIM	Gms.	G	A	Pts.	PIM
			REGULAR SEASON					PLAYOFFS				
90-91—Stratford		OPJHL	48	15	37	52	132	—	—	—	—	—
91-92—Peterborough		OHL	63	17	45	62	90	10	1	8	9	28
92-93—Peterborough		OHL	61	15	62	77	108	21	15	25	40	51
93-94—Hartford		NHL	81	5	25	30	113	—	—	—	—	—
NHL totals			81	5	25	30	113					

P

PRONGER, SEAN
C, CANUCKS

PERSONAL: Born November 30, 1972, in Thunder Bay, Ont. . . . 6-3/195. . . . Shoots left. . . . Full name: Sean James Pronger. . . . Brother of Chris Pronger, defenseman, Hartford Whalers.
COLLEGE: Bowling Green State.
TRANSACTIONS/CAREER NOTES: Selected by Vancouver Canucks in third round (third Canucks pick, 51st overall) of NHL entry draft (June 22, 1991).

Season Team	League		REGULAR SEASON					PLAYOFFS			
		Gms.	G	A	Pts.	PIM	Gms.	G	A	Pts.	PIM
89-90—Thunder Bay Flyers	USHL	48	18	34	52	61	—	—	—	—	—
90-91—Bowling Green State	CCHA	40	3	7	10	30	—	—	—	—	—
91-92—Bowling Green State	CCHA	34	9	7	16	28	—	—	—	—	—
92-93—Bowling Green State	CCHA	39	23	23	46	35	—	—	—	—	—
93-94—Bowling Green State	CCHA	38	17	17	34	38	—	—	—	—	—

PROPP, BRIAN
LW, WHALERS

PERSONAL: Born February 15, 1959, in Lanigan, Sask. . . . 5-10/195. . . . Shoots left. . . . Full name: Brian Philip Propp.
TRANSACTIONS/CAREER NOTES: Selected by Philadelphia Flyers in first round (first Flyers pick, 14th overall) of NHL entry draft (August 9, 1979). . . . Suspended four games by NHL (January 1985). . . . Injured eye (March 4, 1986); missed eight games. . . . Fractured left knee (December 7, 1986). . . . Sprained left knee (December 1987). . . . Traded by Flyers to Boston Bruins for second-round pick (D Terran Sandwith) in 1990 draft (March 2, 1990). . . . Signed as free agent by Minnesota North Stars (July 25, 1990). . . . Injured groin (November 29, 1991); missed eight games. . . . Dislocated shoulder (February 9, 1992); missed 13 games. . . . Sprained knee (March 14, 1992); missed two games. . . . Injured shoulder (April 14, 1992). . . . Assigned to Lugano of Swiss League (November 14, 1992). . . . Signed as free agent by Hartford Whalers (October 4, 1993). . . . Suspended four games and fined $400 by NHL for slashing (February 8, 1994).
HONORS: Named WCHL Rookie of the Year (1976-77). . . . Named to WCHL All-Star second team (1976-77). . . . Named to WCHL All-Star first team (1977-78). . . . Won WHL Player of the Year Award (1978-79). . . . Named to WHL All-Star first team (1978-79). . . . Played in NHL All-Star Game (1980, 1982, 1984, 1986 and 1990).

Season Team	League		REGULAR SEASON					PLAYOFFS			
		Gms.	G	A	Pts.	PIM	Gms.	G	A	Pts.	PIM
75-76—Melville	SAJHL	57	76	92	168	36	—	—	—	—	—
76-77—Brandon	WCHL	72	55	80	135	47	16	†14	12	26	5
77-78—Brandon	WCHL	70	70	*112	*182	200	8	7	6	13	12
78-79—Brandon	WHL	71	*94	*100	*194	127	22	15	23	*38	40
79-80—Philadelphia	NHL	80	34	41	75	54	19	5	10	15	29
80-81—Philadelphia	NHL	79	26	40	66	110	12	6	6	12	32
81-82—Philadelphia	NHL	80	44	47	91	117	4	2	2	4	4
82-83—Philadelphia	NHL	80	40	42	82	72	3	1	2	3	8
83-84—Philadelphia	NHL	79	39	53	92	37	3	0	1	1	6
84-85—Philadelphia	NHL	76	43	53	96	43	19	8	10	18	6
85-86—Philadelphia	NHL	72	40	57	97	47	5	0	2	2	4
86-87—Philadelphia	NHL	53	31	36	67	45	26	12	16	28	10
87-88—Philadelphia	NHL	74	27	49	76	76	7	4	2	6	8
88-89—Philadelphia	NHL	77	32	46	78	37	18	14	9	23	14
89-90—Philadelphia	NHL	40	13	15	28	31	—	—	—	—	—
—Boston	NHL	14	3	9	12	10	20	4	9	13	2
90-91—Minnesota	NHL	79	26	47	73	58	23	8	15	23	28
91-92—Minnesota	NHL	51	12	23	35	49	1	0	0	0	0
92-93—Minnesota	NHL	17	3	3	6	0	—	—	—	—	—
—Lugano	Switzerland	24	21	6	27	32	—	—	—	—	—
—Canadian national team	Int'l	3	3	1	4	2	—	—	—	—	—
93-94—Hartford	NHL	65	12	17	29	44	—	—	—	—	—
NHL totals		1016	425	578	1003	830	160	64	84	148	151

PROSPAL, VACLAV
C, FLYERS

PERSONAL: Born February 17, 1975, in Ceske-Budejovice, Czechoslovakia. . . . 6-2/167. . . . Shoots left.
TRANSACTIONS/CAREER NOTES: Selected by Philadelphia Flyers in third round (second Flyers pick, 71st overall) of NHL entry draft (June 26, 1993).

Season Team	League		REGULAR SEASON					PLAYOFFS			
		Gms.	G	A	Pts.	PIM	Gms.	G	A	Pts.	PIM
91-92—Motor Ceske-Budejovice	Czech. Jrs.	36	16	16	32	12	—	—	—	—	—
92-93—Motor Ceske-Budejovice	Czech. Jrs.					Did not play.					
93-94—Hershey	AHL	55	14	21	35	38	2	0	0	0	2

PROULX, CHRISTIAN
D, CANADIENS

PERSONAL: Born December 10, 1973, in Coaticook, Que. . . . 6-0/190. . . . Shoots left. . . . Name pronounced PROO.
TRANSACTIONS/CAREER NOTES: Selected by Montreal Canadiens in seventh round (seventh Canadiens pick, 164th overall) of NHL entry draft (June 20, 1992).

Season Team	League		REGULAR SEASON					PLAYOFFS			
		Gms.	G	A	Pts.	PIM	Gms.	G	A	Pts.	PIM
90-91—St. Jean	QMJHL	67	1	8	9	73	—	—	—	—	—
91-92—St. Jean	QMJHL	68	1	17	18	180	—	—	—	—	—

P

Season Team	League	Gms.	G	A	Pts.	Pen.	Gms.	G	A	Pts.	Pen.
		REGULAR SEASON					**PLAYOFFS**				
92-93—St. Jean	QMJHL	70	3	34	37	147	4	0	0	0	12
93-94—Fredericton	AHL	70	2	12	14	183	—	—	—	—	—
—Montreal	NHL	7	1	2	3	20	—	—	—	—	—
NHL totals		7	1	2	3	20					

PUPPA, DAREN
G, LIGHTNING

PERSONAL: Born March 23, 1965, in Kirkland Lake, Ont. . . . 6-3/205. . . . Catches right. . . . Full name: Daren James Puppa. . . . Name pronounced POO-puh.
COLLEGE: Rensselaer Polytechnic Institute (N.Y.).
TRANSACTIONS/CAREER NOTES: Selected by Buffalo Sabres in fourth round (sixth Sabres pick, 74th overall) of NHL entry draft (June 8, 1983). . . . Injured knee (February 1986). . . . Fractured left index finger (October 1987). . . . Sprained right wrist (January 14, 1989). . . . Broke right arm (January 27, 1989). . . . Injured back (November 21, 1990); missed nine games. . . . Pulled groin and stomach muscles (February 19, 1991). . . . Fractured arm (November 12, 1991); missed 16 games. . . . Suffered sore knee (January 21, 1993); missed seven games. . . . Traded by Sabres with LW Dave Andreychuk and first-round pick in 1993 draft (D Kenny Jonsson) to Toronto Maple Leafs for G Grant Fuhr and conditional pick in 1995 draft (February 2, 1993). . . . Selected by Florida Panthers in NHL expansion draft (June 24, 1993). . . . Selected by Tampa Bay Lightning in Phase II of NHL expansion draft (June 25, 1993). . . . Suffered from tonsillitis (December 11, 1993); missed two games. . . . Sprained lower back (February 5, 1994); missed two games.
HONORS: Named to AHL All-Star first team (1986-87). . . . Named to THE SPORTING NEWS All-Star second team (1989-90). . . . Named to NHL All-Star second team (1989-90). . . . Played in NHL All-Star Game (1990).

Season Team	League	Gms.	Min.	W	L	T	GA	SO	Avg.	Gms.	Min.	W	L	GA	SO	Avg.
		REGULAR SEASON								**PLAYOFFS**						
83-84—R.P.I.	ECAC	32	1816	24	6	0	89	...	2.94	—	—	—	—	—	—	—
84-85—R.P.I.	ECAC	32	1830	31	1	0	78	0	2.56	—	—	—	—	—	—	—
85-86—Buffalo	NHL	7	401	3	4	0	21	1	3.14	—	—	—	—	—	—	—
—Rochester	AHL	20	1092	8	11	0	79	0	4.34	—	—	—	—	—	—	—
86-87—Buffalo	NHL	3	185	0	2	1	13	0	4.22	—	—	—	—	—	—	—
—Rochester	AHL	57	3129	33	14	0	146	1	*2.80	*16	*944	10	6	*48	*1	3.05
87-88—Rochester	AHL	26	1415	14	8	2	65	2	2.76	2	108	0	1	5	0	2.78
—Buffalo	NHL	17	874	8	6	1	61	0	4.19	3	142	1	1	11	0	4.65
88-89—Buffalo	NHL	37	1908	17	10	6	107	1	3.36	—	—	—	—	—	—	—
89-90—Buffalo	NHL	56	3241	31	16	6	156	1	2.89	6	370	2	4	15	0	2.43
90-91—Buffalo	NHL	38	2092	15	11	6	118	2	3.38	2	81	0	1	10	0	7.41
91-92—Buffalo	NHL	33	1757	11	14	4	114	0	3.89	—	—	—	—	—	—	—
—Rochester	AHL	2	119	0	2	0	9	0	4.54	—	—	—	—	—	—	—
92-93—Buffalo	NHL	24	1306	11	5	4	78	0	3.58	—	—	—	—	—	—	—
—Toronto	NHL	8	479	6	2	0	18	2	2.25	1	20	0	0	1	0	3.00
93-94—Tampa Bay	NHL	63	3653	22	33	6	165	4	2.71	—	—	—	—	—	—	—
NHL totals		286	15896	124	103	34	851	11	3.21	12	613	3	6	37	0	3.62

PURVES, JOHN
RW

PERSONAL: Born February 12, 1968, in Toronto. . . . 6-1/201. . . . Shoots right.
TRANSACTIONS/CAREER NOTES: Selected by Washington Capitals as underage junior in fifth round (sixth Capitals pick, 103rd overall) of NHL entry draft (June 21, 1986). . . . Broke wrist (October 1986). . . . Signed as free agent by Fort Wayne Komets (October 9, 1993).
HONORS: Named to OHL All-Star second team (1988-89).

Season Team	League	Gms.	G	A	Pts.	PIM	Gms.	G	A	Pts.	PIM
		REGULAR SEASON					**PLAYOFFS**				
84-85—Belleville	OHL	55	15	14	29	39	—	—	—	—	—
85-86—Belleville	OHL	16	3	9	12	6	—	—	—	—	—
—Hamilton	OHL	36	13	28	41	36	—	—	—	—	—
86-87—Hamilton	OHL	28	12	11	23	37	9	2	0	2	12
87-88—Hamilton	OHL	64	39	44	83	65	14	7	18	25	4
88-89—Niagara Falls	OHL	5	5	11	16	2	—	—	—	—	—
—North Bay	OHL	42	34	52	86	38	12	14	12	26	16
89-90—Baltimore	AHL	75	29	35	64	12	9	5	7	12	4
90-91—Washington	NHL	7	1	0	1	0	—	—	—	—	—
—Baltimore	AHL	53	22	29	51	27	6	2	3	5	0
91-92—Baltimore	AHL	78	43	46	89	47	—	—	—	—	—
92-93—Kaufbeuren	Germany	43	15	17	32	34	—	—	—	—	—
93-94—Fort Wayne	IHL	69	38	48	86	29	18	10	14	24	12
NHL totals		7	1	0	1	0					

PUSHOR, JAMIE
D, RED WINGS

PERSONAL: Born February 11, 1973, in Lethbridge, Alta. . . . 6-3/192. . . . Shoots right.
TRANSACTIONS/CAREER NOTES: Selected by Detroit Red Wings in second round (second Red Wings pick, 32nd overall) of NHL entry draft (June 22, 1991).

Season Team	League	Gms.	G	A	Pts.	PIM	Gms.	G	A	Pts.	PIM
		REGULAR SEASON					**PLAYOFFS**				
89-90—Lethbridge	WHL	10	0	2	2	2	—	—	—	—	—
90-91—Lethbridge	WHL	71	1	13	14	193	—	—	—	—	—
91-92—Lethbridge	WHL	49	2	15	17	232	5	0	0	0	33
92-93—Lethbridge	WHL	72	6	22	28	200	4	0	1	1	9
93-94—Adirondack	AHL	73	1	17	18	124	12	0	0	0	22

P

QUINN, DAN
C/RW

PERSONAL: Born June 1, 1965, in Ottawa.... 5-11/182.... Shoots left.
TRANSACTIONS/CAREER NOTES: Selected by Calgary Flames as underage junior in first round (first Flames pick, 13th overall) of NHL entry draft (June 8, 1983).... Traded by Flames to Pittsburgh Penguins for C Mike Bullard (November 1986).... Broke left wrist (October 1987).... Traded by Penguins with RW Andrew McBain and C Dave Capuano to Vancouver Canucks for RW Tony Tanti, C Barry Pederson and D Rod Buskas (January 8, 1990).... Bruised shoulder (January 1991).... Traded by Canucks with D Garth Butcher to St. Louis Blues for LW Geoff Courtnall, D Robert Dirk, C Cliff Ronning, LW Sergio Mommesso and fifth-round pick (RW Brian Loney) in 1992 draft (March 5, 1991).... Traded by Blues with C Rod Brind'Amour to Philadelphia Flyers for C Ron Sutter and D Murray Baron (September 22, 1991).... Signed as free agent by Minnesota North Stars (October 5, 1992).... Signed as free agent by Ottawa Senators (March 15, 1993).

			REGULAR SEASON					PLAYOFFS			
Season	Team	League	Gms.	G	A	Pts.	PIM	Gms.	G	A	Pts.	PIM
81-82	Belleville	OHL	67	19	32	51	41	—	—	—	—	—
82-83	Belleville	OHL	70	59	88	147	27	4	2	6	8	2
83-84	Belleville	OHL	24	23	36	59	12	—	—	—	—	—
	Calgary	NHL	54	19	33	52	20	8	3	5	8	4
84-85	Calgary	NHL	74	20	38	58	22	3	0	0	0	0
85-86	Calgary	NHL	78	30	42	72	44	18	8	7	15	10
86-87	Calgary	NHL	16	3	6	9	14	—	—	—	—	—
	Pittsburgh	NHL	64	28	43	71	40	—	—	—	—	—
87-88	Pittsburgh	NHL	70	40	39	79	50	—	—	—	—	—
88-89	Pittsburgh	NHL	79	34	60	94	102	11	6	3	9	10
89-90	Pittsburgh	NHL	41	9	20	29	22	—	—	—	—	—
	Vancouver	NHL	37	16	18	34	27	—	—	—	—	—
90-91	Vancouver	NHL	64	18	31	49	46	—	—	—	—	—
	St. Louis	NHL	14	4	7	11	20	13	4	7	11	32
91-92	Philadelphia	NHL	67	11	26	37	26	—	—	—	—	—
92-93	Minnesota	NHL	11	0	4	4	6	—	—	—	—	—
93-94	Ottawa	NHL	13	7	0	7	6	—	—	—	—	—
NHL totals			**682**	**239**	**367**	**606**	**445**	**53**	**21**	**22**	**43**	**56**

QUINNEY, KEN
RW

PERSONAL: Born May 23, 1965, in New Westminster, B.C.... 5-10/186.... Shoots right.
TRANSACTIONS/CAREER NOTES: Selected by Quebec Nordiques as underage junior in 10th round (ninth Nordiques pick, 203rd overall) of NHL entry draft (June 9, 1984).... Broke wrist (February 1986).... Strained right thumb ligament (December 31, 1990); missed 12 games.... Signed as free agent by Detroit Red Wings (August 1991).... Signed as free agent by Las Vegas Thunder (August 5, 1993).
HONORS: Named to WHL (East) All-Star first team (1984-85).... Named to IHL All-Star first team (1993-94).

			REGULAR SEASON					PLAYOFFS			
Season	Team	League	Gms.	G	A	Pts.	PIM	Gms.	G	A	Pts.	PIM
81-82	Calgary	WHL	63	11	17	28	55	2	0	0	0	15
82-83	Calgary	WHL	71	26	25	51	71	16	6	1	7	46
83-84	Calgary	WHL	71	64	54	118	38	4	5	2	7	0
84-85	Calgary	WHL	56	47	67	114	65	7	6	4	10	15
85-86	Fredericton	AHL	61	11	26	37	34	6	2	2	4	9
86-87	Quebec	NHL	25	2	7	9	16	—	—	—	—	—
	Fredericton	AHL	48	14	27	41	20	—	—	—	—	—
87-88	Fredericton	AHL	58	37	39	76	39	13	3	5	8	35
	Quebec	NHL	15	2	2	4	5	—	—	—	—	—
88-89	Halifax	AHL	72	41	49	90	65	4	3	0	3	0
89-90	Halifax	AHL	44	9	16	25	63	2	0	0	0	2
90-91	Quebec	NHL	19	3	4	7	2	—	—	—	—	—
	Halifax	AHL	44	20	20	40	76	—	—	—	—	—
91-92	Adirondack	AHL	63	31	29	60	33	19	7	12	19	9
92-93	Adirondack	AHL	63	32	34	66	15	10	2	9	11	9
93-94	Las Vegas	IHL	79	*55	53	108	52	5	3	3	6	2
NHL totals			**59**	**7**	**13**	**20**	**23**					

QUINT, DERON
D, JETS

PERSONAL: Born March 12, 1976, in Dover, N.H.... 6-1/182.... Shoots left.
HIGH SCHOOL: Meadowdale (Lynwood, Wash.).
TRANSACTIONS/CAREER NOTES: Selected by Winnipeg Jets in second round (first Jets pick, 30th overall) of NHL entry draft (June 28, 1994).
HONORS: Won WHL Top Draft Choice Award (1993-94).... Named to Can.HL All-Rookie team (1993-94).

			REGULAR SEASON					PLAYOFFS			
Season	Team	League	Gms.	G	A	Pts.	PIM	Gms.	G	A	Pts.	PIM
90-91	Cardigan Prep School	USHS (E)	31	67	54	121	...	—	—	—	—	—
91-92	Cardigan Prep School	USHS (E)	32	111	68	179	...	—	—	—	—	—
92-93	Tabor Academy	N.Y. H.S.	28	15	26	41	30	1	0	2	2	0
93-94	Seattle	WHL	63	15	29	44	47	9	4	12	16	8

QUINTAL, STEPHANE
D, JETS

PERSONAL: Born October 22, 1968, in Boucherville, Que.... 6-3/215.... Shoots right.... Name pronounced KAYN-tahl.
HIGH SCHOOL: Polyvalente de Mortagne (Boucherville, Que.).
TRANSACTIONS/CAREER NOTES: Broke wrist (December 1985).... Selected by

Boston Bruins as underage junior in first round (second Bruins pick, 14th overall) of NHL entry draft (June 13, 1987). . . .
Broke bone near eye (October 1988). . . . Injured knee (January 1989). . . . Sprained right knee (October 17, 1989); missed
eight games. . . . Fractured left ankle (April 9, 1991); missed remainder of playoffs. . . . Traded by Bruins with C Craig Janney to
St. Louis Blues for C Adam Oates (February 7, 1992). . . . Traded by Blues with RW Nelson Emerson to Winnipeg Jets for D Phil
Housley (September 24, 1993). . . . Sprained wrist (January 16, 1994); missed two games. . . . Sprained neck (April 6, 1994);
missed one game.
HONORS: Named to QMJHL All-Star first team (1986-87).

			REGULAR SEASON					PLAYOFFS				
Season	Team	League	Gms.	G	A	Pts.	PIM	Gms.	G	A	Pts.	PIM
85-86	Granby	QMJHL	67	2	17	19	144	—	—	—	—	—
86-87	Granby	QMJHL	67	13	41	54	178	8	0	9	9	10
87-88	Hull	QMJHL	38	13	23	36	138	19	7	12	19	30
88-89	Maine	AHL	16	4	10	14	28	—	—	—	—	—
	Boston	NHL	26	0	1	1	29	—	—	—	—	—
89-90	Boston	NHL	38	2	2	4	22	—	—	—	—	—
	Maine	AHL	37	4	16	20	27	—	—	—	—	—
90-91	Maine	AHL	23	1	5	6	30	—	—	—	—	—
	Boston	NHL	45	2	6	8	89	3	0	1	1	7
91-92	Boston	NHL	49	4	10	14	77	—	—	—	—	—
	St. Louis	NHL	26	0	6	6	32	4	1	2	3	6
92-93	St. Louis	NHL	75	1	10	11	100	9	0	0	0	8
93-94	Winnipeg	NHL	81	8	18	26	119	—	—	—	—	—
	NHL totals		340	17	53	70	468	16	1	3	4	21

QUINTIN, J.F.
LW, SHARKS

PERSONAL: Born May 28, 1969, in St. Jean, Que. . . . 6-0/185. . . . Shoots left. . . . Name pronounced kihn-TAN.
TRANSACTIONS/CAREER NOTES: Fractured knee (October 1985). . . . Selected by Minnesota North Stars in fourth round (fourth North Stars pick, 75th overall) of NHL entry draft (June 17, 1989). . . . Selected by San Jose Sharks in NHL dispersal draft (May 30, 1991).
HONORS: Named to QMJHL All-Star second team (1988-89).

			REGULAR SEASON					PLAYOFFS				
Season	Team	League	Gms.	G	A	Pts.	PIM	Gms.	G	A	Pts.	PIM
86-87	Shawinigan	QMJHL	43	1	9	10	17	—	—	—	—	—
87-88	Shawinigan	QMJHL	70	28	70	98	143	11	5	8	13	26
88-89	Shawinigan	QMJHL	69	52	100	152	105	10	9	15	24	16
89-90	Kalamazoo	IHL	68	20	18	38	38	10	8	4	12	14
90-91	Kalamazoo	IHL	78	31	43	74	64	9	1	5	6	11
91-92	Kansas City	IHL	21	4	6	10	29	13	2	10	12	29
	San Jose	NHL	8	3	0	3	0	—	—	—	—	—
92-93	San Jose	NHL	14	2	5	7	4	—	—	—	—	—
	Kansas City	IHL	64	20	29	49	169	11	2	1	3	16
93-94	Kansas City	IHL	41	14	19	33	117	—	—	—	—	—
	NHL totals		22	5	5	10	4					

RACICOT, ANDRE
G, CANADIENS

PERSONAL: Born June 9, 1969, in Rouyn-Noranda, Que. . . . 5-11/176. . . . Catches left. . . . Name pronounced RAH-sih-KOH.
TRANSACTIONS/CAREER NOTES: Selected by Montreal Canadiens in fourth round (fifth Canadiens pick, 83rd overall) of NHL draft (June 17, 1989). . . . Injured knee (October 20, 1993); missed 11 games.
HONORS: Shared Harry (Hap) Holmes Memorial Trophy with Jean-Claude Bergeron (1989-90). . . . Named to QMJHL All-Star second team (1988-89).
MISCELLANEOUS: Member of Stanley Cup championship team (1993).

			REGULAR SEASON							PLAYOFFS						
Season	Team	League	Gms.	Min.	W	L	T	GA	SO	Avg.	Gms.	Min.	W	L	GA	SO	Avg.
86-87	Longueuil	QMJHL	3	180	1	2	0	19	0	6.33	—	—	—	—	—	—	—
87-88	Hull/Granby	QMJHL	30	1547	15	11	1	105	1	4.07	5	298	1	4	23	0	4.63
88-89	Granby	QMJHL	54	2944	22	24	3	198	0	4.04	4	218	0	4	18	0	4.95
89-90	Sherbrooke	AHL	33	1948	19	11	2	97	1	2.99	5	227	0	4	18	0	4.76
	Montreal	NHL	1	13	0	0	0	3	0	13.85	—	—	—	—	—	—	—
90-91	Fredericton	AHL	22	1252	13	8	1	60	1	2.88	—	—	—	—	—	—	—
	Montreal	NHL	21	975	7	9	2	52	1	3.20	2	12	0	1	2	0	10.00
91-92	Fredericton	AHL	28	1666	14	8	5	86	0	3.10	—	—	—	—	—	—	—
	Montreal	NHL	9	436	0	3	3	23	0	3.17	1	1	0	0	0	0	0.00
92-93	Montreal	NHL	26	1433	17	5	1	81	1	3.39	1	18	0	0	2	0	6.67
93-94	Montreal	NHL	11	500	2	6	2	37	0	4.44	—	—	—	—	—	—	—
	Fredericton	AHL	6	293	1	4	0	16	0	3.28	—	—	—	—	—	—	—
	NHL totals		68	3357	26	23	8	196	2	3.50	4	31	0	1	4	0	7.74

RACINE, YVES
D, CANADIENS

PERSONAL: Born February 7, 1969, in Matane, Que. . . . 6-0/200. . . . Shoots left. . . . Name pronounced EEV ruh-SEEN.
TRANSACTIONS/CAREER NOTES: Selected by Detroit Red Wings as underage junior in first round (first Red Wings pick, 11th overall) of NHL entry draft (June 13, 1987). . . . Injured shoulder

(March 22, 1991); missed four games.... Sprained left shoulder (November 11, 1992); missed four games.... Traded by Red Wings with fourth-round pick in 1994 draft (LW Sebastien Vallee) to Philadelphia Flyers for D Terry Carkner (October 5, 1993).... Tore medial lateral ligament in knee (October 16, 1993); missed 15 games.... Traded by Flyers to Montreal Canadiens for D Kevin Haller (June 29, 1994).

HONORS: Named to QMJHL All-Star first team (1987-88 and 1988-89).... Won Emile (Butch) Bouchard Trophy (1988-89).

			REGULAR SEASON					PLAYOFFS			
Season Team	League	Gms.	G	A	Pts.	PIM	Gms.	G	A	Pts.	PIM
86-87—Longueuil	QMJHL	70	7	43	50	50	20	3	11	14	14
87-88—Victoriaville	QMJHL	69	10	84	94	150	5	0	0	0	13
—Adirondack	AHL	—	—	—	—	—	9	4	2	6	2
88-89—Victoriaville	QMJHL	63	23	85	108	95	18	3	*30	*33	41
—Adirondack	AHL	—	—	—	—	—	2	1	1	2	0
89-90—Detroit	NHL	28	4	9	13	23	—	—	—	—	—
—Adirondack	AHL	46	8	27	35	31	—	—	—	—	—
90-91—Adirondack	AHL	16	3	9	12	10	—	—	—	—	—
—Detroit	NHL	62	7	40	47	33	7	2	0	2	0
91-92—Detroit	NHL	61	2	22	24	94	11	2	1	3	10
92-93—Detroit	NHL	80	9	31	40	80	7	1	3	4	27
93-94—Philadelphia	NHL	67	9	43	52	48					
NHL totals		298	31	145	176	278	25	5	4	9	37

RAGLAN, HERB
RW

PERSONAL: Born August 5, 1967, in Peterborough, Ont.... 6-0/205.... Shoots right.... Son of Clare Raglan, defenseman, Detroit Red Wings and Chicago Blackhawks (1950-51 through 1952-53).

TRANSACTIONS/CAREER NOTES: Selected by St. Louis Blues as underage junior in second round (first Blues pick, 37th overall) of NHL entry draft (June 15, 1985).... Severely sprained ankle (December 1985).... Strained right knee ligaments (November 1987).... Sprained right wrist (October 1988).... Separated left shoulder (November 1988). ... Pulled right groin (February 1989).... Broke right wrist and underwent surgery (November 4, 1989).... Bruised ribs (October 27, 1990).... Pulled left groin (December 1990).... Sprained left knee (February 2, 1991); missed 11 games.... Traded by Blues with D Tony Twist and LW Andy Rymsha to Quebec Nordiques for RW Darin Kimble (February 4, 1991).... Broke nose (November 2, 1991); missed 12 games.... Traded by Nordiques to Tampa Bay Lightning for RW Martin Simard, C Michel Mongeau and RW Steve Tuttle (February 12, 1993).... Signed as free agent by Ottawa Senators (January 1, 1994).... Loaned by Senators to Kalamazoo of IHL (March 22, 1994).

			REGULAR SEASON					PLAYOFFS			
Season Team	League	Gms.	G	A	Pts.	PIM	Gms.	G	A	Pts.	PIM
84-85—Kingston	OHL	58	20	22	42	166	—	—	—	—	—
85-86—Kingston	OHL	28	10	9	19	88	10	5	2	7	30
—St. Louis	NHL	7	0	0	0	5	10	1	1	2	24
86-87—St. Louis	NHL	62	6	10	16	159	4	0	0	0	2
87-88—St. Louis	NHL	73	10	15	25	190	10	1	3	4	11
88-89—St. Louis	NHL	50	7	10	17	144	8	1	2	3	13
89-90—St. Louis	NHL	11	0	1	1	21	—	—	—	—	—
90-91—St. Louis	NHL	32	3	3	6	52	—	—	—	—	—
—Quebec	NHL	15	1	3	4	30	—	—	—	—	—
91-92—Quebec	NHL	62	6	14	20	120	—	—	—	—	—
92-93—Halifax	AHL	28	3	9	12	83	—	—	—	—	—
—Tampa Bay	NHL	2	0	0	0	2	—	—	—	—	—
—Atlanta	IHL	24	4	10	14	139	9	3	3	6	32
93-94—Ottawa	NHL	29	0	0	0	52	—	—	—	—	—
—Kalamazoo	IHL	29	6	11	17	112	5	0	0	0	32
NHL totals		343	33	56	89	775	32	3	6	9	50

RAGNARSSON, MARCUS
D, SHARKS

PERSONAL: Born August 13, 1971, in Ostervala, Sweden.... 6-1/200.... Shoots left.

TRANSACTIONS/CAREER NOTES: Selected by San Jose Sharks in fifth round (fifth Sharks pick, 99th overall) of NHL entry draft (June 20, 1992).

			REGULAR SEASON					PLAYOFFS			
Season Team	League	Gms.	G	A	Pts.	PIM	Gms.	G	A	Pts.	PIM
89-90—Djurgarden	Sweden	13	0	2	2	0	1	0	0	0	0
90-91—Djurgarden	Sweden	35	4	1	5	12	7	0	0	0	6
91-92—Djurgarden	Sweden	40	8	5	13	14	—	—	—	—	—
92-93—Djurgarden	Sweden	35	3	3	6	53	6	0	2	2	0
93-94—Djurgarden	Sweden	19	0	4	4	24	—	—	—	—	—

RAMAGE, ROB
D, FLYERS

PERSONAL: Born January 11, 1959, in Byron, Ont.... 6-2/200.... Shoots right.... Full name: George Robert Ramage.... Name pronounced RAM-ij.

TRANSACTIONS/CAREER NOTES: Signed as underage junior by Birmingham Bulls (July 1978).... Selected by Colorado Rockies in first round (first Rockies pick, first overall) of NHL entry draft (August 9, 1979).... Traded by Rockies to St. Louis Blues for first-round picks in 1982 (C Rocky Trottier) and 1983 (RW John MacLean) drafts (June 9, 1982).... Sprained knee (March 22, 1986).... Suffered tendinitis around left kneecap (November 24, 1986); missed 21 games.... Traded by Blues with G Rick Wamsley to Calgary Flames for RW Brett Hull and LW Steve Bozek

(March 7, 1988).... Suspended eight games by NHL for high-sticking (February 3, 1989).... Traded by Flames to Toronto Maple Leafs for second-round pick (LW Kent Manderville) in 1989 draft (June 16, 1989).... Selected by Minnesota North Stars in NHL expansion draft (May 30, 1991).... Underwent knee surgery (January 23, 1992); missed 38 games.... Selected by Tampa Bay Lightning in NHL expansion draft (June 18, 1992).... Traded by Lightning to Montreal Canadiens for D Eric Charron, D Alain Cote and future considerations (March 20, 1993); Canadiens sent D Donald Dufresne to Lightning to complete deal (June 18, 1993).... Sprained knee (April 7, 1993); missed final three games of regular season.... Traded by Canadiens to Philadelphia Flyers for future considerations (November 27, 1993).

HONORS: Shared Max Kaminsky Trophy with Brad Marsh (1977-78).... Named to OMJHL All-Star first team (1977-78).... Named to WHA All-Star first team (1978-79).... Played in NHL All-Star Game (1981, 1984, 1986 and 1988).

MISCELLANEOUS: Member of Stanley Cup championship teams (1989 and 1993).

			REGULAR SEASON					PLAYOFFS			
Season Team	League	Gms.	G	A	Pts.	PIM	Gms.	G	A	Pts.	PIM
75-76—London	OHA Mj. Jr. A	65	12	31	43	113	5	0	1	1	11
76-77—London	OMJHL	65	15	58	73	177	20	3	11	14	55
77-78—London	OMJHL	59	17	47	64	162	11	4	5	9	29
78-79—Birmingham	WHA	80	12	36	48	165	—	—	—	—	—
79-80—Colorado	NHL	75	8	20	28	135	—	—	—	—	—
80-81—Colorado	NHL	79	20	42	62	193	—	—	—	—	—
81-82—Colorado	NHL	80	13	29	42	201	—	—	—	—	—
82-83—St. Louis	NHL	78	16	35	51	193	4	0	3	3	22
83-84—St. Louis	NHL	80	15	45	60	121	11	1	8	9	32
84-85—St. Louis	NHL	80	7	31	38	178	3	1	3	4	6
85-86—St. Louis	NHL	77	10	56	66	171	19	1	10	11	66
86-87—St. Louis	NHL	59	11	28	39	106	6	2	2	4	21
87-88—St. Louis	NHL	67	8	34	42	127	—	—	—	—	—
—Calgary	NHL	12	1	6	7	37	9	1	3	4	21
88-89—Calgary	NHL	68	3	13	16	156	20	1	11	12	26
89-90—Toronto	NHL	80	8	41	49	202	5	1	2	3	20
90-91—Toronto	NHL	80	10	25	35	173	—	—	—	—	—
91-92—Minnesota	NHL	34	4	5	9	69	—	—	—	—	—
92-93—Tampa Bay	NHL	66	5	12	17	138	—	—	—	—	—
—Montreal	NHL	8	0	1	1	8	7	0	0	0	4
93-94—Montreal	NHL	6	0	1	1	2	—	—	—	—	—
—Philadelphia	NHL	15	0	1	1	14	—	—	—	—	—
WHA totals		80	12	36	48	165					
NHL totals		1044	139	425	564	2224	84	8	42	50	218

RAMSEY, MIKE

D, RED WINGS

PERSONAL: Born December 3, 1960, in Minneapolis.... 6-3/195.... Shoots left.... Full name: Michael Allen Ramsey.

COLLEGE: Minnesota.

TRANSACTIONS/CAREER NOTES: Selected by Buffalo Sabres in first round (first Sabres pick, 11th round) of NHL entry draft (August 9, 1979).... Dislocated thumb (December 4, 1983).... Injured groin (October 1987).... Fractured bone in right hand (November 2, 1988).... Pulled groin (January 12, 1989).... Pulled rib cage muscle (November 26, 1990); missed seven games.... Injured groin (November 22, 1991); missed five games.... Injured groin (January 31, 1992); missed three games.... Injured groin (March 8, 1992); missed three games.... Injured leg (April 12, 1992).... Underwent shoulder surgery (August 8, 1992); missed first nine games of season.... Strained groin (November 7, 1992); missed four games.... Bruised hand (November 18, 1992); missed six games.... Sprained knee (January 29, 1993); missed four games.... Traded by Sabres to Pittsburgh Penguins for LW Bob Errey (March 22, 1993).... Broke toe (November 11, 1993); missed nine games.... Signed as free agent by Detroit Red Wings (August 3, 1994).

HONORS: Played in NHL All-Star Game (1982, 1983, 1985 and 1986).

MISCELLANEOUS: Member of gold-medal-winning U.S. Olympic team (1980).

			REGULAR SEASON					PLAYOFFS			
Season Team	League	Gms.	G	A	Pts.	PIM	Gms.	G	A	Pts.	PIM
78-79—University of Minnesota	WCHA	26	6	11	17	30	—	—	—	—	—
79-80—U.S. national team	Int'l	56	11	22	33	55	—	—	—	—	—
—U.S. Olympic Team	Int'l	7	0	2	2	8	—	—	—	—	—
—Buffalo	NHL	13	1	6	7	6	13	1	2	3	12
80-81—Buffalo	NHL	72	3	14	17	56	8	0	3	3	20
81-82—Buffalo	NHL	80	7	23	30	56	4	1	1	2	14
82-83—Buffalo	NHL	77	8	30	38	55	10	4	4	8	15
83-84—Buffalo	NHL	72	9	22	31	82	3	0	1	1	6
84-85—Buffalo	NHL	79	8	22	30	102	5	0	1	1	23
85-86—Buffalo	NHL	76	7	21	28	117	—	—	—	—	—
86-87—Buffalo	NHL	80	8	31	39	109	—	—	—	—	—
87-88—Buffalo	NHL	63	5	16	21	77	6	0	3	3	29
88-89—Buffalo	NHL	56	2	14	16	84	5	1	0	1	11
89-90—Buffalo	NHL	73	4	21	25	47	6	0	1	1	8
90-91—Buffalo	NHL	71	6	14	20	46	5	1	0	1	12
91-92—Buffalo	NHL	66	3	14	17	67	7	0	2	2	8
92-93—Buffalo	NHL	33	2	8	10	20	—	—	—	—	—
—Pittsburgh	NHL	12	1	2	3	8	12	0	6	6	4
93-94—Pittsburgh	NHL	65	2	2	4	22	1	0	0	0	0
NHL totals		988	76	260	336	954	85	8	24	32	162

RANFORD, BILL
G, OILERS

PERSONAL: Born December 14, 1966, in Brandon, Man. . . . 5-11/185. . . . Catches left.
HIGH SCHOOL: New Westminster (B.C.).
TRANSACTIONS/CAREER NOTES: Selected by Boston Bruins as underage junior in third round (second Bruins pick, 52nd overall) of NHL entry draft (June 15, 1985). . . . Traded by Bruins with LW Geoff Courtnall and second-round pick in 1988 draft (C Petro Koivunen) to Edmonton Oilers for G Andy Moog (March 1988). . . . Sprained ankle (February 14, 1990); missed six games. . . . Strained groin (January 4, 1992); missed two games. . . . Strained hamstring (January 29, 1992); missed five games. . . . Strained right quadriceps (November 12, 1992); missed two games. . . . Strained left hamstring (April 7, 1993); missed two games. . . . Bruised hand (March 23, 1993); missed one game. . . . Strained hamstring (April 5, 1994); missed three games.
HONORS: Named to WHL All-Star second team (1985-86). . . . Won Conn Smythe Trophy (1989-90). . . . Played in NHL All-Star Game (1991).
RECORDS: Shares NHL single-season playoff record for most wins by a goaltender—16 (1990).
MISCELLANEOUS: Member of Stanley Cup championship teams (1988 and 1990).

			REGULAR SEASON								PLAYOFFS						
Season	Team	League	Gms.	Min.	W	L	T	GA	SO	Avg.	Gms.	Min.	W	L	GA	SO	Avg.
83-84	New Westminster	WHL	27	1450	10	14	0	130	0	5.38	1	27	0	0	2	0	4.44
84-85	New Westminster	WHL	38	2034	19	17	0	142	0	4.19	7	309	2	3	26	0	5.05
85-86	New Westminster	WHL	53	2791	17	29	1	225	1	4.84	—	—	—	—	—	—	—
	—Boston	NHL	4	240	3	1	0	10	0	2.50	2	120	0	2	7	0	3.50
86-87	Moncton	AHL	3	180	3	0	0	6	0	2.00	—	—	—	—	—	—	—
	—Boston	NHL	41	2234	16	20	2	124	3	3.33	2	123	0	2	8	0	3.90
87-88	Maine	AHL	51	2856	27	16	6	165	1	3.47	—	—	—	—	—	—	—
	—Edmonton	NHL	6	325	3	0	2	16	0	2.95	—	—	—	—	—	—	—
88-89	Edmonton	NHL	29	1509	15	8	2	88	1	3.50	—	—	—	—	—	—	—
89-90	Edmonton	NHL	56	3107	24	16	9	165	1	3.19	*22	*1401	*16	6	*59	1	2.53
90-91	Edmonton	NHL	60	3415	27	27	3	182	1	3.20	3	135	1	2	8	0	3.56
91-92	Edmonton	NHL	67	3822	27	26	10	228	1	3.58	16	909	8	*8	51	†2	3.37
92-93	Edmonton	NHL	67	3753	17	38	6	240	1	3.84	—	—	—	—	—	—	—
93-94	Edmonton	NHL	71	4070	22	34	11	236	1	3.48	—	—	—	—	—	—	—
NHL totals			401	22475	154	170	45	1289	8	4.19	45	2688	25	20	133	3	2.97

RANHEIM, PAUL
LW, WHALERS

PERSONAL: Born January 25, 1966, in St. Louis. . . . 6-0/195. . . . Shoots right. . . . Full name: Paul Stephen Ranheim. . . . Name pronounced RAN-HIGHM.
HIGH SCHOOL: Edina (Minn.).
COLLEGE: Wisconsin.
TRANSACTIONS/CAREER NOTES: Selected by Calgary Flames in second round (third Flames pick, 38th overall) of NHL entry draft (June 8, 1983). . . . Broke right ankle (December 11, 1990); missed 41 games. . . . Traded by Flames with D Gary Suter and C Ted Drury to Hartford Whalers for C Michael Nylander, D Zarley Zalapski and D James Patrick (March 10, 1994).
HONORS: Named to WCHA All-Star second team (1986-87). . . . Named to NCAA All-America West first team (1987-88). . . . Named to WCHA All-Star first team (1987-88). . . . Won Garry F. Longman Memorial Trophy (1988-89). . . . Won Ken McKenzie Trophy (1988-89). . . . Named to IHL All-Star second team (1988-89).

			REGULAR SEASON				PLAYOFFS				
Season	Team	League	Gms.	G	A	Pts.	PIM	Gms.	G	A	Pts.	PIM
82-83	Edina High School	Minn. H.S.	26	12	25	37	4	—	—	—	—	—
83-84	Edina High School	Minn. H.S.	26	16	24	40	6	—	—	—	—	—
84-85	University of Wisconsin	WCHA	42	11	11	22	40	—	—	—	—	—
85-86	University of Wisconsin	WCHA	33	17	17	34	34	—	—	—	—	—
86-87	University of Wisconsin	WCHA	42	24	35	59	54	—	—	—	—	—
87-88	University of Wisconsin	WCHA	44	36	26	62	63	—	—	—	—	—
88-89	Calgary	NHL	5	0	0	0	0	—	—	—	—	—
	—Salt Lake City	IHL	75	*68	29	97	16	14	5	5	10	8
89-90	Calgary	NHL	80	26	28	54	23	6	1	3	4	2
90-91	Calgary	NHL	39	14	16	30	4	7	2	2	4	0
91-92	Calgary	NHL	80	23	20	43	32	—	—	—	—	—
92-93	Calgary	NHL	83	21	22	43	26	6	0	1	1	0
93-94	Calgary	NHL	67	10	14	24	20	—	—	—	—	—
	—Hartford	NHL	15	0	3	3	2	—	—	—	—	—
NHL totals			369	94	103	197	107	19	3	6	9	2

RATHJE, MIKE
D, SHARKS

PERSONAL: Born May 11, 1974, in Manville, Alta. . . . 6-5/205. . . . Shoots left. . . . Name pronounced RATH-jee.
HIGH SCHOOL: Medicine Hat (Alta.).
TRANSACTIONS/CAREER NOTES: Selected by San Jose Sharks in first round (first Sharks pick, third overall) of NHL entry draft (June 20, 1992). . . . Strained abdomen (February 19, 1994); missed three games. . . . Sprained knee (February 26, 1994); missed four games.
HONORS: Named to Can.HL All-Star second team (1992-93). . . . Named to WHL (East) All-Star second team (1991-92 and 1992-93).

			REGULAR SEASON				PLAYOFFS				
Season	Team	League	Gms.	G	A	Pts.	PIM	Gms.	G	A	Pts.	PIM
90-91	Medicine Hat	WHL	64	1	16	17	28	12	0	4	4	2
91-92	Medicine Hat	WHL	67	11	23	34	109	4	0	1	1	2
92-93	Medicine Hat	WHL	57	12	37	49	103	10	3	3	6	12
	—Kansas City	IHL	—	—	—	—	—	5	0	0	0	12

Season	Team	League	Gms.	G	A	Pts.	Pen.	Gms.	G	A	Pts.	Pen.
93-94—	San Jose	NHL	47	1	9	10	59	1	0	0	0	0
—	Kansas City	IHL	6	0	2	2	0	—	—	—	—	—
NHL totals			47	1	9	10	59	1	0	0	0	0

RAY, ROB

LW, SABRES

PERSONAL: Born June 8, 1968, in Stirling, Ont. . . . 6-0/203. . . . Shoots left.
TRANSACTIONS/CAREER NOTES: Broke jaw (January 1987). . . . Selected by Buffalo Sabres in fifth round (fifth Sabres pick, 97th overall) of NHL entry draft (June 11, 1988). . . . Tore ligament in right knee (April 11, 1993); missed remainder of season.

			REGULAR SEASON					PLAYOFFS				
Season	Team	League	Gms.	G	A	Pts.	PIM	Gms.	G	A	Pts.	PIM
84-85—	Whitby Lawmen	OPJHL	35	5	10	15	318	—	—	—	—	—
85-86—	Cornwall	OHL	53	6	13	19	253	6	0	0	0	26
86-87—	Cornwall	OHL	46	17	20	37	158	5	1	1	2	16
87-88—	Cornwall	OHL	61	11	41	52	179	11	2	3	5	33
88-89—	Rochester	AHL	74	11	18	29	*446	—	—	—	—	—
89-90—	Buffalo	NHL	27	2	1	3	99	—	—	—	—	—
—	Rochester	AHL	43	2	13	15	335	17	1	3	4	*115
90-91—	Rochester	AHL	8	1	1	2	15	—	—	—	—	—
—	Buffalo	NHL	66	8	8	16	*350	6	1	1	2	56
91-92—	Buffalo	NHL	63	5	3	8	354	7	0	0	0	2
92-93—	Buffalo	NHL	68	3	2	5	211	—	—	—	—	—
93-94—	Buffalo	NHL	82	3	4	7	274	7	1	0	1	43
NHL totals			306	21	18	39	1288	20	2	1	3	101

RECCHI, MARK

RW, FLYERS

PERSONAL: Born February 1, 1968, in Kamloops, B.C. . . . 5-10/185. . . . Shoots left. . . . Name pronounced REH-kee.
TRANSACTIONS/CAREER NOTES: Broke ankle (January 1987). . . . Selected by Pittsburgh Penguins in fourth round (fourth Penguins pick, 67th overall) of NHL entry draft (June 11, 1988). . . . Injured left shoulder (December 23, 1990). . . . Sprained right knee (March 30, 1991). . . . Traded by Penguins with D Brian Benning and first-round pick in 1992 draft (LW Jason Bowen) to Philadelphia Flyers for RW Rick Tocchet, D Kjell Samuelsson, G Ken Wregget and third-round pick in 1992 draft (February 19, 1992).
HONORS: Named to WHL (West) All-Star team (1987-88). . . . Named to IHL All-Star second team (1988-89). . . . Named to NHL All-Star second team (1991-92). . . . Played in NHL All-Star Game (1991, 1993, and 1994).
MISCELLANEOUS: Member of Stanley Cup championship team (1991).

			REGULAR SEASON					PLAYOFFS				
Season	Team	League	Gms.	G	A	Pts.	PIM	Gms.	G	A	Pts.	PIM
84-85—	Langley Eagles	BCJHL	51	26	39	65	39	—	—	—	—	—
85-86—	New Westminster	WHL	72	21	40	61	55	—	—	—	—	—
86-87—	Kamloops	WHL	40	26	50	76	63	13	3	16	19	17
87-88—	Kamloops	WHL	62	61	*93	154	75	17	10	*21	†31	18
88-89—	Pittsburgh	NHL	15	1	1	2	0	—	—	—	—	—
—	Muskegon	IHL	63	50	49	99	86	14	7	*14	†21	28
89-90—	Muskegon	IHL	4	7	4	11	2	—	—	—	—	—
—	Pittsburgh	NHL	74	30	37	67	44	—	—	—	—	—
90-91—	Pittsburgh	NHL	78	40	73	113	48	24	10	24	34	33
91-92—	Pittsburgh	NHL	58	33	37	70	78	—	—	—	—	—
—	Philadelphia	NHL	22	10	17	27	18	—	—	—	—	—
92-93—	Philadelphia	NHL	84	53	70	123	95	—	—	—	—	—
93-94—	Philadelphia	NHL	84	40	67	107	46	—	—	—	—	—
NHL totals			415	207	302	509	329	24	10	24	34	33

REDDICK, POKEY

G, PANTHERS

PERSONAL: Born October 6, 1964, in Halifax, N.S. . . . 5-8/170. . . . Catches left.
TRANSACTIONS/CAREER NOTES: Traded by New Westminster Bruins to Brandon Wheat Kings for D Jayson Meyer and D Lee Trim (October 1984). . . . Signed as free agent by Winnipeg Jets (September 27, 1985). . . . Traded by Jets to Edmonton Oilers for future considerations (September 28, 1989). . . . Signed as free agent by Florida Panthers (July 13, 1993).
HONORS: Named to WHL All-Star second team (1983-84). . . . Shared James Norris Memorial Trophy with Rick St. Croix (1985-86). . . . Won N.R. (Bud) Poile Trophy (1992-93).
MISCELLANEOUS: Member of Stanley Cup championship team (1990).

			REGULAR SEASON							PLAYOFFS					
Season	Team	League	Gms.	Min.	W	L	T	GA	SO	Avg.	Gms.	Min.	W	L	GA	SO	Avg.
81-82—	Billings	WHL	1	60	...	...	...	7	0	7.00	—	—	—	—	—	—	—
82-83—	Nanaimo	WHL	*66	*3549	19	38	1	*383	0	6.48	—	—	—	—	—	—	—
83-84—	New Westminster	WHL	50	2930	24	22	2	215	0	4.40	9	542	4	5	53	0	5.87
84-85—	Brandon	WHL	47	2585	14	30	1	243	0	5.64	—	—	—	—	—	—	—
—	Fort Wayne	IHL	10	491	. . .	. . .	. . .	32	2	3.91	4	246	. . .	. . .	17	0	4.15
85-86—	Fort Wayne	IHL	32	1811	15	11	†0	92	†3	3.05	—	—	—	—	—	—	—
86-87—	Winnipeg	NHL	48	2762	21	21	4	149	0	3.24	3	166	0	2	10	0	3.61
87-88—	Winnipeg	NHL	28	1487	9	13	3	102	0	4.12	—	—	—	—	—	—	—
—	Moncton	AHL	9	545	2	6	1	26	0	2.86	—	—	—	—	—	—	—

Season Team	League	REGULAR SEASON								PLAYOFFS						
		Gms.	Min.	W	L	T	GA	SO	Avg.	Gms.	Min.	W	L	GA	SO	Avg.
88-89—Winnipeg	NHL	41	2109	11	17	7	144	0	4.10	—	—	—	—	—	—	—
89-90—Edmonton	NHL	11	604	5	4	2	31	0	3.08	1	2	0	0	0	0	0.00
—Cape Breton	AHL	15	821	9	4	1	54	0	3.95	—	—	—	—	—	—	—
—Phoenix	IHL	3	185	2	1	‡0	7	0	2.27	—	—	—	—	—	—	—
90-91—Edmonton	NHL	2	120	0	2	0	9	0	4.50	—	—	—	—	—	—	—
—Cape Breton	AHL	31	1673	19	10	0	97	2	3.48	2	124	0	2	10	0	4.84
91-92—Cape Breton	AHL	16	765	5	3	3	45	0	3.53	—	—	—	—	—	—	—
—Fort Wayne	IHL	14	787	6	5	‡2	40	1	3.05	7	369	3	4	18	0	2.93
92-93—Fort Wayne	IHL	54	3043	33	16	‡0	156	3	3.08	12	723	*12	0	18	0	*1.49
93-94—Florida	NHL	2	80	0	1	0	8	0	6.00	—	—	—	—	—	—	—
—Cincinnati	IHL	54	2894	31	12	‡6	147	*2	3.05	10	498	6	2	21	†1	2.53
NHL totals		132	7162	46	58	16	443	0	3.71	4	168	0	2	10	0	3.57

REDMOND, KEITH

LW, KINGS

PERSONAL: Born October 25, 1972, in Richmond Hill, Ont.... 6-3/208.... Shoots left.... Full name: Keith Christopher Redmond.
COLLEGE: Bowling Green State.
TRANSACTIONS/CAREER NOTES: Selected by Los Angeles Kings in fourth round (second Kings pick, 79th overall) of NHL entry draft (June 22, 1991).

Season Team	League	REGULAR SEASON					PLAYOFFS				
		Gms.	G	A	Pts.	PIM	Gms.	G	A	Pts.	PIM
88-89—Nepean	COJHL	59	3	12	15	110	—	—	—	—	—
89-90—Nepean	COJHL	40	14	10	24	169	—	—	—	—	—
90-91—Bowling Green State	CCHA	35	1	3	4	72	—	—	—	—	—
91-92—Bowling Green State	CCHA	8	0	0	0	14	—	—	—	—	—
—Belleville	OHL	16	1	7	8	52	—	—	—	—	—
—Detroit	OHL	25	6	12	18	61	7	1	3	4	49
92-93—Muskegon	Col.HL	4	1	0	1	46	—	—	—	—	—
—Phoenix	IHL	53	6	10	16	285	—	—	—	—	—
93-94—Los Angeles	NHL	12	1	0	1	20	—	—	—	—	—
—Phoenix	IHL	43	8	10	18	196	—	—	—	—	—
NHL totals		12	1	0	1	20					

REEKIE, JOE

D, CAPITALS

PERSONAL: Born February 22, 1965, in Victoria, B.C.... 6-3/215.... Shoots left.... Full name: Joseph James Reekie.
TRANSACTIONS/CAREER NOTES: Selected by Hartford Whalers as underage junior in seventh round (eighth Whalers pick, 124th overall) of NHL entry draft (June 8, 1983).... Released by Whalers (June 1984).... Selected by Buffalo Sabres in sixth round (sixth Sabres pick, 119th overall) of NHL entry draft (June 15, 1985).... Injured ankle (March 14, 1987).... Injured shoulder (October 1987).... Broke kneecap (November 15, 1987).... Underwent surgery to left knee (September 1988).... Traded by Sabres to New York Islanders for sixth-round pick (G Bill Pye) in 1989 draft (June 17, 1989).... Sprained right knee (November 1989).... Broke two bones in left hand and suffered facial cuts in automobile accident and underwent surgery (December 7, 1989).... Broke left middle finger (March 21, 1990). ... Injured eye (January 12, 1991); missed six games.... Fractured knuckle on left hand (January 3, 1992); missed 22 games. ... Selected by Tampa Bay Lightning in NHL expansion draft (June 18, 1992).... Broke left leg (January 16, 1993); missed remainder of season.... Traded by Lightning to Washington Capitals for D Enrico Ciccone, third-round pick in 1994 draft and conditional draft pick (March 21, 1994).

Season Team	League	REGULAR SEASON					PLAYOFFS				
		Gms.	G	A	Pts.	PIM	Gms.	G	A	Pts.	PIM
81-82—Nepean	COJHL	16	2	5	7	4	—	—	—	—	—
82-83—North Bay	OHL	59	2	9	11	49	8	0	1	1	11
83-84—North Bay	OHL	9	1	0	1	18	—	—	—	—	—
—Cornwall	OHL	53	6	27	33	166	3	0	0	0	4
84-85—Cornwall	OHL	65	19	63	82	134	9	4	13	17	18
85-86—Rochester	AHL	77	3	25	28	178	—	—	—	—	—
—Buffalo	NHL	3	0	0	0	14	—	—	—	—	—
86-87—Buffalo	NHL	56	1	8	9	82	—	—	—	—	—
—Rochester	AHL	22	0	6	6	52	—	—	—	—	—
87-88—Buffalo	NHL	30	1	4	5	68	2	0	0	0	4
88-89—Rochester	AHL	21	1	2	3	56	—	—	—	—	—
—Buffalo	NHL	15	1	3	4	26	—	—	—	—	—
89-90—New York Islanders	NHL	31	1	8	9	43	—	—	—	—	—
—Springfield	AHL	15	1	4	5	24	—	—	—	—	—
90-91—Capital District	AHL	2	1	0	1	0	—	—	—	—	—
—New York Islanders	NHL	66	3	16	19	96	—	—	—	—	—
91-92—New York Islanders	NHL	54	4	12	16	85	—	—	—	—	—
—Capital District	AHL	3	2	2	4	2	—	—	—	—	—
92-93—Tampa Bay	NHL	42	2	11	13	69	—	—	—	—	—
93-94—Tampa Bay	NHL	73	1	11	12	127	—	—	—	—	—
—Washington	NHL	12	0	5	5	29	11	2	1	3	29
NHL totals		382	14	78	92	639	13	2	1	3	33

REESE, JEFF
G, WHALERS

PERSONAL: Born March 24, 1966, in Brantford, Ont.... 5-9/155.... Catches left.
TRANSACTIONS/CAREER NOTES: Selected by Toronto Maple Leafs as underage junior in fourth round (third Maple Leafs pick, 67th overall) of NHL entry draft (June 9, 1984).... Broke left kneecap (October 23, 1989); missed two months.... Suffered contusion to left kneecap (April 12, 1990)....
Broke transverse processes (March 23, 1991); missed remainder of season.... Traded by Maple Leafs with D Alexander Godynyuk, RW Gary Leeman, D Michel Petit and LW Craig Berube to Calgary Flames for C Doug Gilmour, D Jamie Macoun, LW Kent Manderville, D Ric Nattress and G Rick Wamsley (January 2, 1992).... Lacerated hand; missed first three games of 1992-93 season.... Strained shoulder (October 31, 1993); missed three games.... Traded by Flames with future considerations to Hartford Whalers for D Dan Keczmer (November 19, 1993).... Suffered hip flexor (December 23, 1993); missed six games.
RECORDS: Holds NHL single-game record for most assists by a goaltender—3 (February 10, 1993).

						REGULAR SEASON							PLAYOFFS				
Season	Team	League	Gms.	Min.	W	L	T	GA	SO	Avg.	Gms.	Min.	W	L	GA	SO	Avg.
82-83—Hamilton A's	OJHL	40	2380	...	...	...	176	0	4.44	—	—	—	—	—	—	—
83-84—London	OHL	43	2308	18	19	0	173	0	4.50	6	327	3	3	27	0	4.95
84-85—London	OHL	50	2878	31	15	1	186	1	3.88	8	440	5	2	20	†1	*2.73
85-86—London	OHL	*57	*3281	25	26	3	215	0	3.93	5	299	0	4	25	0	5.02
86-87—Newmarket	AHL	50	2822	11	29	0	193	1	4.10	—	—	—	—	—	—	—
87-88—Newmarket	AHL	28	1587	10	14	3	103	0	3.89	—	—	—	—	—	—	—
—Toronto	NHL	5	249	1	2	1	17	0	4.10	—	—	—	—	—	—	—
88-89—Toronto	NHL	10	486	2	6	1	40	0	4.94	—	—	—	—	—	—	—
—Newmarket	AHL	37	2072	17	14	3	132	0	3.82	—	—	—	—	—	—	—
89-90—Newmarket	AHL	7	431	3	2	2	29	0	4.04	—	—	—	—	—	—	—
—Toronto	NHL	21	1101	9	6	3	81	0	4.41	2	108	1	1	6	0	3.33
90-91—Toronto	NHL	30	1430	6	13	3	92	1	3.86	—	—	—	—	—	—	—
—Newmarket	AHL	3	180	2	1	0	7	0	2.33	—	—	—	—	—	—	—
91-92—Toronto	NHL	8	413	1	5	1	20	1	2.91	—	—	—	—	—	—	—
—Calgary	NHL	12	587	3	2	2	37	0	3.78	—	—	—	—	—	—	—
92-93—Calgary	NHL	26	1311	14	4	1	70	1	3.20	4	209	1	3	17	0	4.88
93-94—Calgary	NHL	1	13	0	0	0	1	0	4.62	—	—	—	—	—	—	—
—Hartford	NHL	19	1086	5	9	3	56	1	3.09	—	—	—	—	—	—	—
NHL totals		132	6676	41	47	15	414	4	3.72	6	317	2	4	23	0	4.35

REICHEL, MARTIN
RW/C, OILERS

PERSONAL: Born November 7, 1973, in Most, Czechoslovakia.... 6-1/183.... Shoots left.... Name pronounced RIGH-kuhl.... Brother of Robert Reichel, center, Calgary Flames.
TRANSACTIONS/CAREER NOTES: Selected by Edmonton Oilers in second round (second Oilers pick, 37th overall) of NHL entry draft (June 20, 1992).

				REGULAR SEASON					PLAYOFFS		
Season	Team	League	Gms.	G	A	Pts.	PIM	Gms.	G	A	Pts.	PIM
90-91—Freiburg	Germany	23	7	8	15	19	—	—	—	—	—
91-92—Freiburg	Germany	27	15	16	31	8	4	1	1	2	4
92-93—Freiburg	Germany	37	13	9	22	27	9	4	4	8	11
93-94—Rosenheim	Germany	20	5	15	20	6	—	—	—	—	—

REICHEL, ROBERT
C, FLAMES

PERSONAL: Born June 25, 1971, in Litvinov, Czechoslovakia.... 5-10/185.... Shoots right.... Name pronounced RIGH-kuhl.... Brother of Martin Reichel, right winger/center in Edmonton Oilers system.
TRANSACTIONS/CAREER NOTES: Selected by Calgary Flames in fourth round (fifth Flames pick, 70th overall) of NHL entry draft (June 17, 1989).... Strained right knee (March 16, 1993); missed three games.
HONORS: Named to Czechoslovakian League All-Star team (1989-90).

				REGULAR SEASON					PLAYOFFS		
Season	Team	League	Gms.	G	A	Pts.	PIM	Gms.	G	A	Pts.	PIM
88-89—Litvinov	Czech.	...	20	31	51	...	—	—	—	—	—
89-90—Litvinov	Czech.	52	49	34	*83	...	—	—	—	—	—
90-91—Calgary	NHL	66	19	22	41	22	6	1	1	2	0
91-92—Calgary	NHL	77	20	34	54	32	—	—	—	—	—
92-93—Calgary	NHL	80	40	48	88	54	6	2	4	6	2
93-94—Calgary	NHL	84	40	53	93	58	7	0	5	5	0
NHL totals		307	119	157	276	166	19	3	10	13	2

REICHERT, CRAIG
RW, MIGHTY DUCKS

PERSONAL: Born May 11, 1974, in Winnipeg.... 6-1/196.... Shoots right.
HIGH SCHOOL: Dr. E.P. Scarlett (Calgary).
TRANSACTIONS/CAREER NOTES: Selected by Mighty Ducks of Anaheim in third round (third Mighty Ducks pick, 67th overall) of NHL entry draft (June 29, 1994).

				REGULAR SEASON					PLAYOFFS		
Season	Team	League	Gms.	G	A	Pts.	PIM	Gms.	G	A	Pts.	PIM
91-92—Spokane	WHL	68	14	30	44	86	4	1	0	1	4
92-93—Red Deer	WHL	66	32	33	65	62	4	3	1	4	2
93-94—Red Deer	WHL	72	52	67	119	153	4	2	2	4	8

REID, DAVID
LW, BRUINS

PERSONAL: Born May 15, 1964, in Toronto.... 6-1/205.... Shoots left.
TRANSACTIONS/CAREER NOTES: Selected by Boston Bruins as underage junior in third round (fourth Bruins pick, 60th overall) of NHL entry draft (June 9, 1982).... Underwent knee surgery (December 1986).... Separated shoulder (November 1987); missed 10 games.... Signed as free agent by

Toronto Maple Leafs (August 1988).... Signed as free agent by Bruins (November 22, 1991).... Suffered from pneumonia (March 1992); missed 10 games.... Injured knee (March 25, 1993); missed remainder of season.

			REGULAR SEASON					PLAYOFFS			
Season	Team	League	Gms.	G	A	Pts.	PIM	Gms.	G	A	Pts.	PIM
81-82—Peterborough		OHL	68	10	32	42	41	9	2	3	5	11
82-83—Peterborough		OHL	70	23	34	57	33	4	3	1	4	0
83-84—Peterborough		OHL	60	33	64	97	12	—	—	—	—	—
—Boston		NHL	8	1	0	1	2	—	—	—	—	—
84-85—Hershey		AHL	43	10	14	24	6	—	—	—	—	—
—Boston		NHL	35	14	13	27	27	5	1	0	1	0
85-86—Moncton		AHL	26	14	18	32	4	—	—	—	—	—
—Boston		NHL	37	10	10	20	10	—	—	—	—	—
86-87—Boston		NHL	12	3	3	6	0	2	0	0	0	0
—Moncton		AHL	40	12	22	34	23	5	0	1	1	0
87-88—Maine		AHL	63	21	37	58	40	10	6	7	13	0
—Boston		NHL	3	0	0	0	0	—	—	—	—	—
88-89—Toronto		NHL	77	9	21	30	22	—	—	—	—	—
89-90—Toronto		NHL	70	9	19	28	9	3	0	0	0	0
90-91—Toronto		NHL	69	15	13	28	18	—	—	—	—	—
91-92—Maine		AHL	12	1	5	6	4	—	—	—	—	—
—Boston		NHL	43	7	7	14	27	15	2	5	7	4
92-93—Boston		NHL	65	20	16	36	10	—	—	—	—	—
93-94—Boston		NHL	83	6	17	23	25	13	2	1	3	2
NHL totals			502	94	119	213	150	38	5	6	11	6

RENBERG, MIKAEL
L.W. FLYERS

PERSONAL: Born May 5, 1972, in Pitea, Sweden.... 6-1/218.... Shoots left.
TRANSACTIONS/CAREER NOTES: Selected by Philadelphia Flyers in second round (third Flyers pick, 40th overall) of NHL entry draft (June 16, 1990).
HONORS: Named to NHL All-Rookie team (1993-94).

			REGULAR SEASON					PLAYOFFS			
Season	Team	League	Gms.	G	A	Pts.	PIM	Gms.	G	A	Pts.	PIM
88-89—Pitea		Sweden	12	6	3	9	...	—	—	—	—	—
89-90—Pitea		Sweden	29	15	19	34	...	—	—	—	—	—
90-91—Lulea		Sweden	29	11	6	17	12	—	—	—	—	—
91-92—Lulea		Sweden	38	8	15	23	20	—	—	—	—	—
92-93—Lulea		Sweden	39	19	13	32	61	11	4	4	8	0
93-94—Philadelphia		NHL	83	38	44	82	36	—	—	—	—	—
NHL totals			83	38	44	82	36					

RHODES, DAMIAN
G. MAPLE LEAFS

PERSONAL: Born May 28, 1969, in St. Paul, Minn.... 6-0/175.... Catches left.
HIGH SCHOOL: Richfield (Minn.).
COLLEGE: Michigan Tech.
TRANSACTIONS/CAREER NOTES: Selected by Toronto Maple Leafs in sixth round (sixth Maple Leafs pick, 112th overall) of NHL entry draft (June 13, 1987).

			REGULAR SEASON							PLAYOFFS						
Season	Team	League	Gms.	Min.	W	L	T	GA	SO	Avg.	Gms.	Min.	W	L	GA	SO	Avg.
85-86—Richfield H.S.		Minn. HS	16	720	...	...	...	56	0	4.67	—	—	—	—	—	—	—
86-87—Richfield H.S.		Minn. HS	19	673	...	...	...	51	1	4.55	—	—	—	—	—	—	—
87-88—Michigan Tech		WCHA	29	1623	16	10	1	114	0	4.21	—	—	—	—	—	—	—
88-89—Michigan Tech		WCHA	37	2216	15	22	0	163	0	4.41	—	—	—	—	—	—	—
89-90—Michigan Tech		WCHA	25	1358	6	17	0	119	0	5.26	—	—	—	—	—	—	—
90-91—Toronto		NHL	1	60	1	0	0	1	0	1.00	—	—	—	—	—	—	—
—Newmarket		AHL	38	2154	8	24	3	144	1	4.01	—	—	—	—	—	—	—
91-92—St. John's		AHL	43	2454	20	16	5	148	0	3.62	6	331	4	1	16	0	2.90
92-93—St. John's		AHL	52	*3074	27	16	8	184	1	3.59	9	538	4	5	37	0	4.13
93-94—Toronto		NHL	22	1213	9	7	3	53	0	2.62	1	0	0	0	0	0	0.00
NHL totals			23	1273	10	7	3	54	0	2.55	1	0	0	0	0	0	0

RICCI, MIKE
C, NORDIQUES

PERSONAL: Born October 27, 1971, in Scarborough, Ont.... 6-0/190.... Shoots left.... Name pronounced REE-CHEE.
TRANSACTIONS/CAREER NOTES: Separated right shoulder (December 1989).... Selected by Philadelphia Flyers in first round (first Flyers pick, fourth overall) of NHL entry draft (June 16, 1990).... Broke right index finger and thumb (October 4, 1990); missed nine games.... Traded by Flyers with G Ron Hextall, C Peter Forsberg, D Steve Duchesne, D Kerry Huffman, first-round pick in 1993 draft (G Jocelyn Thibault), cash and future considerations to Quebec Nordiques for C Eric Lindros (June 20, 1992); Flyers sent LW Chris Simon and first-round pick in 1994 draft (traded to Toronto Maple Leafs) to Nordiques to complete deal (July 21, 1992).... Sprained left wrist (November 3, 1992); missed four games.... Suffered from the flu (January 5, 1993); missed two games.
HONORS: Named to OHL All-Star second team (1988-89).... Won Can.HL Player of the Year Award (1989-90).... Won Red Tilson Trophy (1989-90).... Won William Hanley Trophy (1989-90).... Named to OHL All-Star first team (1989-90).

			REGULAR SEASON					PLAYOFFS			
Season	Team	League	Gms.	G	A	Pts.	PIM	Gms.	G	A	Pts.	PIM
87-88—Peterborough		OHL	41	24	37	61	20	8	5	5	10	4
88-89—Peterborough		OHL	60	54	52	106	43	17	19	16	35	18

Season	Team	League	REGULAR SEASON					PLAYOFFS				
			Gms.	G	A	Pts.	Pen.	Gms.	G	A	Pts.	Pen.
89-90—Peterborough		OHL	60	52	64	116	39	12	5	7	12	26
90-91—Philadelphia		NHL	68	21	20	41	64	—	—	—	—	—
91-92—Philadelphia		NHL	78	20	36	56	93	—	—	—	—	—
92-93—Quebec		NHL	77	27	51	78	123	6	0	6	6	8
93-94—Quebec		NHL	83	30	21	51	113	—	—	—	—	—
NHL totals			306	98	128	226	393	6	0	6	6	8

RICE, STEVE
RW, OILERS

PERSONAL: Born May 26, 1971, in Waterloo, Ont. . . . 6-0/215. . . . Shoots right.
TRANSACTIONS/CAREER NOTES: Underwent knee surgery (October 1986). . . . Selected by New York Rangers in first round (first Rangers pick, 20th overall) of NHL entry draft (June 17, 1989). . . . Suffered back spasms (September 14, 1989). . . . Injured left shoulder (October 1990). . . . Traded by Rangers with C Bernie Nicholls, LW Louie DeBrusk and future considerations to Edmonton Oilers for C Mark Messier and future considerations (October 4, 1991); Rangers traded D David Shaw to Oilers for D Jeff Beukeboom to complete deal (November 12, 1991). . . . Suffered right hip contusion (March 1993); missed two games. . . . Fractured hand (February 12, 1994); missed 16 games.
HONORS: Named to Memorial Cup All-Star team (1989-90). . . . Named to OHL All-Star second team (1990-91). . . . Named to AHL All-Star second team (1992-93).

Season	Team	League	REGULAR SEASON					PLAYOFFS				
			Gms.	G	A	Pts.	PIM	Gms.	G	A	Pts.	PIM
87-88—Kitchener		OHL	59	11	14	25	43	4	0	1	1	0
88-89—Kitchener		OHL	64	36	31	67	42	5	2	1	3	8
89-90—Kitchener		OHL	58	39	37	76	102	16	4	8	12	24
90-91—New York Rangers		NHL	11	1	1	2	4	2	2	1	3	6
—Binghamton		AHL	8	4	1	5	12	5	2	0	2	2
—Kitchener		OHL	29	30	30	60	43	6	5	6	11	2
91-92—Edmonton		NHL	3	0	0	0	2	—	—	—	—	—
—Cape Breton		AHL	45	32	20	52	38	5	4	4	8	10
92-93—Cape Breton		AHL	51	34	28	62	63	14	4	6	10	22
—Edmonton		NHL	28	2	5	7	28	—	—	—	—	—
93-94—Edmonton		NHL	63	17	15	32	36	—	—	—	—	—
NHL totals			105	20	21	41	70	2	2	1	3	6

RICHARD, JEAN-MARC
D

PERSONAL: Born October 8, 1966, in St. Raymond, Que. . . . 5-11/178. . . . Shoots left. . . . Name pronounced ZHAWN-MAHRK rih-SHAHRD.
TRANSACTIONS/CAREER NOTES: Signed as free agent by Quebec Nordiques (April 1987). . . . Loaned to Fort Wayne Komets (March 1991); became free agent when contract expired with Nordiques at end of season. . . . Signed as free agent by Komets (September 1991). . . . Signed as free agent by Las Vegas Thunder (July 8, 1993).
HONORS: Won Emile (Butch) Bouchard Trophy (1986-87). . . . Named to QMJHL All-Star first team (1985-86 and 1986-87). . . . Won Governors Trophy (1991-92). . . . Named to IHL All-Star first team (1991-92 and 1993-94).

Season	Team	League	REGULAR SEASON					PLAYOFFS				
			Gms.	G	A	Pts.	PIM	Gms.	G	A	Pts.	PIM
83-84—Chicoutimi		QMJHL	61	1	20	21	41	—	—	—	—	—
84-85—Chicoutimi		QMJHL	68	10	61	71	57	—	—	—	—	—
85-86—Chicoutimi		QMJHL	72	19	88	107	111	9	3	5	8	14
86-87—Chicoutimi		QMJHL	67	21	81	102	105	16	6	25	31	28
87-88—Fredericton		AHL	68	14	42	56	52	7	2	1	3	4
—Quebec		NHL	4	2	1	3	2	—	—	—	—	—
88-89—Halifax		AHL	57	8	25	33	38	4	1	0	1	4
89-90—Quebec		NHL	1	0	0	0	0	—	—	—	—	—
—Halifax		AHL	40	1	24	25	38	—	—	—	—	—
90-91—Halifax		AHL	80	7	41	48	76	—	—	—	—	—
—Fort Wayne		IHL	1	0	0	0	0	19	3	9	12	8
91-92—Fort Wayne		IHL	82	18	68	86	109	7	0	5	5	20
92-93—San Diego		IHL	6	1	0	1	4	—	—	—	—	—
—Fort Wayne		IHL	52	10	33	43	48	12	6	11	17	6
93-94—Las Vegas		IHL	59	15	33	48	44	5	0	3	3	0
NHL totals			5	2	1	3	2					

RICHARDS, TODD
D

PERSONAL: Born October 20, 1966, in Robbinsdale, Minn. . . . 6-0/190. . . . Shoots right.
HIGH SCHOOL: Armstrong (Plymouth, Minn.).
COLLEGE: Minnesota.
TRANSACTIONS/CAREER NOTES: Selected by Montreal Canadiens in second round (third Canadiens pick, 33rd overall) of NHL entry draft (June 15, 1985). . . . Traded by Canadiens to Hartford Whalers for future considerations (October 1990). . . . Bruised knee (October 14, 1991); missed two games. . . . Signed as free agent by Las Vegas Thunder (July 14, 1993).
HONORS: Named to WCHA All-Star second team (1987-88 and 1988-89). . . . Named to NCAA All-America West second team (1988-89). . . . Named to NCAA All-Tournament team (1988-89). . . . Named to IHL All-Star second team (1993-94).

Season	Team	League	REGULAR SEASON					PLAYOFFS				
			Gms.	G	A	Pts.	PIM	Gms.	G	A	Pts.	PIM
84-85—Armstrong H.S.		Minn. H.S.	24	10	23	33	24	—	—	—	—	—
85-86—University of Minnesota		WCHA	38	6	23	29	38	—	—	—	—	—

R

Season	Team	League	REGULAR SEASON					PLAYOFFS				
			Gms.	G	A	Pts.	Pen.	Gms.	G	A	Pts.	Pen.
86-87—University of Minnesota ...		WCHA	49	8	43	51	70	—	—	—	—	—
87-88—University of Minnesota ...		WCHA	34	10	30	40	26	—	—	—	—	—
88-89—University of Minnesota ...		WCHA	46	6	32	38	60	—	—	—	—	—
89-90—Sherbrooke		AHL	71	6	18	24	73	5	1	2	3	6
90-91—Fredericton		AHL	3	0	1	1	2	—	—	—	—	—
—Springfield		AHL	71	10	41	51	62	14	2	8	10	2
—Hartford		NHL	2	0	4	4	2	6	0	0	0	2
91-92—Hartford		NHL	6	0	0	0	2	5	0	3	3	4
—Springfield		AHL	43	6	23	29	33	8	0	3	3	2
92-93—Springfield		AHL	78	13	42	55	53	9	1	5	6	2
93-94—Las Vegas		IHL	80	11	35	46	122	5	1	4	5	18
NHL totals			8	0	4	4	4	11	0	3	3	6

RICHARDS, TRAVIS
D, STARS

PERSONAL: Born March 22, 1970, in Crystal, Minn. . . . 6-2/195. . . . Shoots right.
COLLEGE: Minnesota.
TRANSACTIONS/CAREER NOTES: Selected by Minnesota North Stars in ninth round (ninth North Stars pick, 169th overall) of NHL entry draft (June 11, 1988). . . . North Stars franchise moved from Minnesota to Dallas and renamed Stars for 1993-94 season.

Season	Team	League	REGULAR SEASON					PLAYOFFS				
			Gms.	G	A	Pts.	PIM	Gms.	G	A	Pts.	PIM
89-90—Minnesota Univ.		WCHA	45	4	24	28	38	—	—	—	—	—
90-91—Minnesota Univ.		WCHA	45	9	25	34	28	—	—	—	—	—
91-92—Minnesota Univ.		WCHA	44	10	23	33	65	—	—	—	—	—
92-93—Minnesota Univ.		WCHA	42	12	26	38	54	—	—	—	—	—
93-94—U.S. national team		Int'l	51	1	11	12	12	—	—	—	—	—
—U.S. Olympic Team		Int'l	8	0	0	0	2	—	—	—	—	—
—Kalamazoo		IHL	19	2	10	12	20	4	1	1	2	0

RICHARDSON, LUKE
D, OILERS

PERSONAL: Born March 26, 1969, in Ottawa. . . . 6-4/210. . . . Shoots left. . . . Full name: Luke Glen Richardson.
TRANSACTIONS/CAREER NOTES: Selected by Toronto Maple Leafs as underage junior in first round (first Maple Leafs pick, seventh overall) of NHL entry draft (June 13, 1987). . . . Traded by Maple Leafs with LW Vincent Damphousse, G Peter Ing, C Scott Thornton and future considerations to Edmonton Oilers for G Grant Fuhr, LW Glenn Anderson and LW Craig Berube (September 19, 1991). . . . Strained clavicular joint (February 11, 1992); missed three games. . . . Suffered from the flu (March 1993); missed one game. . . . Fractured cheekbone (January 7, 1994); missed 15 games.

Season	Team	League	REGULAR SEASON					PLAYOFFS				
			Gms.	G	A	Pts.	PIM	Gms.	G	A	Pts.	PIM
84-85—Ottawa Jr. B		ODHA	35	5	26	31	72	—	—	—	—	—
85-86—Peterborough		OHL	63	6	18	24	57	16	2	1	3	50
86-87—Peterborough		OHL	59	13	32	45	70	12	0	5	5	24
87-88—Toronto		NHL	78	4	6	10	90	2	0	0	0	0
88-89—Toronto		NHL	55	2	7	9	106	—	—	—	—	—
89-90—Toronto		NHL	67	4	14	18	122	5	0	0	0	22
90-91—Toronto		NHL	78	1	9	10	238	—	—	—	—	—
91-92—Edmonton		NHL	75	2	19	21	118	16	0	5	5	45
92-93—Edmonton		NHL	82	3	10	13	142	—	—	—	—	—
93-94—Edmonton		NHL	69	2	6	8	131	—	—	—	—	—
NHL totals			504	18	71	89	947	23	0	5	5	67

RICHER, STEPHANE
D, PANTHERS

PERSONAL: Born April 28, 1966, in Hull, Que. . . . 5-11/190. . . . Shoots right. . . . Full name: Stephane J.G. Richer.
TRANSACTIONS/CAREER NOTES: Signed as free agent by Montreal Canadiens (January 9, 1988). . . . Signed as free agent by Los Angeles Kings (July 11, 1990). . . . Signed as free agent by Canadiens (September 1, 1991). . . . Signed as free agent by Tampa Bay Lightning (July 29, 1992). . . . Traded by Lightning to Boston Bruins for D Bob Beers (October 28, 1992). . . . Selected by Florida Panthers in NHL expansion draft (June 24, 1993). . . . Underwent right shoulder surgery (November 22, 1993); missed three games.
HONORS: Named to AHL All-Star second team (1991-92). . . . Named to IHL All-Star second team (1993-94).

Season	Team	League	REGULAR SEASON					PLAYOFFS				
			Gms.	G	A	Pts.	PIM	Gms.	G	A	Pts.	PIM
83-84—Hull		QMJHL	70	8	38	46	42	—	—	—	—	—
84-85—Hull		QMJHL	67	21	56	77	98	—	—	—	—	—
85-86—Hull		QMJHL	71	14	52	66	166	—	—	—	—	—
86-87—Hull		QMJHL	33	6	22	28	74	8	3	4	7	17
87-88—Baltimore		AHL	22	0	3	3	6	—	—	—	—	—
—Sherbrooke		AHL	41	4	7	11	46	5	1	0	1	10
88-89—Sherbrooke		AHL	70	7	26	33	158	6	1	2	3	18
89-90—Sherbrooke		AHL	60	10	12	22	85	12	4	9	13	16
90-91—Phoenix		IHL	67	11	38	49	48	11	4	6	10	6
—New Haven		AHL	3	0	1	1	0	—	—	—	—	—
91-92—Fredericton		AHL	80	17	47	64	74	7	0	5	5	18

Season	Team	League	REGULAR SEASON					PLAYOFFS				
			Gms.	G	A	Pts.	Pen.	Gms.	G	A	Pts.	Pen.
92-93—Tampa Bay	NHL	3	0	0	0	0	—	—	—	—	—
—Providence	AHL	53	8	29	37	60	—	—	—	—	—
—Boston	NHL	21	1	4	5	18	3	0	0	0	0
93-94—Cincinnati	IHL	66	9	55	64	80	11	2	9	11	26
—Florida	NHL	2	0	1	1	0	—	—	—	—	—
NHL totals			26	1	5	6	18	3	0	0	0	0

RICHER, STEPHANE
RW, DEVILS

R

PERSONAL: Born June 7, 1966, in Buckingham, Que.... 6-2/215.... Shoots right. ... Full name: Stephane Joseph Jean Richer.... Name pronounced REE-shay.
TRANSACTIONS/CAREER NOTES: Selected by Montreal Canadiens as underage junior in second round (third Canadiens pick, 29th overall) of NHL entry draft (June 9, 1984).... Traded by Granby Bisons with LW Greg Choules to Chicoutimi Sagueneens for C Stephane Roy, RW Marc Bureau, Lee Duhemee, Sylvain Demers and D Rene L'Ecuyer (January 1985).... Sprained ankle (November 18, 1985); missed 13 games.... Bruised right hand (March 12, 1988).... Broke right thumb (April 1988).... Sprained right thumb (September 1988).... Suspended 10 games by NHL for slashing (November 16, 1988).... Suffered from the flu (March 15, 1989).... Bruised right shoulder (September 1989).... Bruised left foot (February 1990).... Injured left ankle (April 21, 1990).... Injured knee (December 12, 1990).... Traded by Canadiens with RW Tom Chorske to New Jersey Devils for LW Kirk Muller and G Roland Melanson (September 20, 1991).... Injured groin (October 22, 1991); missed two games.... Injured left knee (March 24, 1992); missed three games.... Injured back (December 6, 1992); missed two games.
HONORS: Named QMJHL Rookie of the Year (1983-84).... Named to QMJHL All-Star second team (1984-85).... Played in NHL All-Star Game (1990).
MISCELLANEOUS: Member of Stanley Cup championship team (1986).

Season	Team	League	REGULAR SEASON					PLAYOFFS				
			Gms.	G	A	Pts.	PIM	Gms.	G	A	Pts.	PIM
83-84—Granby	QMJHL	67	39	37	76	58	3	1	1	2	4
84-85—Granby/Chicoutimi	QMJHL	57	61	59	120	71	12	13	13	26	25
—Montreal	NHL	1	0	0	0	0	—	—	—	—	—
—Sherbrooke	AHL	—	—	—	—	—	9	6	3	9	10
85-86—Montreal	NHL	65	21	16	37	50	16	4	1	5	23
86-87—Sherbrooke	AHL	12	10	4	14	11	—	—	—	—	—
—Montreal	NHL	57	20	19	39	80	5	3	2	5	0
87-88—Montreal	NHL	72	50	28	78	72	8	7	5	12	6
88-89—Montreal	NHL	68	25	35	60	61	21	6	5	11	14
89-90—Montreal	NHL	75	51	40	91	46	9	7	3	10	2
90-91—Montreal	NHL	75	31	30	61	53	13	9	5	14	6
91-92—New Jersey	NHL	74	29	35	64	25	7	1	2	3	0
92-93—New Jersey	NHL	78	38	35	73	44	5	2	2	4	2
93-94—New Jersey	NHL	80	36	36	72	16	20	7	5	12	6
NHL totals			645	301	274	575	447	104	46	30	76	59

RICHTER, BARRY
D, RANGERS

PERSONAL: Born September 11, 1970, in Madison, Wis.... 6-2/203.... Shoots left.... Full name: Barron Patrick Richter.... Son of Pat Richter, tight end, Washington Redskins (1963-1970).
HIGH SCHOOL: Culver Military Academy (Ind.).
COLLEGE: Wisconsin.
TRANSACTIONS/CAREER NOTES: Selected by Hartford Whalers in second round (second Whalers pick, 32nd overall) of NHL entry draft (June 11, 1988).... Traded by Whalers with RW Steve Larmer, LW Nick Kypreos and undisclosed draft pick to New York Rangers for D James Patrick and C Darren Turcotte (November 2, 1993).
HONORS: Named to NCAA All-Tournament team (1991-92).... Named to NCAA All-America West first team (1992-93).... Named to WCHA All-Star first team (1992-93).
MISCELLANEOUS: Member of Stanley Cup championship team (1994).

Season	Team	League	REGULAR SEASON					PLAYOFFS				
			Gms.	G	A	Pts.	PIM	Gms.	G	A	Pts.	PIM
86-87—Culver Military Academy	Indiana H.S.	35	19	26	45	...	—	—	—	—	—
87-88—Culver Military Academy	Indiana H.S.	35	24	29	53	18	—	—	—	—	—
88-89—Culver Military Academy	Indiana H.S.	19	21	29	50	16	—	—	—	—	—
89-90—University of Wisconsin	WCHA	42	13	23	36	26	—	—	—	—	—
90-91—University of Wisconsin	WCHA	43	15	20	35	42	—	—	—	—	—
91-92—University of Wisconsin	WCHA	43	10	29	39	62	—	—	—	—	—
92-93—University of Wisconsin	WCHA	42	14	32	46	74	—	—	—	—	—
93-94—U.S. national team	Int'l	56	7	16	23	50	—	—	—	—	—
—U.S. Olympic Team	Int'l	8	0	3	3	4	—	—	—	—	—
—Binghamton	AHL	21	0	9	9	12	—	—	—	—	—

RICHTER, MIKE
G, RANGERS

PERSONAL: Born September 22, 1966, in Philadelphia.... 5-11/182.... Catches left.... Full name: Michael Thomas Richter.... Name pronounced RIHK-tuhr.
HIGH SCHOOL: Northwood (Lake Placid, N.Y.).
COLLEGE: Wisconsin.
TRANSACTIONS/CAREER NOTES: Selected by New York Rangers in second round (second Rangers pick, 28th overall) of NHL entry draft (June 15, 1985).... Bruised thigh (January 30, 1992); missed 12 games.
HONORS: Won WCHA Rookie of the Year Award (1985-86).... Named to WCHA All-Star second team (1985-86 and 1986-87).

...Played in NHL All-Star Game (1992 and 1994).... Named All-Star Game Most Valuable Player (1994).
MISCELLANEOUS: Member of Stanley Cup championship team (1994).

Season	Team	League	Gms.	Min.	W	L	T	GA	SO	Avg.	Gms.	Min.	W	L	GA	SO	Avg.
84-85—Northwood School	N.Y. H.S.	24	1374	...	...	...	52	2	2.27	—	—	—	—	—	—	—
85-86—Univ. of Wisconsin	WCHA	24	1394	14	9	0	92	1	3.96	—	—	—	—	—	—	—
86-87—Univ. of Wisconsin	WCHA	36	2136	19	16	1	126	0	3.54	—	—	—	—	—	—	—
87-88—U.S. national team	Int'l	29	1559	17	7	2	86	0	3.31	—	—	—	—	—	—	—
—U.S. Olympic Team	Int'l	4	230	2	2	0	15	0	3.91	—	—	—	—	—	—	—
—Colorado	IHL	22	1298	16	5	‡0	68	1	3.14	10	536	5	3	35	0	3.92
88-89—Denver	IHL	*57	3031	23	26	‡0	*217	1	4.30	4	210	0	4	21	0	6.00
—New York Rangers	NHL	—	—	—	—	—	—	—	—	1	58	0	1	4	0	4.14
89-90—New York Rangers	NHL	23	1320	12	5	5	66	0	3.00	6	330	3	2	19	0	3.45
—Flint	IHL	13	782	7	4	‡2	49	0	3.76	—	—	—	—	—	—	—
90-91—New York Rangers	NHL	45	2596	21	13	7	135	0	3.12	6	313	2	4	14	†1	2.68
91-92—New York Rangers	NHL	41	2298	23	12	2	119	3	3.11	7	412	4	2	24	1	3.50
92-93—New York Rangers	NHL	38	2105	13	19	3	134	1	3.82	—	—	—	—	—	—	—
—Binghamton	AHL	5	305	4	0	1	6	0	1.18	—	—	—	—	—	—	—
93-94—New York Rangers	NHL	68	3710	*42	12	6	159	5	2.57	23	1417	*16	7	49	†4	2.07
NHL totals		215	12029	111	61	23	613	9	3.06	43	2530	25	16	110	6	2.61

RIDLEY, MIKE

C, MAPLE LEAFS

PERSONAL: Born July 8, 1963, in Winnipeg.... 6-0/195.... Shoots left.
COLLEGE: Manitoba.
TRANSACTIONS/CAREER NOTES: Signed as free agent by New York Rangers (September 1985).... Traded by Rangers with LW Kelly Miller and RW Bobby Crawford to Washington Capitals for C Bobby Carpenter and second-round pick (RW Jason Prosofsky) in 1989 draft (January 1987).... Suffered collapsed left lung (March 9, 1990); missed six games.... Bruised ribs (April 5, 1990).... Suffered from stomach flu (February 21, 1994); missed one game.... Traded by Capitals with first-round pick in 1994 draft (G Eric Fichaud) to Toronto Maple Leafs for RW Rob Pearson and first-round pick (D Nolan Baumgartner) in 1994 draft (June 28, 1994).
HONORS: Won Senator Joseph A. Sullivan Trophy (1983-84).... Named to CIAU All-Canadian team (1983-84 and 1984-85).... Named to NHL All-Rookie team (1985-86).... Played in NHL All-Star Game (1989).

Season	Team	League	Gms.	G	A	Pts.	PIM	Gms.	G	A	Pts.	PIM
83-84—University of Manitoba	CWUAA	46	39	41	80	...	—	—	—	—	—
84-85—University of Manitoba	CWUAA	30	29	38	67	48	—	—	—	—	—
85-86—New York Rangers	NHL	80	22	43	65	69	16	6	8	14	26
86-87—New York Rangers	NHL	38	16	20	36	20	—	—	—	—	—
—Washington	NHL	40	15	19	34	20	7	2	1	3	6
87-88—Washington	NHL	70	28	31	59	22	14	6	5	11	10
88-89—Washington	NHL	80	41	48	89	49	6	0	5	5	2
89-90—Washington	NHL	74	30	43	73	27	14	3	4	7	8
90-91—Washington	NHL	79	23	48	71	26	11	3	4	7	8
91-92—Washington	NHL	80	29	40	69	38	7	0	11	11	0
92-93—Washington	NHL	84	26	56	82	44	6	1	5	6	0
93-94—Washington	NHL	81	26	44	70	24	11	4	6	10	6
NHL totals		706	256	392	648	339	92	25	49	74	66

RIENDEAU, VINCE

G, BRUINS

PERSONAL: Born April 20, 1966, in St. Hyacinthe, Que.... 5-10/185.... Catches left.... Name pronounced ree-EHN-doh.
COLLEGE: Sherbrooke (Que.).
TRANSACTIONS/CAREER NOTES: Signed as free agent by Montreal Canadiens (October 9, 1985).... Suffered skin rash (November 1987).... Broke leg (April 10, 1988).... Traded by Canadiens with LW Sergio Momesso to St. Louis Blues for LW Jocelyn Lemieux, G Darrell May and second-round pick (D Patrice Brisebois) in 1989 draft (August 9, 1988).... Suffered compound fracture of left little finger (October 4, 1989); missed 10 games.... Pulled groin (February 17, 1991); missed seven games.... Traded by Blues to Detroit Red Wings for D Rick Zombo (October 18, 1991).... Sprained knee (October 25, 1991); missed 59 games.... Strained hip (January 2, 1993); missed six games.... Traded by Red Wings to Boston Bruins for conditional pick in 1995 draft (January 17, 1994).
HONORS: Named to QMJHL All-Star second team (1985-86).... Won Harry (Hap) Holmes Memorial Trophy (1986-87).... Shared Harry (Hap) Holmes Memorial Trophy with Jocelyn Perreault (1987-88).... Named to AHL All-Star second team (1987-88).

Season	Team	League	Gms.	Min.	W	L	T	GA	SO	Avg.	Gms.	Min.	W	L	GA	SO	Avg.
83-84—Verdun	QMJHL	41	2133	...	...	...	147	†2	4.14	—	—	—	—	—	—	—
84-85—Univ. of Sherbrooke	Can. Coll.					Statistics unavailable.										
85-86—Drummondville	QMJHL	57	3336	33	20	3	215	†2	3.87	*23	*1271	10	13	*106	1	5.00
86-87—Sherbrooke	AHL	41	2363	25	14	0	114	2	2.89	13	742	8	5	47	0	3.80
87-88—Sherbrooke	AHL	44	2521	27	13	3	112	*4	*2.67	2	127	0	2	7	0	3.31
—Montreal	NHL	1	36	0	0	0	5	0	8.33	—	—	—	—	—	—	—
88-89—St. Louis	NHL	32	1842	11	15	5	108	0	3.52	—	—	—	—	—	—	—
89-90—St. Louis	NHL	43	2551	17	19	5	149	1	3.50	8	397	3	4	24	0	3.63
90-91—St. Louis	NHL	44	2671	29	9	6	134	3	3.01	13	687	6	7	35	†1	3.06
91-92—St. Louis	NHL	3	157	1	2	0	11	0	4.20	—	—	—	—	—	—	—
—Detroit	NHL	2	87	2	0	0	2	0	1.38	2	73	1	0	4	0	3.29
—Adirondack	AHL	3	179	2	1	0	8	0	2.68	—	—	—	—	—	—	—

Season	Team	League	Gms.	Min.	W	L	T	GA	SO	Avg.	Gms.	Min.	W	L	GA	SO	Avg.
92-93	—Detroit	NHL	22	1193	13	4	2	64	0	3.22	—	—	—	—	—	—	—
93-94	—Detroit	NHL	8	345	2	4	0	23	0	4.00	—	—	—	—	—	—	—
	—Adirondack	AHL	10	583	6	3	0	30	0	3.09	—	—	—	—	—	—	—
	—Boston	NHL	18	976	7	6	1	50	1	3.07	2	120	1	1	8	0	4.00
NHL totals			173	9858	82	59	19	546	5	3.32	25	1277	11	12	71	1	3.34

RIIHIJARVI, JUHA
RW, OILERS

PERSONAL: Born December 15, 1969, in Salla, Finland. . . . 6-3/205. . . . Shoots right. . . . Name pronounced YOO-hah ree-hee-YAHR-vee.
TRANSACTIONS/CAREER NOTES: Selected by Edmonton Oilers in 12th round (11th Oilers pick, 254th overall) of NHL entry draft (June 22, 1991).

Season	Team	League	Gms.	G	A	Pts.	PIM	Gms.	G	A	Pts.	PIM
90-91	—Karpat Oulu	Finland Dv.II	42	29	41	70	34	—	—	—	—	—
91-92	—JyP HT	Finland	38	29	33	62	37	10	4	4	8	10
92-93	—JyP HT	Finland	41	25	31	56	38	9	4	2	6	2
93-94	—Cape Breton	AHL	57	10	15	25	37	—	—	—	—	—

RISIDORE, RYAN
D, WHALERS

PERSONAL: Born April 4, 1976, in Hamilton, Ont. . . . 6-4/192. . . . Shoots left.
HIGH SCHOOL: Bishop MacDonnell (Guelph, Ont.).
TRANSACTIONS/CAREER NOTES: Selected by Hartford Whalers in fifth round (third Whalers pick, 109th overall) of NHL entry draft (June 29, 1994).

Season	Team	League	Gms.	G	A	Pts.	PIM	Gms.	G	A	Pts.	PIM
92-93	—Hamilton Junior B	OHA	41	2	11	13	61	—	—	—	—	—
93-94	—Guelph	OHL	51	2	9	11	39	9	0	0	0	12

RIVERS, JAMIE
D, BLUES

PERSONAL: Born March 16, 1975, in Ottawa. . . . 6-0/180. . . . Shoots left. . . . Brother of Shawn Rivers, defenseman in Tampa Bay Lightning system.
HIGH SCHOOL: Lasalle Secondary (Sudbury, Ont.).
TRANSACTIONS/CAREER NOTES: Selected by St. Louis Blues in third round (second Blues pick, 63rd overall) of NHL entry draft (June 26, 1993).
HONORS: Won Max Kaminsky Award (1993-94). . . . Named to OHL All-Star first team (1993-94). . . . Named to Can.HL All-Star second team (1993-94).

Season	Team	League	Gms.	G	A	Pts.	PIM	Gms.	G	A	Pts.	PIM
90-91	—Ottawa	OHA Jr. A	55	4	30	34	74	—	—	—	—	—
91-92	—Sudbury	OHL	55	3	13	16	20	8	0	0	0	0
92-93	—Sudbury	OHL	62	12	43	55	20	14	7	19	26	4
93-94	—Sudbury	OHL	65	32	*89	121	58	10	1	9	10	14

RIVERS, SHAWN
D, LIGHTNING

PERSONAL: Born January 30, 1971, in Ottawa. . . . 5-10/185. . . . Shoots left. . . . Brother of Jamie Rivers, defenseman in St. Louis Blues system.
COLLEGE: St. Lawrence (N.Y.).
TRANSACTIONS/CAREER NOTES: Signed as free agent by Tampa Bay Lightning (August 13, 1992).

Season	Team	League	Gms.	G	A	Pts.	PIM	Gms.	G	A	Pts.	PIM
88-89	—St. Lawrence University	ECAC	36	3	23	26	20	—	—	—	—	—
89-90	—St. Lawrence University	ECAC	28	3	15	18	31	—	—	—	—	—
90-91	—Sudbury	OHL	66	18	33	51	43	5	2	7	9	0
91-92	—Sudbury	OHL	64	26	54	80	34	11	0	4	4	10
92-93	—Atlanta	IHL	78	9	34	43	101	9	1	3	4	8
	—Tampa Bay	NHL	4	0	2	2	2	—	—	—	—	—
93-94	—Atlanta	IHL	76	6	30	36	88	12	1	4	5	21
NHL totals			4	0	2	2	2					

RIVET, CRAIG
D, CANADIENS

PERSONAL: Born September 13, 1974, in North Bay, Ont. . . . 6-2/172. . . . Shoots right. . . . Name pronounced REE-vay.
TRANSACTIONS/CAREER NOTES: Selected by Montreal Canadiens in third round (fourth Canadiens pick, 68th overall) of NHL entry draft (June 20, 1992).

Season	Team	League	Gms.	G	A	Pts.	PIM	Gms.	G	A	Pts.	PIM
90-91	—Barrie Junior B	OHA	42	9	17	26	55	—	—	—	—	—
91-92	—Kingston	OHL	66	5	21	26	97	—	—	—	—	—
92-93	—Kingston	OHL	64	19	55	74	117	16	5	7	12	39
93-94	—Fredericton	AHL	4	0	2	2	2	—	—	—	—	—
	—Kingston	OHL	61	12	52	64	100	6	0	3	3	6

ROBERGE, MARIO
LW, CANADIENS

PERSONAL: Born January 31, 1964, in Quebec City.... 5-11/193.... Shoots left.... Name pronounced roh-BAIRZH.... Brother of Serge Roberge, right winger, Quebec Nordiques (1990-91).
TRANSACTIONS/CAREER NOTES: Signed as free agent by Sherbrooke Canadiens (January 1988).... Signed as free agent by Montreal Canadiens (October 5, 1988).... Injured thigh (December 22, 1991).... Suspended one off-day and fined $500 by NHL for fighting with taped hand (March 3, 1993).... Suffered hairline fracture of ankle (March 23, 1994); missed remainder of season.
MISCELLANEOUS: Member of Stanley Cup championship team (1993).

Season Team	League	REGULAR SEASON					PLAYOFFS				
		Gms.	G	A	Pts.	PIM	Gms.	G	A	Pts.	PIM
81-82—Quebec	QMJHL	8	0	3	3	2	—	—	—	—	—
82-83—Quebec	QMJHL	69	3	27	30	153	—	—	—	—	—
83-84—Quebec	QMJHL	60	12	28	40	253	—	—	—	—	—
84-85—						Did not play.					
85-86—						Did not play.					
86-87—						Did not play.					
87-88—Port Aux Basques	Nova Scotia	35	25	64	89	152	—	—	—	—	—
88-89—Sherbrooke	AHL	58	4	9	13	249	6	0	2	2	8
89-90—Sherbrooke	AHL	73	13	27	40	247	12	5	2	7	53
90-91—Fredericton	AHL	68	12	27	39	†365	2	0	2	2	5
—Montreal	NHL	5	0	0	0	21	12	0	0	0	24
91-92—Montreal	NHL	20	2	1	3	62	—	—	—	—	—
—Fredericton	AHL	6	1	2	3	20	7	0	2	2	20
92-93—Montreal	NHL	50	4	4	8	142	3	0	0	0	0
93-94—Montreal	NHL	28	1	2	3	55	—	—	—	—	—
NHL totals		103	7	7	14	280	15	0	0	0	24

ROBERTS, DAVID
LW, BLUES

PERSONAL: Born May 28, 1970, in Alameda, Calif.... 6-0/185.... Shoots left.... Full name: David Lance Roberts.... Son of Doug Roberts, defenseman for four NHL teams (1965-66 through 1974-75) and New England Whalers of WHA (1975-76 and 1976-77); and nephew of Gord Roberts, defenseman, Boston Bruins.
HIGH SCHOOL: Avon (Conn.) Old Farms School for Boys.
COLLEGE: Michigan.
TRANSACTIONS/CAREER NOTES: Selected by St. Louis Blues in sixth round (fifth Blues pick, 114th overall) of NHL entry draft (June 17, 1989).
HONORS: Named CCHA Rookie of the Year (1989-90).... Named to CCHA All-Rookie team (1989-90).... Named to NCAA All-America West second team (1990-91).... Named to CCHA All-Star second team (1990-91 and 1992-93).

Season Team	League	REGULAR SEASON					PLAYOFFS				
		Gms.	G	A	Pts.	PIM	Gms.	G	A	Pts.	PIM
87-88—Avon Old Farms H.S.	Conn. H.S.	...	18	39	57	...	—	—	—	—	—
88-89—Avon Old Farms H.S.	Conn. H.S.	...	28	48	76	...	—	—	—	—	—
89-90—University of Michigan	CCHA	42	21	32	53	46	—	—	—	—	—
90-91—University of Michigan	CCHA	43	26	45	71	44	—	—	—	—	—
91-92—University of Michigan	CCHA	44	16	42	58	68	—	—	—	—	—
92-93—University of Michigan	CCHA	40	27	38	65	40	—	—	—	—	—
93-94—U.S. national team	Int'l	49	17	28	45	68	—	—	—	—	—
—U.S. Olympic Team	Int'l	8	1	5	6	4	—	—	—	—	—
—Peoria	IHL	10	4	6	10	4	—	—	—	—	—
—St. Louis	NHL	1	0	0	0	2	3	0	0	0	12
NHL totals		1	0	0	0	2	3	0	0	0	12

ROBERTS, GARY
LW, FLAMES

PERSONAL: Born May 23, 1966, in North York, Ont.... 6-1/190.... Shoots left.
TRANSACTIONS/CAREER NOTES: Selected by Calgary Flames as underage junior in first round (first Flames pick, 12th overall) of NHL entry draft (June 9, 1984).... Injured back (January 1989).... Suffered whiplash (November 9, 1991); missed one game.... Suffered from the flu (January 19, 1993); missed one game.... Suffered left quadricep hematoma (February 16, 1993); missed 25 games.... Suspended one game by NHL for high-sticking (November 19, 1993).... Suspended four games and fined $500 by NHL for two slashing incidents and fined $500 for high-sticking (January 7, 1994).... Fractured thumb (March 20, 1994); missed one game.... Fractured thumb (April 3, 1994); missed last five games of season.
HONORS: Named to OHL All-Star second team (1984-85 and 1985-86).... Played in NHL All-Star Game (1992 and 1993).
MISCELLANEOUS: Member of Stanley Cup championship team (1989).

Season Team	League	REGULAR SEASON					PLAYOFFS				
		Gms.	G	A	Pts.	PIM	Gms.	G	A	Pts.	PIM
82-83—Ottawa	OHL	53	12	8	20	83	5	1	0	1	19
83-84—Ottawa	OHL	48	27	30	57	144	13	10	7	17	*62
84-85—Ottawa	OHL	59	44	62	106	186	5	2	8	10	10
—Moncton	AHL	7	4	2	6	7	—	—	—	—	—
85-86—Ottawa	OHL	24	26	25	51	83	—	—	—	—	—
—Guelph	OHL	23	18	15	33	65	20	18	13	31	43
86-87—Moncton	AHL	38	20	18	38	72	—	—	—	—	—
—Calgary	NHL	32	5	10	15	85	2	0	0	0	4
87-88—Calgary	NHL	74	13	15	28	282	9	2	3	5	29
88-89—Calgary	NHL	71	22	16	38	250	22	5	7	12	57

Season Team	League	REGULAR SEASON					PLAYOFFS				
		Gms.	G	A	Pts.	Pen.	Gms.	G	A	Pts.	Pen.
89-90—Calgary	NHL	78	39	33	72	222	6	2	5	7	41
90-91—Calgary	NHL	80	22	31	53	252	7	1	3	4	18
91-92—Calgary	NHL	76	53	37	90	207	—	—	—	—	—
92-93—Calgary	NHL	58	38	41	79	172	5	1	6	7	43
93-94—Calgary	NHL	73	41	43	84	145	7	2	6	8	24
NHL totals		542	233	226	459	1615	58	13	30	43	216

ROBERTS, GORD
D, BRUINS

PERSONAL: Born October 2, 1957, in Detroit.... 6-1/195.... Shoots left.... Brother of Doug Roberts, defenseman for four NHL teams (1965-66 through 1974-75) and New England Whalers of WHA (1975-76 through 1976-77); and uncle of David Roberts, left winger, St. Louis Blues.

TRANSACTIONS/CAREER NOTES: Signed by New England Whalers (September 1975).... Selected by Montreal Canadiens from Whalers in third round (seventh Canadiens pick, 54th overall) of NHL amateur draft (June 14, 1977).... Selected by Hartford Whalers from Canadiens in NHL expansion draft (June 22, 1979).... Traded by Whalers to Minnesota North Stars for LW Mike Fidler (December 16, 1980).... Bruised hip (April 1984).... Injured foot (November 13, 1985); missed four games.... Dislocated shoulder (October 1986).... Bruised shoulder (January 1988).... Traded by North Stars to Philadelphia Flyers for fourth-round pick (C Jean-Francois Quintin) in 1989 draft (February 8, 1988).... Traded by Flyers to St. Louis Blues for fourth-round pick (LW Reid Simpson) in 1989 draft (March 8, 1988).... Traded by Blues to Pittsburgh Penguins for future considerations; Blues received 11th-round pick in 1992 draft (G Wade Salzman) to complete deal (October 27, 1990).... Signed as free agent by Boston Bruins (June 19, 1992).... Suffered from the flu (December 1992); missed two games.... Injured shoulder (December 1992); missed 11 games.... Injured arm (January 1993); missed three games.... Injured hip (March 1993); missed one game.... Suffered from sore ribs (October 11, 1993); missed seven games.

MISCELLANEOUS: Member of Stanley Cup championship teams (1991 and 1992).

Season Team	League	REGULAR SEASON					PLAYOFFS				
		Gms.	G	A	Pts.	PIM	Gms.	G	A	Pts.	PIM
73-74—Detroit Junior Red Wings	SOJHL	70	25	55	80	340	—	—	—	—	—
74-75—Victoria	WCHL	53	19	45	64	145	12	1	9	10	42
75-76—New England	WHA	77	3	19	22	102	17	2	9	11	36
76-77—New England	WHA	77	13	33	46	169	5	2	2	4	6
77-78—New England	WHA	78	15	46	61	118	14	0	5	5	29
78-79—New England	WHA	79	11	46	57	113	10	0	4	4	10
79-80—Hartford	NHL	80	8	28	36	89	3	1	1	2	2
80-81—Hartford	NHL	27	2	11	13	81	—	—	—	—	—
—Minnesota	NHL	50	6	31	37	94	19	1	5	6	17
81-82—Minnesota	NHL	79	4	30	34	119	4	0	3	3	27
82-83—Minnesota	NHL	80	3	41	44	103	9	1	5	6	14
83-84—Minnesota	NHL	77	8	45	53	132	15	3	7	10	23
84-85—Minnesota	NHL	78	6	36	42	112	9	1	6	7	6
85-86—Minnesota	NHL	76	2	21	23	101	5	0	4	4	8
86-87—Minnesota	NHL	67	3	10	13	68	—	—	—	—	—
87-88—Minnesota	NHL	48	1	10	11	103	—	—	—	—	—
—Philadelphia	NHL	11	1	2	3	15	—	—	—	—	—
—St. Louis	NHL	11	1	3	4	25	10	1	2	3	33
88-89—St. Louis	NHL	77	2	24	26	90	10	1	7	8	8
89-90—St. Louis	NHL	75	3	14	17	140	10	0	2	2	26
90-91—Peoria	IHL	6	0	8	8	4	—	—	—	—	—
—St. Louis	NHL	3	0	1	1	8	—	—	—	—	—
—Pittsburgh	NHL	61	3	12	15	70	24	1	2	3	63
91-92—Pittsburgh	NHL	73	2	22	24	87	19	0	2	2	32
92-93—Boston	NHL	65	5	12	17	105	4	0	0	0	6
93-94—Boston	NHL	59	1	6	7	40	12	0	1	1	8
WHA totals		311	42	144	186	502	46	4	20	24	81
NHL totals		1097	61	359	420	1582	153	10	47	57	273

ROBITAILLE, LUC
LW, PENGUINS

PERSONAL: Born February 17, 1966, in Montreal.... 6-1/190.... Shoots left.... Name pronounced ROH-bih-tigh.

TRANSACTIONS/CAREER NOTES: Selected by Los Angeles Kings as underage junior in ninth round (ninth Kings pick, 171st overall) of NHL entry draft (June 9, 1984).... Suspended four games by NHL games for cross-checking from behind (November 10, 1990).... Underwent surgery to repair slight fracture of right ankle (June 15, 1994).... Traded by Kings to Pittsburgh Penguins for RW Rick Tocchet and second-round pick in 1995 draft (July 29, 1994).

HONORS: Named to QMJHL All-Star second team (1984-85).... Won Can.HL Player of the Year Award (1985-86).... Shared Guy Lafleur Trophy with Sylvain Cote (1985-86).... Named to QMJHL All-Star first team (1985-86).... Named to Memorial Cup All-Star team (1985-86).... Won Calder Memorial Trophy (1986-87).... Named to THE SPORTING NEWS All-Star second team (1986-87 and 1991-92).... Named to NHL All-Star second team (1986-87 and 1991-92).... Named to NHL All-Rookie team (1986-87).... Named to THE SPORTING NEWS All-Star first team (1987-88 through 1990-91 and 1992-93).... Played in NHL All-Star Game (1988-1993).... Named to NHL All-Star first team (1987-88 through 1990-91 and 1992-93).

RECORDS: Holds NHL single-season records for most points by a left-winger—125 (1992-93); and most goals by a left-winger—63 (1992-93).

Season Team	League	REGULAR SEASON					PLAYOFFS				
		Gms.	G	A	Pts.	PIM	Gms.	G	A	Pts.	PIM
83-84—Hull	QMJHL	70	32	53	85	48	—	—	—	—	—
84-85—Hull	QMJHL	64	55	94	149	115	5	4	2	6	27

Season Team	League	REGULAR SEASON					PLAYOFFS				
		Gms.	G	A	Pts.	Pen.	Gms.	G	A	Pts.	Pen.
85-86—Hull	QMJHL	63	68	*123	†191	93	15	17	27	*44	28
86-87—Los Angeles	NHL	79	45	39	84	28	5	1	4	5	2
87-88—Los Angeles	NHL	80	53	58	111	82	5	2	5	7	18
88-89—Los Angeles	NHL	78	46	52	98	65	11	2	6	8	10
89-90—Los Angeles	NHL	80	52	49	101	38	10	5	5	10	10
90-91—Los Angeles	NHL	76	45	46	91	68	12	12	4	16	22
91-92—Los Angeles	NHL	80	44	63	107	95	6	3	4	7	12
92-93—Los Angeles	NHL	84	63	62	125	100	24	9	13	22	28
93-94—Los Angeles	NHL	83	44	42	86	86	—	—	—	—	—
NHL totals		640	392	411	803	562	73	34	41	75	102

R

ROCHE, DAVE
LW, PENGUINS

PERSONAL: Born June 13, 1975, in Lindsay, Ont. . . . 6-4/224. . . . Shoots left. . . . Name pronounced ROHCH.

TRANSACTIONS/CAREER NOTES: Selected by Pittsburgh Penguins in third round (third Penguins pick, 62nd overall) of NHL entry draft (June 26, 1993).

HONORS: Shared Dave Pinkney Trophy with Sandy Allan (1993-94). . . . Won F.W. (Dinty) Moore Trophy (1993-94).

Season Team	League	REGULAR SEASON					PLAYOFFS				
		Gms.	G	A	Pts.	PIM	Gms.	G	A	Pts.	PIM
90-91—Peterborough Jr. B	OHA	40	22	17	39	85	—	—	—	—	—
91-92—Peterborough	OHL	62	10	17	27	105	10	0	0	0	34
92-93—Peterborough	OHL	56	40	60	100	105	21	14	15	29	42
93-94—Peterborough	OHL	34	15	22	37	127	—	—	—	—	—
—Windsor	OHL	29	14	20	37	127	4	1	1	2	15

ROCHEFORT, NORMAND
D

PERSONAL: Born January 28, 1961, in Trois-Rivieres, Que. . . . 6-1/212. . . . Shoots left. . . . Name pronounced ROHSH-fohr. . . . Nephew of Leon Rochefort, right winger, seven NHL teams (1960-61 through 1975-76).

TRANSACTIONS/CAREER NOTES: Selected by Quebec Nordiques as underage junior in second round (first Nordiques pick, 24th overall) of NHL entry draft (June 11, 1980). . . . Injured neck (November 1980). . . . Injured knee; missed parts of 1982-83 season. . . . Sprained ankle (October 19, 1985). . . . Separated shoulder (February 8, 1986). . . . Injured neck and upper back (October 1987). . . . Bruised left foot (January 1988). . . . Sprained right knee (February 1988). . . . Traded by Nordiques with C Jason Lafreniere to New York Rangers for C Walt Poddubny, D Bruce Bell, D Jari Gronstrand and fourth-round pick in 1989 draft (August 1, 1988). . . . Sprained right knee (October 1988). . . . Reinjured knee and underwent surgery (November 9, 1988). . . . Reinjured knee and underwent reconstructive surgery (February 5, 1989). . . . Injured left knee cartilage and underwent surgery (October 6, 1990); missed 18 games. . . . Suffered compressed fracture of second lumbar vertebrae (March 13, 1991). . . . Developed tendinitis in right knee (October 1991); missed 14 games. . . . Suffered infection to right elbow (February 25, 1992); missed four games. . . . Signed as free agent by Tampa Bay Lightning (September 1, 1993).

HONORS: Named to Memorial Cup All-Star team (1978-79). . . . Named to QMJHL All-Star second team (1979-80).

Season Team	League	REGULAR SEASON					PLAYOFFS				
		Gms.	G	A	Pts.	PIM	Gms.	G	A	Pts.	PIM
77-78—Trois-Rivieres	QMJHL	72	9	37	46	36	—	—	—	—	—
78-79—Trois-Rivieres	QMJHL	72	17	57	74	80	13	3	11	14	17
79-80—Trois-Rivieres	QMJHL	20	5	25	30	22	—	—	—	—	—
—Quebec	QMJHL	52	8	39	47	68	5	1	3	4	8
80-81—Quebec	QMJHL	9	2	6	8	14	—	—	—	—	—
—Quebec	NHL	56	3	7	10	51	5	0	0	0	4
81-82—Quebec	NHL	72	4	14	18	115	16	0	2	2	10
82-83—Quebec	NHL	62	6	17	23	40	1	0	0	0	2
83-84—Quebec	NHL	75	2	22	24	47	6	1	0	1	6
84-85—Quebec	NHL	73	3	21	24	74	18	2	1	3	8
85-86—Quebec	NHL	26	5	4	9	30	—	—	—	—	—
86-87—Quebec	NHL	70	6	9	15	46	13	2	1	3	26
87-88—Quebec	NHL	46	3	10	13	49	—	—	—	—	—
88-89—New York Rangers	NHL	11	1	5	6	18	—	—	—	—	—
89-90—Flint	IHL	7	3	2	5	4	—	—	—	—	—
—New York Rangers	NHL	31	3	1	4	24	10	2	1	3	26
90-91—New York Rangers	NHL	44	3	7	10	35	—	—	—	—	—
91-92—New York Rangers	NHL	26	0	2	2	31	—	—	—	—	—
92-93—Eisbaren Berlin	Germany	17	4	2	6	21	—	—	—	—	—
93-94—Tampa Bay	NHL	6	0	0	0	10	—	—	—	—	—
—Atlanta	IHL	65	5	7	12	43	13	0	2	2	6
NHL totals		598	39	119	158	570	69	7	5	12	82

ROENICK, JEREMY
C, BLACKHAWKS

PERSONAL: Born January 17, 1970, in Boston. . . . 6-0/170. . . . Shoots right. . . . Name pronounced ROH-nihk. . . . Brother of Trevor Roenick, right winger in Hartford Whalers system.

HIGH SCHOOL: Thayer Academy (Braintree, Mass.).

TRANSACTIONS/CAREER NOTES: Selected by Chicago Blackhawks in first round (first Blackhawks pick, eighth overall) of NHL entry draft (June 11, 1988). . . . Sprained knee ligaments (January 9, 1989); missed one month.

HONORS: Named to QMJHL All-Star second team (1988-89). . . . Named NHL Rookie of the Year by THE SPORTING NEWS (1989-90). . . . Played in NHL All-Star Game (1991-1994).

Season Team	League	REGULAR SEASON					PLAYOFFS				
		Gms.	G	A	Pts.	PIM	Gms.	G	A	Pts.	PIM
86-87—Thayer Academy	Mass. H.S.	24	31	34	65	...	—	—	—	—	—
87-88—Thayer Academy	Mass. H.S.	...	34	50	84	...	—	—	—	—	—
88-89—Chicago	NHL	20	9	9	18	4	10	1	3	4	7
—Hull	QMJHL	28	34	36	70	14	—	—	—	—	—
89-90—Chicago	NHL	78	26	40	66	54	20	11	7	18	8
90-91—Chicago	NHL	79	41	53	94	80	6	3	5	8	4
91-92—Chicago	NHL	80	53	50	103	98	18	12	10	22	12
92-93—Chicago	NHL	84	50	57	107	86	4	1	2	3	2
93-94—Chicago	NHL	84	46	61	107	125	6	1	6	7	2
NHL totals		425	225	270	495	447	64	29	33	62	35

ROENICK, TREVOR
RW, WHALERS

PERSONAL: Born October 7, 1974, in Derby, Conn. ... 6-1/200. ... Shoots right. ... Brother of Jeremy Roenick, center, Chicago Blackhawks.
HIGH SCHOOL: Thayer Academy (Braintree, Mass.).
COLLEGE: Maine.
TRANSACTIONS/CAREER NOTES: Selected by Hartford Whalers in fourth round (third Whalers pick, 84th overall) of NHL entry draft (June 26, 1993).

Season Team	League	REGULAR SEASON					PLAYOFFS				
		Gms.	G	A	Pts.	PIM	Gms.	G	A	Pts.	PIM
90-91—Thayer Academy	Mass. H.S.	17	10	7	17	0	—	—	—	—	—
91-92—Thayer Academy	Mass. H.S.	26	16	16	32	8	—	—	—	—	—
92-93—Boston	NEJHL	58	61	48	109	94	—	—	—	—	—
93-94—University of Maine	Hockey East	32	4	3	7	18	—	—	—	—	—

ROGLES, CHRIS
G, BLACKHAWKS

PERSONAL: Born January 22, 1969, in St. Louis. ... 5-11/175. ... Catches left.
COLLEGE: Clarkson (N.Y.).
TRANSACTIONS/CAREER NOTES: Signed as free agent by Chicago Blackhawks (June 21, 1993).
HONORS: Won Ken McKenzie Trophy (1993-94).

Season Team	League	REGULAR SEASON								PLAYOFFS						
		Gms.	Min.	W	L	T	GA	SO	Avg.	Gms.	Min.	W	L	GA	SO	Avg.
89-90—Clarkson	ECAC	7	142	1	0	0	7	0	2.96	—	—	—	—	—	—	—
90-91—Clarkson	ECAC	28	1359	16	6	0	76	3	3.36	—	—	—	—	—	—	—
91-92—Clarkson	ECAC	19	998	11	3	0	51	0	3.07	—	—	—	—	—	—	—
92-93—Clarkson	ECAC	27	1482	16	4	4	60	3	2.43	—	—	—	—	—	—	—
93-94—Indianapolis	IHL	44	2421	14	20	†6	147	†2	3.64	—	—	—	—	—	—	—

ROHLOFF, JON
D, BRUINS

PERSONAL: Born October 3, 1969, in Mankato, Minn. ... 6-0/200. ... Shoots right. ... Full name: Jon Richard Rohloff.
HIGH SCHOOL: Grand Rapids (Minn.).
COLLEGE: Minnesota-Duluth.
TRANSACTIONS/CAREER NOTES: Selected by Boston Bruins in ninth round (seventh Bruins pick, 186th overall) of NHL entry draft (June 11, 1988).
HONORS: Named to WCHA All-Star second team (1992-93).

Season Team	League	REGULAR SEASON					PLAYOFFS				
		Gms.	G	A	Pts.	PIM	Gms.	G	A	Pts.	PIM
86-87—Grand Rapids H.S.	Minn. H.S.	21	12	23	35	16	—	—	—	—	—
87-88—Grand Rapids H.S.	Minn. H.S.	23	10	13	23	...	—	—	—	—	—
88-89—Minnesota-Duluth	WCHA	39	1	2	3	44	—	—	—	—	—
89-90—Minnesota-Duluth	WCHA	5	0	1	1	6	2	0	0	0	2
90-91—Minnesota-Duluth	WCHA	32	6	11	17	38	—	—	—	—	—
91-92—Minnesota-Duluth	WCHA	27	9	9	18	48	—	—	—	—	—
92-93—Minnesota-Duluth	WCHA	36	15	19	34	87	—	—	—	—	—
93-94—Providence	AHL	55	12	23	35	59	—	—	—	—	—

ROLSTON, BRIAN
C, DEVILS

PERSONAL: Born February 21, 1973, in Flint, Mich. ... 6-2/185. ... Shoots left.
COLLEGE: Lake Superior State (Mich.).
TRANSACTIONS/CAREER NOTES: Selected by New Jersey Devils in first round (second Devils pick, 11th overall) of NHL entry draft (June 22, 1991). ... Assigned by Devils to U.S. Olympic Team (November 2, 1993).
HONORS: Named to NCAA All-Tournament team (1991-92 and 1992-93). ... Named to NCAA All-America West second team (1992-93). ... Named to CCHA All-Star first team (1992-93).

Season Team	League	REGULAR SEASON					PLAYOFFS				
		Gms.	G	A	Pts.	PIM	Gms.	G	A	Pts.	PIM
89-90—Detroit Compuware	NAJHL	40	36	37	73	57	—	—	—	—	—
90-91—Detroit Compuware	NAJHL	36	49	46	95	14	—	—	—	—	—
91-92—Lake Superior State	CCHA	41	18	28	46	16	—	—	—	—	—
92-93—Lake Superior State	CCHA	39	33	31	64	20	—	—	—	—	—
93-94—U.S. national team	Int'l	41	20	28	48	36	—	—	—	—	—
—U.S. Olympic Team	Int'l	8	7	0	7	8	—	—	—	—	—
—Albany	AHL	17	5	5	10	8	5	1	2	3	0

R

ROMANIUK, RUSS

LW, JETS

PERSONAL: Born May 9, 1970, in Winnipeg.... 6-0/185.... Shoots left.... Full name: Russell James Romaniuk.... Name pronounced ROH-muh-NUHK.
COLLEGE: North Dakota.
TRANSACTIONS/CAREER NOTES: Suffered chip fracture of left knee (December 1987)....
Sprained right shoulder (February 1988).... Selected by Winnipeg Jets in second round (second Jets pick, 31st overall) of NHL entry draft (June 11, 1988).... Fractured knuckle (October 27, 1991); missed six games.... Sprained wrist (December 10, 1991); missed one game.... Sprained knee (November 17, 1992); missed one game.... Sprained ankle (December 17, 1992); missed 10 games.
HONORS: Named to WCHA All-Tournament team (1989-90).... Named to WCHA All-Star first team (1990-91).

Season	Team	League	REGULAR SEASON					PLAYOFFS				
			Gms.	G	A	Pts.	PIM	Gms.	G	A	Pts.	PIM
87-88	St. Boniface	MJHL				Statistics unavailable.						
88-89	Univ. of North Dakota	WCHA	39	17	14	31	32	—	—	—	—	—
89-90	Canadian national team	Int'l	3	1	0	1	0	—	—	—	—	—
	Univ. of North Dakota	WCHA	45	36	15	51	54	—	—	—	—	—
90-91	Univ. of North Dakota	WCHA	39	40	28	68	30	—	—	—	—	—
91-92	Winnipeg	NHL	27	3	5	8	18	—	—	—	—	—
	Moncton	AHL	45	16	15	31	25	10	5	4	9	19
92-93	Winnipeg	NHL	28	3	1	4	22	1	0	0	0	0
	Fort Wayne	IHL	4	2	0	2	7	—	—	—	—	—
	Moncton	AHL	28	18	8	26	40	5	0	4	4	2
93-94	Canadian national team	Int'l	34	8	9	17	17	—	—	—	—	—
	Moncton	AHL	18	16	8	24	24	17	2	6	8	30
	Winnipeg	NHL	24	4	8	12	6	—	—	—	—	—
NHL totals			79	10	14	24	46	1	0	0	0	0

ROMANO, ROBERTO

G, PENGUINS

PERSONAL: Born October 29, 1962, in Montreal.... 5-5/172.... Catches left.
TRANSACTIONS/CAREER NOTES: Traded by Quebec Remparts to Hull Olympics for Dan Sanscartier, Alan Bremner and future considerations (September 1981).... Signed as free agent by Pittsburgh Penguins (September 1983).... Traded by Penguins to Boston Bruins for G Pat Riggin (February 1987).... Left Maine Mariners to play hockey in Italy (December 1987).... Signed as free agent by Pittsburgh Penguins (October 7, 1993).
HONORS: Named to QMJHL All-Star first team (1981-82).

Season	Team	League	REGULAR SEASON							PLAYOFFS						
			Gms.	Min.	W	L	T	GA	SO	Avg.	Gms.	Min.	W	L	GA	SO	Avg.
79-80	Quebec	QMJHL	52	2411	21	17	3	183	0	4.55	3	150	1	1	12	0	4.80
80-81	Quebec	QMJHL	59	3174	24	26	2	233	0	4.40	4	164	1	2	18	0	6.59
81-82	Hull	QMJHL	56	3090	...	...	...	194	1	3.77	13	760	...	...	50	0	3.95
	Quebec	QMJHL	1	60	...	...	...	4	0	4.00	—	—	—	—	—	—	—
82-83	Pittsburgh	NHL	3	155	0	3	0	18	0	6.97	—	—	—	—	—	—	—
	Baltimore	AHL	38	2164	...	...	...	146	0	4.05	9	544	5	3	36	0	3.97
83-84	Pittsburgh	NHL	18	1020	6	11	0	78	1	4.59	—	—	—	—	—	—	—
	Baltimore	AHL	31	1759	23	6	1	106	0	3.62	—	—	—	—	—	—	—
84-85	Pittsburgh	NHL	31	1629	9	17	2	120	1	4.42	—	—	—	—	—	—	—
	Baltimore	AHL	12	719	2	8	2	44	0	3.67	—	—	—	—	—	—	—
85-86	Pittsburgh	NHL	46	2684	21	20	3	159	2	3.55	—	—	—	—	—	—	—
86-87	Moncton	AHL	1	65	0	0	0	3	0	2.77	—	—	—	—	—	—	—
	Boston	NHL	1	60	0	1	0	6	0	6.00	—	—	—	—	—	—	—
	Pittsburgh	NHL	25	1438	9	11	2	87	0	3.63	—	—	—	—	—	—	—
	Baltimore	AHL	5	274	0	3	0	18	0	3.94	—	—	—	—	—	—	—
87-88	Maine	AHL	16	875	5	8	1	52	0	3.57	—	—	—	—	—	—	—
93-94	Cleveland	IHL	11	642	2	7	‡2	45	1	4.21	—	—	—	—	—	—	—
	Pittsburgh	NHL	2	125	1	0	1	3	0	1.44	—	—	—	—	—	—	—
NHL totals			126	7111	1	0	1	471	4	3.97							

RONAN, ED

RW, CANADIENS

PERSONAL: Born March 21, 1968, in Quincy, Mass.... 6-0/197.... Shoots right.
COLLEGE: Boston University.
TRANSACTIONS/CAREER NOTES: Selected by Montreal Canadiens in 11th round (13th Canadiens pick, 227th overall) of NHL entry draft (June 13, 1987).... Suffered concussion (October 6, 1993); missed four games.... Suffered from the flu (March 6, 1994); missed one game.
MISCELLANEOUS: Member of Stanley Cup championship team (1993).

Season	Team	League	REGULAR SEASON					PLAYOFFS				
			Gms.	G	A	Pts.	PIM	Gms.	G	A	Pts.	PIM
87-88	Boston University	Hockey East	31	2	5	7	20	—	—	—	—	—
88-89	Boston University	Hockey East	36	4	11	15	34	—	—	—	—	—
89-90	Boston University	Hockey East	44	17	23	40	50	—	—	—	—	—
90-91	Boston University	Hockey East	41	16	19	35	38	—	—	—	—	—
91-92	Fredericton	AHL	78	25	34	59	82	7	5	1	6	6
	Montreal	NHL	3	0	0	0	0	—	—	—	—	—
92-93	Montreal	NHL	53	5	7	12	20	14	2	3	5	10
	Fredericton	AHL	16	10	5	15	15	5	2	4	6	6
93-94	Montreal	NHL	61	6	8	14	42	7	1	0	1	0
NHL totals			117	11	15	26	62	21	3	3	6	10

RONNING, CLIFF
C, CANUCKS

PERSONAL: Born October 1, 1965, in Vancouver.... 5-8/170.... Shoots left.
HIGH SCHOOL: Burnaby North (B.C.).
TRANSACTIONS/CAREER NOTES: Selected by St. Louis Blues as underage junior in seventh round (ninth Blues pick, 134th overall) of NHL entry draft (June 9, 1984).... Injured groin (November 1988).... Agreed to play in Italy for 1989-90 season (August 1989).... Fractured right index finger (November 12, 1990); missed 12 games.... Traded by Blues with LW Geoff Courtnall, D Robert Dirk, LW Sergio Momesso and fifth-round pick in 1992 draft (RW Brian Loney) to Vancouver Canucks for C Dan Quinn and D Garth Butcher (March 5, 1991).... Sprained hand (January 4, 1993); missed five games.... Separated shoulder (January 8, 1994); missed eight games.
HONORS: Won Stewart (Butch) Paul Memorial Trophy (1983-84).... Named to WHL All-Star second team (1983-84).... Won Most Valuable Player Trophy (1984-85).... Won Bob Brownridge Memorial Trophy (1984-85).... Won Frank Boucher Memorial Trophy (1984-85).... Named to WHL (West) All-Star first team (1984-85).

			REGULAR SEASON					PLAYOFFS			
Season Team	League	Gms.	G	A	Pts.	PIM	Gms.	G	A	Pts.	PIM
82-83—New Westminster	BCJHL	52	82	68	150	42	—	—	—	—	—
83-84—New Westminster	WHL	71	69	67	136	10	9	8	13	21	10
84-85—New Westminster	WHL	70	*89	108	*197	20	11	10	14	24	4
85-86—Canadian national team	Int'l	71	55	63	118	53	—	—	—	—	—
—St. Louis	NHL	—	—	—	—	—	5	1	1	2	2
86-87—Canadian national team	Int'l	26	16	16	32	12	—	—	—	—	—
—St. Louis	NHL	42	11	14	25	6	4	0	1	1	0
87-88—St. Louis	NHL	26	5	8	13	12	—	—	—	—	—
88-89—St. Louis	NHL	64	24	31	55	18	7	1	3	4	0
—Peoria	IHL	12	11	20	31	8	—	—	—	—	—
89-90—Asiago	Italy	42	76	60	136	30	6	7	12	19	4
90-91—St. Louis	NHL	48	14	18	32	10	—	—	—	—	—
—Vancouver	NHL	11	6	6	12	0	6	6	3	9	12
91-92—Vancouver	NHL	80	24	47	71	42	13	8	5	13	6
92-93—Vancouver	NHL	79	29	56	85	30	12	2	9	11	6
93-94—Vancouver	NHL	76	25	43	68	42	24	5	10	15	16
NHL totals		426	138	223	361	160	71	23	32	55	42

RONNQVIST, PETTER
G, SENATORS

PERSONAL: Born February 7, 1973, in Stockholm, Sweden.... 5-10/154.... Catches left.
TRANSACTIONS/CAREER NOTES: Selected by Ottawa Senators (12th Senators pick, 264th overall) in NHL entry draft (June 20, 1992).

			REGULAR SEASON						PLAYOFFS					
Season Team	League	Gms.	Min.	W	L	T	GA	SO	Avg.	Gms.	Min.	W	L	GA SO Avg.
91-92—Nacka	Sweden					Statistics Unavailable.								
92-93—Djurgarden	Sweden	7	380	...	...	...	20	0	3.16	1	60	...	...	5 0 5.00
93-94—Djurgarden	Sweden	12	680	...	...	...	39	0	3.21	—	—	—	—	— — —

ROUSE, BOB
D, MAPLE LEAFS

PERSONAL: Born June 18, 1964, in Surrey, B.C.... 6-2/210.... Shoots right.... Name pronounced ROWZ.
TRANSACTIONS/CAREER NOTES: Selected by Minnesota North Stars as underage junior in fourth round (third North Stars pick, 80th overall) of NHL entry draft (June 9, 1982).... Suffered hip contusions (January 1988).... Traded by North Stars with RW Dino Ciccarelli to Washington Capitals for RW Mike Gartner and D Larry Murphy (March 7, 1989).... Sprained right knee (December 12, 1989); missed eight games.... Traded by Capitals with C Peter Zezel to Toronto Maple Leafs for D Al Iafrate (January 16, 1991).... Broke collarbone (February 16, 1991).... Suspended four games by NHL for stick-swinging incident (October 14, 1993).... Strained knee (December 29, 1993); missed three games.... Tore knee cartilage (January 29, 1994); missed 14 games.
HONORS: Won Top Defenseman Trophy (1983-84).... Named to WHL (East) All-Star first team (1983-84).

			REGULAR SEASON					PLAYOFFS			
Season Team	League	Gms.	G	A	Pts.	PIM	Gms.	G	A	Pts.	PIM
80-81—Billings	WHL	70	0	13	13	116	5	0	0	0	2
81-82—Billings	WHL	71	7	22	29	209	5	0	2	2	10
82-83—Nanaimo	WHL	29	7	20	27	86	—	—	—	—	—
—Lethbridge	WHL	42	8	30	38	82	20	2	13	15	55
83-84—Lethbridge	WHL	71	18	42	60	101	5	0	1	1	28
—Minnesota	NHL	1	0	0	0	0	—	—	—	—	—
84-85—Springfield	AHL	8	0	3	3	6	—	—	—	—	—
—Minnesota	NHL	63	2	9	11	113	—	—	—	—	—
85-86—Minnesota	NHL	75	1	14	15	151	3	0	0	0	2
86-87—Minnesota	NHL	72	2	10	12	179	—	—	—	—	—
87-88—Minnesota	NHL	74	0	12	12	168	—	—	—	—	—
88-89—Minnesota	NHL	66	4	13	17	124	—	—	—	—	—
—Washington	NHL	13	0	2	2	36	6	2	0	2	4
89-90—Washington	NHL	70	4	16	20	123	15	2	3	5	47
90-91—Washington	NHL	47	5	15	20	65	—	—	—	—	—
—Toronto	NHL	13	2	4	6	10	—	—	—	—	—
91-92—Toronto	NHL	79	3	19	22	97	—	—	—	—	—
92-93—Toronto	NHL	82	3	11	14	130	21	3	8	11	29
93-94—Toronto	NHL	63	5	11	16	101	18	0	3	3	29
NHL totals		718	31	136	167	1297	63	7	14	21	111

R

ROUSSEL, DOMINIC
G, FLYERS

PERSONAL: Born February 22, 1970, in Hull, Que. . . . 6-1/190. . . . Catches left. . . . Name pronounced roo-SEHL.
TRANSACTIONS/CAREER NOTES: Selected by Philadelphia Flyers as underage junior in third round (fourth Flyers pick, 63rd overall) of NHL entry draft (June 11, 1988). . . . Pulled groin (November 29, 1992); missed three games. . . . Reinjured groin (December 11, 1992); missed 11 games. . . . Suffered from the flu (March 24, 1994); missed three games.

Season	Team	League	REGULAR SEASON								PLAYOFFS						
			Gms.	Min.	W	L	T	GA	SO	Avg.	Gms.	Min.	W	L	GA	SO	Avg.
87-88	Trois-Rivieres	QMJHL	51	2905	18	25	4	251	0	5.18	—	—	—	—	—	—	—
88-89	Shawinigan	QMJHL	46	2555	24	15	2	171	0	4.02	10	638	6	4	36	0	3.39
89-90	Shawinigan	QMJHL	37	1985	20	14	1	133	0	4.02	2	120	1	1	12	0	6.00
90-91	Hershey	AHL	45	2507	20	14	7	151	1	3.61	7	366	3	4	21	0	3.44
91-92	Hershey	AHL	35	2040	15	11	6	121	1	3.56	—	—	—	—	—	—	—
	Philadelphia	NHL	17	922	7	8	2	40	1	2.60	—	—	—	—	—	—	—
92-93	Philadelphia	NHL	34	1769	13	11	5	111	1	3.76	—	—	—	—	—	—	—
	Hershey	AHL	6	372	0	3	3	23	0	3.71	—	—	—	—	—	—	—
93-94	Philadelphia	NHL	60	3285	29	20	5	183	1	3.34	—	—	—	—	—	—	—
NHL totals			111	5976	49	39	12	334	3	3.35							

ROUSSON, BORIS
G, RANGERS

PERSONAL: Born June 14, 1970, in Val d'Or, Que. . . . 6-2/195. . . . Catches right. . . . Name pronounced roo-SAHN.
TRANSACTIONS/CAREER NOTES: Signed as free agent by New York Rangers (March 31, 1991).
HONORS: Named to QMJHL All-Star second team (1990-91). . . . Shared Harry (Hap) Holmes Memorial Trophy with Corey Hirsch (1992-93).

Season	Team	League	REGULAR SEASON								PLAYOFFS						
			Gms.	Min.	W	L	T	GA	SO	Avg.	Gms.	Min.	W	L	GA	SO	Avg.
87-88	Laval	QMJHL	2	104	0	1	0	14	0	8.08	—	—	—	—	—	—	—
88-89	Laval	QMJHL	22	1187	12	7	0	88	0	4.45	6	295	4	1	15	0	3.05
89-90	Granby	QMJHL	39	2076	10	26	0	158	0	4.57	—	—	—	—	—	—	—
90-91	Granby	QMJHL	*63	*3693	28	25	6	190	2	3.09	—	—	—	—	—	—	—
91-92	Binghamton	AHL	38	2261	16	15	6	123	1	3.26	—	—	—	—	—	—	—
92-93	Binghamton	AHL	31	1847	18	9	4	115	0	3.74	1	20	0	0	2	0	6.00
93-94	Binghamton	AHL	62	3599	26	26	8	232	0	3.87	—	—	—	—	—	—	—

ROY, ANDRE
LW, BRUINS

PERSONAL: Born February 8, 1975, in Port Chester, N.Y. . . . 6-3/178. . . . Shoots left.
TRANSACTIONS/CAREER NOTES: Selected by Boston Bruins in sixth round (fifth Bruins pick, 151st overall) of NHL entry draft (June 29, 1994).

Season	Team	League	REGULAR SEASON					PLAYOFFS				
			Gms.	G	A	Pts.	PIM	Gms.	G	A	Pts.	PIM
93-94	Beauport	QMJHL	33	6	7	13	125	—	—	—	—	—
	Chicoutimi	QMJHL	32	4	14	18	152	25	3	6	9	94

ROY, JEAN-YVES
RW, RANGERS

PERSONAL: Born February 17, 1969, in Rosemere, Que. . . . 5-10/185. . . . Shoots left. . . . Name pronounced ZHAHN-eev WAH.
COLLEGE: Maine.
TRANSACTIONS/CAREER NOTES: Signed as free agent by New York Rangers (July 20, 1992).
HONORS: Named to NCAA All-America East second team (1989-90). . . . Named to Hockey East All-Rookie team (1989-90). . . . Named to NCAA All-America East first team (1990-91 and 1991-92). . . . Named to NCAA All-Tournament team (1990-91). . . . Named to Hockey East All-Star first team (1990-91). . . . Named to Hockey East All-Star second team (1991-92).
MISCELLANEOUS: Member of silver-medal-winning Canadian Olympic team (1994).

Season	Team	League	REGULAR SEASON					PLAYOFFS				
			Gms.	G	A	Pts.	PIM	Gms.	G	A	Pts.	PIM
89-90	University of Maine	Hockey East	46	39	26	65	52	—	—	—	—	—
90-91	University of Maine	Hockey East	43	37	45	82	26	—	—	—	—	—
91-92	University of Maine	Hockey East	35	32	24	56	62	—	—	—	—	—
92-93	Canadian national team	Int'l	23	9	6	15	35	—	—	—	—	—
	Binghamton	AHL	49	13	15	28	21	14	5	2	7	4
93-94	Binghamton	AHL	65	41	24	65	33	—	—	—	—	—
	Canadian national team	Int'l	14	4	2	6	2	—	—	—	—	—
	Canadian Olympic Team	Int'l	8	1	0	1	19	—	—	—	—	—

ROY, PATRICK
G, CANADIENS

PERSONAL: Born October 5, 1965, in Quebec City. . . . 6-0/182. . . . Catches left. . . . Name pronounced WAH.
TRANSACTIONS/CAREER NOTES: Selected by Montreal Canadiens as underage junior in third round (fourth Canadiens pick, 51st overall) of NHL entry draft (June 9, 1984). . . . Suspended eight games by NHL for slashing (October 19, 1987). . . . Sprained medial collateral ligaments in left knee (December 12, 1990); missed nine games. . . . Tore left ankle ligaments (January 27, 1991); missed 14 games. . . . Reinjured left ankle (March 16, 1991). . . . Strained hip flexor (March 6, 1993); missed two games. . . . Suffered stiff neck (December 11, 1993); missed two games. . . . Strained neck (December 22, 1993); missed four games.
HONORS: Won Conn Smythe Trophy (1985-86 and 1992-93). . . . Named to NHL All-Rookie team (1985-86). . . . Shared William

M. Jennings Trophy with Brian Hayward (1986-87 through 1988-89).... Named to NHL All-Star second team (1987-88 and 1990-91).... Named to THE SPORTING NEWS All-Star first team (1988-89, 1989-90, and 1991-92).... Won Trico Goaltender Award (1988-89 and 1989-90).... Named to NHL All-Star first team (1988-89, 1989-90 and 1991-92).... Won Vezina Trophy (1988-89, 1989-90 and 1991-92).... Played in NHL All-Star Game (1988 and 1990-1994).... Named to THE SPORTING NEWS All-Star second team (1990-91).... Won William M. Jennings Trophy (1991-92).

RECORDS: Shares NHL single-season playoff record for most wins by goaltender—16 (1993); most consecutive wins by goaltender—11 (1993).

MISCELLANEOUS: Member of Stanley Cup championship teams (1986 and 1993).

			REGULAR SEASON							PLAYOFFS					
Season Team	League	Gms.	Min.	W	L	T	GA	SO	Avg.	Gms.	Min.	W	L	GA	SO	Avg.
82-83—Granby	QMJHL	54	2808	...	...	...	293	0	6.26	—	—	—	—	—	—	—
83-84—Granby	QMJHL	61	3585	29	29	1	265	0	4.44	4	244	0	4	22	0	5.41
84-85—Granby	QMJHL	44	2463	16	25	1	228	0	5.55	—	—	—	—	—	—	—
—Montreal	NHL	1	20	1	0	0	0	0	0.00	—	—	—	—	—	—	—
—Sherbrooke	AHL	1	60	1	0	0	4	0	4.00	*13	*769	10	3	37	0	*2.89
85-86—Montreal	NHL	47	2651	23	18	3	148	1	3.35	20	1218	*15	5	39	†1	1.92
86-87—Montreal	NHL	46	2686	22	16	6	131	1	2.93	6	330	4	2	22	0	4.00
87-88—Montreal	NHL	45	2586	23	12	9	125	3	2.90	8	430	3	4	24	0	3.35
88-89—Montreal	NHL	48	2744	33	5	6	113	4	*2.47	19	1206	13	6	42	2	*2.09
89-90—Montreal	NHL	54	3173	31	16	5	134	3	2.53	11	641	5	6	26	1	2.43
90-91—Montreal	NHL	48	2835	25	15	6	128	1	2.71	13	785	7	5	40	0	3.06
91-92—Montreal	NHL	67	3935	36	22	8	155	†5	*2.36	11	686	4	7	30	1	2.62
92-93—Montreal	NHL	62	3595	31	25	5	192	2	3.20	20	1293	16	4	46	0	2.13
93-94—Montreal	NHL	68	3867	35	17	11	161	†7	2.50	6	375	3	3	16	0	2.56
NHL totals		486	28092	260	146	59	1287	27	2.75	114	6964	70	42	285	5	2.46

ROY, SIMON
D, OILERS

PERSONAL: Born June 14, 1974, in Montreal.... 6-1/180.... Shoots left.... Name pronounced WAH.

TRANSACTIONS/CAREER NOTES: Selected by Edmonton Oilers in third round (third Oilers pick, 61st overall) of NHL entry draft (June 20, 1992).

		REGULAR SEASON					PLAYOFFS				
Season Team	League	Gms.	G	A	Pts.	PIM	Gms.	G	A	Pts.	PIM
91-92—Shawinigan	QMJHL	63	3	24	27	24	10	1	4	5	9
92-93—Shawinigan	QMJHL	68	5	34	39	56	—	—	—	—	—
93-94—Shawinigan	QMJHL	64	10	46	56	30	5	1	4	5	6

ROY, STEPHANE
C, BLUES

PERSONAL: Born January 26, 1976, in Ste.-Martine, Que.... 5-10/173.... Shoots left.... Name pronounced Stehf-AN Rwah.

TRANSACTIONS/CAREER NOTES: Selected by St. Louis Blues in third round (first Blues pick, 68th overall) of NHL entry draft (June 29, 1994).

		REGULAR SEASON					PLAYOFFS				
Season Team	League	Gms.	G	A	Pts.	PIM	Gms.	G	A	Pts.	PIM
93-94—Val-d'Or	QMJHL	72	25	28	53	116	—	—	—	—	—

RUBACHUK, BRAD
C, SABRES

PERSONAL: Born June 11, 1970, in Winnipeg.... 5-11/180.... Shoots left.... Name pronounced ROO-buh-CHUCK.

TRANSACTIONS/CAREER NOTES: Selected by Buffalo Sabres in 12th round (11th Sabres pick, 250th overall) of NHL entry draft (June 16, 1990).

		REGULAR SEASON					PLAYOFFS				
Season Team	League	Gms.	G	A	Pts.	PIM	Gms.	G	A	Pts.	PIM
88-89—Lethbridge	WHL	66	19	13	32	161	6	3	1	4	25
89-90—Lethbridge	WHL	67	37	36	73	179	16	3	7	10	51
90-91—Lethbridge	WHL	70	64	68	132	237	16	*14	14	28	55
91-92—Rochester	AHL	70	18	16	34	201	13	4	0	4	19
92-93—Rochester	AHL	61	10	15	25	218	12	3	1	4	63
93-94—Rochester	AHL	65	18	18	36	246	4	1	1	2	10

RUCCHIN, STEVE
C, MIGHTY DUCKS

PERSONAL: Born July 4, 1971, in London, Ont.... 6-3/210.... Shoots left.

COLLEGE: Western Ontario.

TRANSACTIONS/CAREER NOTES: Selected by Mighty Ducks of Anaheim in first round (first Mighty Ducks pick, second overall) of NHL supplemental draft (June 28, 1994).

HONORS: Named to OUAA Player of the Year (1993-94).... Named to CIAU All-Star first team (1993-94).

		REGULAR SEASON					PLAYOFFS				
Season Team	League	Gms.	G	A	Pts.	PIM	Gms.	G	A	Pts.	PIM
90-91—Univ. of Western Ontario	OUAA	34	13	16	29	14	—	—	—	—	—
91-92—Univ. of Western Ontario	OUAA	37	28	34	62	36	—	—	—	—	—
92-93—Univ. of Western Ontario	OUAA	34	22	26	48	16	—	—	—	—	—
93-94—Univ. of Western Ontario	OUAA	35	30	23	53	30	—	—	—	—	—

RUCHTY, MATT
D, DEVILS

PERSONAL: Born November 27, 1969, in Kitchener, Ont.... 6-1/210.... Shoots left.... Full name: Matthew Kerry Ruchty.... Name pronounced RUHK-tee.

COLLEGE: Bowling Green State.

TRANSACTIONS/CAREER NOTES: Selected by New Jersey Devils in fourth round (fourth Devils

pick, 65th overall) of NHL entry draft (June 11, 1988).

Season Team	League	Gms.	G	A	Pts.	PIM	Gms.	G	A	Pts.	PIM
		REGULAR SEASON					PLAYOFFS				
87-88—Bowling Green State	CCHA	41	6	15	21	78	—	—	—	—	—
88-89—Bowling Green State	CCHA	43	11	21	32	110	—	—	—	—	—
89-90—Bowling Green State	CCHA	42	28	21	49	135	—	—	—	—	—
90-91—Bowling Green State	CCHA	38	13	18	31	147	—	—	—	—	—
91-92—Utica	AHL	73	9	14	23	250	4	0	0	0	25
92-93—Utica	AHL	74	4	14	18	253	4	0	2	2	15
93-94—Albany	AHL	68	11	11	22	303	5	0	1	1	18

RUCINSKY, MARTIN
LW, NORDIQUES

PERSONAL: Born March 11, 1971, in Most, Czechoslovakia. . . . 6-0/190. . . . Shoots left. . . . Name pronounced roo-SHIHN-skee.

TRANSACTIONS/CAREER NOTES: Selected by Edmonton Oilers in first round (second Oilers pick, 20th overall) of NHL entry draft (June 22, 1991). . . . Traded by Oilers to Quebec Nordiques for G Ron Tugnutt and LW Brad Zavisha (March 10, 1992). . . . Suffered from the flu (February 28, 1993); missed one game. . . . Bruised left buttock (December 3, 1994); missed one game. . . . Sprained right wrist (January 11, 1994); missed one game. . . . Broke left cheek (January 30, 1994); missed four games. . . . Suffered hairline fracture of right wrist (March 7, 1994); missed one game. . . . Suffered hairline fracture of right wrist (March 21, 1994); missed six games. . . . Suffered hairline fracture of right wrist (April 5, 1994); missed one game.

Season Team	League	Gms.	G	A	Pts.	PIM	Gms.	G	A	Pts.	PIM
		REGULAR SEASON					PLAYOFFS				
88-89—CHZ Litvinov	Czech.	3	1	0	1	2	—	—	—	—	—
89-90—CHZ Litvinov	Czech.	47	12	6	18	...	—	—	—	—	—
90-91—CHZ Litvinov	Czech.	49	23	18	41	79	—	—	—	—	—
—Czechoslovakia Jr.	Czech.	7	9	5	14	2	—	—	—	—	—
91-92—Cape Breton	AHL	35	11	12	23	34	—	—	—	—	—
—Edmonton	NHL	2	0	0	0	0	—	—	—	—	—
—Halifax	AHL	7	1	1	2	6	—	—	—	—	—
—Quebec	NHL	4	1	1	2	2	—	—	—	—	—
92-93—Quebec	NHL	77	18	30	48	51	6	1	1	2	4
93-94—Quebec	NHL	60	9	23	32	58	—	—	—	—	—
NHL totals		143	28	54	82	111	6	1	1	2	4

RUFF, JASON
LW, LIGHTNING

PERSONAL: Born January 27, 1970, in Kelowna, B.C. . . . 6-2/200. . . . Shoots left.
TRANSACTIONS/CAREER NOTES: Underwent heel surgery (May 1988). . . . Selected by St. Louis Blues in fifth round (third Blues pick, 96th overall) of NHL entry draft (June 16, 1990). . . . Traded by Blues with third-round pick in 1995 draft and sixth-round pick in 1996 draft to Tampa Bay Lightning for LW Basil McRae and D Doug Crossman (January 28, 1993).
HONORS: Named to WHL (East) All-Star first team (1990-91).

Season Team	League	Gms.	G	A	Pts.	PIM	Gms.	G	A	Pts.	PIM
		REGULAR SEASON					PLAYOFFS				
86-87—Kelowna	BCJHL	45	25	20	45	70	—	—	—	—	—
87-88—Lethbridge	WHL	69	25	22	47	109	—	—	—	—	—
88-89—Lethbridge	WHL	69	42	38	80	127	—	—	—	—	—
89-90—Lethbridge	WHL	72	55	64	119	114	19	9	10	19	18
90-91—Lethbridge	WHL	66	61	75	136	154	16	12	17	29	18
—Peoria	IHL	—	—	—	—	—	5	0	0	0	2
91-92—Peoria	IHL	67	27	45	72	148	10	7	7	14	19
92-93—Peoria	IHL	40	22	21	43	81	—	—	—	—	—
—St. Louis	NHL	7	2	1	3	8	—	—	—	—	—
—Tampa Bay	NHL	1	0	0	0	0	—	—	—	—	—
—Atlanta	IHL	26	11	14	25	90	7	2	1	3	26
93-94—Atlanta	IHL	71	24	25	49	122	14	6	*17	23	41
—Tampa Bay	NHL	6	1	2	3	2	—	—	—	—	—
NHL totals		14	3	3	6	10					

RUMBLE, DARREN
D, SENATORS

PERSONAL: Born January 23, 1969, in Barrie, Ont. . . . 6-1/200. . . . Shoots left. . . . Full name: Darren William Rumble.
HIGH SCHOOL: Eastview (Barrie, Ont.).
TRANSACTIONS/CAREER NOTES: Selected by Philadelphia Flyers as underage junior in first round (first Flyers pick, 20th overall) of NHL entry draft (June 13, 1987). . . . Stretched knee ligaments (November 27, 1988). . . . Selected by Ottawa Senators in NHL expansion draft (June 18, 1992). . . . Bruised thigh (November 29, 1993); missed four games. . . . Injured thumb (March 5, 1994); missed one game.

Season Team	League	Gms.	G	A	Pts.	PIM	Gms.	G	A	Pts.	PIM
		REGULAR SEASON					PLAYOFFS				
85-86—Barrie Jr. B	OHA	46	14	32	46	91	—	—	—	—	—
86-87—Kitchener	OHL	64	11	32	43	44	4	0	1	1	9
87-88—Kitchener	OHL	55	15	50	65	64	—	—	—	—	—
88-89—Kitchener	OHL	46	11	29	40	25	5	1	0	1	2
89-90—Hershey	AHL	57	2	13	15	31	—	—	—	—	—
90-91—Philadelphia	NHL	3	1	0	1	0	—	—	—	—	—
—Hershey	AHL	73	6	35	41	48	3	0	5	5	2

Season Team	League	REGULAR SEASON					PLAYOFFS				
		Gms.	G	A	Pts.	Pen.	Gms.	G	A	Pts.	Pen.
91-92—Hershey	AHL	79	12	54	66	118	6	0	3	3	2
92-93—Ottawa	NHL	69	3	13	16	61	—	—	—	—	—
—New Haven	AHL	2	1	0	1	0	—	—	—	—	—
93-94—Ottawa	NHL	70	6	9	15	116	—	—	—	—	—
—Prince Edward Island	AHL	3	2	0	2	0	—	—	—	—	—
NHL totals		142	10	22	32	177					

RUSHFORTH, PAUL
RW, SABRES

PERSONAL: Born April 22, 1974, in Prince George, B.C. . . . 6-0/188. . . . Shoots right.
HIGH SCHOOL: Chippewa Secondary (North Bay, Ont.).
TRANSACTIONS/CAREER NOTES: Selected by Buffalo Sabres in sixth round (eighth Sabres pick, 131st overall) of NHL entry draft (June 20, 1992).

Season Team	League	REGULAR SEASON					PLAYOFFS				
		Gms.	G	A	Pts.	PIM	Gms.	G	A	Pts.	PIM
89-90—Ottawa	OHA Mj. Jr. A	50	10	7	17	30	—	—	—	—	—
90-91—Ottawa	OHA Mj. Jr. A	38	14	16	30	58	—	—	—	—	—
91-92—North Bay	OHL	65	8	11	19	24	19	0	2	2	6
92-93—North Bay	OHL	21	4	10	14	24	—	—	—	—	—
—Belleville	OHL	36	21	19	40	38	7	7	2	9	4
93-94—Belleville	OHL	63	28	35	63	109	12	6	3	9	8

RUSK, MIKE
D, BLACKHAWKS

PERSONAL: Born April 26, 1975, in Milton, Ont. . . . 6-1/175. . . . Shoots left.
HIGH SCHOOL: Bishop MacDonell (Guelph, Ont.).
TRANSACTIONS/CAREER NOTES: Selected by Chicago Blackhawks in ninth round (10th Blackhawks pick, 232nd overall) of NHL entry draft (June 26, 1993).

Season Team	League	REGULAR SEASON					PLAYOFFS				
		Gms.	G	A	Pts.	PIM	Gms.	G	A	Pts.	PIM
91-92—Muskoka	Jr. A	44	9	24	33	60	—	—	—	—	—
92-93—Guelph	OHL	62	3	15	18	65	5	0	1	1	8
93-94—Guelph	OHL	48	8	26	34	59	9	2	9	11	12

RUSSELL, CAM
D, BLACKHAWKS

PERSONAL: Born January 12, 1969, in Halifax, N.S. . . . 6-4/206. . . . Shoots left.
TRANSACTIONS/CAREER NOTES: Selected by Chicago Blackhawks as underage junior in third round (third Blackhawks pick, 50th overall) of NHL entry draft (June 13, 1987). . . . Suffered from the flu (December 26, 1992); missed one game. . . . Suspended one game by NHL for accumulating three game misconduct penalties (February 11, 1993). . . . Underwent surgery for a herniated disc in neck (March 18, 1994); missed remainder of season.

Season Team	League	REGULAR SEASON					PLAYOFFS				
		Gms.	G	A	Pts.	PIM	Gms.	G	A	Pts.	PIM
85-86—Hull	QMJHL	56	3	4	7	24	15	0	2	2	4
86-87—Hull	QMJHL	66	3	16	19	119	8	0	1	1	16
87-88—Hull	QMJHL	53	9	18	27	141	19	2	5	7	39
88-89—Hull	QMJHL	66	8	32	40	109	9	2	6	8	6
89-90—Indianapolis	IHL	46	3	15	18	114	9	0	1	1	24
—Chicago	NHL	19	0	1	1	27	1	0	0	0	0
90-91—Indianapolis	IHL	53	5	9	14	125	6	0	2	2	30
—Chicago	NHL	3	0	0	0	5	1	0	0	0	0
91-92—Indianapolis	IHL	41	4	9	13	78	—	—	—	—	—
—Chicago	NHL	19	0	0	0	34	12	0	2	2	2
92-93—Chicago	NHL	67	2	4	6	151	4	0	0	0	0
93-94—Chicago	NHL	67	1	7	8	200	—	—	—	—	—
NHL totals		175	3	12	15	417	18	0	2	2	2

RUUTTU, CHRISTIAN
C, BLACKHAWKS

PERSONAL: Born February 20, 1964, in Lappeenranta, Finland. . . . 5-11/192. . . . Shoots left. . . . Name pronounced ROO-TOO.
TRANSACTIONS/CAREER NOTES: Selected by Buffalo Sabres in seventh round (ninth Sabres pick, 134th overall) of NHL entry draft (June 8, 1983). . . . Injured knee (February 1988). . . . Sprained knee (September 1988). . . . Tore pectoral muscle (October 22, 1988). . . . Separated left shoulder (April 5, 1989). . . . Injured leg (January 21, 1992); missed four games. . . . Suffered from the flu (March 16, 1992); missed three games. . . . Traded by Sabres with future considerations to Winnipeg Jets for G Stephane Beauregard (June 15, 1992). . . . Traded by Jets with future considerations to Chicago Blackhawks for G Stephane Beauregard (August 10, 1992). . . . Broke right ankle (1993-94 season); missed 28 games.
HONORS: Named to Finnish League All-Star team (1985-86). . . . Played in NHL All-Star Game (1988).

Season Team	League	REGULAR SEASON					PLAYOFFS				
		Gms.	G	A	Pts.	PIM	Gms.	G	A	Pts.	PIM
82-83—Pori Assat	Finland	36	15	18	33	34	—	—	—	—	—
83-84—Pori Assat	Finland	37	18	42	60	72	9	2	5	7	12
84-85—Pori Assat	Finland	32	14	32	46	34	8	1	6	7	8
85-86—Helsinki IFK	Finland	36	14	42	56	41	10	3	6	9	8
86-87—Buffalo	NHL	76	22	43	65	62	—	—	—	—	—

R

Season Team	League	REGULAR SEASON Gms.	G	A	Pts.	Pen.	PLAYOFFS Gms.	G	A	Pts.	Pen.
87-88—Buffalo	NHL	73	26	45	71	85	6	2	5	7	4
88-89—Buffalo	NHL	67	14	46	60	98	2	0	0	0	0
89-90—Buffalo	NHL	75	19	41	60	66	6	0	0	0	4
90-91—Buffalo	NHL	77	16	34	50	96	6	1	3	4	29
91-92—Buffalo	NHL	70	4	21	25	76	3	0	0	0	6
92-93—Chicago	NHL	84	17	37	54	134	4	0	0	0	2
93-94—Chicago	NHL	54	9	20	29	68	6	0	0	0	2
NHL totals		576	127	287	414	685	33	3	8	11	47

RUZICKA, VLADIMIR

C

PERSONAL: Born June 6, 1963, in Most, Czechoslovakia. . . . 6-3/212. . . . Shoots left. . . . Name pronounced roo-ZEECH-kuh.

TRANSACTIONS/CAREER NOTES: Selected by Toronto Maple Leafs in fourth round (fifth Maple Leafs pick, 73rd overall) of NHL entry draft (June 9, 1982). . . . Rights traded by Maple Leafs to Edmonton Oilers for fourth-round pick (C Greg Walters) in 1990 draft (December 21, 1989). . . . Traded by Oilers to Boston Bruins for D Greg Hawgood (October 22, 1990). . . . Injured left ankle and developed tendinitis (December 29, 1990). . . . Underwent surgery to left ankle tendon (February 12, 1991). . . . Strained groin (December 1992); missed 15 games. . . . Injured ankle (March 1993); missed three games. . . . Injured groin (April 1993); missed six games. . . . Signed as free agent by Ottawa Senators (August 12, 1993). . . . Injured hip (October 16, 1993); missed three games. . . . Injured back (December 28, 1993); missed 11 games.

HONORS: Named Czechoslovakian League Player of the Year (1985-86 and 1987-88). . . . Named to Czechoslovakian League All-Star team (1987-88 and 1989-90).

Season Team	League	REGULAR SEASON Gms.	G	A	Pts.	PIM	PLAYOFFS Gms.	G	A	Pts.	PIM
83-84—Czech. Olympic Team	Int'l	7	4	6	10	0	—	—	—	—	—
84-85—					Statistics unavailable.						
85-86—					Statistics unavailable.						
86-87—CHZ Litvinov	Czech.	32	24	15	39	...	—	—	—	—	—
87-88—Dukla Trencin	Czech.	34	32	21	53	...	—	—	—	—	—
—Czech. Olympic Team	Int'l	8	4	3	7	12	—	—	—	—	—
88-89—Dukla Trencin	Czech.	45	46	38	*84	...	—	—	—	—	—
89-90—CHZ Litvinov	Czech.	32	21	23	44	...	—	—	—	—	—
—Edmonton	NHL	25	11	6	17	10	—	—	—	—	—
90-91—Boston	NHL	29	8	8	16	19	17	2	11	13	0
91-92—Boston	NHL	77	39	36	75	48	13	2	3	5	2
92-93—Boston	NHL	60	19	22	41	38	—	—	—	—	—
93-94—Ottawa	NHL	42	5	13	18	14	—	—	—	—	—
NHL totals		233	82	85	167	129	30	4	14	18	2

RYABCHIKOV, YEVGENI

G, BRUINS

PERSONAL: Born January 16, 1974, in Yaroslavl, U.S.S.R. . . . 5-11/167. . . . Catches left.

TRANSACTIONS/CAREER NOTES: Selected by Boston Bruins in first round (first Bruins pick, 21st overall) of NHL entry draft (June 28, 1994).

HONORS: Named CIS Rookie of the Year (1993-94).

Season Team	League	REGULAR SEASON Gms.	Min.	W	L	T	GA	SO	Avg.	PLAYOFFS Gms.	Min.	W	L	GA	SO	Avg.
93-94—Molot Perm	CIS	28	1572	...	...	...	96	...	3.66	—	—	—	—	—	—	—

RYABYKIN, DMITRI

D, FLAMES

PERSONAL: Born March 24, 1976, in Moscow, U.S.S.R. . . . 6-1/183. . . . Shoots right.

TRANSACTIONS/CAREER NOTES: Selected by Calgary Flames in second round (second Flames pick, 45th overall) of NHL entry draft (June 28, 1994).

Season Team	League	REGULAR SEASON Gms.	G	A	Pts.	PIM	PLAYOFFS Gms.	G	A	Pts.	PIM
93-94—Dynamo-2 Moscow	CIS Div. III				Statistics unavailable.						

RYCHEL, WARREN

LW, KINGS

PERSONAL: Born May 12, 1967, in Tecumseh, Ont. . . . 6-0/190. . . . Shoots left. . . . Full name: Warren Stanley Rychel. . . . Name pronounced RIGH-kuhl.

TRANSACTIONS/CAREER NOTES: Signed as free agent by Chicago Blackhawks (September 19, 1986). . . . Hyperextended left knee (February 1989). . . . Traded by Blackhawks with C Troy Murray to Winnipeg Jets for D Bryan Marchment and D Chris Norton (July 22, 1991). . . . Traded by Jets to Minnesota North Stars for RW Tony Joseph and future considerations (December 30, 1991). . . . Signed as free agent by San Diego Gulls (August 11, 1992). . . . Signed as free agent by Los Angeles Kings (October 3, 1992). . . . Suffered ankle contusion (December 1, 1992); missed 14 games.

Season Team	League	REGULAR SEASON Gms.	G	A	Pts.	PIM	PLAYOFFS Gms.	G	A	Pts.	PIM
83-84—Essex Junior C	OHA	24	11	16	27	86	—	—	—	—	—
84-85—Sudbury	OHL	35	5	8	13	74	—	—	—	—	—
—Guelph	OHL	29	1	3	4	48	—	—	—	—	—
85-86—Guelph	OHL	38	14	5	19	119	—	—	—	—	—
—Ottawa	OHL	29	11	18	29	54	—	—	—	—	—

Season Team	League	Gms.	G	A	Pts.	Pen.	Gms.	G	A	Pts.	Pen.
		REGULAR SEASON					**PLAYOFFS**				
86-87—Ottawa	OHL	28	11	7	18	57	—	—	—	—	—
—Kitchener	OHL	21	5	5	10	39	4	0	0	0	9
87-88—Saginaw	IHL	51	2	7	9	113	1	0	0	0	0
—Peoria	IHL	7	2	1	3	7	—	—	—	—	—
88-89—Saginaw	IHL	50	15	14	29	226	6	0	0	0	51
—Chicago	NHL	2	0	0	0	17	—	—	—	—	—
89-90—Indianapolis	IHL	77	23	16	39	374	14	1	3	4	64
90-91—Indianapolis	IHL	68	33	30	63	338	5	2	1	3	30
—Chicago	NHL	—	—	—	—	—	3	1	3	4	2
91-92—Moncton	AHL	36	14	15	29	211	—	—	—	—	—
—Kalamazoo	IHL	45	15	20	35	165	8	0	3	3	51
92-93—Los Angeles	NHL	70	6	7	13	314	23	6	7	13	39
93-94—Los Angeles	NHL	80	10	9	19	322	—	—	—	—	—
NHL totals		152	16	16	32	653	26	7	10	17	41

SAAL, JASON
G, KINGS

PERSONAL: Born February 1, 1975, in Detroit. . . . 5-9/165. . . . Catches left. . . . Name pronounced SAHL.
TRANSACTIONS/CAREER NOTES: Selected by Los Angeles Kings in fifth round (fifth Kings pick, 117th overall) of NHL entry draft (June 26, 1993).

Season Team	League	Gms.	Min.	W	L	T	GA	SO	Avg.	Gms.	Min.	W	L	GA	SO	Avg.
		REGULAR SEASON								**PLAYOFFS**						
92-93—Detroit	OHL	23	1289	11	8	1	85	0	3.96	3	42	0	0	2	0	2.86
93-94—Detroit	OHL	45	2551	28	11	3	143	0	3.36	7	346	5	0	23	0	3.99

SABOURIN, KEN
D

PERSONAL: Born April 28, 1966, in Scarborough, Ont. . . . 6-3/210. . . . Shoots left. . . . Name pronounced SAB-uhr-ihn.
TRANSACTIONS/CAREER NOTES: Selected by Calgary Flames as underage junior in second round (second Flames pick, 33rd overall) of NHL entry draft (June 9, 1984). . . . Traded by Sault Ste. Marie Greyhounds to Cornwall Royals for Kent Trolley and fifth-round pick in 1986 OHL priority draft (March 1986). . . . Traded by Flames to Washington Capitals for C Paul Fenton (January 24, 1991). . . . Traded by Capitals to Flames for future considerations (December 15, 1992).

Season Team	League	Gms.	G	A	Pts.	PIM	Gms.	G	A	Pts.	PIM
		REGULAR SEASON					**PLAYOFFS**				
82-83—Sault Ste. Marie	OHL	58	0	8	8	90	10	0	0	0	14
83-84—Sault Ste. Marie	OHL	63	7	13	20	157	9	0	1	1	25
84-85—Sault Ste. Marie	OHL	63	5	19	24	139	16	1	4	5	10
85-86—Sault Ste. Marie	OHL	25	1	5	6	77	—	—	—	—	—
—Cornwall	OHL	37	3	12	15	94	6	1	2	3	6
—Moncton	AHL	3	0	0	0	0	6	0	1	1	2
86-87—Moncton	AHL	75	1	10	11	166	6	0	1	1	27
87-88—Salt Lake City	IHL	71	2	8	10	186	16	1	6	7	57
88-89—Calgary	NHL	6	0	1	1	26	1	0	0	0	0
—Salt Lake City	IHL	74	2	18	20	197	11	0	1	1	26
89-90—Calgary	NHL	5	0	0	0	10	—	—	—	—	—
—Salt Lake City	IHL	76	5	19	24	336	11	0	2	2	40
90-91—Salt Lake City	IHL	28	2	15	17	77	—	—	—	—	—
—Calgary	NHL	16	1	3	4	36	—	—	—	—	—
—Washington	NHL	28	1	4	5	81	11	0	0	0	34
91-92—Baltimore	AHL	30	3	8	11	106	—	—	—	—	—
—Washington	NHL	19	0	0	0	48	—	—	—	—	—
92-93—Baltimore	AHL	30	5	14	19	68	—	—	—	—	—
—Salt Lake City	IHL	52	2	11	13	140	—	—	—	—	—
93-94—Milwaukee	IHL	81	6	13	19	279	4	0	0	0	10
NHL totals		74	2	8	10	201	12	0	0	0	34

SACCO, DAVID
RW, MAPLE LEAFS

PERSONAL: Born July 31, 1970, in Medford, Mass. . . . 6-0/190. . . . Shoots right. . . . Full name: David Anthony Sacco. . . . Name pronounced SAK-oh. . . . Brother of Joe Sacco, left winger, Mighty Ducks of Anaheim.
HIGH SCHOOL: Medford (Mass.).
COLLEGE: Boston University.
TRANSACTIONS/CAREER NOTES: Selected by Toronto Maple Leafs in 10th round (ninth Maple Leafs pick, 195th overall) of NHL entry draft (June 11, 1988). . . . Loaned to U.S. Olympic Team (February 27, 1994). . . . Returned to Maple Leafs (March 1, 1994).
HONORS: Named to NCAA All-America East first team (1991-92 and 1992-93). . . . Named to Hockey East All-Star first team (1991-92 and 1992-93).

Season Team	League	Gms.	G	A	Pts.	PIM	Gms.	G	A	Pts.	PIM
		REGULAR SEASON					**PLAYOFFS**				
88-89—Boston University	Hockey East	35	14	29	43	40	—	—	—	—	—
89-90—Boston University	Hockey East	3	0	4	4	2	—	—	—	—	—
90-91—Boston University	Hockey East	40	21	40	61	24	—	—	—	—	—

Season Team	League	Gms.	G	A	Pts.	Pen.		Gms.	G	A	Pts.	Pen.
91-92—Boston University	Hockey East	35	14	33	47	30		—	—	—	—	—
92-93—Boston University	Hockey East	40	25	37	62	86		—	—	—	—	—
93-94—U.S. national team	Int'l	32	8	20	28	88		—	—	—	—	—
—U.S. Olympic Team	Int'l	8	3	5	8	12		—	—	—	—	—
—Toronto	NHL	4	1	1	2	4		—	—	—	—	—
NHL totals		4	1	1	2	4						

SACCO, JOE
LW, MIGHTY DUCKS

PERSONAL: Born February 4, 1969, in Medford, Mass.... 6-1/195.... Shoots left.... Full name: Joseph William Sacco.... Name pronounced SAK-oh.... Brother of David Sacco, center, Toronto Maple Leafs.
HIGH SCHOOL: Medford (Mass.).
COLLEGE: Boston University.
TRANSACTIONS/CAREER NOTES: Selected by Toronto Maple Leafs in fourth round (fourth Maple Leafs pick, 71st overall) of NHL entry draft (June 13, 1987).... Selected by Mighty Ducks of Anaheim in NHL expansion draft (June 24, 1993).

Season Team	League	Gms.	G	A	Pts.	PIM		Gms.	G	A	Pts.	PIM
85-86—Medford H.S.	Mass. H.S.	20	30	30	60	...		—	—	—	—	—
86-87—Medford H.S.	Mass. H.S.	21	22	32	54	...		—	—	—	—	—
87-88—Boston University	Hockey East	34	14	22	36	38		—	—	—	—	—
88-89—Boston University	Hockey East	33	21	19	40	66		—	—	—	—	—
89-90—Boston University	Hockey East	44	28	24	52	70		—	—	—	—	—
90-91—Newmarket	AHL	49	18	17	35	24		—	—	—	—	—
—Toronto	NHL	20	0	5	5	2		—	—	—	—	—
91-92—U.S. national team	Int'l	50	11	26	37	51		—	—	—	—	—
—U.S. Olympic Team	Int'l	8	0	2	2	0		—	—	—	—	—
—Toronto	NHL	17	7	4	11	4		—	—	—	—	—
—St. John's	AHL	—	—	—	—	—		1	1	1	2	0
92-93—Toronto	NHL	23	4	4	8	8		—	—	—	—	—
—St. John's	AHL	37	14	16	30	45		7	6	4	10	2
93-94—Anaheim	NHL	84	19	18	37	61		—	—	—	—	—
NHL totals		144	30	31	61	75						

SAFARIK, RICHARD
LW/RW, SABRES

PERSONAL: Born February 26, 1975, in Nova Zausky, Czechoslovakia.... 6-3/194.... Shoots left.... Name pronounced suh-FAHR-ihk.
TRANSACTIONS/CAREER NOTES: Selected by Buffalo Sabres in fifth round (third Sabres pick, 116th overall) of NHL entry draft (June 26, 1993).

Season Team	League	Gms.	G	A	Pts.	PIM		Gms.	G	A	Pts.	PIM
91-92—Nitra	Czech Dv.II	2	0	0	0	0		—	—	—	—	—
92-93—Nitra	Czech Dv.II	16	0	0	0	2		—	—	—	—	—
93-94—Hull	QMJHL	65	7	14	21	24		19	1	3	4	2

SAKIC, BRIAN
LW

PERSONAL: Born April 9, 1971, in Burnaby, B.C.... 5-10/179.... Shoots left.... Name pronounced SA-kihk.... Brother of Joe Sakic, center, Quebec Nordiques.
TRANSACTIONS/CAREER NOTES: Traded by Swift Current Broncos with RW Wade Smith to Tri-City Americans for LW Murray Duval and D Jason Smith (October 18, 1989).... Broke jaw (March 15, 1990).... Selected by Washington Capitals in fifth round (fifth Capitals pick, 93rd overall) of NHL entry draft (June 16, 1990).... Signed as free agent by New York Rangers (August 13, 1992).
HONORS: Named to WHL All-Star second team (1989-90).... Named to WHL (West) All-Star first team (1990-91).

Season Team	League	Gms.	G	A	Pts.	PIM		Gms.	G	A	Pts.	PIM
87-88—Swift Current	WHL	65	12	37	49	12		—	—	—	—	—
88-89—Swift Current	WHL	71	36	64	100	28		—	—	—	—	—
89-90—Swift Current	WHL	8	6	7	13	4		—	—	—	—	—
—Tri-City	WHL	58	47	92	139	8		—	—	—	—	—
90-91—Tri-City	WHL	69	40	*122	162	19		—	—	—	—	—
91-92—Tri-City	WHL	72	45	*83	128	55		5	4	4	8	14
92-93—Erie	ECHL	51	18	33	51	22		—	—	—	—	—
93-94—Flint	Col.HL	64	39	86	125	30		10	6	7	13	2

SAKIC, JOE
C, NORDIQUES

PERSONAL: Born July 7, 1969, in Burnaby, B.C.... 5-11/185.... Shoots left.... Full name: Joseph Steve Sakic.... Name pronounced SA-kihk.... Brother of Brian Sakic, left winger.
TRANSACTIONS/CAREER NOTES: Selected by Quebec Nordiques as underage junior in first round (second Nordiques pick, 15th overall) of NHL entry draft (June 13, 1987).... Sprained right ankle (November 28, 1988).... Developed bursitis in left ankle (January 21, 1992); missed three games.... Suffered recurrence of bursitis in left ankle (January 30, 1992); missed eight games.... Injured eye (January 2, 1993); missed six games.
HONORS: Won WHL (East) Most Valuable Player Trophy (1986-87).... Won WHL (East) Stewart (Butch) Paul Memorial Trophy (1986-87).... Named to WHL All-Star second team (1986-87).... Won Can.HL Player of the Year Award (1987-88).... Won Four Broncos Memorial Trophy (1987-88).... Shared Bob Clarke Trophy with Theoren Fleury (1987-88).... Won WHL

Player of the Year Award (1987-88).... Named to WHL (East) All-Star first team (1987-88).... Played in NHL All-Star Game (1990-1994).

Season Team	League	REGULAR SEASON					PLAYOFFS				
		Gms.	G	A	Pts.	PIM	Gms.	G	A	Pts.	PIM
86-87—Swift Current	WHL	72	60	73	133	31	4	0	1	1	0
87-88—Swift Current	WHL	64	†78	82	†160	64	10	11	13	24	12
88-89—Quebec	NHL	70	23	39	62	24	—	—	—	—	—
89-90—Quebec	NHL	80	39	63	102	27	—	—	—	—	—
90-91—Quebec	NHL	80	48	61	109	24	—	—	—	—	—
91-92—Quebec	NHL	69	29	65	94	20	—	—	—	—	—
92-93—Quebec	NHL	78	48	57	105	40	6	3	3	6	2
93-94—Quebec	NHL	84	28	64	92	18	—	—	—	—	—
NHL totals		461	215	349	564	153	6	3	3	6	2

SALO, TOMMY
G, ISLANDERS

PERSONAL: Born February 1, 1971, in Surahammar, Sweden.... 5-11/161.... Catches left.
TRANSACTIONS/CAREER NOTES: Selected by New York Islanders in fifth round (fifth Islanders pick, 118th overall) of NHL entry draft (June 26, 1993).
MISCELLANEOUS: Member of gold-medal-winning Swedish Olympic team (1994).

Season Team	League	REGULAR SEASON							PLAYOFFS					
		Gms.	Min.	W	L	T	GA	SO	Avg.	Gms.	Min.	W	L	GA	SO	Avg.
90-91—Vasteras	Sweden	2	100	...	...	...	11	0	6.60	—	—	—	—	—	—	—
91-92—Vasteras	Sweden					Did not play.				—	—	—	—	—	—	—
92-93—Vasteras	Sweden	24	1431	...	...	...	59	2	2.47	—	—	—	—	—	—	—
93-94—Vasteras	Sweden	32	1896	...	...	...	106	...	3.35	—	—	—	—	—	—	—
—Swedish Olympic Team	Int'l	6	370	...	...	...	13	1	2.11	—	—	—	—	—	—	—

SALVADOR, BRYCE
D, LIGHTNING

PERSONAL: Born February 11, 1994, in Brandon, Man.... 6-2/194.... Shoots left.
TRANSACTIONS/CAREER NOTES: Selected by Tampa Bay Lightning in sixth round (sixth Lightning pick, 138th overall) of NHL entry draft (June 29, 1994).

Season Team	League	REGULAR SEASON					PLAYOFFS				
		Gms.	G	A	Pts.	PIM	Gms.	G	A	Pts.	PIM
92-93—Lethbridge	WHL	64	1	4	5	29	4	0	0	0	0
93-94—Lethbridge	WHL	61	4	14	18	36	9	0	1	1	2

SAMUELSSON, KJELL
D, PENGUINS

PERSONAL: Born October 18, 1958, in Tyngsryd, Sweden. ... 6-6/233. ... Shoots right. ... Name pronounced SHEHL SAM-yuhl-suhn.
TRANSACTIONS/CAREER NOTES: Selected by New York Rangers in sixth round (fifth Rangers pick, 119th overall) of NHL entry draft (June 9, 1984). ... Traded by Rangers with second-round pick in 1989 draft (LW Patrik Juhlin) to Philadelphia Flyers for G Bob Froese (December 18, 1986). ... Pulled groin (February 1988). ... Suffered herniated disc (October 1988). ... Bruised hand (March 1989). ... Bruised right shoulder (November 22, 1989); missed 13 games. ... Underwent shoulder surgery (March 1990). ... Traded by Flyers with RW Rick Tocchet, G Ken Wregget and third-round pick in 1992 draft to Pittsburgh Penguins for RW Mark Recchi, D Brian Benning and first-round pick (LW Jason Bowen) in 1992 draft (February 19, 1992). ... Bruised knee (November 27, 1992); missed one game. ... Broke bone in foot (December 1, 1992); missed nine games. ... Fractured cheekbone (December 27, 1992); missed nine games. ... Suffered from the flu (March 18, 1993); missed one game. ... Injured groin (October 19, 1993); missed nine games. ... Injured groin (December 28, 1993); missed 13 games.
HONORS: Played in NHL All-Star Game (1988).
MISCELLANEOUS: Member of Stanley Cup championship team (1992).

Season Team	League	REGULAR SEASON					PLAYOFFS				
		Gms.	G	A	Pts.	PIM	Gms.	G	A	Pts.	PIM
82-83—Tyngsryd	Sweden	32	11	6	17	57	—	—	—	—	—
83-84—Leksand	Sweden	36	6	7	13	59	—	—	—	—	—
84-85—Leksand	Sweden	35	9	5	14	34	—	—	—	—	—
85-86—New York Rangers	NHL	9	0	0	0	10	9	0	1	1	8
—New Haven	AHL	56	6	21	27	87	3	0	0	0	10
86-87—New York Rangers	NHL	30	2	6	8	50	—	—	—	—	—
—Philadelphia	NHL	46	1	6	7	86	26	0	4	4	25
87-88—Philadelphia	NHL	74	6	24	30	184	7	2	5	7	23
88-89—Philadelphia	NHL	69	3	14	17	140	19	1	3	4	24
89-90—Philadelphia	NHL	66	5	17	22	91	—	—	—	—	—
90-91—Philadelphia	NHL	78	9	19	28	82	—	—	—	—	—
91-92—Philadelphia	NHL	54	4	9	13	76	—	—	—	—	—
—Pittsburgh	NHL	20	1	2	3	34	15	0	3	3	12
92-93—Pittsburgh	NHL	63	3	6	9	106	12	0	3	3	2
93-94—Pittsburgh	NHL	59	5	8	13	118	6	0	0	0	26
NHL totals		568	39	111	150	977	94	3	19	22	120

SAMUELSSON, ULF
D, PENGUINS

PERSONAL: Born March 26, 1964, in Fagersta, Sweden.... 6-1/195.... Shoots left. ... Name pronounced UHLF SAM-yuhl-suhn.
TRANSACTIONS/CAREER NOTES: Selected by Hartford Whalers in fourth round (fourth Whalers pick, 67th overall) of NHL entry draft (June 9, 1982).... Suffered from the flu (December 1988); missed nine games.... Tore ligaments in right knee and underwent surgery (August 1989); missed part

of 1989-90 season.... Traded by Whalers with C Ron Francis and D Grant Jennings to Pittsburgh Penguins for C John Cullen, D Zarley Zalapski and RW Jeff Parker (March 4, 1991).... Injured hip flexor (October 29, 1991); missed six games.... Underwent surgery to right elbow (December 1991); missed four games.... Bruised left hand (February 8, 1992); missed one game.... Suffered from the flu (February 1992); missed one game.... Strained shoulder (November 10, 1992); missed two games.... Broke cheekbone (November 27, 1992); missed two games.... Bruised knee (January 1993); missed one game.... Suspended one game by NHL (February 1993).... Suspended three off-days by NHL for stick-swinging incident (March 18, 1993).... Suffered back spasms (April 4, 1993); missed one game.... Injured knee (November 2, 1993); missed one game.... Bruised foot (December 14, 1993); missed two games.

MISCELLANEOUS: Member of Stanley Cup championship teams (1991 and 1992).

Season Team	League	REGULAR SEASON					PLAYOFFS				
		Gms.	G	A	Pts.	PIM	Gms.	G	A	Pts.	PIM
83-84—Leksand	Sweden	36	5	10	15	53	—	—	—	—	—
84-85—Binghamton	AHL	36	5	11	16	92	—	—	—	—	—
—Hartford	NHL	41	2	6	8	83	—	—	—	—	—
85-86—Hartford	NHL	80	5	19	24	174	10	1	2	3	38
86-87—Hartford	NHL	78	2	31	33	162	5	0	1	1	41
87-88—Hartford	NHL	76	8	33	41	159	5	0	0	0	8
88-89—Hartford	NHL	71	9	26	35	181	4	0	2	2	4
89-90—Hartford	NHL	55	2	11	13	167	7	1	0	1	2
90-91—Hartford	NHL	62	3	18	21	174	—	—	—	—	—
—Pittsburgh	NHL	14	1	4	5	37	20	3	2	5	34
91-92—Pittsburgh	NHL	62	1	14	15	206	21	0	2	2	39
92-93—Pittsburgh	NHL	77	3	26	29	249	12	1	5	6	24
93-94—Pittsburgh	NHL	80	5	24	29	199	6	0	1	1	18
NHL totals		696	41	212	253	1791	90	6	15	21	208

SANDERSON, GEOFF
LW, WHALERS

PERSONAL: Born February 1, 1972, in Hay River, N.W.T.... 6-0/185.... Shoots left.

TRANSACTIONS/CAREER NOTES: Selected by Hartford Whalers in second round (second Whalers pick, 36th overall) of NHL entry draft (June 16, 1990).... Bruised shoulder (October 14, 1991); missed one game.... Injured groin (November 13, 1991); missed three games.... Bruised knee (December 7, 1991); missed five games.... Suffered from the flu (February 1, 1994).... Fined $500 by Whalers for involvement in bar brawl (April 1, 1994).

HONORS: Played in NHL All-Star Game (1994).

Season Team	League	REGULAR SEASON					PLAYOFFS				
		Gms.	G	A	Pts.	PIM	Gms.	G	A	Pts.	PIM
88-89—Swift Current	WHL	58	17	11	28	16	12	3	5	8	6
89-90—Swift Current	WHL	70	32	62	94	56	4	1	4	5	8
90-91—Swift Current	WHL	70	62	50	112	57	3	1	2	3	4
—Hartford	NHL	2	1	0	1	0	3	0	0	0	0
—Springfield	AHL	—	—	—	—	—	1	0	0	0	2
91-92—Hartford	NHL	64	13	18	31	18	7	1	0	1	2
92-93—Hartford	NHL	82	46	43	89	28	—	—	—	—	—
93-94—Hartford	NHL	82	41	26	67	42	—	—	—	—	—
NHL totals		230	101	87	188	88	10	1	0	1	2

SANDLAK, JIM
RW, WHALERS

PERSONAL: Born December 12, 1966, in Kitchener, Ont.... 6-4/219.... Shoots right.

TRANSACTIONS/CAREER NOTES: Selected by Vancouver Canucks as underage junior in first round (first Canucks pick, fourth overall) of NHL entry draft (June 15, 1985).... Ruptured ligaments in right thumb (January 1986).... Bruised shoulder (October 1988).... Suffered sore back (November 5, 1991).... Sprained hand (December 1, 1991); missed seven games.... Strained groin (December 31, 1991).... Sprained knee (March 1992); missed seven games.... Strained back and suffered bulging disc (November 18, 1992); missed 17 games.... Sprained hand (April 1, 1993); missed remainder of season.... Traded by Canucks to Hartford Whalers (May 17, 1993); to complete deal in which Canucks sent LW Robert Kron, third-round pick in 1993 draft (D Marek Malik) and future considerations to Whalers for LW Murray Craven and fifth-round pick in 1993 draft (March 22, 1993).... Injured right wrist (October 19, 1993); missed two games.... Broke bone in right foot (October 27, 1993); missed 17 games.... Bruised knee (January 12, 1994); missed eight games.... Injured ankle (February 6, 1994); missed remainder of season.

HONORS: Named to NHL All-Rookie team (1986-87).

Season Team	League	REGULAR SEASON					PLAYOFFS				
		Gms.	G	A	Pts.	PIM	Gms.	G	A	Pts.	PIM
82-83—Kitchener	OHL	38	26	25	51	100	—	—	—	—	—
83-84—London	OHL	68	23	18	41	143	8	1	11	12	13
84-85—London	OHL	58	40	24	64	128	8	3	2	5	14
85-86—London	OHL	16	7	13	20	36	5	2	3	5	24
—Vancouver	NHL	23	1	3	4	10	3	0	1	1	0
86-87—Vancouver	NHL	78	15	21	36	66	—	—	—	—	—
87-88—Vancouver	NHL	49	16	15	31	81	—	—	—	—	—
—Fredericton	AHL	24	10	15	25	47	—	—	—	—	—
88-89—Vancouver	NHL	72	20	20	40	99	6	1	1	2	2
89-90—Vancouver	NHL	70	15	8	23	104	—	—	—	—	—
90-91—Vancouver	NHL	59	7	6	13	125	—	—	—	—	—
91-92—Vancouver	NHL	66	16	24	40	176	13	4	6	10	22

Season Team	League	REGULAR SEASON					PLAYOFFS				
		Gms.	G	A	Pts.	Pen.	Gms.	G	A	Pts.	Pen.
92-93—Vancouver	NHL	59	10	18	28	122	6	2	2	4	4
93-94—Hartford	NHL	27	6	2	8	32	—	—	—	—	—
NHL totals		503	106	117	223	815	28	7	10	17	28

SANDSTROM, TOMAS
RW, PENGUINS

PERSONAL: Born September 4, 1964, in Jakobstad, Finland. . . . 6-2/200. . . . Shoots left.

TRANSACTIONS/CAREER NOTES: Selected by New York Rangers in second round (second Rangers pick, 36th overall) of NHL entry draft (June 9, 1982). . . . Suffered concussion (February 24, 1986). . . . Fractured right ankle (February 11, 1987). . . . Fractured right index finger (November 1987). . . . Traded by Rangers with LW Tony Granato to Los Angeles Kings for C Bernie Nicholls (January 20, 1990). . . . Fractured vertebrae (November 29, 1990); missed 10 games. . . . Partially dislocated shoulder (December 28, 1991); missed 26 games. . . . Fractured left forearm (November 21, 1992); missed 24 games. . . . Fractured jaw (February 28, 1993); missed 21 games. . . . Pulled hamstring (October 26, 1993); missed four games. . . . Traded by Kings to Pittsburgh Penguins for D Marty McSorley and D Jim Paek (February 15, 1994).

HONORS: Named to NHL All-Rookie team (1984-85). . . . Played in NHL All-Star Game (1988 and 1991).

RECORDS: Shares NHL career record for most overtime goals—7.

Season Team	League	REGULAR SEASON					PLAYOFFS				
		Gms.	G	A	Pts.	PIM	Gms.	G	A	Pts.	PIM
82-83—Brynas	Sweden	36	22	14	36	36	—	—	—	—	—
83-84—Brynas	Sweden	...	20	10	30	...	—	—	—	—	—
—Swedish Olympic Team	Int'l	7	2	1	3	6	—	—	—	—	—
84-85—New York Rangers	NHL	74	29	29	58	51	3	0	2	2	0
85-86—New York Rangers	NHL	73	25	29	54	109	16	4	6	10	20
86-87—New York Rangers	NHL	64	40	34	74	60	6	1	2	3	20
87-88—New York Rangers	NHL	69	28	40	68	95	—	—	—	—	—
88-89—New York Rangers	NHL	79	32	56	88	148	4	3	2	5	12
89-90—New York Rangers	NHL	48	19	19	38	100	—	—	—	—	—
—Los Angeles	NHL	28	13	20	33	28	10	5	4	9	19
90-91—Los Angeles	NHL	68	45	44	89	106	10	4	4	8	14
91-92—Los Angeles	NHL	49	17	22	39	70	6	0	3	3	8
92-93—Los Angeles	NHL	39	25	27	52	57	24	8	17	25	12
93-94—Los Angeles	NHL	51	17	24	41	59	—	—	—	—	—
—Pittsburgh	NHL	27	6	11	17	24	6	0	0	0	4
NHL totals		669	296	355	651	907	85	25	40	65	109

SAPOZHNIKOV, ANDREI
D, BRUINS

PERSONAL: Born June 15, 1971, in Chelyabinsk, U.S.S.R. . . . 6-1/185. . . . Shoots left.

TRANSACTIONS/CAREER NOTES: Selected by Boston Bruins in fifth round (fifth Bruins pick, 129th overall) of NHL entry draft (June 26, 1993).

HONORS: Named to CIS All-Star team (1993-94).

Season Team	League	REGULAR SEASON					PLAYOFFS				
		Gms.	G	A	Pts.	PIM	Gms.	G	A	Pts.	PIM
90-91—Traktor Chelyabinsk	USSR	28	0	0	0	14	—	—	—	—	—
91-92—Traktor Chelyabinsk	CIS	43	3	4	7	22	—	—	—	—	—
92-93—Traktor Chelyabinsk	CIS	40	2	7	9	30	8	0	1	1	6
93-94—Traktor Chelyabinsk	CIS	40	4	8	12	34	6	0	0	0	0

SARJEANT, GEOFF
G, BLUES

PERSONAL: Born November 30, 1969, in Orillia, Ont. . . . 5-9/180. . . . Catches left. . . . Full name: Geoff Ian Sarjeant. . . . Name pronounced JAWF SAHR-jehnt.

HIGH SCHOOL: Newmarket (Ont.).

COLLEGE: Michigan Tech.

TRANSACTIONS/CAREER NOTES: Selected by St. Louis Blues in NHL supplemental draft (June 15, 1990).

HONORS: Named to IHL All-Star first team (1993-94).

Season Team	League	REGULAR SEASON							PLAYOFFS						
		Gms.	Min.	W	L	T	GA	SO	Avg.	Gms.	Min.	W	L	GA SO	Avg.
88-89—Michigan Tech	WCHA	6	329	0	3	2	22	0	4.01	—	—	—	—	— —	—
89-90—Michigan Tech	WCHA	19	1043	4	13	0	94	0	5.41	—	—	—	—	— —	—
90-91—Michigan Tech	WCHA	28	1540	6	16	3	97	1	3.78	—	—	—	—	— —	—
91-92—Michigan Tech	WCHA	23	1246	7	13	0	90	1	4.33	—	—	—	—	— —	—
92-93—Peoria	IHL	41	2356	22	14	‡3	130	0	3.31	3	179	0	3	13 0	4.36
93-94—Peoria	IHL	41	2275	25	9	‡2	93	†2	*2.45	4	211	2	2	13 0	3.70

SATAN, MIROSLAV
C

PERSONAL: Born October 22, 1974, in Topolcany, Czechoslovakia. . . . 6-1/176. . . . Shoots left. . . . Name pronounced shuh-TEEN.

TRANSACTIONS/CAREER NOTES: Selected by Edmonton Oilers in fifth round (sixth Oilers pick, 111th overall) of NHL entry draft (June 26, 1993). . . . Signed as free agent by Detroit Vipers (July 27, 1994).

Season Team	League	REGULAR SEASON					PLAYOFFS				
		Gms.	G	A	Pts.	PIM	Gms.	G	A	Pts.	PIM
91-92—VTJ Topolcany	Czech Dv.II	9	2	1	3	6	—	—	—	—	—
—VTJ Topolcany Jrs	Czech. Jrs.	31	30	22	52	...	—	—	—	—	—

Season Team	League	REGULAR SEASON					PLAYOFFS				
		Gms.	G	A	Pts.	Pen.	Gms.	G	A	Pts.	Pen.
92-93—Dukla Trencin	Czech.	38	11	6	17	...	—	—	—	—	—
93-94—Dukla Trencin	Slovakia	30	32	16	48	16	—	—	—	—	—
—Slovakian Olympic team...	Int'l	8	9	0	9	0	—	—	—	—	—

SAVAGE, BRIAN
C, CANADIENS

PERSONAL: Born February 24, 1971, in Sudbury, Ont.... 6-2/191.... Shoots left.
HIGH SCHOOL: Lo-Ellen Park Secondary (Sudbury, Ont.).
COLLEGE: Miami of Ohio.
TRANSACTIONS/CAREER NOTES: Selected by Montreal Canadiens in eighth round (11th Canadiens pick, 171st overall) of NHL entry draft (June 22, 1991).
HONORS: Named to NCAA All-America West second team (1992-93).... Named CCHA Player of the Year (1992-93).... Named to CCHA All-Star first team (1992-93).
MISCELLANEOUS: Member of silver-medal-winning Canadian Olympic team (1994).

Season Team	League	REGULAR SEASON					PLAYOFFS				
		Gms.	G	A	Pts.	PIM	Gms.	G	A	Pts.	PIM
90-91—Miami of Ohio	CCHA	28	5	6	11	26	—	—	—	—	—
91-92—Miami of Ohio	CCHA	40	24	16	40	43	—	—	—	—	—
92-93—Miami of Ohio	CCHA	38	37	21	58	44	—	—	—	—	—
—Canadian national team...	Int'l	9	3	0	3	12	—	—	—	—	—
93-94—Canadian national team...	Int'l	59	22	28	50	44	—	—	—	—	—
—Canadian Olympic Team..	Int'l	8	2	2	4	6	—	—	—	—	—
—Fredericton	AHL	17	12	15	27	4	—	—	—	—	—
—Montreal	NHL	3	1	0	1	0	3	0	2	2	0
NHL totals		3	1	0	1	0	3	0	2	2	0

SAVAGE, REGGIE
RW, NORDIQUES

PERSONAL: Born May 1, 1970, in Montreal.... 5-10/192.... Shoots left.... Full name: Reginald David Savage.
TRANSACTIONS/CAREER NOTES: Selected by Washington Capitals in first round (first Capitals pick, 15th overall) of NHL entry draft (June 11, 1988).... Suspended six games by QMJHL for stick-swinging incident (February 19, 1989).... Traded by Capitals with RW Paul MacDermid to Quebec Nordiques for LW Mike Hough (June 20, 1993).... Suffered charley horse (October 20, 1993); missed one game.... Broke left wrist (February 14, 1994); missed remainder of season.

Season Team	League	REGULAR SEASON					PLAYOFFS				
		Gms.	G	A	Pts.	PIM	Gms.	G	A	Pts.	PIM
87-88—Victoriaville	QMJHL	68	68	54	122	77	5	2	3	5	8
88-89—Victoriaville	QMJHL	54	58	55	113	178	16	15	13	28	52
89-90—Victoriaville	QMJHL	63	51	43	94	79	16	13	10	23	40
90-91—Baltimore	AHL	62	32	29	61	10	6	1	1	2	6
—Washington	NHL	1	0	0	0	0	—	—	—	—	—
91-92—Baltimore	AHL	77	42	28	70	51	—	—	—	—	—
92-93—Baltimore	AHL	40	37	18	55	28	—	—	—	—	—
—Washington	NHL	16	2	3	5	12	—	—	—	—	—
93-94—Quebec	NHL	17	3	4	7	16	—	—	—	—	—
—Cornwall	AHL	33	21	13	34	56	—	—	—	—	—
NHL totals		34	5	7	12	28	—	—	—	—	—

SAVARD, DENIS
C, LIGHTNING

PERSONAL: Born February 4, 1961, in Pointe Gatineau, Que.... 5-10/175.... Shoots right. ... Full name: Denis Joseph Savard.... Name pronounced suh-VAHRD.
TRANSACTIONS/CAREER NOTES: Selected by Chicago Blackhawks as underage junior in first round (first Blackhawks pick, third overall) of NHL entry draft (June 11, 1980).... Strained knee (October 15, 1980).... Broke nose (January 7, 1984).... Injured ankle (October 13, 1984).... Bruised ribs (March 22, 1987).... Broke right ankle (January 21, 1989); missed 19 games.... Sprained left ankle (January 17, 1990).... Broke left index finger (January 26, 1990); missed 17 games.... Traded by Blackhawks to Montreal Canadiens for D Chris Chelios and second-round pick (C Michael Pomichter) in 1991 draft (June 29, 1990).... Suffered sinus infection (January 17, 1991); missed five games.... Injured right thumb (March 16, 1991).... Injured eye (October 30, 1991); missed two games. ... Suffered from the flu (November 22, 1992); missed two games.... Sprained knee (January 2, 1993); missed four games. ... Suspended one game by NHL for game misconduct penalties (January 23, 1993).... Separated shoulder (February 17, 1993); missed 10 games.... Signed as free agent by Tampa Bay Lightning (July 29, 1993).... Suspended four games and fined $500 by NHL for slashing (November 22, 1993).
HONORS: Won Michel Briere Trophy (1979-80).... Named to QMJHL All-Star first team (1979-80).... Named to THE SPORTING NEWS All-Star second team (1982-83).... Named to NHL All-Star second team (1982-83).... Played in NHL All-Star Game (1982-1984, 1986, 1988 and 1991).
RECORDS: Shares NHL record for fastest goal from start of a period—4 seconds (January 12, 1986).
MISCELLANEOUS: Member of Stanley Cup championship team (1993).

Season Team	League	REGULAR SEASON					PLAYOFFS				
		Gms.	G	A	Pts.	PIM	Gms.	G	A	Pts.	PIM
77-78—Montreal	QMJHL	72	37	79	116	22	—	—	—	—	—
78-79—Montreal	QMJHL	70	46	*112	158	88	11	5	6	11	46
79-80—Montreal	QMJHL	72	63	118	181	93	10	7	16	23	8
80-81—Chicago	NHL	76	28	47	75	47	3	0	0	0	0
81-82—Chicago	NHL	80	32	87	119	82	15	11	7	18	52

Season Team	League	REGULAR SEASON					PLAYOFFS				
		Gms.	G	A	Pts.	Pen.	Gms.	G	A	Pts.	Pen.
82-83—Chicago	NHL	78	35	86	121	99	13	8	9	17	22
83-84—Chicago	NHL	75	37	57	94	71	5	1	3	4	9
84-85—Chicago	NHL	79	38	67	105	56	15	9	20	29	20
85-86—Chicago	NHL	80	47	69	116	111	3	4	1	5	6
86-87—Chicago	NHL	70	40	50	90	108	4	1	0	1	12
87-88—Chicago	NHL	80	44	87	131	95	5	4	3	7	17
88-89—Chicago	NHL	58	23	59	82	110	16	8	11	19	10
89-90—Chicago	NHL	60	27	53	80	56	20	7	15	22	41
90-91—Montreal	NHL	70	28	31	59	52	13	2	11	13	35
91-92—Montreal	NHL	77	28	42	70	73	11	3	9	12	8
92-93—Montreal	NHL	63	16	34	50	90	14	0	5	5	4
93-94—Tampa Bay	NHL	74	18	28	46	106	—	—	—	—	—
NHL totals		1020	441	797	1238	1156	137	58	94	152	236

SAVENKO, BOGDAN
RW, BLACKHAWKS

PERSONAL: Born November 20, 1974, in Kiev, U.S.S.R. . . . 6-1/192. . . . Shoots right. . . . Name pronounced BAHG-dahn sah-VEHN-koh.
HIGH SCHOOL: Niagara Falls (Ont.).
TRANSACTIONS/CAREER NOTES: Selected by Chicago Blackhawks in third round (third Blackhawks pick, 54th overall) of NHL entry draft (June 26, 1993).

Season Team	League	REGULAR SEASON					PLAYOFFS				
		Gms.	G	A	Pts.	PIM	Gms.	G	A	Pts.	PIM
90-91—SVSM Kiev	USSR Div. II	40	30	18	48	24	—	—	—	—	—
91-92—Sokol Kiev	CIS	25	3	1	4	4	—	—	—	—	—
92-93—Niagara Falls	OHL	51	29	19	48	15	2	1	0	1	2
93-94—Niagara Falls	OHL	62	42	49	91	22	—	—	—	—	—

SAVOIE, CLAUDE
RW, SENATORS

PERSONAL: Born March 12, 1973, in Montreal. . . . 5-11/200. . . . Shoots right.
TRANSACTIONS/CAREER NOTES: Selected by Ottawa Senators in ninth round (ninth Senators pick, 194th overall) of NHL entry draft (June 20, 1992).

Season Team	League	REGULAR SEASON					PLAYOFFS				
		Gms.	G	A	Pts.	PIM	Gms.	G	A	Pts.	PIM
91-92—Victoriaville	QMJHL	69	39	40	79	140	—	—	—	—	—
92-93—Victoriaville	QMJHL	67	70	61	131	113	6	4	5	9	6
—New Haven	AHL	2	1	1	2	2	—	—	—	—	—
93-94—Prince Edward Island	AHL	77	13	15	28	118	—	—	—	—	—

SCATCHARD, DAVE
C, CANUCKS

PERSONAL: Born February 20, 1976, in Hinton, Alta. . . . 6-2/185. . . . Shoots right.
TRANSACTIONS/CAREER NOTES: Selected by Vancouver Canucks in second round (third Canucks pick, 42nd overall) of NHL entry draft (June 28, 1994).

Season Team	League	REGULAR SEASON					PLAYOFFS				
		Gms.	G	A	Pts.	PIM	Gms.	G	A	Pts.	PIM
92-93—Kimberley	Tier II Jr.A	51	20	23	43	61	—	—	—	—	—
93-94—Portland	WHL	47	9	11	20	46	10	2	1	3	4

SCHLEGEL, BRAD
D, FLAMES

PERSONAL: Born July 22, 1968, in Kitchener, Ont. . . . 5-10/190. . . . Shoots right. . . . Full name: Bradley Wilfred Schlegel. . . . Name pronounced SHLAY-guhl.
TRANSACTIONS/CAREER NOTES: Selected by Washington Capitals in seventh round (eighth Capitals pick, 144th overall) of NHL entry draft (June 17, 1989). . . . Traded by Capitals to Calgary Flames for seventh-round (LW Andrew Brunette) pick in 1993 draft (June 26, 1993). . . . Loaned to Canadian Olympic Team (January 31, 1994); missed 16 games. . . . Pulled groin (October 5, 1993); missed 16 games.
HONORS: Named to OHL All-Star second team (1987-88).
MISCELLANEOUS: Member of silver-medal-winning Canadian Olympic teams (1992 and 1994).

Season Team	League	REGULAR SEASON					PLAYOFFS				
		Gms.	G	A	Pts.	PIM	Gms.	G	A	Pts.	PIM
86-87—London	OHL	65	4	23	27	24	—	—	—	—	—
87-88—London	OHL	66	13	63	76	49	12	8	17	25	6
88-89—Canadian national team	Int'l	60	2	22	24	30	—	—	—	—	—
89-90—Canadian national team	Int'l	61	7	25	32	38	—	—	—	—	—
90-91—Canadian national team	Int'l	53	8	18	26	62	—	—	—	—	—
91-92—Canadian national team	Int'l	61	3	18	21	84	—	—	—	—	—
—Canadian Olympic Team	Int'l	8	1	2	3	4	—	—	—	—	—
—Baltimore	AHL	2	0	1	1	0	—	—	—	—	—
—Washington	NHL	15	0	1	1	0	7	0	1	1	2
92-93—Baltimore	AHL	61	3	20	23	40	7	0	5	5	6
—Washington	NHL	7	0	1	1	6	—	—	—	—	—
93-94—Calgary	NHL	26	1	6	7	4	—	—	—	—	—
—Saint John	AHL	21	2	8	10	6	7	0	1	1	6
—Canadian national team	Int'l	12	0	0	0	8	—	—	—	—	—
—Canadian Olympic Team	Int'l	8	0	0	0	6	—	—	—	—	—
NHL totals		48	1	8	9	10	7	0	1	1	2

S

SCHMIDT, CHRIS
LW, KINGS

PERSONAL: Born March 1, 1976, in Beaverlodge, Alta.... 6-3/193.... Shoots left.
HIGH SCHOOL: Meadowdale (Lynwood, Wash.).
TRANSACTIONS/CAREER NOTES: Selected by Los Angeles Kings in fifth round (fourth Kings pick, 111th overall) of NHL entry draft (June 29, 1994).

Season	Team	League	REGULAR SEASON Gms.	G	A	Pts.	PIM	PLAYOFFS Gms.	G	A	Pts.	PIM
92-93	Seattle	WHL	61	6	7	13	17	5	0	1	1	0
93-94	Seattle	WHL	68	7	17	24	26	9	3	1	4	2

SCHNEIDER, ANDY
LW, SENATORS

PERSONAL: Born March 29, 1972, in Edmonton.... 5-9/170.... Shoots left.
TRANSACTIONS/CAREER NOTES: Signed as free agent by Ottawa Senators (October 9, 1992).

Season	Team	League	REGULAR SEASON Gms.	G	A	Pts.	PIM	PLAYOFFS Gms.	G	A	Pts.	PIM
91-92	Swift Current	WHL	63	44	60	104	120	8	4	9	13	8
92-93	Swift Current	WHL	38	19	66	85	78	17	13	26	39	40
93-94	Prince Edward Island	AHL	61	15	46	61	119	—	—	—	—	—
	Ottawa	NHL	10	0	0	0	15	—	—	—	—	—
NHL totals			**10**	**0**	**0**	**0**	**15**					

SCHNEIDER, MATHIEU
D, CANADIENS

PERSONAL: Born June 12, 1969, in New York.... 5-11/189.... Shoots left.
HIGH SCHOOL: Mount St. Charles Academy (Woonsocket, R.I.).
TRANSACTIONS/CAREER NOTES: Selected by Montreal Canadiens in third round (fourth Canadiens pick, 44th overall) of NHL entry draft (June 13, 1987)....
Bruised left shoulder (February 1990).... Sprained left ankle (January 26, 1991); missed nine games.... Sprained ankle (January 27, 1993); missed 24 games.... Separated shoulder (April 18, 1993); missed seven playoff games.... Injured ankle (December 6, 1993); missed two games.... Underwent arthroscopic elbow surgery (March 29, 1994); missed five games.
HONORS: Named to OHL All-Star first team (1987-88 and 1988-89).
MISCELLANEOUS: Member of Stanley Cup championship team (1993).

Season	Team	League	REGULAR SEASON Gms.	G	A	Pts.	PIM	PLAYOFFS Gms.	G	A	Pts.	PIM
85-86	Mount St. Charles H.S.	R.I.H.S.	19	3	27	30	...	—	—	—	—	—
86-87	Cornwall	OHL	63	7	29	36	75	5	0	0	0	22
87-88	Montreal	NHL	4	0	0	0	2	—	—	—	—	—
	Cornwall	OHL	48	21	40	61	85	11	2	6	8	14
	Sherbrooke	AHL	—	—	—	—	—	3	0	3	3	12
88-89	Cornwall	OHL	59	16	57	73	96	18	7	20	27	30
89-90	Sherbrooke	AHL	28	6	13	19	20	—	—	—	—	—
	Montreal	NHL	44	7	14	21	25	9	1	3	4	31
90-91	Montreal	NHL	69	10	20	30	63	13	2	7	9	18
91-92	Montreal	NHL	78	8	24	32	72	10	1	4	5	6
92-93	Montreal	NHL	60	13	31	44	91	11	1	2	3	16
93-94	Montreal	NHL	75	20	32	52	62	1	0	0	0	0
NHL totals			**330**	**58**	**121**	**179**	**315**	**44**	**5**	**16**	**21**	**71**

SCHULTE, PAXTON
LW, NORDIQUES

PERSONAL: Born July 16, 1972, in Edmonton.... 6-2/217.... Shoots left.... Name pronounced SHUHL-tee.
COLLEGE: North Dakota, then Spokane (Wash.) Falls.
TRANSACTIONS/CAREER NOTES: Selected by Quebec Nordiques in sixth round (seventh Nordiques pick, 124th overall) of NHL entry draft (June 20, 1992).

Season	Team	League	REGULAR SEASON Gms.	G	A	Pts.	PIM	PLAYOFFS Gms.	G	A	Pts.	PIM
89-90	Sherwood Park	AJHL	56	28	38	66	151	—	—	—	—	—
90-91	North Dakota	WCHA	38	2	4	6	32	—	—	—	—	—
91-92	Spokane	WHL	70	42	42	84	222	10	2	8	10	48
92-93	Spokane	WHL	45	38	35	73	142	10	5	6	11	12
93-94	Cornwall	AHL	56	15	15	30	102	—	—	—	—	—
	Quebec	NHL	1	0	0	0	2	—	—	—	—	—
NHL totals			**1**	**0**	**0**	**0**	**2**					

SCHWAB, COREY
G, DEVILS

PERSONAL: Born November 4, 1970, in Battleford, Sask.... 6-0/180.... Catches left.... Name pronounced SHWAHB.
TRANSACTIONS/CAREER NOTES: Selected by New Jersey Devils in 10th round (12th Devils pick, 200th overall) of NHL entry draft (June 16, 1990).

Season	Team	League	REGULAR SEASON Gms.	Min.	W	L	T	GA	SO	Avg.	PLAYOFFS Gms.	Min.	W	L	GA	SO	Avg.
88-89	Seattle	WHL	10	386	2	2	0	31	0	4.82	—						
89-90	Seattle	WHL	27	1150	15	2	1	69	0	3.60	3	49	0	0	2	0	2.45
90-91	Seattle	WHL	58	3289	32	18	3	224	1	4.09	6	382	1	5	25	0	3.93
91-92	Utica	AHL	24	1322	9	12	1	95	1	4.31	—						
	Cincinnati	AHL	8	450	6	0	1	31	0	4.13	9	540	6	3	29	0	3.22

			REGULAR SEASON								PLAYOFFS						
Season	Team	League	Gms.	Min.	W	L	T	GA	SO	Avg.	Gms.	Min.	W	L	GA	SO	Avg.
92-93—Utica		AHL	40	2387	18	16	5	169	2	4.25	1	59	0	1	6	0	6.10
—Cincinnati		IHL	3	185	1	2	0	17	0	5.51	—	—	—	—	—	—	—
93-94—Albany		AHL	51	3059	27	21	3	184	0	3.61	5	298	1	4	20	0	4.02

SCISSONS, SCOTT
C, ISLANDERS

PERSONAL: Born October 29, 1971, in Saskatoon, Sask. . . . 6-1/201. . . . Shoots left. . . . Name pronounced SIH-shuhns.

TRANSACTIONS/CAREER NOTES: Selected by New York Islanders in first round (first Islanders pick, sixth overall) of NHL entry draft (June 16, 1990). . . . Injured right arm in preseason game (October 29, 1990); missed 11 games.

			REGULAR SEASON					PLAYOFFS				
Season	Team	League	Gms.	G	A	Pts.	PIM	Gms.	G	A	Pts.	PIM
88-89—Saskatoon		WHL	71	30	56	86	65	7	0	4	4	16
89-90—Saskatoon		WHL	61	40	47	87	81	10	3	8	11	6
90-91—Saskatoon		WHL	57	24	53	77	61	—	—	—	—	—
—New York Islanders		NHL	1	0	0	0	0	—	—	—	—	—
91-92—Canadian national team		Int'l	27	4	8	12	23	—	—	—	—	—
92-93—Capital District		AHL	43	14	30	44	33	4	0	0	0	0
—New York Islanders		NHL	—	—	—	—	—	1	0	0	0	0
93-94—New York Islanders		NHL	1	0	0	0	0	—	—	—	—	—
—Salt Lake City		IHL	72	10	26	36	123	—	—	—	—	—
NHL totals			2	0	0	0	0	1	0	0	0	0

SELANNE, TEEMU
RW, JETS

PERSONAL: Born July 3, 1970, in Helsinki, Finland. . . . 6-0/181. . . . Shoots right. . . . Name pronounced TAY-moo suh-LAH-nay.

TRANSACTIONS/CAREER NOTES: Selected by Winnipeg Jets in first round (first Jets pick, 10th overall) of NHL entry draft (June 11, 1988). . . . Broke left leg (October 19, 1989). . . . Severed Achilles tendon (January 26, 1994); missed 33 games.

HONORS: Named to Finnish League All-Star team (1990-91 and 1991-92). . . . Named NHL Rookie of the Year by THE SPORTING NEWS (1992-93). . . . Won Calder Memorial Trophy (1992-93). . . . Named to THE SPORTING NEWS All-Star first team (1992-93). . . . Named to NHL All-Star first team (1992-93). . . . Named to NHL All-Rookie team (1992-93). . . . Played in NHL All-Star Game (1993 and 1994).

RECORDS: Holds NHL rookie-season record for most points—132 (1992); goals—76 (1992).

			REGULAR SEASON					PLAYOFFS				
Season	Team	League	Gms.	G	A	Pts.	PIM	Gms.	G	A	Pts.	PIM
87-88—Jokerit		Finland	33	42	23	65	18	5	4	3	7	2
88-89—Jokerit		Finland	34	35	33	68	12	5	7	3	10	4
89-90—Jokerit		Finland	11	4	8	12	0	—	—	—	—	—
90-91—Jokerit		Finland	42	*33	25	58	12	—	—	—	—	—
91-92—Finland Olympic Team		Int'l	8	7	4	11	. . .	—	—	—	—	—
—Jokerit		Finland	44	39	23	62	20	—	—	—	—	—
92-93—Winnipeg		NHL	84	†76	56	132	45	6	4	2	6	2
93-94—Winnipeg		NHL	51	25	29	54	22	—	—	—	—	—
NHL totals			135	101	85	186	67	6	4	2	6	2

SELIVANOV, ALEXANDER
RW, FLYERS

PERSONAL: Born March 23, 1971, in Moscow, U.S.S.R. . . . 6-1/187. . . . Shoots left.

TRANSACTIONS/CAREER NOTES: Selected by Philadelphia Flyers in sixth round (sixth Flyers pick, 140th overall) of NHL entry draft (June 29, 1994).

			REGULAR SEASON					PLAYOFFS				
Season	Team	League	Gms.	G	A	Pts.	PIM	Gms.	G	A	Pts.	PIM
88-89—Spartak Moscow		USSR	1	0	0	0	0	—	—	—	—	—
89-90—Spartak Moscow		USSR	4	0	0	0	0	—	—	—	—	—
90-91—Spartak Moscow		USSR	21	3	1	4	6	—	—	—	—	—
91-92—Spartak Moscow		CIS	31	6	7	13	16	—	—	—	—	—
92-93—Spartak Moscow		CIS	42	12	19	31	16	3	2	0	2	2
93-94—Spartak Moscow		CIS	45	30	11	41	50	6	5	1	6	2

SEMAK, ALEXANDER
C, DEVILS

PERSONAL: Born February 11, 1966, in Ufa, U.S.S.R. . . . 5-10/185. . . . Shoots left. . . . Name pronounced SEE-mahk.

TRANSACTIONS/CAREER NOTES: Selected by New Jersey Devils in 10th round (12th Devils pick, 207th overall) of NHL entry draft (June 11, 1988). . . . Injured shoulder (February 8, 1992); missed seven games. . . . Suffered injury (November 30, 1993); missed two games. . . . Strained knee (December 11, 1993); missed 17 games.

			REGULAR SEASON					PLAYOFFS				
Season	Team	League	Gms.	G	A	Pts.	PIM	Gms.	G	A	Pts.	PIM
87-88—Dynamo Moscow		USSR	47	21	14	35	40	—	—	—	—	—
88-89—Dynamo Moscow		USSR	44	18	10	28	22	—	—	—	—	—
89-90—Dynamo Moscow		USSR	43	23	11	34	33	—	—	—	—	—

S

Season	Team	League	REGULAR SEASON					PLAYOFFS				
			Gms.	G	A	Pts.	Pen.	Gms.	G	A	Pts.	Pen.
90-91—Dynamo Moscow		USSR	46	17	21	38	48	—	—	—	—	—
91-92—Dynamo Moscow		CIS	18	6	11	17	18	—	—	—	—	—
—Utica		AHL	7	3	2	5	0	—	—	—	—	—
—New Jersey		NHL	25	5	6	11	0	1	0	0	0	0
92-93—New Jersey		NHL	82	37	42	79	70	5	1	1	2	0
93-94—New Jersey		NHL	54	12	17	29	22	2	0	0	0	0
NHL totals			161	54	65	119	92	8	1	1	2	0

SEMENOV, ANATOLI
C/LW, MIGHTY DUCKS

PERSONAL: Born March 5, 1962, in Moscow, U.S.S.R. . . . 6-2/190. . . . Shoots left. . . . Name pronounced AN-uh-TOH-lee SEH-muh-nahf.

TRANSACTIONS/CAREER NOTES: Selected by Edmonton Oilers in sixth round (fifth Oilers pick, 120th overall) of NHL entry draft (June 17, 1989). . . . Bruised ribs (March 1, 1991); missed five games. . . . Suffered hairline fracture in left foot (October 1991); missed four games. . . . Suffered concussion (November 1991); missed two games. . . . Injured shoulder (January 4, 1992); missed six games. . . . Sprained ankle (February 28, 1992); missed one game. . . . Selected by Tampa Bay Lightning in NHL expansion draft (June 18, 1992). . . . Traded by Lightning to Vancouver Canucks for C Dave Capuano and fourth-round pick (traded to New Jersey Devils) in 1994 draft (November 3, 1992). . . . Strained knee (January 9, 1993); missed six games. . . . Selected by Mighty Ducks of Anaheim in NHL expansion draft (June 24, 1993). . . . Dislocated elbow (December 7, 1993); missed 21 games. . . . Aggravated elbow injury (January 28, 1994); missed two games.

HONORS: Named to Soviet League All-Star team (1984-85).

MISCELLANEOUS: Member of gold-medal-winning U.S.S.R. Olympic team (1988).

Season	Team	League	REGULAR SEASON					PLAYOFFS				
			Gms.	G	A	Pts.	PIM	Gms.	G	A	Pts.	PIM
79-80—Dynamo Moscow		USSR	8	3	0	3	2	—	—	—	—	—
80-81—Dynamo Moscow		USSR	47	18	14	32	18	—	—	—	—	—
81-82—Dynamo Moscow		USSR	44	12	14	26	28	—	—	—	—	—
82-83—Dynamo Moscow		USSR	44	22	18	40	26	—	—	—	—	—
83-84—Dynamo Moscow		USSR	19	10	5	15	14	—	—	—	—	—
84-85—Dynamo Moscow		USSR	30	17	12	29	32	—	—	—	—	—
85-86—Dynamo Moscow		USSR	32	18	17	35	19	—	—	—	—	—
86-87—Dynamo Moscow		USSR	40	15	29	44	32	—	—	—	—	—
87-88—Dynamo Moscow		USSR	32	17	8	25	22	—	—	—	—	—
88-89—Dynamo Moscow		USSR	31	9	12	21	24	—	—	—	—	—
89-90—Dynamo Moscow		USSR	48	13	20	33	16	—	—	—	—	—
—Edmonton		NHL	—	—	—	—	—	2	0	0	0	0
90-91—Edmonton		NHL	57	15	16	31	26	12	5	5	10	6
91-92—Edmonton		NHL	59	20	22	42	16	8	1	1	2	6
92-93—Tampa Bay		NHL	13	2	3	5	4	—	—	—	—	—
—Vancouver		NHL	62	10	34	44	28	12	1	3	4	0
93-94—Anaheim		NHL	49	11	19	30	12	—	—	—	—	—
NHL totals			240	58	94	152	86	34	7	9	16	12

SEVERYN, BRENT
D, PANTHERS

PERSONAL: Born February 22, 1966, in Vegreville, Alta. . . . 6-2/210. . . . Shoots left. . . . Full name: Brent Leonard Severyn.

COLLEGE: Alberta.

TRANSACTIONS/CAREER NOTES: Selected by Winnipeg Jets in fifth round (fifth Jets pick, 99th overall) of NHL entry draft (June 9, 1984). . . . Injured knee (October 1985). . . . Signed as free agent by Quebec Nordiques (July 15, 1988). . . . Traded by Nordiques to New Jersey Devils for D Dave Marcinyshyn (June 3, 1991). . . . Traded by Devils to Jets for conditional pick in 1994 draft (September 30, 1993). . . . Traded by Jets to Florida Panthers for D Milan Tichy (October 3, 1993). . . . Suffered left eye abrasion (November 23, 1993); missed one game.

HONORS: Named to CWUAA All-Star team (1987-88). . . . Named to AHL All-Star first team (1992-93).

Season	Team	League	REGULAR SEASON					PLAYOFFS				
			Gms.	G	A	Pts.	PIM	Gms.	G	A	Pts.	PIM
82-83—Vegreville		CAJHL	21	20	22	42	10	—	—	—	—	—
83-84—Seattle		WHL	72	14	22	36	49	5	2	1	3	2
84-85—Seattle		WHL	38	8	32	40	54	—	—	—	—	—
—Brandon		WHL	26	7	16	23	57	—	—	—	—	—
85-86—Seattle		WHL	33	11	20	31	164	5	0	4	4	4
—Saskatoon		WHL	9	1	4	5	38	—	—	—	—	—
86-87—University of Alberta		CWUAA	43	7	19	26	171	—	—	—	—	—
87-88—University of Alberta		CWUAA	46	21	29	50	178	—	—	—	—	—
88-89—Halifax		AHL	47	2	12	14	141	—	—	—	—	—
89-90—Quebec		NHL	35	0	2	2	42	—	—	—	—	—
—Halifax		AHL	43	6	9	15	105	6	1	2	3	49
90-91—Halifax		AHL	50	7	26	33	202	—	—	—	—	—
91-92—Utica		AHL	80	11	33	44	211	4	0	1	1	4
92-93—Utica		AHL	77	20	32	52	240	5	0	0	0	35
93-94—Florida		NHL	67	4	7	11	156	—	—	—	—	—
NHL totals			102	4	9	13	198					

SEVIGNY, PIERRE
LW, CANADIENS

PERSONAL: Born September 8, 1971, in Trois-Rivieres, Que. . . . 6-0/189. . . . Shoots left. . . . Name pronounced SEH-vihn-yee.
TRANSACTIONS/CAREER NOTES: Selected by Montreal Canadiens in third round (fourth Canadiens pick, 51st overall) of NHL entry draft (June 17, 1989). . . . Severed knee ligament in off-ice accident (March 25, 1991). . . . Tore knee ligaments (December 6, 1993); missed 23 games.
HONORS: Named to QMJHL All-Star first team (1980-81). . . . Named to QMJHL All-Star second team (1989-90 and 1990-91).

			REGULAR SEASON					PLAYOFFS			
Season Team	League	Gms.	G	A	Pts.	PIM	Gms.	G	A	Pts.	PIM
88-89—Verdun	QMJHL	67	27	43	70	88	—	—	—	—	—
89-90—St. Hyacinthe	QMJHL	67	47	72	119	205	12	8	8	16	42
90-91—St. Hyacinthe	QMJHL	60	36	46	82	203	—	—	—	—	—
91-92—Fredericton	AHL	74	22	37	59	145	7	1	1	2	26
92-93—Fredericton	AHL	80	36	40	76	113	5	1	1	2	2
93-94—Montreal	NHL	43	4	5	9	42	3	0	1	1	0
NHL totals		43	4	5	9	42	3	0	1	1	0

SHANAHAN, BRENDAN
RW/LW, BLUES

PERSONAL: Born January 23, 1969, in Mimico, Ont. . . . 6-3/215. . . . Shoots right. . . . Full name: Brendan Frederick Shanahan.
HIGH SCHOOL: Michael Power/St. Joseph's (Islington, Ont.).
TRANSACTIONS/CAREER NOTES: Bruised tendons in shoulder (January 1987). . . . Selected by New Jersey Devils as underage junior in first round (first Devils pick, second overall) of NHL entry draft (June 13, 1987). . . . Broke nose (December 1987). . . . Suffered back spasms (March 1989). . . . Suspended five games by NHL for stick-fighting (January 13, 1990). . . . Strained lower abdomen (February 1990). . . . Suffered lacerations to lower right side of face and underwent surgery (January 8, 1991); missed five games. . . . Signed as free agent by St. Louis Blues (July 25, 1991); D Scott Stevens awarded to Devils as compensation (September 3, 1991). . . . Pulled groin (October 24, 1992); missed 12 games. . . . Suspended six off-days and fined $500 by NHL for hitting another player in face with his stick (January 7, 1993). . . . Suspended one game by NHL for high-sticking incident (February 23, 1993). . . . Suffered viral infection (November 18, 1993); missed one game. . . . Injured hamstring (March 22, 1994); missed two games.
HONORS: Played in NHL All-Star Game (1994). . . . Named to NHL All-Star first team (1993-94).

			REGULAR SEASON					PLAYOFFS			
Season Team	League	Gms.	G	A	Pts.	PIM	Gms.	G	A	Pts.	PIM
84-85—Mississauga	MTHL	36	20	21	41	26	—	—	—	—	—
85-86—London	OHL	59	28	34	62	70	5	5	5	10	5
86-87—London	OHL	56	39	53	92	128	—	—	—	—	—
87-88—New Jersey	NHL	65	7	19	26	131	12	2	1	3	44
88-89—New Jersey	NHL	68	22	28	50	115	—	—	—	—	—
89-90—New Jersey	NHL	73	30	42	72	137	6	3	3	6	20
90-91—New Jersey	NHL	75	29	37	66	141	7	3	5	8	12
91-92—St. Louis	NHL	80	33	36	69	171	6	2	3	5	14
92-93—St. Louis	NHL	71	51	43	94	174	11	4	3	7	18
93-94—St. Louis	NHL	81	52	50	102	211	4	2	5	7	4
NHL totals		513	224	255	479	1080	46	16	20	36	112

SHANNON, DARRIN
LW, JETS

PERSONAL: Born December 8, 1969, in Barrie, Ont. . . . 6-2/200. . . . Shoots left. . . . Brother of Darryl Shannon, defenseman, Winnipeg Jets.
TRANSACTIONS/CAREER NOTES: Separated right shoulder (November 1986). . . . Dislocated left elbow (November 1987). . . . Separated left shoulder (January 1988). . . . Selected by Pittsburgh Penguins in first round (first Penguins pick, fourth overall) of NHL entry draft (June 11, 1988). . . . Traded by Penguins with D Doug Bodger to Buffalo Sabres for G Tom Barrasso and third-round pick (LW Joe Dziedzic) in 1990 draft (November 12, 1988). . . . Strained knee ligaments (May 1990). . . . Injured jaw (January 8, 1991); missed five games. . . . Traded by Sabres with LW Mike Hartman and D Dean Kennedy to Winnipeg Jets for RW Dave McLlwain, D Gordon Donnelly, fifth-round pick in 1992 draft (LW Yuri Khmylev) and future considerations (October 11, 1991). . . . Injured knee (November 20, 1991). . . . Injured eye (November 25, 1991); missed one game. . . . Sprained leg (December 31, 1991); missed seven games. . . . Strained calf (October 12, 1993); missed five games.
HONORS: Named to OHL All-Scholastic team (1986-87). . . . Won Bobby Smith Trophy (1987-88). . . . Named to Memorial Cup All-Star team (1987-88).

			REGULAR SEASON					PLAYOFFS			
Season Team	League	Gms.	G	A	Pts.	PIM	Gms.	G	A	Pts.	PIM
85-86—Barrie Jr. B	OHA	40	13	22	35	21	—	—	—	—	—
86-87—Windsor	OHL	60	16	67	83	116	14	4	6	10	8
87-88—Windsor	OHL	43	33	41	74	49	12	6	12	18	9
88-89—Windsor	OHL	54	33	48	81	47	4	1	6	7	2
—Buffalo	NHL	3	0	0	0	0	2	0	0	0	0
89-90—Buffalo	NHL	17	2	7	9	4	6	0	1	1	4
—Rochester	AHL	50	20	23	43	25	9	4	1	5	2
90-91—Rochester	AHL	49	26	34	60	56	10	3	5	8	22
—Buffalo	NHL	34	8	6	14	12	6	1	2	3	4
91-92—Buffalo	NHL	1	0	1	1	0	—	—	—	—	—
—Winnipeg	NHL	68	13	26	39	41	7	0	1	1	10
92-93—Winnipeg	NHL	84	20	40	60	91	6	2	4	6	6
93-94—Winnipeg	NHL	77	21	37	58	87	—	—	—	—	—
NHL totals		284	64	117	181	235	27	3	8	11	24

SHANNON, DARRYL
D, JETS

PERSONAL: Born June 21, 1968, in Barrie, Ont. . . . 6-2/195. . . . Shoots left. . . . Brother of Darrin Shannon, left winger, Winnipeg Jets.
TRANSACTIONS/CAREER NOTES: Selected by Toronto Maple Leafs in second round (second Maple Leafs pick, 36th overall) of NHL entry draft (June 21, 1986). . . . Broke right leg and right thumb, bruised chest and suffered slipped disk in automobile accident (June 20, 1990). . . . Signed as free agent with Winnipeg Jets (July 8, 1993).
HONORS: Named to OHL All-Star second team (1986-87). . . . Won Max Kaminsky Trophy (1987-88). . . . Named to OHL All-Star first team (1987-88). . . . Named to Memorial Cup All-Star team (1987-88).

			REGULAR SEASON					PLAYOFFS			
Season Team	League	Gms.	G	A	Pts.	PIM	Gms.	G	A	Pts.	PIM
84-85—Barrie Junior B	OHA	39	5	23	28	50	—	—	—	—	—
85-86—Windsor	OHL	57	6	21	27	52	16	5	6	11	22
86-87—Windsor	OHL	64	23	27	50	83	14	4	8	12	18
87-88—Windsor	OHL	60	16	70	86	116	12	3	8	11	17
88-89—Toronto	NHL	14	1	3	4	6	—	—	—	—	—
—Newmarket	AHL	61	5	24	29	37	5	0	3	3	10
89-90—Newmarket	AHL	47	4	15	19	58	—	—	—	—	—
—Toronto	NHL	10	0	1	1	12	—	—	—	—	—
90-91—Toronto	NHL	10	0	1	1	0	—	—	—	—	—
—Newmarket	AHL	47	2	14	16	51	—	—	—	—	—
91-92—Toronto	NHL	48	2	8	10	23	—	—	—	—	—
92-93—Toronto	NHL	16	0	0	0	11	—	—	—	—	—
—St. John's	AHL	7	1	1	2	4	—	—	—	—	—
93-94—Moncton	AHL	37	1	10	11	62	20	1	7	8	32
—Winnipeg	NHL	20	0	4	4	18	—	—	—	—	—
NHL totals		118	3	17	20	70					

SHANTZ, JEFF
C, BLACKHAWKS

PERSONAL: Born October 10, 1973, in Edmonton. . . . 6-0/185. . . . Shoots right.
HIGH SCHOOL: Robert Usher (Regina, Sask.).
TRANSACTIONS/CAREER NOTES: Selected by Chicago Blackhawks in second round (second Blackhawks pick, 36th overall) of NHL entry draft (June 20, 1992). . . . Bruised right shoulder (1993-94 season); missed six games.
HONORS: Named to WHL (East) All-Star first team (1992-93).

			REGULAR SEASON					PLAYOFFS			
Season Team	League	Gms.	G	A	Pts.	PIM	Gms.	G	A	Pts.	PIM
89-90—Regina	WHL	1	0	0	0	0	—	—	—	—	—
90-91—Regina	WHL	69	16	21	37	22	8	2	2	4	2
91-92—Regina	WHL	72	39	50	89	75	—	—	—	—	—
92-93—Regina	WHL	64	29	54	83	75	13	2	12	14	14
93-94—Chicago	NHL	52	3	13	16	30	6	0	0	0	6
—Indianapolis	IHL	19	5	9	14	20	—	—	—	—	—
NHL totals		52	3	13	16	30	6	0	0	0	6

SHARIFJANOV, VADIM
RW, DEVILS

PERSONAL: Born December 23, 1975, in Ufa, U.S.S.R. . . . 6-0/183. . . . Shoots left. . . . Name pronounced SHARE-in-off.
TRANSACTIONS/CAREER NOTES: Selected by New Jersey Devils in first round (first Devils pick, 25th overall) of NHL entry draft (June 28, 1994).

			REGULAR SEASON					PLAYOFFS			
Season Team	League	Gms.	G	A	Pts.	PIM	Gms.	G	A	Pts.	PIM
92-93—Salavat	CIS	37	6	4	10	16	2	1	0	1	0
93-94—Salavat	CIS	46	10	6	16	36	5	3	0	3	4

SHAW, BRAD
D, SENATORS

PERSONAL: Born April 28, 1964, in Cambridge, Ont. . . . 6-0/190. . . . Shoots right. . . . Full name: Bradley William Shaw.
HIGH SCHOOL: Canterbury (Ottawa), then Eastwood (Kitchner, Ont.).
TRANSACTIONS/CAREER NOTES: Selected by Detroit Red Wings as underage junior in fifth round (fifth Red Wings pick, 86th overall) of NHL entry draft (June 9, 1982). . . . Traded by Red Wings to Hartford Whalers for eighth-round pick (LW Lars Karlsson) in 1984 draft (May 29, 1984). . . . Fractured finger on left hand (February 1988). . . . Broke nose (October 21, 1989). . . . Suffered back spasms (November 12, 1989). . . . Bruised right foot (February 28, 1990). . . . Injured groin (October 28, 1991); missed two games. . . . Injured knee (January 31, 1992); missed four games. . . . Bruised knee (February 29, 1992); missed four games. . . . Injured groin (March 14, 1992); missed three games. . . . Traded by Whalers to New Jersey Devils for future considerations (June 15, 1992). . . . Selected by Ottawa Senators in NHL expansion draft (June 18, 1992). . . . Suffered slight concussion (October 8, 1992); missed two games. . . . Suffered back spasms (December 22, 1993); missed five games. . . . Suffered back spasms (March 4, 1994); missed nine games.
HONORS: Won Max Kaminsky Trophy (1983-84). . . . Named to OHL All-Star first team (1983-84). . . . Won Eddie Shore Plaque (1986-87). . . . Named to AHL All-Star first team (1986-87 and 1987-88). . . . Named to NHL All-Rookie team (1989-90).

			REGULAR SEASON					PLAYOFFS			
Season Team	League	Gms.	G	A	Pts.	PIM	Gms.	G	A	Pts.	PIM
81-82—Ottawa	OHL	68	13	59	72	24	15	1	13	14	4
82-83—Ottawa	OHL	63	12	66	78	24	9	2	9	11	4
83-84—Ottawa	OHL	68	11	71	82	75	13	2	*27	29	9
84-85—Salt Lake City	IHL	44	3	29	32	25	—	—	—	—	—

Season	Team	League	Gms.	G	A	Pts.	Pen.	Gms.	G	A	Pts.	Pen.
	—Binghamton	AHL	24	1	10	11	4	8	1	8	9	6
85-86	—Hartford	NHL	8	0	2	2	4	—	—	—	—	—
	—Binghamton	AHL	64	10	44	54	33	5	0	2	2	6
86-87	—Hartford	NHL	2	0	0	0	0	—	—	—	—	—
	—Binghamton	AHL	77	9	30	39	43	12	1	8	9	2
87-88	—Binghamton	AHL	73	12	50	62	50	4	0	5	5	4
	—Hartford	NHL	1	0	0	0	0	—	—	—	—	—
88-89	—Verice	Italy	35	10	30	40	44	11	4	8	12	13
	—Hartford	NHL	3	1	0	1	0	3	1	0	1	0
	—Canadian national team	Int'l	4	1	0	1	2	—	—	—	—	—
89-90	—Hartford	NHL	64	3	32	35	30	7	2	5	7	0
90-91	—Hartford	NHL	72	4	28	32	29	6	1	2	3	2
91-92	—Hartford	NHL	62	3	22	25	44	3	0	1	1	4
92-93	—Ottawa	NHL	81	7	34	41	34	—	—	—	—	—
93-94	—Ottawa	NHL	66	4	19	23	59	—	—	—	—	—
NHL totals			**359**	**22**	**137**	**159**	**200**	**19**	**4**	**8**	**12**	**6**

SHAW, DAVID
D, BRUINS

PERSONAL: Born May 25, 1964, in St. Thomas, Ont. . . . 6-2/204. . . . Shoots right. **TRANSACTIONS/CAREER NOTES:** Selected by Quebec Nordiques as underage junior in first round (first Nordiques pick, 13th overall) of NHL entry draft (June 9, 1982). . . . Sprained wrist (December 18, 1985). . . . Traded by Nordiques with LW John Ogrodnick to New York Rangers for LW Jeff Jackson and D Terry Carkner (September 30, 1987). . . . Separated shoulder (October 1987). . . . Suspended 12 games by NHL for slashing (October 27, 1988). . . . Bruised shoulder (March 15, 1989). . . . Dislocated right shoulder (November 2, 1989). . . . Reinjured right shoulder (November 22, 1989); missed 10 games. . . . Underwent right shoulder surgery (February 7, 1990). . . . Bruised finger (September 1990). . . . Bruised left big toe (October 31, 1990). . . . Sprained knee (October 20, 1991). . . . Traded by Rangers to Edmonton Oilers for D Jeff Beukeboom (November 12, 1991) to complete deal in which Rangers traded C Bernie Nicholls, LW Louie DeBrusk, RW Steven Rice and future considerations to Oilers for C Mark Messier and future considerations (October 4, 1991). . . . Traded by Oilers to Minnesota North Stars for D Brian Glynn (January 21, 1992). . . . Traded by North Stars to Boston Bruins for future considerations (September 2, 1992). . . . Injured thigh (October 1992); missed one game. . . . Injured foot (December 1992); missed one game. . . . Injured ribs (March 1993); missed five games. . . . Pinched nerve (December 26, 1993); missed three games. . . . Suffered charley horse (January 6, 1994); missed seven games. . . . Injured knee (January 28, 1994); missed 17 games.
HONORS: Named to OHL All-Star first team (1983-84). . . . Named to Memorial Cup All-Star team (1983-84).

Season	Team	League	Gms.	G	A	Pts.	PIM	Gms.	G	A	Pts.	PIM
80-81	—Stratford Junior B	OHA	41	12	19	31	30	—	—	—	—	—
81-82	—Kitchener	OHL	68	6	25	31	99	15	2	2	4	51
82-83	—Kitchener	OHL	57	18	56	74	78	12	2	10	12	18
	—Quebec	NHL	2	0	0	0	0	—	—	—	—	—
83-84	—Kitchener	OHL	58	14	34	48	73	16	4	9	13	12
	—Quebec	NHL	3	0	0	0	0	—	—	—	—	—
84-85	—Guelph	OHL	2	0	0	0	0	—	—	—	—	—
	—Fredericton	AHL	48	7	6	13	73	2	0	0	0	7
	—Quebec	NHL	14	0	0	0	11	—	—	—	—	—
85-86	—Quebec	NHL	73	7	19	26	78	—	—	—	—	—
86-87	—Quebec	NHL	75	0	19	19	69	—	—	—	—	—
87-88	—New York Rangers	NHL	68	7	25	32	100	—	—	—	—	—
88-89	—New York Rangers	NHL	63	6	11	17	88	4	0	2	2	30
89-90	—New York Rangers	NHL	22	2	10	12	22	—	—	—	—	—
90-91	—New York Rangers	NHL	77	2	10	12	89	6	0	0	0	11
91-92	—New York Rangers	NHL	10	0	1	1	15	—	—	—	—	—
	—Edmonton	NHL	12	1	1	2	8	—	—	—	—	—
	—Minnesota	NHL	37	0	7	7	49	7	2	2	4	10
92-93	—Boston	NHL	77	10	14	24	108	4	0	1	1	6
93-94	—Boston	NHL	55	1	9	10	85	13	1	2	3	16
NHL totals			**588**	**36**	**126**	**162**	**722**	**34**	**3**	**7**	**10**	**73**

SHEPPARD, RAY
RW, RED WINGS

PERSONAL: Born May 27, 1966, in Pembroke, Ont. . . . 6-1/190. . . . Shoots right. **TRANSACTIONS/CAREER NOTES:** Selected by Buffalo Sabres as underage junior in third round (third Sabres pick, 60th overall) of NHL entry draft (June 9, 1984). . . . Injured left knee (September 1986); missed Sabres training camp. . . . Bruised back during training camp (September 1988). . . . Lacerated face (November 25, 1988). . . . Lacerated face (November 27, 1988). . . . Suffered from the flu (December 1988). . . . Sprained ankle (January 30, 1989). . . . Injured left knee (March 16, 1990). . . . Traded by Sabres to New York Rangers for future considerations and cash (July 10, 1990). . . . Sprained medial collateral ligaments of right knee (February 18, 1991); missed 13 games. . . . Dislocated left shoulder (March 24, 1991). . . . Signed as free agent by Detroit Red Wings (August 5, 1991). . . . Strained lower abdomen (March 20, 1992); missed five games. . . . Injured knee (October 8, 1992); missed five games. . . . Reinjured knee (October 28, 1992); missed two games. . . . Suffered back spasms (February 13, 1993); missed three games. . . . Strained back (March 2, 1993); missed two games.
HONORS: Won Red Tilson Trophy (1985-86). . . . Won Eddie Powers Memorial Trophy (1985-86). . . . Won Jim Mahon Memorial Trophy (1985-86). . . . Named to OHL All-Star first team (1985-86). . . . Named to NHL All-Rookie team (1987-88).

			REGULAR SEASON					PLAYOFFS			
Season	Team	League	Gms.	G	A	Pts.	PIM	Gms.	G	A	Pts.	PIM
82-83—Brockville		COJHL	48	27	36	63	81	—	—	—	—	—
83-84—Cornwall		OHL	68	44	36	80	69	—	—	—	—	—
84-85—Cornwall		OHL	49	25	33	58	51	9	2	12	14	4
85-86—Cornwall		OHL	63	*81	61	*142	25	6	7	4	11	0
86-87—Rochester		AHL	55	18	13	31	11	15	12	3	15	2
87-88—Buffalo		NHL	74	38	27	65	14	6	1	1	2	2
88-89—Buffalo		NHL	67	22	21	43	15	1	0	1	1	0
89-90—Buffalo		NHL	18	4	2	6	0	—	—	—	—	—
—Rochester		AHL	5	3	5	8	2	17	8	7	15	9
90-91—New York Rangers		NHL	59	24	23	47	21	—	—	—	—	—
91-92—Detroit		NHL	74	36	26	62	27	11	6	2	8	4
92-93—Detroit		NHL	70	32	34	66	29	7	2	3	5	0
93-94—Detroit		NHL	82	52	41	93	26	7	2	1	3	4
NHL totals			444	208	174	382	132	32	11	8	19	10

SHEVALIER, JEFF
LW/C, KINGS

PERSONAL: Born March 14, 1974, in Mississauga, Ont. . . . 5-11/180. . . . Shoots left. . . . Name pronounced shuh-VAHL-yay.
HIGH SCHOOL: Chippewa Secondary (North Bay, Ont.).
TRANSACTIONS/CAREER NOTES: Selected by Los Angeles Kings in fifth round (fourth Kings pick, 111th overall) of NHL entry draft (June 20, 1992).
HONORS: Named to OHL All-Star first team (1993-94).

			REGULAR SEASON					PLAYOFFS			
Season	Team	League	Gms.	G	A	Pts.	PIM	Gms.	G	A	Pts.	PIM
90-91—Oakville Junior B		OHA	5	1	4	5	0	—	—	—	—	—
—Georgetown Junior B		OHA	12	11	11	22	8	—	—	—	—	—
—Acton Junior C		OHA	28	29	31	60	62	—	—	—	—	—
91-92—North Bay		OHL	64	28	29	57	26	21	5	11	16	25
92-93—North Bay		OHL	62	59	54	113	46	2	1	2	3	4
93-94—North Bay		OHL	64	52	49	101	52	17	8	14	22	18

SHTALENKOV, MIKHAIL
G, MIGHTY DUCKS

PERSONAL: Born October 20, 1965, in Moscow, U.S.S.R. . . . 6-2/180. . . . Catches left. . . . Name pronounced mihk-HIGHL shtuh-LEHN-kahf.
TRANSACTIONS/CAREER NOTES: Selected by Mighty Ducks of Anaheim in fifth round (fifth Mighty Ducks pick, 108th overall) of NHL entry draft (June 26, 1993).
HONORS: Named Soviet League Rookie of the Year (1986-87). . . . Won Garry F. Longman Memorial Trophy (1992-93).

			REGULAR SEASON							PLAYOFFS					
Season	Team	League	Gms.	Min.	W	L	T	GA	SO	Avg.	Gms.	Min.	W	L	GA	SO	Avg.
86-87—Dynamo Moscow		USSR	17	893	...	...	...	36	1	2.42	—	—	—	—	—	—	—
87-88—Dynamo Moscow		USSR	25	1302	...	...	...	72	1	3.32	—	—	—	—	—	—	—
88-89—Dynamo Moscow		USSR	4	80	...	...	...	3	0	2.25	—	—	—	—	—	—	—
89-90—Dynamo Moscow		USSR	6	20	...	...	...	1	0	3.00	—	—	—	—	—	—	—
90-91—Dynamo Moscow		USSR	31	1568	...	...	...	56	2	2.14	—	—	—	—	—	—	—
91-92—Dynamo Moscow		CIS	27	1268	...	...	...	45	1	2.13	—	—	—	—	—	—	—
—Unified Olympic Team		Int'l	8	440	...	...	...	12	3	1.64	—	—	—	—	—	—	—
92-93—Milwaukee		IHL	47	2669	26	14	‡5	135	2	3.03	3	209	1	1	11	0	3.16
93-94—San Diego		IHL	28	1616	15	11	‡2	93	0	3.45	—	—	—	—	—	—	—
—Anaheim		NHL	10	543	3	4	1	24	0	2.65	—	—	—	—	—	—	—
NHL totals			10	543	3	4	1	24	0	2.65							

SHUCHUK, GARY
RW/C, KINGS

PERSONAL: Born February 17, 1967, in Edmonton. . . . 5-10/185. . . . Shoots right. . . . Full name: Gary Robert Shuchuk. . . . Name pronounced SHOO-chuhk.
COLLEGE: Wisconsin.
TRANSACTIONS/CAREER NOTES: Selected by Detroit Red Wings in NHL supplemental draft (June 10, 1988). . . . Traded by Red Wings with C Jimmy Carson and RW Marc Potvin to Los Angeles Kings for D Paul Coffey, RW Jim Hiller and C/LW Sylvain Couturier (January 29, 1993). . . . Hyperextended right elbow (February 20, 1993); missed four games. . . . Sprained knee (January 29, 1994); missed 10 games.
HONORS: Won WCHA Most Valuable Player Award (1989-90). . . . Named to NCAA All-America West first team (1989-90). . . . Named to WCHA All-Star first team (1989-90).

			REGULAR SEASON					PLAYOFFS			
Season	Team	League	Gms.	G	A	Pts.	PIM	Gms.	G	A	Pts.	PIM
86-87—University of Wisconsin		WCHA	42	19	11	30	72	—	—	—	—	—
87-88—University of Wisconsin		WCHA	44	7	22	29	70	—	—	—	—	—
88-89—University of Wisconsin		WCHA	46	18	19	37	102	—	—	—	—	—
89-90—University of Wisconsin		WCHA	45	*41	39	*80	70	—	—	—	—	—
90-91—Detroit		NHL	6	1	2	3	6	3	0	0	0	0
—Adirondack		AHL	59	23	24	47	32	—	—	—	—	—
91-92—Adirondack		AHL	79	32	48	80	48	†19	4	9	13	18
92-93—Adirondack		AHL	47	24	53	77	66	—	—	—	—	—
—Los Angeles		NHL	25	2	4	6	16	17	2	2	4	12
93-94—Los Angeles		NHL	56	3	4	7	30	—	—	—	—	—
NHL totals			87	6	10	16	52	20	2	2	4	12

SHULMISTRA, RICH
G, NORDIQUES

PERSONAL: Born April 1, 1971, in Sudbury, Ont.... 6-2/186.... Catches right.
HIGH SCHOOL: LaSalle Secondary (Kingston, Ont.).
COLLEGE: Miami of Ohio.
TRANSACTIONS/CAREER NOTES: Selected by Quebec Nordiques in NHL supplemental draft (June 19, 1992).
HONORS: Named to CCHA All-Star second team (1992-93).

Season Team	League	REGULAR SEASON								PLAYOFFS					
		Gms.	Min.	W	L	T	GA	SO	Avg.	Gms.	Min.	W	L	GA	SO	Avg.
90-91—Miami of Ohio	CCHA	15	920	2	12	2	80	0	5.22	—	—	—	—	—	—	—
91-92—Miami of Ohio	CCHA	19	850	3	5	2	67	0	4.73	—	—	—	—	—	—	—
92-93—Miami of Ohio	CCHA	33	1949	22	6	4	88	...	2.71	—	—	—	—	—	—	—
93-94—Miami of Ohio	CCHA	27	1521	13	12	1	74	0	2.92	—	—	—	—	—	—	—

SIDORKIEWICZ, PETER
G, DEVILS

PERSONAL: Born June 29, 1963, in Dabrown Bialostocka, Poland.... 5-9/180.... Catches left.... Full name: Peter Paul Sidorkiewicz.... Name pronounced sih-DOHR-kuh-VIHCH.
HIGH SCHOOL: O'Neill (Oshawa, Ont.).
TRANSACTIONS/CAREER NOTES: Selected by Washington Capitals as underage junior in fifth round (fifth Capitals pick, 91st overall) of NHL entry draft (June 10, 1981).... Sprained right ankle (March 3, 1991).... Traded by Capitals with C Dean Evason to Hartford Whalers for LW David Jensen (March 1985).... Selected by Ottawa Senators in NHL expansion draft (June 18, 1992).... Traded by Senators with future considerations to New Jersey Devils for G Craig Billington and C/LW Troy Mallette and fourth-round pick (C Cosmo Dupaul) in 1993 draft (June 20, 1993); Senators sent LW Mike Peluso to Devils to complete deal (June 26, 1993).
HONORS: Shared Dave Pinkney Trophy with Jeff Hogg (1982-83).... Named to Memorial Cup All-Star team (1982-83).... Named to AHL All-Star second team (1986-87).... Named to NHL All-Rookie team (1988-89).... Played in NHL All-Star Game (1993).

Season Team	League	REGULAR SEASON								PLAYOFFS					
		Gms.	Min.	W	L	T	GA	SO	Avg.	Gms.	Min.	W	L	GA	SO	Avg.
80-81—Oshawa	OMJHL	7	308	3	3	0	24	0	4.68	5	266	2	2	20	0	4.51
81-82—Oshawa	OHL	29	1553	14	11	1	123	*2	4.75	1	13	0	0	1	0	4.62
82-83—Oshawa	OHL	60	3536	36	20	3	213	0	3.61	*17	*1020	15	1	*60	0	3.53
83-84—Oshawa	OHL	52	2966	28	21	1	205	1	4.15	7	420	3	4	27	†1	3.86
84-85—Fort Wayne	IHL	10	590	4	4	‡2	43	0	4.37	—	—	—	—	—	—	—
—Binghamton	AHL	45	2691	31	9	5	137	3	3.05	8	481	4	4	31	0	3.87
85-86—Binghamton	AHL	49	2819	21	22	3	150	2	*3.19	4	235	1	3	12	0	3.06
86-87—Binghamton	AHL	57	3304	23	16	0	161	4	2.92	13	794	6	7	36	0	*2.72
87-88—Hartford	NHL	1	60	0	1	0	6	0	6.00	—	—	—	—	—	—	—
—Binghamton	AHL	42	2346	19	17	3	144	0	3.68	3	147	0	2	8	0	3.27
88-89—Hartford	NHL	44	2635	22	18	4	133	4	3.03	2	124	0	2	8	0	3.87
89-90—Hartford	NHL	46	2703	19	19	7	161	1	3.57	7	429	3	4	23	0	3.22
90-91—Hartford	NHL	52	2953	21	22	7	164	1	3.33	6	359	2	4	24	0	4.01
91-92—Hartford	NHL	35	1995	9	19	6	111	2	3.34	—	—	—	—	—	—	—
92-93—Ottawa	NHL	64	3388	8	*46	3	*250	0	4.43	—	—	—	—	—	—	—
93-94—New Jersey	NHL	3	130	0	3	0	6	0	2.77	—	—	—	—	—	—	—
—Albany	AHL	15	908	6	7	2	60	0	3.96	—	—	—	—	—	—	—
—Fort Wayne	IHL	11	591	6	3	‡0	27	†2	2.74	18	*1054	10	*6	59	†1	3.36
NHL totals		245	13864	79	128	27	831	8	3.60	15	912	5	10	55	0	3.62

SILLINGER, MIKE
C, RED WINGS

PERSONAL: Born June 29, 1971, in Regina, Sask.... 5-10/191.... Shoots right.... Name pronounced SIHL-ihn-juhr.
TRANSACTIONS/CAREER NOTES: Selected by Detroit Red Wings in first round (first Red Wings pick, 11th overall) of NHL entry draft (June 17, 1989).... Fractured rib in training camp (September 1990).... Suffered from the flu (March 5, 1993); missed three games.... Strained rotator cuff (October 9, 1993); missed four games.
HONORS: Named to WHL All-Star second team (1989-90).... Named to WHL (East) All-Star first team (1990-91).

Season Team	League	REGULAR SEASON				PLAYOFFS			
		Gms.	G	A	Pts.	PIM	Gms.	G	A	Pts.	PIM
87-88—Regina	WHL	67	18	25	43	17	4	2	2	4	0
88-89—Regina	WHL	72	53	78	131	52	—	—	—	—	—
89-90—Regina	WHL	70	57	72	129	41	11	12	10	22	2
—Adirondack	AHL	—	—	—	—	—	1	0	0	0	0
90-91—Regina	WHL	57	50	66	116	42	8	6	9	15	4
—Detroit	NHL	3	0	1	1	0	3	0	1	1	0
91-92—Adirondack	AHL	64	25	41	66	26	15	9	*19	*28	12
—Detroit	NHL	—	—	—	—	—	8	2	2	4	2
92-93—Detroit	NHL	51	4	17	21	16	—	—	—	—	—
—Adirondack	AHL	15	10	20	30	31	11	5	13	18	10
93-94—Detroit	NHL	62	8	21	29	10	—	—	—	—	—
NHL totals		116	12	39	51	26	11	2	3	5	2

SIMON, CHRIS
LW, NORDIQUES

PERSONAL: Born January 30, 1972, in Wawa, Ont.... 6-3/219.... Shoots left.... Name pronounced SIGH-muhn.
TRANSACTIONS/CAREER NOTES: Suspended six games by OHL for shooting the puck in frustration and striking another player (January 20, 1990).... Selected by Philadelphia Flyers in

second round (second Flyers pick, 25th overall) of NHL entry draft (June 16, 1990)... Underwent surgery to repair left rotator cuff and torn muscle (September 1990)... Traded by Flyers with first-round pick in 1994 draft (traded to Toronto Maple Leafs) to Quebec Nordiques (July 21, 1992) to complete deal in which Flyers sent G Ron Hextall, C Mike Ricci, C Peter Forsberg, D Steve Duchesne, first-round pick in 1993 draft (G Jocelyn Thibault) and cash to Nordiques for C Eric Lindros (June 20, 1992)... Suffered from the flu (March 13, 1993); missed one game... Injured back (December 1, 1993); missed 31 games. ... Injured back (February 16, 1994); missed one game... Injured back (March 6, 1994); missed one game... Injured back (March 18, 1994); missed remainder of season.

			REGULAR SEASON					PLAYOFFS			
Season	Team	League	Gms.	G	A	Pts.	PIM	Gms.	G	A	Pts.	PIM
87-88—Sault Ste. Marie		OHA	55	42	36	78	172	—	—	—	—	—
88-89—Ottawa		OHL	36	4	2	6	31	—	—	—	—	—
89-90—Ottawa		OHL	57	36	38	74	146	3	2	1	3	4
90-91—Ottawa		OHL	20	16	6	22	69	17	5	9	14	59
91-92—Ottawa		OHL	2	1	1	2	24	—	—	—	—	—
—Sault Ste. Marie		OHL	31	19	25	44	143	11	5	8	13	49
92-93—Halifax		AHL	36	12	6	18	131	—	—	—	—	—
—Quebec		NHL	16	1	1	2	67	5	0	0	0	26
93-94—Quebec		NHL	37	4	4	8	132	—	—	—	—	—
NHL totals			53	5	5	10	199	5	0	0	0	26

SIMON, JASON
LW, ISLANDERS

PERSONAL: Born March 21, 1969, in Sarnia, Ont... 6-1/190... Shoots left.
TRANSACTIONS/CAREER NOTES: Selected by New Jersey Devils in ninth round (ninth Devils pick, 215th overall) of NHL entry draft (June 26, 1993)... Signed as free agent by Salt Lake Golden Eagles (January 11, 1994).

			REGULAR SEASON					PLAYOFFS			
Season	Team	League	Gms.	G	A	Pts.	PIM	Gms.	G	A	Pts.	PIM
86-87—London		OHL	33	1	2	3	33	—	—	—	—	—
—Sudbury		OHL	26	2	3	5	50	—	—	—	—	—
87-88—Sudbury		OHL	26	5	7	12	35	—	—	—	—	—
—Hamilton		OHL	29	5	13	18	124	11	0	2	2	15
88-89—Windsor		OHL	62	23	39	62	193	4	1	4	5	13
89-90—Utica		AHL	16	3	4	7	28	2	0	0	0	12
—Nashville		ECHL	13	4	3	7	81	5	1	3	4	17
90-91—Johnstown		ECHL	22	11	9	20	55	—	—	—	—	—
—Utica		AHL	50	2	12	14	189	—	—	—	—	—
93-94—Detroit		Col.HL	13	9	16	25	87	—	—	—	—	—
—Salt Lake City		IHL	50	7	7	14	*323	—	—	—	—	—
—New York Islanders		NHL	4	0	0	0	34	—	—	—	—	—
NHL totals			4	0	0	0	34					

SIMON, TODD
C, SABRES

PERSONAL: Born April 21, 1972, in Toronto... 5-10/188... Shoots right.
TRANSACTIONS/CAREER NOTES: Selected by Buffalo Sabres in ninth round (10th Sabres pick, 203rd overall) of NHL entry draft (June 20, 1992).
HONORS: Won Eddie Powers Memorial Trophy (1991-92)... Won Red Tilson Trophy (1991-92).

			REGULAR SEASON					PLAYOFFS			
Season	Team	League	Gms.	G	A	Pts.	PIM	Gms.	G	A	Pts.	PIM
89-90—Niagara Falls		OHL	9	0	1	1	2	11	3	1	4	2
90-91—Niagara Falls		OHL	65	51	74	125	35	14	7	8	15	12
91-92—Niagara Falls		OHL	66	53	93	*146	70	17	17	24	†41	36
92-93—Rochester		AHL	68	27	66	93	54	12	3	14	17	15
93-94—Rochester		AHL	55	33	52	85	79	—	—	—	—	—
—Buffalo		NHL	15	0	1	1	0	5	1	0	1	0
NHL totals			15	0	1	1	0	5	1	0	1	0

SIMPSON, CRAIG
LW, SABRES

PERSONAL: Born February 15, 1967, in London, Ont... 6-2/195... Shoots right... Full name: Craig Andrew Simpson.
COLLEGE: Michigan State.
TRANSACTIONS/CAREER NOTES: Selected by Pittsburgh Penguins in first round (first Penguins pick, second overall) of NHL entry draft (June 15, 1985)... Pulled muscle in right hip (March 1987)... Sprained right wrist (March 14, 1987)... Traded by Penguins with C Dave Hannan, D Chris Joseph and D Moe Mantha to Edmonton Oilers for D Paul Coffey, LW Dave Hunter and RW Wayne Van Dorp (November 24, 1987)... Broke right ankle (December 4, 1988)... Suspended three games by NHL for injuring an opposing player (January 23, 1991)... Bruised chest (November 1991); missed one game... Bruised shoulder (April 18, 1992)... Strained lower back (January 5, 1993); missed four games... Strained lower back (February 23, 1993); missed three games... Suffered protruded disk (March 1993); missed remainder of season. ... Signed as free agent by San Jose Sharks (July 17, 1993); deal invalidated by NHL (July 26, 1993). ... Traded by Oilers to Buffalo Sabres for LW Jozef Cierny and undisclosed draft pick (September 1, 1993)... Suffered sore back (December 1, 1993); missed 42 games.
HONORS: Named to NCAA All-America West first team (1984-85)... Named to CCHA All-Star first team (1984-85).
MISCELLANEOUS: Member of Stanley Cup championship teams (1988 and 1990).

Season Team	League	Gms.	G	A	Pts.	PIM	Gms.	G	A	Pts.	PIM
82-83—London Jr. B	OHA	. . .	48	63	*111	. . .	—	—	—	—	—
83-84—Michigan State	CCHA	30	8	28	36	22	—	—	—	—	—
84-85—Michigan State	CCHA	42	31	53	84	33	—	—	—	—	—
85-86—Pittsburgh	NHL	76	11	17	28	49	—	—	—	—	—
86-87—Pittsburgh	NHL	72	26	25	51	57	—	—	—	—	—
87-88—Pittsburgh	NHL	21	13	13	26	34	—	—	—	—	—
—Edmonton	NHL	59	43	21	64	43	19	13	6	19	26
88-89—Edmonton	NHL	66	35	41	76	80	7	2	0	2	10
89-90—Edmonton	NHL	80	29	32	61	180	22	*16	15	†31	8
90-91—Edmonton	NHL	75	30	27	57	66	18	5	11	16	12
91-92—Edmonton	NHL	79	24	37	61	80	1	0	0	0	0
92-93—Edmonton	NHL	60	24	22	46	36	—	—	—	—	—
93-94—Buffalo	NHL	22	8	8	16	8	—	—	—	—	—
NHL totals		610	243	243	486	633	67	36	32	68	56

SIMPSON, REID
LW, DEVILS

PERSONAL: Born May 21, 1969, in Flin Flon, Man. . . . 6-1/210. . . . Shoots left.
TRANSACTIONS/CAREER NOTES: Selected by Philadelphia Flyers in fourth round (third Flyers pick, 72nd overall) of NHL entry draft (June 17, 1989). . . . Signed as free agent by Minnesota North Stars (December 13, 1992). . . . North Stars franchise moved from Minnesota to Dallas and renamed Stars for 1993-94 season. . . . Traded by Stars with D Roy Mitchell to New Jersey Devils for future considerations (March 21, 1994).

Season Team	League	Gms.	G	A	Pts.	PIM	Gms.	G	A	Pts.	PIM
85-86—Flin Flon	MJHL	40	20	21	41	200	—	—	—	—	—
—New Westminster	WHL	2	0	0	0	0	—	—	—	—	—
86-87—Prince Albert	WHL	47	3	8	11	105	—	—	—	—	—
87-88—Prince Albert	WHL	72	13	14	27	164	10	1	0	1	43
88-89—Prince Albert	WHL	59	26	29	55	264	4	2	1	3	30
89-90—Prince Albert	WHL	29	15	17	32	121	14	4	7	11	34
—Hershey	AHL	28	2	2	4	175	—	—	—	—	—
90-91—Hershey	AHL	54	9	15	24	183	1	0	0	0	0
91-92—Hershey	AHL	60	11	7	18	145	—	—	—	—	—
—Philadelphia	NHL	1	0	0	0	0	—	—	—	—	—
92-93—Kalamazoo	IHL	45	5	5	10	193	—	—	—	—	—
—Minnesota	NHL	1	0	0	0	5	—	—	—	—	—
93-94—Albany	AHL	37	9	5	14	135	5	1	1	2	18
—Kalamazoo	IHL	5	0	0	0	16	—	—	—	—	—
NHL totals		2	0	0	0	5					

SITTLER, RYAN
LW/C, FLYERS

PERSONAL: Born January 28, 1974, in London, Ont. . . . 6-2/185. . . . Shoots left. . . . Son of Darryl Sittler, Hall of Fame center, Toronto Maple Leafs, Philadelphia Flyers and Detroit Red Wings (1970-71 through 1984-85).
HIGH SCHOOL: Nichols School (Buffalo, N.Y.).
COLLEGE: Michigan.
TRANSACTIONS/CAREER NOTES: Selected by Philadelphia Flyers in first round (first Flyers pick, seventh overall) of NHL entry draft (June 20, 1992).

Season Team	League	Gms.	G	A	Pts.	PIM	Gms.	G	A	Pts.	PIM
90-91—Nichols School	N.Y. H.S.	7	8	9	17	8	—	—	—	—	—
—Buffalo	AHAUS	20	25	34	59	26	—	—	—	—	—
91-92—Nichols School	N.Y. H.S.	21	19	29	48	38	—	—	—	—	—
—Buffalo	AHAUS	30	39	54	93	. . .	—	—	—	—	—
92-93—University of Michigan	CCHA	35	9	24	33	43	—	—	—	—	—
93-94—University of Michigan	CCHA	26	9	9	18	14	—	—	—	—	—

SJODIN, TOMMY
D

PERSONAL: Born August 13, 1965, in Sundsvall, Sweden. . . . 5-11/185. . . . Shoots right. . . . Name pronounced shoh-DEEN.
TRANSACTIONS/CAREER NOTES: Selected by Minnesota North Stars in 12th round (10th North Stars pick, 237th overall) of NHL entry draft (June 15, 1985). . . . Injured hand (December 19, 1992); missed one game. . . . Suffered chest contusion (March 14, 1993); missed one game. . . . North Stars franchise moved from Minnesota to Dallas and renamed Stars for 1993-94 season. . . . Traded by Stars with undisclosed draft pick to Quebec Nordiques for G Emmanuel Fernandez (February 13, 1994). . . . Suffered from tonsillitis (April 3, 1994); missed two games.
HONORS: Won Golden Puck Award (1991-92). . . . Named to Swedish League All-Star team (1991-92).

Season Team	League	Gms.	G	A	Pts.	PIM	Gms.	G	A	Pts.	PIM
87-88—Brynas	Sweden	40	6	9	15	28	—	—	—	—	—
88-89—Brynas	Sweden	40	8	11	19	54	—	—	—	—	—
89-90—Brynas	Sweden	40	14	14	28	46	5	0	0	0	2
90-91—Brynas	Sweden	38	12	17	29	79	—	—	—	—	—

Season Team	League	Gms.	G	A	Pts.	Pen.	Gms.	G	A	Pts.	Pen.
		REGULAR SEASON					**PLAYOFFS**				
91-92—Brynas	Sweden	40	6	16	22	46	—	—	—	—	—
—Swedish national team	Int'l	8	0	1	1	6	—	—	—	—	—
—Swedish Olympic Team	Int'l	8	4	1	5	2	—	—	—	—	—
92-93—Minnesota	NHL	77	7	29	36	30	—	—	—	—	—
93-94—Dallas	NHL	7	0	2	2	4	—	—	—	—	—
—Kalamazoo	IHL	38	12	32	44	22	—	—	—	—	—
—Quebec	NHL	22	1	9	10	18	—	—	—	—	—
NHL totals		106	8	40	48	52					

SKALDE, JARROD
C, MIGHTY DUCKS

PERSONAL: Born February 26, 1971, in Niagara Falls, Ont. . . . 6-0/170. . . . Shoots left. . . . Name pronounced SKAHL-dee.

TRANSACTIONS/CAREER NOTES: Selected by New Jersey Devils in second round (third Devils pick, 26th overall) of NHL entry draft (June 17, 1989). . . . Traded by Oshawa Generals to Belleville Bulls for RW Rob Pearson (November 18, 1990). . . . Selected by Mighty Ducks of Anaheim in NHL expansion draft (June 24, 1993).

HONORS: Named to OHL All-Star second team (1990-91).

Season Team	League	Gms.	G	A	Pts.	PIM	Gms.	G	A	Pts.	PIM
		REGULAR SEASON					**PLAYOFFS**				
86-87—Fort Erie Junior B	OHA	41	27	34	61	36	—	—	—	—	—
87-88—Oshawa	OHL	60	12	16	28	24	7	2	1	3	2
88-89—Oshawa	OHL	65	38	38	76	36	6	1	5	6	2
89-90—Oshawa	OHL	62	40	52	92	66	17	10	7	17	6
90-91—New Jersey	NHL	1	0	1	1	0	—	—	—	—	—
—Utica	AHL	3	3	2	5	0	—	—	—	—	—
—Oshawa	OHL	15	8	14	22	14	—	—	—	—	—
—Belleville	OHL	40	30	52	82	21	6	9	6	15	10
91-92—Utica	AHL	62	20	20	40	56	4	3	1	4	8
—New Jersey	NHL	15	2	4	6	4	—	—	—	—	—
92-93—Cincinnati	IHL	4	1	2	3	4	—	—	—	—	—
—Utica	AHL	59	21	39	60	76	5	0	2	2	19
—New Jersey	NHL	11	0	2	2	4	—	—	—	—	—
93-94—San Diego	IHL	57	25	38	63	79	9	3	12	15	10
—Anaheim	NHL	20	5	4	9	10	—	—	—	—	—
NHL totals		47	7	11	18	18					

SKOREPA, ZDENEK
RW, DEVILS

PERSONAL: Born August 10, 1976, in Duchcov, Czechoslovakia. . . . 6-0/187. . . . Shoots left.

TRANSACTIONS/CAREER NOTES: Selected by New Jersey Devils in fourth round (fourth Devils pick, 103rd overall) of NHL entry draft (June 29, 1994).

Season Team	League	Gms.	G	A	Pts.	PIM	Gms.	G	A	Pts.	PIM
		REGULAR SEASON					**PLAYOFFS**				
93-94—Chemopetrol Litvinov	Czech Rep.	20	4	7	11	. . .	4	0	0	0	0

SKRUDLAND, BRIAN
C, PANTHERS

PERSONAL: Born July 31, 1963, in Peace River, Alta. . . . 6-0/196. . . . Shoots left. . . . Name pronounced SKROOD-luhnd. . . . Cousin of Barry Pederson, center for four NHL teams (1980-81 through 1991-92).

TRANSACTIONS/CAREER NOTES: Signed as free agent by Montreal Canadiens (August 1983). . . . Injured groin (February 1988). . . . Strained left knee ligaments (December 27, 1988). . . . Bruised right foot (January 1989). . . . Sprained right ankle (October 7, 1989); missed 21 games. . . . Pulled hip muscle (November 4, 1990); missed six games. . . . Broke foot (January 17, 1991); missed 14 games including All-Star Game. . . . Broke left thumb (October 5, 1991); missed five games. . . . Sprained knee (October 26, 1991); missed 25 games. . . . Broke nose (January 25, 1992); missed eight games. . . . Tore right knee ligaments (October 6, 1992); missed 27 games. . . . Injured shoulder (January 14, 1993); missed one game. . . . Traded by Canadiens to Calgary Flames for RW Gary Leeman (January 28, 1993). . . . Sprained ankle (February 16, 1993); missed four games. . . . Broke thumb (March 2, 1993); missed 12 games. . . . Lacerated right ear (April 11, 1993); missed one game. . . . Selected by Florida Panthers in NHL expansion draft (June 24, 1993). . . . Sprained right ankle (April 4, 1994); missed five games.

HONORS: Won Jack Butterfield Trophy (1984-85).

MISCELLANEOUS: Member of Stanley Cup championship team (1986).

Season Team	League	Gms.	G	A	Pts.	PIM	Gms.	G	A	Pts.	PIM
		REGULAR SEASON					**PLAYOFFS**				
80-81—Saskatoon	WHL	66	15	27	42	97	—	—	—	—	—
81-82—Saskatoon	WHL	71	27	29	56	135	5	0	1	1	2
82-83—Saskatoon	WHL	71	35	59	94	42	6	1	3	4	19
83-84—Nova Scotia	AHL	56	13	12	25	55	12	2	8	10	14
84-85—Sherbrooke	AHL	70	22	28	50	109	17	9	8	17	23
85-86—Montreal	NHL	65	9	13	22	57	20	2	4	6	76
86-87—Montreal	NHL	79	11	17	28	107	14	1	5	6	29
87-88—Montreal	NHL	79	12	24	36	112	11	1	5	6	24
88-89—Montreal	NHL	71	12	29	41	84	21	3	7	10	40
89-90—Montreal	NHL	59	11	31	42	56	11	3	5	8	30

Season Team	League	REGULAR SEASON Gms.	G	A	Pts.	Pen.	PLAYOFFS Gms.	G	A	Pts.	Pen.
90-91—Montreal	NHL	57	15	19	34	85	13	3	10	13	42
91-92—Montreal	NHL	42	3	3	6	36	11	1	1	2	20
92-93—Montreal	NHL	23	5	3	8	55	—	—	—	—	—
—Calgary	NHL	16	2	4	6	10	6	0	3	3	12
93-94—Florida	NHL	79	15	25	40	136	—	—	—	—	—
NHL totals		570	95	168	263	738	107	14	40	54	273

SLANEY, JOHN
D, CAPITALS

PERSONAL: Born February 7, 1972, in St. John's, Nfld. . . . 6-0/185. . . . Shoots left.
TRANSACTIONS/CAREER NOTES: Selected by Washington Capitals in first round (first Capitals pick, ninth overall) of NHL entry draft (June 16, 1990). . . . Sprained right ankle (March 9, 1994); missed six games.
HONORS: Won Max Kaminsky Trophy (1989-90). . . . Named to OHL All-Star first team (1989-90). . . . Named to OHL All-Star second team (1990-91).

Season Team	League	REGULAR SEASON Gms.	G	A	Pts.	PIM	PLAYOFFS Gms.	G	A	Pts.	PIM
88-89—Cornwall	OHL	66	16	43	59	23	18	8	16	24	10
89-90—Cornwall	OHL	64	38	59	97	60	6	0	8	8	11
90-91—Cornwall	OHL	34	21	25	46	28	—	—	—	—	—
91-92—Cornwall	OHL	34	19	41	60	43	6	3	8	11	0
—Baltimore	AHL	6	2	4	6	0	—	—	—	—	—
92-93—Baltimore	AHL	79	20	46	66	60	7	0	7	7	8
93-94—Portland	AHL	29	14	13	27	17	—	—	—	—	—
—Washington	NHL	47	7	9	16	27	11	1	1	2	2
NHL totals		47	7	9	16	27	11	1	1	2	2

SLEGR, JIRI
D, CANUCKS

PERSONAL: Born May 30, 1971, in Litvinov, Czechoslovakia. . . . 6-1/205. . . . Shoots left. . . . Name pronounced YOO-ree SLAY-guhr. . . . Son of Jiri Bubla, defenseman, Vancouver Canucks (1981-82 through 1985-86).
TRANSACTIONS/CAREER NOTES: Selected by Vancouver Canucks in second round (third Canucks pick, 23rd overall) of NHL entry draft (June 16, 1990).
HONORS: Named to Czechoslovakian League All-Star team (1990-91).

Season Team	League	REGULAR SEASON Gms.	G	A	Pts.	PIM	PLAYOFFS Gms.	G	A	Pts.	PIM
88-89—Litvinov	Czech.	8	0	0	0	. . .	—	—	—	—	—
89-90—Litvinov	Czech.	51	4	15	19	. . .	—	—	—	—	—
90-91—Litvinov	Czech.	39	10	33	43	26	—	—	—	—	—
91-92—Litvinov	Czech.	38	7	22	29	30	—	—	—	—	—
—Czech. Olympic Team	Int'l	8	1	1	2	. . .	—	—	—	—	—
92-93—Vancouver	NHL	41	4	22	26	109	5	0	3	3	4
—Hamilton	AHL	21	4	14	18	42	—	—	—	—	—
93-94—Vancouver	NHL	78	5	33	38	86	—	—	—	—	—
NHL totals		119	9	55	64	195	5	0	3	3	4

SMART, RYAN
C, DEVILS

PERSONAL: Born September 22, 1975, in Meadville, Pa. . . . 6-0/170. . . . Shoots right.
HIGH SCHOOL: Meadville (Pa.).
TRANSACTIONS/CAREER NOTES: Selected by New Jersey Devils in sixth round (sixth Devils pick, 134th overall) of NHL entry draft (June 29, 1994).

Season Team	League	REGULAR SEASON Gms.	G	A	Pts.	PIM	PLAYOFFS Gms.	G	A	Pts.	PIM
93-94—Meadville H.S.	Penn. H.S.	46	59	57	116	. . .	—	—	—	—	—

SMEHLIK, RICHARD
D, SABRES

PERSONAL: Born January 23, 1970, in Ostrava, Czechoslovakia. . . . 6-3/208. . . . Shoots left. . . . Name pronounced SHMEHL-ihk.
TRANSACTIONS/CAREER NOTES: Selected by Buffalo Sabres in fifth round (third Sabres pick, 97th overall) of NHL entry draft (June 16, 1990). . . . Injured hip (October 30, 1992); missed two games.

Season Team	League	REGULAR SEASON Gms.	G	A	Pts.	PIM	PLAYOFFS Gms.	G	A	Pts.	PIM
89-90—Vitkovice	Czech.	43	4	3	7	. . .	—	—	—	—	—
90-91—Dukla Jihlava	Czech.	51	4	2	6	22	—	—	—	—	—
91-92—Vitkovice	Czech.	47	9	10	19	. . .	—	—	—	—	—
—Czech. Olympic Team	Int'l	8	0	1	1	2	—	—	—	—	—
92-93—Buffalo	NHL	80	4	27	31	59	8	0	4	4	2
93-94—Buffalo	NHL	84	14	27	41	69	7	0	2	2	10
NHL totals		164	18	54	72	128	15	0	6	6	12

SMITH, ADAM
D, RANGERS

PERSONAL: Born April 24, 1976, in Digby, N.S. . . . 6-0/200. . . . Shoots left.
HIGH SCHOOL: Clover Park (Tacoma, Wash.).
TRANSACTIONS/CAREER NOTES: Selected by New York Rangers in third round (third Rangers pick, 78th overall) of NHL entry draft (June 29, 1994).

Season	Team	League	REGULAR SEASON Gms.	G	A	Pts.	PIM	PLAYOFFS Gms.	G	A	Pts.	PIM
91-92—Kelowna		BCJHL	58	4	4	8	60	—	—	—	—	—
92-93—Tacoma		WHL	67	0	12	12	43	7	0	1	1	4
93-94—Tacoma		WHL	66	4	19	23	119	8	0	0	0	10

SMITH, DERRICK
LW, STARS

PERSONAL: Born January 22, 1965, in Scarborough, Ont. . . . 6-2/215. . . . Shoots left.
TRANSACTIONS/CAREER NOTES: Selected by Philadelphia Flyers as underage junior in third round (second Flyers pick, 44th overall) of NHL entry draft (June 8, 1983). . . . Bruised back (November 1987). . . . Bruised left shoulder (February 1989). . . . Fractured left foot during training camp (September 1989). . . . Sprained right ankle and developed an infected toe (October 30, 1989). . . . Injured ribs (February 20, 1990); missed six games. . . . Claimed by Minnesota North Stars on waivers (October 26, 1991). . . . Injured ankle (December 8, 1991); missed 20 games. . . . Separated shoulder (March 19, 1992); missed five games. . . . North Stars franchise moved from Minnesota to Dallas and renamed Stars for 1993-94 season.
HONORS: Named to IHL All-Star second team (1993-94).

Season	Team	League	REGULAR SEASON Gms.	G	A	Pts.	PIM	PLAYOFFS Gms.	G	A	Pts.	PIM
82-83—Peterborough		OHL	70	16	19	35	47	—	—	—	—	—
83-84—Peterborough		OHL	70	30	36	66	31	8	4	4	8	7
84-85—Philadelphia		NHL	77	17	22	39	31	19	2	5	7	16
85-86—Philadelphia		NHL	69	6	6	12	57	4	0	0	0	10
86-87—Philadelphia		NHL	71	11	21	32	34	26	6	4	10	26
87-88—Philadelphia		NHL	76	16	8	24	104	7	0	0	0	6
88-89—Philadelphia		NHL	74	16	14	30	43	19	5	2	7	12
89-90—Philadelphia		NHL	55	3	6	9	32	—	—	—	—	—
90-91—Philadelphia		NHL	72	11	10	21	37	—	—	—	—	—
91-92—Minnesota		NHL	33	2	4	6	33	7	1	0	1	9
—Kalamazoo		IHL	6	1	5	6	4	—	—	—	—	—
92-93—Kalamazoo		IHL	52	22	13	35	43	—	—	—	—	—
—Minnesota		NHL	9	0	1	1	2	—	—	—	—	—
93-94—Kalamazoo		IHL	77	44	37	81	90	5	0	0	0	18
—Dallas		NHL	1	0	0	0	0	—	—	—	—	—
NHL totals			537	82	92	174	373	82	14	11	25	79

SMITH, GEOFF
D, PANTHERS

PERSONAL: Born March 7, 1969, in Edmonton. . . . 6-3/200. . . . Shoots left. . . . Full name: Geoff Arthur Smith.
HIGH SCHOOL: Harry Ainlay (Edmonton).
COLLEGE: North Dakota.
TRANSACTIONS/CAREER NOTES: Selected by Edmonton Oilers in third round (third Oilers pick, 63rd overall) of NHL entry draft (June 13, 1987). . . . Fractured ankle (October 1988); missed first 10 games of season. . . . Left University of North Dakota and signed to play with Kamloops Blazers (January 1989). . . . Broke jaw (March 1989). . . . Pulled back muscle (February 8, 1991); missed eight games. . . . Bruised shoulder (April 26, 1992). . . . Traded by Oilers to Florida Panthers for third-round (D Corey Neilson) and sixth-round picks in 1994 draft (December 6, 1993). . . . Lacerated left leg (December 10, 1993); missed two games.
HONORS: Named to WHL All-Star first team (1988-89). . . . Named to NHL All-Rookie team (1989-90).
MISCELLANEOUS: Member of Stanley Cup championship team (1990).

Season	Team	League	REGULAR SEASON Gms.	G	A	Pts.	PIM	PLAYOFFS Gms.	G	A	Pts.	PIM
86-87—St. Albert		AJHL	57	7	28	35	101	—	—	—	—	—
87-88—Univ. of North Dakota		WCHA	42	4	12	16	34	—	—	—	—	—
88-89—Kamloops		WHL	32	4	31	35	29	6	1	3	4	12
89-90—Edmonton		NHL	74	4	11	15	52	3	0	0	0	0
90-91—Edmonton		NHL	59	1	12	13	55	4	0	0	0	0
91-92—Edmonton		NHL	74	2	16	18	43	5	0	1	1	6
92-93—Edmonton		NHL	78	4	14	18	30	—	—	—	—	—
93-94—Edmonton		NHL	21	0	3	3	12	—	—	—	—	—
—Florida		NHL	56	1	5	6	38	—	—	—	—	—
NHL totals			362	12	61	73	230	12	0	1	1	6

SMITH, JASON
D, DEVILS

PERSONAL: Born November 2, 1973, in Calgary. . . . 6-3/195. . . . Shoots right.
TRANSACTIONS/CAREER NOTES: Selected by New Jersey Devils in first round (first Devils pick, 18th overall) of NHL entry draft (June 20, 1992).
HONORS: Named to Can.HL All-Rookie team (1991-92). . . . Won Bill Hunter Trophy (1992-93). . . . Named to Can.HL All-Star first team (1992-93). . . . Named to WHL (East) All-Star first team (1992-93).

Season	Team	League	REGULAR SEASON Gms.	G	A	Pts.	PIM	PLAYOFFS Gms.	G	A	Pts.	PIM
90-91—Calgary Canucks		AJHL	45	3	15	18	69	—	—	—	—	—
—Regina		WHL	2	0	0	0	7	—	—	—	—	—
91-92—Regina		WHL	62	9	29	38	168	—	—	—	—	—
92-93—Regina		WHL	64	14	52	66	175	13	4	8	12	39
93-94—New Jersey		NHL	41	0	5	5	43	6	0	0	0	7
—Albany		AHL	20	6	3	9	31	—	—	—	—	—
NHL totals			41	0	5	5	43	6	0	0	0	7

SMITH, STEVE
D, BLACKHAWKS

PERSONAL: Born April 30, 1963, in Glasgow, Scotland. . . . 6-4/215. . . . Shoots left. . . . Full name: James Stephen Smith.
TRANSACTIONS/CAREER NOTES: Selected by Edmonton Oilers as underage junior in sixth round (fifth Oilers pick, 111th overall) of NHL entry draft (June 10, 1981). . . . Strained right shoulder (November 1, 1985). . . . Pulled stomach muscle (February 1986). . . . Separated left shoulder (September 20, 1988). . . . Aggravated shoulder injury (October 1988). . . . Dislocated left shoulder and tore cartilage (January 2, 1989). . . . Underwent surgery to left shoulder (January 23, 1989); missed 45 games. . . . Traded by Oilers to Chicago Blackhawks for D Dave Manson and third-round pick (RW Kirk Maltby) in 1992 draft (September 26, 1991). . . . Pulled rib-cage muscle (December 31, 1991); missed three games. . . . Strained back (December 27, 1992); missed four games. . . . Suspended four games and fined $500 by NHL for slashing (November 22, 1993). . . . Broke left leg (February 24, 1994); missed remainder of season.
HONORS: Played in NHL All-Star Game (1991).
MISCELLANEOUS: Member of Stanley Cup championship teams (1987, 1988 and 1990).

			REGULAR SEASON					PLAYOFFS			
Season Team	League	Gms.	G	A	Pts.	PIM	Gms.	G	A	Pts.	PIM
80-81—London	OMJHL	62	4	12	16	141	—	—	—	—	—
81-82—London	OHL	58	10	36	46	207	4	1	2	3	13
82-83—London	OHL	50	6	35	41	133	3	1	0	1	10
—Moncton	AHL	2	0	0	0	0	—	—	—	—	—
83-84—Moncton	AHL	64	1	8	9	176	—	—	—	—	—
84-85—Nova Scotia	AHL	68	2	28	30	161	5	0	3	3	40
—Edmonton	NHL	2	0	0	0	2	—	—	—	—	—
85-86—Nova Scotia	AHL	4	0	2	2	11	—	—	—	—	—
—Edmonton	NHL	55	4	20	24	166	6	0	1	1	14
86-87—Edmonton	NHL	62	7	15	22	165	15	1	3	4	45
87-88—Edmonton	NHL	79	12	43	55	286	19	1	11	12	55
88-89—Edmonton	NHL	35	3	19	22	97	7	2	2	4	20
89-90—Edmonton	NHL	75	7	34	41	171	22	5	10	15	37
90-91—Edmonton	NHL	77	13	41	54	193	18	1	2	3	45
91-92—Chicago	NHL	76	9	21	30	304	18	1	11	12	16
92-93—Chicago	NHL	78	10	47	57	214	4	0	0	0	10
93-94—Chicago	NHL	57	5	22	27	174	—	—	—	—	—
NHL totals		596	70	262	332	1772	109	11	40	51	242

SMOLINSKI, BRYAN
C, BRUINS

PERSONAL: Born December 27, 1971, in Toledo, O. . . . 6-0/185. . . . Shoots right. . . . Full name: Bryan Anthony Smolinski.
COLLEGE: Michigan State.
TRANSACTIONS/CAREER NOTES: Selected by Boston Bruins in first round (first Bruins pick, 21st overall) of NHL entry draft (June 16, 1990). . . . Injured knee (April 14, 1994); missed one game.
HONORS: Named to CCHA All-Rookie team (1989-90). . . . Named to NCAA All-America West first team (1992-93). . . . Named to CCHA All-Star first team (1992-93).

			REGULAR SEASON					PLAYOFFS			
Season Team	League	Gms.	G	A	Pts.	PIM	Gms.	G	A	Pts.	PIM
87-88—Detroit Little Caesars	MNHL	80	43	77	120	...	—	—	—	—	—
88-89—Stratford Jr. B	OHA	46	32	62	94	132	—	—	—	—	—
89-90—Michigan State	CCHA	39	10	17	27	45	—	—	—	—	—
90-91—Michigan State	CCHA	35	9	12	21	24	—	—	—	—	—
91-92—Michigan State	CCHA	44	30	35	65	59	—	—	—	—	—
92-93—Michigan State	CCHA	40	31	37	*68	93	—	—	—	—	—
—Boston	NHL	9	1	3	4	0	4	1	0	1	2
93-94—Boston	NHL	83	31	20	51	82	13	5	4	9	4
NHL totals		92	32	23	55	82	17	6	4	10	6

SMYTH, GREG
D, BLACKHAWKS

PERSONAL: Born April 23, 1966, in Oakville, Ont. . . . 6-3/212. . . . Shoots right. . . . Name pronounced SMIHTH.
TRANSACTIONS/CAREER NOTES: Selected by Philadelphia Flyers as underage junior in second round (first Flyers pick, 22nd overall) of NHL entry draft (June 9, 1984). . . . Suspended 10 games by OHL for fighting with fans (December 1984). . . . Suspended by London Knights (October 1985). . . . Suspended eight games by OHL (November 7, 1985). . . . Traded by Flyers with third-round pick in 1989 draft (G John Tanner) to Quebec Nordiques for D Terry Carkner (July 25, 1988). . . . Broke two bones in right hand during training camp (September 1988). . . . Suspended eight games by AHL for fighting (December 17, 1988). . . . Injured back (February 15, 1990). . . . Recalled from Halifax by Quebec and refused to report (February 10, 1991). . . . Traded by Nordiques to Calgary Flames for RW Martin Simard (March 10, 1992). . . . Strained stomach (October 6, 1992); missed first four games of season. . . . Injured ribs (December 4, 1992); missed four games. . . . Signed as free agent by Florida Panthers (July 14, 1993). . . . Underwent right elbow surgery (October 6, 1993); missed five games. . . . Traded by Panthers to Toronto Maple Leafs for future considerations (December 7, 1993). . . . Claimed on waivers by Chicago Blackhawks (January 9, 1994). . . . Pulled rib cage muscle (January 27, 1994); missed four games.
HONORS: Named to OHL All-Star second team (1985-86).

			REGULAR SEASON					PLAYOFFS			
Season Team	League	Gms.	G	A	Pts.	PIM	Gms.	G	A	Pts.	PIM
83-84—London	OHL	64	4	21	25	*252	6	1	0	1	24
84-85—London	OHL	47	7	16	23	188	8	2	2	4	27
85-86—London	OHL	46	12	42	54	197	4	1	2	3	28
—Hershey	AHL	2	0	1	1	5	8	0	0	0	60

S

Season Team	League	REGULAR SEASON					PLAYOFFS				
		Gms.	G	A	Pts.	Pen.	Gms.	G	A	Pts.	Pen.
86-87—Hershey	AHL	35	0	2	2	158	2	0	0	0	19
—Philadelphia	NHL	1	0	0	0	0	1	0	0	0	2
87-88—Hershey	AHL	21	0	10	10	102	—	—	—	—	—
—Philadelphia	NHL	48	1	6	7	192	5	0	0	0	38
88-89—Halifax	AHL	43	3	9	12	310	4	0	1	1	35
—Quebec	NHL	10	0	1	1	70	—	—	—	—	—
89-90—Quebec	NHL	13	0	0	0	57	—	—	—	—	—
—Halifax	AHL	49	5	14	19	235	6	1	0	1	52
90-91—Quebec	NHL	1	0	0	0	0	—	—	—	—	—
—Halifax	AHL	56	6	23	29	340	—	—	—	—	—
91-92—Quebec	NHL	29	0	2	2	138	—	—	—	—	—
—Halifax	AHL	9	1	3	4	35	—	—	—	—	—
—Calgary	NHL	7	1	1	2	15	—	—	—	—	—
92-93—Calgary	NHL	35	1	2	3	95	—	—	—	—	—
—Salt Lake City	IHL	5	0	1	1	31	—	—	—	—	—
93-94—Florida	NHL	12	1	0	1	37	—	—	—	—	—
—Toronto	NHL	11	0	1	1	38	—	—	—	—	—
—Chicago	NHL	38	0	0	0	108	6	0	0	0	0
NHL totals		205	4	13	17	750	12	0	0	0	40

SMYTH, KEVIN
LW, WHALERS

PERSONAL: Born November 22, 1973, in Banff, Alta. . . . 6-2/210. . . . Shoots left. . . . Brother of Ryan Smyth, left winger, Edmonton Oilers.
TRANSACTIONS/CAREER NOTES: Selected by Hartford Whalers in fourth round (fourth Whalers pick, 79th overall) of NHL entry draft (June 20, 1992). . . . Bruised spleen (February 11, 1994); missed six games. . . . Injured shoulder (March 22, 1994); missed four games.

Season Team	League	REGULAR SEASON					PLAYOFFS				
		Gms.	G	A	Pts.	PIM	Gms.	G	A	Pts.	PIM
90-91—Moose Jaw	WHL	66	30	45	75	96	6	1	1	2	0
91-92—Moose Jaw	WHL	71	30	55	85	114	4	1	3	4	6
92-93—Moose Jaw	WHL	64	44	38	82	111	—	—	—	—	—
93-94—Springfield	AHL	42	22	27	49	72	6	4	5	9	0
—Hartford	NHL	21	3	2	5	10	—	—	—	—	—
NHL totals		21	3	2	5	10					

SMYTH, RYAN
LW, OILERS

PERSONAL: Born February 21, 1976, in Banff, Alta. . . . 6-1/185. . . . Shoots left. . . . Name pronounced SMITH. . . . Brother of Kevin Smyth, left winger, Hartford Whalers.
HIGH SCHOOL: Vanier Comm. Catholic (Edson, Alta.).
TRANSACTIONS/CAREER NOTES: Selected by Edmonton Oilers in first round (second Oilers pick, sixth overall) of NHL entry draft (June 28, 1994).

Season Team	League	REGULAR SEASON					PLAYOFFS				
		Gms.	G	A	Pts.	PIM	Gms.	G	A	Pts.	PIM
91-92—Moose Jaw	WHL	2	0	0	0	0	—	—	—	—	—
92-93—Moose Jaw	WHL	64	19	14	33	59	—	—	—	—	—
93-94—Moose Jaw	WHL	72	50	55	105	88	—	—	—	—	—

SNELL, CHRIS
D, MAPLE LEAFS

PERSONAL: Born May 12, 1971, in Regina, Sask. . . . 5-10/200. . . . Shoots left.
TRANSACTIONS/CAREER NOTES: Signed as free agent by Toronto Maple Leafs (August 3, 1993).
HONORS: Named to OHL All-Star first team (1989-90). . . . Won Eddie Shore Plaque (1993-94). . . . Named to AHL All-Star first team (1993-94).

Season Team	League	REGULAR SEASON					PLAYOFFS				
		Gms.	G	A	Pts.	PIM	Gms.	G	A	Pts.	PIM
89-90—Ottawa	OHL	63	18	62	80	36	3	2	4	6	4
90-91—Ottawa	OHL	54	23	59	82	58	17	3	14	17	8
91-92—Rochester	AHL	65	5	27	32	66	10	2	1	3	6
92-93—Rochester	AHL	76	14	57	71	83	17	5	8	13	39
93-94—St. John's	AHL	75	22	74	96	92	11	1	15	16	10
—Toronto	NHL	2	0	0	0	2	—	—	—	—	—
NHL totals		2	0	0	0	2					

SNOW, GARTH
G, NORDIQUES

PERSONAL: Born July 28, 1969, in Wrentham, Mass. . . . 6-3/200. . . . Catches left.
HIGH SCHOOL: Mount St. Charles Academy (Woonsocket, R.I.).
COLLEGE: Maine.
TRANSACTIONS/CAREER NOTES: Selected by Quebec Nordiques in sixth round (sixth Nordiques pick, 114th overall) of NHL entry draft (June 13, 1987).
HONORS: Named to NCAA All-Tournament team (1992-93). . . . Named to Hockey East All-Star second team (1992-93).

Season Team	League	REGULAR SEASON							PLAYOFFS					
		Gms.	Min.	W	L	T	GA	SO	Avg.	Gms.	Min.	W	L	GA SO	Avg.
88-89—University of Maine	Hoc. East	5	241	2	2	0	14	1	3.49	—	—	—	—	— —	—
89-90—University of Maine	Hoc. East						Did not play.								
90-91—University of Maine	Hoc. East	25	1290	18	4	0	64	0	2.98	—	—	—	—	— —	—
91-92—University of Maine	Hoc. East	31	1792	25	4	2	73	2	2.44	—	—	—	—	— —	—

Season Team	League	REGULAR SEASON Gms.	Min.	W	L	T	GA	SO	Avg.	PLAYOFFS Gms.	Min.	W	L	GA	SO	Avg.
92-93—University of Maine	Hoc. East	23	1210	21	0	1	42	1	2.08	—	—	—	—	—	—	—
93-94—U.S. national team	Int'l	23	1324	...	...	...	71	...	3.22	—	—	—	—	—	—	—
—Quebec	NHL	5	279	3	2	0	16	0	3.44	—	—	—	—	—	—	—
—U.S. Olympic Team	Int'l	5	299	...	...	...	17	0	3.41	—	—	—	—	—	—	—
—Cornwall	AHL	16	927	6	5	3	51	0	3.30	13	790	8	5	42	0	3.19
NHL totals.............................		5	279	3	2	0	16	0	3.44							

SODERSTROM, TOMMY
G, FLYERS

PERSONAL: Born July 17, 1969, in Stockholm, Sweden. ... 5-9/156. ... Catches left.... Name pronounced SAH-duhr-struhm.
TRANSACTIONS/CAREER NOTES: Selected by Philadelphia Flyers in 11th round (14th Flyers pick, 214th overall) of NHL entry draft (June 16, 1990).... Underwent procedure to correct Wolff-Parkinson-White syndrome (November 3, 1993); missed six games.
HONORS: Named Swedish League Rookie of the Year (1990-91).... Named to Swedish League All-Star team (1991-92).

Season Team	League	REGULAR SEASON Gms.	Min.	W	L	T	GA	SO	Avg.	PLAYOFFS Gms.	Min.	W	L	GA	SO	Avg.
89-90—Djurgarden	Sweden	4	240	...	...	...	14	0	3.50	—	—	—	—	—	—	—
90-91—Djurgarden	Sweden	39	2340	22	12	6	104	3	2.67	7	423	...	...	10	2	1.42
91-92—Djurgarden	Sweden	31	2357	15	8	11	112	...	2.85	—	—	—	—	—	—	—
—Swedish Olympic Team	Int'l	5	296	...	...	...	13	0	2.64	—	—	—	—	—	—	—
92-93—Hershey	AHL	7	373	4	1	0	15	0	2.41	—	—	—	—	—	—	—
—Philadelphia	NHL	44	2512	20	17	6	143	5	3.42	—	—	—	—	—	—	—
93-94—Hershey	AHL	9	462	3	4	1	37	0	4.81	—	—	—	—	—	—	—
—Philadelphia	NHL	34	1736	6	18	4	116	2	4.01	—	—	—	—	—	—	—
NHL totals.............................		78	4248	26	35	10	259	7	3.66							

SOROCHAN, LEE
D, RANGERS

PERSONAL: Born September 9, 1975, in Edmonton. ... 5-11/208. ... Shoots left. ... Name pronounced suh-ROH-kuhn.
HIGH SCHOOL: Gibbons (Alta.).
TRANSACTIONS/CAREER NOTES: Selected by New York Rangers in second round (second Rangers pick, 34th overall) of NHL entry draft (June 26, 1993).

Season Team	League	REGULAR SEASON Gms.	G	A	Pts.	PIM	PLAYOFFS Gms.	G	A	Pts.	PIM
91-92—Lethbridge........................	WHL	67	2	9	11	105	5	0	2	2	6
92-93—Lethbridge........................	WHL	69	8	32	40	208	4	0	1	1	12
93-94—Lethbridge........................	WHL	46	5	27	32	123	9	4	3	7	16

SOUCY, CHRISTIAN
G, BLACKHAWKS

PERSONAL: Born September 14, 1970, in Gatineau, Que. ... 5-11/160. ... Catches left.... Name pronounced SOO-see.
COLLEGE: Vermont.
TRANSACTIONS/CAREER NOTES: Signed as free agent by Chicago Blackhawks (June 21, 1993).
HONORS: Named to NCAA All-America East second team (1991-92).... Named to ECAC All-Star second team (1992-93).

Season Team	League	REGULAR SEASON Gms.	Min.	W	L	T	GA	SO	Avg.	PLAYOFFS Gms.	Min.	W	L	GA	SO	Avg.
89-90—Pembroke	CJHL	47	2721	16	24	4	212	1	4.67	—	—	—	—	—	—	—
90-91—Pembroke	CJHL	54	3109	27	24	1	198	2	3.82	—	—	—	—	—	—	—
91-92—University of Vermont ..	ECAC	30	1783	15	11	3	84	1	2.83	—	—	—	—	—	—	—
92-93—University of Vermont ..	ECAC	29	1708	11	15	3	90	2	3.16	—	—	—	—	—	—	—
93-94—Indianapolis	IHL	46	2302	14	*25	‡1	159	1	4.14	—	—	—	—	—	—	—
—Chicago	NHL	1	3	0	0	0	0	0	0.00	—	—	—	—	—	—	—
NHL totals.............................		1	3	0	0	0	0									0

SOURAY, SHELDON
D, DEVILS

PERSONAL: Born July 13, 1976, in Elk Point, Alta.... 6-3/210.... Shoots left.
TRANSACTIONS/CAREER NOTES: Selected by New Jersey Devils in third round (third Devils pick, 71st overall) of NHL entry draft (June 29, 1994).

Season Team	League	REGULAR SEASON Gms.	G	A	Pts.	PIM	PLAYOFFS Gms.	G	A	Pts.	PIM
92-93—Fort Saskatchewan	AJHL	35	0	12	12	125	—	—	—	—	—
—Tri-City	WHL	2	0	0	0	0	—	—	—	—	—
93-94—Tri-City	WHL	42	3	6	9	122	—	—	—	—	—

SPITZIG, TIM
RW, RED WINGS

PERSONAL: Born April 15, 1974, in Goderich, Ont.... 6-0/195.... Shoots right.
TRANSACTIONS/CAREER NOTES: Selected by Detroit Red Wings in sixth round (seventh Red Wings pick, 152nd overall) of NHL entry draft (June 26, 1993).
HONORS: Won Bobby Smith Trophy (1992-93).

Season Team	League	REGULAR SEASON Gms.	G	A	Pts.	PIM	PLAYOFFS Gms.	G	A	Pts.	PIM
91-92—Kitchener..........................	OHL	62	8	13	21	87	4	0	0	0	2

Season Team	League	REGULAR SEASON					PLAYOFFS				
		Gms.	G	A	Pts.	Pen.	Gms.	G	A	Pts.	Pen.
92-93—Kitchener	OHL	66	39	39	78	127	—	—	—	—	—
93-94—Kitchener	OHL	62	48	38	86	111	5	7	2	9	8

STAIOS, STEVE
D, BLUES

PERSONAL: Born July 28, 1973, in Hamilton, Ont. . . . 6-0/ 183. . . . Shoots right. . . . Name pronounced STAY-ohz.

TRANSACTIONS/CAREER NOTES: Selected by St. Louis Blues in second round (first Blues pick, 27th overall) of NHL entry draft (June 22, 1991).

Season Team	League	REGULAR SEASON					PLAYOFFS				
		Gms.	G	A	Pts.	PIM	Gms.	G	A	Pts.	PIM
89-90—Hamilton Jr. B	OHA	40	9	27	36	66	—	—	—	—	—
90-91—Niagara Falls	OHL	66	17	29	46	115	12	2	3	5	10
91-92—Niagara Falls	OHL	65	11	42	53	122	17	7	8	15	27
92-93—Niagara Falls	OHL	12	4	14	18	30	—	—	—	—	—
—Sudbury	OHL	53	13	44	57	67	11	5	6	11	22
93-94—Peoria	IHL	38	3	9	12	42	—	—	—	—	—

STAJDUHAR, NICK
D, OILERS

PERSONAL: Born December 6, 1974, in Kitchener, Ont. . . . 6-2/ 1195. . . . Shoots left. . . . Name pronounced STAJ-doo-hahr.

TRANSACTIONS/CAREER NOTES: Selected by Edmonton Oilers in first round (second Oilers pick, 16th overall) of NHL entry draft (June 26, 1993).

HONORS: Named to OHL All-Star first team (1993-94).

Season Team	League	REGULAR SEASON					PLAYOFFS				
		Gms.	G	A	Pts.	PIM	Gms.	G	A	Pts.	PIM
90-91—London	OHL	66	3	12	15	39	7	0	0	0	2
91-92—London	OHL	66	6	15	21	62	10	1	4	5	10
92-93—London	OHL	49	15	46	61	58	12	4	11	15	10
93-94—London	OHL	52	34	52	86	58	5	0	2	2	8

STANTON, PAUL
D, BRUINS

PERSONAL: Born June 22, 1967, in Boston. . . . 6-1/200. . . . Shoots right. . . . Full name: Paul Fredrick Stanton.

HIGH SCHOOL: Catholic Memorial (Boston).

COLLEGE: Wisconsin.

TRANSACTIONS/CAREER NOTES: Selected by Pittsburgh Penguins in eighth round (eighth Penguins pick, 149th overall) of NHL entry draft (June 15, 1985). . . . Injured knee ligament (October 31, 1991); missed 16 games. . . . Traded by Penguins to Boston Bruins for third-round pick (LW Greg Crozier) in 1994 draft (October 8, 1993). . . . Suffered from the flu (April 7, 1994); missed one game.

HONORS: Named to NCAA All-America West first team (1987-88). . . . Named to WCHA All-Star first team (1988-89).

MISCELLANEOUS: Member of Stanley Cup championship teams (1991 and 1992).

Season Team	League	REGULAR SEASON					PLAYOFFS				
		Gms.	G	A	Pts.	PIM	Gms.	G	A	Pts.	PIM
83-84—Catholic Memorial H.S.	Mass. H.S.	. . .	15	20	35	. . .	—	—	—	—	—
84-85—Catholic Memorial H.S.	Mass. H.S.	20	16	21	37	17	—	—	—	—	—
85-86—University of Wisconsin	WCHA	36	4	6	10	16	—	—	—	—	—
86-87—University of Wisconsin	WCHA	41	5	17	22	70	—	—	—	—	—
87-88—University of Wisconsin	WCHA	45	9	38	47	98	—	—	—	—	—
88-89—University of Wisconsin	WCHA	45	7	29	36	126	—	—	—	—	—
89-90—Muskegon	IHL	77	5	27	32	61	15	2	4	6	21
90-91—Pittsburgh	NHL	75	5	18	23	40	22	1	2	3	24
91-92—Pittsburgh	NHL	54	2	8	10	62	†21	1	7	8	42
92-93—Pittsburgh	NHL	77	4	12	16	97	1	0	1	1	0
93-94—Boston	NHL	71	3	7	10	54	—	—	—	—	—
NHL totals		277	14	45	59	253	44	2	10	12	66

STAPLETON, MIKE
C/RW, OILERS

PERSONAL: Born May 5, 1966, in Sarnia, Ont. . . . 5-10/ 185. . . . Shoots right. . . . Son of Pat Stapleton, defenseman, Boston Bruins and Chicago Blackhawks (1961-62 through 1972-73); and Chicago Cougars, Indianapolis Racers and Cincinnati Stingers of WHA (1973-74 through 1977-78).

TRANSACTIONS/CAREER NOTES: Selected by Chicago Blackhawks in seventh round (seventh Blackhawks pick, 132nd overall) of NHL entry draft (June 9, 1984). . . . Signed as free agent by Pittsburgh Penguins (September 4, 1992). . . . Claimed on waivers by Edmonton Oilers (February 19, 1994).

Season Team	League	REGULAR SEASON					PLAYOFFS				
		Gms.	G	A	Pts.	PIM	Gms.	G	A	Pts.	PIM
82-83—Strathroy Jr. B	OHA	40	39	38	77	99	—	—	—	—	—
83-84—Cornwall	OHL	70	24	45	69	94	3	1	2	3	4
84-85—Cornwall	OHL	56	41	44	85	68	9	2	4	6	23
85-86—Cornwall	OHL	56	39	65	104	74	6	2	3	5	2
86-87—Canadian national team	Int'l	21	2	4	6	4	—	—	—	—	—
—Chicago	NHL	39	3	6	9	6	4	0	0	0	2
87-88—Saginaw	IHL	31	11	19	30	52	10	5	6	11	10
—Chicago	NHL	53	2	9	11	59	—	—	—	—	—

Season Team	League	REGULAR SEASON					PLAYOFFS				
		Gms.	G	A	Pts.	Pen.	Gms.	G	A	Pts.	Pen.
88-89—Chicago	NHL	7	0	1	1	7	—	—	—	—	—
—Saginaw	IHL	69	21	47	68	162	6	1	3	4	4
89-90—Arvika	Sweden	30	15	18	33	...	—	—	—	—	—
—Indianapolis	IHL	16	5	10	15	6	13	9	10	19	38
90-91—Chicago	NHL	7	0	1	1	2	—	—	—	—	—
—Indianapolis	IHL	75	29	52	81	76	7	1	4	5	0
91-92—Indianapolis	IHL	59	18	40	58	65	—	—	—	—	—
—Chicago	NHL	19	4	4	8	8	—	—	—	—	—
92-93—Pittsburgh	NHL	78	4	9	13	10	4	0	0	0	0
93-94—Pittsburgh	NHL	58	7	4	11	18	—	—	—	—	—
—Edmonton	NHL	23	5	9	14	28	—	—	—	—	—
NHL totals		284	25	43	68	138	8	0	0	0	2

STAROSTENKO, DIMITRI
RW, RANGERS

PERSONAL: Born March 18, 1973, in Minsk, U.S.S.R. .... 6-0/185. .... Shoots left.
TRANSACTIONS/CAREER NOTES: Selected by New York Rangers in fifth round (fifth Rangers pick, 120th overall) of NHL entry draft (June 20, 1992).

Season Team	League	REGULAR SEASON					PLAYOFFS				
		Gms.	G	A	Pts.	PIM	Gms.	G	A	Pts.	PIM
89-90—Dynamo Minsk	USSR	7	0	0	0	2	—	—	—	—	—
90-91—CSKA Moscow	USSR	20	2	1	3	4	—	—	—	—	—
91-92—CSKA Moscow	CIS	32	3	1	4	12	—	—	—	—	—
92-93—CSKA Moscow	CIS	42	15	12	27	22	—	—	—	—	—
93-94—Binghamton	AHL	41	12	9	21	10	—	—	—	—	—

STASTNY, PETER
C, BLUES

PERSONAL: Born September 18, 1956, in Bratislava, Czechoslovakia. .... 6-1/200. .... Shoots left. .... Name pronounced STAST-nee. .... Brother of Anton Stastny, left winger, Quebec Nordiques (1980-81 through 1988-89); and brother of Marian Stastny, right winger, Quebec Nordiques and Toronto Maple Leafs (1981-82 through 1985-86).
TRANSACTIONS/CAREER NOTES: Signed as free agent by Quebec Nordiques (August 26, 1980). .... Injured knee (December 18, 1982). .... Suspended five games by NHL (October 1984). .... Injured lower back (November 1987). .... Sprained left shoulder (December 1988). .... Suffered sore left knee (December 1989). .... Traded by Nordiques to New Jersey Devils for D Craig Wolanin and future considerations; Devils sent D Randy Velischek to Nordiques to complete deal (March 6, 1990). .... Suffered from digestive virus (February 29, 1992); missed eight games. .... Suffered from minor knee sprain and the flu (March 21, 1992); missed five games. .... Missed first five games of regular season due to contract dispute (October 1992). .... Suffered from the flu (January 22, 1993); missed two games. .... Bruised shoulder (March 7, 1993); missed one game. .... Signed as free agent by St. Louis Blues (March 9, 1994).
HONORS: Named to Czechoslovakian League All-Star second team (1977-78). .... Named to Czechoslovakian League All-Star first team (1978-79). .... Named Czechoslovakian League Player of the Year (1979-80). .... Named NHL Rookie of the Year by THE SPORTING NEWS (1980-81). .... Won Calder Memorial Trophy (1980-81). .... Played in NHL All-Star Game (1981, 1982-1984, 1986 and 1988).
RECORDS: Shares NHL single-season record for most assists by a rookie—70 (1980-81). .... Shares NHL single-game record for most points by a rookie—8 (February 22, 1981); most points for road game—8 (February 22, 1981).
STATISTICAL NOTES: One of three players to score 100 points in each of their first six NHL seasons (Wayne Gretzky and Mario Lemieux).

Season Team	League	REGULAR SEASON					PLAYOFFS				
		Gms.	G	A	Pts.	PIM	Gms.	G	A	Pts.	PIM
77-78—Slovan Bratislava	Czech.	44	29	24	53	...	—	—	—	—	—
—Czech. national team	Int'l	16	5	2	7	...	—	—	—	—	—
78-79—Slovan Bratislava	Czech.	44	32	23	55	...	—	—	—	—	—
—Czech. national team	Int'l	18	12	9	21	...	—	—	—	—	—
79-80—Slovan Bratislava	Czech.	40	28	30	58	...	—	—	—	—	—
—Czech. Olympic Team	Int'l	6	7	7	14	6	—	—	—	—	—
80-81—Quebec	NHL	77	39	70	109	37	5	2	8	10	7
81-82—Quebec	NHL	80	46	93	139	91	12	7	11	18	10
82-83—Quebec	NHL	75	47	77	124	78	4	3	2	5	10
83-84—Quebec	NHL	80	46	73	119	73	9	2	7	9	31
84-85—Quebec	NHL	75	32	68	100	95	18	4	19	23	24
85-86—Quebec	NHL	76	41	81	122	60	3	0	1	1	2
86-87—Quebec	NHL	64	24	53	77	43	13	6	9	15	12
87-88—Quebec	NHL	76	46	65	111	69	—	—	—	—	—
88-89—Quebec	NHL	72	35	50	85	117	—	—	—	—	—
89-90—Quebec	NHL	62	24	38	62	24	—	—	—	—	—
—New Jersey	NHL	12	5	6	11	16	6	3	2	5	4
90-91—New Jersey	NHL	77	18	42	60	53	7	3	4	7	2
91-92—New Jersey	NHL	66	24	38	62	42	7	3	7	10	19
92-93—New Jersey	NHL	62	17	23	40	22	5	0	2	2	2
93-94—Slovan Bratislava	Slovakia	4	0	4	4	0	—	—	—	—	—
—Slovakian Olympic team	Int'l	8	5	4	9	9	—	—	—	—	—
—St. Louis	NHL	17	5	11	16	4	4	0	0	0	2
NHL totals		971	449	788	1237	824	93	33	72	105	125

STAUBER, ROBB

G, KINGS

PERSONAL: Born November 25, 1967, in Duluth, Minn. . . . 5-11/180. . . . Catches left. . . . Name pronounced STAW-buhr.
HIGH SCHOOL: Denfeld (Duluth, Minn.).
COLLEGE: Minnesota.
TRANSACTIONS/CAREER NOTES: Selected by Los Angeles Kings in sixth round (fifth Kings pick, 107th overall) of NHL entry draft (June 21, 1986). . . . Twisted left knee and ankle (December 3, 1988); missed 14 games. . . . Injured groin and back (October 1989). . . . Underwent knee surgery (March 1991). . . . Strained shoulder (November 6, 1993); missed four games.
HONORS: Won Hobey Baker Memorial Trophy (1987-88). . . . Won WCHA Most Valuable Player Award (1987-88). . . . Won WCHA Goaltender of the Year Award (1987-88 and 1988-89). . . . Named to NCAA All-America West first team (1987-88). . . . Named to WCHA All-Star first team (1987-88). . . . Named to WCHA All-Star second team (1988-89).

Season Team	League		Gms.	Min.	W	L	T	GA	SO	Avg.	Gms.	Min.	W	L	GA	SO	Avg.
84-85—Duluth Denfeld H.S.	Minn. HS		22	990	...	...	...	37	0	2.24	—	—	—	—	—	—	—
85-86—Duluth Denfeld H.S.	Minn. HS		27	1215	...	...	...	66	0	3.26	—	—	—	—	—	—	—
86-87—Univ. of Minnesota.......	WCHA		20	1072	13	5	0	63	0	3.53	—	—	—	—	—	—	—
87-88—Univ. of Minnesota.......	WCHA		44	2621	34	10	0	119	5	2.72	—	—	—	—	—	—	—
88-89—Univ. of Minnesota.......	WCHA		34	2024	26	8	0	82	0	2.43	—	—	—	—	—	—	—
89-90—New Haven.................	AHL		14	851	6	6	2	43	0	3.03	5	302	2	3	24	0	4.77
—Los Angeles.................	NHL		2	83	0	1	0	11	0	7.95	—	—	—	—	—	—	—
90-91—Phoenix	IHL		4	160	1	2	‡0	11	0	4.13	—	—	—	—	—	—	—
—New Haven.................	AHL		33	1882	13	16	4	115	1	3.67	—	—	—	—	—	—	—
91-92—Phoenix	IHL		22	1242	8	12	‡1	80	0	3.86	—	—	—	—	—	—	—
92-93—Los Angeles.................	NHL		31	1735	15	8	4	111	0	3.84	4	240	3	1	16	0	4.00
93-94—Los Angeles.................	NHL		22	1144	4	11	5	65	1	3.41	—	—	—	—	—	—	—
—Phoenix	IHL		3	121	1	1	‡0	13	0	6.45	—	—	—	—	—	—	—
NHL totals............			55	2962	19	20	9	187	1	3.79	4	240	3	1	16	0	4.00

STEEN, THOMAS

C, JETS

PERSONAL: Born June 8, 1960, in Tocksmark, Sweden. . . . 5-11/185. . . . Shoots left.
TRANSACTIONS/CAREER NOTES: Selected by Winnipeg Jets in fifth round (fifth Jets pick, 103rd overall) of NHL entry draft (June 11, 1979). . . . Lacerated elbow during Canada Cup (September 1981). . . . Injured knee in training camp (October 1981). . . . Suffered protruding disk (December 1989); missed 22 games. . . . Fractured right ankle (November 28, 1990); missed 20 games. . . . Suffered lower back spasms (September 1991); missed first 24 games of season. . . . Suffered ankle contusion (December 1991); missed 10 games. . . . Suffered recurrence of back spasms (January 1992); missed six games. . . . Suffered hip pointer (October 31, 1992); missed one game. . . . Suffered from the flu (February 12, 1993); missed three games. . . . Strained groin (November 26, 1993); missed four games. . . . Strained groin (December 12, 1993); missed four games.
HONORS: Named Swedish League Player of the Year (1980-81).

Season Team	League	Gms.	G	A	Pts.	PIM	Gms.	G	A	Pts.	PIM
76-77—Leksand........................	Sweden	2	1	1	2	2	—	—	—	—	—
77-78—Leksand........................	Sweden	35	5	6	11	30	—	—	—	—	—
78-79—Leksand........................	Sweden	25	13	4	17	35	2	0	0	0	0
—Swedish national team	Int'l	2	0	0	0	0	—	—	—	—	—
79-80—Leksand........................	Sweden	18	7	7	14	14	2	0	0	0	6
80-81—Farjestad......................	Sweden	32	16	23	39	30	7	4	2	6	8
—Swedish national team	Int'l	19	2	5	7	12	—	—	—	—	—
81-82—Winnipeg......................	NHL	73	15	29	44	42	4	0	4	4	2
82-83—Winnipeg......................	NHL	75	26	33	59	60	3	0	2	2	0
83-84—Winnipeg......................	NHL	78	20	45	65	69	3	0	1	1	9
84-85—Winnipeg......................	NHL	79	30	54	84	80	8	2	3	5	17
85-86—Winnipeg......................	NHL	78	17	47	64	76	3	1	1	2	4
86-87—Winnipeg......................	NHL	75	17	33	50	59	10	3	4	7	8
87-88—Winnipeg......................	NHL	76	16	38	54	53	5	1	5	6	2
88-89—Winnipeg......................	NHL	80	27	61	88	80	—	—	—	—	—
89-90—Winnipeg......................	NHL	53	18	48	66	35	7	2	5	7	16
90-91—Winnipeg......................	NHL	58	19	48	67	49	—	—	—	—	—
91-92—Winnipeg......................	NHL	38	13	25	38	29	7	2	4	6	2
92-93—Winnipeg......................	NHL	80	22	50	72	75	6	1	3	4	2
93-94—Winnipeg......................	NHL	76	19	32	51	32	—	—	—	—	—
NHL totals............		919	259	543	802	739	56	12	32	44	62

STERN, RONNIE

RW, FLAMES

PERSONAL: Born January 11, 1967, in Ste. Agatha Des Mont, Que. . . . 6-0/195. . . . Shoots right.
TRANSACTIONS/CAREER NOTES: Selected by Vancouver Canucks as underage junior in fourth round (third Canucks pick, 70th overall) of NHL entry draft (June 21, 1986). . . . Bruised shoulder (April 1989). . . . Suffered laceration near eye and dislocated shoulder (March 19, 1990). . . . Fractured wrist (October 30, 1990); missed 10 weeks. . . . Traded by Canucks with D Kevan Guy and option to switch fourth-round picks in 1992 draft to Calgary Flames for D Dana Murzyn; Flames did not exercise option (March 5, 1991). . . . Suffered back spasms (October 15, 1992); missed 11 games. . . . Broke bone in right foot (October 11, 1993); missed three games. . . . Bruised shoulder (December 7, 1993); missed one game. . . . Bruised shoulder (December 28, 1993); missed six games.

Season Team	League	Gms.	G	A	Pts.	PIM	Gms.	G	A	Pts.	PIM
84-85—Longueuil	QMJHL	67	6	14	20	176	—	—	—	—	—
85-86—Longueuil	QMJHL	70	39	33	72	317	—	—	—	—	—

Season Team	League	REGULAR SEASON					PLAYOFFS				
		Gms.	G	A	Pts.	Pen.	Gms.	G	A	Pts.	Pen.
86-87—Longueuil	QMJHL	56	32	39	71	266	19	11	9	20	55
87-88—Fredericton	AHL	2	1	0	1	4	—	—	—	—	—
—Flint	IHL	55	14	19	33	294	16	8	8	16	94
—Vancouver	NHL	15	0	0	0	52	—	—	—	—	—
88-89—Milwaukee	IHL	45	19	23	42	280	5	1	0	1	11
—Vancouver	NHL	17	1	0	1	49	3	0	1	1	17
89-90—Milwaukee	IHL	26	8	9	17	165	—	—	—	—	—
—Vancouver	NHL	34	2	3	5	208	—	—	—	—	—
90-91—Milwaukee	IHL	7	2	2	4	81	—	—	—	—	—
—Vancouver	NHL	31	2	3	5	171	—	—	—	—	—
—Calgary	NHL	13	1	3	4	69	7	1	3	4	14
91-92—Calgary	NHL	72	13	9	22	338	—	—	—	—	—
92-93—Calgary	NHL	70	10	15	25	207	6	0	0	0	43
93-94—Calgary	NHL	71	9	20	29	243	7	2	0	2	12
NHL totals		323	38	53	91	1337	23	3	4	7	86

STEVENS, JOHN
D, WHALERS

PERSONAL: Born May 4, 1966, in Completon, N.B. . . . 6-1/195. . . . Shoots left.
TRANSACTIONS/CAREER NOTES: Selected by Philadelphia Flyers as underage junior in third round (fifth Flyers pick, 47th overall) of NHL entry draft (June 9, 1984). . . . Underwent knee surgery (September 1984). . . . Signed as free agent by Hartford Whalers (July 16, 1990).

Season Team	League	REGULAR SEASON					PLAYOFFS				
		Gms.	G	A	Pts.	PIM	Gms.	G	A	Pts.	PIM
82-83—Newmarket	OHA	48	2	9	11	111	—	—	—	—	—
83-84—Oshawa	OHL	70	1	10	11	71	7	0	1	1	6
84-85—Oshawa	OHL	45	2	10	12	61	5	0	2	2	4
—Hershey	AHL	3	0	0	0	2	—	—	—	—	—
85-86—Oshawa	OHL	65	1	7	8	146	6	0	2	2	14
—Kalamazoo	IHL	6	0	1	1	8	6	0	3	3	9
86-87—Hershey	AHL	63	1	15	16	131	3	0	0	0	7
—Philadelphia	NHL	6	0	2	2	14	—	—	—	—	—
87-88—Philadelphia	NHL	3	0	0	0	0	—	—	—	—	—
—Hershey	AHL	59	1	15	16	108	—	—	—	—	—
88-89—Hershey	AHL	78	3	13	16	129	12	1	1	2	29
89-90—Hershey	AHL	79	3	10	13	193	—	—	—	—	—
90-91—Hartford	NHL	14	0	1	1	11	—	—	—	—	—
—Springfield	AHL	65	0	12	12	139	18	0	6	6	35
91-92—Springfield	AHL	45	1	12	13	73	11	1	3	4	27
—Hartford	NHL	21	0	4	4	19	—	—	—	—	—
92-93—Springfield	AHL	74	1	19	20	111	15	0	1	1	18
93-94—Springfield	AHL	71	3	9	12	85	3	0	0	0	0
—Hartford	NHL	9	0	3	3	4	—	—	—	—	—
NHL totals		53	0	10	10	48					

STEVENS, KEVIN
LW, PENGUINS

PERSONAL: Born April 15, 1965, in Brockton, Mass. . . . 6-3/217. . . . Shoots left. . . . Full name: Kevin Michael Stevens.
HIGH SCHOOL: Silver Lake (Mass.).
COLLEGE: Boston College.
TRANSACTIONS/CAREER NOTES: Selected by Los Angeles Kings in sixth round (sixth Kings pick, 108th overall) of NHL entry draft (June 8, 1983). . . . Traded by Kings to Pittsburgh Penguins for LW Anders Hakansson (September 9, 1983). . . . Damaged cartilage in left knee (November 5, 1992) and underwent arthroscopic surgery (November 6, 1992); missed nine games. . . . Suspended one game by NHL (March 1993). . . . Suffered from bronchitis (April 3, 1993); missed two games.
HONORS: Named to NCAA All-America East second team (1986-87). . . . Named to Hockey East All-Star first team (1986-87). . . . Named to THE SPORTING NEWS All-Star second team (1990-91 and 1992-93). . . . Named to NHL All-Star second team (1990-91 and 1992-93). . . . Named to THE SPORTING NEWS All-Star first team (1991-92). . . . Named to NHL All-Star first team (1991-92). . . . Played in NHL All-Star Game (1991-1993).
MISCELLANEOUS: Member of Stanley Cup championship teams (1991 and 1992).

Season Team	League	REGULAR SEASON					PLAYOFFS				
		Gms.	G	A	Pts.	PIM	Gms.	G	A	Pts.	PIM
82-83—Silver Lake H.S.	Minn. H.S.	18	24	27	51	...	—	—	—	—	—
83-84—Boston College	ECAC	37	6	14	20	36	—	—	—	—	—
84-85—Boston College	Hockey East	40	13	23	36	36	—	—	—	—	—
85-86—Boston College	Hockey East	42	17	27	44	56	—	—	—	—	—
86-87—Boston College	Hockey East	39	*35	35	70	54	—	—	—	—	—
87-88—U.S. national team	Int'l	44	22	23	45	52	—	—	—	—	—
—U.S. Olympic Team	Int'l	5	1	3	4	2	—	—	—	—	—
—Pittsburgh	NHL	16	5	2	7	8	—	—	—	—	—
88-89—Pittsburgh	NHL	24	12	3	15	19	11	3	7	10	16
—Muskegon	IHL	45	24	41	65	113	—	—	—	—	—
89-90—Pittsburgh	NHL	76	29	41	70	171	—	—	—	—	—
90-91—Pittsburgh	NHL	80	40	46	86	133	24	*17	16	33	53
91-92—Pittsburgh	NHL	80	54	69	123	254	†21	13	15	28	28

Season Team	League	REGULAR SEASON					PLAYOFFS				
		Gms.	G	A	Pts.	Pen.	Gms.	G	A	Pts.	Pen.
92-93—Pittsburgh	NHL	72	55	56	111	177	12	5	11	16	22
93-94—Pittsburgh	NHL	83	41	47	88	155	6	1	1	2	10
NHL totals		431	236	264	500	917	74	39	50	89	129

STEVENS, SCOTT
D, DEVILS

PERSONAL: Born April 1, 1964, in Kitchener, Ont.... 6-2/210.... Shoots left.... Brother of Mike Stevens, center/left winger in New York Rangers system.

TRANSACTIONS/CAREER NOTES: Selected by Washington Capitals as underage junior in first round (first Capitals pick, fifth overall) of NHL entry draft (June 9, 1982).... Bruised right knee (November 6, 1985); missed seven games.... Broke right index finger (December 14, 1986).... Bruised shoulder (April 1988).... Suffered from poison oak (November 1988).... Lacerated face during World Cup (April 21, 1989). ... Broke left foot (December 29, 1989); missed 17 games.... Suspended three games by NHL for scratching (February 27, 1990).... Bruised left shoulder (March 27, 1990).... Dislocated left shoulder (May 3, 1990).... Signed as free agent by St. Louis Blues (July 9, 1990); Blues owed Capitals two first-round draft picks among the top seven over next two years and $100,000 cash; upon failing to get a pick in the top seven in 1991, Blues forfeited their first-round pick in 1991 (LW Trevor Halverson), 1992 (D Sergei Gonchar), 1993 (D Brendan Witt), 1994 and 1995 drafts to Capitals (July 9, 1990).... Awarded to New Jersey Devils as compensation for Blues signing free agent RW/LW Brendan Shanahan (September 3, 1991).... Strained right knee (February 20, 1992); missed 12 games.... Suffered concussion (December 27, 1992); missed three games. ... Strained knee (November 19, 1993); missed one game.

HONORS: Named to NHL All-Rookie team (1982-83).... Named to THE SPORTING NEWS All-Star second team (1987-88).... Named to NHL All-Star first team (1987-88 and 1993-94).... Named to NHL All-Star second team (1991-92).... Played in NHL All-Star Game (1985, 1989, 1991-1994).... Named to THE SPORTING NEWS All-Star first team (1993-94).

Season Team	League	REGULAR SEASON					PLAYOFFS				
		Gms.	G	A	Pts.	PIM	Gms.	G	A	Pts.	PIM
80-81—Kitchener Jr. B	OHA	39	7	33	40	82	—	—	—	—	—
—Kitchener	OHL	1	0	0	0	0	—	—	—	—	—
81-82—Kitchener	OHL	68	6	36	42	158	15	1	10	11	71
82-83—Washington	NHL	77	9	16	25	195	4	1	0	1	26
83-84—Washington	NHL	78	13	32	45	201	8	1	8	9	21
84-85—Washington	NHL	80	21	44	65	221	5	0	1	1	20
85-86—Washington	NHL	73	15	38	53	165	9	3	8	11	12
86-87—Washington	NHL	77	10	51	61	283	7	0	5	5	19
87-88—Washington	NHL	80	12	60	72	184	13	1	11	12	46
88-89—Washington	NHL	80	7	61	68	225	6	1	4	5	11
89-90—Washington	NHL	56	11	29	40	154	15	2	7	9	25
90-91—St. Louis	NHL	78	5	44	49	150	13	0	3	3	36
91-92—New Jersey	NHL	68	17	42	59	124	7	2	1	3	29
92-93—New Jersey	NHL	81	12	45	57	120	5	2	2	4	10
93-94—New Jersey	NHL	83	18	60	78	112	20	2	9	11	42
NHL totals		911	150	522	672	2134	112	15	59	74	297

STEVENSON, TURNER
RW, CANADIENS

PERSONAL: Born May 18, 1972, in Port Alberni, B.C.... 6-3/200.... Shoots right.

TRANSACTIONS/CAREER NOTES: Underwent surgery to remove growth in chest (August 1987).... Injured shoulder (December 1987).... Selected by Montreal Canadiens in first round (first Canadiens pick, 12th overall) of NHL entry draft (June 16, 1990).

HONORS: Named to Can.HL All-Star second team (1991-92).... Named to Memorial Cup All-Star team (1991-92).... Named to WHL (West) All-Star first team (1991-92).

Season Team	League	REGULAR SEASON					PLAYOFFS				
		Gms.	G	A	Pts.	PIM	Gms.	G	A	Pts.	PIM
88-89—Seattle	WHL	69	15	12	27	84	—	—	—	—	—
89-90—Seattle	WHL	62	29	32	61	276	13	3	2	5	35
90-91—Seattle	WHL	57	36	27	63	222	6	1	5	6	15
—Fredericton	AHL	—	—	—	—	—	4	0	0	0	5
91-92—Seattle	WHL	58	20	32	52	304	15	9	3	12	55
92-93—Fredericton	AHL	79	25	34	59	102	5	2	3	5	11
—Montreal	NHL	1	0	0	0	0	—	—	—	—	—
93-94—Fredericton	AHL	66	19	28	47	155	—	—	—	—	—
—Montreal	NHL	2	0	0	0	2	3	0	2	2	0
NHL totals		3	0	0	0	2	3	0	2	2	0

STEWART, CAM
C, BRUINS

PERSONAL: Born September 18, 1971, in Kitchener, Ont.... 5-10/188.... Shoots left.
COLLEGE: Michigan.

TRANSACTIONS/CAREER NOTES: Strained knee ligaments (June 1989).... Selected by Boston Bruins in third round (second Bruins pick, 63rd overall) of NHL entry draft (June 16, 1990).... Fractured finger (November 13, 1993); missed seven games.

Season Team	League	REGULAR SEASON					PLAYOFFS				
		Gms.	G	A	Pts.	PIM	Gms.	G	A	Pts.	PIM
88-89—Elmira Jr. B	OHA	43	38	50	88	138	—	—	—	—	—
89-90—Elmira Jr. B	OHA	46	44	95	139	172	—	—	—	—	—
90-91—University of Michigan	CCHA	44	8	24	32	122	—	—	—	—	—

Season Team	League	REGULAR SEASON					PLAYOFFS				
		Gms.	G	A	Pts.	Pen.	Gms.	G	A	Pts.	Pen.
91-92—University of Michigan	CCHA	44	13	15	28	106	—	—	—	—	—
92-93—University of Michigan	CCHA	39	20	39	59	69	—	—	—	—	—
93-94—Boston	NHL	57	3	6	9	66	8	0	3	3	7
—Providence	AHL	14	3	2	5	5	—	—	—	—	—
NHL totals..................................		57	3	6	9	66	8	0	3	3	7

STEWART, JASON
D, ISLANDERS

PERSONAL: Born April 30, 1976, in St. Paul, Minn. . . . 5-11/185. . . . Shoots right.
HIGH SCHOOL: Simley (Inver Groves Heights, Minn.)
TRANSACTIONS/CAREER NOTES: Selected by New York Islanders in sixth round (seventh Islanders pick, 142nd overall) of NHL entry draft (June 29, 1994).

Season Team	League	REGULAR SEASON					PLAYOFFS				
		Gms.	G	A	Pts.	PIM	Gms.	G	A	Pts.	PIM
93-94—Simley H.S.	Minn. H.S.	23	15	15	30	32	—	—	—	—	—

STEWART, MICHAEL
D, RANGERS

PERSONAL: Born March 30, 1972, in Calgary. . . . 6-2/197. . . . Shoots left. . . . Full name: Michael Donald Stewart.
COLLEGE: Michigan State.
TRANSACTIONS/CAREER NOTES: Selected by New York Rangers in first round (first Rangers pick, 13th overall) of NHL entry draft (June 16, 1990).
HONORS: Named to CCHA All-Rookie team (1989-90).

Season Team	League	REGULAR SEASON					PLAYOFFS				
		Gms.	G	A	Pts.	PIM	Gms.	G	A	Pts.	PIM
89-90—Michigan State................	CCHA	45	2	6	8	45	—	—	—	—	—
90-91—Michigan State................	CCHA	37	3	12	15	58	—	—	—	—	—
91-92—Michigan State................	CCHA	8	1	3	4	6	—	—	—	—	—
92-93—Binghamton	AHL	68	2	10	12	71	1	0	0	0	0
93-94—Binghamton	AHL	79	8	42	50	75	—	—	—	—	—

STILLMAN, CORY
C, FLAMES

PERSONAL: Born December 20, 1973, in Peterborough, Ont. . . . 6-0/185. . . . Shoots left.
HIGH SCHOOL: Herman E. Fawcett (Brantford, Ont.).
TRANSACTIONS/CAREER NOTES: Selected by Calgary Flames in first round (first Flames pick, sixth overall) of NHL entry draft (June 20, 1992).
HONORS: Won Emms Family Award (1990-91).

Season Team	League	REGULAR SEASON					PLAYOFFS				
		Gms.	G	A	Pts.	PIM	Gms.	G	A	Pts.	PIM
89-90—Peterborough Jr. B...........	OHA	41	30	54	84	76	—	—	—	—	—
90-91—Windsor.........................	OHL	64	31	70	101	31	11	3	6	9	8
91-92—Windsor.........................	OHL	53	29	61	90	59	7	2	4	6	8
92-93—Peterborough	OHL	61	25	55	80	55	18	3	8	11	18
—Canadian national team ...	Int'l	1	0	0	0	0	—	—	—	—	—
93-94—Saint John	AHL	79	35	48	83	52	7	2	4	6	16

STOJANOV, ALEX
LW, CANUCKS

PERSONAL: Born April 25, 1973, in Windsor, Ont. . . . 6-4/225. . . . Shoots left. . . . Name pronounced STOY-uh-nahf.
TRANSACTIONS/CAREER NOTES: Dislocated shoulder (July 1989). . . . Selected by Vancouver Canucks in first round (first Canucks pick, seventh overall) of NHL entry draft (June 22, 1991).

Season Team	League	REGULAR SEASON					PLAYOFFS				
		Gms.	G	A	Pts.	PIM	Gms.	G	A	Pts.	PIM
89-90—Dukes of Hamilton	OHL	37	4	4	8	91	—	—	—	—	—
90-91—Dukes of Hamilton	OHL	62	25	20	45	179	4	1	1	2	14
91-92—Guelph	OHL	33	12	15	27	91	—	—	—	—	—
92-93—Guelph	OHL	35	27	28	55	11	—	—	—	—	—
—Newmarket......................	OHL	14	9	7	16	21	7	1	3	4	26
—Hamilton..........................	AHL	4	4	0	4	0	—	—	—	—	—
93-94—Hamilton	AHL	4	0	1	1	5	—	—	—	—	—

STORM, JIM
LW, WHALERS

PERSONAL: Born February 5, 1971, in Detroit. . . . 6-2/200. . . . Shoots left. . . . Full name: James David Storm.
COLLEGE: Michigan Tech.
TRANSACTIONS/CAREER NOTES: Selected by Hartford Whalers in fourth round (fifth Whalers pick, 75th overall) of NHL entry draft (June 22, 1991). . . . Joined U.S. national team (October 6-November 6, 1993).

Season Team	League	REGULAR SEASON					PLAYOFFS				
		Gms.	G	A	Pts.	PIM	Gms.	G	A	Pts.	PIM
88-89—Detroit Compuware..........	NAJHL	60	30	45	75	50	—	—	—	—	—
89-90—Detroit Compuware..........	NAJHL	55	38	73	111	58	—	—	—	—	—
90-91—Michigan Tech	WCHA	36	16	17	33	46	—	—	—	—	—
91-92—Michigan Tech	WCHA	39	25	33	58	12	—	—	—	—	—

Season Team	League	REGULAR SEASON Gms.	G	A	Pts.	Pen.	PLAYOFFS Gms.	G	A	Pts.	Pen.
92-93—Michigan Tech	WCHA	33	22	32	54	30	—	—	—	—	—
93-94—U.S. national team	Int'l	28	8	12	20	14	—	—	—	—	—
—Hartford	NHL	68	6	10	16	27	—	—	—	—	—
NHL totals		68	6	10	16	27					

STORR, JAMIE
G, KINGS

PERSONAL: Born December 28, 1975, in Brampton, Ont. . . . 6-2/192. . . . Catches left.
HIGH SCHOOL: West Hill (Owen Sound, Ont.).
TRANSACTIONS/CAREER NOTES: Selected by Los Angeles Kings in first round (first Kings pick, seventh overall) of NHL entry draft (June 28, 1994).
HONORS: Named to OHL All-Star first team (1993-94).

Season Team	League	REGULAR SEASON Gms.	Min.	W	L	T	GA	SO	Avg.	PLAYOFFS Gms.	Min.	W	L	GA	SO	Avg.
90-91—Brampton	Jr. B	24	1145	...	...	...	91	0	4.77	—	—			—		—
91-92—Owen Sound	OHL	34	1733	...	...	...	128	0	4.43	5	299	...	...	28	0	5.62
92-93—Owen Sound	OHL	41	2362	20	17	3	180	0	4.57	8	454	4	4	35	0	4.63
93-94—Owen Sound	OHL	35	2004	21	11	1	120	1	3.59	9	547	4	5	44	0	4.83
—Can. Olympic Team	Int'l	4	240	...	...	...	10	...	2.50	—	—			—		—

STRACHAN, WAYNE
RW, RANGERS

PERSONAL: Born December 12, 1972, in Fort Frances, Ont. . . . 5-10/185. . . . Shoots right.
COLLEGE: Lake Superior State.
TRANSACTIONS/CAREER NOTES: Selected by New York Rangers in NHL supplemental draft (June 25, 1993).

Season Team	League	REGULAR SEASON Gms.	G	A	Pts.	PIM	PLAYOFFS Gms.	G	A	Pts.	PIM
92-93—Lake Superior State	CCHA	38	20	21	41	44	—	—	—	—	—
93-94—Lake Superior State	CCHA	45	24	23	47	74	—	—	—	—	—

STRAKA, MARTIN
C, PENGUINS

PERSONAL: Born September 3, 1972, in Plzen, Czechoslovakia. . . . 5-10/180. . . . Shoots left. . . . Name pronounced STRAH-kuh.
TRANSACTIONS/CAREER NOTES: Selected by Pittsburgh Penguins in first round (first Penguins pick, 19th overall) of NHL entry draft (June 20, 1992).
HONORS: Named to Czechoslovakian League All-Star team (1991-92).

Season Team	League	REGULAR SEASON Gms.	G	A	Pts.	PIM	PLAYOFFS Gms.	G	A	Pts.	PIM
89-90—Skoda Plzen	Czech.	1	0	3	3	...	—	—	—	—	—
90-91—Skoda Plzen	Czech.	47	7	24	31	6	—	—	—	—	—
91-92—Skoda Plzen	Czech.	50	27	28	55	...	—	—	—	—	—
92-93—Pittsburgh	NHL	42	3	13	16	29	11	2	1	3	2
—Cleveland	IHL	4	4	3	7	0	—	—	—	—	—
93-94—Pittsburgh	NHL	84	30	34	64	24	6	1	0	1	2
NHL totals		126	33	47	80	53	17	3	1	4	4

STROMBERG, MIKA
D, NORDIQUES

PERSONAL: Born February 28, 1970, in Helsinki, Finland. . . . 5-11/178. . . . Shoots left.
TRANSACTIONS/CAREER NOTES: Selected by Quebec Nordiques in 10th round (10th Nordiques pick, 211st overall) of NHL entry draft (June 16, 1990).

Season Team	League	REGULAR SEASON Gms.	G	A	Pts.	PIM	PLAYOFFS Gms.	G	A	Pts.	PIM
88-89—Jokerit	Finland	39	6	12	18	...	—	—	—	—	—
89-90—Jokerit	Finland	42	2	15	17	...	—	—	—	—	—
90-91—Jokerit	Finland	44	4	16	20	38	—	—	—	—	—
91-92—Jokerit	Finland	36	7	14	21	32	—	—	—	—	—
92-93—Jokerit	Finland	16	2	5	7	6	3	1	2	3	4
93-94—Jokerit	Finland	48	17	8	25	53	12	1	3	4	8
—Swedish Olympic Team	Int'l	7	2	2	4	10	—	—	—	—	—

STRUCH, DAVID
C, FLAMES

PERSONAL: Born February 11, 1971, in Calgary. . . . 5-10/180. . . . Shoots left. . . . Name pronounced STROOSH.
TRANSACTIONS/CAREER NOTES: Selected by Calgary Flames in ninth round (ninth Flames pick, 195th overall) of NHL entry draft (June 22, 1991).

Season Team	League	REGULAR SEASON Gms.	G	A	Pts.	PIM	PLAYOFFS Gms.	G	A	Pts.	PIM
88-89—Saskatoon	WHL	66	20	31	51	18	8	2	3	5	6
89-90—Saskatoon	WHL	68	40	37	77	67	10	8	5	13	6
90-91—Saskatoon	WHL	72	45	57	102	69	—	—	—	—	—
91-92—Salt Lake City	IHL	12	4	1	5	8	—	—	—	—	—
—Saskatoon	WHL	47	29	26	55	34	—	—	—	—	—

Season Team	League	REGULAR SEASON Gms.	G	A	Pts.	Pen.	PLAYOFFS Gms.	G	A	Pts.	Pen.
92-93—Salt Lake City..................	IHL	78	20	22	42	73	—	—	—	—	—
93-94—Saint John......................	AHL	58	18	25	43	87	7	0	1	1	4
—Calgary...........................	NHL	4	0	0	0	4	—	—	—	—	—
NHL totals..................................		4	0	0	0	4					

STRUDWICK, JASON
D, ISLANDERS

PERSONAL: Born July 17, 1975, in Edmonton. . . . 6-3/210. . . . Shoots left.
COLLEGE: University College of the Cariboo (Kamloops, B.C.).
TRANSACTIONS/CAREER NOTES: Selected by New York Islanders in third round (third Islanders pick, 63rd overall) of NHL entry draft (June 29, 1994).

Season Team	League	REGULAR SEASON Gms.	G	A	Pts.	PIM	PLAYOFFS Gms.	G	A	Pts.	PIM
93-94—Kamloops	WHL	61	6	8	14	118	19	0	4	4	24

STUMPEL, JOZEF
LW, BRUINS

PERSONAL: Born June 20, 1972, in Nitra, Czechoslovakia. . . . 6-1/190. . . . Shoots right. . . . Name pronounced JOH-sehf STUHM-puhl.
TRANSACTIONS/CAREER NOTES: Selected by Boston Bruins in second round (second Bruins pick, 40th overall) of NHL entry draft (June 22, 1991). . . . Injured shoulder (December 1992); missed nine games. . . . Injured knee (March 17, 1994); missed nine games.

Season Team	League	REGULAR SEASON Gms.	G	A	Pts.	PIM	PLAYOFFS Gms.	G	A	Pts.	PIM
89-90—Nitra	Czech.	38	12	11	23	0	—	—	—	—	—
90-91—Nitra	Czech.	49	23	22	45	14	—	—	—	—	—
91-92—Boston	NHL	4	1	0	1	0	—	—	—	—	—
—Koln	Germany	33	19	18	37	35	—	—	—	—	—
92-93—Providence	AHL	56	31	61	92	26	6	4	4	8	0
—Boston	NHL	13	1	3	4	4	—	—	—	—	—
93-94—Boston	NHL	59	8	15	23	14	13	1	7	8	4
—Providence	AHL	17	5	12	17	4	—	—	—	—	—
NHL totals.................................		76	10	18	28	18	13	1	7	8	4

SULLIVAN, BRIAN
LW, DEVILS

PERSONAL: Born April 23, 1969, in South Windsor, Conn. . . . 6-4/195. . . . Shoots right. . . . Full name: Brian Scott Sullivan.
HIGH SCHOOL: South Windsor (Conn.).
COLLEGE: Northeastern.
TRANSACTIONS/CAREER NOTES: Selected by New Jersey Devils in fourth round (third Devils pick, 65th overall) of NHL entry draft (June 13, 1987). . . . Bruised shoulder (November 1989).

Season Team	League	REGULAR SEASON Gms.	G	A	Pts.	PIM	PLAYOFFS Gms.	G	A	Pts.	PIM
85-86—South Windsor H.S...........	Conn. H.S.	...	39	50	89	...	—	—	—	—	—
86-87—Springfield Jr. B	NEJHL	...	30	35	65	...	—	—	—	—	—
87-88—Northeastern University...	Hockey East	37	20	12	32	18	—	—	—	—	—
88-89—Northeastern University...	Hockey East	34	13	14	27	65	—	—	—	—	—
89-90—Northeastern University...	Hockey East	34	24	21	45	72	—	—	—	—	—
90-91—Northeastern University...	Hockey East	32	17	23	40	75	—	—	—	—	—
91-92—Utica	AHL	70	23	24	47	58	4	0	4	4	6
92-93—Utica	AHL	75	30	27	57	88	5	0	0	0	12
—New Jersey......................	NHL	2	0	1	1	0	—	—	—	—	—
93-94—Albany	AHL	77	31	30	61	140	5	1	1	2	18
NHL totals.................................		2	0	1	1	0					

SULLIVAN, MIKE
LW, FLAMES

PERSONAL: Born February 28, 1968, in Marshfield, Mass. . . . 6-2/190. . . . Shoots left. . . . Full name: Michael Barry Sullivan.
HIGH SCHOOL: Boston College.
COLLEGE: Boston University.
TRANSACTIONS/CAREER NOTES: Selected by New York Rangers in fourth round (fourth Rangers pick, 69th overall) of NHL entry draft (June 13, 1987). . . . Traded by Rangers with D Mark Tinordi, D Paul Jerrard, RW Brett Barnett and third-round pick in 1989 draft (C Murray Garbutt) to Minnesota North Stars for LW Igor Liba, C Brian Lawton and rights to LW Eric Bennett (October 11, 1988). . . . Signed as free agent by San Jose Sharks (August 9, 1991). . . . Sprained left knee (April 6, 1993); missed remainder of season. . . . Claimed on waivers by Calgary Flames (January 6, 1994). . . . Pulled groin (January 29, 1994); missed 13 games. . . . Bruised knee (April 6, 1994); missed one game.

Season Team	League	REGULAR SEASON Gms.	G	A	Pts.	PIM	PLAYOFFS Gms.	G	A	Pts.	PIM
85-86—Boston College H.S...........	Mass. H.S.	22	26	33	59	...	—	—	—	—	—
86-87—Boston College H.S...........	Mass. H.S.	37	13	18	31	18	—	—	—	—	—
87-88—Boston College H.S...........	Mass. H.S.	30	18	22	40	30	—	—	—	—	—
88-89—Boston College H.S...........	Mass. H.S.	36	19	17	36	30	—	—	—	—	—
—Virginia............................	ECHL	2	0	0	0	0	—	—	—	—	—
89-90—Boston University	Hockey East	38	11	20	31	26	—	—	—	—	—
90-91—San Diego	IHL	74	12	23	35	27	—	—	—	—	—

Season Team	League	REGULAR SEASON					PLAYOFFS				
		Gms.	G	A	Pts.	Pen.	Gms.	G	A	Pts.	Pen.
91-92—Kansas City	IHL	10	2	8	10	8	—	—	—	—	—
—San Jose	NHL	64	8	11	19	15	—	—	—	—	—
92-93—San Jose	NHL	81	6	8	14	30	—	—	—	—	—
93-94—San Jose	NHL	26	2	2	4	4	—	—	—	—	—
—Kansas City	IHL	6	3	3	6	0	—	—	—	—	—
—Saint John	AHL	5	2	0	2	4	—	—	—	—	—
—Calgary	NHL	19	2	3	5	6	7	1	1	2	8
NHL totals		190	18	24	42	55	7	1	1	2	8

SUNDBLAD, NIKLAS
RW, FLAMES

PERSONAL: Born January 3, 1973, in Stockholm, Sweden. . . . 6-1/200. . . . Shoots right.

TRANSACTIONS/CAREER NOTES: Selected by Calgary Flames in first round (first Flames pick, 19th overall) of NHL entry draft (June 22, 1991).

Season Team	League	REGULAR SEASON					PLAYOFFS				
		Gms.	G	A	Pts.	PIM	Gms.	G	A	Pts.	PIM
90-91—AIK	Sweden	39	1	3	4	14	—	—	—	—	—
91-92—AIK	Sweden	33	9	2	11	24	3	3	1	4	0
92-93—AIK	Sweden	22	5	4	9	56	—	—	—	—	—
93-94—Saint John	AHL	76	13	19	32	75	4	1	1	2	2

SUNDIN, MATS
RW, MAPLE LEAFS

PERSONAL: Born February 13, 1971, in Sollentuna, Sweden. . . . 6-4/204. . . . Shoots right. . . . Full name: Mats Johan Sundin. . . . Name pronounced SUHN-deen.

TRANSACTIONS/CAREER NOTES: Selected by Quebec Nordiques in first round (first Nordiques pick, first overall) of NHL entry draft (June 17, 1989). . . . Separated right shoulder (January 2, 1993); missed three games. . . . Suspended one game by NHL for second stick-related infraction (March 2, 1993). . . . Traded by Nordiques with D Garth Butcher, LW Todd Warriner and first-round pick in 1994 draft (traded to Washington Capitals who selected D Nolan Baumgartner) to Toronto Maple Leafs for LW Wendel Clark, D Sylvain Lefebvre, RW Landon Wilson and first-round pick (D Jeffrey Kealty) in 1994 draft (June 28, 1994).

HONORS: Named to Swedish League All-Star team (1990-91 and 1991-92).

Season Team	League	REGULAR SEASON					PLAYOFFS				
		Gms.	G	A	Pts.	PIM	Gms.	G	A	Pts.	PIM
88-89—Nacka	Sweden	25	10	8	18	18	—	—	—	—	—
89-90—Djurgarden	Sweden	34	10	8	18	16	8	7	0	7	4
90-91—Quebec	NHL	80	23	36	59	58	—	—	—	—	—
91-92—Quebec	NHL	80	33	43	76	103	—	—	—	—	—
92-93—Quebec	NHL	80	47	67	114	96	6	3	1	4	6
93-94—Quebec	NHL	84	32	53	85	60	—	—	—	—	—
NHL totals		324	135	199	334	317	6	3	1	4	6

SUNDSTROM, NIKLAS
LW, RANGERS

PERSONAL: Born June 6, 1975, in Ornskoldsvik, Sweden. . . . 5-11/183. . . . Shoots left.

TRANSACTIONS/CAREER NOTES: Selected by New York Rangers in first round (first Rangers pick, eighth overall) of NHL entry draft (June 26, 1993).

Season Team	League	REGULAR SEASON					PLAYOFFS				
		Gms.	G	A	Pts.	PIM	Gms.	G	A	Pts.	PIM
91-92—MoDo	Sweden	9	1	3	4	0	—	—	—	—	—
92-93—MoDo	Sweden	40	7	11	18	18	—	—	—	—	—
93-94—MoDo	Sweden	37	7	12	19	28	11	4	3	7	2

SUTER, GARY
D, BLACKHAWKS

PERSONAL: Born June 24, 1964, in Madison, Wis. . . . 6-0/190. . . . Shoots left. . . . Full name: Gary Lee Suter. . . . Name pronounced SOO-tuhr.

COLLEGE: Wisconsin.

TRANSACTIONS/CAREER NOTES: Selected by Calgary Flames in ninth round (ninth Flames pick, 180th overall) of NHL entry draft (June 9, 1984). . . . Stretched knee ligament (December 1986). . . . Suspended first four games of regular season and next six international games in which NHL participates for high-sticking during Canada Cup (September 4, 1987). . . . Injured left knee (February 1988). . . . Pulled hamstring (February 1989). . . . Ruptured appendix (February 22, 1989); missed 16 games. . . . Broke jaw (April 11, 1989). . . . Bruised knee (December 12, 1991); missed 10 games. . . . Injured ribs (March 16, 1993); missed one game. . . . Suffered from the flu (March 30, 1993); missed one game. . . . Torn left knee ligaments (November 4, 1993); missed 33 games. . . . Strained left leg muscle (January 24, 1994); missed 10 games. . . . Traded by Flames with LW Paul Ranheim and C Ted Drury to Hartford Whalers for C Michael Nylander, D Zarley Zalapski and D James Patrick (March 10, 1994). . . . Traded by Hartford with LW Randy Cunneyworth and undisclosed draft pick to Chicago Blackhawks for D Frantisek Kucera and LW Jocelyn Lemieux (March 11, 1994).

HONORS: Named USHL Top Defenseman (1982-83). . . . Named to USHL All-Star first team (1982-83). . . . Won Calder Memorial Trophy (1985-86). . . . Named to NHL All-Rookie team (1985-86). . . . Played in NHL All-Star Game (1986, 1988, 1989 and 1991). . . . Named to THE SPORTING NEWS All-Star first team (1987-88). . . . Named to NHL All-Star second team (1987-88). . . . Named to THE SPORTING NEWS All-Star second team (1988-89).

RECORDS: Shares NHL single-game record for most assists by a defenseman—6 (April 4, 1986).

MISCELLANEOUS: Member of Stanley Cup championship team (1989).

Season	Team	League	REGULAR SEASON Gms.	G	A	Pts.	PIM	PLAYOFFS Gms.	G	A	Pts.	PIM
81-82—Dubuque	USHL	18	3	4	7	32	—	—	—	—	—
82-83—Dubuque	USHL	41	9	10	19	112	—	—	—	—	—
83-84—University of Wisconsin	WCHA	35	4	18	22	68	—	—	—	—	—
84-85—University of Wisconsin	WCHA	39	12	39	51	110	—	—	—	—	—
85-86—Calgary	NHL	80	18	50	68	141	10	2	8	10	8
86-87—Calgary	NHL	68	9	40	49	70	6	0	3	3	10
87-88—Calgary	NHL	75	21	70	91	124	9	1	9	10	6
88-89—Calgary	NHL	63	13	49	62	78	5	0	3	3	10
89-90—Calgary	NHL	76	16	60	76	97	6	0	1	1	14
90-91—Calgary	NHL	79	12	58	70	102	7	1	6	7	12
91-92—Calgary	NHL	70	12	43	55	128	—	—	—	—	—
92-93—Calgary	NHL	81	23	58	81	112	6	2	3	5	8
93-94—Calgary	NHL	25	4	9	13	20	—	—	—	—	—
—Chicago	NHL	16	2	3	5	18	6	3	2	5	6
NHL totals		633	130	440	570	890	55	9	35	44	74

SUTTER, BRENT
C, BLACKHAWKS

PERSONAL: Born June 10, 1962, in Viking, Alta. . . . 5-11/180. . . . Shoots right. . . . Full name: Brent Colin Sutter. . . . Name pronounced SUH-tuhr. . . . Brother of Brian Sutter, left winger, St. Louis Blues (1976-77 through 1987-88) and current head coach, Boston Bruins; brother of Darryl Sutter, left winger, Chicago Blackhawks (1979-80 through 1986-87) and current head coach, Blackhawks; brother of Duane Sutter, right winger, New York Islanders and Blackhawks (1979-80 through 1989-90) and current head coach, Indianapolis Ice of IHL; brother of Rich Sutter, right winger, Chicago Blackhawks; and brother of Ron Sutter, center, New York Islanders.

TRANSACTIONS/CAREER NOTES: Selected by New York Islanders as underage junior in first round (first Islanders pick, 17th overall) of NHL entry draft (June 11, 1980). . . . Damaged tendon and developed infection in right hand (January 1984); missed 11 games. . . . Separated shoulder (March 1985). . . . Bruised left shoulder (October 19, 1985); missed 12 games. . . . Bruised shoulder (December 21, 1985); missed seven games. . . . Strained abductor muscle in right leg (March 1987). . . . Suffered non-displaced fracture of right thumb (December 1987). . . . Lacerated right leg (January 19, 1990). . . . Hospitalized with an infection in right leg after stitches were removed (January 28, 1990); missed seven games. . . . Traded by Islanders with RW Brad Lauer to Chicago Blackhawks for C Adam Creighton and LW Steve Thomas (October 25, 1991). . . . Injured abdomen (March 11, 1992). . . . Broke foot (September 25, 1992); missed 14 games. . . . Bruised index finger (January 19, 1993); missed three games. . . . Injured eye (March 9, 1993); missed two games. . . . Strained back (February 1994); missed five games.

HONORS: Played in NHL All-Star Game (1985).

MISCELLANEOUS: Member of Stanley Cup championship teams (1982 and 1983).

Season	Team	League	REGULAR SEASON Gms.	G	A	Pts.	PIM	PLAYOFFS Gms.	G	A	Pts.	PIM
77-78—Red Deer	AJHL	60	12	18	30	33	—	—	—	—	—
78-79—Red Deer	AJHL	60	42	42	84	79	—	—	—	—	—
79-80—Red Deer	AJHL	59	70	101	171	131	—	—	—	—	—
—Lethbridge	WHL	5	1	0	1	2	—	—	—	—	—
80-81—New York Islanders	NHL	3	2	2	4	0	—	—	—	—	—
—Lethbridge	WHL	68	54	54	108	116	9	6	4	10	51
81-82—Lethbridge	WHL	34	46	34	80	162	—	—	—	—	—
—New York Islanders	NHL	43	21	22	43	114	19	2	6	8	36
82-83—New York Islanders	NHL	80	21	19	40	128	20	10	11	21	26
83-84—New York Islanders	NHL	69	34	15	49	69	20	4	10	14	18
84-85—New York Islanders	NHL	72	42	60	102	51	10	3	3	6	14
85-86—New York Islanders	NHL	61	24	31	55	74	3	0	1	1	2
86-87—New York Islanders	NHL	69	27	36	63	73	5	1	0	1	4
87-88—New York Islanders	NHL	70	29	31	60	55	6	2	1	3	18
88-89—New York Islanders	NHL	77	29	34	63	77	—	—	—	—	—
89-90—New York Islanders	NHL	67	33	35	68	65	5	2	3	5	2
90-91—New York Islanders	NHL	75	21	32	53	49	—	—	—	—	—
91-92—New York Islanders	NHL	8	4	6	10	6	—	—	—	—	—
—Chicago	NHL	61	18	32	50	30	18	3	5	8	22
92-93—Chicago	NHL	65	20	34	54	67	4	1	1	2	4
93-94—Chicago	NHL	73	9	29	38	43	6	0	0	0	2
NHL totals		893	334	418	752	901	116	28	41	69	148

SUTTER, RICH
RW, BLACKHAWKS

PERSONAL: Born December 2, 1963, in Viking, Alta. . . . 5-11/188. . . . Shoots right. . . . Name pronounced SUH-tuhr. . . . Brother of Brian Sutter, left winger, St. Louis Blues (1976-77 through 1987-88) and current head coach, Boston Bruins; brother of Brent Sutter, center, Chicago Blackhawks; brother of Darryl Sutter, left winger, Blackhawks (1979-80 through 1986-87) and current head coach, Blackhawks; brother of Duane Sutter, right winger, New York Islanders and Blackhawks (1979-80 through 1989-90) and current head coach, Indianapolis Ice of IHL; and twin brother of Ron Sutter, center, New York Islanders.

HIGH SCHOOL: Winston Churchill (Lethbridge, Alta.).

TRANSACTIONS/CAREER NOTES: Selected as underage junior by Pittsburgh Penguins in first round (first Penguins pick, 10th overall) of NHL entry draft (June 9, 1982). . . . Traded by Penguins with second-round (D Greg Smyth) and third-round (LW David McLay) picks in 1984 draft to Philadelphia Flyers for C Ron Flockhart, C/LW Mark Taylor, LW Andy Brickley, first-round (RW/C Roger Belanger) and third-round picks in 1984 draft (October 1983). . . . Traded by Flyers with D Dave Richter and third-round pick in 1986 draft to Vancouver Canucks for D J.J. Daigneault, second-round pick in 1986 draft (C Kent Hawley) and fifth-round pick in 1987 draft (June 1986). . . . Lost four teeth (October 23, 1988). . . . Injured lower back (January 17,

1989).... Broke nose (March 24, 1989).... Suspended five games by NHL for slashing (January 27, 1990).... Traded by Canucks with D Harold Snepsts and second-round pick in 1990 draft to Blues for D Adrien Plavsic, first-round pick in 1990 draft (traded to Montreal Canadiens) and second-round pick in 1991 draft (March 6, 1990).... Suffered concussion (November 1, 1991); missed two games.... Selected by Chicago Blackhawks in 1993 waiver draft (October 3, 1993).

| | | | REGULAR SEASON | | | | | PLAYOFFS | | | |
Season	Team	League	Gms.	G	A	Pts.	PIM	Gms.	G	A	Pts.	PIM
79-80	Red Deer	AJHL	60	13	19	32	157	—	—	—	—	—
80-81	Lethbridge	WHL	72	23	18	41	255	9	3	1	4	35
81-82	Lethbridge	WHL	57	38	31	69	263	12	3	3	6	55
82-83	Lethbridge	WHL	64	37	30	67	200	17	14	9	23	43
	Pittsburgh	NHL	4	0	0	0	0	—	—	—	—	—
83-84	Baltimore	AHL	2	0	1	1	0	—	—	—	—	—
	Pittsburgh	NHL	5	0	0	0	0	—	—	—	—	—
	Philadelphia	NHL	70	16	12	28	93	3	0	0	0	15
84-85	Hershey	AHL	13	3	7	10	14	—	—	—	—	—
	Philadelphia	NHL	56	6	10	16	89	11	3	0	3	10
85-86	Philadelphia	NHL	78	14	25	39	199	5	2	0	2	19
86-87	Vancouver	NHL	74	20	22	42	113	—	—	—	—	—
87-88	Vancouver	NHL	80	15	15	30	165	—	—	—	—	—
88-89	Vancouver	NHL	75	17	15	32	122	7	2	1	3	12
89-90	Vancouver	NHL	62	9	9	18	133	—	—	—	—	—
	St. Louis	NHL	12	2	0	2	22	12	2	1	3	39
90-91	St. Louis	NHL	77	16	11	27	122	13	4	2	6	16
91-92	St. Louis	NHL	77	9	16	25	107	6	0	0	0	8
92-93	St. Louis	NHL	84	13	14	27	100	11	0	1	1	10
93-94	Chicago	NHL	83	12	14	26	108	6	0	0	0	2
NHL totals			837	149	163	312	1373	74	13	5	18	131

SUTTER, RON
C, ISLANDERS

PERSONAL: Born December 2, 1963, in Viking, Alta.... 6-0/207.... Shoots right.... Name pronounced SUH-tuhr.... Brother of Brian Sutter, left winger, St. Louis Blues (1976-77 through 1987-88) and current head coach, Boston Bruins; brother of Brent Sutter, center, Chicago Blackhawks; brother of Darryl Sutter, left winger, Blackhawks (1979-80 through 1986-87) and current head coach, Blackhawks; brother of Duane Sutter, right winger, New York Islanders and Blackhawks (1979-80 through 1989-90) and current head coach, Indianapolis Ice of WHL; and twin brother of Rich Sutter, right winger, Chicago Blackhawks.
HIGH SCHOOL: Winston Churchill (Lethbridge, Ont.).
TRANSACTIONS/CAREER NOTES: Selected by Philadelphia Flyers as underage junior in first round (first Flyers pick, fourth overall) of NHL entry draft (June 9, 1982).... Broke ankle (November 27, 1981).... Bruised stress fracture in lower back (January 1987).... Tore rib cartilage (March 1988).... Fractured jaw (October 29, 1988).... Pulled groin (March 1989).... Traded by Flyers with D Murray Baron to St. Louis Blues for C Rod Brind'Amour and C Dan Quinn (September 22, 1991).... Strained ligament in right knee (February 1, 1992); missed 10 games.... Pulled abdomen (September 1992); missed first 18 games of season.... Separated shoulder (March 30, 1993); missed remainder of season. ... Underwent abdominal surgery during off-season; missed nine games.... Traded by Blues with C Bob Bassen and D Garth Butcher to Quebec Nordiques for D Steve Duchesne and RW Denis Chasse (January 23, 1994).... Suffered sore neck (November 16, 1993); missed two games.... Traded by Nordiques with first-round pick in 1994 draft (RW Brett Lindros) to New York Islanders for D Uwe Krupp and first-round pick (D Wade Belak) in 1994 draft (June 28, 1994).

| | | | REGULAR SEASON | | | | | PLAYOFFS | | | |
Season	Team	League	Gms.	G	A	Pts.	PIM	Gms.	G	A	Pts.	PIM
79-80	Red Deer	AJHL	60	12	33	45	44	—	—	—	—	—
80-81	Lethbridge	WHL	72	13	32	45	152	9	2	5	7	29
81-82	Lethbridge	WHL	59	38	54	92	207	12	6	5	11	28
82-83	Lethbridge	WHL	58	35	48	83	98	20	*22	†19	*41	45
	Philadelphia	NHL	10	1	1	2	9	—	—	—	—	—
83-84	Philadelphia	NHL	79	19	32	51	101	3	0	0	0	22
84-85	Philadelphia	NHL	73	16	29	45	94	19	4	8	12	28
85-86	Philadelphia	NHL	75	18	42	60	159	5	0	2	2	10
86-87	Philadelphia	NHL	39	10	17	27	69	16	1	7	8	12
87-88	Philadelphia	NHL	69	8	25	33	146	7	0	1	1	26
88-89	Philadelphia	NHL	55	26	22	48	80	19	1	9	10	51
89-90	Philadelphia	NHL	75	22	26	48	104	—	—	—	—	—
90-91	Philadelphia	NHL	80	17	28	45	92	—	—	—	—	—
91-92	St. Louis	NHL	68	19	27	46	91	6	1	3	4	8
92-93	St. Louis	NHL	59	12	15	27	99	—	—	—	—	—
93-94	St. Louis	NHL	36	6	12	18	46	—	—	—	—	—
	Quebec	NHL	37	9	13	22	44	—	—	—	—	—
NHL totals			755	183	289	472	1134	75	7	30	37	157

SUTTON, KEN
D, SABRES

PERSONAL: Born May 11, 1969, in Edmonton.... 6-0/198.... Shoots left.
TRANSACTIONS/CAREER NOTES: Selected by Buffalo Sabres in fifth round (fourth Sabres pick, 98th overall) of NHL entry draft (June 17, 1989).... Separated shoulder (March 3, 1992); missed six games.... Broke ankle (September 15, 1992); missed first 19 games of season.
HONORS: Named to Memorial Cup All-Star team (1988-89).

| | | | REGULAR SEASON | | | | | PLAYOFFS | | | |
Season	Team	League	Gms.	G	A	Pts.	PIM	Gms.	G	A	Pts.	PIM
87-88	Calgary Canucks	AJHL	53	13	43	56	228	—	—	—	—	—
88-89	Saskatoon	WHL	71	22	31	53	104	8	2	5	7	12

Season Team	League	REGULAR SEASON Gms.	G	A	Pts.	Pen.	PLAYOFFS Gms.	G	A	Pts.	Pen.
89-90—Rochester	AHL	57	5	14	19	83	11	1	6	7	15
90-91—Buffalo	NHL	15	3	6	9	13	6	0	1	1	2
—Rochester	AHL	62	7	24	31	65	3	1	1	2	14
91-92—Buffalo	NHL	64	2	18	20	71	7	0	2	2	4
92-93—Buffalo	NHL	63	8	14	22	30	8	3	1	4	8
93-94—Buffalo	NHL	78	4	20	24	71	4	0	0	0	2
NHL totals		220	17	58	75	185	25	3	4	7	16

SVEHLA, ROBERT
D, FLAMES

PERSONAL: Born January 2, 1969, in Martin, Czechoslovakia. . . . 6-0/185. . . . Shoots left. . . . Name pronounced SVEE-luh.

TRANSACTIONS/CAREER NOTES: Selected by Calgary Flames in fourth round (fourth Flames pick, 78th overall) of NHL entry draft (June 20, 1992).

HONORS: Named Czechoslovakian League Player of the Year (1991-92). . . . Named to Czechoslovakian League All-Star team (1991-92).

MISCELLANEOUS: Member of bronze-medal-winning Czechoslovakian Olympic team (1992).

Season Team	League	REGULAR SEASON Gms.	G	A	Pts.	PIM	PLAYOFFS Gms.	G	A	Pts.	PIM
89-90—Dukla Trencin	Czech.	29	4	3	7	. . .	—	—	—	—	—
90-91—Dukla Trencin	Czech.	58	16	9	25	. . .	—	—	—	—	—
91-92—Dukla Trencin	Czech.	51	23	28	51	0	—	—	—	—	—
—Czech. Olympic Team	Int'l	8	2	1	3	8	—	—	—	—	—
92-93—Malmo	Sweden	40	19	10	29	86	6	0	1	1	0
93-94—Malmo	Sweden	37	14	25	39	*127	10	5	1	6	23
—Slovakian Olympic team	Int'l	8	2	4	6	26	—	—	—	—	—

SVOBODA, PETR
D, SABRES

PERSONAL: Born February 14, 1966, in Most, Czechoslovakia. . . . 6-1/175. . . . Shoots left. . . . Name pronounced svuh-BOH-duh.

TRANSACTIONS/CAREER NOTES: Selected by Montreal Canadiens in first round (first Canadiens pick, fifth overall) of NHL entry draft (June 9, 1984). . . . Suffered back spasms (January 1988). . . . Suffered hip pointer (March 1988). . . . Sprained right wrist (November 21, 1988); missed five games. . . . Injured back (March 1989). . . . Separated shoulder (November 1989). . . . Pulled groin (November 22, 1989). . . . Aggravated groin injury (December 11, 1989); missed 15 games. . . . Bruised left foot (March 11, 1990). . . . Suffered stomach disorder (November 28, 1990); missed five games. . . . Broke left foot (January 15, 1991); missed 15 games. . . . Injured mouth (December 14, 1991). . . . Sprained ankle (February 17, 1992); missed seven games. . . . Traded by Canadiens to Buffalo Sabres for D Kevin Haller (March 10, 1992). . . . Bruised knee (October 28, 1992); missed four games. . . . Tore ligament in right knee (January 17, 1993); missed remainder of season. . . . Injured knee (October 12, 1993); missed three games. . . . Suffered from knee inflammation (October 16, 1993); missed seven games. . . . Sprained left knee (March 17, 1994); missed 12 games.

MISCELLANEOUS: Member of Stanley Cup championship team (1986).

Season Team	League	REGULAR SEASON Gms.	G	A	Pts.	PIM	PLAYOFFS Gms.	G	A	Pts.	PIM
83-84—Czechoslovakia Jr.	Czech.	40	15	21	36	14	—	—	—	—	—
84-85—Montreal	NHL	73	4	27	31	65	7	1	1	2	12
85-86—Montreal	NHL	73	1	18	19	93	8	0	0	0	21
86-87—Montreal	NHL	70	5	17	22	63	14	0	5	5	10
87-88—Montreal	NHL	69	7	22	29	149	10	0	5	5	12
88-89—Montreal	NHL	71	8	37	45	147	21	1	11	12	16
89-90—Montreal	NHL	60	5	31	36	98	10	0	5	5	2
90-91—Montreal	NHL	60	4	22	26	52	2	0	1	1	2
91-92—Buffalo	NHL	13	1	6	7	52	7	1	4	5	6
—Montreal	NHL	58	5	16	21	94	—	—	—	—	—
92-93—Buffalo	NHL	40	2	24	26	59	—	—	—	—	—
93-94—Buffalo	NHL	60	2	14	16	89	3	0	0	0	4
NHL totals		647	44	234	278	961	82	3	32	35	85

SWANSON, BRIAN
C, SHARKS

PERSONAL: Born March 24, 1976, in Eagle River, Alaska. . . . 5-10/180. . . . Shoots left.

TRANSACTIONS/CAREER NOTES: Selected by San Jose Sharks in fifth round (fifth Sharks pick, 115th overall) of NHL entry draft (June 29, 1994).

Season Team	League	REGULAR SEASON Gms.	G	A	Pts.	PIM	PLAYOFFS Gms.	G	A	Pts.	PIM
93-94—Omaha	USHL	47	38	42	80	40	—	—	—	—	—

SWEENEY, BOB
C, SABRES

PERSONAL: Born January 25, 1964, in Boxborough, Mass. . . . 6-3/200. . . . Shoots right. . . . Full name: Robert Emmett Sweeney. . . . Brother of Tim Sweeney, center, Mighty Ducks of Anaheim.

HIGH SCHOOL: Acton (Mass.)-Boxborough.

COLLEGE: Boston College.

TRANSACTIONS/CAREER NOTES: Selected by Boston Bruins in sixth round (sixth Bruins pick, 123rd overall) of NHL entry draft (June 9, 1982). . . . Pulled rib muscle (November 1989); missed six games. . . . Injured left shoulder (April 23, 1991). . . . Sprained knee (February 4, 1992); missed 11 games. . . . Claimed on waivers by Buffalo Sabres and Calgary Flames; NHL

awarded rights to Sabres (October 9, 1992).... Injured rib (November 7, 1993); missed five games.... Injured right knee (March 9, 1994); missed 14 games.... Suspended three games by NHL for fighting (October 11, 1993).
HONORS: Named to NCAA All-America East second team (1984-85).... Named to Hockey East All-Star second team (1984-85).
RECORDS: Shares NHL career record for most overtime goals—7.

Season Team	League	REGULAR SEASON					PLAYOFFS				
		Gms.	G	A	Pts.	PIM	Gms.	G	A	Pts.	PIM
82-83—Boston College	ECAC	30	17	11	28	10	—	—	—	—	—
83-84—Boston College	ECAC	23	14	7	21	10	—	—	—	—	—
84-85—Boston College	Hockey East	44	32	32	64	43	—	—	—	—	—
85-86—Boston College	Hockey East	41	15	24	39	52	—	—	—	—	—
86-87—Boston	NHL	14	2	4	6	21	3	0	0	0	0
—Moncton	AHL	58	29	26	55	81	4	0	2	2	13
87-88—Boston	NHL	80	22	23	45	73	23	6	8	14	66
88-89—Boston	NHL	75	14	14	28	99	10	2	4	6	19
89-90—Boston	NHL	70	22	24	46	93	20	0	2	2	30
90-91—Boston	NHL	80	15	33	48	115	17	4	2	6	45
91-92—Boston	NHL	63	6	14	20	103	14	1	0	1	25
—Maine	AHL	1	1	0	1	0	—	—	—	—	—
92-93—Buffalo	NHL	80	21	26	47	118	8	2	2	4	8
93-94—Buffalo	NHL	60	11	14	25	94	1	0	0	0	0
NHL totals		522	113	152	265	716	96	15	18	33	193

SWEENEY, DON
D, BRUINS

PERSONAL: Born August 17, 1966, in St. Stephen, N.B.... 5-11/170.... Shoots left.... Full name: Donald Clark Sweeney.
COLLEGE: Harvard.
TRANSACTIONS/CAREER NOTES: Selected by Boston Bruins in eighth round (eighth Bruins pick, 166th overall) of NHL entry draft (June 9, 1984).... Bruised left heel (February 22, 1990).... Injured knee (October 12, 1991); missed four games.... Sprained knee (October 5, 1993); missed six games.... Injured ribs (December 15, 1993); missed three games.
HONORS: Named to NCAA All-America East second team (1987-88).... Named to ECAC All-Star first team (1987-88).

Season Team	League	REGULAR SEASON					PLAYOFFS				
		Gms.	G	A	Pts.	PIM	Gms.	G	A	Pts.	PIM
83-84—St. Paul N.B. H.S.	N.B. H.S.	22	33	26	59	...	—	—	—	—	—
84-85—Harvard University	ECAC	29	3	7	10	30	—	—	—	—	—
85-86—Harvard University	ECAC	31	4	5	9	29	—	—	—	—	—
86-87—Harvard University	ECAC	34	7	14	21	22	—	—	—	—	—
87-88—Harvard University	ECAC	30	6	23	29	37	—	—	—	—	—
—Maine	AHL	—	—	—	—	—	6	1	3	4	0
88-89—Maine	AHL	42	8	17	25	24	—	—	—	—	—
—Boston	NHL	36	3	5	8	20	—	—	—	—	—
89-90—Boston	NHL	58	3	5	8	58	21	1	5	6	18
—Maine	AHL	11	0	8	8	8	—	—	—	—	—
90-91—Boston	NHL	77	8	13	21	67	19	3	0	3	25
91-92—Boston	NHL	75	3	11	14	74	15	0	0	0	10
92-93—Boston	NHL	84	7	27	34	68	4	0	0	0	4
93-94—Boston	NHL	75	6	15	21	50	12	2	1	3	4
NHL totals		405	30	76	106	337	71	6	6	12	61

SWEENEY, TIM
C, MIGHTY DUCKS

PERSONAL: Born April 12, 1967, in Boston.... 5-11/185.... Shoots left.... Full name: Timothy Paul Sweeney.... Brother of Bob Sweeney, center, Buffalo Sabres.
HIGH SCHOOL: Weymouth (Mass.).
COLLEGE: Boston College.
TRANSACTIONS/CAREER NOTES: Selected by Calgary Flames in sixth round (seventh Flames pick, 122nd overall) of NHL entry draft (June 15, 1985).... Fractured index finger (January 26, 1988).... Bruised ankle (May 1990).... Signed as free agent by Boston Bruins (September 1992).... Selected by Mighty Ducks of Anaheim in NHL expansion draft (June 24, 1993).... Suffered injury (November 26, 1993); missed four games.
HONORS: Named to NCAA All-America East second team (1988-89).... Named to Hockey East All-Star first team (1988-89). ... Won Ken McKenzie Trophy (1989-90).... Named to IHL All-Star second team (1989-90).... Named to AHL All-Star second team (1992-93).

Season Team	League	REGULAR SEASON					PLAYOFFS				
		Gms.	G	A	Pts.	PIM	Gms.	G	A	Pts.	PIM
83-84—Weymouth North H.S.	Mass. H.S.	23	33	26	59	...	—	—	—	—	—
84-85—Weymouth North H.S.	Mass. H.S.	22	32	56	88	...	—	—	—	—	—
85-86—Boston College	Hockey East	32	8	4	12	8	—	—	—	—	—
86-87—Boston College	Hockey East	38	31	16	47	28	—	—	—	—	—
87-88—Boston College	Hockey East	18	9	11	20	18	—	—	—	—	—
88-89—Boston College	Hockey East	39	29	44	73	26	—	—	—	—	—
89-90—Salt Lake City	IHL	81	46	51	97	32	11	5	4	9	4
90-91—Calgary	NHL	42	7	9	16	8	—	—	—	—	—
—Salt Lake City	IHL	31	19	16	35	8	4	3	3	6	0
91-92—Calgary	NHL	11	1	2	3	4	—	—	—	—	—
—U.S. national team	Int'l	21	9	11	20	10	—	—	—	—	—
—U.S. Olympic Team	Int'l	8	3	4	7	6	—	—	—	—	—

Season Team	League	REGULAR SEASON					PLAYOFFS				
		Gms.	G	A	Pts.	Pen.	Gms.	G	A	Pts.	Pen.
92-93—Providence	AHL	60	41	55	96	32	3	2	2	4	0
—Boston	NHL	14	1	7	8	6	3	0	0	0	0
93-94—Anaheim	NHL	78	16	27	43	49	—	—	—	—	—
NHL totals		145	25	45	70	67	3	0	0	0	0

SYCHRA, MARTIN
C, CANADIENS

PERSONAL: Born June 19, 1974, in Brno, Czechoslovakia. . . . 6-0/176. . . . Shoots right. . . . Name pronounced SEE-kruh.
TRANSACTIONS/CAREER NOTES: Selected by Montreal Canadiens in sixth round (eighth Canadiens pick, 140th overall) of NHL entry draft (June 20, 1992).

Season Team	League	REGULAR SEASON					PLAYOFFS				
		Gms.	G	A	Pts.	PIM	Gms.	G	A	Pts.	PIM
91-92—Zetor Brno	Czech.	13	1	2	3	2	—	—	—	—	—
92-93—Dukla Trencin	Czech.	4	0	1	1	...	—	—	—	—	—
—Dukla Jihlava	Czech.	14	1	1	2	...	—	—	—	—	—
93-94—Kingston	OHL	59	29	32	61	32	6	0	3	3	7

SYDOR, DARRYL
D, KINGS

PERSONAL: Born May 13, 1972, in Edmonton. . . . 6-0/205. . . . Shoots left. . . . Full name: Darryl Marion Sydor. . . . Name pronounced sih-DOHR.
TRANSACTIONS/CAREER NOTES: Selected by Los Angeles Kings in first round (first Kings pick, seventh overall) of NHL entry draft (June 16, 1990). . . . Bruised hip (November 27, 1992); missed two games. . . . Sprained right shoulder (March 15, 1993); missed two games.
HONORS: Named to WHL (West) All-Star first team (1989-90 through 1991-92). . . . Won Bill Hunter Trophy (1990-91). . . . Named to Can.HL All-Star second team (1991-92)

Season Team	League	REGULAR SEASON					PLAYOFFS				
		Gms.	G	A	Pts.	PIM	Gms.	G	A	Pts.	PIM
88-89—Kamloops	WHL	65	12	14	26	86	15	1	4	5	19
89-90—Kamloops	WHL	67	29	66	95	129	17	2	9	11	28
90-91—Kamloops	WHL	66	27	78	105	88	12	3	*22	25	10
91-92—Kamloops	WHL	29	9	39	48	43	17	3	15	18	18
—Los Angeles	NHL	18	1	5	6	22	—	—	—	—	—
92-93—Los Angeles	NHL	80	6	23	29	63	24	3	8	11	16
93-94—Los Angeles	NHL	84	8	27	35	94	—	—	—	—	—
NHL totals		182	15	55	70	179	24	3	8	11	16

SYKORA, MICHAL
D, SHARKS

PERSONAL: Born July 5, 1973, in Pardubice, Czechoslovakia. . . . 6-4/210. . . . Shoots left. . . . Name pronounced sih-KOHR-uh.
TRANSACTIONS/CAREER NOTES: Selected by San Jose Sharks in sixth round (sixth Sharks pick, 123rd overall) of NHL entry draft (June 20, 1992). . . . Strained knee (November 11, 1993); missed four games.
HONORS: Named to Can.HL All-Star second team (1992-93). . . . Named to WHL (West) All-Star first team (1992-93).

Season Team	League	REGULAR SEASON					PLAYOFFS				
		Gms.	G	A	Pts.	PIM	Gms.	G	A	Pts.	PIM
90-91—Pardubice	Czech.	2	0	0	0	0	—	—	—	—	—
91-92—Tacoma	WHL	61	13	23	36	66	4	0	2	2	2
92-93—Tacoma	WHL	70	23	50	73	73	7	4	8	12	2
93-94—San Jose	NHL	22	1	4	5	14	—	—	—	—	—
—Kansas City	IHL	47	5	11	16	30	—	—	—	—	—
NHL totals		22	1	4	5	14					

SYKORA, PETR
C

PERSONAL: Born November 19, 1976, in Plzen, Czechoslovakia. . . . 5-11/172. . . . Shoots left.
TRANSACTIONS/CAREER NOTES: Signed as free agent by Cleveland Lumberjacks (January 31, 1994). . . . Rights traded by Lumberjacks to Detroit Vipers for cash and future considerations (July 27, 1994).

Season Team	League	REGULAR SEASON					PLAYOFFS				
		Gms.	G	A	Pts.	PIM	Gms.	G	A	Pts.	PIM
92-93—Skoda Plzen	Czech.	19	12	5	17	...	—	—	—	—	—
93-94—Skoda Plzen	Czech. Rep.	36	10	8	18	...	—	—	—	—	—
—Cleveland	IHL	13	4	5	9	18	—	—	—	—	—

SYMES, BRAD
D, OILERS

PERSONAL: Born April 26, 1976, in Edmonton. . . . 6-2/210. . . . Shoots left.
TRANSACTIONS/CAREER NOTES: Selected by Edmonton Oilers in third round (fifth Oilers pick, 60th overall) of NHL entry draft (June 29, 1994).

Season Team	League	REGULAR SEASON					PLAYOFFS				
		Gms.	G	A	Pts.	PIM	Gms.	G	A	Pts.	PIM
91-92—Sherwood Park	AJHL	17	3	7	10	92					
92-93—Portland	WHL	68	4	2	6	107	16	0	1	1	7
93-94—Portland	WHL	71	7	15	22	170	7	0	0	0	21

S

TABARACCI, RICK
G, CAPITALS

PERSONAL: Born January 2, 1969, in Toronto.... 5-11/180.... Catches right.... Full name: Richard Stephen Tabaracci.... Name pronounced tab-uh-RA-chee.

TRANSACTIONS/CAREER NOTES: Selected by Pittsburgh Penguins as underage junior in second round (second Penguins pick, 26th overall) of NHL entry draft (June 13, 1987). ... Traded by Penguins with C/LW Randy Cunneyworth and RW Dave McLlwain to Winnipeg Jets for RW Andrew McBain, D Jim Kyte and LW Randy Gilhen (June 17, 1989).... Pulled right hamstring (December 11, 1990); missed seven games.... Strained back (October 10, 1992); missed one game.... Suffered back spasms (December 1, 1992); missed one game.... Suffered back spasms (January 19, 1993); missed seven games.... Traded by Jets to Washington Capitals for G Jim Hrivnak and future considerations (March 22, 1993).... Tore knee ligaments (September 16, 1993); missed seven games.... Slightly sprained knee (February 20, 1994); missed 21 games.

HONORS: Named to OHL All-Star first team (1987-88).... Named to OHL All-Star second team (1988-89).

			REGULAR SEASON								PLAYOFFS						
Season	Team	League	Gms.	Min.	W	L	T	GA	SO	Avg.	Gms.	Min.	W	L	GA	SO	Avg.
85-86—	Markham Jr. B	OHA	40	2176	...	...	...	188	1	5.18	—	—	—	—	—	—	—
86-87—	Cornwall	OHL	*59	*3347	23	32	3	*290	1	5.20	5	303	1	4	26	0	5.15
87-88—	Cornwall	OHL	58	3448	33	18	6	200	†3	3.48	11	642	5	6	37	0	3.46
	—Muskegon	IHL	—	—	—	—	—	—	—	—	1	13	0	0	1	0	4.62
88-89—	Cornwall	OHL	50	2974	24	20	5	*210	1	4.24	18	1080	10	8	65	†1	3.61
	—Pittsburgh	NHL	1	33	0	0	0	4	0	7.27	—	—	—	—	—	—	—
89-90—	Moncton	AHL	27	1580	10	15	2	107	2	4.06	—	—	—	—	—	—	—
	—Fort Wayne	IHL	22	1064	8	9	‡1	73	0	4.12	3	159	1	2	19	0	7.17
90-91—	Moncton	AHL	11	645	4	5	2	41	0	3.81	—	—	—	—	—	—	—
	—Winnipeg	NHL	24	1093	4	9	4	71	1	3.90	—	—	—	—	—	—	—
91-92—	Moncton	AHL	23	1313	10	11	1	80	0	3.66	—	—	—	—	—	—	—
	—Winnipeg	NHL	18	966	6	7	3	52	0	3.23	7	387	3	4	26	0	4.03
92-93—	Winnipeg	NHL	19	959	5	10	0	70	0	4.38	—	—	—	—	—	—	—
	—Moncton	AHL	5	290	2	1	2	18	0	3.72	—	—	—	—	—	—	—
	—Washington	NHL	6	343	3	2	0	10	2	1.75	4	304	1	3	14	0	2.76
93-94—	Portland	AHL	3	177	3	0	0	8	0	2.71	—	—	—	—	—	—	—
	—Washington	NHL	32	1170	13	14	2	91	2	4.67	2	111	0	2	6	0	3.24
NHL totals			**100**	**4564**	**31**	**42**	**9**	**298**	**5**	**3.92**	**13**	**802**	**4**	**9**	**46**	**0**	**3.44**

TAGLIANETTI, PETER
D, PENGUINS

PERSONAL: Born August 15, 1963, in Framingham, Mass.... 6-2/195.... Shoots left.... Full name: Peter Anthony Taglianetti.... Name pronounced TAG-lee-uh-NEH-tee.

COLLEGE: Providence.

TRANSACTIONS/CAREER NOTES: Selected by Winnipeg Jets in third round (fourth Jets pick, 43rd overall) of NHL entry draft (June 8, 1983).... Dislocated shoulder during training camp (October 1985).... Dislocated shoulder (February 20, 1986). ... Underwent surgery to correct recurring shoulder dislocations (March 1986).... Damaged right knee cartilage during training camp and underwent surgery (September 1988).... Injured knee and underwent surgery (October 6, 1989).... Suspended five games by NHL for attempting to injure opposing player (February 20, 1990).... Bruised ribs (April 1990).... Traded by Jets to Minnesota North Stars for future considerations (September 23, 1990).... Traded by North Stars with D Larry Murphy to Pittsburgh Penguins for D Jim Johnson and D Chris Dahlquist (December 11, 1990).... Suffered collapsed lung (February 11, 1991); missed nine games.... Injured back (December 21, 1991); missed two games.... Injured back (March 7, 1992); missed final 15 games of season.... Underwent back surgery (April 5, 1992); missed entire playoffs.... Selected by Tampa Bay Lightning in NHL expansion draft (June 18, 1992).... Suffered concussion (March 20, 1993); missed one game.... Traded by Lightning to Penguins for third-round pick in 1993 draft (March 22, 1993).... Injured neck (November 6, 1993); missed seven games.... Injured back (January 2, 1994); missed three games.... Broke finger (March 6, 1994); missed two games.

HONORS: Named to ECAC All-Star second team (1983-84).... Named to NCAA All-America East second team (1984-85).... Named to Hockey East All-Star first team (1984-85).

MISCELLANEOUS: Member of Stanley Cup championship teams (1991 and 1992).

			REGULAR SEASON					PLAYOFFS			
Season	Team	League	Gms.	G	A	Pts.	PIM	Gms.	G	A	Pts.	PIM
81-82—	Providence College	ECAC	2	0	0	0	2	—	—	—	—	—
82-83—	Providence College	ECAC	43	4	17	21	68	—	—	—	—	—
83-84—	Providence College	ECAC	30	4	25	29	68	—	—	—	—	—
84-85—	Providence College	Hockey East	43	8	21	29	114	—	—	—	—	—
	—Winnipeg	NHL	1	0	0	0	0	1	0	0	0	0
85-86—	Sherbrooke	AHL	24	1	8	9	75	—	—	—	—	—
	—Winnipeg	NHL	18	0	0	0	48	3	0	0	0	2
86-87—	Winnipeg	NHL	3	0	0	0	12	—	—	—	—	—
	—Sherbrooke	AHL	54	5	14	19	104	10	2	5	7	25
87-88—	Winnipeg	NHL	70	6	17	23	182	5	1	1	2	12
88-89—	Winnipeg	NHL	66	1	14	15	226	—	—	—	—	—
89-90—	Moncton	AHL	3	0	2	2	2	—	—	—	—	—
	—Winnipeg	NHL	49	3	6	9	136	5	0	0	0	6
90-91—	Minnesota	NHL	16	0	1	1	14	—	—	—	—	—
	—Pittsburgh	NHL	39	3	8	11	93	19	0	3	3	49
91-92—	Pittsburgh	NHL	44	1	3	4	57	—	—	—	—	—
92-93—	Tampa Bay	NHL	61	1	8	9	150	—	—	—	—	—
	—Pittsburgh	NHL	11	1	4	5	34	11	1	2	3	16
93-94—	Pittsburgh	NHL	60	2	12	14	142	5	0	2	2	16
NHL totals			**438**	**18**	**73**	**91**	**1094**	**49**	**2**	**8**	**10**	**101**

TAMER, CHRIS
D, PENGUINS

PERSONAL: Born November 17, 1970, in Dearborn, Mich. . . . 6-2/185. . . . Shoots left. . . . Full name: Chris Thomas Tamer.
COLLEGE: Michigan.
TRANSACTIONS/CAREER NOTES: Selected by Pittsburgh Penguins in fourth round (third Penguins pick, 68th overall) of NHL entry draft (June 16, 1990). . . . Injured shoulder (March 27, 1994); missed four games.

			REGULAR SEASON					PLAYOFFS				
Season	Team	League	Gms.	G	A	Pts.	PIM	Gms.	G	A	Pts.	PIM
87-88—Redford		NAJHL	40	10	20	30	217	—	—	—	—	—
88-89—Redford		NAJHL	31	6	13	19	79	—	—	—	—	—
89-90—University of Michigan		CCHA	42	2	7	9	147	—	—	—	—	—
90-91—University of Michigan		CCHA	45	8	19	27	130	—	—	—	—	—
91-92—University of Michigan		CCHA	43	4	15	19	*125	—	—	—	—	—
92-93—University of Michigan		CCHA	39	5	18	23	113	—	—	—	—	—
93-94—Cleveland		IHL	53	1	2	3	160	—	—	—	—	—
—Pittsburgh		NHL	12	0	0	0	9	5	0	0	0	2
NHL totals			12	0	0	0	9	5	0	0	0	2

TANCILL, CHRIS
C, STARS

PERSONAL: Born February 7, 1968, in Livonia, Mich. . . . 5-10/185. . . . Shoots left. . . . Full name: Christopher William Tancill.
COLLEGE: Wisconsin.
TRANSACTIONS/CAREER NOTES: Selected by Hartford Whalers in NHL supplemental draft (June 16, 1989). . . . Traded by Whalers to Detroit Red Wings for RW Daniel Shank (December 18, 1991). . . . Signed as free agent by Dallas Stars (August 27, 1993).
HONORS: Named NCAA Tournament Most Valuable Player (1990-91). . . . Named to NCAA All-Tournament team (1990-91). . . . Named to AHL All-Star first team (1991-92 and 1992-93).

			REGULAR SEASON					PLAYOFFS				
Season	Team	League	Gms.	G	A	Pts.	PIM	Gms.	G	A	Pts.	PIM
87-88—University of Wisconsin		WCHA	44	13	14	27	48	—	—	—	—	—
88-89—University of Wisconsin		WCHA	44	20	23	43	50	—	—	—	—	—
89-90—University of Wisconsin		WCHA	45	39	32	71	44	—	—	—	—	—
90-91—Hartford		NHL	9	1	1	2	4	—	—	—	—	—
—Springfield		AHL	72	37	35	72	46	17	8	4	12	32
91-92—Springfield		AHL	17	12	7	19	20	—	—	—	—	—
—Hartford		NHL	10	0	0	0	2	—	—	—	—	—
—Adirondack		AHL	50	36	34	70	42	19	7	9	16	31
—Detroit		NHL	1	0	0	0	0	—	—	—	—	—
92-93—Adirondack		AHL	68	*59	43	102	62	10	7	7	14	10
—Detroit		NHL	4	1	0	1	2	—	—	—	—	—
93-94—Dallas		NHL	12	1	3	4	8	—	—	—	—	—
—Kalamazoo		IHL	60	41	54	95	55	5	0	2	2	8
NHL totals			36	3	4	7	16					

TANNER, JOHN
G, MIGHTY DUCKS

PERSONAL: Born March 17, 1971, in Cambridge, Ont. . . . 6-3/182. . . . Catches left.
TRANSACTIONS/CAREER NOTES: Selected by Quebec Nordiques in third round (fourth Nordiques pick, 54th overall) of NHL entry draft (June 17, 1989). . . . Traded by Peterborough Petes to London Knights for second-round pick in 1990 OHL draft and second- and third-round picks in 1991 OHL draft (January 1990). . . . Traded by Knights to Sudbury Wolves for fourth-round pick in 1991 OHL draft (December 1990). . . . Traded by Nordiques to Mighty Ducks of Anaheim for fourth-round pick in 1995 draft (February 21, 1994).
HONORS: Shared Dave Pinkney Trophy with G Todd Bojcun (1987-88 and 1988-89).

			REGULAR SEASON							PLAYOFFS					
Season	Team	League	Gms.	Min.	W	L	T	GA	SO	Avg.	Gms.	Min.	W	L	GA	SO	Avg.
86-87—New Hamburg Jr. C		OHA	15	889	. . .	. . .	. . .	83	0	5.60	—						
87-88—Peterborough		OHL	26	1532	18	4	3	88	0	3.45	2	98	1	0	3	0	1.84
88-89—Peterborough		OHL	34	1923	22	10	0	107	†2	*3.34	8	369	4	3	23	0	3.74
89-90—Quebec		NHL	1	60	0	1	0	3	0	3.00	—						
—Peterborough		OHL	18	1037	6	8	2	70	0	4.05	—						
—London		OHL	19	1097	12	5	1	53	1	2.90	6	341	2	4	24	0	4.22
90-91—Quebec		NHL	6	228	1	3	1	16	0	4.21	—						
—London		OHL	7	427	3	3	1	29	0	4.07	—						
—Sudbury		OHL	19	1043	10	8	0	60	0	3.45	5	274	1	4	21	0	4.60
91-92—Halifax		AHL	12	672	6	5	1	29	2	2.59	—						
—New Haven		AHL	16	908	7	6	2	57	0	3.77	—						
—Quebec		NHL	14	796	1	7	4	46	1	3.47	—						
92-93—Halifax		AHL	51	2852	20	18	7	199	0	4.19	—						
93-94—Cornwall		AHL	38	2035	14	15	4	123	1	3.63	—						
—San Diego		IHL	13	629	5	3	‡2	37	0	3.53	3	118	0	1	5	0	2.54
NHL totals			21	1084	2	11	5	65	1	3.60							

TARDIF, PATRICE
C, BLUES

PERSONAL: Born October 30, 1970, in Thetford Mines, Que. . . . 6-2/175. . . . Shoots left. . . . Name pronounced TAHR-dihf.
COLLEGE: Champlain Regional (Que.), then Maine.
TRANSACTIONS/CAREER NOTES: Selected by St. Louis Blues in third round (second Blues

pick, 54th overall) of NHL entry draft (June 16, 1990).
HONORS: Named to Hockey East All-Rookie team (1990-91).

Season Team	League	REGULAR SEASON					PLAYOFFS				
		Gms.	G	A	Pts.	PIM	Gms.	G	A	Pts.	PIM
89-90—Champlain Junior College	Can. Coll.	27	58	36	94	36	—	—	—	—	—
90-91—University of Maine	Hockey East	36	13	12	25	18	—	—	—	—	—
91-92—University of Maine	Hockey East	31	18	20	38	14	—	—	—	—	—
92-93—University of Maine	Hockey East	45	23	25	48	22	—	—	—	—	—
93-94—University of Maine	Hockey East	34	18	15	33	42	—	—	—	—	—
—Peoria	IHL	11	4	4	8	21	4	2	0	2	4

TARVAINEN, JUSSI
C, OILERS

PERSONAL: Born May 31, 1976, in Lahti, Finland.... 6-2/187.... Shoots right.
TRANSACTIONS/CAREER NOTES: Selected by Edmonton Oilers in fourth round (seventh Oilers pick, 95th overall) of NHL entry draft (June 29, 1994).

Season Team	League	REGULAR SEASON					PLAYOFFS				
		Gms.	G	A	Pts.	PIM	Gms.	G	A	Pts.	PIM
92-93—Kalpa Juniors...................	Finland Jrs.	17	3	6	9	35	—	—	—	—	—
93-94—Kalpa	Finland	42	3	4	7	20	—	—	—	—	—

TATARINOV, MIKHAIL
D, BRUINS

PERSONAL: Born July 16, 1966, in Penza, U.S.S.R.... 5-10/194.... Shoots left.
... Name pronounced mihk-HIGHL tuh-TAH-rih-nahf.
TRANSACTIONS/CAREER NOTES: Selected by Washington Capitals in 11th round (10th Capitals pick, 225th overall) of NHL entry draft (June 9, 1984).... Traded by Capitals to Quebec Nordiques for second-round pick (D Eric Lavigne) in 1991 draft (June 22, 1991).... Injured ribs (November 16, 1991); missed six games.... Bruised ribs (February 18, 1992); missed five games.... Sprained right thumb (November 11, 1992); missed 15 games.... Injured back (March 15, 1993); missed remainder of season.... Signed as free agent by Boston Bruins (July 30, 1993).... Suffered sore back (October 15, 1993); missed seven games.

Season Team	League	REGULAR SEASON					PLAYOFFS				
		Gms.	G	A	Pts.	PIM	Gms.	G	A	Pts.	PIM
83-84—Sokol Kiev	USSR	38	7	3	10	46	—	—	—	—	—
84-85—Sokol Kiev	USSR	34	3	6	9	54	—	—	—	—	—
85-86—Sokol Kiev	USSR	37	7	5	12	41	—	—	—	—	—
86-87—Dynamo Moscow	USSR	40	10	8	18	43	—	—	—	—	—
87-88—Dynamo Moscow	USSR	30	2	2	4	8	—	—	—	—	—
88-89—Dynamo Moscow	USSR	4	1	0	1	2	—	—	—	—	—
89-90—Dynamo Moscow	USSR	44	11	10	21	34	—	—	—	—	—
90-91—Dynamo Moscow	USSR	11	5	4	9	...	—	—	—	—	—
—Washington	NHL	65	8	15	23	82	—	—	—	—	—
91-92—Quebec	NHL	66	11	27	38	72	—	—	—	—	—
92-93—Quebec	NHL	28	2	6	8	28	—	—	—	—	—
93-94—Boston	NHL	2	0	0	0	0	—	—	—	—	—
—Providence	AHL	3	0	3	3	0	—	—	—	—	—
NHL totals...............................		161	21	48	69	184					

TAYLOR, CHRIS
C, ISLANDERS

PERSONAL: Born March 6, 1972, in Stratford, Ont.... 6-1/190.... Shoots left.... Brother of Tim Taylor, center in Detroit Red Wings system.
TRANSACTIONS/CAREER NOTES: Tore knee ligaments (March 1989).... Selected by New York Islanders in second round (second Islanders pick, 27th overall) of NHL entry draft (June 16, 1990).

Season Team	League	REGULAR SEASON					PLAYOFFS				
		Gms.	G	A	Pts.	PIM	Gms.	G	A	Pts.	PIM
88-89—London	OHL	62	7	16	23	52	15	0	2	2	15
89-90—London	OHL	66	45	60	105	60	6	3	2	5	6
90-91—London	OHL	65	50	78	128	50	7	4	8	12	6
91-92—London	OHL	66	48	74	122	57	10	8	16	24	9
92-93—Capital District................	AHL	77	19	43	62	32	4	0	1	1	2
93-94—Raleigh	ECHL	2	0	0	0	0	—	—	—	—	—
—Salt Lake City...................	IHL	79	21	20	41	38					

TAYLOR, DAVE
RW

PERSONAL: Born December 4, 1955, in Levack, Ont.... 6-0/195.... Shoots right.... Full name: David Andrew Taylor.
HIGH SCHOOL: Levack District (Ont.).
COLLEGE: Clarkson (N.Y.).
TRANSACTIONS/CAREER NOTES: Selected by Los Angeles Kings in 15th round (14th Kings pick, 210th overall) of NHL amateur draft (June 3, 1975).... Pulled back muscle and sprained left knee; missed parts of 1979-80 season.... Sprained shoulder (November 5, 1980).... Broke right wrist (October 29, 1982); missed 33 games.... Injured right knee (January 1983).... Broke wrist at World Championships and underwent surgery (May 28, 1983).... Sprained knee (November 1986).... Injured groin (December 1987).... Tore knee cartilage (January 1989).... Pulled groin (December 13, 1989); missed 15 games.... Suffered knee inflammation (January 1990).... Strained shoulder (April 1990).... Suffered concussion (November 14, 1992); missed 18 games.... Suffered recurring symptoms of previous concussion (February 9, 1993); missed 16 games.... Suffered concussion (January 4, 1994); missed 44 games.... Announced retirement (April 12, 1994).
HONORS: Named ECAC Player of the Year (1976-77).... Named to NCAA All-America East team (1976-77).... Named to THE

SPORTING NEWS All-Star second team (1980-81).... Named to NHL All-Star second team (1980-81).... Played in NHL All-Star Game (1981, 1982, 1986 and 1994).... Won King Clancy Memorial Trophy (1990-91).... Won Bill Masterton Trophy (1990-91).

Season Team	League	REGULAR SEASON					PLAYOFFS				
		Gms.	G	A	Pts.	PIM	Gms.	G	A	Pts.	PIM
74-75—Clarkson	ECAC	...	20	34	54	...	—	—	—	—	—
75-76—Clarkson	ECAC	...	26	33	59	...	—	—	—	—	—
76-77—Clarkson	ECAC	34	41	67	108	...	—	—	—	—	—
—Fort Worth	CHL	7	2	4	6	6	—	—	—	—	—
77-78—Los Angeles	NHL	64	22	21	43	47	2	0	0	0	5
78-79—Los Angeles	NHL	78	43	48	91	124	2	0	0	0	2
79-80—Los Angeles	NHL	61	37	53	90	72	4	2	1	3	4
80-81—Los Angeles	NHL	72	47	65	112	130	4	2	2	4	10
81-82—Los Angeles	NHL	78	39	67	106	130	10	4	6	10	20
82-83—Los Angeles	NHL	46	21	37	58	76	—	—	—	—	—
83-84—Los Angeles	NHL	63	20	49	69	91	—	—	—	—	—
84-85—Los Angeles	NHL	79	41	51	92	132	3	2	2	4	8
85-86—Los Angeles	NHL	76	33	38	71	110	—	—	—	—	—
86-87—Los Angeles	NHL	67	18	44	62	84	5	2	3	5	6
87-88—Los Angeles	NHL	68	26	41	67	129	5	3	3	6	6
88-89—Los Angeles	NHL	70	26	37	63	80	11	1	5	6	19
89-90—Los Angeles	NHL	58	15	26	41	96	6	4	4	8	2
90-91—Los Angeles	NHL	73	23	30	53	148	12	2	1	3	12
91-92—Los Angeles	NHL	77	10	19	29	63	6	1	1	2	20
92-93—Los Angeles	NHL	48	6	9	15	49	22	3	5	8	31
93-94—Los Angeles	NHL	33	4	3	7	28	—	—	—	—	—
NHL totals		1111	431	638	1069	1589	92	26	33	59	145

TAYLOR, TIM
C, RED WINGS

PERSONAL: Born February 6, 1969, in Stratford, Ont.... 6-1/180.... Shoots left.... Full name: Tim Robertson Taylor.... Brother of Chris Taylor, center in New York Islanders system.
TRANSACTIONS/CAREER NOTES: Suffered from mononucleosis (October 1986).... Selected by Washington Capitals in second round (second Capitals pick, 36th overall) of NHL entry draft (June 11, 1988).... Traded by Capitals to Vancouver Canucks for C Eric Murano (January 29, 1993).... Signed as free agent by Detroit Red Wings (July 28, 1993).
HONORS: Won John B. Sollenberger Trophy (1993-94).... Named to AHL All-Star first team (1993-94).

Season Team	League	REGULAR SEASON					PLAYOFFS				
		Gms.	G	A	Pts.	PIM	Gms.	G	A	Pts.	PIM
86-87—London	OHL	34	7	9	16	11	—	—	—	—	—
87-88—London	OHL	64	46	50	96	66	12	9	9	18	26
88-89—London	OHL	61	34	80	114	93	21	*21	25	*46	58
89-90—Baltimore	AHL	74	22	21	43	63	9	2	2	4	13
90-91—Baltimore	AHL	79	25	42	67	75	5	0	1	1	4
91-92—Baltimore	AHL	65	9	18	27	131	—	—	—	—	—
92-93—Baltimore	AHL	41	15	16	31	49	—	—	—	—	—
—Hamilton	AHL	36	15	22	37	37	—	—	—	—	—
93-94—Adirondack	AHL	79	36	*81	117	86	12	2	10	12	12
—Detroit	NHL	1	1	0	1	0	—	—	—	—	—
NHL totals		1	1	0	1	0	—	—	—	—	—

TERRERI, CHRIS
G, DEVILS

PERSONAL: Born November 15, 1964, in Warwick, R.I.... 5-8/160.... Catches left.... Full name: Christopher Arnold Terreri.... Name pronounced tuh-RAIR-ee.
COLLEGE: Providence.
TRANSACTIONS/CAREER NOTES: Selected by New Jersey Devils in fifth round (third Devils pick, 87th overall) of NHL entry draft (June 8, 1983).... Strained knee (October 1986).... Strained lower back (March 21, 1992); missed five games.
HONORS: Named NCAA Tournament Most Valuable Player (1984-85).... Named Hockey East Player of the Year (1984-85). ... Named to NCAA All-Tournament team (1984-85).... Named to NCAA All-America East first team (1984-85).... Named to NCAA All-America East second team (1985-86).... Named to Hockey East All-Star first team (1984-85).

Season Team	League	REGULAR SEASON							PLAYOFFS					
		Gms.	Min.	W	L	T	GA	SO	Avg.	Gms.	Min.	W	L	GA	SO	Avg.
82-83—Providence College	ECAC	11	529	7	1	0	17	2	1.93	—	—	—	—	—	—	—
83-84—Providence College	ECAC	10	391	4	2	0	20	0	3.07	—	—	—	—	—	—	—
84-85—Providence College	Hoc. East	41	2515	15	13	5	131	1	3.13	—	—	—	—	—	—	—
85-86—Providence College	Hoc. East	27	1540	6	16	0	96	0	3.74	—	—	—	—	—	—	—
86-87—Maine	AHL	14	765	4	9	1	57	0	4.47	—	—	—	—	—	—	—
—New Jersey	NHL	7	286	0	3	1	21	0	4.41	—	—	—	—	—	—	—
87-88—U.S. national team	Int'l	26	1430	17	7	2	81	0	3.40	—	—	—	—	—	—	—
—U.S. Olympic Team	Int'l	3	128	1	1	0	14	0	6.56	—	—	—	—	—	—	—
—Utica	AHL	7	399	5	1	0	18	0	2.71	—	—	—	—	—	—	—
88-89—New Jersey	NHL	8	402	0	4	2	18	0	2.69	—	—	—	—	—	—	—
—Utica	AHL	39	2314	20	15	3	132	0	3.42	2	80	0	1	6	0	4.50
89-90—New Jersey	NHL	35	1931	15	12	3	110	0	3.42	4	238	2	2	13	0	3.28

Season Team	League	REGULAR SEASON								PLAYOFFS						
		Gms.	Min.	W	L	T	GA	SO	Avg.	Gms.	Min.	W	L	GA	SO	Avg.
90-91—New Jersey	NHL	53	2970	24	21	7	144	1	2.91	7	428	3	4	21	0	2.94
91-92—New Jersey	NHL	54	3186	22	22	10	169	1	3.18	7	386	3	3	23	0	3.58
92-93—New Jersey	NHL	48	2672	19	21	3	151	2	3.39	4	219	1	3	17	0	4.66
93-94—New Jersey	NHL	44	2340	20	11	4	106	2	2.72	4	200	3	0	9	0	2.70
NHL totals		249	13787	100	94	30	719	6	3.13	26	1471	12	12	83	0	3.39

THEODORE, JOSE
G, CANADIENS

PERSONAL: Born September 13, 1976, in Laval, Que. . . . 5-10/176. . . . Catches right. . . . Name pronounced Hoh-zay Tay-oh-DOR.
TRANSACTIONS/CAREER NOTES: Selected by Montreal Canadiens in second round (second Canadiens pick, 44th overall) of NHL entry draft (June 28, 1994).

Season Team	League	REGULAR SEASON								PLAYOFFS						
		Gms.	Min.	W	L	T	GA	SO	Avg.	Gms.	Min.	W	L	GA	SO	Avg.
92-93—St. Jean	QMJHL	34	1776	12	16	2	112	0	3.78	2	63	0	2	5	0	4.70
93-94—St. Jean	QMJHL	57	3225	20	29	6	194	0	3.61	5	296	1	4	18	1	3.65

THIBAULT, JOCELYN
G, NORDIQUES

PERSONAL: Born January 12, 1975, in Montreal. . . . 5-11/170. . . . Catches left.
TRANSACTIONS/CAREER NOTES: Selected by Quebec Nordiques in first round (first Nordiques pick, 10th overall) of NHL entry draft (June 26, 1993).
HONORS: Named to QMJHL All-Rookie team (1991-92). . . . Won Can.HL Goaltender-of-the-Year Award (1992-93). . . . Won Jacques Plante Trophy (1992-93). . . . Won Michel Briere Trophy (1992-93). . . . Won Marcel Robert Trophy (1992-93). . . . Named to Can.HL All-Star first team (1992-93). . . . Named to QMJHL All-Star first team (1992-93).

Season Team	League	REGULAR SEASON								PLAYOFFS						
		Gms.	Min.	W	L	T	GA	SO	Avg.	Gms.	Min.	W	L	GA	SO	Avg.
91-92—Trois-Rivieres	QMJHL	30	1497	14	7	1	77	0	3.09	3	300	...	...	20	0	4.00
92-93—Sherbrooke	QMJHL	56	3190	34	14	5	159	*3	*2.99	15	883	9	6	57	0	3.87
93-94—Cornwall	AHL	4	240	4	0	0	9	1	2.25	—	—	—	—	—	—	—
—Quebec	NHL	29	1504	8	13	3	83	0	3.31	—	—	—	—	—	—	—
NHL totals		29	1504	8	13	3	83	0	3.31							

THIESSEN, TRAVIS
D, BLACKHAWKS

PERSONAL: Born November 7, 1972, in North Battleford, Sask. . . . 6-3/202. . . . Shoots left. . . . Name pronounced THEE-sehn.
TRANSACTIONS/CAREER NOTES: Selected by Pittsburgh Penguins in third round (third Penguins pick, 67th overall) of NHL entry draft (June 20, 1992). . . . Signed as free agent by Chicago Blackhawks (June 23, 1994).

Season Team	League	REGULAR SEASON					PLAYOFFS				
		Gms.	G	A	Pts.	PIM	Gms.	G	A	Pts.	PIM
90-91—Moose Jaw	WHL	69	4	14	18	80	8	0	0	0	10
91-92—Moose Jaw	WHL	72	9	50	59	112	4	0	2	2	8
92-93—Cleveland	IHL	64	3	7	10	69	4	0	0	0	16
93-94—Cleveland	IHL	74	2	13	15	75	—	—	—	—	—

THOMAS, SCOTT
RW, SABRES

PERSONAL: Born January 18, 1970, in Buffalo, N.Y. . . . 6-2/195. . . . Shoots right. . . . Full name: John Scott Thomas.
HIGH SCHOOL: Nichols (Buffalo, N.Y.).
COLLEGE: Clarkson (N.Y.).
TRANSACTIONS/CAREER NOTES: Selected by Buffalo Sabres in third round (second Sabres pick, 56th overall) of NHL entry draft (June 17, 1989). . . . Broke left thumb (December 1990).
HONORS: Named to ECAC All-Rookie team (1989-90).

Season Team	League	REGULAR SEASON					PLAYOFFS				
		Gms.	G	A	Pts.	PIM	Gms.	G	A	Pts.	PIM
87-88—Nichols	N.Y. H.S.	16	23	39	62	82	—	—	—	—	—
88-89—Nichols	N.Y. H.S.	...	38	52	90	...	—	—	—	—	—
89-90—Clarkson	ECAC	34	19	13	32	95	—	—	—	—	—
90-91—Clarkson	ECAC	40	28	14	42	90	—	—	—	—	—
91-92—Clarkson	ECAC	30	†25	21	46	62	—	—	—	—	—
—Rochester	AHL	—	—	—	—	—	9	0	1	1	17
92-93—Rochester	AHL	66	32	27	59	38	17	8	5	13	6
—Buffalo	NHL	7	1	1	2	15	—	—	—	—	—
93-94—Buffalo	NHL	32	2	2	4	8	—	—	—	—	—
NHL totals		39	3	3	6	23					

THOMAS, STEVE
LW/RW, ISLANDERS

PERSONAL: Born July 15, 1963, in Stockport, England. . . . 5-11/186. . . . Shoots left.
TRANSACTIONS/CAREER NOTES: Signed as free agent by Toronto Maple Leafs (June 1984). . . . Broke wrist during training camp (September 1984). . . . Traded by Maple Leafs with RW Rick Vaive and D Bob McGill to Chicago Blackhawks for LW Al Secord and RW Ed Olczyk (September 3, 1987). . . . Pulled stomach muscle (October 1987). . . . Separated left shoulder (February 20, 1988); underwent surgery (May 1988). . . . Pulled back muscle (October 18, 1988). . . . Separated right shoulder (December 21, 1988). . . .

Underwent surgery to repair chronic shoulder separation problem (January 25, 1989). . . . Strained knee ligaments during training camp (September 1990); missed first 11 games of season. . . . Traded by Blackhawks with C Adam Creighton to New York Islanders for C Brent Sutter and RW Brad Lauer (October 25, 1991). . . . Bruised ribs (March 10, 1992); missed one game. . . . Bruised ribs (November 21, 1992); missed three games. . . . Suffered neck muscle spasms (January 4, 1994); missed five games.

HONORS: Won Dudley (Red) Garrett Memorial Trophy (1984-85). . . . Named to AHL All-Star first team (1984-85).

Season Team	League	REGULAR SEASON					PLAYOFFS				
		Gms.	G	A	Pts.	PIM	Gms.	G	A	Pts.	PIM
81-82—Markham Tier II Jr. A........	OHA	48	68	57	125	113	—	—	—	—	—
82-83—Toronto.............................	OHL	61	18	20	38	42	—	—	—	—	—
83-84—Toronto.............................	OHL	70	51	54	105	77	—	—	—	—	—
84-85—Toronto.............................	NHL	18	1	1	2	2	—	—	—	—	—
—St. Catharines	AHL	64	42	48	90	56	—	—	—	—	—
85-86—St. Catharines	AHL	19	18	14	32	35	—	—	—	—	—
—Toronto.............................	NHL	65	20	37	57	36	10	6	8	14	9
86-87—Toronto.............................	NHL	78	35	27	62	114	13	2	3	5	13
87-88—Chicago	NHL	30	13	13	26	40	3	1	2	3	6
88-89—Chicago	NHL	45	21	19	40	69	12	3	5	8	10
89-90—Chicago	NHL	76	40	30	70	91	20	7	6	13	33
90-91—Chicago	NHL	69	19	35	54	129	6	1	2	3	15
91-92—Chicago	NHL	11	2	6	8	26	—	—	—	—	—
—New York Islanders..........	NHL	71	28	42	70	71	—	—	—	—	—
92-93—New York Islanders..........	NHL	79	37	50	87	111	18	9	8	17	37
93-94—New York Islanders..........	NHL	78	42	33	75	139	4	1	0	1	8
NHL totals.............................		620	258	293	551	828	86	30	34	64	131

THOMLINSON, DAVE
LW, KINGS

PERSONAL: Born October 22, 1966, in Edmonton. . . . 6-1/215. . . . Shoots left.
TRANSACTIONS/CAREER NOTES: Separated shoulder (November 1983). . . . Separated shoulder (November 1984). . . . Selected by Toronto Maple Leafs as underage junior in third round (third Maple Leafs pick, 43rd overall) of NHL entry draft (June 15, 1985). . . . Signed as free agent by St. Louis Blues (July 1987). . . . Bruised foot (February 1990). . . . Signed as free agent by Boston Bruins; Bruins and Blues arranged trade in which Bruins received Thomlinson and D Glen Featherstone for RW Dave Christian, third-round (LW Vitali Prokhorov) and seventh-round (C Lance Burns) picks in 1992 draft (July 1991). . . . Suffered sore back (December 1991). . . . Signed as free agent by New York Rangers (September 4, 1992). . . . Signed as free agent by Los Angeles Kings (July 22, 1993). . . . Fractured hand (February 14, 1994); missed remainder of the season.

Season Team	League	REGULAR SEASON					PLAYOFFS				
		Gms.	G	A	Pts.	PIM	Gms.	G	A	Pts.	PIM
83-84—Brandon............................	WHL	41	17	12	29	62	—	—	—	—	—
84-85—Brandon............................	WHL	26	13	14	27	70	—	—	—	—	—
85-86—Brandon............................	WHL	53	25	20	45	116	—	—	—	—	—
86-87—Brandon............................	WHL	2	0	1	1	9	—	—	—	—	—
—Moose Jaw	WHL	69	44	36	80	126	9	7	3	10	19
87-88—Peoria	IHL	74	27	30	57	56	7	4	3	7	11
88-89—Peoria	IHL	64	27	29	56	154	3	0	1	1	8
89-90—St. Louis	NHL	19	1	2	3	12	—	—	—	—	—
—Peoria	IHL	59	27	40	67	87	5	1	1	2	15
90-91—Peoria	IHL	80	53	54	107	107	11	6	7	13	28
—St. Louis	NHL	3	0	0	0	0	9	3	1	4	4
91-92—Boston	NHL	12	0	1	1	17	—	—	—	—	—
—Maine	AHL	25	9	11	20	36	—	—	—	—	—
92-93—Binghamton	AHL	54	25	35	60	61	12	2	5	7	8
93-94—Los Angeles......................	NHL	7	0	0	0	21	—	—	—	—	—
—Phoenix	IHL	39	10	15	25	70	—	—	—	—	—
NHL totals.............................		41	1	3	4	50	9	3	1	4	4

THOMPSON, BRENT
D, KINGS

PERSONAL: Born January 9, 1971, in Calgary. . . . 6-2/175. . . . Shoots left. . . . Full name: Brenton Keith Thompson.
TRANSACTIONS/CAREER NOTES: Stretched knee ligaments and separated shoulder (September 1987). . . . Selected by Los Angeles Kings in second round (first Kings pick, 39th overall) of NHL entry draft (June 17, 1989). . . . Suffered hip flexor prior to 1992-93 season; missed first six games of season. . . . Strained abdomen (January 23, 1992); missed 17 games.
HONORS: Named to WHL (East) All-Star second team (1990-91).

Season Team	League	REGULAR SEASON					PLAYOFFS				
		Gms.	G	A	Pts.	PIM	Gms.	G	A	Pts.	PIM
88-89—Medicine Hat	WHL	72	3	10	13	160	3	0	0	0	2
89-90—Medicine Hat	WHL	68	10	35	45	167	3	0	1	1	14
90-91—Medicine Hat	WHL	51	5	40	45	87	12	1	7	8	16
—Phoenix	IHL	—	—	—	—	—	4	0	1	1	6
91-92—Phoenix	IHL	42	4	13	17	139	—	—	—	—	—
—Los Angeles......................	NHL	27	0	5	5	89	4	0	0	0	4
92-93—Phoenix	IHL	22	0	5	5	112	—	—	—	—	—
—Los Angeles......................	NHL	30	0	4	4	76	—	—	—	—	—

Season Team	League	REGULAR SEASON					PLAYOFFS				
		Gms.	G	A	Pts.	Pen.	Gms.	G	A	Pts.	Pen.
93-94—Phoenix	IHL	26	1	11	12	118	—	—	—	—	—
—Los Angeles	NHL	24	1	0	1	81	—	—	—	—	—
NHL totals		81	1	9	10	246	4	0	0	0	4

THOMPSON, BRIANE
D. PANTHERS

PERSONAL: Born April 17, 1974, in Peterborough, Ont.... 6-3/205.... Shoots left. **TRANSACTIONS/CAREER NOTES:** Selected by Florida Panthers in eighth round (10th Panthers pick, 187th overall) of NHL entry draft (June 26, 1993).

Season Team	League	REGULAR SEASON					PLAYOFFS				
		Gms.	G	A	Pts.	PIM	Gms.	G	A	Pts.	PIM
90-91—Lindsay Jr. B	OHA	42	5	15	20	40	—	—	—	—	—
91-92—Sault Ste. Marie	OHL	42	0	4	4	17	6	0	0	0	4
92-93—Sault Ste. Marie	OHL	63	2	21	23	57	18	0	6	6	35
93-94—Sault Ste. Marie	OHL	60	5	36	41	136	14	0	3	3	27

THOMSON, JIM
RW, MIGHTY DUCKS

PERSONAL: Born December 30, 1965, in Edmonton.... 6-1/220.... Shoots right. **TRANSACTIONS/CAREER NOTES:** Selected by Washington Capitals as underage junior in ninth round (eighth Capitals pick, 185th overall) of NHL entry draft (June 9, 1984).... Traded by Capitals to Hartford Whalers for D Scot Kleinendorst (March 6, 1989).... Traded by Whalers to New Jersey Devils for RW Chris Cichocki (October 31, 1989).... Signed as free agent by Los Angeles Kings (July 11, 1990).... Fractured foot (January 19, 1991).... Selected by Minnesota North Stars in NHL expansion draft (May 30, 1991). ... Traded by North Stars with D Charlie Huddy, LW Randy Gilhen and fourth-round pick in 1991 draft (D Alexei Zhitnik) to Kings for C Todd Elik (June 22, 1991).... Hyperextended elbow (November 11, 1991); missed four games.... Selected by Ottawa Senators in NHL expansion draft (June 18, 1992).... Traded by Senators with C Marc Fortier to Kings for RW Bob Kudelski and C Shawn McCosh (December 20, 1992).... Selected by Mighty Ducks of Anaheim in NHL expansion draft (June 24, 1993).... Injured shoulder (October 10, 1993); missed remainder of season.... Underwent reconstructive shoulder surgery (December 26, 1993).

Season Team	League	REGULAR SEASON					PLAYOFFS				
		Gms.	G	A	Pts.	PIM	Gms.	G	A	Pts.	PIM
82-83—Markham Waxers	OPJHL	35	6	7	13	81	—	—	—	—	—
83-84—Toronto	OHL	60	10	18	28	68	9	1	0	1	26
84-85—Toronto	OHL	63	23	28	51	122	5	3	1	4	25
—Binghamton	AHL	4	0	0	0	2	—	—	—	—	—
85-86—Binghamton	AHL	59	15	9	24	195	—	—	—	—	—
86-87—Binghamton	AHL	57	13	10	23	*360	10	0	1	1	40
—Washington	NHL	10	0	0	0	35	—	—	—	—	—
87-88—Binghamton	AHL	25	8	9	17	64	4	1	2	3	7
88-89—Baltimore	AHL	41	25	16	41	129	—	—	—	—	—
—Washington	NHL	14	2	0	2	53	—	—	—	—	—
—Hartford	NHL	5	0	0	0	14	—	—	—	—	—
89-90—Binghamton	AHL	8	1	2	3	30	—	—	—	—	—
—Utica	AHL	60	20	23	43	124	4	1	0	1	19
—New Jersey	NHL	3	0	0	0	31	—	—	—	—	—
90-91—New Haven	AHL	27	5	8	13	121	—	—	—	—	—
—Los Angeles	NHL	8	1	0	1	19	—	—	—	—	—
91-92—Los Angeles	NHL	45	1	2	3	162	—	—	—	—	—
—Phoenix	IHL	2	1	0	1	0	—	—	—	—	—
92-93—Ottawa	NHL	15	0	1	1	41	—	—	—	—	—
—Los Angeles	NHL	9	0	0	0	56	1	0	0	0	0
—Phoenix	IHL	14	4	5	9	44	—	—	—	—	—
93-94—Anaheim	NHL	6	0	0	0	5	—	—	—	—	—
NHL totals		115	4	3	7	416	1	0	0	0	0

THORNTON, SCOTT
C, OILERS

PERSONAL: Born January 9, 1971, in London, Ont.... 6-2/200.... Shoots left. **TRANSACTIONS/CAREER NOTES:** Selected by Toronto Maple Leafs in first round (first Maple Leafs pick, third overall) of NHL entry draft (June 17, 1989).... Suspended 12 games by OHL for refusing to leave ice following penalty (February 7, 1990).... Separated shoulder (January 24, 1991); missed eight games.... Traded by Maple Leafs with LW Vincent Damphousse, D Luke Richardson, G Peter Ing and future considerations to Edmonton Oilers for G Grant Fuhr, RW/LW Glenn Anderson and LW Craig Berube (September 19, 1991).... Suffered concussion (November 23, 1991); missed one game.... Sprained ankle (October 6, 1993); missed 13 games. ... Suffered back spasms (November 21, 1993); missed one game.... Suffered wrist contusion (April 14, 1994); missed one game.

Season Team	League	REGULAR SEASON					PLAYOFFS				
		Gms.	G	A	Pts.	PIM	Gms.	G	A	Pts.	PIM
86-87—London Diamonds	OPJHL	31	10	7	17	10	—	—	—	—	—
87-88—Belleville	OHL	62	11	19	30	54	6	0	1	1	2
88-89—Belleville	OHL	59	28	34	62	103	5	1	1	2	6
89-90—Belleville	OHL	47	21	28	49	91	11	2	10	12	15
90-91—Belleville	OHL	3	2	1	3	2	6	0	7	7	14
—Newmarket	AHL	5	1	0	1	4	—	—	—	—	—
—Toronto	NHL	33	1	3	4	30	—	—	—	—	—

Season	Team	League	Gms.	G	A	Pts.	Pen.	Gms.	G	A	Pts.	Pen.
91-92—Edmonton	NHL	15	0	1	1	43	1	0	0	0	0
—Cape Breton	AHL	49	9	14	23	40	5	1	0	1	8
92-93—Cape Breton	AHL	58	23	27	50	102	16	1	2	3	35
—Edmonton	NHL	9	0	1	1	0	—	—	—	—	—
93-94—Edmonton	NHL	61	4	7	11	104	—	—	—	—	—
—Cape Breton	AHL	2	1	1	2	31	—	—	—	—	—
NHL totals		118	5	12	17	177	1	0	0	0	0

TIKKANEN, ESA
LW, BLUES

PERSONAL: Born January 25, 1968, in Helsinki, Finland. . . . 6-1/200. . . . Shoots left. . . . Full name: Esa Kalervo Tikkanen. . . . Name pronounced EHZ-uh TEE-kuh-nehn.

TRANSACTIONS/CAREER NOTES: Selected by Edmonton Oilers in fourth round (fourth Oilers pick, 82nd overall) of NHL entry draft (August 8, 1983). . . . Broke foot (December 10, 1985). . . . Lacerated elbow, developed bursitis and underwent surgery (December 9, 1986). . . . Fractured left wrist (January 1989). . . . Injured right knee (October 28, 1989). . . . Underwent left knee surgery (August 1990); missed first 10 days of training camp. . . . Sprained wrist (December 1, 1991); missed one game. . . . Sprained wrist (December 20, 1991); missed two games. . . . Fractured shoulder (January 4, 1992); missed 37 games. . . . Suffered from the flu (December 1992); missed one game. . . . Suffered elbow infection (February 1993); missed two games. . . . Traded by Oilers to New York Rangers for C Doug Weight (March 17, 1993). . . . Bruised knee (January 14, 1994); missed one game. . . . Traded by Rangers with D Doug Lidster to St. Louis Blues for C Petr Nedved (July 24, 1994); trade arranged as compensation for Blues signing Coach Mike Keenan.

MISCELLANEOUS: Member of Stanley Cup championship team (1985, 1987, 1988, 1990 and 1994).

Season	Team	League	Gms.	G	A	Pts.	PIM	Gms.	G	A	Pts.	PIM
81-82—Regina	WHL	2	0	0	0	0	—	—	—	—	—
82-83—Helsinki Junior IFK	Finland	30	34	31	65	104	4	4	3	7	10
—Helsinki IFK	Finland	—	—	—	—	—	1	0	0	0	2
83-84—Helsinki IFK	Finland	36	19	11	30	30	2	0	0	0	0
—Helsinki Junior IFK	Finland	6	5	9	14	13	4	4	3	7	8
84-85—Helsinki IFK	Finland	36	21	33	54	42	—	—	—	—	—
—Edmonton	NHL	—	—	—	—	—	3	0	0	0	2
85-86—Nova Scotia	AHL	15	4	8	12	17	—	—	—	—	—
—Edmonton	NHL	35	7	6	13	28	8	3	2	5	7
86-87—Edmonton	NHL	76	34	44	78	120	21	7	2	9	22
87-88—Edmonton	NHL	80	23	51	74	153	19	10	17	27	72
88-89—Edmonton	NHL	67	31	47	78	92	7	1	3	4	12
89-90—Edmonton	NHL	79	30	33	63	161	22	13	11	24	26
90-91—Edmonton	NHL	79	27	42	69	85	18	12	8	20	24
91-92—Edmonton	NHL	40	12	16	28	44	16	5	3	8	8
92-93—Edmonton	NHL	66	14	19	33	76	—	—	—	—	—
—New York Rangers	NHL	15	2	5	7	18	—	—	—	—	—
93-94—New York Rangers	NHL	83	22	32	54	114	23	4	4	8	34
NHL totals		620	202	295	497	891	137	55	50	105	207

TILLEY, TOM
D, BLUES

PERSONAL: Born March 28, 1965, in Trenton, Ont. . . . 6-0/190. . . . Shoots right. . . . Full name: Thomas Robert Tilley.

COLLEGE: Michigan State.

TRANSACTIONS/CAREER NOTES: Selected by St. Louis Blues as underage junior in 10th round (13th Blues pick, 196th overall) of NHL entry draft (June 9, 1984). . . . Collapsed on bench during game due to the flu (January 28, 1989). . . . Bruised left shoulder (March 1989). . . . Strained lower back (October 14, 1989); missed eight games. . . . Played in Italy (1991-92 and 1992-93). . . . Signed as free agent by Blues (July 30, 1993). . . . Injured foot (November 3, 1993); missed one game. . . . Injured groin (December 1, 1993); missed six games. . . . Suffered from the flu (December 12, 1993); missed two games. . . . Bruised knee (December 29, 1993); missed three games. . . . Injured groin (February 3, 1994); missed four games. . . . Suffered facial injury (March 23, 1994); missed two games.

HONORS: Named to CCHA All-Star first team (1987-88). . . . Named to IHL All-Star second team (1990-91).

Season	Team	League	Gms.	G	A	Pts.	PIM	Gms.	G	A	Pts.	PIM
83-84—Orillia	OHA	38	16	35	51	113	—	—	—	—	—
84-85—Michigan State	CCHA	37	1	5	6	58	—	—	—	—	—
85-86—Michigan State	CCHA	42	9	25	34	48	—	—	—	—	—
86-87—Michigan State	CCHA	42	7	14	21	46	—	—	—	—	—
87-88—Michigan State	CCHA	46	8	18	26	44	—	—	—	—	—
88-89—St. Louis	NHL	70	1	22	23	47	10	1	2	3	17
89-90—St. Louis	NHL	34	0	5	5	6	—	—	—	—	—
—Salt Lake City	IHL	22	1	8	9	13	—	—	—	—	—
90-91—Peoria	IHL	48	7	38	45	53	13	2	9	11	25
—St. Louis	NHL	22	2	4	6	4	—	—	—	—	—
91-92—Milan	Italy	18	7	13	20	12	12	5	12	17	10
92-93—Milan	Alpenliga	32	5	17	22	21	—	—	—	—	—
—Milan	Italy	14	8	3	11	2	8	1	5	6	4
93-94—St. Louis	NHL	48	1	7	8	32	4	0	1	1	2
NHL totals		174	4	38	42	89	14	1	3	4	19

TINORDI, MARK

D, STARS

PERSONAL: Born May 9, 1966, in Red Deer, Alta.... 6-4/205.... Shoots left.... Name pronounced tuh-NOHR-dee.

TRANSACTIONS/CAREER NOTES: Signed as free agent by New York Rangers (January 4, 1987).... Suffered abdominal pains (January 1988).... Underwent left knee surgery (October 6, 1988).... Traded by Rangers with D Paul Jerrard, C Mike Sullivan, RW Brett Barnett and third-round pick in 1989 draft (C Murray Garbutt) to Minnesota North Stars for LW Igor Liba, C Brian Lawton and rights to LW Eric Bennett (October 11, 1988).... Bruised ribs (December 1988).... Underwent knee surgery (April 1989).... Suspended four games by NHL for cross-checking in a preseason game (September 27, 1989).... Bruised shoulder (December 1989).... Fined $500 by NHL for fighting (December 28, 1989).... Suffered concussion (January 17, 1990); missed six games.... Suspended 10 games by NHL for leaving penalty box to fight during a pre-season game (September 26, 1990).... Suffered from foot palsy (October 15, 1991); missed 17 games.... Sprained knee (January 19, 1993); missed four games.... Broke collarbone (March 16, 1993); missed remainder of season.... North Stars franchise moved from Minnesota to Dallas and renamed Stars for 1993-94 season. ... Suffered from the flu (December 27, 1993); missed one game.... Fractured femur (February 23, 1994); missed 22 games.

HONORS: Named to WHL (East) All-Star first team (1986-87).... Played in NHL All-Star Game (1992).

			REGULAR SEASON					PLAYOFFS				
Season	Team	League	Gms.	G	A	Pts.	PIM	Gms.	G	A	Pts.	PIM
82-83	Lethbridge	WHL	64	0	4	4	50	20	1	1	2	6
83-84	Lethbridge	WHL	72	5	14	19	53	5	0	1	1	7
84-85	Lethbridge	WHL	58	10	15	25	134	4	0	2	2	12
85-86	Lethbridge	WHL	58	8	30	38	139	8	1	3	4	15
86-87	Calgary	WHL	61	29	37	66	148	—	—	—	—	—
	New Haven	AHL	2	0	0	0	2	2	0	0	0	0
87-88	New York Rangers	NHL	24	1	2	3	50	—	—	—	—	—
	Colorado	IHL	41	8	19	27	150	11	1	5	6	31
88-89	Minnesota	NHL	47	2	3	5	107	5	0	0	0	0
	Kalamazoo	IHL	10	0	0	0	35	—	—	—	—	—
89-90	Minnesota	NHL	66	3	7	10	240	7	0	1	1	16
90-91	Minnesota	NHL	69	5	27	32	189	23	5	6	11	78
91-92	Minnesota	NHL	63	4	24	28	179	7	1	2	3	11
92-93	Minnesota	NHL	69	15	27	42	157	—	—	—	—	—
93-94	Dallas	NHL	61	6	18	24	143	—	—	—	—	—
	NHL totals		**399**	**36**	**108**	**144**	**1065**	**42**	**6**	**9**	**15**	**105**

TIPPETT, DAVE

C/LW, FLYERS

PERSONAL: Born August 25, 1961, in Moosomin, Sask.... 5-10/173.... Shoots left.

COLLEGE: North Dakota.

TRANSACTIONS/CAREER NOTES: Signed as free agent by Hartford Whalers (February 29, 1984).... Injured right thumb tendons (October 8, 1989).... Traded by Whalers to Washington Capitals for sixth-round pick (C Jarret Reid) in 1992 draft (September 30, 1990).... Separated shoulder (November 28, 1990); missed 11 games.... Signed as free agent by Pittsburgh Penguins (August 28, 1992).... Fractured thumb (November 20, 1992); missed six games.... Signed as free agent by Philadelphia Flyers (August 2, 1993).... Broke bone in left foot (November 27, 1993); missed eight games.

MISCELLANEOUS: Member of silver-medal-winning Canadian Olympic team (1992).

			REGULAR SEASON					PLAYOFFS				
Season	Team	League	Gms.	G	A	Pts.	PIM	Gms.	G	A	Pts.	PIM
79-80	Prince Albert	SJHL	85	72	95	167	...	—	—	—	—	—
80-81	Prince Albert	SJHL	84	62	93	155	...	—	—	—	—	—
81-82	Univ. of North Dakota	WCHA	43	13	28	41	24	—	—	—	—	—
82-83	Univ. of North Dakota	WCHA	36	15	31	46	44	—	—	—	—	—
83-84	Canadian Olympic Team	Int'l	66	14	19	33	24	—	—	—	—	—
	Hartford	NHL	17	4	2	6	2	—	—	—	—	—
84-85	Hartford	NHL	80	7	12	19	12	—	—	—	—	—
85-86	Hartford	NHL	80	14	20	34	18	10	2	2	4	4
86-87	Hartford	NHL	80	9	22	31	42	6	0	2	2	4
87-88	Hartford	NHL	80	16	21	37	32	6	0	0	0	2
88-89	Hartford	NHL	80	17	24	41	45	4	0	1	1	0
89-90	Hartford	NHL	66	8	19	27	32	7	1	3	4	2
90-91	Washington	NHL	61	6	9	15	24	10	2	3	5	8
91-92	Washington	NHL	30	2	10	12	16	7	0	1	1	0
	Canadian national team	Int'l	1	0	0	0	4	—	—	—	—	—
	Canadian Olympic Team	Int'l	6	1	2	3	10	—	—	—	—	—
92-93	Pittsburgh	NHL	74	6	19	25	56	12	1	4	5	14
93-94	Philadelphia	NHL	73	4	11	15	38	—	—	—	—	—
	NHL totals		**721**	**93**	**169**	**262**	**317**	**62**	**6**	**16**	**22**	**34**

TITOV, GERMAN

C, FLAMES

PERSONAL: Born October 16, 1965, in Borovsk, U.S.S.R.... 6-0/190.... Shoots left.... Name pronounced GUHR-mihn TEE-tahf.

TRANSACTIONS/CAREER NOTES: Selected by Calgary Flames in 10th round (252nd overall) of NHL entry draft (June 26, 1993).... Fractured nose (December 31, 1993); missed four games.... Bruised hand (February 18, 1994); missed two games.... Bruised hand (April 2, 1994); missed one game.

			REGULAR SEASON					PLAYOFFS				
Season	Team	League	Gms.	G	A	Pts.	PIM	Gms.	G	A	Pts.	PIM
82-83	Khimik	USSR	16	0	2	2	4	—	—	—	—	—
83-84	Khimik	USSR						Did not play.				

| | | | REGULAR SEASON | | | | | PLAYOFFS | | | | |
Season Team	League	Gms.	G	A	Pts.	Pen.	Gms.	G	A	Pts.	Pen.
84-85—Khimik	USSR					Did not play.					
85-86—Khimik	USSR					Did not play.					
86-87—Khimik	USSR	23	1	0	1	10	—	—	—	—	—
87-88—Khimik	USSR	39	6	5	11	10	—	—	—	—	—
88-89—Khimik	USSR	44	10	3	13	24	—	—	—	—	—
89-90—Khimik	USSR	44	6	14	20	19	—	—	—	—	—
90-91—Khimik	USSR	45	13	11	24	28	—	—	—	—	—
91-92—Khimik	CIS	42	18	13	31	35	—	—	—	—	—
92-93—TPS	Finland	47	25	19	44	49	—	—	—	—	—
93-94—Calgary	NHL	76	27	18	45	28	7	2	1	3	4
NHL totals		76	27	18	45	28	7	2	1	3	4

TJALLEN, MIKAEL
D, PANTHERS

PERSONAL: Born February 16, 1975, in Ornskoldsvik, Sweden. . . . 6-2/194. . . . Shoots left.

TRANSACTIONS/CAREER NOTES: Selected by Florida Panthers in third round (fourth Panthers pick, 67th overall) of NHL entry draft (June 26, 1993).

| | | | REGULAR SEASON | | | | | PLAYOFFS | | | | |
Season Team	League	Gms.	G	A	Pts.	PIM	Gms.	G	A	Pts.	PIM
91-92—MoDo	Sweden Jr.					Did not play.					
92-93—MoDo	Sweden Jr.					Statistics unavailable.					
93-94—Sundsvall Timra	Swed. Dv.II	24	4	5	9	32	—	—	—	—	—

TKACHENKO, SERGEI
G, CANUCKS

PERSONAL: Born June 6, 1971, in Kiev, U.S.S.R. . . . 6-2/198. . . . Catches left. . . . Name pronounced kuh-CHEHN-koh.

TRANSACTIONS/CAREER NOTES: Selected by Vancouver Canucks in 11th round (ninth Canucks pick, 280th overall) of NHL entry draft (June 20, 1992).

| | | | REGULAR SEASON | | | | | | PLAYOFFS | | | | | |
Season Team	League	Gms.	Min.	W	L	T	GA	SO	Avg.	Gms.	Min.	W	L	GA	SO	Avg.
89-90—Sokol Kiev	USSR	1	10	...	...	...	0	0	0.00	—	—	—	—	—	—	—
90-91—Sokol Kiev	USSR	14	220	...	...	...	14	0	3.82	—	—	—	—	—	—	—
91-92—Sokol Kiev	CIS	24	1305	...	...	...	91	0	4.18	—	—	—	—	—	—	—
92-93—Brantford	Col.HL	4	96	0	1	0	11	0	6.88	—	—	—	—	—	—	—
—Hamilton	AHL	1	60	1	0	0	3	0	3.00	—	—	—	—	—	—	—
93-94—Columbus	ECHL	34	1884	18	7	4	129	0	4.11	4	182	1	2	16	0	5.27
—Hamilton	AHL	2	125	0	1	1	9	0	4.32	—	—	—	—	—	—	—

TKACHUK, KEITH
LW, JETS

PERSONAL: Born March 28, 1972, in Melrose, Mass. . . . 6-2/215. . . . Shoots left. . . . Full name: Keith Matthew Tkachuk. . . . Name pronounced kuh-CHUHK.

HIGH SCHOOL: Malden (Mass.) Catholic.

COLLEGE: Boston University.

TRANSACTIONS/CAREER NOTES: Selected by Winnipeg Jets in first round (first Jets pick, 19th overall) of NHL entry draft (June 16, 1990). . . . Lacerated forearm (November 12, 1993); missed one game.

HONORS: Named to Hockey East All-Rookie team (1990-91).

| | | | REGULAR SEASON | | | | | PLAYOFFS | | | | |
Season Team	League	Gms.	G	A	Pts.	PIM	Gms.	G	A	Pts.	PIM
88-89—Malden Catholic H.S.	Mass. H.S.	21	30	16	46	...	—	—	—	—	—
89-90—Malden Catholic H.S.	Mass. H.S.	6	12	14	26	...	—	—	—	—	—
90-91—Boston University	Hockey East	36	17	23	40	70	—	—	—	—	—
91-92—U.S. national team	Int'l	45	10	10	20	141	—	—	—	—	—
—U.S. Olympic Team	Int'l	8	1	1	2	12	—	—	—	—	—
—Winnipeg	NHL	17	3	5	8	28	7	3	0	3	30
92-93—Winnipeg	NHL	83	28	23	51	201	6	4	0	4	14
93-94—Winnipeg	NHL	84	41	40	81	255	—	—	—	—	—
NHL totals		184	72	68	140	484	13	7	0	7	44

TOCCHET, RICK
RW, KINGS

PERSONAL: Born April 9, 1964, in Scarborough, Ont. . . . 6-0/205. . . . Shoots right. . . . Name pronounced TAH-keht.

TRANSACTIONS/CAREER NOTES: Selected by Philadelphia Flyers as underage junior in sixth round (fifth Flyers pick, 121st overall) of NHL entry draft (June 8, 1983). . . . Bruised right knee (November 23, 1985); missed seven games. . . . Separated left shoulder (February 1988). . . . Suspended 10 games by NHL for injuring an opposing player during a fight (October 27, 1988). . . . Hyperextended right knee (April 21, 1989). . . . Suffered viral infection (November 1989). . . . Tore tendon in left groin area (January 26, 1991); missed five games. . . . Reinjured groin (March 1991); missed five games. . . . Sprained knee (November 29, 1991); missed five games. . . . Bruised heel (January 18, 1991); missed 10 games. . . . Traded by Flyers with G Ken Wregget, D Kjell Samuelsson and third-round pick in 1992 draft to Pittsburgh Penguins for RW Mark Recchi, D Brian Benning and first-round pick (LW Jason Bowen) in 1992 draft (February 19, 1992). . . . Fractured jaw (March 15, 1992); missed three games. . . . Bruised left foot (October 10, 1992); missed two games. . . . Bruised foot (February 8, 1993); missed one game. . . . Bruised ribs (November 13, 1993); missed two games. . . . Suffered back spasms (December 2, 1993); missed two games. . . . Suffered back spasms (December 31, 1993); missed 12 games. . . . Injured back (February 21, 1994); missed one game. . . . Injured back (February 28, 1994); missed 10 games. . . . Underwent back surgery (June 8, 1994). . . . Traded by Penguins with second-round pick in 1995 draft to Los Angeles Kings for LW Luc Robitaille (July 29, 1994).

HONORS: Played in NHL All-Star Game (1989 through 1991 and 1993).
RECORDS: Shares NHL All-Star Game record for fastest goal from start of a period— 19 seconds (1993, second period).
MISCELLANEOUS: Member of Stanley Cup championship team (1992).

Season Team	League	REGULAR SEASON					PLAYOFFS				
		Gms.	G	A	Pts.	PIM	Gms.	G	A	Pts.	PIM
81-82—Sault Ste. Marie	OHL	59	7	15	22	184	11	1	1	2	28
82-83—Sault Ste. Marie	OHL	66	32	34	66	146	16	4	13	17	*67
83-84—Sault Ste. Marie	OHL	64	44	64	108	209	16	*22	14	†36	41
84-85—Philadelphia	NHL	75	14	25	39	181	19	3	4	7	72
85-86—Philadelphia	NHL	69	14	21	35	284	5	1	2	3	26
86-87—Philadelphia	NHL	69	21	26	47	288	26	11	10	21	72
87-88—Philadelphia	NHL	65	31	33	64	301	5	1	4	5	55
88-89—Philadelphia	NHL	66	45	36	81	183	16	6	6	12	69
89-90—Philadelphia	NHL	75	37	59	96	196	—	—	—	—	—
90-91—Philadelphia	NHL	70	40	31	71	150	—	—	—	—	—
91-92—Philadelphia	NHL	42	13	16	29	102	—	—	—	—	—
—Pittsburgh	NHL	19	14	16	30	49	14	6	13	19	24
92-93—Pittsburgh	NHL	80	48	61	109	252	12	7	6	13	24
93-94—Pittsburgh	NHL	51	14	26	40	134	6	2	3	5	20
NHL totals		681	291	350	641	2120	103	37	48	85	362

TODD, KEVIN

C, KINGS

PERSONAL: Born May 4, 1968, in Winnipeg.... 5-10/180.... Shoots left.... Full name: Kevin Lee Todd.
HIGH SCHOOL: Tec Voc (Winnipeg).
TRANSACTIONS/CAREER NOTES: Stretched knee ligaments (December 1985).... Selected by New Jersey Devils as underage junior in seventh round (seventh Devils pick, 129th overall) of NHL entry draft (June 21, 1986).... Injured thigh (October 31, 1992); missed one game.... Reinjured thigh (November 13, 1992); missed three games.... Bruised shoulder (December 15, 1992); missed five games.... Traded by Devils with LW Zdeno Ciger to Edmonton Oilers for C Bernie Nicholls (January 13, 1993).... Separated left shoulder (March 14, 1993); missed remainder of season.... Traded by Oilers to Chicago Blackhawks for D Adam Bennett (October 7, 1993).... Injured knee (November 18, 1993); missed 12 games.... Traded by Blackhawks to Los Angeles Kings for fourth-round pick (D Steve McLaren) in 1994 draft (March 21, 1994).
HONORS: Won Les Cunningham Plaque (1990-91).... Won John B. Sollenberger Trophy (1990-91).... Named to AHL All-Star first team (1990-91).... Named to NHL All-Rookie team (1991-92).

Season Team	League	REGULAR SEASON					PLAYOFFS				
		Gms.	G	A	Pts.	PIM	Gms.	G	A	Pts.	PIM
85-86—Prince Albert	WHL	55	14	25	39	19	20	7	6	13	29
86-87—Prince Albert	WHL	71	39	46	85	92	8	2	5	7	17
87-88—Prince Albert	WHL	72	49	72	121	83	10	8	11	19	27
88-89—New Jersey	NHL	1	0	0	0	0	—	—	—	—	—
—Utica	AHL	78	26	45	71	62	4	2	0	2	6
89-90—Utica	AHL	71	18	36	54	72	5	2	4	6	2
90-91—Utica	AHL	75	37	*81	*118	75	—	—	—	—	—
—New Jersey	NHL	1	0	0	0	0	1	0	0	0	6
91-92—New Jersey	NHL	80	21	42	63	69	7	3	2	5	8
92-93—New Jersey	NHL	30	5	5	10	16	—	—	—	—	—
—Utica	AHL	2	2	1	3	0	—	—	—	—	—
—Edmonton	NHL	25	4	9	13	10	—	—	—	—	—
93-94—Chicago	NHL	35	5	6	11	16	—	—	—	—	—
—Los Angeles	NHL	12	3	8	11	8	—	—	—	—	—
NHL totals		184	38	70	108	119	8	3	2	5	14

TOMLAK, MIKE

LW, WHALERS

PERSONAL: Born October 17, 1964, in Thunder Bay, Ont.... 6-3/205.... Shoots left.... Full name: Michael Ronald Tomlak.
COLLEGE: Western Ontario.
TRANSACTIONS/CAREER NOTES: Selected by Toronto Maple Leafs in 11th round (10th Maple Leafs pick, 208th overall) of NHL entry draft (June 8, 1983).... Signed as free agent by Hartford Whalers (May 28, 1989).... Sprained right wrist (February 9, 1990).... Bruised left foot (January 26, 1992); missed 15 games.... Fractured left leg (March 6, 1992); missed remainder of season and playoffs.
HONORS: Named to CIAU All-Canada team (1986-87).... Named to OUAA All-Star first team (1988-89).

Season Team	League	REGULAR SEASON					PLAYOFFS				
		Gms.	G	A	Pts.	PIM	Gms.	G	A	Pts.	PIM
81-82—Thunder Bay	TBJHL	25	19	26	45	30	—	—	—	—	—
82-83—Cornwall	OHL	70	18	49	67	26	—	—	—	—	—
83-84—Cornwall	OHL	64	24	64	88	21	—	—	—	—	—
84-85—Cornwall	OHL	66	30	70	100	9	—	—	—	—	—
85-86—Univ. of Western Ontario	OUAA	38	28	20	48	45	—	—	—	—	—
86-87—Univ. of Western Ontario	OUAA	38	16	30	46	10	—	—	—	—	—
87-88—Univ. of Western Ontario	OUAA	39	24	52	76	...	—	—	—	—	—
88-89—Univ. of Western Ontario	OUAA	35	16	34	50	...	—	—	—	—	—
89-90—Hartford	NHL	70	7	14	21	48	7	0	1	1	2
90-91—Springfield	AHL	15	4	9	13	15	—	—	—	—	—
—Hartford	NHL	64	8	8	16	55	3	0	0	0	2
91-92—Springfield	AHL	39	16	21	37	24	—	—	—	—	—
—Hartford	NHL	6	0	0	0	0	—	—	—	—	—

Season	Team	League	REGULAR SEASON					PLAYOFFS				
			Gms.	G	A	Pts.	Pen.	Gms.	G	A	Pts.	Pen.
92-93—Springfield		AHL	38	16	21	37	56	5	1	1	2	2
93-94—Springfield		AHL	79	44	56	100	53	4	2	5	7	4
—Hartford		NHL	1	0	0	0	0	—	—	—	—	—
NHL totals			141	15	22	37	103	10	0	1	1	4

TOMLINSON, DAVE
C, JETS

PERSONAL: Born May 8, 1968, in North Vancouver.... 5-11/190.... Shoots left. **COLLEGE:** Boston University.
TRANSACTIONS/CAREER NOTES: Selected by Toronto Maple Leafs in NHL supplemental draft (June 16, 1989).... Traded by Maple Leafs to Florida Panthers for future considerations (August 3, 1993).... Traded by Panthers to Winnipeg Jets for C Jason Cirone (August 3, 1993).

Season	Team	League	REGULAR SEASON					PLAYOFFS				
			Gms.	G	A	Pts.	PIM	Gms.	G	A	Pts.	PIM
87-88—Boston University		Hockey East	34	16	20	36	28	—	—	—	—	—
88-89—Boston University		Hockey East	34	16	30	46	40	—	—	—	—	—
89-90—Boston University		Hockey East	43	15	22	37	53	—	—	—	—	—
90-91—Boston University		Hockey East	41	30	30	60	55	—	—	—	—	—
91-92—St. John's		AHL	75	23	34	57	75	12	4	5	9	6
—Toronto		NHL	3	0	0	0	2	—	—	—	—	—
92-93—St. John's		AHL	70	36	48	84	115	9	1	4	5	8
—Toronto		NHL	3	0	0	0	2	—	—	—	—	—
93-94—Moncton		AHL	39	23	23	46	38	20	6	6	12	24
—Winnipeg		NHL	31	1	3	4	24	—	—	—	—	—
NHL totals			37	1	3	4	28					

TOOKEY, TIM
C

PERSONAL: Born August 29, 1960, in Edmonton.... 5-11/190.... Shoots left.... Full name: Timothy Raymond Tookey.... Name pronounced TOO-kee.
TRANSACTIONS/CAREER NOTES: Selected by Washington Capitals as underage junior in fifth round (fourth Capitals pick, 88th overall) of NHL entry draft (August 9, 1979).... Sprained left ankle (December 30, 1981).... Traded by Capitals to Quebec Nordiques for D Lee Norwood (January 1982).... Suffered concussion (February 1983).... Injured shoulder (April 1983).... Signed as free agent by Pittsburgh Penguins (August 1983).... Signed as free agent by Philadelphia Flyers (August 1985).... Selected by Los Angeles Kings in NHL waiver draft (October 1987).... Placed on recallable waivers by Kings in an attempt to designate him for assignment; claimed by Philadelphia; recalled by Kings and assigned to New Haven (October 1987).... Underwent knee surgery (December 1987).... Traded by Kings to Pittsburgh Penguins for D Patrick Mayer (March 7, 1989).... Signed as free agent by Flyers (July 12, 1989).... Underwent knee surgery (October 1989).... Broke ankle (October 1990); missed two months.... Named player/assistant coach of Providence Bruins (August 3, 1994).
HONORS: Won Jack Butterfield Trophy (1985-86).... Named to AHL All-Star second team (1985-86 and 1991-92).... Won Les Cunningham Plaque (1986-87).... Won John B. Sollenberger Trophy (1986-87).... Named to AHL All-Star first team (1986-87).... Won Fred T. Hunt Memorial Trophy (1992-93).

Season	Team	League	REGULAR SEASON					PLAYOFFS				
			Gms.	G	A	Pts.	PIM	Gms.	G	A	Pts.	PIM
77-78—Portland		WCHL	72	16	15	31	55	8	2	2	4	5
78-79—Portland		WHL	56	33	47	80	55	25	6	14	20	6
79-80—Portland		WHL	70	58	83	141	55	8	2	5	7	4
80-81—Hershey		AHL	47	20	38	58	129	—	—	—	—	—
—Washington		NHL	29	10	13	23	18	—	—	—	—	—
81-82—Washington		NHL	28	8	8	16	35	—	—	—	—	—
—Hershey		AHL	14	4	9	13	10	—	—	—	—	—
—Fredericton		AHL	16	6	10	16	16	—	—	—	—	—
82-83—Quebec		NHL	12	1	6	7	4	—	—	—	—	—
—Fredericton		AHL	53	24	43	67	24	9	5	4	9	0
83-84—Pittsburgh		NHL	8	0	2	2	2	—	—	—	—	—
—Baltimore		AHL	58	16	28	44	25	8	1	1	2	2
84-85—Baltimore		AHL	74	25	43	68	74	15	8	10	18	13
85-86—Hershey		AHL	69	35	*62	97	66	18	†11	8	19	10
86-87—Hershey		AHL	80	51	*73	*124	45	5	5	4	9	0
—Philadelphia		NHL	2	0	0	0	0	10	1	3	4	2
87-88—Los Angeles		NHL	20	1	6	7	8	—	—	—	—	—
—New Haven		AHL	11	6	7	13	2	—	—	—	—	—
88-89—Muskegon		IHL	18	7	14	21	7	8	2	9	11	4
—New Haven		AHL	33	11	18	29	30	—	—	—	—	—
—Los Angeles		NHL	7	2	1	3	4	—	—	—	—	—
89-90—Hershey		AHL	42	18	22	40	28	—	—	—	—	—
90-91—Hershey		AHL	51	17	42	59	43	5	0	5	5	0
91-92—Hershey		AHL	†80	36	69	105	63	6	4	2	6	4
92-93—Hershey		AHL	80	38	70	108	63	—	—	—	—	—
93-94—Hershey		AHL	66	32	57	89	43	11	4	9	13	8
NHL totals			106	22	36	58	71	10	1	3	4	2

TOPOROWSKI, KERRY
RW, BLACKHAWKS

PERSONAL: Born April 9, 1971, in Prince Albert, Sask.... 6-2/212.... Shoots right.... Name pronounced toh-poh-ROW-skee.
TRANSACTIONS/CAREER NOTES: Selected by San Jose Sharks in fourth round (fourth Sharks pick, 67th overall) of NHL entry draft (June 22, 1991)....

Traded by Sharks with second-round pick in 1992 draft to Chicago Blackhawks for D Doug Wilson (September 6, 1991).

Season Team	League	REGULAR SEASON					PLAYOFFS				
		Gms.	G	A	Pts.	PIM	Gms.	G	A	Pts.	PIM
89-90—Spokane	WHL	65	1	13	14	*384	6	0	0	0	37
90-91—Spokane	WHL	65	11	16	27	*505	15	2	2	4	*108
91-92—Indianapolis	IHL	18	1	2	3	206	—	—	—	—	—
92-93—Indianapolis	IHL	17	0	0	0	57	—	—	—	—	—
93-94—Indianapolis	IHL	32	1	4	5	126	—	—	—	—	—
—Las Vegas	IHL	13	1	0	1	129	2	0	0	0	31

TOPOROWSKI, SHAYNE
RW, KINGS

PERSONAL: Born August 6, 1975, in Prince Albert, Sask. . . . 6-2/205. . . . Shoots right.
HIGH SCHOOL: Carlton Comprehensive (Paddockwood, Sask.).
TRANSACTIONS/CAREER NOTES: Selected by Los Angeles Kings in second round (first Kings pick, 42nd overall) of NHL entry draft (June 26, 1993).

Season Team	League	REGULAR SEASON					PLAYOFFS				
		Gms.	G	A	Pts.	PIM	Gms.	G	A	Pts.	PIM
91-92—Prince Albert	WHL	6	2	0	2	2	7	2	1	3	6
92-93—Prince Albert	WHL	72	25	32	57	235	—	—	—	—	—
93-94—Prince Albert	WHL	68	37	45	82	183	—	—	—	—	—

TORMANNEN, ANTTI
RW, SENATORS

PERSONAL: Born September 19, 1970, in Espoo, Finland. . . . 6-1/198. . . . Shoots left.
TRANSACTIONS/CAREER NOTES: Selected by Ottawa Senators in 11th round (10th Senators pick, 274th overall) of NHL entry draft (June 29, 1994).

Season Team	League	REGULAR SEASON					PLAYOFFS				
		Gms.	G	A	Pts.	PIM	Gms.	G	A	Pts.	PIM
91-92—Jokerit	Finland	40	18	11	29	18	—	—	—	—	—
92-93—Jokerit	Finland	21	2	0	2	8	—	—	—	—	—
93-94—Jokerit	Finland	46	20	18	38	46	—	—	—	—	—

TOWNSHEND, GRAEME
RW

PERSONAL: Born October 2, 1965, in Kingston, Jamaica. . . . 6-2/225. . . . Shoots right. . . . Full name: Graeme Scott Townshend. . . . Name pronounced GRAY-ihm TOWN-SEHND.
COLLEGE: Rensselaer Polytechnic Institute (N.Y.).
TRANSACTIONS/CAREER NOTES: Signed as free agent by Boston Bruins (May 12, 1989). . . . Suspended six games by AHL for a pre-game fight (December 15, 1990). . . . Signed as free agent by New York Islanders (September 3, 1991). . . . Signed as free agent by Ottawa Senators (August 24, 1993).

Season Team	League	REGULAR SEASON					PLAYOFFS				
		Gms.	G	A	Pts.	PIM	Gms.	G	A	Pts.	PIM
85-86—R.P.I.	ECAC	29	1	7	8	52	—	—	—	—	—
86-87—R.P.I.	ECAC	31	7	1	8	56	—	—	—	—	—
87-88—R.P.I.	ECAC	32	6	14	20	64	—	—	—	—	—
88-89—R.P.I.	ECAC	31	6	16	22	50	—	—	—	—	—
—Maine	AHL	5	2	1	3	11	—	—	—	—	—
89-90—Boston	NHL	4	0	0	0	7	—	—	—	—	—
—Maine	AHL	64	15	13	28	162	—	—	—	—	—
90-91—Maine	AHL	46	16	10	26	119	2	2	0	2	4
—Boston	NHL	18	2	5	7	12	—	—	—	—	—
91-92—Capital District	AHL	61	14	23	37	94	4	0	2	2	0
—New York Islanders	NHL	7	1	2	3	0	—	—	—	—	—
92-93—Capital District	AHL	67	29	21	50	45	2	0	0	0	0
—New York Islanders	NHL	2	0	0	0	0	—	—	—	—	—
93-94—Prince Edward Island	AHL	56	16	13	29	107	—	—	—	—	—
—Ottawa	NHL	14	0	0	0	9	—	—	—	—	—
NHL totals		45	3	7	10	28					

TRAVERSE, PATRICK
D, SENATORS

PERSONAL: Born March 14, 1974, in Montreal. . . . 6-3/200. . . . Shoots left.
TRANSACTIONS/CAREER NOTES: Selected by Ottawa Senators in third round (third Senators pick, 50th overall) of NHL entry draft (June 20, 1992).

Season Team	League	REGULAR SEASON					PLAYOFFS				
		Gms.	G	A	Pts.	PIM	Gms.	G	A	Pts.	PIM
91-92—Shawinigan	QMJHL	59	3	11	14	12	10	0	0	0	4
92-93—St. Jean	QMJHL	68	6	30	36	24	4	0	1	1	2
—New Haven	AHL	2	0	0	0	2	—	—	—	—	—
93-94—Prince Edward Island	AHL	3	0	1	1	2	—	—	—	—	—
—St. Jean	QMJHL	66	15	37	52	30	5	0	4	4	4

TREBIL, DANIEL
D, DEVILS

PERSONAL: Born April 10, 1974, in Edina, Minn. . . . 6-3/185. . . . Shoots right.
HIGH SCHOOL: Thomas Jefferson (Bloomington, Minn.).
COLLEGE: Minnesota.
TRANSACTIONS/CAREER NOTES: Selected by New Jersey Devils in sixth round (seventh Devils

pick, 138th overall) of NHL entry draft (June 20, 1992).

			REGULAR SEASON					PLAYOFFS				
Season Team	League	Gms.	G	A	Pts.	PIM	Gms.	G	A	Pts.	PIM
89-90—Jefferson HS	Minn. H.S.	22	3	6	9	10	—	—	—	—	—
90-91—Jefferson HS	Minn. H.S.	23	4	12	16	8	—	—	—	—	—
91-92—Jefferson HS	Minn. H.S.	28	7	26	33	6	—	—	—	—	—
92-93—University of Minnesota ...	WCHA	36	2	11	13	16	—	—	—	—	—
93-94—University of Minnesota ...	WCHA	42	1	21	22	24	—	—	—	—	—

TREFILOV, ANDREI
G, FLAMES

PERSONAL: Born August 31, 1969, in Moscow, U.S.S.R. . . . . 6-0/180. . . . Catches left. . . . Name pronounced AHN-dray TREH-fee-lahf.
TRANSACTIONS/CAREER NOTES: Selected by Calgary Flames in 12th round (14th Flames pick, 261st overall) of NHL entry draft (June 22, 1991). . . . Twisted right knee ligament (February 2, 1994); missed 23 games.

			REGULAR SEASON							PLAYOFFS					
Season Team	League	Gms.	Min.	W	L	T	GA	SO	Avg.	Gms.	Min.	W	L	GA SO	Avg.
90-91—Dynamo Moscow	USSR	20	1070	...	...	...	36	0	2.02	—	—	—	—	— —	—
91-92—Dynamo Moscow	CIS	28	1326	...	...	...	35	0	1.58	—	—	—	—	— —	—
—Unified Olympic Team...	Int'l	8	38	...	...	...	2	2	3.16	—	—	—	—	— —	—
92-93—Salt Lake City..............	IHL	44	2536	23	17	†0	135	0	3.19	—	—	—	—	— —	—
—Calgary.........................	NHL	1	65	0	0	1	5	0	4.62	—	—	—	—	— —	—
93-94—Saint John	AHL	28	1629	10	10	7	93	0	3.43	—	—	—	—	— —	—
—Calgary.........................	NHL	11	623	3	4	2	26	2	2.50	—	—	—	—	— —	—
NHL totals...............................		12	688	3	4	3	31	2	2.70						

TRINKA, PAVEL
D, MIGHTY DUCKS

PERSONAL: Born July 27, 1976, in Plzen, Czechoslovakia. . . . 6-3/187. . . . Shoots left.
TRANSACTIONS/CAREER NOTES: Selected by Mighty Ducks of Anaheim in fifth round (fifth Mighty Ducks pick, 106th overall) of NHL entry draft (June 29, 1994).

			REGULAR SEASON					PLAYOFFS				
Season Team	League	Gms.	G	A	Pts.	PIM	Gms.	G	A	Pts.	PIM
93-94—Skoda Plzen.....................	Czech Rep.	12	0	1	1	...	—	—	—	—	—

TROTTIER, BRYAN
C, PENGUINS

PERSONAL: Born July 17, 1956, in Val Marie, Sask. . . . 5-11/195. . . . Shoots left. . . . Full name: Bryan John Trottier. . . . Name pronounced TRAH-chay.
TRANSACTIONS/CAREER NOTES: Selected by New York Islanders from Swift Current Broncos in second round (second Islanders pick, 22nd overall) of NHL amateur draft (May 28, 1974). . . . Sprained left knee (April 1983). . . . Injured left knee (January 1984). . . . Injured knee (October 1984). . . . Fined $1,000 by NHL for being critical of officiating (March 1987). . . . Suffered back spasms (March 1989); missed seven games. . . . Broke left little toe (September 23, 1989). . . . Broke rib (December 13, 1989); missed 12 games. . . . Released by Islanders (July 3, 1990). . . . Signed as free agent by Pittsburgh Penguins (July 20, 1990). . . . Suffered lower back pain (September 1990); missed five pre-season games (September 1990); missed 13 games (November 1990); missed 13 games (January 1991). . . . Sprained right knee (November 30, 1991); missed 14 games. . . . Bruised lower back (March 15, 1992); missed two games. . . . Named assistant coach of Pittsburgh Penguins (June 22, 1993). . . . Injured knee (October 9, 1993); missed one game. . . . Strained muscles behind knee (October 28, 1993); missed six games. . . . Suffered back spasms (January 27, 1994); missed nine games. . . . Suffered back spasms (February 15, 1994); missed remainder of regular season.
HONORS: Won WCHL Most Valuable Player Award (1974-75). . . . Named to WCHL All-Star first team (1974-75). . . . Named NHL Rookie of the Year by THE SPORTING NEWS (1975-76). . . . Won Calder Memorial Trophy (1975-76). . . . Played in NHL All-Star Game (1976, 1978, 1980, 1982, 1983, 1985, 1986 and 1992). . . . Named to THE SPORTING NEWS All-Star first team (1977-78 and 1978-79). . . . Named to NHL All-Star first team (1977-78 and 1978-79). . . . Named NHL Player of the Year by THE SPORTING NEWS (1978-79). . . . Won Hart Memorial Trophy (1978-79). . . . Won Art Ross Trophy (1978-79). . . . Won Conn Smythe Trophy (1979-80). . . . Named to THE SPORTING NEWS All-Star second team (1981-82 and 1983-84). . . . Named to NHL All-Star second team (1981-82 and 1983-84). . . . Won Budweiser/NHL Man of the Year (1987-88). . . . Won King Clancy Memorial Trophy (1988-89).
RECORDS: Holds NHL record for most points in one period—6 (December 23, 1978). . . . Shares NHL record for most goals in one period—4 (February 13, 1982). . . . Holds NHL playoff record for scoring points in most consecutive games—27 (1980-82). . . . Shares NHL record for fastest goal from the start of a game—5 seconds (March 22, 1984). . . . Holds NHL single-season playoff record for scoring points in most consecutive games—18 (1981). . . . Shares NHL single-game playoff records for most shorthanded goals in one period—2; and most shorthanded goals—2 (April 8, 1980).
MISCELLANEOUS: Member of Stanley Cup championship teams (1980-1983, 1991 and 1992).

			REGULAR SEASON					PLAYOFFS				
Season Team	League	Gms.	G	A	Pts.	PIM	Gms.	G	A	Pts.	PIM
72-73—Swift Current...................	WCHL	67	16	29	45	10	—	—	—	—	—
73-74—Swift Current...................	WCHL	68	41	71	112	76	13	7	8	15	8
74-75—Lethbridge.....................	WCHL	67	46	*98	144	103	6	2	5	7	14
75-76—New York Islanders.........	NHL	80	32	63	95	21	13	1	7	8	8
76-77—New York Islanders.........	NHL	76	30	42	72	34	12	2	8	10	2
77-78—New York Islanders.........	NHL	77	46	*77	123	46	7	0	3	3	4
78-79—New York Islanders.........	NHL	76	47	*87	*134	50	10	2	4	6	13
79-80—New York Islanders.........	NHL	78	42	62	104	68	21	†12	17	*29	16
80-81—New York Islanders.........	NHL	73	31	72	103	74	18	11	†18	29	34
81-82—New York Islanders.........	NHL	80	50	79	129	88	19	6	*23	*29	40
82-83—New York Islanders.........	NHL	80	34	55	89	68	17	8	12	20	18

Season Team	League	REGULAR SEASON Gms.	G	A	Pts.	Pen.	PLAYOFFS Gms.	G	A	Pts.	Pen.
83-84—New York Islanders..........	NHL	68	40	71	111	59	21	8	6	14	49
84-85—New York Islanders..........	NHL	68	28	31	59	47	10	4	2	6	8
85-86—New York Islanders..........	NHL	78	37	59	96	72	3	1	1	2	2
86-87—New York Islanders..........	NHL	80	23	64	87	50	14	8	5	13	12
87-88—New York Islanders..........	NHL	77	30	52	82	48	6	0	0	0	10
88-89—New York Islanders..........	NHL	73	17	28	45	44	—	—	—	—	—
89-90—New York Islanders..........	NHL	59	13	11	24	29	4	1	0	1	4
90-91—Pittsburgh	NHL	52	9	19	28	24	23	3	4	7	49
91-92—Pittsburgh	NHL	63	11	18	29	54	21	4	3	7	8
92-93—				Did not play—retired.							
93-94—Pittsburgh	NHL	41	4	11	15	36	2	0	0	0	0
NHL totals................................		1279	524	901	1425	912	221	71	113	184	277

TSULYGIN, NIKOLAI
D, MIGHTY DUCKS

PERSONAL: Born May 29, 1975, in Ufa, U.S.S.R. . . . 6-3/196. . . . Shoots right.
TRANSACTIONS/CAREER NOTES: Selected by Mighty Ducks of Anaheim in second round (second Mighty Ducks pick, 30th overall) of NHL entry draft (June 26, 1993).

Season Team	League	REGULAR SEASON Gms.	G	A	Pts.	PIM	PLAYOFFS Gms.	G	A	Pts.	PIM
92-93—Salavat	CIS	42	5	4	9	21	2	0	0	0	0
93-94—Salavat	CIS	43	0	14	14	24	5	0	1	1	0

TSYGUROV, DENIS
D, SABRES

PERSONAL: Born February 26, 1971, in Chelyabinsk, U.S.S.R. . . . 6-3/198. . . . Shoots left. . . . Name pronounced tsuh-GOOR-ahf.
TRANSACTIONS/CAREER NOTES: Selected by Buffalo Sabres in second round (first Sabres pick, 38th overall) of NHL entry draft (June 26, 1993). . . . Suffered deep thigh bruise (September 25, 1993); missed 11 games.
HONORS: Named to CIS All-Star team (1992-93).

Season Team	League	REGULAR SEASON Gms.	G	A	Pts.	PIM	PLAYOFFS Gms.	G	A	Pts.	PIM
88-89—Traktor Chelyabinsk........	USSR	8	0	0	0	2	—	—	—	—	—
89-90—Traktor Chelyabinsk........	USSR	27	0	1	1	18	—	—	—	—	—
90-91—Traktor Chelyabinsk........	USSR	26	0	1	1	16	—	—	—	—	—
91-92—Lada Togliatti	CIS	29	3	2	5	6	—	—	—	—	—
92-93—Lada Togliatti	CIS	37	7	13	20	29	10	1	1	2	6
93-94—Buffalo	NHL	8	0	0	0	8	—	—	—	—	—
—Rochester	AHL	24	1	10	11	10	1	0	1	1	0
NHL totals................................		8	0	0	0	8					

TUCKER, CHRIS
C, BLACKHAWKS

PERSONAL: Born February 9, 1972, in White Plains, N.Y. . . . 5-11/183. . . . Shoots left. . . . Full name: Christopher Matthew Tucker.
HIGH SCHOOL: Thomas Jefferson (Bloomington, Minn.).
COLLEGE: Wisconsin.
TRANSACTIONS/CAREER NOTES: Selected by Chicago Blackhawks in fourth round (third Blackhawks pick, 79th overall) of NHL entry draft (June 16, 1990).

Season Team	League	REGULAR SEASON Gms.	G	A	Pts.	PIM	PLAYOFFS Gms.	G	A	Pts.	PIM
88-89—Jefferson H.S...................	Minn. H.S.	25	41	23	64	...	—	—	—	—	—
89-90—Jefferson H.S...................	Minn. H.S.	24	24	24	48	...	—	—	—	—	—
90-91—University of Wisconsin ...	WCHA	35	5	6	11	6	—	—	—	—	—
91-92—University of Wisconsin ...	WCHA	38	13	10	23	23	—	—	—	—	—
92-93—University of Wisconsin ...	WCHA	40	10	9	19	12	—	—	—	—	—
93-94—University of Wisconsin ...	WCHA	42	9	19	28	32	—	—	—	—	—

TUCKER, DARCY
C, CANADIENS

PERSONAL: Born March 15, 1975, in Castor, Alta. . . . 5-10/163. . . . Shoots left.
TRANSACTIONS/CAREER NOTES: Selected by Montreal Canadiens in sixth round (eighth Canadiens pick, 151st overall) of NHL entry draft (June 26, 1993).
HONORS: Won Stafford Smythe Memorial Trophy (1993-94). . . . Named to Can.HL All-Star first team (1993-94). . . . Named to WHL (West) All-Star first team (1993-94). . . . Named to Memorial Cup All-Star team (1993-94).

Season Team	League	REGULAR SEASON Gms.	G	A	Pts.	PIM	PLAYOFFS Gms.	G	A	Pts.	PIM
91-92—Kamloops	WHL	26	3	10	13	42	9	0	1	1	16
92-93—Kamloops	WHL	67	31	58	89	155	13	7	6	13	34
93-94—Kamloops	WHL	66	52	88	140	143	19	9	*18	*27	43

TUCKER, JOHN
RW, LIGHTNING

PERSONAL: Born September 29, 1964, in Windsor, Ont. . . . 6-0/200. . . . Shoots right.
TRANSACTIONS/CAREER NOTES: Selected by Buffalo Sabres as underage junior in second round (fourth Sabres pick, 31st overall) of NHL entry draft (June 8, 1983). . . . Broke bone in foot (November 7, 1984). . . . Injured disk (January 28, 1987); underwent surgery following end of

season.... Tore knee ligaments (November 7, 1987).... Injured shoulder (December 1987).... Injured shoulder (February 25, 1988).... Injured back (January 1989); missed 16 games.... Traded by Sabres to Washington Capitals for conditional pick in 1990 draft (January 4, 1990).... Sold by Capitals to Sabres (July 3, 1990).... Traded by Sabres to New York Islanders for future considerations (January 21, 1991).... Signed as free agent by Tampa Bay Lightning (July 21, 1992). ... Injured knee (March 16, 1993); missed six games.... Sprained right knee (November 26, 1993); missed 18 games.
HONORS: Won Red Tilson Trophy (1983-84).... Named to OHL All-Star first team (1983-84).

Season Team	League	REGULAR SEASON					PLAYOFFS				
		Gms.	G	A	Pts.	PIM	Gms.	G	A	Pts.	PIM
81-82—Kitchener	OHL	67	16	32	48	32	15	2	3	5	2
82-83—Kitchener	OHL	70	60	80	140	33	11	5	9	14	10
83-84—Kitchener	OHL	39	40	60	100	25	12	12	18	30	8
—Buffalo	NHL	21	12	4	16	4	3	1	0	1	0
84-85—Buffalo	NHL	64	22	27	49	21	5	1	5	6	0
85-86—Buffalo	NHL	75	31	34	65	39	—	—	—	—	—
86-87—Buffalo	NHL	54	17	34	51	21	—	—	—	—	—
87-88—Buffalo	NHL	45	19	19	38	20	6	7	3	10	18
88-89—Buffalo	NHL	60	13	31	44	31	3	0	3	3	0
89-90—Buffalo	NHL	8	1	2	3	2	—	—	—	—	—
—Washington	NHL	38	9	19	28	10	12	1	7	8	4
90-91—Buffalo	NHL	18	1	3	4	4	—	—	—	—	—
—New York Islanders	NHL	20	3	4	7	4	—	—	—	—	—
91-92—Asiago	Italy				Statistics unavailable.						
92-93—Tampa Bay	NHL	78	17	39	56	69	—	—	—	—	—
93-94—Tampa Bay	NHL	66	17	23	40	28	—	—	—	—	—
NHL totals		547	162	239	401	253	29	10	18	28	22

TUGNUTT, RON
G, CANADIENS

PERSONAL: Born October 22, 1967, in Scarborough, Ont.... 5-11/155.... Catches left.... Full name: Ronald Frederick Bradley Tugnutt.
TRANSACTIONS/CAREER NOTES: Selected by Quebec Nordiques as underage junior in fourth round (fourth Nordiques pick, 81st overall) of NHL entry draft (June 21, 1986).... Sprained ankle (March 1989).... Sprained knee (January 13, 1990).... Injured hamstring (January 29, 1991); missed 11 games.... Traded by Nordiques with LW Brad Zavisha to Edmonton Oilers for LW Martin Rucinsky (March 10, 1992).... Selected by Mighty Ducks of Anaheim in NHL expansion draft (June 24, 1993).... Traded by Mighty Ducks to Montreal Canadiens for C Stephan Lebeau (February 20, 1994).
HONORS: Won F.W. (Dinty) Moore Trophy (1984-85).... Shared Dave Pinkney Trophy with Kay Whitmore (1985-86).... Named to OHL All-Star first team (1986-87).

Season Team	League	REGULAR SEASON							PLAYOFFS						
		Gms.	Min.	W	L	T	GA	SO	Avg.	Gms.	Min.	W	L	GA	SO	Avg.
84-85—Peterborough	OHL	18	938	7	4	2	59	0	3.77	—	—	—	—	—	—	—
85-86—Peterborough	OHL	26	1543	18	7	0	74	1	2.88	3	133	2	0	6	0	2.71
86-87—Peterborough	OHL	31	1891	21	7	2	88	2	*2.79	6	374	3	3	21	1	3.37
87-88—Quebec	NHL	6	284	2	3	0	16	0	3.38	—	—	—	—	—	—	—
—Fredericton	AHL	34	1962	20	9	4	118	1	3.61	4	204	1	2	11	0	3.24
88-89—Quebec	NHL	26	1367	10	10	3	82	0	3.60	—	—	—	—	—	—	—
—Halifax	AHL	24	1368	14	7	2	79	1	3.46	—	—	—	—	—	—	—
89-90—Quebec	NHL	35	1978	5	24	3	152	0	4.61	—	—	—	—	—	—	—
—Halifax	AHL	6	366	1	5	0	23	0	3.77	—	—	—	—	—	—	—
90-91—Halifax	AHL	2	100	0	1	0	8	0	4.80	—	—	—	—	—	—	—
—Quebec	NHL	56	3144	12	†29	10	212	0	4.05	—	—	—	—	—	—	—
91-92—Quebec	NHL	30	1583	6	17	3	106	1	4.02	—	—	—	—	—	—	—
—Halifax	AHL	8	447	3	3	1	30	0	4.03	—	—	—	—	—	—	—
—Edmonton	NHL	3	124	1	1	0	10	0	4.84	2	60	0	0	3	0	3.00
92-93—Edmonton	NHL	26	1338	9	12	2	93	0	4.17	—	—	—	—	—	—	—
93-94—Anaheim	NHL	28	1520	10	15	1	76	1	3.00	—	—	—	—	—	—	—
—Montreal	NHL	8	378	2	3	1	24	0	3.81	1	59	0	1	5	0	5.08
NHL totals		218	11716	57	114	23	771	2	3.95	3	119	0	1	8	0	4.03

TULLY, BRENT
D, CANUCKS

PERSONAL: Born March 26, 1974, in Peterborough, Ont.... 6-3/185.... Shoots right.
HIGH SCHOOL: Thomas A. Stewart (Peterborough, Ont.).
TRANSACTIONS/CAREER NOTES: Selected by Vancouver Canucks in fourth round (fifth Canucks pick, 93rd overall) of NHL entry draft (June 20, 1992).
HONORS: Named to OHL All-Star second team (1992-93).

Season Team	League	REGULAR SEASON					PLAYOFFS				
		Gms.	G	A	Pts.	PIM	Gms.	G	A	Pts.	PIM
90-91—Peterborough Jr. B	OHA	9	3	0	3	23	—	—	—	—	—
—Peterborough	OHL	45	3	5	8	35	2	0	0	0	0
91-92—Peterborough	OHL	65	9	23	32	65	10	0	0	0	2
92-93—Peterborough	OHL	59	15	45	60	81	21	8	24	32	32
93-94—Hamilton	AHL	1	0	0	0	0	1	1	0	1	0
—Peterborough	OHL	37	17	26	43	81	7	5	3	8	12
—Canadian national team	Int'l	1	0	1	1	0	—	—	—	—	—

TURCO, MARTY
G, STARS

PERSONAL: Born August 13, 1975, in Sault Ste. Marie, Ont.... 5-11/175.... Catches left.
TRANSACTIONS/CAREER NOTES: Selected by Dallas Stars in fifth round (fourth Stars pick, 124th overall) of NHL entry draft (June 29, 1994).

Season	Team	League	Gms.	Min.	W	L	T	GA	SO	Avg.	Gms.	Min.	W	L	GA	SO	Avg.
					REGULAR SEASON								PLAYOFFS				
93-94—Cambridge Jr. B		OHA	34	1937	...	...	...	114	0	3.53	—	—	—	—	—	—	—

TURCOTTE, DARREN
C, WHALERS

PERSONAL: Born March 2, 1968, in Boston.... 6-0/178.... Shoots left.... Name pronounced TUHR-kaht.
TRANSACTIONS/CAREER NOTES: Selected by New York Rangers as underage junior in sixth round (sixth Rangers pick, 114th overall) of NHL entry draft (June 21, 1986).... Separated shoulder (October 1987); missed 34 games.... Suffered concussion (March 1989).... Sprained left ankle (October 1989).... Injured knee (April 11, 1990).... Broke left foot (April 27, 1990).... Suffered contusion above left ankle (November 13, 1991); missed two games.... Bruised right foot (March 4, 1992); missed one game.... Reinjured right foot (March 9, 1992); missed two games.... Sprained ankle (January 2, 1993); missed one game.... Suffered hairline fracture in foot (February 10, 1993); missed 11 games.... Traded by Rangers with D James Patrick to Hartford Whalers for RW Steve Larmer, LW Nick Kypreos, and undisclosed draft pick (November 2, 1993).... Underwent medial collateral ligament surgery (December 9, 1993); missed 50 games.
HONORS: Played in NHL All-Star Game (1991).

Season	Team	League	Gms.	G	A	Pts.	PIM	Gms.	G	A	Pts.	PIM
				REGULAR SEASON						PLAYOFFS		
84-85—North Bay		OHL	62	33	32	65	28	8	0	2	2	0
85-86—North Bay		OHL	62	35	37	72	35	10	3	4	7	8
86-87—North Bay		OHL	55	30	48	78	20	18	12	8	20	6
87-88—Colorado		IHL	8	4	3	7	9	6	2	6	8	8
—North Bay		OHL	32	30	33	63	16	4	3	0	3	4
88-89—Denver		IHL	40	21	28	49	32	—	—	—	—	—
—New York Rangers		NHL	20	7	3	10	4	1	0	0	0	0
89-90—New York Rangers		NHL	76	32	34	66	32	10	1	6	7	4
90-91—New York Rangers		NHL	74	26	41	67	37	6	1	2	3	0
91-92—New York Rangers		NHL	71	30	23	53	57	8	4	0	4	6
92-93—New York Rangers		NHL	71	25	28	53	40	—	—	—	—	—
93-94—New York Rangers		NHL	13	2	4	6	13	—	—	—	—	—
—Hartford		NHL	19	2	11	13	4	—	—	—	—	—
NHL totals			344	124	144	268	187	25	6	8	14	10

TURGEON, PIERRE
C, ISLANDERS

PERSONAL: Born August 29, 1969, in Rouyn, Que.... 6-1/203.... Shoots left.... Name pronounced TUHR-zhaw.... Brother of Sylvain Turgeon, left winger, Ottawa Senators.
TRANSACTIONS/CAREER NOTES: Underwent knee surgery (June 1985).... Selected by Buffalo Sabres as underage junior in first round (first Sabres pick, first overall) of NHL entry draft (June 13, 1987).... Traded by Sabres with RW Benoit Hogue, D Uwe Krupp and C Dave McLlwain to New York Islanders for C Pat LaFontaine, LW Randy Wood, D Randy Hillier and future considerations; Sabres later received fourth-round pick (D Dean Melanson) in 1992 draft (October 25, 1991).... Injured right knee (January 3, 1992); missed three games.... Separated shoulder (April 28, 1993); missed six playoff games.... Suffered from tendinitis in right wrist (October 5, 1993); missed one game.... Suffered from the flu (December 29, 1993); missed one game.... Fractured cheekbone (January 26, 1994); missed 12 games.
HONORS: Won Michel Bergeron Trophy (1985-86).... Won Michael Bossy Trophy (1986-87).... Played in NHL All-Star Game (1990, 1993 and 1994).... Won Lady Byng Memorial Trophy (1992-93).

Season	Team	League	Gms.	G	A	Pts.	PIM	Gms.	G	A	Pts.	PIM
				REGULAR SEASON						PLAYOFFS		
85-86—Granby		QMJHL	69	47	67	114	31	—	—	—	—	—
86-87—Granby		QMJHL	58	69	85	154	8	7	9	6	15	15
87-88—Buffalo		NHL	76	14	28	42	34	6	4	3	7	4
88-89—Buffalo		NHL	80	34	54	88	26	5	3	5	8	2
89-90—Buffalo		NHL	80	40	66	106	29	6	2	4	6	2
90-91—Buffalo		NHL	78	32	47	79	26	6	3	1	4	6
91-92—Buffalo		NHL	8	2	6	8	4	—	—	—	—	—
—New York Islanders		NHL	69	38	49	87	16	—	—	—	—	—
92-93—New York Islanders		NHL	83	58	74	132	26	11	6	7	13	0
93-94—New York Islanders		NHL	69	38	56	94	18	4	0	1	1	0
NHL totals			543	256	380	636	179	38	18	21	39	14

TURGEON, SYLVAIN
LW, SENATORS

PERSONAL: Born January 17, 1965, in Noranda, Que.... 6-0/200.... Shoots left.... Full name: Sylvain Dorila Turgeon.... Name pronounced TUHR-zhaw.... Brother of Pierre Turgeon, center, New York Islanders.
TRANSACTIONS/CAREER NOTES: Selected by Hartford Whalers as underage junior in first round (first Whalers pick, second overall) of NHL entry draft (June 8, 1983).... Pulled abdominal muscles (October 1984).... Underwent surgery to repair torn abdominal muscle (November 14, 1986); missed 39 games.... Broke left arm during Team Canada practice (August 11, 1987).... Sprained right knee during training camp (September 1988).... Separated left shoulder (December 21, 1988); missed 36 games.... Burned both eyes from ultra-violet light produced by welder's torch while working on car (February 28, 1989).... Traded by Whalers to New Jersey Devils for RW/LW Pat Verbeek (June 17, 1989).... Aggravated groin injury (March 20, 1990).... Underwent hernia surgery (August 23, 1990); missed first 33 games of season.... Traded by Devils to Montreal Canadiens for RW Claude Lemieux (September 4, 1990).... Broke right kneecap

(February 6, 1991); missed remainder of regular season. . . . Selected by Ottawa Senators in NHL expansion draft (June 18, 1992). . . . Suspended one game by NHL for receiving two major stick fouls in one game (October 23, 1992). . . . Injured groin (February 8, 1993); missed 11 games. . . . Fractured left forearm (October 25, 1993); missed 37 games.
HONORS: Won Des Instructeurs Trophy (1981-82). . . . Won Association of Journalists of Hockey Trophy (1982-83). . . . Named to QMJHL All-Star first team (1982-83). . . . Named to NHL All-Rookie team (1983-84). . . . Played in NHL All-Star Game (1986).

			REGULAR SEASON					PLAYOFFS				
Season	Team	League	Gms.	G	A	Pts.	PIM	Gms.	G	A	Pts.	PIM
81-82	Hull	QMJHL	57	33	40	73	78	14	11	11	22	16
82-83	Hull	QMJHL	67	54	109	163	103	7	8	7	15	10
83-84	Hartford	NHL	76	40	32	72	55	—	—	—	—	—
84-85	Hartford	NHL	64	31	31	62	67	—	—	—	—	—
85-86	Hartford	NHL	76	45	34	79	88	9	2	3	5	4
86-87	Hartford	NHL	41	23	13	36	45	6	1	2	3	4
87-88	Hartford	NHL	71	23	26	49	71	6	0	0	0	4
88-89	Hartford	NHL	42	16	14	30	40	4	0	2	2	4
89-90	New Jersey	NHL	72	30	17	47	81	1	0	0	0	0
90-91	Montreal	NHL	19	5	7	12	20	5	0	0	0	2
91-92	Montreal	NHL	56	9	11	20	39	5	1	0	1	4
92-93	Ottawa	NHL	72	25	18	43	104	—	—	—	—	—
93-94	Ottawa	NHL	47	11	15	26	52	—	—	—	—	—
NHL totals			636	258	218	476	662	36	4	7	11	22

TUTTLE, STEVE
RW

PERSONAL: Born January 5, 1966, in Vancouver. . . . 6-1/180. . . . Shoots right. . . . Full name: Steven Walter Tuttle.
COLLEGE: Wisconsin.
TRANSACTIONS/CAREER NOTES: Selected by St. Louis Blues in sixth round (eighth Blues pick, 113th overall) of NHL entry draft (June 9, 1984). . . . Sprained left knee (December 1988); missed 15 games. . . . Sprained shoulder (February 1989). . . . Traded by Blues with D Rob Robinson, RW Darin Kimble and G Pat Jablonski to Tampa Bay Lightning for future considerations (June 19, 1992). . . . Loaned to Milwaukee Admirals at beginning of 1992-93 season. . . . Traded by Lightning with RW Martin Simard and C Michel Mongeau to Quebec Nordiques for RW Herb Raglan (February 12, 1993). . . . Signed as free agent by Milwaukee Admirals (September 2, 1993).
HONORS: Named to NCAA All-America West second team (1987-88). . . . Named to IHL All-Star first team (1991-92).

			REGULAR SEASON					PLAYOFFS				
Season	Team	League	Gms.	G	A	Pts.	PIM	Gms.	G	A	Pts.	PIM
83-84	Richmond	BCJHL	46	46	34	80	22	—	—	—	—	—
84-85	University of Wisconsin	WCHA	28	3	4	7	0	—	—	—	—	—
85-86	University of Wisconsin	WCHA	32	2	10	12	2	—	—	—	—	—
86-87	University of Wisconsin	WCHA	42	31	21	52	14	—	—	—	—	—
87-88	University of Wisconsin	WCHA	45	27	39	66	18	—	—	—	—	—
88-89	St. Louis	NHL	53	13	12	25	6	6	1	2	3	0
89-90	St. Louis	NHL	71	12	10	22	4	5	0	1	1	2
90-91	St. Louis	NHL	20	3	6	9	2	6	0	3	3	0
	Peoria	IHL	42	24	32	56	8	—	—	—	—	—
91-92	Peoria	IHL	71	43	46	89	22	10	4	8	12	4
92-93	Milwaukee	IHL	51	27	34	61	12	4	0	2	2	2
	Halifax	AHL	22	11	17	28	2	—	—	—	—	—
93-94	Milwaukee	IHL	78	27	44	71	34	4	0	2	2	4
NHL totals			144	28	28	56	12	17	1	6	7	2

TUZZOLINO, TONY
RW, NORDIQUES

PERSONAL: Born October 9, 1975, in Buffalo, N.Y. . . . 6-2/180. . . . Shoots right.
COLLEGE: Michigan State.
TRANSACTIONS/CAREER NOTES: Selected by Quebec Nordiques in fifth round (seventh Nordiques pick, 113th overall) of NHL entry draft (June 29, 1994).

			REGULAR SEASON					PLAYOFFS				
Season	Team	League	Gms.	G	A	Pts.	PIM	Gms.	G	A	Pts.	PIM
91-92	Niagara	NAJHL	45	19	27	46	82	—	—	—	—	—
92-93	Niagara	NAJHL	50	36	41	77	134	—	—	—	—	—
93-94	Michigan State	CCHA	38	4	3	7	50	—	—	—	—	—

TVERDOVSKY, OLEG
D, MIGHTY DUCKS

PERSONAL: Born May 18, 1976, in Donetsk, U.S.S.R. . . . 6-0/183. . . . Shoots left. . . . Name pronounced TEVER-doff-ski.
TRANSACTIONS/CAREER NOTES: Selected by Mighty Ducks of Anaheim in first round (first Mighty Ducks pick, second overall) of NHL entry draft (June 28, 1994).

			REGULAR SEASON					PLAYOFFS				
Season	Team	League	Gms.	G	A	Pts.	PIM	Gms.	G	A	Pts.	PIM
92-93	Soviet Wings	CIS	21	0	1	1	6	6	0	0	0	0
93-94	Soviet Wings	CIS	46	4	10	14	22	3	1	0	1	2

TWIST, TONY
LW, BLUES

PERSONAL: Born May 9, 1968, in Sherwood Park, Alta. . . . 6-0/208. . . . Shoots left. . . . Full name: Anthony Rory Twist.
TRANSACTIONS/CAREER NOTES: Suspended three games and fined $250 by WHL for leaving the penalty box to fight (January 28, 1988). . . . Selected by St. Louis Blues in ninth round (ninth

Blues pick, 177th overall) of NHL entry draft (June 11, 1988).... Suspended 13 games by IHL for checking goaltender after play stopped (December 15, 1990).... Traded by Blues with RW Herb Raglan and LW Andy Rymsha to Quebec Nordiques for RW Darin Kimble (February 4, 1991).... Injured shoulder (December 18, 1993); missed six games.... Hyperextended right elbow (March 30, 1994); missed five games.... Signed as free agent by Blues (August 3, 1994).

			REGULAR SEASON					PLAYOFFS			
Season Team	League	Gms.	G	A	Pts.	PIM	Gms.	G	A	Pts.	PIM
86-87—Saskatoon	WHL	64	0	8	8	181	—	—	—	—	—
87-88—Saskatoon	WHL	55	1	8	9	226	10	1	1	2	6
88-89—Peoria	IHL	67	3	8	11	312	—	—	—	—	—
89-90—St. Louis	NHL	28	0	0	0	124	—	—	—	—	—
—Peoria	IHL	36	1	5	6	200	5	0	1	1	8
90-91—Peoria	IHL	38	2	10	12	244	—	—	—	—	—
—Quebec	NHL	24	0	0	0	104	—	—	—	—	—
91-92—Quebec	NHL	44	0	1	1	164	—	—	—	—	—
92-93—Quebec	NHL	34	0	2	2	64	—	—	—	—	—
93-94—Quebec	NHL	49	0	4	4	101	—	—	—	—	—
NHL totals		179	0	7	7	557					

ULANOV, IGOR
D, JETS

PERSONAL: Born October 1, 1969, in Kraskokamsk, U.S.S.R. ... 6-2/202. ... Shoots right. ... Name pronounced EE-gohr oo-LAH-nahf.

TRANSACTIONS/CAREER NOTES: Selected by Winnipeg Jets in 10th round (eighth Jets pick, 203rd overall) of NHL entry draft (June 22, 1991).... Suffered back spasms (March 7, 1992); missed five games.

			REGULAR SEASON					PLAYOFFS			
Season Team	League	Gms.	G	A	Pts.	PIM	Gms.	G	A	Pts.	PIM
90-91—Khimik	USSR	41	2	2	4	52	—	—	—	—	—
91-92—Khimik	CIS	27	1	4	5	24	—	—	—	—	—
—Winnipeg	NHL	27	2	9	11	67	7	0	0	0	39
—Moncton	AHL	3	0	1	1	16	—	—	—	—	—
92-93—Moncton	AHL	9	1	3	4	26	—	—	—	—	—
—Fort Wayne	IHL	3	0	1	1	29	—	—	—	—	—
—Winnipeg	NHL	56	2	14	16	124	4	0	0	0	4
93-94—Winnipeg	NHL	74	0	17	17	165	—	—	—	—	—
NHL totals		157	4	40	44	356	11	0	0	0	43

USTORF, STEFAN
C, CAPITALS

PERSONAL: Born January 3, 1974, in Kaufbeuren, West Germany. ... 5-11/170. ... Shoots left.

TRANSACTIONS/CAREER NOTES: Selected by Washington Capitals in third round (third Capitals pick, 53rd overall) of NHL entry draft (June 20, 1992).

			REGULAR SEASON					PLAYOFFS			
Season Team	League	Gms.	G	A	Pts.	PIM	Gms.	G	A	Pts.	PIM
91-92—Kaufbeuren	Germany	41	2	22	24	46	—	—	—	—	—
92-93—Kaufbeuren	Germany	37	14	18	32	32	3	1	0	1	10
93-94—Kaufbeuren	Germany	38	10	20	30	21	3	0	0	0	4
—German Olympic team	Int'l	8	1	2	3	2	—	—	—	—	—

VALK, GARRY
LW/RW, MIGHTY DUCKS

PERSONAL: Born November 27, 1967, in Edmonton.... 6-1/205.... Shoots left.... Name pronounced VAHLK.

COLLEGE: North Dakota.

TRANSACTIONS/CAREER NOTES: Selected by Vancouver Canucks in sixth round (fifth Canucks pick, 108th overall) of NHL entry draft (June 13, 1987).... Sprained thumb (November 24, 1991); missed one game.... Sprained shoulder (January 21, 1992); missed eight games.... Sprained knee (February 26, 1993); missed 12 games.... Selected by Mighty Ducks of Anaheim in NHL waiver draft (October 3, 1993).... Suffered concussion (December 5, 1993); missed one game.... Suffered post-concussion syndrome (December 5, 1993); missed four games.

			REGULAR SEASON					PLAYOFFS			
Season Team	League	Gms.	G	A	Pts.	PIM	Gms.	G	A	Pts.	PIM
85-86—Sherwood Park	AJHL	40	20	26	46	116	—	—	—	—	—
86-87—Sherwood Park	AJHL	59	42	44	86	204	—	—	—	—	—
87-88—Univ. of North Dakota	WCHA	38	23	12	35	64	—	—	—	—	—
88-89—Univ. of North Dakota	WCHA	40	14	17	31	71	—	—	—	—	—
89-90—Univ. of North Dakota	WCHA	43	22	17	39	92	—	—	—	—	—
90-91—Vancouver	NHL	59	10	11	21	67	5	0	0	0	20
—Milwaukee	IHL	10	12	4	16	13	3	0	0	0	2
91-92—Vancouver	NHL	65	8	17	25	56	4	0	0	0	5
92-93—Vancouver	NHL	48	6	7	13	77	7	0	1	1	12
—Hamilton	AHL	7	3	6	9	6	—	—	—	—	—
93-94—Anaheim	NHL	78	18	27	45	100	—	—	—	—	—
NHL totals		250	42	62	104	300	16	0	1	1	37

VALLEE, SEBASTIEN
LW, FLYERS

PERSONAL: Born January 2, 1976, in Thetford Mines, Que.... 6-4/180.... Shoots left.... Name pronounced Val-AY.

TRANSACTIONS/CAREER NOTES: Selected by Philadelphia Flyers in fourth round (third Flyers pick, 101st overall) of NHL entry draft (June 29, 1994).

Season	Team	League	Gms.	G	A	Pts.	PIM	Gms.	G	A	Pts.	PIM
91-92—Surrey Jr. A		BCJHL	27	0	1	1	20	—	—	—	—	—
92-93—Surrey Jr. A		BCJHL	60	5	37	42	210	—	—	—	—	—
93-94—Victoriaville		QMJHL	72	17	22	39	22	1	0	0	0	0

VALLIS, LINDSAY
RW, CANADIENS

PERSONAL: Born January 12, 1971, in Winnipeg.... 6-3/207.... Shoots right.
TRANSACTIONS/CAREER NOTES: Selected by Montreal Canadiens in first round (first Canadiens pick, 13th overall) of NHL entry draft (June 17, 1989).

			REGULAR SEASON					PLAYOFFS				
Season	Team	League	Gms.	G	A	Pts.	PIM	Gms.	G	A	Pts.	PIM
87-88—Seattle		WHL	68	31	45	76	65	—	—	—	—	—
88-89—Seattle		WHL	63	21	32	53	48	—	—	—	—	—
89-90—Seattle		WHL	65	34	43	77	68	13	6	5	11	14
90-91—Seattle		WHL	72	41	38	79	119	6	1	3	4	17
—Fredericton		AHL	—	—	—	—	—	7	0	0	0	6
91-92—Fredericton		AHL	71	10	19	29	84	4	0	1	1	7
92-93—Fredericton		AHL	65	18	16	34	38	5	0	2	2	10
93-94—Fredericton		AHL	75	9	30	39	103	—	—	—	—	—
—Montreal		NHL	1	0	0	0	0	—	—	—	—	—
NHL totals			1	0	0	0	0					

VAN ALLEN, SHAUN
C, MIGHTY DUCKS

PERSONAL: Born August 29, 1967, in Shaunavon, Sask.... 6-1/200.... Shoots left.... Full name: Shaun Kelly Van Allen.
HIGH SCHOOL: Walter Murray (Saskatoon, Sask.).
TRANSACTIONS/CAREER NOTES: Selected by Edmonton Oilers in fifth round (fifth Oilers pick, 105th overall) of NHL entry draft (June 13, 1987).... Suffered concussion (January 9, 1993); missed 11 games.... Signed as free agent by Mighty Ducks of Anaheim (July 22, 1993).
HONORS: Named to AHL All-Star second team (1990-91).... Won John B. Sollenberger Trophy (1991-92).... Named to AHL All-Star first team (1991-92).

			REGULAR SEASON					PLAYOFFS				
Season	Team	League	Gms.	G	A	Pts.	PIM	Gms.	G	A	Pts.	PIM
84-85—Swift Current		SAJHL	61	12	20	32	136	—	—	—	—	—
85-86—Saskatoon		WHL	55	12	11	23	43	13	4	8	12	28
86-87—Saskatoon		WHL	72	38	59	97	116	11	4	6	10	24
87-88—Nova Scotia		AHL	19	4	10	14	17	4	1	1	2	4
—Milwaukee		IHL	40	14	28	42	34	—	—	—	—	—
88-89—Cape Breton		AHL	76	32	42	74	81	—	—	—	—	—
89-90—Cape Breton		AHL	61	25	44	69	83	4	0	2	2	8
90-91—Edmonton		NHL	2	0	0	0	0	—	—	—	—	—
—Cape Breton		AHL	76	25	75	100	182	4	0	1	1	8
91-92—Cape Breton		AHL	77	29	*84	*113	80	5	3	7	10	14
92-93—Cape Breton		AHL	43	14	62	76	68	15	8	9	17	18
—Edmonton		NHL	21	1	4	5	6	—	—	—	—	—
93-94—Anaheim		NHL	80	8	25	33	64	—	—	—	—	—
NHL totals			103	9	29	38	70					

VANBIESBROUCK, JOHN
G, PANTHERS

PERSONAL: Born September 4, 1963, in Detroit.... 5-8/172.... Catches left.... Name pronounced van-BEES-bruhk.
TRANSACTIONS/CAREER NOTES: Selected by New York Rangers in fourth round (fifth Rangers pick, 72nd overall) of NHL entry draft (June 10, 1981).... Fractured jaw (October 1987).... Severely lacerated wrist (June 1988).... Underwent knee surgery (May 11, 1990).... Suffered lower back spasms (February 25, 1992); missed 11 games.... Pulled groin (November 2, 1992); missed four games.... Traded by Rangers to Vancouver Canucks for future considerations (June 20, 1993); Canucks sent D Doug Lidster to Rangers to complete deal (June 25, 1993).... Selected by Florida Panthers in NHL expansion draft (June 24, 1993).... Lacerated hand (February 1, 1994); missed seven games.
HONORS: Won F.W. (Dinty) Moore Trophy (1980-81).... Shared Dave Pinkney Trophy with Marc D'Amour (1981-82).... Named to OHL All-Star second team (1982-83).... Shared Tommy Ivan Trophy with D Bruce Affleck (1983-84).... Shared Terry Sawchuk Trophy with Ron Scott (1983-84).... Named to CHL All-Star first team (1983-84).... Won Vezina Trophy (1985-86).... Named to THE SPORTING NEWS All-Star first team (1985-86 and 1993-94).... Named to NHL All-Star first team (1985-86).... Played in NHL All-Star Game (1994).... Named to NHL All-Star second team (1993-94).

			REGULAR SEASON							PLAYOFFS						
Season	Team	League	Gms.	Min.	W	L	T	GA	SO	Avg.	Gms.	Min.	W	L	GA	SO	Avg.
80-81—Sault Ste. Marie		OMJHL	56	2941	31	16	1	203	0	4.14	11	457	3	3	24	1	3.15
81-82—Sault Ste. Marie		OHL	31	1686	12	12	2	102	0	3.63	7	276	1	4	20	0	4.35
—New York Rangers		NHL	1	60	1	0	0	1	0	1.00	—	—	—	—	—	—	—
82-83—Sault Ste. Marie		OHL	*62	3471	39	21	1	209	0	3.61	16	944	7	6	56	†1	3.56
83-84—New York Rangers		NHL	3	180	2	1	0	10	0	3.33	1	0	0	0	0	0	0.00
—Tulsa		CHL	37	2153	20	13	2	124	*3	3.46	4	240	4	0	10	0	*2.50
84-85—New York Rangers		NHL	42	2358	12	24	3	166	1	4.22	1	20	0	0	0	0	0.00
85-86—New York Rangers		NHL	61	3326	31	21	5	184	3	3.32	16	899	8	8	49	†1	3.27
86-87—New York Rangers		NHL	50	2656	18	20	5	161	0	3.64	4	195	1	3	11	1	3.38
87-88—New York Rangers		NHL	56	3319	27	22	7	187	2	3.38							

Season Team	League	REGULAR SEASON Gms.	Min.	W	L	T	GA	SO	Avg.	PLAYOFFS Gms.	Min.	W	L	GA	SO	Avg.
88-89—New York Rangers	NHL	56	3207	28	21	4	197	0	3.69	2	107	0	1	6	0	3.36
89-90—New York Rangers	NHL	47	2734	19	19	7	154	1	3.38	6	298	2	3	15	0	3.02
90-91—New York Rangers	NHL	40	2257	15	18	6	126	3	3.35	1	52	0	0	1	0	1.15
91-92—New York Rangers	NHL	45	2526	27	13	3	120	2	2.85	7	368	2	5	23	0	3.75
92-93—New York Rangers	NHL	48	2757	20	18	7	152	4	3.31	—	—	—	—	—	—	—
93-94—Florida	NHL	57	3440	21	25	11	145	1	2.53	—	—	—	—	—	—	—
NHL totals		506	29326	221	202	58	1603	17	3.17	38	1940	13	20	105	2	3.25

VARADA, VACLAV
RW, SHARKS

PERSONAL: Born April 26, 1976, in Valasske Mezirici, Czechoslovakia.... 6-0/198.... Shoots left.
TRANSACTIONS/CAREER NOTES: Selected by San Jose Sharks in fourth round (fourth Sharks pick, 89th overall) of NHL entry draft (June 29, 1994).

Season Team	League	REGULAR SEASON Gms.	G	A	Pts.	PIM	PLAYOFFS Gms.	G	A	Pts.	PIM
92-93—TJ Vitkovice	Czech.	1	0	0	0	...	—	—	—	—	—
93-94—HC Vitkovice	Czech Rep.	24	6	7	13	...	5	1	1	2	0

VARGA, JOHN
LW, CAPITALS

PERSONAL: Born January 31, 1974, in Chicago.... 5-10/170.... Shoots left.
HIGH SCHOOL: Clover Park (Tacoma, Wash.).
TRANSACTIONS/CAREER NOTES: Selected by Washington Capitals in fifth round (fifth Capitals pick, 119th overall) of NHL entry draft (June 20, 1992).
HONORS: Named to WHL (West) All-Star second team (1993-94).

Season Team	League	REGULAR SEASON Gms.	G	A	Pts.	PIM	PLAYOFFS Gms.	G	A	Pts.	PIM
91-92—Tacoma	WHL	72	25	34	59	93	4	1	2	3	0
92-93—Tacoma	WHL	61	32	32	64	63	7	1	1	2	8
93-94—Tacoma	WHL	65	60	62	122	122	8	2	8	10	14

VARIS, PETRI
LW, SHARKS

PERSONAL: Born May 13, 1969, in Varkaus, Finland.... 6-1/200.... Shoots left.... Name pronounced PEHT-ree VAHR-ihz.
TRANSACTIONS/CAREER NOTES: Selected by San Jose Sharks in sixth round (seventh Sharks pick, 132nd overall) of NHL entry draft (June 26, 1993).
HONORS: Named Finnish Rookie of the Year (1991-92).
MISCELLANEOUS: Member of bronze-medal-winning Finnish Olympic team (1994).

Season Team	League	REGULAR SEASON Gms.	G	A	Pts.	PIM	PLAYOFFS Gms.	G	A	Pts.	PIM
90-91—KooKoo Kouvola	Finland Dv.II	44	20	31	51	42	—	—	—	—	—
91-92—Assat Pori	Finland	36	13	23	36	24	—	—	—	—	—
92-93—Assat Pori	Finland	46	14	35	49	42	8	2	2	4	12
93-94—Jokerit	Finland	31	14	15	29	16	11	3	4	7	6
—Finnish Olympic Team	Int'l	5	1	1	2	2	—	—	—	—	—

VARVIO, JARKKO
LW, STARS

PERSONAL: Born April 28, 1972, in Tampere, Finland.... 5-9/172.... Shoots right.... Name pronounced VAHR-vee-oh.
TRANSACTIONS/CAREER NOTES: Selected by Minnesota North Stars in second round (first North Stars pick, 34th overall) of NHL entry draft (June 20, 1992).... North Stars franchise moved from Minnesota to Dallas and renamed Stars for 1993-94 season.

Season Team	League	REGULAR SEASON Gms.	G	A	Pts.	PIM	PLAYOFFS Gms.	G	A	Pts.	PIM
89-90—Ilves Tampere	Finland	1	0	0	0	0	—	—	—	—	—
90-91—Ilves Tampere	Finland	37	10	7	17	6	—	—	—	—	—
91-92—HPK Hameenlinna	Finland	41	25	9	34	6	—	—	—	—	—
92-93—HPK Hameenlinna	Finland	40	29	19	48	16	12	3	2	5	8
93-94—Dallas	NHL	8	2	3	5	4	—	—	—	—	—
—Kalamazoo	IHL	58	29	16	45	18	1	0	0	0	0
NHL totals		8	2	3	5	4					

VASKE, DENNIS
D, ISLANDERS

PERSONAL: Born October 11, 1967, in Rockford, Ill.... 6-2/211.... Shoots left.... Full name: Dennis James Vaske.... Name pronounced VAS-kee.
HIGH SCHOOL: Armstrong (Plymouth, Minn.).
COLLEGE: Minnesota-Duluth.
TRANSACTIONS/CAREER NOTES: Selected by New York Islanders in second round (second Islanders pick, 38th overall) of NHL entry draft (June 21, 1986).... Lacerated forehead (April 8, 1993); missed three games.... Broke foot (December 19, 1993); missed 13 games.

Season Team	League	REGULAR SEASON Gms.	G	A	Pts.	PIM	PLAYOFFS Gms.	G	A	Pts.	PIM
84-85—Armstrong H.S.	Minn. H.S.	22	5	18	23	...	—	—	—	—	—
85-86—Armstrong H.S.	Minn. H.S.	20	9	13	22	...	—	—	—	—	—
86-87—Minnesota-Duluth	WCHA	33	0	2	2	40	—	—	—	—	—

Season	Team	League		REGULAR SEASON					PLAYOFFS			
			Gms.	G	A	Pts.	Pen.	Gms.	G	A	Pts.	Pen.
87-88—Minnesota-Duluth	WCHA	39	1	6	7	90	—	—	—	—	—
88-89—Minnesota-Duluth	WCHA	37	9	19	28	86	—	—	—	—	—
89-90—Minnesota-Duluth	WCHA	37	5	24	29	72	—	—	—	—	—
90-91—New York Islanders	NHL	5	0	0	0	2	—	—	—	—	—
—Capital District	AHL	67	10	10	20	65	—	—	—	—	—
91-92—Capital District	AHL	31	1	11	12	59	—	—	—	—	—
—New York Islanders	NHL	39	0	1	1	39	—	—	—	—	—
92-93—Capital District	AHL	42	4	15	19	70	—	—	—	—	—
—New York Islanders	NHL	27	1	5	6	32	18	0	6	6	14
93-94—New York Islanders	NHL	65	2	11	13	76	4	0	1	1	2
NHL totals		136	3	17	20	149	22	0	7	7	16

VAUHKONEN, JONNI
RW, BLACKHAWKS

PERSONAL: Born January 1, 1975, in Sounenjoki, Finland.... 6-2/189.... Shoots left.

TRANSACTIONS/CAREER NOTES: Selected by Chicago Blackhawks in fifth round (seventh Blackhawks pick, 128th overall) of NHL entry draft (June 26, 1993).

Season	Team	League		REGULAR SEASON					PLAYOFFS			
			Gms.	G	A	Pts.	PIM	Gms.	G	A	Pts.	PIM
92-93—Reipas Lahti	Finland	41	8	5	13	63	—	—	—	—	—
93-94—Reipas Lahti	Finland	33	2	3	5	22	—	—	—	—	—

VEITCH, DARREN
D

PERSONAL: Born April 24, 1960, in Saskatoon, Sask.... 6-0/200.... Shoots right.... Full name: Darren William Veitch.... Name pronounced VEECH.

TRANSACTIONS/CAREER NOTES: Selected by Washington Capitals in first round (first Capitals pick, fifth overall) of NHL entry draft (June 11, 1980).... Fractured collarbone in three places (October 27, 1982).... Refractured collarbone (February 19, 1983).... Fractured ribs (February 11, 1984).... Bruised ribs (January 1985).... Traded by Capitals to Detroit Red Wings for D John Barrett and D Greg Smith (March 1986).... Injured ankle (March 1988).... Traded by Red Wings to Toronto Maple Leafs for RW Miroslav Frycer (June 1988).... Traded by Maple Leafs to St. Louis Blues for Keith Osborne (March 5, 1991).... Signed as free agent by Moncton Hawks (November 8, 1991).... Signed as free agent by Peoria Rivermen (July 27, 1992).

HONORS: Named to WHL All-Star first team (1979-80).... Named to Memorial Cup All-Star team (1979-80).... Named to AHL All-Star second team (1989-90).... Won Governor's Trophy (1993-94).

Season	Team	League		REGULAR SEASON					PLAYOFFS			
			Gms.	G	A	Pts.	PIM	Gms.	G	A	Pts.	PIM
76-77—Regina Blues	SJHL	60	15	21	36	121	—	—	—	—	—
—Regina	WCHL	1	0	0	0	0	—	—	—	—	—
77-78—Regina	WCHL	71	13	32	45	135	9	0	2	2	4
78-79—Regina	WHL	51	11	36	47	80	—	—	—	—	—
79-80—Regina	WHL	71	29	*93	122	118	18	13	18	31	13
80-81—Hershey	AHL	26	6	22	28	12	10	6	3	9	15
—Washington	NHL	59	4	21	25	46	—	—	—	—	—
81-82—Hershey	AHL	10	5	10	15	16	—	—	—	—	—
—Washington	NHL	67	9	44	53	54	—	—	—	—	—
82-83—Hershey	AHL	5	0	1	1	2	—	—	—	—	—
—Washington	NHL	10	0	8	8	0	—	—	—	—	—
83-84—Washington	NHL	46	6	18	24	17	5	0	1	1	15
—Hershey	AHL	11	1	6	7	4	—	—	—	—	—
84-85—Washington	NHL	75	3	18	21	37	5	0	1	1	4
85-86—Washington	NHL	62	3	9	12	27	—	—	—	—	—
—Detroit	NHL	13	0	5	5	2	—	—	—	—	—
86-87—Detroit	NHL	77	13	45	58	52	12	3	4	7	8
87-88—Detroit	NHL	63	7	33	40	45	11	1	5	6	6
88-89—Newmarket	AHL	33	5	19	24	29	5	0	4	4	4
—Toronto	NHL	37	3	7	10	16	—	—	—	—	—
89-90—Newmarket	AHL	78	13	54	67	30	—	—	—	—	—
90-91—Newmarket	AHL	56	7	28	35	26	—	—	—	—	—
—Toronto	NHL	2	0	1	1	0	—	—	—	—	—
—Peoria	IHL	18	2	14	16	10	19	4	12	16	10
91-92—Moncton	AHL	61	6	23	29	47	11	0	6	6	2
92-93—Peoria	IHL	79	12	37	49	16	4	2	0	2	4
93-94—Peoria	IHL	76	21	54	75	16	6	1	1	2	0
NHL totals		511	48	209	257	296	33	4	11	15	33

V

VERBEEK, PAT
RW, WHALERS

PERSONAL: Born May 24, 1964, in Sarnia, Ont.... 5-9/190.... Shoots right.

TRANSACTIONS/CAREER NOTES: Selected by New Jersey Devils as underage junior in third round (third Devils pick, 43rd overall) of NHL entry draft (June 9, 1982).... Severed left thumb between knuckles in a corn-planting machine on his farm and underwent surgery to have thumb reconnected (May 15, 1985).... Pulled side muscle (March 1987).... Bruised chest (October 28, 1988).... Traded by Devils to Hartford Whalers for LW Sylvain Turgeon (June 17, 1989).... Missed first three games of 1991-92 season due to contract dispute.... Fined $500 by Whalers for involvement in bar brawl (April 1, 1994).

HONORS: Won Emms Family Award (1981-82).... Played in NHL All-Star Game (1991).
STATISTICAL NOTES: Only NHL player ever to lead his team in goals scored and penalty minutes (1989-90 and 1990-91).

Season Team	League	REGULAR SEASON Gms.	G	A	Pts.	PIM	PLAYOFFS Gms.	G	A	Pts.	PIM
80-81—Petrolia Jr. B.	OPJHL	42	44	44	88	155	—	—	—	—	—
81-82—Sudbury	OHL	66	37	51	88	180	—	—	—	—	—
82-83—Sudbury	OHL	61	40	67	107	184	—	—	—	—	—
—New Jersey	NHL	6	3	2	5	8	—	—	—	—	—
83-84—New Jersey	NHL	79	20	27	47	158	—	—	—	—	—
84-85—New Jersey	NHL	78	15	18	33	162	—	—	—	—	—
85-86—New Jersey	NHL	76	25	28	53	79	—	—	—	—	—
86-87—New Jersey	NHL	74	35	24	59	120	—	—	—	—	—
87-88—New Jersey	NHL	73	46	31	77	227	20	4	8	12	51
88-89—New Jersey	NHL	77	26	21	47	189	—	—	—	—	—
89-90—Hartford	NHL	80	44	45	89	228	7	2	2	4	26
90-91—Hartford	NHL	80	43	39	82	246	6	3	2	5	40
91-92—Hartford	NHL	76	22	35	57	243	7	0	2	2	12
92-93—Hartford	NHL	84	39	43	82	197	—	—	—	—	—
93-94—Hartford	NHL	84	37	38	75	177	—	—	—	—	—
NHL totals		**867**	**355**	**351**	**706**	**2034**	**40**	**9**	**14**	**23**	**129**

VERCIK, RUDOLF
LW, RANGERS

PERSONAL: Born March 19, 1976, in Bratislava, Czechoslovakia.... 6-1/189.... Shoots left.
TRANSACTIONS/CAREER NOTES: Selected by New York Rangers in second round (second Rangers pick, 52nd overall) of NHL entry draft (June 29, 1994).

Season Team	League	REGULAR SEASON Gms.	G	A	Pts.	PIM	PLAYOFFS Gms.	G	A	Pts.	PIM
93-94—Slovan Bratislava	Slovakia	17	1	4	5	14	—	—	—	—	—

VERNER, ANDREW
G, OILERS

PERSONAL: Born November 10, 1972, in Weston, Ont.... 6-0/194.... Catches left.
TRANSACTIONS/CAREER NOTES: Selected by Edmonton Oilers in second round (second Oilers pick, 34th overall) of NHL entry draft (June 22, 1991).
HONORS: Named to OHL All-Star second team (1990-91 and 1991-92).

Season Team	League	REGULAR SEASON Gms.	Min.	W	L	T	GA	SO	Avg.	PLAYOFFS Gms.	Min.	W	L	GA	SO	Avg.
89-90—Peterborough	OHL	13	624	7	3	0	38	0	3.65	—	—	—	—	—	—	—
90-91—Peterborough	OHL	46	2523	22	14	7	148	0	3.52	3	185	0	3	15	0	4.86
91-92—Peterborough	OHL	53	3123	*34	13	6	190	1	3.65	10	539	5	5	30	0	3.34
92-93—Cape Breton	AHL	36	1974	17	10	6	126	1	3.83	—	—	—	—	—	—	—
93-94—Cape Breton	AHL	38	2261	11	17	8	175	0	4.64	1	40	0	0	4	0	6.00

VERNON, MIKE
G, RED WINGS

PERSONAL: Born February 24, 1963, in Calgary.... 5-9/170.... Catches left.
TRANSACTIONS/CAREER NOTES: Selected by Calgary Flames in third round (second Flames pick, 56th overall) of NHL entry draft (June 10, 1981).... Injured hip (March 2, 1988).... Suffered back spasms (February 1989).... Suffered back spasms (March 1990); missed 10 games. ... Lacerated forehead (October 25, 1992); missed five games.... Suffered from the flu (November 15, 1993); missed two games.... Twisted knee (December 30, 1993); missed 14 games.... Traded by Flames to Detroit Red Wings for D Steve Chiasson (June 29, 1994).
HONORS: Won WHL Most Valuable Player Trophy (1981-82 and 1982-83).... Won WHL Top Goaltender Trophy (1981-82 and 1982-83).... Won WHL Player of the Year Award (1981-82).... Named to WHL All-Star first team (1981-82 and 1982-83). ... Named to CHL All-Star second team (1983-84).... Named to THE SPORTING NEWS All-Star second team (1988-89).... Named to NHL All-Star second team (1988-89).... Played in NHL All-Star Game (1988-1991 and 1993).
RECORDS: Shares NHL single-season playoff record for most wins by a goaltender—16 (1989).
MISCELLANEOUS: Member of Stanley Cup championship team (1989).

Season Team	League	REGULAR SEASON Gms.	Min.	W	L	T	GA	SO	Avg.	PLAYOFFS Gms.	Min.	W	L	GA	SO	Avg.
80-81—Calgary	WHL	59	3154	33	17	1	198	1	3.77	22	1271	...	...	82	1	3.87
81-82—Calgary	WHL	42	2329	22	14	2	143	*3	*3.68	9	527	...	...	30	0	*3.42
—Oklahoma City	CHL	—	—	—	—	—	—	—	—	1	70	0	1	4	0	3.43
82-83—Calgary	WHL	50	2856	19	18	2	155	*3	*3.26	16	925	9	7	60	0	3.89
—Calgary	NHL	2	100	0	2	0	11	0	6.60	—	—	—	—	—	—	—
83-84—Calgary	NHL	1	11	0	1	0	4	0	21.82	—	—	—	—	—	—	—
—Colorado	CHL	*46	*2648	30	13	2	148	1	*3.35	6	347	2	4	21	0	3.63
84-85—Moncton	AHL	41	2050	10	20	4	134	0	3.92	—	—	—	—	—	—	—
85-86—Salt Lake City	IHL	10	601	...	...	‡...	34	1	3.39	—	—	—	—	—	—	—
—Moncton	AHL	6	374	3	1	2	21	0	3.37	—	—	—	—	—	—	—
—Calgary	NHL	18	921	9	3	3	52	1	3.39	*21	*1229	12	*9	*60	0	2.93
86-87—Calgary	NHL	54	2957	30	21	1	178	1	3.61	5	263	2	3	16	0	3.65
87-88—Calgary	NHL	64	3565	39	16	7	210	1	3.53	9	515	4	4	34	0	3.96
88-89—Calgary	NHL	52	2938	*37	6	5	130	0	2.65	*22	*1381	*16	5	*52	*3	2.26
89-90—Calgary	NHL	47	2795	23	14	9	146	0	3.13	6	342	2	3	19	0	3.33
90-91—Calgary	NHL	54	3121	31	19	3	172	1	3.31	7	427	3	4	21	0	2.95
91-92—Calgary	NHL	63	3640	24	30	9	217	0	3.58	—	—	—	—	—	—	—

V

Season Team	League	REGULAR SEASON								PLAYOFFS						
		Gms.	Min.	W	L	T	GA	SO	Avg.	Gms.	Min.	W	L	GA	SO	Avg.
92-93—Calgary	NHL	64	3732	29	26	9	203	2	3.26	4	150	1	1	15	0	6.00
93-94—Calgary	NHL	48	2798	26	17	5	131	3	2.81	7	466	3	4	23	0	2.96
NHL totals		467	26578	248	155	51	1454	9	3.28	81	4773	43	33	240	3	3.02

VEZINA, STEVE
G, JETS

PERSONAL: Born October 25, 1975, in St. Jean, Que. . . . 5-10/172. . . . Catches left.
TRANSACTIONS/CAREER NOTES: Selected by Winnipeg Jets in sixth round (sixth Jets pick, 143rd overall) of NHL entry draft (June 29, 1994).

Season Team	League	REGULAR SEASON								PLAYOFFS						
		Gms.	Min.	W	L	T	GA	SO	Avg.	Gms.	Min.	W	L	GA	SO	Avg.
92-93—Beauport	QMJHL	19	770	1	13	0	67	0	5.22	—	—	—	—	—	—	—
93-94—Beauport	QMJHL	46	2380	19	15	4	156	0	3.93	10	430	5	4	22	0	3.07

VIAL, DENNIS
D, SENATORS

PERSONAL: Born April 10, 1969, in Sault Ste. Marie, Ont. . . . 6-1/218. . . . Shoots left. . . . Name pronounced vee-AL.
TRANSACTIONS/CAREER NOTES: Suspended three games by OHL for spearing (October 1986). . . . Selected by New York Rangers in sixth round (fifth Rangers pick, 110th overall) of NHL entry draft (June 11, 1988). . . . Suspended indefinitely by OHL for leaving the bench to fight (March 23, 1989). . . . Traded by Rangers with C Kevin Miller and RW Jim Cummins to Detroit Red Wings for RW Joe Kocur and D Per Djoos (March 5, 1991). . . . Injured right knee and ankle (December 7, 1991); missed two games. . . . Traded by Red Wings with D Doug Crossman to Quebec Nordiques for cash (June 15, 1992). . . . Traded by Nordiques to Red Wings for cash (September 9, 1992). . . . Separated right shoulder (January 19, 1993); missed 15 games. . . . Traded by Red Wings to Tampa Bay Lightning for LW Steve Maltais (June 8, 1993). . . . Selected by Mighty Ducks of Anaheim in NHL expansion draft (June 24, 1993). . . . Selected by Ottawa Senators in Phase II of NHL expansion draft (June 25, 1993). . . . Injured left foot (November 10, 1993); missed 12 games. . . . Fractured left hand (December 21, 1993); missed 13 games. . . . Suspended one game and fined $500 by NHL for shooting a puck into opposing team's bench (March 23, 1994).

Season Team	League	REGULAR SEASON					PLAYOFFS				
		Gms.	G	A	Pts.	PIM	Gms.	G	A	Pts.	PIM
85-86—Hamilton	OHL	31	1	1	2	66	—	—	—	—	—
86-87—Hamilton	OHL	53	1	8	9	194	8	0	0	0	8
87-88—Hamilton	OHL	52	3	17	20	229	13	2	2	4	49
88-89—Niagara Falls	OHL	50	10	27	37	230	15	1	7	8	44
89-90—Flint	IHL	79	6	29	35	351	4	0	0	0	10
90-91—Binghamton	AHL	40	2	7	9	250	—	—	—	—	—
—New York Rangers	NHL	21	0	0	0	61	—	—	—	—	—
—Detroit	NHL	9	0	0	0	16	—	—	—	—	—
91-92—Detroit	NHL	27	1	0	1	72	—	—	—	—	—
—Adirondack	AHL	20	2	4	6	107	17	1	3	4	43
92-93—Detroit	NHL	9	0	1	1	20	—	—	—	—	—
—Adirondack	AHL	30	2	11	13	177	11	1	1	2	14
93-94—Ottawa	NHL	55	2	5	7	214	—	—	—	—	—
NHL totals		121	3	6	9	383					

VIITAKOSKI, VESA
LW, FLAMES

PERSONAL: Born February 13, 1971, in Lappeenranta, Finland. . . . 6-3/210. . . . Shoots left. . . . Name pronounced VEH-suh vee-tuh-KAH-skee.
TRANSACTIONS/CAREER NOTES: Selected by Calgary Flames in second round (third Flames pick, 32nd overall) of NHL entry draft (June 16, 1990). . . . Sprained knee (April 13, 1994); missed one game.

Season Team	League	REGULAR SEASON					PLAYOFFS				
		Gms.	G	A	Pts.	PIM	Gms.	G	A	Pts.	PIM
89-90—SaiPa	Finland	44	24	10	34	. . .	—	—	—	—	—
90-91—Tappara	Finland	41	17	23	40	14	—	—	—	—	—
91-92—Tappara	Finland	44	19	19	38	39	—	—	—	—	—
92-93—Tappara	Finland	48	27	27	54	28	—	—	—	—	—
93-94—Calgary	NHL	8	1	2	3	0	—	—	—	—	—
—Saint John	AHL	67	28	39	67	24	5	1	2	3	2
NHL totals		8	1	2	3	0					

VILGRAIN, CLAUDE
RW, FLYERS

PERSONAL: Born March 1, 1963, in Port-au-Prince, Haiti. . . . 6-1/205. . . . Shoots left. . . . Name pronounced VIHL-grayn.
COLLEGE: Moncton (N.B.).
TRANSACTIONS/CAREER NOTES: Selected by Detroit Red Wings in sixth round (sixth Red Wings pick, 107th overall) of NHL entry draft (June 9, 1982). . . . Signed as free agent by Vancouver Canucks (June 18, 1987). . . . Traded by Canucks to New Jersey Devils for C Tim Lenardon (March 7, 1989). . . . Suffered concussion (December 10, 1991); missed two games. . . . Injured groin (January 24, 1992); missed one game. . . . Signed as free agent by Philadelphia Flyers (August 3, 1993).

Season Team	League	REGULAR SEASON					PLAYOFFS				
		Gms.	G	A	Pts.	PIM	Gms.	G	A	Pts.	PIM
80-81—Laval	QMJHL	72	20	31	51	65	—	—	—	—	—
81-82—Laval	QMJHL	58	26	29	55	64	17	14	10	24	22
82-83—Laval	QMJHL	69	46	80	126	72	12	10	4	14	4

V

Season Team	League	REGULAR SEASON					PLAYOFFS				
		Gms.	G	A	Pts.	Pen.	Gms.	G	A	Pts.	Pen.
83-84—University of Moncton......	AUAA	20	11	20	31	8	—	—	—	—	—
84-85—University of Moncton......	AUAA	24	35	28	63	20	—	—	—	—	—
85-86—University of Moncton......	AUAA	19	17	20	37	25	—	—	—	—	—
86-87—Canadian national team ...	Int'l	78	28	42	70	38	—	—	—	—	—
87-88—Canadian national team ...	Int'l	61	21	20	41	41	—	—	—	—	—
—Canadian Olympic Team ..	Int'l	6	0	0	0	0	—	—	—	—	—
—Vancouver........................	NHL	6	1	1	2	0	—	—	—	—	—
88-89—Milwaukee......................	IHL	23	9	13	22	26	—	—	—	—	—
—Utica............................	AHL	55	23	30	53	41	5	0	2	2	2
89-90—New Jersey....................	NHL	6	1	2	3	4	4	0	0	0	0
—Utica............................	AHL	73	37	52	89	32	—	—	—	—	—
90-91—Utica............................	AHL	59	32	46	78	26	—	—	—	—	—
91-92—New Jersey....................	NHL	71	19	27	46	74	7	1	1	2	17
92-93—Cincinnati......................	IHL	57	19	26	45	22	—	—	—	—	—
—New Jersey....................	NHL	4	0	2	2	0	—	—	—	—	—
—Utica............................	AHL	22	6	8	14	4	5	0	1	1	0
93-94—Hershey.......................	AHL	76	30	53	83	45	11	1	6	7	2
—Philadelphia	NHL	2	0	0	0	0	—	—	—	—	—
NHL totals......................................		89	21	32	53	78	11	1	1	2	17

VINCENT, PAUL
C, MAPLE LEAFS

PERSONAL: Born January 4, 1975, in Utica, N.Y.... 6-4/200.... Shoots left.
HIGH SCHOOL: Cushing Academy (Ashburnham, Mass.).
TRANSACTIONS/CAREER NOTES: Selected by Toronto Maple Leafs in sixth round (fourth Maple Leafs pick, 149th overall) of NHL entry draft (June 26, 1993).

Season Team	League	REGULAR SEASON					PLAYOFFS				
		Gms.	G	A	Pts.	PIM	Gms.	G	A	Pts.	PIM
90-91—Cushing Academy............	Mass. H.S.	30	4	2	6	8	—	—	—	—	—
91-92—Cushing Academy............	Mass. H.S.	30	22	41	63	16	—	—	—	—	—
92-93—Cushing Academy............	Mass. H.S.	25	30	32	62	62	—	—	—	—	—
93-94—Seattle	WHL	66	27	26	53	57	8	1	3	4	8

VISHEAU, MARK
D, JETS

PERSONAL: Born June 27, 1973, in Burlington, Ont.... 6-4/197.... Shoots right.... Full name: Mark Andrew Visheau.... Name pronounced VEE-SHOO.
HIGH SCHOOL: Saunders Secondary (London, Ont.).
TRANSACTIONS/CAREER NOTES: Selected by Winnipeg Jets in fourth round (fourth Jets pick, 84th overall) of NHL entry draft (June 20, 1992).

Season Team	League	REGULAR SEASON					PLAYOFFS				
		Gms.	G	A	Pts.	PIM	Gms.	G	A	Pts.	PIM
89-90—Burlington Jr. B................	OHA	42	11	22	33	53	—	—	—	—	—
90-91—London	OHL	59	4	11	15	40	7	0	1	1	6
91-92—London	OHL	66	5	31	36	104	10	0	4	4	27
92-93—London	OHL	62	8	52	60	88	12	0	5	5	26
93-94—Moncton	AHL	48	4	5	9	58	—	—	—	—	—
—Winnipeg	NHL	1	0	0	0	0	—	—	—	—	—
NHL totals......................................		1	0	0	0	0					

VITOLINSH, HARIJS
C, JETS

PERSONAL: Born April 30, 1968, in Riga, U.S.S.R.... 6-3/205.... Shoots left.... Name pronounced HAIR-ihz VEE-toh-LIHNSH.
TRANSACTIONS/CAREER NOTES: Selected by Montreal Canadiens in ninth round (10th Canadiens pick, 188th overall) of NHL entry draft (June 11, 1988).... Returned to draft pool and selected by Winnipeg Jets in ninth round (12th Jets pick, 228th overall) of NHL entry draft (June 26, 1993).

Season Team	League	REGULAR SEASON					PLAYOFFS				
		Gms.	G	A	Pts.	PIM	Gms.	G	A	Pts.	PIM
86-87—Dynamo Riga.......	USSR	17	1	1	2	8	—	—	—	—	—
87-88—Dynamo Riga.......	USSR	30	3	3	6	24	—	—	—	—	—
88-89—Dynamo Riga.......	USSR	36	3	2	5	16	—	—	—	—	—
89-90—Dynamo Riga.......	USSR	45	7	6	13	18	—	—	—	—	—
90-91—Dynamo Riga.......	USSR	46	12	19	31	22	—	—	—	—	—
91-92—Riga	CIS	30	12	5	17	10	—	—	—	—	—
92-93—Chur...................	Switzerland	17	12	6	18	23	—	—	—	—	—
—Thunder Bay	Col.HL	8	6	7	13	12	—	—	—	—	—
—New Haven	AHL	7	6	3	9	4	—	—	—	—	—
93-94—Moncton	AHL	70	28	34	62	41	20	1	3	4	4
—Winnipeg	NHL	8	0	0	0	4	—	—	—	—	—
NHL totals......................................		8	0	0	0	4					

VLASAK, TOMAS
C, KINGS

PERSONAL: Born February 1, 1975, in Prague, Czechoslovakia.... 5-10/161.... Shoots right.
TRANSACTIONS/CAREER NOTES: Selected by Los Angeles Kings in fifth round (sixth Kings pick, 120th overall) of NHL entry draft (June 26, 1993).

Season Team	League	Gms.	G	A	Pts.	PIM	Gms.	G	A	Pts.	PIM
		REGULAR SEASON					PLAYOFFS				
91-92—Slavia Praha Jrs.	Czech. Jrs.	69	49	43	92	24	—	—	—	—	—
92-93—Slavia Praha	Czech Dv.II	31	17	6	23	6	—	—	—	—	—
93-94—Chemopetrol Litvinov	Czech Rep.	41	16	11	27	...	4	0	1	1	0

VOLEK, DAVID
LW/RW, ISLANDERS

PERSONAL: Born August 16, 1966, in Prague, Czechoslovakia.... 6-0/190.... Shoots right....
Name pronounced VAH-lehk.
TRANSACTIONS/CAREER NOTES: Selected by New York Islanders in 10th round (11th Islanders pick, 208th overall) of NHL entry draft (June 9, 1984).... Suspended six months by International Ice Hockey Federation for steroid use (August 1988).... Separated right shoulder (October 1988).... Injured back (November 16, 1991); missed three games.... Strained lower back (February 17, 1992); missed one game.... Pulled rib cage muscles (March 7, 1992); missed two games.... Suffered from the flu (December 13, 1992); missed two games.... Suffered from sore back (1993); missed remainder of season.... Strained hip flexor (December 3, 1993); missed one game.... Suffered herniated disc (January 14, 1994); missed remainder of season.
HONORS: Named to NHL All-Rookie team (1988-89).

Season Team	League	Gms.	G	A	Pts.	PIM	Gms.	G	A	Pts.	PIM
		REGULAR SEASON					PLAYOFFS				
86-87—Sparta Prague.................	Czech.	39	27	25	*52	...	—	—	—	—	—
87-88—Sparta Prague.................	Czech.	30	18	12	30	...	—	—	—	—	—
—Czech. Olympic Team	Int'l	7	1	2	3	2	—	—	—	—	—
88-89—New York Islanders..........	NHL	77	25	34	59	24	—	—	—	—	—
89-90—New York Islanders..........	NHL	80	17	22	39	41	5	1	4	5	0
90-91—New York Islanders..........	NHL	77	22	34	56	57	—	—	—	—	—
91-92—New York Islanders..........	NHL	74	18	42	60	35	—	—	—	—	—
92-93—New York Islanders..........	NHL	56	8	13	21	34	10	4	1	5	2
93-94—New York Islanders..........	NHL	32	5	9	14	10	—	—	—	—	—
NHL totals......................		396	95	154	249	201	15	5	5	10	2

VOLKOV, MIKHAIL
RW, SABRES

PERSONAL: Born March 9, 1972, in Voronezh, U.S.S.R.... 5-10/174.... Shoots left....
Name pronounced VOHL-kahf.
TRANSACTIONS/CAREER NOTES: Selected by the Buffalo Sabres in 11th round (12th Sabres pick, 233rd overall) of NHL entry draft (June 22, 1991).

Season Team	League	Gms.	G	A	Pts.	PIM	Gms.	G	A	Pts.	PIM
		REGULAR SEASON					PLAYOFFS				
89-90—Soviet Wings	USSR	24	0	2	2	4	—	—	—	—	—
90-91—Soviet Wings	USSR	40	8	4	12	8	—	—	—	—	—
91-92—Soviet Wings	CIS	37	3	6	9	16	—	—	—	—	—
92-93—Soviet Wings	CIS	33	9	6	15	11	5	0	1	1	2
93-94—Rochester	AHL	62	12	26	38	28	4	0	2	2	2

VOPAT, JAN
D, WHALERS

PERSONAL: Born March 22, 1973, in Most, Czechoslovakia.... 6-0/198.... Shoots left.
TRANSACTIONS/CAREER NOTES: Selected by Hartford Whalers in third round (third Whalers pick, 57th overall) of NHL entry draft (June 20, 1992).

Season Team	League	Gms.	G	A	Pts.	PIM	Gms.	G	A	Pts.	PIM
		REGULAR SEASON					PLAYOFFS				
90-91—CHZ Litvinov	Czech.	25	1	4	5	4	—	—	—	—	—
91-92—Chemopetrol Litvinov	Czech.	46	4	2	6	6	—	—	—	—	—
92-93—Chemopetrol Litvinov	Czech.	45	12	10	22	...	—	—	—	—	—
93-94—Chemopetrol Litvinov	Czech. Rep.	41	9	19	28	...	4	1	1	2	...
—Czech Republic Olympic ...	Int'l	8	0	1	1	8	—	—	—	—	—

VUJTEK, VLADIMIR
C, OILERS

PERSONAL: Born February 17, 1972, in Ostrava, Severomoravsky, Czechoslovakia. ... 6-1/190.... Shoots left.... Name pronounced VYOO-tehk.
TRANSACTIONS/CAREER NOTES: Selected by Montreal Canadiens in fourth round (fifth Canadiens pick, 73rd overall) of NHL entry draft (June 22, 1991).... Traded by Canadiens with LW Shayne Corson and C Brent Gilchrist to Edmonton Oilers for LW Vincent Damphousse and fourth-round pick (D Adam Wiesel) in 1993 draft (August 27, 1992).... Suffered charley horse (October 6, 1992); missed eight games.... Suspended by Oilers after failing to report to assigned team (January 4, 1993).... Strained lower back (March 17, 1993); missed five games.... Injured shoulder (January 11, 1994); missed seven games.... Injured shoulder and underwent surgery (February 14, 1994); missed remainder of season.
HONORS: Named to WHL (West) All-Star first team (1991-92).

Season Team	League	Gms.	G	A	Pts.	PIM	Gms.	G	A	Pts.	PIM
		REGULAR SEASON					PLAYOFFS				
90-91—Tri-City	WHL	37	26	18	44	25	—	—	—	—	—
91-92—Tri-City	WHL	53	41	61	102	114	—	—	—	—	—
—Montreal...........................	NHL	2	0	0	0	0	—	—	—	—	—
92-93—Edmonton	NHL	30	1	10	11	8	—	—	—	—	—
—Cape Breton	AHL	20	10	9	19	14	1	0	0	0	0
93-94—Edmonton	NHL	40	4	15	19	14	—	—	—	—	—
NHL totals......................		72	5	25	30	22					

VUKOTA, MICK
RW, ISLANDERS

PERSONAL: Born September 14, 1966, in Saskatoon, Sask.... 6-2/215.... Shoots right. ...
Name pronounced vuh-KOH-tuh.
TRANSACTIONS/CAREER NOTES: Signed as free agent by New York Islanders (September 1987). ... Suspended six games by AHL for returning from locker room to fight (November 20,

V

1987).... Suffered sore back (February 1990).... Separated left shoulder (March 18, 1990).... Suspended 10 games by NHL for fighting (April 5, 1990); missed final four games of 1989-90 season and first six games of 1990-91 season.... Injured shoulder; missed first two games of 1992-93 season.... Bruised left hand (October 26, 1993); missed two games.... Suspended 10 games and fined $10,000 by NHL for leaving bench to fight (January 7, 1994).... Suspended two games without pay and fined $500 by NHL for improper conduct in playoff game (May 17, 1994).

Season Team	League	REGULAR SEASON					PLAYOFFS				
		Gms.	G	A	Pts.	PIM	Gms.	G	A	Pts.	PIM
83-84—Winnipeg	WHL	3	1	1	2	10	—	—	—	—	—
84-85—Kelowna Wings	WHL	66	10	6	16	247	—	—	—	—	—
85-86—Spokane	WHL	64	19	14	33	369	9	6	4	10	68
86-87—Spokane	WHL	61	25	28	53	*337	4	0	0	0	40
87-88—New York Islanders	NHL	17	1	0	1	82	2	0	0	0	23
—Springfield	AHL	52	7	9	16	372	—	—	—	—	—
88-89—Springfield	AHL	3	1	0	1	33	—	—	—	—	—
—New York Islanders	NHL	48	2	2	4	237	—	—	—	—	—
89-90—New York Islanders	NHL	76	4	8	12	290	1	0	0	0	17
90-91—Capital District	AHL	2	0	0	0	9	—	—	—	—	—
—New York Islanders	NHL	60	2	4	6	238	—	—	—	—	—
91-92—New York Islanders	NHL	74	0	6	6	293	—	—	—	—	—
92-93—New York Islanders	NHL	74	2	5	7	216	15	0	0	0	16
93-94—New York Islanders	NHL	72	3	1	4	237	4	0	0	0	17
NHL totals		421	14	26	40	1593	22	0	0	0	73

VYBORNY, DAVID
C, OILERS

PERSONAL: Born January 22, 1975, in Jihlava, Czechoslovakia.... 5-10/174.... Shoots left.... Name pronounced vigh-BOHR-nee.
TRANSACTIONS/CAREER NOTES: Selected by Edmonton Oilers in second round (third Oilers pick, 33rd overall) of NHL entry draft (June 26, 1993).
HONORS: Named Czechoslovakian League Rookie of the Year (1991-92).

Season Team	League	REGULAR SEASON					PLAYOFFS				
		Gms.	G	A	Pts.	PIM	Gms.	G	A	Pts.	PIM
90-91—Sparta Prague	Czech.	3	0	0	0	0	—	—	—	—	—
91-92—Sparta Prague	Czech.	32	6	9	15	2	—	—	—	—	—
92-93—Sparta Prague	Czech.	52	20	24	44	...	—	—	—	—	—
93-94—Sparta Prague	Czech Rep.	44	15	20	35	...	7	4	7	11	0

WAITE, JIMMY
G, SHARKS

PERSONAL: Born April 15, 1969, in Sherbrooke, Que.... 6-1/180.... Catches left.... Name pronounced WAYT.
TRANSACTIONS/CAREER NOTES: Selected by Chicago Blackhawks as underage junior in first round (first Blackhawks pick, eighth overall) of NHL entry draft (June 13, 1987).... Broke collarbone (December 6, 1988).... Sprained ankle (October 12, 1991); missed one game.... Loaned to Hershey Bears for part of 1991-92 season.... Traded by Blackhawks to San Jose Sharks for future considerations (June 18, 1993); Sharks sent D Neil Wilkinson to Blackhawks to complete deal (July 9, 1993).... Sprained knee (January 11, 1994); missed two games.... Underwent arthroscopic knee surgery (March 7, 1994); missed eight games.
HONORS: Won Raymond Lagace Trophy (1986-87).... Named to QMJHL All-Star second team (1986-87).... Won James Norris Memorial Trophy (1989-90).... Named to IHL All-Star first team (1989-90).

Season Team	League	REGULAR SEASON								PLAYOFFS						
		Gms.	Min.	W	L	T	GA	SO	Avg.	Gms.	Min.	W	L	GA	SO	Avg.
86-87—Chicoutimi	QMJHL	50	2569	23	17	3	209	†2	4.88	11	576	4	6	54	*1	5.63
87-88—Chicoutimi	QMJHL	36	2000	17	16	1	150	0	4.50	4	222	1	2	17	0	4.59
88-89—Chicago	NHL	11	494	0	7	1	43	0	5.22	—	—	—	—	—	—	—
—Saginaw	IHL	5	304	3	1	‡0	10	0	1.97	—	—	—	—	—	—	—
89-90—Indianapolis	IHL	54	*3207	34	14	‡5	135	*5	*2.53	†10	*602	9	1	19	†1	*1.89
—Chicago	NHL	4	183	2	0	0	14	0	4.59	—	—	—	—	—	—	—
90-91—Indianapolis	IHL	49	2888	26	18	‡4	167	3	3.47	6	369	2	4	20	0	3.25
—Chicago	NHL	1	60	1	0	0	2	0	2.00	—	—	—	—	—	—	—
91-92—Chicago	NHL	17	877	4	7	4	54	0	3.69	—	—	—	—	—	—	—
—Indianapolis	IHL	13	702	4	7	‡1	53	0	4.53	—	—	—	—	—	—	—
—Hershey	AHL	11	631	6	4	1	44	0	4.18	6	360	2	4	19	0	3.17
92-93—Chicago	NHL	20	996	6	7	1	49	2	2.95	—	—	—	—	—	—	—
93-94—San Jose	NHL	15	697	3	7	0	50	0	4.30	2	40	0	0	3	0	4.50
NHL totals		68	3307	16	28	6	212	2	3.85	2	40	0	0	3	0	4.50

WAKALUK, DARCY
G, STARS

PERSONAL: Born March 14, 1966, in Pincher Creek, Alta.... 5-11/180.... Catches left.... Name pronounced WAHK-uh-LUHK.
TRANSACTIONS/CAREER NOTES: Selected by Buffalo Sabres as underage junior in seventh round (seventh Sabres pick, 144th overall) of NHL entry draft (June 9, 1984).... Traded by Sabres to Minnesota North Stars for eighth-round pick in 1991 draft (D Jiri Kuntos) and future considerations (May 26, 1991).... Hyperextended knee (February 17, 1993); missed two games.... North Stars franchise moved from Minnesota to Dallas and renamed Stars for 1993-94 season.
HONORS: Shared Harry (Hap) Holmes Memorial Trophy with David Littman (1990-91).

VW

Season	Team	League	Gms.	Min.	W	L	T	GA	SO	Avg.	Gms.	Min.	W	L	GA	SO	Avg.
83-84—Kelowna Wings	WHL	31	1555	...	...	...	163	0	6.29	—	—	—	—	—	—	—
84-85—Kelowna Wings	WHL	54	3094	19	30	4	244	0	4.73	5	282	1	4	22	0	4.68
85-86—Spokane	WHL	47	2562	21	22	1	224	1	5.25	7	419	3	4	37	0	5.30
86-87—Rochester	AHL	11	545	2	2	0	26	0	2.86	5	141	2	0	11	0	4.68
87-88—Rochester	AHL	55	2763	27	16	3	159	0	3.45	6	328	3	3	22	0	4.02
88-89—Buffalo	NHL	6	214	1	3	0	15	0	4.21	—	—	—	—	—	—	—
—Rochester	AHL	33	1566	11	14	0	97	1	3.72	—	—	—	—	—	—	—
89-90—Rochester	AHL	56	3095	31	16	4	173	2	3.35	†17	*1001	10	6	50	0	*3.00
90-91—Buffalo	NHL	16	630	4	5	3	35	0	3.33	2	37	0	1	2	0	3.24
—Rochester	AHL	26	1363	10	10	3	68	*4	*2.99	9	544	6	3	30	0	3.31
91-92—Minnesota	NHL	36	1905	13	19	1	104	1	3.28	—	—	—	—	—	—	—
—Kalamazoo	IHL	1	60	1	0	‡0	7	0	7.00	—	—	—	—	—	—	—
92-93—Minnesota	NHL	29	1596	10	12	5	97	1	3.65	—	—	—	—	—	—	—
93-94—Dallas	NHL	36	2000	18	9	6	88	3	2.64	5	307	4	1	15	0	2.93
NHL totals		123	6345	46	48	15	339	5	3.21	7	344	4	2	17	0	2.97

WALKER, SCOTT
D, CANUCKS

PERSONAL: Born July 19, 1973, in Montreal.... 5-9/170.... Shoots right.
TRANSACTIONS/CAREER NOTES: Selected by Vancouver Canucks in fifth round (fourth Canucks pick, 124th overall) of NHL entry draft (June 26, 1993).
HONORS: Named to OHL All-Star second team (1992-93).

			REGULAR SEASON					PLAYOFFS				
Season	Team	League	Gms.	G	A	Pts.	PIM	Gms.	G	A	Pts.	PIM
89-90—Kitchener-Cambridge Jr.B	OHA	33	7	27	34	91	—	—	—	—	—
90-91—Cambridge Jr. B	OHA	45	10	27	37	241	—	—	—	—	—
91-92—Owen Sound	OHL	53	7	31	38	128	5	0	7	7	8
92-93—Owen Sound	OHL	57	23	68	91	110	8	1	5	6	16
—Canadian national team	Int'l	2	3	0	3	0	—	—	—	—	—
93-94—Hamilton	AHL	77	10	29	39	272	4	0	1	1	25

WALZ, WES
C, FLAMES

PERSONAL: Born May 15, 1970, in Calgary.... 5-10/185.... Shoots right.... Name pronounced WAHLS.
TRANSACTIONS/CAREER NOTES: Selected by Boston Bruins in third round (third Bruins pick, 57th overall) of NHL entry draft (June 17, 1989).... Traded by Bruins with D Garry Galley and future considerations to Philadelphia Flyers for D Gord Murphy, RW Brian Dobbin and third-round pick (LW Sergei Zholtok) in 1992 draft (January 2, 1992).... Signed as free agent by Calgary Flames (August 31, 1993).
HONORS: Won Jim Piggott Memorial Trophy (1988-89).... Won WHL Player of the Year Award (1989-90).... Named to WHL (East) All-Star first team (1989-90).

			REGULAR SEASON					PLAYOFFS				
Season	Team	League	Gms.	G	A	Pts.	PIM	Gms.	G	A	Pts.	PIM
87-88—Prince Albert	WHL	1	1	1	2	0	—	—	—	—	—
88-89—Lethbridge	WHL	63	29	75	104	32	8	1	5	6	6
89-90—Boston	NHL	2	1	1	2	0	—	—	—	—	—
—Lethbridge	WHL	56	54	86	140	69	19	13	*24	†37	33
90-91—Maine	AHL	20	8	12	20	19	2	0	0	0	21
—Boston	NHL	56	8	8	16	32	2	0	0	0	0
91-92—Boston	NHL	15	0	3	3	12	—	—	—	—	—
—Maine	AHL	21	13	11	24	38	—	—	—	—	—
—Hershey	AHL	41	13	28	41	37	6	1	2	3	0
—Philadelphia	NHL	2	1	0	1	0	—	—	—	—	—
92-93—Hershey	AHL	78	35	45	80	106	—	—	—	—	—
93-94—Calgary	NHL	53	11	27	38	16	6	3	0	3	2
—Saint John	AHL	15	6	6	12	14	—	—	—	—	—
NHL totals		128	21	39	60	60	8	3	0	3	2

WARD, AARON
D, RED WINGS

PERSONAL: Born January 17, 1973, in Windsor, Ont.... 6-2/200.... Shoots right.... Full name: Aaron Christian Ward.
COLLEGE: Michigan.
TRANSACTIONS/CAREER NOTES: Selected by Winnipeg Jets in first round (first Jets pick, fifth overall) of NHL entry draft (June 22, 1991).... Traded by Jets with fourth-round pick in 1993 draft (D John Jakopin) and future considerations to Detroit Red Wings for RW Paul Ysebaert (June 11, 1993); Jets sent RW Alan Kerr to Red Wings to complete deal (June 18, 1993).
HONORS: Named to CCHA All-Rookie Team (1990-91).... Named to CCHA All-Tournament Team (1990-91).

			REGULAR SEASON					PLAYOFFS				
Season	Team	League	Gms.	G	A	Pts.	PIM	Gms.	G	A	Pts.	PIM
88-89—Nepean	COJHL	56	2	17	19	44	—	—	—	—	—
89-90—Nepean	COJHL	52	6	33	39	85	—	—	—	—	—
90-91—University of Michigan	CCHA	46	8	11	19	126	—	—	—	—	—
91-92—University of Michigan	CCHA	42	7	12	19	64	—	—	—	—	—
92-93—University of Michigan	CCHA	30	5	8	13	73	—	—	—	—	—
—Canadian national team	Int'l	4	0	0	0	8	—	—	—	—	—

W

Season Team	League	REGULAR SEASON					PLAYOFFS				
		Gms.	G	A	Pts.	Pen.	Gms.	G	A	Pts.	Pen.
93-94—Detroit	NHL	5	1	0	1	4	—	—	—	—	—
—Adirondack	AHL	58	4	12	16	87	9	2	6	8	6
NHL totals		5	1	0	1	4					

WARD, DIXON
RW. KINGS

PERSONAL: Born September 23, 1968, in Edmonton.... 6-0/195.... Shoots right.
COLLEGE: North Dakota.
TRANSACTIONS/CAREER NOTES: Selected by Vancouver Canucks in seventh round (sixth Canucks pick, 128th overall) of NHL entry draft (June 11, 1988).... Separated left shoulder (December 1990).... Sprained ankle (March 14, 1993); missed four games.... Suspended three games and fined $500 by NHL for checking from behind (October 15, 1993).... Traded by Canucks with future considerations to Los Angeles Kings for C Jimmy Carson (January 8, 1994).
HONORS: Named to WCHA All-Star second team (1990-91 and 1991-92).

Season Team	League	REGULAR SEASON					PLAYOFFS				
		Gms.	G	A	Pts.	PIM	Gms.	G	A	Pts.	PIM
86-87—Red Deer	AJHL	59	46	40	86	153	—	—	—	—	—
87-88—Red Deer	AJHL	51	60	71	131	167	—	—	—	—	—
88-89—Univ. of North Dakota	WCHA	37	8	9	17	26	—	—	—	—	—
89-90—Univ. of North Dakota	WCHA	45	35	34	69	44	—	—	—	—	—
90-91—Univ. of North Dakota	WCHA	43	34	35	69	84	—	—	—	—	—
91-92—Univ. of North Dakota	WCHA	38	33	31	64	90	—	—	—	—	—
92-93—Vancouver	NHL	70	22	30	52	82	9	2	3	5	0
93-94—Vancouver	NHL	33	6	1	7	37	—	—	—	—	—
—Los Angeles	NHL	34	6	2	8	45	—	—	—	—	—
NHL totals		137	34	33	67	164	9	2	3	5	0

WARD, ED
RW. NORDIQUES

PERSONAL: Born November 10, 1969, in Edmonton.... 6-3/205.... Shoots right.... Full name: Edward John Ward.
COLLEGE: Northern Michigan.
TRANSACTIONS/CAREER NOTES: Tore knee cartilage (August 1987).... Selected by Quebec Nordiques in sixth round (seventh Nordiques pick, 108th overall) of NHL entry draft (June 11, 1988).

Season Team	League	REGULAR SEASON					PLAYOFFS				
		Gms.	G	A	Pts.	PIM	Gms.	G	A	Pts.	PIM
86-87—Sherwood Park	AJHL	60	18	28	46	272	—	—	—	—	—
87-88—Northern Michigan Univ.	WCHA	25	0	2	2	40	—	—	—	—	—
88-89—Northern Michigan Univ.	WCHA	42	5	15	20	36	—	—	—	—	—
89-90—Northern Michigan Univ.	WCHA	39	5	11	16	77	—	—	—	—	—
90-91—Northern Michigan Univ.	WCHA	46	13	18	31	109	—	—	—	—	—
91-92—Halifax	AHL	51	7	11	18	65	—	—	—	—	—
—Greensboro	ECHL	12	4	8	12	21	—	—	—	—	—
92-93—Halifax	AHL	70	13	19	32	56	—	—	—	—	—
93-94—Cornwall	AHL	60	12	30	42	65	12	1	3	4	14
—Quebec	NHL	7	1	0	1	5	—	—	—	—	—
NHL totals		7	1	0	1	5					

WARRENER, RHETT
D. PANTHERS

PERSONAL: Born January 27, 1976, in Shaunavon, Sask.... 6-1/209.... Shoots right.
TRANSACTIONS/CAREER NOTES: Selected by Florida Panthers in second round (second Panthers pick, 27th overall) of NHL entry draft (June 28, 1994).

Season Team	League	REGULAR SEASON					PLAYOFFS				
		Gms.	G	A	Pts.	PIM	Gms.	G	A	Pts.	PIM
91-92—Saskatoon	WHL	2	0	0	0	0	—	—	—	—	—
92-93—Saskatoon	WHL	68	2	17	19	100	9	0	0	0	14
93-94—Saskatoon	WHL	61	7	19	26	131	16	0	5	5	33

WARRINER, TODD
LW/C. MAPLE LEAFS

PERSONAL: Born January 3, 1974, in Chatham, Ont.... 6-1/182.... Shoots left.
HIGH SCHOOL: Herman E. Fawcett (Brantford, Ont.).
TRANSACTIONS/CAREER NOTES: Selected by Quebec Nordiques in first round (first Nordiques pick, fourth overall) of NHL entry draft (June 20, 1992).... Traded by Nordiques with C Mats Sundin, D Garth Butcher and first-round pick (traded to Washington Capitals who selected D Nolan Baumgartner) in 1994 draft to Toronto Maple Leafs for LW Wendel Clark, D Sylvain Lefebvre, RW Landon Wilson and first-round pick (D Jeffrey Kealty) in 1994 draft (June 28, 1994).
HONORS: Won Can.HL Top Draft Prospect Award (1991-92).... Won OHL Top Draft Prospect Award (1991-92).... Named to Can.HL All-Star second team (1991-92).... Named to OHL All-Star first team (1991-92).
MISCELLANEOUS: Member of silver-medal-winning Canadian Olympic team (1994).

Season Team	League	REGULAR SEASON					PLAYOFFS				
		Gms.	G	A	Pts.	PIM	Gms.	G	A	Pts.	PIM
88-89—Blenheim Jr. C	OHA	10	1	4	5	0	—	—	—	—	—
89-90—Chatham Jr. B	OHA	40	24	21	45	12	—	—	—	—	—
90-91—Windsor	OHL	57	36	28	64	26	11	6	5	11	12

Season	Team	League	REGULAR SEASON Gms.	G	A	Pts.	Pen.	PLAYOFFS Gms.	G	A	Pts.	Pen.
91-92—Windsor	OHL	50	41	42	83	66	7	5	4	9	6
92-93—Windsor	OHL	23	13	21	34	29	—	—	—	—	—
—Kitchener	OHL	32	19	24	43	35	7	5	14	19	14
93-94—Canadian national team	Int'l	54	12	21	33	33	—	—	—	—	—
—Canadian Olympic Team	Int'l	4	1	1	2	0	—	—	—	—	—
—Kitchener	OHL	—	—	—	—	—	1	0	1	1	0
—Cornwall	AHL	—	—	—	—	—	10	1	4	5	4

WASHBURN, STEVE
C, PANTHERS

PERSONAL: Born April 10, 1975, in Ottawa.... 6-1/178.... Shoots left.
TRANSACTIONS/CAREER NOTES: Selected by Florida Panthers in third round (fifth Panthers pick, 78th overall) of NHL entry draft (June 26, 1993).

Season	Team	League	REGULAR SEASON Gms.	G	A	Pts.	PIM	PLAYOFFS Gms.	G	A	Pts.	PIM
90-91—Gloucester	OPJHL	56	21	30	51	47	—	—	—	—	—
91-92—Ottawa	OHL	59	5	17	22	10	11	2	3	5	4
92-93—Ottawa	OHL	66	20	38	58	54	—	—	—	—	—
93-94—Ottawa	OHL	65	30	50	80	88	17	7	16	23	10

WATT, MIKE
LW/C, OILERS

PERSONAL: Born March 31, 1976, in Seaforth, Ont.... 6-2/210.... Shoots left.
TRANSACTIONS/CAREER NOTES: Selected by Edmonton Oilers in second round (third Oilers pick, 32nd overall) of NHL entry draft (June 28, 1994).

Season	Team	League	REGULAR SEASON Gms.	G	A	Pts.	PIM	PLAYOFFS Gms.	G	A	Pts.	PIM
91-92—Stratford Jr. B	OHA	46	5	26	31	...	—	—	—	—	—
92-93—Stratford Jr. B	OHA	45	20	35	55	100	—	—	—	—	—
93-94—Stratford Jr. B	OHA	48	34	34	68	165	—	—	—	—	—

WATTERS, TIMOTHY
D, KINGS

PERSONAL: Born July 25, 1959, in Kamloops, B.C.... 5-11/185.... Shoots left. ... Full name: Timothy John Watters.
COLLEGE: Michigan Tech.
TRANSACTIONS/CAREER NOTES: Selected by Winnipeg Jets in sixth round (sixth Jets pick, 124th overall) of NHL draft (August 9, 1979).... Pulled hamstring (October 1983).... Broke wrist (December 1984).... Suffered back spasms (February 1986).... Strained knee (December 1987).... Signed as free agent by Los Angeles Kings (July 1988).... Bruised calf (March 1989).... Bruised ankle (December 23, 1989); missed nine games.... Bruised ankle (April 1990).... Bruised ribs (October 14, 1990); missed six games.... Twisted right knee (January 12, 1991).... Injured ankle (October 28, 1991); missed 14 games.... Injured ankle (December 1991).
HONORS: Named to NCAA All-America West team (1980-81).... Named to NCAA All-Tournament team (1980-81).... Named to WCHA All-Star first team (1980-81).

Season	Team	League	REGULAR SEASON Gms.	G	A	Pts.	PIM	PLAYOFFS Gms.	G	A	Pts.	PIM
76-77—Kamloops	BCJHL	60	10	38	48	...	—	—	—	—	—
77-78—Michigan Tech	WCHA	37	1	15	16	47	—	—	—	—	—
78-79—Michigan Tech	WCHA	31	6	21	27	48	—	—	—	—	—
79-80—Canadian national team	Int'l	56	8	21	29	43	—	—	—	—	—
—Canadian Olympic Team	Int'l	6	1	1	2	0	—	—	—	—	—
80-81—Michigan Tech	WCHA	43	12	38	50	36	—	—	—	—	—
81-82—Tulsa	CHL	5	1	2	3	0	—	—	—	—	—
—Winnipeg	NHL	69	2	22	24	97	4	0	1	1	8
82-83—Winnipeg	NHL	77	5	18	23	98	3	0	0	0	2
83-84—Winnipeg	NHL	74	3	20	23	169	3	1	0	1	2
84-85—Winnipeg	NHL	63	2	20	22	74	8	0	1	1	16
85-86—Winnipeg	NHL	56	6	8	14	97	—	—	—	—	—
86-87—Winnipeg	NHL	63	3	13	16	119	10	0	0	0	21
87-88—Winnipeg	NHL	36	0	0	0	106	4	0	0	0	4
—Canadian national team	Int'l	2	0	2	2	0	—	—	—	—	—
—Canadian Olympic Team	Int'l	8	0	1	1	2	—	—	—	—	—
88-89—Los Angeles	NHL	76	3	18	21	168	11	0	1	1	6
89-90—Los Angeles	NHL	62	1	10	11	92	4	0	0	0	6
90-91—Los Angeles	NHL	45	0	4	4	92	7	0	0	0	12
91-92—Los Angeles	NHL	37	0	7	7	92	6	0	0	0	8
—Phoenix	IHL	5	0	3	3	6	—	—	—	—	—
92-93—Phoenix	IHL	31	3	3	6	43	—	—	—	—	—
—Los Angeles	NHL	22	0	2	2	18	22	0	2	2	30
93-94—Los Angeles	NHL	60	1	9	10	67	—	—	—	—	—
NHL totals			740	26	151	177	1289	82	1	5	6	115

WEEKES, KEVIN
G, PANTHERS

PERSONAL: Born April 4, 1975, in Toronto.... 6-0/158.... Catches left. ... Name pronounced WEEKS.
HIGH SCHOOL: West Hill (Ont.) Secondary.
TRANSACTIONS/CAREER NOTES: Selected by Florida Panthers in second round (second Panthers pick, 41st overall) of NHL entry draft (June 26, 1993).

W

Season Team	League	Gms.	Min.	REGULAR SEASON W	L	T	GA	SO	Avg.	PLAYOFFS Gms.	Min.	W	L	GA	SO	Avg.
91-92—St. Michaels Tier II	Jr. A	2	127	...	...	...	11	0	5.20	—	—	—	—	—	—	—
92-93—Owen Sound	OHL	29	1645	9	12	5	143	0	5.22	1	26	0	0	5	0	11.54
93-94—Owen Sound	OHL	34	1974	13	19	1	158	0	4.80	—	—	—	—	—	—	—

WEIGHT, DOUG
C, OILERS

PERSONAL: Born January 21, 1971, in Warren, Mich. . . . 5-11/191. . . . Shoots left. . . . Name pronounced WAYT.
COLLEGE: Lake Superior State (Mich.).
TRANSACTIONS/CAREER NOTES: Selected by New York Rangers in second round (second Rangers pick, 34th overall) of NHL entry draft (June 16, 1990). . . . Sprained elbow (October 14, 1991); missed three games. . . . Damaged ligaments (January 11, 1991). . . . Suspended four off-days and fined $500 by NHL for cross-checking (November 5, 1992). . . . Traded by Rangers to Edmonton Oilers for LW Esa Tikkanen (March 17, 1993).
HONORS: Named to CCHA All-Rookie team (1989-90). . . . Named to NCAA All-America West second team (1990-91). . . . Named to CCHA All-Star first team (1990-91).

Season Team	League	REGULAR SEASON Gms.	G	A	Pts.	PIM	PLAYOFFS Gms.	G	A	Pts.	PIM
88-89—Bloomfield	NAJHL	34	26	53	79	105	—	—	—	—	—
89-90—Lake Superior State	CCHA	46	21	48	69	44	—	—	—	—	—
90-91—Lake Superior State	CCHA	42	29	46	75	86	—	—	—	—	—
—New York Rangers	NHL	—	—	—	—	—	1	0	0	0	0
91-92—New York Rangers	NHL	53	8	22	30	23	7	2	2	4	0
—Binghamton	AHL	9	3	14	17	2	4	1	4	5	6
92-93—New York Rangers	NHL	65	15	25	40	55	—	—	—	—	—
—Edmonton	NHL	13	2	6	8	10	—	—	—	—	—
93-94—Edmonton	NHL	84	24	50	74	47	—	—	—	—	—
NHL totals		215	49	103	152	135	8	2	2	4	0

WEINRICH, ERIC
D, BLACKHAWKS

PERSONAL: Born December 19, 1966, in Roanoke, Va. . . . 6-0/210. . . . Shoots left. . . . Full name: Eric John Weinrich. . . . Name pronounced WIGHN-rihk.
HIGH SCHOOL: North Yarmouth (Maine) Academy.
COLLEGE: Maine.
TRANSACTIONS/CAREER NOTES: Dislocated shoulder (December 1984). . . . Selected by New Jersey Devils in second round (third Devils pick, 32nd overall) of NHL entry draft (June 15, 1985). . . . Traded by Devils with G Sean Burke to Hartford Whalers for RW Bobby Holik, second-round pick in 1993 draft (LW Jay Pandolfo) and future considerations (August 28, 1992). . . . Suffered concussion (November 25, 1992); missed two games. . . . Sprained knee (September 22, 1993); missed five games. . . . Signed as free agent by Hartford Whalers (September 25, 1993). . . . Injured right knee (October 5, 1993); missed five games. . . . Traded with LW Patrick Poulin by Whalers to the Chicago Blackhawks for RW Steve Larmer and D Bryan Marchment (November 2, 1993). . . . Broke jaw (February 24, 1994); missed 17 games.
HONORS: Named to NCAA All-America East second team (1986-87). . . . Named to Hockey East All-Star first team (1986-87). . . . Won Eddie Shore Plaque (1989-90). . . . Named to AHL All-Star first team (1989-90). . . . Named to NHL All-Rookie team (1990-91).

Season Team	League	REGULAR SEASON Gms.	G	A	Pts.	PIM	PLAYOFFS Gms.	G	A	Pts.	PIM
83-84—North Yarmouth Acad.	Maine H.S.	17	23	33	56	...	—	—	—	—	—
84-85—North Yarmouth Acad.	Maine H.S.	20	6	21	27	...	—	—	—	—	—
85-86—University of Maine	Hockey East	34	0	15	15	26	—	—	—	—	—
86-87—University of Maine	Hockey East	41	12	32	44	59	—	—	—	—	—
87-88—University of Maine	Hockey East	8	4	7	11	22	—	—	—	—	—
—U.S. national team	Int'l	39	3	9	12	24	—	—	—	—	—
—U.S. Olympic Team	Int'l	3	0	0	0	24	—	—	—	—	—
88-89—Utica	AHL	80	17	27	44	70	5	0	1	1	8
—New Jersey	NHL	2	0	0	0	0	—	—	—	—	—
89-90—Utica	AHL	57	12	48	60	38	—	—	—	—	—
—New Jersey	NHL	19	2	7	9	11	6	1	3	4	17
90-91—New Jersey	NHL	76	4	34	38	48	7	1	2	3	6
91-92—New Jersey	NHL	76	7	25	32	55	7	0	2	2	4
92-93—Hartford	NHL	79	7	29	36	76	—	—	—	—	—
93-94—Hartford	NHL	8	1	1	2	2	—	—	—	—	—
—Chicago	NHL	54	3	23	26	31	6	0	2	2	6
NHL totals		314	24	119	143	223	26	2	9	11	33

WELLS, CHRIS
C, PENGUINS

PERSONAL: Born November 12, 1975, in Calgary. . . . 6-6/215. . . . Shoots left.
HIGH SCHOOL: Meadowdale (Lynwood, Wash.).
TRANSACTIONS/CAREER NOTES: Selected by Pittsburgh Penguins in first round (first Penguins pick, 24th overall) of NHL entry draft (June 28, 1994).

Season Team	League	REGULAR SEASON Gms.	G	A	Pts.	PIM	PLAYOFFS Gms.	G	A	Pts.	PIM
91-92—Seattle	WHL	64	13	8	21	70	11	0	0	0	15
92-93—Seattle	WHL	63	18	37	55	111	5	2	3	5	4
93-94—Seattle	WHL	69	30	44	74	150	9	6	5	11	23

W

WELLS, JAY
D, RANGERS

PERSONAL: Born May 18, 1959, in Paris, Ont.... 6-1/210.... Shoots left.... Full name: Gordon Jay Wells.

TRANSACTIONS/CAREER NOTES: Selected by Los Angeles Kings in first round (first Kings pick, 16th overall) of NHL entry draft (August 9, 1979).... Broke right hand in team practice (October 16, 1981).... Tore medial collateral ligament in right knee (December 14, 1982).... Sprained ankle (December 1983).... Struck in eye during team practice (February 1987).... Strained lower back (November 1987).... Traded by Kings to Philadelphia Flyers for D Doug Crossman (September 29, 1988).... Bruised right shoulder (October 1988).... Broke knuckle on right hand (January 1989).... Broke toe (November 1989).... Traded by Flyers with fourth-round pick in 1991 draft to Buffalo Sabres for RW Kevin Maguire and second-round pick (RW Mikael Renberg) in 1990 draft (March 5, 1990).... Fractured right ankle (March 6, 1990).... Tore medial collateral ligament of right knee (October 13, 1990); missed 18 games.... Traded by Sabres to New York Rangers for D Randy Moller (March 9, 1992).... Sprained right knee (January 27, 1993); missed 27 games.... Sprained wrist (March 25, 1994); missed one game.... Suffered from the flu (April 2, 1994); missed one game.

HONORS: Named to OMJHL All-Star first team (1978-79).

MISCELLANEOUS: Member of Stanley Cup championship team (1994).

			REGULAR SEASON					PLAYOFFS				
Season Team	League	Gms.	G	A	Pts.	PIM	Gms.	G	A	Pts.	PIM
76-77—Kingston	OMJHL	59	4	7	11	90	—	—	—	—	—
77-78—Kingston	OMJHL	68	9	13	22	195	5	1	2	3	6
78-79—Kingston	OMJHL	48	6	21	27	100	11	2	7	9	29
79-80—Los Angeles	NHL	43	0	0	0	113	4	0	0	0	11
—Binghamton	AHL	28	0	6	6	48	—	—	—	—	—
80-81—Los Angeles	NHL	72	5	13	18	155	4	0	0	0	27
81-82—Los Angeles	NHL	60	1	8	9	145	10	1	3	4	41
82-83—Los Angeles	NHL	69	3	12	15	167	—	—	—	—	—
83-84—Los Angeles	NHL	69	3	18	21	141	—	—	—	—	—
84-85—Los Angeles	NHL	77	2	9	11	185	3	0	1	1	0
85-86—Los Angeles	NHL	79	11	31	42	226	—	—	—	—	—
86-87—Los Angeles	NHL	77	7	29	36	155	5	1	2	3	10
87-88—Los Angeles	NHL	58	2	23	25	159	5	1	2	3	21
88-89—Philadelphia	NHL	67	2	19	21	184	18	0	2	2	51
89-90—Philadelphia	NHL	59	3	16	19	129	—	—	—	—	—
—Buffalo	NHL	1	0	1	1	0	6	0	0	0	12
90-91—Buffalo	NHL	43	1	2	3	86	1	0	1	1	0
91-92—Buffalo	NHL	41	2	9	11	157	—	—	—	—	—
—New York Rangers	NHL	11	0	0	0	24	13	0	2	2	10
92-93—New York Rangers	NHL	53	1	9	10	107	—	—	—	—	—
93-94—New York Rangers	NHL	79	2	7	9	110	23	0	0	0	20
NHL totals		958	45	206	251	2243	92	3	13	16	203

WELSING, ROCKY
D, MIGHTY DUCKS

PERSONAL: Born February 8, 1976, in Beloit, Wis.... 6-3/196.... Shoots left.

TRANSACTIONS/CAREER NOTES: Selected by Mighty Ducks of Anaheim in seventh round (seventh Mighty Ducks pick, 158th overall) of NHL entry draft (June 29, 1994).

			REGULAR SEASON					PLAYOFFS				
Season Team	League	Gms.	G	A	Pts.	PIM	Gms.	G	A	Pts.	PIM
91-92—Wisconsin	USHL	34	1	5	6	110	—	—	—	—	—
92-93—Wisconsin	USHL	63	18	37	55	111	—	—	—	—	—
93-94—Wisconsin	USHL	40	5	21	26	262	—	—	—	—	—

WERENKA, BRAD
D, NORDIQUES

PERSONAL: Born February 12, 1969, in Two Hills, Alta.... 6-2/205.... Shoots left.... Full name: John Bradley Werenka.... Name pronounced wuh-REHN-kuh.

HIGH SCHOOL: Fort Saskatchewan (Alta.).

COLLEGE: Northern Michigan.

TRANSACTIONS/CAREER NOTES: Selected by Edmonton Oilers as underage junior in second round (second Oilers pick, 42nd overall) of NHL entry draft (June 13, 1987).... Tore stomach muscles (October 1988).... Sprained right knee (November 3, 1989).... Loaned by Oilers to Canadian Olympic Team (February 10, 1994).... Traded by Oilers to Quebec Nordiques for G Steve Passmore (March 21, 1994).

HONORS: Named to NCAA All-America West first team (1990-91).... Named to NCAA All-Tournament team (1990-91).... Named to WCHA All-Star first team (1990-91).

MISCELLANEOUS: Member of silver-medal-winning Canadian Olympic team (1994).

			REGULAR SEASON					PLAYOFFS				
Season Team	League	Gms.	G	A	Pts.	PIM	Gms.	G	A	Pts.	PIM
85-86—Fort Saskatchewan	AJHL	29	12	23	35	24	—	—	—	—	—
86-87—Northern Michigan Univ...	WCHA	30	4	4	8	35	—	—	—	—	—
87-88—Northern Michigan Univ...	WCHA	34	7	23	30	26	—	—	—	—	—
88-89—Northern Michigan Univ...	WCHA	28	7	13	20	16	—	—	—	—	—
89-90—Northern Michigan Univ...	WCHA	8	2	5	7	8	—	—	—	—	—
90-91—Northern Michigan Univ...	WCHA	47	20	43	63	36	—	—	—	—	—
91-92—Cape Breton	AHL	66	6	21	27	95	5	0	3	3	6
92-93—Canadian national team ...	Int'l	18	3	7	10	10	—	—	—	—	—
—Edmonton	NHL	27	0	3	3	24	—	—	—	—	—
—Cape Breton	AHL	4	1	1	2	4	16	4	17	21	12
93-94—Cape Breton	AHL	25	6	17	23	19	—	—	—	—	—
—Edmonton	NHL	15	0	4	4	14	—	—	—	—	—
—Canadian national team ...	Int'l	8	2	2	4	8	—	—	—	—	—

W

Season Team	League	REGULAR SEASON					PLAYOFFS				
		Gms.	G	A	Pts.	Pen.	Gms.	G	A	Pts.	Pen.
—Canadian Olympic Team ..	Int'l	8	2	2	4	8	—	—	—	—	—
—Quebec	NHL	11	0	7	7	8	—	—	—	—	—
NHL totals..		53	5	14	19	46					

WESLEY, GLEN
D, BRUINS

PERSONAL: Born October 2, 1968, in Red Deer, Alta.... 6-1/195.... Shoots left.
TRANSACTIONS/CAREER NOTES: Selected by Boston Bruins as underage junior in first round (first Bruins pick, third overall) of NHL entry draft (June 13, 1987).... Sprained left knee (October 1988).... Broke foot (November 24, 1992); missed 14 games.... Injured groin (February 1993); missed one game.... Injured groin (March 1993); missed three games.... Injured groin (April 1993); missed two games.... Injured kidney (March 3, 1994); missed three games.
HONORS: Won WHL West Top Defenseman Trophy (1985-86 and 1986-87).... Named to WHL (West) All-Star first team (1985-86 and 1986-87).... Named to NHL All-Rookie team (1987-88).... Played in NHL All-Star Game (1989).

Season Team	League	REGULAR SEASON					PLAYOFFS				
		Gms.	G	A	Pts.	PIM	Gms.	G	A	Pts.	PIM
83-84—Red Deer	AJHL	57	9	20	29	40	—	—	—	—	—
—Portland	WHL	3	1	2	3	0	—	—	—	—	—
84-85—Portland	WHL	67	16	52	68	76	6	1	6	7	8
85-86—Portland	WHL	69	16	75	91	96	15	3	11	14	29
86-87—Portland	WHL	63	16	46	62	72	20	8	18	26	27
87-88—Boston	NHL	79	7	30	37	69	23	6	8	14	22
88-89—Boston	NHL	77	19	35	54	61	10	0	2	2	4
89-90—Boston	NHL	78	9	27	36	48	21	2	6	8	36
90-91—Boston	NHL	80	11	32	43	78	19	2	9	11	19
91-92—Boston	NHL	78	9	37	46	54	15	2	4	6	16
92-93—Boston	NHL	64	8	25	33	47	4	0	0	0	0
93-94—Boston	NHL	81	14	44	58	64	13	3	3	6	12
NHL totals..		537	77	230	307	421	105	15	32	47	109

WHITE, KAM
D, MAPLE LEAFS

PERSONAL: Born February 13, 1976, in Chicago.... 6-3/195.... Shoots left.
COLLEGE: Lambton (Ont.).
TRANSACTIONS/CAREER NOTES: Selected by Toronto Maple Leafs in sixth round (fifth Maple Leafs pick, 152nd overall) of NHL entry draft (June 29, 1994).

Season Team	League	REGULAR SEASON					PLAYOFFS				
		Gms.	G	A	Pts.	PIM	Gms.	G	A	Pts.	PIM
92-93—Newmarket.......................	OHL	8	0	0	0	8	—	—	—	—	—
—St. Michaels Tier II	Jr. A	32	2	7	9	63	—	—	—	—	—
93-94—Newmarket.......................	OHL	44	0	5	5	125	—	—	—	—	—

WHITE, PETER
C, OILERS

PERSONAL: Born March 15, 1969, in Montreal.... 5-11/200.... Shoots left.... Full name: Peter Toby White.
COLLEGE: Michigan State.
TRANSACTIONS/CAREER NOTES: Selected by Edmonton Oilers in fifth round (fourth Oilers pick, 92nd overall) of NHL entry draft (June 17, 1989).
HONORS: Named to CCHA All-Rookie team (1988-89).... Named CCHA Playoff Most Valuable Player (1989-90).... Named to CCHA All-Tournament team (1989-90).

Season Team	League	REGULAR SEASON					PLAYOFFS				
		Gms.	G	A	Pts.	PIM	Gms.	G	A	Pts.	PIM
87-88—Pembroke	COJHL	56	90	136	226	32	—	—	—	—	—
88-89—Michigan State.................	CCHA	46	20	33	53	17	—	—	—	—	—
89-90—Michigan State.................	CCHA	45	22	40	62	6	—	—	—	—	—
90-91—Michigan State.................	CCHA	37	7	31	38	28	—	—	—	—	—
91-92—Michigan State.................	CCHA	44	26	51	77	32	—	—	—	—	—
92-93—Cape Breton	AHL	64	12	28	40	10	16	3	3	6	12
93-94—Cape Breton	AHL	45	21	49	70	12	5	2	3	5	2
—Edmonton	NHL	26	3	5	8	2	—	—	—	—	—
NHL totals..		26	3	5	8	2					

WHITMORE, KAY
G, CANUCKS

PERSONAL: Born April 10, 1967, in Sudbury, Ont.... 5-11/185.... Catches left.
TRANSACTIONS/CAREER NOTES: Selected by Hartford Whalers as underage junior in second round (second Whalers pick, 26th overall) of NHL entry draft (June 15, 1985).... Traded by Whalers to Vancouver Canucks for G Corrie D'Alessio and conditional pick in 1993 draft (October 1, 1992).
HONORS: Shared Dave Pinkney Trophy with Ron Tugnutt (1985-86).... Named to OHL All-Star first team (1985-86).... Won Jack Butterfield Trophy (1990-91).

Season Team	League	REGULAR SEASON								PLAYOFFS						
		Gms.	Min.	W	L	T	GA	SO	Avg.	Gms.	Min.	W	L	GA	SO	Avg.
83-84—Peterborough	OHL	29	1471	17	8	0	110	0	4.49	—	—	—	—	—	—	—
84-85—Peterborough	OHL	*53	*3077	35	16	2	172	†2	3.35	*17	*1020	10	4	58	0	3.41
85-86—Peterborough	OHL	41	2467	27	12	2	114	†3	*2.77	14	837	8	5	40	0	2.87

— 726 —

Season Team	League	Gms.	Min.	W	L	T	GA	SO	Avg.	Gms.	Min.	W	L	GA	SO	Avg.
86-87—Peterborough	OHL	36	2159	14	17	5	118	1	3.28	7	366	3	3	17	1	2.79
87-88—Binghamton	AHL	38	2137	17	15	4	121	3	3.40	2	118	0	2	10	0	5.08
88-89—Binghamton	AHL	*56	*3200	21	29	4	*241	1	4.52	—	—	—	—	—	—	—
—Hartford	NHL	3	180	2	1	0	10	0	3.33	2	135	0	2	10	0	4.44
89-90—Binghamton	AHL	24	1386	3	19	2	109	0	4.72	—	—	—	—	—	—	—
—Hartford	NHL	9	442	4	2	1	26	0	3.53	—	—	—	—	—	—	—
90-91—Hartford	NHL	18	850	3	9	3	52	0	3.67	—	—	—	—	—	—	—
—Springfield	AHL	33	1916	22	9	1	98	1	3.07	*15	*926	11	4	*37	0	*2.40
91-92—Hartford	NHL	45	2567	14	21	6	155	3	3.62	1	19	0	0	1	0	3.16
92-93—Vancouver	NHL	31	1817	18	8	4	94	1	3.10	—	—	—	—	—	—	—
93-94—Vancouver	NHL	32	1921	18	14	0	113	0	3.53	—	—	—	—	—	—	—
NHL totals		138	7777	59	55	14	450	4	3.47	3	154	0	2	11	0	4.29

WHITNEY, RAY
C, SHARKS

PERSONAL: Born May 8, 1972, in Edmonton. . . . 5-9/160. . . . Shoots right.
TRANSACTIONS/CAREER NOTES: Selected by San Jose Sharks in second round (second Sharks pick, 23rd overall) of NHL entry draft (June 22, 1991). . . . Sprained knee (October 30, 1993); missed 18 games. . . . Suffered from the flu (December 15, 1993); missed one game.
HONORS: Won Four Broncos Memorial Trophy (1990-91). . . . Won Bob Clarke Trophy (1990-91). . . . Won WHL West Player of the Year Award (1990-91). . . . Won George Parsons Trophy (1990-91). . . . Named to Memorial Cup All-Star team (1990-91). . . . Named to WHL (West) All-Star first team (1990-91).

Season Team	League	Gms.	G	A	Pts.	PIM	Gms.	G	A	Pts.	PIM
88-89—Spokane	WHL	71	17	33	50	16	—	—	—	—	—
89-90—Spokane	WHL	71	57	56	113	50	6	3	4	7	6
90-91—Spokane	WHL	72	67	118	*185	36	15	13	18	*31	12
91-92—San Diego	IHL	63	36	54	90	12	4	0	0	0	0
—San Jose	NHL	2	0	3	3	0	—	—	—	—	—
—Koln	Germany	10	3	6	9	4	—	—	—	—	—
92-93—Kansas City	IHL	46	20	33	53	14	12	5	7	12	2
—San Jose	NHL	26	4	6	10	4	—	—	—	—	—
93-94—San Jose	NHL	61	14	26	40	14	14	0	4	4	8
NHL totals		89	18	35	53	18	14	0	4	4	8

WIEMER, JASON
LW, LIGHTNING

PERSONAL: Born April 14, 1976, in Kimberley, B.C. . . . 6-1/215. . . . Shoots left. . . . Name pronounced WEE-mer.
TRANSACTIONS/CAREER NOTES: Selected by Tampa Bay Lightning in first round (first Lightning pick, eighth overall) of NHL entry draft (June 28, 1994).

Season Team	League	Gms.	G	A	Pts.	PIM	Gms.	G	A	Pts.	PIM
91-92—Kimberley	Tier II Jr. A	45	34	33	67	211	—	—	—	—	—
92-93—Portland	WHL	68	18	34	52	159	16	7	3	10	27
93-94—Portland	WHL	72	45	51	96	236	10	4	4	8	32

WIEMER, JIM
D, BRUINS

PERSONAL: Born January 9, 1961, in Sudbury, Ont. . . . 6-4/210. . . . Shoots left. . . . Full name: James Duncan Wiemer. . . . Name pronounced WEE-mer.
TRANSACTIONS/CAREER NOTES: Selected by Buffalo Sabres as underage junior in fourth round (fifth Sabres pick, 83rd overall) of NHL entry draft (June 11, 1980). . . . Traded by Sabres with RW Steve Patrick to New York Rangers for D Chris Renaud and D Dave Maloney (December 6, 1984). . . . Traded by Rangers with rights to D Reijo Ruotsalainen, LW Ville Kentala and LW Clark Donatelli to Edmonton Oilers to complete deal in which Rangers acquired D Don Jackson, D Miroslav Horava and C Mike Golden (October 23, 1986). . . . Traded by Oilers with RW Alan May to Los Angeles Kings for C Brian Wilks and D John English (March 7, 1989). . . . Signed as free agent by Boston Bruins (July 6, 1989). . . . Bruised right leg (November 1989). . . . Pulled groin (January 27, 1992); missed 10 games. . . . Reinjured groin (March 19, 1992); missed six games. . . . Injured groin (December 1992); missed eight games. . . . Injured foot (January 1993); missed two games. . . . Broke foot (January 29, 1993); missed 17 games.
HONORS: Won Eddie Shore Plaque (1985-86). . . . Named to AHL All-Star first team (1985-86).

Season Team	League	Gms.	G	A	Pts.	PIM	Gms.	G	A	Pts.	PIM
78-79—Peterborough	OMJHL	63	15	12	27	50	18	4	4	8	15
79-80—Peterborough	OMJHL	53	17	32	49	63	14	6	9	15	19
80-81—Peterborough	OMJHL	65	41	54	95	102	5	1	2	3	15
81-82—Rochester	AHL	74	19	26	45	57	9	0	4	4	2
82-83—Rochester	AHL	74	15	44	59	43	15	5	15	20	22
—Buffalo	NHL	—	—	—	—	—	1	0	0	0	0
83-84—Buffalo	NHL	64	5	15	20	48	—	—	—	—	—
—Rochester	AHL	12	4	11	15	11	18	3	13	16	20
84-85—Rochester	AHL	13	1	9	10	24	—	—	—	—	—
—New Haven	AHL	33	9	27	36	39	—	—	—	—	—
—Buffalo	NHL	10	3	2	5	4	—	—	—	—	—
—New York Rangers	NHL	22	4	3	7	30	1	0	0	0	0
85-86—New Haven	AHL	73	24	49	73	108	—	—	—	—	—

W

Season	Team	League	Gms.	G	A	Pts.	Pen.	Gms.	G	A	Pts.	Pen.
	—New York Rangers	NHL	7	3	0	3	2	8	1	0	1	6
86-87	—New Haven	AHL	6	0	7	7	6	—	—	—	—	—
	—Nova Scotia	AHL	59	9	25	34	72	5	0	4	4	2
87-88	—Nova Scotia	AHL	57	11	32	43	99	5	1	1	2	14
	—Edmonton	NHL	12	1	2	3	15	2	0	0	0	2
88-89	—Cape Breton	AHL	51	12	29	41	80	—	—	—	—	—
	—Los Angeles	NHL	9	2	3	5	20	10	2	1	3	19
	—New Haven	AHL	3	1	1	2	2	7	2	3	5	2
89-90	—Maine	AHL	6	3	4	7	27	—	—	—	—	—
	—Boston	NHL	61	5	14	19	63	8	0	1	1	4
90-91	—Boston	NHL	61	4	19	23	62	16	1	3	4	14
91-92	—Maine	AHL	3	0	1	1	4	—	—	—	—	—
	—Boston	NHL	47	1	8	9	84	15	1	3	4	14
92-93	—Boston	NHL	28	1	6	7	48	1	0	0	0	4
	—Providence	AHL	4	2	1	3	2	—	—	—	—	—
93-94	—Providence	AHL	35	5	12	17	81	—	—	—	—	—
	—Boston	NHL	4	0	0	0	2	—	—	—	—	—
NHL totals			325	29	72	101	378	62	5	8	13	63

WIESEL, ADAM
D, CANADIENS

PERSONAL: Born January 25, 1975, in Holyoke, Mass. . . . 6-3/201. . . . Shoots right. . . . Name pronounced WEE-zul.
HIGH SCHOOL: South Hadley (Mass.).
TRANSACTIONS/CAREER NOTES: Selected by Montreal Canadiens in fourth round (fourth Canadiens pick, 85th overall) of NHL entry draft (June 26, 1993).

Season	Team	League	Gms.	G	A	Pts.	PIM	Gms.	G	A	Pts.	PIM
90-91	—Springfield Jr. B	NEJHL	43	8	17	25	28	—	—	—	—	—
91-92	—Springfield Jr. B	NEJHL	47	6	13	19	25	—	—	—	—	—
92-93	—Springfield Jr. B	NEJHL	41	11	20	31	34	—	—	—	—	—
93-94	—Clarkson	ECAC	33	3	7	10	28	—	—	—	—	—

WILKIE, BOB
D, FLYERS

PERSONAL: Born February 11, 1969, in Calgary. . . . 6-2/220. . . . Shoots right.
TRANSACTIONS/CAREER NOTES: Selected by Detroit Red Wings as underage junior in second round (third Red Wings pick, 41st overall) of NHL entry draft (June 13, 1987). . . . Fractured kneecap (January 1990). . . . Traded by Red Wings to Philadelphia Flyers for future considerations (February 2, 1993).
HONORS: Named to AHL All-Star second team (1993-94).

Season	Team	League	Gms.	G	A	Pts.	PIM	Gms.	G	A	Pts.	PIM
85-86	—Calgary	WHL	63	8	19	27	56	—	—	—	—	—
86-87	—Swift Current	WHL	65	12	38	50	50	4	1	3	4	2
87-88	—Swift Current	WHL	67	12	68	80	124	10	4	12	16	8
88-89	—Swift Current	WHL	62	18	67	85	89	12	1	11	12	47
89-90	—Adirondack	AHL	58	5	33	38	64	6	1	4	5	2
90-91	—Detroit	NHL	8	1	2	3	2	—	—	—	—	—
	—Adirondack	AHL	43	6	18	24	71	2	1	0	1	2
91-92	—Adirondack	AHL	7	1	4	5	6	16	2	5	7	12
92-93	—Adirondack	AHL	14	0	5	5	20	—	—	—	—	—
	—Fort Wayne	IHL	32	7	14	21	82	12	4	6	10	10
	—Hershey	AHL	28	7	25	32	18	—	—	—	—	—
93-94	—Hershey	AHL	69	8	53	61	100	9	1	4	5	8
	—Philadelphia	NHL	10	1	3	4	8	—	—	—	—	—
NHL totals			18	2	5	7	10					

WILKIE, DAVID
D, CANADIENS

PERSONAL: Born May 30, 1974, in Ellensburg, Wash. . . . 6-2/202. . . . Shoots right.
COLLEGE: Cariboo (B.C.).
TRANSACTIONS/CAREER NOTES: Selected by Montreal Canadiens in first round (first Canadiens pick, 20th overall) of NHL entry draft (June 20, 1992).

Season	Team	League	Gms.	G	A	Pts.	PIM	Gms.	G	A	Pts.	PIM
89-90	—Northwest Americans Jr. B .	WCHL	41	21	27	48	59	—	—	—	—	—
90-91	—Seattle	WHL	25	1	1	2	22	—	—	—	—	—
91-92	—Kamloops	WHL	71	12	28	40	153	16	6	5	11	19
92-93	—Kamloops	WHL	53	11	26	37	109	6	4	2	6	2
93-94	—Kamloops	WHL	27	11	18	29	18	—	—	—	—	—
	—Regina	WHL	29	27	21	48	16	4	1	4	5	4

WILKINSON, DEREK
G, LIGHTNING

PERSONAL: Born July 29, 1974, in Windsor, Ont. . . . 6-0/160. . . . Catches left.
TRANSACTIONS/CAREER NOTES: Selected by Tampa Bay Lightning in eighth round (eighth Lightning pick, 170th overall) of NHL entry draft (June 20, 1992).

W

Season Team	League	REGULAR SEASON Gms.	Min.	W	L	T	GA	SO	Avg.	PLAYOFFS Gms.	Min.	W	L	GA	SO	Avg.
91-92—Detroit	OHL	38	1943	16	17	1	138	1	4.26	7	313	3	2	28	0	5.37
92-93—Detroit	OHL	4	245	1	2	1	18	0	4.41	—	—	—	—	—	—	—
—Belleville	OHL	59	3370	21	24	11	237	0	4.22	7	434	3	4	29	0	4.01
93-94—Belleville	OHL	56	2860	24	16	4	179	2	3.76	12	700	6	†6	39	*1	3.34

WILKINSON, NEIL

D, JETS

PERSONAL: Born August 15, 1967, in Selkirk, Man. . . . 6-3/190. . . . Shoots right. . . . Full name: Neil John Wilkinson.
COLLEGE: Michigan State.
TRANSACTIONS/CAREER NOTES: Suffered concussion and broke nose (January 1986). . . . Selected by Minnesota North Stars in second round (second North Stars pick, 30th overall) of NHL entry draft (June 21, 1986). . . . Twisted knee ligaments during training camp (September 1988). . . . Bruised left instep (November 9, 1989). . . . Strained back (January 1990). . . . Tore left thumb ligaments (March 6, 1991); missed five games. . . . Selected by San Jose Sharks in NHL dispersal draft (May 30, 1991). . . . Injured groin (December 16, 1991); missed four games. . . . Injured eye (January 8, 1992); missed three games. . . . Strained back (February 4, 1992); missed 13 games. . . . Suffered facial contusions (October 28, 1992); missed two games. . . . Strained back (November 10, 1992); missed 14 games. . . . Injured hand (December 18, 1992); missed one game. . . . Strained back (February 10, 1993); missed six games. . . . Traded by Sharks to Chicago Blackhawks (July 9, 1993) to complete deal in which Blackhawks sent G Jimmy Waite to Sharks for future considerations (June 18, 1993). . . . Traded by Blackhawks to Winnipeg Jets for third-round pick in 1995 draft (June 3, 1994).

Season Team	League	REGULAR SEASON Gms.	G	A	Pts.	PIM	PLAYOFFS Gms.	G	A	Pts.	PIM
85-86—Selkirk	MJHL	42	14	35	49	91	—	—	—	—	—
86-87—Michigan State	CCHA	19	3	4	7	18	—	—	—	—	—
87-88—Medicine Hat	WHL	55	11	21	32	157	5	1	0	1	2
88-89—Kalamazoo	IHL	39	5	15	20	96	—	—	—	—	—
89-90—Kalamazoo	IHL	20	6	7	13	62	—	—	—	—	—
—Minnesota	NHL	36	0	5	5	100	7	0	2	2	11
90-91—Kalamazoo	IHL	10	0	3	3	38	—	—	—	—	—
—Minnesota	NHL	50	2	9	11	117	22	3	3	6	12
91-92—San Jose	NHL	60	4	15	19	107	—	—	—	—	—
92-93—San Jose	NHL	59	1	7	8	96	—	—	—	—	—
93-94—Chicago	NHL	72	3	9	12	116	4	0	0	0	0
NHL totals		277	10	45	55	536	33	3	5	8	23

WILLIAMS, DARRYL

LW, KINGS

PERSONAL: Born February 29, 1968, in Mount Pearl, Nfld. . . . 5-11/185. . . . Shoots left. . . . Full name: Darryl Clifford Williams.
TRANSACTIONS/CAREER NOTES: Traded by Hamilton Steelhawks with future considerations to Belleville Bulls for C Keith Gretzky (December 1986). . . . Signed as free agent by Los Angeles Kings (September 1989).

Season Team	League	REGULAR SEASON Gms.	G	A	Pts.	PIM	PLAYOFFS Gms.	G	A	Pts.	PIM
85-86—Victoria	WHL	38	3	2	5	66	—	—	—	—	—
86-87—Hamilton	OHL	24	2	4	6	36	—	—	—	—	—
—Belleville	OHL	34	7	6	13	72	—	—	—	—	—
87-88—Belleville	OHL	63	29	39	68	169	—	—	—	—	—
88-89—New Haven	AHL	15	5	5	10	24	—	—	—	—	—
—Belleville	OHL	45	24	21	45	137	—	—	—	—	—
89-90—New Haven	AHL	51	9	13	22	124	—	—	—	—	—
90-91—New Haven	AHL	57	14	11	25	278	—	—	—	—	—
—Phoenix	IHL	12	2	1	3	53	7	1	0	1	12
91-92—New Haven	AHL	13	0	2	2	69	—	—	—	—	—
—Phoenix	IHL	48	8	19	27	219	—	—	—	—	—
92-93—Phoenix	IHL	61	18	7	25	314	—	—	—	—	—
—Los Angeles	NHL	2	0	0	0	10	—	—	—	—	—
93-94—Phoenix	IHL	52	11	18	29	237	—	—	—	—	—
NHL totals		2	0	0	0	10					

WILLIAMS, DAVID

D, MIGHTY DUCKS

PERSONAL: Born August 25, 1967, in Plainfield, N.J. . . . 6-2/195. . . . Shoots right. . . . Full name: David Andrew Williams.
HIGH SCHOOL: Choate Rosemary Hall (Wallingford, Conn.).
COLLEGE: Dartmouth.
TRANSACTIONS/CAREER NOTES: Selected by New Jersey Devils as underage junior in 12th round (12th Devils pick, 234th overall) of NHL entry draft (June 15, 1985). . . . Signed as free agent by San Jose Sharks (August 9, 1991). . . . Selected by Mighty Ducks of Anaheim in NHL expansion draft (June 24, 1993). . . . Suffered from virus (December 1, 1993); missed three games.
HONORS: Named to NCAA All-America East second team (1988-89). . . . Named to ECAC All-Star first team (1988-89).

Season Team	League	REGULAR SEASON Gms.	G	A	Pts.	PIM	PLAYOFFS Gms.	G	A	Pts.	PIM
86-87—Dartmouth College	ECAC	23	2	19	21	20	—	—	—	—	—
87-88—Dartmouth College	ECAC	25	8	14	22	30	—	—	—	—	—
88-89—Dartmouth College	ECAC	25	4	11	15	28	—	—	—	—	—
89-90—Dartmouth College	ECAC	26	3	12	15	32	—	—	—	—	—

W

Season Team	League	REGULAR SEASON					PLAYOFFS				
		Gms.	G	A	Pts.	Pen.	Gms.	G	A	Pts.	Pen.
90-91—Knoxville	ECHL	38	12	15	27	40	3	0	0	0	4
—Muskegon	IHL	14	1	2	3	4	—	—	—	—	—
91-92—Kansas City	IHL	18	2	3	5	22	—	—	—	—	—
—San Jose	NHL	56	3	25	28	40	—	—	—	—	—
92-93—Kansas City	IHL	31	1	11	12	28	—	—	—	—	—
—San Jose	NHL	40	1	11	12	49	—	—	—	—	—
93-94—San Diego	IHL	16	1	6	7	17	—	—	—	—	—
—Anaheim	NHL	56	5	15	20	42	—	—	—	—	—
NHL totals		152	9	51	60	131					

WILSON, LANDON
RW, NORDIQUES

PERSONAL: Born March 15, 1975, in St. Louis. . . . 6-2/202. . . . Shoots right. . . . Son of Rick Wilson, defenseman, Montreal Canadiens, St. Louis Blues, and Detroit Red Wings (1973-74 through 1976-77).
COLLEGE: North Dakota.
TRANSACTIONS/CAREER NOTES: Selected by Toronto Maple Leafs in first round (second Maple Leafs pick, 19th overall) of NHL entry draft (June 26, 1993). . . . Traded by Maple Leafs with LW Wendel Clark, D Sylvain Lefebvre and first-round pick in 1994 draft (D Jeffrey Kealty) to Quebec Nordiques for C Mats Sundin, D Garth Butcher, LW Todd Warriner and first-round pick (traded to Washington Capitals who selected D Nolan Baumgartner) in 1994 draft (June 28, 1994).
HONORS: Named WCHA Rookie of the Year (1993-94). . . . Named to WCHA All-Rookie team (1993-94).

Season Team	League	REGULAR SEASON					PLAYOFFS				
		Gms.	G	A	Pts.	PIM	Gms.	G	A	Pts.	PIM
92-93—Dubuque	USHL	43	29	36	65	284	—	—	—	—	—
93-94—Univ. of North Dakota	WCHA	35	18	15	33	147					

WILSON, MIKE
D, CANUCKS

PERSONAL: Born February 26, 1975, in Brampton, Ont. . . . 6-5/180. . . . Shoots left.
TRANSACTIONS/CAREER NOTES: Selected by Vancouver Canucks in first round (first Canucks pick, 20th overall) of NHL entry draft (June 26, 1993).
HONORS: Named to Can.HL All-Rookie team (1992-93). . . . Named to OHL All-Rookie team (1992-93).

Season Team	League	REGULAR SEASON					PLAYOFFS				
		Gms.	G	A	Pts.	PIM	Gms.	G	A	Pts.	PIM
91-92—Georgetown Jr. B	OHA	41	9	13	22	65	—	—	—	—	—
92-93—Sudbury	OHL	53	6	7	13	58	14	1	1	2	21
93-94—Sudbury	OHL	60	4	22	26	62	9	1	3	4	8

WILSON, RON
C, CANADIENS

PERSONAL: Born May 13, 1956, in Toronto. . . . 5-9/182. . . . Shoots left. . . . Full name: Ronald Lee Wilson.
TRANSACTIONS/CAREER NOTES: Selected by Montreal Canadiens from St. Catharines Blackhawks in 15th round (15th Canadiens pick, 133rd overall) of NHL amateur draft (June 1, 1976). . . . Sold by Canadiens to Winnipeg Jets (June 1979). . . . Named player/assistant coach of Moncton Golden Flames (May 1988). . . . Traded by Jets to St. Louis Blues for C Doug Evans (January 22, 1990). . . . Injured knee (October 26, 1992); missed three games. . . . Reinjured knee (December 7, 1992); missed two games. . . . Signed as free agent by Canadiens (August 20, 1993).
HONORS: Named to AHL All-Star second team (1988-89).

Season Team	League	REGULAR SEASON					PLAYOFFS				
		Gms.	G	A	Pts.	PIM	Gms.	G	A	Pts.	PIM
74-75—Markham Waxers	OPJHL	43	26	28	54	24	—	—	—	—	—
—Toronto	OHA Mj. Jr. A	16	6	12	18	6	23	9	17	26	6
75-76—St. Catharines	OHA Mj. Jr. A	64	37	62	99	44	4	1	6	7	7
76-77—Nova Scotia	AHL	67	15	21	36	18	6	0	0	0	0
77-78—Nova Scotia	AHL	59	15	25	40	17	11	4	4	8	9
78-79—Nova Scotia	AHL	77	33	42	75	91	10	5	6	11	14
79-80—Winnipeg	NHL	79	21	36	57	28	—	—	—	—	—
80-81—Winnipeg	NHL	77	18	33	51	55	—	—	—	—	—
81-82—Tulsa	CHL	41	20	38	58	22	3	1	0	1	2
—Winnipeg	NHL	39	3	13	16	49	—	—	—	—	—
82-83—Sherbrooke	AHL	65	30	55	85	71	—	—	—	—	—
—Winnipeg	NHL	12	6	3	9	4	3	2	2	4	2
83-84—Winnipeg	NHL	51	3	12	15	12	—	—	—	—	—
—Sherbrooke	AHL	22	10	30	40	16	—	—	—	—	—
84-85—Winnipeg	NHL	75	10	9	19	31	8	4	2	6	2
85-86—Winnipeg	NHL	54	6	7	13	16	1	0	0	0	0
—Sherbrooke	AHL	10	9	8	17	9	—	—	—	—	—
86-87—Winnipeg	NHL	80	3	13	16	13	10	1	2	3	0
87-88—Winnipeg	NHL	69	5	8	13	28	1	0	0	0	2
88-89—Moncton	AHL	80	31	61	92	110	8	1	4	5	20
89-90—Moncton	AHL	47	16	37	53	64	—	—	—	—	—
—St. Louis	NHL	33	3	17	20	23	12	3	5	8	18
90-91—St. Louis	NHL	73	10	27	37	54	7	0	0	0	28
91-92—St. Louis	NHL	64	12	17	29	46	6	0	1	1	0
92-93—St. Louis	NHL	78	8	11	19	44	11	0	0	0	12
93-94—Montreal	NHL	48	2	10	12	12	4	0	0	0	0
NHL totals		832	110	216	326	415	63	10	12	22	64

W

WINDSOR, NICHOLAS
D, NORDIQUES

PERSONAL: Born January 19, 1976, in Granby, Que.... 6-1/165.... Shoots left.
TRANSACTIONS/CAREER NOTES: Selected by Quebec Nordiques in sixth round (eighth Nordiques pick, 139th overall) of NHL entry draft (June 29, 1994).

Season Team	League	REGULAR SEASON					PLAYOFFS				
		Gms.	G	A	Pts.	PIM	Gms.	G	A	Pts.	PIM
93-94—Cornwall	Jr. A	43	13	39	52	121	—	—	—	—	—

WINNES, CHRIS
RW, FLYERS

PERSONAL: Born February 12, 1968, in Ridgefield, Conn.... 6-0/170.... Shoots right.... Name pronounced WIH-nihz.
HIGH SCHOOL: Ridgefield (Conn.), then Northwood (Lake Placid, N.Y.).
COLLEGE: New Hampshire.
TRANSACTIONS/CAREER NOTES: Selected by Boston Bruins in eighth round (ninth Bruins pick, 161st overall) of NHL entry draft (June 13, 1987).... Broke nose (February 23, 1992).... Signed as free agent by Philadelphia Flyers (August 4, 1993).
HONORS: Named to Hockey East All-Freshman team (1987-88).

Season Team	League	REGULAR SEASON					PLAYOFFS				
		Gms.	G	A	Pts.	PIM	Gms.	G	A	Pts.	PIM
85-86—Ridgefield H.S.	Conn. H.S.	24	40	30	70	...	—	—	—	—	—
86-87—Northwood School	N.Y. H.S.	27	25	25	50	...	—	—	—	—	—
87-88—Univ. of New Hampshire	Hockey East	30	17	19	36	28	—	—	—	—	—
88-89—Univ. of New Hampshire	Hockey East	30	11	20	31	22	—	—	—	—	—
89-90—Univ. of New Hampshire	Hockey East	24	10	13	23	12	—	—	—	—	—
90-91—Univ. of New Hampshire	Hockey East	33	15	16	31	24	—	—	—	—	—
—Maine	AHL	7	3	1	4	0	1	0	2	2	0
—Boston	NHL	—	—	—	—	—	1	0	0	0	0
91-92—Maine	AHL	45	12	35	47	30	—	—	—	—	—
—Boston	NHL	24	1	3	4	6	—	—	—	—	—
92-93—Providence	AHL	64	23	36	59	34	4	0	2	2	5
—Boston	NHL	5	0	1	1	0	—	—	—	—	—
93-94—Hershey	AHL	70	29	21	50	20	7	1	3	4	0
—Philadelphia	NHL	4	0	2	2	0	—	—	—	—	—
NHL totals		**33**	**1**	**6**	**7**	**6**	**1**	**0**	**0**	**0**	**0**

WITT, BRENDAN
D, CAPITALS

PERSONAL: Born February 20, 1975, in Humboldt, Sask.... 6-1/205.... Shoots left.
HIGH SCHOOL: Meadowdale (Lynnwood, Wash.).
TRANSACTIONS/CAREER NOTES: Selected by Washington Capitals in first round (first Capitals pick, 11th overall) of NHL entry draft (June 26, 1993).
HONORS: Named to WHL (West) All-Star first team (1992-93 and 1993-94).... Won Bill Hunter Trophy (1993-94).... Named to Can.HL All-Star first team (1993-94).

Season Team	League	REGULAR SEASON					PLAYOFFS				
		Gms.	G	A	Pts.	PIM	Gms.	G	A	Pts.	PIM
90-91—Seattle	WHL	—	—	—	—	—	1	0	0	0	0
91-92—Seattle	WHL	67	3	9	12	212	15	1	1	2	84
92-93—Seattle	WHL	70	2	26	28	239	5	1	2	3	30
93-94—Seattle	WHL	56	8	31	39	235	9	3	8	11	23

WOLANIN, CRAIG
D, NORDIQUES

PERSONAL: Born July 27, 1967, in Grosse Point, Mich.... 6-3/205.... Shoots left.... Name pronounced woh-LAN-ihn.
TRANSACTIONS/CAREER NOTES: Selected by New Jersey Devils as underage junior in first round (first Devils pick, third overall) of NHL entry draft (June 15, 1985).... Bruised left shoulder (October 31, 1985).... Broke left ring finger (February 1, 1986).... Underwent finger surgery (February 19, 1986).... Suffered sore left hip (December 1987).... Sprained right knee (November 15, 1988).... Underwent surgery to right knee (December 1988).... Injured finger (November 22, 1989).... Traded by Devils with future considerations to Quebec Nordiques for C Peter Stastny (March 6, 1990); Devils sent D Randy Velischek to Nordiques to complete deal (August 13, 1990).... Injured knee (April 1, 1990).... Injured groin (October 17, 1991); missed three games.... Injured knee (January 8, 1992); missed four games.... Pulled muscle in right thigh (October 13, 1992); missed 24 games.... Bruised ribs (December 20, 1992); missed six games.... Injured groin (January 16, 1993); missed 28 games.... Pulled groin (April 1, 1993); missed one game.... Strained left groin (October 18, 1993); missed 11 games.... Bruised right knee (November 27, 1993); missed one game.... Strained left hip flexors (January 4, 1994); missed six games.

Season Team	League	REGULAR SEASON					PLAYOFFS				
		Gms.	G	A	Pts.	PIM	Gms.	G	A	Pts.	PIM
84-85—Kitchener	OHL	60	5	16	21	95	4	1	1	2	2
85-86—New Jersey	NHL	44	2	16	18	74	—	—	—	—	—
86-87—New Jersey	NHL	68	4	6	10	109	—	—	—	—	—
87-88—New Jersey	NHL	78	6	25	31	170	18	2	5	7	51
88-89—New Jersey	NHL	56	3	8	11	69	—	—	—	—	—
89-90—Utica	AHL	6	2	4	6	2	—	—	—	—	—
—New Jersey	NHL	37	1	7	8	47	—	—	—	—	—
—Quebec	NHL	13	0	3	3	10	—	—	—	—	—
90-91—Quebec	NHL	80	5	13	18	89	—	—	—	—	—
91-92—Quebec	NHL	69	2	11	13	80	—	—	—	—	—
92-93—Quebec	NHL	24	1	4	5	49	4	0	0	0	4
93-94—Quebec	NHL	63	6	10	16	80	—	—	—	—	—
NHL totals		**532**	**30**	**103**	**133**	**777**	**22**	**2**	**5**	**7**	**55**

W

WOOD, DODY
C/LW, SHARKS

PERSONAL: Born May 8, 1972, in Chetywynd, B.C.... 5-11/180.... Shoots left.
TRANSACTIONS/CAREER NOTES: Selected by San Jose Sharks in third round (fourth Sharks pick, 45th overall) of NHL entry draft (June 22, 1991).

Season	Team	League	REGULAR SEASON					PLAYOFFS				
			Gms.	G	A	Pts.	PIM	Gms.	G	A	Pts.	PIM
89-90	Fort St. John	PCJHL	44	51	73	124	270	—	—	—	—	—
	Seattle	WHL	—	—	—	—	—	5	0	0	0	2
90-91	Seattle	WHL	69	28	37	65	272	6	0	1	1	2
91-92	Seattle	WHL	37	13	19	32	232	—	—	—	—	—
	Swift Current	WHL	3	0	2	2	14	7	2	1	3	37
92-93	Kansas City	IHL	36	3	2	5	216	6	0	1	1	15
	San Jose	NHL	13	1	1	2	71	—	—	—	—	—
93-94	Kansas City	IHL	48	5	15	20	320	—	—	—	—	—
NHL totals			**13**	**1**	**1**	**2**	**71**					

WOOD, RANDY
LW, SABRES

PERSONAL: Born October 12, 1963, in Princeton, N.J.... 6-0/195.... Shoots left.
COLLEGE: Yale.
TRANSACTIONS/CAREER NOTES: Signed as free agent by New York Islanders (August 1986)....
Suspended four games by NHL for stick-swinging incident (October 17, 1989).... Strained right shoulder (March 17, 1990).... Traded by Islanders with C Pat LaFontaine, D Randy Hillier and future considerations to Buffalo Sabres for C Pierre Turgeon, RW Benoit Hogue, D Uwe Krupp and C Dave McIlwain; Sabres received fourth-round pick (D Dean Melanson) in 1992 draft to complete deal (October 25, 1991).
HONORS: Named to ECAC All-Star second team (1984-85).... Named to ECAC All-Star first team (1985-86).

Season	Team	League	REGULAR SEASON					PLAYOFFS				
			Gms.	G	A	Pts.	PIM	Gms.	G	A	Pts.	PIM
82-83	Yale University	ECAC	26	5	14	19	10	—	—	—	—	—
83-84	Yale University	ECAC	18	7	7	14	10	—	—	—	—	—
84-85	Yale University	ECAC	32	25	28	53	23	—	—	—	—	—
85-86	Yale University	ECAC	31	25	30	55	26	—	—	—	—	—
86-87	Springfield	AHL	75	23	24	47	57	—	—	—	—	—
	New York Islanders	NHL	6	1	0	1	4	13	1	3	4	14
87-88	New York Islanders	NHL	75	22	16	38	80	5	1	0	1	6
	Springfield	AHL	1	0	1	1	0	—	—	—	—	—
88-89	Springfield	AHL	1	1	1	2	0	—	—	—	—	—
	New York Islanders	NHL	77	15	13	28	44	—	—	—	—	—
89-90	New York Islanders	NHL	74	24	24	48	39	5	1	1	2	4
90-91	New York Islanders	NHL	76	24	18	42	45	—	—	—	—	—
91-92	New York Islanders	NHL	8	2	2	4	21	—	—	—	—	—
	Buffalo	NHL	70	20	16	36	65	7	2	1	3	6
92-93	Buffalo	NHL	82	18	25	43	77	8	1	4	5	4
93-94	Buffalo	NHL	84	22	16	38	71	6	0	0	0	0
NHL totals			**552**	**148**	**130**	**278**	**446**	**44**	**6**	**9**	**15**	**34**

WOODWARD, ROBERT
LW, CANUCKS

PERSONAL: Born January 15, 1971, in Evanston, Ill.... 6-4/225.... Shoots left.
... Full name: Robert Fairfield Woodward.
HIGH SCHOOL: Deerfield (Ill.).
COLLEGE: Michigan State.
TRANSACTIONS/CAREER NOTES: Bruised kidney playing football (October 1987).... Selected by Vancouver Canucks in second round (second Canucks pick, 29th overall) of NHL entry draft (June 17, 1989).

Season	Team	League	REGULAR SEASON					PLAYOFFS				
			Gms.	G	A	Pts.	PIM	Gms.	G	A	Pts.	PIM
87-88	Deerfield H.S.	Ill. H.S.	25	36	55	91	...	—	—	—	—	—
88-89	Deerfield H.S.	Ill. H.S.	29	46	71	117	12	—	—	—	—	—
89-90	Michigan State	CCHA	44	17	9	26	8	—	—	—	—	—
90-91	Michigan State	CCHA	32	5	13	18	16	—	—	—	—	—
91-92	Michigan State	CCHA	43	14	16	30	64	—	—	—	—	—
92-93	Michigan State	CCHA	36	12	9	21	90	—	—	—	—	—
93-94	Hamilton	AHL	60	11	14	25	45	2	0	0	0	0

WOOLLEY, JASON
D, CAPITALS

PERSONAL: Born July 27, 1969, in Toronto.... 6-0/185.... Shoots left.... Full name: Jason Douglas Woolley.
COLLEGE: Michigan State.
TRANSACTIONS/CAREER NOTES: Selected by Washington Capitals in third round (fourth Capitals pick, 61st overall) of NHL entry draft (June 17, 1989).... Broke wrist (October 12, 1992); missed 24 games.... Tore abdominal muscle (January 2, 1994).
HONORS: Named to CCHA All-Rookie team (1988-89).... Named to NCAA All-America West first team (1990-91).... Named to CCHA All-Star first team (1990-91).
MISCELLANEOUS: Member of silver-medal-winning Canadian Olympic team (1992).

Season	Team	League	REGULAR SEASON					PLAYOFFS				
			Gms.	G	A	Pts.	PIM	Gms.	G	A	Pts.	PIM
87-88	St. Michael's Jr. B	ODHA	31	19	37	56	22	—	—	—	—	—
88-89	Michigan State	CCHA	47	12	25	37	26	—	—	—	—	—

W

Season Team	League	REGULAR SEASON					PLAYOFFS				
		Gms.	G	A	Pts.	Pen.	Gms.	G	A	Pts.	Pen.
89-90—Michigan State	CCHA	45	10	38	48	26	—	—	—	—	—
90-91—Michigan State	CCHA	40	15	44	59	24	—	—	—	—	—
91-92—Canadian national team	Int'l	60	14	30	44	36	—	—	—	—	—
—Canadian Olympic Team	Int'l	8	0	5	5	4	—	—	—	—	—
—Baltimore	AHL	15	1	10	11	6	—	—	—	—	—
—Washington	NHL	1	0	0	0	0	—	—	—	—	—
92-93—Baltimore	AHL	29	14	27	41	22	1	0	2	2	0
—Washington	NHL	26	0	2	2	10	—	—	—	—	—
93-94—Portland	AHL	41	12	29	41	14	9	2	2	4	4
—Washington	NHL	10	1	2	3	4	4	1	0	1	4
NHL totals		37	1	4	5	14	4	1	0	1	4

WORTMAN, KEVIN
D, FLAMES

PERSONAL: Born February 22, 1969, in Sagus, Mass. . . . 6-0/200. . . . Shoots right.
TRANSACTIONS/CAREER NOTES: Selected by Calgary Flames in eighth round (eighth Flames pick, 168th overall) of NHL entry draft (June 20, 1992).
HONORS: Named to IHL All-Star second team (1992-93).

Season Team	League	REGULAR SEASON					PLAYOFFS				
		Gms.	G	A	Pts.	PIM	Gms.	G	A	Pts.	PIM
90-91—American Int'l	NCAA	28	21	25	46	6	—	—	—	—	—
91-92—Salt Lake City	IHL	82	12	34	46	34	5	1	0	1	0
92-93—Salt Lake City	IHL	82	13	50	63	24	—	—	—	—	—
93-94—Saint John	AHL	72	17	32	49	32	7	1	5	6	16
—Calgary	NHL	5	0	0	0	2	—	—	—	—	—
NHL totals		5	0	0	0	2					

WREGGET, KEN
G, PENGUINS

PERSONAL: Born March 25, 1964, in Brandon, Man. . . . 6-1/195. . . . Catches left.
TRANSACTIONS/CAREER NOTES: Selected by Toronto Maple Leafs as underage junior in third round (fourth Maple Leafs pick, 45th overall) of NHL entry draft (June 9, 1982). . . . Injured knee (December 26, 1985). . . . Traded by Maple Leafs to Philadelphia Flyers for two first-round picks (RW Rob Pearson and D Steve Bancroft) in 1989 draft (March 6, 1989). . . . Tore hamstring (November 1, 1989); missed seven games. . . . Pulled hamstring (March 24, 1990). . . . Strained right hip flexor (November 4, 1990); missed 15 games. . . . Traded by Flyers with RW Rick Tocchet, D Kjell Samuelsson and third-round pick in 1992 draft to Pittsburgh Penguins for RW Mark Recchi, D Brian Benning and first-round pick (LW Jason Bowen) in 1992 draft (February 19, 1992). . . . Bruised right knee (February 27, 1993); missed one game. . . . Injured foot (April 4, 1994); missed five games.
HONORS: Won WHL Top Goaltender Trophy (1983-84). . . . Named to WHL (East) All-Star first team (1983-84).
MISCELLANEOUS: Member of Stanley Cup championship team (1992).

Season Team	League	REGULAR SEASON							PLAYOFFS						
		Gms.	Min.	W	L	T	GA	SO	Avg.	Gms.	Min.	W	L	GA	SO	Avg.
81-82—Lethbridge	WHL	36	1713	19	12	0	118	1	4.13	3	84	. . .	. . .	3	0	2.14
82-83—Lethbridge	WHL	48	2696	26	17	1	157	1	3.49	*20	*1154	14	5	58	*1	*3.02
83-84—Lethbridge	WHL	53	*3053	32	20	0	161	0	*3.16	4	210	1	3	18	0	5.14
—Toronto	NHL	3	165	1	1	1	14	0	5.09	—	—	—	—	—	—	—
84-85—Toronto	NHL	23	1278	2	15	3	103	0	4.84	—	—	—	—	—	—	—
—St. Catharines	AHL	12	688	2	8	1	48	0	4.19	—	—	—	—	—	—	—
85-86—St. Catharines	AHL	18	1058	8	9	0	78	1	4.42	—	—	—	—	—	—	—
—Toronto	NHL	30	1566	9	13	4	113	0	4.33	10	607	6	4	32	†1	3.16
86-87—Toronto	NHL	56	3026	22	28	3	200	0	3.97	13	761	7	6	29	1	*2.29
87-88—Toronto	NHL	56	3000	12	35	4	222	2	4.44	2	108	0	1	11	0	6.11
88-89—Toronto	NHL	32	1888	9	20	2	139	0	4.42	—	—	—	—	—	—	—
—Philadelphia	NHL	3	130	1	1	0	13	0	6.00	5	268	2	2	10	0	2.24
89-90—Philadelphia	NHL	51	2961	22	24	3	169	0	3.42	—	—	—	—	—	—	—
90-91—Philadelphia	NHL	30	1484	10	14	3	88	0	3.56	—	—	—	—	—	—	—
91-92—Philadelphia	NHL	23	1259	9	8	3	75	0	3.57	—	—	—	—	—	—	—
—Pittsburgh	NHL	9	448	5	3	0	31	0	4.15	1	40	0	0	4	0	6.00
92-93—Pittsburgh	NHL	25	1368	13	7	2	78	0	3.42	—	—	—	—	—	—	—
93-94—Pittsburgh	NHL	42	2456	21	12	7	138	1	3.37	—	—	—	—	—	—	—
NHL totals		383	21029	136	181	35	1383	3	3.95	31	1784	15	13	86	2	2.89

WREN, BOB
LW, KINGS

PERSONAL: Born September 16, 1974, in Preston, Ont. . . . 5-10/175. . . . Shoots left.
TRANSACTIONS/CAREER NOTES: Selected by Los Angeles Kings in fourth round (third Kings pick, 94th overall) of NHL entry draft (June 26, 1993).
HONORS: Named to OHL All-Star second team (1992-93 and 1993-94).

Season Team	League	REGULAR SEASON					PLAYOFFS				
		Gms.	G	A	Pts.	PIM	Gms.	G	A	Pts.	PIM
90-91—Kingston Jr. B	OHA	32	27	28	55	85	—	—	—	—	—
91-92—Detroit	OHL	62	13	36	49	58	7	3	4	7	19
92-93—Detroit	OHL	63	57	88	145	91	15	4	11	15	20
93-94—Detroit	OHL	57	45	64	109	81	17	12	18	30	20

W

WRIGHT, DARREN
D, BRUINS

PERSONAL: Born January 19, 1976, in Duncan, B.C.... 6-1/182.... Shoots left.
TRANSACTIONS/CAREER NOTES: Selected by Boston Bruins in fifth round (fourth Bruins pick, 125th overall) of NHL entry draft (June 29, 1994).

Season Team	League		REGULAR SEASON					PLAYOFFS			
		Gms.	G	A	Pts.	PIM	Gms.	G	A	Pts.	PIM
91-92—Prince Albert	WHL	2	0	0	0	2	—	—	—	—	—
92-93—Prince Albert	WHL	53	0	4	4	131	—	—	—	—	—
93-94—Prince Albert	WHL	56	0	5	5	151	—	—	—	—	—

WRIGHT, JAMIE
LW, STARS

PERSONAL: Born May 13, 1976, in Kitchener, Ont.... 6-0/172.... Shoots left.
HIGH SCHOOL: Bishop MacDonnell (Guelph, Ont.).
TRANSACTIONS/CAREER NOTES: Selected by Dallas Stars in fourth round (third Stars pick, 98th overall) of NHL entry draft (June 29, 1994).

Season Team	League		REGULAR SEASON					PLAYOFFS			
		Gms.	G	A	Pts.	PIM	Gms.	G	A	Pts.	PIM
91-92—Elmira Jr. B	OHA	44	17	11	28	46	—	—	—	—	—
92-93—Elmira Jr. B	OHA	47	22	32	54	52	—	—	—	—	—
93-94—Guelph	OHL	65	17	15	32	34	8	2	1	3	10

WRIGHT, TYLER
C, OILERS

PERSONAL: Born April 6, 1973, in Canora, Sask.... 5-11/185.... Shoots right.
TRANSACTIONS/CAREER NOTES: Selected by Edmonton Oilers in first round (first Oilers pick, 12th overall) of NHL entry draft (June 22, 1991).

Season Team	League		REGULAR SEASON					PLAYOFFS			
		Gms.	G	A	Pts.	PIM	Gms.	G	A	Pts.	PIM
89-90—Swift Current	WHL	67	14	18	32	119	4	0	0	0	12
90-91—Swift Current	WHL	66	41	51	92	157	3	0	0	0	6
91-92—Swift Current	WHL	63	36	46	82	295	8	2	5	7	16
92-93—Swift Current	WHL	37	24	41	65	76	17	9	17	26	49
—Edmonton	NHL	7	1	1	2	19	—	—	—	—	—
93-94—Cape Breton	AHL	65	14	27	41	160	5	2	0	2	11
—Edmonton	NHL	5	0	0	0	4	—	—	—	—	—
NHL totals		12	1	1	2	23					

YACHMENEV, VITALI
RW, KINGS

PERSONAL: Born January 8, 1975, in Chelyabinsk, U.S.S.R.... 5-9/180.... Shoots left.... Name pronounced YACK-men-ev.
TRANSACTIONS/CAREER NOTES: Selected by Los Angeles Kings in third round (third Kings pick, 59th overall) of NHL entry draft (June 29, 1994).
HONORS: Named Can.HL Rookie of the Year (1993-94).... Won Emms Family Award (1993-94).... Named to Can.HL All-Rookie team (1993-94).... Named to OHL All-Rookie team (1993-94).

Season Team	League		REGULAR SEASON					PLAYOFFS			
		Gms.	G	A	Pts.	PIM	Gms.	G	A	Pts.	PIM
90-91—Traktor Chelyabinsk	USSR	80	88	60	148	72	—	—	—	—	—
91-92—Traktor Chelyabinsk	CIS	80	82	70	152	20	—	—	—	—	—
92-93—Mechel Chelyabinsk	CIS Div. II	51	23	20	43	12	—	—	—	—	—
93-94—North Bay	OHL	66	*61	52	113	18	18	13	19	32	12

YAKE, TERRY
RW, MIGHTY DUCKS

PERSONAL: Born October 22, 1968, in New Westminster, B.C.... 5-11/175.... Shoots right.
TRANSACTIONS/CAREER NOTES: Selected by Hartford Whalers in fourth round (third Whalers pick, 81st overall) of NHL entry draft (June 13, 1987).... Selected by Mighty Ducks of Anaheim in NHL expansion draft (June 24, 1993).

Season Team	League		REGULAR SEASON					PLAYOFFS			
		Gms.	G	A	Pts.	PIM	Gms.	G	A	Pts.	PIM
84-85—Brandon	WHL	11	1	1	2	0	—	—	—	—	—
85-86—Brandon	WHL	72	26	26	52	49	—	—	—	—	—
86-87—Brandon	WHL	71	44	58	102	64	—	—	—	—	—
87-88—Brandon	WHL	72	55	85	140	59	3	4	2	6	7
88-89—Hartford	NHL	2	0	0	0	0	—	—	—	—	—
—Binghamton	AHL	75	39	56	95	57	—	—	—	—	—
89-90—Hartford	NHL	2	0	1	1	0	—	—	—	—	—
—Binghamton	AHL	77	13	42	55	37	—	—	—	—	—
90-91—Hartford	NHL	19	1	4	5	10	6	1	1	2	16
—Springfield	AHL	60	35	42	77	56	15	9	9	18	10
91-92—Hartford	NHL	15	1	1	2	4	—	—	—	—	—
—Springfield	AHL	53	21	34	55	63	8	3	4	7	2
92-93—Springfield	AHL	16	8	14	22	27	—	—	—	—	—
—Hartford	NHL	66	22	31	53	46	—	—	—	—	—
93-94—Anaheim	NHL	82	21	31	52	44	—	—	—	—	—
NHL totals		186	45	68	113	104	6	1	1	2	16

WY

YASHIN, ALEXEI
C, SENATORS

PERSONAL: Born November 5, 1973, in Sverdlovsk, U.S.S.R. . . . . 6-3/215. . . . Shoots left. . . . Name pronounced YA-shihn.
TRANSACTIONS/CAREER NOTES: Selected by Ottawa Senators in first round (first Senators pick, second overall) of NHL entry draft (June 20, 1992). . . . Suffered strep throat (December 4, 1993); missed one game.
HONORS: Named to CIS All-Star team (1992-93). . . . Played in NHL All-Star Game (1994).

Season Team	League	Gms.	G	A	Pts.	PIM	Gms.	G	A	Pts.	PIM
				REGULAR SEASON					PLAYOFFS		
90-91—Avtomobilist Sverdlovsk ..	USSR	26	2	1	3	10	—	—	—	—	—
91-92—Dynamo Moscow	CIS	35	7	5	12	19	—	—	—	—	—
92-93—Dynamo Moscow	CIS	27	10	12	22	18	10	7	3	10	18
93-94—Ottawa............................	NHL	83	30	49	79	22	—	—	—	—	—
NHL totals....................................		83	30	49	79	22					

YAWNEY, TRENT
D, FLAMES

PERSONAL: Born September 29, 1965, in Hudson Bay, Sask. . . . 6-3/195. . . . Shoots left.
TRANSACTIONS/CAREER NOTES: Selected by Chicago Blackhawks as underage junior in third round (second Blackhawks pick, 45th overall) of NHL entry draft (June 9, 1984). . . . Bruised left shoulder (March 1989). . . . Strained right knee (April 24, 1989). . . . Bruised kidney (November 11, 1989). . . . Bruised thigh (January 1990). . . . Strained knee (October 1990). . . . Traded by Blackhawks to Calgary Flames for LW Stephane Matteau (December 16, 1991). . . . Fractured right clavicle (September 26, 1992); missed first 20 games of season. . . . Tore muscle in shoulder (September 9, 1993); missed 25 games.

Season Team	League	Gms.	G	A	Pts.	PIM	Gms.	G	A	Pts.	PIM
				REGULAR SEASON					PLAYOFFS		
81-82—Saskatoon	WHL	6	1	0	1	0	—	—	—	—	—
82-83—Saskatoon	WHL	59	6	31	37	44	6	0	2	2	0
83-84—Saskatoon	WHL	72	13	46	59	81	—	—	—	—	—
84-85—Saskatoon	WHL	72	16	51	67	158	3	1	6	7	7
85-86—Canadian national team ...	Int'l	73	6	15	21	60	—	—	—	—	—
86-87—Canadian national team ...	Int'l	51	4	15	19	37	—	—	—	—	—
87-88—Canadian national team ...	Int'l	60	4	12	16	81	—	—	—	—	—
—Canadian Olympic Team ..	Int'l	8	1	1	2	6	—	—	—	—	—
—Chicago	NHL	15	2	8	10	15	5	0	4	4	8
88-89—Chicago	NHL	69	5	19	24	116	15	3	6	9	20
89-90—Chicago	NHL	70	5	15	20	82	20	3	5	8	27
90-91—Chicago	NHL	61	3	13	16	77	1	0	0	0	0
91-92—Indianapolis	IHL	9	2	3	5	12	—	—	—	—	—
—Calgary	NHL	47	4	9	13	45	—	—	—	—	—
92-93—Calgary........................	NHL	63	1	16	17	67	6	3	2	5	6
93-94—Calgary........................	NHL	58	6	15	21	60	7	0	0	0	16
NHL totals.................................		383	26	95	121	462	54	9	17	26	77

YEGOROV, ALEXEI
C, SHARKS

PERSONAL: Born May 21, 1975, in Leningrad, U.S.S.R. . . . 5-9/174. . . . Shoots left.
TRANSACTIONS/CAREER NOTES: Selected by San Jose Sharks in third round (third Sharks pick, 66th overall) of NHL entry draft (June 29, 1994).

Season Team	League	Gms.	G	A	Pts.	PIM	Gms.	G	A	Pts.	PIM
				REGULAR SEASON					PLAYOFFS		
92-93—SKA St. Petersburg..........	CIS	17	1	2	3	10	6	3	1	4	6
93-94—SKA St. Petersburg..........	CIS	23	5	3	8	18	6	0	0	0	4

YEPANCHINTSEV, VADIM
C, LIGHTNING

PERSONAL: Born March 16, 1976, in Orsk, U.S.S.R. . . . 5-9/165. . . . Shoots left.
TRANSACTIONS/CAREER NOTES: Selected by Tampa Bay Lightning in third round (third Lightning pick, 55th overall) of NHL entry draft (June 29, 1994).

Season Team	League	Gms.	G	A	Pts.	PIM	Gms.	G	A	Pts.	PIM
				REGULAR SEASON					PLAYOFFS		
92-93—Yuzhny Ural					Statistics unavailable.						
93-94—Spartak Moscow..............	CIS	46	6	5	11	16	3	0	1	1	0

YORK, JASON
D, RED WINGS

PERSONAL: Born May 20, 1970, in Nepean, Ont. . . . 6-1/192. . . . Shoots right.
TRANSACTIONS/CAREER NOTES: Selected by Detroit Red Wings in seventh round (sixth Red Wings pick, 129th overall) of NHL entry draft (June 16, 1990).
HONORS: Named to AHL All-Star first team (1993-94).

Season Team	League	Gms.	G	A	Pts.	PIM	Gms.	G	A	Pts.	PIM
				REGULAR SEASON					PLAYOFFS		
89-90—Windsor...........................	OHL	39	9	30	39	38	—	—	—	—	—
—Kitchener..........................	OHL	25	11	25	36	17	17	3	19	22	10
90-91—Windsor...........................	OHL	66	13	80	93	40	11	3	10	13	12
91-92—Adirondack	AHL	49	4	20	24	32	5	0	1	1	0
92-93—Adirondack	AHL	77	15	40	55	86	11	0	3	3	18
—Detroit	NHL	2	0	0	0	0	—	—	—	—	—

Y

Season Team	League	REGULAR SEASON					PLAYOFFS				
		Gms.	G	A	Pts.	Pen.	Gms.	G	A	Pts.	Pen.
93-94—Adirondack	AHL	74	10	56	66	98	12	3	11	14	22
—Detroit	NHL	7	1	2	3	2	—	—	—	—	—
NHL totals		9	1	2	3	2					

YOUNG, JASON
LW, SABRES

PERSONAL: Born December 16, 1972, in Sudbury, Ont.... 5-10/197.... Shoots left.
TRANSACTIONS/CAREER NOTES: Suspended remainder of season by OHL for checking opposing player from behind and breaking his neck (December 4, 1990); reinstated due to career record of 86 penalty minutes in 99 games and because he had no penalties in 71 of the 99 games (March 4, 1991).... Selected by Buffalo Sabres in third round (third Sabres pick, 57th overall) of NHL entry draft (June 22, 1991).
HONORS: Named to WCHA All-Star second team (1992-93).

Season Team	League	REGULAR SEASON					PLAYOFFS				
		Gms.	G	A	Pts.	PIM	Gms.	G	A	Pts.	PIM
89-90—Sudbury	OHL	62	26	47	73	64	—	—	—	—	—
90-91—Sudbury	OHL	37	21	38	59	22	5	0	4	4	10
91-92—Sudbury	OHL	55	26	56	82	49	11	3	2	5	14
92-93—Rochester	AHL	59	20	20	40	60	14	3	4	7	31
93-94—Rochester	AHL	68	17	26	43	84	4	2	2	4	8

YOUNG, SCOTT
RW, NORDIQUES

PERSONAL: Born October 1, 1967, in Clinton, Mass.... 6-0/190.... Shoots right.... Full name: Scott Allen Young.
HIGH SCHOOL: St. Mark's (Southborough, Mass.).
COLLEGE: Boston University.
TRANSACTIONS/CAREER NOTES: Selected by Hartford Whalers in first round (first Whalers pick, 11th overall) of NHL entry draft (June 21, 1986).... Suffered lacerations above right eye (October 8, 1988).... Lacerated face (February 18, 1990).... Traded by Whalers to Pittsburgh Penguins for RW Rob Brown (December 21, 1990).... Traded by Penguins to Quebec Nordiques for D Bryan Fogarty (March 10, 1992).... Injured rib (February 14, 1993); missed one game.... Bruised ribs (February 23, 1993); missed one game.... Sprained right ankle (October 5, 1993); missed eight games.
HONORS: Named Hockey East Rookie of the Year (1985-86).
MISCELLANEOUS: Member of Stanley Cup championship team (1991).

Season Team	League	REGULAR SEASON					PLAYOFFS				
		Gms.	G	A	Pts.	PIM	Gms.	G	A	Pts.	PIM
84-85—St. Marks H.S.	Mass. H.S.	23	28	41	69	...	—	—	—	—	—
85-86—Boston University	Hockey East	38	16	13	29	31	—	—	—	—	—
86-87—Boston University	Hockey East	33	15	21	36	24	—	—	—	—	—
87-88—U.S. Olympic Team	Int'l	59	13	53	66	...	—	—	—	—	—
—Hartford	NHL	7	0	0	0	2	4	1	0	1	0
88-89—Hartford	NHL	76	19	40	59	27	4	2	0	2	4
89-90—Hartford	NHL	80	24	40	64	47	7	2	0	2	2
90-91—Hartford	NHL	34	6	9	15	8	—	—	—	—	—
—Pittsburgh	NHL	43	11	16	27	33	17	1	6	7	2
91-92—U.S. national team	Int'l	10	2	4	6	21	—	—	—	—	—
—U.S. Olympic Team	Int'l	8	2	1	3	2	—	—	—	—	—
—Bolzano	Italy	18	22	17	39	6	—	—	—	—	—
92-93—Quebec	NHL	82	30	30	60	20	6	4	1	5	0
93-94—Quebec	NHL	76	26	25	51	14	—	—	—	—	—
NHL totals		398	116	160	276	151	38	10	7	17	8

YOUNG, WENDELL
G, LIGHTNING

PERSONAL: Born August 1, 1963, in Halifax, N.S.... 5-9/181.... Catches left.
TRANSACTIONS/CAREER NOTES: Selected by Vancouver Canucks as underage junior in fourth round (third Canucks pick, 73rd overall) of NHL entry draft (June 10, 1981). ... Traded by Canucks with third-round pick in 1990 draft (C Kimbi Daniels) to Philadelphia Flyers for D Daryl Stanley and G Darren Jensen (August 28, 1987).... Traded by Flyers with seventh-round pick in 1990 draft (C Mike Valila) to Pittsburgh Penguins for third-round pick (D Chris Therien) in 1990 draft (September 1, 1988). ...Strained ankle (October 1988).... Dislocated right shoulder (February 26, 1991); missed remainder of season.... Fractured right hand (February 5, 1992); missed six games.... Selected by Tampa Bay Lightning in NHL expansion draft (June 18, 1992).... Dislocated shoulder (November 1, 1992); missed five games.... Injured shoulder (March 20, 1993); missed remainder of season.... Injured right shoulder (September 12, 1993); missed 53 games.
HONORS: Won Aldege (Baz) Bastien Trophy (1987-88).... Won Jack Butterfield Trophy (1987-88).... Named to AHL All-Star first team (1987-88).
MISCELLANEOUS: Member of Stanley Cup championship teams (1991 and 1992).

Season Team	League	REGULAR SEASON							PLAYOFFS						
		Gms.	Min.	W	L	T	GA	SO	Avg.	Gms.	Min.	W	L	GA	SO	Avg.
79-80—Cole Harbour	NSJHL	—	1446				94	0	3.90	—	—					
80-81—Kitchener	OMJHL	42	2215	19	15	0	164	1	4.44	14	800	9	1	42	1	3.15
81-82—Kitchener	OHL	*60	*3470	38	17	2	195	1	3.37	15	900	12	1	35	*1	*2.33
82-83—Kitchener	OHL	61	*3611	41	19	0	231	1	3.84	12	720	6	5	43	0	3.58
83-84—Salt Lake City	IHL	20	1094	11	6	‡0	80	0	4.39	4	122	0	2	11	0	5.41
—Fredericton	AHL	11	569	7	3	0	39	1	4.11	—	—					
—Milwaukee	IHL	6	339	...	...	...	17	0	3.01	—	—					

Season Team	League	REGULAR SEASON								PLAYOFFS						
		Gms.	Min.	W	L	T	GA	SO	Avg.	Gms.	Min.	W	L	GA	SO	Avg.
84-85—Fredericton	AHL	22	1242	7	11	3	83	0	4.01	—	—	—	—	—	—	—
85-86—Fredericton	AHL	24	1457	12	8	4	78	0	3.21	—	—	—	—	—	—	—
—Vancouver	NHL	22	1023	4	9	3	61	0	3.58	1	60	0	1	5	0	5.00
86-87—Fredericton	AHL	30	1676	11	16	0	118	0	4.22	—	—	—	—	—	—	—
—Vancouver	NHL	8	420	1	6	1	35	0	5.00	—	—	—	—	—	—	—
87-88—Philadelphia	NHL	6	320	3	2	0	20	0	3.75	—	—	—	—	—	—	—
—Hershey	AHL	51	2922	33	15	1	135	1	2.77	†12	*767	12	0	28	*1	*2.19
88-89—Pittsburgh	NHL	22	1150	12	9	0	92	0	4.80	1	39	0	0	1	0	1.54
—Muskegon	IHL	2	125	...	...	...	7	0	3.36	—	—	—	—	—	—	—
89-90—Pittsburgh	NHL	43	2318	16	20	3	161	1	4.17	—	—	—	—	—	—	—
90-91—Pittsburgh	NHL	18	773	4	6	2	52	0	4.04	—	—	—	—	—	—	—
91-92—Pittsburgh	NHL	18	838	7	6	0	53	0	3.79	—	—	—	—	—	—	—
92-93—Tampa Bay	NHL	31	1591	7	19	2	97	0	3.66	—	—	—	—	—	—	—
—Atlanta	IHL	3	183	3	0	‡0	8	0	2.62	—	—	—	—	—	—	—
93-94—Tampa Bay	NHL	9	480	2	3	1	20	1	2.50	—	—	—	—	—	—	—
NHL totals		177	8913	56	80	12	591	2	3.98	2	99	0	1	6	0	3.64

YSEBAERT, PAUL

LW, BLACKHAWKS

PERSONAL: Born May 15, 1966, in Sarnia, Ont.... 6-1/190.... Shoots left.... Full name: Paul Robert Ysebaert.... Name pronounced IGHS-bahrt.

COLLEGE: Bowling Green State.

TRANSACTIONS/CAREER NOTES: Selected by New Jersey Devils in fourth round (fourth Devils pick, 74th overall) of NHL entry draft (June 9, 1984).... Pulled stomach and groin muscles (December 1988).... Suffered contusion to left thigh (March 1989).... Traded by New Jersey Devils to Detroit Red Wings for D Lee Norwood and future considerations; Devils received fourth-round pick in 1992 draft (D Scott McCabe) to complete deal (November 27, 1990).... Injured knee (December 1991); missed one game.... Suffered from the flu (December 22, 1992); missed one game.... Suffered from the flu (March 5, 1993); missed one game.... Suffered from the flu (March 10, 1993); missed one game.... Traded by Red Wings to Winnipeg Jets for D Aaron Ward, fourth-round pick in 1993 draft and future considerations (June 11, 1993); Jets sent RW Alan Kerr to Red Wings to complete deal (June 18, 1993).... Traded by Jets to Chicago Blackhawks for third-round pick in 1995 draft (March 21, 1994).

HONORS: Named CCHA Rookie of the Year (1984-85).... Named to CCHA All-Star second team (1985-86 and 1986-87).... Won Les Cunningham Plaque (1989-90).... Won John B. Sollenberger Trophy (1989-90).... Named to AHL All-Star first team (1989-90).... Won Alka-Seltzer Plus Award (1991-92).

Season Team	League	REGULAR SEASON					PLAYOFFS				
		Gms.	G	A	Pts.	PIM	Gms.	G	A	Pts.	PIM
83-84—Petrolia Jr. B	OHA	33	35	42	77	20	—	—	—	—	—
84-85—Bowling Green State	CCHA	42	23	32	55	54	—	—	—	—	—
85-86—Bowling Green State	CCHA	42	23	45	68	50	—	—	—	—	—
86-87—Bowling Green State	CCHA	45	27	58	85	44	—	—	—	—	—
—Canadian national team	Int'l	5	1	0	1	4	—	—	—	—	—
87-88—Utica	AHL	78	30	49	79	60	—	—	—	—	—
88-89—Utica	AHL	56	36	44	80	22	5	0	1	1	4
—New Jersey	NHL	5	0	4	4	0	—	—	—	—	—
89-90—New Jersey	NHL	5	1	2	3	0	—	—	—	—	—
—Utica	AHL	74	53	52	*105	61	5	2	4	6	0
90-91—New Jersey	NHL	11	4	3	7	6	—	—	—	—	—
—Detroit	NHL	51	15	18	33	16	2	0	2	2	0
91-92—Detroit	NHL	79	35	40	75	55	10	1	0	1	10
92-93—Detroit	NHL	80	34	28	62	42	7	3	1	4	2
93-94—Winnipeg	NHL	60	9	18	27	18	—	—	—	—	—
—Chicago	NHL	11	5	3	8	8	6	0	0	0	8
NHL totals		302	103	116	219	145	25	4	3	7	20

YULE, STEVE

D, WHALERS

PERSONAL: Born May 27, 1972, in Gleichen, Alta.... 6-0/210.... Shoots right.

TRANSACTIONS/CAREER NOTES: Selected by Hartford Whalers in eighth round (eighth Whalers pick, 163rd overall) of NHL entry draft (June 22, 1991).

Season Team	League	REGULAR SEASON					PLAYOFFS				
		Gms.	G	A	Pts.	PIM	Gms.	G	A	Pts.	PIM
88-89—Kamloops	WHL	65	1	12	13	90	15	0	0	0	17
89-90—Kamloops	WHL	44	4	11	15	99	17	1	4	5	10
90-91—Kamloops	WHL	66	7	16	23	141	6	0	1	1	8
91-92—Kamloops	WHL	61	7	10	17	257	17	2	1	3	37
92-93—Springfield	AHL	38	0	4	4	52	—	—	—	—	—
93-94—Springfield	AHL	61	4	13	17	133	5	0	4	4	8

YUSHKEVICH, DIMITRI

D, FLYERS

PERSONAL: Born November 19, 1971, in Yaroslavl, U.S.S.R.... 5-11/208.... Shoots left.... Name pronounced yoosh-KAY-vihch.

TRANSACTIONS/CAREER NOTES: Selected by Philadelphia Flyers in sixth round (sixth Flyers pick, 122nd overall) of NHL entry draft (June 22, 1991).... Sprained wrist (January 28, 1993); missed two games.... Strained groin (February 18, 1994); missed four games.

Y

Season Team	League	REGULAR SEASON					PLAYOFFS				
		Gms.	G	A	Pts.	PIM	Gms.	G	A	Pts.	PIM
89-90—Torpedo Yaroslavl	USSR	40	2	3	5	...	—	—	—	—	—
90-91—Torpedo Yaroslavl	USSR	41	10	4	14	...	—	—	—	—	—
91-92—Dynamo Moscow	CIS	41	6	7	13	14	—	—	—	—	—
—Unified Olympic Team.......	Int'l	8	1	2	3	4	—	—	—	—	—
92-93—Philadelphia	NHL	82	5	27	32	71	—	—	—	—	—
93-94—Philadelphia	NHL	75	5	25	30	86	—	—	—	—	—
NHL totals.................		157	10	52	62	157					

YZERMAN, STEVE

C, RED WINGS

PERSONAL: Born May 9, 1965, in Cranbrook, B.C. .... 5-11/185. .... Shoots right. .... Name pronounced IGH-zuhr-muhn.

TRANSACTIONS/CAREER NOTES: Selected by Detroit Red Wings as underage junior in first round (first Red Wings pick, fourth overall) of NHL entry draft (June 8, 1983).... Fractured collarbone (January 31, 1986).... Injured ligaments of right knee and underwent surgery (March 1, 1988).... Injured right knee in playoff game (April 8, 1991).... Suffered herniated disc (October 21, 1993); missed 26 games.

HONORS: Named NHL Rookie of the Year by THE SPORTING NEWS (1983-84).... Named to NHL All-Rookie team (1983-84). ... Played in NHL All-Star Game (1984, 1988-1993).... Won Lester B. Pearson Award (1988-89).

STATISTICAL NOTES: Became youngest person (18) to play in NHL All-Star Game (January 31, 1984).

Season Team	League	REGULAR SEASON					PLAYOFFS				
		Gms.	G	A	Pts.	PIM	Gms.	G	A	Pts.	PIM
81-82—Peterborough	OHL	58	21	43	64	65	6	0	1	1	16
82-83—Peterborough	OHL	56	42	49	91	33	4	1	4	5	0
83-84—Detroit	NHL	80	39	48	87	33	4	3	3	6	0
84-85—Detroit	NHL	80	30	59	89	58	3	2	1	3	2
85-86—Detroit	NHL	51	14	28	42	16	—	—	—	—	—
86-87—Detroit	NHL	80	31	59	90	43	16	5	13	18	8
87-88—Detroit	NHL	64	50	52	102	44	3	1	3	4	6
88-89—Detroit	NHL	80	65	90	155	61	6	5	5	10	2
89-90—Detroit	NHL	79	62	65	127	79	—	—	—	—	—
90-91—Detroit	NHL	80	51	57	108	34	7	3	3	6	4
91-92—Detroit	NHL	79	45	58	103	64	11	3	5	8	12
92-93—Detroit	NHL	84	58	79	137	44	7	4	3	7	4
93-94—Detroit	NHL	58	24	58	82	36	3	1	3	4	0
NHL totals.................		815	469	653	1122	512	60	27	39	66	38

ZALAPSKI, ZARLEY

D, FLAMES

PERSONAL: Born April 22, 1968, in Edmonton. .... 6-1/215. .... Shoots left.

TRANSACTIONS/CAREER NOTES: Selected by Pittsburgh Penguins in first round (first Penguins pick, fourth overall) of NHL entry draft (June 21, 1986).... Suffered from Spondylosis, deterioration of the structure of the spine (October 1987).... Tore ligaments in right knee (December 29, 1988).... Broke right collarbone (October 25, 1989).... Sprained right knee (February 24, 1990); missed 13 games. ... Traded by Penguins with C John Cullen and RW Jeff Parker to Hartford Whalers for C Ron Francis, D Ulf Samuelsson and D Grant Jennings (March 4, 1991).... Suffered from the flu (March 3, 1993); missed one game. ... Sprained knee (October 14, 1993); missed 10 games. ... Traded by Hartford Whalers with C Michael Nylander and D James Patrick to Calgary Flames for D Gary Suter, LW Paul Ranheim and C Ted Drury (March 10, 1994).... Bruised thigh (February 16, 1994); missed one game.

HONORS: Named to NHL All-Rookie team (1988-89).... Played in NHL All-Star Game (1993).

Season Team	League	REGULAR SEASON					PLAYOFFS				
		Gms.	G	A	Pts.	PIM	Gms.	G	A	Pts.	PIM
84-85—Fort Saskatchewan	AJHL	23	17	30	47	14	—	—	—	—	—
85-86—Fort Saskatchewan	AJHL	27	20	33	53	46	—	—	—	—	—
—Canadian national team ...	Int'l	32	2	4	6	10	—	—	—	—	—
86-87—Canadian national team ...	Int'l	74	11	29	40	28	—	—	—	—	—
87-88—Canadian national team ...	Int'l	47	3	13	16	32	—	—	—	—	—
—Canadian Olympic Team ..	Int'l	8	1	3	4	2	—	—	—	—	—
—Pittsburgh	NHL	15	3	8	11	7	—	—	—	—	—
88-89—Pittsburgh	NHL	58	12	33	45	57	11	1	8	9	13
89-90—Pittsburgh	NHL	51	6	25	31	37	—	—	—	—	—
90-91—Pittsburgh	NHL	66	12	36	48	59	—	—	—	—	—
—Hartford	NHL	11	3	3	6	6	6	1	3	4	8
91-92—Hartford	NHL	79	20	37	57	120	7	2	3	5	6
92-93—Hartford	NHL	83	14	51	65	94	—	—	—	—	—
93-94—Hartford	NHL	56	7	30	37	56	—	—	—	—	—
—Calgary	NHL	13	3	7	10	18	7	0	3	3	2
NHL totals.................		432	80	230	310	454	31	4	17	21	29

ZAMUNER, ROB

LW/C, LIGHTNING

PERSONAL: Born September 17, 1969, in Oakville, Ont. .... 6-2/210. .... Shoots left. .... Name pronounced ZAM-nuhr.

TRANSACTIONS/CAREER NOTES: Selected by New York Rangers in third round (third Rangers pick, 45th overall) of NHL entry draft (June 17, 1989). .... Signed as free agent by Tampa Bay Lightning (July 14, 1992); Rangers awarded third-round pick in 1993 draft as compensation (July 23, 1992).

Season Team	League	REGULAR SEASON					PLAYOFFS				
		Gms.	G	A	Pts.	PIM	Gms.	G	A	Pts.	PIM
86-87—Guelph	OHL	62	6	15	21	8	—	—	—	—	—
87-88—Guelph	OHL	58	20	41	61	18	—	—	—	—	—
88-89—Guelph	OHL	66	46	65	111	38	7	5	5	10	9
89-90—Flint	IHL	77	44	35	79	32	4	1	0	1	6
90-91—Binghamton	AHL	80	25	58	83	50	9	7	6	13	35
91-92—Binghamton	AHL	61	19	53	72	42	11	8	9	17	8
—New York Rangers	NHL	9	1	2	3	2	—	—	—	—	—
92-93—Tampa Bay	NHL	84	15	28	43	74	—	—	—	—	—
93-94—Tampa Bay	NHL	59	6	6	12	42	—	—	—	—	—
NHL totals		152	22	36	58	118					

ZAVISHA, BRAD
LW/C, OILERS

PERSONAL: Born January 4, 1972, in Hines Creek, Alta. . . . 6-2/205. . . . Shoots left. . . . Name pronounced zuh-VIH-shuh.
TRANSACTIONS/CAREER NOTES: Selected by Quebec Nordiques in third round (third Nordiques pick, 43rd overall) of NHL entry draft (June 16, 1990). . . . Traded by Nordiques with G Ron Tugnutt to Edmonton Oilers for LW Martin Rucinsky (March 10, 1992). . . . Injured knee (September 1992); missed entire 1992-93 season.
HONORS: Named to WHL (East) All-Star first team (1991-92).

Season Team	League	REGULAR SEASON					PLAYOFFS				
		Gms.	G	A	Pts.	PIM	Gms.	G	A	Pts.	PIM
88-89—Seattle	WHL	52	8	13	21	43	—	—	—	—	—
89-90—Seattle	WHL	69	22	38	60	124	13	1	6	7	16
90-91—Seattle	WHL	24	15	12	27	40	—	—	—	—	—
—Portland	WHL	48	25	22	47	41	—	—	—	—	—
91-92—Portland	WHL	11	7	4	11	18	—	—	—	—	—
—Lethbridge	WHL	59	44	40	84	160	5	3	1	4	18
93-94—Cape Breton	AHL	58	19	15	34	114	2	0	0	0	2
—Edmonton	NHL	2	0	0	0	0	—	—	—	—	—
NHL totals		2	0	0	0	0					

ZELEPUKIN, VALERI
RW, DEVILS

PERSONAL: Born September 17, 1968, in Voskresensk, U.S.S.R. . . . 5-11/180. . . . Shoots left. . . . Name pronounced zehl-ih-POO-kihn.
TRANSACTIONS/CAREER NOTES: Selected by New Jersey Devils in 11th round (13th Devils pick, 221st overall) of NHL entry draft (June 22, 1990). . . . Bruised shoulder (January 22, 1993); missed five games. . . . Bruised left shoulder (December 22, 1993); missed one game. . . . Injured chest (April 14, 1994); missed one game.

Season Team	League	REGULAR SEASON					PLAYOFFS				
		Gms.	G	A	Pts.	PIM	Gms.	G	A	Pts.	PIM
84-85—Khimik	USSR	5	0	0	0	2	—	—	—	—	—
85-86—Khimik	USSR	33	2	2	4	10	—	—	—	—	—
86-87—Khimik	USSR	19	1	0	1	4	—	—	—	—	—
87-88—SKA Leningrad	USSR	18	18	6	24	. . .	—	—	—	—	—
—CSKA Moscow	USSR	19	3	1	4	8	—	—	—	—	—
88-89—CSKA Moscow	USSR	17	2	3	5	2	—	—	—	—	—
89-90—Khimik	USSR	46	17	14	31	26	—	—	—	—	—
90-91—Khimik	USSR	46	12	19	31	22	—	—	—	—	—
91-92—Utica	AHL	22	20	9	29	8	—	—	—	—	—
—New Jersey	NHL	44	13	18	31	28	4	1	1	2	2
92-93—New Jersey	NHL	78	23	41	64	70	5	0	2	2	0
93-94—New Jersey	NHL	82	26	31	57	70	20	5	2	7	14
NHL totals		204	62	90	152	168	29	6	5	11	16

ZENT, JASON
LW, ISLANDERS

PERSONAL: Born April 15, 1971, in Buffalo, N.Y. . . . 5-11/180. . . . Shoots left. . . . Full name: Jason William Zent.
HIGH SCHOOL: Nichols School (Buffalo, N.Y.).
COLLEGE: Wisconsin.
TRANSACTIONS/CAREER NOTES: Selected by New York Islanders in third round (third Islanders pick, 44th overall) of NHL entry draft (June 17, 1989). . . . Sprained ankle playing racquetball (January 1991).
HONORS: Named to WCHA All-Rookie team (1990-91). . . . Named to NCAA All-Tournament team (1991-92).

Season Team	League	REGULAR SEASON					PLAYOFFS				
		Gms.	G	A	Pts.	PIM	Gms.	G	A	Pts.	PIM
87-88—Nichols School	N.Y. H.S.	21	20	16	36	28	—	—	—	—	—
88-89—Nichols School	N.Y. H.S.	29	49	32	81	26	—	—	—	—	—
89-90—Nichols School	N.Y. H.S.					Statistics unavailable.					
90-91—University of Wisconsin	WCHA	39	19	18	37	51	—	—	—	—	—
91-92—University of Wisconsin	WCHA	43	27	17	44	134	—	—	—	—	—
92-93—University of Wisconsin	WCHA	40	26	12	38	88	—	—	—	—	—
93-94—University of Wisconsin	WCHA	42	20	21	41	120	—	—	—	—	—

ZETTLER, ROB

D, FLYERS

PERSONAL: Born March 8, 1968, in Sept-Iles, Que.... 6-3/200.... Shoots left.
TRANSACTIONS/CAREER NOTES: Selected by Minnesota North Stars as underage junior in fifth round (fifth North Stars pick, 55th overall) of NHL entry draft (June 21, 1986).... Tore hip flexor (January 21, 1991); missed 11 games.... Selected by San Jose Sharks in NHL dispersal draft (May 30, 1991).... Strained back (October 20, 1992); missed three games.... Injured groin (April 8, 1993); missed one game.... Traded by Sharks to Philadelphia Flyers for C Viacheslav Butsayev (February 1, 1994).

Season Team	League	REGULAR SEASON Gms.	G	A	Pts.	PIM	PLAYOFFS Gms.	G	A	Pts.	PIM
84-85—Sault Ste. Marie	OHL	60	2	14	16	37	—	—	—	—	—
85-86—Sault Ste. Marie	OHL	57	5	23	28	92	—	—	—	—	—
86-87—Sault Ste. Marie	OHL	64	13	22	35	89	4	0	0	0	0
87-88—Sault Ste. Marie	OHL	64	7	41	48	77	6	2	2	4	9
—Kalamazoo	IHL	2	0	1	1	0	7	0	2	2	2
88-89—Minnesota	NHL	2	0	0	0	0	—	—	—	—	—
—Kalamazoo	IHL	80	5	21	26	79	6	0	1	1	26
89-90—Minnesota	NHL	31	0	8	8	45	—	—	—	—	—
—Kalamazoo	IHL	41	6	10	16	64	7	0	0	0	6
90-91—Kalamazoo	IHL	1	0	0	0	2	—	—	—	—	—
—Minnesota	NHL	47	1	4	5	119	—	—	—	—	—
91-92—San Jose	NHL	74	1	8	9	99	—	—	—	—	—
92-93—San Jose	NHL	80	0	7	7	150	—	—	—	—	—
93-94—San Jose	NHL	42	0	3	3	65	—	—	—	—	—
—Philadelphia	NHL	33	0	4	4	69	—	—	—	—	—
NHL totals		**309**	**2**	**34**	**36**	**547**					

ZEZEL, PETER

C, MAPLE LEAFS

PERSONAL: Born April 22, 1965, in Toronto.... 5-11/205.... Shoots left.... Name pronounced ZEH-zehl.
TRANSACTIONS/CAREER NOTES: Selected by Philadelphia Flyers as underage junior in second round (first Flyers pick, 41st overall) of NHL entry draft (June 8, 1983).... Broke hand (November 1984).... Tore medial cartilage in left knee (March 1987).... Sprained right ankle (November 1987).... Separated left shoulder (March 1988).... Traded by Flyers to St. Louis Blues for C Mike Bullard (November 29, 1988).... Pulled groin (December 1988).... Bruised sternum (January 1989).... Sprained right knee (March 5, 1989).... Bruised right hip (March 11, 1990).... Traded by Blues with D Mike Lalor to Washington Capitals for LW Geoff Courtnall (July 13, 1990).... Sprained left ankle (October 23, 1990); missed 23 games.... Reinjured ankle (December 28, 1990); missed two games.... Traded by Capitals with D Bob Rouse to Toronto Maple Leafs for D Al Iafrate (January 16, 1991).... Sprained knee (November 14, 1991); missed five games.... Strained knee (March 5, 1992).... Bruised knee (November 5, 1992); missed five games.... Sprained wrist (January 6, 1993); missed three games.... Sprained neck (March 25, 1993); missed five games.... Injured back (October 16, 1993); missed 41 games.... Suffered back spasms (January 30, 1994); missed one game.
MISCELLANEOUS: Played three games as a striker for Toronto Blizzard in the North American Soccer League (1982).

Season Team	League	REGULAR SEASON Gms.	G	A	Pts.	PIM	PLAYOFFS Gms.	G	A	Pts.	PIM
81-82—Don Mills Flyers	MTHL	40	43	51	94	36	—	—	—	—	—
82-83—Toronto	OHL	66	35	39	74	28	4	2	4	6	0
83-84—Toronto	OHL	68	47	86	133	31	9	7	5	12	4
84-85—Philadelphia	NHL	65	15	46	61	26	19	1	8	9	28
85-86—Philadelphia	NHL	79	17	37	54	76	5	3	1	4	4
86-87—Philadelphia	NHL	71	33	39	72	71	25	3	10	13	10
87-88—Philadelphia	NHL	69	22	35	57	42	7	3	2	5	7
88-89—Philadelphia	NHL	26	4	13	17	15	—	—	—	—	—
—St. Louis	NHL	52	17	36	53	27	10	6	6	12	4
89-90—St. Louis	NHL	73	25	47	72	30	12	1	7	8	4
90-91—Washington	NHL	20	7	5	12	10	—	—	—	—	—
—Toronto	NHL	32	14	14	28	4	—	—	—	—	—
91-92—Toronto	NHL	64	16	33	49	26	—	—	—	—	—
92-93—Toronto	NHL	70	12	23	35	24	20	2	1	3	6
93-94—Toronto	NHL	41	8	8	16	19	18	2	4	6	8
NHL totals		**662**	**190**	**336**	**526**	**370**	**116**	**21**	**39**	**60**	**71**

ZHAMNOV, ALEXEI

C, JETS

PERSONAL: Born October 1, 1970, in Moscow, U.S.S.R.... 6-1/187.... Shoots left.... Name pronounced ZHAHM-nanf.
TRANSACTIONS/CAREER NOTES: Selected by Winnipeg Jets in fourth round (fifth Jets pick, 77th overall) of NHL entry draft (June 16, 1990).... Suffered hip flexor (November 2, 1992); missed two games.... Suffered back spasms (January 27, 1993); missed one game.... Suffered back spasms (February 3, 1993); missed one game.... Suffered back spasms (February 12, 1993); missed 12 games.... Suffered left quad contusion (October 26, 1993); missed three games.... Sprained back (December 27, 1993); missed eight games.... Suffered back spasms (March 19, 1994); missed remainder of season.

Season Team	League	REGULAR SEASON Gms.	G	A	Pts.	PIM	PLAYOFFS Gms.	G	A	Pts.	PIM
88-89—Dynamo Moscow	USSR	4	0	0	0	0	—	—	—	—	—
89-90—Dynamo Moscow	USSR	43	11	6	17	23	—	—	—	—	—
90-91—Dynamo Moscow	USSR	46	16	12	28	24	—	—	—	—	—
91-92—Dynamo Moscow	CIS	39	15	21	36	28	—	—	—	—	—
—Unified Olympic Team	Int'l	8	0	3	3	8	—	—	—	—	—

Season Team	League	REGULAR SEASON					PLAYOFFS				
		Gms.	G	A	Pts.	Pen.	Gms.	G	A	Pts.	Pen.
92-93—Winnipeg	NHL	68	25	47	72	58	6	0	2	2	2
93-94—Winnipeg	NHL	61	26	45	71	62	—	—	—	—	—
NHL totals		129	51	92	143	120	6	0	2	2	2

ZHITNIK, ALEXEI
D, KINGS

PERSONAL: Born October 10, 1972, in Kiev, U.S.S.R. . . . 5-11/180. . . . Shoots left. . . . Name pronounced ZHIHT-nihk.

TRANSACTIONS/CAREER NOTES: Selected by Los Angeles Kings in fourth round (third Kings pick, 81st overall) of NHL entry draft (June 22, 1991). . . . Suffered from the flu (January 12, 1993); missed five games. . . . Suspended one game by NHL for cross-checking (November 30, 1993).

Season Team	League	REGULAR SEASON					PLAYOFFS				
		Gms.	G	A	Pts.	PIM	Gms.	G	A	Pts.	PIM
90-91—Sokol Kiev	USSR	40	1	4	5	46	—	—	—	—	—
91-92—CSKA Moscow	CIS	36	2	7	9	48	—	—	—	—	—
—Unified Olympic Team	Int'l	8	1	0	1	0	—	—	—	—	—
92-93—Los Angeles	NHL	78	12	36	48	80	24	3	9	12	26
93-94—Los Angeles	NHL	81	12	40	52	101	—	—	—	—	—
NHL totals		159	24	76	100	181	24	3	9	12	26

ZHOLTOK, SERGEI
LW, BRUINS

PERSONAL: Born December 2, 1972, in Riga, U.S.S.R. . . . 6-0/185. . . . Shoots left. . . . Name pronounced SAIR-gay ZHOHL-tahk.

TRANSACTIONS/CAREER NOTES: Selected by Boston Bruins in third round (second Bruins pick, 56th overall) of NHL entry draft (June 20, 1992).

Season Team	League	REGULAR SEASON					PLAYOFFS				
		Gms.	G	A	Pts.	PIM	Gms.	G	A	Pts.	PIM
90-91—Dynamo Riga	USSR	39	4	0	4	16	—	—	—	—	—
91-92—Riga	CIS	27	6	3	9	6	—	—	—	—	—
92-93—Providence	AHL	64	31	35	66	57	6	3	5	8	4
—Boston	NHL	1	0	1	1	0	—	—	—	—	—
93-94—Providence	AHL	54	29	33	62	16	—	—	—	—	—
—Boston	NHL	24	2	1	3	2	—	—	—	—	—
NHL totals		25	2	2	4	2	—	—	—	—	—

ZMOLEK, DOUG
D, STARS

PERSONAL: Born November 3, 1970, in Rochester, Minn. . . . 6-2/220. . . . Shoots left. . . . Full name: Doug Allan Zmolek. . . . Name pronounced zuh-MOH-lehk.

HIGH SCHOOL: John Marshall (Rochester, Minn.).

COLLEGE: Minnesota.

TRANSACTIONS/CAREER NOTES: Selected by Minnesota North Stars in first round (first North Stars pick, seventh overall) of NHL entry draft (June 17, 1989). . . . Selected by San Jose Sharks in NHL dispersal draft (May 30, 1991). . . . Traded by Sharks with D Mike Lalor to Dallas Stars for RW Ulf Dahlen and future considerations (March 19, 1994). . . . Sprained thumb (March 12, 1994); missed one game. . . . Separated shoulder (March 31, 1994); missed five games.

HONORS: Named to NCAA All-America West second team (1991-92). . . . Named to WCHA All-Star second team (1991-92).

Season Team	League	REGULAR SEASON					PLAYOFFS				
		Gms.	G	A	Pts.	PIM	Gms.	G	A	Pts.	PIM
87-88—Rochester John Marshall HS	Minn. H.S.	27	4	32	36	...	—	—	—	—	—
88-89—Rochester John Marshall HS	Minn. H.S.	29	17	41	58	...	—	—	—	—	—
89-90—University of Minnesota	WCHA	40	1	10	11	52	—	—	—	—	—
90-91—University of Minnesota	WCHA	42	3	15	18	94	—	—	—	—	—
91-92—University of Minnesota	WCHA	44	6	21	27	88	—	—	—	—	—
92-93—San Jose	NHL	84	5	10	15	229	—	—	—	—	—
93-94—San Jose	NHL	68	0	4	4	122	—	—	—	—	—
—Dallas	NHL	7	1	0	1	11	7	0	1	1	4
NHL totals		159	6	14	20	362	7	0	1	1	4

ZOLOTOV, ROMAN
D, FLYERS

PERSONAL: Born February 13, 1974, in Moscow, U.S.S.R. . . . 6-1/183. . . . Shoots left.

TRANSACTIONS/CAREER NOTES: Selected by Philadelphia Flyers in sixth round (fourth Flyers pick, 127th overall) of NHL entry draft (June 20, 1992).

Season Team	League	REGULAR SEASON					PLAYOFFS				
		Gms.	G	A	Pts.	PIM	Gms.	G	A	Pts.	PIM
91-92—Dynamo Moscow	CIS	1	0	0	0	2	—	—	—	—	—
92-93—Dynamo Moscow	CIS				Statistics unavailable.						
93-94—Dynamo Moscow	CIS	33	0	2	2	20	5	0	1	1	6

ZOMBO, RICK
D, BLUES

PERSONAL: Born May 8, 1963, in Des Plaines, Ill. . . . 6-1/195. . . . Shoots right.

COLLEGE: North Dakota.

TRANSACTIONS/CAREER NOTES: Selected by Detroit Red Wings in eighth round (sixth Red Wings pick, 149th overall) of NHL entry draft (June 10, 1981). . . . Injured knee (December 1984). . . . Injured shoulder (December 1987). . . . Strained knee (December 1988). . . . Suspended three games by NHL for high-sticking (December 27, 1989). . . . Traded by Red Wings to St. Louis Blues for G Vincent Riendeau (October 18, 1991). . . . Fractured bone in left foot (March 14, 1992); missed seven games. . . . Suffered from injury (October 13, 1992); missed one game. . . .

Suspended 10 games by NHL for slashing and shoving linesman (January 13, 1994).
HONORS: Named USHL Best Defenseman (1980-81).... Named to USHL All-Star first team (1980-81).

Season	Team	League	REGULAR SEASON					PLAYOFFS				
			Gms.	G	A	Pts.	PIM	Gms.	G	A	Pts.	PIM
80-81	Austin	USHL	43	10	26	36	73	—	—	—	—	—
81-82	Univ. of North Dakota	WCHA	45	1	15	16	31	—	—	—	—	—
82-83	Univ. of North Dakota	WCHA	33	5	11	16	41	—	—	—	—	—
83-84	Univ. of North Dakota	WCHA	34	7	24	31	40	—	—	—	—	—
84-85	Adirondack	AHL	56	3	32	35	70	—	—	—	—	—
	Detroit	NHL	1	0	0	0	0	—	—	—	—	—
85-86	Adirondack	AHL	69	7	34	41	94	17	0	4	4	40
	Detroit	NHL	14	0	1	1	16	—	—	—	—	—
86-87	Adirondack	AHL	25	0	6	6	22	—	—	—	—	—
	Detroit	NHL	44	1	4	5	59	7	0	1	1	9
87-88	Detroit	NHL	62	3	14	17	96	16	0	6	6	55
88-89	Detroit	NHL	75	1	20	21	106	6	0	1	1	16
89-90	Detroit	NHL	77	5	20	25	95	—	—	—	—	—
90-91	Detroit	NHL	77	4	19	23	55	7	1	0	1	10
91-92	Detroit	NHL	3	0	0	0	15	—	—	—	—	—
	St. Louis	NHL	64	3	15	18	46	6	0	2	2	12
92-93	St. Louis	NHL	71	0	15	15	78	11	0	1	1	12
93-94	St. Louis	NHL	74	2	8	10	85	4	0	0	0	11
NHL totals			562	19	116	135	651	57	1	11	12	125

ZUBOV, SERGEI
D, RANGERS

PERSONAL: Born July 22, 1970, in Moscow, U.S.S.R.... 6-0/195.... Shoots right.... Name pronounced SAIR-gay ZOO-bahf.
TRANSACTIONS/CAREER NOTES: Selected by New York Rangers in fifth round (sixth Rangers pick, 85th overall) of NHL entry draft (June 16, 1990).... Suffered concussion (February 26, 1993); missed one game.
MISCELLANEOUS: Member of Stanley Cup championship team (1994).

Season	Team	League	REGULAR SEASON					PLAYOFFS				
			Gms.	G	A	Pts.	PIM	Gms.	G	A	Pts.	PIM
88-89	CSKA Moscow	USSR	29	1	4	5	10	—	—	—	—	—
89-90	CSKA Moscow	USSR	48	6	2	8	16	—	—	—	—	—
90-91	CSKA Moscow	USSR	41	6	5	11	12	—	—	—	—	—
91-92	CSKA Moscow	CIS	36	4	7	11	6	—	—	—	—	—
	Unified Olympic Team	Int'l	8	0	1	1	0	—	—	—	—	—
92-93	CSKA Moscow	CIS	1	0	1	1	0	—	—	—	—	—
	Binghamton	AHL	30	7	29	36	14	11	5	5	10	2
	New York Rangers	NHL	49	8	23	31	4	—	—	—	—	—
93-94	New York Rangers	NHL	78	12	77	89	39	22	5	14	19	0
	Binghamton	AHL	2	1	2	3	0	—	—	—	—	—
NHL totals			127	20	100	120	43	22	5	14	19	0

NOTE: At deadline, the New York Rangers had not named a head coach for the 1994-95 National Hockey League season. Vancouver President/General Manager/Coach Pat Quinn had not announced whether he would return as the coach of the Canucks for the 1994-95 season.

BOWMAN, SCOTTY
RED WINGS

PERSONAL: Born September 18, 1933, in Montreal. . . . Full name: William Scott Bowman.

HONORS: Inducted into Hall of Fame (1991).

HEAD COACHING RECORD

BACKGROUND: Minor league hockey supervisor, Montreal Canadiens organization (1954-55 through 1956-57). . . . Coach, Team Canada (1976 and 1981). . . . Director of hockey operations/general manager, Buffalo Sabres (1979-80 through 1986-87). . . . Director of player development, Pittsburgh Penguins (1990-91). . . . Director of player personnel (1994-95).

HONORS: Won Jack Adams Award (1976-77). . . . Named NHL Executive of the Year by THE SPORTING NEWS (1979-80).

RECORDS: Holds NHL career regular-season record for wins—880; winning percentage—.654. . . . Holds NHL career playoff record for wins—140; games—226.

							REGULAR SEASON				PLAYOFFS	
Season	Team	League	W	L	T	Pct.	Finish		W	L	Pct.	
67-68—St. Louis		NHL	23	21	14	.517	3rd/Western Division		8	10	.444	
68-69—St. Louis		NHL	37	25	14	.579	1st/Western Division		8	4	.667	
69-70—St. Louis		NHL	37	27	12	.566	1st/Western Division		8	8	.500	
70-71—St. Louis		NHL	13	10	5	.554	2nd/West Division		2	4	.333	
71-72—Montreal		NHL	46	16	16	.692	3rd/East Division		2	4	.333	
72-73—Montreal		NHL	52	10	16	.769	1st/East Division		12	5	.706	
73-74—Montreal		NHL	45	24	9	.635	2nd/East Division		2	4	.333	
74-75—Montreal		NHL	47	14	19	.706	1st/Adams Division		6	5	.545	
75-76—Montreal		NHL	58	11	11	.794	1st/Adams Division		12	1	.923	
76-77—Montreal		NHL	60	8	12	.825	1st/Adams Division		12	2	.857	
77-78—Montreal		NHL	59	10	11	.806	1st/Adams Division		12	3	.800	
78-79—Montreal		NHL	52	17	11	.719	1st/Adams Division		12	4	.750	
79-80—Buffalo		NHL	47	17	16	.688	1st/Adams Division		9	5	.643	
81-82—Buffalo		NHL	18	10	7	.614	3rd/Adams Division		1	3	.250	
82-83—Buffalo		NHL	38	29	13	.556	3rd/Adams Division		6	4	.600	
83-84—Buffalo		NHL	48	25	7	.644	2nd/Adams Division		0	3	.000	
84-85—Buffalo		NHL	38	28	14	.563	3rd/Adams Division		2	3	.400	
85-86—Buffalo		NHL	18	18	1	.500	5th/Adams Division		—	—	—	
86-87—Buffalo		NHL	3	7	2	.333	5th/Adams Division		—	—	—	
91-92—Pittsburgh		NHL	39	32	9	.544	3rd/Adams Division		16	5	.762	
92-93—Pittsburgh		NHL	56	21	7	.726	1st/Patrick Division		7	5	.583	
93-94—Detroit		NHL	46	30	8	.595	1st/Central Division		3	4	.429	
NHL totals (22 years)			**880**	**410**	**234**	**.654**	**NHL totals (20 years)**		**140**	**86**	**.619**	

NOTES:

1968— Defeated Philadelphia in Western Division finals; defeated Minnesota in Stanley Cup semifinals; lost to Montreal in Stanley Cup finals.

1969— Defeated Philadelphia in Stanley Cup quarterfinals; defeated Los Angeles in Stanley Cup semifinals; lost to Montreal in Stanley Cup finals.

1970— Defeated Minnesota in Stanley Cup quarterfinals; defeated Pittsburgh in Stanley Cup quarterfinals; lost to Boston in Stanley Cup finals.

1971— Lost to Minnesota in Stanley Cup quarterfinals.

1972— Lost to New York Rangers in Stanley Cup quarterfinals.

1973— Defeated Buffalo in Stanley Cup quarterfinals; defeated Philadelphia in Stanley Cup semifinals; defeated Chicago in Stanley Cup finals.

1974— Lost to New York Rangers in Stanley Cup quarterfinals.

1975— Defeated Vancouver in Stanley Cup quarterfinals; lost to Buffalo in Stanley Cup semifinals.

1976— Defeated Chicago in Stanley Cup quarterfinals; defeated New York Islanders in Stanley Cup semifinals; defeated Philadelphia in Stanley Cup finals.

1977— Defeated St. Louis in Stanley Cup quarterfinals; defeated New York Islanders in Stanley Cup semifinals; defeated Boston in Stanley Cup finals.

1978— Defeated Detroit in Stanley Cup quarterfinals; defeated Toronto in Stanley Cup semifinals; defeated Boston in Stanley Cup finals.

1979— Defeated Toronto in Stanley Cup quarterfinals; defeated Boston in Stanley Cup semifinals; defeated New York Rangers in Stanley Cup finals.

1980— Defeated Vancouver in Stanley Cup preliminary round; defeated Chicago in Stanley Cup quarterfinals; lost to New York Islanders in Stanley Cup semifinals.

1982— Lost to Boston in Stanley Cup preliminary rounds.

1983— Defeated Montreal in Adams Division semifinals; lost to Boston in Adams Division finals.

1984— Lost to Quebec in Adams Division semifinals.

1985— Lost to Quebec in Adams Division semifinals.

1992— Defeated Washington in Patrick Division semifinals; defeated New York Rangers in Patrick Division finals; defeated Boston in Wales Conference finals; defeated Chicago in Stanley Cup finals.

1993— Defeated New Jersey in Patrick Division semifinals; lost to New York Islanders in Patrick Division finals.

1994— Lost to San Jose in Western Conference quarterfinals.

BOWNESS, RICK
SENATORS

PERSONAL: Born January 25, 1955, in Moncton, N.B. . . . . 6-1/ 185. . . . Shot right. . . . Full name: Richard Gary Bowness. . . . Name pronounced boh-nihz.
HIGH SCHOOL: Halifax (N.S.).
COLLEGE: St. Mary's (N.S.).
TRANSACTIONS/CAREER NOTES: Selected by Atlanta Flames from Montreal Juniors in second round (second Flames pick, 26th overall) of NHL amateur draft (June 3, 1975). . . . Sold by Atlanta Flames to Detroit Red Wings (September 1977). . . . Sold by Red Wings to St. Louis Blues (September 1978). . . . Traded by Blues to Winnipeg Jets for D Craig Norwich (June 19, 1980).
MISCELLANEOUS: Played right wing.

Season Team	League	REGULAR SEASON					PLAYOFFS				
		Gms.	G	A	Pts.	PIM	Gms.	G	A	Pts.	PIM
72-73—Quebec	QMJHL	30	2	7	9	2	—	—	—	—	—
73-74—Montreal	QMJHL	67	25	46	71	95	—	—	—	—	—
74-75—Montreal	QMJHL	71	24	76	100	130	—	—	—	—	—
75-76—Tulsa	CHL	64	25	38	63	160	9	4	3	7	12
—Nova Scotia	AHL	2	0	1	1	0	—	—	—	—	—
—Atlanta	NHL	5	0	0	0	0	—	—	—	—	—
76-77—Tulsa	CHL	39	15	15	30	72	8	0	1	1	20
—Atlanta	NHL	28	0	4	4	29	—	—	—	—	—
77-78—Detroit	NHL	61	8	11	19	76	4	0	0	0	2
78-79—St. Louis	NHL	24	1	3	4	30	—	—	—	—	—
—Salt Lake City	CHL	48	25	28	53	92	10	5	4	9	27
79-80—Salt Lake City	CHL	71	25	46	71	135	13	5	9	14	39
—St. Louis	NHL	10	1	2	3	11	—	—	—	—	—
80-81—Tulsa	CHL	35	12	20	32	82	—	—	—	—	—
—Winnipeg	NHL	45	8	17	25	45	1	0	0	0	0
81-82—Tulsa	CHL	79	34	53	87	201	3	0	2	2	2
82-83—Sherbrooke	AHL	65	17	31	48	117	—	—	—	—	—
NHL totals		173	18	37	55	191	5	0	0	0	2

HEAD COACHING RECORD

BACKGROUND: Player/assistant coach, Sherbrooke, Winnipeg Jets organization (1982-83). . . . Assistant coach, Jets (1983-84 through 1986-87). . . . General manager/coach, Moncton, Jets organization (1987-88).

Season Team	League	REGULAR SEASON					PLAYOFFS		
		W	L	T	Pct.	Finish	W	L	Pct.
87-88—Moncton	AHL	27	45	8	.388	6th/North Division	—	—	—
88-89—Moncton	AHL	37	34	9	.519	3rd/North Division	—	—	—
—Winnipeg	NHL	8	17	3	.339	5th/Smythe Division	—	—	—
89-90—Maine	AHL	31	38	11	.456	5th/North Division	—	—	—
90-91—Maine	AHL	34	34	12	.500	5th/North Division	—	—	—
91-92—Boston	NHL	36	32	12	.525	2nd/Adams Division	8	7	.533
92-93—Ottawa	NHL	10	70	4	.143	6th/Adams Division	—	—	—
93-94—Ottawa	NHL	14	61	9	.220	7th/Northeast Division	—	—	—
NHL totals (4 years)		68	180	28	.297	NHL totals (1 year)	8	7	.533

NOTES:
1992—Defeated Buffalo in Adams Division semifinals; defeated New York Rangers in Adams Division finals; lost to Pittsburgh in Wales Conference finals.

BURNETT, GEORGE
OILERS

PERSONAL: Born March 25, 1962, in Uxbridge, Ont. . . . 6-1/205. . . . Shot right.
HIGH SCHOOL: Sir Wilfrid Laurier (London, Ont.).
COLLEGE: McGill, Que. (degree in physical education).
HONORS: Named to CIAU All-Canadian team (1982-83). . . . Named to QUAA All-Star first team.

Season Team	League	REGULAR SEASON					PLAYOFFS				
		Gms.	G	A	Pts.	PIM	Gms.	G	A	Pts.	PIM
79-80—London	OMJHL	68	14	15	29	21	—	—	—	—	—
80-81—London	OMJHL	67	17	59	76	10	—	—	—	—	—
81-82—London	OHL	68	26	66	92	63	4	1	1	2	2
82-83—McGill University	QUAA	38	21	60	*81	30	—	—	—	—	—
83-84—McGill University	QUAA	43	22	37	59	20	—	—	—	—	—
84-85—McGill University	QUAA	3	2	4	6	0	—	—	—	—	—

HEAD COACHING RECORD

BACKGROUND: Assistant coach, Oshawa Generals of OHL (1989). . . . General manager, Niagara Falls Thunder of OHL (1990-91 and 1991-92).
HONORS: Won Matt Leyden Trophy (1990-91 and 1991-92).

Season Team	League	REGULAR SEASON					PLAYOFFS		
		W	L	T	Pct.	Finish	W	L	Pct.
87-88—Port Perry	OHA Jr. C					Record unavailable.			
88-89—Seneca College	OCAA					Record unavailable.			
89-90—Niagara Falls	OHL	23	39	4	.435	6th/Emms Division	9	7	.563
90-91—Niagara Falls	OHL	39	18	9	.659	2nd/Emms Division	8	6	.571
91-92—Niagara Falls	OHL	39	23	4	.621	2nd/Emms Division	9	8	.529
92-93—Cape Breton	AHL	36	32	12	.525	3rd/Atlantic Division	14	2	.875
93-94—Cape Breton	AHL	32	35	13	.481	4th/Atlantic Division	1	4	.200

NOTES:
1989— Replaced Bill Laforge as coach of Niagara Falls (November 16).
1990— Defeated London in Emms Division quarterfinals; defeated Owen Sound in Emms Division semifinals; lost to Kitchener in Emms Division finals.
1991— Defeated Kitchener in Emms Division quarterfinals; defeated Windsor in Emms Division semifinals; lost to Sault Ste. Marie in Emms Division finals.
1992— Defeated Detroit in Emms Division quarterfinals; defeated London in Emms Division semifinals; lost to Sault Ste. Marie in Emms Division finals.
1993— Defeated Fredericton in Calder Cup divisional semifinals; defeated St. John's in Calder Cup divisional finals; defeated Springfield in Calder Cup league semifinals; defeated Rochester in Calder Cup league finals.
1994— Lost to St. John's in Calder Cup divisional semifinals.

BURNS, PAT
MAPLE LEAFS

PERSONAL: Born April 4, 1952, in St.-Henri, Que.
MISCELLANEOUS: Served 17 years with the Gastineau (Que.) and Ottawa Police Departments before assuming a professional hockey coaching career.

HEAD COACHING RECORD

BACKGROUND: Assistant coach, Canadian national team (1986).... Assistant coach, Canadian national junior team (1987).
HONORS: Named NHL Coach of the Year by THE SPORTING NEWS (1988-89 and 1992-93).... Won Jack Adams Award (1988-89 and 1992-93).

Season	Team	League	W	L	T	Pct.	Finish	W	L	Pct.
									REGULAR SEASON / PLAYOFFS	
83-84	Hull	QMJHL	25	45	0	.357	6th/LeBel Division	—	—	—
84-85	Hull	QMJHL	33	34	1	.493	2nd/LeBel Division	1	4	.200
85-86	Hull	QMJHL	54	18	0	.750	1st/LeBel Division	15	0	1.000
86-87	Hull	QMJHL	26	39	5	.407	4th/LeBel Division	4	4	.500
87-88	Sherbrooke	AHL	42	34	4	.550	3rd/North Division	2	4	.333
88-89	Montreal	NHL	53	18	9	.719	1st/Adams Division	14	7	.667
89-90	Montreal	NHL	41	28	11	.581	3rd/Adams Division	5	6	.455
90-91	Montreal	NHL	39	30	11	.556	2nd/Adams Division	6	7	.462
91-92	Montreal	NHL	41	28	11	.581	1st/Adams Division	4	7	.364
92-93	Toronto	NHL	44	29	11	.589	3rd/Norris Division	11	10	.524
93-94	Toronto	NHL	43	29	12	.583	2nd/Central Division	9	9	.500
NHL totals (6 years)			**261**	**162**	**65**	**.601**	**NHL totals (6 years)**	**49**	**46**	**.516**

NOTES:
1985— Lost to Verdun in President Cup quarterfinals.
1986— Defeated Shawinigan in President Cup quarterfinals; defeated St. Jean in President Cup semifinals; defeated Drummondville in President Cup finals.
1987— Eliminated in President Cup quarterfinal round-robin series.
1988— Lost to Fredericton in Calder Cup quarterfinals.
1989— Defeated Hartford in Adams Division semifinals; defeated Boston in Adams Division finals; defeated Philadelphia in Wales Conference finals; lost to Calgary in Stanley Cup finals.
1990— Defeated Buffalo in Adams Division semifinals; lost to Boston in Adams Division finals.
1991— Defeated Buffalo in Adams Division semifinals; lost to Boston in Adams Division finals.
1992— Defeated Hartford in Adams Division semifinals; lost to Boston in Adams Division finals.
1993— Defeated Detroit in Norris Division semifinals; defeated St. Louis in Norris Division finals; lost to Los Angeles in Campbell Conference finals.
1994— Defeated Chicago in Western Conference quarterfinals; defeated San Jose in Western Conference semifinals; lost to Vancouver in Western Conference finals.

CONSTANTINE, KEVIN
SHARKS

PERSONAL: Born December 27, 1958, in International Falls, Minn....5-10/165. ... Full name: Kevin Lars Constantine.
HIGH SCHOOL: International Falls (Minn.).
COLLEGE: Rensselaer Polytechnic Institute (N.Y.), then Nevada-Reno.
TRANSACTIONS/CAREER NOTES: Selected by Montreal Canadiens in ninth round (11th Canadiens pick, 154th overall) in NHL entry draft (June 15, 1978).... Invited to Canadiens tryout camp (1980).
MISCELLANEOUS: Played goalie.

Season	Team	League	Gms.	Min.	W	L	T	GA	SO	Avg.	Gms.	Min.	W	L	GA	SO	Avg.
						REGULAR SEASON								PLAYOFFS			
77-78	R.P.I.	ECAC	6	229	2	2	0	13	0	3.41	—	—	—	—	—	—	—
78-79	R.P.I.	ECAC	5	233	3	2	0	15	0	3.86	—	—	—	—	—	—	—
79-80	R.P.I.	ECAC	24	1342	11	9	0	89	1	3.98	—	—	—	—	—	—	—

HEAD COACHING RECORD

BACKGROUND: Junior varsity coach, Northwood Prep School in New York (1986-87).... Assistant coach, Kalamazoo, Minnesota North Stars organization (1988-89 through 1990-91).
HONORS: Won Commissioner's Trophy (1991-92).

Season	Team	League	W	L	T	Pct.	Finish	W	L	Pct.
								REGULAR SEASON / PLAYOFFS		
85-86	North Iowa	USHL	17	31	0	.396	6th/USHL	2	3	.400
87-88	Rochester	USHL	39	7	2	.844	T1st/USHL	7	4	.636
91-92	Kansas City	IHL	56	22	4	.707	1st/West Division	12	3	.800
92-93	Kansas City	IHL	46	26	10	.622	2nd/Midwest Division	6	6	.500
93-94	San Jose	NHL	33	35	16	.488	3rd/Pacific Division	7	7	.500
NHL totals (1 year)			**33**	**35**	**16**	**.488**	**NHL totals (1 year)**	**7**	**7**	**.500**

NOTES:
1986— Lost to Sioux City in USHL quarterfinals.
1988— Defeated Sioux City in USHL quarterfinals; defeated St. Paul in USHL semifinals; lost to Thunder Bay in USHL finals. Finished first in USA Jr. A National Championships.
1992— Defeated Salt Lake in Turner Cup quarterfinals; defeated Peoria in Turner Cup semifinals; defeated Muskegon in Turner Cup finals.
1993— Defeated Milwaukee in Turner Cup quarterfinals; lost to San Diego in Turner Cup semifinals.
1994— Defeated Detroit in Western Conference quarterfinals; lost to Toronto in Western Conference semifinals.

CRAWFORD, MARC
NORDIQUES

PERSONAL: Born February 13, 1961, in Belleville, Ont. . . . 5-11/185. . . . Shot left. . . . Full name: Marc Joseph John Crawford. . . . Brother of Bob Crawford right winger with St. Louis Blues, Hartford Whalers, New York Rangers, and Wahington Capitals (1979-80 through 1986-87).

TRANSACTIONS/CAREER NOTES: Selected by Vancouver Canucks in fourth round (third Canucks pick, 70th overall) of NHL entry draft (June 11, 1980). . . . Suspended three games by NHL for leaving the bench to fight (February 3, 1987).

			REGULAR SEASON					PLAYOFFS			
Season Team	League	Gms.	G	A	Pts.	PIM	Gms.	G	A	Pts.	PIM
79-80—Cornwall	OHL	54	27	36	63	127	18	8	20	28	48
80-81—Cornwall	OHL	63	42	57	99	242	19	20	15	35	27
81-82—Dallas	CHL	34	13	21	34	71	—	—	—	—	—
—Vancouver	NHL	40	4	8	12	29	14	1	0	1	11
82-83—Vancouver	NHL	41	4	5	9	28	3	0	1	1	25
—Fredericton	AHL	30	15	9	24	59	9	1	3	4	10
83-84—Vancouver	NHL	19	0	1	1	9	—	—	—	—	—
—Fredericton	AHL	56	9	22	31	96	7	4	2	6	23
84-85—Vancouver	NHL	1	0	0	0	4	—	—	—	—	—
85-86—Vancouver	NHL	54	11	14	25	92	3	0	1	1	8
—Fredericton	AHL	26	10	14	24	55	—	—	—	—	—
86-87—Vancouver	NHL	21	0	3	3	67	—	—	—	—	—
—Fredericton	AHL	25	8	11	19	21	—	—	—	—	—
87-88—Fredericton	AHL	43	5	13	18	90	2	0	0	0	14
88-89—Milwaukee	IHL	53	23	30	53	166	11	2	5	7	26
NHL totals		122	19	31	50	229	20	1	2	3	44

HEAD COACHING RECORD

BACKGROUND: Player/assistant coach, Fredericton Express (1987-88).
HONORS: Won Louis A.R. Pieri award.

		REGULAR SEASON					PLAYOFFS		
Season Team	League	W	L	T	Pct.	Finish	W	L	Pct.
89-90—Cornwall	OHL	24	38	4	.394	6th/Leyden Division	2	4	.333
90-91—Cornwall	OHL	23	42	1	.356	7th/Leyden Division	—	—	—
91-92—St. John's	AHL	39	29	12	.562	2nd/Atlantic Division	11	5	.688
92-93—St. John's	AHL	41	26	13	.594	1st/Atlantic Division	4	5	.444
93-94—St. John's	AHL	45	23	12	.638	1st/Atlantic Division	6	5	.545

NOTES:
1990— Lost to Oshawa in Leyden Division quarterfinals.
1992— Defeated Cape Breton in first round of Calder Cup playoffs; defeated Moncton in second round of Calder Cup playoffs; lost to Adirondack in Calder Cup finals.
1993— Defeated Moncton in first round of Calder Cup playoffs; lost to Cape Breton in second round of Calder Cup playoffs.
1994— Defeated Cape Breton in first round of Calder Cup playoffs; lost to Moncton in second round of Calder Cup playoffs.

CRISP, TERRY
LIGHTNING

PERSONAL: Born May 28, 1943, in Parry Sound, Ont. . . . 5-10/180. . . . Shot left. . . . Full name: Terrance Arthur Crisp.

TRANSACTIONS/CAREER NOTES: Underwent appendectomy and hernia operation; missed part of 1963-64 season. . . . Selected by St. Louis Blues from Boston Bruins in NHL expansion draft (June 6, 1967). . . . Selected by New York Islanders from Blues in expansion draft (June 6, 1972). . . . Traded by Islanders to Philadelphia Flyers for D Jean Potvin and future considerations (March 5, 1973); Islanders received D Glen Irwin to complete deal (May 18, 1973).

MISCELLANEOUS: Played center. . . . Member of Stanley Cup championship teams (1974 and 1975).

			REGULAR SEASON					PLAYOFFS			
Season Team	League	Gms.	G	A	Pts.	PIM	Gms.	G	A	Pts.	PIM
60-61—St. Mary's	OHA			Did not play.							
61-62—Niagara Falls	OHA	50	16	22	38	0	—	—	—	—	—
62-63—Niagara Falls	OHA	50	39	35	74	0	—	—	—	—	—
63-64—Minneapolis	CPHL	42	15	20	35	22	—	—	—	—	—
64-65—Minneapolis	CPHL	70	28	34	62	22	5	0	2	2	0
65-66—Boston	NHL	3	0	0	0	0	—	—	—	—	—
—Oklahoma City	CPHL	61	11	22	33	35	9	1	5	6	0
66-67—Oklahoma City	CPHL	69	31	42	73	37	11	3	7	10	0
67-68—St. Louis	NHL	73	9	20	29	10	18	1	5	6	6
68-69—Kansas City	CHL	4	1	1	2	4	—	—	—	—	—
—St. Louis	NHL	57	6	9	15	14	12	3	4	7	20
69-70—St. Louis	NHL	26	5	6	11	2	16	2	3	5	2
—Buffalo	AHL	51	15	34	49	14	—	—	—	—	—

Season Team	League	REGULAR SEASON					PLAYOFFS				
		Gms.	G	A	Pts.	PIM	Gms.	G	A	Pts.	PIM
70-71—St. Louis	NHL	54	5	11	16	13	6	1	0	1	2
71-72—St. Louis	NHL	75	13	18	31	12	11	1	3	4	2
72-73—New York Islanders	NHL	54	4	16	20	6	—	—	—	—	—
—Philadelphia	NHL	12	1	5	6	2	11	3	2	5	2
73-74—Philadelphia	NHL	71	10	21	31	28	17	2	2	4	4
74-75—Philadelphia	NHL	71	8	19	27	20	9	2	4	6	0
75-76—Philadelphia	NHL	38	6	9	15	28	10	0	5	5	2
76-77—Philadelphia	NHL	2	0	0	0	0	—	—	—	—	—
NHL totals		536	67	134	201	135	110	15	28	43	40

HEAD COACHING RECORD

BACKGROUND: Assistant coach, Philadelphia Flyers (1977-78 and 1978-79). . . . Assistant coach, Canadian national team (1990 through 1992).
HONORS: Won Matt Leyden Trophy (1982-83 and 1984-85). . . . Named NHL Coach of the Year by THE SPORTING NEWS (1987-88).

Season Team	League	REGULAR SEASON					PLAYOFFS		
		W	L	T	Pct.	Finish	W	L	Pct.
79-80—Sault Ste. Marie	OHL	22	45	1	.331	6th/Leyden Division	—	—	—
80-81—Sault Ste. Marie	OHL	47	19	2	.706	1st/Leyden Division	8	7	.526
81-82—Sault Ste. Marie	OHL	40	25	3	.610	2nd/Emms Division	4	6	.423
82-83—Sault Ste. Marie	OHL	48	21	1	.693	1st/Emms Division	7	6	.531
83-84—Sault Ste. Marie	OHL	38	28	4	.571	3rd/Emms Division	8	4	.625
84-85—Sault Ste. Marie	OHL	54	11	1	.826	1st/Emms Division	12	2	.813
85-86—Moncton	AHL	34	34	12	.500	3rd/North Division	5	5	.500
86-87—Moncton	AHL	43	31	6	.575	3rd/North Division	2	4	.333
87-88—Calgary	NHL	48	23	9	.656	1st/Smythe Division	4	5	.444
88-89—Calgary	NHL	54	17	9	.731	1st/Smythe Division	16	6	.727
89-90—Calgary	NHL	42	23	15	.619	1st/Smythe Division	2	4	.333
92-93—Tampa Bay	NHL	23	54	7	.315	6th/Norris Division	—	—	—
93-94—Tampa Bay	NHL	30	43	11	.423	7th/Atlantic Division	—	—	—
NHL totals (5 years)		197	160	51	.607	NHL totals (3 years)	22	15	.595

NOTES:
1981— Sault Ste. Marie had four playoff ties.
1982— Defeated Brantford in Emms Division semifinals; lost to Kitchener in Emms Division finals. Sault Ste. Marie had three playoff ties.
1983— Defeated Brantford in Emms Division semifinals; defeated Kitchener in Emms Division finals; lost to Oshawa in Robertson Cup finals. Sault Ste. Marie had three playoff ties.
1984— Defeated Windsor in Emms Division quarterfinals; defeated Brantford in Emms Division semifinals; lost to Kitchener in Emms Division finals. Sault Ste. Marie had four playoff ties.
1985— Defeated Kitchener in Emms Division quarterfinals; defeated Hamilton in Emms Division finals; defeated Peterborough in Robertson Cup finals. Sault Ste. Marie had two playoff ties.
1986— Defeated Maine in Calder Cup quarterfinals; lost to Adirondack in Calder Cup semifinals.
1987— Lost to Adirondack in Calder Cup quarterfinals.
1988— Defeated Los Angeles in Smythe Division semifinals; lost to Edmonton in Smythe Division finals.
1989— Defeated Vancouver in Smythe Division semifinals; defeated Los Angeles in Smythe Division finals; defeated Chicago in Campbell Conference finals; defeated Montreal in Stanley Cup finals.
1990— Lost to Los Angeles in Smythe Division semifinals.

DEMERS, JACQUES
CANADIENS

PERSONAL: Born August 25, 1944, in Montreal.

HEAD COACHING RECORD

BACKGROUND: Director of player personnel, Chicago Cougars of WHA (1972-73).
HONORS: Won Louis A.R. Pieri Memorial Award (1982-83). . . . Named NHL Coach of the Year by THE SPORTING NEWS (1985-86 and 1986-87). . . . Won Jack Adams Award (1986-87 and 1987-88).

Season Team	League	REGULAR SEASON					PLAYOFFS		
		W	L	T	Pct.	Finish	W	L	Pct.
79-80—Quebec	NHL	25	44	11	.381	5th/Adams Division	—	—	—
81-82—Fredericton	AHL	20	55	5	.281	5th/Northern Division	—	—	—
82-83—Fredericton	AHL	45	27	8	.544	1st/Northern Division	6	6	.500
83-84—St. Louis	NHL	32	41	7	.444	2nd/Norris Division	6	5	.545
84-85—St. Louis	NHL	37	31	12	.538	1st/Norris Division	0	3	.000
85-86—St. Louis	NHL	37	34	9	.519	3rd/Norris Division	10	9	.526
86-87—Detroit	NHL	34	36	10	.488	2nd/Norris Division	9	7	.563
87-88—Detroit	NHL	41	28	11	.581	1st/Norris Division	9	7	.563
88-89—Detroit	NHL	34	34	12	.500	1st/Norris Division	2	4	.333
89-90—Detroit	NHL	28	38	14	.438	5th/Norris Division	—	—	—
92-93—Montreal	NHL	48	30	6	.607	3rd/Adams Division	16	4	.800
93-94—Montreal	NHL	41	29	14	.571	3rd/Northeast Division	3	4	.429
NHL totals (10 years)		357	345	106	.507	NHL totals (8 years)	55	43	.561

NOTES:
1983— Defeated Adirondack in Calder Cup quarterfinals; lost to Maine in Calder Cup semifinals.
1984— Defeated Detroit in Norris Division semifinals; lost to Minnesota in Norris Division finals.
1985— Lost to Minnesota in Norris Division semifinals.

1986— Defeated Minnesota in Norris Division semifinals; defeated Toronto in Norris Division finals; lost to Calgary in Campbell Conference finals.
1987— Defeated Chicago in Norris Division semifinals; defeated Toronto in Norris Division finals; lost to Edmonton in Campbell Conference finals.
1988— Defeated Toronto in Norris Division semifinals; defeated St. Louis in Norris Division finals; lost to Edmonton in Campbell Conference finals.
1989— Lost to Chicago in Norris Division semifinals.
1993— Defeated Quebec in Adams Division semifinals; defeated Buffalo in Adams Division finals; defeated N.Y. Islanders in Wales Conference finals; defeated Los Angeles in Stanley Cup finals.
1994— Lost to Boston in Eastern Conference quarterfinals.

GAINEY, BOB
STARS

PERSONAL: Born December 13, 1953, in Peterborough, Ont. . . . 6-2/195. . . . Shot left. . . . Full name: Robert Michael Gainey.
HIGH SCHOOL: Peterborough (Ont.) Secondaire.
TRANSACTIONS/CAREER NOTES: Selected by Montreal Canadiens from Peterborough TPTs in first round (first Canadiens pick, eighth overall) of NHL amateur draft (May 15, 1973). . . . Separated shoulder; missed part of 1977-78 season. . . . Tore ligaments in left knee (October 5, 1986). . . . Pulled groin (March 14, 1987). . . . Bruised ankle (April 1988). . . . Bruised left foot (October 15, 1988). . . . Broke bone in right foot (January 9, 1989); missed two months. . . . Injured left knee (March 17, 1989). . . . Reinjured left knee (April 5, 1989). . . . Released by Canadiens when he announced he would play the 1989-90 season with Epinal Ecureuils (Squirrels), a second-division team in France.
HONORS: Won Frank J. Selke Award (1977-78 through 1980-81). . . . Played in NHL All-Star Game (1977, 1978, 1980 and 1981). . . . Won Conn Smythe Trophy (1978-79). . . . Inducted into Hall of Fame (1992).
MISCELLANEOUS: Played left wing. . . . Member of Stanley Cup championship teams (1976-1979 and 1986).

			REGULAR SEASON					PLAYOFFS				
Season Team	League	Gms.	G	A	Pts.	PIM		Gms.	G	A	Pts.	PIM
70-71—Peterborough	OHA Jr. A	4	0	0	0	0		—	—	—	—	—
71-72—Peterborough	OHA Mj. Jr. A	4	2	1	3	33		—	—	—	—	—
72-73—Peterborough	OHA Mj. Jr. A	52	22	21	43	99		—	—	—	—	—
73-74—Nova Scotia	AHL	6	2	5	7	4		—	—	—	—	—
—Montreal	NHL	66	3	7	10	34		6	0	0	0	6
74-75—Montreal	NHL	80	17	20	37	49		11	2	4	6	4
75-76—Montreal	NHL	78	15	13	28	57		13	1	3	4	20
76-77—Montreal	NHL	80	14	19	33	41		14	4	1	5	25
77-78—Montreal	NHL	66	15	16	31	57		15	2	7	9	14
78-79—Montreal	NHL	79	20	18	38	44		16	6	10	16	10
79-80—Montreal	NHL	64	14	19	33	32		10	1	1	2	4
80-81—Montreal	NHL	78	23	24	47	36		3	0	0	0	2
81-82—Montreal	NHL	79	21	24	45	24		5	0	1	1	8
82-83—Montreal	NHL	80	12	18	30	43		3	0	0	0	4
83-84—Montreal	NHL	77	17	22	39	41		15	1	5	6	9
84-85—Montreal	NHL	79	19	13	32	40		12	1	3	4	13
85-86—Montreal	NHL	80	20	23	43	20		20	5	5	10	12
86-87—Montreal	NHL	47	8	8	16	19		17	1	3	4	6
87-88—Montreal	NHL	78	11	11	22	14		6	0	1	1	6
88-89—Montreal	NHL	49	10	7	17	34		16	1	4	5	8
89-90—Epinal	France				Statistics unavailable.							
NHL totals		1160	239	262	501	585		182	25	48	73	151

HEAD COACHING RECORD

BACKGROUND: Player/coach for Epinal, a second-division team in France (1989-90). . . . North Stars franchise moved from Minnesota to Dallas and renamed Stars for 1993-94 season.

				REGULAR SEASON				PLAYOFFS		
Season Team	League	W	L	T	Pct.	Finish		W	L	Pct.
90-91—Minnesota	NHL	27	39	14	.425	4th/Norris Division		14	9	.609
91-92—Minnesota	NHL	32	42	6	.438	4th/Norris Division		3	4	.429
92-93—Minnesota	NHL	36	38	10	.488	5th/Norris Division		—	—	—
93-94—Dallas	NHL	42	29	13	.577	3rd/Central Division		5	4	.556
NHL totals (4 years)		137	148	43	.483	NHL totals (3 years)		22	17	.564

NOTES:
1991— Defeated Chicago in Norris Division semifinals; defeated St. Louis in Norris Division finals; defeated Edmonton in Campbell Conference finals; lost to Pittsburgh in Stanley Cup finals.
1992— Lost to Detroit in Norris Division semifinals.
1994— Defeated St. Louis in Western Conference quarterfinals; lost to Vancouver in Western Conference semifinals.

HENNING, LORNE
ISLANDERS

PERSONAL: Born February 23, 1952, in Melfort, Sask. . . . 5-11/185. . . . Shot left. . . . Full name: Lorne Edward Henning.
TRANSACTIONS/CAREER NOTES: Suffered from hepatitis (1971). . . . Selected by Calgary Broncos in WHA draft (February 1972). . . . Selected by New York Islanders from New Westminster Bruins in second round (second Islanders pick, 17th overall) of amateur draft (June 8, 1972). . . . Underwent appendectomy (1974).
RECORDS: Shares NHL playoff record for most shorthanded goals—3 (1980).
MISCELLANEOUS: Played center. . . . Member of Stanley Cup championship teams (1980 and 1981).

Season Team	League	REGULAR SEASON					PLAYOFFS				
		Gms.	G	A	Pts.	PIM	Gms.	G	A	Pts.	PIM
68-69—Estevan	WCHL	60	27	27	54	20	—	—	—	—	—
69-70—Estevan	WCHL	60	40	52	92	33	—	—	—	—	—
70-71—Estevan	WCHL	66	64	66	130	41	—	—	—	—	—
71-72—New Westminster	WCHL	60	51	63	114	29	—	—	—	—	—
72-73—New Haven	AHL	4	0	2	2	2	—	—	—	—	—
—New York Islanders	NHL	63	7	19	26	14	—	—	—	—	—
73-74—New York Islanders	NHL	60	12	15	27	6	—	—	—	—	—
74-75—Fort Worth	CHL	8	4	6	10	4	—	—	—	—	—
—New York Islanders	NHL	60	5	6	11	6	17	0	2	2	0
75-76—New York Islanders	NHL	80	7	10	17	16	13	2	0	2	2
76-77—New York Islanders	NHL	80	13	18	31	10	12	0	1	1	0
77-78—New York Islanders	NHL	79	12	15	27	6	7	0	0	0	4
78-79—New York Islanders	NHL	73	13	20	33	14	10	2	0	2	0
79-80—New York Islanders	NHL	39	3	6	9	6	21	3	4	7	2
80-81—New York Islanders	NHL	9	1	2	3	24	1	0	0	0	0
NHL totals		543	73	111	184	102	81	7	7	14	8

HEAD COACHING RECORD

BACKGROUND: Player/assistant coach, New York Islanders (1980-81).... Assistant coach, New York Islanders (1981-84, 1989-1994).... Served as interim coach of the New York Islanders while Al Arbour was serving a five-game suspension (January 7-14, 1994; team was 2-1-2 during that time).

Season Team	League	REGULAR SEASON					PLAYOFFS		
		W	L	T	Pct.	Finish	W	L	Pct.
84-85—Springfield	AHL	36	40	4	.475	4th/South Division	0	4	.000
85-86—Minnesota	NHL	38	33	9	.531	2nd/Norris Division	2	3	.400
86-87—Minnesota	NHL	30	39	9	.442	5th/Norris Division	—	—	—
93-94—New York Islanders	NHL	2	1	2	.500		—	—	—
NHL totals (3 years)		70	73	20	.491	NHL totals (1 year)	2	3	.400

NOTES:
1986— Lost to St. Louis Blues in Norris Division semifinals.

HOLMGREN, PAUL
WHALERS

PERSONAL: Born December 2, 1955, in St. Paul, Minn.... 6-3/210.... Shoots right.... Full name: Paul Howard Holmgren.
COLLEGE: Minnesota.
TRANSACTIONS/CAREER NOTES: Selected by Edmonton Oilers in fifth round (fifth Oilers pick, 67th overall) of WHA amateur draft (May 1974).... WHA rights traded by Oilers to Minnesota Fighting Saints for future considerations (May 1974).... Selected by Philadelphia Flyers from the University of Minnesota in sixth round (fifth Flyers pick, 108th overall) of NHL amateur draft (June 3, 1975).... Signed by Flyers following demise of Minnesota Fighting Saints (March 1976).... Scratched cornea and underwent eye surgery (1976).... Separated right shoulder; missed parts of 1976-77 and 1977-78 seasons.... Separated shoulder during Team U.S.A. training camp (August 1981).... Suspended five games for assaulting referee (December 12, 1981).... Injured knee (January 1982).... Sprained left knee (October 1983).... Bruised left shoulder (January 1984).... Traded by Flyers to Minnesota North Stars for RW Paul Guay and third-round pick (G Darryl Gilmour) in 1985 draft (February 1984).... Injured shoulder (March 1984).... Underwent shoulder surgery (April 1984).... Separated shoulder (October 1984).... Underwent surgery to left shoulder (December 1984).... Announced retirement as a player to become assistant coach of Flyers (July 1985).
HONORS: Played in NHL All-Star Game (1981).
MISCELLANEOUS: Played right wing.

Season Team	League	REGULAR SEASON					PLAYOFFS				
		Gms.	G	A	Pts.	PIM	Gms.	G	A	Pts.	PIM
73-74—St. Paul Jr. B	OHA	55	22	59	81	183	—	—	—	—	—
74-75—University of Minnesota	WCHA	37	10	21	31	108	—	—	—	—	—
75-76—Johnstown	NAHL	6	3	12	15	12	—	—	—	—	—
—Minnesota	WHA	51	14	16	30	121	—	—	—	—	—
—Richmond	AHL	6	4	4	8	23	—	—	—	—	—
—Philadelphia	NHL	1	0	0	0	2	—	—	—	—	—
76-77—Philadelphia	NHL	59	14	12	26	201	10	1	1	2	25
77-78—Philadelphia	NHL	62	16	18	34	190	12	1	4	5	26
78-79—Philadelphia	NHL	57	19	10	29	168	8	1	5	6	22
79-80—Philadelphia	NHL	74	30	35	65	267	18	10	10	20	47
80-81—Philadelphia	NHL	77	22	37	59	306	12	5	9	14	49
81-82—Philadelphia	NHL	41	9	22	31	183	4	1	2	3	6
82-83—Philadelphia	NHL	77	19	24	43	178	3	0	0	0	6
83-84—Philadelphia	NHL	52	9	13	22	105	—	—	—	—	—
—Minnesota	NHL	11	2	5	7	46	12	0	1	1	6
84-85—Philadelphia	NHL	16	4	3	7	38	3	0	0	0	8
WHA totals		51	14	16	30	121					
NHL totals		527	144	179	323	1684	82	19	32	51	195

HEAD COACHING RECORD
BACKGROUND: Assistant coach, Philadelphia Flyers (1985-86 through 1987-88).

Season Team	League	REGULAR SEASON					PLAYOFFS		
		W	L	T	Pct.	Finish	W	L	Pct.
88-89—Philadelphia	NHL	36	36	8	.500	4th/Patrick Division	10	9	.526
89-90—Philadelphia	NHL	30	39	11	.444	6th/Patrick Division	—	—	—

Season Team	League	W	L	T	Pct.	Finish	W	L	Pct.
90-91—Philadelphia	NHL	33	37	10	.475	5th/Patrick Division	—	—	—
91-92—Philadelphia	NHL	8	14	2	.380		—	—	—
92-93—Hartford	NHL	26	52	6	.345	5th/Adams Division	—	—	—
93-94—Hartford	NHL	4	11	2	.294		—	—	—
NHL totals (6 years)		**137**	**189**	**39**	**.429**	**NHL totals (1 year)**	**10**	**9**	**.526**

NOTES:

1989— Defeated Washington in Patrick Division semifinals; defeated Pittsburgh in Patrick Division finals; lost to Montreal in Wales Conference finals.

1993— Replaced as head coach by Pierre McGuire (November 16), with club in seventh place.

1994— Renamed as head coach (June 28).

JOHNSTON, EDDIE
PENGUINS

PERSONAL: Born November 24, 1935, in Montreal. . . . 6-0/190. . . . Shot left. . . . Full name: Edward Joseph Johnston.

TRANSACTIONS/CAREER NOTES: Drafted by Boston Bruins from Montreal Canadiens (June 1962). . . . Traded by Boston to Toronto Maple Leafs to complete deal in which Boston received G Jacques Plante and Toronto's third-round pick in 1973 amateur draft (C Doug Gibson) for Boston's first-round pick (D Ian Turnbull) in 1973 amateur draft (May 22, 1973). . . . Traded by Toronto to St. Louis Blues for RW Gary Sabourin (May 27, 1974). . . . Sold by St. Louis to Chicago Blackhawks (January 27, 1978).

HONORS: Won EPHL Leading Goalie Award (1960-61).

MISCELLANEOUS: Played goalie.

Season Team	League	Gms.	Min.	W	L	T	GA	SO	Avg.	Gms.	Min.	W	L	GA	SO	Avg.
54-55—Trois Rivieres Flambeaux	QJHL	46	...	...	...	...	169	1	3.67	—	—	—	—	—	—	—
55-56—Chatham	OHA	7	420	...	...	...	31	0	4.43	—	—	—	—	—	—	—
—Amherst	ACSHL	1	60	...	...	...	2	0	2.00	—	—	—	—	—	—	—
56-57—Winnipeg	WHL	50	...	...	...	...	193	2	3.86	—	—	—	—	—	—	—
57-58—Shawinigan Falls	QHL	63	...	...	...	...	230	*5	3.65	14	...	...	...	49	1	3.50
58-59—Edmonton	WHL	49	...	...	...	...	163	1	3.32	3	180	...	...	12	0	4.00
59-60—Johnstown	EHL	63	...	...	...	...	169	4	2.69	—	—	—	—	—	—	—
60-61—Hull-Ottawa	EPHL	70	...	...	...	...	187	*11	*2.67	14	...	...	...	28	0	*2.00
61-62—Spokane	WHL	70	...	...	...	...	237	3	3.30	16	...	...	...	58	*1	3.63
62-63—Boston	NHL	49	2880	11	27	11	196	1	4.08	—	—	—	—	—	—	—
63-64—Boston	NHL	70	*4200	18	*40	12	211	6	3.01	—	—	—	—	—	—	—
64-65—Boston	NHL	47	2820	12	31	4	162	3	3.45	—	—	—	—	—	—	—
65-66—Los Angeles	WHL	5	...	...	...	...	10	1	2.31	—	—	—	—	—	—	—
—Boston	NHL	33	1743	10	19	2	108	1	3.72	—	—	—	—	—	—	—
66-67—Boston	NHL	34	1880	9	21	2	116	0	3.70	—	—	—	—	—	—	—
67-68—Boston	NHL	28	1524	11	8	5	73	...	2.87	—	—	—	—	—	—	—
68-69—Boston	NHL	24	1440	14	6	4	74	2	3.08	1	65	0	1	4	0	3.69
69-70—Boston	NHL	37	2176	16	9	11	108	3	2.98	1	60	0	1	4	0	4.00
70-71—Boston	NHL	38	2280	30	6	2	96	4	2.53	1	60	0	1	7	0	7.00
71-72—Boston	NHL	38	2260	27	8	3	102	2	2.71	7	420	*6	1	13	1	*1.86
72-73—Boston	NHL	45	2510	24	17	1	137	5	3.27	3	160	1	2	9	0	3.38
73-74—Toronto	NHL	26	1516	12	9	4	78	1	3.09	1	60	0	1	6	0	6.00
74-75—St. Louis	NHL	30	1800	12	13	5	93	2	3.10	1	60	0	1	5	0	5.00
75-76—St. Louis	NHL	38	2152	11	17	9	130	1	3.62	—	—	—	—	—	—	—
76-77—St. Louis	NHL	38	2111	13	16	5	108	1	3.07	3	138	0	2	9	0	3.91
77-78—St. Louis	NHL	12	650	5	6	1	45	0	4.15	—	—	—	—	—	—	—
—Chicago	NHL	4	240	1	3	0	17	0	4.25	—	—	—	—	—	—	—
NHL totals		**591**	**34182**	**236**	**256**	**81**	**1854**	**32**	**3.25**	**18**	**1023**	**7**	**10**	**57**	**1**	**3.34**

HEAD COACHING RECORD

BACKGROUND: General manager, Pittsburgh Penguins (1983-84 through 1987-88). . . . Assistant general manager, Penguins (1988-89). . . . Vice president/general manager, Hartford Whalers (1989-90 through 1991-92).

Season Team	League	W	L	T	Pct.	Finish	W	L	Pct.
78-79—New Brunswick	AHL	41	29	19	.575	2nd/Northern Division	2	3	.400
79-80—Chicago	NHL	34	27	19	.544	1st/Smythe Division	4	3	.429
80-81—Pittsburgh	NHL	30	37	13	.456	3rd/Norris Division	2	3	.400
81-82—Pittsburgh	NHL	31	36	13	.469	4th/Patrick Division	2	3	.400
82-83—Pittsburgh	NHL	18	53	9	.281	6th/Patrick Division	—	—	—
93-94—Pittsburgh	NHL	44	27	13	.601	1st/Northeast Division	2	4	.333
NHL totals (5 years)		**157**	**180**	**67**	**.472**	**NHL totals (4 years)**	**9**	**14**	**.391**

NOTES:

1979— Lost to Nova Scotia in Calder Cup quarterfinals.

1980— Defeated St. Louis in Stanley Cup preliminary round; lost to Buffalo in Stanley Cup quarterfinals.

1981— Lost to St. Louis in Stanley Cup preliminary round.

1982— Lost to New York Islanders in Stanley Cup preliminary round.

1994— Lost to Washington in Eastern Conference quarterfinals.

KEENAN, MIKE
BLUES

PERSONAL: Born October 21, 1949, in Whitby, Ont. . . . 5-10/180. . . . Shot right. . . . Full name: Michael Edward Keenan.

HIGH SCHOOL: Denis O'Connor (Ajax, Ont.).

COLLEGE: St. Lawrence (N.Y.).

Season	Team	League	REGULAR SEASON Gms.	G	A	Pts.	PIM	PLAYOFFS Gms.	G	A	Pts.	PIM
69-70	St. Lawrence University...	ECAC	10	0	4	4	32	—	—	—	—	—
70-71	St. Lawrence University...	ECAC	22	4	12	16	35	—	—	—	—	—
71-72	St. Lawrence University...	ECAC	25	13	16	29	52	—	—	—	—	—

HEAD COACHING RECORD

BACKGROUND: Coach, Canadian national junior team (1980).... Coach, NHL All-Star team (1985-86, 1987-88, 1992-93).... Coach, Team Canada (1987).... General manager, Chicago Blackhawks (1989-90 through 1991-92).... General manager/coach, Team Canada (1991).... Coach, Canadian national team (1993)

HONORS: Named NHL Coach of the Year by THE SPORTING NEWS (1984-85).... Won Jack Adams Award (1984-85).

Season	Team	League	REGULAR SEASON W	L	T	Pct.	Finish	PLAYOFFS W	L	Pct.
79-80	Peterborough	OHL	47	20	1	.699	1st/Leyden Division	15	3	.833
80-81	Rochester	AHL	30	42	8	.425	5th/Southern Division	—	—	—
81-82	Rochester	AHL	40	31	9	.556	2nd/Southern Division	4	5	.444
82-83	Rochester	AHL	46	25	9	.631	1st/Southern Division	12	4	.750
83-84	University of Toronto	OUAA	41	5	3	.867	1st/OUAA	9	0	1.000
84-85	Philadelphia	NHL	53	20	7	.706	1st/Patrick Division	12	7	.632
85-86	Philadelphia	NHL	53	23	4	.688	1st/Patrick Division	2	3	.400
86-87	Philadelphia	NHL	46	26	8	.625	1st/Patrick Division	15	11	.577
87-88	Philadelphia	NHL	38	33	9	.513	3rd/Patrick Division	3	4	.429
88-89	Chicago	NHL	27	41	12	.413	4th/Norris Division	9	7	.563
89-90	Chicago	NHL	41	33	6	.550	1st/Norris Division	10	10	.500
90-91	Chicago	NHL	49	23	8	.663	1st/Norris Division	2	4	.333
91-92	Chicago	NHL	36	29	15	.544	2nd/Norris Division	12	6	.667
93-94	New York Rangers	NHL	52	24	8	.667	1st/Atlantic Division	16	7	.696
NHL totals (9 years)			395	252	77	.599	NHL totals (9 years)	81	59	.579

NOTES:
1982— Defeated New Haven in Calder Cup quarterfinals; lost to Binghamton in Calder Cup semifinals.
1983— Defeated Binghamton in Calder Cup quarterfinals; defeated New Haven in Calder Cup semifinals; defeated Maine in Calder Cup finals.
1984— Defeated Guelph in OUAA semifinals; defeated Western Ontario in OUAA finals; defeated New Brunswick in East Regional Qualifying Round; defeated Trois-Rivieres in CIAU Championship Tournament semifinals; defeated Concordia in CIAU Championship Tournament finals.
1985— Defeated New York Rangers in Patrick Division semifinals; defeated New York Islanders in Patrick Division finals; defeated Quebec in Wales Conference finals; lost to Edmonton in Stanley Cup finals.
1986— Lost to New York Rangers in Patrick Division semifinals.
1987— Defeated New York Rangers in Patrick Division semifinals; defeated New York Islanders in Patrick Division finals; defeated Montreal in Wales Conference finals; lost to Edmonton in Stanley Cup finals.
1988— Lost to Washington in Patrick Division semifinals.
1989— Defeated Detroit in Norris Division semifinals; defeated St. Louis in Norris Division finals; lost to Calgary in Campbell Conference finals.
1990— Defeated Minnesota in Norris Division semifinals; defeated St. Louis in Norris Division finals; lost to Edmonton in Campbell Conference finals.
1991— Lost to Minnesota in Norris Division semifinals.
1992— Defeated St. Louis in Norris Division semifinals; defeated Detroit in Norris Division finals; defeated Edmonton in Campbell Conference finals; lost to Pittsburgh in Stanley Cup finals.
1993— Finished fourth in World Championships.
1994— Defeated New York Islanders in Eastern Conference quarterfinals; defeated Washington in Eastern Conference semifinals; defeated New Jersey in Eastern Conference finals; defeated Vancouver in Stanley Cup finals.

KING, DAVE
FLAMES

PERSONAL: Born December 22, 1947, in North Battleford, Sask.

HEAD COACHING RECORD

BACKGROUND: Assistant coach, University of Saskatchewan (1972-73).... Coach, Canadian national junior team (1981-82 and 1982-83).... Assistant coach, Canadian national team (1982).

HONORS: Won Dunc McCallum Memorial Trophy (1977-78).... Named CIAU Coach of the Year (1979-80).

Season	Team	League	REGULAR SEASON W	L	T	Pct.	Finish	PLAYOFFS W	L	Pct.
77-78	Billings	WHL	32	31	9	.507	2nd/Central Division	13	7	.650
78-79	Billings	WHL	38	23	11	.604	1st/Central Division	3	5	.375
79-80	Univ. of Saskatchewan	CIAU	14	15	0	.483	3rd/Canada West	—	—	—
80-81	Univ. of Saskatchewan	CIAU	15	9	0	.625	2nd/Canada West	4	2	.667
81-82	Univ. of Saskatchewan	CIAU	17	7	0	.708	1st/Canada West	4	1	.800
82-83	Univ. of Saskatchewan	CIAU	16	8	0	.667	1st/Canada West	5	0	1.000
83-84	Canadian national team	Int'l					Record unavailable.			
85-86	Canadian national team	Int'l	38	30	5	.555		—	—	—
86-87	Canadian national team	Int'l	49	24	5	.660		—	—	—
87-88	Canadian national team	Int'l	37	27	10	.568		—	—	—
88-89	Canadian national team	Int'l	23	35	6	.406		—	—	—
89-90	Canadian national team	Int'l	36	33	10	.519		—	—	—
90-91	Canadian national team	Int'l	35	20	3	.629		—	—	—
91-92	Canadian national team	Int'l	36	11	8	.727		—	—	—

NHL HEAD COACHES

Season	Team	League	REGULAR SEASON W	L	T	Pct.	Finish	PLAYOFFS W	L	Pct.
92-93	Calgary	NHL	43	30	11	.577	2nd/Smythe Division	2	4	.333
93-94	Calgary	NHL	42	29	13	.577	1st/Pacific Division	3	4	.429
	NHL totals (2 years)		85	59	24	.577	NHL totals (2 year)	5	8	.385

NOTES:

1978— Advanced in Central Division semifinal round-robin tournament; defeated Medicine Hat in Central Division finals; advanced in WHL semifinal round-robin tournament; lost to Westminster in CHL finals.

1981— Defeated Calgary in Canada West Conference finals; defeated Concordia in CIAU tournament finals; defeated Queens in CIAU tournament finals; lost to Moncton in CIAU Championship game.

1982— Defeated Calgary in Canada West Conference finals; defeated Concordia in CIAU tournament finals; defeated Regina in CIAU tournament finals; lost to Moncton in CIAU Championship game.

1983— Defeated Alberta in Canada West Conference finals; defeated Brandon in CIAU tournament finals; defeated Wilfrid Laurier in CIAU tournament finals; defeated Concordia in CIAU Championship game.

1984— Finished fourth in Winter Olympics.

1987— Finished fourth in World Championships.

1988— Finished fourth in Winter Olympics.

1989— Finished second (silver medal) in World Championships.

1990— Finished fourth in World Championships and fourth in Goodwill Games.

1991— Finished second (silver medal) in World Championships.

1992— Finished second (silver medal) in Winter Olympics and seventh in World Championships.

1993— Lost to Los Angeles in Smythe Division semifinals.

1994— Lost to Vancouver in Western Conference quarterfinals.

LEMAIRE, JACQUES
DEVILS

PERSONAL: Born September 7, 1945, in Ville LaSalle, Quebec.... 5-10/180.... Shot left.... Full name: Jacques Gerard Lemaire.
HONORS: Inducted into Hall of Fame (1984).
MISCELLANEOUS: Played center and left wing.

Season	Team	League	REGULAR SEASON Gms.	G	A	Pts.	PIM	PLAYOFFS Gms.	G	A	Pts.	PIM
62-63	Lachine	QJHL	42	41	63	104	...	—	—	—	—	—
63-64	Montreal Jr. Canadiens	OHA Jr. A	42	25	30	55	...	—	—	—	—	—
64-65	Montreal Jr. Canadiens	OHA Jr. A	56	25	47	72	...	—	—	—	—	—
	Quebec	AHL	1	0	0	0	0	—	—	—	—	—
65-66	Montreal Jr. Canadiens	OHA Jr. A	48	41	52	93	69	—	—	—	—	—
66-67	Houston	CPHL	69	19	30	49	19	6	0	1	1	0
67-68	Montreal	NHL	69	22	20	42	16	13	7	6	13	6
68-69	Montreal	NHL	75	29	34	63	29	14	4	2	6	6
69-70	Montreal	NHL	69	32	28	60	16	—	—	—	—	—
70-71	Montreal	NHL	78	28	28	56	18	20	9	10	19	17
71-72	Montreal	NHL	77	32	49	81	26	6	2	1	3	2
72-73	Montreal	NHL	77	44	51	95	16	17	7	13	20	2
73-74	Montreal	NHL	66	29	38	67	10	6	0	4	4	2
74-75	Montreal	NHL	80	36	56	92	20	11	5	7	12	4
75-76	Montreal	NHL	61	20	32	52	20	13	3	3	6	2
76-77	Montreal	NHL	75	34	41	75	22	14	7	12	19	6
77-78	Montreal	NHL	75	36	61	97	14	15	6	8	14	10
78-79	Montreal	NHL	50	24	31	55	10	16	11	12	23	6
	NHL totals		852	366	469	835	217	145	61	78	139	63

HEAD COACHING RECORD

BACKGROUND: Assistant coach, University of Plattsburgh (1981-82).... Assistant coach, Montreal Canadiens (October 1982 - February 1983).... Assistant to managing director/director of hockey personnel, Canadiens (1985-86 through 1987-88).... Assistant to managing director/managing director of Verdun, Canadiens organization (1988-89).... Assistant to managing director, Canadiens (1989-90 and 1990-91).... Assistant to managing director/managing director of Fredericton, Canadiens organization (1991-92 and 1992-93).... Served as interim coach of Montreal Canadiens while Jacques Demers was hospitalized with chest pains (March 10 and 11, 1993; team was 1-1 during that time).
HONORS: Named NHL Coach of the Year by THE SPORTING NEWS (1993-94).... Won Jack Adams Award (1993-94).

Season	Team	League	REGULAR SEASON W	L	T	Pct.	Finish	PLAYOFFS W	L	Pct.
79-80	Sierre	Swiss					Record unavailable.			
80-81	Sierre	Swiss					Record unavailable.			
82-83	Longueuil	QMJHL	37	29	4	.557	3rd/LeBel Division	8	7	.533
83-84	Montreal	NHL	7	10	0	.412	4th/Adams Division	9	6	.600
84-85	Montreal	NHL	41	27	12	.588	1st/Adams Division	6	6	.500
93-94	New Jersey	NHL	47	25	12	.631	2nd Atlantic Division	11	9	.55
	NHL totals (3 years)		95	62	24	.591	NHL totals (3 years)	26	21	.553

NOTES:

1983— Defeated Chicoutimi in President Cup quarterfinals; defeated Laval in President Cup semifinals; lost to Verdun in President Cup finals.

1984— Defeated Boston in Adams Division semifinals; defeated Quebec in Adams Division finals; lost to New York Islanders in Wales Conference finals.

1985— Defeated Boston in Adams Division semifinals; lost to Quebec in Adams Division finals.

1994— Defeated Buffalo in Eastern Conference quarterfinals; defeated Boston in Eastern Conference semifinals; lost to New York Rangers in Eastern Conference finals.

MELROSE, BARRY
KINGS

PERSONAL: Born July 15, 1956, in Kelvington, Sask. . . . 6-1/201. . . . Shot right. . . . Full name: Barry James Melrose.
TRANSACTIONS/CAREER NOTES: Selected by Montreal Canadiens from Kamloops Chiefs in second round (fourth Canadiens pick, 36th overall) of NHL amateur draft (June 1, 1976). . . . Selected by Cincinnati Stingers in WHA amateur player draft (June 1976). . . . Signed by Stingers (September 1976). . . . Claimed by Quebec Nordiques in WHA dispersal draft (June 1979). . . . Selected by Canadiens in NHL reclaim draft (June 1979). . . . Selected by Winnipeg Jets in NHL expansion draft (June 1979). . . . Claimed on waivers by Toronto Maple Leafs (November 30, 1980). . . . Signed as free agent by Detroit Red Wings (July 5, 1983). . . . Injured knee (March 1986). . . . Underwent leg surgery (September 1986).
MISCELLANEOUS: Played defense.

Season	Team	League	REGULAR SEASON					PLAYOFFS				
			Gms.	G	A	Pts.	PIM	Gms.	G	A	Pts.	PIM
73-74	Weyburn	SJHL	50	2	19	21	162	—	—	—	—	—
74-75	Kamloops	WCHL	70	6	18	24	95	6	1	1	2	21
75-76	Kamloops	WCHL	72	12	49	61	112	12	4	6	10	14
76-77	Springfield	AHL	23	0	3	3	17	—	—	—	—	—
	Cincinnati	WHA	29	1	4	5	8	2	0	0	0	0
77-78	Cincinnati	WHA	69	2	9	11	113	—	—	—	—	—
78-79	Cincinnati	WHA	80	2	14	16	222	3	0	1	1	8
79-80	Winnipeg	NHL	74	4	6	10	124	—	—	—	—	—
80-81	Winnipeg	NHL	18	1	1	2	40	—	—	—	—	—
	Toronto	NHL	57	2	5	7	166	3	0	1	1	15
81-82	Toronto	NHL	64	1	5	6	186	—	—	—	—	—
82-83	St. Catharines	AHL	25	1	10	11	106	—	—	—	—	—
	Toronto	NHL	52	2	5	7	68	4	0	1	1	23
83-84	Detroit	NHL	21	0	1	1	74	—	—	—	—	—
	Adirondack	AHL	16	2	1	3	226	—	—	—	—	—
84-85	Adirondack	AHL	72	3	13	16	226	—	—	—	—	—
85-86	Adirondack	AHL	57	4	4	8	204	—	—	—	—	—
	Detroit	NHL	14	0	0	0	70	—	—	—	—	—
86-87	Adirondack	AHL	55	4	9	13	170	11	1	2	3	107
	WHA totals		178	5	27	32	343	5	0	1	1	8
	NHL totals		300	10	23	33	728	7	0	2	2	38

HEAD COACHING RECORD

BACKGROUND: General manager, Adirondack, Detroit Red Wings organization (1990-91 and 1991-92).

Season	Team	League	REGULAR SEASON				Finish	PLAYOFFS		
			W	L	T	Pct.		W	L	Pct.
87-88	Medicine Hat	WHL	44	22	6	.653	2nd/East Division	12	4	.750
88-89	Seattle	WHL	33	35	4	.486	5th/West Division	—	—	—
89-90	Adirondack	AHL	42	27	11	.594	2nd/South Division	2	4	.333
90-91	Adirondack	AHL	33	37	10	.475	5th/South Division	1	1	.500
91-92	Adirondack	AHL	40	36	4	.525	2nd/Northern Division	14	5	.737
92-93	Los Angeles	NHL	39	35	10	.524	3rd/Smythe Division	13	11	.542
93-94	Los Angeles	NHL	27	45	12	.393	5th/Pacific Division	—	—	—
	NHL totals (2 years)		66	80	22	.458	**NHL totals (1 year)**	13	11	.542

NOTES:
1988—Defeated Prince Albert in East Division quarterfinals; defeated Saskatoon in East Division finals; defeated Kamloops in WHL finals.
1990—Lost to Baltimore in Calder Cup quarterfinals.
1991—Lost to Hershey in Calder Cup qualifying round.
1992—Defeated New Haven in Northern Division semifinals; defeated Springfield in Northern Division finals; defeated Rochester in Calder Cup pre-finals series; defeated St. John's in Calder Cup finals.
1993—Defeated Calgary in Smythe Division semifinals; defeated Vancouver in Smythe Division finals; defeated Toronto in Campbell Conference finals; lost to Montreal in Stanley Cup finals.

MUCKLER, JOHN
SABRES

PERSONAL: Born April 13, 1934, in Midland, Ont. . . . 6-1/200. . . . Shot left. . . . Full name: John Ernest Muckler.
MISCELLANEOUS: Played defense.

Season	Team	League	REGULAR SEASON					PLAYOFFS				
			Gms.	G	A	Pts.	PIM	Gms.	G	A	Pts.	PIM
49-50	Detroit	IHL	32	3	4	7	24	—	—	—	—	—
50-51	Windsor	OJHA				Statistics unavailable.		—	—	—	—	—
51-52	Windsor	OJHA	48	2	3	5	. . .	—	—	—	—	—
52-53	Windsor	OJHA				Statistics unavailable.		—	—	—	—	—
53-54	Guelph	OJHA				Statistics unavailable.		—	—	—	—	—
54-55	Chatham	OHA	7	0	1	1	. . .	—	—	—	—	—
	Belleville	OHA				Statistics unavailable.		—	—	—	—	—
55-56	Baltimore	EHL	62	11	34	45	82	—	—	—	—	—

HEAD COACHING RECORD

BACKGROUND: Director of player personnel, New York Rangers (1966-67). . . . Scout, Vancouver Canucks (1979-80 and 1980-81). . . . Assistant coach, Edmonton Oilers (1982-83 and 1984-85). . . . Co-coach, Oilers (1985-86 through 1988-89). . . . Director of hockey operations, Buffalo Sabres (1991-92). . . . General manager, Sabres (1993-94 through present).
HONORS: Named EHL Coach of the Year (1964-65). . . . Won Louis A.R. Pieri Trophy (1974-75). . . . Won Jake Milford Trophy with Jack Evans (1978-79).

NHL HEAD COACHES

Season	Team	League	REGULAR SEASON					PLAYOFFS		
			W	L	T	Pct.	Finish	W	L	Pct.
59-60—New York Rovers	....	EHL	18	41	1	.308		—	—	—
60-61—New York Rovers	....	EHL	18	45	1	.289		—	—	—
61-62—Long Island	....	EHL	26	41	1	.390		—	—	—
62-63—Long Island	....	EHL					Record unavailable.			
63-64—Long Island	....	EHL	32	24	6	.565		—	—	—
64-65—Long Island	....	EHL	42	29	1	.590		—	—	—
65-66—Long Island	....	EHL	46	23	3	.660		—	—	—
68-69—Memphis	....	CHL	3	5	1	.389	4th/Northern Division	—	—	—
68-69—Minnesota	....	NHL	6	23	6	.257	6th/West Division	—	—	—
71-72—Cleveland	....	AHL	32	34	10	.487	4th/Western Division	2	4	.333
72-73—Cleveland-Jacksonville	..	AHL	23	44	9	.362	5th/Western Division	—	—	—
73-74—Providence	....	AHL	38	26	12	.579	2nd/Northern Division	9	6	.600
74-75—Providence	....	AHL	43	21	12	.645	1st/North Division	2	4	.333
75-76—Providence	....	AHL	34	34	8	.500	3rd/North Division	0	3	.000
76-77—Rhode Island	....	AHL	21	30	2	.415	6th/AHL	—	—	—
78-79—Dallas	....	CHL	45	28	3	.612	2nd/CHL	8	1	.889
81-82—Wichita	....	CHL	44	33	3	.569	1st/Southern Division	3	4	.429
89-90—Edmonton	....	NHL	38	28	14	.563	2nd/Smythe Division	16	4	.800
90-91—Edmonton	....	NHL	37	37	6	.500	3rd/Smythe Division	9	9	.500
91-92—Buffalo	....	NHL	22	22	8	.500	3rd/Adams Division	3	4	.429
92-93—Buffalo	....	NHL	38	36	10	.512	4th/Adams Division	4	4	.500
93-94—Buffalo	....	NHL	43	32	9	.565	4th/Northeast Division	3	4	.429
NHL totals (6 years)	....		184	178	53	.507	**NHL totals (5 years)**	35	25	.583

NOTES:
1972— Lost to Baltimore in Calder Cup semifinals.
1974— Defeated Nova Scotia in Calder Cup quarterfinals; defeated New Haven in Calder Cup semifinals; lost to Hershey in Calder Cup finals.
1975— Lost to Springfield in Calder Cup quarterfinals.
1976— Lost to Rochester in Calder Cup quarterfinals.
1979— Defeated Kansas City in Adams Cup semifinals; defeated Salt Lake City in Adams Cup finals.
1982— Defeated Nashville in Adams Cup quarterfinals; lost to Indianapolis in Adams Cup semifinals.
1990— Defeated Winnipeg in Smythe Division semifinals; defeated Los Angeles in Smythe Division finals; defeated Chicago in Campbell Conference finals; defeated Boston in Stanley Cup finals.
1991— Defeated Calgary in Smythe Division semifinals; defeated Los Angeles in Smythe Division finals; lost to Minnesota in Campbell Conference finals.
1992— Lost to Boston in Adams Division semifinals.
1993— Defeated Boston in Adams Division semifinals; lost to Montreal in Adams Division finals.
1994— Lost to New Jersey in Eastern Conference quarterfinals.

MURRAY, TERRY
FLYERS

PERSONAL: Born July 20, 1950, in Shawville, Que. ... 6-2/190. ... Shot right. ... Full name: Terry Rodney Murray. ... Brother of Bryan Murray, general manager, Florida Panthers.
HIGH SCHOOL: Shawville (Que.).
TRANSACTIONS/CAREER NOTES: Selected by Oakland Seals from Ottawa 67's in seventh round (seventh Seals pick, 88th overall) of amateur draft (June 11, 1970). ... Loaned to Boston Braves (February 1972). ... Broke leg (1973-74). ... Traded by Philadelphia Flyers with RW Dave Kelly, RW Steve Coates and LW Bob Ritchie to Detroit Red Wings for D Mike Korney and D Rick LaPointe (February 1977). ... Sold by Red Wings to Flyers (November 1977). ... Selected by Washington Capitals in NHL waiver draft (October 1981).
HONORS: Won Eddie Shore Plaque (1977-78 and 1978-79). ... Named to AHL All-Star first team (1975-76, 1977-78 and 1978-79).
MISCELLANEOUS: Played defense.

Season	Team	League	REGULAR SEASON					PLAYOFFS				
			Gms.	G	A	Pts.	PIM	Gms.	G	A	Pts.	PIM
67-68—Ottawa	....	OHA Jr. A	52	0	4	4	59	—	—	—	—	—
68-69—Ottawa	....	OHA Jr. A	50	1	16	17	39	—	—	—	—	—
69-70—Ottawa	....	OHA Jr. A	50	4	24	28	43	—	—	—	—	—
70-71—Providence	....	AHL	57	1	22	23	47	10	0	1	1	5
71-72—Baltimore	....	AHL	30	0	5	5	13	—	—	—	—	—
—Boston		AHL	9	0	0	0	0	—	—	—	—	—
—Oklahoma City		CPHL	17	1	1	2	19	6	0	0	0	2
72-73—Salt Lake City	....	WHL	39	3	8	11	30	9	0	6	6	14
—California		NHL	23	0	3	3	4	—	—	—	—	—
73-74—California		NHL	58	0	12	12	48	—	—	—	—	—
74-75—Salt Lake City	....	CHL	62	5	30	35	122	11	2	2	4	30
—California		NHL	9	0	2	2	8	—	—	—	—	—
75-76—Richmond		AHL	67	8	48	56	95	6	1	4	5	2
—Philadelphia		NHL	3	0	0	0	2	6	0	1	1	0
76-77—Philadelphia	....	NHL	36	0	13	13	14	—	—	—	—	—
—Detroit		NHL	23	0	7	7	10	—	—	—	—	—
77-78—Philadelphia	....	AHL	7	2	1	3	13	—	—	—	—	—
—Maine		AHL	68	9	40	49	53	12	1	7	8	28
78-79—Philadelphia	....	NHL	5	0	0	0	0	—	—	—	—	—
—Maine		AHL	55	14	23	37	14	10	1	5	6	6

Season	Team	League	Gms.	G	A	Pts.	PIM	Gms.	G	A	Pts.	PIM
			REGULAR SEASON					PLAYOFFS				
79-80	Maine	AHL	68	3	19	22	26	12	2	2	4	10
80-81	Maine	AHL	2	0	1	1	0	—	—	—	—	—
	Philadelphia	NHL	71	1	17	18	53	12	2	1	3	10
81-82	Washington	NHL	74	3	22	25	60	—	—	—	—	—
	NHL totals		302	4	76	80	199	18	2	2	4	10

HEAD COACHING RECORD

BACKGROUND: Assistant coach, Washington Capitals (1982-83 through 1987-1988).

Season	Team	League	W	L	T	Pct.	Finish	W	L	Pct.
			REGULAR SEASON					PLAYOFFS		
88-89	Baltimore	AHL	30	46	4	.400	6th/South Division	—	—	—
89-90	Baltimore	AHL	26	17	1	.646		—	—	—
	Washington	NHL	18	14	2	.559	3rd/Patrick Division	8	7	.533
90-91	Washington	NHL	37	36	7	.506	3rd/Patrick Division	5	6	.455
91-92	Washington	NHL	45	27	8	.613	2nd/Patrick Division	3	4	.429
92-93	Washington	NHL	43	34	7	.554	2nd/Patrick Division	2	4	.333
93-94	Washington	NHL	20	23	4	.468		—	—	—
	NHL totals (5 years)		163	134	28	.545	NHL totals (4 years)	18	21	.461

NOTES:
1990— Defeated New Jersey in Patrick Division semifinals; defeated New York Rangers in Patrick Division finals; lost to Boston in Wales Conference finals.
1991— Defeated New York Rangers in Patrick Division semifinals; lost to Pittsburgh in Patrick Division finals.
1992— Lost to Pittsburgh in Patrick Division semifinals.
1993— Lost to New York Islanders in Patrick Division semifinals.
1994— Replaced as head coach by Jim Schoenfeld (January 27), with club in fifth place. Loaned to Florida Panthers (February 18) to coach Cincinnati Cyclones of IHL.

NEILSON, ROGER
PANTHERS

PERSONAL: Born June 16, 1934, in Toronto.
COLLEGE: McMaster (Ont.).

HEAD COACHING RECORD

BACKGROUND: Scout, Peterborough, Montreal Canadiens organization (1964-65 through 1966-67).... Assistant coach, Buffalo Sabres (1979-80).... Assistant coach, Vancouver Canucks (1981-82).... Assistant coach, Chicago Blackhawks (1984-85 through 1986-87).... Scout, Blackhawks (1987-88 and 1988-89).

Season	Team	League	W	L	T	Pct.	Finish	W	L	Pct.
			REGULAR SEASON					PLAYOFFS		
66-67	Peterborough	OHA	7	8	3	.472		—	—	—
67-68	Peterborough	OHA	13	30	11	.343	8th/OHA	—	—	—
68-69	Peterborough	OHA	27	18	9	.583	3rd/OHA	4	6	.400
69-70	Peterborough	OHA	29	13	12	.648	2nd/OHA	2	4	.333
70-71	Peterborough	OHA	41	13	8	.726	1st/OHA	1	4	.200
71-72	Peterborough	OHA	34	20	9	.611	3rd/OHA	13	2	.824
72-73	Peterborough	OHA	42	13	8	.730	2nd/OHA	9	4	.639
73-74	Peterborough	OHA	35	21	14	.600	3rd/OHA	7	7	.500
74-75	Peterborough	OHA	37	20	13	.621	2nd/OHA	5	4	.545
75-76	Peterborough	OHA	18	37	11	.356	6th/Leyden Division	—	—	—
76-77	Dallas	CHL	35	25	16	.565	2nd/CHL	1	4	.200
77-78	Toronto	NHL	41	29	10	.575	3rd/Adams Division	6	7	.462
78-79	Toronto	NHL	34	33	13	.506	3rd/Adams Division	2	4	.333
79-80	Buffalo	NHL	14	6	6	.654	1st/Adams Division	—	—	—
80-81	Buffalo	NHL	39	20	21	.619	1st/Adams Division	4	4	.500
81-82	Vancouver	NHL	4	0	1	.900	2nd/Smythe Division	11	6	.647
82-83	Vancouver	NHL	30	35	15	.469	3rd/Smythe Division	1	3	.250
83-84	Vancouver	NHL	17	26	5	.406	3rd/Smythe Division	—	—	—
	Los Angeles	NHL	8	17	3	.339	5th/Smythe Division	—	—	—
89-90	New York Rangers	NHL	36	31	13	.531	1st/Patrick Division	5	5	.500
90-91	New York Rangers	NHL	36	31	13	.531	2nd/Patrick Division	2	4	.333
91-92	New York Rangers	NHL	50	25	5	.656	1st/Patrick Division	6	7	.462
92-93	New York Rangers	NHL	19	17	4	.525		—	—	—
93-94	Florida Panthers	NHL	33	34	17	.494	5th/Atlantic Division	—	—	—
	NHL totals (12 years)		361	304	126	.536	NHL totals (8 years)	37	40	.429

NOTES:
1969— Defeated London in OHA quarterfinals; lost to Montreal in OHA semifinals.
1970— Lost to London in OHA quarterfinals.
1971— Lost to Toronto in OHA quarterfinals.
1972— Defeated St. Catherines in OHA quarterfinals; defeated Toronto in OHA semifinals; defeated Ottawa in OHA finals; lost to Cornwall in Memorial Cup finals. Peterborough had two playoff ties.
1973— Defeated Oshawa in OHA quarterfinals; defeated London in OHA semifinals; lost to Toronto in OHA finals. Peterborough had five playoff ties.
1974— Defeated Oshawa in OHA quarterfinals; defeated Kitchener in OHA semifinals; lost to St. Catherines in OHA finals. Peterborough had four playoff ties.
1975— Defeated Oshawa in OHA quarterfinals; lost to Hamilton in OHA finals. Peterborough had two playoff ties.
1977— Lost to Tulsa in Adams Cup semifinals.

1978— Defeated Los Angeles in Stanley Cup preliminary round; defeated New York Islanders in Stanley Cup quarterfinals; lost to Montreal in Stanley Cup semifinals.
1979— Defeated Atlanta in Stanley Cup preliminary round; lost to Montreal in Stanley Cup quarterfinals.
1981— Defeated Vancouver in Stanley Cup preliminary round; lost to Minnesota in Stanley Cup quarterfinals.
1982— Defeated Calgary in Smythe Division semifinals; defeated Los Angeles in Smythe Division finals; defeated Chicago in Campbell Conference finals; lost to New York Islanders in Stanley Cup finals.
1983— Lost to Calgary in Smythe Division semifinals.
1990— Defeated New York Islanders in Patrick Division semifinals; lost to Washington in Patrick Division finals.
1991— Lost to Washington in Patrick Division semifinals.
1992— Defeated New Jersey in Patrick Division semifinals; lost to Pittsburgh in Patrick Division finals.

PADDOCK, JOHN
JETS

PERSONAL: Born June 9, 1954, in Brandon, Man.... 6-3/192.... Shot right.... Full name: Alvin John Paddock.... Name pronounced PA-dihk.
HIGH SCHOOL: Rivers (Man.) Collegiate.
TRANSACTIONS/CAREER NOTES: Selected by Washington Capitals from Brandon Wheat Kings in third round (third Capitals pick, 37th overall) of NHL amateur draft (May 28, 1974).... Traded by Capitals to Philadelphia Flyers to complete earlier deal for LW Bob Sirois (September 1976).... Dislocated shoulder (1977-78).... Dislocated right elbow (1979-80).... Sold by Flyers to Quebec Nordiques (August 1980).... Signed as free agent by New Jersey Devils (August 1983).
MISCELLANEOUS: Played right wing.

			REGULAR SEASON					PLAYOFFS				
Season Team	League	Gms.	G	A	Pts.	PIM	Gms.	G	A	Pts.	PIM
72-73—Brandon	WCHL	11	3	2	5	6	—	—	—	—	—
73-74—Brandon	WCHL	68	34	49	83	228	—	—	—	—	—
74-75—Richmond	AHL	72	26	22	48	206	7	5	3	8	38
75-76—Richmond	AHL	42	11	14	25	98	8	0	3	3	5
—Washington	NHL	8	1	1	2	12	—	—	—	—	—
76-77—Springfield	AHL	61	13	16	29	106	—	—	—	—	—
—Philadelphia	NHL	5	0	0	0	9	—	—	—	—	—
77-78—Maine	AHL	61	8	12	20	152	8	0	0	0	25
78-79—Maine	AHL	79	30	37	67	275	10	*9	1	10	13
79-80—Philadelphia	NHL	32	3	7	10	36	3	2	0	2	0
80-81—Maine	AHL	22	8	7	15	53	8	10	6	16	48
—Quebec	NHL	32	2	5	7	25	2	0	0	0	0
81-82—Maine	AHL	39	6	10	16	123	3	0	1	1	18
82-83—Maine	AHL	69	30	23	53	188	13	2	2	4	18
—Philadelphia	NHL	10	2	1	3	4	—	—	—	—	—
83-84—Maine	AHL	17	3	6	9	34	—	—	—	—	—
NHL totals		87	8	14	22	86	5	2	0	2	0

HEAD COACHING RECORD

BACKGROUND: Assistant general manager, Philadelphia Flyers (1989-90).
HONORS: Shared Louis A.R. Pieri Memorial Award with Mike Milbury (1987-88).

		REGULAR SEASON					PLAYOFFS		
Season Team	League	W	L	T	Pct.	Finish	W	L	Pct.
83-84—Maine	AHL	33	36	11	.481	3rd/North Division	12	5	.706
84-85—Maine	AHL	38	32	10	.538	1st/North Division	5	6	.454
85-86—Hershey	AHL	48	29	3	.619	1st/South Division	10	8	.555
86-87—Hershey	AHL	43	36	1	.544	4th/South Division	1	4	.200
87-88—Hershey	AHL	50	27	3	.644	1st/South Division	12	0	1.000
88-89—Hershey	AHL	40	30	10	.563	2nd/South Division	7	5	.583
90-91—Binghamton	AHL	44	30	6	.588	2nd/South Division	4	6	.400
91-92—Winnipeg	NHL	33	32	15	.506	4th/Smythe Division	3	4	.429
92-93—Winnipeg	NHL	40	37	7	.518	4th/Smythe Division	2	4	.333
93-94—Winnipeg	NHL	24	51	9	.339	6th/Central Division	—	—	—
NHL totals (3 years)		97	120	31	.453	**NHL totals (2 years)**	5	8	.385

NOTES:
1984— Defeated Adirondack in Calder Cup quarterfinals; defeated Nova Scotia in Calder Cup semifinals; defeated Rochester in Calder Cup finals.
1985— Defeated Maine in Calder Cup quarterfinals; lost to Sherbrooke in Calder Cup semifinals.
1986— Defeated New Haven in Calder Cup quarterfinals; defeated St. Catherines in Calder Cup semifinals; lost to Adirondack in Calder Cup finals.
1987— Lost to Rochester in Calder Cup quarterfinals.
1988— Defeated Binghamton in Calder Cup quarterfinals; defeated Adirondack in Calder Cup semifinals; defeated Fredericton in Calder Cup finals.
1989— Defeated Utica in Calder Cup quarterfinals; lost to Adirondack in Calder Cup semifinals.
1991— Defeated Adirondack in Calder Cup qualifying round; defeated Baltimore in Calder Cup quarterfinals; lost to Rochester in Calder Cup semifinals.
1992— Lost to Vancouver in Smythe Division semifinals.
1993— Lost to Vancouver in Smythe Division semifinals.

QUINN, PAT
CANUCKS

PERSONAL: Born January 29, 1943, in Hamilton, Ont.... 6-3/215.... Shot left.... Full name: John Brian Patrick Quinn.
HIGH SCHOOL: Central (Hamilton, Ont.).
COLLEGE: UC San Diego, then Delaware (attended law school).

TRANSACTIONS/CAREER NOTES: Suspended eight games for stick-swinging (November 1960).... Loaned by Detroit Red Wings to Tulsa Oilers for 1964-65 season.... Broke ankle (1965).... Selected by Montreal Canadiens from Red Wings in intraleague draft (June 1966).... Sold by Canadiens to St. Louis Blues (June 1967).... Loaned to Oilers for 1967-68 season.... Sold by Blues to Toronto Maple Leafs for rights to LW Dickie Moore (March 1968).... Selected by Vancouver Canucks in NHL expansion draft (June 1970).... Selected by Atlanta Flames in NHL expansion draft (June 1972).... Broke leg (1976).
MISCELLANEOUS: Played defense.

Season Team	League	REGULAR SEASON					PLAYOFFS				
		Gms.	G	A	Pts.	PIM	Gms.	G	A	Pts.	PIM
58-59—Hamilton Jr. A.	OHA	20	0	1	1	...	—	—	—	—	—
59-60—Hamilton Jr. A.	OHA	27	0	1	1	...	—	—	—	—	—
60-61—Hamilton Jr. B	OHA					Statistics unavailable.					
61-62—						Unknown.					
62-63—Edmonton	CAHL					Statistics unavailable.					
63-64—Knoxville	EHL	72	6	31	37	217	3	0	0	0	9
64-65—Tulsa	CPHL	70	3	32	35	202	—	—	—	—	—
65-66—Memphis	CPHL	67	2	16	18	135	—	—	—	—	—
66-67—Houston	CPHL	15	0	3	3	66	—	—	—	—	—
—Seattle	WHL	35	1	3	4	49	5	0	0	0	2
67-68—Tulsa	CPHL	51	3	15	18	178	11	1	4	5	19
68-69—Tulsa	CHL	17	0	6	6	25	—	—	—	—	—
—Toronto	NHL	40	2	7	9	95	4	0	0	0	13
69-70—Tulsa	CHL	2	0	1	1	6	—	—	—	—	—
—Toronto	NHL	59	0	5	5	88	—	—	—	—	—
70-71—Vancouver	NHL	76	2	11	13	149	—	—	—	—	—
71-72—Vancouver	NHL	57	2	3	5	63	—	—	—	—	—
72-73—Atlanta	NHL	78	2	18	20	113	—	—	—	—	—
73-74—Atlanta	NHL	77	5	27	32	94	4	0	0	0	6
74-75—Atlanta	NHL	80	2	19	21	156	—	—	—	—	—
75-76—Atlanta	NHL	80	2	11	13	134	2	0	1	1	2
76-77—Atlanta	NHL	59	1	12	13	58	1	0	0	0	0
NHL totals		606	18	113	131	950	11	0	1	1	21

HEAD COACHING RECORD

BACKGROUND: Assistant coach, Philadelphia Flyers (1977-78).... Coach, Team Canada (1986).... President/general manager, Vancouver Canucks (1987-88 through present).
HONORS: Named NHL Coach of the Year by THE SPORTING NEWS (1979-80 and 1991-92).... Won Jack Adams Award (1979-80 and 1991-92).

Season Team	League	REGULAR SEASON					PLAYOFFS		
		W	L	T	Pct.	Finish	W	L	Pct.
78-79—Philadelphia	NHL	18	8	4	.667	2nd/Patrick Division	3	5	.375
79-80—Philadelphia	NHL	48	12	20	.725	1st/Patrick Division	13	6	.684
80-81—Philadelphia	NHL	41	24	15	.606	2nd/Patrick Division	6	6	.500
81-82—Philadelphia	NHL	34	29	9	.535	3rd/Patrick Division	—	—	—
84-85—Los Angeles	NHL	34	32	14	.513	4th/Smythe Division	0	3	.000
85-86—Los Angeles	NHL	23	49	8	.338	5th/Smythe Division	—	—	—
86-87—Los Angeles	NHL	18	20	4	.476	4th/Smythe Division	—	—	—
90-91—Vancouver	NHL	9	13	4	.423	4th/Smythe Division	2	4	.333
91-92—Vancouver	NHL	42	26	12	.600	1st/Smythe Division	6	7	.462
92-93—Vancouver	NHL	46	29	9	.601	1st/Smythe Division	6	6	.500
93-94—Vancouver	NHL	41	40	3	.506	2nd/Pacific Division	15	9	.625
NHL totals (11 years)		354	282	102	.549	**NHL totals (8 years)**	51	46	.526

NOTES:
1979— Defeated Vancouver in Stanley Cup preliminary round; lost to New York Rangers in Stanley Cup quarterfinals.
1980— Defeated Edmonton in Stanley Cup preliminary round; defeated New York Rangers in Stanley Cup quarterfinals; defeated Minnesota in Stanley Cup semifinals; lost to New York Islanders in Stanley Cup finals.
1985— Lost to Edmonton in Smythe Division semifinals.
1991— Lost to Los Angeles in Smythe Division semifinals.
1992— Defeated Winnipeg in Smythe Division semifinals; lost to Edmonton in Smythe Division finals.
1993— Defeated Winnipeg in Smythe Division semifinals; lost to Los Angeles in Smythe Division finals.
1994— Defeated Calgary in Western Conference quarterfinals; defeated Dallas in Western Conference semifinals; defeated Toronto in Western Conference finals; lost to New York Rangers in Stanley Cup finals.

SCHOENFELD, JIM
CAPITALS

PERSONAL: Born September 4, 1952, in Galt, Ont. ... 6-2/208. ... Shot left. ... Full name: James Grant Schoenfeld.
TRANSACTIONS/CAREER NOTES: Traded by London Knights with D Ken Southwick and RW Rick Kehoe to Hamilton Red Wings for D Gary Geldhart, RW Gordon Brooks, LW Dave Gilmour and Mike Craig (December 1969).... Traded by Red Wings to Niagara Falls Flyers for C Russ Friesen and D Mike Healey (January 1971).... Selected by New York Raiders in WHA player selection draft (February 1972).... Selected by Buffalo Sabres in first round (first Sabres pick, fifth overall) of NHL amateur draft (June 8, 1972).... Damaged nerve in leg (1972); underwent corrective surgery following season.... Ruptured spinal disc (1973); missed most of season.... Underwent back surgery (1973).... Broke left foot (1974).... Suffered from mononucleosis (1975).... Suffered from viral pneumonia (1976).... Broke right foot (1978).... Separated shoulder (1978).... Strained knee (1978).... Injured hand and suffered from the flu (December 1980); missed nine games.... Broke left little finger (September 1981).... Broke metatarsal bone in right foot (October 18, 1981).... Traded by Buffalo Sabres with RW Danny Gare, G Bob Sauve and C Derek Smith to Detroit Red Wings for C Dale McCourt, RW Mike Foligno, C Brent Peterson and future considerations (December 1981)....

Separated ribs (October 1982).... Released by Red Wings (June 1983).... Signed as free agent by Boston Bruins (August 1983).... Fractured and separated left shoulder (November 11, 1983); underwent surgery.... Injured shoulder (February 27, 1984).... Announced retirement (September 1984).... Recalled to active player status by Sabres (December 19, 1984).... Stress fracture in right foot (January, 1985); missed 13 games.... Announced retirement (June 1985).

HONORS: Named to the NHL All-Star second team (1979-80).... Played in NHL All-Star Game (1976-77 and 1979-80).

MISCELLANEOUS: Played defense.

Season Team	League	REGULAR SEASON					PLAYOFFS				
		Gms.	G	A	Pts.	PIM	Gms.	G	A	Pts.	PIM
69-70—London	OHA Mj. Jr. A	16	1	4	5	81	—	—	—	—	—
—Hamilton Jr. A.	OHA	32	2	12	14	54	—	—	—	—	—
70-71—Hamilton Jr. A.	OHA	25	3	19	22	120	—	—	—	—	—
—Niagara Falls	OHA	30	3	9	12	85	—	—	—	—	—
71-72—Niagara Falls	OHA	40	6	46	52	*225	—	—	—	—	—
72-73—Buffalo	NHL	66	4	15	19	178	6	2	1	3	4
73-74—Cincinnati	AHL	2	0	2	2	4	—	—	—	—	—
—Buffalo	NHL	28	1	8	9	56	—	—	—	—	—
74-75—Buffalo	NHL	68	1	19	20	184	17	1	4	5	38
75-76—Buffalo	NHL	56	2	22	24	114	8	0	3	3	33
76-77—Buffalo	NHL	65	7	25	32	97	6	0	0	0	12
77-78—Buffalo	NHL	60	2	20	22	89	8	0	1	1	28
78-79—Buffalo	NHL	46	8	17	25	67	3	0	1	1	0
79-80—Buffalo	NHL	77	9	27	36	72	14	0	3	3	18
80-81—Buffalo	NHL	71	8	25	33	110	8	0	0	0	14
81-82—Buffalo	NHL	13	3	2	5	30	—	—	—	—	—
—Detroit	NHL	39	5	9	14	69	—	—	—	—	—
82-83—Detroit	NHL	57	1	10	11	18	—	—	—	—	—
83-84—Boston	NHL	39	0	2	2	20	—	—	—	—	—
84-85—Buffalo	NHL	34	0	3	3	28	5	0	0	0	4
NHL totals		**719**	**51**	**204**	**255**	**1132**	**75**	**3**	**13**	**16**	**151**

HEAD COACHING RECORD

Season Team	League	REGULAR SEASON					PLAYOFFS		
		W	L	T	Pct.	Finish	W	L	Pct.
84-85—Rochester	AHL	17	6	2	.720	3rd/South Division	—	—	—
85-86—Buffalo	NHL	19	19	5	.500	5th/Adams Division	—	—	—
87-88—New Jersey	NHL	17	12	1	.583	6th/Patrick Division	11	9	.550
88-89—New Jersey	NHL	27	41	12	.413	5th/Patrick Division	—	—	—
89-90—New Jersey	NHL	6	6	2	.500		—	—	—
93-94—Washington	NHL	19	12	6	.595	3rd/Atlantic Division	5	6	.455
NHL totals (4 years)		**88**	**90**	**26**	**.495**	**NHL totals (1 year)**	**16**	**15**	**.516**

NOTES:

1988— Defeated New York Islanders in Patrick Division semifinals; defeated Washington in Patrick Division final; lost to Boston in Campbell Conference finals.

1994— Defeated Pittsburgh Penguins in Eastern Conference quarterfinals; lost to New York Rangers in Eastern Conference semifinals.

SUTTER, BRIAN
BRUINS

PERSONAL: Born October 7, 1956, in Viking, Alta.... 5-11/172.... Shot left.... Full name: Brian Louis Allen Sutter.... Name pronounced suh-tuhr.... Brother of Darryl Sutter, left winger, Chicago Blackhawks (1979-80 through 1986-87) and current head coach, Blackhawks; brother of Brent Sutter, center, Blackhawks; brother of Ron Sutter, center, New York Islanders; brother of Rich Sutter, right winger, Chicago Blackhawks; and brother of Duane Sutter, right winger, New York Islanders and Blackhawks (1979-80 through 1989-90) and current head coach, Indianapolis Ice of IHL.

TRANSACTIONS/CAREER NOTES: Selected by St. Louis Blues from Lethbridge Broncos in second round (second Blues pick, 20th overall) of NHL amateur draft (June 1, 1976).... Suffered hairline fracture of pelvis (November 3, 1983).... Broke left shoulder (January 16, 1986).... Reinjured left shoulder (March 8, 1986).... Damaged left shoulder muscle (November 1986).... Sprained ankle (November 1987).... Retired as player and signed as head coach of Blues (June 1988).

HONORS: Played in NHL All-Star Game (1982, 1983 and 1985).

MISCELLANEOUS: Played left wing.

Season Team	League	REGULAR SEASON					PLAYOFFS				
		Gms.	G	A	Pts.	PIM	Gms.	G	A	Pts.	PIM
72-73—Red Deer	AJHL	51	27	40	67	54	—	—	—	—	—
73-74—Red Deer	AJHL	59	42	54	96	139	—	—	—	—	—
74-75—Lethbridge	WCHL	53	34	47	81	134	6	0	1	1	39
75-76—Lethbridge	WCHL	72	36	56	92	233	7	3	4	7	45
76-77—Kansas City	CHL	38	15	23	38	47	—	—	—	—	—
—St. Louis	NHL	35	4	10	14	82	4	1	0	1	14
77-78—St. Louis	NHL	78	9	13	22	123	—	—	—	—	—
78-79—St. Louis	NHL	77	41	39	80	165	—	—	—	—	—
79-80—St. Louis	NHL	71	23	35	58	156	3	0	0	0	4
80-81—St. Louis	NHL	78	35	34	69	232	11	6	3	9	77
81-82—St. Louis	NHL	74	39	36	75	239	10	8	6	14	49
82-83—St. Louis	NHL	79	46	30	76	254	4	2	1	3	10
83-84—St. Louis	NHL	76	32	51	83	162	11	1	5	6	22
84-85—St. Louis	NHL	77	37	37	74	121	3	2	1	3	2
85-86—St. Louis	NHL	44	19	23	42	87	9	1	2	3	22

Season	Team	League	REGULAR SEASON Gms.	G	A	Pts.	PIM	PLAYOFFS Gms.	G	A	Pts.	PIM
86-87—St. Louis		NHL	14	3	3	6	18	—	—	—	—	—
87-88—St. Louis		NHL	76	15	22	37	147	10	0	3	3	49
NHL totals			779	303	333	636	1786	65	21	21	42	249

HEAD COACHING RECORD

BACKGROUND: Assistant coach, Team Canada (1991).
HONORS: Won Jack Adams Trophy (1990-91).

Season	Team	League	W	L	T	Pct.	Finish	PLAYOFFS W	L	Pct.
88-89—St. Louis		NHL	33	35	12	.488	2nd/Norris Division	5	5	.500
89-90—St. Louis		NHL	37	34	9	.519	2nd/Norris Division	7	5	.583
90-91—St. Louis		NHL	47	22	11	.656	2nd/Norris Division	6	7	.462
91-92—St. Louis		NHL	36	33	11	.519	3rd/Norris Division	2	4	.333
92-93—Boston		NHL	51	26	7	.649	1st/Adams Division	0	4	.000
93-94—Boston		NHL	42	29	13	.577	2nd/Northeast Division	6	7	.462
NHL totals (6 years)			246	179	63	.569	NHL totals (6 years)	26	32	.448

NOTES:
1989— Defeated Minnesota in Norris Division semifinals; lost to Chicago in Norris Division finals.
1990— Defeated Toronto in Norris Division semifinals; lost to Chicago in Norris Division finals.
1991— Defeated Detroit in Norris Division semifinals; lost to Minnesota in Norris Division finals.
1992— Lost to Chicago in Norris Division semifinals.
1993— Lost to Buffalo in Adams Division semifinals.
1994— Defeated Montreal in Eastern Conferece Quarterfinals; lost to New Jersey in Eastern Conference semifinals.

SUTTER, DARRYL
BLACKHAWKS

PERSONAL: Born August 19, 1958, in Viking, Alta. . . . 5-10/163. . . . Shot left. . . . Name pronounced SUH-tuhr. . . . Brother of Brian Sutter, left winger, St. Louis Blues (1976-77 through 1987-88) and current head coach, Boston Bruins; brother of Duane Sutter, right winger, New York Islanders and Chicago Blackhawks (1979-80 through 1989-90) and current head coach, Indianapolis Ice of IHL; brother of Rich Sutter, right winger, Blackhawks; brother of Ron Sutter, center, New York Islanders; and brother of Brent Sutter, center, Blackhawks.
TRANSACTIONS/CAREER NOTES: Selected by Chicago Blackhawks in 11th round (11th Blackhawks pick, 179th overall) of NHL amateur draft (June 1978). . . . Lacerated left elbow, developed infection and underwent surgery (November 27, 1981). . . . Broke nose (November 7, 1982). . . . Broke ribs (November 1983). . . . Fracture left cheekbone and injured left eye (January 2, 1984). . . . Underwent arthroscopic surgery to right knee (September 1984). . . . Bruised ribs (October 1984). . . . Broke left ankle (December 26, 1984). . . . Separated right shoulder and underwent surgery (November 13, 1985); missed 30 games. . . . Injured knee (February 1987). . . . Retired as player and signed as assistant coach of Blackhawks (June 1987).
HONORS: Named top rookie of Japan National League (1978-79). . . . Won Dudley (Red) Garrett Memorial Trophy (1979-80). . . . Named to AHL All-Star second team (1979-80).
MISCELLANEOUS: Played left wing.

Season	Team	League	REGULAR SEASON Gms.	G	A	Pts.	PIM	PLAYOFFS Gms.	G	A	Pts.	PIM
74-75—Red Deer		AJHL	60	16	20	36	43	—	—	—	—	—
75-76—Red Deer		AJHL	60	43	93	136	82	—	—	—	—	—
76-77—Red Deer		AJHL	56	55	78	133	131	—	—	—	—	—
—Lethbridge		WCHL	1	1	0	1	0	15	3	7	10	13
77-78—Lethbridge		WCHL	68	33	48	81	119	8	4	9	13	2
78-79—New Brunswick		AHL	19	7	6	13	6	5	1	2	3	0
—Iwakura		Japan	20	28	13	41	0	—	—	—	—	—
79-80—New Brunswick		AHL	69	35	31	66	69	12	6	6	12	8
—Chicago		NHL	8	2	0	2	2	7	3	1	4	2
80-81—Chicago		NHL	76	40	22	62	86	3	3	1	4	2
81-82—Chicago		NHL	40	23	12	35	31	3	0	1	1	2
82-83—Chicago		NHL	80	31	30	61	53	13	4	6	10	8
83-84—Chicago		NHL	59	20	20	40	44	5	1	1	2	0
84-85—Chicago		NHL	49	20	18	38	12	15	12	7	19	12
85-86—Chicago		NHL	50	17	10	27	44	3	1	2	3	0
86-87—Chicago		NHL	44	8	6	14	16	2	0	0	0	0
NHL totals			406	161	118	279	288	51	24	19	43	26

HEAD COACHING RECORD

BACKGROUND: Assistant coach, Chicago Blackhawks (1987-88). . . . Associate coach, Blackhawks (1991-92).
HONORS: Won Commissioner's Trophy (1989-90).

Season	Team	League	W	L	T	Pct.	Finish	PLAYOFFS W	L	Pct.
88-89—Saginaw		IHL	46	26	10	.622	2nd/East Division	2	4	.333
89-90—Indianapolis		IHL	53	21	8	.695	1st/West Division	12	2	.857
90-91—Indianapolis		IHL	48	29	5	.616	2nd/East Division	3	4	.429
92-93—Chicago		NHL	47	25	12	.631	1st/Norris Division	0	4	.000
93-94—Chicago		NHL	39	36	9	.518	5th/Central Division	2	4	.333
NHL totals (2 years)			86	61	21	.574	NHL totals (2 years)	2	8	.200

NOTES:
1989— Lost to Fort Wayne in Turner Cup quarterfinals.

1990— Defeated Peoria in Turner Cup quarterfinals; defeated Salt Lake City in Turner Cup semifinals; defeated Muskegon in Turner Cup finals.
1991— Lost to Fort Wayne in Turner Cup quarterfinals.
1993— Lost to St. Louis in Norris Division semifinals.
1994— Lost to Toronto in Western Conference quarterfinals.

WILSON, RON
MIGHTY DUCKS

PERSONAL: Born May 28, 1955, in Windsor, Ont.... 5-11/175.... Shot right.... Full name: Ronald Lawrence Wilson.... Son of Larry Wilson, forward, Detroit Red Wings and Chicago Blawkhawks (1949-50 through 1955-56).
COLLEGE: Providence.
TRANSACTIONS/CAREER NOTES: Selected by Toronto Maple Leafs in seventh round (seventh Maple Leafs pick, 132nd overall) in NHL entry draft (June 3, 1975).... Loaned by Davos club to Minnesota North Stars for remainder of NHL season and playoffs (March 1985).... Loaned by Davos club to Minnesota North Stars for remainder of NHL season and playoffs (March 1986). ... Traded by Davos to Minnesota North Stars for Craig Levie (May 1986).... Separated shoulder (March 9, 1987).
HONORS: Named to NCAA All-America East first team (1974-75 and 1975-76).
MISCELLANEOUS: Played defense.

Season	Team	League	REGULAR SEASON					PLAYOFFS				
			Gms.	G	A	Pts.	PIM	Gms.	G	A	Pts.	PIM
73-74—	Providence	ECAC	26	16	22	38	...	—	—	—	—	—
74-75—	Providence	ECAC	27	26	61	87	12	—	—	—	—	—
	—U.S. national team	Int'l	27	5	32	37	42	—	—	—	—	—
75-76—	Providence	ECAC	28	19	47	66	44	—	—	—	—	—
76-77—	Providence	ECAC	30	17	42	59	62	—	—	—	—	—
	—Dallas	CHL	4	1	0	1	2	—	—	—	—	—
77-78—	Dallas	CHL	67	31	38	69	18	—	—	—	—	—
	—Toronto	NHL	13	2	1	3	0	—	—	—	—	—
78-79—	New Brunswick	AHL	31	11	20	31	13	—	—	—	—	—
	—Toronto	NHL	5	0	2	2	2	—	—	—	—	—
79-80—	New Brunswick	AHL	43	20	43	63	10	—	—	—	—	—
80-81—	Davos HC	Switzerland				Statistics unavailable.						
81-82—	Davos HC	Switzerland				Statistics unavailable.						
82-83—	Davos HC	Switzerland				Statistics unavailable.						
83-84—	Davos HC	Switzerland				Statistics unavailable.						
84-85—	Davos HC	Switzerland				Statistics unavailable.						
	—Minnesota	NHL	13	4	8	12	2	—	—	—	—	—
85-86—	Davos HC	Switzerland				Statistics unavailable.						
	—Minnesota	NHL	11	1	3	4	8	—	—	—	—	—
86-87—	Minnesota	NHL	65	12	29	41	36	—	—	—	—	—
87-88—	Minnesota	NHL	24	2	12	14	16	—	—	—	—	—
NHL totals			**131**	**21**	**55**	**76**	**64**					

HEAD COACHING RECORD

BACKGROUND: Assistant coach, Milwaukee, Vancouver Canucks organization (1989-90).... Served as interim coach of Milwaukee while Ron Lapointe was hospitalized for cancer treatments (February and March 1990; team went 9-10).... Assistant coach, Vancouver Canucks (1990-91 through 1992-93).

Season	Team	League	REGULAR SEASON					PLAYOFFS		
			W	L	T	Pct.	Finish	W	L	Pct.
93-94—	Anaheim	NHL	33	46	5	.423	4th/Pacific Division	—	—	—